A-Z BIG LON[DON]

CONTENTS

Key to Map Pages	2-3
Map Pages @ approx. 4¼" to 1 mile	4-156
Large Scale Map Pages @ 8½" to 1 mile	157-173
Railway Connections Map	174-175
West End Cinema & Theatre Maps	176
Index to Streets, Areas & selected Places of Interest	177-283
Index to Hospitals & Hospices	284-286
Index to Stations	287-288
Underground Railway Map	Back Cover

REFERENCE

Symbol	Example
Motorway	M1
A Road	A2
Under Construction	
Proposed	
B Road	B408
Dual Carriageway	
One Way Street	→

Traffic flow on A Roads is indicated by a heavy line on the drivers' left.

Symbol	Example
Junction Name	MARBLE ARCH
Restricted Access	
Pedestrianized Road	
Track & Footpath	
Residential Walkway	
Railway	Tunnel, Level Crossing
Stations:	
National Rail Network	
Docklands Light Railway	DLR
Underground Station	is the registered trade mark of Transport for London
Croydon Tramlink	Tunnel, Stop

The boarding of Tramlink trams at stops may be limited to a single direction, indicated by the arrow.

Symbol	Example
Map Continuation	62 — Large Scale Map Pages 160
Built Up Area	BANK STREET
House Numbers A & B Roads only	51 22 19 48
Church or Chapel	†
Fire Station	■
Hospital	H
Information Centre	i
National Grid Reference	530
Police Station	▲
Post Office	★
Toilet with facilities for the Disabled	
Educational Establishment	
Hospital or Hospice	
Industrial Building	
Leisure or Recreational Facility	
Place of Interest	
Public Building	
Shopping Centre or Market	
Other Selected Buildings	

SCALE

Pages 4-156
4¼ inches to 1 Mile

0 — ¼ — ½ — ¾ Mile
0 — 250 — 500 — 750 Metres — 1 Kilometre

1:14,908
10.79cm to 1 mile
6.71cm to 1 km

Geographers' A-Z Map Company Limited

Head Office : Fairfield Road, Borough Green, Sevenoaks, Kent TN15 8PP Tel: 01732 781000 (General Enquires & Trade Sales)
Showrooms : 44 Gray's Inn Road, London WC1X 8HX Tel: 020 7440 9500 (Retail Sales)
www.a-zmaps.co.uk

Ordnance Survey® This product includes mapping data licensed from Ordnance Survey® with the permission of the Controller of Her Majesty's Stationery Office.

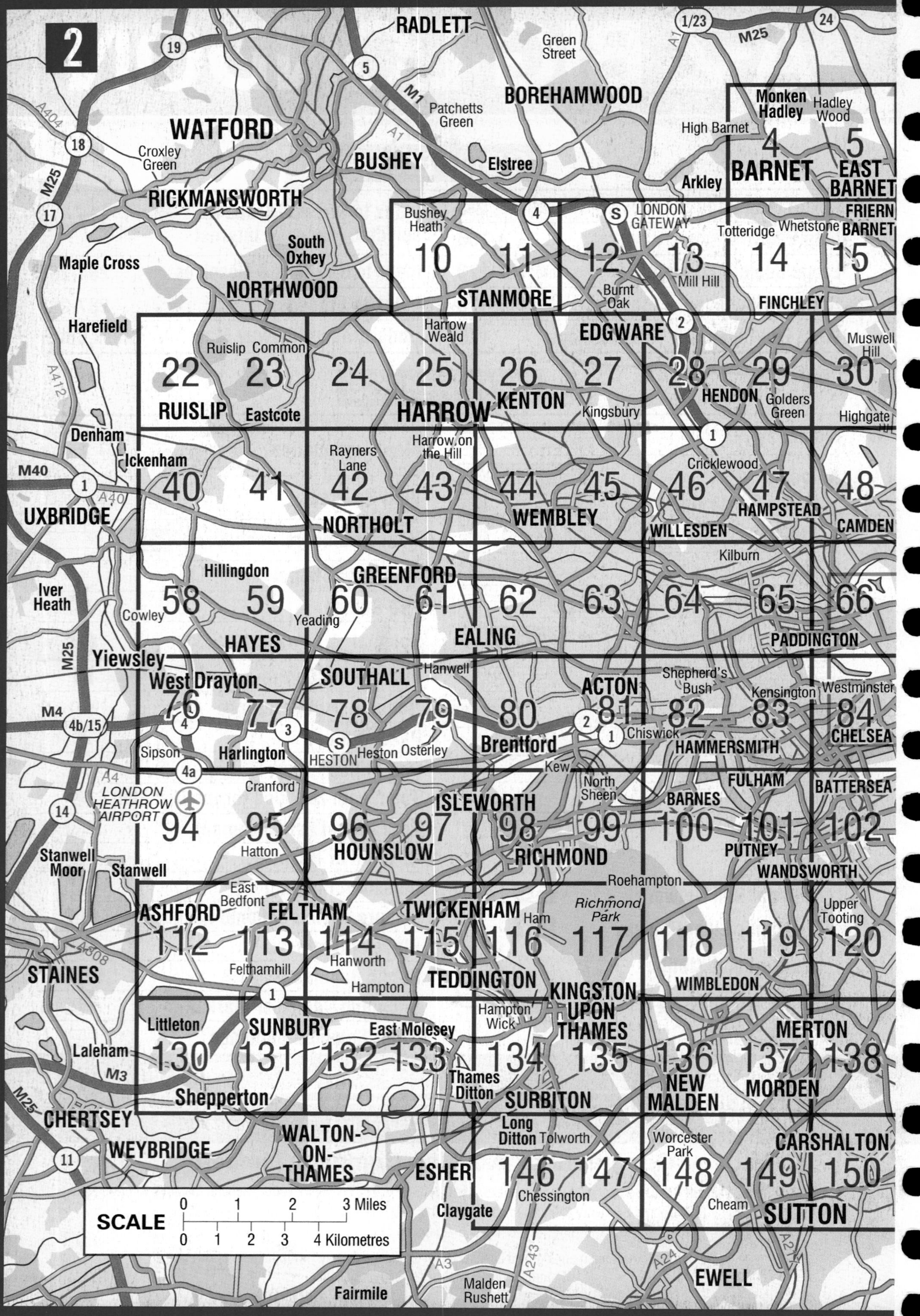

RADLETT
Green Street
BOREHAMWOOD
WATFORD
Croxley Green
Patchetts Green
BUSHEY
Elstree
High Barnet
Monken Hadley
Hadley Wood
4
5
BARNET
EAST BARNET
Arkley
RICKMANSWORTH
Bushey Heath
LONDON GATEWAY
FRIERN BARNET
Totteridge
Whetstone
10
11
12
13
14
15
Maple Cross
South Oxhey
NORTHWOOD
STANMORE
Burnt Oak
Mill Hill
FINCHLEY
Harefield
Harrow Weald
EDGWARE
Muswell Hill
Ruislip Common
22
23
24
25
26
27
28
29
30
RUISLIP
Eastcote
HARROW
KENTON
Kingsbury
HENDON
Golders Green
Highgate
Denham
Rayners Lane
Harrow on the Hill
Ickenham
Cricklewood
40
41
42
43
44
45
46
47
48
UXBRIDGE
NORTHOLT
WEMBLEY
WILLESDEN
HAMPSTEAD
CAMDEN
Hillingdon
GREENFORD
Kilburn
Iver Heath
58
59
60
61
62
63
64
65
66
Cowley
Yeading
HAYES
EALING
PADDINGTON
Yiewsley
West Drayton
SOUTHALL
Hanwell
ACTON
Shepherd's Bush
Kensington
Westminster
76
77
78
79
80
81
82
83
84
CHELSEA
Chiswick
HAMMERSMITH
Sipson
Harlington
HESTON
Heston
Osterley
Brentford
Kew
North Sheen
FULHAM
BATTERSEA
Cranford
LONDON HEATHROW AIRPORT
ISLEWORTH
BARNES
94
95
96
97
98
99
100
101
102
Hatton
HOUNSLOW
RICHMOND
PUTNEY
Stanwell Moor
Stanwell
WANDSWORTH
Roehampton
East Bedfont
Richmond Park
Upper Tooting
ASHFORD
FELTHAM
TWICKENHAM
Ham
112
113
114
115
116
117
118
119
120
Hanworth
Felthamhill
STAINES
Hampton
TEDDINGTON
WIMBLEDON
KINGSTON UPON THAMES
Hampton Wick
Littleton
SUNBURY
East Molesey
MERTON
Laleham
130
131
132
133
134
135
136
137
138
Thames Ditton
NEW MALDEN
MORDEN
Shepperton
SURBITON
CHERTSEY
Long Ditton
Tolworth
Worcester Park
CARSHALTON
WEYBRIDGE
WALTON-ON-THAMES
ESHER
146
147
148
149
150
Chessington
Cheam
SUTTON
Claygate
EWELL
Fairmile
Malden Rushett
M1
M25
M4
M40
M3
A1
A404
A412
A40
A4
A308
A3
A243
A24
A2
1/23
24
19
18
17
14
11
4b/15
4a
S
SCALE
0 1 2 3 Miles
0 1 2 3 4 Kilometres

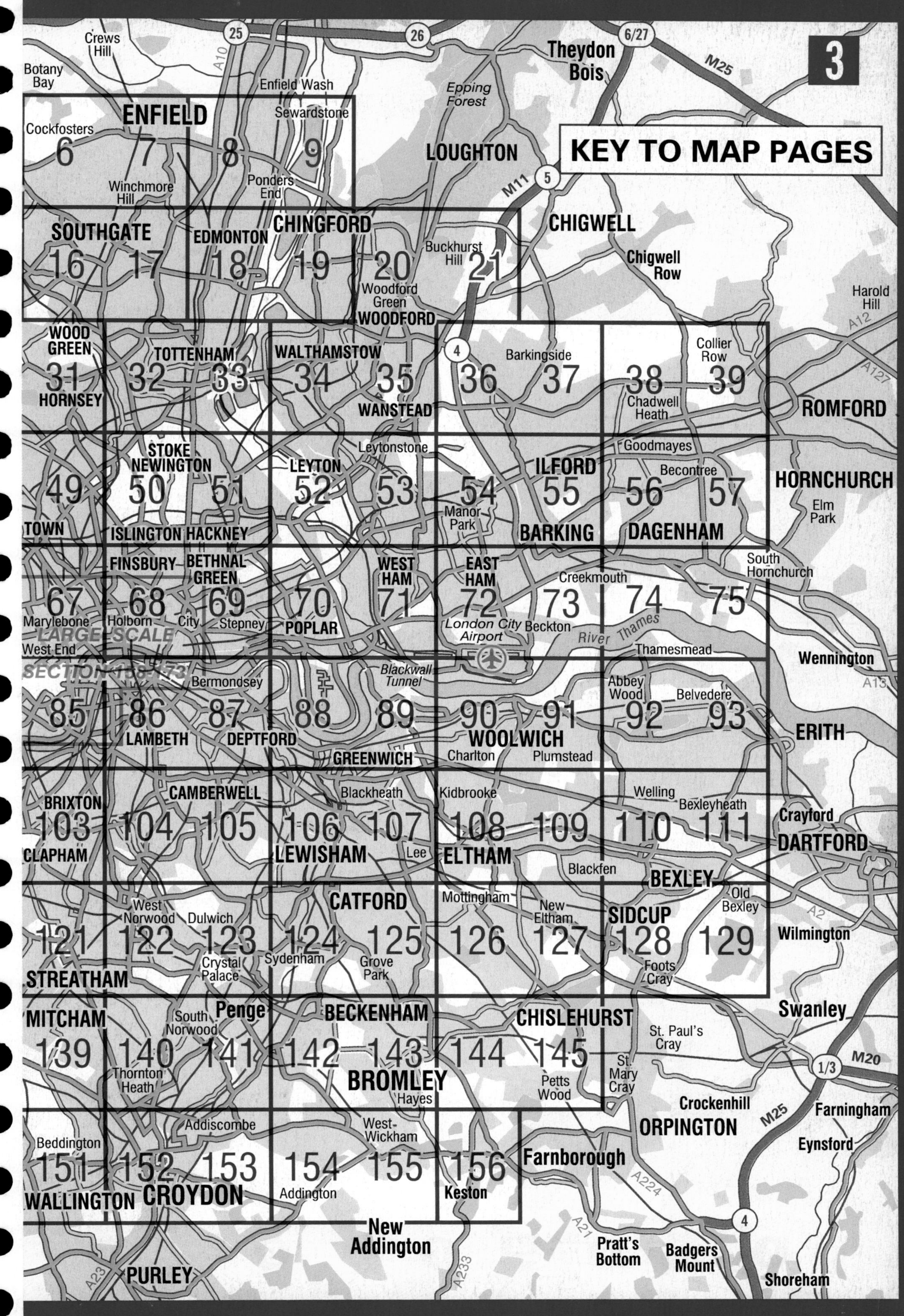

KEY TO MAP PAGES

3

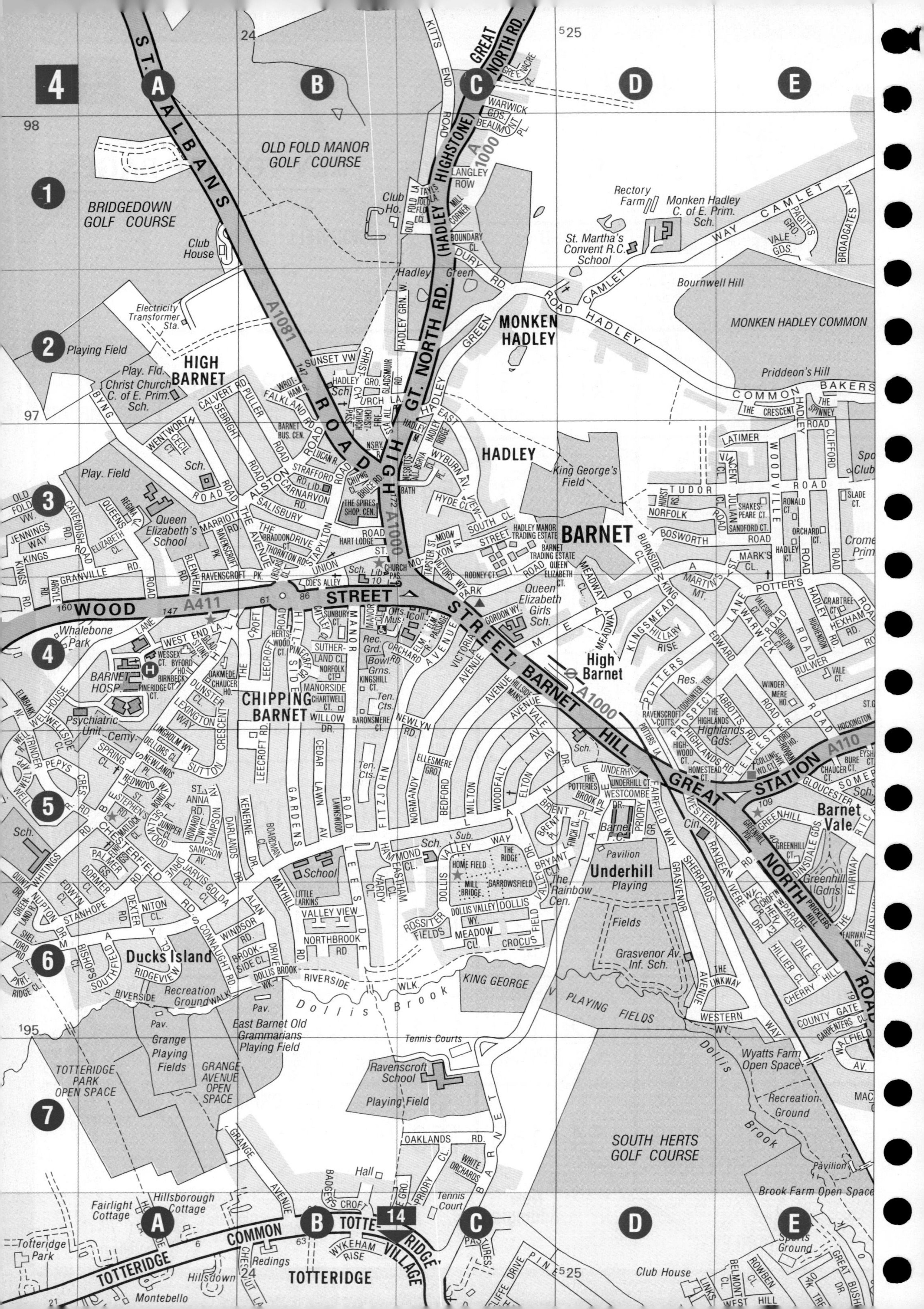

A
B
C
D
E
1
2
3
4
5
6
7
98
97
195
24
525
ST. ALBANS ROAD
A1081
GREAT NORTH RD.
GT. NORTH RD.
(HADLEY HIGHSTONE)
A1000
OLD FOLD MANOR GOLF COURSE
BRIDGEDOWN GOLF COURSE
Club House
Club Ho.
KITTS END ROAD
WARWICK GDS.
BEAUMONT PL.
LANGLEY ROW
MILL CORNER
BOUNDARY CL.
DURY RD.
Rectory Farm
Monken Hadley C. of E. Prim. Sch.
St. Martha's Convent R.C. School
CAMLET WAY
VALE GDS.
BROADGATES AV.
Bournwell Hill
MONKEN HADLEY COMMON
MONKEN HADLEY
HADLEY ROAD
Hadley Green
Electricity Transformer Sta.
Playing Field
Play. Fld.
HIGH BARNET
Christ Church C. of E. Prim. Sch.
SUNSET VW.
Priddeon's Hill
COMMON
BAKERS
THE CRESCENT
THE SPINNEY
HADLEY ROAD
LATIMER
CLIFFORD
Spo Club
HADLEY
King George's Field
Play. Field
Queen Elizabeth's School
OLD FOLD VW.
JENNINGS WAY
KINGS RD.
CAVENDISH ROAD
QUEENS
ELIZABETH CL.
CALVERT RD.
SEBRIGHT
PULLER
WENTWORTH
CECIL
STRAFFORD RD.
CARNARVON RD.
ALSTON ROAD
SALISBURY
BARNET BUS. CEN.
THE SPIRES SHOP. CEN.
HYDE CL.
VIEW
SOUTH CL.
HADLEY MANOR TRADING ESTATE
BARNET
BARNET TRADING ESTATE
TUDOR
NORFOLK
BOSWORTH
ROAD
MARK'S CL.
BURNSIDE CL.
POTTER'S
Crome Prim
GRANVILLE RD.
RAVENSCROFT PK.
BLENHEIM
WOOD STREET
A411
STREET
HIGH STREET
BARNET HILL
A1000
Whalebone Park
WEST END LA.
BARNET HOSP.
Psychiatric Unit
Cemy.
CHIPPING BARNET
Queen Elizabeth Girls Sch.
High Barnet
MEADWAY
KINGSMEAD
HILLARY RISE
Res.
Highlands Gds.
GREAT NORTH ROAD
STATION
A110
Barnet Vale
GREENHILL
Greenhill Gdns.
LEECROFT RD.
CEDAR LAWN AV.
FITZJOHN AV.
NORMANDY AV.
BEDFORD
MILTON
WOODFALL
ELTON
WESTCOMBE DR.
Barnet F.C.
Pavilion
Underhill
Playing Fields
Grasvenor Av. Inf. Sch.
PLAYING FIELDS
SHERRARDS WAY
WESTERN WAY
School
Sch.
DOLLIS VALLEY WAY
HOME FIELD
The Rainbow Cen.
VALLEY VIEW
NORTHBROOK RD
ROSSITER FIELDS
MEADOW CL.
CROCUS
Ducks Island
RIDGEVIEW
Recreation Ground
RIVERSIDE WALK
Dollis Brook
KING GEORGE
East Barnet Old Grammarians Playing Field
Pav.
Grange Playing Fields
TOTTERIDGE PARK OPEN SPACE
GRANGE AVENUE OPEN SPACE
Tennis Courts
Ravenscroft School
Playing Field
OAKLANDS RD.
Hall
Tennis Court
SOUTH HERTS GOLF COURSE
Wyatts Farm Open Space
Recreation Ground
Pavilion
Brook Farm Open Space
Fairlight Cottage
Hillsborough Cottage
Totteridge Park
TOTTERIDGE COMMON
Redings
Hillsdown
Montebello
14
TOTTERIDGE VILLAGE
WYKEHAM RISE
TOTTERIDGE
Club House
Sports Ground

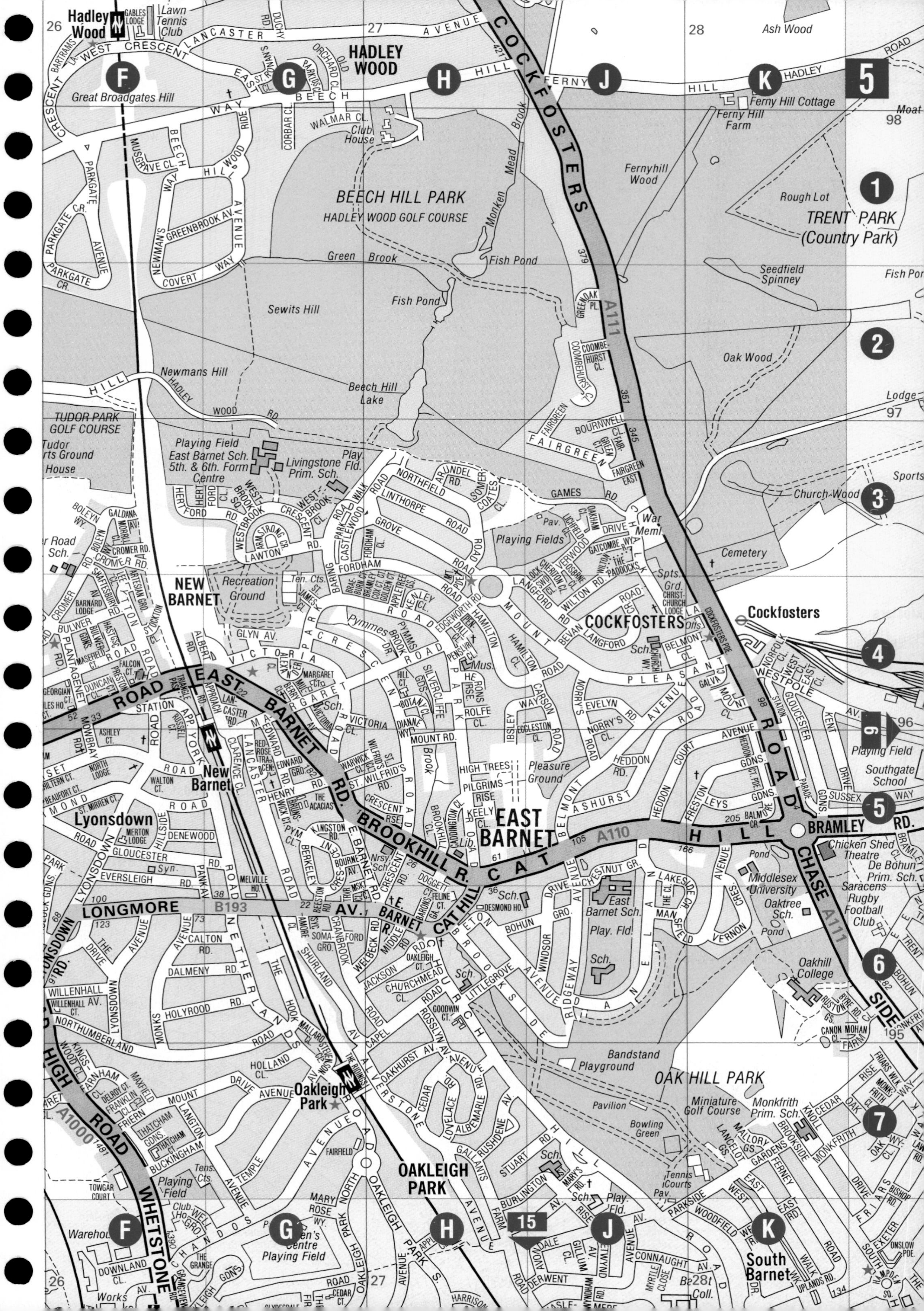

HADLEY WOOD
BEECH HILL PARK
HADLEY WOOD GOLF COURSE
TRENT PARK
(Country Park)
NEW BARNET
COCKFOSTERS
EAST BARNET
Lyonsdown
OAK HILL PARK
OAKLEIGH PARK
South Barnet

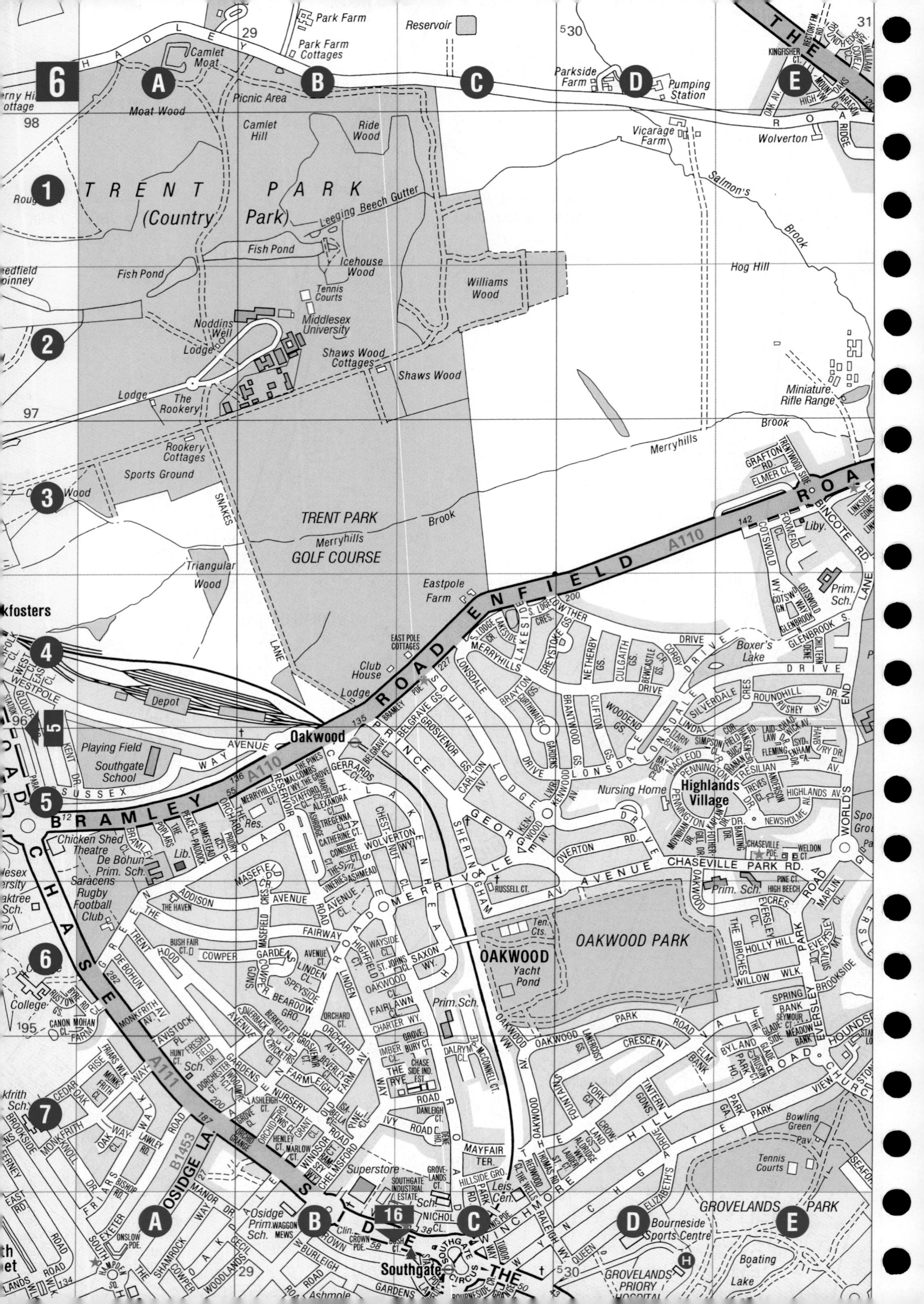
TRENT PARK (Country Park)
Camlet Moat
Moat Wood
Picnic Area
Camlet Hill
Ride Wood
Park Farm
Park Farm Cottages
Reservoir
Parkside Farm
Pumping Station
Vicarage Farm
Wolverton
Leeging Beech Gutter
Fish Pond
Icehouse Wood
Tennis Courts
Williams Wood
Middlesex University
Noddins Well
Lodge
Shaws Wood Cottages
Shaws Wood
The Rookery
Rookery Cottages
Sports Ground
Salmon's Brook
Hog Hill
Miniature Rifle Range
Merryhills Brook
TRENT PARK GOLF COURSE
Triangular Wood
Eastpole Farm
East Pole Cottages
Club House
Depot
Oakwood
Playing Field
Southgate School
ENFIELD ROAD A110
BRAMLEY ROAD
CHASE SIDE A111
Chicken Shed Theatre
De Bohun Prim. Sch.
Saracens Rugby Football Club
Highlands Village
Nursing Home
Boxer's Lake
OAKWOOD PARK
OAKWOOD
Yacht Pond
Prim. Sch.
Superstore
Southgate Industrial Estate
Osidge Prim. Sch.
Southgate
Bourneside Sports Centre
GROVELANDS PARK
GROVELANDS PRIORY HOSPITAL
Boating Lake
Bowling Green
Tennis Courts
Pav.
Liby.
Prim. Sch.
College
Leis. Cen.

5
16

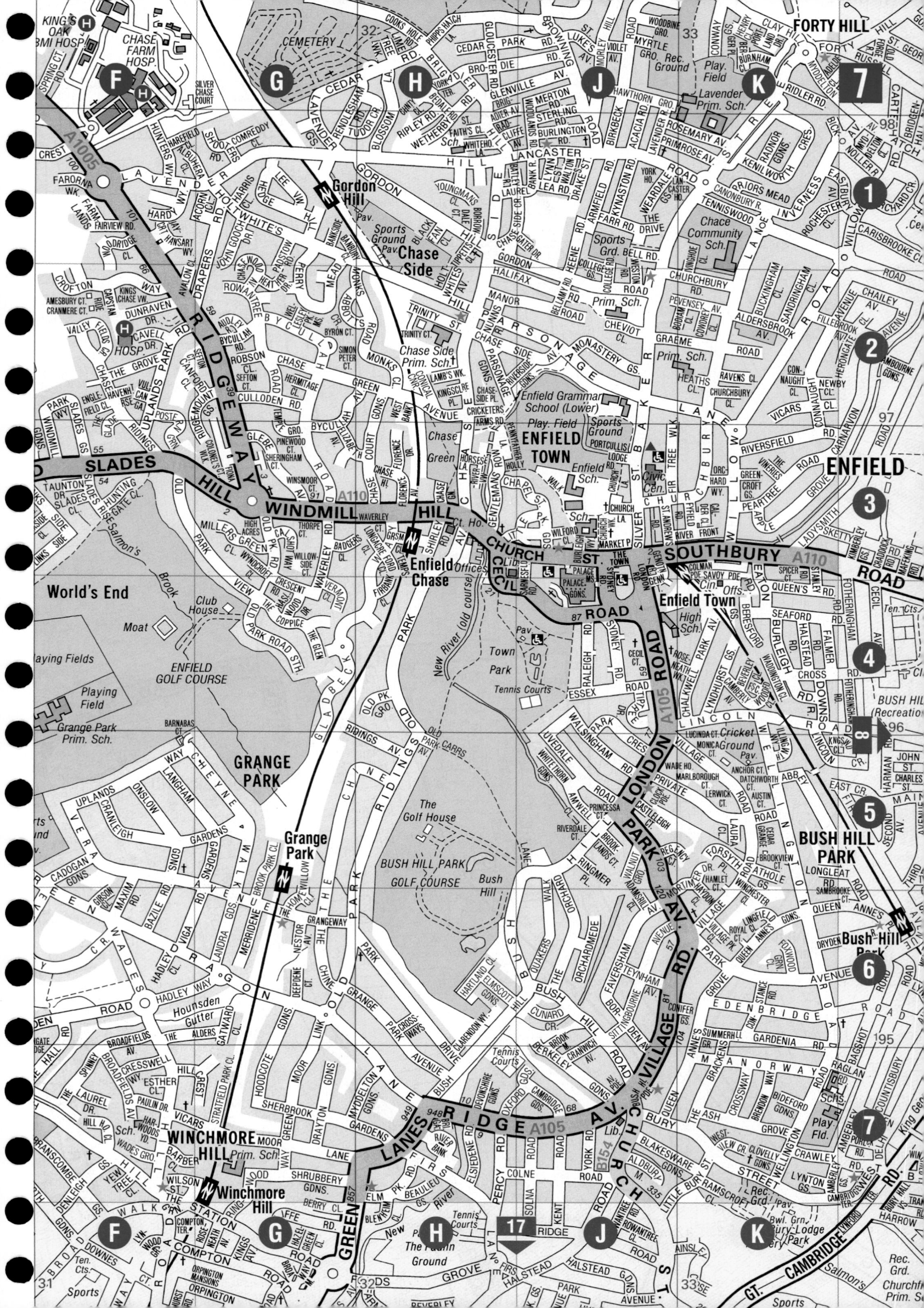

7
FORTY HILL
ENFIELD
ENFIELD TOWN
Enfield Town
Enfield Chase
Gordon Hill
Grange Park
Winchmore Hill
Bush Hill Park
BUSH HILL PARK
WINCHMORE HILL
GRANGE PARK
World's End
Chase Side
CHASE FARM HOSP.
KING'S OAK BMI HOSP.
CEMETERY
ENFIELD GOLF COURSE
BUSH HILL PARK GOLF COURSE
The Golf House
Town Park
Chase Green
Enfield Grammar School (Lower)
Chace Community Sch.
Lavender Prim. Sch.
Chase Side Prim. Sch.
Grange Park Prim. Sch.
Winchmore Hill Prim. Sch.
Civic Cen.
Cricket Ground
New River (old course)
Salmon's Brook
Moat
Playing Fields
Playing Field
RIDGEWAY
SLADES HILL
WINDMILL HILL
CHURCH ST.
CECIL ROAD
SOUTHBURY ROAD
LONDON ROAD
PARK AV.
VILLAGE RD.
RIDGE AV.
GREEN LANES
LANCASTER RD.
BAKER ST.
CHASE SIDE
GORDON HILL
PARSONAGE LA.
CHURCHBURY LA.
LINCOLN RD.
OLD PARK RIDINGS
DRAGON RD.
BUSH HILL
CHURCH ST.
GT. CAMBRIDGE RD.
A1005
A110
A105
B154
17
8
96
97
98
195
1
2
3
4
5
6
7
F
G
H
J
K
31
32
33

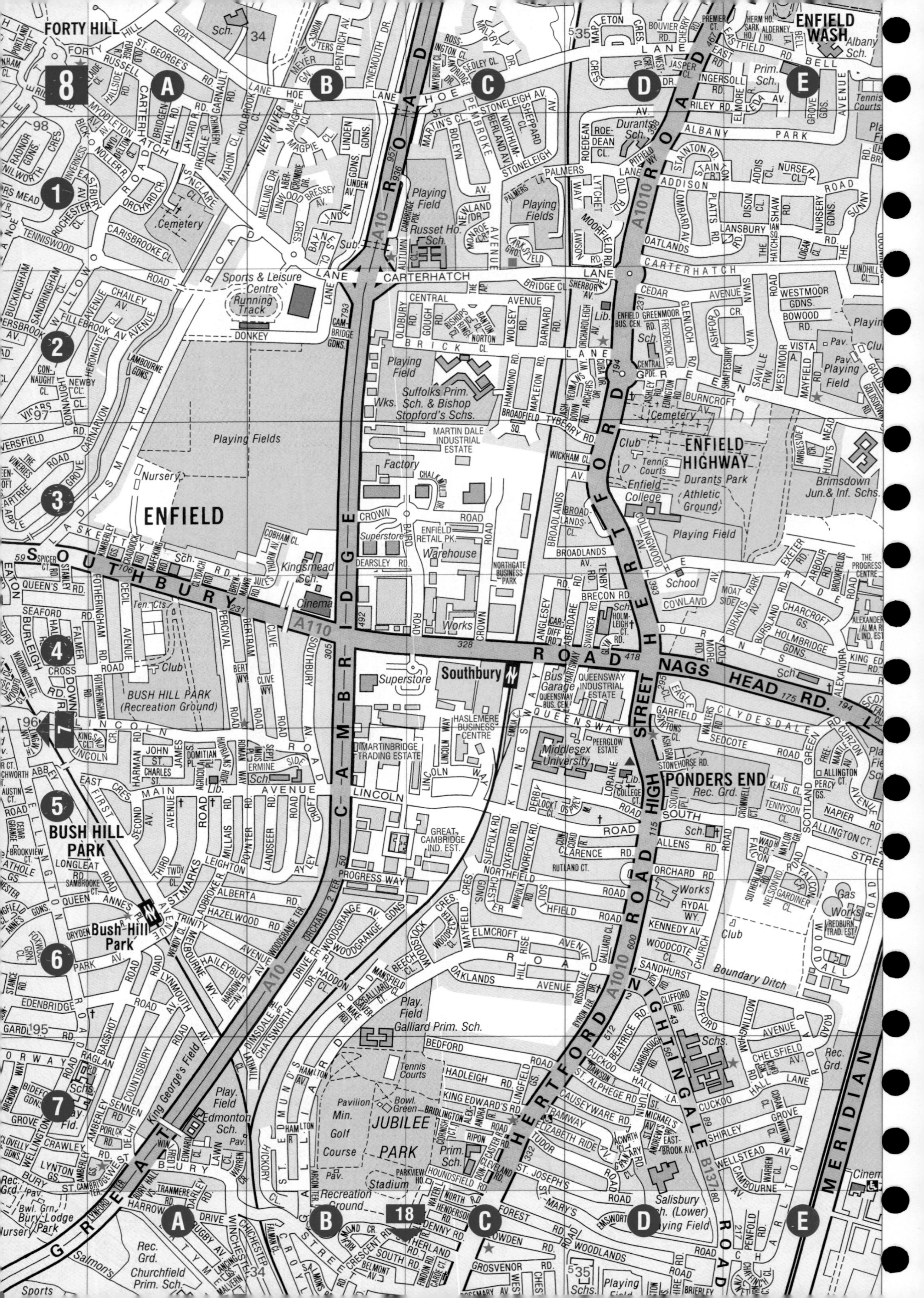

8
FORTY HILL
ENFIELD WASH
ENFIELD
ENFIELD HIGHWAY
PONDERS END
BUSH HILL PARK
Bush Hill Park
JUBILEE PARK
Southbury
SOUTHBURY ROAD
A110
A10
A1010
GREAT CAMBRIDGE ROAD
HERTFORD ROAD
HIGH STREET
NAGS HEAD RD.
CARTERHATCH LANE
HOE LANE
BULLSMOOR LANE
NIGHTINGALE ROAD
MERIDIAN
LINCOLN ROAD
QUEENSWAY
Middlesex University
Sports & Leisure Centre
Running Track
Playing Fields
Cemetery
Durants Park
Enfield College
Brimsdown Jun.& Inf. Schs.
MARTIN DALE INDUSTRIAL ESTATE
ENFIELD RETAIL PK.
NORTHGATE BUSINESS PARK
HASLEMERE BUSINESS CENTRE
MARTINBRIDGE TRADING ESTATE
GREAT CAMBRIDGE IND. EST.
QUEENSWAY INDUSTRIAL ESTATE
BUSH HILL PARK (Recreation Ground)
Suffolks Prim. Sch. & Bishop Stopford's Schs.
Galliard Prim. Sch.
Edmonton Sch.
Salisbury Sch. (Lower)
Boundary Ditch
7
18
34
535
A B C D E
1 2 3 4 5 6 7

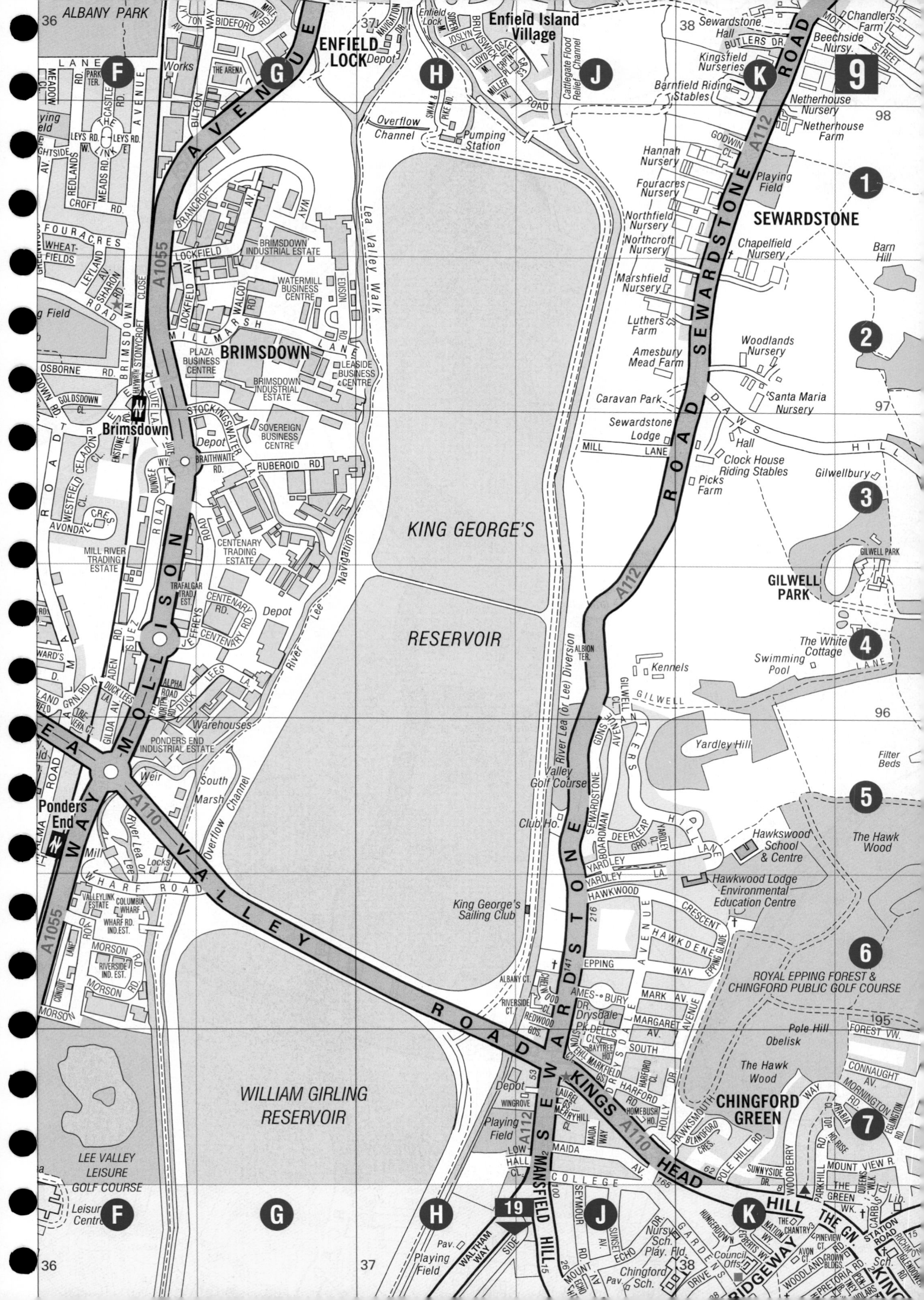

9
ALBANY PARK
ENFIELD LOCK
Enfield Island Village
Depot
Cattlegate Flood Relief Channel
Sewardstone Hall
BUTLERS DR.
Chandlers Farm
Beechside Nursy.
MOTT STREET
Kingsfield Nurseries
Barnfield Riding Stables
Netherhouse Nursery
Netherhouse Farm
GODWIN CL.
Hannah Nursery
Fouracres Nursery
Playing Field
Northfield Nursery
Northcroft Nursery
Chapelfield Nursery
SEWARDSTONE
Barn Hill
Marshfield Nursery
Luthers Farm
Amesbury Mead Farm
Woodlands Nursery
Caravan Park
Santa Maria Nursery
Sewardstone Lodge
DAWS HILL
Hall
MILL LANE
Clock House Riding Stables
Gilwellbury
Picks Farm
GILWELL PARK
The White Cottage
Swimming Pool
Kennels
GILWELL LANE
Yardley Hill
Filter Beds
The Hawk Wood
Hawkswood School & Centre
Hawkwood Lodge Environmental Education Centre
ROYAL EPPING FOREST & CHINGFORD PUBLIC GOLF COURSE
Pole Hill Obelisk
The Hawk Wood
CHINGFORD GREEN
FOREST VW.
CONNAUGHT AV.
MORNINGTON RD.
KING GEORGE'S
RESERVOIR
King George's Sailing Club
Valley Golf Course
Club Ho.
River Lea (or Lee) Diversion
Overflow Channel
Pumping Station
Lea Valley Walk
River Lee Navigation
SEWARDSTONE ROAD
A112
A1055
MOLLISON AVENUE
BRIMSDOWN
Brimsdown
BRIMSDOWN INDUSTRIAL ESTATE
WATERMILL BUSINESS CENTRE
PLAZA BUSINESS CENTRE
LEASIDE BUSINESS CENTRE
SOVEREIGN BUSINESS CENTRE
CENTENARY TRADING ESTATE
TRAFALGAR TRAD. EST.
MILL RIVER TRADING ESTATE
PONDERS END INDUSTRIAL ESTATE
Warehouses
Depot
Works
MILLMARSH LANE
RUBEROID RD.
LOCKFIELD AV.
OSBORNE RD.
FOURACRES
CROFT RD.
Ponders End
South Marsh
Weir
Locks
Mill
WHARF ROAD
VALLEYLINK ESTATE
COLUMBIA WHARF
WHARF RD. IND.EST.
RIVERSIDE IND. EST.
MORSON RD.
A110
LEA VALLEY ROAD
KINGS HEAD HILL
WILLIAM GIRLING RESERVOIR
LEE VALLEY LEISURE GOLF COURSE
Leisure Centre
MANSFIELD HILL
WALTHAM WAY
Playing Field
Depot
COLLEGE
Nursy. Sch.
Play. Fld.
Chingford Sch.
Council Offs.
RIDGEWAY
STATION ROAD
F G H J K
1 2 3 4 5 6 7
36 37 38
98 97 96 195
19

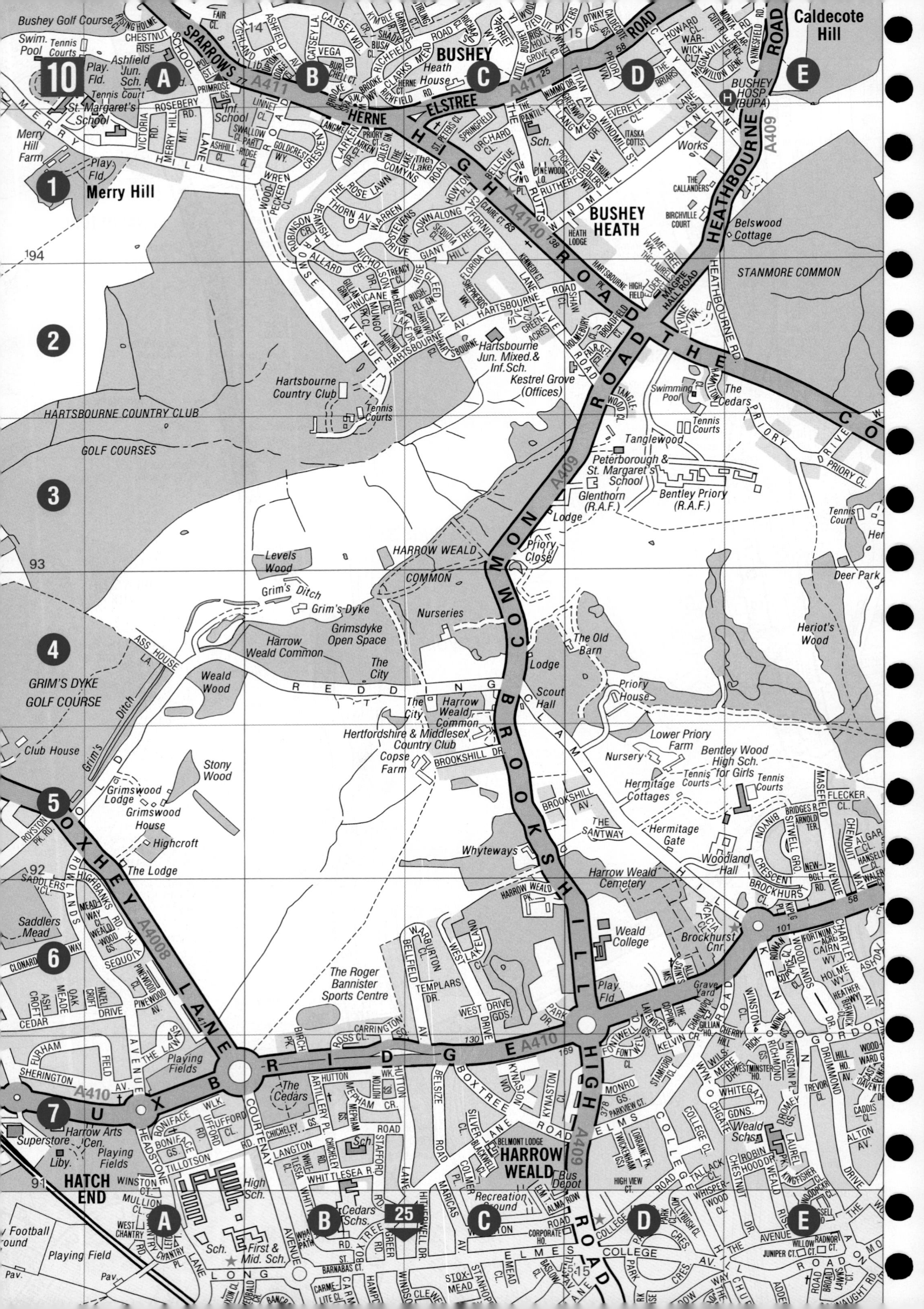

10
Bushey Golf Course
Swim. Pool
Tennis Courts
Play. Fld.
Ashfield Jun. Sch.
Tennis Court
St. Margaret's School
Merry Hill Farm
Merry Hill
CHESTNUT RISE
SCHOOL
ROSEBERY RD.
VICTORIA RD.
MERRY HILL MT.
MERRY HILL
PRIMROSE GS.
Inf. School
SPARROWS
A411
HERNE
ELSTREE
HIGH ROAD
BUSHEY
Heath House
CATSEY LA.
CATSEY WD.
VEGA RD.
ASHFIELD AV.
RICHFIELD
CLARKS MEAD
PRIORY VW.
CLAY LANE
HOWARD CL.
THE BRIARS
EVERETT CL.
WINDMILL ST.
ITASKA COTTS.
Works
BUSHEY HOSP. (BUPA)
Caldecote Hill
HEATHBOURNE ROAD
A409
THE CALLANDERS
BIRCHVILLE COURT
BUSHEY HEATH
HEATH LODGE
Belswood Cottage
STANMORE COMMON
A4140
ROSE LAWN
THORN AV.
WARREN
ALLARD CR.
NICHOLSON DR.
FINUCANE
HARTSBOURNE AV.
Hartsbourne Jun. Mixed & Inf. Sch.
Kestrel Grove (Offices)
Hartsbourne Country Club
Tennis Courts
HARTSBOURNE COUNTRY CLUB
GOLF COURSES
COMMON ROAD
THE COMMON
Swimming Pool
The Cedars
Tennis Courts
Tanglewood
Peterborough & St. Margaret's School
Bentley Priory (R.A.F.)
Glenthorn (R.A.F.)
Lodge
PRIORY DRIVE
PRIORY CL.
Tennis Court
Priory Close
HARROW WEALD
COMMON
Levels Wood
Grim's Ditch
Grim's Dyke
Grimsdyke Open Space
Nurseries
Harrow Weald Common
The City
The Old Barn
Lodge
Deer Park
Heriot's Wood
GRIM'S DYKE GOLF COURSE
ASS HOUSE LA.
Weald Wood
REDDING
Scout Hall
Priory House
CLAMP HILL
Harrow Weald Common
Hertfordshire & Middlesex Country Club
Copse Farm
BROOKSHILL DR.
BROOKSHILL
Lower Priory Farm
Bentley Wood High Sch. for Girls
Nursery
Tennis Courts
Hermitage Cottages
Club House
Stony Wood
Grimswood Lodge
Grimswood House
Highcroft
The Lodge
OXHEY LANE
A4008
BROOKSHILL AV.
THE SANTWAY
Hermitage Gate
Whyteways
Woodland Hall
Harrow Weald Cemetery
HARROW WEALD PK.
Weald College
Brockhurst Cnr.
Saddlers Mead
SEQUOIA PK.
The Roger Bannister Sports Centre
TEMPLARS DR.
WEST DRIVE GDS.
Play. Fld.
Grave Yard
KENTON LANE
GORDON AV.
A410
UXBRIDGE RD.
HIGH ROAD
CEDAR DRIVE
Playing Fields
The Cedars
SHERINGTON AV.
Superstore
Harrow Arts Cen.
Playing Fields
Liby.
HATCH END
High Sch.
Sch.
First & Mid. Sch.
Cedars Schs.
25
BELMONT LODGE
HARROW WEALD
Bus Depot
Recreation Ground
ELMS ROAD
COLLEGE AV.
Weald Schs.
Football Ground
Playing Field
LONG ELMES

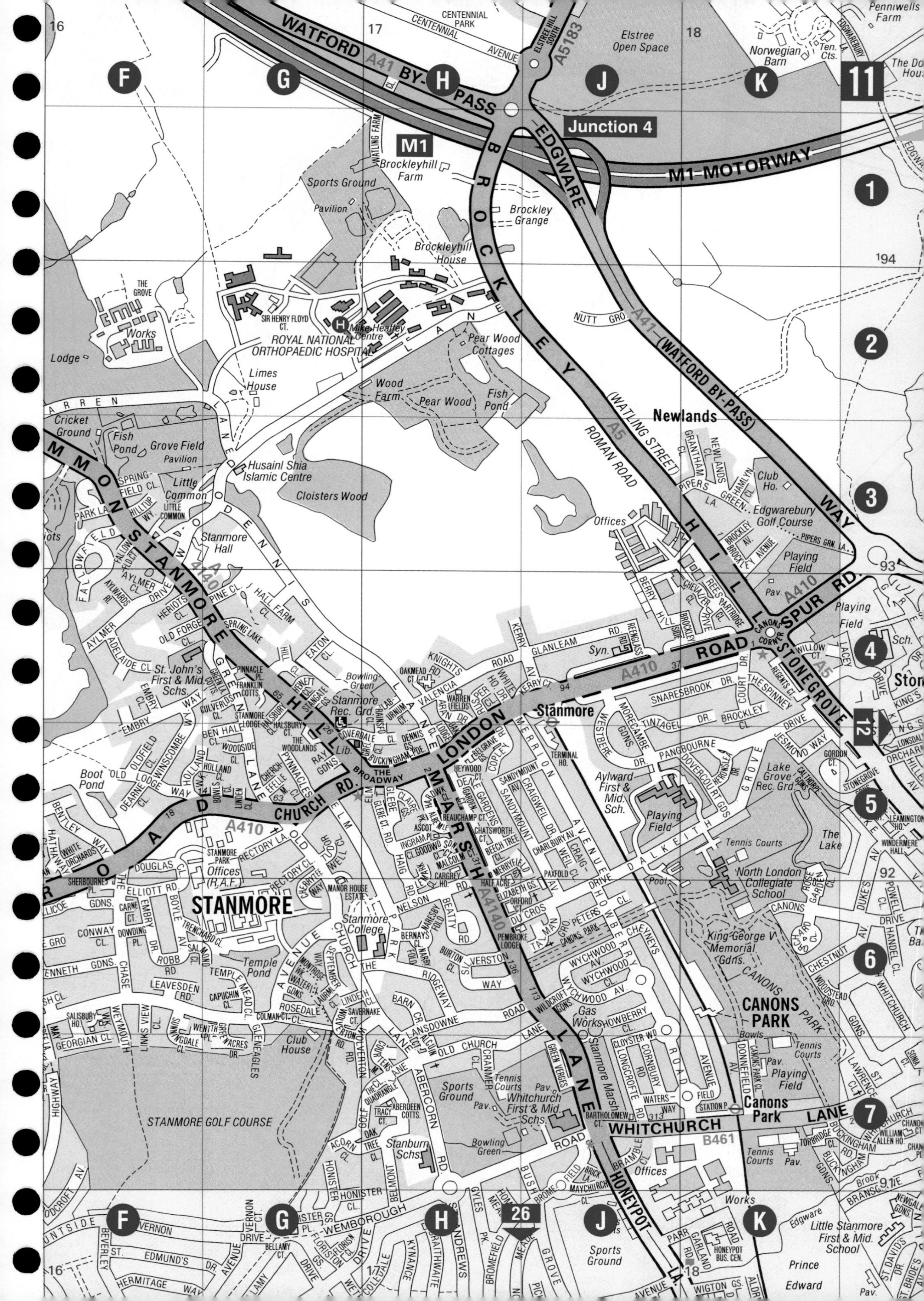
WATFORD BY-PASS
A41
Junction 4
M1
M1-MOTORWAY
EDGWARE
A5183
Elstree Open Space
Norwegian Barn
Penniwells Farm
Brockleyhill Farm
Sports Ground
Pavilion
Brockley Grange
Brockleyhill House
BROCKLEY HILL
ROYAL NATIONAL ORTHOPAEDIC HOSPITAL
Works
Lodge
Limes House
Pear Wood Cottages
Wood Farm
Pear Wood
Fish Pond
Cricket Ground
Grove Field
Little Common
Husaini Shia Islamic Centre
Cloisters Wood
Stanmore Hall
A41 (WATFORD BY-PASS)
(WATLING STREET)
A5 ROMAN ROAD
Newlands
Club Ho.
Edgwarebury Golf Course
Offices
Playing Field
SPUR RD.
A410
STONEGROVE
LONDON ROAD
Stanmore
STANMORE HILL
A4140
St. John's First & Mid. Schs.
Stanmore Rec. Grd.
THE BROADWAY
CHURCH RD.
MARSH
Boot Pond
Aylward First & Mid. Sch.
Lake Grove Rec. Grd.
The Lake
North London Collegiate School
STANMORE
Stanmore College
Temple Pond
King George V Memorial Gdns.
CANONS PARK
Gas Works
Club House
STANMORE GOLF COURSE
Sports Ground
Whitchurch First & Mid. Schs.
Stanmore Marsh
Canons Park
WHITCHURCH LANE
B461
HONEYPOT
Stanburn Schs.
Tennis Courts
Little Stanmore First & Mid. School
Sports Ground
Prince Edward
26
12
F G H J K
1 2 3 4 5 6 7
16 17 18
194 93 92 91

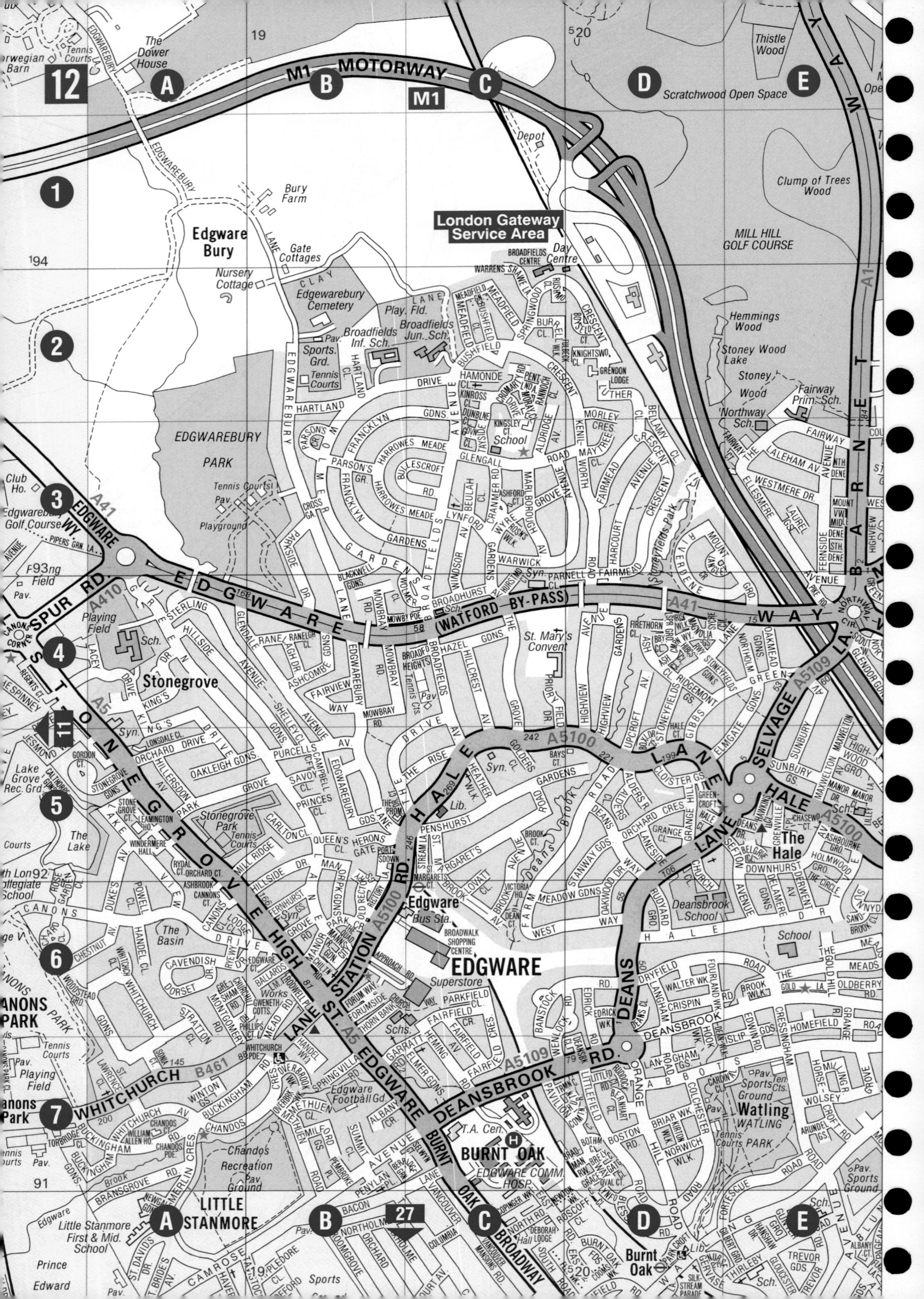
12
M1 MOTORWAY
M1
Scratchwood Open Space
Thistle Wood
The Dower House
Clump of Trees Wood
London Gateway Service Area
Edgware Bury
Bury Farm
MILL HILL GOLF COURSE
Edgwarebury Cemetery
Hemmings Wood
Stoney Wood Lake
EDGWAREBURY PARK
A41
EDGWARE WAY (WATFORD BY-PASS)
A410 SPUR RD.
Stonegrove
St. Mary's Convent
A5100
A5109
SELVAGE LA
The Hale
Stonegrove Park
EDGWARE
Superstore
Edgware Bus Sta.
Deansbrook School
WHITCHURCH LA
B461
EDGWARE RD.
DEANSBROOK RD.
BURNT OAK
EDGWARE COMM. HOSP.
Watling
Chandos Recreation Ground
LITTLE STANMORE
Little Stanmore First & Mid. School
Canons Park
Burnt Oak
BURNT OAK BROADWAY
11
27

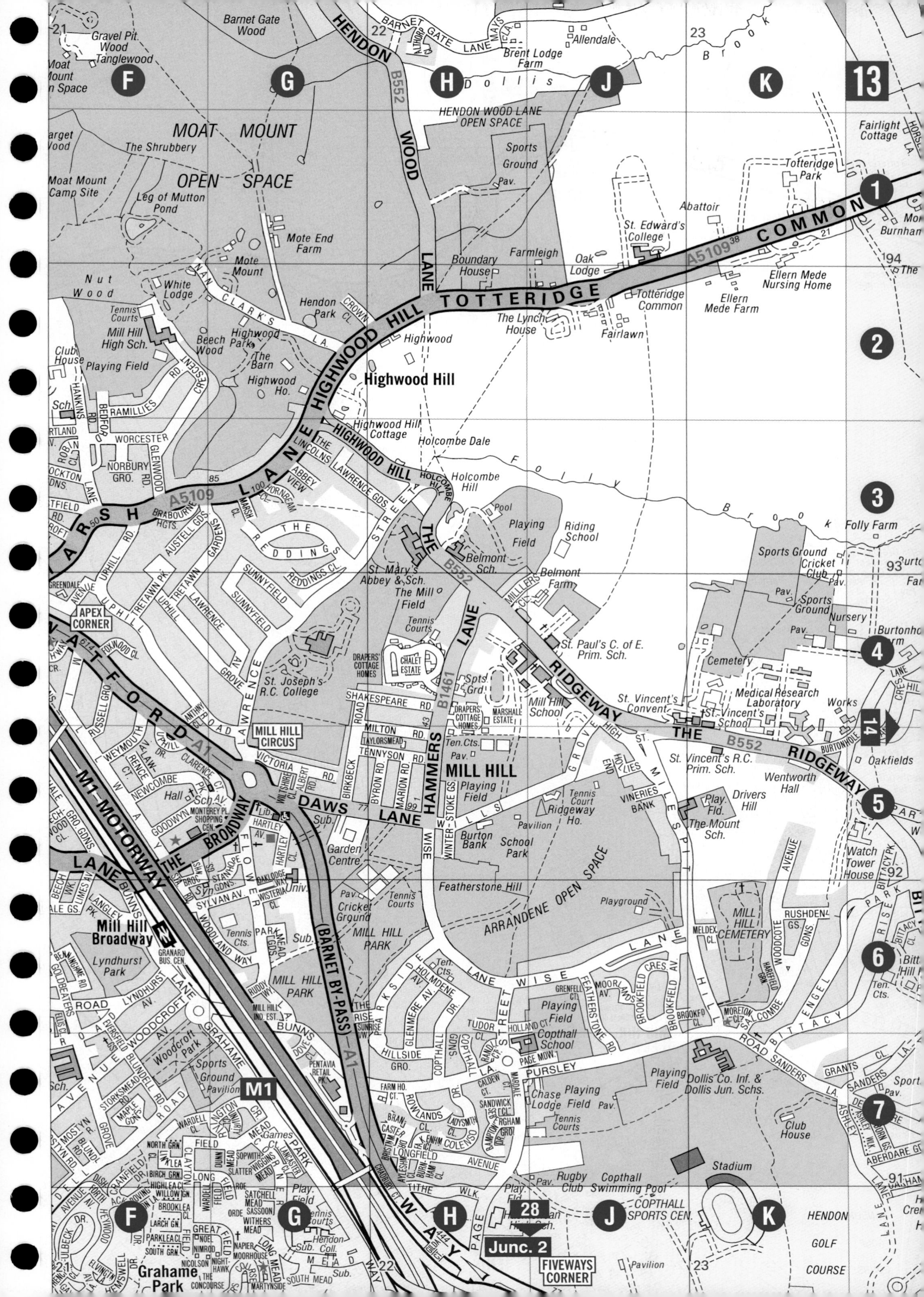
13
F
G
H
J
K
1
2
3
4
5
6
7
14
28
M1
Junc. 2
Gravel Pit Wood
Tanglewood
Barnet Gate Wood
Moat Mount Open Space
HENDON WOOD LANE
B552
BARNET GATE LANE
Brent Lodge Farm
Allendale
Dollis Brook
HENDON WOOD LANE OPEN SPACE
Sports Ground
Pav.
Fairlight Cottage
Totteridge Park
MOAT MOUNT OPEN SPACE
The Shrubbery
Moat Mount Camp Site
Leg of Mutton Pond
Mote End Farm
Mote Mount
Abattoir
St. Edward's College
TOTTERIDGE COMMON
A5109
Boundary House
Farmleigh
Oak Lodge
Ellern Mede Nursing Home
Ellern Mede Farm
Totteridge Common
The Lynch House
Fairlawn
Nut Wood
White Lodge
NAN CLARK'S LA.
Hendon Park
CROWN CL.
HIGHWOOD HILL
Highwood
Highwood Hill
Tennis Courts
Mill Hill High Sch.
Beech Wood
Highwood Park
The Barn
Highwood Ho.
Club House
Playing Field
RAMILLIES RD.
WORCESTER
NORBURY GRO.
GLENWOOD RD.
Highwood Hill Cottage
Holcombe Dale
Folly Brook
Holcombe Hill
HOLCOMBE HILL
THE LINCOLNS
LAWRENCE GDS.
ABBEY VIEW
MARSH LANE
HORNBEAM
THE REDDINGS
REDDINGS CL.
Playing Field
Riding School
Folly Farm
Sports Ground
Cricket Club
Pav.
Belmont Sch.
Belmont Farm
St. Mary's Abbey & Sch.
The Mill Field
THE RIDGEWAY
B552
Sports Ground
Nursery
Burtonhole Farm
AUSTELL GDS.
TRETAWN GDNS.
TRETAWN PK.
UPHILL RD.
LAWRENCE ST.
SUNNYFIELD
APEX CORNER
WATFORD WAY
A1
Tennis Courts
DRAPERS' COTTAGE HOMES
CHALET ESTATE
St. Paul's C. of E. Prim. Sch.
Cemetery
Medical Research Laboratory
Works
St. Joseph's R.C. College
SHAKESPEARE RD.
MILTON RD.
TAYLORSMEAD
TENNYSON RD.
B1461
HAMMERS LANE
Spts. Grd.
MARSHALL ESTATE
Mill Hill School
St. Vincent's Convent
St. Vincent's School
Oakfields
St. Vincent's R.C. Prim. Sch.
Wentworth Hall
Drivers Hill
MILL HILL CIRCUS
VICTORIA RD.
DAWS LANE
BIRKBECK RD.
BYRON RD.
MARION RD.
MILL HILL
Playing Field
Tennis Court
Ridgeway Ho.
VINERIES BANK
Play. Fld.
The Mount Sch.
Pavilion
Burton Bank
School Park
WISE LANE
Lib.
HARTLEY AV.
MONTEREY PL. SHOPPING CEN.
THE BROADWAY
M1 MOTORWAY
Hall
Sch.
Sub.
Garden Centre
ARRANDENE OPEN SPACE
Watch Tower House
Featherstone Hill
Playground
MILL HILL CEMETERY
Mill Hill Broadway
BUNNS LANE
SYLVAN AV.
Univ.
Pav.
Cricket Ground
Tennis Courts
WOODLAND WAY
Tennis Cts.
MILL HILL PARK
(BARNET BY-PASS)
Lyndhurst Park
GRANARD BUS. CEN.
Ten. Cts.
HOLMDENE AV.
PARKSIDE
GLENMERE AV.
FEATHERSTONE RD.
BROOKFIELD AV.
Playing Field
LYNDHURST AV.
WOODCROFT AV.
MILL HILL IND. EST.
Woodcroft Park
Sports Ground
Pavilion
GRAHAME PARK WAY
PENTAVIA RETAIL PK.
TUDOR CL.
HOLLAND CT.
Copthall School
HILLSIDE GRO.
PAGE MDW.
PURSLEY RD.
Playing Field
Dollis Co. Inf. & Dollis Jun. Schs.
BITTACY HILL
SANDERS LA.
Chase Lodge
Playing Field
Pav.
Tennis Courts
Club House
ROWLANDS
COLENSO DR.
LONGFIELD AV.
Stadium
ABERDARE GDNS.
Rugby Club
Copthall Swimming Pool
COPTHALL SPORTS CEN.
HENDON GOLF COURSE
Games Ct.
Play. Field
Tennis Courts
Hendon Sub. Coll.
SOUTH MEAD
Grahame Park
THE CONCOURSE
Pavilion
FIVEWAYS CORNER
Sub.
22
23
21
91
92
93
94

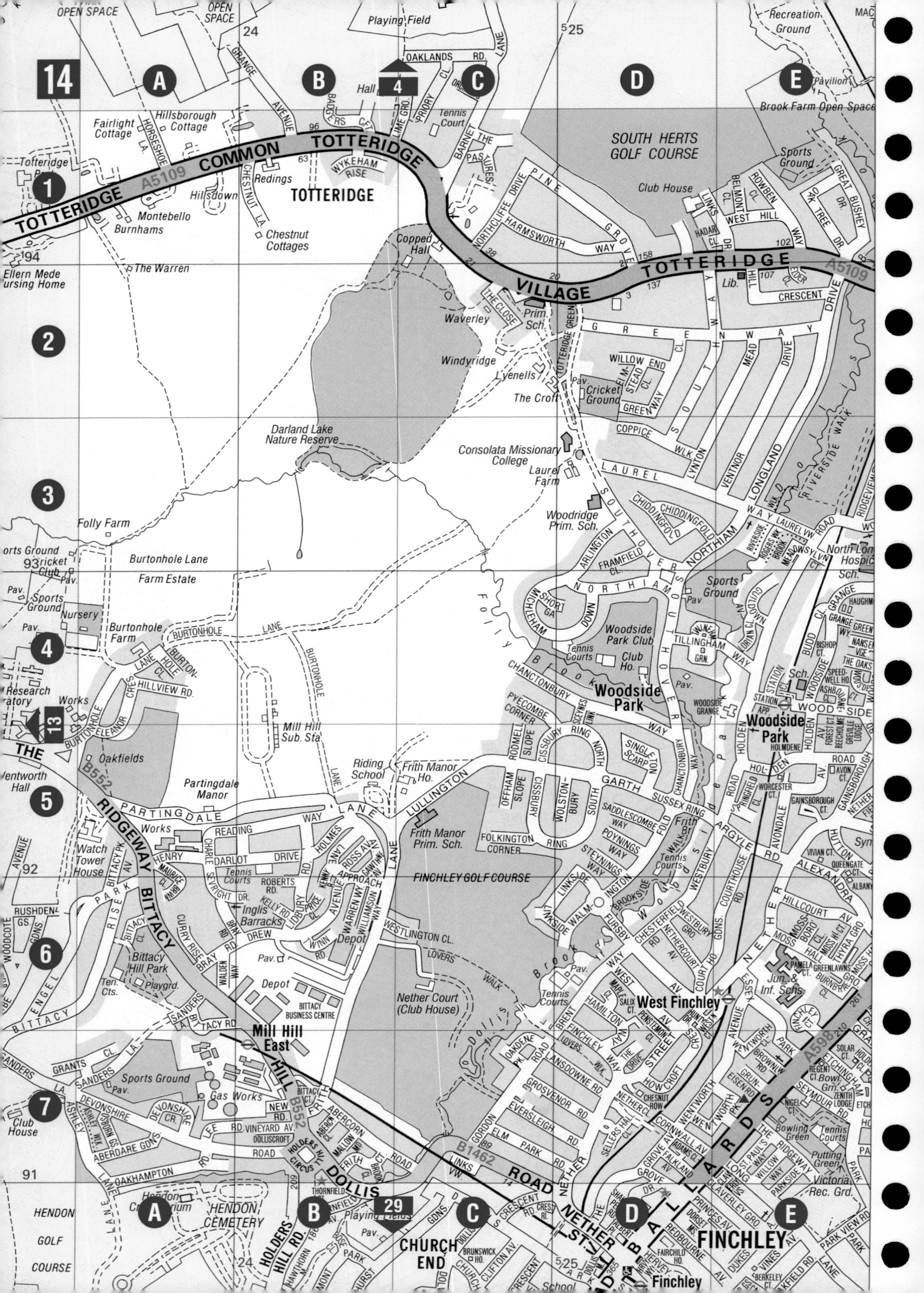

TOTTERIDGE COMMON
A5109
TOTTERIDGE
TOTTERIDGE VILLAGE
SOUTH HERTS GOLF COURSE
Club House
Brook Farm Open Space
Recreation Ground
Playing Field
Darland Lake Nature Reserve
Burtonhole Lane Farm Estate
Folly Farm
Burtonhole Farm
Copped Hall
Consolata Missionary College
Laurel Farm
Woodridge Prim. Sch.
Woodside Park Club
Woodside Park
Frith Manor Ho.
Riding School
Partingdale Manor
Oakfields
Mill Hill Sub. Sta.
Frith Manor Prim. Sch.
FINCHLEY GOLF COURSE
Nether Court (Club House)
Inglis Barracks
Bittacy Hill Park
Mill Hill East
Gas Works
Sports Ground
West Finchley
HENDON CEMETERY
HENDON GOLF COURSE
CHURCH END
FINCHLEY
Victoria Rec. Grd.
Finchley
BALLARDS
A598
B552
B1462
RIDGEWAY
BITTACY HILL
NETHER ST.
DOLLIS RD.
BALLARDS LA.
4
13
29

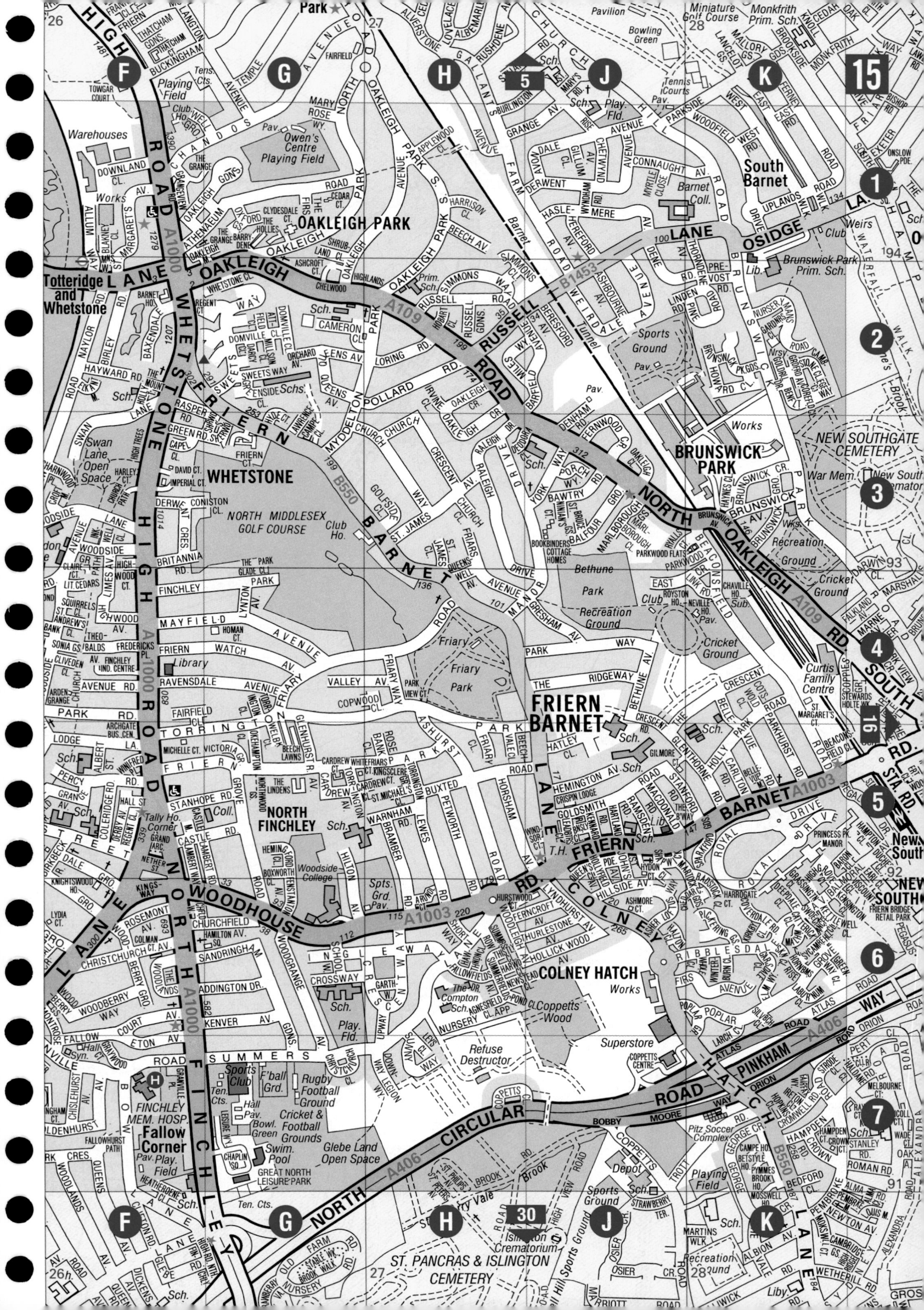

15
26
27
28
F
G
H
J
K
1
2
3
4
5
6
7
5
16
30
OAKLEIGH PARK
Totteridge and Whetstone
WHETSTONE
NORTH MIDDLESEX GOLF COURSE
South Barnet
Barnet Coll.
BRUNSWICK PARK
NEW SOUTHGATE CEMETERY
Brunswick Park Prim. Sch.
Bethune Park
Recreation Ground
Friary Park
FRIERN BARNET
NORTH FINCHLEY
Woodside College
Tally Ho. Corner
COLNEY HATCH
Coppetts Wood
Refuse Destructor
Superstore
FINCHLEY MEM. HOSP.
Fallow Corner
Glebe Land Open Space
GREAT NORTH LEISURE PARK
Owen's Centre Playing Field
Swan Lane Open Space
ST. PANCRAS & ISLINGTON CEMETERY
Islington Crematorium
Works
Warehouses
Playing Field
Sports Ground
Cricket Ground
Curtis Family Centre
OAKLEIGH ROAD NORTH
OAKLEIGH ROAD SOUTH
RUSSELL ROAD
FRIERN BARNET ROAD
FRIERN BARNET LANE
FRIERN BARNET RD.
COLNEY HATCH LANE
WOODHOUSE ROAD
HIGH ROAD
WHETSTONE HIGH ROAD
NORTH CIRCULAR ROAD
PINKHAM WAY
OSIDGE LANE
OAKLEIGH LANE
BRUNSWICK PARK
A1000
A109
A1003
A406
B550
B1453

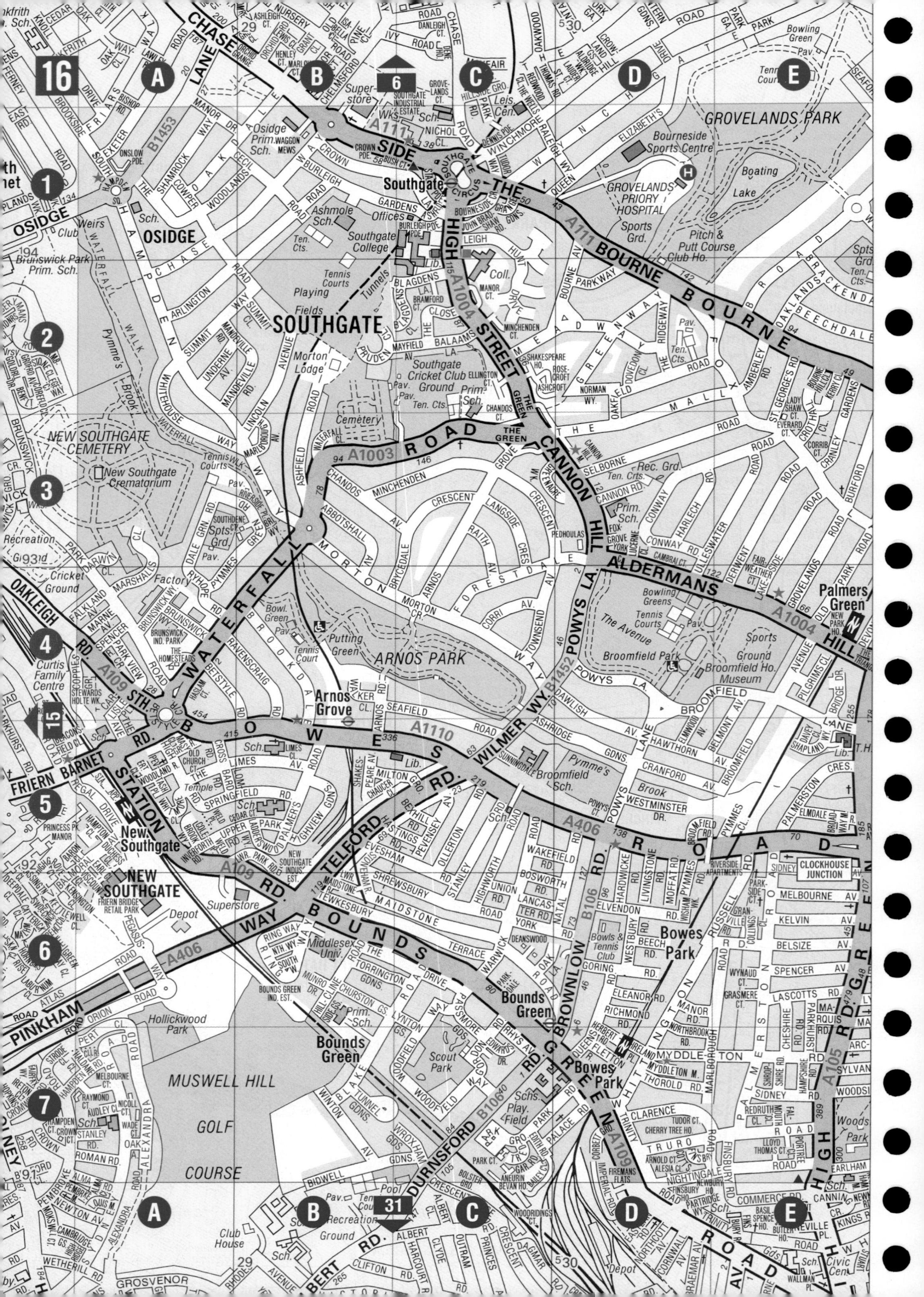

16
A
B
C
D
E
1
2
3
4
5
6
7
6
15
31
SOUTHGATE
Southgate
OSIDGE
NEW SOUTHGATE
New Southgate
Arnos Grove
ARNOS PARK
Bounds Green
Bowes Park
Palmers Green
GROVELANDS PARK
Boating Lake
GROVELANDS PRIORY HOSPITAL
Bourneside Sports Centre
Pitch & Putt Course
Southgate College
Southgate Cricket Club Ground
NEW SOUTHGATE CEMETERY
New Southgate Crematorium
Broomfield Park
Broomfield Ho. Museum
Pymme's Brook
Broomfield Sch.
Middlesex Univ.
Scout Park
MUSWELL HILL GOLF COURSE
Hollickwood Park
Curtis Family Centre
Cricket Ground
Recreation Ground
Brunswick Park Prim. Sch.
Superstore
FRIERN BRIDGE RETAIL PARK
BOUNDS GREEN IND. EST.
CLOCKHOUSE JUNCTION
CHASE SIDE
THE BOURNE
BOURNE HILL
HIGH STREET
CANNON HILL
ALDERMANS HILL
WATERFALL ROAD
BOWES ROAD
TELFORD RD.
BOUNDS GREEN RD.
PINKHAM WAY
FRIERN BARNET RD.
OAKLEIGH RD. STH.
STATION RD.
POWYS LA.
WILMER WY.
BROWNLOW RD.
DURNSFORD RD.
PYMMES RD.
GREEN LANES
HIGH RD.
SOUTHGATE CIRCUS
ARNOS RD.
BROOKDALE
A111
A1004
A1003
A1110
A109
A406
A105
B1453
B1452
B106

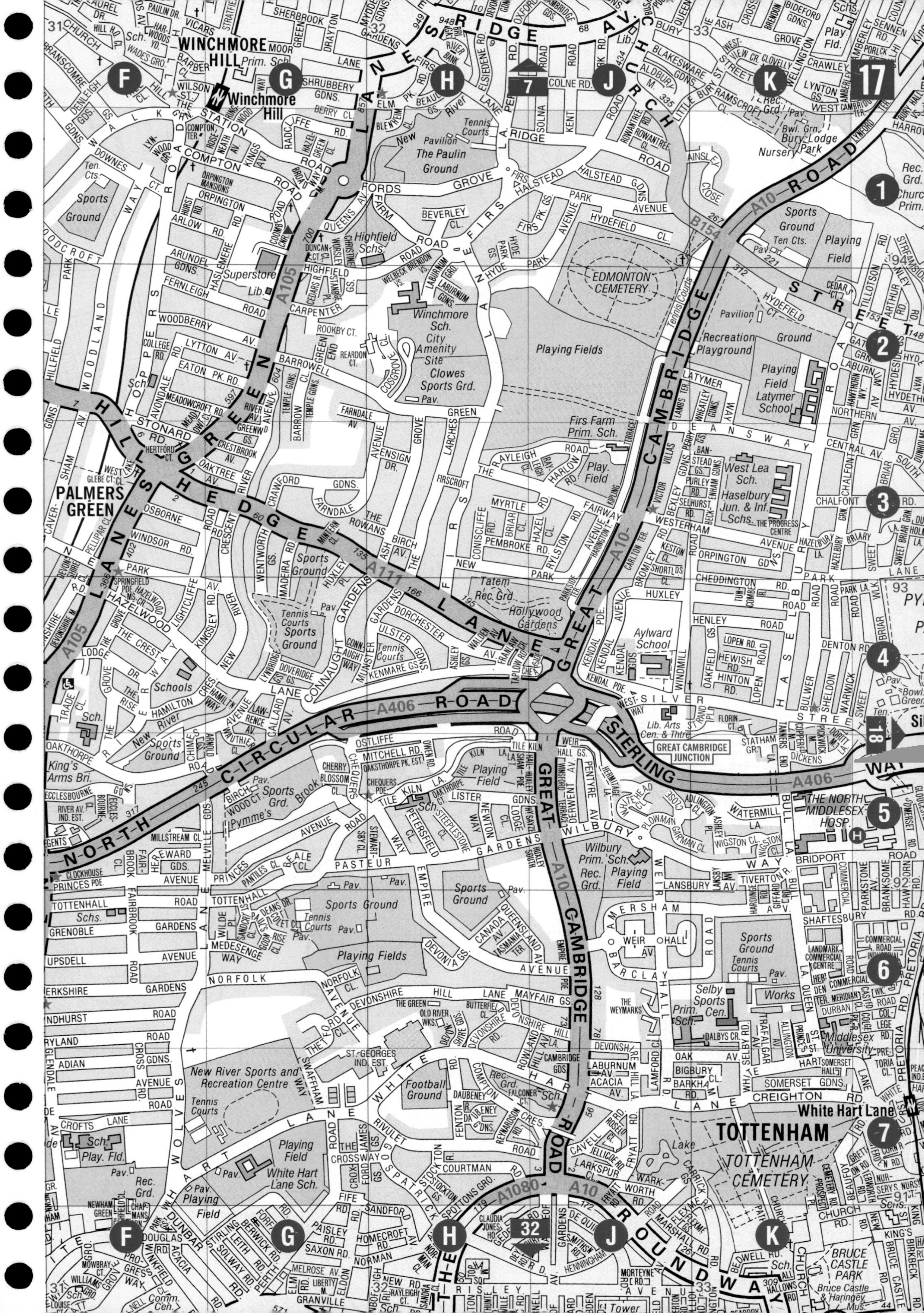

17
F
G
H
J
K
1
2
3
4
5
6
7
7
18
32
WINCHMORE HILL
Winchmore Hill
PALMERS GREEN
TOTTENHAM
White Hart Lane
RIDGE AV.
CHURCH ST.
GREEN LANES
HEDGE LANE
GREAT CAMBRIDGE ROAD
NORTH CIRCULAR ROAD
STERLING WAY
ROUNDWAY
WHITE HART LANE
SILVER STREET
FORE STREET
A10
A105
A111
A406
A1080
B154
Edmonton Cemetery
Playing Fields
Winchmore Sch.
City Amenity Site
Clowes Sports Grd.
The Paulin Ground
Pavilion
Bury Lodge Park
Nursery
Highfield Schs.
Superstore
Lib.
Firs Farm Prim. Sch.
Play. Field
Tatem Rec. Grd.
Hollywood Gardens
Aylward School
West Lea Sch.
Haselbury Jun. & Inf. Schs.
Latymer School
Recreation Ground
Playground
Sports Ground
Tennis Courts
Schools
New River Sports Ground
King's Arms Bri.
Pymme's Brook
Great Cambridge Junction
Lib. Arts Cen. & Thtre
The North Middlesex Hosp.
Wilbury Prim. Sch.
Rec. Grd.
Weir Hall
Selby Sports Cen.
Prim. Sch.
Works
Middlesex University
New River Sports and Recreation Centre
Football Ground
White Hart Lane Sch.
Tottenham Cemetery
Lake
Bruce Castle Park
Bruce Castle & Haringey Mus.
Tower

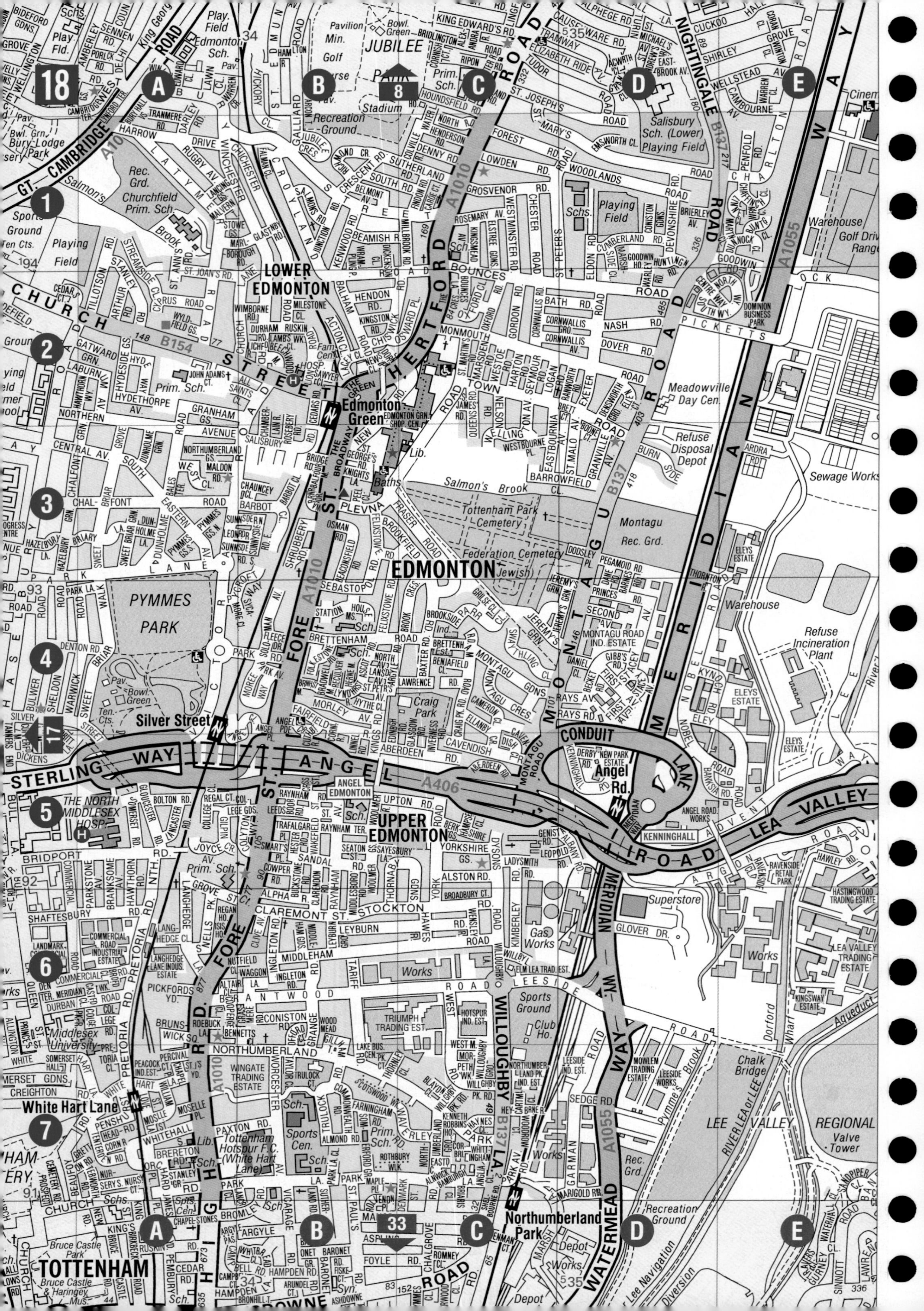
18
A
B
C
D
E
1
2
3
4
5
6
7
8
17
33
LOWER EDMONTON
EDMONTON
UPPER EDMONTON
TOTTENHAM
JUBILEE PARK
PYMMES PARK
Edmonton Green
Silver Street
White Hart Lane
Angel Rd.
Northumberland Park
ANGEL EDMONTON
THE NORTH MIDDLESEX HOSP.
Tottenham Park Cemetery
Federation Cemetery (Jewish)
Montagu Rec. Grd.
Craig Park
Salmon's Brook
Tottenham Hotspur F.C. (White Hart Lane)
Middlesex University
Bruce Castle Park
Bruce Castle & Haringey Mus.
Meadowville Day Cen.
Refuse Disposal Depot
Refuse Incineration Plant
Sewage Works
Superstore
Gas Works
Sports Ground
Recreation Ground
LEE VALLEY REGIONAL
Valve Tower
Chalk Bridge
Aqueduct
Lee Navigation
Diversion
Pymme's Brook
RIVER LEA or LEE
GT. CAMBRIDGE ROAD
CHURCH STREET
HERTFORD ROAD
FORE ST.
HIGH RD.
STERLING WAY
ANGEL ROAD
CONDUIT LANE
LEA VALLEY ROAD
MERIDIAN WAY
MONTAGU ROAD
WATERMEAD WAY
WILLOUGHBY LA.
NIGHTINGALE ROAD
PICKETTS LOCK
ADVENT WAY
LEESIDE ROAD
A10
A1010
A406
A1055
B137
B154

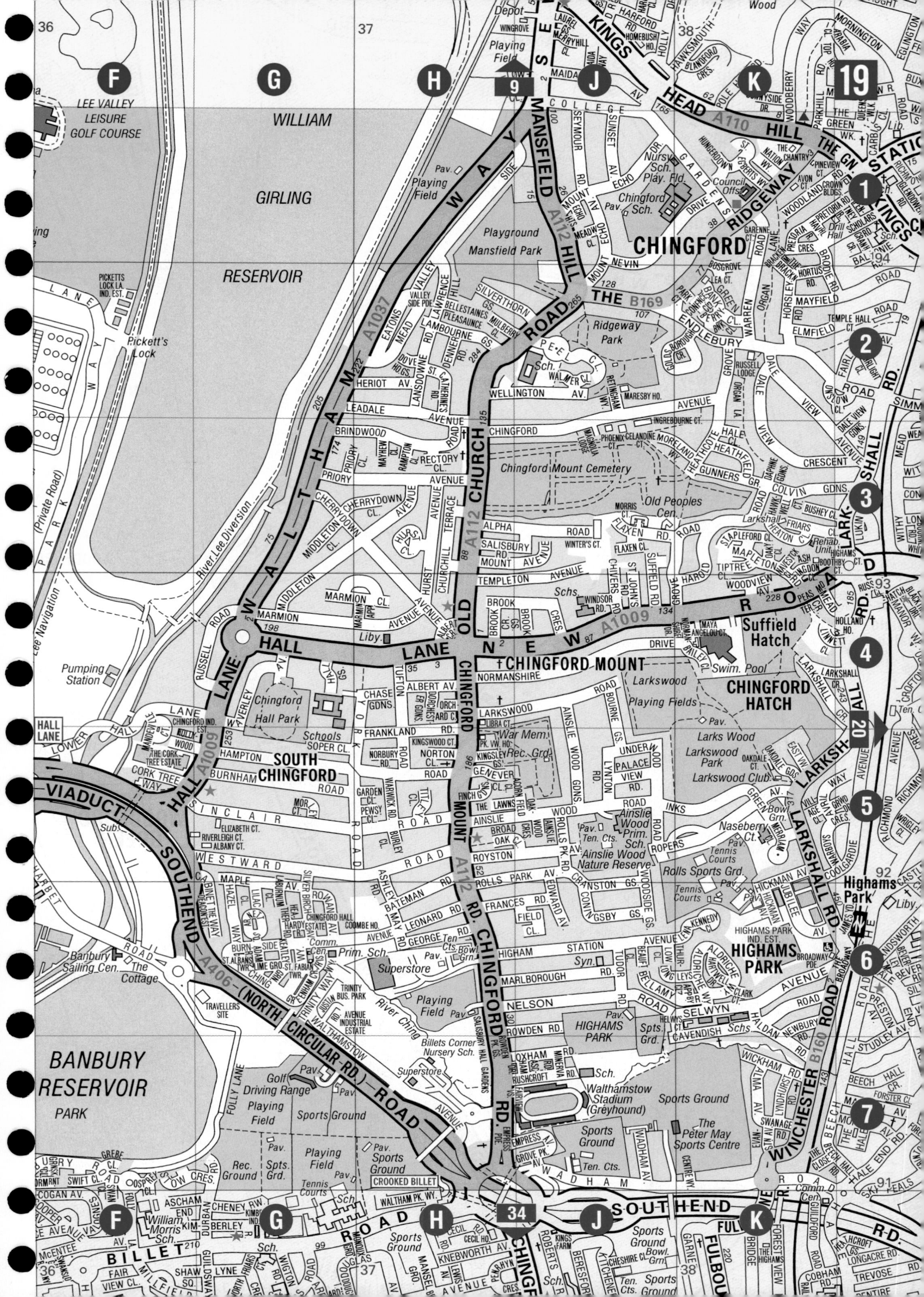

19
36
37
38
F
G
H
J
K
1
2
3
4
5
6
7
9
20
34
LEE VALLEY LEISURE GOLF COURSE
WILLIAM GIRLING RESERVOIR
PICKETTS LOCK LA. IND. EST.
Pickett's Lock
PARK WAY
(Private Road)
River Lee Diversion
Lee Navigation
Pumping Station
HALL LANE
LOWER HALL LANE
VIADUCT
BANBURY RESERVOIR
BANBURY PARK
Banbury Sailing Cen.
The Cottage
TRAVELLERS SITE
NORTH CIRCULAR ROAD
SOUTHEND ROAD
A406
WALTHAM WAY
A1037
A1009
HALL LANE
NEW ROAD
MANSFIELD HILL
A112
KINGS HEAD HILL
A110
RIDGEWAY
THE RIDGEWAY
B169
CHINGFORD
OLD CHURCH ROAD
CHINGFORD MOUNT
CHINGFORD MOUNT RD.
CHINGFORD RD.
SOUTH CHINGFORD
CHINGFORD HATCH
HIGHAMS PARK
LARKSHALL RD.
WINCHESTER ROAD
B160
COLLEGE GARDENS
Playing Field
Playground
Mansfield Park
Ridgeway Park
Chingford Sch.
Council Offs.
Nursy. Sch.
Chingford Mount Cemetery
Old Peoples Cen.
Suffield Hatch
Swim. Pool
Larkswood Playing Fields
Larks Wood
Larkswood Park
Larkswood Club
Chingford Hall Park
War Mem. Rec. Grd.
Ainslie Wood Prim. Sch.
Ainslie Wood Nature Reserve
Rolls Sports Grd.
Tennis Courts
Naseberry Ct.
HIGHAMS PARK IND. EST.
Highams Park
Superstore
Prim. Sch.
River Ching
TRINITY BUS. PARK
AVENUE INDUSTRIAL ESTATE
Billets Corner Nursery Sch.
Golf Driving Range
Sports Ground
Rec. Ground
Walthamstow Stadium (Greyhound)
The Peter May Sports Centre
CROOKED BILLET
WALTHAM PK. WY.
BILLET ROAD
WADHAM
FULBOURNE
William Morris Sch.
Wood
Depot
Liby.
Sch.
Schs.
Syn.
Comm. Cen.

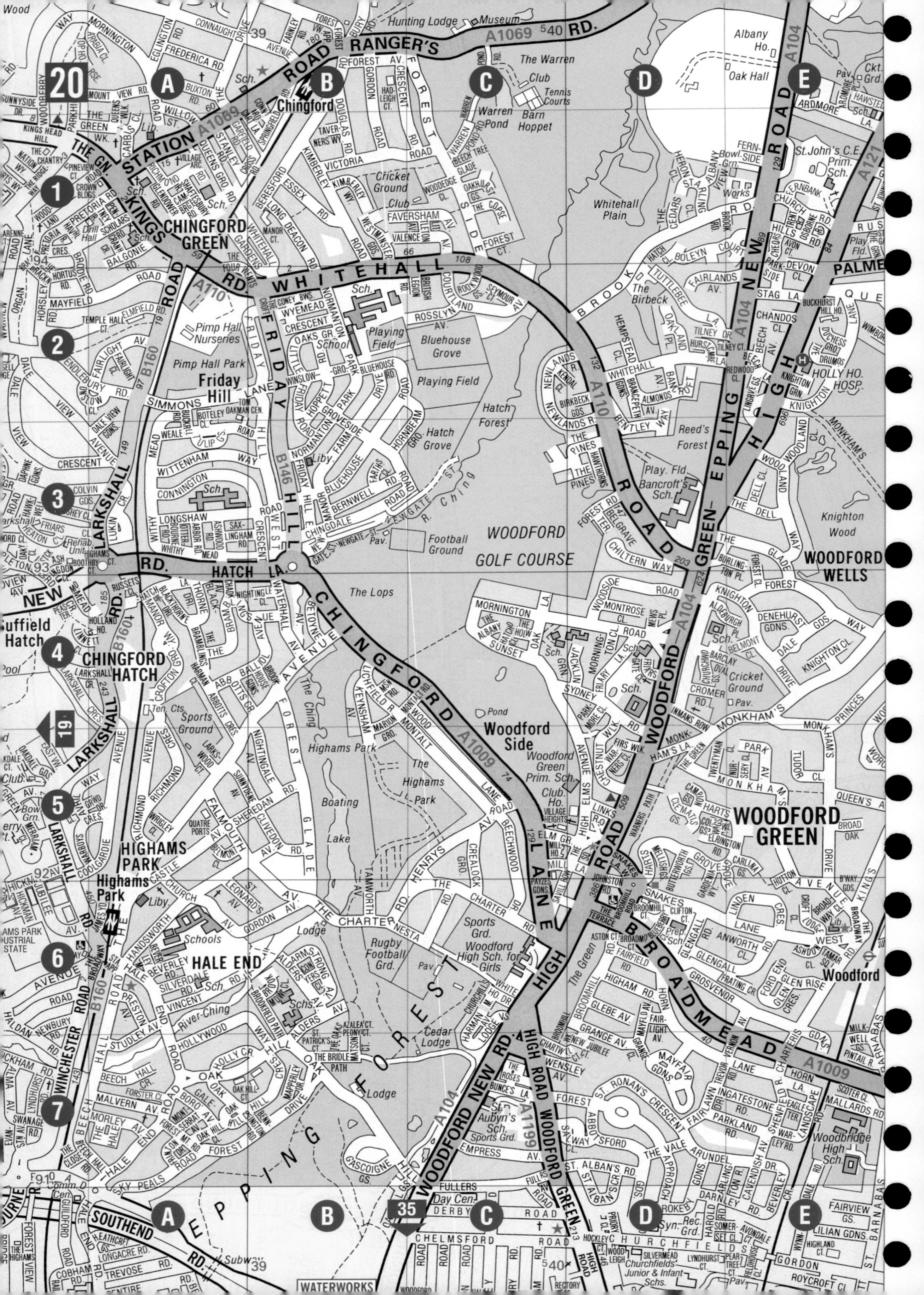

20
19
35
A
B
C
D
E
1
2
3
4
5
6
7
RANGER'S RD.
A1069
STATION ROAD
Chingford
CHINGFORD GREEN
KINGS ROAD
THE GN.
Hunting Lodge
Museum
The Warren
Club
Tennis Courts
Warren Pond
Barn Hoppet
Albany Ho.
Oak Hall
Whitehall Plain
Cricket Ground
Club
WHITEHALL RD.
A110
FRIDAY HILL
Friday Hill
Pimp Hall Nurseries
Pimp Hall Park
Playing Field
Bluehouse Grove
Hatch Forest
Hatch Grove
Football Ground
R. Ching
WOODFORD GOLF COURSE
The Lops
LARKSHALL RD.
B160
B146
HATCH LA.
NEW RD.
CHINGFORD HATCH
Sports Ground
CHINGFORD LANE
A1009
Highams Park
Boating Lake
The Highams Park
The Ching
Woodford Side
Woodford Green Prim. Sch.
HIGHAMS PARK
HALE END
Schools
Rugby Football Grd.
Sports Grd.
Woodford High Sch. for Girls
Cedar Lodge
Lodge
EPPING FOREST
HIGH ROAD
WOODFORD NEW RD.
A104
A1199
HIGH ROAD WOODFORD GREEN
BROADMEAD
WOODFORD GREEN
WOODFORD WELLS
Knighton Wood
Reed's Forest
Play. Fld.
Bancroft's Sch.
The Birbeck
HOLLY HO. HOSP.
EPPING NEW ROAD
HIGH ROAD
WOODFORD GREEN
Cricket Ground
Woodford
Woodbridge High Sch.
St. Aubyn's Sch.
CHELMSFORD ROAD
CHURCHFIELDS
SOUTHEND RD.
WINCHESTER ROAD
WATERWORKS
Churchfields Junior & Infant Schs.

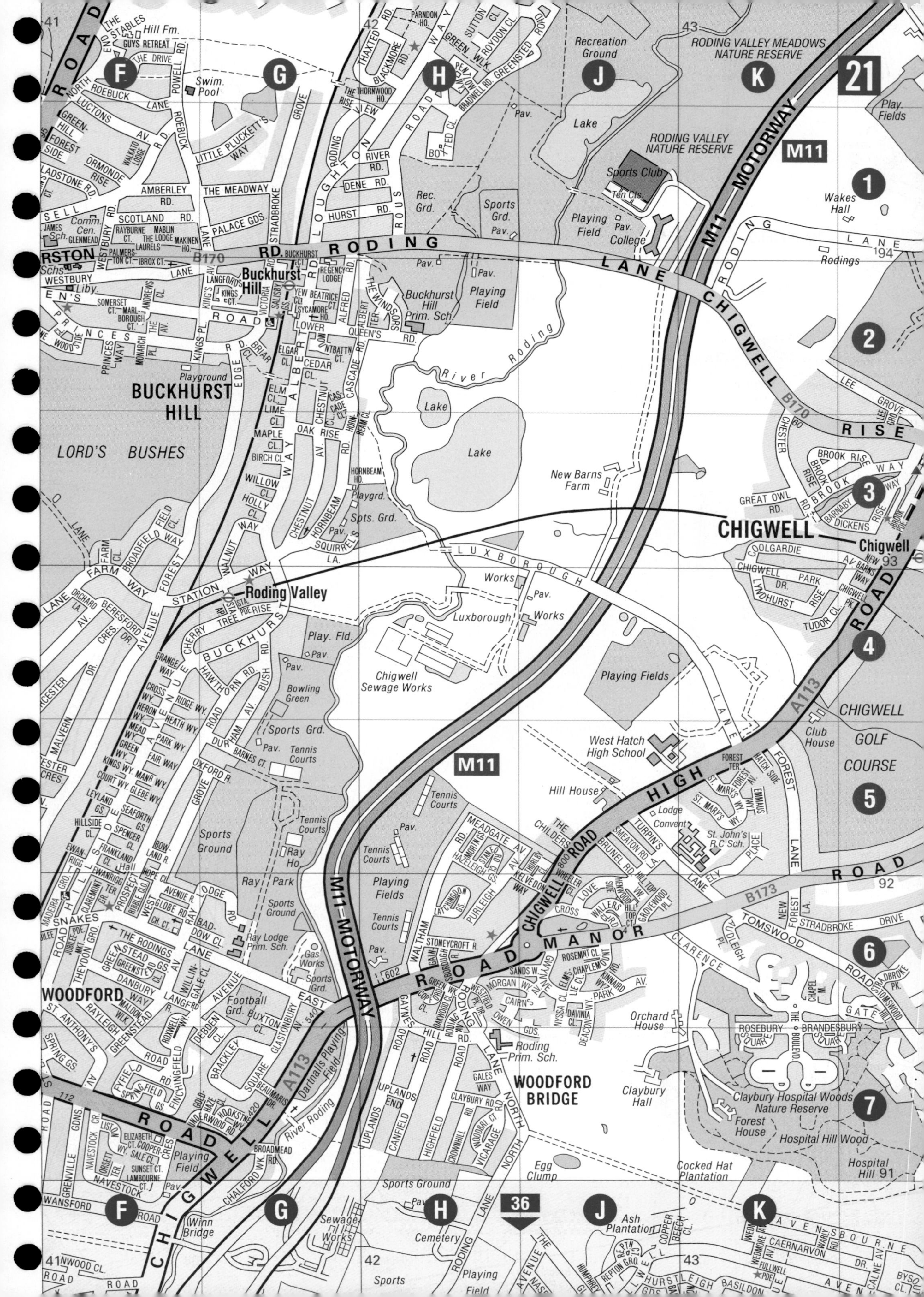
21
BUCKHURST HILL
Buckhurst Hill
LORD'S BUSHES
Roding Valley
CHIGWELL
Chigwell
WOODFORD
WOODFORD BRIDGE
M11 MOTORWAY
M11
RODING LANE
CHIGWELL LANE
CHIGWELL RISE
HIGH ROAD
MANOR ROAD
CHIGWELL ROAD
LUXBOROUGH LANE
RODING VALLEY MEADOWS NATURE RESERVE
RODING VALLEY NATURE RESERVE
Recreation Ground
Lake
Sports Club
Playing Field
College
Rodings
Wakes Hall
Play Fields
River Roding
Chigwell Sewage Works
Luxborough
Works
Playing Fields
New Barns Farm
West Hatch High School
Hill House
CHIGWELL GOLF COURSE
Club House
St. John's R.C Sch.
Convent
Ray Park
Sports Ground
Ray Lodge Prim. Sch.
Gas Works
Football Grd.
Roding Prim. Sch.
Orchard House
Claybury Hall
Claybury Hospital Woods Nature Reserve
Forest House
Hospital Hill Wood
Hospital Hill
Egg Clump
Cocked Hat Plantation
Ash Plantation
Cemetery
Sewage Works
Winn Bridge
Dartnalls Playing Field
Buckhurst Hill Prim. Sch.
Playground
36

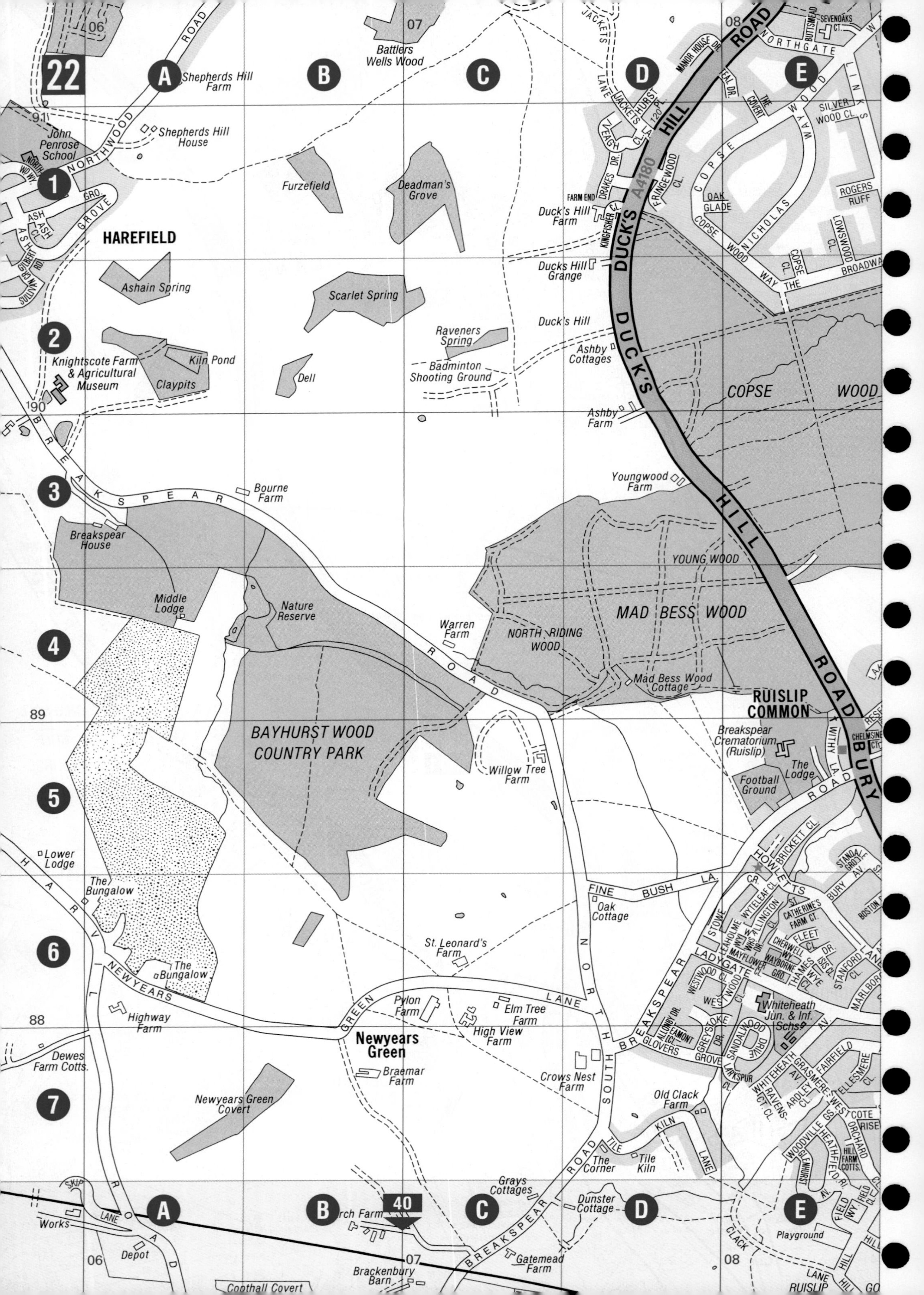
A
B
C
D
E
1
2
3
4
5
6
7
06
07
08
91
190
89
88
Battlers Wells Wood
Shepherds Hill Farm
Shepherds Hill House
John Penrose School
NORTHWOOD ROAD
HAREFIELD
GROVE
ASH CL.
Ashain Spring
Furzefield
Deadman's Grove
Scarlet Spring
Raveners Spring
Dell
Knightscote Farm & Agricultural Museum
Kiln Pond
Claypits
Badminton Shooting Ground
JACKETS LANE
DUCK'S HILL ROAD
A4180
MANOR HOUSE DR.
NORTHGATE
SEVENOAKS CT.
THE COVERT
SILVER WOOD CL.
LINKS WAY
COPSE WOOD WAY
OAK GLADE
NICHOLAS WAY
ROGERS RUFF
LOWSWOOD CL.
COPSE CL.
THE BROADWAY
DRAKES DR.
VEAGH CL.
FRINGEWOOD CL.
KINGFISHER CL.
FARM END
Duck's Hill Farm
Ducks Hill Grange
Duck's Hill
Ashby Cottages
Ashby Farm
COPSE WOOD
BREAKSPEAR ROAD
Bourne Farm
Breakspear House
Middle Lodge
Nature Reserve
Warren Farm
Youngwood Farm
YOUNG WOOD
MAD BESS WOOD
NORTH RIDING WOOD
Mad Bess Wood Cottage
RUISLIP COMMON
Breakspear Crematorium (Ruislip)
The Lodge
Football Ground
WITHY LA.
BURY ROAD
BAYHURST WOOD COUNTRY PARK
Willow Tree Farm
Lower Lodge
The Bungalow
HAREFIELD ROAD
NEWYEARS GREEN LANE
Highway Farm
Dewes Farm Cotts.
FINE BUSH LA.
Oak Cottage
St. Leonard's Farm
Pylon Farm
Elm Tree Farm
High View Farm
Newyears Green
Braemar Farm
Crows Nest Farm
NORTH BREAKSPEAR ROAD
SOUTH BREAKSPEAR ROAD
Newyears Green Covert
Old Clack Farm
TILE KILN LANE
The Corner
Tile Kiln
Grays Cottages
Dunster Cottage
HOWLETTS LA.
BRICKETT CL.
LADYGATE LA.
WESTWOOD CL.
GLOVERS GROVE
SANDALWOOD DRIVE
Whiteheath Jun. & Inf. Schs.
WHITEHEATH AV.
GRASMERE AV.
FAIRFIELD AV.
ELLESMERE CL.
WOODVILLE GDNS.
HEATHFIELD RI.
ORCHARD CL.
HILL FARM COTTS.
Playground
CLACK LANE
RUISLIP
SKIP LANE
Works
Depot
Gatemead Farm
Brackenbury Barn
Coothall Covert
40

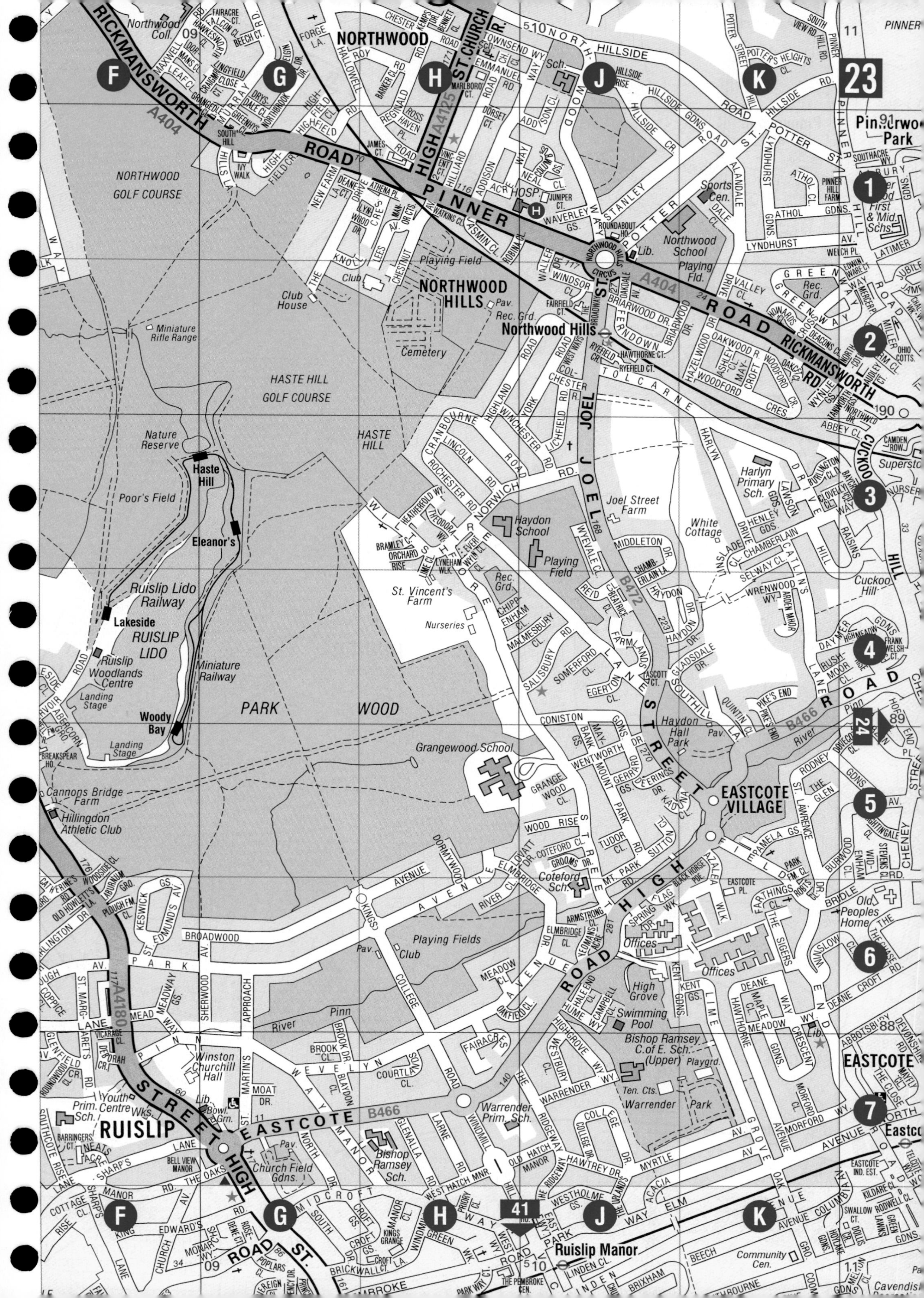
23
NORTHWOOD
Northwood Coll.
RICKMANSWORTH ROAD
A404
PINNER ROAD
HIGH ST.
A4125
CHURCH RD.
NORTH HILLSIDE
HILLSIDE ROAD
POTTER ST.
Pinner Wood Park
PINNER HILL RD.
Sports Cen.
Northwood School Playing Fld.
Northwood Hills Circus
NORTHWOOD HILLS
Northwood Hills
NORTHWOOD GOLF COURSE
HASTE HILL GOLF COURSE
HASTE HILL
Miniature Rifle Range
Club House
Playing Field
Cemetery
Rec. Grd.
Nature Reserve
Haste Hill
Poor's Field
Eleanor's
Ruislip Lido Railway
Lakeside
RUISLIP LIDO
Ruislip Woodlands Centre
Landing Stage
Miniature Railway
Woody Bay
PARK WOOD
Grangewood School
Cannons Bridge Farm
Hillingdon Athletic Club
St. Vincent's Farm
Nurseries
Haydon School
Playing Field
JOEL STREET
B472
Joel Street Farm
Harlyn Primary Sch.
White Cottage
Cuckoo Hill
CUCKOO HILL
Haydon Hall Park
B466
River Pinn
EASTCOTE VILLAGE
HIGH ROAD
FIELD END ROAD
Coteford Sch.
Offices
High Grove
Swimming Pool
Bishop Ramsey C.of E. Sch. (Upper)
Warrender Park
Old Peoples Home
EASTCOTE
Eastcote
AVENUE
Playing Fields
Club
Winston Churchill Hall
Youth Centre
Prim. Sch.
RUISLIP
HIGH STREET
A4180
EASTCOTE ROAD
Church Field Gdns.
Bishop Ramsey Sch.
Warrender Prim. Sch.
Ruislip Manor
Community Cen.
EASTCOTE IND. EST.
24
41
F G H J K
1 2 3 4 5 6 7

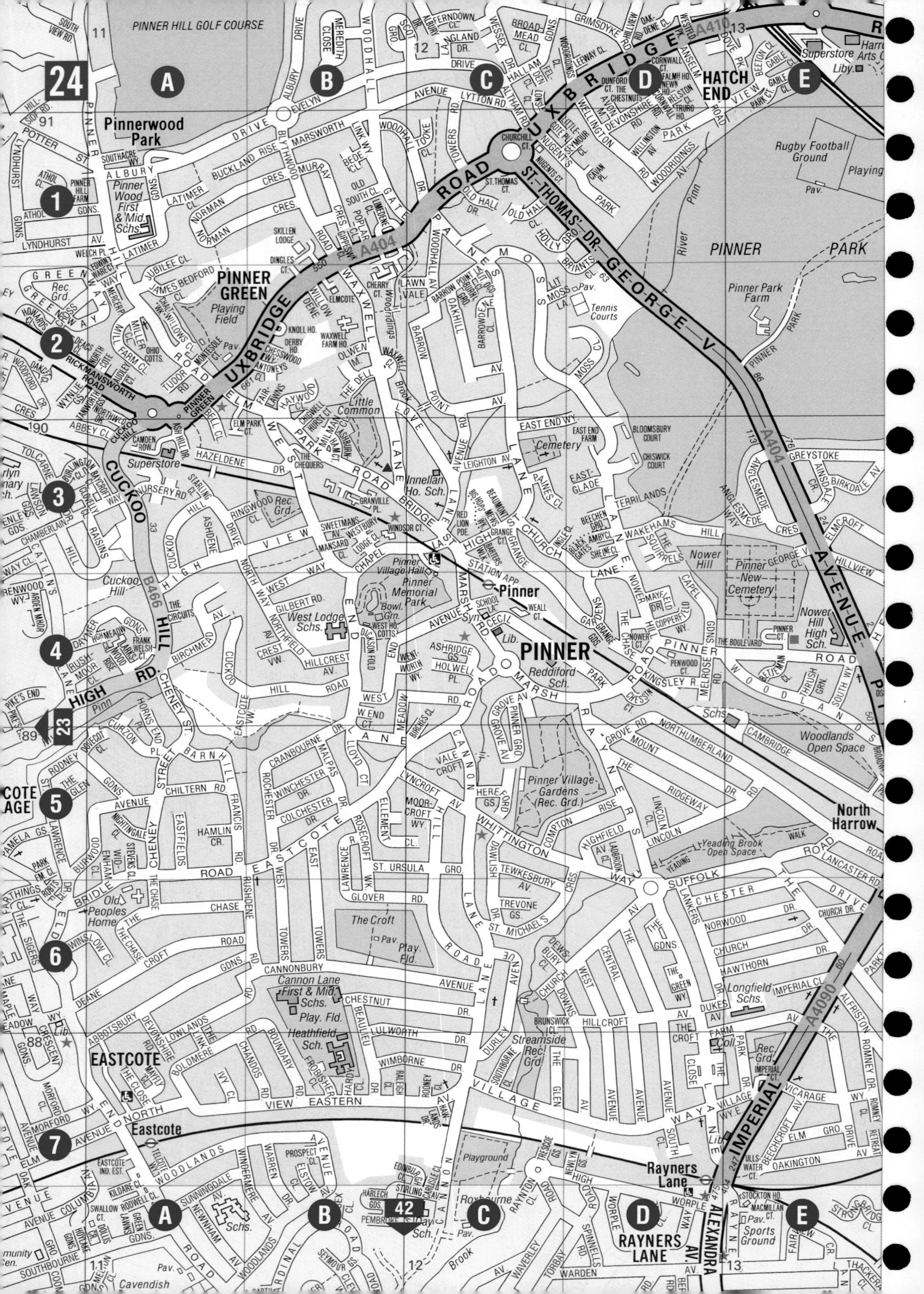

24
23
42
PINNER HILL GOLF COURSE
Pinnerwood Park
PINNER GREEN
HATCH END
PINNER
PINNER PARK
Pinner Park Farm
Rugby Football Ground
North Harrow
EASTCOTE
Eastcote
Rayners Lane
RAYNERS LANE
Pinner Memorial Park
Pinner Village Gardens (Rec. Grd.)
Yeading Brook Open Space
Woodlands Open Space
Pinner New Cemetery
Nower Hill
Little Common
Cuckoo Hill
UXBRIDGE ROAD
ST. THOMAS' DR.
GEORGE V AVENUE
CUCKOO HILL
HIGH RD.
RICKMANSWORTH ROAD
BRIDGE ST.
MARSH RD.
EASTCOTE ROAD
CANNON LANE
RAYNERS LANE
IMPERIAL DR.
ALEXANDRA AV.
A404
A410
A4090
B466

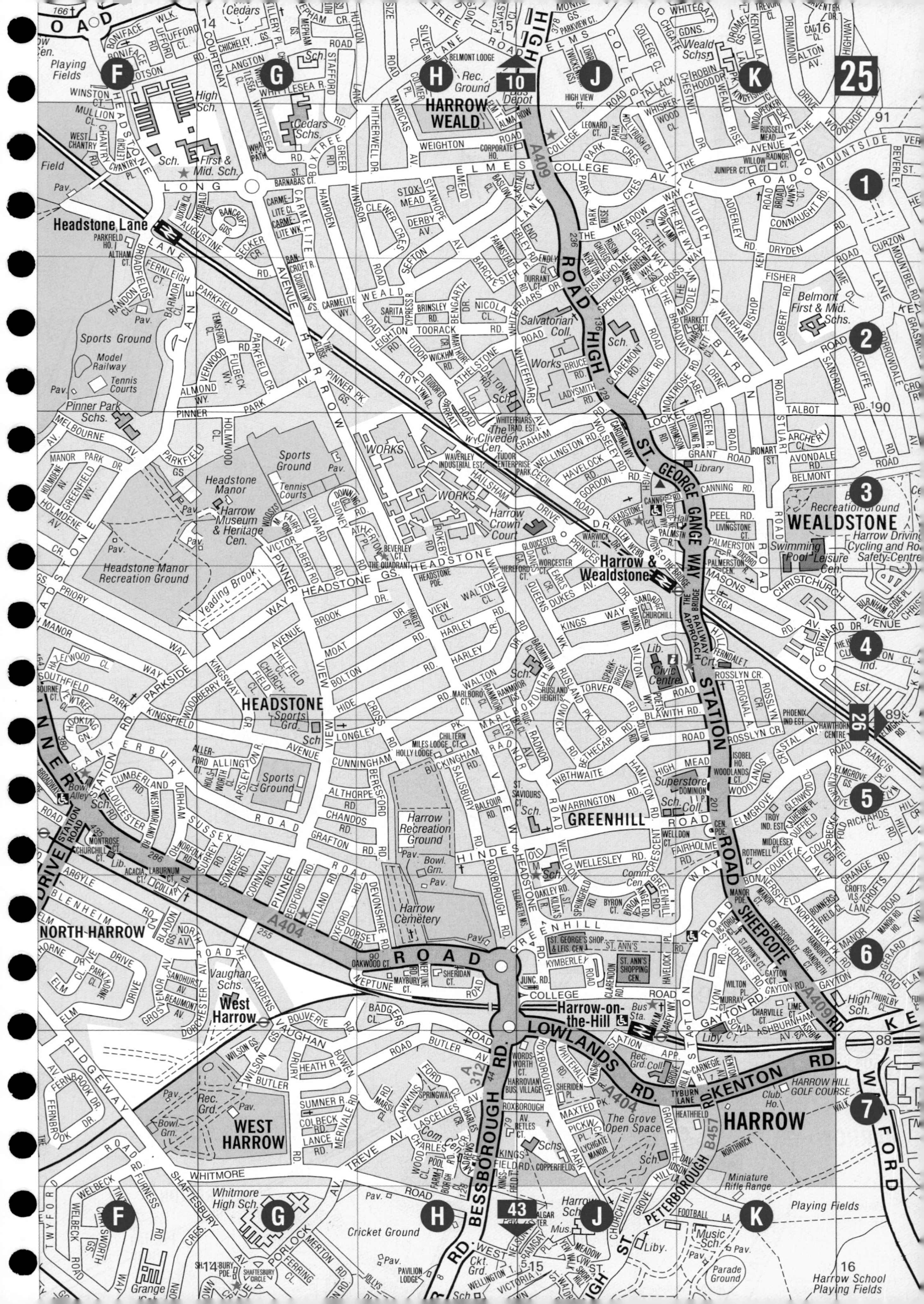

25
HARROW WEALD
Headstone Lane
Sports Ground
Model Railway
Pinner Park Schs.
Headstone Manor
Harrow Museum & Heritage Cen.
Headstone Manor Recreation Ground
Salvatorian Coll.
Harrow Crown Court
Harrow & Wealdstone
WEALDSTONE
Recreation Ground
Harrow Driving Cycling and Road Safety Centre
Swimming Pool
Leisure Cen.
Civic Centre
HEADSTONE
Harrow Recreation Ground
Harrow Cemetery
GREENHILL
NORTH HARROW
West Harrow
WEST HARROW
Harrow-on-the-Hill
The Grove Open Space
HARROW
HARROW HILL GOLF COURSE
Whitmore High Sch.
Cricket Ground
Playing Fields
Harrow School Playing Fields
Miniature Rifle Range
10
43
26

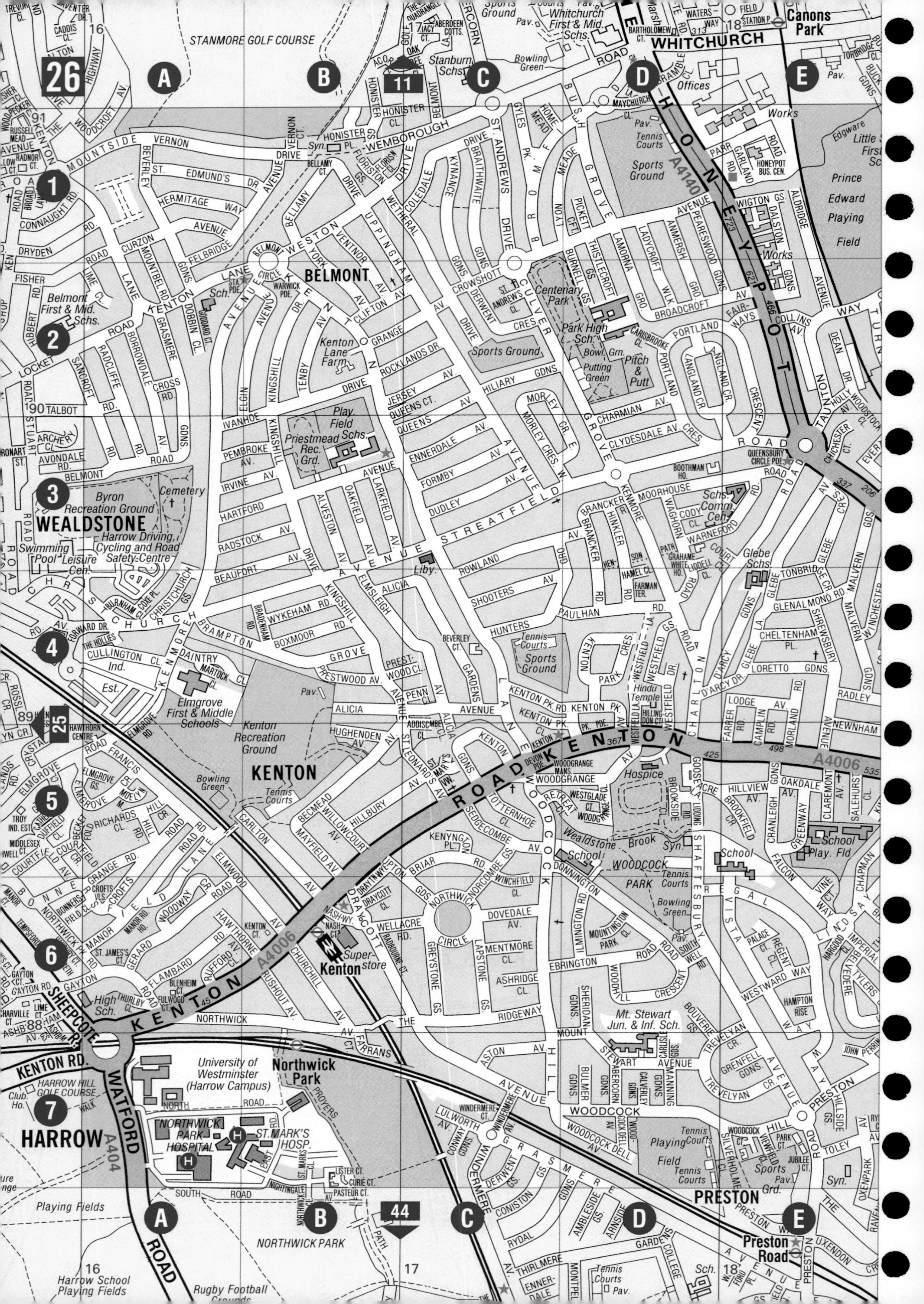

26
11
44
25
A
B
C
D
E
1
2
3
4
5
6
7
16
17
18
STANMORE GOLF COURSE
Whitchurch First & Mid. Schs.
Canons Park
WHITCHURCH
Stanburn Schs.
Offices
Works
Prince Edward Playing Field
HONEYPOT LANE
A4140
Sports Ground
Tennis Courts
HONEYPOT BUS. CEN.
WEMBOROUGH
MOUNTSIDE
VERNON DRIVE
BELMONT
Belmont First & Mid. Schs.
Kenton Lane Farm
Centenary Park
Park High Sch.
Pitch & Putt
Putting Green
Sports Ground
Play Field
Priestmead Rec. Grd.
Schs.
QUEENSBURY CIRCLE PDE.
Schs. Comm. Cen.
Glebe Schs.
WEALDSTONE
Byron Recreation Ground
Cemetery
Harrow Driving, Cycling and Road Safety Centre
Swimming Pool
Leisure Cen.
STREATFIELD AVENUE
Liby.
CHRISTCHURCH AVENUE
Elmgrove First & Middle Schools
Kenton Recreation Ground
KENTON
Bowling Green
Tennis Courts
Hindu Temple
Hospice
KENTON ROAD
A4006
Wealdstone Brook
School
WOODCOCK PARK
Bowling Green
School Play. Fld.
Kenton
Super-store
NORTHWICK CIRCLE
High Sch.
SHEEPCOTE RD.
KENTON RD.
HARROW HILL GOLF COURSE
HARROW
WATFORD ROAD
A404
University of Westminster (Harrow Campus)
Northwick Park
NORTHWICK PARK HOSPITAL
ST. MARK'S HOSP.
Mt. Stewart Jun. & Inf. Sch.
WOODCOCK HILL
Playing Field
Tennis Courts
PRESTON
Preston Road
Playing Fields
NORTHWICK PARK
Harrow School Playing Fields
Rugby Football Grounds

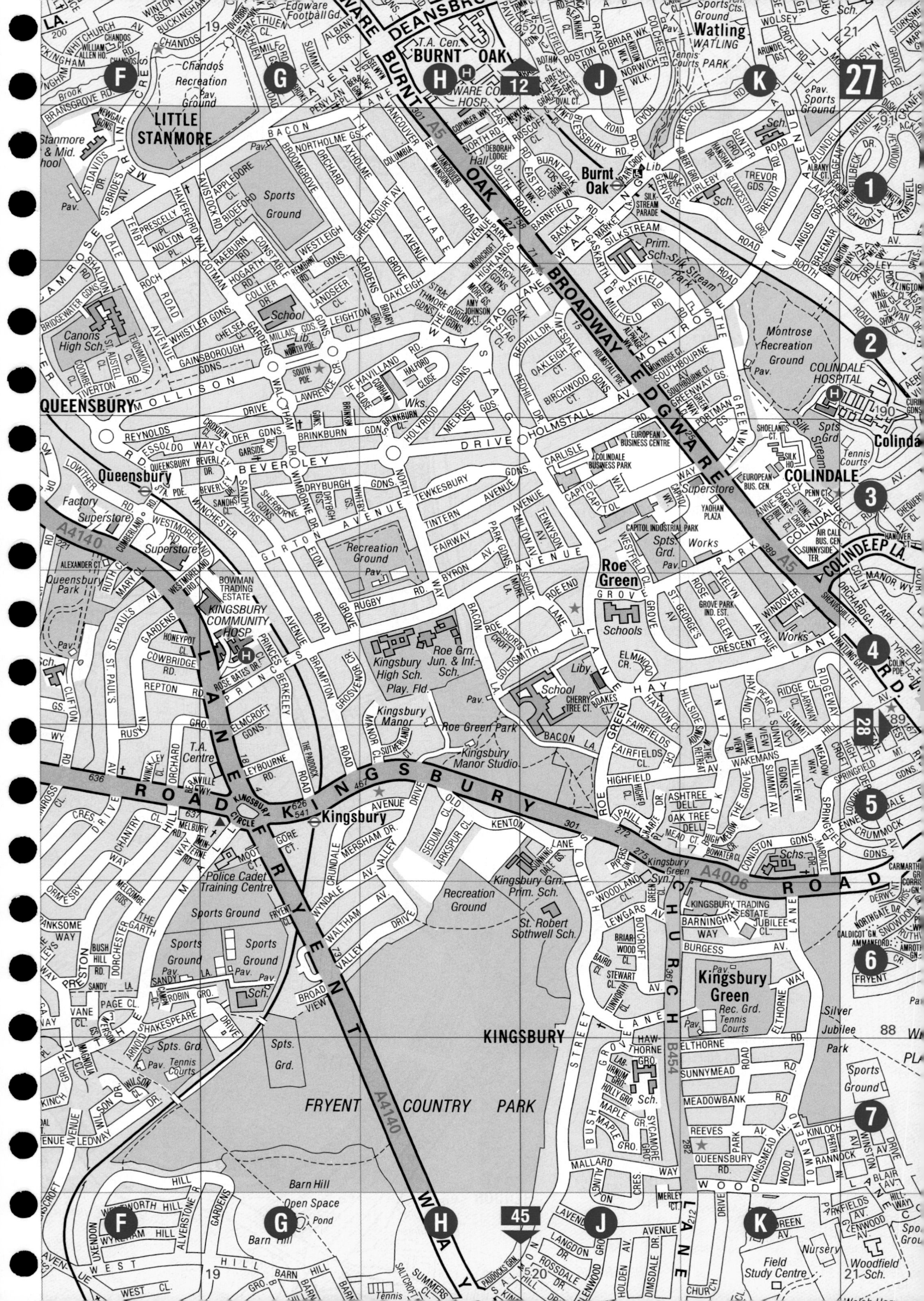
27
BURNT OAK
T.A. Cen.
LITTLE STANMORE
Chandos Recreation Ground
Stanmore & Mid. School
Canons High Sch.
Sports Ground
School
Lib.
QUEENSBURY
Queensbury
Factory
Superstore
A4140
Queensbury Park
BOWMAN TRADING ESTATE
KINGSBURY COMMUNITY HOSP
Burnt Oak
Lib
SILK-STREAM PARADE
Prim. Sch.
Silk Stream Park
BROADWAY
EDGWARE
Montrose Recreation Ground
COLINDALE HOSPITAL
COLINDALE
Colindale
EUROPEAN BUSINESS CENTRE
COLINDALE BUSINESS PARK
Superstore
YAOHAN PLAZA
CAPITOL INDUSTRIAL PARK
Spts. Grd.
Works
Roe Green
Schools
GROVE PARK IND. EST.
COLINDEEP LA.
A5
Recreation Ground
Kingsbury High Sch. Play. Fld.
Roe Grn. Jun. & Inf. Sch.
Kingsbury Manor
Roe Green Park
Kingsbury Manor Studio
School
T.A. Centre
KINGSBURY
ROAD
Kingsbury
KINGSBURY CIRCLE
Police Cadet Training Centre
Sports Ground
Recreation Ground
Kingsbury Grn. Prim. Sch.
St. Robert Sothwell Sch.
Kingsbury Green
A4006
KINGSBURY TRADING ESTATE
Kingsbury Green Rec. Grd.
Silver Jubilee Park
FRYENT COUNTRY PARK
FRYENT WAY
A4140
Barn Hill Open Space
Pond
Barn Hill
Spts. Grd.
Sch.
B454
CHURCH LANE
Field Study Centre
Nursery
Woodfield Sch.
12
45
28
F
G
H
J
K
1
2
3
4
5
6
7
19
20
21
88
89
90

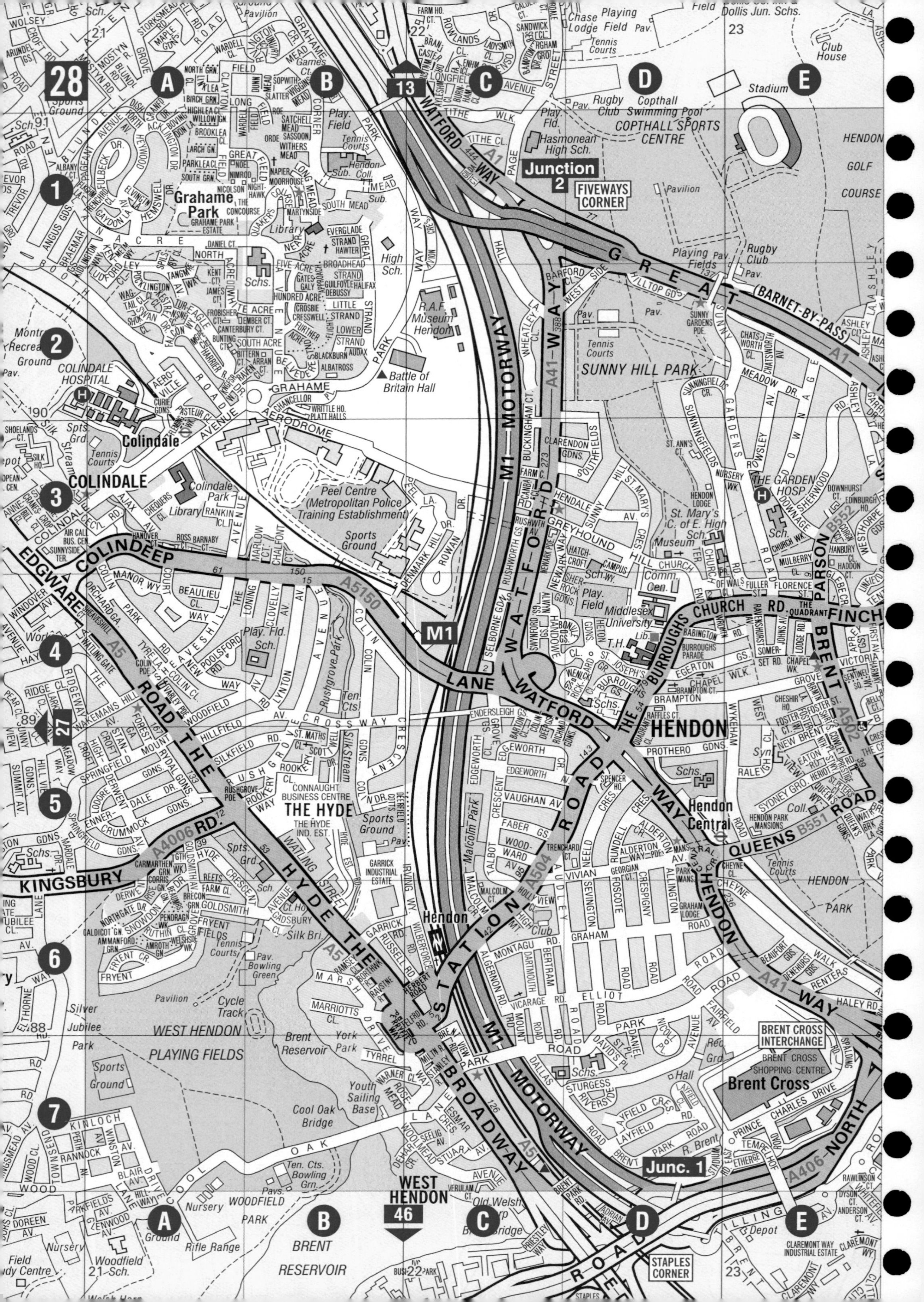
28
A
B
C
D
E
1
2
3
4
5
6
7
13
27
46
Grahame Park
Colindale
COLINDALE
COLINDALE HOSPITAL
Peel Centre (Metropolitan Police Training Establishment)
R.A.F. Museum Hendon
Battle of Britain Hall
Junction 2
FIVEWAYS CORNER
COPTHALL SPORTS CENTRE
HENDON GOLF COURSE
SUNNY HILL PARK
GREAT (BARNET-BY-PASS)
M1 MOTORWAY
WATFORD WAY
COLINDEEP LANE
EDGWARE ROAD
THE HYDE
HENDON
Hendon Central
Middlesex University
QUEENS ROAD
BURROUGHS
CHURCH RD.
HENDON WAY
STATION ROAD
KINGSBURY RD.
WEST HENDON PLAYING FIELDS
Brent Reservoir
BRENT RESERVOIR
WOODFIELD PARK
Brent Cross
BRENT CROSS INTERCHANGE
Junc. 1
NORTH CIRCULAR ROAD
STAPLES CORNER
WEST HENDON
BROADWAY
Hendon

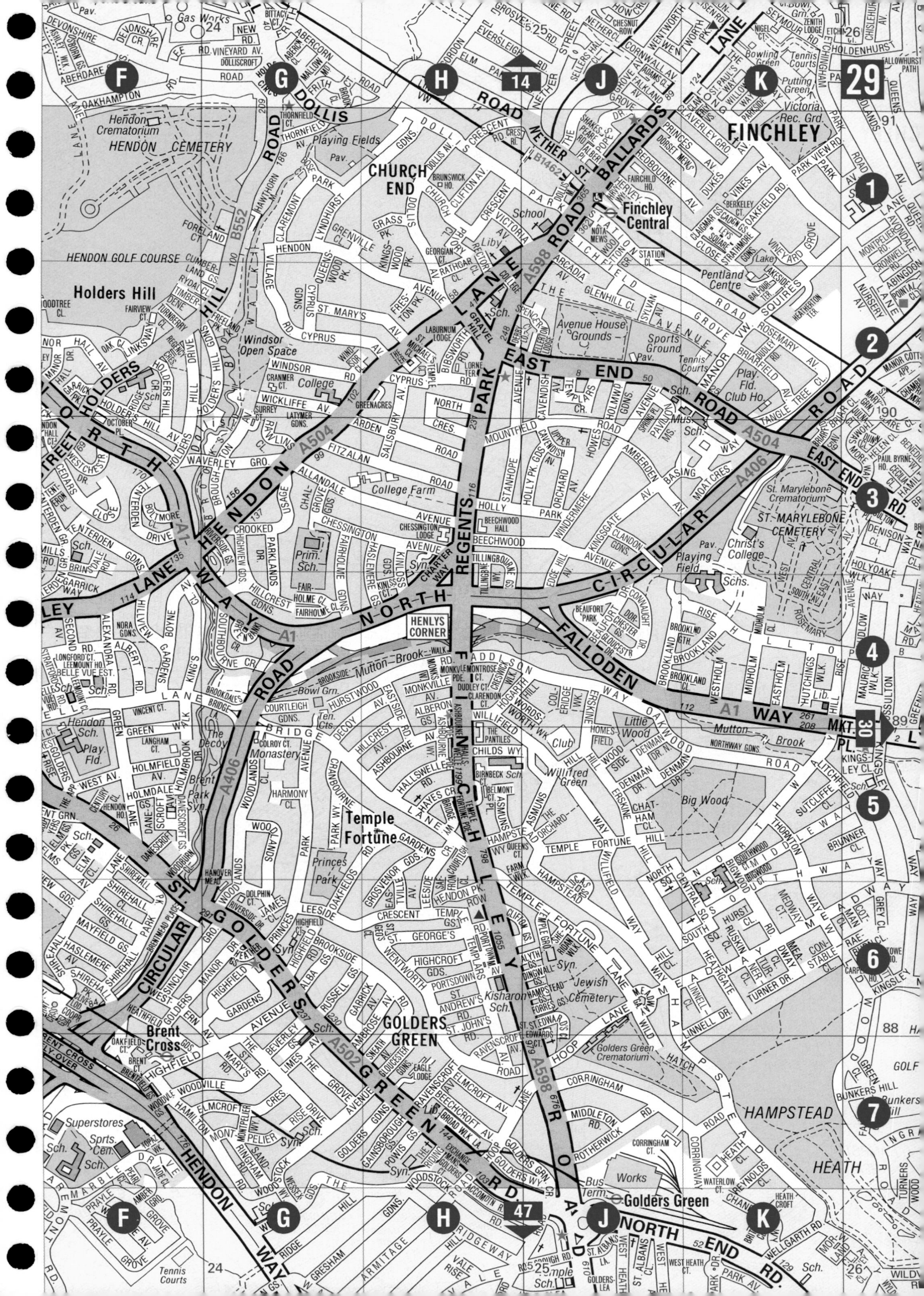

29
14
47
30
F
G
H
J
K
1
2
3
4
5
6
7
24
25
26
FINCHLEY
CHURCH END
Finchley Central
Holders Hill
HENDON GOLF COURSE
Hendon Crematorium
HENDON CEMETERY
Windsor Open Space
College Farm
HENLYS CORNER
Temple Fortune
GOLDERS GREEN
Golders Green
Brent Cross
HAMPSTEAD
HEATH
Big Wood
Little Wood
Golders Green Crematorium
Jewish Cemetery
St. Marylebone Crematorium
ST. MARYLEBONE CEMETERY
Christ's College
Avenue House Grounds
Sports Ground
Victoria Rec. Grd.
Pentland Centre
Princes Park
The Decoy
Superstores
Mutton Brook
NORTH CIRCULAR ROAD
FALLODEN WAY
HENDON WAY
GOLDERS GREEN RD.
FINCHLEY RD.
REGENTS PARK ROAD
EAST END ROAD
BALLARDS LANE
HENDON LANE
DOLLIS ROAD
NETHER ST.
HOLDERS HILL
NORTH END RD.
A1
A406
A504
A598
A502
A41
B552
B1462

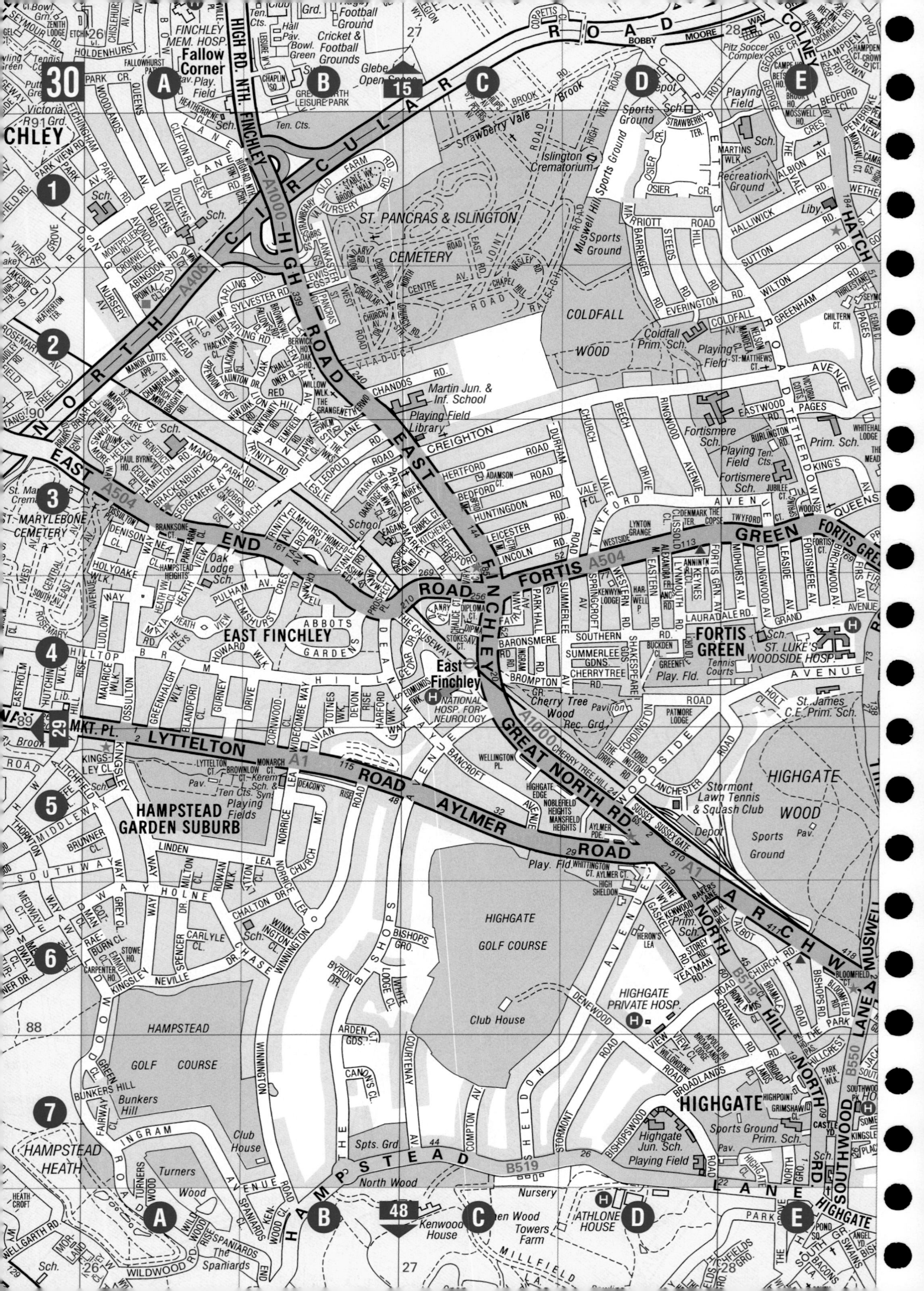

Fallow Corner
NORTH CIRCULAR ROAD
A406
HIGH RD. NTH. FINCHLEY
A1000
HIGH ROAD
EAST FINCHLEY
EAST END ROAD
A504
FORTIS GREEN
FORTIS GREEN
ST. PANCRAS & ISLINGTON CEMETERY
Islington Crematorium
COLDFALL WOOD
Muswell Hill Sports Ground
Sports Ground
Glebe Open Space
Strawberry Vale
Martin Jun. & Inf. School
Playing Field
Library
Fortismere Sch.
St. LUKE'S WOODSIDE HOSP.
East Finchley
NATIONAL HOSP. FOR NEUROLOGY
Cherry Tree Wood
GREAT NORTH RD.
LYTTELTON ROAD
A1
AYLMER ROAD
ARCHWAY ROAD
HAMPSTEAD GARDEN SUBURB
HIGHGATE WOOD
Stormont Lawn Tennis & Squash Club
HIGHGATE GOLF COURSE
Club House
HIGHGATE PRIVATE HOSP.
HIGHGATE
HAMPSTEAD GOLF COURSE
Bunkers Hill
HAMPSTEAD HEATH
Turners Wood
HAMPSTEAD LANE
B519
North Wood
Kenwood House
Ken Wood Towers Farm
ATHLONE HOUSE
The Spaniards
NORTH HILL
B550
SOUTHWOOD LANE
MUSWELL HILL
St. MARYLEBONE CEMETERY
ABBOTS GARDENS
HIGHGATE ROAD
MUSWELL HILL ROAD
A B C D E
1 2 3 4 5 6 7
15
29
48

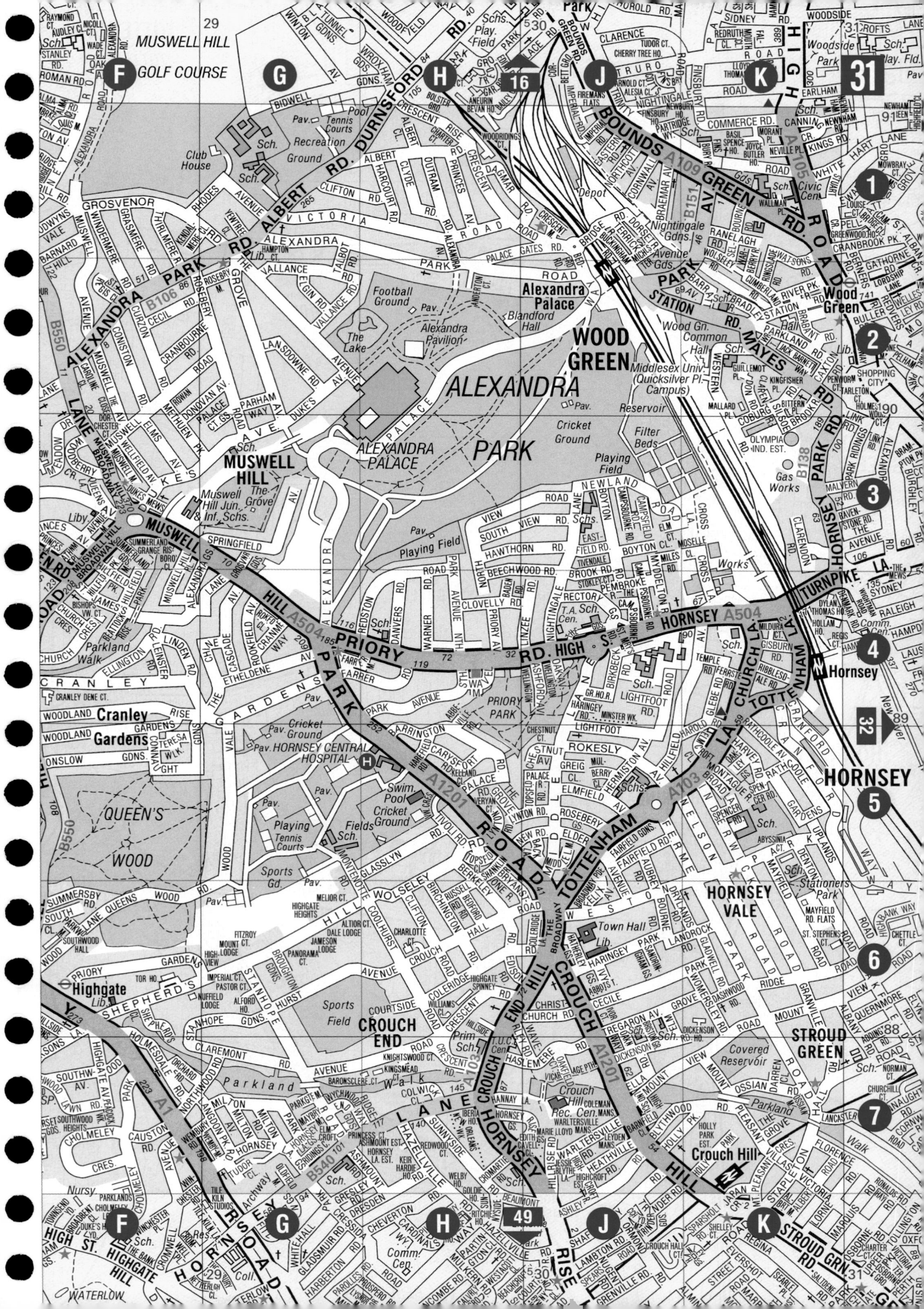

31
16
49
32
F
G
H
J
K
1
2
3
4
5
6
7
MUSWELL HILL
GOLF COURSE
ALEXANDRA PARK RD.
ALBERT RD.
DURNSFORD RD.
Recreation Ground
Club House
VICTORIA ROAD
ALEXANDRA PARK ROAD
PALACE GATES RD.
BOUNDS GREEN RD.
A109
A105
HIGH ROAD
Wood Green
WOOD GREEN
Alexandra Palace
Blandford Hall
Alexandra Pavilion
The Lake
Football Ground
ALEXANDRA
PARK
ALEXANDRA PALACE
Cricket Ground
Playing Field
Reservoir
Filter Beds
Middlesex Univ. (Quicksilver Pl. Campus)
Wood Gn. Common
STATION RD.
MAYES RD.
Gas Works
Nightingale Gdns.
Depot
MUSWELL HILL
MUSWELL HILL BROADWAY
MUSWELL HILL
A504
PRIORY RD.
HIGH ST.
HORNSEY
A504
TURNPIKE LA.
Hornsey
HORNSEY
PRIORY PARK
PARK ROAD
A1201
HORNSEY CENTRAL HOSPITAL
Cricket Ground
Playing Tennis Courts
Swim. Pool
Cricket Ground
Sports Gd.
QUEEN'S WOOD
Cranley Gardens
QUEENS WOOD RD.
WOLSELEY RD.
TOTTENHAM LA.
A103
HORNSEY VALE
Stationers Park
Town Hall
The Broadway
CROUCH END HILL
CROUCH HILL
CROUCH END
Sports Field
Parkland Walk
HORNSEY LANE
B540
Highgate
HIGHGATE HILL
HORNSEY RISE
HORNSEY ROAD
A1
STROUD GREEN
Covered Reservoir
Crouch Hill
STROUD GRN. RD.
B550
B106
B151
B138

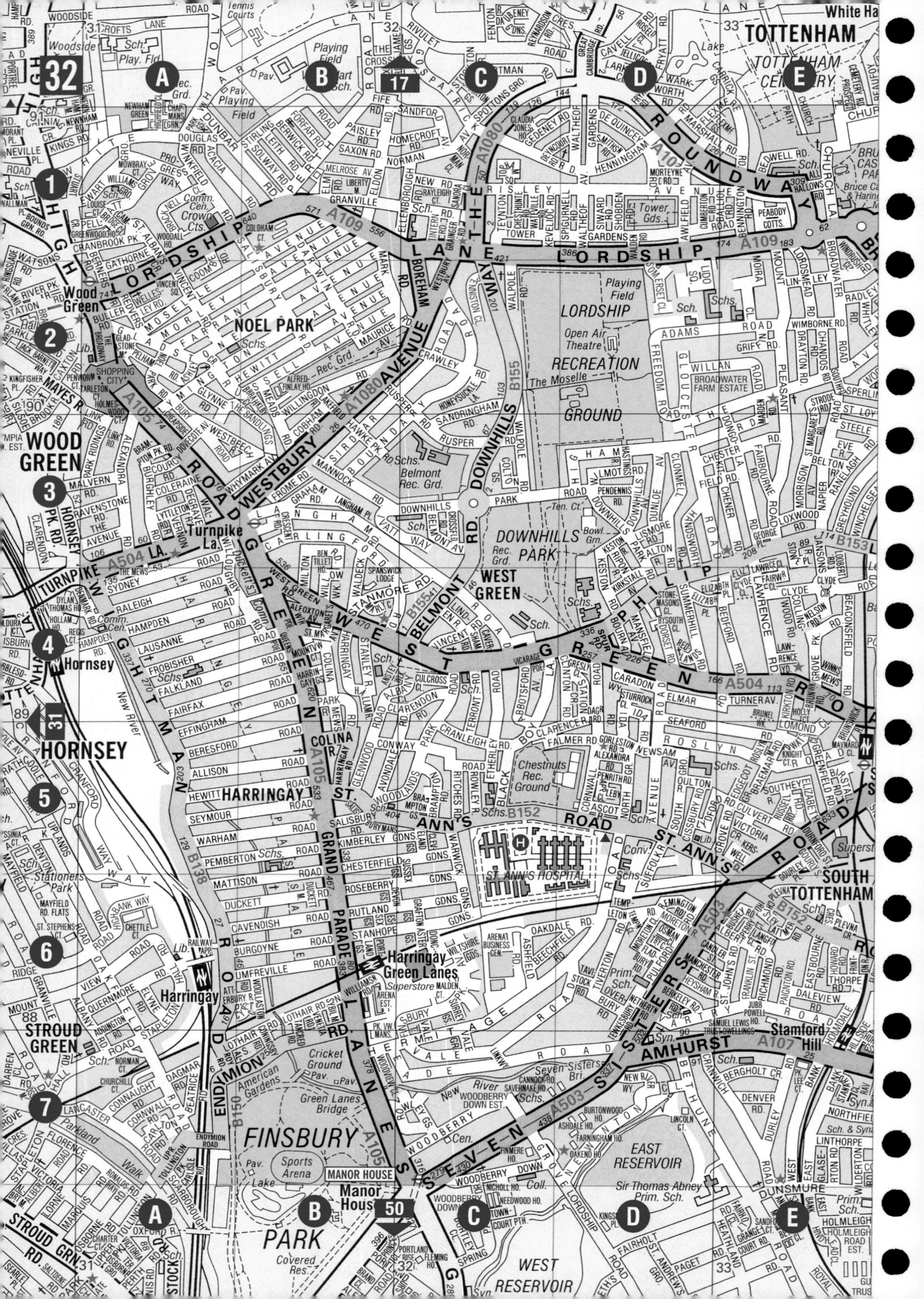

32
17
33
31
50
A
B
C
D
E
1
2
3
4
5
6
7
TOTTENHAM
TOTTENHAM CEMETERY
WOOD GREEN
Wood Green
NOEL PARK
LORDSHIP RECREATION GROUND
Playing Field
Open Air Theatre
The Moselle
BROADWATER FARM ESTATE
DOWNHILLS PARK
WEST GREEN
HORNSEY
Hornsey
HARRINGAY
Harringay
Harringay Green Lanes
STROUD GREEN
FINSBURY PARK
Sports Arena
MANOR HOUSE
Manor House
EAST RESERVOIR
WEST RESERVOIR
SOUTH TOTTENHAM
Stamford Hill
ST. ANN'S HOSPITAL
Chestnuts Rec. Ground
Belmont Rec. Grd.
Stationers Park
American Gardens
Cricket Ground
Green Lanes Bridge
New River
Parkland Walk
Seven Sisters Bri.
WOODBERRY DOWN EST.
Sir Thomas Abney Prim. Sch.
Covered Res.
Superstore
SHOPPING CITY
LORDSHIP LANE A109
ROUNDWAY A1080
THE WAY
WESTBURY AVENUE A1080
DOWNHILLS WAY B155
WEST GREEN ROAD A504
PHILIP LANE
TURNPIKE LA. A504
Turnpike La.
WIGHTMAN ROAD B138
GREEN LANES A105
GRAND PARADE
ST. ANN'S ROAD B152
ST. ANN'S ROAD
SEVEN SISTERS ROAD A503
AMHURST PARK A107
ENDYMION ROAD
HIGH ROAD
HORNSEY PK. RD.
STROUD GRN. RD.
HERMITAGE ROAD
VALE ROAD
WOODBERRY DOWN
LORDSHIP PARK
BETHUNE ROAD

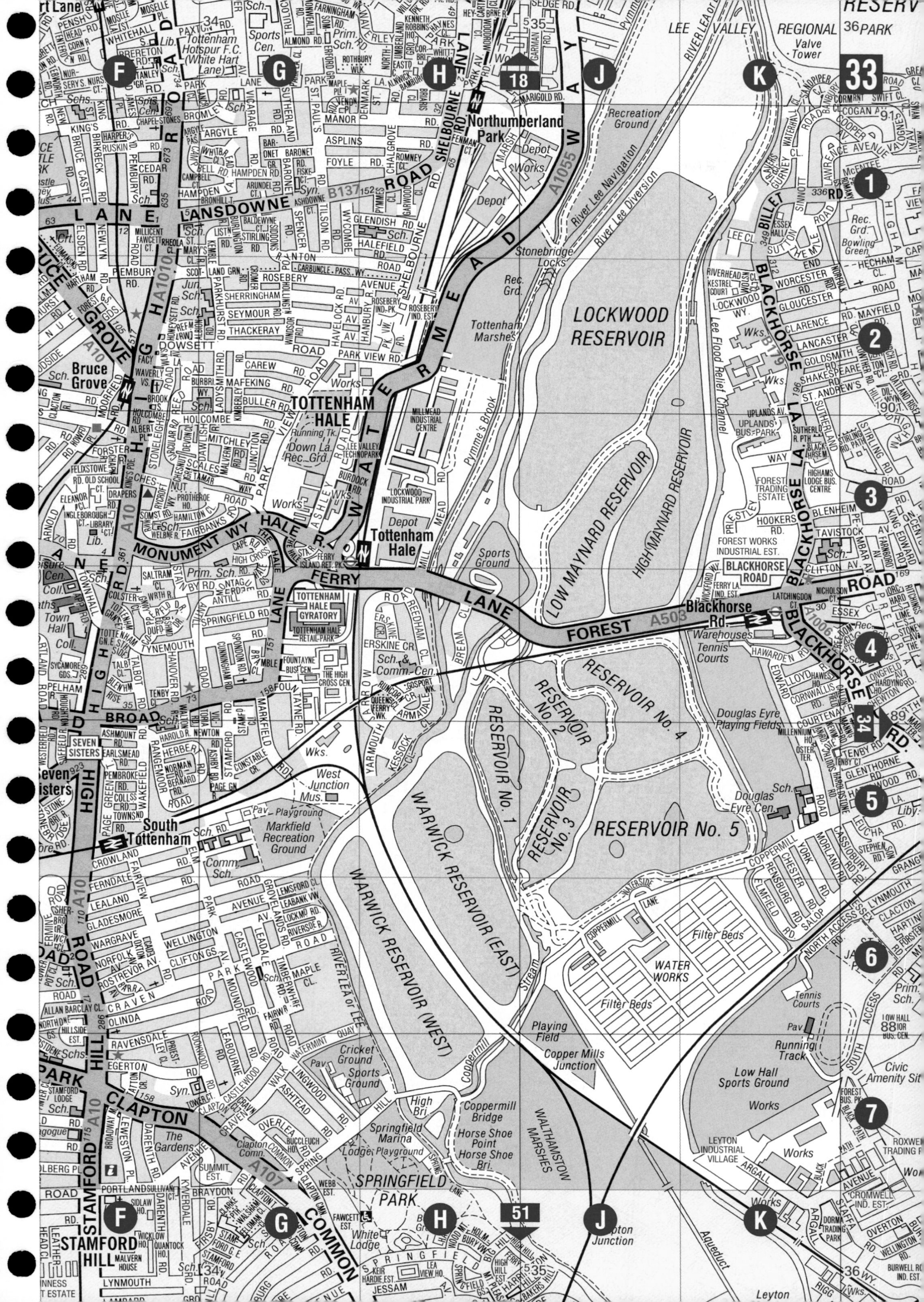

33
18
51
34
TOTTENHAM HALE
Tottenham Hale
Northumberland Park
Bruce Grove
South Tottenham
Seven Sisters
STAMFORD HILL
Blackhorse Rd.
LEE VALLEY REGIONAL PARK
LOCKWOOD RESERVOIR
LOW MAYNARD RESERVOIR
HIGH MAYNARD RESERVOIR
RESERVOIR No. 1
RESERVOIR No. 2
RESERVOIR No. 3
RESERVOIR No. 4
RESERVOIR No. 5
WARWICK RESERVOIR (EAST)
WARWICK RESERVOIR (WEST)
WALTHAMSTOW MARSHES
SPRINGFIELD PARK
Tottenham Marshes
Markfield Recreation Ground
WATER WORKS
Filter Beds
Low Hall Sports Ground
LEYTON INDUSTRIAL VILLAGE
Tottenham Hotspur F.C. (White Hart Lane)
WATERMEAD WAY
FERRY LANE
FOREST ROAD
BLACKHORSE LANE
HIGH ROAD
STAMFORD HILL
CLAPTON COMMON
LANSDOWNE ROAD
MONUMENT WY
BROAD LANE
A10
A503
A1055
A107
A1006
B137
B179
HA1010

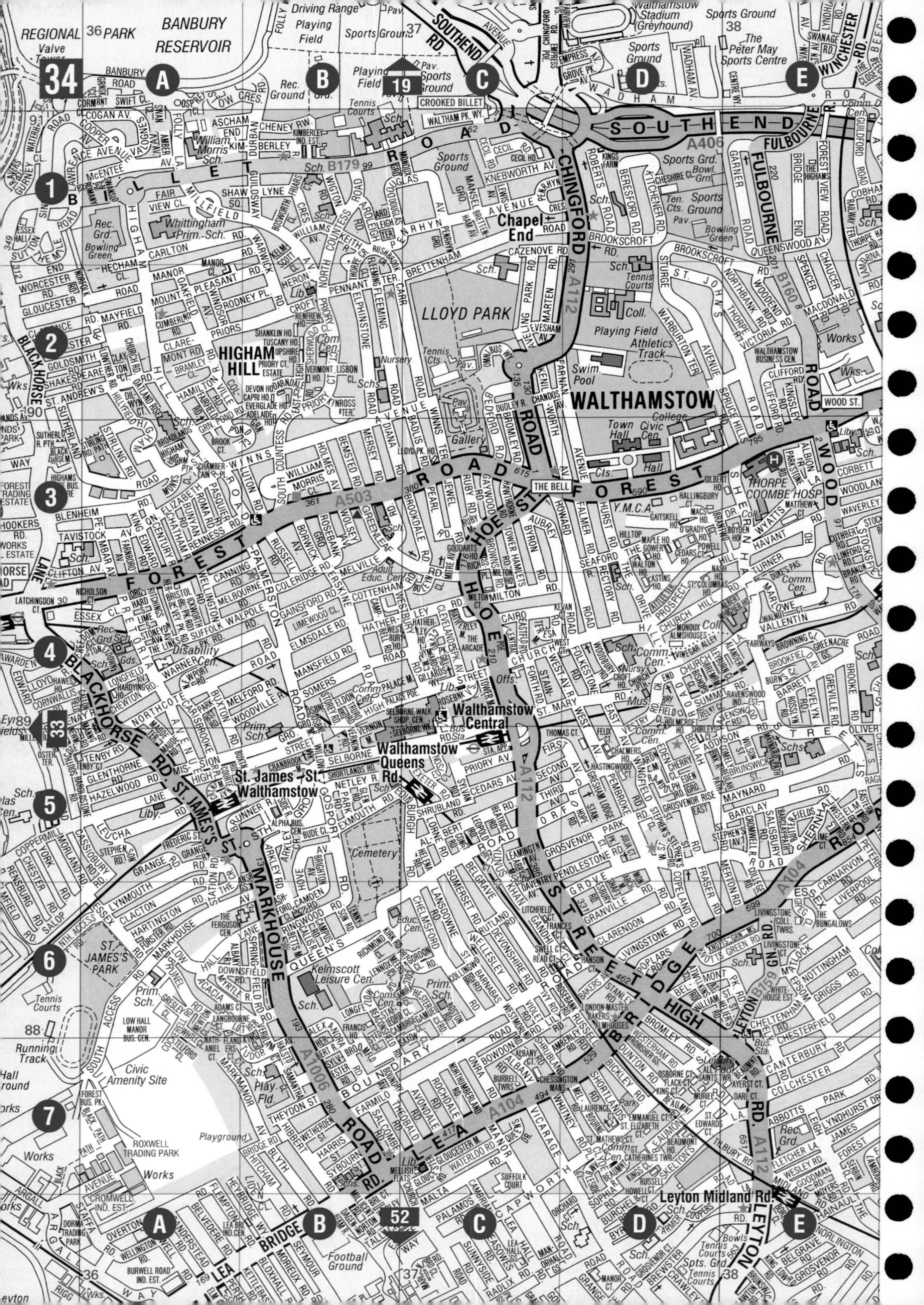

34
REGIONAL PARK
BANBURY RESERVOIR
Valve Tower
Driving Range
Playing Field
Sports Ground
Walthamstow Stadium (Greyhound)
The Peter May Sports Centre
19
CROOKED BILLET
SOUTHEND RD.
SOUTHEND
A406
FULBOURNE RD.
WADHAM
BILLET ROAD
B179
CHINGFORD ROAD
A112
Chapel End
LLOYD PARK
Playing Field
Athletics Track
Swim. Pool
WALTHAMSTOW
Town Hall
Civic Cen.
College
Gallery
HIGHAM HILL
Whittingham Prim. Sch.
BLACKHORSE LANE
FOREST ROAD
A503
THE BELL
THORPE COOMBE HOSP.
WOOD ST.
HOE ST.
Walthamstow Central
Walthamstow Queens Rd.
St. James St. Walthamstow
ST. JAMES'S ST.
BLACKHORSE RD.
MARKHOUSE RD.
A1006
Cemetery
Kelmscott Leisure Cen.
ST. JAMES'S PARK
Running Track
Civic Amenity Site
Playground
ROXWELL TRADING PARK
LEA BRIDGE
33
52
HIGH STREET
HIGH RD. LEYTON
B159
A104
LEA BRIDGE ROAD
ESSEX RD.
Leyton Midland Rd.
Football Ground
Tennis Courts
CROMWELL IND. EST.
BURWELL ROAD IND. EST.
A B C D E
1 2 3 4 5 6 7
36 37 38
88 89 90 91

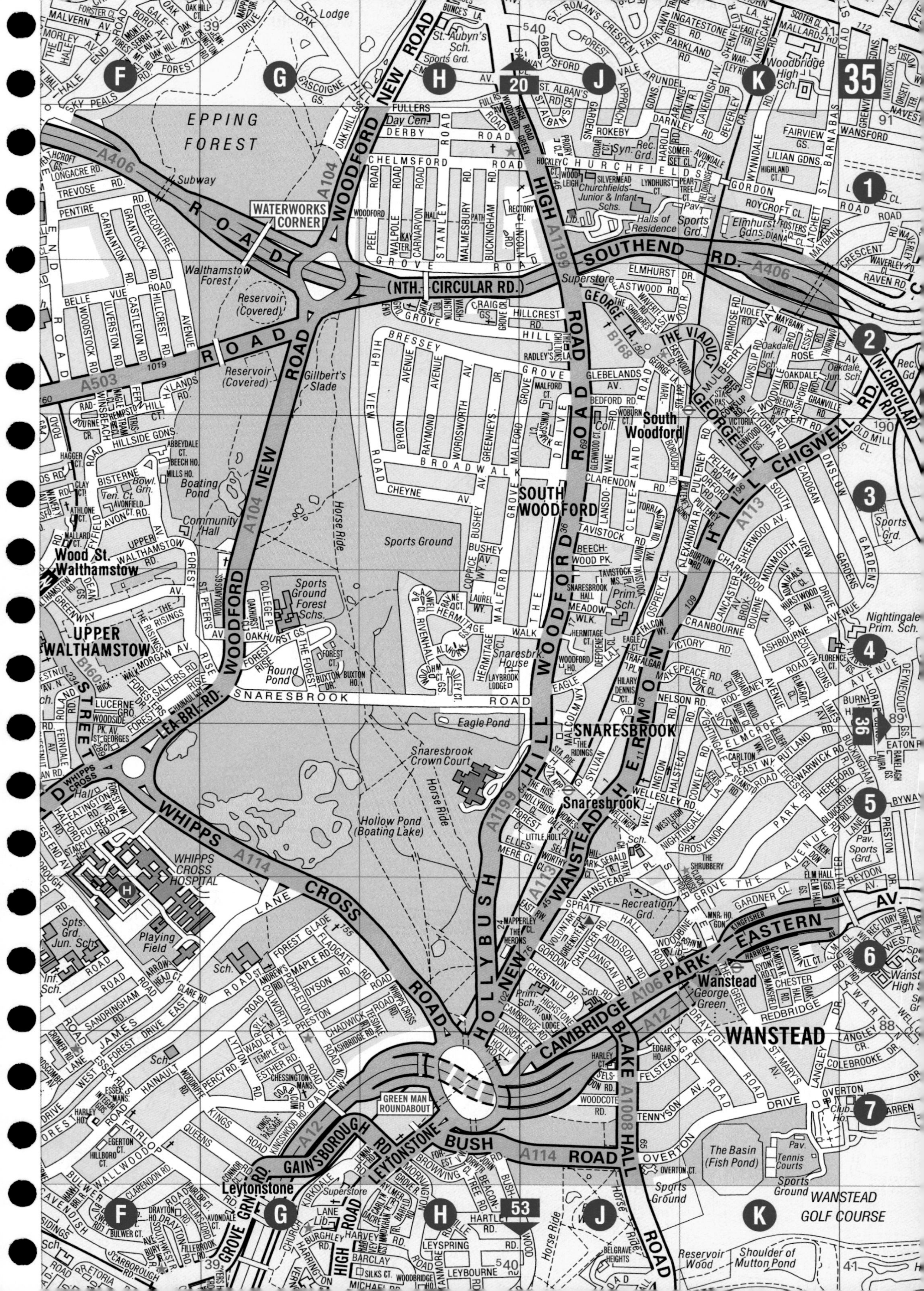

35
20
36
53
F
G
H
J
K
1
2
3
4
5
6
7
EPPING FOREST
A406
ROAD
WATERWORKS CORNER
WOODFORD NEW ROAD
A104
SOUTHEND RD.
(NTH. CIRCULAR RD.)
Walthamstow Forest
Reservoir (Covered)
A503
Gilbert's Slade
NEW ROAD
HIGH ROAD WOODFORD GREEN
A1199
CHELMSFORD ROAD
DERBY ROAD
GROVE ROAD
Fullers Day Cen.
St. Aubyn's Sch.
Sports Grd.
St. Alban's
Churchfields' Junior & Infant Schs.
Halls of Residence
Sports Grd.
Elmhurst Gdns.
Woodbridge High Sch.
FAIRVIEW GS.
LILIAN GDNS.
WANSFORD
GORDON
ROYCROFT CL.
CRESCENT
Superstore
GEORGE LA.
B168
THE VIADUCT
BRESSEY
BROADWALK
CHEYNE AV.
SOUTH WOODFORD
South Woodford
Coll.
GLEBELANDS AV.
CLARENDON RD.
TAVISTOCK RD.
CHIGWELL
A113
HIGH ROAD
WOODFORD
CHARNWOOD
MONMOUTH
CRANBOURNE RD.
Nightingale Prim. Sch.
Sports Grd.
Oakdale Inf. Sch.
Oakdale Jun. Sch.
(N. CIRCULAR) RD.
OLD MILL CL.
Boating Pond
Community Hall
Sports Ground
Horse Ride
Sports Ground Forest Schs.
Wood St. Walthamstow
UPPER WALTHAMSTOW
B160
STREET
WOODFORD
LEA BRI. RD.
SNARESBROOK ROAD
Round Pond
Snaresbrk. House
Eagle Pond
SNARESBROOK
Snaresbrook
Snaresbrook Crown Court
Hollow Pond (Boating Lake)
HERMON HILL
WANSTEAD
A1199
HOLLYBUSH HILL
NEW WANSTEAD
A113
WHIPPS CROSS ROAD
A114
WHIPPS CROSS HOSPITAL
Playing Field
LANE
Recreation Grd.
THE AVENUE
GROSVENOR
THE SHRUBBERY
EASTERN AV.
PARK
Wanstead
George Green
WANSTEAD
A106
CAMBRIDGE PARK
A12
BLAKE HALL ROAD
A1008
GREEN MAN ROUNDABOUT
BUSH ROAD
A114
LEYTONSTONE
GAINSBOROUGH RD.
HIGH ROAD
Leytonstone
Superstore
Lib.
GROVE GRN. RD.
OVERTON DRIVE
The Basin (Fish Pond)
Pav. Tennis Courts
Sports Ground
WANSTEAD GOLF COURSE
Sports Ground
Reservoir Wood
Shoulder of Mutton Pond
Club Ho.
JAMES LANE
FOREST DRIVE EAST
HAINAULT RD.
KINGS ROAD
QUEENS ROAD
FAIRLOP ROAD
WALLWOOD RD.
CAVENDISH
BULWER
Sch.
Sch.
Prim. Sch.
Spts. Grd. Jun. Sch.
Inf. Sch.
Pav. Sports Grd.
REDBRIDGE
ST. MARY'S AV.
LANGLEY
COLEBROOKE
TENNYSON AV.
39
540
41
39
540
41

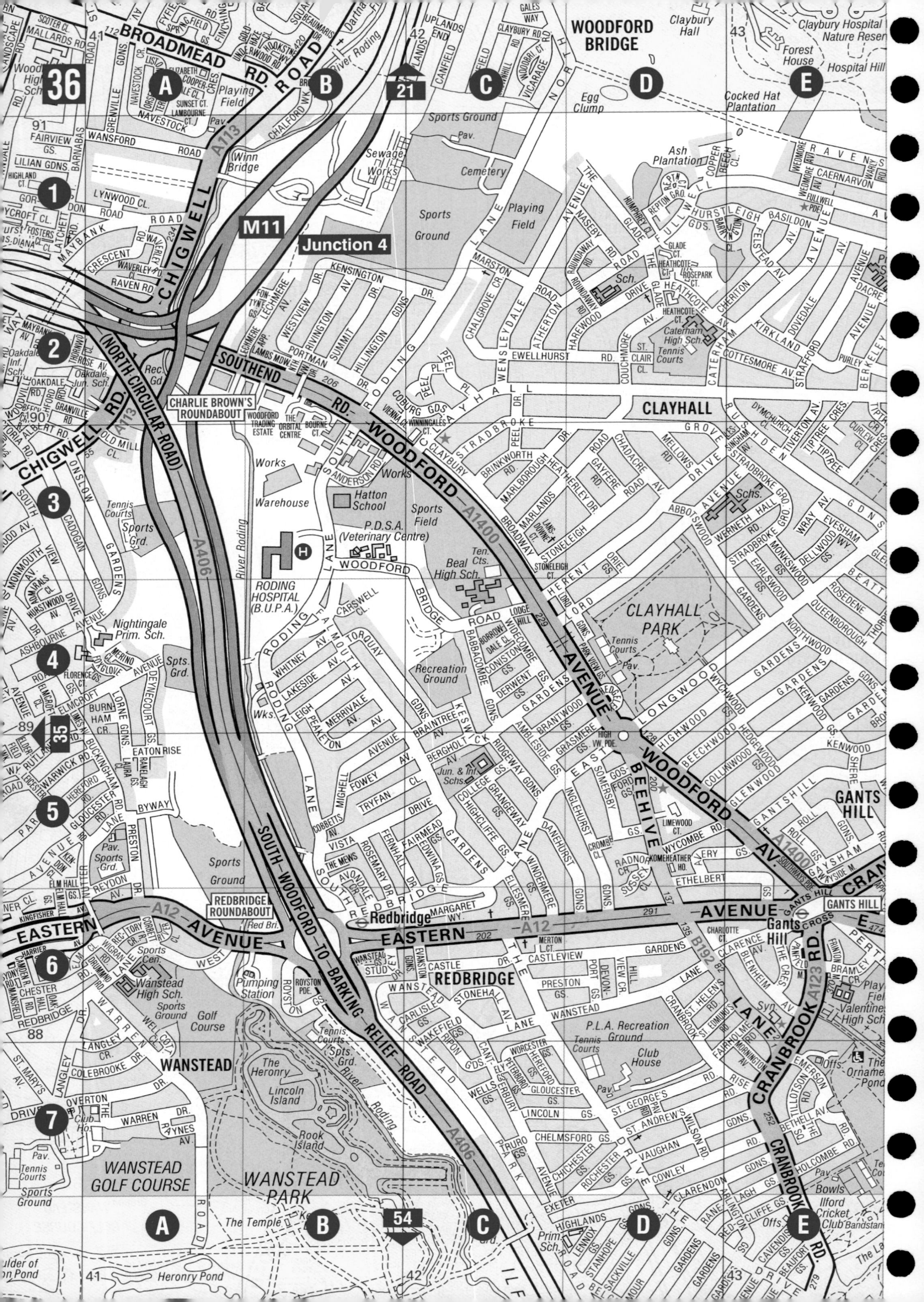
36
WOODFORD BRIDGE
CLAYHALL
CLAYHALL PARK
GANTS HILL
REDBRIDGE
WANSTEAD
WANSTEAD GOLF COURSE
WANSTEAD PARK
M11
Junction 4
CHARLIE BROWN'S ROUNDABOUT
REDBRIDGE ROUNDABOUT
RODING HOSPITAL (B.U.P.A.)
21
35
54

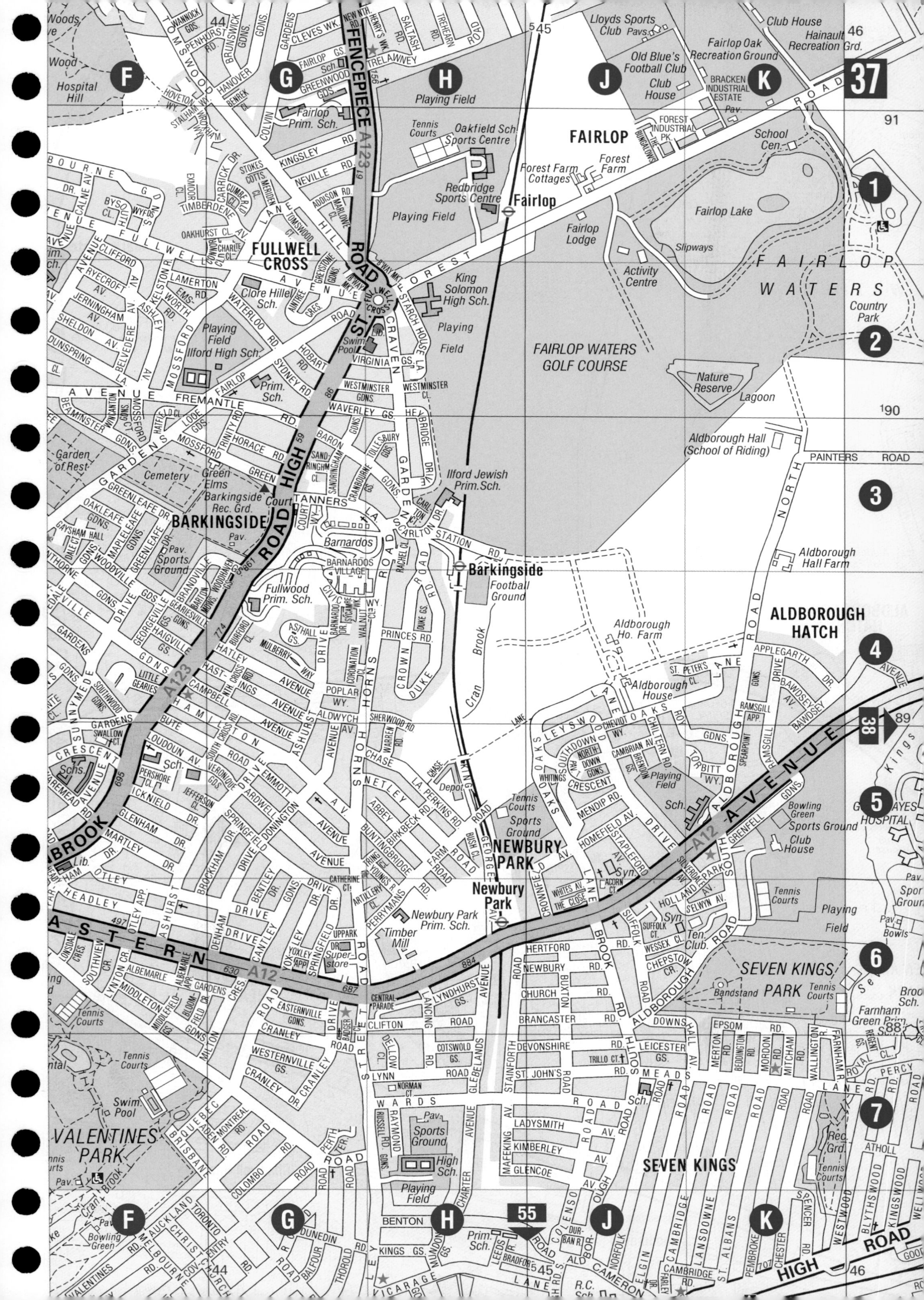
37
FAIRLOP
Fairlop
FULLWELL CROSS
BARKINGSIDE
Barkingside
NEWBURY PARK
Newbury Park
ALDBOROUGH HATCH
SEVEN KINGS
VALENTINES PARK
SEVEN KINGS PARK
FAIRLOP WATERS
Country Park
FAIRLOP WATERS GOLF COURSE
Fairlop Lake
Slipways
Activity Centre
Nature Reserve
Lagoon
Fairlop Lodge
Forest Farm Cottages
Forest Farm
FOREST INDUSTRIAL PK.
BRACKEN INDUSTRIAL ESTATE
School Cen.
Lloyds Sports Club
Club House
Hainault Recreation Grd.
Fairlop Oak Recreation Ground
Old Blue's Football Club
Playing Field
Tennis Courts
Oakfield Sch. Sports Centre
Redbridge Sports Centre
Fairlop Prim. Sch.
King Solomon High Sch.
Clore Hillel Sch.
Ilford High Sch.
Ilford Jewish Prim.Sch.
Barnardos
BARNARDOS VILLAGE
Fullwood Prim. Sch.
Cemetery
Garden of Rest
Barkingside Rec. Grd.
Pav. Sports Ground
Football Ground
Aldborough Hall (School of Riding)
Aldborough Hall Farm
Aldborough Ho. Farm
Aldborough House
Cran Brook
Newbury Park Prim. Sch.
Timber Mill
Super-store
Sports Ground
Bowling Green
Club House
Bandstand
Swim. Pool
High Sch.
Prim. Sch.
Hospital Hill
FENCEPIECE A123 ROAD
HIGH ROAD
EASTERN A12 AVENUE
FOREST ROAD
HAINAULT ROAD
PAINTERS ROAD
NORTH ROAD
STATION RD.
HORNS ROAD
ALDBOROUGH ROAD SOUTH
HIGH ROAD
F G H J K
1 2 3 4 5 6 7
44 45 46
91 90 89 88
38
55

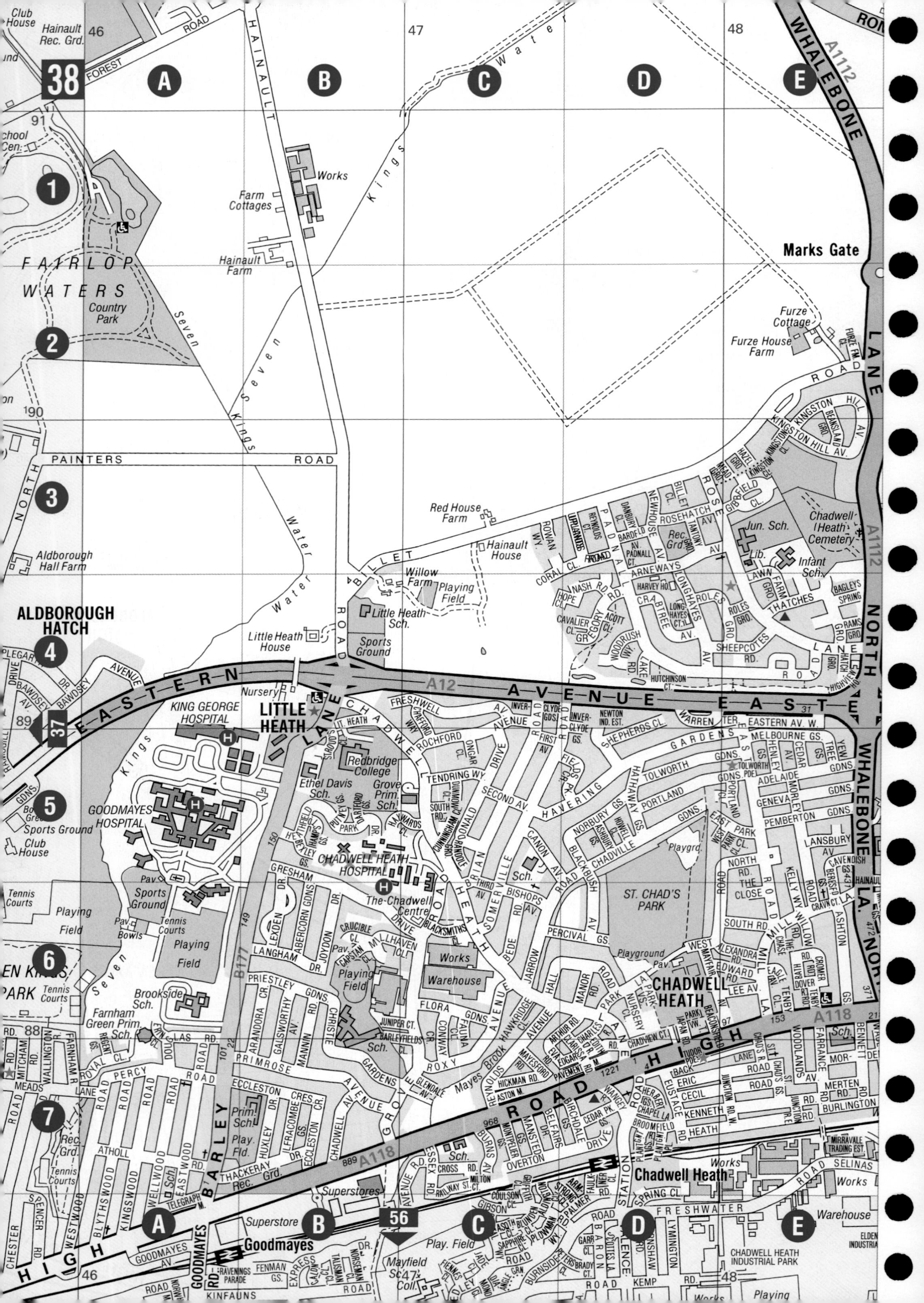
Club House
Hainault Rec. Grd.
46
47
48
FOREST ROAD
HAINAULT ROAD
Water
Kings
A
B
C
D
E
WHALEBONE
A1112
91
School Cen.
1
Works
Farm Cottages
Hainault Farm
FAIRLOP WATERS
Country Park
Seven
2
Marks Gate
Furze Cottage
Furze House Farm
FURZE FM. CL.
ROAD
LANE
190
PAINTERS ROAD
NORTH
3
KINGSTON HILL AV.
KINGSTON HILL
Red House Farm
Aldborough Hall Farm
Hainault House
Willow Farm
Playing Field
BILLET ROAD
ROSE LANE
ROSEHATCH AV.
NEWHOUSE AV.
PADNALL
Rec. Grd.
Jun. Sch.
Chadwell Heath Cemetery
Lib.
Infant Sch.
ARNEWAYS
CORAL CL.
NASH RD.
CAVALIER CL.
GREGORY RD.
CRABTREE AV.
ROLES GRO.
THATCHES
SHEEPCOTES LANE
WOODRUSH WY.
HUTCHINSON CT.
ALDBOROUGH HATCH
Little Heath Sch.
Little Heath House
Sports Ground
4
BAWDSEY AVENUE
EASTERN AVENUE EAST
A12
Nursery
LITTLE HEATH
KING GEORGE HOSPITAL
89
37
FRESHWELL AV.
ROCHFORD
ONGAR CL.
AVENUE
FIRST AV.
NEWTON IND. EST.
WARREN
EASTERN AV. W.
MELBOURNE GS.
SHEPHERDS CL.
GARDENS
TOLWORTH
Redbridge College
Ethel Davis Sch.
Grove Prim. Sch.
TENDRING WY.
SECOND AV.
HAVERING
PORTLAND
ADELAIDE
GENEVA
PEMBERTON
LANSBURY AV.
5
GOODMAYES HOSPITAL
Sports Ground
Club House
CHADWELL HEATH HOSPITAL
The Chadwell Centre
NORBURY GS.
HATHAWAY GS.
EAST PARK CL.
Playgrd.
CHADVILLE
BLACKBUSH AV.
BISHOPS AV.
THIRD AV.
SOMERVILLE
Sch.
NORTH RD.
THE CLOSE
KELLY WY.
CAVENDISH GS.
HAINAULT
Tennis Courts
Playing Field
Sports Ground
Tennis Courts
Pav.
Bowls
Playing Field
GRESHAM
LEXDEN DR.
ABERCORN GDNS.
JOYDON DR.
LANGHAM DR.
ST. CHAD'S PARK
PERCIVAL
SOUTH RD.
MILLWILLOW
ASHTON
CRUCIBLE CL.
MILLHAVEN CL.
BLACKSMITHS CL.
Works
Warehouse
Playing Field
6
SEVEN KINGS PARK
Tennis Courts
Brookside Sch.
Farnham Green Prim. Sch.
B177
PRIESTLEY GDNS.
ARANDORA CR.
GALSWORTHY AV.
MANNIN RD.
CHRISTIE
JUNIPER CT.
BARLEYFIELDS CL.
FLORA GDNS.
CONWAY
BEDE
JARROW
HALL
MANOR RD.
Playground
WEST MAYFAIR
ALEXANDRA RD.
EDWARD
LEE AV.
CHADWELL HEATH
PARK VW.
BEACONSFIELD
97
153
A118
Sch.
88
MEADS LANE
MITCHAM
WALLINGTON RD.
FARNHAM RD.
REGENT GS.
ROYAL CL.
PERCY ROAD
DOUGLAS RD.
PRIMROSE ROAD
ECCLESTON CRES.
GARDENS
ROXY
GLENDALE AV.
Mayes Brook
HAWKRIDGE
AVENUE
REYNOLDS AV.
HICKMAN RD
ASTON M.
MAYESFORD RD.
PAVEMENT
1221
HIGH ROAD
CHADVIEW CT.
TUDOR PDE.
BACK LANE
ERIC
CECIL
KENNETH RD.
HEATH
EUSTACE
BURLINGTON
WOODLANDS AV.
FARRANCE
MERTEN RD.
BENNETT
7
Rec. Grd.
Tennis Courts
ATHOLL
WELLWOOD RD.
EASTWOOD RD.
BARLEY LANE
Prim. Sch.
Play. Fld.
HUXLEY DR.
ILFRACOMBE GS.
ECCLESTON CR.
CHADWELL AVENUE
GROVE
THACKERAY
Rec. Grd.
889
Superstores
ESSEX RD.
CROSS RD.
MILTON CT.
RAILWAY ST.
968
BURNS AV.
MONTPELIER GS.
MANSTED GS.
BELFAIRS DR.
BIRCHDALE GS.
CEDAR PK. GS.
OVERTON
DRIVE
Chadwell Heath
Works
MIRRAVALE TRADING EST.
SELINAS ROAD
Works
Warehouse
TELEGRAPH M.
SPENCER
BLYTHSWOOD
KINGSWOOD
WESTWOOD
CHESTER RD.
56
Superstore
Goodmayes
GOODMAYES AV.
HIGH
46
GOODMAYES RD.
FENMAN GS.
EXPRESS DR.
RAVENINGS PARADE
KINFAUNS ROAD
Play. Field
Mayfield Sch.
47
Coll.
COULSON CL.
GIBSON CL.
STATION
SPRING CL.
FRESHWATER ROAD
LYMINGTON
BURNSIDE
BARON
KEMP ROAD
Works
48
CHADWELL HEATH INDUSTRIAL PARK
Playing
ELDEN INDUSTRIAL

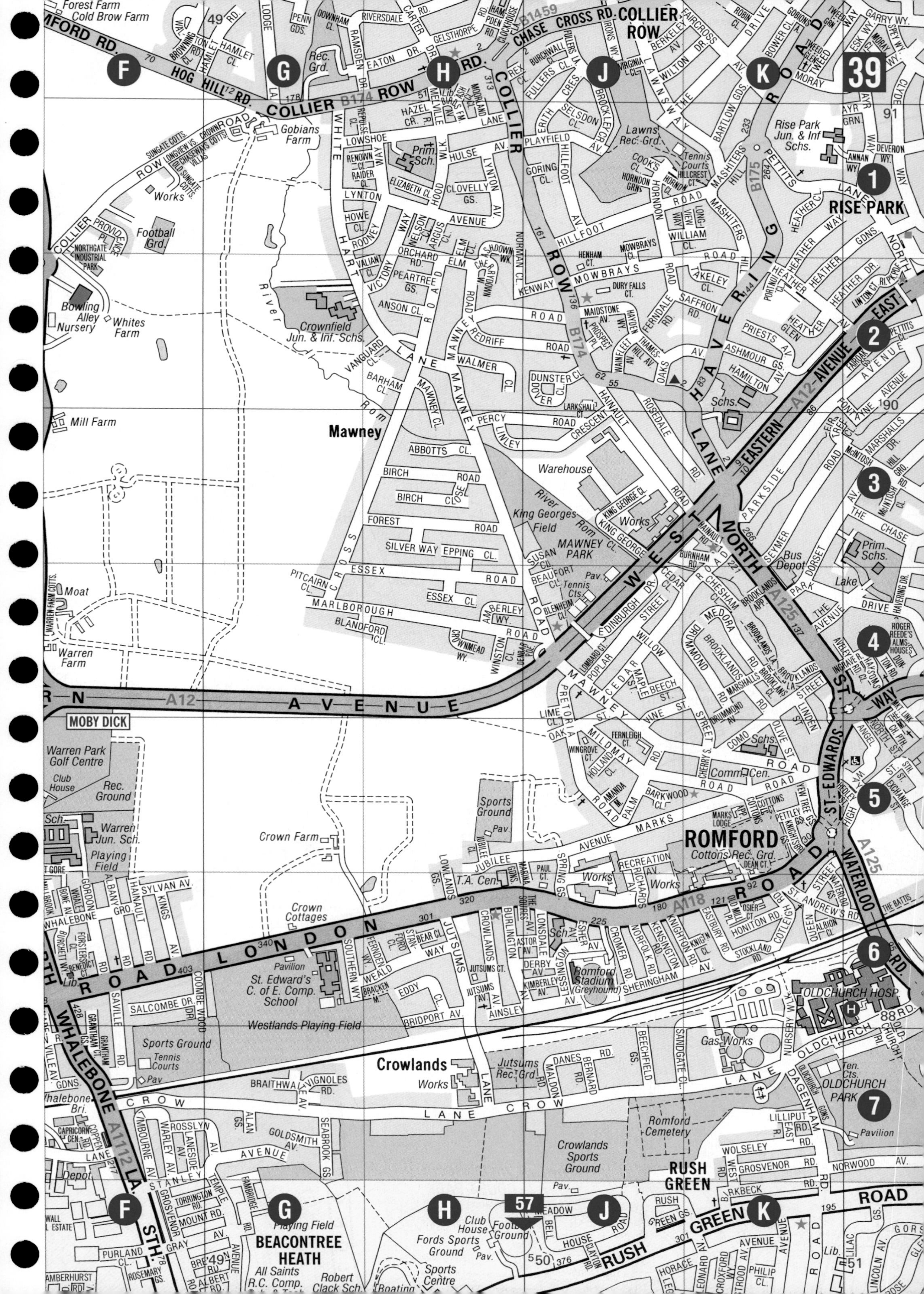
39
Forest Farm
Cold Brow Farm
COLLIER ROW
CHASE CROSS RD.
HOG HILL RD.
COLLIER ROW RD.
COLLIER ROW LA.
Gobians Farm
Works
Football Grd.
NORTHGATE INDUSTRIAL PARK
Bowling Alley
Nursery
Whites Farm
Mill Farm
Moat
Warren Farm
River Rom
Crownfield Jun. & Inf. Schs.
Mawney
MAWNEY RD.
CROSS RD.
FOREST ROAD
ESSEX ROAD
MARLBOROUGH RD.
King Georges Field
MAWNEY PARK
Warehouse
Works
Lawns Rec. Grd.
Tennis Courts
Rise Park Jun. & Inf Schs.
RISE PARK
PETTITS LANE
HAVERING RD.
EASTERN AVENUE
A12
WEST
NORTH STREET
Bus Depot
Prim. Schs.
Lake
ROGER REEDE'S ALMS-HOUSES
ST. EDWARDS WAY
WATERLOO RD.
A125
A118
MOBY DICK
Warren Park Golf Centre
Club House
Rec. Ground
Warren Jun. Sch.
Playing Field
Crown Farm
Crown Cottages
Sports Ground
T.A. Cen.
ROMFORD
Cottons Rec. Grd.
Comm. Cen.
LONDON ROAD
St. Edward's C. of E. Comp. School
Westlands Playing Field
Romford Stadium (Greyhound)
Crowlands
Works
Jutsums Rec. Grd.
Gas Works
OLDCHURCH HOSP.
OLDCHURCH PARK
CROW LANE
Romford Cemetery
Crowlands Sports Ground
RUSH GREEN
RUSH GREEN ROAD
WHALEBONE LA.
A1112
BEACONTREE HEATH
Playing Field
Club House
Football Ground
Fords Sports Ground
Sports Centre
All Saints R.C. Comp.
Robert Clack Sch.
57
49
50
51
90
91
F
G
H
J
K
1
2
3
4
5
6
7

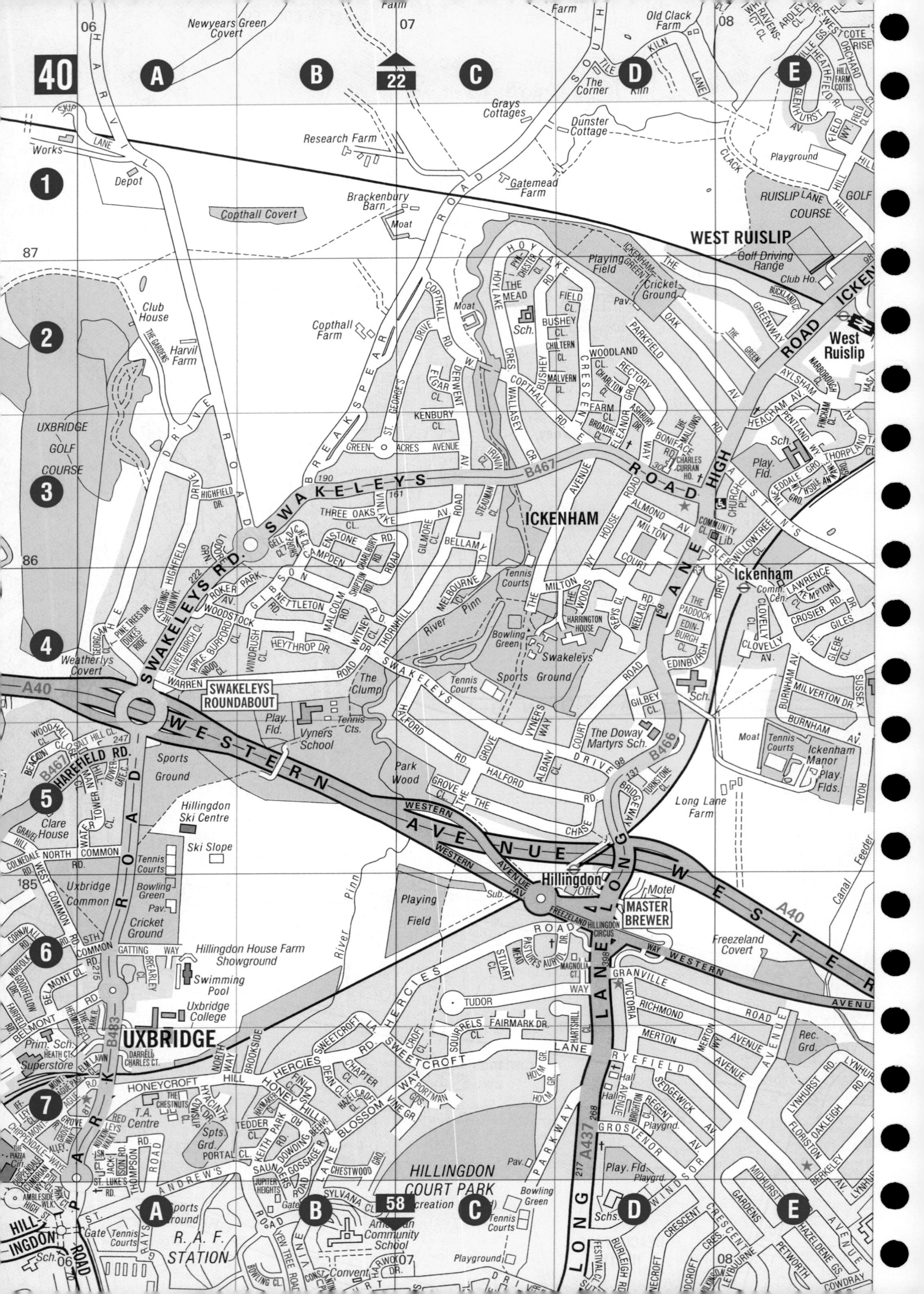
22
58
WEST RUISLIP
West Ruislip
ICKENHAM
Ickenham
UXBRIDGE
HILLINGDON COURT PARK
Hillingdon
SWAKELEYS ROUNDABOUT
MASTER BREWER
Uxbridge Golf Course
Ruislip Golf Course
Copthall Covert
Research Farm
Brackenbury Barn
Gatemead Farm
Grays Cottages
Dunster Cottage
Old Clack Farm
Newyears Green Covert
Harvil Farm
Copthall Farm
Swakeleys
Vyners School
Hillingdon Ski Centre
Hillingdon House Farm Showground
Uxbridge College
Uxbridge Common
Long Lane Farm
Freezeland Covert
Ickenham Manor
The Doway Martyrs Sch.
R. A. F. STATION
American Community School
SWAKELEYS ROAD
WESTERN AVENUE
LONG LANE
HIGH ROAD
PARK ROAD
HARVIL ROAD
BREAKSPEAR ROAD SOUTH
HERCIES ROAD
A40
B467
B466
B483
A437

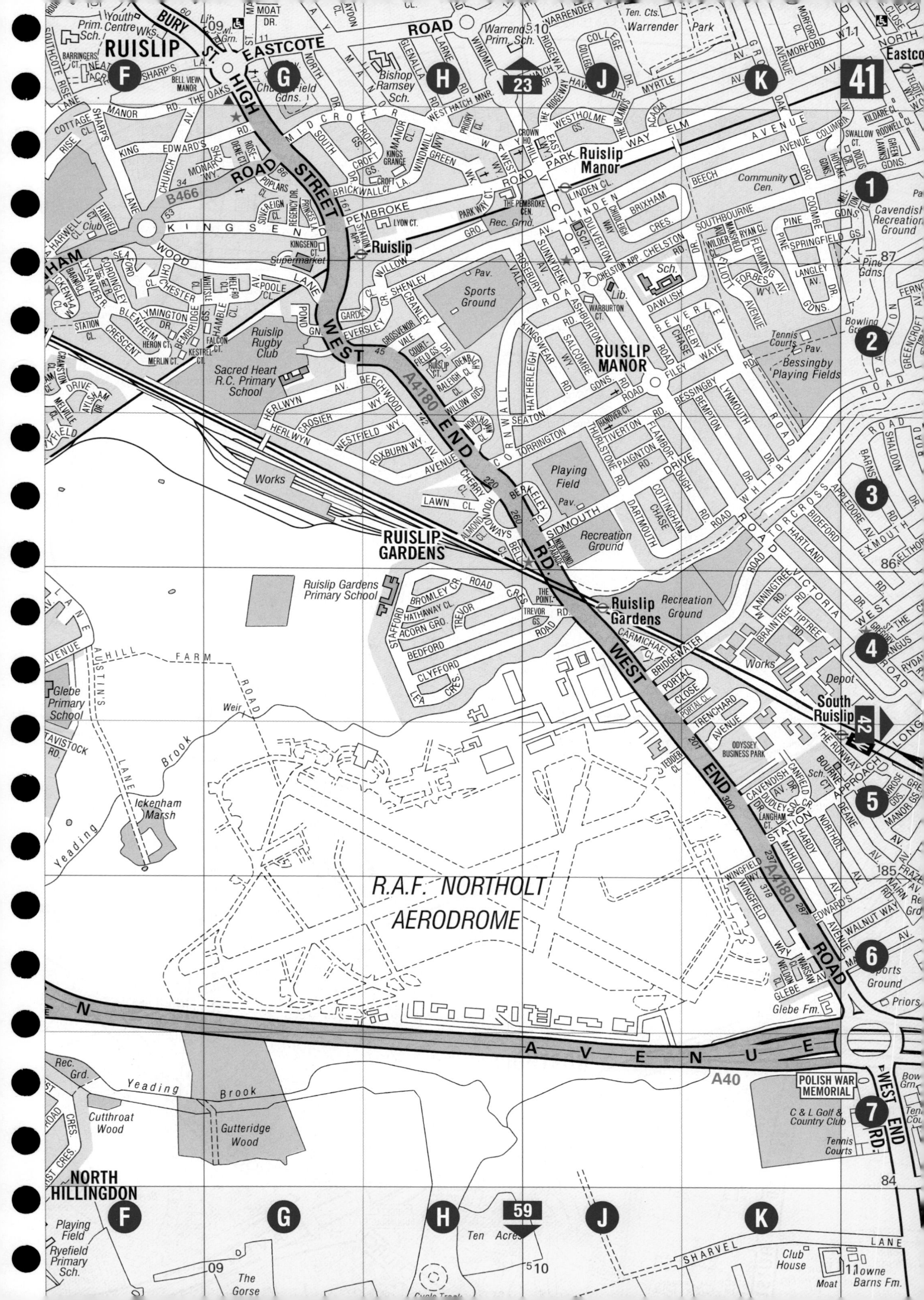

41
RUISLIP
EASTCOTE
Ruislip Manor
RUISLIP MANOR
Ruislip
RUISLIP GARDENS
Ruislip Gardens
South Ruislip
R.A.F. NORTHOLT AERODROME
NORTH HILLINGDON
HIGH STREET
WEST END ROAD
A4180
B466
A40
AVENUE
Sports Ground
Ruislip Rugby Club
Sacred Heart R.C. Primary School
Ruislip Gardens Primary School
Bishop Ramsey Sch.
Works
Playing Field
Recreation Ground
Bessingby Playing Fields
Cavendish Recreation Ground
Community Cen.
Supermarket
Ickenham Marsh
Glebe Primary School
Cutthroat Wood
Gutteridge Wood
Yeading Brook
POLISH WAR MEMORIAL
C & L Golf & Country Club
ODYSSEY BUSINESS PARK
Glebe Fm.
Ten Acres
Club House
Towne Barns Fm.
SHARVEL LANE
23
42
59
F
G
H
J
K
1
2
3
4
5
6
7

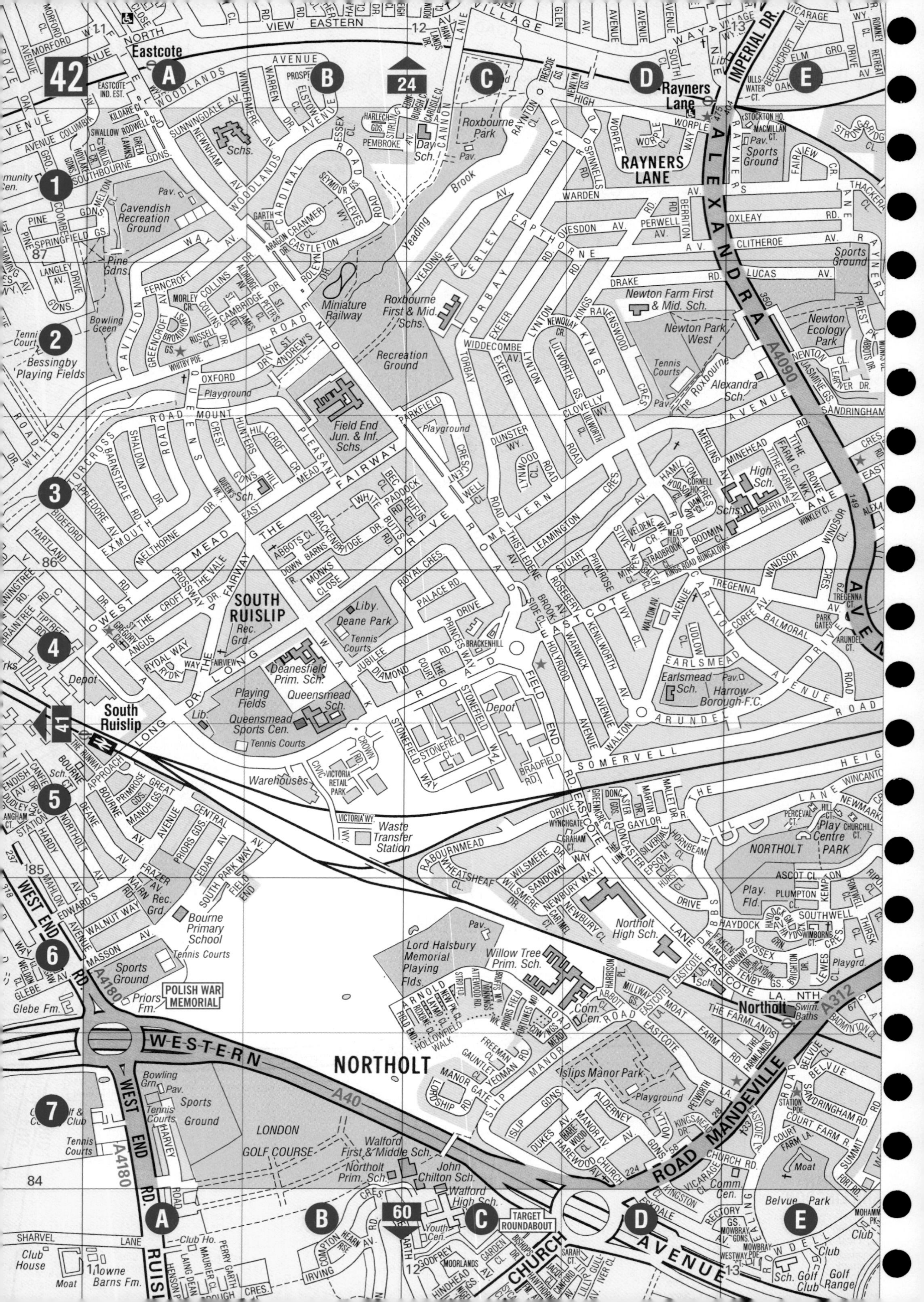

42
Eastcote
A
B
C
D
E
24
Rayners Lane
RAYNERS LANE
ALEXANDRA AV.
A4090
IMPERIAL DR.
Sports Ground
Cavendish Recreation Ground
Pav.
Schs.
Day Sch.
Roxbourne Park
Yeading Brook
Miniature Railway
Roxbourne First & Mid. Schs.
Recreation Ground
Newton Farm First & Mid. Sch.
Newton Park West
Tennis Courts
Alexandra Sch.
Newton Ecology Park
The Roxbourne
Bowling Green
Bessingby Playing Fields
Pine Gdns.
Field End Jun. & Inf. Schs.
Playground
High Sch.
Queen's Sch.
SOUTH RUISLIP
Rec. Grd.
Liby.
Deane Park
Tennis Courts
Deanesfield Prim. Sch.
Queensmead Sch.
Playing Fields
Queensmead Sports Cen.
Lib.
Depot
South Ruislip
41
Warehouses
Victoria Retail Park
Waste Transfer Station
Earlsmead Sch.
Harrow Borough F.C.
Northolt High Sch.
NORTHOLT PARK
Play Centre
Play. Fld.
Bourne Primary School
Tennis Courts
Sports Ground
POLISH WAR MEMORIAL
Priors Fm.
Glebe Fm.
Lord Halsbury Memorial Playing Flds.
Willow Tree Prim. Sch.
Com. Cen.
Northolt
Swim. Baths
A312
WESTERN
A40
NORTHOLT
A4180
WEST END RD.
Islips Manor Park
Playground
Bowling Grn
Sports Ground
LONDON GOLF COURSE
Walford First & Middle Sch.
Northolt Prim. Sch.
John Chilton Sch.
Walford High Sch.
Youth Cen.
60
TARGET ROUNDABOUT
ROAD MANDEVILLE
Comm. Cen.
Belvue Park
Moat
Club House
Towne Barns Fm.
Golf Club
Golf Range
CHURCH AVENUE
1
2
3
4
5
6
7
84
85
86
87
11
12
13

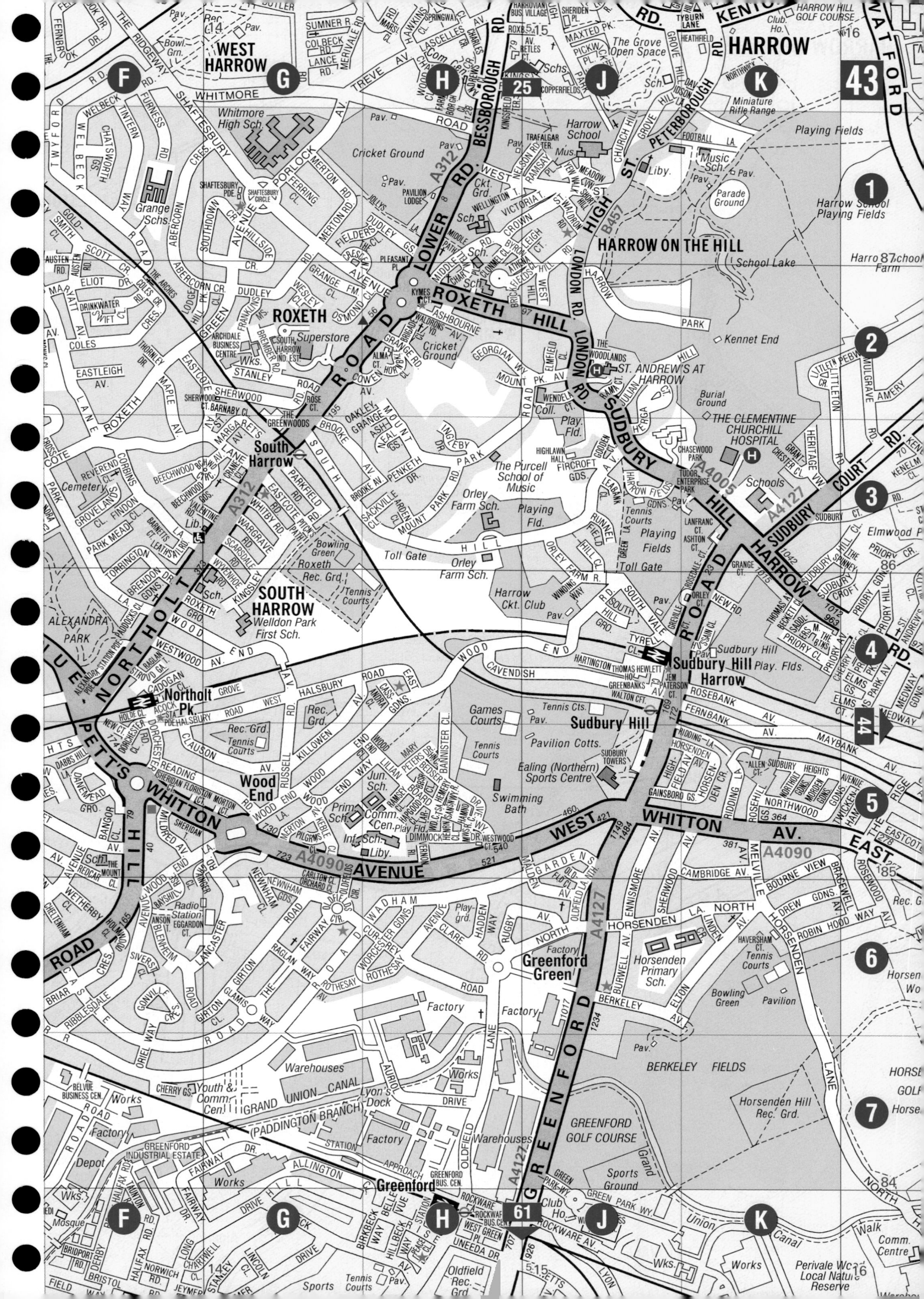
WEST HARROW
HARROW
HARROW ON THE HILL
ROXETH
SOUTH HARROW
South Harrow
Northolt Pk.
Sudbury Hill Harrow
Sudbury Hill
Wood End
Greenford Green
Greenford
F
G
H
J
K
1
2
3
4
5
6
7
25
44
61
Whitmore High Sch.
Cricket Ground
Harrow School
Harrow School Playing Fields
Playing Fields
Miniature Rifle Range
Parade Ground
School Lake
Kennet End
ST. ANDREW'S AT HARROW
THE CLEMENTINE CHURCHILL HOSPITAL
Burial Ground
Schools
The Purcell School of Music
Orley Farm Sch.
Playing Fld.
Toll Gate
Harrow Ckt. Club
Superstore
Cemetery
ALEXANDRA PARK
Welldon Park First Sch.
Roxeth Rec. Grd.
Games Courts
Tennis Courts
Pavilion Cotts.
Ealing (Northern) Sports Centre
Swimming Bath
Horsenden Primary Sch.
Radio Station
Factory
Warehouses
GRAND UNION CANAL
(PADDINGTON BRANCH)
Lyon's Dock
GREENFORD INDUSTRIAL ESTATE
GREENFORD GOLF COURSE
Sports Ground
BERKELEY FIELDS
Horsenden Hill Rec. Grd.
Bowling Green
Pavilion
Mosque
Oldfield Rec. Grd.
Perivale Wood Local Nature Reserve
A312
A4005
A4127
A4090
B457
LOWER RD.
ROXETH HILL
LONDON RD.
SUDBURY HILL
HARROW ROAD
NORTHOLT ROAD
WHITTON AVENUE
WEST WHITTON AV.
EAST
GREENFORD ROAD
WHITMORE ROAD
BESSBOROUGH RD.
HIGH ST.
SUDBURY COURT RD.
WATFORD

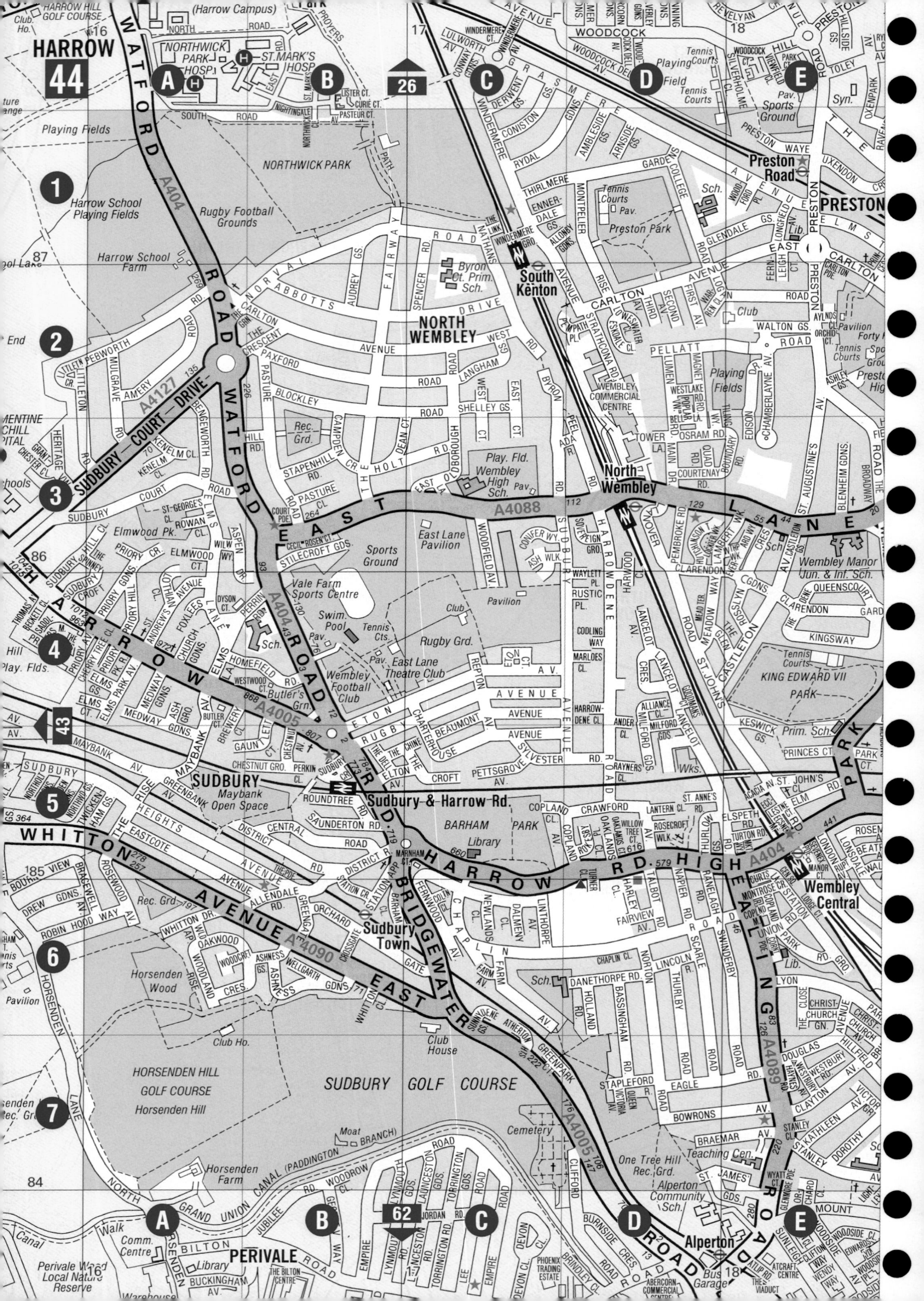
NORTHWICK PARK
Rugby Football Grounds
Harrow School Playing Fields
Harrow School Farm
NORTH WEMBLEY
South Kenton
Preston Road
PRESTON
Preston Park
North Wembley
Sports Ground
Vale Farm Sports Centre
East Lane Pavilion
Wembley Football Club
SUDBURY
Maybank Open Space
Sudbury & Harrow Rd.
Sudbury Town
BARHAM PARK
KING EDWARD VII PARK
Wembley Central
Wembley Manor Jun. & Inf. Sch.
HORSENDEN HILL GOLF COURSE
Horsenden Hill
Horsenden Wood
SUDBURY GOLF COURSE
One Tree Hill Rec. Grd.
Alperton
PERIVALE
GRAND UNION CANAL (PADDINGTON BRANCH)
WATFORD ROAD
EAST LANE
HARROW ROAD
WHITTON AVENUE EAST
EALING ROAD
BRIDGEWATER ROAD
SUDBURY COURT DRIVE
A404
A4088
A4005
A4090
A4089
A4127

26
43
62

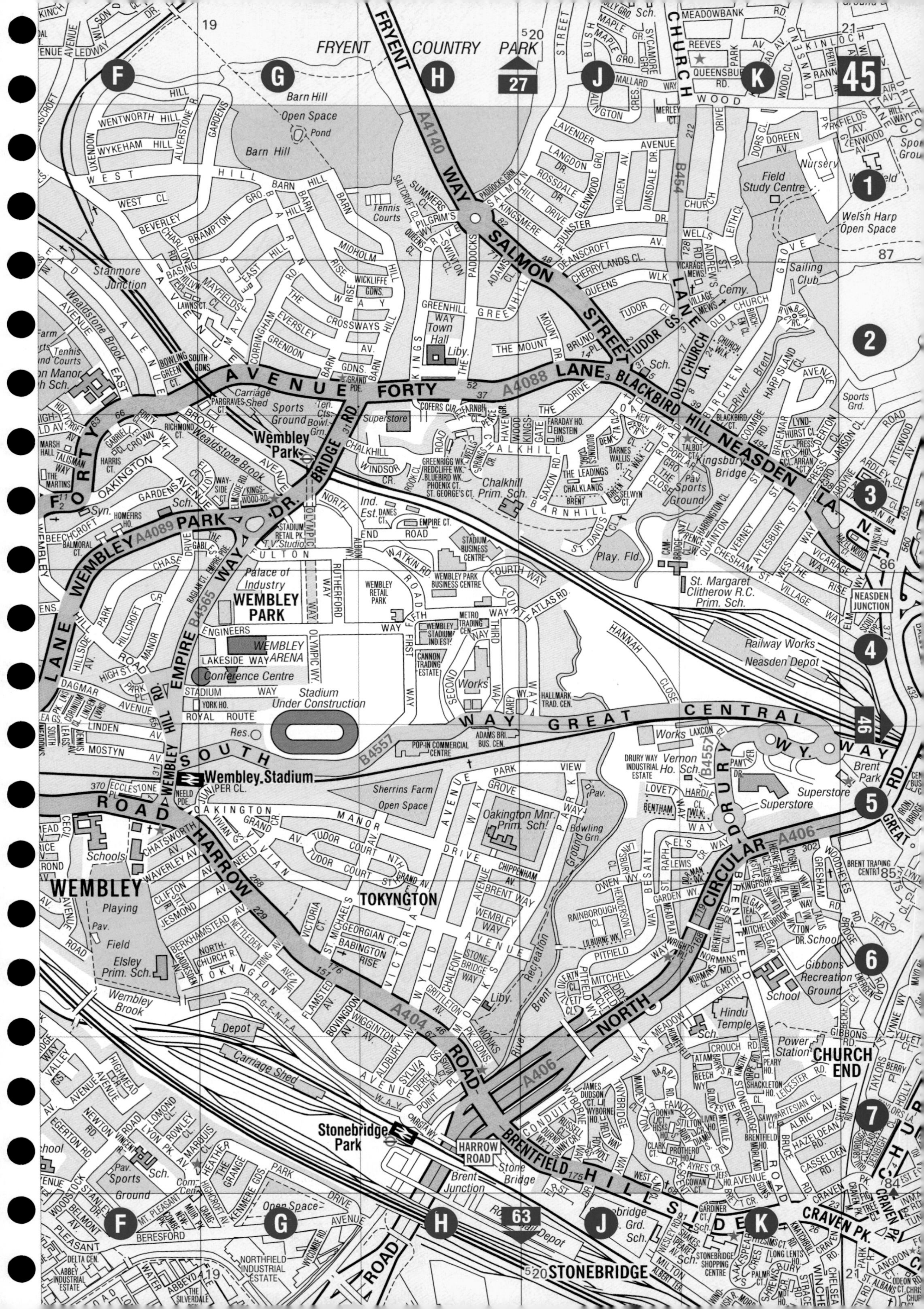
FRYENT COUNTRY PARK
Barn Hill
Open Space
Barn Hill
WEMBLEY PARK
Wembley Park
Palace of Industry
WEMBLEY ARENA
Conference Centre
Stadium Under Construction
Wembley Stadium
Sherrins Farm Open Space
Oakington Mnr. Prim. Sch.
TOKYNGTON
WEMBLEY
Playing Field
Elsley Prim. Sch.
Stonebridge Park
HARROW ROAD
STONEBRIDGE
CHURCH END
Kingsbury Bridge
Welsh Harp Open Space
Field Study Centre
Railway Works
Neasden Depot
NEASDEN JUNCTION
Brent Park
Superstore
Hindu Temple
Power Station
Gibbons Recreation Ground
St. Margaret Clitherow R.C. Prim. Sch.
Chalkhill Prim. Sch.
Stanmore Junction
A4140
A4088
A4089
B4565
B4557
A404
A406
B454
27
46
63

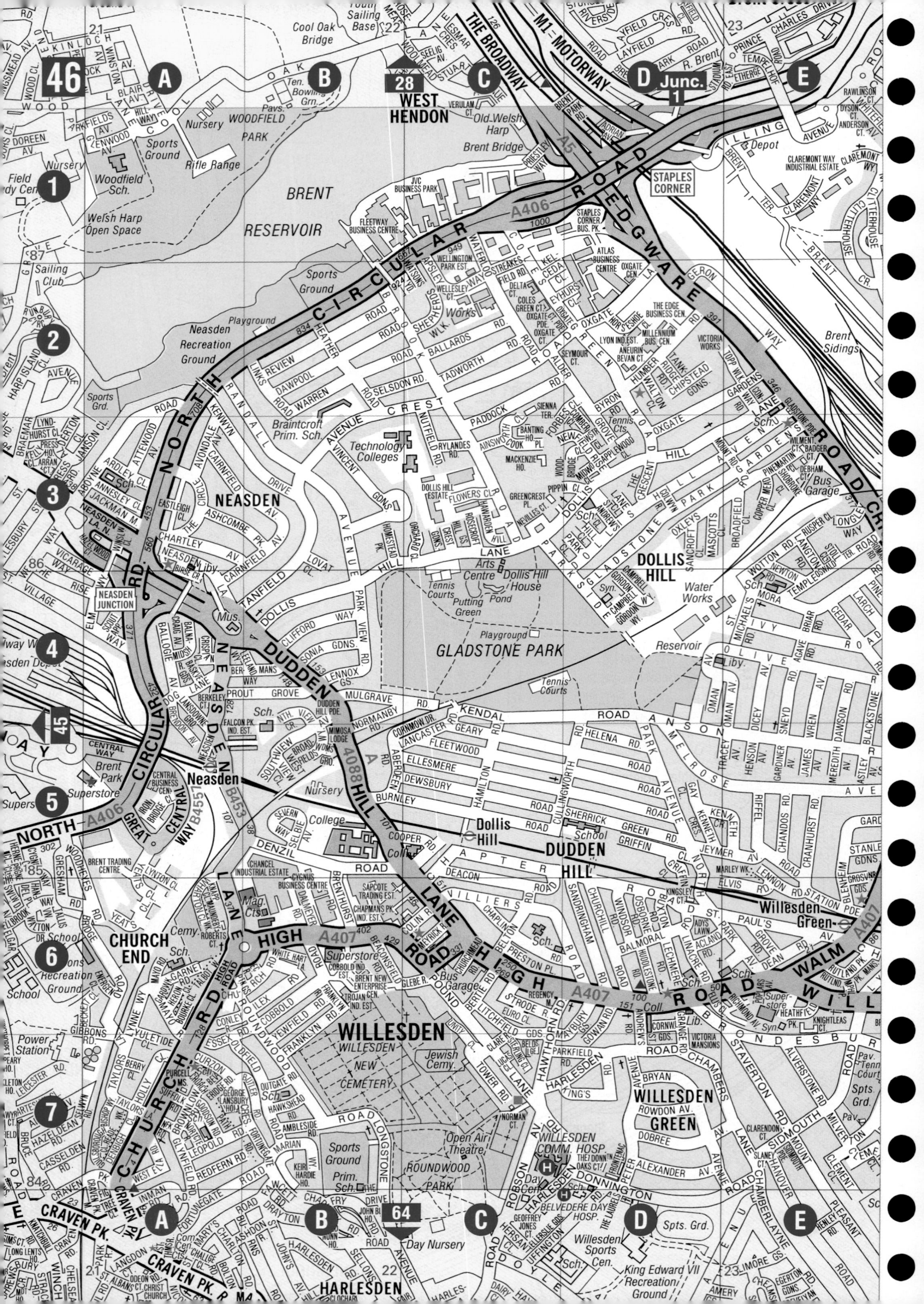
A
B
C
D
E
1
2
3
4
5
6
7
28
45
64
Junc. 1
WEST HENDON
Cool Oak Bridge
Youth Sailing Base
WOODFIELD PARK
Woodfield Sch.
Welsh Harp Open Space
Sailing Club
Nursery
Sports Ground
Rifle Range
Old Welsh Harp
Brent Bridge
BRENT RESERVOIR
M1 MOTORWAY
THE BROADWAY
STAPLES CORNER
CLAREMONT WAY INDUSTRIAL ESTATE
Depot
Brent Sidings
NORTH CIRCULAR ROAD
EDGWARE ROAD
A406
A5
JVC BUSINESS PARK
FLEETWAY BUSINESS CENTRE
STAPLES CORNER BUS. PK.
ATLAS BUSINESS CENTRE
THE EDGE BUSINESS CEN.
MILLENNIUM BUS. CEN.
VICTORIA WORKS
Works
Neasden Recreation Ground
Playground
Sports Grd.
Braintcroft Prim. Sch.
Technology Colleges
DOLLIS HILL ESTATE
NEASDEN
NEASDEN JUNCTION
Mus.
Liby.
DOLLIS HILL
Arts Centre
Dollis Hill House
Tennis Courts
Putting Green
Pond
Water Works
Reservoir
GLADSTONE PARK
Bus Garage
DUDDEN HILL LANE
A4088
FALCON PK. IND. EST.
MIMOSA LODGE
Brent Park
Superstore
Neasden
Nursery
College
Dollis Hill
DUDDEN HILL
BRENT TRADING CENTRE
CHANCEL INDUSTRIAL ESTATE
CYGNUS BUSINESS CENTRE
SAPCOTE TRADING EST.
CHAPMANS PK. IND. EST.
CHURCH END
Cemy.
HIGH ROAD
A407
Recreation Ground
School
Power Station
WILLESDEN
WILLESDEN NEW CEMETERY
Jewish Cemy.
ROUNDWOOD PARK
Open Air Theatre
Sports Ground
Prim. Sch.
Willesden Green
WILLESDEN GREEN
WILLESDEN COMM. HOSP.
BELVEDERE DAY HOSP.
Willesden Sports Cen.
King Edward VII Recreation Ground
Spts. Grd.
Day Nursery
HARLESDEN
CRAVEN PK.
CHURCH RD.

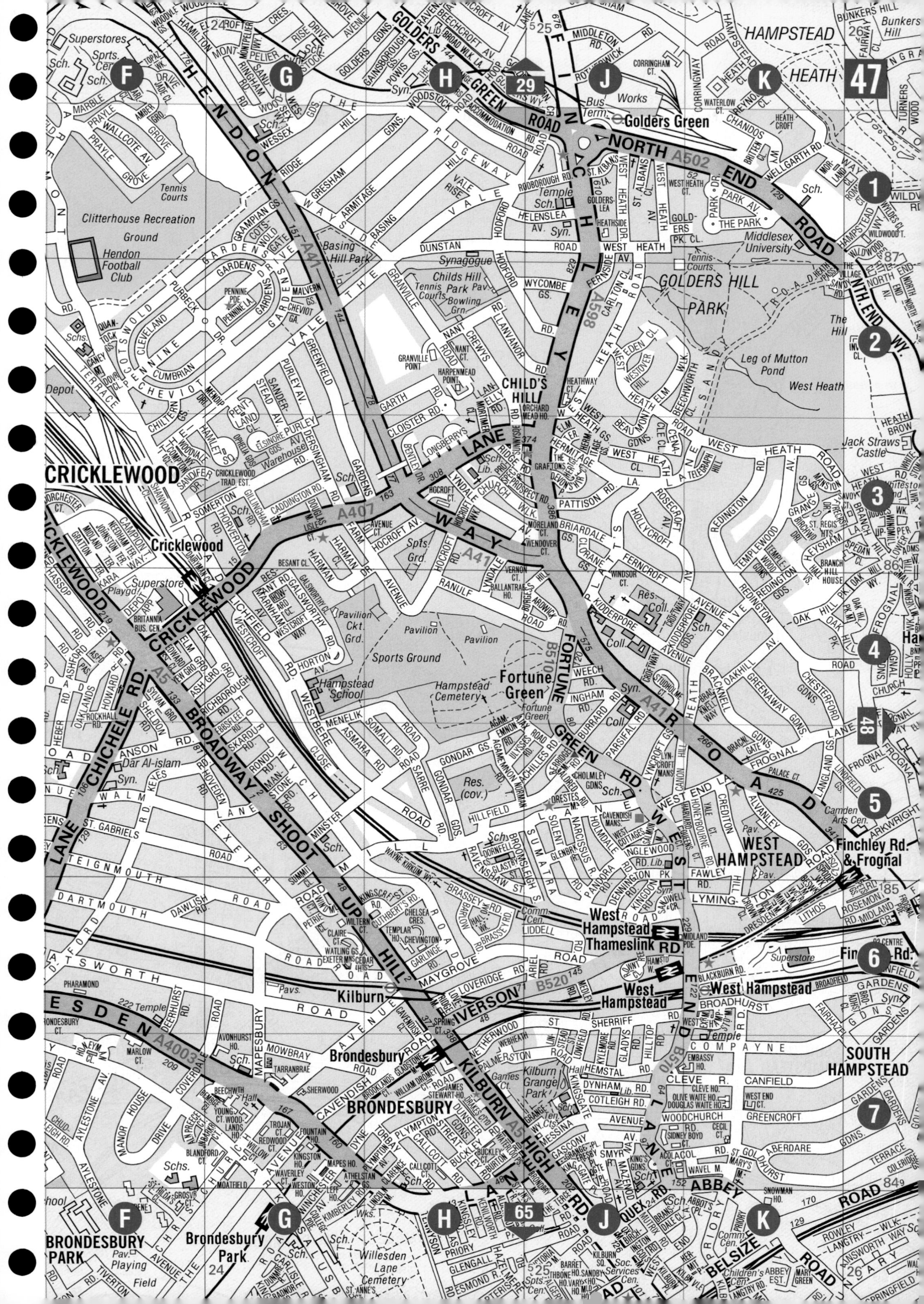
47
HAMPSTEAD
HEATH
Bunkers Hill
Golders Green
NORTH END ROAD
A502
GOLDERS HILL PARK
Leg of Mutton Pond
West Heath
The Hill
Jack Straws Castle
Middlesex University
CHILD'S HILL
FINCHLEY ROAD
A598
HENDON WAY
A41
Clitterhouse Recreation Ground
Hendon Football Club
Tennis Courts
Basing Hill Park
Childs Hill Park
Synagogue
CRICKLEWOOD
Cricklewood
CRICKLEWOOD BROADWAY
A407
A5
CHICHELE RD.
SHOOT UP HILL
Dar Al-islam
Sports Ground
Hampstead School
Hampstead Cemetery
Fortune Green
FORTUNE GREEN RD.
B510
WEST END LANE
WEST HAMPSTEAD
West Hampstead Thameslink
West Hampstead
Kilburn
B520
IVERSON RD.
Brondesbury
BRONDESBURY
KILBURN HIGH RD.
Kilburn Grange Park
SOUTH HAMPSTEAD
Finchley Rd. & Frognal
Camden Arts Cen.
WILLESDEN LANE
A4003
Willesden Lane Cemetery
BRONDESBURY PARK
Brondesbury Park
ABBEY ROAD
BELSIZE ROAD
29
48
65
F
G
H
J
K
1
2
3
4
5
6
7

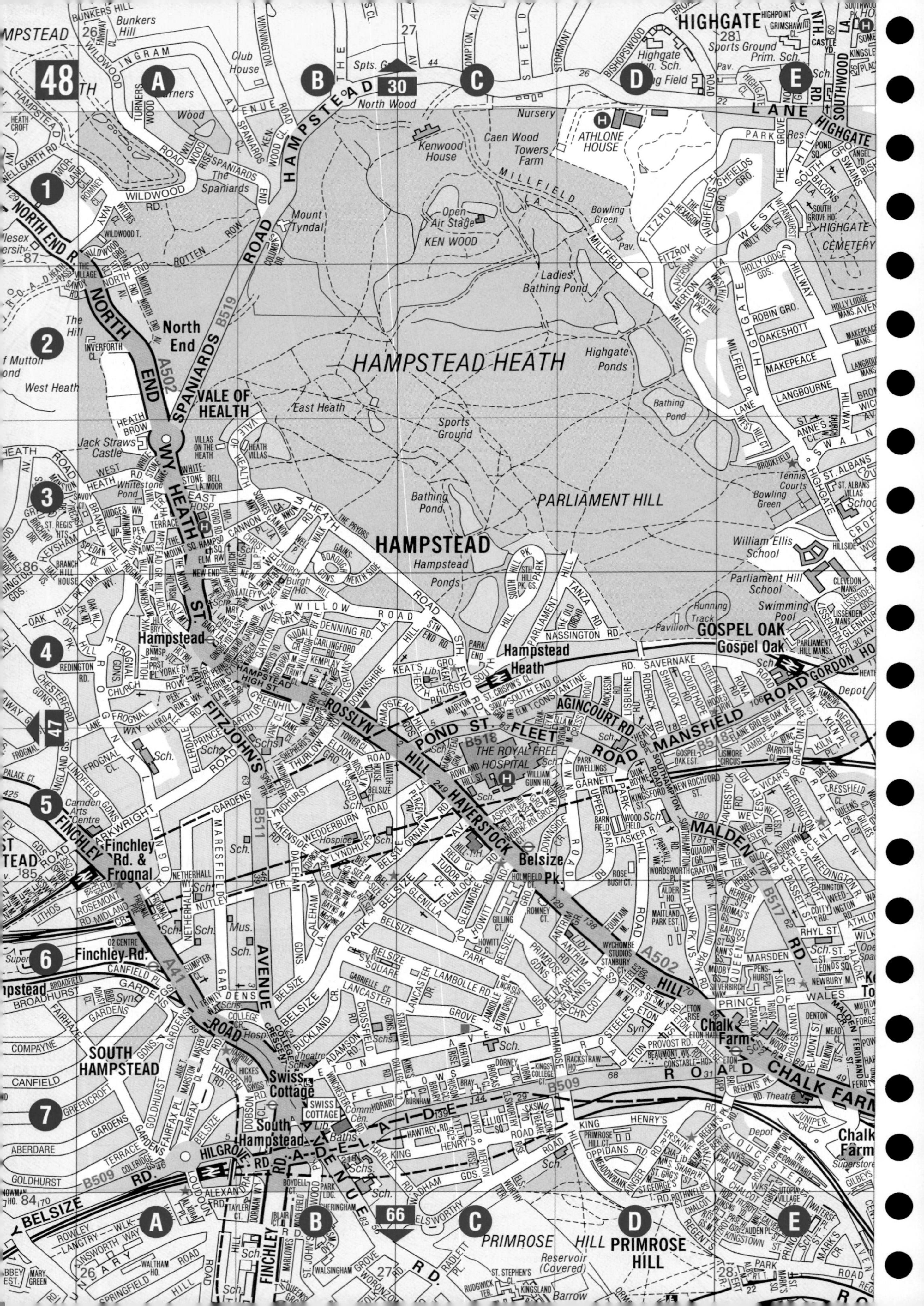
HIGHGATE
HAMPSTEAD HEATH
HAMPSTEAD
PARLIAMENT HILL
GOSPEL OAK
Gospel Oak
VALE OF HEALTH
North End
KEN WOOD
Kenwood House
ATHLONE HOUSE
Caen Wood Towers Farm
Highgate Ponds
Ladies' Bathing Pond
Hampstead Ponds
Hampstead Heath
THE ROYAL FREE HOSPITAL
Belsize Pk.
Chalk Farm
Swiss Cottage
SOUTH HAMPSTEAD
South Hampstead
Finchley Rd. & Frognal
Finchley Rd.
PRIMROSE HILL
HIGHGATE CEMETERY
William Ellis School
Parliament Hill School
Jack Straws Castle
West Heath
The Hill
Whitestone Pond
Spaniards
North Wood
HAMPSTEAD LANE
SPANIARDS ROAD
NORTH END ROAD
HEATH ST.
FITZJOHN'S AVENUE
ROSSLYN HILL
HAVERSTOCK HILL
FINCHLEY ROAD
ADELAIDE ROAD
CHALK FARM ROAD
MALDEN RD.
AGINCOURT RD.
FLEET ROAD
MANSFIELD ROAD
GORDON HOUSE ROAD
HIGHGATE WEST HILL
MILLFIELD LA.
A502
B519
B518
B511
A41
B509
B517
30
47
66
A
B
C
D
E
1
2
3
4
5
6
7

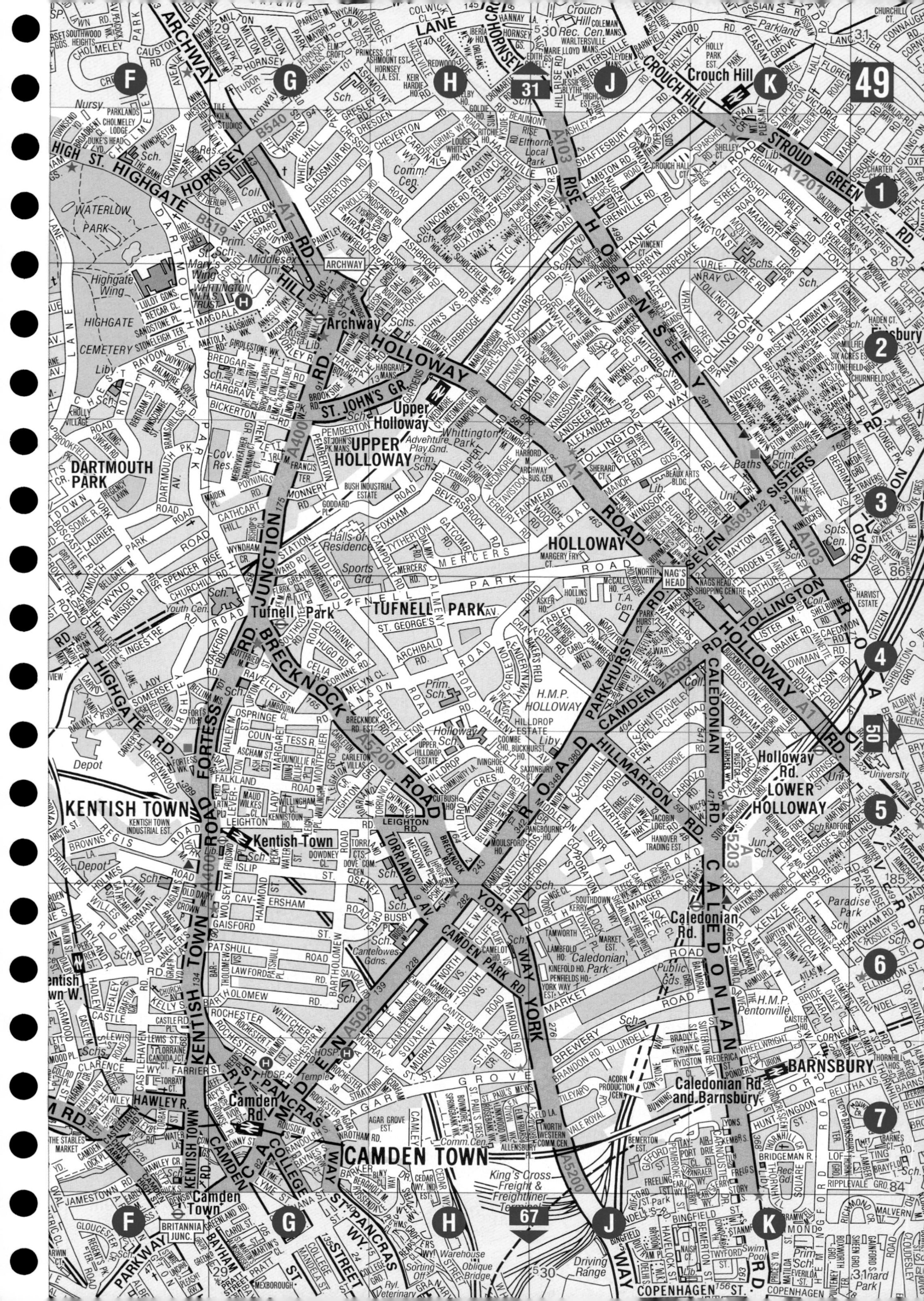

49
F
G
H
J
K
31
67
50
1
2
3
4
5
6
7
ARCHWAY
HORNSEY LANE
Crouch Hill
CROUCH HILL
STROUD GREEN
HIGHGATE HILL
HIGH ST.
HORNSEY LANE
WATERLOW PARK
HIGHGATE CEMETERY
Highgate Wing
WHITTINGTON N.H.S. TRUST
Middlesex Uni.
Archway
HOLLOWAY RD.
ST. JOHN'S GR.
Upper Holloway
UPPER HOLLOWAY
Whittington Park
DARTMOUTH PARK
DARTMOUTH PARK HILL
HORNSEY RISE
HORNSEY RD.
Elthorne Local Park
HOLLOWAY
NAG'S HEAD
NAGS HEAD SHOPPING CENTRE
SEVEN SISTERS RD.
TOLLINGTON RD.
JUNCTION RD.
TUFNELL PARK
Tufnell Park
Sports Grd.
Halls of Residence
BRECKNOCK ROAD
H.M.P. HOLLOWAY
HILLDROP ESTATE
CAMDEN RD.
PARKHURST RD.
HILLMARTON RD.
CALEDONIAN RD.
Holloway Rd.
LOWER HOLLOWAY
KENTISH TOWN
Kentish Town
KENTISH TOWN RD.
FORTESS RD.
HIGHGATE RD.
YORK WAY
CAMDEN PARK RD.
Caledonian Rd.
Caledonian Park
H.M.P. Pentonville
Paradise Park
BARNSBURY
Caledonian Rd and Barnsbury
ST. PANCRAS WY.
CAMDEN TOWN
Camden Rd.
Camden Town
King's Cross Freight & Freightliner Terminal
AGAR GROVE
COPENHAGEN ST.
PARKWAY
BRITANNIA JUNC.
Driving Range

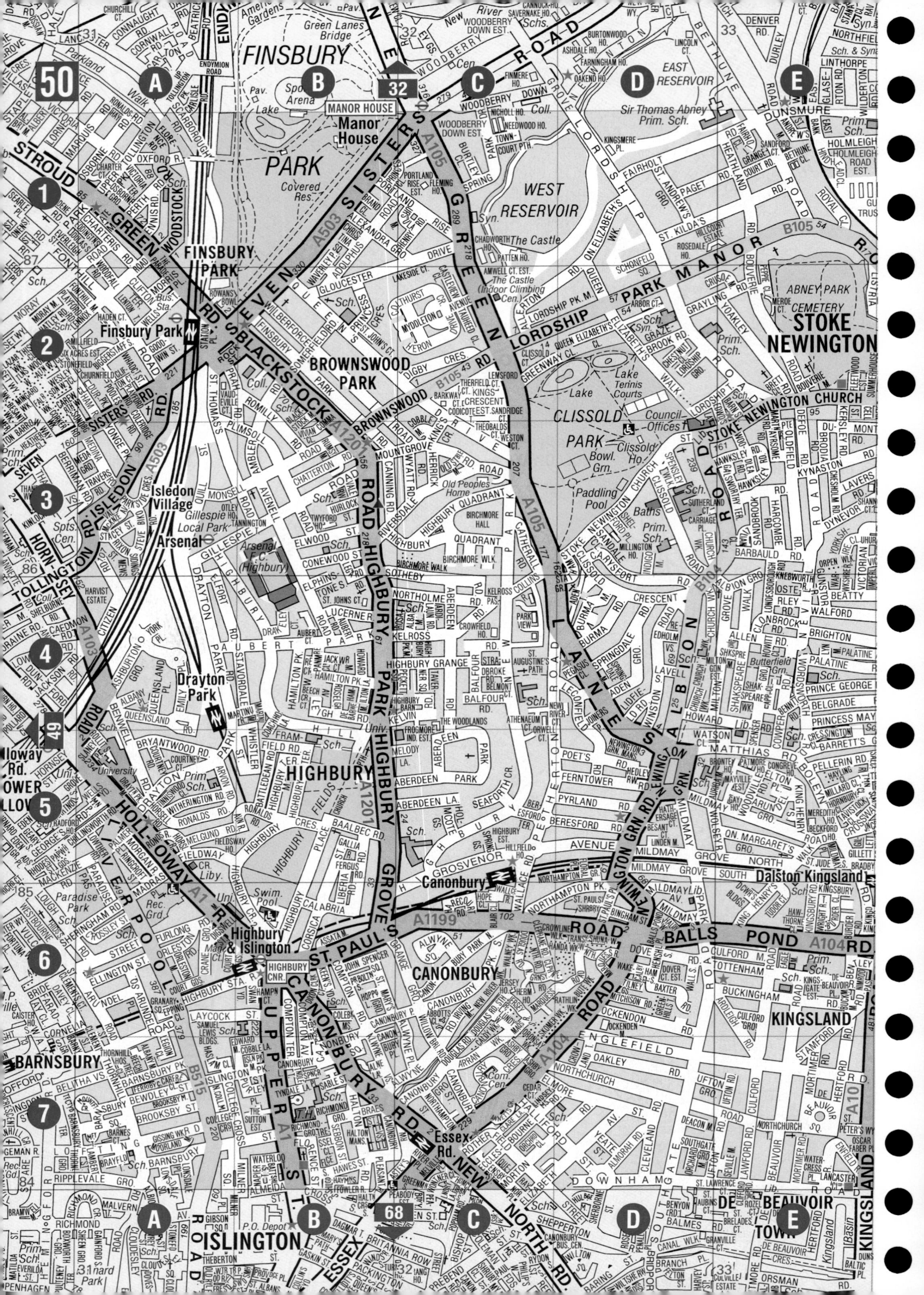

50
32
49
68
A
B
C
D
E
1
2
3
4
5
6
7
FINSBURY
PARK
Manor House
MANOR HOUSE
Green Lanes Bridge
WEST RESERVOIR
EAST RESERVOIR
The Castle
FINSBURY PARK
Finsbury Park
SEVEN SISTERS RD.
BLACKSTOCK RD.
BROWNSWOOD PARK
LORDSHIP PARK
MANOR RD.
STOKE NEWINGTON
STOKE NEWINGTON CHURCH ST.
ABNEY PARK CEMETERY
CLISSOLD PARK
Lake
Council Offices
Clissold Ho.
Paddling Pool
GREEN LANES
A105
A503
A1201
A1199
A104
A103
A1
B105
B104
B515
A10
STROUD GREEN RD.
WOODSTOCK RD.
ISLEDON RD.
Isledon Village
Arsenal
Arsenal F.C. (Highbury)
Drayton Park
HOLLOWAY RD.
LIVERPOOL RD.
HIGHBURY
HIGHBURY PARK
HIGHBURY GROVE
HIGHBURY QUADRANT
HIGHBURY NEW PARK
ALBION RD.
NEWINGTON GRN.
MILDMAY
BALLS POND RD.
Dalston Kingsland
Canonbury
CANONBURY
CANONBURY RD.
ST. PAUL'S RD.
Highbury & Islington
HIGHBURY CNR.
UPPER ST.
ESSEX RD.
Essex Rd.
NEW NORTH RD.
KINGSLAND
DE BEAUVOIR TOWN
KINGSLAND RD.
BARNSBURY
ISLINGTON

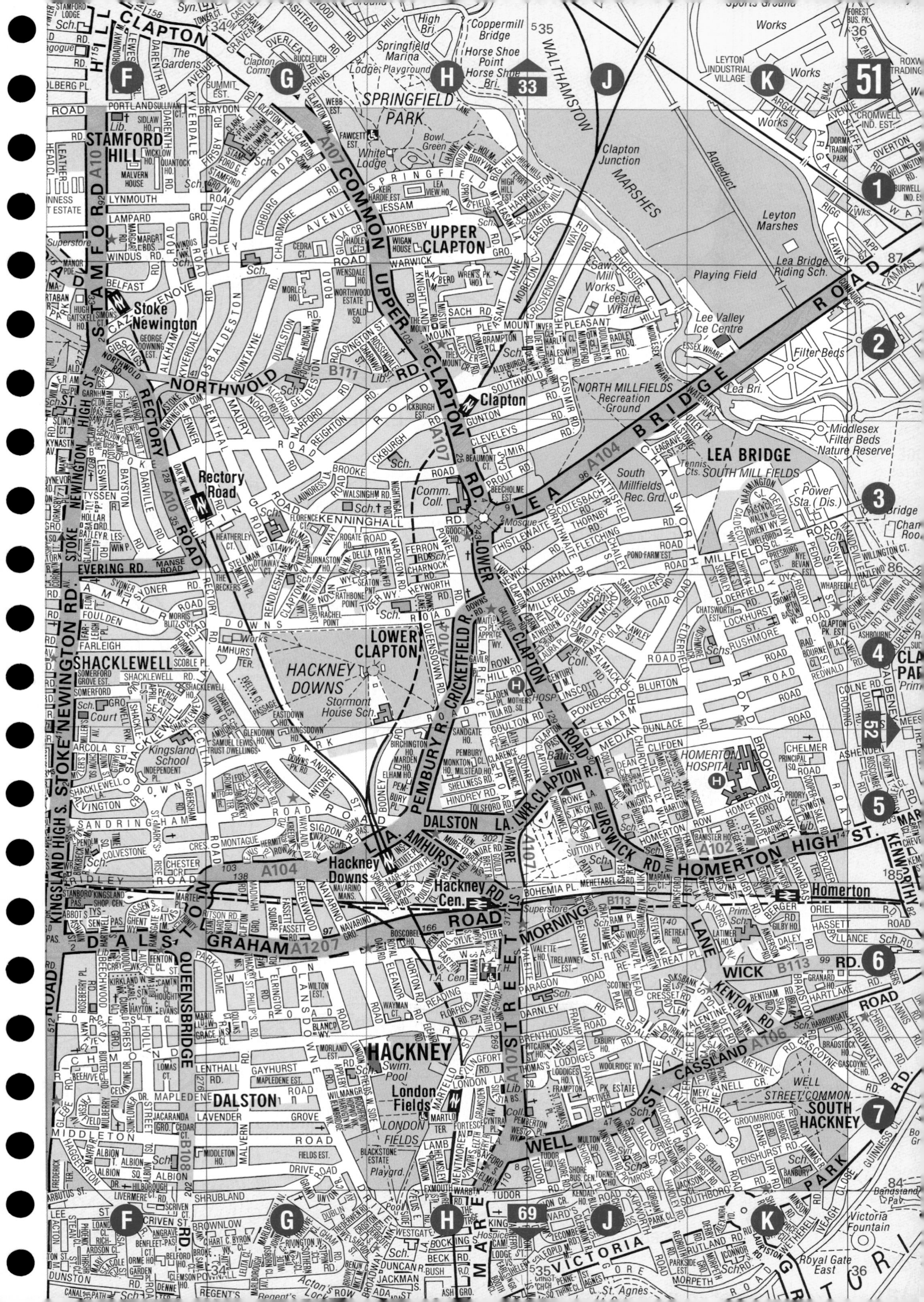

51
33
52
69
F
G
H
J
K
1
2
3
4
5
6
7
CLAPTON
STAMFORD HILL
Stoke Newington
UPPER CLAPTON
SPRINGFIELD PARK
Springfield Marina
Coppermill Bridge
Horse Shoe Point
WALTHAMSTOW
Clapton Junction
MARSHES
Leyton Marshes
LEYTON INDUSTRIAL VILLAGE
Works
Playing Field
Lea Bridge Riding Sch.
Lee Valley Ice Centre
Filter Beds
Middlesex Filter Beds Nature Reserve
LEA BRIDGE ROAD
LEA BRIDGE
NORTH MILLFIELDS Recreation Ground
South Millfields Rec. Grd.
SOUTH MILL FIELDS
Power Sta. (Dis.)
NORTHWOLD RD
Clapton
Rectory Road
LOWER CLAPTON
HACKNEY DOWNS
Stormont House Sch.
SHACKLEWELL
Kingsland School
HOMERTON HOSPITAL
HOMERTON HIGH ST.
Homerton
Hackney Downs
Hackney Cen.
DALSTON
HACKNEY
London Fields
LONDON FIELDS
SOUTH HACKNEY
WELL STREET COMMON
STOKE NEWINGTON RD.
KINGSLAND HIGH S.
GRAHAM ROAD
MORNING LANE
MARE STREET
WICK RD.
CASSLAND RD.
VICTORIA
Victoria Fountain
Royal Gate East
A10
A107
A104
A102
A106
A1207
B111
B113
B108

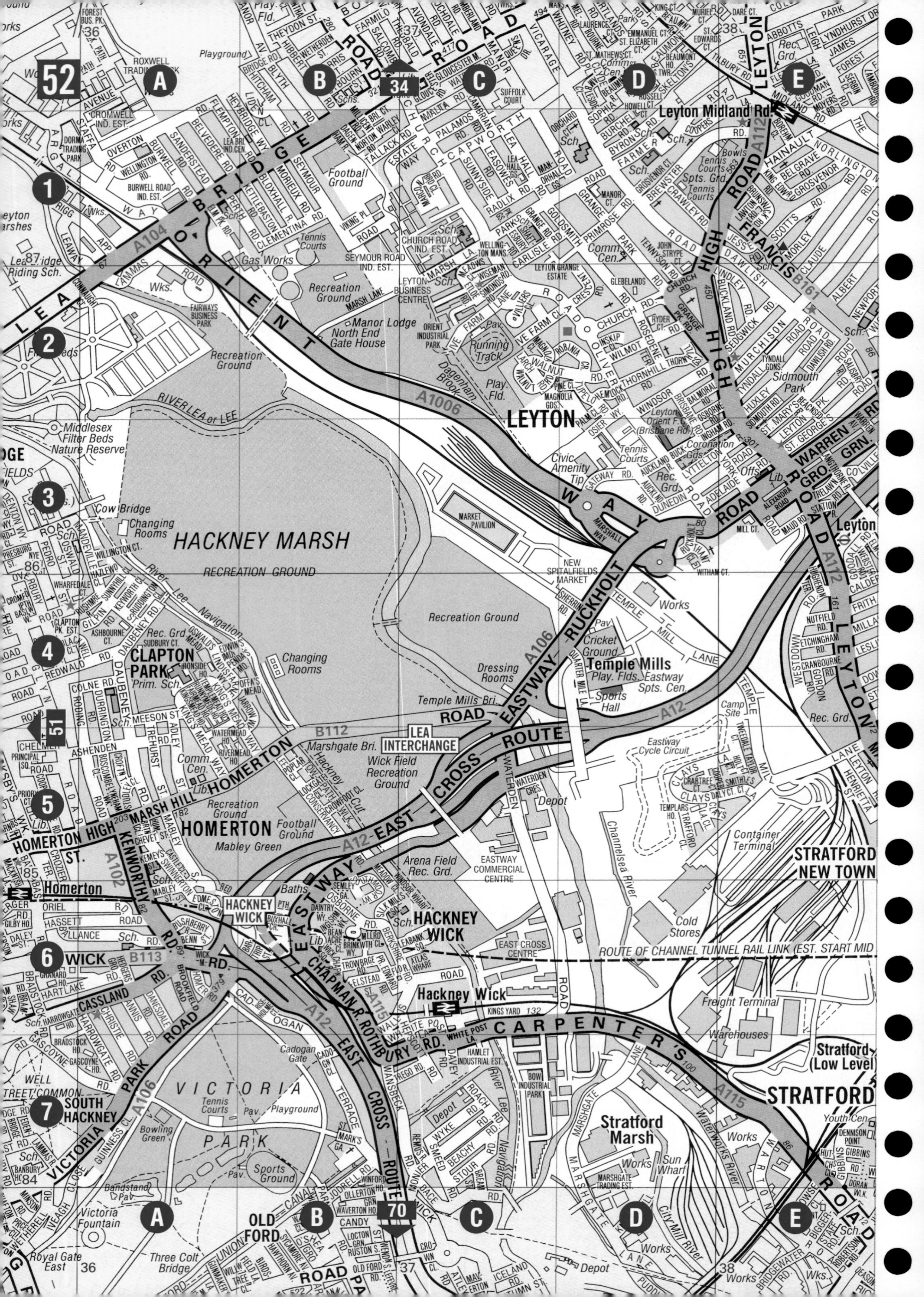

52
A
B
C
D
E
1
2
3
4
5
6
7
34
51
70
LEYTON
HACKNEY MARSH
RECREATION GROUND
CLAPTON PARK
HOMERTON
HACKNEY WICK
SOUTH HACKNEY
VICTORIA PARK
OLD FORD
STRATFORD
STRATFORD NEW TOWN
Stratford Marsh
Temple Mills
Leyton Midland Rd.
Hackney Wick
Homerton
Stratford (Low Level)
LEA BRIDGE ROAD
ORIENT WAY
RUCKHOLT ROAD
EASTWAY
EAST CROSS ROUTE
HOMERTON HIGH ST.
CARPENTER'S RD.
HIGH ROAD
LEYTON ROAD
A104
A1006
A106
A12
A102
A115
A112
B112
B113
LEA INTERCHANGE
Middlesex Filter Beds Nature Reserve
Lee Navigation
RIVER LEA or LEE
Dagenham Brook
Channelsea River
Waterworks River
City Mill River
Cow Bridge
Temple Mills Bri.
Marshgate Bri.
Wick Field Recreation Ground
Arena Field Rec. Grd.
Mabley Green
New Spitalfields Market
Market Pavilion
Eastway Cycle Circuit
Container Terminal
Freight Terminal
Warehouses
Cold Stores
ROUTE OF CHANNEL TUNNEL RAIL LINK (EST. START MID
Manor Lodge North End Gate House
Leyton Orient F.C. (Brisbane Rd.)
Civic Amenity Tip
Running Track
Sports Hall
Cricket Ground
Eastway Commercial Centre
East Cross Centre
Bow Industrial Park
Hamlet Industrial Est.
Marshgate Trading Est.
Sun Wharf
Sidmouth Park
Leyton Grange Estate
Three Colt Bridge
Royal Gate East
Victoria Fountain
Cadogan Gate
Bowling Green
Sports Ground
Bandstand
Gas Works
Riding Sch.

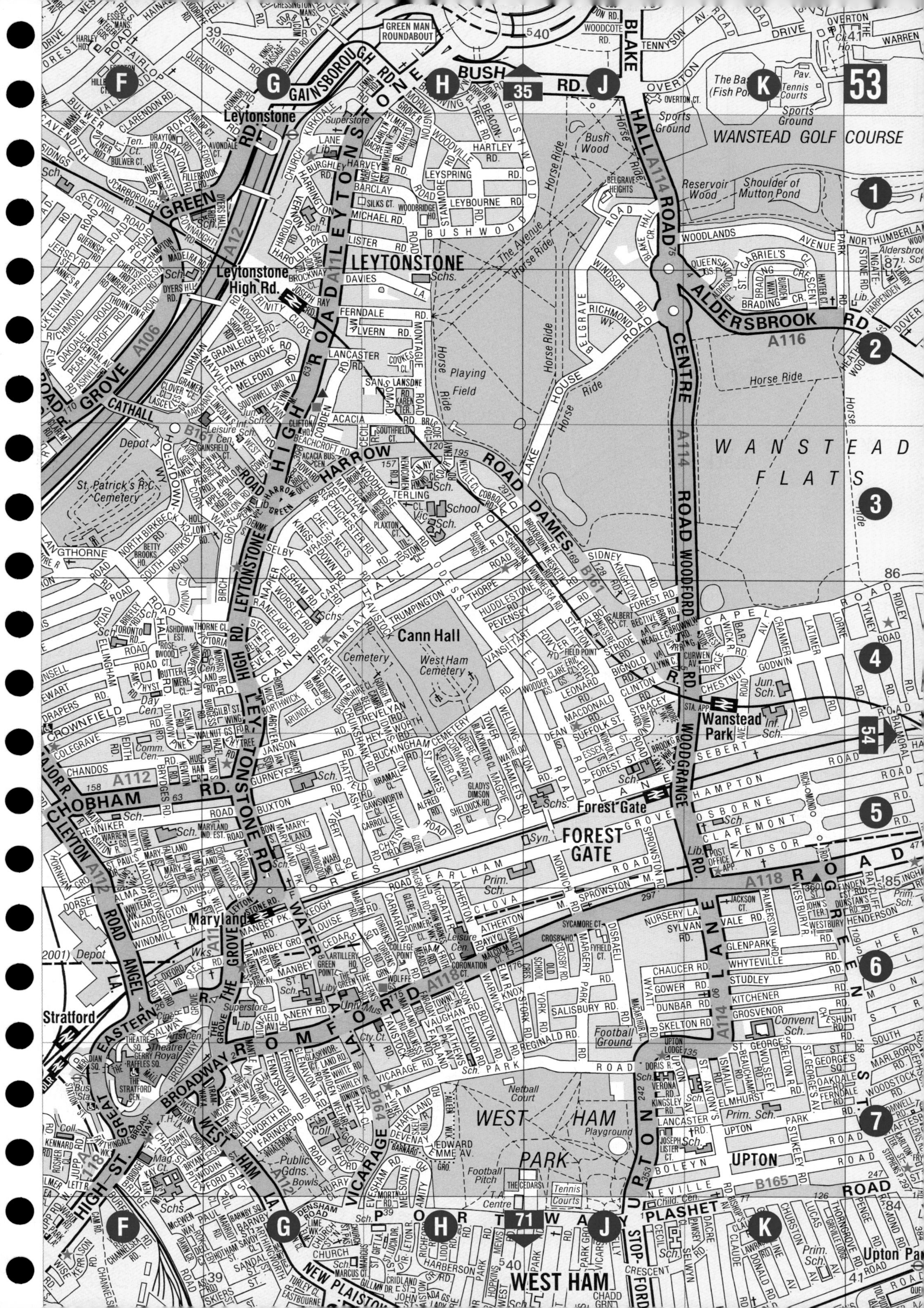

GREEN MAN ROUNDABOUT
BUSH RD.
35
BLAKE HALL ROAD
A114
WANSTEAD GOLF COURSE
Bush Wood
Reservoir Wood
Shoulder of Mutton Pond
Sports Ground
Leytonstone
LEYTONSTONE
Leytonstone High Rd.
LEYTONSTONE HIGH ROAD
A11
GAINSBOROUGH RD.
GREEN
A12
GROVE ROAD
A106
CATHALL
ALDERSBROOK RD.
A116
CENTRE ROAD
WOODFORD ROAD
WANSTEAD FLATS
Playing Field
Horse Ride
LAKE HOUSE ROAD
HARROW ROAD
DAMES ROAD
B161
St. Patrick's R.C. Cemetery
Cann Hall
West Ham Cemetery
Cemetery
CANN HALL ROAD
Wanstead Park
54
CHOBHAM RD.
A112
LEYTON ROAD
Forest Gate
FOREST GATE
WOODGRANGE RD.
A118
ROMFORD ROAD
Maryland
Stratford
THE GROVE
BROADWAY
GREAT EASTERN ROAD
ANGEL LA.
WEST HAM LA.
HIGH ST.
VICARAGE LA.
B164
WEST HAM PARK
Playground
Football Pitch
Netball Court
Tennis Courts
THE CEDARS
PORTWAY
71
UPTON LANE
UPTON
PLASHET ROAD
B165
Football Ground
GREEN ST.
WEST HAM
Upton Park
NEW PLAISTOW RD.
F
G
H
J
K
1
2
3
4
5
6
7

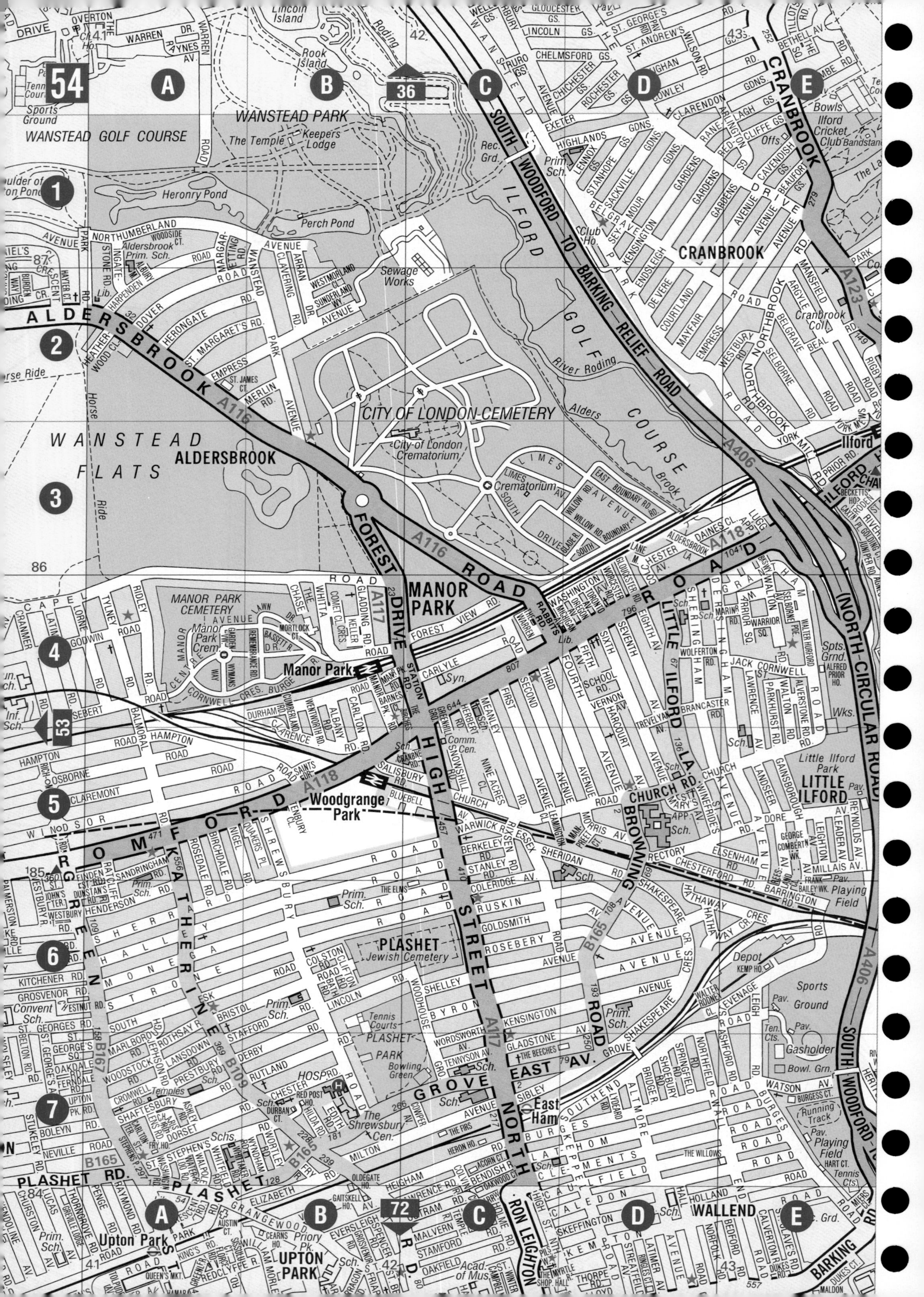
WANSTEAD PARK
WANSTEAD GOLF COURSE
Heronry Pond
Perch Pond
The Temple
Keepers Lodge
Sewage Works
CITY OF LONDON CEMETERY
City of London Crematorium
WANSTEAD FLATS
ALDERSBROOK
ALDERSBROOK ROAD
ILFORD GOLF COURSE
River Roding
Alders Brook
SOUTH WOODFORD TO BARKING RELIEF ROAD
CRANBROOK
Ilford
MANOR PARK
MANOR PARK CEMETERY
Manor Park
ROMFORD ROAD
Woodgrange Park
LITTLE ILFORD
Little Ilford Park
PLASHET
Jewish Cemetery
PLASHET PARK
HIGH STREET NORTH
East Ham
WALLEND
UPTON PARK
Upton Park
GREEN STREET
KATHERINE ROAD
PLASHET ROAD
NORTH CIRCULAR ROAD
Sports Ground
Gasholder
Running Track
Playing Field
BARKING ROAD
36
53
72

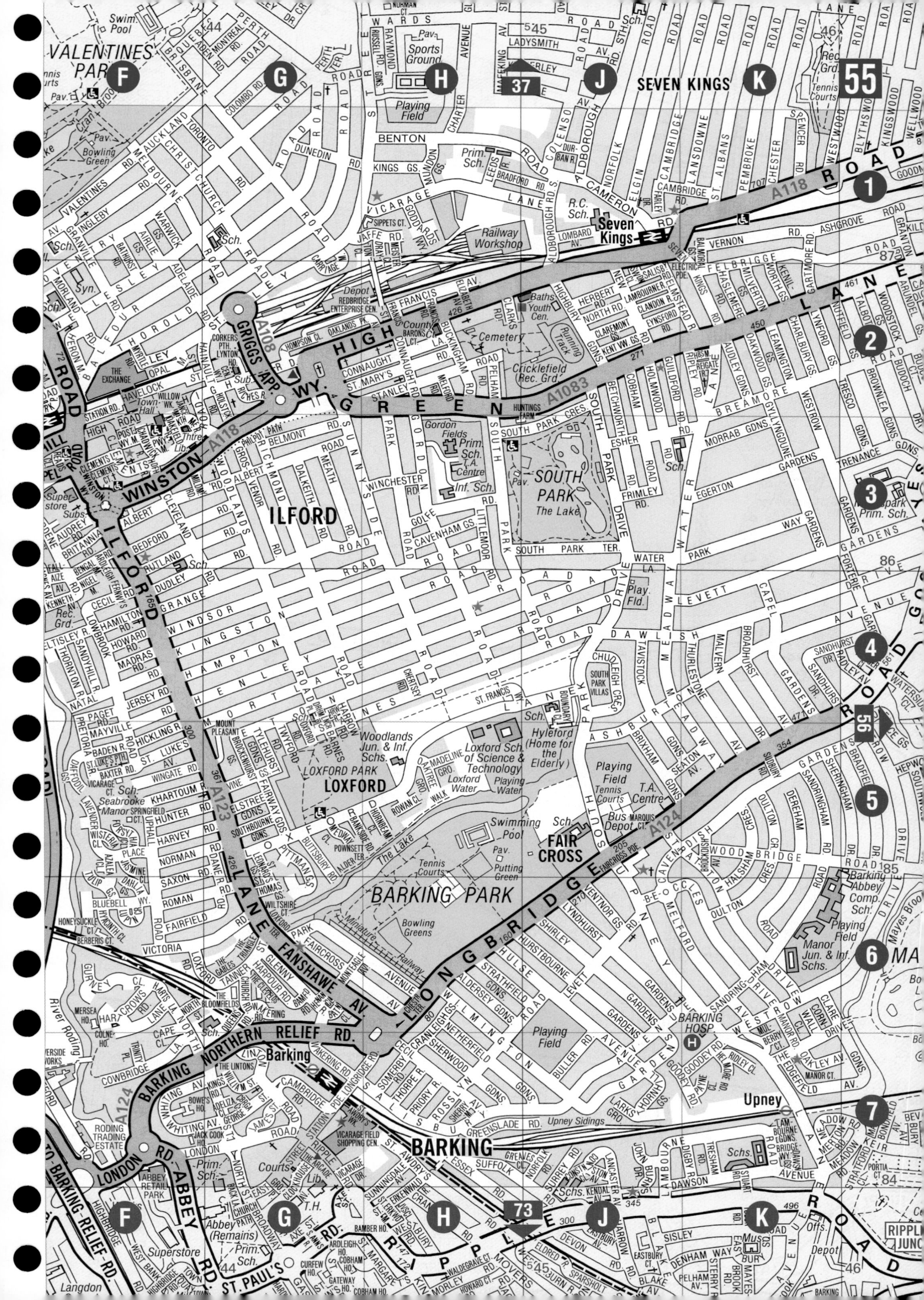
55
VALENTINES PARK
SEVEN KINGS
ILFORD
SOUTH PARK
The Lake
LOXFORD
BARKING PARK
FAIR CROSS
BARKING
Barking
Upney
Seven Kings
37
56
73
F
G
H
J
K
1
2
3
4
5
6
7
44
45
46
84
85
86
87
HIGH ROAD
GREEN LANE
HIGH WY.
WINSTON WY.
ILFORD LANE
LONGBRIDGE ROAD
FANSHAWE AV.
BARKING NORTHERN RELIEF RD.
LONDON RD.
ABBEY RD.
RIPPLE ROAD
VICARAGE LANE
CAMERON RD.
SOUTH PARK DRIVE
MEADWAY
LEVETT
DAWLISH
ASHBURTON
BREAMORE
EGERTON
WESTROW
GRIGGS APP.
A118
A1083
A108
A123
A124
Sports Ground
Playing Field
Railway Workshop
Cemetery
Running Track
Cricklefield Rec. Grd.
Gordon Fields Prim. Sch.
T.A. Centre
Inf. Sch.
Woodlands Jun. & Inf. Schs.
LOXFORD PARK
Loxford Sch. of Science & Technology
Hyleford (Home for the Elderly)
Swimming Pool
Tennis Courts
Putting Green
Bowling Greens
Miniature Railway
Bus Depot
BARKING HOSP.
Manor Jun. & Inf. Schs.
Barking Abbey Comp. Sch.
Upney Sidings
Abbey (Remains)
Superstore
VICARAGE FIELD SHOPPING CEN.
RODING TRADING ESTATE
ABBEY RETAIL PARK
THE EXCHANGE
Town Hall
Baths Youth Cen.
REDBRIDGE ENTERPRISE CEN.
Depot
Play. Fld.
Rec. Grd.
Bowling Green
Swim. Pool
River Roding

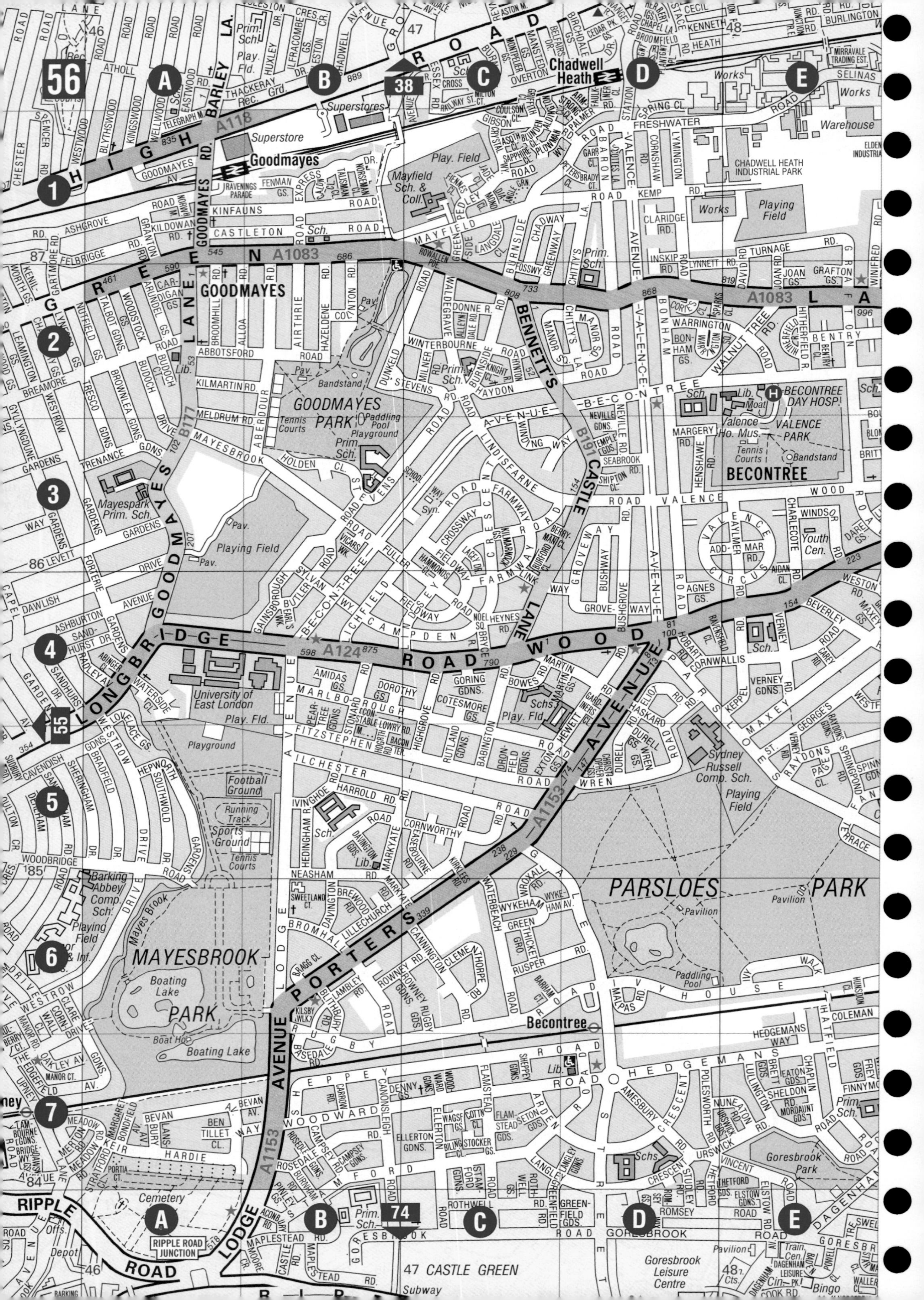

56
A
B
C
D
E
1
2
3
4
5
6
7
38
74
55
HIGH ROAD
A118
Goodmayes
Superstore
Superstores
Chadwell Heath
GREEN LANE
A1083
GOODMAYES
GOODMAYES LANE
BARLEY LA.
B177
Mayfield Sch. & Coll.
Play. Field
CHADWELL HEATH INDUSTRIAL PARK
Warehouse
Works
Playing Field
GOODMAYES PARK
Tennis Courts
Paddling Pool
Playground
Bandstand
BENNETTS CASTLE LANE
B191
BECONTREE AVENUE
VALENCE AVENUE
BECONTREE DAY HOSP.
VALENCE PARK
Valence Ho. Mus.
BECONTREE
Mayespark Prim. Sch.
Playing Field
LONGBRIDGE ROAD
A124
WOOD LANE
University of East London
Play. Fld.
Football Ground
Running Track
Sports Ground
Tennis Courts
Barking Abbey Comp. Sch.
MAYESBROOK PARK
Mayes Brook
Boating Lake
Boat Ho.
Sydney Russell Comp. Sch.
PARSLOES PARK
Pavilion
Paddling Pool
PORTERS AVENUE
A1153
Becontree
LODGE AVENUE
Goresbrook Park
Cemetery
RIPPLE ROAD
RIPPLE ROAD JUNCTION
GORESBROOK ROAD
47 CASTLE GREEN
Subway
Goresbrook Leisure Centre
DAGENHAM
Youth Cen.

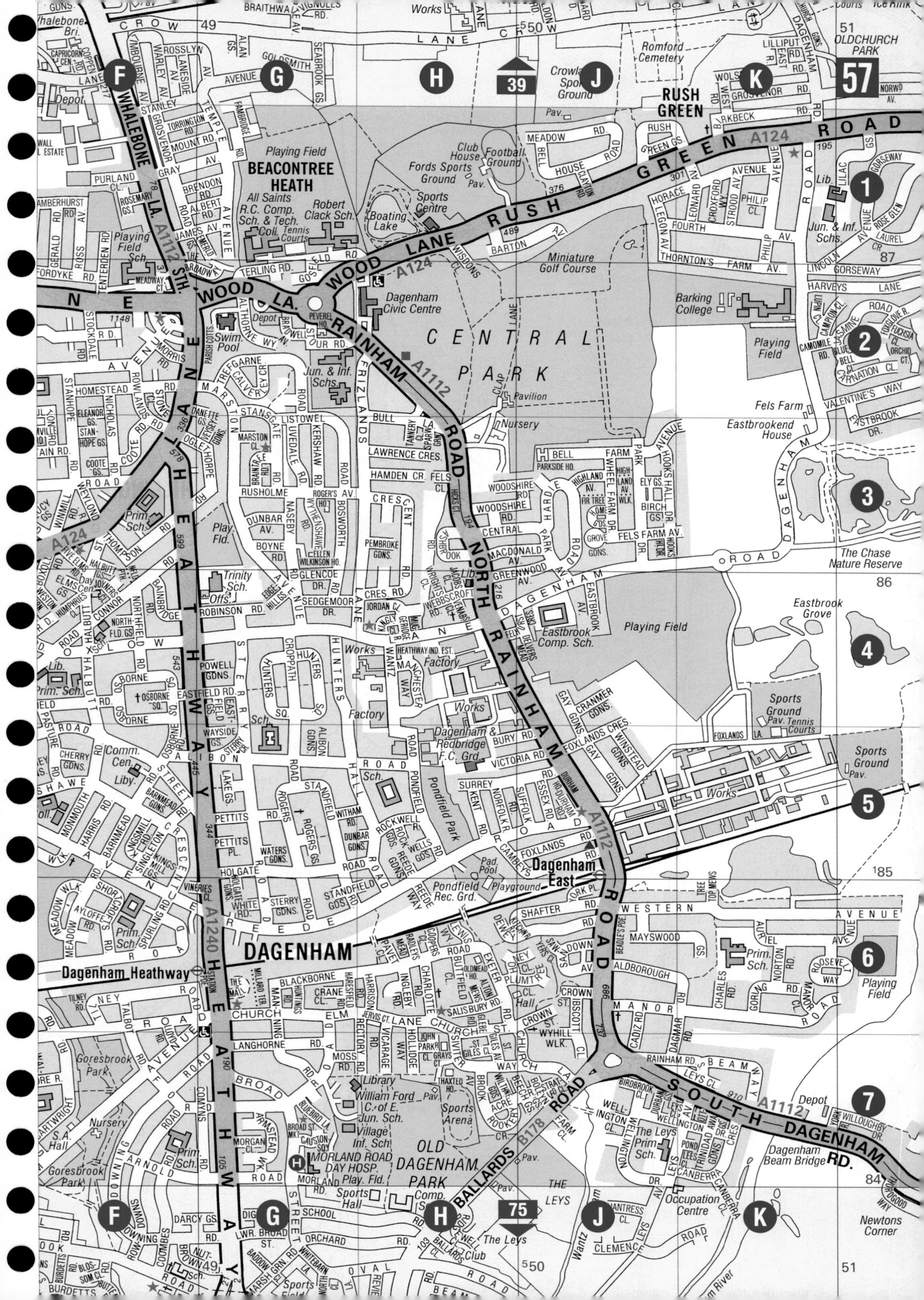
57
39
75
F
G
H
J
K
1
2
3
4
5
6
7
49
50
51
84
85
86
87
OLDCHURCH PARK
RUSH GREEN
Romford Cemetery
Crowlands Sports Ground
WHALEBONE LA.
CROW LANE
GOLDSMITH AVENUE
BEACONTREE HEATH
Playing Field
All Saints R.C. Comp. Sch. & Tech. Coll.
Robert Clack Sch.
Boating Lake
Sports Centre
Fords Sports Ground
Club House
Football Ground
RUSH GREEN ROAD
A124
WOOD LANE
WOOD LA.
NEW ROAD
Miniature Golf Course
Dagenham Civic Centre
CENTRAL PARK
Pavilion
Nursery
RAINHAM ROAD
A1112
RAINHAM ROAD NORTH
Barking College
Playing Field
Fels Farm
Eastbrookend House
DAGENHAM ROAD
The Chase Nature Reserve
Eastbrook Grove
Playing Field
Eastbrook Comp. Sch.
Sports Ground
Pav.
Tennis Courts
Works
Factory
Dagenham & Redbridge F.C. Grd.
Pondfield Park
Pondfield Rec. Grd.
Playground
Dagenham East
DAGENHAM
Dagenham Heathway
HEATHWAY
A1240
REEDE ROAD
LOWEN ROAD
CHURCH ELM LANE
CHURCH ST.
Goresbrook Park
Nursery
S.A. Hall
Prim. Sch.
Library
William Ford C. of E. Jun. Sch.
Village Inf. Sch.
MORLAND ROAD DAY HOSP.
Play. Fld.
OLD DAGENHAM PARK
Sports Arena
Sports Hall
Comp. Sch.
BALLARDS ROAD
B178
THE LEYS
The Leys
Occupation Centre
The Leys Prim. Sch.
Depot
SOUTH DAGENHAM RD.
Dagenham Beam Bridge
BEAM WAY
Newtons Corner
WESTERN AVENUE
AVENUE
MANOR ROAD
ALDBOROUGH
MAYSWOOD
Playing Field
Club

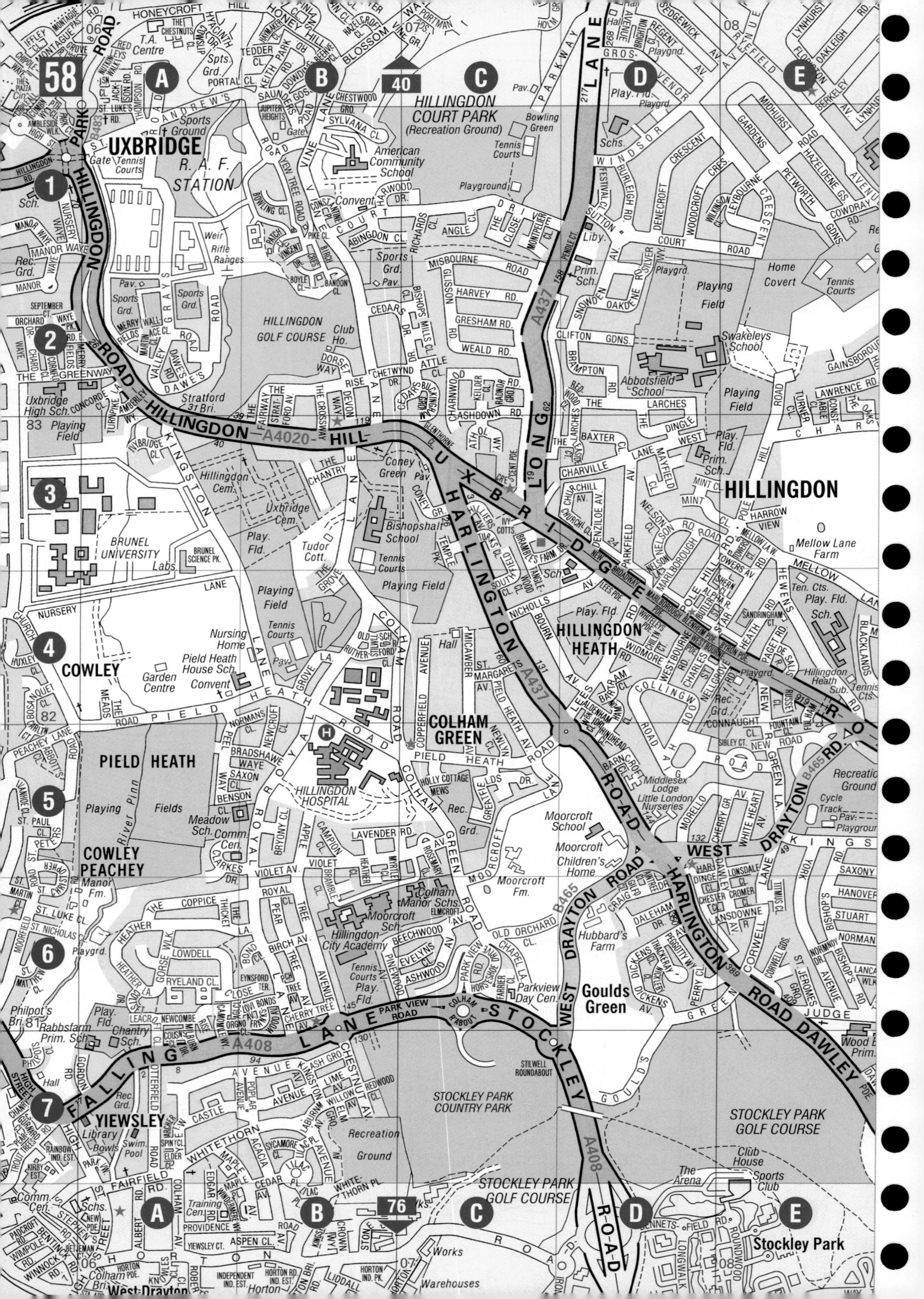
40
76
A
B
C
D
E
1
2
3
4
5
6
7
UXBRIDGE
R.A.F. STATION
HILLINGDON COURT PARK
(Recreation Ground)
American Community School
HILLINGDON GOLF COURSE
Club Ho.
Rifle Ranges
Sports Ground
T.A. Centre
Convent
Bowling Green
Tennis Courts
Playground
Play. Fld.
Liby.
Prim. Sch.
Playing Field
Swakeleys School
Abbotsfield School
Home Covert
HILLINGDON
Mellow Lane Farm
Uxbridge High Sch.
Playing Field
Stratford Bri.
HILLINGDON HILL
A4020
Hillingdon Cem.
Uxbridge Cem.
BRUNEL UNIVERSITY
BRUNEL SCIENCE PK.
Labs.
Coney Green
Bishopshalt School
Tudor Cott.
Tennis Courts
Playing Field
UXBRIDGE ROAD
HARLINGTON ROAD
LONG LANE
A437
Nursing Home
Pield Heath House Sch.
Convent
Garden Centre
COWLEY
HILLINGDON HEATH
Hillingdon Heath Sub.
COLHAM GREEN
HILLINGDON HOSPITAL
Middlesex Lodge
Little London Nurseries
Recreation Ground
Cycle Track
PIELD HEATH
Playing Fields
River Pinn
Meadow Sch.
Comm. Cen.
COWLEY PEACHEY
Manor Fm.
Moorcroft School
Moorcroft Children's Home
Moorcroft Fm.
Colham Manor Schs.
Moorcroft Sch.
Hillingdon City Academy
Hubbard's Farm
WEST DRAYTON ROAD
B465
Goulds Green
Parkview Day Cen.
Tennis Courts
Play. Fld.
Philpot's Bri.
Rabbsfarm Prim. Sch.
Chantry Sch.
FALLING LANE
A408
STOCKLEY ROAD
COLHAM R'ABOUT
STILWELL ROUNDABOUT
STOCKLEY PARK COUNTRY PARK
STOCKLEY PARK GOLF COURSE
Club House
The Arena
Sports Club
Stockley Park
DAWLEY ROAD
YIEWSLEY
Library
Bowls
Swim. Pool
Rec. Grd.
Recreation Ground
RAINBOW IND. EST.
KIRBY EST.
Comm. Cen.
Schs.
Training Cen.
HORTON ROAD
Works
Warehouses
INDEPENDENT IND. EST.
HORTON RD. IND. EST.
HORTON IND. PK.
Colham Bri.
West Drayton
Horton

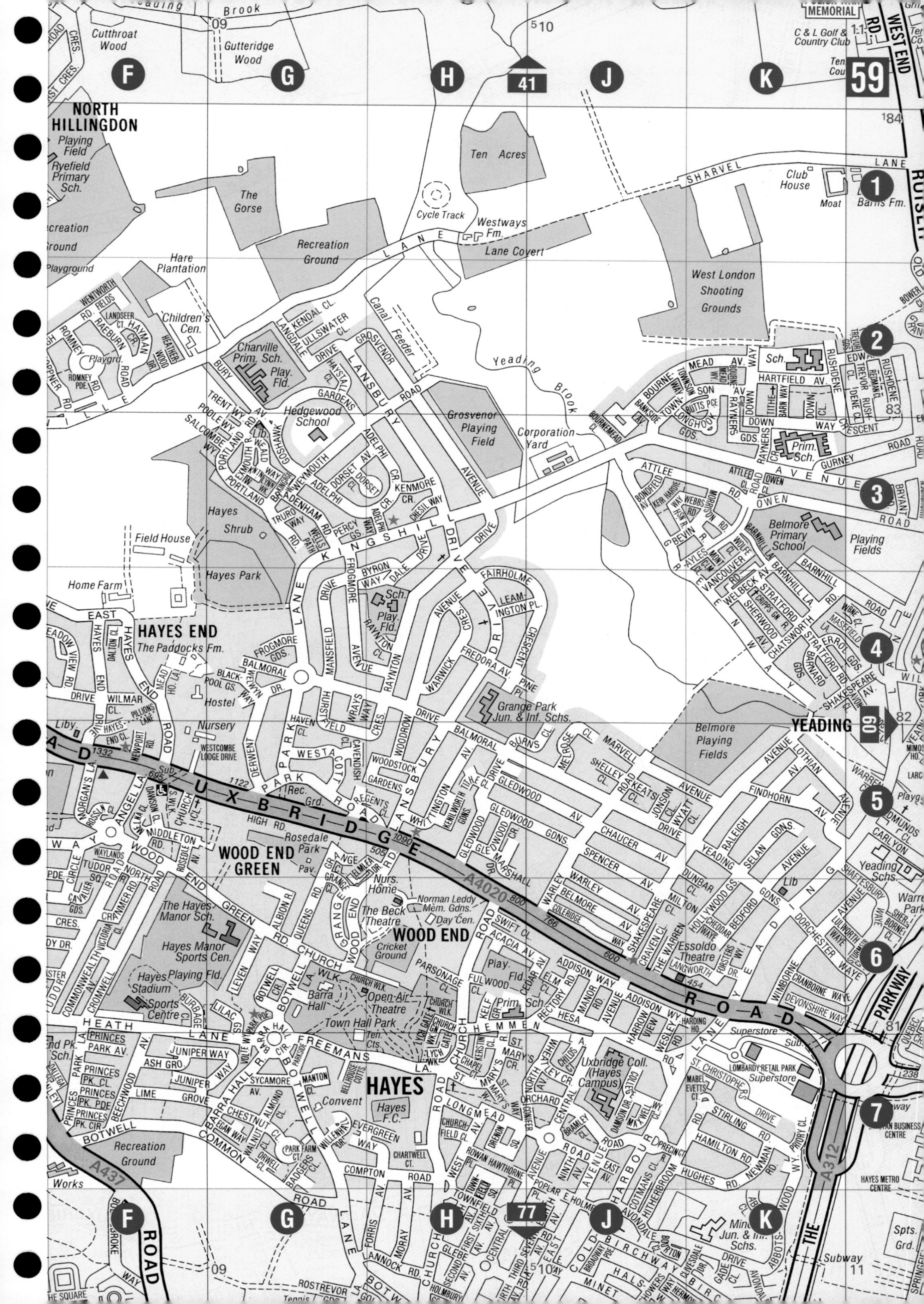
F
G
H
J
K
41
77
60
1
2
3
4
5
6
7
NORTH HILLINGDON
HAYES END
WOOD END GREEN
WOOD END
HAYES
YEADING
Cutthroat Wood
Gutteridge Wood
Brook
C & L Golf & Country Club
MEMORIAL
WEST END RD.
Ten Acres
The Gorse
Recreation Ground
Cycle Track
Westways Fm.
Lane Covert
SHARVEL LANE
Club House
Moat
Barns Fm.
West London Shooting Grounds
Hare Plantation
Children's Cen.
Playing Field
Ryefield Primary Sch.
Playground
Charville Prim. Sch.
Play. Fld.
Hedgewood School
Canal Feeder
Yeading Brook
Grosvenor Playing Field
Corporation Yard
Belmore Primary School
Playing Fields
Hayes Shrub
Field House
Hayes Park
Home Farm
The Paddocks Fm.
Hostel
Nursery
Grange Park Jun. & Inf. Schs.
Belmore Playing Fields
UXBRIDGE ROAD
A4020
Rosedale Park
Pav.
Nurs. Home
Norman Leddy Mem. Gdns.
The Beck Theatre
Day Cen.
Cricket Ground
The Hayes Manor Sch.
Hayes Manor Sports Cen.
Hayes Stadium
Playing Fld.
Sports Centre
Barra Hall
Open-Air Theatre
Town Hall Park
Ten. Cts.
Prim. Sch.
Uxbridge Coll. (Hayes Campus)
Essoldo Theatre
Superstore
Lombardy Retail Park
Yeading Schs.
Lib
Convent
Hayes F.C.
Recreation Ground
Works
A437
A312
THE PARKWAY
Mina Jun. & Inf. Schs.
Spts. Grd.
Subway
KINGSHILL DRIVE
LANSBURY DRIVE
HEATH LANE
FREEMANS LA.
BOTWELL COMMON ROAD
CHURCH ROAD
COMPTON ROAD
YEADING LANE
ROAD

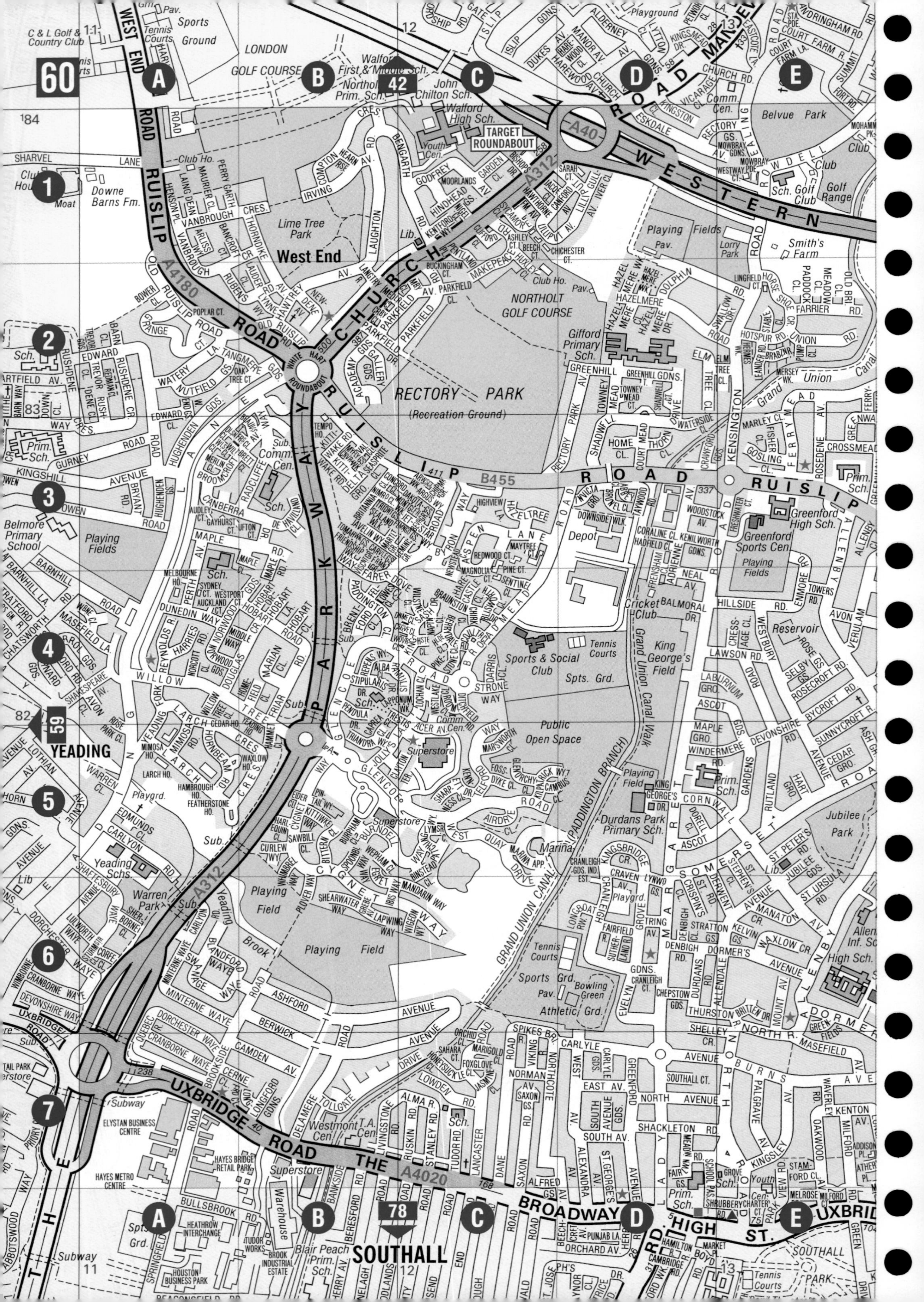

60
A
B
C
D
E
1
2
3
4
5
6
7
42
59
78
C & L Golf & Country Club
Sports Ground
LONDON GOLF COURSE
Walford First & Middle Sch.
Northolt Prim. Sch.
John Chilton Sch.
Walford High Sch.
TARGET ROUNDABOUT
Downe Barns Fm.
Moat
Lime Tree Park
West End
WEST END ROAD
RUISLIP ROAD
A4180
SHARVEL LANE
CHURCH ROAD
A312
A40
WESTERN
Belvue Park
Golf Club
Golf Range
Smith's Farm
Playing Fields
NORTHOLT GOLF COURSE
Gifford Primary Sch.
RECTORY PARK
(Recreation Ground)
RUISLIP ROAD
B455
Greenford High Sch.
Greenford Sports Cen.
Grand Union Canal
WHITE HART ROUNDABOUT
PARKWAY
YEADING
Belmore Primary School
Playing Fields
Yeading Schs.
Warren Park
Sports & Social Club
Tennis Courts
Spts. Grd.
King George's Field
Grand Union Canal Walk
Public Open Space
Superstore
Marina
GRAND UNION CANAL (PADDINGTON BRANCH)
Durdans Park Primary Sch.
Jubilee Park
Reservoir
Playing Field
Yeading Brook
Sports Grd.
Bowling Green
Athletic Grd.
UXBRIDGE ROAD
THE BROADWAY
A4020
HIGH ST.
SOUTHALL
Elystan Business Centre
Hayes Bridge Retail Park
Hayes Metro Centre
Heathrow Interchange
Brook Industrial Estate
Houston Business Park
Westmont T.A. Cen.
Blair Peach Prim. Sch.
Warehouse
Subway
11
12
13
82
83
84

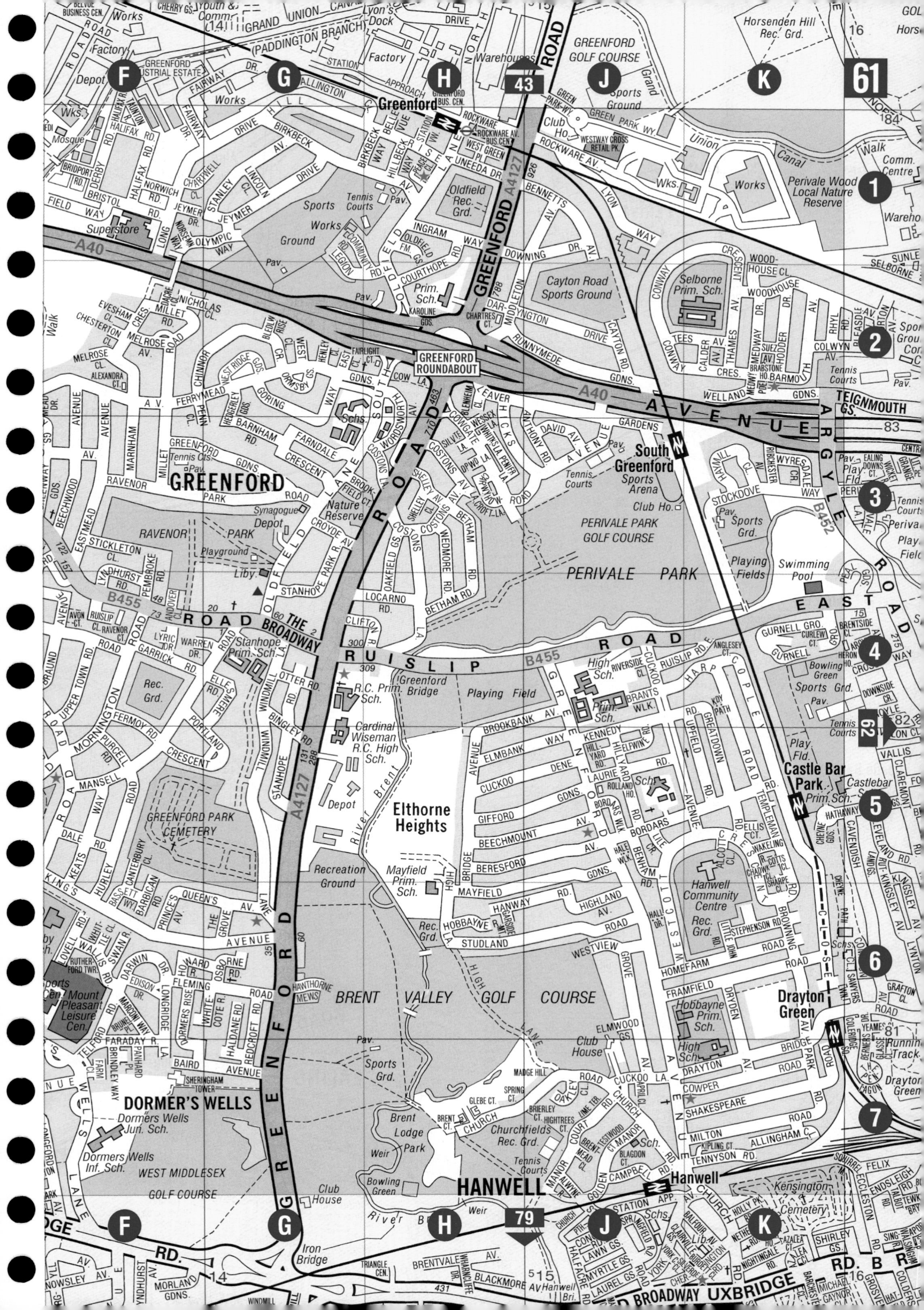

61
43
79
62
F
G
H
J
K
1
2
3
4
5
6
7
GREENFORD
Greenford
GREENFORD ROUNDABOUT
South Greenford
Castle Bar Park
Drayton Green
Hanwell
HANWELL
Elthorne Heights
DORMER'S WELLS
PERIVALE PARK
PERIVALE PARK GOLF COURSE
BRENT VALLEY GOLF COURSE
GREENFORD GOLF COURSE
WEST MIDDLESEX GOLF COURSE
GREENFORD PARK CEMETERY
RAVENOR PARK
Perivale Wood Local Nature Reserve
Horsenden Hill Rec. Grd.
GRAND UNION CANAL (PADDINGTON BRANCH)
GREENFORD ROAD
A4127
A40
WESTERN AVENUE
ARGYLE ROAD
RUISLIP ROAD
RUISLIP ROAD EAST
B455
B452
OLDFIELD LANE
CUCKOO AVENUE
UXBRIDGE ROAD
BROADWAY
Brent Lodge Park
Hanwell Community Centre
Mount Pleasant Leisure Cen.

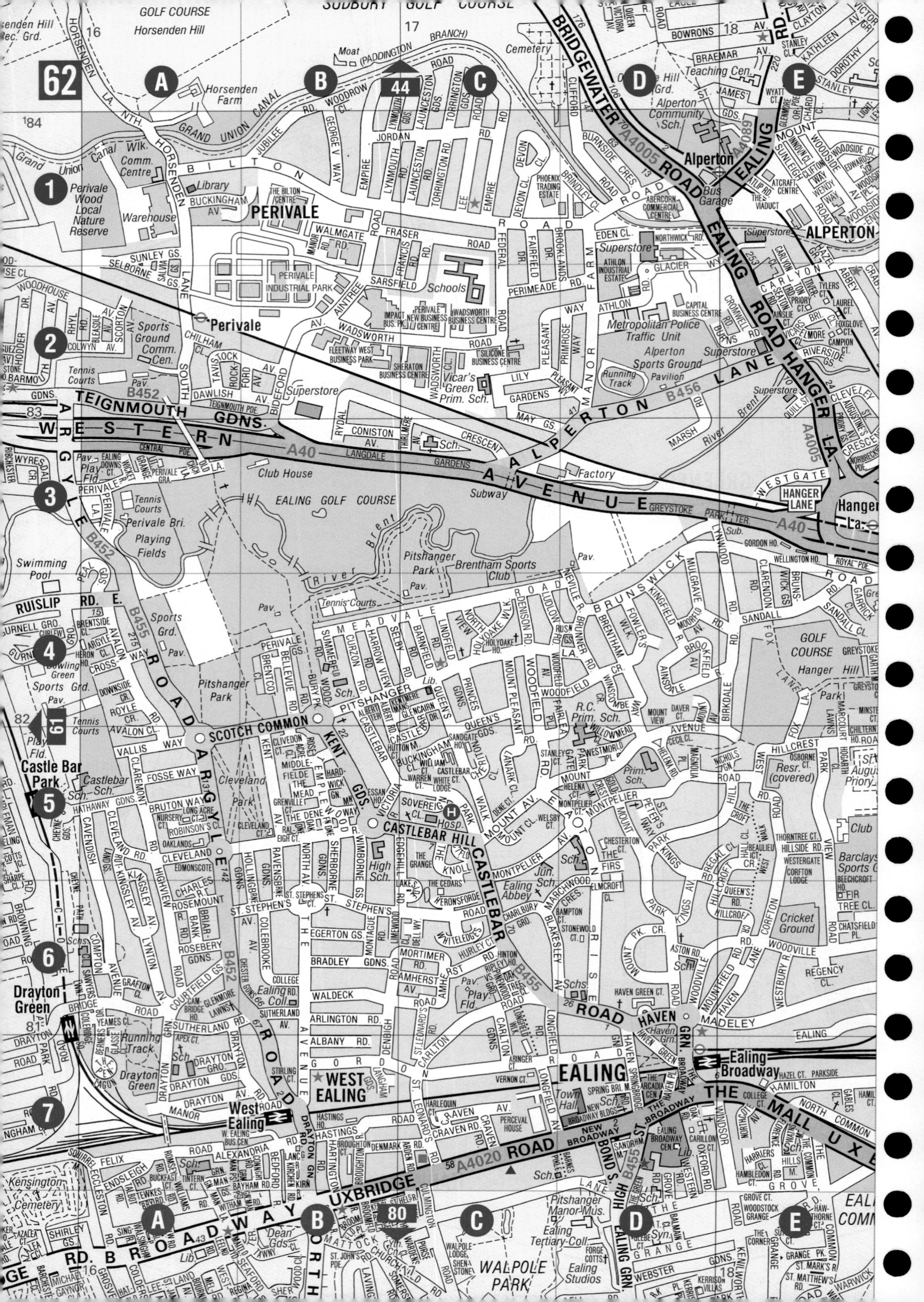
62
44
61
80
A
B
C
D
E
1
2
3
4
5
6
7
16
17
18
84
83
82
81
GOLF COURSE
Horsenden Hill
SUDBURY GOLF COURSE
Horsenden Farm
GRAND UNION CANAL
(PADDINGTON BRANCH)
Moat
Cemetery
BRIDGEWATER ROAD
BOWRONS AV.
BRAEMAR AV.
Teaching Cen.
Alperton Community Sch.
A4005
A4089
Alperton
EALING ROAD
Bus Garage
ALPERTON
Perivale Wood Local Nature Reserve
Comm. Centre
Library
Warehouse
BILTON ROAD
BUCKINGHAM AV.
PERIVALE
THE BILTON CENTRE
PHOENIX TRADING ESTATE
ABERCORN COMMERCIAL CENTRE
WALMGATE RD.
FRASER ROAD
SARSFIELD
Schools
PERIVALE INDUSTRIAL PARK
IMPACT BUS. PK.
PERIVALE NEW BUSINESS CENTRE
WADSWORTH BUSINESS CENTRE
FLEETWAY WEST BUSINESS PARK
SHERATON BUSINESS CENTRE
SILICONE BUSINESS CENTRE
WADSWORTH
PERIMEADE RD.
ATHLON INDUSTRIAL ESTATE
CAPITAL BUSINESS CENTRE
Superstore
Metropolitan Police Traffic Unit
Alperton Sports Ground
Running Track
Pavilion
HANGER LANE
Perivale
Sports Ground Comm. Cen.
Tennis Courts
B452
TEIGNMOUTH GDNS.
WESTERN AVENUE
A40
ALPERTON LANE
B456
Vicar's Green Prim. Sch.
Club House
Factory
EALING GOLF COURSE
Subway
River Brent
HANGER LANE
Hanger La.
Perivale Bri. Playing Fields
Swimming Pool
Pitshanger Park
Brentham Sports Club
Tennis Courts
RUISLIP RD. E.
B455
Sports Grd.
Bowling Green
Sports Grd.
GOLF COURSE Hanger Hill
Park
SCOTCH COMMON
ARGYLE ROAD
KENT GDNS.
PITSHANGER LA.
R.C. Prim. Sch.
Castle Bar Park
Castlebar Sch.
Cleveland Park
CASTLEBAR HILL
High Sch.
Hosp.
Resr. (covered)
Club
Barclays Sports G.
Cricket Ground
Ealing Abbey
Jun. Sch.
B455
Drayton Green
Running Track
Ealing Coll.
HAVEN GRN.
Haven Grn.
EALING
Ealing Broadway
WEST EALING
West Ealing
Town Hall
THE MALL
UXBRIDGE ROAD
A4020
NEW BROADWAY
EALING BROADWAY CEN.
HIGH ST.
Kensington Cemetery
BROADWAY
Dean Gdns.
Pitshanger Manor Mus.
Ealing Tertiary Coll.
WALPOLE PARK
Ealing Studios
EALING GRN.
EALING COMMON

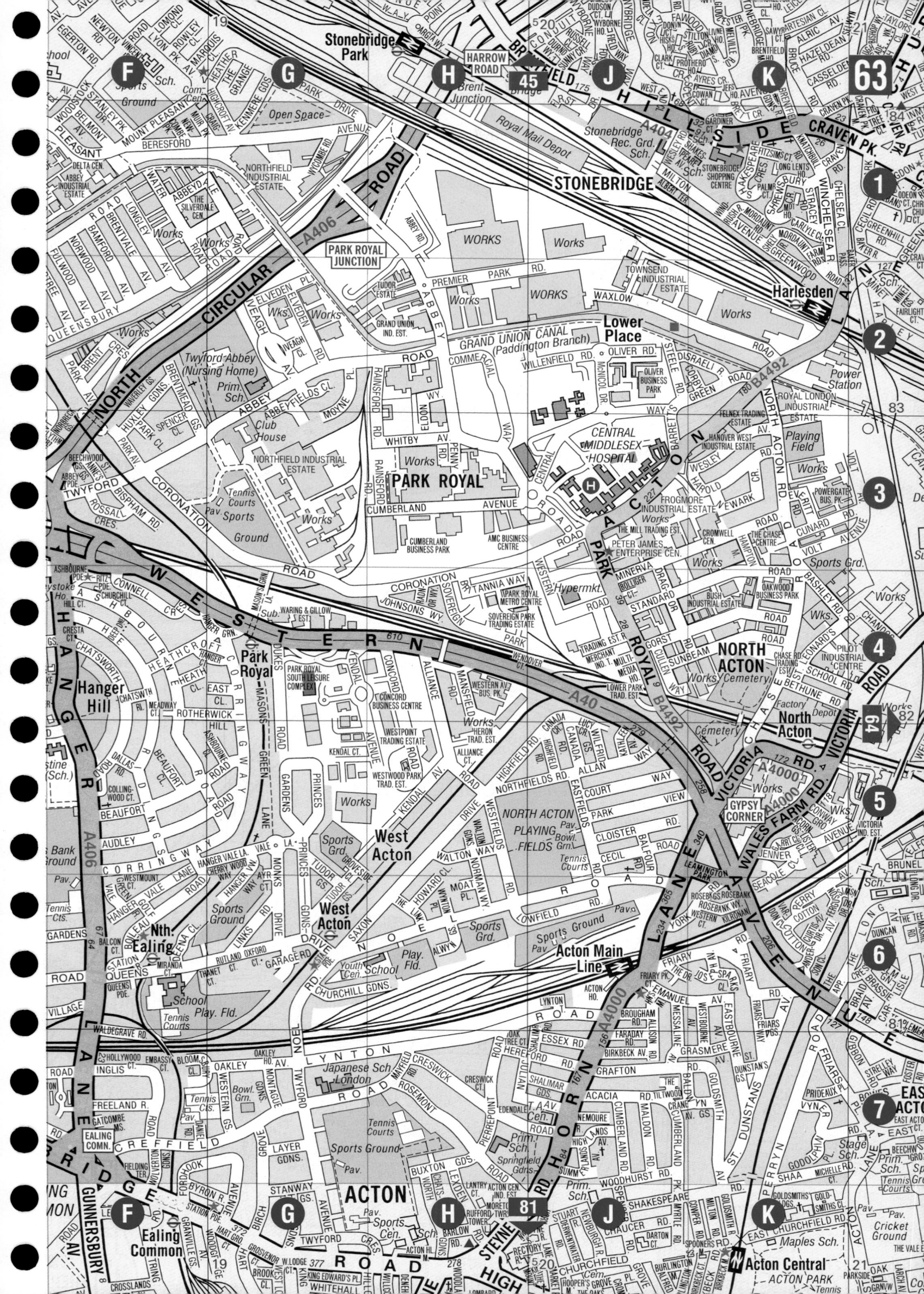
63
19
20
21
F
G
H
J
K
1
2
3
4
5
6
7
Stonebridge Park
HARROW ROAD
45
Brent Junction
HILLSIDE
CRAVEN PK.
A404
Royal Mail Depot
Stonebridge Rec. Grd. Sch.
STONEBRIDGE
STONEBRIDGE SHOPPING CENTRE
NORTH CIRCULAR ROAD
A406
NORTHFIELD INDUSTRIAL ESTATE
PARK ROYAL JUNCTION
Open Space
Sports Ground
BERESFORD
MOUNT PLEASANT
PLEASANT
QUEENSBURY
ABBEY INDUSTRIAL ESTATE
THE SILVERDALE CEN.
WORKS
Works
PREMIER PARK RD.
TUDOR ESTATE
GRAND UNION IND. EST.
TOWNSEND INDUSTRIAL ESTATE
WAXLOW
Harlesden
Lower Place
GRAND UNION CANAL (Paddington Branch)
OLIVER RD.
OLIVER BUSINESS PARK
WILLENFIELD RD.
B4492
Power Station
ROYAL LONDON INDUSTRIAL ESTATE
Twyford Abbey (Nursing Home)
Club House
NORTHFIELD INDUSTRIAL ESTATE
PARK ROYAL
CENTRAL MIDDLESEX HOSPITAL
ACTON LANE
FELNEX TRADING ESTATE
HANOVER WEST INDUSTRIAL ESTATE
Playing Field
NORTH ACTON RD.
FROGMORE INDUSTRIAL ESTATE
POWERGATE BUS. PK.
TWYFORD
CORONATION
Tennis Courts
CUMBERLAND AVENUE
CUMBERLAND BUSINESS PARK
AMC BUSINESS CENTRE
THE MILL TRADING EST.
PETER JAMES ENTERPRISE CEN.
CROMWELL CEN.
THE CHASE CENTRE
Sports Grd.
WESTERN AVENUE
A40
PARK ROYAL METRO CENTRE
SOVEREIGN PARK TRADING ESTATE
Hypermkt.
BUSH INDUSTRIAL ESTATE
OAKWOOD BUSINESS PARK
Park Royal
PARK ROYAL SOUTH LEISURE COMPLEX
CONCORD BUSINESS CENTRE
WESTERN AV. BUS. PK.
HERON TRAD. EST.
LOWER PARK TRAD. EST.
NORTH ACTON
Cemetery
PILOT INDUSTRIAL CENTRE
VICTORIA ROAD
North Acton
64
Hanger Hill
HANGER LANE
WESTPOINT TRADING ESTATE
WESTWOOD PARK TRAD. EST.
KENDAL CT.
GYPSY CORNER
A4000
WALES FARM RD.
VICTORIA IND. EST.
NORTH ACTON PLAYING FIELDS
West Acton
Sports Grd.
West Acton
Nth. Ealing
Sports Ground
School
Play. Fld.
Acton Main Line
Youth Cen.
HORN LANE
Japanese Sch. London
LYNTON
CRESWICK
EALING COMN.
Tennis Courts
Sports Ground
ACTON
Springfield Gdns.
EAST ACTON
Ealing Common
GUNNERSBURY AV.
81
HIGH ST.
CHURCHFIELD
Acton Central
ACTON PARK
Maples Sch.
Cricket Ground
TWYFORD CRES.
ROAD

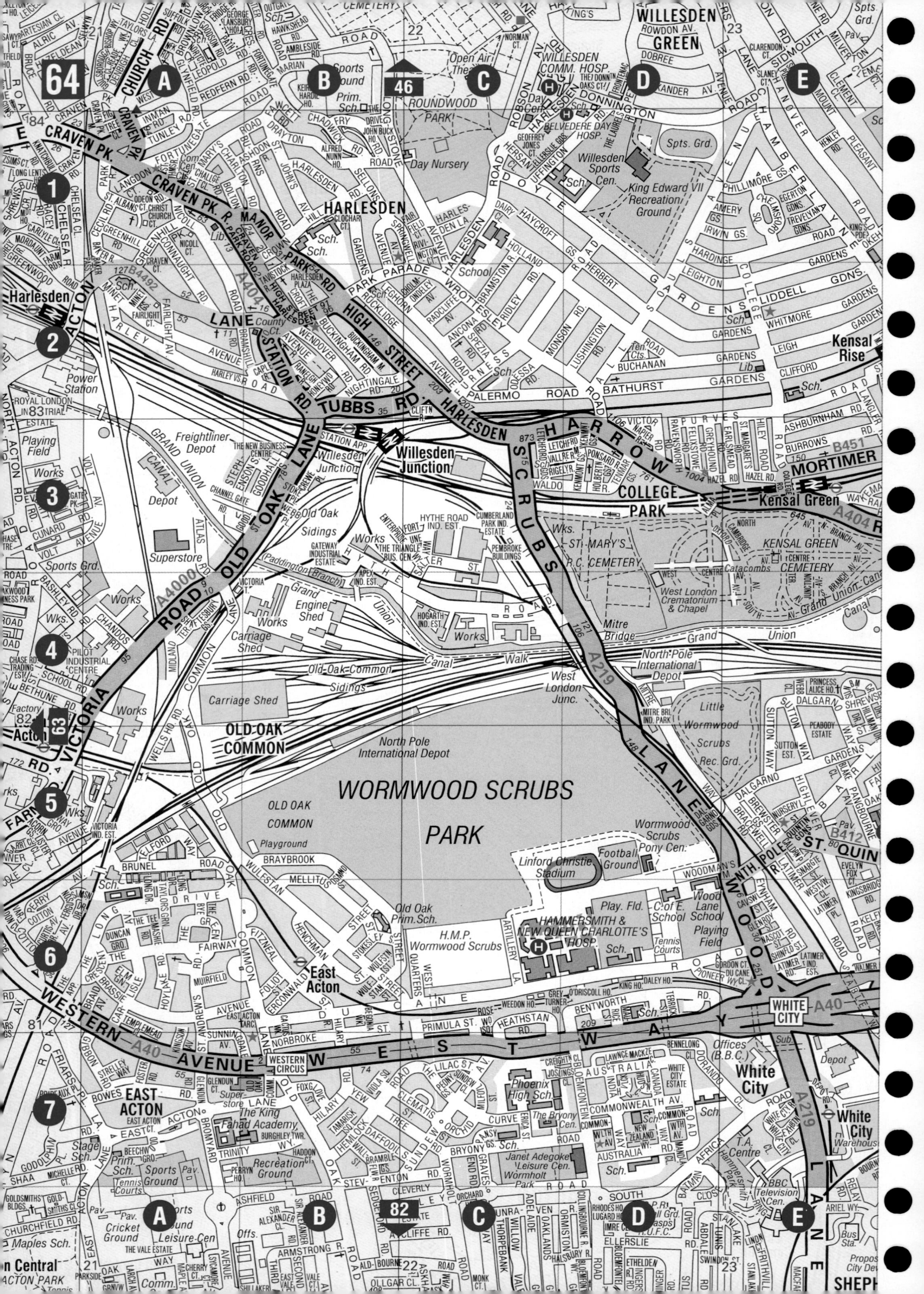
64
46
82
63
WILLESDEN GREEN
HARLESDEN
COLLEGE PARK
Kensal Green
Kensal Rise
Harlesden
Willesden Junction
WORMWOOD SCRUBS PARK
OLD OAK COMMON
EAST ACTON
East Acton
White City
WHITE CITY
Willesden Comm. Hosp.
Willesden Sports Cen.
King Edward VII Recreation Ground
Roundwood Park
St. Mary's R.C. Cemetery
Kensal Green Cemetery
West London Crematorium & Chapel
Little Wormwood Scrubs Rec. Grd.
Linford Christie Stadium
Hammersmith & New Queen Charlotte's Hosp.
H.M.P. Wormwood Scrubs
North Pole International Depot
Freightliner Depot
Grand Union Canal
Old Oak Sidings
Old Oak Common Sidings
Carriage Shed
Power Station
Superstore
Phoenix High Sch.
Janet Adegoke Leisure Cen.
Wormholt Park
The King Fahad Academy
BBC Television Cen.
Offices (B.B.C.)
Mitre Bridge
West London Junc.
CRAVEN PK. RD.
HIGH STREET
HARLESDEN RD.
TUBBS RD.
STATION RD.
OLD OAK LANE
OLD OAK COMMON LANE
SCRUBS LANE
HARROW ROAD
VICTORIA ROAD
WESTERN AVENUE
WESTWAY
WOOD LANE
DU CANE ROAD
MORTIMER RD.
ACTON LANE
A404
A4000
A219
A40
B451
B412
B4492
A
B
C
D
E
1
2
3
4
5
6
7
21
22
23
81
82
83
84

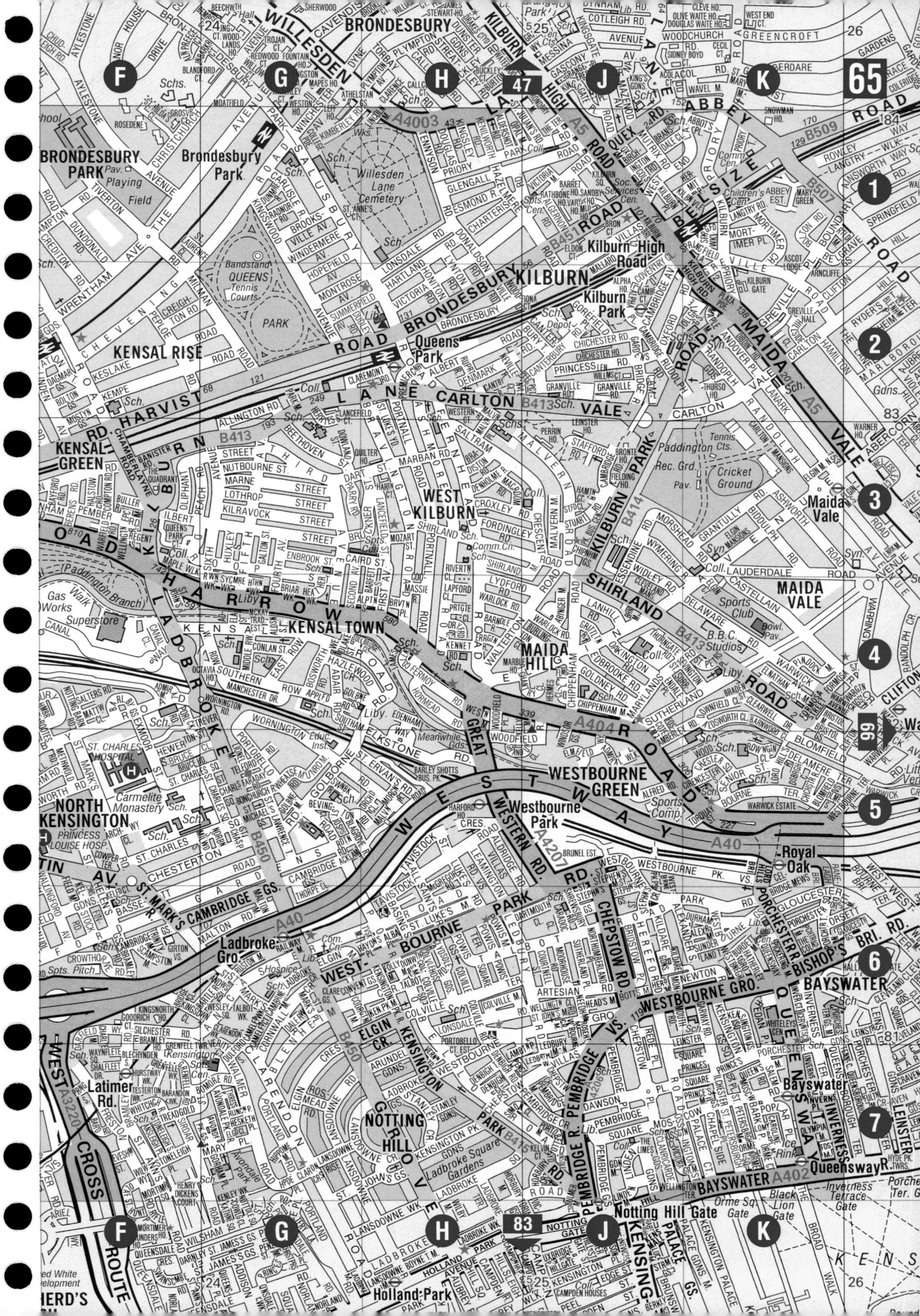

BRONDESBURY
WILLESDEN
KILBURN
47
BRONDESBURY PARK
Brondesbury Park
Willesden Lane Cemetery
BELSIZE
ABBEY ROAD
QUEENS PARK
Queens Park
KILBURN
Kilburn High Road
Kilburn Park
KENSAL RISE
HARVIST ROAD
CARLTON VALE
KENSAL GREEN
WEST KILBURN
Paddington Rec. Grd.
Cricket Ground
Maida Vale
MAIDA VALE
MAIDA VALE
SHIRLAND ROAD
HARROW ROAD
KENSAL TOWN
MAIDA HILL
LADBROKE GROVE
WESTBOURNE GREEN
WESTWAY
Westbourne Park
Royal Oak
NORTH KENSINGTON
ST. CHARLES HOSPITAL
Carmelite Monastery
PRINCESS LOUISE HOSP.
Ladbroke Gro
WESTBOURNE GRO.
BAYSWATER
Bayswater
Latimer Rd.
NOTTING HILL
Ladbroke Square Gardens
WEST CROSS ROUTE
BAYSWATER
Queensway
Notting Hill Gate
Holland Park
83
99
F
G
H
J
K
1
2
3
4
5
6
7
24
25
26

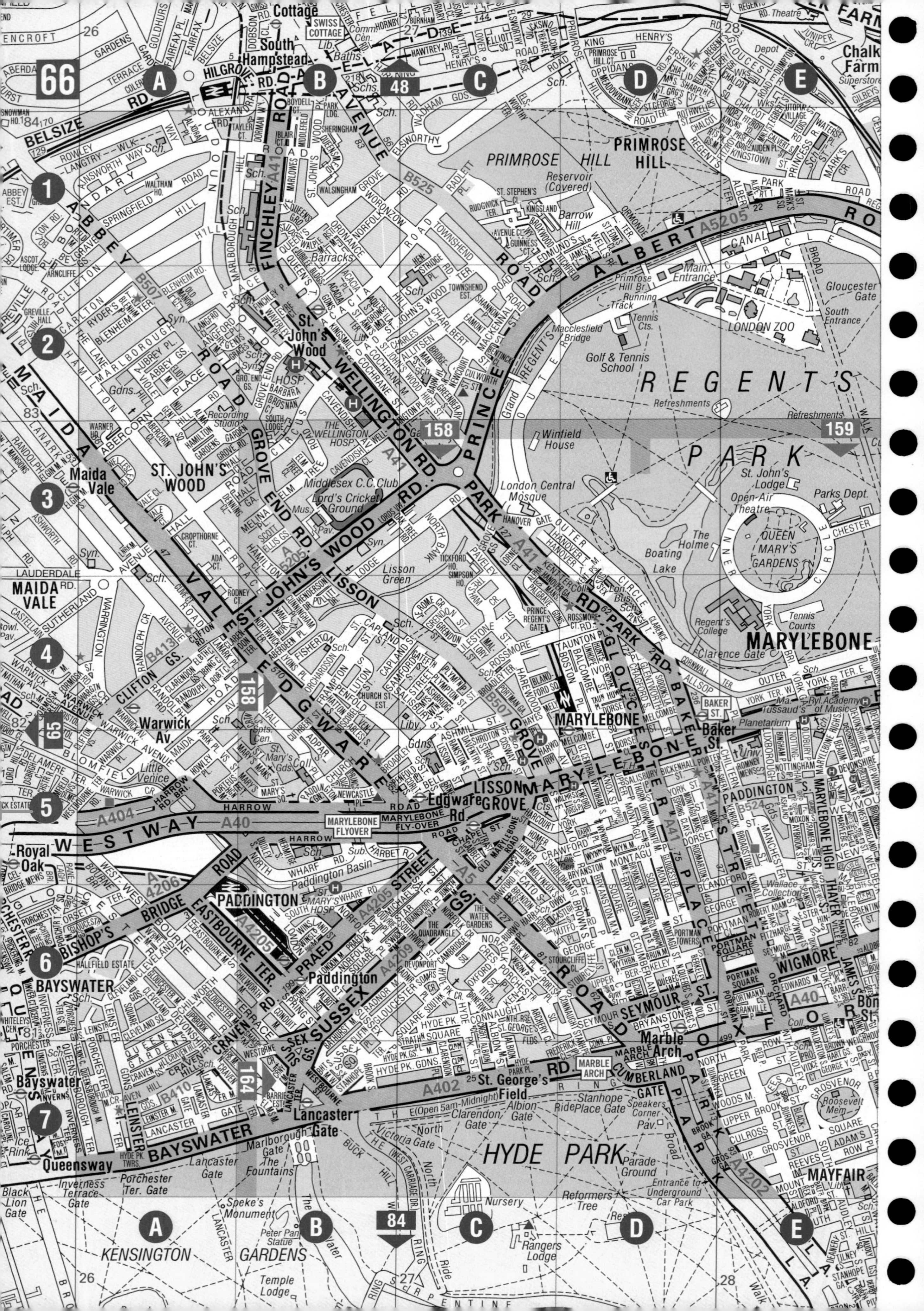

A
B
C
D
E
1
2
3
4
5
6
7
48
158
159
65
164
84
26
27
28
Swiss Cottage
South Hampstead
Belsize Rd.
Hilgrove Rd.
Finchley Road
Avenue Road
Elsworthy
Primrose Hill
Primrose Hill
Reservoir (Covered)
Barrow Hill
Chalk Farm
Abbey Road
Boundary Rd.
Springfield Road
Hill Road
Marlborough Place
St. John's Wood
Wellington Rd.
Prince Albert Road
Albert Road
A5205
A41
B525
B507
Barracks
Main Entrance
Primrose Hill Br
Running Track
Tennis Cts.
Macclesfield Bridge
Golf & Tennis School
London Zoo
Gloucester Gate
South Entrance
Regent's Park
Refreshments
Winfield House
St. John's Lodge
Parks Dept.
Open-Air Theatre
Queen Mary's Gardens
The Holme
Boating Lake
London Central Mosque
Hanover Gate
Outer Circle
Inner Circle
Regent's College
Tennis Courts
Clarence Gate
Marylebone
Maida Vale
Lauderdale Rd.
Clifton Gs.
Warwick Av.
Little Venice
Grove End Rd.
Lord's Cricket Ground
Middlesex C.C. Club
The Wellington Hosp.
St. John's Wood Rd.
Lisson Grove
Lisson Green
Edgware Road
Edgware Rd
Park Road
Baker Street
Baker St.
Marylebone Road
Madame Tussaud's
Ryl. Academy of Music
Planetarium
Gloucester Place
Dorset Sq.
Westway
A40
A404
Harrow Road
Marylebone Fly-Over
Marylebone Flyover
Royal Oak
Paddington
Paddington Basin
Bishop's Bridge Road
Praed St.
Sussex Gdns.
Eastbourne Ter.
Hallfield Estate
Bayswater
Bayswater Road
Queensway
Lancaster Gate
Marble Arch
Cumberland Gate
Oxford Street
A5
A4205
A4206
A4209
A402
A4202
Connaught Sq.
Bryanston Sq.
Montagu Sq.
Portman Square
Seymour St.
Wigmore St.
Manchester Sq.
Wallace Collection
Paddington St.
Marylebone High St.
Park Lane
Speakers Corner
Stanhope Place Gate
Albion Gate
Clarendon Gate
Victoria Gate
Marlborough Gate
The Fountains
Hyde Park
Parade Ground
Reformers Tree
Nursery
Rangers Lodge
Entrance to Underground Car Park
Kensington Gardens
Speke's Monument
Peter Pan Statue
Temple Lodge
Long Water
The Ring
North Carriage Dr.
Buck Hill Walk
Serpentine
Black Lion Gate
Inverness Terrace Gate
Porchester Ter. Gate
Lancaster Gate
Ice Rink
Grosvenor Square
Roosevelt Mem.
Mayfair
Upper Brook St.
Upper Grosvenor St.
Mount St.

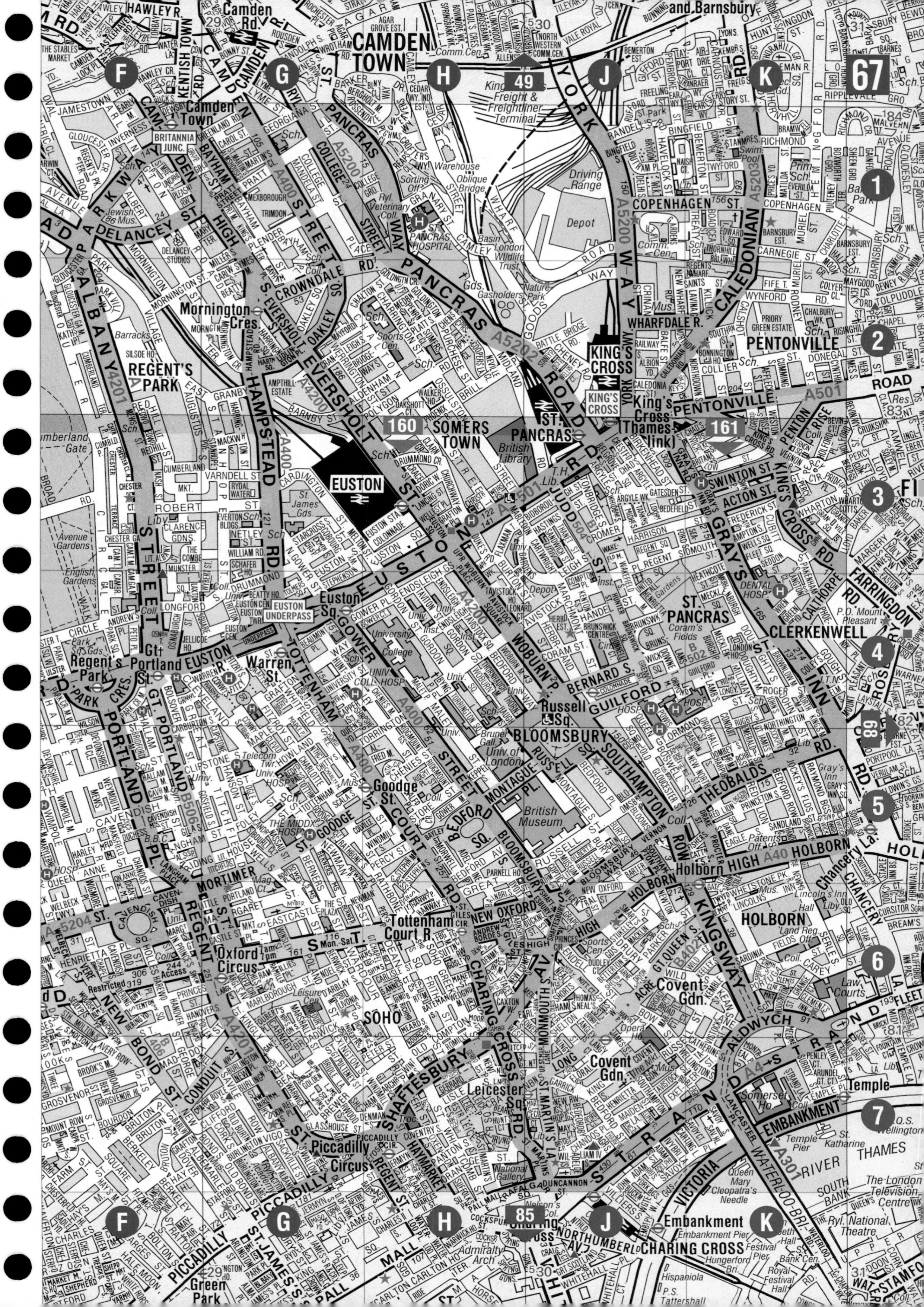
67
CAMDEN TOWN
Camden Town
Camden Rd.
KENTISH TOWN
BRITANNIA JUNC.
Mornington Cres.
REGENT'S PARK
SOMERS TOWN
EUSTON
Euston
Euston Sq.
EUSTON UNDERPASS
KING'S CROSS
King's Cross (Thameslink)
ST. PANCRAS
PENTONVILLE
CLERKENWELL
BLOOMSBURY
Russell Sq.
British Museum
British Library
HOLBORN
Holborn
Covent Gdn.
SOHO
Tottenham Court R.
Goodge St.
Warren St.
Great Portland St.
Regent's Park
Oxford Circus
Piccadilly Circus
Leicester Sq.
Charing Cross
CHARING CROSS
Embankment
Temple
Green Park
King's Cross Freight & Freightliner Terminal
Driving Range
Depot
Camley St. Nature Park
Gasholders
London Wildlife Trust
St. Pancras Hospital
National Gallery
Admiralty Arch
Nelson's Col.
Cleopatra's Needle
Somerset Ho.
Law Courts
Lincoln's Inn
Gray's Inn
Coram's Fields
University College
Univ. of London
RIVER THAMES
SOUTH BANK
Royal Festival Hall
Ryl. National Theatre
Hungerford Bri.
Waterloo Bri.
Embankment Pier
Temple Pier
49
85
160
161
68
F
G
H
J
K
1
2
3
4
5
6
7
A5200
A5202
A5203
A501
A4200
A400
A4201
A40
A4
A301
A5204
B506
B502
B504
B402
PARKWAY
DELANCEY ST.
ALBANY ST.
HAMPSTEAD RD.
EVERSHOLT ST.
PANCRAS WAY
PANCRAS RD.
YORK WAY
CALEDONIAN RD.
COPENHAGEN ST.
PENTONVILLE RD.
KING'S CROSS RD.
GRAY'S INN RD.
FARRINGDON RD.
EUSTON RD.
CROWNDALE RD.
GOWER ST.
TOTTENHAM COURT RD.
WOBURN PL.
SOUTHAMPTON ROW
THEOBALDS RD.
GUILFORD ST.
BERNARD ST.
JUDD ST.
KINGSWAY
HIGH HOLBORN
NEW OXFORD ST.
SHAFTESBURY AV.
CHARING CROSS RD.
OXFORD ST.
REGENT ST.
PORTLAND PL.
GT. PORTLAND ST.
MORTIMER ST.
GOODGE ST.
BEDFORD SQ.
RUSSELL SQ.
NEW BOND ST.
CONDUIT ST.
PICCADILLY
HAYMARKET
STRAND
ALDWYCH
VICTORIA EMBANKMENT
NORTHUMBERLAND AV.
ST. MARTIN'S LA.
MONMOUTH ST.
LONG ACRE
THE MALL
PALL MALL
ST. JAMES'S ST.
CHANCERY LA.
FLEET ST.

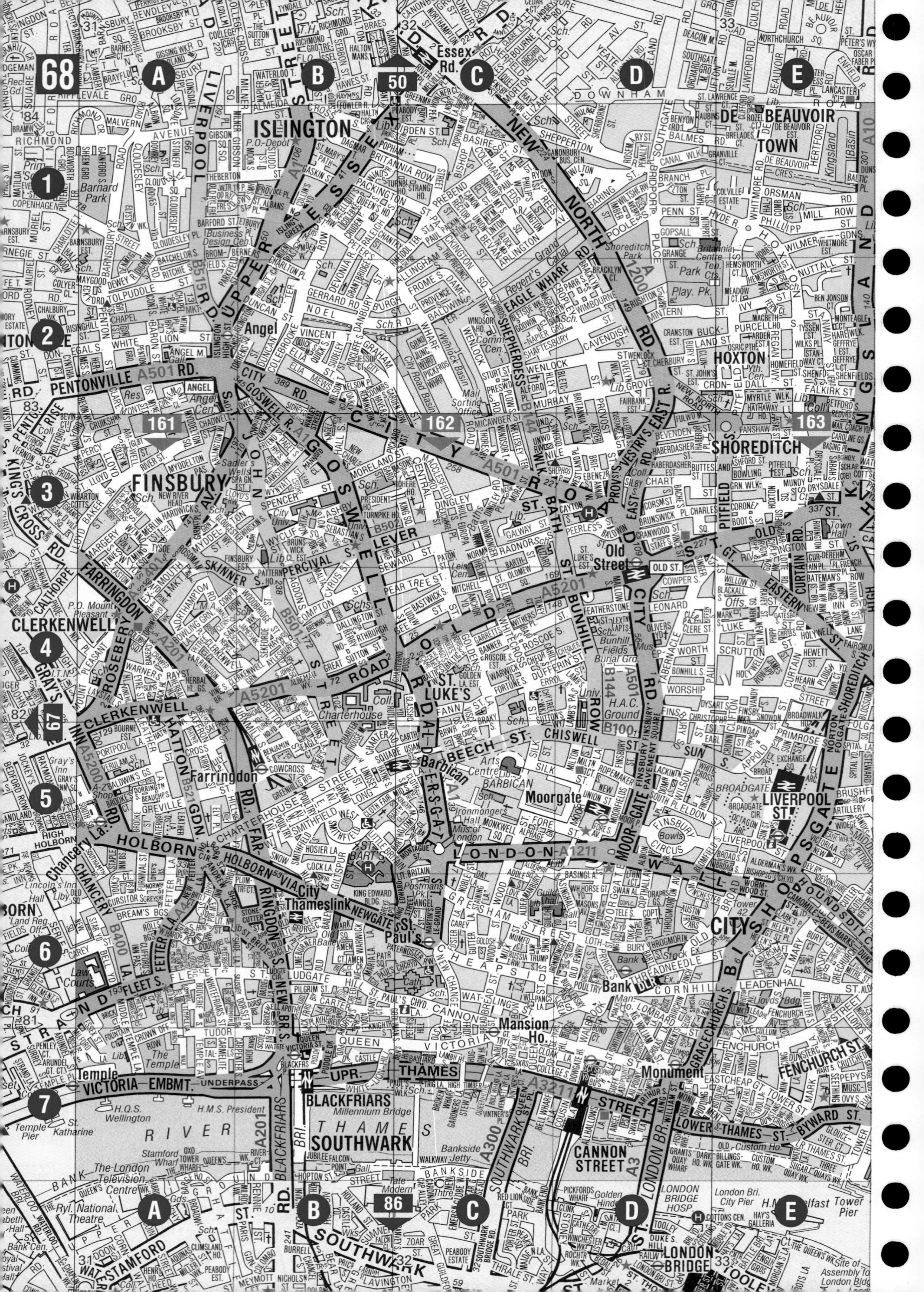

68
A
B
C
D
E
50
86
161
162
163
67
1
2
3
4
5
6
7
ISLINGTON
DE BEAUVOIR TOWN
Angel
HOXTON
FINSBURY
SHOREDITCH
CLERKENWELL
ST. LUKE'S
Farringdon
Barbican
Moorgate
LIVERPOOL ST.
CITY
Old Street
Bank
Mansion Ho.
Monument
CANNON STREET
BLACKFRIARS
SOUTHWARK
LONDON BRIDGE
Temple
RIVER THAMES
PENTONVILLE RD.
CITY RD.
GOSWELL RD.
NEW NORTH RD.
OLD ST.
CLERKENWELL RD.
HOLBORN
FLEET ST.
STRAND
VICTORIA EMBMT.
UPR. THAMES ST.
LOWER THAMES ST.
LONDON WALL
CHEAPSIDE
CORNHILL
BISHOPSGATE
KINGSLAND RD.
Essex Rd.
Thameslink
St. Paul's

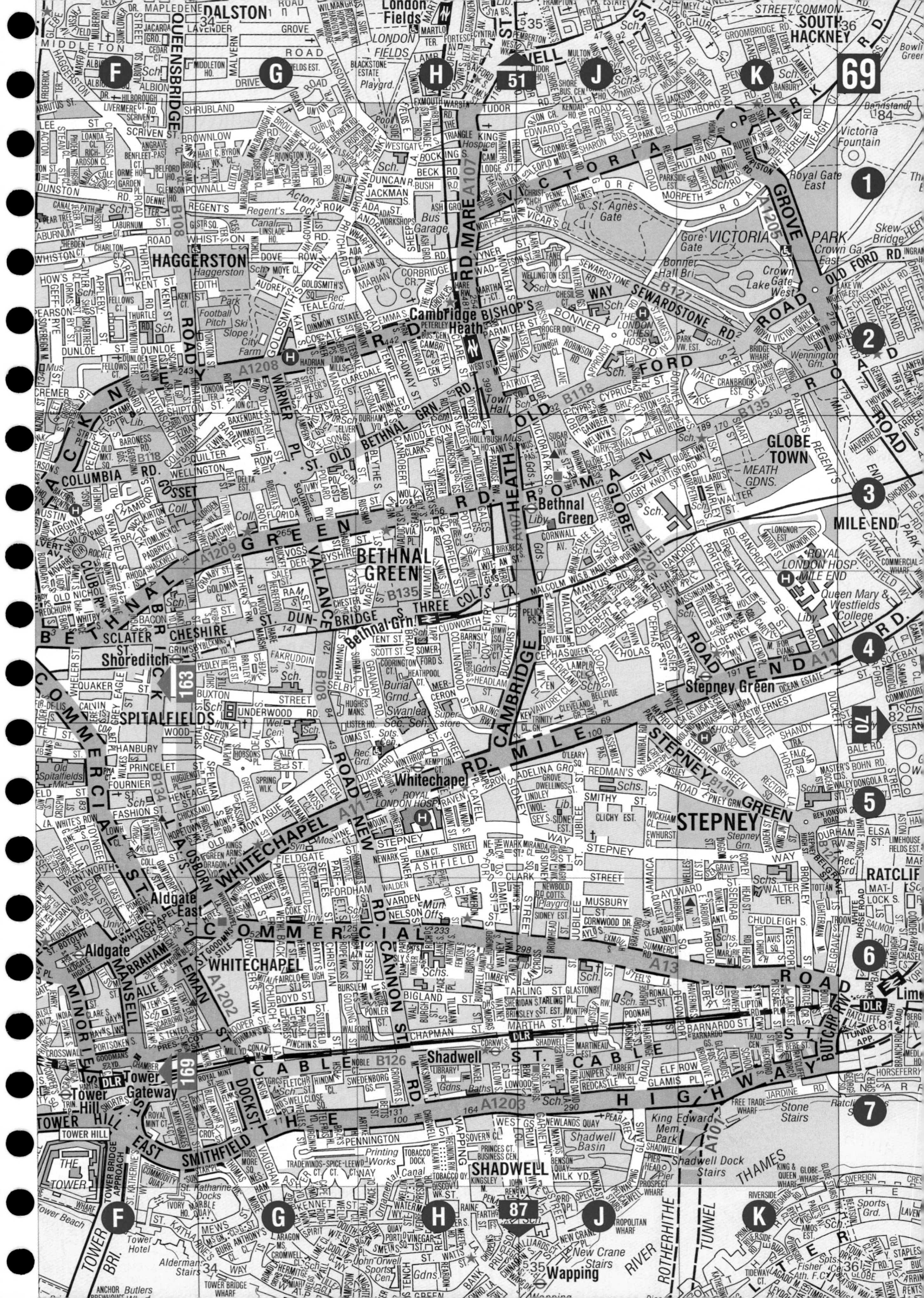
69
DALSTON
London Fields
SOUTH HACKNEY
F
G
H
J
K
51
VICTORIA PARK
HAGGERSTON
Cambridge Heath
BISHOP'S WAY
SEWARDSTONE RD.
OLD FORD RD.
GLOBE TOWN
Bethnal Green
BETHNAL GREEN
MILE END
Queen Mary & Westfields College
Shoreditch
163
SPITALFIELDS
Stepney Green
70
Whitechapel
ROYAL LONDON HOSP.
STEPNEY
RATCLIFF
Aldgate East
Aldgate
WHITECHAPEL
COMMERCIAL RD.
Tower Gateway
169
Tower Hill
TOWER HILL
THE TOWER
Shadwell
SHADWELL
CABLE ST.
THE HIGHWAY
King Edward Mem. Park
Shadwell Basin
RIVER THAMES
ROTHERHITHE TUNNEL
87
Wapping
MILE END RD.
WHITECHAPEL RD.
CAMBRIDGE HEATH RD.
MARE ST.
HACKNEY RD.
QUEENSBRIDGE RD.
GREEN RD.
ROMAN RD.
1
2
3
4
5
6
7
34
35
36

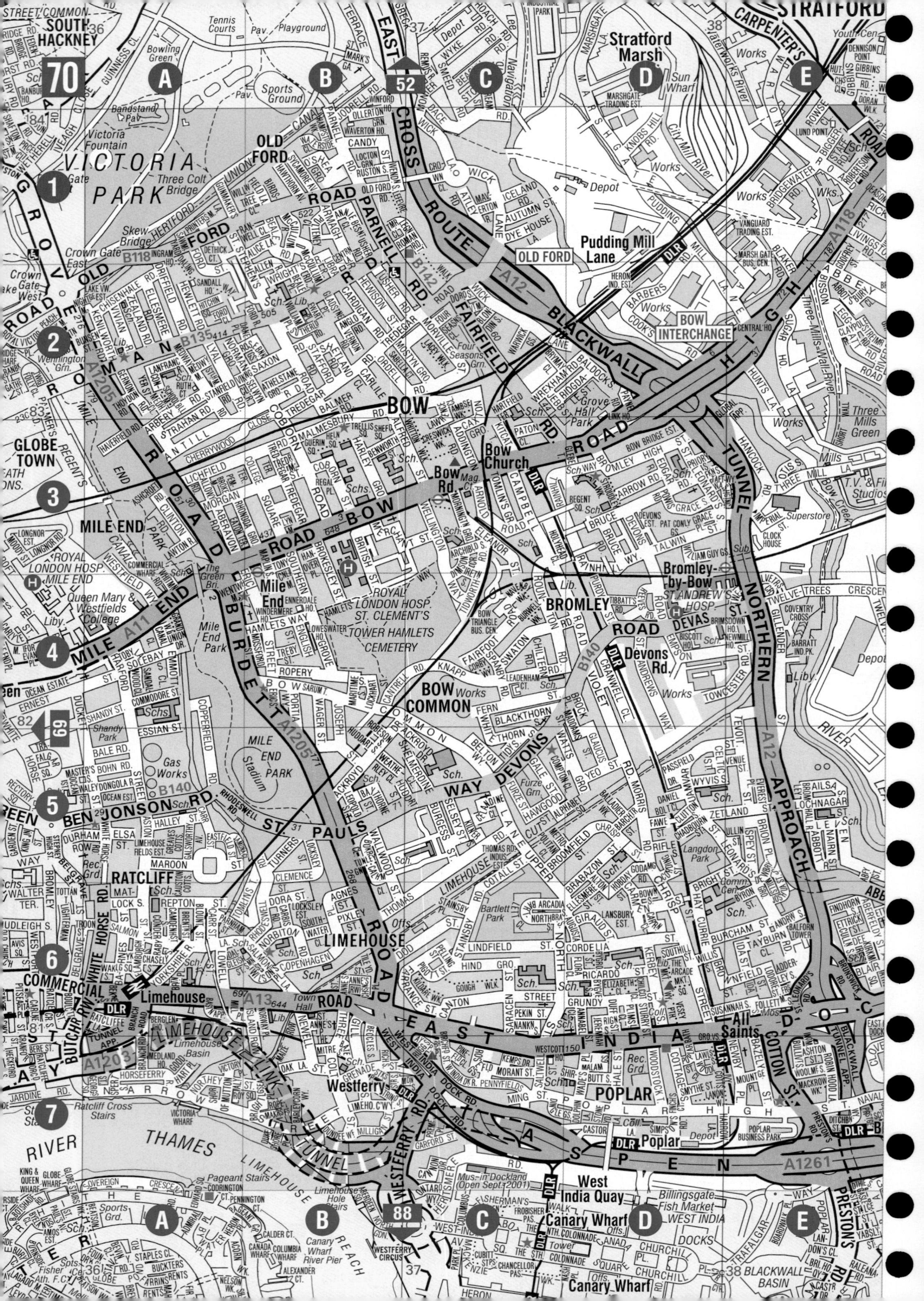
70
52
69
88
SOUTH HACKNEY
VICTORIA PARK
Victoria Fountain
Three Colt Bridge
Skew Bridge
Crown Gate East
Crown Gate West
Bowling Green
Bandstand
Sports Ground
Tennis Courts
Playground
OLD FORD
OLD FORD ROAD
ROMAN ROAD
GROVE ROAD
PARNELL RD
FAIRFIELD RD
EAST CROSS ROUTE
BLACKWALL TUNNEL NORTHERN APPROACH
OLD FORD
Pudding Mill Lane
Stratford Marsh
STRATFORD
CARPENTER'S RD
BOW INTERCHANGE
BOW
Bow Church
Bow Rd.
BOW ROAD
HIGH ST.
Grove Hall Park
Four Seasons Grn.
GLOBE TOWN
MILE END
MILE END ROAD
ROYAL LONDON HOSP. MILE END
Queen Mary & Westfields College
Mile End Park
Mile End
MILE END PARK Stadium
BURDETT ROAD
ROYAL LONDON HOSP. ST. CLEMENT'S
TOWER HAMLETS CEMETERY
BOW COMMON
BOW COMMON LA.
DEVONS ROAD
Devons Rd.
BROMLEY
Bromley-by-Bow
ST. ANDREW'S HOSP.
Three Mills Green
Langdon Park
BEN JONSON RD.
ST. PAULS WAY
RATCLIFF
LIMEHOUSE
Limehouse
Limehouse Basin
COMMERCIAL ROAD
EAST INDIA DOCK RD.
LIMEHOUSE LINK TUNNEL
Westferry
WESTFERRY RD.
POPLAR
Poplar
All Saints
ASPEN WAY
POPLAR HIGH ST.
West India Quay
Canary Wharf
Billingsgate Fish Market
WEST INDIA DOCKS
Mus. in Dockland (Open Sept. 2001)
Canary Wharf River Pier
RIVER THAMES
LIMEHOUSE REACH
Ratcliff Cross Stairs
Pageant Stairs
Limehouse Hole Stairs
BLACKWALL BASIN
Bartlett Park
Shandy Park
Gas Works
A12
A11
A13
A1205
A1261
A118
B118
B135
B140
B142
DLR

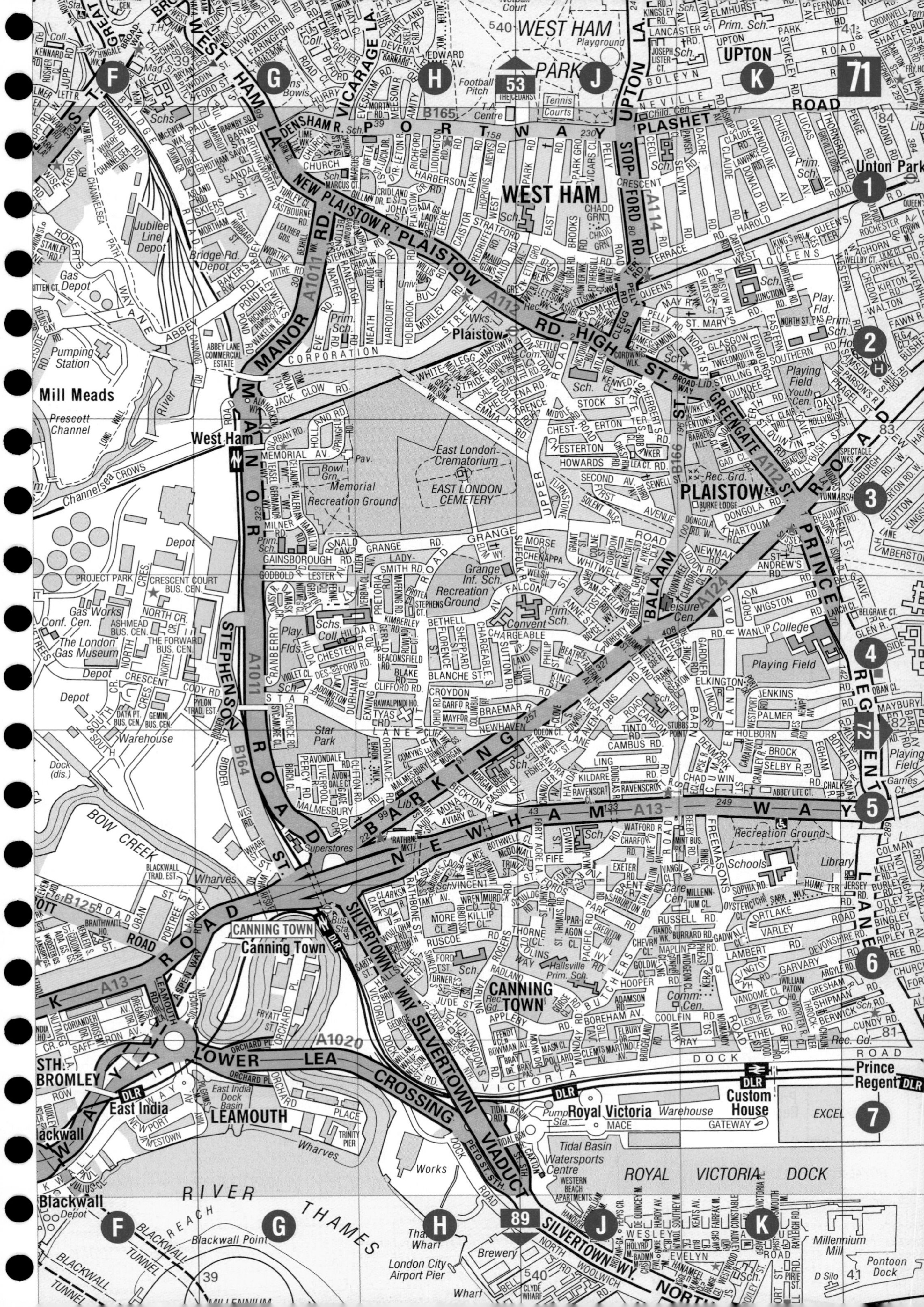

71
53
72
89
F
G
H
J
K
1
2
3
4
5
6
7
WEST HAM
PARK
WEST HAM
UPTON
Upton Park
PLAISTOW
CANNING TOWN
LEAMOUTH
STH. BROMLEY
Blackwall
Mill Meads
Prescott Channel
West Ham
Canning Town
CANNING TOWN
East India
Royal Victoria
Custom House
Prince Regent
Plaistow
PORTWAY
PLASHET ROAD
UPTON LA.
STOPFORD RD
PLAISTOW RD.
NEW PLAISTOW R.
HIGH ST.
MANOR RD
MANOR ROAD
STEPHENSON ST.
BARKING ROAD
NEWHAM WAY
PRINCE REGENT LANE
GREENGATE ST.
BALAAM ST.
SILVERTOWN WAY
SILVERTOWN WY.
LOWER LEA CROSSING
VICTORIA DOCK ROAD
VIADUCT
VICARAGE LA.
WEST HAM LA.
ABBEY ROAD
ABBEY LANE
CORPORATION
CHANNELSEA ROAD
A1011
A112
A114
A124
A13
A1020
B164
B165
B166
B125
East London Crematorium
EAST LONDON CEMETERY
Memorial Recreation Ground
Grange Recreation Ground
Star Park
Jubilee Line Depot
Bridge Rd. Depot
Gas Depot
Pumping Station
The London Gas Museum
Gas Works
PROJECT PARK
CRESCENT COURT BUS. CEN.
BOW CREEK
RIVER THAMES
BLACKWALL REACH
Blackwall Point
BLACKWALL TUNNEL
ROYAL VICTORIA DOCK
Tidal Basin Watersports Centre
London City Airport Pier
Millennium Mill
Pontoon Dock
EXCEL
Warehouse
Wharves
Works
Brewery
Playing Field
Recreation Ground
Leisure Cen.
College
Schools
Library
Superstores
Football Pitch
Tennis Courts

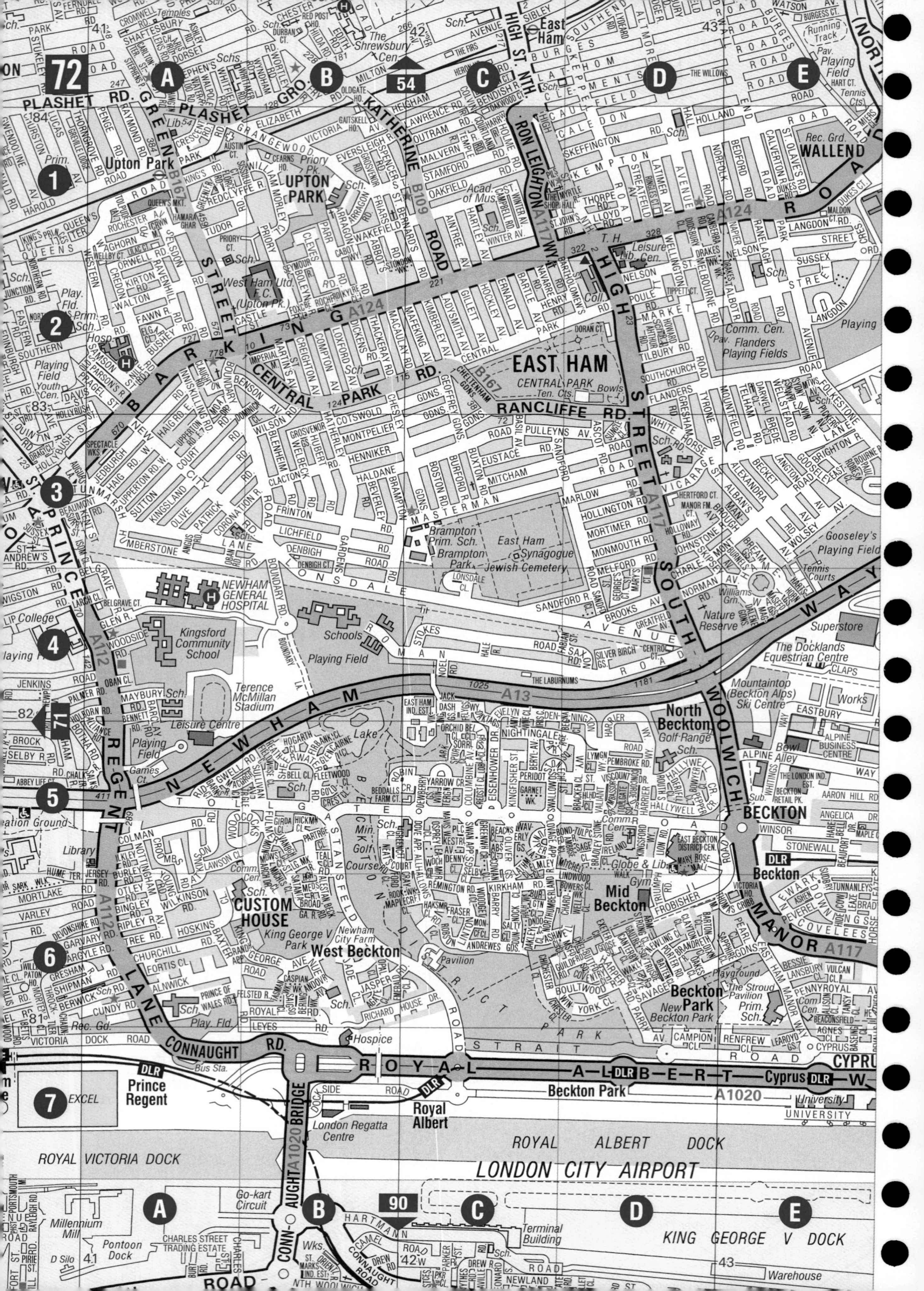

54
Upton Park
UPTON PARK
East Ham
WALLEND
EAST HAM
CENTRAL PARK
PLASHET RD.
PLASHET GRO.
GREEN STREET
KATHERINE ROAD
HIGH ST. NTH
RON LEIGHTON WAY
BARKING ROAD
HIGH STREET SOUTH
CENTRAL PARK RD.
RANCLIFFE RD.
West Ham Utd. F.C. (Upton Pk.)
East Ham Synagogue
Jewish Cemetery
Brampton Park
NEWHAM GENERAL HOSPITAL
Kingsford Community School
Terence McMillan Stadium
Leisure Centre
Playing Field
Schools
NEWHAM WAY
A13
North Beckton
Golf Range
Mountaintop (Beckton Alps) Ski Centre
The Docklands Equestrian Centre
Superstore
Nature Reserve
Gooseley's Playing Field
Flanders Playing Fields
WOOLWICH MANOR WAY
BECKTON
Beckton
Mid Beckton
CUSTOM HOUSE
King George V Park
West Beckton
Newham City Farm
Beckton Park
New Beckton Park
REGENT
LANE
PRINCE
CONNAUGHT RD.
ROYAL ALBERT
Prince Regent
EXCEL
Royal Albert
Beckton Park
Cyprus
A1020
London Regatta Centre
ROYAL VICTORIA DOCK
ROYAL ALBERT DOCK
LONDON CITY AIRPORT
Go-kart Circuit
Millennium Mill
Pontoon Dock
CHARLES STREET TRADING ESTATE
CONNAUGHT BRIDGE
Terminal Building
KING GEORGE V DOCK
Warehouse
90
71

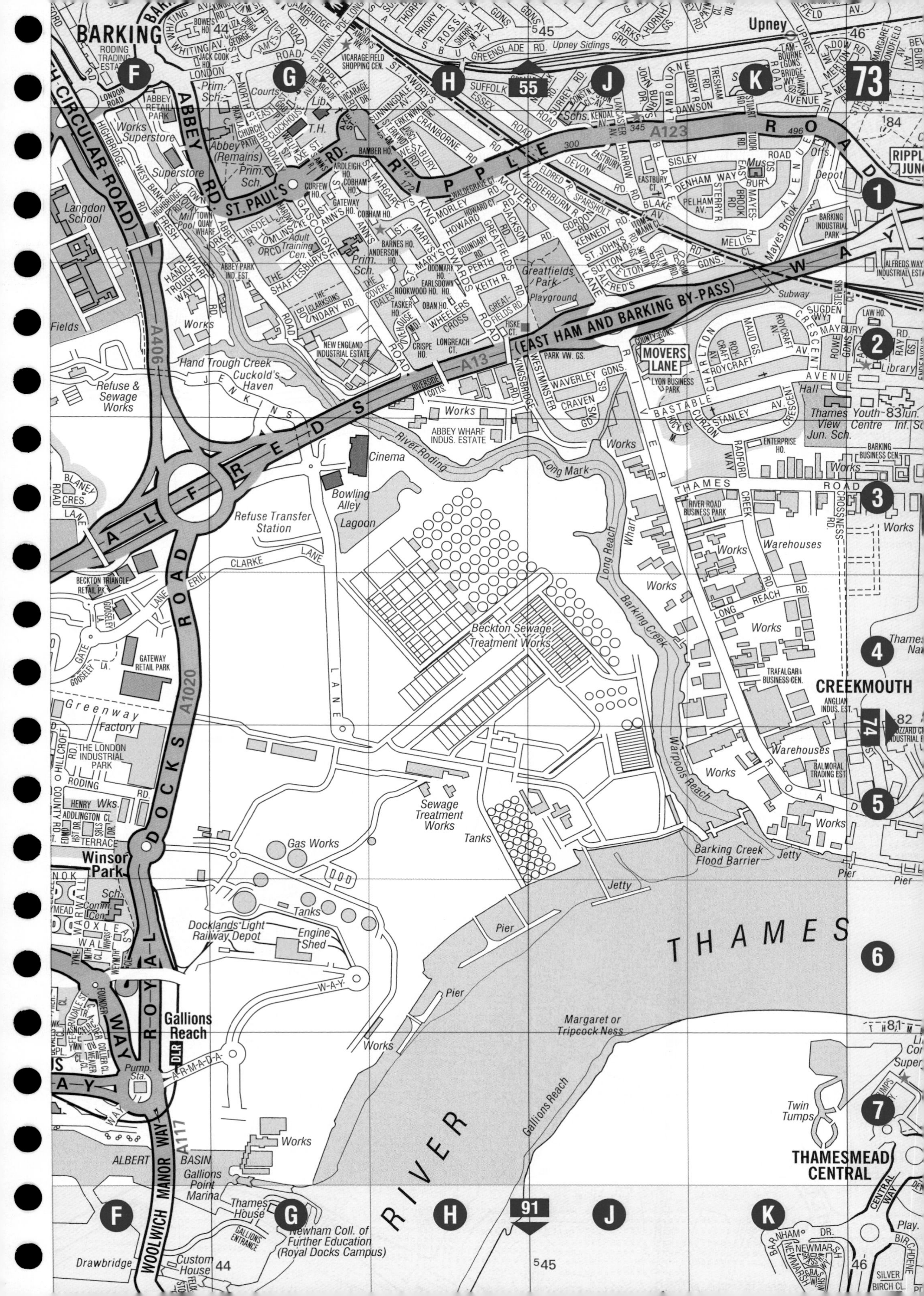
BARKING
Upney
CREEKMOUTH
THAMESMEAD CENTRAL
Winsor Park
Gallions Reach
RIPPLE ROAD
A123
ST. PAUL'S RD.
ABBEY RD.
NORTH CIRCULAR ROAD
A406
ALFREDS WAY
A13
(EAST HAM AND BARKING BY-PASS)
DOCKS ROAD
A1020
ROYAL DOCKS ROAD
WOOLWICH MANOR WAY
A117
ARMADA WAY
MOVERS LANE
RIVER ROAD
THAMES ROAD
CREEK RD.
LONG REACH RD.
Beckton Sewage Treatment Works
Sewage Treatment Works
Gas Works
Tanks
Docklands Light Railway Depot
Engine Shed
River Roding
Barking Creek
Long Reach
Warpools Reach
Barking Creek Flood Barrier
Jetty
Pier
THAMES
RIVER
Gallions Reach
Margaret or Tripcock Ness
Twin Tumps
Refuse & Sewage Works
Refuse Transfer Station
Cinema
Bowling Alley
Lagoon
Hand Trough Creek
Cuckold's Haven
Long Mark
ABBEY WHARF INDUS. ESTATE
NEW ENGLAND INDUSTRIAL ESTATE
RIVER ROAD BUSINESS PARK
TRAFALGAR BUSINESS CEN.
ANGLIAN INDUS. EST.
BALMORAL TRADING EST.
BARKING BUSINESS CEN.
BARKING INDUSTRIAL PARK
LYON BUSINESS PARK
BECKTON TRIANGLE RETAIL PK.
GATEWAY RETAIL PARK
THE LONDON INDUSTRIAL PARK
RODING TRADING ESTATE
ABBEY RETAIL PARK
Greatfields Park
Langdon School
Thames View Jun. Sch.
Youth Centre
Greenway
ALBERT BASIN
Gallions Point Marina
Thames House
Newham Coll. of Further Education (Royal Docks Campus)
Drawbridge
Custom House
55
74
91
F G H J K
1 2 3 4 5 6 7
44 45 46

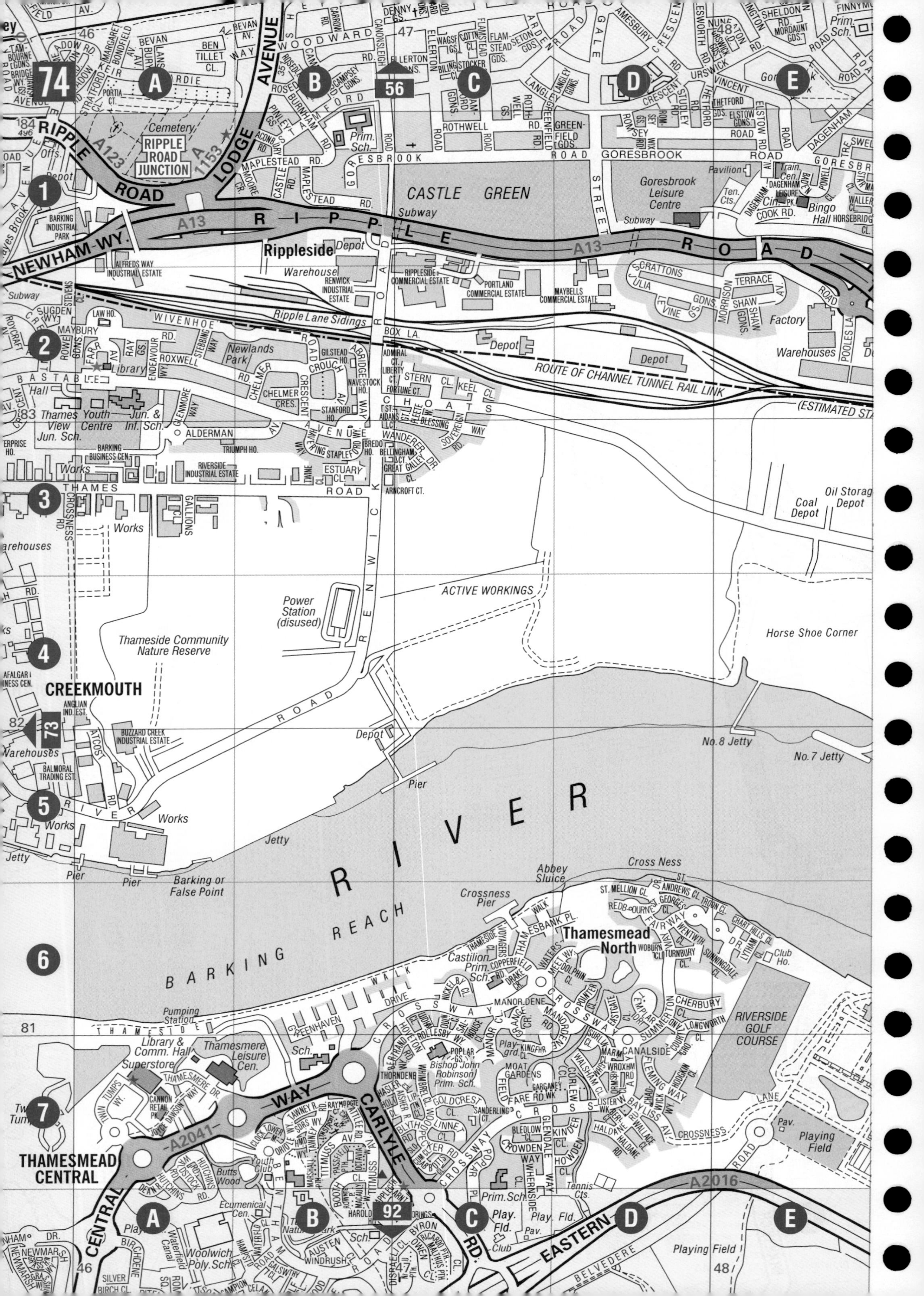

74
56
92
73
A
B
C
D
E
1
2
3
4
5
6
7
46
47
48
81
82
83
184
RIPPLE ROAD JUNCTION
Cemetery
RIPPLE ROAD
LODGE AVENUE
A123
A 1153
A13
Rippleside
Subway
CASTLE GREEN
GORESBROOK ROAD
Goresbrook Leisure Centre
Bingo Hall
Factory
Warehouses
Depot
Ripple Lane Sidings
ROUTE OF CHANNEL TUNNEL RAIL LINK
(ESTIMATED STA
NEWHAM WY.
BARKING INDUSTRIAL PARK
ALFREDS WAY INDUSTRIAL ESTATE
RENWICK INDUSTRIAL ESTATE
RIPPLESIDE COMMERCIAL ESTATE
PORTLAND COMMERCIAL ESTATE
MAYBELLS COMMERCIAL ESTATE
Newlands Park
Library
Thames View Jun. Sch.
Youth Centre
Jun. & Inf. Sch.
BARKING BUSINESS CEN.
RIVERSIDE INDUSTRIAL ESTATE
THAMES ROAD
RENWICK ROAD
Works
Coal Depot
Oil Storage Depot
ACTIVE WORKINGS
Power Station (disused)
Thameside Community Nature Reserve
CREEKMOUTH
BUZZARD CREEK INDUSTRIAL ESTATE
BALMORAL TRADING EST.
RIVER RD.
Horse Shoe Corner
No.8 Jetty
No.7 Jetty
Pier
Jetty
Barking or False Point
RIVER
BARKING REACH
Abbey Sluice
Cross Ness
Crossness Pier
Thamesmead North
Castilion Prim. Sch.
RIVERSIDE GOLF COURSE
Club Ho.
Pumping Station
THAMESIDE WALK
Library & Comm. Hall
Thamesmere Leisure Cen.
Superstore
Bishop John Robinson Prim. Sch.
CANALSIDE
CROSSWAY
CARLYLE WAY
A2041
A2016
EASTERN WAY
THAMESMEAD CENTRAL
Butts Wood
Woolwich Poly. Sch.
Ecumenical Cen.
Prim. Sch.
Play. Fld.
Playing Field
Tennis Cts.
CROSSNESS RD.

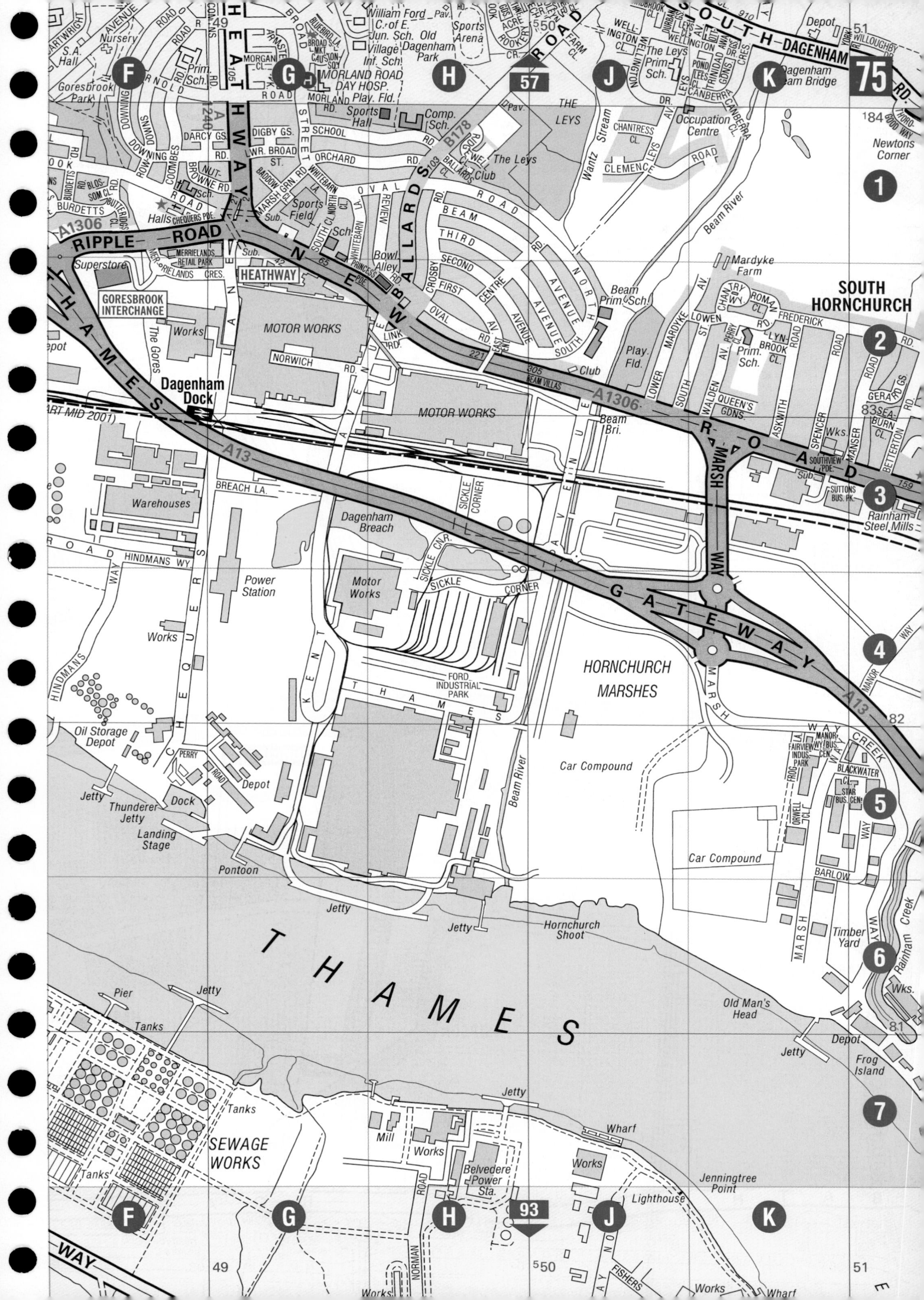

75
57
93
F
G
H
J
K
1
2
3
4
5
6
7
49
550
51
184
83
82
81
SOUTH DAGENHAM
SOUTH HORNCHURCH
Newtons Corner
Dagenham Beam Bridge
Occupation Centre
Mardyke Farm
THE LEYS
The Leys
Club
Wantz Stream
Beam River
Beam Prim. Sch.
The Leys Prim. Sch.
William Ford C. of E. Jun. Sch.
Old Village Inf. Sch.
Dagenham Park
Sports Arena
MORLAND ROAD DAY HOSP.
Play. Fld.
Sports Hall
Comp. Sch.
Goresbrook Park
Nursery
S.A. Hall
Prim. Sch.
Sports Field
Bowl. Alley
RIPPLE ROAD
A1306
HEATHWAY
B178
BALLARDS
NEW ROAD
MARSH WAY
GATEWAY
A13
A1240
Superstore
MERRIELANDS RETAIL PARK
GORESBROOK INTERCHANGE
The Gores
Works
MOTOR WORKS
NORWICH RD.
Dagenham Dock
Beam Bri.
Warehouses
BREACH LA.
Dagenham Breach
SICKLE CORNER
Motor Works
Power Station
HINDMANS WY.
CHEQUERS
KENT AVENUE
FORD INDUSTRIAL PARK
THAMES
HORNCHURCH MARSHES
Car Compound
Beam River
Rainham Steel Mills
SUTTONS BUS. PK.
Oil Storage Depot
Jetty
Thunderer Jetty
Landing Stage
Dock
Depot
Pontoon
Hornchurch Shoot
Timber Yard
Rainham Creek
Wks.
Old Man's Head
Frog Island
Pier
Tanks
SEWAGE WORKS
Mill
Works
Belvedere Power Sta.
Wharf
Jenningtree Point
Lighthouse
WAY

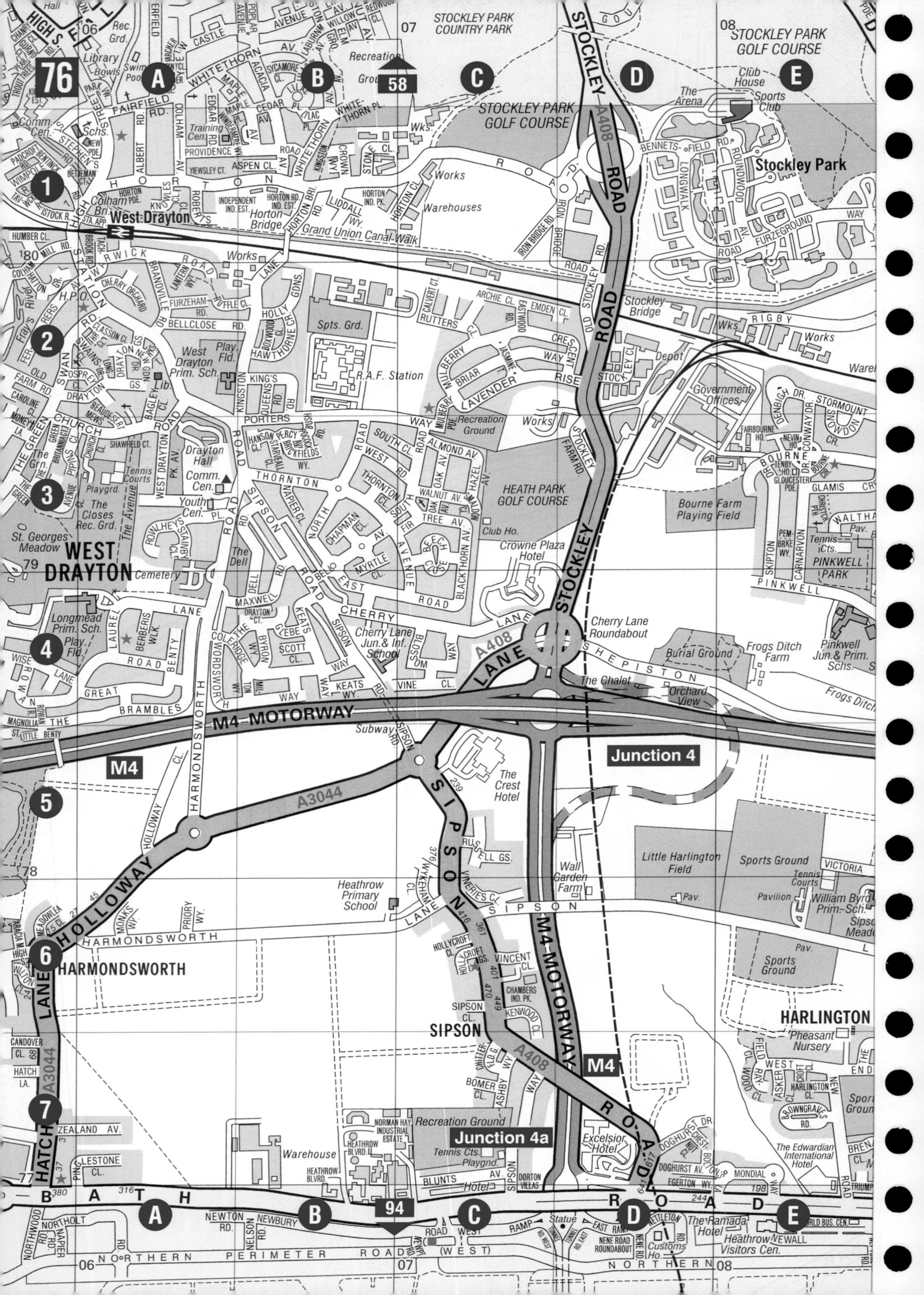

58
94
STOCKLEY PARK COUNTRY PARK
STOCKLEY PARK GOLF COURSE
Stockley Park
Club House
Sports Club
The Arena
WEST DRAYTON
West Drayton
HARMONDSWORTH
SIPSON
HARLINGTON
STOCKLEY ROAD
A408
M4 MOTORWAY
M4
Junction 4
Junction 4a
A3044
HOLLOWAY LANE
HATCH LANE
SIPSON ROAD
SIPSON LANE
HARMONDSWORTH LANE
CHERRY LANE
SHEPISTON LANE
HORTON ROAD
BATH ROAD
NORTHERN PERIMETER ROAD (WEST)
Cherry Lane Roundabout
Grand Union Canal Walk
Horton Bridge
R.A.F. Station
HEATH PARK GOLF COURSE
Crowne Plaza Hotel
The Crest Hotel
Excelsior Hotel
The Ramada Hotel
The Edwardian International Hotel
Heathrow Visitors Cen.
Customs Ho.
Government Offices
Bourne Farm Playing Field
PINKWELL PARK
Little Harlington Field
Sports Ground
Wall Garden Farm
Frogs Ditch Farm
Burial Ground
Heathrow Primary School
Recreation Ground
Warehouses
Works
Cemetery
Longmead Prim. Sch.
West Drayton Prim. Sch.
Drayton Hall
St. Georges Meadow
The Closes Rec. Grd.
Cherry Lane Jun.& Inf. School
Pinkwell Jun.& Prim. Schs.
William Byrd Prim. Sch.
Pheasant Nursery
NORMAN HAY INDUSTRIAL ESTATE
Stockley Bridge

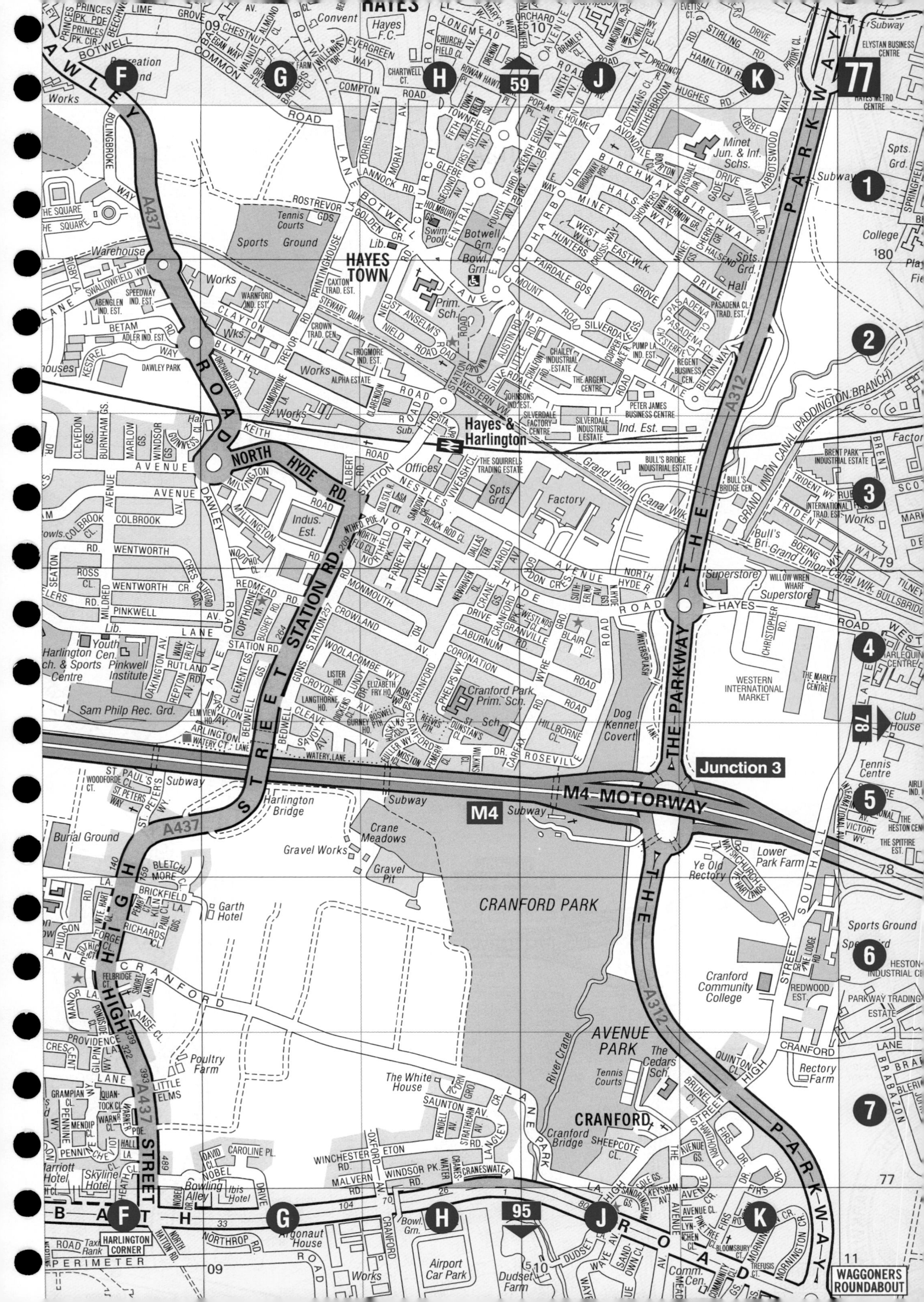

HAYES
77
59
95
78
F
G
H
J
K
1
2
3
4
5
6
7
09
10
11
77
78
79
80
180
Hayes F.C.
Convent
LONGMEAD
PRINCES PK. PDE
PRINCES PK. CIR
BOTWELL COMMON
LIME GROVE
CHESTNUT
EVERGREEN WAY
COMPTON ROAD
CHARTWELL CT.
STIRLING DRIVE
HAMILTON RD.
HUGHES RD.
ELYSTAN BUSINESS CENTRE
HAYES METRO CENTRE
Subway
Recreation Ground
Works
BOLINGBROKE WAY
DAWLEY ROAD
A437
THE SQUARE
ROSTREVOR GDS.
Tennis Courts
Sports Ground
Warehouse
HAYES TOWN
Lib.
Swim. Pool
Botwell Grn.
Bowl. Grn.
Prim. Sch.
Minet Jun. & Inf. Schs.
Spts. Grd.
College
BIRCHWAY
MINET
COLDHARBOUR LANE
PUMP LANE
SILVERDALE
FAIRDALE GDS
PASADENA CL. TRAD. EST.
PUMP LA. IND. EST.
REGENT BUSINESS CEN.
THE ARGENT CENTRE
PETER JAMES BUSINESS CENTRE
CHAILEY INDUSTRIAL ESTATE
SILVERDALE INDUSTRIAL ESTATE
Ind. Est.
A312
THE PARKWAY
GRAND UNION CANAL (PADDINGTON BRANCH)
SWALLOWFIELD WY.
SPEEDWAY IND. EST.
ABENGLEN IND. EST.
WARNFORD IND. EST.
CLAYTON
BETAM
ADLER IND. EST.
DAWLEY PARK
KESTREL WAY
BLYTH
GRAMOPHONE LA.
Works
ALPHA ESTATE
FROGMORE IND. EST.
CROWN TRAD. CEN.
CAXTON TRAD. EST.
STEWART QUAY
PRINTINGHOUSE LANE
Hayes & Harlington
KEITH
NORTH HYDE RD.
Offices
THE SQUIRRELS TRADING ESTATE
BULL'S BRIDGE INDUSTRIAL ESTATE
BRENT PARK INDUSTRIAL ESTATE
Grand Union
Canal Wlk.
Factory
Spts. Grd.
Indus. Est.
NESTLES AVENUE
BULL'S BRIDGE CEN.
INTERNATIONAL TRAD. EST.
Works
TRIDENT WAY
Bull's Bri.
BOEING WAY
Grand Union Canal Wlk.
BULLSBRIDGE
Superstore
WILLOW WREN WHARF
HAYES ROAD
NORTH HYDE ROAD
STATION RD.
STATION ROAD
CLEVEDON GS.
BURNHAM GS.
MARLOW GS.
WINDSOR GS.
AVENUE
COLBROOK
WENTWORTH
ROSS CL.
SEATON
MILDRED
PINKWELL
LANE
Lib.
Youth Cen.
Harlington Sch. & Sports Centre
Pinkwell Institute
Sam Philp Rec. Grd.
REDMEAD RD.
MONMOUTH
CROWLAND
WOOLACOMBE WY.
CROYDE
LAURNUM
CORONATION
GRANVILLE
BLAIR CL.
Cranford Park Prim. Sch.
St. Sch.
HILLBORNE CL.
ROSEVILLE
WATERY LANE
Dog Kennel Covert
WESTERN INTERNATIONAL MARKET
THE MARKET CENTRE
HARLEQUIN CENTRE
Club House
Tennis Centre
Junction 3
M4 MOTORWAY
M4
Subway
ST. PAUL'S
ST. PETERS WAY
Harlington Bridge
HIGH STREET
Burial Ground
Crane Meadows
Gravel Works
Gravel Pit
CRANFORD PARK
Ye Old Rectory
Lower Park Farm
SOUTHALL LANE
THE VICTORY
THE HESTON CEN.
THE SPITFIRE EST.
Sports Ground
HESTON INDUSTRIAL CE.
REDWOOD EST.
PARKWAY TRADING ESTATE
Cranford Community College
BLETCHMORE CL.
BRICKFIELD LA.
Garth Hotel
CRANFORD LANE
MANOR LA.
PROVIDENCE
Poultry Farm
The White House
AVENUE PARK
River Crane
Tennis Courts
The Cedars Sch.
CRANFORD
Cranford Bridge
SHEEPCOTE CL.
QUINTON CL.
HIGH STREET
Rectory Farm
BRABAZON
CRANFORD LANE
LITTLE ELMS
GRAMPIAN CL.
PENNINE WY.
MENDIP CL.
CAROLINE PL.
DAVID CL.
Marriott Hotel
Skyline Hotel
Bowling Alley
Ibis Hotel
WINCHESTER RD.
MALVERN RD
WINDSOR PK. RD.
CRANESWATER
SAUNTON AV.
BATH ROAD
HARLINGTON CORNER
Taxi Rank
NORTHROP RD.
PERIMETER ROAD
Argonaut House
Bowl. Grn.
Airport Car Park
Works
Dudset Farm
Comm. Cen.
WAGGONERS ROUNDABOUT

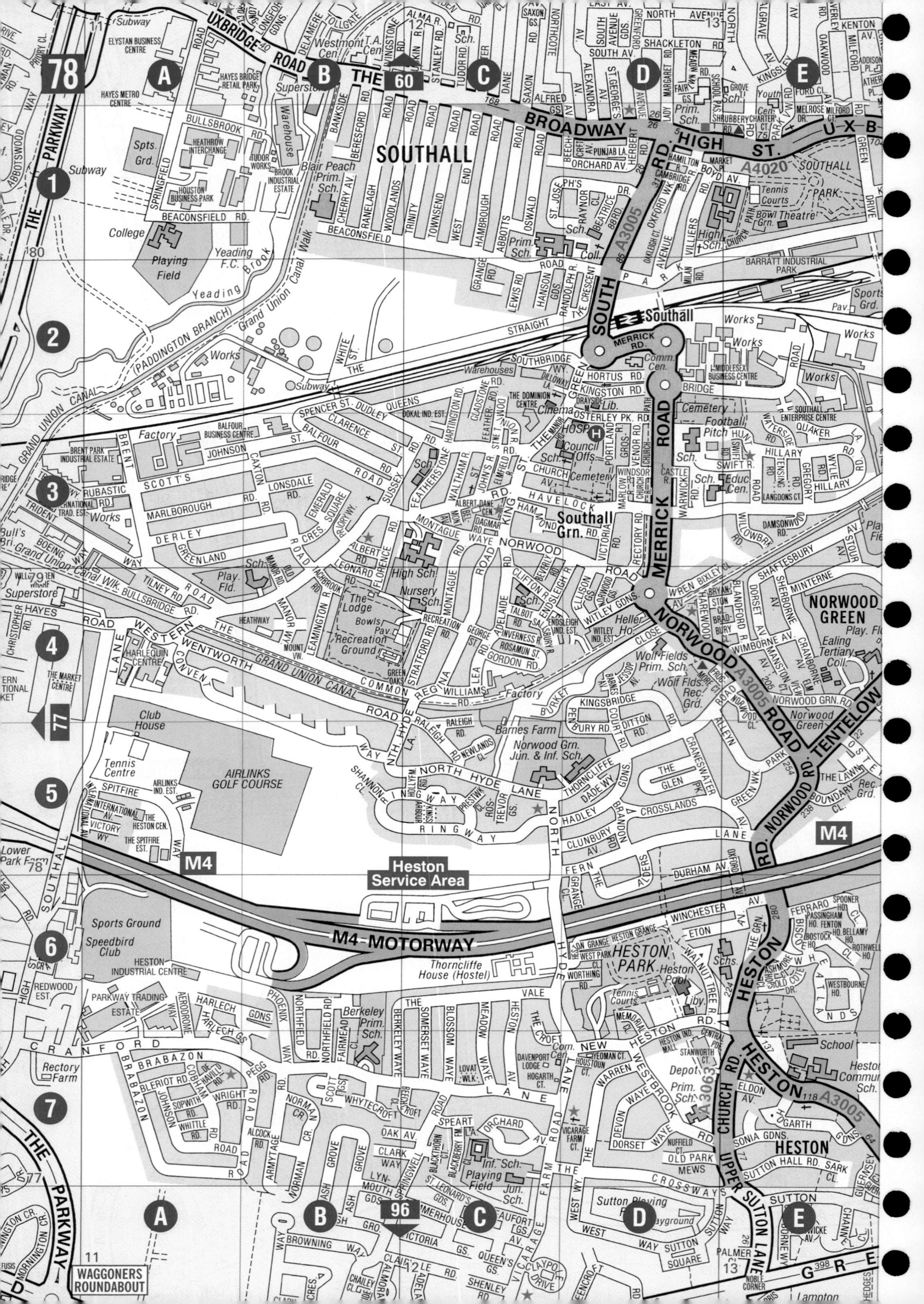

78
60
77
96
SOUTHALL
NORWOOD GREEN
HESTON
Southall Grn.
UXBRIDGE ROAD
THE BROADWAY
HIGH ST.
SOUTH RD.
MERRICK ROAD
NORWOOD ROAD
TENTELOW LA.
HESTON RD.
NORTH HYDE LANE
NORTH HYDE LA.
HAYES ROAD
WESTERN ROAD
THE PARKWAY
CRANFORD LANE
M4-MOTORWAY
M4
Heston Service Area
GRAND UNION CANAL
Grand Union Canal Walk
(PADDINGTON BRANCH)
Yeading Brook
Yeading F.C.
AIRLINKS GOLF COURSE
Club House
Tennis Centre
Sports Ground
Speedbird Club
HESTON INDUSTRIAL CENTRE
PARKWAY TRADING ESTATE
Rectory Farm
HESTON PARK
Heston Pool
Liby.
Sutton Playing Fld.
Playground
Thorncliffe House (Hostel)
Barnes Farm
Norwood Grn. Jun. & Inf. Sch.
Recreation Ground
The Lodge
High Sch.
Nursery Sch.
Cemetery
Football Pitch
Southall
Comm. Cen.
Lib.
Cinema
Council Offs.
HOSP.
Wolf Fields Prim. Sch.
Wolf Flds. Rec. Grd.
Norwood Green
Ealing Tertiary Coll.
Heston Community Sch.
Berkeley Prim. Sch.
Blair Peach Prim. Sch.
College
Playing Field
ELYSTAN BUSINESS CENTRE
HAYES BRIDGE RETAIL PARK
HAYES METRO CENTRE
HEATHROW INTERCHANGE
HOUSTON BUSINESS PARK
BROOK INDUSTRIAL ESTATE
BRENT PARK INDUSTRIAL ESTATE
BALFOUR BUSINESS CENTRE
MIDDLESEX BUSINESS CENTRE
SOUTHALL ENTERPRISE CENTRE
BARRATT INDUSTRIAL PARK
HARLEQUIN CENTRE
THE MARKET CENTRE
SOUTHALL PARK
Bowl Theatre
A4020
A3005
A3063
WAGGONERS ROUNDABOUT
A B C D E
1 2 3 4 5 6 7

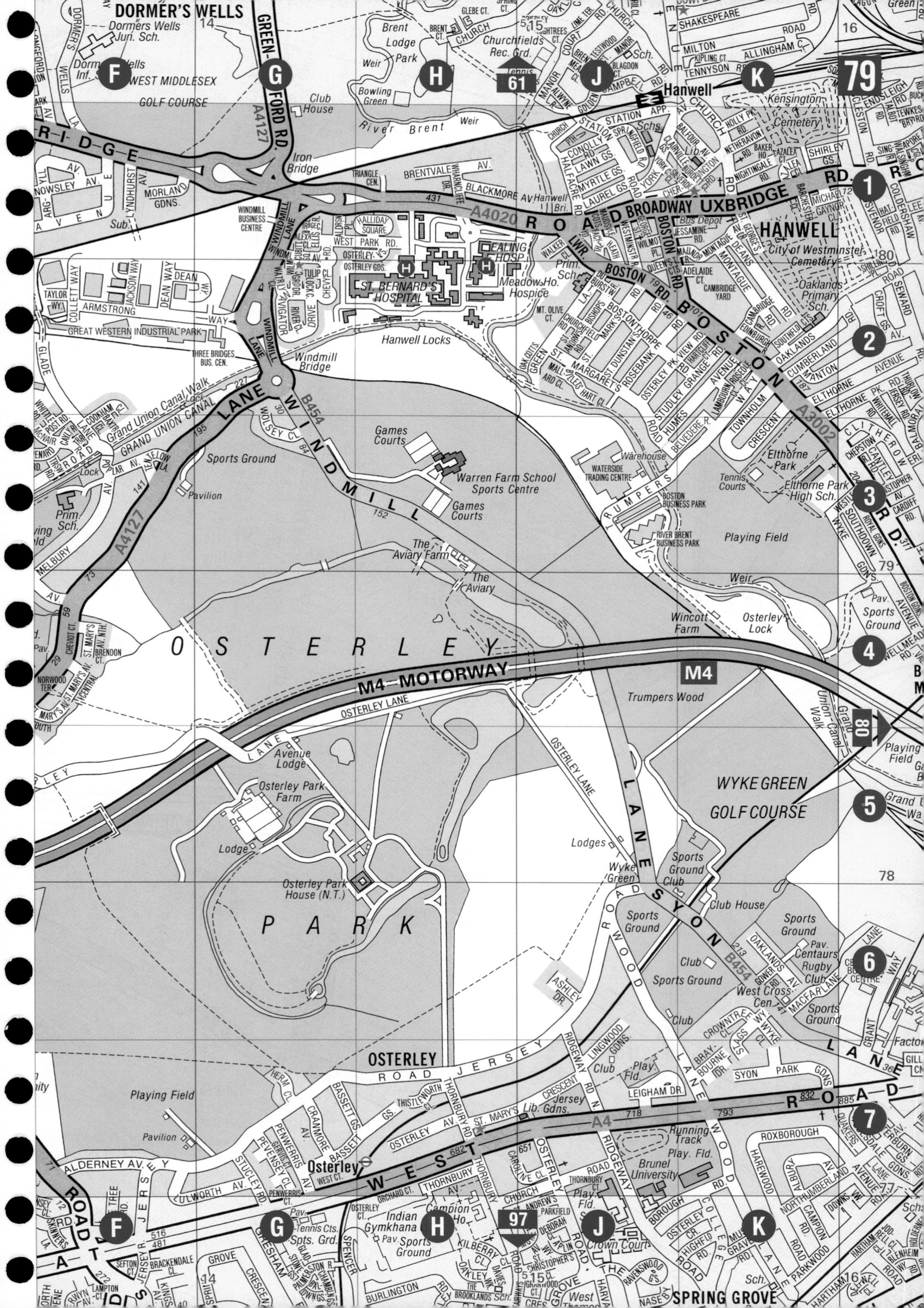

DORMER'S WELLS
Dormers Wells Jun. Sch.
WEST MIDDLESEX GOLF COURSE
GREENFORD RD.
A4127
Brent Lodge Park
Churchfields Rec. Grd.
Hanwell
HANWELL
Kensington Cemetery
City of Westminster Cemetery
UXBRIDGE ROAD
BROADWAY
A4020
ST. BERNARD'S HOSPITAL
EALING HOSP.
Meadows Ho. Hospice
Hanwell Locks
Windmill Bridge
GREAT WESTERN INDUSTRIAL PARK
Grand Union Canal Walk
GRAND UNION CANAL
BOSTON RD.
A3002
Oaklands Primary Sch.
Elthorne Park
Elthorne Park High Sch.
WINDMILL LANE
B454
Games Courts
Warren Farm School Sports Centre
Sports Ground
The Aviary Farm
The Aviary
WATERSIDE TRADING CENTRE
BOSTON BUSINESS PARK
RIVER BRENT BUSINESS PARK
Playing Field
Wincott Farm
Osterley Lock
OSTERLEY
M4 MOTORWAY
M4
Trumpers Wood
OSTERLEY LANE
Avenue Lodge
Osterley Park Farm
Osterley Park House (N.T.)
PARK
WYKE GREEN GOLF COURSE
SYON LANE
Wyke Green
Centaurs Rugby Club
West Cross Cen.
OSTERLEY
JERSEY ROAD
Playing Field
Osterley
GREAT WEST ROAD
A4
Brunel University
Running Track
Indian Gymkhana Sports Ground
Crown Court
SPRING GROVE
F G H J K
1 2 3 4 5 6 7
14 15 16
61 79 80 97
78

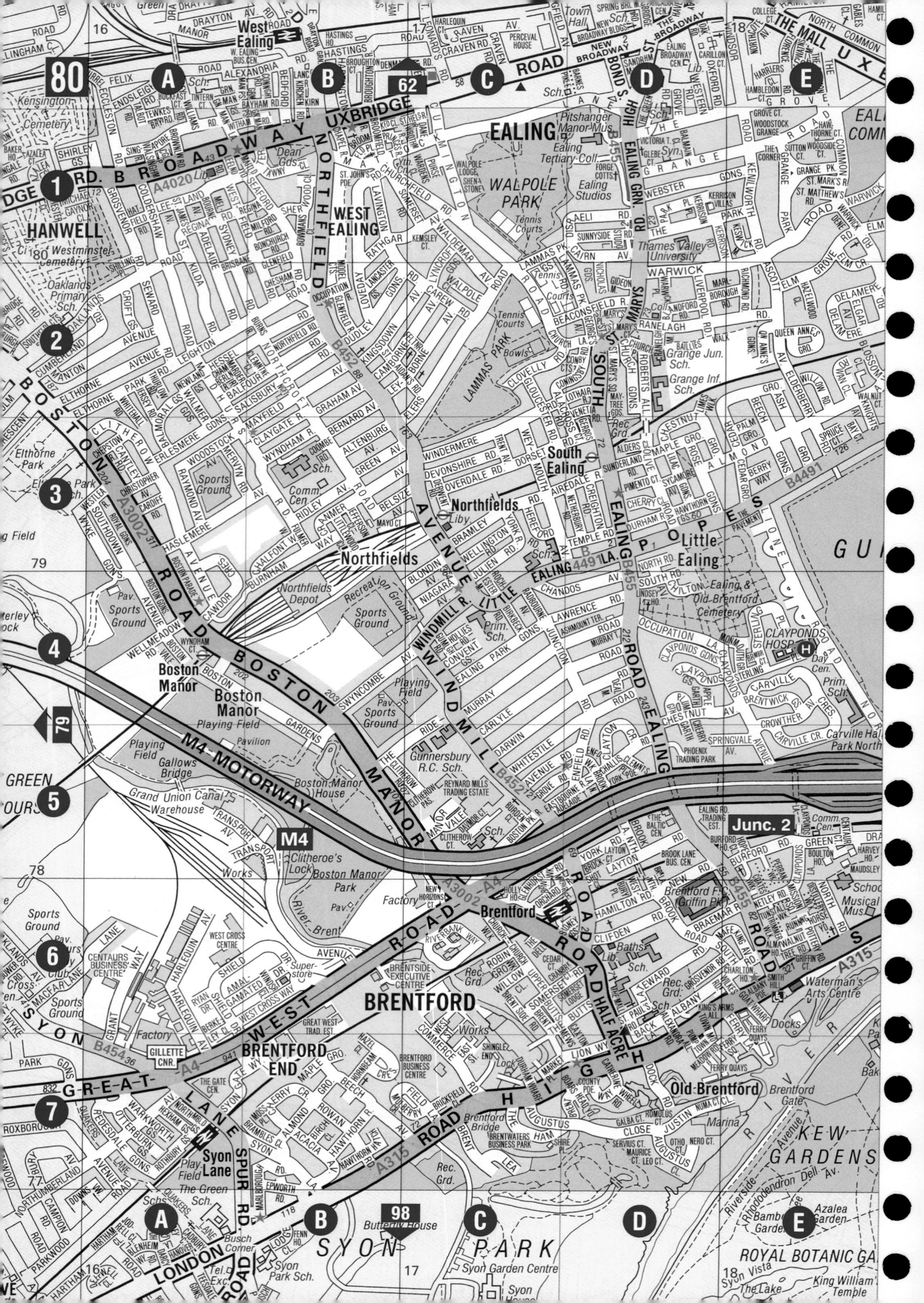

80
A
B
C
D
E
1
2
3
4
5
6
7
62
79
98
16
17
18
79
78
77
West Ealing
EALING
WEST EALING
HANWELL
South Ealing
Northfields
Little Ealing
Boston Manor
BRENTFORD
BRENTFORD END
Old Brentford
Syon Lane
SYON PARK
KEW GARDENS
ROYAL BOTANIC GARDENS
UXBRIDGE ROAD
BROADWAY
NEW BROADWAY
THE MALL
NORTHFIELD AVENUE
BOSTON ROAD
BOSTON MANOR ROAD
M4 MOTORWAY
GREAT WEST ROAD
HIGH ROAD
LONDON ROAD
SOUTH EALING ROAD
POPES LA.
ST. MARYS RD.
WINDMILL ROAD
LITTLE EALING LA.
HALF ACRE
SYON LANE
A4020
A3002
B452
B455
B4491
B454
A4
A315
M4
Junc. 2
WALPOLE PARK
Pitshanger Manor Mus.
Ealing Tertiary Coll.
Ealing Studios
Thames Valley University
Kensington Cemetery
Westminster Cemetery
Oaklands Primary Sch.
Elthorne Park
Lammas Park
Northfields Depot
Recreation Ground
Sports Ground
Playing Field
Gunnersbury R.C. Sch.
Grange Jun. Sch.
Grange Inf. Sch.
Ealing & Old Brentford Cemetery
CLAYPONDS HOSP.
Boston Manor House
Boston Manor Park
Grand Union Canal
Gallows Bridge
Clitheroe's Lock
River Brent
Brentford F.C. Griffin Pk.
Waterman's Arts Centre
Brentford Bridge
Syon Garden Centre
Butterfly House
Syon Park Sch.
Bamboo Garden
Azalea Garden
Rhododendron Dell
Syon Vista
The Lake
King William's Temple
Brentford Gate
Marina
Docks
GILLETTE CNR.
Busch Corner

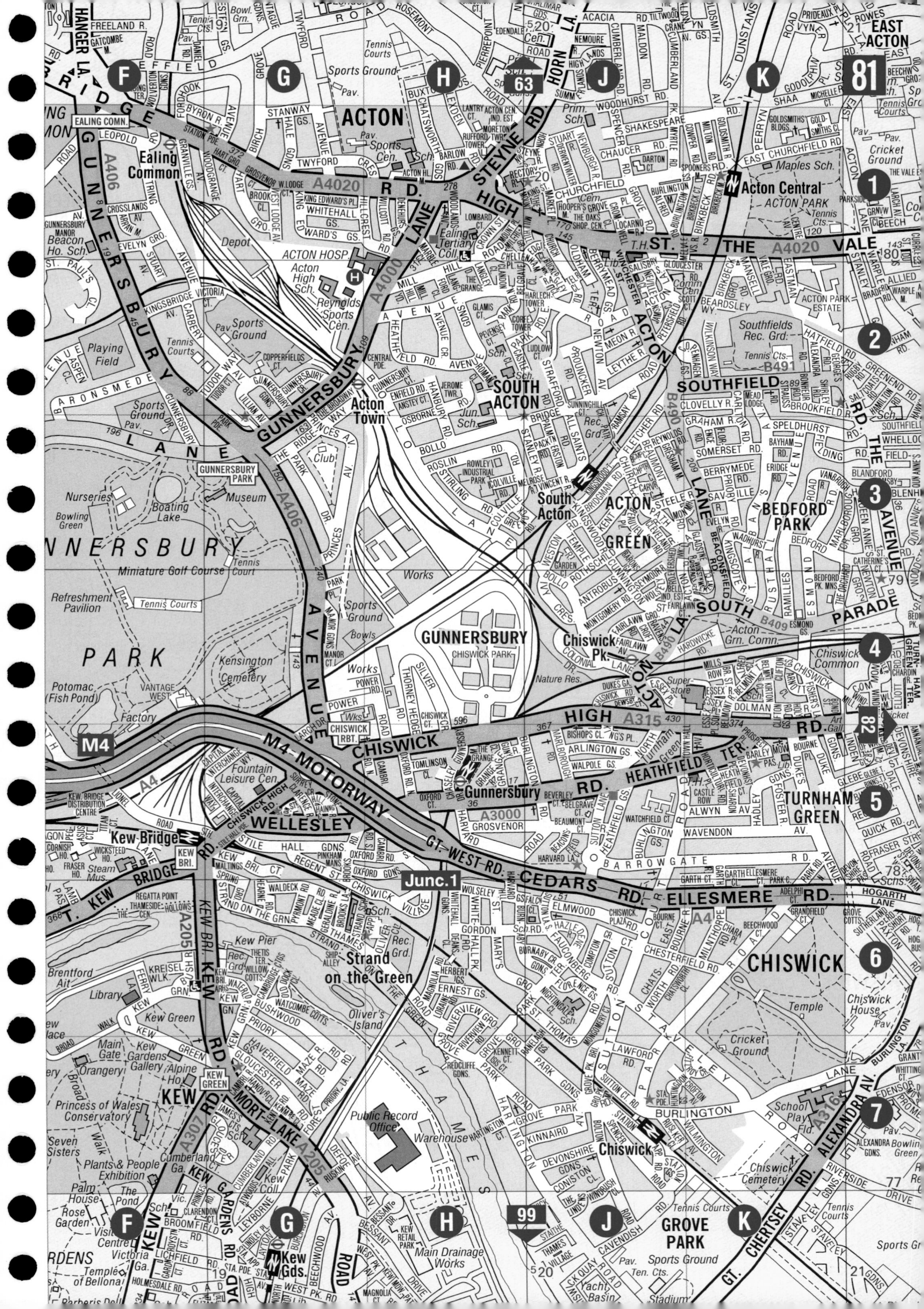
81
ACTON
EAST ACTON
Ealing Common
Acton Central
ACTON PARK
SOUTH ACTON
Acton Town
South Acton
ACTON GREEN
BEDFORD PARK
SOUTHFIELD RD.
GUNNERSBURY
GUNNERSBURY PARK
Chiswick Pk.
Gunnersbury
TURNHAM GREEN
CHISWICK
Kew Bridge
Strand on the Green
KEW
Chiswick
GROVE PARK
Kew Gds.
M4 MOTORWAY
CHISWICK HIGH RD.
GT. WEST RD.
CEDARS RD.
ELLESMERE RD.
Junc.1
THE VALE
HIGH ST.
Public Record Office
Oliver's Island
Kew Pier
Brentford Ait
Chiswick House
Chiswick Cemetery
63
82
99
F
G
H
J
K
1
2
3
4
5
6
7

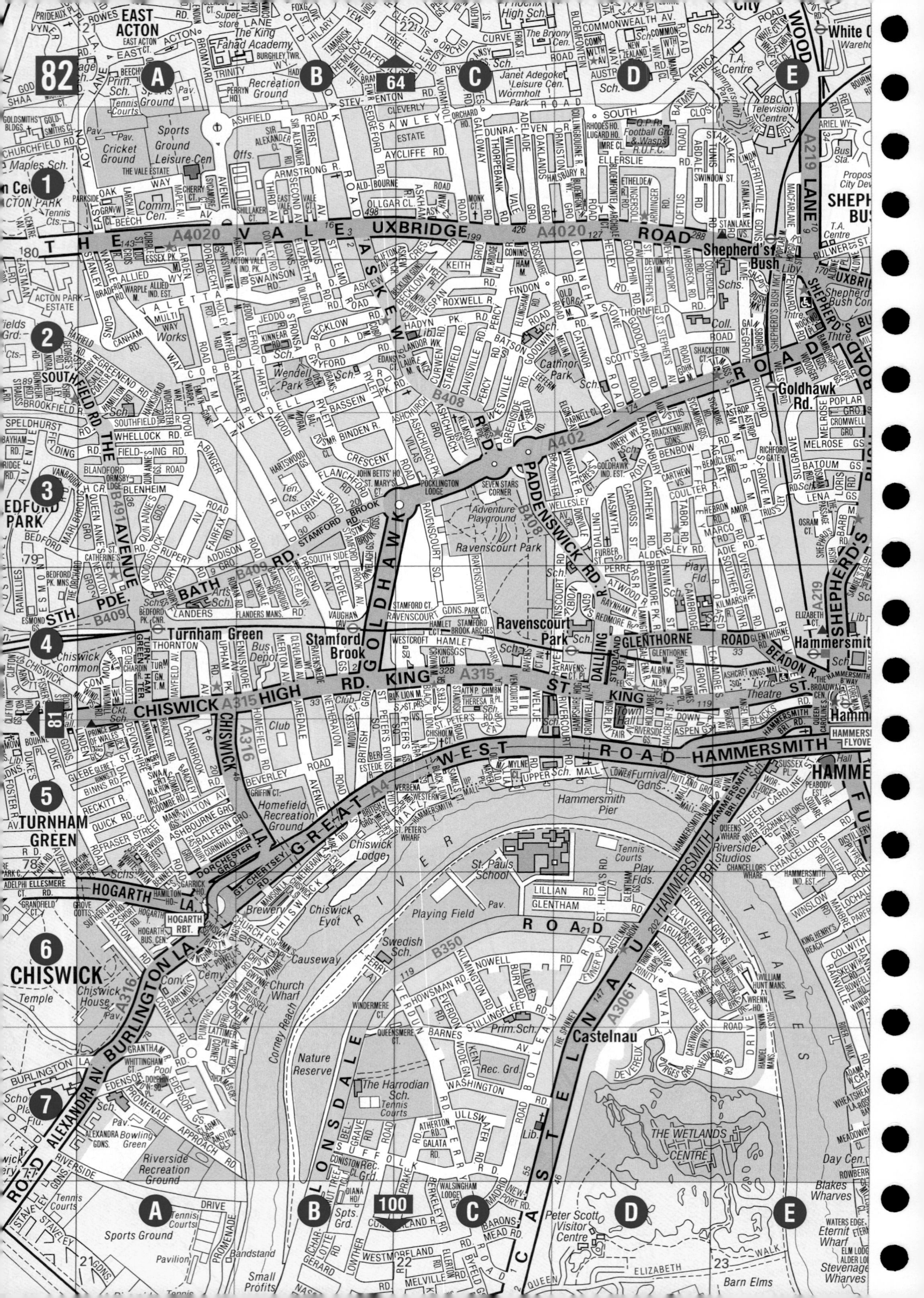
EAST ACTON
64
A
B
C
D
E
1
2
3
4
5
6
7
THE VALE
UXBRIDGE ROAD
A4020
Shepherd's Bush
Goldhawk Rd.
GOLDHAWK ROAD
A402
B408
Ravenscourt Park
Turnham Green
Stamford Brook
Ravenscourt Park
CHISWICK HIGH RD.
KING ST.
A315
A316
GREAT WEST ROAD
HAMMERSMITH
A4
BEDFORD PARK
TURNHAM GREEN
CHISWICK
HOGARTH LA.
HOGARTH RBT.
BURLINGTON LA.
ALEXANDRA AV.
Chiswick House
Chiswick Eyot
RIVER THAMES
Hammersmith Pier
St. Pauls School
Playing Field
B350
LONSDALE
CASTELNAU
A306
Castelnau
THE WETLANDS CENTRE
Peter Scott Visitor Centre
Nature Reserve
The Harrodian Sch.
Riverside Recreation Ground
Sports Ground
Homefield Recreation Ground
Riverside Studios
Lyric Theatre
Town Hall
Adventure Playground
Cathnor Park
Wendell Park
Wormholt Park
Q.P.R. Football Grd. & Wasps R.U.F.C.
BBC Television Centre
White City
WOOD LANE
A219
SHEPHERD'S BUSH
Blakes Wharves
Stevenage Wharves
81
100
21
22
23
78
79
80

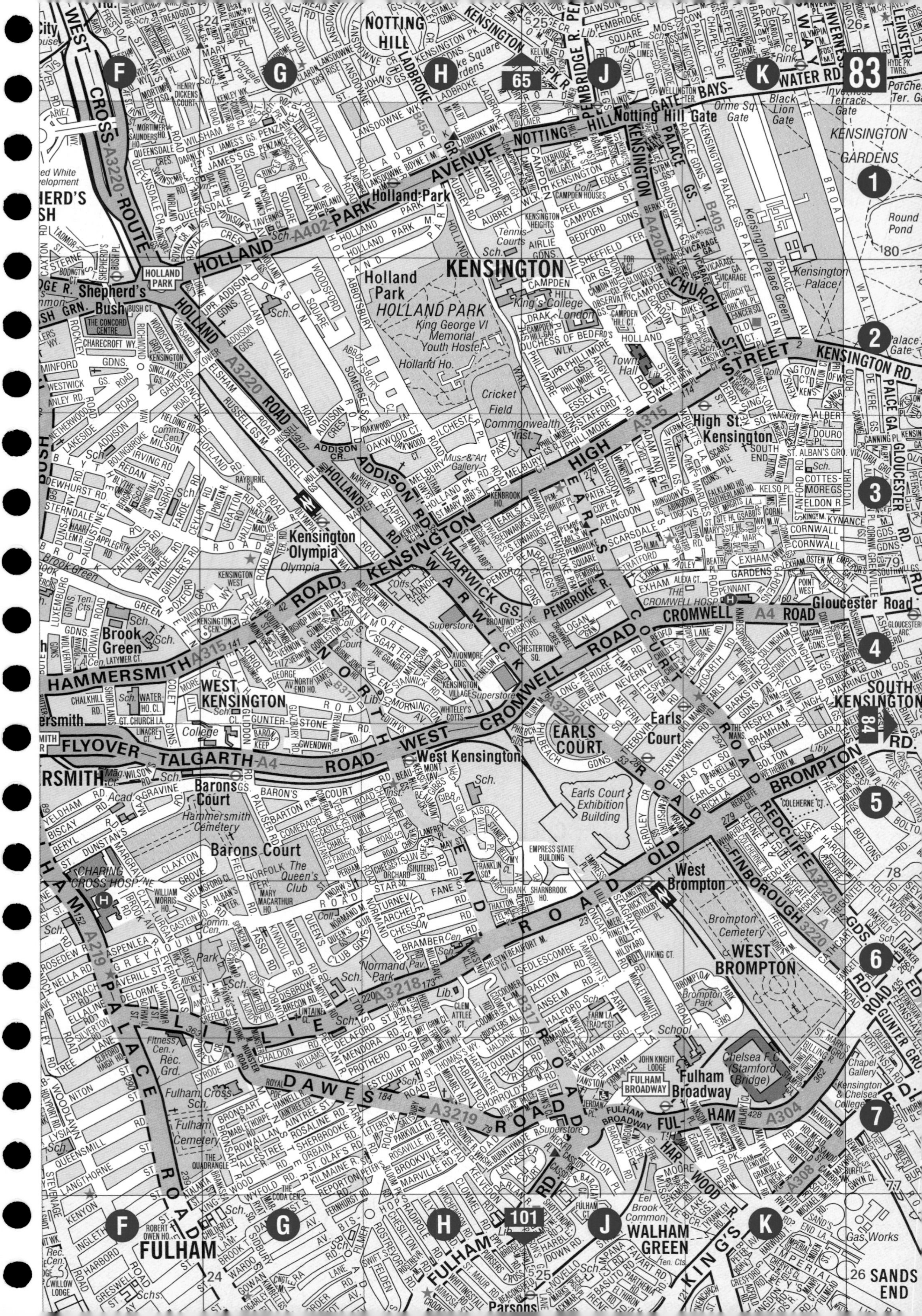

83
65
84
101
F
G
H
J
K
1
2
3
4
5
6
7
24
25
26
NOTTING HILL
Notting Hill Gate
NOTTING HILL GATE
BAYSWATER RD.
KENSINGTON GARDENS
Round Pond
Kensington Palace
KENSINGTON RD.
KENSINGTON
Holland Park
HOLLAND PARK
King George VI Memorial Youth Hostel
Holland Ho.
Cricket Field
Commonwealth Inst.
King's College London
Town Hall
HOLLAND PARK AVENUE
HOLLAND ROAD
HOLLAND
Shepherd's Bush
SHEPHERD'S BUSH
WEST CROSS ROUTE
A3220
A402
A4204
B405
A315
KENSINGTON HIGH STREET
KENSINGTON CHURCH STREET
High St. Kensington
Kensington Olympia
Olympia
Brook Green
HAMMERSMITH ROAD
WEST KENSINGTON
West Kensington
NORTH END ROAD
WARWICK ROAD
CROMWELL ROAD
WEST CROMWELL ROAD
A4
Gloucester Road
SOUTH KENSINGTON
Superstore
EARLS COURT
Earls Court
EARLS COURT ROAD
Earls Court Exhibition Building
EMPRESS STATE BUILDING
FLYOVER
TALGARTH ROAD
Barons Court
Hammersmith Cemetery
The Queen's Club
CHARING CROSS HOSP.
BROMPTON ROAD
REDCLIFFE GDNS.
FINBOROUGH ROAD
OLD BROMPTON ROAD
West Brompton
WEST BROMPTON
Brompton Cemetery
LILLIE ROAD
A3218
Normand Park
DAWES ROAD
A3219
FULHAM PALACE ROAD
A219
Fulham Cross Sch.
Fulham Cemetery
FULHAM BROADWAY
Fulham Broadway
Chelsea F.C. (Stamford Bridge)
FULHAM ROAD
A304
A308
Kensington & Chelsea College
Eel Brook Common
WALHAM GREEN
KING'S ROAD
FULHAM
Gas Works
SANDS END
Parsons

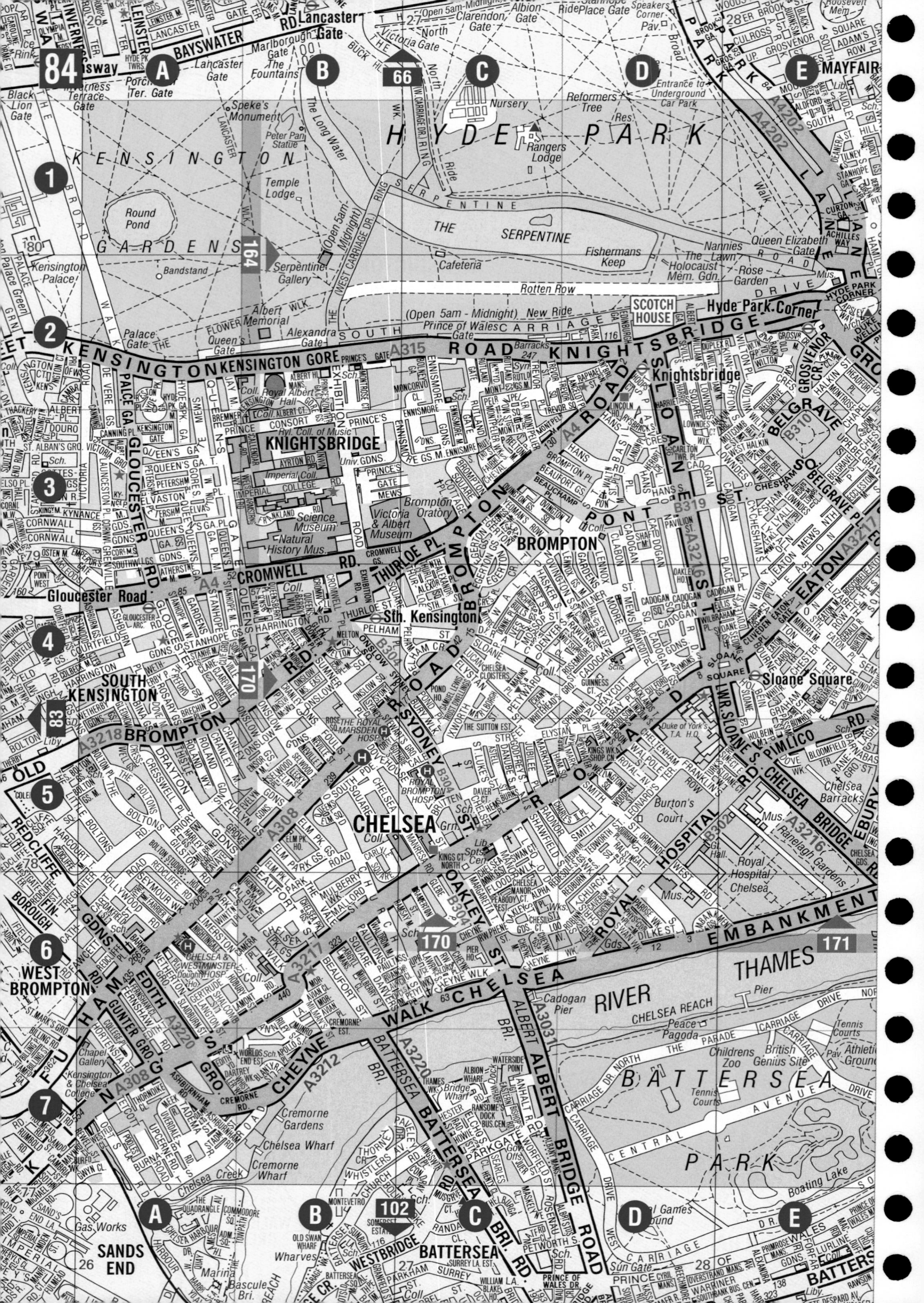
A
B
C
D
E
66
MAYFAIR
HYDE PARK
KENSINGTON GARDENS
Round Pond
Kensington Palace
Bandstand
Speke's Monument
Peter Pan Statue
The Long Water
Temple Lodge
The Fountains
Marlborough Gate
Lancaster Gate
Victoria Gate
Clarendon Gate
Albion Gate
Speakers Corner
Reformers Tree
Rangers Lodge
Nursery
THE SERPENTINE
Serpentine Gallery
Cafeteria
Fishermans Keep
Nannies Lawn
The Holocaust Mem. Gdn.
Rose Garden
Queen Elizabeth Gate
Rotten Row
SCOTCH HOUSE
Hyde Park Corner
Albert Memorial
Alexandra Gate
Queen's Gate
Palace Gate
164
1
2
3
4
5
6
7
KENSINGTON ROAD
KENSINGTON GORE
KNIGHTSBRIDGE
Knightsbridge
Coll. Royal Albert Hall
Ryl. Coll. of Music
KNIGHTSBRIDGE
Imperial Coll.
IMPERIAL COLLEGE
Science Museum
Natural History Mus.
Victoria & Albert Museum
Brompton Oratory
BROMPTON
BROMPTON ROAD
BELGRAVE SQ.
CROMWELL RD.
Gloucester Road
Sth. Kensington
SOUTH KENSINGTON
83
170
A3218 BROMPTON
THE ROYAL MARSDEN HOSP.
ROYAL BROMPTON HOSP.
CHELSEA
Sloane Square
PIMLICO RD.
Burton's Court
Royal Hospital Chelsea
Ranelagh Gardens
Chelsea Barracks
CHELSEA BRIDGE
EMBANKMENT
171
WEST BROMPTON
CHELSEA & WESTMINSTER HOSP.
FULHAM RD.
CHEYNE WALK
Cadogan Pier
RIVER THAMES
CHELSEA REACH
Peace Pagoda
Childrens Zoo
BATTERSEA PARK
Tennis Courts
Boating Lake
ALBERT BRIDGE ROAD
BATTERSEA BRI. RD.
Cremorne Gardens
Chelsea Wharf
Cremorne Wharf
Chelsea Creek
Gas Works
SANDS END
BATTERSEA
102
Kensington & Chelsea College
Chapel Gallery

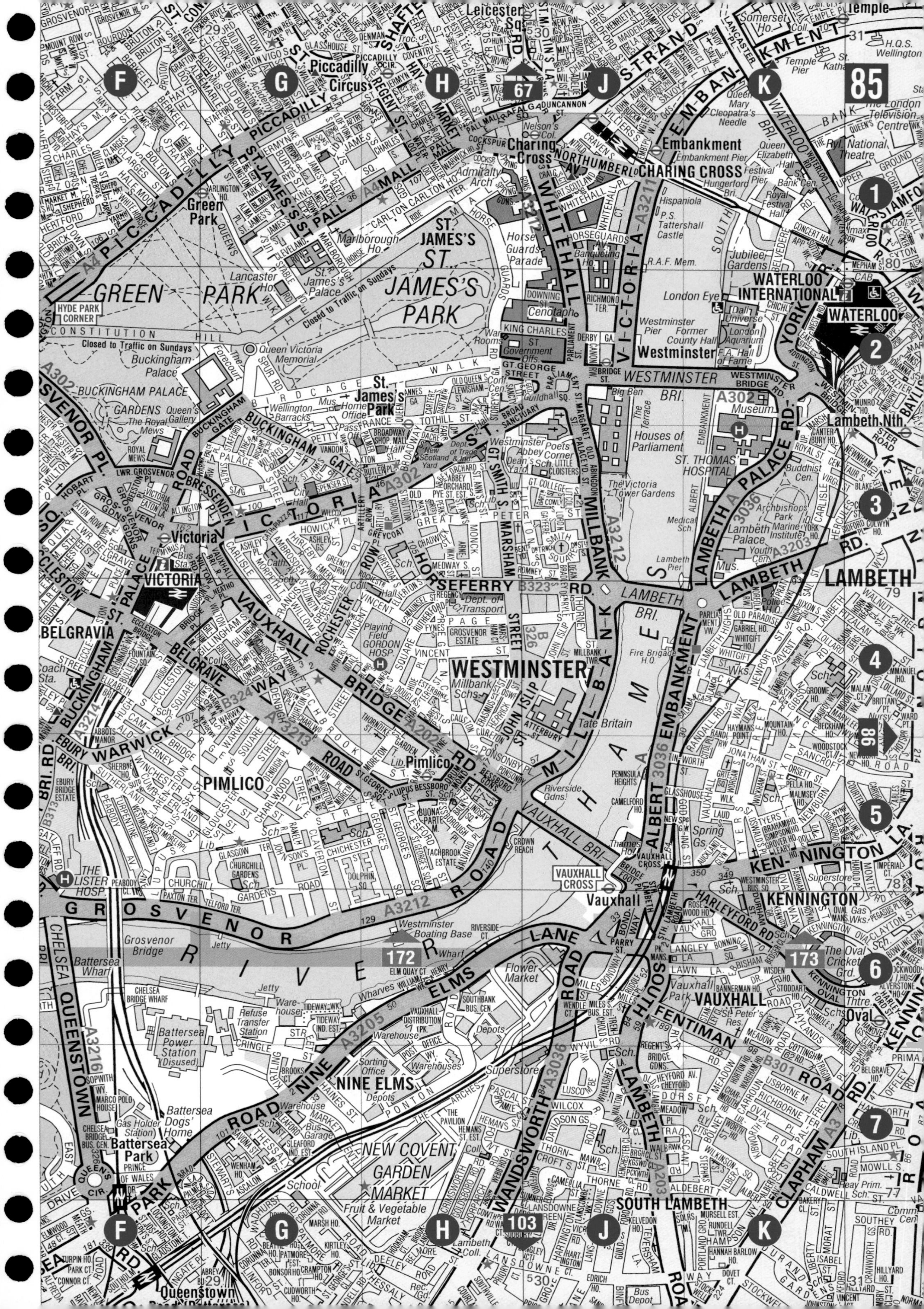

F
G
H
J
K
67
Piccadilly Circus
Leicester Sq
Charing Cross
Embankment
CHARING CROSS
Temple
Somerset Ho.
Waterloo Bri.
The London Television Centre
Ryl. National Theatre
Queen Elizabeth Hall
Royal Festival Hall
Hungerford Bri.
Jubilee Gardens
London Eye
WATERLOO INTERNATIONAL
WATERLOO
Westminster
County Hall
GREEN PARK
Green Park
ST. JAMES'S PARK
St. James's Palace
Marlborough Ho.
Lancaster Ho.
Buckingham Palace
BUCKINGHAM PALACE GARDENS
Queen Victoria Memorial
Wellington Barracks
St. James's Park
Horse Guards Parade
Cenotaph
Downing St.
HYDE PARK CORNER
CONSTITUTION HILL
Closed to Traffic on Sundays
PICCADILLY
THE MALL
WHITEHALL
VICTORIA
Victoria
VICTORIA STREET
Big Ben
Houses of Parliament
Westminster Abbey
WESTMINSTER BRIDGE
St. Thomas' Hospital
Lambeth Palace
LAMBETH BRI.
LAMBETH
Lambeth Nth.
HORSEFERRY RD.
MILLBANK
Tate Britain
WESTMINSTER
BELGRAVIA
PIMLICO
Pimlico
VAUXHALL BRIDGE RD.
VAUXHALL BRI.
Vauxhall
VAUXHALL CROSS
ALBERT EMBANKMENT
KENNINGTON
The Oval Cricket Grd.
Oval
VAUXHALL
Vauxhall Park
GROSVENOR ROAD
RIVER THAMES
Grosvenor Bridge
172
173
NINE ELMS LANE
NINE ELMS
Battersea Power Station (Disused)
Battersea Dogs' Home
Battersea Park
NEW COVENT GARDEN MARKET
Fruit & Vegetable Market
WANDSWORTH ROAD
SOUTH LAMBETH
SOUTH LAMBETH ROAD
CLAPHAM ROAD
QUEENSTOWN ROAD
Queenstown
CHELSEA BRIDGE
103
86
1
2
3
4
5
6
7

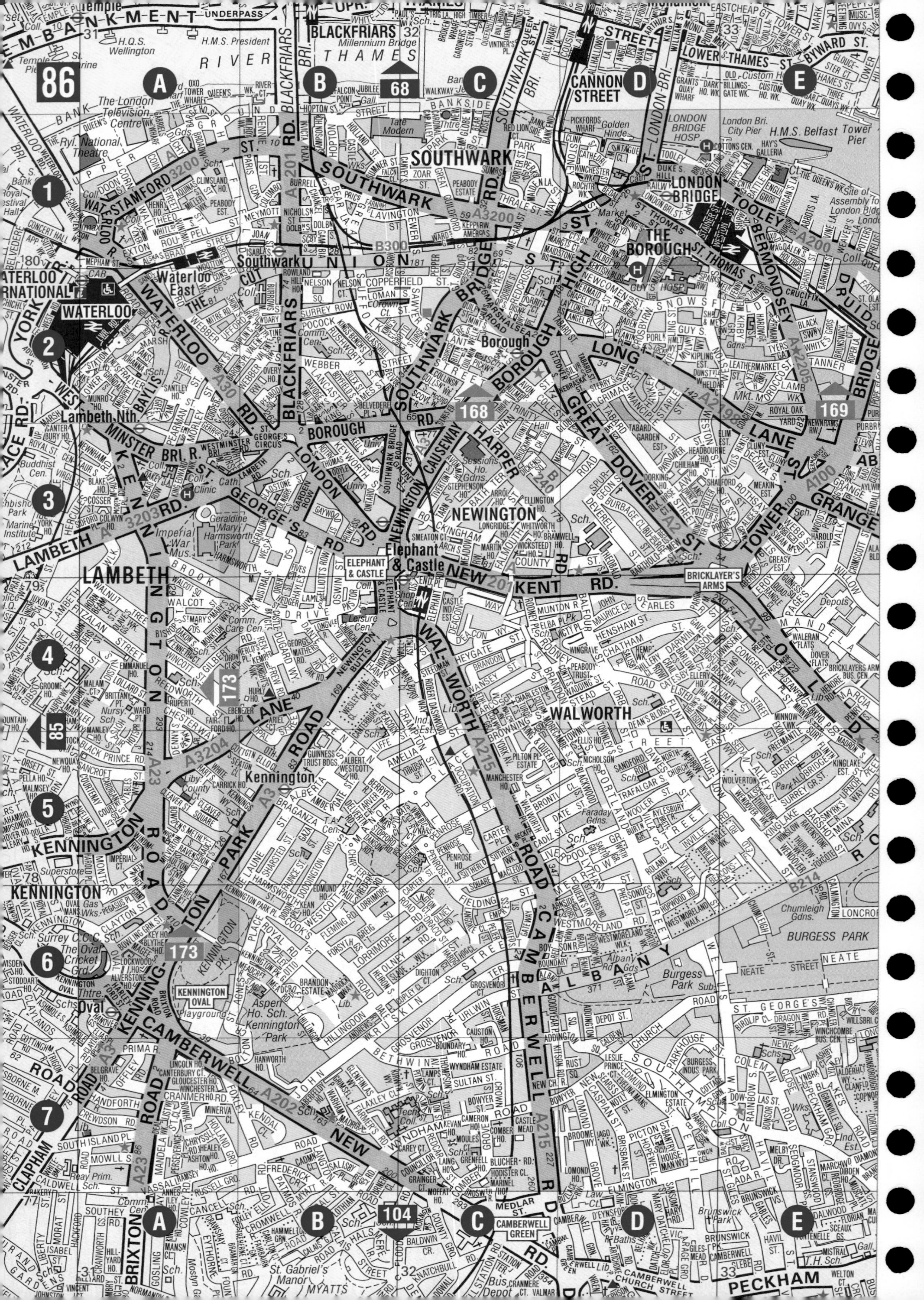

86
A
B
C
D
E
68
RIVER THAMES
BLACKFRIARS
Millennium Bridge
CANNON STREET
LOWER THAMES ST.
BYWARD ST.
H.Q.S. Wellington
H.M.S. President
The London Television Centre
Ryl. National Theatre
Tate Modern
BANKSIDE
Golden Hinde
London Bri. City Pier
H.M.S. Belfast
Tower Pier
SOUTHWARK
STAMFORD ST.
SOUTHWARK ST.
LONDON BRIDGE
TOOLEY ST.
THE BOROUGH
GUY'S HOSP.
BERMONDSEY ST.
UNION ST.
Southwark
Waterloo East
WATERLOO INTERNATIONAL
WATERLOO
THE CUT
WATERLOO RD.
BLACKFRIARS RD.
SOUTHWARK BRIDGE RD.
BOROUGH HIGH ST.
LONG LANE
Borough
168
169
Lambeth Nth.
WESTMINSTER BRI. RD.
ST. GEORGE'S CIRCUS
BOROUGH RD.
LONDON RD.
GREAT DOVER ST.
HARPER RD.
NEWINGTON CAUSEWAY
NEWINGTON
ST. GEORGE'S RD.
Imperial War Mus.
Geraldine Mary Harmsworth Park
LAMBETH RD.
LAMBETH
KENNINGTON RD.
ELEPHANT & CASTLE
Elephant & Castle
NEW KENT RD.
BRICKLAYER'S ARMS
TOWER BRIDGE RD.
GRANGE RD.
OLD KENT RD.
WALWORTH RD.
WALWORTH
KENNINGTON LANE
173
85
KENNINGTON PARK RD.
Kennington
A3204
A23
A3
A215
A2
A100
A200
A3200
A201
A202
EAST ST.
KENNINGTON
Surrey C.C.C. The Oval Cricket Grd.
KENNINGTON OVAL
Kennington Park
CAMBERWELL RD.
CAMBERWELL NEW RD.
ALBANY RD.
Burgess Park
BURGESS PARK
NEATE STREET
ST. GEORGE'S WAY
SOUTHAMPTON WAY
WYNDHAM ESTATE
CAMBERWELL GREEN
104
BRIXTON RD.
CLAPHAM RD.
PECKHAM
St. Gabriel's Manor
31
32
33
1
2
3
4
5
6
7

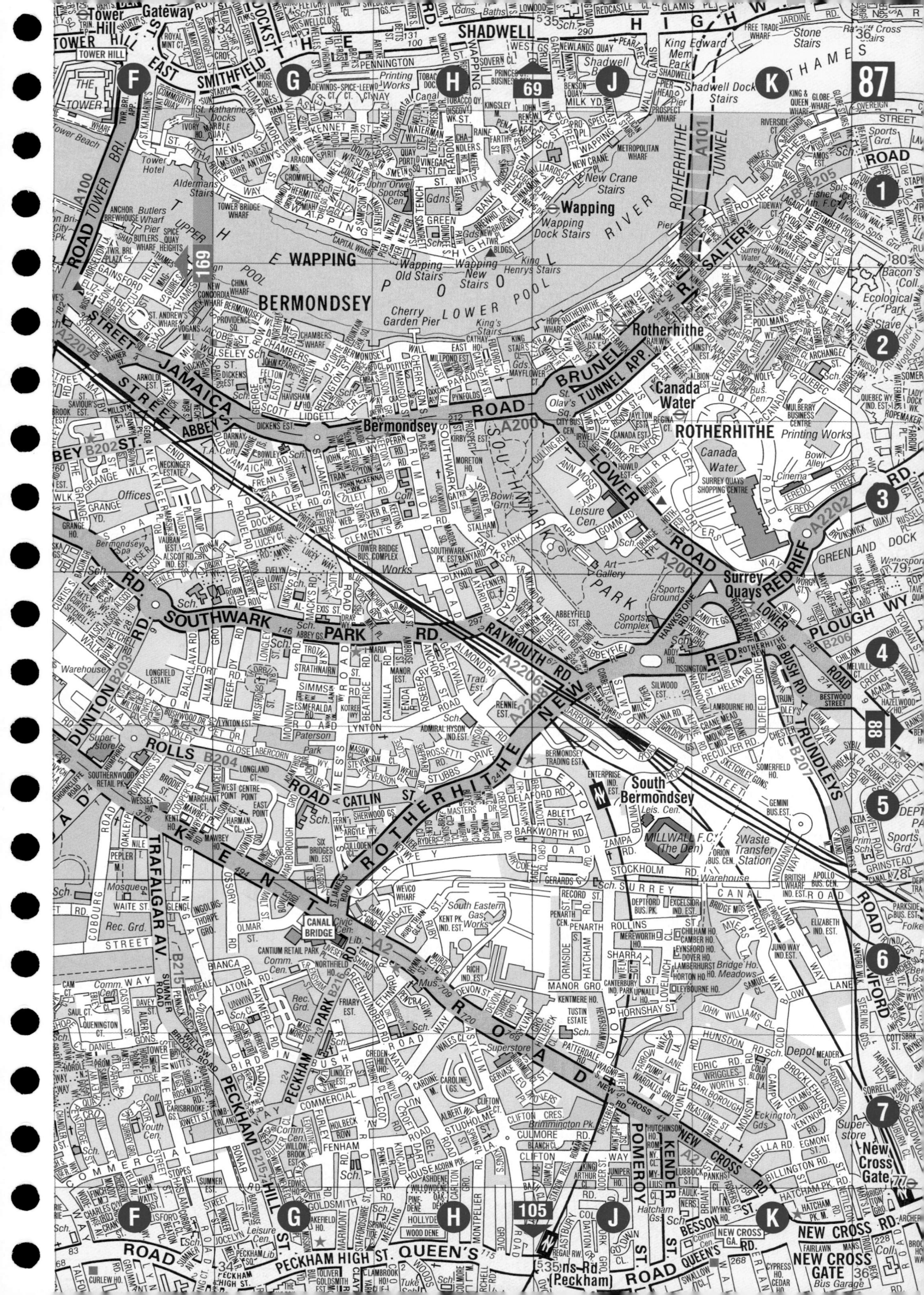
87
Tower Hill
Gateway
TOWER HILL
THE TOWER
SHADWELL
EAST SMITHFIELD
WAPPING
HIGHWAY
THAMES
Shadwell Dock Stairs
King Edward Mem. Park
Wapping
Wapping Dock Stairs
New Crane Stairs
RIVER
POOL
UPPER POOL
LOWER POOL
BERMONDSEY
Cherry Garden Pier
ROTHERHITHE TUNNEL
A101
A100
TOWER BRI. ROAD
Butlers Wharf
Rotherhithe
BRUNEL RD.
TUNNEL APP.
SALTER RD.
JAMAICA ROAD
STREET
ABBEY ST.
A2207
A200
Bermondsey
Canada Water
ROTHERHITHE
SOUTHWARK PARK
LOWER ROAD
Surrey Quays
REDRIFF RD.
GREENLAND DOCK
PLOUGH WY.
SOUTHWARK PARK RD.
RAYMOUTH RD.
A2206
A2208
NEW ROTHERHITHE
ROLLS RD.
DUNTON RD.
CATLIN ST.
South Bermondsey
MILLWALL F.C. (The Den)
TRUNDLEYS RD.
SURREY CANAL ROAD
KENT ROAD
OLD
TRAFALGAR AV.
CANAL BRIDGE
A2
ASYLUM ROAD
PECKHAM PARK RD.
PECKHAM HILL ST.
COMMERCIAL WAY
NEW CROSS RD.
New Cross Gate
NEW CROSS GATE
PECKHAM HIGH ST.
QUEEN'S ROAD
69
169
88
105
1
2
3
4
5
6
7
F
G
H
J
K

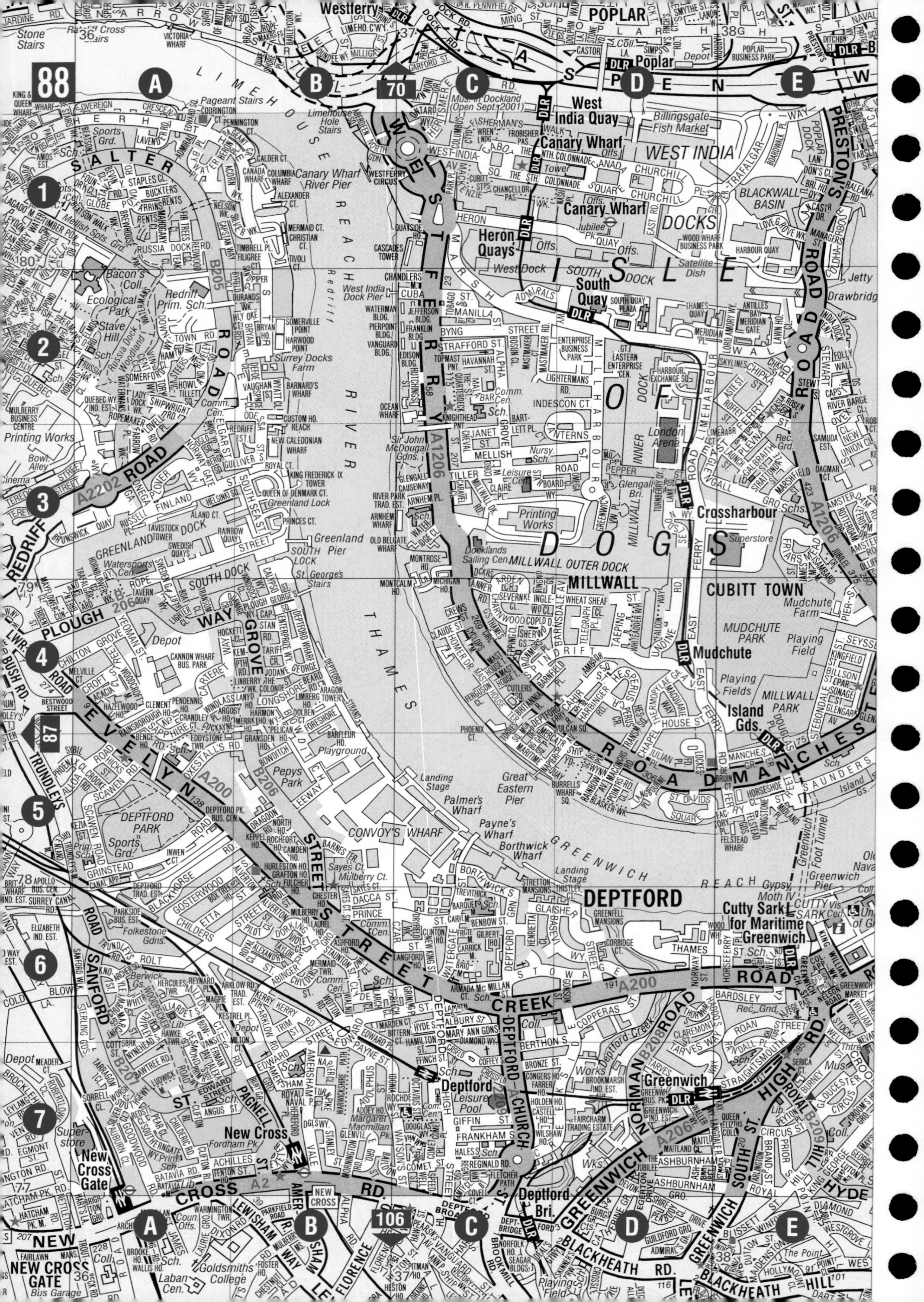

88
A
B
C
D
E
1
2
3
4
5
6
7
70
87
106
Westferry
POPLAR
Poplar
West India Quay
Billingsgate Fish Market
Canary Wharf
WEST INDIA
Canary Wharf River Pier
Limehouse Hole Stairs
Pageant Stairs
Stone Stairs
Ratcliff Cross Stairs
LIMEHOUSE REACH
SALTER ROAD
Bacon's Coll.
Ecological Park
Stave Hill
Redriff Prim. Sch.
Surrey Docks Farm
Printing Works
Bowl. Alley
Cinema
REDRIFF ROAD
Greenland Dock
Greenland Pier
South Lock
St. George's Stairs
South Dock
PLOUGH WAY
GROVE STREET
Depot
Heron Quays
South Quay
West Dock
ISLE OF DOGS
Blackwall Basin
DOCKS
London Arena
Crossharbour
Superstore
MILLWALL OUTER DOCK
MILLWALL
Dockland Sailing Cen.
CUBITT TOWN
Mudchute Farm
MUDCHUTE PARK
Mudchute
Playing Field
Playing Fields
MILLWALL PARK
Island Gds.
MANCHESTER ROAD
WESTFERRY ROAD
EAST FERRY RD.
Greenwich Foot Tunnel
RIVER THAMES
Sir John McDougall Gdns.
Landing Stage
Palmer's Wharf
Great Eastern Pier
Payne's Wharf
Borthwick Wharf
GREENWICH REACH
Greenwich Pier
Gypsy Moth IV
Cutty Sark for Maritime Greenwich
CONVOY'S WHARF
Pepys Park
Playground
DEPTFORD PARK
Sports Grd.
EVELYN STREET
DEPTFORD
DEPTFORD STREET
CREEK ROAD
Deptford Creek
Deptford
Deptford Leisure Pool
Deptford Bri.
DEPTFORD CHURCH ST.
Greenwich
NORMAN ROAD
GREENWICH HIGH RD.
GREENWICH SOUTH ST.
Folkestone Gdns.
New Cross
New Cross Gate
NEW CROSS RD.
NEW CROSS GATE
Goldsmiths' College
Laban Cen.
BLACKHEATH RD.
BLACKHEATH HILL
TRUNDLEYS ROAD
SANFORD STREET
LEWISHAM WAY
A200
A206
A1206
A2202
A2
B205
B206
B207
B208
B209
DLR

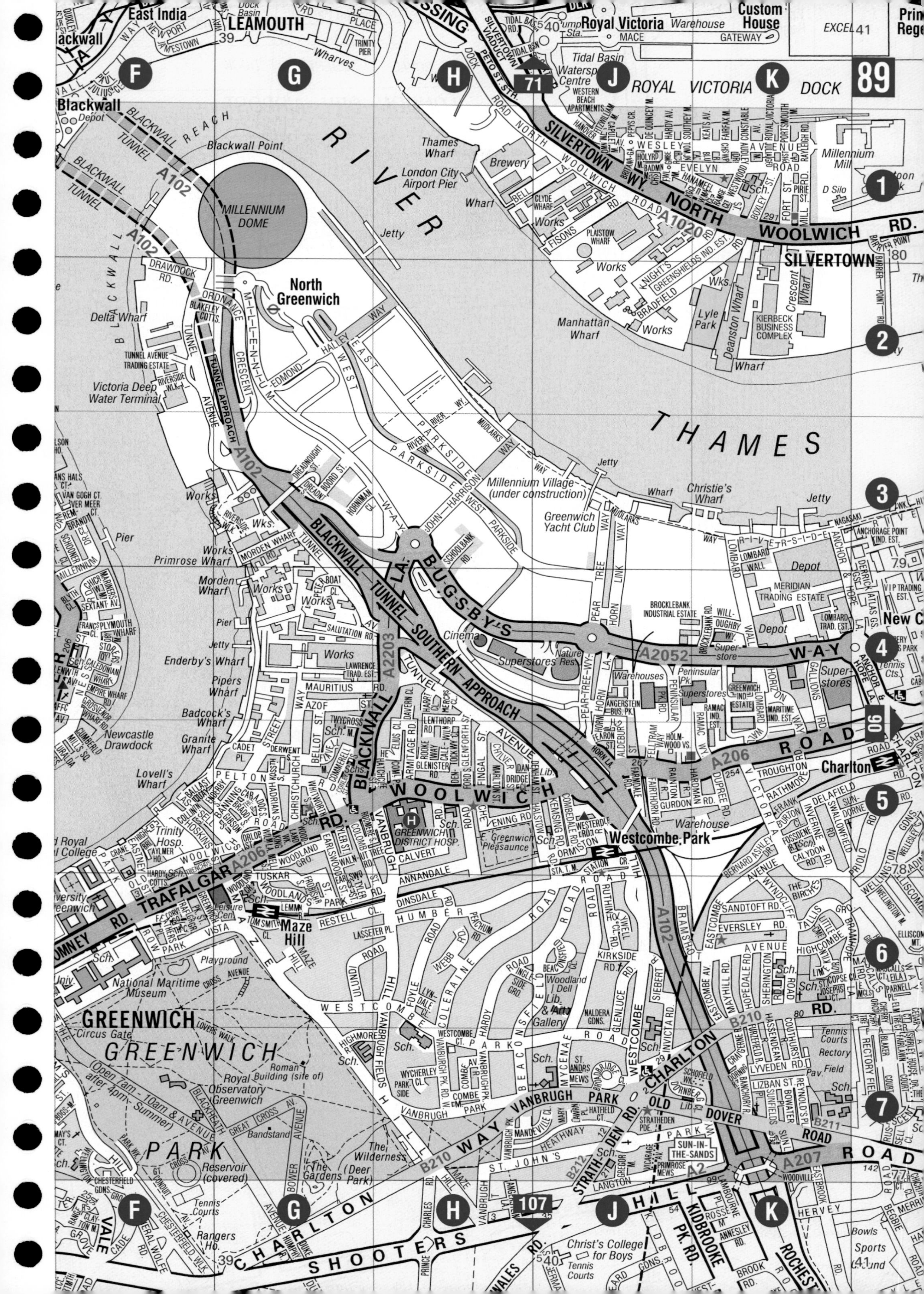
East India
Blackwall
LEAMOUTH
Wharves
TRINITY PIER
Royal Victoria
Custom House
Warehouse
MACE
GATEWAY
EXCEL
Tidal Basin
Watersports Centre
WESTERN BEACH APARTMENTS
71
ROYAL VICTORIA DOCK
F
G
H
J
K
BLACKWALL REACH
BLACKWALL TUNNEL
Blackwall Point
RIVER
THAMES
Thames Wharf
London City Airport Pier
Brewery
Wharf
Jetty
MILLENNIUM DOME
A102
SILVERTOWN WY.
NORTH WOODLICH RD.
A1020
WOOLWICH ROAD
Millennium Mill
D Silo
1
2
3
4
5
6
7
SILVERTOWN
Works
FISONS
PLAISTOW WHARF
Crescent Wharf
KIERBECK BUSINESS COMPLEX
Lyle Park
Deanston Wharf
Manhattan Wharf
North Greenwich
DRAWDOCK RD.
Delta Wharf
TUNNEL AVENUE TRADING ESTATE
Victoria Deep Water Terminal
MILLENNIUM WAY
TUNNEL APPROACH
EDMOND
HALLEY
WEST PARKSIDE
Millennium Village (under construction)
Greenwich Yacht Club
Christie's Wharf
Pier
Primrose Wharf
Morden Wharf
Enderby's Wharf
Pipers Wharf
Badcock's Wharf
Granite Wharf
Newcastle Drawdock
Lovell's Wharf
BLACKWALL TUNNEL SOUTHERN APPROACH
BUGSBY'S WAY
A2052
A2203
Cinema
Superstores
Nature Res.
Warehouses
Peninsular Pk.
MERIDIAN TRADING ESTATE
Depot
BROCKLEBANK INDUSTRIAL ESTATE
New C
90
A206
WOOLWICH RD.
ROAD
Charlton
Westcombe Park
Warehouse
GREENWICH DISTRICT HOSP.
Greenwich Pleasaunce
Trinity Hosp.
Royal Naval College
TRAFALGAR RD.
ROMNEY RD.
Maze Hill
Leisure Cen.
A102
National Maritime Museum
Playground
GREENWICH
GREENWICH PARK
Circus Gate
(Open 7am - 10am & after 4pm - Summer)
Royal Observatory Greenwich
Roman Building (site of)
Bandstand
Reservoir (covered)
The Wilderness (Deer Park)
The Gardens
Rangers Ho.
Tennis Courts
WESTCOMBE PARK RD.
VANBRUGH PARK
Woodland Dell
Lib. & Art Gallery
CHARLTON
OLD DOVER ROAD
B210
B211
A207
A2
SUN-IN-THE-SANDS
107
SHOOTERS HILL
CHARLTON WAY
Christ's College for Boys
KIDBROOKE PK. RD.
ROCHESTER
Bowls
Sports Ground
Tennis Courts
Rectory Field

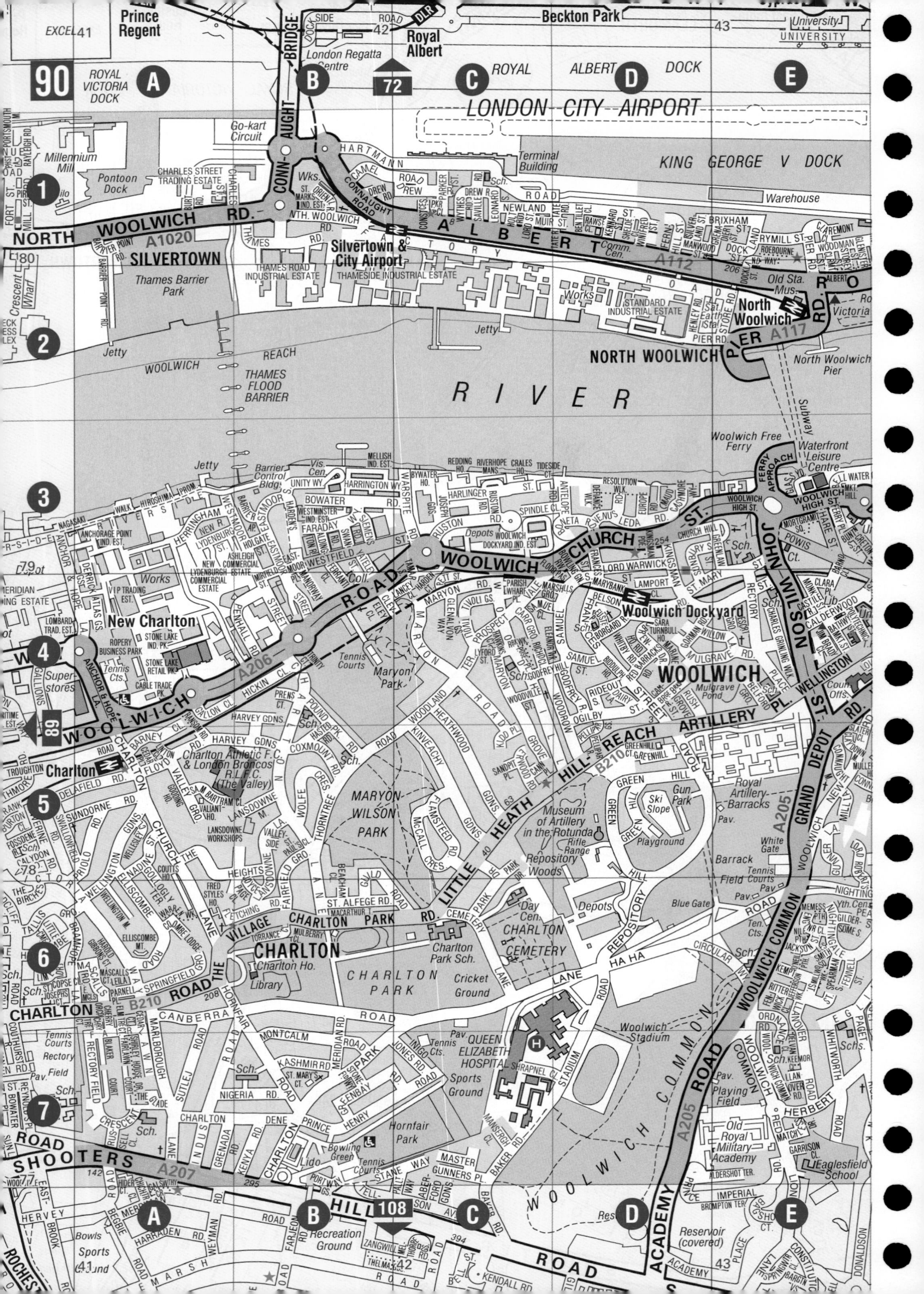

Prince Regent
EXCEL
Beckton Park
Royal Albert
London Regatta Centre
72
ROYAL VICTORIA DOCK
ROYAL ALBERT DOCK
LONDON CITY AIRPORT
KING GEORGE V DOCK
Terminal Building
Warehouse
Go-kart Circuit
Millennium Mill
Pontoon Dock
CHARLES STREET TRADING ESTATE
CONNAUGHT BRIDGE
HARTMANN ROAD
NORTH WOOLWICH RD.
A1020
SILVERTOWN
Thames Barrier Park
THAMES ROAD INDUSTRIAL ESTATE
Silvertown & City Airport
THAMESIDE INDUSTRIAL ESTATE
ALBERT ROAD
A112
FACTORY ROAD
STANDARD INDUSTRIAL ESTATE
Old Sta. Mus.
North Woolwich
PIER RD.
A117
NORTH WOOLWICH
North Woolwich Pier
Jetty
WOOLWICH REACH
THAMES FLOOD BARRIER
RIVER
Subway
Woolwich Free Ferry
Waterfront Leisure Centre
Barrier Control Bldg.
HARRINGTON WY.
BOWATER
WOOLWICH HIGH ST.
WOOLWICH CHURCH ST.
WOOLWICH DOCKYARD IND. EST.
Woolwich Dockyard
WOOLWICH
ANCHORAGE POINT IND. EST.
New Charlton
STONE LAKE IND. PK.
ROPERY BUSINESS PARK
STONE LAKE RETAIL PK.
CABLE TRADE PK.
Super-stores
WOOLWICH ROAD
A206
89
Charlton
Charlton Athletic F.C. & London Broncos R.L.F.C. (The Valley)
Maryon Park
MARYON-WILSON PARK
Mulgrave Pond
ARTILLERY PL.
JOHN WILSON ST.
GRAND DEPOT RD.
A205
Royal Artillery Barracks
Museum of Artillery in the Rotunda
Rifle Range
Gun Park
Ski Slope
Playground
Repository Woods
Barrack Field
White Gate
Blue Gate
Depots
LITTLE HEATH
HILL REACH
B210
CHARLTON PARK RD.
CHARLTON
Charlton Ho.
Library
CHARLTON PARK
Charlton Park Sch.
Cricket Ground
CHARLTON CEMETERY
Day Cen.
WOOLWICH COMMON
HA HA RD.
QUEEN ELIZABETH HOSPITAL
Woolwich Stadium
Sports Ground
Hornfair Park
Bowling Green
Lido
Old Royal Military Academy
Eaglesfield School
SHOOTERS HILL ROAD
A207
108
Recreation Ground
Bowls
Reservoir (covered)
ACADEMY ROAD
A
B
C
D
E
1
2
3
4
5
6
7

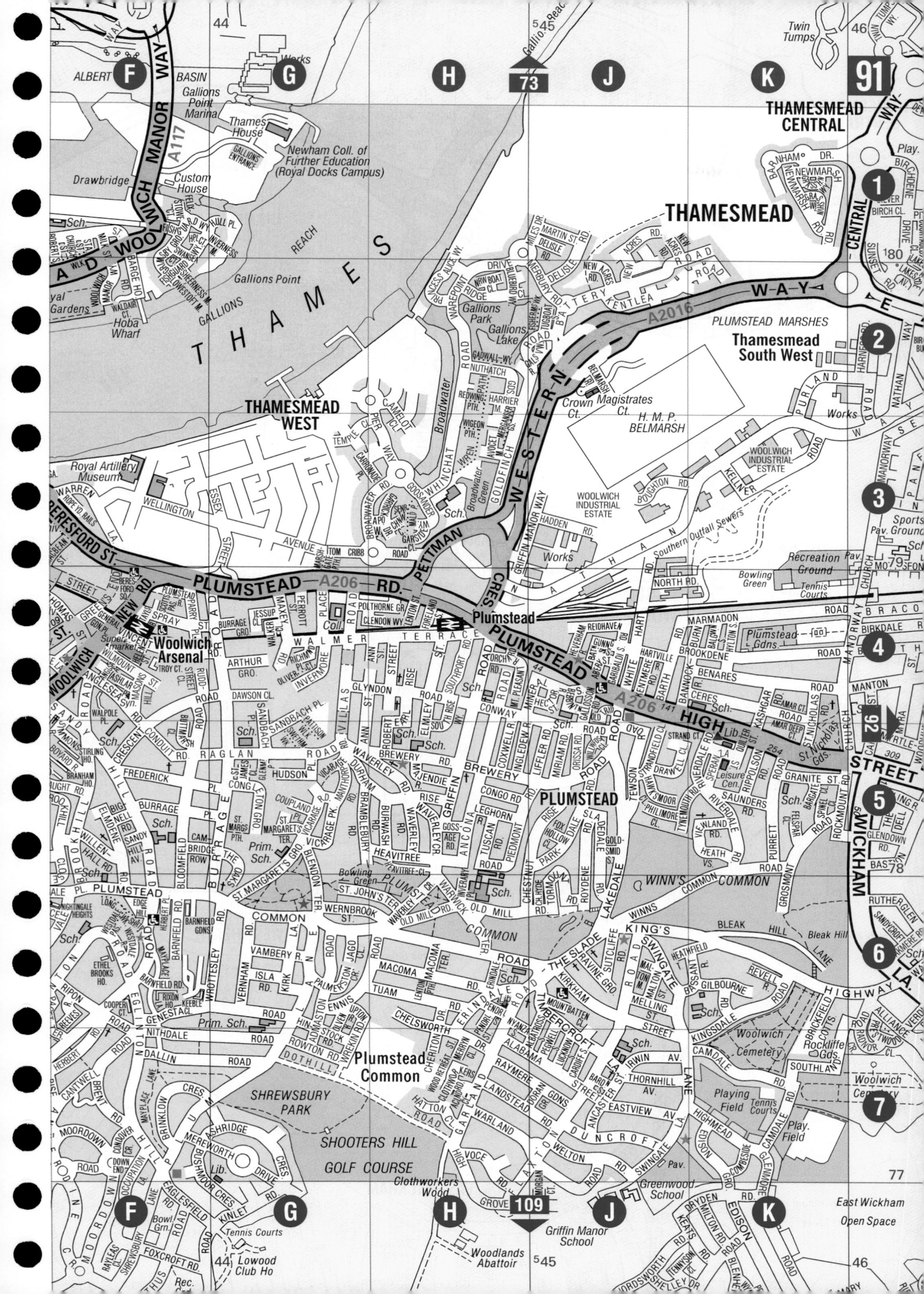
91
73
92
109
F
G
H
J
K
1
2
3
4
5
6
7
44
45
46
77
78
79
THAMESMEAD CENTRAL
THAMESMEAD
Thamesmead South West
THAMESMEAD WEST
PLUMSTEAD MARSHES
THAMES
GALLIONS
REACH
Gallions Point
ALBERT
BASIN
Gallions Point Marina
Thames House
Newham Coll. of Further Education (Royal Docks Campus)
Custom House
Drawbridge
Hoba Wharf
WOOLWICH MANOR WAY
A117
Royal Artillery Museum
Gallions Park
Gallions Lake
Broadwater
Broadwater Green
WESTERN WAY
A2016
Crown Ct.
Magistrates Ct.
H. M. P. BELMARSH
WOOLWICH INDUSTRIAL ESTATE
Works
Southern Outfall Sewers
Recreation Ground
Bowling Green
Tennis Courts
PLUMSTEAD RD.
A206
Plumstead
Woolwich Arsenal
PLUMSTEAD HIGH STREET
WALMER TERRACE
PLUMSTEAD
Plumstead Gdns.
WINN'S COMMON
PLUMSTEAD COMMON
Plumstead Common
SHREWSBURY PARK
SHOOTERS HILL GOLF COURSE
Clothworkers Wood
Woodlands Abattoir
Greenwood School
Griffin Manor School
Woolwich Cemetery
Rockliffe Gds.
Bleak Hill
Playing Field
Play. Field
East Wickham Open Space
Lowood Club Ho
Tennis Courts
WICKHAM LA.
HIGHWAY
BLEAK HILL LANE
KING'S HIGHWAY
WOOLWICH RD.
SHREWSBURY LANE
Sch.
Prim. Sch.
Lib.
Leisure Cen.

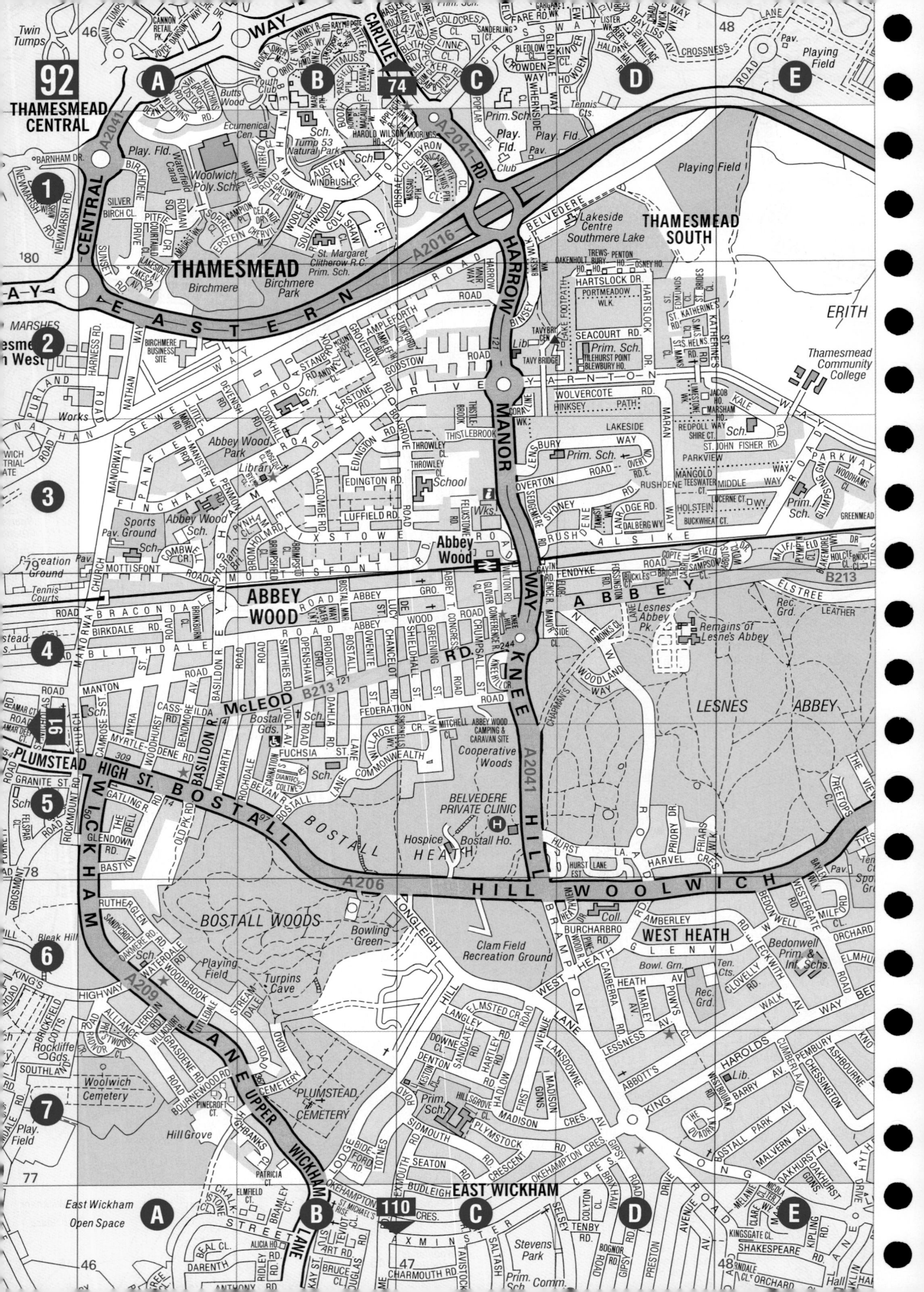
92
THAMESMEAD CENTRAL
Twin Tumps
A
B
C
D
E
1
2
3
4
5
6
7
46
47
48
180
79
78
77
74
91
110
THAMESMEAD
Birchmere
Birchmere Park
THAMESMEAD SOUTH
Lakeside Centre
Southmere Lake
Playing Field
ERITH
Thamesmead Community College
MARSHES
Birchmere Business Site
Works
Abbey Wood Park
Library
Abbey Wood Sch.
Sports Pav. Ground
Recreation Ground
Tennis Courts
ABBEY WOOD
Abbey Wood
Lesnes Abbey Pk.
Remains of Lesne's Abbey
LESNES ABBEY
Rec. Grd.
Cooperative Woods
BELVEDERE PRIVATE CLINIC
Hospice
Bostall Ho.
BOSTALL HEATH
BOSTALL WOODS
Bowling Green
Clam Field Recreation Ground
Turpins Cave
Playing Field
WEST HEATH
Bowl. Grn.
Bedonwell Prim. & Inf. Schs.
Woolwich Cemetery
PLUMSTEAD CEMETERY
Hill Grove
Rockliffe Gds.
Bleak Hill
EAST WICKHAM
East Wickham Open Space
Stevens Park
EASTERN WAY
A2016
A2041
A206
A209
B213
HARROW MANOR WAY
KNEE HILL
CENTRAL WAY
CARLYLE RD.
BOSTALL HILL
WOOLWICH RD.
PLUMSTEAD HIGH ST.
WICKHAM LANE
UPPER WICKHAM LANE
McLEOD RD.
ABBEY RD.
YARNTON WAY
RIVER WAY
SEWELL RD.
MOTTISFONT ROAD
FELIXSTOWE ROAD
ALSIKE RD.
FENDYKE
ELSTREE
CROSSWAY
KING HAROLDS WAY
LONG LANE
AXMINSTER CRES.
OKEHAMPTON CRES.
BRAMPTON RD.
LONGLEIGH LANE
WEST HEATH RD.
GLENVIEW
BLITHDALE RD.
BRACONDALE RD.
BIRKDALE RD.
MANORWAY
FINCHALE RD.
PANFIELD RD.
HARTSLOCK DR.
WOLVERCOTE RD.
LAKESIDE

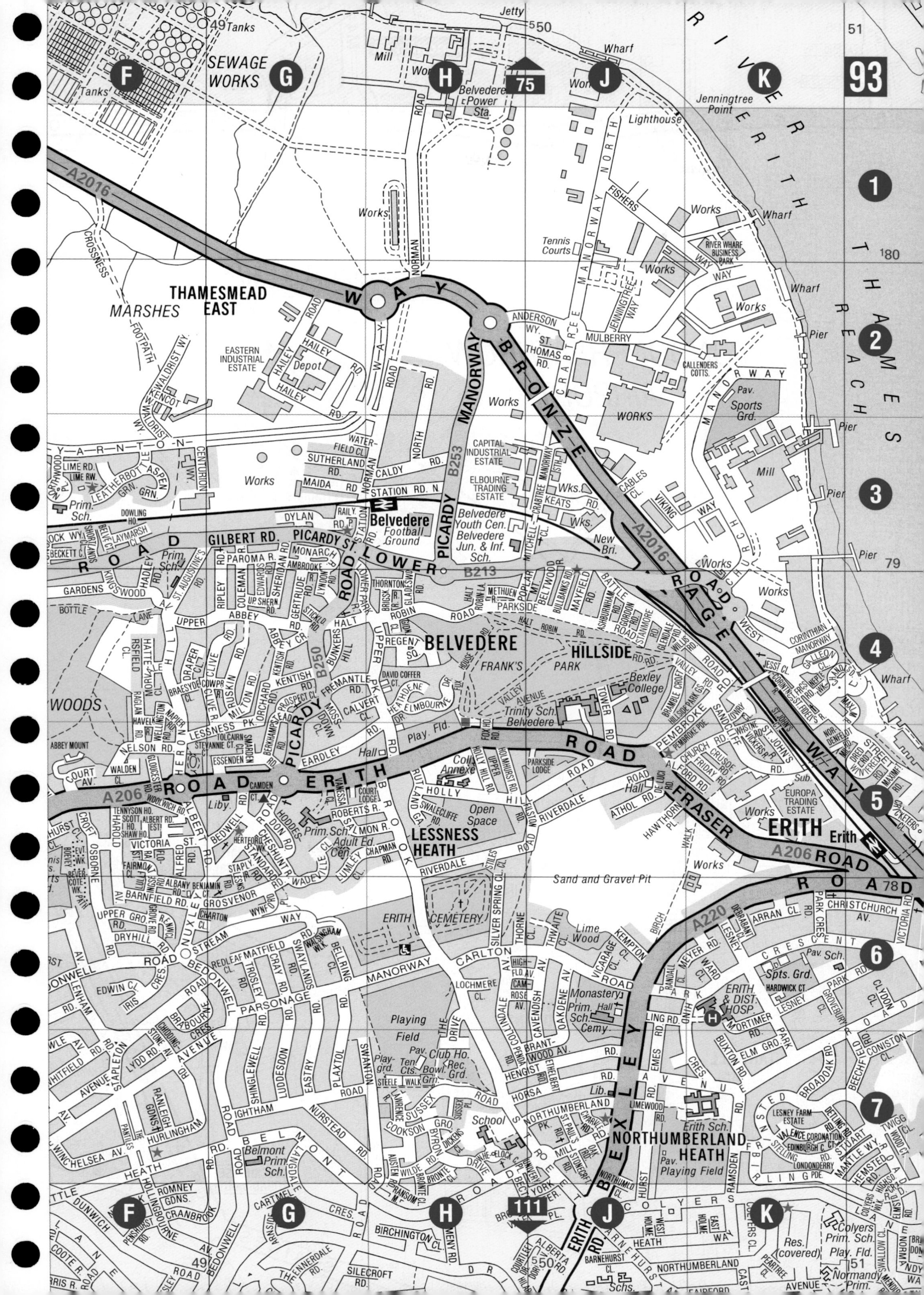
RIVER THAMES
ERITH REACH
SEWAGE WORKS
THAMESMEAD EAST
MARSHES
Belvedere Power Sta.
Jennintree Point
Lighthouse
Works
Wharf
Pier
Jetty
Mill
WORKS
Sports Grd.
EASTERN INDUSTRIAL ESTATE
CAPITAL INDUSTRIAL ESTATE
ELBOURNE TRADING ESTATE
RIVER WHARF BUSINESS PARK
A2016
WAY
BRONZE
MANORWAY
B253
Belvedere
Football Ground
Belvedere Youth Cen.
Belvedere Jun. & Inf. Sch.
LOWER
B213
BELVEDERE
HILLSIDE
FRANK'S PARK
Bexley College
Trinity Sch. Belvedere
PICARDY
B250
ERITH ROAD
A206
LESSNESS HEATH
Open Space
FRASER ROAD
ERITH
EUROPA TRADING ESTATE
Sand and Gravel Pit
ERITH CEMETERY
Lime Wood
A220
ERITH & DIST. HOSP.
Monastery Prim. Sch.
Playing Field
NORTHUMBERLAND HEATH
Erith Sch.
Belmont Prim. Sch.
BEXLEY
Colyers Prim. Sch.
WOODS
LESNEY FARM ESTATE
75
111
F
G
H
J
K
1
2
3
4
5
6
7
49
50
51
180
79
78

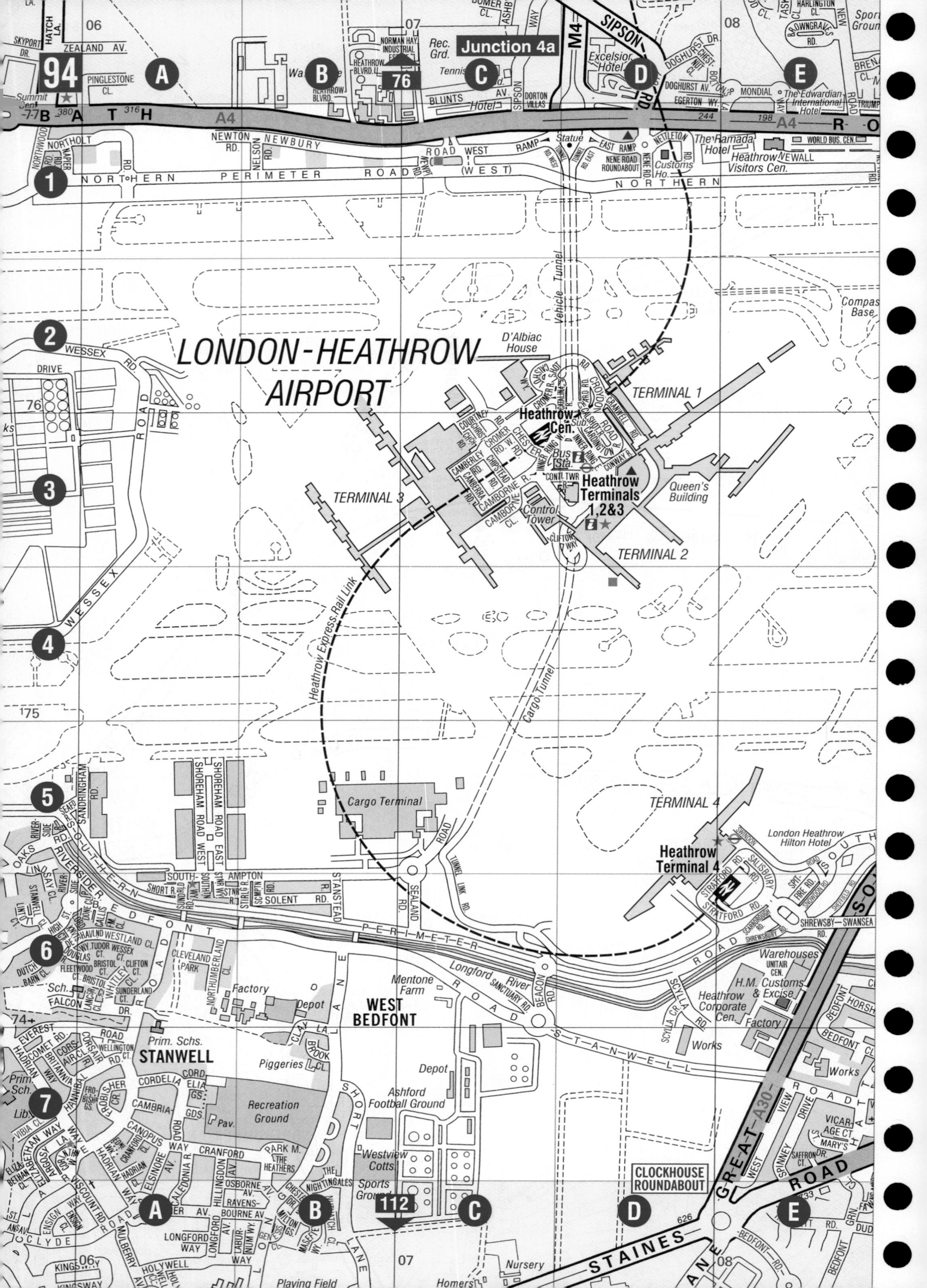

LONDON-HEATHROW AIRPORT

94

Junction 4a

TERMINAL 1

TERMINAL 3

Heathrow Cen.

Heathrow Terminals 1, 2 & 3

TERMINAL 2

Queen's Building

Control Tower

Heathrow Express Rail Link

Cargo Tunnel

Cargo Terminal

TERMINAL 4

Heathrow Terminal 4

London Heathrow Hilton Hotel

WEST BEDFONT

STANWELL

Recreation Ground

Ashford Football Ground

CLOCKHOUSE ROUNDABOUT

STAINES

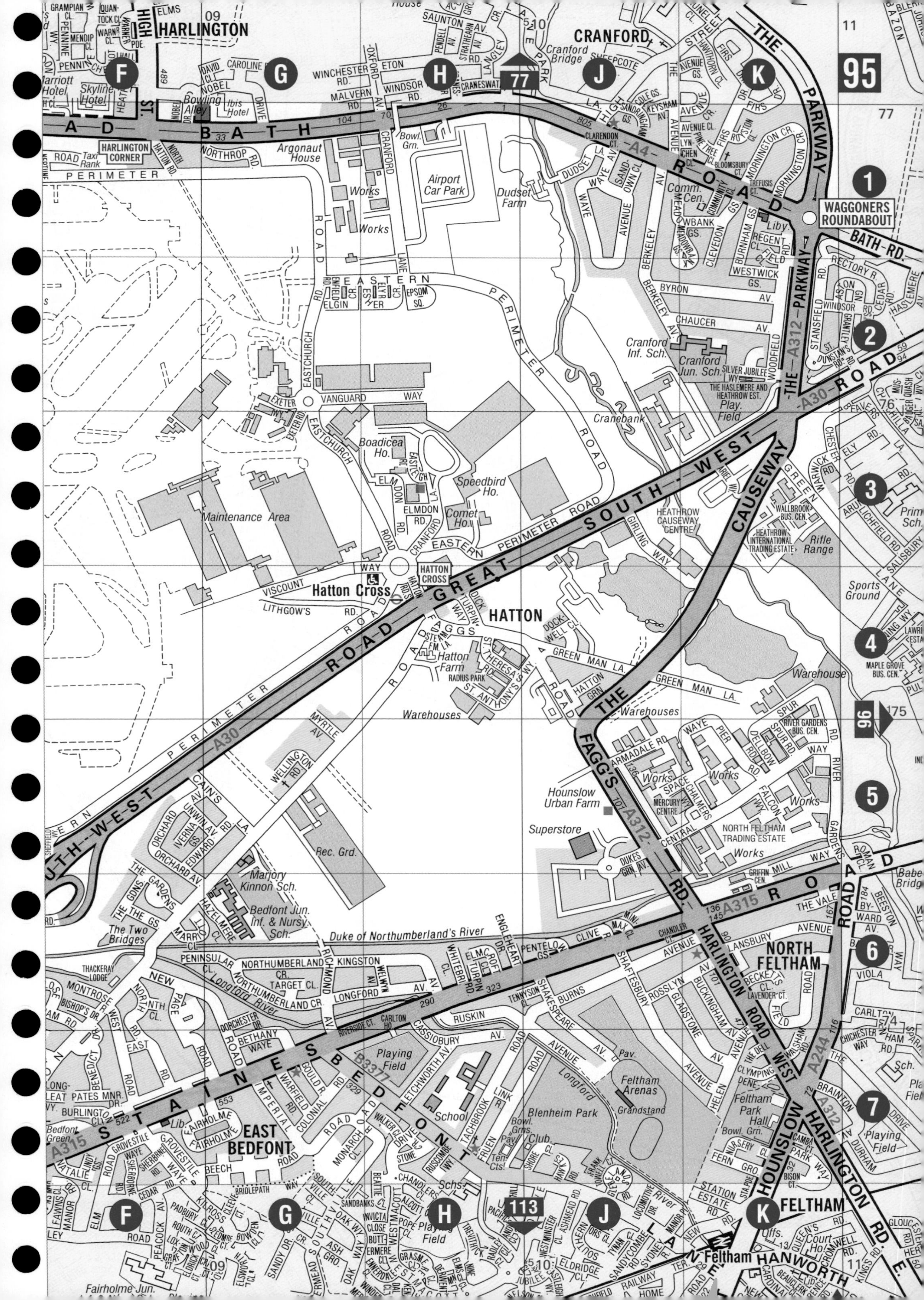
95
HARLINGTON
CRANFORD
Cranford Bridge
BATH ROAD
A4 ROAD
THE PARKWAY
WAGGONERS ROUNDABOUT
BATH RD.
HARLINGTON CORNER
Argonaut House
Airport Car Park
Dudset Farm
Skyline Hotel
Ibis Hotel
Bowling Alley
Marriott Hotel
Works
NORTHROP RD.
PERIMETER ROAD
EASTERN PERIMETER ROAD
EASTCHURCH RD.
VANGUARD WAY
Boadicea Ho.
Speedbird Ho.
Comet Ho.
Maintenance Area
Hatton Cross
HATTON CROSS
VISCOUNT WAY
LITHGOW'S RD.
HATTON
GREAT SOUTH WEST ROAD
A30 ROAD
A312 PARKWAY
Cranford Inf. Sch.
Cranford Jun. Sch.
THE HASLEMERE AND HEATHROW EST.
Play. Field
Cranebank
HEATHROW CAUSEWAY CENTRE
HEATHROW INTERNATIONAL TRADING ESTATE
Rifle Range
Sports Ground
THE CAUSEWAY
MAPLE GROVE BUS. CEN.
Warehouse
Warehouses
GREEN MAN LA.
Hatton Farm
RADIUS PARK
FAGG'S RD.
A312
Hounslow Urban Farm
Superstore
RIVER GARDENS BUS. CEN.
NORTH FELTHAM TRADING ESTATE
GRIFFIN CEN.
A315 ROAD
Rec. Grd.
Marjory Kinnon Sch.
Bedfont Jun. Inf. & Nursy. Sch.
The Two Bridges
Duke of Northumberland's River
Longford River
NORTH FELTHAM
HARLINGTON ROAD WEST
STAINES ROAD
BEDFONT ROAD
B3377
Playing Field
School
Blenheim Park
Feltham Arenas
Grandstand
Feltham Park Hall
EAST BEDFONT
Bedfont Green
A315
FELTHAM
Feltham
HANWORTH
HOUNSLOW ROAD
HARLINGTON RD. E.
A244
Playing Field
Fairholme Jun.
F
G
H
J
K
1
2
3
4
5
6
7
77
113
96
09
10
11
175

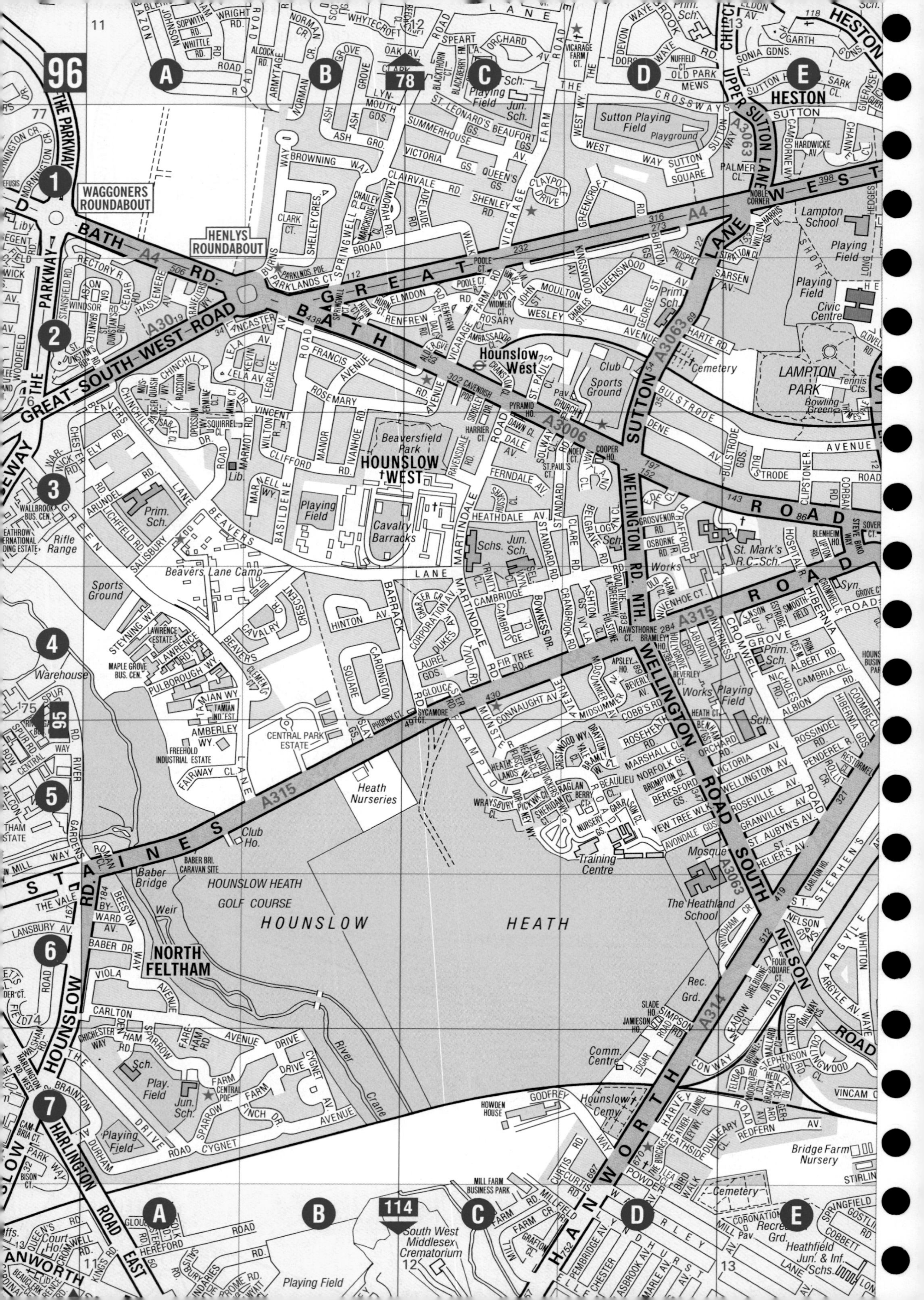

78
HESTON
Sutton Playing Field
Playground
WAGGONERS ROUNDABOUT
HENLYS ROUNDABOUT
GREAT SOUTH-WEST ROAD
GREAT WEST ROAD
BATH RD.
A4
A30
A3006
A3063
A315
A314
Hounslow West
HOUNSLOW WEST
Beaversfield Park
Cavalry Barracks
Playing Field
Sports Ground
Lampton School
Civic Centre
LAMPTON PARK
Cemetery
BULSTRODE AVENUE
WELLINGTON RD. NTH.
WELLINGTON ROAD SOUTH
SUTTON LANE
STAINES ROAD
HOUNSLOW ROAD
Beavers Lane Camp
Rifle Range
Warehouse
CENTRAL PARK ESTATE
FREEHOLD INDUSTRIAL ESTATE
Heath Nurseries
HOUNSLOW HEATH GOLF COURSE
HOUNSLOW HEATH
NORTH FELTHAM
Baber Bridge
BABER BRI. CARAVAN SITE
Weir
River Crane
Training Centre
Mosque
The Heathland School
Rec. Grd.
Comm. Centre
Hounslow Cemy.
MILL FARM BUSINESS PARK
South West Middlesex Crematorium
Playing Field
Bridge Farm Nursery
Heathfield Jun. & Inf. Schs.
HANWORTH ROAD
HARLINGTON ROAD EAST
NELSON ROAD
95
114

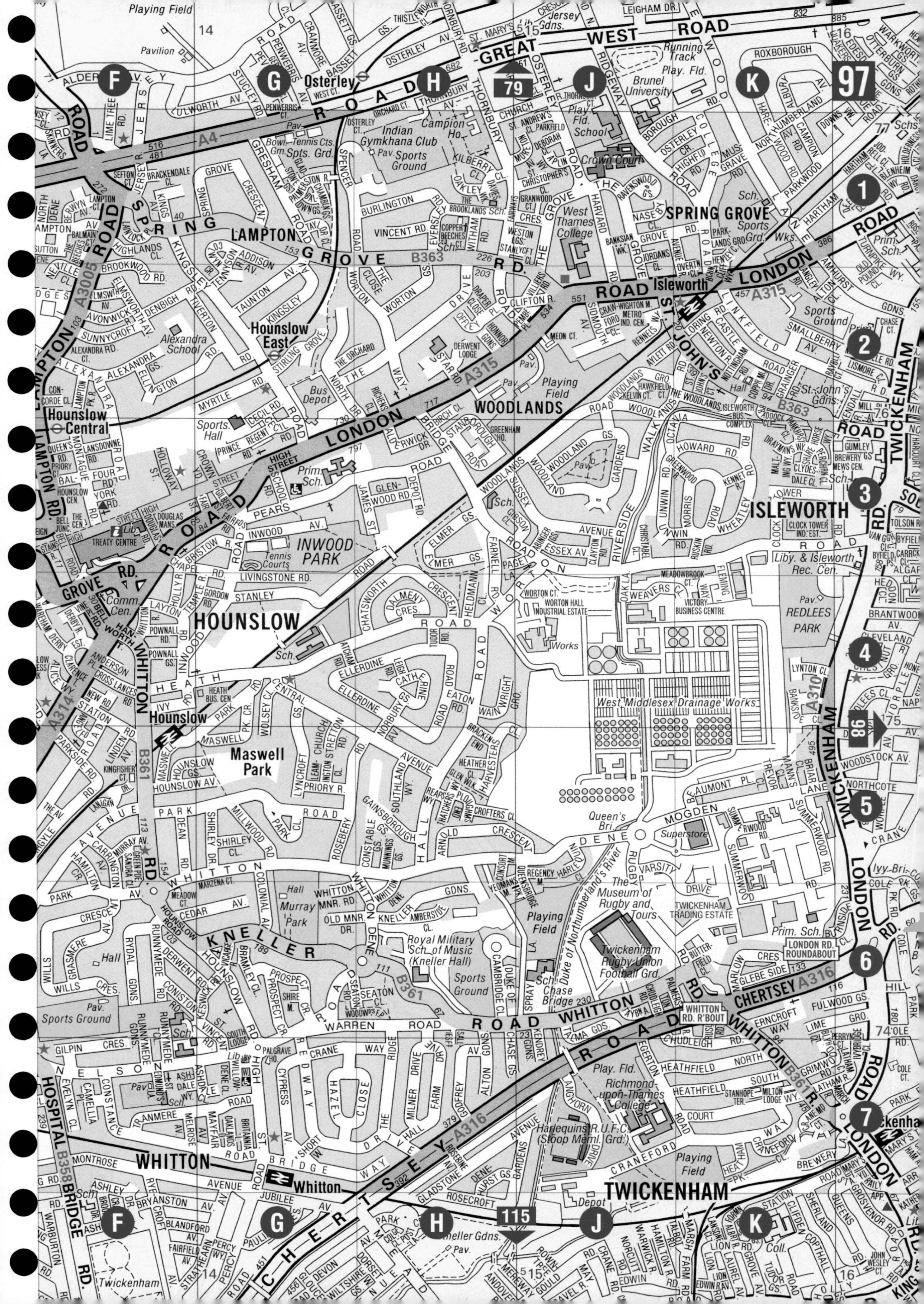

97
79
115
86
F
G
H
J
K
1
2
3
4
5
6
7
14
15
16
GREAT WEST ROAD
A4
Osterley
Playing Field
Pavilion
Indian Gymkhana Club
Sports Ground
Campion Ho.
Brunel University
Running Track
Play. Fld.
Crown Court
SPRING GROVE
Sports Grd.
LAMPTON
SPRING GROVE RD.
B363
Hounslow East
Alexandra School
West Thames College
Isleworth
LONDON ROAD
A315
ST. JOHN'S
Sports Ground
Bus Depot
Playing Field
WOODLANDS
Hounslow Central
Sports Hall
HIGH STREET
Prim. Sch.
INWOOD PARK
Tennis Courts
ISLEWORTH
Clock Tower Ind. Est.
Liby. & Isleworth Rec. Cen.
REDLEES PARK
HOUNSLOW
Worton Hall Industrial Estate
Victory Business Centre
Works
West Middlesex Drainage Works
Hounslow
Maswell Park
B361
A314
A3005
A310
TWICKENHAM RD.
MOGDEN LANE
Superstore
Queen's Bri.
Duke of Northumberland's River
The Museum of Rugby and Tours
Twickenham Trading Estate
Twickenham Rugby Union Football Grd.
LONDON RD. ROUNDABOUT
Murray Park
Royal Military Sch. of Music (Kneller Hall)
Sports Ground
Playing Field
KNELLER ROAD
WHITTON ROAD
WHITTON RD. R'BOUT
CHERTSEY ROAD
A316
Sports Ground
Play. Fld.
Richmond-upon-Thames College
Harlequins R.U.F.C. (Stoop Meml. Grd.)
Playing Field
WHITTON
Whitton
TWICKENHAM
Depot
Kneller Gdns.
HOSPITAL BRIDGE RD.
B358
Twickenham

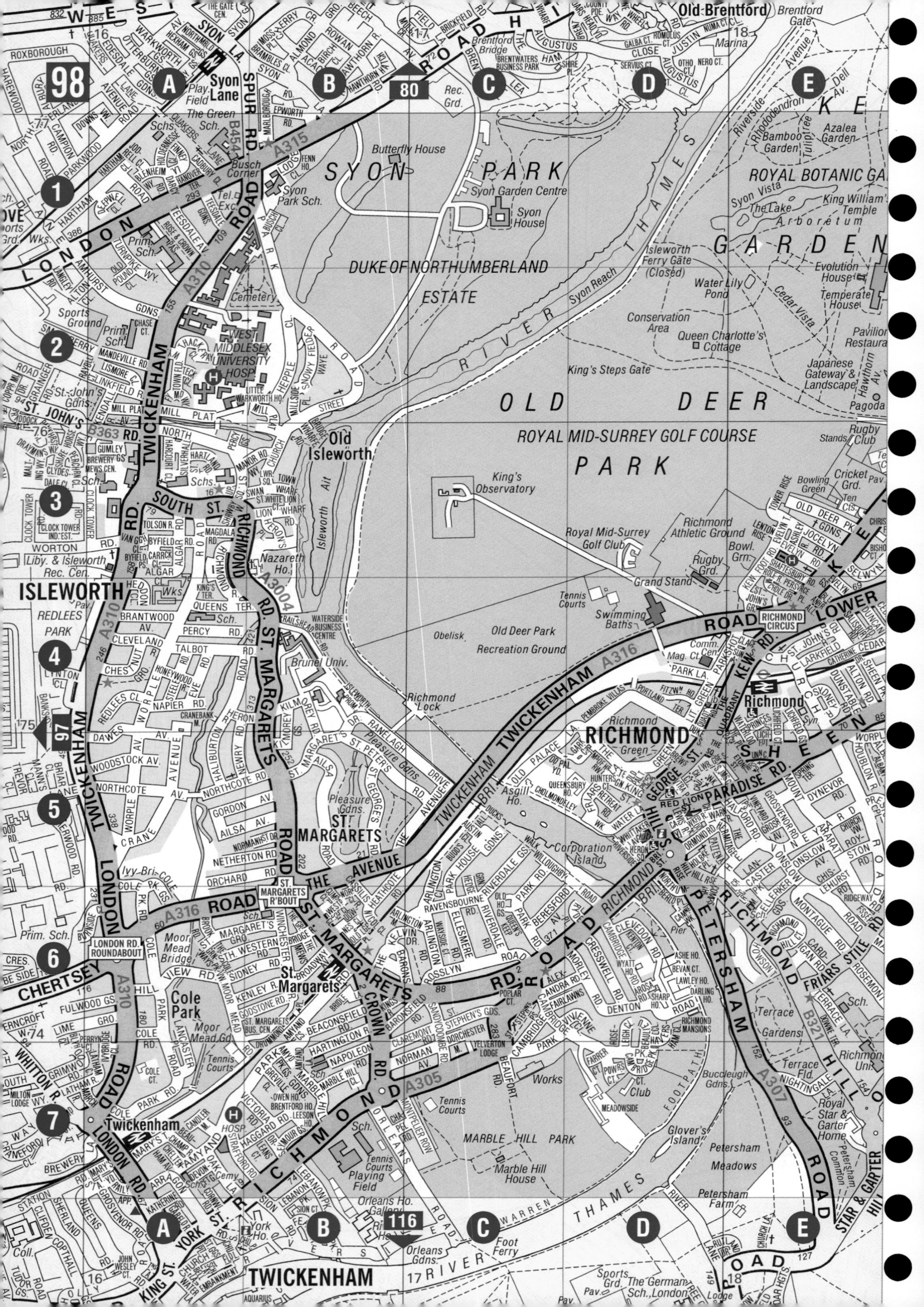
Old Brentford
Brentford Gate
Syon Lane
80
Brentford Bridge
Brentwaters Business Park
SYON PARK
Butterfly House
Syon Garden Centre
Syon House
Syon Park Sch.
Busch Corner
ROYAL BOTANIC GARDENS
Syon Vista
The Lake
King William's Temple
Arboretum
Bamboo Garden
Azalea Garden
Rhododendron Dell
LONDON ROAD
A315
A310
TWICKENHAM ROAD
DUKE OF NORTHUMBERLAND ESTATE
Cemetery
WEST MIDDLESEX UNIVERSITY HOSP.
RIVER THAMES
Syon Reach
Isleworth Ferry Gate (Closed)
Water Lily Pond
Conservation Area
Queen Charlotte's Cottage
Cedar Vista
Evolution House
Temperate House
Pavilion Restaurant
Japanese Gateway & Landscape
Pagoda
King's Steps Gate
OLD DEER PARK
ROYAL MID-SURREY GOLF COURSE
Old Isleworth
Isleworth Ait
King's Observatory
Royal Mid-Surrey Golf Club
Richmond Athletic Ground
Rugby Grd.
Grand Stand
Rugby Club
Cricket Grd.
Bowling Green
ISLEWORTH
Liby. & Isleworth Rec. Cen.
REDLEES PARK
SOUTH ST.
RICHMOND RD.
A3004
ST. MARGARETS RD.
Nazareth Ho.
Brunel Univ.
Waterside Business Centre
Swimming Baths
Tennis Courts
Obelisk
Old Deer Park Recreation Ground
TWICKENHAM ROAD
A316
RICHMOND CIRCUS
LOWER MORTLAKE RD.
KEW RD.
Richmond
RICHMOND
Richmond Green
Richmond Lock
Pleasure Gdns.
ST. MARGARETS
THE AVENUE
ST. MARGARETS R'BOUT
LONDON RD. ROUNDABOUT
A316 ROAD
CHERTSEY ROAD
Cole Park
Moor Mead Bridge
Moor Mead Gd.
St. Margarets
Asgill Ho.
Corporation Island
HILL ST.
GEORGE ST.
PARADISE RD.
SHEEN RD.
RICHMOND ROAD
PETERSHAM RD.
A307
ST. MARGARETS RD.
CROWN RD.
RICHMOND RD.
A305
Twickenham
MARBLE HILL PARK
Marble Hill House
Orleans Ho. Gallery
Orleans Gdns.
Buccleugh Gdns.
Glover's Island
Petersham Meadows
Petersham Farm
Petersham Common
Terrace Gardens
Terrace Fld.
Royal Star & Garter Home
Richmond Hill
FRIARS STILE RD.
B321
RIVER THAMES
Foot Ferry
TWICKENHAM
KING ST.
YORK ST.
Sports Grd.
The German Sch., London
STAR & GARTER HILL
97
116

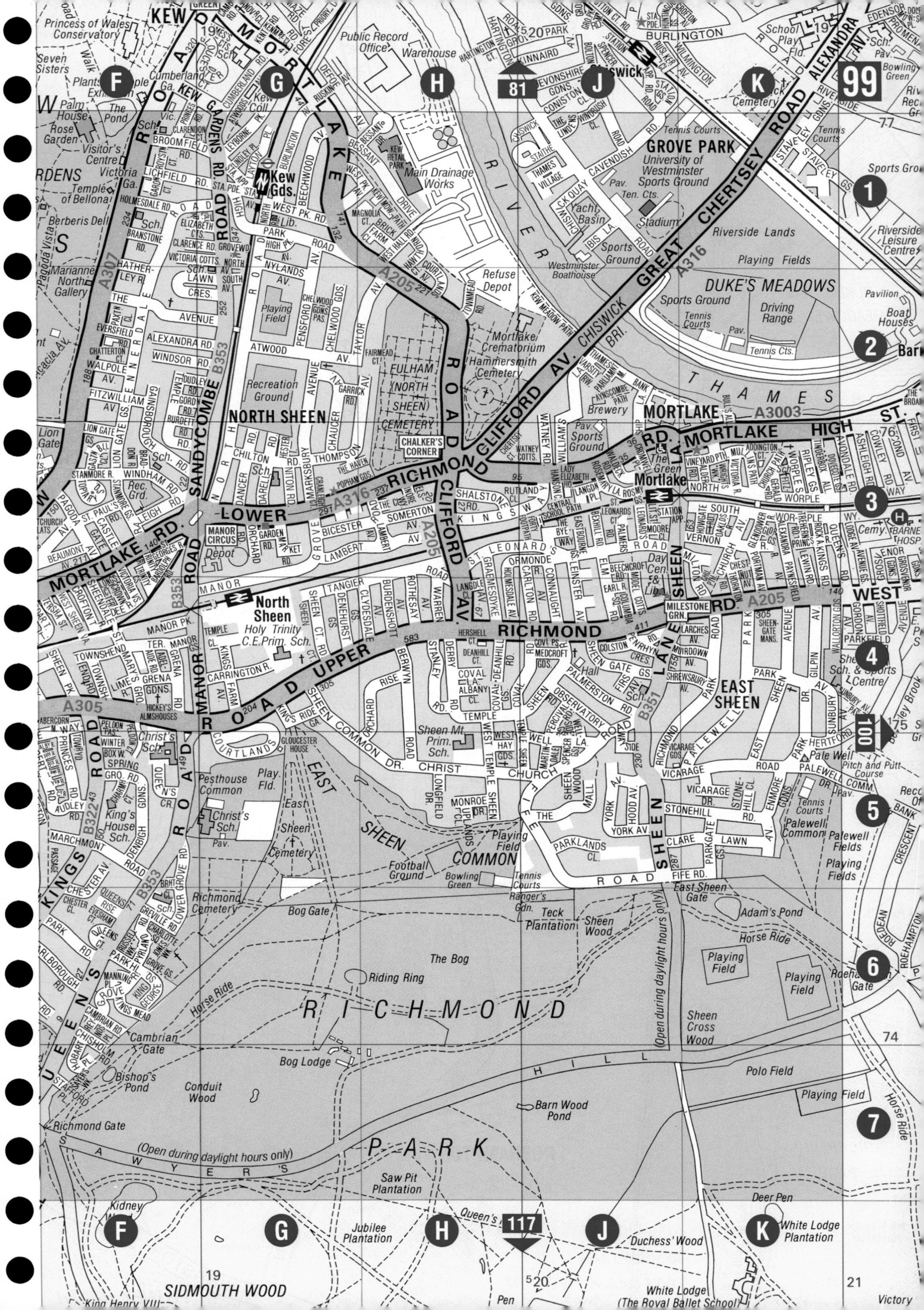
99
KEW
MORTLAKE
GROVE PARK
University of Westminster Sports Ground
DUKE'S MEADOWS
RIVER THAMES
NORTH SHEEN
Mortlake Crematorium
Hammersmith Cemetery
FULHAM (NORTH SHEEN) CEMETERY
CHALKER'S CORNER
North Sheen
EAST SHEEN
EAST SHEEN COMMON
RICHMOND PARK
Richmond Cemetery
East Sheen Cemetery
Sheen Cross Wood
Polo Field
Richmond Gate
Sidmouth Wood
White Lodge (The Royal Ballet School)
81
100
117

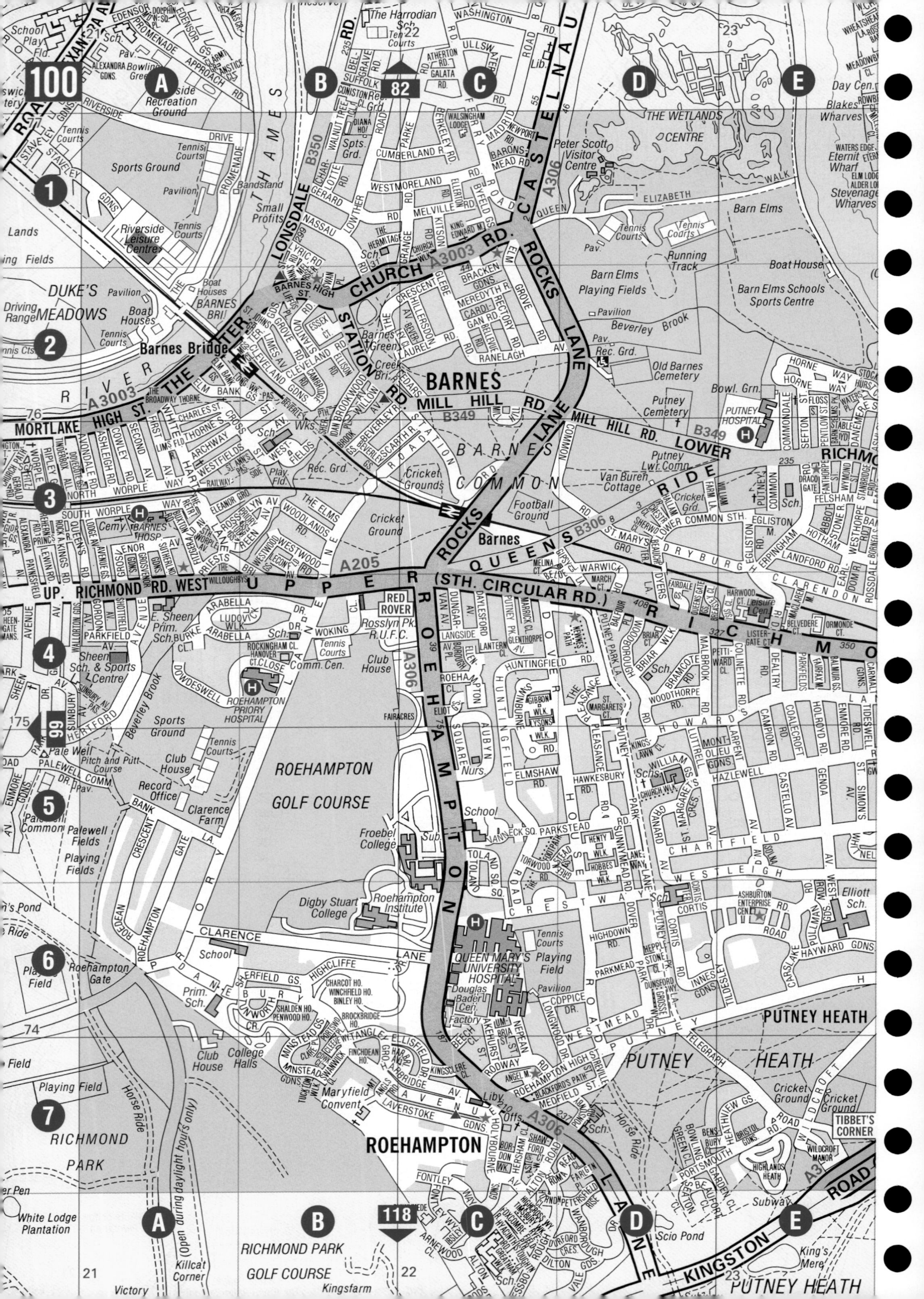

A
B
C
D
E
82
1
2
3
4
5
6
7
99
118
Barnes Bridge
BARNES
Barnes
MORTLAKE HIGH ST.
UP. RICHMOND RD. WEST
UPPER RICHMOND RD.
(STH. CIRCULAR RD.)
CHURCH RD.
CASTELNAU
ROCKS LANE
LONSDALE RD.
STATION RD.
MILL HILL RD.
LOWER RICHMOND RD.
QUEENS RIDE
ROEHAMPTON LANE
THE WETLANDS CENTRE
Peter Scott Visitor Centre
Barn Elms Playing Fields
Barn Elms Schools Sports Centre
Old Barnes Cemetery
Putney Cemetery
PUTNEY HOSPITAL
BARNES COMMON
Cricket Grounds
Football Ground
Riverside Recreation Ground
Sports Ground
Riverside Leisure Centre
DUKE'S MEADOWS
RIVER THAMES
ROEHAMPTON GOLF COURSE
Roehampton Institute
Digby Stuart College
Froebel College
QUEEN MARY'S UNIVERSITY HOSPITAL
ROEHAMPTON PRIORY HOSPITAL
Rosslyn Pk. R.U.F.C.
ROEHAMPTON
RICHMOND PARK
RICHMOND PARK GOLF COURSE
White Lodge Plantation
Killcat Corner
(Open during daylight hours only)
Horse Ride
PUTNEY HEATH
TIBBET'S CORNER
KINGSTON ROAD
Scio Pond
King's Mere
Roehampton Gate
Palewell Common
Palewell Fields Playing Fields
Sheen Sch. & Sports Centre
E. Sheen Prim. Sch.
Record Office
Clarence Farm
College Halls
Maryfield Convent
A3003
A205
A306
B349
B350
B306
A3
21
22
23
74
75
76
175

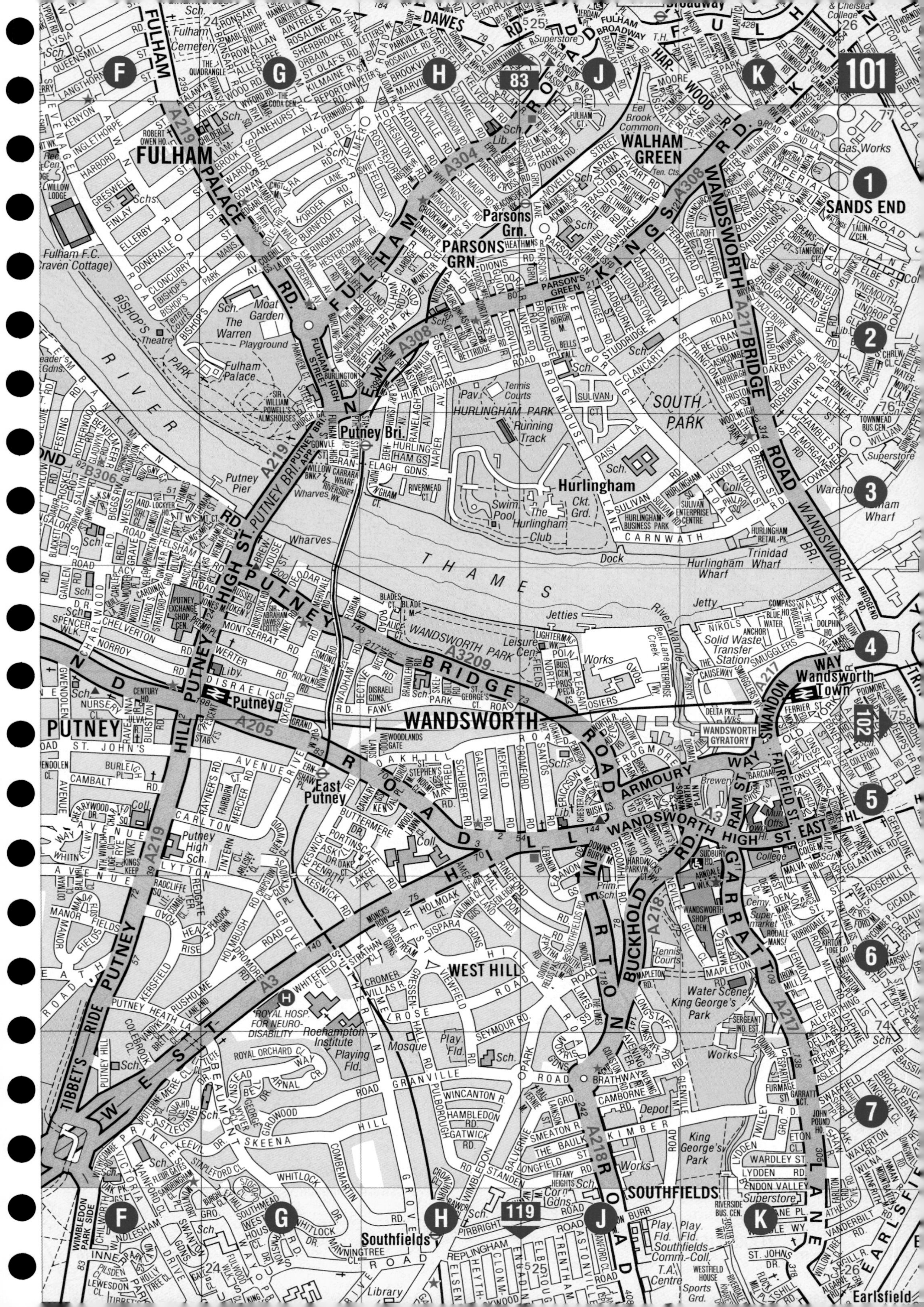

FULHAM
FULHAM PALACE RD.
Fulham Cemetery
Fulham F.C. (Craven Cottage)
Bishop's Park
The Warren
Moat Garden
Playground
Fulham Palace
RIVER
THAMES
Putney Pier
Putney Bri.
Hurlingham Park
Running Track
Hurlingham
The Hurlingham Club
South Park
Parsons Grn.
PARSONS GRN
WALHAM GREEN
Eel Brook Common
KINGS RD.
WANDSWORTH BRIDGE RD.
SANDS END
Gas Works
Hurlingham Wharf
Trinidad Wharf
Wandsworth Park
WANDSWORTH
Wandsworth Town
WANDSWORTH GYRATORY
PUTNEY
Putney
East Putney
PUTNEY HIGH ST.
PUTNEY BRIDGE RD.
UPPER RICHMOND RD.
WEST HILL
WANDSWORTH HIGH ST.
GARRATT LANE
BUCKHOLD RD.
MERTON RD.
King George's Park
SOUTHFIELDS
Southfields
PUTNEY HEATH
TIBBET'S RIDE
Roehampton Institute Playing Fld.
ROYAL HOSP. FOR NEURO-DISABILITY
Earlsfield
83
102
119

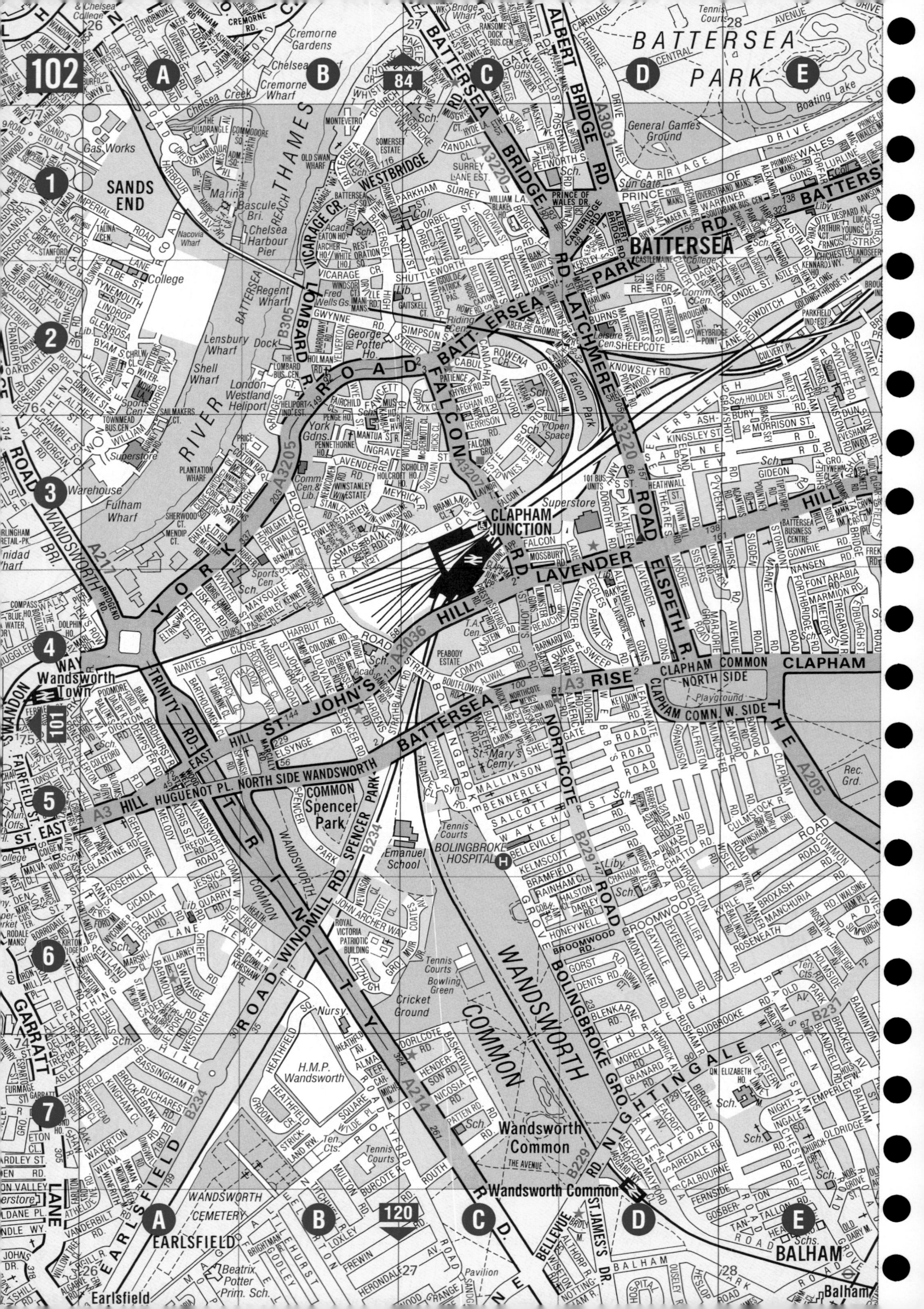
BATTERSEA PARK
BATTERSEA
SANDS END
RIVER THAMES
CHELSEA REACH
Cremorne Gardens
Chelsea Creek
Gas Works
Chelsea Harbour Pier
Bascule Bri.
Lensbury Wharf
Shell Wharf
London Westland Heliport
Regent Wharf
Plantation Wharf
Fulham Wharf
Warehouse
Superstore
CLAPHAM JUNCTION
Falcon Park
Open Space
General Games Ground
Boating Lake
Sun Gate
Wandsworth Town
Spencer Park
Emanuel School
BOLINGBROKE HOSPITAL
St. Mary's Cemy.
WANDSWORTH COMMON
Wandsworth Common
H.M.P. Wandsworth
Cricket Ground
Tennis Courts
Bowling Green
WANDSWORTH CEMETERY
EARLSFIELD
Earlsfield
BALHAM
Balham
Beatrix Potter Prim. Sch.
Pavilion
YORK ROAD
BATTERSEA PARK RD.
BATTERSEA BRIDGE RD.
ALBERT BRIDGE RD.
LATCHMERE ROAD
LAVENDER HILL
ST. JOHN'S HILL
BATTERSEA RISE
CLAPHAM COMMON NORTH SIDE
CLAPHAM COMM. W. SIDE
NORTHCOTE ROAD
BOLINGBROKE GRO.
NIGHTINGALE LANE
TRINITY ROAD
WINDMILL RD.
SPENCER PARK
EARLSFIELD
GARRATT LANE
WANDSWORTH BRI. ROAD
EAST HILL
WANDSWORTH COMMON NORTH SIDE
A3 A205 A214 A217 A3031 A3036 A3205 A3207 A3220 B229 B231 B234 B305
A B C D E
1 2 3 4 5 6 7
84
101
120
26 27 28

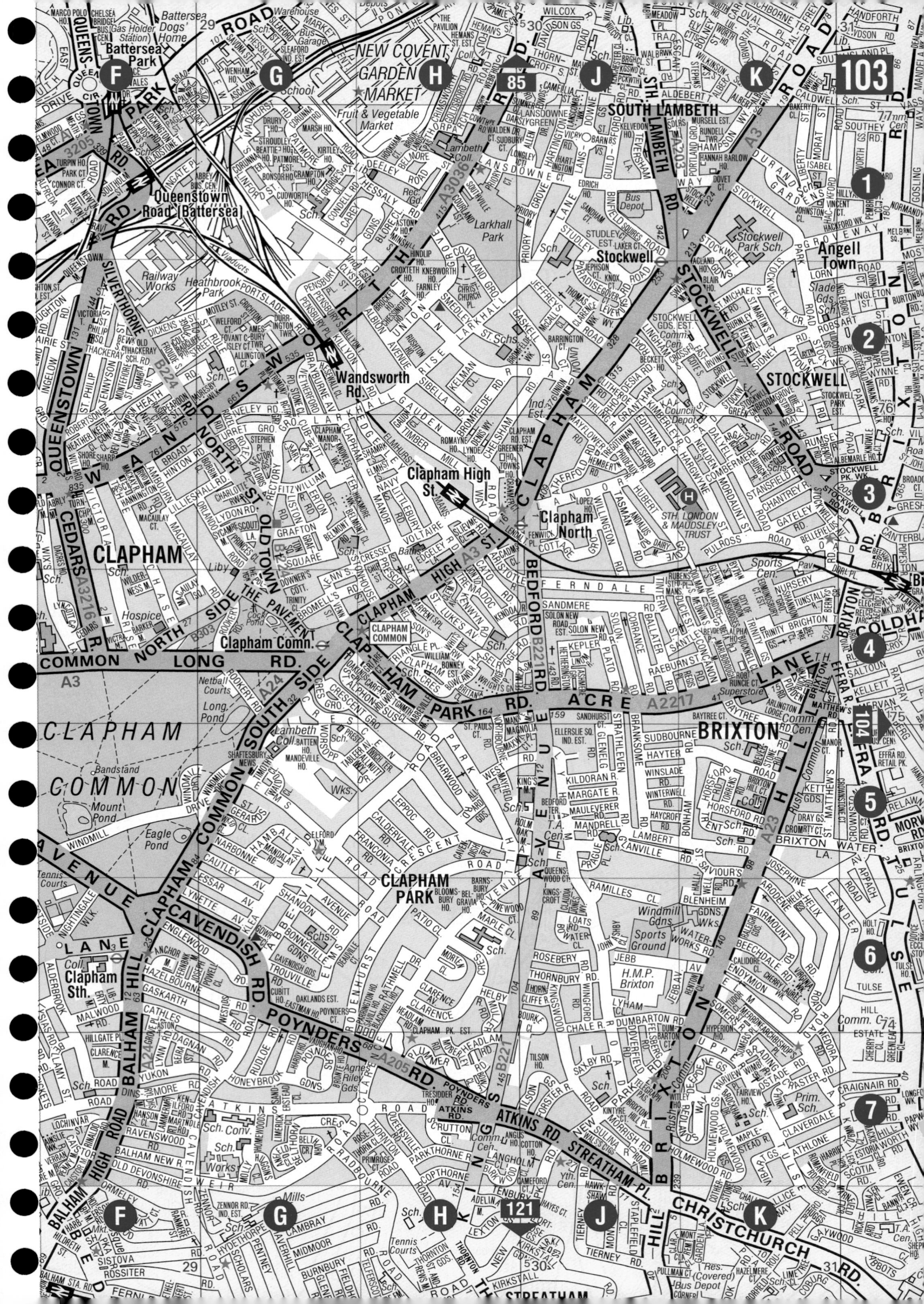

103
F
G
H
J
K
85
29
30
31
Battersea Park
Battersea Dogs' Home
Battersea Gas Holder Station
NEW COVENT GARDEN MARKET
Fruit & Vegetable Market
SOUTH LAMBETH
Queenstown Road (Battersea)
Railway Works
Heathbrook Park
Larkhall Park
Lambeth Coll.
Bus Depot
Stockwell
Stockwell Park Sch.
Angell Town
Slade Gds.
Wandsworth Rd.
STOCKWELL
1
2
3
4
5
6
7
Clapham High St.
Clapham North
STH. LONDON & MAUDSLEY TRUST
CLAPHAM
Hospice
Clapham Comm.
CLAPHAM COMMON
Sports Cen.
BRIXTON
Superstore
104
CLAPHAM COMMON
Bandstand
Mount Pond
Eagle Pond
Tennis Courts
Long Pond
Netball Courts
CLAPHAM PARK
Windmill Gdns.
Sports Ground
H.M.P. Brixton
Clapham Sth.
121
Tennis Courts
Res. (Covered)
Bus Depot
STREATHAM
QUEENSTOWN RD.
WANDSWORTH RD.
CLAPHAM RD.
STOCKWELL RD.
SOUTH LAMBETH RD.
LONG RD.
COMMON NORTH SIDE
CLAPHAM COMMON SOUTH SIDE
CLAPHAM PARK RD.
ACRE LANE
BEDFORD RD.
KING'S AVENUE
BRIXTON HILL
CAVENDISH RD.
POYNDERS RD.
ATKINS RD.
STREATHAM PL.
CHRISTCHURCH RD.
BALHAM HIGH ROAD
CLAPHAM COMMON WEST SIDE
NIGHTINGALE LANE
TULSE HILL
LARKHALL RISE
A3
A24
A3036
A203
A2217
A23
A205
B221
B224
A3216

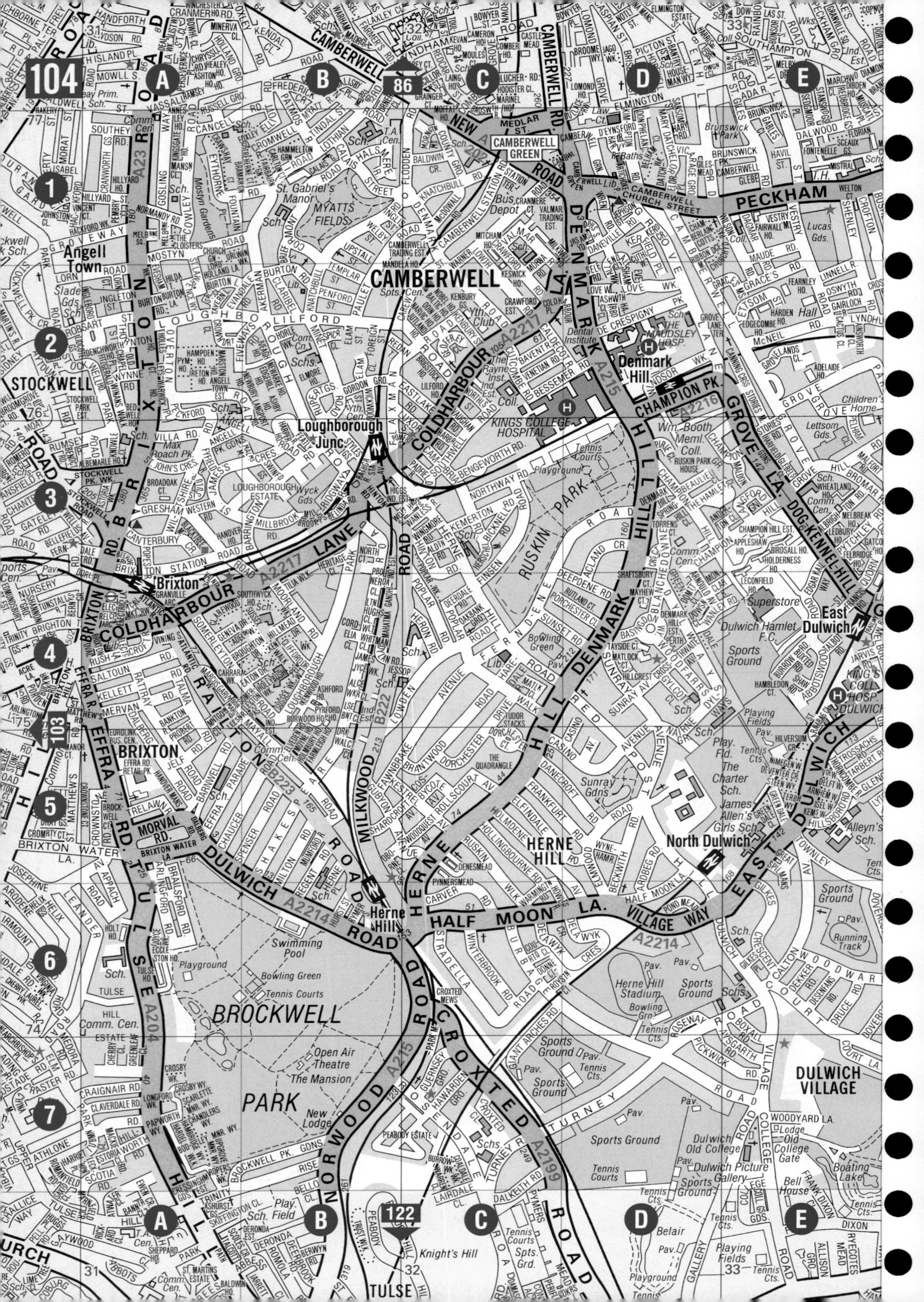

A
B
C
D
E
1
2
3
4
5
6
7
86
103
122
CAMBERWELL
CAMBERWELL GREEN
Angell Town
STOCKWELL
BRIXTON
Brixton
Loughborough Junc.
Denmark Hill
East Dulwich
North Dulwich
Herne Hill
HERNE HILL
DULWICH VILLAGE
BROCKWELL
PARK
RUSKIN PARK
PECKHAM
KINGS COLLEGE HOSPITAL
THE MAUDSLEY HOSP.
KING'S COLL. HOSP.
Myatts Fields
Lucas Gds.
Brunswick Park
Dulwich Hamlet F.C.
Sports Ground
Herne Hill Stadium
Dulwich Old College
Dulwich Picture Gallery
James Allen's Girls Sch.
The Charter Sch.
Alleyn's Sch.
Swimming Pool
Bowling Green
Tennis Courts
Open Air Theatre
The Mansion
New Lodge
Belair
Knight's Hill
Playground
Superstore
Sunray Gdns.
Boating Lake
Bell House
Old College Gate
PEABODY ESTATE
LOUGHBOROUGH ESTATE
CHAMPION HILL EST.
COLDHARBOUR LANE A2217
BRIXTON ROAD A23
DENMARK HILL A215
CAMBERWELL CHURCH STREET
CHAMPION PK. A2216
GROVE LA.
DOG KENNEL HILL
HALF MOON LA.
VILLAGE WAY A2214
DULWICH ROAD A2214
EAST DULWICH GROVE
NORWOOD ROAD A215
CROXTED ROAD A2199
TULSE HILL A204
EFFRA RD.
RAILTON ROAD B223
MILKWOOD ROAD B222
HERNE HILL
FERNDENE ROAD
RED POST HILL
COLLEGE ROAD
TURNEY ROAD
NEW ROAD
BRIXTON WATER LA.
LOUGHBOROUGH ROAD
FLAXMAN ROAD
SUNRAY AV.
31
32
33

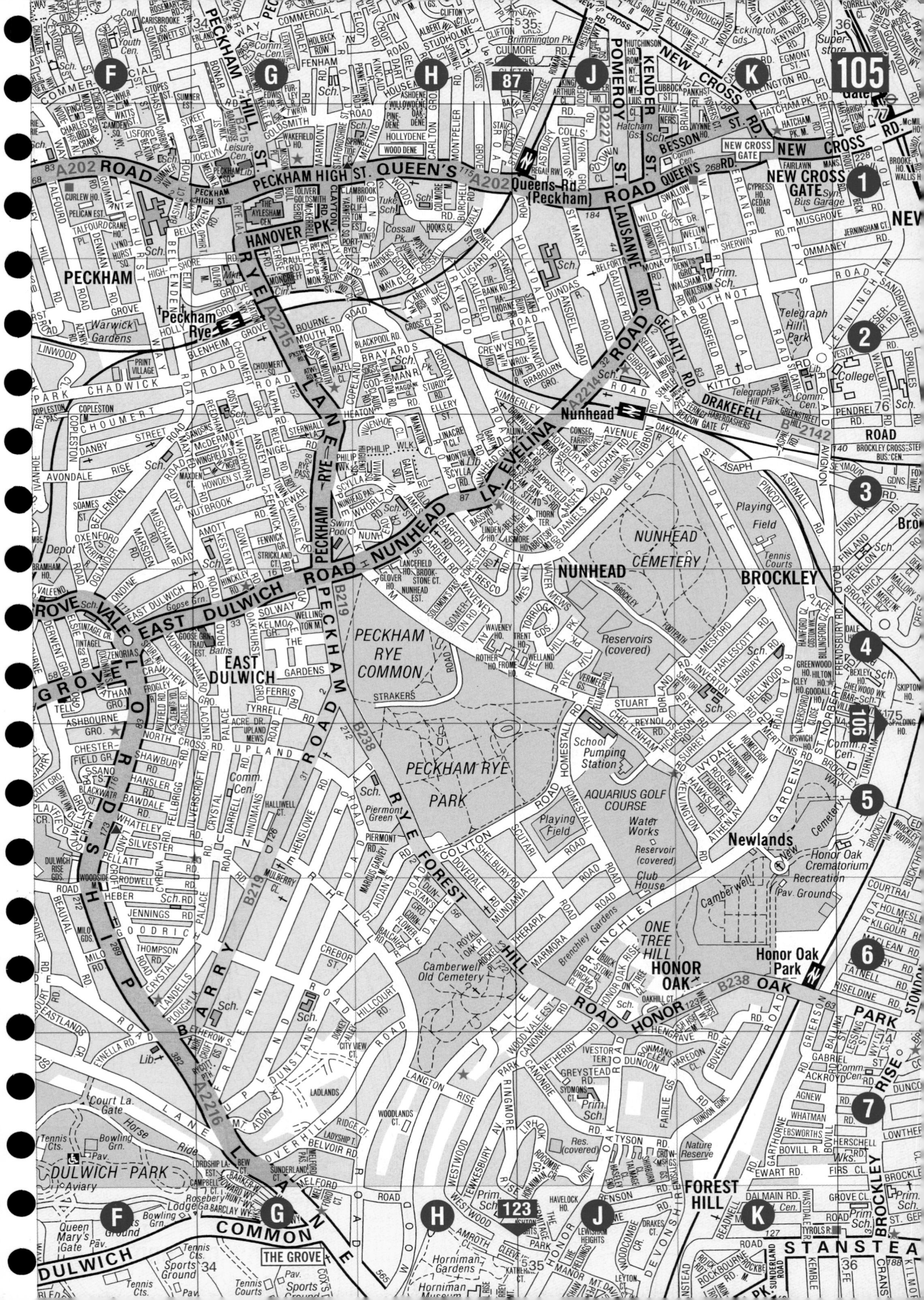

105
F
G
H
J
K
1
2
3
4
5
6
7
87
123
106
34
35
36
PECKHAM
PECKHAM HIGH ST.
QUEEN'S ROAD
A202
Queens Rd. (Peckham)
NEW CROSS GATE
NEW CROSS
HANOVER PK.
RYE LANE
A2215
Peckham Rye
NUNHEAD
Nunhead
NUNHEAD CEMETERY
EVELINA RD.
A2214
LAUSANNE RD.
POMEROY ST.
BROCKLEY
Telegraph Hill Park
DRAKEFELL ROAD
B2142
EAST DULWICH ROAD
EAST DULWICH
GROVE VALE
LORDSHIP LANE
A2216
PECKHAM RYE
PECKHAM RYE COMMON
PECKHAM RYE PARK
B219
B238
FOREST HILL
AQUARIUS GOLF COURSE
Reservoirs (covered)
Pumping Station
Water Works
Newlands
Honor Oak Crematorium
Camberwell New Cemetery
Camberwell Old Cemetery
ONE TREE HILL
HONOR OAK
Honor Oak Park
HONOR OAK ROAD
BARRY ROAD
DULWICH PARK
DULWICH COMMON
Court La. Gate
Horse Ride
Bowling Grn.
Queen Mary's Gate
THE GROVE
Horniman Gardens
Horniman Museum
STANSTEAD
Playing Field
Tennis Courts
Nature Reserve
Warwick Gardens
Goose Grn.
Baths
Swim. Pool
College
Bus Garage
Superstore
Brimmington Pk.
Hatcham Gs.
Leisure Cen.
Cossall Pk.
Tuke Sch.
Piermont Green
Club House

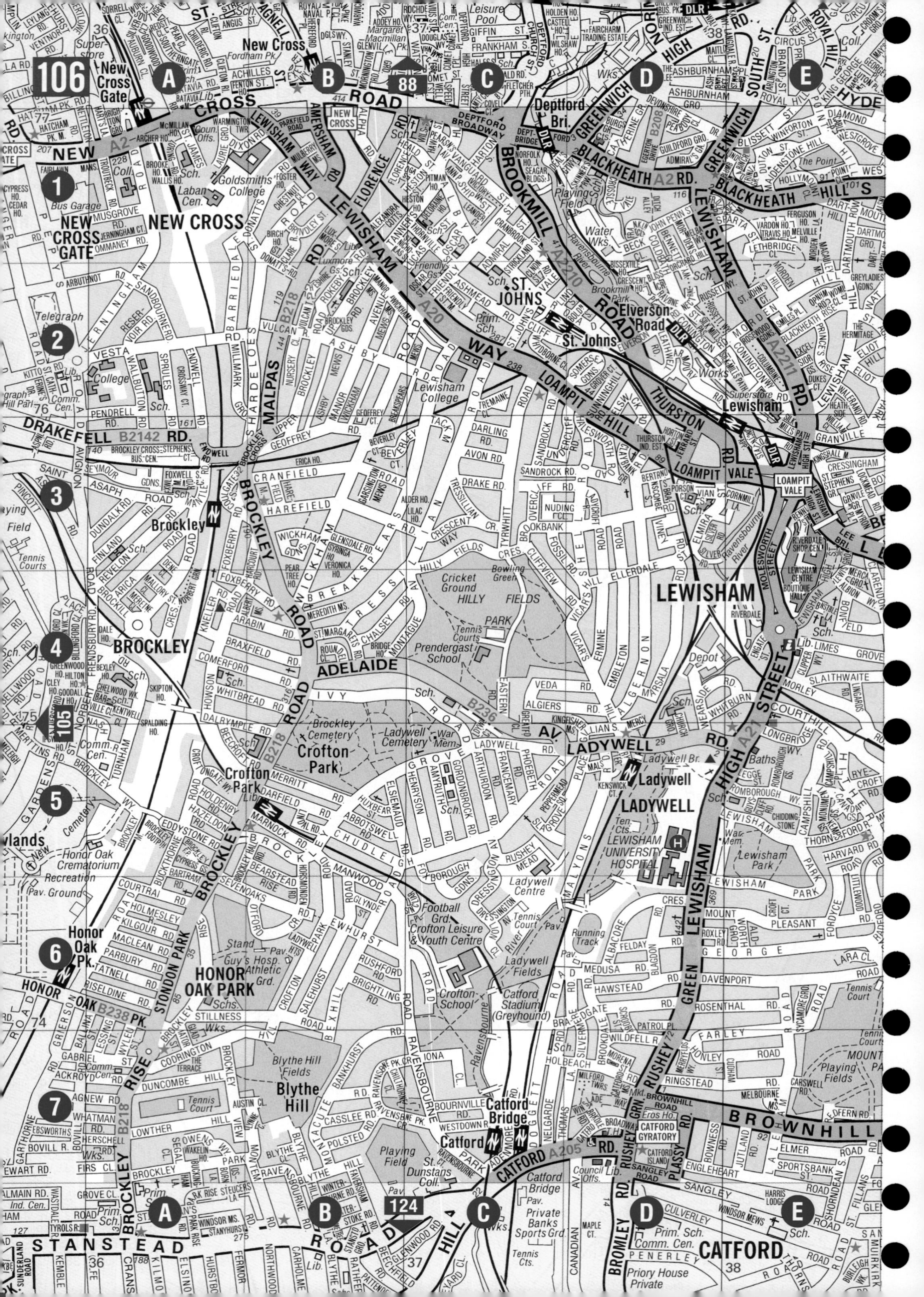

88
105
124
NEW CROSS
New Cross Gate
New Cross
NEW CROSS GATE
Goldsmiths College
Laban Cen.
Deptford Bri.
ST. JOHNS
St. Johns
Elverson Road
Lewisham
Lewisham College
BROCKLEY
Brockley
Telegraph Hill Park
Crofton Park
Brockley Cemetery
Ladywell Cemetery
HILLY FIELDS
Cricket Ground
Prendergast School
LEWISHAM
Ladywell
LADYWELL
LEWISHAM UNIVERSITY HOSPITAL
Lewisham Park
Ladywell Fields
Running Track
Football Grd. Crofton Leisure & Youth Centre
Crofton School
Catford Stadium (Greyhound)
Honor Oak Pk.
HONOR OAK PARK
Honor Oak Crematorium
Guy's Hosp. Athletic Grd.
Blythe Hill Fields
Blythe Hill
Catford Bridge
Catford
CATFORD GYRATORY
Private Banks Sports Grd.
Playing Field
Playing Fields
CATFORD
NEW CROSS ROAD
LEWISHAM WAY
BROCKMILL ROAD
LOAMPIT HILL
LOAMPIT VALE
THURSTON RD.
BLACKHEATH HILL
BLACKHEATH RD.
GREENWICH HIGH RD.
DRAKEFELL RD.
BROCKLEY ROAD
ADELAIDE AV.
LADYWELL RD.
LEWISHAM HIGH STREET
RUSHEY GREEN
STONDON PARK
BROCKLEY RISE
HONOR OAK PK.
BROWNHILL RD.
CATFORD RD.
STANSTEAD ROAD
A2
A20
A21
A205
A2210
A2211
B218
B236
B238
B2142

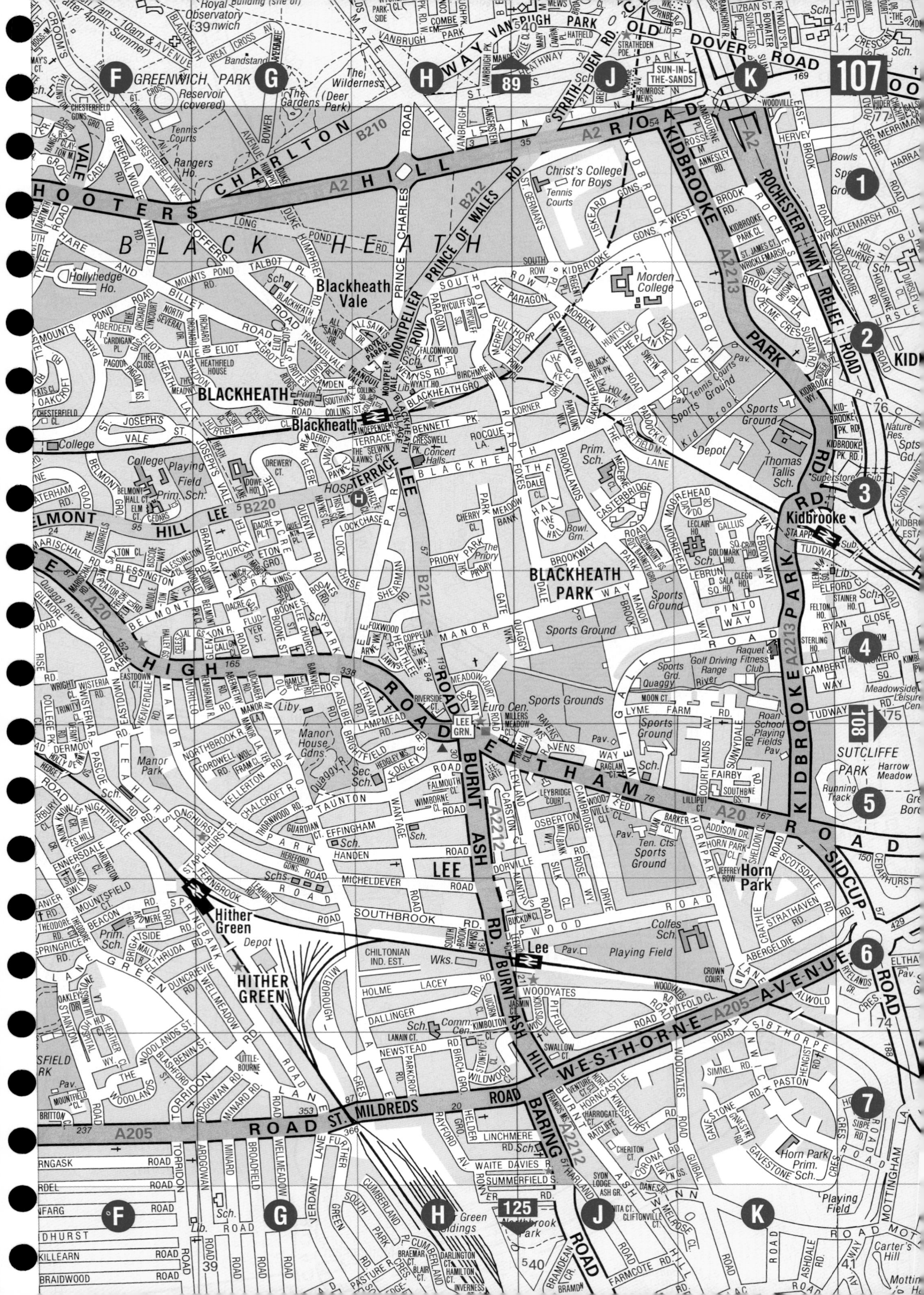

GREENWICH PARK
Reservoir (covered)
The Wilderness (Deer Park)
VANBRUGH PARK
OLD DOVER ROAD
SUN-IN-THE-SANDS
89
CHARLTON ROAD
SHOOTERS HILL
B L A C K H E A T H
Christ's College for Boys
KIDBROOKE PARK ROAD
ROCHESTER WAY RELIEF ROAD
PRINCE CHARLES ROAD
PRINCE OF WALES RD.
Blackheath Vale
BLACKHEATH
Blackheath
Morden College
A2213
Hollyhedge Ho.
BELMONT HILL
LEE TERRACE
LEE HIGH ROAD
BLACKHEATH PARK
Sports Ground
Kidbrooke
Thomas Tallis Sch.
Quaggy River
A20
Manor House Gdns.
Manor Park
LEE
BURNT ASH ROAD
ELTHAM ROAD
SIDCUP ROAD
108
175
SUTCLIFFE PARK
Horn Park
Hither Green
HITHER GREEN
Lee
Colfes Sch.
Playing Field
WESTHORNE AVENUE
A205
ST. MILDREDS ROAD
BARING ROAD
125
MOTTINGHAM

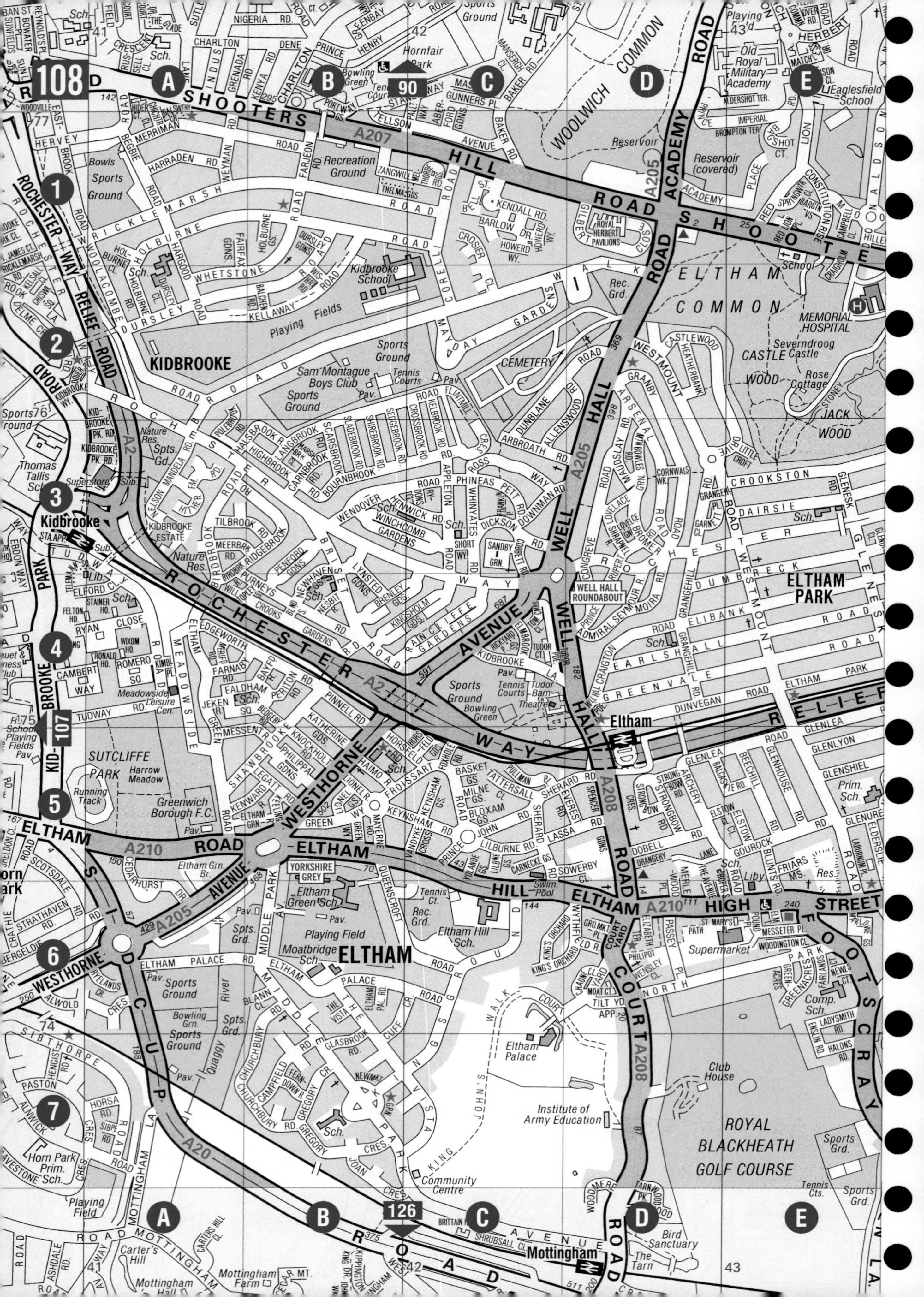

108
90
126
107
KIDBROOKE
ELTHAM
ELTHAM PARK
ELTHAM COMMON
WOOLWICH COMMON
SHOOTERS HILL ROAD
ROCHESTER WAY
ROCHESTER WAY RELIEF ROAD
WELL HALL ROAD
ELTHAM HIGH STREET
ELTHAM HILL
ELTHAM ROAD
WESTHORNE AVENUE
SIDCUP ROAD
COURT ROAD
FOOTSCRAY ROAD
MOTTINGHAM ROAD
KIDBROOKE PARK ROAD
Kidbrooke
Eltham
Mottingham
Eltham Palace
Royal Blackheath Golf Course
Memorial Hospital
Severndroog Castle
Castle Wood
Jack Wood
Sutcliffe Park
Well Hall Roundabout
Institute of Army Education
Kidbrooke School
Eltham Hill Sch.
Old Royal Military Academy
Eaglesfield School
Recreation Ground
Playing Fields
Cemetery
Greenwich Borough F.C.
Harrow Meadow
Running Track
Community Centre
Bird Sanctuary
The Tarn
Hornfair Park
Thomas Tallis Sch.
Sam Montague Boys Club
Tudor Barn Theatre
Club House
43

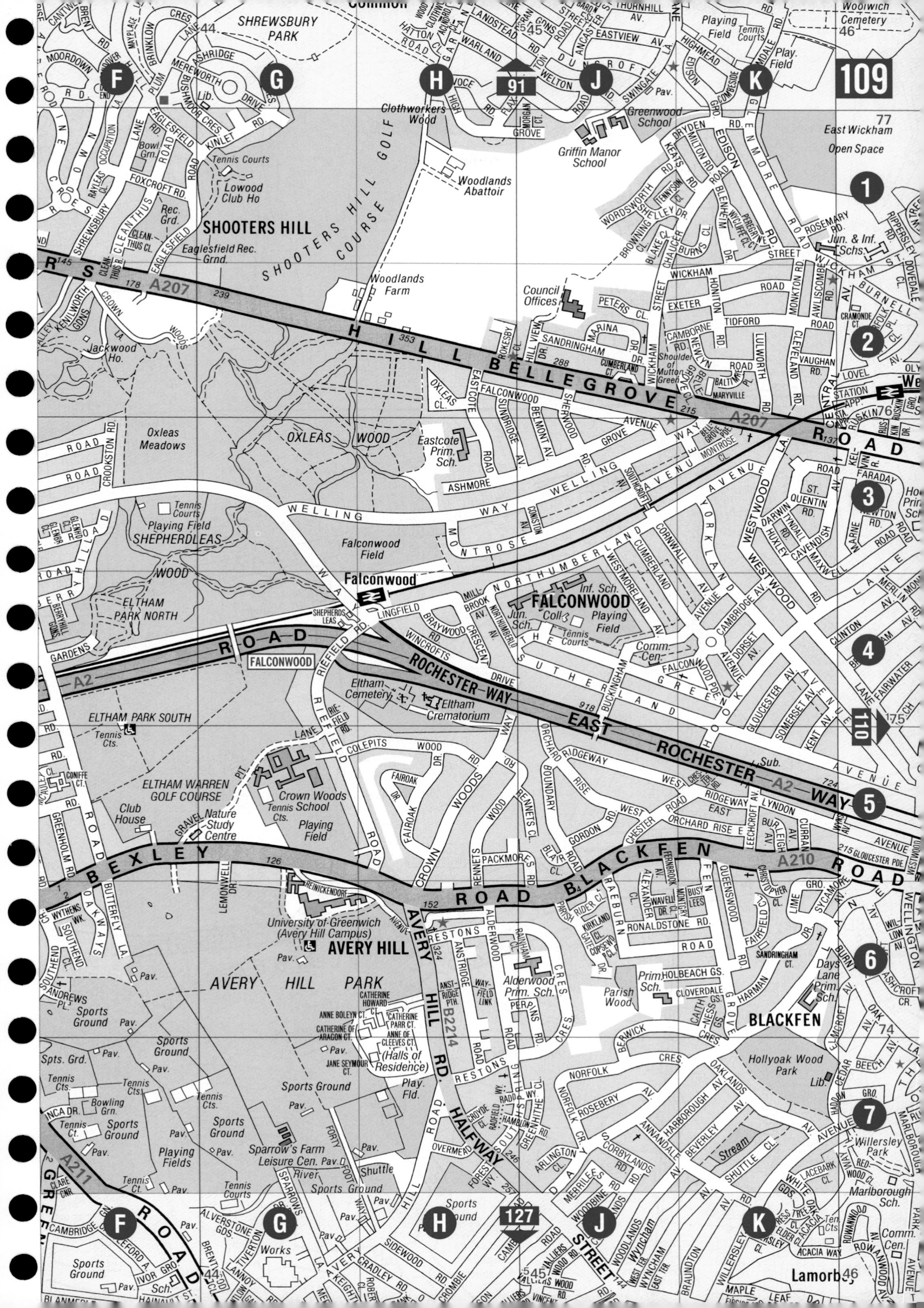
SHREWSBURY PARK
Woolwich Cemetery
Playing Field
Clothworkers Wood
Greenwood School
Griffin Manor School
East Wickham Open Space
Woodlands Abattoir
Lowood Club Ho
SHOOTERS HILL
Eaglesfield Rec. Grnd.
SHOOTERS HILL GOLF COURSE
Woodlands Farm
Council Offices
Jackwood Ho.
SHOOTERS HILL
BELLEGROVE ROAD
A207
Shoulder of Mutton Green
Oxleas Meadows
OXLEAS WOOD
Eastcote Prim. Sch.
WELLING WAY
Playing Field
SHEPHERDLEAS WOOD
Falconwood Field
Falconwood
ELTHAM PARK NORTH
FALCONWOOD
Jun. Sch.
Coll.
Inf. Sch.
Playing Field
Tennis Courts
Comm. Cen.
ROCHESTER WAY
EAST ROCHESTER WAY
A2
Eltham Cemetery
Eltham Crematorium
ELTHAM PARK SOUTH
ELTHAM WARREN GOLF COURSE
Club House
Nature Study Centre
Crown Woods School
Playing Field
BEXLEY ROAD
BLACKFEN ROAD
A210
University of Greenwich (Avery Hill Campus)
AVERY HILL
AVERY HILL PARK
AVERY HILL RD.
B2214
Alderwood Prim. Sch.
Parish Wood
Prim. Sch.
Days Lane Prim. Sch.
BLACKFEN
Hollyoak Wood Park
Lib.
Sports Ground
Sports Ground
Spts. Grd.
Bowling Grn.
Playing Fields
Sports Ground
Sparrow's Farm Leisure Cen.
HALFWAY STREET
Play. Fld.
River Shuttle
Stream
Willersley Park
Marlborough Sch.
A211
Sports Ground
Works
Comm. Cen.
Lamorbey
91
110
127
F G H J K
1 2 3 4 5 6 7

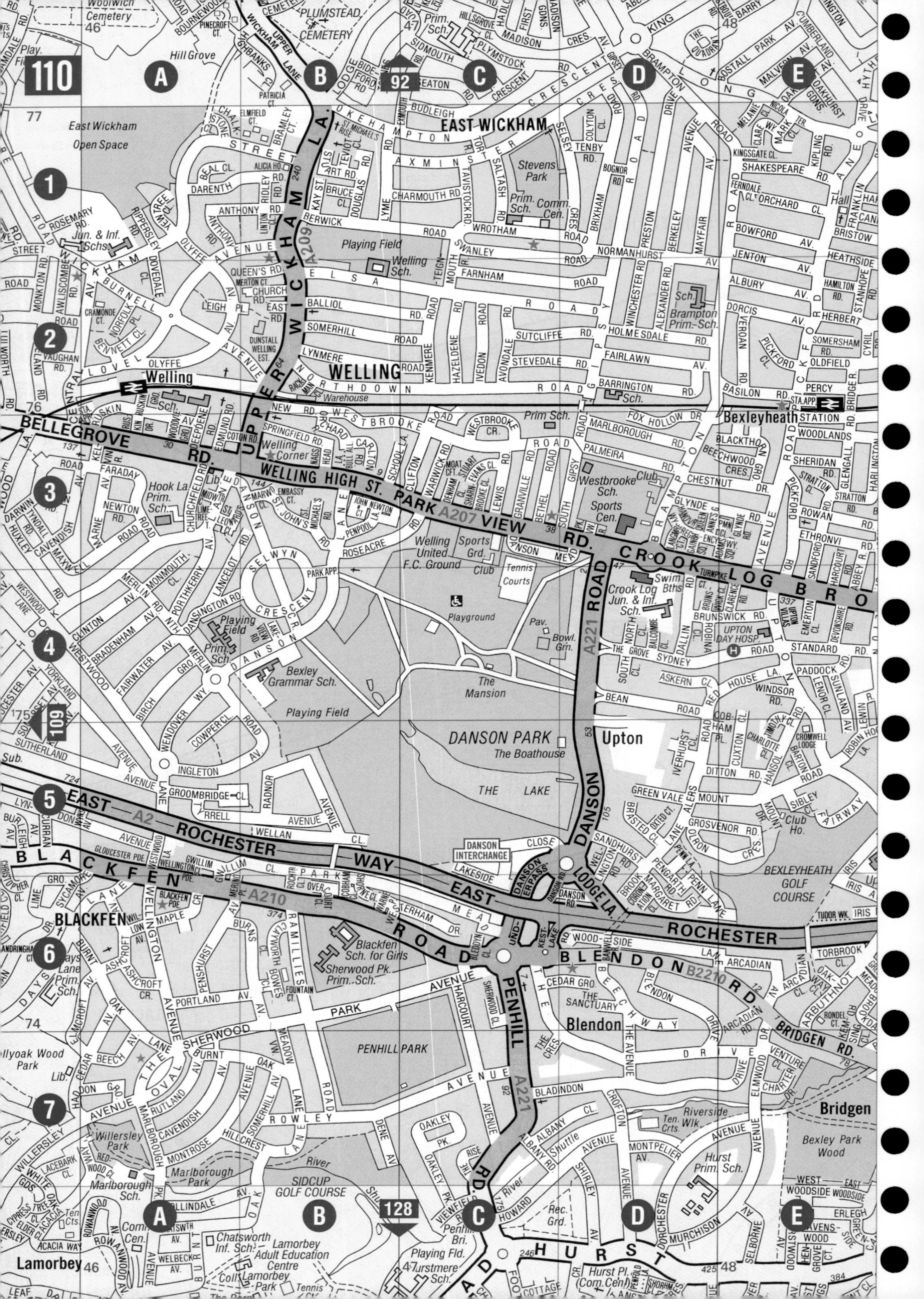
EAST WICKHAM
WELLING
Welling
Bexleyheath
Upton
DANSON PARK
The Boathouse
THE LAKE
The Mansion
BLACKFEN
Blendon
Bridgen
Lamorbey
East Wickham Open Space
Playing Field
Welling Sch.
Bexley Grammar Sch.
Welling United F.C. Ground
BEXLEYHEATH GOLF COURSE
SIDCUP GOLF COURSE
PENHILL PARK
Bexley Park Wood
DANSON INTERCHANGE
UPPER WICKHAM LA.
WELLING HIGH ST.
PARK VIEW RD.
BELLEGROVE RD.
CROOK LOG
DANSON ROAD
EAST ROCHESTER WAY
BLACKFEN ROAD
ROCHESTER
BLENDON RD.
PENHILL RD.
BRIDGEN RD.
HURST RD.
A209
A207
A221
A2
A210
B2210
92
109
128

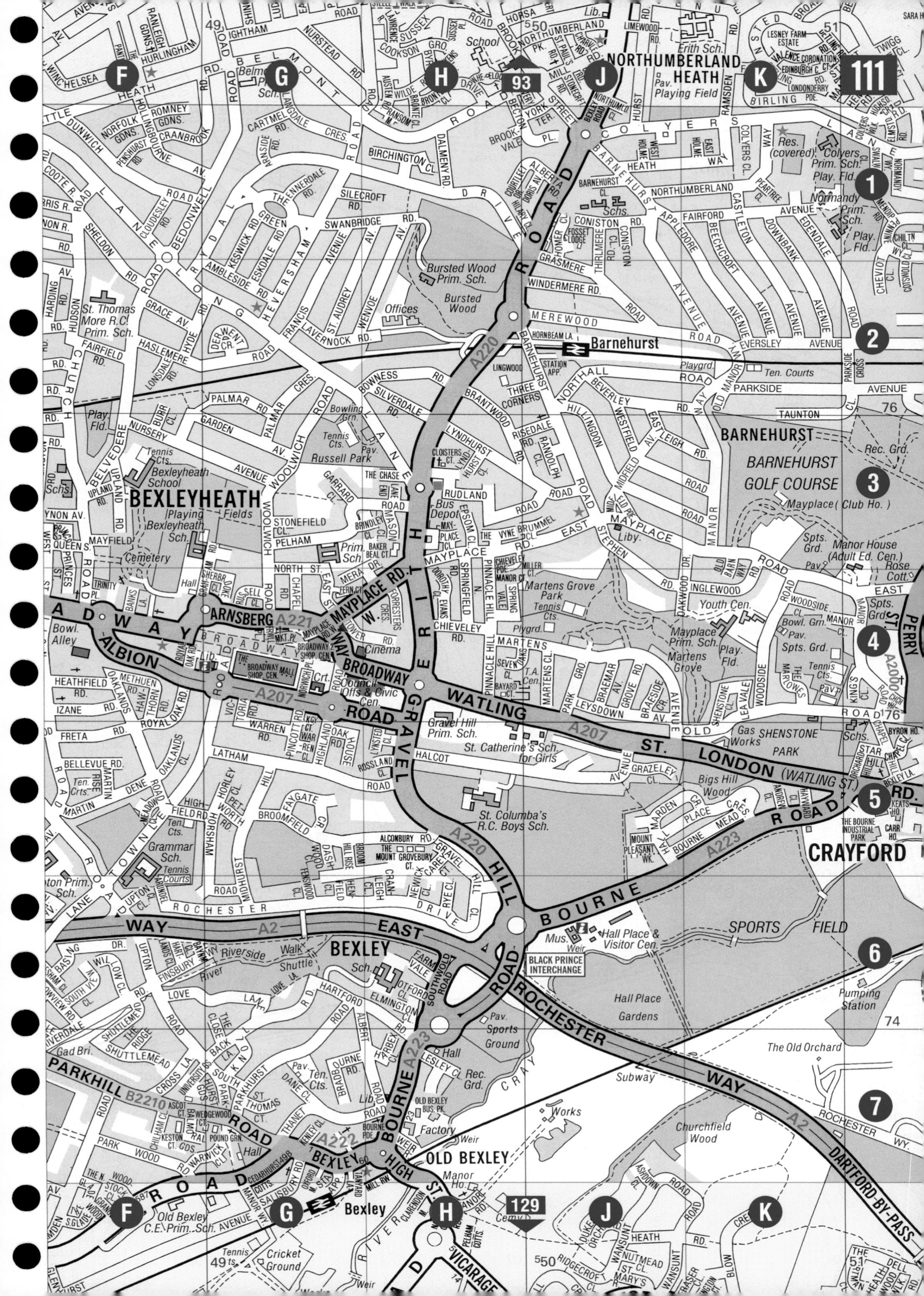

NORTHUMBERLAND HEATH
Erith Sch.
Playing Field
Lesney Farm Estate
93
Colyers Prim. Sch.
Normandy Prim. Sch.
Bursted Wood Prim. Sch.
Bursted Wood
St. Thomas More R.C. Prim. Sch.
Barnehurst
BARNEHURST
BARNEHURST GOLF COURSE
Mayplace (Club Ho.)
Manor House (Adult Ed. Cen.)
BEXLEYHEATH
Bexleyheath School
Playing Fields
Bexleyheath Sch.
Cemetery
Russell Park
Martens Grove Park
Mayplace Prim. Sch.
Youth Cen.
The Broadway Mall Shop. Cen.
Broadway Shop. Cen.
Council Offs & Civic Cen.
Cinema
Bus Depot
Gravel Hill Prim. Sch.
St. Catherine's Sch. for Girls
St. Columba's R.C. Boys Sch.
Bigs Hill Wood
Shenstone Park
The Bourne Industrial Park
CRAYFORD
Grammar Sch.
BEXLEY
Hall Place & Visitor Cen.
Black Prince Interchange
Sports Field
Hall Place Gardens
Pumping Station
The Old Orchard
Sports Ground
Churchfield Wood
OLD BEXLEY
Bexley
Old Bexley C.E. Prim. Sch.
Cricket Ground
129
A2
A220
A221
A207
A223
A222
B2210
A2000
WATLING ST.
LONDON RD. (WATLING ST.)
BROADWAY
GRAVEL HILL
BOURNE RD.
ROCHESTER WAY
DARTFORD-BY-PASS
BEXLEY RD.
PARKHILL ROAD
BARNEHURST RD.
COLYERS LA.
MAYPLACE RD.
ALBION ROAD
ARNSBERG WAY
F G H J K
1 2 3 4 5 6 7

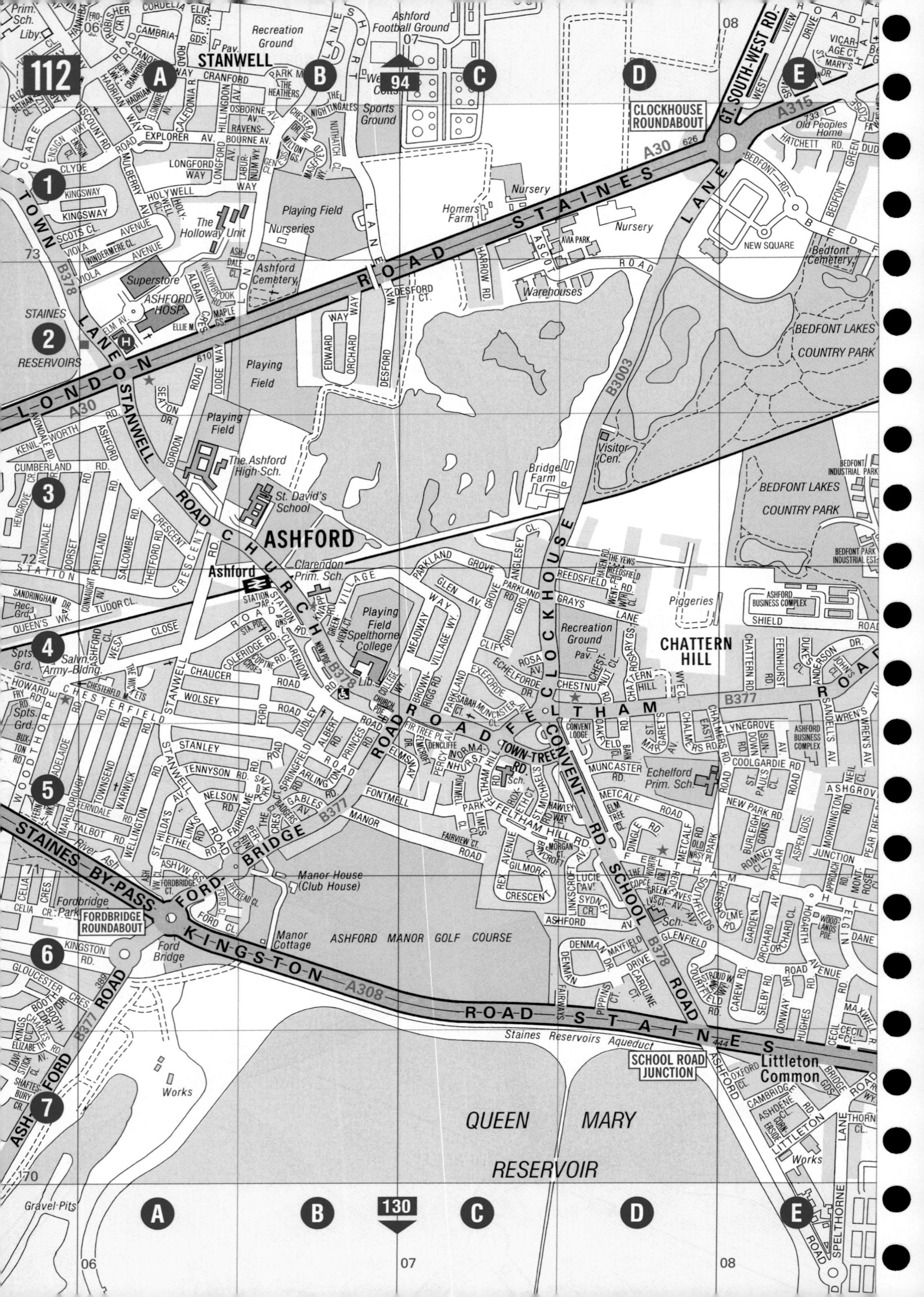
STANWELL
Recreation Ground
Ashford Football Ground
Sports Ground
94
CLOCKHOUSE ROUNDABOUT
GT. SOUTH-WEST RD.
A315
Old Peoples Home
HATCHETT RD.
BEDFONT RD.
NEW SQUARE
Bedfont Cemetery
BEDFONT LAKES COUNTRY PARK
BEDFONT INDUSTRIAL PARK
BEDFONT PARK INDUSTRIAL EST.
ASHFORD BUSINESS COMPLEX
SHIELD ROAD
CHATTERN HILL
Piggeries
A30
LONDON ROAD
STAINES ROAD
CLOCKHOUSE LANE
B3003
Nursery
Homers Farm
AVIA PARK
Warehouses
Visitor Cen.
Bridge Farm
STAINES RESERVOIRS
The Holloway Unit
Superstore
ASHFORD HOSP.
Ashford Cemetery
Playing Field
Nurseries
The Ashford High Sch.
St. David's School
ASHFORD
Ashford
Clarendon Prim. Sch.
Spelthorne College
Lib.
CHURCH ROAD
STATION ROAD
STANWELL ROAD
B378
B377
FELTHAM ROAD
FELTHAM HILL RD.
TOWN TREE RD.
CONVENT RD.
SCHOOL RD.
Recreation Ground
Echelford Prim. Sch.
Sch.
STAINES-BY-PASS
FORDBRIDGE ROUNDABOUT
FORD BRIDGE ROAD
Fordbridge Park
Ford Bridge
Manor House (Club House)
Manor Cottage
ASHFORD MANOR GOLF COURSE
KINGSTON ROAD
A308
Staines Reservoirs Aqueduct
SCHOOL ROAD JUNCTION
Littleton Common
QUEEN MARY RESERVOIR
Works
Gravel Pits
SPELTHORNE LANE
130
A B C D E
1 2 3 4 5 6 7
06 07 08
70 71 72 73

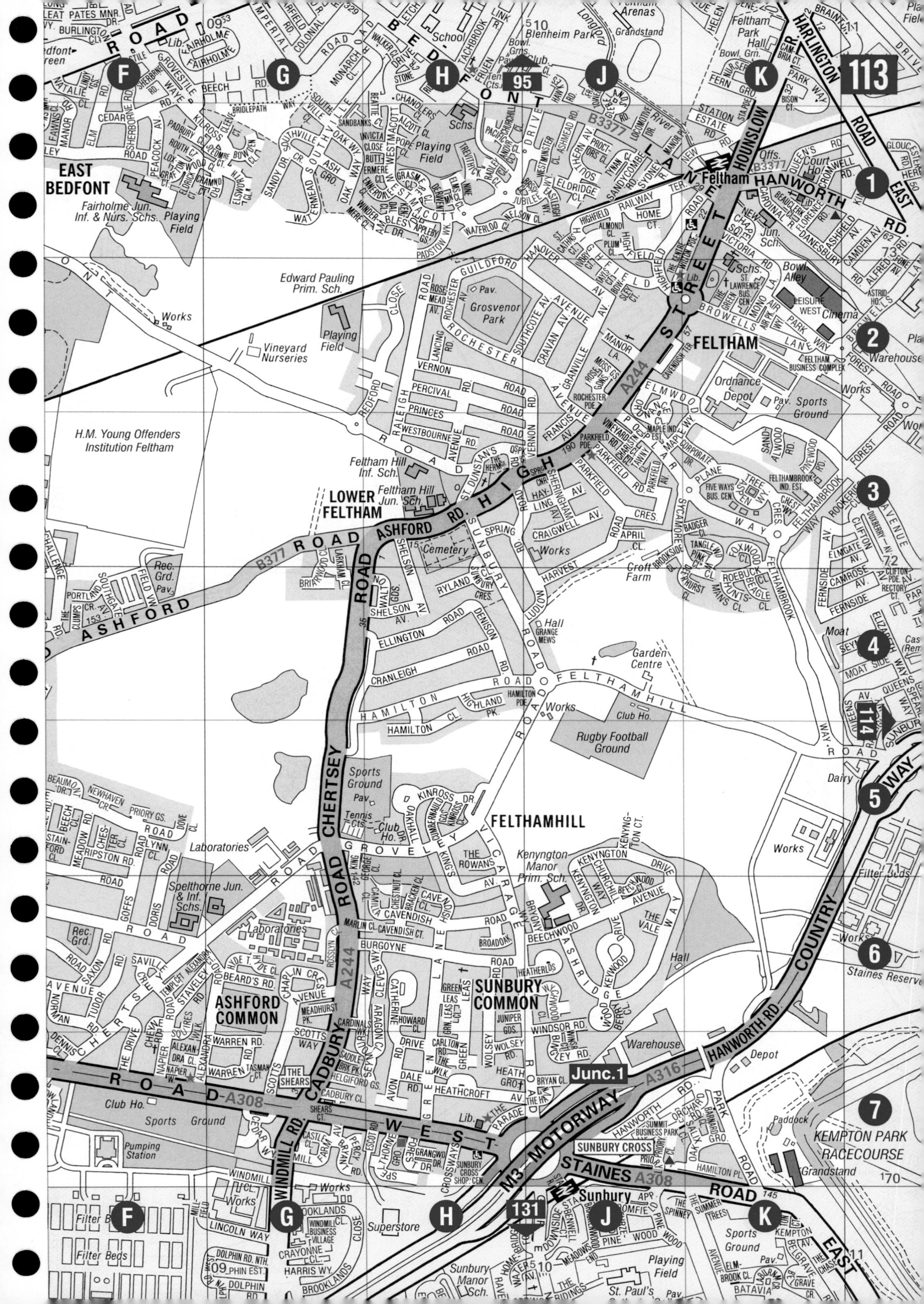
95
EAST BEDFONT
Fairholme Jun. Inf. & Nurs. Schs.
Playing Field
Edward Pauling Prim. Sch.
Vineyard Nurseries
Works
H.M. Young Offenders Institution Feltham
Grosvenor Park
Feltham
FELTHAM
HANWORTH RD.
HOUNSLOW RD.
HIGH STREET
A244
B3377
Leisure West Cinema
Bowl. Alley
Ordnance Depot
Sports Ground
Warehouse
FELTHAMBROOK IND. EST.
FIVE WAYS BUS. CEN.
LOWER FELTHAM
Feltham Hill Inf. Sch.
Feltham Hill Jun. Sch.
ASHFORD ROAD
B377
Cemetery
Croft Farm
Garden Centre
FELTHAM HILL ROAD
Rugby Football Ground
Club Ho.
CHERTSEY ROAD
FELTHAMHILL
Kenyngton Manor Prim. Sch.
Laboratories
Spelthorne Jun. & Inf. Schs.
ASHFORD COMMON
SUNBURY COMMON
STAINES ROAD WEST
A308
Junc.1
M3 MOTORWAY
A316
HANWORTH RD.
COUNTRY WAY
114
SUNBURY CROSS
STAINES ROAD EAST
Sunbury
131
Superstore
Pumping Station
Filter Beds
Sports Ground
Dairy
Depot
KEMPTON PARK RACECOURSE
Grandstand
Paddock
Staines Reservoir
Sunbury Manor Sch.
St. Paul's
Playing Field
F G H J K
1 2 3 4 5 6 7

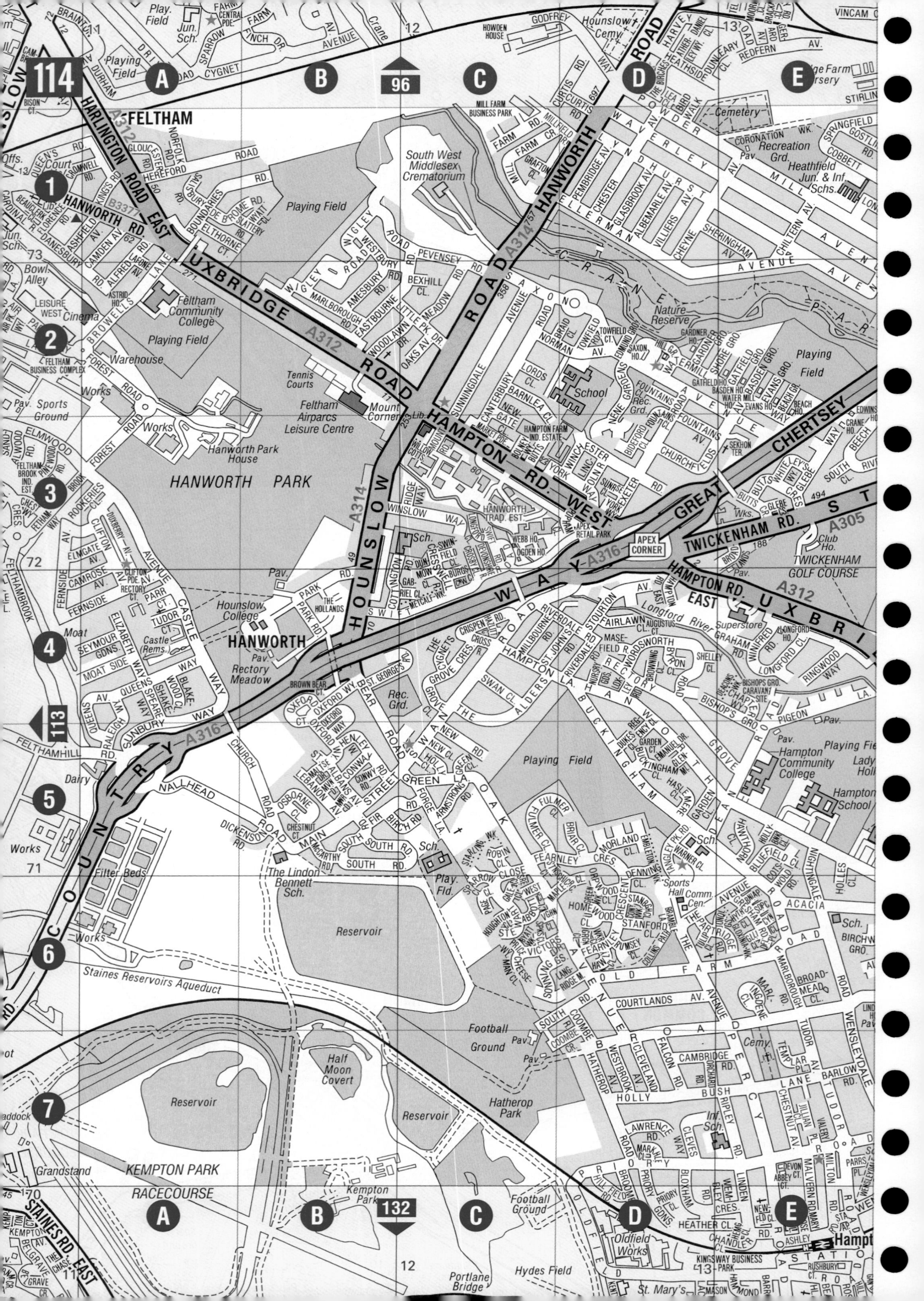

114
96
132
113
A
B
C
D
E
1
2
3
4
5
6
7
12
13
FELTHAM
HANWORTH
HANWORTH PARK
Hanworth Park House
Hounslow College
Feltham Community College
Feltham Airparcs Leisure Centre
Mount Corner
South West Middlesex Crematorium
Mill Farm Business Park
Howden House
Hounslow Cemy.
Playing Field
Tennis Courts
Warehouse
Works
Sports Ground
Bowl Alley
Leisure West Cinema
Feltham Business Complex
Feltham Brook Ind. Est.
Castle (Rems.)
Moat
Rectory Meadow
Dairy
Filter Beds
Staines Reservoirs Aqueduct
The Lindon Bennett Sch.
Reservoir
Half Moon Covert
Football Ground
Hatherop Park
Kempton Park
KEMPTON PARK RACECOURSE
Grandstand
Portlane Bridge
Hydes Field
Oldfield Works
Kingsway Business Park
Hanworth Trad. Est.
Apex Retail Park
APEX CORNER
Hampton Farm Ind. Estate
School
Nature Reserve
Recreation Grd.
Heathfield Jun. & Inf. Schs.
Cemetery
TWICKENHAM GOLF COURSE
Club Ho.
Superstore
Longford River
Bishops Gro. Caravan Site
Hampton Community College
Hampton School
Lady Holl
Sports Hall
Comm. Cen.
Cemy.
Inf. Sch.
Play. Fld.
Rec. Grd.
UXBRIDGE ROAD
HARLINGTON ROAD EAST
HANWORTH RD.
HANWORTH ROAD
HOUNSLOW ROAD
HAMPTON RD. WEST
HAMPTON RD. EAST
GREAT CHERTSEY
TWICKENHAM RD.
COUNTRY WAY
A312
A314
A316
A305
B3377
CRANE PARK
CRANE AVENUE
STAINES RD. EAST
OLD FARM ROAD
PRIORY ROAD
PERCY ROAD
BUCKINGHAM ROAD
WORTHING
HAMPTON LA.
OAK AVENUE
ACACIA ROAD
BEAR ROAD
CHURCH ROAD
SWAN ROAD
MAIN STREET
NALLHEAD ROAD
SUNBURY WAY
CASTLE WAY
FOREST ROAD
POWDER MILL LANE
WAVERLEY
LYNDHURST
STATION

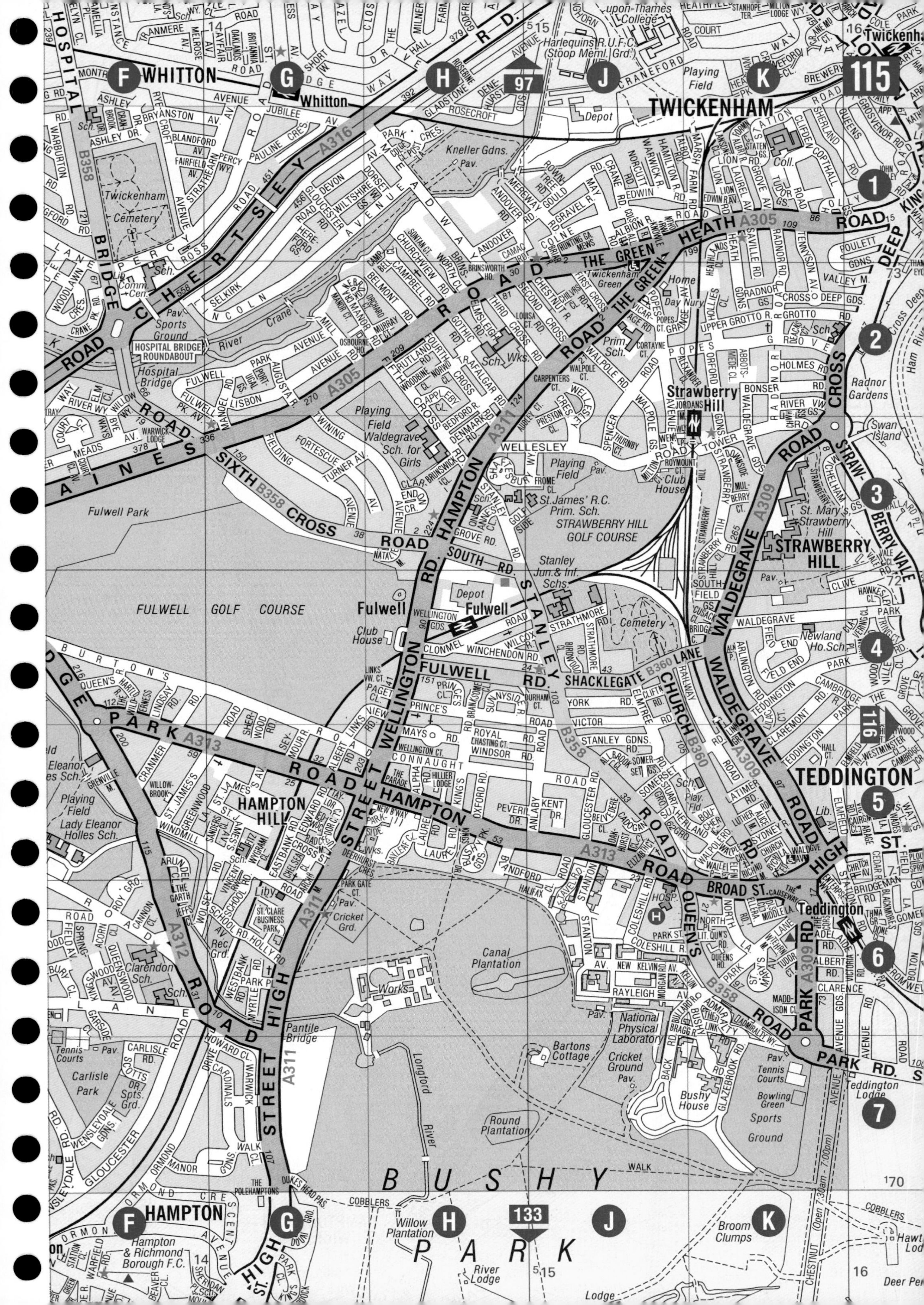

115
WHITTON
TWICKENHAM
Twickenham Cemetery
Kneller Gdns.
Twickenham Green
Strawberry Hill
STRAWBERRY HILL
STRAWBERRY HILL GOLF COURSE
St. Mary's Strawberry Hill
Radnor Gardens
Swan Island
Fulwell
Fulwell Park
FULWELL GOLF COURSE
HAMPTON HILL
TEDDINGTON
Teddington
HAMPTON
Hampton & Richmond Borough F.C.
Canal Plantation
National Physical Laboratory
Bushy House
Round Plantation
Pantile Bridge
Longford River
Willow Plantation
Broom Clumps
BUSHY PARK
Harlequins R.U.F.C. (Stoop Meml. Grd.)
Hospital Bridge Roundabout
Teddington Lodge
Sports Ground
97
116
133

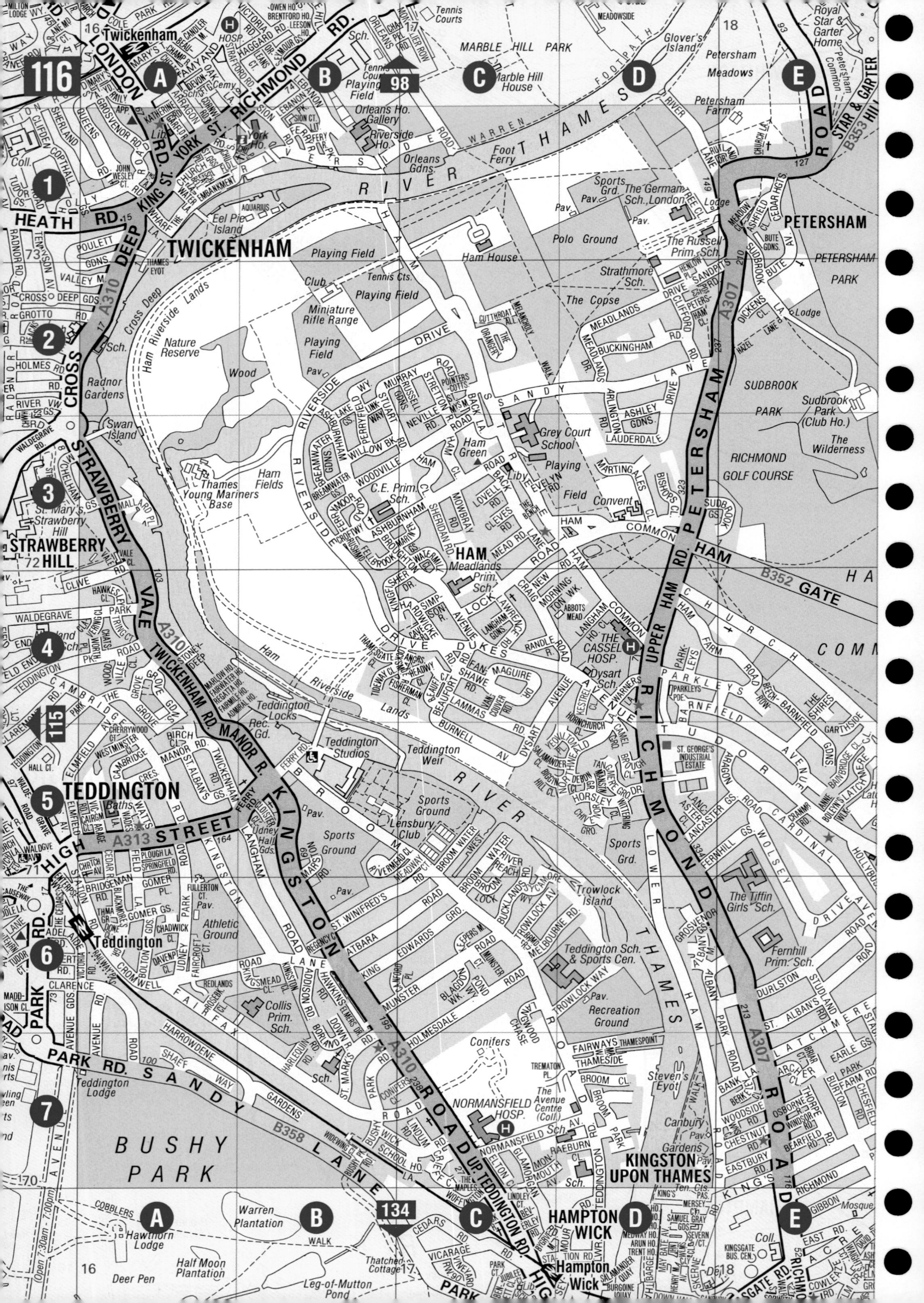

116
98
115
134
A
B
C
D
E
1
2
3
4
5
6
7
16
17
18
Twickenham
TWICKENHAM
MARBLE HILL PARK
Marble Hill House
Orleans Ho. Gallery
Riverside Ho.
Orleans Gdns.
York Ho.
Glover's Island
Petersham Meadows
Petersham Farm
Royal Star & Garter Home
Petersham Common
RIVER THAMES
Foot Ferry
WARREN FOOTPATH
Eel Pie Island
Ham House
Playing Field
Polo Ground
Sports Grd.
The German Sch., London
The Russell Prim. Sch.
Strathmore Sch.
The Copse
PETERSHAM
PETERSHAM PARK
SUDBROOK PARK
Sudbrook Park (Club Ho.)
The Wilderness
RICHMOND GOLF COURSE
Miniature Rifle Range
Tennis Cts.
Nature Reserve
Ham Riverside Lands
Cross Deep
Radnor Gardens
Swan Island
Wood
Ham Fields
Thames Young Mariners Base
Grey Court School
Ham Green
C.E. Prim. Sch.
Convent
HAM
Meadlands Prim. Sch.
The Cassel Hosp.
Dysart Sch.
St. George's Industrial Estate
Sports Grd.
The Tiffin Girls' Sch.
Fernhill Prim. Sch.
STRAWBERRY HILL
St. Mary's, Strawberry Hill
Teddington Locks
Rec. Gd.
Teddington Studios
Teddington Weir
Riverside Lands
Sports Ground
Lensbury Club
Trowlock Island
Teddington Sch. & Sports Cen.
Recreation Ground
TEDDINGTON
Teddington
Athletic Ground
Collis Prim. Sch.
Conifers
Steven's Eyot
NORMANSFIELD HOSP.
The Avenue Centre (Coll.)
Canbury Gardens
KINGSTON UPON THAMES
HAMPTON WICK
Hampton Wick
BUSHY PARK
Teddington Lodge
Hawthorn Lodge
Warren Plantation
Half Moon Plantation
Deer Pen
Thatched Cottage
Leg-of-Mutton Pond
(Open 7:30am - 7:00pm)
RICHMOND RD.
LONDON RD.
YORK ST.
KING ST.
HEATH RD.
CROSS DEEP
STRAWBERRY VALE
TWICKENHAM RD.
MANOR R.
KINGSTON ROAD
UP. TEDDINGTON RD.
A310
A313
A307
B352
B353
B358
HIGH STREET
PARK RD.
SANDY LANE
HAM COMMON
HAM GATE
UPPER HAM RD.
PETERSHAM RD.
RICHMOND ROAD
SANDY LANE
RIVERSIDE DRIVE
DUKES AVENUE
LOWER HAM RD.
STAR & GARTER HILL
CHURCH RD.
TUDOR DRIVE
LATCHMERE
CARDINAL AVE.
KING'S RD.

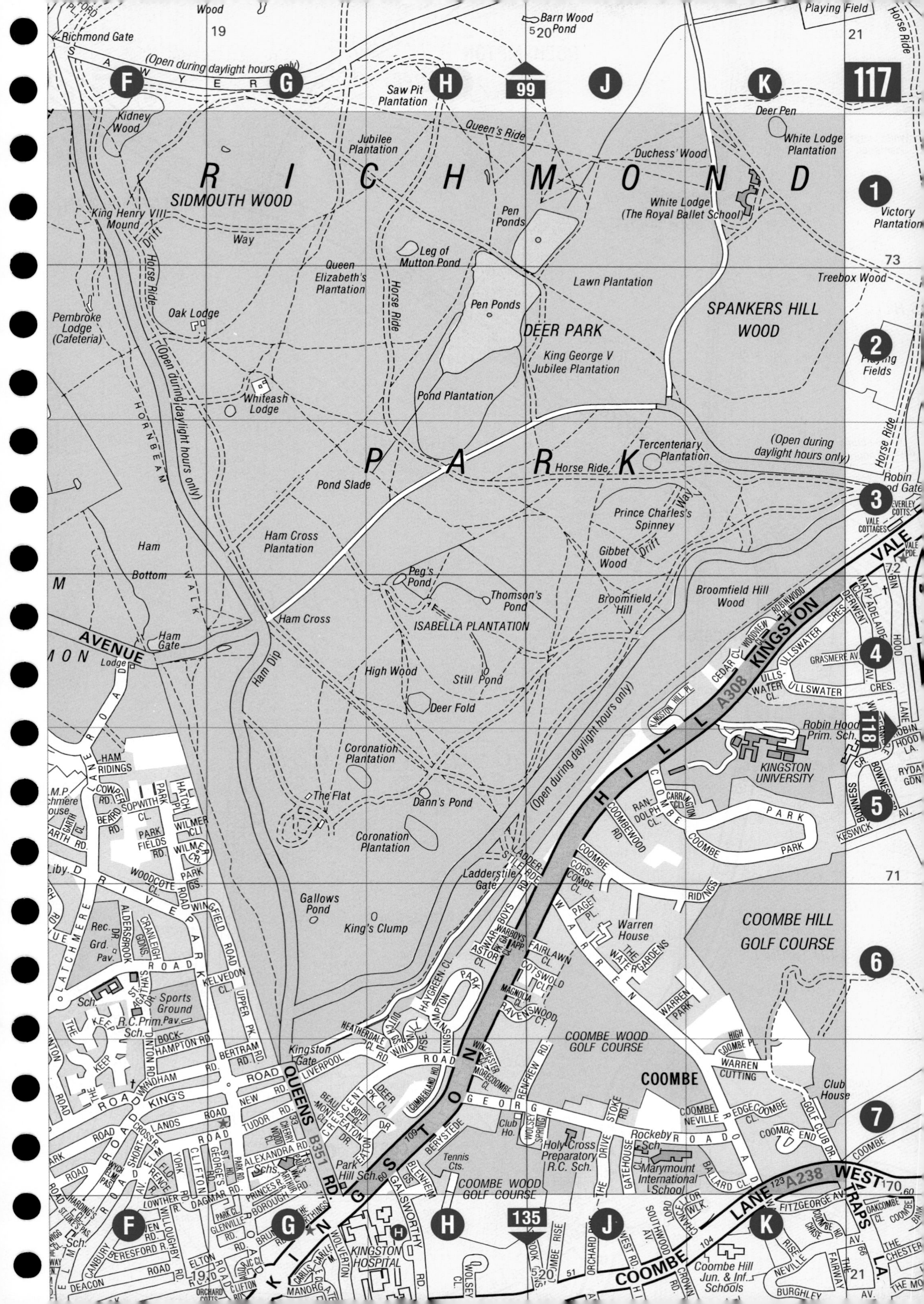
RICHMOND PARK
SIDMOUTH WOOD
Richmond Gate
Kidney Wood
King Henry VIII Mound
Pembroke Lodge (Cafeteria)
Oak Lodge
Whiteash Lodge
Saw Pit Plantation
Jubilee Plantation
Queen's Ride
Queen Elizabeth's Plantation
Leg of Mutton Pond
Pen Ponds
Duchess' Wood
White Lodge (The Royal Ballet School)
Deer Pen
White Lodge Plantation
Victory Plantation
Treebox Wood
Lawn Plantation
SPANKERS HILL WOOD
DEER PARK
King George V Jubilee Plantation
Pond Plantation
Playing Fields
Playing Field
Barn Wood Pond
Tercentenary Plantation
(Open during daylight hours only)
Horse Ride
Robin Hood Gate
Pond Slade
Prince Charles's Spinney
Gibbet Wood
Ham Cross Plantation
Ham Bottom
Ham Cross
Ham Gate
Ham Dip
Peg's Pond
Thomson's Pond
ISABELLA PLANTATION
Broomfield Hill
Broomfield Hill Wood
High Wood
Still Pond
Deer Fold
Coronation Plantation
The Flat
Dann's Pond
Ladderstile Gate
Gallows Pond
King's Clump
Kingston Gate
HORNBEAM WALK
KINGSTON HILL
KINGSTON VALE
Robin Hood Prim. Sch.
KINGSTON UNIVERSITY
COOMBE PARK
COOMBE HILL GOLF COURSE
Warren House
COOMBE WOOD GOLF COURSE
COOMBE
Club House
Holy Cross Preparatory R.C. Sch.
Rockeby Sch.
Marymount International School
Park Hill Sch.
KINGSTON HOSPITAL
Coombe Hill Jun. & Inf. Schools
QUEENS RD.
KING'S ROAD
LIVERPOOL ROAD
GEORGE ROAD
WARREN ROAD
COOMBE LANE WEST
TRAPS LA.
Sports Ground
R.C. Prim. Sch.
Rec. Grd.
PARK FIELDS
HAM RIDINGS
Tennis Cts.

99
118
135

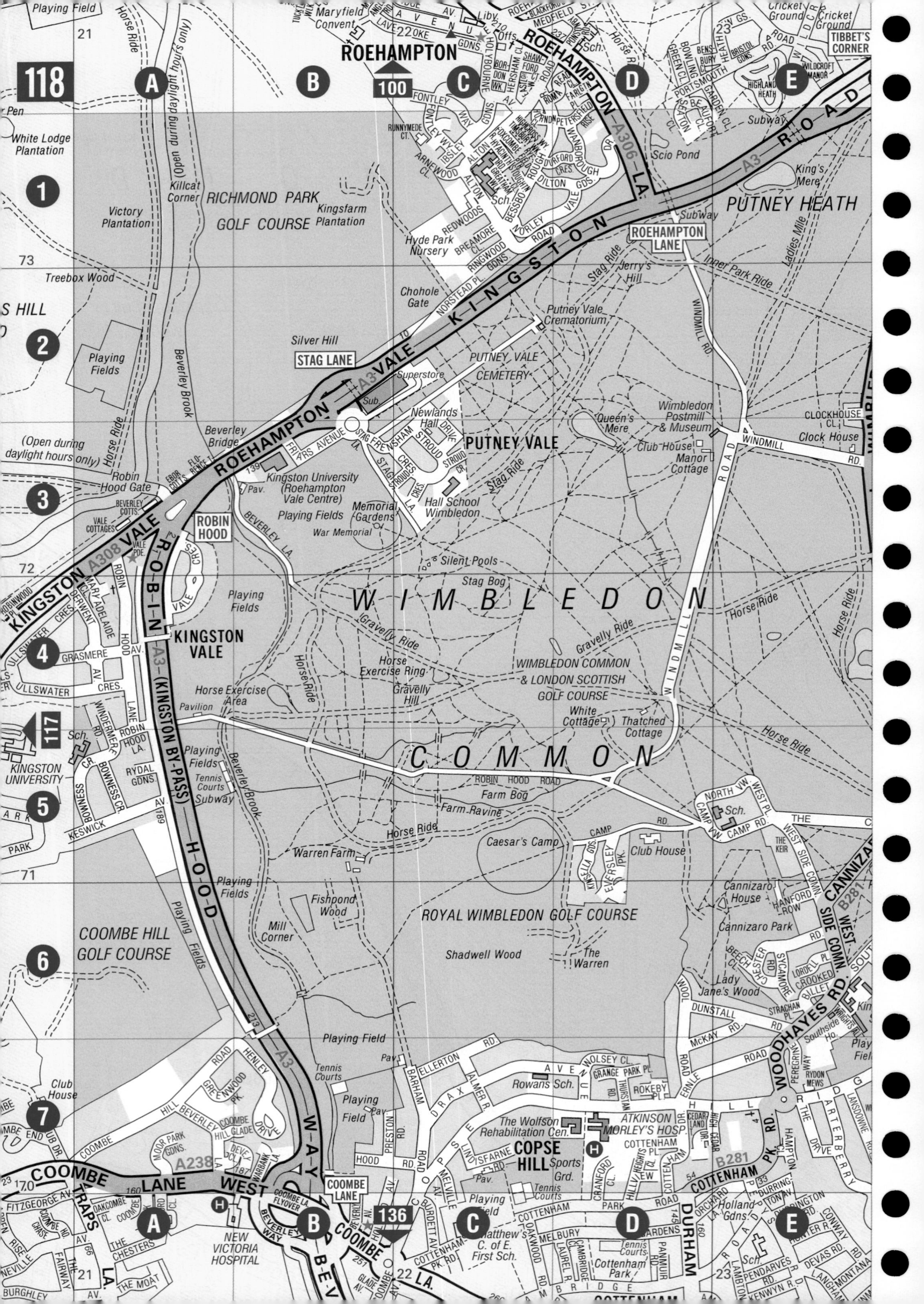
ROEHAMPTON
100
RICHMOND PARK GOLF COURSE
Killcat Corner
Victory Plantation
Kingsfarm Plantation
White Lodge Plantation
Treebox Wood
Playing Fields
Beverley Brook
Horse Ride
(Open during daylight hours only)
Robin Hood Gate
Beverley Bridge
Silver Hill
STAG LANE
KINGSTON VALE
ROEHAMPTON VALE
ROEHAMPTON LANE
PUTNEY HEATH
Scio Pond
King's Mere
TIBBET'S CORNER
Hyde Park Nursery
Chohole Gate
Putney Vale Crematorium
PUTNEY VALE CEMETERY
Superstore
Newlands Hall
PUTNEY VALE
Kingston University (Roehampton Vale Centre)
Memorial Gardens
War Memorial
Hall School Wimbledon
ROBIN HOOD
Queen's Mere
Wimbledon Postmill & Museum
Club House
Manor Cottage
Jerry's Hill
Stag Ride
Inner Park Ride
Clock House
Silent Pools
Stag Bog
WIMBLEDON COMMON
Gravelly Ride
Horse Exercise Ring
Gravelly Hill
WIMBLEDON COMMON & LONDON SCOTTISH GOLF COURSE
White Cottage
Thatched Cottage
Horse Exercise Area
Pavilion
KINGSTON VALE
117
KINGSTON UNIVERSITY
ROBIN HOOD (KINGSTON BY-PASS)
Farm Bog
Farm Ravine
Caesar's Camp
Warren Farm
Club House
Fishpond Wood
Mill Corner
ROYAL WIMBLEDON GOLF COURSE
Shadwell Wood
The Warren
Cannizaro House
Cannizaro Park
Lady Jane's Wood
COOMBE HILL GOLF COURSE
Playing Field
Tennis Courts
Rowans Sch.
The Wolfson Rehabilitation Cen.
ATKINSON MORLEY'S HOSP.
COPSE HILL
Sports Grd.
COOMBE LANE WEST
COOMBE LANE
136
NEW VICTORIA HOSPITAL
St. Matthew's C. of E. First Sch.
Cottenham Park
Holland Gdns.
DURHAM RD.
WOODHAYES RD.
CANNIZARO RD.
A3
A306
A308
A238
B281
21
22
23
73
72
71
170
A B C D E
1 2 3 4 5 6 7

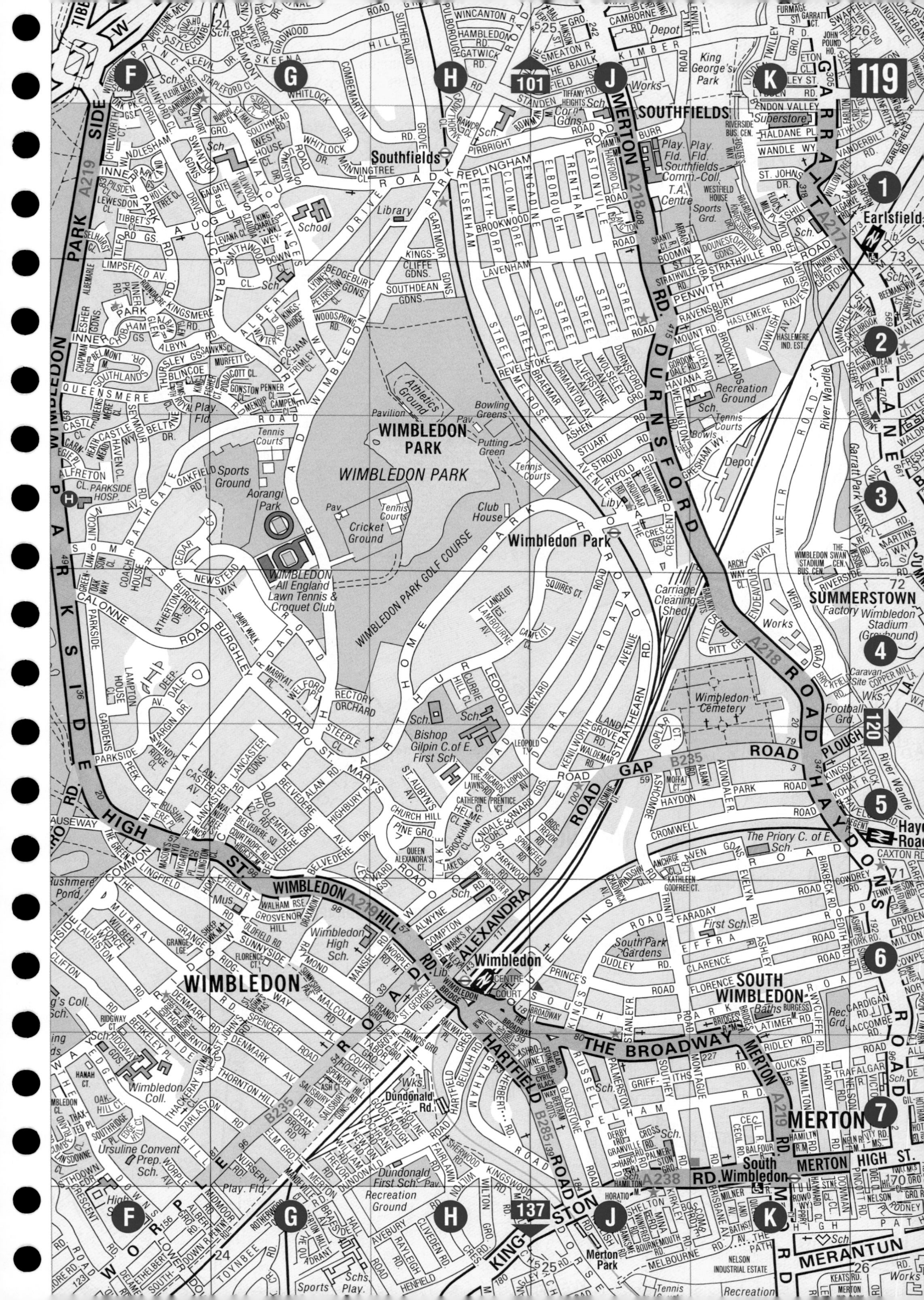

SOUTHFIELDS
Southfields
King George's Park
Superstore
Earlsfield
Play. Fld.
Southfields Comm. Coll.
T.A. Centre
Sports Grd.
Recreation Ground
Tennis Courts
Depot
River Wandle
WIMBLEDON PARK
WIMBLEDON PARK
Athletics Ground
Pavilion
Bowling Greens
Putting Green
Club House
Cricket Ground
WIMBLEDON PARK GOLF COURSE
Wimbledon Park
WIMBLEDON
All England Lawn Tennis & Croquet Club
Aorangi Park
Sports Ground
PARKSIDE HOSP.
Carriage Cleaning Shed
SUMMERSTOWN
Factory
Wimbledon Stadium (Greyhound)
Caravan Site
Football Grd.
Wimbledon Cemetery
Bishop Gilpin C. of E. First Sch.
The Priory C. of E. Sch.
First Sch.
South Park Gardens
SOUTH WIMBLEDON
Baths
Rec. Grd.
MERTON
MERTON HIGH ST.
South Wimbledon
Haydons Road
WIMBLEDON
Wimbledon
Wimbledon High Sch.
Wimbledon Coll.
Ursuline Convent Prep. Sch.
Rushmere Pond
Mus.
Lib.
Dundonald Rd.
Dundonald First Sch.
Recreation Ground
Merton Park
NELSON INDUSTRIAL ESTATE
PARKSIDE
WIMBLEDON PARK SIDE
A219
A218
A217
A238
B235
B285
HIGH ST.
WIMBLEDON HILL RD.
ALEXANDRA RD.
THE BROADWAY
HARTFIELD RD.
KINGSTON ROAD
DURNSFORD RD.
MERTON RD.
GARRATT LANE
HAYDONS ROAD
PLOUGH LANE
GAP ROAD
ARTHUR RD.
HOME PARK RD.
WORPLE RD.
QUEENSMERE RD.
VICTORIA DRIVE
REPLINGHAM RD.
MERANTUN WAY
F
G
H
J
K
1
2
3
4
5
6
7
101
120
137
24
25
26

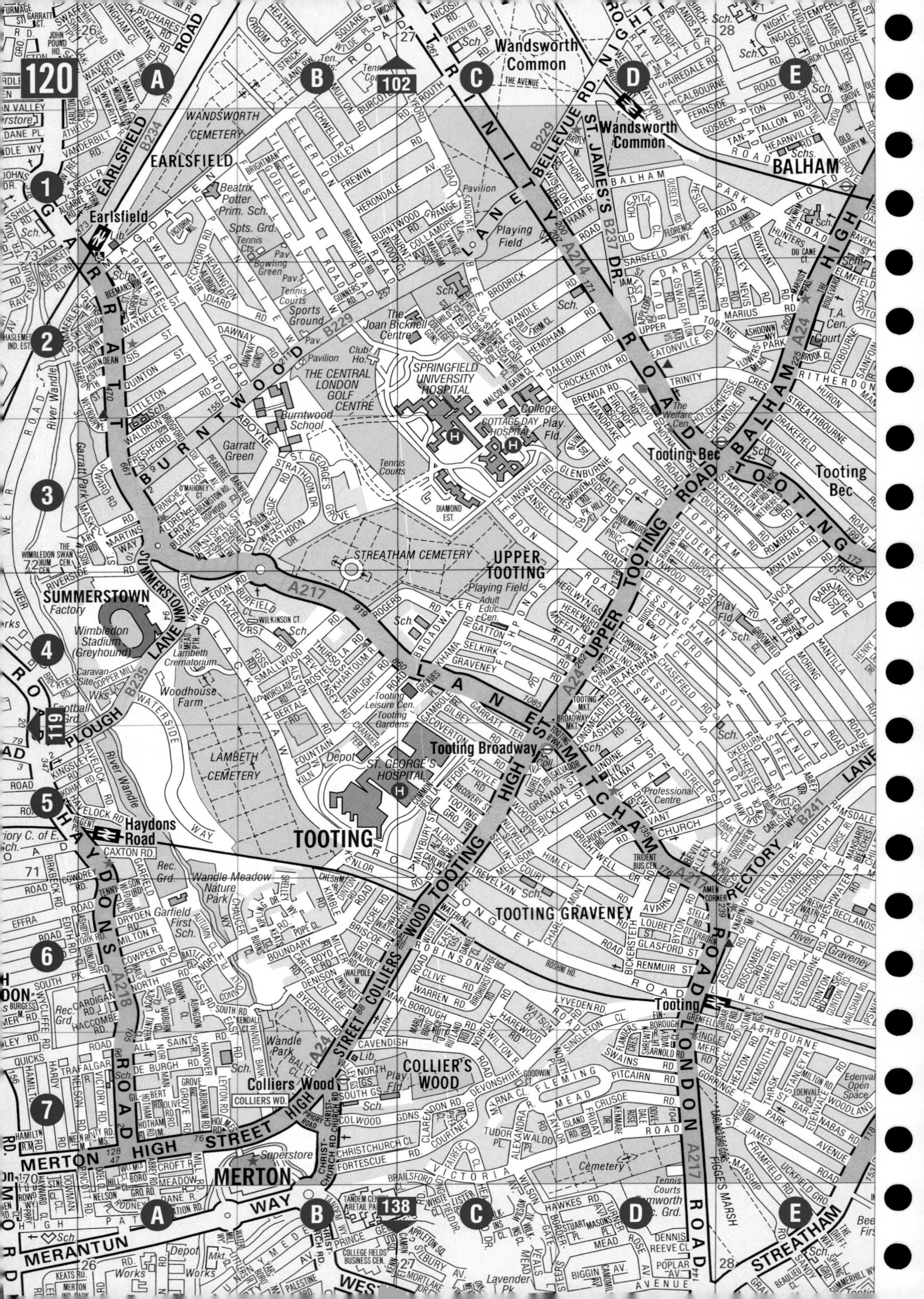

102
Wandsworth Common
WANDSWORTH CEMETERY
EARLSFIELD
Earlsfield
BALHAM
Beatrix Potter Prim. Sch.
The Joan Bicknell Centre
THE CENTRAL LONDON GOLF CENTRE
SPRINGFIELD UNIVERSITY HOSPITAL
COTTAGE DAY HOSPITAL
Burntwood School
Garratt Green
Garratt Park
River Wandle
Tooting Bec
STREATHAM CEMETERY
UPPER TOOTING
SUMMERSTOWN
Wimbledon Stadium (Greyhound)
Lambeth Crematorium
Woodhouse Farm
LAMBETH CEMETERY
Tooting Leisure Cen.
Tooting Gardens
Tooting Broadway
ST. GEORGE'S HOSPITAL
TOOTING
Haydons Road
Wandle Meadow Nature Park
Garfield First Sch.
TOOTING GRAVENEY
Tooting
Wandle Park
Colliers Wood
COLLIER'S WOOD
Superstore
MERTON
Cemetery
119
138
BURNTWOOD
TRINITY ROAD
UPPER TOOTING ROAD
BALHAM HIGH ROAD
TOOTING BEC ROAD
MITCHAM ROAD
TOOTING HIGH ST.
COLLIERS WOOD HIGH STREET
MERTON HIGH STREET
HAYDONS ROAD
GARRATT LANE
PLOUGH LANE
SUMMERSTOWN
LONDON ROAD
STREATHAM
MERANTUN WAY

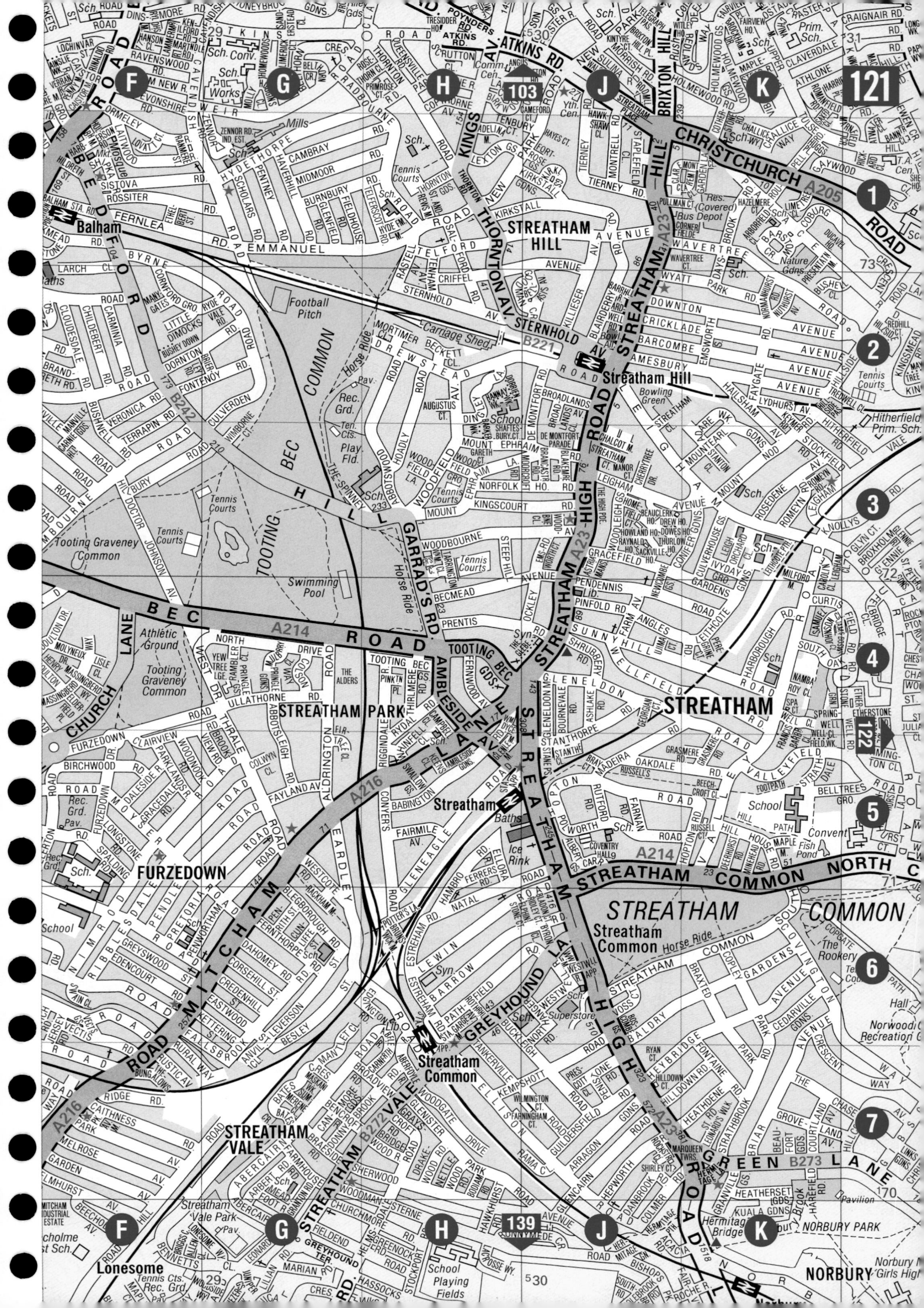

F
G
H
J
K
103
1
2
3
4
5
6
7
122
139
29
530
31
72
73
71
Balham
BEDFORD HILL
RAVENSWOOD RD.
ATKINS RD.
CHRISTCHURCH ROAD
A205
BRIXTON HILL
STREATHAM HILL
KINGS AVENUE
THORNTON AV.
EMMANUEL RD.
STERNHOLD AV.
B221
Streatham Hill
STREATHAM HIGH ROAD
A23
LEIGHAM AVENUE
Football Pitch
Carriage Shed
TOOTING BEC COMMON
Tooting Graveney Common
Swimming Pool
Tennis Courts
BEC ROAD
A214
GARRAD'S RD.
TOOTING BEC GDS.
STREATHAM PARK
STREATHAM
FURZEDOWN
CHURCH LANE
Athletic Ground
A216
MITCHAM ROAD
Streatham
Baths
Ice Rink
STREATHAM COMMON NORTH
STREATHAM COMMON
Streatham Common
Horse Ride
The Rookery
Norwood Recreation G
GREYHOUND LA.
Superstore
STREATHAM VALE
B272
Streatham Common
GREEN LANE
B273
Hermitage Bridge
NORBURY PARK
NORBURY
Norbury Girls High
Streatham Vale Park
Lonesome
MITCHAM INDUSTRIAL ESTATE
School Playing Fields
Pavilion
Hitherfield Prim. Sch.
Convent
School
Fish Pond

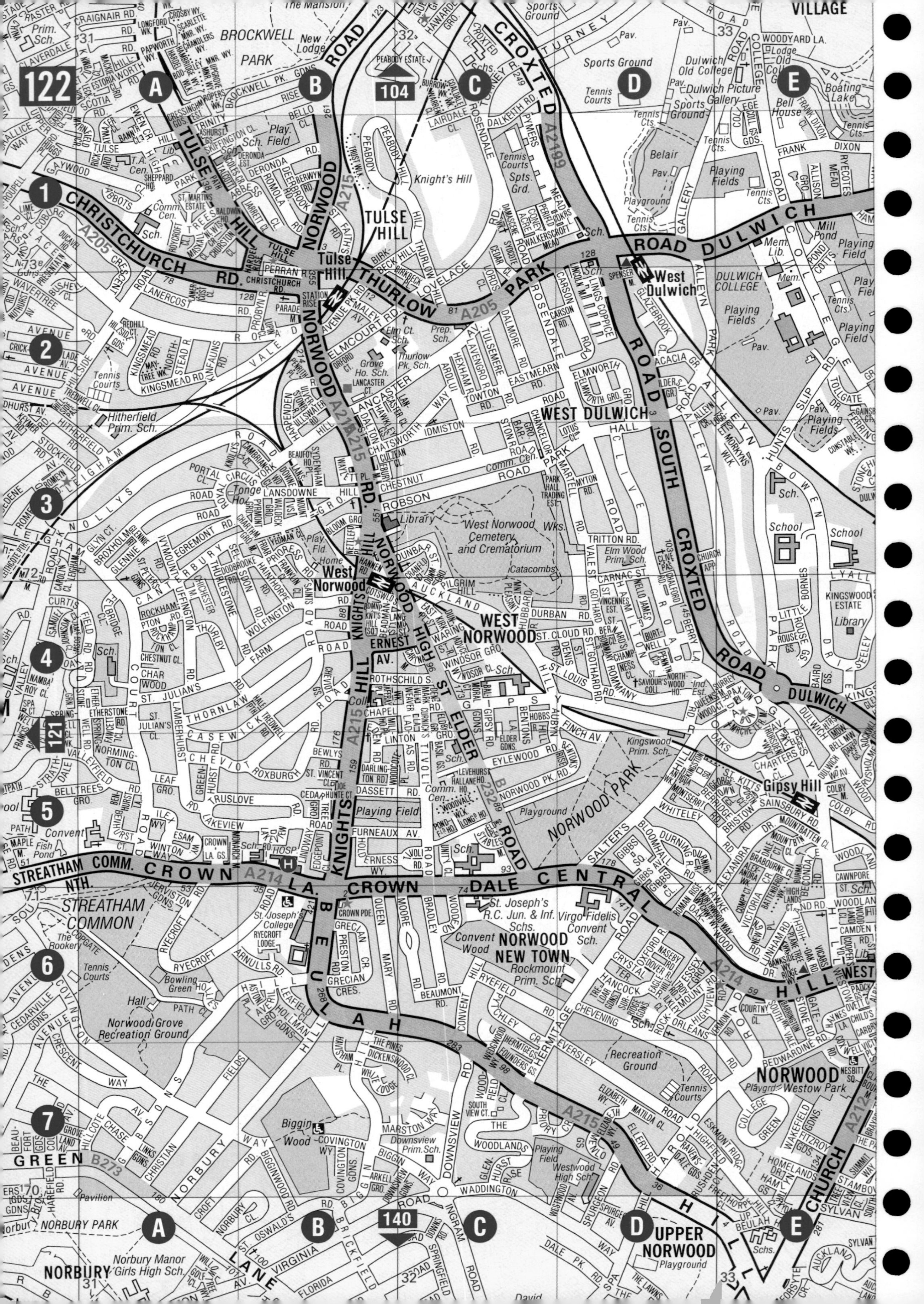

122
104
121
140
A
B
C
D
E
1
2
3
4
5
6
7
VILLAGE
BROCKWELL PARK
The Mansion
New Lodge
Prim. Sch.
PEABODY ESTATE
Sports Ground
Tennis Courts
Dulwich Old College
Dulwich Picture Gallery
Bell House
Boating Lake
Belair
Playing Fields
Knight's Hill
TULSE HILL
Tulse Hill
West Dulwich
DULWICH COLLEGE
CHRISTCHURCH RD.
A205
THURLOW PARK
DULWICH ROAD
CROXTED ROAD
A2199
SOUTH CROXTED ROAD
NORWOOD ROAD
TULSE HILL
A215
WEST DULWICH
Hitherfield Prim. Sch.
Tonge Ho.
Library
West Norwood Cemetery and Crematorium
Catacombs
Elm Wood Prim. Sch.
West Norwood
WEST NORWOOD
KNIGHTS HILL
NORWOOD HIGH ST
ELDER ROAD
B232
Kingswood Prim. Sch.
KINGSWOOD ESTATE
Gipsy Hill
NORWOOD PARK
Playing Field
STREATHAM COMM. NTH.
CROWN LA.
A214
CROWN DALE
CENTRAL HILL
WESTOW HILL
STREATHAM COMMON
St. Joseph's College
St. Joseph's R.C. Jun. & Inf. Schs.
Virgo Fidelis Convent Sch.
Convent Wood
NORWOOD NEW TOWN
Rockmount Prim. Sch.
Norwood Grove Recreation Ground
Recreation Ground
BEULAH HILL
NORWOOD
Westow Park
Biggin Wood
Downsview Prim. Sch.
Westwood High Sch.
GREEN LANE
B273
NORBURY PARK
Norbury Manor Girls High Sch.
NORBURY
UPPER NORWOOD
Playground
CHURCH RD.
A212

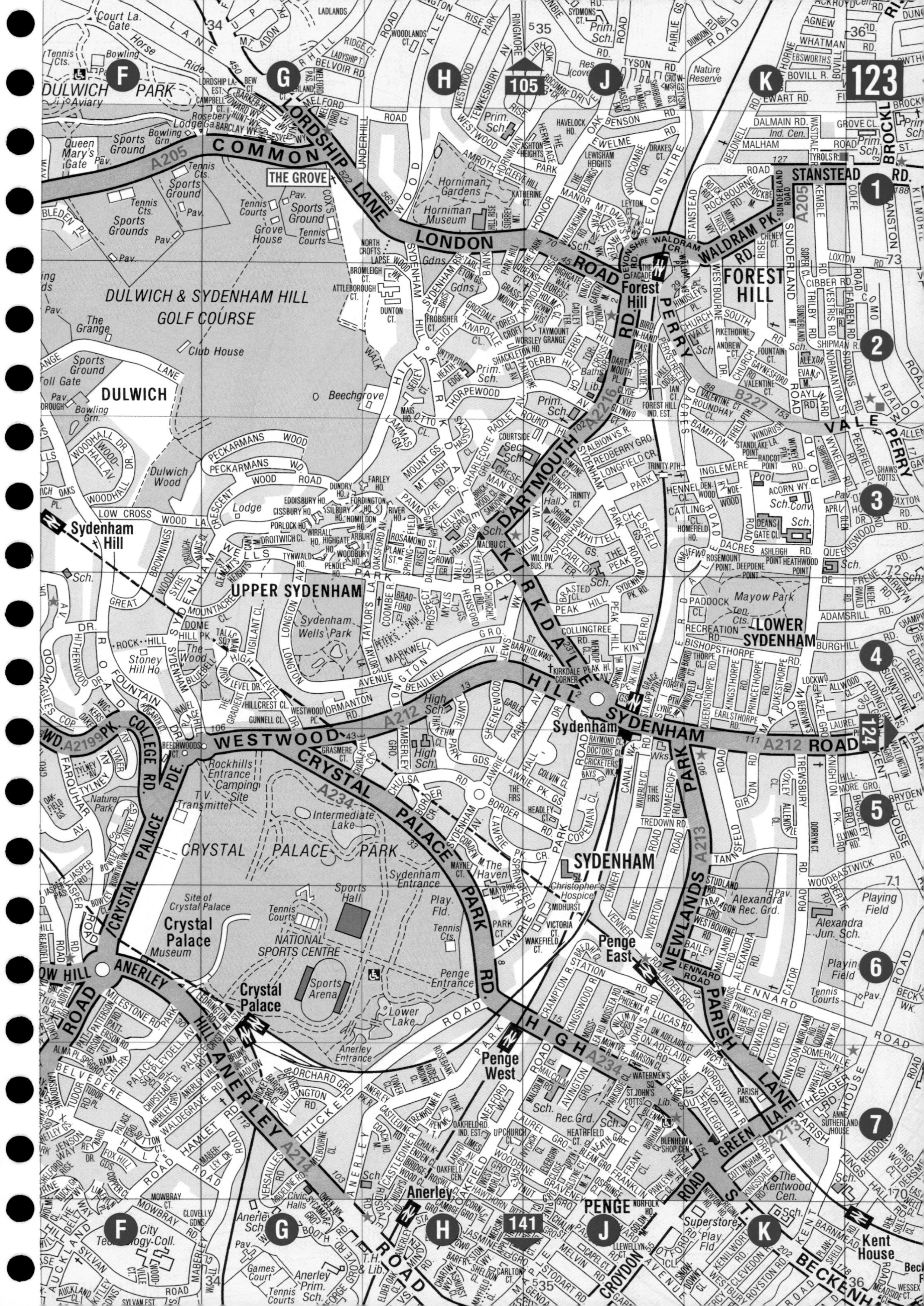
DULWICH PARK
DULWICH & SYDENHAM HILL GOLF COURSE
DULWICH
Dulwich Wood
Sydenham Hill
UPPER SYDENHAM
Sydenham Wells Park
CRYSTAL PALACE PARK
Crystal Palace
NATIONAL SPORTS CENTRE
Sports Arena
Horniman Gardens
Horniman Museum
FOREST HILL
Forest Hill
LOWER SYDENHAM
Mayow Park
Sydenham
SYDENHAM
Penge East
Penge West
PENGE
Anerley
Kent House
COMMON
LONDON ROAD
LORDSHIP LANE
DARTMOUTH RD.
KIRKDALE
SYDENHAM HILL
SYDENHAM ROAD
WESTWOOD HILL
CRYSTAL PALACE PARK RD.
HIGH ST.
NEWLANDS PARK
PARISH LANE
ANERLEY HILL
ANERLEY ROAD
WALDRAM PK.
STANSTEAD RD.
PERRY VALE
THE GROVE
105
124
141
F
G
H
J
K
1
2
3
4
5
6
7
34
35
36

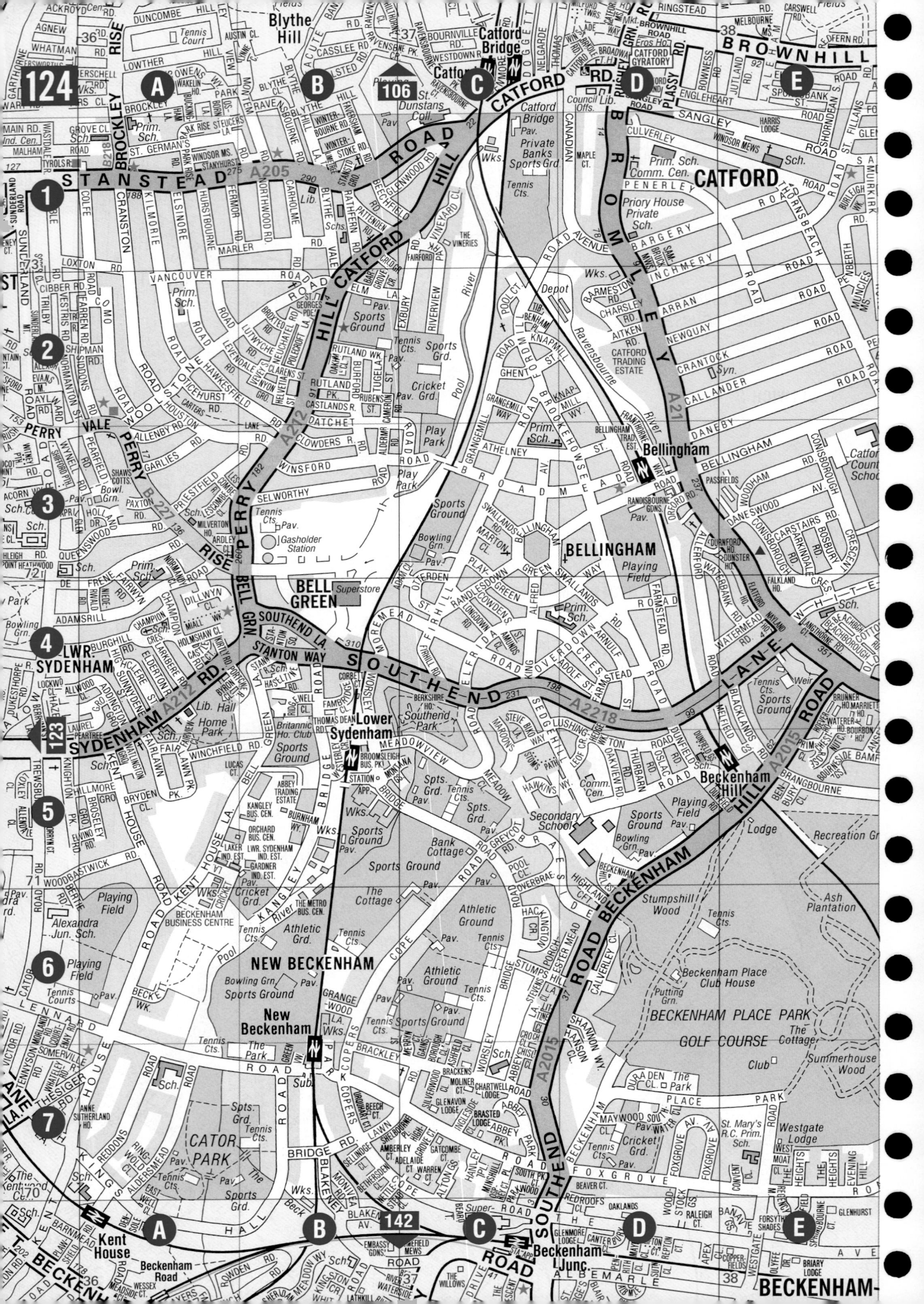

Blythe Hill
Catford Bridge
Catford
CATFORD
STANSTEAD ROAD
CATFORD HILL
BROMLEY ROAD
BROWNHILL ROAD
CATFORD GYRATORY
Bellingham
BELLINGHAM
BELL GREEN
PERRY HILL
PERRY RISE
LWR. SYDENHAM
SYDENHAM RD.
SOUTHEND LANE
Lower Sydenham
NEW BECKENHAM
New Beckenham
BECKENHAM HILL ROAD
Beckenham Hill
BECKENHAM PLACE PARK
GOLF COURSE
CATOR PARK
Kent House
Beckenham Road
Beckenham Junc.
SOUTHEND ROAD
BECKENHAM
Gasholder Station
Superstore
Sports Ground
Playing Field
Stumpshill Wood
Ash Plantation
Summerhouse Wood
Beckenham Place Club House
106
123
142

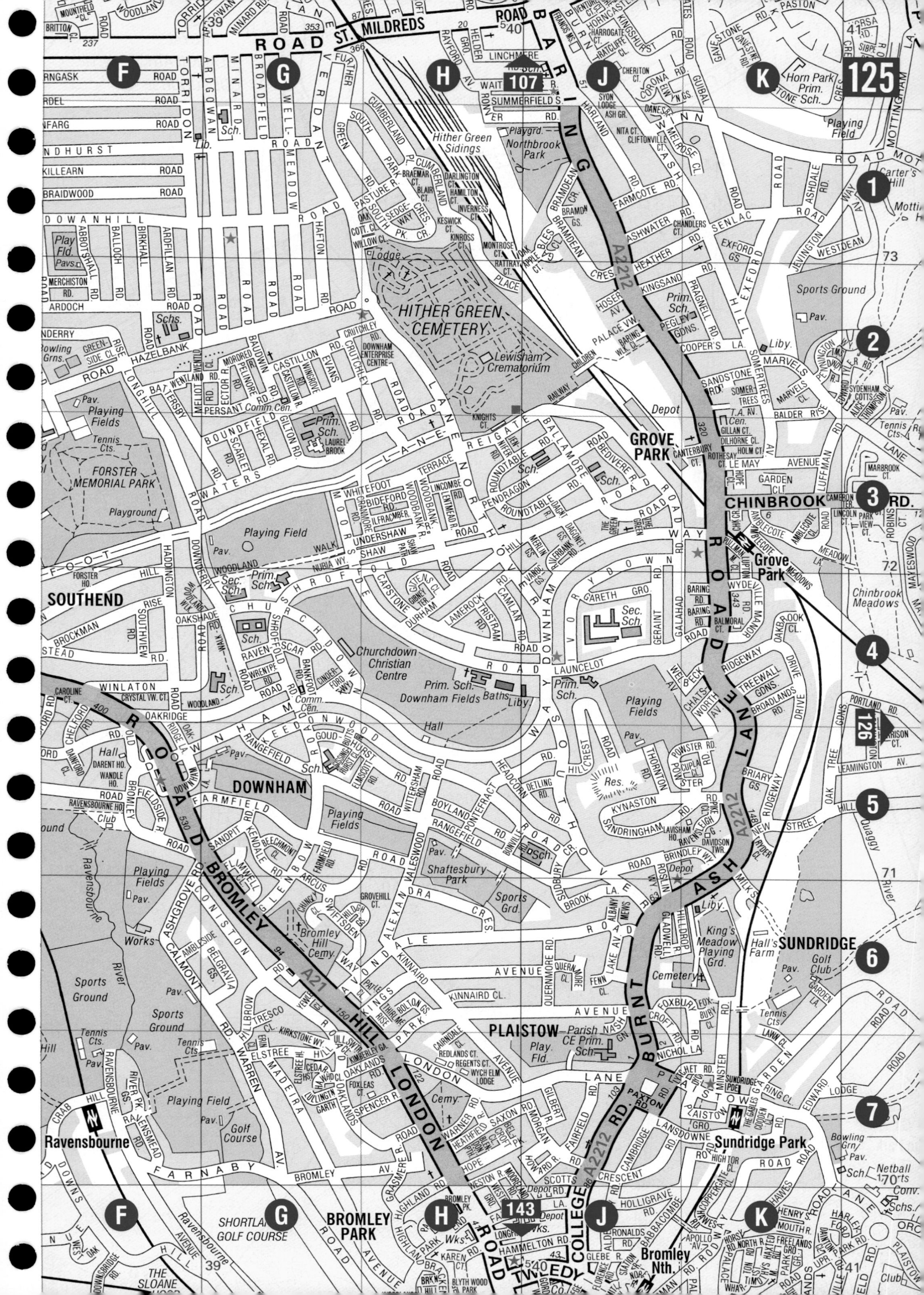

125
107
126
143
F
G
H
J
K
1
2
3
4
5
6
7
HITHER GREEN CEMETERY
Lewisham Crematorium
Hither Green Sidings
GROVE PARK
SOUTHEND
DOWNHAM
PLAISTOW
SUNDRIDGE
Sundridge Park
Ravensbourne
Bromley Nth.
BROMLEY PARK
FORSTER MEMORIAL PARK
Churchdown Christian Centre
Shaftesbury Park
King's Meadow Playing Grd.
Chinbrook Meadows
Sports Ground
Golf Course
SHORTLANDS GOLF COURSE
ROAD ST. MILDREDS
BARING ROAD
BURNT ASH LANE
BURNT ASH HILL
BROMLEY ROAD
LONDON ROAD
CHINBROOK RD.
WHITEFOOT LANE
A2212
A21

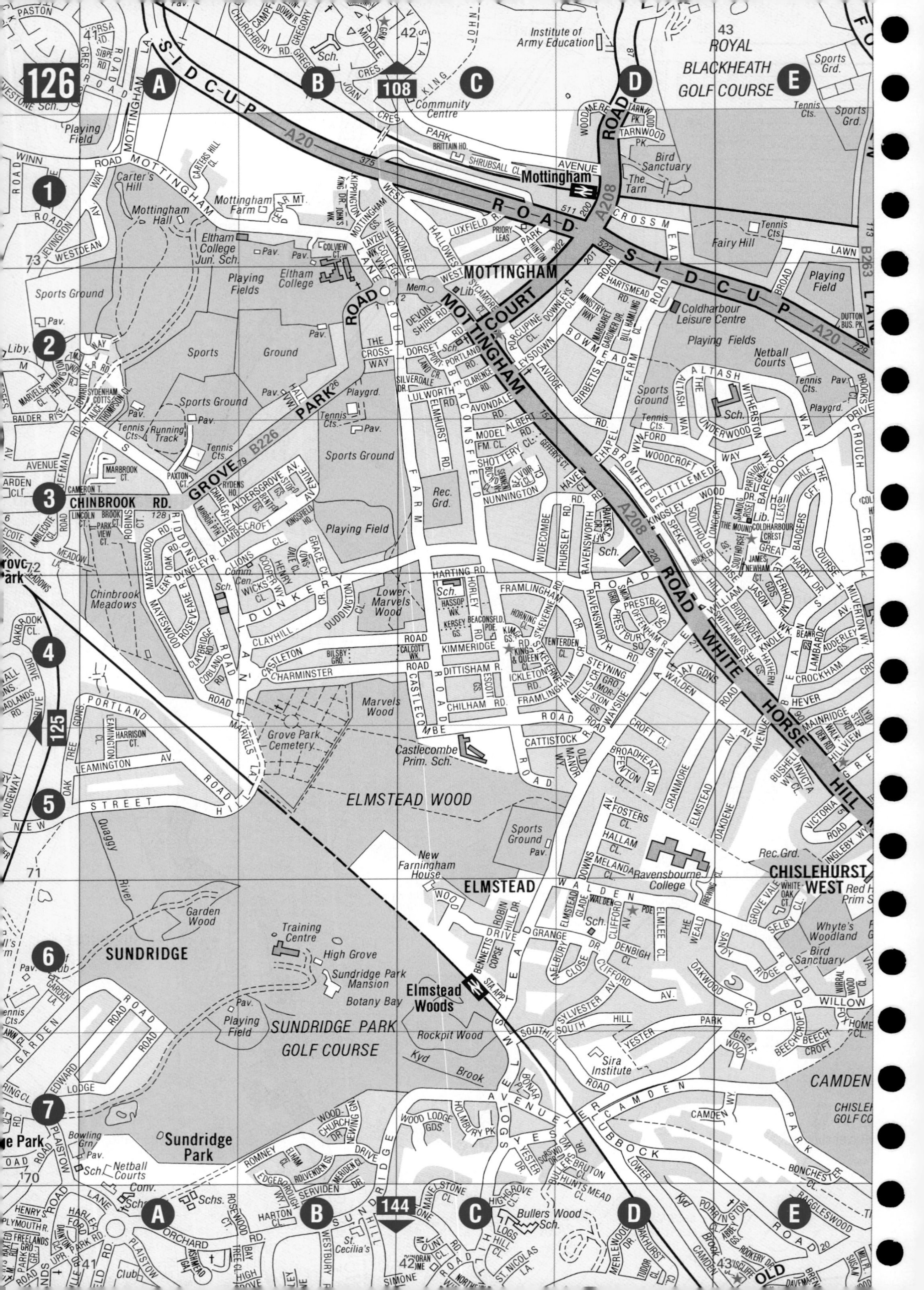

126
108
144
125
A
B
C
D
E
1
2
3
4
5
6
7
SIDCUP ROAD
A20
A208
B226
B263
MOTTINGHAM
Mottingham
Mottingham Farm
Mottingham Hall
Carter's Hill
Eltham College Jun. Sch.
Eltham College
Institute of Army Education
ROYAL BLACKHEATH GOLF COURSE
Community Centre
Bird Sanctuary
The Tarn
Fairy Hill
Coldharbour Leisure Centre
Playing Fields
Netball Courts
Sports Ground
Playing Field
Running Track
Rec. Grd.
GROVE PARK
CHINBROOK RD.
Chinbrook Meadows
DUNKERY RD.
Lower Marvels Wood
Marvels Wood
Grove Park Cemetery
Castlecombe Prim. Sch.
ELMSTEAD WOOD
New Farningham House
ELMSTEAD
Ravensbourne College
CHISLEHURST WEST
Whyte's Woodland
Bird Sanctuary
SUNDRIDGE
Garden Wood
Training Centre
High Grove
Sundridge Park Mansion
Botany Bay
Elmstead Woods
Rockpit Wood
SUNDRIDGE PARK GOLF COURSE
Kyd Brook
Sundridge Park
Quaggy River
Sira Institute
CAMDEN
Bullers Wood Sch.
WHITE HORSE HILL
MOTTINGHAM LANE
MOTTINGHAM ROAD
COURT ROAD
WHITE HORSE ROAD
BEACONSFIELD RD.
FARM
FRAMLINGHAM CR.
MARVELS LA.
NEW STREET
PORTLAND
LEAMINGTON AV.
ELMSTEAD LA.
SOUTHILL RD.
CAMDEN PARK RD.
YESTER RD.
WOOD LODGE GDS.
SUNDRIDGE AV.
PLAISTOW LANE
ORCHARD RD.
St. Cecilia's

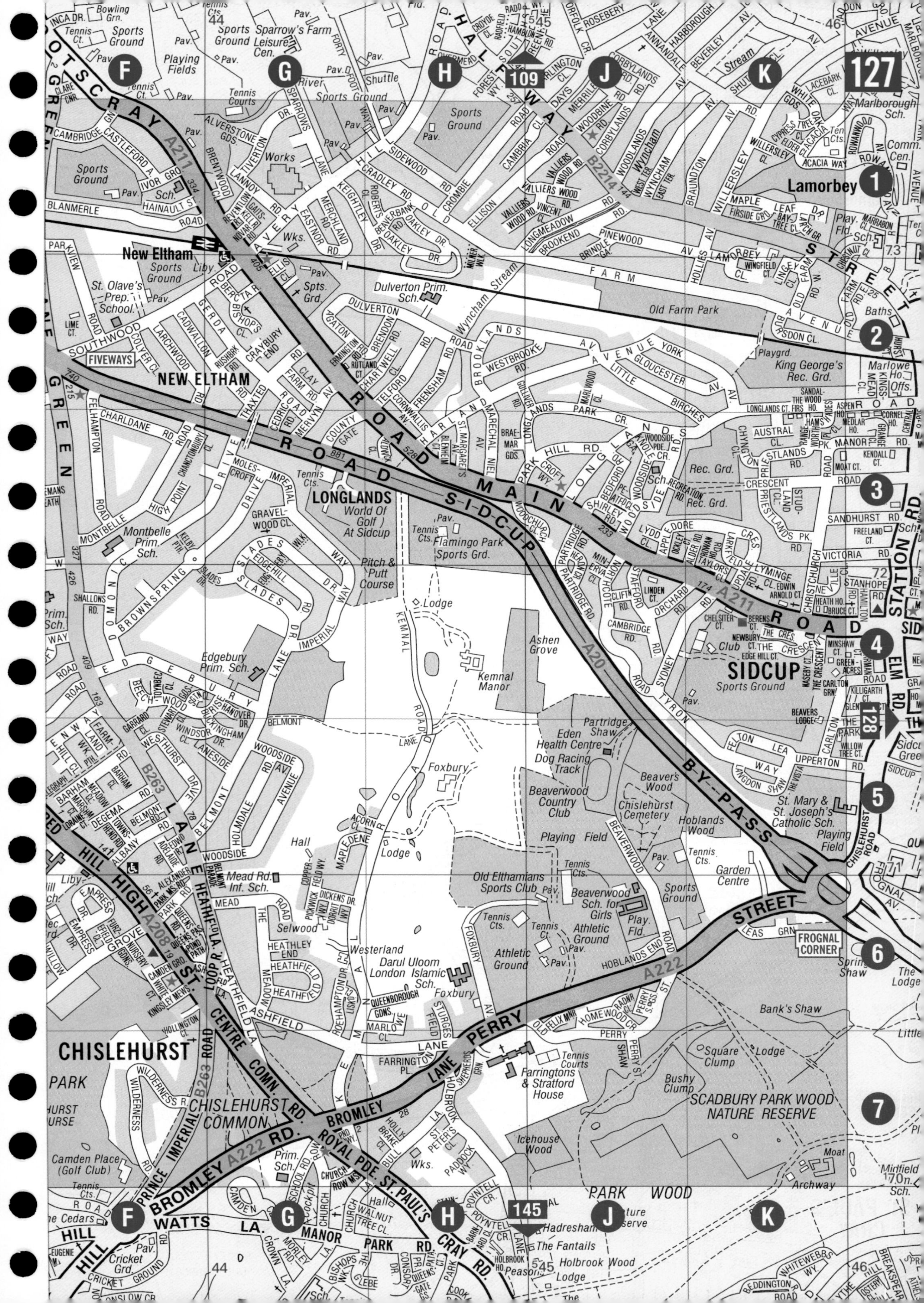
F
G
H
J
K
109
1
2
3
4
5
6
7
128
145
44
45
46
Lamorbey
New Eltham
NEW ELTHAM
LONGLANDS
SIDCUP
CHISLEHURST
CHISLEHURST COMMON
FIVEWAYS
FROGNAL CORNER
SIDCUP ROAD
SIDCUP BY-PASS
MAIN ROAD
CRAY ROAD
HALFWAY STREET
STATION RD.
PERRY LANE
BROMLEY LANE
BROMLEY RD.
FARM AVENUE
STREET
A211
A20
A222
A208
B263
B2214
Sports Ground
Sparrow's Farm Sports Ground Leisure Cen.
Playing Fields
Shuttle River
Works
Sports Ground
Marlborough Sch.
Comm. Cen.
Old Farm Park
King George's Rec. Grd.
Dulverton Prim. Sch.
New Eltham Sports Ground
St. Olave's Prep. School
Spts. Grd.
Wyncham Stream
World Of Golf / At Sidcup
Pitch & Putt Course
Flamingo Park Sports Grd.
Rec. Grd.
Montbelle Prim. Sch.
Edgebury Prim. Sch.
Ashen Grove
Kemnal Manor
Foxbury
Eden Health Centre
Dog Racing Track
Beaverwood Country Club
Chislehurst Cemetery
Beaver's Wood
Hoblands Wood
Partridge Shaw
St. Mary & St. Joseph's Catholic Sch.
Playing Field
Garden Centre
Old Elthamians Sports Club
Beaverwood Sch. for Girls
Athletic Ground
Mead Rd. Inf. Sch.
Selwood
Westerland
Darul Uloom London Islamic Sch.
Hall
Lodge
Farringtons & Stratford House
Square Clump
Bushy Clump
Bank's Shaw
SCADBURY PARK WOOD NATURE RESERVE
Icehouse Wood
Camden Place (Golf Club)
Prim. Sch.
Cricket Grd.
PARK WOOD
Hadresham
The Fantails
Holbrook Wood Lodge
Archway
Moat
Spring Shaw
The Lodge
Sidcup Sports Ground
Club
Baths
Marlowe Ho. Offs.

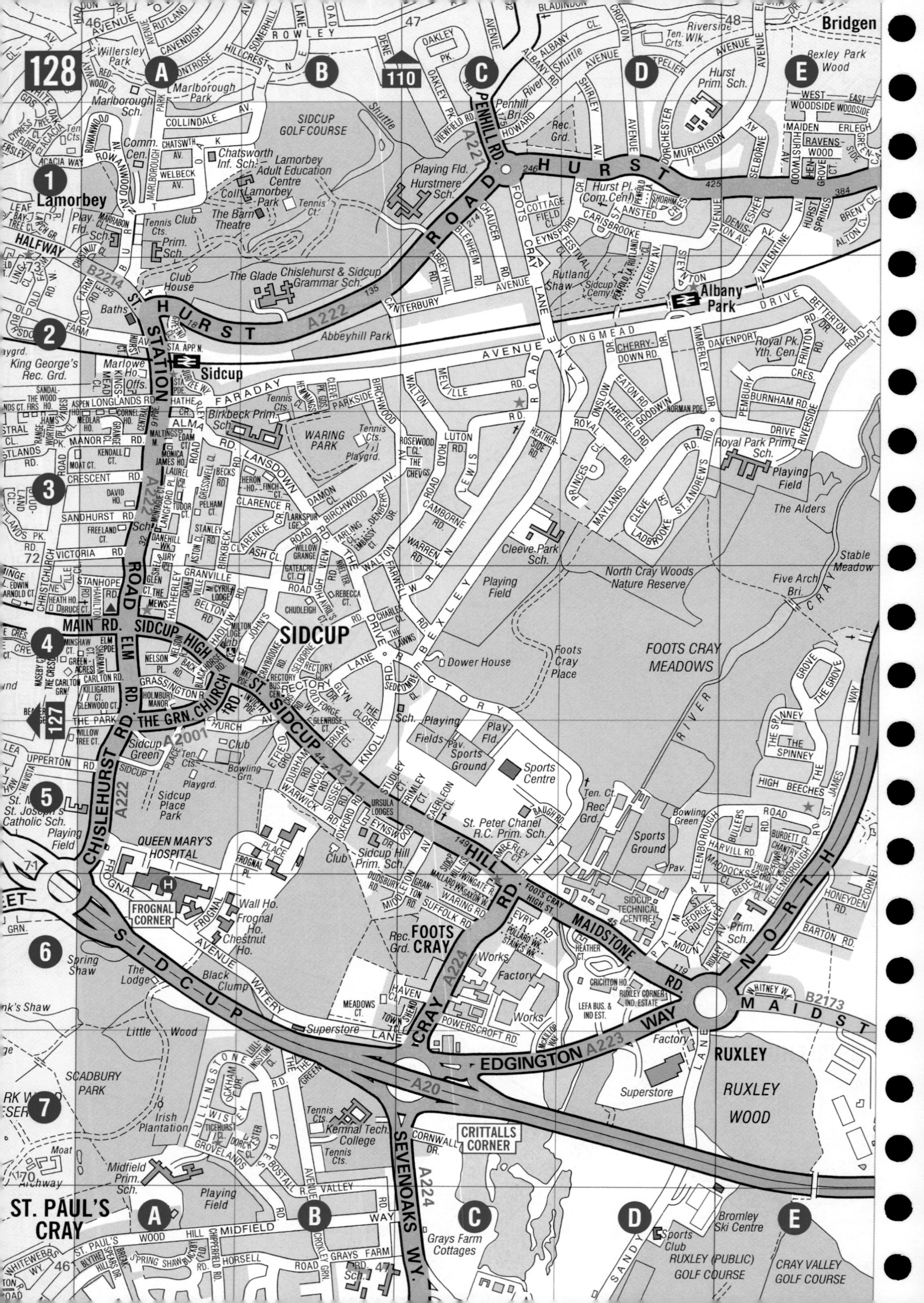
128
110
127
A
B
C
D
E
1
2
3
4
5
6
7
Bridgen
Bexley Park Wood
Hurst Prim. Sch.
Lamorbey
Halfway
Willersley Park
Marlborough Park
Marlborough Sch.
SIDCUP GOLF COURSE
Chatsworth Inf. Sch.
Lamorbey Adult Education Centre
Coll. Lamorbey Park
The Barn Theatre
Tennis Club
Prim. Sch.
Club House
The Glade
Chislehurst & Sidcup Grammar Sch.
Playing Fld.
Hurstmere Sch.
Penhill Bri.
Rec. Grd.
Hurst Pl. (Com. Cen.)
Rutland Shaw
Sidcup Cemy.
Albany Park
HURST ROAD
PENHILL RD.
A221
A222
B2214
Abbeyhill Park
King George's Rec. Grd.
Marlowe Ho. Offs.
Sidcup
STATION ROAD
Birkbeck Prim. Sch.
WARING PARK
Royal Pk. Yth. Cen.
Royal Park Prim. Sch.
Playing Field
The Alders
Cleeve Park Sch.
North Cray Woods Nature Reserve
Stable Meadow
Five Arch Bri.
SIDCUP
Dower House
Foots Cray Place
FOOTS CRAY MEADOWS
Playing Fields
Play. Fld.
Sports Ground
Sports Centre
St. Peter Chanel R.C. Prim. Sch.
Sidcup Hill Prim. Sch.
Sidcup Green
Sidcup Place Park
St. Joseph's Catholic Sch.
QUEEN MARY'S HOSPITAL
FROGNAL CORNER
Wall Ho.
Frognal Ho.
Chestnut Ho.
Spring Shaw
The Lodge
Black Clump
SIDCUP BY-PASS
Superstore
Little Wood
SCADBURY PARK
Irish Plantation
Moat
Archway
Midfield Prim. Sch.
Playing Field
ST. PAUL'S CRAY
FOOTS CRAY
Rec. Grd.
Works
Factory
SIDCUP TECHNICAL CENTRE
RUXLEY CORNER IND. ESTATE
LEFA BUS. & IND EST.
MAIDSTONE RD.
A211
A224
A223
A20
B2173
EDGINGTON WAY
NORTH CRAY RD.
RUXLEY
RUXLEY WOOD
Kemnal Tech. College
CRITTALLS CORNER
SEVENOAKS WY.
Grays Farm Cottages
Bromley Ski Centre
Sports Club
RUXLEY (PUBLIC) GOLF COURSE
CRAY VALLEY GOLF COURSE
RIVER CRAY
Bowling Green
Prim. Sch.

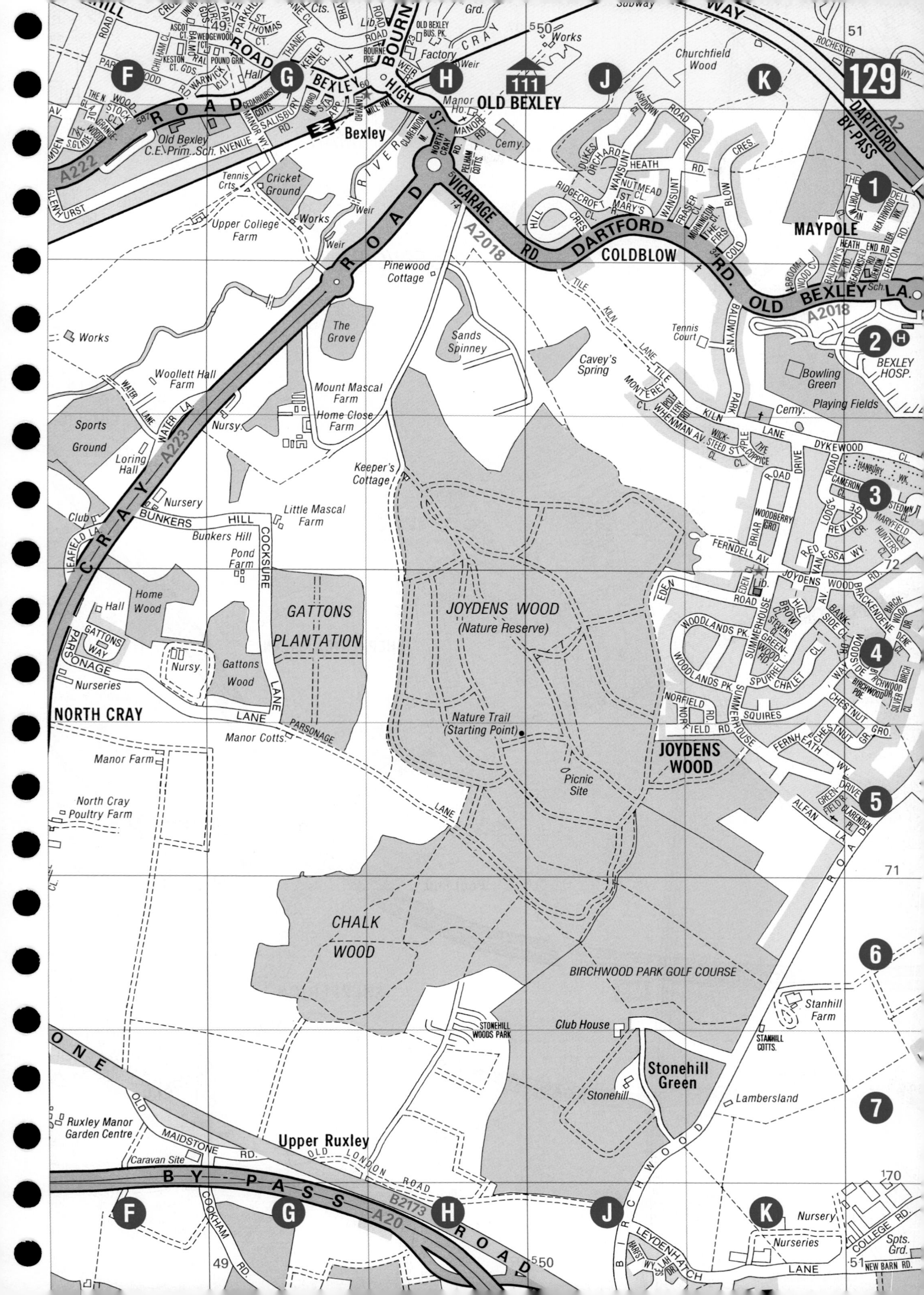

F **G** **H** **J** **K**

111 **OLD BEXLEY**

1

MAYPOLE

COLDBLOW

2
BEXLEY HOSP.

3

4

5

6

7

Bexley

Old Bexley C.E. Prim. Sch.

Tennis Crts.

Cricket Ground

Works

Weir

Upper College Farm

Weir

Pinewood Cottage

The Grove

Sands Spinney

Cavey's Spring

Woollett Hall Farm

Mount Mascal Farm

Home Close Farm

Sports Ground

Loring Hall

Nursy.

Club

BUNKERS HILL

Bunkers Hill Pond Farm

Little Mascal Farm

Keeper's Cottage

JOYDENS WOOD
(Nature Reserve)

JOYDENS WOOD

GATTONS WAY

Nursy.

Home Wood

Hall

GATTONS PLANTATION

Gattons Wood

Nature Trail
(Starting Point)

Picnic Site

NORTH CRAY

Manor Cotts.

Manor Farm

North Cray Poultry Farm

CHALK WOOD

BIRCHWOOD PARK GOLF COURSE

Stanhill Farm

Stonehill Woods Park

Club House

STANHILL COTTS.

Stonehill Green

Stonehill

Lambersland

Ruxley Manor Garden Centre

Caravan Site

MAIDSTONE RD.

Upper Ruxley

BY-PASS ROAD

College Rd.

Nursery

Nurseries

LEYDENHATCH LANE

Spts. Grd.

NEW BARN RD.

F **G** **H** **J** **K**

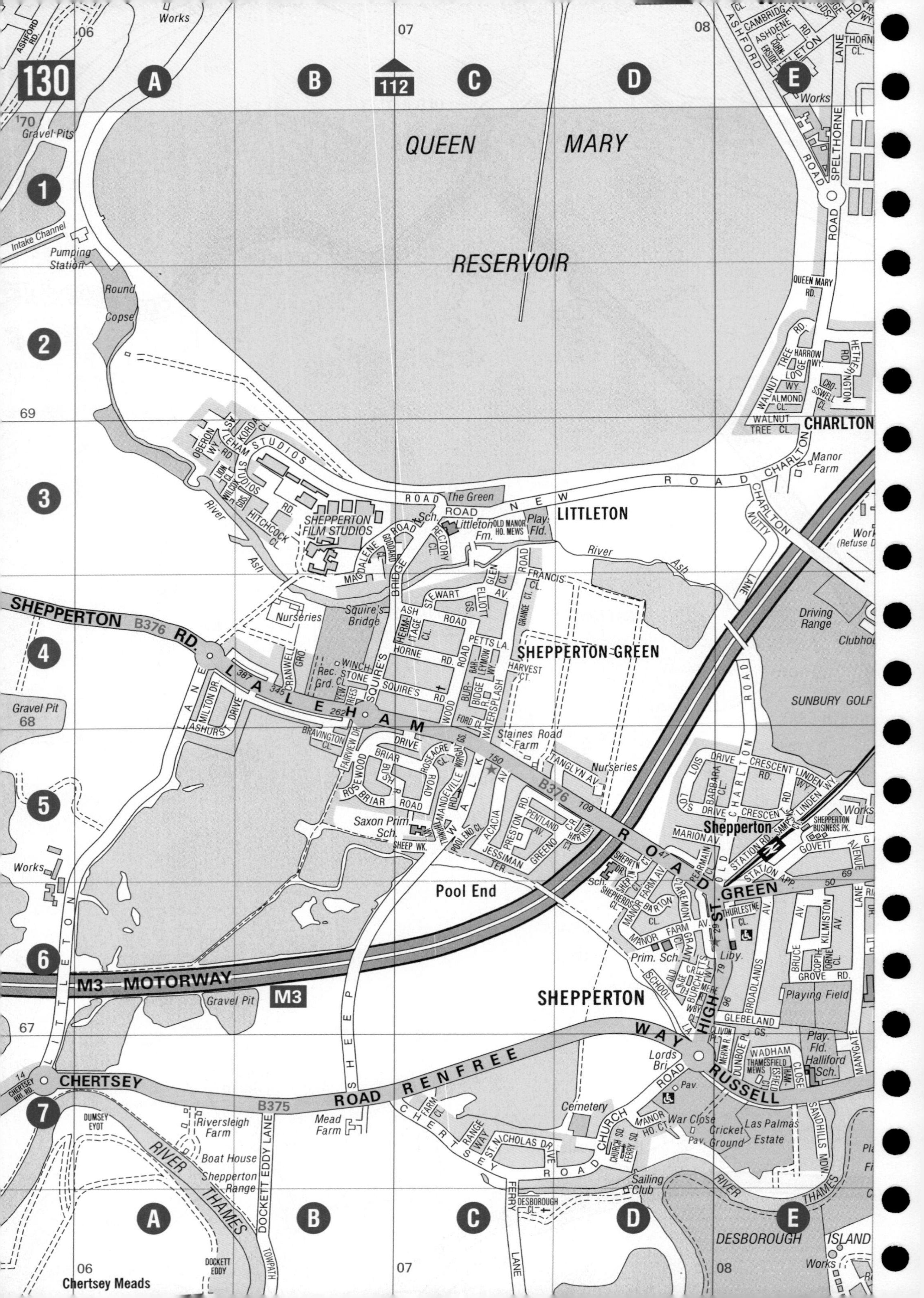

130

A · B · C · D · E

QUEEN MARY

RESERVOIR

Works

Gravel Pits

Intake Channel

Pumping Station

Round Copse

CHARLTON

Manor Farm

Works (Refuse D...)

Driving Range

Clubhou...

SUNBURY GOLF

SHEPPERTON FILM STUDIOS

STUDIOS

LITTLETON

The Green

SHEPPERTON GREEN

Shepperton

SHEPPERTON BUSINESS PK.

SHEPPERTON

Saxon Prim. Sch.

Pool End

M3 MOTORWAY

Gravel Pit

CHERTSEY

ROAD RENFREE WAY

RUSSELL

DESBOROUGH

ISLAND

RIVER THAMES

Chertsey Meads

DESBOROUGH

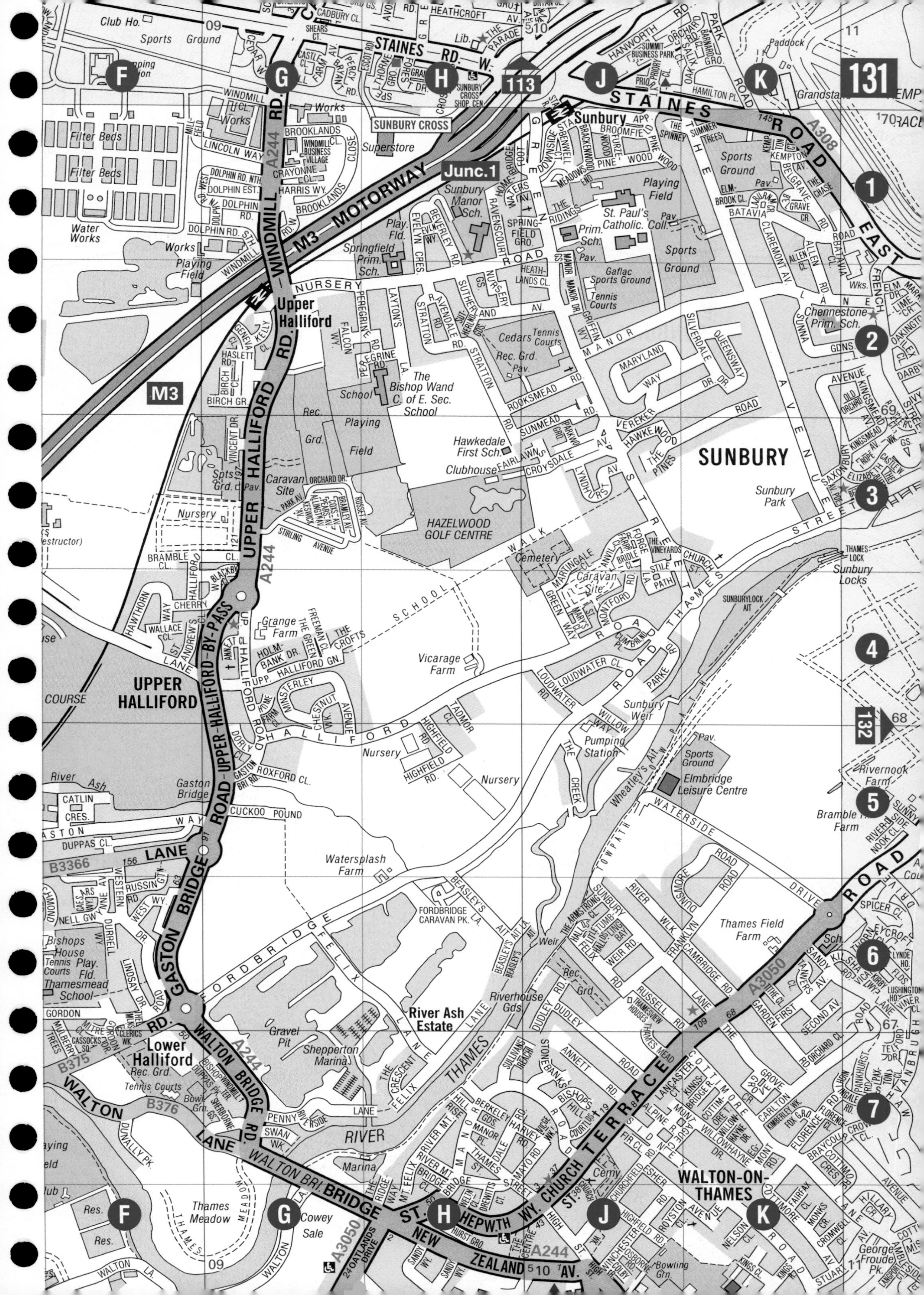

131
113
132
SUNBURY
UPPER HALLIFORD
Upper Halliford
Lower Halliford
WALTON-ON-THAMES
Sunbury
SUNBURY CROSS
M3 MOTORWAY
M3
Junc.1
A244
A308
A3050
B3366
B375
B376
STAINES RD. W.
STAINES ROAD EAST
WINDMILL RD.
UPPER HALLIFORD RD.
UPPER HALLIFORD BY-PASS
GASTON BRIDGE ROAD
WALTON BRIDGE RD.
WALTON BRIDGE
NEW ZEALAND AV.
CHURCH ST.
THAMES ST.
NURSERY RD.
MANOR LANE
GREEN ST.
HALLIFORD ROAD
FORDBRIDGE RD.
FELIX LANE
SCHOOL WALK
SUNBURY ROAD
TERRACE
CHURCH WY.
AVENUE
ROAD
RIVER THAMES
Sunbury Locks
Sunbury Weir
Elmbridge Leisure Centre
HAZELWOOD GOLF CENTRE
Sunbury Park
Sunbury Manor Sch.
St. Paul's Catholic Coll.
The Bishop Wand C. of E. Sec. School
Springfield Prim. Sch.
Chennestone Prim. Sch.
Hawkedale First Sch.
Thamesmead School
River Ash Estate
Shepperton Marina
Thames Meadow
Gravel Pit
Filter Beds
Water Works
Superstore
Playing Field
Sports Ground
Cemetery
Nursery
Pumping Station
Caravan Site
Vicarage Farm
Grange Farm
Watersplash Farm
Thames Field Farm
Riverneok Farm
Bramble Hill Farm
F
G
H
J
K
1
2
3
4
5
6
7
09
10
11
67
68
69

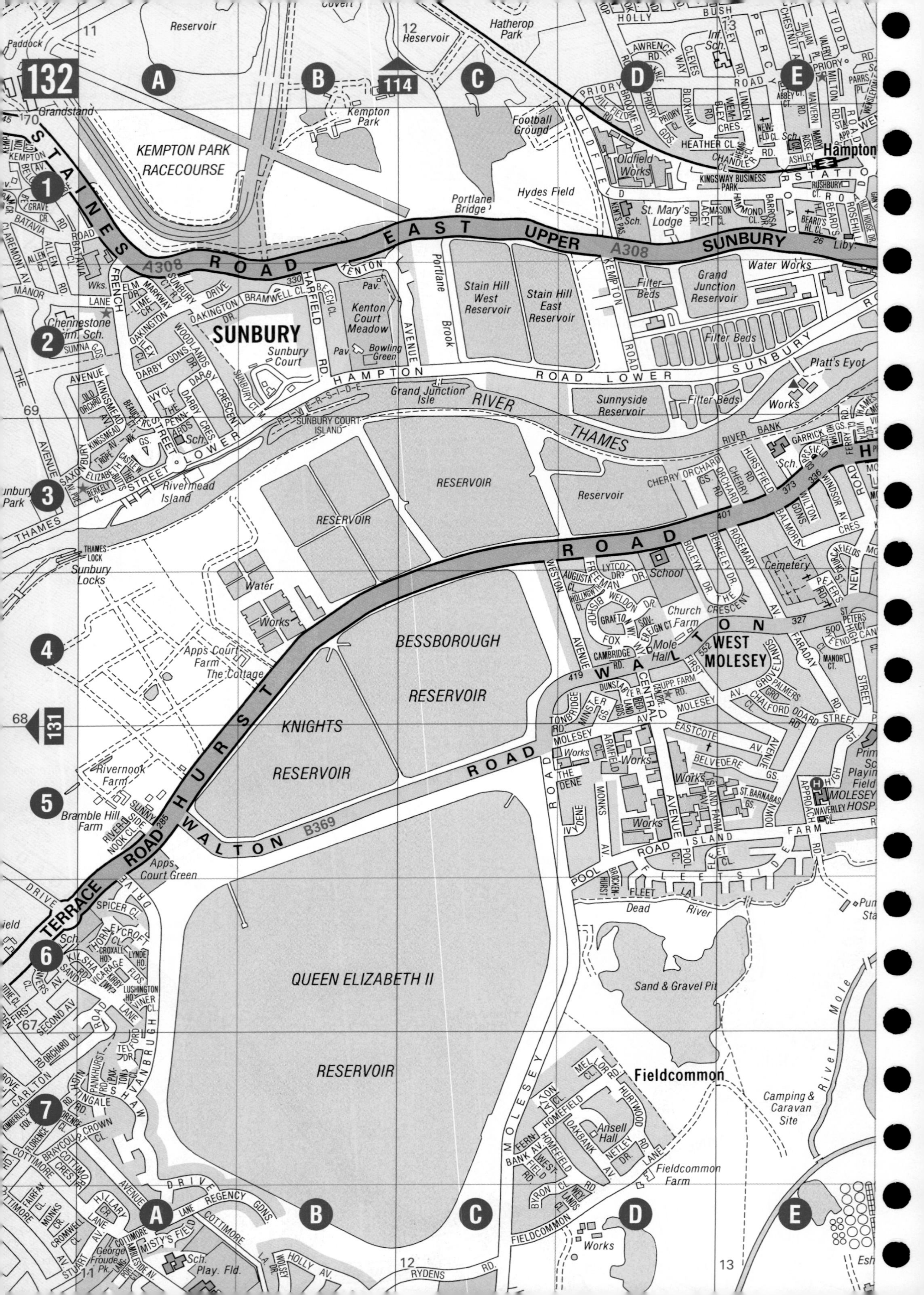
Reservoir
Hatherop Park
Reservoir
114
Kempton Park
KEMPTON PARK RACECOURSE
Grandstand
Football Ground
Oldfield Works
Hydes Field
Portlane Bridge
St. Mary's Lodge
Hampton
STAINES ROAD
A308
EAST UPPER SUNBURY ROAD
Water Works
Grand Junction Reservoir
Filter Beds
Stain Hill West Reservoir
Stain Hill East Reservoir
Kenton Court Meadow
Bowling Green
Portlane Brook
SUNBURY
Sunbury Court
Chennestone Prim. Sch.
HAMPTON ROAD LOWER SUNBURY
Platt's Eyot
Grand Junction Isle
RIVER THAMES
Sunnyside Reservoir
Filter Beds
Works
SUNBURY COURT ISLAND
Rivermead Island
RESERVOIR
Reservoir
THAMES LOCK
Sunbury Locks
Water Works
Apps Court Farm
The Cottage
BESSBOROUGH RESERVOIR
KNIGHTS RESERVOIR
HURST ROAD
Cemetery
Church Farm
Mole Hall
WEST MOLESEY
WALTON ROAD
MOLESEY HOSP.
Riverncok Farm
Bramble Hill Farm
WALTON ROAD
B369
Apps Court Green
TERRACE ROAD
Dead River
Sand & Gravel Pit
QUEEN ELIZABETH II RESERVOIR
Fieldcommon
River Mole
Camping & Caravan Site
Ansell Hall
Fieldcommon Farm
Works
131
George Froude Pk.
RYDENS RD.

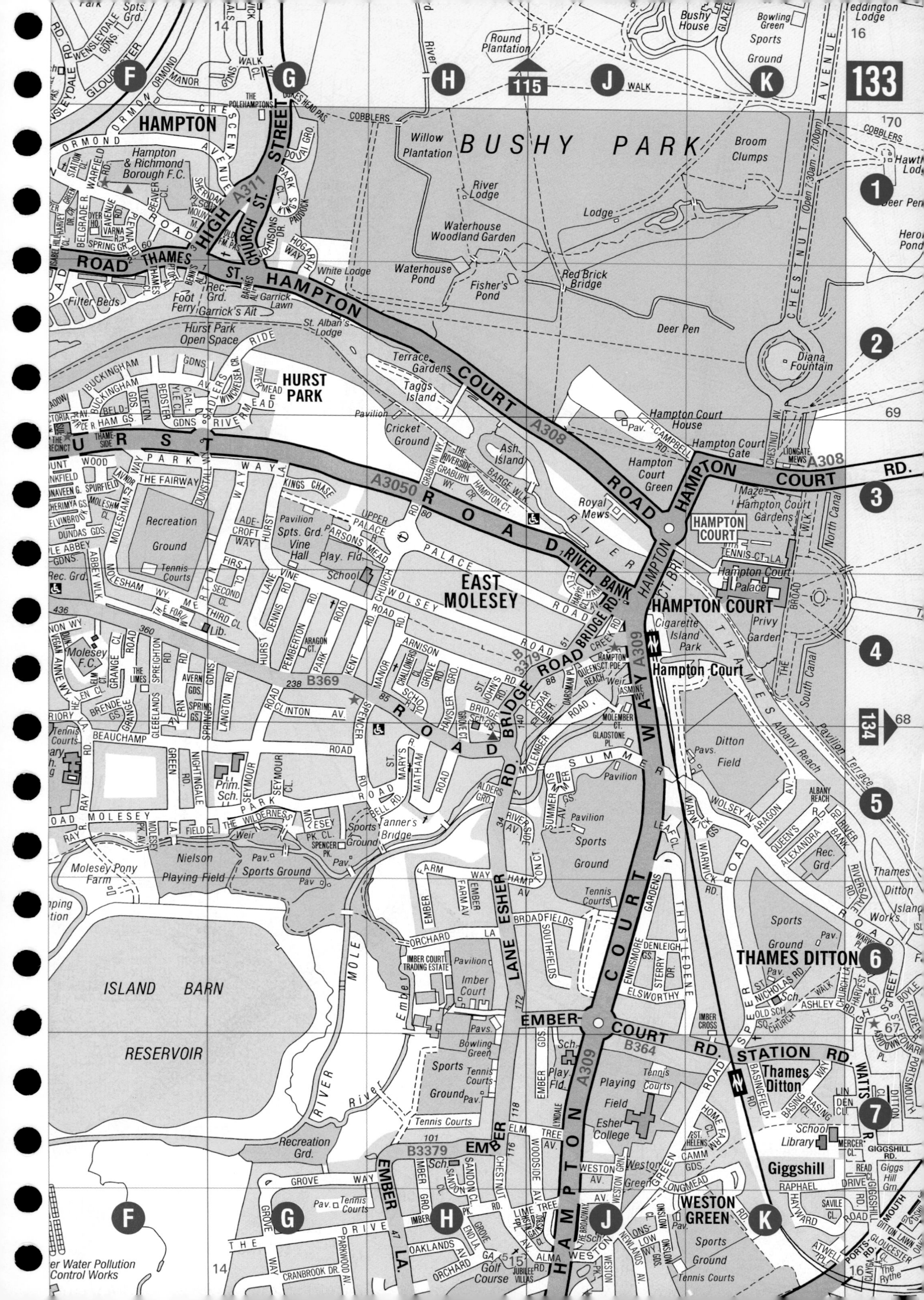

F G H 115 J K

HAMPTON

BUSHY PARK

Willow Plantation

Round Plantation

Bushy House

Bowling Green Sports Ground

Teddington Lodge

16

170

COBBLERS

Hawth Lod.

1

Deer Pen

River Lodge

Waterhouse Woodland Garden

Waterhouse Pond

Fisher's Pond

Red Brick Bridge

Lodge

Broom Clumps

Heron Pond

White Lodge

Deer Pen

2

St. Alban's Lodge

Hurst Park Open Space

Terrace Gardens

Taggs Island

Diana Fountain

69

HURST PARK

Pavilion

Cricket Ground

Ash Island

BARGE WLK.

Hampton Court House

Hampton Court Green

Hampton Court Gate

LIONGATE MEWS

A308 RD.

3

Recreation Ground

Tennis Courts

Pavilion

Spts. Grd. Vine Hall

Play. Fld.

School

Royal Mews

Maze

Hampton Court Gardens

North Canal

EAST MOLESEY

HAMPTON COURT

Cigarette Island Park

Hampton Court

Hampton Court Palace

Privy Garden

South Canal

4

Molesey F.C.

The Limes

Ditton Field

Pavs.

Albany Reach

134 68

5

Prim. Sch.

The Wilderness

Sports Ground

Tanner's Bridge

Pavilion

Sports Ground

Queen's

Alexandra

Rec. Grd.

Thames Ditton Island Works

Nielson Playing Field

Sports Ground

Molesey Pony Farm

Tennis Courts

Sports Ground

Pav.

THAMES DITTON

6

ISLAND BARN RESERVOIR

Imber Court Trading Estate

Pavilion

Imber Court

Pavs.

Broadfields

Southfields

Tennis Courts

Old Sch.

Thames Ditton

Giggshill

67

7

Recreation Grd.

Bowling Green

Sports Ground

Tennis Courts

Golf Course

Tennis Courts

Esher College

Playing Field

Tennis Courts

Weston Green

WESTON GREEN

School

Library

Giggshill

Sports Ground

Tennis Courts

16

er Water Pollution Control Works

14

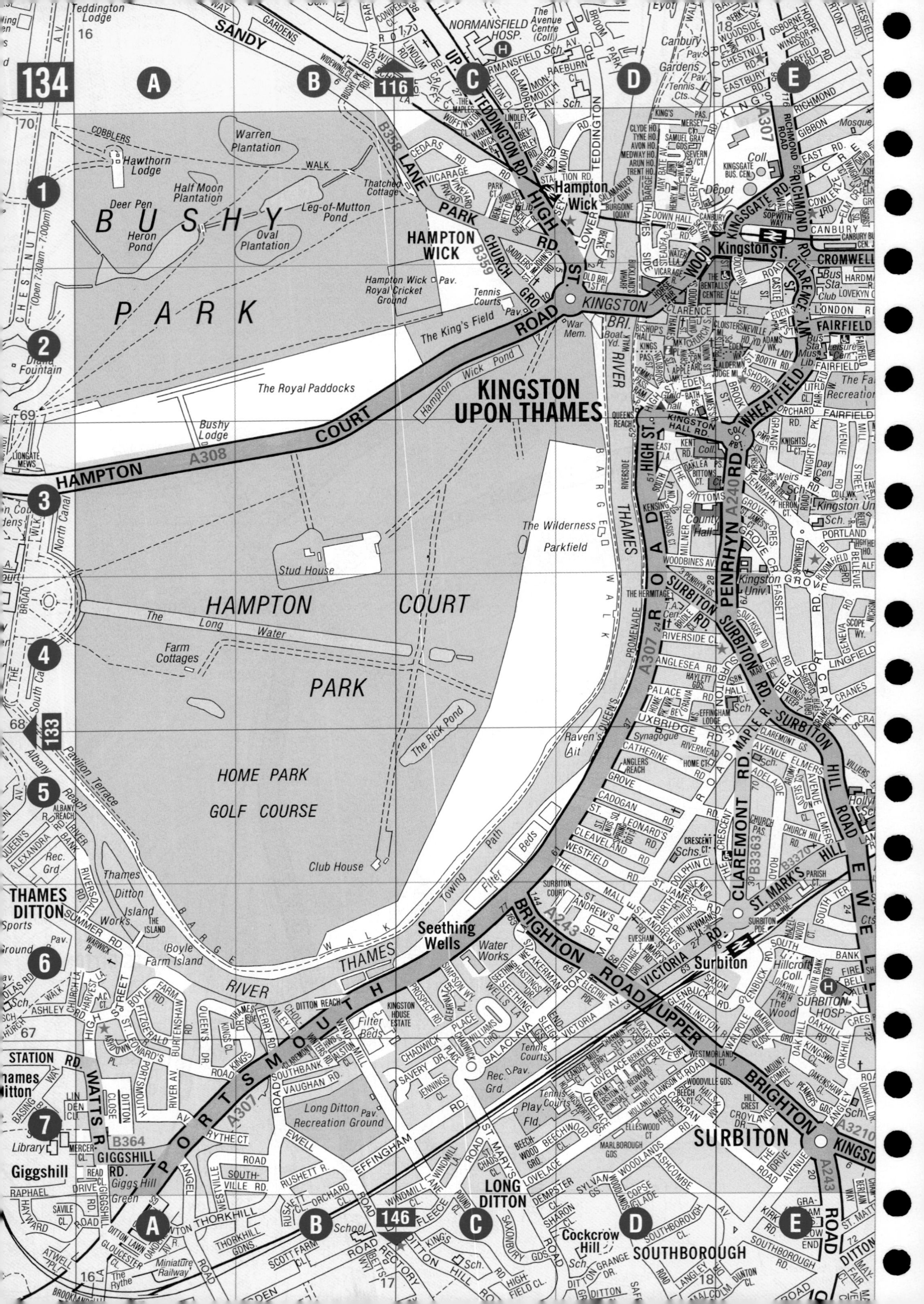
BUSHY PARK
HAMPTON WICK
KINGSTON UPON THAMES
HAMPTON COURT PARK
HOME PARK GOLF COURSE
THAMES DITTON
Seething Wells
SURBITON
LONG DITTON
SOUTHBOROUGH
Cockcrow Hill
Giggshill
The Royal Paddocks
Stud House
The Long Water
Warren Plantation
Hawthorn Lodge
Half Moon Plantation
Leg-of-Mutton Pond
Heron Pond
Oval Plantation
Diana Fountain
Bushy Lodge
The King's Field
Hampton Wick Pond
The Wilderness
Parkfield
Farm Cottages
The Rick Pond
Club House
Thames Ditton Island
Boyle Farm Island
Raven's Ait
Long Ditton Recreation Ground
NORMANSFIELD HOSP.
HAMPTON COURT ROAD
PORTSMOUTH ROAD
BRIGHTON ROAD
RIVER THAMES
116
133
146

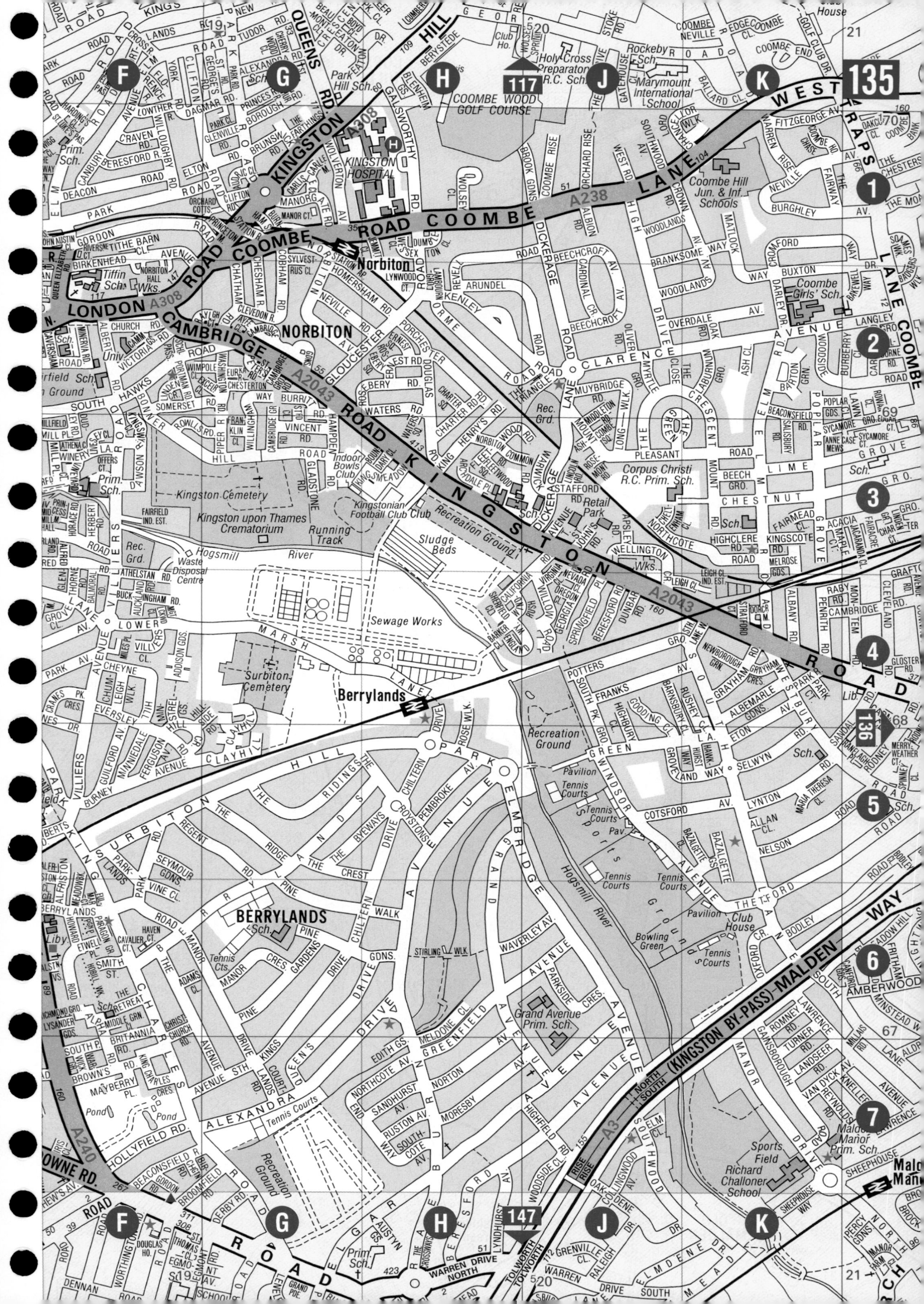

135
117
147
136
F
G
H
J
K
1
2
3
4
5
6
7
KINGSTON HILL
QUEENS RD.
COOMBE WOOD GOLF COURSE
Holy Cross Preparatory R.C. Sch.
Marymount International School
Rockeby Sch.
COOMBE LANE WEST
KINGSTON HOSPITAL
Park Hill Sch.
COOMBE ROAD
A238
A308
LONDON ROAD
Norbiton
NORBITON
CAMBRIDGE ROAD
A2043
KINGSTON ROAD
Tiffin Sch.
Coombe Hill Jun. & Inf. Schools
Coombe Girls' Sch.
CLARENCE AVENUE
LANGLEY AVENUE
COOMBE LANE
Corpus Christi R.C. Prim. Sch.
Kingston Cemetery
Kingston upon Thames Crematorium
FAIRFIELD IND. EST.
Indoor Bowls Club
Kingstonian Football Club
Running Track
Recreation Ground
Sludge Beds
Retail Park
Rec. Grd.
Hogsmill River
Waste Disposal Centre
Sewage Works
LOWER MARSH LANE
Surbiton Cemetery
Berrylands
PARK AVENUE
THE ROYSTONS
Recreation Ground
Pavilion
Tennis Courts
Sports Ground
Bowling Green
Club House
BERRYLANDS Sch.
GRAND AVENUE
ELMBRIDGE AVENUE
Grand Avenue Prim. Sch.
ALEXANDRA DRIVE
Tennis Courts
Recreation Ground
KINGSTON BY-PASS
MALDEN WAY
A3
Sports Field
Richard Challoner School
Malden Manor Prim. Sch.
EWELL ROAD
A240
HOLLYFIELD RD.
WARREN DRIVE NORTH
TOLWORTH
SURBITON HILL PARK
VILLIERS AVENUE
ELMDENE

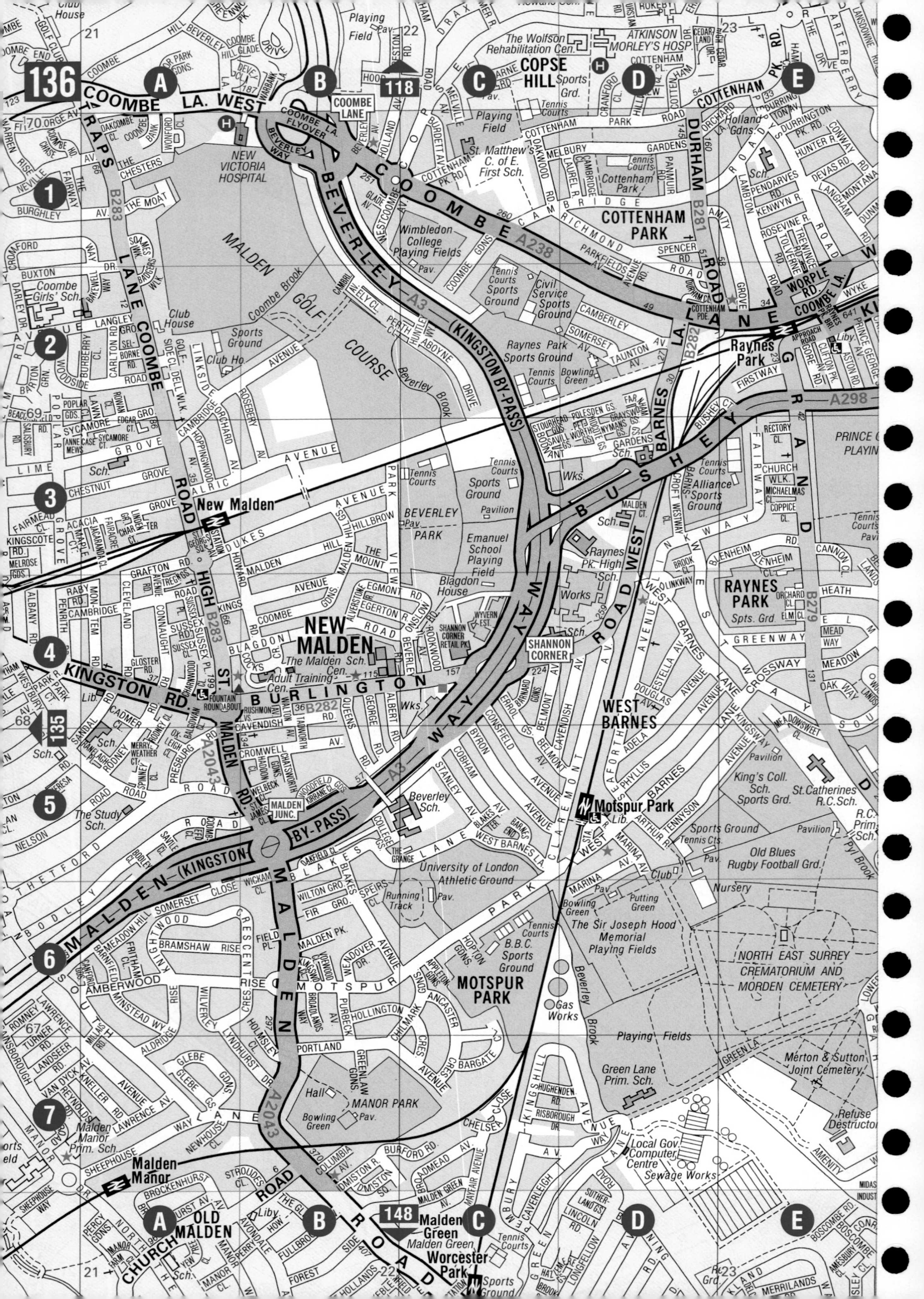
COOMBE LA. WEST
NEW VICTORIA HOSPITAL
COPSE HILL
The Wolfson Rehabilitation Cen.
ATKINSON MORLEY'S HOSP.
COTTENHAM PARK
COOMBE A238
BEVERLEY A3 (KINGSTON BY-PASS)
MALDEN GOLF COURSE
Coombe Girls' Sch.
Wimbledon College Playing Fields
Civil Service Sports Ground
Raynes Park Sports Ground
Raynes Park
New Malden
NEW MALDEN
KINGSTON RD.
BURLINGTON
BEVERLEY PARK
Emanuel School Playing Field
Raynes Pk. High Sch.
SHANNON CORNER
WEST BARNES
RAYNES PARK
BUSHEY RD. A298
Motspur Park
MALDEN JUNC.
MALDEN RD. A2043
University of London Athletic Ground
The Sir Joseph Hood Memorial Playing Fields
NORTH EAST SURREY CREMATORIUM AND MORDEN CEMETERY
King's Coll. Sch. Sports Grd.
St. Catherines R.C. Sch.
Old Blues Rugby Football Grd.
B.B.C. Sports Ground
MOTSPUR PARK
Gas Works
MANOR PARK
Green Lane Prim. Sch.
Merton & Sutton Joint Cemetery
Local Gov. Computer Centre
Sewage Works
Malden Manor
OLD MALDEN
Malden Green
Worcester Park
Malden Manor Prim. Sch.
The Study Sch.
Beverley Sch.
The Malden Sch. Cen.
Adult Training Cen.
Blagdon House

118
135
148

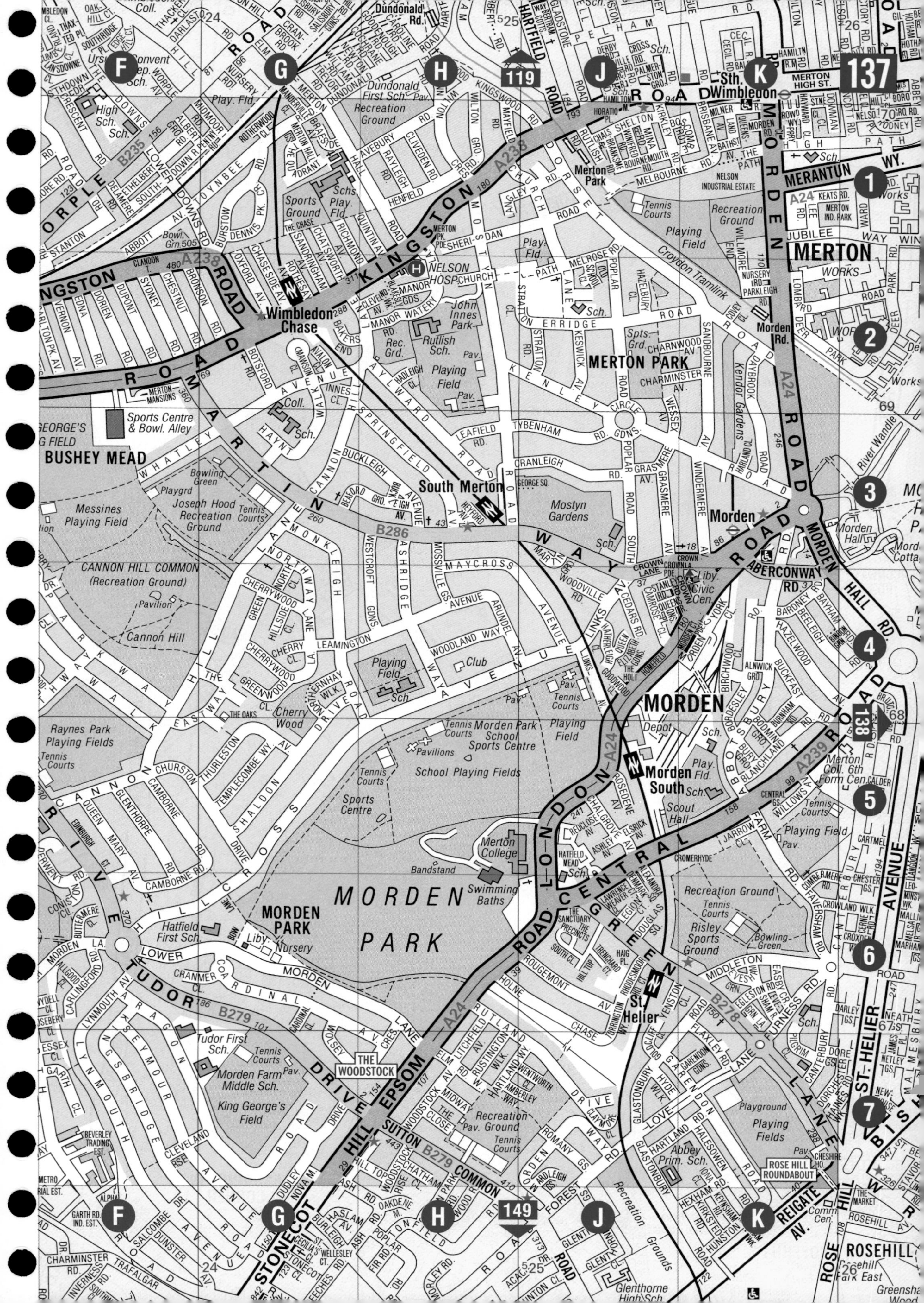

F
G
H
J
K
119
149
138
1
2
3
4
5
6
7
24
25
26
MERTON
MERTON PARK
MORDEN
MORDEN PARK
BUSHEY MEAD
ROSEHILL
KINGSTON ROAD
MARTIN WAY
MORDEN ROAD
LONDON ROAD
CENTRAL ROAD
EPSOM ROAD
STONECOT HILL
SUTTON COMMON ROAD
TUDOR DRIVE
MORDEN HALL ROAD
ST. HELIER AVENUE
Wimbledon Chase
South Merton
Morden South
Morden
Morden Rd.
Merton Park
Dundonald Rd.
Sth. Wimbledon
St. Helier
Cannon Hill Common (Recreation Ground)
Joseph Hood Recreation Ground
Messines Playing Field
Raynes Park Playing Fields
Morden Park School Sports Centre
School Playing Fields
Merton College
Swimming Baths
John Innes Park
Mostyn Gardens
Kendor Gardens
Sports Centre & Bowl. Alley
Rutlish Sch.
King George's Field
Morden Farm Middle Sch.
Tudor First Sch.
Hatfield First Sch.
Risley Sports Ground
Recreation Ground
Abbey Prim. Sch.
Croydon Tramlink
NELSON HOSP.
NELSON INDUSTRIAL ESTATE
MERTON IND. PARK
ROSE HILL ROUNDABOUT
THE WOODSTOCK
Glenthorne High Sch.

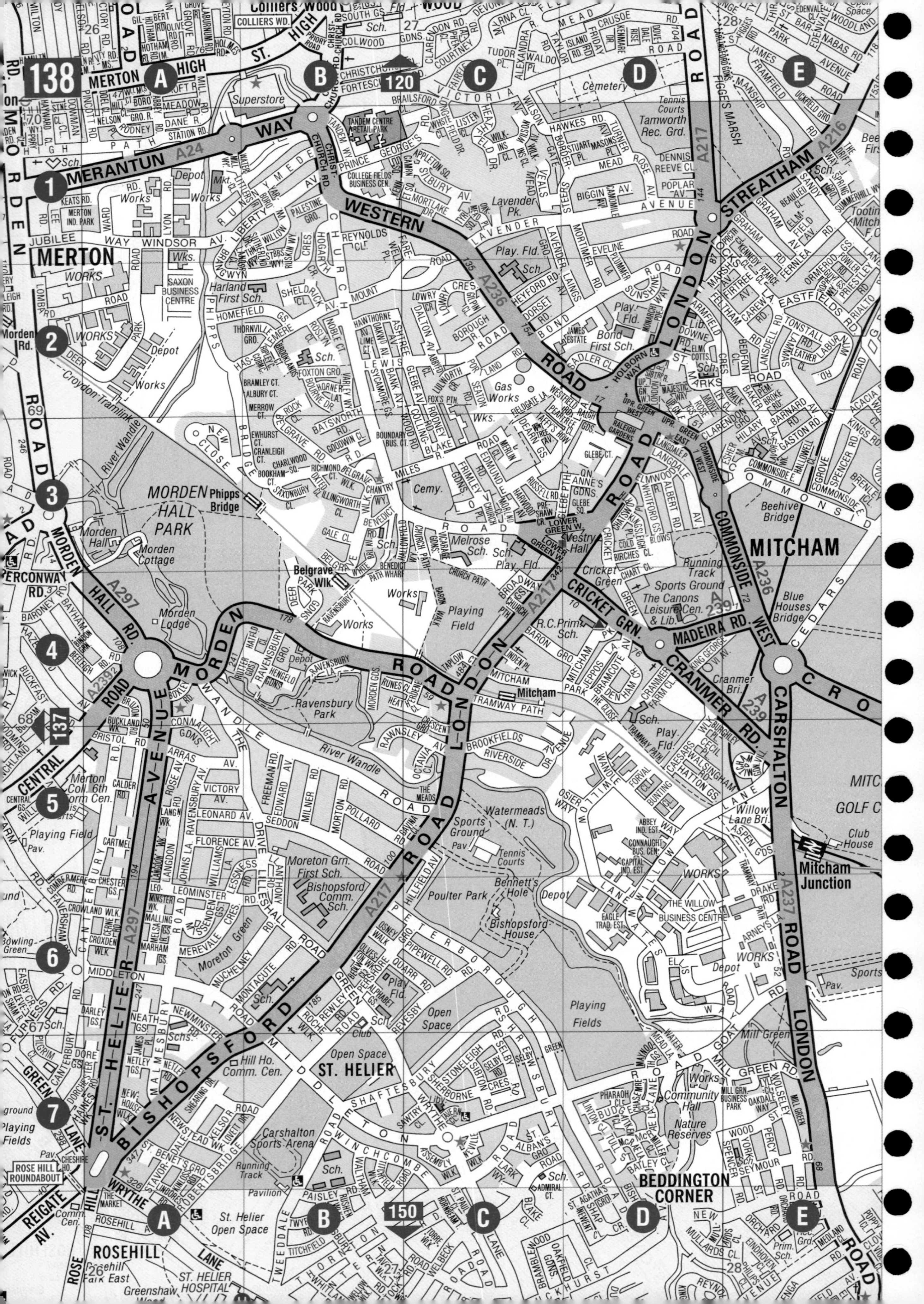

138
Colliers Wood
COLLIERS WD.
120
A
B
C
D
E
1
2
3
4
5
6
7
MERTON
MERANTUN WAY
A24
Superstore
TANDEM CENTRE RETAIL PARK
WESTERN ROAD
A236
LAVENDER AVENUE
Lavender Pk.
Cemetery
Tamworth Rec. Grd.
FIGGES MARSH
A217
STREATHAM ROAD
A216
LONDON ROAD
MITCHAM
Harland First Sch.
SAXON BUSINESS CENTRE
Morden Rd.
Croydon Tramlink
River Wandle
MORDEN HALL PARK
Phipps Bridge
Morden Hall
Morden Cottage
Morden Lodge
MORDEN HALL RD.
A297
A239
MORDEN ROAD
Belgrave Wlk.
Cemy.
Gas Works
Bond First Sch.
Vestry Hall
Cricket Green
CRICKET GRN.
Running Track
Sports Ground
The Canons Leisure Cen. & Lib.
COMMONSIDE WEST
Beehive Bridge
Blue Houses Bridge
MADEIRA RD.
CRANMER RD.
Cranmer Bri.
Mitcham
TRAMWAY PATH
Ravensbury Park
Playing Field
R.C.Prim. Sch.
137
CENTRAL RD.
Merton Coll. 6th Form Cen.
Playing Field
ST. HELIER AVENUE
Watermeads (N. T.)
Sports Ground
Tennis Courts
Poulter Park
Bennett's Hole
Bishopsford House
Moreton Grn. First Sch.
Bishopsford Comm. Sch.
Moreton Green
BISHOPSFORD ROAD
Playing Fields
Open Space
ST. HELIER
Hill Ho. Comm. Cen.
Carshalton Sports Arena
Running Track
Pavilion
ROSE HILL ROUNDABOUT
REIGATE AV.
WRYTHE LANE
St. Helier Open Space
ROSEHILL
ST. HELIER HOSPITAL
150
BEDDINGTON CORNER
Community Hall
Nature Reserves
Mill Green
CARSHALTON ROAD
A237
LONDON ROAD
Mitcham Junction
Willow Lane Bri.
ABBEY IND. EST.
CONNAUGHT BUS. CEN.
CAPITAL IND. EST.
THE WILLOW BUSINESS CENTRE
WORKS
Depot
Club House
MITCHAM GOLF C
Sports

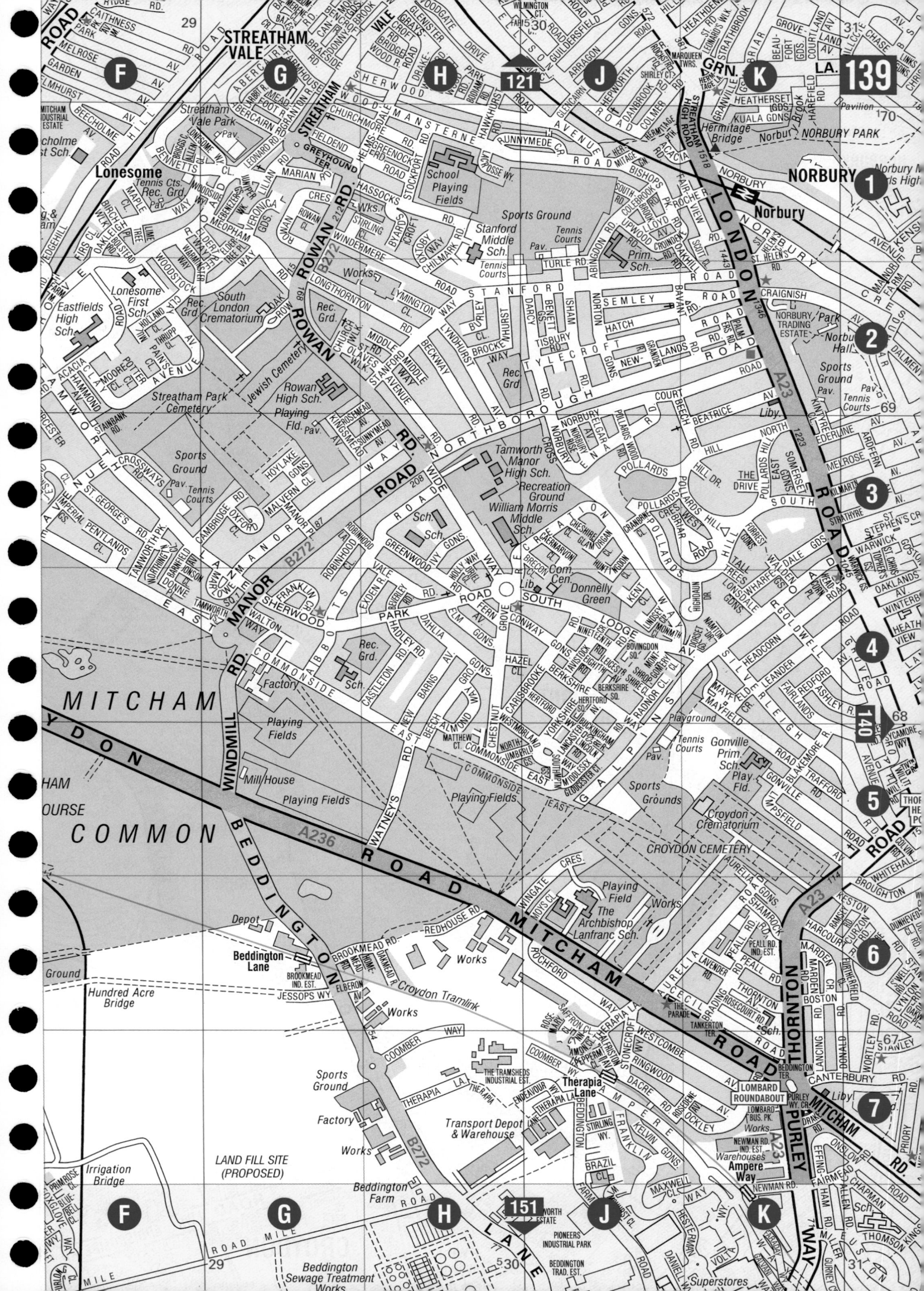

139
STREATHAM VALE
F
G
H
J
K
121
NORBURY
Norbury
1
2
3
4
5
6
7
Streatham Vale Park
Lonesome
Lonesome First Sch.
Eastfields High Sch.
South London Crematorium
Streatham Park Cemetery
Jewish Cemetery
Rowan High Sch.
School Playing Fields
Sports Ground
Stanford Middle Sch.
Tennis Courts
Tamworth Manor High Sch.
Recreation Ground
William Morris Middle Sch.
Donnelly Green
NORBURY PARK
NORBURY TRADING ESTATE
Norbury Hall
Sports Ground
MITCHAM
COMMON
Playing Fields
Mill House
Factory
Croydon Crematorium
CROYDON CEMETERY
Gonville Prim. Sch.
Sports Grounds
The Archbishop Lanfranc Sch.
Playing Field
Works
Beddington Lane
Hundred Acre Bridge
Croydon Tramlink
THE TRAMSHEDS INDUSTRIAL EST.
Therapia Lane
Transport Depot & Warehouse
LAND FILL SITE (PROPOSED)
Irrigation Bridge
Beddington Farm
Beddington Sewage Treatment Works
Ampere Way
LOMBARD ROUNDABOUT
Superstores
PIONEERS INDUSTRIAL PARK
BEDDINGTON TRAD. EST.
151
140
LONDON ROAD
MITCHAM ROAD
STREATHAM HIGH ROAD
THORNTON ROAD
PURLEY WAY
NORTHBOROUGH ROAD
MANOR ROAD
ROWAN RD.
BEDDINGTON LANE
WINDMILL RD.
COMMONSIDE EAST
A23
A236
B272
29
30
31
70
69
68
67

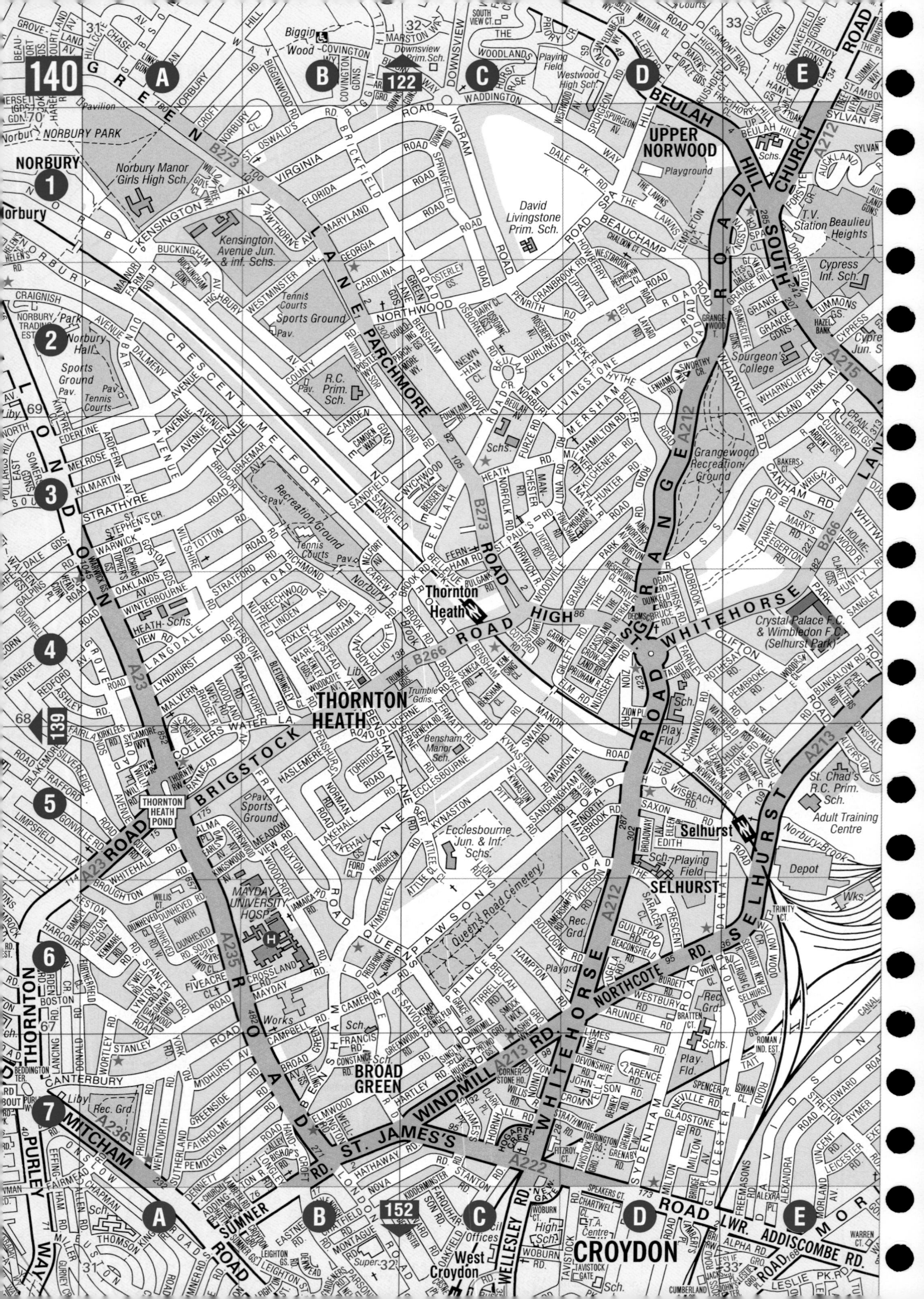
A
B
C
D
E
1
2
3
4
5
6
7
122
139
152
NORBURY
Norbury
NORBURY PARK
Norbury Manor Girls High Sch.
Kensington Avenue Jun. & Inf. Schs.
Norbury Hall
Sports Ground
Tennis Courts
R.C. Prim. Sch.
Recreation Ground
Biggin Wood
Downsview Prim.Sch.
David Livingstone Prim. Sch.
UPPER NORWOOD
Playground
Westwood High Sch.
Spurgeon's College
Grangewood Recreation Ground
Cypress Inf. Sch.
Beaulieu Heights
T.V. Station
Thornton Heath
THORNTON HEATH
Crystal Palace F.C. & Wimbledon F.C. (Selhurst Park)
Bensham Manor Sch.
THORNTON HEATH POND
Ecclesbourne Jun. & Inf. Schs.
Queen's Road Cemetery
MAYDAY UNIVERSITY HOSP.
Selhurst
SELHURST
Playing Field
St. Chad's R.C. Prim. Sch.
Adult Training Centre
Depot
Wks.
BROAD GREEN
CROYDON
West Croydon
High Sch.
T.A. Centre
GREEN LANE
PARCHMORE ROAD
BEULAH HILL
SOUTH NORWOOD HILL
CHURCH ROAD
BRIGSTOCK ROAD
HIGH STREET
WHITEHORSE LANE
WHITEHORSE ROAD
ST. JAMES'S RD.
WINDMILL RD.
LONDON ROAD
WITCHAM ROAD
PURLEY WAY
NORTHCOTE RD.
SELHURST ROAD
LWR. ADDISCOMBE RD.
A23
A212
A213
A215
A222
A235
A236
B266
B273

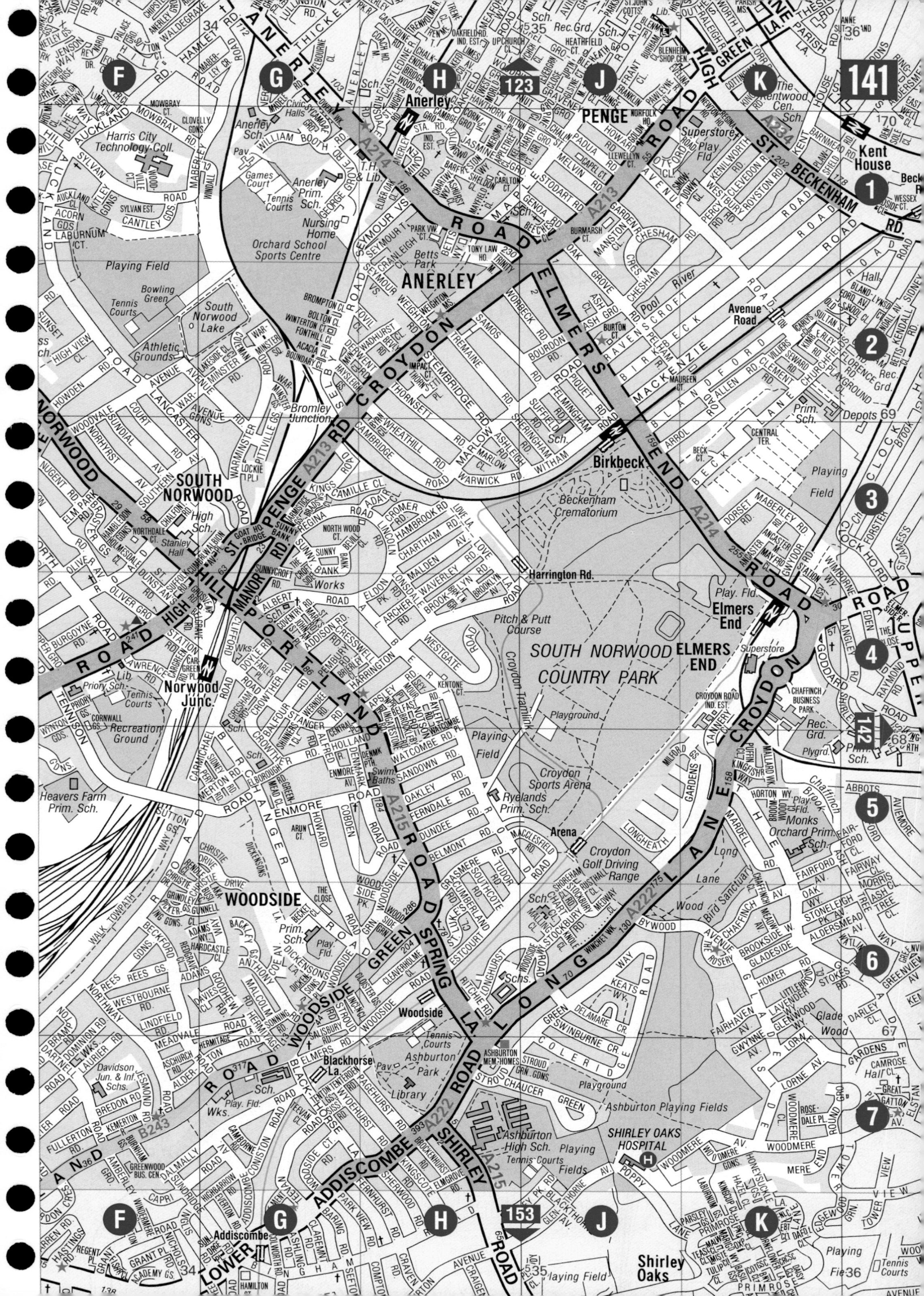

141
F
G
H
J
K
123
153
142
1
2
3
4
5
6
7
34
35
36
67
68
69
170
PENGE
ANERLEY
SOUTH NORWOOD
WOODSIDE
Anerley
Kent House
Birkbeck
Elmers End
Norwood Junc.
Woodside
Blackhorse La.
Arena
Harrington Rd.
Avenue Road
Addiscombe
Shirley Oaks
SOUTH NORWOOD COUNTRY PARK
Beckenham Crematorium
Harris City Technology Coll.
South Norwood Lake
Bromley Junction
Croydon Sports Arena
Croydon Golf Driving Range
Ashburton Park
Ashburton Playing Fields
Ashburton High Sch.
SHIRLEY OAKS HOSPITAL
Croydon Tramlink
Pitch & Putt Course
Heavers Farm Prim. Sch.
Ryelands Prim. Sch.
Monks Orchard Prim. Sch.
Davidson Jun. & Inf. Schs.
Anerley Prim. Sch.
Orchard School Sports Centre
Recreation Ground
Playing Field
Betts Park
Library
CROYDON RD
ELMERS END ROAD
PORTLAND ROAD
WOODSIDE GREEN
SPRING LA
LONG LANE
ADDISCOMBE ROAD
SHIRLEY ROAD
PENGE RD
HIGH STREET
ANERLEY RD
ST. BECKENHAM RD.
A213
A214
A215
A222
A234
B243

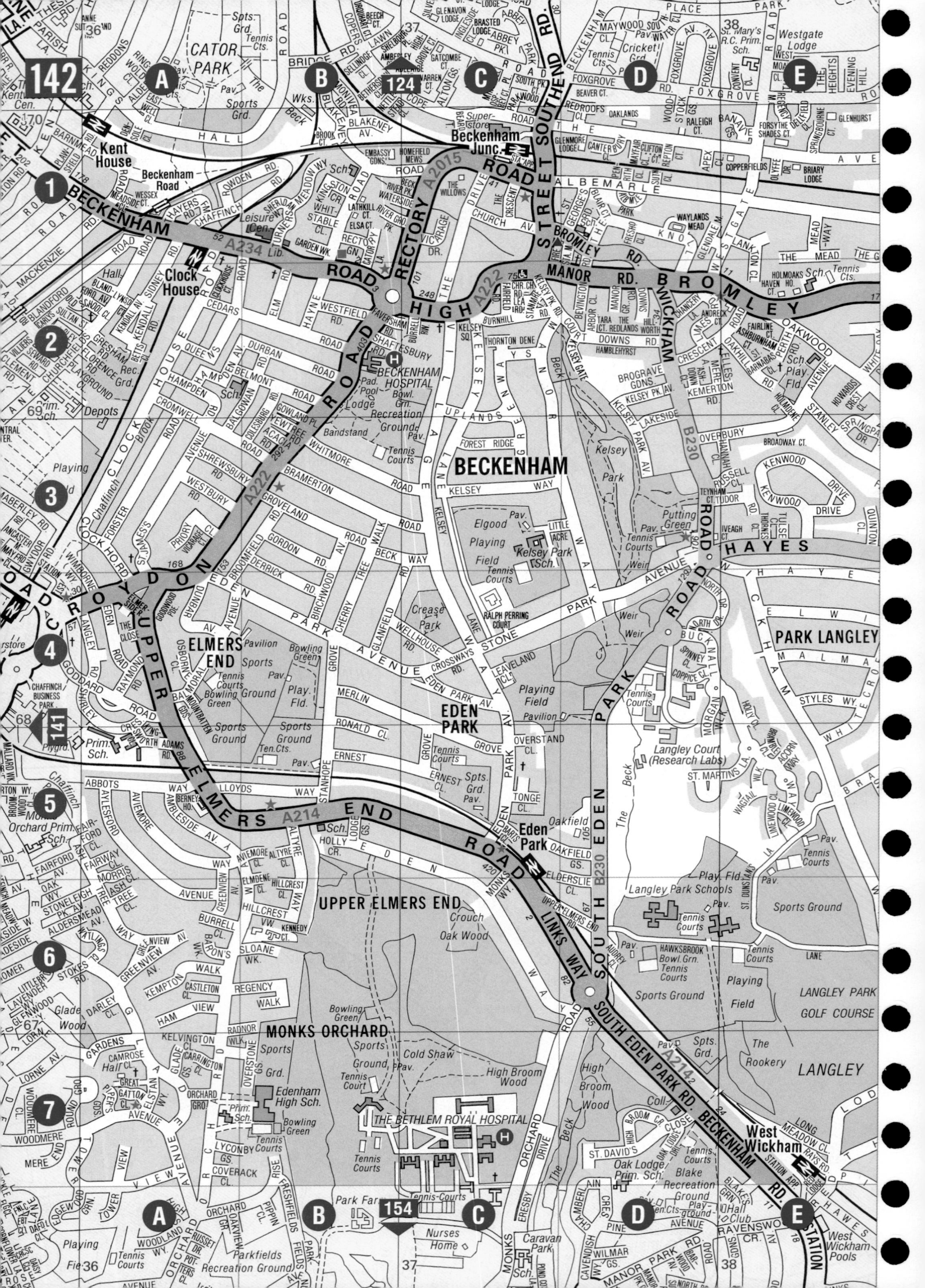

142
124
141
154
A
B
C
D
E
1
2
3
4
5
6
7
36
37
38
BECKENHAM
ELMERS END
EDEN PARK
PARK LANGLEY
UPPER ELMERS END
MONKS ORCHARD
LANGLEY
West Wickham
Kent House
Beckenham Road
Clock House
Beckenham Junc.
Eden Park
CATOR PARK
Kelsey Park
Crease Park
Elgood Playing Field
Kelsey Park Sch.
Beckenham Hospital
Recreation Ground
Langley Court (Research Labs)
Langley Park Schools
LANGLEY PARK GOLF COURSE
THE BETHLEM ROYAL HOSPITAL
Edenham High Sch.
Crouch Oak Wood
High Broom Wood
High Broom Wood
Cold Shaw
The Rookery
Glade Wood
Oak Lodge Prim. Sch.
Blake Recreation Ground
Parkfields Recreation Ground
Nurses Home
Caravan Park
Monks Orchard Prim. Sch.
West Wickham Pools
BECKENHAM ROAD
CROYDON ROAD
UPPER ELMERS END
ELMERS END ROAD
HIGH STREET
SOUTHEND ROAD
RECTORY ROAD
MANOR RD.
BROMLEY RD.
WICKHAM ROAD
HAYES
PARK ROAD
SOUTH EDEN PARK RD.
LINKS WAY
BECKENHAM RD.
A234
A222
A2015
A214
B230

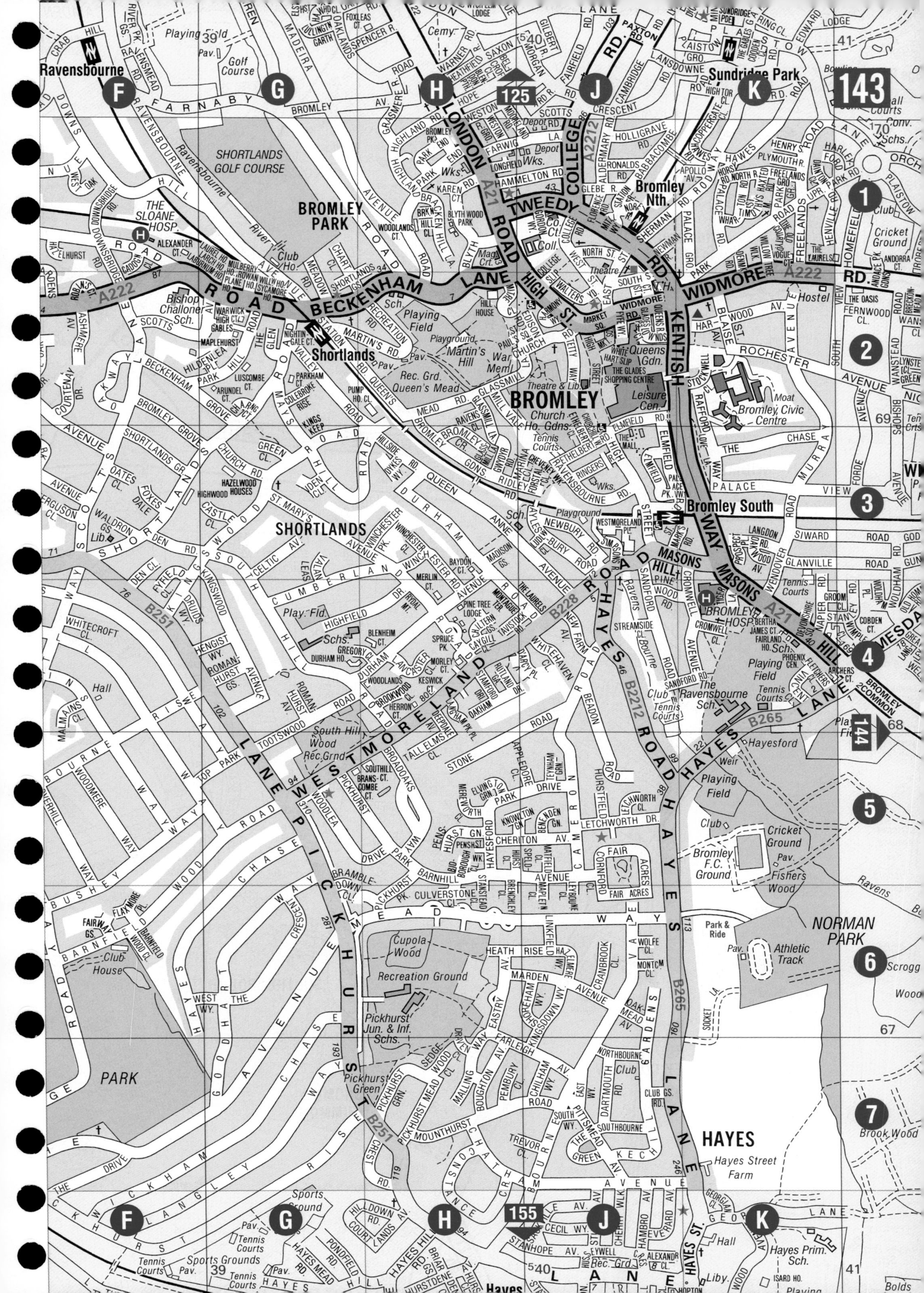
Ravensbourne
Sundridge Park
125
SHORTLANDS GOLF COURSE
THE SLOANE HOSP.
BROMLEY PARK
Bromley Nth.
TWEEDY
A21 ROAD
LONDON
COLLEGE
A2212
WIDMORE
RD.
A222
ROAD
BECKENHAM
LANE
Bishop Challoner Sch.
Shortlands
Martin's Hill
Rec. Grd. Queen's Mead
BROMLEY
Church Ho. Gdns.
The Glades Shopping Centre
Leisure Cen.
Queens Gdn.
KENTISH
WAY
Bromley Civic Centre
Moat
Bromley South
SHORTLANDS
MASONS HILL
A21
BROMLEY HOSP.
B228
B251
WESTMORELAND ROAD
HAYES ROAD
B2212
B265
HAYES LANE
The Ravensbourne Sch.
South Hill Wood Rec.Grnd
Hayesford
144
Playing Field
Cricket Ground
Bromley F.C. Ground
Fishers Wood
NORMAN PARK
Athletic Track
Park & Ride
Cupola Wood
Recreation Ground
Pickhurst Jun. & Inf. Schs.
Pickhurst Green
PICKHURST LANE
PARK
HAYES
Hayes Street Farm
Brook Wood
155
Hayes Prim. Sch.
Sports Ground
Sports Grounds
Tennis Courts
1
2
3
4
5
6
7
F
G
H
J
K
39
40
41
67
68
69

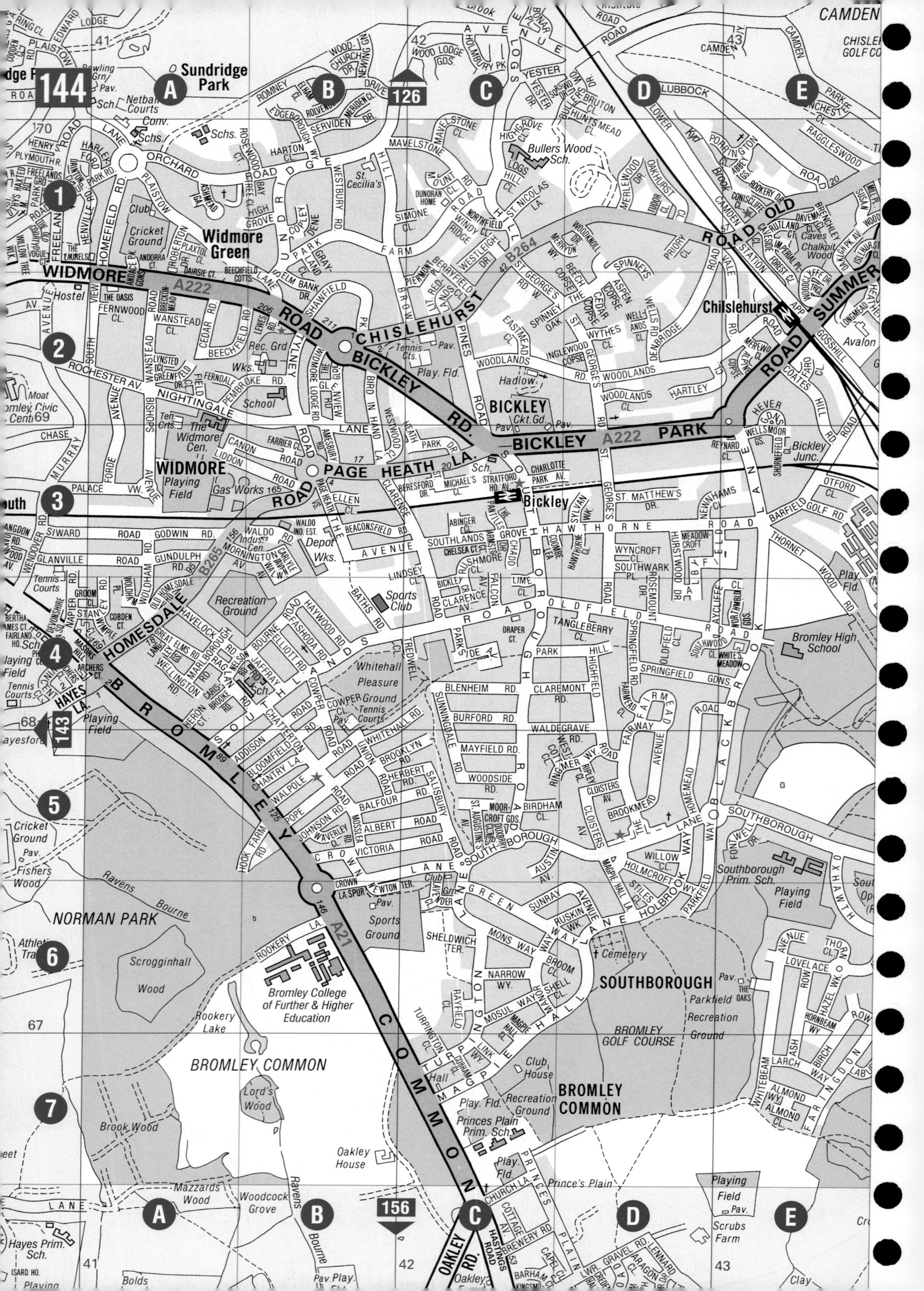
144
A
B
C
D
E
1
2
3
4
5
6
7
126
143
156
41
42
43
67
68
69
170
CAMDEN
CHISLEHURST GOLF CO.
Sundridge Park
Netball Courts
Conv.
Schs.
Sch.
Pav.
ORCHARD
PLAISTOW LANE
SUNDRIDGE AVENUE
HOMEFIELD RD.
Club
Cricket Ground
Widmore Green
WIDMORE ROAD
A222
Hostel
THE OASIS
FERNWOOD CL.
WANSTEAD CL.
CEDAR RD.
BEECHFIELD RD.
Rec. Grd.
Wks.
School
ROCHESTER AV.
NIGHTINGALE
The Widmore Cen.
WIDMORE
Playing Field
Gas Works
PALACE VW.
CHASE
MURRAY
Moat
Bromley Civic Centre
SIWARD ROAD
GODWIN RD.
GLANVILLE ROAD
GUNDULPH RD.
Tennis Courts
HOMESDALE
B265
Recreation Ground
Waldo Indus. Cen.
MORNINGTON AV.
Depot Wks.
BICKLEY RD.
CHISLEHURST ROAD
Tennis Cts.
Pav.
Play. Fld.
PAGE HEATH LA.
BIRD IN HAND LA.
WESTWOOD CL.
LANE
Sch.
Bickley
BICKLEY
Ckt. Gd.
Hadlow
WOODLANDS RD.
BICKLEY PARK
ST. GEORGE'S RD.
HAWTHORNE ROAD
ST. MATTHEW'S DR.
Bullers Wood Sch.
YESTER
LUBBOCK
LOWER CAMDEN
OLD ROAD
SUMMER
Chislehurst
Caves
Chalkpit Wood
Avalon
Bickley Junc.
OTFORD CL.
BARFIELD
GOLF RD.
THORNET WOOD RD.
Play. Fld.
Bromley High School
BLACKBROOK LANE
OLDFIELD ROAD
TANGLEBERRY CL.
PARK HILL
SPRINGFIELD GDNS.
Sports Club
BATHS RD.
Whitehall Pleasure Ground
Tennis Courts
BLENHEIM RD.
BURFORD RD.
MAYFIELD RD.
WOODSIDE RD.
CLAREMONT RD.
WALDEGRAVE RD.
SUNNINGDALE RD.
BROMLEY COMMON
A21
Playing Field
Cricket Ground
Fishers Wood
Ravens Bourne
NORMAN PARK
Athletic Track
Scrogginhall Wood
Rookery Lake
Bromley College of Further & Higher Education
Sports Ground
Lord's Wood
Brook Wood
Oakley House
Mazzards Wood
Woodcock Grove
Hayes Prim. Sch.
SOUTHBOROUGH
SOUTHBOROUGH LANE
Southborough Prim. Sch.
Cemetery
Parkfield Recreation Ground
BROMLEY GOLF COURSE
Club House
Recreation Ground
Princes Plain Prim. Sch.
Prince's Plain
Playing Field
Scrubs Farm
OAKLEY RD.
HASTINGS ROAD
CHURCH LA.
MAGPIE HALL LA.
HOLBROOK WY

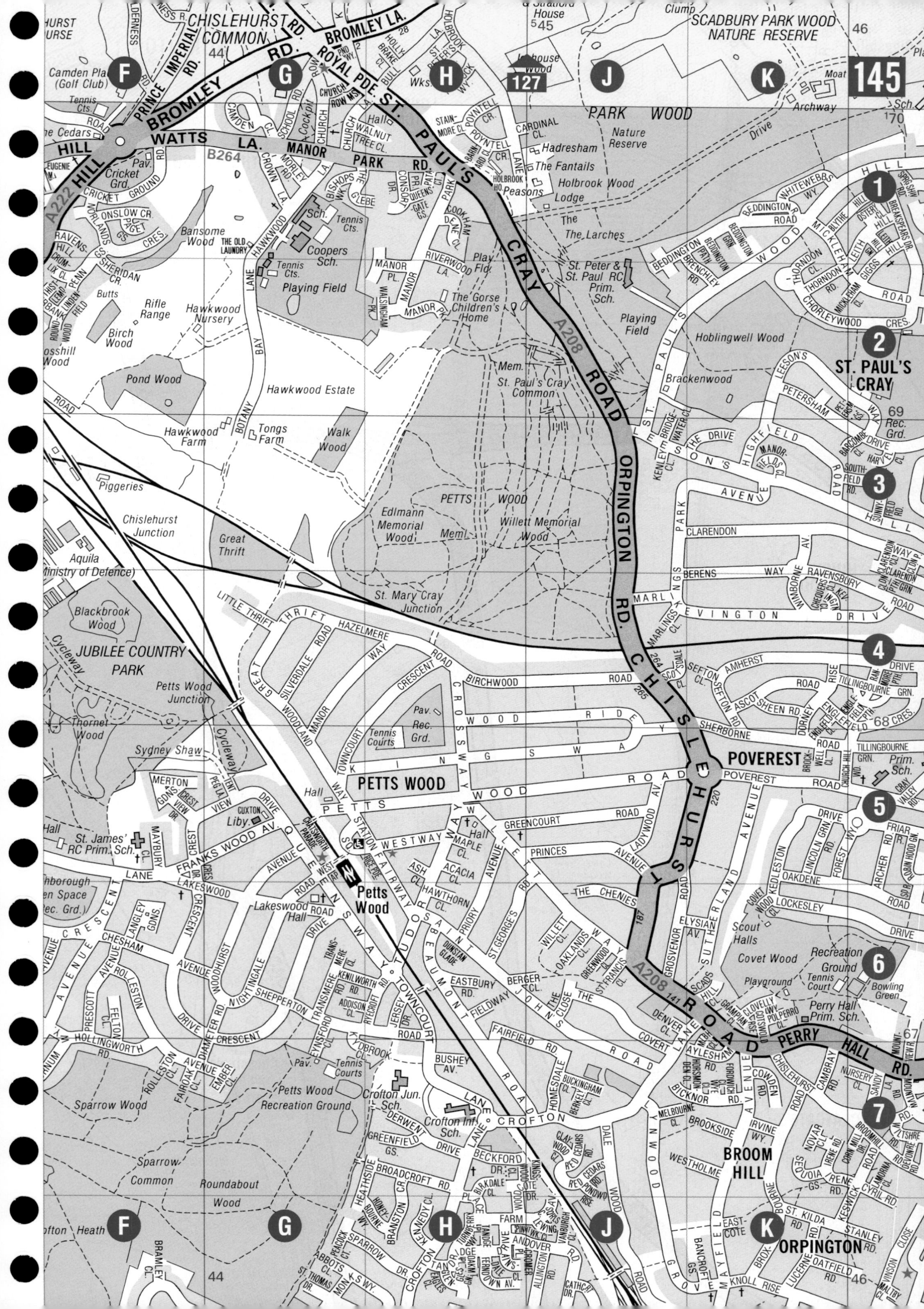

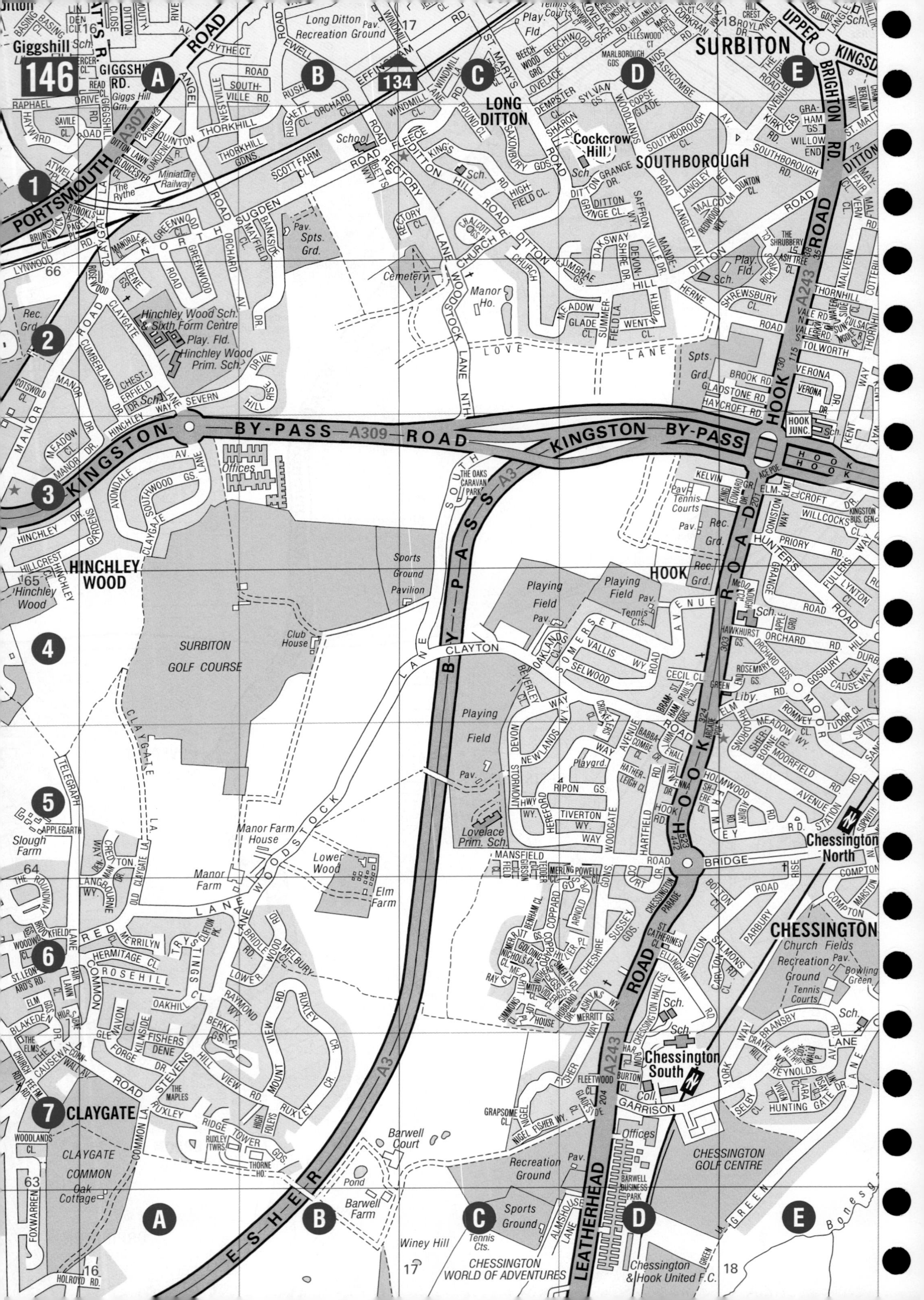

SURBITON
LONG DITTON
SOUTHBOROUGH
Cockcrow Hill
Giggshill
HINCHLEY WOOD
HOOK
CHESSINGTON
CLAYGATE
SURBITON GOLF COURSE
KINGSTON BY-PASS A309 ROAD
KINGSTON BY-PASS
PORTSMOUTH ROAD
ESHER BY-PASS A3
LEATHERHEAD ROAD A243
HOOK ROAD
Chessington North
Chessington South
CHESSINGTON GOLF CENTRE
CHESSINGTON WORLD OF ADVENTURES
Chessington & Hook United F.C.
CLAYGATE COMMON
Long Ditton Recreation Ground
Hinchley Wood Sch. & Sixth Form Centre
Hinchley Wood Prim. Sch.
Lovelace Prim. Sch.
Manor Farm House
Lower Wood
Elm Farm
Barwell Court
Barwell Farm
Winey Hill
Church Fields Recreation Ground
134

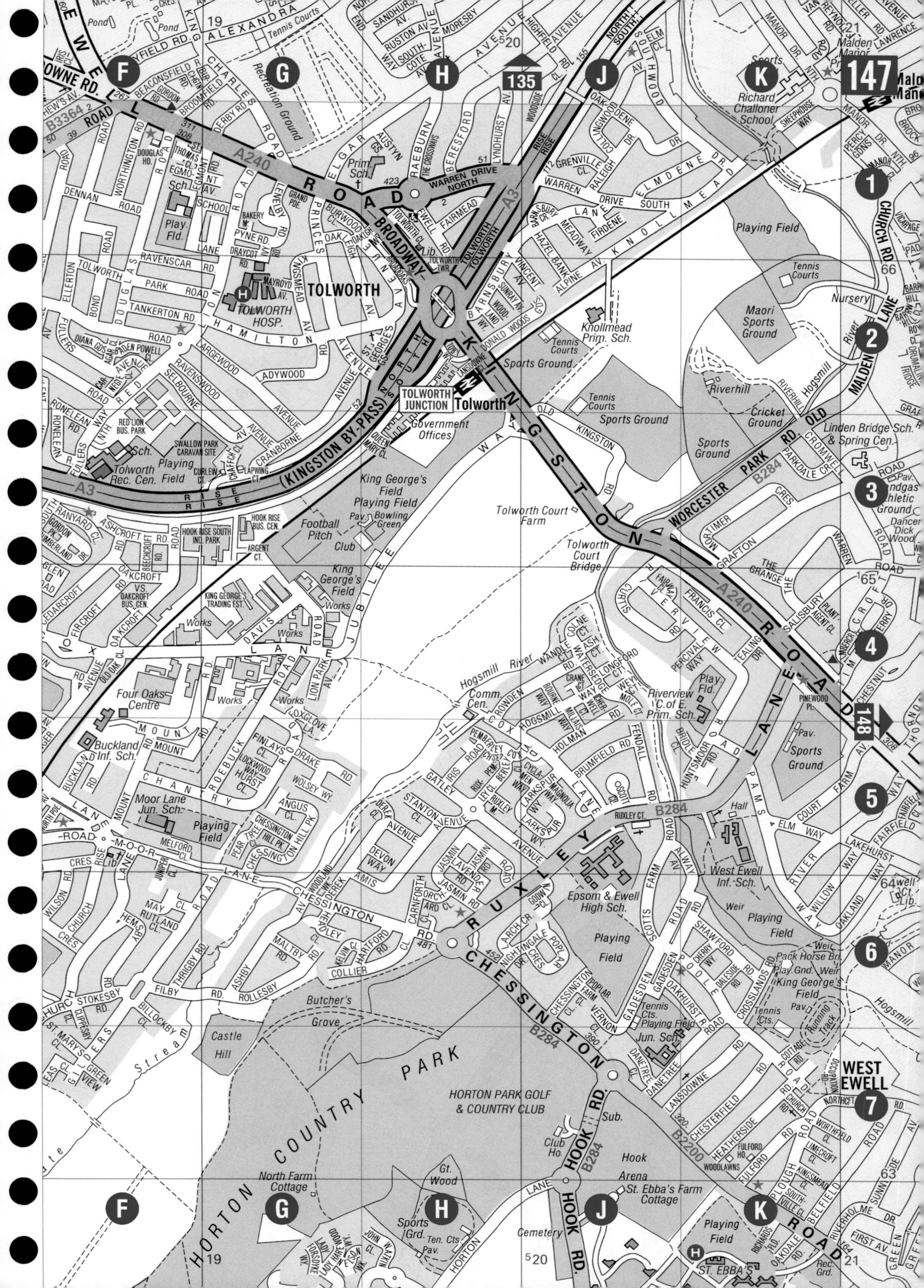
F
G
H
135
J
K
147
1
2
3
4
5
6
7
148
19
20
21
TOLWORTH
Tolworth Hosp.
Tolworth Junction
Tolworth
Government Offices
King George's Field Playing Field
Tolworth Rec. Cen.
Tolworth Court Farm
Tolworth Court Bridge
Knollmead Prim. Sch.
Maori Sports Ground
Richard Challoner School
Riverhill
Cricket Ground
Sports Ground
Linden Bridge Sch. & Spring Cen.
Playing Field
Four Oaks Centre
Buckland Inf. Sch.
Moor Lane Jun. Sch.
Riverview C. of E. Prim. Sch.
Epsom & Ewell High Sch.
West Ewell Inf. Sch.
Hogsmill River
Castle Hill
Butcher's Grove
HORTON COUNTRY PARK
HORTON PARK GOLF & COUNTRY CLUB
North Farm Cottage
Gt. Wood
St. Ebba's Farm Cottage
Hook Arena
Cemetery
WEST EWELL
KINGSTON ROAD
KINGSTON BY-PASS
A3
A240
B284
B2200
B3364
RUXLEY LANE
CHESSINGTON ROAD
WORCESTER PARK RD.
HOOK RD.
MALDEN LANE
CHURCH RD.

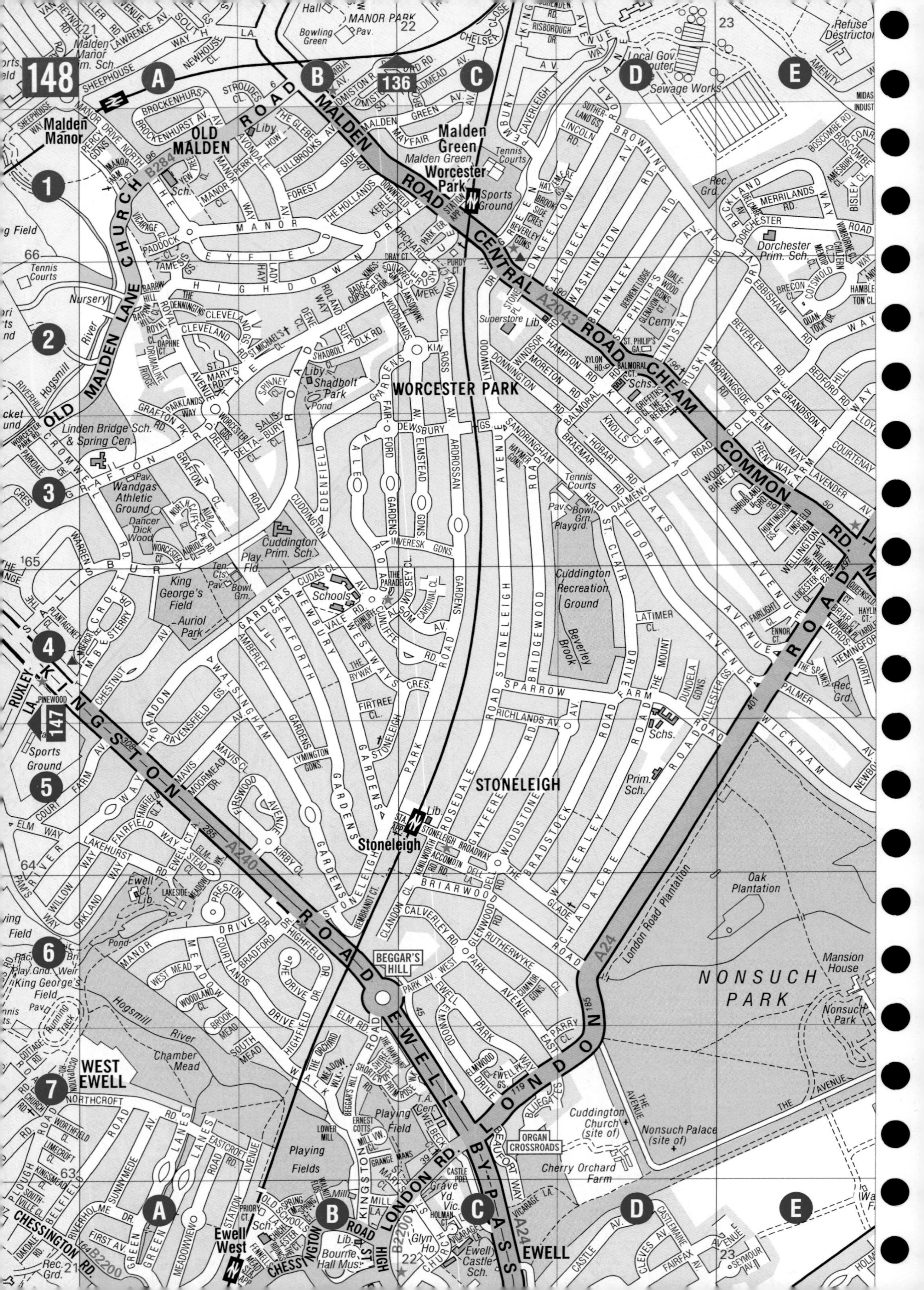

Malden Manor
OLD MALDEN
Malden Green
Worcester Park
WORCESTER PARK
Cuddington Prim. Sch.
King George's Field
Cuddington Recreation Ground
Dorchester Prim. Sch.
STONELEIGH
Stoneleigh
WEST EWELL
Ewell West
EWELL
NONSUCH PARK
Nonsuch Palace (site of)
Cherry Orchard Farm
Cuddington Church (site of)
Oak Plantation
London Road Plantation
Mansion House
Sewage Works
Refuse Destructor
Wandgas Athletic Ground
Hogsmill River
Chamber Mead
Playing Fields
Bourne Hall Mus.
BEGGAR'S HILL
ORGAN CROSSROADS
MALDEN ROAD
CENTRAL ROAD
CHEAM COMMON ROAD
KINGSTON ROAD
EWELL BY-PASS
LONDON ROAD
A2043
A240
A24
B284
B2200

136
147

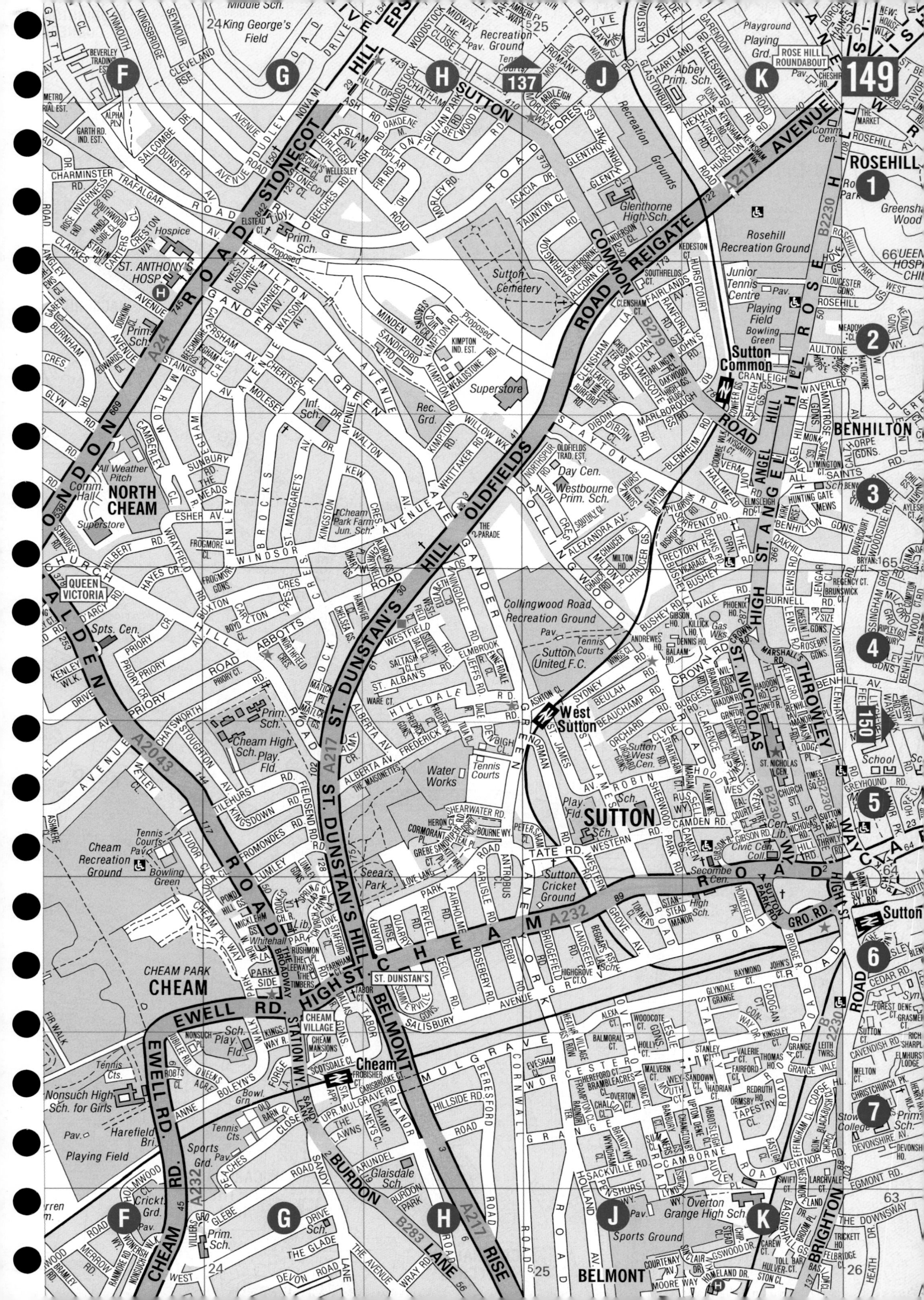
149
137
150
F
G
H
J
K
1
2
3
4
5
6
7
24
25
26
ROSEHILL
BENHILTON
NORTH CHEAM
CHEAM
SUTTON
BELMONT
Sutton Common
West Sutton
Cheam
Sutton
STONECOT HILL
LONDON ROAD
MALDEN ROAD
OLDFIELDS ROAD
ST. DUNSTAN'S HILL
REIGATE AVENUE
COMMON ROAD
ANGEL HILL
ST. NICHOLAS WAY
THROWLEY WAY
HIGH ST.
CHEAM ROAD
EWELL RD.
BELMONT RISE
BURDON LANE
BRIGHTON ROAD
Sutton Cemetery
Rosehill Recreation Ground
Collingwood Road Recreation Ground
Cheam Recreation Ground
CHEAM PARK
Superstore
Sutton United F.C.
Glenthorne High Sch.
Cheam High Sch.
Nonsuch High Sch. for Girls
Overton Grange High Sch.
Sutton Cricket Ground
Seears Park
Water Works
ST. ANTHONY'S HOSP.
King George's Field

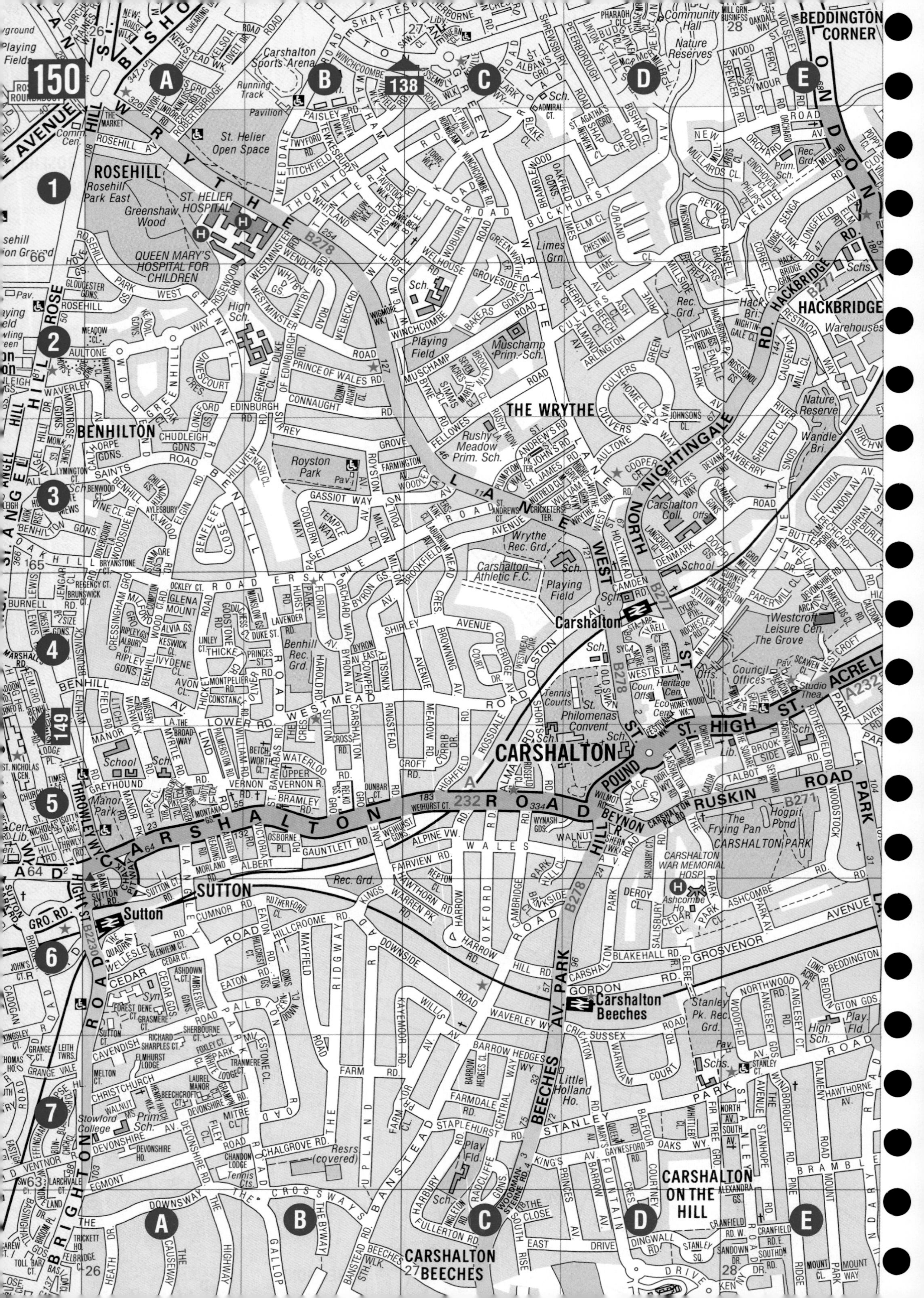

150
138
149
BEDDINGTON CORNER
ROSEHILL
Rosehill Park East
Greenshaw Wood
ST. HELIER HOSPITAL
QUEEN MARY'S HOSPITAL FOR CHILDREN
St. Helier Open Space
Carshalton Sports Arena
Running Track
Pavilion
Community Hall
Nature Reserves
BENHILTON
THE WRYTHE
Muschamp Prim. Sch.
Playing Field
Rushy Meadow Prim. Sch.
Royston Park
Limes Grn.
HACKBRIDGE
Warehouses
Nature Reserve
Wandle Bri.
Carshalton Coll.
Wrythe Rec. Grd.
Carshalton Athletic F.C.
Carshalton
Benhill Rec. Grd.
Westcroft Leisure Cen.
The Grove
Council Offices
Studio Thea.
Heritage Cen.
St. Philomenas Convent
CARSHALTON
Manor Park
SUTTON
Sutton
The Frying Pan
Hogpit Pond
CARSHALTON PARK
CARSHALTON WAR MEMORIAL HOSP.
Ashcombe Ho.
Carshalton Beeches
Stanley Pk. Rec. Grd.
Little Holland Ho.
High Sch.
Stowford College
Resrs (covered)
Tennis Cts.
CARSHALTON ON THE HILL
CARSHALTON BEECHES
B278
B277
B271
A232
B2230
A
B
C
D
E
1
2
3
4
5
6
7
26
27
28
63
64
65
66

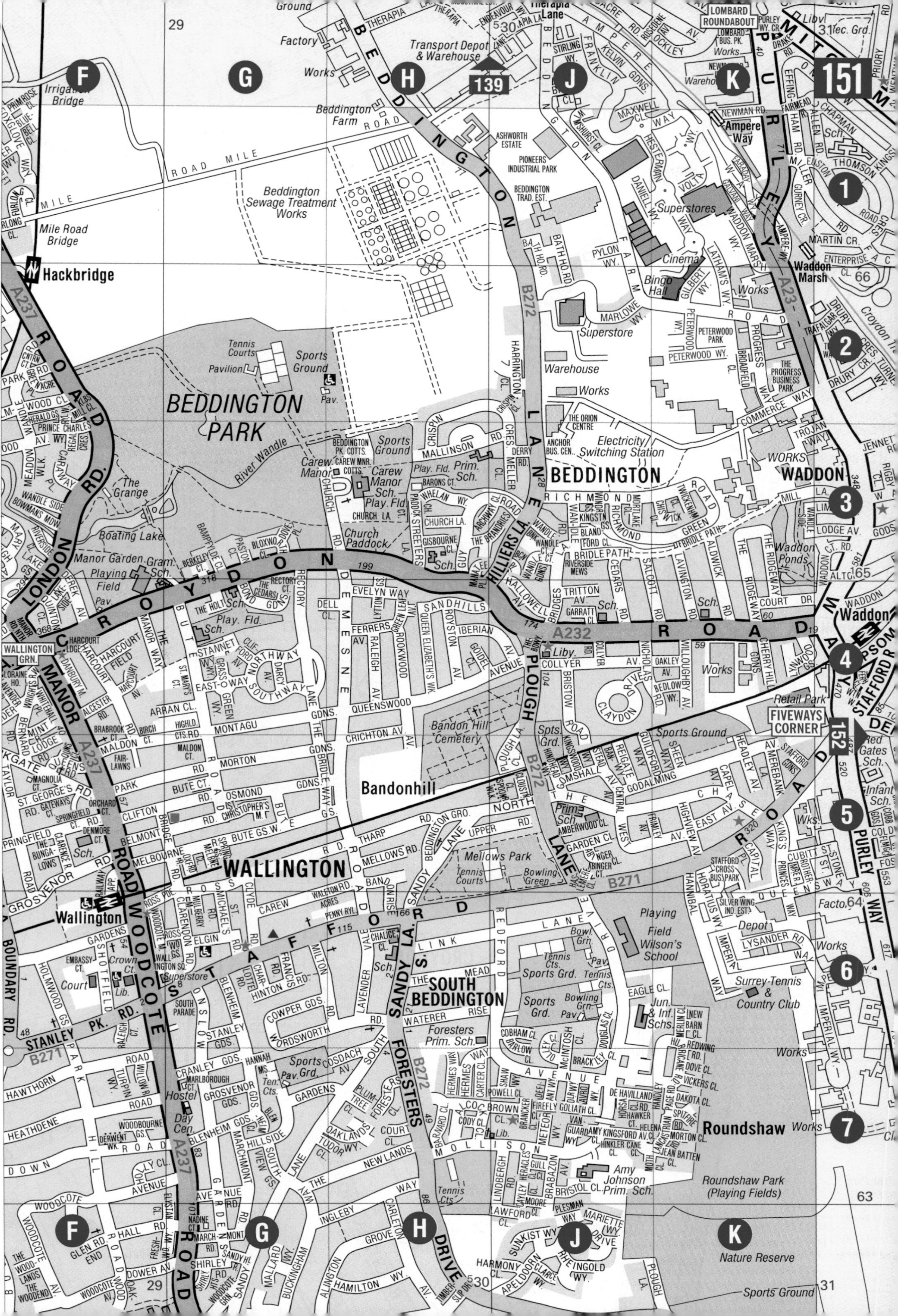
F
G
H
J
K
1
2
3
4
5
6
7
29
30
31
139
152
BEDDINGTON PARK
BEDDINGTON
WALLINGTON
SOUTH BEDDINGTON
WADDON
Bandonhill
Roundshaw
Hackbridge
Wallington
Waddon
Waddon Marsh
Ampere Way
Therapia Lane
LOMBARD ROUNDABOUT
FIVEWAYS CORNER
Beddington Sewage Treatment Works
Beddington Farm
Mile Road Bridge
Irrigation Bridge
Transport Depot & Warehouse
Superstores
Superstore
Cinema
Bingo Hall
Electricity Switching Station
Bandon Hill Cemetery
Mellows Park
Carew Manor
Church Paddock
Boating Lake
The Grange
River Wandle
Manor Garden Playing Field
Playing Field Wilson's School
Surrey Tennis & Country Club
Roundshaw Park (Playing Fields)
Nature Reserve
Amy Johnson Prim. Sch.
Foresters Prim. Sch.
Waddon Ponds
Retail Park
Red Gates Sch.
LONDON ROAD
CROYDON ROAD
MANOR ROAD
WOODCOTE ROAD
BEDDINGTON LANE
PLOUGH LANE
STAFFORD ROAD
PURLEY WAY
SANDY LANE
FORESTERS DRIVE
A237
A232
A23
B272
B271

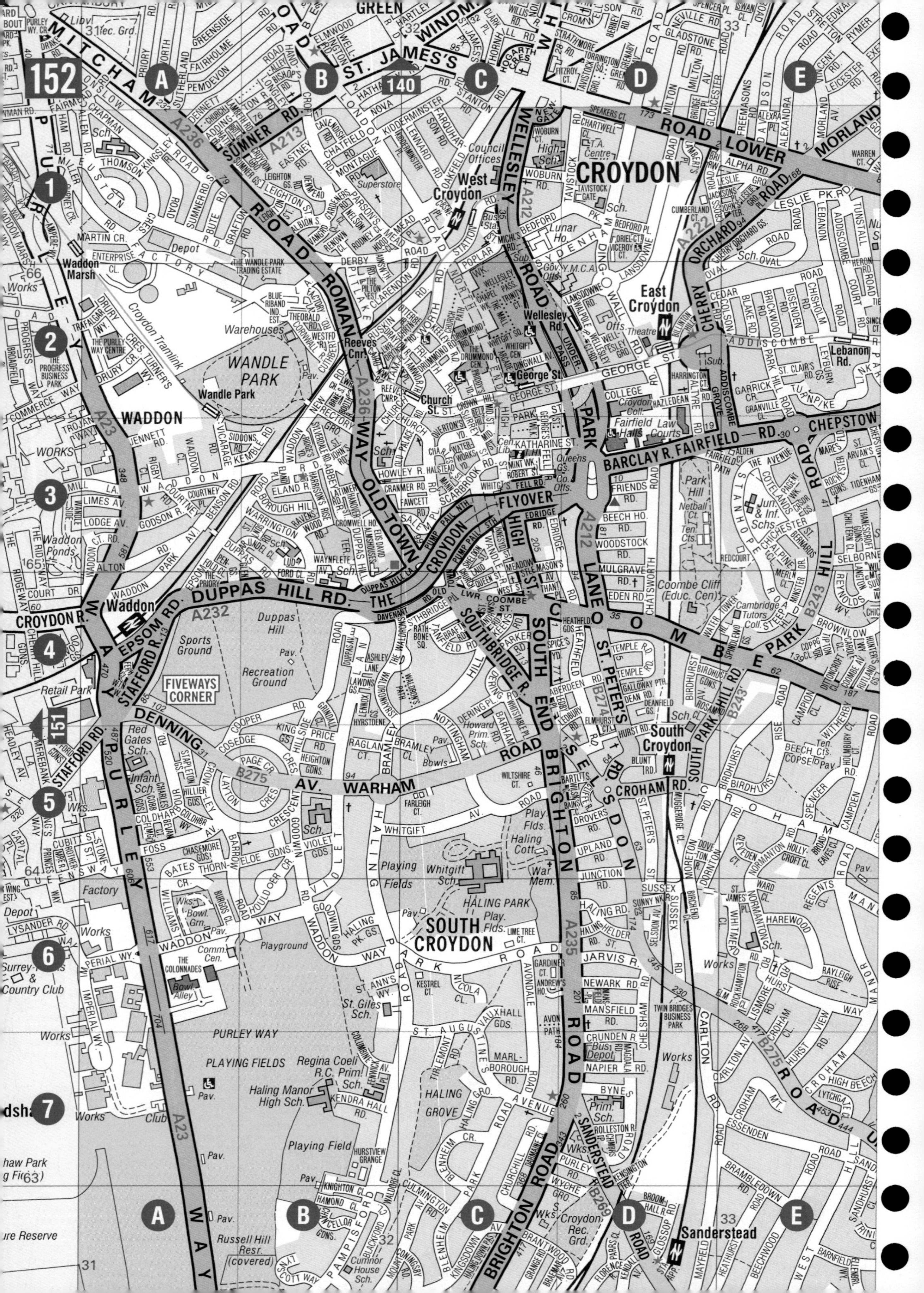
A
B
C
D
E
1
2
3
4
5
6
7
140
151
CROYDON
West Croydon
East Croydon
South Croydon
SOUTH CROYDON
WADDON
Waddon
Waddon Marsh
Sanderstead
WANDLE PARK
Wandle Park
Reeves Cnr.
Church St.
George St.
Wellesley Rd.
Lebanon Rd.
Croydon Tramlink
Warehouses
Depot
Works
Factory
Superstore
Council Offices
Fairfield Halls
Law Courts
Croydon Coll.
Coombe Cliff (Educ. Cen.)
Cambridge Tutors Coll.
Duppas Hill
Sports Ground
Recreation Ground
FIVEWAYS CORNER
Retail Park
Red Gates Sch.
Playing Fields
Whitgift Sch.
HALING PARK
HALING GROVE
PURLEY WAY PLAYING FIELDS
Playground
Regina Coeli R.C. Prim. Sch.
Haling Manor High Sch.
St. Giles Sch.
Playing Field
Russell Hill Resr. (covered)
Croydon Rec. Grd.
Bus Depot
Surrey Country Club
MITCHAM ROAD
ST. JAMES'S
SUMNER RD.
ROMAN WAY
OLD TOWN
FLYOVER
WELLESLEY ROAD
PARK LANE
DUPPAS HILL RD.
DENNING AV.
WARHAM ROAD
PURLEY WAY
BRIGHTON ROAD
SOUTH END
SELSDON ROAD
COOMBE ROAD
PARK HILL
FAIRFIELD RD.
BARCLAY R.
LOWER ADDISCOMBE ROAD
CHERRY ORCHARD ROAD
SOUTH PARK HILL RD.
CROHAM ROAD
CROYDON R.
STAFFORD RD.
EPSOM RD.
WADDON WAY
PARK ROAD
A23
A232
A236
A212
A213
A222
A235
B243
B274
B275
B269

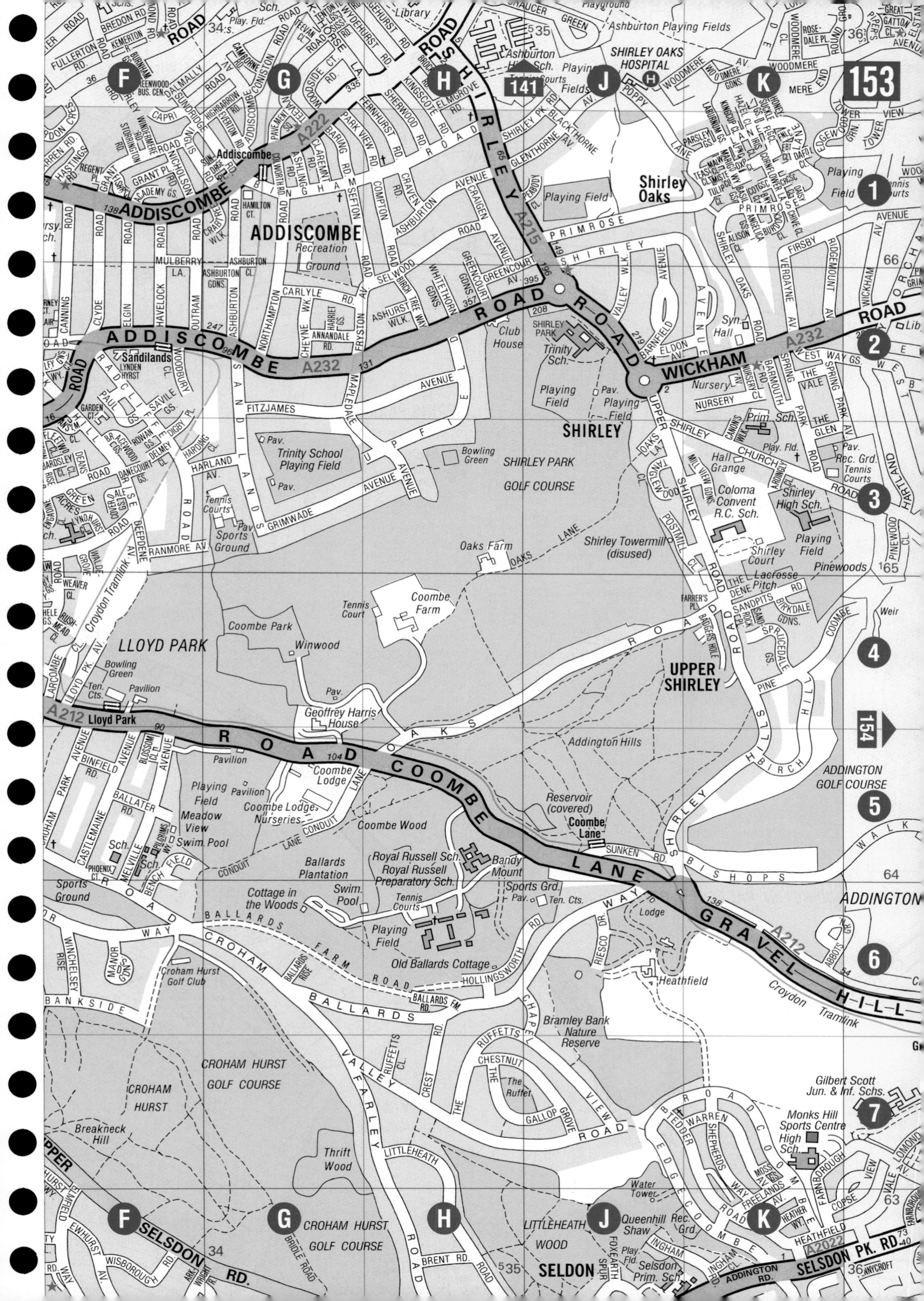
ADDISCOMBE
Addiscombe
Sandilands
LLOYD PARK
Lloyd Park
SHIRLEY
UPPER SHIRLEY
Shirley Oaks
SHIRLEY OAKS HOSPITAL
SHIRLEY PARK GOLF COURSE
ADDINGTON GOLF COURSE
ADDINGTON
CROHAM HURST GOLF COURSE
SELSDON
Addington Hills
Coombe Wood
Shirley Towermill (disused)
Coombe Farm
Oaks Farm
Trinity School Playing Field
Bramley Bank Nature Reserve
Croham Hurst Golf Club
Breakneck Hill
Thrift Wood
LITTLEHEATH WOOD
Queenhill Shaw
Croydon Tramlink
ADDISCOMBE ROAD
WICKHAM ROAD
SHIRLEY ROAD
COOMBE ROAD
COOMBE LANE
GRAVEL HILL
SELSDON RD.
SELSDON PK. RD.
A222
A232
A215
A212
A2022
141
154

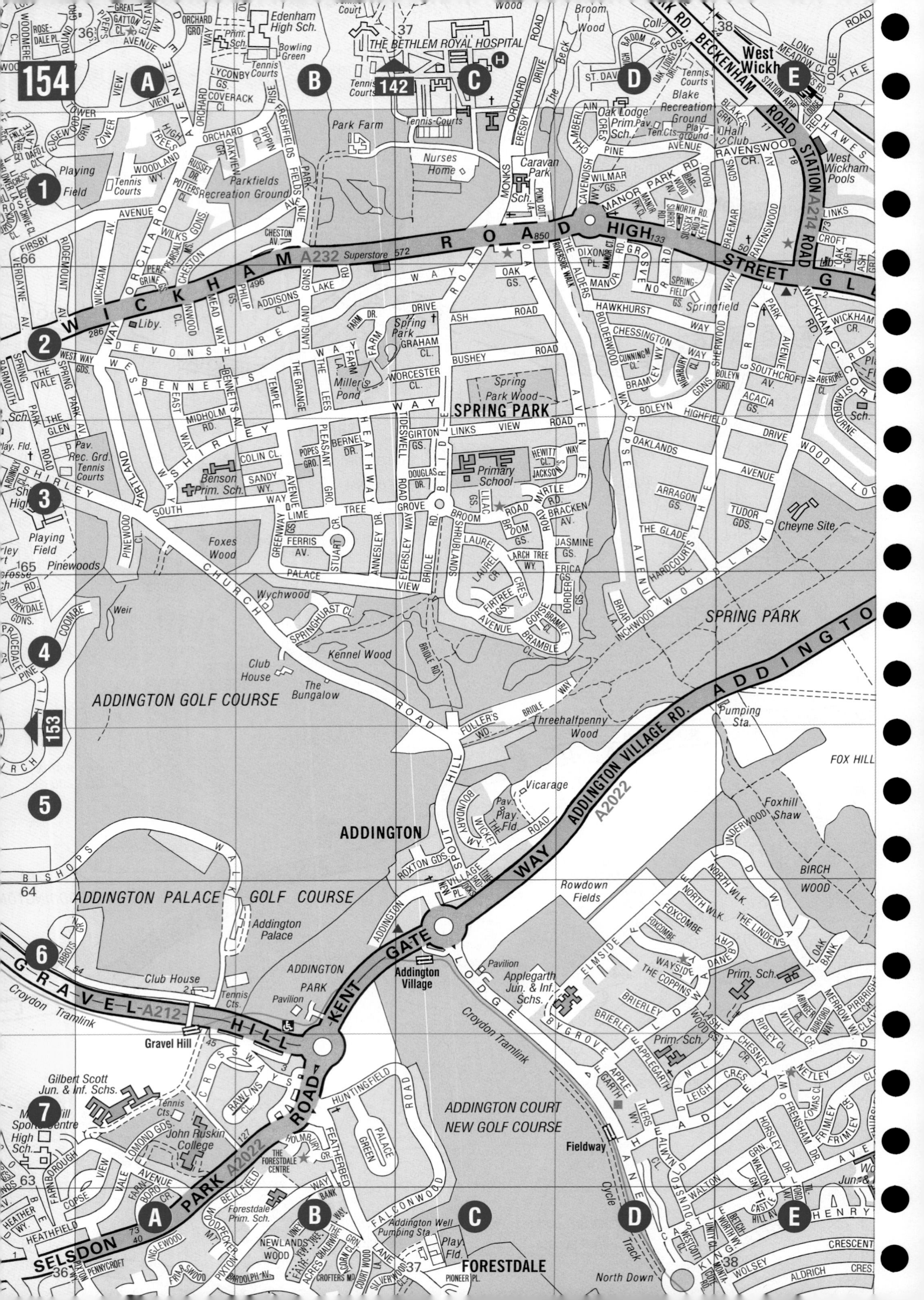

SPRING PARK
ADDINGTON
ADDINGTON GOLF COURSE
ADDINGTON PALACE GOLF COURSE
ADDINGTON COURT NEW GOLF COURSE
FORESTDALE
West Wickham
WICKHAM ROAD
HIGH STREET
ADDINGTON VILLAGE RD.
KENT GATE WAY
GRAVEL HILL
SELSDON PARK ROAD
The Bethlem Royal Hospital
Parkfields Recreation Ground
Spring Park Wood
Foxes Wood
Kennel Wood
Threehalfpenny Wood
Addington Palace
Addington Village
Gravel Hill
Fieldway
Croydon Tramlink
Cheyne Site
Foxhill Shaw
Birch Wood
Rowdown Fields
Applegarth Jun. & Inf. Schs.
Gilbert Scott Jun. & Inf. Schs.
John Ruskin College
Forestdale Prim. Sch.
Addington Well Pumping Sta.
Edenham High Sch.
Benson Prim. Sch.
Oak Lodge Prim. Sch.
Blake Recreation Ground

142
153

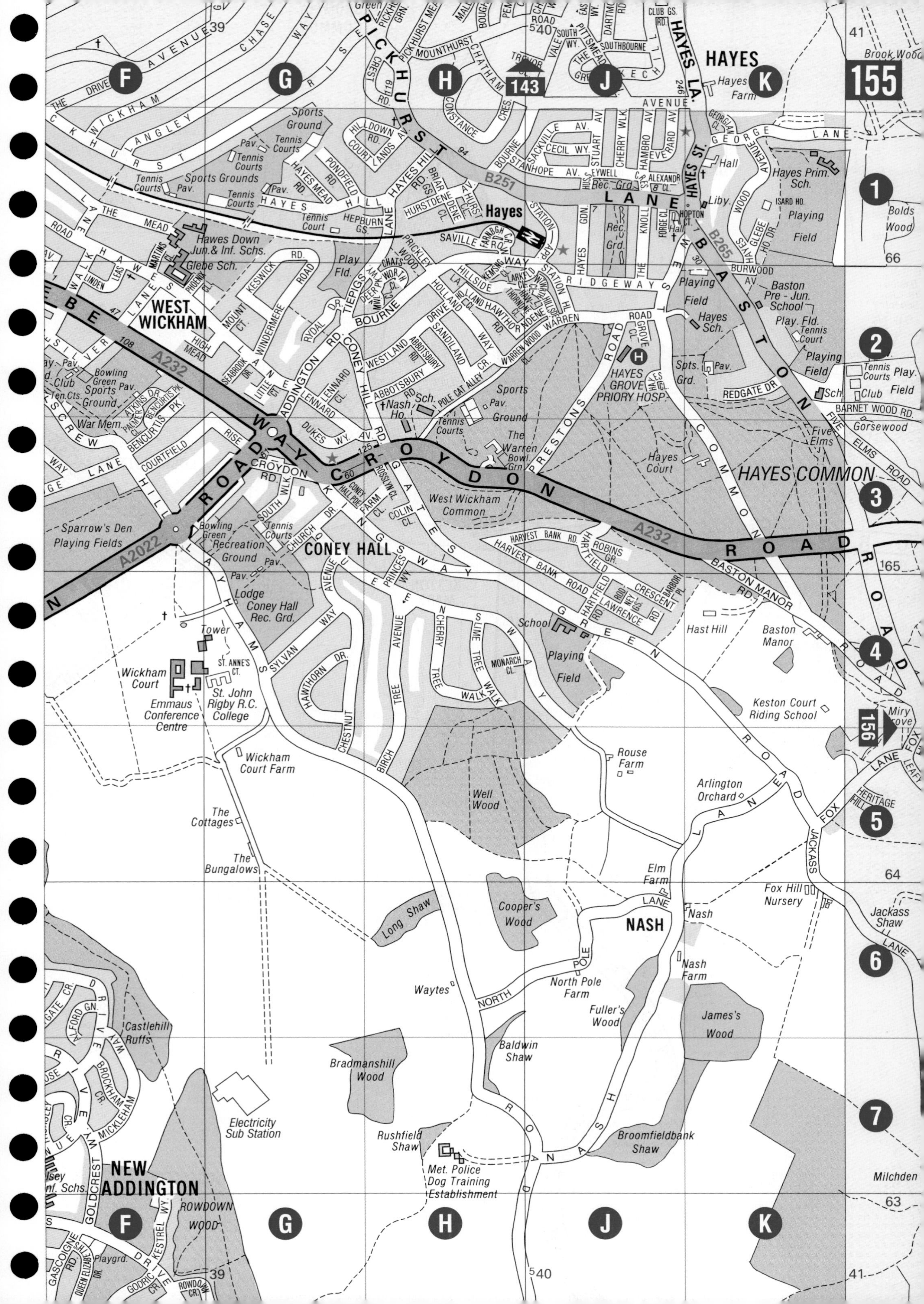
HAYES
WEST WICKHAM
CONEY HALL
HAYES COMMON
NASH
NEW ADDINGTON
Hayes
Hayes Farm
Hayes Prim. Sch.
Hawes Down Jun.& Inf. Schs.
Glebe Sch.
Sports Grounds
Sparrow's Den Playing Fields
Coney Hall Rec. Grd.
Wickham Court
Emmaus Conference Centre
St. John Rigby R.C. College
Wickham Court Farm
HAYES GROVE PRIORY HOSP.
West Wickham Common
Hayes Court
Baston Pre - Jun. School
Hayes Sch.
Baston Manor
Hast Hill
Keston Court Riding School
Rouse Farm
Arlington Orchard
Well Wood
Elm Farm
Cooper's Wood
Long Shaw
Nash Farm
North Pole Farm
Fuller's Wood
James's Wood
Baldwin Shaw
Bradmanshill Wood
Broomfieldbank Shaw
Rushfield Shaw
Met. Police Dog Training Establishment
Electricity Sub Station
Castlehill Ruffs
Rowdown Wood
Fox Hill Nursery
Jackass Shaw
Milchden
Bolds Wood
Gorsewood
Five Elms
CROYDON ROAD
A232
A2022
B251
B265
HAYES LANE
BASTON ROAD
143
156

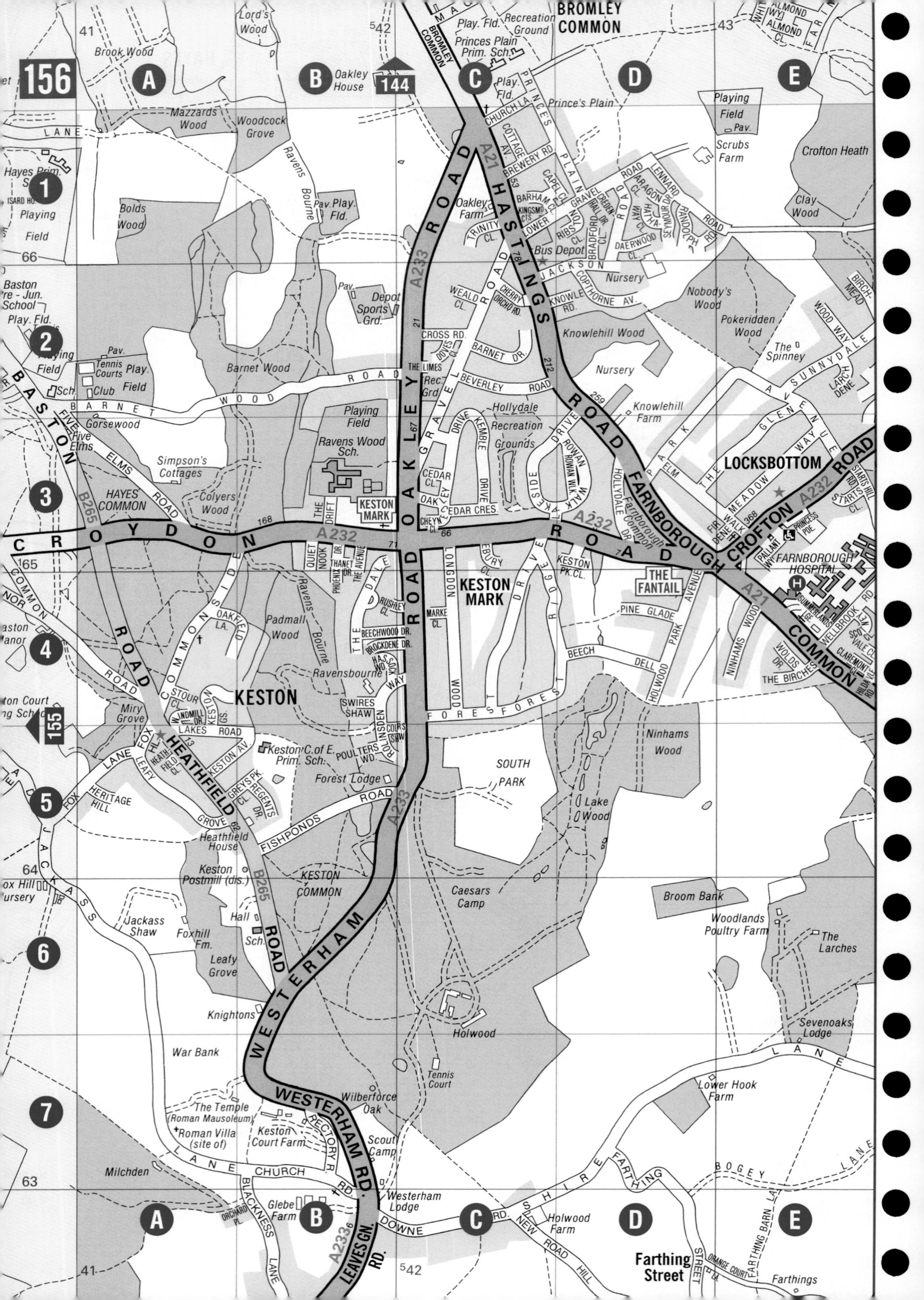
BROMLEY COMMON
Recreation Ground
Princes Plain Prim. Sch.
Lord's Wood
Brook Wood
Mazzards Wood
Woodcock Grove
Oakley House
144
Prince's Plain
Playing Field
Scrubs Farm
Crofton Heath
Hayes Prim. Sch.
Bolds Wood
Ravens Bourne
Oakley Farm
Clay Wood
Bus Depot
Nursery
Nobody's Wood
Pokeridden Wood
Knowlehill Wood
Baston Manor Jun. School
Depot Sports Grd.
Barnet Wood
The Spinney
Gorsewood
Five Elms
Simpson's Cottages
Playing Field
Ravens Wood Sch.
Hollydale Recreation Grounds
Knowlehill Farm
LOCKSBOTTOM
HAYES COMMON
Colyers Wood
KESTON MARK
CROYDON ROAD
A232
OAKLEY ROAD
A233
HASTINGS ROAD
A21
FARNBOROUGH COMMON
CROFTON ROAD
THE FANTAIL
FARNBOROUGH HOSPITAL
KESTON MARK
Padmall Wood
Ravensbourne
KESTON
Miry Grove
155
Swires Shaw
Keston C.of E. Prim. Sch.
Forest Lodge
Ninhams Wood
SOUTH PARK
Lake Wood
Heathfield House
Keston Postmill (dis.)
KESTON COMMON
Caesars Camp
Broom Bank
Woodlands Poultry Farm
The Larches
Jackass Shaw
Foxhill Fm.
Leafy Grove
Knightons
Holwood
Sevenoaks Lodge
War Bank
WESTERHAM ROAD
Tennis Court
Lower Hook Farm
The Temple (Roman Mausoleum)
Roman Villa (site of)
Keston Court Farm
Wilberforce Oak
Scout Camp
Milchden
Glebe Farm
Westerham Lodge
Holwood Farm
Farthing Street
Farthings
CHURCH LANE
DOWNE RD.
SHIRE LANE
BOGEY LANE
NEW ROAD HILL
LEAVES GN. RD.
HEATHFIELD ROAD
FISHPONDS ROAD
FOREST RIDGE
BARNET WOOD ROAD
BASTON ROAD
LANE

LARGE SCALE SECTION

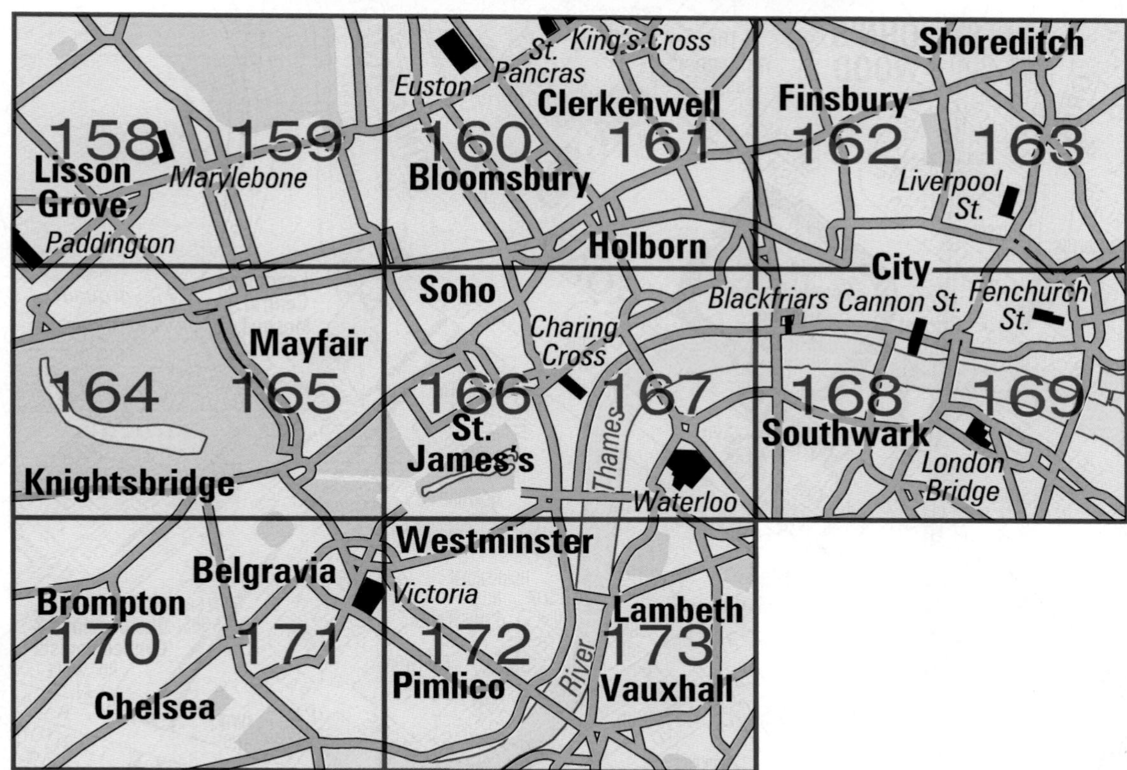

158 Lisson Grove *Paddington* *Marylebone*	159
160 Bloomsbury *Euston* *St. Pancras* King's Cross Clerkenwell	161 Holborn
162 Finsbury *Liverpool St.* Shoreditch	163
164 Knightsbridge	165 Mayfair
166 Soho St. James's *Charing Cross*	167 *Thames* City Blackfriars Cannon St. Fenchurch St. Waterloo
168 Southwark	169 London Bridge
170 Brompton Chelsea	171 Belgravia *Victoria*
172 Westminster Pimlico *River*	173 Lambeth Vauxhall

REFERENCE

A Road	A41	**Church or Chapel**	†
B Road	B524	**Fire Station**	■
Dual Carriageway		**Information Centre**	🛈
		National Grid Reference	$^5 27$
One Way Street	→	**Police Station**	▲
Traffic flow on A Roads is indicated by a heavy line on the drivers' left.		**Post Office**	★
		National Rail Network	⇌
B' road / Minor road	→	**Docklands Light Railway**	DLR
House Numbers	37 3	**Underground Station**	is the registered trade mark of Transport for London
A & B Roads only	20 14	**Educational Establishment**	
Restricted Access		**Hospital or Hospice**	
Pedestrianized Road		**Industrial Building**	
Footpath	- - - - - -	**Leisure or Recreational Facility**	
Residential Walkway	· · · · · · ·	**Place of Interest**	
		Open to the Public	
Page Continuation	Large Scale Map Pages	**Public Building**	
	▲166 ▲66	**Shopping Centre or Market**	
		Other Selected Building	

SCALE

8½ inches to 1 mile   **1:7454**   **13.4cm to 1km**

0 50 100 200 300 Yards ¼ ½ Mile

0 50 100 200 300 400 500 750 Metres 1 Kilometre

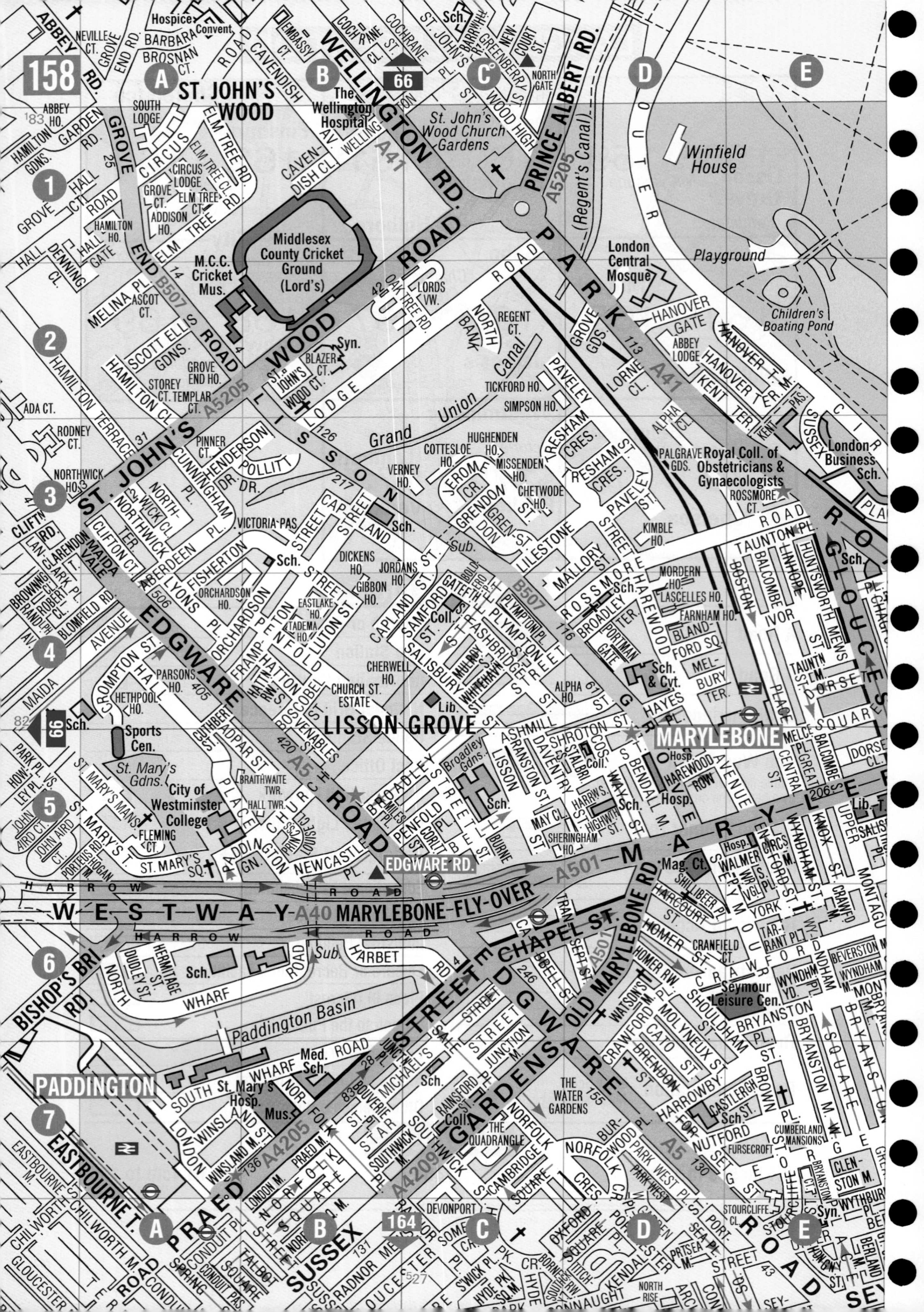
ST. JOHN'S WOOD
LISSON GROVE
MARYLEBONE
PADDINGTON
EDGWARE RD.
Middlesex County Cricket Ground (Lord's)
M.C.C. Cricket Mus.
Winfield House
London Central Mosque
Children's Boating Pond
Playground
Royal Coll. of Obstetricians & Gynaecologists
London Business Sch.
St. John's Wood Church Gardens
The Wellington Hospital
Grand Union Canal
Paddington Basin
St. Mary's Hosp.
City of Westminster College
Seymour Leisure Cen.
Sports Cen.
St. Mary's Gdns.
THE WATER GARDENS
THE QUADRANGLE
WESTWAY A40 MARYLEBONE FLY-OVER
ST. JOHN'S WOOD ROAD A5205
WELLINGTON RD. A41
PRINCE ALBERT RD. A5205 (Regent's Canal)
PARK ROAD A41
EDGWARE ROAD A5
MARYLEBONE RD A501
PRAED STREET A4205
SUSSEX GARDENS A4209
GLOUCESTER PL.
LISSON GROVE B507
GROVE END ROAD B507
OLD MARYLEBONE RD
CHAPEL ST.
HARROW ROAD
BISHOP'S BRI. RD.
EASTBOURNE T.
66
164
82
183
527

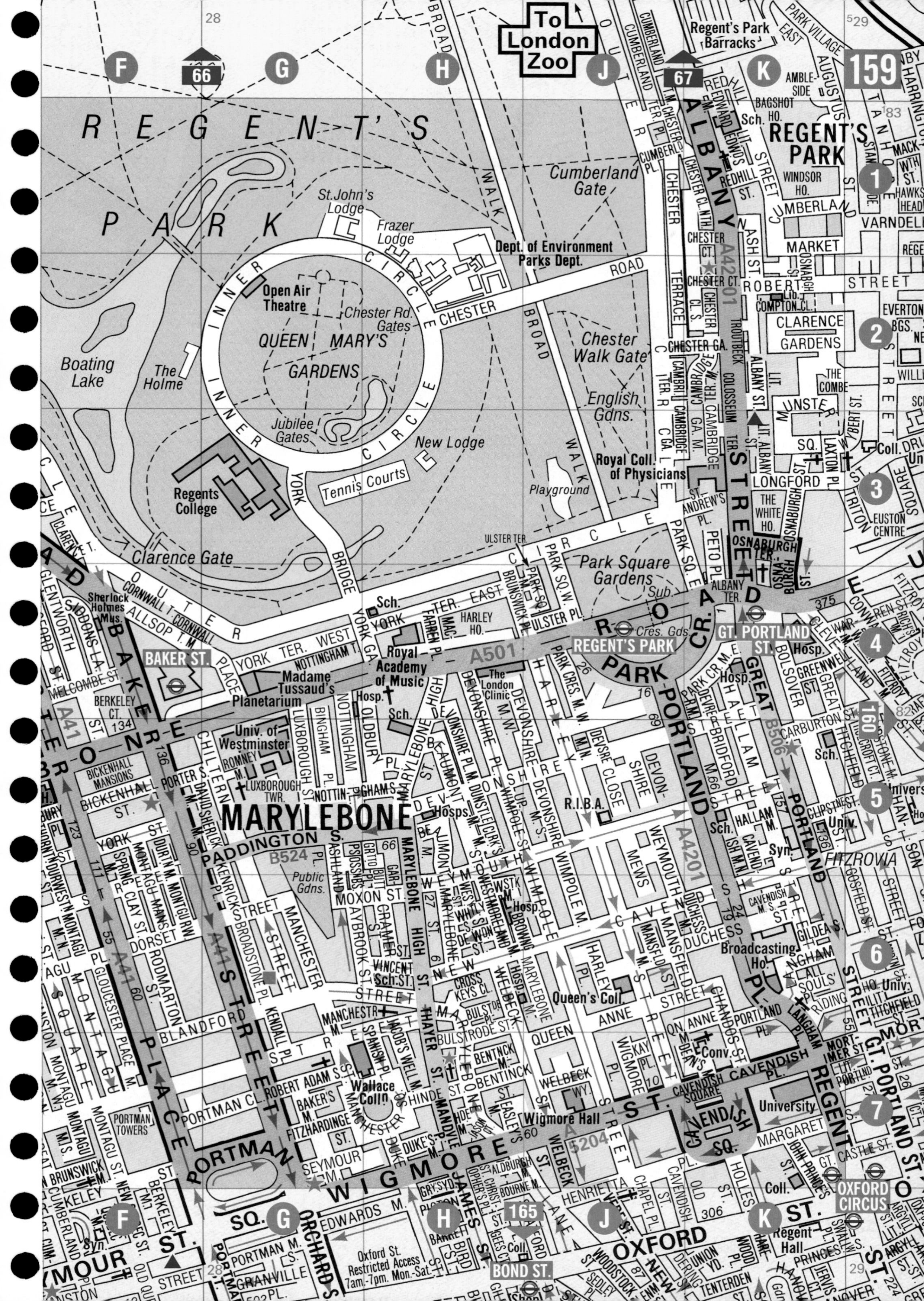

159
To London Zoo
Regent's Park Barracks
REGENT'S PARK
PARK
Cumberland Gate
St. John's Lodge
Frazer Lodge
Dept. of Environment Parks Dept.
CHESTER ROAD
Open Air Theatre
Chester Rd. Gates
QUEEN MARY'S GARDENS
INNER CIRCLE
Boating Lake
The Holme
Chester Walk Gate
English Gdns.
Jubilee Gates
New Lodge
Tennis Courts
Regents College
Royal Coll. of Physicians
Playground
Clarence Gate
OUTER CIRCLE
YORK BRIDGE
Park Square Gardens
Sherlock Holmes Mus.
BAKER ST.
Madame Tussaud's
Planetarium
Royal Academy of Music
The London Clinic
REGENT'S PARK
GT. PORTLAND ST.
PARK CRESCENT
A501
MARYLEBONE ROAD
EUSTON ROAD
Univ. of Westminster
MARYLEBONE
R.I.B.A.
PADDINGTON ST.
Public Gdns.
MARYLEBONE HIGH ST.
WEYMOUTH ST.
NEW CAVENDISH STREET
HARLEY ST.
WIMPOLE ST.
PORTLAND PLACE
GREAT PORTLAND STREET
FITZROVIA
Broadcasting Ho.
Queen's Coll.
QUEEN ANNE STREET
WIGMORE ST.
Wigmore Hall
Wallace Colln.
CAVENDISH SQ.
University
MARGARET ST.
REGENT ST.
OXFORD CIRCUS
OXFORD ST.
BOND ST.
PORTMAN SQ.
BAKER STREET
GLOUCESTER PLACE
MONTAGU SQUARE
BLANDFORD ST.
MANCHESTER SQ.
Oxford St. Restricted Access 7am.-7pm. Mon.-Sat.
Regent Hall

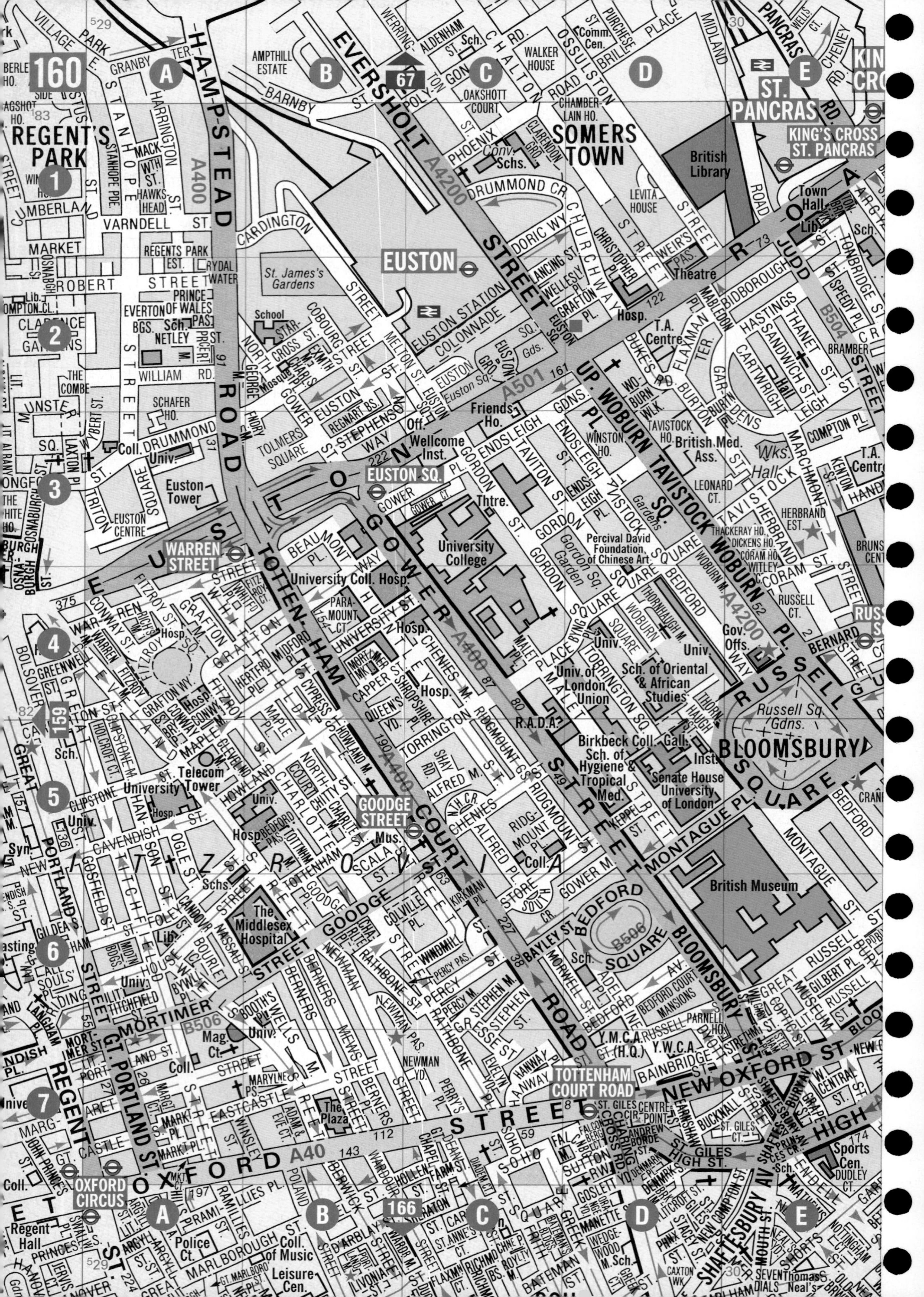

160
67
159
166
A
B
C
D
E
1
2
3
4
5
6
7
REGENT'S PARK
SOMERS TOWN
BLOOMSBURY
FITZROVIA
St. PANCRAS
KING'S CROSS ST. PANCRAS
British Library
EUSTON
EUSTON SQ.
WARREN STREET
GOODGE STREET
TOTTENHAM COURT ROAD
OXFORD CIRCUS
HAMPSTEAD ROAD
EVERSHOLT STREET
EUSTON ROAD
TOTTENHAM COURT ROAD
GOWER STREET
WOBURN PL.
UP. WOBURN PL.
TAVISTOCK SQ.
RUSSELL SQUARE
BEDFORD SQUARE
BLOOMSBURY ST.
NEW OXFORD ST.
OXFORD STREET
GOODGE STREET
GT. PORTLAND ST.
REGENT ST.
PORTLAND PL.
MORTIMER ST.
CLEVELAND ST.
CHARLOTTE ST.
MALET ST.
GORDON SQ.
ENDSLEIGH GDNS.
DRUMMOND CR.
CARDINGTON ST.
OSSULSTON ST.
CHALTON ST.
MIDLAND RD.
JUDD ST.
MARCHMONT ST.
HUNTER ST.
BRUNSWICK SQ.
MONTAGUE PL.
GREAT RUSSELL ST.
ST. GILES HIGH ST.
SHAFTESBURY AV.
CHARING CROSS RD.
SOHO SQUARE
A400
A4200
A501
A40
B506
B504
St. James's Gardens
Euston Tower
Euston Centre
University College
University Coll. Hosp.
Telecom Tower
The Middlesex Hospital
British Museum
Senate House University of London
Sch. of Oriental & African Studies
Birkbeck Coll. Sch. of Hygiene & Tropical Med.
R.A.D.A.
Percival David Foundation of Chinese Art
Wellcome Inst.
Friends Ho.
British Med. Ass.
Russell Sq. Gdns.
Gordon Sq. Garden
Y.M.C.A. (H.Q.)
Y.W.C.A.
Centre Point
The Plaza
Sports Cen.
Police Ct.
Coll. of Music
Leisure Cen.
Regent Hall
Town Hall
Theatre

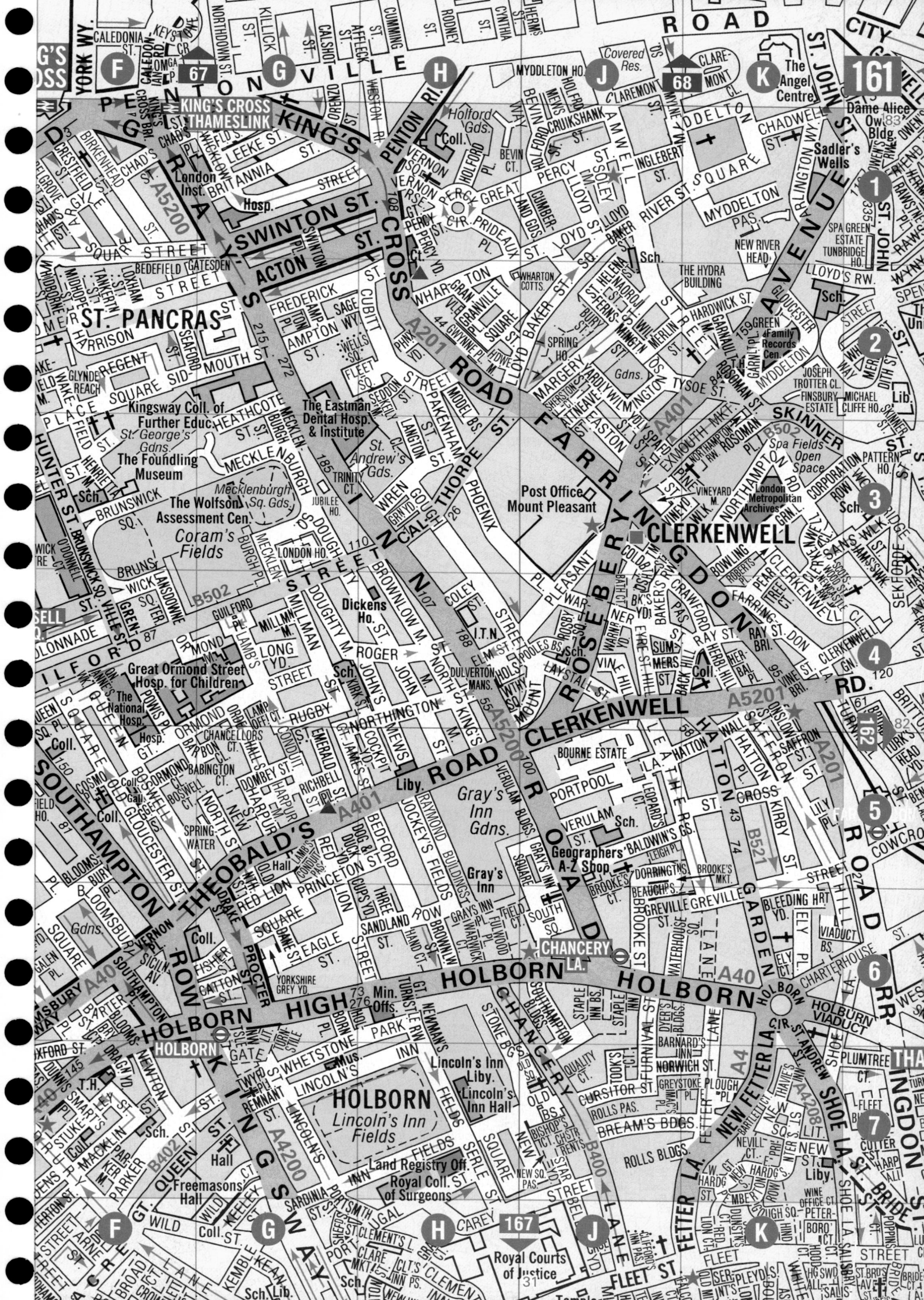
PENTONVILLE ROAD
KING'S CROSS THAMESLINK
KING'S CROSS ROAD
GRAY'S INN ROAD
A5200
ST. PANCRAS
SWINTON ST.
ACTON ST.
London Inst.
Hosp.
Kingsway Coll. of Further Educ.
St. George's Gdns.
The Foundling Museum
The Wolfson Assessment Cen.
Coram's Fields
Mecklenburgh Sq. Gdns.
MECKLENBURGH SQ.
BRUNSWICK SQ.
HUNTER ST.
The Eastman Dental Hosp. & Institute
St. Andrew's Gds.
Dickens Ho.
DOUGHTY ST.
GUILFORD ST.
Great Ormond Street Hosp. for Children
The National Hosp.
QUEEN SQUARE
SOUTHAMPTON ROW
THEOBALD'S ROAD
A401
Gray's Inn Gdns.
Gray's Inn
CLERKENWELL ROAD
A5201
FARRINGDON ROAD
A201
ROSEBERY AVENUE
Post Office Mount Pleasant
CLERKENWELL
London Metropolitan Archives
Spa Fields Open Space
SKINNER ST.
Family Records Cen.
Sadler's Wells
ST. JOHN ST.
The Angel Centre
Dame Alice Owen's Bldg.
Holford Gds.
Coll.
THE HYDRA BUILDING
NEW RIVER HEAD
MYDDELTON SQUARE
AMWELL ST.
LLOYD BAKER ST.
Covered Res.
MYDDLETON HO.
PHOENIX PL.
MOUNT PLEASANT
I.T.N.
BOURNE ESTATE
Geographers' A-Z Shop
HATTON GARDEN
LEATHER LA.
B521
HOLBORN
HOLBORN VIADUCT
HOLBORN CIR.
CHARTERHOUSE ST.
A40
HIGH HOLBORN
CHANCERY LA.
CHANCERY LANE
Min. Offs.
KINGSWAY
A4200
HOLBORN
Lincoln's Inn Fields
Lincoln's Inn Liby.
Lincoln's Inn Hall
Land Registry Off.
Royal Coll. of Surgeons
Freemasons' Hall
B402
B400
Royal Courts of Justice
FLEET ST.
NEW FETTER LA.
FETTER LA.
A4
A4208
SHOE LA.
ST. BRIDE ST.
Temple
Mus.
Liby.
Sch.
RED LION SQUARE
BLOOMSBURY SQUARE
GT. QUEEN ST.
LONG ACRE
B502
67
68
167
162
F G H J K
1 2 3 4 5 6 7

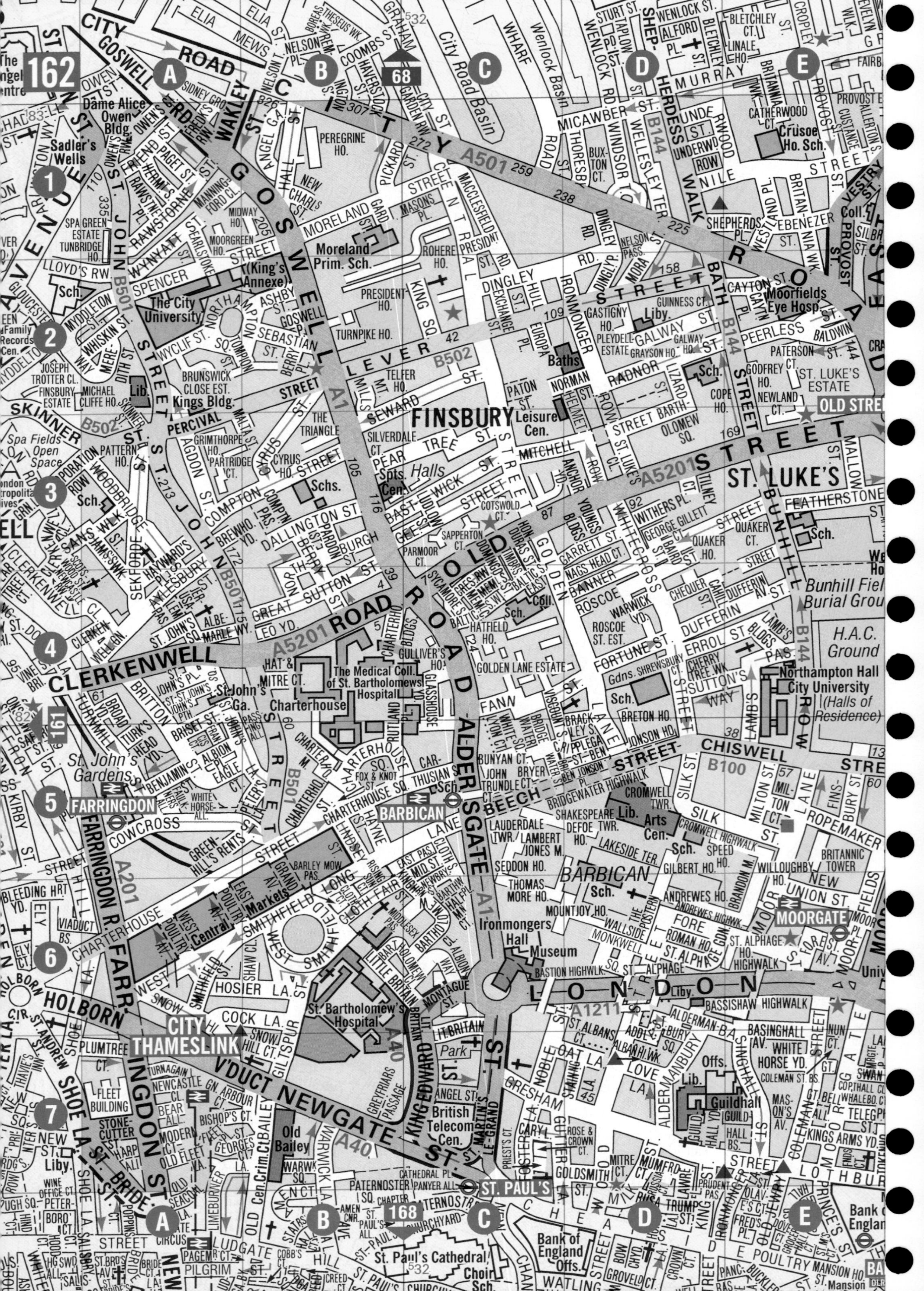
162
A
B
C
D
E
1
2
3
4
5
6
7
68
168
161
CITY ROAD
GOSWELL ROAD
City Road Basin
Wenlock Basin
WHARF
WENLOCK ST.
SHEPHERDESS WALK
MURRAY
CATHERWOOD
Crusoe Ho. Sch.
A501
B144
B501
B502
B100
A5201
A1
A1211
A40
A201
Dame Alice Owen Bldg.
Sadler's Wells
ST. JOHN ST.
SPA GREEN ESTATE
TUNBRIDGE HO.
LLOYD'S RW.
The City University
Family Records Cen.
JOSEPH TROTTER CL.
FINSBURY ESTATE
MICHAEL CLIFFE HO.
SKINNER ST.
Spa Fields Open Space
WAKLEY ST.
PEREGRINE HO.
MORELAND ST.
Moreland Prim. Sch.
MACCLESFIELD RD.
PRESIDENT HO.
KING SQ.
TURNPIKE HO.
LEVER STREET
SEBASTIAN ST.
BRUNSWICK CLOSE EST.
Kings Bldg.
PERCIVAL
NORTHAMPTON SQ.
SPENCER
(King's Annexe)
DINGLEY RD.
NILE
SHEPHERDS PL.
EBENEZER
Moorfields Eye Hosp.
GALWAY ST.
PEERLESS
Liby.
Baths
RADNOR
ST. LUKE'S ESTATE
OLD STREET
ST. LUKE'S
FINSBURY
Leisure Cen.
MITCHELL
PEAR TREE ST.
SEWARD
THE TRIANGLE
Spts. Cen.
Halls
Schs.
COMPTON
DALLINGTON ST.
GREAT SUTTON ST.
OLD STREET
BUNHILL ROW
FEATHERSTONE
Bunhill Fields Burial Ground
H.A.C. Ground
Northampton Hall City University (Halls of Residence)
FORTUNE ST.
DUFFERIN ST.
ROSCOE
WHITECROSS ST.
GOLDEN LANE ESTATE
CHISWELL STREET
CLERKENWELL ROAD
The Medical Coll. of St. Bartholomew's Hospital
Charterhouse
CHARTERHOUSE SQ.
ST. JOHN ST.
St. John's Gardens
FARRINGDON
COWCROSS
BARBICAN
ALDERSGATE ST.
BEECH STREET
CROMWELL TWR.
Lib.
Arts Cen.
SILK ST.
ROPEMAKER
BRITANNIC TOWER
BARBICAN
MOORGATE
Ironmongers Hall
Museum
LONDON WALL
BASSISHAW HIGHWALK
Central Markets
SMITHFIELD
WEST SMITHFIELD
CLOTH FAIR
LONG LA.
St. Bartholomew's Hospital
HOSIER LA.
COCK LA.
HOLBORN
HOLBORN CIR.
CHARTERHOUSE
FARRINGDON R.
CITY THAMESLINK
V'DUCT
NEWGATE ST.
KING EDWARD ST.
GREYFRIARS PASSAGE
British Telecom Cen.
Old Bailey
WARWICK LA.
ST. MARTIN'S LE GRAND
ST. PAUL'S
Guildhall
Offs.
GRESHAM
CHEAPSIDE
WOOD ST.
MILK ST.
Bank of England Offs.
St. Paul's Cathedral
Choir Sch.
PATERNOSTER SQ.
LUDGATE HILL
LUDGATE CIRCUS
FLEET BUILDING
SHOE LA.
NEW ST.
ST. BRIDE ST.
FARRINGDON ST.
POULTRY
LOTHBURY
COLEMAN ST.
BASINGHALL AV.
WHITE HORSE YD.
WATLING ST.
532

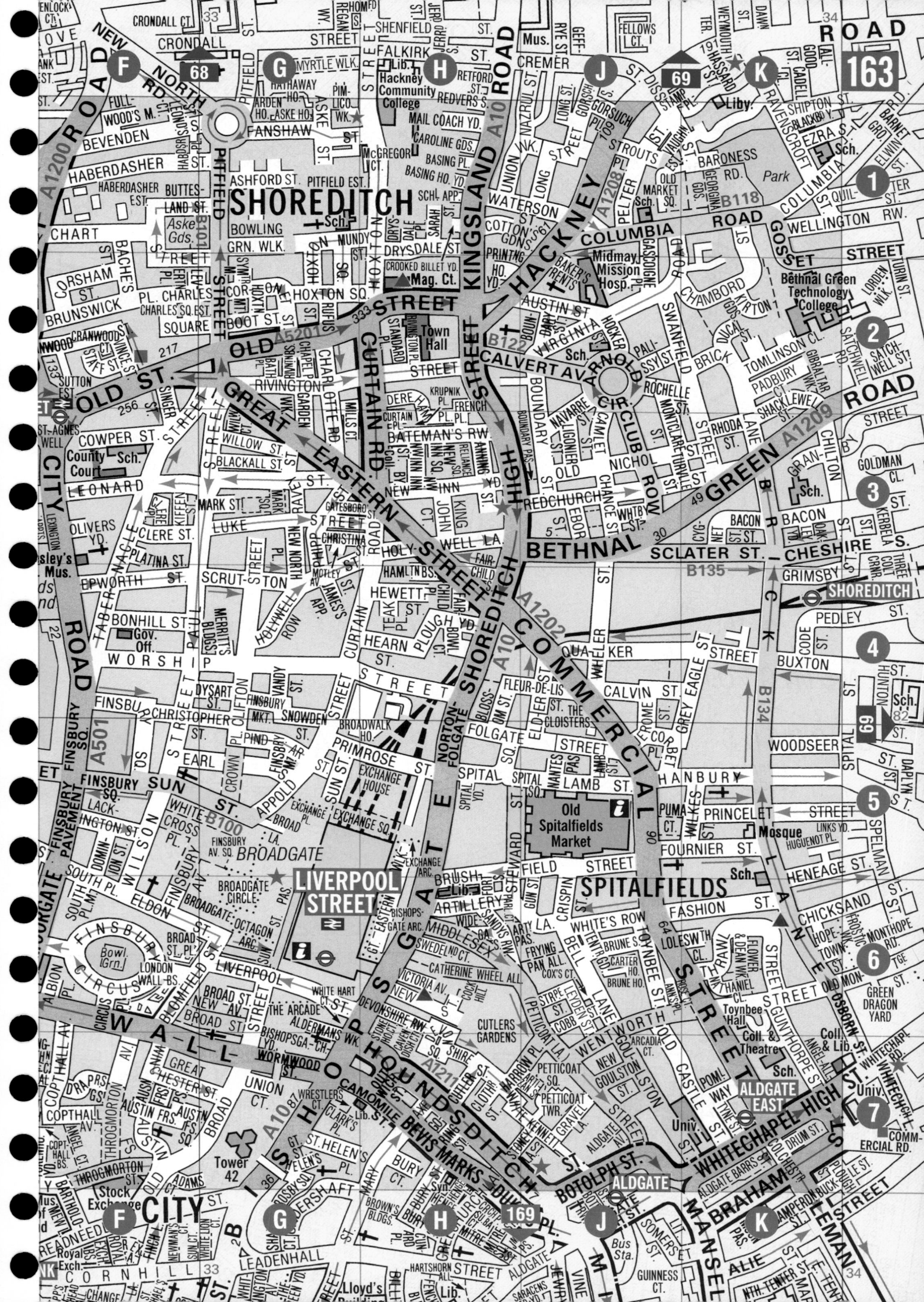

SHOREDITCH
SPITALFIELDS
CITY
BROADGATE
LIVERPOOL STREET
Old Spitalfields Market
Hackney Community College
Bethnal Green Technology College
Midmay Mission Hosp.
Tower 42
Stock Exchange
KINGSLAND ROAD
HACKNEY ROAD
OLD ST.
GREAT EASTERN STREET
SHOREDITCH HIGH STREET
COMMERCIAL STREET
BETHNAL GREEN ROAD
BRICK LANE
BISHOPSGATE
HOUNDSDITCH
WHITECHAPEL HIGH ST.
CITY ROAD
LONDON WALL
COLUMBIA ROAD
68
69
169

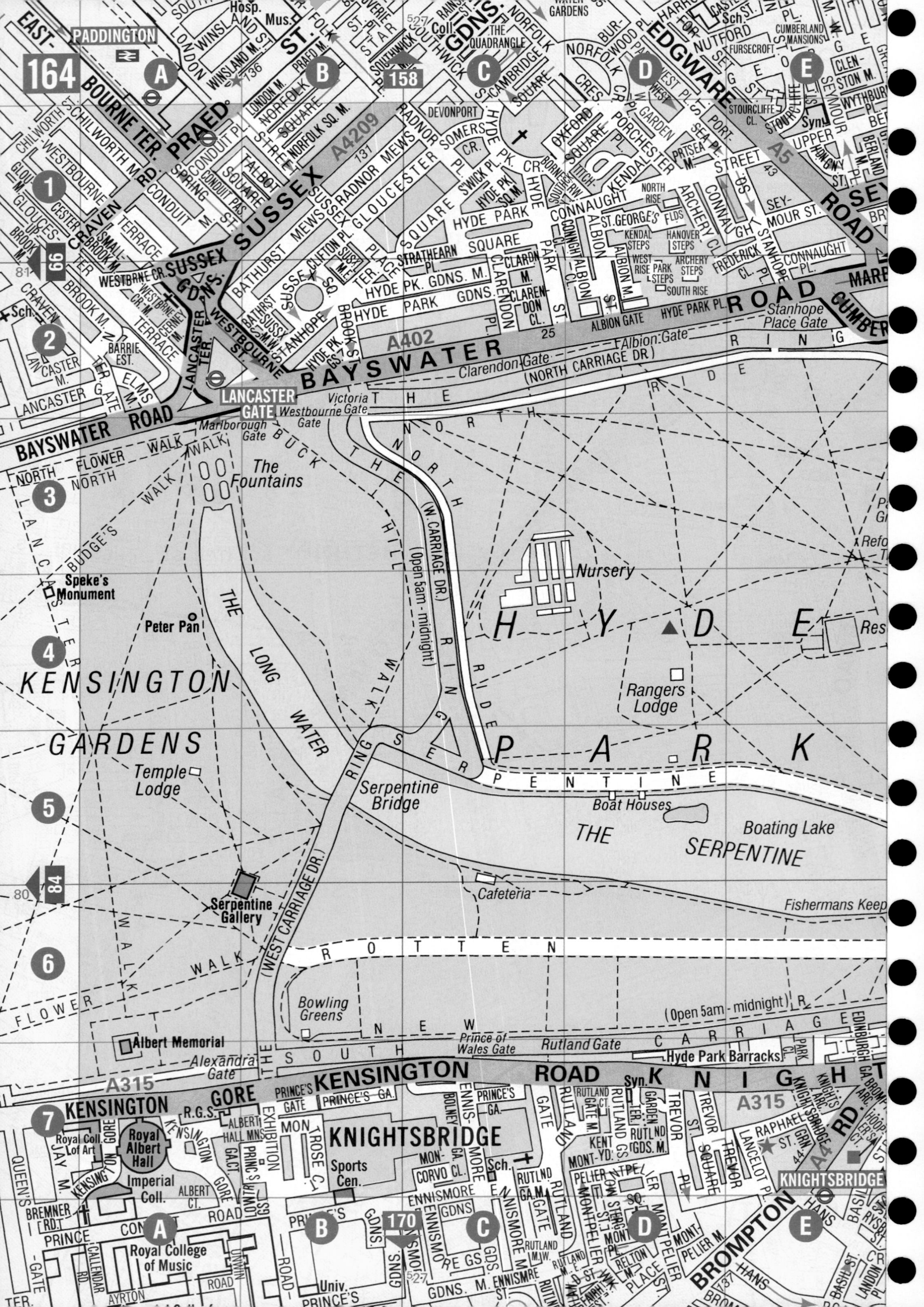
PADDINGTON
EAST-BOURNE TER.
PRAED ST.
SUSSEX GDNS.
A4209
158
GLOUCESTER SQUARE
HYDE PARK SQUARE
CONNAUGHT ST.
EDGWARE RD.
A5
SEYMOUR ST.
BAYSWATER ROAD
A402
LANCASTER GATE
Victoria Gate
Westbourne Gate
Marlborough Gate
Clarendon Gate
Albion Gate
Stanhope Place Gate
99
THE RING
NORTH RIDE
THE FLOWER WALK
The Fountains
THE LONG WATER
Speke's Monument
Peter Pan
KENSINGTON GARDENS
Temple Lodge
Nursery
HYDE PARK
Rangers Lodge
SERPENTINE RD.
Serpentine Bridge
Boat Houses
THE SERPENTINE
Boating Lake
Cafeteria
Fishermans Keep
84
Serpentine Gallery
ROTTEN ROW
(WEST CARRIAGE DR.)
(W. CARRIAGE DR.)
(Open 5am - midnight)
Bowling Greens
Albert Memorial
Alexandra Gate
Prince of Wales Gate
Rutland Gate
SOUTH CARRIAGE DR.
Hyde Park Barracks
KENSINGTON ROAD
KNIGHTSBRIDGE
A315
KENSINGTON GORE
Royal Albert Hall
Royal Coll. of Art
Imperial Coll.
Royal College of Music
Sports Cen.
A4
BROMPTON RD.
170
1
2
3
4
5
6
7
A
B
C
D
E

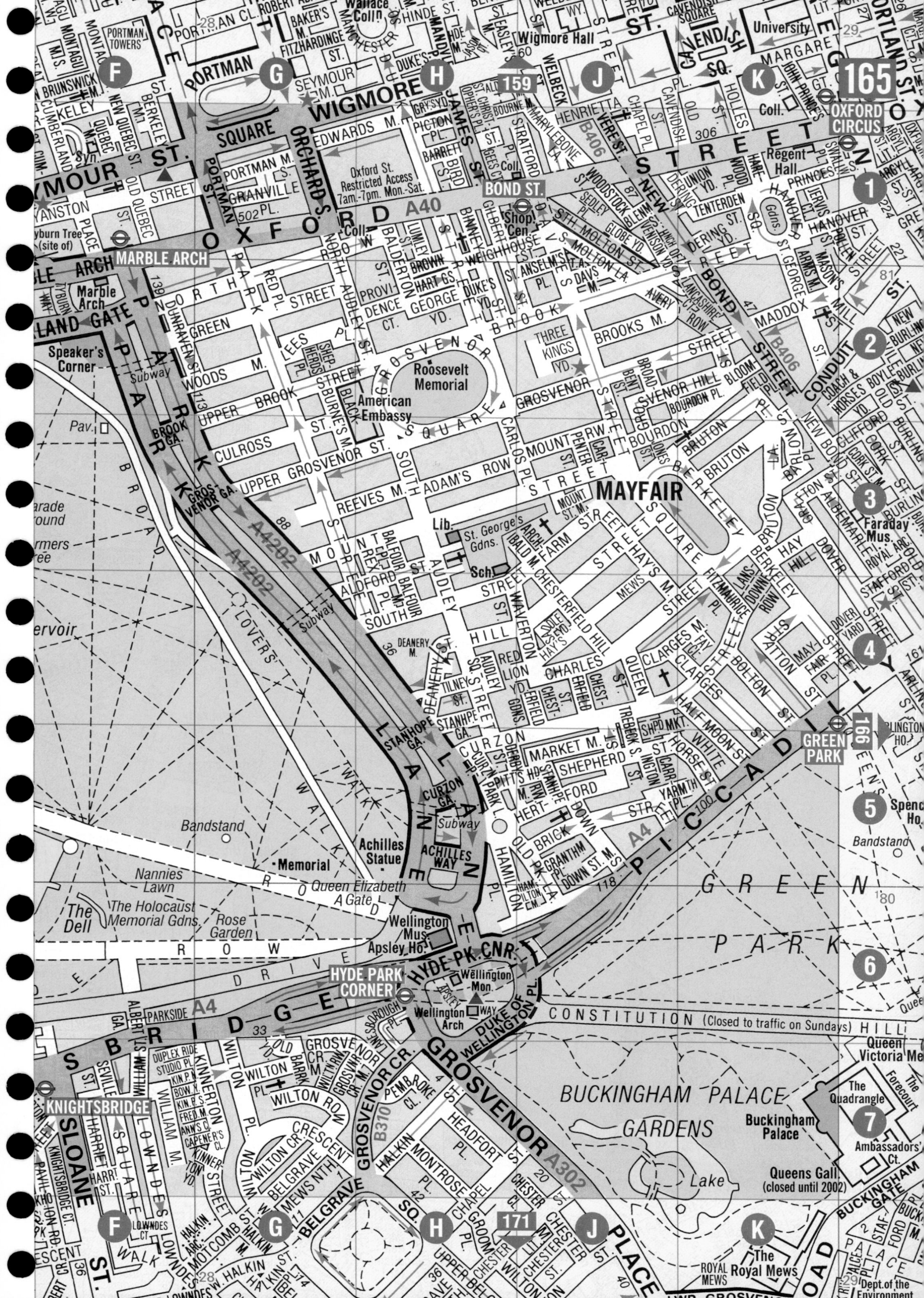
165
OXFORD CIRCUS
OXFORD STREET A40
MARBLE ARCH
BOND ST.
GREEN PARK
HYDE PARK CORNER
KNIGHTSBRIDGE
MAYFAIR
Wallace Colln.
Wigmore Hall
University
Regent Hall
Oxford St. Restricted Access 7am.-7pm. Mon.-Sat.
Tyburn Tree (site of)
Marble Arch
Speaker's Corner
Roosevelt Memorial
American Embassy
Faraday Mus.
PORTMAN SQUARE
WIGMORE ST.
SEYMOUR ST.
ORCHARD ST.
JAMES ST.
NEW BOND STREET
CAVENDISH SQ.
HANOVER SQ.
GROSVENOR SQUARE
BERKELEY SQUARE
PARK LANE
NORTH ROW
UPPER BROOK STREET
UPPER GROSVENOR ST.
SOUTH AUDLEY ST.
MOUNT STREET
CURZON ST.
PICCADILLY
CONDUIT ST.
BRUTON ST.
DAVIES ST.
BROOK ST.
ALBEMARLE ST.
DOVER ST.
HALF MOON ST.
CLARGES ST.
HAMILTON PL.
HYDE PK. CNR.
KNIGHTSBRIDGE
GROSVENOR PLACE
GROSVENOR CRESCENT
BELGRAVE SQ.
WILTON CRESCENT
SLOANE ST.
LOWNDES SQUARE
DUKE OF WELLINGTON PL.
CONSTITUTION HILL (Closed to traffic on Sundays)
A4202
A4
A302
B310
B406
Achilles Statue
Memorial
Bandstand
Nannies Lawn
The Dell
The Holocaust Memorial Gdns.
Rose Garden
Queen Elizabeth Gate
Wellington Mus.
Apsley Ho.
Wellington Mon.
Wellington Arch
GREEN PARK
BUCKINGHAM PALACE GARDENS
Lake
Buckingham Palace
The Quadrangle
The Forecourt
Queen Victoria Mem.
Ambassadors' Ct.
Queens Gall. (closed until 2002)
The Royal Mews
ROYAL MEWS
BUCKINGHAM GATE
Dept. of the Environment
159
166
171
F G H J K
1 2 3 4 5 6 7

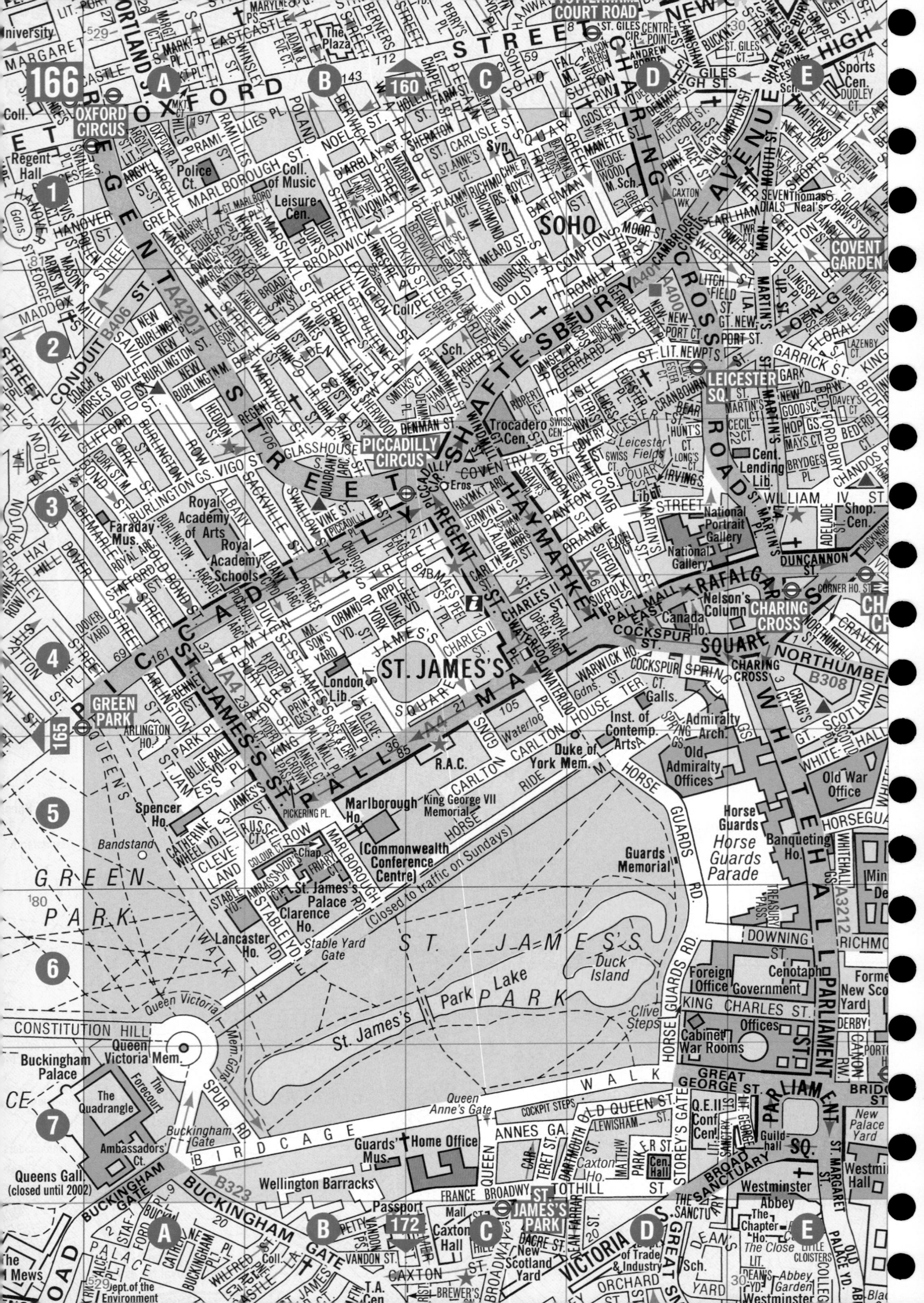
166
A
B
C
D
E
1
2
3
4
5
6
7
160
165
172
OXFORD CIRCUS
OXFORD ST.
REGENT ST.
PICCADILLY CIRCUS
PICCADILLY
SHAFTESBURY AVENUE
CHARING CROSS ROAD
LEICESTER SQ.
COVENT GARDEN
SOHO
HAYMARKET
TRAFALGAR SQUARE
CHARING CROSS
WHITEHALL
PARLIAMENT ST.
ST. JAMES'S SQUARE
PALL MALL
ST. JAMES'S ST.
GREEN PARK
ST. JAMES'S PARK
THE MALL
BIRDCAGE WALK
CONSTITUTION HILL
HORSE GUARDS RD.
GREAT GEORGE ST.
BROAD SANCTUARY
VICTORIA ST.
BUCKINGHAM GATE
TOTTENHAM COURT ROAD
NEW OXFORD ST.
HIGH HOLBORN
LONG ACRE
GARRICK ST.
COVENTRY ST.
JERMYN ST.
VIGO ST.
CONDUIT ST.
GREAT MARLBOROUGH ST.
BROADWICK ST.
OLD COMPTON ST.
GERRARD ST.
WILLIAM IV ST.
DUNCANNON ST.
NORTHUMBERLAND AVE.
Regent Hall
Police Ct.
Coll. of Music
Leisure Cen.
Royal Academy of Arts
Royal Academy Schools
Faraday Mus.
Trocadero Cen.
Eros
National Portrait Gallery
National Gallery
Nelson's Column
Canada Ho.
London Lib.
R.A.C.
Inst. of Contemp. Arts
Duke of York Mem.
Admiralty Arch.
Old Admiralty Offices
Old War Office
Horse Guards
Horse Guards Parade
Banqueting Ho.
Guards Memorial
Spencer Ho.
Bandstand
Marlborough Ho.
King George VII Memorial
(Commonwealth Conference Centre)
St. James's Palace
Clarence Ho.
Lancaster Ho.
Stable Yard Gate
(Closed to traffic on Sundays)
Duck Island
Lake
Queen Victoria Mem.
Buckingham Palace
The Quadrangle
The Forecourt
Ambassadors' Ct.
Queens Gall (closed until 2002)
Buckingham Gate
Queen Anne's Gate
Wellington Barracks
Guards' Mus.
Home Office
Foreign Office
Government Offices
Cabinet War Rooms
Cenotaph
Downing St.
King Charles St.
Q.E.II Conf. Cen.
Guildhall
Westminster Abbey
Westminster Hall
New Palace Yard
Passport
Caxton Hall
Caxton Ho.
New Scotland Yard
ST. JAMES'S PARK
Dept. of Trade & Industry
Dept. of the Environment
The Chapter Ho.
The Close
Abbey Garden
Cent. Lending Lib.
Shop. Cen.
Sports Cen.

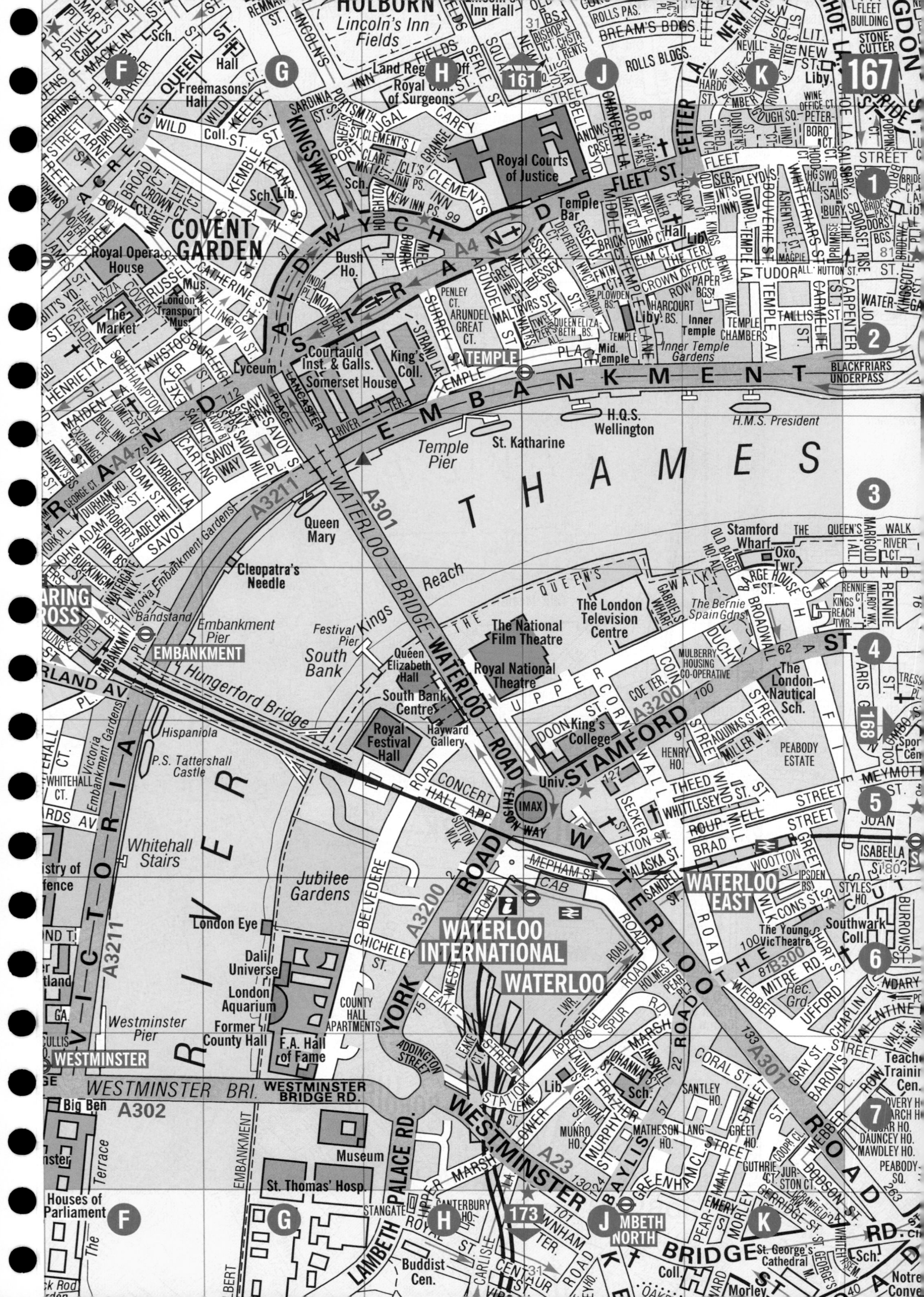
HOLBORN
Lincoln's Inn Fields
COVENT GARDEN
Royal Opera House
Royal Courts of Justice
Somerset House
King's Coll.
Courtauld Inst. & Galls.
TEMPLE
EMBANKMENT
BLACKFRIARS UNDERPASS
H.Q.S. Wellington
H.M.S. President
Temple Pier
St. Katharine
THAMES
Queen Mary
Cleopatra's Needle
Embankment Pier
Festival Pier
Kings Reach
South Bank
The National Film Theatre
Royal National Theatre
Queen Elizabeth Hall
South Bank Centre
Hayward Gallery
Royal Festival Hall
The London Television Centre
Stamford Wharf
Oxo Twr.
The London Nautical Sch.
PEABODY ESTATE
King's College
STAMFORD
WATERLOO BRIDGE
WATERLOO ROAD
IMAX
WATERLOO EAST
WATERLOO INTERNATIONAL
WATERLOO
The Young Vic Theatre
Southwark Coll.
Jubilee Gardens
London Eye
Dali Universe
London Aquarium
Former County Hall
F.A. Hall of Fame
COUNTY HALL APARTMENTS
Whitehall Stairs
Westminster Pier
WESTMINSTER
WESTMINSTER BRI.
WESTMINSTER BRIDGE RD.
Big Ben
Houses of Parliament
St. Thomas' Hosp.
Museum
LAMBETH PALACE RD.
YORK ROAD
VICTORIA EMBANKMENT
RIVER
Hungerford Bridge
Hispaniola
P.S. Tattershall Castle
Victoria Embankment Gardens
Bandstand
STRAND
ALDWYCH
FLEET ST.
KINGSWAY
Temple Bar
Inner Temple
Inner Temple Gardens
Mid. Temple
Lyceum
London Transport Mus.
The Market
Freemasons Hall
Bush Ho.
Buddist Cen.
St. George's Cathedral
LAMBETH NORTH
Morley Coll.
161
168
173
A4
A301
A3211
A3200
A302
A23
B300
1 2 3 4 5 6 7
F G H J K

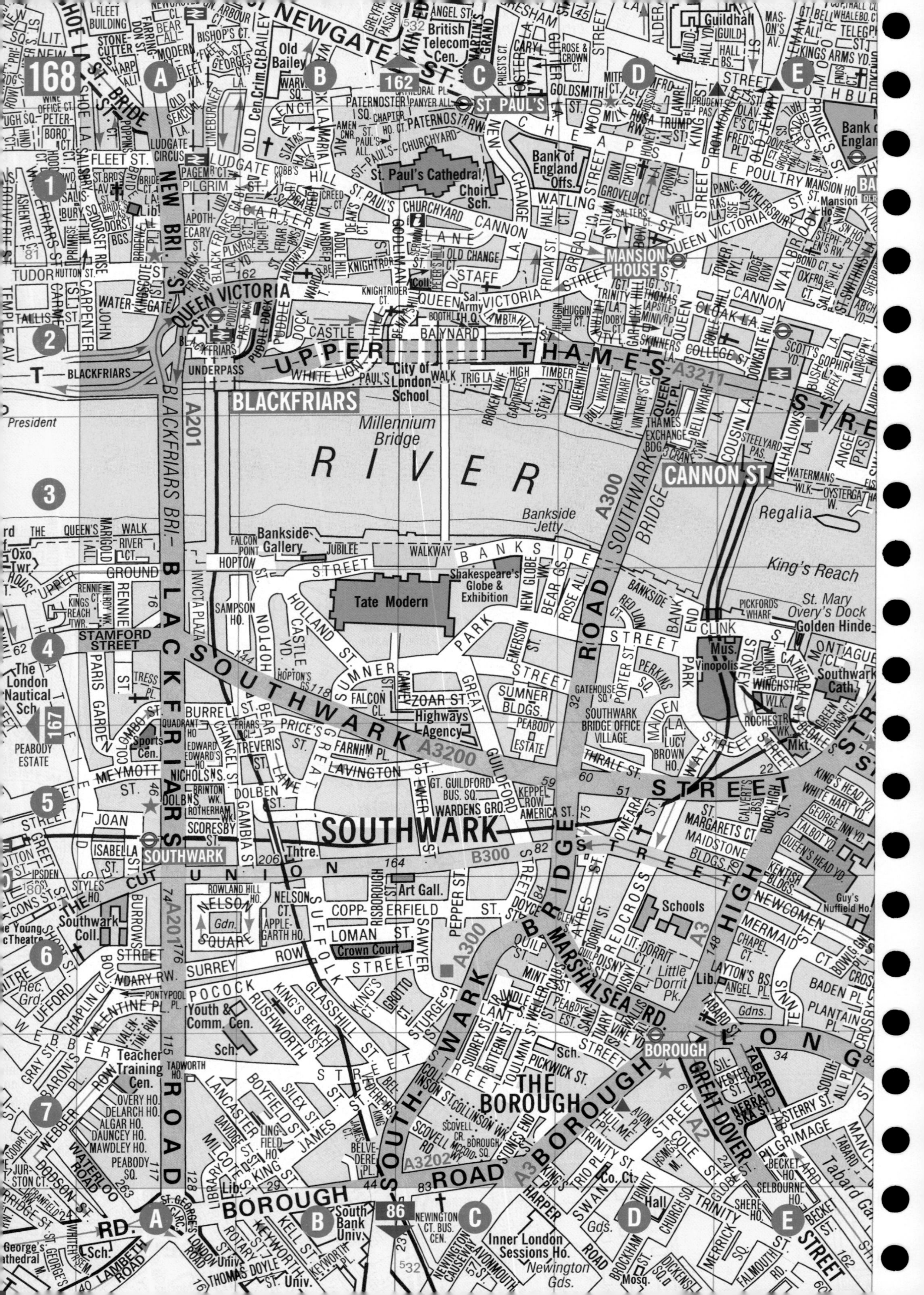
168
A
B
C
D
E
1
2
3
4
5
6
7
162
167
86
NEWGATE ST.
Old Bailey
British Telecom Cen.
Guildhall
ST. PAUL'S
St. Paul's Cathedral
Choir Sch.
Bank of England Offs.
Bank of England
CHEAPSIDE
POULTRY
FLEET ST.
LUDGATE CIRCUS
LUDGATE HILL
NEW BRI. ST.
QUEEN VICTORIA ST.
CANNON ST.
WATLING ST.
MANSION HOUSE
UPPER THAMES ST.
BLACKFRIARS
BLACKFRIARS UNDERPASS
City of London School
Millennium Bridge
RIVER
President
Bankside Jetty
Bankside Gallery
Tate Modern
Shakespeare's Globe & Exhibition
CANNON ST.
Regalia
King's Reach
St. Mary Overy's Dock
Golden Hinde
Southwark Cath.
Vinopolis
Mus.
CLINK ST.
BANKSIDE
HOPTON ST.
SUMNER ST.
PARK ST.
SOUTHWARK ST.
A3200
SOUTHWARK BRIDGE RD.
A300
SOUTHWARK BRIDGE
BLACKFRIARS RD.
BLACKFRIARS BRI.
A201
STAMFORD STREET
The London Nautical Sch.
Sports Cen.
PEABODY ESTATE
Highways Agency
SOUTHWARK
B300
UNION ST.
THE CUT
Art Gall.
Crown Court
Southwark Coll.
The Young Vic Theatre
NELSON SQUARE
Gdn.
Youth & Comm. Cen.
Teacher Training Cen.
SURREY ROW
BOROUGH HIGH ST.
A3
MARSHALSEA RD.
Little Dorrit Pk.
Schools
Guy's Nuffield Ho.
LONG LANE
BOROUGH
THE BOROUGH
GREAT DOVER ST.
A2
BOROUGH RD.
A3202
LAMBETH RD.
South Bank Univ.
Inner London Sessions Ho.
Newington Gds.
Tabard Gdns.
WATERLOO RD.
St. George's Cathedral

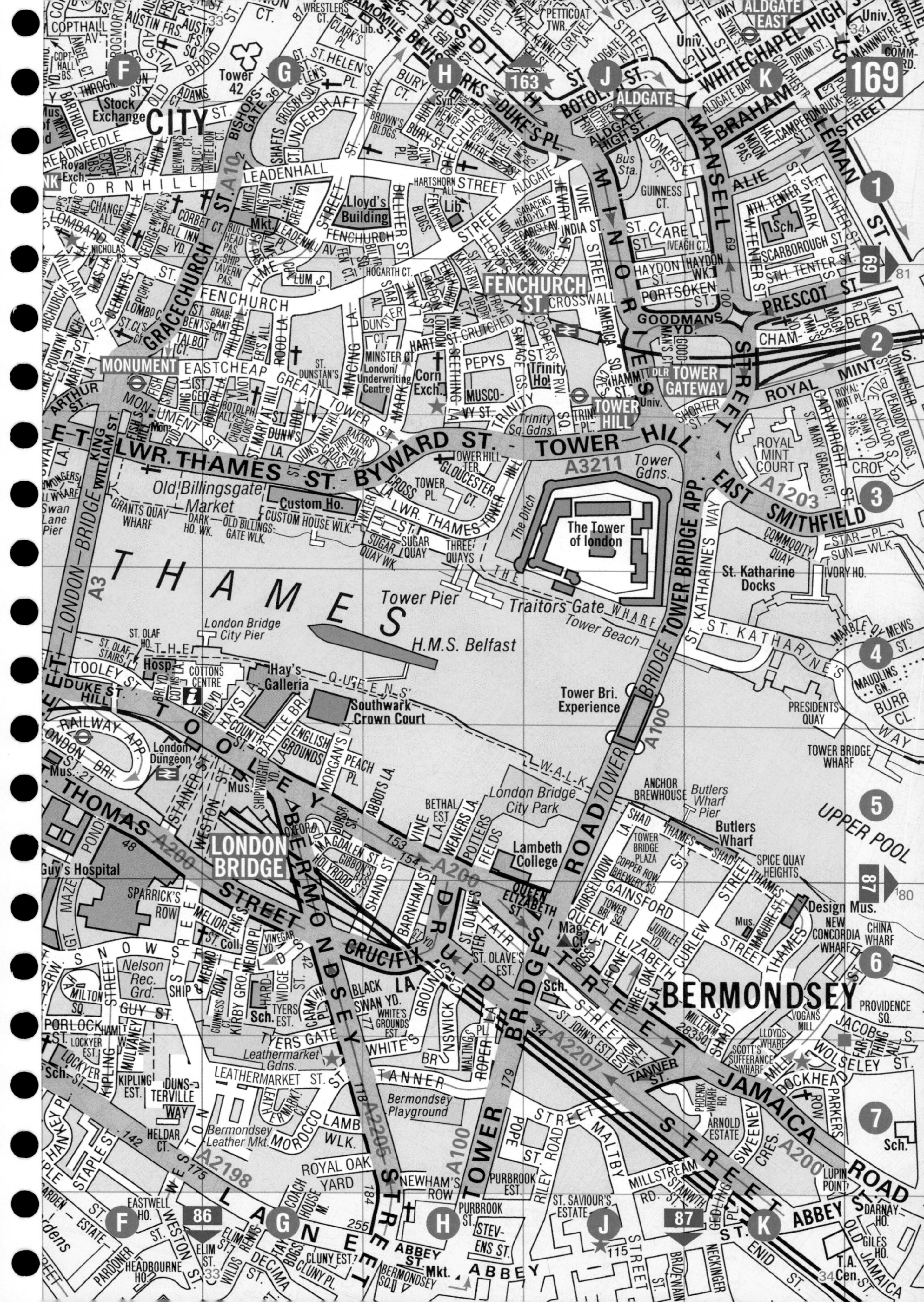

CITY
THAMES
Tower of London
H.M.S. Belfast
Tower Pier
St. Katharine Docks
LONDON BRIDGE
TOWER HILL
FENCHURCH ST.
ALDGATE
MONUMENT
TOWER GATEWAY
BERMONDSEY
Guy's Hospital
Southwark Crown Court
Hay's Galleria
Lloyd's Building
Stock Exchange
Tower 42
Custom Ho.
Old Billingsgate Market
Tower Bri. Experience
London Bridge City Park
Butlers Wharf
Design Mus.
UPPER POOL
LWR. THAMES ST.
BYWARD ST.
TOOLEY ST.
TOWER BRIDGE ROAD
JAMAICA ROAD
EAST SMITHFIELD
MINORIES
LEADENHALL
FENCHURCH
GRACECHURCH
BISHOPSGATE
WHITECHAPEL HIGH

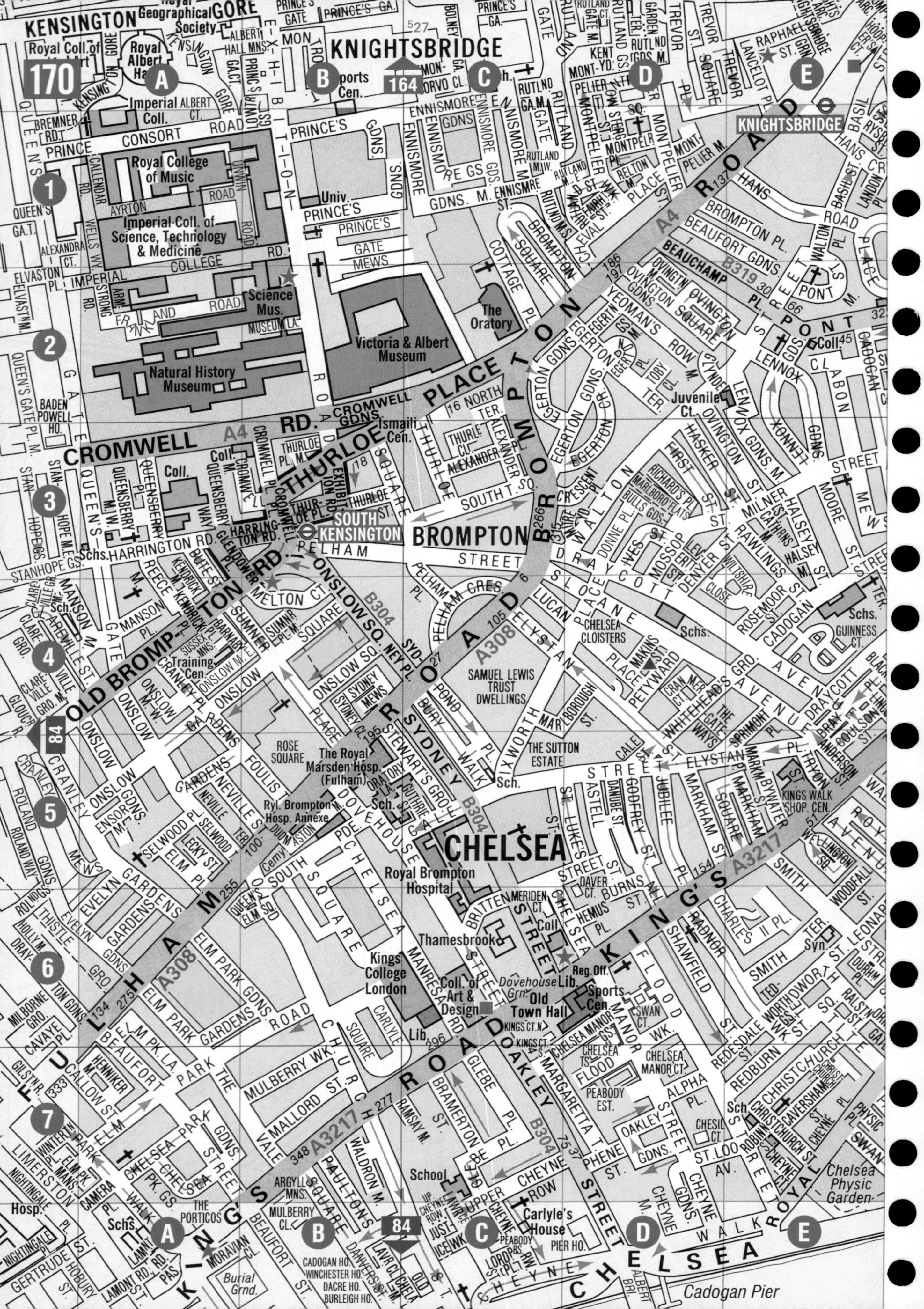
KENSINGTON
KNIGHTSBRIDGE
164
Royal Geographical Society
Royal Coll. of Art
Royal Albert Hall
Imperial Coll.
Sports Cen.
KNIGHTSBRIDGE
PRINCE CONSORT ROAD
Royal College of Music
Imperial Coll. of Science, Technology & Medicine
IMPERIAL COLLEGE RD.
Science Mus.
Natural History Museum
Victoria & Albert Museum
The Oratory
Univ.
PRINCE'S GATE MEWS
ENNISMORE GDNS.
BROMPTON ROAD
A4
B319
BEAUCHAMP PL.
PONT ST.
Juvenile Ct.
CROMWELL RD.
CROMWELL GDNS.
THURLOE PLACE
Ismaili Cen.
QUEEN'S GATE
SOUTH KENSINGTON
BROMPTON
HARRINGTON RD.
PELHAM STREET
OLD BROMPTON RD.
B304
A308
ONSLOW SQUARE
SLOANE AVENUE
CHELSEA CLOISTERS
SAMUEL LEWIS TRUST DWELLINGS
THE SUTTON ESTATE
ELYSTAN STREET
Schs.
GUINNESS CT.
Training Cen.
The Royal Marsden Hosp. (Fulham)
Ryl. Brompton Hosp. Annexe
ROSE SQUARE
KINGS WALK SHOP. CEN.
CHELSEA
Royal Brompton Hospital
A3217
KING'S ROAD
Thamesbrook
Kings College London
Coll. of Art & Design
Dovehouse Grn.
Old Town Hall
Reg. Off.
Lib.
Sports Cen.
CHELSEA MANOR CT.
PEABODY EST.
FULHAM ROAD
ELM PARK GARDENS
EVELYN GARDENS
MULBERRY WK.
MALLORD ST.
CARLYLE SQUARE
Hosp.
Schs
THE PORTICOS
Burial Grnd.
School
Carlyle's House
PIER HO.
CADOGAN HO.
WINCHESTER HO.
DACRE HO.
BURLEIGH HO.
ROYAL HOSPITAL RD.
Chelsea Physic Garden
CHEYNE WALK
CHELSEA EMBANKMENT
ALBERT BRI.
Cadogan Pier
84
A B C D E
1 2 3 4 5 6 7

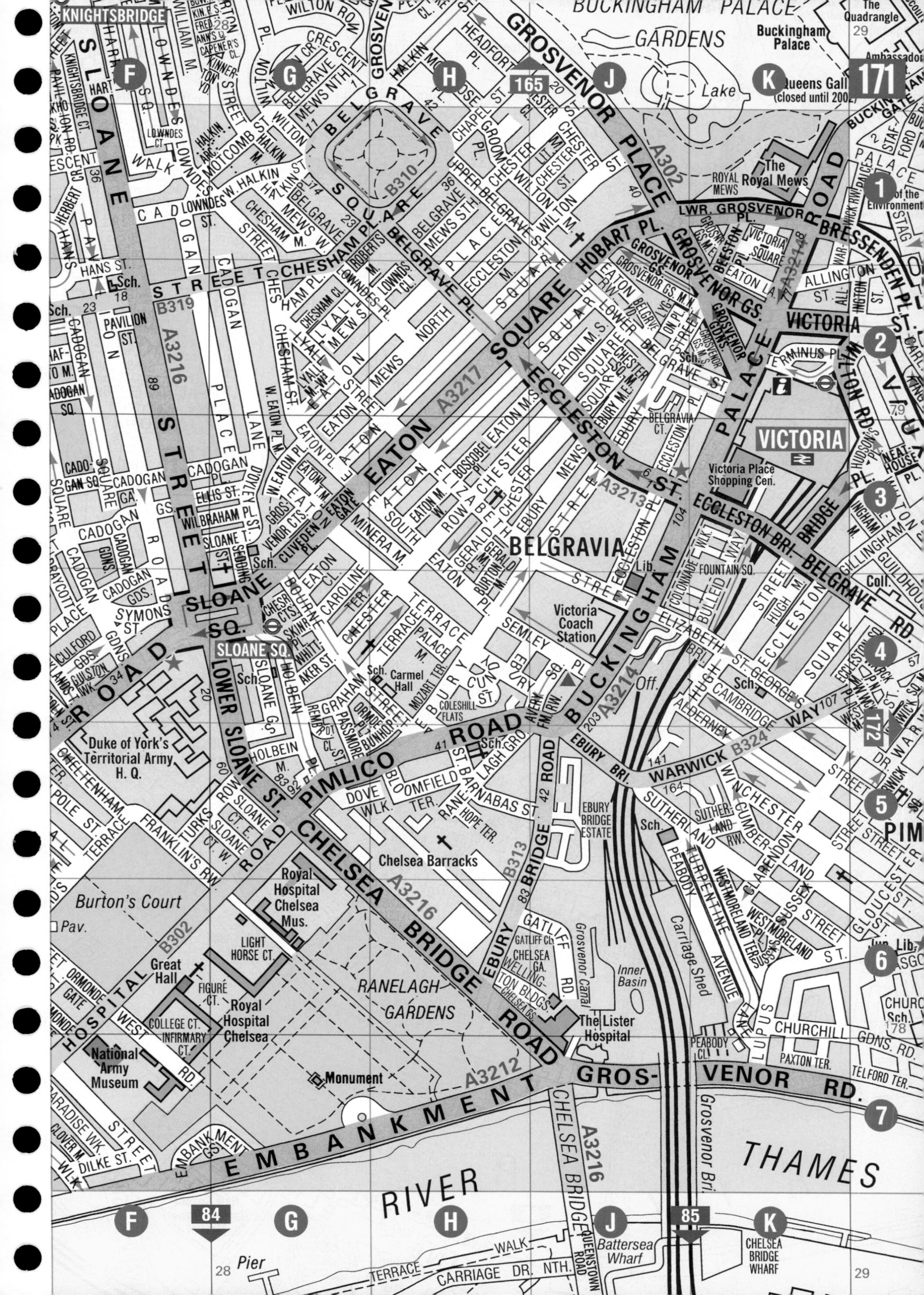
KNIGHTSBRIDGE
BUCKINGHAM PALACE GARDENS
Buckingham Palace
The Quadrangle
Queens Gall. (closed until 2002)
Lake
The Royal Mews
ROYAL MEWS
GROSVENOR PLACE
BELGRAVE SQUARE
SLOANE STREET
CHESHAM PLACE
EATON SQUARE
ECCLESTON ST.
BUCKINGHAM PALACE ROAD
VICTORIA
Victoria Place Shopping Cen.
BELGRAVIA
Victoria Coach Station
SLOANE SQ.
PIMLICO ROAD
LOWER SLOANE ST.
CHELSEA BRIDGE ROAD
EBURY BRIDGE ROAD
Duke of York's Territorial Army H. Q.
Burton's Court
Chelsea Barracks
Royal Hospital Chelsea
Royal Hospital Chelsea Mus.
Great Hall
National Army Museum
RANELAGH GARDENS
Monument
The Lister Hospital
EBURY BRIDGE ESTATE
Grosvenor Canal
Inner Basin
Carriage Shed
WARWICK WAY
GROSVENOR RD.
EMBANKMENT
RIVER THAMES
CHELSEA BRIDGE
Battersea Wharf
CHELSEA BRIDGE WHARF
Pier
CARRIAGE DR. NTH.
165
172
84
85
F
G
H
J
K
1
2
3
4
5
6
7
28
29

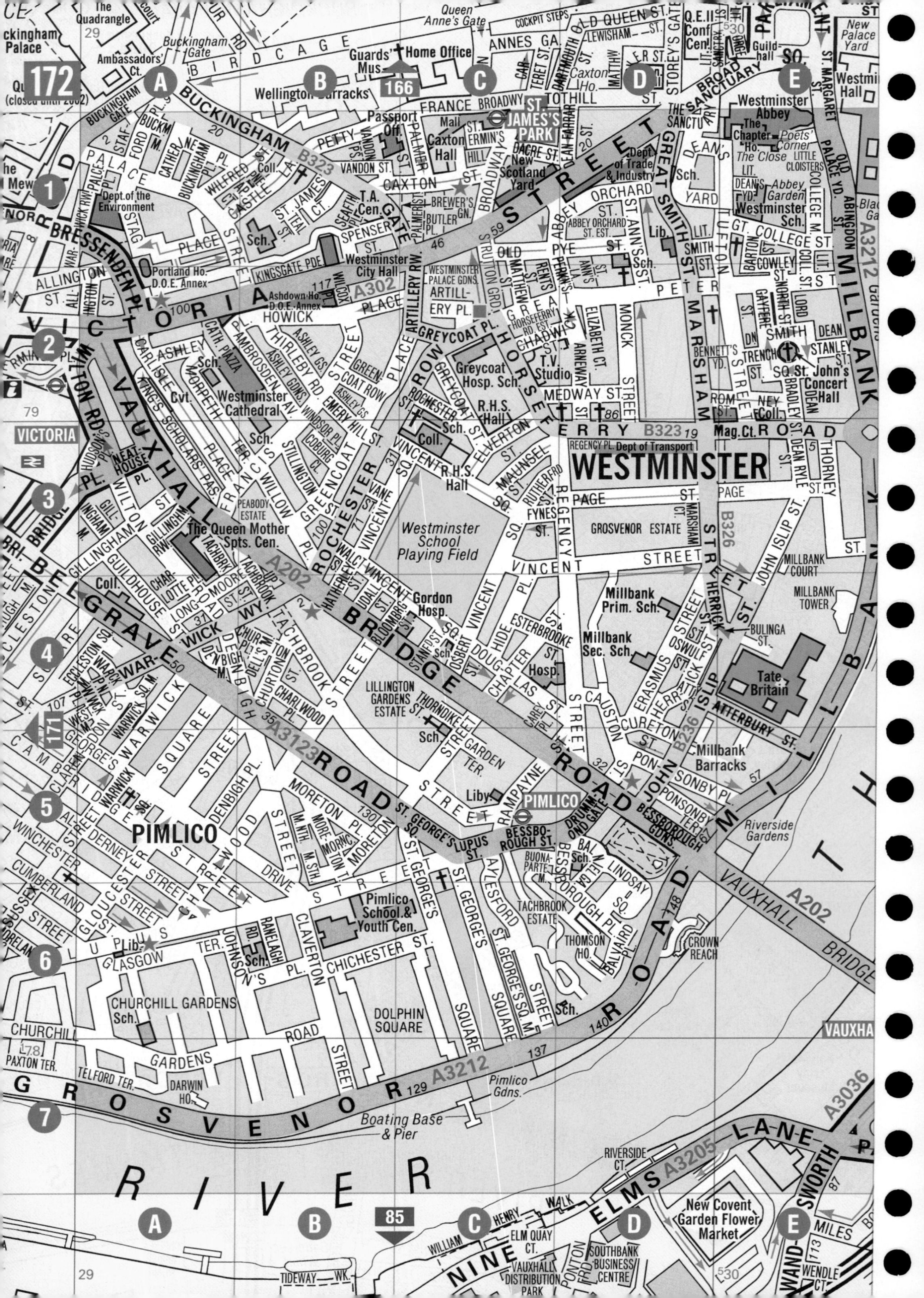

WESTMINSTER
PIMLICO
VICTORIA
RIVER THAMES
Westminster Abbey
Westminster Cathedral
Tate Britain
Westminster School Playing Field
Wellington Barracks
Home Office
Guards' Mus.
St. James's Park
New Scotland Yard
Caxton Hall
Dept. of Trade & Industry
Dept. of the Environment
Westminster City Hall
Greycoat Hosp. Sch.
R.H.S. Hall
Dept of Transport
Millbank Tower
Millbank Barracks
Pimlico School & Youth Cen.
Churchill Gardens
Dolphin Square
Lillington Gardens Estate
Tachbrook Estate
Grosvenor Estate
The Queen Mother Spts. Cen.
St. John's Concert Hall
Riverside Gardens
New Covent Garden Flower Market
Southbank Business Centre
Vauxhall Distribution Park
Boating Base & Pier
Pimlico Gdns.
Crown Reach
Q.E.II Conf. Cen.
New Palace Yard
Westminster Hall
VICTORIA STREET
VAUXHALL BRIDGE ROAD
BELGRAVE ROAD
GROSVENOR ROAD
MILLBANK
NINE ELMS LANE
WANDSWORTH ROAD
HORSEFERRY ROAD
BIRDCAGE WALK
BUCKINGHAM GATE
A302
A202
A3212
A3213
A3205
A3036
B323
B326
B236
166
171
85

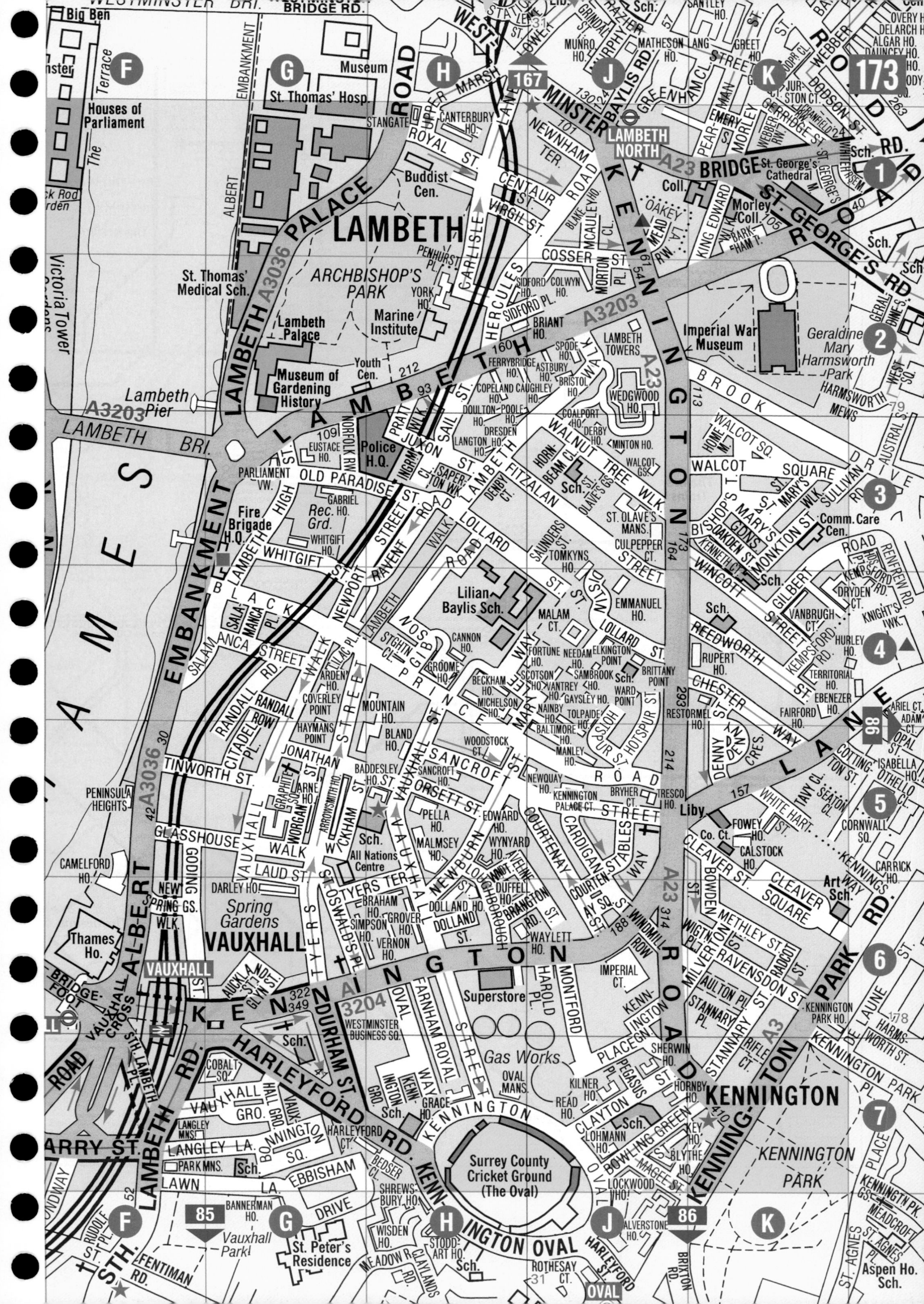
LAMBETH
VAUXHALL
KENNINGTON
Archbishop's Park
Lambeth Palace
Museum of Gardening History
Imperial War Museum
Geraldine Mary Harmsworth Park
Surrey County Cricket Ground (The Oval)
Gas Works
Spring Gardens
Kennington Park
Vauxhall Park
St. Thomas' Hosp.
Houses of Parliament
Big Ben
Lambeth North
Vauxhall
Oval
Lambeth Pier
Lambeth Bri.
Victoria Tower Gardens
Albert Embankment
Lambeth Road
Kennington Road
Kennington Lane
Kennington Park Road
Harleyford Road
St. George's Road
Lollard Street
Black Prince Road
Lilian Baylis Sch.
Fire Brigade H.Q.
Police H.Q.
Marine Institute
Buddist Cen.
St. Thomas' Medical Sch.
St. George's Cathedral
Morley Coll.
Superstore
St. Peter's Residence
A3203
A3036
A23
A3
A3204
167
85
86
98
178
F G H J K
1 2 3 4 5 6 7

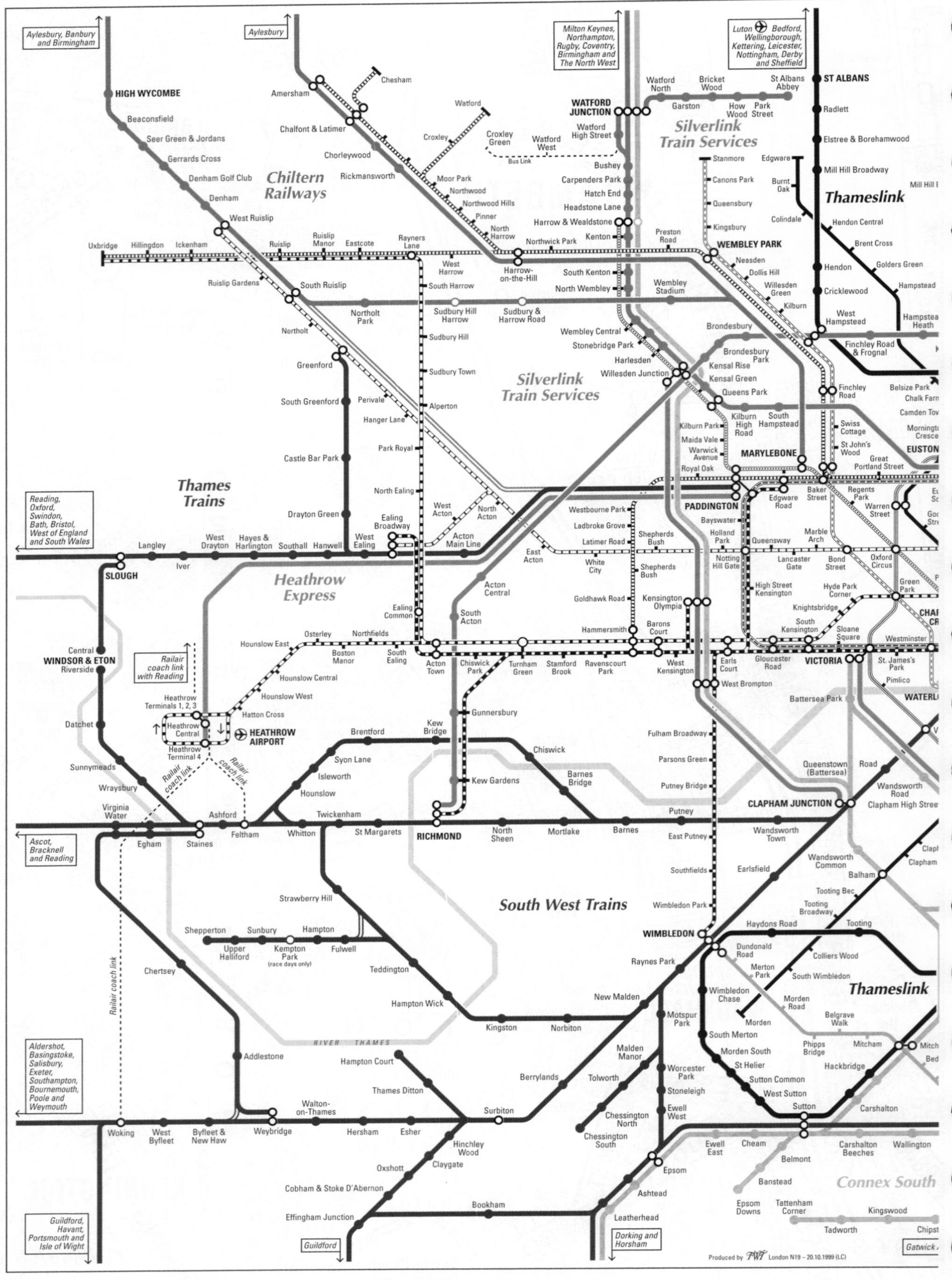

Aylesbury, Banbury and Birmingham
Aylesbury
Milton Keynes, Northampton, Rugby, Coventry, Birmingham and The North West
Luton Bedford, Wellingborough, Kettering, Leicester, Nottingham, Derby and Sheffield
HIGH WYCOMBE
Beaconsfield
Seer Green & Jordans
Gerrards Cross
Denham Golf Club
Denham
West Ruislip
Chiltern Railways
Amersham
Chesham
Chalfont & Latimer
Chorleywood
Rickmansworth
Watford
Croxley
Croxley Green
Watford West
Bus Link
Moor Park
Northwood
Northwood Hills
Pinner
North Harrow
Watford North
Bricket Wood
St Albans Abbey
Garston
How Wood
Park Street
WATFORD JUNCTION
Watford High Street
Bushey
Carpenders Park
Hatch End
Headstone Lane
Harrow & Wealdstone
Kenton
Silverlink Train Services
Stanmore
Canons Park
Queensbury
Kingsbury
Edgware
Burnt Oak
Colindale
ST ALBANS
Radlett
Elstree & Borehamwood
Mill Hill Broadway
Mill Hill E
Thameslink
Hendon Central
Brent Cross
Golders Green
Hendon
Cricklewood
Hampstead
West Hampstead
Hampstead Heath
Uxbridge
Hillingdon
Ickenham
Ruislip
Ruislip Manor
Eastcote
Rayners Lane
West Harrow
Harrow-on-the-Hill
Northwick Park
Preston Road
WEMBLEY PARK
Neasden
Dollis Hill
Willesden Green
Kilburn
Ruislip Gardens
South Ruislip
South Harrow
South Kenton
North Wembley
Wembley Stadium
Northolt
Northolt Park
Sudbury Hill Harrow
Sudbury & Harrow Road
Wembley Central
Stonebridge Park
Harlesden
Willesden Junction
Brondesbury
Brondesbury Park
Kensal Rise
Kensal Green
Queens Park
Finchley Road & Frognal
Finchley Road
Belsize Park
Chalk Farm
Camden Tov
Greenford
Sudbury Hill
Sudbury Town
Silverlink Train Services
South Greenford
Perivale
Hanger Lane
Alperton
Park Royal
Kilburn Park
Maida Vale
Warwick Avenue
Kilburn High Road
South Hampstead
Swiss Cottage
St John's Wood
Morningt Cresce
EUSTON
Great Portland Street
Castle Bar Park
MARYLEBONE
Royal Oak
Thames Trains
North Ealing
Reading, Oxford, Swindon, Bath, Bristol, West of England and South Wales
Drayton Green
Ealing Broadway
West Acton
North Acton
Westbourne Park
Ladbroke Grove
Latimer Road
PADDINGTON
Bayswater
Edgware Road
Baker Street
Regents Park
Warren Street
Langley
West Drayton
Hayes & Harlington
Southall
Hanwell
West Ealing
Acton Main Line
East Acton
Shepherds Bush
White City
Shepherds Bush
Holland Park
Notting Hill Gate
Queensway
Marble Arch
Lancaster Gate
Bond Street
Oxford Circus
Iver
SLOUGH
Heathrow Express
Acton Central
Goldhawk Road
Kensington Olympia
High Street Kensington
Hyde Park Corner
Green Park
Ealing Common
South Acton
Knightsbridge
South Kensington
Sloane Square
Hammersmith
Barons Court
Westminster
Osterley
Northfields
Hounslow East
Boston Manor
South Ealing
Acton Town
Chiswick Park
Turnham Green
Stamford Brook
Ravenscourt Park
West Kensington
Earls Court
Gloucester Road
VICTORIA
St James's Park
Pimlico
Central
WINDSOR & ETON
Riverside
Railair coach link with Reading
Hounslow Central
Hounslow West
West Brompton
Battersea Park
WATERL
Heathrow Terminals 1, 2, 3
Hatton Cross
Datchet
Heathrow Central
HEATHROW AIRPORT
Heathrow Terminal 4
Brentford
Kew Bridge
Gunnersbury
Fulham Broadway
Sunnymeads
Syon Lane
Isleworth
Chiswick
Parsons Green
Queenstown Road (Battersea)
Wraysbury
Railair coach link
Railair coach link
Hounslow
Kew Gardens
Barnes Bridge
Putney Bridge
Wandsworth Road
Virginia Water
Ashford
Twickenham
Putney
CLAPHAM JUNCTION
Clapham High Street
Egham
Staines
Feltham
Whitton
St Margarets
RICHMOND
North Sheen
Mortlake
Barnes
East Putney
Wandsworth Town
Ascot, Bracknell and Reading
Southfields
Earlsfield
Wandsworth Common
Clapham
Balham
Strawberry Hill
Tooting Bec
Tooting Broadway
South West Trains
Wimbledon Park
Haydons Road
Tooting
Shepperton
Sunbury
Hampton
Upper Halliford
Kempton Park (race days only)
Fulwell
WIMBLEDON
Dundonald Road
Colliers Wood
Merton Park
South Wimbledon
Raynes Park
Chertsey
Teddington
Railair coach link
Wimbledon Chase
Morden Road
Thameslink
New Malden
Hampton Wick
Morden
Belgrave Walk
Motspur Park
Kingston
Norbiton
South Merton
Mitcham
Mitch
Phipps Bridge
Morden South
Hackbridge
Bed
Aldershot, Basingstoke, Salisbury, Exeter, Southampton, Bournemouth, Poole and Weymouth
River Thames
Addlestone
Hampton Court
Malden Manor
St Helier
Worcester Park
Berrylands
Tolworth
Sutton Common
Thames Ditton
Stoneleigh
West Sutton
Walton-on-Thames
Surbiton
Ewell West
Sutton
Carshalton
Chessington North
Chessington South
Woking
West Byfleet
Byfleet & New Haw
Weybridge
Hersham
Esher
Hinchley Wood
Ewell East
Cheam
Carshalton Beeches
Wallington
Belmont
Claygate
Oxshott
Epsom
Connex South
Banstead
Cobham & Stoke D'Abernon
Ashtead
Bookham
Effingham Junction
Leatherhead
Epsom Downs
Tattenham Corner
Kingswood
Tadworth
Chipst
Guildford, Havant, Portsmouth and Isle of Wight
Guildford
Dorking and Horsham
Gatwick
Produced by TWT London N19 – 20.10.1999 (LC)

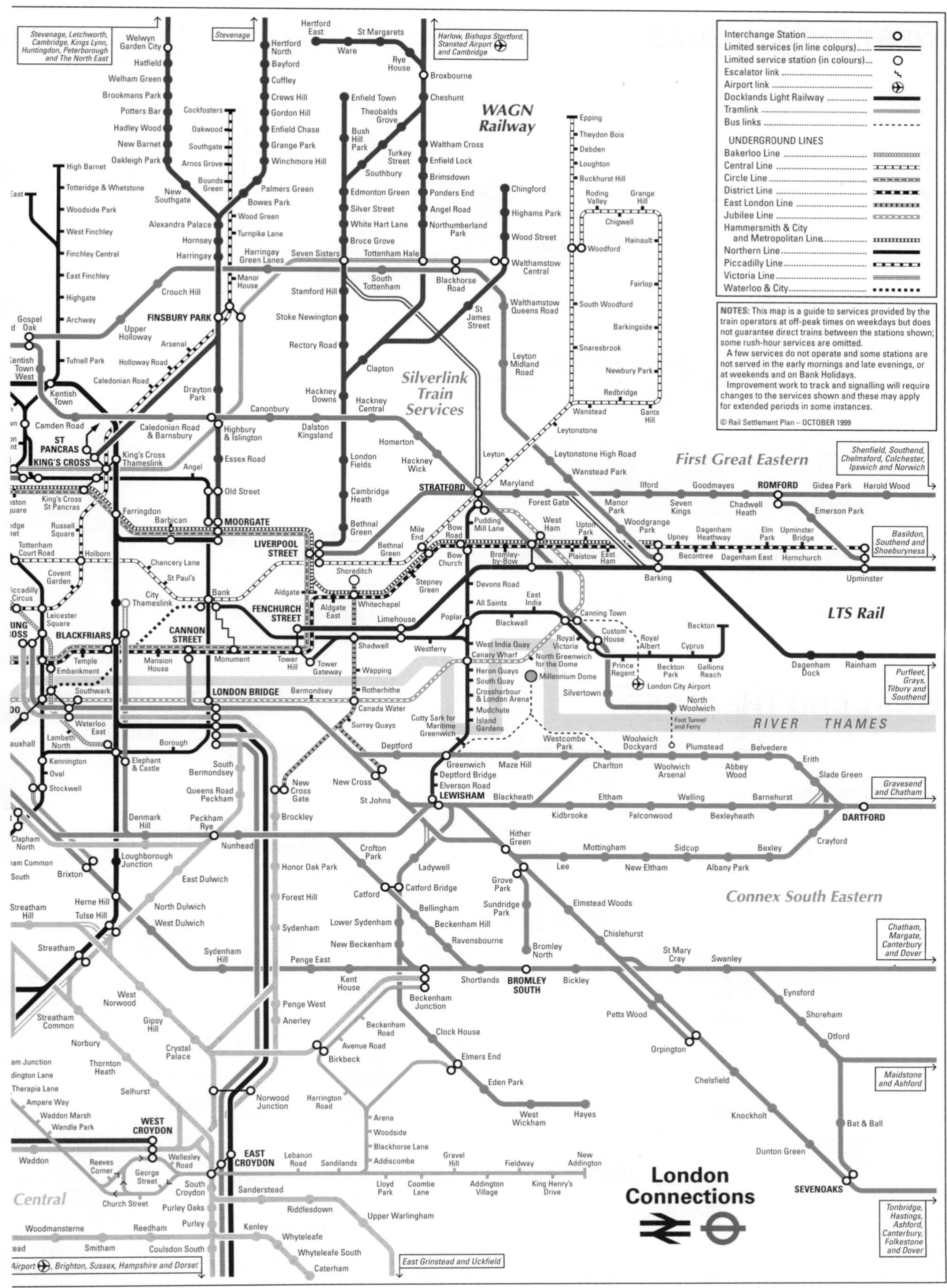
Interchange Station
Limited service (in line colours)
Limited service station (in colours)
Escalator link
Airport link
Docklands Light Railway
Tramlink
Bus links
UNDERGROUND LINES
Bakerloo Line
Central Line
Circle Line
District Line
East London Line
Jubilee Line
Hammersmith & City and Metropolitan Line
Northern Line
Piccadilly Line
Victoria Line
Waterloo & City
NOTES: This map is a guide to services provided by the train operators at off-peak times on weekdays but does not guarantee direct trains between the stations shown; some rush-hour services are omitted.
A few services do not operate and some stations are not served in the early mornings and late evenings, or at weekends and on Bank Holidays.
Improvement work to track and signalling may result in changes to the services shown and these may apply for extended periods in some instances.
© Rail Settlement Plan – OCTOBER 1999
WAGN Railway
Silverlink Train Services
First Great Eastern
LTS Rail
Connex South Eastern
Central
RIVER THAMES
London Connections
Stevenage, Letchworth, Cambridge, Kings Lynn, Huntingdon, Peterborough and The North East
Stevenage
Harlow, Bishops Stortford, Stansted Airport and Cambridge
Shenfield, Southend, Chelmsford, Colchester, Ipswich and Norwich
Basildon, Southend and Shoeburyness
Purfleet, Grays, Tilbury and Southend
Gravesend and Chatham
Chatham, Margate, Canterbury and Dover
Maidstone and Ashford
Tonbridge, Hastings, Ashford, Canterbury, Folkestone and Dover
East Grinstead and Uckfield
Airport, Brighton, Sussex, Hampshire and Dorset
Welwyn Garden City
Hatfield
Welham Green
Brookmans Park
Potters Bar
Hadley Wood
New Barnet
Oakleigh Park
High Barnet
Totteridge & Whetstone
Woodside Park
West Finchley
Finchley Central
East Finchley
Highgate
Archway
Tufnell Park
Kentish Town
Kentish Town West
Gospel Oak
Camden Road
Cockfosters
Oakwood
Southgate
Arnos Grove
Bounds Green
New Southgate
Alexandra Palace
Hornsey
Harringay
Crouch Hill
Upper Holloway
FINSBURY PARK
Arsenal
Holloway Road
Caledonian Road
Drayton Park
Caledonian Road & Barnsbury
ST PANCRAS
KING'S CROSS
King's Cross Thameslink
Angel
Highbury & Islington
Essex Road
Old Street
Hertford North
Bayford
Cuffley
Crews Hill
Gordon Hill
Enfield Chase
Grange Park
Winchmore Hill
Palmers Green
Bowes Park
Wood Green
Turnpike Lane
Harringay Green Lanes
Manor House
Hertford East
Ware
St Margarets
Rye House
Broxbourne
Cheshunt
Enfield Town
Theobalds Grove
Bush Hill Park
Turkey Street
Southbury
Waltham Cross
Enfield Lock
Brimsdown
Ponders End
Angel Road
Northumberland Park
Edmonton Green
Silver Street
White Hart Lane
Bruce Grove
Seven Sisters
Tottenham Hale
South Tottenham
Blackhorse Road
Stamford Hill
Stoke Newington
Rectory Road
Clapton
Hackney Downs
Hackney Central
Canonbury
Dalston Kingsland
Homerton
Hackney Wick
London Fields
Cambridge Heath
Bethnal Green
Chingford
Highams Park
Wood Street
Walthamstow Central
Walthamstow Queens Road
St James Street
Leyton Midland Road
Leyton
Epping
Theydon Bois
Debden
Loughton
Buckhurst Hill
Roding Valley
Grange Hill
Chigwell
Hainault
Woodford
Fairlop
South Woodford
Barkingside
Snaresbrook
Newbury Park
Redbridge
Wanstead
Gants Hill
Leytonstone
Leytonstone High Road
Wanstead Park
STRATFORD
Maryland
Forest Gate
Manor Park
Ilford
Seven Kings
Goodmayes
Chadwell Heath
ROMFORD
Gidea Park
Harold Wood
Emerson Park
Woodgrange Park
Upton Park
East Ham
West Ham
Plaistow
Upney
Barking
Dagenham Heathway
Becontree
Dagenham East
Elm Park
Hornchurch
Upminster Bridge
Upminster
Euston Square
King's Cross St Pancras
Farringdon
Barbican
MOORGATE
LIVERPOOL STREET
Russell Square
Tottenham Court Road
Holborn
Chancery Lane
St Paul's
Covent Garden
Leicester Square
Piccadilly Circus
City Thameslink
Bank
BLACKFRIARS
CANNON STREET
Mansion House
Monument
Temple
Embankment
Tower Hill
FENCHURCH STREET
Aldgate
Aldgate East
Shoreditch
Whitechapel
Mile End
Bow Road
Pudding Mill Lane
Bow Church
Bromley-by-Bow
Stepney Green
Devons Road
All Saints
Limehouse
Poplar
East India
Blackwall
Canning Town
Custom House
Royal Victoria
Royal Albert
Beckton Park
Cyprus
Gallions Reach
Beckton
Prince Regent
London City Airport
North Woolwich
Foot Tunnel and Ferry
Silvertown
Westferry
West India Quay
Canary Wharf
North Greenwich for the Dome
Millennium Dome
Heron Quays
South Quay
Crossharbour & London Arena
Mudchute
Island Gardens
Cutty Sark for Maritime Greenwich
Shadwell
Wapping
Rotherhithe
Canada Water
Surrey Quays
Tower Gateway
LONDON BRIDGE
Bermondsey
Southwark
Waterloo East
Lambeth North
Borough
Elephant & Castle
Kennington
Oval
Stockwell
Vauxhall
South Bermondsey
Queens Road Peckham
Peckham Rye
Denmark Hill
New Cross Gate
New Cross
St Johns
Deptford
Greenwich
Deptford Bridge
Elverson Road
LEWISHAM
Maze Hill
Westcombe Park
Charlton
Woolwich Dockyard
Woolwich Arsenal
Plumstead
Abbey Wood
Belvedere
Erith
Slade Green
Blackheath
Eltham
Welling
Barnehurst
Kidbrooke
Falconwood
Bexleyheath
DARTFORD
Crayford
Hither Green
Mottingham
Sidcup
Bexley
Lee
New Eltham
Albany Park
Clapham North
Clapham Common
Clapham South
Brixton
Loughborough Junction
East Dulwich
Nunhead
Brockley
Honor Oak Park
Crofton Park
Forest Hill
Catford
Catford Bridge
Ladywell
Grove Park
Sundridge Park
Bellingham
Beckenham Hill
Ravensbourne
Bromley North
Elmstead Woods
Chislehurst
St Mary Cray
Swanley
Streatham Hill
Herne Hill
Tulse Hill
North Dulwich
West Dulwich
Sydenham
Lower Sydenham
New Beckenham
Sydenham Hill
Penge East
Streatham
Kent House
Shortlands
BROMLEY SOUTH
Bickley
Beckenham Junction
Penge West
Anerley
West Norwood
Gipsy Hill
Streatham Common
Norbury
Crystal Palace
Thornton Heath
Beckenham Road
Avenue Road
Birkbeck
Clock House
Elmers End
Eden Park
West Wickham
Hayes
Petts Wood
Orpington
Chelsfield
Knockholt
Dunton Green
SEVENOAKS
Eynsford
Shoreham
Otford
Bat & Ball
Mitcham Junction
Beddington Lane
Therapia Lane
Ampere Way
Waddon Marsh
Wandle Park
Selhurst
WEST CROYDON
Norwood Junction
Harrington Road
Arena
Woodside
Blackhorse Lane
Addiscombe
Lebanon Road
Sandilands
EAST CROYDON
Waddon
Reeves Corner
George Street
Wellesley Road
Church Street
South Croydon
Sanderstead
Purley Oaks
Purley
Riddlesdown
Kenley
Whyteleafe
Whyteleafe South
Caterham
Upper Warlingham
Lloyd Park
Coombe Lane
Gravel Hill
Addington Village
Fieldway
King Henry's Drive
New Addington
Woodmansterne
Reedham
Smitham
Coulsdon South

WEST END CINEMAS

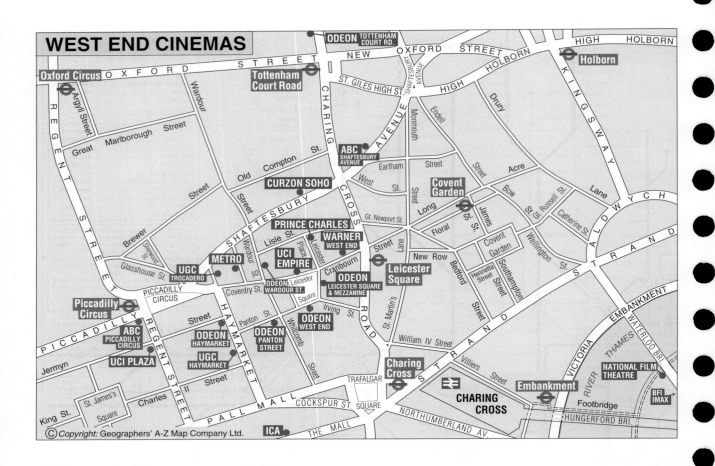

Oxford Circus · OXFORD STREET · Argyll Street · Wardour · Great Marlborough Street · Street · Brewer · Sherwood · Glasshouse St. · **Piccadilly Circus** · REGENT STREET · **ABC PICCADILLY CIRCUS** · **UCI PLAZA** · Jermyn · King St. · St. James's Square · Charles · PALL MALL

ODEON TOTTENHAM COURT RD. · NEW OXFORD STREET · HIGH HOLBORN · **Holborn** · KINGSWAY · Drury · HIGH HOLBORN · **Tottenham Court Road** · ST. GILES HIGH ST. · CHARING CROSS · SHAFTESBURY AVENUE · Monmouth · Endell · **ABC SHAFTESBURY AVENUE** · Earlham · Street · Acre · Lane · **CURZON SOHO** · West St. · Street · **Covent Garden** · Bow · St. Gt. Russell St. · Catherine St. · **PRINCE CHARLES** · Lisle St. · Gt. Newport St. · Long · James St. · St. · Wellington St. · **WARNER WEST END** · **UCI EMPIRE** · Leicester Place · Cranbourn · Street · Lane · New Row · Covent Garden · Henrietta Street · Southampton Street · **METRO** · **UGC TROCADERO** · Coventry St. · **ODEON WARDOUR ST.** · Leicester Square · **ODEON LEICESTER SQUARE & MEZZANINE** · **Leicester Square** · Bedford · STRAND · ALDWYCH · **ODEON HAYMARKET** · **ODEON PANTON STREET** · **ODEON WEST END** · Irving St. · St. Martin's · William IV Street · **UGC HAYMARKET** · Panton St. · Whitcomb Street · HAYMARKET · Street · **Charing Cross** · STRAND · Villiers Street · EMBANKMENT · WATERLOO BRI. · THAMES · **Embankment** · **NATIONAL FILM THEATRE** · TRAFALGAR SQUARE · **CHARING CROSS** · Footbridge · **BFI IMAX** · COCKSPUR ST. · NORTHUMBERLAND AV. · HUNGERFORD BRI. · **ICA** · THE MALL

© Copyright: Geographers' A-Z Map Company Ltd.

WEST END THEATRES

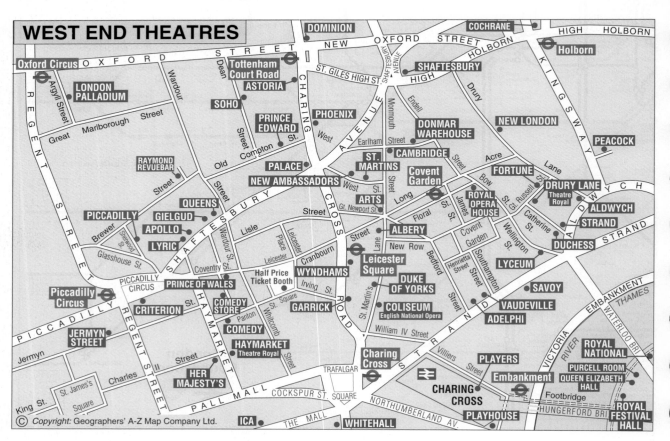

Oxford Circus · OXFORD STREET · Argyll Street · **LONDON PALLADIUM** · Wardour · Great Marlborough Street · Street · **RAYMOND REVUEBAR** · Street · Brewer · Sherwood · Glasshouse St. · **PICCADILLY** · **GIELGUD** · **APOLLO** · **LYRIC** · **QUEENS** · **Piccadilly Circus** · PICCADILLY CIRCUS · REGENT STREET · **CRITERION** · **JERMYN STREET** · Jermyn · King St. · St. James's Square · Charles · PALL MALL

DOMINION · NEW OXFORD STREET · **COCHRANE** · HIGH HOLBORN · **Holborn** · KINGSWAY · Dean · **Tottenham Court Road** · ST. GILES HIGH ST. · HIGH · **SHAFTESBURY** · **ASTORIA** · SHAFTESBURY AVENUE · Monmouth · Endell · Drury · **SOHO** · **PHOENIX** · West · Earlham · Street · **DONMAR WAREHOUSE** · **NEW LONDON** · **PRINCE EDWARD** · Compton St. · Street · **CAMBRIDGE** · Acre · Lane · **PEACOCK** · Old · **PALACE** · **ST. MARTINS** · Street · **FORTUNE** · **NEW AMBASSADORS** · West St. · **Covent Garden** · **ROYAL OPERA HOUSE** · St. Gt. Russell St. · **DRURY LANE** · Theatre Royal · **ARTS** · Gt. Newport St. · Long · James · Bow · Catherine St. · **ALDWYCH** · **STRAND** · Street · Floral · St. · St. · Wellington St. · **DUCHESS** · STRAND · **QUEENS** · Lisle · Leicester Place · **ALBERY** · New Row · Covent Garden · **LYCEUM** · Cranbourn · Street · Lane · Henrietta Street · Southampton Street · Coventry St. · Leicester · **WYNDHAMS** · **Leicester Square** · Bedford · **SAVOY** · **PRINCE OF WALES** · Half Price Ticket Booth · **GARRICK** · Irving St. · **DUKE OF YORKS** · D · **VAUDEVILLE** · **COMEDY STORE** · Panton St. · Square · **COLISEUM** English National Opera · **ADELPHI** · **CRITERION** · St. · Whitcomb · St. Martin's · William IV Street · EMBANKMENT · THAMES · **COMEDY** · HAYMARKET · Street · **Charing Cross** · STRAND · **PLAYERS** · **Embankment** · WATERLOO BRI. · **HAYMARKET** Theatre Royal · **ROYAL NATIONAL** · **HER MAJESTY'S** · TRAFALGAR SQUARE · Villiers Street · **PURCELL ROOM** · **QUEEN ELIZABETH HALL** · King St. · St. James's Square · Charles · PALL MALL · COCKSPUR ST. · **CHARING CROSS** · NORTHUMBERLAND AV. · Footbridge · **ROYAL FESTIVAL HALL** · **ICA** · THE MALL · **WHITEHALL** · **PLAYHOUSE** · HUNGERFORD BRI.

© Copyright: Geographers' A-Z Map Company Ltd.

INDEX

Including Streets, Places & Areas, Industrial Estates, Selected Subsidiary Addresses, Junction Names and Selected Places of Interest.

HOW TO USE THIS INDEX

1. Each street name is followed by its Postal District (or, if outside the London Postal Districts, by its Posttown or Postal Locality), and then by its map reference; e.g. Abbeville Rd. *SW4* —6G **103** is in the South West 4 Postal District and is found in square 6G on page **103**. The page number being shown in bold type. A strict alphabetical order is followed in which Av., Rd., St. etc. (though abbreviated) are read in full and as part of the street name; e.g. Abbotsmede Clo. appears after Abbots Mead but before Abbots Pk.
2. Streets and a selection of Subsidiary names not shown on the Maps, appear in this index in *Italics* with the thoroughfare to which it is connected shown in brackets; e.g. *Abbey Ct. SE17 —5C 86 (off Macleod St.)*
3. Places and areas are shown in the index in **bold type** the map reference referring to the actual map square in which the town or area is located and not to the place name; e.g. **Abbey Wood. —4C 92**
4. An example of a selected place of interest is **Admiralty Arch. —1H 85 (4D 166)**
5. Map references shown in brackets; e.g. Abbey Orchard St. *SW1* —3H **85** (1D **172**) refer to entries that also appear on the large scale pages **158-173**.

GENERAL ABBREVIATIONS

All : Alley
App : Approach
Arc : Arcade
Av : Avenue
Bk : Back
Boulevd : Boulevard
Bri : Bridge
B'way : Broadway
Bldgs : Buildings
Bus : Business
Cvn : Caravan
Cen : Centre
Chu : Church
Chyd : Churchyard
Circ : Circle
Cir : Circus
Clo : Close
Comn : Common
Cotts : Cottages
Ct : Court
Cres : Crescent
Cft : Croft
Dri : Drive
E : East
Embkmt : Embankment
Est : Estate
Fld : Field
Gdns : Gardens
Gth : Garth
Ga : Gate
Gt : Great
Grn : Green
Gro : Grove
Ho : House
Ind : Industrial
Info : Information
Junct : Junction
La : Lane
Lit : Little
Lwr : Lower
Mc : Mac
Mnr : Manor
Mans : Mansions
Mkt : Market
Mdw : Meadow
M : Mews
Mt : Mount
Mus : Museum
N : North
Pal : Palace
Pde : Parade
Pk : Park
Pas : Passage
Pl : Place
Quad : Quadrant
Res : Residential
Ri : Rise
Rd : Road
Shop : Shopping
S : South
Sq : Square
Sta : Station
St : Street
Ter : Terrace
Trad : Trading
Up : Upper
Va : Vale
Vw : View
Vs : Villas
Vis : Visitors
Wlk : Walk
W : West
Yd : Yard

POSTTOWN AND POSTAL LOCALITY ABBREVIATIONS

Ashf : Ashford
Bark : Barking
B'side : Barkingside
B'hurst : Barnehurst
Barn : Barnet
Beck : Beckenham
Bedd : Beddington
Bedf : Bedfont
Belm : Belmont
Belv : Belvedere
Bex : Bexley
Bexh : Bexleyheath
Borwd : Borehamwood
Bren : Brentford
Brim : Brimsdown
Brom : Bromley
Buck H : Buckhurst Hill
Bush : Bushey
Bus H : Bushey Heath
Cars : Carshalton
Chad H : Chadwell Heath
Cheam : Cheam
Cher : Chertsey
Chess : Chessington
Chig : Chigwell
Chst : Chislehurst
Clay : Claygate
Cockf : Cockfosters
Col R : Collier Row
Cran : Cranford
Cray : Crayford
Croy : Croydon
Dag : Dagenham
Dart : Dartford
Dit H : Ditton Hill
E Barn : East Barnet
Eastc : Eastcote
E Mol : East Molesey
Edgw : Edgware
Els : Elstree
Enf : Enfield
Eps : Epsom
Eri : Erith
Esh : Esher
Ewe : Ewell
Farnb : Farnborough
Felt : Feltham
Frog : Frogmore
Gnfd : Greenford
Hack : Hackbridge
Ham : Ham
Hamp : Hampton
Hamp H : Hampton Hill
Hamp W : Hampton Wick
Hanw : Hanworth
Hare : Harefield
Harm : Harmondsworth
Harr : Harrow
Har W : Harrow Weald
H End : Hatch End
Hayes : Hayes (Kent)
Hay : Hayes (Middlesex)
H'row : Heathrow
H'row A : London Heathrow Airport
High Bar : High Barnet
Hil : Hillingdon
Hin W : Hinchley Wood
Houn : Hounslow
Ick : Ickenham
Ilf : Ilford
Iswth : Isleworth
Kent : Kenton
Kes : Keston
Kew : Kew
King T : Kingston Upon Thames
Lale : Laleham
L Hth : Little Heath
Lou : Loughton
Mawn : Mawneys
Mitc : Mitcham
Mit J : Mitcham Junction
Mord : Morden
New Ad : New Addington
New Bar : New Barnet
N Mald : New Malden
N Har : North Harrow
N'holt : Northolt
N Hth : Northumberland Heath
N'wd : Northwood
Orp : Orpington
Pet W : Petts Wood
Pinn : Pinner
Pot B : Potters Bar
Purl : Purley
Rain : Rainham
Rich : Richmond
Ridg : Ridgeway, The
Romf : Romford
Ruis : Ruislip
Rush G : Rush Green
St M : St Mary Cray
St P : St Pauls Cray
Shep : Shepperton
Short : Shortlands
Sidc : Sidcup
S'hall : Southall
S Croy : South Croydon
S Harr : South Harrow
S Ruis : South Ruislip
Stai : Staines
Stan : Stanmore
Stanw : Stanwell
S'leigh : Stoneleigh
Sun : Sunbury-On-Thames
Surb : Surbiton
Sutt : Sutton
Swan : Swanley
Tedd : Teddington
Th Dit : Thames Ditton
T Hth : Thornton Heath
Twic : Twickenham
Uxb : Uxbridge
Wall : Wallington
Wal X : Waltham Cross
W on T : Walton-On-Thames
Warl : Warlingham
W'stone : Wealdstone
Well : Welling
Wemb : Wembley
W Dray : West Drayton
W Ewe : West Ewell
W Mol : West Molesey
W W'ck : West Wickham
Wey : Weybridge
Whit : Whitton
Wok : Woking
Wfd G : Woodford Green
Wor Pk : Worcester Park
Yiew : Yiewsley

INDEX

1 Owen St. EC1 —2B 68 (1A 162)
(off Owen St.)
101 Bus. Units. *SW11* —3D **102**
198 Gallery. —6B 104
(off Railton Rd.)
3 Cranes Wlk. *EC4* —3D **168**

Aaron Hill Rd. *E6* —5E **72**
Abady Ho. SW1 —4H 85 (3D 172)
(off Page St.)
Abberley M. *SW4* —3F **103**
Abbess Clo. *E6* —5C **72**
Abbess Clo. *SW2* —1B **122**
Abbeville M. *SW4* —4H **103**
Abbeville Rd. *N8* —4H **31**
Abbeville Rd. *SW4* —6G **103**
Abbey Av. *Wemb* —2E **62**
Abbey Bus. Cen. *SW8* —1G **103**
Abbey Clo. *Hay* —1K **77**
Abbey Clo. *N'holt* —3D **60**
Abbey Clo. *Pinn* —3K **23**
Abbey Ct. NW8 —2A 66
(off Abbey Rd.)
Abbey Ct. SE17 —5C 86
(off Macleod St.)
Abbey Ct. *Hamp* —7E **114**
Abbey Cres. *Belv* —4G **93**
Abbeydale Ct. *E17* —3F **35**
Abbeydale Ct. S'hall —6F 61
(off Dormers Ri.)
Abbeydale Rd. *Wemb* —1F **63**
Abbey Dri. *SW17* —5E **120**
Abbey Est. *NW8* —1K **65**
Abbeyfield Clo. *Mitc* —2C **138**
Abbeyfield Est. *SE16* —4J **87**
Abbeyfield Rd. *SE16* —4J **87**
(in two parts)
Abbeyfields Clo. *NW10* —3G **63**
Abbey Gdns. *NW8* —2A **66**
Abbey Gdns. *SE16* —4G **87**
Abbey Gdns. *W6* —6G **83**
Abbey Gdns. *Chst* —1E **144**
Abbey Gro. *SE2* —4B **92**
Abbey Hill Rd. *Sidc* —2C **128**
Abbey Ho. E15 —2G 71
(off Baker's Row)
Abbey Ho. *NW8* —1A **158**
Abbey Ind. Est. *Mitc* —5D **138**
Abbey Ind. Est. *Wemb* —1F **63**
Abbey La. *E15* —2E **70**
Abbey La. *Beck* —7C **124**
Abbey La. Commercial Est. *E15* —2G **71**
Abbey Life Ct. *E16* —5K **71**
Abbey Lodge. NW8 —2D **158**
Abbey M. *E17* —5C **34**
Abbey Mt. *Belv* —5F **93**
Abbey Orchard St. *SW1* —3H **85** (1D **172**)
Abbey Orchard St. Est. *SW1* —3H **85** (1D **172**)
Abbey Pde. SW19 —7A 120
(off Merton High St.)
Abbey Pde. *W5* —3F **63**
Abbey Pk. *Beck* —7C **124**
Abbey Retail Pk. *Bark* —7F **55**
Abbey Rd. *E15* —2F **71**
Abbey Rd. *NW6 & NW8* —7K **47** (1A **158**)
Abbey Rd. *NW10* —1H **63**
Abbey Rd. *SW19* —7A **120**
Abbey Rd. *Bark* —7F **55**
Abbey Rd. *Belv* —4D **92**
Abbey Rd. *Bexh* —4E **110**
Abbey Rd. *Croy* —3B **152**
Abbey Rd. *Enf* —5K **7**
Abbey Rd. *Ilf* —5H **37**
Abbey St. *E13* —4J **71**
Abbey St. *SE1* —3E **86** (7H **169**)
Abbey Ter. *SE2* —4C **92**
Abbey Trad. Est. *SE26* —5B **124**
Abbey Vw. *NW7* —3G **13**
Abbey Wlk. *W Mol* —3F **133**
Abbey Wharf Ind. Est. *Bark* —3H **73**
Abbey Wood. —4C 92
Abbey Wood Camping & Cvn. Site. *SE2* —4C **92**
Abbey Wood Rd. *SE2* —4B **92**
Abbot Ct. SW8 —7J 85
(off Hartington Rd.)
Abbot Ho. *E14* —7D **70**
Abbotsbury Clo. *E15* —2E **70**
Abbotsbury Gdns. *Pinn* —7A **24**
Abbotsbury M. *SE15* —3J **105**
Abbotsbury Rd. *W14* —2G **83**
Abbotsbury Rd. *Brom* —2H **155**
Abbotsbury Rd. *Mord* —-5K **137**
Abbots Clo. *Orp* —7G **145**
Abbots Clo. *Ruis* —3B **42**
Abbots Dri. *Harr* —2E **42**
Abbotsford Av. *N15* —4C **32**
Abbotsford Gdns. *Wfd G* —7D **20**
Abbotsford Rd. *Ilf* —2A **56**
Abbots Gdns. *N2* —4B **30**
Abbots Grn. *Croy* —6K **153**
Abbotshade Rd. *SE16* —1K **87**
Abbotshall Av. *N14* —3B **16**
Abbotshall Rd. *SE6* —1F **125**
Abbot's Ho. *W14* —3H **83**
Abbots La. *SE1* —1E **86** (5H **169**)
Abbotsleigh Clo. *Sutt* —7K **149**
Abbotsleigh Rd. *SW16* —4G **121**
Abbots Mnr. *SW1* —4F **85** (5J **171**)
Abbots Mead. *Rich* —4D **116**
Abbotsmede Clo. *Twic* —2K **115**
Abbots Pk. *SW2* —1A **122**
Abbot's Pl. *NW6* —1K **65**
Abbot's Rd. *E6* —1B **72**
Abbots Rd. *Edgw* —7D **12**
Abbots Ter. *N8* —6J **31**
Abbotstone Rd. *SW15* —3E **100**
Abbot St. *E8* —6F **51**
Abbots Wlk. *W8* —3K **83**
Abbotswell Rd. *SE4* —5B **106**
Abbotswood Clo. *Belv* —3E **92**
Abbotswood Gdns. *Ilf* —3D **36**
Abbotswood Rd. *SE22* —4E **104**
Abbotswood Rd. *SW16* —3H **121**
Abbotswood Way. *Hay* —1K **77**
Abbott Av. *SW20* —1F **137**
Abbott Clo. *Hamp* —6C **114**
Abbott Clo. *N'holt* —6D **42**
Abbott Rd. *E14* —5E **70**
(in two parts)
Abbottsbury Clo. *W14* —2G **83**
Abbotts Clo. *SE28* —7C **74**
Abbotts Clo. *N1* —6C **50**
Abbotts Clo. *Romf* —3H **39**
Abbott's Clo. *Uxb* —5A **58**
Abbotts Cres. *E4* —4A **20**
Abbotts Cres. *Enf* —2G **7**
Abbotts Dri. *Wemb* —2B **44**
Abbotts Ho. SW1 —5H 85 (6C 172)
(off Aylesford St.)
Abbotts Pk. Rd. *E10* —7E **34**
Abbotts Rd. *Mitc* —4G **139**
(in two parts)
Abbotts Rd. *New Bar* —4E **4**
Abbotts Rd. *S'hall* —1C **78**
Abbotts Rd. *Sutt* —4G **149**
Abbott's Wlk. *Bexh* —7D **92**
Abbotts Wharf. *E14* —6C **70**
Abby Pk. Ind. Est. *Bark* —2G **73**
Abchurch La. *EC4* —7D **68** (2F **169**)
(in two parts)
Abchurch Yd. *EC4* —2E **168**
Abdale Rd. *W12* —1D **82**
Abel Ho. SE11 —6A 86 (7K 173)
(off Kennington Rd.)
Abenglen Ind. Est. *Hay* —2F **77**
Aberavon Rd. *E3* —3A **70**
Abercairn Rd. *SW16* —7G **121**
Aberconway Rd. *Mord* —4K **137**
Abercorn Clo. *NW7* —7B **14**
Abercorn Clo. *NW8* —3A **66**
Abercorn Commercial Cen. *Wemb* —1D **62**
Abercorn Cres. *Harr* —1F **43**
Abercorn Gdns. *Harr* —7D **26**
Abercorn Gdns. *Romf* —6B **38**
Abercorn Gro. *Ruis* —4F **23**
Abercorn Ho. SE10 —7D 88
(off Tarves Way)
Abercorn Mans. NW8 —2A 66
(off Abercorn Pl.)
Abercorn M. *Rich* —4F **99**
Abercorn Pl. *NW8* —3A **66**
Abercorn Rd. *NW7* —7B **14**
Abercorn Rd. *Stan* —7H **11**
Abercorn Way. *SE1* —5G **87**
Abercrombie Dri. *Enf* —1B **8**
Abercrombie St. *SW11* —2C **102**
Aberdare Clo. *W W'ck* —2E **154**
Aberdare Gdns. *NW6* —7K **47**
Aberdare Gdns. *NW7* —7A **14**
Aberdare Rd. *Enf* —4D **8**
Aberdeen Cotts. *Stan* —7H **11**
Aberdeen Ct. W9 —4A 66 (4A 158)
(off Maida Va.)
Aberdeen La. *N5* —5C **50**
Aberdeen Mans. WC1 —4J 67 (3E 160)
(off Kenton St.)
Aberdeen Pde. N18 —5C 18
(off Aberdeen Rd.)
Aberdeen Pk. *N5* —5C **50**
Aberdeen Pl. *NW8* —4B **66**
Aberdeen Rd. *N5* —4C **50**
Aberdeen Rd. *N18* —5B **18**
(in two parts)
Aberdeen Rd. *NW10* —5B **46**
Aberdeen Rd. *Croy* —4C **152**
Aberdeen Rd. *Harr* —2K **25**
Aberdeen Sq. *E14* —1B **88**
Aberdeen Ter. *SE3* —2F **107**
Aberdour Rd. *Ilf* —3B **56**
Aberdour St. *SE1* —4E **86**
Aberfeldy Ho. *SE5* —7B **86**
(in two parts)
Aberfeldy St. *E14* —6E **70**
(in two parts)
Aberford Gdns. *SE18* —1C **108**
Aberfoyle Rd. *SW16* —6H **121**
(in two parts)
Abergeldie Rd. *SE12* —6K **107**
Abernethy Rd. *SE13* —4G **107**
Abersham Rd. *E8* —5F **51**
Abery St. *SE18* —4J **91**
Abingdon. W14 —4H 83
(off Kensington Village)
Abingdon Clo. *NW1* —6H **49**
Abingdon Clo. SE1 —4F 87
(off Bushwood Dri.)
Abingdon Clo. *SW19* —6A **120**
Abingdon Clo. *Uxb* —1B **58**
Abingdon Ct. W8 —3J 83
(off Abingdon Vs.)
Abingdon Gdns. *W8* —3J **83**
Abingdon Ho. E2 —4F 69 (3J 163)
(off Boundary St.)
Abingdon Lodge. *W8* —3J **83**
Abingdon Rd. *N3* —2A **30**
Abingdon Rd. *SW16* —2J **139**
Abingdon Rd. *W8* —3J **83**
Abingdon St. *SW1* —3J **85** (1E **172**)
Abingdon Vs. *W8* —3J **83**
Abinger Clo. *Bark* —4A **56**
Abinger Clo. *Brom* —3C **144**
Abinger Clo. *New Ad* —6E **154**
Abinger Clo. *Wall* —5J **151**
Abinger Ct. *W5* —7C **62**
Abinger Ct. *Wall* —5J **151**
Abinger Gdns. *Iswth* —3J **97**
Abinger Gro. *SE8* —6B **88**

Abinger Ho.—Albion Clo.

Abinger Ho. SE1 —2D 86 (7E 168)
(off Gt. Dover St.)
Abinger M. W9 —4J 65
Abinger Rd. W4 —3A 82
Ablett St. SE16 —5J 87
Abney Gdns. N16 —2F 51
Aboyne Dri. SW20 —2C 136
Aboyne Rd. NW10 —3A 46
Aboyne Rd. SW17 —3B 120
Abridge Way. Bark —2B 74
Abyssinia Clo. SW11 —4C 102
Abyssinia Ct. N8 —5K 31
Abyssinia Rd. SW11 —4C 102
Acacia Av. N17 —7J 17
Acacia Av. Bren —7B 80
Acacia Av. Hay —6H 59
Acacia Av. Ruis —1J 41
Acacia Av. Shep —5C 130
Acacia Av. Wemb —5E 44
Acacia Av. W Dray —7B 58
Acacia Bus. Cen. E11 —3G 53
Acacia Clo. SE8 —4A 88
Acacia Clo. SE20 —2G 141
Acacia Clo. Orp —5H 145
Acacia Clo. Stan —6D 10
Acacia Ct. Harr —5F 25
Acacia Dri. Sutt —1J 149
Acacia Gdns. NW8 —2B 66
Acacia Gdns. W W'ck —2E 154
Acacia Gro. SE21 —2D 122
Acacia Gro. N Mald —3K 135
Acacia Ho. N22 —1A 32
(off Douglas Rd.)
Acacia M. W Dray —6A 76
Acacia Pl. NW8 —2B 66
Acacia Rd. E11 —2G 53
Acacia Rd. E17 —6A 34
Acacia Rd. N22 —1A 32
Acacia Rd. NW8 —2B 66
Acacia Rd. SW16 —1J 139
Acacia Rd. W3 —7J 63
Acacia Rd. Beck —3B 142
Acacia Rd. Enf —1J 7
Acacia Rd. Hamp —6E 114
Acacia Rd. Mitc —2E 138
Acacias, The. Barn —5G 5
Acacia Way. Sidc —1K 127
Academy Bldgs. N1 —1G 163
Academy Gdns. Croy —1F 153
Academy Gdns. N'holt —2B 60
Academy Ho. E3 —5D 70
Academy Pl. SE18 —1D 108
Academy Rd. SE18 —1D 108
Acanthus Dri. SE1 —5G 87
Acanthus Rd. SW11 —3E 102
Accommodation Rd. NW11 —1H 47
Accommodation Rd. Wor Pk —5C 148
A.C. Court. Th Dit —6A 134
Ace Pde. Chess —3E 146
Acer Av. Hay —5C 60
Acfold Rd. SW6 —1K 101
Achilles Clo. SE1 —5G 87
Achilles Rd. NW6 —5J 47
Achilles St. SE14 —7A 88
Achilles Way. W1 —1E 84 (5H 165)
Acklam Rd. W10 —5G 65
(in two parts)
Acklington Dri. NW9 —1A 28
Ackmar Rd. SW6 —1J 101
Ackroyd Dri. E3 —5C 70
Ackroyd Rd. SE23 —7K 105
Acland Clo. SE18 —7H 91
Acland Cres. SE5 —3D 104
Acland Ho. SW9 —1K 103
Acland Rd. NW2 —6D 46
Acock Gro. N'holt —4F 43
Acol Ct. NW6 —7J 47
Acol Cres. Ruis —5K 41
Acol Rd. NW6 —7J 47
Aconbury Rd. Dag —1B 74
Acorn Clo. E4 —5J 19
Acorn Clo. Chst —5G 127
Acorn Clo. Enf —1G 7
Acorn Clo. Hamp —6F 115
Acorn Clo. Stan —7G 11
Acorn Ct. E6 —7C 54
Acorn Ct. Ilf —6J 37
Acorn Gdns. SE19 —1F 141
Acorn Gdns. W3 —5K 63
Acorn Gro. Hay —7H 77
Acorn Gro. Ruis —4H 41
Acorn Pde. SE15 —7H 87
Acorn Production Cen. N7 —7J 49
Acorn Wlk. SE16 —1A 88
Acorn Way. SE23 —3K 123
Acorn Way. Beck —5E 142
Acre Dri. SE22 —4G 105
Acrefield Ho. NW4 —4F 29
(off Belle Vue Est.)
Acre Path. N'holt —6C 42
(off Arnold Rd.)
Acre Rd. SW19 —6B 120
Acre Rd. Dag —7H 57
Acre Rd. King T —1E 134
Acre Way. N'wd —1H 23
Acris St. SW18 —5A 102
Acton. —1J 81
Acton Central Ind. Est. W3 —1H 81
Acton Clo. N9 —2B 18
Acton Green. —3J 81
Acton Hill M. W3 —1H 81
Acton Ho. E8 —1F 69
(off Lee St.)
Acton La. NW10 —3J 63
Acton La. W3 & W4 —2J 81
(in three parts)
Acton M. E8 —1F 69
Acton Pk. Est. W3 —2K 81
Acton St. WC1 —3K 67 (2G 161)
Acton Va. Ind. Pk. W3 —1B 82
Acuba Rd. SW18 —2K 119
Acworth Clo. N9 —7D 8
Acworth Ho. SE18 —6F 91
(off Barnfield Rd.)
Ada Ct. N1 —1C 68
(off Packington St.)
Ada Ct. NW8 —3A 66 (2A 158)
Ada Gdns. E14 —6F 71
Ada Gdns. E15 —1H 71
Ada Ho. E2 —1G 69
(off Ada Pl.)
Adair Clo. SE25 —3H 141
Adair Rd. W10 —4G 65
Adair Tower. W10 —4G 65
(off Appleford Rd.)
Adam & Eve Ct. W1 —7B 160
Adam & Eve M. W8 —3J 83
Adam Clo. SE6 —4B 124
Adam Ct. SE11 —4K 173
Adam Ct. SW7 —4A 84
(off Gloucester Rd.)
Adam Rd. E4 —6G 19
Adams Bri. Bus. Cen. Wemb —5H 45
Adams Clo. N3 —7D 14
Adams Clo. NW9 —2H 45
Adams Clo. Surb —6F 135
Adams Ct. E17 —6A 34
Adams Ct. EC2 —6E 68 (7F 163)
Adams Gdns. Est. SE16 —2J 87
Adams Ho. E14 —6F 71
Adamson Ct. N2 —3C 30
Adamson Rd. E16 —6J 71
Adamson Rd. NW3 —7B 48
Adams Pl. E14 —1D 88
(off N. Colonnade, The)
Adams Pl. N7 —5K 49
Adamsrill Clo. Enf —6J 7
Adamsrill Rd. SE26 —4K 123
Adams Rd. N17 —2D 32
Adams Rd. Beck —5A 142
Adam's Row. W1 —7E 66 (3H 165)
Adams Sq. Bexh —3E 110
Adam St. WC2 —7J 67 (3F 167)
Adams Wlk. King T —2E 134
Adams Way. Croy —6F 141
Adam Wlk. SW6 —7E 82
(off Crabtree La.)
Ada Pl. E2 —1G 69
Adare Wlk. SW16 —3K 121
Ada Rd. SE5 —7E 86
Ada Rd. Wemb —3D 44
Adastral Ho. WC1 —5K 67
(off New North St.)
Ada St. E8 —1H 69
Ada Workshops. E8 —1H 69
Adderley Gdns. SE9 —4E 126
Adderley Gro. SW11 —5E 102
Adderley Rd. Harr —1K 25
Adderley St. E14 —6E 70
Addey Ho. SE8 —7B 88
Addington. —5C 154
Addington Ct. SW14 —3K 99
Addington Dri. N12 —6G 15
Addington Gro. SE26 —4A 124
Addington Ho. SW9 —2K 103
(off Stockwell Rd.)
Addington Rd. E3 —3C 70
Addington Rd. E16 —4G 71
Addington Rd. N4 —6A 32
Addington Rd. Croy —1A 152
Addington Rd. S Croy —7K 153
Addington Rd. W W'ck —4E 154
Addington Sq. SE5 —6D 86
(in two parts)
Addington St. SE1 —2K 85 (7H 167)
Addington Village Rd. Croy —6B 154
(in two parts)
Addis Clo. Enf —1E 8
Addiscombe. —1G 153
Addiscombe Av. Croy —1G 153
Addiscombe Clo. Harr —5C 26
Addiscombe Ct. Rd. Croy —1E 152
Addiscombe Gro. Croy —2E 152
Addiscombe Rd. Croy —2E 152
Addisland Ct. W14 —2G 83
(off Holland Vs. Rd.)
Addison Av. N14 —6A 6
Addison Av. W11 —1G 83
Addison Av. Houn —1G 97
Addison Bri. Pl. W14 —4H 83
Addison Clo. N'wd —1J 23
Addison Clo. Orp —6G 145
Addison Cres. W14 —3G 83
Addison Dri. SE12 —5K 107
Addison Gdns. W14 —3F 83
Addison Gdns. Surb —4F 135
Addison Gro. W4 —3A 82
Addison Ho. NW8 —1A 158
Addison Pl. SE25 —4G 141
Addison Pl. W11 —1G 83
Addison Pl. S'hall —7E 60
Addison Rd. E11 —6J 35
Addison Rd. E17 —5D 34
Addison Rd. SE25 —4G 141
Addison Rd. W14 —2G 83
Addison Rd. Brom —5A 144
Addison Rd. Enf —1D 8
Addison Rd. Ilf —1G 37
Addison Rd. Tedd —6B 116
Addisons Clo. Croy —2B 154
Addison Ter. W4 —4J 81
(off Chiswick Rd.)
Addison Way. NW11 —4H 29
Addison Way. Hay —6J 59
Addison Way. N'wd —1H 23
Addle Hill. EC4 —6B 68 (1B 168)
Addle St. EC2 —6C 68 (7D 162)
Addmar Rd. Dag —3D 56
Addy Ho. SE16 —4J 87
Adecroft Way. W Mol —3G 133
Adela Av. N Mald —5D 136
Adelaide Av. SE4 —4B 106
Adelaide Clo. Enf —1K 7
Adelaide Clo. Stan —4F 11
Adelaide Ct. NW8 —2A 66
(off Abercorn Pl.)
Adelaide Ct. W7 —2K 79
Adelaide Ct. Beck —7B 124
Adelaide Gdns. Romf —5E 38
Adelaide Gro. W12 —1C 82
Adelaide Ho. E15 —2H 71
Adelaide Ho. E17 —2B 34
Adelaide Ho. SE5 —2E 104
Adelaide Ho. W11 —6H 65
(off Portobello Rd.)
Adelaide Rd. E10 —3D 52
Adelaide Rd. NW3 —7B 48
Adelaide Rd. SW18 —5J 101
Adelaide Rd. W13 —1A 80
Adelaide Rd. Ashf —5A 112
Adelaide Rd. Chst —5F 127
Adelaide Rd. Houn —1C 96
Adelaide Rd. Ilf —2F 55
Adelaide Rd. Rich —4F 99
Adelaide Rd. S'hall —4C 78
Adelaide Rd. Surb —5E 134
Adelaide Rd. Tedd —6K 115
Adelaide Rd. W on T —7J 131
Adelaide St. WC2 —7J 67 (3E 166)
Adelaide Ter. Bren —5D 80
Adelaide Wlk. SW9 —4A 104
Adela St. W10 —4G 65
Adelina Gro. E1 —5J 69
Adelina M. SW12 —1H 121
Adeline Pl. WC1 —5H 67 (6D 160)
Adeliza Clo. Bark —7G 55
Adelphi Ct. W4 —6K 81
Adelphi Cres. Hay —3G 59
Adelphi Ter. WC2 —7J 67 (3F 167)
Adelphi Way. Hay —3H 59
Adeney Clo. W6 —6F 83
Aden Gro. N16 —4D 50
Adenmore Rd. SE6 —7C 106
Aden Rd. Enf —4F 9
Aden Rd. Ilf —7G 37
Aden Ter. N16 —4D 50
Adeyfield Ho. EC1 —3D 68 (2F 163)
(off Cranwood St.)
Adie Rd. W6 —3E 82
Adine Rd. E13 —4K 71
Adler Ind. Est. Hay —2F 77
Adler St. E1 —6G 69
Adley St. E5 —5A 52
Adlington Clo. N18 —5K 17
Admaston Rd. SE18 —7G 91
Admiral Ct. SW10 —1A 102
(off Admiral Sq.)
Admiral Ct. W1 —5E 66 (6G 159)
(off Blandford St.)
Admiral Ct. Bark —2B 74
Admiral Ct. Cars —1C 150
Admiral Ho. SW1 —4G 85 (3B 172)
(off Willow Pl.)
Admiral Ho. Tedd —4A 116
Admiral Hyson Ind. Est. SE16 —5H 87
Admiral M. W10 —4F 65
Admiral Pl. SE16 —1A 88
Admirals Clo. E18 —4K 35
Admirals Ct. E6 —6F 73
(off Trader Rd.)
Admirals Ct. SE1 —1F 87 (5J 169)
(off Horselydown La.)
Admiral Seymour Rd. SE9 —4D 108
Admiral's Ga. SE10 —1D 106
Admirals Pl. E14 —2C 88
Admiral Sq. SW10 —1A 102
Admiral St. SE8 —2C 106
Admirals Wlk. NW3 —3A 48
Admiralty Arch. —1H 85 (4D 166)
Admiralty Clo. SE8 —7C 88
Admiralty Rd. Tedd —6K 115
Admiralty Way. Tedd —6K 115
Admiral Wlk. W9 —5J 65
Adolf St. SE6 —4D 124
Adolphus Rd. N4 —2B 50
Adolphus St. SE8 —7B 88
Adpar St. W2 —5B 66 (5A 158)
Adrian Av. NW2 —1D 46
Adrian Boult Ho. E2 —3H 69
(off Mansford St.)
Adrian Ho. N1 —1K 67
(off Barnsbury Est.)
Adrian Ho. SW8 —7J 85
(off Wyvil Rd.)
Adrian M. SW10 —6K 83
Adriatic Building. E14 —7A 70
Adrienne Av. S'hall —4D 60
Adstock Ho. N1 —7B 50
(off Sutton Est., The)
Advance Rd. SE27 —4C 122
Adventurers Ct. E14 —7F 71
Advent Way. N18 —5E 18
Adys Lawn. NW2 —6D 46
Ady's Rd. SE15 —3F 105
Aegon Ho. E14 —3D 88
(off Lanark Sq.)
Aerodrome Rd. NW9 & NW4 —2B 28
Aerodrome Way. Houn —6A 78
Aeroville. NW9 —2A 28
Affleck St. N1 —2K 67 (1G 161)
Afghan Rd. SW11 —2C 102
Afsil Ho. EC1 —5A 68 (6K 161)
(off Viaduct Bldgs.)
Agamemnon Rd. NW6 —4H 47
Agar Clo. Surb —2F 147
Agar Gro. NW1 —7G 49
Agar Gro. Est. NW1 —7H 49
Agar Pl. NW1 —7G 49
Agar St. WC2 —7J 67 (3E 166)
Agate Clo. E16 —6B 72
Agate Rd. W6 —3E 82
Agatha Clo. E1 —1H 87
Agaton Rd. SE9 —2G 127
Agave Rd. NW2 —4E 46
Agdon St. EC1 —4B 68 (3A 162)
Agincourt Rd. NW3 —4D 48
Agnes Av. Ilf —4E 54
Agnes Clo. E6 —7E 72
Agnesfield Clo. N12 —6H 15
Agnes Gdns. Dag —4D 56
Agnes Ho. W11 —7F 65
(off St Ann's Rd.)
Agnes Rd. W3 —1B 82
Agnes St. E14 —6B 70
Agnew Rd. SE23 —7K 105
Agricola Pl. Enf —5A 8
Aidan Clo. Dag —3E 56
Aigburth Mans. SW9 —7A 86
(off Mowll St.)
Aileen Wlk. E15 —7H 53
Ailsa Av. Twic —5A 98
Ailsa Rd. Twic —5B 98
Ailsa St. E14 —5E 70
Ainger M. NW3 —7D 48
(off Ainger Rd., in two parts)
Ainger Rd. NW3 —7D 48
Ainsdale. NW1 —2G 67 (1A 160)
(off Harrington St.)
Ainsdale Clo. Orp —7H 145
Ainsdale Cres. Pinn —3E 24
Ainsdale Dri. SE1 —5G 87
Ainsdale Rd. W5 —4D 62
Ainsley Av. Romf —6H 39
Ainsley Clo. N9 —1K 17
Ainsley St. E2 —3H 69
Ainslie Ct. Wemb —2E 62
Ainslie Wlk. SW12 —7F 103
Ainslie Wood Cres. E4 —5J 19
Ainslie Wood Gdns. E4 —4J 19
Ainslie Wood Rd. E4 —5H 19
Ainsty Est. SE16 —2K 87
Ainsty St. SE16 —2J 87
Ainsworth Clo. NW2 —3C 46
Ainsworth Clo. SE15 —2E 104
Ainsworth Ho. NW8 —1K 65
Ainsworth Rd. E9 —7J 51
Ainsworth Rd. Croy —1B 152
Ainsworth Way. NW8 —1A 66
Aintree Av. E6 —1C 72
Aintree Clo. Uxb —6D 58
Aintree Cres. Ilf —2G 37
Aintree Est. SW6 —7G 83
(off Aintree St.)
Aintree Rd. Gnfd —2B 62
Aintree St. SW6 —7G 83
Airbourne Ho. Wall —4G 151
(off Maldon Rd.)
Air Call Bus. Cen. NW9 —3K 27
Aird Ho. SE1 —3C 86
(off Rockingham St.)
Airdrie Clo. N1 —7K 49
Airdrie Clo. Hay —5C 60
Airedale Av. W4 —4B 82
Airedale Av. S. W4 —5B 82
Airedale Rd. SW12 —7D 102
Airedale Rd. W5 —3C 80
Airlie Gdns. W8 —1J 83
Airlie Gdns. Ilf —1F 55
Airlinks Ind. Est. Houn —5A 78
Air Pk. Way. Felt —2K 113
Air St. W1 —7G 67 (3B 166)
Airthrie Rd. Ilf —2B 56
Aisgill Av. W14 —5H 83
(in two parts)
Aisher Rd. SE28 —7C 74
Aislibie Rd. SE12 —4G 107
Aiten Pl. W6 —4C 82
Aithan Ho. E14 —6B 70
Aitken Clo. E8 —1G 69
Aitken Clo. Mitc —7D 138
Aitken Rd. SE6 —2D 124
Ajax Av. NW9 —3A 28
Ajax Rd. NW6 —4H 47
Akabusi Clo. Croy —6G 141
Akbar Ho. E14 —4D 88
Akehurst St. SW15 —6C 100
Akenside Rd. NW3 —5B 48
Akerman Rd. SW9 —2B 104
Akerman Rd. Surb —6C 134
Alabama St. SE18 —7H 91
Alacross Rd. W5 —2C 80
Alandale Dri. Pinn —1K 23
Aland Ct. SE16 —3A 88
Alander M. E17 —4E 34
Alan Dri. Barn —6B 4
Alan Gdns. Romf —7G 39
Alan Hocken Way. E15 —2G 71
Alan Preece Ct. NW6 —7F 47
Alan Rd. SW19 —5G 119
Alanthus Clo. SE12 —6J 107
Alaska Bldgs. SE1 —3F 87
Alaska St. SE1 —1A 86 (5J 167)
Alba Clo. Hay —4B 60
Albacore Cres. SE13 —6D 106
Alba Gdns. NW11 —6G 29
Albain Cres. Ashf —2A 112
Alban Highwalk. EC2 —7D 162
(in two parts)
Albany. N12 —6E 14
Albany. W1 —7G 67 (3A 166)
Albany Clo. N15 —4B 32
Albany Clo. SW14 —4H 99
Albany Clo. Bex —7C 110
Albany Clo. Uxb —5C 40
Albany Ct. E4 —6H 9
(Sewardstone Rd.)
Albany Ct. E4 —5G 19
(Westward Rd.)
Albany Ct. E10 —7C 34
Albany Ct. NW8 —2B 66 (1A 158)
(off Abbey Rd.)
Albany Ct. NW9 —1K 27
Albany Courtyard. W1 —7G 67 (3B 166)
Albany Cres. Edgw —7B 12
Albany Mans. SW11 —7C 84
Albany M. N1 —7A 50
Albany M. SE5 —6C 86
Albany M. Brom —6J 125
Albany M. King T —6D 116
Albany M. Sutt —5K 149
Albany Pde. Bren —6E 80
Albany Pk. Av. Enf —1D 8
Albany Pk. Rd. King T —6D 116
Albany Pas. Rich —5E 98
Albany Pl. N7 —4A 50
Albany Reach. Th Dit —5K 133
Albany Rd. E10 —7C 34
Albany Rd. E12 —4B 54
Albany Rd. E17 —6A 34
Albany Rd. N4 —6A 32
Albany Rd. N18 —5D 18
Albany Rd. SE5 —6D 86
Albany Rd. SW19 —5K 119
Albany Rd. W13 —7B 62
Albany Rd. Belv —6F 93
Albany Rd. Bex —7C 110
Albany Rd. Bren —6D 80
Albany Rd. Chst —5F 127
Albany Rd. N Mald —4K 135
Albany Rd. Rich —5F 99
Albany Rd. Romf —6F 39
Albany St. NW1 —2F 67 (1K 159)
Albany Ter. NW1 —4F 67
(off Marylebone Rd.)
Albany Ter. Rich —5F 99
(off Albany Pas.)
Albany, The. Wfd G —4C 20
Albany Vw. Buck H —1D 20
Alba Pl. W11 —6H 65
Albatross. NW9 —2B 28
Albatross Ct. SE8 —6B 88
(off Childers St.)
Albatross St. SE18 —7J 91
Albatross Way. SE16 —2K 87
Albemarle. SW19 —2F 119
Albemarle App. Ilf —6F 37
Albemarle Av. Twic —1D 114
Albemarle Gdns. Ilf —6F 37
Albemarle Gdns. N Mald —4K 135
Albemarle Ho. SW9 —3A 104
Albemarle Pk. Beck —1D 142
Albemarle Pk. Stan —5H 11
Albemarle Rd. Beck —1D 142
Albemarle Rd. E Barn —7H 5
Albemarle St. W1 —7F 67 (3K 165)
Albemarle Way. EC1 —4B 68 (4A 162)
Alberon Gdns. NW11 —4H 29
Alberta Av. Sutt —4G 149
Alberta Est. SE17 —5B 86
(off Alberta St.)
Alberta Ho. E14 —1E 88
Alberta Rd. Enf —6A 8
Alberta Rd. Eri —1J 111
Alberta St. SE17 —5B 86
Albert Av. E4 —4H 19
Albert Av. SW8 —7K 85
Albert Barnes Ho. SE1 —3C 86
(off New Kent Rd.)
Albert Bigg Point. E15 —2E 70
(off Godfrey St.)
Albert Bri. SW3 & SW11 —6C 84 (7D 170)
Albert Bri. Rd. SW11 —7C 84
Albert Carr Gdns. SW16 —5J 121
Albert Clo. E9 —1H 69
Albert Clo. N22 —1H 31
Albert Cotts. E1 —5G 69
(off Deal St.)
Albert Ct. E7 —4J 53
Albert Ct. SW7 —3B 84 (7A 164)
Albert Ct. Ga. SW1 —7E 164
Albert Cres. E4 —4H 19
Albert Dane Cen. S'hall —3C 78
Albert Dri. SW19 —2G 119
Albert Embkmt. SE1 —3K 85
(Lambeth Pal. Rd.)
Albert Embkmt. SE1 —5J 85 (6F 173)
(Vauxhall Cross)
Albert Gdns. E1 —6K 69
Albert Ga. SW1 —2D 84 (6F 165)
Albert Gray Ho. SW10 —7B 84
(off Worlds End Est.)
Albert Gro. SW20 —1F 137
Albert Hall Mans. SW7 —2B 84 (7A 164)
(in two parts)
Albert Ho. E18 —3K 35
(off Albert Rd.)
Albert Memorial. —2B 84 (7A 164)
Albert M. E14 —7A 70
Albert M. N4 —1K 49
Albert M. SE4 —4B 106
Albert M. W8 —3A 84
Albert Pl. N3 —1J 29
Albert Pl. N17 —3F 33
Albert Pl. W8 —3K 83
Albert Rd. E10 —2E 52
Albert Rd. E16 —1C 90
Albert Rd. E17 —5C 34
Albert Rd. E18 —3K 35
Albert Rd. N4 —1K 49
Albert Rd. N15 —6E 32
Albert Rd. N22 —1G 31
Albert Rd. NW4 —4F 29
Albert Rd. NW6 —2H 65
Albert Rd. NW7 —5G 13
Albert Rd. SE9 —3C 126
Albert Rd. SE20 —6K 123
Albert Rd. SE25 —4G 141
Albert Rd. W5 —4H 61
Albert Rd. Ashf —5B 112
Albert Rd. Barn —4F 5
Albert Rd. Belv —5F 93
Albert Rd. Bex —6G 111
Albert Rd. Brom —5B 144
Albert Rd. Buck H —2G 21
Albert Rd. Dag —1G 57
Albert Rd. Hamp H —5G 115
Albert Rd. Harr —3G 25
Albert Rd. Hay —3G 77
Albert Rd. Houn —4E 96
Albert Rd. Ilf —3F 55
Albert Rd. King T —2F 135
Albert Rd. Mitc —3D 138
Albert Rd. N Mald —4B 136
Albert Rd. Rich —5E 98
Albert Rd. S'hall —3B 78
Albert Rd. Sutt —5B 150
Albert Rd. Tedd —6K 115
Albert Rd. Twic —1K 115
Albert Rd. W Dray —1A 76
Albert Rd. Est. Belv —5F 93
Albert Sq. E15 —5G 53
Albert Sq. SW8 —7K 85
Albert Starr Ho. SE8 —4K 87
(off Bush Rd.)
Albert St. N12 —5F 15
Albert St. NW1 —1F 67
Albert Studios. SW11 —1D 102
Albert Ter. NW1 —1E 66
Albert Ter. NW10 —1J 63
Albert Ter. W5 —4B 62
Albert Ter. Buck H —2H 21
Albert Ter. M. NW1 —1E 66
Albert Victoria Ho. N22 —1A 32
(off Pellatt Gro.)
Albert Wlk. E16 —2E 90
Albert Way. SE15 —7H 87
Albert Westcott Ho. SE17 —5B 86
Albert Whicker Ho. E17 —4E 34
Albert Yd. SE19 —6E 122
Albion Av. N10 —1E 30
Albion Av. SW8 —2H 103
Albion Clo. W2 —7C 66 (2D 164)
Albion Clo. Romf —6K 39

Albion Dri.—Alverston Gdns.

Albion Dri. E8 —7F 51
(in two parts)
Albion Est. SE16 —2K 87
Albion Gdns. W6 —4D 82
Albion Ga. W2 —2D 164
(in two parts)
Albion Gro. N16 —4E 50
Albion Ho. E16 —1F 91
(off Church St.)
Albion M. N1 —1A 68
Albion M. W2 —7C 66 (2D 164)
Albion M. W6 —4D 82
Albion Pl. EC1 —5B 68 (5A 162)
Albion Pl. EC2 —5D 68 (6F 163)
Albion Pl. SE25 —3G 141
Albion Pl. W6 —4D 82
Albion Rd. E17 —3E 34
Albion Rd. N16 —4D 50
Albion Rd. N17 —2G 33
Albion Rd. Bexh —4F 111
Albion Rd. Hay —6G 59
Albion Rd. Houn —4E 96
Albion Rd. King T —1J 135
Albion Rd. Sutt —6B 150
Albion Rd. Twic —1J 115
Albion Sq. E8 —7F 51
Albion St. SE16 —2J 87
Albion St. W2 —6C 66 (1D 164)
Albion St. Croy —1B 152
Albion Ter. E4 —4J 9
Albion Ter. E8 —7F 51
Albion Vs. Rd. SE26 —3J 123
Albion Way. EC1 —5C 68 (6C 162)
Albion Way. SE13 —4E 106
Albion Way. Wemb —3G 45
Albion Wharf. SW11 —7C 84
Albion Yd. N1 —2J 67
Albrighton Rd. SE22 —3E 104
Albuhera Clo. Enf —1F 7
Albury Av. Bexh —2E 110
Albury Av. Iswth —7K 79
Albury Clo. Hamp —6F 115
Albury Ct. Mitc —2B 138
Albury Ct. N'holt —3A 60
(off Canberra Dri.)
Albury Ct. Sutt —4A 150
Albury Dri. Pinn —1A 24
Albury Ho. SE1 —2B 86 (7B 168)
(off Boyfield St.)
Albury M. E12 —2A 54
Albury Rd. Chess —5E 146
Albury St. SE8 —6C 88
Albyfield. Brom —4D 144
Albyn Rd. SE8 —1C 106
Alcester Cres. E5 —2H 51
Alcester Rd. Wall —4F 151
Alcock Clo. Wall —7H 151
Alcock Rd. Houn —7B 78
Alconbury. Bexh —5H 111
Alconbury Rd. E5 —2G 51
Alcorn Clo. Sutt —2J 149
Alcott Clo. W7 —5K 61
Alcott Clo. Felt —1H 113
Alcuin Ct. Stan —7H 11
Aldam Pl. N16 —2F 51
Aldborough Ct. Ilf —5K 37
(off Aldborough Rd. N.)
Aldborough Hatch. —4K 37
Aldborough Rd. Dag —6J 57
Aldborough Rd. N. Ilf —5K 37
Aldborough Rd. S. Ilf —1J 55
(in two parts)
Aldbourne Rd. W3 —1B 82
(in two parts)
Aldbridge St. SE17 —5E 86
Aldburgh M. W1 —6E 66 (7H 159)
(in two parts)
Aldbury Av. Wemb —7H 45
Aldbury Ho. SW3 —4C 84 (5C 170)
(off Ixworth Pl.)
Aldbury M. N9 —7J 7
Aldebert Ter. SW8 —7J 85
Aldeburgh Clo. E5 —2H 51
Aldeburgh Pl. Wfd G —4D 20
Aldeburgh St. SE10 —5J 89
Alden Av. E15 —3H 71
Alden Ct. Croy —3E 152
Aldenham Dri. Uxb —4D 58
Aldenham Ho. NW1 —2G 67 (1B 160)
(off Aldenham St.)
Aldenham St. NW1 —2G 67 (1C 160)
Alden Ho. E8 —1H 69
(off Duncan Rd.)
Aldensley Rd. W6 —3D 82
Alderbrook Rd. SW12 —6F 103
Alderbury Rd. SW13 —6C 82
Alder Clo. SE15 —6F 87
Alder Gro. NW2 —2C 46
Aldergrove Gdns. Houn —2C 96
Alderholt Way. SE15 —7E 86
Alder Ho. NW3 —6D 48
Alder Ho. SE4 —3C 106
Alder Ho. SE15 —6F 87
(off Alder Clo.)
Alder Lodge. SW6 —1E 100
Alderman Av. Bark —3A 74
Aldermanbury. EC2 —6C 68 (7D 162)
Aldermanbury Sq. EC2
—5C 68 (6D 162)
Alderman Judge Mall. King T
—2E 134
Aldermans Hill. N13 —4D 16
Aldermans Wlk. EC2
—5E 68 (6G 163)
Aldermary Rd. Brom —1J 143
Alder M. N19 —2G 49
Aldermoor Rd. SE6 —3B 124
Alderney Av. Houn —7F 79
Alderney Gdns. N'holt —7D 42
Alderney Ho. Enf —1E 8
Alderney Rd. E1 —4K 69
Alderney St. SW1 —4F 85 (4K 171)
Alder Rd. SW14 —3K 99
Alder Rd. Sidc —3K 127
Alders Av. Wfd G —6B 20
Aldersbrook. —2K 53
Aldersbrook Av. Enf —2K 7
Aldersbrook Dri. King T —6F 117
Aldersbrook La. E12 —3D 54
Aldersbrook Rd. E11 & E12 —2K 53
Alders Clo. E11 —2K 53
Alders Clo. W5 —3D 80
Alders Clo. Edgw —5D 12
Aldersey Gdns. Bark —6H 55
Aldersford Clo. SE4 —5K 105
Aldersgate St. EC1 —5C 68 (5C 162)
Alders Gro. E Mol —5H 133
Aldersgrove Av. SE9 —3B 126
Aldershot Rd. NW6 —1H 65
Aldershot Ter. SE18 —7E 90
Aldersmead Av. Croy —6K 141
Aldersmead Rd. Beck —7A 124
Alderson Pl. S'hall —1G 79
Alderson St. W10 —4G 65
Alders Rd. Edgw —5D 12
Alders, The. N21 —6F 7
Alders, The. SW16 —4G 121
Alders, The. Felt —4C 114
Alders, The. Houn —6D 78
Alders, The. W W'ck —1D 154
Alderton Clo. NW10 —3K 45
Alderton Cres. NW4 —5D 28
Alderton Rd. SE24 —3C 104
Alderton Rd. Croy —7F 141
Alderton Way. NW4 —5D 28
Alderville Rd. SW6 —2H 101
Alder Wlk. Ilf —5G 55
Alderwick Dri. Houn —3H 97
Alderwood Rd. SE9 —6H 109
Aldford Ho. W1 —1E 84 (4G 165)
(off Park St.)
Aldford St. W1 —1E 84 (4H 165)
Aldgate. (Junct.) —6F 69
Aldgate. E1 —6F 69
(off Whitechapel High St.)
Aldgate. EC3 —6E 68 (1H 169)
Aldgate Av. E1 —6F 69 (7J 163)
Aldgate Barrs. E1 —7K 163
Aldgate High St. EC3
—6F 69 (1J 169)
Aldgate Triangle. E1 —6G 69
(off Coke St.)
Aldham Ho. SE4 —2B 106
Aldine Ct. W12 —2E 82
(off Aldine St.)
Aldine Pl. W12 —2E 82
Aldine St. W12 —2E 82
Aldington Clo. Dag —1C 56
Aldington Ct. E8 —7G 51
(off Lansdowne Dri.)
Aldington Rd. SE18 —3B 90
Aldis M. SW17 —5C 120
Aldis St. SW17 —5C 120
Aldred Rd. NW6 —5J 47
Aldren Rd. SW17 —3A 120
Aldriche Way. E4 —6K 19
Aldrich Gdns. Sutt —3H 149
Aldrich Ter. SW18 —2A 120
Aldrick Ho. N1 —1K 67
(off Barnsbury Est.)
Aldridge Av. Edgw —3C 12
Aldridge Av. Ruis —2A 42
Aldridge Av. Stan —1E 26
Aldridge Ri. N Mald —7A 136
Aldridge Rd. Vs. W11 —5H 65
Aldridge Wlk. N14 —7D 6
Aldrington Rd. SW16 —5G 121
Aldsworth Clo. W9 —4K 65
Aldwick Clo. SE9 —3H 127
Aldwick Rd. Croy —3K 151
Aldworth Gro. SE13 —6E 106
Aldworth Rd. E15 —7G 53
Aldwych. WC2 —6K 67 (2G 167)
Aldwych Av. Ilf —4G 37
Aldwyn Ho. SW8 —7J 85
(off Davidson Gdns.)
Alers Rd. Bexh —5D 110
Alesia Clo. N22 —7D 16
Alestan Beck Rd. E16 —6B 72
Alexa Ct. W8 —4J 83
Alexa Ct. Sutt —6J 149
Alexander Av. NW10 —7D 46
Alexander Clo. Barn —4G 5
Alexander Clo. Brom —1J 155
Alexander Clo. Sidc —6J 109
Alexander Clo. S'hall —1G 79
Alexander Clo. Twic —2J 115
Alexander Ct. SE16 —1B 88
Alexander Ct. Beck —1F 143
Alexander Ct. Stan —3F 27
Alexander Evans M. SE23 —2K 123
Alexander Fleming Mus. —7B 158
Alexander Ho. E14 —3C 88
Alexander M. W2 —6K 65
Alexander Pl. SW7 —4C 84 (3C 170)
Alexander Rd. N19 —3J 49
Alexander Rd. Bexh —2D 110
Alexander Rd. Chst —6F 127
Alexander Sq. SW3 —4C 84 (3C 170)
Alexander St. W2 —6J 65
Alexander Studios. SW11 —4B 102
(off Haydon Way)
Alexandra Av. N22 —1H 31
Alexandra Av. SW11 —1E 102
Alexandra Av. W4 —7K 81
Alexandra Av. Harr —1D 42
Alexandra Av. S'hall —7D 60
Alexandra Av. Sutt —3J 149
Alexandra Clo. SE8 —6B 88
Alexandra Clo. Ashf —7F 113
Alexandra Clo. Harr —3E 42
Alexandra Cotts. SE14 —1B 106
Alexandra Ct. N14 —5B 6
Alexandra Ct. SW7 —1A 170
Alexandra Ct. W2 —7K 65
(off Moscow Rd.)
Alexandra Ct. W9 —4A 66
(off Maida Va.)
Alexandra Ct. Ashf —6F 113
Alexandra Ct. Gnfd —2F 61
Alexandra Ct. Houn —2F 97
Alexandra Cres. Brom —6H 125
Alexandra Dri. SE19 —5E 122
Alexandra Dri. Surb —7G 135
Alexandra Gdns. N10 —4F 31
Alexandra Gdns. W4 —7A 82
Alexandra Gdns. Cars —7E 150
Alexandra Gdns. Houn —2F 97
Alexandra Gro. N4 —1B 50
Alexandra Gro. N12 —5E 14
Alexandra Mans. SW3 —6B 84 (7A 170)
(off Moravian Clo.)
Alexandra M. N2 —3D 30
Alexandra M. SW19 —6H 119
Alexandra Palace. —2H 31
Alexandra Pal. Way. N22 —4G 31
Alexandra Pde. Harr —4F 43
Alexandra Pk. Rd. N10 —2F 31
Alexandra Pk. Rd. N22 —1G 31
Alexandra Pl. NW8 —1A 66
Alexandra Pl. SE25 —5D 140
Alexandra Pl. Croy —1E 152
Alexandra Rd. E6 —3E 72
Alexandra Rd. E10 —3E 52
Alexandra Rd. E17 —6B 34
Alexandra Rd. E18 —3K 35
Alexandra Rd. N8 —3A 32
Alexandra Rd. N9 —7C 8
Alexandra Rd. N10 —1F 31
Alexandra Rd. N15 —5D 32
Alexandra Rd. NW4 —4F 29
Alexandra Rd. NW8 —1A 66
Alexandra Rd. SE26 —6K 123
Alexandra Rd. SW14 —3K 99
Alexandra Rd. SW19 —6H 119
Alexandra Rd. W4 —2K 81
Alexandra Rd. Ashf —7F 113
Alexandra Rd. Bren —6D 80
Alexandra Rd. Chad H —6E 38
Alexandra Rd. Croy —1E 152
Alexandra Rd. Enf —4E 8
Alexandra Rd. Houn —2F 97
Alexandra Rd. King T —7G 117
Alexandra Rd. Mitc —7C 120
Alexandra Rd. Rich —2F 99
Alexandra Rd. Th Dit —5K 133
Alexandra Rd. Twic —6C 98
Alexandra Rd. Ind. Est. Enf —4E 8
Alexandra Sq. Mord —5J 137
Alexandra St. E16 —5J 71
Alexandra St. SE14 —7A 88
Alexandra Ter. E14 —5D 88
Alexandra Wlk. SE19 —5E 122
Alexandra Yd. E9 —1K 69
Alexandria Rd. W13 —7A 62
Alexis St. SE16 —4G 87
Alfan La. Dart —5K 129
Alfearn Rd. E5 —4J 51
Alford Ct. N1 —2C 68 (1D 162)
(in two parts)
Alford Grn. New Ad —6F 155
Alford Ho. N6 —6G 31
Alford Pl. N1 —2C 68 (1D 162)
Alford Rd. Eri —5J 93
Alfoxton Av. N8 —4B 32
Alfreda St. SW11 —1F 103
Alfred Clo. W4 —4K 81
Alfred Finlay Ho. N22 —2B 32
Alfred Gdns. S'hall —7C 60
Alfred Ho. E9 —5A 52
(off Homerton Rd.)
Alfred Ho. E12 —7C 54
(off Tennyson Av.)
Alfred M. W1 —5H 67 (5C 160)
Alfred Nunn Ho. NW10 —1B 64
Alfred Pl. WC1 —5H 67 (5C 160)
Alfred Prior Ho. E12 —4E 54
Alfred Rd. E15 —5H 53
Alfred Rd. SE25 —5G 141
Alfred Rd. W2 —5J 65
Alfred Rd. W3 —1J 81
Alfred Rd. Belv —5F 93
Alfred Rd. Buck H —2G 21
Alfred Rd. Felt —2A 114
Alfred Rd. King T —3E 134
Alfred Rd. Sutt —5A 150
Alfred's Gdns. Bark —2J 73
Alfred St. E3 —3B 70
Alfreds Way. Bark —3F 73
Alfred's Way Ind. Est. Bark —2A 74
Alfreton Clo. SW19 —3F 119
Alfriston. Surb —6F 135
Alfriston Av. Croy —7J 139
Alfriston Av. Harr —6E 24
Alfriston Clo. Surb —5F 135
Alfriston Rd. SW11 —5D 102
Algar Clo. Iswth —3A 98
Algar Clo. Stan —5E 10
Algar Ho. SE1 —7A 168
Algar Rd. Iswth —3A 98
Algarve Rd. SW18 —1K 119
Algernon Rd. NW4 —6C 28
Algernon Rd. NW6 —1J 65
Algernon Rd. SE13 —4D 106
Algiers Rd. SE13 —4C 106
Alibon Gdns. Dag —5G 57
Alibon Rd. Dag —5F 57
Alice Ct. SW15 —4H 101
Alice Gilliatt Ct. W14 —6H 83
(off Star Rd.)
Alice La. E3 —1B 70
Alice M. Tedd —5K 115
Alice Owen Technology Cen. EC1 —3B 68
Alice Shepherd Ho. E14 —2E 88
Alice St. SE1 —3E 86
(in two parts)
Alice Thompson Clo. SE12 —2A 126
Alice Walker Clo. SE24 —4B 104
Alice Way. Houn —4F 97
Alicia Av. Harr —4B 26
Alicia Clo. Harr —5C 26
Alicia Gdns. Harr —4B 26
Alicia Ho. Well —1B 110
Alie St. E1 —6F 69 (1K 169)
Alington Cres. NW9 —7J 27
Alington Gro. Wall —7G 151
Alison Clo. E6 —6E 72
Alison Clo. Croy —1K 153
Alison Ct. SE1 —5G 87
Aliwal Rd. SW11 —4C 102
Alkerden Rd. W4 —5A 82
Alkham Rd. N16 —2F 51
Allan Barclay Clo. N15 —6F 33
Allan Clo. N Mald —5K 135
Allandale Av. N3 —3G 29
Allanson Ct. E10 —2C 52
(off Leyton Grange Est.)
Allan Way. W3 —5J 63
Allard Cres. Bus H —1B 10
Allard Gdns. SW4 —5H 103
Allardyce St. SW4 —4K 103
Allbrook Clo. Tedd —5J 115
Allcroft Rd. NW5 —5E 48
Allenby Clo. Gnfd —3E 60
Allenby Rd. SE23 —3A 124
Allenby Rd. S'hall —6E 60
Allen Clo. Mitc —1F 139
Allen Clo. Sun —1K 131
Allen Ct. E17 —6C 34
(off Yunus Khan Clo.)
Allen Ct. Gnfd —5K 43
Allendale Av. S'hall —6E 60
Allendale Clo. SE5 —2D 104
Allendale Clo. SE26 —5K 123
Allendale Rd. Gnfd —6B 44
Allen Edwards Dri. SW8 —1J 103
Allenford Ho. SW15 —6B 100
(off Tunworth Cres.)
Allen Rd. E3 —2B 70
Allen Rd. N16 —4E 50
Allen Rd. Beck —2K 141
Allen Rd. Croy —1A 152
Allen Rd. Sun —1K 131
Allensbury Pl. NW1 —7H 49
Allens Rd. Enf —5D 8
Allen St. W8 —3J 83
Allenswood Rd. SE9 —3C 108
Allerford Ct. Harr —5G 25
Allerford Rd. SE6 —3D 124
Allerton Ho. N1 —3D 68 (1E 162)
(off Provost Est.)
Allerton Rd. N16 —2C 50
Allerton St. N1 —3D 68 (1E 162)
Allerton Wlk. N7 —2K 49
Allestree Rd. SW6 —7G 83
Alleyn Cres. SE21 —2D 122
Alleyndale Rd. Dag —2C 56
Alleyn Ho. SE1 —3D 86
(off Burbage Clo.)
Alleyn Pk. SE21 —2D 122
Alleyn Pk. S'hall —5E 78
Alleyn Rd. SE21 —3D 122
Allfarthing La. SW18 —6K 101
Allgood Clo. Mord —6F 137
Allgood St. E2 —2F 69 (1K 163)
Allhallows La. EC4 —7D 68 (3E 168)
Allhallows Rd. E6 —5C 72
All Hallows Rd. N17 —1E 32
Alliance Clo. Wemb —4D 44
Alliance Ct. W3 —5H 63
Alliance Rd. E13 —5A 72
Alliance Rd. SE18 —6A 92
Alliance Rd. W3 —4H 63
Allied Ind. Est. W3 —2A 82
Allied Way. W3 —2A 82
Allingham Clo. W7 —7K 61
Allingham St. N1 —2C 68
Allington Av. N17 —6K 17
Allington Av. Shep —3G 131
Allington Clo. SW19 —5F 119
Allington Clo. Gnfd —7G 43
Allington Ct. SW1 —3F 85 (2K 171)
(off Allington St.)
Allington Ct. SW8 —2G 103
Allington Ct. Enf —5E 8
(in two parts)
Allington Rd. NW4 —5D 28
Allington Rd. W10 —3G 65
Allington Rd. Harr —5G 25
Allington St. SW1 —3F 85 (2K 171)
Allison Clo. SE10 —1E 106
Allison Gro. SE21 —1E 122
Allison Rd. N8 —5A 32
Allison Rd. W3 —6J 63
Alliston Ho. E2 —3F 69 (2K 163)
(off Gibraltar Wlk.)
Allitsen Rd. NW8 —2C 66
(in two parts)
Allnutt Way. SW4 —5H 103
Alloa Rd. SE8 —5K 87
Alloa Rd. Ilf —2A 56
Allom Ho. W11 —7G 65
(off Clarendon Rd.)
Allonby Dri. Ruis —7D 22
Allonby Gdns. Wemb —1C 44
Alloway Rd. E3 —3A 70
Allport Ho. SE5 —3D 104
(off Denmark Hill)
All Saints Clo. N9 —2B 18
All Saints Ct. Houn —1B 96
(off Springwell Rd.)
All Saints Dri. SE3 —2G 107
All Saints Ho. W11 —5H 65
All Saints M. Harr —6D 10
All Saints Pas. SW18 —5J 101
All Saints Rd. SW19 —7A 120
(in two parts)
All Saints Rd. W3 —3J 81
All Saints Rd. W11 —5H 65
All Saints Rd. Sutt —3K 149
All Saints St. N1 —2K 67
All Saints Tower. E10 —7D 34
All Seasons Ct. E1 —1G 87
(off Aragon M.)
Allsop Pl. NW1 —4D 66 (4F 159)
All Souls Av. NW10 —2D 64
All Souls' Pl. W1 —5F 67 (6K 159)
Allum Way. N20 —1F 15
Allwood Clo. SE26 —4K 123
Alma Av. E4 —7K 19
Almack Rd. E5 —4J 51
Alma Clo. N10 —1F 31
Alma Ct. Harr —2H 43
Alma Cres. Sutt —5G 149
Alma Gro. SE1 —4F 87
Alma Ho. Bren —6E 80
Alma Pl. NW10 —3D 64
Alma Pl. SE19 —7F 123
Alma Pl. T Hth —5A 140
Alma Rd. N10 —7A 16
Alma Rd. SW18 —4A 102
Alma Rd. Cars —5C 150
Alma Rd. Enf —5F 9
Alma Rd. Esh —7J 133
Alma Rd. Sidc —3A 128
Alma Rd. S'hall —7C 60
Alma Rd. Ind. Est. Enf —4E 8
Alma Row. Harr —1H 25
Alma Sq. NW8 —2A 66
Alma St. E15 —6F 53
Alma St. NW5 —6F 49
Alma Ter. SW18 —7B 102
Alma Ter. W8 —3J 83
Almeida St. N1 —1B 68
Almeida Theatre. —1B 68
Almeric Rd. SW11 —4D 102
Almer Rd. SW20 —7C 118
Almington St. N4 —1K 49
Almond Av. W5 —3D 80
Almond Av. Cars —2D 150
Almond Av. Uxb —3D 40
Almond Av. W Dray —3C 76
Almond Clo. SE15 —2G 105
Almond Clo. Brom —7E 144
Almond Clo. Felt —1J 113
Almond Clo. Hay —7G 59
Almond Clo. Ruis —3H 41
Almond Clo. Shep —2E 130
Almond Gro. Bren —7B 80
Almond Rd. N17 —7B 18
Almond Rd. SE16 —4H 87
Almonds Av. Buck H —2D 20
Almondsbury Ct. SE15 —7E 86
(off Newent Clo.)
Almond Way. Brom —7E 144
Almond Way. Harr —2F 25
Almond Way. Mitc —5H 139
Almorah Rd. N1 —7D 50
Almorah Rd. Houn —1B 96
Almshouse La. Chess —7C 146
Alnmouth Ct. S'hall —6G 61
(off Fleming Rd.)
Alnwick. N17 —7C 18
Alnwick Gro. Mord —4K 137
Alnwick Rd. E16 —6A 72
Alnwick Rd. SE12 —6K 107
Alperton. —2E 62
Alperton La. Gnfd & Wemb —3C 62
Alperton St. W10 —4H 65
Alphabet Gdns. Cars —6B 138
Alphabet Sq. E3 —5C 70
Alpha Bus. Cen. E17 —5B 34
Alpha Clo. NW1 —4C 66 (3D 158)
Alpha Est. Hay —2G 77
Alpha Gro. E14 —2C 88
Alpha Ho. NW6 —2J 65
Alpha Ho. NW8 —4C 158
Alpha Ho. SW9 —4K 103
Alpha Pl. NW6 —2J 65
Alpha Pl. SW3 —6C 84 (7D 170)
Alpha Pl. Mord —1F 149
Alpha Rd. E4 —3H 19
Alpha Rd. N18 —6B 18
Alpha Rd. SE14 —1B 106
Alpha Rd. Croy —1E 152
Alpha Rd. Enf —4F 9
Alpha Rd. Surb —6F 135
Alpha Rd. Tedd —5H 115
Alpha Rd. Uxb —4D 58
Alpha St. SE15 —2G 105
Alphea Clo. SW19 —7C 120
Alpine Av. Surb —2J 147
Alpine Bus. Cen. E6 —5E 72
Alpine Clo. Croy —3E 152
Alpine Copse. Brom —2E 144
Alpine Rd. SE16 —4J 87
(in two parts)
Alpine Rd. W on T —7J 131
Alpine Vw. Cars —5C 150
Alpine Wlk. Stan —2D 10
Alpine Way. E6 —5E 72
Alric Av. NW10 —7K 45
Alric Av. N Mald —3A 136
Alroy Rd. N4 —7A 32
Alsace Rd. SE17 —5E 86
Alscot Rd. SE1 —4F 87
(in two parts)
Alscot Rd. Ind. Est. SE1 —3F 87
Alscot Way. SE1 —4F 87
Alsike Rd. SE2 & Eri —3D 92
Alsom Av. Wor Pk —4C 148
Alston Clo. Surb —7B 134
Alston Rd. N18 —5C 18
Alston Rd. SW17 —4B 120
Alston Rd. Barn —3B 4
Altair Clo. N17 —6A 18
Altash Way. SE9 —2D 126
Altenburg Av. W13 —3B 80
Altenburg Gdns. SW11 —4D 102
Alt Gro. SW19 —7H 119
Altham Ct. Harr —1F 25
Altham Rd. Pinn —1C 24
Althea St. SW6 —2K 101
Althorne Gdns. E18 —4H 35
Althorne Way. Dag —2G 57
Althorp Clo. Barn —1H 13
Althorpe M. SW11 —1B 102
Althorpe Rd. Harr —5G 25
Althorp Rd. SW17 —1D 120
Altior Ct. N6 —6G 31
Altmore Av. E6 —7D 54
Alton Av. Stan —7E 10
Alton Clo. Bex —1E 128
Alton Clo. Iswth —2K 97
Alton Gdns. Beck —7C 124
Alton Gdns. Twic —7H 97
Alton Rd. N17 —3D 32
Alton Rd. SW15 —1C 118
Alton Rd. Croy —3A 152
Alton Rd. Rich —4E 98
Alton St. E14 —5D 70
Altyre Clo. Beck —5B 142
Altyre Rd. Croy —2D 152
Altyre Way. Beck —5B 142
Aluna Ct. SE15 —3J 105
Alvanley Gdns. NW6 —5K 47
Alverstone Av. SW19 —2J 119
Alverstone Av. Barn & E Barn —7H 5
Alverstone Gdns. SE9 —1G 127
Alverstone Ho. SE11 —6A 86 (7J 173)
Alverstone Rd. E12 —4E 54
Alverstone Rd. NW2 —7E 46
Alverstone Rd. N Mald —4B 136
Alverstone Rd. Wemb —1F 45
Alverston Gdns. SE25 —5E 140

Alverton St.—Arden Cres.

Alverton St. SE8 —5B 88
(in two parts)
Alveston Av. Harr —3B 26
Alvey St. SE17 —5E 86
Alvia Gdns. Sutt —4A 150
Alvington Cres. E8 —5F 51
Alway Av. Eps —5K 147
Alwold Cres. SE12 —6K 107
Alwyn Av. W4 —5K 81
Alwyn Clo. New Ad —7D 154
Alwyne La. N1 —7B 50
Alwyne Pl. N1 —6C 50
Alwyne Rd. N1 —7C 50
Alwyne Rd. SW19 —6H 119
Alwyne Rd. W7 —7J 61
Alwyne Sq. N1 —6C 50
Alwyne Vs. N1 —7B 50
Alwyn Gdns. NW4 —4C 28
Alwyn Gdns. W3 —6H 63
Alyth Gdns. NW11 —6J 29
Amalgamated Dri. Bren —6A 80
Amanda M. Romf —5J 39
Amar Ct. SE18 —4K 91
Amar Deep Ct. SE18 —5K 91
Amazon St. E1 —6G 69
Ambassador Clo. Houn —2C 96
Ambassador Gdns. E6 —5D 72
Ambassadors' Ct. SW1 —5B 166
Ambassador Sq. E14 —4D 88
Amber Av. E17 —1A 34
Amberden Av. N3 —3J 29
Ambergate St. SE17 —5B 86
Amber Gro. NW2 —1F 47
Amberley Clo. Pinn —3D 24
Amberley Ct. Beck —7B 124
Amberley Ct. Sidc —5C 128
Amberley Gdns. Enf —7K 7
Amberley Gdns. Eps —4B 148
Amberley Gro. SE26 —5H 123
Amberley Gro. Croy —7F 141
Amberley Rd. E10 —7C 34
Amberley Rd. N13 —2E 16
Amberley Rd. SE2 —6D 92
Amberley Rd. W9 —5J 65
Amberley Rd. Buck H —1F 21
Amberley Rd. Enf —7A 8
Amberley Way. Houn —5A 96
Amberley Way. Mord —7H 137
Amberley Way. Romf —4H 39
Amberley Way. Uxb —2A 58
Amberside Clo. Iswth —6H 97
Amberwood Clo. Wall —5J 151
Amberwood Ri. N Mald —6A 136
Amblecote Clo. SE12 —3K 125
Amblecote Meadows. SE12 —3K 125
Amblecote Rd. SE12 —3K 125
Ambler Rd. N4 —3B 50
Ambleside. NW1 —1K 159
Ambleside. Brom —6F 125
Ambleside Av. SW16 —4H 121
Ambleside Av. Beck —5A 142
Ambleside Av. W on T —7A 132
Ambleside Clo. E9 —5J 51
Ambleside Clo. E10 —7D 34
Ambleside Cres. Enf —3E 8
Ambleside Dri. Felt —1H 113
Ambleside Gdns. SW16 —5H 121
Ambleside Gdns. Ilf —4C 36
Ambleside Gdns. Sutt —6A 150
Ambleside Gdns. Wemb —1D 44
Ambleside Point. SE15 —7J 87
(off Tustin Est.)
Ambleside Rd. NW10 —7B 46
Ambleside Rd. Bexh —2G 111
Ambleside Wlk. Uxb —1A 58
Ambrooke Rd. Belv —3G 93
Ambrosden Av. SW1
—3G 85 (2B 172)
Ambrose Av. NW11 —7G 29
Ambrose Clo. E6 —5D 72
Ambrose Ho. E14 —5C 70
Ambrose M. SW11 —2D 102
Ambrose St. SE16 —4H 87
Ambrose Wlk. E3 —2C 70
AMC Bus. Cen. NW10 —3H 63
Amelia St. SE17 —5C 86
Amen Corner. EC4 —6B 68 (1B 168)
Amen Corner. SW17 —6D 120
Amen Ct. EC4 —6B 68 (1B 168)
Amenity Way. Mord —7E 136
America Sq. EC3 —7F 69 (2J 169)
America St. SE1 —1C 86 (5C 168)
Amerland Rd. SW18 —5H 101
Amersham Av. N18 —6J 17
Amersham Gro. SE14 —7B 88
Amersham Rd. SE14 —1B 106
Amersham Rd. Croy —6C 140
Amersham Va. SE14 —7B 88
Amery Gdns. NW10 —1E 64
Amery Ho. SE17 —5E 86
(off Kinglake St.)
Amery Rd. Harr —2A 44
Amesbury Av. SW2 —2J 121
Amesbury Clo. Wor Pk —1E 148
Amesbury Ct. Enf —2F 7
Amesbury Dri. E4 —6J 9
Amesbury Rd. Brom —3B 144
Amesbury Rd. Dag —7D 56
Amesbury Rd. Felt —2B 114
Amesbury Tower. SW8 —2G 103
Ames Cotts. E14 —5A 70
Amethyst Rd. E15 —4F 53
Amherst Av. W13 —6C 62
Amherst Dri. Orp —4K 145
Amherst Gdns. W13 —6C 62
(off Amherst Rd.)
Amherst Rd. W13 —6C 62
Amhurst Gdns. Iswth —2A 98
Amhurst Pk. N16 —7D 32
Amhurst Pas. E8 —5G 51
Amhurst Rd. E8 —5H 51
Amhurst Rd. N16 & E8 —4F 51
Amhurst Ter. E8 —4G 51
Amhurst Wlk. SE28 —1A 92
Amias Ho. EC1 —4C 68 (3C 162)
(off Central St.)
Amidas Gdns. Dag —4B 56
Amiel St. E1 —4J 69
Amies St. SW11 —3D 102
Amigo Ho. SE1 —3A 86 (1K 173)
(off Morley St.)
Amina Way. SE16 —3G 87
Amis Av. Eps —6H 147
Amity Gro. SW20 —1D 136
Amity Rd. E15 —7H 53
Ammanford Grn. NW9 —6A 28
Amner Rd. SW11 —6E 102
Amor Rd. W6 —3E 82
Amory Ho. N1 —1K 67
(off Barnsbury Est.)
Amos Est. SE16 —1K 87
Amott Rd. SE15 —3G 105
Amoy Pl. E14 —6B 70
(in two parts)
Ampere Way. Croy —7J 139
(in two parts)
Ampleforth Rd. SE2 —2B 92
Ampthill Est. NW1 —2G 67 (1B 160)
Ampton Pl. WC1 —3K 67 (2G 161)
Ampton St. WC1 —3K 67 (2G 161)
Amroth Clo. SE23 —1H 123
Amroth Grn. NW9 —6A 28
Amstel Ct. SE15 —7F 87
(off Garnies Clo.)
Amsterdam Rd. E14 —3E 88
Amundsen Ct. E14 —5C 88
Amunsden Ho. NW10 —7K 45
(off Stonebridge Pk.)
Amwell Clo. Enf —5J 7
Amwell Ct. Est. N16 —2C 50
Amwell St. N1 —3A 68 (1J 161)
Amyand Cotts. Twic —6B 98
Amyand La. Twic —7B 98
Amyand Pk. Gdns. Twic —7B 98
Amyand Pk. Rd. Twic —7A 98
Amy Clo. Wall —7J 151
Amy Johnson Ct. Edgw —2H 27
Amyruth Rd. SE4 —5C 106
Amy Warne Clo. E6 —4C 72
Anatola Rd. N19 —2F 49
Ancaster Cres. N Mald —6C 136
Ancaster M. Beck —3K 141
Ancaster Rd. Beck —3K 141
Ancaster St. SE18 —7J 91
Anchor. SW18 —4K 101
Anchorage Clo. SW19 —5J 119
Anchorage Ho. E14 —7F 71
(off Clove Cres.)
Anchorage Ho. E14 —2B 88
(off Cuba St.)
Anchorage Point Ind. Est. SE7 —3A 90
Anchor & Hope La. SE7 —3K 89
Anchor Brewhouse. SE1
—1F 87 (5J 169)
Anchor Bus. Cen. Croy —3J 151
Anchor Ct. SW1 —4H 85 (4C 172)
(off Vauxhall Bri. Rd.)
Anchor Ct. Enf —5K 7
Anchor Ho. E16 —6A 72
(off Prince Regent La.)
Anchor Ho. EC1 —4C 68 (3C 162)
(off Old St.)
Anchor M. SW12 —6F 103
Anchor St. SE16 —4H 87
Anchor Wharf. E3 —5D 70
Anchor Yd. EC1 —4C 68 (3D 162)
Ancill Clo. W6 —6G 83
Ancona Rd. NW10 —2C 64
Ancona Rd. SE18 —5H 91
Andace Pk. Gdns. Brom —2A 144
Andalus Rd. SW9 —3J 103
Ander Clo. Wemb —4D 44
Anderson Clo. N21 —5E 6
Anderson Clo. W3 —6K 63
Anderson Clo. Sutt —1J 149
Anderson Ct. NW2 —1E 46
Anderson Dri. Ashf —4E 112
Anderson Ho. Bark —2H 73
Anderson Pl. Houn —4F 97
Anderson Rd. E9 —6K 51
Anderson Rd. Wfd G —3B 36
Anderson Sq. N1 —1B 68
(off Gaskin St.)
Anderson St. SW3 —5D 84 (5E 170)
Anderson Way. Belv —2J 93
Anderton Clo. SE5 —3D 104
Anderton Ct. N22 —2H 31
Andorra Ct. Brom —1A 144
Andover Av. E16 —6B 72
Andover Clo. Felt —1H 113
Andover Clo. Gnfd —4F 61
Andover Pl. NW6 —2K 65
Andover Rd. N7 —2K 49
Andover Rd. Orp —7H 145
Andover Rd. Twic —1H 115
Andoversford Ct. SE15 —6E 86
(off Bibury Clo.)
Andreck Ct. Beck —2D 142
Andre St. E8 —5G 51
Andrew Borde St. WC2 —6H 67 (7D 160)
Andrew Clo. Dart —5K 111
Andrew Ct. SE23 —2K 123
Andrewes Gdns. E6 —6C 72
Andrewes Highwalk. EC2 —6D 162
Andrewes Ho. EC2 —6D 162
Andrewes Ho. Sutt —4J 149
Andrew Pl. SW8 —7H 85
Andrews Clo. Buck H —2F 21
Andrews Clo. Harr —7H 25
Andrews Clo. Wor Pk —2F 149
Andrews Crosse. WC2 —1J 167
Andrew's Ho. S Croy —6C 152
Andrews Pl. SE9 —6F 109
Andrew's Rd. E8 —1H 69
Andrew St. E14 —6E 70
Andrews Wlk. SE17 —6B 86
Andwell Clo. SE2 —2B 92
Anerley. —2H 141
Anerley Gro. SE19 —7F 123
Anerley Hill. SE19 —6F 123
Anerley Pk. SE20 —7G 123
Anerley Pk. Rd. SE20 —7H 123
Anerley Rd. SE19 & SE20 —7G 123
Anerley Sta. Rd. SE20 —1H 141
Anerley St. SW11 —2D 102
Anerley Va. SE19 —7F 123
Aneurin Bevan Ct. NW2 —2D 46
Aneurin Bevan Ho. N11 —7C 16
Anfield Clo. SW12 —7G 103
Angel. (Junct.) —2A 68
Angela Davies Ind. Est. SE24 —4B 104
Angel All. E1 —7K 163
Angel Cen., The. N1 —2A 68
(off St John St.)
Angel Clo. N18 —5A 18
Angel Corner Pde. N18 —4B 18
Angel Ct. EC2 —6D 68 (7F 163)
Angel Ct. SW1 —1G 85 (5B 166)
Angel Edmonton. (Junct.) —5B 18
Angelfield. Houn —4F 97
Angel Ga. EC1 —3B 68 (1B 162)
(in three parts)
Angel Hill. Sutt —3K 149
(in two parts)
Angel Hill Dri. Sutt —3K 149
Angelica Clo. W Dray —6B 58
Angelica Dri. E6 —5E 72
Angelica Gdns. Croy —1K 153
Angel La. E15 —6F 53
Angel La. Hay —5F 59
Angell Pk. Gdns. SW9 —3A 104
Angell Rd. SW9 —3A 104
Angell Town. —1A 104
Angell Town Est. SW9 —2A 104
Angel M. E1 —7H 69
Angel M. N1 —2A 68
Angel M. SW15 —7C 100
Angel Pas. EC4 —7D 68 (3E 168)
Angel Pl. N18 —4B 18
Angel Pl. SE1 —2D 86 (6E 168)
Angel Rd. N18 —5B 18
Angel Rd. Harr —6J 25
Angel Rd. Th Dit —7A 134
Angel Rd. Works. N18 —5D 18
Angel Sq. N1 —2A 68
Angel St. EC1 —6C 68 (7C 162)
Angel Wlk. W6 —4E 82
Angel Way. Romf —5K 39
Angel Yd. N6 —1E 48
Angerstein Bus. Pk. SE10 —4J 89
Angerstein La. SE3 —1H 107
Anglebury. W2 —6J 65
(off Talbot Rd.)
Angle Clo. Uxb —1C 58
Angle Grn. Dag —1C 56
Anglers Clo. Rich —4C 116
Angler's La. NW5 —6F 49
Anglers Reach. Surb —5D 134
Anglers, The. King T —3D 134
(off High St.)
Anglesea Av. SE18 —4F 91
Anglesea Rd. SE18 —4F 91
Anglesea Rd. King T —4D 134
Anglesey Clo. Ashf —3C 112
Anglesey Ct. W7 —4K 61
Anglesey Ct. Rd. Cars —6E 150
Anglesey Gdns. Cars —6E 150
Anglesey Ho. E14 —6C 70
Anglesey Rd. Enf —4C 8
Anglesmede Cres. Pinn —3E 24
Anglesmede Way. Pinn —3E 24
Angles Rd. SW16 —4J 121
Anglia Clo. N17 —7C 18
Anglia Ct. Dag —1D 56
(off Spring Clo.)
Anglia Ho. E14 —6A 70
Anglian Ind. Est. Bark —4K 73
Anglian Rd. E11 —3F 53
Anglia Wlk. E6 —1E 72
(off Napier Rd.)
Anglo Rd. E3 —2B 70
Angrave Ct. E8 —1F 69
(off Scriven St.)
Angrave Pas. E8 —1F 69
Angus Clo. Chess —5G 147
Angus Dri. Ruis —4A 42
Angus Gdns. NW9 —1K 27
Angus Ho. SW2 —7H 103
Angus Rd. E13 —3A 72
Angus St. SE14 —7A 88
Anhalt Rd. SW11 —7C 84
Ankerdine Cres. SE18 —7F 91
Anlaby Rd. Tedd —5J 115
Anley Rd. W6 —2F 83
Anmersh Gro. Stan —1D 26
Annabel Clo. E14 —6D 70
Anna Clo. E8 —1F 69
Annandale Gro. Uxb —3E 40
Annandale Rd. SE10 —6H 89
Annandale Rd. W4 —5A 82
Annandale Rd. Croy —2G 153
Annandale Rd. Sidc —7J 109
Anna Neagle Clo. E7 —4J 53
Annan Way. Romf —1K 39
Anne Boleyn Ct. SE9 —6H 109
Anne Boleyn's Wlk. King T —5E 116
Anne Boleyn's Wlk. Sutt —7F 149
Anne Case M. N Mald —3K 135
Anne of Cleeves Ct. SE9 —7H 109
Annesley Av. NW9 —3K 27
Annesley Clo. NW10 —3A 46
Annesley Dri. Croy —3B 154
Annesley Ho. SW9 —1A 104
Annesley Rd. SE3 —1K 107
Annesley Wlk. N19 —2G 49
Anne St. E13 —4J 71
Anne Sutherland Ho. Beck —7A 124
Annett Clo. Shep —4G 131
Annette Clo. Harr —2J 25
Annette Rd. N7 —3K 49
(in two parts)
Annett Rd. W on T —7J 131
Annetts Cres. N1 —7C 50
Anne Way. W Mol —4F 133
Annie Besant Clo. E3 —1B 70
Annie Taylor Ho. E12 —4E 54
(off Walton Rd.)
Anning St. EC2 —4E 68 (3H 163)
Annington Rd. N2 —3D 30
Annis Rd. E9 —6A 52
Ann La. SW10 —6B 84
Ann Moss Way. SE16 —3J 87
Ann's Clo. SW1 —7F 165
Ann's Pl. E1 —6J 163
Ann St. SE18 —5G 91
(in two parts)
Annsworthy Av. T Hth —3D 140
Annsworthy Cres. SE25 —2D 140
Ansar Gdns. E17 —5B 34
Ansdell Rd. SE15 —2J 105
Ansdell St. W8 —3K 83
Ansdell Ter. W8 —3K 83
Ansell Gro. Cars —1E 150
Ansell Rd. SW17 —3C 120
Anselm Clo. Croy —3F 153
Anselm Rd. SW6 —6J 83
Anselm Rd. Pinn —1D 24
Ansford Rd. Brom —5E 124
Ansleigh Pl. W11 —7F 65
Anson Clo. Romf —2H 39
Anson Ho. SW1 —6G 85 (7A 172)
(off Churchill Gdns.)
Anson Rd. N19 —4G 49
Anson Rd. NW2 —4D 46
Anson Ter. N'holt —6F 43
Anstey Ct. W3 —2H 81
Anstey Rd. SE15 —3G 105
Anstey Wlk. N15 —4B 32
Anstice Clo. W4 —7A 82
Anstridge Path. SE9 —6H 109
Anstridge Rd. SE9 —6H 109
Antelope Rd. SE18 —3D 90
Anthony Clo. NW7 —4F 13
Anthony Cope Ct. N1 —3D 68 (1F 163)
(off Chart St.)
Anthony Ho. NW1 —4C 66 (4C 158)
(off Ashbridge St.)
Anthony Rd. SE25 —6G 141
Anthony Rd. Gnfd —3J 61
Anthony Rd. Well —1A 110
Anthony St. E1 —6H 69
Antigua Wlk. SE19 —5D 122
Antilles Bay. E14 —2E 88
Antill Rd. E3 —3A 70
Antill Rd. N15 —4G 33
Antill Ter. E1 —6K 69
Antlers Hill. E4 —5J 9
Anton Cres. Sutt —3J 149
Antoneys Clo. Pinn —2B 24
Anton St. E8 —5G 51
Antrim Gro. NW3 —6D 48
Antrim Rd. NW3 —6D 48
Antrobus Clo. Sutt —5H 149
Antrobus Rd. W4 —4J 81
Anvil Clo. SW16 —7G 121
Anvil Rd. Sun —3J 131
Anworth Clo. Wfd G —6E 20
Apeldoorn Dri. Wall —7J 151
Apex Clo. Beck —1D 142
Apex Corner. (Junct.) —4E 12
(Edgware)
Apex Corner. (Junct.) —3D 114
(Hanworth)
Apex Ct. W13 —7A 62
Apex Ind. Est. NW10 —4B 64
Apex Pde. NW7 —4E 12
(off Selvage La.)
Apex Retail Pk. Felt —3D 114
Aphrodite Ct. E14 —4C 88
Aplin Way. Iswth —1J 97
Apollo Av. Brom —1K 143
Apollo Bus. Cen. SE8 —5K 87
Apollo Ct. E1 —7G 69
(off Thomas More St.)
Apollo Ho. N6 —7E 30
Apollo Ho. SW10 —7B 84
(off Riley St.)
Apollo Pl. E11 —3G 53
Apollo Pl. SW10 —7B 84
Apollo Way. SE28 —3H 91
Apostle Way. T Hth —2B 140
Apothecary St. EC4 —6B 68 (1A 168)
Appach Rd. SW2 —5A 104
Apple Blossom Ct. SW8 —7H 85
(off Pascal St.)
Appleby Clo. E4 —6K 19
Appleby Clo. N15 —5D 32
Appleby Clo. Twic —2H 115
Appleby Gdns. Felt —1H 113
Appleby Rd. E8 —7G 51
Appleby Rd. E16 —6H 71
Appleby St. E2 —2F 69
Appledore Av. Bexh —1J 111
Appledore Av. Ruis —3K 41
Appledore Clo. SW17 —2D 120
Appledore Clo. Brom —5H 143
Appledore Clo. Edgw —1G 27
Appledore Cres. Sidc —3J 127
Appleford Ho. W10 —4G 65
(off Bosworth Rd.)
Appleford Rd. W10 —4G 65
Apple Gth. Bren —4D 80
Applegarth. Clay —5A 146
Applegarth. New Ad —7D 154
(in two parts)
Applegarth Dri. Ilf —4K 37
Applegarth Ho. SE1 —6B 168
Applegarth Ho. SE15 —7G 87
(off Bird in Bush Rd.)
Applegarth Rd. SE28 —1B 92
Applegarth Rd. W14 —3F 83
Apple Gro. Chess —4E 146
Apple Gro. Enf —3K 7
Apple Mkt. King T —2D 134
Apple Rd. E11 —3G 53
Appleshaw Ho. SE5 —3E 104
Appleton Gdns. N Mald —6C 136
Appleton Rd. SE3 —3C 108
Appleton Sq. Mitc —1C 138
Apple Tree Av. Uxb & W Dray —5B 58
Appletree Clo. SE20 —1H 141
Appletree Gdns. Barn —4H 5
Apple Tree Yd. SW1 —1G 85 (4B 166)
Applewood Clo. N20 —1H 15
(in two parts)
Applewood Clo. NW2 —3D 46
Applewood Clo. Ick —4A 40
Appold St. EC2 —5E 68 (5G 163)
Apprentice Way. E5 —4H 51
Approach Clo. N16 —4E 50
Approach Rd. E2 —2J 69
Approach Rd. SW20 —2E 136
Approach Rd. Ashf —6E 112
Approach Rd. Barn —4G 5
Approach Rd. Edgw —6B 12
Approach Rd. W Mol —5E 132
Approach, The. NW4 —5F 29
Approach, The. W3 —6K 63
Approach, The. Enf —2C 8
Aprey Gdns. NW4 —4E 28
April Clo. W7 —7J 61
April Clo. Felt —3J 113
April Ct. E2 —2G 69
(off Teale St.)
April Glen. SE23 —3K 123
April St. E8 —4F 51
Apsley Clo. Harr —5G 25
Apsley Ho. NW8 —2B 66
(off Finchley Rd.)
Apsley Ho. Houn —4D 96
Apsley Rd. SE25 —4H 141
Apsley Rd. N Mald —3J 135
Apsley Way. NW2 —2C 46
Apsley Way. W1 —2E 84 (6H 165)
(in two parts)
Aquarius. Twic —1B 116
Aquila St. NW8 —2B 66
Aquinas St. SE1 —1A 86 (5K 167)
Arabella Dri. SW15 —4A 100
Arabia Clo. E4 —7K 9
Arabin Rd. SE4 —4A 106
Aragon Av. Th Dit —5K 133
Aragon Clo. Brom —1D 156
Aragon Clo. Enf —1E 6
Aragon Clo. Sun —6H 113
Aragon Ct. E Mol —4G 133
Aragon Dri. Ruis —1B 42
Aragon M. E1 —1G 87
Aragon Rd. King T —5E 116
Aragon Rd. Mord —6F 137
Aragon Tower. SE8 —4B 88
Arandora Cres. Romf —7B 38
Aran Dri. Stan —4H 11
Arapiles Ho. E14 —6F 71
Arbery Rd. E3 —3A 70
Arbon Ct. N1 —1C 68
(off Linton St.)
Arbor Clo. Beck —2D 142
Arbor Ct. N16 —2D 50
Arborfield Clo. SW2 —1K 121
Arborfield Ho. E14 —7C 70
Arbor Rd. E4 —3A 20
Arbour Rd. Enf —3E 8
Arbour Sq. E1 —6K 69
Arbroath Rd. SE9 —3C 108
Arbury Ct. SE20 —1H 141
Arbury Ter. SE26 —3G 123
Arbuthnot La. Bex —6E 110
Arbuthnot Rd. SE14 —2K 105
Arbutus St. E8 —1F 69
Arcade. Croy —2C 152
Arcade Pde. Chess —5D 146
Arcade, The. E14 —6D 70
Arcade, The. E17 —4C 34
Arcade, The. EC2 —6G 163
Arcade, The. Bark —7G 55
Arcadia Av. N3 —2J 29
Arcadia Cen., The. W5 —7D 62
Arcadia Clo. Cars —4E 150
Arcadia Ct. E1 —7J 163
Arcadian Av. Bex —6E 110
Arcadian Clo. Bex —6E 110
Arcadian Gdns. N22 —7E 16
Arcadian Rd. Bex —6E 110
Arcadia St. E14 —6C 70
Archangel St. SE16 —2K 87
Archbishop's Pl. SW2 —7K 103
Archdale Bus. Cen. Harr —2G 43
Archdale Ct. W12 —1D 82
Archdale Ho. SE1 —3E 86 (7G 169)
(off Long La.)
Archdale Pl. N Mald —3H 135
Archdale Rd. SE22 —5F 105
Archel Rd. W14 —6H 83
Archer Clo. King T —7E 116
Archer Ho. SE14 —1A 106
Archer Ho. SW11 —1B 102
Archer Ho. W11 —7H 65
(off Westbourne Gro.)
Archer Ho. W13 —1B 80
(off Sherwood Clo.)
Archer M. Hamp H —6G 115
Archer Rd. SE25 —4H 141
Archer Rd. Orp —5K 145
Archers Ct. Brom —4K 143
Archers Dri. Enf —2D 8
Archers Lodge. SE16 —5G 87
(off Culloden Clo.)
Archer Sq. SE14 —6A 88
Archer St. W1 —7H 67 (2C 166)
Archer Ter. W Dray —7A 58
Archery Clo. W2 —6C 66 (1D 164)
Archery Clo. Harr —3K 25
Archery Rd. SE9 —5D 108
Archery Steps. W2 —2D 164
Arches Bus. Cen., The. S'hall —2D 78
(off Merrick Rd.)
Arches, The. NW1 —7F 49
Arches, The. SW8 —7H 85
Arches, The. WC2 —1J 85
(off Villiers St.)
Arches, The. Harr —2F 43
Archgate Bus. Cen. N12 —5F 15
Archibald M. W1 —7E 66 (3J 165)
Archibald Rd. N7 —4H 49
Archibald St. E3 —3C 70
Archie Clo. W Dray —2C 76
Arch St. SE1 —3C 86
Archway. (Junct.) —2G 49
Archway Bus. Cen. N19 —3H 49
Archway Clo. N19 —2G 49
Archway Clo. SW19 —3K 119
Archway Clo. W10 —5F 65
Archway Clo. Wall —3H 151
Archway Mall. N19 —2G 49
Archway Rd. N6 & N19 —6E 30
Archway St. SW13 —3A 100
Arcola St. E8 —5F 51
Arcon Ter. N9 —7B 8
Arctic St. NW5 —5F 49
Arcus Rd. Brom —6G 125
Ardbeg Rd. SE24 —5D 104
Arden Clo. Harr —3H 43
Arden Ct. Gdns. N2 —6B 30
Arden Cres. E14 —4C 88

Arden Cres.—Ashmere Gro.

Arden Cres. Dag —7C 56
Arden Est. N1 —2E 68
Arden Grange. N12 —4F 15
Arden Ho. N1 —1G 163
Arden Ho. SE11 —4G 173
Arden Ho. SW9 —2J 103
(off Grantham Rd.)
Arden M. E17 —5D 34
Arden Mhor. Pinn —4K 23
Arden Rd. N3 —3H 29
Arden Rd. W13 —7C 62
Ardent Clo. SE25 —3E 140
Ardfern Av. SW16 —3A 140
Ardfillan Rd. SE6 —1F 125
Ardgowan Rd. SE6 —7G 107
(in two parts)
Ardilaun Rd. N5 —4C 50
Ardingly Clo. Croy —3K 153
Ardleigh Gdns. Sutt —7J 137
Ardleigh Ho. Bark —1G 73
Ardleigh M. Ilf —3F 55
Ardleigh Rd. E17 —1B 34
Ardleigh Rd. N1 —6E 50
Ardleigh Ter. E17 —1B 34
Ardley Clo. NW10 —3A 46
Ardley Clo. SE6 —3A 124
Ardley Clo. Ruis —7E 22
Ardlui Rd. SE27 —2C 122
Ardmay Gdns. Surb —5E 134
Ardmere Rd. SE13 —6F 107
Ardmore La. Buck H —1E 20
Ardmore Pl. Buck H —1E 20
Ardoch Rd. SE6 —2F 125
Ardra Rd. N9 —3E 18
Ardrossan Gdns. Wor Pk —3C 148
Ardshiel Clo. SW15 —3F 101
Ardwell Av. Ilf —5G 37
Ardwell Rd. SW2 —2J 121
Ardwick Rd. NW2 —4J 47
Arena Bus. Cen. N4 —6C 32
Arena Est. N4 —6B 32
Arena, The. Enf —1G 9
Ares Ct. E14 —4C 88
Arethusa Ho. E14 —4C 88
Argali Ho. Eri —3E 92
(off Kale Rd.)
Argall Av. E10 —7K 33
Argall Way. E10 —1K 51
Argenta Way. NW10 —7H 45
Argenta Way. Wemb & NW10 —6G 45
Argent Cen., The. Hay —2J 77
Argent Ct. Chess —3G 147
Argon M. SW6 —7J 83
Argon Rd. N18 —5E 18
Argosy Ho. SE8 —4A 88
Argosy La. Stanw —7A 94
Argus Clo. Romf —1H 39
Argus Way. N'holt —3C 60
Argyle Av. Houn —6E 96
(in two parts)
Argyle Clo. W13 —4A 62
Argyle Ho. E14 —3E 88
Argyle Pas. N17 —1F 33
Argyle Pl. W6 —4D 82
Argyle Rd. E1 —4K 69
Argyle Rd. E15 —4G 53
Argyle Rd. E16 —6K 71
Argyle Rd. N12 —5E 14
Argyle Rd. N17 —1G 33
Argyle Rd. N18 —4B 18
Argyle Rd. Barn —4A 4
Argyle Rd. Gnfd & W13 —3K 61
Argyle Rd. Harr —6F 25
Argyle Rd. Houn —5F 97
Argyle Rd. Ilf —2E 54
Argyle Sq. WC1 —3J 67 (1F 161)
Argyle St. NW1 —3J 67 (1E 160)
Argyle Wlk. WC1 —3J 67 (2F 161)
Argyle Way. SE16 —5G 87
(off St James Rd.)
Argyll Av. S'hall —1F 79
Argyll Clo. SW9 —3K 103
Argyll Gdns. Edgw —2H 27
Argyll Mans. SW3 —6B 84 (7B 170)
Argyll Mans. W14 —4G 83
(off Hammersmith Rd.)
Argyll Rd. W8 —2J 83
Argyll St. W1 —6G 67 (1A 166)
Arica Rd. SE4 —4A 106
Ariel Ct. SE11 —4B 86 (4K 173)
Ariel Rd. NW6 —6J 47
Ariel Way. W12 —1E 82
Ariel Way. Houn —3K 95
Aristotle Rd. SW4 —3H 103
Arkell Gro. SE19 —7B 122
Arkindale Rd. SE6 —3E 124
Arkley Cres. E17 —5B 34
Arkley Rd. E17 —5B 34
Arklow Ho. SE5 —6D 86
(off Albany Rd.)
Arklow M. Surb —2E 146
Arklow Rd. SE14 —6B 88
Arklow Rd. Trad. Est. SE14 —6A 88
Arkwright Ho. SW2 —7J 103
(off Streatham Pl.)
Arkwright Rd. NW3 —5A 48
Arkwright Rd. S Croy —7F 153
Arlesey Clo. SW15 —5G 101
Arlesford Rd. SW9 —3J 103
Arlingford Rd. SW2 —5A 104
Arlington. N12 —3D 14
Arlington Av. N1 —1C 68
(in two parts)
Arlington Clo. SE13 —5F 107
Arlington Clo. Sidc —7J 109
Arlington Clo. Sutt —2J 149
Arlington Clo. Twic —6C 98
Arlington Ct. W3 —2H 81
(off Mill Hill Rd.)
Arlington Ct. Hay —5G 77
Arlington Dri. Cars —2D 150
Arlington Dri. Ruis —6F 23
Arlington Gdns. W4 —5J 81
Arlington Gdns. Ilf —1E 54
Arlington Ho. EC1 —3A 68 (1K 161)
(off Arlington Way)
Arlington Ho. SE8 —6B 88
(off Evelyn St.)
Arlington Ho. SW1 —1G 85 (4A 166)
Arlington Lodge. SW2 —4K 103
Arlington M. Twic —6B 98
Arlington Pk. Mans. W4 —5J 81
(off Sutton La. N.)
Arlington Pas. Tedd —4K 115
Arlington Pl. SE10 —7E 88
Arlington Rd. N14 —2A 16
Arlington Rd. NW1 —1F 67
Arlington Rd. W13 —6B 62
Arlington Rd. Ashf —5B 112
Arlington Rd. Rich —2D 116
Arlington Rd. Surb —6D 134
Arlington Rd. Tedd —4K 115
Arlington Rd. Twic —6C 98
Arlington Rd. Wfd G —1J 35
Arlington Sq. N1 —1C 68
Arlington St. SW1 —1G 85 (4A 166)
Arlington Way. EC1 —3A 68 (1K 161)
Arliss Way. N'holt —1A 60
Arlow Rd. N21 —1F 17
Armada Ct. SE8 —6C 88
Armadale Clo. N17 —4H 33
Armadale Rd. SW6 —7J 83
Armadale Rd. Felt —5J 95
Armada Way. E6 —7F 73
Armagh Rd. E3 —1B 70
Armfield Clo. W Mol —5D 132
Armfield Cres. Mitc —2D 138
Armfield Rd. Enf —1J 7
Arminger Rd. W12 —1D 82
Armistice Gdns. SE25 —3G 141
Armitage Rd. NW11 —1G 47
Armitage Rd. SE10 —5H 89
Armour Clo. N7 —6K 49
Armoury Rd. SE8 —2D 106
Armoury Way. SW18 —5J 101
Armstead Wlk. Dag —7G 57
Armstrong Av. Wfd G —6B 20
Armstrong Clo. E6 —6D 72
Armstrong Clo. Brom —3C 144
Armstrong Clo. Dag —7D 38
Armstrong Clo. Pinn —6J 23
Armstrong Clo. W on T —6J 131
Armstrong Cres. Cockf —3G 5
Armstrong Rd. SW7 —3B 84 (2A 170)
Armstrong Rd. W3 —1B 82
Armstrong Rd. Felt —5C 114
Armstrong Way. S'hall —2F 79
Armytage Rd. Houn —7B 78
Arnal Cres. SW18 —7G 101
Arncliffe. NW6 —2K 65
Arncliffe Clo. N11 —6K 15
Arncroft Ct. Bark —3B 74
Arndale Wlk. SW18 —5K 101
Arne Ho. SE11 —5G 173
Arne St. WC2 —6J 67 (1F 167)
Arnett Sq. E4 —6G 19
Arne Wlk. SE3 —4H 107
Arneways Av. Romf —3D 38
Arneway St. SW1 —3H 85 (2D 172)
Arnewood Clo. SW15 —1C 118
Arneys La. Mitc —6E 138
Arngask Rd. SE6 —7F 107
Arnhem Pl. E14 —3C 88
Arnhem Way. SE22 —5E 104
Arnhem Wharf. E14 —3B 88
Arnison Rd. E Mol —4H 133
Arnold Cir. E2 —3F 69 (2J 163)
Arnold Clo. Harr —7F 27
Arnold Ct. N22 —7D 16
Arnold Cres. Iswth —5H 97
Arnold Dri. Chess —6D 146
Arnold Est. SE1 —2F 87 (7K 169)
(in two parts)
Arnold Gdns. N13 —5G 17
Arnold Ho. SE3 —7A 90
(off Shooters Hill Rd.)
Arnold Ho. SE17 —5B 86
(off Doddington Gro.)
Arnold Mans. W14 —6H 83
(off Queen's Club Gdns.)
Arnold Rd. E3 —3C 70
Arnold Rd. N15 —3F 33
Arnold Rd. SW17 —7D 120
Arnold Rd. Dag —7F 57
Arnold Rd. N'holt —6C 42
Arnold Ter. Stan —5E 10
Arnos Gro. N14 —4C 16
Arnos Gro. Ct. N11 —5B 16
(off Palmer's Rd.)
Arnos Rd. N11 —4B 16
Arnot Ho. SE5 —7C 86
(off Comber Gro.)
Arnott Clo. SE28 —1C 92
Arnott Clo. W4 —4K 81
Arnould Av. SE5 —4D 104
Arnsberga Way. Bexh —4G 111
Arnside Gdns. Wemb —1D 44
Arnside Rd. Bexh —1G 111
Arnside St. SE17 —6D 86
Arnulf St. SE6 —4D 124
Arnulls Rd. SW16 —6B 122
Arodene Rd. SW2 —6K 103
Arosa Rd. Twic —6D 98
(in two parts)
Arpley Sq. SE20 —7J 123
(off High St.)
Arragon Gdns. SW16 —7J 121
Arragon Gdns. W W'ck —3D 154
Arragon Rd. E6 —1B 72
Arragon Rd. SW18 —1J 119
Arragon Rd. Twic —7A 98
Arran Clo. Eri —6K 93
Arran Clo. Wall —4F 151
Arran Ct. NW9 —2B 28
Arran Ct. NW10 —3K 45
Arran Dri. E12 —1B 54
Arran Ho. E14 —1E 88
Arran M. W5 —1F 81
Arran Rd. SE6 —2D 124
Arran Wlk. N1 —7C 50
Arras Av. Mord —5A 138
Arrol Ho. SE1 —3C 86
Arrol Rd. Beck —3J 141
Arrow Ct. SW5 —4J 83
(off W. Cromwell Rd.)
Arrowhead Ct. E11 —6F 35
Arrow Rd. E3 —3D 70
Arrowscout Wlk. N'holt —3C 60
Arrowsmith Ho. SE11 —5G 173
Arsenal F.C. —3B 50
Arsenal Rd. SE9 —2D 108
Artemis Ct. E14 —4C 88
Arterberry Rd. SW20 —7E 118
Artesian Clo. NW10 —7K 45
Artesian Gro. Barn —4F 5
Artesian Rd. W2 —6J 65
Artesian Wlk. E11 —3G 53
Arthingworth St. E15 —1G 71
Arthur Ct. SW11 —1E 102
Arthur Ct. W2 —6K 65
(off Queensway)
Arthur Ct. W10 —6F 65
(off Silchester Rd.)
Arthur Deakin Ho. E1 —5G 69 (5K 163)
(off Hunton St.)
Arthurdon Rd. SE4 —5C 106
Arthur Gro. SE18 —4G 91
Arthur Henderson Ho. SW6 —2H 101
(off Fulham Rd.)
Arthur Horsley Wlk. E7 —5H 53
(off Tower Hamlets Rd.)
Arthur Rd. E6 —2D 72
Arthur Rd. N7 —4K 49
Arthur Rd. N9 —2A 18
Arthur Rd. SW19 —5H 119
Arthur Rd. King T —7G 117
Arthur Rd. N Mald —5D 136
Arthur Rd. Romf —6C 38
Arthur St. EC4 —7D 68 (2F 169)
Artichoke Hill. E1 —7H 69
Artichoke M. SE5 —1D 104
(off Artichoke Pl.)
Artichoke Pl. SE5 —1D 104
Artillery Clo. Ilf —6G 37
Artillery Ho. E15 —6G 53
Artillery Ho. SE18 —5E 90
(off Connaught M.)
Artillery La. E1 —5E 68 (6H 163)
Artillery La. W12 —6C 64
Artillery Pas. E1 —6J 163
Artillery Pl. SE18 —5D 90
Artillery Pl. SW1 —3H 85 (2C 172)
Artillery Pl. Harr —7B 10
Artillery Row. SW1 —3G 85 (2C 172)
Artisan Clo. E6 —6F 73
Artizan St. E1 —7J 163
Arun Ct. SE25 —5G 141
Arundel Av. Mord —4H 137
Arundel Bldgs. SE1 —3E 86
(off Swan Mead)
Arundel Clo. E15 —4G 53
Arundel Clo. SW11 —5C 102
Arundel Clo. Bex —6F 111
Arundel Clo. Croy —3B 152
Arundel Clo. Hamp H —5F 115
Arundel Ct. N12 —6H 15
Arundel Ct. N17 —1G 33
Arundel Ct. SW3 —5C 84 (5D 170)
(off Jubilee Pl.)
Arundel Ct. Short —2G 143
Arundel Ct. S Harr —4E 42
Arundel Dri. Harr —4D 42
Arundel Dri. Wfd G —7D 20
Arundel Gdns. N21 —1F 17
Arundel Gdns. W11 —7H 65
Arundel Gdns. Edgw —7E 12
Arundel Gdns. Ilf —2A 56
Arundel Gt. Ct. WC2 —7K 67 (2H 167)
Arundel Gro. N16 —5E 50
Arundel Ho. W3 —2H 81
(off Park Rd. N.)
Arundel Mans. SW6 —1H 101
(off Kelvedon Rd.)
Arundel Pl. N1 —6A 50
Arundel Rd. Cockf —3H 5
Arundel Rd. Croy —6D 140
Arundel Rd. Houn —3A 96
Arundel Rd. King T —2H 135
Arundel Rd. Sutt —7H 149
Arundel Sq. N7 —6A 50
Arundel St. WC2 —7K 67 (2H 167)
Arundel Ter. SW13 —6D 82
Arun Ho. King T —1D 134
Arvon Rd. N5 —5A 50
(in two parts)
Asa Ct. Hay —3H 77
Ascalon Ho. SW8 —7G 85
(off Thessaly Rd.)
Ascalon St. SW8 —7G 85
Ascham Dri. E4 —7J 19
Ascham End. E17 —1A 34
Ascham St. NW5 —5G 49
Aschurch Rd. Croy —7F 141
Ascot Clo. N'holt —5E 42
Ascot Ct. NW8 —2A 158
Ascot Ct. Bex —7F 111
Ascot Gdns. S'hall —5D 60
Ascot Ho. NW1 —3F 67 (1K 159)
(off Redhill St.)
Ascot Ho. W9 —4J 65
(off Harrow Rd.)
Ascot Lodge. NW6 —1K 65
Ascot Pl. Stan —5H 11
Ascot Rd. E6 —3D 72
Ascot Rd. N15 —5D 32
Ascot Rd. N18 —4B 18
Ascot Rd. SW17 —6E 120
Ascot Rd. Felt —1C 112
Ascot Rd. Orp —4K 145
Ascott Av. W5 —2E 80
Ascott Clo. Pinn —4J 23
Ashbourne Av. E18 —4K 35
Ashbourne Av. N20 —2J 15
Ashbourne Av. NW11 —5H 29
Ashbourne Av. Bexh —7E 92
Ashbourne Av. Harr —2H 43
Ashbourne Clo. N12 —4E 14
Ashbourne Clo. W5 —5G 63
Ashbourne Ct. E5 —4A 52
Ashbourne Ct. N12 —4E 14
(off Ashbourne Clo.)
Ashbourne Gro. NW7 —5E 12
Ashbourne Gro. SE22 —4F 105
Ashbourne Gro. W4 —5A 82
Ashbourne Pde. NW11 —4H 29
Ashbourne Pde. W5 —4F 63
Ashbourne Rd. W5 —4F 63
Ashbourne Rd. Mitc —7E 120
Ashbourne Ter. SW19 —7H 119
Ashbourne Way. NW11 —4H 29
Ashbridge Rd. E11 —7G 35
Ashbridge St. NW8 —4C 66 (4C 158)
Ashbrook. Edgw —6A 12
Ashbrook Rd. N19 —1H 49
Ashbrook Rd. Dag —3H 57
Ashburn Gdns. SW7 —4A 84
Ashburnham Av. Harr —6K 25
Ashburnham Clo. N2 —3B 30
Ashburnham Ct. Beck —2E 142
Ashburnham Ct. Pinn —3B 24
Ashburnham Gdns. Harr —6K 25
Ashburnham Gro. SE10 —7D 88
Ashburnham Mans. SW10 —7A 84
(off Ashburnham Rd.)
Ashburnham Pl. SE10 —7D 88
Ashburnham Retreat. SE10 —7D 88
Ashburnham Rd. NW10 —3E 64
Ashburnham Rd. SW10 —7A 84
Ashburnham Rd. Belv —4J 93
Ashburnham Rd. Rich —3B 116
Ashburnham Tower. SW10 —7B 84
(off Worlds End Est.)
Ashburn Pl. SW7 —4A 84
Ashburton Av. Croy —1H 153
Ashburton Av. Ilf —5J 55
Ashburton Clo. Croy —1G 153
Ashburton Enterprise Cen. SW15 —6E 100
Ashburton Gdns. Croy —2G 153
Ashburton Gro. N7 —4A 50
Ashburton Ho. W9 —4H 65
(off Fernhead Rd.)
Ashburton Memorial Homes. Croy —7H 141
Ashburton Rd. E16 —6J 71
Ashburton Rd. Croy —2G 153
Ashburton Rd. Ruis —2J 41
Ashburton Ter. E13 —2J 71
Ashbury Dri. Uxb —3D 40
Ashbury Gdns. Romf —5D 38
Ashbury Pl. SW19 —6A 120
Ashbury Rd. SW11 —3D 102
Ashby Av. Chess —6G 147
Ashby Ct. NW8 —4B 66 (3B 158)
(off Pollitt Dri.)
Ashby Gro. N1 —7C 50
Ashby Ho. N1 —7C 50
(off Essex Rd.)
Ashby Ho. SW9 —2B 104
Ashby M. SE4 —2B 106
Ashby Rd. N15 —5G 33
Ashby Rd. SE4 —2B 106
Ashby St. EC1 —3B 68 (2B 162)
Ashby Wlk. Croy —6C 140
Ashby Way. W Dray —7C 76
Ashchurch Gro. W12 —3C 82
Ashchurch Pk. Vs. W12 —3C 82
Ashchurch Ter. W12 —3C 82
Ash Clo. SE20 —2J 141
Ash Clo. Cars —2D 150
Ash Clo. Edgw —4D 12
Ash Clo. Hare —1A 22
Ash Clo. N Mald —2K 135
Ash Clo. Orp —5H 145
Ash Clo. Romf —1H 39
Ash Clo. Sidc —3B 128
Ash Clo. Stan —6F 11
Ashcombe Av. Surb —7D 134
Ashcombe Gdns. Edgw —4B 12
Ashcombe Pk. NW2 —3A 46
Ashcombe Rd. SW19 —5J 119
Ashcombe Rd. Cars —6E 150
Ashcombe Sq. N Mald —3J 135
Ashcombe St. SW6 —2K 101
Ash Ct. NW5 —5G 49
Ash Ct. SW19 —7G 119
Ash Ct. W1 —6D 66 (7E 158)
(off Harrowby St.)
Ash Ct. Eps —4J 147
Ashcroft. N14 —2C 16
Ash Cft. Pinn —6A 10
Ashcroft Av. Sidc —6A 110
Ashcroft Ct. N20 —2G 15
Ashcroft Cres. Sidc —6A 110
Ashcroft Rd. E3 —3A 70
Ashcroft Rd. Chess —3F 147
Ashcroft Sq. W6 —4E 82
Ashdale Clo. Stai —2A 112
Ashdale Clo. Twic —7G 97
Ashdale Gro. Stan —6E 10
Ashdale Ho. N4 —7D 32
Ashdale Rd. SE12 —1K 125
Ashdale Way. Twic —7F 97
Ashdene. SE15 —7H 87
Ashdene. Pinn —3A 24
Ashdene Clo. Ashf —7E 112
Ashdon Clo. Wfd G —6E 20
Ashdon Rd. NW10 —1B 64
Ashdown. W13 —5B 62
(off Clivedon Ct.)
Ashdown Clo. Beck —2D 142
Ashdown Clo. Bex —7J 111
Ashdown Ct. Sutt —6A 150
Ashdown Cres. NW5 —5E 48
Ashdowne Ct. N17 —1G 33
Ashdown Est. E11 —4F 53
Ashdown Ho. SW1 —3G 85
(off Victoria St.)
Ashdown Pl. Th Dit —7A 134
Ashdown Rd. Enf —2D 8
Ashdown Rd. King T —2E 134
Ashdown Rd. Uxb —2C 58
Ashdown Wlk. E14 —4C 88
(off Copeland Dri.)
Ashdown Wlk. Romf —1H 39
Ashdown Way. SW17 —2E 120
Ashe Ho. Twic —6D 98
Ashenden. SE1 —4C 86
(off Deacon Way)
Ashenden Rd. E5 —5A 52
Ashen Gro. SW19 —3J 119
Ashentree Ct. EC4 —1K 167
Asher Loftus Way. N11 —6J 15
Asher Way. E1 —7G 69
Ashfield Av. Bush —1B 10
Ashfield Av. Felt —1K 113
Ashfield Clo. Beck —7C 124
Ashfield Clo. Rich —1E 116
Ashfield Ho. W14 —5H 83
Ashfield La. Chst —6F 127
(in three parts)
Ashfield Pde. N14 —1C 16
Ashfield Rd. N4 —6C 32
Ashfield Rd. N14 —3B 16
Ashfield Rd. W3 —1B 82
Ashfield St. E1 —5H 69
Ashfield Yd. E1 —5J 69
Ashford. —4B 112
Ashford Av. N8 —4J 31
Ashford Av. Ashf —6D 112
Ashford Av. Hay —6B 60
Ashford Bus. Complex. Ashf —5E 112
(Sandell's Av.)
Ashford Bus. Complex. Ashf —4E 112
(Shield Rd.)
Ashford Clo. E17 —6B 34
Ashford Clo. Ashf —4A 112
Ashford Common. —7F 113
Ashford Ct. Edgw —3C 12
Ashford Cres. Ashf —3A 112
Ashford Cres. Enf —2D 8
Ashford Ho. SE8 —6B 88
Ashford Ho. SW9 —4B 104
Ashford Pas. NW2 —4F 47
Ashford Rd. E6 —7E 54
Ashford Rd. E18 —2K 35
Ashford Rd. NW2 —4F 47
Ashford Rd. Ashf —7E 112
Ashford Rd. Felt —4F 113
Ashford St. N1 —3E 68 (1G 163)
Ash Gro. E8 —1H 69
(in two parts)
Ash Gro. N13 —3H 17
Ash Gro. NW2 —4F 47
Ash Gro. SE12 —1J 125
Ash Gro. SE20 —2J 141
Ash Gro. W5 —2E 80
Ash Gro. Enf —7K 7
Ash Gro. Felt —1G 113
Ash Gro. Hare —1A 22
Ash Gro. Hay —7F 59
Ash Gro. Houn —1B 96
Ash Gro. S'hall —5E 60
Ash Gro. Wemb —4A 44
Ash Gro. W Dray —7B 58
Ash Gro. W W'ck —2E 154
Ashgrove Ct. W9 —5J 65
(off Elmfield Way)
Ashgrove Ho. SW1 —5H 85 (5D 172)
(off Lindsay Sq.)
Ashgrove Rd. Ashf —5E 112
Ashgrove Rd. Brom —6F 125
Ashgrove Rd. Ilf —1K 55
Ash Hill Clo. Bush —1A 10
Ash Hill Dri. Pinn —3A 24
Ash Ho. E14 —2E 88
Ash Ho. SE1 —4F 87
(off Longfield Est.)
Ash Ho. W10 —4G 65
(off Heather Wlk.)
Ashingdon Clo. E4 —3K 19
Ashington Rd. SW6 —2H 101
Ashlake Rd. SW16 —4J 121
Ashland Pl. W1 —5E 66 (5G 159)
Ashlar Pl. SE18 —4F 91
Ashleigh Commercial Est. SE7 —3A 90
Ashleigh Ct. N14 —7B 6
Ashleigh Ct. W5 —4D 80
(off Murray Rd.)
Ashleigh Gdns. Sutt —2K 149
Ashleigh Point. SE23 —3K 123
Ashleigh Rd. SE20 —3H 141
Ashleigh Rd. SW14 —3A 100
Ashley Av. Ilf —2F 37
Ashley Av. Mord —5J 137
Ashley Clo. NW4 —2E 28
Ashley Clo. Pinn —2K 23
Ashley Ct. NW4 —2E 28
Ashley Ct. NW9 —2B 28
(off Guilfoyle)
Ashley Ct. SW1 —3G 85 (2A 172)
(off Morpeth Ter.)
Ashley Ct. Barn —5F 5
Ashley Ct. N'holt —1C 60
Ashley Cres. N22 —2A 32
Ashley Cres. SW11 —3E 102
Ashley Dri. Iswth —6J 79
Ashley Dri. Twic —1F 115
Ashley Gdns. N13 —4H 17
Ashley Gdns. SW1 —3G 85 (2B 172)
(in three parts)
Ashley Gdns. Rich —2D 116
Ashley Gdns. Wemb —2E 44
Ashley La. NW4 —7K 13
(in two parts)
Ashley La. Croy —4B 152
Ashley Pl. SW1 —3G 85 (2A 172)
(in two parts)
Ashley Rd. E4 —6H 19
Ashley Rd. E7 —7A 54
Ashley Rd. N17 —3G 33
Ashley Rd. N19 —1J 49
Ashley Rd. SW19 —6K 119
Ashley Rd. Enf —2D 8
Ashley Rd. Hamp —1E 132
Ashley Rd. Rich —3E 98
Ashley Rd. Th Dit —6K 133
Ashley Rd. T Hth —4K 139
Ashley Wlk. NW7 —7A 14
Ashling Rd. Croy —1G 153
Ashlin Rd. E15 —4F 53
Ashlone Rd. SW15 —3E 100
Ashlyns Way. Chess —6D 146
Ashmead. N14 —5B 6
Ashmead Bus. Cen. E3 —4F 71
Ashmead Ga. Brom —1A 144
Ashmead Ho. E9 —5A 52
(off Homerton Rd.)
Ashmead Rd. SE8 —2C 106
Ashmead Rd. Felt —1J 113
Ashmere Av. Beck —2F 143
Ashmere Clo. Sutt —5F 149
Ashmere Gro. SW2 —4J 103

Ashmill St.—Ayton Ho.

Ashmill St. NW1 —5C 66 (5C 158)
Ashmole Pl. SW8 —6K 85
(in two parts)
Ashmole St. SW8 —6K 85 (7H 173)
Ashmore. NW1 —7H 49
(off Agar Gro.)
Ashmore Ct. N11 —6J 15
Ashmore Ct. Houn —6E 78
Ashmore Gro. Well —3H 109
Ashmore Ho. W14 —3G 83
(off Russell Rd.)
Ashmore Rd. W9 —2H 65
Ashmount Est. N19 —7H 31
Ashmount Rd. N6 —7G 31
Ashmount Rd. N15 —5F 33
Ashmount Ter. W5 —4D 80
Ashmour Gdns. Romf —2K 39
Ashneal Gdns. Harr —3H 43
Ashness Gdns. Gnfd —6B 44
Ashness Rd. SW11 —5D 102
Ashpark Ho. E14 —6B 70
Ashridge Clo. Harr —6C 26
Ashridge Ct. N14 —5B 6
Ashridge Ct. S'hall —6G 61
(off Redcroft Rd.)
Ashridge Cres. SE18 —7G 91
Ashridge Gdns. N13 —5C 16
Ashridge Gdns. Pinn —4C 24
Ashridge Way. Mord —3H 137
Ashridge Way. Sun —6J 113
Ash Rd. E15 —5G 53
Ash Rd. Croy —2C 154
Ash Rd. Shep —4C 130
Ash Rd. Sutt —7G 137
Ash Row. Brom —7E 144
Ashtead Rd. E5 —7G 33
Ashton Clo. Sutt —4J 149
Ashton Ct. Harr —3K 43
Ashton Gdns. Houn —4D 96
Ashton Gdns. Romf —6E 38
Ashton Heights. SE23 —1J 123
Ashton Ho. SW9 —7A 86
Ashton Rd. E15 —5F 53
Ashton St. E14 —7E 70
Ashtree Av. Mitc —2B 138
Ash Tree Clo. Croy —6A 142
Ash Tree Clo. Surb —2E 146
Ashtree Dell. NW9 —5K 27
Ash Tree Way. Croy —5K 141
Ashurst Clo. SE20 —1H 141
Ashurst Dri. Ilf —6F 37
Ashurst Dri. Shep —5A 130
Ashurst Gdns. SW2 —1A 122
Ashurst Rd. N12 —5H 15
Ashurst Rd. Barn —5J 5
Ashurst Wlk. Croy —2H 153
Ashvale Rd. SW17 —5D 120
Ash Vw. Clo. Ashf —6A 112
Ash Vw. Gdns. Ashf —5A 112
Ashville Rd. E11 —2F 53
Ash Wlk. Wemb —3C 44
Ashwater Rd. SE12 —1J 125
Ashway Cen., The. King T —1E 134
Ashwell Clo. E6 —6C 72
Ashwin St. E8 —6F 51
Ashwood Av. Uxb —6C 58
Ashwood Gdns. Hay —4H 77
Ashwood Gdns. New Ad —6D 154
Ashwood Rd. E4 —3A 20
Ashworth Clo. SE5 —2D 104
Ashworth Est. Croy —1J 151
Ashworth Mans. W9 —3K 65
(off Elgin Av.)
Ashworth Rd. W9 —3K 65
Aske Ho. N1 —1G 163
(in two parts)
Asker Ho. N7 —4J 49
Askern Clo. Bexh —4D 110
Aske St. N1 —3E 68 (1G 163)
Askew Cres. W12 —2B 82
Askew Est. W12 —1B 82
(off Uxbridge Rd.)
Askew Rd. W12 —1B 82
Askham Ct. W12 —1C 82
Askham Rd. W12 —1C 82
Askill Dri. SW15 —5G 101
Askwith Rd. Rain —3K 75
Asland Rd. E15 —1G 71
Aslett St. SW18 —7K 101
Asmara Rd. NW2 —5G 47
Asmuns Hill. NW11 —5J 29
Asmuns Pl. NW11 —5H 29
Asolando Dri. SE17 —4C 86
(off King and Queen St.)
Aspen Clo. N19 —2G 49
Aspen Clo. W5 —2F 81
Aspen Clo. W Dray —1B 76
Aspen Copse. Brom —2D 144
Aspen Dri. Wemb —3A 44
Aspen Gdns. W6 —5D 82
Aspen Gdns. Ashf —5E 112
Aspen Gdns. Mitc —5E 138
Aspen Grn. Eri —3F 93
Aspen Ho. Sidc —3A 128
Aspen La. N'holt —3C 60
Aspenlea Rd. W6 —6F 83
Aspen Lodge. W8 —3K 83
Aspen Way. E14 —7D 70
Aspen Way. Felt —3K 113
Aspern Gro. NW3 —5C 48
Aspinall Rd. SE4 —3K 105
Aspinden Rd. SE16 —4H 87
Aspley Rd. SW18 —5K 101
Asplins Rd. N17 —1G 33
Asquith Clo. Dag —1C 56
Assam St. E1 —6G 69
Assata M. N1 —6B 50
Assembly Pas. E1 —5J 69
Assembly Wlk. Cars —7C 138
Ass Ho. La. Harr —4A 10
Astall Clo. Harr —1J 25
Astbury Ho. SE11 —2J 173
Astbury Rd. SE15 —1J 105
Astell St. SW3 —5C 84 (5D 170)
Aste St. E14 —2E 88
Astey's Row. N1 —7C 50
Asthall Gdns. Ilf —4G 37
Astins Ho. E17 —4D 34
Astleham Rd. Shep —3A 130
Astle St. SW11 —2E 102
Astley Av. NW2 —5E 46
Astley Ho. SE1 —5F 87
(off Rowcross St.)
Aston Av. Harr —7C 26
Aston Clo. Sidc —3A 128
Aston Ct. Wfd G —6D 20
Aston Grn. Houn —2A 96
Aston Ho. SW8 —1H 103
Aston Ho. W11 —7H 65
(off Westbourne Gro.)
Aston M. Romf —7C 38
Aston Pl. SW16 —6B 122
Aston Rd. SW20 —2E 136
Aston Rd. W5 —6D 62
Aston St. E14 —5A 70
Aston Ter. SW12 —6F 103
Astonville St. SW18 —1J 119
Astor Av. Romf —6J 39
Astor Clo. King T —6H 117
Astoria Mans. SW16 —3J 121
Astoria Wlk. SW9 —3A 104
Astrid Ho. Felt —2A 114
Astrop M. W6 —3E 82
Astrop Ter. W6 —2E 82
Astwood M. SW7 —4A 84
Asylum Rd. SE15 —7H 87
Atalanta St. SW6 —7F 83
Atbara Rd. Tedd —6B 116
Atcham Rd. Houn —4G 97
Atcost Rd. Bark —5A 74
Atcraft Cen. Wemb —1E 62
Atheldene Rd. SW18 —1K 119
Athelney St. SE6 —3C 124
Athelstane Gro. E3 —2B 70
Athelstane M. N4 —1A 50
Athelstan Gdns. NW6 —7G 47
Athelstan Rd. King T —4F 135
Athelstan Way. Orp —1K 145
Athelstone Rd. Harr —2H 25
Athena Clo. Harr —2H 43
Athena Clo. King T —3F 135
Athenaeum Ct. N5 —4C 50
Athenaeum Pl. N10 —3F 31
Athenaeum Rd. N20 —1F 15
Athena Pl. N'wd —1H 23
Athenia Ho. E14 —6F 71
Athenlay Rd. SE15 —5K 105
Athens Gdns. W9 —4J 65
(off Harrow Rd.)
Atherden Rd. E5 —4J 51
Atherfold Rd. SW9 —3J 103
Atherley Way. Houn —7D 96
Atherstone Ct. W2 —5K 65
(off Delamere Ter.)
Atherstone M. SW7 —4A 84
Atherton Dri. SW19 —4F 119
Atherton Heights. Wemb —6C 44
Atherton M. E7 —6H 53
Atherton Pl. Harr —3H 25
Atherton Pl. S'hall —7E 60
Atherton Rd. E7 —6H 53
Atherton Rd. SW13 —7C 82
Atherton Rd. Ilf —2C 36
Atherton St. SW11 —2C 102
Athlone Clo. E5 —5H 51
Athlone Ct. E17 —3F 35
Athlone Rd. SW2 —7K 103
Athlone St. NW5 —6E 48
Athlon Ind. Est. Wemb —1D 62
Athlon Rd. Wemb —2D 62
Athol Clo. Pinn —1K 23
Athole Gdns. Enf —5K 7
Athol Gdns. Pinn —1K 23
Atholl Ho. W9 —3A 66
(off Maida Va.)
Atholl Rd. Ilf —7A 38
Athol Rd. Eri —5J 93
Athol Sq. E14 —6E 70
Athol Way. Uxb —3C 58
Atkin Building. WC1 —5K 67
(off Raymond Bldgs.)
Atkins Dri. W W'ck —2F 155
Atkinson Ct. E10 —7D 34
(off Kings Clo.)
Atkinson Ho. E2 —2G 69
(off Pritchards Rd.)
Atkinson Ho. E13 —4H 71
(off Sutton Rd.)
Atkinson Ho. SE17 —4D 86
(off Catesby St.)
Atkinson Rd. E16 —5A 72
Atkins Rd. E10 —6D 34
Atkins Rd. SW12 —7G 103
Atlantic Ct. E14 —7F 71
Atlantic Rd. SW9 —4A 104
Atlas Bus. Cen. NW2 —1D 46
Atlas Gdns. SE7 —4A 90
Atlas M. E8 —6F 51
Atlas M. N7 —6K 49
Atlas Rd. E13 —2J 71
Atlas Rd. N11 —7K 15
Atlas Rd. NW10 —3A 64
Atlas Rd. Wemb —4J 45
Atlas Wharf. E9 —6C 52
Atley Rd. E3 —1C 70
Atlip Rd. Wemb —1E 62
Atney Rd. SW15 —4G 101
Atterbury Rd. N4 —6A 32
Atterbury St. SW1 —4J 85 (4D 172)
Attewood Av. NW10 —3A 46
Attewood Rd. N'holt —6C 42
Attfield Clo. N20 —2G 15
Attilburgh Ho. SE1 —3F 87 (7J 169)
(off Abbey St.)
Attleborough Ct. SE26 —2G 123
Attle Clo. Uxb —2C 58
Attlee Clo. Hay —3K 59
Attlee Clo. T Hth —5C 140
Attlee Rd. SE28 —7B 74
Attlee Rd. Hay —3J 59
Attlee Ter. E17 —4D 34
Attneave St. EC1 —3A 68 (2J 161)
Atwater Clo. SW2 —1A 122
Atwell Clo. E10 —6D 34
Atwell Pl. Th Dit —7K 133
Atwell Rd. SE15 —2G 105
Atwood Av. Rich —2G 99
Atwood Rd. W6 —4D 82
Atwoods All. Rich —1G 99
Aubert Ct. N5 —4B 50
Aubert Pk. N5 —4B 50
Aubert Rd. N5 —4B 50
Aubrey Beardsley Ho. SW1 —4G 85 (4B 172)
(off Vauxhall Bri. Rd.)
Aubrey Mans. NW1 —5C 66 (5C 158)
(off Lisson St.)
Aubrey Moore Point. E15 —2E 70
(off Abbey La.)
Aubrey Pl. NW8 —2A 66
Aubrey Rd. E17 —3C 34
Aubrey Rd. N8 —5J 31
Aubrey Rd. W8 —1H 83
Aubrey Wlk. W8 —1H 83
Auburn Clo. SE14 —7A 88
Aubyn Hill. SE27 —4C 122
Aubyn Sq. SW15 —5C 100
Auckland Clo. SE19 —1F 141
Auckland Ct. Hay —4A 60
Auckland Gdns. SE19 —1E 140
Auckland Hill. SE27 —4C 122
Auckland Ho. W12 —7D 64
(off White City Est.)
Auckland Ri. SE19 —1E 140
Auckland Rd. E10 —3D 52
Auckland Rd. SE19 —1F 141
Auckland Rd. SW11 —4C 102
Auckland Rd. Ilf —1F 55
Auckland Rd. King T —4F 135
Auckland St. SE11 —5K 85 (6G 173)
Audax. NW9 —2B 28
Auden Pl. NW1 —1E 66
(in two parts)
Auden Pl. Cheam —4E 148
Audleigh Pl. Chig —6K 21
Audley Clo. N10 —7A 16
Audley Clo. SW11 —3E 102
Audley Ct. E18 —4H 35
Audley Ct. N'holt —3A 60
Audley Ct. Pinn —2A 24
Audley Ct. Twic —3H 115
Audley Dri. E16 —1K 89
Audley Gdns. Ilf —2K 55
Audley Pl. Sutt —7K 149
Audley Rd. NW4 —5C 28
Audley Rd. W5 —5F 63
Audley Rd. Enf —2G 7
Audley Rd. Rich —5F 99
Audley Sq. W1 —1E 84 (4H 165)
Audrey Clo. Beck —6D 142
Audrey Gdns. Wemb —2B 44
Audrey Rd. Ilf —3F 55
Audrey St. E2 —2G 69
Audric Clo. King T —1G 135
Augurs La. E13 —3K 71
Augusta Clo. W Mol —4D 132
Augusta Rd. Twic —2G 115
Augusta St. E14 —6D 70
Augustine Rd. W14 —3F 83
Augustine Rd. Harr —1F 25
Augustus Clo. W12 —2D 82
Augustus Clo. Bren —7C 80
Augustus Ct. SW16 —2H 121
Augustus Ct. Felt —4D 114
Augustus Ho. NW1 —2G 67 (1A 160)
(off Augustus St.)
Augustus Rd. SW19 —1F 119
Augustus St. NW1 —2F 67 (1K 159)
Aultone Way. Cars —3D 150
Aultone Way. Sutt —2K 149
Aulton Pl. SE11 —5A 86 (6K 173)
Aurelia Gdns. Croy —5K 139
Aurelia Rd. Croy —6J 139
Auriel Av. Dag —6K 57
Auriga M. N1 —5D 50
Auriol Clo. Wor Pk —3A 148
Auriol Dri. Gnfd —7H 43
Auriol Dri. Uxb —6C 40
Auriol Pk. Rd. Wor Pk —3A 148
Auriol Rd. W14 —4G 83
Aurora Ho. E14 —6D 70
Austell Gdns. NW7 —3F 13
Austen Clo. SE28 —1B 92
Austen Ho. NW6 —3J 65
(off Cambridge Rd.)
Austen Rd. Eri —7H 93
Austen Rd. Harr —2F 43
Austin Av. Brom —5C 144
Austin Clo. SE23 —7A 106
Austin Clo. Twic —5C 98
Austin Ct. E6 —1A 72
Austin Ct. SE15 —3G 105
(off Philip Wlk.)
Austin Ct. Enf —5K 7
Austin Friars. EC2 —6D 68 (7F 163)
(in two parts)
Austin Friars Pas. EC2 —7F 163
Austin Friars Sq. EC2 —7F 163
Austin Rd. SW11 —1E 102
Austin Rd. Hay —2H 77
Austin's La. Uxb —3E 40
(in two parts)
Austin St. E2 —3F 69 (2J 163)
Austin Ter. SE1 —3A 86 (1K 173)
Austral Clo. Sidc —3K 127
Australia Rd. W12 —7D 64
Austral St. SE11 —4B 86 (3K 173)
Austyn Gdns. Surb —1H 147
Autumn Clo. SW19 —6A 120
Autumn Clo. Enf —1B 8
Autumn St. E3 —1C 70
Avalon Clo. SW20 —2G 137
Avalon Clo. W13 —5A 62
Avalon Clo. Enf —2F 7
Avalon Rd. SW6 —1K 101
Avalon Rd. W13 —4A 62
Avarn Rd. SW17 —6D 120
Avebury Ct. N1 —1D 68
(off Imber St.)
Avebury Pk. Surb —7D 134
Avebury Rd. E11 —1F 53
Avebury Rd. SW19 —1H 137
Avebury St. N1 —1D 68
Aveley Mans. Bark —7F 55
(off Whiting Av.)
Aveley Rd. Romf —4K 39
Aveline St. SE11 —5A 86 (5H 173)
Aveling Pk. Rd. E17 —2C 34
Ave Maria La. EC4 —6B 68 (1B 168)
Avenell Rd. N5 —3B 50
Avenfield Ho. W1 —7D 66 (2F 165)
(off Park La.)
Avening Rd. SW18 —7J 101
Avening Ter. SW18 —7J 101
Avenons Rd. E13 —4J 71
Avenue Clo. N14 —6B 6
Avenue Clo. NW8 —1C 66
(in two parts)
Avenue Clo. Houn —1K 95
Avenue Clo. W Dray —3A 76
Avenue Ct. N14 —6B 6
Avenue Ct. NW2 —3H 47
Avenue Ct. SW3 —4D 84 (4E 170)
(off Draycott Av.)
Avenue Cres. W3 —2H 81
Avenue Cres. Houn —1K 95
Avenue Elmers. Surb —5E 134
Avenue Gdns. SE25 —2G 141
Avenue Gdns. SW14 —3A 100
Avenue Gdns. W3 —2H 81
Avenue Gdns. Houn —7K 77
Avenue Gdns. Tedd —7K 115
Avenue Ho. NW8 —2C 66
(off Allitsen Rd.)
Avenue Ind. Est. E4 —6G 19
Avenue Lodge. NW8 —7B 48
(off Avenue Rd.)
Avenue Mans. NW3 —5K 47
(off Finchley Rd.)
Avenue M. N10 —3F 31
Avenue Pde. N21 —7J 7
Avenue Pde. Sun —3K 131
Avenue Pk. Rd. SE27 —2B 122
Avenue Rd. E7 —4K 53
Avenue Rd. N6 —7G 31
Avenue Rd. N12 —4F 15
Avenue Rd. N14 —7B 6
Avenue Rd. N15 —5D 32
Avenue Rd. NW3 & NW8 —7B 48
Avenue Rd. NW10 —2B 64
Avenue Rd. SE25 —2F 141
Avenue Rd. SW16 —2H 139
Avenue Rd. SW20 —2D 136
Avenue Rd. W3 —2H 81
Avenue Rd. SE20 & Beck —1J 141
Avenue Rd. Belv —4J 93
Avenue Rd. Bexh —3E 110
Avenue Rd. Bren —5C 80
Avenue Rd. Chad H —1C 56
Avenue Rd. Eri —7J 93
Avenue Rd. Felt —3H 113
Avenue Rd. Hamp —1F 133
Avenue Rd. Iswth —1K 97
Avenue Rd. King T —3E 134
Avenue Rd. N Mald —4A 136
Avenue Rd. Pinn —3C 24
Avenue Rd. S'hall —1D 78
Avenue Rd. Tedd —7A 116
Avenue Rd. Wall —7G 151
Avenue Rd. Wfd G —6F 21
Avenue S. Surb —7G 135
Avenue Ter. N Mald —3J 135
Avenue, The. E4 —6A 20
Avenue, The. E11 —6K 35
Avenue, The. N3 —2J 29
Avenue, The. N8 —3A 32
Avenue, The. N10 —2G 31
Avenue, The. N11 —5A 16
Avenue, The. N17 —3D 32
Avenue, The. NW6 —1F 65
Avenue, The. SE9 —5D 108
Avenue, The. SE10 —7F 89
Avenue, The. SW4 —5E 102
Avenue, The. SW18 —7C 102
Avenue, The. W4 —3A 82
Avenue, The. W13 —6B 62
Avenue, The. Barn —3B 4
Avenue, The. Beck —1D 142
Avenue, The. Bex —7D 110
Avenue, The. Brom —3B 144
Avenue, The. Cars —7E 150
Avenue, The. Cran —1J 95
Avenue, The. Croy —3E 152
Avenue, The. Eps & Sutt —7D 148
Avenue, The. Hamp —6D 114
Avenue, The. Harr —1K 25
Avenue, The. Houn —5F 97
Avenue, The. Ick —4C 40
Avenue, The. Kes —4B 156
Avenue, The. Pinn —7D 24
Avenue, The. Rich —2F 99
Avenue, The. Romf —4K 39
Avenue, The. St P —7B 128
Avenue, The. Sun —1K 131
Avenue, The. Surb —6F 135
Avenue, The. Sutt —7G 149
Avenue, The. Twic —5B 98
Avenue, The. Wemb —1E 44
Avenue, The. W W'ck —7G 143
Avenue, The. Wor Pk —2B 148
Averil Gro. SW16 —6B 122
Averill St. W6 —6F 83
Avern Gdns. W Mol —4F 133
Avern Rd. W Mol —4F 133
Avery Farm Row. SW1 —4E 84 (4J 171)
Avery Gdns. Ilf —5D 36
Avery Hill. —6H 109
Avery Hill Rd. SE9 —6H 109
Avery Row. W1 —7F 67 (2J 165)
Avia Pk. Felt —1D 112
Aviary Clo. E16 —5H 71
Aviemore Clo. Beck —5B 142
Aviemore Way. Beck —5A 142
Avignon Rd. SE4 —3K 105
Avington Ct. SE1 —4E 86
(off Old Kent Rd.)
Avington Gro. SE20 —7J 123
Avington Way. SE15 —7F 87
Avion Cres. NW9 —1C 28
Avis Sq. E1 —6K 69
Avoca Rd. SW17 —4E 120
Avocet Clo. SE1 —5G 87
Avocet M. SE28 —3H 91
Avon Clo. Hay —4A 60
Avon Clo. Sutt —4A 150
Avon Clo. Wor Pk —2C 148
Avon Ct. E4 —1K 19
Avon Ct. N12 —5E 14
Avon Ct. Buck H —1E 20
Avon Ct. Gnfd —4F 61
Avondale Av. N12 —5E 14
Avondale Av. NW2 —3A 46
Avondale Av. Barn —1J 15
Avondale Av. Esh —3A 146
Avondale Av. Wor Pk —1B 148
Avondale Ct. E11 —1G 53
Avondale Ct. E16 —5G 71
Avondale Ct. E18 —1K 35
Avondale Cres. Enf —3F 9
Avondale Cres. Ilf —5B 36
Avondale Dri. Hay —1J 77
Avondale Gdns. Houn —5D 96
Avondale Ho. SE1 —5G 87
(off Avondale Sq.)
Avondale Pk. Gdns. W11 —7G 65
Avondale Pk. Rd. W11 —7G 65
Avondale Ri. SE15 —3F 105
Avondale Rd. E16 —5G 71
Avondale Rd. E17 —7C 34
Avondale Rd. N3 —1A 30
Avondale Rd. N13 —2F 17
Avondale Rd. N15 —5B 32
Avondale Rd. SE9 —2C 126
Avondale Rd. SW14 —3A 100
Avondale Rd. SW19 —5K 119
Avondale Rd. Ashf —3A 112
Avondale Rd. Brom —6G 125
Avondale Rd. Harr —3K 25
Avondale Rd. S Croy —6C 152
Avondale Rd. Well —2C 110
Avondale Sq. SE1 —5G 87
Avonfield Ct. E17 —2F 35
Avon Ho. W8 —3J 83
(off Allen St.)
Avon Ho. W14 —4H 83
(off Avonmore Rd.)
Avon Ho. King T —1D 134
Avonhurst Ho. NW2 —7G 47
Avonley Rd. SE14 —7J 87
Avon M. Pinn —1D 24
Avonmore Gdns. W14 —4H 83
Avonmore Pl. W14 —4G 83
(off Avonmore Rd.)
Avonmore Rd. W14 —4G 83
Avonmouth St. SE1 —3C 86 (7C 168)
Avon Path. S Croy —6C 152
Avon Pl. SE1 —2C 86 (7D 168)
Avon Rd. E17 —3F 35
Avon Rd. SE4 —3C 106
Avon Rd. Gnfd —4E 60
Avon Rd. Sun —7H 113
Avon Way. E18 —3J 35
Avonwick Rd. Houn —2F 97
Avril Way. E4 —5K 19
Avro Way. Wall —7J 151
Awlfield Av. N17 —1D 32
Awliscombe Rd. Well —2K 109
Axe St. Bark —1G 73
(in two parts)
Axholme Av. Edgw —1G 27
Axminster Cres. Well —1C 110
Axminster Rd. N7 —3J 49
Aybrook St. W1 —5E 66 (6G 159)
Aycliffe Clo. Brom —4D 144
Aycliffe Rd. W12 —1C 82
Ayerst Ct. E10 —7E 34
Aylands Clo. Wemb —2E 44
Aylesbury Clo. E7 —6H 53
Aylesbury Ct. Sutt —3A 150
Aylesbury Ho. SE15 —6G 87
(off Friary Est.)
Aylesbury Rd. SE17 —5D 86
Aylesbury Rd. Brom —3J 143
Aylesbury St. EC1 —4B 68 (4A 162)
Aylesbury St. NW10 —3K 45
Aylesford Av. Beck —5A 142
Aylesford Ho. SE1 —2D 86 (7F 169)
(off Long La.)
Aylesford St. SW1 —5H 85 (5C 172)
Aylesham Cen., The. SE15 —1G 105
Aylesham Clo. NW7 —7H 13
Aylesham Rd. Orp —7K 145
Ayles Rd. Hay & N'holt —3K 59
Aylestone Av. NW6 —7F 47
Aylett Rd. SE25 —4H 141
Aylett Rd. Iswth —2J 97
Ayley Cft. Enf —5B 8
Ayliffe Clo. King T —2G 135
Aylmer Clo. Stan —4F 11
Aylmer Ct. N2 —5D 30
Aylmer Dri. Stan —4F 11
Aylmer Ho. SE10 —5F 89
Aylmer Pde. N2 —5D 30
Aylmer Rd. E11 —1H 53
Aylmer Rd. N2 —5C 30
Aylmer Rd. W12 —2B 82
Aylmer Rd. Dag —3E 56
Ayloffe Rd. Dag —6F 57
Aylsham Dri. Uxb —2E 40
Aylton Est. SE16 —2J 87
Aylward Rd. SE23 —2K 123
Aylward Rd. SW20 —2H 137
Aylwards Ri. Stan —4F 11
Aylward St. E1 —6J 69
(in two parts)
Aylwin Est. SE1 —3E 86
Aynhoe Mans. W14 —4F 83
(off Aynhoe Rd.)
Aynhoe Rd. W14 —4F 83
Aynscombe Path. SW14 —2J 99
Ayr Ct. W3 —6G 63
Ayres Clo. E13 —3J 71
Ayres Cres. NW10 —7K 45
Ayres St. SE1 —2C 86 (6D 168)
Ayr Grn. Romf —1K 39
Ayrsome Rd. N16 —3E 50
Ayrton Rd. SW7 —3B 84 (1A 170)
Ayr Way. Romf —1K 39
Aysgarth Ct. Sutt —3K 149
Aysgarth Rd. SE21 —7E 104
Ayton Ho. SE5 —7D 86
(off Edmund St.)

Aytoun Pl.—Barningham Way

Aytoun Pl. SW9 —2K 103
Aytoun Rd. SW9 —2K 103
Azalea Clo. W7 —1K 79
Azalea Clo. Ilf —5F 55
Azalea Ct. W7 —1K 79
Azalea Ct. Wfd G —6B 20
Azalea Wlk. Pinn —5K 23
Azania M. NW5 —6F 49
Azenby Rd. SE15 —2F 105
Azof St. SE10 —4G 89

Baalbec Rd. N5 —5B 50
Babbacombe Clo. Chess —5D 146
Babbacombe Gdns. Ilf —4C 36
Babbacombe Rd. Brom —1J 143
Baber Bri. Cvn. Site. Felt —5A 96
Baber Dri. Felt —6A 96
Babington Ct. WC1 —5G 161
Babington Ho. SE1 —2C 86 (6D 168)
(off Disney St.)
Babington Ri. Wemb —6G 45
Babington Rd. NW4 —4D 28
Babington Rd. SW16 —5H 121
Babington Rd. Dag —5C 56
Babmaes St. SW1 —7H 67 (3C 166)
Bacchus Wlk. N1 —2E 68
(off Regan Way)
Bache's St. N1 —3D 68
Back All. EC3 —1H 169
Bk. Church La. E1 —6G 69
Back Hill. EC1 —4A 68 (4K 161)
Backhouse Pl. SE17 —4E 86
Back La. N8 —5J 31
Back La. NW3 —4A 48
Back La. Bark —1G 73
Back La. Bex —7G 111
Back La. Bren —6D 80
Back La. Edgw —1J 27
Back La. Rich —2C 116
(in two parts)
Back La. Romf —7D 38
Backley Gdns. SE25 —6G 141
Back Rd. Sidc —4A 128
Back Rd. Tedd —7J 115
Bacon Gro. SE1 —3F 87
Bacon La. NW9 —4H 27
Bacon La. Edgw —1G 27
Bacons La. N6 —1E 48
Bacon St. E1 & E2 —4F 69 (3K 163)
Bacon Ter. Dag —5B 56
Bacton St. E2 —3J 69
Baddesley Ho. SE11 —5H 173
Baddow Clo. Dag —1G 75
Baddow Clo. Wfd G —6G 21
Baddow Wlk. N1 —1C 68
(off New N. Rd.)
Baden Pl. SE1 —2D 86 (6E 168)
Baden Powell Clo. Dag —1E 74
Baden Powell Clo. Surb —2F 147
Baden Powell Ho. SW7 —2A 170
Baden Powell Ho. Belv —3G 93
Baden Rd. N8 —4H 31
Baden Rd. Ilf —5F 55
Badger Clo. Felt —3K 113
Badger Clo. Houn —3A 96
Badger Clo. Ilf —6G 37
Badger Ct. NW2 —3E 46
Badgers Clo. Ashf —5B 112
Badgers Clo. Enf —3G 7
Badgers Clo. Harr —6H 25
Badgers Clo. Hay —7G 59
Badgers Copse. Wor Pk —2B 148
Badgers Cft. N20 —7B 4
Badgers Cft. SE9 —3E 126
Badgers Hole. Croy —4K 153
Badgers Wlk. N Mald —2A 136
Badlis Rd. E17 —3C 34
Badminton Clo. Harr —4J 25
Badminton Clo. N'holt —6E 42
Badminton M. E16 —1J 89
Badminton Rd. SW12 —6E 102
Badsworth Rd. SE5 —1C 104
Baffin Way. E14 —1E 88
(off Blackwall Way)
Bagley Clo. W Dray —2A 76
Bagley's La. SW6 —1K 101
Bagleys Spring. Romf —4E 38
Bagnigge Ho. WC1 —3A 68 (2J 161)
(off Margery St.)
Bagshot Ct. SE18 —1E 108
Bagshot Ho. NW1 —1K 159
Bagshot Rd. Enf —7A 8
Bagshot St. SE17 —5E 86
Baildon St. SE8 —7B 88
Bailey Clo. E4 —4K 19
Bailey Clo. N11 —7C 16
Bailey M. W4 —6H 81
(off Hervert Gdns.)
Bailey Pl. SE26 —6K 123
Baillies Wlk. W5 —2D 80
Bainbridge Clo. Rich —5E 116
Bainbridge Rd. Dag —4F 57
Bainbridge St. WC1 —6H 67 (7D 160)
Baines Clo. S Croy —5D 152
Baird Av. S'hall —7F 61
Baird Clo. E10 —1C 52
Baird Clo. NW9 —6J 27
Baird Gdns. SE19 —4E 122
Baird Ho. W12 —7D 64
(off White City Est.)
Baird Memorial Cotts. N14 —2C 16
(off Balaams La.)
Baird Rd. Enf —3C 8
Baird St. EC1 —4C 68 (3D 162)
Baizdon Rd. SE3 —2G 107
Baker Beal Ct. Bexh —3H 111
Baker Ho. W7 —1K 79
Baker La. Mitc —2E 138
Baker Pass. NW10 —1A 64
Baker Rd. NW10 —1A 64
Baker Rd. SE18 —7C 90
Bakers Av. E17 —6D 34
Bakers Ct. SE25 —3E 140
Bakers End. SW20 —2G 137
Baker's Fld. N7 —4J 49
Bakers Gdns. Cars —2C 150
Bakers Hall Ct. EC3 —3G 169
Bakers Hill. E5 —1J 51
Bakers Hill. New Bar —2E 4
Bakers Ho. W5 —1D 80
(off Grove, The)
Bakers La. N6 —6D 30
Baker's M. W1 —6E 66 (7G 159)
Bakers Pas. NW3 —4A 48
(off Heath St.)
Baker's Rents. E2 —3F 69 (2J 163)
Baker's Row. E15 —2G 71
Baker's Row. EC1 —4A 68 (4J 161)
Baker Street. (Junct.) —5D 66
Baker St. NW1 & W1 —4D 66 (4F 159)
Baker St. Enf —3J 7
Baker's Yd. EC1 —4J 161
Bakery Clo. SW9 —7K 85
Bakery M. Surb —1G 147
Bakery Path. Edgw —6C 12
(off St Margaret's Rd.)
Bakery Pl. SW11 —4D 102
Bakewell Way. N Mald —2A 136
Balaam Ho. Sutt —4J 149
Balaams La. N14 —2C 16
Balaam St. E13 —4J 71
Balaclava Rd. SE1 —4F 87
Balaclava Rd. Surb —7C 134
Balcaskie Rd. SE9 —5D 108
Balchen Rd. SE3 —2B 108
Balchier Rd. SE22 —6H 105
Balcombe Clo. Bexh —4D 110
Balcombe Ho. NW1 —4C 66 (3E 158)
(off Taunton Pl.)
Balcombe St. NW1 —4D 66 (3E 158)
Balcon Ct. W5 —6F 63
Balcorne St. E9 —7J 51
Balder Ri. SE12 —2K 125
Balderton Flats. W1 —6E 66 (1H 165)
(off Balderton St.)
Balderton St. W1 —6E 66 (1H 165)
Baldewyne Ct. N17 —1G 33
Baldock St. E3 —2D 70
Baldry Gdns. SW16 —6J 121
Baldwin Cres. SE5 —1C 104
Baldwin Gdns. Houn —1G 97
Baldwin Ho. SW2 —1A 122
Baldwin's Gdns. EC1 —5A 68 (5J 161)
Baldwin St. EC1 —3D 68 (2E 162)
Baldwin Ter. N1 —2C 68
Baldwyn Gdns. W3 —7K 63
Baldwyn's Pk. Bex —2K 129
Baldwyn's Rd. Bex —2K 129
Bale Rd. E1 —5A 70
Bales Ter. N9 —3A 18
Balfern Gro. W4 —5A 82
Balfern St. SW11 —2C 102
Balfe St. N1 —2J 67
Balforn Tower. E14 —6E 70
Balfour Av. W7 —1K 79
Balfour Bus. Cen. S'hall —3A 78
Balfour Gro. N20 —3J 15
Balfour Ho. W10 —5F 65
(off St Charles Sq.)
Balfour M. N9 —3B 18
Balfour M. W1 —1E 84 (4H 165)
Balfour Pl. SW15 —4D 100
Balfour Pl. W1 —7E 66 (3H 165)
Balfour Rd. N5 —4C 50
Balfour Rd. SE25 —5G 141
Balfour Rd. SW19 —7K 119
Balfour Rd. W3 —5J 63
Balfour Rd. W13 —2A 80
Balfour Rd. Brom —5B 144
Balfour Rd. Cars —7D 150
Balfour Rd. Harr —5H 25
Balfour Rd. Houn —3F 97
Balfour Rd. Ilf —2F 55
Balfour Rd. S'hall —3B 78
Balfour St. SE17 —4D 86
Balfour Ter. N3 —2K 29
Balfron Tower. E14 —6E 70
Balgonie Rd. E4 —1A 20
Balgowan Clo. N Mald —5A 136
Balgowan Rd. Beck —3A 142
Balgowan St. SE18 —4K 91
Balham. —1F 121
Balham Continental Mkt. SW12 —1F 121
(off Shipka Rd.)
Balham Gro. SW12 —7E 102
Balham High Rd. SW17 & SW12 —3E 120
Balham Hill. SW12 —7F 103
Balham New Rd. SW12 —7F 103
Balham Pk. Rd. SW12 —1D 120
Balham Rd. N9 —2B 18
Balham Sta. Rd. SW12 —1F 121
Balin Ho. SE1 —2D 86 (6E 168)
(off Long La.)
Balkan Wlk. E1 —7H 69
Balladier Wlk. E14 —5D 70
Ballamore Rd. Brom —3J 125
Ballance Rd. E9 —6K 51
Ballantine St. SW18 —4A 102
Ballantrae Ho. NW2 —4H 47
Ballard Clo. King T —7K 117
Ballards Clo. Dag —1H 75
Ballards Farm Rd. S Croy & Croy —6G 153
(in two parts)
Ballards La. N3 & N12 —1J 29
Ballards M. Edgw —6B 12
Ballards Ri. S Croy —6G 153
Ballards Rd. NW2 —2C 46
Ballards Rd. Dag —2H 75
Ballards Way. S Croy & Croy —6G 153
Ballast Quay. SE10 —5F 89
Ballater Rd. SW2 —4J 103
Ballater Rd. S Croy —5F 153
Ball Ct. EC3 —6D 68 (1F 169)
(off Cornhill)
Ballina St. SE23 —7K 105
Ballin Ct. E14 —2E 88
Ballingdon Rd. SW11 —6E 102
Balliol Av. E4 —4B 20
Balliol Rd. N17 —1E 32
Balliol Rd. W10 —6E 64
Balliol Rd. Well —2B 110
Balloch Rd. SE6 —1F 125
Ballogie Av. NW10 —4A 46
Ballow Clo. SE5 —7E 86
Ball's Pond Pl. N1 —6D 50
Balls Pond Rd. N1 —6D 50
Balmain Clo. W5 —1D 80
Balmain Ct. Houn —1F 97
Balmer Rd. E3 —2B 70
Balmes Rd. N1 —1D 68
Balmoral Av. N11 —6K 15
Balmoral Av. Beck —4A 142
Balmoral Clo. SW15 —6F 101
Balmoral Ct. SE12 —4K 125
Balmoral Ct. SE27 —4C 122
Balmoral Ct. Sutt —7J 149
Balmoral Ct. Wemb —3F 45
Balmoral Ct. Wor Pk —2D 148
Balmoral Cres. W Mol —3E 132
Balmoral Dri. Hay —4G 59
Balmoral Dri. S'hall —4D 60
Balmoral Gdns. W13 —3A 80
Balmoral Gdns. Bex —7F 111
Balmoral Gdns. Ilf —1K 55
Balmoral Gro. N7 —6K 49
Balmoral Ho. E14 —3D 88
Balmoral Ho. W14 —4G 83
(off Windsor Way)
Balmoral M. W12 —3B 82
Balmoral Rd. E7 —4A 54
Balmoral Rd. E10 —2D 52
Balmoral Rd. NW2 —6D 46
Balmoral Rd. Harr —4E 42
Balmoral Rd. King T —4F 135
Balmoral Rd. Wor Pk —3D 148
Balmoral Trad. Est. Bark —5K 73
Balmore Cres. Barn —5K 5
Balmore St. N19 —2F 49
Balmuir Gdns. SW15 —4E 100
Balnacraig Av. NW10 —4A 46
Balniel Ga. SW1 —5H 85 (5D 172)
Balsam Ho. E14 —7D 70
Baltic Cen., The. Bren —5D 80
Baltic Clo. SW19 —7B 120
Baltic Ct. SE16 —2K 87
Baltic Ho. SE5 —2C 104
Baltic Pl. N1 —1E 68
Baltic St. E. EC1 —4C 68 (4C 162)
Baltic St. W. EC1 —4C 68 (4C 162)
Baltimore Ho. SE11 —5J 173
Baltimore Pl. Well —2K 109
Balvaird Pl. SW1 —5H 85 (6D 172)
Balvernie Gro. SW18 —7H 101
Balvernie M. SW18 —7J 101
Bamber Ho. Bark —1H 73
Bamborough Gdns. W12 —2E 82
Bamburgh. N17 —7C 18
Bamford Av. Wemb —1F 63
Bamford Ct. E15 —5D 52
Bamford Rd. Bark —6G 55
Bamford Rd. Brom —5E 124
Bampfylde Clo. Wall —3G 151
Bampton Ct. W5 —6D 62
Bampton Dri. NW7 —7H 13
Bampton Rd. SE23 —3K 123
Banavie Gdns. Beck —1E 142
Banbury Clo. Enf —1G 7
Banbury Ct. WC2 —2E 166
Banbury Ct. Sutt —7J 149
Banbury Ho. E9 —7K 51
Banbury Rd. E9 —7K 51
Banbury Rd. E17 —7E 18
Banbury St. SW11 —2C 102
Banbury Wlk. N'holt —2E 60
(off Brabazon Rd.)
Banchory Rd. SE3 —7K 89
Bancroft Av. N2 —5C 30
Bancroft Av. Buck H —2D 20
Bancroft Clo. Ashf —5C 112
Bancroft Ct. SW8 —7J 85
(off Allen Edwards Dri.)
Bancroft Ct. N'holt —1A 60
Bancroft Gdns. Harr —1G 25
Bancroft Gdns. Orp —7K 145
Bancroft Rd. E1 —3J 69
Bancroft Rd. Harr —2G 25
Bandon Clo. Uxb —2B 58
Bandonhill. —5H 151
Bandon Ri. Wall —5H 151
Bangalore St. SW15 —3E 100
Bangor Clo. N'holt —5F 43
Banim St. W6 —4D 82
Banister Ho. E9 —5K 51
Banister Ho. W10 —3G 65
(off Bruckner St.)
Banister Rd. W10 —3F 65
Bank Av. Mitc —2B 138
Bank Bldgs. E4 —6A 20
(off Avenue, The)
Bank End. SE1 —1C 86 (4D 168)
Bankfoot Rd. Brom —4G 125
Bankhurst Rd. SE6 —7B 106
Bank La. SW15 —5A 100
Bank La. King T —7E 116
Bank M. Sutt —6A 150
Bank of England. —6D 68 (1E 168)
Bank of England Mus. —1F 169
Bank of England Offices. EC4 —6C 68
(off New Change)
Banks Ho. SE1 —3C 86
(off Rockingham St.)
Banksian Wlk. Iswth —1J 97
Banksia Rd. N18 —5D 18
Bankside. SE1 —7C 68 (3C 168)
(in two parts)
Bankside. Enf —1G 7
Bankside. S'hall —1B 78
Bankside. S Croy —6F 153
Bankside Art Gallery. —7B 68 (3B 168)
Bankside Av. N'holt —2J 59
Bankside Clo. Bex —4K 129
Bankside Clo. Cars —6C 150
Bankside Clo. Iswth —4K 97
Bankside Dri. Th Dit —1B 146
Bankside Rd. Ilf —5G 55
Bankside Way. SE19 —6E 122
Banks La. Bexh —4F 111
Banks Way. E12 —3E 54
Bank, The. N6 —1F 49
Bankton Rd. SW2 —4A 104
Bankwell Rd. SE13 —4G 107
Bannerman Ho. SW8 —6K 85 (7G 173)
Banner St. EC1 —4C 68 (4D 162)
Banning St. SE10 —5G 89
Bannister Clo. SW2 —1A 122
Bannister Clo. Gnfd —5H 43
Bannockburn Rd. SE18 —4J 91
Banqueting House. —1J 85 (5E 166)
Banstead Gdns. N9 —3K 17
Banstead Rd. Cars —7B 150
Banstead Rd. S. Sutt —7B 150
Banstead St. SE15 —3J 105
Banstead Way. Wall —5J 151
Banstock Rd. Edgw —6C 12
Banting Dri. N21 —5E 6
Banting Ho. NW2 —3C 46
Bantock Ho. W10 —3G 65
(off Third Av.)
Banton Clo. Enf —2C 8
Bantry St. SE5 —7D 86
Banwell Rd. Bex —6D 110
Banyard Rd. SE16 —3H 87
Baptist Gdns. NW5 —6E 48
Barandon Wlk. W11 —7F 65
Barbara Brosnan Ct. NW8 —2B 66 (1A 158)
Barbara Clo. Shep —5D 130
Barbara Hucklesby Clo. N22 —2B 32
Barbauld Rd. N16 —3E 50
Barber Clo. N21 —7F 7
Barbers All. E13 —3K 71
Barbers Rd. E15 —2D 70
Barbican. EC2 —5C 68
(off Beech St.)
Barbican Arts Cen. —5C 68 (5D 162)
Barbican Rd. Gnfd —6F 61
Barb M. W6 —3E 82
Barbon Clo. WC1 —5K 67 (5F 161)
Barbot Clo. N9 —3B 18
Barchard St. SW18 —5K 101
Barchester Clo. W7 —1K 79
Barchester Rd. Harr —2H 25
Barchester St. E14 —5D 70
Barclay Clo. SW6 —7J 83
Barclay Oval. Wfd G —4D 20
Barclay Path. E17 —5E 34
Barclay Rd. E11 —1H 53
Barclay Rd. E13 —4A 72
Barclay Rd. E17 —5E 34
Barclay Rd. N18 —6J 17
Barclay Rd. SW6 —7J 83
Barclay Rd. Croy —3D 152
Barclay Way. SE22 —1G 123
Barcombe Av. SW2 —2J 121
Barcombe Clo. Orp —3K 145
Bardell Ho. SE1 —2G 87 (7K 169)
(off Dickens Est.)
Barden St. SE18 —7J 91
Bardfield Av. Romf —3D 38
Bardney Rd. Mord —4K 137
Bardolph Rd. N7 —4J 49
Bardolph Rd. Rich —3F 99
Bard Rd. W10 —7F 65
Bardsey Wlk. N1 —6C 50
(off Douglas Rd. N.)
Bardsley Clo. Croy —3F 153
Bardsley La. SE10 —6E 88
Barfett St. W10 —4H 65
Barfield Av. N20 —2J 15
Barfield Rd. E11 —1H 53
Barfield Rd. Brom —3E 144
Barfleur Ho. SE8 —5B 88
Barford Clo. NW4 —2C 28
Barford St. N1 —1A 68
Barforth Rd. SE15 —3H 105
Barfreston Way. SE20 —1H 141
Bargate Clo. SE18 —5K 91
Bargate Clo. N Mald —7C 136
Barge Ho. Rd. E16 —2F 91
Barge Ho. St. SE1 —1A 86 (4K 167)
Bargery Rd. SE6 —1D 124
Barge Wlk. E Mol —3H 133
Barge Wlk. Hamp W —1D 134
Barge Wlk. King T —3D 134
Bargrove Clo. SE20 —7G 123
Bargrove Cres. SE6 —2B 124
Barham Clo. Brom —1C 156
Barham Clo. Chst —5F 127
Barham Clo. Romf —2H 39
Barham Clo. Wemb —6B 44
Barham Ho. SE17 —5E 86
(off Kinglake St.)
Barham Rd. SW20 —7C 118
Barham Rd. Chst —5F 127
Barham Rd. S Croy —4C 152
Baring Clo. SE12 —2J 125
Baring Ho. E14 —6C 70
Baring Rd. SE12 —7J 107
Baring Rd. Cockf —4G 5
Baring Rd. Croy —1G 153
Baring St. N1 —1D 68
Barker Clo. N Mald —4K 135
Barker Clo. N'wd —1H 23
Barker Dri. NW1 —7G 49
Barker M. SW4 —4F 103
Barkers Arc. W8 —2K 83
Barker St. SW10 —6A 84
Barker Wlk. SW16 —3H 121
Barker Way. SE22 —7G 105
Barkham Rd. N17 —7J 17
Barkham Ter. SE1 —1K 173
Barking. —7G 55
Barking Bus. Cen. Bark —3A 74
Barking Ind. Pk. Bark —1K 73
Barking Northern Relief Rd. Bark —7F 55
Barking Railway. —6H 55
Barking Rd. E13 & E6 —2A 72
Barking Rd. E16 & E13 —5H 71
Barkingside. —3G 37
Bark Pl. W2 —7K 65
Barkston Gdns. SW5 —4K 83
Barkway Ct. N4 —2C 50
Barkwood Clo. Romf —5J 39
Barkworth Rd. SE16 —5H 87
Barlborough St. SE14 —7K 87
Barlby Gdns. W10 —4F 65
Barlby Rd. W10 —5E 64
Barleycorn Way. E14 —7B 70
(in two parts)
Barleyfields Clo. Romf —6B 38
Barley La. Ilf & Romf —7A 38
Barley Mow Pas. EC1 —5B 162
Barley Mow Pas. W4 —5K 81
Barleymow Way. Shep —4C 130
Barley Shotts Bus. Pk. W10 —5H 65
Barlings Ho. SE4 —4K 105
(off Frendsbury Rd.)
Barlow Clo. Wall —6J 151
Barlow Dri. SE18 —1C 108
Barlow Ho. N1 —3D 68 (1E 162)
(off Provost Est.)
Barlow Ho. W11 —7G 65
(off Walmer Rd.)
Barlow Pl. W1 —7F 67 (3K 165)
Barlow Rd. NW6 —6H 47
Barlow Rd. W3 —1H 81
Barlow Rd. Hamp —7E 114
Barlow St. SE17 —4D 86
Barlow Way. Rain —5K 75
Barmeston Rd. SE6 —2D 124
Barmor Clo. Harr —2F 25
Barmouth Av. Gnfd —2K 61
Barmouth Rd. SW18 —6A 102
Barmouth Rd. Croy —2K 153
Barnabas Ct. N21 —4F 7
Barnabas Rd. E9 —5K 51
Barnaby Clo. Harr —2G 43
Barnaby Ct. NW9 —3A 28
Barnaby Ct. SE16 —2G 87
(off Scott Lidgett Cres.)
Barnaby Pl. SW7 —4A 170
Barnaby Way. Chig —3K 21
Barnard Clo. SE18 —4E 90
Barnard Clo. Chst —1H 145
Barnard Clo. Sun —7K 113
Barnard Clo. Wall —7H 151
Barnard Gdns. Hay —4K 59
Barnard Gdns. N Mald —4C 136
Barnard Gro. E15 —7H 53
Barnard Hill. N10 —1F 31
Barnard Lodge. W9 —5J 65
(off Admiral Wlk.)
Barnard Lodge. New Bar —4F 5
Barnard M. SW11 —4C 102
Barnardo Dri. Ilf —4G 37
Barnardo Gdns. E1 —7K 69
Barnardo St. E1 —6K 69
Barnardos Village. B'side —3G 37
Barnard Rd. SW11 —4C 102
Barnard Rd. Enf —2C 8
Barnard Rd. Mitc —3E 138
Barnard's Inn. EC4 —6K 161
Barnard's Wharf. SE16 —2B 88
Barnbrough. NW1 —1G 67
(off Camden St.)
Barnby Sq. E15 —1G 71
Barnby St. E15 —1G 71
Barnby St. NW1 —2G 67 (1B 160)
Barn Clo. NW5 —5H 49
(off Torriano Av.)
Barn Clo. Ashf —5D 112
Barn Clo. N'holt —2A 60
Barn Cres. Stan —6H 11
Barncroft Clo. Uxb —5D 58
Barnehurst. —3J 111
Barnehurst Av. Eri & Bexh —1J 111
Barnehurst Clo. Eri —1J 111
Barnehurst Rd. Bexh —2J 111
Barn Elms Pk. SW15 —3E 100
Barnes. —2B 100
Barnes All. Hamp —2G 133
Barnes Av. SW13 —7C 82
Barnes Av. S'hall —4D 78
Barnes Clo. E12 —4B 54
Barnes Ct. N1 —7A 50
Barnes Ct. Wfd G —5G 21
Barnes End. N Mald —5C 136
Barnes High St. SW13 —2B 100
Barnes Ho. Bark —1H 73
Barnes Pikle. W5 —7D 62
Barnes Rd. N18 —4D 18
Barnes St. E14 —6A 70
Barnes Ter. SE8 —5B 88
Barnes Wallis Ct. Wemb —3J 45
Barnet. —3B 4
Barnet Bus. Cen. Barn —3B 4
Barnet By-Pass. NW7 —6G 13
Barnet Dri. Brom —2C 156
Barnet F.C. —5D 4
Barnet Ga. La. Barn —1H 13
Barnet Gro. E2 —3G 69 (1K 163)
Barnet Hill. Barn —4C 4
Barnet Ho. N20 —2F 15
Barnet La. N20 & Barn —1C 14
Barnet Mus. —4B 4
Barnet Trad. Est. High Bar —3C 4
Barnetts Ct. Harr —3F 43
Barnett St. E1 —6H 69
Barnet Vale. —5E 4
Barnet Way. NW7 —3E 12
Barnet Wood Rd. Brom —2A 156
Barney Clo. SE7 —5A 90
Barn Fld. NW3 —5D 48
Barnfield. N Mald —6A 136
Barnfield Av. Croy —2J 153
Barnfield Av. King T —4D 116
Barnfield Av. Mitc —4F 139
Barnfield Clo. N4 —7J 31
Barnfield Clo. SW17 —3B 120
Barnfield Gdns. SE18 —6F 91
Barnfield Gdns. King T —4E 116
Barnfield Pl. E14 —4C 88
Barnfield Rd. SE18 —6F 91
(in two parts)
Barnfield Rd. W5 —4C 62
Barnfield Rd. Belv —6F 93
Barnfield Rd. Edgw —1J 27
Barnfield Rd. S Croy —7E 152
Barnfield Wood Clo. Beck —6F 143
Barnfield Wood Rd. Beck —6F 143
Barnham Dri. SE28 —1K 91
Barnham Rd. Gnfd —3G 61
Barnham St. SE1 —2E 86 (6H 169)
Barnhill. Pinn —5A 24
Barn Hill. Wemb —1G 45
Barnhill Av. Brom —5H 143
Barnhill La. Hay —3K 59
Barnhill Rd. Hay —3K 59
Barnhill Rd. Wemb —3J 45
Barningham Way. NW9 —6K 27

Barnlea Clo. Felt —2C 114
Barnmead Gdns. Dag —5F 57
Barnmead Rd. Beck —1K 141
Barnmead Rd. Dag —5F 57
Barn M. S Harr —3E 42
Barn Ri. Wemb —1G 45
Barnsbury. —7K 49
Barnsbury Clo. N Mald —4J 135
Barnsbury Cres. Surb —1J 147
Barnsbury Est. N1 —1K 67
(in two parts)
Barnsbury Gro. N7 —7K 49
Barnsbury Ho. SW4 —6H 103
Barnsbury La. Surb —2H 147
Barnsbury Pk. N1 —7A 50
Barnsbury Rd. N1 —2A 68
Barnsbury Sq. N1 —7A 50
Barnsbury St. N1 —7A 50
Barnsbury Ter. N1 —7K 49
Barnscroft. SW20 —3D 136
Barnsdale Av. E14 —4C 88
Barnsdale Rd. W9 —4H 65
Barnsley St. E1 —4H 69
Barnstable La. SE13 —4E 106
Barnstaple Ho. SE12 —5H 107
(off Taunton Rd.)
Barnstaple Rd. Ruis —3A 42
Barnston Wlk. N1 —1C 68
(off Popham St.)
Barn St. N16 —2E 50
Barn Way. Wemb —1G 45
Barnwell Rd. SW2 —5A 104
Barnwood Clo. W9 —4K 65
Barnwood Clo. Ruis —2F 41
Baron Clo. N11 —5K 15
Baroness Rd. E2 —3F 69 (1K 163)
Baronet Gro. N17 —1G 33
Baronet Rd. N17 —1G 33
Baron Gdns. Ilf —3G 37
Baron Gro. Mitc —4C 138
Baron Rd. Dag —1D 56
Baronsclere Ct. N6 —7G 31
Barons Court. —5G 83
Barons Ct. Ilf —2H 55
Barons Ct. Wall —3H 151
Baron's Ct. Rd. W14 —5G 83
Barons Court Theatre. —5G 83
Baronsfield Rd. Twic —6B 98
Barons Ga. W4 —3J 81
Barons Ga. Barn —6H 5
Barons Keep. W14 —5G 83
Barons Mead. Harr —4J 25
Baronsmead Rd. SW13 —1C 100
Baronsmede. W5 —2F 81
Baronsmere Ct. Barn —4B 4
Baronsmere Rd. N2 —4C 30
Baron's Pl. SE1 —2A 86 (7K 167)
Barons, The. Twic —6B 98
Baron St. N1 —2A 68
Baron's Wlk. Croy —6A 142
Baron Wlk. E16 —5H 71
Baron Wlk. Mitc —4C 138
Barque M. SE8 —6C 88
Barrack Rd. Houn —4B 96
Barra Hall Cir. Hay —7G 59
Barra Hall Rd. Hay —7G 59
Barratt Av. N22 —2K 31
Barratt Ho. N1 —7B 50
(off Sable St.)
Barratt Ind. Pk. E3 —4E 70
Barratt Ind. Pk. S'hall —2E 78
Barratt Way. Harr —2H 25
Barrenger Rd. N10 —1D 30
Barret Ho. NW6 —1J 65
Barret Ho. SW9 —3K 103
(off Benedict Rd.)
Barrett Ho. SE17 —5C 86
(off Browning St.)
Barrett Rd. E17 —4E 34
Barrett's Grn. Rd. NW10 —3J 63
Barrett's Gro. N16 —5E 50
Barrett St. W1 —6E 66 (1H 165)
Barrhill Rd. SW2 —2J 121
Barrie Ct. New Bar —5F 5
(off Lyonsdown Rd.)
Barriedale. SE14 —2A 106
Barrie Est. W2 —7B 66 (2A 164)
Barrie Ho. W2 —7A 66
(off Lancaster Ga.)
Barrie Ho. W3 —2J 81
(off Castle Clo.)
Barrier App. SE7 —3B 90
Barrier Point Rd. E16 —1A 90
Barringers Ct. Ruis —7F 23
Barringer Sq. SW17 —4E 120
Barrington Clo. NW5 —5E 48
Barrington Clo. Ilf —1D 36
Barrington Ct. NW5 —5E 48
Barrington Ct. SW4 —2J 103
Barrington Ct. W3 —2H 81
(off Cheltenham Pl.)
Barrington Rd. E12 —6E 54
Barrington Rd. N8 —5H 31
Barrington Rd. SW9 —3B 104
Barrington Rd. Bexh —2D 110
Barrington Rd. Sutt —2J 149
Barrington Vs. SE18 —1E 108
Barrington Wlk. SE19 —6E 122
Barrosa Dri. Hamp —1E 132
Barrow Av. Cars —7D 150
Barrow Clo. N21 —3G 17
Barrow Ct. SE6 —1H 125
(off Cumberland Pk.)
Barrowdene Clo. Pinn —2C 24
Barrowell Grn. N21 —2G 17
Barrowfield Clo. N9 —3C 18
Barrowgate Rd. W4 —5J 81
Barrow Hedges Clo. Cars —7C 150
Barrow Hedges Way. Cars —7C 150
Barrowhill. Wor Pk —2A 148
Barrowhill Clo. Wor Pk —2A 148
Barrow Hill Est. NW8 —2C 66
(off Barrow Hill Rd.)
Barrow Hill Rd. NW8
—2C 66 (1C 158)
Barrow Point Av. Pinn —2C 24
Barrow Point La. Pinn —2C 24
Barrow Rd. SW16 —6H 121
Barrow Rd. Croy —5A 152
Barrow Wlk. Bren —6C 80
Barrs Rd. NW10 —7K 45
Barry Av. N15 —6F 33
Barry Av. Bexh —7E 92
Barrydene. N20 —1G 15
Barry Rd. E6 —6C 72
Barry Rd. NW10 —7J 45
Barry Rd. SE22 —6G 105
Barset Rd. SE15 —3J 105
(in three parts)
Barson Clo. SE20 —7J 123
Barston Rd. SE27 —3C 122
Barstow Cres. SW2 —1K 121
Barter St. WC1 —5J 67 (6F 161)
Barters Wlk. Pinn —3C 24
Bartholomew Clo. EC1 —5C 68 (6B 162)
(in two parts)
Bartholomew Clo. SW18 —4A 102
Bartholomew Ct. E14 —7F 71
Bartholomew Ct. EC1 —4C 68 (3D 162)
(off Old St.)
Bartholomew Ct. Edgw —7J 11
Bartholomew La. EC2 —6D 68 (1F 169)
Bartholomew Pl. EC1 —6C 162
Bartholomew Rd. NW5 —6G 49
Bartholomew Sq. E1 —4H 69
Bartholomew Sq. EC1
—4C 68 (3D 162)
Bartholomew St. SE1 —3D 86
Bartholomew Vs. NW5 —6G 49
Barth Rd. SE18 —4J 91
Bartle Av. E6 —2C 72
Bartle Rd. W11 —6G 65
Bartlett Clo. E14 —6C 70
Bartlett Ct. EC4 —6A 68 (7K 161)
Bartlett Houses. Dag —7H 57
(off Vicarage Rd.)
Bartletts Pas. EC4 —6A 68
(off Fetter La.)
Bartlett St. S Croy —5D 152
Bartlett Ter. Croy —2A 154
Bartlow Gdns. Romf —1K 39
Barton Av. Romf —1H 57
Barton Clo. E6 —6D 72
Barton Clo. E9 —5J 51
Barton Clo. NW4 —4C 28
Barton Clo. SE15 —3H 105
Barton Clo. Bexh —5E 110
Barton Clo. Shep —6D 130
Barton Ct. W14 —5G 83
(off Baron's Ct. Rd.)
Barton Grn. N Mald —2K 135
Barton Ho. N1 —7B 50
(off Sable St.)
Barton Ho. SW6 —3K 101
(off Wandsworth Bri. Rd.)
Barton Meadows. Ilf —4F 37
Barton Rd. W14 —5G 83
Barton Rd. Sidc —6E 128
Barton St. SW1 —3J 85 (1E 172)
Bartonway. NW8 —1B 66
(off Queen's Ter.)
Bartram Clo. Uxb —4D 58
Bartram Rd. SE4 —5A 106
Bartrams La. Barn —1F 5
Bartrip St. E9 —6B 52
Barts Clo. Beck —5C 142
Barville Clo. SE4 —4A 106
Barwell Bus Pk. Chess —7D 146
Barwell Ho. E2 —4G 69
(off Menotti St.)
Barwick Ho. W3 —2J 81
(off Strafford Rd.)
Barwick Rd. E7 —4K 53
Barwood Av. W W'ck —1D 154
Basden Gro. Felt —2E 114
Basden Ho. Felt —2E 114
Basedale Rd. Dag —7B 56
Baseing Clo. E6 —7E 72
Basevi Way. SE8 —6C 88
Bashley Rd. NW10 —4K 63
Basil Av. E6 —3C 72
Basildene Rd. Houn —3B 96
Basildon Av. Ilf —1E 36
Basildon Clo. Sutt —7K 149
Basildon Ct. W1 —5E 66 (5H 159)
(off Devonshire Rd.)
Basildon Rd. SE2 —5A 92
Basil Gdns. SE27 —5C 122
Basil Gdns. Croy —1K 153
Basil Ho. SW8 —7J 85
(off Wyvil Rd.)
Basilon Rd. Bexh —2E 110
Basil Spence Ho. N22 —1K 31
Basil St. SW3 —3D 84 (1E 170)
Basin App. E14 —6A 70
Basing Clo. Th Dit —7K 133
Basing Ct. SE15 —1F 105
Basingdon Way. SE5 —4D 104
Basing Dri. Bex —6F 111
Basingfield Rd. Th Dit —7K 133
Basinghall Av. EC2 —6D 68 (7E 162)
Basinghall Gdns. Sutt —7K 149
Basinghall St. EC2 —6D 68 (7E 162)
Basing Hill. NW11 —1H 47
Basing Hill. Wemb —2F 45
Basing Ho. Bark —1H 73
(off St Margarets)
Basing Ho. Yd. E2 —3E 68 (1H 163)
Basing Pl. E2 —3E 68 (1H 163)
Basing St. W11 —6H 65
Basing Way. N3 —3J 29
Basing Way. Th Dit —7K 133
Basire St. N1 —1C 68
Baskerville Gdns. NW10 —4A 46
Baskerville Rd. SW18 —7C 102
Basket Gdns. SE9 —5C 108
Baslow Clo. Harr —1H 25
Baslow Wlk. E5 —4K 51
Basnett Rd. SW11 —3E 102
Bassano St. SE22 —5F 105
Bassant Rd. SE18 —6K 91
Bassein Pk. Rd. W12 —2B 82
Bassett Gdns. Iswth —7G 79
Bassett Rd. E7 —4B 54
Bassett Rd. W10 —6F 65
Bassett St. NW5 —6E 48
Bassett's Way. Orp —4E 156
Bassett Way. Gnfd —6F 61
Bassingbourn Ho. N1 —7A 50
(off Sutton Est., The)
Bassingham Rd. SW18 —7A 102
Bassingham Rd. Wemb —6D 44
Bassishaw Highwalk. EC2 —6D 162
Basswood Clo. SE15 —3H 105
Bastable Av. Bark —2J 73
Basterfield Ho. EC1 —4C 68 (4C 162)
(off Golden La. Est.)
Bastion Highwalk. EC2 —6C 162
Bastion Ho. EC2 —5C 68
(off London Wall)
Bastion Rd. SE2 —5A 92
Baston Mnr. Rd. Brom —3K 155
Baston Rd. Brom —1K 155
Bastwick St. EC1 —4C 68 (3C 162)
Basuto Rd. SW6 —1J 101
Batavia Clo. Sun —1K 131
Batavia Ho. SE14 —7A 88
(off Batavia Rd.)
Batavia M. SE14 —7A 88
Batavia Rd. SE14 —7A 88
Batavia Rd. Sun —1K 131
Batchelor St. N1 —1A 68
Bateman Clo. Bark —6G 55
Bateman Ho. SE11 —6B 86
(off Brandon Est.)
Bateman Rd. E4 —6H 19
Bateman's Bldgs. W1 —1C 166
Bateman's Row. EC2
—4E 68 (3H 163)
Bateman St. W1 —6H 67 (1C 166)
Bates Cres. SW16 —7G 121
Bates Cres. Croy —5A 152
Bateson St. SE18 —4J 91
Bates Point. E13 —1J 71
(off Pelly Rd.)
Bate St. E14 —7B 70
Bath Clo. SE15 —7H 87
Bath Ct. EC1 —4J 161
Bath Ct. SE26 —3G 123
(off Droitwich Clo.)
Bathgate Rd. SW19 —3F 119
Bath Gro. E2 —2G 69 (1K 163)
(off Horatio St.)
Bath Ho. E2 —4G 69
(off Ramsey St.)
Bath Ho. SE1 —3C 86
(off Bath Ter.)
Bath Ho. Rd. Croy —1J 151
Bath Pas. King T —2D 134
Bath Pl. EC2 —3E 68 (2G 163)
Bath Pl. W6 —5E 82
(off Fulham Pal. Rd.)
Bath Pl. Barn —3C 4
Bath Rd. E7 —6B 54
Bath Rd. N9 —2C 18
Bath Rd. W4 —4A 82
Bath Rd. Hay & H'row A —1G 95
Bath Rd. Houn —1A 96
Bath Rd. Romf —6E 38
Baths App. SW6 —7H 83
Baths Rd. Brom —4B 144
Bath St. EC1 —3C 68 (2D 162)
Bath Ter. SE1 —3C 86
Bathurst Av. SW19 —1K 137
Bathurst Gdns. NW10 —2D 64
Bathurst M. W2 —6B 66 (2B 164)
Bathurst Rd. Ilf —1F 55
Bathurst St. W2 —7B 66 (2B 164)
Bathway. SE18 —4E 90
Batley Clo. Mitc —7D 138
Batley Pl. N16 —3F 51
Batley Rd. N16 —3F 51
Batley Rd. Enf —1H 7
Batman Clo. W12 —1D 82
Batoum Gdns. W6 —3E 82
Batson Ho. E1 —6G 69
(off Fairclough St.)
Batson St. W12 —2C 82
Batsworth Rd. Mitc —3B 138
Battenberg Wlk. SE19 —6E 122
Batten Clo. E6 —6D 72
Batten Ho. SW4 —5G 103
Batten Ho. W10 —3G 65
(off Third Av.)
Batten St. SW11 —3C 102
Battersby Rd. SE6 —2F 125
Battersea. —1E 102
Battersea Bri. SW3 & SW11 —7B 84
Battersea Bri. Rd. SW11 —7C 84
Battersea Bus. Cen. SW11 —3E 102
Battersea Chu. Rd. SW11 —1B 102
Battersea Dogs' Home. —7F 85
Battersea High St. SW11 —1B 102
(in two parts)
Battersea Pk. —7E 84
Battersea Pk. Children's Zoo. —7E 84
Battersea Pk. Rd. SW11 & SW8
—2C 102
Battersea Ri. SW11 —5C 102
Battersea Sq. SW11 —1B 102
Battery Rd. SE28 —2J 91
Battishill St. N1 —7B 50
Battis, The. Romf —6K 39
Battlebridge Ct. N1 —2J 67
(off Wharfdale Rd.)
Battle Bri. La. SE1 —1E 86 (5G 169)
Battle Bri. Rd. NW1 —2J 67
Battle Clo. SW19 —6A 120
Battledean Rd. N5 —5B 50
Battle Ho. SE15 —6G 87
(off Haymerle Rd.)
Battle Rd. Belv & Eri —4J 93
Batty St. E1 —6G 69
Baudene M. NW4 —4D 28
(off Burroughs, The)
Baudwin Rd. SE6 —2G 125
Baugh Rd. Sidc —5C 128
Baulk, The. SW18 —7J 101
Bavant Rd. SW16 —2J 139
Bavaria Rd. N19 —2J 49
(in two parts)
Bavent Rd. SE5 —2C 104
Bawdale Rd. SE22 —5F 105
Bawdsey Av. Ilf —4K 37
Bawtree Rd. SE14 —7A 88
Bawtry Rd. N20 —3J 15
Baxendale. N20 —2F 15
Baxendale St. E2 —3G 69
Baxter Clo. S'hall —3F 79
Baxter Clo. Uxb —3D 58
Baxter Rd. E16 —6A 72
Baxter Rd. N1 —6D 50
Baxter Rd. N18 —4C 18
Baxter Rd. Ilf —5F 55
Bayard Ct. Bexh —4H 111
(off Watling St.)
Bay Ct. W5 —3E 80
Baycroft Clo. Pinn —3A 24
Baydon Ct. Short —3H 143
Bayer Ho. EC1 —4C 68 (4C 162)
(off Golden La. Est.)
Bayfield Ho. SE4 —4K 105
(off Coston Wlk.)
Bayfield Rd. SE9 —4B 108
Bayford M. E8 —7H 51
(off Bayford St.)
Bayford Rd. NW10 —3F 65
Bayford St. E8 —7H 51
Bayford St. Ind. Est. E9 —7A 52
Baygrove M. Hamp W —1C 134
Bayham Pl. NW1 —1G 67
Bayham Rd. W4 —3K 81
Bayham Rd. W13 —7B 62
Bayham Rd. Mord —4K 137
Bayham St. NW1 —1G 67
Bayhurst Wood Country Pk. —5B 22
Bayleaf Clo. Hamp H —5H 115
Bayley St. W1 —5H 67 (6C 160)
Bayley Wlk. SE2 —5E 92
Baylis Rd. SE1 —2A 86 (7J 167)
Bayliss Av. SE28 —7D 74
Bayliss Clo. N21 —5D 6
Baynard St. EC4 —7C 68
Bayne Clo. E6 —6D 72
Baynes Clo. Enf —1B 8
Baynes M. NW3 —6B 48
Baynes St. NW1 —7G 49
Baynham Clo. Bex —6F 111
Bayonne Rd. W6 —6G 83
Bays Clo. SE26 —5J 123
Bays Ct. Edgw —5C 12
Bayshill Ri. N'holt —6F 43
Bayston Rd. N16 —3F 51
Bayswater. —7A 66
Bayswater Rd. W2 —7K 65 (3A 164)
Baythorne St. E3 —5B 70
Bayton Ct. E8 —7G 51
(off Lansdowne Dri.)
Bay Tree Clo. Brom —1B 144
Baytree Clo. Sidc —1K 127
Baytree Ct. SW2 —4K 103
Baytree Ho. E4 —7J 9
Baytree Rd. SW2 —4K 103
Bazalgette Clo. N Mald —5K 135
Bazalgette Gdns. N Mald —5K 135
Bazalgette Ho. NW8 —4B 66 (3B 158)
(off Orchardson St.)
Bazeley Ho. SE1 —2B 86 (7A 168)
(off Library St.)
Bazely St. E14 —7E 70
Bazile Rd. N21 —6F 7
Beacham Clo. SE7 —5B 90
Beachborough Rd. Brom —4E 124
Beachcroft Rd. E11 —3G 53
Beachcroft Way. N19 —1H 49
Beach Gro. Felt —2E 114
Beach Ho. SW5 —5J 83
(off Philbeach Gdns.)
Beach Ho. Felt —2E 114
Beachy Rd. E3 —7C 52
Beacon Clo. Uxb —5A 40
Beacon Ga. SE14 —3K 105
Beacon Gro. Cars —4E 150
Beacon Hill. N7 —5J 49
Beacon Ho. E14 —5D 88
Beacon Pl. Croy —3J 151
Beacon Rd. SE13 —6F 107
Beacon Rd. H'row A —6C 94
Beacons Clo. E6 —5C 72
Beaconsfield Clo. N11 —5K 15
Beaconsfield Clo. SE3 —6J 89
Beaconsfield Clo. W4 —5J 81
Beaconsfield Pde. SE9 —4C 126
Beaconsfield Rd. E10 —2E 52
Beaconsfield Rd. E16 —4H 71
Beaconsfield Rd. E17 —6B 34
Beaconsfield Rd. N9 —3B 18
Beaconsfield Rd. N11 —3K 15
Beaconsfield Rd. N15 —4E 32
Beaconsfield Rd. NW10 —6B 46
Beaconsfield Rd. SE3 —7H 89
Beaconsfield Rd. SE9 —2C 126
Beaconsfield Rd. SE17 —5D 86
Beaconsfield Rd. W4 —3K 81
Beaconsfield Rd. W5 —2C 80
Beaconsfield Rd. Bex —2K 129
Beaconsfield Rd. Brom —3B 144
Beaconsfield Rd. Croy —6D 140
Beaconsfield Rd. Hay —1A 78
Beaconsfield Rd. N Mald —2K 135
Beaconsfield Rd. S'hall —1B 78
Beaconsfield Rd. Surb —7F 135
Beaconsfield Rd. Twic —6B 98
Beaconsfield Ter. Romf —6D 38
Beaconsfield Ter. Rd. W14 —3G 83
Beaconsfield Wlk. E6 —6E 72
Beaconsfield Wlk. SW6 —1H 101
Beacontree Av. E17 —1F 35
Beacontree Heath. —2G 57
Beacontree Rd. E11 —1H 53
Beadle's Pde. Dag —6J 57
Beadlow Clo. Cars —6B 138
Beadman St. SE27 —4B 122
Beadnell Rd. SE23 —1K 123
Beadon Rd. W6 —4E 82
Beadon Rd. Brom —4J 143
Beaford Gro. SW20 —3G 137
Beagle Clo. Felt —4K 113
Beak St. W1 —7G 67 (2B 166)
Beal Clo. Well —1A 110
Beale Clo. N13 —5G 17
Beale Pl. E3 —2B 70
Beale Rd. E3 —1B 70
Beal Rd. Ilf —2E 54
Beam Av. Dag —1H 75
Beaminster Gdns. Ilf —2F 37
Beaminster Ho. SW8 —7K 85
(off Dorset Rd.)
Beamish Dri. Bus H —1B 10
Beamish Rd. N9 —1B 18
Beam Vs. Dag —2J 75
Beamway. Dag —7K 57
Beanacre Clo. E9 —6B 52
Bean Rd. Bexh —4D 110
Beanshaw. SE9 —4E 126
Beansland Gro. Romf —2E 38
Bear All. EC4 —6B 68 (7A 162)
Bear Clo. Romf —6H 39
Beardell St. SE19 —6F 123
Beardow Gro. N14 —6B 6
Beard Rd. SE8 —4B 88
Beard Rd. King T —5F 117
Beardsfield. E13 —2J 71
Beard's Hill. Hamp —1E 132
Beard's Hill Clo. Hamp —1E 132
Beardsley Ter. Dag —5B 56
(off Fitzstephen Rd.)
Beardsley Way. W3 —2K 81
Beard's Rd. Ashf —6G 113
Bearfield Rd. King T —7E 116
Bear Gdns. SE1 —1C 86 (4C 168)
Bear La. SE1 —1B 86 (4B 168)
Bear Rd. Felt —4B 114
Bearsted Ri. SE4 —5B 106
Bearsted Ter. Beck —1C 142
Bear St. WC2 —7H 67 (2D 166)
Beasley's Ait. Sun —6H 131
Beasley's Ait La. Sun —6H 131
Beaton Clo. SE15 —1F 105
Beatrice Av. SW16 —3K 139
Beatrice Av. Wemb —5E 44
Beatrice Clo. E13 —4J 71
Beatrice Clo. Pinn —4J 23
Beatrice Ct. Buck H —2G 21
Beatrice Pl. W8 —3K 83
Beatrice Rd. E17 —5C 34
Beatrice Rd. N4 —7A 32
Beatrice Rd. N9 —7D 8
Beatrice Rd. SE1 —4G 87
Beatrice Rd. Rich —5F 99
Beatrice Rd. S'hall —1D 78
Beatrix Ho. SW5 —5K 83
(off Old Brompton Rd.)
Beatson Wlk. SE16 —1A 88
(in two parts)
Beattie Clo. Felt —7H 95
Beattie Ho. SW8 —1G 103
Beattock Ri. N10 —4F 31
Beatty Ho. E14 —2C 88
(off Admirals Way)
Beatty Ho. NW1 —4G 67 (3A 160)
Beatty Ho. SW1 —5G 85 (6B 172)
(off Dolphin Sq.)
Beatty Rd. N16 —4E 50
Beatty Rd. Stan —6H 11
Beatty St. NW1 —2G 67
Beattyville Gdns. Ilf —4E 36
Beauchamp Clo. W4 —3J 81
Beauchamp Ct. Stan —5H 11
Beauchamp Pl. SW3 —3C 84 (1D 170)
Beauchamp Rd. E7 —7K 53
Beauchamp Rd. SE19 —1D 140
Beauchamp Rd. SW11 —4C 102
Beauchamp Rd. Sutt —4J 149
Beauchamp Rd. Twic —7A 98
Beauchamp Rd. W Mol & E Mol —5F 133
Beauchamp St. EC1 —5A 68 (6J 161)
Beauchamp Ter. SW15 —3D 100
Beauclerc Ct. Sun —2A 132
Beauclerc Rd. W6 —3D 82
Beauclerk Clo. Felt —1K 113
Beauclerk Ho. SW16 —3J 121
Beaudesert M. W Dray —2A 76
Beaufort Av. Harr —4A 26
Beaufort Clo. E4 —6J 19
Beaufort Clo. SW15 —7D 100
Beaufort Clo. W5 —5F 63
Beaufort Clo. Romf —4J 39
Beaufort Ct. N11 —5A 16
(off Limes Av., The)
Beaufort Ct. New Bar —5F 5
Beaufort Ct. Rich —4C 116
Beaufort Dri. E6 —5E 72
Beaufort Dri. NW11 —4J 29
Beaufort Gdns. NW4 —6E 28
Beaufort Gdns. SW3 —3C 84 (1D 170)
Beaufort Gdns. SW16 —7K 121
Beaufort Gdns. Houn —1C 96
Beaufort Gdns. Ilf —1E 54
Beaufort Ho. E14 —2C 88
Beaufort Ho. SW1 —5H 85 (6C 172)
(off Aylesford St.)
Beaufort M. SW6 —6H 83
Beaufort Pk. NW11 —4J 29
Beaufort Rd. W5 —5F 63
Beaufort Rd. King T —4E 134
Beaufort Rd. Rich —4C 116
Beaufort Rd. Ruis —2F 41
Beaufort Rd. Twic —7C 98
Beaufort St. SW3 —6B 84 (7A 170)
Beaufort Ter. E14 —5E 88
Beaufort Way. Eps —7C 148
Beaufoy Ho. SE27 —3B 122
Beaufoy Ho. SW8 —7K 85
(off Rita Rd.)
Beaufoy Rd. N17 —7K 17
Beaufoy Wlk. SE11 —4K 85
Beaulieu Av. E16 —1K 89
Beaulieu Av. SE26 —4H 123
Beaulieu Clo. NW9 —4A 28
Beaulieu Clo. SE5 —3D 104
Beaulieu Clo. Houn —5D 96
Beaulieu Clo. Mitc —1E 138
Beaulieu Clo. Twic —6D 98
Beaulieu Ct. W5 —5E 62
Beaulieu Dri. Pinn —6B 24
Beaulieu Gdns. N21 —7H 7
Beaulieu Pl. W4 —3J 81
Beaumanor Gdns. SE9 —4E 126
Beaumaris Dri. Wfd G —7G 21
Beaumaris Grn. NW9 —6A 28
Beaumaris Tower. W3 —2H 81
(off Park Rd. N.)
Beaumont. W14 —4H 83
(off Avonmore Rd.)

Beaumont Av.—Belvedere Strand

Beaumont Av. W14 —5H 83
Beaumont Av. Harr —6F 25
Beaumont Av. Rich —3F 99
Beaumont Av. Wemb —5C 44
Beaumont Bldgs. WC2 —6J 67 (1F 167)
(off Martlett Ct.)
Beaumont Clo. King T —7G 117
Beaumont Ct. E5 —3H 51
Beaumont Ct. W1 —5E 66 (5H 159)
(off Beaumont St.)
Beaumont Ct. W4 —5J 81
Beaumont Cres. W14 —5H 83
Beaumont Dri. Ashf —5F 113
Beaumont Gdns. NW3 —3J 47
Beaumont Gro. E1 —4K 69
Beaumont Ho. E10 —7D 34
Beaumont Ho. E15 —1H 71
(off John St.)
Beaumont Lodge. E8 —6G 51
(off Greenwood Rd.)
Beaumont M. W1 —5E 66 (5H 159)
Beaumont M. Pinn —3C 24
Beaumont Pl. W1 —4G 67 (3B 160)
Beaumont Pl. Barn —1C 4
Beaumont Pl. Iswth —5K 97
Beaumont Ri. N19 —1H 49
Beaumont Rd. E10 —7D 34
(in three parts)
Beaumont Rd. E13 —3K 71
Beaumont Rd. SE19 —6C 122
Beaumont Rd. SW19 —7G 101
Beaumont Rd. W4 —3J 81
Beaumont Rd. Orp —6H 145
Beaumont Sq. E1 —5K 69
Beaumont St. W1 —5E 66 (5H 159)
Beaumont Ter. SE13 —7G 107
(off Wellmeadow Rd.)
Beaumont Wlk. NW3 —7D 48
Beauvais Ter. N'holt —3B 60
Beauval Rd. SE22 —6F 105
Beaux Arts Building. N7 —3J 49
Beaverbank Rd. SE9 —1H 127
Beaver Clo. SE20 —7G 123
Beaver Clo. Hamp —1F 133
Beaver Ct. Beck —7D 124
Beaver Gro. N'holt —3C 60
Beavers Cres. Houn —4A 96
Beavers La. Houn —2A 96
Beavers Lodge. Sidc —4K 127
Beaverwood Rd. Chst —5J 127
Beavor Gro. W6 —5C 82
(off Beavor La.)
Beavor La. W6 —5C 82
Bebbington Rd. SE18 —4J 91
Beccles Dri. Bark —6J 55
Beccles St. E14 —6B 70
Bec Clo. Ruis —3B 42
Bechervaise Ct. E10 —1D 52
(off Leyton Grange Est.)
Beck Clo. SE13 —1D 106
Beck Ct. Beck —3K 141
Beckenham. —1C 142
Beckenham Bus. Cen. Beck —6A 124
Beckenham Crematorium. Beck —3J 141
Beckenham Gdns. N9 —3K 17
Beckenham Gro. Brom —2F 143
Beckenham Hill Est. Beck —5D 124
Beckenham Hill Rd. Beck & SE6 —6D 124
Beckenham La. Brom —2G 143
Beckenham Pl. Pk. Beck —7D 124
Beckenham Rd. Beck —1K 141
Beckenham Rd. W W'ck —7D 142
Beckers, The. N16 —4G 51
Becket Av. E6 —3E 72
Becket Clo. SE25 —6G 141
Becket Clo. SW19 —7K 119
(off High Path)
Becket Fold. Harr —5K 25
Becket Ho. SE1 —7E 168
Becket Rd. N18 —4D 18
Becket St. SE1 —3D 86 (7E 168)
Beckett Clo. NW10 —6A 46
Beckett Clo. SW16 —2H 121
Beckett Clo. Belv —3F 93
Beckett Ho. SW9 —2J 103
Becketts Clo. Felt —6K 95
Becketts Ho. Ilf —3E 54
Becketts Pl. Hamp W —1D 134
Beckett Wlk. Beck —6A 124
Beckfoot. NW1 —2G 67 (1B 160)
(off Ampthill Est.)
Beckford Dri. Orp —7H 145
Beckford Ho. N16 —5E 50
Beckford Pl. SE17 —5C 86
Beckford Rd. Croy —6F 141
Beckham Ho. SE11 —4K 85 (4H 173)
Beck La. Beck —3K 141
Becklow Gdns. W12 —2C 82
(off Becklow Rd.)
Becklow M. W12 —2C 82
(off Becklow Rd.)
Becklow Rd. W12 —2B 82
(in two parts)
Beck River Pk. Beck —1C 142
Beck Rd. E8 —1H 69
Becks Rd. Sidc —3A 128
Beck Theatre, The. —6H 59
Beckton. —6D 72
Beckton Park. —6D 72
Beckton Retail Pk. E6 —5E 72
Beckton Rd. E16 —5H 71
Beckton Triangle Retail Pk. E6 —4F 73
Beck Way. Beck —3B 142
Beckway Rd. SW16 —2H 139
Beckway St. SE17 —4E 86
(in two parts)
Beckwith Rd. SE24 —5D 104
Beclands Rd. SW17 —6E 120
Becmead Av. SW16 —4H 121
Becmead Av. Harr —5B 26
Becondale Rd. SE19 —5E 122
Becontree. —2E 56
Becontree Av. Dag —4B 56
Bective Pl. SW15 —4H 101
Bective Rd. E7 —4J 53
Bective Rd. SW15 —4H 101
Becton Pl. Eri —7H 93
Bedale Rd. Enf —1H 7
Bedale St. SE1 —1D 86 (5E 168)
Beddalls Farm Ct. E6 —5B 72
Beddington. —3J 151
Beddington Corner. —7E 138
Beddington Farm Rd. Croy —7J 139
Beddington Gdns. Cars & Wall —6E 150
(in two parts)
Beddington Grn. Orp —1K 145
Beddington Gro. Wall —5H 151
Beddington La. Croy —5G 139
Beddington Pk. Cotts. Wall —3H 151
Beddington Path. St P —1K 145
Beddington Rd. Ilf —7K 37
Beddington Rd. Orp —1J 145
Beddington Ter. Croy —7K 139
Beddington Trad. Est. Croy —1J 151
Bede Clo. Pinn —1B 24
Bedefield. WC1 —3J 67 (2F 161)
Bede Ho. SE4 —1B 106
Bedens Rd. Sidc —6E 128
Bede Rd. Romf —6C 38
Bedfont Clo. Felt —6E 94
Bedfont Clo. Mitc —2E 138
Bedfont Grn. Clo. Felt —1E 112
Bedfont Ind. Pk. Ashf —3E 112
Bedfont Lakes Country Pk. —2E 112
Bedfont La. Felt —7H 95
Bedfont Pk. Ind. Est. Ashf —3E 112
Bedfont Rd. Felt —1E 112
Bedfont Rd. Stanw —6A 94
Bedford Av. WC1 —5H 67 (6D 160)
Bedford Av. Barn —5C 4
Bedford Av. Hay —6K 59
Bedfordbury. WC2 —7J 67 (2E 166)
Bedford Clo. N10 —7K 15
Bedford Clo. W4 —6A 82
Bedford Corner. W4 —4A 82
(off South Pde.)
Bedford Ct. WC2 —7J 67 (3E 166)
(in two parts)
Bedford Ct. Mans. WC1 —6D 160
Bedford Gdns. W8 —1J 83
Bedford Hill. SW12 & SW16 —1F 121
Bedford Ho. SW4 —4J 103
(off Solon New Rd. Est.)
Bedford M. N2 —3C 30
Bedford Park. —3K 81
Bedford Pk. Croy —1C 152
Bedford Pk. Corner. W4 —4A 82
Bedford Pk. Mans. W4 —4K 81
Bedford Pas. SW6 —7G 83
(off Dawes Rd.)
Bedford Pas. W1 —5G 67 (5B 160)
Bedford Pl. WC1 —5J 67 (5E 160)
Bedford Pl. Croy —1D 152
Bedford Rd. E6 —1E 72
Bedford Rd. E17 —2C 34
Bedford Rd. E18 —2J 35
Bedford Rd. N2 —3C 30
Bedford Rd. N8 —6H 31
Bedford Rd. N9 —7C 8
Bedford Rd. N15 —4E 32
Bedford Rd. N22 —1J 31
Bedford Rd. NW7 —2F 13
Bedford Rd. SW4 —4J 103
Bedford Rd. W4 —3K 81
Bedford Rd. W13 —7B 62
Bedford Rd. Harr —6G 25
Bedford Rd. Ilf —3F 55
Bedford Rd. Ruis —4H 41
Bedford Rd. Sidc —3J 127
Bedford Rd. Twic —3H 115
Bedford Rd. Wor Pk —2E 148
Bedford Row. WC1 —5K 67 (5H 161)
Bedford Sq. WC1 —5H 67 (6D 160)
Bedford St. WC2 —7J 67 (2E 166)
Bedford Ter. SW4 —5J 103
Bedford Way. WC1 —4H 67 (4D 160)
Bedgebury Gdns. SW19 —2G 119
Bedgebury Rd. SE9 —4B 108
Bedivere Rd. Brom —3J 125
Bedlow Way. Croy —4K 151
Bedmond Ho. SW3 —5C 84 (5C 170)
(off Ixworth Pl.)
Bedonwell Rd. SE2 & Belv —6E 92
Bedonwell Rd. Belv —6E 92
Bedonwell Rd. Bexh —1F 111
Bedser Clo. SE11 —6K 85 (7H 173)
Bedser Clo. T Hth —3C 140
Bedser Dri. Gnfd —5H 43
Bedster Gdns. W Mol —2F 133
Bedwardine Rd. SE19 —7E 122
Bedwell Ct. Romf —7D 38
(off Broomfield Rd.)
Bedwell Gdns. Hay —5G 77
(in two parts)
Bedwell Ho. SW9 —2A 104
Bedwell Rd. N17 —1E 32
Bedwell Rd. Belv —5G 93
Beeby Rd. E16 —5K 71
Beech Av. N20 —1H 15
Beech Av. W3 —1A 82
Beech Av. Bren —7B 80
Beech Av. Buck H —2E 20
Beech Av. Ruis —1K 41
Beech Av. Sidc —7A 110
Beech Clo. N9 —6B 8
Beech Clo. SE8 —6C 88
Beech Clo. SW15 —7C 100
Beech Clo. SW19 —6E 118
Beech Clo. Ashf —5F 113
Beech Clo. Cars —2D 150
Beech Clo. Sun —2B 132
Beech Clo. W Dray —3C 76
Beech Copse. Brom —1D 144
Beech Copse. S Croy —5E 152
Beech Ct. W1 —6D 66 (7E 158)
(off Harrowby St.)
Beech Ct. Beck —7B 124
Beech Ct. N'holt —1C 60
Beech Ct. N'wd —1G 23
Beech Ct. Surb —7D 134
Beech Cres. Ct. N5 —4B 50
Beechcroft. Chst —7E 126
Beechcroft Av. NW11 —7H 29
Beechcroft Av. Bexh —1K 111
Beechcroft Av. Harr —7E 24
Beechcroft Av. N Mald —1J 135
Beechcroft Av. S'hall —1D 78
Beechcroft Clo. SW16 —5K 121
Beechcroft Clo. Houn —7C 78
Beechcroft Ct. NW11 —7H 29
(off Beechcroft Av.)
Beechcroft Ct. Sutt —7A 150
Beechcroft Gdns. Wemb —3F 45
Beechcroft Ho. W5 —5E 62
Beechcroft Rd. E18 —2K 35
Beechcroft Rd. SW14 —3J 99
Beechcroft Rd. SW17 —2C 120
Beechcroft Rd. Chess —3F 147
Beechdale. N21 —2E 16
Beechdale Rd. SW2 —6K 103
Beech Dell. Kes —4D 156
Beech Dri. N2 —2D 30
Beechen Cliff Way. Iswth —2K 97
Beechen Gro. Pinn —3D 24
Beechen Pl. SE23 —2K 123
Beeches Av. Cars —7C 150
Beeches Clo. SE20 —1J 141
Beeches Rd. SW17 —3C 120
Beeches Rd. Sutt —1G 149
Beeches, The. E12 —7C 54
Beeches, The. Houn —1F 97
Beeches Wlk. Cars —7B 150
Beechfield Cotts. Brom —2A 144
Beechfield Gdns. Romf —7J 39
Beechfield Rd. N4 —6C 32
Beechfield Rd. SE6 —1B 124
Beechfield Rd. Brom —2A 144
Beechfield Rd. Eri —7K 93
Beech Gdns. EC2 —5C 68
(off Beech St.)
Beech Gdns. W5 —2E 80
Beech Gdns. Dag —7J 57
Beech Gro. Mitc —5H 139
(in two parts)
Beech Gro. N Mald —3K 135
Beech Hall Cres. E4 —7A 20
Beech Hall Rd. E4 —7K 19
Beech Haven Ct. Dart —5K 111
(off London Rd.)
Beech Hill. Barn —1G 5
Beech Hill Av. Barn —1F 5
Beech Ho. E17 —3F 35
Beech Ho. Rd. Croy —3D 152
Beechhill Rd. SE9 —5E 108
Beech La. Buck H —2E 20
Beech Lawns. N12 —5G 15
Beechmont Clo. Brom —5G 125
Beechmore Gdns. Sutt —2F 149
Beechmore Rd. SW11 —1D 102
Beechmount Av. W7 —5H 61
Beecholme. N12 —5E 14
Beecholme Av. Mitc —1F 139
Beecholme Est. E5 —3H 51
Beech Rd. N11 —6D 16
Beech Rd. SW16 —2J 139
Beech Rd. Felt —7G 95
Beech Row. Ham —4E 116
Beech St. EC2 —5C 68 (5C 162)
Beech St. Romf —4J 39
Beech Tree Clo. N1 —7A 50
Beech Tree Clo. Stan —5H 11
Beech Tree Glade. E4 —1C 20
Beech Tree Pl. Sutt —5K 149
Beechvale Clo. N12 —5H 15
Beech Wlk. NW7 —6F 13
Beech Way. NW10 —7K 45
Beechway. Bex —6D 110
Beech Way. Twic —3E 114
Beechwood Av. N3 —3H 29
Beechwood Av. Gnfd —3F 61
Beechwood Av. Harr —3F 43
Beechwood Av. Hay —7F 59
Beechwood Av. Rich —1G 99
Beechwood Av. Ruis —2H 41
Beechwood Av. Sun —6J 113
Beechwood Av. T Hth —4B 140
Beechwood Av. Uxb —6C 58
Beechwood Circ. Harr —3F 43
Beechwood Clo. N2 —4D 30
(off Western Rd.)
Beechwood Clo. NW7 —5F 13
Beechwood Clo. Surb —7C 134
Beechwood Ct. W4 —6K 81
Beechwood Ct. Cars —4D 150
Beechwood Ct. Sun —6J 113
Beechwood Cres. Bexh —3D 110
Beechwood Dri. Kes —4B 156
Beechwood Dri. Wfd G —5C 20
Beechwood Gdns. NW10 —3F 63
Beechwood Gdns. Harr —3F 43
Beechwood Gdns. Ilf —5D 36
Beechwood Gro. W3 —7A 64
Beechwood Gro. Surb —7C 134
Beechwood Hall. N3 —3H 29
Beechwood Ho. E2 —2G 69
(off Teale St.)
Beechwood M. N9 —2B 18
Beechwood Pk. E18 —3J 35
Beechwood Ri. Chst —4F 127
Beechwood Rd. E8 —6F 51
Beechwood Rd. N8 —4H 31
Beechwood Rd. S Croy —7E 152
Beechwoods Ct. SE19 —5F 123
Beechworth. NW6 —7G 47
Beechworth Clo. NW3 —2J 47
Beecroft Rd. SE4 —5A 106
Beehive Clo. E8 —7F 51
Beehive Clo. Uxb —7B 40
Beehive La. Ilf —5D 36
Beehive Pl. SW9 —3A 104
Beeleigh Rd. Mord —4K 137
Beemans Row. SW18 —2A 120
Bee Pas. EC3 —6E 68
(off Lime St.)
Beeston Clo. E8 —5G 51
Beeston Ho. SE1 —3D 86
(off Burbage Clo.)
Beeston Pl. SW1 —3F 85 (1K 171)
Beeston Rd. Barn —6G 5
Beeston Way. Felt —6A 96
Beethoven St. W10 —3G 65
Beeton Clo. Pinn —1E 24
Begbie Rd. SE3 —1A 108
Beggar's Hill. (Junct.) —6B 148
Beggar's Hill. Eps —7B 148
Beggars Roost La. Sutt —6J 149
Begonia Clo. E6 —5D 72
Begonia Pl. Hamp —6E 114
Begonia Wlk. W12 —6B 64
Beira St. SW12 —7F 103
Bekesbourne St. E14 —6A 70
Belcroft Clo. Brom —7H 125
Beldanes Lodge. NW10 —7C 46
Beldham Gdns. W Mol —2F 133
Belfairs Dri. Romf —7C 38
Belfast Rd. N16 —2F 51
Belfast Rd. SE25 —4H 141
Belfield Rd. Eps —7K 147
Belfont Wlk. N7 —4J 49
(in two parts)
Belford Gro. SE18 —4E 90
Belford Ho. E8 —1F 69
Belfort Rd. SE15 —2J 105
Belfry Clo. SE16 —5H 87
Belgrade Rd. N16 —4E 50
Belgrade Rd. Hamp —1F 133
Belgrave Clo. N14 —5B 6
Belgrave Clo. NW7 —5E 12
Belgrave Clo. W3 —2H 81
Belgrave Ct. E13 —4A 72
Belgrave Ct. W4 —5J 81
Belgrave Cres. Sun —1K 131
Belgrave Gdns. N14 —4C 6
Belgrave Gdns. NW8 —1K 65
Belgrave Gdns. Stan —5H 11
Belgrave Heights. E11 —1J 53
Belgrave Ho. SW9 —7A 86
Belgrave M. N. SW1 —2E 84 (7G 165)
Belgrave M. S. SW1 —3E 84 (1H 171)
Belgrave M. W. SW1 —3E 84 (1G 171)
Belgrave Pl. SW1 —3E 84 (1H 171)
Belgrave Rd. E10 —1E 52
Belgrave Rd. E11 —2J 53
Belgrave Rd. E13 —4A 72
Belgrave Rd. E17 —5C 34
Belgrave Rd. SE25 —4F 141
Belgrave Rd. SW1 —4F 85 (4K 171)
Belgrave Rd. SW13 —7B 82
Belgrave Rd. Houn —3D 96
Belgrave Rd. Ilf —1D 54
Belgrave Rd. Mitc —3B 138
Belgrave Rd. Sun —1K 131
Belgrave Sq. SW1 —3E 84 (1G 171)
Belgrave St. E1 —5K 69
Belgrave Ter. Wfd G —3D 20
Belgrave Wlk. Mitc —3B 138
Belgrave Yd. SW1 —2J 171
Belgravia. —3E 84 (2H 171)
Belgravia Clo. Barn —3C 4
Belgravia Ct. SW1 —2J 171
Belgravia Gdns. Brom —6G 125
Belgravia Ho. SW1 —3E 84 (1G 171)
(off Halkin Pl.)
Belgravia Ho. SW4 —6H 103
Belgravia M. King T —4D 134
Belgravia Workshops. N19 —2J 49
(off Marlborough Rd.)
Belgrove St. NW1 —3J 67 (1F 161)
Belham Wlk. SE5 —1D 104
Belinda Rd. SW9 —3B 104
Belitha Vs. N1 —7K 49
Bellamy Clo. E14 —2C 88
Bellamy Clo. W14 —5H 83
Bellamy Clo. Edgw —2D 12
Bellamy Clo. Uxb —3C 40
Bellamy Ct. Stan —1B 26
Bellamy Dri. Stan —1B 26
Bellamy Ho. Houn —6E 78
Bellamy Rd. E4 —6J 19
Bellamy Rd. Enf —2J 7
Bellamy St. SW12 —7F 103
Bellasis Av. SW2 —2J 121
Bell Av. W Dray —4B 76
Bell Clo. Pinn —2A 24
Bell Clo. Ruis —3H 41
Bellclose Rd. W Dray —2A 76
Bell Ct. NW4 —4E 28
Bell Dri. SW18 —7G 101
Bellefields Rd. SW9 —3K 103
Bellegrove Clo. Well —2K 109
Bellegrove Pde. Well —3K 109
Bellegrove Rd. Well —2J 109
Bellenden Rd. SE15 —1F 105
Bellestaines Pleasaunce. E4 —2H 19
Belleville Rd. SW11 —5C 102
Belle Vue. Gnfd —1H 61
Belle Vue Est. NW4 —4F 29
Bellevue La. Bus H —1C 10
Bellevue M. N11 —5K 15
Bellevue Pk. T Hth —3C 140
Bellevue Pl. E1 —4J 69
Belle Vue Rd. E17 —2F 35
Bellevue Rd. N11 —4K 15
Belle Vue Rd. NW4 —4F 29
Bellevue Rd. SW13 —2C 100
Bellevue Rd. SW17 —1C 120
Bellevue Rd. W13 —4B 62
Bellevue Rd. Bexh —5F 111
Bellevue Rd. King T —3E 134
(in two parts)
Bellew St. SW17 —3A 120
Bell Farm Av. Dag —3J 57
Bellfield. Croy —7A 154
Bellfield Av. Harr —6C 10
Bellflower Clo. E6 —5C 72
Bell Gdns. E10 —1C 52
(off Church Rd.)
Bellgate M. NW5 —4F 49
Bell Green. —4A 124
Bell Grn. SE26 —4B 124
Bell Grn. La. SE26 —5B 124
Bell Hill. Croy —2C 152
Bellhouse Cotts. Hay —7G 59
Bell Ho. Rd. Romf —1J 57
Bellina M. NW5 —4F 49
Bell Ind. Est. W4 —4J 81
Bellingham. —3D 124
Bellingham. N17 —7C 18
(off Park La.)
Bellingham Ct. Bark —3B 74
Bellingham Grn. SE6 —3C 124
Bellingham Rd. SE6 —3D 124
Bellingham Trad. Est. SE6 —3D 124
Bell Inn Yd. EC3 —6D 68 (1F 169)
Bell Junct. Houn —3F 97
Bell La. E1 —5F 69 (6J 163)
Bell La. E16 —1H 89
Bell La. NW4 & NW11 —4F 29
Bell La. Enf —1E 8
Bell La. Twic —1A 116
Bell La. Wemb —3D 44
Bell Mdw. SE19 —5E 122
Bell Moor. NW3 —3A 48
(off E. Heath Rd.)
Bello Clo. SE24 —7B 104
Bellot St. SE10 —5G 89
Bellring Clo. Belv —6G 93
Bell Rd. E Mol —5H 133
Bell Rd. Enf —1J 7
Bell Rd. Houn —3F 97
Bells All. SW6 —2J 101
Bells Hill. Barn —5A 4
Bell St. NW1 —5C 66 (5C 158)
Bell St. SE18 —1C 108
Bell, The. (Junct.) —3C 34
Belltrees Gro. SW16 —5K 121
Bell Vw. Mnr. Ruis —7F 23
Bell Water Ga. SE18 —3E 90
Bell Wharf La. EC4 —7C 68 (3D 168)
Bellwood Rd. SE15 —4K 105
Bell Yd. WC2 —6A 68 (1J 167)
Belmarsh Rd. SE28 —2J 91
Belmont. —2A 26
Belmont Av. N9 —1B 18
Belmont Av. N13 —5E 16
Belmont Av. N17 —3C 32
Belmont Av. Barn —5J 5
Belmont Av. N Mald —4C 136
Belmont Av. S'hall —3C 78
Belmont Av. Well —2J 109
Belmont Av. Wemb —1F 63
Belmont Circ. Harr —1B 26
Belmont Clo. E4 —5A 20
Belmont Clo. N20 —1E 14
Belmont Clo. SW4 —3G 103
Belmont Clo. Cockf —4J 5
Belmont Clo. Uxb —6A 40
Belmont Clo. Wfd G —4E 20
Belmont Ct. N5 —4C 50
Belmont Ct. NW11 —5H 29
Belmont Gro. SE13 —3F 107
Belmont Gro. W4 —4K 81
Belmont Hall Ct. SE13 —3F 107
Belmont Hill. SE13 —3E 106
Belmont La. Chst —5F 127
(in two parts)
Belmont La. Stan —1C 26
Belmont Lodge. Har W —7C 10
Belmont M. SW19 —2F 119
Belmont Pde. Chst —5G 127
Belmont Pk. SE13 —4F 107
Belmont Pk. Clo. SE13 —4G 107
Belmont Pk. Rd. E10 —6D 34
Belmont Ri. Sutt —6H 149
Belmont Rd. N15 & N17 —4C 32
Belmont Rd. SE25 —5H 141
Belmont Rd. SW4 —3G 103
Belmont Rd. W4 —4K 81
Belmont Rd. Beck —2A 142
Belmont Rd. Chst —5F 127
Belmont Rd. Eri —7G 93
Belmont Rd. Harr —3K 25
Belmont Rd. Ilf —3G 55
Belmont Rd. Twic —2H 115
Belmont Rd. Wall —5F 151
Belmont St. NW1 —7E 48
Belmont Ter. W4 —4K 81
Belmore Av. Hay —6J 59
Belmore La. N7 —5H 49
Belmore St. SW8 —1H 103
Beloe Clo. SW15 —4C 100
Belsham St. E9 —6J 51
Belsize Av. N13 —6E 16
Belsize Av. NW3 —6B 48
Belsize Av. W13 —3B 80
Belsize Ct. NW3 —5B 48
Belsize Ct. Garages. NW3 —5B 48
(off Belsize La.)
Belsize Cres. NW3 —5B 48
Belsize Gdns. Sutt —4K 149
Belsize Gro. NW3 —6C 48
Belsize La. NW3 —6B 48
Belsize M. NW3 —6B 48
Belsize Pk. NW3 —6B 48
Belsize Pk. Gdns. NW3 —6B 48
Belsize Pk. M. NW3 —6B 48
Belsize Pl. NW3 —5B 48
Belsize Rd. NW6 —1J 65
Belsize Rd. Harr —7C 10
Belsize Sq. NW3 —6B 48
Belsize Ter. NW3 —6B 48
Belson Rd. SE18 —4D 90
Beltane Dri. SW19 —3F 119
Belthorn Cres. SW12 —7G 103
Belton Rd. E7 —7K 53
Belton Rd. E11 —4G 53
Belton Rd. N17 —3E 32
Belton Rd. NW2 —6C 46
Belton Rd. Sidc —4A 128
Belton Way. E3 —5C 70
Beltran Rd. SW6 —2K 101
Beltwood Rd. Belv —4J 93
Belvedere. —3H 93
Belvedere Av. SW19 —5G 119
Belvedere Av. Ilf —2F 37
Belvedere Bldgs. SE1 —2B 86 (7B 168)
Belvedere Clo. Tedd —5J 115
Belvedere Ct. SW15 —4E 100
Belvedere Ct. Belv —3F 93
Belvedere Dri. SW19 —5G 119
Belvedere Gdns. W Mol —5D 132
Belvedere Gro. SW19 —5G 119
Belvedere M. SE15 —3J 105
Belvedere Pl. SE1 —2B 86 (7B 168)
Belvedere Pl. SW2 —4K 103
Belvedere Rd. E10 —1A 52
Belvedere Rd. SE1 —1K 85 (6H 167)
Belvedere Rd. SE2 —1C 92
Belvedere Rd. SE19 —7F 123
Belvedere Rd. W7 —3K 79
Belvedere Rd. Bexh —3F 111
Belvedere Sq. SW19 —5G 119
Belvedere Strand. NW9 —2B 28

A-Z Big London 185

Belvedere, The—Billing Pl.

Belvedere, The. SW10 —1A 102
(off Chelsea Harbour)
Belvedere Way. Harr —6E 26
Belvoir Clo. SE9 —3C 126
Belvoir Rd. SE22 —7G 105
Belvue Bus. Cen. N'holt —7F 43
Belvue Clo. N'holt —7E 42
Belvue Rd. N'holt —7E 42
Bembridge Clo. NW6 —7G 47
Bembridge Gdns. Ruis —2F 41
Bembridge Ho. SE8 —4B 88
(off Longshore)
Bemersyde Point. E13 —3K 71
(off Dongola Rd. W.)
Bemerton Est. N1 —7J 49
Bemerton St. N1 —1K 67
Bemish Rd. SW15 —3F 101
Bempton Dri. Ruis —2K 41
Bemsted Rd. E17 —3B 34
Benares Rd. SE18 —4K 91
Benbow Rd. W6 —3D 82
Benbow St. SE8 —6C 88
Benbury Clo. Brom —5E 124
Bence Ho. SE8 —5A 88
Bench Fld. S Croy —6F 153
Bench, The. Rich —3C 116
Bencroft Rd. SW16 —7G 121
Bencurtis Pk. W W'ck —3F 155
Bendall M. NW1 —5D 158
Bendemeer Rd. SW15 —3F 101
Benden Ho. SE13 —5E 106
(off Monument Gdns.)
Bendish Rd. E6 —7C 54
Bendmore Av. SE2 —5A 92
Bendon Valley. SW18 —7K 101
Benedict Clo. Belv —3E 92
Benedict Ct. Romf —6F 39
Benedict Dri. Felt —7F 95
Benedict Rd. SW9 —3K 103
Benedict Rd. Mitc —3B 138
Benedict Way. N2 —3A 30
Benedict Wharf. Mitc —3B 138
Benenden Grn. Brom —5J 143
Benett Gdns. SW16 —2J 139
Ben Ezra Ct. SE17 —4C 86
(off Asolando Dri.)
Benfleet Clo. Sutt —3A 150
Benfleet Ct. E8 —1F 69
Benfleet Way. N11 —2K 15
Bengal Ct. EC3 —6D 68 (1F 169)
(off Birchin La.)
Bengal Rd. Ilf —4F 55
Bengarth Dri. Harr —2H 25
Bengarth Rd. N'holt —1C 60
Bengeworth Rd. SE5 —3C 104
Bengeworth Rd. Harr —2A 44
Ben Hale Clo. Stan —5G 11
Benham Clo. SW11 —3B 102
Benham Clo. Chess —6C 146
Benham Gdns. Houn —5D 96
Benham Rd. W7 —5J 61
Benham's Pl. NW3 —4A 48
Benhill Av. Sutt —4K 149
Benhill Rd. SE5 —7D 86
Benhill Rd. Sutt —3A 150
Benhill Wood Rd. Sutt —3A 150
Benhilton. —2K 149
Benhilton Gdns. Sutt —3K 149
Benhurst Ct. SW16 —5A 122
Benhurst La. SW16 —5A 122
Benin St. SE13 —7F 107
Benjafield Clo. N18 —4C 18
Benjamin Clo. E8 —1G 69
Benjamin Ct. Belv —6F 93
Benjamin St. EC1 —5B 68 (5A 162)
Ben Jonson Ct. N1 —2E 68
Ben Jonson Ho. EC2 —5D 162
Ben Jonson Pl. EC2 —5D 162
Ben Jonson Rd. E1 —5K 69
Benledi St. E14 —6F 71
Bennelong Clo. W12 —7D 64
Bennerley Rd. SW11 —5C 102
Bennets Fld. Rd. Uxb —1D 76
Bennet's Hill. EC4 —7C 68 (2B 168)
Bennet St. SW1 —1G 85 (4A 166)
Bennett Clo. Hamp W —1C 134
Bennett Clo. N'wd —1H 23
Bennett Clo. Well —2A 110
Bennett Ct. N7 —3K 49
Bennett Gro. SE13 —1D 106
Bennett Ho. SW1 —4H 85 (3D 172)
(off Page St.)
Bennett Pk. SE3 —3H 107
Bennett Rd. E13 —4A 72
Bennett Rd. N16 —4E 50
Bennett Rd. Romf —6E 38
Bennetts Av. Croy —2A 154
Bennetts Av. Gnfd —1J 61
Bennett's Castle La. Dag —2C 56
Bennetts Clo. N17 —6A 18
Bennetts Clo. Mitc —1F 139
Bennetts Copse. Chst —6C 126
Bennett St. W4 —6A 82
Bennetts Way. Croy —2A 154
Bennett's Yd. SW1 —3H 85 (2D 172)
Benningholme Rd. Edgw —6F 13
Bennington Rd. E4 —7B 20
Bennington Rd. N17 —1E 32
Benn's All. Hamp —2F 133
Benn St. E9 —6A 52
Benns Wlk. Rich —4E 98
(off Michelsdale Dri.)
Benrek Clo. Ilf —1G 37
Bensbury Clo. SW15 —7D 100
Bensham Clo. T Hth —4C 140
Bensham Gro. T Hth —2C 140
Bensham La. T Hth & Croy —4B 140
Bensham Mnr. Rd. T Hth —4C 140
Bensley Clo. N11 —5J 15
Ben Smith Way. SE16 —3G 87
Benson Av. E6 —2A 72
Benson Clo. Houn —4E 96
Benson Clo. Uxb —5A 58
Benson Ho. E2 —4F 69 (3J 163)
(off Ligonier St.)
Benson Ho. SE1 —1B 86 (5K 167)
(off Hatfields)
Benson Quay. E1 —7J 69
Benson Rd. SE23 —1J 123
Benson Rd. Croy —3A 152
Bentall Cen., The. King T —2D 134
Bentfield Gdns. SE9 —3B 126
Benthal Rd. N16 —3G 51
Bentham Ct. N1 —7C 50
(off Ecclesbourne Rd.)
Bentham Ct. SE1 —3D 86
(off Falmouth Rd.)
Bentham Rd. E9 —6K 51
Bentham Rd. SE28 —7B 74
Bentham Wlk. NW10 —5J 45
Ben Tillet Clo. E16 —1D 90
Ben Tillet Clo. Bark —7A 56
Ben Tillet Ho. N15 —3B 32
Bentinck Clo. NW8 —2C 66
Bentinck M. W1 —6E 66 (7H 159)
Bentinck Rd. W Dray —1A 76
Bentinck St. W1 —6E 66 (7H 159)
Bentley Dri. NW2 —3H 47
Bentley Dri. Ilf —6G 37
Bentley Ho. SE5 —1E 104
(off Peckham Rd.)
Bentley Rd. N1 —6E 50
Bentley Way. Stan —5F 11
Bentley Way. Wfd G —3D 20
Benton Rd. Ilf —1H 55
Bentons La. SE27 —4C 122
Benton's Ri. SE27 —5D 122
Bentry Clo. Dag —2E 56
Bentry Rd. Dag —2E 56
Bentworth Ct. E2 —4G 69 (3K 163)
(off Granby St.)
Bentworth Rd. W12 —6D 64
Benville Ho. SW8 —7K 85
(off Oval Pl.)
Benwell Ct. Sun —1J 131
Benwell Rd. N7 —4A 50
Benwick Clo. SE16 —4H 87
Benwood Ct. Sutt —3A 150
Benworth St. E3 —3B 70
Benyon Ct. N1 —1E 68
(off De Beauvoir Est.)
Benyon Ho. EC1 —3A 68 (1K 161)
(off Myddelton Pas.)
Benyon Rd. N1 —1D 68
Berberis Ct. Ilf —6F 55
Berberis Ho. E3 —5C 70
Berberis Wlk. W Dray —4A 76
Berber Pl. E14 —7C 70
Berber Rd. SW11 —5D 102
Berberry Clo. Edgw —4D 12
Bercta Rd. SE9 —2G 127
Berenger Tower. SW10 —7B 84
(off Worlds End Est.)
Berenger Wlk. SW10 —7B 84
(off Worlds End Est.)
Berens Ct. Sidc —4K 127
Berens Rd. NW10 —3F 65
Berens Way. Chst —3K 145
Beresford Av. N20 —2J 15
Beresford Av. W7 —5H 61
Beresford Av. Surb —1H 147
Beresford Av. Twic —6C 98
Beresford Av. Wemb —1F 63
Beresford Dri. Brom —3B 144
Beresford Dri. Wfd G —4F 21
Beresford Gdns. Enf —4K 7
Beresford Gdns. Houn —5D 96
Beresford Gdns. Romf —5E 38
Beresford Rd. E4 —1B 20
Beresford Rd. E17 —1D 34
Beresford Rd. N2 —3C 30
Beresford Rd. N5 —5D 50
Beresford Rd. N8 —5A 32
Beresford Rd. Harr —5H 25
Beresford Rd. King T —1F 135
Beresford Rd. N Mald —4J 135
Beresford Rd. S'hall —1B 78
Beresford Rd. Sutt —7H 149
Beresford Sq. SE18 —4F 91
Beresford St. SE18 —3F 91
Beresford Ter. N5 —5C 50
Berestede Rd. W4 —5B 82
Bere St. E1 —7K 69
Bergen Ho. SE5 —2C 104
(off Carew St.)
Bergen Sq. SE16 —3A 88
Berger Clo. Orp —6H 145
Berger Rd. E9 —6K 51
Berghem M. W14 —3F 83
Bergholt Av. Ilf —5C 36
Bergholt Cres. N16 —7E 32
Bergholt M. NW1 —7G 49
Berglen Ct. E14 —6A 70
Berglen Ho. E14 —6A 70
Bering Sq. E14 —5C 88
Bering Wlk. E16 —6B 72
Berisford M. SW18 —6A 102
Berkeley Av. Bexh —1D 110
Berkeley Av. Gnfd —6J 43
Berkeley Av. Houn —1J 95
Berkeley Av. Ilf —2E 36
Berkeley Av. Romf —1J 39
Berkeley Clo. Bren —6A 80
Berkeley Clo. King T —7E 116
Berkeley Clo. Orp —7J 145
Berkeley Clo. Ruis —3J 41
Berkeley Clo. Twic —3J 115
(off Wellesley Rd.)
Berkeley Ct. N3 —1K 29
Berkeley Ct. N14 —6B 6
Berkeley Ct. NW1 —4F 159
Berkeley Ct. NW10 —4A 46
Berkeley Ct. NW11 —7H 29
(off Ravenscroft Av.)
Berkeley Ct. W5 —7C 62
(off Gordon Rd.)
Berkeley Ct. Surb —7D 134
Berkeley Ct. Wall —3G 151
Berkeley Cres. Barn —5G 5
Berkeley Dri. W Mol —3D 132
Berkeley Gdns. N21 —7J 7
Berkeley Gdns. W8 —1J 83
Berkeley Gdns. Clay —6A 146
Berkeley Gdns. W on T —7H 131
Berkeley Ho. Bren —6D 80
(off Albany Rd.)
Berkeley M. W1 —6D 66 (1F 165)
Berkeley Pl. SW19 —6F 119
Berkeley Rd. E12 —5C 54
Berkeley Rd. N8 —5H 31
Berkeley Rd. N15 —6D 32
Berkeley Rd. NW9 —4G 27
Berkeley Rd. SW13 —1C 100
Berkeley Rd. Uxb —7E 40
Berkeley Sq. W1 —7F 67 (3K 165)
Berkeley St. W1 —7F 67 (3K 165)
Berkeley Wlk. N4 —2K 49
(off Durham Rd.)
Berkeley Waye. Houn —6B 78
Berkely Clo. Sun —3A 132
Berkhampstead Rd. Belv —5G 93
Berkhamsted Av. Wemb —6F 45
Berkley Gro. NW1 —7E 48
Berkley Rd. NW1 —7D 48
Berkshire Ct. W7 —4K 61
(off Copley Clo.)
Berkshire Gdns. N13 —6F 17
Berkshire Gdns. N18 —5C 18
Berkshire Ho. SE6 —4C 124
Berkshire Rd. E9 —6B 52
Berkshire Sq. Mitc —4J 139
Berkshire Way. Mitc —4J 139
Bermans Way. NW10 —4A 46
Bermondsey. —2G 87 (7K 169)
Bermondsey Sq. SE1
—3E 86 (7H 169)
Bermondsey St. SE1 —1E 86 (5G 169)
Bermondsey Trad. Est. SE16 —5J 87
Bermondsey Wall E. SE16 —2G 87
Bermondsey Wall W. SE16 —2G 87
Bernal Clo. SE28 —7D 74
Bernard Ashley Dri. SE7 —5K 89
Bernard Av. W13 —3B 80
Bernard Cassidy St. E16 —5H 71
Bernard Gdns. SW19 —5H 119
Bernard Mans. WC1 —4J 67 (4E 160)
Bernard Rd. N15 —5F 33
Bernard Rd. Romf —7J 39
Bernard Rd. Wall —4F 151
Bernard Shaw Ct. NW1 —7G 49
(off St Pancras Way)
Bernard St. WC1 —4J 67 (4E 160)
Bernard Sunley Ho. SW9 —7A 86
(off S. Island Pl.)
Bernays Clo. Stan —6H 11
Bernays Gro. SW9 —4K 103
Bernel Dri. Croy —3B 154
Berne Rd. T Hth —5C 140
Berners Dri. W13 —7A 62
Berners Ho. N1 —2A 68
(off Barnsbury Est.)
Berners M. W1 —5G 67 (6B 160)
Berners Pl. W1 —6G 67 (7B 160)
Berners Rd. N1 —1B 68
Berners Rd. N22 —1A 32
Berners St. W1 —5G 67 (6B 160)
Berner Ter. E1 —6G 69
(off Fairclough St.)
Berney Ho. Beck —5A 142
Berney Rd. Croy —7D 140
Bernhart Clo. Edgw —7D 12
Bernville Way. Harr —5F 27
Bernwell Rd. E4 —3B 20
Berridge Grn. Edgw —7B 12
Berridge M. NW6 —5J 47
Berridge Rd. SE19 —5D 122
Berriman Rd. N7 —3K 49
Berriton Rd. Harr —1D 42
Berrybank Clo. E4 —2K 19
Berry Clo. N21 —1G 17
Berry Clo. NW10 —7A 46
Berry Ct. Houn —5D 96
Berrydale Rd. Hay —4C 60
Berryfield Clo. E17 —4D 34
Berryfield Clo. Brom —1C 144
Berryfield Rd. SE17 —5B 86
Berryhill. SE9 —4F 109
Berry Hill. Stan —4J 11
Berryhill Gdns. SE9 —4F 109
Berrylands. —6G 135
Berrylands. SW20 —3E 136
Berrylands. Surb —6F 135
Berrylands Rd. Surb —6F 135
Berry La. SE21 —4D 122
Berryman Clo. Dag —3C 56
Berryman's La. SE26 —4K 123
Berrymead Gdns. W3 —1J 81
Berrymede Rd. W4 —3K 81
Berry Pl. EC1 —3B 68 (2B 162)
Berry St. EC1 —4B 68 (3B 162)
Berry Way. W5 —3E 80
Bertal Rd. SW17 —4B 120
Bertha Hollamby Ct. Sidc —5C 128
(off Sidcup Hill)
Bertha James Ct. Brom —4K 143
Berthons Gdns. E17 —5F 35
(off Wood St.)
Berthon St. SE8 —7C 88
Bertie Rd. NW10 —6C 46
Bertie Rd. SE26 —6K 123
Bertram Cotts. SW19 —7J 119
Bertram Rd. NW4 —6C 28
Bertram Rd. Enf —4B 8
Bertram Rd. King T —7G 117
Bertram St. N19 —2F 49
Bertrand Ho. SW16 —3J 121
(off Leigham Av.)
Bertrand St. SE13 —3D 106
Bertrand Way. SE28 —7B 74
Bert Rd. T Hth —5C 140
Bert Way. Enf —4A 8
Berwick Av. Hay —6B 60
Berwick Clo. Stan —6E 10
Berwick Cres. Sidc —7J 109
Berwick Ho. N2 —2B 30
Berwick Rd. E16 —6K 71
Berwick Rd. N22 —1B 32
Berwick Rd. Well —1B 110
Berwick St. W1 —6G 67 (7B 160)
Berwyn Av. Houn —1F 97
Berwyn Rd. SE24 —1B 122
Berwyn Rd. Rich —4H 99
Beryl Av. E6 —5C 72
Beryl Rd. W6 —5F 83
Berystede. King T —7H 117
Besant Clo. NW2 —3G 47
Besant Ct. N1 —5D 50
Besant Ho. NW8 —1A 66
(off Boundary Rd.)
Besant Rd. NW2 —4G 47
Besant Wlk. N7 —2K 49
Besant Way. NW10 —5J 45
Besford Ho. E2 —2G 69
(off Pritchard's Rd.)
Besley St. SW16 —6G 121
Bessant Dri. Rich —1G 99
Bessborough Gdns. SW1
—5H 85 (5D 172)
Bessborough Pl. SW1 —5H 85 (5D 172)
Bessborough Rd. SW15 —1C 118
Bessborough Rd. Harr —1H 43
Bessborough St. SW1 —5H 85 (5C 172)
Bessemer Ct. NW1 —7G 49
(off Rochester Sq.)
Bessemer Rd. SE5 —2C 104
Bessie Lansbury Clo. E6 —6E 72
Bessingby Rd. Ruis —2K 41
Bessingham Wlk. SE4 —4K 105
(off Aldersford Clo.)
Besson St. SE14 —1J 105
Bessy St. E2 —3J 69
Bestwood St. SE8 —4K 87
Beswick M. NW6 —6K 47
Betam Rd. Hay —2F 77
Beta Pl. SW9 —4K 103
Betchworth Clo. Sutt —5B 150
Betchworth Rd. Ilf —2J 55
Betchworth Way. New Ad —7E 154
Bethal Est. SE1 —5H 169
Betham Rd. Gnfd —4H 61
Bethany Waye. Felt —7G 95
Bethecar Rd. Harr —5J 25
Bethell Av. E16 —4H 71
Bethell Av. Ilf —7E 36
Bethel Rd. Well —3C 110
Bethersden Clo. Beck —7B 124
Bethersden Ho. SE17 —5E 86
(off Kinglake St.)
Bethlehem Ho. E14 —7B 70
Bethnal Green. —3H 69
Bethnal Green Mus. of Childhood.
—3J 69
Bethnal Grn. Rd. E1 & E2
—4F 69 (3J 163)
Bethune Av. N11 —4J 15
Bethune Clo. N16 —1E 50
Bethune Rd. N16 —7D 32
Bethune Rd. NW10 —4K 63
Bethwin Rd. SE5 —7B 86
Betjeman Clo. Pinn —4E 24
Betjeman Ct. W Dray —1A 76
Betony Clo. Croy —1K 153
Betoyne Av. E4 —4B 20
Betsham Ho. SE1 —2D 86 (6E 168)
(off Newcomen St.)
Betstyle Cir. N11 —4A 16
Betstyle Ho. N10 —7K 15
Betstyle Rd. N11 —4A 16
Betterton Dri. Sidc —2E 128
Betterton Ho. WC2 —6J 67 (1F 167)
(off Betterton St.)
Betterton Rd. Rain —3K 75
Betterton St. WC2 —6J 67 (1E 166)
Bettons Pk. E15 —1G 71
Bettridge Rd. SW6 —2H 101
Betts Clo. Beck —2A 142
Betts Ho. E1 —7H 69
(off Betts St.)
Betts M. E17 —6B 34
Betts Rd. E16 —7K 71
Betts St. E1 —7H 69
Betts Way. SE20 —1H 141
Betts Way. Surb —1B 146
Betty Brooks Ho. E11 —3F 53
Betty May Gray Ho. E14 —4E 88
Beulah Av. T Hth —2C 140
Beulah Clo. Edgw —3C 12
Beulah Cres. T Hth —2C 140
Beulah Gro. Croy —6C 140
Beulah Hill. SE19 —6B 122
Beulah Path. E17 —5E 34
Beulah Rd. E17 —5D 34
Beulah Rd. SW19 —7H 119
Beulah Rd. Sutt —4J 149
Beulah Rd. T Hth —3C 140
Bevan Av. Bark —7A 56
Bevan Ct. Croy —5A 152
Bevan Ho. WC1 —5J 67 (5F 161)
(off Boswell St.)
Bevan Ho. Twic —6D 98
Bevan Rd. SE2 —5B 92
Bevan Rd. Barn —4J 5
Bevan St. N1 —1C 68
Bev Callender Clo. SW8 —3F 103
Bevenden St. N1 —3D 68 (1F 163)
Bevercote Wlk. Belv —6F 93
Beverley Av. SW20 —1B 136
Beverley Av. Houn —4D 96
Beverley Av. Sidc —7K 109
Beverley Clo. N21 —1H 17
Beverley Clo. SW11 —4B 102
Beverley Clo. SW13 —2C 100
Beverley Clo. Chess —4C 146
Beverley Clo. Enf —4K 7
Beverley Cotts. SW15 —3A 118
Beverley Ct. N2 —4D 30
(off Western Rd.)
Beverley Ct. N14 —7B 6
Beverley Ct. SE4 —3B 106
Beverley Ct. W4 —5J 81
Beverley Ct. Harr —3H 25
Beverley Ct. Houn —4D 96
Beverley Ct. Kent —4C 26
Beverley Cres. Wfd G —1K 35
Beverley Dri. Edgw —3G 27
Beverley Gdns. NW11 —7G 29
Beverley Gdns. SW13 —3B 100
Beverley Gdns. Stan —1A 26
Beverley Gdns. Wemb —1F 45
Beverley Gdns. Wor Pk —1C 148
Beverley Ho. Brom —5F 125
(off Brangbourne Rd.)
Beverley La. SW15 —3B 118
Beverley La. King T —7A 118
Beverley M. E4 —6A 20
Beverley Path. SW13 —2B 100
Beverley Rd. E4 —6A 20
Beverley Rd. E6 —3B 72
Beverley Rd. SE20 —2H 141
Beverley Rd. SW13 —3B 100
Beverley Rd. W4 —5B 82
Beverley Rd. Bexh —2J 111
Beverley Rd. Brom —2C 156
Beverley Rd. Dag —4E 56
Beverley Rd. King T —1C 134
Beverley Rd. Mitc —4H 139
Beverley Rd. N Mald —4C 136
Beverley Rd. Ruis —2J 41
Beverley Rd. S'hall —4C 78
Beverley Rd. Sun —1H 131
Beverley Rd. Wor Pk —2E 148
Beverley Trad. Est. Mord —7F 137
Beverley Way. SW20 & N Mald
—1B 136
Beversbrook Rd. N19 —3H 49
Beverstone Rd. SW2 —5K 103
Beverstone Rd. T Hth —4A 140
Beverston M. W1 —6E 158
Bevill Allen Clo. SW17 —5D 120
Bevill Clo. SE25 —3G 141
Bevin Clo. SE16 —1A 88
Bevin Ct. WC1 —3K 67 (1H 161)
Bevington Rd. W10 —5G 65
Bevington Rd. Beck —2D 142
Bevington St. SE16 —2G 87
Bevin Rd. Hay —3J 59
Bevin Sq. SW17 —3D 120
Bevin Way. WC1 —2A 68 (1J 161)
Bevis Marks. EC3 —6E 68 (7H 163)
Bewcastle Gdns. Enf —4D 6
Bew Ct. SE22 —7G 105
Bewdley St. N1 —7A 50
Bewick St. SW8 —2F 103
Bewley St. E1 —7J 69
Bewlys Rd. SE27 —5B 122
Bexhill Clo. Felt —2C 114
Bexhill Rd. N11 —5C 16
Bexhill Rd. SE4 —6B 106
Bexhill Rd. SW14 —3J 99
Bexhill Wlk. E15 —1G 71
Bexley. —7G 111
Bexley Gdns. N9 —3J 17
Bexley Gdns. Chad H —5B 38
Bexley Hall Place Vis. Cen. —6J 111
Bexleyheath. —4G 111
Bexley High St. Bex —7G 111
Bexley Ho. SE4 —4A 106
Bexley La. Dart —5K 111
Bexley La. Sidc —4C 128
Bexley Local Studies & Archive Cen.
—6J 111
Bexley Rd. SE9 —5F 109
Bexley Rd. Eri —1J 111
(in two parts)
Beynon Rd. Cars —5D 150
Bianca Rd. SE15 —6G 87
Bibsworth Rd. N3 —2H 29
Bibury Clo. SE15 —6E 86
(in two parts)
Bicester Rd. Rich —3G 99
Bickenhall Mans. NW1 —5F 159
(in two parts)
Bickenhall St. W1 —5D 66 (5F 159)
Bickersteth Rd. SW17 —6D 120
Bickerton Rd. N19 —2G 49
Bickley. —3C 144
Bickley Cres. Brom —4C 144
Bickley Pk. Rd. Brom —3C 144
Bickley Rd. E10 —7D 34
Bickley Rd. Brom —2B 144
Bickley St. SW17 —5C 120
Bicknell Ho. E1 —6G 69
(off Ellen St.)
Bicknell Rd. SE5 —3C 104
Bicknoller Rd. Enf —1K 7
Bicknor Rd. Orp —7J 145
Bidborough Clo. Brom —5H 143
Bidborough St. WC1 —3J 67 (2E 160)
Biddenden Way. SE9 —4E 126
Bidder St. E16 —5G 71
(in two parts)
Biddesden Ho. SW3 —4D 84 (4E 170)
(off Cadogan St.)
Biddestone Rd. N7 —4K 49
Biddulph Ho. SE18 —4D 90
Biddulph Mans. W9 —3K 65
(off Elgin Av.)
Biddulph Rd. W9 —3K 65
Bideford Av. Gnfd —2B 62
Bideford Clo. Edgw —1G 27
Bideford Clo. Felt —3D 114
Bideford Gdns. Enf —7K 7
Bideford Rd. Brom —3H 125
Bideford Rd. Enf —1G 9
Bideford Rd. Ruis —3K 41
Bideford Rd. Well —7B 92
Bidwell Gdns. N11 —7B 16
Bidwell St. SE15 —1H 105
Big Ben. —2J 85 (7F 167)
Bigbury Clo. N17 —7J 17
Biggerstaff Rd. E15 —1E 70
Biggerstaff St. N4 —2A 50
Biggin Av. Mitc —1D 138
Biggin Hill. SE19 —1B 140
Biggin Hill Clo. King T —5C 116
Biggin Way. SE19 —7B 122
Bigginwood Rd. SW16 —7B 122
Biggs Row. SW15 —3F 101
Big Hill. E5 —1H 51
Bigland St. E1 —6H 69
Bignell Rd. SE18 —5F 91
Bignold Rd. E7 —4J 53
Bigwood Ct. NW11 —5K 29
Bigwood Rd. NW11 —5K 29
Bilberry Ho. E3 —5C 70
Billet Clo. Romf —3D 38
Billet Rd. E17 —1K 33
Billet Rd. Romf —3B 38
Billets Hart Clo. W7 —2J 79
Bill Hamling Clo. SE9 —2D 126
Billing Clo. Dag —7C 56
Billingford Clo. SE4 —4K 105
Billingley. NW1 —1G 67
(off Pratt St.)
Billing Pl. SW10 —7K 83

Billing Rd.—Blomfield St.

Billing Rd. SW10 —7K 83
Billingsgate Fish Market. —1D 88
Billingsgate Rd. E14 —7C 70
Billing St. SW6 —7K 83
Billington Hill. Croy —2D 152
Billington Rd. SE14 —7K 87
Billiter Sq. EC3 —1H 169
Billiter St. EC3 —6E 68 (1H 169)
Bill Nicholson Way. N17 —7A 18
(off High Rd.)
Billockby Clo. Chess —6F 147
Billson St. E14 —4E 88
Bilsby Gro. SE9 —4B 126
Bilsby Lodge. Wemb —3J 45
(off Chalklands)
Bilton Cen., The. Gnfd —1B 62
Bilton Rd. Gnfd —1A 62
Bilton Towers. W1 —6D 66 (1F 165)
(off Gt. Cumberland Pl.)
Bilton Way. Enf —1F 9
Bilton Way. Hay —2K 77
Bina Gdns. SW5 —4A 84
Bincote Rd. Enf —3E 6
Binden Rd. W12 —3B 82
Bindon Grn. Mord —4K 137
Binfield Rd. SW8 —1J 103
Binfield Rd. S Croy —5F 153
Bingfield St. N1 —1J 67
(in two parts)
Bingham Ct. N1 —7B 50
(off Halton Rd.)
Bingham Pl. W1 —5E 66 (5G 159)
Bingham Rd. Croy —1G 153
Bingham St. N1 —6D 50
Bingley Rd. E16 —6A 72
Bingley Rd. Gnfd —4G 61
Bingley Rd. Sun —7J 113
Binley Ho. SW15 —6B 100
Binney St. W1 —6E 66 (1H 165)
Binnie Ho. SE1 —3C 86
(off Bath Ter.)
Binns Rd. W4 —5A 82
Binns Ter. W4 —5A 82
Binsey Wlk. SE2 —2C 92
Binstead Clo. Hay —5C 60
Binyon Cres. Stan —5E 10
Birbetts Rd. SE9 —2D 126
Bircham Path. SE4 —4K 105
(off Aldersford Clo.)
Birchanger Rd. SE25 —5G 141
Birch Av. N13 —3H 17
Birch Av. W Dray —6B 58
Birch Clo. E16 —5G 71
Birch Clo. N19 —2G 49
Birch Clo. SE15 —2G 105
(off Bournemouth Clo.)
Birch Clo. Bren —7B 80
Birch Clo. Buck H —3G 21
Birch Clo. Houn —2H 97
Birch Clo. Romf —3H 39
Birch Clo. Shep —2G 131
Birch Clo. Tedd —5A 116
Birch Ct. Wall —4F 151
Birch Cres. Uxb —1B 58
Birchdale Gdns. Romf —7D 38
Birchdale Rd. E7 —5A 54
Birchdene Dri. SE28 —1A 92
Birchen Clo. NW9 —2K 45
Birchend Clo. S Croy —6D 152
Birchen Gro. NW9 —2K 45
Birches Clo. Mitc —3D 138
Birches Clo. Pinn —5C 24
Birches, The. E12 —4C 54
Birches, The. N21 —6E 6
Birches, The. SE7 —6K 89
Birches, The. Houn —7D 96
Birches, The. Orp —4E 156
Birchfield Ho. E14 —7C 70
Birchfield St. E14 —7C 70
Birch Gdns. Dag —3J 57
Birch Grn. NW9 —7F 13
Birch Gro. E11 —4G 53
Birch Gro. SE12 —7H 107
Birch Gro. W3 —1G 81
Birch Gro. Shep —2G 131
Birch Gro. Well —4A 110
Birch Hill. Croy —5K 153
Birch Ho. N22 —1A 32
(off Acacia Rd.)
Birch Ho. SE14 —1B 106
Birch Ho. SW2 —6A 104
(off Tulse Hill)
Birch Ho. W10 —4G 65
(off Droop St.)
Birchington Clo. Bexh —1H 111
Birchington Ct. NW6 —1K 65
(off W. End La.)
Birchington Ho. E5 —5H 51
Birchington Rd. N8 —6H 31
Birchington Rd. NW6 —1J 65
Birchington Rd. Surb —7F 135
Birchin La. EC3 —6D 68 (1F 169)
Birchlands Av. SW12 —7D 102
Birchmead. Orp —2E 156
Birchmead Av. Pinn —4A 24
Birchmere Bus. Site. SE28 —2A 92
Birchmere Lodge. SE16 —5H 87
(off Sherwood Gdns.)
Birchmere Row. SE3 —2H 107
Birchmore Hall. N5 —3C 50
Birchmore Wlk. N5 —3C 50
Birch Pk. Harr —7B 10
Birch Rd. Felt —5B 114
Birch Rd. Romf —3H 39
Birch Row. Brom —7E 144
Birch Tree Av. W W'ck —5H 155
Birch Tree Way. Croy —2H 153
Birch Va. Ct. NW8 —4B 66 (3B 158)
(off Pollitt Dri.)
Birchville Ct. Bus H —1D 10
Birch Wlk. Eri —6J 93
Birch Wlk. Mitc —1F 139
Birchway. Hay —1J 77
Birchwood Av. N10 —3E 30
Birchwood Av. Beck —4B 142
Birchwood Av. Sidc —2B 128
Birchwood Av. Wall —3E 150
Birchwood Clo. Mord —4K 137
Birchwood Ct. N13 —5G 17
Birchwood Ct. Edgw —2J 27
Birchwood Dri. NW3 —3K 47
Birchwood Dri. Dart —4K 129
Birchwood Gro. Hamp —6E 114
Birchwood Pde. Dart —4K 129
Birchwood Rd. SW17 —5F 121
Birchwood Rd. Orp —4H 145
Birdbrook Clo. Dag —7J 57
Birdbrook Ho. N1 —7C 50
(off Popham Rd.)
Birdbrook Rd. SE3 —4A 108
Birdcage Wlk. SW1 —2G 85 (7A 166)
Birdham Clo. Brom —5C 144
Birdhurst Av. S Croy —4D 152
Birdhurst Gdns. S Croy —4D 152
Birdhurst Ri. S Croy —5E 152
Birdhurst Rd. SW18 —5A 102
Birdhurst Rd. SW19 —6C 120
Birdhurst Rd. S Croy —5E 152
Bird in Bush Rd. SE15 —7G 87
Bird in Hand La. Brom —2B 144
Bird-in-Hand Pas. SE23 —2J 123
Bird in Hand Yd. NW3 —4A 48
Birdlip Clo. SE15 —6E 86
Birdsall Ho. SE5 —3E 104
Birds Farm Av. Romf —1H 39
Birdsfield La. E3 —1B 70
Bird St. W1 —6E 66 (1H 165)
Bird Wlk. Twic —1D 114
Birdwood Clo. Tedd —4J 115
Birkbeck Av. W3 —7J 63
Birkbeck Av. Gnfd —1G 61
Birkbeck Ct. W3 —1K 81
Birkbeck Gdns. Wfd G —2D 20
Birkbeck Gro. W3 —2K 81
Birkbeck Hill. SE21 —1B 122
Birkbeck M. E8 —5F 51
Birkbeck M. W3 —1K 81
Birkbeck Pl. SE21 —2C 122
Birkbeck Rd. E8 —5F 51
Birkbeck Rd. N8 —4J 31
Birkbeck Rd. N12 —5F 15
Birkbeck Rd. N17 —1F 33
Birkbeck Rd. NW7 —5G 13
Birkbeck Rd. SW19 —5K 119
Birkbeck Rd. W3 —1K 81
Birkbeck Rd. W5 —4C 80
Birkbeck Rd. Beck —2J 141
Birkbeck Rd. Enf —1J 7
Birkbeck Rd. Ilf —5H 37
Birkbeck Rd. Romf —1K 57
Birkbeck Rd. Sidc —3A 128
Birkbeck St. E2 —3H 69
Birkbeck Way. Gnfd —1H 61
Birkdale Av. Pinn —3E 24
Birkdale Clo. SE16 —5H 87
Birkdale Clo. Orp —7H 145
Birkdale Ct. S'hall —6G 61
(off Redcroft Rd.)
Birkdale Gdns. Croy —4K 153
Birkdale Rd. SE2 —4A 92
Birkdale Rd. W5 —4E 62
Birkenhead Av. King T —2F 135
Birkenhead St. WC1 —3J 67 (1F 161)
Birkhall Rd. SE6 —1F 125
Birkwood Clo. SW12 —7H 103
Birley Lodge. NW8 —2B 66
(off Acacia Rd.)
Birley Rd. N20 —2F 15
Birley St. SW11 —2E 102
Birling Rd. Eri —7K 93
Birnam Rd. N4 —2K 49
Birnbeck Ct. NW11 —5H 29
Birnbeck Ct. Barn —4A 4
Birrell Ho. SW9 —2K 103
(off Stockwell Rd.)
Birse Cres. NW10 —3A 46
Birstall Rd. N15 —5E 32
Biscay Rd. W6 —5F 83
Biscoe Clo. Houn —6E 78
Biscoe Way. SE13 —3F 107
Biscott Ho. E3 —4D 70
Bisenden Rd. Croy —2E 152
Bisham Clo. Cars —1D 150
Bisham Gdns. N6 —1E 48
Bishop Ct. N12 —4E 14
Bishop Ct. Rich —3E 98
Bishop Duppas Pk. Shep —7G 131
Bishop Fox Way. W Mol —4D 132
Bishop Ken Rd. Harr —2K 25
Bishop King's Rd. W14 —4G 83
Bishop Rd. N14 —7A 6
Bishop's Av. E13 —1K 71
Bishop's Av. SW6 —2F 101
Bishops Av. Brom —2A 144
Bishops Av. Romf —6C 38
Bishops Av., The. N2 —6B 30
Bishop's Bri. Rd. W2 —6K 65 (6A 158)
Bishops Clo. E17 —4D 34
Bishop's Clo. N19 —3G 49
Bishop's Clo. SE9 —2G 127
Bishops Clo. W4 —5J 81
Bishops Clo. Barn —6A 4
Bishops Clo. Enf —2C 8
Bishops Clo. Rich —3D 116
Bishop's Clo. Sutt —3J 149
Bishops Clo. Uxb —2C 58
Bishop's Ct. EC4 —7A 162
Bishops Ct. W2 —6K 65
(off Bishop's Bri. Rd.)
Bishop's Ct. WC2 —7J 161
Bishopsdale Ho. NW6 —1J 65
(off Kilburn Va.)
Bishop's Dri. Felt —6F 95
Bishops Dri. N'holt —1C 60
Bishopsford Rd. Mord —7A 138
Bishopsgate. EC2 —6E 68 (1G 169)
Bishopsgate Arc. EC2 —6H 163
Bishopsgate Chu. Yd. EC2
—5E 68 (7G 163)
Bishopsgate Institute & Libraries
—6H 163
Bishops Grn. Brom —1K 143
(off Up. Park Rd.)
Bishops Gro. N2 —6C 30
Bishop's Gro. Hamp —4D 114
Bishops Gro. Cvn. Site. Hamp —4E 114
Bishop's Hall. King T —2D 134
Bishops Hill. W on T —7J 131
Bishops Ho. SW8 —7J 85
Bishop's Mans. SW6 —2F 101
(in two parts)
Bishops Mead. SE5 —7C 86
(off Camberwell Rd.)
Bishop's Pk. Rd. SW6 —2F 101
Bishops Pk. Rd. SW16 —1J 139
Bishops Rd. N6 —6E 30
Bishops Rd. SW6 —1G 101
Bishop's Rd. SW11 —7C 84
Bishops Rd. W7 —2J 79
Bishop's Rd. Croy —7B 140
Bishop's Rd. Hay —6E 58
Bishop's Ter. SE11 —4A 86 (3K 173)
Bishopsthorpe Rd. SE26 —4K 123
Bishop St. N1 —1C 68
Bishops Vw. Ct. N10 —4F 31
Bishops Wlk. Chst —1G 145
Bishops Wlk. Croy —5K 153
Bishops Wlk. Pinn —3C 24
Bishop's Way. E2 —2H 69
Bishopswood Rd. N6 —7D 30
Bishop Way. NW10 —7A 46
Bishop Wilfred Wood Clo. SE15 —2G 105
Bishop Wilfred Wood Ct. E13 —2A 72
(off Pragel St.)
Bisley Clo. Wor Pk —1E 148
Bison Ct. Felt —7K 95
Bispham Rd. NW10 —3F 63
Bissextile Ho. SE8 —2D 106
Bisson Rd. E15 —2E 70
Bisterne Av. E17 —3F 35
Bittacy Bus. Cen. NW7 —6B 14
Bittacy Clo. NW7 —6A 14
Bittacy Ct. NW7 —7B 14
Bittacy Hill. NW7 —6A 14
Bittacy Pk. Av. NW7 —5A 14
Bittacy Ri. NW7 —6K 13
Bittacy Rd. NW7 —6A 14
Bittern Clo. Hay —5B 60
Bittern Ct. NW9 —2A 28
Bittern Ct. SE8 —6C 88
Bittern Ho. SE1 —2C 86 (7C 168)
(off Gt. Suffolk St.)
Bittern Pl. N22 —2K 31
Bittern St. SE1 —2C 86 (7C 168)
Bittoms Ct. King T —3D 134
Bittoms, The. King T —3D 134
(in two parts)
Bixley Clo. S'hall —4D 78
Blackall St. EC2 —4E 68 (3G 163)
Blackberry Clo. Shep —4G 131
Blackberry Farm Clo. Houn —7C 78
Blackberry Fld. Orp —7A 128
Blackbird Ct. NW9 —2K 45
Blackbird Hill. NW9 —2J 45
Blackbird Yd. E2 —3F 69 (1K 163)
Blackborne Rd. Dag —6G 57
Black Boy La. N15 —5C 32
Blackbrook La. Brom —5D 144
Blackburn. NW9 —2B 28
Blackburne's M. W1 —7E 66 (2G 165)
Blackburn Rd. NW6 —6K 47
Blackbush Av. Romf —5D 38
Blackbush Clo. Sutt —7K 149
Blackdown Clo. N2 —2A 30
Blackett St. SW15 —3F 101
Black Fan Clo. Enf —1H 7
Blackfen. —6A 110
Blackfen Pde. Sidc —6A 110
Blackfen Rd. Sidc —6J 109
Blackford Clo. S Croy —7B 152
Blackford's Path. SW15 —7C 100
Blackfriars Bri. SE1 & EC4
—7B 68 (2A 168)
Blackfriars Ct. EC4 —2A 168
Black Friars La. EC4 —6B 68 (2A 168)
(in two parts)
Blackfriars Pas. EC4 —7B 68 (2A 168)
Blackfriars Rd. SE1 —2B 86 (4A 168)
Blackfriars Underpass. EC4
—7A 68 (2A 168)
Black Gates. Pinn —3D 24
Blackheath. —2H 107
Blackheath Av. SE10 —7F 89
Blackheath Bus. Est. SE10 —1E 106
(off Blackheath Hill)
Blackheath Gro. SE3 —2H 107
Blackheath Hill. SE10 —1E 106
Blackheath Park. —4J 107
Blackheath Pk. SE3 —3H 107
Blackheath Ri. SE13 —2E 106
Blackheath Rd. SE10 —1D 106
Blackheath Vale. —2H 107
Blackheath Va. SE3 —2G 107
Blackheath Village. SE3 —2H 107
Black Horse Ct. SE1 —3D 86
(off Gt. Dover St.)
Blackhorse La. E17 —2K 33
Black Horse La. Croy —7G 141
Blackhorse M. E17 —3K 33
Black Horse Pde. Eastc —5K 23
Blackhorse Road. (Junct.) —4K 33
Blackhorse Rd. E17 —4K 33
Blackhorse Rd. SE8 —6A 88
Blackhorse Rd. Sidc —4A 128
Blacklands Dri. Hay —4E 58
Blacklands Rd. SE6 —4E 124
Blacklands Ter. SW3 —4D 84 (4E 170)
Black Lion La. W6 —4C 82
Black Lion M. W6 —4C 82
Blackmans Yd. E2 —4G 69 (3K 163)
(off Grimsby St.)
Blackmore Av. S'hall —1H 79
Blackmore Ho. N1 —1K 67
(off Barnsbury Est.)
Blackmore Rd. Buck H —1H 21
Blackmore's Gro. Tedd —6A 116
Blackmore Tower. W3 —3J 81
(off Stanley Rd.)
Blackness La. Kes —7B 156
Black Path. E10 —7A 34
Blackpool Gdns. Hay —4G 59
Blackpool Rd. SE15 —2H 105
Black Prince Interchange.
(Junct.) —6H 111
Black Prince Rd. SE1 & SE11
—4K 85 (4G 173)
Black Rod Clo. Hay —3H 77
Blackshaw Rd. SW17 —4A 120
Blacksmiths Clo. Romf —6C 38
Blacksmiths Ho. E17 —4C 34
(off Gillards M.)
Blacks Rd. W6 —5E 82
Blackstock M. N4 —2B 50
Blackstock Rd. N4 & N5 —2B 50
Blackstone Est. E8 —7H 51
Blackstone Ho. SW1 —5G 85 (6A 172)
(off Churchill Gdns.)
Blackstone Rd. NW2 —5E 46
Black Swan Yd. SE1 —2E 86 (6H 169)
Blackthorn Av. W Dray —4C 76
Blackthorn Ct. Houn —7C 78
Blackthorne Av. Croy —1J 153
Blackthorne Ct. SE15 —7F 87
(off Cator St.)
Blackthorne Ct. S'hall —1F 79
(off Dormers Wells La.)
Blackthorne Dri. E4 —4A 20
Blackthorn Gro. Bexh —3E 110
Blackthorn St. E3 —4C 70
Blacktree M. SW9 —3A 104
Blackwall. —7E 70
Blackwall La. SE10 —5G 89
(in two parts)
Blackwall Trad. Est. E14 —5F 71
Blackwall Tunnel. E14 & SE10 —1F 89
(in two parts)
Blackwall Tunnel App. E14 —7E 70
Blackwall Tunnel Northern App.
E3 & E14 —2C 70
Blackwall Tunnel Northern App. E14
—4E 70
Blackwall Tunnel Southern App. SE10
—3G 89
Blackwall Way. E14 —7E 70
Blackwater Clo. E7 —4H 53
Blackwater Clo. Rain —5K 75
Blackwater Ho. NW8 —5B 66 (5B 158)
(off Church St.)
Blackwater St. SE22 —5F 105
Blackwell Clo. E5 —4K 51
Blackwell Clo. Harr —7C 10
Blackwell Gdns. Edgw —4B 12
Blackwell Ho. SW4 —6H 103
Blackwood St. SE17 —5D 86
Blade M. SW15 —4H 101
Blades Ct. SW15 —4H 101
Blades Ho. SE11 —6A 86
(off Kennington Oval)
Bladindon Dri. Bex —7C 110
Bladon Ct. SW16 —6J 121
Bladon Gdns. Harr —6F 25
Blagdens Clo. N14 —2C 16
Blagdens La. N14 —2C 16
Blagdon Ct. W7 —7J 61
Blagdon Rd. SE13 —6D 106
Blagdon Rd. N Mald —4B 136
Blagdon Wlk. Tedd —6C 116
Blagrove Rd. W10 —5G 65
Blair Av. NW9 —7A 28
Blair Clo. N1 —6C 50
Blair Clo. Hay —4J 77
Blair Clo. Sidc —5J 109
Blair Ct. NW8 —1B 66
Blair Ct. SE6 —1H 125
Blair Ct. Beck —1D 142
Blairderry Rd. SW2 —2J 121
Blair Ho. SW9 —2K 103
Blair St. E14 —6E 70
Blake Av. Bark —1J 73
Blake Clo. W10 —5E 64
Blake Clo. Cars —1C 150
Blake Clo. Well —1J 109
Blake Ct. NW6 —3J 65
(off Stafford Clo.)
Blakeden Dri. Clay —6A 146
Blake Gdns. SW6 —1K 101
Blake Hall Cres. E11 —1J 53
Blake Hall Rd. E11 —7J 35
Blakehall Rd. Cars —6D 150
Blake Ho. E14 —2C 88
(off Admirals Way)
Blake Ho. SE1 —3A 86 (1J 173)
Blakeley Cotts. SE10 —2F 89
Blakemore Rd. SW16 —3J 121
Blakemore Rd. T Hth —5K 139
Blakemore Way. Belv —3E 92
Blakeney Av. Beck —1B 142
Blakeney Clo. E8 —5G 51
Blakeney Clo. N20 —1F 15
Blakeney Clo. NW1 —7H 49
Blakeney Rd. Beck —7B 124
Blakenham Rd. SW17 —4D 120
Blaker Ct. SE7 —7A 90
(in two parts)
Blake Rd. E16 —4H 71
Blake Rd. N11 —7B 16
Blake Rd. Croy —2E 152
Blake Rd. Mitc —3C 138
Blaker Rd. E15 —1E 70
Blakes Av. N Mald —5B 136
Blake's Grn. W W'ck —1E 154
Blakes La. N Mald —5B 136
Blakesley Av. W5 —6C 62
Blakesley Wlk. SW20 —2H 137
Blake's Rd. SE15 —7E 86
Blakes Ter. N Mald —5C 136
Blakesware Gdns. N9 —7J 7
Blakewood Clo. Felt —4A 114
Blanchard Clo. SE9 —3C 126
Blanchard Ho. Twic —6D 98
(off Clevedon Rd.)
Blanchard Way. E8 —6G 51
Blanch Clo. SE15 —7J 87
Blanchedowne. SE5 —4D 104
Blanche St. E16 —4H 71
Blanchland Rd. Mord —5K 137
Blandfield Rd. SW12 —7E 102
Blandford Av. Beck —2A 142
Blandford Av. Twic —1F 115
Blandford Clo. N2 —4A 30
Blandford Clo. Croy —3J 151
Blandford Clo. Romf —4G 39
Blandford Ct. E8 —7E 50
(off St Peter's Way)
Blandford Ct. NW6 —7F 47
Blandford Cres. E4 —7K 9
Blandford Ho. SW8 —7K 85
(off Richborne Ter.)
Blandford Rd. W4 —3A 82
Blandford Rd. W5 —2D 80
Blandford Rd. Beck —3J 141
Blandford Rd. S'hall —4E 78
Blandford Rd. Tedd —5H 115
Blandford Sq. NW1 —4C 66 (4D 158)
Blandford St. W1 —6D 66 (7F 159)
Blandford Waye. Hay —6A 60
Bland Ho. SE11 —5H 173
Bland St. SE9 —4B 108
Blaney Cres. E6 —3F 73
Blanmerle Rd. SE9 —1F 127
Blann Clo. SE9 —6B 108
Blantyre St. SW10 —7B 84
Blantyre Tower. SW10 —7B 84
(off Blantyre St.)
Blantyre Wlk. SW10 —7B 84
(off Worlds End Est.)
Blashford. NW3 —7D 48
(off Adelaide Rd.)
Blashford St. SE13 —7F 107
Blasker Wlk. E14 —5D 88
Blawith Rd. Harr —4J 25
Blaxland Ho. W12 —7D 64
(off White City Est.)
Blaydon Clo. N17 —7C 18
Blaydon Clo. Ruis —7G 23
Blaydon Ct. N'holt —6E 42
Blazer Ct. NW8 —2B 158
Bleak Hill La. SE18 —6K 91
Blean Gro. SE20 —7J 123
Bleasdale Av. Gnfd —2A 62
Blechynden St. W10 —7F 65
Bleddyn Clo. Sidc —6C 110
Bledlow Clo. SE28 —7C 74
Bledlow Ho. NW8 —4B 66 (4B 158)
(off Capland St.)
Bledlow Ri. Gnfd —2G 61
Bleeding Heart Yd. EC1 —6K 161
Blegborough Rd. SW16 —6G 121
Blemundsbury. WC1 —5K 67 (5G 161)
(off Dombey St.)
Blendon. —6D 110
Blendon Dri. Bex —6D 110
Blendon Path. Brom —7H 125
Blendon Rd. Bex —6D 110
Blendon Row. SE17 —4D 86
(off Townley St.)
Blendon Ter. SE18 —5G 91
Blendworth Way. SE15 —7E 86
(off Clanfield Way)
Blenheim Av. Ilf —6E 36
Blenheim Clo. N21 —1H 17
Blenheim Clo. SW20 —3E 136
Blenheim Clo. Gnfd —2H 61
Blenheim Clo. Romf —4J 39
Blenheim Clo. Wall —7G 151
Blenheim Ct. N19 —2J 49
Blenheim Ct. Brom —4H 143
Blenheim Ct. Kent —6A 26
Blenheim Ct. Sidc —3H 127
Blenheim Ct. Sutt —6A 150
Blenheim Cres. W11 —7G 65
Blenheim Cres. Ruis —2F 41
Blenheim Cres. S Croy —7C 152
Blenheim Dri. Well —1K 109
Blenheim Gdns. NW2 —6E 46
Blenheim Gdns. SW2 —6K 103
Blenheim Gdns. King T —7H 117
Blenheim Gdns. Wall —6G 151
Blenheim Gdns. Wemb —3E 44
Blenheim Gro. SE15 —2G 105
Blenheim Ho. Houn —3E 96
Blenheim Pde. Uxb —4D 58
Blenheim Pk. Rd. S Croy —7C 152
Blenheim Pas. NW8 —2A 66
(in two parts)
Blenheim Ri. N15 —4F 33
Blenheim Rd. E6 —3B 72
Blenheim Rd. E15 —4G 53
Blenheim Rd. E17 —3K 33
Blenheim Rd. NW8 —2A 66
Blenheim Rd. SE20 —7J 123
Blenheim Rd. SW20 —3E 136
Blenheim Rd. W4 —3A 82
Blenheim Rd. Barn —3A 4
Blenheim Rd. Brom —4C 144
Blenheim Rd. Harr —6F 25
Blenheim Rd. N'holt —6F 43
Blenheim Rd. Sidc —1C 128
Blenheim Rd. Sutt —3J 149
Blenheim Shop. Cen. SE20 —7J 123
Blenheim St. W1 —6F 67 (1J 165)
Blenheim Ter. NW8 —2A 66
Blenheim Way. Iswth —1A 98
Blenkarne Rd. SW11 —6D 102
Bleriot. NW9 —2B 28
(off Belvedere Strand)
Bleriot Rd. Houn —7A 78
Blessbury Rd. Edgw —1J 27
Blessington Clo. SE13 —3F 107
Blessington Rd. SE13 —3F 107
Blessing Way. Bark —3C 74
Bletchingley Clo. T Hth —4B 140
Bletchley Ct. N1 —1E 162
(in two parts)
Bletchley St. N1 —2D 68 (1D 162)
Bletchmore Clo. Hay —5F 77
Bletsoe Wlk. N1 —2C 68
Blewbury Ho. SE2 —2D 92
Blincoe Clo. SW19 —2F 119
Bliss Cres. SE13 —2D 106
Blissett St. SE10 —1E 106
Blisworth Clo. Hay —4C 60
Blisworth Ho. E2 —1G 69
(off Whiston Rd.)
Blithbury Rd. Dag —6B 56
Blithdale Rd. SE2 —4A 92
Blithfield St. W8 —3K 83
Blockley Rd. Wemb —2B 44
Bloemfontein Av. W12 —1D 82
Bloemfontein Rd. W12 —7D 64
Bloemfontein Way. W12 —1D 82
Blomfield Ct. W9 —4A 66 (3A 158)
(off Lanark Pl.)
Blomfield Rd. W9 —5K 65 (4A 158)
Blomfield St. EC2 —5D 68 (6F 163)

Blomfield Vs.—Boxgrove Rd.

Blomfield Vs. W2 —5K 65
Blomville Rd. Dag —3E 56
Blondel St. SW11 —2E 102
Blondin Av. W5 —4C 80
Blondin St. E3 —2C 70
Bloomburg St. SW1 —4H 85 (4B 172)
Bloomfield Ct. N6 —6E 30
Bloomfield Cres. Ilf —6F 37
Bloomfield Ho. E1 —5G 69 (off Old Montague St.)
Bloomfield Pl. W1 —2K 165
Bloomfield Rd. N6 —6E 30
Bloomfield Rd. SE18 —6F 91
Bloomfield Rd. Brom —5B 144
Bloomfield Rd. King T —4E 134
Bloomfields, The. Bark —6G 55
Bloomfield Ter. SW1 —5E 84 (5H 171)
Bloom Gro. SE27 —3B 122
Bloomhall Rd. SE19 —5D 122
Bloom Pk. Rd. SW6 —7H 83
Bloomsbury. —5J 67 (5E 160)
Bloomsbury Clo. W5 —7F 63
Bloomsbury Ct. WC1 —6F 161
Bloomsbury Ct. Houn —1K 95
Bloomsbury Ct. Pinn —3D 24
Bloomsbury Ho. SW4 —6H 103
Bloomsbury Pl. SW18 —5A 102
Bloomsbury Pl. WC1 —5J 67 (5F 161)
Bloomsbury Sq. WC1 —5J 67 (6F 161)
Bloomsbury St. WC1 —5H 67 (6D 160)
Bloomsbury Way. WC1 —5J 67 (6E 160)
Blore Clo. SW8 —1H 103
Blore Ct. W1 —1C 166
Blossom Clo. W5 —2E 80
Blossom Clo. Dag —1F 75
Blossom Clo. S Croy —5F 153
Blossom La. Enf —1H 7
Blossom St. E1 —4E 68 (4H 163)
Blossom Way. Uxb —7B 40
Blossom Way. W Dray —4C 76
Blossom Waye. Houn —6C 78
Blount Ho. E14 —5A 70
Blount St. E14 —5A 70
Bloxam Gdns. SE9 —5C 108
Bloxhall Rd. E10 —1B 52
Bloxham Cres. Hamp —7D 114
Bloxworth Clo. Wall —3G 151
Blucher Rd. SE5 —7C 86
Blue Anchor All. Rich —4E 98
Blue Anchor La. SE16 —4G 87
Blue Anchor Yd. E1 —7G 69 (3K 169)
Blue Ball Yd. SW1 —1G 85 (5A 166)
Bluebell Av. E12 —5B 54
Bluebell Clo. E9 —1J 69
Bluebell Clo. SE26 —4F 123
Bluebell Clo. Rush G —2K 57
Bluebell Clo. Wall —1F 151
Bluebell Way. Ilf —6F 55
Blueberry Clo. Wfd G —6D 20
Bluebird La. Dag —7G 57
Bluebird Wlk. Wemb —3H 45
Bluebird Way. SE28 —2H 91
Bluefield Clo. Hamp —5E 114
Bluegates. Ewe —7C 148
Bluehouse Rd. E4 —2B 20
Blue Riband Ind. Est. Croy —2B 152
Blue Water. SW18 —4K 101
Blundell Ho. SE14 —7A 88 (off Goodwood Rd.)
Blundell Rd. Edgw —1K 27
Blundell St. N7 —7J 49
Blunden Clo. Dag —1C 56
Blunt Rd. S Croy —5D 152
Blunts Av. W Dray —7C 76
Blunts Rd. SE9 —5E 108
Blurton Rd. E5 —4J 51
Blydon Ct. N21 —5E 6 (off Chaseville Pk. Rd.)
Blyth Clo. E14 —4F 89
Blyth Clo. Twic —6K 97
Blythe Clo. SE6 —7B 106
Blythe Hill. —7B 106
Blythe Hill. SE6 —7B 106
Blythe Hill. Orp —1K 145
Blythe Hill La. SE6 —7B 106
Blythe Ho. SE11 —6A 86 (7J 173)
Blythe M. W14 —3F 83
Blythendale Ho. E2 —2G 69 (off Mansford St.)
Blythe Rd. W14 —3F 83
Blythe St. E2 —3H 69
Blythe Va. SE6 —1B 124
Blyth Hill Pl. SE6 —7D 106
Blyth Rd. E17 —7B 34
Blyth Rd. SE28 —7C 74
Blyth Rd. Brom —1H 143
Blyth Rd. Hay —2G 77
Blythswood Rd. Ilf —1A 56
Blyth Wood Pk. Brom —1H 143
Blythwood Rd. N4 —7J 31
Blythwood Rd. Pinn —1B 24
Boades M. NW3 —4B 48
Boadicea St. N1 —1K 67
Boakes Clo. NW9 —4J 27
Boardman Av. E4 —5J 9
Boardman Clo. Barn —5B 4
Boardwalk Pl. E14 —1E 88
Boarhound. NW9 —2B 28 (off Further Acre)
Boarley Ho. SE17 —4E 86 (off Massinger St.)
Boars Head Yd. Bren —7D 80
Boathouse Wlk. SE15 —7F 87 (in two parts)
Boat Lifter Way. SE16 —4A 88
Bob Anker Clo. E13 —3J 71
Bobbin Clo. SW4 —3G 103
Bobby Moore Way. N12 —7J 15
Bob Marley Way. SE24 —4A 104
Bockhampton Rd. King T —7F 117
Bocking St. E8 —1H 69
Boddicott Clo. SW19 —2G 119
Boddington Ho. SE14 —1J 105 (off Pomeroy St.)
Boddys Bri. SE1 —1A 86 (4K 167) (off Hatfields)
Bodeney Ho. SE5 —1E 104 (off Peckham Rd.)
Boden Ho. E1 —5G 69 (5K 163) (off Woodseer St.)
Bodiam Clo. Enf —2K 7
Bodiam Rd. SW16 —7H 121
Bodington Ct. W12 —2F 83
Bodley Clo. N Mald —5A 136
Bodley Mnr. Way. SW2 —7A 104
Bodley Rd. N Mald —6K 135
Bodmin. NW9 —2B 28 (off Further Acre)
Bodmin Clo. Harr —3D 42
Bodmin Gro. Mord —5K 137
Bodmin Pl. SE27 —4B 122
Bodmin St. SW18 —1J 119
Bodnant Gdns. SW20 —3C 136
Bodney Rd. E8 —5H 51
Boeing Way. S'hall —3K 77
Boevey Path. Belv —5F 93
Bogey La. Orp —7E 156
Bognor Rd. Well —1D 110
Bohemia Pl. E8 —6J 51
Bohn Rd. E1 —5A 70
Bohun Gro. Barn —6H 5
Boileau Pde. W5 —6F 63 (off Boileau Rd.)
Boileau Rd. SW13 —7C 82
Boileau Rd. W5 —6F 63
Bolden St. SE8 —2D 106
Boldero Pl. NW8 —4C 158
Bolderwood Way. W W'ck —2D 154
Boldmere Rd. Pinn —7A 24
Boleyn Av. Enf —1C 8
Boleyn Clo. E17 —4C 34
Boleyn Ct. Buck H —1D 20
Boleyn Dri. Ruis —2B 42
Boleyn Dri. W Mol —3D 132
Boleyn Gdns. Dag —7J 57
Boleyn Gdns. W W'ck —2D 154
Boleyn Gro. W W'ck —2E 154
Boleyn Rd. E6 —2B 72
Boleyn Rd. E7 —7J 53
Boleyn Rd. N16 —5E 50
Boleyn Way. Barn —3F 5
Bolina Rd. SE16 —5J 87
Bolingbroke Gro. SW11 —4C 102
Bolingbroke Rd. W14 —3F 83
Bolingbroke Wlk. SW11 —1B 102
Bolingbroke Way. Hay —1F 77
Bolliger Ct. NW10 —4J 63
Bollo Bri. Rd. W3 —3H 81
Bollo Ct. W3 —3J 81 (off Bollo Bri. Rd.)
Bollo La. W3 & W4 —2H 81
Bolney Ga. SW7 —2C 84 (7C 164)
Bolney St. SW8 —7K 85
Bolney Way. Felt —3C 114
Bolsover St. W1 —4F 67 (4K 159)
Bolstead Rd. Mitc —1F 139
Bolster Gro. N22 —7C 16
Bolt Ct. EC4 —6A 68 (1K 167)
Boltmore Clo. NW4 —3F 29
Bolton Clo. SE20 —2G 141
Bolton Clo. Chess —6D 146
Bolton Cres. SE5 —7B 86
Bolton Gdns. NW10 —2F 65
Bolton Gdns. SW5 —5K 83
Bolton Gdns. Brom —6H 125
Bolton Gdns. Tedd —6A 116
Bolton Gdns. M. SW10 —5A 84
Bolton Ho. SE10 —5G 89 (off Trafalgar Rd.)
Bolton Pl. NW8 —1K 65 (off Bolton Rd.)
Bolton Rd. E15 —6H 53
Bolton Rd. N18 —5A 18
Bolton Rd. NW8 —1K 65
Bolton Rd. NW10 —1A 64
Bolton Rd. W4 —7J 81
Bolton Rd. Chess —6D 146
Bolton Rd. Harr —4G 25
Boltons Ct. SW5 —5K 83 (off Old Brompton Rd.)
Bolton's La. Hay —7D 76
Boltons Pl. SW5 —5A 84
Boltons, The. SW10 —5A 84
Boltons, The. Wemb —4K 43
Bolton St. W1 —1F 85 (4K 165)
Bolton Studios. SW10 —5A 84
Bolton Wlk. N4 —2K 49 (off Durham Rd.)
Bombay St. SE16 —4H 87
Bomer Clo. W Dray —7C 76
Bomore Rd. W11 —7G 65
Bonar Pl. Chst —7C 126
Bonar Rd. SE15 —7G 87
Bonchester Clo. Chst —7E 126
Bonchurch Clo. Sutt —7K 149
Bonchurch Rd. W10 —5G 65
Bonchurch Rd. W13 —1B 80
Bond Clo. W Dray —6B 58
Bond Ct. EC4 —7D 68 (2E 168)
Bondfield Av. Hay —3J 59
Bondfield Rd. E6 —5D 72
Bond Gdns. Wall —4G 151
Bond Ho. NW6 —2H 65 (off Rupert Rd.)
Bond Ho. SE14 —7A 88 (off Goodwood Rd.)
Bonding Yd. Wlk. SE16 —3A 88
Bond Rd. Mitc —2C 138
Bond Rd. Surb —2F 147
Bond St. E15 —5G 53
Bond St. W4 —4K 81
Bond St. W5 —7D 62
Bondway. SW8 —6J 85 (7G 173)
Boneta Rd. SE18 —3D 90
Bonfield Rd. SE13 —4E 106
Bonham Gdns. Dag —2D 56
Bonham Rd. SW2 —5K 103
Bonham Rd. Dag —2D 56
Bonheur Rd. W4 —2K 81
Bonhill St. EC2 —4D 68 (4F 163)
Boniface Gdns. Harr —7A 10
Boniface Rd. Uxb —3D 40
Boniface Wlk. Harr —7A 10
Bonington Ho. N1 —2K 67
Bon Marche Ter. M. SE27 —4E 122
Bonner Hill Rd. King T —2F 135 (in two parts)
Bonner Rd. E2 —2J 69
Bonnersfield Clo. Harr —6K 25
Bonnersfield La. Harr —6K 25
Bonner St. E2 —2J 69
Bonneville Gdns. SW4 —6G 103
Bonnington Ct. N'holt —2B 60 (off Gallery Gdns.)
Bonnington Sq. SW8 —6K 85 (7G 173)
Bonny St. NW1 —7G 49
Bonser Rd. Twic —2K 115
Bonsor Ho. SW8 —1G 103
Bonsor St. SE5 —7E 86
Bonville Gdns. NW4 —4D 28
Bonville Rd. Brom —5H 125
Bookbinders Cottage Homes. N20 —3J 15
Booker Clo. E14 —5B 70
Booker Rd. N18 —5B 18
Bookham Ct. SW19 —3B 138
Boone Ct. N9 —3D 18
Boones Rd. SE13 —4G 107
Boone St. SE13 —4G 107
Boord St. SE10 —3G 89
Boothby Ct. E4 —3K 19
Boothby Rd. N19 —2H 49
Booth Clo. E9 —1H 69
Booth Clo. SE28 —1B 92
Booth Dri. Stai —6A 112
Booth La. EC4 —2C 168
Boothman Ho. Kent —3D 26
Booth Rd. NW9 —2K 27
Booth Rd. Croy —2B 152
Booth's Pl. W1 —5G 67 (6B 160)
Boot Pde. Edgw —6B 12 (off High St.)
Boot St. N1 —3E 68 (2G 163)
Bordars Rd. W7 —5J 61
Bordars Wlk. W7 —5J 61
Borden Av. Enf —6J 7
Border Cres. SE26 —5H 123
Border Gdns. Croy —4D 154
Bordergate. Mitc —1C 138
Border Rd. SE26 —5H 123
Bordesley Rd. Mord —5K 137
Bordeston Ct. Bren —7C 80 (off Augustus Clo.)
Bordon Wlk. SW15 —7C 100
Boreas Wlk. N1 —1B 162
Boreham Av. E16 —6J 71
Boreham Clo. E10 —1E 52
Boreham Rd. N22 —2C 32
Borgard Rd. SE18 —4D 90
Borland Rd. SE15 —4J 105
Borland Rd. Tedd —7B 116
Borneo St. SW15 —3E 100
Borough High St. SE1 —2C 86 (7D 168)
Borough Hill. Croy —3B 152
Borough Rd. SE1 —3B 86 (7B 168)
Borough Rd. Iswth —1J 97
Borough Rd. King T —1G 135
Borough Rd. Mitc —2C 138
Borough Sq. SE1 —7C 168
Borough, The. —2D 86 (6E 168)
Borrett Clo. SE17 —5C 86
Borrodaile Rd. SW18 —6K 101
Borrowdale. NW1 —3G 67 (2A 160) (off Robert St.)
Borrowdale Av. Harr —2A 26
Borrowdale Clo. Ilf —4C 36
Borrowdale Ct. Enf —1H 7
Borthwick M. E15 —4G 53
Borthwick Rd. E15 —4G 53
Borthwick Rd. NW9 —6B 28
Borthwick St. SE8 —5C 88
Borwick Av. E17 —3B 34
Bosanquet Clo. Uxb —4A 58
Bosbury Rd. SE6 —3E 124
Boscastle Rd. NW5 —3F 49
Boscobel Ho. E8 —6H 51
Boscobel Pl. SW1 —4E 84 (3H 171)
Boscobel St. NW8 —4B 66 (4B 158)
Boscombe Av. E10 —7F 35
Boscombe Clo. E5 —5A 52
Boscombe Gdns. SW16 —6J 121
Boscombe Rd. SW17 —6E 120
Boscombe Rd. SW19 —1K 137
Boscombe Rd. W12 —1C 82
Boscombe Rd. Wor Pk —1E 148
Bose Clo. N3 —1G 29
Bosgrove. E4 —2K 19
Boss Ho. SE1 —2F 87 (6J 169) (off Boss St.)
Boss St. SE1 —2F 87 (6J 169)
Bostall Hill. SE2 —5A 92
Bostall La. SE2 —5B 92
Bostall Mnr. Way. SE2 —4B 92
Bostall Pk. Av. Bexh —7E 92
Bostall Rd. Orp —7B 128
Bostock Ho. Houn —6E 78
Boston Bus. Pk. W7 —3J 79
Boston Gdns. W4 —6A 82
Boston Gdns. W7 —4A 80
Boston Gdns. Bren —4A 80
Boston Gro. Ruis —6E 22
Boston Manor. —4A 80
Boston Manor House. —5B 80
Boston Mnr. Rd. Bren —4B 80
Boston Pde. W7 —3A 80
Boston Pk. Rd. Bren —5C 80
Boston Pl. NW1 —4D 66 (4E 158)
Boston Rd. E6 —3C 72
Boston Rd. E17 —6C 34
Boston Rd. W7 —1J 79
Boston Rd. Croy —6K 139
Boston Rd. Edgw —7D 12
Bostonthorpe Rd. W7 —2J 79
Boston Va. W7 —4A 80
Bosun Clo. E14 —2C 88
Boswell Ct. W14 —3F 83 (off Blythe Rd.)
Boswell Ct. WC1 —5J 67 (5F 161)
Boswell Ho. WC1 —5J 67 (5F 161) (off Boswell St.)
Boswell Path. Hay —4H 77
Boswell Rd. T Hth —4C 140
Boswell St. WC1 —5J 67 (5F 161)
Bosworth Clo. E17 —1B 34
Bosworth Ho. W10 —4G 65 (off Bosworth Rd.)
Bosworth Rd. N11 —6C 16
Bosworth Rd. W10 —4G 65
Bosworth Rd. Barn —3D 4
Bosworth Rd. Dag —3G 57
Botany Bay La. Chst —3G 145
Botany Clo. Barn —4H 5
Boteley Clo. E4 —2A 20
Botham Clo. Edgw —7D 12
Botha Rd. E13 —5K 71
Bothwell Clo. E16 —5H 71
Bothwell St. SW6 —6F 83
Botolph All. EC3 —2G 169
Botolph La. EC3 —7E 68 (3G 169)
Botsford Rd. SW20 —2G 137
Botts M. W2 —6J 65
Botwell Comn. Rd. Hay —7F 59
Botwell Cres. Hay —6G 59
Botwell La. Hay —7G 59
Boucher Clo. Tedd —5K 115
Bouchier Ho. N2 —2B 30
Boughton Av. Brom —7H 143
Boughton Ho. SE1 —2D 86 (6E 168) (off Tennis St.)
Boughton Rd. SE28 —3J 91
Boulcott St. E1 —6K 69
Boulevard, The. SW17 —2E 120
Boulevard, The. SW18 —4K 101
Boulevard, The. Pinn —4E 24
Boulevard, The. Wfd G —6K 21
Boulogne Ho. SE1 —3F 87 (7J 169) (off Abbey St.)
Boulogne Rd. Croy —6C 140
Boulter Ho. SE14 —1J 105 (off Kender St.)
Boulton Ho. Bren —5E 80
Boulton Rd. Dag —2E 56
Boultwood Rd. E6 —6D 72
Bounces La. N9 —2C 18
Bounces Rd. N9 —2C 18
Boundaries Rd. SW12 —2D 120
Boundaries Rd. Felt —1A 114
Boundary Av. E17 —7B 34
Boundary Bus. Ct. Mitc —3B 138
Boundary Clo. SE25 —2G 141
Boundary Clo. Barn —1C 4
Boundary Clo. Ilf —4J 55
Boundary Clo. King T —3H 135
Boundary Clo. S'hall —5E 78
Boundary Ct. N18 —6A 18 (off Snells Pk.)
Boundary Ho. SE5 —7C 86
Boundary La. E13 —3B 72
Boundary La. SE5 —6C 86
Boundary M. NW8 —1A 66 (off Boundary Rd.)
Boundary Pas. E1 —4F 69 (3J 163)
Boundary Rd. E13 —2A 72
Boundary Rd. E17 —7B 34
Boundary Rd. N2 —1B 30
Boundary Rd. N9 —6D 8
Boundary Rd. N22 —3B 32
Boundary Rd. NW8 —1K 65
Boundary Rd. SW19 —6B 120
Boundary Rd. Bark —2G 73 (in two parts)
Boundary Rd. Cars & Wall —6F 151
Boundary Rd. Pinn —7B 24
Boundary Rd. Sidc —5J 109
Boundary Rd. Wemb —3E 44
Boundary Row. SE1 —2B 86 (6A 168)
Boundary St. E2 —3F 69 (2J 163) (in two parts)
Boundary Way. Croy —5C 154
Boundfield Rd. SE6 —3G 125
Bounds Green. —6C 16
Bounds Grn. Ct. N11 —6C 16 (off Bounds Grn. Rd.)
Bounds Grn. Ind. Est. N11 —6B 16
Bounds Grn. Rd. N11 & N22 —6B 16
Bourbon Ho. SE6 —5E 124
Bourchier St. W1 —7H 67 (2C 166) (in two parts)
Bourdon Pl. W1 —2K 165
Bourdon Rd. SE20 —2J 141
Bourdon St. W1 —7F 67 (3J 165)
Bourke Clo. NW10 —6A 46
Bourke Clo. SW4 —6J 103
Bourlet Clo. W1 —5G 67 (6A 160)
Bourn Av. N15 —4D 32
Bourn Av. Uxb —4C 58
Bournbrook Rd. SE3 —3B 108
Bourne Av. N14 —2D 16
Bourne Av. Barn —5G 5
Bourne Av. Hay —3E 76
Bourne Av. Ruis —5A 42
Bourne Cir. Hay —3E 76
Bourne Ct. W4 —6J 81
Bourne Ct. S Ruis —5K 41
Bourne Ct. Wfd G —3B 36
Bourne Dri. Mitc —2B 138
Bourne Est. EC1 —5A 68 (5J 161)
Bourne Gdns. E4 —4J 19
Bourne Hall Mus. —7B 148
Bourne Hill. N14 —1D 16
Bourne Hill Clo. N13 —2E 16
Bourne Ind. Pk., The. Dart —5K 111
Bourne Mead. Bex —5J 111
Bournemead Av. N'holt —2J 59
Bournemead Clo. N'holt —3J 59
Bournemead Way. N'holt —2K 59
Bourne M. W1 —6E 66 (1H 165)
Bournemouth Clo. SE15 —2G 105
Bournemouth Rd. SE15 —2G 105
Bournemouth Rd. SW19 —1J 137
Bourne Pde. Bex —7H 111
Bourne Pl. W4 —5K 81
Bourne Rd. E7 —3H 53
Bourne Rd. N8 —6J 31
Bourne Rd. Bex & Dart —7H 111
Bourne Rd. Brom —4B 144
Bournes Ho. N15 —6E 32 (off Chisley Rd.)
Bourneside Cres. N14 —1C 16
Bourneside Gdns. SE6 —5E 124
Bourne St. SW1 —4E 84 (4G 171)
Bourne St. Croy —2B 152
Bourne Ter. W2 —5K 65
Bourne, The. N14 —1C 16
Bourne Va. Brom —1H 155
Bournevale Rd. SW16 —4J 121
Bourne Vw. Gnfd —6K 43
Bourne Way. Brom —2H 155
Bourne Way. Eps —4J 147
Bourne Way. Sutt —5H 149
Bournewood Rd. SE18 —7A 92
Bournville Rd. SE6 —7C 106
Bournwell Clo. Barn —3J 5
Bourton Clo. Hay —1J 77
Bousfield Rd. SE14 —2K 105
Boutflower Rd. SW11 —4C 102
Boutique Hall. SE13 —4E 106
Bouverie Gdns. Harr —6D 26
Bouverie M. N16 —2E 50
Bouverie Pl. W2 —6B 66 (7B 158)
Bouverie Rd. N16 —2E 50
Bouverie Rd. Harr —6G 25
Bouverie St. EC4 —6A 68 (1K 167)
Boveney Rd. SE23 —7K 105
Bovill Rd. SE23 —7K 105
Bovingdon Av. Wemb —6G 45
Bovingdon Clo. N19 —2G 49
Bovingdon La. NW9 —1A 28
Bovingdon Rd. SW6 —1K 101
Bovingdon Sq. Mitc —4J 139
Bow. —3C 70
Bowater Clo. NW9 —5K 27
Bowater Clo. SW2 —6J 103
Bowater Ho. EC1 —4C 68 (4C 162) (off Golden La. Est.)
Bowater Pl. SE3 —7K 89
Bowater Rd. SE18 —3B 90
Bow Bri. Est. E3 —3D 70
Bow Chyd. EC4 —1D 168
Bow Common. —5C 70
Bow Comn. La. E3 —4B 70
Bowden Clo. Felt —1G 113
Bowden St. SE11 —5A 86 (6K 173)
Bowditch. SE8 —4B 88 (in two parts)
Bowdon Rd. E17 —7C 34
Bowen Dri. SE21 —3E 122
Bowen Rd. Harr —7G 25
Bowen St. E14 —6D 70
Bower Av. SE10 —1G 107
Bower Clo. N'holt —2A 60
Bower Clo. Romf —1K 39
Bower Ct. E4 —1K 19 (off Ridgeway, The)
Bowerdean St. SW6 —1K 101
Bowerman Av. SE14 —6A 88
Bowerman Ct. N19 —2H 49 (off St John's Way)
Bower St. E1 —6K 69
Bowers Wlk. E6 —6D 72
Bowes Clo. Sidc —6B 110
Bowe's Ho. Bark —7F 55
Bowes-Lyon Hall. E16 —1J 89 (off Wesley Av., in two parts)
Bowes Park. —7D 16
Bowes Rd. N11 & N13 —5B 16
Bowes Rd. W3 —7A 64
Bowes Rd. Dag —4C 56
Bowfell Rd. W6 —6E 82
Bowford Av. Bexh —1E 110
Bowhill Clo. SW9 —7A 86
Bowie Clo. SW4 —7H 103
Bow Ind. Pk. E15 —7C 52
Bow Interchange. (Junct.) —2D 70
Bowland Rd. SW4 —4H 103
Bowland Rd. Wfd G —5F 21
Bowland Yd. SW1 —7F 165
Bow La. EC4 —6C 68 (1D 168)
Bow La. N12 —7F 15
Bow La. Mord —6G 137
Bowl Ct. EC2 —4E 68 (4H 163)
Bowles Rd. SE1 —6G 87
Bowley Clo. SE19 —6F 123
Bowley Ho. SE16 —3G 87
Bowley La. SE19 —5F 123
Bowling Clo. Uxb —1B 58
Bowling Grn. Clo. SW15 —7D 100
Bowling Grn. Ct. Wemb —2F 45
Bowling Grn. La. EC1 —4A 68 (3K 161)
Bowling Grn. Pl. SE1 —2D 86 (6E 168)
Bowling Grn. Row. SE18 —3D 90
Bowling Grn. St. SE11 —6A 86 (7J 173)
Bowling Grn. Wlk. N1 —3E 68 (1G 163)
Bowls Clo. Stan —5G 11
Bowman Av. E16 —7H 71
Bowman M. SW18 —1H 119
Bowman's Bldgs. NW1 —5C 66 (5C 158) (off Penfold St.)
Bowmans Clo. W13 —1B 80
Bowmans Lea. SE23 —7J 105
Bowmans Mdw. Wall —3F 151
Bowman's M. E1 —7G 69
Bowman's M. N7 —3J 49
Bowman's Pl. N7 —3J 49
Bowman Trad. Est. NW9 —4G 27
Bowmead. SE9 —2D 126
Bowmore Wlk. NW1 —7H 49
Bowness Clo. E8 —6F 51 (off Beechwood Rd.)
Bowness Cres. SW15 —5A 118
Bowness Dri. Houn —4C 96
Bowness Ho. SE15 —7J 87 (off Hillbeck Clo.)
Bowness Rd. SE6 —7D 106
Bowness Rd. Bexh —2H 111
Bowood Rd. SW11 —5E 102
Bowood Rd. Enf —2E 8
Bow Rd. E3 —3B 70
Bowrons Av. Wemb —7D 44
Bowry Ho. E14 —5B 70
Bowsley Ct. Felt —2J 113
Bowsprit Point. E14 —3C 88
Bow St. E15 —5G 53
Bow St. WC2 —6J 67 (1F 167)
Bow Triangle Bus. Cen. E3 —4C 70
Bowyer Clo. E6 —5D 72
Bowyer Ho. N1 —1E 68 (off Whitmore Est.)
Bowyer Pl. SE5 —7C 86
Bowyer St. SE5 —7C 86
Boxall Rd. SE21 —6E 104
Boxelder Clo. Edgw —5D 12
Boxgrove Rd. SE2 —2B 92

Box La. Bark —2B 74
Boxley Rd. Mord —4A 138
Boxley St. E16 —1K 89
Boxmoor Ho. W11 —1F 83
(off Queensdale Cres.)
Boxmoor Rd. Harr —4B 26
Boxoll Rd. Dag —4F 57
Boxted Clo. Buck H —1H 21
Box Tree Ho. SE8 —6A 88
Boxtree La. Harr —1G 25
Boxtree Rd. Harr —7C 10
Boxwood Clo. W Dray —2B 76
Boxworth Clo. N12 —5G 15
Boxworth Gro. N1 —1K 67
Boyard Rd. SE18 —5F 91
Boyce Ho. W10 —3H 65
(off Bruckner St.)
Boyce Way. E13 —4J 71
Boycroft Av. NW9 —6J 27
Boyd Av. S'hall —1D 78
Boyd Clo. King T —7G 117
Boydell Ct. NW8 —7B 48
(in two parts)
Boyden Ho. E17 —3E 34
Boyd Rd. SW19 —6B 120
Boyd St. E1 —6G 69
Boyfield St. SE1 —2B 86 (7B 168)
Boyland Rd. Brom —5H 125
Boyle Av. Stan —6F 11
Boyle Clo. Uxb —2B 58
Boyle Farm Rd. Th Dit —6A 134
Boyle St. W1 —7G 67 (2A 166)
Boyne Av. NW4 —4F 29
Boyne Rd. SE13 —3E 106
Boyne Rd. Dag —3G 57
Boyne Ter. M. W11 —1H 83
Boyseland Ct. Edgw —2D 12
Boyson Rd. SE5 —6C 86
(in two parts)
Boyson Wlk. SE17 —6D 86
Boyton Clo. E1 —4J 69
Boyton Clo. N8 —3J 31
Boyton Ho. NW8 —2B 66
(off Wellington Rd.)
Boyton Rd. N8 —3J 31
Brabant Ct. EC3 —2G 169
Brabant Rd. N22 —2K 31
Brabazon Av. Wall —7J 151
Brabazon Rd. Houn —7A 78
Brabazon Rd. N'holt —2E 60
Brabazon St. E14 —6D 70
Brabner Ho. E2 —3G 69 (1K 163)
(off Wellington Row)
Brabourne Clo. SE19 —5E 122
Brabourne Cres. Bexh —6F 93
Brabourne Heights. NW7 —3F 13
Brabourne Ri. Beck —5E 142
Brabourn Gro. SE15 —2J 105
Brabrook Ct. Wall —4F 151
Brabstone Ho. Gnfd —2K 61
Bracer Ho. N1 —2E 68
(off Whitmore Est.)
Bracewell Av. Gnfd —5K 43
Bracewell Rd. W10 —5E 64
Bracewood Gdns. Croy —3F 153
Bracey M. N19 —2J 49
Bracey St. N4 —2J 49
Bracken Av. SW12 —6E 102
Bracken Av. Croy —3C 154
Brackenbridge Dri. Ruis —3B 42
Brackenbury. N4 —1A 50
(off Osborne Rd.)
Brackenbury Gdns. W6 —3D 82
Brackenbury Rd. N2 —3A 30
Brackenbury Rd. W6 —3D 82
Bracken Clo. E6 —5D 72
Bracken Clo. Sun —6H 113
Bracken Clo. Twic —7E 96
Brackendale. N21 —2E 16
Brackendale Clo. Houn —1F 97
Brackendene. Dart —4K 129
Bracken End. Iswth —5H 97
Brackenfield Clo. E5 —3H 51
Bracken Gdns. SW13 —2C 100
Brackenhill. Ruis —4C 42
Bracken Hill Clo. Brom —1H 143
Bracken Hill La. Brom —1H 143
Bracken Ho. E3 —5C 70
Bracken Ind. Est. Ilf —1K 37
Bracken M. E4 —1K 19
Bracken M. Romf —6H 39
Brackens. Beck —7C 124
Brackens, The. Enf —7K 7
Bracken, The. E4 —2K 19
Brackenwood. Sun —1J 131
Brackenwood Lodge. Barn —4D 4
(off Prospect Rd.)
Brackley Clo. Wall —7J 151
Brackley Ct. NW8 —4B 66 (3B 158)
(off Henderson Dri.)
Brackley Rd. W4 —5A 82
Brackley Rd. Beck —7B 124
Brackley Sq. Wfd G —7G 21
Brackley St. EC1 —4C 68 (5D 162)
Brackley Ter. W4 —5A 82
Bracklyn Ct. N1 —2D 68
(in three parts)
Bracklyn St. N1 —2D 68
Bracknell Clo. N22 —1A 32
Bracknell Gdns. NW3 —4K 47
Bracknell Ga. NW3 —5K 47
Bracknell Way. NW3 —4K 47
Bracondale Rd. SE2 —4A 92
Bradbourne Rd. Bex —7G 111
Bradbourne St. SW6 —2J 101
Bradbury Clo. S'hall —4D 78
Bradbury M. N16 —5E 50
(off Bradbury St.)
Bradbury St. N16 —5E 50
Braddock Clo. Iswth —2K 97
Braddon Ct. Barn —3B 4
Braddon Rd. Rich —3F 99
Braddyll St. SE10 —5G 89
Bradenham. SE17 —6D 86
(off Bradenham Clo.)
Bradenham Av. Well —4A 110
Bradenham Clo. SE17 —6D 86
Bradenham Rd. Harr —4B 26
Bradenham Rd. Hay —3G 59
Braden St. W9 —4K 65
Bradfield Ct. NW1 —7F 49
(off Hawley Rd.)
Bradfield Dri. Bark —5A 56
Bradfield Rd. E16 —2J 89
Bradfield Rd. Ruis —5C 42
Bradford Clo. N17 —6A 18
Bradford Clo. SE26 —4H 123
Bradford Clo. Brom —1D 156
Bradford Dri. Eps —6B 148
Bradford Rd. W3 —2A 82
Bradford Rd. Ilf —1H 55
Bradgate Rd. SE6 —6D 106
Brading Cres. E11 —2K 53
Brading Rd. SW2 —7K 103
Brading Rd. Croy —6K 139
Brading Ter. W12 —3C 82
Bradiston Rd. W9 —3H 65
Bradley Clo. N7 —6J 49
Bradley Gdns. W13 —6B 62
Bradley Ho. E2 —2G 69
(off Claredale St.)
Bradley Ho. SE16 —4J 87
(off Raymouth Rd.)
Bradley M. SW17 —1D 120
Bradley Rd. N22 —2K 31
Bradley Rd. SE19 —6C 122
Bradley's Clo. N1 —2A 68
Bradley Stone Rd. E6 —5D 72
Bradman Row. Edgw —7D 12
Bradmead. SW8 —7F 85
Bradmore Pk. Rd. W6 —4D 82
Bradshaw Clo. SW19 —6J 119
Bradshawe Waye. Uxb —5B 58
Bradshaws Clo. SE25 —3G 141
Bradstock Ho. E9 —7K 51
Bradstock Rd. E9 —6K 51
Bradstock Rd. Eps —5C 148
Brad St. SE1 —1A 86 (5K 167)
Bradwell Av. Dag —2G 57
Bradwell Clo. E18 —4H 35
Bradwell Ho. NW6 —1K 65
(off Mortimer Cres.)
Bradwell M. N18 —4B 18
Bradwell Rd. Buck H —1H 21
Brady Ct. Dag —1D 56
Bradymead. E6 —6E 72
Brady St. E1 —4H 69
Braeburn Ct. Barn —4G 5
Braemar Av. N22 —1J 31
Braemar Av. NW10 —3K 45
Braemar Av. SW19 —2J 119
Braemar Av. Bexh —4J 111
Braemar Av. T Hth —3A 140
Braemar Av. Wemb —7D 44
Braemar Ct. SE6 —1H 125
Braemar Gdns. NW9 —1K 27
Braemar Gdns. Sidc —3H 127
Braemar Gdns. W W'ck —1E 154
Braemar Ho. W9 —3A 66
(off Maida Va.)
Braemar Rd. E13 —4H 71
Braemar Rd. N15 —5E 32
Braemar Rd. Bren —6D 80
Braemar Rd. Wor Pk —3D 148
Braemer Clo. SE16 —5H 87
(off Masters Dri.)
Braeside. Beck —5C 124
Braeside Av. SW19 —1G 137
Braeside Cres. Bexh —4J 111
Braeside Rd. SW16 —7G 121
Braes St. N1 —7B 50
Braesyde Clo. Belv —4F 93
Brafferton Rd. Croy —4C 152
Braganza St. SE17 —5B 86
Bragg Clo. Dag —6B 56
Bragg Rd. Tedd —6J 115
Braham Ho. SE11 —5K 85 (6H 173)
Braham St. E1 —6F 69 (1K 169)
Braid Av. W3 —6A 64
Braid Clo. Felt —2D 114
Braid Ho. SE10 —1E 106
(off Blackheath Hill)
Braidwood Pas. EC1 —5C 68 (5C 162)
(off Aldersgate St.)
Braidwood Rd. SE6 —1F 125
Brailsford Clo. SW19 —7C 120
Brailsford Rd. SW2 —5A 104
Brainton Av. Felt —7K 95
Braintree Av. Ilf —4C 36
Braintree Rd. Dag —3G 57
Braintree Rd. Ruis —4K 41
Braintree St. E2 —3J 69
Braithwaite Av. Romf —7G 39
Braithwaite Gdns. Stan —1C 26
Braithwaite Ho. E14 —6F 71
Braithwaite Ho. EC1 —4D 68 (3E 162)
(off Bunhill Row)
Braithwaite Rd. Enf —3G 9
Braithwaite Tower. W2 —5B 158
Bramah Grn. SW9 —1A 104
Bramah Tea & Coffee Mus. —6K 169
Bramalea Clo. N6 —6E 30
Bramall Clo. E15 —5H 53
Bramall Ct. N7 —5K 49
(off George's Rd.)
Bramber. WC1 —2E 160
Bramber Ct. W5 —4E 80
Bramber Rd. N12 —5H 15
Bramber Rd. W14 —6H 83
Brambleacres Clo. Sutt —7J 149
Bramblebury Rd. SE18 —5G 91
Bramble Clo. N15 —4G 33
Bramble Clo. Beck —5E 142
Bramble Clo. Croy —4C 154
Bramble Clo. Shep —3F 131
Bramble Clo. Stan —7J 11
Bramble Clo. Uxb —6B 58
Bramble Cft. Eri —4J 93
Brambledown Clo. W W'ck —5G 143
Brambledown Rd. Cars & Wall —7E 150
Brambledown Rd. S Croy —7E 152
Bramble Gdns. W12 —7B 64
Bramble Ho. E3 —5C 70
Bramble La. Hamp —6D 114
Brambles Clo. Iswth —7B 80
Brambles Farm Dri. Uxb —3C 58
Brambles, The. SW19 —5H 119
(off Woodside)
Brambles, The. W Dray —4A 76
Bramblewood Clo. Cars —1C 150
Bramblings, The. E4 —4A 20
Bramcote Av. Mitc —4D 138
Bramcote Gro. SE16 —5J 87
Bramcote Rd. SW15 —4D 100
Bramdean Cres. SE12 —1J 125
Bramdean Gdns. SE12 —1J 125
Bramerton Rd. Beck —3B 142
Bramerton St. SW3 —6C 84 (7C 170)
Bramfield Ct. N4 —3C 50
(off Queens Dri.)
Bramfield Rd. SW11 —6C 102
Bramford Ct. N14 —2C 16
Bramford Rd. SW18 —4A 102
Bramham Gdns. SW5 —5K 83
Bramham Gdns. Chess —4D 146
Bramham Ho. SE15 —3F 105
Bramhope La. SE7 —6K 89
Bramlands Clo. SW11 —3C 102
Bramley Av. Shep —3G 131
Bramley Clo. E17 —2A 34
Bramley Clo. N14 —5A 6
Bramley Clo. Eastc —3H 23
Bramley Clo. Hay —7J 59
Bramley Clo. Orp —7F 145
Bramley Clo. S Croy —5C 152
Bramley Clo. Twic —6G 97
Bramley Ct. E4 —1K 19
(off Ridgeway, The)
Bramley Ct. Barn —4H 5
Bramley Ct. Mitc —2B 138
Bramley Ct. S'hall —7G 61
(off Baird Av.)
Bramley Ct. Well —1B 110
Bramley Cres. SW8 —7H 85
Bramley Cres. Ilf —6E 36
Bramley Hill. S Croy —5B 152
Bramley Ho. SW15 —6B 100
(off Tunworth Cres.)
Bramley Ho. W10 —6F 65
Bramley Ho. Houn —4D 96
Bramley Pde. N14 —4B 6
Bramley Rd. N14 —5K 5
Bramley Rd. W5 —3C 80
Bramley Rd. W10 —6F 65
Bramley Rd. Cheam —7F 149
Bramley Rd. Sutt —5B 150
Bramley Way. Houn —5D 96
Bramley Way. W W'ck —2D 154
Brampton. WC1 —5K 67 (6G 161)
(off Red Lion Sq.)
Brampton Clo. E5 —2H 51
Brampton Ct. NW4 —4D 28
Brampton Gdns. N15 —5C 32
Brampton Gro. NW4 —4D 28
Brampton Gro. Harr —4A 26
Brampton Gro. Wemb —1G 45
Brampton La. NW4 —4E 28
Brampton Pk. Rd. N8 —3A 32
Brampton Rd. E6 —3B 72
Brampton Rd. N15 —5C 32
Brampton Rd. NW9 —4G 27
Brampton Rd. SE2 & Bexh —6C 92
Brampton Rd. Croy —7F 141
Brampton Rd. Uxb —2D 58
Bramshaw Ri. N Mald —6A 136
Bramshaw Rd. E9 —6K 51
Bramshill Gdns. NW5 —3F 49
Bramshill Rd. NW10 —2B 64
Bramshot Av. SE7 —6J 89
Bramshurst. NW8 —1K 65
(off Abbey Rd.)
Bramston Rd. NW10 —2C 64
Bramston Rd. SW17 —3A 120
Bramwell Clo. Sun —2B 132
Bramwell Ho. SE1 —3C 86
Bramwell Ho. SW1 —5G 85 (6A 172)
(off Churchill Gdns.)
Bramwell M. N1 —1K 67
Brancaster Dri. NW7 —7H 13
Brancaster Rd. E12 —4D 54
Brancaster Rd. SW16 —3J 121
Brancaster Rd. Ilf —6J 37
Brancepeth Gdns. Buck H —2D 20
Branch Hill. NW3 —3A 48
Branch Hill Ho. NW3 —3K 47
Branch Pl. N1 —1D 68
Branch Rd. E14 —7A 70
Branch St. SE5 —7E 86
Brancker Clo. Wall —7J 151
Brancker Rd. Harr —3D 26
Brancroft Way. Enf —1F 9
Brand Clo. N4 —1B 50
Brandesbury Sq. Wfd G —7K 21
Brandlehow Rd. SW15 —4H 101
Brandon. NW9 —2B 28
(off Further Acre)
Brandon Est. SE17 —6B 86
Brandon Ho. Beck —5D 124
(off Beckenham Hill Rd.)
Brandon Mans. W14 —6G 83
(off Queen's Club Gdns.)
Brandon M. EC2 —6E 162
Brandon Rd. E17 —4E 34
Brandon Rd. N7 —7J 49
Brandon Rd. S'hall —5D 78
Brandon Rd. Sutt —4K 149
Brandon St. SE17 —4C 86
(in three parts)
Brandram M. SE13 —4G 107
(off Brandram Rd.)
Brandram Rd. SE13 —3G 107
Brandreth Ct. Harr —6K 25
Brandreth Rd. E6 —6D 72
Brandreth Rd. SW17 —2F 121
Brandries, The. Wall —3H 151
Brand St. SE10 —7E 88
Brandville Gdns. Ilf —4F 37
Brandville Rd. W Dray —2A 76
Brandy Way. Sutt —7J 149
Brangbourne Rd. Brom —5E 124
Brangton Rd. SE11 —5K 85 (6H 173)
Brangwyn Ct. W14 —3G 83
(off Blythe Rd.)
Brangwyn Cres. SW19 —1A 138
Branham Ho. SE18 —5F 91
Branksea St. SW6 —7G 83
Branksome Av. N18 —6A 18
Branksome Clo. Tedd —4H 115
Branksome Ho. SW8 —7K 85
(off Meadow Rd.)
Branksome Rd. SW2 —5J 103
Branksome Rd. SW19 —1J 137
Branksome Way. Harr —6F 27
Branksome Way. N Mald —1J 135
Branksome Ct. N2 —3A 30
Bransby Rd. Chess —6E 146
Branscombe. NW1 —1G 67
(off Plender St.)
Branscombe Ct. Brom —5H 143
Branscombe Gdns. N21 —7F 7
Branscombe St. SE13 —3D 106
Bransdale Clo. NW6 —1J 65
Bransgrove Rd. Edgw —1F 27
Branston Cres. Orp —7H 145
Branstone Rd. Rich —1F 99
Brants Wlk. W7 —4J 61
Brantwood Av. Eri —7J 93
Brantwood Av. Iswth —4A 98
Brantwood Clo. E17 —3D 34
Brantwood Gdns. Enf —4D 6
Brantwood Gdns. Ilf —4C 36
Brantwood Ho. SE5 —7C 86
(off Wyndam Est.)
Brantwood Rd. N17 —6B 18
Brantwood Rd. SE24 —5C 104
Brantwood Rd. Bexh —2H 111
Brantwood Rd. S Croy —7C 152
Brasenose Dri. SW13 —6E 82
Brasher Clo. Gnfd —5H 43
Brassett Point. E15 —1G 71
(off Abbey Rd.)
Brassey Clo. Felt —1J 113
Brassey Ho. E14 —4D 88
Brassey Rd. NW6 —6H 47
Brassey Sq. SW11 —3E 102
Brassie Av. W3 —6A 64
Brass Tally All. SE16 —2K 87
Brasted Clo. SE26 —4J 123
Brasted Clo. Bexh —5D 110
Brasted Lodge. SE20 —7C 124
Brathay. NW1 —2G 67 (1B 160)
(off Ampthill Est.)
Brathway Rd. SW18 —7J 101
Bratley St. E1 —4G 69
Bratten Ct. Croy —6D 140
Braund Av. Gnfd —4F 61
Braundton Av. Sidc —1K 127
Braunston Dri. Hay —4C 60
Bravington Clo. Shep —5B 130
Bravington Pl. W9 —4H 65
Bravington Rd. W9 —2H 65
Brawne Ho. SE17 —6B 86
(off Brandon Est.)
Braxfield Rd. SE4 —4A 106
Braxted Pk. SW16 —6K 121
Bray. NW3 —7C 48
Brayards Rd. SE15 —2H 105
Brayards Rd. Est. SE15 —2J 105
(off Brayards Rd.)
Braybourne Dri. Iswth —7K 79
Braybrooke Gdns. SE19 —7E 122
Braybrook St. W12 —5B 64
Brayburne Av. SW4 —2G 103
Bray Ct. SW16 —5J 121
Braycourt Av. W on T —7K 131
Bray Cres. SE16 —2K 87
Braydon Rd. N16 —1G 51
Bray Dri. E16 —7H 71
Brayfield Ter. N1 —7A 50
Brayford Sq. E1 —6J 69
Bray Pas. E16 —7J 71
Bray Pl. SW3 —4D 84 (4E 170)
Bray Rd. NW7 —6A 14
Brayton Gdns. Enf —4C 6
Braywood Rd. SE9 —4H 109
Brazil Clo. Bedd —7J 139
Breach La. Dag —3G 75
Bread St. EC4 —6C 68 (1D 168)
(in two parts)
Breakspear Crematorium. Ruis —5E 22
Breakspear Ho. Ruis —5F 23
Breakspear Rd. Ruis —7D 22
Breakspear Rd. N. Hare —3A 22
Breakspear Rd. S. Uxb & Hare —3B 40
Breakspears Dri. Orp —1K 145
Breakspears M. SE4 —2B 106
Breakspears Rd. SE4 —4B 106
Bream Clo. N17 —4H 33
Bream Gdns. E6 —3E 72
Breamore Clo. SW15 —1C 118
Breamore Ho. SE15 —7G 87
(off Friary Est.)
Breamore Rd. Ilf —2K 55
Bream's Bldgs. EC4 —6A 68 (7J 161)
Bream St. E3 —7C 52
Breamwater Gdns. Rich —3B 116
Brearley Clo. Edgw —7D 12
Brearley Clo. Uxb —6A 40
Breasley Clo. SW15 —4D 100
Breasy Pl. NW4 —4D 28
(off Burroughs Gdns.)
Brechin Pl. SW7 —4A 84
Brecknock Rd. N19 & N7 —4G 49
Brecknock Rd. Est. N19 —4G 49
Breckonmead. Brom —2A 144
Brecon Clo. Mitc —3J 139
Brecon Clo. Wor Pk —2E 148
Brecon Grn. NW9 —6A 28
Brecon Ho. W2 —6A 66
(off Hallfield Est.)
Brecon M. NW5 —5H 49
Brecon Rd. W6 —6G 83
Brecon Rd. Enf —4D 8
Brede Clo. E6 —3E 72
Bredel Ho. E14 —5C 70
Bredgar Rd. N19 —2G 49
Bredhurst Clo. SE20 —6J 123
Bredo Ho. Bark —3B 74
Bredon Rd. Croy —7F 141
Breer St. SW6 —3K 101
Breezers Ct. E1 —7G 69
(off Highway, The)
Breezer's Hill. E1 —7G 69
Brember Rd. Harr —2G 43
Bremer M. E17 —4D 34
Bremner Rd. SW7 —3A 84 (1A 170)
Brenchley Clo. Brom —6H 143
Brenchley Clo. Chst —1E 144
Brenchley Gdns. SE23 —6J 105
Brenchley Rd. Orp —2K 145
Brenda Rd. SW17 —2D 120
Brende Gdns. W Mol —4F 133
Brendon Av. NW10 —4A 46
Brendon Clo. Hay —7E 76
Brendon Ct. S'hall —4F 79
Brendon Gdns. Harr —4F 43
Brendon Gdns. Ilf —5J 37
Brendon Gro. N2 —2A 30
Brendon Rd. SE9 —2H 127
Brendon Rd. Dag —1F 57
Brendon St. W1 —6C 66 (7D 158)
Brendon Vs. N21 —1H 17
Brendon Way. Enf —7K 7
Brenley Clo. Mitc —3E 138
Brenley Gdns. SE9 —4B 108
Brenley Ho. SE1 —2D 86 (6E 168)
(off Tennis St.)
Brennand Ct. N19 —3G 49
Brent Clo. Bex —1E 128
Brentcot Clo. W13 —4B 62
Brent Ct. NW11 —7F 29
Brent Ct. W7 —7H 61
Brent Cres. NW10 —2F 63
Brent Cross. —7E 28
Brent Cross Fly-Over. NW2 —7F 29
Brent Cross Gdns. NW4 —6F 29
Brent Cross Interchange. (Junct.) —7F 29
Brent Cross Shop. Cen. NW4 —7E 28
Brentfield. NW10 —7H 45
Brentfield Clo. NW10 —6K 45
Brentfield Gdns. NW2 —7F 29
Brentfield Ho. NW10 —7K 45
Brentfield Rd. NW10 —6K 45
Brentford. —6D 80
Brentford Bus. Cen. Bren —7C 80
Brentford Clo. Hay —4B 60
Brentford End. —7B 80
Brentford F.C. —6D 80
Brentford Ho. Twic —7B 98
Brentford Musical Mus. —6E 80
Brent Grn. NW4 —5E 28
Brent Grn. Wlk. Wemb —3J 45
Brentham Way. W5 —4D 62
Brenthouse Rd. E9 —7J 51
Brenthurst Rd. NW10 —6B 46
Brent Lea. Bren —7C 80
Brentmead Clo. W7 —7J 61
Brentmead Gdns. NW10 —2F 63
Brentmead Pl. NW11 —6F 29
Brent New Enterprise Cen. NW10 —6B 46
Brenton St. E14 —6A 70
Brent Pk. Ind. Est. W7 —3K 77
Brent Pk. Rd. NW9 & NW4 —7D 28
(in two parts)
Brent Pl. Barn —5C 4
Brent Rd. E16 —6J 71
Brent Rd. SE18 —7F 91
Brent Rd. Bren —6C 80
Brent Rd. S'hall —3A 78
Brent Rd. S Croy —7H 153
Brent Side. Bren —6C 80
Brentside Clo. W13 —4A 62
Brentside Executive Cen. Bren —6B 80
Brent St. NW4 —4E 28
Brent Ter. NW2 —1E 46
(in two parts)
Brent Trad. Cen. NW10 —5A 46
Brentvale Av. S'hall —1H 79
Brentvale Av. Wemb —1F 63
Brent Vw. Rd. NW9 —6C 28
Brentwaters Bus. Pk. Bren —7C 80
Brent Way. N3 —6D 14
Brent Way. Bren —7D 80
Brent Way. Wemb —6H 45
Brentwick Gdns. Bren —4E 80
Brentwood Clo. SE9 —1G 127
Brentwood Ho. SE18 —7B 90
(off Portway Gdns.)
Brentwood Lodge. NW4 —5F 29
(off Holmdale Gdns.)
Brereton Rd. N17 —7A 18
Bressenden Pl. SW1 —3F 85 (1K 171)
Bressey Av. Enf —1B 8
Bressey Gro. E18 —2H 35
Breton Highwalk. EC2 —5C 68
(off Golden La.)
Breton Ho. EC1 —4D 162
Breton Ho. SE1 —3F 87 (7J 169)
(off Abbey St.)
Brett Clo. N16 —2E 50
Brett Clo. N'holt —3B 60
Brett Ct. N9 —2D 18
Brett Cres. NW10 —1K 63
Brettell St. SE17 —5D 86
Brettenham Av. E17 —1C 34
Brettenham Rd. E17 —2C 34
Brettenham Rd. N18 —4B 18
Brett Gdns. Dag —7E 56
Brett Ho. Clo. SW15 —7F 101
Brettinghurst. SE1 —5G 87
(off Avondale Sq.)
Brett Pas. E8 —5H 51
Brett Rd. E8 —5H 51
Brewer's Grn. SW1 —1C 172
Brewer's Hall Garden. EC2
(off London Wall) —5C 68 (6D 162)
Brewers La. Rich —5D 98
Brewer St. W1 —7G 67 (2B 166)
Brewery Clo. Wemb —5A 44
Brewery Ind. Est., The. N1 —2C 68 (1D 162)
Brewery La. Twic —7K 97
Brewery M. Cen. Iswth —3A 98
Brewery Rd. N7 —7J 49
Brewery Rd. SE18 —5H 91
Brewery Rd. Brom —1C 156
Brewery Sq. SE1 —5J 169
Brewhouse La. E1 —1H 87
Brewhouse Rd. SE18 —4D 90
Brewhouse St. SW15 —3G 101
Brewhouse Wlk. SE16 —1A 88
Brewhouse Yd. EC1 —4B 68 (3A 162)

Brewood Rd.—Brockshot Clo.

Brewood Rd. Dag —6B 56
Brewster Gdns. W10 —5E 64
Brewster Ho. E14 —7B 70
Brewster Ho. SE1 —4F 87
(off Dunton Rd.)
Brewster Rd. E10 —1D 52
Brian Rd. Romf —5C 38
Briant Ho. SE1 —2J 173
Briants Clo. Pinn —2D 24
Briant St. SE14 —1K 105
Briar Av. SW16 —7K 121
Briarbank Rd. W13 —6A 62
Briar Clo. N2 —3K 29
Briar Clo. N13 —3H 17
Briar Clo. Buck H —2G 21
Briar Clo. Hamp —5D 114
Briar Clo. Iswth —5K 97
Briar Ct. SW15 —4D 100
Briar Ct. Sutt —4E 148
Briar Cres. N'holt —6F 43
Briardale Gdns. NW3 —3J 47
Briarfield Av. N2 —3K 29
Briarfield Av. N3 —2K 29
Briar Gdns. Brom —1H 155
Briaris Clo. N17 —7C 18
Briar La. Croy —4D 154
Briar Rd. NW2 —4E 46
Briar Rd. SW16 —3J 139
Briar Rd. Bex —3K 129
Briar Rd. Harr —5C 26
Briar Rd. Shep —5B 130
Briar Rd. Twic —1J 115
Briars, The. Bush —1D 10
Briar Wlk. SW15 —4D 100
Briar Wlk. W10 —4G 65
Briar Wlk. Edgw —7D 12
Briar Way. W Dray —2C 76
Briarwood Clo. NW9 —6J 27
Briarwood Clo. Felt —4G 113
Briarwood Ct. Wor Pk —1C 148
(off Avenue, The)
Briarwood Dri. N'wd —2J 23
Briarwood Rd. SW4 —5H 103
Briarwood Rd. Eps —6C 148
Briary Clo. NW3 —7C 48
Briary Ct. Sidc —5B 128
Briary Gdns. Brom —5K 125
Briary Gro. Edgw —2H 27
Briary La. N9 —3A 18
Briary Lodge. Beck —1E 142
Brickbarn Clo. SW10 —7A 84
(off King's Barn)
Brick Ct. EC4 —1A 68 (1J 167)
Brickett Clo. Ruis —5E 22
Brick Farm Clo. Rich —1H 99
Brickfield Clo. Bren —7C 80
Brickfield Cotts. SE18 —7K 91
Brickfield La. Hay —6F 77
Brickfield Rd. SW19 —4K 119
Brickfield Rd. T Hth —1B 140
Brickfields. Harr —2H 43
(in two parts)
Brickfields Way. W Dray —3B 76
Brick La. E2 & E1 —3F 69 (2K 163)
Brick La. Enf —2C 8
Brick La. Stan —7J 11
Bricklayers Arms. (Junct.) —3D 86
Bricklayers Arms Bus. Cen. SE1 —4E 86
Brick St. W1 —1F 85 (5J 165)
Brickwall La. Ruis —1G 41
Brickwood Clo. SE26 —3H 123
Brickwood Rd. Croy —2E 152
Brideale Clo. SE15 —6F 87
Bride Ct. EC4 —1A 168
Bride La. EC4 —6B 68 (1A 168)
Bridel M. N1 —1B 68
(off Colebrook Row)
Bride St. N7 —6K 49
Bridewain St. SE1 —3F 87 (7J 169)
(in two parts)
Bridewell Pl. E1 —1H 87
Bridewell Pl. EC4 —6B 68 (1A 168)
Bridford M. W1 —5F 67 (5K 159)
Bridge App. NW1 —7E 48
Bridge Av. W6 —4E 82
Bridge Av. W7 —5H 61
Bridge Clo. W10 —6F 65
Bridge Clo. Enf —2C 8
Bridge Clo. Tedd —4K 115
Bridge Clo. W on T —7H 131
Bridge Ct. E10 —1B 52
Bridge Dri. N13 —4E 16
Bridge End. E17 —1E 34
Bridgefield Rd. Sutt —6J 149
Bridgefoot. SE1 —5J 85 (6F 173)
Bridgefoot. Sun —1H 131
Bridge Gdns. Ashf —7E 112
Bridge Gdns. E Mol —4H 133
Bridge Ga. N21 —7H 7
Bridge Ho. E9 —6K 51
(off Shepherds La.)
Bridge Ho. NW3 —7E 48
(off Adelaide Rd.)
Bridge Ho. SE4 —4B 106
Bridge Ho. SW1 —5F 85 (5J 171)
Bridge Ho. Sutt —6K 149
(off Bridge Rd.)
Bridgehouse Ct. SE1 —2B 86 (7A 168)
Bridge Ho. Quay. E14 —1E 88
Bridgeland Rd. E16 —7J 71
Bridge La. NW11 —4G 29
Bridge La. SW11 —1C 102
Bridgeman Rd. N1 —7K 49
Bridgeman Rd. Tedd —6A 116
Bridgeman St. NW8 —2C 66
Bridge Meadows. SE14 —6K 87
Bridgen. —7E 110
Bridgend Rd. SW18 —4A 102
Bridgenhall Rd. Enf —1A 8
Bridgen Rd. Bex —7E 110
Bridge Pde. N21 —7H 7
(off Ridge Av.)
Bridgepark. SW18 —5J 101
Bridge Pl. SW1 —4F 85 (3K 171)
Bridge Pl. Croy —1D 152
Bridgeport Pl. E1 —1G 87
Bridge Rd. E6 —7D 54
Bridge Rd. E15 —7F 53
Bridge Rd. E17 —7B 34
Bridge Rd. N9 —3B 18
Bridge Rd. N22 —1J 31
Bridge Rd. NW10 —6A 46
Bridge Rd. Beck —7B 124
Bridge Rd. Bexh —2E 110
Bridge Rd. Chess —5E 146
Bridge Rd. E Mol —4H 133
Bridge Rd. Houn & Iswth —3H 97
Bridge Rd. S'hall —2D 78
Bridge Rd. Sutt —6K 149
Bridge Rd. Twic —6B 98
Bridge Rd. Wall —5F 151
Bridge Rd. Wemb —3G 45
Bridge Row. Croy —1D 152
Bridges Ct. SW11 —3B 102
(in two parts)
Bridges Ho. SE5 —7D 86
(off Elmington Est.)
Bridgeside Ho. N1 —2C 68
(off Wharf Rd.)
Bridges La. Croy —4J 151
Bridges Pl. SW6 —1H 101
Bridges Rd. SW19 —6K 119
Bridges Rd. Stan —5E 10
Bridges Rd. M. SW19 —6K 119
Bridge St. SW1 —2J 85 (7E 166)
Bridge St. W4 —4K 81
Bridge St. Pinn —3C 24
Bridge St. Rich —5D 98
Bridge St. W on T —7G 131
Bridge Ter. E15 —7F 53
(in two parts)
Bridge, The. Harr —4K 25
Bridgetown Clo. SE19 —5E 122
Bridge Vw. W6 —5E 82
Bridgewalk Heights. SE1
(off Weston St.) —2D 86 (6F 169)
Bridgewater Clo. Chst —3J 145
Bridgewater Gdns. Edgw —2F 27
Bridgewater Highwalk. EC2 —5C 162
Bridgewater Rd. E15 —1E 70
Bridgewater Rd. Ruis —4J 41
Bridgewater Rd. Wemb —6C 44
Bridgewater Sq. EC2 —5C 68 (5C 162)
Bridgewater St. EC2 —5C 68 (5C 162)
Bridge Way. N11 —3B 16
Bridge Way. NW11 —5H 29
Bridgeway. Bark —7K 55
Bridge Way. Twic —7G 97
Bridge Way. Uxb —5D 40
Bridge Way. Wemb —7E 44
Bridgeway St. NW1 —2G 67
Bridge Wharf. E2 —2K 69
Bridge Wharf Rd. Iswth —3B 98
Bridgewood Clo. SE20 —7H 123
Bridgewood Rd. SW16 —7H 121
Bridgewood Rd. Wor Pk —4C 148
Bridge Yd. SE1 —1D 86 (4F 169)
Bridgford St. SW18 —3A 120
Bridgman Rd. W4 —3J 81
Bridgnorth Ho. SE15 —6G 87
(off Friary Est.)
Bridgwater Ho. W2 —6A 66
(off Hallfield Est.)
Bridle Clo. Eps —5K 147
Bridle Clo. King T —4D 134
Bridle Clo. Sun —3J 131
Bridle La. W1 —7G 67 (2B 166)
Bridle La. Twic —6B 98
Bridle Path. Croy —3J 151
(in two parts)
Bridle Path, The. E4 —7B 20
Bridlepath Way. Felt —1G 113
Bridle Rd. Clay —6B 146
Bridle Rd. Croy —3C 154
(in two parts)
Bridle Rd. Pinn —6K 23
Bridle Rd. S Croy —7G 153
Bridle Way. Croy —4C 154
Bridleway, The. Wall —5G 151
Bridlington Rd. N9 —7C 8
Bridport. SE17 —5D 86
(off Date St.)
Bridport Av. Romf —6H 39
Bridport Ho. N1 —1D 68
(off Bridport Pl.)
Bridport Pl. N1 —1D 68
(in two parts)
Bridport Rd. N18 —5K 17
Bridport Rd. Gnfd —1F 61
Bridport Rd. T Hth —3A 140
Bridstow Pl. W2 —6J 65
Brief St. SE5 —1B 104
Brierfield. NW1 —1G 67
(off Arlington Rd.)
Brierley. New Ad —6D 154
(in two parts)
Brierley Av. N9 —1D 18
Brierley Clo. SE25 —4G 141
Brierley Ct. W7 —7J 61
Brierley Rd. E11 —4F 53
Brierley Rd. SW12 —2G 121
Brierly Gdns. E2 —2J 69
Brigade Clo. Harr —2H 43
Brigade St. SE3 —2H 107
Brigadier Av. Enf —1H 7
Brigadier Hill. Enf —1H 7
Briggeford Clo. E5 —2G 51
Briggs Clo. Mitc —1F 139
Briggs Ho. E2 —3F 69 (1K 163)
(off Chambord St.)
Bright Clo. Belv —4D 92
Brightfield Rd. SE12 —5G 107
Brightling Rd. SE4 —6B 106
Brightlingsea Pl. E14 —7B 70
Brightman Rd. SW18 —1B 120
Brighton Av. E17 —5B 34
Brighton Bldgs. SE1 —3E 86
(off Tower Bri. Rd.)
Brighton Clo. Uxb —7D 40
Brighton Dri. N'holt —6E 42
Brighton Gro. SE14 —1A 106
Brighton Rd. E6 —3E 72
(in two parts)
Brighton Rd. N2 —2A 30
Brighton Rd. N16 —4E 50
Brighton Rd. S Croy —5C 152
Brighton Rd. Surb —6C 134
Brighton Ter. SW9 —4K 103
Brightside Rd. SE13 —6F 107
Brightside, The. Enf —1E 8
Bright St. E14 —6D 70
Brightwell Clo. Croy —1A 152
Brightwell Cres. SW17 —5D 120
Brig M. SE8 —6C 88
Brigstock Ho. SE5 —2C 104
Brigstock Rd. Belv —4H 93
Brigstock Rd. T Hth —5A 140
Brill Pl. NW1 —2H 67 (1D 160)
Brim Hill. N2 —4A 30
Brimpsfield Clo. SE2 —3B 92
Brimsdown. —2F 9
Brimsdown Av. Enf —2F 9
Brimsdown Ho. E3 —4D 70
Brimsdown Ind. Est. Brim —2G 9
Brimsdown Ind. Est. Enf —1G 9
Brimstone Ho. E15 —7G 53
(off Victoria St.)
Brindle Ga. Sidc —1J 127
Brindley Clo. Bexh —3G 111
Brindley Clo. Gnfd —1D 62
Brindley St. SE14 —1B 106
Brindley Way. Brom —5J 125
Brindley Way. S'hall —7F 61
Brindwood Rd. E4 —3G 19
Brinkburn Clo. SE2 —4A 92
Brinkburn Clo. Edgw —3H 27
Brinkburn Gdns. Edgw —3G 27
Brinkley Rd. Wor Pk —2D 148
Brinklow Cres. SE18 —7F 91
Brinklow Ho. W2 —5K 65
(off Torquay St.)
Brinkworth Rd. Ilf —3C 36
Brinkworth Way. E9 —6B 52
Brinsdale Rd. NW4 —3F 29
Brinsley Rd. Harr —2H 25
Brinsley St. E1 —6H 69
Brinsworth Clo. Twic —1H 115
Brinsworth Ho. Twic —2H 115
Brinton Wlk. SE1 —5A 168
Brion Pl. E14 —5E 70
Brisbane Av. SW19 —1K 137
Brisbane Rd. E10 —2D 52
Brisbane Rd. W13 —2A 80
Brisbane Rd. Ilf —7F 37
Brisbane St. SE5 —7D 86
Briscoe Clo. E11 —2H 53
Briscoe Rd. SW19 —6B 120
Briset Rd. SE9 —3B 108
Briset St. EC1 —5B 68 (5A 162)
Briset Way. N7 —2K 49
Bristol Clo. Stanw —6A 94
Bristol Clo. Wall —7J 151
Bristol Ct. Stanw —6A 94
Bristol Gdns. SW15 —7E 100
Bristol Gdns. W9 —4K 65
Bristol Ho. SE11 —2J 173
Bristol Ho. Bark —7A 56
(off Margaret Bondfield Av.)
Bristol M. W9 —4K 65
Bristol Pk. Rd. E17 —4A 34
Bristol Rd. E7 —6A 54
Bristol Rd. Gnfd —1F 61
Bristol Rd. Mord —5A 138
Briston Gro. N8 —6J 31
Briston M. NW7 —7H 13
Bristow Rd. SE19 —5E 122
Bristow Rd. Bexh —1E 110
Bristow Rd. Croy —4J 151
Bristow Rd. Houn —3G 97
Britain Vis. Cen. —4C 166
Britania Bus. Cen. NW2 —4F 47
Britannia Bri. E14 —6B 70
Britannia Clo. SW4 —4H 103
Britannia Clo. N'holt —3B 60
Britannia Ct. W Dray —3A 76
Britannia Ga. E16 —1J 89
Britannia Junction. (Junct.) —1F 67
Britannia La. Twic —7G 97
Britannia Rd. E14 —4C 88
Britannia Rd. N12 —3F 15
Britannia Rd. SW6 —7K 83
(in two parts)
Britannia Rd. Ilf —3F 55
Britannia Rd. Surb —7F 135
Britannia Row. N1 —1B 68
Britannia St. WC1 —3K 67 (1G 161)
Britannia Wlk. N1 —2D 68 (1E 162)
(in two parts)
Britannia Way. NW10 —4H 63
Britannia Way. SW6 —7K 83
(off Britannia Rd.)
Britannia Way. Stanw —7A 94
Britannic Highwalk. EC2 —5D 68
(off Moor La.)
Britannic Tower. EC2 —5E 162
British Gro. W4 —5B 82
British Gro. Pas. W4 —5B 82
British Gro. S. W4 —5B 82
British Legion Rd. E4 —2C 20
British Library. —3H 67 (1D 160)
British Mus. —5J 67 (6E 160)
British St. E3 —3B 70
British Telecom Cen. EC1 —6C 68
(off Newgate St.)
British Wharf Ind. Est. SE14 —5K 87
Britley Ho. E14 —6B 70
Brittain Ho. SE9 —1C 126
Brittain Rd. Dag —3E 56
Brittany Point. SE11 —4A 86 (4J 173)
Britten Clo. NW11 —1K 47
Britten Ct. E15 —2F 71
Britten Dri. S'hall —6E 60
Britten St. SW3 —5C 84 (6C 170)
Britton Clo. SE6 —7F 107
Britton St. EC1 —4B 68 (4A 162)
Brixham Cres. Ruis —1J 41
Brixham Gdns. Ilf —5J 55
Brixham Rd. Well —1D 110
Brixham St. E16 —1E 90
Brixton. —4K 103
Brixton Est. Edgw —2H 27
Brixton Hill. SW2 —7J 103
Brixton Hill Ct. SW2 —5K 103
Brixton Hill Pl. SW2 —7J 103
Brixton Oval. SW9 —4A 104
Brixton Rd. SE11 —6A 86 (7J 173)
Brixton Rd. SW9 & SE11 —4A 104
Brixton Sta. Rd. SW9 —3A 104
Brixton Water La. SW2 —5K 103
Broadacre Clo. Uxb —3D 40
Broadbent Clo. N6 —1F 49
Broadbent St. W1 —7F 67 (2J 165)
Broadbridge Clo. SE3 —7J 89
Broadbury Ct. N18 —6C 18
Broad Comn. Est. N16 —1G 51
(off Osbaldeston Rd.)
Broadcoombe. S Croy —7J 153
Broad Ct. WC2 —6J 67 (1F 167)
Broadcroft Av. Stan —2D 26
Broadcroft Rd. Orp —7H 145
Broadeaves Clo. S Croy —5E 152
Broadfield. NW6 —6K 47
Broadfield Clo. NW2 —3E 46
Broadfield Clo. Croy —2K 151
Broadfield Ct. Bus H —2D 10
Broadfield Ct. N Har —1F 25
(off Broadfields)
Broadfield Heights. NW7 —4C 12
Broadfield La. NW1 —7J 49
Broadfield Rd. SE6 —7G 107
Broadfields. E Mol —6J 133
Broadfields. Harr —2F 25
Broadfields Av. N21 —6F 7
Broadfields Av. Edgw —4C 12
Broadfields Cen. Edgw —1C 12
Broadfield Sq. Enf —2C 8
Broadfields Way. NW10 —5B 46
Broadfield Way. Buck H —3F 21
Broadgate. EC2 —5E 68
(off Broadgate Cir.)
Broadgate Circ. EC2 —6G 163
Broadgate Rd. E16 —6B 72
Broadgates Av. Barn —1E 4
Broadgates Ct. SE11 —5A 86 (6K 173)
(off Cleaver St.)
Broadgates Rd. SW18 —1B 120
Broad Green. —7B 140
Broad Grn. Av. Croy —7B 140
Broadhead Strand. NW9 —2B 28
Broadheath Dri. Chst —5D 126
Broadhinton Rd. SW4 —3F 103
Broadhurst Av. Edgw —4C 12
Broadhurst Av. Ilf —4K 55
Broadhurst Clo. NW6 —6A 48
Broadhurst Clo. Rich —5F 99
Broadhurst Gdns. NW6 —6K 47
Broadhurst Gdns. Ruis —2A 42
Broadlands. E17 —3A 34
Broadlands. Hanw —3E 114
Broadlands Av. SW16 —2J 121
Broadlands Av. Enf —3C 8
Broadlands Av. Shep —6E 130
Broadlands Clo. N6 —7E 30
Broadlands Clo. SW16 —2J 121
Broadlands Clo. Enf —3D 8
Broadlands Ct. Rich —7G 81
(off Kew Gdns. Rd.)
Broadlands Lodge. N6 —7D 30
Broadlands Rd. N6 —7D 30
Broadlands Rd. Brom —4K 125
Broadlands Way. N Mald —6B 136
Broad La. EC2 —5E 68 (5G 163)
(in two parts)
Broad La. N8 —5K 31
Broad La. N15 —4F 33
Broad La. Hamp —7D 114
Broad Lawn. SE9 —2E 126
Broadlawns Ct. Harr —1K 25
Broadley St. W2 —5B 66 (5B 158)
Broadley Ter. NW1 —4C 66 (4D 158)
Broadmayne. SE17 —5D 86
(off Portland St.)
Broadmead. SE6 —3C 124
Broadmead. W14 —4G 83
Broadmead Av. Wor Pk —7C 136
Broadmead Clo. Hamp —6E 114
Broadmead Clo. Pinn —1C 24
Broadmead Ct. Wfd G —6D 20
Broadmead Rd. Hay & N'holt —4C 60
Broadmead Rd. Wfd G —6D 20
Broadoak. Sun —6H 113
Broad Oak. Wfd G —5E 20
Broad Oak Clo. E4 —5H 19
Broadoak Ct. SW9 —3A 104
Broadoak Ho. NW6 —1K 65
(off Mortimer Cres.)
Broadoak Rd. Eri —7K 93
Broadoaks. Surb —2H 147
Broadoaks Way. Brom —5H 143
Broad Sanctuary. SW1 —2H 85 (7D 166)
Broadstone Ho. SW8 —7K 85
(off Dorset Rd.)
Broadstone Pl. W1 —5E 66 (6G 159)
Broad St. Dag —7G 57
Broad St. Tedd —6K 115
Broad St. Av. EC2 —5E 68 (6G 163)
Broad St. Mkt. Dag —7G 57
Broad St. Pl. EC2 —6F 163
Broad Vw. NW9 —6G 27
Broadview Rd. SW16 —7H 121
Broadwalk. E18 —3H 35
Broad Wlk. N21 —2E 16
Broad Wlk. NW1 —1E 66 (1H 159)
Broad Wlk. SE3 —2A 108
Broad Wlk. W1 —7D 66 (3F 165)
Broadwalk. Harr —5E 24
Broad Wlk. Houn —1B 96
Broad Wlk. Rich —7F 81
Broadwalk Ct. W8 —1J 83
(off Palace Gdns. Ter.)
Broadwalk Ho. EC2 —4E 68 (5G 163)
Broadwalk Ho. SW7 —2A 84
(off Broadwalk Ho.)
Broad Wlk. La. NW11 —7H 29
Broadwalk Shop. Cen. Edgw —6C 12
Broad Wlk., The. W8 —1K 83
Broad Wlk., The. E Mol —4K 133
Broadwalk, The. N'wd —2E 22
Broadwall. SE1 —1A 86 (4K 167)
Broadwater Farm Est. N17 —2D 32
Broadwater Rd. N17 —1E 32
Broadwater Rd. SE28 —3H 91
Broadwater Rd. SW17 —4C 120
Broadway. E13 —2K 71
Broadway. E15 —7F 53
(in two parts)
Broadway. SW1 —3H 85 (7C 166)
Broadway. W7 —1J 79
Broadway. W13 —1A 80
Broadway. Bark —1G 73
Broadway. Bexh —4E 110
Broadway. Surb —1H 147
Broadway Arc. W6 —4E 82
(off Hammersmith B'way.)
Broadway Av. Croy —5D 140
Broadway Av. Twic —6B 98
Broadway Cen., The. W6 —4E 82
Broadway Clo. Wfd G —6E 20
Broadway Ct. SW19 —6J 119
Broadway Ct. Beck —3E 142
Broadway Gdns. Mitc —4C 138
Broadway Gdns. Wfd G —6E 20
Broadway Ho. E8 —1H 69
Broadway Ho. Brom —5F 125
(off Bromley Rd.)
Broadway Mkt. E8 —1H 69
Broadway Mkt. SW17 —4D 120
Broadway Mkt. Ilf —2H 37
(in two parts)
Broadway Mkt. M. E8 —1G 69
Broadway M. N13 —5E 16
Broadway M. N16 —7F 33
Broadway M. N21 —1G 17
Broadway Pde. E4 —6K 19
Broadway Pde. N8 —6J 31
Broadway Pde. Harr —5F 25
Broadway Pde. Hay —1J 77
Broadway Pl. SW19 —6H 119
Broadway Shop. Cen. Bexh —4G 111
Broadway Shop. Mall. SW1 —3H 85
Broadway, The. E4 —6A 20
Broadway, The. N8 —6J 31
Broadway, The. N9 —3B 18
Broadway, The. N11 —5K 15
(off Stanford Rd.)
Broadway, The. N14 —1C 16
(off Southgate Cir.)
Broadway, The. N22 —2A 32
Broadway, The. NW7 —7H 13
(off Colenso Dri.)
Broadway, The. NW7 —5F 13
(Watford Way)
Broadway, The. NW9 —6B 28
Broadway, The. SW14 —2A 100
Broadway, The. SW19 —6H 119
Broadway, The. W3 —2G 81
Broadway, The. W5 —7D 62
Broadway, The. Cheam —6G 149
Broadway, The. Croy —4J 151
Broadway, The. Dag —2F 57
Broadway, The. Gnfd —4G 61
Broadway, The. N'wd —2J 23
Broadway, The. S'hall —7B 60
Broadway, The. Stan —5H 11
Broadway, The. Sutt —5A 150
Broadway, The. Th Dit —7J 133
Broadway, The. W'stone —2J 25
Broadway, The. Wemb —3E 44
Broadway, The. Wfd G —6E 20
Broadwell Ct. Houn —1B 96
(off Springwell Rd.)
Broadwick St. W1 —7G 67 (2B 166)
Broadwood Av. Ruis —6G 23
Broadwood Ter. W14 —4H 83
(off Warwick Rd.)
Broad Yd. EC1 —4B 68 (4A 162)
Brocas Clo. NW3 —7C 48
Brockbridge Ho. SW15 —6B 100
Brockdene Dri. Kes —4B 156
Brockdish Av. Bark —5K 55
Brockenhurst. W Mol —5D 132
Brockenhurst Av. Wor Pk —1A 148
Brockenhurst Gdns. NW7 —5F 13
Brockenhurst Gdns. Ilf —5G 55
Brockenhurst M. N18 —4B 18
Brockenhurst Rd. Croy —7H 141
Brockenhurst Way. SW16 —2H 139
Brocket Ho. SW8 —2H 103
Brockham Clo. SW19 —5H 119
Brockham Cres. New Ad —7F 155
Brockham Dri. SW2 —7K 103
Brockham Dri. Ilf —6F 37
Brockham Ho. NW1 —1G 67
(off Bayham Pl.)
Brockham Ho. SW2 —7K 103
(off Brockham Dri.)
Brockham St. SE1 —3C 86 (7D 168)
Brockhurst Clo. Stan —6E 10
Brockill Cres. SE4 —4A 106
Brocklebank Ho. E16 —1E 90
(off Glenister St.)
Brocklebank Ind. Est. SE7 —4J 89
Brocklebank Rd. SE7 —4K 89
Brocklebank Rd. SW18 —7A 102
Brocklehurst St. SE14 —7K 87
Brocklesby Rd. SE25 —4H 141
Brockley. —4B 106
Brockley Av. Stan —3K 11
Brockley Clo. Stan —4K 11
Brockley Cres. Romf —1J 39
Brockley Cross. SE4 —3A 106
Brockley Cross Bus. Cen. SE4 —3A 106
Brockley Footpath. SE4 —5A 106
(in two parts)
Brockley Footpath. SE15 —4J 105
Brockley Gdns. SE4 —2B 106
Brockley Gro. SE4 —5B 106
Brockley Hall Rd. SE4 —5A 106
Brockley Hill. Stan —1H 11
Brockley M. SE4 —5A 106
Brockley Pk. SE23 —7A 106
Brockley Ri. SE23 —1A 124
Brockley Rd. SE4 —3B 106
Brockley Side. Stan —4K 11
Brockley Vw. SE23 —7A 106
Brockley Way. SE4 —5K 105
Brockman Ri. Brom —4F 125
Brockmer Ho. E1 —7H 69
(off Crowder St.)
Brock Pl. E3 —4D 70
Brock Rd. E13 —5K 71
Brocks Dri. Sutt —3G 149
Brockshot Clo. Bren —5D 80

Brock St.—Buckingham St.

Brock St. SE15 —3J 105
Brockway Clo. E11 —2G 53
Brockwell Clo. Orp —5K 145
Brockwell Ct. SW2 —5A 104
Brockwell Ho. SE11 —6K 85 (7H 173)
(off Vauxhall St.)
Brockwell Pk. Gdns. SE24 —7A 104
Brodia Rd. N16 —3E 50
Brodie Ho. SE1 —5F 87
(off Cooper's Rd.)
Brodie Rd. E4 —1K 19
Brodie Rd. Enf —1H 7
Brodie St. SE1 —5F 87
Brodlove La. E1 —7K 69
Brodrick Gro. SE2 —4B 92
Brodrick Rd. SW17 —2C 120
Brograve Gdns. Beck —2D 142
Broken Wharf. EC4 —7C 68 (2C 168)
Brokesley St. E3 —3B 70
Broke Wlk. E8 —1F 69
Bromar Rd. SE5 —3E 104
Bromefield. Stan —1C 26
Bromell's Rd. SW4 —4G 103
Brome Rd. SE9 —3D 108
Bromfelde Rd. SW4 —3H 103
Bromfelde Wlk. SW4 —2H 103
Bromfield St. N1 —1A 68
Bromhall Rd. Dag —6B 56
Bromhead St. E1 —6J 69
Bromhedge. SE9 —3D 126
Bromholm Rd. SE2 —3B 92
Bromleigh Ct. SE23 —2G 123
Bromleigh Ho. SE1 —3F 87 (7J 169)
(off Abbey St.)
Bromley. —3D 70
(Bow)
Bromley. —2J 143
(Chislehurst)
Bromley Av. Brom —7G 125
Bromley Common. —1C 156
Bromley Comn. Brom —4A 144
Bromley Cres. Brom —3H 143
Bromley Cres. Ruis —4H 41
Bromley F.C. —5K 143
Bromley Gdns. Brom —3H 143
Bromley Gro. Brom —2F 143
Bromley Hall Rd. E14 —5E 70
Bromley High St. E3 —3D 70
Bromley Hill. Brom —6G 125
Bromley Ind. Cen. Brom —3B 144
(off Waldo Rd.)
Bromley La. Chst —7G 127
Bromley Park. —1G 143
Bromley Pk. Brom —1H 143
Bromley Pl. W1 —5G 67 (5A 160)
Bromley Rd. E10 —6D 34
Bromley Rd. E17 —3C 34
Bromley Rd. N17 —1F 33
Bromley Rd. N18 —3J 17
Bromley Rd. SE6 & Brom —1D 124
Bromley Rd. Beck & Short —1D 142
Bromley Rd. Chst —1F 145
Bromley St. E1 —5K 69
Brompton. —3C 84 (2D 170)
Brompton Arc. SW1 —7E 164
Brompton Clo. SE20 —2G 141
Brompton Clo. Houn —5D 96
Brompton Gro. N2 —4C 30
Brompton Pk. Cres. SW6 —6K 83
Brompton Pl. SW3 —3C 84 (1D 170)
Brompton Rd. SW3 & SW1
—4C 84 (3C 170)
Brompton Sq. SW3 —3C 84 (1C 170)
Brompton Ter. SE18 —1D 108
Bromwich Av. N6 —2E 48
Bromyard Av. W3 —7A 64
Bron Ct. NW6 —1J 65
Brondesbury. —7H 47
Brondesbury Ct. NW2 —6F 47
Brondesbury M. NW6 —7J 47
Brondesbury Park. —1G 65
Brondesbury Pk. NW2 & NW6 —6D 46
Brondesbury Rd. NW6 —2H 65
Brondesbury Vs. NW6 —2H 65
Bronhill Ter. N17 —1G 33
Bronsart Rd. SW6 —7G 83
Bronson Rd. SW20 —2F 137
Bronte Clo. E7 —4J 53
Bronte Clo. Eri —7H 93
Bronte Clo. Ilf —4E 36
Bronte Ho. N16 —5E 50
Bronte Ho. NW6 —3J 65
(off Cambridge Rd.)
Bronte Ho. SW4 —7G 103
Bronti Clo. SE17 —5C 86
Bronwen Ct. NW8 —3B 66 (2A 158)
(off Grove End Rd.)
Bronze Age Way. Belv & Eri —2H 93
Bronze St. SE8 —7C 88
Brook Av. Dag —7H 57
Brook Av. Edgw —6C 12
Brook Av. Wemb —3G 45
Brookbank Av. W7 —5H 61
Brookbank Rd. SE13 —3C 106
Brook Clo. NW7 —7B 14
Brook Clo. SW17 —2E 120
Brook Clo. SW20 —3D 136
Brook Clo. W5 —1G 81
Brook Clo. Ruis —7G 23
Brook Clo. Stanw —7B 94
Brook Ct. E11 —3G 53
Brook Ct. E15 —5D 52
(off Clays La.)
Brook Ct. E17 —3A 34
Brook Ct. SE12 —3A 126
Brook Ct. Beck —1B 142
Brook Ct. Edgw —5C 12
Brook Cres. E4 —4H 19
Brook Cres. N9 —4C 18
Brookdale. N11 —4B 16
Brookdale Rd. E17 —3C 34
Brookdale Rd. SE6 —7D 106
(in two parts)
Brookdale Rd. Bex —6E 110
Brookdales. NW4 —4G 29
Brookdene Rd. SE18 —4J 91
Brook Dri. SE11 —3A 86 (2K 173)
Brook Dri. Harr —4G 25
Brook Dri. Ruis —7G 23
Brooke Av. Harr —3G 43
Brooke Clo. Bush —1B 10
Brooke Ho. SE14 —1A 106
Brookehowse Rd. SE6 —2C 124
Brookend Rd. Sidc —1J 127
Brooke Rd. E5 —3G 51
Brooke Rd. E17 —4E 34
Brooke Rd. N16 —3F 51
Brooke's Ct. WC1 —5A 68 (6J 161)
Brooke's Mkt. EC1 —5K 161
Brooke St. EC1 —5A 68 (6J 161)
Brooke Way. Bush —1B 10
Brookfield. N6 —3E 48
Brookfield Av. E17 —4E 34
Brookfield Av. NW7 —6J 13
Brookfield Av. W5 —4D 62
Brookfield Av. Sutt —4C 150
Brookfield Clo. NW7 —6J 13
Brookfield Ct. Gnfd —3G 61
Brookfield Cres. NW7 —6J 13
Brookfield Cres. Harr —5E 26
Brookfield Gdns. Clay —6A 146
Brookfield Pk. NW5 —3F 49
Brookfield Path. Wfd G —6B 20
Brookfield Rd. E9 —6A 52
Brookfield Rd. N9 —3B 18
Brookfield Rd. W4 —2K 81
Brookfields. Enf —4E 8
Brookfields Av. Mitc —5C 138
Brook Gdns. E4 —4J 19
Brook Gdns. SW13 —3B 100
Brook Gdns. King T —1J 135
Brook Ga. W1 —7D 66 (3F 165)
Brook Green. —4F 83
Brook Grn. W6 —3F 83
Brookhill Clo. SE18 —5F 91
Brookhill Clo. E Barn —5H 5
Brookhill Rd. SE18 —6F 91
Brookhill Rd. Barn & E Barn —5H 5
Brookhouse Gdns. E4 —4B 20
Brook Houses. NW1 —2G 67
(off Cranleigh St.)
Brook Ind. Est. Hay —1B 78
Brooking Rd. E7 —5J 53
Brookland Clo. NW11 —4J 29
Brookland Gth. NW11 —4J 29
Brookland Hill. NW11 —4K 29
Brookland Ri. NW11 —4J 29
Brooklands App. Romf —4K 39
Brooklands Av. SW19 —2K 119
Brooklands Av. Sidc —2H 127
Brooklands Clo. Romf —4K 39
Brooklands Clo. Sun —1G 131
Brooklands Ct. N21 —5J 7
Brooklands Ct. NW6 —7H 47
Brooklands Ct. Mitc —2B 138
Brooklands Dri. Gnfd —1C 62
Brooklands La. Romf —4K 39
Brooklands Pk. SE3 —3J 107
Brooklands Pas. SW8 —1H 103
Brooklands Rd. Romf —4K 39
Brooklands Rd. Th Dit —1A 146
Brooklands, The. Iswth —1H 97
Brook La. SE3 —2K 107
Brook La. Bex —6D 110
Brook La. Brom —6J 125
Brook La. Bus. Cen. Bren —5D 80
Brook La. N. Bren —5D 80
(in two parts)
Brooklea Clo. NW9 —1A 28
Brook Lodge. Romf —4K 39
(off Brooklands Rd.)
Brooklyn Av. SE25 —4H 141
Brooklyn Clo. Cars —2C 150
Brooklyn Gro. SE25 —4H 141
Brooklyn Rd. SE25 —4H 141
Brooklyn Rd. Brom —5B 144
Brookmarsh Ind. Est. SE8 —7D 88
Brook Mead. Eps —6A 148
Brookmead Av. Brom —5D 144
Brookmead Ind. Est. Croy —6G 139
Brook Mdw. N12 —3E 14
Brook Mdw. Clo. Wfd G —6B 20
Brookmead Rd. Croy —6G 139
Brook M. WC2 —6H 67 (1D 166)
Brook M. N. W2 —7A 66 (2A 164)
Brookmill Rd. SE8 —1C 106
Brook Pde. Chig —3K 21
Brook Pk. Clo. N21 —5G 7
Brook Pas. SW6 —7J 83
Brook Pl. Barn —5D 4
Brook Ri. Chig —3K 21
Brook Rd. N2 —7H 15
Brook Rd. N8 —4J 31
Brook Rd. N22 —3K 31
Brook Rd. NW2 —2B 46
Brook Rd. Buck H —2D 20
Brook Rd. Ilf —6J 37
Brook Rd. Surb —2E 146
Brook Rd. T Hth —4C 140
Brook Rd. Twic —6A 98
Brook Rd. S. Bren —6D 80
Brooks Av. E6 —4D 72
Brooksbank St. E9 —6J 51
Brooksby M. N1 —7A 50
Brooksby St. N1 —7A 50
Brooksby's Wlk. E9 —5K 51
Brooks Clo. SE9 —2E 126
Brooks Ct. SW8 —7G 85
Brookscroft. E17 —3D 34
(off Forest Rd.)
Brookscroft Rd. E17 —1D 34
(in two parts)
Brookshill. Harr —5C 10
Brookshill Av. Harr —5C 10
Brookshill Dri. Harr —5C 10
Brookside. N21 —6E 6
Brookside. Cars —5E 150
Brookside. E Barn —6H 5
Brookside. Orp —7K 145
Brookside. Uxb —7B 40
Brookside Clo. Barn —6B 4
Brookside Clo. Felt —3J 113
Brookside Clo. Kent —5D 26
Brookside Clo. S Harr —4C 42
Brookside Cres. Wor Pk —1C 148
Brookside Rd. N9 —4C 18
(in two parts)
Brookside Rd. N19 —2G 49
Brookside Rd. NW11 —6G 29
Brookside Rd. Hay —7A 60
Brookside S. E Barn —7K 5
Brookside Wlk. N12 —6D 14
Brookside Wlk. NW11 —4G 29
Brookside Way. Croy —6K 141
Brooks La. W4 —6G 81
Brooks M. W1 —7F 67 (2J 165)
Brooks Rd. E13 —1J 71
Brooks Rd. W4 —5G 81
Brookstone Ct. SE15 —4H 105
Brook St. N17 —2F 33
Brook St. W1 —7F 67 (2J 165)
Brook St. W2 —7B 66 (2B 164)
Brook St. Belv & Eri —5H 93
Brook St. King T —2E 134
Brooksville Av. NW6 —1G 65
Brooks Wlk. N3 —3G 29
Brook Va. Eri —1H 111
Brookview Ct. Enf —5K 7
Brookview Rd. SW16 —5G 121
Brookville Rd. SW6 —7H 83
Brook Wlk. N2 —1B 30
Brook Wlk. Edgw —6E 12
Brookway. SE3 —3J 107
Brook Way. Chig —3K 21
Brookwood Av. SW13 —2B 100
Brookwood Clo. Brom —4H 143
Brookwood Ho. SE1 —2B 86 (7B 168)
(off Webber St.)
Brookwood Rd. SW18 —1H 119
Brookwood Rd. Houn —2F 97
Broom Clo. Brom —6C 144
Broom Clo. Tedd —7D 116
Broomcroft Av. N'holt —3A 60
Broome Rd. Hamp —7D 114
Broome Way. SE5 —7D 86
Broomfield. E17 —7B 34
Broomfield. NW1 —7E 48
(off Ferdinand St.)
Broomfield. Sun —1J 131
Broomfield Av. N13 —5E 16
Broomfield Ct. SE16 —3G 87
(off Ben Smith Way)
Broomfield Ho. SE17 —4E 86
(off Massinger St.)
Broomfield Ho. Stan —3F 11
(off Stanmore Hill)
Broomfield House Mus. —4D 16
Broomfield La. N13 —4D 16
Broomfield Pl. W13 —1B 80
Broomfield Rd. N13 —5D 16
Broomfield Rd. W13 —1B 80
Broomfield Rd. Beck —3A 142
Broomfield Rd. Bexh —5G 111
Broomfield Rd. Rich —1F 99
Broomfield Rd. Romf —7D 38
Broomfield Rd. Surb —1F 147
Broomfield Rd. Tedd —6C 116
Broomfield St. E14 —5C 70
Broom Gdns. Croy —3C 154
Broomgrove Gdns. Edgw —1G 27
Broomgrove Rd. SW9 —2K 103
Broomhall Rd. S Croy —7D 152
Broom Hill. —7K 145
Broomhill Ct. Wfd G —6D 20
Broom Hill Ri. Bexh —5G 111
Broomhill Rd. SW18 —5J 101
Broomhill Rd. Ilf —2A 56
Broomhill Rd. Orp —7K 145
Broomhill Rd. Wfd G —6D 20
(in two parts)
Broomhill Wlk. Wfd G —6C 20
Broomhouse La. SW6 —2J 101
Broomhouse Rd. SW6 —2J 101
Broomloan La. Sutt —2J 149
Broom Lock. Tedd —6C 116
Broom Mead. Bexh —6G 111
Broom Pk. Tedd —7D 116
Broom Rd. Croy —3C 154
Broom Rd. Tedd —5B 116
Broomsleigh Bus. Pk. SE26 —5B 124
Broomsleigh St. NW6 —5H 47
Broom Water. Tedd —6C 116
Broom Water W. Tedd —5C 116
Broomwood Clo. Bex —2K 129
Broomwood Clo. Croy —5K 141
Broomwood Rd. SW11 —6D 102
Broseley Gro. SE26 —5A 124
Broster Gdns. SE25 —3F 141
Brougham Rd. E8 —1G 69
Brougham Rd. W3 —6J 63
Brougham St. SW11 —2D 102
Brough Clo. SW8 —7J 85
Brough Clo. King T —5D 116
Broughton Av. N3 —3G 29
Broughton Av. Rich —3B 116
Broughton Ct. W13 —7B 62
Broughton Dri. SW9 —4A 104
Broughton Gdns. N6 —6G 31
Broughton Rd. SW6 —2K 101
Broughton Rd. W13 —7B 62
Broughton Rd. T Hth —6A 140
Broughton St. SW8 —2E 102
Broughton St. Ind. Est. SW11 —2E 102
Brouncker Rd. W3 —2J 81
Browells La. Felt —2K 113
Brown Bear Ct. Felt —4B 114
Brown Clo. Wall —7J 151
Brownfield Area. E14 —6E 70
Brownfield St. E14 —6D 70
Browngraves Rd. Hay —7E 76
Brown Hart Gdns. W1 —7E 66 (2H 165)
Brownhill Rd. SE6 —7D 106
Browning Av. W7 —6K 61
Browning Av. Sutt —4C 150
Browning Av. Wor Pk —1D 148
Browning Clo. E17 —4E 34
Browning Clo. W9 —4A 66 (4A 158)
Browning Clo. Col R —1F 39
Browning Clo. Hamp —4D 114
Browning Clo. Well —1J 109
Browning M. W1 —5F 67 (6H 159)
Browning Rd. E11 —7H 35
Browning Rd. E12 —5D 54
Browning Rd. Enf —1J 7
Browning St. SE17 —5C 86
Browning Way. Houn —1B 96
Brownlea Gdns. Ilf —2A 56
Brownlow Ct. N2 —5A 30
Brownlow Ct. N11 —6D 16
(off Brownlow Rd.)
Brownlow Ho. SE16 —2G 87
(off George Row)
Brownlow M. WC1 —4K 67 (4H 161)
Brownlow Rd. E7 —4J 53
Brownlow Rd. E8 —1F 69
Brownlow Rd. N3 —7E 14
Brownlow Rd. N11 —6D 16
Brownlow Rd. NW10 —7A 46
Brownlow Rd. W13 —1A 80
Brownlow Rd. Croy —4E 152
Brownlow St. WC1 —5K 67 (6H 161)
Brownrigg Rd. Ashf —4C 112
Browns Arc. W1 —7G 67
(off Regent St.)
Brown's Bldgs. EC3 —6E 68 (1H 169)
Browns La. NW5 —5F 49
Brownspring Dri. SE9 —4F 127
Browns Rd. E17 —3C 34
Brown's Rd. Surb —7F 135
Brown St. W1 —6D 66 (7E 158)
Brownswell Rd. N2 —2B 30
Brownswood Park. —2B 50
Brownswood Rd. N4 —3B 50
Broxash Rd. SW11 —6E 102
Broxbourne Av. E18 —4K 35
Broxbourne Rd. E7 —3J 53
Broxbourne Rd. Orp —7K 145
Broxholme Ho. SW6 —1K 101
(off Harwood Rd.)
Broxholm Rd. SW16 —3A 122
Broxted Rd. SE23 —2B 124
Broxwood Way. NW8 —1C 66
Bruce Av. Shep —6E 130
Bruce Castle Ct. N17 —1F 33
(off Lordship La.)
Bruce Castle Mus. —1E 32
Bruce Castle Rd. N17 —1F 33
Bruce Clo. W10 —5F 65
Bruce Clo. Well —1B 110
Bruce Ct. Sidc —4K 127
Bruce Gdns. N20 —3J 15
Bruce Gro. N17 —1E 32
Bruce Hall M. SW17 —4E 120
Bruce Ho. W10 —5F 65
Bruce Rd. E3 —3D 70
Bruce Rd. NW10 —7K 45
Bruce Rd. SE25 —4D 140
Bruce Rd. Barn —3B 4
Bruce Rd. Harr —2J 25
Bruce Rd. Mitc —7E 120
Bruckner St. W10 —3G 65
Brudenell Rd. SW17 —3D 120
Bruffs Mdw. N'holt —6C 42
Bruges Pl. NW1 —7G 49
(off Randolph St.)
Brumfield Rd. Eps —5J 147
Brummel Clo. Bexh —3J 111
Brune Ho. E1 —6J 163
Brunei Gallery. —5H 67 (5D 160)
Brunel Clo. SE19 —6F 123
Brunel Clo. Houn —7K 77
Brunel Clo. N'holt —3D 60
Brunel Est. W2 —5J 65
Brunel Ho. E14 —5D 88
Brunel Pl. S'hall —6F 61
Brunel Rd. E17 —6A 34
Brunel Rd. SE16 —2J 87
Brunel Rd. W3 —5A 64
Brunel Rd. Wfd G —5J 21
Brunel Science Pk. Uxb —3A 58
Brunel St. E16 —6H 71
Brunel Wlk. N15 —4E 32
Brunel Wlk. Twic —7E 96
Brune St. E1 —5F 69 (6J 163)
Brunlees Ho. SE1 —3C 86
(off Bath Ter.)
Brunner Clo. NW11 —5K 29
Brunner Ho. SE6 —4E 124
Brunner Rd. E17 —5A 34
Brunner Rd. W5 —4D 62
Bruno Pl. NW9 —2J 45
Brunswick Av. N11 —3K 15
(in two parts)
Brunswick Cen. WC1 —4J 67 (3E 160)
Brunswick Clo. Bexh —4D 110
Brunswick Clo. Pinn —6C 24
Brunswick Clo. Th Dit —1A 146
Brunswick Clo. Twic —3H 115
Brunswick Clo. Est. EC1
—3B 68 (2A 162)
Brunswick Ct. EC1 —3B 68 (2A 162)
(off Tompion St.)
Brunswick Ct. SE1 —2E 86 (7H 169)
Brunswick Ct. SW1 —4H 85 (4D 172)
(off Regency St.)
Brunswick Ct. Barn —5G 5
Brunswick Ct. Sutt —4K 149
Brunswick Cres. N11 —3K 15
Brunswick Gdns. W5 —4E 62
Brunswick Gdns. W8 —1J 83
Brunswick Gdns. Ilf —1G 37
Brunswick Gro. N11 —3K 15
Brunswick Ho. E2 —2F 69
(off Thurtle Rd.)
Brunswick Ho. N3 —1H 29
Brunswick Ind. Pk. N11 —4A 16
Brunswick Mans. WC1 —4J 67 (3F 161)
(off Handel St.)
Brunswick M. SW16 —6H 121
Brunswick M. W1 —6D 66 (7F 159)
Brunswick Park. —3K 15
Brunswick Pk. SE5 —1E 104
Brunswick Pk. Gdns. N11 —2K 15
Brunswick Pk. Rd. N11 —2K 15
Brunswick Pl. N1 —3D 68 (2F 163)
Brunswick Pl. NW1 —4E 66 (4H 159)
Brunswick Pl. SE19 —7G 123
Brunswick Quay. SE16 —3K 87
Brunswick Rd. E10 —1E 52
Brunswick Rd. E14 —6E 70
Brunswick Rd. N15 —4E 32
(in two parts)
Brunswick Rd. W5 —4D 62
Brunswick Rd. Bexh —4D 110
Brunswick Rd. Enf —1H 9
Brunswick Rd. King T —1G 135
Brunswick Rd. Sutt —4K 149
Brunswick Sq. N17 —6A 18
Brunswick Sq. WC1 —4J 67 (3F 161)
Brunswick St. E17 —5E 34
Brunswick Vs. SE5 —1E 104
Brunswick Way. N11 —4A 16
Brunton Pl. E14 —6A 70
Brushfield St. EC2 —5E 68 (5H 163)
(in two parts)
Brussels Rd. SW11 —4B 102
Bruton Clo. Chst —7D 126
Bruton La. W1 —7F 67 (3K 165)
Bruton Pl. W1 —7F 67 (3K 165)
Bruton Rd. Mord —4A 138
Bruton St. W1 —7F 67 (3K 165)
Bruton Way. W13 —5A 62
Brutus Ct. SE11 —4B 86
(off Kennington La.)
Bryan Av. NW10 —7D 46
Bryan Clo. Sun —7J 113
Bryan Ho. SE16 —2B 88
Bryan Rd. SE16 —2B 88
Bryan's All. SW6 —2K 101
Bryanston Av. Twic —1F 115
Bryanston Clo. S'hall —4D 78
Bryanston Ct. W1 —7E 158
(in two parts)
Bryanstone Ct. Sutt —3A 150
Bryanstone Rd. N8 —6H 31
Bryanston Mans. W1 —5D 66 (5E 158)
(off York St.)
Bryanston M. E. W1 —5D 66 (6E 158)
Bryanston M. W. W1 —5D 66 (6E 158)
Bryanston Pl. W1 —5D 66 (6E 158)
Bryanston Sq. W1 —6D 66 (6E 158)
Bryanston St. W1 —6D 66 (1E 164)
Bryant Clo. Barn —5C 4
Bryant Ct. E2 —2F 69
(off Whiston Rd., in two parts)
Bryant Rd. N'holt —3A 60
Bryant St. E15 —7F 53
Bryantwood Rd. N7 —5A 50
Brycedale Cres. N14 —4B 16
Bryce Rd. Dag —4C 56
Bryden Clo. SE26 —5A 124
Brydges Pl. WC2 —7J 67 (3E 166)
Brydges Rd. E15 —5F 53
Brydon Wlk. N1 —1J 67
Bryer Ct. EC2 —5C 162
Bryet Rd. N7 —3J 49
Bryher Ct. SE11 —5J 173
Brymay Clo. E3 —2C 70
Brynmaer Rd. SW11 —1D 102
Brynmawr Rd. Enf —4A 8
Bryony Clo. Uxb —5B 58
Bryony Rd. W12 —7C 64
Bryony Way. Sun —6J 113
Buccleugh Ho. E5 —7G 33
Buchanan Clo. N21 —5E 6
Buchanan Ct. SE16 —4K 87
(off Worgan St.)
Buchanan Gdns. NW10 —2D 64
Buchan Rd. SE15 —3J 105
Bucharest Rd. SW18 —7A 102
Buckden Clo. N2 —4D 30
Buckden Clo. SE12 —6J 107
Buckfast Ct. W13 —7A 62
Buckfast Rd. Mord —4K 137
Buckfast St. E2 —3G 69
Buck Hill Wlk. W2 —7B 66 (3B 164)
Buckhold Rd. SW18 —6J 101
Buckhurst Av. Cars —1C 150
Buckhurst Ct. Buck H —2G 21
(off Albert Rd.)
Buckhurst Hill. —2G 21
Buckhurst Hill Ho. Buck H —2E 20
Buckhurst Ho. N7 —5H 49
Buckhurst St. E1 —4H 69
Buckhurst Ter. Buck H —1G 21
Buckhurst Way. Buck H —4G 21
Buckingham Arc. WC2 —3E 166
Buckingham Av. N20 —7F 5
Buckingham Av. Felt —6K 95
Buckingham Av. Gnfd —1A 62
Buckingham Av. T Hth —1A 140
Buckingham Av. Well —4J 109
Buckingham Av. W Mol —2F 133
Buckingham Chambers. SW1
(off Greencoat Pl.) —4G 85 (3B 172)
Buckingham Clo. W5 —5C 62
Buckingham Clo. Enf —2K 7
Buckingham Clo. Hamp —5D 114
Buckingham Clo. Orp —7J 145
Buckingham Ct. NW4 —3C 28
Buckingham Ct. W7 —4K 61
(off Copley Clo.)
Buckingham Ct. N'holt —2C 60
Buckingham Dri. Chst —4G 127
Buckingham Gdns. Edgw —7A 12
Buckingham Gdns. T Hth —2A 140
Buckingham Gdns. W Mol —2F 133
Buckingham Ga. SW1 —3G 85 (1A 172)
Buckingham Gro. Uxb —2C 58
Buckingham La. SE23 —7A 106
Buckingham Mans. NW6 —5K 47
(off W. End La.)
Buckingham M. N1 —6E 50
Buckingham M. NW10 —2B 64
Buckingham M. SW1 —1A 172
Buckingham Palace. —2F 85 (6K 165)
Buckingham Pal. Rd. SW1
—4F 85 (4J 171)
Buckingham Pde. Stan —5H 11
Buckingham Pl. SW1 —3G 85 (1A 172)
Buckingham Rd. E10 —3D 52
Buckingham Rd. E11 —5A 36
Buckingham Rd. E15 —5H 53
Buckingham Rd. E18 —1H 35
Buckingham Rd. N1 —6E 50
Buckingham Rd. N22 —1J 31
Buckingham Rd. NW10 —2B 64
Buckingham Rd. Edgw —7A 12
Buckingham Rd. Hamp —4D 114
Buckingham Rd. Harr —5H 25
Buckingham Rd. Ilf —2H 55
Buckingham Rd. King T —4F 135
Buckingham Rd. Mitc —4J 139
Buckingham Rd. Rich —2D 116
Buckingham St. WC2 —7J 67 (4F 167)

Buckland Ct.—Byculla Rd.

Buckland Ct. N1 —2E 68
(off St Johns Est.)
Buckland Ct. Ick —2E 40
Buckland Cres. NW3 —7B 48
Buckland Ri. Pinn —1A 24
Buckland Rd. E10 —2E 52
Buckland Rd. Chess —5F 147
Bucklands Rd. Tedd —6C 116
Buckland St. N1 —2D 68
Buckland's Wharf. King T —2D 134
Buckland Wlk. W3 —2J 81
Buckland Wlk. Mord —4A 138
Buckland Way. Wor Pk —1E 148
Buck La. NW9 —5K 27
Bucklebury. NW1 —4G 67 (3A 160)
(off Stanhope St.)
Buckleigh Av. SW20 —3G 137
Buckleigh Rd. SW16 —6H 121
Buckleigh Way. SE19 —7F 123
Buckler Gdns. SE9 —3D 126
Bucklers All. SW6 —6H 83
(in two parts)
Bucklersbury. EC4 —1E 168
(in two parts)
Bucklersbury Pas. EC4 —6D 68 (1E 168)
Buckler's Way. Cars —3D 150
Buckles Ct. Belv —4D 92
Buckle St. E1 —6F 69 (7K 163)
Buckley Ct. NW6 —7H 47
Buckley Rd. NW6 —7H 47
Buckmaster Clo. SW9 —3A 104
(off Stockwell Pk. Rd.)
Buckmaster Ho. N7 —4K 49
Buckmaster Rd. SW11 —4C 102
Bucknall St. WC1 —6J 67 (7D 160)
Bucknall Way. Beck —4D 142
Bucknell Clo. SW9 —4K 103
Buckner Rd. SW2 —4K 103
Bucknill Ho. SW1 —5F 85 (5J 171)
(off Ebury Bri. Rd.)
Buckrell Rd. E4 —2A 20
Buckridge Ho. EC1 —5A 68 (5J 161)
(off Portpool La.)
Buckstone Clo. SE23 —6J 105
Buckstone Rd. N18 —5B 18
Buck St. NW1 —7F 49
Buckters Rents. SE16 —1A 88
Buckthorne Rd. SE4 —5A 106
Buckthorn Ho. Sidc —3K 127
(off Longlands Rd.)
Buck Wlk. E17 —4F 35
Buckwheat Ct. Eri —3D 92
Budd Clo. N12 —4E 14
Buddings Circ. Wemb —3J 45
Budd's All. Twic —5C 98
Bude Clo. E17 —5B 34
Budge La. Mitc —7D 138
Budge Row. EC4 —7D 68 (1E 168)
Budge's Wlk. W2 —3A 164
Budleigh Cres. Well —1C 110
Budleigh Ho. SE15 —7G 87
(off Bird in Bush Rd.)
Budoch Ct. Ilf —2A 56
Budoch Dri. Ilf —2A 56
Buer Rd. SW6 —2G 101
Bugsby's Way. SE10 & SE7 —4H 89
Bulbarrow. NW8 —1K 65
(off Abbey Rd.)
Bulganak Rd. T Hth —4C 140
Bullace Row. SE5 —1D 104
Bull All. Well —3B 110
Bullard Rd. Tedd —6J 115
Bullard's Pl. E2 —3K 69
Bullbanks Rd. Belv —4J 93
Bulleid Way. SW1 —4F 85 (4K 171)
Bullen St. SW11 —2C 102
Buller Clo. SE15 —7G 87
Buller Rd. N17 —2G 33
Buller Rd. N22 —2A 32
Buller Rd. NW10 —3F 65
Buller Rd. Bark —7J 55
Buller Rd. T Hth —2D 140
Bullers Clo. Sidc —5E 128
Bullers Wood Dri. Chst —7D 126
Bullescroft Rd. Edgw —3B 12
Bullingham Mans. W8 —2J 83
(off Pitt St. La.)
Bull Inn Ct. WC2 —3F 167
Bullivant St. E14 —7E 70
Bull La. N18 —5K 17
Bull La. Chst —7H 127
Bull La. Dag —3H 57
Bull Rd. E15 —2H 71
Bullrush Clo. Croy —6E 140
Bull's All. SW14 —2K 99
Bull's Bri. Cen. Hay —3K 77
Bull's Bri. Ind. Est. Hay —3J 77
Bullsbridge Rd. S'hall —4A 78
Bullsbrook Rd. Hay —1A 78
Bulls Gdns. SW3 —4C 84 (3D 170)
(in two parts)
Bulls Head Pas. EC3 —1G 169
Bull Wharf La. EC4 —7C 68 (3D 168)
Bull Yd. SE15 —1G 105
Bulmer Gdns. Harr —7D 26
Bulmer M. W11 —7J 65
Bulmer Pl. W11 —1J 83
Bulow Est. SW6 —1K 101
(off Pearscroft Rd.)
Bulstrode Av. Houn —2D 96
Bulstrode Gdns. Houn —3E 96
Bulstrode Pl. W1 —5E 66 (6H 159)
Bulstrode Rd. Houn —3E 96
Bulstrode St. W1 —6E 66 (7H 159)
Bulwer Ct. E11 —1F 53
Bulwer Ct. Rd. E11 —1F 53
Bulwer Gdns. Barn —4F 5
Bulwer Rd. E11 —7F 35
Bulwer Rd. N18 —4K 17
Bulwer Rd. Barn —4E 4
Bulwer St. W12 —1E 82
Bunce's La. Wfd G —7C 20
Bungalow Rd. SE25 —4E 140
Bungalows, The. E10 —6E 34
Bungalows, The. SW16 —7F 121
Bungalows, The. Ilf —1J 37
Bungalows, The. Wall —5F 151
Bunhill Row. EC1 —4D 68 (3E 162)
Bunhouse Pl. SW1 —5E 84 (5H 171)
Bunkers Hill. NW11 —7A 30
Bunkers Hill. Belv —4G 93
Bunkers Hill. Sidc —3F 129
Bunning Way. N7 —7J 49
Bunns La. NW7 —6F 13
(in two parts)
Bunsen St. E3 —2A 70
Buntingbridge Rd. Ilf —5H 37
Bunting Clo. N9 —1E 18
Bunting Clo. Mitc —5D 138
Bunting Ct. NW9 —2A 28
Bunton St. SE18 —3E 90
Bunyan Ct. EC2 —5C 162
Bunyan Rd. E17 —3A 34
Buonaparte M. SW1 —5H 85 (5C 172)
Burbage Clo. SE1 —3D 86
Burbage Clo. Hay —6F 59
Burbage Ho. N1 —1D 68
(off Poole St.)
Burbage Rd. SE24 & SE21 —6C 104
Burberry Clo. N Mald —2A 136
Burbidge Rd. Shep —4C 130
Burbridge Way. N17 —2G 33
Burcham St. E14 —6D 70
Burcharbro Rd. SE2 —6D 92
Burchell Ct. Bush —1B 10
Burchell Ho. SE11 —5K 85 (5H 173)
(off Jonathan St.)
Burchell Rd. E10 —1D 52
Burchell Rd. SE15 —1H 105
Burchetts Way. Shep —6D 130
Burchett Way. Romf —6F 39
Burchwall Clo. Romf —1J 39
Burcote Rd. SW18 —7B 102
Burden Clo. Bren —5C 80
Burden Ho. SW8 —7J 85
(off Thorncroft St.)
Burdenshott Av. Rich —4H 99
Burden Way. E11 —2K 53
Burder Clo. N1 —6E 50
Burder Rd. N1 —6E 50
Burdett Av. SW20 —1C 136
Burdett Clo. W7 —1K 79
Burdett Clo. Sidc —5E 128
Burdett M. NW3 —6B 48
Burdett M. W2 —6K 65
Burdett Rd. E3 & E14 —4A 70
Burdett Rd. Croy —6D 140
Burdett Rd. Rich —2F 99
Burdetts Rd. Dag —1F 75
Burdock Clo. Croy —1K 153
Burdock Rd. N17 —3G 33
Burdon La. Sutt —7G 149
Burdon Pk. Sutt —7H 149
Bure Ct. New Bar —5E 4
Burfield Clo. SW17 —4B 120
Burford Clo. Dag —3C 56
Burford Clo. Ilf —4G 37
Burford Clo. Uxb —4A 40
Burford Gdns. N13 —3E 16
Burford Ho. Bren —5D 80
Burford Rd. E6 —3C 72
Burford Rd. E15 —1F 71
Burford Rd. SE6 —2B 124
Burford Rd. Bren —5E 80
Burford Rd. Brom —4C 144
Burford Rd. Sutt —2J 149
Burford Rd. Wor Pk —7B 136
Burford Wlk. SW6 —7A 84
Burford Way. New Ad —6E 154
Burge Rd. E7 —4B 54
Burges Gro. SW13 —7D 82
Burges Rd. E6 —7C 54
Burgess Av. NW9 —6K 27
Burgess Clo. Felt —4C 114
Burgess Ct. E6 —7E 54
Burgess Ct. S'hall —6F 61
(off Fleming Rd.)
Burgess Hill. NW2 —4J 47
Burgess Ind. Pk. SE5 —7D 86
Burgess M. SW19 —6K 119
Burgess Pk. —6E 86
Burgess Rd. E6 —7E 54
Burgess Rd. E15 —4G 53
Burgess Rd. Sutt —4K 149
Burgess St. E14 —5C 70
Burge St. SE1 —3D 86
Burghill Rd. SE26 —4A 124
Burghley Av. N Mald —1K 135
Burghley Hall Clo. SW19 —1G 119
Burghley Pl. Mitc —5D 138
Burghley Rd. E11 —1G 53
Burghley Rd. N8 —3A 32
Burghley Rd. NW5 —4F 49
Burghley Rd. SW19 —4F 119
Burghley Tower. W3 —7B 64
Burgh St. N1 —2B 68
Burgoine Quay. King T —1D 134
Burgon St. EC4 —6B 68 (1B 168)
Burgos Clo. Croy —6A 152
Burgos Gro. SE10 —1D 106
Burgoyne Rd. N4 —6B 32
Burgoyne Rd. SE25 —4F 141
Burgoyne Rd. SW9 —3K 103
Burgoyne Rd. Sun —6H 113
Burham Clo. SE20 —7J 123
Burhill Gro. Pinn —2C 24
Burke Clo. SW15 —4A 100
Burke Lodge. E13 —3K 71
Burke St. E16 —5H 71
Burket Clo. S'hall —4C 78
Burland Rd. SW11 —5D 102
Burleigh Av. Sidc —5K 109
Burleigh Av. Wall —3E 150
Burleigh Gdns. N14 —1B 16
Burleigh Gdns. Ashf —5E 112
Burleigh Ho. SW3 —7B 170
Burleigh Ho. W10 —5G 65
(off St Charles Sq.)
Burleigh Pde. N14 —1C 16
Burleigh Pl. SW15 —5F 101
Burleigh Rd. Enf —4K 7
Burleigh Rd. Sutt —1G 149
Burleigh Rd. Uxb —1D 58
Burleigh St. WC2 —7K 67 (2G 167)
Burleigh Wlk. SE6 —1E 124
Burleigh Way. Enf —3J 7
Burley Clo. E4 —5H 19
Burley Clo. SW16 —2H 139
Burley Rd. E16 —6A 72
Burlington Arc. W1 —7G 67 (3A 166)
Burlington Av. Rich —1G 99
Burlington Av. Romf —6H 39
Burlington Clo. E6 —6C 72
Burlington Clo. W9 —4J 65
Burlington Clo. Felt —7F 95
Burlington Clo. Orp —2E 156
Burlington Clo. Pinn —3K 23
Burlington Gdns. SW6 —2G 101
Burlington Gdns. W1 —7G 67 (3A 166)
Burlington Gdns. W3 —1J 81
Burlington Gdns. W4 —5J 81
Burlington Gdns. Romf —7E 38
Burlington La. W4 —7J 81
Burlington M. SW15 —5H 101
Burlington M. W3 —1J 81
Burlington Pl. SW6 —2G 101
Burlington Pl. Wfd G —3E 20
Burlington Ri. E Barn —1H 15
Burlington Rd. N10 —3E 30
Burlington Rd. N17 —1G 33
Burlington Rd. SW6 —2G 101
Burlington Rd. W4 —5J 81
Burlington Rd. Enf —1J 7
Burlington Rd. Isleworth —1H 97
Burlington Rd. N Mald —4B 136
Burlington Rd. T Hth —2C 140
Burma M. N16 —4D 50
Burma Rd. N16 —4D 50
Burmarsh Ct. SE20 —1J 141
Burma Ter. SE19 —5E 122
Burmester Rd. SW17 —3A 120
Burnaby Cres. W4 —6J 81
Burnaby Gdns. W4 —6H 81
Burnaby St. SW10 —7A 84
Burnard Pl. N7 —5K 49
Burnaston Ho. E5 —3G 51
Burnbrae Clo. N12 —6E 14
Burnbury Rd. SW12 —1G 121
Burncroft Av. Enf —2D 8
Burndell Way. Hay —5B 60
Burne Jones Ho. W14 —4G 83
(off N. End Rd.)
Burnell Av. Rich —5C 116
Burnell Av. Well —2A 110
Burnell Gdns. Stan —2D 26
Burnell Rd. Sutt —4K 149
Burnell Wlk. SE1 —5F 87
(off Abingdon Clo.)
Burnels Av. E6 —3E 72
Burness Clo. N7 —6K 49
Burne St. NW1 —5C 66 (5C 158)
Burnett Clo. E9 —5J 51
Burnett Ho. SE13 —2E 106
(off Lewisham Hill)
Burney Av. Surb —5F 135
Burney St. SE10 —7E 88
Burnfoot Av. SW6 —1G 101
Burnham. NW3 —7C 48
Burnham Av. Uxb —4E 40
Burnham Clo. NW7 —7H 13
Burnham Clo. SE1 —4F 87
Burnham Clo. Enf —1K 7
Burnham Clo. W'stone —4A 26
Burnham Ct. W2 —7K 65
(off Moscow Rd.)
Burnham Cres. E11 —4A 36
Burnham Dri. Wor Pk —2F 149
Burnham Gdns. Croy —7F 141
Burnham Gdns. Hay —3F 77
Burnham Gdns. Houn —1K 95
Burnham Rd. E4 —5G 19
Burnham Rd. Dag —7B 56
Burnham Rd. Mord —4K 137
Burnham Rd. Romf —3K 39
Burnham Rd. Sidc —2E 128
Burnham St. E2 —3J 69
Burnham St. King T —1G 135
Burnham Way. SE26 —5B 124
Burnham Way. W13 —4B 80
Burnhill Clo. SE15 —7H 87
Burnhill Rd. Beck —2C 142
Burnley Rd. NW10 —5B 46
Burnley Rd. SW9 —2K 103
Burnsall St. SW3 —5C 84 (6D 170)
Burns Av. Chad H —7C 38
Burns Av. Felt —6J 95
Burns Av. Sidc —6B 110
Burns Av. S'hall —7E 60
Burns Clo. E17 —4E 34
Burns Clo. SW19 —6B 120
Burns Clo. Hay —5H 59
Burns Clo. Well —1K 109
Burns Ho. SE17 —5B 86
(off Doddington Gro.)
Burn Side. N9 —3D 18
Burnside Av. E4 —6G 19
Burnside Clo. SE16 —1K 87
Burnside Clo. Barn —3D 4
Burnside Clo. Twic —6A 98
Burnside Cres. Wemb —1D 62
Burnside Rd. Dag —2C 56
Burns Rd. NW10 —1B 64
Burns Rd. SW11 —2D 102
Burns Rd. W13 —2B 80
Burns Rd. Wemb —2E 62
Burns Way. Houn —2B 96
Burnt Ash Hill. SE12 —6H 107
(in two parts)
Burnt Ash La. Brom —7J 125
Burnt Ash Rd. SE12 —5H 107
Burnthwaite Rd. SW6 —7H 83
Burnt Oak. —1J 27
Burnt Oak B'way. Edgw —7C 12
Burnt Oak Fields. Edgw —1J 27
Burnt Oak La. Sidc —6A 110
Burntwood Clo. SW18 —1C 120
Burntwood Grange Rd. SW18 —1B 120
Burntwood La. SW17 —3A 120
Burntwood Vw. SE19 —5F 123
Buross St. E1 —6H 69
Burpham Clo. Hay —5B 60
Burrage Ct. SE16 —4K 87
(off Worgan St.)
Burrage Gro. SE18 —4G 91
Burrage Pl. SE18 —5F 91
Burrage Rd. SE18 —6G 91
Burrard Rd. E16 —6K 71
Burrard Rd. NW6 —5J 47
Burr Clo. E1 —1G 87 (4K 169)
Burr Clo. Bexh —3F 111
Burrell Clo. Croy —6A 142
Burrell Clo. Edgw —2C 12
Burrell Row. Beck —2C 142
Burrell St. SE1 —1B 86 (4A 168)
Burrell's Wharf Sq. E14 —5D 88
Burrells Wharf Sq. E14 —5D 88
Burrell Towers. E10 —7C 34
Burritt Rd. King T —2G 135
Burrmill Ct. SE16 —3K 87
(off Worgan St.)
Burroughs Gdns. NW4 —4D 28
Burroughs Pde. NW4 —4D 28
Burroughs, The. NW4 —4D 28
Burrow Ho. SW9 —2A 104
(off Stockwell Pk. Rd.)
Burrow Rd. SE22 —4E 104
Burrows M. SE1 —2B 86 (6A 168)
Burrows Rd. NW10 —3E 64
Burrow Wlk. SE21 —7C 104
Burr Rd. SW18 —1J 119
Bursar St. SE1 —5G 169
Bursdon Clo. Sidc —2K 127
Bursland Rd. Enf —4E 8
Burslem St. E1 —6G 69
Burstock Rd. SW15 —4G 101
Burston Rd. SW15 —5F 101
Burstow Rd. SW20 —1G 137
Burtenshaw Rd. Th Dit —7A 134
Burtley Clo. N4 —1C 50
Burton Bank. N1 —7D 50
(off Yeate St.)
Burton Clo. Chess —7D 146
Burton Clo. T Hth —3D 140
Burton Ct. SE20 —2J 141
Burton Ct. SW3 —5D 84 (5F 171)
(off Turks Row, in two parts)
Burton Gdns. Houn —1D 96
Burton Gro. SE17 —5D 86
Burtonhole Clo. NW7 —4A 14
Burtonhole La. NW7 —5K 13
Burton Ho. SE16 —2H 87
(off Cherry Garden St.)
Burton La. SW9 —2A 104
(in two parts)
Burton M. SW1 —4E 84 (4H 171)
Burton Pl. WC1 —4H 67 (2D 160)
Burton Rd. E18 —3K 35
Burton Rd. NW6 —7H 47
Burton Rd. SW9 —2B 104
(Akerman Rd.)
Burton Rd. SW9 —2A 104
(Brixton Rd.)
Burton Rd. King T —7E 116
Burton's Rd. Hamp H —4F 115
Burton St. WC1 —3H 67 (2D 160)
Burtonwood Ho. N4 —7D 32
Burt Rd. E16 —1A 90
Burtt Ho. N1 —3E 68 (1G 163)
(off Aske St.)
Burtwell La. SE27 —4D 122
Burwash Ho. SE1 —2D 86 (7F 169)
(off Kipling Est.)
Burwash Rd. SE18 —5H 91
Burwell Av. Gnfd —6J 43
Burwell Clo. E1 —6H 69
Burwell Rd. E10 —1A 52
Burwell Rd. Ind. Est. E10 —1A 52
Burwell Wlk. E3 —4C 70
Burwood Av. Brom —2K 155
Burwood Av. Pinn —5K 23
Burwood Clo. Surb —1G 147
Burwood Ho. SW9 —4B 104
Burwood Pl. W2 —6C 66 (7D 158)
Bury Av. Hay —2G 59
Bury Av. Ruis —6E 22
Bury Clo. SE16 —1K 87
Bury Ct. EC3 —6E 68 (7H 163)
Bury Gro. Mord —5K 137
Bury Hall Vs. N9 —7A 8
Bury Pl. WC1 —5J 67 (6E 160)
Bury Rd. E4 —1B 20
Bury Rd. N22 —2A 32
Bury Rd. Dag —5H 57
Bury St. EC3 —6E 68 (1H 169)
Bury St. N9 —7A 8
Bury St. SW1 —1G 85 (4B 166)
Bury St. Ruis —5E 22
Bury St. W. N9 —7J 7
Bury Wlk. SW3 —4C 84 (4C 170)
Busbridge Ho. E14 —5C 70
Busby M. NW5 —6H 49
Busby Pl. NW5 —6H 49
Busch Clo. Isleworth —1B 98
Bushbaby Clo. SE1 —3E 86
Bushberry Rd. E9 —6A 52
Bush Clo. Ilf —5H 37
Bush Cotts. SW18 —5J 101
Bush Ct. N14 —1C 16
Bush Ct. W12 —2F 83
Bushell Clo. SW2 —2K 121
Bushell Grn. Bus H —2C 10
Bushell St. E1 —1G 87
Bushell Way. Chst —5E 126
Bushey. —1A 10
Bushey Av. E18 —3H 35
Bushey Av. Orp —7H 145
Bushey Clo. E4 —3K 19
Bushey Clo. Uxb —2C 40
Bushey Ct. SW20 —3D 136
Bushey Down. SW12 —2F 121
Bushey Heath. —1C 10
Bushey Hill Rd. SE5 —1E 104
Bushey La. Sutt —4J 149
Bushey Mead. —2F 137
Bushey Rd. E13 —2A 72
Bushey Rd. N15 —6E 32
Bushey Rd. SW20 —3D 136
Bushey Rd. Croy —2C 154
Bushey Rd. Hay —4G 77
Bushey Rd. Ick & Uxb —2C 40
Bushey Rd. Sutt —4J 149
Bushey Way. Beck —6F 143
Bush Fair Ct. N14 —6A 6
Bushfield Clo. Edgw —2C 12
Bushfield Cres. Edgw —2C 12
Bush Gro. NW9 —7J 27
Bush Gro. Stan —1D 26
Bushgrove Rd. Dag —4D 56
Bush Hill. N21 —7H 7
Bush Hill Pde. N9 —7J 7
Bush Hill Park. —6A 8
Bush Hill Rd. N21 —6J 7
Bush Hill Rd. Harr —6F 27
Bush Ind. Est. N19 —3G 49
Bush Ind. Est. NW10 —4K 63
Bush La. EC4 —7D 68 (2E 168)
Bushmead Clo. N15 —4F 33
Bushmoor Cres. SE18 —7F 91
Bushnell Rd. SW17 —2F 121
Bush Rd. E8 —1H 69
Bush Rd. E11 —7H 35
Bush Rd. SE8 —4K 87
Bush Rd. Buck H —4G 21
Bush Rd. Rich —6F 81
Bush Rd. Shep —5B 130
Bushway. Dag —4D 56
Bushwood. E11 —1H 53
Bushwood Dri. SE1 —4F 87
Bushwood Rd. Rich —6G 81
Bushy Ct. King T —1C 134
(off Up. Teddington Rd.)
Bushy Lees. Sidc —6K 109
Bushy Pk. Gdns. Tedd —5H 115
Bushy Pk. Rd. Tedd —7B 116
(in two parts)
Bushy Rd. Tedd —6K 115
Butcher Row. E14 & E1 —7K 69
Butchers Rd. E16 —6J 71
Bute Av. Rich —2E 116
Bute Ct. Wall —5G 151
Bute Gdns. W6 —4F 83
Bute Gdns. Rich —1E 116
Bute Gdns. Wall —5G 151
Bute Gdns. W. Wall —5G 151
Bute Rd. Croy —1A 152
Bute Rd. Ilf —5F 37
Bute Rd. Wall —4G 151
Bute St. SW7 —4B 84 (3A 170)
Bute Wlk. N1 —6D 50
Butfield Ho. E9 —6J 51
(off Stevens Av.)
Butler Av. Harr —7H 25
Butler Ct. Wemb —4A 44
Butler Ho. E14 —6B 70
Butler Pl. SW1 —1C 172
Butler Rd. NW10 —7B 46
Butler Rd. Dag —4B 56
Butler Rd. Harr —7G 25
Butlers & Colonial Wharf. SE1
(off Shad Thames) —2F 87 (6K 169)
Butlers Dri. E4 —1K 9
Butler St. E2 —3J 69
Butler St. Uxb —4D 58
Butlers Wharf. SE1 —6K 169
Butley Ct. E3 —2A 70
(off Ford St.)
Butterfield Clo. N17 —6H 17
Butterfield Clo. SE16 —2H 87
Butterfield Clo. Twic —6K 97
Butterfields. E17 —5E 34
Butterfield Sq. E6 —6D 72
Butterfly La. SE9 —6F 109
Butterfly Wlk. SE5 —2D 104
(off Denmark Hill)
Butter Hill. Cars —3E 150
Butteridges Clo. Dag —1F 75
Buttermere. NW1 —3F 67 (1K 159)
(off Augustus St.)
Buttermere Clo. E15 —4F 53
Buttermere Clo. SE1 —4F 87
Buttermere Clo. Felt —1H 113
Buttermere Clo. Mord —6F 137
Buttermere Ct. NW8 —1B 66
(off Boundary Rd.)
Buttermere Dri. SW15 —5G 101
Buttermere Wlk. E8 —6F 51
Butterwick. W6 —4F 83
Butterworth Gdns. Wfd G —6D 20
Buttesland St. N1 —3D 68 (1F 163)
Buttfield Clo. Dag —6H 57
Buttmarsh Clo. SE18 —5F 91
Buttsbury Rd. Ilf —5G 55
(in two parts)
Butts Cotts. Felt —3C 114
Butts Cres. Hanw —3E 114
Buttsmead. N'wd —1E 22
Butts Piece. N'holt —2K 59
Butts Rd. Brom —5G 125
Butts, The. Bren —6C 80
Butts, The. Sun —3A 132
Buxhall Cres. E9 —6B 52
Buxted Rd. E8 —7F 51
Buxted Rd. N12 —5H 15
Buxted Rd. SE22 —4E 104
Buxton Clo. Wfd G —6G 21
Buxton Ct. N1 —1D 162
(in two parts)
Buxton Cres. Sutt —4G 149
Buxton Dri. E11 —4G 35
Buxton Dri. N Mald —2K 135
Buxton Gdns. W3 —7H 63
Buxton Ho. E11 —4G 35
Buxton Rd. E4 —1A 20
Buxton Rd. E6 —3C 72
Buxton Rd. E15 —5G 53
Buxton Rd. E17 —4A 34
Buxton Rd. N19 —1H 49
Buxton Rd. NW2 —6D 46
Buxton Rd. SW14 —3A 100
Buxton Rd. Ashf —5A 112
Buxton Rd. Eri —7K 93
Buxton Rd. Ilf —6J 37
Buxton Rd. T Hth —5B 140
Buxton St. E1 —4F 69 (4K 163)
Buzzard Creek Ind. Est. Bark —5A 74
Byam St. SW6 —2A 102
Byards Ct. SE16 —4K 87
(off Worgan St.)
Byards Cft. SW16 —1H 139
Byatt Wlk. Hamp —6C 114
Bychurch End. Tedd —5K 115
Bycroft Rd. S'hall —4E 60
Bycroft St. SE20 —7K 123
Bycullah Av. Enf —3G 7
Bycullah Rd. Enf —2G 7

Byegrove Rd.—Canal Rd.

Byegrove Rd. SW19 —6B 120
Byelands Clo. SE16 —1K 87
Bye, The. W3 —6A 64
Byeways. Twic —3F 115
Byeways, The. Surb —5G 135
Byeway, The. SW14 —3J 99
Bye Way, The. Harr —1J 25
Byfeld Gdns. SW13 —1C 100
Byfield Clo. SE16 —2B 88
Byfield Pas. Iswth —3A 98
Byfield Rd. Iswth —3A 98
Byford Clo. E15 —7G 53
Byford Ho. Barn —4A 4
Bygrove. New Ad —6C 154
Bygrove St. E14 —6D 70
(in two parts)
Byland Clo. N21 —7E 6
Bylands Clo. SE2 —3B 92
Byne Rd. SE26 —6J 123
Byne Rd. Cars —2C 150
Bynes Rd. S Croy —7D 152
Byng Pl. WC1 —4H 67 (4D 160)
Byng Rd. Barn —2A 4
Byng St. E14 —2C 88
Bynon Av. Bexh —3F 111
Byre Rd. N14 —6A 6
Byrne Rd. SW12 —1F 121
Byron Av. E12 —6C 54
Byron Av. E18 —3H 35
Byron Av. NW9 —4H 27
Byron Av. Houn —2J 95
Byron Av. N Mald —5C 136
Byron Av. Sutt —4B 150
Byron Av. E. Sutt —4B 150
Byron Clo. E8 —1G 69
Byron Clo. SE20 —3H 141
Byron Clo. SE26 —4A 124
Byron Clo. SE28 —1C 92
Byron Clo. SW16 —6J 121
Byron Clo. Hamp —4D 114
Byron Clo. W on T —7C 132
Byron Ct. E11 —4K 35
(off Makepeace Rd.)
Byron Ct. NW6 —7A 48
(off Fairfax Rd.)
Byron Ct. W7 —4A 80
(off Boston Rd.)
Byron Ct. W9 —4J 65
(off Lanhill Rd.)
Byron Ct. WC1 —4K 67 (3G 161)
(off Mecklenburgh Sq.)
Byron Ct. Enf —2G 7
Byron Ct. Harr —6J 25
Byron Dri. N2 —6B 30
Byron Dri. Eri —7H 93
Byron Gdns. Sutt —4B 150
Byron Hill Rd. Harr —1H 43
Byron M. NW3 —5D 48
Byron M. W9 —4J 65
Byron Pde. Uxb —4E 58
Byron Rd. E10 —1D 52
Byron Rd. E17 —3C 34
Byron Rd. NW2 —2D 46
Byron Rd. NW7 —5H 13
Byron Rd. W5 —1F 81
Byron Rd. Harr —6J 25
Byron Rd. W'stone —2K 25
Byron Rd. Wemb —2C 44
Byron St. E14 —6E 70
Byron Ter. N9 —6D 8
Byron Way. Hay —4H 59
Byron Way. N'holt —3C 60
Byron Way. W Dray —4B 76
Bysouth Clo. N15 —4D 32
Bysouth Clo. Ilf —1F 37
Bythorn St. SW9 —3K 103
Byton Rd. SW17 —6D 120
Byward Av. Felt —6A 96
Byward St. EC3 —7E 68 (3H 169)
Bywater Ho. SE18 —3C 90
Bywater Pl. SE16 —1A 88
Bywater St. SW3 —5D 84 (5E 170)
Byway. E11 —5A 36
Byway, The. Eps —4B 148
Byway, The. Sutt —7B 150
Bywell Pl. W1 —6A 160
Bywood Av. Croy —6J 141
Byworth Wlk. N19 —1J 49

Cabbell St. NW1 —5C 66 (6C 158)
Cabinet War Rooms. —2H 85 (6D 166)
Cabinet Way. E4 —6G 19
Cable Ho. WC1 —3A 68 (1J 161)
(off Gt. Percy St.)
Cable Pl. SE10 —1E 106
Cables Clo. Belv —3J 93
Cable St. E1 —7G 69
Cable Trade Pk. SE7 —4A 90
Cabot Ct. SE16 —4K 87
(off Worgan St.)
Cabot Sq. E14 —1C 88
Cabot Way. E6 —1B 72
Cab Rd. SE1 —6J 167
Cabul Rd. SW11 —2C 102
Caci Ho. W14 —4H 83
(off Avonmore Rd.)
Cactus Clo. SE15 —2E 104
Cactus Wlk. W12 —6B 64
Cadbury Clo. Iswth —1A 98
Cadbury Clo. Sun —7G 113
Cadbury Rd. Sun —7G 113
Cadbury Way. SE16 —3F 87
(in two parts)
Caddington Clo. Barn —5H 5
Caddington Rd. NW2 —3G 47
Caddis Clo. Stan —7E 10
Cadell Clo. E2 —2F 69 (1K 163)
Cade Rd. SE10 —1F 107
Cader Rd. SW18 —6A 102
Cadet Dri. SE1 —4F 87
Cadet Pl. SE10 —5G 89
Cadiz Ct. Dag —7K 57
(off Rainham Rd. S.)
Cadiz Rd. Dag —7J 57
Cadiz St. SE17 —5C 86
Cadley Ter. SE23 —2J 123
Cadman Clo. SW9 —7B 86
Cadman Ct. W4 —5H 81
(off Chaseley Dri.)
Cadmer Clo. N Mald —4A 136
Cadmore Ho. N1 —7B 50
(off Sutton Est., The)
Cadmus Clo. SW4 —3H 103
Cadnam Lodge. E14 —3E 88
Cadogan Clo. E9 —7B 52
Cadogan Clo. Beck —1F 143
Cadogan Clo. Harr —4F 43
Cadogan Clo. Tedd —5J 115
Cadogan Ct. SW3 —4D 84 (4E 170)
(off Draycott Av.)
Cadogan Ct. Sutt —6K 149
Cadogan Gdns. E18 —3K 35
Cadogan Gdns. N3 —1K 29
Cadogan Gdns. N21 —5F 7
Cadogan Gdns. SW3 —4D 84 (3F 171)
Cadogan Ga. SW1 —4D 84 (3F 171)
Cadogan Ho. SW3 —7B 170
Cadogan La. SW1 —3E 84 (2G 171)
Cadogan Pl. SW1 —3D 84 (1F 171)
Cadogan Rd. Surb —5D 134
Cadogan Sq. SW1 —3D 84 (2E 170)
Cadogan St. SW3 —4D 84 (4E 170)
Cadogan Ter. E9 —6B 52
Cadoxton Av. N15 —6F 33
Cadwallon Rd. SE9 —2F 127
Caedmon Rd. N7 —4K 49
Caerleon Clo. Sidc —5C 128
Caerleon Ter. SE2 —4B 92
Caernarvon Clo. Mitc —3J 139
Caernarvon Dri. Ilf —1E 36
Caernarvon Ho. W2 —6A 66
(off Hallfield Est.)
Caesars Wlk. Mitc —5D 138
Caesars Way. Shep —6F 131
Cahill St. EC1 —4C 68 (4D 162)
Cahir St. E14 —4D 88
Cain Ct. W5 —5C 62
(off Castlebar M.)
Caine Ho. W3 —2H 81
(off Hanbury Rd.)
Cain's La. Felt —5G 95
Caird St. W10 —3G 65
Cairn Av. W5 —1D 80
Cairndale Clo. Brom —7H 125
Cairnfield Av. NW2 —3A 46
Cairngorm Clo. Tedd —5A 116
Cairns Av. Wfd G —6H 21
Cairns Rd. SW11 —5C 102
Cairn Way. Stan —6E 10
Cairo New Rd. Croy —2B 152
Cairo Rd. E17 —4C 34
Caister Ho. N7 —6K 49
Caistor Ho. E15 —1H 71
(off Caistor Pk. Rd.)
Caistor M. SW12 —7F 103
Caistor Pk. Rd. E15 —1H 71
Caistor Rd. SW12 —7F 103
Caithness Gdns. Sidc —6K 109
Caithness Ho. N1 —1K 67
(off Twyford St.)
Caithness Rd. W14 —3F 83
Caithness Rd. Mitc —7F 121
Calabria Rd. N5 —6B 50
Calais Ga. SE5 —1B 104
Calais St. SE5 —1B 104
Calbourne Rd. SW12 —7D 102
Calcott Ct. W14 —3G 83
(off Blythe Rd.)
Calcott Wlk. SE9 —4C 126
Caldbeck Av. Wor Pk —2C 148
Caldecot Rd. SE5 —2C 104
Caldecott Way. E5 —3K 51
Calder Av. Gnfd —2K 61
Calder Clo. Enf —3K 7
Calder Ct. SE16 —1B 88
Calder Gdns. Edgw —3G 27
Calderon Ho. NW8 —2C 66
(off Townshend Est.)
Calderon Pl. W10 —5E 64
Calderon Rd. E11 —4E 52
Calder Rd. Mord —5A 138
Caldervale Rd. SW4 —5H 103
Calderwood St. SE18 —4E 90
Caldew Ct. NW7 —7H 13
Caldew St. SE5 —7D 86
Caldicot Grn. NW9 —6A 28
Caldwell St. SW9 —7K 85
Caldy Rd. Belv —3H 93
Caldy Wlk. N1 —7C 50
Caleb St. SE1 —2C 86 (6C 168)
Caledonia Ct. Bark —2C 74
(off Keel Clo.)
Caledonia Ho. E14 —6A 70
Caledonian Clo. Ilf —1B 56
Caledonian Rd. N7 & N1 —4K 49 (1F 161)
Caledonian Wharf. E14 —4F 89
Caledonia Rd. Stai —1A 112
Caledonia St. N1 —2J 67 (1F 161)
Caledon Rd. E6 —1D 72
Caledon Rd. Wall —4E 150
Cale St. SW3 —5C 84 (5C 170)
Caletock Way. SE10 —5H 89
Calgarth. NW1 —2G 67 (1B 160)
(off Ampthill Est.)
Caliban Tower. N1 —2E 68
(off Arden Est.)
Calico Row. SW11 —3A 102
Calidore Clo. SW2 —6K 103
California La. Bus H & Bush —1C 10
California Pl. Bush —1C 10
(off High Rd.)
California Rd. N Mald —4H 135
Callaby Ter. N1 —6D 50
Callaghan Clo. SE13 —4G 107
Callaghan Cotts. E1 —5J 69
(off Lindley St.)
Callander Rd. SE6 —2D 124
Callanders, The. Bush —1D 10
Callard Av. N13 —4G 17
Callcott Ct. NW6 —7H 47
Callcott Rd. NW6 —7H 47
Callcott St. W8 —1J 83
Callendar Rd. SW7 —3B 84 (1A 170)
Callenders Cotts. Belv —2K 93
Callingham Clo. E14 —5B 70
Callis Farm Clo. Stanw —6A 94
Callis Rd. E17 —6B 34
Callonfield. E17 —4K 33
Callow St. SW3 —6B 84 (7A 170)
Callum Welch Ho. EC1 —4C 68 (4C 162)
(off Goswell Rd.)
Calmington Rd. SE5 —6E 86
Calmont Rd. Brom —6F 125
Calne Av. Ilf —1F 37
Calonne Rd. SW19 —4F 119
Calshot Ho. N1 —2K 67
(off Priory Grn. Est.)
Calshot Rd. H'row A —2C 94
(in two parts)
Calshot St. N1 —2K 67 (1G 161)
Calshot Way. Enf —3G 7
Calshot Way. H'row A —2C 94
(in two parts)
Calstock. NW1 —1H 67
(off Royal College St.)
Calstock Ho. SE11 —5K 173
Calthorpe Gdns. Edgw —5K 11
Calthorpe Gdns. Sutt —3A 150
Calthorpe St. WC1 —4K 67 (3H 161)
Calton Av. SE21 —6E 104
Calton Rd. New Bar —6F 5
Calverley Clo. Beck —6D 124
Calverley Cres. Dag —2G 57
Calverley Gdns. Harr —7D 26
Calverley Gro. N19 —1H 49
Calverley Rd. Eps —6C 148
Calvert Av. E1 —3E 68 (2H 163)
Calvert Clo. Belv —4G 93
Calvert Clo. Sidc —6E 128
Calverton. SE5 —6E 86
(off Albany Rd.)
Calverton Rd. E6 —1E 72
Calvert Rd. SE10 —5H 89
Calvert Rd. Barn —2A 4
Calvert's Bldgs. SE1 —1D 86 (5E 168)
Calvert St. NW1 —1E 66
Calvin St. E1 —4F 69 (4J 163)
Calydon Rd. SE7 —5K 89
Calypso Way. SE16 —3B 88
Camac Rd. Twic —1H 115
Cambalt Rd. SW15 —5F 101
Camber Ho. SE15 —6J 87
Camberley Av. SW20 —2D 136
Camberley Av. Enf —4K 7
Camberley Clo. Sutt —3F 149
Camberley Ho. NW1 —2F 67
(off Redhill St.)
Camberley Rd. H'row A —3C 94
Cambert Way. SE3 —4K 107
Camberwell. —1D 104
Camberwell Chu. St. SE5 —1D 104
Camberwell Glebe. SE5 —1E 104
Camberwell Green. (Junct.) —1D 104
Camberwell Grn. SE5 —1D 104
Camberwell Gro. SE5 —1D 104
Camberwell New Rd. SE5 —6A 86
Camberwell Pl. SE5 —1C 104
Camberwell Rd. SE17 & SE5 —6C 86
Camberwell Sta. Rd. SE5 —1C 104
Camberwell Trad. Est. SE5 —1B 104
Cambeys Rd. Dag —5H 57
Camborne Av. W13 —2B 80
Camborne Clo. H'row A —3C 94
Camborne Rd. SW18 —7J 101
Camborne Rd. Croy —7G 141
Camborne Rd. Mord —5F 137
Camborne Rd. Sidc —3C 128
Camborne Rd. Sutt —7J 149
Camborne Rd. Well —2J 109
Camborne Way. Houn —1E 96
Cambourne Av. N9 —7E 8
Cambourne M. W11 —6G 65
(off St Mark's Rd.)
Cambourne Rd. H'row A —3C 94
Cambourne Wlk. Rich —6D 98
Cambrai Ct. N13 —3D 16
Cambray Rd. SW12 —1G 121
Cambray Rd. Orp —7K 145
Cambria Clo. Houn —4E 96
Cambria Clo. Sidc —1H 127
Cambria Ct. Felt —7K 95
Cambria Gdns. Stai —7A 94
(in two parts)
Cambria Ho. E14 —6A 70
Cambria Ho. SE26 —4G 123
(off High Level Dri.)
Cambrian Av. Ilf —5J 37
Cambrian Clo. SE27 —3B 122
Cambrian Grn. NW9 —5A 28
(off Snowden Dri.)
Cambrian Rd. E10 —7C 34
Cambrian Rd. Rich —6F 99
Cambria Rd. SE5 —3C 104
Cambria St. SW6 —7K 83
Cambridge Av. NW6 —2J 65
Cambridge Av. NW10 —3E 64
Cambridge Av. Gnfd —5K 43
Cambridge Av. N Mald —3A 136
(in two parts)
Cambridge Av. Well —4K 109
Cambridge Barracks Rd. SE18 —4D 90
Cambridge Cir. WC2 —6H 67 (1D 166)
Cambridge Clo. E17 —6B 34
Cambridge Clo. N22 —1A 32
Cambridge Clo. NW10 —3J 45
Cambridge Clo. SW20 —1D 136
Cambridge Clo. Houn —4C 96
Cambridge Cotts. Kew & Rich —6G 81
Cambridge Ct. N15 —7E 32
(off Amhurst Pk.)
Cambridge Ct. NW6 —2J 65
(in three parts)
Cambridge Ct. W2 —5C 66 (6C 158)
(off Edgware Rd.)
Cambridge Cres. E2 —2H 69
Cambridge Cres. Tedd —5A 116
Cambridge Dri. SE12 —5J 107
Cambridge Dri. Ruis —2A 42
Cambridge Gdns. N10 —1E 30
Cambridge Gdns. N17 —7J 17
Cambridge Gdns. N21 —7J 7
Cambridge Gdns. NW6 —2J 65
Cambridge Gdns. W10 —6F 65
Cambridge Gdns. Enf —2B 8
Cambridge Gdns. King T —2G 135
Cambridge Ga. NW1 —4F 67 (3J 159)
Cambridge Ga. M. NW1 —4F 67 (3K 159)
Cambridge Grn. SE9 —1F 127
Cambridge Gro. SE20 —1H 141
Cambridge Gro. W6 —4D 82
Cambridge Gro. Rd. King T —3G 135
(in two parts)
Cambridge Heath Rd. E1 & E2 —5H 69
Cambridge Ho. W13 —6A 62
Cambridge Lodge Vs. E8 —1H 69
Cambridge Pde. Enf —1B 8
Cambridge Pk. E11 —7J 35
Cambridge Pk. Twic —6C 98
Cambridge Pk. Ct. Twic —7D 98
Cambridge Pk. Rd. E11 —7H 35
Cambridge Pl. W8 —2K 83
Cambridge Rd. E4 —1A 20
Cambridge Rd. E11 —6H 35
Cambridge Rd. NW6 —2J 65
(in two parts)
Cambridge Rd. SE20 —3H 141
Cambridge Rd. SW11 —1D 102
Cambridge Rd. SW13 —2B 100
Cambridge Rd. SW20 —1C 136
Cambridge Rd. W7 —2K 79
Cambridge Rd. Ashf —7E 112
Cambridge Rd. Bark —7G 55
Cambridge Rd. Brom —7J 125
Cambridge Rd. Cars —6C 150
Cambridge Rd. Hamp —7D 114
Cambridge Rd. Harr —5E 24
Cambridge Rd. Houn —4C 96
Cambridge Rd. Ilf —1J 55
Cambridge Rd. King T —2F 135
Cambridge Rd. Mitc —3G 139
Cambridge Rd. N Mald —4A 136
Cambridge Rd. Rich —7G 81
Cambridge Rd. Sidc —4J 127
Cambridge Rd. S'hall —1D 78
Cambridge Rd. Tedd —4K 115
Cambridge Rd. Twic —6D 98
Cambridge Rd. W on T —6K 131
Cambridge Rd. W Mol —4D 132
Cambridge Rd. N. W4 —5H 81
Cambridge Rd. S. W4 —5H 81
Cambridge Row. SE18 —5F 91
Cambridge Sq. W2 —6C 66 (7C 158)
Cambridge St. SW1 —4F 85 (4K 171)
Cambridge Ter. N9 —7K 7
Cambridge Ter. NW1 —3F 67 (2J 159)
Cambridge Ter. M. NW1 —3F 67 (2K 159)
Cambridge Yd. W7 —2K 79
Cambstone Clo. N11 —2K 15
Cambus Clo. Hay —5C 60
Cambus Rd. E16 —5J 71
Cam Ct. SE15 —6F 87
Camdale Rd. SE18 —7K 91
Camden Arts Cen. —5A 48
Camden Av. Felt —1A 114
Camden Av. Hay —7B 60
Camden Clo. Chst —1G 145
Camden Ct. NW1 —7G 49
(off Rousden St.)
Camden Ct. Belv —5G 93
Camden Gdns. NW1 —7F 49
Camden Gdns. Sutt —5K 149
Camden Gdns. T Hth —3B 140
Camden Gro. Chst —6F 127
Camden High St. NW1 —7F 49
Camden Hill Rd. SE19 —6E 122
Camden Ho. SE8 —5B 88
Camdenhurst St. E14 —6A 70
Camden La. N7 —5H 49
Camden Lock Market. —7F 49
Camden Lock Pl. NW1 —7F 49
Camden M. NW1 —7G 49
Camden Pk. Rd. NW1 —6H 49
Camden Pk. Rd. Chst —7D 126
Camden Passage. —2B 68
Camden Pas. N1 —1B 68
(in two parts)
Camden Rd. E11 —6K 35
Camden Rd. E17 —6B 34
Camden Rd. NW1 & N7 —7G 49
Camden Rd. Bex —1F 129
Camden Rd. Cars —4D 150
Camden Rd. Sutt —5K 149
Camden Row. SE3 —2G 107
Camden Row. Pinn —3A 24
Camden Sq. NW1 —7H 49
Camden Sq. SE15 —1F 105
Camden St. NW1 —7G 49
Camden Studios. NW1 —1G 67
(off Camden St.)
Camden Ter. NW1 —6H 49
Camden Town. —1F 67
Camden Wlk. N1 —1B 68
(in two parts)
Camden Way. Chst —7D 126
Camden Way. T Hth —3B 140
Cameford Ct. SW12 —7J 103
Camelford. NW1 —1G 67
(off Royal College St.)
Camelford Ct. W11 —6G 65
Camelford Ho. SE1 —5J 85 (5F 173)
Camelford Wlk. W11 —6G 65
Camel Gro. King T —5D 116
Camellia Ho. SE8 —7B 88
(off Idonia St.)
Camellia Pl. Twic —7F 97
Camellia St. SW8 —7J 85
Camelot Clo. SE28 —2H 91
Camelot Clo. SW19 —4H 119
Camelot Ho. NW1 —6H 49
Camel Rd. E16 —1B 90
Camera Pl. SW10 —6B 84 (7A 170)
Cameret Ct. W14 —2F 83
(off Holland Rd.)
Cameron Clo. N18 —4C 18
Cameron Clo. N20 —2G 15
Cameron Clo. Bex —3K 129
Cameron Ho. NW8 —2C 66
(off St John's Wood Ter.)
Cameron Ho. SE5 —7C 86
Cameron Pl. E1 —6H 69
Cameron Rd. SE6 —2B 124
Cameron Rd. Brom —5J 143
Cameron Rd. Croy —6B 140
Cameron Rd. Ilf —1J 55
Cameron Sq. Mitc —1C 138
Cameron Ter. SE12 —3K 125
Camerton Clo. E8 —6F 51
Camilla Clo. Sun —6H 113
Camilla Rd. SE16 —4H 87
Camille Clo. SE25 —3G 141
Camlan Rd. Brom —4H 125
Camlet St. E2 —4F 69 (3J 163)
Camlet Way. Barn —2D 4
Camley St. NW1 —7H 49
Camm Gdns. King T —2F 135
Camm Gdns. Th Dit —7K 133
Camomile Av. Mitc —1D 138
Camomile Rd. Rush G —2K 57
Camomile St. EC3 —6E 68 (7H 163)
Camomile Way. W Dray —6A 58
Campana Rd. SW6 —1J 101
Campania Building. E1 —7K 69
(off Jardine Rd.)
Campbell Av. Ilf —4F 37
Campbell Clo. SE18 —1E 108
Campbell Clo. SW16 —4H 121
Campbell Clo. Ruis —6J 23
Campbell Clo. Twic —2H 115
Campbell Ct. N17 —1F 33
Campbell Ct. SE21 —7G 105
Campbell Ct. SW7 —3A 84
(off Gloucester Rd.)
Campbell Cft. Edgw —5B 12
Campbell Gordon Way. NW2 —4D 46
Campbell Ho. SW1 —5G 85 (6A 172)
(off Churchill Gdns.)
Campbell Ho. W12 —7D 64
(off White City Est.)
Campbell Rd. E3 —3C 70
Campbell Rd. E6 —1C 72
Campbell Rd. E15 —4H 53
Campbell Rd. E17 —4B 34
Campbell Rd. N17 —1F 33
Campbell Rd. W7 —7J 61
Campbell Rd. Croy —7B 140
Campbell Rd. E Mol —3J 133
Campbell Rd. Twic —2H 115
Campbell Wlk. N1 —1J 67
(off Outram Pl.)
Campdale Rd. N7 —3H 49
Campden Cres. Dag —4B 56
Campden Cres. Wemb —3B 44
Campden Gro. W8 —2J 83
Campden Hill. W8 —2J 83
Campden Hill Ct. W8 —2J 83
Campden Hill Gdns. W8 —1J 83
Campden Hill Ga. W8 —2J 83
Campden Hill Mans. W8 —1J 83
(off Kensington Church St.)
Campden Hill Pl. W11 —1H 83
Campden Hill Rd. W11 —1J 83
Campden Hill Sq. W11 —1H 83
Campden Ho. NW6 —7B 48
Campden Ho. W8 —1J 83
Campden Ho. Clo. W8 —2J 83
Campden Houses. W8 —1J 83
(off Peel St.)
Campden Rd. S Croy —5E 152
Campden Rd. Uxb —3B 40
Campden St. W8 —1J 83
Campe Ho. N10 —7K 15
Campen Clo. SW19 —2G 119
Camperdown Ho. Wall —6F 151
(off Stanley Pk. Rd.)
Camperdown St. E1 —6F 69 (1K 169)
Campfield Rd. SE9 —7B 108
Campion Clo. E6 —7D 72
Campion Clo. Croy —4E 152
Campion Clo. Harr —6F 27
Campion Clo. Rush G —2K 57
Campion Clo. Uxb —5B 58
Campion Ct. Wemb —2E 62
Campion Gdns. Wfd G —5D 20
Campion Pl. SE28 —1A 92
Campion Rd. SW15 —4E 100
Campion Rd. Iswth —1K 97
Campion Ter. NW2 —3F 47
Campion Way. Edgw —4D 12
Camplin Rd. Harr —5E 26
Camplin St. SE14 —7K 87
Camp Rd. SW19 —5D 118
(in two parts)
Campsbourne Rd. N8 —3J 31
(in two parts)
Campsbourne, The. N8 —4J 31
Campsey Gdns. Dag —7B 56
Campsey Rd. Dag —7B 56
Campsfield Rd. N8 —3J 31
Campshill Pl. SE13 —5E 106
Campshill Rd. SE13 —5E 106
Campus Rd. E17 —6B 34
Campus Way. NW4 —3D 28
Camp Vw. SW19 —5D 118
Cam Rd. E15 —1F 71
Camrose Av. Edgw —2F 27
Camrose Av. Eri —6H 93
Camrose Av. Felt —4A 114
Camrose Clo. Croy —7A 142
Camrose Clo. Mord —4J 137
Camrose St. SE2 —5A 92
Canada Av. N18 —6H 17
Canada Cres. W3 —5J 63
Canada Est. SE16 —3J 87
Canada Gdns. SE13 —5E 106
Canada Rd. W3 —5J 63
Canada Sq. E14 —1D 88
Canada St. SE16 —2K 87
Canada Way. W12 —7D 64
Canada Wharf. SE16 —1B 88
Canadian Av. SE6 —1D 124
Canal App. SE8 —5A 88
Canal Bridge. (Junct.) —6G 87
Canal Building. N1 —2C 68
(off Shepherdess Wlk.)
Canal Clo. E1 —4A 70
Canal Clo. W10 —4F 65
Canal Gro. SE15 —6H 87
Canal Path. E2 —1F 69
Canal Rd. E3 —4A 70

Canalside—Casselden Rd.

Canalside. SE28 —7D 74
Canal St. SE5 —6D 86
Canal Wlk. N1 —1D 68
Canal Wlk. SE25 —6E 140
Canal Wlk. SE26 —5J 123
Canal Way. W10 —4F 65
Canary Wharf. —1D 88
Canberra Clo. NW4 —3C 28
Canberra Clo. Dag —7K 57
Canberra Cres. Dag —7K 57
Canberra Dri. N'holt —3A 60
Canberra Rd. E6 —1D 72
Canberra Rd. SE7 —6A 90
Canberra Rd. Bexh —6D 92
Canberra Rd. H'row A —3C 94
Canbury Av. King T —1F 135
Canbury Bus. Cen. King T —1E 134
Canbury Bus. Pk. King T —1E 134
Canbury M. SE26 —3G 123
Canbury Pk. Rd. King T —1E 134
Canbury Pas. King T —1D 134
Cancell Rd. SW9 —1A 104
Candahar Rd. SW11 —2C 102
Candida Ct. NW1 —7F 49
Candler M. Twic —7A 98
Candler St. N15 —6D 32
Candover Clo. W Dray —7A 76
Candover St. W1 —5G 67 (6A 160)
Candy St. E3 —1B 70
Cane Clo. Wall —7J 151
(in two parts)
Caney M. NW2 —2F 47
Canfield Dri. Ruis —5K 41
Canfield Gdns. NW6 —7K 47
Canfield Ho. N15 —6E 32
(off Albert Rd.)
Canfield Pl. NW6 —6A 48
Canfield Rd. Wfd G —7H 21
Canford Av. N'holt —1D 60
Canford Clo. Enf —2F 7
Canford Gdns. N Mald —6A 136
Canford Pl. Tedd —6C 116
Canford Rd. SW11 —5E 102
Canham Rd. SE25 —3E 140
Canham Rd. W3 —2A 82
Canmore Gdns. SW16 —7G 121
Cann Hall. —4G 53
Cann Hall Rd. E11 —4G 53
Cann Ho. W14 —3G 83
(off Russell Rd.)
Canning Cres. N22 —1K 31
Canning Cross. SE5 —2E 104
Canning Ho. W12 —7D 64
(off White City Est.)
Canning Pas. W8 —3A 84
(in two parts)
Canning Pl. W8 —3A 84
Canning Pl. M. W8 —3A 84
(off Canning Pl.)
Canning Rd. E15 —2F 71
Canning Rd. E17 —4A 34
Canning Rd. N5 —3B 50
Canning Rd. Croy —2F 153
Canning Rd. Harr —3J 25
Cannington Rd. Dag —6C 56
Canning Town. —6H 71
Canning Town. (Junct.) —5G 71
Cannizaro Rd. SW19 —6E 118
Cannock Ho. N4 —7C 32
Cannonbury Av. Pinn —6B 24
Cannon Clo. SW20 —3E 136
Cannon Clo. Hamp —6F 115
Cannon Dri. E14 —7C 70
Cannon Hill. N14 —3D 16
Cannon Hill. NW6 —5J 47
Cannon Hill La. SW20 —5F 137
Cannon Hill M. N14 —3D 16
Cannon Ho. SE11 —4H 173
Cannon La. NW3 —3B 48
Cannon La. Pinn —5C 24
Cannon Pl. NW3 —3B 48
Cannon Pl. SE7 —5C 90
Cannon Retail Pk. SE28 —7A 74
Cannon Rd. N14 —3D 16
Cannon Rd. Bexh —1E 110
Cannon St. EC4 —6C 68 (1C 168)
Cannon St. Rd. E1 —6H 69
Cannon Trad. Est. Wemb —4H 45
Cannon Way. W Mol —4E 132
Cannon Wharf Bus. Pk. SE8 —4A 88
Cannon Workshops. E14 —7C 70
Canon Av. Romf —5C 38
Canonbie Rd. SE23 —7J 105
Canonbury. —6C 50
Canonbury Bus. Cen. N1 —1D 68
Canonbury Ct. N1 —7B 50
(off Hawes St.)
Canonbury Cres. N1 —7C 50
Canonbury Gro. N1 —7C 50
Canonbury La. N1 —7B 50
Canonbury Pk. N. N1 —6C 50
Canonbury Pk. S. N1 —6C 50
Canonbury Pl. N1 —6B 50
(in two parts)
Canonbury Rd. N1 —6B 50
Canonbury Rd. Enf —1K 7
Canonbury Sq. N1 —7B 50
Canonbury St. N1 —7C 50
Canonbury Vs. N1 —7B 50
Canon Mohan Clo. N14 —6K 5
Canon Rd. Brom —3A 144
Canon Row. SW1 —2J 85 (7E 166)
(in two parts)
Canon's Clo. N2 —7B 30
Canons Clo. Edgw —6A 12
Canons Corner. Edgw —4K 11
Canons Ct. Edgw —6A 12
Canons Dri. Edgw —6K 11
Canonsleigh Rd. Dag —7B 56
Canons Park. —6K 11
Canons Pk. Stan —6J 11
Canons Pk. Clo. Edgw —7K 11
Canon St. N1 —1C 68
Canon's Wlk. Croy —3K 153
Canopus Way. Stai —7A 94
Canrobert St. E2 —2H 69
Cantelowes Rd. NW1 —6H 49
Canterbury Av. Ilf —7C 36
Canterbury Av. Sidc —2B 128
Canterbury Clo. E6 —6D 72
Canterbury Clo. SE5 —2C 104
(off Lilford Rd.)
Canterbury Clo. Beck —1D 142
Canterbury Clo. Gnfd —5F 61
Canterbury Ct. NW6 —2J 65
Canterbury Ct. NW9 —2A 28
Canterbury Ct. SE12 —3K 125
Canterbury Cres. SW9 —3A 104
Canterbury Gro. SE27 —4A 122
Canterbury Ho. SE1 —3K 85 (1H 173)
Canterbury Ho. SW9 —7A 86
Canterbury Ho. Bark —7A 56
(off Margaret Bondfield Av.)
Canterbury Ind. Pk. SE15 —6J 87
Canterbury Pl. SE17 —5B 86
Canterbury Rd. E10 —7E 34
Canterbury Rd. NW6 —2H 65
(in two parts)
Canterbury Rd. Croy —7K 139
Canterbury Rd. Felt —2C 114
Canterbury Rd. Harr —5F 25
Canterbury Rd. Mord —7K 137
Canterbury Ter. NW6 —2J 65
Cantium Retail Pk. SE1 —6G 87
Cantley Gdns. SE19 —1F 141
Cantley Gdns. Ilf —6G 37
Cantley Rd. W7 —3A 80
Canton St. E14 —6C 70
Cantrell Rd. E3 —4B 70
Cantwell Rd. SE18 —7F 91
Canute Gdns. SE16 —4K 87
Canvey St. SE1 —1C 86 (4C 168)
Cape Clo. Bark —7F 55
Cape Henry Ct. E14 —7F 71
Cape Ho. E8 —6F 51
(off Dalston La.)
Capel Av. Wall —5K 151
Capel Clo. N20 —3F 15
Capel Clo. Brom —1C 156
Capel Ct. EC2 —6D 68
(off Bartholomew La.)
Capel Ct. SE20 —1J 141
Capel Gdns. Ilf —4K 55
Capel Gdns. Pinn —4D 24
Capel Rd. E7 & E12 —4K 53
Capel Rd. Barn —6H 5
Capener's Clo. SW1 —7F 165
Capern Rd. SW18 —1A 120
Cape Rd. N17 —3G 33
Cape Yd. E1 —7G 69
(off Kennet St.)
Capital Bus. Cen. Wemb —2D 62
Capital Ind. Est. Belv —3H 93
Capital Ind. Est. Mitc —5D 138
Capital Interchange Way. Bren —5G 81
Capital Pl. Croy —5K 151
Capital Wharf. E1 —1G 87
Capitol Ind. Pk. NW9 —3J 27
Capitol Way. NW9 —3J 27
Capland Ho. NW8 —4B 66 (3B 158)
(off Capland St.)
Capland St. NW8 —4B 66 (3B 158)
Caple Ho. SW10 —7A 84
(off King's Rd.)
Caple Rd. NW10 —2B 64
Capper St. W1 —4G 67 (4B 160)
Caprea Clo. Hay —5B 60
Capricorn Cen. Dag —7F 39
Capri Ho. E17 —2B 34
Capri Rd. Croy —1F 153
Capstan Clo. Romf —6B 38
Capstan Ho. E14 —7F 71
(off Clove Cres.)
Capstan Ho. E14 —4E 88
(off Stebondale St.)
Capstan Ride. Enf —2F 7
Capstan Rd. SE8 —4B 88
Capstan Sq. E14 —2E 88
Capstan Way. SE16 —1A 88
Capstone Rd. Brom —4H 125
Capthorne Av. Harr —1C 42
Capuchin Clo. Stan —6G 11
Capulet M. E16 —1J 89
Capworth St. E10 —1C 52
Caradoc Clo. W2 —6J 65
Caradoc Evans Clo. N11 —5A 16
(off Springfield Rd.)
Caradoc St. SE10 —5G 89
Caradon Clo. E11 —1G 53
Caradon Way. N15 —4D 32
Caravel Clo. E14 —3C 88
Caravelle Gdns. N'holt —3B 60
Caravel M. SE8 —6C 88
Caraway Clo. E13 —5K 71
Caraway Heights. E14 —7E 70
(off Poplar High St.)
Caraway Pl. Wall —3F 151
Carberry Rd. SE19 —6E 122
Carbery Av. W3 —2F 81
Carbis Clo. E4 —1A 20
Carbis Rd. E14 —6B 70
Carbuncle Pas. Way. N17 —2G 33
Carburton St. W1 —5F 67 (5K 159)
Cardale St. E14 —3E 88
Carden Rd. SE15 —3H 105
Cardiff Ho. SE15 —6G 87
(off Friary Est.)
Cardiff Rd. W7 —3A 80
Cardiff Rd. Enf —4C 8
Cardiff St. SE18 —7J 91
Cardigan Ct. W7 —4K 61
(off Copley Clo.)
Cardigan Gdns. Ilf —2A 56
Cardigan Pl. SE3 —2F 107
Cardigan Rd. E3 —2B 70
Cardigan Rd. SW13 —2C 100
Cardigan Rd. SW19 —6A 120
Cardigan Rd. Rich —6E 98
Cardigan St. SE11 —5A 86 (5J 173)
Cardigan Wlk. N1 —7C 50
(off Ashby Gro.)
Cardinal Av. King T —5E 116
Cardinal Av. Mord —6G 137
Cardinal Bourne St. SE1 —3D 86
Cardinal Cap All. SE1
—1C 86 (3C 168)
Cardinal Clo. Chst —1H 145
Cardinal Clo. Edgw —7E 12
Cardinal Clo. Mord —6G 137
Cardinal Clo. Wor Pk —4C 148
Cardinal Ct. E1 —7G 69
(off Thomas More St.)
Cardinal Cres. N Mald —2J 135
Cardinal Pl. SW15 —4F 101
Cardinal Rd. Felt —1K 113
Cardinal Rd. Ruis —1B 42
Cardinals Wlk. Hamp —7G 115
Cardinals Wlk. Sun —6G 113
Cardinals Way. N19 —1H 49
Cardinal Way. Harr —3J 25
Cardine M. SE15 —7H 87
Cardington Rd. H'row A —3D 94
Cardington Sq. Houn —4B 96
Cardington St. NW1 —3G 67 (1B 160)
Cardozo Rd. N7 —5J 49
Cardrew Av. N12 —5G 15
Cardrew Clo. N12 —5H 15
Cardrew Ct. N12 —5G 15
Cardross St. W6 —3D 82
Cardwell Rd. N7 —4J 49
Carew Clo. N7 —2K 49
Carew Ct. Sutt —7K 149
Carew Manor & Dovecote. —3H 151
Carew Mnr. Cotts. Wall —3H 151
Carew Rd. N17 —2G 33
Carew Rd. W13 —2C 80
Carew Rd. Ashf —6E 112
Carew Rd. Mitc —2E 138
Carew Rd. T Hth —4B 140
Carew Rd. Wall —6G 151
Carew St. SE5 —2C 104
Carey Ct. SE5 —7C 86
Carey Ct. Bexh —5H 111
Carey Gdns. SW8 —1G 103
Carey La. EC2 —6C 68 (7C 162)
Carey Mans. SW1 —4H 85 (3C 172)
(off Rutherford St.)
Carey Pl. SW1 —4C 172
Carey Rd. Dag —4E 56
Carey St. WC2 —6K 67 (1H 167)
Carey Way. Wemb —4H 45
Carfax Pl. SW4 —4H 103
Carfax Rd. Hay —5H 77
Carfree Clo. N1 —7A 50
Cargill Rd. SW18 —1K 119
Cargreen Pl. SE25 —4F 141
Cargreen Rd. SE25 —4F 141
Cargrey Ho. Stan —5H 11
Carholme Rd. SE23 —1B 124
Carillon Ct. W5 —7D 62
Carina M. SE27 —4C 122
Carisbrooke Av. Bex —1D 128
Carisbrooke Clo. Enf —1A 8
Carisbrooke Clo. Stan —2D 26
Carisbrooke Ct. W3 —2J 81
(off Brouncker Rd.)
Carisbrooke Ct. Cheam —7H 149
Carisbrooke Ct. N'holt —1D 60
(off Eskdale Av.)
Carisbrooke Gdns. SE15 —7F 87
Carisbrooke Rd. E17 —4A 34
Carisbrooke Rd. Brom —4A 144
Carisbrooke Rd. Mitc —4H 139
Carker's La. NW5 —5F 49
Carleton Av. Wall —7H 151
Carleton Clo. Esh —7H 133
Carleton Gdns. N19 —5G 49
Carleton Rd. N7 —5H 49
Carleton Vs. NW5 —5G 49
Carlile Clo. E3 —2B 70
Carlina Gdns. Wfd G —5E 20
Carlingford Gdns. Mitc —7D 120
Carlingford Rd. N8 —3B 32
Carlingford Rd. NW3 —4B 48
Carlingford Rd. Mord —6F 137
Carlisle Av. EC3 —6F 69 (1J 169)
Carlisle Av. W3 —6A 64
Carlisle Clo. King T —1G 135
Carlisle Clo. Pinn —1C 42
Carlisle Gdns. Harr —7D 26
Carlisle Gdns. Ilf —6C 36
Carlisle La. SE1 —3K 85 (2H 173)
Carlisle Mans. SW1 —4G 85 (3A 172)
(off Carlisle Pl.)
Carlisle M. King T —1G 135
Carlisle Pl. N11 —4A 16
Carlisle Pl. SW1 —3G 85 (2A 172)
Carlisle Rd. E10 —1C 52
Carlisle Rd. N4 —7A 32
Carlisle Rd. NW6 —1G 65
Carlisle Rd. NW9 —3J 27
Carlisle Rd. Hamp —7F 115
Carlisle Rd. Sutt —6H 149
Carlisle St. W1 —6H 67 (1C 166)
Carlisle Wlk. E8 —6F 51
Carlisle Way. SW17 —5E 120
Carlos Pl. W1 —7E 66 (3H 165)
Carlow St. NW1 —2G 67
Carlton Av. N14 —5C 6
Carlton Av. Felt —6A 96
Carlton Av. Harr —5B 26
Carlton Av. Hay —4G 77
Carlton Av. S Croy —7E 152
Carlton Av. E. Wemb —2D 44
Carlton Av. W. Wemb —2B 44
Carlton Clo. NW3 —2J 47
Carlton Clo. Chess —6D 146
Carlton Clo. Edgw —5B 12
Carlton Clo. N'holt —5G 43
Carlton Ct. SE20 —1H 141
Carlton Ct. SW9 —1B 104
Carlton Ct. W9 —2K 65
(off Maida Va.)
Carlton Ct. Ilf —3H 37
Carlton Ct. Uxb —5A 58
Carlton Cres. Sutt —4G 149
Carlton Dri. SW15 —5F 101
Carlton Dri. Ilf —3H 37
Carlton Gdns. SW1 —1H 85 (5C 166)
Carlton Gdns. W5 —6C 62
Carlton Grn. Sidc —4K 127
Carlton Gro. SE15 —1H 105
Carlton Hill. NW8 —2K 65
Carlton Ho. NW6 —2J 65
(off Canterbury Ter., in five parts)
Carlton Ho. Felt —6H 95
Carlton Ho. Ter. SW1 —1H 85 (5C 166)
Carlton Lodge. N4 —7A 32
(off Carlton Rd.)
Carlton Mans. NW6 —7J 47
(off W. End La.)
Carlton Mans. W9 —3K 65
Carlton Pde. Wemb —2E 44
Carlton Pk. Av. SW20 —2F 137
Carlton Rd. E11 —1H 53
Carlton Rd. E12 —4B 54
Carlton Rd. E17 —1A 34
Carlton Rd. N4 —7A 32
Carlton Rd. N11 —5K 15
Carlton Rd. SW14 —3J 99
Carlton Rd. W4 —2K 81
Carlton Rd. W5 —7C 62
Carlton Rd. Eri —6H 93
Carlton Rd. N Mald —2A 136
Carlton Rd. Sidc —5K 127
Carlton Rd. S Croy —6D 152
Carlton Rd. Sun —7H 113
Carlton Rd. W on T —7K 131
Carlton Rd. Well —3B 110
Carlton Sq. E1 —4K 69
(in two parts)
Carlton St. SW1 —7H 67 (3C 166)
Carlton Ter. E7 —7A 54
Carlton Ter. E11 —5K 35
Carlton Ter. N18 —3J 17
Carlton Ter. SE26 —3J 123
Carlton Tower Pl. SW1
—3D 84 (1F 171)
Carlton Va. NW6 —2H 65
Carlwell St. SW17 —5C 120
Carlyle Av. Brom —3B 144
Carlyle Av. S'hall —7D 60
Carlyle Clo. N2 —6A 30
Carlyle Clo. NW10 —1K 63
Carlyle Clo. W Mol —2F 133
Carlyle Ct. SW6 —1K 101
(off Maltings Pl.)
Carlyle Ct. SW10 —1A 102
(off Chelsea Harbour)
Carlyle Gdns. S'hall —7D 60
Carlyle M. E1 —4K 69
Carlyle Pl. SW15 —4F 101
Carlyle Rd. E12 —4C 54
Carlyle Rd. SE28 —7B 74
Carlyle Rd. W5 —5C 80
Carlyle Rd. Croy —2G 153
Carlyle's House. —7C 170
Carlyle Sq. SW3 —5B 84 (6B 170)
Carlyon Av. Harr —4D 42
Carlyon Clo. Wemb —1E 62
Carlyon Rd. Hay —5A 60
(in two parts)
Carlyon Rd. Wemb —2E 62
Carlys Clo. Beck —2K 141
Carmalt Gdns. SW15 —4E 100
Carmarthen Ct. W7 —4K 61
(off Copley Clo.)
Carmarthen Grn. NW9 —5A 28
Carmarthen Pl. SE1 —2E 86 (6G 169)
Carmel Ct. W8 —2K 83
(off Holland St.)
Carmelite Clo. Harr —1G 25
Carmelite Rd. Harr —1G 25
Carmelite St. EC4 —7A 68 (2K 167)
Carmelite Wlk. Harr —1G 25
Carmelite Way. Harr —2G 25
Carmen St. E14 —6D 70
Carmichael Clo. SW11 —3B 102
Carmichael Clo. Ruis —4J 41
Carmichael Ct. SW13 —2B 100
(off Grove Rd.)
Carmichael Ho. E14 —7E 70
Carmichael M. SW18 —7B 102
Carmichael Rd. SE25 —5F 141
Carminia Rd. SW17 —2F 121
Carnaby St. W1 —6G 67 (1A 166)
Carnac St. SE27 —4D 122
Carnanton Rd. E17 —1F 35
Carnarvon Av. Enf —3A 8
Carnarvon Dri. Hay —3E 76
Carnarvon Rd. E10 —5E 34
Carnarvon Rd. E15 —6H 53
Carnarvon Rd. E18 —1H 35
Carnarvon Rd. Barn —3B 4
Carnation Clo. Rush G —2K 57
Carnation St. SE2 —5B 92
Carnbrook Rd. SE3 —3B 108
Carnecke Gdns. SE9 —5C 108
Carnegie Clo. Surb —2F 147
Carnegie Pl. SW19 —3F 119
Carnegie Rd. Harr —7K 25
Carnegie St. N1 —1K 67
Carnforth Clo. Eps —6K 147
Carnforth Rd. SW16 —7H 121
Carnie Hall. SW17 —3F 121
Carnoustie Dri. N1 —7K 49
(in two parts)
Carnwath Rd. SW6 —3J 101
Caroe Ct. N9 —1C 18
Carolina Clo. E15 —5G 53
Carolina Rd. T Hth —2B 140
Caroline Clo. N10 —2F 31
Caroline Clo. SW16 —3K 121
Caroline Clo. W2 —7K 65
(off Bayswater Rd.)
Caroline Clo. Croy —4E 152
Caroline Clo. Isleworth —7H 79
Caroline Ct. SE6 —4F 125
Caroline Ct. Ashf —6D 112
Caroline Ct. Stan —6F 11
Caroline Gdns. E2 —3E 68 (1H 163)
Caroline Gdns. SE15 —7H 87
Caroline Pl. SW11 —2E 102
Caroline Pl. W2 —7K 65
Caroline Pl. Hay —7G 77
Caroline Pl. M. W2 —7K 65
Caroline Rd. SW19 —7H 119
Caroline St. E1 —6K 69
Caroline Ter. SW1 —4E 84 (4G 171)
Caroline Wlk. W6 —6G 83
(off Lillie Rd.)
Carol St. NW1 —1G 67
Carpenter Gdns. N21 —2G 17
Carpenter Ho. E14 —5C 70
Carpenter Ho. NW11 —6A 30
Carpenters Clo. Barn —6E 4
Carpenters Ct. NW1 —1G 67
(off Pratt St.)
Carpenters Ct. Twic —2J 115
Carpenters M. N7 —5J 49
Carpenters Pl. SW4 —4H 103
Carpenter's Rd. E15 —6C 52
Carpenter St. W1 —7F 67 (3J 165)
Carradale Ho. E14 —6E 70
Carrara Wlk. SE24 —4A 104
Carrara Wharf. SW6 —3G 101
Carr Gro. SE18 —4C 90
Carr Ho. Dart —5K 111
Carriage Dri. E. SW11 —7E 84
Carriage Dri. N. SW11 —7D 84 (7H 171)
(in two parts)
Carriage Dri. S. SW11 —1D 102
Carriage Dri. W. SW11 —7D 84
Carriage M. Ilf —2G 55
Carriage Pl. N16 —3D 50
Carrick Clo. Iswth —3A 98
Carrick Dri. Ilf —1G 37
Carrick Gdns. N17 —7K 17
Carrick Ho. N7 —6K 49
(off Caledonian Rd.)
Carrick Ho. SE11 —5K 173
Carrick M. SE8 —6C 88
Carrill Way. Belv —4D 92
Carrington Av. Houn —5F 97
Carrington Clo. Croy —7A 142
Carrington Clo. King T —5J 117
Carrington Gdns. E7 —4J 53
Carrington Ho. W1 —1F 85 (5J 165)
(off Carrington St.)
Carrington Rd. Rich —4G 99
Carrington Sq. Harr —6B 10
Carrington St. W1 —1F 85 (5J 165)
Carrol Clo. NW5 —4F 49
Carroll Clo. E15 —5H 53
Carroll Ct. W3 —3H 81
(off Osborne Rd.)
Carroll Ho. W2 —7B 66 (2A 164)
(off Craven Ter.)
Carronade Pl. SE28 —3G 91
Carron Clo. E14 —6D 70
Carroun Rd. SW8 —7K 85
Carroway La. Gnfd —3H 61
Carrow Rd. Dag —7B 56
Carr Rd. E17 —2B 34
Carr Rd. N'holt —6E 42
Carrs La. N21 —5H 7
Carr St. E14 —6A 70
(in two parts)
Carshalton. —4E 150
Carshalton Athletic F.C. —4C 150
Carshalton Beeches. —7C 150
Carshalton Gro. Sutt —4B 150
Carshalton On The Hill. —7E 150
Carshalton Pk. Rd. Cars —5D 150
Carshalton Pl. Cars —5E 150
Carshalton Rd. Mit J & Mitc —4E 138
Carshalton Rd. Sutt & Cars —5A 150
Carslake Rd. SW15 —6E 100
Carson Rd. E16 —4J 71
Carson Rd. SE21 —2D 122
Carson Rd. Cockf —4J 5
Carstairs Rd. SE6 —3E 124
Carston Clo. SE12 —5H 107
Carswell Clo. Ilf —4B 36
Carswell Rd. SE6 —7E 106
Carter Clo. Wall —7H 151
Carter Ct. EC4 —1A 168
Carter Dri. Romf —1H 39
Carteret St. SW1 —2H 85 (7C 166)
Carteret Way. SE8 —4A 88
Carterhatch La. Enf —1A 8
Carterhatch Rd. Enf —1D 8
Carter Ho. E1 —6J 163
Carter La. EC4 —6B 68 (1B 168)
Carter Pl. SE17 —5C 86
Carter Rd. E13 —1K 71
Carter Rd. SW19 —6B 120
Carters Clo. NW5 —5H 49
(off Torriano Av.)
Carters Clo. Wor Pk —2F 149
Carters Hill Clo. SE9 —1A 126
Carters La. SE23 —2A 124
Carter St. SE17 —6C 86
Carter's Yd. SW18 —5J 101
Carthew Rd. W6 —3D 82
Carthew Vs. W6 —3D 82
Carthusian St. EC1 —5C 68 (5C 162)
Cartier Circ. E14 —1D 88
Carting La. WC2 —7J 67 (3F 167)
Cart La. E4 —1B 20
Cartmel. NW1 —3G 67 (1A 160)
(off Hampstead Rd.)
Cartmel Clo. N17 —7C 18
Cartmel Ct. N'holt —6C 42
Cartmel Rd. Bexh —1G 111
Carton Ho. SE16 —7K 169
Carton Ho. W11 —1F 83
(off St Ann's Rd.)
Cartwright Gdns. WC1 —3J 67 (2E 160)
Cartwright Ho. SE1 —3C 86
(off County St.)
Cartwright Rd. Dag —7F 57
Cartwright St. E1 —7F 69 (2K 169)
Cartwright Way. SW13 —7D 82
Carvel Ho. E14 —5E 88
Carver Clo. W4 —3J 81
Carver Rd. SE24 —6C 104
Carville Cres. Bren —4E 80
Cary Rd. E11 —4G 53
Carysfort Rd. N8 —5H 31
Carysfort Rd. N16 —3D 50
Casby Ho. SE16 —3G 87
(off Marine St.)
Cascade Av. N10 —4G 31
Cascade Clo. Buck H —2G 21
Cascade Rd. Buck H —2G 21
Cascades Tower. E14 —1C 88
Casella Rd. SE14 —7K 87
Casewick Rd. SE27 —5A 122
Casimir Rd. E5 —2J 51
Casino Av. SE24 —5C 104
Caspian St. SE5 —7D 86
Caspian Wlk. E16 —6B 72
Cassandra Clo. N'holt —4H 43
Casselden Rd. NW10 —7K 45

Chalcroft Rd. SE13 —5G 107
Chaldon Ct. SE19 —1D 140
Chaldon Rd. SW6 —7G 83
Chale Rd. SW2 —6J 103
Chalet Clo. Bex —4K 129
Chalet Est. NW7 —4H 13
Chalfont Av. Wemb —6H 45
Chalfont Ct. NW1 —4D 66 (4F 159)
(off Baker St.)
Chalfont Ct. NW9 —3B 28
Chalfont Ct. Harr —6K 25
(off Northwick Pk. Rd.)
Chalfont Grn. N9 —3K 17
Chalfont Ho. SE16 —3H 87
(off Keetons Rd.)
Chalfont Rd. N9 —3K 17
Chalfont Rd. SE25 —3F 141
Chalfont Rd. Hay —2J 77
Chalfont Wlk. Pinn —2A 24
Chalfont Way. W13 —3B 80
Chalford Clo. W Mol —4E 132
Chalford Rd. SE21 —4D 122
Chalford Wlk. Wfd G —1B 36
Chalgrove Av. Mord —5J 137
Chalgrove Cres. Ilf —2C 36
Chalgrove Gdns. N3 —3G 29
Chalgrove Rd. N17 —1H 33
Chalgrove Rd. Sutt —7B 150
Chalice Clo. Wall —6H 151
Chalice Ct. N2 —4C 30
Chalkenden Clo. SE20 —7H 123
Chalker's Corner. (Junct.) —3H 99
Chalk Farm. —7E 48
Chalk Farm Rd. NW1 —7E 48
Chalkhill Rd. W6 —4F 83
Chalkhill Rd. Wemb —3G 45
(in two parts)
Chalklands. Wemb —3J 45
Chalk La. Barn & Cockf —3J 5
Chalkley Clo. Mitc —2D 138
Chalkmill Dri. Enf —3C 8
Chalk Pit Way. Sutt —6A 150
Chalk Rd. E13 —5K 71
Chalkstone Clo. Well —1A 110
Chalkwell Pk. Av. Enf —4K 7
Challenge Clo. NW10 —1A 64
Challenge Rd. Ashf —3F 113
Challice Way. SW2 —1K 121
Challin St. SE20 —1J 141
Challis Rd. Bren —5D 80
Challoner Clo. N2 —2B 30
Challoner Cres. W14 —5H 83
Challoners Clo. E Mol —4H 133
Challoner St. W14 —5H 83
Chalmers Ho. E17 —5D 34
Chalmers Rd. Ashf —5D 112
Chalmers Rd. E. Ashf —4D 112
Chalmers Wlk. SE17 —6B 86
(off Hillingdon St.)
Chalmers Way. Felt —5K 95
Chalsey Rd. SE4 —4B 106
Chalton Dri. N2 —6B 30
Chalton Ho. NW1 —3H 67 (1C 160)
(off Chalton St.)
Chalton St. NW1 —2G 67 (1C 160)
(in three parts)
Chamberlain Clo. SE28 —3H 91
Chamberlain Cotts. SE5 —1D 104
Chamberlain Cres. W W'ck —1D 154
Chamberlain Gdns. Houn —1G 97
Chamberlain Ho. NW1 —1D 160
Chamberlain Ho. SE1 —2A 86 (7J 167)
(off Westminster Bri. Rd.)
Chamberlain La. Pinn —4J 23
Chamberlain Pl. E17 —3A 34
Chamberlain Rd. N2 —2A 30
Chamberlain Rd. N9 —3B 18
Chamberlain Rd. W13 —2A 80
Chamberlain St. NW1 —7D 48
Chamberlain Wlk. Felt —4C 114
(off Swift Rd.)
Chamberlain Way. Pinn —3K 23
Chamberlain Way. Surb —7E 134
Chamberlayne Av. Wemb —3E 44
Chamberlayne Rd. NW10 —1E 64
Chambers Gdns. N2 —1B 30
Chambers Ind. Pk. W Dray —6C 76
Chambers La. NW10 —7D 46
Chambers Pl. S Croy —7D 152
Chambers Rd. N7 —4J 49
Chambers St. SE16 —2G 87
Chambers, The. SW10 —1A 102
(off Chelsea Harbour)
Chamber St. E1 —7F 69 (2K 169)
Chambers Wharf. SE16 —2G 87
Chambon Pl. W6 —4C 82
Chambord St. E2 —3F 69 (1K 163)
Chamomile Ct. E17 —6C 34
(off Yunus Khan Clo.)
Champion Cres. SE26 —4A 124
Champion Gro. SE5 —3D 104
Champion Hill. SE5 —3D 104
Champion Hill Est. SE5 —3E 104
Champion Pk. SE5 —2D 104
Champion Rd. SE26 —4A 124
Champlain Ho. W12 —7D 64
(off White City Est.)
Champness Clo. SE27 —4D 122
Champneys Clo. Sutt —7H 149
Chancel Ind. Est. NW10 —5B 46
Chancellor Gdns. S Croy —7B 152
Chancellor Gro. SE21 —2C 122
Chancellor Pas. E14 —1C 88
Chancellor Pl. NW9 —2B 28
Chancellors Ct. WC1 —5G 161
Chancellor's Rd. W6 —5E 82
Chancellor's St. W6 —5E 82
Chancellors Wharf. W6 —5E 82
Chancelot Rd. SE2 —4B 92
Chancel St. SE1 —1B 86 (5A 168)
Chancery La. WC2 —6A 68 (6H 161)
Chancery La. Beck —2D 142
Chance St. E2 & E1 —4F 69 (3J 163)
Chanctonbury Clo. SE9 —3F 127
Chanctonbury Gdns. Sutt —7K 149
Chanctonbury Way. N12 —4C 14
Chandler Av. E16 —5J 71
Chandler Clo. Hamp —1E 132
Chandler Ct. Felt —6J 95
Chandlers Clo. Felt —7H 95
Chandlers Ct. SE12 —1K 125
Chandlers Dri. Eri —4K 93
Chandlers M. E14 —2C 88
Chandler St. E1 —1H 87
Chandlers Way. SW2 —7A 104
Chandler Way. SE15 —7F 87
(Diamond St.)
Chandler Way. SE15 —6E 86
(St George's Way)
Chandlery Ho. E1 —6G 69
(off Bk. Church La.)
Chandlery, The. SE1 —3A 86 (1K 173)
(off Gerridge St.)
Chandon Lodge. Sutt —7A 150
Chandos Av. E17 —2C 34
Chandos Av. N14 —3B 16
Chandos Av. N20 —1F 15
Chandos Av. W5 —4C 80
Chandos Clo. Buck H —2E 20
Chandos Ct. N14 —2C 16
Chandos Ct. Edgw —7A 12
Chandos Cres. Edgw —7A 12
Chandos Pde. Edgw —7A 12
Chandos Pl. WC2 —7J 67 (3E 166)
Chandos Rd. E15 —5F 53
Chandos Rd. N2 —2B 30
Chandos Rd. N17 —2E 32
Chandos Rd. NW2 —5E 46
Chandos Rd. NW10 —4A 64
Chandos Rd. Harr —5G 25
Chandos Rd. Pinn —7B 24
Chandos St. W1 —5F 67 (6K 159)
Chandos Way. NW11 —1K 47
Change All. EC3 —6D 68 (1F 169)
Channel Clo. Houn —1E 96
Channel Ga. Rd. NW10 —3A 64
Channel Islands Est. N1 —6C 50
(off Guernsey Rd.)
Channelsea Path. E15 —1F 71
Channelsea Rd. E15 —1F 71
Chantress Clo. Dag —1J 75
Chantrey Rd. SW9 —3K 103
Chantry Clo. W9 —4H 65
Chantry Clo. Enf —1H 7
Chantry Clo. Harr —5F 27
Chantry Clo. Sidc —5E 128
Chantry Clo. W Dray —7A 58
Chantry La. Brom —5B 144
Chantry Pl. Harr —1F 25
Chantry Rd. Chess —5F 147
Chantry Rd. Harr —1F 25
Chantry Sq. W8 —3K 83
Chantry St. N1 —1B 68
Chantry, The. E4 —1K 19
Chantry, The. Uxb —3B 58
Chantry Way. Mitc —3B 138
Chantry Way. Rain —2K 75
Chant Sq. E15 —7F 53
Chant St. E15 —7F 53
Chapel Clo. Dart —5K 111
Chapel Ct. N2 —3C 30
Chapel Ct. SE1 —2D 86 (6E 168)
Chapel Ct. Hay —7H 59
Chapel End. —1C 34
Chapel Farm Rd. SE9 —3D 126
Chapel Hill. N2 —2C 30
Chapel Hill. Dart —5K 111
Chapel Ho. St. E14 —5D 88
Chapel La. Pinn —3B 24
Chapel La. Romf —7D 38
Chapel La. Uxb —6C 58
Chapel Mkt. N1 —2A 68
Chapel M. Wfd G —6K 21
Chapel Path. E11 —6K 35
(off Woodbine Pl.)
Chapel Pl. EC2 —3E 68 (2G 163)
Chapel Pl. N1 —2A 68
Chapel Pl. N17 —7A 18
Chapel Pl. W1 —6F 67 (1J 165)
Chapel Rd. SE27 —4B 122
Chapel Rd. W13 —1B 80
Chapel Rd. Bexh —4G 111
Chapel Rd. Houn —3F 97
Chapel Rd. Ilf —3E 54
Chapel Rd. Twic —7B 98
Chapel Side. W2 —7K 65
Chapel Stones. N17 —1F 33
Chapel St. SW1 —3E 84 (1H 171)
Chapel St. W2 —5C 66 (6C 158)
Chapel St. Enf —3H 7
Chapel Vw. S Croy —6J 153
Chapel Wlk. NW4 —4D 28
(in two parts)
Chapel Wlk. Croy —2C 152
Chapel Way. N7 —3K 49
Chapel Yd. SW18 —5J 101
(off Wandsworth High St.)
Chaplemount Rd. Wfd G —6J 21
Chaplin Clo. SE1 —2A 86 (6K 167)
Chaplin Clo. Wemb —6D 44
Chaplin Cres. Sun —6G 113
Chaplin Rd. E15 —2H 71
Chaplin Rd. N17 —3F 33
Chaplin Rd. NW2 —6C 46
Chaplin Rd. Dag —7E 56
Chaplin Rd. Wemb —6C 44
Chaplin Sq. N12 —7G 15
Chapman Clo. W Dray —3B 76
Chapman Cres. Harr —6E 26
Chapman Rd. E9 —6B 52
Chapman Rd. Belv —5H 93
Chapman Rd. Croy —1A 152
Chapmans Grn. N22 —1A 32
Chapman's La. SE2 & Belv —4C 92
Chapmans Pk. Ind. Est. NW10 —6B 46
Chapman Sq. SW19 —2F 119
Chapman St. E1 —7H 69
Chapman Ter. N22 —1B 32
(off Perth Rd.)
Chapone Pl. W1 —1C 166
Chapter Chambers. SW1
(off Chapter St.) —4H 85 (4C 172)
Chapter Clo. W4 —3J 81
Chapter Clo. Uxb —7B 40
Chapter Ho. Ct. EC4 —1B 168
Chapter Rd. NW2 —5C 46
Chapter Rd. SE17 —5B 86
Chapter St. SW1 —4H 85 (4C 172)
Chapter Way. Hamp —4E 114
Chara Pl. W4 —6K 81
Charcot Ho. SW15 —6B 100
Charcroft Ct. W14 —2F 83
(off Minford Gdns.)
Charcroft Gdns. Enf —4E 8
Chardin Rd. W4 —4A 82
Chardmore Rd. N16 —1G 51
Chard Rd. H'row A —2D 94
Chardwell Clo. E6 —6D 72
Charecroft Way. W12 —2F 83
Charfield Ct. W9 —4K 65
(off Shirland Rd.)
Charford Rd. E16 —5J 71
Chargeable La. E13 —4H 71
Chargeable St. E16 —4H 71
Chargrove Clo. SE16 —2K 87
Charing Ct. Short —2G 143
Charing Cross. SW1 —4E 166
Charing Cross Rd. WC2
—6H 67 (7D 160)
Charing Ho. SE1 —2A 86 (6K 167)
(off Windmill Wlk.)
Charlbert Ct. NW8 —2C 66
(off Charlbert St.)
Charlbert St. NW8 —2C 66
Charlbury Av. Stan —5J 11
Charlbury Gdns. Ilf —2K 55
Charlbury Gro. W5 —6C 62
Charlbury Rd. Uxb —3B 40
Charldane Rd. SE9 —3F 127
Charlecote Gro. SE26 —3H 123
Charlecote Rd. Dag —3E 56
Charlemont Rd. E6 —4D 72
Charles Barry Clo. SW4 —3G 103
Charles Bradlaugh Ho. N17 —7C 18
(off Haynes Clo.)
Charles Clo. Sidc —4B 128
Charles Cobb Gdns. Croy —5A 152
Charles Coveney Rd. SE5 —1F 105
Charles Cres. Harr —7H 25
(in two parts)
Charles Curran Ho. Uxb —3D 40
Charles Dickens Ho. E2 —3G 69
(off Mansford St.)
Charle Sevright Dri. NW7 —5A 14
Charlesfield. SE9 —3A 126
Charles Flemwell M. E16 —1J 89
Charles Gardner Ct. N1 —3D 68 (1F 163)
(off Haberdasher Est.)
Charles Grinling Wlk. SE18 —4E 90
Charles Harrod Ct. SW13 —6E 82
(off Somerville Av.)
Charles Hocking Ho. W3 —2J 81
(off Bollo Bri. Rd.)
Charles Ho. N17 —7A 18
(off Love La.)
Charles La. NW8 —2C 66
Charles MacKenzie Ho. SE16 —4G 87
(off Linsey St.)
Charles Pl. NW1 —3G 67 (2B 160)
Charles Rd. E7 —7A 54
Charles Rd. SW19 —1J 137
Charles Rd. W13 —6A 62
Charles Rd. Dag —6K 57
Charles Rd. Romf —6D 38
Charles Rd. Stai —6A 112
Charles Rowan Ho. WC1
(off Margery St.) —3A 68 (2J 161)
Charles II Pl. SW3 —5D 84 (6E 170)
Charles II St. SW1 —1H 85 (4C 166)
Charles Simmons Ho. WC1
(off Margery St.) —3K 67 (2J 161)
Charles Sq. N1 —3D 68 (2F 163)
Charles Sq. Est. N1 —2F 163
Charles St. E16 —1A 90
Charles St. SW13 —2A 100
Charles St. W1 —1F 85 (4J 165)
Charles St. Croy —3C 152
Charles St. Enf —5A 8
Charles St. Houn —2D 96
Charles St. Uxb —4D 58
Charles St. Trad. Est. E16 —1A 90
Charleston Clo. Felt —3J 113
Charleston St. SE17 —4C 86
Charles Townsend Ho. EC1 —3B 68
(off Finsbury Est.)
Charles Uton Ct. E8 —4G 51
Charles Whincup Rd. E16 —1K 89
Charlesworth Ho. E14 —6C 70
Charleville Cir. SE26 —5G 123
Charleville Mans. W14 —5G 83
(off Charleville Rd.)
Charleville Rd. W14 —5G 83
Charlie Brown's Roundabout. (Junct.)
—2A 36
Charlie Chaplin Wlk. SE1
—1K 85 (5H 167)
Charlieville Rd. Eri —7J 93
Charlmont Rd. SW17 —6C 120
Charlotte Clo. Bexh —5E 110
Charlotte Clo. Ilf —1G 37
Charlotte Ct. N8 —6H 31
Charlotte Ct. SE17 —4E 86
(off Old Kent Rd.)
Charlotte Ct. Ilf —6D 36
Charlotte Despard Av. SW11 —1E 102
Charlotte M. W1 —5G 67 (5B 160)
Charlotte M. W10 —6F 65
Charlotte M. W14 —4G 83
Charlotte Pk. Av. Brom —3C 144
Charlotte Pl. NW9 —5J 27
Charlotte Pl. SW1 —4G 85 (4A 172)
Charlotte Pl. W1 —5G 67 (6B 160)
Charlotte Rd. EC2 —3E 68 (2G 163)
Charlotte Rd. SW13 —1B 100
Charlotte Rd. Dag —6H 57
Charlotte Rd. Wall —6G 151
Charlotte Row. SW4 —3G 103
Charlotte Sq. Rich —6F 99
Charlotte St. W1 —5G 67 (5B 160)
Charlotte Ter. N1 —1K 67
Charlow Clo. SW6 —2A 102
Charlton. —2E 130
(Shepperton)
Charlton. —6B 90
(Woolwich)
Charlton Athletic F.C. —5A 90
Charlton Chu. La. SE7 —5A 90
Charlton Clo. Uxb —2D 40
Charlton Ct. E2 —1F 69
Charlton Cres. Bark —2K 73
Charlton Dene. SE7 —7A 90
Charlton Ho. Bren —6E 80
Charlton King's Rd. NW5 —5H 49
Charlton La. SE7 —4B 90
Charlton La. Shep —3E 130
Charlton Pk. La. SE7 —7B 90
Charlton Pk. Rd. SE7 —6B 90
Charlton Pl. N1 —2B 68
Charlton Rd. N9 —1E 18
Charlton Rd. NW10 —1A 64
Charlton Rd. SE3 & SE7 —7J 89
Charlton Rd. Harr —4D 26
Charlton Rd. Shep —3E 130
Charlton Rd. Wemb —1F 45
Charlton Way. SE3 —1G 107
Charlwood. Croy —7B 154
Charlwood Clo. Harr —6D 10
Charlwood Ho. SW1 —4H 85 (4C 172)
(off Vauxhall Bri. Rd.)
Charlwood Houses. WC1
(off Midhope St.) —3J 67 (2F 161)
Charlwood Pl. SW1 —4G 85 (4B 172)
Charlwood Rd. SW15 —4F 101
Charlwood Sq. Mitc —3B 138
Charlwood St. SW1 —5G 85 (6A 172)
(in two parts)
Charlwood Ter. SW15 —4F 101
Charmans Ho. SW8 —7J 85
(off Wandsworth Rd.)
Charmian Av. Stan —3D 26
Charminster Av. SW19 —2J 137
Charminster Ct. Surb —7D 134
Charminster Rd. SE9 —4B 126
Charminster Rd. Wor Pk —1F 149
Charmouth Ct. Rich —5F 99
Charmouth Ho. SW8 —7K 85
Charmouth Rd. Well —1C 110
Charnock Rd. E5 —3H 51
Charnwood Av. SW19 —2J 137
Charnwood Clo. N Mald —4A 136
Charnwood Dri. E18 —3K 35
Charnwood Gdns. E14 —4C 88
Charnwood Pl. N20 —3F 15
Charnwood Rd. SE25 —5D 140
Charnwood Rd. Uxb —2C 58
Charnwood St. E5 —2H 51
Charrington Rd. Croy —2C 152
Charrington St. NW1 —2H 67
Charsley Rd. SE6 —2D 124
Chart Clo. Brom —1G 143
Chart Clo. Croy —6J 141
Chart Clo. Mitc —4D 138
Charter Av. Ilf —1H 55
Charter Ct. N4 —1A 50
Charter Ct. N22 —1H 31
Charter Ct. N Mald —3A 136
Charter Ct. S'hall —1E 78
Charter Cres. Houn —4C 96
Charter Dri. Bex —7E 110
Charter Ho. WC2 —6J 67 (1F 167)
(off Crown Ct.)
Charter Ho. Sutt —6K 149
(off Mulgrave Rd.)
Charterhouse Av. Wemb —4C 44
Charterhouse Bldgs. EC1
—4C 68 (4B 162)
Charterhouse M. EC1 —5B 68 (5B 162)
Charterhouse Sq. EC1
—5B 68 (5B 162)
Charterhouse St. EC1
—5A 68 (6K 161)
Charteris Rd. N4 —1A 50
Charteris Rd. NW6 —1H 65
Charteris Rd. Wfd G —7E 20
Charter Rd. King T —3H 135
Charter Rd., The. Wfd G —6B 20
Charters Clo. SE19 —5E 122
Charter Sq. King T —2H 135
Charter Way. N3 —4H 29
Charter Way. N14 —6B 6
Chartes Ho. SE1 —3E 86 (7H 169)
(off Stevens St.)
Chartfield Av. SW15 —5D 100
Chartfield Sq. SW15 —5F 101
Chartham Ct. SW9 —3A 104
(off Canterbury Cres.)
Chartham Gro. SE27 —3B 122
Chartham Ho. SE1 —3D 86 (7F 169)
(off Weston St.)
Chartham Rd. SE25 —3H 141
Chart Hills Clo. SE28 —6E 74
Chart Ho. E14 —5D 88
Chartley Av. NW2 —3A 46
Chartley Av. Stan —6E 10
Charton Clo. Belv —6F 93
Chartres Ct. Gnfd —2H 61
Chartridge. SE17 —6D 86
(off Westmoreland Rd.)
Chart St. N1 —3D 68 (1F 163)
Chartwell Clo. SE9 —2H 127
Chartwell Clo. Croy —1D 152
Chartwell Clo. Gnfd —1F 61
Chartwell Ct. Barn —4B 4
Chartwell Ct. Hay —7H 59
Chartwell Ct. Wfd G —7C 20
Chartwell Gdns. Sutt —3G 149
Chartwell Lodge. Beck —7C 124
Chartwell Pl. Harr —2H 43
Chartwell Pl. Sutt —3H 149
Chartwell Way. SE20 —1H 141
Charville Ct. Harr —6K 25
Charville La. Hay —3E 58
Charville La. W. Uxb —3D 58
Char Wood. SW16 —4A 122
Chase Bank Ct. N14 —6B 6
(off Avenue Rd.)
Chase Cen., The. NW10 —3K 63
Chase Ct. Iswth —2A 98
Chase Ct. Gdns. Enf —3H 7
Chase Cross Rd. Romf —1J 39
Chasefield Rd. SW17 —4D 120
Chase Gdns. E4 —4H 19
Chase Gdns. Twic —7H 97
Chase Grn. Enf —3H 7
Chase Grn. Av. Enf —2G 7
Chase Hill. Enf —3H 7
Chase La. Ilf —5H 37
(in two parts)
Chaseley Dri. W4 —5H 81
Chaseley St. E14 —6A 70
Chasemore Clo. Mitc —7D 138
Chasemore Gdns. Croy —5A 152
Chasemore Ho. SW6 —7G 83
Chase Ridings. Enf —2F 7
Chase Rd. N14 —5B 6
Chase Rd. NW10 —4K 63
Chase Rd. Trad. Est. NW10 —4K 63
Chase Side. —2H 7
Chase Side. N14 —6K 5
Chase Side. Enf —3H 7
Chaseside Av. SW20 —1G 137
Chase Side Av. Enf —2H 7
Chase Side Cres. Enf —1H 7
Chase Side Pl. Enf —2H 7
Chase Side Works Ind. Est. N14
—7C 6
Chase, The. E12 —4B 54
Chase, The. SW4 —3F 103
Chase, The. SW16 —7K 121
Chase, The. SW20 —1G 137
Chase, The. Bexh —3H 111
Chase, The. Brom —3K 143
Chase, The. Chad H —6E 38
Chase, The. Eastc —6A 24
Chase, The. Edgw —1H 27
Chase, The. Pinn —4D 24
Chase, The. Romf —3K 39
Chase, The. Stan —6F 11
Chase, The. Sun —1K 131
Chase, The. Uxb —5C 40
Chase, The. Wall —5J 151
Chaseville Pde. N21 —5E 6
Chaseville Pk. Rd. N21 —5D 6
Chase Way. N14 —2A 16
Chaseways Vs. Romf —1F 39
Chasewood Av. Enf —2G 7
Chasewood Ct. NW7 —5E 12
Chasewood Pk. Harr —3K 43
Chaston St. NW5 —5E 48
(off Grafton Ter.)
Chatfield Rd. SW11 —3A 102
Chatfield Rd. Croy —1B 152
Chatham Av. Brom —7H 143
Chatham Clo. NW11 —5J 29
Chatham Clo. Sutt —7H 137
Chatham Pl. E9 —6J 51
Chatham Rd. E17 —3A 34
Chatham Rd. E18 —2H 35
Chatham Rd. SW11 —6D 102
Chatham Rd. King T —2G 135
Chatham St. SE17 —4D 86
Chatsfield Pl. W5 —6E 62
Chatsworth Av. NW4 —2E 28
Chatsworth Av. SW20 —1G 137
Chatsworth Av. Brom —4K 125
Chatsworth Av. Sidc —1A 128
Chatsworth Av. Wemb —5F 45
Chatsworth Clo. NW4 —2E 28
Chatsworth Clo. W4 —6J 81
Chatsworth Clo. W W'ck —2H 155
Chatsworth Ct. W8 —4J 83
(off Pembroke Rd.)
Chatsworth Ct. Stan —5H 11
Chatsworth Cres. Houn —4H 97
Chatsworth Dri. Enf —7B 8
Chatsworth Est. E5 —4K 51
Chatsworth Gdns. W3 —1H 81
Chatsworth Gdns. Harr —1F 43
Chatsworth Gdns. N Mald —5B 136
Chatsworth Lodge. W4 —5K 81
(off Bourne Pl.)
Chatsworth Pde. Orp —5G 145
Chatsworth Pl. Mitc —3D 138
Chatsworth Pl. Tedd —4A 116
Chatsworth Ri. W5 —4F 63
Chatsworth Rd. E5 —3J 51
Chatsworth Rd. E15 —5H 53
Chatsworth Rd. NW2 —6E 46
Chatsworth Rd. W4 —6J 81
Chatsworth Rd. W5 —4F 63
Chatsworth Rd. Croy —4D 152
Chatsworth Rd. Hay —4K 59
Chatsworth Rd. Sutt —5F 149
Chatsworth Way. SE27 —3B 122
Chattern Hill. —4D 112
Chattern Hill. Ashf —4D 112
Chattern Rd. Ashf —4E 112
Chatterton Ct. Rich —2F 99
Chatterton M. N4 —3B 50
(off Chatterton Rd.)
Chatterton Rd. N4 —3B 50
Chatterton Rd. Brom —4B 144
Chatto Rd. SW11 —5D 102
Chaucer Av. Hay —5J 59
Chaucer Av. Houn —2K 95
Chaucer Av. Rich —3G 99
Chaucer Clo. N11 —5B 16
Chaucer Ct. New Bar —5E 4
Chaucer Dri. SE1 —4F 87
Chaucer Gdns. Sutt —3J 149
(in two parts)
Chaucer Grn. Croy —7H 141
Chaucer Ho. SW1 —5G 85 (6A 172)
(off Churchill Gdns.)
Chaucer Ho. Barn —4A 4
Chaucer Ho. Sutt —3J 149
(off Chaucer Gdns.)
Chaucer Mans. W14 —6G 83
(off Queen's Club Gdns.)
Chaucer Rd. E7 —6J 53
Chaucer Rd. E11 —6J 35
Chaucer Rd. E17 —2E 34
Chaucer Rd. SE24 —5A 104
Chaucer Rd. W3 —1J 81
Chaucer Rd. Ashf —4A 112
Chaucer Rd. Sidc —1C 128
Chaucer Rd. Sutt —4J 149
Chaucer Rd. Well —1J 109
Chaucer Way. SW19 —6A 120
Chaulden Ho. EC1 —3D 68 (2F 163)
(off Cranwood St.)
Chauncey Clo. N9 —3B 18
Chaundrye Clo. SE9 —6D 108
Chauntler Clo. E16 —6K 71
Chaville Ho. N11 —4K 15

Cheadle Ct.—Chiltons, The

Cheadle Ct. NW8 —4B 66 (3B 158)
Cheadle Ho. E14 —6B 70
Cheam. —6G 149
Cheam Comn. Rd. Wor Pk —2D 148
Cheam Mans. Sutt —7G 149
Cheam Pk. Way. Sutt —6G 149
Cheam Rd. Sutt —6H 149
Cheam St. SE15 —3J 105
Cheam Village. (Junct.) —6G 149
Cheapside. EC2 —6C 68 (1D 168)
Cheapside. N13 —4J 17
Cheapside. N22 —3A 32
Chearsley. SE17 —4C 86
(off Deacon Way)
Cheddar Clo. N11 —6J 15
Cheddar Waye. Hay —6K 59
Cheddington Ho. E2 —1G 69
(off Whiston Rd.)
Cheddington Rd. N18 —3K 17
Chedworth Clo. E16 —6H 71
Cheeseman Clo. Hamp —6C 114
Cheesemans Ter. W14 —5H 83
(in two parts)
Chelford Rd. Brom —5F 125
Chelmer Cres. Bark —2B 74
Chelmer Rd. E9 —5K 51
Chelmsford Clo. E6 —6D 72
Chelmsford Clo. W6 —6F 83
Chelmsford Ct. N14 —7C 6
(off Chelmsford Rd.)
Chelmsford Gdns. Ilf —7C 36
Chelmsford Ho. N7 —4K 49
(off Holloway Rd.)
Chelmsford Rd. E11 —1F 53
Chelmsford Rd. E17 —6C 34
Chelmsford Rd. E18 —1H 35
Chelmsford Rd. N14 —7B 6
Chelmsford Sq. NW10 —1E 64
Chelmsine Ct. Ruis —5E 22
Chelsea. —5C 84 (6C 170)
Chelsea Bri. SW1 & SW8 —6F 85 (7J 171)
Chelsea Bri. Bus. Cen. SW8 —7F 85
Chelsea Bri. Rd. SW1 —5E 84 (5G 171)
Chelsea Bri. Wharf. SW8 —6F 85 (7K 171)
Chelsea Cloisters. SW3 —4C 84 (4D 170)
Chelsea Clo. NW10 —1K 63
Chelsea Clo. Edgw —2G 27
Chelsea Clo. Hamp H —5G 115
Chelsea Clo. Wor Pk —7C 136
Chelsea Ct. Brom —3C 144
Chelsea Cres. NW2 —6H 47
Chelsea Cres. SW10 —1A 102
Chelsea Embkmt. SW3 —6C 84 (7D 170)
Chelsea Farm Ho. Studios. SW10
(off Milman's St.) —6B 84
Chelsea F.C. —7K 83
Chelsea Gdns. SW1 —5E 84 (6H 171)
Chelsea Gdns. Sutt —4G 149
Chelsea Ga. SW1 —6H 171
Chelsea Harbour Design Cen. SW10 —1A 102
Chelsea Harbour Dri. SW10 —1A 102
Chelsea Lodge. SW3 —6D 84 (7F 171)
(off Tite St.)
Chelsea Mnr. Ct. SW3 —6C 84 (7D 170)
Chelsea Mnr. Gdns. SW3 —5C 84 (6D 170)
Chelsea Mnr. St. SW3 —5C 84 (6D 170)
Chelsea Pk. Gdns. SW3 —6B 84 (7A 170)
Chelsea Physic Garden. —6D 84 (7E 170)
Chelsea Reach Tower. SW10 —7B 84
(off Worlds End Est.)
Chelsea Sq. SW3 —5B 84 (5B 170)
Chelsea Studios. SW6 —7K 83
(off Fulham Rd.)
Chelsea Towers. SW3 —7D 170
Chelsea Village. SW6 —7K 83
(off Fulham Rd.)
Chelsea Wharf. SW10 —7B 84
(off Lots Rd.)
Chelsfield Av. N9 —7E 8
Chelsfield Gdns. SE26 —3J 123
Chelsfield Grn. N9 —7E 8
Chelsfield Ho. SE17 —4E 86
(off Massinger St.)
Chelsham Rd. SW4 —3H 103
Chelsham Rd. S Croy —7D 152
Chelsiter Ct. Sidc —4K 127
Chelston App. Ruis —2J 41
Chelston Rd. Ruis —1J 41
Chelsworth Dri. SE18 —6H 91
Cheltenham Av. Twic —7A 98
Cheltenham Clo. N Mald —3J 135
Cheltenham Clo. N'holt —6F 43
Cheltenham Ct. Stan —5H 11
(off Marsh La.)
Cheltenham Gdns. E6 —2C 72
Cheltenham Pl. W3 —1H 81
Cheltenham Pl. Harr —4E 26
Cheltenham Rd. E10 —6E 34
Cheltenham Rd. SE15 —4J 105
Cheltenham Ter. SW3 —5D 84 (5F 171)
Chelverton Rd. SW15 —4F 101
Chelwood. N20 —2G 15
Chelwood Clo. E4 —6J 9
Chelwood Gdns. Rich —2G 99
Chelwood Gdns. Pas. Rich —2G 99
Chelwood Ho. W2 —6B 66 (1B 164)
(off Gloucester Sq.)
Chelwood Wlk. SE4 —4A 106
Chenappa Clo. E13 —3J 71
Chenduit Way. Stan —5E 10
Cheney Ct. SE23 —1K 123
Cheney Rd. NW1 —2J 67 (1E 160)
Cheney Row. E17 —1B 34
Cheneys Rd. E11 —3G 53
Cheney St. Pinn —4A 24
Chenies Ho. W4 —7B 82
(off Corney Reach Way)
Chenies M. WC1 —4H 67 (4C 160)
Chenies Pl. NW1 —2H 67
Chenies St. WC1 —5H 67 (5C 160)
Chenies, The. NW1 —2H 67
(off Pancras Rd.)
Chenies, The. Orp —6J 145
Cheniston Gdns. W8 —3K 83
Chepstow Clo. SW15 —6G 101
Chepstow Corner. W2 —6J 65
(off Pembridge Vs.)
Chepstow Ct. W11 —7J 65
(off Chepstow Cres.)
Chepstow Cres. W11 —7J 65
Chepstow Cres. Ilf —6J 37
Chepstow Gdns. S'hall —6D 60
Chepstow Pl. W2 —6J 65
Chepstow Ri. Croy —3E 152
Chepstow Rd. W2 —6J 65
Chepstow Rd. W7 —3A 80
Chepstow Rd. Croy —3E 152
Chepstow Vs. W11 —7H 65
Chepstow Way. SE15 —7F 87
Chequers. Buck H —1E 20
Chequers Clo. NW9 —3A 28
Chequers Clo. Orp —4K 145
Chequers Ct. EC1 —4D 68 (3E 162)
(off Chequer St.)
Chequers Ho. NW8 —4C 66 (3C 158)
(off Jerome Cres.)
Chequers La. Dag —5F 75
Chequers Pde. N13 —5H 17
Chequers Pde. SE9 —6D 108
(off Eltham High St.)
Chequers Pde. Dag —1F 75
Chequers, The. Pinn —3B 24
Chequer St. EC1 —4C 68 (4D 162)
(in two parts)
Chequers Way. N13 —5G 17
Cherbury Clo. SE28 —6D 74
Cherbury Ct. N1 —2D 68
(off St John's Est.)
Cherbury St. N1 —2D 68
Cherchefelle M. Stan —5G 11
Cherimoya Gdns. W Mol —3F 133
Cherington Rd. W7 —1J 79
Cheriton Av. Brom —5H 143
Cheriton Av. Ilf —2D 36
Cheriton Clo. W5 —5C 62
Cheriton Clo. Barn —3J 5
Cheriton Ct. SE12 —7J 107
Cheriton Dri. SE18 —7H 91
Cheriton Sq. SW17 —2E 120
Cherry Av. S'hall —1B 78
Cherry Blossom Clo. N13 —5G 17
Cherry Clo. E17 —5D 34
Cherry Clo. SW2 —7A 104
Cherry Clo. W5 —3D 80
Cherry Clo. Cars —2D 150
Cherry Clo. Mord —4G 137
Cherry Clo. Ruis —3H 41
Cherry Ct. W3 —1A 82
Cherry Ct. Pinn —2B 24
Cherry Cres. Bren —7B 80
Cherrydown Av. E4 —3G 19
Cherrydown Clo. E4 —3H 19
Cherrydown Rd. Sidc —2D 128
Cherrydown Wlk. Romf —2H 39
Cherry Gdns. Dag —5F 57
Cherry Gdns. N'holt —7F 43
Cherry Garden St. SE16 —2H 87
Cherry Gth. Bren —5D 80
Cherry Gro. Hay —1K 77
Cherry Gro. Uxb —5E 58
Cherry Hill. Harr —6E 10
Cherry Hill. New Bar —6E 4
Cherry Hill Gdns. Croy —4K 151
Cherrylands Clo. NW9 —2J 45
Cherry La. W Dray —4B 76
Cherry Laurel Wlk. SW2 —6K 103
Cherry Orchard. SE7 —6A 90
Cherry Orchard. W Dray —2A 76
Cherry Orchard Gdns. Croy —1D 152
Cherry Orchard Gdns. W Mol —3D 132
Cherry Orchard Rd. Brom —2C 156
Cherry Orchard Rd. Croy —2D 152
Cherry Orchard Rd. W Mol —3E 132
Cherry Rd. Enf —1D 8
Cherry St. Romf —5K 39
Cherry Tree Av. W Dray —6B 58
Cherry Tree Clo. E9 —1J 69
Cherry Tree Clo. Wemb —4A 44
Cherry Tree Ct. NW9 —4J 27
Cherry Tree Ct. SE7 —6A 90
Cherrytree Dri. SW16 —3J 121
Cherry Tree Hill. N2 —5C 30
Cherry Tree Ho. N22 —7D 16
Cherry Tree Ri. Buck H —4F 21
Cherry Tree Rd. E15 —5G 53
Cherry Tree Rd. N2 —4D 30
Cherry Tree Wlk. EC1 —4C 68 (4D 162)
Cherry Tree Wlk. Beck —4B 142
Cherry Tree Wlk. W W'ck —4H 155
Cherrytree Way. Stan —6G 11
Cherry Wlk. Brom —1J 155
Cherry Way. Eps —6K 147
Cherry Way. Shep —4F 131
Cherrywood Clo. E3 —3A 70
Cherry Wood Clo. King T —7G 117
Cherrywood Ct. Tedd —5A 116
Cherrywood Dri. SW15 —5F 101
Cherrywood La. Mord —4G 137
Cherry Wood Way. W5 —5G 63
Chertsey Bri. Rd. Cher —7A 130
Chertsey Ct. SW14 —3H 99
Chertsey Dri. Sutt —2G 149
Chertsey Rd. E11 —2F 53
Chertsey Rd. Ashf & Sun —7F 113
Chertsey Rd. Felt —5G 113
Chertsey Rd. Ilf —4H 55
Chertsey Rd. Shep —7A 130
Chertsey Rd. Twic —2J 115
Chertsey St. SW17 —5E 120
Chervil Clo. Felt —3J 113
Chervil M. SE28 —1B 92
Cherwell Ct. Eps —4J 147
Cherwell Ho. NW8 —4B 158
Cherwell Way. Ruis —6E 22
Cheryls Clo. SW6 —1K 101
Cheseman St. SE26 —3H 123
Chesfield Rd. King T —7E 116
Chesham Av. Orp —6F 145
Chesham Clo. SW1 —2G 171
Chesham Clo. Romf —4K 39
Chesham Cres. SE20 —1J 141
Chesham Flats. W1 —7E 66 (2H 165)
(off Brown Hart Gdns.)
Chesham M. SW1 —1G 171
Chesham Pl. SW1 —3E 84 (2G 171)
(in two parts)
Chesham Rd. SE20 —2J 141
Chesham Rd. SW19 —5B 120
Chesham Rd. King T —2G 135
Chesham St. NW10 —3K 45
Chesham St. SW1 —3E 84 (2G 171)
Chesham Ter. W13 —2B 80
Cheshire Clo. E17 —1D 34
Cheshire Clo. SE4 —2B 106
Cheshire Clo. Mitc —3J 139
Cheshire Ct. EC4 —6A 68 (1K 167)
(off Fleet St.)
Cheshire Gdns. Chess —6D 146
Cheshire Ho. Mord —7K 137
Cheshire Rd. N22 —7E 16
Cheshire St. E2 —4F 69 (3K 163)
Cheshir Ho. NW4 —4E 28
Chesholm Rd. N16 —3E 50
Cheshunt Ho. NW6 —1K 65
(off Mortimer Cres.)
Cheshunt Rd. E7 —6K 53
Cheshunt Rd. Belv —5G 93
Chesil Ct. E2 —2J 69
Chesil Ct. SW3 —7D 170
Chesilton Rd. SW6 —1H 101
Chesil Way. Hay —3H 59
Chesley Gdns. E6 —2B 72
Chesney Ct. W9 —4J 65
(off Shirland Rd.)
Chesney Cres. New Ad —7E 154
Chesney Ho. SE13 —4F 107
(off Mercator Rd.)
Chesney St. SW11 —1E 102
Chesnut Gro. N17 —3F 33
Chesnut Rd. N17 —3F 33
Chesnut Row. N3 —7D 14
Chessholme Rd. Ashf —6E 112
Chessing Ct. N2 —3D 30
(off Fortis Grn.)
Chessington. —5F 147
Chessington Av. N3 —3G 29
Chessington Av. Bexh —5E 92
Chessington Clo. Eps —6J 147
Chessington Ct. N3 —3H 29
(off Charter Way)
Chessington Ct. Pinn —4D 24
Chessington Hall Gdns. Chess —7D 146
Chessington Hill Pk. Chess —5G 147
Chessington Ho. SW8 —2H 103
Chessington Lodge. N3 —3H 29
Chessington Mans. E10 —7C 34
Chessington Mans. E11 —7G 35
Chessington Pde. Chess —6D 146
Chessington Rd. Eps & Ewe —6G 147
Chessington Way. W W'ck —2D 154
Chesson Rd. W14 —6H 83
Chesswood Way. Pinn —2B 24
Chestbrook Ct. Enf —5K 7
(off Forsyth Pl.)
Chester Av. Rich —6F 99
Chester Av. Twic —1D 114
Chester Clo. SW1 —2F 85 (7J 165)
Chester Clo. SW13 —3D 100
Chester Clo. Ashf —5F 113
Chester Clo. Rich —6F 99
Chester Clo. Sutt —2J 149
Chester Clo. Uxb —6D 58
Chester Clo. N. NW1 —3F 67 (1K 159)
Chester Clo. S. NW1 —3F 67 (2K 159)
Chester Cotts. SW1 —4G 171
Chester Ct. NW1 —3F 67 (1K 159)
Chester Ct. SE8 —5K 87
Chester Cres. E8 —5F 51
Chester Dri. Harr —6D 24
Chesterfield Clo. SE13 —2F 107
Chesterfield Dri. Esh —2A 146
Chesterfield Flats. Barn —5A 4
(off Bells Hill)
Chesterfield Gdns. N4 —5B 32
Chesterfield Gdns. SE10 —1F 107
Chesterfield Gdns. W1 —1F 85 (4J 165)
Chesterfield Gro. SE22 —5F 105
Chesterfield Hill. W1 —1F 85 (4J 165)
Chesterfield Ho. W1 —1E 84 (4H 165)
(off Chesterfield Gdns.)
Chesterfield Lodge. N21 —7E 6
(off Church Hill)
Chesterfield M. Ashf —4A 112
Chesterfield Rd. E10 —6E 34
Chesterfield Rd. N3 —6D 14
Chesterfield Rd. W4 —6J 81
Chesterfield Rd. Ashf —4A 112
Chesterfield Rd. Barn —5A 4
Chesterfield Rd. Eps —7K 147
Chesterfield St. W1 —1F 85 (4J 165)
Chesterfield Wlk. SE10 —1F 107
Chesterfield Way. SE15 —7J 87
Chesterfield Way. Hay —2J 77
Chesterford Gdns. NW3 —4K 47
Chesterford Ho. SE18 —1B 108
(off Tellson Av.)
Chesterford Rd. E12 —5D 54
Chester Gdns. W13 —6B 62
Chester Gdns. Enf —6C 8
Chester Gdns. Mord —6A 138
Chester Ga. NW1 —3F 67 (2J 159)
Chester Ho. SE8 —6B 88
Chester Ho. SW1 —4F 85 (3J 171)
(off Eccleston Pl.)
Chester Ho. SW9 —7A 86
(off Brixton Rd.)
Chesterman Ct. W4 —7A 82
(off Corney Reach Way)
Chester M. SW1 —3F 85 (1J 171)
Chester Pl. NW1 —3F 67 (1J 159)
Chester Rd. E7 —7B 54
Chester Rd. E11 —6K 35
Chester Rd. E16 —4G 71
Chester Rd. E17 —5K 33
Chester Rd. N9 —1C 18
Chester Rd. N17 —3D 32
Chester Rd. N19 —2F 49
Chester Rd. NW1 —3E 66 (2H 159)
Chester Rd. SW19 —6E 118
Chester Rd. Chig —3K 21
Chester Rd. Houn —3K 95
Chester Rd. Ilf —1K 55
Chester Rd. H'row A —3C 94
Chester Rd. N'wd —1H 23
Chester Rd. Sidc —5J 109
Chester Row. SW1 —4E 84 (4G 171)
Chester Sq. SW1 —4E 84 (3H 171)
Chester Sq. M. SW1 —2J 171
Chesters, The. N Mald —1A 136
Chester St. E2 —4G 69
Chester St. SW1 —3E 84 (1H 171)
Chester Ter. NW1 —3F 67 (1J 159)
(in three parts)
Chester Ter. Bark —6H 55
Chesterton Clo. SW18 —5J 101
Chesterton Clo. Gnfd —2F 61
Chesterton Ct. W3 —3H 81
(off Hanbury Rd.)
Chesterton Ct. W5 —5D 62
Chesterton Dri. Stai —1B 112
Chesterton Rd. E13 —3J 71
Chesterton Rd. W10 —5F 65
Chesterton Sq. W8 —4J 83
Chesterton Ter. E13 —3J 71
Chesterton Ter. King T —2G 135
Chester Way. SE11 —4A 86 (4K 173)
Chesthunte Rd. N17 —1C 32
Chestnut All. SW6 —6H 83
Chestnut Av. E7 —4K 53
Chestnut Av. N8 —5J 31
Chestnut Av. SW14 —3K 99
Chestnut Av. Bren —4D 80
Chestnut Av. Buck H —3G 21
Chestnut Av. E Mol & Tedd —3K 133
Chestnut Av. Edgw —6K 11
Chestnut Av. Eps —4A 148
Chestnut Av. Esh —7H 133
Chestnut Av. Hamp —7E 114
Chestnut Av. N'wd —2H 23
Chestnut Av. Wemb —5B 44
Chestnut Av. W Dray —7B 58
Chestnut Av. W W'ck —5G 155
Chestnut Av. N. E17 —4F 35
Chestnut Av. S. E17 —5E 34
Chestnut Clo. N14 —5B 6
Chestnut Clo. N16 —2D 50
Chestnut Clo. SE6 —5E 124
Chestnut Clo. SE14 —1B 106
Chestnut Clo. SW16 —4A 122
Chestnut Clo. Ashf —4D 112
Chestnut Clo. Buck H —3G 21
Chestnut Clo. Cars —1D 150
Chestnut Clo. Hay —7G 59
Chestnut Clo. Sidc —1A 128
Chestnut Clo. Sun —6H 113
Chestnut Clo. W Dray —7D 76
Chestnut Ct. N8 —5J 31
Chestnut Ct. SW6 —6H 83
Chestnut Ct. W8 —3K 83
Chestnut Ct. Felt —5B 114
Chestnut Dri. E11 —6J 35
Chestnut Dri. Bexh —3D 110
Chestnut Dri. Harr —7E 10
Chestnut Dri. Pinn —6B 24
Chestnut Gro. SE20 —7H 123
Chestnut Gro. SW12 —7E 102
Chestnut Gro. W5 —3D 80
Chestnut Gro. Barn —5J 5
Chestnut Gro. Dart —4K 129
Chestnut Gro. Iswth —4A 98
Chestnut Gro. Mitc —5H 139
Chestnut Gro. N Mald —3K 135
Chestnut Gro. S Croy —7H 153
Chestnut Gro. Wemb —5A 44
Chestnut Ho. W4 —4A 82
(off Orchard, The)
Chestnut La. N20 —1B 14
Chestnut Ri. SE18 —6H 91
Chestnut Ri. Bush —1A 10
Chestnut Rd. SE27 —3B 122
Chestnut Rd. SW20 —2F 137
Chestnut Rd. Ashf —4D 112
Chestnut Rd. King T —7E 116
Chestnut Rd. Twic —2J 115
Chestnuts, The. N5 —4C 50
(off Highbury Grange)
Chestnuts, The. Pinn —1D 24
Chestnuts, The. Uxb —7A 40
Chestnut Ter. Sutt —4K 149
Chestnut Wlk. Shep —4G 131
Chestnut Wlk. Wfd G —5D 20
Chestnut Way. Felt —3K 113
Cheston Av. Croy —2A 154
Chestwood Gro. Uxb —7B 40
Chettle Clo. SE1 —3D 86
(off Spurgeon St.)
Chettle Ct. N8 —6A 32
Chetwode Ho. NW8 —3C 158
Chetwode Rd. SW17 —3D 120
Chetwood Wlk. E6 —5C 72
(off Greenwich Cres.)
Chetwynd Av. E Barn —1J 15
Chetwynd Dri. Uxb —2B 58
Chetwynd Rd. NW5 —4F 49
Chevalier Clo. Stan —4K 11
Cheval Pl. SW7 —3C 84 (1D 170)
Cheval St. E14 —3C 88
Cheveney Wlk. Brom —3J 143
Chevening Rd. NW6 —2F 65
Chevening Rd. SE10 —5H 89
Chevening Rd. SE19 —6D 122
Chevenings, The. Sidc —3C 128
Cheverell Ho. E2 —2G 69
(off Pritchard's Rd.)
Cheverton Rd. N19 —1H 49
Chevet St. E9 —5A 52
Chevington. NW2 —6H 47
Cheviot. N17 —7C 18
(off Northumberland Gro.)
Cheviot Clo. Bexh —2K 111
Cheviot Clo. Enf —2J 7
Cheviot Clo. Hay —7F 77
Cheviot Ct. S'hall —4F 79
Cheviot Gdns. NW2 —2F 47
Cheviot Gdns. SE27 —4B 122
Cheviot Ga. NW2 —2G 47
Cheviot Rd. SE27 —5A 122
Cheviot Way. Ilf —4J 37
Chevron Clo. E16 —6J 71
Chevy Rd. S'hall —2G 79
Chewton Rd. E17 —4A 34
Cheylesmore Ho. SW1 —5F 85 (6J 171)
(off Ebury Bri. Rd.)
Cheyne Av. E18 —3H 35
Cheyne Av. Twic —1D 114
Cheyne Clo. NW4 —5E 28
Cheyne Clo. Brom —3C 156
Cheyne Ct. SW3 —6D 84 (7E 170)
Cheyne Gdns. SW3 —6C 84 (7D 170)
Cheyne Gdns. W13 —5K 61
Cheyne Hill. Surb —4F 135
Cheyne M. SW3 —6C 84 (7D 170)
Cheyne Path. W7 —5K 61
Cheyne Pl. SW3 —6D 84 (7E 170)
Cheyne Rd. Ashf —7F 113
Cheyne Row. SW3 —6C 84 (7C 170)
Cheyne Wlk. N21 —5G 7
Cheyne Wlk. NW4 —6E 28
Cheyne Wlk. SW10 & SW3
(in three parts) —7B 84 (7C 170)
Cheyne Wlk. Croy —2G 153
Cheyneys Av. Edgw —6J 11
Chichele Gdns. Croy —4E 152
Chichele Rd. NW2 —5F 47
Chicheley Gdns. Harr —7B 10
(in two parts)
Chicheley Rd. Harr —7B 10
Chicheley St. SE1 —2K 85 (6H 167)
Chichester Av. Ruis —2F 41
Chichester Clo. E6 —6C 72
Chichester Clo. SE3 —7A 90
Chichester Clo. Hamp —6D 114
Chichester Ct. Edgw —6B 12
(off Whitchurch La.)
Chichester Ct. Eps —7B 148
Chichester Ct. N'holt —1C 60
Chichester Ct. Stan —3E 26
Chichester Gdns. Ilf —7C 36
Chichester Ho. NW6 —2J 65
Chichester Ho. SW9 —7A 86
(off Brixton Rd.)
Chichester M. SE27 —4A 122
Chichester Rents. WC2 —7J 161
Chichester Rd. E11 —3G 53
Chichester Rd. N9 —1B 18
Chichester Rd. NW6 —2J 65
Chichester Rd. W2 —5K 65
Chichester Rd. Croy —3E 152
Chichester St. SW1 —5G 85 (6B 172)
Chichester Way. E14 —4F 89
Chichester Way. Felt —7A 96
Chicksand Ho. E1 —5G 69 (5K 163)
(off Chicksand St.)
Chicksand St. E1 —5F 69 (6K 163)
(in two parts)
Chiddingfold. N12 —3D 14
Chiddingstone. SE13 —5E 106
Chiddingstone Av. Bexh —7F 93
Chiddingstone St. SW6 —2J 101
Chieveley Pde. Bexh —4H 111
(off Chieveley Rd.)
Chieveley Pde. Bexh —3H 111
(Mayplace Rd. E.)
Chieveley Rd. Bexh —4H 111
Chignell Pl. W13 —1A 80
Chigwell Hill. E1 —7H 69
Chigwell Hurst Ct. Pinn —3B 24
Chigwell Pk. Chig —4K 21
Chigwell Pk. Dri. Chig —3K 21
Chigwell Ri. Chig —2K 21
Chigwell Rd. E18 & Wfd G —3K 35
Chilcot Clo. E14 —6D 70
Childebert Rd. SW17 —2F 121
Childeric Rd. SE14 —7A 88
Childerley St. SW6 —1G 101
Childers St. SE8 —6A 88
Childers, The. Wfd G —5J 21
Childs Ct. Hay —7J 59
Child's Hill. —3J 47
Childs Hill Wlk. NW2 —3H 47
(off Cricklewood La.)
Child's La. SE19 —6E 122
Child's Pl. SW5 —4J 83
Child's St. SW5 —4J 83
Child's Wlk. SW5 —4J 83
Childs Way. NW11 —5H 29
Chilham Clo. Bex —7F 111
Chilham Clo. Gnfd —2A 62
Chilham Ho. SE1 —3D 86
Chilham Ho. SE15 —6J 87
Chilham Rd. SE9 —4C 126
Chilham Way. Brom —7J 143
Chilianwalla Memorial. —7G 171
Chillerton Rd. SW17 —5E 120
Chillingworth Gdns. Twic —3K 115
Chillingworth Rd. N7 —5A 50
Chilmark Gdns. N Mald —6C 136
Chilmark Rd. SW16 —2H 139
Chiltern Av. Twic —1E 114
Chiltern Clo. Croy —3E 152
Chiltern Clo. Uxb —2C 40
Chiltern Clo. Wor Pk —1E 148
Chiltern Ct. N10 —2E 30
Chiltern Ct. NW1 —4D 66 (4F 159)
(off Baker St.)
Chiltern Ct. Harr —5H 25
Chiltern Ct. New Bar —5F 5
Chiltern Ct. Uxb —4D 58
Chiltern Dene. Enf —4E 6
Chiltern Dri. Surb —6G 135
Chiltern Gdns. NW2 —3F 47
Chiltern Gdns. Brom —4H 143
Chiltern Ho. SE17 —6D 86
(off Portland St.)
Chiltern Ho. W5 —5E 62
Chiltern Rd. E3 —4C 70
Chiltern Rd. Ilf —5J 37
Chiltern Rd. Pinn —5A 24
Chiltern St. W1 —5E 66 (5G 159)
Chiltern Way. Wfd G —3D 20
Chilthorne Clo. SE6 —7B 106
Chilton Av. W5 —4D 80
Chilton Ct. N22 —7D 16
(off Truro Rd.)
Chilton Gro. SE8 —4K 87
Chiltonian Ind. Est. SE12 —6H 107
Chilton Rd. Edgw —6B 12
Chilton Rd. Rich —3G 99
Chiltons, The. E18 —2J 35

Chilton St.—Claredale Ho.

Chilton St. E2 —4F 69 (3K 163)
Chilvers Clo. Twic —2J 115
Chilver St. SE10 —5H 89
Chilworth Ct. SW19 —1F 119
Chilworth Gdns. Sutt —3A 150
Chilworth M. W2 —6B 66 (1A 164)
Chilworth St. W2 —6A 66 (1A 164)
Chimes Av. N13 —5F 17
Chimney Ct. E1 —1H 87
(off Brewhouse La.)
China Ct. E1 —1H 87
(off Asher Way)
China M. SW2 —7K 103
China Wharf. SE16 —2G 87 (6K 169)
Chinbrook Cres. SE12 —3K 125
Chinbrook Rd. SE12 —3K 125
Chinchilla Dri. Houn —2A 96
Chine, The. N10 —4G 31
Chine, The. N21 —6G 7
Chine, The. Wemb —5B 44
Ching Ct. WC2 —6J 67 (1E 166)
(off Monmouth St.)
Chingdale Rd. E4 —3B 20
Chingford. —1K 19
Chingford Av. E4 —3H 19
Chingford Green. —1A 20
Chingford Hall Est. E4 —6G 19
Chingford Hatch. —4A 20
Chingford Ind. Est. E4 —4F 19
Chingford La. Wfd G —4B 20
Chingford Mount. —4H 19
Chingford Mt. Rd. E4 —4H 19
Chingford Rd. E4 —6H 19
Chingford Rd. E17 —1D 34
Chingley Clo. Brom —6G 125
Ching Way. E4 —6G 19
(in two parts)
Chinnery Clo. Enf —1A 8
Chinnock's Wharf. E14 —7A 70
Chinnor Cres. Gnfd —2F 61
Chipka St. E14 —2E 88
(in two parts)
Chipley St. SE14 —6A 88
Chipmunk Gro. N'holt —3C 60
Chippendale All. Uxb —7A 40
Chippendale Ho. SW1 —5F 85 (6K 171)
(off Churchill Gdns.)
Chippendale St. E5 —3K 51
Chippendale Waye. Uxb —7A 40
Chippenham Av. Wemb —5H 45
Chippenham Clo. Pinn —4H 23
Chippenham Gdns. NW6 —3J 65
Chippenham M. W9 —4J 65
Chippenham Rd. W9 —4J 65
Chipperfield Ho. SW3 —5C 84 (5C 170)
(off Ixworth Pl.)
Chipperfield Rd. Orp & St P —7A 128
Chipping Barnet. —4B 4
Chipping Clo. Barn —3B 4
Chipstead Av. T Hth —4B 140
Chipstead Clo. SE19 —7F 123
Chipstead Clo. Sutt —7K 149
Chipstead Gdns. NW2 —2D 46
Chipstead Rd. H'row A —3C 94
Chipstead St. SW6 —1J 101
Chip St. SW4 —3H 103
Chirk Clo. Hay —4C 60
Chisenhale Rd. E3 —2A 70
Chisholm Ct. W6 —5C 82
Chisholm Rd. Croy —2E 152
Chisholm Rd. Rich —6F 99
Chisledon Wlk. E9 —6B 52
(off Osborne Rd.)
Chislehurst. —6F 127
Chislehurst Av. N12 —7F 15
Chislehurst Caves. —1E 144
Chislehurst Rd. Brom & Chst —2B 144
Chislehurst Rd. Orp —4J 145
Chislehurst Rd. Rich —5E 98
Chislehurst Rd. Sidc —5A 128
Chislehurst West. —5E 126
Chislet Clo. Beck —7C 124
Chisley Rd. N15 —6E 32
Chiswell Sq. SE3 —2K 107
Chiswell St. EC1 —5C 68 (5E 162)
Chiswick. —6K 81
Chiswick Bri. SW14 & W4 —2J 99
Chiswick Clo. Croy —3K 151
Chiswick Comn. Rd. W4 —4K 81
Chiswick Ct. W4 —4H 81
Chiswick Ct. Pinn —3D 24
Chiswick High Rd. Bren & W4 —5G 81
(in two parts)
Chiswick House. —6A 82
Chiswick La. W4 —5A 82
Chiswick La. S. W4 —6B 82
Chiswick Mall. W4 & W6 —6B 82
Chiswick Pk. W4 —4H 81
Chiswick Plaza. W4 —6J 81
Chiswick Quay. W4 —1J 99
Chiswick Rd. N9 —2B 18
Chiswick Rd. W4 —4J 81
Chiswick Roundabout. (Junct.) —5G 81
Chiswick Sq. W4 —6A 82
Chiswick Staithe. W4 —1J 99
Chiswick Ter. W4 —4J 81
Chiswick Village. W4 —6G 81
Chiswick Wharf. W4 —6B 82
Chitterfield Ga. W Dray —7C 76
Chitty's La. Dag —2D 56
Chitty St. W1 —5G 67 (5B 160)
Chivalry Rd. SW11 —5C 102
Chive Clo. Croy —1K 153
Chivenor Gro. King T —5D 116
Chivers Rd. E4 —3J 19
Choats Rd. Bark & Dag —2C 74
Chobham Gdns. SW19 —2F 119
Chobham Rd. E15 —5F 53
Cholmeley Cres. N6 —7F 31
Cholmeley Lodge. N6 —1F 49
Cholmeley Pk. N6 —1F 49
Cholmley Gdns. NW6 —5J 47
Cholmley Rd. Th Dit —6B 134
Cholmondeley Av. NW10 —2C 64
Cholmondeley Wlk. Rich —5C 98
(in two parts)
Choppin's Ct. E1 —1H 87
Chopwell Clo. E15 —7F 53
Chorleywood Cres. Orp —2K 145
Choumert Gro. SE15 —2G 105
Choumert Rd. SE15 —3F 105
Choumert Sq. SE15 —2G 105
Chow Sq. E8 —5F 51
Chrisp St. E14 —5D 70
(in two parts)
Christabel Clo. Iswth —3J 97
Christchurch Av. N12 —6F 15
Christchurch Av. NW6 —1F 65
Christchurch Av. Eri —6K 93
Christchurch Av. Harr —4K 25
Christchurch Av. Tedd —5A 116
Christchurch Av. Wemb —6E 44
Christchurch Clo. N12 —7G 15
Christchurch Clo. SW19 —7B 120
Christchurch Ct. NW10 —1A 64
Christchurch Ct. Hay —4A 60
(off Dunedin Way)
Christchurch Flats. Rich —3E 98
Christchurch Gdns. Harr —4A 26
Christchurch Grn. Wemb —6E 44
Christchurch Hill. NW3 —3B 48
Christchurch Ho. SW2 —1K 121
(off Christchurch Rd.)
Christchurch La. Barn —2B 4
Christchurch Lodge. Barn —4J 5
Christchurch Pk. Sutt —7A 150
Christchurch Pas. NW3 —3A 48
Christchurch Pas. High Bar —2B 4
Christchurch Path. Hay —3E 76
Christchurch Pl. SW8 —2H 103
Christchurch Rd. N8 —6J 31
Christchurch Rd. SW2 —1K 121
Christ Chu. Rd. SW14 —5H 99
Christchurch Rd. SW19 —7B 120
Christ Chu. Rd. Beck —2C 142
Christchurch Rd. Ilf —1F 55
Christchurch Rd. H'row A —3C 94
Christchurch Rd. Sidc —4K 127
Christchurch Rd. Surb —6F 135
Christchurch Sq. E9 —1J 69
Christchurch St. SW3 —6D 84 (7E 170)
Christchurch Ter. SW3 —7E 170
Christchurch Way. SE10 —5G 89
Christian Ct. SE16 —1B 88
Christian Fields. SW16 —7A 122
Christian Pl. E1 —6G 69
(off Burslem St.)
Christian St. E1 —6G 69
Christie Ct. N19 —2J 49
Christie Dri. Croy —5G 141
Christie Gdns. Romf —6B 38
Christie Rd. E9 —6A 52
Christina Sq. N4 —1B 50
Christina St. EC2 —4E 68 (3G 163)
Christine Worsley Clo. N21 —1G 17
Christopher Av. W7 —3A 80
Christopher Clo. SE16 —2K 87
Christopher Clo. Sidc —5K 109
Christopher Gdns. Dag —5D 56
Christopher Ho. Sidc —2A 128
(off Station Rd.)
Christopher Pl. NW1 —3H 67 (1D 160)
Christopher Rd. S'hall —4K 77
Christophers M. W11 —1G 83
Christopher St. EC2 —4D 68 (4F 163)
Chryssell Rd. SW9 —7A 86
Chubworthy St. SE14 —6A 88
Chudleigh. Sidc —4B 128
Chudleigh Cres. Ilf —4J 55
Chudleigh Gdns. Sutt —3A 150
Chudleigh Rd. NW6 —7F 47
Chudleigh Rd. SE4 —5B 106
Chudleigh Rd. Twic —6J 97
(in two parts)
Chudleigh St. E1 —6K 69
Chudleigh Way. Ruis —1J 41
Chulsa Rd. SE26 —5H 123
Chumleigh St. SE5 —6E 86
Chumleigh Wlk. Surb —4F 135
Church All. Croy —1A 152
Church App. SE21 —3D 122
Church Av. E4 —6A 20
Church Av. N2 —2B 30
Church Av. NW1 —6F 49
Church Av. SW14 —3K 99
Church Av. Beck —1C 142
Church Av. N'holt —7D 42
Church Av. Pinn —6C 24
Church Av. Ruis —1F 41
Church Av. Sidc —5A 128
Church Av. S'hall —3C 78
Churchbank. E17 —4C 34
(off Teresa M.)
Churchbury Clo. Enf —2K 7
Churchbury La. Enf —3J 7
Churchbury Rd. SE9 —7A 108
Churchbury Rd. Enf —2K 7
Church Cloisters. EC3 —3G 169
Church Clo. N20 —3H 15
Church Clo. W8 —2K 83
Church Clo. Edgw —5D 12
Church Clo. Hay —5F 59
Church Clo. Houn —2C 96
Church Clo. N'wd —1H 23
Church Clo. W Dray —3A 76
Church Ct. Rich —5D 98
Church Ct. Wfd G —6F 21
Church Cres. E9 —7K 51
Church Cres. N3 —1H 29
Church Cres. N10 —4F 31
Church Cres. N20 —3H 15
Churchcroft Clo. SW12 —7E 102
Churchdown. Brom —4G 125
Church Dri. NW9 —1K 45
Church Dri. Harr —6E 24
Church Dri. W W'ck —3G 155
Church Elm La. Dag —6G 57
Church End. —1H 29
(Finchley)
Church End. —6A 46
(Willesden)
Church End. E17 —4D 34
Church End. NW4 —3D 28
Church Entry. EC4 —1B 168
Church Est. Almshouses. Rich —4F 99
(off Sheen Rd.)
Church Farm House Mus. —3D 28
Church Farm La. Sutt —6G 149
Churchfield Av. N12 —6G 15
Churchfield Clo. Harr —4G 25
Churchfield Clo. Hay —7H 59
Churchfield Mans. SW6 —2H 101
(off New King's Rd.)
Churchfield Rd. W3 —1J 81
Churchfield Rd. W7 —2J 79
Churchfield Rd. W13 —1B 80
Churchfield Rd. W on T —7J 131
Churchfield Rd. Well —3A 110
Churchfields. E18 —1J 35
Churchfields. SE10 —6E 88
Churchfields. W Mol —3E 132
Churchfields Av. Felt —3D 114
Churchfields Rd. Beck —2K 141
Churchfield Way. N12 —6F 15
Church Gdns. W5 —2D 80
Church Gdns. Wemb —4A 44
Church Gth. N19 —2H 49
(off St John's Gro.)
Church Ga. SW6 —3G 101
Church Grn. SW9 —1A 104
Church Grn. Hay —6H 59
Church Gro. SE13 —5D 106
Church Gro. King T —1C 134
Church Hill. E17 —4C 34
Church Hill. N21 —7E 6
Church Hill. SE18 —3D 90
Church Hill. SW19 —5H 119
Church Hill. Cars —5D 150
Church Hill. Cray —4K 111
Church Hill. Harr —1J 43
Church Hill Rd. E17 —4D 34
Church Hill Rd. Barn & E Barn —6H 5
Church Hill Rd. Surb —5E 134
Church Hill Rd. Sutt —3F 149
Church Hill Wood. Orp —5K 145
Church Ho. SW1 —3H 85
(off Gt. Smith St.)
Church Hyde. SE18 —6J 91
Churchill Av. Harr —6B 26
Churchill Av. Uxb —3D 58
Churchill Clo. Felt —1H 113
Churchill Clo. Uxb —3D 58
Churchill Ct. N4 —7A 32
Churchill Ct. W5 —4F 63
Churchill Ct. N'holt —5E 42
Churchill Ct. Pinn —1C 24
Churchill Ct. S Harr —5F 25
Churchill Gdns. SW1 —6A 172
(in three parts)
Churchill Gdns. W3 —6G 63
Churchill Gdns. Rd. SW1 —5F 85 (6K 171)
Churchill Pl. E14 —1D 88
Churchill Pl. Harr —4J 25
Churchill Rd. E16 —6A 72
Churchill Rd. NW2 —6D 46
Churchill Rd. NW5 —4F 49
Churchill Rd. Edgw —6A 12
Churchill Rd. S Croy —7C 152
Churchills M. Wfd G —6C 20
Churchill Ter. E4 —4H 19
Churchill Theatre. —2J 143
Churchill Wlk. E9 —5J 51
Churchill Way. Brom —2J 143
Churchill Way. Sun —5J 113
Church La. E11 —1G 53
Church La. E17 —4D 34
Church La. N2 —3B 30
Church La. N8 —4K 31
Church La. N9 —2B 18
Church La. N17 —1E 32
Church La. NW9 —6J 27
Church La. SW17 —5D 120
Church La. SW19 —1H 137
Church La. W5 —2C 80
Church La. Brom —1C 156
Church La. Chess —6F 147
Church La. Chst —1G 145
Church La. Dag —7J 57
Church La. Enf —3J 7
Church La. Harr —1K 25
Church La. Pinn —3C 24
Church La. Rich —1E 116
Church La. Tedd —5K 115
Church La. Th Dit —6K 133
Church La. Twic —1A 116
Church La. Wall —3H 151
Churchley Rd. SE26 —4H 123
Church Manorway. SE2 —5A 92
Church Manorway. Eri —3K 93
Church Mead. SE5 —7C 86
(off Camberwell Rd.)
Churchmead Clo. E Barn —6H 5
Church Mdw. Surb —2C 146
Churchmead Rd. NW10 —6C 46
Churchmore Rd. SW16 —1G 139
Church Mt. N2 —5B 30
Chu. Paddock Ct. Wall —3H 151
Church Pde. Ashf —4B 112
Church Pas. EC2 —6C 68
(off Guildhall Yd.)
Church Pas. Barn —3B 4
Church Pas. Surb —5E 134
Church Pas. Twic —1B 116
Church Path. E11 —5J 35
Church Path. E17 —4D 34
Church Path. N5 —5B 50
Church Path. N12 —4F 15
Church Path. N17 —1E 32
Church Path. NW10 —7A 46
Church Path. SW14 —4K 99
(in two parts)
Church Path. SW19 —2H 137
Church Path. W3 & W4 —2J 81
(in two parts)
Church Path. W7 —1J 79
Church Path. Bark —1G 73
Church Path. Barn —4B 4
Church Path. Croy —2C 152
Church Path. Mitc —3C 138
(in two parts)
Church Path. Romf —5K 39
Church Path. S'hall —1E 78
(UB1)
Church Path. S'hall —3D 78
(UB2)
Church Pl. SW1 —7G 67 (3B 166)
Church Pl. W5 —2D 80
Church Pl. Ick —3E 40
Church Pl. Mitc —3C 138
Church Ri. SE23 —2K 123
Church Ri. Chess —6F 147
Church Rd. E10 —1C 52
Church Rd. E12 —5C 54
Church Rd. E17 —2A 34
Church Rd. N6 —6E 30
Church Rd. N17 —1E 32
(in two parts)
Church Rd. NW4 —4D 28
Church Rd. NW10 —7A 46
Church Rd. SE19 —1E 140
Church Rd. SW13 —2B 100
Church Rd. SW19 —5G 119
(High St.)
Church Rd. W3 —1J 81
Church Rd. W7 —7H 61
Church Rd. SW19 & Mitc —1B 138
(Western Rd.)
Church Rd. Ashf —3B 112
Church Rd. Bark —6G 55
Church Rd. Bexh —2F 111
Church Rd. Brom —2J 143
Church Rd. Buck H —1E 20
Church Rd. Cran —5K 77
Church Rd. Croy —3C 152
(in two parts)
Church Rd. E Mol —4H 133
Church Rd. Enf —6D 8
Church Rd. Eri —5K 93
Church Rd. Felt —5B 114
Church Rd. Ham & Rich —4D 116
Church Rd. Hay —1H 77
Church Rd. Houn —7E 78
Church Rd. Ilf —6J 37
Church Rd. Iswth —1H 97
Church Rd. Kes —7B 156
Church Rd. King T —2F 135
Church Rd. N'holt —2B 60
Church Rd. N'wd —1H 23
Church Rd. Rich —4E 98
Church Rd. Shep —7D 130
Church Rd. Short —3G 143
Church Rd. Sidc —4A 128
Church Rd. S'hall —3D 78
Church Rd. Stan —5G 11
Church Rd. Surb —1C 146
Church Rd. Sutt —6G 149
Church Rd. Tedd —4J 115
Church Rd. Uxb —4A 58
Church Rd. Wall —3G 151
Church Rd. Well —2B 110
Church Rd. W Dray —3A 76
Church Rd. W Ewe —7G 147
Church Rd. Wor Pk —1A 148
Church Rd. Almshouses. E10 —2D 52
(off Church Rd.)
Church Rd. Ind. Est. E10 —1C 52
Church Rd. N. N2 —2B 30
Church Rd. S. N2 —2B 30
Church Row. NW3 —4A 48
Church Row. Chst —1G 145
Church Row M. Chst —7G 127
Church Sq. Shep —7D 130
Church St. E15 —1G 71
Church St. E16 —1F 91
Church St. N9 —7J 7
Church St. W2 & NW8 —5B 66 (5B 158)
Church St. W4 —6B 82
Church St. Croy —3B 152
Church St. Dag —6H 57
Church St. Enf —3H 7
Church St. Hamp —1G 133
Church St. Iswth —3B 98
Church St. King T —2D 134
Church St. Sun —3K 131
Church St. Sutt —5K 149
Church St. Twic —1A 116
Church St. W on T —7J 131
Church St. Est. NW8 —4B 66 (4B 158)
(in two parts)
Church St. N. E15 —1G 71
Church St. Pas. E15 —1G 71
Church Stretton Rd. Houn —5G 97
Church Ter. NW4 —3D 28
Church Ter. SE13 —3G 107
Church Ter. Rich —5D 98
Church Va. N2 —3D 30
Church Va. SE23 —2K 123
Church Vw. Rich —5E 98
Churchview Rd. Twic —1H 115
Church Wlk. N6 —3E 48
Church Wlk. N16 —3D 50
(in three parts)
Church Wlk. NW2 —3H 47
Church Wlk. NW4 —3E 28
Church Wlk. NW9 —2K 45
Church Wlk. SW13 —1C 100
Church Wlk. SW15 —5D 100
Church Wlk. SW16 —2G 139
Church Wlk. SW20 —3E 136
Church Wlk. Bren —6C 80
(in two parts)
Church Wlk. Enf —3J 7
Church Wlk. Hay —6G 59
(in three parts)
Church Wlk. Rich —5D 98
Church Wlk. Th Dit —6K 133
Church Wlk. W on T —7J 131
Churchward Ho. W14 —5H 83
(off Ivatt Pl.)
Church Way. N20 —3H 15
Churchway. NW1 —3H 67 (1D 160)
(in two parts)
Church Way. Barn —4J 5
Church Way. Edgw —6B 12
Churchwell Path. E9 —5J 51
Churchwood Gdns. Wfd G —4D 20
Churchyard Pas. SE5 —2D 104
Churchyard Row. SE11 —4B 86
Churnfield. N4 —2A 50
Churston Av. E13 —1K 71
Churston Clo. SW2 —1A 122
Churston Dri. Mord —5F 137
Churston Gdns. N11 —6B 16
Churton Pl. SW1 —4G 85 (4B 172)
Churton St. SW1 —4G 85 (4B 172)
Chusan Pl. E14 —6B 70
Chute Ho. SW9 —2A 104
(off Stockwell Pk. Rd.)
Chyngton Clo. Sidc —3K 127
Cibber Rd. SE23 —2K 123
Cicada Rd. SW18 —6A 102
Cicely Ho. NW8 —2B 66
(off Cochrane St.)
Cicely Rd. SE15 —1G 105
Cinderford Way. Brom —4G 125
Cinnamon Clo. Croy —7J 139
Cinnamon Row. SW11 —3A 102
Cinnamon St. E1 —1H 87
Cinnamon Wharf. SE1 —6K 169
Cintra Pk. SE19 —7F 123
Circle Gdns. SW19 —2J 137
Circle, The. NW2 —3A 46
Circle, The. NW7 —6E 12
Circle, The. SE1 —2F 87 (6J 169)
(off Queen Elizabeth St.)
Circuits, The. Pinn —4A 24
Circular Rd. N2 —2B 30
Circular Rd. N17 —3F 33
Circular Way. SE18 —6D 90
Circus Lodge. NW8 —1A 158
Circus M. W1 —5E 158
Circus Pl. EC2 —5D 68 (6F 163)
Circus Rd. NW8 —3B 66 (1A 158)
Circus St. SE10 —7E 88
Cirencester St. W2 —5K 65
Cissbury Ho. SE26 —3G 123
Cissbury Ring N. N12 —5C 14
Cissbury Ring S. N12 —5C 14
Cissbury Rd. N15 —5D 32
Citadel Pl. SE11 —5K 85 (5G 173)
Citizen Rd. N7 —4A 50
City Bus. Cen. SE16 —3J 87
City Central Est. EC1 —3C 68 (2C 162)
(off Seward St.)
City Garden Row. N1 —2B 68 (1B 162)
City Harbour. E14 —3D 88
City Heights. SE1 —1E 86 (5H 169)
(off Weavers La.)
City Ho. Wall —1E 150
(off Corbet Clo.)
City of London. —6D 68 (7E 162)
City of London Almshouses. SW9 —4K 103
City of London Crematorium. E12 —3C 54
City Pavilion. EC1 —5B 68 (5A 162)
(off Britton St.)
City Rd. EC1 —2B 68 (1A 162)
City Tower. EC2 —5D 68 (6E 162)
(off Basinghall St.)
City Vw. Ct. SE22 —7G 105
Civic Way. B'side & Ilf —4G 37
Civic Way. Ruis —5B 42
Clabon M. SW1 —3D 84 (2E 170)
Clack La. Ruis —1E 40
Clack St. SE16 —2J 87
Clacton Rd. E13 —3B 72
Clacton Rd. E17 —6A 34
Clacton Rd. N17 —2F 33
Claigmar Gdns. N3 —1K 29
Claire Ct. N12 —4F 15
Claire Ct. NW2 —6G 47
Claire Ct. Bush —1C 10
Claire Gdns. Stan —5H 11
Claire Ho. Edgw —2J 27
(off Burnt Oak B'way.)
Claire Pl. E14 —3C 88
Clairvale Rd. Houn —1B 96
Clairview Rd. SW16 —5F 121
Clairville Gdns. W7 —1J 79
Clairville Point. SE23 —3K 123
(off Dacres Rd.)
Clamp Hill. Stan —4C 10
Clancarty Rd. SW6 —2J 101
Clandeboye Ho. E15 —1H 71
(off John St.)
Clandon Clo. W3 —2H 81
Clandon Clo. Eps —6B 148
Clandon Gdns. N3 —3J 29
Clandon Ho. SE1 —2B 86 (7B 168)
(off Webber St.)
Clandon Rd. Ilf —2J 55
Clandon St. SE8 —2C 106
Clandon Ter. SW20 —2F 137
Clanfield Way. SE15 —7E 86
Clanricarde Gdns. W2 —7J 65
Clapham. —4G 103
Clapham Common. (Junct.) —4H 103
Clapham Comn. N. Side. SW4 —4D 102
Clapham Comn. S. Side. SW4 —6F 103
Clapham Comn. W. Side. SW4 —4D 102
(in two parts)
Clapham Cres. SW4 —4H 103
Clapham High St. SW4 —4H 103
Clapham Junction. —3C 102
Clapham Junct. App. SW11 —3C 102
Clapham Mnr. Ct. SW4 —3G 103
Clapham Mnr. St. SW4 —3G 103
Clapham Park. —6H 103
Clapham Pk. Est. SW4 —6H 103
Clapham Pk. Rd. SW4 —4G 103
Clapham Pk. Ter. SW4 —5J 103
(off Kings Av.)
Clapham Rd. SW4 —3J 103
Clapham Rd. Est. SW4 —3J 103
Clap La. Dag —2H 57
Claps Ga. La. E6 —4E 72
Clapton Comn. E5 —7F 33
Clapton Park. —4K 51
Clapton Pk. Est. E5 —4K 51
Clapton Pas. E5 —5J 51
Clapton Sq. E5 —5J 51
Clapton Ter. N16 —1G 51
Clapton Way. E5 —4G 51
Clara Grant Ho. E14 —3C 88
Clara Nehab Ho. NW11 —5H 29
(off Leeside Cres.)
Clara Pl. SE18 —4E 90
Clare Clo. N2 —3A 30
Clare Corner. SE9 —7F 109
Clare Ct. WC1 —3J 67 (2F 161)
(off Judd St.)
Claredale Ho. E2 —2H 69
(off Claredale St.)

198 A-Z Big London

Claredale St.—Cloth Fair

Claredale St. E2 —2G 69
Clare Gdns. E7 —4J 53
Clare Gdns. W11 —6G 65
Clare Gdns. Bark —6K 55
Clare La. N1 —7C 50
Clare Lawn Av. SW14 —5J 99
Clare Mkt. WC2 —6K 67 (1H 167)
Clare M. SW6 —7K 83
Claremont. Shep —6D 130
Claremont Av. Harr —5E 26
Claremont Av. N Mald —5C 136
Claremont Av. Sun —1K 131
Claremont Clo. E16 —1E 90
Claremont Clo. N1 —2A 68 (1K 161)
Claremont Clo. SW2 —1J 121
Claremont Clo. Orp —4E 156
Claremont Gdns. Ilf —2J 55
Claremont Gdns. Surb —5E 134
Claremont Gro. W4 —7A 82
Claremont Gro. Wfd G —6F 21
Claremont Pk. N3 —1G 29
Claremont Rd. E7 —5K 53
Claremont Rd. E11 —3F 53
Claremont Rd. E17 —2A 34
Claremont Rd. N6 —7G 31
Claremont Rd. NW2 —7F 29
Claremont Rd. W9 —2G 65
Claremont Rd. W13 —5A 62
Claremont Rd. Brom —4C 144
Claremont Rd. Croy —1G 153
Claremont Rd. Harr —2J 25
Claremont Rd. Surb —5E 134
Claremont Rd. Tedd —5K 115
Claremont Rd. Twic —1D 98
Claremont Sq. N1 —2A 68 (1J 161)
Claremont St. E16 —2E 90
Claremont St. N18 —6B 18
Claremont St. SE10 —6D 88
Claremont Ter. Surb —7B 134
Claremont Way. NW2 —1E 46
(in two parts)
Claremont Way Ind. Est. NW2 —1E 46
Clarence Av. SW4 —7H 103
Clarence Av. Brom —4C 144
Clarence Av. Ilf —6E 36
Clarence Av. N Mald —2J 135
Clarence Clo. Barn —5G 5
Clarence Clo. Bus H —1E 10
Clarence Ct. NW7 —5F 13
Clarence Cres. SW4 —6H 103
Clarence Cres. Sidc —3B 128
Clarence Gdns. NW1 —3F 67 (2K 159)
Clarence Ga. Wfd G —6J 21
(in four parts)
Clarence Ga. Gdns. NW1 —4D 66
(off Glentworth St.)
Clarence House. —6B 166
Clarence La. SW15 —6A 100
Clarence M. E5 —5H 51
Clarence M. SE16 —1K 87
Clarence M. SW12 —7F 103
Clarence Pas. NW1 —2J 67
Clarence Pl. E5 —5H 51
Clarence Rd. E5 —4H 51
Clarence Rd. E12 —4B 54
Clarence Rd. E16 —4G 71
Clarence Rd. E17 —2K 33
Clarence Rd. N15 —5C 32
Clarence Rd. N22 —7D 16
Clarence Rd. NW6 —7H 47
Clarence Rd. SE9 —2C 126
Clarence Rd. SW19 —6K 119
Clarence Rd. W4 —5G 81
Clarence Rd. Bexh —4E 110
Clarence Rd. Brom —3B 144
Clarence Rd. Croy —7D 140
Clarence Rd. Enf —5D 8
Clarence Rd. Rich —1F 99
Clarence Rd. Sidc —3B 128
Clarence Rd. Sutt —5K 149
Clarence Rd. Tedd —6K 115
Clarence Rd. Wall —5F 151
Clarence St. King T —2D 134
(in three parts)
Clarence St. Rich —4E 98
Clarence St. S'hall —3B 78
Clarence Ter. NW1 —4D 66 (3F 159)
Clarence Ter. Houn —4F 97
Clarence Wlk. SW4 —2J 103
Clarence Way. NW1 —7F 49
Clarenden Pl. Dart —5K 129
Clarendon Clo. E9 —7J 51
Clarendon Clo. W2 —7C 66 (2C 164)
Clarendon Clo. Orp —3K 145
Clarendon Ct. NW2 —7E 46
Clarendon Ct. NW11 —4H 29
Clarendon Ct. Beck —1D 142
(off Albemarle Rd.)
Clarendon Ct. Houn —1J 95
Clarendon Ct. Rich —1F 99
Clarendon Cres. Twic —3H 115
Clarendon Cross. W11 —7G 65
Clarendon Dri. SW15 —4E 100
Clarendon Flats. W1 —6E 66 (1H 165)
(off Balderton St.)
Clarendon Gdns. NW4 —3C 28
Clarendon Gdns. W9 —4A 66
Clarendon Gdns. Ilf —7D 36
Clarendon Gdns. Wemb —3D 44
Clarendon Grn. Orp —4K 145
Clarendon Gro. NW1 —3H 67 (1C 160)
Clarendon Gro. Mitc —3D 138
Clarendon Ho. NW1 —2G 67
(off Werrington St.)
Clarendon M. W2 —7C 66 (2C 164)
Clarendon M. Bex —1H 129
Clarendon Path. Orp —4K 145
(in two parts)
Clarendon Pl. W2 —7C 66 (2C 164)
Clarendon Ri. SE13 —4E 106
Clarendon Rd. E11 —1F 53
Clarendon Rd. E17 —6D 34
Clarendon Rd. E18 —3J 35
Clarendon Rd. N8 —3K 31
Clarendon Rd. N15 —4C 32
Clarendon Rd. N18 —6B 18
Clarendon Rd. N22 —2K 31
Clarendon Rd. SW19 —7C 120
Clarendon Rd. W5 —4E 62
Clarendon Rd. W11 —7G 65
Clarendon Rd. Ashf —4B 112
Clarendon Rd. Croy —2B 152
Clarendon Rd. Harr —6J 25
Clarendon Rd. Hay —2H 77
Clarendon Rd. Wall —6G 151
Clarendon St. SW1 —5F 85 (5K 171)
Clarendon Ter. W9 —4A 66 (3A 158)
Clarendon Wlk. W11 —6G 65
Clarendon Way. N21 —6H 7
Clarendon Way. Chst & St M —3K 145
Clarens St. SE6 —2B 124
Clare Pl. SW15 —7B 100
Clare Rd. E11 —6F 35
Clare Rd. NW10 —7C 46
Clare Rd. SE14 —1B 106
Clare Rd. Gnfd —6H 43
Clare Rd. Houn —3D 96
Clare Rd. Stai & Stanw —1A 112
Clare St. E2 —2H 69
Claret Gdns. SE25 —3E 140
Clareville Gro. SW7 —4A 84 (4A 170)
Clareville Gro. M. SW7 —4A 170
Clareville St. SW7 —4A 84
Clare Way. Bexh —1E 110
Clarewood Ct. W1 —5D 66 (6E 158)
(off Seymour Pl.)
Clarewood Wlk. SW9 —4A 104
Clarges M. W1 —1F 85 (4J 165)
Clarges St. W1 —1F 85 (4K 165)
Claribel Rd. SW9 —2B 104
Clarice Way. Wall —7J 151
Claridge Ct. SW6 —2H 101
Claridge Rd. Dag —1D 56
Clarion Ho. SW1 —5G 85 (5B 172)
(off Moreton Pl.)
Clarion Ho. W1 —6H 67 (1C 166)
(off St Anne's Ct.)
Clarissa Ho. E14 —6D 70
Clarissa Rd. Romf —7D 38
Clarissa St. E8 —1F 69
Clark Ct. NW10 —7J 45
Clarke Mans. Bark —7K 55
(off Upney La.)
Clarke Path. N16 —1G 51
Clarkes Av. Wor Pk —1F 149
Clarkes Dri. Uxb —5A 58
Clarke's M. W1 —5E 66 (5H 159)
Clarks Mead. Bush —1B 10
Clarkson Rd. E16 —6H 71
Clarkson Row. NW1 —2G 67
(off Mornington Ter.)
Clarksons, The. Bark —2G 73
Clarkson St. E2 —3H 69
Clark's Pl. EC2 —6E 68 (7G 163)
Clarks Rd. Ilf —2H 55
Clark St. E1 —5H 69
Clark Way. Houn —7B 78
Classon Clo. W Dray —2A 76
Claude Rd. E10 —2E 52
Claude Rd. E13 —1K 71
Claude Rd. SE15 —2H 105
Claude St. E14 —4C 88
Claudia Jones Ho. N17 —1C 32
Claudia Jones Way. SW2 —6J 103
Claudia Pl. SW19 —1G 119
Claughton Rd. E13 —2A 72
Clauson Av. N'holt —5F 43
Clavell St. SE10 —6E 88
Claverdale Rd. SW2 —7K 103
Clavering Av. SW13 —6D 82
Clavering Clo. Twic —4A 116
Clavering Ho. SE13 —4F 107
(off Blessington Rd.)
Clavering Ind. Est. N9 —2D 18
(off Montagu Rd.)
Clavering Rd. E12 —1B 54
Claverley Gro. N3 —1K 29
Claverley Vs. N3 —7E 14
Claverton St. SW1 —5G 85 (6B 172)
Clave St. E1 —1J 87
Claxton Gro. W6 —5F 83
Claxton Path. SE4 —4K 105
(off Coston Wlk.)
Clay Av. Mitc —2F 139
Claybank Gro. SE13 —3D 106
Claybourne M. SE19 —7E 122
Claybridge Rd. SE12 —4A 126
Claybrook Clo. N2 —3B 30
Claybrook Rd. W6 —6F 83
Claybury. Bush —1A 10
Claybury B'way. Ilf —3C 36
Claybury Rd. Wfd G —7H 21
Clay Ct. E17 —3F 35
Claydon. SE17 —4C 86
(off Deacon Way)
Claydon Dri. Croy —4J 151
Claydon Ho. NW4 —2F 29
(off Holders Hill Rd.)
Claydon Ho. SE28 —6D 74
(off St Georges Clo.)
Claydown M. SE18 —5E 90
Clay Farm Rd. SE9 —2G 127
Claygate Cres. New Ad —6E 154
Claygate La. Esh —2A 146
(in two parts)
Claygate La. Th Dit —1A 146
Claygate Rd. W13 —3B 80
Clayhall. —2D 36
Clayhall Av. Ilf —3C 36
Clay Hill. Enf —1K 7
Clayhill. Surb —5G 135
Clayhill Cres. SE9 —4B 126
Claylands Pl. SW8 —7A 86
Claylands Rd. SW8 —6K 85 (7H 173)
Clay La. Bus H —1D 10
Clay La. Edgw —2B 12
Clay La. Stanw —7B 94
Claymore Clo. Mord —7J 137
Claypole Ct. E17 —5C 34
(off Yunus Khan Clo.)
Claypole Dri. Houn —1C 96
Claypole Rd. E15 —2E 70
Clayponds Av. W5 & Bren —4D 80
Clayponds Gdns. W5 —4D 80
(in two parts)
Clayponds La. Bren —5E 80
Clays La. E15 —5D 52
Clays La. Clo. E15 —5D 52
Clay St. W1 —5D 66 (6F 159)
Clayton Av. Wemb —7E 44
Clayton Clo. E6 —6D 72
Clayton Ct. E17 —2A 34
Clayton Cres. Bren —5D 80
Clayton Fld. NW9 —7F 13
Clayton M. SE10 —1F 107
Clayton Rd. SE15 —1G 105
Clayton Rd. Chess —4C 146
Clayton Rd. Hay —2G 77
Clayton Rd. Iswth —3J 97
Clayton Rd. Romf —1J 57
Clayton St. SE11 —6A 86 (7J 173)
Clayton Ter. Hay —5C 60
Claywood Clo. Orp —7J 145
Clayworth Clo. Sidc —6B 110
Cleanthus Clo. SE18 —1F 109
Cleanthus Rd. SE18 —2F 109
(in two parts)
Clearbrook Way. E1 —6J 69
Clearwater Pl. Surb —6C 134
Clearwater Ter. W11 —2G 83
(off Lorne Gdns.)
Clearwell Dri. W9 —4K 65
Cleave Av. Hay —4G 77
Cleaveland Rd. Surb —5D 134
Cleaverholme Clo. SE25 —6H 141
Cleaver Ho. NW3 —7D 48
Cleaver Sq. SE11 —5A 86 (6K 173)
Cleaver St. SE11 —5A 86 (5K 173)
Cleeve Ct. Felt —1G 113
Cleeve Hill. SE23 —1H 123
Cleeve Pk. Gdns. Sidc —2B 128
Cleeve Way. SW15 —7B 100
Cleeve Workshops. E2 —3E 68 (2H 163)
(off Boundary St.)
Clegg Ho. SE3 —4K 107
Clegg St. E1 —1H 87
Clegg St. E13 —2J 71
Clematis Gdns. Wfd G —5D 20
Clematis St. W12 —7C 64
Clem Attlee Ct. SW6 —6H 83
Clem Attlee Pde. SW6 —6H 83
(off N. End Rd.)
Clemence Rd. Dag —1J 75
Clemence St. E14 —5B 70
Clement Av. SW4 —4H 103
Clement Clo. NW6 —7E 46
Clement Clo. W4 —4K 81
Clement Gdns. Hay —4G 77
Clementhorpe Rd. Dag —6C 56
Clement Ho. SE8 —4A 88
Clementina Rd. E10 —1B 52
Clementine Clo. W13 —2B 80
Clement Rd. SW19 —5G 119
Clement Rd. Beck —2K 141
Clement's Av. E16 —7J 71
Clements Ct. Houn —4B 96
Clements Ct. Ilf —3F 55
Clement's Inn. WC2 —6K 67 (1H 167)
Clement's Inn Pas. WC2 —1H 167
Clements La. EC4 —7D 68 (2F 169)
Clements La. Ilf —3F 55
Clements Pl. Bren —5D 80
Clements Rd. E6 —7C 54
Clement's Rd. SE16 —3G 87
Clements Rd. Ilf —3F 55
Clemson Ho. E8 —1F 69
(off Queensbridge Rd.)
Clendon Way. SE18 —4G 91
Clennam St. SE1 —2C 86 (6D 168)
Clensham Ct. Sutt —2J 149
Clensham La. Sutt —2J 149
Clenston M. W1 —6D 66 (7E 158)
Cleopatra's Needle. —7K 67 (3G 167)
Clephane Rd. N1 —6C 50
Clephane Rd. N. N1 —6C 50
Clere Pl. EC2 —4D 68 (3F 163)
Clere St. EC2 —4D 68 (3F 163)
Clerics Wlk. Shep —7F 131
Clerkenwell. —4A 68 (4A 162)
Clerkenwell Clo. EC1 —4A 68 (3K 161)
(in two parts)
Clerkenwell Grn. EC1 —4A 68 (4K 161)
Clerkenwell Rd. EC1 —4A 68 (4J 161)
Clermont Rd. E9 —1J 69
Clevedon Ct. S Croy —5E 152
Clevedon Clo. N16 —3F 51
Clevedon Gdns. Hay —3F 77
Clevedon Gdns. Houn —1K 95
Clevedon Mans. NW5 —4E 48
Clevedon Pas. N16 —2F 51
Clevedon Rd. SE20 —1K 141
Clevedon Rd. King T —2G 135
Clevedon Rd. Twic —6D 98
(in two parts)
Cleve Ho. NW6 —7K 47
Cleveland Av. SW20 —2H 137
Cleveland Av. W4 —4B 82
Cleveland Av. Hamp —7D 114
Cleveland Ct. W13 —5B 62
Cleveland Gdns. N4 —5C 32
Cleveland Gdns. NW2 —2F 47
Cleveland Gdns. SW13 —2B 100
Cleveland Gdns. W2 —6A 66
Cleveland Gdns. Wor Pk —2A 148
Cleveland Gro. E1 —4J 69
Cleveland Ho. N2 —2B 30
(off Grange, The)
Cleveland La. N9 —7C 8
Cleveland Mans. SW9 —7A 86
(off Mowll St.)
Cleveland Mans. W9 —4J 65
Cleveland M. W1 —5G 67 (5A 160)
Cleveland Pk. Stai —6A 94
Cleveland Pk. Av. E17 —4C 34
Cleveland Pk. Cres. E17 —4C 34
Cleveland Pl. SW1 —1G 85 (4B 166)
Cleveland Ri. Mord —7F 137
Cleveland Rd. E18 —3J 35
Cleveland Rd. N1 —7D 50
Cleveland Rd. SW13 —2B 100
Cleveland Rd. W4 —3J 81
Cleveland Rd. W13 —5A 62
Cleveland Rd. Ilf —3F 55
Cleveland Rd. Iswth —4A 98
Cleveland Rd. N Mald —4A 136
Cleveland Rd. Well —2K 109
Cleveland Rd. Wor Pk —2A 148
Cleveland Row. SW1 —1G 85 (5A 166)
Cleveland Sq. W2 —6A 66
Clevelands, The. Bark —6G 55
Cleveland St. W1 —4F 67 (4K 159)
Cleveland Ter. W2 —6A 66
Cleveland Way. E1 —4J 69
Cleveley Clo. SE7 —4B 90
Cleveley Cres. W5 —2E 62
Cleveleys Rd. E5 —3H 51
Cleverly Est. W12 —1C 82
Cleve Rd. NW6 —7K 47
Cleve Rd. Sidc —3D 128
Cleves Av. Eps —7D 148
Cleves Rd. E6 —1B 72
Cleves Rd. Rich —3C 116
Cleves Wlk. Ilf —1G 37
Cleves Way. Hamp —7D 114
Cleves Way. Ruis —1B 42
Cleves Way. Sun —6H 113
Clewer Ct. E10 —1C 52
(off Leyton Grange Est.)
Clewer Cres. Harr —1H 25
Clewer Ho. SE2 —2D 92
(off Wolvercote Rd.)
Cley Ho. SE4 —4K 105
Clichy Est. E1 —5J 69
Clifden Rd. E5 —5J 51
Clifden Rd. Bren —6D 80
Clifden Rd. Twic —1K 115
Cliffe Rd. S Croy —5D 152
Cliffe Wlk. Sutt —5A 150
(off Greyhound Rd.)
Clifford Av. SW14 —3H 99
(in two parts)
Clifford Av. Chst —6D 126
Clifford Av. Ilf —1F 37
Clifford Av. Wall —4G 151
Clifford Clo. N'holt —1C 60
Clifford Ct. W2 —5K 65
(off Westbourne Pk. Vs.)
Clifford Dri. SW9 —4B 104
Clifford Gdns. NW10 —2E 64
Clifford Gdns. Hay —4G 77
Clifford Gro. Ashf —4C 112
Clifford Haigh Ho. SW6 —7F 83
Clifford Ho. W14 —4H 83
(off Edith Vs.)
Clifford Rd. E16 —4H 71
Clifford Rd. E17 —2E 34
Clifford Rd. N1 —1E 68
Clifford Rd. N9 —6D 8
Clifford Rd. SE25 —4G 141
Clifford Rd. Barn —3E 4
Clifford Rd. Houn —3B 96
Clifford Rd. Rich —2D 116
Clifford Rd. Wemb —7D 44
Clifford's Inn Pas. WC2 —6A 68 (1J 167)
Clifford St. W1 —7G 67 (3A 166)
Clifford Way. NW10 —4B 46
Cliff Rd. NW1 —6H 49
Cliffsend Ho. SW9 —1A 104
(off Cowley Rd.)
Cliff Ter. SE8 —2C 106
Cliffview Rd. SE13 —3C 106
Cliff Vs. NW1 —6H 49
Cliff Wlk. E16 —5H 71
(in two parts)
Clifton Av. E17 —3K 33
Clifton Av. N3 —1H 29
Clifton Av. W12 —1B 82
Clifton Av. Felt —3A 114
Clifton Av. Stan —2B 26
Clifton Av. Wemb —6F 45
Clifton Ct. N4 —2A 50
Clifton Ct. NW8 —3A 158
Clifton Ct. SE15 —7H 87
Clifton Ct. Beck —1D 142
Clifton Ct. Stanw —6A 94
Clifton Ct. Wfd G —6D 20
Clifton Cres. SE15 —7H 87
Clifton Est. SE15 —1H 105
Clifton Gdns. N15 —6F 33
Clifton Gdns. NW11 —6H 29
Clifton Gdns. W4 —4K 81
(in two parts)
Clifton Gdns. W9 —4A 66
Clifton Gdns. Enf —4D 6
Clifton Gdns. Uxb —2D 58
Clifton Gro. E8 —6G 51
Clifton Hill. NW6 —2K 65
Clifton Ho. E2 —4F 69 (3J 163)
(off Club Row)
Clifton Ho. E11 —2G 53
Clifton Pde. Felt —4A 114
Clifton Pk. Av. SW20 —2E 136
Clifton Pl. SE16 —2J 87
Clifton Pl. W2 —6B 66 (1B 164)
Clifton Ri. SE14 —7A 88
(in two parts)
Clifton Rd. E7 —6B 54
Clifton Rd. E16 —5G 71
Clifton Rd. N3 —1A 30
Clifton Rd. N8 —6H 31
Clifton Rd. N22 —1G 31
Clifton Rd. NW10 —2C 64
Clifton Rd. SE25 —4E 140
Clifton Rd. SW19 —6F 119
Clifton Rd. W9 —4A 66 (3A 158)
Clifton Rd. Gnfd —4G 61
Clifton Rd. Harr —4F 27
Clifton Rd. Ilf —6H 37
Clifton Rd. Iswth —2J 97
Clifton Rd. King T —7F 117
Clifton Rd. Sidc —4J 127
Clifton Rd. S'hall —4C 78
Clifton Rd. Tedd —4J 115
Clifton Rd. Wall —5F 151
Clifton Rd. Well —3C 110
Clifton St. EC2 —5E 68 (5G 163)
Clifton Ter. N4 —2A 50
Clifton Vs. W9 —5A 66
Cliftonville Ct. SE12 —1J 125
Clifton Wlk. W6 —4D 82
(off King St.)
Clifton Way. SE15 —7H 87
Clifton Way. H'row A —3D 94
Clifton Way. Wemb —1E 62
Climsland Ho. SE1 —1A 86 (4K 167)
Clinch Ct. E16 —5J 71
(off Plymouth Rd.)
Cline Rd. N11 —6B 16
Clinger Ct. N1 —1E 68
Clink Exhibition, The. —4E 168
Clink St. SE1 —1D 86 (4E 168)
Clink Wharf. SE1 —1D 86 (4E 168)
(off Clink St.)
Clinton Av. E Mol —4G 133
Clinton Av. Well —4A 110
Clinton Ho. SE8 —6C 88
Clinton Rd. E3 —3A 70
Clinton Rd. E7 —4J 53
Clinton Rd. N15 —4D 32
Clipper Clo. SE16 —2K 87
Clipper Ho. E14 —5E 88
Clipper Way. SE13 —4E 106
Clippesby Clo. Chess —6F 147
Clipstone M. W1 —5G 67 (5A 160)
Clipstone Rd. Houn —3E 96
Clipstone St. W1 —5F 67 (5K 159)
Clissold Clo. N2 —3D 30
Clissold Ct. N4 —2C 50
Clissold Cres. N16 —3D 50
Clissold Rd. N16 —3D 50
Clitheroe Av. Harr —1E 42
Clitheroe Rd. SW9 —2J 103
Clitherow Av. W7 —3A 80
Clitherow Ct. Bren —5C 80
Clitherow Pas. Bren —5C 80
Clitherow Rd. Bren —5B 80
Clitterhouse Cres. NW2 —1E 46
Clitterhouse Rd. NW2 —1E 46
Clive Av. N18 —6B 18
Clive Ct. W9 —4A 66
(off Maida Va.)
Cliveden Clo. N12 —4F 15
Cliveden Pl. SW1 —4E 84 (3G 171)
Cliveden Pl. Shep —6E 130
Cliveden Rd. SW19 —1H 137
Clivedon Ct. W13 —5B 62
Clivedon Rd. E4 —5B 20
Clive Lloyd Ho. N15 —5C 32
(off Woodlands Pk. Rd.)
Clive Lodge. NW4 —6F 29
Clive Pas. SE21 —3D 122
Clive Rd. SE21 —3D 122
Clive Rd. SW19 —6C 120
Clive Rd. Belv —4G 93
Clive Rd. Enf —4B 8
Clive Rd. Felt —6J 95
Clive Rd. Twic —4K 115
Clivesdale Dri. Hay —1K 77
Clive Way. Enf —4B 8
Cloak La. EC4 —7C 68 (2D 168)
Clochar Ct. NW10 —1B 64
Clock Ho. E3 —3E 70
Clock Ho. E17 —4F 35
(off Wood St.)
Clockhouse Av. Bark —1G 73
Clockhouse Clo. SW19 —2E 118
Clockhouse Ct. Beck —2A 142
Clockhouse La. Ashf & Felt —4C 112
Clockhouse La. Romf —1H 39
Clock House Pde. E11 —5K 35
Clockhouse Pde. N13 —5F 17
Clockhouse Pl. SW15 —6G 101
Clock Ho. Rd. Beck —3A 142
Clockhouse Roundabout. (Junct.) —1D 112
Clock Pde. Enf —5J 7
Clock Pl. SE11 —4B 86
(off Newington Butts)
Clock Tower Ind. Est. Iswth —3K 97
Clock Tower M. N1 —1C 68
Clock Tower M. SE28 —7B 74
Clock Tower Pl. N7 —6J 49
Clock Tower Rd. Iswth —3K 97
Cloister Clo. Tedd —5B 116
Cloister Gdns. SE25 —6H 141
Cloister Gdns. Edgw —5D 12
Cloister Rd. NW2 —3H 47
Cloister Rd. W3 —5J 63
Cloisters Av. Brom —5D 144
Cloisters Bus. Cen. SW8 —7F 85
(off Battersea Pk. Rd.)
Cloisters Ct. Bexh —3H 111
Cloisters Mall. King T —2E 134
Cloisters, The. E1 —4J 163
Cloisters, The. SW9 —1A 104
Clonard Way. Pinn —6A 10
Clonbrock Rd. N16 —4E 50
Cloncurry St. SW6 —2F 101
Clonmel Clo. Harr —2H 43
Clonmell Rd. N17 —3D 32
Clonmel Rd. SW6 —7H 83
Clonmel Rd. Tedd —4H 115
Clonmore St. SW18 —1H 119
Clorane Gdns. NW3 —3J 47
Close, The. E4 —7K 19
Close, The. N10 —2F 31
Close, The. N14 —2C 16
Close, The. N20 —2C 14
Close, The. SE3 —2F 107
Close, The. SE25 —6G 141
Close, The. Beck —4A 142
Close, The. Bex —6G 111
Close, The. Cars —7C 150
Close, The. E Barn —6J 5
Close, The. Eastc —7A 24
Close, The. Harr —2G 25
Close, The. Ilf —6J 37
Close, The. Iswth —2H 97
Close, The. Mitc —4D 138
Close, The. N Mald —2J 135
Close, The. Orp —6J 145
Close, The. Pinn —7D 24
Close, The. Rich —3H 99
Close, The. Romf —6E 38
Close, The. Sidc —4B 128
Close, The. Surb —6E 134
Close, The. Sutt —7H 137
Close, The. Uxb —1C 58
Close, The. Wemb —6E 44
(HA0)
Close, The. Wemb —3J 45
(HA9)
Cloth Ct. EC1 —6B 162
Cloth Fair. EC1 —5B 68 (6B 162)

Clothier St.—Combside

Clothier St. E1 —6E 68 (7H 163)
Cloth St. EC1 —5C 68 (5C 162)
Clothworkers Rd. SE18 —7H 91
Cloudesdale Rd. SW17 —2F 121
Cloudesley Pl. N1 —1A 68
Cloudesley Rd. N1 —1A 68
(in two parts)
Cloudesley Rd. Bexh —1F 111
Cloudesley Sq. N1 —1A 68
Cloudesley St. N1 —1A 68
Clouston Clo. Wall —5J 151
Clova Rd. E7 —6H 53
Clove Cres. E14 —7F 71
Clove Hitch Quay. SW11 —3A 102
Clovelly Av. NW9 —4B 28
Clovelly Av. Uxb —4E 40
Clovelly Clo. Pinn —3K 23
Clovelly Clo. Uxb —4E 40
Clovelly Gdns. SE19 —1F 141
Clovelly Gdns. Enf —7K 7
Clovelly Gdns. Romf —1H 39
Clovelly Ho. W2 —6A 66
(off Hallfield Est.)
Clovelly Rd. N8 —4H 31
Clovelly Rd. W4 —2K 81
Clovelly Rd. W5 —2C 80
Clovelly Rd. Bexh —6E 92
Clovelly Rd. Houn —2E 96
Clovelly Way. E1 —6J 69
Clovelly Way. Orp —6K 145
Clovelly Way. S Harr —2D 42
Clover Clo. E11 —2F 53
Cloverdale Gdns. Sidc —6K 109
Clover M. SW3 —6D 84 (7F 171)
Clover Way. Wall —1E 150
Clove St. E13 —4J 71
Clowders Rd. SE6 —3B 124
Clowser Clo. Sutt —5A 150
Cloysters Grn. E1 —1G 87
Cloyster Wood. Edgw —7J 11
Club Gdns. Rd. Hayes —7J 143
Club Row. E2 & E1 —4F 69 (3J 163)
Clumps, The. Ashf —4F 113
Clunbury Av. S'hall —5D 78
Clunbury St. N1 —2D 68
Cluny Est. SE1 —3E 86 (7G 169)
Cluny M. SW5 —4J 83
Cluny Pl. SE1 —3E 86 (7G 169)
Cluse Ct. N1 —2C 68
(off St Peters St., in two parts)
Clutton St. E14 —5D 70
Clydach Rd. Enf —4A 8
Clyde Cir. N15 —4E 32
Clyde Ct. NW1 —2H 67
(off Hampden Clo.)
Clyde Flats. SW6 —7H 83
(off Rhylston Rd.)
Clyde Ho. King T —1D 134
Clyde Pl. E10 —7D 34
Clyde Rd. N15 —4E 32
Clyde Rd. N22 —1H 31
Clyde Rd. Croy —2F 153
Clyde Rd. Stai & Stanw —1A 112
Clyde Rd. Sutt —5J 149
Clyde Rd. Wall —6G 151
Clydesdale. Enf —4E 8
Clydesdale Av. Stan —3D 26
Clydesdale Clo. Iswth —3K 97
Clydesdale Ct. N20 —1G 15
Clydesdale Gdns. Rich —4H 99
Clydesdale Ho. W11 —6H 65
(off Clydesdale Rd.)
Clydesdale Ho. Eri —2E 92
(off Kale Rd.)
Clydesdale Rd. W11 —6H 65
Clyde St. SE8 —6B 88
Clyde Ter. SE23 —2J 123
Clyde Va. SE23 —2J 123
Clyde Way. Romf —1K 39
Clyde Wharf. E16 —1J 89
Clydon Clo. Eri —6K 93
Clyfford Rd. Ruis —4H 41
Clymping Dene. Felt —7K 95
Clynes Ho. Dag —3G 57
(off Uvedale Rd.)
Clyston St. SW8 —2G 103
Coach & Horses Yd. W1 —7G 67 (2K 165)
Coach Ho. La. N5 —4B 50
Coach Ho. La. SW19 —4F 119
Coach Ho. M. SE1 —2E 86 (7G 169)
Coach Ho. M. SE20 —7H 123
Coach Ho. M. SE23 —6K 105
Coach Ho. Yd. NW3 —4A 48
(off Hampstead High St.)
Coach Ho. Yd. SW18 —4K 101
Coach Yd. M. N19 —1J 49
Coaldale Wlk. SE21 —7C 104
Coalecroft Rd. SW15 —4E 100
Coalport Ho. SE11 —2J 173
Coates Av. SW18 —6C 102
Coates Hill Rd. Brom —2E 144
Coate St. E2 —2G 69
Coates Wlk. Bren —6E 80
Cobalt Sq. SW8 —7G 173
Cobbett Rd. SE9 —3C 108
Cobbett Rd. Twic —1E 114
Cobbetts Av. Ilf —5B 36
Cobbett St. SW8 —7K 85
Cobble La. N1 —7B 50
Cobble M. N4 —3C 50
Cobblers Wlk. Hamp & Tedd —1G 133
(in two parts)
Cobblestone Pl. Croy —1C 152
Cobbold Ct. SW1 —4H 85 (3C 172)
(off Elverton St.)
Cobbold Ind. Est. NW10 —6B 46
Cobbold M. W12 —2B 82
Cobbold Rd. E11 —3H 53
Cobbold Rd. NW10 —6B 46
Cobbold Rd. W12 —2A 82
Cobb's Ct. EC4 —1B 168
Cobb's Rd. Houn —4D 96
Cobb St. E1 —5F 69 (6J 163)
Cobden Ct. Brom —4A 144
Cobden Ho. E2 —3G 69
(off Nelson Gdns.)
Cobden Ho. NW1 —2G 67
(off Arlington Rd.)
Cobden M. SE26 —5H 123
Cobden Rd. E11 —3G 53
Cobden Rd. SE25 —5G 141
Cobham Av. N Mald —5C 136
Cobham Clo. SW11 —6C 102
Cobham Clo. Brom —7C 144
Cobham Clo. Edgw —2H 27
Cobham Clo. Enf —3B 8
Cobham Clo. Sidc —6B 110
Cobham Clo. Wall —6J 151
Cobham Ct. Mitc —2B 138
Cobham Ho. Bark —1G 73
(in two parts)
Cobham M. NW1 —7H 49
Cobham Pl. Bexh —5D 110
Cobham Rd. E17 —1E 34
Cobham Rd. N22 —3B 32
Cobham Rd. Houn —7A 78
Cobham Rd. Ilf —2J 55
Cobham Rd. King T —2G 135
Cobland Rd. SE12 —4A 126
Coborn Rd. E3 —2B 70
Coborn St. E3 —3B 70
Cobourg Rd. SE5 —6F 87
Cobourg St. NW1 —3G 67 (2B 160)
Coburg Clo. SW1 —3B 172
Coburg Cres. SW2 —1K 121
Coburg Gdns. Ilf —2B 36
Coburg Rd. N22 —2K 31
Cochrane Clo. NW8 —1B 158
Cochrane Ct. E10 —1C 52
(off Leyton Grange Est.)
Cochrane Ho. E14 —2C 88
(off Admirals Way)
Cochrane M. NW8 —2B 66
Cochrane Rd. SW19 —7G 119
Cochrane St. NW8 —2B 66 (1B 158)
Cockayne Way. SE8 —4A 88
Cockburn Ho. SW1 —5H 85 (6D 172)
(off Aylesford St.)
Cockcrow Hill. —1D 146
Cockerell Rd. E17 —7A 34
Cockfosters. —4J 5
Cockfosters Pde. Barn —4K 5
Cock Hill. E1 —5E 68 (6H 163)
Cock La. EC1 —5B 68 (6A 162)
Cockpit Steps. SW1 —7C 166
Cockpit Yd. WC1 —5K 67 (5H 161)
Cocks Cres. N Mald —4B 136
Cockspur Ct. SW1 —1H 85 (4D 166)
Cockspur St. SW1 —1H 85 (4D 166)
Cocksure La. Sidc —3G 129
Coda Cen., The. SW6 —7G 83
Code St. E1 —4F 69 (4K 163)
Codicote Ter. N4 —2C 50
Codling Clo. E1 —1G 87
Codling Way. Wemb —4D 44
Codrington Ct. E1 —4H 69
Codrington Ct. SE16 —7A 70
Codrington Hill. SE23 —7A 106
Codrington M. W11 —6G 65
Cody Clo. Harr —3D 26
Cody Clo. Wall —7H 151
Cody Rd. E16 —4F 71
Coe Av. SE25 —6G 141
Coe's All. Barn —4B 4
Cofers Circ. Wemb —2H 45
Coffey St. SE8 —7C 88
Cogan Av. E17 —1A 34
Coin St. SE1 —1A 86 (4J 167)
(in two parts)
Coity Rd. NW5 —6E 48
Cokers La. SE21 —1D 122
Coke St. E1 —6G 69
Colas M. NW6 —1J 65
Colbeck M. SW5 —4K 83
Colbeck Rd. Harr —7G 25
Colberg Pl. N16 —7F 33
Colborne Ho. E14 —7C 70
Colborne Way. Wor Pk —3E 148
Colbrook Av. Hay —3F 77
Colbrook Clo. Hay —3F 77
Colburn Way. Sutt —3B 150
Colby M. SE19 —5E 122
Colby Rd. SE19 —5E 122
Colby Rd. W on T —7J 131
Colchester Av. E12 —4D 54
Colchester Dri. Pinn —5B 24
Colchester Rd. E10 —7E 34
Colchester Rd. E17 —6C 34
Colchester Rd. Edgw —7D 12
Colchester Rd. N'wd —2J 23
Colchester St. E1 —6F 69 (7K 163)
Coldbath Sq. EC1 —4A 68 (3J 161)
Coldbath St. SE13 —1D 106
(in two parts)
Coldblow. —1J 129
Cold Blow Cres. Bex —1K 129
Cold Blow La. SE14 —7K 87
(in two parts)
Cold Blows. Mitc —3D 138
Coldershaw Rd. W13 —1A 80
Coldfall Av. N10 —2E 30
Coldham Ct. N22 —1B 32
Coldharbour. E14 —2E 88
Coldharbour Crest. SE9 —3E 126
Coldharbour La. SW9 & SE5 —4A 104
Coldharbour La. Hay —1J 77
Coldharbour Pl. SE5 —2C 104
Coldharbour Rd. Croy —5A 152
Coldharbour Way. Croy —5A 152
Coldstream Gdns. SW18 —6H 101
Colebeck M. N1 —6B 50
Colebert Av. E1 —4J 69
Colebrook Clo. SW15 —7F 101
Colebrook Ct. SW3 —4C 84 (4D 170)
(off Makins St.)
Colebrooke Av. W13 —6B 62
Colebrooke Ct. Sidc —4B 128
(off Granville Rd.)
Colebrooke Dri. E11 —7A 36
Colebrooke Pl. N1 —1B 68
Colebrooke Ri. Brom —2G 143
Colebrooke Row. EC1 —2B 68
Colebrook Ho. E14 —6D 70
Colebrook Rd. SW16 —1J 139
Colebrook Way. N11 —5A 16
Coleby Path. SE5 —7D 86
Colechurch Ho. SE1 —5G 87
(off Avondale Sq.)
Cole Clo. SE28 —1B 92
Cole Ct. Twic —7A 98
Coledale Dri. Stan —1C 26
Coleford Rd. SW18 —5A 102
Cole Gdns. Houn —7J 77
Colegrave Rd. E15 —5F 53
Colegrove Rd. SE15 —6F 87
Coleherne Ct. SW5 —5K 83
Coleherne Mans. SW5 —5K 83
(off Old Brompton Rd.)
Coleherne M. SW10 —5K 83
Coleherne Rd. SW10 —5K 83
Colehill Gdns. SW6 —2G 101
Colehill La. SW6 —1G 101
Cole Ho. SE1 —2A 86 (7J 167)
(off Baylis Rd.)
Coleman Clo. SE25 —2G 141
Coleman Fields. N1 —1C 68
Coleman Mans. N8 —7J 31
Coleman Rd. SE5 —7E 86
Coleman Rd. Belv —4G 93
Coleman Rd. Dag —6E 56
Colemans Heath. SE9 —3E 126
Coleman St. EC2 —6D 68 (7E 162)
Coleman St. Bldgs. EC2 —7E 162
Colenso Dri. NW7 —7H 13
Colenso Rd. E5 —4J 51
Colenso Rd. Ilf —1J 55
Cole Park. —6A 98
Cole Pk. Gdns. Twic —5A 98
Cole Pk. Rd. Twic —6A 98
Cole Pk. Vw. Twic —6A 98
Colepits Wood Rd. SE9 —5G 109
Coleraine Rd. N8 —3A 32
Coleraine Rd. SE3 —6H 89
Coleridge Av. E12 —6C 54
Coleridge Av. Sutt —4C 150
Coleridge Clo. SW8 —2F 103
Coleridge Ct. W14 —3F 83
(off Blythe Rd.)
Coleridge Ct. New Bar —5E 4
(off Station Rd.)
Coleridge Gdns. NW6 —7A 48
Coleridge Ho. SE17 —5C 86
(off Browning St.)
Coleridge Ho. SW1 —5G 85 (6B 172)
(off Churchill Gdns.)
Coleridge La. N8 —6J 31
Coleridge Rd. E17 —4B 34
Coleridge Rd. N4 —2A 50
Coleridge Rd. N8 —6H 31
Coleridge Rd. N12 —5F 15
Coleridge Rd. Ashf —4A 112
Coleridge Rd. Croy —7J 141
Coleridge Sq. W13 —6A 62
Coleridge Wlk. NW11 —4J 29
Coleridge Way. Hay —6J 59
Coleridge Way. W Dray —4A 76
Cole Rd. Twic —6A 98
Colesburg Rd. Beck —3B 142
Coles Cres. Harr —2F 43
Coles Grn. Bus H —1B 10
Coles Grn. Ct. NW2 —2C 46
Coles Grn. Rd. NW2 —1C 46
Coleshill Flats. SW1 —4H 171
Coleshill Rd. Tedd —6J 115
Colestown St. SW11 —2C 102
Cole St. SE1 —2C 86 (7D 168)
Colesworth Ho. Edgw —2J 27
(off Burnt Oak B'way.)
Colet Clo. N13 —6G 17
Colet Gdns. W14 —4F 83
Colet Ho. SE17 —5B 86
(off Doddington Gro.)
Coley St. WC1 —4K 67 (4H 161)
Colfe & Hatcliffe Glebe. SE13 —5E 106
(off Lewisham High St.)
Colfe Rd. SE23 —1A 124
Colham Av. W Dray —1A 76
Colham Green. —5C 58
Colham Grn. Rd. Uxb —5C 58
Colham Mill Rd. W Dray —2A 76
Colham Rd. Uxb —4B 58
Colham Roundabout. Uxb —6C 58
Colina M. N15 —4B 32
Colina Rd. N8 —5B 32
Colin Clo. NW9 —4A 28
Colin Clo. Croy —3B 154
Colin Clo. W W'ck —3H 155
Colin Cres. NW9 —4B 28
Colindale. —3K 27
Colindale Av. NW9 —3K 27
Colindale Bus. Pk. NW9 —3J 27
Colindeep Gdns. NW4 —4C 28
Colindeep La. NW9 & NW4 —3A 28
Colin Dri. NW9 —5B 28
Colinette Rd. SW15 —4E 100
Colin Gdns. NW9 —4B 28
Colin Pde. NW9 —4A 28
Colin Pk. Rd. NW9 —4A 28
Colin Rd. NW10 —6C 46
Colinton Rd. Ilf —2B 56
Colin Winter Ho. E1 —4J 69
(off Nicholas Rd.)
Coliston Pas. SW18 —7J 101
Coliston Rd. SW18 —7J 101
Collamore Av. SW18 —1C 120
Collapit Clo. Harr —6F 25
Collard Pl. NW1 —7F 49
Collards Almshouses. E17 —5E 34
(off Maynard Rd.)
College App. SE10 —6E 88
College Av. Harr —1J 25
College Clo. E5 —5J 51
College Clo. N18 —5A 18
College Clo. Harr —7D 10
College Clo. Twic —1H 115
College Ct. SW3 —6F 171
College Ct. W5 —7E 62
College Ct. W6 —5E 82
(off Queen Caroline St.)
College Ct. Enf —5D 8
College Cres. NW3 —6A 48
(in two parts)
College Cross. N1 —7A 50
College Dri. Ruis —7J 23
College E. E1 —5F 69
College Fields Bus. Cen. SW19 —1B 138
College Gdns. E4 —7J 9
College Gdns. N18 —5A 18
College Gdns. SE21 —1E 122
College Gdns. SW17 —2C 120
(in three parts)
College Gdns. Enf —1J 7
College Gdns. Ilf —5C 36
College Gdns. N Mald —5B 136
College Grn. SE19 —7E 122
College Gro. NW1 —1G 67
College Hill. EC4 —7C 68 (2D 168)
College Hill Rd. Harr —7D 10
College La. NW5 —4F 49
College Mans. NW6 —1G 65
(off Winchester Av.)
College M. N1 —7A 50
(in two parts)
College M. SW1 —1E 172
College M. SW18 —5K 101
College of Arms. —2C 168
College Pde. NW6 —1G 65
College Park. —3D 64
College Pk. Clo. SE13 —4F 107
College Pk. Rd. N17 —6A 18
College Pl. E17 —4G 35
College Pl. NW1 —1G 67
College Pl. SW10 —7A 84
College Point. E15 —6H 53
College Rd. E17 —5E 34
College Rd. N17 —6A 18
College Rd. N21 —2F 17
College Rd. NW10 —2E 64
College Rd. SE21 & SE19 —7E 104
College Rd. SW19 —6B 120
College Rd. W13 —6B 62
College Rd. Brom —1J 143
College Rd. Croy —2D 152
College Rd. Enf —2J 7
College Rd. Harr —6J 25
College Rd. Har W —1J 25
College Rd. Iswth —1K 97
College Rd. Swan —7K 129
College Rd. Wemb —1D 44
College Roundabout. King T —3E 134
College Row. E9 —5K 51
College Slip. Brom —1J 143
College St. EC4 —7C 68 (2D 168)
College Ter. E3 —3B 70
College Ter. N3 —2H 29
College Vw. SE9 —1B 126
College Wlk. King T —3E 134
College Way. Ashf —4B 112
College Way. Hay —7J 59
College Yd. NW5 —4F 49
Collent St. E9 —6J 51
Colless Rd. N15 —5F 33
Collett Rd. SE16 —3G 87
Collett Way. S'hall —2F 79
Collier Clo. E6 —7F 73
Collier Clo. Eps —6G 147
Collier Dri. Edgw —2G 27
Collier Row. —1H 39
Collier Row La. Romf —1H 39
Collier Row Rd. Romf —1F 39
Colliers Shaw. Kes —5B 156
Collier St. N1 —2K 67
Colliers Water La. T Hth —5A 140
Collier's Wood. —7B 120
Colliers Wood. (Junct.) —7B 120
Collindale Av. Eri —7H 93
Collindale Av. Sidc —1A 128
Collingbourne Rd. W12 —1D 82
Collingham Gdns. SW5 —4K 83
Collingham Pl. SW5 —4K 83
Collingham Rd. SW5 —4K 83
Collings Clo. N22 —6E 16
Collington St. SE10 —5F 89
Collingtree Rd. SE26 —4J 123
Collingwood Av. N10 —3E 30
Collingwood Av. Surb —1J 147
Collingwood Clo. SE20 —1H 141
Collingwood Clo. Twic —7E 96
Collingwood Ct. W5 —5F 63
Collingwood Ct. New Bar —5E 4
Collingwood Ho. SW1 —5H 85 (6C 172)
(off Dolphin Sq.)
Collingwood Ho. W1 —5G 67 (5A 160)
(off Clipstone St.)
Collingwood Rd. E17 —6C 34
Collingwood Rd. N15 —4E 32
Collingwood Rd. Mitc —3C 138
Collingwood Rd. Sutt —3J 149
Collingwood Rd. Uxb —4D 58
Collingwood St. E1 —4H 69
Collins Av. Stan —2E 26
Collins Ct. E8 —6G 51
Collins Dri. Ruis —2A 42
Collins Ho. E15 —1H 71
(off John St.)
Collinson Ct. SE1 —2C 86 (7C 168)
(off Gt. Suffolk St.)
Collinson Ho. SE15 —7G 87
(off Peckham Pk. Rd.)
Collinson St. SE1 —2C 86 (7C 168)
Collinson Wlk. SE1 —2C 86 (7C 168)
Collins Path. Hamp —6D 114
Collins Rd. N5 —4C 50
Collins Sq. SE3 —2H 107
Collins St. SE3 —2G 107
(in two parts)
Collin's Yd. N1 —1B 68
Collinwood Av. Enf —3D 8
Collinwood Gdns. Ilf —5D 36
Collis All. Twic —1J 115
Collis Rd. SE15 —1J 105
Collyer Av. Croy —4J 151
Collyer Pl. SE15 —1G 105
Collyer Rd. Bedd —4J 151
Colman Ct. N12 —6F 15
Colman Ct. Stan —6G 11
Colman Pde. Enf —3K 7
Colman Rd. E16 —5A 72
Colmans Wharf. E14 —5D 70
Colmar Clo. E1 —4K 69
Colmer Pl. Harr —7C 10
Colmer Rd. SW16 —1J 139
Colmore M. SE15 —1H 105
Colmore Rd. Enf —4D 8
Colnbrook St. SE1 —3B 86
Colne Ct. W7 —6H 61
(off Hobbayne Rd.)
Colne Ct. Eps —4J 147
Colnedale Rd. Uxb —5A 40
Colne Ho. Bark —7F 55
Colne Rd. E5 —4A 52
Colne Rd. N21 —7J 7
Colne Rd. Twic —1J 115
Colne St. E13 —3J 71
Colney Hatch. —6J 15
Colney Hatch La. N11 & N10 —6J 15
Cologne Rd. SW11 —4B 102
Colombo Rd. Ilf —1G 55
Colombo St. SE1 —1B 86 (5A 168)
Colomb St. SE10 —5G 89
Colonel's Wlk. Enf —3G 7
Colonial Av. Twic —6G 97
Colonial Dri. W4 —4J 81
Colonial Rd. Felt —7G 95
Colonnade. WC1 —4J 67 (4F 161)
Colonnades, The. W2 —6K 65
Colonnades, The. Croy —6A 152
Colonnade, The. SE8 —4B 88
Colonnade Wlk. SW1 —4F 85 (4J 171)
Colosseum Ter. NW1 —2K 159
Colour Ct. SW1 —5B 166
Colroy Ct. NW11 —5G 29
Colson Rd. Croy —2E 152
Colson Way. SW16 —4G 121
Colsterworth Rd. N15 —4F 33
(in two parts)
Colston Av. Cars —4C 150
Colston Ct. Cars —4D 150
(off West St.)
Colston Rd. E7 —6B 54
Colston Rd. SW14 —4J 99
Colthurst Cres. N4 —2B 50
Coltman Ho. E14 —6A 70
Coltman Ho. SE10 —6E 88
(off Welland St.)
Coltness Cres. SE2 —5B 92
Colton Gdns. N17 —3C 32
Colton Rd. Harr —5J 25
Coltsfoot Dri. W Dray —6A 58
Colt St. E14 —7B 70
Columbas. E14 —1C 88
Columbas Dri. NW3 —1B 48
Columbia Av. Edgw —1H 27
Columbia Av. Ruis —1K 41
Columbia Av. Wor Pk —7B 136
Columbia Ct. SE16 —3J 87
(off Surrey Quays Rd.)
Columbia Rd. E2 —3F 69 (1J 163)
Columbia Rd. E16 —4H 71
Columbia Sq. SW14 —4J 99
Columbia Wharf. SE16 —1B 88
Columbia Wharf. Enf —6F 9
Columbine Av. E6 —5C 72
Columbine Av. S Croy —7B 152
Columbine Way. SE13 —2E 106
Columbus Courtyard. E14 —1C 88
Columbus Gdns. N'wd —1J 23
Colva Wlk. N19 —2F 49
Colvestone Cres. E8 —5F 51
Colview Ct. SE9 —1B 126
Colville Est. N1 —1E 68
Colville Est. W. E2 —3F 69
(off Turin St.)
Colville Gdns. W11 —6H 65
(in two parts)
Colville Houses. W11 —6H 65
Colville M. W11 —6H 65
Colville Pl. W1 —5G 67 (6B 160)
Colville Rd. E11 —3E 52
Colville Rd. E17 —2A 34
Colville Rd. N9 —1C 18
Colville Rd. W3 —3H 81
Colville Rd. W11 —6H 65
Colville Sq. W11 —6H 65
Colville Sq. M. W11 —6H 65
Colville Ter. W11 —6H 65
Colvin Clo. SE26 —5J 123
Colvin Gdns. E4 —3K 19
Colvin Gdns. E18 —4K 35
Colvin Gdns. Ilf —1G 37
Colvin Rd. E6 —7C 54
Colvin Rd. T Hth —5A 140
Colwall Gdns. Wfd G —5D 20
Colwell Rd. SE22 —5F 105
Colwick Clo. N6 —7H 31
Colwith Rd. W6 —6E 82
Colwood Gdns. SW19 —7B 120
Colworth Gro. SE17 —4C 86
Colworth Rd. E11 —6G 35
Colworth Rd. Croy —1G 153
Colwyn Av. Gnfd —2K 61
Colwyn Clo. SW16 —5G 121
Colwyn Cres. Houn —1G 97
Colwyn Grn. NW9 —6A 28
(off Snowden Dri.)
Colwyn Ho. SE1 —3A 86 (2J 173)
Colwyn Rd. NW2 —3D 46
Colwyn Way. N18 —5B 18
Colyer Clo. N1 —2K 67
Colyer Clo. SE9 —2F 127
Colyers Clo. Eri —1K 111
Colyers La. Eri —1J 111
Colyers Wlk. Eri —1K 111
Colyton Clo. Well —1D 110
Colyton Clo. Wemb —6C 44
Colyton Rd. SE22 —5H 105
Combe Av. SE3 —7H 89
Combedale Rd. SE10 —5J 89
Combemartin Rd. SW18 —7G 101
Combe M. SE3 —7H 89
Comber Clo. NW2 —3D 46
Comber Gro. SE5 —7C 86
Comber Ho. SE5 —7C 86
Combermere Rd. SW9 —3K 103
Combermere Rd. Mord —6K 137
Comberton Rd. E5 —2H 51
Combeside. SE18 —7K 91

Corelli Rd.—Cranbrook St.

Corelli Rd. SE3 —2C 108
Corfe Av. Harr —4E 42
Corfe Clo. Hay —6A 60
Corfe Ho. SW8 —7K 85
(off Dorset Rd.)
Corfe Tower. W3 —2H 81
Corfield Rd. N21 —5E 6
Corfield St. E2 —3H 69
Corfton Lodge. W5 —5E 62
Corfton Rd. W5 —6E 62
Coriander Av. E14 —6F 71
Cories Clo. Dag —2D 56
Corinium Clo. Wemb —4F 45
Corinne Rd. N19 —4G 49
Corinthian Manorway. Eri —4K 93
Corinthian Rd. Eri —4K 93
Corinthian Way. Stanw —7A 94
Corkers Path. Ilf —2G 55
Corker Wlk. N7 —2K 49
Corkran Rd. Surb —7D 134
Corkscrew Hill. W W'ck —2E 154
Cork Sq. E1 —1H 87
Cork St. W1 —7G 67 (3A 166)
Cork St. M. W1 —3A 166
Cork Tree Est., The. E4 —5F 19
Cork Tree Ho. SE27 —5B 122
(off Lakeview Rd.)
Cork Tree Way. E4 —5F 19
Corlett St. NW1 —5C 66 (5C 158)
Cormont Rd. SE5 —1B 104
Cormorant Clo. E17 —7F 19
Cormorant Ct. SE8 —6B 88
(off Pilot Clo.)
Cormorant Pl. Sutt —5H 149
Cormorant Rd. E7 —5H 53
Cornbury Ho. SE8 —6B 88
(off Evelyn St.)
Cornbury Rd. Edgw —7J 11
Cornel Ho. Sidc —3A 128
Cornelia Ho. Twic —6D 98
(off Denton Rd.)
Cornelia St. N7 —6K 49
Cornell Building. E1 —6G 69
(off Coke St.)
Cornell Clo. Sidc —6E 128
Cornell Ho. S Harr —3D 42
Cornercroft. Sutt —5F 149
(off Wickham Av.)
Corner Fielde. SW2 —1K 121
Corner Grn. SE3 —2J 107
Corner Ho. St. WC2 —4E 166
Corner Mead. NW9 —7G 13
Cornerside. Ashf —7E 112
Cornerstone Ho. Croy —7C 140
Corner, The. W5 —1E 80
Corney Reach Way. W4 —7A 82
Corney Rd. W4 —6A 82
Cornfield Clo. Uxb —2A 58
Cornflower La. Croy —1K 153
Cornflower Ter. SE22 —6H 105
Cornford Clo. Brom —5J 143
Cornford Gro. SW12 —2F 121
Cornhill. EC3 —6D 68 (1F 169)
Cornish Ct. N9 —7C 8
Cornish Gro. SE20 —1H 141
Cornish Ho. SE17 —6B 86
(off Brandon Est.)
Cornish Ho. Bren —5F 81
Corn Mill Dri. Orp —7K 145
Cornmill La. SE13 —3E 106
Cornmow Dri. NW10 —5B 46
Cornshaw Rd. Dag —1D 56
Cornthwaite Rd. E5 —3J 51
Cornwall Av. E2 —3J 69
Cornwall Av. N3 —7D 14
Cornwall Av. N22 —1J 31
Cornwall Av. Clay —7A 146
Cornwall Av. S'hall —5D 60
Cornwall Av. Well —3J 109
Cornwall Clo. Bark —6K 55
Cornwall Ct. W7 —4K 61
(off Copley Clo.)
Cornwall Ct. Pinn —1D 24
Cornwall Cres. W11 —6G 65
Cornwall Dri. Orp —7C 128
Cornwall Gdns. NW10 —6D 46
Cornwall Gdns. SE25 —4F 141
Cornwall Gdns. SW7 —3K 83
Cornwall Gdns. Wlk. SW7 —3K 83
Cornwall Gro. W4 —5A 82
Cornwallis Av. N9 —2C 18
Cornwallis Av. SE9 —2H 127
Cornwallis Ct. SW8 —1J 103
(off Lansdowne Grn.)
Cornwallis Gro. N9 —2C 18
Cornwallis Ho. W12 —7D 64
(off India Way)
Cornwallis Rd. E17 —4K 33
Cornwallis Rd. N9 —2C 18
Cornwallis Rd. N19 —2J 49
Cornwallis Rd. Dag —4D 56
Cornwallis Sq. N19 —2J 49
Cornwallis Wlk. SE9 —3D 108
Cornwall Mans. SW10 —7A 84
(off Cremorne Rd.)
Cornwall M. S. SW7 —3A 84
Cornwall M. W. SW7 —3K 83
Cornwall Rd. N4 —7A 32
Cornwall Rd. N15 —5D 32
Cornwall Rd. N18 —5B 18
Cornwall Rd. SE1 —1A 86 (4J 167)
Cornwall Rd. Croy —2B 152
Cornwall Rd. Harr —6G 25
Cornwall Rd. Pinn —1D 24
Cornwall Rd. Ruis —3H 41
Cornwall Rd. Sutt —7H 149
Cornwall Rd. Twic —7A 98
Cornwall Rd. Uxb —6A 40
Cornwall Sq. SE11 —5K 173
Cornwall St. E1 —7H 69
Cornwall Ter. NW1 —4D 66 (4F 159)
Cornwall Ter. M. NW1 —4F 159
Corn Way. E11 —3F 53
Cornwell Cres. E7 —4A 54
Cornwood Clo. N2 —5B 30
Cornwood Dri. E1 —6J 69
Cornworthy Rd. Dag —5C 56
Corona Rd. SE12 —7J 107
Coronation Av. N16 —4F 51
Coronation Clo. Bex —6D 110
Coronation Clo. Ilf —4G 37
Coronation Ct. E15 —6H 53
Coronation Ct. Eri —7K 93
Coronation Rd. E13 —3A 72
Coronation Rd. NW10 —3F 63
Coronation Rd. Hay —4H 77
Coronation Wlk. Twic —1E 114
Coronet Pde. Wemb —6E 44
Coronet St. N1 —3E 68 (2G 163)
Corporate Dri. Felt —3K 113
Corporate Ho. Har W —1H 25
Corporation Av. Houn —4C 96
Corporation Row. EC1 —4A 68 (3K 161)
Corporation St. E15 —2G 71
Corporation St. N7 —5J 49
Corrance Rd. SW2 —4J 103
Corri Av. N14 —4C 16
Corrib Ct. N13 —3E 16
Corrib Dri. Sutt —5C 150
Corrigan Clo. NW4 —3E 28
Corringham Ct. NW11 —7J 29
Corringham Rd. NW11 —7J 29
Corringham Rd. Wemb —2G 45
Corringway. NW11 —7K 29
Corringway. W5 —4G 63
Corris Grn. NW9 —5A 28
Corry Ho. E14 —7D 70
Corsair Clo. Stai —7A 94
Corsair Rd. Stai —7A 94
Corscombe Clo. King T —5J 117
Corsehill St. SW16 —6G 121
Corsham St. N1 —3D 68 (2F 163)
Corsica St. N1 —6B 50
Corsley Way. E9 —6B 52
(off Osborne Rd.)
Cortayne Ct. Twic —2J 115
Cortayne Rd. SW6 —2H 101
Cortis Rd. SW15 —6D 100
Cortis Ter. SW15 —6D 100
Corunna Rd. SW8 —1G 103
Corunna Ter. SW8 —1G 103
Corvette Sq. SE10 —6F 89
Corwell Gdns. Uxb —6E 58
Corwell La. Uxb —6E 58
(in two parts)
Coryton Path. W9 —4H 65
(off Ashmore Rd.)
Cosbycote Av. SE24 —5C 104
Cosdach Av. Wall —7H 151
Cosedge Cres. Croy —5A 152
Cosgrove Clo. N21 —2H 17
Cosgrove Clo. Hay —4C 60
Cosgrove Ho. E2 —1G 69
(off Whiston Rd.)
Cosmo Pl. WC1 —5J 67 (5F 161)
Cosmur Clo. W12 —3B 82
Cossall Wlk. SE15 —2H 105
Cosser St. SE1 —3A 86 (1J 173)
Costa St. SE15 —2G 105
Costons Av. Gnfd —3H 61
Costons La. Gnfd —3H 61
Coston Wlk. SE4 —4K 105
Cosway Mans. NW1 —5C 66 (5D 158)
(off Shroton St.)
Cosway St. NW1 —5C 66 (5D 158)
Cotall St. E14 —5C 70
Coteford Clo. Pinn —5J 23
Coteford St. SW17 —4D 120
Cotelands. Croy —3E 152
Cotesbach Rd. E5 —3J 51
Cotes Ho. NW8 —4C 66 (4C 158)
(off Broadley St.)
Cotesmore Gdns. Dag —4C 56
Cotford Rd. T Hth —4C 140
Cotham St. SE17 —4C 86
Cotherstone Rd. SW2 —1K 121
Cotleigh Av. Bex —2D 128
Cotleigh Rd. NW6 —7J 47
Cotleigh Rd. Romf —6K 39
Cotman Clo. NW11 —6A 30
Cotman Clo. SW15 —6F 101
Cotman Gdns. Edgw —2G 27
Cotman Ho. NW8 —2C 66
(off Townshend Est.)
Cotman Ho. N'holt —2B 60
(off Academy Gdns.)
Cotman M. Dag —5C 56
(off Highgrove Rd.)
Cotmans Clo. Hay —1J 77
Coton Rd. Well —3A 110
Cotsford Av. N Mald —5J 135
Cotswold Clo. N11 —4K 15
Cotswold Clo. Hin W —2A 146
Cotswold Clo. King T —6J 117
Cotswold Ct. EC1 —3C 162
Cotswold Ct. Gnfd —2K 61
(off Hodder Dri.)
Cotswold Gdns. E6 —3B 72
Cotswold Gdns. NW2 —2F 47
Cotswold Gdns. Ilf —7H 37
Cotswold Ga. NW2 —1G 47
Cotswold Grn. Enf —4E 6
Cotswold M. SW11 —1B 102
Cotswold Ri. Orp —6K 145
Cotswold Rd. Hamp —6E 114
Cotswold St. SE27 —4B 122
Cotswold Way. Enf —3E 6
Cotswold Way. Wor Pk —2E 148
Cottage Av. Brom —1C 156
Cottage Clo. E1 —4J 69
(off Mile End Rd.)
Cottage Clo. Ruis —1F 41
Cottage Fld. Clo. Sidc —1C 128
Cottage Grn. SE5 —7D 86
Cottage Gro. SW9 —3J 103
Cottage Gro. Surb —6D 134
Cottage Pl. SW3 —3C 84 (1C 170)
Cottage Rd. Eps —7K 147
Cottage St. E14 —7D 70
Cottage Wlk. N16 —3F 51
Cottenham Dri. SW20 —7D 118
Cottenham Pde. SW20 —2D 136
Cottenham Park. —1D 136
Cottenham Pk. Rd. SW20 —1C 136
(in two parts)
Cottenham Pl. SW20 —7D 118
Cottenham Rd. E17 —4B 34
Cotterill Rd. Surb —2E 146
Cottesbrook St. SE14 —7A 88
Cottesloe Ho. NW8 —3C 158
Cottesloe M. SE1 —3A 86 (1K 173)
(off Emery St.)
Cottesmore Av. Ilf —2E 36
Cottesmore Ct. W8 —3K 83
(off Stanford Rd.)
Cottesmore Gdns. W8 —3K 83
Cottimore Av. W on T —7K 131
Cottimore Cres. W on T —7K 131
Cottimore La. W on T —7K 131
Cottimore Ter. W on T —7K 131
Cottingham Chase. Ruis —3J 41
Cottingham Rd. SE20 —7K 123
Cottingham Rd. SW8 —7K 85
Cottington Rd. Felt —4B 114
Cottington St. SE11
—5A 86 (5K 173)
Cotton Av. W3 —6K 63
Cotton Clo. Dag —7C 56
Cottongrass Clo. Croy —1K 153
Cotton Hill. Brom —4E 124
Cotton Ho. SW2 —7J 103
Cotton Row. SW11 —3A 102
Cottons App. Romf —5K 39
Cottons Cen. SE1 —1E 86 (4G 169)
Cottons Ct. Romf —5K 39
Cotton's Gdns. E2 —3E 68 (1H 163)
Cottons La. SE1 —1D 86 (4F 169)
Cotton St. E14 —7E 70
Cotts Clo. W7 —5K 61
Couchmore Av. Ilf —2D 36
Coulgate St. SE4 —3A 106
Coulson Clo. Dag —1C 56
Coulson St. SW3 —5D 84 (5E 170)
Coulter Clo. Hay —4C 60
Coulter Rd. W6 —3D 82
Coulthurst Ct. SW16 —7J 121
(off Heybridge Av.)
Councillor St. SE5 —7C 86
Counter Ct. SE1 —1D 86
(off Borough High St.)
Counter St. SE1 —5G 169
Countess Rd. NW5 —5G 49
Countisbury Av. Enf —7A 8
Country Way. Hanw —6K 113
County Gdns. Bark —2J 73
County Ga. SE9 —3G 127
County Ga. New Bar —6E 4
County Gro. SE5 —1C 104
County Hall Apartments. SE1
—6G 167
County Pde. Bren —7D 80
County Rd. E6 —5F 73
County Rd. T Hth —2B 140
County St. SE1 —3C 86
Coupland Pl. SE18 —5G 91
Courcy Rd. N8 —3A 32
Courland Gro. SW8 —1H 103
Courland St. SW8 —1H 103
(in two parts)
Course, The. SE9 —3E 126
Courtauld Clo. SE28 —1A 92
Courtauld Ho. E2 —1G 69
(off Goldsmiths Row)
Courtauld Institute Galleries.
—2G 167
Courtauld Rd. N19 —1J 49
Court Av. Belv —5F 93
Court Clo. Harr —3E 26
Court Clo. Twic —3F 115
Court Clo. Wall —7H 151
Court Clo. Av. Twic —3F 115
Court Cres. Chess —5D 146
Court Downs Rd. Beck —2D 142
Court Dri. Croy —4K 151
Court Dri. Stan —4K 11
Court Dri. Sutt —4C 150
Court Dri. Uxb —1B 58
Courtenay Av. N6 —7C 30
Courtenay Av. Harr —7B 10
Courtenay Av. Sutt —7J 149
Courtenay Dri. Beck —2F 143
Courtenay Gdns. Harr —2G 25
Courtenay M. E17 —5A 34
Courtenay Pl. E17 —5A 34
Courtenay Rd. E11 —3H 53
Courtenay Rd. E17 —4K 33
Courtenay Rd. SE20 —6K 123
Courtenay Rd. Wemb —3D 44
Courtenay Rd. Wor Pk —3E 148
Courtenay Sq. SE11 —5A 86 (6J 173)
Courtenay St. SE11 —5A 86 (5J 173)
Courtens M. Stan —7H 11
Court Farm Av. Eps —5K 147
Court Farm La. N'holt —7E 42
Court Farm Rd. SE9 —2B 126
Court Farm Rd. N'holt —7E 42
Courtfield. W5 —5C 62
Courtfield Av. Harr —5K 25
Courtfield Cres. Harr —5K 25
Courtfield Gdns. SW5 —4K 83
Courtfield Gdns. W13 —6A 62
Courtfield Gdns. Ruis —2H 41
Courtfield Ho. WC1 —5A 68 (5J 161)
(off Baldwins Gdns.)
Courtfield M. SW5 —4A 84
Courtfield Ri. W W'ck —3F 155
Courtfield Rd. SW7 —4A 84
Courtfield Rd. Ashf —6D 112
Court Gdns. N7 —6A 50
(in two parts)
Courthill Rd. SE13 —4E 106
Courthope Ho. SW8 —7J 85
(off Hartington Rd.)
Courthope Rd. NW3 —4D 48
Courthope Rd. SW19 —5G 119
Courthope Rd. Gnfd —2H 61
Courthope Vs. SW19 —7G 119
Court Ho. Gdns. N3 —6D 14
Courthouse Rd. N12 —6E 14
Courtland Av. E4 —2C 20
Courtland Av. NW7 —3E 12
Courtland Av. SW16 —7K 121
Courtland Av. Ilf —2D 54
Courtland Gro. SE28 —7D 74
Courtland Rd. E6 —1C 72
Courtlands. Rich —5G 99
Courtlands. W on T —7J 131
Courtlands Av. SE12 —5K 107
Courtlands Av. Brom —1G 155
Courtlands Av. Hamp —6D 114
Courtlands Av. Rich —2H 99
Courtlands Clo. Ruis —7H 23
Courtlands Dri. Eps —6A 148
Courtlands Rd. Surb —7G 135
Court La. SE21 —6E 104
Court La. Gdns. SE21 —7E 104
Courtleet Dri. Eri —1H 111
Courtleigh. NW11 —5H 29
Courtleigh Gdns. NW11 —4G 29
Court Lodge. Belv —5G 93
Courtman Rd. N17 —7H 17
Court Mead. N'holt —3D 60
Courtmead Clo. SE24 —6C 104
Courtnell St. W2 —6J 65
Courtney Clo. SE19 —6E 122
Courtney Ct. N7 —5A 50
Courtney Cres. Cars —7D 150
Courtney Ho. NW4 —3E 28
(off Mulberry Clo.)
Courtney Ho. W14 —3G 83
(off Russell Rd.)
Courtney Pl. Croy —3A 152
Courtney Rd. N7 —5A 50
Courtney Rd. SW19 —7C 120
Courtney Rd. Croy —3A 152
Courtney Rd. H'row A —3C 94
Court Pde. Wemb —3B 44
(in two parts)
Courtrai Rd. SE23 —6A 106
Court Rd. SE9 —6D 108
Court Rd. SE25 —2F 141
Court Rd. S'hall —4D 78
Court Rd. Uxb —5D 40
Courtside. N8 —6H 31
Courtside. SE26 —3H 123
Court St. E1 —5H 69
Court St. Brom —2J 143
Court, The. Ruis —4C 42
Courtville Ho. W10 —3G 65
(off Third Av.)
Court Way. NW9 —4A 28
Court Way. W3 —5J 63
Court Way. Ilf —3G 37
Court Way. Twic —7K 97
Court Way. Wfd G —5F 21
Court Yd. SE9 —6C 108
Courtyard, The. N1 —7K 49
Courtyard, The. NW1 —7E 48
Cousin La. EC4 —7D 68 (3E 168)
Cousins Clo. W Dray —7A 58
Couthurst Rd. SE3 —6K 89
Coutts Av. Chess —5E 146
Coutt's Cres. NW5 —3E 48
Coutts Ho. SE7 —5A 90
Couzens Ho. E3 —5B 70
Coval Gdns. SW14 —4H 99
Coval La. SW14 —4H 99
Coval Pas. SW14 —4J 99
Coval Rd. SW14 —4H 99
Covelees Wall. E6 —6E 72
Covell Ct. SE8 —7C 88
Covell Ct. Enf —1E 6
(off Ridgeway, The)
Covent Garden. —7J 67 (2F 167)
Covent Garden. —7J 67 (2F 167)
Covent Garden. WC2
—7J 67 (2F 167)
Coventry Clo. E6 —6D 72
Coventry Clo. NW6 —2J 65
Coventry Cross. E3 —4E 70
Coventry Hall. SW16 —5J 121
Coventry Rd. E1 & E2 —4H 69
Coventry Rd. SE25 —4G 141
Coventry Rd. Ilf —2F 55
Coventry St. W1 —7H 67 (3C 166)
Coverack Clo. N14 —6B 6
Coverack Clo. Croy —7A 142
Coverdale Clo. Stan —5G 11
Coverdale Gdns. Croy —3F 153
Coverdale Rd. N11 —6K 15
Coverdale Rd. NW2 —7F 47
Coverdale Rd. W12 —2D 82
Coverdales, The. Bark —2H 73
Coverley Clo. E1 —5G 69
Coverley Point. SE11 —4G 173
Coverton Rd. SW17 —5C 120
Covert, The. SE19 —7F 123
(off Fox Hill)
Covert, The. N'wd —1E 22
Covert, The. Orp —6J 145
Covert Way. Barn —2F 5
Covet Wood Clo. Orp —6K 145
Covey Clo. SW19 —2K 137
Covington Gdns. SW16 —7B 122
Covington Way. SW16 —6K 121
(in two parts)
Cowan Clo. E6 —5C 72
Cowan Ct. NW10 —7K 45
Cowbridge La. Bark —7F 55
Cowbridge Rd. Harr —4F 27
Cowcross St. EC1 —5B 68 (5A 162)
Cowdenbeath Path. N1 —1K 67
Cowden Rd. Orp —7K 145
Cowden St. SE6 —4C 124
Cowdray Rd. Uxb —1E 58
Cowdrey Clo. Enf —2K 7
Cowdrey Rd. SW19 —5K 119
Cowdry Rd. E9 —6A 52
Cowen Av. Harr —2H 43
Cowgate Rd. Gnfd —3H 61
Cowick Rd. SW17 —4D 120
Cowings Mead. N'holt —6C 42
Cowland Av. Enf —4D 8
Cow La. Gnfd —2H 61
Cow Leaze. E6 —6E 72
Cowleaze Rd. King T —1E 134
Cowley La. E11 —3G 53
Cowley Peachey. —6A 58
Cowley Pl. NW4 —5E 28
Cowley Rd. E11 —5K 35
Cowley Rd. SW9 —1A 104
Cowley Rd. SW14 —3A 100
Cowley Rd. W3 —1B 82
Cowley Rd. Ilf —7D 36
Cowley St. SW1 —3J 85 (1E 172)
Cowling Clo. W11 —1G 83
Cowper Av. E6 —7C 54
Cowper Av. Sutt —4B 150
Cowper Clo. Brom —4B 144
Cowper Clo. Well —5A 110
Cowper Gdns. N14 —6A 6
Cowper Gdns. Wall —6G 151
Cowper Ho. SE17 —5C 86
(off Browning St.)
Cowper Ho. SW1 —5H 85 (6C 172)
(off Aylesford St.)
Cowper Rd. N14 —1A 16
Cowper Rd. N16 —5E 50
Cowper Rd. N18 —5B 18
Cowper Rd. SW19 —6A 120
Cowper Rd. W3 —1K 81
Cowper Rd. W7 —7K 61
Cowper Rd. Belv —4F 93
Cowper Rd. Brom —4B 144
Cowper Rd. King T —5F 117
Cowper's Ct. EC3 —1F 169
Cowper St. EC2 —4D 68 (3F 163)
Cowper Ter. W10 —5F 65
Cowslip Clo. Uxb —7A 40
Cowslip Rd. E18 —2K 35
Cowthorpe Rd. SW8 —1H 103
Cox Ct. Barn —4H 5
Coxe Pl. W'stone —4A 26
Cox Ho. W6 —6G 83
(off Field Rd.)
Cox La. Chess —4F 147
Cox La. Eps —5H 147
Coxmount Rd. SE7 —5B 90
Coxs Av. Shep —3G 131
Cox's Ct. E1 —6J 163
Coxson Way. SE1 —2F 87 (7J 169)
Cox's Wlk. SE21 & SE26 —1G 123
Coxwell Rd. SE18 —5H 91
Coxwell Rd. SE19 —7E 122
Coxwold Path. Chess —7E 146
Crab Hill. Beck —7F 125
Crabtree Av. Romf —4D 38
Crabtree Av. Wemb —2E 62
Crabtree Clo. E2 —2F 69
Crabtree Ct. E15 —5D 52
Crabtree Ct. New Bar —4E 4
Crabtree La. SW6 —7E 82
(in two parts)
Crabtree Manorway N. Belv —2J 93
Crabtree Manorway S. Belv —3J 93
Crabtree Wlk. SE15 —1F 105
(off Peckham Rd.)
Crabtree Wlk. Croy —1G 153
Craddock Rd. Enf —3A 8
Craddock St. NW5 —6E 48
Cradley Rd. SE9 —1H 127
Crafts Council. —2A 68
Cragie Ho. SE1 —4F 87
(off Balaclava Rd.)
Craig Dri. Uxb —6D 58
Craigen Av. Croy —1H 153
Craigerne Rd. SE3 —7K 89
Craig Gdns. E18 —2H 35
Craigholm. SE18 —2E 108
Craigmore Ct. N'wd —1G 23
Craigmuir Pk. Wemb —1F 63
Craignair Rd. SW2 —7A 104
Craignish Av. SW16 —2K 139
Craig Pk. Rd. N18 —4C 18
Craig Rd. Rich —4C 116
Craig's Ct. SW1 —1J 85 (4E 166)
Craigton Rd. SE9 —4D 108
Craigweil Clo. Stan —5J 11
Craigweil Dri. Stan —5J 11
Craigwell Av. Felt —3J 113
Craik Ct. NW6 —2H 65
(off Carlton Va.)
Crail Row. SE17 —4D 86
Crales Ho. SE18 —3C 90
Cramer St. W1 —5E 66 (6H 159)
Crammond Clo. W6 —6G 83
Cramond Ct. Felt —1G 113
Cramonde Ct. Well —2A 110
Crampton Ho. SW8 —1G 103
Crampton Rd. SE20 —6J 123
Crampton St. SE17 —4C 86
Cranberry Clo. N'holt —2B 60
Cranberry La. E16 —4G 71
Cranborne Av. S'hall —4E 78
Cranborne Av. Surb —3G 147
Cranborne Rd. Bark —1H 73
Cranborne Waye. Hay —6K 59
(in two parts)
Cranbourn All. WC2 —7H 67
(off Cranbourn St.)
Cranbourne Av. E11 —4K 35
Cranbourne Clo. SW16 —3J 139
Cranbourne Dri. Pinn —5B 24
Cranbourne Gdns. NW11 —5G 29
Cranbourne Gdns. Ilf —3G 37
Cranbourne Rd. E12 —5C 54
Cranbourne Rd. E15 —4E 52
Cranbourne Rd. N10 —2F 31
Cranbourne Rd. N'wd —3H 23
Cranbourn Ho. SE16 —2H 87
(off Marigold St.)
Cranbourn Pas. SE16 —2H 87
(off Wilson Gro.)
Cranbourn Pl. SE16 —2H 87
Cranbourn St. WC2 —7H 67 (2D 166)
Cranbrook. —1D 54
Cranbrook. NW1 —1G 67
(off Camden St.)
Cranbrook Clo. Brom —6J 143
Cranbrook Ct. Bren —6C 80
Cranbrook Dri. Esh —7G 133
Cranbrook Dri. Twic —1F 115
Cranbrook Est. E2 —2K 69
Cranbrook M. E17 —5B 34
Cranbrook Pk. N22 —1A 32
Cranbrook Ri. Ilf —6D 36
Cranbrook Rd. SE8 —1C 106
Cranbrook Rd. SW19 —7G 119
Cranbrook Rd. W4 —5A 82
Cranbrook Rd. Barn —6G 5
Cranbrook Rd. Bexh —1F 111
Cranbrook Rd. Houn —4D 96
Cranbrook Rd. Ilf —7E 36
Cranbrook Rd. T Hth —2C 140
Cranbrook St. E2 —2K 69

Cranbury Rd.—Cross La.

Cranbury Rd. SW6 —2K 101
Crandley Ct. SE8 —4A 88
Crane Av. W3 —7J 63
Crane Av. Iswth —5A 98
Cranebank M. Twic —4A 98
Cranebrook. Twic —2G 115
Crane Clo. Dag —6G 57
Crane Clo. Harr —3G 43
Crane Ct. EC4 —6A 68 (1K 167)
Crane Ct. Eps —4J 147
Craneford Clo. Twic —7K 97
Craneford Way. Twic —7J 97
Crane Gdns. Hay —4H 77
Crane Gro. N7 —6A 50
Crane Ho. SE15 —1F 105
Crane Ho. Felt —3E 114
Crane Lodge Rd. Houn —6K 77
Cranemead. SE16 —4K 87
Crane Mead Ct. Twic —7K 97
Crane Pk. Rd. Twic —2F 115
Crane Rd. Twic —1J 115
Cranesbill Clo. NW9 —3K 27
Cranes Dri. Surb —4E 134
Cranes Pk. Surb —4E 134
Cranes Pk. Av. Surb —4E 134
Cranes Pk. Cres. Surb —4F 135
Crane St. SE10 —5F 89
Crane St. SE15 —1F 105
Craneswater. Hay —7H 77
Craneswater Pk. S'hall —5D 78
Crane Way. Twic —7G 97
Cranfield Clo. SE27 —3C 122
Cranfield Ct. W1 —6D 158
Cranfield Dri. NW9 —7F 13
Cranfield Ho. WC1 —5E 160
Cranfield Rd. SE4 —3B 106
Cranfield Rd. E. Cars —7E 150
Cranfield Rd. W. Cars —7D 150
Cranfield Row. SE1 —1K 173
Cranford. —1J 95
Cranford Av. N13 —5D 16
Cranford Av. Stai —7A 94
Cranford Clo. SW20 —7D 118
Cranford Clo. Stai —7A 94
Cranford Cotts. E1 —7K 69
(off Cranford St.)
Cranford Dri. Hay —4H 77
Cranford La. Hay —6F 77
Cranford La. H'row —1H 95
(in two parts)
Cranford La. Houn —7K 77
Cranford Pk. Rd. Hay —4H 77
Cranford St. E1 —7K 69
Cranford Way. N8 —4K 31
Cranhurst Rd. NW2 —5E 46
Cranleigh Clo. SE20 —2H 141
Cranleigh Clo. Bex —6H 111
Cranleigh Ct. Mitc —3B 138
Cranleigh Ct. Rich —3G 99
Cranleigh Ct. S'hall —6D 60
Cranleigh Gdns. N21 —5F 7
Cranleigh Gdns. SE25 —3E 140
Cranleigh Gdns. Bark —7H 55
Cranleigh Gdns. Harr —5E 26
Cranleigh Gdns. King T —6F 117
Cranleigh Gdns. S'hall —6D 60
Cranleigh Gdns. Sutt —2K 149
Cranleigh Gdns. Ind. Est. S'hall —5D 60
Cranleigh Houses. NW1 —2G 67
(off Cranleigh St.)
Cranleigh M. SW11 —2C 102
Cranleigh Rd. N15 —5C 32
Cranleigh Rd. SW19 —3J 137
Cranleigh Rd. Felt —4H 113
Cranleigh St. NW1 —2G 67
Cranley Dene Ct. N10 —4F 31
Cranley Dri. Ilf —7G 37
Cranley Dri. Ruis —2H 41
Cranley Gardens. —4F 31
Cranley Gdns. N10 —4F 31
Cranley Gdns. N13 —3E 16
Cranley Gdns. SW7 —5A 84 (5A 170)
Cranley Gdns. Wall —7G 151
Cranley M. SW7 —5A 84 (5A 170)
Cranley Pde. SE9 —4C 126
(off Beaconsfield Rd.)
Cranley Pl. SW7 —4B 84 (4A 170)
Cranley Rd. E13 —5K 71
Cranley Rd. Ilf —6G 37
Cranmer Av. W13 —3B 80
Cranmer Clo. Mord —6F 137
Cranmer Clo. Ruis —1B 42
Cranmer Clo. Stan —7H 11
Cranmer Ct. N3 —2G 29
Cranmer Ct. SW3 —4C 84 (4D 170)
Cranmer Ct. SW4 —3H 103
Cranmere Ct. SE5 —1C 104
Cranmere Ct. Enf —2F 7
Cranmer Farm Clo. Mitc —4D 138
Cranmer Gdns. Dag —4J 57
Cranmer Ho. SW9 —7A 86
(off Brixton Rd.)
Cranmer Rd. E7 —4K 53
Cranmer Rd. SW9 —7A 86
Cranmer Rd. Croy —3B 152
Cranmer Rd. Edgw —3C 12
Cranmer Rd. Hamp H —5F 115
Cranmer Rd. Hay —6F 59
Cranmer Rd. King T —5E 116
Cranmer Rd. Mitc —4D 138
Cranmer Ter. SW17 —5B 120
Cranmore Av. Iswth —7G 79
Cranmore Rd. Brom —3H 125
Cranmore Rd. Chst —5D 126
Cranmore Way. N10 —4G 31
Cranston Clo. Houn —2C 96
Cranston Clo. Uxb —2F 41
Cranston Est. N1 —2D 68
Cranston Gdns. E4 —6J 19
Cranston Rd. SE23 —1A 124
Cranswick Rd. SE16 —5H 87
Crantock Rd. SE6 —2D 124
Cranwell Clo. E3 —4D 70
Cranwell Gro. Shep —4B 130
Cranwell Rd. H'row A —2D 94
Cranwich Av. N21 —7J 7
Cranwich Rd. N16 —7D 32
Cranwood Ct. EC1 —2F 163
Cranwood St. EC1 —3D 68 (2F 163)
Cranworth Cres. E4 —1A 20
Cranworth Gdns. SW9 —1A 104
Craster Rd. SW2 —7K 103
Crathie Rd. SE12 —6K 107
Cravan Av. Felt —2J 113
Craven Av. W5 —7C 62
Craven Av. S'hall —5D 60
Craven Clo. N16 —7G 33
Craven Clo. Hay —6J 59
Craven Ct. NW10 —1A 64
Craven Ct. Romf —6E 38
Craven Gdns. SW19 —5J 119
Craven Gdns. Bark —2J 73
Craven Gdns. Ilf —2H 37
Craven Hill. W2 —7A 66
Craven Hill Gdns. W2 —7A 66
(in two parts)
Craven Hill M. W2 —7A 66
Craven Lodge. W2 —7A 66
(off Craven Hill)
Craven M. SW11 —3E 102
Craven Pk. NW10 —1K 63
Craven Pk. M. NW10 —1A 64
Craven Pk. Rd. N15 —6F 33
Craven Pk. Rd. NW10 —1A 64
Craven Pas. WC2 —1J 85 (4E 166)
(off Craven St.)
Craven Rd. NW10 —1K 63
Craven Rd. W2 —7A 66 (2A 164)
Craven Rd. W5 —7C 62
Craven Rd. Croy —1H 153
Craven Rd. King T —1F 135
Craven St. WC2 —1J 85 (4E 166)
Craven Ter. W2 —7A 66 (2A 164)
Craven Wlk. N16 —7G 33
Crawford Av. Wemb —5D 44
Crawford Bldgs. W1 —5C 66 (6D 158)
(off Homer St.)
Crawford Clo. Iswth —2J 97
Crawford Est. SE5 —2C 104
Crawford Gdns. N13 —3G 17
Crawford Gdns. N'holt —3D 60
Crawford Mans. W1 —5C 66 (6D 158)
(off Crawford St.)
Crawford M. W1 —5D 66 (6E 158)
Crawford Pas. EC1 —4A 68 (4K 161)
Crawford Pl. W2 —6C 66 (7D 158)
Crawford Point. E16 —6H 71
(off Wouldham Rd.)
Crawford Rd. SE5 —1C 104
Crawford St. W1 —5C 66 (6E 158)
Crawley Rd. E10 —1D 52
Crawley Rd. N22 —2C 32
Crawley Rd. Enf —7K 7
Crawshay Ct. SW9 —1A 104
Crawthew Gro. SE22 —4F 105
Craybrooke Rd. Sidc —4B 128
Craybury End. SE9 —2G 127
Crayford Clo. E6 —6B 72
Crayford Ho. SE1 —2D 86 (7F 169)
(off Long La.)
Crayford Rd. N7 —4H 49
Crayke Hill. Chess —7E 146
Crayle Ho. EC1 —4B 68 (3B 162)
(off Malta St.)
Crayonne Clo. Sun —1G 131
Cray Rd. Belv —6G 93
Cray Rd. Sidc —6C 128
Cray Valley Rd. Orp —5K 145
Crealock Gro. Wfd G —5C 20
Crealock St. SW18 —6K 101
Creasy Est. SE1 —3E 86
Crebor St. SE22 —6G 105
Credenhall Dri. Brom —1D 156
Credenhill Ho. SE15 —7H 87
Credenhill St. SW16 —6G 121
Crediton Hill. NW6 —5K 47
Crediton Rd. E16 —6J 71
Crediton Rd. NW10 —1F 65
Crediton Way. Clay —5A 146
Credon Rd. E13 —2A 72
Credon Rd. SE16 —5H 87
Creechurch La. EC3 —6E 68 (1H 169)
(in two parts)
Creechurch Pl. EC3 —1H 169
Creed Ct. EC4 —1B 168
Creed La. EC4 —6B 68 (1B 168)
Creek Ho. W14 —3G 83
(off Russell Rd.)
Creekmouth. —4K 73
Creek Rd. SE8 & SE10 —6C 88
Creek Rd. Bark —3K 73
Creek Rd. E Mol —4J 133
Creekside. SE8 —7D 88
Creek, The. Sun —5J 131
Creek Way. Rain —5K 75
Creeland Gro. SE6 —1B 124
Crefeld Clo. SW6 —6G 83
Creffield Rd. W5 & W3 —7F 63
Creighton Av. E6 —2B 72
Creighton Av. N2 & N10 —3C 30
Creighton Clo. W12 —7C 64
Creighton Rd. N17 —7K 17
Creighton Rd. NW6 —2F 65
Creighton Rd. W5 —3D 80
Cremer Bus. Cen. E2 —2F 69 (1J 163)
(off Cremer St.)
Cremer St. E2 —2F 69 (1J 163)
Cremorne Est. SW10 —6B 84
Cremorne Rd. SW10 —7A 84
Crescent. EC3 —7F 69 (2J 169)
Crescent Ct. Surb —5D 134
Crescent Ct. Bus. Cen. E16 —4F 71
Crescent Dri. Orp —6F 145
Crescent E. Barn —1F 5
Crescent Gdns. SW19 —3J 119
Crescent Gdns. Ruis —7K 23
Crescent Gro. SW4 —4G 103
Crescent Gro. Mitc —4C 138
Crescent Ho. EC1 —4C 68 (4C 162)
(off Golden La. Est.)
Crescent Ho. SE8 —2D 106
Crescent La. SW4 —4G 103
Crescent M. N22 —1J 31
Crescent Pde. Uxb —3C 58
Crescent Pl. SW3 —4C 84 (3D 170)
Crescent Ri. N3 —1H 29
Crescent Ri. N22 —1H 31
Crescent Ri. Barn —5H 5
Crescent Rd. E4 —1B 20
Crescent Rd. E6 —1A 72
Crescent Rd. E10 —2D 52
Crescent Rd. E13 —1J 71
Crescent Rd. E18 —1A 36
Crescent Rd. N3 —1H 29
Crescent Rd. N8 —6H 31
Crescent Rd. N9 —1B 18
Crescent Rd. N11 —4J 15
Crescent Rd. N15 —3B 32
Crescent Rd. N22 —1H 31
Crescent Rd. SE18 —5F 91
Crescent Rd. SW20 —1F 137
Crescent Rd. Barn —4G 5
Crescent Rd. Beck —2D 142
Crescent Rd. Brom —7J 125
Crescent Rd. Dag —3H 57
Crescent Rd. Enf —4G 7
Crescent Rd. King T —7G 117
Crescent Rd. Shep —5E 130
Crescent Rd. Sidc —3K 127
Crescent Row. EC1 —4C 68 (4C 162)
Crescent Stables. SW15 —5G 101
Crescent St. N1 —7K 49
Crescent, The. E17 —6A 34
Crescent, The. N9 —2C 18
Crescent, The. N11 —4K 15
Crescent, The. NW2 —3D 46
Crescent, The. SE7 —7A 90
Crescent, The. SW13 —2B 100
Crescent, The. SW19 —3J 119
Crescent, The. W3 —6A 64
Crescent, The. Ashf —5B 112
Crescent, The. Barn —2E 4
Crescent, The. Beck —1C 142
Crescent, The. Bex —7C 110
Crescent, The. Croy —6D 140
Crescent, The. Harr —1G 43
Crescent, The. Hay —7F 77
Crescent, The. Ilf —6E 36
Crescent, The. N Mald —3J 135
Crescent, The. Shep —7H 131
Crescent, The. Sidc —4K 127
Crescent, The. S'hall —2D 78
Crescent, The. Surb —5E 134
Crescent, The. Sutt —5B 150
Crescent, The. Wemb —2B 44
Crescent, The. W Mol —4E 132
Crescent, The. W W'ck —6G 143
Crescent Way. N12 —6H 15
Crescent Way. SE4 —3C 106
Crescent Way. SW16 —6K 121
Crescent W. Barn —1F 5
Crescent Wood Rd. SE26 —3G 123
Cresford Rd. SW6 —1K 101
Crespigny Rd. NW4 —6D 28
Cressage Clo. S'hall —4F 61
Cressage Ho. Bren —6E 80
(off Ealing Rd.)
Cressal Ho. E14 —3C 88
Cresset Rd. E9 —6J 51
Cresset St. SW4 —3H 103
Cressfield Clo. NW5 —5E 48
Cressida Rd. N19 —1G 49
Cressingham Gdns. Est. SW2 —7A 104
Cressingham Gro. Sutt —4A 150
Cressingham Rd. SE13 —3E 106
Cressingham Rd. Edgw —6E 12
Cressington Clo. N16 —5E 50
Cresswell. NW9 —2B 28
Cresswell Gdns. SW5 —5A 84
Cresswell Pk. SE3 —3H 107
Cresswell Pl. SW10 —5A 84
Cresswell Rd. SE25 —4G 141
Cresswell Rd. Felt —3C 114
Cresswell Rd. Twic —6D 98
Cresswell Way. N21 —7F 7
Cressy Ct. E1 —5J 69
Cressy Ct. W6 —3D 82
Cressy Houses. E1 —5J 69
(off Hannibal Rd.)
Cressy Pl. E1 —5J 69
Cressy Rd. NW3 —5D 48
Cresta Ct. W5 —4F 63
Cresta Ho. NW3 —7B 48
Crestbrook Av. N13 —3G 17
Crestbrook Pl. N13 —3G 17
(off Green Lanes)
Crest Ct. NW4 —5E 28
Crest Dri. Enf —1D 8
Crestfield St. NW1 —3J 67 (1F 161)
Crest Gdns. Ruis —3A 42
Creston Way. Wor Pk —1F 149
Crest Rd. NW2 —2C 46
Crest Rd. Brom —7H 143
Crest Rd. S Croy —7H 153
Crest, The. N13 —4F 17
Crest, The. NW4 —5E 28
Crest, The. Surb —5G 135
Crest Vw. Pinn —4B 24
Crest Vw. Dri. Orp —5F 145
Crestway. SW15 —6C 100
Crestwood Way. Houn —5C 96
Creswick Ct. W3 —7H 63
Creswick Rd. W3 —7H 63
Creswick Wlk. E3 —3C 70
Creswick Wlk. NW11 —4H 29
Creton St. SE18 —3E 90
Crewdson Rd. SW9 —7A 86
Crewe Pl. NW10 —3B 64
Crews St. E14 —4C 88
Crewys Rd. NW2 —2H 47
Crewys Rd. SE15 —2H 105
Crichton Av. Wall —5H 151
Crichton Ho. Sidc —6D 128
Crichton Rd. Cars —6D 150
Crichton St. SW8 —2G 103
Cricketers Arms Rd. Enf —2H 7
Cricketers Clo. N14 —7B 6
Cricketers Clo. Chess —3D 146
Cricketers Clo. Eri —5K 93
Cricketers Ct. SE11 —4B 86
(off Kennington La.)
Cricketers M. SW18 —5K 101
Cricketers Ter. Cars —3C 150
Cricketers Wlk. SE26 —5J 123
Cricketfield Rd. E5 —4H 51
Cricket Grn. Mitc —3D 138
Cricket Ground Rd. Chst —1F 145
(in two parts)
Cricket La. Beck —6A 124
Cricklade Av. SW2 —2J 121
Cricklewood. —3G 47
Cricklewood B'way. NW2 —3E 46
Cricklewood La. NW2 —4F 47
Cricklewood Trad. Est. NW2 —3G 47
Cridland St. E15 —1H 71
Crieff Ct. Tedd —7C 116
Crieff Rd. SW18 —6A 102
Criffel Av. SW2 —2H 121
Crimscott St. SE1 —3E 86
Crimsworth Rd. SW8 —1H 103
Crinan St. N1 —2J 67
Cringle St. SW8 —7G 85
Cripplegate St. EC2 —5C 68 (5D 162)
Cripps Grn. Hay —4K 59
Crispe Ho. N1 —1K 67
(off Barnsbury Est.)
Crispe Ho. Bark —2H 73
Crispen Rd. Felt —4C 114
Crispian Clo. NW10 —4A 46
Crispin Clo. Croy —2J 151
Crispin Cres. Croy —3H 151
Crispin Lodge. N11 —5J 15
Crispin Rd. Edgw —6D 12
Crispin St. E1 —5F 69 (6J 163)
Crisp Rd. W6 —5E 82
Cristowe Rd. SW6 —2H 101
Criterion M. N19 —2H 49
Crittalls Corner. (Junct.) —7C 128
Crockerton Rd. SW17 —2D 120
Crockham Way. SE9 —4E 126
Crocus Clo. Croy —1K 153
Crocus Fld. Barn —6C 4
Croft Av. W W'ck —1E 154
Croft Clo. NW7 —3F 13
Croft Clo. Belv —5F 93
Croft Clo. Chst —5D 126
Croft Clo. Hay —7E 76
Croft Clo. Uxb —7C 40
Croft Ct. SE13 —6E 106
Croft Ct. Ruis —1H 41
Croftdown Rd. NW5 —3E 48
Croft End Clo. Chess —3F 147
(off Ashcroft Rd.)
Crofters Clo. Iswth —5H 97
Crofters Way. NW1 —1H 67
Croft Gdns. W7 —2A 80
Croft Gdns. Ruis —1G 41
Croft Ho. E17 —4D 34
Croft Ho. W10 —3G 65
(off Third Av.)
Croft Lodge Clo. Wfd G —6E 20
Croft M. N12 —3F 15
Crofton Av. W4 —7K 81
Crofton Av. Bex —7D 110
Croftongate Way. SE4 —5A 106
Crofton Gro. E4 —4A 20
Crofton Park. —5B 106
Crofton Pk. Rd. SE4 —6B 106
Crofton Rd. E13 —4K 71
Crofton Rd. SE5 —1E 104
Crofton Rd. Orp —3E 156
Crofton Ter. E5 —5A 52
Crofton Ter. Rich —4F 99
Crofton Way. Barn —6E 4
Crofton Way. Enf —2F 7
Croft Rd. SW16 —1A 140
Croft Rd. SW19 —7A 120
Croft Rd. Brom —6J 125
Croft Rd. Enf —1F 9
Croft Rd. Sutt —5C 150
Crofts Ho. E2 —2G 69
(off Teale St.)
Croftside, The. SE25 —3G 141
Crofts La. N22 —7F 17
Crofts Rd. Harr —6A 26
Crofts St. E1 —7G 69 (3K 169)
Crofts, The. Shep —4G 131
Croft St. SE8 —4A 88
Crofts Vs. Harr —6A 26
Croft, The. E4 —2B 20
Croft, The. NW10 —2B 64
Croft, The. W5 —5E 62
Croft, The. Barn —4B 4
Croft, The. Houn —6C 78
Croft, The. Pinn —7D 24
Croft, The. Ruis —4A 42
Croft, The. Wemb —5C 44
Croftway. NW3 —4J 47
Croftway. Rich —3B 116
Croft Way. Sidc —3J 127
Crogsland Rd. NW1 —7E 48
Croham Clo. S Croy —7E 152
Croham Mnr. Rd. S Croy —7E 152
Croham Mt. S Croy —7E 152
Croham Pk. Av. S Croy —5E 152
Croham Rd. S Croy —5D 152
Croham Valley Rd. S Croy —6G 153
Croindene Rd. SW16 —1J 139
Crokesley Ho. Edgw —2J 27
(off Burnt Oak B'way.)
Cromartie Rd. N19 —7H 31
Cromarty Ct. SW2 —5K 103
Cromarty Rd. Edgw —2C 12
Cromberdale Ct. N17 —1G 33
(off Spencer Rd.)
Crombie Clo. Ilf —5D 36
Crombie M. SW11 —2C 102
Crombie Rd. Sidc —1H 127
Crome Ho. N'holt —2C 60
(off Parkfield Dri.)
Cromer Clo. Uxb —6E 58
Cromerhyde. Mord —5K 137
Cromer Pl. Orp —7J 145
Cromer Rd. E10 —7F 35
Cromer Rd. N17 —2G 33
Cromer Rd. SE25 —3H 141
Cromer Rd. SW17 —6E 120
Cromer Rd. Chad H —6E 38
Cromer Rd. H'row A —2C 94
Cromer Rd. New Bar —4F 5
Cromer Rd. Romf —6J 39
Cromer Rd. Wfd G —4D 20
Cromer Rd. W. H'row A —3C 94
Cromer St. WC1 —3J 67 (2E 160)
Cromer Ter. E8 —5G 51
Cromer Vs. Rd. SW18 —6H 101
Cromford Path. E5 —4K 51
Cromford Rd. SW18 —5J 101
Cromford Way. N Mald —1K 135
Cromlix Clo. Chst —2F 145
Crompton Ho. SE1 —3C 86
(off County St.)
Crompton Ho. W2 —4B 66 (4A 158)
(off Hall Pl.)
Crompton Pl. Enf —1H 9
Crompton St. W2 —4B 66 (4A 158)
Cromwell Av. N6 —1F 49
Cromwell Av. W6 —5D 82
Cromwell Av. Brom —4K 143
Cromwell Av. N Mald —5B 136
Cromwell Cen. NW10 —3K 63
Cromwell Cen., The. Dag —7F 39
(off Selinas La.)
Cromwell Clo. E1 —1G 87
Cromwell Clo. N2 —4B 30
Cromwell Clo. W3 —1J 81
(in two parts)
Cromwell Clo. Brom —4K 143
Cromwell Clo. W on T —7K 131
Cromwell Ct. Enf —5E 8
Cromwell Cres. W8 —4J 83
Cromwell Gdns. SW7 —3B 84 (2B 170)
Cromwell Gro. W6 —3E 82
Cromwell Highwalk. EC2 —5D 162
Cromwell Ho. Croy —3B 152
Cromwell Ind. Est. E10 —1A 52
Cromwell Lodge. Bexh —5E 110
Cromwell M. SW7 —4B 84 (3B 170)
Cromwell Pl. EC2 —5C 68
(off Beech St.)
Cromwell Pl. N6 —1F 49
Cromwell Pl. SW7 —4B 84 (3B 170)
Cromwell Pl. SW14 —3J 99
Cromwell Rd. E7 —7A 54
Cromwell Rd. E17 —6E 34
Cromwell Rd. N3 —1A 30
Cromwell Rd. N10 —7K 15
(in two parts)
Cromwell Rd. SW5 & SW7 —4J 83 (3A 170)
Cromwell Rd. SW9 —1B 104
Cromwell Rd. SW19 —5J 119
Cromwell Rd. Beck —2A 142
Cromwell Rd. Croy —7D 140
Cromwell Rd. Felt —1K 113
Cromwell Rd. Hay —6F 59
Cromwell Rd. Houn —4E 96
Cromwell Rd. King T —1E 134
Cromwell Rd. Tedd —6A 116
Cromwell Rd. Wemb —2E 62
Cromwell Rd. Wor Pk —3K 147
Cromwell St. Houn —4E 96
Cromwell Tower. EC2 —5D 162
Crondace Rd. SW6 —1J 101
Crondall Ct. N1 —1F 163
Crondall St. N1 —2D 68 (1F 163)
Crone Ct. NW6 —2H 65
(off Denmark Rd.)
Cronin St. SE15 —7F 87
Crooked Billet. (Junct.) —1C 34
Crooked Billet. SW19 —6E 118
Crooked Billet Yd. E2 —3E 68 (2H 163)
Crooked Usage. N3 —3G 29
Crooke Rd. SE8 —5A 88
Crookham Rd. SW6 —1H 101
Crook Log. Bexh —3D 110
Crookston Rd. SE9 —3E 108
Croombs Rd. E16 —5A 72
Croom's Hill. SE10 —7E 88
Croom's Hill Gro. SE10 —7E 88
Cropley Ct. N1 —2D 68
(off Cropley St., in two parts)
Cropley St. N1 —2D 68 (1E 162)
Croppath Rd. Dag —4G 57
Cropthorne Ct. W9 —3A 66
Crosbie. NW9 —2B 28
Crosbie Ho. E17 —3E 34
(off Prospect Hill)
Crosby Clo. Felt —3C 114
Crosby Ct. SE1 —6E 168
Crosby Ho. E7 —6J 53
Crosby Ho. E14 —3E 88
Crosby Rd. E7 —6J 53
Crosby Rd. Dag —2H 75
Crosby Row. SE1 —2D 86 (7E 168)
Crosby Sq. EC3 —6E 68 (1G 169)
Crosby Wlk. E8 —6F 51
Crosby Wlk. SW2 —7A 104
Crosby Way. SW2 —7A 104
Crosier Clo. SE3 —1C 108
Crosier Rd. Ick —4E 40
Crosier Way. Ruis —3G 41
Crosland Pl. SW11 —3E 102
Cross Av. SE10 —6F 89
Crossbow Ho. W13 —1B 80
(off Sherwood Clo.)
Crossbrook Rd. SE3 —2C 108
Cross Clo. SE15 —2H 105
Cross Deep. Twic —2K 115
Cross Deep Gdns. Twic —2K 115
Crossfield Ho. W11 —7G 65
(off Mary Pl.)
Crossfield Rd. N17 —3C 32
Crossfield Rd. NW3 —6B 48
Crossfield St. SE8 —7C 88
Crossford St. SW9 —2K 103
Cross Ga. Edgw —3B 12
Crossgate. Gnfd —6B 44
Cross Keys Clo. N9 —2B 18
(off Green, The)
Cross Keys Clo. N9 —2B 18
(off Lacey Clo.)
Cross Keys Clo. W1 —5E 66 (6H 159)
Cross Keys Sq. EC1 —5C 68
(off Lit. Britain)
Cross Lances Rd. Houn —4F 97
Crossland Rd. T Hth —6B 140
Crosslands Av. W5 —1F 81
Crosslands Av. S'hall —5D 78
Crosslands Rd. Eps —6K 147
Cross La. EC3 —7E 68 (3G 169)
Cross La. N8 —3K 31
(in two parts)

Cross La.—Daleham Dri.

Cross La. Bex —7F 111
Crossleigh Ct. SE14 —7B 88
(off New Cross Rd.)
Crosslet St. SE17 —4D 86
Crosslet Va. SE10 —1D 106
Crossley St. N7 —6A 50
Crossmead. SE9 —1D 126
Crossmead Av. Gnfd —3E 60
Crossmount Ho. SE5 —7C 86
(off Bowyer St.)
Crossness Footpath. Eri —1F 93
Crossness La. SE28 —7D 74
Crossness Rd. Bark —3K 73
Cross Rd. E4 —1A 20
Cross Rd. N11 —5A 16
Cross Rd. N22 —7F 17
Cross Rd. SW19 —7J 119
Cross Rd. Brom —2C 156
Cross Rd. Chad H —7C 38
Cross Rd. Croy —1D 152
Cross Rd. Enf —4K 7
Cross Rd. Felt —4C 114
Cross Rd. Harr —4H 25
Cross Rd. King T —7F 117
Cross Rd. Mawn & Romf —4G 39
Cross Rd. Sidc —4B 128
Cross Rd. S Harr —3F 43
Cross Rd. Sutt —5B 150
Cross Rd. W'stone —2A 26
Cross Rd. Wfd G —6J 21
Cross St. N1 —1B 68
Cross St. N18 —5B 18
Cross St. SE5 —3D 104
Cross St. SW13 —2A 100
Cross St. Hamp H —5G 115
Crossthwaite Av. SE5 —4D 104
Crosswall. EC3 —7F 69 (2J 169)
Crossway. N12 —6G 15
Crossway. N16 —5E 50
Crossway. NW9 —4B 28
Crossway. SE28 —7B 74
Crossway. SW20 —4E 136
Crossway. W13 —4A 62
Crossway. Dag —3C 56
Crossway. Enf —7K 7
Crossway. Hay —1J 77
Crossway. Orp —4H 145
Cross Way. Pinn —2K 23
Crossway. Ruis —4A 42
Cross Way. Wfd G —4F 21
Crossway Ct. SE4 —2A 106
Crossways. N21 —6H 7
Crossways. S Croy —7A 154
Crossways. Sun —7H 113
Crossways. Sutt —7B 150
Crossways Rd. Beck —4C 142
Crossways Rd. Mitc —3F 139
Crossways Ter. E5 —4J 51
Crossways, The. Houn —7D 78
Crossways, The. Surb —1H 147
Crossways, The. Wemb —2G 45
Crossway, The. N22 —7G 17
Crossway, The. SE9 —2B 126
Cross Way, The. Harr —2J 25
Crossway, The. Uxb —2B 58
Crosswell Clo. Shep —2E 130
Croston St. E8 —1G 69
Crothall Clo. N13 —3E 16
Crouch Av. Bark —2B 74
Crouch Clo. Beck —6C 124
Crouch Cft. SE9 —3E 126
Crouch End. —7H 31
Crouch End Hill. N8 —7H 31
Crouch Hall Ct. N19 —1J 49
Crouch Hall Rd. N8 —6H 31
Crouch Hill. N8 & N4 —6J 31
Crouchman's Clo. SE26 —3F 123
Crouch Rd. NW10 —7K 45
Crowborough Rd. SW17 —6E 120
Crowden Way. SE28 —7C 74
Crowder St. E1 —7H 69
Crowfield Ho. N5 —4C 50
Crowfoot Clo. E9 —5B 52
Crowhurst Clo. SW9 —2A 104
Crowhurst Ho. SW9 —2K 103
(off Aytoun Rd.)
Crowland Av. Hay —4G 77
Crowland Gdns. N14 —7D 6
Crowland Ho. NW8 —1A 66
(off Springfield Rd.)
Crowland Rd. N15 —5F 33
Crowland Rd. T Hth —4D 140
Crowlands Av. Romf —6H 39
Crowland Ter. N1 —7D 50
Crowland Wlk. Mord —6K 137
Crow La. Romf —7F 39
Crowley Cres. Croy —5A 152
Crowline Wlk. N1 —6C 50
Crowmarsh Gdns. SE23 —7J 105
Crown Arc. King T —2D 134
Crownbourne Ct. Sutt —4K 149
(off St Nicholas Way)
Crown Bldgs. E4 —1A 20
Crown Clo. E3 —1C 70
Crown Clo. NW6 —6K 47
Crown Clo. NW7 —2G 13
Crown Clo. Hay —2H 77
Crown Clo. W on T —7A 132
Crown Clo. Bus. Cen. E3 —1C 70
(off Crown Clo.)
Crown Cotts. Romf —1G 39
Crown Ct. EC4 —1D 168
Crown Ct. N10 —7K 15
Crown Ct. SE12 —6K 107
Crown Dale. SE19 —6B 122
Crowndale Ct. NW1 —2H 67
(off Crowndale Ct.)
Crowndale Rd. NW1 —2G 67
Crownfield Av. Ilf —6J 37
Crownfield Rd. E15 —4F 53
Crown Hill. Croy —2C 152
Crown Hill Rd. NW10 —1B 64
Crownhill Rd. Wfd G —7H 21
Crown Ho. Ruis —1J 41
Crown La. N14 —1B 16
Crown La. SW16 —5A 122
Crown La. Brom —5B 144
Crown La. Chst —1G 145
Crown La. Mord —4J 137
Crown La. Gdns. SW16 —5A 122
Crown La. Spur. Brom —6B 144
Crown Lodge. SW3 —4C 84 (4D 170)
Crownmead Way. Romf —4H 39
Crown M. E13 —1A 72
Crown M. W6 —4C 82
Crown Office Row. EC4 —7A 68 (2J 167)
Crown Pde. N14 —1B 16
Crown Pde. SE19 —6B 122
Crown Pde. Mord —3J 137
Crown Pas. SW1 —1G 85 (5B 166)
Crown Pas. King T —2D 134
Crown Pl. EC2 —5E 68 (5G 163)
Crown Pl. NW5 —6F 49
Crown Reach. SW1 —5H 85 (6D 172)
Crown Rd. N10 —7K 15
Crown Rd. Enf —4C 8
Crown Rd. Ilf —4H 37
Crown Rd. Mord —4K 137
Crown Rd. N Mald —1J 135
Crown Rd. Ruis —5B 42
Crown Rd. Sutt —4K 149
Crown Rd. Twic —6B 98
Crownstone Ct. SW2 —5A 104
Crownstone Rd. SW2 —5A 104
Crown St. SE5 —7C 86
Crown St. W3 —1H 81
Crown St. Dag —6J 57
(in two parts)
Crown St. Harr —1H 43
Crown Ter. N14 —1C 16
(off Crown La.)
Crown Ter. Rich —4F 99
Crown Trad. Cen. Hay —2G 77
Crowntree Clo. Iswth —6K 79
Crown Wlk. Wemb —3F 45
Crown Way. W Dray —1B 76
Crown Wharf. E14 —1E 88
Crown Woods. SE18 —2F 109
Crown Woods Way. SE9 —5H 109
Crown Yd. Houn —3G 97
Crowshott Av. Stan —2C 26
Crows Rd. E15 —3F 71
Crows Rd. Bark —6F 55
Crowther Av. Bren —4E 80
Crowther Rd. SE25 —5G 141
Crowthorne Clo. SW18 —7H 101
Crowthorne Rd. W10 —6F 65
Croxall Ho. W on T —6A 132
Croxden Clo. Edgw —3G 27
Croxden Wlk. Mord —6A 138
Croxford Gdns. N22 —7G 17
Croxford Way. Romf —1K 57
Croxley Grn. Orp —7B 128
Croxley Rd. W9 —3H 65
Croxted Clo. SE21 —7C 104
Croxted M. SE24 —6C 104
Croxted Rd. SE24 & SE21 —6C 104
Croxteth Ho. SW8 —2H 103
Croyde Av. Gnfd —3G 61
Croyde Av. Hay —4G 77
Croyde Clo. Sidc —7H 109
Croydon. —2C 152
Croydon. N17 —2D 32
(off Gloucester Rd.)
Croydon Crematorium. Croy —5K 139
Croydon Flyover, The. Croy —3C 152
Croydon Gro. Croy —1B 152
Croydon Ho. SE1 —1A 86 (6K 167)
(off Wootton St.)
Croydon Rd. E13 —4H 71
Croydon Rd. SE20 —2H 141
Croydon Rd. Beck —5K 141
Croydon Rd. Brom & Kes —3A 156
Croydon Rd. H'row A —2D 94
Croydon Rd. Mitc & Bedd —4E 138
Croydon Rd. Wall & Croy —4F 151
Croydon Rd. W W'ck & Brom —3G 155
Croydon Rd. Ind. Est. Beck —4K 141
Croyland Rd. N9 —1B 18
Croylands Dri. Surb —7E 134
Croysdale Av. Sun —3J 131
Crozier Ho. SE3 —3K 107
Crozier Ho. SW8 —7K 85
(off Wilkinson St.)
Crozier Ter. E9 —5K 51
Crucible Clo. Romf —6B 38
Crucifix La. SE1 —2E 86 (6H 169)
Cruden Ho. SE5 —6B 86
(off Brandon Est.)
Cruden St. N1 —1B 68
Cruikshank Ho. NW8 —2C 66
(off Townshend Rd.)
Cruikshank Rd. E15 —4G 53
Cruikshank St. WC1 —3A 68 (1J 161)
Crummock Gdns. NW9 —5A 28
Crumpsall St. SE2 —4C 92
Crundale Av. NW9 —5G 27
Crunden Rd. S Croy —7D 152
Crusader Gdns. Croy —3E 152
Crusoe M. N16 —2D 50
Crusoe Rd. Eri —5K 93
Crusoe Rd. Mitc —7D 120
Crutched Friars. EC3 —7E 68 (2H 169)
Crutchley Rd. SE6 —2G 125
Crystal Palace. —6F 123
Crystal Palace F.C. —4E 140
Crystal Palace Mus. —6F 123
Crystal Palace National Sports Centre. —6G 123
Crystal Pal. Pde. SE19 —6F 123
Crystal Pal. Pk. Rd. SE26 —5G 123
Crystal Pal. Rd. SE22 —6F 105
Crystal Pal. Sta. Rd. SE19 —6G 123
Crystal Ter. SE19 —6D 122
Crystal Vw. Ct. Brom —4F 125
Crystal Way. Dag —1C 56
Crystal Way. Harr —5K 25
Cuba Dri. Enf —2D 8
Cuba St. E14 —2C 88
Cubitt Ho. SW4 —6G 103
Cubitt Sq. S'hall —1G 79
Cubitt Steps. E14 —1C 88
Cubitt St. WC1 —3K 67 (2H 161)
Cubitt St. Croy —5K 151
Cubitt's Yd. WC2 —2F 167
Cubitt Ter. SW4 —3G 103
Cubitt Town. —4E 88
Cuckoo Av. W7 —4J 61
Cuckoo Dene. W7 —5H 61
Cuckoo Hall La. N9 —7D 8
Cuckoo Hall Rd. N9 —7D 8
Cuckoo Hill. Pinn —3A 24
Cuckoo Hill Dri. Pinn —3A 24
Cuckoo Hill Rd. Pinn —4A 24
Cuckoo La. W7 —7J 61
Cuckoo Pound. Shep —5G 131
Cudas Clo. Eps —4B 148
Cuddington. SE17 —4C 86
(off Deacon Way)
Cuddington Av. Wor Pk —3B 148
Cudham St. SE6 —7E 106
Cudworth Ho. SW8 —1G 103
Cudworth St. E1 —4H 69
Cuff Cres. SE9 —6B 108
Cuff Point. E2 —3F 69 (1J 163)
(off Columbia Rd.)
Culford Gdns. SW3 —4D 84 (4F 171)
Culford Gro. N1 —6E 50
Culford Mans. SW3 —4D 84 (4F 171)
Culford M. N1 —6E 50
Culford Rd. N1 —7E 50
(in two parts)
Culgaith Gdns. Enf —4D 6
Culham Ho. E2 —3F 69 (2J 163)
(off Palissy St.)
Cullen Way. NW10 —4J 63
Culling Rd. SE16 —3J 87
Cullington Clo. Harr —4A 26
Cullingworth Rd. NW10 —5C 46
Culloden Clo. SE1 —5G 87
Culloden Rd. Enf —2G 7
Culloden St. E14 —6E 70
Cullum St. EC3 —7E 68 (2G 169)
Cullum Welch Ct. N1 —3D 68 (1F 163)
(off Haberdasher St.)
Culmington Pde. W13 —1C 80
(off Culmington Rd.)
Culmington Rd. W13 —1C 80
Culmington Rd. S Croy —7C 152
Culmore Rd. SE15 —7H 87
Culmstock Rd. SW11 —5E 102
Culpeper Ho. E14 —6A 70
Culpepper Ct. SE11 —3J 173
Culross Bldgs. N1 —2J 67
(off Battle Bri. Rd.)
Culross Clo. N15 —4C 32
Culross St. W1 —7E 66 (3G 165)
Culsac Rd. Surb —2E 146
Culverden Rd. SW12 —2G 121
Culver Gro. Stan —2C 26
Culverhouse. WC1 —5K 67 (6G 161)
(off Red Lion Sq.)
Culverhouse Gdns. SW16 —3K 121
Culverlands Clo. Stan —4G 11
Culverley Rd. SE6 —1D 124
Culvers Av. Cars —2D 150
Culvers Retreat. Cars —1D 150
Culverstone Clo. Hayes —6H 143
Culvers Way. Cars —2D 150
Culvert Pl. SW11 —2E 102
Culvert Rd. N15 —5E 32
Culvert Rd. SW11 —2D 102
Culworth Ho. NW8 —2C 66
(off Allitsen Rd.)
Culworth St. NW8 —2C 66
Culzean Clo. SE27 —3B 122
Cumberland Av. NW10 —3H 63
Cumberland Av. Well —3J 109
Cumberland Bus. Pk. NW10 —3H 63
Cumberland Clo. E8 —6F 51
Cumberland Clo. SW20 —7F 119
Cumberland Clo. Ilf —1G 37
Cumberland Clo. Twic —6B 98
Cumberland Ct. SW1 —5F 85 (5K 171)
(off Cumberland St.)
Cumberland Ct. Croy —1D 152
Cumberland Ct. Harr —3J 25
(off Princes Dri.)
Cumberland Ct. Well —2J 109
Cumberland Cres. W14 —4G 83
(in two parts)
Cumberland Dri. Bexh —7E 92
Cumberland Dri. Chess —3F 147
Cumberland Dri. Esh —2A 146
Cumberland Gdns. NW4 —2G 29
Cumberland Gdns. WC1 —3A 68 (1J 161)
Cumberland Ga. W1 —7D 66 (2E 164)
Cumberland Ho. N9 —1D 18
(off Cumberland Rd.)
Cumberland Ho. King T —7H 117
Cumberland Mans. W1 —7E 158
Cumberland Mkt. NW1 —3F 67 (1K 159)
Cumberland Mills Sq. E14 —5F 89
Cumberland Pk. W3 —7J 63
Cumberland Pk. Ind. Est. NW10 —3C 64
Cumberland Pl. NW1 —3F 67 (1J 159)
Cumberland Pl. SE6 —1H 125
Cumberland Pl. Sun —4J 131
Cumberland Rd. E12 —4B 54
Cumberland Rd. E13 —5K 71
Cumberland Rd. E17 —2A 34
Cumberland Rd. N9 —1D 18
Cumberland Rd. N22 —2K 31
Cumberland Rd. SE25 —6H 141
Cumberland Rd. SW13 —1B 100
Cumberland Rd. W3 —7J 63
Cumberland Rd. W7 —2K 79
Cumberland Rd. Ashf —3A 112
Cumberland Rd. Brom —4G 143
Cumberland Rd. Harr —5F 25
Cumberland Rd. Rich —7G 81
Cumberland Rd. Stan —3F 27
Cumberland St. SW1 —5F 85 (5K 171)
Cumberland Ter. NW1 —2F 67 (1J 159)
Cumberland Ter. M. NW1 —1J 159
Cumberland Vs. W3 —7J 63
(off Cumberland Rd.)
Cumberlow Av. SE25 —3F 141
Cumbernauld Gdns. Sun —5H 113
Cumberton Rd. N17 —1D 32
Cumbrae Gdns. Surb —2D 146
Cumbrian Gdns. NW2 —2F 47
Cumbrian Way. Uxb —7A 40
Cumming St. N1 —2K 67 (1H 161)
Cumnor Clo. SW9 —2K 103
(off Robsart St.)
Cumnor Gdns. Eps —6C 148
Cumnor Rd. Sutt —6A 150
Cunard Cres. N21 —6J 7
Cunard Pl. EC3 —6E 68 (1H 169)
Cunard Rd. NW10 —3K 63
Cunard Wlk. SE16 —4K 87
Cundy Rd. E16 —6A 72
Cundy St. SW1 —4E 84 (4H 171)
Cunliffe Pde. Eps —4B 148
Cunliffe Rd. Eps —4B 148
Cunliffe St. SW16 —6G 121
Cunningham Clo. Romf —5C 38
Cunningham Clo. W W'ck —2D 154
Cunningham Ho. SE5 —7D 86
(off Elmington Est.)
Cunningham Pk. Harr —5G 25
Cunningham Pl. NW8 —4B 66 (3A 158)
Cunningham Rd. N15 —4G 33
Cunnington St. W4 —3J 81
Cupar Rd. SW11 —1E 102
Cupola Clo. Brom —5K 125
Cureton St. SW1 —4H 85 (4D 172)
Curfew Ho. Bark —1G 73
Curie Ct. Harr —7B 26
Curie Gdns. NW9 —2A 28
Curlew Clo. SE28 —7D 74
Curlew Clo. Ilf —3E 36
Curlew Ct. W13 —4K 61
Curlew Ct. Surb —3G 147
Curlew Ho. SE4 —4A 106
(off St Norbert Rd.)
Curlew Ho. SE15 —1F 105
Curlew St. SE1 —2F 87 (6K 169)
Curlew Way. Hay —5B 60
Curnick's La. SE27 —4C 122
Curran Av. Sidc —5K 109
Curran Av. Wall —3E 150
Curran Ho. SW3 —4C 84 (4C 170)
(off Lucan Pl.)
Currey Rd. Gnfd —6H 43
Curricle St. W3 —1A 82
Currie Hill Clo. SW19 —4H 119
Currie Ho. E14 —6F 71
Curry Ri. NW7 —6A 14
Cursitor St. WC2 —6A 68 (7J 161)
Curtain Pl. EC2 —3H 163
Curtain Rd. EC2 —4E 68 (2H 163)
(in two parts)
Curthwaite Gdns. Enf —4C 6
Curtis Dri. W3 —6K 63
Curtis Fld. Rd. SW16 —4K 121
Curtis Ho. SE17 —5D 86
(off Morecambe St.)
Curtis La. Wemb —5E 44
Curtis Rd. Eps —4J 147
Curtis Rd. Houn —7D 96
Curtis St. SE1 —4F 87
Curtis Way. SE1 —4F 87
Curtis Way. SE28 —7B 74
Curtlington Ho. Edgw —2J 27
(off Burnt Oak B'way.)
Curve, The. W12 —7C 64
Curwen Av. E7 —4K 53
Curwen Rd. W12 —2C 82
Curzon Av. Enf —5E 8
Curzon Av. Stan —1A 26
Curzon Ct. SW6 —1K 101
(off Maltings Pl.)
Curzon Cres. NW10 —7A 46
Curzon Cres. Bark —2K 73
Curzon Ga. W1 —1E 84 (5H 165)
Curzon Pl. W1 —1E 84 (5H 165)
Curzon Pl. Pinn —5A 24
Curzon Rd. N10 —2F 31
Curzon Rd. W5 —4B 62
Curzon Rd. T Hth —6A 140
Curzon St. W1 —1E 84 (5H 165)
Cusack Clo. Twic —4K 115
Custance Ho. N1 —2D 68 (1E 162)
(off Provost Est.)
Custance St. N1 —3D 68 (1E 162)
Custom House. —6A 72
Custom House. —7E 68 (3G 169)
Custom Ho. Reach. SE16 —2B 88
Custom Ho. Wlk. EC3 —7E 68 (3G 169)
Cutbush Ho. N7 —5H 49
Cutcombe Rd. SE5 —2C 104
Cuthberga St. Bark —7G 55
(off George St.)
Cuthbert Gdns. SE25 —3E 140
Cuthbert Harrowing Ho. EC1
(off Golden La. Est.) —4C 68 (4C 162)
Cuthbert Ho. W2 —5B 66 (5A 158)
(off Hall Pl.)
Cuthbert Rd. E17 —3E 34
Cuthbert Rd. N18 —5B 18
Cuthbert Rd. Croy —2B 152
Cuthbert St. W2 —5B 66 (5A 158)
Cuthill Wlk. SE5 —1D 104
Cutlers Gdns. E1 —6H 163
Cutlers Sq. E14 —4C 88
Cutler St. E1 —6E 68 (7H 163)
Cut, The. SE1 —2A 86 (6K 167)
Cutthroat All. Rich —2C 116
Cutty Sark Clipper Ship. —6E 88
Cutty Sark Gdns. SE10 —6E 88
(off King William Wlk.)
Cuxton. Pet W —5G 145
Cuxton Clo. Bexh —5E 110
Cyclamen Clo. Hamp —6E 114
Cyclamen Way. Eps —5J 147
Cyclops M. E14 —4C 88
Cygnet Av. Felt —7A 96
Cygnet Clo. NW10 —5K 45
Cygnets, The. Felt —4C 114
Cygnet St. E1 —4F 69 (3K 163)
Cygnet Way. Hay —5B 60
Cygnus Bus. Cen. NW10 —5B 46
Cymbeline Ct. Harr —6K 25
(off Gayton Rd.)
Cynthia St. N1 —2K 67 (1H 161)
Cyntra Pl. E8 —7H 51
Cypress Av. Twic —7G 97
Cypress Gdns. SE4 —5A 106
Cypress Ho. SE14 —1K 105
Cypress Pl. W1 —4G 67 (4B 160)
Cypress Rd. SE25 —2E 140
Cypress Rd. Harr —2H 25
Cypress Tree Clo. Sidc —1K 127
Cyprus. —7E 72
Cyprus Av. N3 —2G 29
Cyprus Clo. N4 —6B 32
Cyprus Gdns. N3 —2G 29
Cyprus Pl. E2 —2J 69
Cyprus Pl. E6 —7E 72
Cyprus Rd. N3 —2H 29
Cyprus Rd. N9 —2A 18
Cyprus St. E2 —2J 69
(in two parts)
Cyrena Rd. SE22 —6F 105
Cyril Lodge. Sidc —4A 128
Cyril Mans. SW11 —1D 102
Cyril Rd. Bexh —2E 110
Cyril Rd. Orp —7K 145
Cyrus Ho. EC1 —4B 68 (3B 162)
Cyrus St. EC1 —3B 162
Czar St. SE8 —6C 88

Dabbs Hill La. N'holt —6D 42
(in two parts)
Dabbs La. EC1 —4A 68 (4K 161)
(off Farringdon Rd.)
Dabin Cres. SE10 —1E 106
Dacca St. SE8 —6B 88
Dace Rd. E3 —1C 70
Dacre Av. Ilf —2E 36
Dacre Clo. Gnfd —2F 61
Dacre Gdns. SE13 —4G 107
Dacre Ho. SW3 —7B 170
Dacre Pk. SE13 —3G 107
Dacre Pl. SE13 —3G 107
Dacre Rd. E11 —1H 53
Dacre Rd. E13 —1K 71
Dacre Rd. Croy —7J 139
Dacres Ho. SW4 —3F 103
Dacres Rd. SE23 —2K 123
Dacre St. SW1 —3H 85 (1C 172)
Dade Way. S'hall —5D 78
Daerwood Clo. Brom —1D 156
Daffodil Clo. Croy —1K 153
Daffodil Gdns. Ilf —5F 55
Daffodil Pl. Hamp —6E 114
Daffodil St. W12 —7B 64
Dafforne Rd. SW17 —3E 120
Dagenham. —6G 57
Dagenham & Redbridge F.C. —5H 57
Dagenham Av. Dag —1E 74
(in two parts)
Dagenham Leisure Pk. Dag —1E 74
Dagenham Rd. E10 —1B 52
Dagenham Rd. Dag & Romf —4H 57
Dagenham Rd. Rain —7K 57
Dagenham Rd. Romf & Rush G —7K 39
Dagleish St. E14 —6A 70
Dagmar Av. Wemb —4F 45
Dagmar Ct. E14 —3E 88
Dagmar Gdns. NW10 —2F 65
Dagmar M. S'hall —3C 78
(off Dagmar Rd.)
Dagmar Pas. N1 —1B 68
(off Cross St.)
Dagmar Rd. N4 —7A 32
Dagmar Rd. N15 —4D 32
Dagmar Rd. N22 —1H 31
Dagmar Rd. SE5 —1E 104
Dagmar Rd. SE25 —5E 140
Dagmar Rd. Dag —7J 57
Dagmar Rd. King T —1F 135
Dagmar Rd. S'hall —3C 78
Dagmar Ter. N1 —1B 68
Dagnall Pk. SE25 —6E 140
Dagnall Rd. SE25 —5E 140
Dagnall St. SW11 —2D 102
Dagnan Rd. SW12 —7F 103
Dagonet Gdns. Brom —3J 125
Dagonet Rd. Brom —3J 125
Dahlia Gdns. Ilf —6F 55
Dahlia Gdns. Mitc —4H 139
Dahlia Rd. SE2 —4B 92
Dahomey Rd. SW16 —6G 121
Daimler Way. Wall —7J 151
Dain Ct. W8 —4J 83
(off Lexham Gdns.)
Daines Clo. E12 —3D 54
Dainford Clo. Brom —5F 125
Dainton Clo. Brom —1K 143
Daintry Clo. Harr —4A 26
Daintry Way. E9 —6B 52
Dairsie Ct. Brom —2A 144
Dairsie Rd. SE9 —3E 108
Dairy Clo. NW10 —1C 64
Dairy Clo. Brom —7K 125
Dairy Clo. T Hth —2C 140
Dairy La. SE18 —4D 90
Dairyman Clo. NW2 —3F 47
Dairy M. SW9 —3J 103
Dairy Wlk. SW19 —4G 119
Daisy Clo. Croy —1K 153
Daisy Dobbings Wlk. N19 —7J 31
(off Jessie Blythe La.)
Daisy La. SW6 —3J 101
Daisy Rd. E16 —4G 71
Daisy Rd. E18 —2K 35
Dakota Clo. Wall —7K 151
Dakota Gdns. E6 —4C 72
Dakota Gdns. N'holt —3C 60
Dalberg Rd. SW2 —4A 104
(in two parts)
Dalberg Way. SE2 —3D 92
Dalby Rd. SW18 —4A 102
Dalbys Cres. N17 —6K 17
Dalby St. NW5 —6F 49
Dalcross Rd. Houn —2C 96
Dale Av. Edgw —1F 27
Dale Av. Houn —3C 96
Dalebury Rd. SW17 —2D 120
Dale Clo. SE3 —3J 107
Dale Clo. New Bar —6E 4
Dale Clo. Pinn —1K 23
Dale Dri. Hay —4H 59
Dale Gdns. Wfd G —4E 20
Dale Grn. Rd. N11 —3A 16
Dale Gro. N12 —5F 15
Daleham Dri. Uxb —6D 58

Dell Clo.—Dinton Ho.

Dell Clo. Wall —4G 151
Dell Clo. Wfd G —3E 20
Dell Farm Rd. Ruis —5F 23
Dellfield Clo. Beck —1E 142
Dell La. Eps —5C 148
Dellors Clo. Barn —5A 4
Dellow Clo. Ilf —7H 37
Dellow St. E1 —7H 69
Dell Rd. Eps —6C 148
Dell Rd. W Dray —4B 76
Dells Clo. E4 —7J 9
Dells Clo. Tedd —6K 115
Dell's M. SW1 —4B 172
Dell, The. SE2 —5A 92
Dell, The. SE19 —1F 141
Dell, The. Bex —1K 129
Dell, The. Bren —6C 80
Dell, The. Felt —7K 95
Dell, The. Pinn —2B 24
Dell, The. Wemb —5B 44
Dell, The. Wfd G —3E 20
Dell Wlk. N Mald —2A 136
Dell Way. W13 —6C 62
Dellwood Gdns. Ilf —3E 36
Delmaine Ho. E14 —6A 70
Delmare Clo. SW9 —4K 103
Delme Cres. SE3 —2K 107
Delmerend Ho. SW3 —5C 84 (5C 170)
(off Sutton Est., The)
Delmey Clo. Croy —3F 153
Deloraine Ho. SE8 —1C 106
Delorme St. W6 —6F 83
Delroy Ct. N20 —7F 5
Delta Building. E14 —6E 70
Delta Cen. Wemb —1F 63
Delta Clo. Wor Pk —3B 148
Delta Ct. NW2 —2C 46
Delta Est. E2 —3G 69
Delta Gro. N'holt —3B 60
Delta Pk. SW18 —4K 101
Delta Rd. Wor Pk —3A 148
Delta St. E2 —3G 69 (1K 163)
De Luci Rd. Eri —5J 93
De Lucy St. SE2 —4B 92
Delvan Clo. SE18 —7E 90
Delvers Mead. Dag —4J 57
Delverton Ho. SE17 —5B 86
(off Delverton Rd.)
Delverton Rd. SE17 —5B 86
Delvino Rd. SW6 —1J 101
Demesne Rd. Wall —4H 151
Demeta Clo. Wemb —3J 45
De Montfort Pde. SW16 —3J 121
De Montfort Rd. SW16 —3J 121
De Morgan Rd. SW6 —3K 101
Dempster Clo. Surb —1C 146
Dempster Rd. SW18 —5A 102
Denbar Pde. Romf —4H 39
Denberry Dri. Sidc —3B 128
Denbigh Clo. NW10 —7A 46
Denbigh Clo. W11 —7H 65
Denbigh Clo. Chst —6D 126
Denbigh Clo. Ruis —2H 41
Denbigh Clo. S'hall —6D 60
Denbigh Clo. Sutt —5H 149
Denbigh Ct. E6 —3B 72
Denbigh Ct. W7 —5K 61
(off Copley Clo.)
Denbigh Dri. Hay —2E 76
Denbigh Gdns. Rich —5F 99
Denbigh Ho. SW1 —3D 84 (1F 171)
Denbigh Ho. W11 —7H 65
(off Westbourne Gro.)
Denbigh M. SW1 —4A 172
Denbigh Pl. SW1 —5G 85 (5A 172)
Denbigh Rd. E6 —3B 72
Denbigh Rd. W11 —7H 65
Denbigh Rd. W13 —7B 62
Denbigh Rd. Houn —2F 97
Denbigh Rd. S'hall —6D 60
Denbigh St. SW1 —4G 85 (4A 172)
(in two parts)
Denbigh Ter. W11 —7H 65
Denbridge Rd. Brom —2D 144
Denby Ct. SE11 —3H 173
Dence Ho. E2 —3G 69 (2K 163)
(off Turin St.)
Denchworth Ho. SW9 —2A 104
Dencliffe. Ashf —5C 112
Den Clo. Beck —3F 143
Dene Av. Houn —3D 96
Dene Av. Sidc —7B 110
Dene Clo. SE4 —3A 106
Dene Clo. Brom —1H 155
Dene Clo. Dart —4K 129
Dene Clo. Wor Pk —2B 148
Dene Ct. W5 —5C 62
Denecroft Cres. Uxb —1D 58
Dene Gdns. Stan —5H 11
Dene Gdns. Th Dit —2A 146
Denehurst Gdns. NW4 —6E 28
Denehurst Gdns. W3 —1H 81
Denehurst Gdns. Rich —4G 99
Denehurst Gdns. Twic —7H 97
Denehurst Gdns. Wfd G —4E 20
Dene Rd. N11 —1J 15
Dene Rd. Buck H —1G 21
Denesmead. SE24 —5C 104
Dene, The. W13 —5B 62
Dene, The. Croy —4K 153
Dene, The. Wemb —4E 44
Dene, The. W Mol —5D 132
Denewood. New Bar —5F 5
Denewood Rd. N6 —6D 30
Denford St. SE10 —5H 89
Dengie Wlk. N1 —1C 68
(off Basire St.)
Denham Clo. Well —3C 110
Denham Ct. SE26 —3H 123
(off Kirkdale)
Denham Ct. S'hall —7G 61
(off Baird Av.)
Denham Cres. Mitc —4D 138
Denham Dri. Ilf —6G 37
Denham Ho. W12 —7D 64
(off White City Est.)
Denham Rd. N20 —3J 15
Denham Rd. Felt —7A 96
Denham St. SE10 —5J 89
Denham Way. Bark —1K 73
Denholme Rd. W9 —3H 65
Denison Clo. N2 —3A 30
Denison Ho. E14 —6C 70
Denison Rd. SW19 —6B 120
Denison Rd. W5 —4C 62
Denison Rd. Felt —4H 113
Deniston Av. Bex —1E 128
Denis Way. SW4 —3H 103
Denland Ho. SW8 —7K 85
(off Dorset Rd.)
Denleigh Gdns. N21 —7F 7
Denleigh Gdns. Th Dit —6J 133
Denman Dri. NW11 —5J 29
Denman Dri. Ashf —6D 112
Denman Dri. Clay —5A 146
Denman Dri. N. NW11 —5J 29
Denman Dri. S. NW11 —5J 29
Denman Pl. W1 —2C 166
Denman Rd. SE15 —1F 105
Denman St. W1 —7H 67 (3C 166)
Denmark Av. SW19 —7G 119
Denmark Ct. Mord —6J 137
Denmark Gdns. Cars —3D 150
Denmark Gro. N1 —2A 68
Denmark Hill. SE5 —1D 104
Denmark Hill Dri. NW9 —3C 28
Denmark Hill Est. SE5 —4D 104
Denmark Mans. SE5 —2C 104
(off Coldharbour La.)
Denmark Path. SE25 —5H 141
Denmark Pl. WC2 —6H 67 (7D 160)
Denmark Rd. N8 —4A 32
Denmark Rd. NW6 —2H 65
(in two parts)
Denmark Rd. SE5 —1C 104
Denmark Rd. SE25 —5G 141
Denmark Rd. SW19 —6F 119
Denmark Rd. W13 —7B 62
Denmark Rd. Brom —1K 143
Denmark Rd. Cars —3D 150
Denmark Rd. King T —3E 134
Denmark Rd. Twic —3H 115
Denmark St. E11 —3G 53
Denmark St. E13 —5K 71
Denmark St. N17 —1H 33
Denmark St. WC2 —6H 67 (7D 160)
Denmark Ter. N2 —3D 30
Denmark Wlk. SE27 —4C 122
Denmead Ho. SW15 —6B 100
(off Highcliffe Dri.)
Denmead Rd. Croy —1B 152
Denmead Way. SE15 —7F 87
(off Pentridge St.)
Denmore Ct. Wall —5F 151
Dennan Rd. Surb —1F 147
Dennard Way. Farnb —4E 156
Denner Rd. E4 —2H 19
Denne Ter. E8 —1F 69
Dennett Rd. Croy —1A 152
Dennetts Gro. SE14 —1J 105
Denning Av. Croy —4A 152
Denning Clo. NW8 —3A 66 (1A 158)
Denning Clo. Hamp —5D 114
Denning Point. E1 —6F 69 (7K 163)
(off Commercial St.)
Denning Rd. NW3 —4B 48
Dennington Clo. E5 —2J 51
Dennington Pk. Rd. NW6 —6J 47
Denningtons, The. Wor Pk —2A 148
Dennis Av. Wemb —5F 45
Dennis Clo. Ashf —7F 113
Dennis Gdns. Stan —5H 11
Dennis Ho. Sutt —4J 149
Dennis La. Stan —3G 11
Dennison Gro. SW14 —3K 99
Dennison Point. E15 —7E 52
Dennis Pde. N14 —1C 16
Dennis Pk. Cres. SW20 —1G 137
Dennis Reeve Clo. Mitc —1D 138
Dennis Rd. E Mol —4G 133
Denny Clo. E6 —5C 72
Denny Cres. SE11 —5A 86 (5K 173)
Denny Gdns. Dag —7B 56
Denny Rd. N9 —1C 18
Denny St. SE11 —5A 86 (5K 173)
Den Rd. Brom —3F 143
Densham Ho. NW8 —2B 66 (1B 158)
(off Cochrane St.)
Densham Rd. E15 —1G 71
Densole Clo. Beck —1A 142
Denstone Ho. SE15 —6G 87
(off Haymerle Rd.)
Densworth Gro. N9 —2D 18
Dent Ho. SE17 —4E 86
(off Tatum St.)
Denton. NW1 —6E 48
Denton Ho. N1 —7B 50
(off Halton Rd.)
Denton Rd. N8 —5K 31
Denton Rd. N18 —4K 17
Denton Rd. Bex —2K 129
Denton Rd. Twic —6D 98
Denton Rd. Well —7C 92
Denton St. SW18 —6K 101
Denton Ter. Bex —2K 129
Denton Way. E5 —3K 51
Dents Rd. SW11 —6D 102
Denver Clo. Orp —6J 145
Denver Rd. N16 —7E 32
Denwood. SE23 —3K 123
Denyer St. SW3 —4C 84 (4D 170)
Denys Ho. EC1 —5A 68 (5J 161)
(off Bourne Est.)
Denziloe Av. Uxb —3D 58
Denzil Rd. NW10 —5B 46
Deodar Rd. SW15 —4G 101
Deodora Clo. N20 —3H 15
Depot App. NW2 —4F 47
Depot Rd. W12 —7E 64
Depot Rd. Houn —3H 97
Depot St. SE5 —6D 86
Deptford. —7C 88
Deptford Bri. SE8 —1C 106
Deptford B'way. SE8 —1C 106
Deptford Chu. St. SE8 —6C 88
Deptford Ferry Rd. E14 —4C 88
Deptford Grn. SE8 —6C 88
Deptford High St. SE8 —6C 88
Deptford Pk. Bus. Cen. SE8 —5A 88
Deptford Strand. SE8 —4B 88
Deptford Trad. Est. SE8 —5A 88
Deptford Wharf. SE8 —4B 88
(in two parts)
De Quincey Ho. SW1 —5G 85 (6A 172)
(off Lupus St.)
De Quincey M. E16 —1J 89
De Quincey Rd. N17 —1D 32
Derby Av. N12 —5F 15
Derby Av. Harr —1H 25
Derby Av. Romf —6J 39
Derby Est. Houn —4F 97
Derby Ga. SW1 —2J 85 (6E 166)
(in two parts)
Derby Hill. SE23 —2J 123
Derby Hill Cres. SE23 —2J 123
Derby Ho. SE11 —3J 173
Derby Ho. Pinn —2B 24
Derby Lodge. N3 —2H 29
Derby Lodge. WC1 —3K 67 (1G 161)
(off Britannia St.)
Derby Rd. E7 —7B 54
Derby Rd. E9 —1K 69
Derby Rd. E18 —1H 35
Derby Rd. N18 —5D 18
Derby Rd. SW14 —4H 99
Derby Rd. SW19 —7J 119
Derby Rd. Croy —1B 152
Derby Rd. Enf —5C 8
Derby Rd. Gnfd —1F 61
Derby Rd. Houn —4F 97
Derby Rd. Surb —1G 147
Derby Rd. Sutt —6H 149
Derbyshire St. E2 —3G 69
(in two parts)
Derby St. W1 —1E 84 (5H 165)
Dereham Ho. SE4 —4K 105
(off Frendsbury Rd.)
Dereham Pl. EC2 —3E 68 (2H 163)
(in two parts)
Dereham Rd. Bark —5K 55
Derek Av. Eps —6G 147
Derek Av. Wall —4F 151
Derek Av. Wemb —7H 45
Derek Clo. Ewe —5H 147
Derek Walcott Clo. SE24 —5B 104
Dericote St. E8 —1H 69
Deridene Clo. Stanw —6A 94
Derifall Clo. E6 —5D 72
Dering Pl. Croy —4C 152
Dering Rd. Croy —4C 152
Dering St. W1 —6F 67 (1J 165)
Dering Yd. W1 —6F 67 (1K 165)
Derinton Rd. SW17 —4D 120
Derley Rd. S'hall —3A 78
Dermody Gdns. SE13 —5F 107
Dermody Rd. SE13 —5F 107
Deronda Est. SW2 —1B 122
Deronda Rd. SE24 —1B 122
Deroy Clo. Cars —6D 150
Derrick Gdns. SE7 —3A 90
Derrick Rd. Beck —3B 142
Derry Rd. Croy —3J 151
Derry St. W8 —2K 83
Dersingham Av. E12 —4D 54
Dersingham Rd. NW2 —3G 47
Derwent. NW1 —3G 67 (2A 160)
(off Robert St.)
Derwent Av. N18 —5J 17
Derwent Av. NW7 —6E 12
Derwent Av. NW9 —5A 28
Derwent Av. SW15 —4A 118
Derwent Av. Barn —1J 15
Derwent Av. Uxb —2C 40
Derwent Clo. Felt —1H 113
Derwent Cres. N12 —3F 15
Derwent Cres. Bexh —2G 111
Derwent Cres. Stan —2C 26
Derwent Dri. Hay —5G 59
Derwent Dri. Orp —7H 145
Derwent Gdns. Ilf —4C 36
Derwent Gdns. Wemb —7C 26
Derwent Gro. SE22 —4F 105
Derwent Ho. E3 —4B 70
(off Southern Gro.)
Derwent Ho. SE20 —2H 141
(off Derwent Rd.)
Derwent Ho. SW7 —4A 84 (3A 170)
(off Cromwell Rd.)
Derwent Lodge. Iswth —2H 97
Derwent Lodge. Wor Pk —2D 148
Derwent Ri. NW9 —6A 28
Derwent Rd. N13 —4E 16
Derwent Rd. SE20 —2G 141
Derwent Rd. SW20 —5F 137
Derwent Rd. W5 —3C 80
Derwent Rd. S'hall —6D 60
Derwent Rd. Twic —6F 97
Derwent St. SE10 —5G 89
Derwent Wlk. Wall —7F 151
Derwentwater Rd. W3 —1J 81
Derwent Yd. W13 —3C 80
(off Derwent Rd.)
De Salis Rd. Uxb —4E 58
Desborough Clo. W2 —5K 65
(off Bourne Ter.)
Desborough Clo. Shep —7C 130
Desborough Ho. W14 —6H 83
(off N. End Rd.)
Desenfans Rd. SE21 —6E 104
Desford Ct. Ashf —2C 112
Desford Rd. E16 —4G 71
Desford Way. Ashf —2B 112
Design Mus. —6K 169
Desmond Ho. Barn —6H 5
Desmond St. SE14 —7A 88
Despard Rd. N19 —1G 49
Dethick Ct. E3 —1A 70
Detling Ho. SE17 —4E 86
(off Congreve St.)
Detling Rd. Brom —5J 125
Detling Rd. Eri —7K 93
Detmold Rd. E5 —2J 51
Devalls Clo. E6 —7F 73
Devana End. Cars —3D 150
Devas Rd. SW20 —1E 136
Devas St. E3 —4D 70
Devenay Rd. E15 —7H 53
Devenish Rd. SE2 —2A 92
Deventer Cres. SE22 —5E 104
De Vere Gdns. W8 —2A 84
De Vere Gdns. Ilf —2D 54
Deverell St. SE1 —3D 86
De Vere M. W8 —3A 84
(off De Vere Gdns.)
Devereux Ct. WC2 —1J 167
Devereux La. SW13 —7D 82
Devereux Rd. SW11 —6D 102
Deveron Way. Romf —1K 39
Devey Clo. King T —7B 118
Devitt Ho. E14 —7D 70
Devizes St. N1 —1D 68
(off Avebury St.)
Devon Av. Twic —1G 115
Devon Clo. N17 —3F 33
Devon Clo. Buck H —2E 20
Devon Clo. Gnfd —1C 62
Devon Ct. W7 —5K 61
(off Copley Clo.)
Devon Ct. Hamp —7E 114
Devoncroft Gdns. Twic —7A 98
Devon Gdns. N4 —6B 32
Devon Ho. E17 —2B 34
Devonhurst Pl. W4 —5K 81
Devonia Gdns. N18 —6H 17
Devonia Rd. N1 —2B 68
Devon Mans. SE1 —2F 87 (6J 169)
(off Tooley St.)
Devon Pde. Harr —5C 26
Devonport. W2 —6C 66 (1C 164)
Devonport Gdns. Ilf —6D 36
Devonport M. W12 —2D 82
Devonport Rd. W12 —1D 82
Devonport St. E1 —6K 69
Devon Ri. N2 —4B 30
Devon Rd. Bark —1J 73
Devon Rd. Sutt —7G 149
Devons Est. E3 —3D 70
Devonshire Av. Sutt —7A 150
Devonshire Clo. E15 —4G 53
Devonshire Clo. N13 —3F 17
Devonshire Clo. W1 —5F 67 (5J 159)
Devonshire Ct. WC1 —5J 67 (5F 161)
(off Boswell St.)
Devonshire Ct. Pinn —1D 24
(off Devonshire Rd.)
Devonshire Cres. NW7 —7A 14
Devonshire Dri. SE10 —7D 88
Devonshire Dri. Surb —1D 146
Devonshire Gdns. N17 —6H 17
Devonshire Gdns. N21 —7H 7
Devonshire Gdns. W4 —7J 81
Devonshire Gro. SE15 —6H 87
Devonshire Hill La. N17 —6G 17
(in two parts)
Devonshire Ho. SE1 —3C 86
(off Bath Ter.)
Devonshire Ho. SW1 —5H 85 (5D 172)
(off Lindsay Sq.)
Devonshire Ho. Sutt —7A 150
Devonshire Ho. Bus. Cen. Brom
(off Devonshire Sq.) —4K 143
Devonshire M. N13 —4F 17
Devonshire M. W4 —5A 82
Devonshire M. N. W1 —5F 67 (5J 159)
Devonshire M. S. W1 —5F 67 (5J 159)
Devonshire M. W. W1 —4E 66 (4H 159)
Devonshire Pas. W4 —5A 82
Devonshire Pl. NW1 —4E 66 (4H 159)
Devonshire Pl. NW2 —3J 47
Devonshire Pl. W8 —3K 83
Devonshire Pl. M. W1 —5E 66 (4H 159)
Devonshire Rd. E16 —6K 71
Devonshire Rd. E17 —6C 34
Devonshire Rd. N9 —1D 18
Devonshire Rd. N13 —4E 16
Devonshire Rd. N17 —6H 17
Devonshire Rd. NW7 —7A 14
Devonshire Rd. SE9 —2C 126
Devonshire Rd. SE23 —1J 123
Devonshire Rd. SW19 —7C 120
Devonshire Rd. W4 —5A 82
Devonshire Rd. W5 —3C 80
Devonshire Rd. Bexh —4E 110
Devonshire Rd. Cars —4E 150
Devonshire Rd. Croy —7D 140
Devonshire Rd. Eastc —6A 24
Devonshire Rd. Felt —3C 114
Devonshire Rd. Harr —6H 25
Devonshire Rd. Ilf —7J 37
Devonshire Rd. Orp —7K 145
Devonshire Rd. Pinn —1D 24
Devonshire Rd. S'hall —5E 60
Devonshire Rd. Sutt —7A 150
Devonshire Row. EC2
—5E 68 (6H 163)
Devonshire Row M. W1 —4K 159
Devonshire Sq. EC2 —6E 68 (6H 163)
Devonshire Sq. Brom —4K 143
Devonshire St. W1 —5E 66 (5H 159)
Devonshire St. W4 —5A 82
Devonshire Ter. W2 —6A 66
Devonshire Way. Croy —2A 154
Devonshire Way. Hay —6K 59
Devons Rd. E3 —5C 70
(in two parts)
Devon St. SE15 —6H 87
Devon Way. Chess —5C 146
Devon Way. Eps —5H 147
Devon Way. Uxb —2B 58
Devon Waye. Houn —7D 78
Devon Wharf. E14 —5E 70
De Walden Ho. NW8 —2C 66
(off Allitsen Rd.)
De Walden St. W1 —5E 66 (6H 159)
Dewar St. SE15 —3G 105
Dewberry Gdns. E6 —5C 72
Dewberry St. E14 —5E 70
Dewey Rd. N1 —2A 68
Dewey Rd. Dag —6H 57
Dewey St. SW17 —5D 120
Dewhurst Rd. W6 —3F 83
Dewsbury Clo. Pinn —6C 24
Dewsbury Ct. W4 —4J 81
Dewsbury Gdns. Wor Pk —3C 148
Dewsbury Rd. NW10 —5C 46
Dewsbury Ter. NW1 —1F 67
Dexter Ho. Eri —3E 92
(off Kale Rd.)
Dexter Rd. Barn —6A 4
Deyncourt Rd. N17 —1C 32
Deynecourt Gdns. E11 —4A 36
D'Eynsford Rd. SE5 —1D 104
Dhonau Ho. SE1 —4F 87
(off Longfield Est.)
Diadem Ct. W1 —7C 160
Dial Wlk., The. W8 —2K 83
(off Broad Wlk., The)
Diameter Rd. Orp —7F 145
Diamond Clo. Dag —1C 56
Diamond Est. SW17 —3C 120
Diamond Rd. Ruis —4B 42
Diamond St. NW10 —7K 45
Diamond St. SE5 —7E 86
Diamond Ter. SE10 —1E 106
Diamond Way. SE8 —6C 88
Diana Clo. E18 —1K 35
Diana Clo. SE8 —6B 88
Diana Gdns. Surb —2F 147
Diana Ho. SW13 —1B 100
Diana Rd. E17 —3B 34
Dianne Way. Barn —4H 5
Dianthus Clo. SE2 —5B 92
Dibden Ho. SE5 —7E 86
Dibden St. N1 —1C 68
Dibdin Clo. Sutt —3J 149
Dibdin Ho. NW6 —2K 65
(in two parts)
Dibdin Rd. Sutt —3J 149
Dicey Av. NW2 —4E 46
Dickens Av. N3 —1A 30
Dickens Av. Uxb —6D 58
Dickens Clo. Eri —7H 93
Dickens Clo. Hay —4G 77
Dickens Clo. Rich —2E 116
Dickens Ct. E11 —4J 35
(off Makepeace Rd.)
Dickens Dri. Chst —6G 127
Dickens Est. SE1 —2G 87
(George Row)
Dickens Est. SE16 —3G 87
(Jamaica Rd.)
Dickens' House. —4H 161
Dickens Ho. NW6 —3J 65
(off Malvern Rd.)
Dickens Ho. NW8 —3B 158
Dickens Ho. SE17 —5B 86
(off Doddington Gro.)
Dickens Ho. W9 —4J 65
(off Malvern Rd.)
Dickens Ho. WC1 —3E 160
Dickens La. N18 —5K 17
Dickens M. EC1 —5B 68 (5A 162)
(off Turnmill St.)
Dickenson Clo. N9 —1B 18
Dickenson Ho. N8 —6K 31
Dickenson Rd. N8 —7J 31
Dickenson Rd. Felt —5A 114
Dickensons La. SE25 —5G 141
(in two parts)
Dickensons Pl. SE25 —6G 141
Dickens Ri. Chig —3K 21
Dickens Rd. E6 —2B 72
Dickens Sq. SE1 —3C 86 (7D 168)
Dickens St. SW8 —2F 103
Dickerage La. N Mald —3J 135
Dickerage Rd. King T & N Mald —1J 135
Dicksee Ho. NW8 —4B 66 (4A 158)
(off Lyons Pl.)
Dickson Fold. Pinn —4B 24
Dickson Rd. SE9 —3C 108
Dick Turpin Way. Felt —4H 95
Didsbury Clo. E6 —1D 72
Digby Bus. Cen. E9 —6K 51
(off Digby Rd.)
Digby Cres. N4 —2C 50
Digby Gdns. Dag —1G 75
Digby Mans. W6 —5D 82
(off Hammersmith Bri. Rd.)
Digby Pl. Croy —3F 153
Digby Rd. E9 —6K 51
Digby Rd. Bark —7K 55
Digby St. E2 —3J 69
Diggon St. E1 —5K 69
Dighton Ct. SE17 —6C 86
(off John Ruskin St.)
Dighton Rd. SW18 —5A 102
Dignum St. N1 —2A 68
Digswell St. N7 —6A 50
Dilhorne Clo. SE12 —3K 125
Dilke St. SW3 —6D 84 (7F 171)
Dilloway La. S'hall —2C 78
Dillwyn Clo. SE26 —4A 124
Dilston Clo. N'holt —3A 60
Dilston Gro. SE16 —4J 87
Dilton Gdns. SW15 —1C 118
Dilwyn Ct. E17 —2A 34
Dimes Pl. W6 —4D 82
Dimmock Dri. Gnfd —5H 43
Dimond Clo. E7 —4J 53
Dimsdale Dri. NW9 —1J 45
Dimsdale Dri. Enf —7B 8
Dimsdale Wlk. E13 —2J 71
Dimson Cres. E3 —3C 70
Dingle Gdns. E14 —7C 70
Dingle Rd. Ashf —5D 112
Dingles Ct. Pinn —1B 24
Dingle, The. Uxb —3D 58
Dingley La. SW16 —2H 121
Dingley Pl. EC1 —3C 68 (2D 162)
Dingley Rd. EC1 —3C 68 (2C 162)
Dingwall Av. Croy & New Ad —2C 152
Dingwall Gdns. NW11 —6J 29
Dingwall Rd. SW18 —7A 102
Dingwall Rd. Cars —7D 150
Dingwall Rd. Croy —1D 152
Dinmont Est. E2 —2G 69
Dinmont Ho. E2 —2G 69
(off Pritchard's Rd.)
Dinmont St. E2 —2H 69
Dinsdale Gdns. SE25 —5E 140
Dinsdale Gdns. New Bar —5E 4
Dinsdale Rd. SE3 —6H 89
Dinsmore Rd. SW12 —7F 103
Dinton Ho. NW8 —4C 66 (3C 158)
(off Lilestone St.)

Dinton Rd.—Drayton Ho.

Dinton Rd. SW19 —6B 120
Dinton Rd. King T —7F 117
Diploma Av. N2 —4C 30
Diploma Ct. N2 —4C 30
Dirleton Rd. E15 —1H 71
Disbrowe Rd. W6 —6G 83
Discovery Bus. Pk. SE16 —3G 87
(off St James's Rd.)
Discovery Ho. E14 —7E 70
Discovery Wlk. E1 —1H 87
Dishforth La. NW9 —7F 13
Disley Ct. S'hall —6F 61
(off Howard Rd.)
Disney Pl. SE1 —2C 86 (6D 168)
Disney St. SE1 —2C 86 (6D 168)
Dison Clo. Enf —1E 8
Disraeli Clo. SE28 —1C 92
Disraeli Clo. W4 —3K 81
Disraeli Gdns. SW15 —4H 101
Disraeli Rd. E7 —6J 53
Disraeli Rd. NW10 —2K 63
Disraeli Rd. SW15 —4G 101
Disraeli Rd. W5 —1D 80
Diss St. E2 —3F 69 (1J 163)
Distaff La. EC4 —7C 68 (2C 168)
Distillery La. W6 —5E 82
Distillery Rd. W6 —5E 82
Distillery Wlk. Bren —6E 80
Distin St. SE11 —4A 86 (4J 173)
District Rd. Wemb —5B 44
Ditch All. SE10 —1D 106
Ditchburn St. E14 —7E 70
Ditchfield Rd. Hay —4C 60
Ditchley Ct. W7 —5K 61
(off Templeman Rd.)
Dittisham Rd. SE9 —4C 126
Ditton Clo. Th Dit —7A 134
Dittoncroft Clo. Croy —4E 152
Ditton Grange Clo. Surb —1D 146
Ditton Grange Dri. Surb —1D 146
Ditton Hill. Surb —1C 146
Ditton Hill Rd. Surb —1C 146
Ditton Lawn. Th Dit —1A 146
Ditton Pl. SE20 —1H 141
Ditton Reach. Th Dit —6B 134
Ditton Rd. Bexh —5D 110
Ditton Rd. S'hall —5D 78
Ditton Rd. Surb —2D 146
Divis Way. SW15 —6D 100
(off Dover Pk. Dri.)
Dixon Clark Ct. N1 —6B 50
Dixon Clo. E6 —6D 72
Dixon Pl. W W'ck —1D 154
Dixon Rd. SE14 —1A 106
Dixon Rd. SE25 —3E 140
Dixon's All. SE16 —2H 87
Dobbin Clo. Harr —2A 26
Dobell Rd. SE9 —5D 108
Dobree Av. NW10 —7D 46
Dobson Clo. NW6 —7B 48
Dobson Ho. SE5 —7D 86
(off Edmund St.)
Doby Ct. EC4 —2D 168
Dockers Tanner Rd. E14 —4C 88
Dockett Eddy. Cher —7A 130
Dockett Eddy La. Shep —7B 130
Dockhead. SE1 —2F 87 (7K 169)
Dockhead Wharf. SE1 —2F 87 (7K 169)
(off Shad Thames)
Dock Hill Av. SE16 —1K 87
Dockland St. E16 —1E 90
(in two parts)
Dockley Rd. SE16 —3G 87
Dockley Rd. Ind. Est. SE16 —3G 87
(off Dockley Rd.)
Dock Rd. E16 —7H 71
Dock Rd. Bren —7D 80
Dockside Rd. E16 —7B 72
Dock St. E1 —7G 69
Dockwell Clo. Felt —4J 95
Doctor Johnson Av. SW17 —3F 121
Doctors Clo. SE26 —5J 123
Docwra's Bldgs. N1 —6E 50
Dodbrooke Rd. SE27 —3A 122
Doddington Gro. SE17 —6B 86
Doddington Pl. SE17 —6B 86
Dodsley Pl. N9 —3D 18
Dodson St. SE1 —2A 86 (7K 167)
Dod St. E14 —6B 70
Doebury Wlk. SE18 —6A 92
(off Prestwood Clo.)
Doel Clo. SW19 —7A 120
Dog and Duck Yd. WC1 —5G 161
Doggett Rd. SE6 —7C 106
Doggetts Courts. Barn —5H 5
Doghurst Av. Hay —7D 76
Doghurst Dri. W Dray —7D 76
Dog Kennel Hill. SE5 —3E 104
Dog Kennel Hill Est. SE22 —3E 104
(off Albrighton Rd.)
Dog La. NW10 —4A 46
Doherty Rd. E13 —4J 71
Dokal Ind. Est. S'hall —3C 78
Dolben Ct. SE8 —4B 88
Dolben St. SE1 —1B 86 (5A 168)
(in two parts)
Dolby Rd. SW6 —2H 101
Dolland Ho. SE11 —6H 173
Dolland St. SE11 —5K 85 (6H 173)
Dollar Bay. E14 —2E 88
Dollary Pde. King T —3H 135
(off Kingston Rd.)
Dollis Av. N3 —1H 29
Dollis Brook Wlk. Barn —6B 4
Dollis Cres. Ruis —1A 42
Dolliscroft. NW7 —7B 14
Dollis Hill. —2D 46
Dollis Hill Av. NW2 —3D 46
Dollis Hill Est. NW2 —3C 46
Dollis Hill La. NW2 —4B 46
Dollis M. N3 —1J 29
Dollis Pk. N3 —1H 29
Dollis Rd. NW7 & N3 —7B 14
Dollis Valley Way. Barn —6C 4
Dolman Clo. N3 —1A 30
Dolman Rd. W4 —4K 81
Dolman St. SW4 —4K 103
Dolphin Clo. SE16 —2K 87
Dolphin Clo. SE28 —6D 74
Dolphin Clo. Surb —5D 134
Dolphin Ct. NW11 —6G 29
Dolphin Ct. SE8 —6B 88
(off Wotton Rd.)
Dolphin Est. Sun —1G 131
Dolphin Ho. SW18 —4K 101
Dolphin La. E14 —7D 70
Dolphin Rd. N'holt —2D 60
Dolphin Rd. Sun —1G 131
Dolphin Rd. N. Sun —1G 131
Dolphin Rd. S. Sun —1G 131
Dolphin Rd. W. Sun —1G 131
Dolphin Sq. SW1 —5G 85 (6B 172)
Dolphin Sq. W4 —7A 82
Dolphin St. King T —2E 134
Dolphin Tower. SE8 —6B 88
(off Abinger Gro.)
Dombey Ho. SE1 —2G 87 (7K 169)
(off Wolseley St.)
Dombey Ho. W11 —1F 83
(off St Ann's Rd.)
Dombey St. WC1 —5K 67 (5G 161)
(in two parts)
Dome Hill Pk. SE26 —4F 123
Domett Clo. SE5 —4D 104
Domfe Pl. E5 —4J 51
Domingo St. EC1 —4C 68 (3C 162)
Dominica Clo. E13 —3A 72
Dominion Bus. Pk. N9 —2E 18
Dominion Cen., The. S'hall —2C 78
Dominion Ho. E14 —5D 88
Dominion Pde. Harr —5K 25
Dominion Rd. Croy —7F 141
Dominion Rd. S'hall —2C 78
Dominion St. EC2 —5D 68 (5F 163)
Domitian Pl. Enf —5A 8
Domonic Dri. SE9 —4F 127
Domville Clo. N20 —2G 15
Donald Dri. Romf —5C 38
Donald Hunter Ho. E7 —5K 53
(off Post Office App., in two parts)
Donald Rd. E13 —1K 71
Donald Rd. Croy —7K 139
Donaldson Rd. NW6 —1H 65
Donaldson Rd. SE18 —1E 108
Donald Woods Gdns. Surb —2H 147
Doncaster Dri. N'holt —5D 42
Doncaster Gdns. N4 —6C 32
Doncaster Gdns. N'holt —5D 42
Doncaster Rd. N9 —7C 8
Donegal St. N1 —2K 67
Doneraile Ho. SW1 —5F 85 (6J 171)
(off Ebury Bri. Rd.)
Doneraile St. SW6 —2F 101
Dongola Rd. E1 —5A 70
Dongola Rd. E13 —3K 71
Dongola Rd. N17 —3E 32
Dongola Rd. W. E13 —3K 71
Donington Av. Ilf —5G 37
Donkey All. SE22 —7G 105
Donkey La. Enf —2B 8
Donnatt's Rd. SE14 —1B 106
Donne Ct. SE24 —6C 104
Donnefield Av. Edgw —7K 11
Donne Ho. E14 —6C 70
Donnelly Ct. SW6 —7G 83
(off Dawes Rd.)
Donne Pl. SW3 —4C 84 (3D 170)
Donne Pl. Mitc —4F 139
Donne Rd. Dag —2C 56
Donnington Ct. NW1 —7F 49
(off Castlehaven Rd.)
Donnington Ct. NW10 —7D 46
Donnington Rd. NW10 —7D 46
Donnington Rd. Harr —5D 26
Donnington Rd. Wor Pk —2C 148
Donnybrook Rd. SW16 —7G 121
Donoghue Cotts. E14 —5A 70
(off Maroon St.)
Donovan Av. N10 —2F 31
Donovan Ct. NW10 —7J 45
Donovan Ct. SW10 —5B 84 (6A 170)
(off Drayton Gdns.)
Don Phelan Clo. SE5 —1D 104
Doone Clo. Tedd —6A 116
Doon St. SE1 —1A 86 (5J 167)
Dora Ho. E14 —6B 70
Dora Ho. W11 —7F 65
(off St Ann's Rd.)
Doral Way. Cars —5D 150
Doran Ct. E6 —2D 72
Dorando Clo. W12 —7D 64
Doran Gro. SE18 —7J 91
Doran Mnr. N2 —5D 30
(off Gt. North Rd.)
Doran Wlk. E15 —7E 52
Dora Rd. SW19 —5J 119
Dora St. E14 —6B 70
Dorchester Av. N13 —4H 17
Dorchester Av. Bex —1D 128
Dorchester Av. Harr —6G 25
Dorchester Clo. N'holt —5F 43
Dorchester Clo. Orp —7B 128
Dorchester Ct. E18 —1H 35
(off Buckingham Rd.)
Dorchester Ct. N1 —7E 50
(off Englefield Rd.)
Dorchester Ct. N10 —3F 31
Dorchester Ct. N14 —7A 6
Dorchester Ct. NW2 —3F 47
Dorchester Ct. SE24 —5C 104
Dorchester Dri. SE24 —5C 104
Dorchester Dri. Felt —6G 95
Dorchester Gdns. E4 —4H 19
Dorchester Gdns. NW11 —4J 29
Dorchester Gro. W4 —5A 82
Dorchester M. N Mald —4K 135
Dorchester M. Twic —6C 98
Dorchester Rd. Mord —7K 137
Dorchester Rd. N'holt —5F 43
Dorchester Rd. Wor Pk —1E 148
Dorchester Ter. NW2 —3F 47
(off Grattpn Ter.)
Dorchester Way. Harr —6F 27
Dorchester Waye. Hay —6K 59
(in two parts)
Dorcis Av. Bexh —2E 110
Dordrecht Rd. W3 —1A 82
Dore Av. E12 —5E 54
Doreen Av. NW9 —1K 45
Doreen Capstan Ho. E11 —3G 53
(off Apollo Pl.)
Dore Gdns. Mord —7K 137
Dorell Clo. S'hall —5D 60
Doria Rd. SW6 —2H 101
Doric Way. NW1 —3H 67 (1C 160)
Dorien Rd. SW20 —2F 137
Dorinda St. N7 —6A 50
Doris Av. Eri —1J 111
Doris Emmerton Ct. SW11 —4A 102
Doris Rd. E7 —7J 53
Doris Rd. Ashf —6F 113
Doritt M. N18 —5K 17
Dorking Clo. SE8 —6B 88
Dorking Clo. Wor Pk —2F 149
Dorking Ct. N17 —1G 33
(off Hampden La.)
Dorking Ho. SE1 —3D 86
Dorlcote Rd. SW18 —7C 102
Dorly Clo. Shep —5G 131
Dorman Pl. N9 —2B 18
Dormans Clo. N'wd —1F 23
Dorman Wlk. NW10 —5K 45
Dorman Way. NW8 —1B 66
Dorma Trad. Pk. E10 —1K 51
Dormay St. SW18 —5K 101
Dormer Clo. E15 —6H 53
Dormer Clo. Barn —5A 4
Dormer's Av. S'hall —6E 60
Dormers Ri. S'hall —6F 61
Dormer's Wells. —7F 61
Dormer's Wells La. S'hall —6E 60
Dormstone Ho. SE17 —4E 86
(off Beckway St.)
Dormywood. Ruis —5H 23
Dornberg Clo. SE3 —7J 89
Dornberg Rd. SE3 —7K 89
Dorncliffe Rd. SW6 —2G 101
Dorney. NW3 —7C 48
Dorney Ri. Orp —4K 145
Dorney Way. Houn —5C 96
Dornfell St. NW6 —5H 47
Dornton Rd. SW12 —2F 121
Dornton Rd. S Croy —6D 152
Dorothy Av. Wemb —7E 44
Dorothy Evans Clo. Bexh —4H 111
Dorothy Gdns. Dag —4B 56
Dorothy Pettingell Ho. Sutt —3K 149
(off Angel Hill)
Dorothy Rd. SW11 —3D 102
Dorrell Pl. SW9 —3A 104
Dorrien Wlk. SW16 —2H 121
Dorrington Ct. SE25 —1E 140
Dorrington St. EC1 —5A 68 (5J 161)
Dorrit Ho. W11 —1F 83
(off St Ann's Rd.)
Dorrit St. SE1 —6D 168
Dorrit Way. Chst —6G 127
Dorryn Ct. SE26 —5K 123
Dors Clo. NW9 —1K 45
Dorset Av. Hay —3G 59
Dorset Av. Romf —4K 39
Dorset Av. S'hall —4E 78
Dorset Av. Well —4K 109
Dorset Bldgs. EC4 —6B 68 (1A 168)
Dorset Clo. NW1 —5D 66 (5E 158)
Dorset Clo. Hay —3G 59
Dorset Ct. N1 —7E 50
(off Hertford Rd.)
Dorset Ct. W7 —5K 61
(off Copley Clo.)
Dorset Ct. N'wd —1H 23
Dorset Dri. Edgw —6A 12
Dorset Gdns. Mitc —4K 139
Dorset Ho. NW1 —4D 66 (5F 159)
(off Gloucester Pl.)
Dorset M. N3 —1J 29
Dorset Pl. E15 —6F 53
Dorset Ri. EC4 —6B 68 (1A 168)
Dorset Rd. E7 —7A 54
Dorset Rd. N15 —4D 32
Dorset Rd. N22 —1J 31
Dorset Rd. SE9 —2C 126
Dorset Rd. SW8 —7J 85
Dorset Rd. SW19 —1J 137
Dorset Rd. W5 —3C 80
Dorset Rd. Ashf —3A 112
Dorset Rd. Beck —3K 141
Dorset Rd. Harr —6G 25
Dorset Rd. Mitc —2C 138
Dorset Sq. NW1 —4D 66 (4E 158)
Dorset St. W1 —5D 66 (6F 159)
Dorset Way. Twic —1H 115
Dorset Way. Uxb —2B 58
Dorset Waye. Houn —7D 78
Dorton Clo. SE15 —7E 86
Dorton Vs. W Dray —7C 76
Dorville Cres. W6 —3D 82
Dorville Rd. SE12 —5H 107
Dothill Rd. SE18 —7G 91
Douai Gro. Hamp —1G 133
Doughty Ho. SW10 —6A 84
(off Netherton Gro.)
Doughty M. WC1 —4K 67 (4G 161)
Doughty St. WC1 —4K 67 (3G 161)
Douglas Av. E17 —1B 34
Douglas Av. N Mald —4D 136
Douglas Av. Wemb —7E 44
Douglas Clo. Stan —5F 11
Douglas Clo. Wall —6J 151
Douglas Ct. NW6 —7J 47
(off Quex Rd.)
Douglas Cres. Hay —4A 60
Douglas Dri. Croy —3C 154
Douglas Est. N1 —6C 50
(off Marquess Rd.)
Douglas Ho. Surb —1F 147
Douglas Johnstone Ho. SW6 —6H 83
(off Clem Attlee Ct.)
Douglas Mans. Houn —3F 97
Douglas M. NW2 —3G 47
Douglas Pl. E14 —4E 88
Douglas Pl. SW1 —4H 85 (4C 172)
(off Douglas St.)
Douglas Rd. E4 —1B 20
Douglas Rd. E16 —5J 71
Douglas Rd. N1 —7C 50
Douglas Rd. N22 —1A 32
Douglas Rd. NW6 —1H 65
Douglas Rd. Houn —3F 97
Douglas Rd. Ilf —7A 38
Douglas Rd. King T —2H 135
Douglas Rd. Stanw —6A 94
Douglas Rd. Surb —2F 147
Douglas Rd. Well —1B 110
Douglas Rd. N. N1 —6C 50
Douglas Rd. S. N1 —6C 50
Douglas Robinson Ct. SW16 —7J 121
(off Streatham High Rd.)
Douglas Sq. Mord —6J 137
Douglas St. SW1 —4H 85 (4C 172)
Douglas Ter. E17 —1B 34
Douglas Waite Ho. NW6 —7J 47
Douglas Way. SE8 —7C 88
Douglas Way. SE14 —7B 88
(in two parts)
Doulton Ho. SE11 —2H 173
Doulton M. NW6 —6K 47
Dounesforth Gdns. SW18 —1K 119
Douro Pl. W8 —3K 83
Douro St. E3 —2C 70
Douthwaite Sq. E1 —1G 87
Dove App. E6 —5C 72
Dove Clo. NW7 —7G 13
Dove Clo. N'holt —4B 60
Dove Clo. Wall —7K 151
Dove Commercial Cen. NW5 —5G 49
Dovecot Clo. Pinn —5A 24
Dovecote Av. N22 —3A 32
Dovecote Gdns. SW14 —3K 99
Dove Ct. EC2 —1E 168
Dovedale Av. Harr —6C 26
Dovedale Av. Ilf —2E 36
Dovedale Clo. Well —2A 110
Dovedale Ri. Mitc —7D 120
Dovedale Rd. SE22 —5H 105
Dovedon Clo. N14 —2D 16
Dovehouse Ct. N'holt —3B 60
(off Kittiwake Rd.)
Dove Ho. Gdns. E4 —2H 19
Dovehouse Mead. Bark —2H 73
Dovehouse St. SW3 —5B 84 (5B 170)
Dove M. SW5 —4A 84
Dove Pk. Pinn —1E 24
Dover Clo. NW2 —2F 47
Dover Clo. Romf —2J 39
Dovercourt Av. T Hth —5A 140
Dovercourt Est. N1 —6D 50
Dovercourt Gdns. Stan —5K 11
Dovercourt La. Sutt —3A 150
Dovercourt Rd. SE22 —6E 104
Doverfield Rd. SW2 —7J 103
Dover Flats. SE1 —4E 86
Dover Gdns. Cars —3D 150
Dover Ho. SE15 —6J 87
Dover Ho. Rd. SW15 —4C 100
Doveridge Gdns. N13 —4G 17
Dove Rd. N1 —6D 50
Dove Row. E2 —1G 69
Dover Pk. Dri. SW15 —6D 100
Dover Patrol. SE3 —2K 107
Dover Rd. E12 —2A 54
Dover Rd. N9 —2D 18
Dover Rd. SE19 —6D 122
Dover Rd. Romf —6E 38
Dover St. W1 —7F 67 (3K 165)
Dover Ter. Rich —2F 99
(off Sandycombe Rd.)
Dover Yd. W1 —4A 166
Doves Clo. Brom —2C 156
Doves Yd. N1 —1A 68
Doveton Rd. S Croy —5D 152
Doveton St. E1 —4J 69
Dove Wlk. SW1 —5E 84 (5G 171)
Dovey Lodge. N1 —7A 50
(off Bewdley St.)
Dowanhill Rd. SE6 —1F 125
Dowdeswell Clo. SW15 —4A 100
Dowding Ho. N6 —7E 30
(off Hillcrest)
Dowding Pl. Stan —6F 11
Dowding Rd. Uxb —7B 40
Dowdney Clo. NW5 —5G 49
Dowe Ho. SE3 —3G 107
Dower Av. Wall —7F 151
Dowes Ho. SW16 —3J 121
Dowgate Hill. EC4 —7D 68 (2E 168)
Dowland St. W10 —3G 65
Dowlas St. SE5 —7E 86
Dowler Ho. E1 —6G 69
(off Burslem St.)
Dowling Ho. Belv —3F 93
Dowman Clo. SW19 —1K 137
Downage. NW4 —3E 28
Downalong. Bus H —1C 10
Downbank Av. Bexh —1K 111
Down Barns Rd. Ruis —3B 42
Downbury M. SW18 —5J 101
Down Clo. N'holt —2K 59
Downderry Rd. Brom —3F 125
Downe Clo. Well —7C 92
Down End. SE18 —7F 91
Downend Ct. SE15 —6E 86
(off Longhope Clo.)
Downe Rd. Kes —7C 156
Downe Rd. Mitc —2D 138
Downer's Cottage. SW4 —4G 103
Downes Clo. Twic —6B 98
Downes Ct. N21 —1F 17
Downe Ter. Rich —6E 98
Downfield. Wor Pk —1B 148
Downfield Clo. W9 —4K 65
Down Hall Rd. King T —1D 134
Downham. —5F 125
Downham Clo. Romf —1G 39
Downham Enterprise Cen. SE6 —2H 125
Downham La. Brom —5F 125
Downham Rd. N1 —7D 50
Downham Way. Brom —5F 125
Downhills Av. N17 —3D 32
Downhills Pk. Rd. N17 —3C 32
Downhills Way. N17 —3C 32
Downhurst Av. NW7 —5E 12
Downhurst Ct. NW4 —3E 28
Downing Clo. Harr —3G 25
Downing Dri. Gnfd —1H 61
Downing Rd. Dag —1F 75
Downings. E6 —6E 72
Downing St. SW1 —2J 85 (6E 166)
Downland Clo. N20 —1F 15
Downleys Clo. SE9 —2C 126
Downman Rd. SE9 —3C 108
Down Pl. W6 —4D 82
Down Rd. Tedd —6B 116
Downs Av. Chst —5D 126
Downs Av. Pinn —6C 24
Downsbridge Rd. Beck —1F 143
Downsell Rd. E15 —4E 52
Downsfield Rd. E17 —6A 34
Downshall Av. Ilf —6J 37
Downs Hill. Beck —7F 125
Downshire Hill. NW3 —4B 48
Downside. Sun —1J 131
Downside. Twic —3K 115
Downside Clo. SW19 —6A 120
Downside Cres. NW3 —5C 48
Downside Cres. W13 —4A 62
Downside Rd. Sutt —6B 150
Downside Wlk. Bren —6D 80
(off Windmill Rd.)
Downside Wlk. N'holt —3D 60
Downs La. E5 —4H 51
Downs Pk. Rd. E8 & E5 —5F 51
Downs Rd. E5 —4G 51
Downs Rd. Beck —2D 142
(in two parts)
Downs Rd. Enf —4K 7
Downs Rd. T Hth —1C 140
Downs, The. SW20 —7F 119
Down St. W1 —1F 85 (5J 165)
Down St. W Mol —5E 132
Down St. M. W1 —1F 85 (5J 165)
Downs Vw. Iswth —1K 97
Downsview Gdns. SE19 —7B 122
Downsview Rd. SE19 —7C 122
Downsway, The. Sutt —7A 150
Downton Av. SW2 —2J 121
Downtown Rd. SE16 —2A 88
Downway. N12 —7H 15
Down Way. N'holt —3K 59
Dowrey St. N1 —1A 68
Dowsett Rd. N17 —2F 33
Dowson Clo. SE5 —4D 104
Doyce St. SE1 —2C 86 (6C 168)
Doyle Gdns. NW10 —1C 64
Doyle Rd. SE25 —4G 141
D'Oyley St. SW1 —4E 84 (3G 171)
Doynton St. N19 —2F 49
Draco Ga. SW15 —3E 100
Draco St. SE17 —6C 86
Dragmire La. Mitc —3B 138
Dragonfly Clo. E13 —3K 71
Dragon Rd. SE15 —6E 86
Dragon Yd. WC1 —7F 161
Dragoon Rd. SE8 —5B 88
Dragor Rd. NW10 —4J 63
Drake Clo. SE16 —2K 87
Drake Cres. SE28 —6C 74
Drakefell Rd. SE14 & SE4 —2K 105
Drakefield Rd. SW17 —3E 120
Drake Hall. E16 —1K 89
(off Wesley Av., in two parts)
Drake Ho. SW1 —6H 85 (7C 172)
(off Dolphin Sq.)
Drakeland Ho. W9 —4H 65
(off Fernhead Rd.)
Drakeley Ct. N5 —4B 50
Drake Rd. SE4 —3C 106
Drake Rd. Chess —5G 147
Drake Rd. Croy —7K 139
Drake Rd. Harr —2D 42
Drake Rd. Mitc —6E 138
Drakes Ct. SE23 —1J 123
Drakes Courtyard. NW6 —7H 47
Drakes Dri. N'wd —1D 22
Drake St. WC1 —5K 67 (6G 161)
Drake St. Enf —1J 7
Drakes Wlk. E6 —1D 72
(in two parts)
Drakewood Rd. SW16 —7H 121
Draper Clo. Belv —4F 93
Draper Clo. Iswth —2H 97
Draper Ct. Brom —4C 144
Draper Ho. SE1 —4B 86
(off Elephant & Castle)
Draper Pl. N1 —1B 68
(off Dagmar Ter.)
Drapers' Cottage Homes. NW7 —4H 13
(in two parts)
Drapers Gdns. EC2 —6D 68 (7F 163)
Drapers Rd. E15 —4F 53
Drapers Rd. N17 —3F 33
Drapers Rd. Enf —2G 7
Drappers Way. SE16 —4G 87
Draven Clo. Brom —7H 143
Drawdock Rd. SE10 —2F 89
Drawell Clo. SE18 —5J 91
Drax Av. SW20 —7C 118
Draycot Rd. E11 —6K 35
Draycot Rd. Surb —1G 147
Draycott Av. SW3 —4C 84 (3D 170)
Draycott Av. Harr —6B 26
Draycott Clo. Harr —6B 26
Draycott Pl. SW3 —4D 84 (4E 170)
Draycott Ter. SW3 —4D 84 (4F 171)
Dray Ct. Wor Pk —1B 148
Drayford Clo. W9 —4H 65
Dray Gdns. SW2 —5K 103
Draymans Way. Iswth —3K 97
Drayside M. S'hall —2D 78
Drayson M. W8 —2J 83
Drayton Av. W13 —7A 62
Drayton Bri. Rd. W7 & W13 —7K 61
Drayton Clo. Houn —5D 96
Drayton Clo. Ilf —1H 55
Drayton Ct. W Dray —4B 76
Drayton Gdns. N21 —7G 7
Drayton Gdns. SW10 —5A 84 (6A 170)
Drayton Gdns. W13 —7A 62
Drayton Gdns. W Dray —2A 76
Drayton Grn. W13 —7A 62
Drayton Grn. Rd. W13 —7B 62
Drayton Gro. W13 —7A 62
Drayton Ho. E11 —1F 53

Drayton Pk.—Earldom Rd.

Drayton Pk. N5 —4A 50
Drayton Pk. M. N5 —5A 50
Drayton Rd. E11 —1F 53
Drayton Rd. N17 —2E 32
Drayton Rd. NW10 —1B 64
Drayton Rd. W13 —7A 62
Drayton Rd. Croy —2B 152
Drayton Waye. Harr —6B 26
Dreadnought St. SE10 —3G 89
Drenon Sq. Hay —7H 59
Dresden Clo. NW6 —6K 47
Dresden Ho. SE11 —3H 173
Dresden Rd. N19 —1G 49
Dressington Av. SE4 —6C 106
Drew Av. NW7 —6B 14
Drewery Ct. SE3 —3G 107
Drewett Ho. E1 —6G 69
(off Christian St.)
Drew Gdns. Gnfd —6K 43
Drew Ho. SW16 —3J 121
Drewitts Ct. W on T —7H 131
Drew Rd. E16 —1B 90
(in three parts)
Drewstead Rd. SW16 —2H 121
Driffield Ct. NW9 —1A 28
(off Pageant Av.)
Driffield Rd. E3 —2A 70
Drift, The. Brom —3B 156
Driftway, The. Mitc —1E 138
Drinkwater Ho. SE5 —7D 86
(off Picton St.)
Drinkwater Rd. Harr —2F 43
Drive Ct. Edgw —5B 12
Drive Mans. SW6 —2G 101
(off Fulham Rd.)
Drive, The. E4 —1A 20
Drive, The. E17 —3D 34
Drive, The. E18 —4J 35
Drive, The. N2 —5D 30
Drive, The. N3 —7D 14
Drive, The. N7 —6K 49
Drive, The. N11 —6C 16
Drive, The. NW10 —1B 64
Drive, The. NW11 —7G 29
Drive, The. SW6 —2G 101
Drive, The. SW16 —3K 139
Drive, The. SW20 —7E 118
Drive, The. W3 —6J 63
Drive, The. Ashf —7F 113
Drive, The. Bark —7K 55
Drive, The. Beck —2C 142
Drive, The. Bex —6C 110
Drive, The. Buck H —1F 21
Drive, The. Chst —3K 145
Drive, The. Col R —1K 39
Drive, The. Edgw —5B 12
Drive, The. Enf —1J 7
Drive, The. Eps —6B 148
Drive, The. Eri —7H 93
Drive, The. Esh —7G 133
Drive, The. Felt —7A 96
Drive, The. Harr —7E 24
Drive, The. High Bar —3B 4
Drive, The. Houn & Iswth —2H 97
Drive, The. Ilf —6C 36
Drive, The. King T —7J 117
Drive, The. Mord —5A 138
Drive, The. New Bar —6F 5
Drive, The. N'wd —2G 23
Drive, The. Sidc —3B 128
Drive, The. Surb —7E 134
Drive, The. T Hth —4D 140
Drive, The. Uxb —3A 40
Drive, The. Wemb —2J 45
Drive, The. W W'ck —7F 143
Driveway, The. E17 —6D 34
(off Hoe St.)
Droitwich Clo. SE26 —3G 123
Dromey Gdns. Harr —7E 10
Dromore Rd. SW15 —6G 101
Dronfield Gdns. Dag —5C 56
Droop St. W10 —3F 65
Drovers Pl. SE15 —7J 87
Drovers Rd. S Croy —5D 152
Druce Rd. SE21 —6E 104
Druid St. SE1 —2E 86 (6H 169)
Druids Way. Brom —4F 143
Drumaline Ridge. Wor Pk —2A 148
Drummond Av. Romf —4K 39
Drummond Cen. Croy —2C 152
Drummond Cres. NW1 —3H 67 (1C 160)
Drummond Dri. Stan —7E 10
Drummond Ga. SW1 —5H 85 (5D 172)
Drummond Ho. E2 —2G 69
(off Goldsmiths Row)
Drummond Pl. Twic —7B 98
Drummond Rd. E11 —6A 36
Drummond Rd. SE16 —3H 87
Drummond Rd. Croy —2C 152
(in two parts)
Drummond Rd. Romf —4K 39
Drummonds, The. Buck H —2E 20
Drummond St. NW1 —4G 67 (3A 160)
Drum St. E1 —6F 69 (7K 163)
Drury Cres. Croy —2A 152
Drury Ho. SW8 —1G 103
Drury La. WC2 —6J 67 (7F 161)
Drury Rd. Harr —7G 25
Drury Way. NW10 —5K 45
Drury Way Ind. Est. NW10 —5J 45
Dryad St. SW15 —3F 101
Dryburgh Gdns. NW9 —3G 27
Dryburgh Ho. SW1 —5F 85 (5K 171)
(off Abbots Mnr.)
Dryburgh Rd. SW15 —3D 100
Dryden Av. W7 —6K 61
Dryden Ct. SE11 —4B 86 (4K 173)
Dryden Mans. W14 —6G 83
(off Queen's Club Gdns.)
Dryden Rd. SW19 —6A 120
Dryden Rd. Enf —6K 7
Dryden Rd. Harr —1K 25
Dryden Rd. Well —1K 109
Dryden St. WC2 —6J 67 (1F 167)
Dryfield Clo. NW10 —6J 45
Dryfield Rd. Edgw —6D 12
Dryfield Wlk. SE8 —6C 88
Dryhill Rd. Belv —6F 93
Drylands Rd. N8 —6J 31
Drysdale Av. E4 —7J 9
Drysdale Clo. N'wd —1G 23
Drysdale Ho. N1 —3E 68 (1H 163)
(off Drysdale St.)
Drysdale Pl. N1 —3E 68 (1H 163)
Drysdale St. N1 —3E 68 (1H 163)
Dublin Av. E8 —1G 69
Dublin Ct. S Harr —2H 43
(off Northolt Rd.)
Du Burstow Ter. W7 —2J 79
Ducal St. E2 —3F 69 (2K 163)
Du Cane Clo. W12 —6E 64
Du Cane Ct. SW17 —1E 120
Du Cane Rd. W12 —6B 64
Ducavel Ho. SW2 —1K 121
Duchess Clo. N11 —5A 16
Duchess Clo. Sutt —4A 150
Duchess Gro. Buck H —2E 20
Duchess M. W1 —5F 67 (6K 159)
Duchess of Bedford Ho. W8 —2J 83
(off Duchess of Bedford's Wlk.)
Duchess of Bedford's Wlk. W8 —2J 83
Duchess St. W1 —5F 67 (6K 159)
Duchy Rd. Barn —1G 5
Duchy St. SE1 —1A 86 (4K 167)
(in two parts)
Ducie St. SW4 —4K 103
Duckett M. N4 —6B 32
Duckett Rd. N4 —6A 32
Duckett St. E1 —4K 69
Ducking Stool Ct. Romf —4K 39
Duck La. W1 —1C 166
Duck Lees La. Enf —4F 9
Duck's Hill Rd. N'wd & Ruis —1D 22
Ducks Island. —6A 4
Ducks Wlk. Twic —5C 98
Du Cros Dri. Stan —6J 11
Du Cros Rd. W3 —1A 82
Dudden Hill. —5D 46
Dudden Hill La. NW10 —4B 46
Dudden Hill Pde. NW10 —4B 46
Duddington Clo. SE9 —4B 126
Dudley Av. Harr —3C 26
Dudley Ct. NW11 —4H 29
Dudley Ct. W1 —6D 66 (1E 164)
(off Up. Berkeley St.)
Dudley Ct. WC2 —6J 67 (7E 160)
Dudley Dri. Mord —1G 149
Dudley Dri. Ruis —5K 41
Dudley Gdns. W13 —2B 80
Dudley Gdns. Harr —1H 43
Dudley Ho. W2 —5B 66 (6A 158)
(off N. Wharf Rd.)
Dudley Rd. E17 —2C 34
Dudley Rd. N3 —2K 29
Dudley Rd. NW6 —2G 65
Dudley Rd. SW19 —6J 119
Dudley Rd. Ashf —5B 112
Dudley Rd. Felt —1E 112
Dudley Rd. Harr —2G 43
Dudley Rd. Ilf —4F 55
Dudley Rd. King T —3F 135
Dudley Rd. Rich —2F 99
Dudley Rd. S'hall —2B 78
Dudley Rd. W on T —6J 131
Dudley St. W2 —5B 66 (6A 158)
Dudlington Rd. E5 —2J 51
Dudmaston M. SW3 —5B 170
Dudsbury Rd. Sidc —6B 128
Dudset La. Houn —1J 95
Duffell Ho. SE11 —6H 173
Dufferin Av. EC1 —4E 162
Dufferin Ct. EC1 —4D 68 (4E 162)
(off Dufferin St.)
Dufferin St. EC1 —4C 68 (4D 162)
Duffield Clo. Harr —5K 25
Duffield Dri. N15 —4F 33
Duff St. E14 —6D 70
Dufour's Pl. W1 —6G 67 (1B 166)
Dugard Way. SE11 —4B 86
Duke Gdns. Ilf —4H 37
Duke Humphrey Rd. SE3 —1G 107
(in two parts)
Duke of Cambridge Clo. Twic —6H 97
Duke of Edinburgh Rd. Sutt —2B 150
Duke of Wellington Pl. SW1 —2E 84 (6H 165)
Duke of York Column. —5D 166
Duke of York St. SW1 —1G 85 (4B 166)
Duke Rd. W4 —5K 81
Duke Rd. Ilf —4H 37
Dukes Av. N3 —1K 29
Duke's Av. N10 —3F 31
Duke's Av. W4 —5K 81
Duke's Av. Edgw —6A 12
Dukes Av. Harr —4J 25
Dukes Av. Houn —4C 96
Dukes Av. N Mald —3B 136
Dukes Av. N Har —6D 24
Dukes Av. N'holt —7C 42
Dukes Av. Rich & King T —4C 116
Dukes Clo. Ashf —4E 112
Dukes Clo. Hamp —5D 114
Dukes Ct. E6 —1E 72
Dukes Ct. SE13 —2E 106
Dukes Ga. W4 —4J 81
Dukes Grn. Av. Felt —5J 95
Dukes Head Pas. Hamp —7G 115
Duke's Head Yd. N6 —1F 49
Duke Shore Pl. E14 —7B 70
Duke Shore Wharf. E14 —7B 70
Duke's Ho. SW1 —4H 85 (3D 172)
(off Vincent St.)
Dukes La. W8 —2K 83
Dukes M. N10 —3F 31
Duke's M. W1 —7H 159
Dukes Orchard. Bex —1J 129
Duke's Pas. E17 —4E 34
Duke's Pl. EC3 —6E 68 (1H 169)
Dukes Ride. Uxb —4A 40
Dukes Rd. E6 —1E 72
Duke's Rd. NW1 —3H 67 (2D 160)
Dukes Rd. W3 —4G 63
Dukesthorpe Rd. SE26 —4K 123
Duke St. SW1 —1G 85
Duke St. W1 —6E 66 (4B 166)
Duke St. Rich —4D 98
Duke St. Sutt —4B 150
Duke St. Hill. SE1 —1D 86 (4F 169)
Duke St. Mans. W1 —6E 66 (1H 165)
(off Duke St.)
Dukes Way. W W'ck —3G 155
Duke's Yd. W1 —7E 66 (2H 165)
Dulas St. N4 —1K 49
Dulford St. W11 —7G 65
Dulka Rd. SW11 —5D 102
Dulverton. NW1 —1G 67
(off Royal College St.)
Dulverton Mans. WC1 —4H 161
Dulverton Rd. SE9 —2G 127
Dulverton Rd. Ruis —1J 41
Dulwich. —2E 122
Dulwich Comn. SE21 & SE22 —1E 122
Dulwich Hamlet F.C. —4E 104
Dulwich Lawn Clo. SE22 —5F 105
Dulwich Oaks Pl. SE21 —3E 122
Dulwich Picture Gallery. —7E 104
Dulwich Ri. Gdns. SE22 —5F 105
Dulwich Rd. SE24 —5A 104
Dulwich Village. —7E 104
Dulwich Village. SE21 —6D 104
Dulwich Wood Av. SE19 —4E 122
Dulwich Wood Pk. SE19 —4E 122
Dumain Ct. SE11 —4B 86
(off Opal St.)
Dumbarton Ct. SW2 —6J 103
Dumbarton Rd. SW2 —6J 103
Dumbleton Clo. King T —1H 135
Dumbreck Rd. SE9 —4D 108
Dumont Rd. N16 —3E 50
Dumpton Pl. NW1 —7E 48
Dumsey Eyot. Cher —7A 130
Dunally Pk. Shep —7F 131
Dunbar Av. SW16 —2A 140
Dunbar Av. Beck —4A 142
Dunbar Av. Dag —3G 57
Dunbar Clo. Hay —6K 59
Dunbar Gdns. Dag —5G 57
Dunbar Rd. E7 —6J 53
Dunbar Rd. N22 —1A 32
Dunbar Rd. N Mald —4J 135
Dunbar St. SE27 —3C 122
Dunbar Wharf. E14 —7B 70
Dunblane Clo. Edgw —2C 12
Dunblane Rd. SE9 —3C 108
Dunboe Pl. Shep —7E 130
Dunboyne Rd. NW3 —5D 48
Dunbridge Ho. SW15 —6B 100
(off Highcliffe Dri.)
Dunbridge St. E2 —4G 69
Duncan Clo. Barn —4F 5
Duncan Ct. N21 —1G 17
Duncan Gro. W3 —6A 64
Duncan Ho. SW1 —5G 85 (6B 172)
(off Dolphin Sq.)
Duncannon Ho. SW1 —5H 85 (6D 172)
(off Lindsay Sq.)
Duncannon St. WC2 —7J 67 (3E 166)
Duncan Rd. E8 —1H 69
Duncan Rd. Rich —4E 98
Duncan St. N1 —2B 68
Duncan Ter. N1 —2B 68
(in two parts)
Duncombe Hill. SE23 —7A 106
Duncombe Rd. N19 —1H 49
Duncrievie Rd. SE13 —6F 107
Duncroft. SE18 —7J 91
Dundalk Rd. SE4 —3A 106
Dundas Gdns. W Mol —3F 133
Dundas Rd. SE15 —2J 105
Dundee Ho. W9 —3A 66
(off Maida Va.)
Dundee Rd. E13 —2K 71
Dundee Rd. SE25 —5H 141
Dundee St. E1 —1H 87
Dundee Way. Enf —3F 9
Dundee Wharf. E14 —7B 70
Dundela Gdns. Wor Pk —4D 148
Dundonald Clo. E6 —6C 72
Dundonald Ho. E14 —2D 88
Dundonald Rd. NW10 —1F 65
Dundonald Rd. SW19 —7G 119
Dundry Ho. SE26 —3G 123
Dunedin Ho. E16 —1D 90
(off Manwood St.)
Dunedin Rd. E10 —3D 52
Dunedin Rd. Ilf —1G 55
Dunedin Way. Hay —4A 60
Dunelm Gro. SE27 —3C 122
Dunelm St. E1 —6K 69
Dunfield Gdns. SE6 —5D 124
Dunfield Rd. SE6 —5D 124
(in two parts)
Dunford Ct. Pinn —1D 24
Dunford Rd. N7 —4K 49
Dungarvan Av. SW15 —4C 100
Dunheved Clo. T Hth —6A 140
Dunheved Rd. N. T Hth —6A 140
Dunheved Rd. S. T Hth —6A 140
Dunheved Rd. W. T Hth —6A 140
Dunholme Grn. N9 —3A 18
Dunholme La. N9 —3A 18
Dunholme Rd. N9 —3A 18
Dunkeld Ho. E14 —6F 71
Dunkeld Rd. SE25 —4D 140
Dunkeld Rd. Dag —2B 56
Dunkery Rd. SE9 —4B 126
Dunkirk St. SE27 —4C 122
Dunlace Rd. E5 —4J 51
Dunleary Clo. Houn —7D 96
Dunley Dri. New Ad —7D 154
Dunloe Av. N17 —3D 32
Dunloe Ct. E2 —2F 69
(off Dawson St.)
Dunloe St. E2 —2F 69
Dunlop Pl. SE16 —3F 87
Dunmore Point. E2 —3F 69 (2J 163)
(off Gascoigne Pl.)
Dunmore Rd. NW6 —1G 65
Dunmore Rd. SW20 —1E 136
Dunmow Clo. Felt —3C 114
Dunmow Clo. Romf —5C 38
Dunmow Ho. SE11 —5K 85 (5H 173)
(off Newburn St.)
Dunmow Rd. E15 —4F 53
Dunmow Wlk. N1 —1C 68
(off Popham St.)
Dunnage Cres. SE16 —4A 88
Dunnico Ho. SE17 —5E 86
(off East St.)
Dunn Mead. NW9 —7G 13
Dunnock Clo. E6 —6C 72
Dunnock Clo. N9 —1E 18
Dunn's Pas. WC1 —7F 161
Dunn St. E8 —5F 51
Dunollie Pl. NW5 —5G 49
Dunollie Rd. NW5 —5G 49
Dunoon Gdns. SE23 —7K 105
Dunoon Ho. N1 —1K 67
(off Bemerton Est.)
Dunoon Rd. SE23 —7J 105
Dunoran Home. Brom —1C 144
Dunraven Dri. Enf —2F 7
Dunraven Rd. W12 —1C 82
Dunraven St. W1 —7D 66 (2F 165)
Dunsany Rd. W14 —3F 83
Dunsfold Way. New Ad —7D 154
Dunsford Way. SW15 —6D 100
Dunsmore Clo. Hay —4C 60
Dunsmore Rd. W on T —6K 131
Dunsmure Rd. N16 —1E 50
Dunspring La. Ilf —2F 37
Dunstable M. W1 —5E 66 (5H 159)
Dunstable Rd. Rich —4E 98
Dunstable Rd. W Mol —4D 132
Dunstall Rd. SW20 —6D 118
Dunstall Way. W Mol —3F 133
Dunstall Welling Est. Well —2B 110
Dunstan Clo. N2 —3A 30
Dunstan Glade. Orp —6H 145
Dunstan Houses. E1 —5J 69
(off Stepney Grn.)
Dunstan Rd. NW11 —1H 47
Dunstan's Gro. SE22 —6H 105
Dunstan's Rd. SE22 —7G 105
Dunster Av. Mord —1F 149
Dunster Clo. Barn —4A 4
Dunster Clo. Romf —2J 39
Dunster Ct. EC3 —7E 68 (2H 169)
Dunster Dri. NW9 —1J 45
Dunster Gdns. NW6 —7H 47
Dunster Ho. SE6 —3E 124
Dunsterville Way. SE1 —2D 86 (7F 169)
Dunster Way. Harr —3C 42
Dunston Rd. E8 —1F 69
Dunston Rd. SW11 —2E 102
Dunston St. E8 —1E 68
Dunton Clo. Surb —1E 146
Dunton Ct. SE23 —2H 123
Dunton Rd. E10 —7D 34
Dunton Rd. SE1 —5F 87
Dunton Rd. Romf —4K 39
Duntshill Rd. SW18 —1K 119
Dunvegan Clo. W Mol —4F 133
Dunvegan Rd. SE9 —4D 108
Dunwich Rd. Bexh —1F 111
Dunworth M. W11 —6H 65
Duplex Ride. SW1 —2D 84 (7F 165)
Dupont Rd. SW20 —2F 137
Duppas Av. Croy —4B 152
Duppas Clo. Shep —5F 131
Duppas Hill La. Croy —4B 152
Duppas Hill Rd. Croy —4A 152
Duppas Hill Ter. Croy —3B 152
Duppas Rd. Croy —3A 152
Dupree Rd. SE7 —5K 89
Duraden Clo. Beck —7D 124
Durand Clo. Cars —1D 150
Durand Gdns. SW9 —1K 103
Durands Wlk. SE16 —2B 88
Durand Way. NW10 —7J 45
Durants Pk. Av. Enf —4E 8
Durants Rd. Enf —4D 8
Durant St. E2 —2G 69
Durban Ct. E7 —7B 54
Durban Gdns. Dag —7J 57
Durban Rd. E15 —3G 71
Durban Rd. E17 —1B 34
Durban Rd. N17 —6K 17
Durban Rd. SE27 —4C 122
Durban Rd. Beck —2B 142
Durban Rd. Ilf —1J 55
Durbin Rd. Chess —4E 146
Durdan Cotts. S'hall —6D 60
(off Denbigh Rd.)
Durdans Rd. S'hall —6D 60
Durell Gdns. Dag —5D 56
Durell Rd. Dag —5D 56
Durfey Ho. SE5 —7D 86
(off Edmund St.)
Durford Cres. SW15 —1D 118
Durham Av. Brom —4H 143
Durham Av. Houn —5D 78
Durham Av. Wfd G —5G 21
Durham Clo. SW20 —2D 136
Durham Ct. NW6 —2J 65
(off Kilburn Pk. Rd., in two parts)
Durham Ct. Tedd —4J 115
Durham Hill. Brom —4H 125
Durham Ho. Bark —7A 56
(off Margaret Bondfield Av.)
Durham Ho. Brom —4G 143
Durham Ho. Dag —5J 57
Durham Ho. St. WC2 —3F 167
Durham Pl. SW3 —5D 84 (6E 170)
Durham Pl. Ilf —4G 55
Durham Ri. SE18 —5G 91
Durham Rd. E12 —4B 54
Durham Rd. E16 —4G 71
Durham Rd. N2 —3C 30
Durham Rd. N7 —2K 49
Durham Rd. N9 —2B 18
Durham Rd. SW20 —1D 136
Durham Rd. W5 —3D 80
Durham Rd. Brom —3H 143
Durham Rd. Dag —5J 57
Durham Rd. Felt —7A 96
Durham Rd. Harr —5F 25
Durham Rd. Sidc —5B 128
Durham Row. E1 —5K 69
Durham St. SE11 —6K 85 (6G 173)
Durham Ter. W2 —6K 65
Durham Wharf. Bren —7C 80
Durham Yd. E2 —3H 69
Durley Av. Pinn —7C 24
Durley Rd. N16 —7E 32
Durlston Rd. E5 —2G 51
Durlston Rd. King T —6E 116
Durnford Ho. SE6 —3E 124
Durnford St. N15 —5E 32
Durnford St. SE10 —6E 88
Durning Rd. SE19 —5D 122
Durnsford Av. SW19 —2J 119
Durnsford Rd. N11 —1H 31
Durnsford Rd. SW19 —2J 119
Durrant Ct. Har W —2J 25
Durrell Rd. SW6 —1H 101
Durrell Way. Shep —6F 131
Durrels Ho. W14 —4H 83
(off Warwick Rd.)
Durrington Av. SW20 —7E 118
Durrington Pk. Rd. SW20 —1E 136
Durrington Rd. E5 —4A 52
Durrington Tower. SW8 —2G 103
Durrisdeer Ho. NW2 —4H 47
(off Lyndale)
Dursley Clo. SE3 —2A 108
Dursley Ct. SE15 —7E 86
(off Lydney Clo.)
Dursley Gdns. SE3 —1B 108
Dursley Rd. SE3 —2A 108
Durward St. E1 —5H 69
Durweston M. W1 —5F 159
Durweston St. W1 —5D 66 (6F 159)
Dury Falls Ct. Romf —2J 39
Dury Rd. Barn —1C 4
Dutch Barn Clo. Stanw —6A 94
Dutch Gdns. King T —6H 117
Dutch Yd. SW18 —5J 101
Duthie St. E14 —7E 70
Dutton Bus. Pk. SE9 —2E 126
Dutton St. SE10 —1E 106
Duxberry Av. Felt —3A 114
Duxberry Clo. Brom —5C 144
Duxford Ho. SE2 —2D 92
(off Wolvercote Rd.)
Dye Ho. La. E3 —1C 70
Dyer Ho. Hamp —1F 133
Dyer's Bldgs. EC1 —5A 68 (6J 161)
Dyers Hall Rd. E11 —1G 53
Dyers Hill Rd. E11 —2F 53
Dyers La. SW15 —4D 100
Dykes Way. Brom —3H 143
Dykewood Clo. Bex —3K 129
Dylan Rd. SE24 —4B 104
Dylan Rd. Belv —3G 93
Dylan Thomas Ho. N8 —4K 31
Dylways. SE5 —4D 104
Dymchurch Clo. Ilf —2E 36
Dymes Path. SW19 —2F 119
Dymock Ct. SE15 —7E 86
(off Lydney Clo.)
Dymock St. SW6 —3K 101
Dyneley Rd. SE12 —3A 126
Dyne Rd. NW6 —7G 47
Dynevor Rd. N16 —3E 50
Dynevor Rd. Rich —5E 98
Dynham Rd. NW6 —7J 47
Dyott St. WC1 —6H 67 (7D 160)
Dysart Av. King T —5C 116
Dysart St. EC2 —4D 68 (4G 163)
Dyson Ct. NW2 —1E 46
Dyson Ct. Wemb —4A 44
Dyson Ho. SE10 —5H 89
(off Blackwall La.)
Dyson Rd. E11 —6G 35
Dyson Rd. E15 —6H 53
Dysons Rd. N18 —5C 18

Eade Rd. N4 —7C 32
Eagans Clo. N2 —3B 30
Eagle Av. Romf —6E 38
Eagle Clo. SE16 —5J 87
Eagle Clo. Enf —4D 8
Eagle Clo. Wall —6J 151
Eagle Ct. E11 —4J 35
Eagle Ct. EC1 —5B 68 (5A 162)
Eagle Dri. NW9 —2A 28
Eagle Hill. SE19 —6D 122
Eagle La. E11 —4J 35
Eagle Lodge. NW11 —7H 29
Eagle M. N1 —6E 50
Eagle Pl. SW1 —3B 166
Eagle Pl. SW7 —5A 84
(off Rolandway)
Eagle Rd. Wemb —7D 44
Eaglesfield Rd. SE18 —1F 109
Eagle St. WC1 —5K 67 (6G 161)
Eagle Ter. Wfd G —7E 20
Eagle Trad. Est. Mitc —6D 138
Eagle Wharf Ct. SE1 —1F 87 (5J 169)
(off Lafone St.)
Eagle Wharf E. E14 —7A 70
(off Narrow St.)
Eagle Wharf Rd. N1 —2C 68
Eagle Wharf W. E14 —7A 70
(off Narrow St.)
Eardham Sq. SE9 —4A 108
Ealing. —7D 62
Ealing B'way. Cen. W5 —7D 62
Ealing Common. (Junct.) —7F 63
Ealing Downs Ct. Gnfd —3A 62
Ealing Grn. W5 —1D 80
Ealing Pk. Gdns. W5 —4C 80
Ealing Rd. Bren —4D 80
Ealing Rd. N'holt —1E 60
Ealing Rd. Wemb —6E 44
Ealing Rd. Trad. Est. Bren —5D 80
Ealing Village. W5 —6E 62
Eamont Clo. Ruis —7D 22
Eamont Ct. NW8 —2C 66
(off Eamont St.)
Eamont St. NW8 —2C 66
Eardley Cres. SW5 —5J 83
Eardley Rd. SW16 —6G 121
Eardley Rd. Belv —5G 93
Earl Clo. N11 —5A 16
Earldom Rd. SW15 —4E 100

Earle Gdns.—Egan Way

Earle Gdns. King T —7E 116
Earlham Gro. E7 —5H 53
Earlham Gro. N22 —7E 16
Earlham St. WC2 —6J 67 (1D 166)
Earl Ho. NW1 —4C 66 (4D 158)
(off Lisson Gro.)
Earlom Ho. WC1 —3A 68 (2J 161)
(off Margery St.)
Earl Ri. SE18 —5H 91
Earl Rd. SW14 —4J 99
Earls Court. —5J 83
Earl's Court Exhibition Building. —5J 83
Earls Ct. Gdns. SW5 —4K 83
Earls Ct. Rd. W8 & SW5 —3J 83
Earl's Ct. Sq. SW5 —5K 83
Earls Cres. Harr —4J 25
Earlsdown Ho. Bark —2H 73
Earlsferry Way. N1 —7J 49
(in two parts)
Earlsfield. —1A 120
Earlsfield Rd. SW18 —1A 120
Earlshall Rd. SE9 —4D 108
Earlsmead. Harr —4D 42
Earlsmead Rd. N15 —5F 33
Earlsmead Rd. NW10 —3E 64
Earls Ter. W8 —3H 83
Earlsthorpe M. SW12 —6E 102
Earlsthorpe Rd. SE26 —4K 123
Earlstoke St. EC1 —3B 68 (1A 162)
Earlston Gro. E9 —1H 69
Earl St. EC2 —5D 68 (5G 163)
Earls Wlk. W8 —3J 83
Earl's Wlk. Dag —4B 56
Earlswood Av. T Hth —5A 140
Earlswood Clo. SE10 —6G 89
Earlswood Gdns. Ilf —3E 36
Earlswood St. SE10 —5G 89
Early M. NW1 —1F 67
Earnshaw St. WC2 —6H 67 (7D 160)
Earsby St. W14 —4G 83
(in three parts)
Easby Cres. Mord —6K 137
Easebourne Rd. Dag —5C 56
Easley's M. W1 —7H 159
East Acton. —7A 64
E. Acton Arc. W3 —6A 64
E. Acton Ct. W3 —7A 64
E. Acton La. W3 —1A 82
E. Arbour St. E1 —6K 69
East Av. E12 —7C 54
East Av. E17 —4D 34
East Av. N2 —4K 29
East Av. Hay —2H 77
East Av. S'hall —7D 60
East Av. Wall —5K 151
East Bank. N16 —7E 32
Eastbank Rd. Hamp H —5G 115
East Barnet. —6H 5
E. Barnet Rd. Barn —4G 5
E. Beckton District Cen. E6 —5D 72
East Bedfont. —7F 95
East Block. SE1 —2K 85
(off York Rd.)
E. Boundary Rd. E12 —3D 54
Eastbourne Av. W3 —6K 63
Eastbourne Gdns. SW14 —3J 99
Eastbourne M. W2 —6A 66 (7A 158)
Eastbourne Rd. E6 —3E 72
(in two parts)
Eastbourne Rd. E15 —1G 71
Eastbourne Rd. N15 —6E 32
Eastbourne Rd. SW17 —6E 120
Eastbourne Rd. W4 —6J 81
Eastbourne Rd. Bren —5C 80
Eastbourne Rd. Felt —2B 114
Eastbourne Ter. W2 —6A 66 (7A 158)
Eastbournia Av. N9 —3C 18
Eastbrook Av. N9 —7D 8
Eastbrook Av. Dag —4J 57
Eastbrook Dri. Romf —3K 57
Eastbrook Rd. SE3 —1K 107
Eastbury Av. Bark —1J 73
Eastbury Av. Enf —1A 8
Eastbury Ct. Bark —1J 73
Eastbury Ct. New Bar —5F 5
(off Lyonsdown Rd.)
Eastbury Gro. W4 —5A 82
Eastbury Rd. E6 —4E 72
Eastbury Rd. King T —7E 116
Eastbury Rd. Orp —6H 145
Eastbury Rd. Romf —6K 39
Eastbury Sq. Bark —1K 73
Eastbury Ter. E1 —4K 69
Eastcastle St. W1 —6G 67 (7A 160)
Eastcheap. EC3 —7E 68 (2G 169)
E. Churchfield Rd. W3 —1K 81
Eastchurch Rd. H'row A —2G 95
East Clo. W5 —4G 63
East Clo. Barn —4K 5
East Clo. Gnfd —2G 61
Eastcombe Av. SE7 —6K 89
Eastcote. —7K 23
Eastcote. Orp —7K 145
Eastcote Av. Gnfd —5A 44
Eastcote Av. Harr —2F 43
Eastcote Av. W Mol —5D 132
Eastcote Ind. Est. Ruis —7A 24
Eastcote La. Harr —4C 42
Eastcote La. N'holt —5D 42
(in two parts)
Eastcote La. N. N'holt —6D 42
Eastcote Rd. Harr —3G 43
Eastcote Rd. Pinn —5B 24
Eastcote Rd. Ruis —7G 23
Eastcote Rd. Well —2H 109
Eastcote St. SW9 —2K 103
Eastcote Vw. Pinn —4A 24
Eastcote Village. —5K 23
East Ct. Wemb —2C 44
East Cres. N11 —4J 15
East Cres. Enf —5A 8
Eastcroft Rd. Eps —7A 148
E. Cross Cen. E15 —6C 52
E. Cross Route. E9 & E3 —7B 52
Eastdown Ct. SE13 —4F 107
Eastdown Ho. E8 —4G 51
Eastdown Pk. SE13 —4F 107
East Dri. Cars —7C 150
E. Duck Lees La. Enf —4F 9
East Dulwich. —4F 105
E. Dulwich Gro. SE22 —5E 104
E. Dulwich Rd. SE22 & SE15 —4F 105
E. End Farm. Pinn —3D 24
E. End Rd. N3 & N2 —2J 29
E. End Way. Pinn —3C 24
E. Entrance. Dag —2H 75
Eastern Av. E11 & Ilf —6K 35
Eastern Av. Pinn —7B 24
Eastern Av. E. Romf —3K 39
Eastern Av. W. Romf —4E 38
(in two parts)
Eastern Ind. Est. Eri —2G 93
Eastern Perimeter Rd. H'row A —2H 95
Eastern Rd. E13 —2K 71
Eastern Rd. E17 —5E 34
Eastern Rd. N2 —3D 30
Eastern Rd. N22 —1J 31
Eastern Rd. SE4 —4C 106
Easternville Gdns. Ilf —6G 37
Eastern Way. SE28 —2A 92
E. Ferry Rd. E14 —4D 88
Eastfield Gdns. Dag —4G 57
Eastfield Rd. E17 —4C 34
Eastfield Rd. N8 —3J 31
Eastfield Rd. Dag —4F 57
Eastfield Rd. Enf —1E 8
Eastfields. Pinn —5A 24
Eastfields Rd. W3 —5J 63
Eastfields Rd. Mitc —2E 138
Eastfield St. E14 —5A 70
East Finchley. —4C 30
East Gdns. SW17 —6C 120
Eastgate Clo. SE28 —6D 74
Eastglade. Pinn —3D 24
East Ham. —1D 72
E. Ham and Barking By-Pass. Bark —2J 73
Eastham Clo. Barn —5C 4
E. Ham Ind. Est. E6 —4C 72
E. Ham Mnr. Way. E6 —6E 72
E. Harding St. EC4 —6A 68 (7K 161)
E. Heath Rd. NW3 —3A 48
East Hill. SW18 —5K 101
East Hill. Wemb —2G 45
Eastholm. NW11 —4K 29
East Holme. Eri —1K 111
East Holme. Hay —1J 77
E. India Bldgs. E14 —7C 70
E. India Dock Ho. E14 —6E 70
E. India Dock Rd. E14 —6C 70
E. India Dock Wall Rd. E14 —7F 71
Eastlake Ho. NW8 —4B 158
Eastlake Rd. SE5 —2C 104
Eastlands Cres. SE21 —6F 105
East La. SE16 —2G 87
(Chambers St.)
East La. SE16 —2G 87
(Scott Lidgett Cres., in two parts)
East La. King T —3D 134
East La. Wemb —3B 44
Eastlea M. E16 —4G 71
Eastleigh Av. Harr —2F 43
Eastleigh Clo. NW2 —3A 46
Eastleigh Clo. Sutt —7K 149
Eastleigh Rd. E17 —2B 34
Eastleigh Rd. Bexh —3J 111
Eastleigh Rd. H'row A —3H 95
Eastleigh Wlk. SW15 —7C 100
Eastleigh Way. Felt —1J 113
East London Crematorium. E13 —3H 71
Eastman Ho. SW4 —6G 103
Eastman Rd. W3 —2K 81
East Mascalls. SE7 —6A 90
East Mead. Ruis —3B 42
Eastmead Av. Gnfd —3F 61
Eastmead Clo. Brom —2C 144
Eastmearn Rd. SE27 —2C 122
East Molesey. —4H 133
Eastmoor Pl. SE7 —3B 90
Eastmoor St. SE7 —3B 90
E. Mount St. E1 —5H 69
Eastney Rd. Croy —1B 152
Eastney St. SE10 —5F 89
Eastnor Rd. SE9 —1G 127
Easton St. WC1 —4A 68 (3J 161)
East Pk. Clo. Romf —5D 38
East Parkside. SE10 —2G 89
East Pas. EC1 —5C 162
East Pier. E1 —1H 87
East Pl. SE27 —4C 122
East Point. SE1 —5G 87
E. Poultry Av. EC1 —5B 68 (6A 162)
East Ramp. H'row A —1D 94
East Rd. E15 —1J 71
East Rd. EC1 —3D 68 (2E 162)
East Rd. N2 —1C 30
East Rd. SW19 —6A 120
East Rd. Barn —1K 15
East Rd. Chad H —5E 38
East Rd. Edgw —1H 27
East Rd. Enf —1D 8
East Rd. Felt —7F 95
East Rd. Harr —7B 26
East Rd. King T —1E 134
East Rd. Rush G —7K 39
East Rd. Well —2B 110
East Rd. W Dray —4B 76
E. Rochester Way. Sidc & Bex —4J 109
East Row. E11 —6J 35
East Row. W10 —4G 65
Eastry Av. Brom —6H 143
Eastry Ho. SW8 —7J 85
(off Hartington Rd.)
Eastry Rd. Eri —7G 93
East Sheen. —4J 99
E. Sheen Av. SW14 —5K 99
Eastside Rd. NW11 —4H 29
East Smithfield. E1 —7F 69 (3K 169)
East St. SE17 —5C 86
East St. Bark —1G 73
East St. Bexh —4G 111
East St. Bren —7C 80
East St. Brom —2J 143
E. Surrey Gro. SE15 —7F 87
E. Tenter St. E1 —6F 69 (1K 169)
East Ter. Sidc —1J 127
East Towers. Pinn —5B 24
East Va. W3 —1B 82
East Vw. E4 —5K 19
East Vw. Barn —2C 4
Eastview Av. SE18 —7J 91
Eastville Av. NW11 —6H 29
East Wlk. E Barn —7K 5
East Wlk. Hay —1J 77
Eastway. E9 —6B 52
(in two parts)
East Way. E11 —5K 35
East Way. Brom —7J 143
East Way. Croy —2A 154
East Way. Hay —1J 77
Eastway. Mord —5F 137
East Way. Ruis —1J 41
Eastway. Wall —4G 151
Eastway Commercial Cen. E15 —5C 52
Eastwell Clo. Beck —7A 124
Eastwell Ho. SE1 —7F 169
East Wickham. —1C 110
Eastwood Clo. E18 —2J 35
Eastwood Clo. N17 —7C 18
Eastwood Rd. E18 —2J 35
Eastwood Rd. N10 —2E 30
Eastwood Rd. Ilf —7A 38
Eastwood Rd. W Dray —2C 76
E. Woodside. Bex —1E 128
Eastwood St. SW16 —6G 121
Eatington Rd. E10 —5F 35
Eaton Clo. SW1 —4E 84 (4G 171)
Eaton Clo. Stan —4G 11
Eaton Dri. SW9 —4B 104
Eaton Dri. King T —7G 117
Eaton Dri. Romf —1H 39
Eaton Garages. NW3 —6C 48
Eaton Gdns. Dag —7E 56
Eaton Ga. SW1 —4E 84 (3G 171)
Eaton Gro. N19 —3H 49
Eaton Ho. SW11 —1B 102
Eaton La. SW1 —3F 85 (2K 171)
Eaton Mans. SW1 —4E 84 (4G 171)
(off Bourne St.)
Eaton M. N. SW1 —4E 84 (3G 171)
Eaton M. S. SW1 —4E 84 (3H 171)
Eaton M. W. SW1 —4E 84 (3H 171)
Eaton Pk. Rd. N13 —2F 17
Eaton Pl. SW1 —4E 84 (2G 171)
Eaton Ri. E11 —5A 36
Eaton Ri. W5 —5D 62
Eaton Rd. NW4 —5E 28
Eaton Rd. Enf —3K 7
Eaton Rd. Houn —4H 97
Eaton Rd. Sidc —2D 128
Eaton Rd. Sutt —6A 150
Eaton Row. SW1 —3F 85 (2J 171)
Eatons Mead. E4 —2H 19
Eaton Sq. SW1 —4E 84 (3G 171)
Eaton Ter. E3 —3A 70
Eaton Ter. SW1 —4E 84 (3G 171)
Eaton Ter. M. SW1 —3G 171
Eatonville Rd. SW17 —2D 120
Eatonville Vs. SW17 —2D 120
Ebbisham Dri. SW8 —6K 85 (7G 173)
Ebbisham Rd. Wor Pk —2E 148
Ebbsfleet Rd. NW2 —5G 47
Ebdon Way. SE3 —3K 107
Ebenezer Ho. SE11 —4B 86 (4K 173)
Ebenezer St. N1 —3D 68 (1E 162)
Ebenezer Wlk. SW16 —1G 139
Ebley Clo. SE15 —6F 87
Ebner St. SW18 —5K 101
Ebor Cotts. SW15 —3A 118
Ebor St. E1 —4F 69 (3J 163)
Ebrington Rd. Harr —6D 26
Ebsworth St. SE23 —7K 105
Eburne Rd. N7 —3J 49
Ebury Bri. SW1 —5F 85 (5J 171)
Ebury Bri. Est. SW1 —5F 85 (5J 171)
Ebury Bri. Rd. SW1 —5E 84 (6H 171)
Ebury Clo. Kes —3C 156
Ebury M. SE27 —3B 122
Ebury M. SW1 —4F 85 (3J 171)
Ebury M. E. SW1 —3F 85 (2J 171)
Ebury Sq. SW1 —4E 84 (4H 171)
Ebury St. SW1 —4E 84 (4H 171)
Ecclesbourne Clo. N13 —5F 17
Ecclesbourne Gdns. N13 —5F 17
Ecclesbourne Rd. N1 —7C 50
Ecclesbourne Rd. T Hth —5C 140
Eccles Rd. SW11 —4D 102
Eccleston Bri. SW1 —4F 85 (3K 171)
Eccleston Clo. Cockf —4J 5
Eccleston Cres. Romf —7B 38
Ecclestone Ct. Wemb —5E 44
Ecclestone M. Wemb —5E 44
Ecclestone Pl. Wemb —5E 45
Eccleston Ho. SW2 —6A 104
Eccleston M. SW1 —3E 84 (2H 171)
Eccleston Pl. SW1 —4F 85 (3J 171)
Eccleston Rd. W13 —7A 62
Eccleston Sq. SW1 —4F 85 (4K 171)
Eccleston Sq. M. SW1 —4F 85 (4K 171)
Eccleston St. SW1 —3F 85 (2J 171)
Echelforde Dri. Ashf —4C 112
Echo Heights. E4 —1J 19
Eckford St. N1 —2A 68
Eckington Ho. N15 —6D 32
(off Fladbury Rd.)
Eckstein Rd. SW11 —4C 102
Eclipse Rd. E13 —5K 71
Ector Rd. SE6 —2G 125
Edam Ct. Sidc —3A 128
Edans Ct. W12 —2B 82
Edbrooke Rd. W9 —4J 65
Eddington St. N4 —1A 50
Eddisbury Ho. SE26 —3G 123
Eddiscombe Rd. SW6 —2H 101
Eddy Clo. Romf —6H 39
Eddystone Rd. SE4 —5A 106
Eddystone Tower. SE8 —5A 88
Eddystone Wlk. Stai —7A 94
Ede Clo. Houn —3D 96
Edenbridge Clo. SE16 —5H 87
(off Masters Dri.)
Edenbridge Rd. E9 —7K 51
Edenbridge Rd. Enf —6K 7
Eden Clo. NW3 —2J 47
Eden Clo. W8 —3J 83
Eden Clo. Bex —4K 129
Eden Clo. Wemb —1D 62
Edencourt Rd. SW16 —6F 121
Edendale. W3 —7H 63
Edendale Rd. Bexh —1K 111
Edenfield Gdns. Wor Pk —3B 148
Eden Gro. E17 —5D 34
Eden Gro. N7 —5K 49
Edenham Way. W10 —4H 65
Eden Ho. NW8 —4C 66 (4C 158)
(off Church St.)
Edenhurst Av. SW6 —3H 101
Eden M. SW17 —3A 120
Eden Park. —5C 142
Eden Pk. Av. Beck —4A 142
(in two parts)
Eden Rd. E17 —5D 34
Eden Rd. SE27 —4B 122
Eden Rd. Beck —4A 142
Eden Rd. Bex —4J 129
Eden Rd. Croy —4D 152
Edensor Gdns. W4 —7A 82
Edensor Rd. W4 —7A 82
Eden St. King T —2D 134
Edenvale Clo. Mitc —7E 120
Edenvale Rd. Mitc —7E 120
Edenvale St. SW6 —2K 101
Eden Wlk. King T —2E 134
Eden Way. Beck —5B 142
Ederline Av. SW16 —3K 139
Edgar Ct. N Mald —2A 136
Edgar Ho. E9 —5A 52
(off Homerton Rd.)
Edgar Ho. E11 —7J 35
Edgar Ho. SW8 —7J 85
(off Wyvil Rd.)
Edgar Kail Way. SE22 —4E 104
Edgarley Ter. SW6 —1G 101
Edgar Rd. E3 —3D 70
Edgar Rd. Houn —7D 96
Edgar Rd. Romf —7D 38
Edgar Rd. W Dray —7A 58
Edgeborough Way. Brom —7B 126
Edgebury. Chst —4F 127
Edgebury Wlk. Chst —4G 127
Edge Bus. Cen., The. NW2 —2D 46
Edgecombe Ho. SE5 —2E 104
Edgecoombe. S Croy —7J 153
Edgecoombe Clo. King T —7K 117
Edgecote Clo. W3 —1J 81
Edgecot Gro. N15 —5E 32
Edgefield Av. Bark —7K 55
Edgefield Ct. Bark —7K 55
(off Edgefield Av.)
Edgefoot Gro. N15 —5E 32
Edge Hill. SE18 —6F 91
Edge Hill. SW19 —7F 119
Edge Hill Av. N3 —4J 29
Edge Hill Ct. SW19 —7F 119
Edge Hill Ct. Sidc —4K 127
Edgehill Gdns. Dag —4G 57
Edgehill Ho. SW9 —2B 104
Edgehill Rd. W13 —5C 62
Edgehill Rd. Chst —3G 127
Edgehill Rd. Mitc —1F 139
Edgeley La. SW4 —3H 103
Edgeley Rd. SW4 —3H 103
Edgel St. SW18 —4K 101
Edgepoint Clo. SE27 —5B 122
Edge St. W8 —1J 83
Edgewood Grn. Croy —1K 153
Edgeworth Av. NW4 —5C 28
Edgeworth Clo. NW4 —5C 28
Edgeworth Ct. Barn —4H 5
(off Fordham Rd.)
Edgeworth Cres. NW4 —5C 28
Edgeworth Ho. NW8 —1A 66
(off Boundary Rd.)
Edgeworth Rd. SE9 —4A 108
Edgeworth Rd. Cockf —4H 5
Edgington Rd. SW16 —6H 121
Edgington Way. Sidc —7C 128
Edgson Ho. SW1 —5F 85 (5J 171)
(off Ebury Bri. Rd.)
Edgware. —6B 12
Edgware Bury. —1A 12
Edgwarebury Gdns. Edgw —5B 12
Edgwarebury La. Els & Edgw —1A 12
(in three parts)
Edgware Ct. Edgw —6B 12
Edgware Rd. NW2 —1D 46
Edgware Rd. NW9 —2J 27
Edgware Rd. W2 —4B 66 (4A 158)
Edgware Way. Edgw —4A 12
Edgware Way. Els —1J 11
Edinburgh Clo. E2 —2J 69
Edinburgh Clo. Pinn —7B 24
Edinburgh Clo. Uxb —4D 40
Edinburgh Ct. SW20 —5F 137
Edinburgh Ct. Eri —7K 93
Edinburgh Ct. King T —3E 134
(off Watersplash Clo.)
Edinburgh Dri. Romf —4J 39
Edinburgh Dri. Uxb —4D 40
Edinburgh Ga. SW1 —2D 84 (6E 164)
Edinburgh Ho. NW4 —3E 28
Edinburgh Ho. W9 —3K 65
(off Maida Va.)
Edinburgh Rd. E13 —2K 71
Edinburgh Rd. E17 —5C 34
Edinburgh Rd. N18 —5B 18
Edinburgh Rd. W7 —2K 79
Edinburgh Rd. Sutt —2A 150
Edington. NW5 —6E 48
Edington Rd. SE2 —3B 92
Edington Rd. Enf —2D 8
Edison Building. E14 —2C 88
Edison Clo. E17 —5C 34
Edison Dri. S'hall —6F 61
Edison Dri. Wemb —3E 44
Edison Gro. SE18 —7K 91
Edison Ho. Wemb —3J 45
(off Barnhill Rd.)
Edison Rd. N8 —6H 31
Edison Rd. Brom —2J 143
Edison Rd. Enf —2G 9
Edison Rd. Well —1K 109
Edis St. NW1 —1E 66
Edith Brinson Ho. E14 —6F 71
Edith Cavell Clo. N19 —7J 31
Edith Gdns. Surb —7H 135
Edith Gro. SW10 —6A 84
Edith Ho. W6 —5E 82
(off Queen Caroline St.)
Edithna St. SW9 —3J 103
Edith Neville Cotts. NW1 —3H 67 (1C 160)
Edith Rd. E6 —7B 54
Edith Rd. E15 —5F 53
Edith Rd. N11 —7C 16
Edith Rd. SE25 —5D 140
Edith Rd. SW19 —6K 119
Edith Rd. W14 —4G 83
Edith Rd. Romf —7D 38
Edith Row. SW6 —1K 101
Edith St. E2 —2G 69
Edith Summerskill Ho. SW6 —7H 83
(off Clem Attlee Est.)
Edith Ter. SW10 —7A 84
Edith Vs. W14 —4H 83
Edith Yd. SW10 —7A 84
Edmansons Clo. N17 —1F 33
Edmeston Clo. E9 —6A 52
Edmond Ct. SE14 —1J 105
Edmonscote. W13 —5A 62
Edmonton. —4B 18
Edmonton Grn. Shop. Cen. N9 —2B 18
Edmund Halley Way. SE10 —2G 89
Edmund Ho. SE17 —6B 86
Edmund Hurst Dri. E6 —5F 73
Edmund Rd. Mitc —3C 138
Edmund Rd. Well —3A 110
Edmundsbury Ct. Est. SW9 —4K 103
Edmunds Clo. Hay —5A 60
Edmund St. SE5 —7D 86
Edmunds Wlk. N2 —4C 30
Ednam Ho. SE15 —6G 87
(off Haymerle Rd.)
Edna Rd. SW20 —2F 137
Edna St. SW11 —1C 102
Edred Ho. E9 —4A 52
(off Lindisfarne Way)
Edrich Ho. SW4 —1J 103
Edric Ho. SW1 —4H 85 (3D 172)
(off Page St.)
Edrick Rd. Edgw —6D 12
Edrick Wlk. Edgw —6D 12
Edric Rd. SE14 —7K 87
Edridge Rd. Croy —3C 152
Edward Av. E4 —6J 19
Edward Av. Mord —5B 138
Edward Bond Ho. WC1 —3J 67 (2F 161)
(off Cromer St.)
Edward Clo. N9 —7A 8
Edward Clo. NW2 —4F 47
Edward Clo. Hamp H —5G 115
Edward Clo. N'holt —3A 60
Edward Ct. E16 —5J 71
Edward Dodd Ct. N1 —3D 68 (1F 163)
(off Haberdasher St.)
Edward Edward's Ho. SE1 —5A 168
Edwardes Pl. W8 —3H 83
Edwardes Sq. W8 —3H 83
Edward Gro. Barn —5G 5
Edward Ho. SE11 —5H 173
Edward Mann Clo. E1 —6K 69
(off Caroline St.)
Edward Mans. Bark —7K 55
(off Upney La.)
Edward M. NW1 —3F 67 (1K 159)
Edward Pl. SE8 —6B 88
Edward Rd. E17 —4K 33
Edward Rd. SE20 —7K 123
Edward Rd. Barn —5G 5
Edward Rd. Brom —7K 125
Edward Rd. Chst —5F 127
Edward Rd. Croy —7E 140
Edward Rd. Felt —5F 95
Edward Rd. Hamp H —5G 115
Edward Rd. Harr —3G 25
Edward Rd. N'holt —2A 60
Edward Rd. Romf —6E 38
Edward's Av. Ruis —6K 41
Edwards Clo. Wor Pk —2F 149
Edwards Cotts. N1 —6B 50
Edwards Dri. N11 —7C 16
Edward's La. N16 —2D 50
Edwards M. N1 —7B 50
Edwards M. W1 —6E 66 (1G 165)
Edward Sq. N1 —1K 67
Edward Sq. SE16 —1A 88
Edwards Rd. Belv —4G 93
Edward St. E16 —4J 71
Edward St. SE14 —7A 88
Edwards Yd. Wemb —1E 62
Edward Temme Av. E15 —7H 53
Edward Tyler Rd. SE12 —2A 126
Edward Way. Ashf —2B 112
Edwina Gdns. Ilf —5C 36
Edwin Arnold Ct. Sidc —4K 127
Edwin Av. E6 —2E 72
(in two parts)
Edwin Clo. Bexh —6F 93
Edwin Pl. Croy —1E 152
Edwin Rd. Edgw —6E 12
Edwin Rd. Twic —1J 115
(in two parts)
Edwin's Mead. E9 —4A 52
Edwinstray Ho. Felt —2E 114
Edwin St. E1 —4J 69
Edwin St. E16 —5J 71
Edwin Ware Ct. Pinn —2A 24
Edwis Ho. SE15 —7G 87
Edwyn Clo. Barn —6A 4
Effie Pl. SW6 —7J 83
Effie Rd. SW6 —7J 83
Effingham Clo. Sutt —7K 149
Effingham Lodge. King T —4D 134
Effingham Rd. N8 —5A 32
Effingham Rd. SE12 —5G 107
Effingham Rd. Croy —7K 139
Effingham Rd. Surb —7B 134
Effort St. SW17 —5C 120
Effra Ct. SW2 —5K 103
(off Brixton Hill)
Effra Pde. SW2 —5A 104
Effra Rd. SW2 —4A 104
Effra Rd. SW19 —6K 119
Effra Rd. Retail Pk. SW2 —5A 104
Egan Way. Hay —7G 59

A-Z Big London 209

Egbert St.—Elmwood Clo.

Egbert St. NW1 —1E 66
Egbury Ho. SW15 —6B 100
(off Tangley Gro.)
Egerton Clo. Pinn —4J 23
Egerton Ct. E11 —7F 35
Egerton Cres. SW3 —4C 84 (3D 170)
Egerton Dri. SE10 —1D 106
Egerton Gdns. NW4 —4D 28
Egerton Gdns. NW10 —1E 64
Egerton Gdns. SW3 —4C 84 (2C 170)
Egerton Gdns. W13 —6B 62
Egerton Gdns. Ilf —3K 55
Egerton Gdns. M. SW3 —3C 84 (2D 170)
Egerton Pl. SW3 —3C 84 (2D 170)
Egerton Rd. N16 —7F 33
Egerton Rd. SE25 —3E 140
Egerton Rd. N Mald —4B 136
Egerton Rd. Twic —7J 97
Egerton Rd. Wemb —7F 45
Egerton Ter. SW3 —3C 84 (2D 170)
Egerton Way. Hay —7D 76
Eggardon Ct. N'holt —6F 43
Egham Clo. SW19 —2G 119
Egham Clo. Sutt —2G 149
Egham Cres. Sutt —3G 149
Egham Rd. E13 —5K 71
Eglantine Rd. SW18 —5A 102
Egleston Rd. Mord —6K 137
Eglington Ct. SE17 —6C 86
Eglington Rd. E4 —1A 20
Eglinton Hill. SE18 —6F 91
Eglinton Rd. SE18 —6E 90
Egliston M. SW15 —3E 100
Egliston Rd. SW15 —3E 100
Eglon M. NW1 —7D 48
Egmont Av. Surb —1F 147
Egmont Rd. N Mald —4B 136
Egmont Rd. Surb —1F 147
Egmont Rd. Sutt —7A 150
Egmont Rd. W on T —7K 131
Egmont St. SE14 —7K 87
Egremont Ho. SE13 —2D 106
(off Russett Way)
Egremont Rd. SE27 —3A 122
Egret Way. Hay —5B 60
Eider Clo. E7 —5H 53
Eider Clo. Hay —5B 60
Eighteenth Rd. Mitc —4J 139
Eighth Av. E12 —4D 54
Eighth Av. Hay —1J 77
Eileen Rd. SE25 —5D 140
Eileen Wilkinson Ho. SW6 —6H 83
(off Clem Attlee Ct.)
Eindhoven Clo. Cars —1E 150
Einstein Ho. Wemb —3J 45
Eisenhower Dri. E6 —5C 72
Elaine Gro. NW5 —5E 48
Elam Clo. SE5 —2B 104
Elam St. SE5 —2B 104
Elan Ct. E1 —5H 69
Eland Pl. Croy —3B 152
Eland Rd. SW11 —3D 102
Eland Rd. Croy —3B 152
Elba Pl. SE17 —4C 86
Elberon Av. Croy —6G 139
Elbe St. SW6 —2A 102
Elborough Rd. SE25 —5G 141
Elborough St. SW18 —1J 119
Elbourne Ct. SE16 —3K 87
(off Worgan St.)
Elbourne Trad. Est. Belv —3H 93
Elbourn Ho. SW3 —5C 84 (5C 170)
(off Cale St.)
Elbury Dri. E16 —6J 71
Elcho St. SW11 —7C 84
Elcot Av. SE15 —7H 87
Eldenwall Ind. Est. Dag —1E 56
Elder Av. N8 —5J 31
Elderberry Gro. SE27 —4C 122
Elderberry Rd. W5 —2E 80
Elder Clo. N20 —2E 14
Elder Clo. Sidc —1K 127
Elder Clo. W Dray —7A 58
Elder Ct. Bush —2D 10
Elderfield Ho. E14 —7C 70
Elderfield Pl. SW17 —4F 121
Elderfield Rd. E5 —4K 51
Elderfield Wlk. E11 —5K 35
Elderflower Way. E15 —7G 53
Elder Gdns. SE27 —5C 122
Elder Oak Clo. SE20 —1H 141
Elder Oak Ct. SE20 —1H 141
(off Anerley Ct.)
Elder Rd. SE27 —4C 122
Elderslie Clo. Beck —5C 142
Elderslie Rd. SE9 —5E 108
Elder St. E1 —4F 69 (5J 163)
(in two parts)
Elderton Rd. SE26 —4A 124
Eldertree Pl. Mitc —1G 139
Eldertree Way. Mitc —1G 139
Elder Wlk. N1 —1B 68
(off Popham St.)
Elderwood Pl. SE27 —5C 122
Eldon Av. Croy —2J 153
Eldon Av. Houn —7E 78
Eldon Ct. NW6 —1J 65
Eldon Gro. NW3 —5B 48
Eldon Pk. SE25 —4H 141
Eldon Rd. E17 —4B 34
Eldon Rd. N9 —1D 18
Eldon Rd. N22 —1B 32
Eldon Rd. W8 —3K 83
Eldon St. EC2 —5D 68 (6F 163)
Eldon Way. NW10 —3H 63
Eldred Rd. Bark —1J 73
Eldrick Ct. Felt —1F 113
Eldridge Clo. Felt —1J 113
Eldridge Ct. SE16 —3G 87
Eleanora Ter. Sutt —5A 150
(off Lind Rd.)
Eleanor Clo. N15 —3F 33
Eleanor Clo. SE16 —2K 87
Eleanor Cres. NW7 —5A 14
Eleanor Gdns. Barn —5A 4
Eleanor Gdns. Dag —2F 57
Eleanor Gro. SW13 —3A 100
Eleanor Gro. Ick & Uxb —3D 40
Eleanor Rd. E8 —6H 51
Eleanor Rd. E15 —6H 53
Eleanor Rd. N11 —6D 16
Eleanor St. E3 —3C 70
Eleanor Wlk. SE18 —4C 90
Electric Av. SW9 —4A 104
Electric La. SW9 & SW2 —4A 104
(in two parts)
Electric Pde. E18 —2J 35
(off George La.)
Electric Pde. Ilf —2J 55
Electric Pde. Surb —6D 134
Elephant & Castle. (Junct.) —3B 86
Elephant & Castle. SE1 —4B 86
Elephant La. SE16 —2J 87
Elephant Rd. SE17 —4C 86
Elers Rd. W13 —2C 80
Elers Rd. Hay —4F 77
Eley Rd. N18 —4D 18
Eleys Est. N9 —3E 18
(Meridian Way)
Eleys Est. N18 —5E 18
(Advent Way)
Eleys Est. N18 —4E 18
(Kynoch Rd.)
Elfindale Rd. SE24 —5C 104
Elfin Gro. Tedd —5K 115
Elford Clo. SE3 —4K 107
Elford M. SW4 —5G 103
Elfort Rd. N5 —4A 50
Elfrida Cres. SE6 —4C 124
Elf Row. E1 —7J 69
Elfwine Rd. W7 —5J 61
Elgar. N8 —3J 31
(off Boyton Clo.)
Elgar Av. NW10 —6K 45
(in two parts)
Elgar Av. SW16 —3J 139
Elgar Av. W5 —2E 80
Elgar Av. Surb —1G 147
Elgar Clo. E13 —2A 72
Elgar Clo. SE8 —7C 88
Elgar Clo. Buck H —2G 21
Elgar Clo. Uxb —2C 40
Elgar Ct. W14 —3G 83
(off Blythe Rd.)
Elgar Ho. NW6 —7A 48
Elgar Ho. SW1 —5F 85 (6K 171)
(off Churchill Gdns.)
Elgar St. SE16 —3A 88
Elgin Av. W9 —4H 65
Elgin Av. W12 —2D 82
Elgin Av. Ashf —6E 112
Elgin Av. Harr —2B 26
Elgin Ct. W9 —4K 65
Elgin Cres. W11 —7G 65
Elgin Cres. H'row A —2G 95
Elgin Dri. N'wd —1G 23
Elgin Est. W9 —4J 65
(off Elgin Av.)
Elgin Ho. E14 —6D 70
Elgin Mans. W9 —3K 65
Elgin M. W11 —6G 65
Elgin M. N. W9 —3K 65
Elgin M. S. W9 —3K 65
Elgin Rd. N22 —2G 31
Elgin Rd. Croy —2F 153
Elgin Rd. Ilf —1J 55
Elgin Rd. Sutt —3A 150
Elgin Rd. Wall —6G 151
Elgood Clo. W11 —7G 65
Elgood Ho. NW8 —2B 66
(off Wellington Rd.)
Elham Clo. Brom —7B 126
Elham Ho. E5 —5H 51
Elia M. N1 —2B 68 (1A 162)
Elias Pl. SW8 —6A 86
Elia St. N1 —2B 68 (1B 162)
Elibank Rd. SE9 —4D 108
Elim Est. SE1 —3E 86 (7G 169)
Elim St. SE1 —7F 169
(in two parts)
Elim Way. E13 —3H 71
Eliot Bank. SE23 —2H 123
Eliot Cotts. SE3 —2G 107
Eliot Dri. Harr —2F 43
Eliot Gdns. SW15 —4C 100
Eliot Hill. SE13 —2E 106
Eliot M. NW8 —2A 66
Eliot Pk. SE13 —2E 106
Eliot Pl. SE3 —2G 107
Eliot Rd. Dag —4D 56
Eliot Va. SE3 —2F 107
Elis David Almshouses. Croy —3B 152
Elizabethan Clo. Stanw —7A 94
Elizabethan Way. Stanw —7A 94
Elizabeth Av. N1 —1C 68
Elizabeth Av. Enf —3G 7
Elizabeth Av. Ilf —2H 55
Elizabeth Av. Stai —7A 112
Elizabeth Barnes Ct. SW6 —2K 101
Elizabeth Blackwell Ho. N22 —1A 32
(off Progress Way)
Elizabeth Bri. SW1 —4F 85 (4J 171)
Elizabeth Clo. E14 —6D 70
Elizabeth Clo. W9 —4A 66
Elizabeth Clo. Barn —3A 4
Elizabeth Clo. Romf —1H 39
Elizabeth Clo. Sutt —4H 149
Elizabeth Clyde Clo. N15 —4E 32
Elizabeth Cotts. Kew —1F 99
Elizabeth Ct. E4 —5G 19
Elizabeth Ct. SW1 —2D 172
Elizabeth Ct. SW10 —6B 84
Elizabeth Ct. W6 —4E 82
Elizabeth Ct. Tedd —5J 115
Elizabeth Ct. Wfd G —7F 21
Elizabeth Fry Ho. Hay —4H 77
Elizabeth Fry Rd. E8 —7H 51
Elizabeth Gdns. W3 —1B 82
Elizabeth Gdns. Stan —6H 11
Elizabeth Gdns. Sun —3A 132
Elizabeth Garrett Anderson Ho. Belv —3G 93
(off Ambrook Rd.)
Elizabeth Ho. SE11 —4A 86 (4K 173)
(off Reedworth St.)
Elizabeth Ind. Est. SE14 —6K 87
Elizabeth M. NW3 —6C 48
Elizabeth M. Harr —6J 25
Elizabeth Newcomen Ho. SE1 —2D 86 (6E 168)
(off Newcomen St.)
Elizabeth Pl. N15 —4D 32
Elizabeth Ride. N9 —7C 8
Elizabeth Rd. E6 —1B 72
Elizabeth Rd. N15 —5E 32
Elizabeth Sq. SE16 —7A 70
(off Sovereign Cres.)
Elizabeth St. SW1 —4E 84 (3H 171)
Elizabeth Ter. SE9 —6D 108
Elizabeth Way. SE19 —7D 122
Elizabeth Way. Felt —4A 114
Elkanet M. N20 —2F 15
Elkington Point. SE11 —4J 173
Elkington Rd. E13 —4K 71
Elkstone Ct. SE15 —6E 86
(off Birdlip Clo.)
Elkstone Rd. W10 —5H 65
Ellaline Rd. W6 —6F 83
Ella M. NW3 —4D 48
Ellanby Cres. N18 —4C 18
Elland Ho. E14 —6B 70
Elland Rd. SE15 —4J 105
Ella Rd. N8 —7J 31
Ellement Clo. Pinn —5B 24
Ellena Ct. N14 —3D 16
(off Conway Rd.)
Ellenborough Ho. W12 —7D 64
(off White City Est.)
Ellenborough Pl. SW15 —4C 100
Ellenborough Rd. N22 —1C 32
Ellenborough Rd. Sidc —5D 128
Ellenbridge Way. S Croy —7E 152
Ellen Clo. Brom —3B 144
Ellen Ct. E4 —1K 19
(off Ridgeway, The)
Ellen Ct. N9 —2D 18
Ellen St. E1 —6G 69
Ellen Webb Dri. W'stone —3J 25
Ellen Wilkinson Ho. Dag —3G 57
Elleray Rd. Tedd —6K 115
Ellerby St. SW6 —1F 101
Ellerdale Clo. NW3 —4A 48
Ellerdale Rd. NW3 —5A 48
Ellerdale St. SE13 —4D 106
Ellerdine Rd. Houn —4G 97
Ellerker Gdns. Rich —6E 98
Ellerman Av. Twic —1D 114
Ellerslie Gdns. NW10 —1C 64
Ellerslie Rd. W12 —1D 82
Ellerslie Sq. Ind. Est. SW2 —5J 103
Ellerton Gdns. Dag —7C 56
Ellerton Lodge. N3 —2J 29
Ellerton Rd. SW13 —1C 100
Ellerton Rd. SW18 —1B 120
Ellerton Rd. SW20 —7C 118
Ellerton Rd. Dag —7C 56
Ellerton Rd. Surb —2F 147
Ellery Ho. SE17 —4D 86
Ellery Rd. SE19 —7D 122
Ellery St. SE15 —2H 105
Ellesmere Av. NW7 —3E 12
Ellesmere Av. Beck —2D 142
Ellesmere Clo. E11 —5H 35
Ellesmere Clo. Ruis —7E 22
Ellesmere Ct. W4 —5K 81
Ellesmere Gdns. Ilf —5C 36
Ellesmere Gro. Barn —5C 4
Ellesmere Rd. E3 —2A 70
Ellesmere Rd. NW10 —5C 46
Ellesmere Rd. W4 —6J 81
Ellesmere Rd. Gnfd —4G 61
Ellesmere Rd. Twic —6C 98
Ellesmere St. E14 —6D 70
Elleswood Ct. Surb —7D 134
Ellie M. Ashf —2A 112
Ellingfort Rd. E8 —7H 51
Ellingham Rd. E15 —4F 53
Ellingham Rd. W12 —2C 82
Ellingham Rd. Chess —6F 146
Ellington Ct. N14 —2C 16
Ellington Ho. SE1 —3C 86
Ellington Rd. N10 —4F 31
Ellington Rd. Felt —4H 113
Ellington Rd. Houn —2F 97
Ellington St. N7 —6A 50
Elliot Clo. E15 —7G 53
Elliot Ho. W1 —5C 66 (6D 158)
(off Molyneux St.)
Elliot Rd. NW4 —6D 28
Elliott Av. Ruis —2K 41
Elliott Clo. Wemb —3G 45
Elliott Gdns. Shep —4C 130
Elliott Rd. SW9 —1B 104
Elliott Rd. W4 —4A 82
Elliott Rd. Brom —4B 144
Elliott Rd. Stan —6F 11
Elliott Rd. T Hth —4B 140
Elliott's Pl. N1 —1B 68
Elliott Sq. NW3 —7C 48
Elliotts Row. SE11 —4B 86
Ellis Clo. NW10 —6D 46
Ellis Clo. SE9 —2G 127
Ellis Clo. Edgw —6F 13
Elliscombe Mt. SE7 —6A 90
Elliscombe Rd. SE7 —5A 90
Ellis Ct. W7 —5K 61
Ellisfield Dri. SW15 —7C 100
Ellis Franklin Ct. NW8 —2A 66
(off Abbey Rd.)
Ellis Ho. SE17 —5D 86
(off Brandon St.)
Ellison Gdns. S'hall —4D 78
Ellison Ho. SE13 —2D 106
(off Lewisham Rd.)
Ellison Rd. SW13 —2B 100
Ellison Rd. SW16 —7H 121
Ellison Rd. Sidc —1H 127
Ellis Rd. Mitc —6D 138
Ellis Rd. S'hall —1G 79
Ellis St. SW1 —4E 84 (3F 171)
Ellora Rd. SW16 —5H 121
Ellsworth St. E2 —3H 69
Ellwood Ct. W9 —4K 65
(off Clearwell Dri.)
Elmar Rd. N15 —4D 32
Elm Av. W5 —1E 80
Elm Av. Ashf —2A 112
Elm Av. Ruis —1J 41
Elm Bank. N14 —7D 6
Elmbank Av. Barn —4A 4
Elm Bank Dri. Brom —2B 144
Elm Bank Gdns. SW13 —2A 100
Elmbank Way. W7 —5H 61
Elmbourne Dri. Belv —4H 93
Elmbourne Rd. SW17 —3E 120
Elmbridge Av. Surb —5H 135
Elmbridge Clo. Ruis —6J 23
Elmbridge Dri. Ruis —5H 23
Elmbridge Wlk. E8 —7G 51
Elmbrook Clo. Sun —1K 131
Elmbrook Gdns. SE9 —4C 108
Elmbrook Rd. Sutt —4H 149
Elm Clo. E11 —6K 35
Elm Clo. N19 —2G 49
Elm Clo. NW4 —5F 29
Elm Clo. SW20 —4E 136
Elm Clo. Buck H —2G 21
Elm Clo. Cars —1D 150
Elm Clo. Harr —6F 25
Elm Clo. Hay —6J 59
Elm Clo. Romf —1H 39
Elm Clo. S Croy —6E 152
Elm Clo. Surb —7J 135
Elm Clo. Twic —2F 115
Elmcote. Pinn —2B 24
Elm Cotts. Mitc —2D 138
Elm Ct. EC4 —1J 167
Elm Ct. SE13 —3F 107
Elm Ct. W Mol —4F 133
Elmcourt Rd. SE27 —2B 122
Elm Cres. W5 —2E 80
Elm Cres. King T —1E 134
Elmcroft. N6 —7G 31
Elmcroft Av. E11 —5K 35
Elmcroft Av. N9 —6C 8
Elmcroft Av. NW11 —7H 29
Elmcroft Av. Sidc —7K 109
Elmcroft Clo. E11 —4K 35
Elmcroft Clo. N8 —5K 31
Elmcroft Clo. W5 —6D 62
Elmcroft Clo. Chess —3E 146
Elmcroft Clo. Felt —6H 95
Elmcroft Cres. NW11 —7G 29
Elmcroft Cres. Harr —3E 24
Elmcroft Dri. Ashf —5C 112
Elmcroft Dri. Chess —3E 146
Elmcroft Gdns. NW9 —4G 27
Elmcroft St. E5 —4J 51
Elmcroft Ter. Uxb —6C 58
Elmdale Rd. N13 —5E 16
Elmdene. Surb —1J 147
Elmdene Clo. Beck —6B 142
Elmdene Rd. SE18 —5F 91
Elmdon Rd. Houn —2B 96
Elmdon Rd. H'row A —3H 95
Elm Dri. Harr —6F 25
Elm Dri. Sun —2A 132
Elmer Clo. Enf —3E 6
Elmer Gdns. Edgw —7C 12
Elmer Gdns. Iswth —3H 97
Elmer Ho. NW1 —5C 66 (5C 158)
(off Broadley St.)
Elmer Rd. SE6 —7E 106
Elmers Dri. Tedd —6B 116
Elmers End. —4A 142
Elmers End Rd. SE20 & Beck —2J 141
Elmerside Rd. Beck —4A 142
Elmers Rd. SE25 —7G 141
Elmfield Av. N8 —5J 31
Elmfield Av. Mitc —1E 138
Elmfield Av. Tedd —5K 115
Elmfield Clo. Harr —2J 43
Elmfield Ct. Well —1B 110
Elmfield Ho. N2 —2B 30
(off Grange, The)
Elmfield Pk. Brom —3J 143
Elmfield Rd. E4 —2K 19
Elmfield Rd. E17 —6K 33
Elmfield Rd. N2 —3B 30
Elmfield Rd. SW17 —2E 120
Elmfield Rd. Brom —2J 143
Elmfield Rd. S'hall —3C 78
Elmfield Way. W9 —5J 65
Elmfield Way. S Croy —7F 153
Elm Friars Wlk. NW1 —7H 49
Elm Gdns. N2 —3A 30
Elm Gdns. Clay —6A 146
Elm Gdns. Mitc —4H 139
Elmgate Av. Felt —3K 113
Elmgate Gdns. Edgw —5D 12
Elm Grn. W3 —6A 64
Elm Gro. N8 —6J 31
Elm Gro. NW2 —4F 47
Elm Gro. SE15 —2F 105
Elm Gro. SW19 —7G 119
Elm Gro. Eri —7K 93
Elm Gro. Harr —7E 24
Elm Gro. King T —1E 134
Elm Gro. Sutt —4K 149
Elm Gro. W Dray —7B 58
Elm Gro. Wfd G —5C 20
Elmgrove Cres. Harr —5K 25
Elmgrove Gdns. Harr —5A 26
Elm Gro. Pde. Wall —3E 150
Elm Gro. Rd. SW13 —1C 100
Elm Gro. Rd. W5 —2E 80
Elmgrove Rd. Croy —7H 141
Elmgrove Rd. Harr —5K 25
Elmgrove Rd. Kent —5A 26
Elm Hall Gdns. E11 —5K 35
(in two parts)
Elm Ho. E14 —2E 88
Elm Ho. W10 —4G 65
(off Briar Wlk.)
Elmhurst. Belv —6E 92
Elmhurst Av. N2 —3B 30
Elmhurst Av. Mitc —7F 121
Elmhurst Ct. Croy —4D 152
Elmhurst Dri. E18 —2J 35
Elmhurst Lodge. Sutt —7A 150
Elmhurst Mans. SW4 —3H 103
Elmhurst Rd. E7 —7K 53
Elmhurst Rd. N17 —2F 33
Elmhurst Rd. SE9 —2C 126
Elmhurst St. SW4 —3H 103
Elmington Clo. Bex —6H 111
Elmington Est. SE5 —7D 86
Elmington Rd. SE5 —7D 86
Elmira St. SE13 —3D 106
Elm La. SE6 —2B 124
Elm Lawn Clo. Uxb —7A 40
Elmlea Dri. Hay —5G 59
Elm Lea Trad. Est. N17 —6C 18
Elmlee Clo. Chst —6D 126
Elmley Clo. E6 —5C 72
Elmley St. SE18 —5H 91
(in two parts)
Elm Lodge. SW6 —1E 100
Elmore Clo. Wemb —2E 62
Elmore Ho. SW9 —2B 104
Elmore Rd. E11 —3E 52
Elmore Rd. Enf —1E 8
Elmore St. N1 —7C 50
Elm Pde. Sidc —4A 128
Elm Pk. SW2 —6K 103
Elm Pk. Stan —5G 11
Elm Pk. Av. N15 —5F 33
Elm Pk. Chambers. SW10 —5B 84 (6A 170)
Elm Pk. Ct. Pinn —3A 24
Elm Pk. Gdns. NW4 —5F 29
Elm Pk. Gdns. SW10 —5B 84 (6A 170)
Elm Pk. Ho. SW10 —5B 84 (6A 170)
Elm Pk. La. SW3 —5B 84 (6A 170)
Elm Pk. Mans. SW10 —7A 170
Elm Pk. Rd. E10 —1A 52
Elm Pk. Rd. N3 —7C 14
Elm Pk. Rd. N21 —7H 7
Elm Pk. Rd. SE25 —3F 141
Elm Pk. Rd. SW3 —6B 84 (7A 170)
Elm Pk. Rd. Pinn —2A 24
Elm Pas. Barn —4C 4
Elm Pl. SW7 —5B 84 (5A 170)
Elm Quay Ct. SW8 —6H 85 (7C 172)
Elm Rd. E7 —6H 53
Elm Rd. E11 —2F 53
Elm Rd. E17 —5E 34
Elm Rd. N22 —1B 32
Elm Rd. SW14 —3J 99
Elm Rd. Barn —4C 4
Elm Rd. Beck —2B 142
Elm Rd. Chess —4E 146
Elm Rd. Eps —6B 148
Elm Rd. Felt —1F 113
Elm Rd. King T —1F 135
Elm Rd. N Mald —2K 135
Elm Rd. Romf —2H 39
Elm Rd. Sidc —4A 128
Elm Rd. T Hth —4D 140
Elm Rd. Wall —1E 150
Elm Rd. Wemb —5E 44
Elm Rd. W. Sutt —7H 137
Elm Row. NW3 —3A 48
Elms Av. N10 —3F 31
Elms Av. NW4 —5F 29
Elmscott Gdns. N21 —6H 7
Elmscott Rd. Brom —5G 125
Elms Ct. Wemb —4A 44
Elms Cres. SW4 —6G 103
Elmsdale Rd. E17 —4B 34
Elms Gdns. Dag —4F 57
Elms Gdns. Wemb —4A 44
Elmshaw Rd. SW15 —5C 100
Elmshurst Cres. N2 —4B 30
Elmside. New Ad —6D 154
Elmside Rd. Wemb —3G 45
Elms La. Wemb —3A 44
Elmsleigh Av. Harr —4B 26
Elmsleigh Ct. Sutt —3K 149
Elmsleigh Ho. Twic —2H 115
(off Staines Rd.)
Elmsleigh Rd. Twic —2H 115
Elmslie Clo. Wfd G —6J 21
Elmslie Point. E3 —5B 70
Elms M. W2 —7B 66 (2A 164)
Elms Pk. Av. Wemb —4A 44
Elms Rd. SW4 —5G 103
Elms Rd. Harr —7D 10
Elmstead. —6D 126
Elmstead Av. Chst —5D 126
Elmstead Av. Wemb —1E 44
Elmstead Clo. N20 —2D 14
Elmstead Clo. Eps —5A 148
Elmstead Gdns. Wor Pk —3C 148
Elmstead Glade. Chst —6D 126
Elmstead La. Chst —7C 126
Elmstead Rd. Eri —1K 111
Elmstead Rd. Ilf —2J 55
Elmsted Cres. Well —6C 92
Elms, The. E12 —6B 54
Elms, The. SW13 —3B 100
Elms, The. Clay —7A 146
Elmstone Rd. SW6 —1J 101
Elm St. WC1 —4K 67 (4H 161)
Elmsway. Ashf —5C 112
Elmsworth Av. Houn —2F 97
Elm Ter. NW2 —3J 47
Elm Ter. NW3 —4C 48
Elm Ter. SE9 —6E 108
Elm Ter. Harr —1H 25
Elm Ter. Stan —5H 11
Elmton Ct. NW8 —4B 66 (3A 158)
(off Cunningham Pl.)
Elmton Way. E5 —3G 51
Elm Tree Av. Esh —7H 133
Elm Tree Clo. NW8 —3B 66 (1A 158)
Elm Tree Clo. Ashf —5D 112
Elm Tree Clo. N'holt —2D 60
Elm Tree Ct. NW8 —1A 158
Elm Tree Ct. SE7 —6A 90
Elm Tree Rd. NW8 —3B 66 (1A 158)
Elmtree Rd. Tedd —4J 115
Elm Vw. Ct. S'hall —4E 78
Elm Vw. Ho. Hay —4G 77
Elm Wlk. NW3 —2J 47
Elm Wlk. SW20 —4E 136
Elm Wlk. Orp —3D 156
Elm Way. N11 —6K 15
Elm Way. NW10 —4A 46
Elm Way. Eps —5K 147
Elm Way. Wor Pk —3E 148
Elmwood Av. N13 —5D 16
Elmwood Av. Felt —2J 113
Elmwood Av. Harr —5A 26
Elmwood Clo. Eps —7C 148
Elmwood Clo. Wall —2F 151

Elmwood Ct. E10 —1C 52
(off Goldsmith Rd.)
Elmwood Ct. SW11 —1F 103
Elmwood Ct. Wemb —3A 44
Elmwood Cres. NW9 —4J 27
Elmwood Dri. Bex —7E 110
Elmwood Dri. Eps —6C 148
Elmwood Gdns. W7 —6J 61
Elmwood Rd. SE24 —5D 104
Elmwood Rd. W4 —6J 81
Elmwood Rd. Croy —7B 140
Elmwood Rd. Mitc —3D 138
Elmworth Gro. SE21 —2D 122
Elnathan M. W9 —4K 65
Elphinstone Ct. SW16 —6J 121
Elphinstone Rd. E17 —2B 34
Elphinstone St. N5 —4B 50
Elrington Rd. E8 —6G 51
Elrington Rd. Wfd G —5D 20
Elsa Ct. Beck —1B 142
Elsa Rd. Well —2B 110
Elsa St. E1 —5A 70
Elsdale St. E9 —6J 51
Elsden M. E2 —2J 69
Elsden Rd. N17 —1F 33
Elsenham Rd. E12 —5E 54
Elsenham St. SW18 —1H 119
Elsham Rd. E11 —3G 53
Elsham Rd. W14 —2G 83
Elsham Ter. W14 —3G 83
(off Elsham Rd.)
Elsiedene Rd. N21 —7H 7
Elsie La. Ct. W2 —5J 65
(off Westbourne Pk. Vs.)
Elsiemaud Rd. SE4 —5B 106
Elsie Rd. SE22 —4F 105
Elsinore Av. Stai —7A 94
Elsinore Gdns. NW2 —3G 47
Elsinore Ho. N1 —1A 68
(off Denmark Gro.)
Elsinore Rd. SE23 —1A 124
Elsinore Way. Rich —3H 99
Elsley Rd. SW11 —3D 102
Elsmore Ho. SE5 —2C 104
(off Denmark Rd.)
Elspeth Rd. SW11 —4D 102
Elspeth Rd. Wemb —5E 44
Elsrick Av. Mord —5J 137
Elstan Way. Croy —7A 142
Elstead Ct. Sutt —1G 149
Elstead Ho. SW2 —7K 103
(off Redlands Way)
Elsted St. SE17 —4D 86
Elstow Clo. SE9 —5D 108
(in two parts)
Elstow Clo. Ruis —7B 24
Elstow Gdns. Dag —1E 74
Elstow Rd. Dag —7E 56
Elstree Gdns. N9 —1C 18
Elstree Gdns. Belv —4E 92
Elstree Gdns. Ilf —5G 55
Elstree Hill. Brom —7G 125
Elstree Hill S. Els —1J 11
Elstree Rd. Bus H & Bush —1C 10
Elswick Rd. SE13 —2D 106
Elswick St. SW6 —2A 102
Elsworth Clo. Felt —1G 113
Elsworthy. Th Dit —6J 133
Elsworthy Ri. NW3 —7C 48
Elsworthy Rd. NW3 —1C 66
Elsworthy Ter. NW3 —7C 48
Elsynge Rd. SW18 —5B 102
Eltham. —6D 108
Eltham Crematorium. SE9 —4H 109
Eltham Grn. SE9 —5B 108
Eltham Grn. Rd. SE9 —4A 108
Eltham High St. SE9 —6D 108
Eltham Hill. SE9 —5B 108
Eltham Palace. —7C 108
Eltham Pal. Rd. SE9 —6A 108
Eltham Park. —4E 108
Eltham Pk. Gdns. SE9 —4E 108
Eltham Rd. SE12 & SE9 —5H 107
Elthiron Rd. SW6 —1J 101
Elthorne Av. W7 —2K 79
Elthorne Ct. Felt —1A 114
Elthorne Heights. —5H 61
Elthorne Pk. Rd. W7 —2K 79
Elthorne Rd. N19 —2H 49
Elthorne Rd. NW9 —7K 27
Elthorne Way. NW9 —6K 27
Elthruda Rd. SE13 —6F 107
Eltisley Rd. Ilf —4F 55
Elton Av. Barn —5C 4
Elton Av. Gnfd —6J 43
Elton Av. Wemb —5B 44
Elton Clo. King T —7C 116
Elton Ho. E3 —1B 70
(off Candy St.)
Elton Pl. N16 —5E 50
Elton Rd. King T —1F 135
Eltringham St. SW18 —4A 102
Elvaston M. SW7 —3A 84 (2A 170)
Elvaston Pl. SW7 —3A 84 (2A 170)
Elveden Ho. SE24 —5B 104
Elveden Pl. NW10 —2G 63
Elveden Rd. NW10 —2G 63
Elvendon Rd. N13 —6D 16
Elver Gdns. E2 —3G 69
(off St Peter's Clo.)
Elverson Rd. SE8 —2D 106
Elverton St. SW1 —4H 85 (3C 172)
Elvington Grn. Brom —5H 143
Elvington La. NW9 —1A 28
Elvino Rd. SE26 —5A 124
Elvis Rd. NW2 —6E 46
Elwill Way. Beck —4E 142
Elwin St. E2 —3G 69 (1K 163)
Elwood St. N5 —3B 50
Elworth Ho. SW8 —7K 85
(off Oval Pl.)
Elwyn Gdns. SE12 —7J 107
Ely Clo. N Mald —2B 136
Ely Cotts. SW8 —7K 85
Ely Ct. EC1 —6K 161
Ely Ct. NW6 —2J 65
(off Chichester Rd., in two parts)
Ely Gdns. Dag —3J 57
Ely Gdns. Ilf —7C 36
Ely Ho. SE15 —7G 87
(off Friary Est.)
Elyne Rd. N4 —6A 32
Ely Pl. EC1 —5A 68 (6K 161)
Ely Pl. Wfd G —6K 21
Ely Rd. E10 —6E 34
Ely Rd. Croy —5D 140
Ely Rd. Houn —3A 96
Ely Rd. H'row A —2H 95
Elysian Av. Orp —6K 145
Elysium Pl. SW6 —2H 101
(off Elysium St.)
Elysium St. SW6 —2H 101
Elystan Bus. Cen. Hay —7A 60
Elystan Clo. Wall —7G 151
Elystan Pl. SW3 —5C 84 (5D 170)
Elystan St. SW3 —4C 84 (4C 170)
Elystan Wlk. N1 —1A 68
Emanuel Av. W3 —6J 63
Emanuel Dri. Hamp —5D 114
Embankment. SW15 —2F 101
Embankment Gdns. SW3 —6D 84 (7F 171)
Embankment Pl. WC2 —1J 85 (4F 167)
Embankment, The. Twic —1A 116
Embassy Ct. N11 —6C 16
(off Bounds Grn. Rd.)
Embassy Ct. NW8 —1B 158
Embassy Ct. W5 —7F 63
Embassy Ct. Sidc —3B 128
Embassy Ct. Wall —6F 151
Embassy Ct. Well —3B 110
Embassy Gdns. Beck —1B 142
Embassy Ho. NW6 —7K 47
Emba St. SE16 —2G 87
Ember Clo. Orp —7G 145
Ember Ct. NW9 —2A 28
Embercourt Rd. Th Dit —6J 133
Ember Farm Av. E Mol —6H 133
Ember Farm Way. E Mol —6H 133
Ember Gdns. Th Dit —7J 133
Ember La. Esh & E Mol —7H 133
Emberton. SE17 —6E 86
(off Albany Rd.)
Emberton Ct. EC1 —3B 68 (2A 162)
(off Tompion St.)
Embleton Rd. SE13 —4D 106
Embleton Wlk. Hamp —5D 114
Embley Point. E5 —4H 51
(off Tiger Way)
Embroidery Bus. Cen. Wfd G —2B 36
(off Southend Rd.)
Embry Clo. Stan —4F 11
Embry Dri. Stan —6F 11
Embry Way. Stan —5F 11
Emden Clo. W Dray —2C 76
Emden St. SW6 —1K 101
Emerald Clo. E16 —6B 72
Emerald Gdns. Dag —1G 57
Emerald Sq. S'hall —3B 78
Emerald St. WC1 —5K 67 (5G 161)
Emerson Gdns. Harr —6F 27
Emerson Rd. Ilf —7E 36
Emerson St. SE1 —1C 86 (4C 168)
Emerton Clo. Bexh —4E 110
Emery Hill St. SW1 —3G 85 (2B 172)
Emery St. SE1 —3A 86 (1K 173)
Emes Rd. Eri —7J 93
Emilia Clo. Enf —5C 8
Emily Pl. N7 —4A 50
Emily St. E16 —6H 71
(off Jude St.)
Emlyn Gdns. W12 —2A 82
Emlyn Rd. W12 —2A 82
Emmanuel Ct. E10 —7D 34
Emmanuel Ho. SE11 —4A 86 (4J 173)
Emmanuel Rd. SW12 —1G 121
Emmanuel Rd. N'wd —1H 23
Emma Rd. E13 —2H 71
Emma St. E2 —2H 69
Emmaus Way. Chig —5K 21
Emminster. NW6 —1K 65
(off Abbey Rd.)
Emmott Av. Ilf —5G 37
Emmott Clo. E1 —4A 70
Emmott Clo. NW11 —6A 30
Emms Pas. King T —2D 134
Emperor's Ga. SW7 —3A 84
Empire Av. N18 —5H 17
Empire Ct. Wemb —3H 45
Empire Pde. N18 —6J 17
Empire Pde. Wemb —3G 45
Empire Rd. Gnfd —1B 62
Empire Sq. N7 —3J 49
Empire Sq. SE20 —7K 123
(off High St.)
Empire Way. Wemb —4F 45
Empire Wharf. E3 —1A 70
(off Old Ford Rd.)
Empire Wharf Rd. E14 —4F 89
Empress Av. E4 —7J 19
Empress Av. E12 —2A 54
Empress Av. Ilf —2D 54
Empress Av. Wfd G —7C 20
Empress Dri. Chst —6F 127
Empress Pde. E4 —7H 19
Empress Pl. SW6 —5J 83
Empress State Building. W14 —5J 83
Empress St. SE17 —6C 86
Empson St. E3 —4D 70
Emsworth Clo. N9 —1D 18
Emsworth Ct. SW16 —3J 121
Emsworth Rd. Ilf —2F 37
Emsworth St. SW2 —2K 121
Emu Rd. SW8 —2F 103
Ena Rd. SW16 —3J 139
Enbrook St. W10 —3G 65
Endale Clo. Cars —2D 150
Endeavour Way. SW19 —4K 119
Endeavour Way. Bark —2A 74
Endeavour Way. Croy —7J 139
Endell St. WC2 —6J 67 (7E 160)
Enderby St. SE10 —5F 89
Enderley Clo. Harr —2J 25
Enderley Rd. Harr —1J 25
Endersleigh Gdns. NW4 —4C 28
Endlebury Rd. E4 —2K 19
Endlesham Rd. SW12 —7E 102
Endsleigh Gdns. WC1 —4H 67 (3C 160)
Endsleigh Gdns. Ilf —2D 54
Endsleigh Gdns. Surb —6C 134
Endsleigh Ind. Est. S'hall —4C 78
Endsleigh Pl. WC1 —4H 67 (3D 160)
Endsleigh Rd. W13 —7A 62
Endsleigh Rd. S'hall —4C 78
Endsleigh St. WC1 —4H 67 (3D 160)
End Way. Surb —7G 135
Endwell Rd. SE4 —2A 106
Endymion Rd. N4 —7A 32
Endymion Rd. SW2 —6K 103
Energen Clo. NW10 —6A 46
Enfield. —3J 7
Enfield Bus. Cen. Enf —2D 8
Enfield Cloisters. N1 —3E 68 (1G 163)
(off Fanshaw St.)
Enfield Highway. —2E 8
Enfield Ho. SW9 —2J 103
(off Stockwell Rd.)
Enfield Island Village. —1H 9
Enfield Retail Pk. Enf —3C 8
Enfield Rd. N1 —7E 50
Enfield Rd. W3 —2H 81
Enfield Rd. Bren —5D 80
Enfield Rd. Enf —4C 6
Enfield Rd. H'row A —2G 95
Enfield Town. —3J 7
Enfield Wlk. Bren —5D 80
Enford St. W1 —5D 66 (5E 158)
Engadine Clo. Croy —3F 153
Engadine St. SW18 —1H 119
Engate St. SE13 —4E 106
Engel Pk. NW7 —6K 13
Engine Ct. SW1 —1G 85 (5B 166)
(off St James' Pal.)
Engineer Clo. SE18 —6E 90
Engineers Way. Wemb —4G 45
England's La. NW3 —6D 48
England Way. N Mald —4H 135
Englefield. NW1 —3G 67 (2A 160)
(off Clarence Gdns.)
Englefield Clo. Croy —6C 140
Englefield Clo. Enf —2F 7
Englefield Clo. Orp —5K 145
Englefield Cres. Orp —4K 145
Englefield Path. Orp —4K 145
Englefield Rd. N1 —7D 50
Engleheart Dri. Felt —6H 95
Engleheart Rd. SE6 —7D 106
Englewood Rd. SW12 —6F 103
English Grounds. SE1 —1E 86 (5G 169)
English St. E3 —4B 70
Enid St. SE16 —3F 87 (7K 169)
Enmore Av. SE25 —5G 141
Enmore Gdns. SW14 —5K 99
Enmore Rd. SE25 —5G 141
Enmore Rd. SW15 —4E 100
Enmore Rd. S'hall —4E 60
Ennerdale. NW1 —3G 67 (1A 160)
(off Ennerdale)
Ennerdale Av. Stan —3C 26
Ennerdale Clo. Felt —1H 113
Ennerdale Clo. Sutt —4H 149
Ennerdale Dri. NW9 —5A 28
Ennerdale Gdns. Wemb —1C 44
Ennerdale Ho. E3 —4B 70
Ennerdale Rd. Bexh —1G 111
Ennerdale Rd. Rich —2F 99
Ennersdale Rd. SE13 —5F 107
Ennis Ho. E14 —6D 70
Ennismore Av. W4 —4B 82
Ennismore Av. Gnfd —6J 43
Ennismore Gdns. SW7 —2C 84 (7C 164)
Ennismore Gdns. Th Dit —6J 133
Ennismore Gdns. M. SW7 —3C 84 (1C 170)
Ennismore M. SW7 —3C 84 (7C 164)
Ennismore St. SW7 —3C 84 (1C 170)
Ennis Rd. N4 —1A 50
Ennis Rd. SE18 —6G 91
Ennor Ct. Sutt —4E 148
Ensbury Ho. SW8 —7K 85
(off Carroun Rd.)
Ensign Clo. Stanw —1A 112
Ensign Dri. N13 —3H 17
Ensign Ho. E14 —2C 88
Ensign Ind. Cen. E1 —7G 69
(off Ensign St.)
Ensign St. E1 —7G 69
Ensign Way. Stanw —1A 112
Enslin Rd. SE9 —7E 108
Ensor M. SW7 —5B 84 (5A 170)
Enstone Rd. Enf —3F 9
Enstone Rd. Uxb —3B 40
Enterprise Bus. Pk. E14 —2D 88
Enterprise Cen., The. Beck —5A 124
(off Cricket La.)
Enterprise Clo. Croy —1A 152
Enterprise Ho. E14 —5D 88
Enterprise Ho. Bark —3K 73
Enterprise Ind. Est. SE16 —5J 87
Enterprise Way. NW10 —3B 64
Enterprise Way. SW18 —4J 101
Enterprise Way. Tedd —6K 115
Enterprize Way. SE8 —4B 88
Epcot M. NW10 —3F 65
Epirus M. SW6 —7J 83
Epirus Rd. SW6 —7H 83
Epping Clo. E14 —4C 88
Epping Clo. Romf —3H 39
Epping Glade. E4 —6K 9
Epping New Rd. Buck H & Lou —2E 20
Epping Pl. N1 —6A 50
Epping Way. E4 —6J 9
Epple Rd. SW6 —1H 101
Epsom Clo. Bexh —3H 111
Epsom Clo. N'holt —5D 42
Epsom Rd. E10 —6E 34
Epsom Rd. Croy —4A 152
Epsom Rd. Ilf —6K 37
Epsom Rd. Sutt & Mord —7H 137
Epsom Sq. H'row A —2H 95
Epstein Rd. SE28 —1A 92
Epworth Rd. Iswth —7B 80
Epworth St. EC1 —4D 68 (4F 163)
Equity Sq. E2 —3F 69 (2K 163)
(off Shacklewell St.)
Erasmus St. SW1 —4H 85 (4D 172)
Erconwald St. W12 —6B 64
Eresby Dri. Beck —1C 154
Eresby Ho. SW7 —2C 84 (7D 164)
(off Rutland Ga.)
Eresby Pl. NW6 —7J 47
Erica Gdns. Croy —3D 154
Erica Ho. N22 —1A 32
(off Acacia Rd.)
Erica Ho. SE4 —3B 106
Erica St. W12 —7C 64
Eric Clarke La. Bark —4F 73
Eric Clo. E7 —4J 53
Ericcson Clo. SW18 —5J 101
Eric Fletcher Ct. N1 —7C 50
(off Essex Rd.)
Eric Rd. E7 —4J 53
Eric Rd. NW10 —6B 46
Eric Rd. Romf —7D 38
Ericson Ho. SE13 —4F 107
(off Blessington Rd.)
Eric St. E3 —4B 70
(in two parts)
Eric Wilkins Ho. SE1 —5G 87
(off Old Kent Rd.)
Eridge Rd. NW10 —7A 46
Eridge Rd. W4 —3K 81
Erin Clo. Brom —7G 125
Erin Clo. Ilf —6A 38
Erindale. SE18 —6H 91
Erindale Ter. SE18 —6H 91
Erith Cres. Romf —1J 39
Erith Rd. Belv & Eri —5G 93
Erith Rd. Bexh & N Hth —4H 111
Erlanger Rd. SE14 —1K 105
Erlesmere Gdns. W7 —3A 80
Ermine Clo. Houn —2A 96
Ermine Rd. N15 —6F 33
Ermine Rd. SE13 —4D 106
Ermine Side. Enf —5B 8
Ermington Rd. SE9 —2G 127
Ernald Av. E6 —2C 72
Erncroft Way. Twic —6K 97
Ernest Av. SE27 —4B 122
Ernest Clo. Beck —5C 142
Ernest Cotts. Eps —7B 148
Ernest Gdns. W4 —6H 81
Ernest Gro. Beck —5B 142
Ernest Harriss Ho. W9 —4J 65
(off Elgin Av.)
Ernest Rd. King T —2H 135
Ernest Sq. King T —2H 135
Ernest St. E1 —4K 69
Ernle Rd. SW20 —7D 118
Ernshaw Pl. SW15 —5G 101
Eros. —7H 67 (3C 166)
Eros Ho. Shops. SE23 —7A 106
(off Brockley Pk.)
Erpingham Rd. SW15 —3E 100
Erridge Rd. SW19 —2J 137
Errington Rd. W9 —4H 65
Errol Gdns. Hay —4K 59
Errol Gdns. N Mald —4C 136
Errol St. EC1 —4C 68 (4D 162)
Erskine Clo. Sutt —3C 150
Erskine Cres. N17 —4H 33
Erskine Hill. NW11 —4J 29
Erskine Ho. SW1 —5G 85 (6A 172)
(off Churchill Gdns.)
Erskine M. NW3 —7D 48
(off Erskine Rd.)
Erskine Rd. E17 —4B 34
Erskine Rd. NW3 —7D 48
Erskine Rd. Sutt —4B 150
Erwood Rd. SE7 —5C 90
Esam Way. SW16 —5A 122
Escot Rd. Sun —7H 113
Escott Gdns. SE9 —4C 126
Escreet Gro. SE18 —4E 90
Esher Av. Romf —6J 39
Esher Av. Sutt —3F 149
Esher Av. W on T —7J 131
Esher By-Pass. Clay —7B 146
Esher Clo. Bex —1E 128
Esher Cres. H'row A —2H 95
Esher Gdns. SW19 —2F 119
Esher M. Mitc —3E 138
Esher Rd. E Mol —6H 133
Esher Rd. Ilf —3J 55
Eskdale. NW1 —2G 67 (1A 160)
(off Stanhope St.)
Eskdale Av. N'holt —1D 60
Eskdale Clo. Wemb —2D 44
Eskdale Rd. Bexh —2G 111
Eskmont Ridge. SE19 —7D 122
Esk Rd. E13 —4J 71
Esk Way. Romf —1K 39
Esmar Cres. NW9 —7C 28
Esmeralda Rd. SE1 —4G 87
Esmond Ct. W8 —3K 83
(off Ansdell St.)
Esmond Gdns. W4 —4K 81
Esmond Rd. NW6 —1H 65
Esmond Rd. W4 —4K 81
Esmond St. SW15 —4G 101
Esparto St. SW18 —7K 101
Essan Ho. W5 —5B 62
Essenden Rd. Belv —5G 93
Essenden Rd. S Croy —7E 152
Essendine Rd. W9 —3J 65
Essex Av. Iswth —3J 97
Essex Clo. E17 —4A 34
Essex Clo. Mord —7F 137
Essex Clo. Romf —4H 39
Essex Clo. Ruis —1B 42
Essex Ct. EC4 —1J 167
Essex Ct. SW13 —2B 100
Essex Gdns. N4 —6B 32
Essex Gro. SE19 —6D 122
Essex Hall. E17 —1K 33
Essex Ho. E14 —6D 70
Essex Mans. E11 —7F 35
Essex Pk. N3 —6E 14
Essex Pk. M. W3 —1A 82
Essex Pl. W4 —4J 81
(in two parts)
Essex Pl. Sq. W4 —4K 81
Essex Rd. E4 —1B 20
Essex Rd. E10 —6E 34
Essex Rd. E12 —5C 54
Essex Rd. E17 —6A 34
Essex Rd. E18 —2K 35
Essex Rd. N1 —1B 68
Essex Rd. NW10 —7A 46
Essex Rd. W3 —7J 63
Essex Rd. W4 —4K 81
(in two parts)
Essex Rd. Bark —7H 55
Essex Rd. Chad H —7C 38
Essex Rd. Dag —5J 57
Essex Rd. Enf —4J 7
Essex Rd. Romf —4H 39
Essex Rd. S. E11 —7F 35
Essex St. E7 —5J 53
Essex St. SE18 —3G 91
Essex St. WC2 —6A 68 (1J 167)
Essex Vs. W8 —2J 83
Essex Wharf. E5 —2K 51
Essian St. E1 —5A 70
Essoldo Way. Edgw —3F 27
Estate Way. E10 —1B 52
Estcourt Rd. SE25 —6H 141
Estcourt Rd. SW6 —7H 83
Estella Av. N Mald —4D 136
Estella Ho. W11 —7F 65
(off St Ann's Rd.)
Estelle Rd. NW3 —4D 48
Esterbrooke St. SW1 —4H 85 (4C 172)
Este Rd. SW11 —3C 102
Esther Clo. N21 —7F 7
Esther Rd. E11 —7G 35
Estoria Clo. SW2 —7A 104
Estorick Collection of Modern Italian Art. —6B 50
(off Canonbury Sq.)
Estreham Rd. SW16 —6H 121
Estridge Clo. Houn —4E 96
Estuary Clo. Bark —3B 74
Eswyn Rd. SW17 —4D 120
Etal Ho. N1 —7B 50
(off Sutton Est., The)
Etcetera Theatre. —7F 49
Etchingham Ct. N3 —7E 14
Etchingham Pk. Rd. N3 —7E 14
Etchingham Rd. E15 —4E 52
Eternit Wlk. SW6 —1E 100
Etfield Gro. Sidc —5B 128
Ethelbert Clo. Brom —3J 143
Ethelbert Gdns. Ilf —5D 36
Ethelbert Rd. SW20 —1F 137
Ethelbert Rd. Brom —3J 143
Ethelbert Rd. Eri —7J 93
Ethelbert St. SW12 —1F 121
Ethel Brooks Ho. SE18 —6F 91
Ethelburga St. SW11 —1C 102
Etheldene Av. N10 —4G 31
Ethelden Rd. W12 —1D 82
Ethel Rd. E16 —6K 71
Ethel Rd. Ashf —5A 112
Ethel St. SE17 —4C 86
Etheridge Rd. NW4 —7E 28
Etherley Rd. N15 —5C 32
Etherow St. SE22 —7G 105
Etherstone Grn. SW16 —4A 122
Etherstone Rd. SW16 —4A 122
Ethnard Rd. SE15 —6H 87
Ethronvi Rd. Bexh —3E 110
Etloe Rd. E10 —2C 52
Eton Av. N12 —7F 15
Eton Av. NW3 —7B 48
Eton Av. Barn —6H 5
Eton Av. Houn —6D 78
Eton Av. N Mald —5K 135
Eton Av. Wemb —4B 44
Eton Clo. SW18 —7K 101
Eton College Rd. NW3 —6D 48
Eton Ct. Wemb —4C 44
Eton Gro. NW9 —3G 27
Eton Gro. SE13 —3G 107
Eton Hall. NW3 —6D 48
Eton Ho. N5 —4B 50
(off Leigh Rd.)
Eton Mnr. Ct. E10 —2C 52
(off Leyton Grange Est.)
Eton Pl. NW3 —7E 48
Eton Ri. NW3 —6D 48
Eton Rd. NW3 —7D 48
Eton Rd. Hay —7H 77
Eton Rd. Ilf —4G 55
Eton St. Rich —5E 98
Eton Vs. NW3 —6D 48
Etta St. SE8 —6A 88
Ettrick St. E14 —6E 70
(in two parts)
Etwell Pl. Surb —6F 135
Eugene Cotter Ho. SE17 —4D 86
(off Tatum St.)
Eugenia Rd. SE16 —4J 87
Eugenie M. Chst —1F 145
Eureka Rd. King T —2G 135
Euro Clo. NW10 —6C 46
Eurolink Bus. Cen. SW2 —5A 104
Europa Pl. EC1 —3C 68 (2C 162)
Europa Trad. Est. Eri —5K 93
European Bus. Cen. NW9 —3J 27
(in two parts)
Europe Rd. SE18 —3D 90
Eustace Ho. SE1 —3G 173
Eustace Pl. SE18 —4D 90
Eustace Rd. E6 —3C 72
Eustace Rd. SW6 —7J 83
Eustace Rd. Romf —7D 38
Euston Cen. NW1 —4G 67 (3A 160)
(in two parts)
Euston Gro. NW1 —2C 160
Euston Rd. NW1 & N1 —4F 67 (3A 160)
Euston Rd. Croy —1A 152
Euston Sq. NW1 —3H 67 (3A 160)
(in two parts)
Euston Sta. Colonnade. NW1 —3H 67 (2C 160)
Euston St. NW1 —3G 67 (2B 160)
Euston Tower. NW1 —4G 67
Euston Underpass. —4G 67
Evandale Rd. SW9 —2A 104

Evangelist Rd.—Faraday Mus.

Evangelist Rd. NW5 —4F 49
Evans Clo. E8 —6F 51
Evans Gro. Felt —2E 114
Evans Ho. SW8 —7H 85
(off Wandsworth Rd.)
Evans Ho. W12 —7D 64
(off White City Est.)
Evans Ho. Felt —2E 114
Evans Rd. SE6 —2G 125
Evanston Av. E4 —7K 19
Evanston Gdns. Ilf —6C 36
Eva Rd. Romf —7C 38
Evelina Mans. SE5 —7D 86
Evelina Rd. SE15 —3J 105
Evelina Rd. SE20 —7J 123
Eveline Rd. Mitc —1D 138
Evelyn Av. NW9 —4K 27
Evelyn Av. Ruis —7G 23
Evelyn Clo. Twic —7F 97
Evelyn Ct. E8 —4G 51
Evelyn Ct. N1 —2D 68 (1E 162)
(off Evelyn Wlk., in two parts)
Evelyn Cres. Sun —1H 131
Evelyn Denington Ct. N1 —7B 50
(off Upper St.)
Evelyn Denington Rd. E6 —4C 72
Evelyn Dri. Pinn —1B 24
Evelyn Fox Ct. W10 —5E 64
Evelyn Gdns. SW7 —5A 84 (6A 170)
Evelyn Gdns. Rich —4E 98
Evelyn Gro. W5 —1F 81
Evelyn Gro. S'hall —6D 60
Evelyn Ho. W12 —2B 82
(off Cobbold Rd.)
Evelyn Lowe Est. SE16 —3G 87
Evelyn Mans. SW1 —3G 85 (2A 172)
(off Carlisle Pl.)
Evelyn Mans. W14 —6G 83
(off Queen's Club Gdns.)
Evelyn Rd. E16 —1J 89
Evelyn Rd. E17 —4E 34
Evelyn Rd. SW19 —5K 119
Evelyn Rd. W4 —3K 81
Evelyn Rd. Cockf —4J 5
Evelyn Rd. Ham —3C 116
Evelyn Rd. Rich —3E 98
Evelyns Clo. Uxb —6C 58
Evelyn St. SE8 —4A 88
Evelyn Ter. Rich —3E 98
Evelyn Wlk. N1 —2D 68 (1E 162)
Evelyn Way. Sun —1H 131
Evelyn Way. Wall —4H 151
Evelyn Yd. W1 —6H 67 (7C 160)
Evening Hill. Beck —7E 124
Evenlode Ho. SE2 —2C 92
Evenwood Clo. SW15 —5G 101
Everard Av. Brom —1J 155
Everard Ct. N13 —3E 16
Everard Ho. E1 —6G 69
(off Boyd St.)
Everard Way. Wemb —3E 44
Everatt Clo. SW18 —6H 101
Everdon Rd. SW13 —6C 82
Everest Pl. E14 —5E 70
Everest Rd. SE9 —5D 108
Everest Rd. Stanw —7A 94
Everett Clo. Bus H —1D 10
Everett Clo. Pinn —3H 23
Everett Ho. SE17 —5D 86
Everett Wlk. Belv —5F 93
Everglade Ho. E17 —2B 34
Everglade Strand. NW9 —1B 28
Evergreen Clo. SE20 —7J 123
Evergreen Way. Hay —7G 59
Everilda St. N1 —1K 67
Evering Rd. N16 & E5 —3F 51
Everington Rd. N10 —2D 30
Everington St. W6 —6F 83
(in two parts)
Everitt Rd. NW10 —3K 63
Everleigh St. N4 —1K 49
Eve Rd. E11 —4G 53
Eve Rd. E15 —2G 71
Eve Rd. N17 —3E 32
Eve Rd. Iswth —4A 98
Eversfield Gdns. NW7 —6F 13
Eversfield Rd. Rich —2F 99
Evershed Wlk. W4 —3J 81
Eversholt St. NW1 —2G 67 (1B 160)
Evershot Rd. N4 —1K 49
Eversleigh Rd. E6 —1B 72
Eversleigh Rd. N3 —7C 14
Eversleigh Rd. SW11 —3D 102
Eversleigh Rd. Barn & New Bar —5F 5
Eversley Av. Bexh —2K 111
Eversley Av. Wemb —2G 45
Eversley Clo. N21 —6E 6
Eversley Cres. N21 —6E 6
Eversley Cres. Iswth —1H 97
Eversley Cres. Ruis —2G 41
Eversley Ho. E2 —3G 69 (2K 163)
(off Gossett St.)
Eversley Mt. N21 —6E 6
Eversley Pk. SW19 —6D 118
Eversley Pk. Rd. N21 —6E 6
Eversley Rd. SE7 —6K 89
Eversley Rd. SE19 —7D 122
Eversley Rd. Surb —4F 135
Eversley Way. Croy —4C 154
Everthorpe Rd. SE15 —3F 105
Everton Bldgs. NW1 —3G 67 (2A 160)
Everton Dri. Stan —3E 26
Everton Rd. Croy —1G 153
Evesham Av. E17 —2C 34
Evesham Clo. Gnfd —2F 61
Evesham Clo. Sutt —7J 149
Evesham Ct. W13 —1A 80
(off Tewkesbury Rd.)
Evesham Ct. Rich —6F 99
Evesham Grn. Mord —6K 137
Evesham Ho. NW8 —1A 66
(off Abbey Rd.)
Evesham Rd. E15 —7H 53
Evesham Rd. N11 —5B 16
Evesham Rd. Mord —6K 137
Evesham St. W11 —7F 65
Evesham Ter. Surb —6D 134
Evesham Wlk. SE5 —2D 104
Evesham Wlk. SW9 —2A 104
Evesham Way. SW11 —3E 102
Evesham Way. Ilf —3E 36
Evry Rd. Sidc —6C 128
Ewald Rd. SW6 —2H 101
Ewanrigg Ter. Wfd G —5F 21
Ewart Gro. N22 —1A 32
Ewart Pl. E3 —2B 70
Ewart Rd. SE23 —7K 105
Ewe Clo. N7 —6J 49
Ewell. —7B 148
Ewell By-Pass. Eps —7C 148
Ewell Ct. Av. Eps & Ewe —5A 148
Ewellhurst Rd. Ilf —2C 36
Ewell Pk. Gdns. Eps —7C 148
Ewell Pk. Way. Ewe —6C 148
Ewell Rd. Cheam & Sutt —7F 149
Ewell Rd. Dit H —6E 134
Ewell Rd. Surb —7B 134
Ewelme Rd. SE23 —1J 123
Ewen Cres. SW2 —7A 104
Ewen Ho. N1 —1K 67
(off Barnsbury Est.)
Ewer St. SE1 —1C 86 (5C 168)
Ewhurst Av. S Croy —7F 153
Ewhurst Clo. E1 —5J 69
Ewhurst Ct. Mitc —3B 138
Ewhurst Rd. SE4 —6B 106
Exbury Ho. E9 —7J 51
Exbury Ho. SW1 —5H 85 (5C 172)
(off Rampayne St.)
Exbury Rd. SE6 —2C 124
Excel. —7K 71
Excel Ct. WC2 —3D 166
Excelsior Clo. King T —2G 135
Excelsior Gdns. SE13 —2E 106
Exchange Arc. EC2 —5E 68 (5H 163)
Exchange Building. E1 —4F 69 (4J 163)
(off Commercial St.)
Exchange Clo. N11 —2K 15
Exchange Ct. WC2 —7J 67 (3F 167)
Exchange Ho. EC2 —5H 163
Exchange Mans. NW11 —7H 29
Exchange Pl. EC2 —5E 68 (5G 163)
Exchange Sq. EC2 —5E 68 (5G 163)
Exchange St. EC1 —3C 68 (2C 162)
Exchange St. Romf —5K 39
Exchange, The. Ilf —2F 55
Exeforde Av. Ashf —4C 112
Exeter Clo. E6 —6D 72
Exeter Ct. NW6 —2J 65
(off Cambridge Rd.)
Exeter Ct. Surb —5E 134
Exeter Gdns. Ilf —1C 54
Exeter Ho. SE15 —6G 87
(off Friary Est.)
Exeter Ho. W2 —6A 66
(off Hallfield Est.)
Exeter Ho. Bark —7A 56
(off Margaret Bondfield Av.)
Exeter Ho. Felt —2D 114
(off Watermill Way)
Exeter Mans. NW2 —6G 47
Exeter M. NW6 —6K 47
Exeter M. SW6 —7J 83
Exeter Rd. E16 —5J 71
Exeter Rd. E17 —5C 34
Exeter Rd. N9 —2D 18
Exeter Rd. N14 —1A 16
Exeter Rd. NW2 —5G 47
Exeter Rd. Croy —7E 140
Exeter Rd. Dag —6H 57
Exeter Rd. Enf —3E 8
Exeter Rd. Felt —3D 114
Exeter Rd. Harr —2C 42
Exeter Rd. H'row A —3G 95
Exeter Rd. Well —2J 109
Exeter St. WC2 —7J 67 (2F 167)
Exeter Way. SE14 —7B 88
Exeter Way. H'row A —2G 95
Exford Gdns. SE12 —1K 125
Exford Rd. SE12 —2K 125
Exhibition Clo. W12 —7E 64
Exhibition Rd. SW7 —2B 84 (7B 164)
Exmoor Clo. Ilf —1F 37
Exmoor St. W10 —4F 65
Exmouth Ho. E14 —4D 88
Exmouth Ho. EC1 —4A 68 (3J 161)
(off Pine St.)
Exmouth Mkt. EC1 —4A 68 (3J 161)
Exmouth M. NW1 —3G 67 (2B 160)
Exmouth Pl. E8 —7H 51
Exmouth Rd. E17 —5B 34
Exmouth Rd. Hay —3G 59
Exmouth Rd. Ruis —3A 42
Exmouth Rd. Well —1C 110
Exmouth St. E1 —6J 69
Exning Rd. E16 —4H 71
Exonbury. NW8 —1K 65
(off Abbey Rd.)
Exon St. SE17 —5E 86
Explorer Av. Stai —1A 112
Express Dri. Ilf —1B 56
Express Newspapers. SE1 —1B 86
(off Blackfriars Rd.)
Express Wharf. E14 —2C 88
Exton Cres. NW10 —7J 45
Exton Gdns. Dag —5C 56
Exton St. SE1 —1A 86 (5J 167)
Eyebright Clo. Croy —1K 153
Eyhurst Clo. NW2 —2C 46
Eylewood Rd. SE27 —5C 122
Eynella Rd. SE22 —7F 105
Eynham Rd. W12 —6E 64
Eynsford Clo. Orp —7G 145
Eynsford Cres. Bex —1C 128
Eynsford Ho. SE1 —2D 86 (7E 168)
(off Crosby Row)
Eynsford Ho. SE15 —6J 87
Eynsford Ho. SE17 —4E 86
(off Beckway St.)
Eynsford Rd. Ilf —2J 55
Eynsford Ter. W Dray —6B 58
Eynsham Dri. SE2 —4J 93
Eynswood Dri. Sidc —5B 128
Eyot Gdns. W6 —5B 82
Eyot Grn. W4 —5B 82
Eyre Ct. NW8 —2B 66
Eyre St. Hill. EC1 —4A 68 (4J 161)
Eysham Ct. New Bar —5E 4
Eythorne Rd. SW9 —1A 104
Ezra St. E2 —3F 69 (1K 163)

Faber Gdns. NW4 —5C 28
Fabian Rd. SW6 —7H 83
Fabian St. E6 —4D 72
Facade, The. SE23 —2J 123
Factory La. N17 —2F 33
Factory La. Croy —1A 152
Factory Pl. E14 —5E 88
Factory Rd. E16 —1B 90
Factory Sq. SW16 —6J 121
(off Streatham High Rd.)
Factory Yd. W7 —1J 79
Fagg's Rd. Felt —4H 95
Fairacre. N Mald —3A 136
Fairacres. SW15 —4B 100
Fair Acres. Brom —5J 143
Fair Acres. Croy —7B 154
Fairacres. Ruis —7H 23
Fairbairn Grn. SW9 —1B 104
Fairbank Av. Orp —2E 156
Fairbank Est. N1 —2D 68 (1E 162)
Fairbanks Rd. N17 —3F 33
Fairbourne Ho. Hay —3E 76
Fairbourne Rd. N17 —3E 32
Fairbridge Rd. N19 —2H 49
Fairbrook Clo. N13 —5F 17
Fairbrook Rd. N13 —6F 17
Fairburn Ct. SW15 —5G 101
Fairburn Ho. W14 —5H 83
(off Ivatt Pl.)
Fairby Ho. SE1 —4F 87
(off Longfield Est.)
Fairby Rd. SE12 —5K 107
Faircharm Trad. Est. SE8 —7D 88
Fairchild Clo. SW11 —2B 102
Fairchild Ho. N1 —3E 68 (1G 163)
(off Fanshaw St.)
Fairchild Ho. N3 —1J 29
Fairchild Pl. EC2 —4H 163
Fairchild St. EC2 —4E 68 (3H 163)
Fair Clo. Bush —1A 10
Fairclough St. E1 —6G 69
Faircroft Ct. Tedd —6A 116
Fair Cross. —5J 55
Faircross Av. Bark —6G 55
Faircross Av. Romf —1K 39
Faircross Pde. Bark —5J 55
Fairdale Gdns. SW15 —4D 100
Fairdale Gdns. Hay —2J 77
Fairey Av. Hay —4H 77
Fairfax Clo. W on T —7K 131
Fairfax Gdns. SE3 —1A 108
Fairfax M. E16 —1K 89
Fairfax M. SW15 —4E 100
Fairfax Pl. NW6 —7A 48
Fairfax Rd. N8 —4A 32
Fairfax Rd. NW6 —7A 48
Fairfax Rd. W4 —3A 82
Fairfax Rd. Tedd —6A 116
Fairfax Way. N10 —7K 15
Fairfield. N20 —7G 5
Fairfield. NW1 —1G 67
(off Arlington Rd.)
Fairfield Av. NW4 —6D 28
Fairfield Av. Edgw —6C 12
Fairfield Av. Ruis —7E 22
Fairfield Av. Twic —1F 115
Fairfield Clo. N12 —4F 15
Fairfield Clo. Enf —4E 8
Fairfield Clo. Ewe —5A 148
Fairfield Clo. Mitc —7C 120
Fairfield Clo. Sidc —6K 109
Fairfield Ct. NW10 —1C 64
Fairfield Ct. N'wd —2J 23
Fairfield Ct. Ruis —1F 41
Fairfield Cres. Edgw —6C 12
Fairfield Dri. SW18 —5K 101
Fairfield Dri. Gnfd —1C 62
Fairfield Dri. Harr —3G 25
Fairfield E. King T —2E 134
Fairfield Gdns. N8 —5J 31
Fairfield Gro. SE7 —6B 90
Fairfield Halls & Ashcroft Theatre. —3D 152
Fairfield Ind. Est. King T —3F 135
Fairfield N. King T —2E 134
Fairfield Path. Croy —3D 152
Fairfield Pl. King T —3E 134
Fairfield Rd. E3 —2C 70
Fairfield Rd. E17 —2A 34
Fairfield Rd. N8 —5J 31
Fairfield Rd. N18 —4B 18
Fairfield Rd. Beck —2C 142
Fairfield Rd. Bexh —2F 111
Fairfield Rd. Brom —7J 125
Fairfield Rd. Croy —3D 152
Fairfield Rd. Ilf —6F 55
Fairfield Rd. King T —2E 134
Fairfield Rd. Orp —6H 145
Fairfield Rd. S'hall —6D 60
Fairfield Rd. W Dray —7A 58
Fairfield Rd. Wfd G —6D 20
Fairfields Clo. NW9 —5J 27
Fairfields Cres. NW9 —4J 27
Fairfield S. King T —2E 134
Fairfields Rd. Houn —3G 97
Fairfield St. SW18 —5K 101
Fairfield Way. Barn —5D 4
Fairfield Way. Eps —5A 148
Fairfield W. King T —2E 134
Fairfoot Rd. E3 —4C 70
Fairford. SE6 —1C 124
Fairford Av. Bexh —1K 111
Fairford Av. Croy —5K 141
Fairford Clo. Croy —5A 142
Fairford Ct. Sutt —7K 149
Fairford Gdns. Wor Pk —2B 148
Fairford Ho. SE11 —4A 86 (4K 173)
Fairgreen. Barn —3J 5
Fairgreen Ct. Barn —3J 5
Fairgreen E. Barn —3J 5
Fairgreen Rd. T Hth —5B 140
Fairhaven Av. Croy —6K 141
Fairhazel Gdns. NW6 —6K 47
Fairholme. Felt —7F 95
Fairholme Clo. N3 —4G 29
Fairholme Cres. Hay —4H 59
Fairholme Gdns. N3 —3G 29
Fairholme Rd. W14 —5G 83
Fairholme Rd. Ashf —5A 112
Fairholme Rd. Croy —7A 140
Fairholme Rd. Harr —5K 25
Fairholme Rd. Ilf —7D 36
Fairholme Rd. Sutt —6H 149
Fairholt Clo. N16 —1E 50
Fairholt Rd. N16 —1D 50
Fairholt St. SW7 —3C 84 (1D 170)
Fairland Ho. Brom —4K 143
Fairland Rd. E15 —6H 53
Fairlands Av. Buck H —2D 20
Fairlands Av. Sutt —2J 149
Fairlands Av. T Hth —4K 139
Fairlands Ct. SE9 —6E 108
Fairlawn. SE7 —7A 90
Fairlawn Av. N2 —4C 30
Fairlawn Av. W4 —4J 81
Fairlawn Av. Bexh —2D 110
Fairlawn Clo. N14 —6B 6
Fair Lawn Clo. Clay —6A 146
Fairlawn Clo. Felt —4D 114
Fairlawn Clo. King T —6J 117
Fairlawn Ct. SE7 —7A 90
(in two parts)
Fairlawn Ct. W4 —4J 81
Fairlawn Dri. Wfd G —7D 20
Fairlawn Gdns. S'hall —7D 60
Fairlawn Gro. W4 —4J 81
Fairlawn Mans. SE14 —1K 105
Fairlawn Pk. SE26 —5A 124
Fairlawn Rd. SW19 —7H 119
Fairlawns. Pinn —2B 24
Fairlawns. Sun —3H 131
Fairlawns. Twic —6C 98
Fairlawns. Wall —5F 151
Fairlea Pl. W5 —4C 62
Fairlie Gdns. SE23 —7J 105
Fairlight Av. E4 —2A 20
Fairlight Av. NW10 —2A 64
Fairlight Av. Wfd G —6D 20
Fairlight Clo. E4 —2A 20
Fairlight Clo. Wor Pk —4E 148
Fairlight Ct. NW10 —2A 64
Fairlight Ct. Gnfd —2G 61
Fairlight Rd. SW17 —4B 120
Fairline Ct. Beck —2E 142
Fairlop. —1J 37
Fairlop Ct. E11 —1F 53
Fairlop Gdns. Ilf —1G 37
Fairlop Rd. E11 —7F 35
Fairlop Rd. Ilf —2G 37
Fairman Ter. Kent —4D 26
Fairmark Dri. Uxb —6C 40
Fairmead. Brom —4D 144
Fairmead. Surb —1H 147
Fairmead Clo. Brom —4D 144
Fairmead Clo. Houn —7B 78
Fairmead Clo. N Mald —3K 135
Fairmead Ct. Rich —2H 99
Fairmead Cres. Edgw —3D 12
Fairmead Gdns. Ilf —5C 36
Fairmead Ho. E9 —4A 52
Fairmead Rd. N19 —3H 49
Fairmead Rd. Croy —7K 139
Fairmile Av. SW16 —5H 121
Fairmile Ho. Tedd —4A 116
Fairmont Clo. Belv —5F 93
Fairmount Rd. SW2 —6K 103
Fairoak Clo. Orp —7F 145
Fairoak Dri. SE9 —5H 109
Fairoak Gdns. Romf —2K 39
Fairseat Clo. Bus H —2D 10
Fairstead Wlk. N1 —1C 68
(off Popham St.)
Fair St. SE1 —2E 86 (6H 169)
Fair St. Houn —3G 97
Fairthorn Rd. SE7 —5J 89
Fairview. Ruis —4A 42
Fairview Av. Wemb —6D 44
Fairview Clo. E17 —1A 34
Fairview Clo. SE26 —5A 124
Fairview Ct. NW4 —2F 29
Fairview Ct. Ashf —5C 112
Fairview Cres. Harr —1E 42
Fairview Dri. Shep —5B 130
Fairview Gdns. Wfd G —1K 35
Fairview Ho. SW2 —7K 103
Fairview Ind. Pk. Rain —5K 75
Fairview Pl. SW2 —7K 103
Fairview Rd. N15 —5F 33
Fairview Rd. SW16 —1K 139
Fairview Rd. Enf —1F 7
Fairview Rd. Sutt —5B 150
Fairview Vs. E4 —7J 19
Fairview Way. Edgw —4B 12
Fairwall Ho. SE5 —1E 104
Fairwater Av. Well —4A 110
Fairwater Ho. Tedd —4A 116
Fairway. SW20 —3E 136
Fairway. Bexh —5E 110
Fairway. Orp —5H 145
Fair Way. Wfd G —5F 21
Fairway Av. NW9 —3H 27
Fairway Clo. NW11 —7A 30
Fairway Clo. Croy —5A 142
Fairway Clo. Eps —4J 147
Fairway Clo. Houn —5A 96
Fairway Ct. NW7 —3E 12
Fairway Ct. New Bar —6E 4
Fairway Dri. SE28 —6D 74
Fairway Dri. Gnfd —7F 43
Fairway Gdns. Beck —6F 143
Fairway Gdns. Ilf —5G 55
Fairways. E17 —4E 34
Fairways. Ashf —6D 112
Fairways. Iswth —1J 97
Fairways. Stan —2E 26
Fairways. Tedd —7D 116
Fairways Bus. Pk. E10 —2A 52
Fairway, The. N13 —3H 17
Fairway, The. N14 —6A 6
Fairway, The. NW7 —3E 12
Fairway, The. W3 —6A 64
Fairway, The. Brom —5D 144
Fairway, The. New Bar —6E 4
Fairway, The. N Mald —1K 135
Fairway, The. N'holt —6G 43
Fairway, The. Ruis —4A 42
Fairway, The. Uxb —2B 58
Fairway, The. Wemb —3B 44
Fairway, The. W Mol —3F 133
Fairweather Clo. N15 —4E 32
Fairweather Ct. N13 —3E 16
Fairweather Rd. N16 —6G 33
Fairwyn Rd. SE26 —4A 124
Fakenham Clo. NW7 —7H 13
Fakenham Clo. N'holt —6D 42
Fakruddin St. E1 —4G 69
Falcon. WC1 —5J 67 (5F 161)
(off Old Gloucester St.)
Falcon Av. Brom —4C 144
Falconberg Ct. W1 —6H 67 (7D 160)
Falconberg M. W1 —6H 67 (7D 160)
Falcon Clo. SE1 —1B 86 (4B 168)
Falcon Clo. W4 —6J 81
Falcon Clo. N'wd —1G 23
Falcon Ct. E18 —3K 35
(off Albert Rd.)
Falcon Ct. EC4 —6A 68 (1K 167)
Falcon Ct. N1 —2B 68
(off City Garden Row)
Falcon Ct. New Bar —4F 5
Falcon Ct. Ruis —2G 41
Falcon Cres. Enf —5E 8
Falcon Dri. Stanw —6A 94
Falconer Ct. N17 —7H 17
Falconer Wlk. N7 —2K 49
Falcon Gro. SW11 —3C 102
Falcon Ho. E14 —5D 88
Falcon La. SW11 —3C 102
Falcon Lodge. W9 —5J 65
(off Admiral Wlk.)
Falcon Pk. Ind. Est. NW10 —4A 46
Falcon Point. SE1 —7B 68 (3B 168)
Falcon Rd. SW11 —2C 102
Falcon Rd. Enf —5E 8
Falcon Rd. Hamp —7D 114
Falcon St. E13 —4H 71
Falcon Ter. SW11 —3C 102
Falcon Way. E11 —4J 35
Falcon Way. E14 —4D 88
Falcon Way. NW9 —2A 28
Falcon Way. Felt —5K 95
Falcon Way. Harr —5E 26
Falcon Way. Sun —2G 131
Falconwood. —4K 109
Falconwood. (Junct.) —4G 109
Falconwood. SE9 —4G 109
Falconwood Av. Well —2H 109
Falconwood Ct. SE3 —2H 107
Falconwood Pde. Well —4J 109
Falconwood Rd. Croy —7B 154
Falcourt Clo. Sutt —5K 149
Falkirk Ho. W9 —2K 65
(off Maida Va.)
Falkirk St. N1 —2E 68 (1H 163)
Falkland Av. N3 —7D 14
Falkland Av. N11 —4A 16
Falkland Ho. SE6 —4E 124
Falkland Ho. W8 —3K 83
Falkland Ho. W14 —5H 83
(off Edith Vs.)
Falkland Pk. Av. SE25 —3E 140
Falkland Pl. NW5 —5G 49
Falkland Rd. N8 —4A 32
Falkland Rd. NW5 —5G 49
Falkland Rd. Barn —2B 4
Fallaize Av. Ilf —4F 55
Falling La. W Dray & Uxb —7A 58
Falloden Way. NW11 —4J 29
Fallodon Ho. W11 —5H 65
(off St Luke's Rd.)
Fallow Corner. —7F 15
Fallow Ct. SE16 —5G 87
(off Argyle Way)
Fallow Ct. Av. N12 —7F 15
Fallowfield. Stan —4F 11
Fallowfield Ct. Stan —3F 11
Fallowfields Dri. N12 —6H 15
Fallowhurst Path. N12 —7F 15
Fallows Clo. N2 —2B 30
Fallsbrook Rd. SW16 —6F 121
Falman Clo. N9 —1B 18
Falmer Rd. E17 —3D 34
Falmer Rd. N15 —5C 32
Falmer Rd. Enf —4K 7
Falmouth Av. E4 —5A 20
Falmouth Clo. N22 —7E 16
Falmouth Clo. SE12 —5H 107
Falmouth Gdns. Ilf —4B 36
Falmouth Ho. SE11 —5A 86 (5K 173)
(off Seaton Clo.)
Falmouth Ho. W2 —7C 66 (2C 164)
(off Clarendon Pl.)
Falmouth Ho. Pinn —1D 24
Falmouth Rd. SE1 —3C 86 (7E 168)
Falmouth St. E15 —5F 53
Falstaff Ct. SE11 —4B 86
(off Opal St.)
Falstaff Ho. N1 —2E 68 (1G 163)
(off Arden Est.)
Falstaff M. Hamp H —5H 115
Fambridge Clo. SE26 —4B 124
Fambridge Ct. Romf —5K 39
(off Marks Rd.)
Fambridge Rd. Dag —1G 57
Fane Ho. E2 —1J 69
Fane St. W14 —6H 83
Fan Mus. —7E 88
Fann St. EC1 & EC2 —4C 68 (4C 162)
(in two parts)
Fanshawe Av. Bark —6G 55
Fanshawe Cres. Dag —5E 56
Fanshawe Rd. Rich —4C 116
Fanshaw St. N1 —3E 68 (1G 163)
Fantail, The. (Junct.) —3D 156
Fanthorpe St. SW15 —3E 100
Faraday Av. Sidc —2A 128
Faraday Clo. N7 —6K 49
Faraday Ho. E14 —7B 70
Faraday Ho. Wemb —3J 45
Faraday Mans. W14 —6G 83
(off Queen's Club Gdns.)
Faraday Mus. —7G 67 (3A 166)

Faraday Rd.—Fine Bush La.

Faraday Rd. E15 —6H 53
Faraday Rd. SW19 —6J 119
Faraday Rd. W3 —7J 63
Faraday Rd. W10 —5G 65
Faraday Rd. S'hall —7F 61
Faraday Rd. Well —3A 110
Faraday Rd. W Mol —4E 132
Faraday Way. SE18 —3B 90
Faraday Way. Croy —1K 151
Fareham Rd. Felt —7A 96
Fareham St. W1 —6H 67 (7C 160)
Farewell Pl. Mitc —1C 138
Faringdon Av. Brom —7E 144
Faringford Rd. E15 —7G 53
Farjeon Ho. NW3 —7B 48
(off Hilgrove Rd.)
Farjeon Rd. SE3 —1B 108
Farleigh Av. Brom —7H 143
Farleigh Ct. S Croy —5C 152
Farleigh Pl. N16 —4F 51
Farleigh Rd. N16 —4F 51
Farley Ct. NW1 —4D 66 (4G 159)
(off Allsop Pl.)
Farley Dri. Ilf —1J 55
Farley Ho. SE26 —3H 123
Farley Pl. SE25 —4G 141
Farley Rd. SE6 —7D 106
Farley Rd. S Croy —7G 153
Farlington Pl. SW15 —7D 100
Farlow Rd. SW15 —3F 101
Farlton Rd. SW18 —1K 119
Farman Gro. N'holt —3B 60
Farm Av. NW2 —3G 47
Farm Av. SW16 —4J 121
Farm Av. Harr —7D 24
Farm Av. Wemb —6C 44
Farmborough Clo. Harr —7H 25
Farm Clo. N14 —6A 6
Farm Clo. NW4 —3C 28
Farm Clo. SW6 —7J 83
Farm Clo. Buck H —3F 21
Farm Clo. Dag —7J 57
Farm Clo. Shep —7C 130
Farm Clo. S'hall —7F 61
Farm Clo. Sutt —7B 150
Farm Clo. Uxb —2D 40
Farm Clo. W W'ck —3H 155
Farmcote Rd. SE12 —1J 125
Farm Ct. NW4 —3C 28
Farmdale Rd. SE10 —5J 89
Farmdale Rd. Cars —7C 150
Farm Dri. Croy —2B 154
Farm End. N'wd —1D 22
Farmer Rd. E10 —1D 52
Farmer's Rd. SE5 —7B 86
Farmer St. W11 —1J 83
Farmfield Rd. Brom —5G 125
Farm Ho. Ct. NW7 —7H 13
Farmhouse Rd. SW16 —7G 121
Farmilo Rd. E17 —7B 34
Farmington Av. Sutt —3B 150
Farmlands. Enf —1F 7
Farmlands. Pinn —4J 23
Farmlands, The. N'holt —7E 42
Farmland Wlk. Chst —5F 127
Farm La. SW6 —6J 83
Farm La. Croy —2B 154
Farm La. Trad. Est. SW6 —6J 83
Farmleigh. N14 —7B 6
Farmleigh Ho. SW9 —5B 104
Farm M. Mitc —2F 139
Farm Pl. W8 —1J 83
Farm Rd. N21 —1H 17
Farm Rd. NW10 —1K 63
Farm Rd. Edgw —6C 12
Farm Rd. Houn —1C 114
Farm Rd. Mord —5K 137
Farm Rd. Sutt —7B 150
Farmstead Rd. SE6 —4D 124
Farmstead Rd. Harr —1H 25
Farm St. W1 —7F 67 (3J 165)
Farm Va. Bex —6H 111
Farm Wlk. NW11 —5H 29
Farm Way. Buck H —4F 21
Farmway. Dag —3C 56
Farm Way. Wor Pk —3E 148
Farnaby Ho. W10 —3H 65
(off Bruckner St.)
Farnaby Rd. SE9 —4A 108
Farnaby Rd. Brom —7F 125
Farnan Av. E17 —2C 34
Farnan Rd. SW16 —5J 121
Farnborough Av. E17 —3A 34
Farnborough Av. S Croy —7K 153
Farnborough Clo. Wemb —2H 45
Farnborough Comn. Orp —3D 156
Farnborough Cres. Brom —1H 155
Farnborough Cres. S Croy —7A 154
Farnborough Way. SE15 —7E 86
Farncombe St. SE16 —2G 87
Farndale Av. N13 —3G 17
Farndale Cres. Gnfd —3G 61
Farndale Ho. NW6 —1K 65
(off Kilburn Va.)
Farnell M. SW5 —5K 83
Farnell Rd. Isleth —3H 97
Farnham Clo. N20 —7F 5
Farnham Ct. S'hall —7G 61
(off Redcroft Rd.)
Farnham Ct. Sutt —6G 149
Farnham Gdns. SW20 —2D 136
Farnham Ho. NW1 —4D 158
Farnham Pl. SE1 —1B 86 (5B 168)
Farnham Rd. Ilf —7K 37
Farnham Rd. Well —2C 110
Farnham Royal. SE11 —5K 85 (6H 173)
Farningham Ct. SW16 —7H 121
Farningham Ho. N4 —7D 32
Farningham Rd. N17 —7B 18
Farnley Ho. SW8 —2H 103
Farnley Rd. E4 —1B 20
Farnley Rd. SE25 —4D 140
Farnworth Ho. E14 —4F 89
Faro Clo. Brom —2E 144
Faroe Rd. W14 —3F 83
Farorna Wlk. Enf —1F 7
Farquhar Rd. SE19 —5F 123
Farquhar Rd. SW19 —3J 119
Farquharson Rd. Croy —1C 152
Farrance Rd. Romf —6E 38
Farrance St. E14 —6B 70
Farrans Ct. Harr —7B 26
Farrant Av. N22 —2A 32
Farr Av. Bark —2A 74
Farren Rd. SE23 —2A 124
Farrer Ct. Twic —7D 98
Farrer Ho. SE8 —7C 88
Farrer M. N8 —4G 31
Farrer Rd. N8 —4G 31
Farrer Rd. Harr —5E 26
Farrer's Pl. Croy —4K 153
Farrier Clo. Brom —3B 144
Farrier Clo. Sun —3J 131
Farrier Clo. Uxb —6C 58
Farrier Rd. N'holt —2E 60
Farriers Ho. EC1 —4C 68 (4D 162)
(off Errol St.)
Farrier St. NW1 —7F 49
Farrier Wlk. SW10 —6A 84
Farringdon La. EC1 —4A 68 (4K 161)
Farringdon Rd. EC1 —4A 68 (3J 161)
Farringdon St. EC4 —5B 68 (6A 162)
Farrington Pl. Chst —7H 127
Farrins Rents. SE16 —1A 88
Farrow La. SE14 —7J 87
Farrow Pl. SE16 —3A 88
Farr Rd. Enf —1J 7
Farthingale Wlk. E15 —7F 53
Farthing All. SE1 —2G 87 (7K 169)
Farthing Barn La. Orp —7E 156
Farthing Fields. E1 —1H 87
Farthings Clo. E4 —3B 20
Farthings Clo. Pinn —6K 23
Farthings, The. King T —1G 135
Farthing Street. —7D 156
Farthing St. Orp —7D 156
Farwell Rd. Sidc —4B 128
Farwig La. Brom —1H 143
Fashion St. E1 —5F 69 (6K 163)
Fashoda Rd. Brom —4B 144
Fassett Rd. E8 —6G 51
Fassett Rd. King T —4E 134
Fassett Sq. E8 —6G 51
Fauconberg Ct. W4 —6J 81
(off Fauconberg Rd.)
Fauconberg Rd. W4 —6J 81
Faulkner Clo. Dag —7D 38
Faulkners All. EC1 —5B 68 (5A 162)
Faulkner St. SE14 —1J 105
Fauna Clo. Romf —6C 38
Faunce Ho. SE17 —6B 86
(off Doddington Gro.)
Faunce St. SE17 —5B 86
Favart Rd. SW6 —1J 101
Faversham Av. E4 —1B 20
Faversham Av. Enf —6J 7
Faversham Ho. NW1 —1G 67
(off Bayham Pl.)
Faversham Ho. SE17 —5E 86
(off Kinglake St.)
Faversham Rd. SE6 —7B 106
Faversham Rd. Beck —2B 142
Faversham Rd. Mord —6K 137
Fawcett Clo. SW11 —2B 102
Fawcett Clo. SW16 —5A 122
Fawcett Est. E5 —1G 51
Fawcett Rd. NW10 —7B 46
Fawcett Rd. Croy —3C 152
Fawcett St. SW10 —6A 84
Fawe Pk. Rd. SW15 —4H 101
Fawe St. E14 —5D 70
Fawkham Ho. SE1 —4F 87
(off Longfield Est.)
Fawley Lodge. E14 —4F 89
Fawley Rd. NW6 —5K 47
Fawnbrake Av. SE24 —5B 104
Fawn Rd. E13 —2A 72
Fawns Mnr. Clo. Felt —1E 112
Fawns Mnr. Rd. Felt —1F 113
Fawood Av. NW10 —7J 45
Faygate Cres. Bexh —5G 111
Faygate Rd. SW2 —2K 121
Fayland Av. SW16 —5G 121
Fearnley Cres. Hamp —5C 114
Fearnley Ho. SE5 —2E 104
Fearon St. SE10 —5J 89
Featherbed La. Croy & Warl —7B 154
Feathers Pl. SE10 —6F 89
Featherstone Av. SE23 —2H 123
Featherstone Ho. Hay —5A 60
Featherstone Ind. Est. S'hall —2C 78
(off Straight, The)
Featherstone Rd. NW7 —6J 13
Featherstone Rd. S'hall —3C 78
Featherstone St. EC1 —4D 68 (3E 162)
Featherstone Ter. S'hall —3C 78
Featley Rd. SW9 —3B 104
Federal Rd. Gnfd —1C 62
Federation Rd. SE2 —4B 92
Fee Farm Rd. Clay —7A 146
Felbridge Av. Stan —1A 26
Felbridge Clo. SW16 —4A 122
Felbridge Clo. Sutt —7K 149
Felbridge Ct. Felt —1K 113
(off High St.)
Felbridge Ct. Hay —6F 77
Felbridge Ho. SE22 —3E 104
Felbrigge Rd. Ilf —2K 55
Felday Rd. SE13 —6D 106
Felden Clo. Pinn —1C 24
Felden St. SW6 —1H 101
Feldman Clo. N16 —1G 51
Felgate M. W6 —4D 82
Felhampton Rd. SE9 —2F 127
Felhurst Cres. Dag —4H 57
Feline Ct. Barn —6H 5
Felix Av. N8 —6J 31
Felix Ct. E17 —5D 34
Felix La. Shep —6G 131
Felix Mnr. Chst —6J 127
Felix Rd. W13 —7A 62
Felix Rd. W on T —6J 131
Felixstowe Ct. E16 —1F 91
Felixstowe Rd. N9 —3B 18
Felixstowe Rd. N17 —3F 33
Felixstowe Rd. NW10 —3D 64
Felixstowe Rd. SE2 —3B 92
Felix St. E2 —2H 69
Fellbrigg Rd. SE22 —5F 105
Fellbrigg St. E1 —4H 69
Fellbrook. Rich —3B 116
Fellowes Clo. Hay —4B 60
Fellowes Rd. Cars —3C 150
Fellows Ct. E2 —2F 69 (1J 163)
(in four parts)
Fellows Rd. NW3 —7B 48
Fell Rd. Croy —3C 152
Felltram Way. SE7 —5J 89
Fell Wlk. Edgw —1J 27
Felmersham Clo. SW4 —4J 103
Felmingham Rd. SE20 —2J 141
Felnex Trad. Est. NW10 —2K 63
Felsberg Rd. SW2 —6J 103
Fels Clo. Dag —3H 57
Fels Farm Av. Dag —3J 57
Felsham Rd. SW15 —3E 100
Felspar Clo. SE18 —5K 91
Felstead Av. Ilf —1E 36
Felstead Gdns. E14 —5E 88
Felstead Rd. E9 —6B 52
Felstead Rd. E11 —7J 35
Felstead St. E9 —6B 52
Felstead Wharf. E14 —5E 88
Felsted Rd. E16 —6B 72
Feltham. —2J 113
Feltham Av. E Mol —4J 133
Felthambrook Ind. Est. Felt —3K 113
Felthambrook Way. Felt —3K 113
Feltham Bus. Complex. Felt —2K 113
Felthamhill. —5H 113
Feltham Hill Rd. Ashf —5C 112
Felthamhill Rd. Felt —4J 113
Feltham Rd. Ashf —4C 112
Feltham Rd. Mitc —2D 138
Felton Clo. Orp —6F 145
Felton Gdns. Bark —1J 73
Felton Ho. N1 —1D 68
(off Colville Est.)
Felton Ho. SE3 —4K 107
Felton Lea. Sidc —5K 127
Felton Rd. W13 —2C 80
Felton Rd. Bark —2J 73
Felton St. N1 —1D 68
Fencepiece Rd. Chig —1G 37
Fenchurch Av. EC3 —6E 68 (1G 169)
Fenchurch Bldgs. EC3 —6E 68 (1H 169)
Fenchurch Pl. EC3 —6E 68 (2H 169)
Fenchurch St. EC3 —7E 68 (2G 169)
Fen Ct. EC3 —6E 68 (2G 169)
Fendall Rd. Eps —5J 147
Fendall St. SE1 —3E 86
(in two parts)
Fendt Clo. E16 —6H 71
Fendyke Rd. Belv —4D 92
Fenelon Pl. W14 —4H 83
Fen Gro. Sidc —5K 109
Fenham Rd. SE15 —7G 87
Fenman Ct. N17 —1H 33
Fenman Gdns. Ilf —1B 56
Fenn Clo. Brom —6J 125
Fennel Clo. E16 —4G 71
Fennel Clo. Croy —1K 153
Fennells Mead. Eps —7B 148
Fennell St. SE18 —6E 90
Fenner Clo. SE16 —4H 87
Fenner Sq. SW11 —3B 102
Fenn Ho. Isleth —1B 98
Fenning St. SE1 —2E 86 (6G 169)
Fenn St. E9 —5J 51
Fenstanton. N4 —1K 49
(off Marquis Rd.)
Fenstanton Av. N12 —6G 15
Fen St. E16 —7H 71
Fenswood Clo. Bex —6G 111
Fentiman Rd. SW8 —6J 85 (7F 173)
Fenton Clo. E8 —6F 51
Fenton Clo. SW9 —2K 103
Fenton Clo. Chst —5D 126
Fenton House. —4A 48
(off Windmill Hill)
Fenton Ho. SE14 —7A 88
Fenton Ho. Houn —6E 78
Fenton Rd. N17 —7H 17
Fentons Av. E13 —3K 71
Fenton St. E1 —6H 69
Fenwick Clo. SE18 —6E 90
Fenwick Gro. SE15 —3G 105
Fenwick Pl. SW9 —3J 103
Fenwick Pl. S Croy —7B 152
Fenwick Rd. SE15 —3G 105
Ferby Ct. SE9 —3H 127
(off Main Rd.)
Ferdinand Pl. NW1 —7E 48
Ferdinand St. NW1 —7E 48
Ferguson Av. Surb —5F 135
Ferguson Cen., The. E17 —6A 34
Ferguson Clo. E14 —4C 88
Ferguson Clo. Brom —3F 143
Ferguson Dri. W3 —6K 63
Ferguson Ho. SE10 —1E 106
Fergus Rd. N5 —5B 50
Fermain Ct. E. N1 —1E 68
(off De Beauvoir Est.)
Fermain Ct. N. N1 —1E 68
(off De Beauvoir Est.)
Fermain Ct. W. N1 —1E 68
(off De Beauvoir Est.)
Ferme Pk. Rd. N8 & N4 —5J 31
Fermor Rd. SE23 —1A 124
Fermoy Rd. W9 —4H 65
Fermoy Rd. Gnfd —4F 61
Fern Av. Mitc —4H 139
Fernbank. Buck H —1E 20
Fernbank Av. W on T —7C 132
Fernbank Av. Wemb —4K 43
Fernbank M. SW12 —6F 103
Fernbrook Av. Sidc —5J 109
Fernbrook Cres. SE13 —6G 107
(off Fernbrook Rd.)
Fernbrook Dri. Harr —7F 25
Fernbrook Rd. SE13 —6G 107
Ferncliff Rd. E8 —5G 51
Fern Clo. N1 —2E 68
Fern Ct. SE14 —2K 105
Fern Ct. Bexh —4G 111
Ferncroft Av. N12 —6J 15
Ferncroft Av. NW3 —3J 47
Ferncroft Av. Ruis —2A 42
Ferndale. Brom —2A 144
Ferndale Av. E17 —5F 35
Ferndale Av. Houn —3C 96
Ferndale Clo. Bexh —1E 110
Ferndale Rd. E7 —7K 53
Ferndale Rd. E11 —2G 53
Ferndale Rd. N15 —6F 33
Ferndale Rd. SE25 —5H 141
Ferndale Rd. SW4 & SW9 —4J 103
Ferndale Rd. Ashf —5A 112
Ferndale Rd. Romf —2J 39
Ferndale St. E6 —7F 73
Ferndale Ter. Harr —4K 25
Ferndell Av. Bex —3K 129
Fern Dene. W13 —5B 62
Ferndene Rd. SE24 —4C 104
Fernden Way. Romf —6H 39
Ferndown. N'wd —2J 23
Ferndown Av. Orp —7H 145
Ferndown Clo. Pinn —1C 24
Ferndown Clo. Sutt —6B 150
Ferndown Ct. S'hall —6G 61
(off Haldane Rd.)
Ferndown Lodge. E14 —3E 88
Ferndown Rd. SE9 —7B 108
Ferney Meade Way. Isleth —2A 98
Ferney Rd. E Barn —7K 5
Fern Gro. Felt —7K 95
Fernhall Dri. Ilf —5B 36
Fernham Rd. T Hth —3C 140
Fernhead Rd. W9 —2H 65
Fernheath Way. Dart —5K 129
Fernhill Ct. E17 —2F 35
Fernhill Gdns. King T —5D 116
Fernhill St. E16 —1D 90
Fernholme Rd. SE15 —5K 105
Fernhurst Gdns. Edgw —6B 12
Fernhurst Rd. SW6 —1G 101
Fernhurst Rd. Ashf —4E 112
Fernhurst Rd. Croy —7H 141
Fern La. Houn —5D 78
Fernlea Rd. SW12 —1F 121
Fernlea Rd. Mitc —2E 138
Fernleigh Clo. Croy —4A 152
Fernleigh Ct. Harr —2F 25
Fernleigh Ct. Romf —5J 39
Fernleigh Ct. Wemb —2E 44
Fernleigh Rd. N21 —2F 17
Fernsbury St. WC1 —3A 68 (2J 161)
Fernshaw Clo. SW10 —6A 84
Fernshaw Rd. SW10 —6A 84
Fernside. NW11 —2J 47
Fernside. Buck H —1E 20
Fernside Av. NW7 —3E 12
Fernside Av. Felt —4K 113
Fernside Ct. NW4 —2F 29
(off Holders Hill Rd.)
Fernside Rd. SW12 —1D 120
Ferns Rd. E15 —6H 53
Fern St. E3 —4C 70
Fernthorpe Rd. SW16 —6G 121
Ferntower Rd. N5 —5D 50
Fern Wlk. SE1 —5G 87
(off Argyle Way)
Fern Wlk. Ashf —5A 112
Fernways. Ilf —4F 55
Fernwood. Croy —7A 154
Fernwood Av. SW16 —4H 121
Fernwood Av. Wemb —6C 44
Fernwood Clo. Brom —2A 144
Fernwood Cres. N20 —3J 15
Ferny Hill. Barn —1J 5
Ferranti Clo. SE18 —3B 90
Ferraro Clo. Houn —6E 78
Ferrers Av. Wall —4H 151
Ferrers Av. W Dray —2A 76
Ferrers Rd. SW16 —5H 121
Ferrestone Rd. N8 —4K 31
Ferriby Clo. N1 —7A 50
Ferrier Ind. Est. SW18 —4K 101
(off Ferrier St.)
Ferrier Point. E16 —5J 71
(off Forty Acre La.)
Ferrier St. SW18 —4K 101
Ferring Clo. Harr —1G 43
Ferrings. SE21 —3E 122
Ferris Av. Croy —3B 154
Ferris Rd. SE22 —4G 105
Ferron Rd. E5 —3H 51
Ferry App. SE18 —3E 90
Ferrybridge Ho. SE11 —2H 173
Ferrydale Lodge. NW4 —4E 28
(off Church Rd.)
Ferry Ho. E5 —1H 51
(off High Hill Ferry)
Ferry Island Retail Pk. N17 —3G 33
Ferry La. N17 —4G 33
Ferry La. SW13 —6B 82
Ferry La. Bren —6E 80
Ferry La. Rich —6F 81
Ferry La. Shep —7C 130
Ferry La. Ind. Est. E17 —4K 33
Ferrymead Av. Gnfd —3E 60
Ferrymead Dri. Gnfd —2E 60
Ferrymead Gdns. Gnfd —2F 61
Ferrymoor. Rich —3B 116
Ferry Pl. SE18 —3E 90
Ferry Quays. Bren —7D 80
(in two parts)
Ferry Rd. SW13 —7C 82
Ferry Rd. Tedd —5B 116
Ferry Rd. Th Dit —6B 134
Ferry Rd. Twic —1B 116
Ferry Rd. W Mol —3E 132
Ferry Sq. Bren —7E 80
Ferry Sq. Shep —7D 130
Ferry St. E14 —5E 88
Festing Rd. SW15 —3F 101
Festival Clo. Bex —1D 128
Festival Clo. Uxb —1D 58
Festival Wlk. Cars —5D 150
Fetter La. EC4 —6A 68 (1K 167)
(in two parts)
Fettes Ho. NW8 —2B 66
(off Cochrane St.)
Ffinch St. SE8 —7C 88
Field Clo. E4 —6J 19
Field Clo. Brom —2A 144
Field Clo. Buck H —3F 21
Field Clo. Chess —5C 146
Field Clo. Hay —7E 76
Field Clo. Houn —1K 95
Field Clo. Ruis —1E 40
Field Clo. Uxb —2D 40
Field Clo. W Mol —5F 133
Fieldcommon. —7D 132
Fieldcommon La. W on T —7C 132
Field Ct. SW19 —3J 119
Field Ct. WC1 —5K 67 (6H 161)
Field End. N'holt —6C 42
Field End. Ruis —6A 42
Field End. Twic —4K 115
Fieldend Rd. SW16 —1G 139
Field End Rd. Eastc & Pinn —5K 23
Fielders Clo. Enf —4K 7
Fielders Clo. Harr —1G 43
Fieldfare Rd. SE28 —7C 74
Fieldgate La. Mitc —2C 138
Fieldgate Mans. E1 —5G 69
(off Fieldgate St., in two parts)
Fieldgate St. E1 —5G 69
Fieldhouse Clo. E18 —1K 35
Fieldhouse Rd. SW12 —1G 121
Fielding Av. Twic —3G 115
Fielding Ho. NW6 —3J 65
(off Cambridge Rd.)
Fielding Ho. W4 —6A 82
(off Devonshire Rd.)
Fielding M. SW13 —6D 82
(off Jenner Pl.)
Fielding Rd. W4 —3K 81
Fielding Rd. W14 —3F 83
Fieldings, The. SE23 —1J 123
Fielding St. SE17 —6C 86
Fielding Ter. W5 —7F 63
Field La. Bren —7C 80
Field La. Tedd —5A 116
Field Mead. NW7 —7F 13
Field Pl. N Mald —6B 136
Field Point. E7 —4J 53
Field Rd. E7 —4H 53
Field Rd. N17 —3D 32
Field Rd. W6 —5G 83
Field Rd. Felt —6K 95
Fieldsend Rd. Sutt —5G 149
Fields Est. E8 —7G 51
Fieldside Rd. Brom —5F 125
Fields Pk. Cres. Romf —5D 38
Field St. WC1 —3K 67 (1G 161)
Fieldsway Ho. N5 —5A 50
Fieldview. SW18 —1B 120
Field Vw. Felt —4F 113
Fieldview Cotts. N14 —2C 16
(off Balaams La.)
Field Way. NW10 —7J 45
Fieldway. Dag —3C 56
Field Way. Gnfd —1F 61
Fieldway. New Ad —7D 154
Fieldway. Orp —6H 145
Field Way. Ruis —1E 40
Fieldway Cres. N5 —5A 50
Fiennes Clo. Dag —1C 56
Fifehead Clo. Ashf —6A 112
Fife Rd. E16 —5J 71
Fife Rd. N22 —7G 17
Fife Rd. SW14 —5J 99
Fife Rd. King T —2E 134
(in two parts)
Fife Ter. N1 —2K 67
Fifield Path. SE23 —3K 123
Fifth Av. E12 —4D 54
Fifth Av. W10 —3G 65
Fifth Av. Hay —1H 77
Fifth Cross Rd. Twic —2H 115
Fifth Way. Wemb —4H 45
Figges Rd. Mitc —7E 120
Fig Tree Clo. NW10 —1A 64
Figure Ct. SW3 —6F 171
Filanco Ct. W7 —1K 79
(off Uxbridge Rd.)
Filby Rd. Chess —6F 147
Filey Av. N16 —1G 51
Filey Clo. Sutt —7A 150
Filey Waye. Ruis —2J 41
Filigree Ct. SE16 —1B 88
Fillebrook Av. Enf —2K 7
Fillebrook Rd. E11 —1F 53
Filmer Rd. SW6 —1G 101
Filston Rd. Eri —5J 93
Finborough Ho. SW10 —6A 84
(off Fawcett St.)
Finborough Rd. SW10 —5K 83
Finborough Rd. SW17 —6D 120
Finborough Theatre, The. —6K 83
Finchale Rd. SE2 —3A 92
Fincham Clo. Uxb —3E 40
Finch Av. SE27 —4D 122
Finch Clo. NW10 —6K 45
Finch Clo. Barn —5D 4
Finch Ct. Sidc —3B 128
Finchdean Ho. SW15 —7B 100
Finch Dri. Felt —7B 96
Finch Gdns. E4 —5H 19
Finchingfield Av. Wfd G —7F 21
Finch La. EC3 —6D 68 (1F 169)
Finchley. —1J 29
Finchley Ct. N3 —6E 14
Finchley Ind. Est. N12 —4F 15
Finchley La. NW4 —4E 28
Finchley Pk. N12 —4F 15
Finchley Pl. NW8 —2B 66
Finchley Rd. NW3 —1J 47
Finchley Rd. NW8 —1B 66
Finchley Rd. NW11 & NW2 —4H 29
Finchley Way. N3 —7D 14
Finch Lodge. W2 —5J 65
(off Admiral Wlk.)
Finch M. SE15 —1F 105
Finch's Ct. E14 —7D 70
Finden Rd. E7 —5A 54
Findhorn Av. Hay —5K 59
Findhorn St. E14 —6E 70
Findon Clo. SW18 —6J 101
Findon Clo. Harr —3F 43
Findon Rd. N9 —1C 18
Findon Rd. W12 —2C 82
Fine Bush La. Hare —6D 22

Fingal St. SE10 —5H 89
Fingest Ho. NW8 —4C 66 (3C 158)
(off Lilestone St.)
Finians Clo. Uxb —7B 40
Finland Rd. SE4 —3A 106
Finland St. SE16 —3A 88
Finlays Clo. Chess —5G 147
Finlay St. SW6 —1F 101
Finmere Ho. N4 —7C 32
Finnemore Ho. N1 —1C 68
(off Britannia Row)
Finney La. Iswth —1A 98
Finn Ho. N1 —3D 68 (1F 163)
(off Bevenden St.)
Finnis St. E2 —3H 69
Finnymore Rd. Dag —7E 56
Finsbury. —3A 68 (2K 161)
Finsbury Av. EC2 —5D 68 (6F 163)
(in two parts)
Finsbury Av. Sq. EC2 —5G 163
Finsbury Cir. EC2 —5D 68 (6F 163)
Finsbury Cotts. N22 —7D 16
Finsbury Est. EC1 —3A 68 (2K 161)
Finsbury Ho. N22 —1J 31
Finsbury Mkt. EC2 —4E 68 (4G 163)
(in two parts)
Finsbury Park. —1A 50
Finsbury Pk. Av. N4 —6C 32
Finsbury Pk. Rd. N4 —2B 50
Finsbury Pavement. EC2
—5D 68 (5F 163)
Finsbury Rd. N22 —7E 16
Finsbury Sq. EC2 —5D 68 (4F 163)
Finsbury St. EC2 —5D 68 (5E 162)
Finsbury Way. Bex —6F 111
Finsen Rd. SE5 —4C 104
Finstock Rd. W10 —6F 65
Finucane Ri. Bus H —2B 10
Finwhale Ho. E14 —3D 88
Fiona Ct. NW6 —2J 65
Fiona Ct. Enf —3G 7
Firbank Clo. E16 —5B 72
Firbank Clo. Enf —4H 7
Firbank Rd. SE15 —2H 105
Fir Clo. W on T —7J 131
Fircroft Gdns. Harr —3J 43
Fircroft Rd. SW17 —2D 120
Fircroft Rd. Chess —4F 147
Fir Dene. Orp —3D 156
Firdene. Surb —1J 147
Fire Bell La. Surb —6E 134
Firecrest Dri. NW3 —3K 47
Firefly Clo. Wall —7J 151
Firefly Gdns. E6 —4C 72
Firemans Flats. N22 —7D 16
Fire Sta. All. High Bar —3B 4
Fire Sta. M. Beck —1C 142
Firethorn Clo. Edgw —4D 12
Fir Gro. N Mald —6B 136
Firhill Rd. SE6 —4C 124
Fir Ho. W10 —4G 65
(off Droop St.)
Fir Rd. Felt —5B 114
Fir Rd. Sutt —1H 149
Firs Av. N10 —3E 30
Firs Av. N11 —6J 15
Firs Av. SW14 —4J 99
Firsby Av. Croy —1K 153
Firsby Rd. N16 —1G 51
Firs Clo. N10 —4E 30
Firs Clo. SE23 —7A 106
Firs Clo. Mitc —1F 139
Firscroft. N13 —3H 17
Firs Dri. Houn —7K 77
Firs Ho. N22 —1A 32
(off Acacia Rd.)
Firside Gro. Sidc —1K 127
Firs La. N13 & N21 —3H 17
Firs La. N21 —7H 7
Firs Pk. Av. N21 —1H 17
Firs Pk. Gdns. N21 —1H 17
First Av. E12 —4C 54
First Av. E13 —3J 71
First Av. E17 —5C 34
First Av. N18 —4D 18
First Av. NW4 —4E 28
First Av. SW14 —3A 100
First Av. W3 —1B 82
First Av. W10 —4H 65
First Av. Bexh —7C 92
First Av. Dag —2H 75
First Av. Enf —5A 8
First Av. Eps —7A 148
First Av. Hay —1H 77
First Av. Romf —5C 38
First Av. W on T —6K 131
First Av. Wemb —2D 44
First Av. W Mol —4D 132
First Clo. W Mol —3G 133
First Cross Rd. Twic —2J 115
First Dri. NW10 —7J 45
Firs, The. E6 —7C 54
Firs, The. N20 —1G 15
Firs, The. SE26 —5H 123
(Lawrie Pk. Gdns.)
Firs, The. SE26 —5J 123
(Venner Rd.)
Firs, The. W5 —5D 62
Firs, The. Bex —1K 129
Firs, The. Sidc —3K 127
First St. SW3 —4C 84 (3D 170)
Firstway. SW20 —2E 136
First Way. Wemb —4H 45
Firs Wlk. Wfd G —5D 20
Firswood Av. Eps —5A 148
Firth Gdns. SW6 —1G 101
Firth Ho. E2 —3G 69
(off Barnet Gro.)
Firtree Av. Mitc —2E 138
Fir Tree Av. W Dray —3C 76
Firtree Clo. SW16 —5G 121
Fir Tree Clo. W5 —6E 62
Firtree Clo. Ewe —4B 148
Fir Tree Clo. Romf —3K 39
Firtree Gdns. Croy —4C 154
Fir Tree Gro. Cars —7D 150
Fir Tree Pl. Ashf —5C 112
Fir Tree Rd. Houn —4C 96
Fir Trees Clo. SE16 —1A 88

Fir Tree Wlk. Dag —3J 57
Fir Tree Wlk. Enf —3J 7
Fir Wlk. Sutt —6F 149
Fishemans Wlk. E14 —1C 88
Fisher Athletic F.C. —1K 87
Fisher Clo. Croy —1F 153
Fisher Clo. Gnfd —3E 60
Fisher Ho. N1 —1A 68
(off Barnsbury Est.)
Fisherman Clo. Rich —4B 116
Fishermans Dri. SE16 —2K 87
Fisherman's Pl. W4 —6B 82
Fisherman's Wlk. E14 —1C 88
Fishermans Wlk. SE28 —2J 91
Fisher Rd. Harr —2K 25
Fisher's Clo. SW16 —3H 121
Fishers Ct. SE14 —1K 105
Fishers Dene. Clay —7A 146
Fisher's La. W4 —4K 81
Fisher St. E16 —5J 71
Fisher St. WC1 —5K 67 (6G 161)
Fishers Way. Belv —1J 93
Fisherton St. NW8 —4B 66 (4A 158)
Fishguard Way. E16 —1F 91
(in two parts)
Fishmongers Hall Wharf. EC4 —3E 168
Fishponds Rd. SW17 —4C 120
Fishponds Rd. Kes —5B 156
Fish St. Hill. EC3 —7D 68 (3F 169)
Fish Wharf. EC3 —7D 68
(off Lwr. Thames St.)
Fiske Ct. N17 —1G 33
Fiske Ct. Bark —2H 73
Fisons Rd. E16 —1J 89
Fitzalan Rd. N3 —3G 29
Fitzalan St. SE11 —4A 86 (3H 173)
Fitzgeorge Av. W14 —4G 83
Fitzgeorge Av. N Mald —1K 135
Fitzgerald Av. SW14 —3A 100
Fitzgerald Ct. E10 —1D 52
(off Leyton Grange Est.)
Fitzgerald Ho. E14 —6D 70
Fitzgerald Ho. SW9 —2A 104
Fitzgerald Rd. E11 —5J 35
Fitzgerald Rd. SW14 —3K 99
Fitzgerald Rd. Th Dit —6A 134
Fitzhardinge Ho. W1 —6E 66 (7G 159)
(off Portman Sq.)
Fitzhardinge St. W1 —6E 66 (7G 159)
Fitzhugh Gro. SW18 —6B 102
Fitzjames Av. W14 —4G 83
Fitzjames Av. Croy —2G 153
Fitzjohn Av. Barn —5B 4
Fitzjohn's Av. NW3 —4A 48
Fitzmaurice Pl. W1 —1F 85 (4K 165)
Fitzneal St. W3 —6B 64
Fitzrovia. —5K 159
Fitzroy Clo. N6 —1D 48
Fitzroy Ct. N6 —6G 31
Fitzroy Ct. W1 —4B 160
Fitzroy Ct. Croy —7D 140
Fitzroy Cres. W4 —7K 81
Fitzroy Gdns. SE19 —7E 122
Fitzroy Ho. E14 —5B 70
Fitzroy Ho. SE1 —5F 87
(off Coopers La.)
Fitzroy M. W1 —4A 160
Fitzroy Pk. N6 —1D 48
Fitzroy Rd. NW1 —1E 66
Fitzroy Sq. W1 —4G 67 (4A 160)
Fitzroy St. W1 —4G 67 (4A 160)
(in two parts)
Fitzroy Yd. NW1 —1E 66
Fitzsimmons Ct. NW10 —1K 63
Fitzstephen Rd. Dag —5B 56
Fitzwarren Gdns. N19 —1G 49
Fitzwilliam Av. Rich —2F 99
Fitzwilliam Heights. SE23 —2J 123
Fitzwilliam Ho. Rich —4D 98
Fitzwilliam M. E16 —1J 89
Fitzwilliam Rd. SW4 —3G 103
Fitzwygram Clo. Hamp H —5G 115
Five Acre. NW9 —2B 28
Fiveacre Clo. T Hth —6A 140
Five Bell All. E14 —6B 70
Five Elms Rd. Brom —2K 155
Five Elms Rd. Dag —3F 57
Fives Ct. SE11 —3B 86
Fiveways. (Junct.) —2F 127
Fiveways. SE9 —2F 127
Five Ways Bus. Cen. Felt —3K 113
Fiveways Corner. (Junct.) —1C 28
(Barnet)
Fiveways Corner. (Junct.) —4A 152
(Croydon)
Fiveways Rd. SW9 —2A 104
Flack Ct. E10 —7D 34
Fladbury Rd. N15 —6D 32
Fladgate Rd. E11 —6G 35
Flag Clo. Croy —1K 153
Flag Wlk. Pinn —6J 23
Flambard Rd. Harr —6A 26
Flamborough Ho. SE15 —1G 105
(off Clayton Rd.)
Flamborough Rd. Ruis —3J 41
Flamborough St. E14 —6A 70
Flamborough Wlk. E14 —6A 70
Flamingo Ct. SE8 —7C 88
(off Hamilton St.)
Flamingo Gdns. N'holt —3C 60
Flamstead Gdns. Dag —7C 56
Flamstead Ho. SW3 —5C 84 (5C 170)
(off Cale St.)
Flamstead Rd. Dag —7C 56
Flamsted Av. Wemb —6G 45
Flamsteed Rd. SE7 —5C 90
Flanchford Rd. W12 —3B 82
Flanders Ct. E17 —7A 34
Flanders Cres. SW17 —7D 120
Flanders Mans. W4 —4B 82
Flanders Rd. E6 —2D 72
Flanders Rd. W4 —4A 82
Flanders Way. E9 —6K 51
Flank St. E1 —7G 69
Flansham Ho. E14 —6B 70
Flask Wlk. NW3 —4A 48
Flatford Ho. SE6 —4E 124
Flatiron Yd. SE1 —1C 86 (5D 168)
(off Union St.)

Flavell M. SE10 —5G 89
Flaxen Clo. E4 —3J 19
Flaxen Rd. E4 —3J 19
Flaxley Rd. Mord —6K 137
Flaxman Ct. W1 —1C 166
Flaxman Ct. WC1 —3H 67 (2D 160)
Flaxman Ct. Belv —5G 93
(off Hoddesdon Rd.)
Flaxman Ho. W4 —5A 82
(off Devonshire St.)
Flaxman Rd. SE5 —3B 104
Flaxman Ter. WC1 —3H 67 (2D 160)
Flaxmore Pl. Beck —6F 143
Flaxton Rd. SE18 —1H 109
Flecker Clo. Stan —5E 10
Fleece Dri. N9 —4B 18
Fleece Rd. Surb —1C 146
Fleece Wlk. N7 —6J 49
Fleeming Clo. E17 —2B 34
Fleeming Rd. E17 —2B 34
Fleetbank Ho. EC4 —6A 68 (1K 167)
(off Salisbury Sq.)
Fleet Building. EC4 —7A 162
Fleet Clo. Ruis —6E 22
Fleet Clo. W Mol —5D 132
Fleetfield. WC1 —3J 67 (1F 161)
(off Birkenhead St.)
Fleet La. W Mol —6D 132
Fleet Pl. EC4 —7A 162
(in two parts)
Fleet Rd. NW3 —5C 48
Fleetside. W Mol —5D 132
Fleet Sq. WC1 —3K 67 (2H 161)
Fleet St. EC4 —6A 68 (1J 167)
Fleet St. Hill. E1 —4G 69
Fleetway. WC1 —3J 67 (1F 161)
(off Birkenhead St.)
Fleetway Bus. Cen. NW2 —1B 46
Fleetway W. Bus. Pk. Gnfd —2B 62
Fleetwood Clo. E16 —5B 72
Fleetwood Clo. Chess —7D 146
Fleetwood Clo. Croy —3F 153
Fleetwood Ct. E6 —5D 72
(off Evelyn Dennington Rd.)
Fleetwood Ct. Stanw —6A 94
Fleetwood Rd. NW10 —5C 46
Fleetwood Rd. King T —3H 135
Fleetwood Sq. King T —3H 135
Fleetwood St. N16 —2E 50
Fleming. N8 —3J 31
(off Boyton Clo.)
Fleming Clo. W9 —4J 65
Fleming Ct. W2 —5A 158
Fleming Ct. Croy —5A 152
Fleming Dri. N21 —5E 6
Fleming Ho. N4 —1C 50
Fleming Ho. SE16 —2G 87
(off George Row)
Fleming Ho. Wemb —3J 45
(off Barnhill Rd.)
Fleming Lodge. W2 —5J 65
(off Admiral Wlk.)
Fleming Mead. Mitc —7C 120
Fleming Rd. SE17 —6B 86
Fleming Rd. S'hall —6F 61
Fleming Wlk. NW9 —3A 28
Fleming Way. SE28 —7D 74
Fleming Way. Iswth —4K 97
Flemming Av. Ruis —1K 41
Flempton Rd. E10 —1A 52
Fletcher Bldgs. WC2 —6J 67 (1F 167)
(off Martlett Ct.)
Fletcher Clo. E6 —6F 73
Fletcher La. E10 —7E 34
Fletcher Path. SE8 —7C 88
Fletcher Rd. W4 —3J 81
Fletchers Clo. Brom —4K 143
Fletcher St. E1 —7G 69
Fletching Rd. E5 —3J 51
Fletching Rd. SE7 —6A 90
Fletton Rd. N11 —7D 16
Fleur-de-Lis St. E1 —4F 69 (4H 163)
(in two parts)
Fleur Gates. SW19 —7F 101
Flexmere Rd. N17 —1D 32
Flight App. NW9 —2B 28
Flimwell Clo. Brom —5G 125
Flintmill Cres. SE3 —2C 108
(in three parts)
Flinton St. SE17 —5E 86
Flint St. SE17 —4D 86
Flitcroft St. WC2 —6H 67 (1D 166)
Flitton Ho. N1 —7B 50
(off Sutton Est., The)
Flock Mill Pl. SW18 —1K 119
Flockton St. SE16 —2G 87
Flodden Rd. SE5 —1C 104
Flood La. Twic —1A 116
Flood Pas. SE18 —3C 90
Flood St. SW3 —5C 84 (6D 170)
Flood Wlk. SW3 —6C 84 (7D 170)
Flora Clo. E14 —6D 70
Flora Gdns. W6 —4D 82
(off Albion Gdns.)
Flora Gdns. Romf —6C 38
Floral Pl. N1 —5D 50
Floral St. WC2 —7J 67 (2E 166)
Flora St. Belv —5F 93
Florence Av. Enf —3H 7
Florence Av. Mord —5A 138
Florence Clo. W on T —7K 131
Florence Ct. E5 —3G 51
Florence Ct. E11 —4K 35
Florence Ct. N1 —7B 50
(off Florence St.)
Florence Ct. SW19 —6G 119
Florence Ct. W9 —3A 66
(off Maida Va.)
Florence Dri. Enf —3H 7
Florence Elson Clo. E12 —3E 54
(off Grantham Rd.)
Florence Gdns. W4 —6J 81
Florence Ho. W11 —7F 65
Florence Mans. NW4 —5D 28
(off Vivian Av.)
Florence Nightingale Mus.
—2K 85 (7G 167)
Florence Rd. E6 —1A 72
Florence Rd. E13 —2H 71

Florence Rd. N4 —7K 31
(in two parts)
Florence Rd. SE2 —4C 92
Florence Rd. SE14 —1B 106
Florence Rd. SW19 —6K 119
Florence Rd. W4 —3K 81
Florence Rd. W5 —7E 62
Florence Rd. Beck —2A 142
Florence Rd. Brom —1J 143
Florence Rd. Felt —1K 113
Florence Rd. King T —7F 117
Florence Rd. S'hall —4B 78
Florence Rd. W on T —7K 131
Florence St. E16 —4H 71
Florence St. N1 —7B 50
Florence St. NW4 —4E 28
Florence Ter. SE14 —1B 106
Florence Ter. SW15 —3A 118
Florence Way. SW12 —1D 120
Florey Lodge. W9 —5J 65
(off Admiral Wlk.)
Florfield Pas. E8 —6H 51
(off Florfield Rd.)
Florfield Rd. E8 —6H 51
Florian. SE5 —1E 104
Florian Av. Sutt —4B 150
Florian Rd. SW15 —4G 101
Florida Clo. Bus H —2C 10
Florida Ct. Brom —4H 143
(off Westmoreland Rd.)
Florida Rd. T Hth —1B 140
Florida St. E2 —3G 69
Florin Ct. N18 —4K 17
Florin Ct. SE1 —2F 87 (7J 169)
(off Tanner St.)
Floris Pl. SW4 —3G 103
Floriston Av. Uxb —7E 40
Floriston Clo. Stan —1B 26
Floriston Ct. N'holt —5F 43
Floriston Gdns. Stan —1B 26
Floss St. SW15 —2E 100
Flower & Dean Wlk. E1 —5F 69 (6K 163)
(in two parts)
Flower La. NW7 —5G 13
Flowerpot Clo. N15 —6F 33
Flowers Clo. NW2 —3C 46
Flowersmead. SW17 —2E 120
Flowers M. N19 —2G 49
Flower Wlk., The. SW7 —2A 84 (6A 164)
Floyd Rd. SE7 —5A 90
Fludyer St. SE13 —4G 107
Foley St. W1 —5G 67 (6A 160)
Folgate St. E1 —5E 68 (5H 163)
(in two parts)
Foliot Ho. N1 —2K 67
(off Priory Grn. Est.)
Foliot St. W3 —6B 64
Folkestone Ct. N'holt —5F 43
(off Newmarket Av.)
Folkestone Rd. E6 —2E 72
Folkestone Rd. E17 —4D 34
Folkestone Rd. N18 —4B 18
Folkingham La. NW9 —1K 27
Folkington Corner. N12 —5C 14
Folland. NW9 —2B 28
(off Hundred Acre)
Follett Ho. SW10 —7B 84
(off Worlds End Est.)
Follett St. E14 —6E 70
Follingham Ct. N1 —3E 68 (1H 163)
(off Drysdale Pl.)
Folly La. E17 —1A 34
(in two parts)
Folly M. W11 —6H 65
Folly Wall. E14 —2E 88
Fontaine Rd. SW16 —7K 121
Fontarabia Rd. SW11 —4E 102
Fontayne Av. Romf —2K 39
Fontenelle Gdns. SE5 —1E 104
Fontenoy Ho. SE11 —4B 86
(off Kennington La.)
Fontenoy Rd. SW12 —2F 121
Fonteyne Gdns. Wfd G —2B 36
Fonthill Clo. SE20 —2G 141
Fonthill M. N4 —2K 49
Fonthill Rd. N4 —1K 49
Font Hills. N2 —2A 30
Fontley Way. SW15 —7C 100
Fontmell Clo. Ashf —5C 112
Fontmell Pk. Ashf —5B 112
Fontwell Clo. Harr —7D 10
Fontwell Clo. N'holt —6E 42
Fontwell Dri. Brom —5E 144
Football Association Hall of Fame.
—2K 85 (7G 167)
Football La. Harr —1K 43
Footpath, The. SW15 —6C 100
Foots Cray. —6C 128
Foots Cray High St. Sidc —6C 128
Foots Cray La. Sidc —1C 128
Footscray Rd. SE9 —6E 108
Forbes Clo. NW2 —3C 46
Forbes St. E1 —6G 69
Forbes Way. Ruis —2K 41
Forburg Rd. N16 —1G 51
Fordbridge Cvn. Pk. Sun —6H 131
Fordbridge Ct. Ashf —6A 112
Fordbridge Rd. Ashf —6A 112
Fordbridge Rd. Sun —6G 131
Fordbridge Roundabout. (Junct.)
—6A 112
Ford Clo. E3 —2A 70
Ford Clo. Ashf —6A 112
Ford Clo. Harr —7H 25
Ford Clo. Shep —4C 130
Ford Clo. T Hth —5B 140
Forde Av. Brom —3A 144
Fordel Rd. SE6 —1F 125
Ford End. Wfd G —6E 20
Fordham Clo. Barn —3H 5
Fordham Rd. Barn —3G 5
Fordham St. E1 —6G 69
Fordhook Av. W5 —1F 81
Ford Ho. Barn —5E 4
Ford Ind. Pk. Dag —4H 75
Fordingley Rd. W9 —3H 65
Fordington Ho. SE26 —3G 123
Fordington Rd. N6 —5D 30
Fordmill Rd. SE6 —2C 124

Ford Rd. E3 —2B 70
Ford Rd. Ashf —4B 112
Ford Rd. Dag —7F 57
Fords Gro. N21 —1H 17
Fords Pk. Rd. E16 —5J 71
Ford Sq. E1 —5H 69
Ford St. E3 —1A 70
Ford St. E16 —6H 71
Fordwich Clo. Orp —7K 145
Fordwych Rd. NW2 —4G 47
Fordyce Rd. SE13 —6E 106
Fordyke Rd. Dag —2F 57
Foreign St. SE5 —2B 104
Foreland Ct. NW4 —1F 29
Foreland Ho. W11 —7G 65
(off Walmer Rd.)
Foreland St. SE18 —4H 91
Foreman Ct. W6 —4E 82
Foreman Ct. Twic —1K 115
Foreshore. SE8 —4B 88
Forest App. E4 —1B 20
Forest App. Wfd G —7D 20
Forest Av. E4 —1B 20
Forest Av. Chig —5K 21
Forest Bus. Pk. E17 —7A 34
Forest Clo. E11 —5J 35
Forest Clo. Chst —1E 144
Forest Clo. Wfd G —3E 20
Forest Ct. E4 —1C 20
Forest Ct. N12 —5E 14
Forest Cft. SE23 —2H 123
Forestdale. —7B 154
Forestdale. N14 —4C 16
Forestdale Cen., The. Croy —7B 154
Forest Dene Ct. Sutt —6A 150
Forest Dri. E12 —3B 54
Forest Dri. Kes —4C 156
Forest Dri. Sun —7H 113
Forest Dri. Wfd G —7A 20
Forest Dri. E. E11 —7F 35
Forest Dri. W. E11 —7E 34
Forest Edge. Buck H —4F 21
Forester Rd. SE15 —3H 105
Foresters Clo. Wall —7H 151
Foresters Cres. Bexh —4H 111
Foresters Dri. E17 —4F 35
Foresters Dri. Wall —7H 151
Forest Gdns. N17 —2F 33
Forest Gate. —5K 53
Forest Ga. NW9 —4A 28
Forest Glade. E4 —4B 20
Forest Glade. E11 —6G 35
Forest Gro. E8 —6F 51
Forest Hill. —2J 123
Forest Hill Bus. Cen. SE23 —2J 123
(off Clyde Va.)
Forest Hill Ind. Est. SE23 —2J 123
Forest Hill Rd. SE22 & SE23 —5H 105
Forestholme Clo. SE23 —2J 123
Forest Ind. Pk. Ilf —1J 37
Forest La. E15 & E7 —5G 53
Forest La. Chig —5K 21
Forest Lodge. SE26 —3J 123
(off Dartmouth Rd.)
Forest Mt. Rd. E4 —7A 20
Forest Point. E7 —5K 53
(off Windsor Rd.)
Fore St. EC2 —5C 68 (6D 162)
Fore St. N18 & N9 —6A 18
Fore St. Pinn —3H 23
Fore St. Av. EC2 —5D 68 (6E 162)
Forest Ridge. Beck —3C 142
Forest Ridge. Kes —4C 156
Forest Ri. E17 —3F 35
(in two parts)
Forest Rd. E7 —4J 53
Forest Rd. E8 —6F 51
Forest Rd. E11 —7F 35
Forest Rd. N9 —1C 18
Forest Rd. N17 & E17 —4J 33
Forest Rd. Felt —2A 114
Forest Rd. Ilf —2H 37
Forest Rd. Rich —7G 81
Forest Rd. Romf —3H 39
Forest Rd. Sutt —1J 149
Forest Rd. Wfd G —3D 20
Forest Side. E4 —1C 20
Forest Side. E7 —4K 53
Forest Side. Buck H —1F 21
Forest Side. Wor Pk —1B 148
Forest St. E7 —5J 53
Forest Ter. Chig —5K 21
Forest, The. E11 —4G 35
Forest Trad. Est. E17 —3K 33
Forest Vw. E4 —7K 9
Forest Vw. E11 —7H 35
Forest Vw. Av. E10 —5F 35
Forest Vw. Rd. E12 —4C 54
Forest Vw. Rd. E17 —1E 34
Forest Way. N19 —2G 49
Forest Way. Orp —5K 145
Forest Way. Sidc —7H 109
Forest Way. Wfd G —4E 20
Forest Works Ind. Est. E17 —3K 33
Forfar Rd. N22 —1B 32
Forfar Rd. SW11 —1E 102
Forge Clo. Brom —1J 155
Forge Clo. Hay —6F 77
Forge Cotts. W5 —1D 80
Forge Dri. Clay —7A 146
Forge La. Felt —5C 114
Forge La. N'wd —1G 23
Forge La. Sun —3J 131
Forge La. Sutt —7G 149
Forge Pl. NW1 —6E 48
Forman Pl. N16 —4F 51
Formby Av. Stan —3C 26
Formby Ct. N7 —5A 50
(off Morgan Rd.)
Former County Hall.
—2K 85 (6G 167)
Formosa St. W9 —4K 65
Formunt Clo. E16 —5H 71
Forres Gdns. NW11 —6J 29
Forrester Path. SE26 —4J 123
Forrest Gdns. SW16 —3K 139
Forris Av. Hay —1H 77
Forset Ct. W2 —6C 66 (7D 158)
(off Harrowby St.)

Forset St. W1 —6C 66 (7D 158)
Forstal Clo. Brom —3J 143
Forster Clo. E4 —7A 20
Forster Ho. Brom —4F 125
Forster Rd. E17 —6A 34
Forster Rd. N17 —3F 33
Forster Rd. SW12 —7J 103
Forster Rd. Beck —3A 142
Forsters Clo. Romf —6F 39
Forsters Way. Hay —6K 59
Forston St. N1 —2C 68
Forsyte Cres. SE19 —1E 140
Forsythe Shades Ct. Beck —1E 142
Forsyth Gdns. SE17 —6B 86
Forsyth Ho. SW1 —5G 85 (5B 172)
(off Tachbrook St.)
Forsythia Clo. Ilf —5F 55
Forsyth Pl. Enf —5K 7
Forterie Gdns. Ilf —3A 56
Fortescue Av. E8 —7H 51
Fortescue Av. Twic —3G 115
Fortescue Rd. SW19 —7B 120
Fortescue Rd. Edgw —1K 27
Fortess Gro. NW5 —5G 49
Fortess Rd. NW5 —5F 49
Fortess Wlk. NW5 —5F 49
Fortess Yd. NW5 —4F 49
Forthbridge Rd. SW11 —4E 102
Fortis Clo. E16 —6A 72
Fortis Ct. N10 —3E 30
Fortis Green. —4D 30
Fortis Grn. N2 & N10 —4C 30
Fortis Grn. Av. N2 —3D 30
Fortis Grn. Rd. N10 —3E 30
Fortismere Av. N10 —3E 30
Fortnam Rd. N19 —2H 49
Fortnum's Acre. Stan —6E 10
Fort Rd. SE1 —4F 87
Fort Rd. N'holt —7E 42
Fortrose Gdns. SW2 —1J 121
Fort St. E1 —5E 68 (6H 163)
Fort St. E16 —1K 89
Fortuna Clo. N7 —6K 49
Fortune Ct. Bark —2C 74
Fortunegate Rd. NW10 —1A 64
Fortune Green. —4J 47
Fortune Grn. Rd. NW6 —4J 47
Fortune Ho. EC1 —4C 68 (4D 162)
(off Fortune St.)
Fortune Ho. SE11 —4J 173
Fortunes Mead. N'holt —6C 42
Fortune St. EC1 —4C 68 (4D 162)
Fortune Wlk. SE28 —3H 91
(off Broadwater Rd.)
Fortune Way. NW10 —3C 64
Forty Acre La. E16 —5J 71
Forty Av. Wemb —3F 45
Forty Clo. Wemb —3F 45
Forty Footpath. SW14 —3J 99
Forty Foot Way. SE9 —7G 109
Forty Hill. —1K 7
Forty Hill. Enf —1K 7
Forty La. Wemb —2H 45
Forum Magnus Sq. SE1
(off York Rd.) —2K 85 (6H 167)
Forumside. Edgw —6B 12
Forum, The. W Mol —4F 133
Forum Way. Edgw —6B 12
Forval Clo. Mitc —5D 138
Forward Bus. Cen. E16 —4F 71
Forward Dri. Harr —4K 25
Fosbrooke Ho. SW8 —7J 85
(off Davidson Gdns.)
Fosbury M. W2 —7K 65
Foscote M. W9 —4J 65
Foscote Rd. NW4 —6D 28
Foskett Rd. SW6 —2H 101
Foss Av. Croy —5A 152
Fossdene Rd. SE7 —5K 89
Fossdyke Clo. Hay —5C 60
Fosset Lodge. Bexh —1J 111
Fosse Way. W13 —5A 62
Fossil Rd. SE13 —3C 106
Fossington Rd. Belv —4D 92
Foss Rd. SW17 —4B 120
Fossway. Dag —2C 56
Foster Ct. NW1 —7G 49
(off Royal College St.)
Foster Ct. NW4 —4E 28
Foster Ho. SE14 —1B 106
Foster La. EC2 —6C 68 (7C 162)
Foster Rd. E13 —4J 71
Foster Rd. W3 —7A 64
Foster Rd. W4 —5K 81
Fosters Clo. E18 —1K 35
Fosters Clo. Chst —5D 126
Foster St. NW4 —4E 28
Foster's Way. SW18 —1K 119
Foster Wlk. NW4 —4E 28
Fothergill Clo. E13 —2J 71
Fothergill Dri. N21 —5D 6
Fotheringham Rd. Enf —4A 8
Foubert's Pl. W1 —6G 67 (1A 166)
Foulden Rd. N16 —4F 51
Foulden Ter. N16 —4F 51
Foulis Ter. SW7 —5B 84 (5B 170)
Foulser Rd. SW17 —3D 120
Foulsham Rd. T Hth —3C 140
Founder Clo. E6 —6F 73
Founders Ct. EC2 —7E 162
Founders Gdns. SE19 —7C 122
Founders Ho. SW1 —5H 85 (6C 172)
(off Aylesford St.)
Foundling Ct. WC1 —4J 67
(off Brunswick Cen.)
Foundry Clo. SE16 —1A 88
Foundry Ho. E14 —5D 70
Foundry M. NW1 —3B 160
Foundry Pl. SW18 —7K 101
Fountain Clo. Uxb —5E 58
Fountain Ct. EC4 —7A 68 (2J 167)
Fountain Ct. SE23 —2K 123
Fountain Ct. SW1 —4F 85 (4J 171)
(off Buckingham Pal. Rd.)
Fountain Ct. Sidc —6B 110
Fountain Dri. SE19 —4F 123
Fountain Dri. Cars —7D 150
Fountain Grn. Sq. SE16 —2G 87
Fountain Ho. NW6 —7G 47
Fountain Ho. W1 —1E 84 (4G 165)
(off Park St.)
Fountain M. N5 —4C 50
(off Highbury Grange)
Fountain M. NW3 —6D 48
Fountain Pl. SW9 —1A 104
Fountain Rd. SW17 —5B 120
Fountain Rd. T Hth —3C 140
Fountain Roundabout. N Mald —4A 136
Fountains Av. Felt —3D 114
Fountains Clo. Felt —2D 114
(in two parts)
Fountains Cres. N14 —7D 6
Fountain Sq. SW1 —4F 85 (3K 171)
Fountains, The. N3 —7E 14
(off Ballards La.)
Fountayne Bus. Cen. N15 —4G 33
Fountayne Rd. N15 —4G 33
Fountayne Rd. N16 —2G 51
Fount St. SW8 —7H 85
Fouracres. Enf —1F 9
Fourland Wlk. Edgw —6D 12
Fournier St. E1 —5F 69 (5J 163)
Four Seasons Clo. E3 —2C 70
Four Seasons Cres. Sutt —2H 149
Four Sq. Ct. Houn —6E 96
Fourth Av. E12 —4D 54
Fourth Av. W10 —4G 65
Fourth Av. Hay —1H 77
Fourth Av. Romf —1K 57
Fourth Cross Rd. Twic —2H 115
Fourth Way. Wemb —4H 45
Four Wents, The. E4 —1A 20
Fovant Ct. SW8 —2G 103
Fowey Av. Ilf —5B 36
Fowey Clo. E1 —1H 87
Fowey Ho. SE11 —5K 173
Fowler Clo. SW11 —3B 102
Fowler Ho. N15 —5D 32
(off South Gro)
Fowler Rd. E7 —4J 53
Fowler Rd. N1 —1B 68
Fowler Rd. Mitc —2E 138
Fowlers Clo. Sidc —5E 128
Fowler's Wlk. W5 —4D 62
Fownes St. SW11 —3C 102
Fox & Knot St. EC1 —5B 162
Foxberry Rd. SE4 —3A 106
Foxborough Gdns. SE4 —5C 106
Foxbourne Rd. SW17 —2E 120
Foxbury Av. Chst —6H 127
Foxbury Clo. Brom —6K 125
Foxbury Rd. Brom —6J 125
Fox Clo. E1 —4J 69
Fox Clo. E16 —5J 71
Foxcombe. New Ad —6D 154
(in two parts)
Foxcombe Clo. E6 —2B 72
Foxcombe Rd. SW15 —1C 118
Foxcote. SE5 —5E 86
Foxcroft. WC1 —2K 67 (1H 161)
(off Penton Ri.)
Foxcroft Rd. SE18 —1F 109
Foxearth Spur. S Croy —7J 153
Foxes Dale. SE3 —3J 107
Foxes Dale. Brom —3F 143
Foxfield. NW1 —1F 67
(off Arlington Rd.)
Foxglove Clo. S'hall —7C 60
Foxglove Ct. Wemb —2E 62
Foxglove Gdns. E11 —4A 36
Foxglove La. Chess —4G 147
Foxglove Rd. Rush G —2K 57
Foxglove St. W12 —7B 64
Foxglove Way. Wall —1F 151
Foxgrove. N14 —3D 16
Fox Gro. W on T —7K 131
Foxgrove Av. Beck —7D 124
Foxgrove Rd. Beck —7D 124
Foxham Rd. N19 —3H 49
Fox Hill. SE19 —7F 123
Fox Hill. Kes —5A 156
Fox Hill Gdns. SE19 —7F 123
Foxhole Rd. SE9 —5C 108
Fox Hollow Clo. SE18 —5J 91
Fox Hollow Dri. Bexh —3D 110
Foxholt Gdns. NW10 —7J 45
Foxhome Clo. Chst —6E 126
Fox Ho. Rd. Belv —4H 93
(in two parts)
Foxlands Cres. Dag —5J 57
Foxlands La. Dag —5K 57
Foxlands Rd. Dag —5J 57
Fox La. N13 —2E 16
Fox La. W5 —4E 62
(in two parts)
Fox La. Kes —5K 155
Foxleas Ct. Brom —7G 125
Foxlees. Wemb —4A 44
Foxley Clo. E8 —5G 51
Foxley Ct. Sutt —7A 150
Foxley Rd. SW9 —7A 86
Foxley Rd. T Hth —4B 140
Foxley Sq. SW9 —1B 104
Foxmead Clo. Enf —3E 6
Foxmore St. SW11 —1D 102
Fox Rd. E16 —5H 71
Fox's Path. Mitc —2C 138
Foxton Gro. Mitc —2B 138
Foxton Ho. E16 —2E 90
(off Albert Rd.)
Foxwarren. Clay —7A 146
Foxwell M. SE4 —3A 106
Foxwell St. SE4 —3A 106
Foxwood Clo. NW7 —4F 13
Foxwood Clo. Felt —3K 113
Foxwood Grn. Clo. Enf —6K 7
Foxwood Rd. SE3 —4H 107
Foyle Rd. N17 —1G 33
Foyle Rd. SE3 —6H 89
Framfield Clo. N12 —3D 14
Framfield Ct. Enf —6K 7
(off Queen Annes Gdns.)
Framfield Rd. N5 —5B 50
Framfield Rd. W7 —6J 61
Framfield Rd. Mitc —7E 120
Framlingham Clo. E5 —2J 51
Framlingham Cres. SE9 —4C 126
Frampton. NW1 —7H 49
(off Wrotham Rd.)
Frampton Clo. Sutt —7J 149
Frampton Ct. W3 —2J 81
(off Cheltenham Pl.)
Frampton Ho. NW8 —4B 66 (4B 158)
(off Frampton St.)
Frampton Pk. Est. E9 —7J 51
Frampton Pk. Rd. E9 —6J 51
Frampton Rd. Houn —5C 96
Frampton St. NW8 —4B 66 (4B 158)
Francemary Rd. SE4 —5C 106
Frances Ct. E17 —6C 34
Frances Rd. E4 —6H 19
Frances St. SE18 —3D 90
Franche Ct. Rd. SW17 —3A 120
Francis Av. Bexh —2G 111
Francis Av. Felt —3J 113
Francis Av. Ilf —2H 55
Francis Barber Clo. SW16 —5K 121
Franciscan Rd. SW17 —5D 120
Francis Chichester Way. SW11 —1E 102
Francis Clo. E14 —4F 89
Francis Clo. Eps —4K 147
Francis Clo. Shep —4C 130
Francis Ct. EC1 —5A 162
Francis Ct. NW7 —5G 13
(off Watford Way)
Francis Gro. SW19 —6H 119
(in two parts)
Francis Ho. E17 —6B 34
Francis Ho. N1 —1E 68
(off Colville Est.)
Francis M. SE12 —7J 107
Francis Rd. E10 —1E 52
Francis Rd. N2 —4D 30
Francis Rd. Croy —7B 140
Francis Rd. Gnfd —2B 62
Francis Rd. Harr —5A 26
Francis Rd. Houn —2B 96
Francis Rd. Ilf —2H 55
Francis Rd. Pinn —5A 24
Francis Rd. Wall —6G 151
Francis St. E15 —5G 53
Francis St. SW1 —4G 85 (3A 172)
Francis St. Ilf —2H 55
Francis Ter. N19 —3G 49
Francis Wlk. N1 —1K 67
Francklyn Gdns. Edgw —3B 12
Franconia Rd. SW4 —5H 103
Frank Bailey Wlk. E12 —5E 54
Frank Beswick Ho. SW6 —6H 83
(off Clem Attlee Ct.)
Frank Burton Clo. SE7 —5K 89
Frank Dixon Clo. SE21 —7E 104
Frank Dixon Way. SE21 —1E 122
Frankfurt Rd. SE24 —5C 104
Frankham Ho. SE8 —7C 88
(off Frankham St.)
Frankham St. SE8 —7C 88
Frank Ho. SW8 —7J 85
(off Wyvil Rd.)
Frankland Clo. SE16 —3H 87
Frankland Clo. Wfd G —5F 21
Frankland Rd. E4 —5H 19
Frankland Rd. SW7 —3B 84 (2A 170)
Franklin Building. E14 —2C 88
Franklin Clo. N20 —7F 5
Franklin Clo. SE13 —1D 106
Franklin Clo. SE27 —3B 122
Franklin Clo. King T —3G 135
Franklin Cotts. Stan —4G 11
Franklin Cres. Mitc —4G 139
Franklin Pas. SE9 —3C 108
Franklin Rd. SE20 —7J 123
Franklin Rd. Bexh —1E 110
Franklins M. Harr —2G 43
Franklin Sq. W14 —5H 83
Franklin's Row. SW3 —5D 84 (5F 171)
Franklin St. E3 —3D 70
Franklin St. N15 —6E 32
Franklin Way. Croy —7J 139
Franklyn Rd. NW10 —6B 46
Franklyn Rd. W on T —6J 131
Franks Av. N Mald —4J 135
Frank Soskice Ho. SW6 —6H 83
(off Clem Attlee Ct.)
Frank St. E13 —4J 71
Franks Wood Av. Orp —5F 145
Frankswood Av. W Dray —6B 58
Frank Towell Ct. Felt —7J 95
Frank Welsh Ct. Pinn —4A 24
Franlaw Cres. N13 —4H 17
Fransfield Gro. SE26 —3H 123
Frans Hals Ct. E14 —3E 88
Frant Clo. SE20 —7J 123
Franthorne Way. SE6 —2D 124
Frant Rd. T Hth —5B 140
Fraser Clo. E6 —6C 72
Fraser Clo. Bex —1J 129
Fraser Ct. E14 —5E 88
Fraser Ho. Bren —5F 81
Fraser Rd. E17 —5D 34
Fraser Rd. N9 —3C 18
Fraser Rd. Eri —5J 93
Fraser Rd. Gnfd —1B 62
Fraser St. W4 —5A 82
Frating Cres. Wfd G —6E 20
Frazer Av. Ruis —5A 42
Frazier St. SE1 —2A 86 (7J 167)
Frean St. SE16 —3G 87
Frearson Ho. WC1 —3K 67 (1H 161)
(off Penton Ri.)
Freda Corbett Clo. SE15 —7G 87
Frederica Rd. E4 —1A 20
Frederica St. N7 —7K 49
Frederick Clo. W2 —7D 66 (2D 164)
Frederick Clo. Sutt —4H 149
Frederick Cres. SW9 —7B 86
Frederick Cres. Enf —2D 8
Frederick Gdns. Croy —6B 140
Frederick Gdns. Sutt —4H 149
Frederick Pl. SE18 —5F 91
Frederick Rd. SE17 —6B 86
Frederick Rd. Rain —2K 75
Frederick Rd. Sutt —5H 149
Frederick's Pl. EC2 —6D 68 (1E 168)
Fredericks Pl. N12 —4F 15
Frederick Sq. SE16 —7A 70
(off Sovereign Cres.)
Frederick's Row. EC1 —3B 68 (1A 162)
Frederick St. WC1 —3K 67 (2G 161)
Frederick Ter. E8 —7F 51
Frederic M. SW1 —7F 165
Frederic St. E17 —5A 34
Fredora Av. Hay —4H 59
Fred Styles Ho. SE7 —6A 90
Fred White Wlk. N7 —6J 49
Freedom Clo. E17 —4K 33
Freedom Rd. N17 —2D 32
Freedom St. SW11 —2D 102
Freegrove Rd. N7 —5J 49
(in two parts)
Freehold Ind. Cen. Houn —5A 96
Freeland Ct. Sidc —3A 128
Freeland Pk. NW4 —2G 29
Freeland Rd. W5 —7F 63
Freelands Av. S Croy —7K 153
Freelands Gro. Brom —1K 143
Freelands Rd. Brom —1K 143
Freeling Ho. NW8 —1B 66
(off Dorman Way)
Freeling St. N1 —7J 49
(in two parts)
Freeman Clo. N'holt —7C 42
Freeman Clo. Shep —4G 131
Freeman Dri. W Mol —4D 132
Freeman Rd. Mord —5B 138
Freemans La. Hay —7G 59
Freemantle Av. Enf —5E 8
Freemantle St. SE17 —5E 86
Freemasons Rd. E16 —5K 71
Freemasons Rd. Croy —1E 152
Freethorpe Clo. SE19 —7D 122
Free Trade Wharf. E1 —7K 69
Freezeland Way. Hil & Uxb —6D 40
Freke Rd. SW11 —3E 102
Fremantle Rd. Belv —4G 93
Fremantle Rd. Ilf —2F 37
Fremont St. E9 —1H 69
French Ordinary Ct. EC3 —2H 169
French Pl. E1 —3E 68 (2H 163)
French St. Sun —2A 132
Frendsbury Rd. SE4 —4A 106
Frensham Clo. S'hall —4D 60
Frensham Dri. SW15 —3B 118
Frensham Dri. New Ad —7E 154
Frensham Rd. SE9 —2H 127
Frensham St. SE15 —6G 87
Frere St. SW11 —2C 102
Freshfield Av. E8 —7F 51
Freshfield Clo. SE13 —4F 107
Freshfield Dri. N14 —7A 6
Freshfields. Croy —1B 154
Freshford St. SW17 —3A 120
Freshwater Clo. SW17 —6E 120
Freshwater Ct. W1 —5C 66 (6D 158)
(off Crawford St.)
Freshwater Ct. S'hall —3E 60
Freshwater Rd. SW17 —6E 120
Freshwater Rd. Dag —1D 56
Freshwell Av. Romf —4C 38
Fresh Wharf Rd. Bark —1F 73
Freshwood Clo. Beck —1D 142
Freshwood Way. Wall —7F 151
Freston Gdns. Barn —5K 5
Freston Pk. N3 —2H 29
Freston Rd. W10 & W11 —7F 65
Freta Rd. Bexh —5F 111
Freud Mus., The. —6A 48
(off Maresfield Gdns.)
Frewell Ho. EC1 —5A 68
(off Bourne Est.)
Frewing Clo. Chst —6D 126
Frewin Rd. SW18 —1B 120
Friar M. SE27 —3B 122
Friar Rd. Hay —4B 60
Friar Rd. Orp —5K 145
Friars Av. N20 —3H 15
Friars Av. SW15 —3B 118
Friars Clo. E4 —3K 19
Friars Clo. SE1 —5B 168
Friars Clo. N'holt —3B 60
Friars Ct. E17 —1B 34
Friars Gdns. W3 —6K 63
Friars Ga. Clo. Wfd G —4D 20
Friars La. Rich —5D 98
Friars Mead. E14 —3E 88
Friars M. SE9 —5E 108
Friars Pl. La. W3 —7K 63
Friars Rd. E6 —1B 72
Friars Stile Pl. Rich —6E 98
Friars Stile Rd. Rich —6E 98
Friar St. EC4 —6B 68 (1B 168)
Friars Wlk. N14 —7A 6
Friars Wlk. SE2 —5D 92
Friars Way. W3 —6K 63
Friary Clo. N12 —5H 15
Friary Ct. SW1 —5B 166
Friary Est. SE15 —6G 87
(in two parts)
Friary La. Wfd G —4D 20
Friary Pk. Ct. W3 —6J 63
Friary Rd. N12 —4G 15
Friary Rd. SE15 —7G 87
Friary Rd. W3 —6J 63
Friary Way. N12 —4H 15
Friday Hill. —2B 20
Friday Hill. E4 —2B 20
Friday Hill E. E4 —3B 20
Friday Hill W. E4 —2B 20
Friday Rd. Eri —5K 93
Friday Rd. Mitc —7D 120
Friday St. EC4 —7C 68 (2C 168)
Frideswide Pl. NW5 —5G 49
Friendly Pl. SE13 —1D 106
Friendly St. SE8 —2C 106
Friendly St. M. SE8 —2C 106
Friendship Wlk. N'holt —3B 60
Friends Rd. Croy —3D 152
Friend St. EC1 —3B 68 (1A 162)
Friern Barnet. —5J 15
Friern Barnet La. N20 & N11 —2G 15
Friern Barnet Rd. N11 —5J 15
Friern Bri. Retail Pk. N11 —6A 16
Friern Ct. N20 —3G 15
Friern Mt. Dri. N20 —7F 5
Friern Pk. N12 —5F 15
Friern Rd. SE22 —7G 105
Friern Watch Av. N12 —4F 15
Frigate Ho. E14 —4E 88
Frigate M. SE8 —6C 88
Frimley Av. Wall —5J 151
Frimley Clo. SW19 —2G 119
Frimley Clo. New Ad —7E 154
Frimley Ct. Sidc —5C 128
Frimley Cres. New Ad —7E 154
Frimley Gdns. Mitc —3C 138
Frimley Rd. Chess —5D 146
Frimley Rd. Ilf —3J 55
Frimley Way. E1 —4K 69
Fringewood Clo. N'wd —1D 22
Frinsted Rd. Eri —7K 93
Frinton Ct. W13 —5B 62
(off Hardwick Grn.)
Frinton Dri. Wfd G —7A 20
Frinton M. Ilf —6E 36
Frinton Rd. E6 —3B 72
Frinton Rd. N15 —6E 32
Frinton Rd. SW17 —6E 120
Frinton Rd. Sidc —2E 128
Friston St. SW6 —2K 101
Friswell Pl. Bexh —4G 111
Fritham Clo. N Mald —6A 136
Frith Ct. NW7 —7B 14
Frith Ho. NW8 —4B 66 (4B 158)
(off Frampton St.)
Frith La. NW7 —7B 14
Frith Rd. E11 —4E 52
Frith Rd. Croy —2C 152
Frith St. W1 —6H 67 (1C 166)
Frithville Gdns. W12 —1E 82
Frizlands La. Dag —2H 57
Frobisher Clo. Pinn —7B 24
Frobisher Ct. NW9 —2A 28
Frobisher Ct. SE23 —2H 123
Frobisher Ct. W12 —2E 82
(off Lime Gro.)
Frobisher Ct. Sutt —7G 149
Frobisher Cres. EC2 —5C 68
(off Beech St.)
Frobisher Cres. Stai —7A 94
Frobisher Gdns. E10 —7D 34
Frobisher Gdns. Stai —7A 94
Frobisher Ho. SW1 —6H 85 (7C 172)
(off Dolphin Sq.)
Frobisher Pas. E14 —1C 88
Frobisher Rd. E6 —6D 72
Frobisher Rd. N8 —4A 32
Frobisher St. SE10 —6G 89
Frog La. Frog —5K 75
Frogley Rd. SE22 —4F 105
Frogmore. SW18 —5J 101
Frogmore Av. Hay —4G 59
Frogmore Clo. Sutt —3F 149
Frogmore Ct. S'hall —4D 78
Frogmore Gdns. Hay —4G 59
Frogmore Gdns. Sutt —4G 149
Frogmore Ind. Est. N5 —5C 50
Frogmore Ind. Est. NW10 —3J 63
Frogmore Ind. Est. Hay —2G 77
Frognal. NW3 —4A 48
Frognal Av. Harr —4K 25
Frognal Av. Sidc —6A 128
Frognal Clo. NW3 —5A 48
Frognal Corner. (Junct.) —6K 127
Frognal Ct. NW3 —6A 48
Frognal Gdns. NW3 —4A 48
Frognal La. NW3 —5K 47
Frognal Pde. NW3 —6A 48
Frognal Pl. Sidc —6A 128
Frognal Ri. NW3 —3A 48
Frognal Way. NW3 —4A 48
Froissart Rd. SE9 —5B 108
Frome Ho. SE15 —4H 105
Frome Rd. N15 —3B 32
Frome St. N1 —2C 68
Fromondes Rd. Sutt —5G 149
Frontenac. NW10 —7D 46
Frostic Wlk. E1 —6K 163
Froude St. SW8 —2F 103
Fruen Rd. Felt —7H 95
Fruiterers Pas. EC4 —3D 168
Fryatt Rd. N17 —7J 17
(in two parts)
Fryatt St. E14 —6G 71
Fryent Clo. NW9 —6G 27
Fryent Country Pk. —7H 27
Fryent Cres. NW9 —6A 28
Fryent Fields. NW9 —6A 28
Fryent Gro. NW9 —6A 28
Fryent Way. NW9 —5G 27
Fry Ho. E7 —7A 54
Frying Pan All. E1 —6J 163
Fry Rd. E6 —7B 54
Fry Rd. NW10 —1B 64
Fry Rd. Ashf —4A 112
Fryston Av. Croy —2G 153
Fuchsia Clo. Rush G —2K 57
Fuchsia St. SE2 —5B 92
Fulbeck Dri. NW9 —1A 28
Fulbeck Rd. N19 —4G 49
Fulbeck Wlk. Edgw —2C 12
Fulbeck Way. Harr —2G 25
Fulbourne Rd. E17 —1E 34
Fulbourne St. E1 —5H 69
Fulbrook M. N19 —4G 49
Fulcher Ho. N1 —1E 68
(off Colville Ho.)
Fulcher Ho. SE8 —5B 88
Fulford Ho. Eps —7K 147
Fulford Rd. Eps —7K 147
Fulford St. SE16 —2H 87
Fulham. —2G 101
Fulham Broadway. (Junct.) —5H 65
Fulham B'way. SW6 —7J 83
Fulham Clo. Uxb —4E 58
Fulham Ct. SW6 —1J 101
Fulham F.C. —1F 101
Fulham High St. SW6 —2G 101
Fulham Pal. Rd. W6 & SW6 —5E 82
Fulham Pk. Gdns. SW6 —2H 101
Fulham Pk. Rd. SW6 —2H 101
Fulham Rd. SW6 —2G 101
Fulham Rd. SW10 & SW3 —6A 84

Fullbrooks Av.—George Comberton Wlk.

Fullbrooks Av. Wor Pk —1B 148
Fuller Clo. E2 —3K 163
Fuller Rd. Dag —3B 56
Fullers Av. E18 —7C 20
Fullers Av. Surb —2F 147
Fullers Clo. Romf —1J 39
Fuller's Griffin Brewery & Vis. Cen. —6B 82
Fullers La. Romf —1J 39
Fullers Rd. E18 —7C 20
Fuller St. NW4 —4E 28
Fullers Way N. Surb —3F 147
Fullers Way S. Chess —4E 146
Fuller's Wood. Croy —5C 154
Fullerton Ct. Tedd —6A 116
Fullerton Rd. SW18 —5K 101
Fullerton Rd. Cars —7C 150
Fullerton Rd. Croy —7F 141
Fuller Way. Hay —5H 77
Fullwell Av. Ilf —1D 36
Fullwell Cross. Ilf —2H 37
Fullwell Pde. Ilf —1E 36
Fullwood's M. N1 —3D 68 (1F 163)
Fulmar Ct. Surb —6F 135
Fulmead St. SW6 —1K 101
Fulmer Clo. Hamp —5C 114
Fulmer Ho. NW8 —4C 66 (4C 158)
(off Mallory St.)
Fulmer Rd. E16 —5B 72
Fulmer Way. W13 —3B 80
Fulready Rd. E10 —5F 35
Fulstone Clo. Houn —4D 96
Fulthorp Rd. SE3 —2H 107
Fulton M. W2 —7A 66
(off Porchester Ter.)
Fulton Rd. Wemb —3G 45
Fulwell. —4H 115
Fulwell Ct. S'hall —7G 61
(off Baird Av.)
Fulwell Cross. —2G 37
Fulwell Pk. Av. Twic —2F 115
Fulwell Rd. Tedd —4H 115
Fulwood Av. Wemb —2F 63
Fulwood Clo. Hay —6H 59
Fulwood Ct. Kent —6A 26
Fulwood Gdns. Twic —6K 97
Fulwood Pl. WC1 —5K 67 (6H 161)
Fulwood Wlk. SW19 —1G 119
Furber St. W6 —3D 82
Furham Fld. Pinn —7A 10
Furley Ho. SE15 —7G 87
(off Peckham Pk. Rd.)
Furley Rd. SE15 —7G 87
Furlong Clo. Wall —1F 151
Furlong Path. N'holt —6C 42
(off Arnold Rd.)
Furlong Rd. N7 —6A 50
Furmage St. SW18 —7K 101
Furneaux Av. SE27 —5B 122
Furness Ho. SW1 —5F 85 (5J 171)
(off Abbots Mnr.)
Furness Rd. NW10 —2C 64
Furness Rd. SW6 —2K 101
Furness Rd. Harr —7F 25
Furness Rd. Mord —6K 137
Furnival Mans. W1 —5G 67 (6A 160)
(off Wells St.)
Furnival St. EC4 —6A 68 (7J 161)
Furrow La. E9 —5J 51
Fursby Av. N3 —6D 14
Furscroft. W1 —7E 158
Further Acre. NW9 —2B 28
Furtherfield Clo. Croy —6A 140
Further Grn. Rd. SE6 —7G 107
Furzedown. —5F 121
Furzedown Dri. SW17 —5F 121
Furzedown Rd. SW17 —5F 121
Furze Farm Clo. Romf —2E 38
Furzefield Clo. Chst —6F 127
Furzefield Rd. SE3 —6K 89
Furzeground Way. Uxb —1E 76
Furzeham Rd. W Dray —2A 76
Furze Rd. T Hth —3C 140
Furze St. E3 —5C 70
Furzewood. Sun —1J 131
Fye Foot La. EC4 —7C 68 (2C 168)
(off Queen Victoria St., in two parts)
Fyfe Way. Brom —2J 143
Fyfield. N4 —2A 50
(off Six Acres Est.)
Fyfield Clo. Brom —4F 143
Fyfield Ct. E7 —6J 53
Fyfield Ho. E6 —1C 72
(off Ron Leighton Way)
Fyfield Rd. E17 —3F 35
Fyfield Rd. SW9 —3A 104
Fyfield Rd. Enf —3K 7
Fyfield Rd. Wfd G —7F 21
Fynes St. SW1 —4H 85 (3C 172)

Gable Clo. Pinn —1E 24
Gable Ct. SE26 —4H 123
Gables Av. Ashf —5B 112
Gables Clo. SE5 —1E 104
Gables Clo. SE12 —1J 125
Gables Lodge. Barn —1F 5
Gables, The. N10 —3E 30
(off Fortis Grn.)
Gables, The. Bark —6G 55
Gables, The. Brom —7K 125
Gables, The. Wemb —3G 45
Gabriel Clo. Felt —4C 114
Gabriel Ho. SE11 —4K 85 (3G 173)
Gabrielle Clo. Wemb —3F 45
Gabrielle Ct. NW3 —6B 48
Gabriel St. SE23 —7K 105
Gabriels Wharf. SE1 —1A 86 (4J 167)
Gad Clo. E13 —3K 71
Gaddesden Av. Wemb —6F 45
Gaddesden Ho. EC1 —3D 68 (2F 163)
(off Cranwood St.)
Gadebridge Ho. SW3 —5C 84 (5C 170)
(off Cale St.)
Gade Clo. Hay —1K 77
Gadesden Rd. Eps —6J 147
(in two parts)
Gadsbury Clo. NW9 —6B 28
Gadsden Ho. W10 —4G 65
(off Hazlewood Cres.)
Gadwall Clo. E16 —6K 71
Gadwall Way. SE28 —2H 91
Gage Rd. E16 —5G 71
Gage St. WC1 —5J 67 (5F 161)
Gainford St. N1 —1A 68
Gainsboro Gdns. Gnfd —5J 43
Gainsborough Av. E12 —5E 54
Gainsborough Clo. Beck —7C 124
Gainsborough Clo. Esh —7J 133
Gainsborough Ct. N12 —5E 14
Gainsborough Ct. SE21 —2E 122
Gainsborough Ct. W4 —5H 81
(off Chaseley Dri.)
Gainsborough Ct. W12 —2E 82
Gainsborough Gdns. NW3 —3B 48
Gainsborough Gdns. NW11 —7H 29
Gainsborough Gdns. Edgw —2F 27
Gainsborough Gdns. Iswth —5H 97
Gainsborough Ho. SW1
(off Erasmus St.) —4H 85 (4D 172)
Gainsborough Ho. Dag —4B 56
(off Gainsborough Rd.)
Gainsborough Lodge. Harr —5K 25
(off Hindes Rd.)
Gainsborough Mans. W14 —6G 83
(off Queen's Club Gdns.)
Gainsborough M. SE26 —3H 123
Gainsborough Rd. E11 —7G 35
Gainsborough Rd. E15 —3G 71
Gainsborough Rd. N12 —5E 14
Gainsborough Rd. W4 —4B 82
Gainsborough Rd. Dag —4B 56
Gainsborough Rd. Hay —2E 58
Gainsborough Rd. N Mald —6K 135
Gainsborough Rd. Rich —2F 99
Gainsborough Rd. Wfd G —6H 21
Gainsborough Sq. Bexh —3D 110
Gainsborough Ter. Sutt —7H 149
(off Belmont Ri.)
Gainsborough Tower. N'holt —2B 60
(off Academy Gdns.)
Gainsfield Ct. E11 —3G 53
Gainsford Rd. E17 —4B 34
Gainsford St. SE1 —2F 87 (6J 169)
Gairloch Ho. NW1 —7H 49
(off Stratford Vs.)
Gairloch Rd. SE5 —2E 104
Gaisford St. NW5 —6G 49
Gaitskell Ct. SW11 —2C 102
Gaitskell Ho. E6 —1B 72
Gaitskell Ho. E17 —3D 34
Gaitskell Ho. SE17 —6E 86
(off Villa St.)
Gaitskell Rd. SE9 —1G 127
Galahad Rd. Brom —4J 125
Galata Rd. SW13 —7C 82
Galatea Sq. SE15 —3H 105
Galba Ct. Bren —7D 80
Galbraith St. E14 —3E 88
Galdana Av. Barn —3F 5
Galeborough Av. Wfd G —7A 20
Gale Clo. Hamp —6C 114
Gale Clo. Mitc —3B 138
Galena Rd. W6 —4D 82
Galen Pl. WC1 —5J 67 (6F 161)
Galesbury Rd. SW18 —6A 102
Gales Gdns. E2 —3H 69
Gale St. E3 —5C 70
Gale St. Dag —5C 56
Gales Way. Wfd G —7H 21
Galgate Clo. SW19 —1F 119
Gallants Farm Rd. E Barn —7H 5
Galleon Clo. SE16 —2K 87
Galleon Clo. Eri —4K 93
Galleon Ho. E14 —4E 88
Gallery Ct. SE1 —2D 86 (7E 168)
(off Pilgrimage St.)
Gallery Ct. SW10 —6A 84
Gallery Gdns. N'holt —2B 60
Gallery Rd. SE21 —1D 122
Galleywall Rd. SE16 —4H 87
Galliard Clo. N9 —6D 8
Galliard Ct. N9 —6B 8
Galliard Rd. N9 —7B 8
Gallia Rd. N5 —5B 50
Gallions Clo. Bark —3A 74
Gallions Entrance. E16 —1G 91
Gallions Rd. SE7 —4K 89
(in two parts)
Gallions Vw. Rd. SE28 —2J 91
Galliver Pl. E5 —4H 51
Gallon Clo. SE7 —4A 90
Gallop, The. S Croy —7H 153
Gallosson Rd. SE18 —4J 91
Galloway Path. Croy —4D 152
Galloway Rd. W12 —1C 82
Gallus Clo. N21 —6E 6
Gallus Sq. SE3 —3K 107
Galpin's Rd. T Hth —5J 139
Galsworthy Clo. NW2 —4G 47
Galsworthy Av. E14 —5A 70
Galsworthy Av. Romf —7B 38
Galsworthy Clo. SE28 —1B 92
Galsworthy Ct. W3 —3H 81
(off Bollo Bri. Rd.)
Galsworthy Cres. SE3 —1A 108
Galsworthy Ho. W11 —6G 65
Galsworthy Rd. NW2 —4G 47
Galsworthy Rd. King T —7H 117
Galsworthy Ter. N16 —3E 50
Galton St. W10 —3G 65
Galva Clo. Barn —4K 5
Galvani Way. Croy —1K 151
Galveston Rd. SW15 —5H 101
Galway Clo. SE16 —5H 87
(off Masters Dri.)
Galway Ho. EC1 —2D 162
Galway St. EC1 —3C 68 (2D 162)
Galy. NW9 —2B 28
Gambetta St. SW8 —2F 103
Gambia St. SE1 —1B 86 (5B 168)
Gambier Ho. EC1 —3C 68 (2D 162)
(off Mora St.)
Gambole Rd. SW17 —4C 120
Games Rd. Barn —3J 5
Gamlen Rd. SW15 —4F 101
Gamuel Clo. E17 —6C 34
Gander Grn. Cres. Hamp —1E 132
Gander Grn. La. Sutt —2G 149
Gandhi Clo. E17 —6C 34
Gandolfi St. SE15 —6E 86
Ganton St. W1 —7G 67 (2A 166)
Gants Hill. —6E 36
Gants Hill. (Junct.) —6E 36
Gantshill Cres. Ilf —5E 36
Gants Hill Cross. Ilf —6E 36
Gap Rd. SW19 —5J 119
Garage Rd. W3 —6G 63
Garbett Ho. SE17 —6B 86
(off Doddington Gro.)
Garbutt Pl. W1 —5E 66 (5H 159)
Garden Av. Bexh —3G 111
Garden Av. Mitc —7F 121
Garden City. Edgw —6B 12
Garden Clo. E4 —5H 19
Garden Clo. SE12 —3K 125
Garden Clo. SW15 —7E 100
Garden Clo. Ashf —6E 112
Garden Clo. Hamp —5D 114
Garden Clo. N'holt —1C 60
Garden Clo. Ruis —2G 41
Garden Clo. Wall —5J 151
Garden Ct. W4 —3J 81
Garden Ct. WC2 —2J 167
Garden Ct. Croy —2F 153
Garden Ct. Hamp —5D 114
Garden Ct. Rich —1F 99
Garden Ct. Stan —5H 11
Gardener Gro. Felt —2D 114
Gardeners Clo. N11 —2K 15
Gardeners Rd. Croy —1B 152
Garden Ho. N2 —2B 30
(off Grange, The)
Gardenia Rd. Enf —6K 7
Gardenia Way. Wfd G —6D 20
Garden La. SW2 —1K 121
Garden La. Brom —6K 125
Garden M. W2 —7J 65
Garden Pl. E8 —1F 69
Garden Rd. NW8 —3A 66 (1A 158)
Garden Rd. SE20 —1J 141
Garden Rd. Brom —7K 125
Garden Rd. Rich —3G 99
Garden Rd. W on T —6K 131
Garden Row. SE1 —3B 86
Gardens, The. N8 —4J 31
(in two parts)
Gardens, The. SE22 —4G 105
Gardens, The. Beck —1E 142
Gardens, The. Felt —5F 95
Gardens, The. Harr —6G 25
Gardens, The. Pinn —6D 24
Gardens, The. Uxb —2A 40
Garden St. E1 —5K 69
Garden Ter. SW1 —5H 85 (5C 172)
Garden Ter. SW7 —7D 164
Garden Vw. E7 —4A 54
Garden Wlk. EC2 —3E 68 (2G 163)
Garden Wlk. Beck —1B 142
Garden Way. NW10 —6J 45
Gardiner Av. NW2 —5E 46
Gardiner Clo. Enf —6E 8
Gardiner Ct. NW10 —1K 63
Gardiner Ct. S Croy —6C 152
Gardiners Clo. Dag —4D 56
Gardner Clo. E11 —6K 35
Gardner Ho. Felt —2D 114
Gardner Ho. S'hall —7B 60
(off Broadway, The)
Gardner Ind. Est. SE26 —5B 124
Gardner Rd. E13 —4K 71
Gardners La. EC4 —7C 68 (2C 168)
Gardnor Rd. NW3 —4B 48
Gard St. EC1 —3B 68 (1B 162)
Garendon Gdns. Mord —7K 137
Garendon Rd. Mord —7K 137
Garenne Ct. E4 —1K 19
Gareth Clo. Wor Pk —2F 149
Gareth Ct. SW16 —3H 121
Gareth Gro. Brom —4J 125
Garfield. Enf —5J 7
(off Private Rd.)
Garfield M. SW11 —3E 102
Garfield Rd. E4 —1A 20
Garfield Rd. E13 —4H 71
Garfield Rd. SW11 —3E 102
Garfield Rd. SW19 —5A 120
Garfield Rd. Enf —4D 8
Garfield Rd. Twic —1A 116
Garford St. E14 —7C 70
Garganey Ct. NW10 —6K 45
(off Elgar Av.)
Garganey Wlk. SE28 —7C 74
Garibaldi St. SE18 —4J 91
Garland Rd. SE18 —7H 91
Garland Rd. Stan —1E 26
Garlick Hill. EC4 —7C 68 (2D 168)
Garlies Rd. SE23 —3A 124
Garlinge Rd. NW2 —6H 47
Garman Clo. N18 —5J 17
Garman Rd. N17 —7D 18
Garnault M. EC1 —2K 161
Garnault Pl. EC1 —3A 68 (2K 161)
Garnault Rd. Enf —1A 8
Garner Clo. Dag —1D 56
Garner Rd. E17 —1E 34
Garner St. E2 —2G 69
Garnet Rd. NW10 —6A 46
Garnet Rd. T Hth —4C 140
Garnet St. E1 —7J 69
Garnett Clo. SE9 —3D 108
Garnett Rd. NW3 —5D 48
Garnett Way. E17 —1A 34
(off Swansland Gdns.)
Garnet Wlk. E6 —5C 72
Garnham Clo. N16 —2F 51
Garnham St. N16 —2F 51
Garnies Clo. SE15 —7F 87
Garrad's Rd. SW16 —3H 121
Garrard Clo. Bexh —3G 111
Garrard Clo. Chst —5F 127
Garrard Wlk. NW10 —6A 46
Garratt Clo. Croy —4J 151
Garratt Ct. SW18 —7K 101
Garratt La. SW18 & SW17 —6K 101
Garratt Rd. Edgw —7B 12
Garratts Rd. Bush —1B 10
Garratt Ter. SW17 —4C 120
Garrett Clo. W3 —5K 63
Garrett St. EC1 —4C 68 (3D 162)
Garrick Av. NW11 —6G 29
Garrick Clo. SW18 —4A 102
Garrick Clo. W5 —4E 62
Garrick Clo. Rich —5D 98
Garrick Cres. Croy —2E 152
Garrick Dri. NW4 —2E 28
Garrick Dri. SE28 —3H 91
Garrick Gdns. W Mol —3E 132
Garrick Ho. W1 —1F 85 (5J 165)
Garrick Ho. W4 —6A 82
Garrick Ind. Est. NW9 —5B 28
Garrick Pk. NW4 —2F 29
Garrick Rd. NW9 —6B 28
Garrick Rd. Gnfd —4F 61
Garrick Rd. Rich —2G 99
Garrick St. WC2 —7J 67 (2E 166)
Garrick Way. NW4 —4F 29
Garrick Yd. WC2 —2E 166
Garrison Clo. SE18 —7E 90
Garrison Clo. Houn —5D 96
Garrison La. Chess —7D 146
Garrowsfield. Barn —6C 4
Garry Way. Romf —1K 39
Garsdale Clo. N11 —6K 15
Garsdale Ter. W14 —5H 83
Garside Ct. SE28 —3H 91
Garside Clo. Hamp —6F 115
Garsington M. SE4 —3B 106
Garson Ho. W2 —7B 66 (2A 164)
(off Gloucester Ter.)
Garston Ho. N1 —7B 50
(off Sutton Est., The)
Garter Way. SE16 —2K 87
Garth Clo. W4 —5K 81
Garth Clo. King T —5F 117
Garth Clo. Mord —7F 137
Garth Clo. Ruis —1B 42
Garth Ct. W4 —5K 81
Garth Ct. Harr —6K 25
(off Northwick Pk. Rd.)
Garth M. W5 —4E 62
Garthorne Rd. SE23 —7K 105
Garth Rd. NW2 —2H 47
Garth Rd. W4 —5K 81
Garth Rd. King T —5F 117
Garth Rd. Mord —6E 136
Garth Rd. Ind. Est. Mord —1F 149
Garthside. Ham —5E 116
Garth, The. Hamp —6F 115
Garth, The. Harr —6F 27
Garthway. N12 —6H 15
Gartmoor Gdns. SW19 —1H 119
Gartmore Rd. Ilf —2K 55
Garton Pl. SW18 —6A 102
Gartons Clo. Enf —4D 8
Gartons Way. SW11 —3A 102
Garvary Rd. E16 —6K 71
Garway Rd. W2 —6K 65
Garwood Clo. N17 —1H 33
Gascoigne Gdns. Wfd G —7B 20
Gascoigne Pl. E2 —3F 69 (1J 163)
(in two parts)
Gascoigne Rd. Bark —1G 73
Gascoigne Rd. New Ad —7F 155
Gascony Av. NW6 —7J 47
Gascoyne Ho. E9 —7A 52
Gascoyne Rd. E9 —7K 51
Gaselee St. E14 —7E 70
Gaskarth Rd. SW12 —6F 103
Gaskarth Rd. Edgw —1J 27
Gaskell Rd. N6 —6D 30
Gaskell St. SW4 —2J 103
Gaskin St. N1 —1B 68
Gaspar Clo. SW5 —4K 83
(off Courtfield Gdns.)
Gaspar M. SW5 —4K 83
Gassiot Rd. SW17 —4D 120
Gassiot Way. Sutt —3B 150
Gastein Rd. W6 —6F 83
Gastigny Ho. EC1 —2D 162
Gaston Bell Clo. Rich —3F 99
Gaston Bri. Rd. Shep —6F 131
Gaston Rd. Mitc —3E 138
Gaston Way. Shep —5F 131
Gataker St. SE16 —3H 87
Gatcombe Ct. Beck —7C 124
Gatcombe Ho. SE22 —3E 104
Gatcombe M. W5 —7F 63
Gatcombe Rd. E16 —1J 89
Gatcombe Rd. N19 —3H 49
Gatcombe Way. Barn —3J 5
Gateacre Ct. Sidc —4B 128
Gate Cen., The. Bren —7A 80
Gateforth St. NW8 —4C 66 (4C 158)
Gate Hill Ct. W11 —1H 83
(off Ladbroke Ter.)
Gatehouse Clo. King T —7J 117
Gatehouse Sq. SE1 —4D 168
Gateley Ho. SE4 —4K 105
(off Coston Wlk.)
Gateley Rd. SW9 —3K 103
Gate Lodge. W9 —5J 65
Gate M. SW7 —7D 164
Gater Dri. Enf —1J 7
Gates. NW9 —2B 28
Gatesborough St. EC2 —4E 68 (3G 163)
Gates Ct. SE17 —5C 86
Gatesden. WC1 —3J 67 (2G 161)
Gates Grn. Rd. W W'ck —3H 155
Gateside Rd. SW17 —3D 120
Gatestone Rd. SE19 —6E 122
Gate St. WC2 —6K 67 (7G 161)
Gate Theatre, The. —1J 83
Gateway. SE17 —6C 86
Gateway Arc. N1 —2B 68
Gateway Ho. Bark —1G 73
Gateway Ind. Est. NW10 —3B 64
Gateway M. E8 —5F 51
Gateway Retail Pk. E6 —4F 73
Gateway Rd. E10 —3D 52
Gateways Ct. Wall —5F 151
Gateways, The. SW3 —4D 170
Gateways, The. Rich —4D 98
(off Park La.)
Gatfield Gro. Felt —2E 114
Gatfield Ho. Felt —2E 114
Gathorne Rd. N22 —2A 32
Gathorne St. E2 —2K 69
Gatley Av. Eps —5H 147
Gatliff Clo. SW1 —6J 171
Gatliff Rd. SW1 —5F 85 (6J 171)
(in two parts)
Gatling Rd. SE2 —5A 92
Gatting Clo. Edgw —7D 12
Gatting Way. Uxb —6A 40
Gattis Wharf. N1 —2J 67
(off New Wharf Rd.)
Gatton Rd. SW17 —4C 120
Gattons Way. Sidc —4F 129
Gatward Clo. N21 —6G 7
Gatward Grn. N9 —2A 18
Gatwick Ho. E14 —6B 70
Gatwick Rd. SW18 —7H 101
Gauden Clo. SW4 —3H 103
Gauden Rd. SW4 —2H 103
Gaumont Ter. W12 —2E 82
(off Lime Gro.)
Gauntlet. NW9 —2B 28
(off Five Acre)
Gauntlet Clo. N'holt —7C 42
Gauntlett Ct. Wemb —5B 44
Gauntlett Rd. Sutt —5B 150
Gaunt St. SE1 —3C 86
Gautrey Rd. SE15 —2J 105
Gautrey Sq. E6 —6D 72
Gavel St. SE17 —4D 86
Gavestone Cres. SE12 —7K 107
Gavestone Rd. SE12 —7K 107
Gaviller Pl. E5 —4H 51
Gavina Clo. Mord —5C 138
Gawber St. E2 —3J 69
Gawsworth Clo. E15 —5H 53
Gawthorne Av. NW7 —5B 14
Gay Clo. NW2 —5D 46
Gaydon Ho. W2 —5K 65
(off Bourne Ter.)
Gaydon La. NW9 —1A 28
Gayfere Rd. Eps —5C 148
Gayfere Rd. Ilf —3D 36
Gayfere St. SW1 —3J 85 (2E 172)
Gayford Rd. W12 —2B 82
Gay Gdns. Dag —4J 57
Gay Ho. N1 —5E 50
Gayhurst. SE17 —6D 86
(off Hopwood Rd.)
Gayhurst Ct. N'holt —3A 60
Gayhurst Ho. NW8 —4C 66 (3C 158)
(off Mallory St.)
Gayhurst Rd. E8 —7G 51
Gaylor Rd. N'holt —5D 42
Gaymead. NW8 —1K 65
(off Abbey Rd.)
Gaynesford Rd. SE23 —2K 123
Gaynesford Rd. Cars —7D 150
Gaynes Hill Rd. Wfd G —6H 21
Gay Rd. E15 —2F 71
Gaysham Av. Ilf —5E 36
Gaysham Hall. Ilf —3F 37
Gaysley Ho. SE11 —4J 173
Gay St. SW15 —3F 101
Gaythorne St. E3 —5B 70
Gayton Ct. Harr —6K 25
Gayton Cres. NW3 —4B 48
Gayton Rd. NW3 —4B 48
Gayton Rd. SE2 —3C 92
Gayton Rd. Harr —6K 25
Gayville Rd. SW11 —6D 102
Gaywood Clo. SW2 —1K 121
Gaywood Rd. E17 —3C 34
Gaywood St. SE1 —3B 86
Gaza St. SE17 —5B 86
Gaze Ho. E14 —6F 71
Gearies ville Gdns. Ilf —4F 37
Geary Rd. NW10 —5C 46
Geary St. N7 —5K 49
Geddes Pl. Bexh —4G 111
Gedeney Rd. N17 —1C 32
Gedling Pl. SE1 —3F 87 (7K 169)
Geere Rd. E15 —1H 71
Gees Ct. W1 —6E 66 (1H 165)
Gee St. EC1 —4C 68 (3C 162)
Geffery's Ct. SE9 —3C 126
Geffrye Ct. N1 —2E 68
Geffrye Est. N1 —2E 68
Geffrye Mus. —2F 69 (1J 163)
Geffrye St. E2 —2F 69 (1J 163)
Geldart Rd. SE15 —7H 87
Geldeston Rd. E5 —2G 51
Gellatly Rd. SE14 —2J 105
Gell Clo. Uxb —3B 40
Gelsthorpe Rd. Romf —1H 39
Gemini Bus. Cen. E16 —4F 71
Gemini Bus. Est. SE14 —5K 87
Gemini Ct. E1 —7G 69
(off Vaughan Way)
Gemini Gro. N'holt —3C 60
General Gordon Pl. SE18 —4F 91
General Wolfe Rd. SE10 —1F 107
Genesis Clo. Stanw —1B 112
Genesta Rd. SE18 —6F 91
Geneva Clo. Shep —2G 131
Geneva Dri. SW9 —4A 104
Geneva Gdns. Romf —5E 38
Geneva Rd. King T —4E 134
Geneva Rd. T Hth —5C 140
Genever Clo. E4 —5H 19
Genista Rd. N18 —5C 18
Genoa Av. SW15 —5E 100
Genoa Rd. SE20 —1J 141
Genotin Rd. Enf —3J 7
Genotin Ter. Enf —4J 7
Gentlemans Row. Enf —3H 7
Gentry Gdns. E13 —4J 71
Geoffrey Clo. SE5 —2C 104
Geoffrey Ct. SE4 —2B 106
Geoffrey Gdns. E6 —2C 72
Geoffrey Ho. SE1 —3D 86 (7F 169)
(off Pardoner St.)
Geoffrey Jones Ct. NW10 —1C 64
Geoffrey Rd. SE4 —3B 106
Geographers A-Z Shop. —5A 68 (5J 161)
George Beard Rd. SE8 —4B 88
George Comberton Wlk. E12 —5E 54

George Ct.—Glenthorne Clo.

George Ct. WC2 —3F 167
George Cres. N10 —7K 15
George Downing Est. N16 —2F 51
George Eliot Ho. SW1 —4G 85 (4B 172)
(off Vauxhall Bri. Rd.)
George Elliston Ho. SE1 —5G 87
(off Old Kent Rd.)
George Eyre Ho. NW8 —2B 66
(off Cochrane St.)
George V Av. Pinn —2D 24
George V Clo. Pinn —3E 24
George V Way. Gnfd —1B 62
George Gange Way. Harr —3K 25
George Gillett Ct. EC1 —3D 162
George Gro. Rd. SE20 —1G 141
George Inn Yd. SE1 —1D 86 (5E 168)
George La. E18 —2J 35
(in two parts)
George La. SE13 —6D 106
George La. Brom —1K 155
George Lansbury Ho. N22 —1A 32
(off Progress Way)
George Lansbury Ho. NW10 —7A 46
George Lindgren Ho. SW6 —7H 83
(off Clem Attlee Ct.)
George Loveless Ho. E2
(off Diss St.) —3F 69 (1K 163)
George Lowe Ct. W2 —5K 65
(off Bourne Ter.)
George Mathers Rd. SE11 —4B 86
George M. NW1 —2B 160
George M. Enf —3J 7
(off Town, The)
George Peabody Ct. NW1
(off Bell St.) —5C 66 (5C 158)
George Pl. N17 —3E 32
George Rd. E4 —6H 19
George Rd. King T —7H 117
(in two parts)
George Rd. N Mald —4B 136
George Row. SE16 —2G 87
George Sq. SW19 —3J 137
George's Rd. N7 —5K 49
George's Sq. SW6 —6H 83
(off N. End Rd.)
George St. E16 —6H 71
George St. W1 —6D 66 (7E 158)
George St. W7 —1J 79
George St. Bark —7G 55
George St. Croy —2C 152
George St. Houn —2D 96
George St. Rich —5D 98
George St. S'hall —4C 78
George Tingle Ho. SE1 —3F 87
(off Grange Wlk.)
Georgetown Clo. SE19 —5E 122
Georgette Pl. SE10 —7E 88
Georgeville Gdns. Ilf —4F 37
George Wyver Clo. SW19 —7G 101
George Yd. EC3 —6D 68 (1F 169)
George Yd. W1 —7E 66 (2H 165)
Georgiana St. NW1 —1G 67
Georgian Clo. Brom —1K 155
Georgian Clo. Stan —7F 11
Georgian Clo. Uxb —4A 40
Georgian Ct. E9 —1J 69
Georgian Ct. N3 —1H 29
Georgian Ct. NW4 —5D 28
Georgian Ct. SW16 —4J 121
Georgian Ct. New Bar —4F 5
Georgian Ct. Wemb —6G 45
Georgian Way. Harr —2H 43
Georgia Rd. N Mald —4J 135
Georgia Rd. T Hth —1B 140
Georgina Gdns. E2 —3F 69 (1K 163)
Geraint Rd. Brom —4J 125
Geraldine Rd. SW18 —5A 102
Geraldine Rd. W4 —6G 81
Geraldine St. SE11 —3B 86 (2K 173)
Gerald M. SW1 —3H 171
Gerald Rd. E16 —4H 71
Gerald Rd. SW1 —4E 84 (3H 171)
Gerald Rd. Dag —2F 57
Gerard Av. Houn —7E 96
Gerard Gdns. Rain —2K 75
Gerard Rd. SW13 —1B 100
Gerard Rd. Harr —6A 26
Gerards Clo. SE16 —5J 87
Gerda Rd. SE9 —2G 127
Germander Way. E15 —3G 71
Gernon Rd. E3 —2A 70
Geron Way. NW2 —2D 46
Gerrard Gdns. Pinn —5J 23
Gerrard Pl. W1 —7H 67 (2D 166)
Gerrard Rd. N1 —2B 68
Gerrards Clo. N14 —5B 6
Gerrards Ct. W5 —3D 80
Gerrard St. W1 —7H 67 (2D 166)
Gerridge Ct. SE1 —3A 86 (1K 173)
(off Gerridge St.)
Gerridge St. SE1 —3A 86 (1K 173)
Gerry Raffles Sq. E15 —7F 53
Gertrude Rd. Belv —4G 93
Gertrude St. SW10 —6A 84 (7A 170)
Gervase Clo. Wemb —3J 45
Gervase Rd. Edgw —1J 27
Gervase St. SE15 —7H 87
Gervis Ct. Houn —7G 79
Ghent St. SE6 —2C 124
Ghent Way. E8 —6F 51
Giant Arches Rd. SE24 —7C 104
Giant Tree Hill. Bus H —1C 10
Gibbfield Clo. Romf —3E 38
Gibbings Ho. SE1 —2B 86 (7B 168)
(off King James St.)
Gibbins Rd. E15 —7E 52
(in three parts)
Gibbon Ho. NW8 —4B 66 (4B 158)
(off Fisherton St.)
Gibbon Rd. SE15 —2J 105
Gibbon Rd. W3 —7A 64
Gibbon Rd. King T —1E 134
Gibbon's Rents. SE1 —5G 169
Gibbons Rd. NW10 —6A 46
Gibbon Wlk. SW15 —4C 100
Gibbs Av. SE19 —5D 122
Gibbs Clo. SE19 —6D 122
Gibbs Grn. W14 —5H 83
(in three parts)
Gibbs Grn. Edgw —4D 12
Gibb's Rd. N18 —4D 18
Gibbs Sq. SE19 —5D 122
Gibney Ter. Brom —4H 125
Gibraltar Wlk. E2 —2K 163
Gibson Clo. E1 —4J 69
Gibson Clo. N21 —6F 7
Gibson Clo. Chess —5C 146
Gibson Clo. Isw th —3J 97
Gibson Gdns. N16 —2F 51
Gibson Ho. Sutt —4J 149
Gibson Rd. SE11 —4K 85 (4H 173)
Gibson Rd. Dag —1C 56
Gibson Rd. Sutt —5K 149
Gibson Rd. Uxb —4B 40
Gibsons Hill. SW16 —7A 122
Gibson Sq. N1 —1A 68
Gibson St. SE10 —5G 89
Gideon Clo. Belv —4H 93
Gideon M. W5 —2D 80
Gideon Rd. SW11 —3E 102
Giesbach Rd. N19 —2H 49
Giffard Rd. N18 —6K 17
Giffin St. SE8 —7C 88
Gifford Gdns. W7 —5H 61
Gifford Ho. SW1 —5G 85 (6A 172)
(off Churchill Gdns.)
Gifford St. N1 —7J 49
Gift La. E15 —1H 71
Giggshill. —7A 134
Giggs Hill. Orp —2K 145
Giggshill Gdns. Th Dit —1A 146
Giggshill Rd. Th Dit —7A 134
Gilbert Bri. EC2 —5C 68
(off Barbican)
Gilbert Clo. SE18 —1D 108
Gilbert Clo. SW19 —7K 119
(off High Path)
Gilbert Ct. W5 —6F 63
(off Green Va.)
Gilbert Gro. Edgw —1K 27
Gilbert Ho. E17 —3D 34
Gilbert Ho. EC2 —5D 162
Gilbert Ho. SE8 —6C 88
Gilbert Ho. SW1 —5F 85 (6K 171)
(off Churchill Gdns.)
Gilbert Ho. SW8 —7J 85
(off Wyvil Rd.)
Gilbert Pl. WC1 —5J 67 (6E 160)
Gilbert Rd. SE11 —4A 86 (4K 173)
Gilbert Rd. SW19 —7A 120
Gilbert Rd. Belv —3G 93
Gilbert Rd. Brom —7J 125
Gilbert Rd. Hare —2A 22
Gilbert Rd. Pinn —4B 24
Gilbert Sheldon Ho. W2
(off Edgware Rd.) —5B 66 (5B 158)
Gilbertson Ho. E14 —3C 88
Gilbert St. E15 —4G 53
Gilbert St. W1 —6E 66 (1H 165)
Gilbert St. Houn —3G 97
Gilbert Way. Croy —2K 151
Gilbey Clo. Uxb —4D 40
Gilbey Rd. SW17 —4C 120
Gilbeys Yd. NW1 —7E 48
Gilbourne Rd. SE18 —6K 91
Gilda Av. Enf —5F 9
Gilda Ct. NW7 —1C 28
Gilda Cres. N16 —1G 51
Gildea Clo. Pinn —1E 24
Gildea St. W1 —5F 67 (6K 159)
Gilden Cres. NW5 —5E 48
Gildersome St. SE18 —6E 90
Gilders Rd. Chess —7F 147
Giles Coppice. SE19 —4F 123
Giles Ho. SE16 —7K 169
Gilesmead. SE5 —1D 104
Gilfrid Clo. Uxb —6D 58
Gilkes Cres. SE21 —6E 104
Gilkes Pl. SE21 —6E 104
Gillan Ct. SE12 —3K 125
Gillan Grn. Bus H —2B 10
Gillards M. E17 —4C 34
Gillards Way. E17 —4C 34
Gill Av. E16 —6J 71
Gillender St. E3 & E14 —4E 70
Gillender St. E14 —4E 70
Gillespie Rd. N5 —3A 50
Gillett Av. E6 —2C 72
Gillette Corner. (Junct.) —7A 80
Gillett Ho. N8 —3J 31
(off Campsfield Rd.)
Gillett Pl. N16 —5E 50
Gillett Rd. T Hth —4D 140
Gillett St. N16 —5E 50
Gillfoot. NW1 —2G 67 (1A 160)
(off Hampstead Rd.)
Gillham Ter. N17 —6B 18
Gillian Ho. Har W —6D 10
Gillian Pk. Rd. Sutt —1H 149
Gillian St. SE13 —5D 106
Gillies St. NW5 —5E 48
Gilling Ct. NW3 —6C 48
Gillingham M. SW1 —4G 85 (3A 172)
Gillingham Rd. NW2 —3G 47
Gillingham Row. SW1 —4G 85 (3A 172)
Gillingham St. SW1 —4G 85 (3A 172)
Gillings Ct. Barn —4B 4
(off Wood St.)
Gillison Wlk. SE16 —3H 87
Gillman Dri. E15 —1H 71
Gillman Ho. E2 —2G 69
(off Pritchard's Rd.)
Gill St. E14 —6B 70
Gillum Clo. E Barn —1J 15
Gilmore Clo. Uxb —3C 40
Gilmore Ct. N11 —5J 15
Gilmore Cres. Ashf —5C 112
Gilmore Rd. SE13 —4F 107
Gilpin Av. SW14 —4K 99
Gilpin Clo. Mitc —2C 138
Gilpin Cres. N18 —5A 18
Gilpin Cres. Twic —7F 97
Gilpin Rd. E5 —4A 52
Gilpin Way. Hay —7F 77
Gilray Ho. W2 —7B 66 (2A 164)
(off Gloucester Ter.)
Gilsland Rd. T Hth —4D 140
Gilstead Ho. Bark —2B 74
Gilstead Rd. SW6 —2K 101
Gilston Rd. SW10 —5A 84 (7A 170)
Gilton Rd. SE6 —3G 125
Giltspur St. EC1 —6B 68 (7B 162)
Gilwell Clo. E4 —4J 9
Gilwell La. E4 —4J 9
Gilwell Park. —4K 9
Gilwell Pk. E4 —3K 9
Ginsburg Yd. NW3 —4A 48
Gippeswyck Clo. Pinn —1B 24
Gipsy Hill. SE19 —4E 122
Gipsy La. SW15 —3D 100
Gipsy Rd. SE27 —4C 122
Gipsy Rd. Well —7D 92
Gipsy Rd. Gdns. SE27 —4C 122
Giralda Clo. E16 —5B 72
Giraud St. E14 —6D 70
Girdler's Rd. W14 —4F 83
Girdlestone Wlk. N19 —2G 49
Girdwood Rd. SW18 —7G 101
Girling Ho. N1 —1E 68
(off Colville Est.)
Girling Way. Felt —3J 95
Gironde Rd. SW6 —7H 83
Girtin Ho. N'holt —2B 60
(off Academy Gdns.)
Girton Av. NW9 —3G 27
Girton Clo. N'holt —6G 43
Girton Gdns. Croy —3C 154
Girton Rd. SE26 —5K 123
Girton Rd. N'holt —6G 43
Girton Vs. W10 —6F 65
Gisbourne Clo. Wall —3H 151
Gisburn Ho. SE15 —6G 87
(off Friary Est.)
Gisburn Rd. N8 —4K 31
Gissing Wlk. N1 —7A 50
Gittens Clo. Brom —4H 125
Given Wilson Wlk. E13 —2H 71
Glacier Way. Wemb —2D 62
Gladbeck Way. Enf —4G 7
Gladding Rd. E12 —4B 54
Glade Clo. Surb —2D 146
Glade Ct. Ilf —1D 36
Glade Gdns. Croy —7A 142
Glade La. S'hall —2F 79
Glade Rd. E12 —3D 54
Gladeside. N21 —6E 6
Gladeside. Croy —6K 141
Gladeside Clo. Chess —7D 146
Gladesmore Rd. N15 —6F 33
Glades Pl. Brom —2J 143
Glades Shop. Cen., The. Brom —2J 143
Gladeswood Rd. Belv —4H 93
Glade, The. N20 —3G 15
Glade, The. N21 —7E 6
Glade, The. SE7 —7A 90
Glade, The. Brom —2B 144
Glade, The. Croy —6A 142
Glade, The. Enf —3F 7
Glade, The. Eps —6C 148
Glade, The. Ilf —1D 36
Glade, The. Sutt —7G 149
Glade, The. W W'ck —3D 154
Glade, The. Wfd G —3E 20
Gladiator St. SE23 —7A 106
Glading Ter. N16 —3F 51
Gladioli Clo. Hamp —6E 114
Gladsdale Dri. Pinn —4K 23
Gladsmuir Rd. N19 —1G 49
Gladsmuir Rd. Barn —2B 4
Gladstone Av. E12 —7C 54
Gladstone Av. N22 —2A 32
Gladstone Av. Felt —6J 95
Gladstone Av. Twic —1H 115
Gladstone Ct. SW1 —4H 85 (4D 172)
(off Regency St.)
Gladstone Gdns. Houn —1G 97
Gladstone Ho. E14 —6C 70
Gladstone M. N22 —2A 32
Gladstone M. NW6 —7H 47
Gladstone M. SE20 —7J 123
Gladstone Pde. NW2 —2E 46
Gladstone Pk. Gdns. NW2 —3D 46
Gladstone Pl. E3 —2B 70
Gladstone Pl. Barn —4A 4
Gladstone Pl. E Mol —5J 133
Gladstone Rd. SW19 —7J 119
Gladstone Rd. W4 —3K 81
Gladstone Rd. Buck H —1F 21
Gladstone Rd. Croy —7D 140
Gladstone Rd. King T —3G 135
Gladstone Rd. S'hall —2C 78
Gladstone Rd. Surb —2D 146
Gladstone St. SE1 —3B 86
Gladstone Ter. SE27 —5C 122
(off Bentons La.)
Gladstone Ter. SW8 —1F 103
Gladstone Way. Harr —3J 25
Gladwell Rd. N8 —6K 31
Gladwell Rd. Brom —6J 125
Gladwin Ho. NW1 —2G 67 (1B 160)
(off Cranleigh St.)
Gladwyn Rd. SW15 —3F 101
Gladys Dimson Ho. E7 —5H 53
Gladys Rd. NW6 —7J 47
Glaisher St. SE8 —6C 88
Glamis Ct. W3 —2H 81
Glamis Cres. Hay —3E 76
Glamis Pl. E1 —7J 69
Glamis Rd. E1 —7J 69
Glamis Way. N'holt —6G 43
Glamorgan Clo. Mitc —3J 139
Glamorgan Ct. W7 —5K 61
(off Copley Clo.)
Glamorgan Rd. King T —7C 116
Glanfield Rd. Beck —4B 142
Glanleam Rd. Stan —4J 11
Glanville Rd. SW2 —5J 103
Glanville Rd. Brom —3K 143
Glasbrook Av. Twic —1D 114
Glasbrook Rd. SE9 —7B 108
Glaserton Rd. N16 —7E 32
Glasford St. SW17 —6D 120
Glasfryn Ct. Harr —2H 43
(off Roxeth Hill)
Glasfryn Ho. Harr —2H 43
(off Roxeth Hill)
Glasgow Ho. W9 —2K 65
(off Maida Va.)
Glasgow Rd. E13 —2K 71
Glasgow Rd. N18 —5C 18
Glasgow Ter. SW1 —5G 85 (6A 172)
Glasier Ct. E15 —7G 53
Glasse Clo. W13 —7A 62
Glasshill St. SE1 —2B 86 (6B 168)
Glasshouse Fields. E1 —7K 69
Glasshouse St. W1 —7G 67 (3B 166)
Glasshouse Wlk. SE1 —5J 85 (5F 173)
Glasshouse Yd. EC1 —4C 68 (4C 162)
Glasslyn Rd. N8 —5H 31
Glassmill La. Brom —2H 143
(in two parts)
Glass St. E2 —4H 69
Glass Yd. SE18 —3E 90
Glastonbury Av. Wfd G —7G 21
Glastonbury Ct. W13 —1A 80
(off Talbot Rd.)
Glastonbury Ho. SE12 —5H 107
(off Wantage Rd.)
Glastonbury Ho. SW1 —5F 85 (5J 171)
(off Abbots Mnr.)
Glastonbury Pl. E1 —6J 69
Glastonbury Rd. N9 —1B 18
Glastonbury Rd. Mord —7J 137
Glastonbury St. NW6 —5H 47
Glaston Ct. W5 —1D 80
(off Grange Rd.)
Glaucus St. E3 —5D 70
Glazbury Rd. W14 —4G 83
Glazebrook Clo. SE21 —2D 122
Glazebrook Rd. Tedd —7K 115
Glebe Av. Enf —3G 7
Glebe Av. Harr —4E 26
Glebe Av. Mitc —2C 138
Glebe Av. Ruis —6K 41
Glebe Av. Uxb —3E 40
Glebe Av. Wfd G —6D 20
Glebe Clo. W4 —5A 82
Glebe Clo. Uxb —4E 40
Glebe Cotts. Felt —3E 114
Glebe Ct. N13 —3F 17
Glebe Ct. SE3 —3G 107
(off Glebe, The)
Glebe Ct. W5 —1D 80
Glebe Ct. W7 —7H 61
Glebe Ct. Mitc —3D 138
Glebe Ct. Stan —5H 11
Glebe Cres. NW4 —4E 28
Glebe Cres. Harr —3E 26
Glebe Gdns. N Mald —7A 136
Glebe Ho. Dri. Brom —1K 155
Glebe Hyrst. SE19 —4E 122
Glebeland Gdns. Shep —6E 130
Glebelands. E10 —2D 52
Glebelands. W Mol —5F 133
Glebelands Av. E18 —2J 35
Glebelands Av. Ilf —7H 37
Glebelands Clo. SE5 —3E 104
Glebelands Rd. Felt —1J 113
Glebe La. Harr —4E 26
Glebe Path. Mitc —3D 138
Glebe Pl. SW3 —6C 84 (7C 170)
Glebe Rd. E8 —7F 51
Glebe Rd. N3 —1A 30
Glebe Rd. N8 —4K 31
Glebe Rd. NW10 —6C 46
Glebe Rd. SW13 —2C 100
Glebe Rd. Brom —1J 143
Glebe Rd. Cars —6D 150
Glebe Rd. Dag —6H 57
Glebe Rd. Hay —1H 77
Glebe Rd. Stan —5H 11
Glebe Rd. Sutt —7G 149
Glebe Side. Twic —6K 97
Glebe Sq. Mitc —3D 138
Glebe St. W4 —5A 82
Glebe Ter. E3 —3D 70
Glebe Ter. W4 —5A 82
Glebe, The. SE3 —3G 107
Glebe, The. SW16 —4H 121
Glebe, The. Chst —1G 145
Glebe, The. W Dray —4B 76
Glebe, The. Wor Pk —1B 148
Glebe Way. Hanw —3E 114
Glebe Way. W W'ck —2E 154
Glebe Way. Wfd G —5F 21
Gledhow Gdns. SW5 —4A 84
Gledstanes Rd. W14 —5G 83
Gledwood Av. Hay —5H 59
Gledwood Cres. Hay —5H 59
Gledwood Dri. Hay —5H 59
Gledwood Gdns. Hay —5H 59
Gleed Av. Bus H —2C 10
Glegg Pl. SW15 —4F 101
Glenaffric Av. E14 —4F 89
Glen Albyn Rd. SW19 —2F 119
Glenallan Ho. W14 —4H 83
(off N. End Cres.)
Glenalla Rd. Ruis —7H 23
Glenalmond Rd. Harr —4E 26
Glenalvon Way. SE18 —4C 90
Glena Mt. Sutt —4A 150
Glenarm Rd. E5 —4J 51
Glen Av. Ashf —4C 112
Glenavon Clo. Clay —6A 146
Glenavon Ct. Wor Pk —2D 148
Glenavon Lodge. Beck —7C 124
Glenavon Rd. E15 —7G 53
Glenbarr Clo. SE9 —3F 109
Glenbow Rd. Brom —6G 125
Glenbrook N. Enf —4E 6
Glenbrook Rd. NW6 —5J 47
Glenbrook S. Enf —4E 6
Glenbuck Rd. Surb —6D 134
Glenburnie Rd. SW17 —3D 120
Glencairn Dri. W5 —4C 62
Glencairne Clo. E16 —5B 72
Glencairn Rd. SW16 —1J 139
Glen Clo. Shep —4C 130
Glencoe Av. Ilf —7H 37
Glencoe Dri. Dag —4G 57
Glencoe Mans. SW9 —7A 86
(off Mowll St.)
Glencoe Rd. Hay —5B 60
Glen Ct. Sidc —4A 128
Glen Cres. Wfd G —6E 20
Glendale Av. N22 —7F 17
Glendale Av. Edgw —4A 12
Glendale Av. Romf —7C 38
Glendale Clo. SE9 —3E 108
Glendale Dri. SW19 —5H 119
Glendale Gdns. Wemb —1D 44
Glendale M. Beck —1D 142
Glendale Rd. Eri —4J 93
Glendale Way. SE28 —7C 74
Glendall St. SW9 —4K 103
Glendarvon St. SW15 —3F 101
Glendevon Clo. Edgw —3C 12
Glendish Rd. N17 —1H 33
Glendor Gdns. NW7 —4E 12
Glendower Gdns. SW14 —3K 99
Glendower Pl. SW7 —4B 84 (3A 170)
Glendower Rd. E4 —1A 20
Glendower Rd. SW14 —3K 99
Glendown Ho. E8 —5G 51
Glendown Rd. SE2 —5A 92
Glendun Ct. W3 —7A 64
Glendun Rd. W3 —7A 64
Gleneagle M. SW16 —5H 121
Gleneagle Rd. SW16 —5H 121
Gleneagles. W13 —5B 62
(off Malvern Way)
Gleneagles. Stan —7G 11
Gleneagles Clo. SE16 —5H 87
(off Ryder Dri.)
Gleneagles Clo. Orp —7H 145
Gleneagles Grn. Orp —7H 145
Gleneagles Tower. S'hall —6G 61
(off Fleming Rd.)
Gleneldon M. SW16 —4J 121
Gleneldon Rd. SW16 —4J 121
Glenelg Rd. SW2 —5J 103
Glenesk Rd. SE9 —3E 108
Glenfarg Rd. SE6 —1E 124
Glenfield Cres. Ruis —7F 23
Glenfield Rd. SW12 —1G 121
Glenfield Rd. W13 —2B 80
Glenfield Rd. Ashf —6D 112
Glenfield Ter. W13 —2B 80
Glenfinlas Way. SE5 —7B 86
Glenforth St. SE10 —5H 89
Glengall Gro. E14 —3D 88
Glengall Pas. NW6 —1J 65
(off Priory Pk. Rd., in two parts)
Glengall Rd. NW6 —1H 65
Glengall Rd. SE15 —5F 87
Glengall Rd. Bexh —3E 110
Glengall Rd. Edgw —3C 12
Glengall Rd. Wfd G —6D 20
Glengall Ter. SE15 —6F 87
Glen Gdns. Croy —3A 152
Glengariff Mans. SW9 —7A 86
(off S. Island Pl.)
Glengarnock Av. E14 —4E 88
Glengarry Rd. SE22 —5E 104
Glenham Dri. Ilf —5F 37
Glenhead Clo. SE9 —3F 109
Glenhill Clo. N3 —2J 29
Glen Ho. E16 —1E 90
(off Storey St.)
Glenhouse Rd. SE9 —5E 108
Glenhurst. Beck —1E 142
Glenhurst Av. NW5 —4E 48
Glenhurst Av. Bex —1F 129
Glenhurst Av. Ruis —7E 22
Glenhurst Ri. SE19 —7C 122
Glenhurst Rd. N12 —5G 15
Glenhurst Rd. Bren —6C 80
Glenilla Rd. NW3 —6C 48
Glenister Pk. Rd. SW16 —7H 121
Glenister Rd. SE10 —5H 89
Glenister St. E16 —1E 90
Glenkerry Ho. E14 —6E 70
Glenlea Rd. SE9 —5D 108
Glenloch Rd. NW3 —6C 48
Glenloch Rd. Enf —2D 8
Glenluce Rd. SE3 —6J 89
Glenlyon Rd. SE9 —5E 108
Glenmead. Buck H —1F 21
Glenmere Av. NW7 —7H 13
Glenmill. Hamp —5D 114
Glenmore Lawns. W13 —6A 62
Glenmore Lodge. Beck —1D 142
Glenmore Pde. Wemb —1E 62
Glenmore Rd. NW3 —6C 48
Glenmore Rd. Well —7K 91
Glenmore Way. Bark —2A 74
Glenmount Path. SE18 —5G 91
Glennie Ho. SE10 —1E 106
(off Blackheath Hill)
Glennie Rd. SE27 —3A 122
Glenny Rd. Bark —6G 55
Glenorchy Clo. Hay —5C 60
Glenparke Rd. E7 —6K 53
Glenridding. NW1 —2G 67 (1B 160)
(off Ampthill Est.)
Glen Ri. Wfd G —6E 20
Glen Rd. E13 —4A 72
Glen Rd. E17 —5B 34
Glen Rd. Chess —4F 147
Glen Rd. End. Wall —7F 151
Glenrosa St. SW6 —2A 102
Glenrose Ct. Sidc —5B 128
Glensdale Rd. SE4 —3B 106
Glenshaw Mans. SW9 —7A 86
(off Brixton Rd.)
Glenshiel Rd. SE9 —5E 108
Glentanner Way. SW17 —3B 120
Glen Ter. E14 —2E 88
Glentham Gdns. SW13 —6D 82
Glentham Rd. SW13 —6C 82
Glen, The. Brom —2G 143
Glen, The. Croy —3K 153
Glen, The. Eastc —5K 23
Glen, The. Enf —4G 7
Glen, The. Orp —3D 156
Glen, The. Pinn —7C 24
Glen, The. S'hall —5D 78
Glen, The. Wemb —4E 44
Glenthorne Av. Croy —1H 153
Glenthorne Clo. Sutt —1J 149
Glenthorne Clo. Uxb —3C 58

Glenthorne Gdns. Ilf —3E 36
Glenthorne Gdns. Sutt —1J 149
Glenthorne M. W6 —4D 82
Glenthorne Rd. E17 —5A 34
Glenthorne Rd. N11 —5J 15
Glenthorne Rd. W6 —4D 82
Glenthorne Rd. King T —4F 135
Glenthorpe Av. SW15 —4C 100
Glenthorpe Rd. Mord —5F 137
Glenton Rd. SE13 —4G 107
Glentworth St. NW1 —4D 66 (4F 159)
Glenure Rd. SE9 —5E 108
Glenview. SE2 —6D 92
Glenview Rd. Brom —2B 144
Glenville Av. Enf —1H 7
Glenville Gro. SE8 —7B 88
Glenville M. SW18 —7K 101
Glenville Rd. King T —1G 135
Glen Wlk. Iswth —5H 97
Glenwood Av. NW9 —1A 46
Glenwood Clo. Harr —5K 25
Glenwood Ct. E18 —3J 35
Glenwood Ct. Sidc —4A 128
Glenwood Gdns. Ilf —5E 36
Glenwood Gro. NW9 —1J 45
Glenwood Rd. N15 —5B 32
Glenwood Rd. NW7 —3F 13
Glenwood Rd. SE6 —1B 124
Glenwood Rd. Eps —6C 148
Glenwood Rd. Houn —3H 97
Glenwood Way. Croy —6K 141
Glenworth Av. E14 —4F 89
Gliddon Rd. W14 —4G 83
Glimpsing Grn. Eri —3E 92
Glisson Rd. Uxb —2C 58
Global App. E3 —2D 70
Globe Ind. Est. SE16 —1A 88
Globe Rd. E2 & E1 —3J 69
(in two parts)
Globe Rd. E15 —5H 53
Globe Rd. Wfd G —6F 21
Globe Rope Wlk. E14 —4D 88
Globe Stairs. SE16 —7K 69
Globe St. SE1 —3D 86 (7E 168)
Globe Ter. E2 —3J 69
Globe Town. —3K 69
Globe Town Mkt. E2 —3K 69
Globe Wharf. SE16 —7K 69
Globe Yd. W1 —1J 165
Glossop Rd. S Croy —7D 152
Gloster Rd. N Mald —4A 136
Gloucester Arc. SW7 —4A 84
Gloucester Av. NW1 —7E 48
Gloucester Av. Sidc —2J 127
Gloucester Av. Well —4K 109
Gloucester Cir. SE10 —7E 88
Gloucester Clo. NW10 —7K 45
Gloucester Clo. Th Dit —1A 146
Gloucester Ct. EC3 —7E 68 (3H 169)
Gloucester Ct. NW11 —7H 29
(off Golders Grn. Rd.)
Gloucester Ct. W7 —5K 61
(off Copley Clo.)
Gloucester Ct. Harr —3J 25
Gloucester Ct. Mitc —5J 139
Gloucester Ct. Rich —7G 81
Gloucester Cres. NW1 —1F 67
Gloucester Cres. Stai —6A 112
Gloucester Dri. N4 —2B 50
Gloucester Dri. NW11 —4J 29
Gloucester Gdns. NW11 —7H 29
Gloucester Gdns. W2 —6A 66
Gloucester Gdns. Cockf —4K 5
Gloucester Gdns. Ilf —7C 36
Gloucester Gdns. Sutt —2K 149
Gloucester Ga. NW1 —2F 67
(in two parts)
Gloucester Ga. M. NW1 —2F 67
Gloucester Gro. Edgw —1K 27
Gloucester Ho. NW6 —2J 65
(off Cambridge Rd.)
Gloucester Ho. SE5 —7A 86
Gloucester Ho. Rich —5G 99
Gloucester M. E10 —7C 34
Gloucester M. W2 —6A 66 (1A 164)
Gloucester M. W. W2 —6A 66
Gloucester Pde. Hay —3E 76
Gloucester Pde. Sidc —5A 110
Gloucester Pl. NW1 & W1 —4D 66 (4E 158)
Gloucester Pl. M. W1 —5D 66 (6F 159)
Gloucester Rd. E10 —7C 34
Gloucester Rd. E11 —5K 35
Gloucester Rd. E12 —3D 54
Gloucester Rd. E17 —2K 33
Gloucester Rd. N17 —2D 32
Gloucester Rd. N18 —5A 18
Gloucester Rd. SW7 —3A 84 (4A 170)
Gloucester Rd. W3 —2J 81
Gloucester Rd. W5 —2C 80
Gloucester Rd. Barn —5E 4
Gloucester Rd. Belv —5F 93
Gloucester Rd. Croy —1D 152
Gloucester Rd. Enf —1H 7
Gloucester Rd. Felt —1A 114
Gloucester Rd. Hamp —7F 115
Gloucester Rd. Harr —5F 25
Gloucester Rd. Houn —4C 96
Gloucester Rd. King T —2G 135
Gloucester Rd. Rich —7G 81
Gloucester Rd. Tedd —5J 115
Gloucester Rd. Twic —1G 115
Gloucester Sq. E2 —1G 69
Gloucester Sq. W2 —6B 66 (1B 164)
Gloucester St. SW1 —5G 85 (6A 172)
Gloucester Ter. N14 —1C 16
(off Crown La.)
Gloucester Ter. W2 —6K 65 (1A 164)
Gloucester Wlk. W8 —2J 83
Gloucester Way. EC1 —3A 68 (2K 161)
Glover Clo. SE2 —4C 92
Glover Dri. N18 —6D 18
Glover Ho. NW6 —7A 48
Glover Ho. SE15 —4H 105
Glover Rd. Pinn —6B 24
Glovers Gro. Ruis —7D 22
Gloxinia Wlk. Hamp —6E 114
Glycena Rd. SW11 —3D 102
Glyn Av. Barn —4G 5
Glyn Clo. SE25 —2E 140
Glyn Ct. SW16 —3A 122
Glyndale Grange. Sutt —6K 149
Glyndebourne Ct. N'holt —3A 60
(off Canberra Dri.)
Glynde M. SW3 —2D 170
Glynde Reach. WC1 —2F 161
Glynde Rd. Bexh —3D 110
Glynde St. SE4 —6B 106
Glyndon Rd. SE18 —4G 91
Glyn Dri. Sidc —4B 128
Glynfield Rd. NW10 —7A 46
Glynne Rd. N22 —2A 32
Glyn Rd. E5 —3K 51
Glyn Rd. Enf —4D 8
Glyn Rd. Wor Pk —2F 149
Glyn St. SE11 —5K 85 (6G 173)
Glynwood Ct. SE23 —2J 123
Goater's All. SW6 —7H 83
(off Dawes Rd.)
Goat Ho. Bri. SE25 —3G 141
Goat La. Enf —1A 8
Goat Rd. Mitc —7E 138
Goat Wharf. Bren —6E 80
Gobions Av. Romf —1K 39
Godalming Av. Wall —5J 151
Godalming Rd. E14 —5D 70
Godbold Rd. E15 —4G 71
Goddard Clo. Shep —3B 130
Goddard Ct. W'stone —2A 26
Goddard Pl. N19 —3G 49
Goddard Rd. Beck —4K 141
Goddards Way. Ilf —1H 55
Goddarts Ho. E17 —3C 34
Godfrey Av. N'holt —1C 60
Godfrey Av. Twic —7H 97
Godfrey Hill. SE18 —4C 90
Godfrey Ho. EC1 —2E 162
Godfrey Rd. SE18 —4D 90
Godfrey St. E15 —2E 70
Godfrey St. SW3 —5C 84 (5D 170)
Godfrey Way. Houn —7C 96
Goding St. SE11 —5J 85 (5F 173)
Godley Rd. SW18 —1B 120
Godliman St. EC4 —6B 68 (1B 168)
Godman Rd. SE15 —2H 105
Godolphin Clo. N13 —6G 17
Godolphin Pl. W3 —7K 63
Godolphin Rd. W12 —1D 82
(in two parts)
Godson Rd. Croy —3A 152
Godstone Ho. SE1 —3D 86 (7F 169)
(off Pardoner St.)
Godstone Rd. Sutt —4A 150
Godstone Rd. Twic —6B 98
Godstow Rd. SE2 —2B 92
Godwin Clo. E4 —1K 9
Godwin Clo. N1 —2C 68
Godwin Clo. Eps —6J 147
Godwin Ct. NW1 —2G 67
(off Chalton St.)
Godwin Ho. NW6 —2K 65
(off Tollgate Gdns., in three parts)
Godwin Rd. E7 —4K 53
Godwin Rd. Brom —3A 144
Goffers Rd. SE3 —1G 107
Goffs Rd. Ashf —6F 113
Goidel Clo. Wall —4H 151
Golborne Gdns. W10 —4G 65
Golborne Ho. W10 —4G 65
(off Adair Rd.)
Golborne M. W10 —5G 65
Golborne Rd. W10 —5G 65
Golda Clo. Barn —6A 4
Goldbeaters Gro. Edgw —6F 13
Goldcliff Clo. Mord —7J 137
Goldcrest Clo. E16 —5B 72
Goldcrest Clo. SE28 —7C 74
Goldcrest M. W5 —5D 62
Goldcrest Way. Bush —1B 10
Goldcrest Way. New Ad —7F 155
Golden Ct. Barn —4H 5
Golden Ct. Rich —5D 98
Golden Cres. Hay —1H 77
Golden Cross M. W11 —6H 65
(off Portobello Rd.)
Golden Hinde Educational Mus. —1D 86 (4E 168)
Golden Hind Pl. SE8 —4B 88
(off Grove St.)
Golden La. EC1 —4C 68 (3C 162)
Golden La. Est. EC1 —4C 68 (4C 162)
Golden Mnr. W7 —7J 61
Golden M. SE20 —1J 141
Golden Pde. E17 —3E 34
(off Wood St.)
Golden Plover Clo. E16 —6J 71
Golden Sq. W1 —7G 67 (2B 166)
Golden Yd. NW3 —4A 48
(off Holly Mt.)
Golders Clo. Edgw —5C 12
Golders Ct. NW11 —7H 29
Golders Gdns. NW11 —7G 29
Golders Green. —6G 29
Golders Green Crematorium. NW11 —7J 29
Golders Grn. Cres. NW11 —7H 29
Golders Grn. Rd. NW11 —6G 29
Golders Mnr. Dri. NW11 —6F 29
Golders Pk. Clo. NW11 —1J 47
Golders Ri. NW4 —5F 29
Golders Way. NW11 —7H 29
Golderton. NW4 —4D 28
(off Prince of Wales Clo.)
Goldeslea. NW11 —1J 47
Goldfinch Rd. SE28 —3H 91
Goldhawk Ind. Est. W6 —3D 82
Goldhawk M. W12 —2D 82
Goldhawk Rd. W6 & W12 —4B 82
Goldhaze Clo. Wfd G —7G 21
Gold Hill. Edgw —6E 12
Goldhurst Gdns. NW6 —7A 48
Goldhurst Ter. NW6 —7K 47
Goldie Ho. N19 —7H 31
Golding Clo. Chess —6C 146
Golding Ct. Ilf —3E 54
Golding St. E1 —6G 69
Golding Ter. E1 —6G 69
Golding Ter. SW11 —2E 102
Goldington Ct. NW1 —1H 67
(off Royal College St.)
Goldington Cres. NW1 —2H 67
Goldington St. NW1 —2H 67
Gold La. Edgw —6E 12
Goldman Clo. E2 —4G 69 (3K 163)
Goldmark Ho. SE3 —3K 107
Goldney Rd. W9 —4J 65
Goldrill Dri. N11 —2K 15
Goldsborough Cres. E4 —2J 19
Goldsborough Ho. E14 —5D 88
Goldsborough Rd. SW8 —1H 103
Goldsdown Clo. Enf —2F 9
Goldsdown Rd. Enf —2E 8
Goldsmid St. SE18 —5J 91
Goldsmith Av. E12 —6C 54
Goldsmith Av. NW9 —5A 28
Goldsmith Av. W3 —7K 63
Goldsmith Av. Romf —7G 39
Goldsmith Clo. Harr —1F 43
Goldsmith Ct. WC2 —6J 67 (7F 161)
(off Stukeley St.)
Goldsmith La. NW9 —4H 27
Goldsmith Rd. E10 —1C 52
Goldsmith Rd. E17 —2K 33
Goldsmith Rd. N11 —5J 15
Goldsmith Rd. SE15 —1G 105
Goldsmith Rd. W3 —1K 81
Goldsmith's Bldgs. W3 —1K 81
Goldsmiths Clo. W3 —1K 81
Goldsmith's Pl. NW6 —1K 65
(off Springfield La.)
Goldsmith's Row. E2 —2G 69
Goldsmith's Sq. E2 —2G 69
Goldsmith St. EC2 —6C 68 (7D 162)
Goldsworthy Gdns. SE16 —5J 87
Goldthorpe. NW1 —1G 67
(off Camden St.)
Goldwell Ho. SE22 —3E 104
Goldwell Rd. T Hth —4K 139
Goldwin Clo. SE14 —1J 105
Goldwing Clo. E16 —6J 71
Golf Clo. Stan —7H 11
Golf Clo. T Hth —1A 140
Golf Club Dri. King T —7K 117
Golfe Rd. Ilf —3H 55
Golf Rd. W5 —6F 63
Golf Rd. Brom —3E 144
Golf Side. Twic —3H 115
Golfside Clo. N20 —3H 15
Golfside Clo. N Mald —2A 136
Goliath Clo. Wall —7J 151
Gollogly Ter. SE7 —5A 90
Gomer Gdns. Tedd —6A 116
Gomer Pl. Tedd —6A 116
Gomm Rd. SE16 —3J 87
Gomshall Av. Wall —5J 151
Gondar Gdns. NW6 —5H 47
Gonson St. SE8 —6D 88
Gonston Clo. SW19 —2G 119
Gonville Cres. N'holt —6F 43
Gonville Rd. T Hth —5K 139
Gonville St. SW6 —3G 101
Gooch Ho. E5 —3H 51
Gooch Ho. EC1 —5A 68 (5J 161)
(off Portpool La.)
Goodall Ho. SE4 —4K 105
Goodall Rd. E11 —3E 52
Gooden Ct. Harr —3J 43
Goodenough Rd. SW19 —7H 119
Goodey Rd. Bark —7J 55
Goodge Pl. W1 —5G 67 (6B 160)
Goodge St. W1 —5G 67 (6B 160)
Goodhall St. NW10 —3B 64
(in two parts)
Goodhart Pl. E14 —7A 70
Good Hart Pl. E14 —7A 70
Goodhart Way. W W'ck —7G 143
Goodhew Rd. Croy —6G 141
Gooding Clo. N Mald —4J 135
Goodinge Clo. N7 —6J 49
Gooding Ho. SE7 —5A 90
Goodman Cres. SW2 —2J 121
Goodman Rd. E10 —7E 34
Goodman's Ct. E1 —2J 169
Goodmans Ct. Wemb —4D 44
Goodman's Stile. E1 —6G 69 (7K 163)
Goodmans Yd. EC3 —7F 69 (2J 169)
Goodmayes. —1A 56
Goodmayes Av. Ilf —1A 56
Goodmayes La. Ilf —4A 56
Goodmayes Rd. Ilf —1A 56
Goodrich Ct. W10 —6F 65
Goodrich Rd. SE22 —6F 105
Goodson Rd. NW10 —7A 46
Goodson St. N1 —2A 68
Goods Way. NW1 —2J 67
Goodway Gdns. E14 —6F 71
Goodwill Ho. E14 —7D 70
Goodwin Clo. SE16 —3F 87
Goodwin Clo. Mitc —3B 138
Goodwin Ct. N8 —3J 31
(off Campsbourne Rd.)
Goodwin Ct. SW19 —7C 120
Goodwin Ct. Barn —6H 5
Goodwin Dri. Sidc —3D 128
Goodwin Gdns. Croy —6B 152
Goodwin Ho. N9 —1D 18
Goodwin Rd. N9 —1E 18
Goodwin Rd. W12 —2C 82
Goodwin Rd. Croy —5B 152
Goodwins Ct. WC2 —7J 67 (2E 166)
Goodwin St. N4 —2A 50
Goodwood Clo. Mord —4J 137
Goodwood Clo. Stan —5H 11
Goodwood Ct. W1 —5F 67 (5K 159)
(off Devonshire St.)
Goodwood Dri. N'holt —6E 42
Goodwood Pde. Beck —4A 142
Goodwood Rd. SE14 —7A 88
Goodwyn Av. NW7 —5F 13
Goodwyns Va. N10 —1E 30
Goodyear Ho. N2 —2B 30
(off Grange, The)
Goodyear Pl. SE5 —6C 86
Goodyer Ho. SW1 —5H 85 (5C 172)
(off Tachbrook St.)
Goodyers Gdns. NW4 —5F 29
Goosander Way. SE28 —3H 91
Gooseacre La. Harr —5D 26
Goose Grn. Trad. Est. SE22 —4F 105
Gooseley La. E6 —3E 72
(in two parts)
Goosens Clo. Sutt —5A 150
Goose Sq. E6 —6D 72
Gophir La. EC4 —7D 68 (2E 168)
Gopsall St. N1 —1D 68
Gordon Av. E4 —6B 20
Gordon Av. SW14 —4A 100
Gordon Av. Stan —7E 10
Gordon Av. Twic —5A 98
Gordonbrock Rd. SE4 —5C 106
Gordon Clo. E17 —6C 34
Gordon Clo. N19 —1G 49
Gordon Ct. W12 —6E 64
Gordon Ct. Edgw —5K 11
Gordon Cres. Croy —1E 152
Gordon Cres. Hay —3J 77
Gordondale Rd. SW19 —2J 119
Gordon Dri. Shep —7F 131
Gordon Gdns. Edgw —2H 27
Gordon Gro. SE5 —2B 104
Gordon Hill. Enf —1H 7
Gordon Ho. E1 —7J 69
(off Glamis Rd.)
Gordon Ho. W5 —3E 62
Gordon Ho. Rd. NW5 —4E 48
Gordon Mans. WC1 —4H 67 (4C 160)
(off Torrington Pl.)
Gordon Pl. W8 —2J 83
Gordon Rd. E4 —1B 20
Gordon Rd. E11 —6J 35
Gordon Rd. E15 —4E 52
Gordon Rd. E18 —1K 35
Gordon Rd. N3 —7C 14
Gordon Rd. N9 —2C 18
Gordon Rd. N11 —7C 16
Gordon Rd. SE15 —2H 105
Gordon Rd. W4 —6H 81
Gordon Rd. W13 & W5 —7B 62
Gordon Rd. Ashf —3A 112
Gordon Rd. Bark —1J 73
Gordon Rd. Beck —3B 142
Gordon Rd. Belv —4J 93
Gordon Rd. Cars —6D 150
Gordon Rd. Chad H & Romf —6F 39
Gordon Rd. Enf —1H 7
Gordon Rd. Harr —3J 25
Gordon Rd. Houn —4G 97
Gordon Rd. Ilf —3H 55
Gordon Rd. King T —1F 135
Gordon Rd. Rich —2F 99
Gordon Rd. Shep —6F 131
Gordon Rd. Sidc —5J 109
Gordon Rd. S'hall —4C 78
Gordon Rd. Surb —7F 135
Gordon Rd. W Dray —7A 58
Gordon Sq. WC1 —4H 67 (3C 160)
Gordon St. E13 —3J 71
Gordon St. WC1 —4H 67 (3C 160)
Gordon Way. Barn —4C 4
Gordon Way. Brom —1J 143
Gore Ct. NW9 —5G 27
Gorefield Ho. NW6 —2J 65
(off Canterbury Rd.)
Gorefield Pl. NW6 —2J 65
Gore Rd. E9 —1J 69
Gore Rd. SW20 —2E 136
Goresbrook Interchange. (Junct.) —2F 75
Goresbrook Rd. Dag —1B 74
Gore St. SW7 —3A 84
Gorham Pl. W11 —7G 65
Goring Clo. Romf —1J 39
Goring Gdns. Dag —4C 56
Goring Rd. N11 —6D 16
Goring Rd. Dag —6K 57
Goring St. EC3 —7H 163
Goring Way. Gnfd —2G 61
Gorleston Rd. N15 —5D 32
Gorleston St. W14 —4G 83
(in two parts)
Gorman Rd. SE18 —4D 90
Gorringe Pk. Av. Mitc —7D 120
Gorse Clo. E16 —6J 71
Gorsefield Ho. E14 —7C 70
Gorse Ri. SW17 —5E 120
Gorse Rd. Croy —4C 154
Gorse Wlk. W Dray —6A 58
Gorseway. Romf —1K 57
Gorst Rd. NW10 —4J 63
Gorst Rd. SW11 —6D 102
Gorsuch Pl. E2 —3F 69 (1J 163)
Gorsuch St. E2 —2F 69 (1J 163)
Gosberton Rd. SW12 —1D 120
Gosbury Hill. Chess —4E 146
Gosfield Rd. Dag —2G 57
Gosfield St. W1 —5G 67 (6A 160)
Gosford Gdns. Ilf —5D 36
Goshawk Gdns. Hay —3G 59
Goslett Yd. WC2 —6H 67 (1D 166)
Gosling Clo. Gnfd —3E 60
Gosling Ct. SE8 —6B 88
(off Wotton Rd.)
Gosling Way. SW9 —1A 104
Gospatrick Rd. N17 —7H 17
Gospel Oak. —4E 48
Gospel Oak Est. NW5 —5D 48
Gosport Rd. E17 —5B 34
Gosport Wlk. N17 —4H 33
Gosport Way. SE15 —7F 87
Gossage Rd. SE18 —5H 91
Gossage Rd. Uxb —7B 40
Gosset St. E2 —3F 69 (1K 163)
Gosshill Rd. Chst —2E 144
Gossington Clo. Chst —4F 127
Gosterwood St. SE8 —6A 88
Gostling Rd. Twic —1E 114
Goston Gdns. T Hth —3A 140
Goswell Pl. EC1 —2B 162
Goswell Rd. EC1 —2B 68 (1A 162)
Gothic Cotts. Enf —2H 7
(off Chase Grn. Av.)
Gothic Ct. SE5 —7C 86
(off Wyndham Rd.)
Gothic Ct. Hay —6F 77
Gothic Rd. Twic —2H 115
Gottfried M. NW5 —4G 49
Goudhurst Rd. Brom —5G 125
Gough Ho. N1 —1B 68
(off Windsor St.)
Gough Rd. E15 —4H 53
Gough Rd. Enf —2C 8
Gough Sq. EC4 —6A 68 (7K 161)
Gough St. WC1 —4K 67 (3H 161)
Gough Wlk. E14 —6C 70
Goulden Ho. SW11 —2C 102
Goulding Gdns. T Hth —2C 140
Gould Rd. Felt —7G 95
Gould Rd. Twic —1J 115
Goulds Green. —6D 58
Gould's Grn. Uxb —7D 58
Gould Ter. E8 —5H 51
Goulston St. E1 —6F 69 (7J 163)
Goulton Rd. E5 —4H 51
Gourley Pl. N15 —5E 32
Gourley St. N15 —5E 32
Gourock Rd. SE9 —5E 108
Govan St. E2 —1G 69
Gover Ct. SW4 —2J 103
Govett Av. Shep —5E 130
Govier Clo. E15 —7G 53
Gowan Av. SW6 —1G 101
Gowan Ho. E2 —3F 69 (2K 163)
(off Chambord St.)
Gowan Rd. NW10 —6D 46
Gower Clo. SW4 —6G 103
Gower Ct. WC1 —4H 67 (3C 160)
Gower Ho. E17 —3D 34
Gower Ho. SE17 —5C 86
Gower M. WC1 —5H 67 (6D 160)
Gower M. Mans. WC1 —5H 67 (5D 160)
(off Gower M.)
Gower Pl. WC1 —4H 67 (3B 160)
Gower Rd. E7 —6J 53
Gower Rd. Iswth —6K 79
Gower St. WC1 —4G 67 (3B 160)
Gower's Wlk. E1 —6G 69
Gowland Pl. Beck —2B 142
Gowlett Rd. SE15 —3G 105
Gowrie Rd. SW11 —3E 102
Graburn Way. E Mol —3H 133
Grace Av. Bexh —2F 111
Gracechurch St. EC3 —7D 68 (2F 169)
Grace Clo. SE9 —3B 126
Grace Clo. Edgw —7D 12
Gracedale Rd. SW16 —5F 121
Gracefield Gdns. SW16 —3J 121
Grace Ho. SE11 —7H 173
Grace Jones Clo. E8 —6G 51
Grace Path. SE26 —4J 123
Grace Pl. E3 —3D 70
Grace Rd. Croy —6C 140
Graces All. E1 —7G 69
Graces M. NW8 —2A 66
Grace's M. SE5 —2D 104
Grace's Rd. SE5 —2E 104
Grace St. E3 —3D 70
Gradient, The. SE26 —4G 123
Graeme Rd. Enf —2J 7
Graemesdyke Av. SW14 —3H 99
Grafely Way. SE15 —7F 87
Grafton Clo. W13 —6A 62
Grafton Clo. Houn —1C 114
Grafton Clo. Wor Pk —3A 148
Grafton Ct. Felt —1F 113
Grafton Cres. NW1 —6F 49
Grafton Gdns. N4 —6C 32
Grafton Gdns. Dag —2E 56
Grafton Ho. SE8 —5B 88
Grafton M. N1 —2C 68
(off Frome St.)
Grafton M. W1 —4G 67 (4A 160)
Grafton Pk. Rd. Wor Pk —2A 148
Grafton Pl. NW1 —3H 67 (2D 160)
Grafton Rd. NW5 —5E 48
Grafton Rd. W3 —7J 63
Grafton Rd. Croy —1A 152
Grafton Rd. Dag —1E 56
Grafton Rd. Enf —3E 6
Grafton Rd. Harr —5G 25
Grafton Rd. N Mald —3A 136
Grafton Rd. Wor Pk —3K 147
Grafton Sq. SW4 —3G 103
Graftons, The. NW2 —3J 47
Grafton St. W1 —7F 67 (3K 165)
Grafton Ter. NW5 —5D 48
Grafton Way. W1 & WC1 —4G 67 (4A 160)
Grafton Way. W Mol —4D 132
Grafton Yd. NW5 —6F 49
Graham Av. W13 —2B 80
Graham Av. Mitc —1E 138
Graham Clo. Croy —2C 154
Graham Ct. N'holt —5D 42
Grahame Park. —1B 28
Grahame Pk. Est. NW9 —1A 28
Grahame Pk. Way. NW7 & NW9 —7G 13
Grahame White Ho. Kent —3D 26
Graham Gdns. Surb —1E 146
Graham Ho. N9 —1D 18
(off Cumberland Rd.)
Graham Lodge. NW4 —6D 28
Graham Mans. Bark —7A 56
(off Lansbury Av.)
Graham Rd. E8 —6G 51
Graham Rd. E13 —3J 71
Graham Rd. N15 —3B 32
Graham Rd. NW4 —6D 28
Graham Rd. SW19 —7H 119
Graham Rd. W4 —3K 81
Graham Rd. Bexh —4G 111
Graham Rd. Hamp —4E 114
Graham Rd. Harr —3J 25
Graham Rd. Mitc —1E 138
Graham St. N1 —2B 68 (1C 162)
Graham Ter. SW1 —4E 84 (4G 171)
Graham Ter. Sidc —6B 110
(off Westerham Dri.)
Grainger Clo. N'holt —5F 43
Grainger Ct. SE5 —7C 86
Grainger Rd. N22 —1C 32
Grainger Rd. Iswth —2K 97
Gramer Clo. E11 —2F 53
Gramophone La. Hay —2G 77
Grampian Clo. Hay —7F 77
Grampian Clo. Orp —6K 145

Grampian Gdns.—Greenock Rd.

Grampian Gdns. NW2 —1G 47
Grampians, The. W12 —2F 83
(off Shepherd's Bush Rd.)
Grampion Clo. Sutt —7A 150
Granada St. SW17 —5C 120
Granard Av. SW15 —5D 100
Granard Bus. Cen. NW7 —6F 13
Granard Ho. E9 —6K 51
Granard Rd. SW12 —7D 102
Granary Clo. N9 —7D 8
Granary Rd. E1 —4H 69
Granary Sq. N1 —6A 50
Granary St. NW1 —1H 67
Granby Pl. SE1 —2A 86 (7J 167)
(off Station App. Rd.)
Granby Rd. SE9 —2D 108
Granby St. E2 —4G 69 (3K 163)
(in two parts)
Granby Ter. NW1 —2G 67 (1A 160)
Grand Arc. N12 —5F 15
Grand Av. EC1 —5B 68 (5B 162)
(in two parts)
Grand Av. N10 —4E 30
Grand Av. Surb —5H 135
Grand Av. Wemb —5G 45
Grand Av. E. Wemb —5H 45
Grand Depot Rd. SE18 —5E 90
Grand Dri. SW20 —2E 136
Grand Dri. S'hall —2G 79
Granden Rd. SW16 —2J 139
Grandfield Ct. W4 —6K 81
Grandison Rd. SW11 —5D 102
Grandison Rd. Wor Pk —2E 148
Grand Junct. Wharf. N1 —2C 68
Grand Pde. N4 —5B 32
Grand Pde. SW14 —4J 99
(off Up. Richmond Rd. W.)
Grand Pde. Surb —1G 147
Grand Pde. Wemb —2G 45
Grand Pde. M. SW15 —5G 101
Grand Union Cen. W10 —4F 65
(off West Row)
Grand Union Clo. W9 —5H 65
Grand Union Cres. E8 —1G 69
Grand Union Ind. Est. NW10 —2H 63
Grand Union Wlk. NW1 —7F 49
(off Kentish Town Rd.)
Grand Vitesse Ind. Cen. SE1
(off Dolben St.) —1B 86 (5B 168)
Grand Wlk. E1 —4A 70
Granfield St. SW11 —1B 102
Grange Av. N12 —5F 15
Grange Av. N20 —7B 4
Grange Av. SE25 —2E 140
Grange Av. E Barn —1H 15
Grange Av. Stan —2B 26
Grange Av. Twic —2J 115
Grange Av. Wfd G —6D 20
Grangecliffe Gdns. SE25 —2E 140
Grange Clo. Edgw —5D 12
Grange Clo. Hay —5G 59
Grange Clo. Houn —6D 78
Grange Clo. Sidc —3A 128
Grange Clo. W Mol —4F 133
Grange Clo. Wfd G —7D 20
Grange Ct. NW10 —3A 46
(off Neasden La.)
Grange Ct. WC2 —6K 67 (1H 167)
Grange Ct. Harr —3K 43
Grange Ct. N'holt —2A 60
Grange Ct. Pinn —3C 24
Grange Ct. Shep —4C 130
Grange Ct. Sutt —7K 149
Grangecourt Rd. N16 —1E 50
Grange Cres. SE28 —6C 74
Grangedale Clo. N'wd —1G 23
Grange Dri. Chst —6C 126
Grange Farm Clo. Harr —2G 43
Grangefield. NW1 —7H 49
(off Marquis Rd.)
Grange Gdns. N14 —1C 16
Grange Gdns. NW3 —3K 47
Grange Gdns. SE25 —2E 140
Grange Gdns. Pinn —3C 24
Grange Gro. N1 —6C 50
Grange Hill. SE25 —2E 140
Grange Hill. Edgw —5D 12
Grangehill Pl. SE9 —3D 108
Grangehill Rd. SE9 —4D 108
Grange Ho. SE1 —3F 87
Grange La. SE21 —2F 123
Grange Lodge. SW19 —6F 119
Grange Mans. Eps —7B 148
Grange M. Felt —4J 113
Grangemill Rd. SE6 —3C 124
Grangemill Way. SE6 —2C 124
Grange Mus. of Community History. —4A 46
Grange Park. —6G 7
Grange Pk. W5 —1E 80
Grange Pk. Av. N21 —6H 7
Grange Pk. Pl. SW20 —7D 118
Grange Pk. Rd. E10 —1D 52
Grange Pk. Rd. T Hth —4D 140
Grange Pl. NW6 —7J 47
Grange Rd. E10 —1C 52
Grange Rd. E13 —3H 71
Grange Rd. E17 —5A 34
(in two parts)
Grange Rd. N6 —6E 30
Grange Rd. N17 & N18 —6B 18
Grange Rd. NW10 —6D 46
Grange Rd. SE1 —3E 86
Grange Rd. SW13 —1C 100
Grange Rd. W4 —5H 81
Grange Rd. W5 —1D 80
Grange Rd. Chess —4E 146
Grange Rd. Edgw —6E 12
Grange Rd. Harr —5A 26
Grange Rd. Hay —6G 59
Grange Rd. Ilf —4F 55
Grange Rd. King T —3E 134
Grange Rd. S'hall —2C 78
Grange Rd. S Croy —7C 152
Grange Rd. S Harr —2H 43
Grange Rd. Sutt —7J 149
Grange Rd. T Hth & SE25 —4D 140
Grange Rd. W Mol —4F 133
Grange St. N1 —1D 68
Grange, The. E17 —5A 34
(off Grange Rd.)
Grange, The. N2 —2B 30
Grange, The. N20 —1G 15
(Athenaeum Rd.)
Grange, The. N20 —1F 15
(Chandos Av.)
Grange, The. SE1 —3F 87
Grange, The. SW19 —6F 119
Grange, The. W3 —2H 81
Grange, The. W4 —5H 81
Grange, The. W13 —5C 62
Grange, The. W14 —4H 83
Grange, The. Croy —2B 154
Grange, The. N Mald —5B 136
Grange, The. Wemb —7G 45
Grange, The. Wor Pk —3K 147
Grange Va. Sutt —7K 149
Grangeview Rd. N20 —1F 15
Grange Wlk. SE1 —3E 86
Grange Wlk. M. SE1 —3E 86
(off Grange Wlk.)
Grange Way. N12 —4E 14
Grange Way. NW6 —7J 47
Grange Way. Wfd G —4F 21
Grangeway Gdns. Ilf —5C 36
Grangeway, The. N21 —6G 7
Grangewood. Bex —1F 129
Grangewood Clo. Pinn —5J 23
Grangewood Dri. Sun —7H 113
Grangewood La. Beck —6B 124
Grangewood St. E6 —1B 72
Grangewood Ter. SE25 —2D 140
Grange Yd. SE1 —3F 87
Granham Gdns. N9 —2A 18
Granite St. SE18 —5K 91
Granleigh Rd. E11 —2G 53
Gransden Av. E8 —7H 51
Gransden Ho. SE8 —5B 88
Gransden Rd. W12 —2B 82
Grantbridge St. N1 —2B 68
Grantchester. King T —2G 135
(off St Peters Rd.)
Grantchester Clo. Harr —3K 43
Grant Clo. N14 —7B 6
Grant Clo. Shep —6D 130
Grant Ct. E4 —1K 19
(off Ridgeway, The)
Grantham Clo. Edgw —3K 11
Grantham Ct. Romf —7F 39
Grantham Gdns. Romf —6F 39
Grantham Ho. SE15 —6G 87
(off Friary Est.)
Grantham Pl. W1 —1F 85 (5J 165)
Grantham Rd. E12 —4E 54
Grantham Rd. SW9 —2J 103
Grantham Rd. W4 —7A 82
Grantley Rd. Houn —2A 96
Grantley St. E1 —3K 69
Grantock Rd. E17 —1F 35
Granton Rd. SW16 —1G 139
Granton Rd. Ilf —1A 56
Granton Rd. Sidc —6C 128
Grant Pl. Croy —1F 153
Grant Rd. SW11 —4B 102
Grant Rd. Croy —1F 153
Grant Rd. Harr —3K 25
Grants Clo. NW7 —7K 13
Grants Quay Wharf. EC3 —7D 68 (3F 169)
Grant St. E13 —3J 71
Grant St. N1 —2A 68
Grantully Rd. W9 —3K 65
Grant Way. Iswth —6A 80
Granville Arc. SW9 —4A 104
Granville Av. N9 —3D 18
Granville Av. Felt —2J 113
Granville Av. Houn —5E 96
Granville Clo. Croy —2E 152
Granville Ct. N1 —1E 68
(off Colville Est.)
Granville Ct. SE14 —7A 88
(off Nynehead St.)
Granville Gdns. SW16 —1K 139
Granville Gdns. W5 —1F 81
Granville Gro. SE13 —3E 106
Granville Ho. E14 —6C 70
Granville M. Sidc —4A 128
Granville Pk. SE13 —3E 106
Granville Pl. N12 —7F 15
Granville Pl. SW6 —7K 83
Granville Pl. W1 —6E 66 (1G 165)
Granville Pl. Pinn —3B 24
Granville Point. NW2 —2H 47
Granville Rd. E17 —6D 34
Granville Rd. E18 —2K 35
Granville Rd. N4 —6K 31
Granville Rd. N12 —7F 15
Granville Rd. N13 —6E 16
Granville Rd. N22 —1B 32
Granville Rd. NW2 —2H 47
Granville Rd. NW6 —2J 65
(in two parts)
Granville Rd. SW18 —7H 101
Granville Rd. SW19 —7J 119
Granville Rd. Barn —4A 4
Granville Rd. Hay —4H 77
Granville Rd. Ilf —1F 55
Granville Rd. Sidc —4A 128
Granville Rd. Uxb —6D 40
Granville Rd. Well —3C 110
Granville Sq. SE15 —7E 86
Granville Sq. WC1 —3K 67 (2H 161)
Granville St. WC1 —3K 67 (2H 161)
Granwood Ct. Iswth —1J 97
Grape St. WC2 —6J 67 (7E 160)
Graphite Sq. SE11 —5K 85 (5G 173)
Grapsome Clo. Chess —7C 146
Grasdene Rd. SE18 —7A 92
Grasmere. NW1 —3F 67 (2K 159)
(off Osnaburgh St.)
Grasmere Av. SW15 —4K 117
Grasmere Av. SW19 —3J 137
Grasmere Av. W3 —7K 63
Grasmere Av. Houn —6F 97
Grasmere Av. Orp —3E 156
Grasmere Av. Ruis —7E 22
Grasmere Av. Wemb —7C 26
Grasmere Clo. Felt —1H 113
Grasmere Ct. N22 —6E 16
Grasmere Ct. SE26 —5G 123
Grasmere Ct. Sutt —6A 150
Grasmere Gdns. Harr —2A 26
Grasmere Gdns. Ilf —5D 36
Grasmere Gdns. Orp —3E 156
Grasmere Point. SE15 —7J 87
(off Old Kent Rd.)
Grasmere Rd. E13 —2J 71
Grasmere Rd. N10 —1F 31
Grasmere Rd. N17 —6B 18
Grasmere Rd. SE25 —6H 141
Grasmere Rd. SW16 —5K 121
Grasmere Rd. Bexh —2J 111
Grasmere Rd. Brom —1H 143
Grasmere Rd. Orp —3E 156
Grasshaven Way. SE28 —1K 91
(in two parts)
Grassington Clo. N11 —6K 15
Grassington Rd. Sidc —4A 128
Grassmount. SE23 —2H 123
Grass Pk. N3 —1H 29
Grass Way. Wall —4G 151
Grasvenor Av. Barn —5D 4
Gratton Rd. W14 —3G 83
Gratton Ter. NW2 —3F 47
Gravel Hill. N3 —2H 29
Gravel Hill. Bexh —5H 111
Gravel Hill. Croy —6K 153
Gravel Hill. Uxb —5A 40
Gravel Hill Clo. Bexh —5H 111
Gravel La. E1 —6F 69 (7J 163)
Gravel Pit La. SE9 —5F 109
Gravel Rd. Brom —3C 156
Gravel Rd. Twic —1J 115
Gravelwood Clo. Chst —3G 127
Gravenel Gdns. SW17 —5C 120
(off Nutwell St.)
Graveney Gro. SE20 —7J 123
Graveney Rd. SW17 —4C 120
Gravesend Rd. W12 —7C 64
Gray Av. Dag —1F 57
Grayham Cres. N Mald —4K 135
Grayham Rd. N Mald —4K 135
Gray Ho. SE17 —5C 86
Grayland Clo. Brom —1B 144
Grayling Clo. E16 —4G 71
Grayling Ct. W5 —1D 80
(off Grange Rd.)
Grayling Rd. N16 —2D 50
Grayling Sq. E2 —3G 69
(off Nelson Gdns.)
Grays Ct. Dag —7H 57
Grayscroft Rd. SW16 —7H 121
Grays Farm Rd. Orp —7B 128
Grayshott Rd. SW11 —2E 102
Gray's Inn. —5K 67 (5H 161)
Gray's Inn Bldgs. EC1 —4A 68 (4J 161)
(off Rosebery Av.)
Gray's Inn Pl. WC1 —5K 67 (6H 161)
Gray's Inn Rd. WC1 —3J 67 (1F 161)
Gray's Inn Sq. WC1 —5K 67 (5J 161)
Grays La. Ashf —4D 112
Grayson Ho. EC1 —2D 162
Grays Rd. Uxb —2A 58
Gray St. SE1 —2A 86 (7K 167)
Grayswood Gdns. SW20 —2D 136
Gray's Yd. W1 —1H 165
Graywood Ct. N12 —7F 15
Grazebrook Rd. N16 —2D 50
Grazeley Clo. Bexh —5J 111
Grazeley Ct. SE19 —5E 122
Gt. Acre Ct. SW4 —4H 103
Gt. Arthur Ho. EC1 —4C 68 (4C 162)
(off Golden La. Est.)
Gt. Bell All. EC2 —6D 68 (7E 162)
Great Benty. W Dray —4A 76
Great Brownings. SE21 —4F 123
Gt. Bushey Dri. N20 —1E 14
Gt. Cambridge Ind. Est. Enf —5C 8
Great Cambridge Junction. (Junct.) —5J 17
Gt. Cambridge Rd. N18 & Enf —4J 17
Gt. Castle St. W1 —6F 67 (7K 159)
Gt. Central Av. Ruis —5A 42
Gt. Central St. NW1 —5D 66 (5E 158)
Gt. Central Way. NW10 —5A 46
Gt. Central Way. Wemb & NW10 —4J 45
Gt. Chapel St. W1 —6H 67 (7C 160)
Gt. Chertsey Rd. W4 —2J 99
Gt. Chertsey Rd. Felt —3D 114
Gt. Church La. W6 —4F 83
Gt. College St. SW1 —3J 85 (1E 172)
Great Cft. WC1 —3J 67 (2F 161)
(off Cromer St.)
Gt. Cross Av. SE10 —7F 89
(in three parts)
Gt. Cumberland M. W1 —6D 66 (1E 164)
Gt. Cumberland Pl. W1 —6D 66 (7E 158)
Gt. Dover St. SE1 —2C 86 (7D 168)
Greatdown Rd. W7 —4K 61
Gt. Eastern Bldgs. E1 —5G 69
(off Fieldgate St.)
Gt. Eastern Enterprise Cen. E14 —2D 88
Gt. Eastern Rd. E15 —7F 53
Gt. Eastern St. EC2 —3E 68 (2G 163)
Gt. Eastern Wlk. EC2 —6H 163
Gt. Eastern Wharf. SW11 —7C 84
Gt. Elms Rd. Brom —4A 144
Great Fld. NW9 —1A 28
Greatfield Av. E6 —4D 72
Greatfield Clo. N19 —4G 49
Greatfield Clo. SE4 —4C 106
Greatfields Dri. Uxb —5C 58
Greatfields Rd. Bark —1H 73
Gt. Fleete Way. Bark —2C 74
Gt. Galley Clo. Bark —3B 74
Gt. Gatton Clo. Croy —7A 142
Gt. George St. SW1 —2H 85 (7D 166)
Gt. Guildford Bus. Sq. SE1 —5C 168
Gt. Guildford St. SE1 —1C 86 (4C 168)
Greatham Wlk. SW15 —1C 118
Gt. Harry Dri. SE9 —3E 126
Gt. James St. WC1 —5K 67 (5G 161)
Gt. Marlborough St. W1 —6G 67 (1A 166)
Gt. Maze Pond. SE1 —2D 86 (5F 169)
(in two parts)
Gt. Newport St. WC2 —7J 67 (2E 166)
Gt. New St. EC4 —6A 68 (7K 161)
Gt. N. Leisure Pk. N12 —7G 15
Gt. North Rd. N2 & N6 —5C 30
Gt. North Rd. Barn —2C 4
Gt. North Rd. New Bar —5D 4
Gt. North Way. NW4 —2D 28
Greatorex Ho. E1 —5G 69
(off Greatorex St.)
Greatorex St. E1 —5G 69
Gt. Ormond St. WC1 —5J 67 (5F 161)
Gt. Owl Rd. Chig —3K 21
Gt. Percy St. WC1 —3K 67 (1H 161)
Gt. Peter St. SW1 —3H 85 (2C 172)
Gt. Portland St. W1 —4F 67 (4K 159)
Gt. Pulteney St. W1 —7G 67 (2B 166)
Gt. Queen St. WC2 —6J 67 (1F 167)
Gt. Russell St. WC1 —6H 67 (7D 160)
Gt. St Helen's. EC3 —6E 68 (7G 163)
Gt. St Thomas Apostle. EC4 —7C 68 (2D 168)
Gt. Scotland Yd. SW1 —1J 85 (5E 166)
Gt. Smith St. SW1 —3H 85 (1D 172)
Gt. South W. Rd. Bedf & Felt —7E 94
Great Spilmans. SE22 —5E 104
Great Strand. NW9 —1B 28
Gt. Suffolk St. SE1 —1B 86 (5B 168)
Gt. Sutton St. EC1 —4B 68 (4B 162)
Gt. Swan All. EC2 —6D 68 (7E 162)
(in two parts)
Great Thrift. Orp —4G 145
Gt. Titchfield St. W1 —4F 67 (4K 159)
Gt. Tower St. EC3 —7E 68 (2G 169)
Gt. Trinity La. EC4 —7C 68 (2D 168)
Great Turnstile. WC1 —5K 67 (6H 161)
Gt. Western Ind. Pk. S'hall —2F 79
Gt. Western Rd. W9 & W11 —5H 65
Gt. West Rd. W4 & W6 —5B 82
Gt. West Rd. Houn & Iswth —2B 96
Gt. West Rd. Iswth —7A 80
Gt. West Trad. Est. Bren —6B 80
Gt. Winchester St. EC2 —6D 68 (7F 163)
Gt. Windmill St. W1 —7H 67 (2C 166)
Greatwood. Chst —7E 126
Great Yd. SE1 —6H 169
Greaves Clo. Bark —7H 55
Greaves Cotts. E14 —5A 70
Greaves Pl. SW17 —4C 120
Greaves Tower. SW10 —7A 84
(off Worlds End Est.)
Grebe Av. Hay —6B 60
Grebe Clo. E7 —5H 53
Grebe Clo. E17 —7F 19
Grebe Ct. E14 —2E 88
Grebe Ct. SE8 —6B 88
(off Dorking Clo.)
Grebe Ct. Sutt —5H 149
Grebe Ter. King T —3E 134
Grecian Cres. SE19 —6B 122
Greek Ct. W1 —6H 67 (1D 166)
Greek St. W1 —6H 67 (1D 166)
Greenacre Clo. Barn —1C 4
Greenacre Clo. N'holt —5D 42
Greenacre Gdns. E17 —4E 34
Greenacre Pl. Hack —2F 151
Greenacres. N3 —2H 29
Greenacres. SE9 —6E 108
Greenacres. Bus H —2C 10
Green Acres. Croy —3F 153
Greenacres. Sidc —4A 128
Greenacres Av. Uxb —3B 40
Greenacres Dri. Stan —6G 11
Greenacre Sq. SE16 —2K 87
Greenacre Wlk. N14 —3C 16
Grn. Arbour Ct. EC4 —6B 68 (7A 162)
(off Old Bailey)
Green Av. NW7 —4E 12
Green Av. W13 —3B 80
Greenaway Gdns. NW3 —4K 47
Greenaway Ho. NW8 —1A 66
(off Boundary Rd.)
Greenaway Ho. WC1 —3A 68 (2J 161)
(off Fernsbury St.)
Green Bank. E1 —1H 87
Greenbank. N12 —4E 14
Greenbank Av. Wemb —5A 44
Green Bank Clo. E4 —2K 19
Greenbank Cres. NW4 —4G 29
Greenbanks. Harr —4J 43
Greenbay Rd. SE7 —7B 90
Greenberry St. NW8 —2C 66 (1C 158)
Greenbrook Av. Barn —1F 5
Green Clo. E15 —1G 71
Green Clo. NW9 —6J 27
Green Clo. NW11 —7A 30
Green Clo. Brom —3G 143
Green Clo. Cars —2D 150
Green Clo. Felt —5C 114
Greencoat Mans. SW1 —3G 85 (2B 172)
(off Greencoat Row)
Greencoat Pl. SW1 —4G 85 (2B 172)
Greencoat Row. SW1 —3G 85 (2B 172)
Greencourt Av. Croy —2H 153
Greencourt Av. Edgw —1H 27
Greencourt Gdns. Croy —1H 153
Greencourt Rd. Orp —5H 145
Greencrest Pl. NW2 —3C 46
Greencroft. Edgw —5D 12
Greencroft Av. Ruis —2A 42
Greencroft Clo. E6 —5B 72
Greencroft Gdns. NW6 —7K 47
Greencroft Gdns. Enf —3K 7
Greencroft Rd. Houn —1D 96
Greendale. NW7 —4F 13
Green Dale. SE5 —4D 104
Green Dale. SE22 —5E 104
Grn. Dale Clo. SE22 —5E 104
Grn. Dragon Ct. SE1 —4E 168
Grn. Dragon La. N21 —6F 7
Grn. Dragon La. Bren —5E 80
Grn. Dragon Yd. E1 —5G 69 (6K 163)
Green Dri. S'hall —1E 78
Greene Ho. SE1 —3D 86
(off Burbage Clo.)
Green End. N21 —2G 17
Green End. Chess —4E 146
Greenend Rd. W4 —2A 82
Greener Ho. SW4 —3H 103
Greenfell Mans. SE8 —6D 88
Greenfield Av. Surb —7H 135
Greenfield Dri. N2 —4D 30
Greenfield Dri. Brom —2A 144
Greenfield Gdns. NW2 —2G 47
Greenfield Gdns. Dag —1D 74
Greenfield Gdns. Orp —7H 145
Greenfield Rd. E1 —5G 69
Greenfield Rd. N15 —5E 32
Greenfield Rd. Dag —7C 56
Greenfield Rd. Dart —5K 129
Greenfields. S'hall —6E 60
Greenfield Way. Harr —3F 25
Greenford. —3G 61
Greenford Av. W7 —4J 61
Greenford Av. S'hall —7D 60
Greenford Bus. Cen. Gnfd —7H 43
Greenford Gdns. Gnfd —3F 61
Greenford Green. —6J 43
Greenford Ind. Est. N'holt —7F 43
Greenford Rd. S'hall & Gnfd —1G 79
Greenford Rd. Sutt —4K 149
(in two parts)
Greenford Roundabout. (Junct.) —2H 61
Greengate. Gnfd —6B 44
Greengate Lodge. E13 —2K 71
(off Hollybush St.)
Greengate St. E13 —2K 71
Greenhalgh Wlk. N2 —4A 30
Greenham Clo. SE1 —2A 86 (7J 167)
Greenham Cres. E4 —6G 19
Greenham Ho. Houn —3H 97
Greenham Rd. N10 —2E 30
Greenhaven Dri. SE28 —6B 74
Greenheath Bus. Cen. E2 —4H 69
(off Three Colts La.)
Green Hedge. Twic —5C 98
Greenheys Clo. N'wd —1G 23
Greenheys Dri. E18 —3H 35
Greenhill. —5J 25
Greenhill. NW3 —4B 48
Green Hill. SE18 —5D 90
Greenhill. Buck H —1F 21
Greenhill. Sutt —2A 150
Greenhill. Wemb —2H 45
Greenhill Ct. SE18 —5D 90
Greenhill Ct. New Bar —5E 4
Greenhill Gdns. N'holt —2D 60
Greenhill Gro. E12 —4C 54
Greenhill Pde. New Bar —5E 4
Greenhill Pk. NW10 —1A 64
Greenhill Pk. New Bar —5E 4
Greenhill Rd. NW10 —1A 64
Greenhill Rd. Harr —6J 25
Greenhill's Rents. EC1 —5B 68 (5A 162)
Greenhills Ter. N1 —6D 50
Greenhill Ter. SE18 —5D 90
Greenhill Ter. N'holt —2D 60
Greenhill Way. Harr —6J 25
Greenhill Way. Wemb —2H 45
Greenhithe Clo. Sidc —7J 109
Greenholm Rd. SE9 —5F 109
Grn. Hundred Rd. SE15 —6G 87
Greenhurst Rd. SE27 —5A 122
Greening St. SE2 —4C 92
Greenland Cres. S'hall —3A 78
Greenland M. SE8 —5K 87
Greenland Pl. NW1 —1F 67
Greenland Quay. SE16 —4K 87
Greenland Rd. NW1 —1G 67
Greenland Rd. Barn —6A 4
Greenland St. NW1 —1F 67
Green La. NW4 —4F 29
Green La. SE20 —7K 123
Green La. W7 —2J 79
Green La. SE9 & Chst —1F 127
Green La. SW16 & T Hth —7K 121
Green La. Chess —7D 146
(in two parts)
Green La. Edgw —4A 12
Green La. Felt —5C 114
Green La. Harr —3J 43
Green La. Houn —3K 95
Green La. Ilf & Dag —2H 55
Green La. Mord —7E 136
(Battersea Cemetery)
Green La. Mord —6J 137
(Morden)
Green La. N Mald —5J 135
Green La. Shep —6E 130
Green La. Stan —4G 11
Green La. Sun —7H 113
Green La. Uxb —5E 58
Green La. W Mol —5F 133
Green La. Wor Pk —1C 148
Green La. Cotts. Stan —4G 11
Green La. Gdns. T Hth —2C 140
Green Lanes. N8 & N4 —3B 32
Green Lanes. N13 & N21 —3F 17
Green Lanes. Eps —7A 148
(in two parts)
Greenlaw Ct. W5 —6D 62
(off Mount Pk. Rd.)
Greenlaw Gdns. N Mald —7B 136
Greenlawns. N12 —6E 14
Green Lawns. Ruis —1A 42
Greenlaw St. SE18 —3E 90
Green Leaf Av. Wall —4H 151
Greenleaf Clo. SW2 —7A 104
Greenleafe Dri. Ilf —3F 37
Greenleaf Rd. E6 —1A 72
Greenleaf Rd. E17 —3B 34
Green Leas. Sun —6H 113
Green Leas Clo. Sun —6H 113
Greenleaves Ct. Ashf —6D 112
Green Man Gdns. W13 —7A 62
Green Man La. W13 —7A 62
Green Man La. Felt —4J 95
Green Man Pas. W13 —7A 62
(in two parts)
Green Man Roundabout. (Junct.) —7H 35
Greenman St. N1 —7C 50
Greenmead. Eri —3E 92
Greenmead Clo. SE25 —5G 141
Green Moor Link. N21 —7G 7
Greenmoor Rd. Enf —2D 8
Greenoak Clo. Cockf —2J 5
Green Oaks. S'hall —4B 78
Greenoak Way. SW19 —4F 119
Greenock Rd. SW16 —1H 139
Greenock Rd. W3 —3H 81

Greeno Cres.—Guildhall Library

Greeno Cres. Shep —5C 130
Green Pde. Houn —5F 97
Green Pk. —2F 85 (5K 165)
Greenpark Ct. Wemb —7C 44
Grn. Park Way. Gnfd —7J 43
Green Point. E15 —6G 53
Grn. Pond Clo. E17 —3A 34
Grn. Pond Rd. E17 —3A 34
Greenrigg Wlk. Wemb —3H 45
Green Rd. N14 —6A 6
Green Rd. N20 —3F 15
Green's Ct. W1 —2C 166
Green's End. SE18 —4F 91
Greenshank Clo. E17 —7F 19
Greenshields Ind. Est. E16 —2J 89
Greenside. Bex —1E 128
Green Side. Dag —1C 56
Greenside Clo. N20 —2G 15
Greenside Clo. SE6 —2F 125
Greenside Rd. W12 —3C 82
Greenside Rd. Croy —7A 140
Greenslade Rd. Bark —7H 55
Greenstead Av. Wfd G —7F 21
Greenstead Clo. Wfd G —6F 21
Greenstead Gdns. SW15 —5D 100
Greenstead Gdns. Wfd G —6F 21
Greensted Rd. Lou —1H 21
Greenstone M. E11 —6J 35
Green St. E7 & E13 —6K 53
Green St. W1 —7E 66 (2G 165)
Green St. Enf —2D 8
Green St. Sun —1J 131
Greenstreet Hill. SE14 —2K 105
Green Ter. EC1 —3A 68 (2K 161)
Green, The. E4 —1K 19
Green, The. E11 —6K 35
Green, The. E15 —6G 53
Green, The. N9 —2B 18
Green, The. N14 —2C 16
Green, The. N17 —6H 17
Green, The. N21 —7F 7
Green, The. SW19 —5F 119
Green, The. W3 —6A 64
Green, The. W5 —1D 80
Green, The. Bexh —1G 111
Green, The. Brom —3J 125
(in two parts)
Green, The. Buck H —1E 20
Green, The. Cars —4E 150
Green, The. Croy —7B 154
Green, The. Felt —2K 113
Green, The. Hayes —7J 143
Green, The. Houn —6E 78
Green, The. Ick —2E 40
Green, The. Mord —4G 137
Green, The. N Mald —3K 135
Green, The. Orp —4E 156
Green, The. Rich —5D 98
Green, The. St P —7B 128
Green, The. Shep —4G 131
Green, The. Sidc —4A 128
Green, The. S'hall —3C 78
Green, The. Sutt —3K 149
Green, The. Twic —1J 115
Green, The. Well —4J 109
Green, The. Wemb —2A 44
Green, The. W Dray —3A 76
Green, The. Wfd G —5D 20
Green Va. W5 —6F 63
Green Va. Bexh —5D 110
Greenvale Rd. SE9 —4D 108
Green Verges. Stan —7J 11
Green Vw. Chess —7F 147
Greenview Av. Beck —6A 142
Greenview Av. Croy —6A 142
Greenview Clo. W3 —1A 82
Greenview Ct. Ashf —4B 112
Green Wlk. NW4 —5F 29
Green Wlk. SE1 —3E 86
Green Wlk. Hamp —6D 114
Green Wlk. Lou —1H 21
Green Wlk. Ruis —1H 41
Green Wlk. S'hall —5E 78
Green Wlk. Wfd G —6H 21
Green Wlk., The. E4 —1A 20
Greenway. N14 —2D 16
Greenway. N20 —2D 14
Green Way. SE9 —5B 108
Greenway. SW20 —4E 136
Green Way. Brom —6C 144
Greenway. Chst —5E 126
Greenway. Dag —2C 56
Greenway. Hay —3J 59
Greenway. Kent —5E 26
Greenway. Pinn —2K 23
Green Way. Sun —4J 131
Greenway. Wall —4G 151
Greenway. Wfd G —5F 21
Greenway Av. E17 —4F 35
Greenway Clo. N4 —2C 50
Greenway Clo. N11 —6K 15
Greenway Clo. N15 —4F 33
Greenway Clo. N20 —2D 14
Greenway Clo. NW9 —2K 27
Greenway Gdns. NW9 —2K 27
Greenway Gdns. Croy —3B 154
Greenway Gdns. Gnfd —3E 60
Greenway Gdns. Harr —2J 25
Greenways. Beck —3C 142
Greenways, The. Twic —6A 98
Greenway, The. NW9 —2K 27
Greenway, The. Houn —4D 96
Greenway, The. Ick —2E 40
Green Way, The. Pinn —6D 24
Greenway, The. Uxb —2A 58
Green Way, The. W'stone —1J 25
Greenwell St. W1 —4F 67 (4K 159)
Greenwich. —7E 88
Greenwich Bus. Pk. SE10 —7D 88
Greenwich Chu. St. SE10 —6E 88
Greenwich Cres. E6 —5C 72
Greenwich Gateway Vis. Cen. —6E 88
Greenwich High Rd. SE10 —1D 106
Greenwich Ind. Est. SE7 —4K 89
Greenwich Ind. Est. SE10 —7D 88
Greenwich Mkt. SE10 —6E 88
Greenwich Pk. —7G 89
Greenwich Pk. St. SE10 —6F 89
Greenwich S. St. SE10 —1D 106
Greenwich Vw. Pl. E14 —3D 88
Greenwood Av. Dag —4H 57
Greenwood Av. Enf —2F 9
Greenwood Bus. Cen. Croy —7F 141
Greenwood Clo. Bus H —1D 10
Greenwood Clo. Mord —4G 137
Greenwood Clo. Orp —6J 145
Greenwood Clo. Sidc —2A 128
Greenwood Clo. Th Dit —1A 146
Greenwood Dri. E4 —5A 20
Greenwood Gdns. N13 —3G 17
Greenwood Gdns. Ilf —1G 37
Greenwood Ho. N22 —1A 32
Greenwood Ho. SE4 —4K 105
Greenwood La. Hamp H —5F 115
Greenwood Mans. Bark —7A 56
(off Lansbury Av.)
Greenwood Pk. King T —7A 118
Greenwood Pl. NW5 —5F 49
Greenwood Rd. E8 —6G 51
Greenwood Rd. E13 —2H 71
Greenwood Rd. Bex —4K 129
Greenwood Rd. Croy —7B 140
Greenwood Rd. Iswth —3K 97
Greenwood Rd. Mitc —3H 139
Greenwood Rd. Th Dit —1A 146
Greenwoods, The. S Harr —3G 43
Greenwood Ter. NW10 —1K 63
Green Wrythe Cres. Cars —1C 150
Green Wrythe La. Cars —6B 138
Green Yd. WC1 —3H 161
Green Yd., The. EC3 —1G 169
Greer Rd. Harr —1G 25
Greet Ho. SE1 —7K 167
Greet St. SE1 —1A 86 (5K 167)
Greg Clo. E10 —6E 34
Gregory Clo. Brom —4G 143
Gregory Cres. SE9 —7B 108
Gregory Pl. W8 —2K 83
Gregory Rd. Romf —4D 38
Gregory Rd. S'hall —3E 78
Greig Clo. N8 —5J 31
Greig Ter. SE17 —6B 86
Grenaby Av. Croy —7D 140
Grenaby Rd. Croy —7D 140
Grenada Ho. E14 —7B 70
Grenada Rd. SE7 —7A 90
Grenade St. E14 —7B 70
Grenadier St. E16 —1E 90
Grena Gdns. Rich —4F 99
Grena Rd. Rich —4F 99
Grendon Gdns. Wemb —2G 45
Grendon Ho. E9 —7J 51
(off Shore Pl.)
Grendon Ho. N1 —2K 67
(off Priory Grn. Est.)
Grendon Lodge. Edgw —2D 12
Grendon St. NW8 —4C 66 (3C 158)
Grenfell Ct. NW7 —6J 13
Grenfell Gdns. Harr —7E 26
Grenfell Gdns. Ilf —5K 37
Grenfell Ho. SE5 —7C 86
Grenfell Rd. SW17 —6D 120
Grenfell Rd. W11 —7F 65
Grenfell Tower. W11 —7F 65
Grenfell Wlk. W11 —7F 65
Grennell Clo. Sutt —2B 150
Grennell Rd. Sutt —2A 150
Grenoble Gdns. N13 —6F 17
Grenville Clo. N3 —1G 29
Grenville Clo. Surb —1J 147
Grenville Ct. W13 —5B 62
Grenville Gdns. Wfd G —1A 36
Grenville Ho. SW1 —6H 85 (7C 172)
(off Dolphin Sq.)
Grenville M. SW7 —4A 84
(off Harrington Gdns.)
Grenville M. Hamp —5F 115
Grenville Pl. NW7 —5E 12
Grenville Pl. SW7 —3A 84
Grenville Rd. N19 —1J 49
Grenville St. WC1 —4J 67 (4F 161)
Gresham Av. N20 —4J 15
Gresham Clo. Bex —6E 110
Gresham Clo. Enf —3H 7
Gresham Dri. Romf —5B 38
Gresham Gdns. NW11 —1G 47
Gresham Lodge. E17 —5D 34
Gresham M. W4 —3J 81
Gresham Rd. E6 —2D 72
Gresham Rd. E16 —6K 71
Gresham Rd. NW10 —5K 45
Gresham Rd. SE25 —4G 141
Gresham Rd. SW9 —3A 104
Gresham Rd. Beck —2A 142
Gresham Rd. Edgw —6A 12
Gresham Rd. Hamp —6E 114
Gresham Rd. Houn —1G 97
Gresham Rd. Uxb —2C 58
Gresham St. EC2 —6C 68 (7C 162)
Gresham Way. SW19 —3K 119
Gresley Clo. E17 —6A 34
Gresley Clo. N15 —4D 32
Gresley Rd. N19 —1G 49
Gressenhall Rd. SW18 —6H 101
Gresse St. W1 —6H 67 (6C 160)
Gresswell Clo. Sidc —3A 128
Greswell St. SW6 —1F 101
Gretton Rd. N17 —7A 18
Greville Clo. Twic —7B 98
Greville Ct. Harr —4J 43
Greville Hall. NW6 —2K 65
Greville Lodge. E13 —1K 71
Greville Lodge. N12 —5E 14
Greville Lodge. Edgw —4C 12
(off Broadhurst Av.)
Greville M. NW6 —1K 65
(off Greville Rd.)
Greville Pl. NW6 —2K 65
Greville Rd. E17 —4E 34
Greville Rd. NW6 —2K 65
Greville Rd. Rich —6F 99
Greville St. EC1 —5A 68 (6J 161)
(in two parts)
Grey Clo. NW11 —6A 30
Greycoat Gdns. SW1 —3H 85 (2C 172)
(off Greycoat St.)
Greycoat Pl. SW1 —3H 85 (2C 172)
Greycoat St. SW1 —3H 85 (2C 172)
Greycot Rd. Beck —5C 124
Grey Eagle St. E1 —4F 69 (4K 163)
Greyfell Clo. Stan —5H 11
Greyfriars. SE26 —3G 123
(off Wells Pk. Rd.)
Greyfriars Pas. EC1 —6B 68 (7B 162)
Greyhound Commercial Cen., The. Dart —5K 111
Greyhound Ct. WC2 —7K 67 (2H 167)
Greyhound Hill. NW4 —3C 28
Greyhound La. SW16 —6H 121
Greyhound Mans. W6 —6G 83
(off Greyhound Rd.)
Greyhound Rd. N15 —3E 32
Greyhound Rd. NW10 —3D 64
Greyhound Rd. W6 & W14 —6F 83
Greyhound Rd. Sutt —5A 150
Greyhound Ter. SW16 —1G 139
Grey Ho. W12 —7D 64
(off White City Est.)
Greyladies Gdns. SE10 —2E 106
Greys Pk. Clo. Kes —5B 156
Greystead Rd. SE23 —7J 105
Greystoke Av. Pinn —3E 24
Greystoke Ct. W5 —4E 62
Greystoke Dri. Ruis —7D 22
Greystoke Gdns. W5 —4E 62
Greystoke Gdns. Enf —4C 6
Greystoke Ho. SE15 —6G 87
(off Peckham Pk. Rd.)
Greystoke Lodge. W5 —4F 63
(off Hanger La.)
Greystoke Pk. Ter. W5 —3D 62
Greystoke Pl. EC4 —6A 68 (7J 161)
Greystone Gdns. Harr —6C 26
Greystone Gdns. Ilf —2G 37
Greystone Path. E11 —7H 35
(off Mornington Rd.)
Greyswood St. SW16 —6F 121
Grey Turner Ho. W12 —6C 64
Grierson Rd. SE23 —7K 105
Griffin Cen. Felt —5K 95
Griffin Cen., The. King T —2D 134
(off Market Pl.)
Griffin Clo. NW10 —5D 46
Griffin Ct. W4 —5B 82
Griffin Ct. Bren —6E 80
Griffin Ho. E14 —6D 70
Griffin Mnr. Way. SE28 —3H 91
Griffin Rd. N17 —2E 32
Griffin Rd. SE18 —5H 91
Griffin Way. Sun —2J 131
Griffith Clo. Dag —7C 38
Griffiths Clo. Wor Pk —2D 148
Griffiths Rd. SW19 —7J 119
Griggs App. Ilf —2G 55
Grigg's Pl. SE1 —3E 86
(off Grange Rd.)
Griggs Rd. E10 —6E 34
Grilse Clo. N9 —4C 18
Grimaldi Ho. N1 —2K 67
(off Priory Grn. Est.)
Grimsby Gro. E16 —2F 91
Grimsby St. E2 —4F 69 (4K 163)
Grimsel Path. SE5 —7B 86
Grimshaw Clo. N6 —7E 30
Grimston Rd. SW6 —2H 101
Grimthorpe Ho. EC1 —3A 162
Grimwade Av. Croy —3G 153
Grimwade Clo. SE15 —3J 105
Grimwood Rd. Twic —7K 97
Grindall Clo. Croy —4B 152
Grindal St. SE1 —2A 86 (7J 167)
Grindleford Av. N11 —2K 15
Grindley Gdns. Croy —6F 141
Grindley Ho. E3 —5B 70
Grinling Pl. SE8 —6C 88
Grinstead Rd. SE8 —5A 88
Grisedale. NW1 —3G 67 (1A 160)
(off Cumberland Mkt.)
Grittleton Av. Wemb —6H 45
Grittleton Rd. W9 —4J 65
Grizedale Ter. SE23 —2H 123
Grocer's Hall Ct. EC2 —6D 68 (1E 168)
Grocer's Hall Gdns. EC2 —1E 168
Grogan Clo. Hamp —6D 114
Groombridge Clo. Well —5A 110
Groombridge Rd. E9 —7K 51
Groom Clo. Brom —4K 143
Groom Cres. SW18 —7B 102
Groome Ho. SE11 —4K 85 (4H 173)
Groomfield Clo. SW17 —4E 120
Groom Pl. SW1 —3E 84 (1H 171)
Grooms Dri. Pinn —5J 23
Grosmont Rd. SE18 —6K 91
Grosse Way. SW15 —6D 100
Grosvenor Av. N5 —5C 50
Grosvenor Av. SW14 —3A 100
Grosvenor Av. Cars —6D 150
Grosvenor Av. Harr —6F 25
Grosvenor Av. Hay —2H 59
Grosvenor Av. Rich —5E 98
Grosvenor Cotts. SW1 —4E 84 (3G 171)
Grosvenor Ct. E10 —1D 52
Grosvenor Ct. N14 —7B 6
Grosvenor Ct. NW6 —1F 65
Grosvenor Ct. NW7 —5E 12
(off Hale La.)
Grosvenor Ct. SE5 —6C 86
Grosvenor Ct. W3 —1G 81
Grosvenor Ct. W5 —7E 62
(off Grove, The)
Grosvenor Ct. Mans. W2 —6D 66 (1E 164)
(off Edgware Rd.)
Grosvenor Cres. NW9 —4G 27
Grosvenor Cres. SW1 —2E 84 (7H 165)
Grosvenor Cres. Uxb —7D 40
Grosvenor Cres. M. SW1 —2E 84 (7G 165)
Grosvenor Est. SW1 —4H 85 (3D 172)
Grosvenor Gdns. E6 —3B 72
Grosvenor Gdns. N10 —3G 31
Grosvenor Gdns. N14 —5C 6
Grosvenor Gdns. NW2 —6E 46
Grosvenor Gdns. NW11 —6H 29
Grosvenor Gdns. SW1 —3F 85 (1J 171)
Grosvenor Gdns. SW14 —3A 100
Grosvenor Gdns. King T —6D 116
Grosvenor Gdns. Wall —7G 151
Grosvenor Gdns. Wfd G —6D 20
Grosvenor Gdns. M. E. SW1 —1K 171
Grosvenor Gdns. M. N. SW1 —2J 171
Grosvenor Gdns. M. S. SW1 —2K 171
Grosvenor Ga. W1 —7E 66 (3G 165)
Grosvenor Hill. SW19 —6G 119
Grosvenor Hill. W1 —7F 67 (2J 165)
Grosvenor Hill Ct. W1 —7F 67 (2J 165)
(off Bourdon St.)
Grosvenor Pde. W5 —1G 81
(off Uxbridge Rd.)
Grosvenor Pk. SE5 —7C 86
Grosvenor Pk. Rd. E17 —5C 34
Grosvenor Pl. SW1 —2E 84 (7H 165)
Grosvenor Ri. E. E17 —5D 34
Grosvenor Rd. E6 —1B 72
Grosvenor Rd. E7 —6K 53
Grosvenor Rd. E10 —1E 52
Grosvenor Rd. E11 —5K 35
Grosvenor Rd. N3 —7C 14
Grosvenor Rd. N9 —1C 18
Grosvenor Rd. N10 —1F 31
Grosvenor Rd. SE25 —4F 141
Grosvenor Rd. SW1 —6F 85 (7J 171)
Grosvenor Rd. W4 —5H 81
Grosvenor Rd. W7 —1A 80
Grosvenor Rd. Belv —6G 93
Grosvenor Rd. Bexh —5D 110
Grosvenor Rd. Bren —6D 80
Grosvenor Rd. Dag —1F 57
Grosvenor Rd. Houn —3D 96
Grosvenor Rd. Ilf —3G 55
Grosvenor Rd. Orp —6J 145
Grosvenor Rd. Rich —5E 98
Grosvenor Rd. Romf —7K 39
Grosvenor Rd. S'hall —3D 78
Grosvenor Rd. Twic —1A 116
Grosvenor Rd. Wall —6F 151
Grosvenor Rd. W W'ck —1D 154
Grosvenor Sq. W1 —7E 66 (2H 165)
Grosvenor St. W1 —7F 67 (2J 165)
Grosvenor Ter. SE5 —7C 86
Grosvenor Va. Ruis —2H 41
Grosvenor Way. E5 —2J 51
Grosvenor Wharf Rd. E14 —4F 89
Grotes Bldgs. SE3 —2G 107
Grote's Pl. SE3 —2G 107
Groton Rd. SW18 —2K 119
Grotto Ct. SE1 —2B 86 (6B 168)
Grotto Pas. W1 —5E 66 (5H 159)
Grotto Rd. Twic —2K 115
Grove Av. N3 —7D 14
Grove Av. N10 —2G 31
Grove Av. W7 —6J 61
Grove Av. Pinn —4C 24
Grove Av. Sutt —6J 149
Grove Av. Twic —1K 115
Grovebury Clo. Eri —6K 93
Grovebury Ct. N14 —7C 6
Grovebury Ct. Bexh —5H 111
Grovebury Rd. SE2 —2B 92
Grove Clo. N14 —7B 6
Grove Clo. SE23 —1A 124
Grove Clo. Brom —2J 155
Grove Clo. Felt —4C 114
Grove Clo. King T —4F 135
Grove Clo. Uxb —5C 40
Grove Cotts. W4 —6A 82
Grove Ct. NW8 —1A 158
Grove Ct. SW10 —5A 84 (6A 170)
(off Drayton Gdns.)
Grove Ct. W5 —1E 80
Grove Ct. E Mol —4H 133
Grove Ct. Houn —4E 96
Grove Cres. E18 —2H 35
Grove Cres. NW9 —4J 27
Grove Cres. Felt —4C 114
Grove Cres. King T —3E 134
Grove Cres. W on T —7K 131
Grove Cres. Rd. E15 —6F 53
Grovedale Rd. N19 —2H 49
Grove Dwellings. E1 —5J 69
Grove End. E18 —2H 35
Grove End. NW5 —4F 49
Grove End Gdns. NW8 —2B 66
Grove End Ho. NW8 —2A 158
Grove End La. Esh —7H 133
Grove End Rd. NW8 —2B 66 (1A 158)
Grovefield. N11 —4A 16
(off Coppies Gro.)
Grove Footpath. Surb —4E 134
Grove Gdns. NW4 —5C 28
Grove Gdns. NW8 —3C 66 (2D 158)
Grove Gdns. Dag —3J 57
Grove Gdns. Enf —1E 8
Grove Gdns. Rich —6F 99
Grove Gdns. Tedd —4A 116
Grove Grn. Rd. E10 —3E 52
Grove Hall Ct. NW8 —3A 66 (1A 158)
Grove Hill. E18 —2H 35
Grove Hill. Harr —7J 25
Grovehill Ct. Brom —6H 125
Grove Hill Rd. SE5 —3E 104
Grove Hill Rd. Harr —7K 25
Grove Ho. SW3 —6C 84 (7D 170)
Grove Ho. Rd. N8 —4J 31
Groveland Av. SW16 —7K 121
Groveland Ct. EC4 —1D 168
Groveland Rd. Beck —3B 142
Grovelands. W Mol —4E 132
Grovelands Clo. SE5 —2E 104
Grovelands Clo. Harr —3F 43
Grovelands Ct. N14 —7C 6
Grovelands Rd. N13 —4E 16
Grovelands Rd. N15 —6G 33
Grovelands Rd. Orp —7A 128
Groveland Way. N Mald —5J 135
Grove La. SE5 —1D 104
Grove La. King T —4E 134
Grove La. Uxb —4B 58
Grove La.Ter. SE5 —2D 104
Groveley Rd. Sun —5H 113
Grove Mkt. Pl. SE9 —6D 108
Grove M. W6 —3E 82
Grove Mill Pl. Cars —3E 150
Grove Park. —3K 125
(Bromley)
Grove Park. —1J 99
(Chiswick)
Grove Pk. E11 —6K 35
Grove Pk. NW9 —4J 27
Grove Pk. SE5 —2E 104
Gro. Park Av. E4 —7J 19
Gro. Park Bri. W4 —7J 81
Gro. Park Gdns. W4 —7H 81
Gro. Park Ind. Est. NW9 —4K 27
Gro. Park M. W4 —7J 81
Gro. Park Rd. N15 —4E 32
Gro. Park Rd. SE9 —3A 126
Gro. Park. Rd. W4 —7H 81
Gro. Park Ter. W4 —7H 81
Grove Pas. E2 —2H 69
Grove Pl. NW3 —3B 48
Grove Pl. SW12 —7F 103
Grove Pl. W3 —1J 81
Grove Pl. Bark —7G 55
Grover Ct. SE13 —2D 106
Grover Ho. SE11 —5K 85 (6H 173)
Grove Rd. E3 —1K 69
Grove Rd. E4 —4K 19
Grove Rd. E11 —7H 35
Grove Rd. E17 —6D 34
Grove Rd. E18 —2H 35
Grove Rd. N11 —5A 16
Grove Rd. N12 —5G 15
Grove Rd. N15 —5E 32
Grove Rd. NW2 —6E 46
Grove Rd. SW13 —2B 100
Grove Rd. SW19 —7A 120
Grove Rd. W3 —1J 81
Grove Rd. W5 —7D 62
Grove Rd. Belv —6F 93
Grove Rd. Bexh —4J 111
Grove Rd. Bren —5C 80
Grove Rd. Chad H & Romf —7B 38
Grove Rd. Cockf —3H 5
Grove Rd. E Mol —4H 133
Grove Rd. Edgw —6B 12
Grove Rd. Houn —4E 96
Grove Rd. Iswth —1J 97
Grove Rd. Mitc —3E 138
(in two parts)
Grove Rd. Pinn —5D 24
Grove Rd. Rich —6F 99
Grove Rd. Shep —6E 130
Grove Rd. Surb —5D 134
Grove Rd. Sutt —6J 149
Grove Rd. T Hth —4A 140
Grove Rd. Twic —3H 115
Grove Rd. Uxb —7A 40
Groveside Clo. W3 —5G 63
Groveside Clo. Cars —2C 150
Groveside Rd. E4 —2B 20
Grovestile Waye. Felt —7F 95
Grove St. N18 —5A 18
Grove St. SE8 —4B 88
Grove Ter. NW5 —3F 49
Grove Ter. S'hall —7E 60
Grove Ter. Tedd —4A 116
Grove Ter. M. NW5 —3F 49
Grove, The. (Junct.) —1G 123
Grove, The. E15 —6G 53
Grove, The. N3 —1J 29
Grove, The. N4 —7K 31
Grove, The. N6 —1E 48
Grove, The. N8 —5H 31
Grove, The. N13 —4F 17
(in two parts)
Grove, The. N14 —5B 6
Grove, The. NW9 —5K 27
Grove, The. NW11 —7G 29
Grove, The. W5 —1D 80
Grove, The. Bexh —4D 110
Grove, The. Edgw —4C 12
Grove, The. Enf —2F 7
Grove, The. Gnfd —6G 61
Grove, The. Iswth —1J 97
Grove, The. Sidc —4E 128
Grove, The. Stan —2F 11
Grove, The. Tedd —4A 116
Grove, The. Twic —6B 98
Grove, The. Uxb —4B 58
(UB8)
Grove, The. Uxb —5C 40
(UB10)
Grove, The. W on T —7K 131
Grove, The. W W'ck —3D 154
Grove Va. SE22 —4F 105
Grove Va. Chst —6E 126
Grove Vs. E14 —7D 70
Groveway. SW9 —1K 103
Groveway. Dag —4D 56
Grove Way. Esh —7G 133
Grove Way. Uxb —7A 40
Grove Way. Wemb —5H 45
Grovewood. Rich —1G 99
Grovewood Pl. Wfd G —6J 21
Grummant Rd. SE15 —1F 105
Grundy St. E14 —6D 70
Gruneisen Rd. N3 —7E 14
Guardian Ct. SE12 —5G 107
Guard's Mus. —2G 85 (7B 166)
Gubyon Av. SE24 —5B 104
Guerin Sq. E3 —3B 70
Guernsey Clo. Houn —7E 78
Guernsey Gro. SE24 —7C 104
Guernsey Ho. N1 —6C 50
(off Douglas Rd. N.)
Guernsey Ho. Enf —1E 8
(off Eastfield Rd.)
Guernsey Rd. E10 —1F 53
Guernsey Rd. N1 —6C 50
Guibal Rd. SE12 —7K 107
Guildersfield Rd. SW16 —7J 121
Guildford Av. Felt —2H 113
Guildford Gro. SE10 —1D 106
Guildford Ho. E6 —6D 72
Guildford Rd. E17 —1E 34
Guildford Rd. SW8 —1J 103
Guildford Rd. Croy —6D 140
Guildford Rd. Ilf —2J 55
Guildford Way. Wall —5J 151
Guildhall. —6C 68 (7D 162)
Guildhall Bldgs. EC2 —7E 162
Guildhall Library. —6C 68 (7D 162)

Guildhall Offices—Hampstead Way

Guildhall Offices. EC2 —6C 68
(off Basinghall St.)
Guildhall Yd. EC2 —7D 162
Guildhouse St. SW1 —4G 85 (3A 172)
Guildown Av. N12 —4E 14
Guild Rd. SE7 —6B 90
Guildsway. E17 —1B 34
Guilford Av. Surb —5F 135
Guilford Pl. WC1 —4K 67 (4G 161)
Guilford St. WC1 —4J 67 (4E 160)
Guilfoyle. NW9 —2B 28
Guillemot Pl. N22 —2K 31
Guilsborough Clo. NW10 —7A 46
Guinness Clo. E9 —7A 52
Guinness Clo. Hay —3F 77
Guinness Ct. E1 —1J 169
Guinness Ct. EC1 —2D 162
Guinness Ct. NW8 —1C 66
Guinness Ct. SE1 —6G 169
Guinness Ct. SW3 —4D 84 (4E 170)
Guinness Ct. Croy —2F 153
Guinness Sq. SE1 —4E 86
Guinness Trust Bldgs. SE11 —5B 86
Guinness Trust Bldgs. W6 —5F 83
(off Fulham Pal. Rd.)
Guinness Trust Est. E15 —1H 71
Guinness Trust Est. N16 —1E 50
Guion Rd. SW6 —2H 101
Gulland Wlk. N1 —6C 50
(off Oronsay Wlk.)
Gull Clo. Wall —7J 151
Gulliver Clo. N'holt —1D 60
Gulliver Rd. Sidc —2H 127
Gulliver's Ho. EC1 —4C 162
Gulliver St. SE16 —3A 88
Gulston Wlk. SW3 —4F 171
Gumleigh Rd. W5 —4C 80
Gumley Gdns. Iswth —3A 98
Gundulph Rd. Brom —3A 144
Gunmaker's La. E3 —1A 70
Gunnell Clo. SE26 —4G 123
Gunnell Clo. Croy —6F 141
Gunner La. SE18 —5E 90
Gunnersbury. —5H 81
Gunnersbury Av. W5 & W3 —1F 81
Gunnersbury Clo. W4 —5H 81
Gunnersbury Ct. W3 —2H 81
Gunnersbury Cres. W3 —2G 81
Gunnersbury Dri. W5 —2F 81
Gunnersbury Gdns. W3 —2G 81
Gunnersbury La. W3 —3G 81
Gunnersbury Mnr. W5 —1F 81
Gunnersbury M. W4 —5H 81
Gunnersbury Park. (Junct.) —3G 81
Gunnersbury Pk. Mus. —3G 81
Gunners Gro. E4 —3K 19
Gunners Rd. SW18 —2B 120
Gunning St. SE18 —4J 91
Gunpowder Sq. EC4 —6A 68 (7K 161)
(off Gough Sq., in two parts)
Gunstor Rd. N16 —4E 50
Gun St. E1 —5F 69 (6J 163)
Gunter Gro. SW10 —6A 84
Gunter Gro. Edgw —1K 27
Gunterstone Rd. W14 —4G 83
Gunthorpe St. E1 —5F 69 (6K 163)
Gunton Rd. E5 —3H 51
Gunton Rd. SW17 —6E 120
Gunwhale Clo. SE16 —1K 87
Gun Wharf Bus. Cen. E3 —1A 70
(off Old Ford Rd.)
Gurdon Ho. E14 —6C 70
Gurdon Rd. SE7 —5J 89
Gurnard Clo. W Dray —7A 58
Gurnell Gro. W13 —4K 61
Gurney Clo. E15 —5G 53
Gurney Clo. E17 —1K 33
Gurney Clo. Bark —6F 55
Gurney Cres. Croy —1K 151
Gurney Dri. N2 —4A 30
Gurney Ho. E2 —2G 69
(off Goldsmith Row)
Gurney Ho. Hay —4G 77
Gurney Rd. E15 —5G 53
Gurney Rd. SW6 —3A 102
Gurney Rd. Cars —4E 150
Gurney Rd. N'holt —3K 59
Guthrie Ct. SE1 —7K 167
Guthrie St. SW3 —5B 84 (5C 170)
Gutter La. EC2 —6C 68 (7C 162)
Guyatt Gdns. Mitc —2E 138
Guy Barnett Gro. SE3 —3J 107
Guy Rd. Wall —3H 151
Guyscliff Rd. SE13 —5E 106
Guys Retreat. Buck H —1F 21
Guy St. SE1 —2D 86 (6F 169)
Gwalior Rd. SW15 —4F 101
Gwendolen Av. SW15 —4F 101
Gwendolen Clo. SW15 —5F 101
Gwendoline Av. E13 —1K 71
Gwendwr Rd. W14 —5G 83
Gweneth Cotts. Edgw —6B 12
Gwillim Clo. Sidc —5A 110
Gwilym Maries Ho. E2 —3H 69
(off Blythe St.)
Gwydor Rd. Beck —3K 141
Gwydyr Rd. Brom —3H 143
Gwyn Clo. SW6 —7A 84
Gwynne Av. Croy —7K 141
Gwynne Clo. W4 —6B 82
Gwynne Ho. WC1 —3A 68 (2J 161)
(off Lloyd Baker St.)
Gwynne Pk. Av. Wfd G —6J 21
Gwynne Pl. WC1 —3K 67 (2H 161)
Gwynne Rd. SW11 —2B 102
Gylcote Clo. SE5 —4D 104
Gyles Pk. Stan —1C 26
Gyllyngdune Gdns. Ilf —2K 55
Gypsy Corner. (Junct.) —5K 63

H

Haarlem Rd. W14 —3F 83
Haberdasher Est. N1 —3D 68 (1F 163)
Haberdasher Pl. N1 —3D 68 (1F 163)
Haberdashers Ct. SE14 —3K 105
Haberdasher St. N1 —3D 68 (1F 163)
Habington Ho. SE5 —7D 86
(off Notley St.)
Haccombe Rd. SW19 —6A 120
Hackbridge. —2E 150
Hackbridge Grn. Wall —2E 150
Hackbridge Pk. Gdns. Cars —2D 150
Hackbridge Rd. Wall —2E 150
Hackford Rd. SW9 —1K 103
Hackford Wlk. SW9 —1K 103
Hackington Cres. Beck —6C 124
Hacklington Ct. New Bar —4E 4
Hackney. —6H 51
Hackney Gro. E8 —6H 51
Hackney Rd. E2 —3E 68 (2J 163)
Hackney Wick. —6C 52
Hackney Wick. (Junct.) —6B 52
Hadar Clo. N20 —1D 14
Hadden Rd. SE28 —3J 91
Hadden Way. Gnfd —6H 43
Haddington Ct. SE10 —7D 88
(off Tarves Way)
Haddington Rd. Brom —3F 125
Haddon Clo. Enf —6B 8
Haddon Clo. N Mald —5B 136
Haddon Ct. NW4 —3E 28
Haddon Ct. W3 —7B 64
Haddon Fld. SE8 —4K 87
Haddon Gro. Sidc —7K 109
Haddon Rd. Sutt —4K 149
Haddo St. SE10 —6D 88
Haden Ct. N4 —2A 50
Hadfield Clo. S'hall —3D 60
Hadfield Ho. E1 —6G 69
(off Ellen St.)
Hadleigh Clo. E1 —4J 69
Hadleigh Clo. SW20 —2H 137
Hadleigh Ct. E4 —4F 13
Hadleigh Ho. E1 —4J 69
Hadleigh Rd. N9 —7C 8
Hadleigh St. E2 —3J 69
Hadleigh Wlk. E6 —6C 72
Hadley. —3C 4
Hadley Clo. N21 —6F 7
Hadley Comn. Barn —2D 4
Hadley Ct. N16 —1G 51
Hadley Ct. New Bar —3E 4
Hadley Gdns. W4 —5K 81
Hadley Gdns. S'hall —5D 78
Hadley Grn. Rd. Barn —2C 4
Hadley Grn. W. Barn —2C 4
Hadley Gro. Barn —2B 4
Hadley Highstone. Barn —1C 4
Hadley Mnr. Trad. Est. Barn —3C 4
Hadley M. Barn —3C 4
Hadley Pde. Barn —3B 4
(off High St.)
Hadley Ridge. Barn —3C 4
Hadley Rd. Barn —2E 4
Hadley Rd. Barn & Enf —1K 5
Hadley Rd. Belv —4F 93
Hadley Rd. Mitc —4H 139
Hadley St. NW1 —6F 49
(in two parts)
Hadley Way. N21 —6F 7
Hadley Wood. —1F 5
Hadley Wood Rd. Barn —2F 5
Hadlow Ho. SE17 —5E 86
(off Kinglake Est.)
Hadlow Pl. SE19 —7G 123
Hadlow Rd. Sidc —4A 128
Hadlow Rd. Well —7C 92
Hadrian Clo. Stai —7A 94
Hadrian Clo. Wall —7J 151
Hadrian Ct. Sutt —7K 149
Hadrian Est. E2 —2G 69
(off Hackney Rd.)
Hadrians Ride. Enf —5A 8
Hadrian St. SE10 —5G 89
Hadrian Way. Stai & Stanw —7A 94
(in two parts)
Hadstock Ho. NW1 —3H 67 (1D 160)
(off Ossulston St.)
Hadyn Pk. Ct. W12 —2C 82
(off Curwen Rd.)
Hadyn Pk. Rd. W12 —2C 82
Hafer Rd. SW11 —4D 102
Hafton Rd. SE6 —1G 125
Haggard Rd. Twic —7B 98
Hagger Ct. E17 —3F 35
Haggerston. —2F 69
Haggerston Rd. E8 & E2 —7F 51
Hague St. E2 —3G 69
Ha Ha Rd. SE18 —6D 90
Haig Ho. E2 —2G 69 (1K 163)
(off Shipton St.)
Haig Pl. Mord —6J 137
Haig Rd. Stan —5H 11
Haig Rd. Uxb —5D 58
Haig Rd. E. E13 —3A 72
Haig Rd. W. E13 —3A 72
Haigville Gdns. Ilf —4F 37
Hailes Clo. SW19 —6A 120
Haileybury Av. Enf —6A 8
Hailey Rd. Eri —2G 93
Hailsham Av. SW2 —2K 121
Hailsham Clo. Surb —7D 134
Hailsham Cres. Bark —6K 55
Hailsham Dri. Harr —3H 25
Hailsham Rd. SW17 —6E 120
Hailsham Ter. N18 —5J 17
Haimo Rd. SE9 —5B 108
Hainault Ct. E17 —4F 35
Hainault Gore. Romf —5E 38
Hainault Rd. E11 —1E 52
Hainault Rd. Chad H —6F 39
Hainault Rd. Col R & Romf —2J 39
Hainault Rd. Romf —1B 38
Hainault St. SE9 —1F 127
Hainault St. Ilf —2G 55
Haines St. SW8 —7G 85
Haines Wlk. Mord —7K 137
Hainford Clo. SE4 —4K 105
Haining Clo. W4 —5G 81
Hainthorpe Rd. SE27 —3B 122
Hainton Clo. E1 —6H 69
Halberd M. E5 —2H 51
Halbutt Gdns. Dag —3F 57
Halbutt St. Dag —4F 57
Halcomb St. N1 —1E 68
Halcot Av. Bexh —5H 111
Halcrow St. E1 —5H 69
Halcyon. Enf —5K 7
(off Private Rd.)
Haldane Clo. N10 —7A 16
Haldane Pl. SW18 —1K 119
Haldane Rd. E6 —3B 72
Haldane Rd. SE28 —7D 74
Haldane Rd. SW6 —7H 83
Haldane Rd. S'hall —7G 61
Haldan Rd. E4 —6K 19
Haldon Rd. SW18 —6H 101
Hale Clo. E4 —3K 19
Hale Clo. Edgw —5D 12
Hale Ct. Edgw —5D 12
Hale Dri. NW7 —6D 12
Hale End. —6A 20
Hale End Clo. Ruis —6J 23
Hale End Rd. E4 —6A 20
Halefield Rd. N17 —1H 33
Hale Gdns. N17 —4G 33
Hale Gdns. W3 —1G 81
Hale Gro. Gdns. NW7 —5F 13
Hale Ho. SW1 —5H 85 (5D 172)
(off Lindsay Sq.)
Hale La. NW7 —5E 12
Hale La. Edgw —5C 12
Hale Path. SE27 —4B 122
Hale Rd. E6 —4C 72
Hale Rd. N17 —3G 33
Halesowen Rd. Mord —7K 137
Hales Prior. N1 —2K 67 (1G 161)
(off Calshot St.)
Hales St. SE8 —7C 88
Hale St. E14 —7D 70
Halesworth Clo. E5 —2J 51
Halesworth Rd. SE13 —3D 106
Hale, The. —5E 12
Hale, The. E4 —7A 20
Hale, The. N17 —3G 33
Hale Wlk. W7 —5J 61
Haley Rd. NW4 —6E 28
Half Acre. Bren —6D 80
Half Acre. Stan —6H 11
Half Acre Rd. W7 —1J 79
Half Moon Ct. EC1 —6C 162
Half Moon Cres. N1 —2K 67
(in two parts)
Half Moon La. SE24 —6C 104
Half Moon Pas. E1 —6F 69 (1K 169)
(in two parts)
Half Moon St. W1 —1F 85 (4K 165)
Halford Clo. Edgw —2H 27
Halford Rd. E10 —5F 35
Halford Rd. SW6 —6J 83
Halford Rd. Rich —5E 98
Halford Rd. Uxb —4C 40
Halfway St. Sidc —7H 109
Haliburton Rd. Twic —5A 98
Haliday Ho. N1 —6D 50
(off Mildmay St.)
Haliday Wlk. N1 —6D 50
Halidon Clo. E9 —5J 51
Halifax. NW9 —2B 28
Halifax Clo. Tedd —6J 115
Halifax Rd. Enf —2H 7
Halifax Rd. Gnfd —1F 61
Halifax St. SE26 —3H 123
Halifield Dri. Belv —3E 92
Haling Down Pas. Purl —7C 152
(in two parts)
Haling Gro. S Croy —7C 152
Haling Pk. Gdns. S Croy —6B 152
Haling Pk. Rd. S Croy —5B 152
Haling Rd. S Croy —6D 152
Haliwell Ho. NW6 —1K 65
(off Mortimer Cres.)
Halkin Arc. SW1 —3D 84 (1F 171)
(in two parts)
Halkin M. SW1 —3E 84 (1G 171)
Halkin Pl. SW1 —3E 84 (1G 171)
Halkin St. SW1 —2E 84 (7H 165)
Hallam Clo. Chst —5D 126
Hallam Ct. W1 —5F 67 (5K 159)
(off Hallam St.)
Hallam Gdns. Pinn —1C 24
Hallam Ho. SW1 —5G 85 (6B 172)
(off Churchill Gdns.)
Hallam M. W1 —5F 67 (5K 159)
Hallam Rd. N15 —4B 32
Hallam Rd. SW13 —3D 100
Hallam St. W1 —4F 67 (4K 159)
Hallane Ho. SE27 —5C 122
Hall Clo. W5 —5E 62
Hall Ct. Tedd —5K 115
Hall Dri. SE26 —5J 123
Hall Dri. W7 —6J 61
Halley Gdns. SE13 —4F 107
Halley Ho. E2 —2G 69
(off Pritchards Rd.)
Halley Rd. E7 & E12 —6A 54
Halley St. E14 —5A 70
Hall Farm Clo. Stan —4G 11
Hall Farm Dri. Twic —7H 97
Hallfield Est. W2 —6A 66
(in two parts)
Hall Gdns. E4 —4G 19
Hall Ga. NW8 —3B 66 (1A 158)
Halliards, The. W on T —6J 131
Halliday Sq. S'hall —1H 79
Halliford Clo. Shep —4F 131
Halliford Rd. Shep & Sun —5G 131
Halliford St. N1 —7C 50
Hallingbury Ct. E17 —3D 34
Halliwell Ct. SE22 —5G 105
Halliwell Rd. SW2 —6K 103
Halliwick Ct. Pde. N12 —6J 15
(off Woodhouse Rd.)
Halliwick Rd. N10 —1E 30
Hall Lane. (Junct.) —5E 18
Hall La. E4 —5F 19
Hall La. NW4 —1C 28
Hall La. Hay —7F 77
Hallmark Trad. Cen. Wemb —4J 45
Hallmead Rd. Sutt —3K 149
Hall Oak Wlk. NW6 —6H 47
Hallowell Av. Croy —4J 151
Hallowell Clo. Mitc —3E 138
Hallowell Rd. N'wd —1G 23
Hallowfield Way. Mitc —3C 138
Hall Place. —6J 111
Hall Pl. W2 —4B 66 (4A 158)
(in two parts)
Hall Pl. Cres. Bex —5J 111
Hall Place Mus. —6J 111
Hall Rd. E6 —1D 72
Hall Rd. E15 —4F 53
Hall Rd. NW8 —3A 66 (1A 158)
Hall Rd. Chad H —6C 38
Hall Rd. Iswth —5H 97
Hall Rd. Wall —7F 151
Hallside Rd. Enf —1A 8
Hall St. EC1 —3B 68 (1B 162)
Hall St. N12 —5F 15
Hallsville Rd. E16 —6H 71
Hallswelle Pde. NW11 —5H 29
Hallswelle Rd. NW11 —5H 29
Hall, The. SE3 —3J 107
Hall Tower. W2 —5B 158
Hall Vw. SE9 —2B 126
Hallywell Cres. E6 —5D 72
Halons Rd. SE9 —7E 108
Halpin Pl. SE17 —4D 86
Halsbrook Rd. SE3 —3A 108
Halsbury Clo. Stan —4G 11
Halsbury Ct. Stan —5G 11
Halsbury Rd. W12 —1D 82
Halsbury Rd. E. N'holt —4G 43
Halsbury Rd. W. N'holt —5F 43
Halsend. Hay —1K 77
Halsey M. SW3 —4D 84 (3E 170)
Halsey St. SW3 —4D 84 (3E 170)
Halsmere Rd. SE5 —1B 104
Halstead Clo. Croy —3C 152
Halstead Ct. E17 —7B 34
Halstead Ct. N1 —2D 68 (1F 163)
(off Fairbank Est.)
Halstead Gdns. N21 —1J 17
Halstead Rd. E11 —5J 35
Halstead Rd. N21 —1J 17
Halstead Rd. Enf —4K 7
Halston Clo. SW11 —6D 102
Halstow Rd. NW10 —3F 65
Halstow Rd. SE10 —5J 89
Halsway. Hay —1J 77
Halton Clo. N11 —6J 15
Halton Cross St. N1 —1B 68
Halton Mans. N1 —7B 50
Halton Pl. N1 —1C 68
Halton Rd. N1 —7B 50
Halt Robin La. Belv —4H 93
Halt Robin Rd. Belv —4G 93
(in two parts)
Halyard Ho. E14 —3E 88
Ham. —3C 116
Hamara Ghar. E13 —1A 72
Hambalt Rd. SW4 —5G 103
Hamble Clo. Ruis —2G 41
Hambledon Pl. SE21 —1E 122
Hambledon. SE17 —6D 86
(off Villa St.)
Hambledon Clo. Uxb —4D 58
Hambledon Ct. SE22 —4E 104
Hambledon Ct. W5 —7E 62
Hambledon Gdns. SE25 —3F 141
Hambledon Rd. SW18 —7H 101
Hambledown Rd. Sidc —7H 109
Hambleyhrst. Beck —2D 142
Hamble St. SW6 —3K 101
Hambleton Clo. Wor Pk —2E 148
Hamble Wlk. N'holt —2E 60
(off Brabazon Rd.)
Hambley Ho. SE16 —4H 87
(off Camilla Rd.)
Hamblin Ho. S'hall —7C 60
(off Broadway, The)
Hambridge Way. SW2 —7A 104
Hambro Av. Brom —1J 155
Hambrook Rd. SE25 —3H 141
Hambro Rd. SW16 —6H 121
Hambrough Ho. Hay —5A 60
Hambrough Rd. S'hall —1C 78
Ham Clo. Rich —3C 116
(in two parts)
Ham Comn. Rich —3D 116
Hamden Cres. Dag —3H 57
Hamel Clo. Harr —4D 26
Hame Way. E6 —4E 72
Ham Farm Rd. Rich —4D 116
Hamfrith Rd. E15 —6H 53
Ham Ga. Av. Rich —3D 116
Ham House. —1C 116
Hamilton Av. N9 —7B 8
Hamilton Av. Ilf —4F 37
Hamilton Av. Romf —2K 39
Hamilton Av. Surb —2G 147
Hamilton Av. Sutt —2G 149
Hamilton Bldgs. EC2 —4H 163
Hamilton Clo. N17 —3F 33
Hamilton Clo. NW8 —3B 66 (2A 158)
Hamilton Clo. SE16 —2A 88
Hamilton Clo. Cockf —4H 5
Hamilton Clo. Felt —5H 113
Hamilton Clo. Stan —2D 10
Hamilton Ct. SE6 —1H 125
Hamilton Ct. SW15 —3G 101
Hamilton Ct. W5 —7E 62
Hamilton Ct. W9 —3A 66
(off Maida Va.)
Hamilton Ct. Croy —1G 153
Hamilton Cres. N13 —4F 17
Hamilton Cres. Harr —3D 42
Hamilton Cres. Houn —5F 97
Hamilton Gdns. NW8 —3A 66 (1A 158)
Hamilton Ho. E14 —5D 88
Hamilton Ho. NW8 —1A 158
Hamilton Ho. W4 —6A 82
Hamilton La. N5 —4B 50
Hamilton M. SW18 —1J 119
Hamilton M. SW19 —7J 119
Hamilton M. W1 —2F 85 (6J 165)
Hamilton Pde. Felt —4H 113
Hamilton Pk. N5 —4B 50
Hamilton Pk. W. N5 —4B 50
Hamilton Pl. W1 —1E 84 (5H 165)
Hamilton Pl. Sun —7K 113
Hamilton Rd. E15 —3G 71
Hamilton Rd. E17 —2A 34
Hamilton Rd. N2 —3A 30
Hamilton Rd. N9 —7B 8
Hamilton Rd. NW10 —5C 46
Hamilton Rd. NW11 —7F 29
Hamilton Rd. SE27 —4D 122
Hamilton Rd. SW19 —7K 119
Hamilton Rd. W4 —2A 82
Hamilton Rd. W5 —7E 62
Hamilton Rd. Bexh —2E 110
Hamilton Rd. Bren —6D 80
Hamilton Rd. Cockf —4H 5
Hamilton Rd. Felt —4H 113
Hamilton Rd. Harr —5J 25
Hamilton Rd. Hay —7K 59
Hamilton Rd. Ilf —4F 55
Hamilton Rd. Sidc —4A 128
Hamilton Rd. S'hall —1D 78
Hamilton Rd. T Hth —3D 140
Hamilton Rd. Twic —1J 115
Hamilton Rd. Ind. Est. SE27 —4D 122
(off Hamilton Rd.)
Hamilton Rd. M. SW19 —7K 119
Hamilton Sq. N12 —6G 15
Hamilton Sq. SE1 —6F 169
Hamilton St. SE8 —6C 88
Hamilton Ter. NW8 —2K 65 (2A 158)
Hamilton Way. N3 —6D 14
Hamilton Way. N13 —4G 17
Hamilton Way. Wall —7H 151
Hamlea Clo. SE12 —5J 107
Hamlet Clo. SE13 —4G 107
Hamlet Clo. Romf —1G 39
Hamlet Ct. SE11 —5B 86
(off Opal St.)
Hamlet Ct. W6 —4C 82
Hamlet Ct. Enf —5K 7
Hamlet Gdns. W6 —4C 82
Hamlet Ind. Est. E9 —7C 52
Hamlet Rd. SE19 —7F 123
Hamlet Rd. Romf —1G 39
Hamlet Sq. NW2 —3G 47
Hamlets Way. E3 —4B 70
(in two parts)
Hamlet, The. SE5 —3D 104
Hamlet Way. SE1 —2D 86 (6F 169)
Hamlin Cres. Pinn —5A 24
Hamlyn Clo. Edgw —3K 11
Hamlyn Gdns. SE19 —7E 122
Hammelton Grn. SW9 —1B 104
Hammelton Rd. Brom —1H 143
Hammerfield Ho. SW3 —5C 84 (5D 170)
(off Marlborough St.)
Hammers La. NW7 —5H 13
Hammersmith. —4E 82
Hammersmith Bri. SW13 & W6 —6D 82
Hammersmith Bri. Rd. W6 —5E 82
(in two parts)
Hammersmith Broadway. (Junct.) —4E 82
Hammersmith B'way. W6 —4E 82
Hammersmith Flyover.(Junct.) —5E 82
Hammersmith Flyover. W6 —5E 82
Hammersmith Gro. W6 —2E 82
Hammersmith Ind. Est. W6 —6E 82
Hammersmith Rd. W6 & W14 —4F 83
Hammersmith Ter. W6 —5C 82
Hammet Clo. Hay —5B 60
Hammett St. EC3 —7F 69 (2J 169)
Hammond Av. Mitc —2F 139
Hammond Clo. Barn —5B 4
Hammond Clo. Gnfd —5H 43
Hammond Clo. Hamp —1E 132
Hammond Ct. E10 —2D 52
Hammond Ct. E17 —5A 34
(off Maude Rd.)
Hammond Ho. E14 —3C 88
Hammond Ho. SE14 —7J 87
(off Lubbock St.)
Hammond Lodge. W9 —5J 65
(off Admiral Wlk.)
Hammond Rd. Enf —2C 8
Hammond Rd. S'hall —3C 78
Hammonds Clo. Dag —3C 56
Hammond St. NW5 —6G 49
Hammond Way. SE28 —7B 74
Hamond Clo. S Croy —7B 152
Hamonde Clo. Edgw —2C 12
Hamond Sq. N1 —2E 68
(off Hoxton St.)
Ham Pk. Rd. E15 & E7 —7H 53
Hampden Av. Beck —2A 142
Hampden Clo. NW1 —2H 67
Hampden Ct. N10 —7K 15
Hampden Gurney St. W1 —6D 66 (1E 164)
Hampden Ho. SW9 —2A 104
Hampden La. N17 —1F 33
Hampden Rd. N8 —4A 32
Hampden Rd. N10 —7K 15
Hampden Rd. N17 —1G 33
Hampden Rd. N19 —2H 49
Hampden Rd. Beck —2A 142
Hampden Rd. Harr —1G 25
Hampden Rd. King T —3G 135
Hampden Rd. Romf —1H 39
Hampden Sq. N14 —1A 16
Hampden Way. N14 —1A 16
Hampshire Clo. N18 —5C 18
Hampshire Hog La. W6 —5D 82
Hampshire Rd. N22 —7E 16
Hampshire St. NW5 —6H 49
Hampson Way. SW8 —1K 103
Hampstead. —4B 48
Hampstead Clo. SE28 —1B 92
Hampstead Gdns. NW11 —6J 29
Hampstead Gdns. Chad H —5B 38
Hampstead Garden Suburb. —5A 30
Hampstead Grn. NW3 —5C 48
Hampstead Gro. NW3 —3A 48
Hampstead Heath. —2C 48
Hampstead Heights. N2 —3A 30
Hampstead High St. NW3 —4B 48
Hampstead Hill Gdns. NW3 —4B 48
Hampstead La. NW3 & N6 —1B 48
Hampstead Mus. —4B 48
(off New End Sq.)
Hampstead Rd. NW1 —2G 67 (1A 160)
Hampstead Sq. NW3 —3A 48
Hampstead Theatre Club. —7B 48
Hampstead Wlk. E3 —1B 70
Hampstead Way. NW11 —5H 29

Hampstead W.—Hartland Rd.

Hampstead W. NW6 —6J 47
Hampton. —1F 133
Hampton & Richmond Borough F.C. —1F 133
Hampton Clo. N11 —5A 16
Hampton Clo. NW6 —3J 65
Hampton Clo. SW20 —7E 118
Hampton Court. —4J 133
Hampton Court. (Junct.) —3J 133
Hampton Ct. N1 —6B 50
Hampton Ct. N22 —1G 31
Hampton Ct. Av. E Mol —6H 133
Hampton Ct. Cres. E Mol —3H 133
Hampton Court Palace. —4K 133
Hampton Ct. Pde. E Mol —4J 133
Hampton Ct. Rd. Hamp —2G 133
Hampton Farm Ind. Est. Felt —3C 114
Hampton Hill. —5G 115
Hampton Ho. Bexh —2H 111
(off Erith Rd.)
Hampton La. Felt —4C 114
Hampton M. NW10 —3K 63
Hampton Ri. Harr —6E 26
Hampton Rd. E4 —5G 19
Hampton Rd. E7 —5K 53
Hampton Rd. E11 —1F 53
Hampton Rd. Croy —6C 140
Hampton Rd. Ilf —4G 55
Hampton Rd. Tedd —5H 115
Hampton Rd. Twic —3H 115
Hampton Rd. Wor Pk —2C 148
Hampton Rd. E. Felt & Hanw —4D 114
Hampton Rd. W. Felt —3C 114
Hampton St. SE17 & SE1 —4B 86
Hampton Wick. —1C 134
Ham Ridings. Rich —5F 117
Hamshades Clo. Sidc —3K 127
Ham St. Rich —1B 116
Ham, The. Bren —7C 80
Ham Vw. Croy —6A 142
Ham Yd. W1 —7H 67 (2C 166)
Hanah Ct. SW19 —7F 119
Hanameel St. E16 —1K 89
Hanbury Clo. NW4 —3E 28
Hanbury Ct. Harr —6K 25
Hanbury Dri. N21 —5E 6
Hanbury Ho. E1 —5G 69
(off Hanbury St.)
Hanbury Ho. SW8 —7J 85
(off Regent's Bri. Gdns.)
Hanbury M. N1 —1C 68
Hanbury Rd. N17 —2H 33
Hanbury Rd. W3 —2H 81
Hanbury St. E1 —5F 69 (5K 163)
Hanbury Wlk. Bex —3K 129
Hancock Rd. E3 —3E 70
Hancock Rd. SE19 —6D 122
Handa Wlk. N1 —6D 50
Hand Ct. WC1 —5K 67 (6H 161)
Handcroft Rd. Croy —7B 140
Handel Clo. Edgw —6A 12
Handel Mans. SW13 —7E 82
Handel Mans. WC1 —4J 67 (3F 161)
(off Handel St.)
Handel Pde. Edgw —7B 12
(off Whitchurch La.)
Handel Pl. NW10 —6K 45
Handel St. WC1 —4J 67 (3E 160)
Handel Way. Edgw —7B 12
Handen Rd. SE12 —5G 107
Handforth Rd. SW9 —7A 86
Handforth Rd. Ilf —3F 55
Handley Page Rd. Wall —7K 151
Handley Rd. E9 —7J 51
Handowe Clo. NW4 —4C 28
Handside Clo. Wor Pk —1F 149
Hands Wlk. E16 —6J 71
Handsworth Av. E4 —6A 20
Handsworth Rd. N17 —3D 32
Handtrough Way. Bark —2F 73
Hanford Clo. SW18 —1J 119
Hanford Row. SW19 —6E 118
Hanger Ct. W5 —4F 63
Hanger Grn. W5 —4G 63
Hanger Hill. —4F 63
Hanger Lane. (Junct.) —3E 62
Hanger La. W5 —2E 62
Hanger Va. La. W5 —6F 63
(in two parts)
Hanger Vw. Way. W3 —6G 63
Hanging Sword All. EC4 —1K 167
Hankey Pl. SE1 —2D 86 (7F 169)
Hankins La. NW7 —2F 13
Hanley Gdns. N4 —1K 49
Hanley Pl. Beck —7C 124
Hanley Rd. N4 —1J 49
Hanmer Wlk. N7 —2K 49
Hannah Barlow Ho. SW8 —1K 103
Hannah Clo. NW10 —4J 45
Hannah Clo. Beck —3E 142
Hannah Mary Way. SE1 —4G 87
Hannah M. Wall —7G 151
Hannay La. N8 —7H 31
Hannay Wlk. SW16 —2H 121
Hannell Rd. SW6 —7G 83
Hannen Rd. SE27 —3B 122
Hannibal Rd. E1 —5J 69
Hannibal Rd. Stai & Stanw —7A 94
Hannibal Way. Croy —5K 151
Hannington Point. E9 —6B 52
(off Eastway)
Hannington Rd. SW4 —3F 103
Hanover Av. E16 —1J 89
Hanover Av. Felt —1J 113
Hanover Circ. Hay —6E 58
Hanover Clo. Rich —7G 81
Hanover Clo. Sutt —4G 149
Hanover Ct. NW9 —3A 28
Hanover Ct. SW15 —4B 100
Hanover Ct. W12 —1C 82
(off Uxbridge Rd.)
Hanover Ct. Ruis —3J 41
Hanover Dri. Chst —4G 127
Hanover Flats. W1 —7E 66 (2H 165)
(off Binney St.)
Hanover Gdns. SE11 —6A 86
Hanover Gdns. Ilf —1G 37
Hanover Ga. NW8 & NW1 —3C 66 (2D 158)
Hanover Ga. Mans. NW1 —4C 66 (3D 158)
Hanover Ho. NW8 —2C 66
(off St John's Wood High St.)
Hanover Ho. SW9 —3A 104
Hanover Mans. SW2 —5A 104
Hanover Mead. NW11 —5G 29
Hanover Pk. SE15 —1G 105
Hanover Pl. E3 —3B 70
Hanover Pl. WC2 —6J 67 (1F 167)
Hanover Rd. N15 —4F 33
Hanover Rd. NW10 —7E 46
Hanover Rd. SW19 —7A 120
Hanover Sq. W1 —6F 67 (1K 165)
Hanover Steps. W2 —1D 164
Hanover St. W1 —6F 67 (1K 165)
Hanover St. Croy —3B 152
Hanover Ter. NW1 —3C 66 (2E 158)
Hanover Ter. Iswth —1A 98
Hanover Ter. M. NW1 —3C 66 (2D 158)
Hanover Trad. Est. N7 —5J 49
Hanover Way. Bexh —3D 110
Hanover W. Ind. Est. NW10 —3K 63
Hanover Yd. N1 —2C 68
(off Noel Rd.)
Hansard M. W14 —2F 83
(in two parts)
Hansart Way. Enf —1F 7
Hans Cres. SW1 —3D 84 (1E 170)
Hanselin Clo. Stan —5E 10
Hansen Dri. N21 —5E 6
Hanshaw Dri. Edgw —1K 27
Hansler Gro. E Mol —4H 133
Hansler Rd. SE22 —5F 105
Hansol Rd. Bexh —5E 110
Hanson Clo. SW12 —7F 103
Hanson Clo. SW14 —3J 99
Hanson Clo. Beck —6D 124
Hanson Clo. W Dray —3B 76
Hanson Ct. E17 —6D 34
Hanson Gdns. S'hall —2C 78
Hanson St. W1 —5G 67 (5A 160)
Hans Pl. SW1 —3D 84 (1F 171)
Hans Rd. SW3 —3D 84 (1E 170)
Hans St. SW1 —3D 84 (2F 171)
Hanway Pl. W1 —6H 67 (7C 160)
Hanway Rd. W7 —6H 61
Hanway St. W1 —6H 67 (7C 160)
Hanwell. —1K 79
Hanworth. —4B 114
Hanworth Ho. SE5 —7B 86
(in two parts)
Hanworth Rd. Felt —1K 113
Hanworth Rd. Hamp —4D 114
Hanworth Rd. Houn —1C 114
Hanworth Rd. Sun —7J 113
(in two parts)
Hanworth Ter. Houn —4F 97
Hanworth Trad. Est. Felt —3C 114
Hapgood Clo. Gnfd —5H 43
Harad's Pl. E1 —7G 69
Harben Pde. NW3 —7A 48
Harben Rd. NW6 —7A 48
Harberson Rd. E15 —1H 71
Harberson Rd. SW12 —1F 121
Harberton Rd. N19 —1G 49
Harbet Rd. N18 & E4 —5F 19
Harbet Rd. W2 —5B 66 (6B 158)
Harbex Clo. Bex —7H 111
Harbinger Rd. E14 —4D 88
Harbledown Ho. SE1 —2D 86 (7E 168)
(off Manciple St.)
Harbledown Rd. SW6 —1J 101
Harbord Clo. SE5 —2D 104
Harbord St. SW6 —1F 101
Harborough Av. Sidc —7J 109
Harborough Rd. SW16 —4K 121
Harbour Av. SW10 —1A 102
Harbour Exchange Sq. E14 —2D 88
Harbour Quay. E14 —1E 88
Harbour Rd. SE5 —3C 104
Harbour Yd. SW10 —1A 102
Harbridge Av. SW15 —7B 100
Harbury Rd. Cars —7C 150
Harbut Rd. SW11 —4B 102
Harcombe Rd. N16 —3E 50
Harcourt Av. E12 —4D 54
Harcourt Av. Edgw —3D 12
Harcourt Av. Sidc —6C 110
Harcourt Av. Wall —4F 151
Harcourt Bldgs. EC4 —2J 167
Harcourt Clo. Iswth —3A 98
Harcourt Fld. Wall —4F 151
Harcourt Lodge. Wall —4F 151
Harcourt Rd. E15 —2H 71
Harcourt Rd. N22 —1H 31
Harcourt Rd. SE4 —3B 106
Harcourt Rd. SW19 —7J 119
Harcourt Rd. Bexh —4E 110
Harcourt Rd. T Hth —6K 139
Harcourt Rd. Wall —4F 151
Harcourt St. NW1 —5C 66 (6D 158)
Harcourt Ter. SW10 —5K 83
Hardcastle Clo. Croy —6G 141
Hardcourts Clo. W W'ck —4D 154
Hardel Ri. SW2 —1B 122
Hardel Wlk. SW2 —7A 104
Harden Ct. SE7 —4C 90
Harden Ho. SE5 —2E 104
Harden's Manorway. SE7 —3B 90
(in three parts)
Harders Rd. SE15 —2H 105
Hardess St. SE24 —3C 104
Hardie Clo. NW10 —5K 45
Hardie Rd. Dag —3J 57
Harding Clo. SE17 —6C 86
Harding Clo. Croy —3F 153
Hardinge Clo. Uxb —5D 58
Hardinge La. E1 —6J 69
Hardinge Rd. N18 —6K 17
Hardinge Rd. NW10 —1D 64
Hardinge St. E1 —6J 69
Harding Ho. Hay —6K 59
Harding Rd. Bexh —2F 111
Harding's Clo. King T —1F 135
Hardings La. SE20 —6K 123
Hardman Rd. SE7 —5K 89
Hardman Rd. King T —2E 134
Hardwick Clo. Stan —5H 11
Hardwick Ct. Eri —6K 93
Hardwicke Av. Houn —1E 96
Hardwicke M. WC1 —3A 68 (2H 161)
(off Lloyd Baker M.)
Hardwicke Rd. N13 —6D 16
Hardwicke Rd. W4 —4K 81
Hardwicke Rd. Rich —4C 116
Hardwicke St. Bark —1G 73
Hardwick Grn. W13 —5B 62
Hardwick Ho. NW8 —4C 66 (3D 158)
(off Lilestone St.)
Hardwick St. EC1 —3A 68 (2K 161)
Hardwicks Way. SW18 —5J 101
Hardwidge St. SE1 —2E 86 (6G 169)
Hardy Av. E16 —1J 89
Hardy Av. Ruis —5K 41
Hardy Clo. SE16 —2K 87
Hardy Clo. Barn —6B 4
Hardy Clo. Pinn —7B 24
Hardy Cotts. SE10 —6F 89
Hardy Ho. SW4 —7G 103
Hardying Ho. E17 —4A 34
Hardy Rd. E4 —6G 19
Hardy Rd. SE3 —7H 89
Hardy Rd. SW19 —7K 119
Hardys Clo. E Mol —4J 133
Hardy Way. Enf —1F 7
Hare & Billet Rd. SE3 —1F 107
Harebell Dri. E6 —5E 72
Harecastle Clo. Hay —4C 60
Hare Ct. EC4 —6A 68 (1J 167)
Harecourt Rd. N1 —6C 50
Haredale Rd. SE24 —4C 104
Haredon Clo. SE23 —7K 105
Harefield Clo. Enf —1F 7
Harefield Grn. NW7 —6K 13
Harefield M. SE4 —3B 106
Harefield Rd. N8 —5H 31
Harefield Rd. SE4 —3B 106
Harefield Rd. SW16 —7K 121
Harefield Rd. Sidc —3D 128
Harefield Rd. Uxb —5A 40
Hare Marsh. E2 —4G 69
Hare Pl. EC4 —6A 68
(off Pleydell St.)
Hare Row. E2 —2H 69
Haresfield Rd. Dag —6G 57
Hare St. SE18 —3E 90
Hare Wlk. N1 —2E 68
Harewood Av. NW1 —4C 66 (4D 158)
Harewood Av. N'holt —7D 42
Harewood Clo. N'holt —7D 42
Harewood Dri. Ilf —2D 36
Harewood Pl. W1 —6F 67 (1K 165)
Harewood Rd. SW19 —6C 120
Harewood Rd. Iswth —7K 79
Harewood Rd. S Croy —6E 152
Harewood Row. NW1 —5C 66 (5D 158)
Harewood Ter. S'hall —4D 78
Harfield Gdns. SE5 —3E 104
Harfield Rd. Sun —2B 132
Harfleur Ct. SE11 —4B 86
(off Opal St.)
Harford Clo. E4 —7J 9
Harford Ho. SE5 —6C 86
(off Bethwin Rd.)
Harford Ho. W11 —5H 65
Harford M. N19 —3H 49
Harford Rd. E4 —7J 9
Harford St. E1 —4A 70
Harford Wlk. N2 —4B 30
Harfst Way. Swan —7J 129
Hargood Clo. Harr —6E 26
Hargood Rd. SE3 —1A 108
Hargrave Mans. N19 —2H 49
Hargrave Pk. N19 —2G 49
Hargrave Pl. NW5 —5H 49
Hargrave Rd. N19 —2G 49
Hargraves Ho. W12 —7D 64
(off White City Est.)
Hargwyne St. SW9 —3K 103
Haringey Pk. N8 —6J 31
Haringey Pas. N8 —4A 32
Haringey Rd. N8 —4J 31
Harington Ter. N18 —3J 17
Harkett Clo. Harr —2K 25
Harkett Ct. W'stone —2K 25
Harkness Ho. E1 —6G 69
(off Christian St.)
Harland Av. Croy —3F 153
Harland Av. Sidc —3H 127
Harland Clo. SW19 —3K 137
Harland Rd. SE12 —1J 125
Harlech Gdns. Houn —6A 78
Harlech Gdns. Pinn —1B 42
Harlech Rd. N14 —3D 16
Harlech Tower. W3 —2J 81
Harlequin Av. Bren —6A 80
Harlequin Cen. S'hall —4A 78
Harlequin Clo. Hay —5B 60
Harlequin Clo. Iswth —5J 97
Harlequin Ct. NW10 —6K 45
(off Mitchellbrook Way)
Harlequin Ct. W5 —7C 62
Harlequin Ho. Eri —3E 92
(off Kale Rd.)
Harlequin Rd. Tedd —7B 116
Harlequins R.U.F.C. —7J 97
Harlescott Rd. SE15 —4K 105
Harlesden. —2B 64
Harlesden Gdns. NW10 —1B 64
Harlesden La. NW10 —1C 64
Harlesden Plaza. NW10 —2B 64
Harlesden Rd. NW10 —1C 64
Harleston Clo. E5 —2J 51
Harley Clo. Wemb —6D 44
Harley Ct. E11 —7J 35
Harley Ct. N20 —3F 15
Harley Ct. Harr —4H 25
Harley Cres. Harr —4H 25
Harleyford. Brom —1K 143
Harleyford Ct. SE11 —7G 173
Harleyford Mnr. W3 —1J 81
(off Edgecote Clo.)
Harleyford Rd. SE11 —6K 85 (7G 173)
Harleyford St. SE11 —6A 86 (7J 173)
Harley Gdns. SW10 —5A 84
Harley Gro. E3 —3B 70
Harley Ho. E11 —7F 35
Harley Ho. NW1 —4H 159
Harley Pl. W1 —5F 67 (6J 159)
Harley Rd. NW3 —7B 48
Harley Rd. NW10 —2A 64
Harley Rd. Harr —4H 25
Harley St. W1 —4F 67 (4J 159)
Harley Vs. NW10 —2A 64
Harling Ct. SW11 —2D 102
Harlinger St. SE18 —3C 90
Harlington. —6F 77
Harlington Clo. Hay —7E 76
Harlington Rd. Bexh —3E 110
Harlington Rd. Uxb —3C 58
Harlington Rd. E. Felt —7K 95
Harlington Rd. W. Felt —6K 95
Harlowe Clo. E8 —1G 69
Harlowe Ho. E8 —1F 69
(off Clarissa St.)
Harlow Mans. Bark —7F 55
(off Whiting Av.)
Harlow Rd. N13 —3J 17
Harlyn Dri. Pinn —3K 23
Harlynwood. SE5 —7C 86
(off Wyndham Rd.)
Harman Av. Wfd G —6C 20
Harman Clo. E4 —4A 20
Harman Clo. NW2 —3G 47
Harman Clo. SE1 —5G 87
Harman Dri. NW2 —3G 47
Harman Dri. Sidc —6K 109
Harman Rd. Enf —5A 8
Harmondsworth La. W Dray —6A 76
Harmondsworth Rd. W Dray —5A 76
Harmon Ho. SE8 —4B 88
Harmont Ho. W1 —5F 67 (6J 159)
(off Harley St.)
Harmony Clo. NW11 —5G 29
Harmony Clo. Wall —7H 151
Harmony Way. NW4 —4E 28
Harmony Way. Brom —2J 143
Harmood Gro. NW1 —7F 49
Harmood Pl. NW1 —7F 49
Harmood St. NW1 —6F 49
Harmsworth M. SE1 —3A 86 (2K 173)
Harmsworth St. SE17 —5B 86 (6K 173)
Harmsworth Way. N20 —1C 14
Harness Rd. SE28 —2A 92
Harold Av. Belv —5F 93
Harold Av. Hay —3H 77
Harold Ct. SE16 —2K 87
Harold Est. SE1 —3E 86
Harold Gibbons Ct. SE7 —6A 90
Harold Laski Ho. EC1 —3B 68 (2B 162)
(off Percival St.)
Harold Maddison Ho. SE17 —5B 86
(off Alberta St.)
Harold Pl. SE11 —5A 86 (6J 173)
Harold Rd. E4 —4K 19
Harold Rd. E11 —1G 53
Harold Rd. E13 —1K 71
Harold Rd. N8 —5K 31
Harold Rd. N15 —5F 33
Harold Rd. NW10 —3K 63
Harold Rd. SE19 —7D 122
Harold Rd. Sutt —4B 150
Harold Rd. Wfd G —1J 35
Haroldstone Rd. E17 —5K 33
Harold Wilson Ho. SE28 —1B 92
Harold Wilson Ho. SW6 —6H 83
(off Clem Attlee Ct.)
Harp All. EC4 —6B 68 (7A 162)
Harp Bus. Cen. NW2 —1C 46
(off Apsley Way)
Harpenden Rd. E12 —2A 54
Harpenden Rd. SE27 —3B 122
Harpenmead Point. NW2 —2H 47
Harper Clo. N14 —5B 6
Harper Ho. SW9 —3B 104
Harper Rd. E6 —6D 72
Harper Rd. SE1 —3C 86 (7D 168)
Harper's Yd. N17 —1F 33
Harp Island Clo. NW10 —2K 45
Harp La. EC3 —7E 68 (3G 169)
Harpley Sq. E1 —4J 69
Harpour Rd. Bark —6G 55
Harp Rd. W7 —4K 61
Harpsden St. SW11 —1E 102
Harpur M. WC1 —5K 67 (5G 161)
Harpur St. WC1 —5K 67 (5G 161)
Harraden Rd. SE3 —1A 108
Harrier Av. E11 —6K 35
Harrier Ct. Houn —3C 96
Harrier M. SE28 —2H 91
Harrier Rd. NW9 —2A 28
Harriers Clo. W5 —7E 62
Harrier Way. E6 —5D 72
Harries Rd. Hay —4A 60
Harriet Clo. E8 —1G 69
Harriet Gdns. Croy —2G 153
Harriet Ho. SW6 —7K 83
(off Wandon Rd.)
Harriet St. SW1 —2D 84 (7F 165)
Harriet Tubman Clo. SW2 —7K 103
Harriet Wlk. SW1 —2D 84 (7F 165)
Harriet Way. Bush —1C 10
Harringay. —5B 32
Harringay Gdns. N8 —4B 32
Harringay Rd. N15 —5B 32
(in two parts)
Harrington Clo. NW10 —3K 45
Harrington Clo. Croy —2J 151
Harrington Ct. W10 —3H 65
Harrington Ct. Croy —2D 152
Harrington Gdns. SW7 —4K 83
Harrington Hill. E5 —1H 51
Harrington Ho. NW1 —3G 67 (1A 160)
(off Harrington St.)
Harrington Ho. Uxb —4D 40
Harrington Rd. E11 —1G 53
Harrington Rd. SE25 —4G 141
Harrington Rd. SW7 —4B 84 (3A 170)
Harrington Sq. NW1 —2G 67
Harrington St. NW1 —2G 67 (1A 160)
(in two parts)
Harrington Way. SE18 —3B 90
Harriott Clo. SE10 —4H 89
Harris Bldgs. E1 —6G 69
(off Burslem St.)
Harris Clo. Enf —1G 7
Harris Clo. Houn —1E 96
Harris Ct. Wemb —3F 45
Harris Ho. SW9 —3A 104
(off St James's Cres.)
Harris Lodge. SE6 —1E 124
Harrison Clo. N20 —1H 15
Harrison Ct. Shep —5D 130
Harrison Ho. SE17 —5D 86
(off Brandon St.)
Harrison Rd. Dag —6H 57
Harrison's Ri. Croy —3B 152
Harrison St. WC1 —3J 67 (2F 161)
Harris Rd. Bexh —1E 110
Harris Rd. Dag —5F 57
Harris St. E17 —7B 34
Harris St. SE5 —7D 86
Harris Way. Sun —1G 131
Harrogate Ct. N11 —6K 15
Harrogate Ct. SE12 —7J 107
Harrogate Ct. SE26 —3G 123
(off Droitwich Clo.)
Harrold Ho. NW3 —7A 48
Harrold Ho. NW6 —7A 48
Harrold Rd. Dag —5B 56
Harrovian Bus. Village. Harr —7J 25
Harrow. —6J 25
Harrow Av. Enf —6A 8
Harroway Rd. SW11 —2B 102
Harrow Borough F.C. —4E 42
Harrowby St. W2 —6C 66 (7D 158)
Harrow Clo. Chess —7D 146
Harrowdene Clo. Wemb —4D 44
Harrowdene Gdns. Tedd —6A 116
Harrowdene Rd. Wemb —3D 44
Harrow Dri. N9 —1A 18
Harrowes Meade. Edgw —3B 12
Harrow Fields Gdns. Harr —3J 43
Harrowgate Ho. E9 —6K 51
Harrowgate Rd. E9 —6A 52
Harrow Grn. E11 —3G 53
Harrow La. E14 —7E 70
Harrow Lodge. NW8 —4B 66 (3A 158)
(off Northwick Ter.)
Harrow Mnr. Way. SE2 —1C 92
Harrow Mus. & Heritage Cen. —3G 25
Harrow On The Hill. —1J 43
Harrow Pk. Harr —2J 43
Harrow Pl. E1 —6E 68 (7H 163)
Harrow Road. (Junct.) —7H 45
Harrow Rd. E6 —1C 72
Harrow Rd. E11 —3G 53
Harrow Rd. NW10 —3C 64
Harrow Rd. W2 & NW1 —5A 66 (6A 158)
(in two parts)
Harrow Rd. W10 & W9 —4G 65
Harrow Rd. Bark —1J 73
Harrow Rd. Cars —6C 150
Harrow Rd. Felt —2C 112
Harrow Rd. Ilf —4G 55
Harrow Rd. Wemb —4K 43
(HA0)
Harrow Rd. Wemb —5G 45
(HA9)
Harrow Rd. Bri. W2 —5A 66
Harrow School Old Speech Room Gallery. (off High St., Harrow School) —1J 43
Harrow St. NW1 —5D 158
Harrow Vw. Harr —2G 25
Harrow Vw. Hay —6J 59
Harrow Vw. Uxb —3E 58
Harrow Vw. Rd. W5 —4B 62
Harrow Way. Shep —2E 130
Harrow Weald. —1J 25
Harrow Weald Pk. Harr —6C 10
Harry Hinkins Ho. SE17 —5C 86
(off Bronti Clo.)
Harry Lambourn Ho. SE15 —7H 87
(off Gervase St.)
Hartcliff Ct. W7 —2K 79
Hart Ct. E6 —7E 54
Harte Rd. Houn —2D 96
Hartfield Av. N'holt —2K 59
Hartfield Cres. SW19 —7H 119
Hartfield Cres. W W'ck —3J 155
Hartfield Gro. SE20 —1J 141
Hartfield Ho. N'holt —2K 59
(off Hartfield Av.)
Hartfield Rd. SW19 —7H 119
Hartfield Rd. Chess —5D 146
Hartfield Rd. W W'ck —4J 155
Hartfield Ter. E3 —2C 70
Hartford Av. Harr —3A 26
Hartford Rd. Bex —6G 111
Hartford Rd. Eps —6H 147
Hart Gro. W5 —1G 81
Hart Gro. S'hall —5E 60
Hart Gro. Ct. W5 —1G 81
Hartham Clo. N7 —5J 49
Hartham Clo. Iswth —1A 98
Hartham Rd. N7 —5J 49
Hartham Rd. N17 —2F 33
Hartham Rd. Iswth —1K 97
Harting Rd. SE9 —3C 126
Hartington Clo. Harr —4J 43
Hartington Corner. (Junct.) —1F 95
Hartington Ct. SW8 —1J 103
Hartington Ct. W4 —7H 81
Hartington Ho. SW1 —5H 85 (5D 172)
(off Drummond Ga.)
Hartington Rd. E16 —6K 71
Hartington Rd. E17 —6A 34
Hartington Rd. SW8 —1J 103
Hartington Rd. W4 —7H 81
Hartington Rd. W13 —7B 62
Hartington Rd. S'hall —3C 78
Hartington Rd. Twic —7B 98
Hartismere Rd. SW6 —7H 83
Hartlake Rd. E9 —6K 51
Hartland. NW1 —1G 67
(off Royal College St.)
Hartland Clo. N21 —6H 7
Hartland Clo. Edgw —2B 12
Hartland Ct. N11 —5J 15
(off Hartland Rd.)
Hartland Dri. Edgw —2B 12
Hartland Dri. Ruis —3K 41
Hartland Rd. E15 —7H 53
Hartland Rd. N11 —5J 15
Hartland Rd. NW1 —7F 49

Hartland Rd.—Hazelwood Ct.

Hartland Rd. NW6 —2H 65
Hartland Rd. Hamp H —4F 115
Hartland Rd. Iswth —3A 98
Hartland Rd. Mord —7J 137
Hartlands Clo. Bex —6F 111
Hartlands, The. Houn —6K 77
Hartland Way. Croy —3A 154
Hartland Way. Mord —7H 137
Hartlepool Ct. E16 —1F 91
Hartley Av. E6 —1C 72
Hartley Av. NW7 —5G 13
Hartley Clo. NW7 —5G 13
Hartley Clo. Brom —2D 144
Hartley Ho. SE1 —4F 87
(off Longfield Est.)
Hartley Rd. E11 —1H 53
Hartley Rd. Croy —7C 140
Hartley Rd. Well —7C 92
Hartley St. E2 —3J 69
(in two parts)
Hart Lodge. High Bar —3B 4
Hartmann Rd. E16 —1B 90
Hartnoll St. N7 —5K 49
Harton Clo. Brom —1B 144
Harton Rd. N9 —2C 18
Harton St. SE8 —1C 106
Hartop Point. SW6 —7G 83
(off Pellant Rd.)
Hartsbourne Av. Bus H —2B 10
Hartsbourne Clo. Bus H —2C 10
Hartsbourne Ct. S'hall —6G 61
(off Fleming Rd.)
Hartsbourne Pk. Bush —2D 10
Hartsbourne Rd. Bus H —2C 10
Harts Gro. Wfd G —5D 20
Hartshill Clo. Uxb —7D 40
Hartshorn All. EC3 —1H 169
Hartshorn Gdns. E6 —4E 72
Hart's La. SE14 —1A 106
Harts La. Bark —6F 55
Hartslock Dri. SE2 —2D 92
Hartsmead Rd. SE9 —2D 126
Hart St. EC3 —7E 68 (2H 169)
Hartsway. Enf —4D 8
Hartswood Gdns. W12 —3B 82
Hartswood Rd. W12 —2B 82
Hartsworth Clo. E13 —2H 71
Hartville Rd. SE18 —4J 91
Hartwell Dri. E4 —6K 19
Hartwell St. E8 —6F 51
Hartwood Grn. Bush —2C 10
Harvard Ct. NW6 —5K 47
Harvard Hill. W4 —6H 81
Harvard Ho. SE17 —6B 86
(off Doddington Gro.)
Harvard La. W4 —5J 81
Harvard Rd. SE13 —5E 106
Harvard Rd. W4 —5H 81
Harvard Rd. Iswth —1J 97
Harvel Clo. Orp —3K 145
Harvel Cres. SE2 —5D 92
Harvest Bank Rd. W W'ck —3H 155
Harvest Ct. Shep —4C 130
Harvesters Clo. Iswth —5H 97
Harvest La. Th Dit —6A 134
Harvest Rd. Felt —4J 113
Harvey Ct. E17 —5C 34
Harvey Dri. Hamp —1F 133
Harvey Gdns. E11 —1H 53
Harvey Gdns. SE7 —5A 90
Harvey Ho. N1 —1D 68
(off Colville Est.)
Harvey Ho. SW1 —5H 85 (6D 172)
(off Aylesford St.)
Harvey Ho. Bren —5E 80
Harvey Ho. Romf —4D 38
Harvey Lodge. W9 —5J 65
(off Admiral Wlk.)
Harvey Point. E16 —5J 71
(off Fife Rd.)
Harvey Rd. E11 —1G 53
Harvey Rd. N8 —5K 31
Harvey Rd. SE5 —1D 104
(in two parts)
Harvey Rd. Houn —7D 96
Harvey Rd. Ilf —5F 55
Harvey Rd. N'holt —7A 42
Harvey Rd. Uxb —2C 58
Harvey Rd. W on T —7H 131
Harvey's Bldgs. WC2 —7J 67 (3F 167)
Harveys La. Romf —2K 57
Harvey St. N1 —1D 68
Harvill Rd. Sidc —5E 128
Harvil Rd. Hare & Ick —5A 22
Harvington Wlk. E8 —7G 51
Harvist Est. N7 —4A 50
Harvist Rd. NW6 —2F 65
Harwell Clo. Ruis —1F 41
Harwell Pas. N2 —4D 30
Harwood Av. Brom —2K 143
Harwood Av. Mitc —3C 138
Harwood Clo. N12 —6H 15
Harwood Clo. Wemb —4D 44
Harwood Ct. N1 —1D 68
(off Colville Est.)
Harwood Ct. SW15 —4E 100
Harwood Dri. Uxb —1B 58
Harwood Point. SE16 —2B 88
Harwood Rd. SW6 —7J 83
Harwoods Yd. N21 —7F 7
Harwood Ter. SW6 —1K 101
Haselbury Rd. N18 & N9 —4K 17
Haseley End. SE23 —7J 105
Haselrigge Rd. SW4 —4H 103
Haseltine Rd. SE26 —4B 124
Haselwood Dri. Enf —4G 7
Haskard Rd. Dag —4D 56
Hasker St. SW3 —4C 84 (3D 170)
Haslam Av. Sutt —1G 149
Haslam Clo. N1 —7A 50
Haslam Clo. Uxb —2E 40
Haslam Ct. N11 —4A 16
Haslam St. SE15 —7F 87
Haslemere and Heathrow Est., The. Houn —2K 95
Haslemere Av. NW4 —6F 29
Haslemere Av. SW18 —2K 119
Haslemere Av. W7 & W13 —3A 80
Haslemere Av. Barn —1J 15
Haslemere Av. Houn —2A 96
Haslemere Av. Mitc —2B 138
Haslemere Bus. Cen. Enf —4C 8
Haslemere Clo. Hamp —5D 114
Haslemere Clo. Wall —5J 151
Haslemere Gdns. N3 —3H 29
Haslemere Ind. Est. SW18 —2K 119
Haslemere Rd. N8 —7H 31
Haslemere Rd. N21 —2G 17
Haslemere Rd. Bexh —2F 111
Haslemere Rd. Ilf —2K 55
Haslemere Rd. T Hth —5B 140
Hasler Clo. SE28 —7B 74
Haslers Wharf. E3 —1A 70
(off Old Ford Rd.)
Haslett Rd. Shep —2G 131
Hasluck Gdns. New Bar —6E 4
Hassard St. E2 —2F 69 (1K 163)
Hassendean Rd. SE3 —6K 89
Hassett Rd. E9 —6K 51
Hassocks Clo. SE26 —3H 123
Hassocks Rd. SW16 —1H 139
Hassock Wood. Kes —4B 156
Hassop Rd. NW2 —4F 47
Hassop Wlk. SE9 —4C 126
Hasted Rd. SE7 —5B 90
Hastings Av. Ilf —4G 37
Hastings Clo. SE15 —7G 87
Hastings Clo. Barn —4F 5
Hastings Ct. Tedd —5H 115
Hastings Dri. Surb —6C 134
Hastings Ho. SE18 —4D 90
(off Mulgrave Rd.)
Hastings Ho. W12 —7D 64
(off White City Est.)
Hastings Ho. W13 —7B 62
Hastings Ho. WC1 —3J 67 (2E 160)
(off Hastings St.)
Hastings Rd. N11 —5B 16
Hastings Rd. N17 —3D 32
Hastings Rd. W13 —7B 62
Hastings Rd. Brom —1C 156
Hastings Rd. Croy —1F 153
Hastings St. WC1 —3J 67 (2E 160)
Hastingwood Ct. E17 —5D 34
Hastingwood Trad. Est. N18 —6E 18
Hastoe Clo. Hay —4C 60
Hat & Mitre Ct. EC1 —4B 162
Hatcham M. Bus. Cen. SE14 —1K 105
Hatcham Pk. M. SE14 —1K 105
Hatcham Pk. Rd. SE14 —1K 105
Hatcham Rd. SE15 —6J 87
Hatchard Rd. N19 —2H 49
Hatchcliffe St. SE10 —5H 89
Hatchcroft. NW4 —3D 28
Hatch End. —1D 24
Hatchett Rd. Felt —1E 112
Hatchfield Ho. N15 —6E 32
(off Albert Rd.)
Hatch Gro. Romf —4E 38
Hatch La. E4 —4A 20
(in two parts)
Hatch La. W Dray —7A 76
Hatch Pl. King T —5F 117
Hatch Rd. SW16 —2J 139
Hatch Side. Chig —5K 21
Hatch, The. Enf —1E 8
Hatchwood Clo. Wfd G —4C 20
Hatcliffe Clo. SE3 —3H 107
Hatfield Clo. SE14 —7K 87
Hatfield Clo. Ilf —3F 37
Hatfield Clo. Mitc —4B 138
Hatfield Ct. SE3 —7J 89
Hatfield Ct. N'holt —3A 60
(off Canberra Dri.)
Hatfield Ho. EC1 —4C 68 (4C 162)
(off Golden La. Est.)
Hatfield Mead. Mord —5J 137
Hatfield Rd. E15 —5G 53
Hatfield Rd. W4 —2K 81
Hatfield Rd. W13 —1A 80
Hatfield Rd. Dag —6E 56
Hatfields. SE1 —1A 86 (4K 167)
Hathaway Clo. Brom —1D 156
Hathaway Clo. Ruis —4H 41
Hathaway Clo. Stan —5F 11
Hathaway Cres. E12 —6D 54
Hathaway Gdns. W13 —5A 62
Hathaway Gdns. Romf —5D 38
Hathaway Ho. N1 —2E 68 (1G 163)
Hathaway Rd. Croy —7B 140
Hatherleigh Clo. Chess —5D 146
Hatherleigh Clo. Mord —4J 137
Hatherleigh Rd. Ruis —2J 41
Hatherley Ct. W2 —6K 65
(off Hatherley Gro.)
Hatherley Cres. Sidc —2A 128
Hatherley Gdns. E6 —3B 72
Hatherley Gdns. N8 —6J 31
Hatherley Gro. W2 —6K 65
Hatherley Ho. E17 —4C 34
Hatherley M. E17 —4C 34
Hatherley Rd. E17 —4B 34
Hatherley Rd. Rich —1F 99
Hatherley Rd. Sidc —4A 128
Hatherley St. SW1 —4G 85 (4B 172)
Hathern Gdns. SE9 —4E 126
Hatherop Rd. Hamp —7D 114
Hathersage Ct. N1 —5D 50
Hathorne Clo. SE15 —2H 105
Hathway St. SE15 —2K 105
Hathway Ter. SE15 —2K 105
(off Hathway St.)
Hatley Av. Ilf —4G 37
Hatley Clo. N11 —5J 15
Hatley Rd. N7 —2K 49
Hatteraick St. SE16 —2J 87
Hattersfield Clo. Belv —4F 93
Hatton. —4H 95
Hatton Clo. SE18 —7H 91
Hatton Cross. (Junct.) —4H 95
Hatton Garden. EC1 —5A 68 (5K 161)
Hatton Gdns. Mitc —5D 138
Hatton Grn. Felt —4J 95
Hatton Gro. W Dray —2A 76
Hatton Pl. EC1 —5A 68 (5K 161)
Hatton Rd. Bedf & Felt —7E 94
Hatton Rd. Croy —1A 152
Hatton Rd. S. Felt —4H 95
Hatton Row. NW8 —4B 158
Hatton St. NW8 —4B 66 (4B 158)
Hatton Wall. EC1 —5A 68 (5K 161)
Haughmond. N12 —4E 14
Haunch of Venison Yd. W1 —6F 67 (1J 165)
Hauteville Ct. Gdns. W6 —3B 82
(off South Side)
Havana Rd. SW19 —2J 119
Havannah St. E14 —2C 88
Havant Rd. E17 —3E 34
Havelock Clo. W12 —7D 64
Havelock Ct. S'hall —3D 78
(off Havelock Rd.)
Havelock Ho. SE23 —1J 123
Havelock Pl. Harr —6J 25
Havelock Rd. N17 —2G 33
Havelock Rd. SW19 —5A 120
Havelock Rd. Belv —4F 93
Havelock Rd. Brom —4A 144
Havelock Rd. Croy —2F 153
Havelock Rd. Harr —3J 25
Havelock Rd. S'hall —3C 78
Havelock St. N1 —1J 67
Havelock St. Ilf —2F 55
Havelock Ter. SW8 —1F 103
Havelock Wlk. SE23 —1J 123
Haven Clo. SE9 —3D 126
Haven Clo. SW19 —3F 119
Haven Clo. Hay —4G 59
Haven Clo. Sidc —6C 128
Haven Ct. Beck —2E 142
Haven Ct. Surb —6F 135
Haven Grn. W5 —6D 62
Haven Grn. Ct. W5 —6D 62
Havenhurst Ri. Enf —2F 7
Haven La. W5 —6E 62
Haven Lodge. Enf —6K 7
(off Village Rd.)
Haven M. E3 —5B 70
Haven Pl. W5 —7D 62
Havenpool. NW8 —1K 65
(off Abbey Rd.)
Haven Rd. Ashf —3D 112
Haven St. NW1 —7F 49
Haven, The. N14 —6A 6
Haven, The. Rich —3G 99
Haven, The. Sun —7J 113
Haven Wood. Wemb —3H 45
Haverfield Gdns. Rich —7G 81
Haverfield Rd. E3 —3A 70
Haverford Way. Edgw —1F 27
Haverhill Rd. E4 —1K 19
Haverhill Rd. SW12 —1G 121
Havering Dri. Romf —4K 39
Havering Gdns. Romf —5C 38
Havering St. E1 —6K 69
Havering Way. Bark —3B 74
Haversham Clo. Twic —6D 98
Haversham Ct. Gnfd —6K 43
Haversham Pl. N6 —2D 48
Haverstock Hill. NW3 —5C 48
Haverstock Pl. EC1 —3B 68 (1B 162)
(off Haverstock St.)
Haverstock Rd. NW5 —5E 48
Haverstock St. N1 —2B 68 (1B 162)
Havil St. SE5 —7E 86
Havisham Ho. SE16 —2G 87
Havisham Pl. SE19 —7B 122
Hawarden Gro. SE24 —7C 104
Hawarden Hill. NW2 —3C 46
Hawarden Rd. E17 —4K 33
Hawbridge Rd. E11 —1F 53
Hawes Ho. E17 —4K 33
Hawes La. W W'ck —1E 154
Hawes Rd. N18 —6C 18
Hawes Rd. Brom —1K 143
(in two parts)
Hawes St. N1 —7B 50
Hawgood St. E3 —5C 70
Hawkdene. E4 —6J 9
Hawke Ct. Hay —4A 60
(off Perth Av.)
Hawke Pk. Rd. N22 —3B 32
Hawke Pl. SE16 —2K 87
Hawker Clo. Wall —7J 151
Hawke Rd. SE19 —6D 122
Hawkesbury Rd. SW15 —5D 100
Hawkesfield Rd. SE23 —2A 124
Hawkesley Clo. Twic —4A 116
Hawkes Rd. Felt —7J 95
Hawkes Rd. Mitc —1D 138
Hawkesworth Clo. N'wd —1G 23
Hawke Tower. SE14 —6A 88
Hawkewood Rd. Sun —3J 131
Hawkfield Ct. Iswth —2J 97
Hawkhurst Gdns. Chess —4E 146
Hawkhurst Rd. SW16 —1H 139
Hawkhurst Way. N Mald —5K 135
Hawkhurst Way. W W'ck —2D 154
Hawkinge. N17 —2D 32
(off Gloucester Rd.)
Hawkins Clo. NW7 —5E 12
Hawkins Clo. Harr —7H 25
Hawkins Ct. SE18 —4C 90
Hawkins Ho. SE8 —6C 88
(off New King St.)
Hawkins Ho. SW1 —6G 85 (7B 172)
(off Dolphin Sq.)
Hawkins Rd. Tedd —6B 116
Hawkins Way. SE6 —5C 124
Hawkley Gdns. SE27 —2B 122
Hawkridge Clo. Romf —6C 38
Hawksbrook La. Beck —6D 142
(in two parts)
Hawkshaw Clo. SW2 —7J 103
Hawkshead. NW1 —1A 160
Hawkshead Clo. Brom —7G 125
Hawkshead Rd. NW10 —7B 46
Hawkshead Rd. W4 —2A 82
Hawkslade Rd. SE15 —5K 105
Hawksley Rd. N16 —3E 50
Hawks M. SE10 —7E 88
Hawksmoor Clo. E6 —6C 72
Hawksmoor Clo. SE18 —5J 91
Hawksmoor M. E1 —7H 69
Hawksmoor Pl. E2 —4G 69
(off Cheshire St.)
Hawksmoor St. W6 —6F 83
Hawksmouth. E4 —7K 9
Hawks Pas. King T —2F 135
(off Fairfield Rd.)
Hawks Rd. King T —2F 135
Hawkstone Rd. SE16 —4J 87
Hawkwell Ct. E4 —3K 19
Hawkwell Wlk. N1 —1C 68
(off Maldon Rd.)
Hawkwood Cres. E4 —6J 9
Hawkwood La. Chst —1G 145
Hawkwood Mt. E5 —1H 51
Hawlands Dri. Pinn —7C 24
Hawley Clo. Hamp —6D 114
Hawley Cres. NW1 —7F 49
Hawley M. NW1 —7F 49
Hawley Rd. N18 —5E 18
Hawley Rd. NW1 —7F 49
(in three parts)
Hawley St. NW1 —7F 49
Hawley Way. Ashf —5C 112
Hawstead Rd. SE6 —6D 106
Hawsted. Buck H —1E 20
Hawter. NW9 —1B 28
Hawthorn Av. E3 —1B 70
Hawthorn Av. N13 —5D 16
Hawthorn Cen. Harr —5K 25
Hawthorn Clo. Hamp —5E 114
Hawthorn Clo. Houn —7K 77
Hawthorn Clo. Orp —6H 145
Hawthorn Cotts. Well —3A 110
(off Hook La.)
Hawthorn Ct. Pinn —2A 24
(off Rickmansworth Rd.)
Hawthorn Ct. Rich —1H 99
Hawthorn Cres. SW17 —5E 120
Hawthornden Clo. N12 —6H 15
Hawthorndene Clo. Brom —2H 155
Hawthorndene Rd. Brom —2H 155
Hawthorn Dri. Harr —6E 24
Hawthorn Dri. W W'ck —4G 155
Hawthorne Av. Cars —7E 150
Hawthorne Av. Harr —6A 26
Hawthorne Av. Mitc —2B 138
Hawthorne Av. Ruis —6K 23
Hawthorne Av. T Hth —1B 140
Hawthorne Clo. N1 —6E 50
Hawthorne Clo. Brom —3D 144
Hawthorne Clo. Sutt —2A 150
Hawthorne Ct. W5 —1E 80
Hawthorne Ct. N'wd —2J 23
Hawthorne Cres. W Dray —2B 76
Hawthorne Farm Av. N'holt —1C 60
Hawthorne Gro. NW9 —7J 27
Hawthorne Ho. SW1 —5G 85 (6B 172)
(off Churchill Gdns.)
Hawthorne M. Gnfd —6G 61
Hawthorne Pl. Hay —7H 59
Hawthorne Rd. E17 —3C 34
Hawthorne Rd. Brom —3C 144
Hawthorn Gdns. W5 —3D 80
Hawthorn Gro. SE20 —7H 123
Hawthorn Gro. Enf —1J 7
Hawthorn Hatch. Bren —7B 80
Hawthorn M. NW7 —1G 29
Hawthorn Pl. Eri —5J 93
Hawthorn Rd. N8 —3H 31
Hawthorn Rd. N18 —6A 18
Hawthorn Rd. NW10 —7C 46
Hawthorn Rd. Bexh —4F 111
Hawthorn Rd. Bren —7B 80
Hawthorn Rd. Buck H —4G 21
Hawthorn Rd. Sutt —6C 150
Hawthorn Rd. Wall —7F 151
Hawthorns. Wfd G —3D 20
Hawthorns, The. Eps —7B 148
Hawthorn Wlk. W10 —4G 65
Hawthorn Way. N9 —2K 17
Hawthorn Way. Shep —4F 131
Hawtrey Av. N'holt —2B 60
Hawtrey Dri. Ruis —7J 23
Hawtrey Rd. NW3 —7C 48
Haxted Rd. Brom —1K 143
Hay Clo. E15 —7G 53
Haycroft Gdns. NW10 —1C 64
Haycroft Rd. SW2 —5J 103
Haycroft Rd. Surb —2D 146
Hay Currie St. E14 —6D 70
Hayday Rd. E16 —5J 71
Haydens M. W3 —6J 63
Hayden's Pl. W11 —6H 65
Hayden Way. Romf —2J 39
Haydock Av. N'holt —6E 42
Haydock Grn. N'holt —6E 42
Haydock Grn. Flats. N'holt —6E 42
(off Haydock Grn.)
Haydon Clo. NW9 —4J 27
Haydon Clo. Enf —6K 7
Haydon Dri. Pinn —4J 23
Haydon Pk. Rd. SW19 —5J 119
Haydon Rd. Dag —2C 56
Haydons Rd. SW19 —5K 119
Haydon St. EC3 —7F 69 (2J 169)
Haydon Wlk. E1 —6F 69 (1K 169)
Haydon Way. SW11 —4B 102
Hayes. —1J 155
(Bromley)
Hayes. —6G 59
(Hillingdon)
Hayes Bri. Retail Cen. Hay —7A 60
Hayes Chase. W W'ck —6F 143
Hayes Clo. Brom —2J 155
Hayes Ct. SE5 —7C 86
(off Camberwell New Rd.)
Hayes Ct. SW2 —1J 121
Hayes Cres. NW11 —5H 29
Hayes Cres. Sutt —4F 149
Hayes End. —5F 59
Hayes End Clo. Hay —5F 59
Hayes End Dri. Hay —4F 59
Hayes End Rd. Hay —4F 59
Hayes F.C. —7H 59
Hayesford Pk. Dri. Brom —5H 143
Hayes Garden. Brom —2J 155
Hayes Hill. Brom —1G 155
Hayes Hill Rd. Brom —1H 155
Hayes La. Beck —3E 142
Hayes La. Brom —5J 143
Hayes Mead Rd. Brom —1G 155
Hayes Metro Cen. Hay —7A 60
Hayes Pl. NW1 —4C 66 (4D 158)
Hayes Rd. Brom —4J 143
Hayes Rd. S'hall —4K 77
Hayes St. Brom —1K 155
Hayes Town. —2H 77
Hayes Way. Beck —4E 142
Hayes Wood Av. Brom & Hayes —1K 155
Hayfield Pas. E1 —4J 69
Hayfield Yd. E1 —4J 69
Haygarth Pl. SW19 —5F 119
Haygreen Clo. King T —6H 117
Hay Hill. W1 —7F 67 (3K 165)
Hayland Clo. NW9 —4K 27
Hay La. NW9 —4J 27
Hayles Bldgs. SE11 —4B 86
(off Elliotts Row)
Hayles St. SE11 —4B 86
Haylett Gdns. King T —4D 134
Hayling Av. Felt —3J 113
Hayling Clo. N16 —5E 50
Hayling Ct. Sutt —4E 148
Haymaker Clo. Uxb —7B 40
Hayman Cres. Hay —2F 59
Haymans Point. SE11 —4K 85 (4G 173)
Hayman St. N1 —7B 50
Haymarket. SW1 —7H 67 (3C 166)
Haymarket Arc. SW1 —3C 166
Haymer Gdns. Wor Pk —3C 148
Haymerle Ho. SE15 —6G 87
(off Haymerle Rd.)
Haymerle Rd. SE15 —6G 87
Haymill Clo. Gnfd —3K 61
Hayne Ho. W11 —1G 83
(off Penzance Pl.)
Hayne Rd. Beck —2B 142
Haynes Clo. N11 —3K 15
Haynes Clo. N17 —7C 18
Haynes Clo. SE3 —3G 107
Haynes La. SE19 —6E 122
Haynes Rd. Wemb —7E 44
Hayne St. EC1 —5B 68 (5B 162)
Haynt Wlk. SW20 —3G 137
Hay's Galleria. SE1 —1E 86 (4G 169)
Hays La. SE1 —1E 86 (4G 169)
Haysleigh Gdns. SE20 —2G 141
Hay's M. W1 —1F 85 (4J 165)
Haysoms Clo. Romf —4K 39
Haystall Clo. Hay —2G 59
Hay St. E2 —1G 69
Hayter Ct. E11 —2K 53
Hayter Rd. SW2 —5J 103
Hayton Clo. E8 —6F 51
Hayward Clo. SW19 —7K 119
Hayward Clo. Dart —5K 111
Hayward Ct. SW9 —2J 103
(off Clapham Rd.)
Hayward Gallery. —4H 167
Hayward Gdns. SW15 —6E 100
Hayward Rd. N20 —2F 15
Hayward Rd. Th Dit —7K 133
Haywards Clo. Chad H —5B 38
Hayward's Pl. EC1 —4B 68 (3A 162)
Haywards Yd. SE4 —5B 106
(off Lindal Rd.)
Haywood Clo. Pinn —2B 24
Haywood Lodge. N11 —6D 16
(off Oak La.)
Haywood Rd. Brom —4B 144
Hayworth Clo. Enf —2F 9
Hazel Av. W Dray —3C 76
Hazel Bank. SE25 —2E 140
Hazel Bank. Surb —1J 147
Hazelbank Rd. SE6 —2F 125
Hazelbourne Rd. SW12 —6F 103
Hazelbury Clo. SW19 —2J 137
Hazelbury Grn. N9 —3K 17
Hazelbury La. N9 —3K 17
Hazel Clo. N13 —3J 17
Hazel Clo. N19 —2G 49
Hazel Clo. SE15 —2G 105
Hazel Clo. Bren —7B 80
Hazel Clo. Croy —7K 141
Hazel Clo. Mitc —4H 139
Hazel Clo. Twic —7G 97
Hazel Ct. W5 —7E 62
Hazel Cres. Romf —1H 39
Hazel Cft. Pinn —6A 10
Hazelcroft Clo. Uxb —7B 40
Hazeldean Rd. NW10 —7K 45
Hazeldene Dri. Pinn —3A 24
Hazeldene Gdns. Uxb —1E 58
Hazeldene Rd. Ilf —2B 56
Hazeldene Rd. Well —2C 110
Hazeldon Rd. SE4 —5A 106
Hazeleigh Gdns. Wfd G —5H 21
Hazel Gdns. Edgw —4C 12
Hazelgreen Clo. N21 —1G 17
Hazel Gro. SE26 —4K 123
Hazel Gro. Orp —2E 156
Hazel Gro. Romf —3E 38
Hazel Gro. Wemb —1E 62
Hazelhurst. Beck —1F 143
Hazelhurst Ct. SE6 —5E 124
(off Beckenham Hill Rd.)
Hazelhurst Rd. SW17 —4A 120
Hazel La. Rich —2E 116
Hazellville Rd. N19 —7H 31
Hazelmere Clo. Felt —6G 95
Hazelmere Clo. N'holt —2D 60
Hazelmere Ct. SW2 —1K 121
Hazelmere Dri. N'holt —2D 60
Hazelmere Rd. NW6 —1H 65
Hazelmere Rd. N'holt —2D 60
Hazelmere Rd. Orp —4G 145
Hazelmere Wlk. N'holt —2D 60
Hazelmere Way. Brom —6J 143
Hazel Rd. E15 —5G 53
Hazel Rd. NW10 —3D 64
(in two parts)
Hazeltree La. N'holt —3C 60
Hazel Wlk. Brom —6E 144
Hazel Way. E4 —6G 19
Hazel Way. SE1 —4F 87
Hazelwood Av. Mord —4K 137
Hazelwood Clo. W5 —2E 80
Hazelwood Clo. Harr —4F 25
Hazelwood Ct. N13 —4F 17
(off Hazelwood La.)

Hazelwood Ct. NW10 —3A 46
Hazelwood Ct. Surb —6E 134
Hazelwood Cres. N13 —4F 17
Hazelwood Dri. Pinn —2K 23
Hazelwood Ho. SE8 —4A 88
Hazelwood Houses. Short —3G 143
Hazelwood La. N13 —4F 17
Hazelwood Rd. E17 —5A 34
Hazelwood Rd. Enf —6A 8
Hazlebury Rd. SW6 —2K 101
Hazledean Rd. Croy —2D 152
Hazledene Rd. W4 —6J 81
Hazlemere Gdns. Wor Pk —1C 148
Hazlewell Rd. SW15 —5E 100
Hazlewood Clo. E5 —3A 52
Hazlewood Cres. W10 —4G 65
Hazlewood Tower. W10 —4G 65
(off Golborne Gdns.)
Hazlitt Clo. Felt —4C 114
Hazlitt M. W14 —3G 83
Hazlitt Rd. W14 —3G 83
Heacham Av. Uxb —3E 40
Headbourne Ho. SE1 —7F 169
Headcorn Pl. T Hth —4K 139
Headcorn Rd. N17 —7A 18
Headcorn Rd. Brom —5H 125
Headcorn Rd. T Hth —4K 139
Headfort Pl. SW1 —2E 84 (7H 165)
Headington Rd. SW18 —2A 120
Headlam Rd. SW4 —6H 103
(in two parts)
Headlam St. E1 —4H 69
Headley App. Ilf —5F 37
Headley Av. Wall —5K 151
Headley Clo. Eps —6G 147
Headley Ct. SE26 —5J 123
Headley Dri. Ilf —6F 37
Headley Dri. New Ad —7D 154
Head's M. W11 —6J 65
Headstone. —4G 25
Headstone Dri. Harr —3H 25
Headstone Gdns. Harr —4G 25
Headstone La. Harr —7A 10
Headstone Pde. Harr —4H 25
Headstone Rd. Harr —5J 25
Head St. E1 —6K 69
(in two parts)
Headway Clo. Rich —4C 116
Heald St. SE14 —1C 106
Healey Ho. SW9 —7A 86
Healey St. NW1 —6F 49
Hearne Rd. W4 —6G 81
Hearn Ri. N'holt —1B 60
Hearn's Bldgs. SE17 —4D 86
Hearn St. EC2 —4E 68 (4H 163)
Hearnville Rd. SW12 —1E 120
Heatham Pk. Twic —7K 97
Heath Av. Bexh —6D 92
Heathbourne Rd. Bus H & Stan —1D 10
Heath Brow. NW3 —3A 48
Heath Bus. Cen. Houn —4G 97
Heath Clo. NW11 —7K 29
Heath Clo. W5 —4F 63
Heath Clo. Hay —7F 77
Heathcock Ct. WC2 —7J 67 (3F 167)
(off Exchange Ct.)
Heathcote Av. Ilf —2D 36
Heathcote Ct. Ilf —1D 36
(in two parts)
Heathcote Gro. E4 —3K 19
Heathcote Rd. Twic —6B 98
Heathcote St. WC1 —4K 67 (3G 161)
Heath Ct. Houn —4D 96
Heath Ct. Uxb —7A 40
Heathcroft. NW11 —1K 47
Heathcroft. W5 —4F 63
Heathcroft Av. Sun —7H 113
Heathcroft Gdns. E17 —1F 35
Heathdale Av. Houn —3C 96
Heathdene Dri. Belv —4H 93
Heathdene Rd. SW16 —7K 121
Heathdene Rd. Wall —7F 151
Heath Dri. NW3 —4K 47
Heath Dri. SW20 —4E 136
Heath Dri. Sutt —7A 150
Heathedge. SE26 —2H 123
Heath End Rd. Bex —1K 129
Heather Av. Romf —2K 39
Heatherbank. SE9 —2D 108
Heatherbank. Chst —2E 144
Heather Clo. E6 —6E 72
Heather Clo. N7 —3K 49
Heather Clo. SE13 —7F 107
Heather Clo. SW8 —3F 103
Heather Clo. Hamp —1D 132
Heather Clo. Iswth —5H 97
Heather Clo. Romf —1K 39
Heather Clo. Uxb —5B 58
Heather Ct. Sidc —6D 128
Heatherdale Clo. King T —6G 117
Heatherdene Clo. N12 —7F 15
Heatherdene Clo. Mitc —4B 138
Heather Dri. Enf —2G 7
Heather Dri. Romf —2K 39
Heatherfield Pk. Dri. Romf —5B 38
Heatherfold Way. Pinn —3H 23
Heather Gdns. NW11 —6G 29
Heather Gdns. Romf —2K 39
Heather Gdns. Sutt —6J 149
Heather Glen. Romf —2K 39
Heather Ho. E14 —6E 70
Heatherlands. Sun —6J 113
Heather La. W Dray —6A 58
Heatherley Ct. E5 —3G 51
Heatherley Dri. Ilf —3C 36
Heather Pk. Dri. Wemb —7G 45
Heather Pk. Pde. Wemb —7F 45
(off Heather Pk. Dri.)
Heather Rd. E4 —6G 19
Heather Rd. NW2 —2B 46
Heather Rd. SE12 —2J 125
Heatherset Gdns. SW16 —7K 121
Heatherside Rd. Eps —7K 147
Heatherside Rd. Sidc —3C 128
Heathers, The. Stai —7B 94
Heatherton Ter. N3 —2K 29
Heather Wlk. W10 —4G 65
Heather Wlk. Edgw —5C 12
Heather Wlk. Twic —7E 96
(off Stephenson Rd.)
Heather Way. Romf —2K 39
Heather Way. S Croy —7K 153
Heather Way. Stan —6E 10
Heatherwood Clo. E12 —2A 54
Heatherwood Dri. Hay —2F 59
Heathfield. E4 —3K 19
Heathfield. Chst —6G 127
Heathfield. Harr —7K 25
Heathfield Av. SW18 —7B 102
Heathfield Clo. E16 —5B 72
Heathfield Clo. Kes —5A 156
Heathfield Ct. SE20 —7J 123
Heathfield Ct. W4 —5K 81
Heathfield Dri. Mitc —1C 138
Heathfield Gdns. NW11 —6F 29
Heathfield Gdns. SE3 —2G 107
(off Baizdon Rd.)
Heathfield Gdns. SW18 —6B 102
Heathfield Gdns. W4 —5J 81
Heathfield Gdns. Croy —4D 152
Heathfield Ho. SE3 —2G 107
Heathfield La. Chst —6F 127
Heathfield N. Twic —7J 97
Heathfield Pk. NW2 —6E 46
Heathfield Ri. Ruis —7E 22
Heathfield Rd. SW18 —6A 102
Heathfield Rd. W3 —2H 81
Heathfield Rd. Bexh —4F 111
Heathfield Rd. Brom —7H 125
Heathfield Rd. Croy —4D 152
Heathfield Rd. Kes —5A 156
Heathfields Ct. Houn —5C 96
Heathfield S. Twic —7K 97
Heathfield Sq. SW18 —7B 102
Heathfield St. W11 —7G 65
(off Portland Rd.)
Heathfield Ter. SE18 —6J 91
Heathfield Ter. W4 —5J 81
Heathfield Va. S Croy —7K 153
Heath Gdns. Twic —1K 115
Heathgate. NW11 —6K 29
Heathgate Pl. NW3 —5D 48
Heath Gro. SE20 —7J 123
Heath Gro. Sun —7H 113
Heath Ho. Sidc —4K 127
Heath Hurst Rd. NW3 —4C 48
Heathland Rd. N16 —1E 50
Heathlands Clo. Sun —2J 131
Heathlands Clo. Twic —2K 115
Heathlands Way. Houn —5C 96
Heath La. SE3 —2F 107
(in two parts)
Heathlee Rd. SE3 —4H 107
Heathley End. Chst —6G 127
Heath Lodge. Bush —1D 10
Heathmans Rd. SW6 —1H 101
Heath Mead. SW19 —3F 119
Heath Pk. Dri. Brom —3C 144
Heath Pas. NW3 —1A 48
Heathpool Ct. E1 —4H 69
(off Brady St.)
Heath Ri. SW15 —6F 101
Heath Ri. Brom —6H 143
Heath Rd. SW8 —2F 103
Heath Rd. Bex —1J 129
Heath Rd. Harr —7G 25
Heath Rd. Houn —4F 97
Heath Rd. Romf —7D 38
Heath Rd. T Hth —3C 140
Heath Rd. Twic —1K 115
Heath Rd. Uxb —4E 58
Heathrow Airport. —3D 94
Heathrow Boulevd. W Dray —7B 76
Heathrow Causeway Cen. Houn —3J 95
Heathrow Interchange. (Junct.) —7A 60
Heathrow Interchange. Hay —1A 78
Heathrow International Trad. Est. Houn —3K 95
Heaths Clo. Enf —2K 7
Heath Side. NW3 —4B 48
Heathside. NW11 —1J 47
Heathside. SE13 —2E 106
Heathside. Houn —7D 96
Heathside. Orp —7G 145
Heathside Av. Bexh —1E 110
Heathstan Rd. W12 —6C 64
Heath St. NW3 —3A 48
Heath, The. W7 —1J 79
Heath Vw. N2 —4A 30
Heathview. NW5 —4E 48
Heath Vw. Clo. N2 —4A 30
Heathview Dri. SE2 —6D 92
Heathview Gdns. SW15 —7E 100
Heathview Rd. T Hth —4A 140
Heath Vs. NW3 —3B 48
Heath Vs. SE18 —5K 91
Heathville Rd. N19 —7J 31
Heathwall St. SW11 —3D 102
Heathway. (Junct.) —1G 75
Heathway. SE3 —7J 89
Heathway. Croy —3B 154
Heathway. Dag —3F 57
Heath Way. Eri —1J 111
Heathway. S'hall —4B 78
Heath Way. Wfd G —5F 21
Heathway Ct. NW11 —2J 47
Heathway Ind. Est. Dag —4H 57
Heathwood Gdns. SE7 —4C 90
Heathwood Point. SE23 —3K 123
Heathwood Wlk. Bex —1K 129
Heaton Clo. E4 —3K 19
Heaton Rd. SE15 —2H 105
Heaton Rd. Mitc —7E 120
Heaver Rd. SW11 —3B 102
Heavitree Clo. SE18 —5H 91
Heavitree Rd. SE18 —5H 91
(in two parts)
Hebden Ct. E2 —1F 69
Hebden Ter. N17 —6K 17
Hebdon Rd. SW17 —3C 120
Heber Mans. W14 —6G 83
(off Queen's Club Gdns.)
Heber Rd. NW2 —5F 47
Heber Rd. SE22 —6F 105
Hebron Rd. W6 —3E 82
Hecham Clo. E17 —2A 34
Heckfield Pl. SW6 —7J 83
Heckford Ho. E14 —6D 70
Heckford St. E1 —7K 69
Heckford St. Bus. Cen. E1 —7K 69
(off Heckford St.)
Hector. NW9 —1B 28
(off Five Acre)
Hector Peterson Ho. Wemb —7F 27
(off Wilson Dri.)
Hector St. SE18 —4J 91
Heddington Gro. N7 —5K 49
Heddon Clo. Iswth —4A 98
Heddon Ct. Av. Barn —5J 5
Heddon Ct. Pde. Barn —5K 5
Heddon Rd. Cockf —5J 5
Heddon St. W1 —7G 67 (2A 166)
(in two parts)
Hedgegate Ct. W11 —6H 65
(in two parts)
Hedge Hill. Enf —1G 7
Hedge La. N13 —3G 17
Hedgemans Rd. Dag —7D 56
Hedgemans Way. Dag —6E 56
Hedgerley Gdns. Gnfd —2G 61
Hedgers Gro. E9 —6A 52
Hedger St. SE11 —4B 86
Hedge Wlk. SE6 —5D 124
Hedgewood Gdns. Ilf —5E 36
Hedgley. Ilf —4D 36
Hedgley M. SE12 —5H 107
Hedgley St. SE12 —5H 107
Hedingham Clo. N1 —7C 50
Hedingham Rd. Dag —5B 56
Hedley Ho. E14 —3E 88
Hedley Rd. Twic —7E 96
Hedley Row. N5 —5D 50
Hedley St. Romf —5K 39
Hedsor Ho. E2 —4F 69 (3J 163)
(off Ligonier St.)
Heenan Clo. Bark —6G 55
Heene Rd. Enf —1J 7
Hega Ho. E14 —5E 70
Heidegger Cres. SW13 —7D 82
Heigham Rd. E6 —1B 72
Heighton Gdns. Croy —5B 152
Heights Clo. SW20 —7D 118
Heights, The. SE7 —5A 90
Heights, The. Beck —7E 124
(in two parts)
Heights, The. N'holt —5D 42
Heiron St. SE17 —6B 86
Helby Rd. SW4 —6H 103
Heldar Ct. SE1 —2D 86 (7F 169)
Helder Gro. SE12 —7H 107
Helder St. S Croy —6D 152
Heldmann Clo. Houn —4H 97
Helena Clo. Wall —7J 151
Helena Ct. W5 —5D 62
Helena Pl. E9 —1H 69
Helena Rd. E13 —2H 71
Helena Rd. E17 —5C 34
Helena Rd. NW10 —5D 46
Helena Rd. W5 —5D 62
Helena Sq. SE16 —7A 70
(off Sovereign Cres.)
Helen Av. Felt —7K 95
Helen Clo. N2 —3A 30
Helen Clo. W Mol —4F 133
Helen Gladstone Ho. SE1
(off Surrey Row) —2B 86 (6A 168)
Helen Mackay Ho. E14 —6F 71
Helenslea Av. NW11 —1J 47
Helen's Pl. E2 —3J 69
Helen St. SE18 —4F 91
Helen Taylor Ho. SE16 —3G 87
(off Evelyn Lowe Est.)
Helford Clo. Ruis —2G 41
Helgiford Gdns. Sun —7G 113
Heliport Ind. Est. SW11 —2B 102
Helix Gdns. SW2 —6K 103
Helix Rd. SW2 —6K 103
Hellings St. E1 —1G 87
Helme Clo. SW19 —5H 119
Helmet Row. EC1 —4C 68 (3D 162)
(in two parts)
Helmore Rd. Bark —7K 55
Helmsdale Clo. Hay —4C 60
Helmsdale Ho. NW6 —2K 65
(off Carlton Va.)
Helmsdale Rd. SW16 —1H 139
Helmsley Pl. E8 —7H 51
Helmsley St. E8 —7H 51
Helsby Ct. NW8 —4B 66 (3A 158)
(off Pollitt Dri.)
Helsinki Sq. SE16 —3A 88
Helston. NW1 —2G 67
(off Camden St.)
Helston Clo. Pinn —1D 24
Helston Ct. N15 —5E 32
(off Culvert Rd.)
Helston Ho. SE11 —5A 86 (5K 173)
(off Kennings Way)
Helvetia St. SE6 —2B 124
Helwys Ct. E4 —6J 19
Hemans St. SW8 —7H 85
Hemans St. Est. SW8 —7H 85
Hemberton Rd. SW9 —3J 103
Hemery Rd. Gnfd —5H 43
Hemingford Clo. N12 —5G 15
Hemingford Rd. N1 —1K 67
Hemingford Rd. Sutt —4E 148
Heming Rd. Edgw —7C 12
Hemington Av. N11 —5J 15
Hemingway Clo. NW5 —4E 48
Hemlock Rd. E10 —2D 52
Hemlock Rd. W12 —7B 64
(in two parts)
Hemmen La. Hay —6H 59
Hemming Clo. Hamp —1E 132
Hemmings Clo. Sidc —2B 128
Hemming St. E1 —4G 69
Hempstead Clo. Buck H —2D 20
Hempstead Rd. E17 —3F 35
Hemp Wlk. SE17 —4D 86
Hemsby Rd. Chess —6F 147
Hemstal Rd. NW6 —7J 47
Hemsted Rd. Eri —7K 93
Hemswell Dri. NW9 —1A 28
Hemsworth Ct. N1 —2E 68
Hemsworth St. N1 —2E 68
Hemus Pl. SW3 —5C 84 (6D 170)
Henchman St. W12 —6B 64
Hendale Av. NW4 —3D 28
Henderson Clo. NW10 —6J 45
Henderson Dri. NW8 —4B 66 (3A 158)
Henderson Ho. Dag —3G 57
(off Kershaw Rd.)
Henderson Rd. E7 —6A 54
Henderson Rd. N9 —1C 18
Henderson Rd. SW18 —7C 102
Henderson Rd. Croy —6D 140
Henderson Rd. Hay —3J 59
Hendham Rd. SW17 —2C 120
Hendon. —5D 28
Hendon Av. N3 —1G 29
Hendon Crematorium. NW4 —1F 29
Hendon F.C. —1F 47
Hendon Hall Ct. NW4 —3F 29
Hendon Ho. NW4 —5F 29
Hendon La. N3 —3G 29
Hendon Lodge. NW4 —3D 28
Hendon Pk. Mans. NW4 —5E 28
Hendon Pk. Row. NW11 —6H 29
Hendon Rd. N9 —2B 18
Hendon Way. NW4 & NW2 —6D 28
Hendon Wood La. NW7 —1G 13
Hendren Clo. Gnfd —5H 43
Hendre Rd. SE1 —4E 86
Hendrick Av. SW12 —7D 102
Heneage La. EC3 —6E 68 (1H 169)
Heneage Pl. EC3 —6E 68 (1H 169)
Heneage St. E1 —5F 69 (5K 163)
Henfield Clo. N19 —1G 49
Henfield Clo. Bex —6G 111
Henfield Rd. SW19 —1H 137
Hengelo Gdns. Mitc —4B 138
Hengist Rd. SE12 —7K 107
Hengist Rd. Eri —7H 93
Hengist Way. Brom —4G 143
Hengrave Rd. SE23 —6J 105
Hengrove Ct. Bex —1E 128
Hengrove Cres. Ashf —3A 112
Henham Ct. Romf —2J 39
Henley Av. Sutt —3G 149
Henley Clo. Gnfd —2G 61
Henley Clo. Iswth —1K 97
Henley Ct. N14 —7B 6
Henley Dri. SE1 —4F 87
Henley Dri. King T —7B 118
Henley Gdns. Pinn —3K 23
Henley Gdns. Romf —5E 38
Henley Ho. E2 —4F 69 (3K 163)
(off Swanfield St.)
Henley Prior. N1 —2K 67 (1G 161)
(off Collier St.)
Henley Rd. E16 —2D 90
Henley Rd. N18 —4K 17
Henley Rd. NW10 —1E 64
Henley Rd. Ilf —4G 55
Henley St. SW11 —2E 102
Henley Way. Felt —5B 114
Henlow Pl. Rich —2D 116
Henlys Corner. (Junct.) —4H 29
Henlys Roundabout. (Junct.) —1A 96
Hennel Clo. SE23 —3J 123
Henniker Gdns. E6 —3B 72
Henniker M. SW3 —6B 84 (7A 170)
Henniker Point. E15 —5G 53
(off Leytonstone Rd.)
Henniker Rd. E15 —5F 53
Henningham Rd. N17 —1D 32
Henning St. SW11 —1C 102
Henrietta Clo. SE8 —6C 88
Henrietta Ho. N15 —6E 32
(off St Ann's Rd.)
Henrietta Ho. W6 —5E 82
(off Queen Caroline St.)
Henrietta M. WC1 —4J 67 (3F 161)
Henrietta Pl. W1 —6F 67 (1J 165)
Henrietta St. E15 —5E 52
Henrietta St. WC2 —7J 67 (2F 167)
Henriques St. E1 —6G 69
Henry Addlington Clo. E6 —5F 73
Henry Clo. Enf —1K 7
Henry Cooper Way. SE9 —3B 126
Henry Darlot Dri. NW7 —5A 14
Henry Dickens Ct. W11 —7F 65
Henry Doulton Dri. SW17 —4E 120
Henry Hatch Wlk. Sutt —7A 150
Henry Ho. SE1 —1A 86 (5J 167)
Henry Ho. SW8 —7J 85
(off Wyvil Rd.)
Henry Jackson Rd. SW15 —3F 101
Henry Macaulay Av. King T —1D 134
Henry Peters Dri. Tedd —5J 115
Henry Rd. E6 —2C 72
Henry Rd. N4 —1C 50
Henry Rd. Barn —5G 5
Henrys Av. Wfd G —5C 20
Henryson Rd. SE4 —5C 106
Henry St. Brom —1K 143
Henry's Wlk. Ilf —1H 37
Henry Wise Ho. SW1 —4G 85 (4B 172)
(off Vauxhall Bri. Rd.)
Hensford Gdns. SE26 —4H 123
Henshall St. N1 —6D 50
Henshawe Rd. Dag —3D 56
Henshaw St. SE17 —4D 86
Henslowe Rd. SE22 —5G 105
Henslow Ho. SE15 —7G 87
(off Peckham Pk. Rd.)
Henson Av. NW2 —5E 46
Henson Path. Harr —3D 26
Henson Pl. N'holt —1A 60
Henstridge Pl. NW8 —1C 66
Henty Clo. SW11 —7C 84
Henty Wlk. SW15 —5D 100
Henville Rd. Brom —1K 143
Henwick Rd. SE9 —3B 108
Henwood Side. Wfd G —6J 21
Hepburn Gdns. Brom —1G 155
Hepburn M. SW11 —5D 102
Hepple Clo. Iswth —2B 98
Hepplestone Clo. SW15 —6D 100
Hepscott Rd. E9 —6C 52
Hepworth Ct. N1 —1B 68
(off Gaskin St.)
Hepworth Ct. NW3 —5C 48
Hepworth Gdns. Bark —5A 56
Hepworth Rd. SW16 —7J 121
Hepworth Way. W on T —7H 131
Heracles. NW9 —1B 28
(off Five Acre)
Heracles Clo. Wall —7J 151
Hera Ct. E14 —4C 88
Herald Gdns. Wall —2F 151
Herald's Pl. SE11 —4B 86 (3K 173)
Herald St. E2 —4H 69
Herbal Hill. EC1 —4A 68 (4K 161)
Herbal Hill Gdns. EC1 —4A 68 (4K 161)
Herbal Pl. EC1 —4A 68 (4K 161)
(off Herbal Hill)
Herbert Cres. SW1 —3D 84 (1F 171)
Herbert Gdns. NW10 —2D 64
Herbert Gdns. W4 —6H 81
Herbert Gdns. Romf —7D 38
Herbert Ho. E1 —6F 69 (7J 163)
(off Old Castle St.)
Herbert Morrison Ho. SW6 —6H 83
(off Clem Attlee Ct.)
Herbert Pl. SE18 —6F 91
Herbert Rd. E12 —4C 54
Herbert Rd. E17 —7B 34
Herbert Rd. N11 —7D 16
Herbert Rd. N15 —5F 33
Herbert Rd. NW9 —6C 28
Herbert Rd. SE18 —7E 90
(in two parts)
Herbert Rd. SW19 —7H 119
(in two parts)
Herbert Rd. Bexh —2E 110
Herbert Rd. Brom —5B 144
Herbert Rd. Ilf —2J 55
Herbert Rd. King T —3F 135
Herbert Rd. S'hall —1D 78
Herbert St. E13 —2J 71
Herbert St. NW5 —6E 48
Herbrand Est. WC1 —3E 160
Herbrand St. WC1 —4J 67 (3E 160)
Hercies Rd. Uxb —7B 40
Hercules Pl. N7 —3J 49
(in two parts)
Hercules Rd. SE1 —3K 85 (2H 173)
Hercules St. N7 —3J 49
Hercules Tower. SE14 —6A 88
Hercules Wharf. E14 —7G 71
Hercules Yd. N7 —3J 49
Hereford Av. Barn —1J 15
Hereford Bldgs. SW3 —6B 84 (7B 170)
Hereford Ct. W7 —5K 61
(off Copley Clo.)
Hereford Ct. Harr —4J 25
Hereford Ct. Sutt —7J 149
Hereford Gdns. SE13 —5G 107
Hereford Gdns. Ilf —7C 36
Hereford Gdns. Pinn —5C 24
Hereford Gdns. Twic —1G 115
Hereford Ho. NW6 —2J 65
(off Carlton Va.)
Hereford Ho. SW3 —3C 84 (1D 170)
(off Old Brompton Rd.)
Hereford Ho. SW10 —7K 83
(off Fulham Rd.)
Hereford M. W2 —6J 65
Hereford Pl. SE14 —7B 88
Hereford Retreat. SE15 —7G 87
Hereford Rd. E11 —5K 35
Hereford Rd. W2 —6J 65
Hereford Rd. W3 —7H 63
Hereford Rd. W5 —3C 80
Hereford Rd. Felt —1A 114
Hereford Sq. SW7 —4A 84
Hereford St. E2 —4G 69
Hereford Way. Chess —5C 146
Herent Dri. Ilf —4C 36
Hereward Gdns. N13 —5F 17
Hereward Rd. SW17 —4D 120
Herga Ct. Harr —3J 43
Herga Rd. Harr —4K 25
Heriot Av. E4 —2H 19
Heriot Rd. NW4 —5E 28
Heriots Clo. Stan —4F 11
Heritage Clo. SW9 —3B 104
Heritage Hill. Kes —5A 156
Heritage Vw. Harr —3K 43
Herlwyn Av. Ruis —2G 41
Herlwyn Gdns. SW17 —4D 120
Herm Clo. Iswth —7G 79
Hermes Clo. W9 —4J 65
Hermes St. N1 —2A 68 (1J 161)
Hermes Wlk. N'holt —2E 60
Hermes Way. Wall —7H 151
Herm Ho. N1 —6C 50
Herm Ho. Enf —1E 8
Hermiston Av. N8 —5J 31
Hermitage Clo. E18 —4H 35
Hermitage Clo. Clay —6A 146
Hermitage Clo. Enf —2G 7
Hermitage Clo. Shep —4C 130
Hermitage Ct. E1 —1G 87
(off Knighten St.)
Hermitage Ct. E18 —4J 35
Hermitage Ct. NW2 —3J 47
Hermitage Gdns. NW2 —3J 47
Hermitage Gdns. SE19 —7C 122
Hermitage Grn. SW16 —1J 139
Hermitage La. N18 —5J 17
Hermitage La. NW2 —3J 47
Hermitage La. SE25 —6G 141
(in two parts)
Hermitage La. SW16 —7K 121
Hermitage La. Croy & SE25 —7G 141
Hermitage Path. SW16 —1J 139
Hermitage Rd. N4 & N15 —7B 32
Hermitage Rd. SE19 —7C 122
Hermitage Row. E8 —5G 51
Hermitage St. W2 —5B 66 (6A 158)
Hermitage, The. SE13 —2E 106
Hermitage, The. SE23 —1J 123
Hermitage, The. SW13 —1B 100
Hermitage, The. Felt —3H 113
Hermitage, The. King T —4D 134
Hermitage, The. Rich —5E 98
Hermitage, The. Uxb —6A 40
Hermitage Wlk. E18 —4H 35
Hermitage Wall. E1 —1G 87

Hermitage Way—Hill Farm Rd.

Hermitage Way. Stan —1A 26
Hermit Pl. NW6 —1K 65
Hermit Rd. E16 —5H 71
Hermit St. EC1 —3B 68 (1A 162)
Hermon Gro. Hay —1J 77
Hermon Hill. E11 & E18 —5J 35
Herndon Rd. SW18 —5A 102
Herne Clo. NW10 —5K 45
Herne Ct. Bush —1B 10
Herne Hill. —5C 104
Herne Hill. SE24 —6C 104
Herne Hill Ho. SE24 —6B 104
(off Railton Rd.)
Herne Hill Rd. SE24 —3C 104
Herne Hill Stadium. —4D 104
Herne M. N18 —4B 18
Herne Pl. SE24 —5B 104
Herne Rd. Surb —2D 146
Heron Clo. E17 —2B 34
Heron Clo. NW10 —6A 46
Heron Clo. Buck H —1D 20
Heron Clo. Sutt —5H 149
Heron Ct. E14 —3E 88
Heron Ct. Brom —4A 144
Heron Ct. King T —3E 134
Heron Ct. Ruis —2F 41
Heron Cres. Sidc —3J 127
Herondale Av. SW18 —1B 120
Heron Dri. N4 —2C 50
Herongate Clo. Enf —2A 8
Herongate Rd. E12 —2A 54
Heron Hill. Belv —5F 93
Heron Ho. E6 —7C 54
Heron Ho. NW8 —2C 66 (1C 158)
(off Barrow Hill Est.)
Heron Ho. W13 —4A 62
Heron Ho. Sidc —3B 128
Heron Ind. Est. E15 —2D 70
Heron M. Ilf —2F 55
Heron Pl. SE16 —1A 88
Heron Pl. W1 —6E 66 (7H 159)
(off Thayer St.)
Heron Quay. E14 —1C 88
Heron Rd. SE24 —4C 104
Heron Rd. Croy —2E 152
Heron Rd. Twic —4A 98
Heronsforde. W13 —6C 62
Herons Ga. Edgw —5B 12
Heron's Lea. N6 —6D 30
Heronslea Dri. Stan —5K 11
Heron's Pl. Iswth —3B 98
Heron Sq. Rich —5D 98
Herons Ri. New Bar —4H 5
Herons, The. E11 —6H 35
Heron Trad. Est. W3 —5H 63
Heron Way. Wfd G —4F 21
Herrick Rd. N5 —3C 50
Herrick St. SW1 —4H 85 (4D 172)
Herries St. W10 —2G 65
Herringham Rd. SE7 —3A 90
Herron Ct. Short —4H 143
Hersant Clo. NW10 —1C 64
Herschell M. SE5 —3C 104
Herschell Rd. SE23 —7A 106
Hersham Clo. SW15 —7C 100
Hershell Ct. SW14 —4H 99
Hertford Av. SW14 —5K 99
Hertford Clo. Barn —3G 5
Hertford Ct. E6 —3D 72
(off Vicarage La.)
Hertford Ct. N13 —3F 17
Hertford Pl. W1 —4G 67 (4B 160)
Hertford Rd. N1 —1E 68
(in two parts)
Hertford Rd. N2 —3C 30
Hertford Rd. N9 & Wal X —2C 18
Hertford Rd. Bark —7E 54
Hertford Rd. Barn —3F 5
Hertford Rd. Ilf —6J 37
Hertford Sq. Mitc —4J 139
Hertford St. W1 —1F 85 (5J 165)
Hertford Wlk. Belv —5G 93
Hertford Way. Mitc —4J 139
Hertslet Rd. N7 —3K 49
Hertsmere Ho. E14 —7C 70
Hertsmere Rd. E14 —1C 88
Hertswood Ct. Barn —4B 4
Hervey Clo. N3 —1J 29
Hervey Pk. Rd. E17 —4A 34
Hervey Rd. SE3 —1K 107
Hervey Way. N3 —1J 29
Hesa Rd. Hay —6J 59
Hesewall Clo. SW4 —2G 103
Hesketh Pl. W11 —7G 65
Hesketh Rd. E7 —3J 53
Heslop Rd. SW12 —1D 120
Hesper M. SW5 —4K 83
Hesperus Clo. E14 —4D 88
Hesperus Cres. E14 —4D 88
Hessel Rd. W13 —2A 80
Hessel St. E1 —6H 69
Hestercombe Av. SW6 —2G 101
Hesterman Way. Croy —1K 151
Hester Rd. N18 —5B 18
Hester Rd. SW11 —7C 84
Hester Ter. Rich —3G 99
Heston. —7E 78
Heston Av. Houn —6C 78
Heston Cen., The. Houn —5A 78
Heston Grange. Houn —6D 78
Heston Grange La. Houn —6D 78
Heston Ho. SE8 —1C 106
Heston Ind. Cen. Houn —6A 78
Heston Ind. Mall. Houn —7D 78
Heston Rd. Houn —7E 78
Heston St. SE14 —1C 106
Hetherington Rd. SW4 —4J 103
Hetherington Rd. Shep —2E 130
Hetherington Way. Uxb —4A 40
Hethpool Ho. W2 —4A 158
Hetley Gdns. SE19 —7F 123
Hetley Ho. W12 —2D 82
(off Hetley Rd.)
Hetley Rd. W12 —1D 82
Heton Gdns. NW4 —4D 28
Hevelius Clo. SE10 —5H 89
Hever Cft. SE9 —4E 126
Hever Gdns. Brom —2E 144
Heverham Rd. SE18 —4J 91
Heversham Ho. SE15 —6J 87
Heversham Rd. Bexh —2G 111
Hewens Rd. Uxb —4E 58
Hewer St. W10 —5F 65
Hewett Clo. Stan —4G 11
Hewett Rd. Dag —5D 56
Hewett St. EC2 —4E 68 (4H 163)
Hewish Rd. N18 —4K 17
Hewison St. E3 —2B 70
Hewitt Av. N22 —2B 32
Hewitt Clo. Croy —3C 154
Hewitt Rd. N8 —5A 32
Hewlett Rd. E3 —2A 70
Hexagon, The. N6 —1D 48
Hexal Rd. SE6 —3G 125
Hexham Gdns. Iswth —7A 80
Hexham Rd. SE27 —2C 122
Hexham Rd. Barn —4E 4
Hexham Rd. Mord —1K 149
Heybourne Rd. N17 —7C 18
Heybridge Av. SW16 —7J 121
Heybridge Dri. Ilf —2H 37
Heybridge Way. E10 —7A 34
Heydon Ho. SE14 —1J 105
(off Kender St.)
Heyford Av. SW8 —7J 85
Heyford Av. SW20 —3H 137
Heyford Rd. Mitc —2C 138
Heyford Ter. SW8 —7J 85
Heygate St. SE17 —4C 86
Heylyn Sq. E3 —3B 70
Heynes Rd. Dag —4C 56
Heysham La. NW3 —3K 47
Heysham Rd. N15 —6D 32
Heythorp St. SW18 —1H 119
Heythrop Dri. Ick —4B 40
Heywood Av. NW9 —1A 28
Heywood Ct. Stan —5H 11
Heyworth Rd. E5 —4H 51
Heyworth Rd. E15 —5H 53
Hibbert Rd. E17 —7B 34
Hibbert Rd. Harr & W'stone —2K 25
Hibbert St. SW11 —3B 102
Hibernia Gdns. Houn —4E 96
Hibernia Point. SE2 —2D 92
(off Wolvercote Rd.)
Hibernia Rd. Houn —4E 96
Hibiscus Clo. Edgw —4D 12
Hichisson Rd. SE15 —5J 105
Hickes Ho. NW6 —7B 48
Hickey's Almshouses. Rich —4F 99
Hickin Clo. SE7 —4B 90
Hickin St. E14 —3E 88
Hickleton. NW1 —1G 67
(off Camden St.)
Hickling Rd. Ilf —5F 55
Hickman Av. E4 —6K 19
Hickman Clo. E16 —5B 72
Hickman Rd. Romf —7C 38
Hickmore Wlk. SW4 —3H 103
Hickory Clo. N9 —7B 8
Hicks Av. Gnfd —3H 61
Hicks Clo. SW11 —3C 102
Hicks Ct. Dag —3H 57
Hicks St. SE8 —5A 88
Hidcote Gdns. SW20 —3D 136
Hide. E6 —6E 72
Hide Pl. SW1 —4H 85 (4C 172)
Hider Ct. SE3 —7A 90
Hide Rd. Harr —4G 25
Hides St. N7 —6K 49
Hide Tower. SW1 —4H 85 (4C 172)
(off Regency St.)
Higgins Ho. N1 —1E 68
(off Colville Est.)
Higginson Ho. NW3 —7D 48
Higgins Wlk. Hamp —6C 114
(off Abbott Clo.)
Higgs Ind. Est. SE24 —3B 104
High Acres. Enf —3G 7
Higham Hill. —2A 34
Higham Hill Rd. E17 —1A 34
Higham Path. E17 —3A 34
Higham Pl. E17 —3A 34
Higham Rd. N17 —3D 32
Higham Rd. Wfd G —6D 20
Highams Ct. E4 —3A 20
Highams Lodge Bus. Cen. E17 —3K 33
Highams Park. —6A 20
Highams Pk. Ind. Est. E4 —6K 19
Higham Sta. Av. E4 —6H 19
Highams, The. E17 —1E 34
Higham St. E17 —3A 34
Highbanks Clo. Well —7B 92
Highbanks Rd. Pinn —6A 10
Highbank Way. N8 —6A 32
High Barnet. —2A 4
Highbarrow Rd. Croy —1G 153
High Beech. N21 —6E 6
High Beech. S Croy —7E 152
High Beeches. Sidc —5E 128
High Birch Ct. New Bar —4H 5
(off Park Rd.)
High Bri. SE10 —5F 89
Highbridge Rd. Bark —1F 73
Highbrook Rd. SE3 —3B 108
High Broom Cres. W W'ck —7D 142
Highbury. —4B 50
Highbury Av. T Hth —2A 140
Highbury Barn. N5 —4C 50
Highbury Clo. N Mald —4J 135
Highbury Clo. W W'ck —2D 154
Highbury Corner. (Junct.) —6B 50
Highbury Cres. N5 —5B 50
Highbury Est. N5 —5C 50
Highbury Gdns. Ilf —2J 55
Highbury Grange. N5 —4C 50
Highbury Gro. N5 —5B 50
Highbury Hill. N5 —3A 50
Highbury M. N7 —6A 50
Highbury New Pk. N5 —5C 50
Highbury Pk. N5 —3B 50
Highbury Pk. M. N5 —4C 50
Highbury Pl. N5 —6B 50
Highbury Quad. N5 —3C 50
Highbury Rd. SW19 —5G 119
Highbury Sta. Rd. N1 —6A 50
Highbury Ter. N5 —5B 50
Highbury Ter. M. N5 —5B 50
High Cedar Dri. SW20 —7E 118
Highclere Rd. N Mald —3K 135
Highclere St. SE26 —4A 124
Highcliffe. W13 —5B 62
(off Clivedon Ct.)
Highcliffe Dri. SW15 —6B 100
Highcliffe Gdns. Ilf —5C 36
Highcombe. SE7 —6K 89
Highcombe Clo. SE9 —1B 126
High Coombe Pl. King T —6K 117
High Cft. NW9 —5A 28
Highcroft Av. Wemb —7G 45
Highcroft Est. N19 —7J 31
Highcroft Gdns. NW11 —6H 29
Highcroft Rd. N19 —7J 31
High Cross Cen., The. N15 —4G 33
High Cross Rd. N17 —3G 33
Highcross Way. SW15 —1C 118
Highdaun Dri. SW16 —4K 139
Highdown. Wor Pk —2A 148
Highdown Rd. SW15 —6D 100
High Dri. N Mald —1J 135
High Elms. Wfd G —5D 20
Highfield. Bus H —2D 10
Highfield. Felt —1J 113
Highfield Av. NW9 —5J 27
Highfield Av. NW11 —7F 29
Highfield Av. Eri —6H 93
Highfield Av. Gnfd —5J 43
Highfield Av. Pinn —5D 24
Highfield Av. Wemb —3F 45
Highfield Clo. N22 —1A 32
Highfield Clo. NW9 —5J 27
Highfield Clo. SE13 —6F 107
Highfield Clo. N'wd —1G 23
Highfield Clo. Surb —1C 146
Highfield Ct. N14 —6B 6
Highfield Ct. NW11 —6G 29
Highfield Cres. N'wd —1G 23
Highfield Dri. Brom —4G 143
Highfield Dri. Eps —6B 148
Highfield Dri. Ick & Uxb —4A 40
Highfield Dri. W W'ck —2D 154
Highfield Gdns. NW11 —6G 29
Highfield Hill. SE19 —7D 122
Highfield Rd. N21 —2G 17
Highfield Rd. NW11 —6G 29
Highfield Rd. W3 —5H 63
Highfield Rd. Bexh —5F 111
Highfield Rd. Brom —4D 144
Highfield Rd. Chst —3K 145
Highfield Rd. Felt —2J 113
Highfield Rd. Iswth —1K 97
Highfield Rd. N'wd —1G 23
Highfield Rd. Sun —5H 131
Highfield Rd. Surb —7J 135
Highfield Rd. Sutt —5C 150
Highfield Rd. W on T —7J 131
Highfield Rd. Wfd G —7H 21
Highfields. Sutt —2J 149
Highfields Gro. N6 —1D 48
High Foleys. Clay —7B 146
High Gables. Brom —2G 143
Highgate. —1F 49
Highgate Av. N6 —7F 31
Highgate Cemetery. —2F 49
Highgate Clo. N6 —7E 30
Highgate Edge. N2 —5C 30
Highgate Heights. N6 —6G 31
Highgate High St. N6 —1E 48
Highgate Hill. N6 & N19 —1F 49
Highgate Ho. SE26 —3G 123
Highgate Rd. N6 —3E 48
Highgate Spinney. N8 —6H 31
Highgate Wlk. SE23 —2J 123
Highgate W. Hill. N6 —2E 48
High Gro. SE18 —7H 91
High Gro. Brom —1B 144
Highgrove Clo. N11 —5K 15
Highgrove Clo. Chst —1C 144
Highgrove Ct. Beck —7C 124
Highgrove Ct. Sutt —6J 149
Highgrove M. Cars —3D 150
Highgrove Rd. Dag —5C 56
Highgrove Way. Ruis —6J 23
High Hill Est. E5 —1H 51
High Hill Ferry. E5 —1H 51
High Holborn. WC1 —6J 67 (7E 160)
Highland Av. W7 —6J 61
Highland Av. Dag —3J 57
Highland Cotts. Wall —4G 151
Highland Ct. E18 —1K 35
Highland Cft. Beck —5D 124
Highland Dri. Bush —1A 10
Highland Pk. Felt —4H 113
Highland Rd. SE19 —6E 122
Highland Rd. Bexh —5G 111
Highland Rd. Brom —1H 143
Highland Rd. N'wd —2H 23
Highlands. N20 —2H 15
Highlands Av. N21 —5E 6
Highlands Av. W3 —7J 63
Highlands Clo. N4 —7J 31
Highlands Clo. Houn —1F 97
Highlands Ct. SE19 —6E 122
Highlands Gdns. Ilf —1D 54
Highlands Heath. SW15 —7E 100
Highlands Rd. Barn —5D 4
Highlands, The. Barn —4D 4
Highlands, The. Edgw —2H 27
Highlands Village. —5E 6
Highland Ter. SE13 —3D 106
(off Claybank Gro.)
High La. W7 —5H 61
(in two parts)
Highlawn Hall. Harr —3J 43
Highlea Clo. NW9 —7F 13
High Level Dri. SE26 —4G 123
Highlever Rd. W10 —5E 64
Highmead. N18 —5B 18
(off Alpha Rd.)
Highmead. SE18 —7K 91
High Mead. Harr —5J 25
High Mead. W W'ck —2F 155
Highmead Cres. Wemb —7F 45
High Mdw. Clo. Pinn —4A 24
High Mdw. Cres. NW9 —5K 27
High Meads Rd. E16 —6B 72
Highmore Rd. SE3 —7G 89
High Mt. NW4 —6C 28
High Oaks. Enf —1E 6
High Pde., The. SW16 —3J 121
High Pk. Av. Rich —1G 99
High Pk. Rd. Rich —1G 99
High Path. SW19 —1K 137
Highpoint. N6 —7E 30
High Point. SE9 —3F 127
High Ridge. N10 —1F 31
High Ridge Pl. Enf —1E 6
(off Oak Av.)
High Rd. E18 —1J 35
High Rd. N11 —7A 16
High Rd. N15 & N17 —5F 33
High Rd. N22 —1K 31
High Rd. NW10 —6A 46
High Rd. Buck H & Lou —2E 20
High Rd. Bus H & Bush —1C 10
High Rd. Chig —5K 21
High Rd. Eastc —6J 23
High Rd. Harr —7D 10
High Rd. Hay —5G 59
High Rd. Ick —3D 40
High Rd. Ilf & Romf —3F 55
(in five parts)
High Rd. Romf —7D 38
High Rd. Wemb —5D 44
High Rd. E. Finchley. N2 —1B 30
High Rd. Leyton. E10 & E15 —6D 34
High Rd. Leytonstone. E11 & E15 —4G 53
High Rd. N. Finchley. N12 —3F 15
High Rd. Whetstone. N20 —7F 5
High Rd. Woodford Grn. Wfd G —6C 20
High Sheldon. N6 —6D 30
Highshore Rd. SE15 —2F 105
(in two parts)
Highstead Cres. Eri —1K 111
Highstone Av. E11 —6J 35
Highstone Ct. E11 —6H 35
(off New Wanstead)
Highstone Mans. NW1 —7G 49
(off Camden Rd.)
High St. E11 —5J 35
High St. E13 —2J 71
High St. E15 —2E 70
High St. E17 —5A 34
High St. N8 —4J 31
High St. N14 —1C 16
High St. NW7 —5J 13
High St. SE20 —6J 123
High St. SE25 —4F 141
High St. SW19 —7B 120
(Colliers Wood)
High St. SW19 —5F 119
(Wimbledon)
High St. W3 —1H 81
High St. W5 —1D 80
High St. B'side —3G 37
High St. Barn —3B 4
High St. Beck —2C 142
High St. Bren —7C 80
High St. Brom —2J 143
High St. Cars —5E 150
High St. Cheam —6G 149
High St. Chst —6F 127
High St. Cran —1J 95
High St. Croy —2C 152
(in two parts)
High St. Edgw —6B 12
High St. Enf —5D 8
High St. Ewe —7B 148
High St. Felt —3H 113
High St. Hamp —1G 133
High St. Hamp H —6G 115
High St. Hamp W —1C 134
High St. Harm —6A 76
High St. Harr —1J 43
(HA1)
High St. Harr —2J 25
(HA3)
High St. Hay —6F 77
High St. Houn —3F 97
High St. King T —3D 134
High St. N Mald —4A 136
High St. N'wd —1H 23
High St. Pinn —3C 24
High St. Romf —5K 39
High St. Ruis —7G 23
High St. Shep —6D 130
High St. S'hall —1D 78
High St. Stanw —6A 94
High St. Sutt —4K 149
High St. Tedd —5K 115
High St. Th Dit —6A 134
High St. T Hth —4C 140
High St. Uxb —1A 58
High St. W on T —7J 131
High St. W'stone —2J 25
High St. Wemb —4F 45
High St. W Dray —7A 58
High St. W Mol —4E 132
High St. W W'ck —1D 154
High St. Whit —7G 97
High St. Harlesden. NW10 —2B 64
High St. M. SW19 —5G 119
High St. N. E12 & E6 —5C 54
High St. S. E6 —2D 72
High Timber St. EC4 —7C 68 (2C 168)
High Tor Clo. Brom —7K 125
High Trees. N20 —3F 15
High Trees. SW2 —1A 122
High Trees. Barn —5H 5
High Trees. Croy —1A 154
Hightrees Ct. W7 —7J 61
Highview. N6 —6G 31
Highview. NW7 —3E 12
Highview. N'holt —3C 60
High Vw. Pinn —4A 24
Highview Av. Edgw —4D 12
Highview Av. Wall —5K 151
High Vw. Clo. SE19 —2F 141
High Vw. Ct. Har W —7D 10
Highview Gdns. N3 —3G 29
Highview Gdns. N11 —5B 16
Highview Gdns. Edgw —4D 12
Highview Ho. Romf —4E 38
High Vw. Pde. Ilf —5D 36
High Vw. Rd. E18 —2H 35
High Vw. Rd. N2 —1D 30
Highview Rd. SE19 —6D 122
Highview Rd. W13 —5A 62
High Vw. Rd. Sidc —4B 128
Highway, The. E1 & E14 —7G 69
Highway, The. Stan —1K 25
Highway, The. Sutt —7A 150
Highway Trad. Cen., The. E1 —7K 69
(off Heckford St.)
Highwood. Short —3G 143
Highwood Av. N12 —4F 15
Highwood Ct. N12 —3F 15
Highwood Ct. Barn —5D 4
Highwood Gdns. Ilf —5D 36
Highwood Gro. NW7 —5E 12
Highwood Hill. —3G 13
Highwood Hill. NW7 —2G 13
Highwood Rd. N19 —3J 49
High Worple. Harr —7D 24
Highworth Rd. N11 —6C 16
Highworth St. NW1 —5D 158
Hilary Av. Mitc —3E 138
Hilary Clo. E11 —5J 35
Hilary Clo. SW6 —7K 83
Hilary Clo. Eri —1H 111
Hilary Dennis Ct. E11 —4J 35
Hilary Rd. W12 —6B 64
(in two parts)
Hilbert Rd. Sutt —3F 149
Hilborough Ct. E8 —7F 51
Hilda Ct. Surb —7D 134
Hilda Rd. E6 —7B 54
Hilda Rd. E16 —4G 71
Hilda Ter. SW9 —2A 104
Hilda Va. Clo. Orp —4E 156
Hilda Va. Rd. Orp —4E 156
Hildenborough Gdns. Brom —6G 125
Hildenborough Ho. Beck —7B 124
(off Bethersden Clo.)
Hildenlea Pl. Brom —2F 143
Hildreth St. SW12 —1F 121
Hildyard Rd. SW6 —6J 83
Hiley Rd. NW10 —3E 64
Hilgrove Rd. NW6 —7A 48
Hiliary Gdns. Stan —2C 26
Hillary. N8 —3J 31
(off Boyton Clo.)
Hillary Cres. W on T —7A 132
Hillary Ri. Barn —4D 4
Hillary Rd. S'hall —3E 78
Hillbeck Clo. SE15 —7J 87
Hillbeck Way. Gnfd —1H 61
Hillborne Clo. Hay —5J 77
Hillboro Ct. E11 —7F 35
Hillborough Clo. SW19 —7A 120
Hillbrook Rd. SW17 —3D 120
Hill Brow. Brom —1B 144
Hillbrow. N Mald —3B 136
Hill Brow Clo. Bex —4K 129
Hillbrow Rd. Brom —7G 125
Hillbury Av. Harr —5B 26
Hillbury Rd. SW17 —3F 121
Hill Clo. NW2 —3D 46
Hill Clo. NW11 —6J 29
Hill Clo. Chst —5F 127
Hill Clo. Harr —3J 43
Hill Clo. Stan —4G 11
Hillcote Av. SW16 —7A 122
Hill Ct. W5 —4F 63
Hill Ct. Barn —4H 5
Hill Ct. N'holt —5E 42
Hillcourt Av. N12 —6E 14
Hillcourt Est. N16 —1D 50
Hillcourt Rd. SE22 —6H 105
Hill Cres. N20 —2E 14
Hill Cres. Bex —1J 129
Hill Cres. Harr —5A 26
Hill Cres. Surb —5F 135
Hill Cres. Wor Pk —2E 148
Hillcrest. N6 —7E 30
Hillcrest. N21 —7F 7
Hillcrest. SE5 —4D 104
Hillcrest. Sidc —7A 110
Hill Crest. Surb —7E 134
Hillcrest Av. NW11 —5H 29
Hillcrest Av. Edgw —4C 12
Hillcrest Av. Pinn —4B 24
Hillcrest Clo. SE26 —4G 123
Hillcrest Clo. Beck —6B 142
Hillcrest Ct. Romf —1K 39
Hillcrest Ct. Sutt —6B 150
Hillcrest Gdns. N3 —4G 29
Hillcrest Gdns. NW2 —3C 46
Hillcrest Gdns. Esh —3A 146
Hillcrest Rd. E17 —2F 35
Hillcrest Rd. E18 —2J 35
Hillcrest Rd. W3 —1G 81
Hillcrest Rd. W5 —5E 62
Hillcrest Rd. Brom —5J 125
Hillcrest Vw. Beck —6B 142
Hillcroft Av. Pinn —6D 24
Hillcroft Cres. W5 —6E 62
Hillcroft Cres. Ruis —3B 42
Hillcroft Cres. Wemb —4F 45
Hillcroft Rd. E6 —5F 73
Hillcroome Rd. Sutt —6B 150
Hillcross Av. Mord —6F 137
Hilldale Rd. Sutt —4H 149
Hilldown Ct. SW16 —7J 121
Hilldown Rd. SW16 —7J 121
Hilldown Rd. Brom —1G 155
Hill Dri. NW9 —1J 45
Hill Dri. SW16 —3K 139
Hilldrop Cres. N7 —5H 49
Hilldrop Est. N7 —4H 49
Hilldrop La. N7 —5H 49
Hilldrop Rd. N7 —5H 49
Hilldrop Rd. Brom —6K 125
Hillend. SE18 —1E 108
Hillersden Ho. SW1 —5F 85 (5J 171)
(off Ebury Bri. Rd.)
Hillersdon Av. SW13 —2C 100
Hillersdon Av. Edgw —5A 12
Hillery Clo. SE17 —4D 86
Hill Farm Cotts. Ruis —7E 22
Hill Farm Rd. W10 —5E 64
Hill Farm Rd. Uxb —4F 41

Hillfield Av.—Holmewood Gdns.

Hillfield Av. N8 —5J 31
Hillfield Av. NW9 —5A 28
Hillfield Av. Mord —6C 138
Hillfield Av. Wemb —7E 44
Hillfield Clo. Harr —4G 25
Hillfield Ct. NW3 —5C 48
Hillfield Ho. N5 —5C 50
Hillfield Pk. N10 —4F 31
Hillfield Pk. N21 —2F 17
Hillfield Pk. M. N10 —4F 31
Hillfield Rd. NW6 —5H 47
Hill Fld. Rd. Hamp —7D 114
Hillfoot Av. Romf —1J 39
Hillfoot Rd. Romf —1J 39
Hillgate Pl. SW12 —7F 103
Hillgate Pl. W8 —1J 83
Hillgate St. W11 —1J 83
Hill Gro. Felt —2D 114
Hill Gro. Romf —3K 39
Hill Ho. E5 —1H 51
(off Harrington Hill)
Hill Ho. Brom —2H 143
Hillhouse Av. Stan —7E 10
Hill Ho. Clo. N21 —7F 7
Hill Ho. Dri. Hamp —1E 132
Hill Ho. Rd. SW16 —5K 121
Hilliard Rd. N'wd —1H 23
Hilliards Ct. E1 —1J 87
Hillier Clo. New Bar —6E 4
Hillier Gdns. Croy —5A 152
Hillier Lodge. Tedd —5H 115
Hillier Pl. Chess —6D 146
Hillier Rd. SW11 —6D 102
Hilliers Av. Uxb —3C 58
Hilliers La. Croy —3J 151
Hillingdon. —3C 58
Hillingdon Av. Stai —1A 112
Hillingdon Cir. Hil —6D 40
Hillingdon Ct. Harr —4D 26
Hillingdon Heath. —4D 58
Hillingdon Hill. Uxb —2A 58
Hillingdon Rd. Bexh —2J 111
Hillingdon Rd. Uxb —1A 58
Hillingdon St. SE5 & SE17 —6B 86
(in two parts)
Hillington Gdns. Wfd G —2B 36
Hill La. Ruis —1E 40
Hillman Clo. Uxb —5A 40
Hillman Dri. W10 —4E 64
Hillman St. E8 —6H 51
Hillmarton Rd. N7 —5J 49
Hillmead Dri. SW9 —4B 104
Hillmore Ct. SE13 —3F 107
(off Belmont Hill)
Hillmore Gro. SE26 —5A 124
Hill Path. SW16 —5K 121
Hillreach. SE18 —5D 90
Hill Ri. N9 —6C 8
Hill Ri. NW11 —4K 29
Hill Ri. SE23 —1H 123
Hill Ri. Esh —2B 146
Hill Ri. Gnfd —7G 43
Hill Ri. Rich —5D 98
Hill Ri. Ruis —1E 40
Hill Ri. W on T —7H 131
Hillrise Mans. N19 —7J 31
(off Warltersville Rd.)
Hillrise Rd. N19 —7J 31
Hill Rd. N10 —1D 30
Hill Rd. NW8 —3A 66
Hill Rd. Cars —6C 150
Hill Rd. Harr —5A 26
Hill Rd. Mitc —1F 139
Hill Rd. Pinn —5C 24
Hill Rd. Sutt —5K 149
Hill Rd. Wemb —3B 44
Hillsboro' Rd. SE22 —5E 104
Hillsborough Ct. NW6 —1K 65
(off Mortimer Cres.)
Hillsgrove Clo. Well —7C 92
Hillside. —4J 93
Hillside. N8 —6H 31
Hillside. NW5 —3E 48
Hillside. NW9 —4K 27
Hillside. NW10 —7J 45
Hillside. SW19 —6F 119
Hillside. Eri —4J 93
Hillside. New Bar —5F 5
Hillside Av. N11 —6J 15
Hillside Av. Wemb —4F 45
Hillside Av. Wfd G —6F 21
Hillside Clo. NW8 —2K 65
Hillside Clo. Mord —4G 137
Hillside Clo. Wfd G —5F 21
Hillside Cres. Harr —1G 43
Hillside Cres. N'wd —1J 23
Hillside Dri. Edgw —6B 12
Hillside Est. N15 —6F 33
Hillside Gdns. E17 —3F 35
Hillside Gdns. N6 —6F 31
Hillside Gdns. N11 —6B 16
Hillside Gdns. SW2 —2A 122
Hillside Gdns. Barn —4B 4
Hillside Gdns. Edgw —4A 12
Hillside Gdns. Harr —7E 26
Hillside Gdns. N'wd —1J 23
Hillside Gdns. Wall —7G 151
Hillside Gro. N14 —7C 6
Hillside Gro. NW7 —7H 13
Hillside La. Brom —2H 155
(in two parts)
Hillside Mans. Barn —4C 4
Hillside Pas. SW16 —2K 121
Hillside Ri. N'wd —1J 23
Hillside Rd. N16 —7E 32
Hillside Rd. SW2 —2K 121
Hillside Rd. W5 —5E 62
Hillside Rd. Brom —3H 143
Hillside Rd. Croy —5B 152
Hillside Rd. N'wd —1J 23
Hillside Rd. Pinn —1K 23
Hillside Rd. S'hall —4E 60
Hillside Rd. Surb —4F 135
Hillside Rd. Sutt —7H 149
Hills La. N'wd —1G 23
Hillsleigh Rd. W8 —1H 83
Hills M. W5 —7E 62
Hills Pl. W1 —6G 67 (1A 166)
Hills Rd. Buck H —1E 20
Hillstowe St. E5 —3J 51
Hill St. W1 —1E 84 (4H 165)
Hill St. Rich —5D 98
Hilltop. E17 —3D 34
Hilltop. NW11 —4K 29
Hill Top. Mord —6J 137
Hill Top. Sutt —7H 137
Hilltop Ct. NW8 —7A 48
(off Alexandra Rd.)
Hill Top Ct. Wfd G —6J 21
Hilltop Gdns. NW4 —2D 28
Hilltop Rd. NW6 —7J 47
Hill Top Vw. Wfd G —6J 21
Hilltop Way. Stan —3F 11
Hillview. SW20 —7D 118
Hillview Av. Harr —5E 26
Hillview Clo. Wemb —2F 45
Hill Vw. Cres. Ilf —6D 36
Hill Vw. Dri. Well —2J 109
Hillview Gdns. NW4 —4F 29
Hill Vw. Gdns. NW9 —5K 27
Hillview Gdns. Harr —3E 24
Hillview Rd. NW7 —4A 14
Hillview Rd. Chst —5E 126
Hill Vw. Rd. Clay —7A 146
Hillview Rd. Sutt —3A 150
Hill Vw. Rd. Twic —6A 98
Hillway. N6 —2E 48
Hillway. NW9 —1A 46
Hillwood Ho. NW1 —2G 67 (1B 160)
(off Polygon Rd.)
Hillworth. Beck —2D 142
Hillworth Rd. SW2 —7A 104
Hillyard Ho. SW9 —1A 104
Hillyard Rd. W7 —5J 61
Hillyard St. SW9 —1A 104
Hillyfield. E17 —2A 34
Hilly Fields Cres. SE4 —3C 106
Hilsea St. E5 —4J 51
Hilton Av. N12 —5G 15
Hilton Ho. SE4 —4K 105
Hilversum Cres. SE22 —5E 104
Himley Rd. SW17 —5C 120
Hinchinbrook Ho. NW6 —1K 65
(off Mortimer Cres.)
Hinchley Clo. Esh —4A 146
Hinchley Dri. Esh —3A 146
Hinchley Way. Esh —3A 146
Hinckley Rd. SE15 —4G 105
Hind Ct. EC4 —6A 68 (1K 167)
Hind Cres. Eri & N Hth —6K 93
Hinde Ho. W1 —6E 66 (7H 159)
(off Hinde St.)
Hinde M. W1 —7H 159
Hindes Rd. Harr —5H 25
Hinde St. W1 —6E 66 (7H 159)
Hind Gro. E14 —6C 70
Hindhead Clo. N16 —1E 50
Hindhead Clo. Uxb —5D 58
Hindhead Gdns. N'holt —1C 60
Hindhead Way. Wall —5J 151
Hindlip Ho. SW8 —1H 103
Hindmans Rd. SE22 —5G 105
Hindmans Way. Dag —4F 75
Hindmarsh Clo. E1 —7G 69
Hindrey Rd. E5 —5H 51
Hindsley's Pl. SE23 —2J 123
Hinkler Clo. Wall —7J 151
(in two parts)
Hinkler Rd. Harr —3D 26
Hinksey Path. SE2 —2D 92
Hinstock. NW6 —1K 65
(off Belsize Rd.)
Hinstock Rd. SE18 —6G 91
Hinton Av. Houn —4B 96
Hinton Clo. SE9 —1C 126
Hinton Ct. E10 —2D 52
(off Leyton Grange Est.)
Hinton Ho. W5 —6C 62
Hinton Rd. N18 —4K 17
Hinton Rd. SW9 —3B 104
Hinton Rd. Wall —6G 151
Hippodrome M. W11 —7G 65
Hippodrome Pl. W11 —7G 65
Hiroshima Promenade. SE7 —3A 90
Hissocks Ho. NW10 —7J 45
(off Stilton Cres.)
Hitcham Rd. E17 —7B 34
Hitchcock Clo. Shep —3B 130
Hitchin Sq. E3 —2A 70
Hitherbroom Rd. Hay —1J 77
Hither Farm Rd. SE3 —3A 108
Hitherfield Rd. SW16 —2K 121
Hitherfield Rd. Dag —2E 56
Hither Green. —6G 107
Hither Grn. La. SE13 —5E 106
Hitherwell Dri. Harr —1H 25
Hitherwood Dri. SE19 —4F 123
Hive Clo. Bus H —2C 10
Hive Rd. Bus H —2C 10
HMS Belfast. —1E 86 (4H 169)
Hoadly Rd. SW16 —3H 121
Hobart Clo. N20 —2H 15
Hobart Clo. Hay —4B 60
Hobart Dri. Hay —4B 60
Hobart Gdns. T Hth —3D 140
Hobart La. Hay —4B 60
Hobart Pl. SW1 —3F 85 (1J 171)
Hobart Pl. Rich —7F 99
Hobart Rd. Dag —4D 56
Hobart Rd. Hay —4B 60
Hobart Rd. Ilf —2G 37
Hobart Rd. Wor Pk —3D 148
Hobbayne Rd. W7 —6H 61
Hobbes Wlk. SW15 —5D 100
Hobbs Ct. SE1 —2F 87 (6K 169)
(off Mill St.)
Hobbs Grn. N2 —3H 30
Hobbs M. Ilf —2K 55
Hobbs Pl. N1 —1E 68
Hobbs Pl. Est. N1 —1E 68
(off Hobbs Pl.)
Hobbs Rd. SE27 —4C 122
Hobday St. E14 —6D 70
Hobill Wlk. Surb —6F 135
Hoblands End. Chst —6J 127
Hobson's Pl. E1 —5G 69
Hobury St. SW10 —6A 84 (7A 170)
Hocker St. E2 —3F 69 (2J 163)
Hockett Clo. SE8 —4A 88
Hockley Av. E6 —2C 72
Hockley Ct. E18 —1J 35
Hockley M. Bark —3J 73
Hocroft Av. NW2 —3H 47
Hocroft Ct. NW2 —3H 47
Hocroft Rd. NW2 —3H 47
Hocroft Wlk. NW2 —3H 47
Hodder Dri. Gnfd —2K 61
Hoddesdon Rd. Belv —5G 93
Hodes Row. NW3 —4E 48
Hodford Rd. NW11 —1H 47
Hodgkin Clo. SE28 —7D 74
Hodister Clo. SE5 —7C 86
Hodnet Gro. SE16 —4K 87
Hodson Clo. Harr —3D 42
Hoecroft Ct. Enf —1D 8
(off Hoe La.)
Hoe La. Enf —1B 8
Hoe St. E17 —4C 34
Hoever Ho. SE6 —4E 124
Hofland Rd. W14 —3G 83
Hogan M. W2 —5A 66 (5A 158)
Hogan Way. E5 —2G 51
Hogarth Av. Ashf —6E 112
Hogarth Bus. Cen. W4 —6A 82
Hogarth Clo. E16 —5B 72
Hogarth Clo. W5 —5E 62
Hogarth Ct. E1 —6G 69
(off Batty St.)
Hogarth Ct. EC3 —6E 68 (2H 169)
Hogarth Ct. NW1 —7G 49
(off St Pancras Way)
Hogarth Ct. SE19 —4F 123
Hogarth Ct. Houn —7C 78
Hogarth Cres. SW19 —1B 138
Hogarth Cres. Croy —7C 140
Hogarth Gdns. Houn —7E 78
Hogarth Hill. NW11 —4H 29
Hogarth Ho. SW1 —4H 85 (4D 172)
(off Erasmus St.)
Hogarth Ho. N'holt —2B 60
(off Gallery Gdns.)
Hogarth Ind. Est. NW10 —4C 64
Hogarth La. W4 —6A 82
Hogarth Pl. SW5 —4K 83
(off Hogarth Rd.)
Hogarth Rd. SW5 —4K 83
Hogarth Rd. Dag —5B 56
Hogarth Rd. Edgw —2G 27
Hogarth Roundabout. (Junct.) —6A 82
Hogarth's House. —6A 82
Hogarth Ter. W4 —6A 82
Hogarth Way. Hamp —1G 133
Hog Hill Rd. Romf —1F 39
Hogshead Pas. E1 —7H 69
(off Pennington St.)
Hogsmill Wlk. King T —3E 134
(off Penrhyn Rd.)
Hogsmill Way. Eps —5J 147
Holbeach Gdns. Sidc —6J 109
Holbeach M. SW12 —1F 121
Holbeach Rd. SE6 —7C 106
Holbeck Row. SE15 —7G 87
Holbein Ho. SW1 —5E 84 (5G 171)
(off Holbein M.)
Holbein M. SW1 —5E 84 (5G 171)
Holbein Pl. SW1 —4E 84 (4G 171)
Holbein Ter. Dag —4C 56
(off Marlborough Rd.)
Holberton Gdns. NW10 —3D 64
Holborn. —5A 68 (6J 161)
Holborn. EC1 —5A 68 (6J 161)
Holborn Cir. EC1 —5A 68 (6K 161)
Holborn Pl. WC2 —6G 161
Holborn Rd. E13 —5K 71
Holborn Viaduct. EC1
—5A 68 (6K 161)
Holborn Way. Mitc —2D 138
Holbrook Clo. N19 —1F 49
Holbrook Clo. Enf —1A 8
Holbrooke Ct. N7 —3J 49
Holbrooke Pl. Rich —5D 98
Holbrook Ho. Chst —1H 145
Holbrook La. Chst —7H 127
Holbrook Rd. E15 —2H 71
Holbrook Way. Brom —6D 144
Holburne Clo. SE3 —1A 108
Holburne Gdns. SE3 —1B 108
Holburne Rd. SE3 —1A 108
Holcombe Hill. NW7 —3H 13
Holcombe Ho. SW9 —3J 103
(off Landor Rd.)
Holcombe Pl. SE4 —3A 106
(off S. Asaph Rd.)
Holcombe Rd. N17 —3F 33
(in two parts)
Holcombe Rd. Ilf —7E 36
Holcombe St. W6 —4D 82
Holcote Clo. Belv —3E 92
Holcroft Ct. W1 —5A 160
Holcroft Ho. SW11 —3B 102
Holcroft Rd. E9 —7J 51
Holden Av. N12 —5E 14
Holden Av. NW9 —1J 45
Holdenby Rd. SE4 —5A 106
Holden Clo. Dag —3B 56
Holden Ho. N1 —1C 68
(off Prebend St.)
Holden Ho. SE8 —7C 88
Holdenhurst Av. N12 —7F 15
Holden Rd. N12 —5E 14
Holden St. SW11 —2E 102
Holder Clo. N3 —7E 14
Holdernesse Clo. Iswth —1A 98
Holdernesse Rd. SW17 —3D 120
Holderness Ho. SE5 —3E 104
Holderness Way. SE27 —5B 122
Holders Hill. —2F 29
Holder's Hill Av. NW4 —2F 29
Holders Hill Cir. NW7 —7B 14
Holders Hill Cres. NW4 —2F 29
Holders Hill Dri. NW4 —3F 29
Holder's Hill Gdns. NW4 —2G 29
Holders Hill Rd. NW4 & NW7 —2F 29
Holford Ho. SE16 —4H 87
(off Camilla Rd.)
Holford M. WC1 —1J 161
Holford Pl. WC1 —3K 67 (1H 161)
Holford Rd. NW3 —3A 48
Holford St. WC1 —3K 67 (1J 161)
Holford Yd. WC1 —2A 68
Holgate Av. SW11 —3B 102
Holgate Gdns. Dag —6G 57
Holgate Rd. Dag —5G 57
Holgate St. SE7 —3B 90
Hollam Ho. N8 —4K 31
Holland Av. SW20 —1B 136
Holland Av. Sutt —7J 149
Holland Clo. Brom —2H 155
Holland Clo. New Bar —7G 5
Holland Clo. Romf —5J 39
Holland Clo. Stan —5G 11
Holland Ct. E17 —4E 34
(off Evelyn Rd.)
Holland Ct. NW7 —6H 13
Holland Ct. Surb —7D 134
Holland Dri. SE23 —3A 124
Holland Gdns. W14 —3G 83
Holland Gro. SW9 —7A 86
Holland Ho. E4 —4A 20
Holland Park. —1H 83
Holland Park. (Junct.) —2F 83
Holland Pk. —2H 83
Holland Pk. W11 —1G 83
Holland Pk. Av. W11 —2G 83
Holland Pk. Av. Ilf —6J 37
Holland Pk. Gdns. W14 —2G 83
Holland Pk. M. W11 —1G 83
Holland Pk. Rd. W14 —3H 83
Holland Pk. Theatre. —2H 83
Holland Pas. N1 —1C 68
(off Basire St.)
Holland Pl. W8 —2K 83
(off Kensington Chu. St.)
Holland Pl. Chambers. W8 —2K 83
(off Pitt St. La.)
Holland Ri. Ho. SW9 —7K 85
(off Clapham Rd.)
Holland Rd. E6 —1D 72
Holland Rd. E15 —3G 71
Holland Rd. NW10 —1C 64
Holland Rd. SE25 —5G 141
Holland Rd. W14 —2F 83
Holland Rd. Wemb —6D 44
Hollands, The. Felt —4B 114
Hollands, The. Wor Pk —1B 148
Holland St. SE1 —1B 86 (4B 168)
Holland St. W8 —2J 83
Holland Vs. Rd. W14 —2G 83
Holland Wlk. N19 —1H 49
Holland Wlk. W8 —1H 83
(off Holland Pk. Av.)
Holland Wlk. Stan —5F 11
Holland Way. Brom —2H 155
Hollar Rd. N16 —3F 51
Hollen St. W1 —6H 67 (7C 160)
Holles Clo. Hamp —6E 114
Holles Ho. SW9 —2A 104
Holles St. W1 —6F 67 (7K 159)
Holley Rd. W3 —2A 82
Hollick Wood Av. N12 —6J 15
Holliday Sq. SW11 —3B 102
(off Fowler Clo.)
Hollidge Way. Dag —7H 57
Hollies Av. Sidc —2K 127
Hollies Clo. SW16 —6A 122
Hollies Clo. Twic —2K 115
Hollies End. NW7 —5J 13
Hollies Rd. W5 —4C 80
Hollies, The. E11 —5J 35
(off New Wanstead)
Hollies, The. N20 —1G 15
Hollies, The. Harr —4A 26
Hollies Way. SW12 —7E 102
Holligrave Rd. Brom —1J 143
Hollingbourne Av. Bexh —1F 111
Hollingbourne Gdns. W13 —5B 62
Hollingbourne Rd. SE24 —5C 104
Hollingsworth Ct. Surb —7D 134
Hollingsworth Rd. Croy —6H 153
Hollington Ct. Chst —6F 127
Hollington Cres. N Mald —6B 136
Hollington Rd. E6 —3D 72
Hollington Rd. N17 —2G 33
Hollingworth Clo. W Mol —4D 132
Hollingworth Rd. Orp —6F 145
Hollins Ho. N7 —4J 49
Hollisfield. WC1 —3J 67 (2F 161)
(off Cromer St.)
Hollman Gdns. SW16 —6B 122
Holloway. —3J 49
Holloway Clo. W Dray —5A 76
Holloway Ho. NW2 —3E 46
Holloway La. W Dray —6A 76
Holloway Rd. E6 —3D 72
Holloway Rd. E11 —3F 53
Holloway Rd. N7 —4K 49
Holloway Rd. N19 & N7 —2H 49
Holloway St. Houn —3F 97
Hollowfield Wlk. N'holt —7C 42
Hollows, The. Bren —6F 81
Hollow, The. Wfd G —4C 20
Holly Av. Stan —2E 26
Holly Av. W on T —7B 132
Hollybank Clo. Hamp —5E 114
Hollyberry La. NW3 —4A 48
Hollybrake Clo. Chst —7H 127
Hollybush Clo. E11 —5J 35
Hollybush Clo. Harr —1J 25
Hollybush Gdns. E2 —3H 69
Hollybush Hill. E11 —6H 35
Hollybush Hill. NW3 —4A 48
Hollybush Ho. E2 —3H 69
Holly Bush La. Hamp —7D 114
Hollybush Pl. E2 —3H 69
Hollybush Rd. King T —5E 116
Hollybush Steps. NW3 —4A 48
(off Holly Mt.)
Hollybush St. E13 —3K 71
Holly Bush Va. NW3 —4A 48
Hollybush Wlk. SW9 —4B 104
Holly Clo. NW10 —7A 46
Holly Clo. Beck —4E 142
Holly Clo. Buck H —3G 21
Holly Clo. Felt —5C 114
Holly Clo. Wall —7F 151
Holly Cottage M. Uxb —5C 58
Holly Ct. N15 —4E 32
Holly Ct. Sidc —4B 128
(off Sidcup Hill)
Holly Ct. Sutt —7J 149
Holly Cres. Beck —5B 142
Holly Cres. Wfd G —7A 20
Hollycroft Av. NW3 —3J 47
Hollycroft Av. Wemb —2F 45
Hollycroft Clo. S Croy —5E 152
Hollycroft Clo. W Dray —6C 76
Hollycroft Gdns. W Dray —6C 76
Hollydale Clo. N'holt —4F 43
Hollydale Dri. Brom —3D 156
Hollydale Rd. SE15 —1J 105
Holly Dene. SE15 —1H 105
Hollydown Way. E11 —3F 53
Holly Dri. E4 —7J 9
Holly Farm Rd. S'hall —5C 78
Hollyfield Av. N11 —5J 15
Hollyfield Rd. Surb —7F 135
Holly Gdns. W Dray —2B 76
Holly Gro. NW9 —7J 27
Holly Gro. SE15 —2F 105
Hollygrove. Bush —1C 10
Holly Gro. Pinn —1C 24
Hollygrove Clo. Houn —4D 96
Holly Hedge Ter. SE13 —5F 107
Holly Hill. N21 —6E 6
Holly Hill. NW3 —4A 48
Holly Hill Rd. Belv & Eri —5H 93
Holly Ho. W10 —4G 65
(off Hawthorn Wlk.)
Holly Ho. Iswth —6C 80
Holly Lodge. Harr —5H 25
Holly Lodge Gdns. N6 —2E 48
Holly Lodge Mans. N6 —2E 48
Hollymead. Cars —3D 150
Holly M. SW10 —6A 170
Holly Mt. NW3 —4A 48
Hollymount Clo. SE10 —1E 106
Holly Pk. N3 —3H 29
Holly Pk. N4 —7J 31
(in two parts)
Holly Pk. Est. N4 —7K 31
Holly Pk. Gdns. N3 —3J 29
Holly Pk. Rd. N11 —5K 15
Holly Pk. Rd. W7 —1K 79
Holly Pl. NW3 —4A 48
(off Holly Berry La.)
Holly Rd. E11 —7H 35
Holly Rd. W4 —4K 81
Holly Rd. Hamp & Hamp H —6G 115
Holly Rd. Houn —4F 97
Holly Rd. Twic —1K 115
Holly St. E8 —7F 51
Holly Ter. N6 —1E 48
Holly Ter. N20 —2F 15
Holly Tree Clo. SW19 —1F 119
Holly Tree Ho. SE4 —3B 106
(off Brockley Rd.)
Hollytree Pde. Sidc —6C 128
(off Sidcup Hill)
Holly Vw. Clo. NW4 —6C 28
Holly Village. N6 —2F 49
Holly Wlk. NW3 —4A 48
Holly Wlk. Enf —3H 7
Holly Way. Mitc —4H 139
Hollywood Ct. W5 —7F 63
Hollywood Gdns. Hay —6K 59
Hollywood M. SW10 —6A 84
Hollywood Rd. E4 —5F 19
Hollywood Rd. SW10 —6A 84
Hollywood Way. Wfd G —7A 20
Holman Ct. Ewe —7C 148
Holman Hunt Ho. W6 —5G 83
(off Field Rd.)
Holman Rd. SW11 —2B 102
Holman Rd. Eps —5J 147
Holmbank Dri. Shep —4G 131
Holmbridge Gdns. Enf —4E 8
Holmbrook. NW1 —2G 67
(off Eversholt St.)
Holmbrook Dri. NW4 —5F 29
Holmbury Ct. SW17 —3D 120
Holmbury Ct. S Croy —5E 152
Holmbury Gdns. Hay —1H 77
Holmbury Gro. Croy —7B 154
Holmbury Ho. SE24 —5B 104
Holmbury Mnr. Sidc —4A 128
Holmbury Pk. Brom —7C 126
Holmbury Vw. E5 —1H 51
Holmbush Rd. SW15 —6G 101
Holmcote Gdns. N5 —5C 50
Holm Ct. SE12 —3K 125
Holmcroft Ho. E17 —4D 34
Holmcroft Way. Brom —5D 144
Holmdale Gdns. NW4 —5F 29
Holmdale Rd. NW6 —5J 47
Holmdale Rd. Chst —5G 127
Holmdale Ter. N15 —7E 32
Holmdene. N12 —5E 14
Holmdene Av. NW7 —6H 13
Holmdene Av. SE24 —5C 104
Holmdene Av. Harr —3F 25
Holmdene Clo. Beck —2E 142
Holmead Rd. SW6 —7K 83
Holmebury Clo. Bush —2D 10
Holme Lacey Rd. SE12 —6H 107
Holme Rd. E6 —1C 72
Holmes Av. E17 —3B 34
Holmes Av. NW7 —5B 14
Holmesdale Av. SW14 —3H 99
Holmesdale Clo. SE25 —3F 141
Holmesdale Ho. NW6 —1J 65
(off Kilburn Va.)
Holmesdale Rd. N6 —7F 31
Holmesdale Rd. Bexh —2D 110
Holmesdale Rd. Croy & SE25 —5D 140
Holmesdale Rd. Rich —1F 99
Holmesdale Rd. Tedd —7C 116
Holmesley Rd. SE23 —6A 106
Holmes Pl. SW10 —6A 84
Holmes Rd. NW5 —5F 49
Holmes Rd. SW19 —7A 120
Holmes Rd. Twic —2K 115
Holmes Ter. SE1 —6J 167
Holmeswood Ct. N22 —2A 32
Holme Way. Stan —6E 10
Holmewood Gdns. SW2 —7K 103

Holmewood Rd.—Hugh M.

Holmewood Rd. SE25 —3E 140
Holmewood Rd. SW2 —7J 103
Holmfield Av. NW4 —5F 29
Holmfield Ct. NW3 —5C 48
Holm Gro. Uxb —7C 40
Holmhurst Rd. Belv —5H 93
Holmleigh Ct. Enf —4D 8
Holmleigh Rd. N16 —1E 50
Holmleigh Rd. Est. N16 —1E 50
Holmoak Clo. SW15 —6H 101
Holm Oak M. SW4 —5J 103
Holmoaks Ho. Beck —2E 142
Holmsdale Ho. E14 —7D 70
Holmsdale Ho. N11 —4A 16
(off Coppies Gro.)
Holmshaw Clo. SE26 —4A 124
Holmside Rd. SW12 —6E 102
Holmsley Clo. N Mald —6B 136
Holmsley Ho. SW15 —7B 100
(off Tangley Gro.)
Holmstall Av. Edgw —3J 27
Holmstall Pde. Edgw —2J 27
Holm Wlk. SE3 —2J 107
Holmwood Clo. Harr —3G 25
Holmwood Clo. N'holt —6F 43
Holmwood Clo. Sutt —7F 149
Holmwood Gdns. N3 —2J 29
Holmwood Gdns. Wall —6F 151
Holmwood Gro. NW7 —5E 12
Holmwood Rd. Chess —5D 146
Holmwood Rd. Ilf —2J 55
Holmwood Vs. SE7 —5J 89
Holne Chase. N2 —6A 30
Holne Chase. Mord —6H 137
Holness Rd. E15 —6H 53
Holroyd Rd. SW15 —4E 100
Holroyd Rd. Clay —7A 146
Holst Ct. SE1 —3A 86 (1J 173)
(off Westminster Bri. Rd.)
Holstein Way. Eri —3D 92
Holst Mans. SW13 —6E 82
Holstock Rd. Ilf —2G 55
Holsworth Clo. Harr —5G 25
Holsworthy Sq. WC1 —4H 161
Holsworthy Way. Chess —5C 146
Holt Clo. N10 —4E 30
Holt Clo. SE28 —7B 74
Holt Ct. E15 —5E 52
Holt Ho. SW2 —6A 104
Holton St. E1 —4K 69
Holt Rd. E16 —1C 90
Holt Rd. Wemb —3B 44
Holt, The. Mord —4J 137
Holt, The. Wall —4G 151
Holtwhites Av. Enf —2H 7
Holtwhite's Hill. Enf —1G 7
Holwell Pl. Pinn —4C 24
Holwood Pk. Av. Orp —4D 156
Holwood Pl. SW4 —4H 103
Holybourne Av. SW15 —7C 100
Holyhead Clo. E3 —3C 70
Holyhead Clo. E6 —5D 72
Holy Oake Ct. SE16 —2B 88
Holyoake Ho. W5 —4C 62
Holyoake Wlk. N2 —3A 30
Holyoake Wlk. W5 —4C 62
Holyoak Rd. SE11 —4B 86
Holyport Rd. SW6 —7F 83
Holyrood Av. Harr —4C 42
Holyrood Gdns. Edgw —3H 27
Holyrood M. E16 —1J 89
(off Badminton M.)
Holyrood Rd. New Bar —6F 5
Holyrood St. SE1 —1E 86 (5G 169)
Holywell Clo. SE3 —6J 89
Holywell Clo. SE16 —5H 87
Holywell Clo. Stai —1A 112
Holywell La. EC2 —4E 68 (3H 163)
Holywell Row. EC2 —4E 68 (4G 163)
Holywell Way. Stai —1A 112
Homan Ct. N12 —4G 15
Homebush Ho. E4 —7J 9
Home Clo. Cars —2D 150
Home Clo. N'holt —3D 60
Home Ct. Felt —1J 113
Home Ct. Surb —5D 134
Homecroft Rd. N22 —1C 32
Homecroft Rd. SE26 —5J 123
Home Farm Clo. Shep —4G 131
Home Farm Clo. Th Dit —7K 133
Homefarm Rd. W7 —6J 61
Home Fld. Barn —5C 4
Homefield. Mord —4J 137
Homefield Av. Ilf —5J 37
Homefield Clo. NW10 —6J 45
Homefield Clo. Hay —4B 60
Homefield Ct. SW16 —3J 121
Homefield Gdns. N2 —3B 30
Homefield Gdns. Mitc —2A 138
Homefield Ho. SE23 —3K 123
Homefield M. Beck —1C 142
Homefield Pk. Sutt —6K 149
Homefield Rd. SW19 —6F 119
Homefield Rd. W4 —4B 82
Homefield Rd. Brom —1A 144
Homefield Rd. Edgw —6E 12
Homefield Rd. W on T —7C 132
Homefield Rd. Wemb —4A 44
Homefield St. N1 —2E 68 (1G 163)
Homefirs Ho. Wemb —3F 45
Home Gdns. Dag —3J 57
Homelands Dri. SE19 —7E 122
Homeleigh Rd. SE15 —5K 105
Home Mead. Stan —1C 26
Homemead Rd. Brom —5D 144
Homemead Rd. Croy —6G 139
Home Pk. Pde. King T —2D 134
(off High St.)
Home Pk. Rd. SW19 —4H 119
Home Pk. Wlk. King T —4D 134
Homer Clo. Bexh —1J 111
Homer Dri. E14 —4C 88
Home Rd. SW11 —2C 102
Homer Rd. E9 —6A 52
Homer Rd. Croy —6K 141
Homer Row. W1 —5C 66 (6D 158)
Homersham Rd. King T —2G 135
Homer St. NW1 —5C 66 (6D 158)
Homerton. —5K 51
Homerton Gro. E9 —5K 51
Homerton High St. E9 —5K 51
Homerton Rd. E9 —5A 52
Homerton Row. E9 —5J 51
Homerton Ter. E9 —6J 51
(in two parts)
Homesdale Clo. E11 —5J 35
Homesdale Rd. Brom —4A 144
Homesdale Rd. Orp —7J 145
Homesfield. NW11 —5J 29
Homestall Rd. SE22 —5J 105
Homestead Ct. Barn —5D 4
Homestead Paddock. N14 —5A 6
Homestead Pk. NW2 —3B 46
Homestead Rd. SW6 —7H 83
Homestead Rd. Dag —2F 57
Homesteads, The. N11 —4A 16
Homewaters Av. Sun —1H 131
Homewillow Clo. N21 —6G 7
Homewood Clo. Hamp —6D 114
Homewood Cres. Chst —6J 127
Homewoods. SW12 —7G 103
Homildon Ho. SE26 —3G 123
Honduras St. EC1 —4C 68 (3C 162)
Honeybourne Rd. NW6 —5K 47
Honeybourne Way. Orp —7H 145
Honeybrook Rd. SW12 —7G 103
Honey Clo. Dag —6H 57
Honeycroft Hill. Uxb —7A 40
Honeyden Rd. Sidc —6E 128
Honey Hill. Uxb —7B 40
Honey La. EC2 —1D 168
Honeyman Clo. NW6 —7F 47
(in two parts)
Honeymead. N8 —3J 31
(off Campsfield Rd.)
Honeypot Bus. Cen. Stan —1E 26
Honeypot Clo. NW9 —4F 27
Honeypot La. Stan & NW9 —7J 11
Honeysett Rd. N17 —2F 33
Honeysuckle Clo. S'hall —7C 60
Honeysuckle Ct. E12 —6F 55
Honeysuckle Gdns. Croy —7K 141
Honeysuckle La. N22 —2C 32
Honeywell Rd. SW11 —6D 102
Honeywood Heritage Cen. —4D 150
Honeywood Rd. NW10 —2B 64
Honeywood Rd. Iswth —4A 98
Honeywood Wlk. Cars —4D 150
Honister Clo. Stan —1B 26
Honister Gdns. Stan —7G 11
Honister Pl. Stan —1B 26
Honiton Gdns. SE15 —2J 105
(off Gibbon Rd.)
Honiton Rd. NW6 —2H 65
Honiton Rd. Romf —6K 39
Honiton Rd. Well —2K 109
Honley Rd. SE6 —7D 106
Honnor Gdns. Iswth —2H 97
Honor Oak. —6J 105
Honor Oak Crematorium. SE23 —5A 106
Honor Oak Park. —7A 106
Honor Oak Pk. SE23 —6J 105
Honor Oak Ri. SE23 —6J 105
Honor Oak Rd. SE23 —1J 123
Hood Av. N14 —6A 6
Hood Av. SW14 —5J 99
Hood Clo. Croy —1B 152
Hoodcote Gdns. N21 —7G 7
Hood Ct. EC4 —1K 167
Hood Ho. SE5 —7D 86
(off Elmington Est.)
Hood Ho. SW1 —5H 85 (6C 172)
(off Dolphin Sq.)
Hood Rd. SW20 —7B 118
Hood Wlk. Romf —1H 39
Hook. —4D 146
Hookers Rd. E17 —3K 33
Hook Farm Rd. Brom —5B 144
Hookham Ct. SW8 —1H 103
Hooking Grn. Harr —5F 25
Hook Junction. (Junct.) —3E 146
Hook La. Well —5K 109
Hook Ri. Bus. Cen. Chess —3G 147
Hook Ri. N. Surb —3E 146
Hook Ri. S. Surb —3E 146
Hook Ri. S. Ind. Pk. Chess —3F 147
Hook Rd. Chess & Surb —5D 146
Hook Rd. Eps —7J 147
Hooks Clo. SE15 —1H 105
Hookshall Dri. Dag —3J 57
Hookstone Way. Wfd G —7G 21
Hooks Way. SE22 —1G 123
Hook, The. New Bar —6G 5
Hook Wlk. Edgw —6D 12
Hooper Rd. E16 —6J 71
Hooper's Ct. SW3 —2D 84 (7E 164)
Hooper's M. W3 —1J 81
Hooper Sq. E1 —6G 69
(off Hooper St.)
Hooper St. E1 —6G 69
Hoop La. NW11 —7H 29
(in two parts)
Hope Clo. N1 —6C 50
Hope Clo. SE12 —3K 125
Hope Clo. Bren —5E 80
Hope Clo. Chad H —4D 38
Hope Clo. Sutt —5A 150
Hope Clo. Wfd G —6F 21
Hopedale Rd. SE7 —6K 89
Hopefield Av. NW6 —2G 65
Hope Pk. Brom —7H 125
Hopes Clo. Houn —6E 78
Hope St. SW11 —3B 102
Hopetown St. E1 —5F 69 (6K 163)
Hopewell St. SE5 —7D 86
Hope Wharf. SE16 —2J 87
Hop Gdns. WC2 —7J 67 (3E 166)
Hopgood St. W12 —1E 82
Hopkins Clo. N10 —7K 15
Hopkins Ho. E14 —6C 70
Hopkins M. E15 —1H 71
Hopkinsons Pl. NW1 —1E 66
Hopkins St. W1 —6G 67 (1B 166)
Hoppers Rd. N13 & N21 —2F 17
Hoppett Rd. E4 —2B 20
Hopping La. N1 —6B 50
Hoppingwood Av. N Mald —3A 136
Hoppner Rd. Hay —2F 59
Hopton Ct. Hayes —1K 155
Hopton Gdns. N Mald —6C 136
Hopton Rd. SW16 —5J 121
Hopton's Gdns. SE1 —4B 168
Hopton St. SE1 —1B 86 (4B 168)
Hopwood Clo. SW17 —3A 120
Hopwood Rd. SE17 —6D 86
Hopwood Wlk. E8 —7G 51
Horace Av. Romf —1J 57
Horace Rd. E7 —4K 53
Horace Rd. Ilf —3G 37
Horace Rd. King T —3F 135
Horatio Ho. E2 —2F 69 (1K 163)
(off Horatio St.)
Horatio Pl. E14 —2E 88
(off Preston's Rd.)
Horatio Pl. SW19 —1J 137
Horatio St. E2 —2F 69 (1K 163)
(in two parts)
Horatius Way. Croy —5K 151
Horbury Cres. W11 —7J 65
Horbury M. W11 —7H 65
Horder Rd. SW6 —1G 101
Hordle Promenade E. SE15 —7F 87
Hordle Promenade N. SE15 —7F 87
Hordle Promenade S. SE15 —7F 87
(off Quarley Way)
Hordle Promenade W. SE15 —7E 86
(off Clanfield Way)
Horizon Building. E14 —7C 70
(off Hertsmere Rd.)
Horizon Way. SE7 —4K 89
Horle Wlk. SW9 —2B 104
Horley Clo. Bexh —5G 111
Horley Rd. SE9 —4C 126
Hormead Rd. W9 —4H 65
Hornbeam Clo. NW7 —3G 13
Hornbeam Clo. SE11 —4A 86 (3J 173)
Hornbeam Clo. Buck H —3G 21
Hornbeam Clo. Ilf —5H 55
Hornbeam Clo. N'holt —5D 42
Hornbeam Cres. Bren —7B 80
Hornbeam Gro. E4 —3B 20
Hornbeam Ho. Buck H —3G 21
Hornbeam La. Bexh —2J 111
Hornbeam Rd. Buck H —3G 21
Hornbeam Rd. Hay —5A 60
Hornbeams Ri. N11 —6K 15
Hornbeam Ter. Cars —1C 150
Hornbeam Wlk. Rich —2F 117
Hornbeam Way. Brom —6E 144
Hornblower Clo. SE16 —3A 88
Hornbuckle Clo. Harr —2H 43
Hornby Clo. NW3 —7B 48
Hornby Ho. SE11 —7J 173
Horncastle Clo. SE12 —7J 107
Horncastle Rd. SE12 —7J 107
Hornchurch. N17 —2D 32
(off Gloucester Rd.)
Hornchurch Clo. King T —4D 116
Horndean Clo. SW15 —1C 118
Horndon Clo. Romf —1J 39
Horndon Grn. Romf —1J 39
Horndon Rd. Romf —1J 39
Horner Ho. N1 —1E 68
(off Whitmore Est.)
Horner La. Mitc —2B 138
Horne Rd. Shep —4C 130
Horne Way. SW15 —2E 100
Hornfair Rd. SE7 —6A 90
Horniman Clo. SE10 —3G 89
Horniman Dri. SE23 —1H 123
Horniman Mus. —1H 123
Horning Clo. SE9 —4C 126
Horn La. SE10 —5J 89
(in three parts)
Horn La. W3 —7J 63
(in two parts)
Horn La. Wfd G —6D 20
Horn Park. —5K 107
Horn Pk. Clo. SE12 —5K 107
Hornpark La. SE12 —5K 107
Horns End Pl. Pinn —4A 24
Hornsey. —4J 31
Hornsey La. N6 —1F 49
Hornsey La. Est. N19 —7H 31
Hornsey La. Gdns. N6 —7G 31
Hornsey Pk. Rd. N8 —3K 31
Hornsey Ri. N19 —7H 31
Hornsey Ri. Gdns. N19 —7H 31
Hornsey Rd. N19 & N7 —1J 49
Hornsey St. N7 —5K 49
Hornsey Vale. —5K 31
Hornshay St. SE15 —6J 87
Horns Rd. Ilf —4H 37
Hornton Ct. W8 —2J 83
(off Kensington High St.)
Hornton Pl. W8 —2K 83
Hornton St. W8 —2J 83
Horsa Clo. Wall —7J 151
Horsa Rd. SE12 —7A 108
Horsa Rd. Eri —7H 93
Horse & Dolphin Yd. W1 —2D 166
Horsebridge Clo. Dag —1E 74
Horsecroft Rd. Edgw —7E 12
Horse Fair. King T —2D 134
Horseferry Pl. SE10 —6E 88
Horseferry Rd. E14 —7A 70
Horseferry Rd. SW1 —3H 85 (2C 172)
Horseferry Rd. Est. SW1 —2C 172
Horseguards Av. SW1 —1J 85 (5E 166)
Horse Guards Rd. SW1 —1H 85 (5D 166)
Horse Leaze. E6 —6E 72
Horsell Rd. N5 —5A 50
(in two parts)
Horsell Rd. Orp —7B 128
Horselydown La. SE1 —2F 87 (6J 169)
Horselydown Mans. SE1 —2F 87 (6J 169)
(off Lafone St.)
Horsemongers M. SE1 —7D 168
Horsenden Av. Gnfd —5K 43
Horsenden Cres. Gnfd —5K 43
Horsenden La. Gnfd —6J 43
Horsenden La. N. Gnfd —6K 43
Horsenden La. S. Gnfd —1A 62
Horse Ride. SW1 —5C 166
Horseshoe Clo. E14 —5E 88
Horseshoe Clo. NW2 —2D 46
Horse Shoe Cres. N'holt —2E 60
Horseshoe Dri. Uxb —6C 58
Horse Shoe Grn. Sutt —2K 149
Horseshoe La. N20 —1A 14
Horseshoe La. Enf —3H 7
Horseshoe Wharf. SE1 —1D 86 (4E 168)
(off Clink St.)
Horse Yd. N1 —1B 68
(off Essex Rd.)
Horsfeld Gdns. SE9 —5C 108
Horsfeld Rd. SE9 —5B 108
Horsfield Ho. N1 —7C 50
(off Northampton St.)
Horsford Rd. SW2 —5K 103
Horsham Av. N12 —5H 15
Horsham Ct. N17 —1G 33
(off Lansdowne Rd.)
Horsham Rd. Bexh —5G 111
Horsham Rd. Felt —6E 94
Horsley Dri. King T —5D 116
Horsley Dri. New Ad —7E 154
Horsley Rd. E4 —2K 19
Horsley Rd. Brom —1K 143
Horsley St. SE17 —6D 86
Horsman Ho. SE5 —6C 86
(off Bethwin Rd.)
Horsman St. SE5 —6C 86
Horsmonden Clo. Orp —7K 145
Horsmonden Rd. SE4 —5B 106
Hortensia Ho. SW10 —7A 84
(off Hortensia Rd.)
Hortensia Rd. SW10 —7A 84
Horticultural Pl. W4 —5K 81
Horton Av. NW2 —4G 47
Horton Bri. Rd. W Dray —1B 76
Horton Clo. W Dray —1C 76
Horton Country Pk. —7H 147
Horton Ho. SE15 —6J 87
Horton Ho. SW8 —7K 85
Horton Ho. W6 —5G 83
(off Field Rd.)
Horton Ind. Pk. W Dray —1B 76
Horton La. Eps —7H 147
Horton Pde. W Dray —1A 76
Horton Rd. E8 —6H 51
Horton Rd. W Dray —1A 76
Horton Rd. Ind. Est. W Dray —1B 76
Horton St. SE13 —3D 106
Horton Way. Croy —5K 141
Hortus Rd. E4 —2K 19
Hortus Rd. S'hall —2D 78
Horwood Ho. NW8 —4C 66 (3D 158)
(off Paveley St.)
Hosack Rd. SW17 —2E 120
Hoser Av. SE12 —2J 125
Hosier La. EC1 —5B 68 (6A 162)
Hoskins Clo. E16 —6A 72
Hoskins Clo. Hay —5H 77
Hoskins St. SE10 —5F 89
Hospital Bri. Rd. Twic —7F 97
Hospital Bridge Roundabout. (Junct.) —2F 115
Hospital Rd. E9 —5K 51
Hospital Rd. Houn —3E 96
Hospital Way. SE13 —7F 107
Hotham Clo. W Mol —3E 132
Hotham Rd. SW15 —3E 100
Hotham Rd. SW19 —7A 120
Hotham Rd. M. SW19 —7A 120
Hotham St. E15 —1G 71
Hothfield Pl. SE16 —3J 87
Hotspur Ind. Est. N17 —6C 18
Hotspur Rd. N'holt —2E 60
Hotspur St. SE11 —4A 86 (5J 173)
Houblon Rd. Rich —5E 98
Houghton Clo. E8 —6F 51
Houghton Clo. Hamp —6C 114
Houghton Rd. N15 —4F 33
Houghton St. WC2 —6K 67 (1H 167)
(in two parts)
Houlder Cres. Croy —6B 152
Houndsden Rd. N21 —6E 6
Houndsditch. EC3 —6E 68 (7H 163)
Houndsfield Rd. N9 —7C 8
Hounslow. —3F 97
Hounslow Av. Houn —5F 97
Hounslow Bus. Pk. Houn —4F 97
Hounslow Cen. Houn —3F 97
Hounslow Gdns. Houn —5F 97
Hounslow Rd. Felt —1K 113
Hounslow Rd. Hanw —4B 114
Hounslow Rd. Twic —6F 97
Hounslow Urban Farm. —5J 95
(off Fagg's Rd.)
Hounslow West. —2C 96
Houseman Way. SE5 —7D 86
Houses of Parliament. —3J 85 (1F 173)
Houston Bus. Pk. Hay —1A 78
Houston Pl. Esh —7H 133
Houston Rd. SE23 —2A 124
Houstoun Ct. Houn —7D 78
Hove Av. E17 —5B 34
Hoveden Rd. NW2 —5G 47
Hove Gdns. Sutt —1K 149
Hoveton Rd. SE28 —6C 74
Hoveton Way. Ilf —1F 37
Howard Av. Bex —1C 128
Howard Clo. N11 —2K 15
Howard Clo. NW2 —4G 47
Howard Clo. W3 —6H 63
Howard Clo. Bus H —1D 10
Howard Clo. Hamp —7G 115
Howard Clo. Sun —6H 113
Howard Ct. Bark —1H 73
Howard Ho. SE8 —6B 88
(off Evelyn St.)
Howard Ho. SW1 —5G 85 (6B 172)
(off Dolphin Sq.)
Howard Ho. SW9 —3B 104
(off Barrington Rd.)
Howard Ho. W1 —4F 67 (4K 159)
(off Cleveland St.)
Howard M. N5 —4B 50
Howard Rd. E6 —2D 72
Howard Rd. E11 —3G 53
Howard Rd. E17 —3C 34
Howard Rd. N15 —6E 32
Howard Rd. N16 —4D 50
Howard Rd. NW2 —4F 47
Howard Rd. SE20 —1J 141
Howard Rd. SE25 —5G 141
Howard Rd. Ashf —4A 112
Howard Rd. Bark —1H 73
Howard Rd. Brom —7J 125
Howard Rd. Ilf —4F 55
Howard Rd. Iswth —3K 97
Howard Rd. N Mald —3A 136
Howard Rd. S'hall —6F 61
Howard Rd. Surb —6F 135
Howards Clo. Pinn —2K 23
Howards Crest Clo. Beck —2E 142
Howard's La. SW15 —4D 100
Howards Rd. E13 —3J 71
Howard St. Th Dit —7B 134
Howard Wlk. N2 —4A 30
Howard Way. SE22 —7G 105
Howard Way. Barn —5A 4
Howarth Ct. E15 —5D 52
Howarth Rd. SE2 —5A 92
Howberry Clo. Edgw —6J 11
Howberry Rd. Stan & Edgw —6J 11
Howberry Rd. T Hth —1D 140
Howbury Rd. SE15 —3J 105
Howcroft Cres. N3 —7D 14
Howcroft La. Gnfd —3H 61
Howden Clo. SE28 —7D 74
Howden Ho. Houn —7C 96
Howden Rd. SE25 —2F 141
Howden St. SE15 —3G 105
Howe Clo. Romf —1G 39
Howell Clo. Romf —5D 38
Howell Ct. E10 —7D 34
Howell Wlk. SE17 —4B 86
Howerd Way. SE18 —1C 108
(in two parts)
Howes Clo. N3 —3J 29
Howeth Ct. N11 —6J 15
(off Ribblesdale Av.)
Howfield Pl. N17 —3F 33
Howgate Rd. SW14 —3K 99
Howick Pl. SW1 —3G 85 (2B 172)
Howie St. SW11 —7C 84
Howitt Clo. N16 —4E 50
Howitt Clo. NW3 —6C 48
Howitt Rd. NW3 —6C 48
Howland Est. SE16 —3J 87
Howland Ho. SW16 —3J 121
Howland M. E. W1 —5G 67 (5B 160)
Howland St. W1 —5G 67 (5A 160)
Howland Way. SE16 —2A 88
Howletts La. Ruis —5E 22
Howlett's Rd. SE24 —6C 104
Howley Pl. W2 —5A 66 (5A 158)
Howley Rd. Croy —3B 152
Howsman Rd. SW13 —6C 82
Howson Rd. SE4 —4A 106
Howson Ter. Rich —6E 98
How's St. E2 —2F 69
Howton Pl. Bus H —1C 10
Hoxton. —2E 68
Hoxton Hall Theatre. —2E 68
Hoxton Mkt. N1 —2G 163
Hoxton Sq. N1 —3E 68 (2G 163)
Hoxton St. N1 —1E 68 (2G 163)
Hoylake Cres. Ick & Uxb —2C 40
Hoylake Gdns. Mitc —3G 139
Hoylake Gdns. Ruis —1K 41
Hoylake Rd. W3 —6A 64
Hoyland Clo. SE15 —7H 87
Hoyle Rd. SW17 —5C 120
Hoy St. E16 —6H 71
Hubbard Dri. Chess —6D 146
Hubbard Rd. SE27 —4C 122
Hubbard St. E15 —1G 71
Huberd Ho. SE1 —3D 86 (7F 169)
(off Manciple St.)
Hubert Clo. SW19 —1A 138
(off Nelson Gro. Rd.)
Hubert Gro. SW9 —3J 103
Hubert Ho. NW8 —4C 66 (4C 158)
Hubert Rd. E6 —3B 72
Hucknall Ct. NW8 —4B 66 (3A 158)
(off Cunningham Pl.)
Huddart St. E3 —5B 70
(in two parts)
Huddleston Clo. E2 —2J 69
Huddlestone Rd. E7 —4H 53
Huddlestone Rd. NW2 —6D 46
Huddleston Rd. N7 —3G 49
Hudson. NW9 —1B 28
(off Near Acre)
Hudson Clo. W12 —7D 64
Hudson Ct. E14 —5C 88
Hudson Pl. SE18 —5G 91
Hudson Rd. Bexh —2F 111
Hudson Rd. Hay —6F 77
Hudson's Pl. SW1 —3A 172
Huggin Ct. EC4 —2C 168
Huggin Hill. EC4 —7C 68 (2D 168)
Huggins Pl. SW2 —1K 121
Hughan Rd. E15 —5F 53
Hugh Astor Ct. SE1 —3B 86 (7B 168)
(off Keyworth St.)
Hugh Clark Ho. W13 —1A 80
(off Singapore Rd.)
Hugh Dalton Av. SW6 —6H 83
Hughenden Av. Harr —5B 26
Hughenden Gdns. N'holt —3A 60
(in two parts)
Hughenden Ho. NW8 —3C 158
Hughenden Rd. Wor Pk —7C 136
Hughendon. New Bar —4E 4
Hughendon Ter. E15 —4E 52
Hughes Ct. N7 —5H 49
Hughes Ho. SE17 —4B 86
(off Peacock St.)
Hughes Mans. E1 —4G 69
Hughes M. SW11 —5D 102
Hughes Rd. Ashf —6E 112
Hughes Rd. Hay —7K 59
Hughes Ter. E16 —5H 71
(off Clarkson Rd.)
Hughes Wlk. Croy —7C 140
Hugh Gaitskell Clo. SW6 —6H 83
Hugh Gaitskell Ho. N16 —2F 51
Hugh Herland Ho. King T —3E 134
Hugh M. SW1 —4F 85 (4K 171)

Isambard M.—Jubilee Mkt.

Isambard M. E14 —3E 88
Isambard Pl. SE16 —1J 87
Isard Ho. Hayes —1K 155
Isel Way. SE22 —5E 104
Isham Rd. SW16 —2J 139
Isis Clo. SW15 —4E 100
Isis Clo. Ruis —6E 22
Isis Ct. W4 —7H 81
Isis Ho. N18 —6A 18
Isis Ho. NW8 —4B 66 (4B 158)
(off Church St. Est.)
Isis St. SW18 —2A 120
Island Farm Av. W Mol —5D 132
Island Farm Rd. W Mol —5D 132
Island Rd. Mitc —7D 120
Island Row. E14 —6B 70
Island, The. Th Dit —6A 134
Isla Rd. SE18 —6G 91
Islay Gdns. Houn —5B 96
Islay Wlk. N1 —6C 50
Isleden Ho. N1 —1C 68
(off Prebend St.)
Isledon Rd. N7 —3A 50
Isledon Village. —3A 50
Islehurst Clo. Chst —1E 144
Isleworth. —3A 98
Isleworth Bus. Complex. Iswth —2K 97
Isleworth Promenade. Twic —4B 98
Isley Ct. SW8 —2G 103
Islington. —7B 50
Islington Crematorium. N2 —1D 30
Islington Grn. N1 —1B 68
Islington High St. N1 —2A 68
(in two parts)
Islington Pk. M. N1 —7B 50
Islington Pk. St. N1 —7A 50
Islip Gdns. Edgw —7E 12
Islip Gdns. N'holt —7C 42
Islip Mnr. Rd. N'holt —7C 42
Islip St. NW5 —5G 49
Ismailia Rd. E7 —7K 53
Isobel Ho. Harr —5K 25
Isom Clo. E13 —3K 71
Itaska Cotts. Bush —1D 10
Ivanhoe Clo. Uxb —5A 58
Ivanhoe Dri. Harr —3A 26
Ivanhoe Rd. SE5 —3F 105
Ivanhoe Rd. Houn —3B 96
Ivatt Pl. W14 —5H 83
Ivatt Way. N17 —3B 32
Iveagh Av. NW10 —2G 63
Iveagh Clo. E9 —1K 69
Iveagh Clo. NW10 —2G 63
Iveagh Clo. N'wd —1D 22
Iveagh Ct. E1 —1J 169
Iveagh Ct. Beck —3E 142
Iveagh Ho. SW9 —2B 104
Iveagh Ho. SW10 —7A 84
(off King's Rd.)
Iveagh Ter. NW10 —2G 63
(off Iveagh Av.)
Ivedon Rd. Well —2C 110
Ive Farm Clo. E10 —2C 52
Ive Farm La. E10 —2C 52
Iveley Rd. SW4 —2G 103
Ivere Dri. New Bar —6E 4
Iverhurst Clo. Bexh —5D 110
Iverna Ct. W8 —3J 83
Iverna Gdns. W8 —3J 83
Iverna Gdns. Felt —5F 95
Iverson Rd. NW6 —6H 47
Ivers Way. New Ad —7D 154
Ives Rd. E16 —5G 71
Ives St. SW3 —4C 84 (3D 170)
Ivestor Ter. SE23 —7J 105
Ivimey St. E2 —3G 69
Ivinghoe Clo. Enf —1K 7
Ivinghoe Ho. N7 —5H 49
Ivinghoe Rd. Dag —5B 56
Ivor Ct. N8 —6J 31
Ivor Ct. NW1 —4D 66 (3E 158)
(off Gloucester Pl.)
Ivor Gro. SE9 —1F 127
Ivories, The. N1 —7C 50
(off Northampton St.)
Ivor Pl. NW1 —4D 66 (4E 158)
Ivor St. NW1 —7G 49
Ivory Ct. Felt —2J 113
Ivorydown. Brom —4J 125
Ivory Ho. E1 —1F 87 (3K 169)
Ivory Sq. SW11 —3A 102
Ivybridge Clo. Twic —7A 98
Ivybridge Clo. Uxb —3A 58
Ivybridge Ct. Chst —1E 144
(off Old Hill)
Ivybridge La. WC2 —7J 67 (3F 167)
Ivychurch Clo. SE20 —7J 123
Ivychurch La. SE17 —5F 87
Ivy Clo. Harr —4D 42
Ivy Clo. Pinn —7A 24
Ivy Clo. Sun —2A 132
Ivy Cotts. E14 —7D 70
Ivy Cotts. Uxb —3C 58
Ivy Ct. SE16 —5G 87
(off Argyle Way)
Ivy Cres. W4 —4J 81
Ivydale Rd. SE15 —3K 105
Ivydale Rd. Cars —2D 150
Ivyday Gro. SW16 —3K 121
Ivydene. W Mol —5D 132
Ivydene Clo. Sutt —4A 150
Ivy Gdns. N8 —6J 31
Ivy Gdns. Mitc —3H 139
Ivyhouse Rd. Dag —6D 56
Ivyhouse Rd. Uxb —3D 40
Ivy La. Houn —4D 96
Ivymount Rd. SE27 —3A 122
Ivy Rd. E16 —6J 71
Ivy Rd. E17 —6C 34
Ivy Rd. N14 —7B 6
Ivy Rd. NW2 —4E 46
Ivy Rd. SE4 —4B 106
Ivy Rd. SW17 —5C 120
Ivy Rd. Houn —4F 97
Ivy Rd. Surb —1G 147
Ivy St. N1 —2E 68
Ivy Wlk. Dag —6E 56
Ivy Wlk. N'wd —1G 23

Ixworth Pl. SW3 —5C 84 (5C 170)
Izane Rd. Bexh —4F 111

Jacaranda Clo. N Mald —3A 136
Jacaranda Gro. E8 —7F 51
Jackass La. Kes —5K 155
Jack Barnett Way. N22 —2K 31
Jack Clow Rd. E15 —2G 71
Jack Cook Ho. Bark —7F 55
Jack Cornwell St. E12 —4E 54
Jack Dash Ho. E14 —2E 88
Jack Dash Way. E6 —4C 72
Jacklin Grn. Wfd G —4D 20
Jackman M. NW10 —3A 46
Jackman St. E8 —1H 69
Jackson Clo. E9 —7J 51
Jackson Clo. Uxb —7A 40
Jackson Ct. E7 —6K 53
Jackson Rd. N7 —4K 49
Jackson Rd. Bark —1H 73
Jackson Rd. Barn —6H 5
Jackson Rd. Brom —2D 156
Jackson Rd. Uxb —7A 40
Jacksons La. N6 —7E 30
Jacksons Pl. Croy —1D 152
Jackson St. SE18 —6E 90
Jackson's Way. Croy —3C 154
Jackson Way. S'hall —2F 79
Jack Walker Ct. N5 —4B 50
Jacob Ho. Eri —2D 92
Jacobin Lodge. N7 —5J 49
Jacobs Clo. Dag —4H 57
Jacobs Ho. E13 —3A 72
(off New City Rd.)
Jacob St. SE1 —2G 87 (6K 169)
Jacob's Well M. W1 —5E 66 (6H 159)
Jacqueline Clo. N'holt —1C 60
Jacqueline Creft Ter. N6 —6E 30
(off Grange Rd.)
Jacqueline Vs. E17 —5E 34
(off Shernhall St.)
Jade Clo. E16 —6B 72
Jade Clo. NW2 —7F 29
Jade Clo. Dag —1C 56
Jade Ter. NW6 —7A 48
Jaffe Rd. Ilf —1H 55
Jaffray Pl. SE27 —4B 122
Jaffray Rd. Brom —4B 144
Jaggard Way. SW12 —7D 102
Jago Clo. SE18 —6G 91
Jago Wlk. SE5 —7D 86
Jamaica Rd. SE1 & SE16 —2F 87 (7K 169)
Jamaica Rd. T Hth —6B 140
Jamaica St. E1 —6J 69
James Anderson Ct. N1 —2E 68
(off Kingsland Rd.)
James Av. NW2 —5E 46
James Av. Dag —1F 57
James Bedford Clo. Pinn —2A 24
James Boswell Clo. SW16 —4K 121
James Brine Ho. E2 —3F 69 (1K 163)
(off Ravenscroft St.)
James Clo. E13 —2J 71
James Clo. NW11 —6G 29
James Collins Clo. W9 —4H 65
James Ct. N1 —1C 68
(off Raynor Pl.)
James Ct. NW9 —2A 28
James Ct. N'holt —2C 60
(off Church Rd.)
James Ct. N'wd —1H 23
James Dudson Ct. NW10 —7J 45
James Est. Mitc —2D 138
James Gdns. N22 —7G 17
James Hammett Ho. E2 —3F 69 (1K 163)
(off Ravenscroft St.)
James Joyce Wlk. SE24 —4B 104
James La. E10 & E11 —7E 34
James Newman Ct. SE9 —3E 126
Jameson Clo. W3 —2J 81
Jameson Ho. SE11 —5K 85 (5G 173)
(off Glasshouse Wlk.)
Jameson Lodge. N6 —6G 31
Jameson St. W8 —1J 83
James Pl. N17 —1F 33
James's Cotts. Rich —7G 81
James Stewart Ho. NW6 —7H 47
James St. W1 —6E 66 (1H 165)
James St. WC2 —7J 67 (1F 167)
James St. Bark —7G 55
James St. Enf —5A 8
James St. Houn —3H 97
James Stroud Ho. SE17 —5C 86
(off Bronti Clo.)
James Ter. SW14 —3K 99
(off Church Path)
Jamestown Rd. NW1 —1F 67
Jamestown Way. E14 —7F 71
James Yd. E4 —6A 20
Jamieson Ho. Houn —6D 96
Jamuna Clo. E14 —5A 70
Jane Austen Hall. E16 —1K 89
(off Wesley Av., in two parts)
Jane Austen Ho. SW1 —5G 85 (6A 172)
(off Churchill Gdns.)
Jane Seymour Ct. SE9 —7G 109
Jane St. E1 —6H 69
Janet St. E14 —3C 88
Janeway Pl. SE16 —2H 87
Janeway St. SE16 —2G 87
Janice M. Ilf —2F 55
Jansen Wlk. SW11 —3B 102
Janson Clo. E15 —5G 53
Janson Clo. NW10 —3A 46
Janson Rd. E15 —5G 53
Jansons Rd. N15 —3E 32
Japan Cres. N4 —1K 49
Japan Rd. Chad H & Romf —6D 38
Jardine Rd. E1 —7K 69
Jarrett Clo. SW2 —1B 122
Jarrow Clo. Mord —5K 137
Jarrow Rd. N17 —4H 33
Jarrow Rd. SE16 —4J 87
Jarrow Rd. Romf —6C 38
Jarrow Way. E9 —4B 52
Jarvis Clo. Bark —1H 73

Jarvis Clo. Barn —5A 4
Jarvis Rd. SE22 —4E 104
Jarvis Rd. S Croy —6D 152
Jashoda Ho. SE18 —5E 90
(off Connaught M.)
Jasmin Clo. N'wd —1H 23
Jasmin Ct. SE12 —6H 107
Jasmine Clo. Ilf —5F 55
Jasmine Clo. Orp —2E 156
Jasmine Clo. S'hall —7C 60
Jasmine Ct. SW19 —5J 119
Jasmine Gdns. Croy —3D 154
Jasmine Gdns. Harr —2E 42
Jasmine Gro. SE20 —1H 141
Jasmine Rd. Rush G —2K 57
Jasmine Ter. W Dray —2C 76
Jasmine Way. E Mol —4J 133
Jasmin Lodge. SE16 —5H 87
(off Sherwood Gdns.)
Jasmin Rd. Eps —5H 147
Jason Ct. W1 —7H 159
Jason Wlk. SE9 —4E 126
Jasper Clo. Enf —1D 8
Jasper Pas. SE19 —6F 123
Jasper Rd. E16 —6B 72
Jasper Rd. SE19 —5F 123
Jasper Wlk. N1 —3D 68 (1E 162)
Java Wharf. SE1 —6K 169
Javelin Way. N'holt —3B 60
Jaycroft. Enf —1F 7
Jay Gdns. Chst —4D 126
Jay M. SW7 —2A 84 (7A 164)
Jean Batten Clo. Wall —7K 151
Jean Darling Ho. SW10 —6B 84
(off Cremorne Est.)
Jebb Av. SW2 —6J 103
(in two parts)
Jebb St. E3 —2C 70
Jedburgh Rd. E13 —3A 72
Jedburgh St. SW11 —4E 102
Jeddo M. W3 —2B 82
Jeddo Rd. W12 —2B 82
Jefferson Building. E14 —2C 88
Jefferson Clo. W13 —3B 80
Jefferson Clo. Ilf —5F 37
Jefferson Wlk. SE18 —6E 90
Jeffrey Row. SE12 —5K 107
Jeffrey's Pl. NW1 —7G 49
Jeffreys Rd. SW4 —2J 103
Jeffreys Rd. Enf —4F 9
Jeffrey's St. NW1 —7G 49
Jeffries Ho. NW10 —7K 45
Jeffs Clo. Hamp —6F 115
Jeffs Rd. Sutt —4H 149
Jeger Av. E2 —1F 69
Jeken Rd. SE9 —4A 108
Jelf Rd. SW2 —5A 104
Jellicoe Gdns. Stan —6E 10
Jellicoe Ho. E2 —2G 69 (1K 163)
(off Ropley St.)
Jellicoe Ho. NW1 —4F 67 (4K 159)
Jellicoe Rd. E13 —4J 71
Jellicoe Rd. N17 —7J 17
Jemmett Clo. King T —1H 135
Jem Paterson Ct. Harr —4J 43
Jengar Clo. Sutt —4K 149
Jenkins La. Bark —2G 73
Jenkins Rd. E13 —4K 71
Jenner Av. W3 —5K 63
Jenner Ho. WC1 —4J 67 (3F 161)
(off Hunter St.)
Jenner Pl. SW13 —6D 82
Jenner Rd. N16 —3F 51
Jennett Rd. Croy —3A 152
Jennifer Ho. SE11 —4A 86 (4K 173)
(off Reedworth St.)
Jennifer Rd. Brom —3H 125
Jenningsbury Ho. SW3 —5C 84 (5D 170)
(off Marlborough St.)
Jennings Clo. Surb —7C 134
Jennings Rd. SE22 —6F 105
Jennings Way. Barn —3A 4
Jenningtree Way. Belv —2J 93
Jenny Hammond Clo. E11 —3H 53
Jenson Way. SE19 —7F 123
Jenton Av. Bexh —1E 110
Jephson Ct. SW4 —2J 103
Jephson Ho. SE17 —6B 86
(off Doddington Gro.)
Jephson Rd. E7 —7A 54
Jephson St. SE5 —1D 104
Jephtha Rd. SW18 —6J 101
Jeppos La. Mitc —4D 138
Jepson Ho. SW6 —1K 101
(off Pearscroft Rd.)
Jerdan Pl. SW6 —7J 83
Jeremiah St. E14 —6D 70
Jeremy Bentham Ho. E2 —3G 69
(off Mansford St.)
Jeremy's Grn. N18 —4C 18
Jermyn St. SW1 —1G 85 (4A 166)
(in two parts)
Jerningham Av. Ilf —2F 37
Jerningham Ct. SE14 —1A 106
Jerningham Rd. SE14 —2A 106
Jerome Cres. NW8 —4C 66 (3C 158)
Jerome Ho. NW1 —5C 66 (5D 158)
(off Lisson Gro.)
Jerome Ho. SW7 —4B 84 (3A 170)
(off Glendower Pl.)
Jerome St. E1 —5J 163
Jerome Tower. W3 —2H 81
Jerrard St. SE13 —3D 106
Jerrold St. N1 —2E 68 (1H 163)
Jersey Av. Stan —2B 26
Jersey Dri. Orp —6H 145
Jersey Ho. N1 —6C 50
Jersey Ho. Enf —1E 8
(off Eastfield Rd.)
Jersey Rd. E11 —1F 53
Jersey Rd. E16 —6A 72
Jersey Rd. N1 —6C 50
Jersey Rd. SW17 —6F 121
Jersey Rd. W7 —2A 80
Jersey Rd. Houn & Iswth —1F 97
Jersey Rd. Ilf —4F 55
Jersey St. E2 —3H 69
Jerusalem Pas. EC1 —4B 68 (4A 162)

Jervis Bay Ho. E14 —6F 71
Jervis Ct. W1 —1K 165
Jervis Ct. Dag —6H 57
Jerviston Gdns. SW16 —6A 122
Jerwood Space Art Gallery. —6B 168
Jesmond Av. Wemb —6F 45
Jesmond Clo. Mitc —3F 139
Jesmond Rd. Croy —7F 141
Jesmond Way. Stan —5K 11
Jessam Av. E5 —1H 51
Jessamine Rd. W7 —1K 79
Jessel Ho. SW1 —4H 85 (3D 172)
(off Page St.)
Jessel Ho. WC1 —3J 67 (2E 160)
(off Judd St.)
Jessel Mans. W14 —6G 83
(off Queen's Club Gdns.)
Jesse Rd. E10 —1E 52
Jessett Clo. Eri —4K 93
Jessica Rd. SW18 —6A 102
Jessie Blythe La. N19 —7J 31
Jessiman Ter. Shep —5C 130
Jesson Ho. SE17 —4D 86
(off Orb St.)
Jessop Av. S'hall —4D 78
Jessop Ct. N1 —2B 68
Jessop Rd. SE24 —4B 104
Jessop Sq. E14 —1C 88
Jessops Way. Croy —6G 139
Jessup Clo. SE18 —4G 91
Jetstar Way. N'holt —3C 60
Jevington Way. SE12 —1K 125
Jewel Rd. E17 —3C 34
Jewish Mus. —1F 67
Jewish Mus., The. —2K 29
(off East End Rd.)
Jewry St. EC3 —6F 69 (1J 169)
Jew's Row. SW18 —4K 101
Jews Wlk. SE26 —4H 123
Jeymer Av. NW2 —5D 46
Jeymer Dri. Gnfd —1F 61
(in two parts)
Jeypore Pas. SW18 —6A 102
Jeypore Rd. SW18 —7A 102
Jillian Clo. Hamp —7E 114
Jim Bradley Clo. SE18 —4E 90
Jim Griffiths Ho. SW6 —6H 83
(off Clem Attlee Ct.)
Joan Cres. SE9 —7B 108
Joan Gdns. Dag —2E 56
Joan Rd. Dag —2E 56
Joan St. SE1 —1B 86 (5A 168)
Jocelin Ho. N1 —1K 67
(off Barnsbury Est.)
Jocelyn Rd. Rich —3E 98
Jocelyn St. SE15 —1G 105
Jockey's Fields. WC1 —5K 67 (5H 161)
Jodane St. SE8 —4B 88
Jodrell Clo. Iswth —1A 98
Jodrell Rd. E3 —1B 70
Joe Hunte Ct. SE27 —5B 122
Joel St. N'wd & Pinn —2J 23
Johanna St. SE1 —2A 86 (7J 167)
John Adams Ct. N9 —2A 18
John Adam St. WC2 —7J 67 (3F 167)
John Aird Ct. W2 —5A 158
(in two parts)
John Archer Way. SW18 —6B 102
John Ashby Clo. SW2 —6J 103
John Austin Clo. King T —1F 135
John Baird Ct. SE26 —4K 123
John Barker Ct. NW6 —7G 47
John Barnes Wlk. E15 —6H 53
John Betts' Ho. W12 —3B 82
John Bradshaw Rd. N14 —1C 16
John Brent Ho. SE8 —4K 87
(off Bush Rd.)
John Buck Ho. NW10 —1B 64
John Burns Dri. Bark —7J 55
John Campbell Rd. N16 —5E 50
John Carpenter St. EC4 —7B 68 (2A 168)
John Cartwright Ho. E2 —3H 69
(off Old Bethnal Grn. Rd.)
John Drinkwater Clo. E11 —7H 35
John Felton Rd. SE16 —2G 87
John Fielden Ho. E2 —3H 69
(off Canrobert St.)
John Fisher St. E1 —7G 69 (2K 169)
John Gooch Dri. Enf —1G 7
John Harrison Way. SE10 —3H 89
John Islip St. SW1 —4H 85 (5D 172)
John Kennedy Ct. N1 —6D 50
(off Newington Grn. Rd.)
John Knight Lodge. SW6 —7J 83
(off Vanston Pl.)
John Lamb Ct. Harr —1J 25
John Masefield Ho. N15 —6D 32
(off Fladbury Rd.)
John Maurice Clo. SE17 —4D 86
John McDonald Ho. E14 —3E 88
John McKenna Wlk. SE16 —3G 87
John Newton Ct. Well —3B 110
John Parker Clo. Dag —7H 57
John Parker Sq. SW11 —3B 102
John Parry Ct. N1 —2E 68
(off Hare Wlk.)
John Penn St. SE13 —1D 106
John Perrin Pl. Harr —7E 26
John Pound Ho. SW18 —7K 101
John Prince's St. W1 —6F 67 (7K 159)
John Pritchard Ho. E1 —4G 69
(off Buxton St.)
John Ratcliffe Ho. NW6 —3J 65
(off Chippenham Gdns.)
John Rennie Wlk. E1 —1H 87
John Roll Way. SE16 —3G 87
John Ruskin St. SE5 —7B 86
John's Av. NW4 —4E 28
John's Clo. Ashf —4E 112
John's Ct. Sutt —6K 149
John Scurr Ho. E14 —6A 70
John Silkin La. SE8 —4K 87
John's La. Mord —5A 138
John's M. WC1 —4K 67 (4H 161)
John Smith Av. SW6 —7H 83
Johnson Clo. E8 —1G 69

Johnson Ho. E2 —3G 69
(off Roberta St.)
Johnson Ho. NW1 —2G 67
(off Cranleigh St.)
Johnson Ho. SW1 —4E 84 (4H 171)
(off Cundy St.)
Johnson Lodge. W2 —5J 65
(off Admiral Wlk.)
Johnson Mans. W14 —6G 83
(off Queen's Club Gdns.)
Johnson Rd. Brom —5B 144
Johnson Rd. Croy —7D 140
Johnson Rd. Houn —7A 78
Johnsons Clo. Cars —2D 150
Johnson's Ct. EC4 —6A 68 (1K 167)
Johnsons Dri. Hamp —1G 133
Johnsons Ind. Est. Hay —2H 77
Johnson's Pl. SW1 —5G 85 (6A 172)
Johnson St. E1 —7J 69
Johnson St. S'hall —3A 78
Johnsons Way. NW10 —4H 63
John Spencer Sq. N1 —6B 50
John's Pl. E1 —6H 69
John's Ter. Croy —1E 152
Johnston Clo. SW9 —1K 103
Johnstone Ho. SE13 —3F 107
(off Belmont Hill)
Johnstone Rd. E6 —3D 72
Johnston Rd. Wfd G —6D 20
John Strachey Ho. SW6 —6H 83
(off Clem Attlee Ct.)
John St. E15 —1H 71
John St. SE25 —4G 141
John St. WC1 —4K 67 (4H 161)
John St. Enf —5A 8
John St. Houn —2C 96
John Strype Ct. E10 —1D 52
John Trundle Ct. EC2 —5C 162
John Trundle Highwalk. EC2
(off Beech St.) —5C 68 (5C 162)
John Tucker Ho. E14 —3C 88
John Watkin Clo. Eps —7H 147
John Wesley Ct. Twic —1A 116
John Wesley Highwalk. EC1 —5C 68
(off Barbican)
John Wheatley Ho. SW6 —6H 83
(off Clem Attlee Ct.)
John Williams Clo. SE14 —6K 87
John Williams Clo. King T —1D 134
John Wilson St. SE18 —3E 90
John Woolley Clo. SE13 —4G 107
Joiners Arms Yd. SE5 —1D 104
Joiners Pl. N5 —4D 50
Joint Rd. N2 —1C 30
Jollys La. Harr —1H 43
Jollys La. Hay —5B 60
Jonathan St. SE11 —5K 85 (5G 173)
Jones Ho. E14 —6F 71
Jones M. SW15 —4G 101
Jones Rd. E13 —5K 71
Jones St. W1 —7F 67 (3J 165)
Jones Wlk. Rich —6F 99
Jonquil Gdns. Hamp —6E 114
Jonson Clo. Hay —5J 59
Jonson Clo. Mitc —4F 139
Jonson Ho. SE1 —3D 86
(off Burbage Clo.)
Jordan Clo. Dag —4H 57
Jordan Clo. Harr —3D 42
Jordan Ho. N1 —1D 68
(off Colville Est.)
Jordan Ho. SE4 —4K 105
(off St Norbert Rd.)
Jordan Rd. Gnfd —1B 62
Jordans Clo. Iswth —1J 97
Jordans Ho. NW8 —3B 158
Jordans M. Twic —2J 115
Joseph Av. W3 —6K 63
Joseph Conrad Ho. SW1
(off Tachbrook St.) —4G 85 (4B 172)
Joseph Ct. N15 —6E 32
(off Amhurst Pk.)
Josephine Av. SW2 —5K 103
Joseph Irwin Ho. E14 —7B 70
Joseph Lister Ct. E7 —7J 53
Joseph Powell Clo. SW12 —6F 103
Joseph Ray Rd. E11 —2G 53
Joseph St. E3 —4B 70
Joseph Trotter Clo. EC1 —2K 161
Joshua St. E14 —5E 70
Joslings Clo. W12 —7C 64
Joslyn Clo. Enf —1H 9
Josseline Ct. E3 —2A 70
(off Ford St.)
Joubert St. SW11 —2D 102
Jowett St. SE15 —7F 87
Joyce Av. N18 —5A 18
Joyce Butler Ho. N22 —1K 31
Joyce Dawson Way. SE28 —7A 74
Joyce Page Clo. SE7 —6B 90
Joyce Wlk. SW2 —6A 104
Joydens Wood. —4K 129
Joydens Wood Rd. Bex —4K 129
Joydon Dri. Romf —6B 38
Joyners Clo. Dag —4F 57
Joystone Ct. New Bar —4H 5
(off Park Rd.)
Jubb Powell Ho. N15 —6E 32
Jubilee Av. E4 —6K 19
Jubilee Av. Romf —5H 39
Jubilee Av. Twic —1G 115
Jubilee Bldgs. NW8 —1B 66
(off Queen's Ter.)
Jubilee Clo. NW9 —6K 27
Jubilee Clo. King T —1C 134
Jubilee Clo. Pinn —2A 24
Jubilee Clo. Romf —5H 39
Jubilee Ct. N10 —3E 30
Jubilee Ct. Harr —7E 26
Jubilee Ct. Houn —3G 97
(off Bristow Rd.)
Jubilee Cres. E14 —3E 88
Jubilee Cres. N9 —1B 18
Jubilee Dri. Ruis —4B 42
Jubilee Gdns. S'hall —5E 60
Jubilee Ho. SE11 —4A 86 (4K 173)
(off Reedworth St.)
Jubilee Ho. WC1 —3G 161
Jubilee Mkt. Wfd G —6F 21

Kenwrick Ho.—Kings Rd.

Kenwrick Ho. N1 —1K 67
(off Barnsbury Est.)
Kenwyn Dri. NW2 —2A 46
Kenwyn Lodge. N2 —4D 30
Kenwyn Rd. SW4 —4H 103
Kenwyn Rd. SW20 —1E 136
Kenya Rd. SE7 —7B 90
Kenyngton Ct. Sun —5J 113
Kenyngton Dri. Sun —5J 113
Kenyngton Pl. Harr —5C 26
Kenyon Mans. W14 —6G 83
(off Queen's Club Gdns.)
Kenyon St. SW6 —1F 101
Keogh Rd. E15 —6G 53
Keple Pl. SW13 —6D 82
Kepler Rd. SW4 —4J 103
Keppel Ho. SE8 —5B 88
Keppel Rd. E6 —7D 54
Keppel Rd. Dag —4E 56
Keppel Row. SE1 —1C 86 (5C 168)
Keppel St. WC1 —5H 67 (5D 160)
Kerbela St. E2 —4G 69 (3K 163)
Kerbey St. E14 —6D 70
Kerfield Cres. SE5 —1D 104
Kerfield Pl. SE5 —1D 104
Kerridge Ct. N1 —6E 50
(off Balls Pond Rd.)
Kerrison Pl. W5 —1D 80
Kerrison Rd. E15 —1F 71
Kerrison Rd. SW11 —3C 102
Kerrison Rd. W5 —1D 80
Kerrison Vs. W5 —1D 80
Kerry. N7 —6J 49
Kerry Av. Stan —4H 11
Kerry Clo. E16 —6K 71
Kerry Clo. N13 —2E 16
Kerry Ct. Stan —4J 11
Kerry Path. SE14 —6B 88
Kerry Rd. SE14 —6B 88
Kersey Gdns. SE9 —4C 126
Kersfield Rd. SW15 —6F 101
Kershaw Clo. SW18 —6B 102
Kershaw Rd. Dag —3G 57
Kersley M. SW11 —1D 102
Kersley Rd. N16 —2E 50
Kersley St. SW11 —2D 102
Kerstin Clo. Hay —7H 59
Kerswell Clo. N15 —5E 32
Kerwick Clo. N7 —7J 49
Keslake Mans. NW10 —2F 65
(off Station Ter.)
Keslake Rd. NW6 —2F 65
Kessock Clo. N17 —5H 33
Kestlake Rd. Bex —6C 110
Keston. —5A 156
Keston Av. Kes —5A 156
Keston Clo. N18 —3J 17
Keston Clo. Well —7C 92
Keston Ct. Bex —7F 111
Keston Gdns. Kes —4A 156
Keston Ho. SE17 —5E 86
(off Kinglake St.)
Keston Mark. —4C 156
Keston Mark. (Junct.) —3C 156
Keston Pk. Clo. Kes —3D 156
Keston Rd. N17 —3D 32
Keston Rd. SE15 —3G 105
Keston Rd. T Hth —6A 140
Kestrel Av. E6 —5C 72
Kestrel Av. SE24 —5B 104
Kestrel Clo. NW9 —2A 28
Kestrel Clo. NW10 —5K 45
Kestrel Clo. King T —4D 116
Kestrel Ct. E17 —2K 33
Kestrel Ct. SE8 —6B 88
(off Abinger Gro.)
Kestrel Ct. Ruis —2F 41
Kestrel Ct. S Croy —6C 152
Kestrel Ho. EC1 —3C 68 (1C 162)
(off Pickard St.)
Kestrel Pl. SE14 —6A 88
Kestrel Way. Hay —2F 77
Kestrel Way. New Ad —7F 155
Keswick Av. SW15 —5A 118
Keswick Av. SW19 —2J 137
Keswick Av. Shep —3G 131
Keswick Clo. Sutt —4A 150
Keswick Ct. SE6 —1H 125
Keswick Ct. Short —4H 143
Keswick Gdns. Ilf —4C 36
Keswick Gdns. Ruis —6F 23
Keswick Gdns. Wemb —4E 44
Keswick Ho. SE5 —2C 104
Keswick M. W5 —1E 80
Keswick Rd. SW15 —5G 101
Keswick Rd. Bexh —1G 111
Keswick Rd. Orp —7K 145
Keswick Rd. Twic —6G 97
Keswick Rd. W W'ck —2G 155
Kettering St. SW16 —6G 121
Kett Gdns. SW2 —5K 103
Kettlebaston Rd. E10 —1B 52
Kettleby Ho. SW9 —3B 104
(off Barrington Rd.)
Kettlewell Clo. N11 —6K 15
Kevan Ct. E17 —4C 34
Kevan Ho. SE5 —7C 86
Keveloc Rd. N17 —1C 32
Kevin Clo. Houn —2B 96
Kevington Clo. Orp —4K 145
Kevington Dri. Chst & Orp —4J 145
Kew. —7G 81
Kew Bridge. (Junct.) —5F 81
Kew Bri. Bren & Kew —6F 81
Kew Bri. Arches. Rich —6G 81
Kew Bri. Ct. W4 —5G 81
Kew Bri. Distribution Cen. Bren —5F 81
Kew Bri. Rd. Bren —6F 81
Kew Bridge Steam Mus. —5F 81
Kew Cres. Sutt —3G 149
Kew Foot Rd. Rich —4E 98
Kew Gardens Plants & People Exhibition. —7F 81
Kew Gdns. Rd. Rich —7F 81
Kew Green. —7G 81
Kew Grn. Rich —6F 81
Kew Mdw. Path. Rich —1H 99
(in two parts)
Kew Palace. —7E 80
Kew Retail Pk. Rich —1H 99
Kew Rd. Rich —6G 81
Keybridge Ho. SW8 —6J 85 (7F 173)
(off Miles St.)
Key Clo. E1 —4J 69
Keyes Ho. SW1 —5H 85 (6C 172)
(off Dolphin Sq.)
Keyes Rd. NW2 —5F 47
Key Ho. SE11 —6A 86 (7K 173)
Keymer Rd. SW2 —2K 121
Keynes Clo. N2 —4D 30
Keynsham Av. Wfd G —4B 20
Keynsham Gdns. SE9 —5C 108
Keynsham Rd. SE9 —5B 108
Keynsham Rd. Mord —1K 149
Keynsham Wlk. Mord —1K 149
Keyse Rd. SE1 —3F 87
Keysham Av. Houn —1J 95
Keystone Cres. N1 —2J 67 (1F 161)
Keywood Dri. Sun —6J 113
Keyworth Clo. E5 —4A 52
Keyworth Pl. SE1 —7B 168
Keyworth St. SE1 —3B 86 (7B 168)
Kezia St. SE8 —5A 88
Khama Rd. SW17 —4C 120
Khartoum Rd. E13 —3K 71
Khartoum Rd. SW17 —4B 120
Khartoum Rd. Ilf —5F 55
Khyber Rd. SW11 —2C 102
Kibworth St. SW8 —7K 85
Kidbrooke. —2K 107
Kidbrooke Est. SE3 —3A 108
Kidbrooke Gdns. SE3 —2J 107
Kidbrooke Gro. SE3 —1J 107
Kidbrooke La. SE9 —4C 108
Kidbrooke Pk. Clo. SE3 —1K 107
Kidbrooke Pk. Rd. SE3 —1K 107
Kidbrooke Way. SE3 —2K 107
Kidderminster Pl. Croy —1B 152
Kidderminster Rd. Croy —1B 152
Kidderpore Av. NW3 —4J 47
Kidderpore Gdns. NW3 —4J 47
Kidd Pl. SE7 —5C 90
Kidlington Way. NW9 —2K 27
Kierbeck Bus. Complex. E16 —2K 89
Kier Hardie Ct. NW10 —7B 46
Kiffen St. EC2 —4D 68 (3F 163)
Kilberry Clo. Iswth —1H 97
Kilbrennan Ho. E14 —6E 70
Kilburn. —1J 65
Kilburn Bri. NW6 —1J 65
Kilburn Ga. NW6 —2K 65
Kilburn High Rd. NW6 —7H 47
Kilburn La. W10 & W9 —3F 65
Kilburn Pk. Rd. NW6 —3J 65
Kilburn Pl. NW6 —1J 65
Kilburn Priory. NW6 —1K 65
Kilburns Mill Clo. Wall —2F 151
Kilburn Sq. NW6 —1J 65
Kilburn Va. NW6 —1K 65
Kilburn Va. Est. NW6 —1K 65
(off Kilburn Va.)
Kildare Clo. Ruis —1A 42
Kildare Gdns. W2 —6J 65
Kildare Rd. E16 —5J 71
Kildare Ter. W2 —6J 65
Kildare Wlk. E14 —6C 70
Kildoran Rd. SW2 —5J 103
Kildowan Rd. Ilf —1A 56
Kilgour Rd. SE23 —6A 106
Kilkie St. SW6 —2A 102
Killarney Rd. SW18 —6A 102
Killearn Rd. SE6 —1F 125
Killester Gdns. Wor Pk —4D 148
Killick Ho. Sutt —4K 149
Killick St. N1 —2K 67 (1G 161)
Killieser Av. SW2 —2J 121
Killigarth Ct. Sidc —4A 128
Killip Clo. E16 —6H 71
Killowen Av. N'holt —5G 43
Killowen Rd. E9 —6K 51
Killyon Rd. SW8 —2G 103
Killyon Ter. SW8 —2G 103
Kilmaine Rd. SW6 —7G 83
Kilmarnock Gdns. Dag —3C 56
Kilmarsh Rd. W6 —4E 82
Kilmartin Av. SW16 —3A 140
Kilmartin Rd. Ilf —2A 56
Kilmington Rd. SW13 —6C 82
Kilmiston Av. Shep —6E 130
Kilmore Ho. E14 —6D 70
Kilmorey Gdns. Twic —5B 98
Kilmorey Rd. Twic —4B 98
Kilmorie Rd. SE23 —1A 124
Kilmuir Ho. SW1 —4E 84 (4H 171)
(off Bury St.)
Kiln Clo. Hay —6F 77
Kiln Ct. E14 —7B 70
Kilner Ho. SE11 —7J 173
Kilner St. E14 —5C 70
Kiln M. SW17 —5B 120
Kiln Pl. NW5 —5E 48
Kilnside. Clay —7A 146
Kilpatrick Way. Hay —5C 60
Kilravock St. W10 —3G 65
Kilronan. W3 —6K 63
Kilross Rd. Felt —1F 113
Kilsby Wlk. Dag —6B 56
Kilsha Rd. W on T —6A 132
Kimbell Gdns. SW6 —1G 101
Kimbell Pl. SE3 —4A 108
Kimberley Av. E6 —2C 72
Kimberley Av. SE15 —2H 105
Kimberley Av. Ilf —7H 37
Kimberley Av. Romf —6J 39
Kimberley Dri. Sidc —2D 128
Kimberley Gdns. N4 —5B 32
Kimberley Gdns. Enf —3A 8
Kimberley Ga. Brom —7G 125
Kimberley Ho. E14 —3E 88
Kimberley Ind. Est. E17 —1B 34
Kimberley Rd. E4 —1B 20
Kimberley Rd. E11 —2F 53
Kimberley Rd. E16 —4H 71
Kimberley Rd. E17 —1A 34
Kimberley Rd. N17 —2G 33
Kimberley Rd. N18 —6C 18
Kimberley Rd. NW6 —1G 65
Kimberley Rd. SW9 —2J 103
Kimberley Rd. Beck —2K 141
Kimberley Rd. Croy —6B 140
Kimberley Wlk. W on T —7K 131
Kimberley Way. E4 —1B 20
Kimber Rd. SW18 —7J 101
Kimble Cres. Bush —1B 10
Kimble Ho. NW8 —3D 158
Kimble Rd. SW19 —6B 120
Kimbolton Clo. SE12 —6H 107
Kimbolton Ct. SW3 —4C 84 (4C 170)
(off Fulham Rd.)
Kimbolton Row. SW3 —4C 84
(off Fulham Rd.)
Kimmeridge Gdns. SE9 —4C 126
Kimmeridge Rd. SE9 —4C 126
Kimpton Ind. Est. Sutt —2H 149
Kimpton Rd. SE5 —1D 104
Kimpton Rd. Sutt —2H 149
Kinburn St. SE16 —2K 87
Kincaid Rd. SE15 —7H 87
Kincardine Gdns. W9 —4J 65
(off Harrow Rd.)
Kinch Gro. Wemb —7F 27
Kinder Clo. SE28 —7D 74
Kinder Ho. N1 —2D 68
(off Cranston Est.)
Kindersley Ho. E1 —6G 69
(off Pinchin St.)
Kinder St. E1 —6H 69
Kinefold Ho. N7 —6J 49
Kinfauns Rd. SW2 —2A 122
Kinfauns Rd. Ilf —2A 56
King Alfred Av. SE6 —4C 124
(in two parts)
King & Queen Clo. SE9 —4C 126
King & Queen St. SE17 —5C 86
King & Queen Wharf. SE16 —7K 69
King Arthur Clo. SE15 —7J 87
King Charles Ct. SE17 —6B 86
(off Royal Rd.)
King Charles Cres. Surb —7F 135
King Charles Ho. SW6 —7K 83
(off Wandon Rd.)
King Charles Rd. Surb —5F 135
King Charles St. SW1 —2H 85 (6D 166)
King Charles Ter. E1 —7H 69
(off Sovereign Clo.)
King Charles Wlk. SW19 —1G 119
King Ct. E10 —7D 34
Kingcup Clo. Croy —7K 141
King David La. E1 —7J 69
Kingdon Ho. E14 —3E 88
Kingdon Rd. NW6 —6J 47
King Edward Building. EC1 —6B 68 (7C 162)
King Edward Dri. Chess —3E 146
King Edward Mans. E8 —1H 69
(off Mare St.)
King Edward Mans. SW6 —7J 83
(off Fulham Rd.)
King Edward M. SW13 —1C 100
King Edward Rd. E10 —1E 52
King Edward Rd. E17 —3A 34
King Edward Rd. Barn —4D 4
King Edward's Gdns. W3 —1G 81
King Edwards Gro. Tedd —6B 116
King Edward's Pl. W3 —1G 81
King Edward's Rd. E8 —1H 69
King Edward's Rd. N9 —7C 8
King Edwards Rd. Bark —1H 73
King Edward's Rd. Enf —4E 8
King Edward's Rd. Ruis —1F 41
King Edward St. EC1 —6C 68 (7C 162)
King Edward III M. SE16 —2H 87
King Edward Wlk. SE1 —3A 86 (1K 173)
Kingfield Rd. W5 —4D 62
Kingfield St. E14 —4E 88
Kingfisher Av. E11 —6K 35
Kingfisher Clo. SE28 —7C 74
Kingfisher Clo. Har W —7E 10
Kingfisher Clo. N'wd —1D 22
Kingfisher Ct. E14 —2E 88
Kingfisher Ct. SW19 —2F 119
Kingfisher Ct. Enf —1E 6
Kingfisher Ct. Houn —5F 97
Kingfisher Dri. Rich —4B 116
Kingfisher M. SE13 —4C 106
Kingfisher Pl. N22 —2K 31
Kingfisher St. E6 —5C 72
Kingfisher Wlk. NW9 —2A 28
Kingfisher Way. NW10 —6K 45
Kingfisher Way. Beck —5K 141
King Frederick IX Tower. SE16 —3B 88
King Gdns. Croy —5B 152
King George Av. E16 —6A 72
King George Av. Ilf —5H 37
King George Clo. Romf —3J 39
King George Clo. Sun —5G 113
King George's Dri. S'hall —5D 60
King George VI Av. Mitc —4D 138
King George's Trad. Est. Chess —4G 147
King George St. SE10 —7E 88
Kingham Clo. SW18 —7A 102
Kingham Clo. W11 —2G 83
(off Holland Pk. Av.)
King Harolds Way. Bexh & Belv —7D 92
King Henry's Dri. New Ad —7D 154
King Henry's Reach. W6 —6E 82
King Henry's Rd. NW3 —7C 48
King Henry's Rd. King T —3H 135
King Henry St. N16 —5E 50
King Henry's Wlk. N1 —6E 50
King Henry Ter. E1 —7H 69
(off Sovereign Clo.)
Kinghorn St. EC1 —5C 68 (6C 162)
King Ho. W12 —6D 64
King James Ct. SE1 —7B 168
King James St. SE1 —2B 86 (7B 168)
King John Ct. EC2 —4E 68 (3H 163)
King John St. E1 —5K 69
King John's Wlk. SE9 —7C 108
(Middle Pk. Av.)
King John's Wlk. SE9 —1B 126
(Mottingham La.)
Kinglake Est. SE17 —5E 86
Kinglake St. SE17 —5E 86
(in two parts)
Kingly Ct. W1 —2B 166
Kingly St. W1 —6G 67 (1A 166)
Kingsand Rd. SE12 —2J 125
Kings Arbour. S'hall —5C 78
King's Arms All. Bren —6D 80
Kings Arms Ct. E1 —6K 163
Kings Arms Yd. EC2 —6D 68 (7E 162)
Kingsash Dri. Hay —4C 60
King's Av. N10 —3E 30
Kings Av. N21 —1G 17
Kings Av. SW12 & SW4 —1H 121
Kings Av. W5 —6D 62
Kings Av. Brom —6H 125
King's Av. Buck H —2G 21
King's Av. Cars —7C 150
King's Av. Gnfd —5F 61
Kings Av. Houn —1F 97
Kings Av. N Mald —4A 136
Kings Av. Romf —6F 39
King's Av. Sun —5H 113
King's Av. Wfd G —6E 20
King's Bench St. SE1 —2B 86 (6B 168)
King's Bench Wlk. EC4 —6A 68 (1K 167)
Kingsbridge Av. W5 —2F 81
Kingsbridge Ct. E14 —3C 88
(off Dockers Tanner Rd.)
Kingsbridge Cres. S'hall —5D 60
Kingsbridge Rd. W10 —6E 64
Kingsbridge Rd. Bark —2H 73
Kingsbridge Rd. Mord —6F 137
Kingsbridge Rd. S'hall —5D 78
Kingsbridge Rd. W on T —7K 131
Kingsbridge Way. Hay —3G 59
Kingsbury. —7K 27
Kingsbury Circ. NW9 —5G 27
Kingsbury Green. —5J 27
Kingsbury Rd. N1 —6E 50
Kingsbury Rd. NW9 —5G 27
Kingsbury Ter. N1 —6E 50
Kingsbury Trad. Est. NW9 —6K 27
Kings Chase. E Mol —3G 133
Kings Chase Vw. Ridg —2F 7
Kingsclere Clo. SW15 —7C 100
Kingsclere Ct. N12 —5H 15
Kingsclere Pl. Enf —2H 7
Kingscliffe Gdns. SW19 —1H 119
Kings Clo. E10 —7D 34
King's Clo. NW4 —4F 29
King's Clo. Dart —4K 111
Kings Clo. Stai —7A 112
Kings Clo. Th Dit —6A 134
Kings Clo. W on T —7K 131
Kings College Ct. NW3 —7C 48
King's College Rd. NW3 —7C 48
Kings College Rd. Ruis —6H 23
Kingscote Farm Agricultural Mus. —2A 22
Kingscote Rd. W4 —3K 81
Kingscote Rd. Croy —7H 141
Kingscote Rd. N Mald —3K 135
Kingscote St. EC4 —7B 68 (2A 168)
King's Ct. E13 —1K 71
Kings Ct. NW8 —1D 66
(off Prince Albert Rd.)
King's Ct. SE1 —2B 86 (6B 168)
Kings Ct. W6 —4C 82
Kings Ct. Buck H —2G 21
Kings Ct. N. SW3 —6C 170
Kingscourt Rd. SW16 —3H 121
Kings Ct. S. SW3 —6C 170
King's Cres. N4 —3C 50
Kings Cres. Est. N4 —2C 50
Kingscroft. SW4 —6J 103
Kingscroft Rd. NW2 —6H 47
King's Cross. —2J 67
Kings Cross. (Junct.) —3J 67
King's Cross Bri. N1 —3J 67 (1F 161)
(off Gray's Inn Rd.)
King's Cross Rd. WC1 —3K 67 (1G 161)
Kingsdale Gdns. W11 —1F 83
Kingsdale Rd. SE18 —7K 91
Kingsdale Rd. SE20 —7K 123
Kingsdown Av. W3 —7A 64
Kingsdown Av. W13 —2B 80
Kingsdown Av. S Croy —7C 152
Kingsdown Clo. SE16 —5H 87
(off Masters Dri.)
Kingsdown Clo. W10 —6F 65
Kingsdowne Rd. Surb —7E 134
Kingsdown Ho. E8 —5G 51
Kingsdown Rd. E11 —3G 53
Kingsdown Rd. N19 —2J 49
Kingsdown Rd. Sutt —5G 149
Kingsdown Way. Brom —7J 143
King's Dri. Edgw —4A 12
Kings Dri. Surb —7G 135
Kings Dri. Tedd —5H 115
Kings Dri. Th Dit —7B 134
Kings Dri. Wemb —2H 45
Kingsend. Ruis —1F 41
Kingsend Ct. Ruis —1G 41
Kings Farm. E17 —1D 34
Kings Farm Av. Rich —4G 99
Kingsfield Av. Harr —4F 25
Kingsfield Ho. SE9 —3B 126
Kingsfield Rd. Harr —7H 25
Kingsfield Ter. Harr —1H 43
Kingsford Av. Wall —7J 151
Kingsford St. NW5 —5D 48
Kingsford Way. E6 —5D 72
King's Gdns. NW6 —7J 47
Kings Gdns. Ilf —1H 55
Kings Gth. M. SE23 —2J 123
Kingsgate. Wemb —3J 45
Kingsgate Av. N3 —3J 29
Kingsgate Bus. Cen. King T —1E 134
Kingsgate Clo. Bexh —1E 110
Kingsgate Est. N1 —6E 50
Kingsgate Ho. SW9 —1A 104
Kingsgate Mans. WC1 —5K 67
(off Red Lion Sq.)
Kingsgate Pde. SW1 —2B 172
Kingsgate Pl. NW6 —7J 47
Kingsgate Rd. NW6 —7J 47
Kingsgate Rd. King T —1E 134
Kings Grange. Ruis —1H 41
Kingsground. SE9 —7B 108
King's Gro. SE15 —7H 87
(in two parts)
Kingshall M. SE13 —3E 106
Kings Hall Rd. Beck —7A 124
Kings Head Hill. E4 —7J 9
Kings Head Pas. SW4 —4H 103
(off Clapham Pk. Rd.)
Kings Head Theatre. —1B 68
King's Head Yd. SE1 —1D 86 (5E 168)
King's Highway. SE18 —6J 91
Kingshill. SE17 —4C 86
Kingshill Av. Harr —4B 26
Kingshill Av. Hay & N'holt —3G 59
Kingshill Av. Wor Pk —7C 136
Kingshill Ct. Barn —4B 4
Kingshill Dri. Harr —2B 26
Kingshold Rd. E9 —7J 51
Kingsholm Gdns. SE9 —4B 108
Kings Ho. SW8 —7J 85
(off S. Lambeth Rd.)
Kingshurst Rd. SE12 —7J 107
Kings Keep. SW15 —5F 101
Kings Keep. Brom —3G 143
Kings Keep. King T —4E 134
Kingsland. —6E 50
Kingsland. NW8 —1C 66
Kingsland Grn. E8 —6E 50
Kingsland High St. E8 —6F 51
Kingsland Pas. E8 —6E 50
Kingsland Rd. E2 & E8 —3E 68 (2H 163)
Kingsland Rd. E13 —3A 72
Kingsland Shop. Cen. E8 —6F 51
Kings La. Sutt —6B 150
Kingslawn Clo. SW15 —5D 100
Kingsleigh Pl. Mitc —3D 138
Kingsleigh Wlk. Brom —4H 143
Kingsley Av. W13 —5A 62
Kingsley Av. Houn —2G 97
Kingsley Av. S'hall —7E 60
Kingsley Av. Sutt —4B 150
Kingsley Clo. N2 —5A 30
Kingsley Clo. Dag —4H 57
Kingsley Ct. NW10 —6D 46
Kingsley Ct. Bexh —5G 111
Kingsley Ct. Edgw —3C 12
Kingsley Ct. Sutt —7K 149
Kingsley Ct. Wor Pk —2B 148
(off Avenue, The)
Kingsley Dri. Wor Pk —2B 148
Kingsley Flats. SE1 —4E 86
(off Old Kent Rd.)
Kingsley Gdns. E4 —5H 19
Kingsley Ho. SW3 —6B 84
(off Beaufort St.)
Kingsley Mans. W14 —6G 83
(off Greyhound Rd.)
Kingsley M. E1 —7H 69
Kingsley M. W8 —3K 83
Kingsley M. Chst —6F 127
Kingsley Pl. N6 —7E 30
Kingsley Rd. E7 —7J 53
Kingsley Rd. E17 —2E 34
Kingsley Rd. N13 —4F 17
Kingsley Rd. NW6 —1H 65
Kingsley Rd. SW19 —5K 119
Kingsley Rd. Croy —1A 152
Kingsley Rd. Harr —4G 43
Kingsley Rd. Houn —1F 97
Kingsley Rd. Ilf —1G 37
Kingsley Rd. Pinn —4D 24
Kingsley St. SW11 —3D 102
Kingsley Way. NW11 —6A 30
Kingsley Wood Dri. SE9 —3D 126
Kingslyn Cres. SE19 —1E 140
Kings Mall. W6 —4E 82
Kingsman Pde. SE18 —3D 90
Kingsman St. SE18 —3D 90
Kingsmead. Barn —4D 4
Kings Mead. Rich —6F 99
Kingsmead Av. N9 —1C 18
Kingsmead Av. NW9 —7K 27
Kingsmead Av. Mitc —3G 139
Kingsmead Av. Sun —2A 132
Kingsmead Av. Surb —2G 147
Kingsmead Av. Wor Pk —2D 148
Kingsmead Clo. Eps —7K 147
Kingsmead Clo. Sidc —2A 128
Kingsmead Clo. Tedd —6B 116
Kingsmead Cotts. Brom —1C 156
Kingsmead Ct. N6 —7H 31
Kingsmead Dri. N'holt —7D 42
Kingsmead Ho. E9 —4A 52
Kingsmeadow. King T —3H 135
Kingsmead Rd. SW2 —2A 122
King's Mead Way. E9 —4A 52
Kingsmere Clo. SW15 —3F 101
Kingsmere Pk. NW9 —1H 45
Kingsmere Pl. N16 —1D 50
Kingsmere Rd. SW19 —2F 119
King's M. SW4 —5J 103
King's M. WC1 —4K 67 (4H 161)
Kingsmill. NW8 —2B 66
(off Kingsmill Ter.)
Kingsmill Gdns. Dag —5F 57
Kingsmill Ho. SW3 —5C 84 (5D 170)
(off Marlborough St.)
Kingsmill Rd. Dag —5F 57
Kingsmill Ter. NW8 —2B 66
Kingsnorth Ho. W10 —6F 65
Kingsnympton Pk. King T —7H 117
King's Orchard. SE9 —6C 108
King's Paddock. Hamp —1G 133
Kings Pde. N17 —3F 33
King's Pde. NW10 —1E 64
Kings Pde. W12 —3C 82
King's Pde. Cars —3D 150
(off Wrythe La.)
King's Pde. Edgw —5B 12
(off Edgwarebury La.)
Kingspark Ct. E18 —3J 35
Kings Pas. E11 —7G 35
Kings Pas. King T —2D 134
King's Pas. King T —1D 134
King's Pl. SE1 —2C 86 (7C 168)
King's Pl. W4 —5J 81
Kings Pl. Buck H —2F 21
King Sq. EC1 —3C 68 (2C 162)
King's Quay. SW10 —1A 102
(off Chelsea Harbour)
Kings Reach Tower. SE1 —4K 167
Kings Ride Ga. Rich —4G 99
Kingsridge. SW19 —2G 119
Kings Rd. E4 —1A 20

King's Rd.—Lamberhurst Rd.

King's Rd. E6 —1A 72
Kings Rd. E11 —7G 35
King's Rd. N17 —1F 33
Kings Rd. N18 —5B 18
Kings Rd. N22 —1K 31
King's Rd. NW10 —7D 46
Kings Rd. SE25 —3G 141
King's Rd. SW6 & SW10 —7K 83 (7A 170)
Kings Rd. SW14 —3K 99
Kings Rd. SW19 —6J 119
Kings Rd. W5 —5D 62
Kings Rd. Bark —7G 55
Kings Rd. Barn —3A 4
Kings Rd. Felt —1A 114
Kings Rd. Harr —2D 42
King's Rd. King T —1E 134
Kings Rd. Mitc —3E 138
Kings Rd. Rich —6F 99
King's Rd. Surb —1C 146
King's Rd. Tedd —5H 115
Kings Rd. Twic —6B 98
King's Rd. W Dray —2B 76
Kings Rd. Bungalows. S Harr —4D 42
King's Scholars' Pas. SW1 —2A 172
King Stairs Clo. SE16 —2H 87
King's Ter. NW1 —1G 67
King's Ter. Iswth —4A 98
Kingsthorpe Rd. SE26 —4K 123
Kingston Av. Felt —6G 95
Kingston Av. Sutt —3G 149
Kingston Av. W Dray —7B 58
(in two parts)
Kingston Bri. King T —2D 134
Kingston Bus. Cen. Chess —3E 146
Kingston By-Pass. SW15 & SW20 —4A 118
Kingston By-Pass. Surb & N Mald —3D 146
Kingston Clo. N'holt —1D 60
Kingston Clo. Romf —3E 38
(in two parts)
Kingston Clo. Tedd —6B 116
Kingston Cres. Beck —1B 142
Kingston Gdns. Croy —3J 151
Kingston Hall Rd. King T —3D 134
Kingston Hill. King T —1G 135
Kingston Hill Av. Romf —3E 38
Kingston Hill Pl. King T —4J 117
Kingston Ho. NW6 —7G 47
Kingston Ho. E. SW7 —2C 84 (7C 164)
(off Prince's Ga.)
Kingston Ho. Est. Surb —6B 134
Kingston Ho. N. SW7 —2C 84 (7C 164)
(off Prince's Ga.)
Kingston Ho. S. SW7 —2C 84 (7C 164)
(off Ennismore Gdns.)
Kingstonian F.C. —3G 135
Kingston La. Tedd —5A 116
Kingston La. Uxb —3A 58
Kingston La. W Dray —2B 76
Kingston Mus. —2E 134
Kingston Pl. Harr —7E 10
Kingston Rd. N9 —2B 18
Kingston Rd. SW15 & SW19 —2C 118
Kingston Rd. SW20 & SW19 —2F 137
Kingston Rd. Barn —5G 5
Kingston Rd. Eps —7B 148
Kingston Rd. Ilf —4F 55
Kingston Rd. King T & N Mald —3H 135
Kingston Rd. S'hall —2D 78
Kingston Rd. Stai & Ashf —6A 112
(in two parts)
Kingston Rd. Surb & Eps —2H 147
Kingston Rd. Tedd —5B 116
Kingston Sq. SE19 —5D 122
Kingston Upon Thames. —2E 134
Kingston upon Thames Crematorium. King T —3G 135
Kingston Vale. —4A 118
Kingston Va. SW15 —4K 117
Kingstown St. NW1 —1E 66
(in two parts)
King St. E13 —4J 71
King St. EC2 —6C 68 (1D 168)
King St. N2 —3B 30
King St. N17 —1F 33
King St. SW1 —1G 85 (5B 166)
King St. W3 —1J 81
King St. W6 —4C 82
King St. WC2 —7J 67 (2E 166)
King St. Rich —5D 98
King St. S'hall —3C 78
King St. Twic —1A 116
King St. Pde. Twic —1A 116
(off King St.)
Kings Wlk. Shop. Cen. SW3 —5D 84 (5E 170)
Kingswater Pl. SW11 —7C 84
Kingsway. N12 —6F 15
Kingsway. SW14 —3H 99
Kingsway. WC2 —6K 67 (7G 161)
King's Way. Croy —5K 151
Kingsway. Enf —5C 8
Kings Way. Harr —4J 25
Kingsway. Hay —5E 58
Kingsway. N Mald —4E 136
Kingsway. Orp —5H 145
Kingsway. Stai —1A 112
Kingsway. Wemb —4E 44
Kingsway. W W'ck —3G 155
Kings Way. Wfd G —5F 21
Kingsway Bus. Pk. Hamp —1D 132
Kingsway Cres. Harr —4G 25
Kingsway Est. N18 —6E 18
Kingsway Mans. WC1 —5K 67 (6G 161)
(off Red Lion Sq.)
Kingsway Pl. EC1 —4A 68 (3K 161)
(off Corporation Row)
Kingsway Rd. Sutt —7G 149
Kingswear Rd. NW5 —3F 49
Kingswear Rd. Ruis —2J 41
Kingswood Av. NW6 —1G 65
Kingswood Av. Belv —4F 93
Kingswood Av. Brom —3G 143
Kingswood Av. Hamp —6F 115
Kingswood Av. Houn —1D 96
Kingswood Av. T Hth —5A 140
Kingswood Clo. N20 —7F 5
Kingswood Clo. SW8 —7J 85
Kingswood Clo. Enf —5K 7
Kingswood Clo. N Mald —6B 136
Kingswood Clo. Orp —7J 145
Kingswood Clo. Surb —7E 134
Kingswood Ct. E4 —5H 19
Kingswood Ct. NW6 —7J 47
(off W. End La.)
Kingswood Dri. SE19 —4E 122
Kingswood Dri. Cars —1D 150
Kingswood Dri. Sutt —7K 149
Kingswood Est. SE21 —4E 122
Kingswood Pk. N3 —1H 29
Kingswood Pl. SE13 —4G 107
Kingswood Rd. E11 —7G 35
Kingswood Rd. SE20 —6J 123
Kingswood Rd. SW2 —6J 103
Kingswood Rd. SW19 —7H 119
Kingswood Rd. W4 —3J 81
Kingswood Rd. Brom & Short —4F 143
Kingswood Rd. Ilf —1A 56
Kingswood Rd. Wemb —3G 45
Kingswood Ter. W4 —3J 81
Kingswood Way. Wall —5J 151
Kingsworth Clo. Beck —5A 142
Kingsworthy Clo. King T —3F 135
Kings Yd. E9 —6C 52
Kings Yd. SW15 —3E 100
(off Lwr. Richmond Rd.)
Kingthorpe Rd. NW10 —7K 45
Kingthorpe Ter. NW10 —6K 45
Kington Ho. NW6 —1K 65
(off Mortimer Cres.)
Kingward Ho. E1 —5G 69
(off Hanbury St.)
King William IV Gdns. SE20 —6J 123
King William La. SE10 —5G 89
King William St. EC4 —6D 68 (1E 168)
King William Wlk. SE10 —6E 88
(in two parts)
Kingwood Rd. SW6 —1G 101
Kinlet Rd. SE18 —1G 109
Kinloch Dri. NW9 —7K 27
Kinloch St. N7 —3K 49
Kinloss Ct. N3 —4H 29
Kinloss Gdns. N3 —3H 29
Kinloss Rd. Cars —7A 138
Kinnaird Av. W4 —7J 81
Kinnaird Av. Brom —6H 125
Kinnaird Clo. Brom —6H 125
Kinnaird Way. Wfd G —6J 21
Kinnear Rd. W12 —2B 82
Kinnerton Pl. N. SW1 —7F 165
Kinnerton Pl. S. SW1 —7F 165
Kinnerton St. SW1 —2E 84 (7G 165)
Kinnerton Yd. SW1 —7G 165
Kinnoul Rd. W6 —6G 83
Kinross Av. Wor Pk —2C 148
Kinross Clo. Edgw —2C 12
Kinross Clo. Harr —5F 27
Kinross Clo. Sun —5H 113
Kinross Ct. SE6 —1H 125
Kinross Dri. Sun —5H 113
Kinross Ter. E17 —2B 34
Kinsale Rd. SE15 —3G 105
Kinsella Gdns. SW19 —5D 118
Kinsham Ho. E2 —4G 69
(off Ramsey St.)
Kintore Way. SE1 —4F 87
Kintyre Clo. SW16 —2K 139
Kintyre Ct. SW2 —7J 103
Kintyre Ho. E14 —1E 88
Kinveachy Gdns. SE7 —5C 90
Kinver Rd. SE26 —4J 123
Kipling Ct. W7 —7K 61
Kipling Dri. SW19 —6B 120
Kipling Est. SE1 —2D 86 (7F 169)
Kipling Ho. SE5 —7D 86
(off Elmington Est.)
Kipling Pl. Stan —6E 10
Kipling Rd. Bexh —1E 110
Kipling St. SE1 —2D 86 (7F 169)
Kipling Ter. N9 —3J 17
Kipling Tower. W3 —3J 81
(off Palmerston Rd.)
Kippington Dri. SE9 —1B 126
Kirby Clo. Eps —5B 148
Kirby Est. SE16 —3H 87
Kirby Est. W Dray —7A 58
Kirby Gro. SE1 —2E 86 (6G 169)
Kirby St. EC1 —5A 68 (5K 161)
Kirby Way. W on T —6A 132
Kirchen Rd. W13 —7B 62
Kirkby Clo. N11 —6K 15
Kirkdale. SE26 —2H 123
Kirkdale Corner. SE26 —4J 123
Kirkdale Rd. E11 —1G 53
Kirkeby Ho. EC1 —5A 68 (5J 161)
(off Leather La.)
Kirkfield Clo. W13 —1B 80
Kirkham Rd. E6 —6C 72
Kirkham St. SE18 —6J 91
Kirkland Av. Ilf —2E 36
Kirkland Clo. Sidc —6J 109
Kirkland Ho. E14 —5D 88
(off St Davids Sq.)
Kirkland Ho. E14 —5D 88
(off Westferry Rd.)
Kirkland Wlk. E8 —6F 51
Kirk La. SE18 —6G 91
Kirkleas Rd. Surb —1E 146
Kirklees Rd. Dag —5C 56
Kirklees Rd. T Hth —5A 140
Kirkley Rd. SW19 —1J 137
Kirkman Pl. W1 —6C 160
Kirkmichael Rd. E14 —6E 70
Kirk Ri. Sutt —3K 149
Kirk Rd. E17 —6B 34
Kirkside Rd. SE3 —6J 89
Kirk's Pl. E14 —5B 70
Kirkstall Av. N17 —4D 32
Kirkstall Gdns. SW2 —1J 121
Kirkstall Rd. SW2 —1H 121
Kirksted Rd. Mord —1K 149
Kirkstone. NW1 —3G 67 (1A 160)
(off Harrington St.)
Kirkstone Way. Brom —7G 125
Kirk St. WC1 —4G 161
Kirkton Rd. N15 —4E 32
Kirkwall Pl. E2 —3J 69
Kirkwood La. NW1 —7E 48
Kirkwood Rd. SE15 —2H 105
Kirn Rd. W13 —7B 62
Kirrane Clo. N Mald —5B 136
Kirtley Ho. SW8 —1G 103
Kirtley Rd. SE26 —4A 124
Kirtling St. SW8 —7G 85
Kirton Clo. W4 —4K 81
Kirton Gdns. E2 —3F 69 (2K 163)
(in two parts)
Kirton Lodge. SW18 —6K 101
Kirton Rd. E13 —2A 72
Kirton Wlk. Edgw —7D 12
Kirwyn Way. SE5 —7B 86
Kitcat Ter. E3 —3C 70
Kitchener Rd. E7 —6K 53
Kitchener Rd. E17 —1D 34
Kitchener Rd. N2 —3C 30
Kitchener Rd. N17 —3E 32
Kitchener Rd. Dag —6H 57
Kitchener Rd. T Hth —3D 140
Kite Pl. E2 —3G 69
(off Lampern St.)
Kite Yd. SW11 —1D 102
(off Cambridge Rd.)
Kitley Gdns. SE19 —1F 141
Kitson Rd. SE5 —7D 86
Kitson Rd. SW13 —1C 100
Kittiwake Pl. Sutt —5H 149
Kittiwake Rd. N'holt —3B 60
Kittiwake Way. Hay —5B 60
Kitto Rd. SE14 —2K 105
Kitts End Rd. Barn —1C 4
Kiver Rd. N19 —2H 49
Klea Av. SW4 —6G 103
Klein's Wharf. E14 —3C 88
Knapdale Clo. SE23 —2H 123
Knapmill Rd. SE6 —2C 124
Knapmill Way. SE6 —2D 124
Knapp Clo. NW10 —6A 46
Knapp Rd. E3 —4C 70
Knapp Rd. Ashf —4B 112
Knapton M. SW17 —6E 120
Knaresborough Dri. SW18 —1K 119
Knaresborough Pl. SW5 —4K 83
Knatchbull Rd. NW10 —1K 63
Knatchbull Rd. SE5 —2B 104
Knebworth Av. E17 —1C 34
Knebworth Ho. SW8 —2H 103
Knebworth Rd. N16 —4E 50
Knee Hill. SE2 —4C 92
Kneehill Cres. SE2 —4C 92
Kneller Gdns. Iswth —6H 97
Kneller Ho. N'holt —2B 60
(off Academy Gdns.)
Kneller Rd. SE4 —4A 106
Kneller Rd. N Mald —7A 136
Kneller Rd. Twic —6G 97
Knight Clo. Dag —2C 56
Knight Ct. E4 —1K 19
(off Ridgeway, The)
Knight Ct. N15 —5E 32
Knighten St. E1 —1H 87
Knighthead Point. E14 —2C 88
Knight Ho. SE17 —4E 86
(off Huntsman St.)
Knightland Rd. E5 —2H 51
Knightleas Ct. NW2 —6E 46
Knighton Clo. Romf —6K 39
Knighton Clo. S Croy —7B 152
Knighton Clo. Wfd G —4E 20
Knighton Dri. Wfd G —4E 20
Knighton Grn. Buck H —2E 20
Knighton La. Buck H —2E 20
Knighton Pk. Rd. SE26 —5K 123
Knighton Rd. E7 —3J 53
Knighton Rd. Romf —6J 39
Knightrider Ct. EC4 —2B 168
Knightrider St. EC4 —6B 68 (2B 168)
Knights Arc. SW1 —7E 164
Knights Av. W5 —2E 80
Knightsbridge. —2C 84 (7E 164)
Knightsbridge. SW7 & SW1 —2D 84 (7D 164)
Knightsbridge Ct. SW1 —7F 165
Knightsbridge Gdns. Romf —5K 39
Knightsbridge Grn. SW1
(in two parts) —2D 84 (7E 164)
Knights Clo. E9 —5J 51
Knights Ct. Brom —3H 125
Knights Ct. King T —3E 134
Knights Hill. SE27 —5B 122
Knight's Hill Sq. SE27 —4B 122
Knights Ho. SW8 —7J 85
(off S. Lambeth Rd.)
Knights La. N9 —3B 18
Knight's Pk. King T —3E 134
Knight's Rd. E16 —2J 89
Knights Rd. Stan —4H 11
Knights Wlk. SE11 —4B 86 (4K 173)
(in two parts)
Knightswood Clo. Edgw —2D 12
Knightswood Ct. N6 —7H 31
Knightswood Ho. N12 —6F 15
Knightwood Cres. N Mald —6A 136
Knivet Rd. SW6 —6J 83
Knobs Hill Rd. E15 —1D 70
Knockholt Rd. SE9 —5B 108
Knole Clo. Croy —6J 141
Knole Ct. N'holt —3A 60
(off Broomcroft Av.)
Knole Ga. Sidc —3J 127
Knole, The. SE9 —4E 126
Knoll Cres. N'wd —1G 23
(in two parts)
Knoll Dri. N14 —7K 5
Knoll Ho. NW8 —2A 66
(off Carlton Hill)
Knoll Ho. Pinn —2B 24
Knollmead. Surb —1J 147
Knoll Ri. Orp —7K 145
Knoll Rd. SW18 —5A 102
Knoll Rd. Bex —7G 111
Knoll Rd. Sidc —5B 128
Knolls Clo. Wor Pk —3D 148
Knoll, The. W13 —5C 62
Knoll, The. Beck —1D 142
Knoll, The. Brom —2J 155
Knollys Clo. SW16 —3A 122
Knolly's Ho. WC1 —4J 67 (3E 160)
(off Tavistock Pl.)
Knollys Rd. SW16 —3K 121
Knottisford St. E2 —3J 69
Knotts Grn. M. E10 —6D 34
Knotts Grn. Rd. E10 —6D 34
Knowle Av. Bexh —7E 92
Knowle Clo. SW9 —3A 104
Knowle Rd. Brom —2D 156
Knowle Rd. Twic —1J 115
Knowles Clo. W Dray —1A 76
Knowles Ct. Harr —6K 25
(off Gayton Rd.)
Knowles Hill Cres. SE13 —5F 107
Knowles Wlk. SW4 —3G 103
Knowlton Grn. Brom —5H 143
Knowlton Ho. SW9 —1A 104
(off Cowley Rd.)
Knowsley Av. S'hall —1F 79
Knowsley Rd. SW11 —2D 102
Knox Ct. SW4 —2J 103
Knox Rd. E7 —6H 53
Knox St. NW1 —5D 66 (5E 158)
Knoyle St. SE14 —6A 88
Koblenz Ho. N8 —3J 31
(off Newland Rd.)
Kohat Rd. SW19 —5K 119
Komeheather Ho. Ilf —5D 36
Korda Clo. Shep —3B 130
Kossuth St. SE10 —5G 89
Kotree Way. SE1 —4G 87
Kramer M. SW5 —5J 83
Kreedman Wlk. E8 —5G 51
Kreisel Wlk. Rich —6F 81
Kristina Ct. Sutt —6J 149
(off Overton Rd.)
Krupnik Pl. EC2 —2H 163
Kuala Gdns. SW16 —1K 139
Kubrick Bus. Est. E7 —4K 53
(off Station App.)
Kuhn Way. E7 —5J 53
Kydbrook Clo. Orp —7G 145
Kylemore Clo. E6 —2B 72
Kylemore Rd. NW6 —7J 47
Kylestrome Ho. SW1 —4E 84 (4H 171)
(off Cundy St.)
Kymberley Rd. Harr —6J 25
Kymes Ct. S Harr —2H 43
Kynance Gdns. Stan —1C 26
Kynance M. SW7 —3K 83
Kynance Pl. W8 —3A 84
Kynaston Av. N16 —3F 51
Kynaston Av. T Hth —5C 140
Kynaston Clo. Harr —7C 10
Kynaston Cres. T Hth —5C 140
Kynaston Rd. N16 —3E 50
Kynaston Rd. Brom —5J 125
Kynaston Rd. Enf —1J 7
Kynaston Rd. T Hth —5C 140
Kynaston Wood. Harr —7C 10
Kynnersley Clo. Cars —3D 150
Kynoch Rd. N18 —4D 18
Kyrle Rd. SW11 —6E 102
Kyverdale Rd. N16 —1F 51

Laburnum Av. N9 —2A 18
Laburnum Av. N17 —7J 17
Laburnum Av. Sutt —3C 150
Laburnum Av. W Dray —7B 58
Laburnum Clo. E4 —6G 19
Laburnum Clo. N11 —6K 15
Laburnum Clo. SE15 —7J 87
Laburnum Ct. E2 —1F 69
(in two parts)
Laburnum Ct. SE16 —2J 87
(off Albion St.)
Laburnum Ct. SE19 —1F 141
Laburnum Ct. Harr —6F 25
Laburnum Ct. Stan —4H 11
Laburnum Cres. Sun —1K 131
Laburnum Gdns. N21 —2H 17
Laburnum Gdns. Croy —7K 141
Laburnum Gro. N21 —2H 17
Laburnum Gro. NW9 —7J 27
Laburnum Gro. Houn —4D 96
Laburnum Gro. N Mald —2K 135
Laburnum Gro. Ruis —6F 23
Laburnum Gro. S'hall —4D 60
Laburnum Ho. Brom —1F 143
Laburnum Lodge. N3 —2H 29
Laburnum Pl. SE9 —5E 108
Laburnum Rd. SW19 —7A 120
Laburnum Rd. Hay —4H 77
Laburnum Rd. Mitc —2E 138
Laburnums, The. E6 —4C 72
Laburnum St. E2 —1F 69
Laburnum Way. Brom —7E 144
Laburnum Way. Stai —1B 112
Lacebark Clo. Sidc —7K 109
Lacey Clo. N9 —2B 18
Lacey Dri. Edgw —4A 12
Lacey Dri. Hamp —1D 132
Lacey Wlk. E3 —2C 70
Lackington St. EC2 —5D 68 (5F 163)
Lackland Ho. SE1 —5F 87
(off Rowcross St.)
Lacland Ho. SW10 —7B 84
(off Worlds End Est.)
Lacock Clo. SW19 —6A 120
Lacock Ct. W13 —1A 80
(off Singapore Rd.)
Lacon Ho. WC1 —5K 67
(off Theobalds Rd.)
Lacon Rd. SE22 —4G 105
Lacrosse Way. SW16 —1H 139
Lacy Dri. Dag —3C 56
Lacy Rd. SW15 —4F 101
Ladas Rd. SE27 —4C 122
Ladbroke Cres. W11 —6G 65
Ladbroke Gdns. W11 —7H 65
Ladbroke Gro. W10 & W11 —4F 65
Ladbroke Gro. Ho. W11 —7H 65
Ladbroke M. W11 —1G 83
Ladbroke Rd. W11 —1H 83
Ladbroke Rd. Enf —6A 8
Ladbroke Sq. W11 —7H 65
Ladbroke Ter. W11 —7H 65
Ladbroke Wlk. W11 —1H 83
Ladbrook Clo. Pinn —5D 24
Ladbrooke Cres. Sidc —3D 128
Ladbrook Rd. SE25 —4D 140
Ladderstile Ride. King T —5H 117
Ladderswood Way. N11 —5B 16
Ladlands. SE22 —7G 105
Lady Booth Rd. King T —2E 134
Ladycroft Rd. SE13 —3D 106
Ladycroft Wlk. Stan —1D 26
Lady Dock Wlk. SE16 —2A 88
Lady Elizabeth Ho. SW14 —3J 99
Lady Forsdyke Way. Eps —7G 147
Ladygate La. Ruis —6D 22
Lady Harewood Way. Eps —1G 147
Lady Hay. Wor Pk —2B 148
Lady Margaret Rd. NW5 & N19 —5G 49
Lady Margaret Rd. S'hall —7D 60
Lady Micos Almshouses. E1 —6J 69
(off Aylward St.)
Lady Sarah Ho. N11 —6J 15
(off Asher Loftus Way)
Lady Shaw Ct. N13 —2E 16
Ladyship Ter. SE22 —7G 105
Ladysmith Av. E6 —2C 72
Ladysmith Av. Ilf —7J 37
Ladysmith Clo. NW7 —7H 13
Ladysmith Rd. E16 —3H 71
Ladysmith Rd. N17 —2G 33
Ladysmith Rd. N18 —5C 18
Ladysmith Rd. SE9 —6E 108
Ladysmith Rd. Enf —3K 7
(in two parts)
Ladysmith Rd. Harr —2J 25
Lady Somerset Rd. NW5 —4F 49
Ladywell. —5D 106
Ladywell Clo. SE4 —5C 106
Ladywell Heights. SE4 —6B 106
Ladywell Rd. SE13 —5C 106
Ladywell St. E15 —1H 71
Ladywood Av. Orp —5J 145
Ladywood Rd. Surb —2G 147
Lafone Av. Felt —2A 114
Lafone St. SE1 —2F 87 (6J 169)
Lagado M. SE16 —1K 87
Laidlaw Dri. N21 —5E 6
Laing Dean. N'holt —1A 60
Laing Ho. SE5 —7C 86
Laings Av. Mitc —2D 138
Lainlock Pl. Houn —1F 97
Lainson St. SW18 —7J 101
Lairdale Clo. SE21 —1C 122
Laird Ho. SE5 —7C 86
(off Redcar St.)
Lairs Clo. N7 —5J 49
Laitwood Rd. SW12 —1F 121
Lakanal. SE5 —1E 104
(off Dalwood St.)
Lake Av. Brom —6J 125
Lake Bus. Cen. N17 —7B 18
Lake Clo. SW19 —5H 119
Lakedale Rd. SE18 —6J 91
Lake Dri. Bush —2C 10
Lakefield Clo. SE20 —7H 123
Lakefield Rd. N22 —2B 32
Lake Footpath. SE2 —2D 92
Lake Gdns. Dag —5G 57
Lake Gdns. Rich —2B 116
Lake Gdns. Wall —3F 151
Lakehall Gdns. T Hth —5B 140
Lakehall Rd. T Hth —5B 140
Lake Ho. SE1 —2C 86 (7C 168)
(off Southwark Bri. Rd.)
Lake Ho. Rd. E11 —3J 53
Lakehurst Rd. Eps —5A 148
Lakeland Clo. Harr —6C 10
Lakenheath. N14 —5C 6
Laker Ct. SW4 —1J 103
Laker Ind. Est. SE26 —5A 124
(off Kent Ho. La.)
Lake Rd. SW19 —5H 119
Lake Rd. Croy —2B 154
Lake Rd. Romf —4D 38
Laker Pl. SW15 —6G 101
Lakeside. N3 —2K 29
Lakeside. W13 —6C 62
Lakeside. Beck —3D 142
Lakeside. Enf —4C 6
Lakeside. Eps —6A 148
Lakeside. Wall —4F 151
Lakeside Av. SE28 —2A 92
Lakeside Av. Ilf —4B 36
Lakeside Clo. SE25 —2G 141
Lakeside Clo. Ruis —4E 22
Lakeside Clo. Sidc —5C 110
Lakeside Ct. N4 —2C 50
Lakeside Cres. Barn —5J 5
Lakeside Dri. Brom —3C 156
Lakeside Rd. N13 —4E 16
Lakeside Rd. W14 —3F 83
Lakeside Ter. EC2 —5D 162
Lakeside Way. SE2 —3D 92
Lakeside Way. Wemb —4G 45
Lakes Rd. Kes —5A 156
Lakeswood Rd. Orp —6F 145
Lake, The. Bush —1C 10
Lake Vw. Edgw —5A 12
Lake Vw. Ct. SW1 —3F 85 (1K 171)
(off Bressenden Pl.)
Lake Vw. Est. E3 —2A 70
Lakeview Rd. SE27 —5A 122
Lakeview Rd. Well —4B 110
Lake Vw. Ter. N18 —4A 18
(off Sweet Briar Wlk.)
Lakis Clo. NW3 —4A 48
Laleham Av. NW7 —3E 12
Laleham Ho. E2 —4F 69 (3J 163)
(off Camlet St.)
Laleham Rd. SE6 —7E 106
Laleham Rd. Shep —4B 130
Lalor St. SW6 —2G 101
Lambarde Av. SE9 —4E 126
Lamb Ct. E14 —7A 70
(off Narrow St.)
Lamberhurst Ho. SE15 —6J 87
Lamberhurst Rd. SE27 —4A 122
Lamberhurst Rd. Dag —1F 57

Lambert Av.—Lattimer Pl.

Lambert Av. Rich —3G 99
Lambert Ct. Eri —6J 93
(off Park Cres.)
Lambert Jones M. EC2 —5C 162
Lambert Lodge. Bren —5D 80
(off Layton Rd.)
Lambert Rd. E16 —6K 71
Lambert Rd. N12 —5G 15
Lambert Rd. SW2 —5J 103
Lambert's Pl. Croy —1D 152
Lamberts Rd. Surb —5E 134
Lambert St. N1 —7A 50
Lambert Wlk. Wemb —3D 44
Lambert Way. N12 —5F 15
Lambeth. —3K 85 (2G 173)
Lambeth Bri. SW1 & SE1 —4J 85 (3F 173)
Lambeth Crematorium. SW17 —4A 120
Lambeth High St. SE1 —4K 85 (4G 173)
Lambeth Hill. EC4 —7C 68 (2C 168)
Lambeth Pal. Rd. SE1 —3K 85 (2G 173)
Lambeth Rd. SE1 & SE11 —4K 85 (3G 173)
Lambeth Rd. Croy —7A 140
Lambeth Towers. SE1 —2J 173
Lambeth Wlk. SE11 —4K 85 (4H 173)
(in two parts)
Lambfold Ho. N7 —6J 49
Lamb La. E8 —7H 51
Lamble St. NW5 —5E 48
Lambley Rd. Dag —6B 56
Lambolle Pl. NW3 —6C 48
Lambolle Rd. NW3 —6C 48
Lambourn Clo. NW5 —4G 49
Lambourn Clo. W7 —2K 79
Lambourne Av. SW19 —4H 119
Lambourne Ct. Wfd G —7F 21
Lambourne Gdns. E4 —2H 19
Lambourne Gdns. Bark —7K 55
Lambourne Gdns. Enf —2A 8
Lambourne Ho. NW8 —5B 66 (5B 158)
(off Broadley St.)
Lambourne Ho. SE16 —4K 87
Lambourne Pl. SE3 —1K 107
Lambourne Rd. E11 —7E 34
Lambourne Rd. Bark —7J 55
Lambourne Rd. Ilf —2J 55
Lambourn Gro. King T —2H 135
Lambourn Rd. SW8 —3F 103
Lamb Pas. Bren —6F 81
Lambrook Ho. SE15 —1G 105
Lambrook Ter. SW6 —1G 101
Lamb's Bldgs. EC1 —4D 68 (4E 162)
Lamb's Clo. N9 —2B 18
Lamb's Conduit Pas. WC1 —5G 161
Lamb's Conduit St. WC1 —4K 67 (4G 161)
(in three parts)
Lambscroft Av. SE9 —3A 126
Lambs Mdw. Wfd G —2B 36
Lamb's M. N1 —1B 68
Lamb's Pas. EC1 —4D 68 (5E 162)
Lambs Ter. N9 —2J 17
Lamb St. E1 —5E 68 (5J 163)
Lamb's Wlk. Enf —2H 7
Lambton Pl. W11 —7H 65
Lambton Rd. N19 —1J 49
Lambton Rd. SW20 —1E 136
Lamb Wlk. SE1 —2E 86 (7G 169)
LAMDA Theatre. —4J 83
Lamerock Rd. Brom —4H 125
Lamerton Rd. Ilf —2F 37
Lamerton St. SE8 —6C 88
Lamford Clo. N17 —7J 17
Lamington St. W6 —4D 82
Lamlash St. SE11 —4B 86
Lammas Av. Mitc —2E 138
Lammas Grn. SE26 —3H 123
Lammas Pk. Gdns. W5 —1C 80
Lammas Pk. Rd. W5 —2D 80
Lammas Rd. E9 —7K 51
Lammas Rd. E10 —2A 52
Lammas Rd. Rich —4C 116
Lammermoor Rd. SW12 —7F 103
Lamont Rd. SW10 —6B 84 (7A 170)
Lamont Rd. Pas. SW10 —7A 170
Lamorbey. —1K 127
Lamorbey Clo. Sidc —1K 127
Lamorna Clo. E17 —2E 34
Lamorna Clo. Orp —7K 145
Lamorna Gro. Stan —1D 26
Lampard Gro. N16 —1F 51
Lampern Sq. E2 —3G 69
Lampeter Sq. W6 —6G 83
Lamplighter Clo. E1 —4J 69
Lampmead Rd. SE12 —5H 107
Lamp Office Ct. WC1 —4G 161
Lamport Clo. SE18 —4D 90
Lamps Ct. SE5 —7C 86
Lampton. —1F 97
Lampton Av. Houn —1F 97
Lampton Ct. Houn —1F 97
Lampton Ho. Clo. SW19 —4F 119
Lampton Pk. Rd. Houn —2F 97
Lampton Rd. Houn —2F 97
Lanacre Av. NW9 —1K 27
Lanain Ct. SE12 —7H 107
Lanark Clo. W5 —5C 62
Lanark Ct. N'holt —5E 42
(off Newmarket Av.)
Lanark Ho. SE1 —5G 87
(off Old Kent Rd.)
Lanark Mans. W9 —4A 66
(off Lanark Rd.)
Lanark M. W9 —3A 66
Lanark Pl. W9 —4A 66 (3A 158)
Lanark Rd. W9 —2K 65
Lanark Sq. E14 —3D 88
Lanata Wlk. Hay —4B 60
(off Alba Clo.)
Lanbury Rd. SE15 —4K 105
Lancashire Ct. W1 —2K 165
Lancaster Av. E18 —4K 35
Lancaster Av. SE27 —2B 122
Lancaster Av. SW19 —5F 119
Lancaster Av. Bark —7J 55
Lancaster Av. Barn —1G 5
Lancaster Av. Mitc —5J 139
Lancaster Clo. N1 —7E 50
Lancaster Clo. N17 —7B 18
Lancaster Clo. NW9 —7G 13
Lancaster Clo. SE27 —2B 122
Lancaster Clo. W2 —7K 65
(off St Petersburgh Pl.)
Lancaster Clo. Brom —4H 143
Lancaster Clo. Croy —2J 151
Lancaster Clo. King T —5D 116
Lancaster Clo. Stanw —6A 94
Lancaster Cotts. Rich —6E 98
Lancaster Ct. SE27 —2B 122
Lancaster Ct. SW6 —7H 83
Lancaster Ct. W2 —7A 66 (2A 164)
(off Lancaster Ga.)
Lancaster Ct. Sutt —7J 149
(off Mulgrave Rd.)
Lancaster Ct. W on T —7J 131
Lancaster Dri. E14 —1E 88
Lancaster Dri. NW3 —6C 48
Lancaster Gdns. SW19 —5G 119
Lancaster Gdns. W13 —2B 80
Lancaster Gdns. King T —5D 116
Lancaster Ga. W2 —7A 66 (2A 164)
Lancaster Gro. NW3 —6B 48
Lancaster Hall. E16 —1J 89
(off Wesley Av., in two parts)
Lancaster Ho. Enf —1J 7
Lancaster Lodge. W11 —6G 65
(off Lancaster Rd.)
Lancaster M. SW18 —5K 101
Lancaster M. W2 —7A 66 (2A 164)
Lancaster M. Rich —6E 98
Lancaster Pk. Rich —5E 98
Lancaster Pl. SW19 —5F 119
Lancaster Pl. WC2 —7K 67 (2G 167)
Lancaster Pl. Houn —2A 96
Lancaster Pl. Ilf —5G 55
Lancaster Pl. Twic —6A 98
Lancaster Rd. E7 —7J 53
Lancaster Rd. E11 —2G 53
Lancaster Rd. E17 —2K 33
Lancaster Rd. N4 —7K 31
Lancaster Rd. N11 —6C 16
Lancaster Rd. N18 —5A 18
Lancaster Rd. NW10 —5C 46
Lancaster Rd. SE25 —2F 141
Lancaster Rd. SW19 —5F 119
Lancaster Rd. W11 —6G 65
Lancaster Rd. Barn —4G 5
(in two parts)
Lancaster Rd. Enf —1J 7
Lancaster Rd. Harr —5E 24
Lancaster Rd. N'holt —6G 43
Lancaster Rd. S'hall —7C 60
Lancaster Stables. NW3 —6C 48
Lancaster St. SE1 —2B 86 (7A 168)
Lancaster Ter. W2 —7B 66 (2A 164)
Lancaster Wlk. W2 —1A 84 (3A 164)
Lancaster Wlk. Hay —6E 58
Lancastrian Rd. Wall —7K 151
Lancefield Ct. W10 —2G 65
Lancefield Ho. SE15 —3H 105
Lancefield St. W10 —3H 65
Lancell St. N16 —2E 50
Lancelot Av. Wemb —4D 44
Lancelot Cres. Wemb —4D 44
Lancelot Gdns. E Barn —7K 5
Lancelot Pl. SW7 —2D 84 (7E 164)
Lancelot Rd. Well —4A 110
Lancelot Rd. Wemb —4D 44
Lance Rd. Harr —7G 25
Lancer Sq. W8 —2K 83
Lancey Clo. SE7 —4C 90
Lanchester Ct. W2 —6D 66 (1E 164)
(off Seymour St.)
Lanchester Rd. N6 —5D 30
Lancing Gdns. N9 —1A 18
Lancing Rd. W13 —7B 62
Lancing Rd. Croy —7K 139
Lancing Rd. Felt —2H 113
Lancing Rd. Ilf —6H 37
Lancing St. NW1 —3H 67 (2C 160)
Lancresse Ct. N1 —1E 68
(off De Beauvoir Est.)
Landcroft Rd. SE22 —5F 105
Landells Rd. SE22 —6F 105
Landford Rd. SW15 —3E 100
Landgrove Rd. SW19 —5J 119
Landin Ho. E14 —6C 70
Landleys Fld. NW5 —5H 49
(off Long Mdw.)
Landmann Way. SE14 —5K 87
Landmark Commercial Cen. N18 —6K 17
Landon Pl. SW1 —3D 84 (1E 170)
Landon's Clo. E14 —1E 88
Landons Clo. E14 —1E 88
Landon Wlk. E14 —7D 70
Landon Way. Ashf —6D 112
Landor Rd. SW4 —3J 103
Landor Wlk. W12 —2C 82
Landra Gdns. N21 —6G 7
Landrake. NW1 —1G 67
(off Plender St.)
Landridge Dri. Enf —1C 8
Landridge Rd. SW6 —2H 101
Landrock Rd. N8 —6J 31
Landscape Rd. Wfd G —7E 20
Landseer Av. E12 —5E 54
Landseer Clo. SW19 —1A 138
Landseer Clo. Edgw —2G 27
Landseer Ct. Hay —2F 59
Landseer Ho. NW8 —4B 66 (3B 158)
(off Frampton St.)
Landseer Ho. SW1 —4H 85 (4D 172)
(off Herrick St.)
Landseer Ho. SW11 —1E 102
Landseer Ho. N'holt —2B 60
(off Parkfield Dri.)
Landseer Rd. N19 —3J 49
(in two parts)
Landseer Rd. Enf —5B 8
Landseer Rd. N Mald —7K 135
Landseer Rd. Sutt —6J 149
Landstead Rd. SE18 —7H 91
Landulph Ho. SE11 —5A 86 (5K 173)
(off Kennings Way)
Landward Ct. W1 —6C 66 (7D 158)
(off Harrowby St.)
Lane App. NW7 —5B 14
Lane Clo. NW2 —3D 46
Lane End. SW15 —6F 101
Lane End. Bexh —3H 111
Lane Gdns. Bus H —1D 10
Lane M. E12 —3D 54
Lanercost Clo. SW2 —2A 122
Lanercost Gdns. N14 —7D 6
Lanercost Rd. SW2 —2A 122
Lanesborough Pl. SW1 —6H 165
Laneside. Chst —5F 127
Laneside. Edgw —5D 12
Laneside Av. Dag —7F 39
Lane, The. NW8 —2A 66
Lane, The. SE3 —3J 107
Laneway. SW15 —5D 100
Laney Ho. EC1 —5A 68
(off Leather La.)
Lanfranc Ct. Harr —3K 43
Lanfranc Rd. E3 —2A 70
Lanfrey Pl. W14 —5H 83
Langbourne Av. N6 —2E 48
Langbourne Ct. E17 —6A 34
Langbourne Mans. N6 —2E 48
Langbourne Pl. E14 —5D 88
Langbourne Way. Clay —6A 146
Langbrook Rd. SE3 —3B 108
Langcroft Clo. Cars —3D 150
Langdale. NW1 —3G 67 (1A 160)
(off Stanhope St.)
Langdale Av. Mitc —3D 138
Langdale Clo. SE17 —6C 86
Langdale Clo. SW14 —4H 99
Langdale Clo. Dag —1C 56
Langdale Clo. Orp —3E 156
Langdale Cres. Bexh —7G 93
Langdale Dri. Hay —2G 59
Langdale Gdns. Gnfd —3B 62
Langdale Ho. SW1 —5G 85 (6A 172)
(off Churchill Gdns.)
Langdale Pde. Mitc —3D 138
Langdale Rd. SE10 —7E 88
Langdale Rd. T Hth —4A 140
Langdale St. E1 —6H 69
Langdon Ct. EC1 —2B 68 (1B 162)
(off City Rd.)
Langdon Ct. NW10 —1A 64
Langdon Cres. E6 —2E 72
Langdon Dri. NW9 —1J 45
Langdon Ho. E14 —6E 70
Langdon Pk. Rd. N6 —7G 31
Langdon Pl. SW14 —3J 99
Langdon Rd. E6 —1E 72
Langdon Rd. Brom —3K 143
Langdon Rd. Mord —5A 138
Langdons Ct. S'hall —3E 78
Langdon Shaw. Sidc —5K 127
Langdon Wlk. Mord —5A 138
Langdon Way. SE1 —4G 87
Langford Clo. E8 —5G 51
Langford Clo. N15 —6E 32
Langford Clo. NW8 —2A 66
Langford Clo. W3 —2H 81
Langford Ct. NW8 —2A 66
(off Abbey Rd.)
Langford Cres. Cockf —4J 5
Langford Grn. SE5 —3E 104
Langford Ho. SE8 —6C 88
Langford Pl. NW8 —2A 66
Langford Pl. Sidc —3A 128
Langford Rd. SW6 —2K 101
Langford Rd. Cockf —4J 5
Langford Rd. Wfd G —6F 21
Langfords. Buck H —2G 21
Langham Clo. N15 —3B 32
(off Langham Rd.)
Langham Ct. NW4 —5F 29
Langham Ct. Ruis —5K 41
Langham Dri. Romf —6B 38
Langham Gdns. N21 —5F 7
Langham Gdns. W13 —7B 62
Langham Gdns. Edgw —7D 12
Langham Gdns. Rich —4C 116
Langham Gdns. Wemb —2C 44
Langham Ho. Clo. Rich —4D 116
Langham Mans. SW5 —5K 83
(off Earl's Ct. Sq.)
Langham Pl. N15 —3B 32
Langham Pl. W1 —5F 67 (6K 159)
Langham Pl. W4 —6A 82
Langham Rd. N15 —3B 32
Langham Rd. SW20 —1E 136
Langham Rd. Edgw —6D 12
Langham Rd. Tedd —5B 116
Langham St. W1 —5F 67 (6K 159)
Langhedge Clo. N18 —6A 18
Langhedge La. N18 —6A 18
Langhedge La. Ind. Est. N18 —6A 18
Langholm Clo. SW12 —7H 103
Langholme. Bush —1B 10
Langhorn Dri. Twic —7J 97
Langhorne Ct. NW8 —7B 48
(off Dorman Way)
Langhorne Rd. Dag —7G 57
Lang Ho. SW8 —7J 85
(off Hartington Rd.)
Langland Cres. Stan —2D 26
Langland Dri. Pinn —1C 24
Langland Gdns. NW3 —5K 47
Langland Gdns. Croy —2B 154
Langland Ho. SE5 —7D 86
(off Edmund St.)
Langler Rd. NW10 —2E 64
Langley Av. Ruis —2K 41
Langley Av. Surb —1D 146
Langley Av. Wor Pk —1F 149
Langley Ct. WC2 —7J 67 (2E 166)
Langley Cres. E11 —7A 36
Langley Cres. Dag —7C 56
Langley Cres. Edgw —3D 12
Langley Cres. Hay —7H 77
Langley Dri. E11 —7K 35
Langley Dri. W3 —2H 81
Langley Gdns. Brom —4A 144
Langley Gdns. Dag —7D 56
Langley Gdns. Orp —6F 145
Langley Gro. N Mald —2A 136
Langley La. SW8 —6J 85 (7F 173)
Langley Mans. SW8 —7F 173
Langley Pk. NW7 —6F 13
Langley Pk. Rd. Sutt —5A 150
Langley Rd. SW19 —1H 137
Langley Rd. Beck —4A 142
Langley Rd. Iswth —2K 97
Langley Rd. Surb —7E 134
Langley Rd. Well —6C 92
Langley Row. Barn —1C 4
Langley St. WC2 —6J 67 (1E 166)
Langley Way. W W'ck —1F 155
Langmead Dri. Bus H —1D 10
Langmead St. SE27 —4B 122
Langmore Ct. Bexh —3D 110
Langmore Ho. E1 —6G 69
(off Stutfield St.)
Langport Ct. W on T —7A 112
Langport Ho. SW9 —2B 104
Langridge M. Hamp —6D 114
Langroyd Rd. SW17 —2D 120
Langside Av. SW15 —4C 100
Langside Cres. N14 —3C 16
Langston Hughes Clo. SE24 —4B 104
Lang St. E1 —4J 69
Langthorn Ct. EC2 —6D 68 (7E 162)
Langthorne Ct. SE6 —4E 124
Langthorne Ho. Hay —4G 77
Langthorne Rd. E11 —3E 52
Langthorne St. SW6 —7F 83
Langton Av. E6 —3E 72
Langton Av. N20 —7F 5
Langton Clo. WC1 —4K 67 (3H 161)
Langton Ho. SE11 —3H 173
Langton Pl. SW18 —1J 119
Langton Ri. SE23 —7H 105
Langton Rd. NW2 —3E 46
Langton Rd. SW9 —7B 86
Langton Rd. Harr —7B 10
Langton Rd. W Mol —4G 133
Langton St. SW10 —6A 84
Langton Way. SE3 —1H 107
Langton Way. Croy —3E 152
Langtry Pl. SW6 —6J 83
Langtry Rd. NW8 —1K 65
Langtry Rd. N'holt —2B 60
Langtry Wlk. NW8 —1K 65
Langwood Chase. Tedd —6C 116
Langworth Dri. Hay —6J 59
Lanhill Rd. W9 —4J 65
Lanier Rd. SE13 —6F 107
Lanigan Dri. Houn —5F 97
Lankaster Gdns. N2 —1B 30
Lankers Dri. Harr —6D 24
Lankton Clo. Beck —1E 142
Lannock Rd. Hay —1H 77
Lannoy Point. SW6 —7G 83
(off Pellant Rd.)
Lannoy Rd. SE9 —1G 127
Lanrick Ho. E14 —6F 71
Lanrick Rd. E14 —6F 71
Lanridge Rd. SE2 —3D 92
Lansbury Av. N18 —5J 17
Lansbury Av. Bark —7A 56
Lansbury Av. Felt —6K 95
Lansbury Av. Romf —5E 38
Lansbury Clo. NW10 —5J 45
Lansbury Dri. Hay —2G 59
Lansbury Est. E14 —6D 70
Lansbury Gdns. E14 —6F 71
Lansbury Rd. Enf —1E 8
Lansbury Way. N18 —5K 17
Lanscombe Wlk. SW8 —1J 103
Lansdell Ho. SW2 —6A 104
(off Tulse Hill)
Lansdell Rd. Mitc —2E 138
Lansdowne Av. Bexh —7D 92
Lansdowne Av. Orp —7F 145
Lansdowne Clo. SW20 —7F 119
Lansdowne Clo. Surb —2H 147
Lansdowne Clo. Twic —1K 115
Lansdowne Ct. W11 —7G 65
(off Lansdowne Ri.)
Lansdowne Ct. Ilf —3C 36
Lansdowne Ct. Wor Pk —2C 148
Lansdowne Cres. W11 —7G 65
Lansdowne Dri. E8 —6G 51
Lansdowne Gdns. SW8 —1J 103
Lansdowne Grn. SW8 —1J 103
Lansdowne Gro. NW10 —4A 46
Lansdowne Hill. SE27 —3B 122
Lansdowne La. SE7 —6B 90
Lansdowne M. SE7 —5B 90
Lansdowne M. W11 —1H 83
Lansdowne Pl. SE1 —3D 86
Lansdowne Pl. SE19 —7F 123
Lansdowne Ri. W11 —7G 65
Lansdowne Rd. E4 —2H 19
Lansdowne Rd. E11 —2H 53
Lansdowne Rd. E17 —6C 34
Lansdowne Rd. E18 —3J 35
Lansdowne Rd. N3 —7D 14
Lansdowne Rd. N10 —2G 31
Lansdowne Rd. N17 —1F 33
Lansdowne Rd. SW19 —7E 118
Lansdowne Rd. W11 —7G 65
Lansdowne Rd. Brom —7J 125
Lansdowne Rd. Croy —2C 152
Lansdowne Rd. Eps —7J 147
Lansdowne Rd. Harr —7J 25
Lansdowne Rd. Houn —3F 97
Lansdowne Rd. Ilf —1K 55
Lansdowne Rd. Stan —6H 11
Lansdowne Rd. Uxb —6E 58
Lansdowne Row. W1 —1F 85 (4K 165)
Lansdowne Ter. WC1 —4J 67 (4F 161)
Lansdowne Wlk. W11 —1H 83
Lansdowne Way. SW8 —1H 103
Lansdowne Wood Clo. SE27 —3B 122
Lansdowne Workshops. SE7 —5A 90
Lansdown Rd. E7 —7A 54
Lansdown Rd. Sidc —3B 128
Lansfield Av. N18 —4B 18
Lantern Clo. SW15 —4C 100
Lantern Clo. Wemb —5D 44
Lanterns Ct. E14 —2D 88
Lantern Way. W Dray —2A 76
Lant Ho. SE1 —2C 86 (7C 168)
(off Toulmin St.)
Lant St. SE1 —2C 86 (6C 168)
Lanvanor Rd. SE15 —2J 105
Lanyard Ho. SE8 —4B 88
Lapford Clo. W9 —4H 65
Lapponum Wlk. Hay —4B 60
Lapse Wood Wlk. SE23 —1H 123
Lapstone Gdns. Harr —6C 26
Lapwing Ct. Surb —3G 147
Lapwing Tower. SE8 —6B 88
(off Abinger Gro., in two parts)
Lapwing Way. Hay —6B 60
Lapworth. N11 —4A 16
(off Coppies Gro.)
Lapworth Ct. W2 —5K 65
(off Chichester Rd.)
Lara Clo. SE13 —6E 106
Lara Clo. Chess —7E 146
Larbert Rd. SW16 —7G 121
Larch Av. W3 —1A 82
Larch Clo. E13 —4K 71
Larch Clo. N11 —7K 15
Larch Clo. N19 —2G 49
Larch Clo. SE8 —6B 88
Larch Clo. SW12 —2F 121
Larch Cres. Eps —6H 147
Larch Cres. Hay —5A 60
Larch Dene. Orp —2E 156
Larch Dri. W4 —5G 81
Larches Av. SW14 —4K 99
Larches, The. N13 —3H 17
Larches, The. Uxb —3D 58
Larch Grn. NW9 —1A 28
Larch Gro. Sidc —1K 127
Larch Ho. W10 —4G 65
(off Rowan Wlk.)
Larch Ho. Brom —1G 143
Larch Ho. Hay —5A 60
Larch Rd. E10 —2C 52
Larch Rd. NW2 —4E 46
Larch Tree Way. Croy —3C 154
Larchvale Ct. Sutt —7K 149
Larch Way. Brom —7E 144
Larchwood Rd. SE9 —2F 127
Larcombe Clo. Croy —4F 153
Larcombe Ct. Sutt —7K 149
(off Worcester Rd.)
Larcom St. SE17 —4C 86
Larden Rd. W3 —1A 82
Largewood Av. Surb —2G 147
Larissa St. SE17 —5D 86
Larkbere Rd. SE26 —4A 124
Larken Clo. Bush —1B 10
Larken Dri. Bush —1B 10
Larkfield Av. Harr —3B 26
Larkfield Clo. Brom —2H 155
Larkfield Rd. Rich —4E 98
Larkfield Rd. Sidc —3K 127
Larkhall La. SW4 —2H 103
Larkhall Ri. SW4 —3G 103
Larkham Clo. Felt —3G 113
Lark Row. E2 —1J 69
Larksfield Gro. Enf —1C 8
Larks Gro. Bark —7J 55
Larkshall Ct. Romf —2J 39
Larkshall Cres. E4 —4K 19
Larkshall Rd. E4 —5K 19
Larkspur Clo. E6 —5C 72
Larkspur Clo. N17 —7J 17
Larkspur Clo. NW9 —5K 27
Larkspur Clo. Ruis —7E 22
Larkspur Gro. Edgw —4D 12
Larkspur Lodge. Sidc —3B 128
Larkspur Way. Eps —5J 147
Larkswood Ct. E4 —5A 20
Larkswood Ri. Pinn —4A 24
Larkswood Rd. E4 —4H 19
Lark Way. Cars —7C 138
Larkway Clo. NW9 —4K 27
Larnach Rd. W6 —6F 83
Larne Rd. Ruis —7H 23
Larpent Av. SW15 —5E 100
Larwood Clo. Gnfd —5H 43
Lascelles Av. Harr —7H 25
Lascelles Clo. E11 —2F 53
Lascelles Ho. NW1 —4D 158
Lascotts Rd. N22 —6E 16
Laseron Ho. N15 —4F 33
(off Tottenham Grn. E.)
Lassa Rd. SE9 —5C 108
Lassell St. SE10 —5F 89
Lasseter Pl. SE3 —6G 89
Latchett Rd. E18 —1K 35
Latchingdon Ct. E17 —4K 33
Latchingdon Gdns. Wfd G —6H 21
Latchmere Clo. Rich —5E 116
Latchmere La. King T —6F 117
Latchmere Pas. SW11 —2C 102
Latchmere Rd. SW11 —2D 102
Latchmere Rd. King T —7E 116
Latchmere St. SW11 —2D 102
Lateward Rd. Bren —6D 80
Latham Clo. E6 —5C 72
Latham Clo. Twic —7A 98
Latham Ct. W14 —4J 83
(off W. Cromwell Rd.)
Latham Ct. N'holt —3B 60
(off Seasprite Clo.)
Latham Rd. Bexh —5G 111
Latham Rd. Twic —7K 97
Latham's Way. Croy —1K 151
Lathkill Clo. Enf —7B 8
Lathkill Ct. Beck —1B 142
Lathom Rd. E6 —7C 54
Latimer Av. E6 —1D 72
Latimer Clo. Pinn —1A 24
Latimer Clo. Wor Pk —4D 148
Latimer Gdns. Pinn —1A 24
Latimer Ho. E9 —6K 51
Latimer Ho. W11 —7H 65
(off Kensington Pk. Rd.)
Latimer Ind. Est. W10 —6E 64
Latimer Pl. W10 —6E 64
Latimer Rd. E7 —4K 53
Latimer Rd. N15 —6E 32
Latimer Rd. SW19 —6K 119
Latimer Rd. W10 —5E 64
(in two parts)
Latimer Rd. Barn —3E 4
Latimer Rd. Croy —3B 152
Latimer Rd. Tedd —5K 115
Latona Rd. SE15 —6G 87
Lattimer Pl. W4 —7A 82

Latton Clo.—Lenton Path

Latton Clo. W on T —7C 132
Latymer Ct. W6 —4F 83
Latymer Gdns. N3 —2G 29
Latymer Rd. N9 —1A 18
Latymer Way. N9 —2K 17
Lauder Clo. N'holt —2B 60
Lauder Ct. N14 —7D 6
Lauderdale Dri. Rich —3D 116
Lauderdale Mans. W9 —3K 65
(off Lauderdale Rd., in two parts)
Lauderdale Pl. EC2 —5C 68
(off Beech St.)
Lauderdale Rd. W9 —3K 65
Lauderdale Tower. EC2 —5C 162
Laud St. SE11 —5K 85 (5G 173)
Laud St. Croy —3C 152
Laughton Rd. N'holt —1B 60
Launcelot Rd. Brom —4J 125
Launcelot St. SE1 —2A 86 (7J 167)
Launceston Gdns. Gnfd —1C 62
Launceston Pl. W8 —3A 84
Launceston Rd. Gnfd —1C 62
Launch St. E14 —3E 88
Laundress La. N16 —3G 51
Laundry La. N1 —1C 68
Laundry Rd. W6 —6G 83
Laura Clo. E11 —5A 36
Laura Clo. Enf —5K 7
Lauradale Rd. N2 —4D 30
Laura Pl. E5 —4J 51
Laurel Av. Twic —1K 115
Laurel Bank Gdns. SW6 —2H 101
Laurel Bank Rd. Enf —1H 7
Laurel Bank Vs. W7 —1J 79
(off Lwr. Boston Rd.)
Laurelbrook. SE6 —3G 125
Laurel Clo. N19 —2G 49
Laurel Clo. SW17 —5C 120
Laurel Clo. Sidc —3A 128
Laurel Ct. Wemb —2E 62
Laurel Cres. Croy —3C 154
Laurel Cres. Romf —1K 57
Laurel Dri. N21 —7F 7
Laurel Gdns. E4 —7J 9
Laurel Gdns. NW7 —3E 12
Laurel Gdns. W7 —1J 79
Laurel Gdns. Houn —4C 96
Laurel Gro. SE20 —7H 123
Laurel Gro. SE26 —4K 123
Laurel Ho. SE8 —6B 88
Laurel Ho. Brom —1G 143
Laurel La. W Dray —4A 76
Laurel Mnr. Sutt —7A 150
Laurel Pk. Harr —7E 10
Laurel Rd. SW13 —2C 100
Laurel Rd. SW20 —1D 136
Laurel Rd. Hamp H —5H 115
Laurels, The. NW10 —1D 64
Laurels, The. Brom —4J 143
(Durham Rd.)
Laurels, The. Brom —1K 143
(Freelands Rd.)
Laurels, The. Buck H —1F 21
Laurels, The. Bush —2D 10
Laurel St. E8 —6F 51
Laurel Vw. N12 —3E 14
Laurel Way. E18 —4H 35
Laurel Way. N20 —3D 14
Laurence Ct. E10 —7D 34
Laurence M. W12 —2C 82
Laurence Pountney Hill. EC4 —7D 68 (2E 168)
Laurence Pountney La. EC4 —7D 68 (2E 168)
Laurie Gro. SE14 —1A 106
Laurie Ho. SE1 —3B 86
(off St George's Rd.)
Laurie Rd. W7 —5J 61
Laurier Rd. NW5 —3F 49
Laurier Rd. Croy —7F 141
Laurimel Clo. Stan —6G 11
Laurino Pl. Bush —2B 10
Lauriston Rd. E9 —7J 51
Lauriston Rd. SW19 —6F 119
Lausanne Rd. N8 —4A 32
Lausanne Rd. SE15 —1J 105
Lavell St. N16 —4D 50
Lavender Av. NW9 —1J 45
Lavender Av. Mitc —1C 138
Lavender Av. Wor Pk —3E 148
Lavender Clo. SW3 —6B 84 (7B 170)
Lavender Clo. Brom —6C 144
Lavender Clo. Cars —4F 151
Lavender Ct. Felt —6K 95
Lavender Ct. W Mol —3F 133
Lavender Gdns. SW11 —4D 102
Lavender Gdns. Enf —1G 7
Lavender Gdns. Har W —6D 10
Lavender Gro. E8 —7G 51
Lavender Gro. Mitc —1C 138
Lavender Hill. SW11 —4C 102
Lavender Hill. Enf —1F 7
Lavender Pl. Ilf —5F 55
Lavender Ri. W Dray —2C 76
Lavender Rd. SE16 —1A 88
Lavender Rd. SW11 —3B 102
Lavender Rd. Cars —4E 150
Lavender Rd. Croy —6K 139
Lavender Rd. Enf —1J 7
Lavender Rd. Eps —5H 147
Lavender Rd. Sutt —4B 150
Lavender Rd. Uxb —5B 58
Lavender Sq. E11 —3F 53
Lavender St. E15 —6G 53
Lavender Sweep. SW11 —4D 102
Lavender Ter. SW11 —3C 102
Lavender Va. Wall —6H 151
Lavender Wlk. SW11 —4D 102
Lavender Wlk. Mitc —3E 138
Lavender Way. Croy —6K 141
Lavendon Ho. NW8 —4C 66 (3D 158)
(off Paveley St.)
Lavengro Rd. SE27 —2C 122
Lavenham Rd. SW18 —2H 119
Lavernock Rd. Bexh —2G 111
Lavers Rd. N16 —3E 50
Laverstoke Gdns. SW15 —7B 100
Laverton M. SW5 —4K 83
Laverton Pl. SW5 —4K 83
Lavidge Rd. SE9 —2C 126
Lavina Gro. N1 —2K 67
Lavington Rd. W13 —1B 80
Lavington Rd. Croy —3K 151
Lavington St. SE1 —1B 86 (5B 168)
Lavisham Ho. Brom —5J 125
Lawdons Gdns. Croy —4B 152
Lawford Clo. Wall —7J 151
Lawford Rd. N1 —7E 50
Lawford Rd. NW5 —6G 49
Lawford Rd. W4 —7J 81
Law Ho. Bark —2A 74
Lawless Ho. E14 —7E 70
Lawless St. E14 —7D 70
Lawley Ho. Twic —6D 98
Lawley Rd. N14 —7A 6
Lawley St. E5 —4J 51
Lawn Clo. N9 —7A 8
Lawn Clo. Brom —7K 125
Lawn Clo. N Mald —2A 136
Lawn Clo. Ruis —3H 41
Lawn Cres. Rich —2G 99
Lawn Dri. E7 —4B 54
Lawn Farm Gro. Romf —4E 38
Lawn Gdns. W7 —1J 79
Lawn Ho. Clo. E14 —2E 88
Lawn La. SW8 —6J 85 (7F 173)
Lawn Rd. NW3 —5D 48
Lawn Rd. Beck —7B 124
Lawns Ct. Wemb —2F 45
Lawnside. SE3 —4H 107
Lawns, The. E4 —5H 19
Lawns, The. SE3 —3H 107
Lawns, The. SE19 —1D 140
Lawns, The. SW19 —5H 119
Lawns, The. Pinn —7A 10
Lawns, The. Sidc —4B 128
Lawns, The. Sutt —7G 149
Lawnsway. Romf —1J 39
Lawnswood. Barn —5B 4
Lawn Ter. SE3 —3G 107
Lawn, The. S'hall —5E 78
Lawn Va. Pinn —2C 24
Lawrence Av. E12 —4E 54
Lawrence Av. E17 —1K 33
Lawrence Av. N13 —4G 17
Lawrence Av. NW7 —4F 13
Lawrence Av. N Mald —6K 135
Lawrence Bldgs. N16 —3F 51
Lawrence Campe Clo. N20 —3G 15
Lawrence Clo. E3 —3C 70
Lawrence Clo. N15 —3E 32
Lawrence Clo. W12 —7D 64
Lawrence Ct. NW7 —5F 13
Lawrence Ct. W3 —3J 81
(off Stanley Rd.)
Lawrence Cres. Dag —3H 57
Lawrence Cres. Edgw —2G 27
Lawrence Dri. Uxb —4E 40
Lawrence Est. Houn —4A 96
Lawrence Gdns. NW7 —3G 13
Lawrence Hill. E4 —2H 19
Lawrence Ho. SW1 —4H 85 (4D 172)
(off Cureton St.)
Lawrence La. EC2 —6C 68 (7D 162)
Lawrence Pde. Iswth —3B 98
(off Lower Sq.)
Lawrence Pl. N1 —1J 67
(off Brydon Wlk.)
Lawrence Rd. E6 —1C 72
Lawrence Rd. E13 —1K 71
Lawrence Rd. N15 —4E 32
Lawrence Rd. N18 —4C 18
(in two parts)
Lawrence Rd. SE25 —4F 141
Lawrence Rd. W5 —4C 80
Lawrence Rd. Eri —7H 93
Lawrence Rd. Hamp —7D 114
Lawrence Rd. Hay —2E 58
Lawrence Rd. Houn —4A 96
Lawrence Rd. Pinn —6B 24
Lawrence Rd. Rich —4C 116
Lawrence Rd. W W'ck —4J 155
Lawrence St. E16 —5H 71
Lawrence St. NW7 —4G 13
Lawrence St. SW3 —6C 84 (7C 170)
Lawrence Trad. Est. SE10 —4G 89
Lawrence Way. NW10 —3K 45
Lawrence Weaver Clo. Mord —6J 137
Lawrence Yd. N15 —4E 32
Lawrie Pk. Av. SE26 —5H 123
Lawrie Pk. Cres. SE26 —5H 123
Lawrie Pk. Gdns. SE26 —4H 123
Lawrie Pk. Rd. SE26 —6H 123
Lawson Clo. E16 —5A 72
Lawson Clo. SW19 —3F 119
Lawson Ct. N4 —1K 49
(off Lorne Rd.)
Lawson Ct. Surb —7D 134
Lawson Gdns. Pinn —3K 23
Lawson Ho. SE18 —6E 90
(off Nightingale Pl.)
Lawson Ho. W12 —7D 64
(off White City Est.)
Lawson Rd. Enf —1D 8
Lawson Rd. S'hall —4E 60
Law St. SE1 —3D 86
Lawton Rd. E3 —3A 70
Lawton Rd. E10 —1E 52
Lawton Rd. Cockf —3G 5
Laxcon Clo. NW10 —5K 45
Laxfield Ct. E8 —1G 69
(off Pownall Rd.)
Laxford Ho. SW1 —4E 84 (4H 171)
(off Cundy St.)
Laxley Clo. SE5 —7B 86
Laxton Pl. NW1 —4F 67 (3K 159)
Layard Rd. SE16 —4H 87
Layard Rd. Enf —1A 8
Layard Rd. T Hth —2D 140
Layard Sq. SE16 —4H 87
Laybourne Ho. E14 —2C 88
(off Admirals Way)
Laybrook Lodge. E18 —4H 35
Laycock St. N1 —6A 50
Layer Gdns. W3 —7G 63
Layfield Clo. NW4 —7D 28
Layfield Cres. NW4 —7D 28
Layfield Rd. NW4 —7D 28
Layhams Rd. W W'ck & Kes —3F 155
Laymarsh Clo. Belv —3F 93
Laymead Clo. N'holt —6C 42
Laystall Ct. WC1 —4A 68 (4J 161)
(off Mt. Pleasant)
Laystall St. EC1 —4A 68 (4J 161)
Layton Ct. Bren —5D 80
Layton Cres. Croy —5A 152
Layton Pl. Kew —1G 99
Layton Rd. Bren —5D 80
Layton Rd. Houn —4F 97
Layton's Bldgs. SE1 —2D 86 (6E 168)
Layton's La. Sun —2H 131
Layzell Wlk. SE9 —1B 126
Lazar Wlk. N7 —2K 49
Lazenby Ct. WC2 —2E 166
Leabank Clo. Harr —3J 43
Leabank Sq. E9 —6C 52
Leabank Vw. N15 —6G 33
Lea Bon Ct. E15 —1H 71
(off Plaistow Gro.)
Leabourne Rd. N16 —7G 33
Lea Bridge. —3K 51
Lea Bri. Ind. Cen. E10 —1A 52
Lea Bri. Rd. E5 & E10 —3J 51
Lea Bri. Rd. E10 —7C 34
Lea Clo. Twic —7D 96
Lea Ct. E4 —2K 19
Lea Ct. E13 —3J 71
Lea Cres. Ruis —4H 41
Leacroft Av. SW12 —7D 102
Leacroft Clo. W Dray —6A 58
Leadale Av. E4 —2H 19
Leadale Rd. N15 & N16 —6G 33
Leadbeaters Clo. N11 —5J 15
Leadbetter Ct. NW10 —7K 45
(off Melville Rd.)
Leadenhall Market. —6E 68 (1G 169)
Leadenhall Mkt. EC3 —6E 68
(off Leadenhall Pl.)
Leadenhall Pl. EC3 —6E 68 (1G 169)
Leadenhall St. EC3 —6E 68 (1G 169)
Leadenham Ct. E3 —4C 70
Leader Av. E12 —5E 54
Leadings, The. Wemb —3J 45
Leaf Clo. N'wd —1F 23
Leaf Clo. Th Dit —5J 133
Leaf Gro. SE27 —5A 122
Leafield Clo. SW16 —6B 122
Leafield La. Sidc —3F 129
Leafield Rd. SW20 —3H 137
Leafield Rd. Sutt —2J 149
Leafy Gro. Kes —5A 156
Leafy Oak Rd. SE12 —4A 126
Leafy Way. Croy —2F 153
Lea Gdns. Wemb —4F 45
Leagrave St. E5 —3J 51
Lea Hall Gdns. E10 —1C 52
Lea Hall Rd. E10 —1C 52
Leaholme Way. Ruis —6E 22
Lea Ho. NW8 —4C 66 (4C 158)
(off Salisbury St.)
Leahurst Rd. SE13 —5F 107
Lea Interchange. (Junct.) —5C 52
Leake Ct. SE1 —2K 85 (7H 167)
Leake St. SE1 —2K 85 (6H 167)
(in two parts)
Lealand Rd. N15 —6F 33
Leamington Av. E17 —5C 34
Leamington Av. Brom —5A 126
Leamington Av. Mord —4G 137
Leamington Clo. E12 —5C 54
Leamington Clo. Brom —4A 126
Leamington Clo. Houn —5G 97
Leamington Cres. Harr —3C 42
Leamington Gdns. Ilf —2K 55
Leamington Ho. Edgw —5A 12
Leamington Pk. W3 —5K 63
Leamington Pl. Hay —4H 59
Leamington Rd. S'hall —4B 78
Leamington Rd. Vs. W11 —5H 65
Leamore St. W6 —4E 82
Leamouth. —7G 71
Leamouth Rd. E14 —6F 71
Leander Ct. SE8 —1C 106
Leander Ct. Surb —7D 134
Leander Rd. SW2 —6K 103
Leander Rd. N'holt —2E 60
Leander Rd. T Hth —4K 139
Lea Pk. Trad. Est. E10 —1B 52
(off Warley Clo.)
Leapold M. E9 —1J 69
Learner Dri. Harr —2E 42
Lea Rd. Beck —2C 142
Lea Rd. Enf —1J 7
Lea Rd. S'hall —4C 78
Learoyd Gdns. E6 —7E 72
Leary Ho. SE11 —5K 85 (6H 173)
Leas Clo. Chess —7F 147
Leas Dale. SE9 —3E 126
Leas Grn. Chst —6K 127
Leaside Av. N10 —3E 30
Leaside Bus. Cen. Enf —2G 9
Leaside Ct. Uxb —3D 58
Leaside Mans. N10 —3E 30
(off Fortis Grn.)
Leaside Rd. E5 —1J 51
Leasowes Rd. E10 —1C 52
Leatherbottle Grn. Eri —3F 93
Leather Bottle La. Belv —4E 92
Leather Clo. Mitc —2E 138
Leatherdale St. E1 —4J 69
(in two parts)
Leather Gdns. E15 —1G 71
Leatherhead Clo. N16 —1F 51
Leatherhead Rd. Chess —7D 146
Leather La. EC1 —5A 68 (5J 161)
(in two parts)
Leathermarket Ct. SE1 —2E 86 (7G 169)
Leathermarket St. SE1 —2E 86 (7G 169)
Leathersellers Clo. Barn —3B 4
Leathsail Rd. Harr —3F 43
Leathwaite Rd. SW11 —4D 102
Leathwell Rd. SE8 —2D 106
Lea Va. Dart —4K 111
Lea Valley Rd. Enf & E4 —5F 9
Lea Valley Trad. Est. N18 —6E 18
Lea Valley Viaduct. N18 & E4 —5E 18
Leaveland Clo. Beck —4C 142
Leaver Gdns. Gnfd —2H 61
Leavesden Rd. Stan —6F 11
Leaves Grn. Rd. Kes —7B 156
Lea Vw. Ho. E5 —1H 51
Leaway. E10 —1K 51
Lebanon Av. Felt —5B 114
Lebanon Gdns. SW18 —6J 101
Lebanon Pk. Twic —7B 98
Lebanon Rd. SW18 —5J 101
Lebanon Rd. Croy —1E 152
Lebrun Sq. SE3 —4K 107
Lebus Ho. NW8 —2C 66 (1C 158)
(off Cochrane St.)
Le Caye Apartments. E14 —4F 89
Lechmere App. Wfd G —2A 36
Lechmere Av. Wfd G —2B 36
Lechmere Rd. NW2 —6D 46
Leckford Rd. SW18 —2A 120
Leckhampton Pl. SW2 —7A 104
Leckwith Av. Bexh —6E 92
Lecky St. SW7 —5B 84 (5A 170)
Leclair Ho. SE3 —3K 107
Leconfield Av. SW13 —3B 100
Leconfield Ho. SE5 —4E 104
Leconfield Rd. N5 —4D 50
Leda Av. Enf —1E 8
Ledam Ho. EC1 —5A 68 (5J 161)
(off Bourne Est.)
Leda Rd. SE18 —3D 90
Ledbury Ho. SE22 —3E 104
Ledbury Ho. W11 —6H 65
(off Colville Rd.)
Ledbury M. N. W11 —7J 65
Ledbury M. W. W11 —7J 65
Ledbury Pl. Croy —4C 152
Ledbury Rd. W11 —6H 65
Ledbury Rd. Croy —4D 152
Ledbury St. SE15 —7G 87
Ledrington Rd. SE19 —6G 123
Ledway Dri. Wemb —7F 27
Lee. —5H 107
Lee Av. Romf —6E 38
Lee Bri. SE13 —3E 106
Leechcroft Av. Sidc —5K 109
Leechcroft Rd. Wall —3E 150
Lee Chu. St. SE13 —4G 107
Lee Clo. E17 —1K 33
Lee Clo. Barn —4F 5
Lee Conservancy Rd. E9 —5B 52
Lee Ct. SE13 —4F 107
Leecroft Rd. Barn —5B 4
Leeds Pl. N4 —1K 49
Leeds Rd. Ilf —1H 55
Leeds St. N18 —5B 18
Leefern Rd. W12 —2C 82
Leegate. SE12 —5H 107
Lee Green. (Junct.) —5H 107
Lee Gro. Chig —2K 21
Lee High Rd. SE13 & SE12 —3E 106
Lee Ho. EC2 —5C 68
(off Monkwell Sq.)
Leeke St. WC1 —3K 67 (1G 161)
Leeland Rd. W13 —1A 80
Leeland Ter. W13 —1A 80
Leeland Way. NW10 —4B 46
Leemount Clo. NW4 —4F 29
Leemount Ho. NW4 —4F 29
Lee Pk. SE3 —4H 107
Lee Pk. Way. N18 & N9 —4E 18
Leerdam Dri. E14 —3E 88
Lee Rd. NW7 —7A 14
Lee Rd. SE3 —3H 107
Lee Rd. SW19 —1K 137
Lee Rd. Enf —6B 8
Lee Rd. Gnfd —1C 62
Lees Av. N'wd —1H 23
Lees Ct. W1 —7E 66 (2G 165)
(off Lees Pl.)
Leeside. Barn —5B 4
Leeside Cres. NW11 —6G 29
Leeside Ind. Est. N17 —7D 18
Leeside Rd. N17 —6C 18
Leeside Works. N17 —7D 18
Leeson Ho. Twic —7B 98
Leeson Rd. SE24 —4A 104
Leesons Hill. Chst & St M —3J 145
Leeson's Way. Orp —2K 145
Lees Pde. Uxb —4D 58
Lees Pl. W1 —7E 66 (2G 165)
Lees Rd. Uxb —4D 58
Lees, The. Croy —2B 154
Lee St. E8 —1F 69
Lee Ter. SE3 —3G 107
Lee Valley Ice Centre. —2K 51
Lee Valley Leisure Centre. —1F 19
Lee Valley Technopark. N17 —3G 33
Lee Vw. Enf —1G 7
Leeward Ct. E1 —7G 69
Leeward Gdns. SW19 —5G 119
Leeway. SE8 —5B 88
Leeway Clo. H End —1D 24
Leeways, The. Sutt —6G 149
Leewood Clo. SE12 —6J 107
Lefa Bus. & Ind. Est. Sidc —6D 128
Lefevre Wlk. E3 —1B 70
Leff Ho. NW6 —1G 65
Lefroy Ho. SE1 —2C 86 (7C 168)
(off Southward Bri. Rd.)
Lefroy Rd. W12 —2B 82
Legard Rd. N5 —3B 50
Legatt Rd. SE9 —5B 108
Leggatt Rd. E15 —2E 70
Legge St. SE13 —5E 106
Leghorn Rd. NW10 —2B 64
Leghorn Rd. SE18 —5H 91
Legion Clo. N1 —7A 50
Legion Ct. Mord —6J 137
Legion Rd. Gnfd —1G 61
Legion Ter. E3 —1B 70
Legion Way. N12 —7H 15
Legon Av. Romf —1J 57
Legrace Av. Houn —2B 96
Leicester Av. Mitc —4J 139
Leicester Clo. Wor Pk —4E 148
Leicester Ct. WC2 —2D 166
Leicester Ct. Twic —6D 98
(off Clevedon Rd.)
Leicester Gdns. Ilf —7J 37
Leicester Ho. SW9 —3B 104
(off Loughborough Rd.)
Leicester M. N2 —3C 30
Leicester Pl. WC2 —7H 67 (2D 166)
Leicester Rd. E11 —5K 35
Leicester Rd. N2 —3C 30
Leicester Rd. NW10 —7K 45
Leicester Rd. Barn & New Bar —5E 4
Leicester Rd. Croy —7E 140
Leicester Sq. WC2 —7H 67 (3D 166)
Leicester St. WC2 —7H 67 (2D 166)
Leigham Av. SW16 —3J 121
Leigham Clo. SW16 —3K 121
Leigham Ct. Rd. SW16 —2J 121
Leigham Dri. Iswth —7J 79
Leigham Hall Pde. SW16 —3J 121
(off Streatham High Rd.)
Leigham Va. SW16 & SW2 —3K 121
Leigh Av. Ilf —4B 36
Leigh Clo. N Mald —4J 135
Leigh Clo. Ind. Est. N Mald —4K 135
Leigh Ct. Harr —1J 43
Leigh Cres. New Ad —7D 154
Leigh Gdns. NW10 —2E 64
Leigh Hunt Dri. N14 —1C 16
Leigh Orchard Clo. SW16 —3K 121
Leigh Pl. EC1 —5A 68 (5J 161)
Leigh Pl. Well —2A 110
Leigh Rd. E6 —6E 54
Leigh Rd. E10 —7E 34
Leigh Rd. N5 —4B 50
Leigh Rd. Houn —4H 97
Leigh St. WC1 —3J 67 (2E 160)
Leighton Av. E12 —5E 54
Leighton Av. Pinn —3C 24
Leighton Clo. Edgw —2G 27
Leighton Cres. NW5 —5G 49
Leighton Gdns. NW10 —2D 64
Leighton Gdns. Croy —1B 152
Leighton Gro. NW5 —5G 49
Leighton Ho. SW1 —4H 85 (4D 172)
(off John Islip St.)
Leighton House Art Gallery. —3H 83
Leighton House Mus. —3H 83
Leighton Mans. W14 —6G 83
(off Greyhound Rd.)
Leighton Pl. NW5 —5G 49
Leighton Rd. NW5 —5G 49
Leighton Rd. W13 —2A 80
Leighton Rd. Enf —5A 8
Leighton Rd. Har W —2H 25
Leighton St. Croy —1B 152
Leila Parnell Pl. SE7 —6A 90
Leinster Av. SW14 —3J 99
Leinster Ct. NW6 —3J 65
Leinster Gdns. W2 —6A 66
Leinster Ho. NW6 —3J 65
Leinster M. W2 —7A 66
Leinster Pl. W2 —6A 66
Leinster Rd. N10 —4F 31
Leinster Sq. W2 —6J 65
Leinster Ter. W2 —7A 66
Leisure Way. N12 —7G 15
Leisure West. Felt —2K 113
Leith Clo. NW9 —1K 45
Leithcote Gdns. SW16 —4K 121
Leithcote Path. SW16 —3K 121
Leith Hill. Orp —1K 145
Leith Hill Grn. Orp —1K 145
Leith Mans. W9 —3K 65
(off Grantully Rd.)
Leith Rd. N22 —1B 32
Leith Towers. Sutt —7K 149
Lela Av. Houn —2A 96
Lelita Clo. E8 —1G 69
Lely Ho. N'holt —2B 60
(off Academy Gdns.)
Leman Pas. E1 —6G 69
(off Leman St.)
Leman St. E1 —6F 69 (1K 169)
Lemark Clo. Stan —6H 11
Le May Av. SE12 —3K 125
Lemmon Rd. SE10 —6G 89
Lemna Rd. E11 —7H 35
Lemonwell Dri. SE9 —6G 109
Lemsford Clo. N15 —6G 33
Lemsford Ct. N4 —2C 50
Lemuel St. SW18 —6A 102
Lena Gdns. W6 —3E 82
Lena Kennedy Clo. E4 —6K 19
Lenanton Steps. E14 —2C 88
Len Clifton Ho. SE18 —4D 90
(off Cambridge Barracks Rd.)
Lendal Ter. SW4 —3H 103
Lenelby Rd. Surb —1G 147
Len Freeman Pl. SW6 —6H 83
Lenham Ho. SE1 —3D 86 (7F 169)
(off Long La.)
Lenham Rd. SE12 —4H 107
Lenham Rd. Bexh —6F 93
Lenham Rd. Sutt —4K 149
Lenham Rd. T Hth —2D 140
Lennard Av. W W'ck —2G 155
Lennard Clo. W W'ck —2G 155
Lennard Rd. SE20 & Beck —6K 123
Lennard Rd. Brom —1D 156
Lennard Rd. Croy —1C 152
Lennon Rd. NW2 —5E 46
Lennox Gdns. NW10 —4B 46
Lennox Gdns. SW1 —3D 84 (2E 170)
Lennox Gdns. Croy —4B 152
Lennox Gdns. Ilf —1D 54
Lennox Gdns. M. SW1 —3D 84 (2E 170)
Lennox Ho. Belv —3G 93
(off Picardy St.)
Lennox Ho. Twic —6D 98
(off Clevedon Rd.)
Lennox Rd. E17 —6B 34
Lennox Rd. N4 —2K 49
Lenor Clo. Bexh —4E 110
Lensbury Way. SE2 —3C 92
Lens Rd. E7 —7A 54
Lenthall Ho. SW1 —5G 85 (6B 172)
(off Churchill Gdns.)
Lenthall Rd. E8 —7G 51
Lenthorp Rd. SE10 —4H 89
Lentmead Rd. Brom —3H 125
Lenton Path. SE18 —6H 91

Lenton Ri.—Linksway

Lenton Ri. Rich —3E 98
Lenton Rd. SE18 —4H 91
Len Williams Ct. NW6 —2J 65
Leo Ct. Bren —7D 80
Leof Cres. SE6 —5D 124
Leominster Rd. Mord —6A 138
Leominster Wlk. Mord —6A 138
Leonard Av. Mord —5A 138
Leonard Av. Romf —1K 57
Leonard Ct. WC1 —3D 160
Leonard Ct. Har W —1J 25
Leonard Rd. E4 —6H 19
Leonard Rd. E7 —4J 53
Leonard Rd. N9 —3A 18
Leonard Rd. SW16 —1G 139
Leonard Rd. S'hall —3B 78
Leonard Robbins Path. SE28 —7B 74
(off Tawney Rd.)
Leonard's Rd. E14 —5E 70
Leonard St. E16 —1C 90
Leonard St. EC1 —4D 68 (3F 163)
Leonora Ho. W9 —4A 66
(off Lanark Rd.)
Leontine Clo. SE15 —7G 87
Leopards Ct. EC1 —5J 161
Leopold Av. SW19 —5H 119
Leopold Bldgs. E2 —3F 69 (1J 163)
(off Columbia Rd.)
Leopold M. E9 —1J 69
Leopold Rd. E17 —5C 34
Leopold Rd. N2 —3B 30
Leopold Rd. N18 —5C 18
Leopold Rd. NW10 —7A 46
Leopold Rd. SW19 —4H 119
Leopold Rd. W5 —1F 81
Leopold St. E3 —5B 70
Leopold Ter. SW19 —5H 119
Leo St. SE15 —7H 87
Leo Yd. EC1 —4B 162
Leppoc Rd. SW4 —5H 103
Leroy St. SE1 —4E 86
Lerry Clo. W14 —6H 83
Lerwick Ct. Enf —5K 7
Lescombe Clo. SE23 —3A 124
Lescombe Rd. SE23 —3A 124
Lesley Clo. Bex —7H 111
Leslie Gdns. Sutt —6J 149
Leslie Gro. Croy —1E 152
Leslie Gro. Pl. Croy —1E 152
Leslie Pk. Rd. Croy —1E 152
Leslie Prince Ct. SE5 —7D 86
Leslie Rd. E11 —4E 52
Leslie Rd. E16 —6K 71
Leslie Rd. N2 —3B 30
Leslie Smith Sq. SE18 —6E 90
Lesnes Abbey. —4D 92
Lesney Farm Est. Eri —7K 93
Lesney Pk. Eri —6K 93
Lesney Pk. Rd. Eri —6K 93
Lessar Av. SW4 —6G 103
Lessingham Av. SW17 —4D 120
Lessingham Av. Ilf —3E 36
Lessing St. SE23 —7A 106
Lessington Av. Romf —6J 39
Lessness Av. Bexh —7D 92
Lessness Heath. —5G 93
Lessness Pk. Belv —5F 93
Lessness Rd. Belv —6G 93
Lessness Rd. Mord —6A 138
Lester Av. E15 —4G 71
Leswin Pl. N16 —3F 51
Leswin Rd. N16 —3F 51
Letchford Gdns. NW10 —3C 64
Letchford M. NW10 —3C 64
Letchford Ter. Harr —1F 25
Letchworth Av. Felt —7H 95
Letchworth Clo. Brom —5J 143
Letchworth Dri. Brom —5J 143
Letchworth St. SW17 —4D 120
Lethbridge Clo. SE13 —1E 106
Letterstone Rd. SW6 —7H 83
Lettice St. SW6 —1H 101
Lett Rd. E15 —7F 53
Lettsom St. SE5 —2E 104
Lettsom Wlk. E13 —2J 71
Leucha Rd. E17 —5A 34
Levana Clo. SW19 —1G 119
Levehurst Ho. SE27 —5C 122
Levendale Rd. SE23 —2A 124
Levenhurst Way. SW4 —2J 103
Leven Rd. E14 —5E 70
Leven Way. Hay —6G 59
Leverett St. SW3 —4C 84 (3D 170)
Leverholme Gdns. SE9 —3E 126
Leverington Pl. N1 —2F 163
Leverson St. SW16 —6G 121
Leverstock Ho. SW3 —5C 84 (5D 170)
(off Cale St.)
Lever St. EC1 —3B 68 (2B 162)
Leverton Pl. NW5 —5G 49
Leverton St. NW5 —5G 49
Levett Gdns. Ilf —4K 55
Levett Rd. Bark —6J 55
Levine Gdns. Bark —2D 74
Levison Way. N19 —1H 49
Levita Ho. NW1 —1D 160
(in two parts)
Lewes Clo. N'holt —6E 42
Lewesdon Clo. SW19 —1F 119
Lewes Ho. SE1 —2E 86 (6H 169)
Lewes Ho. SE15 —6G 87
(off Friary Est.)
Lewes Rd. N12 —5H 15
Lewes Rd. Brom —2B 144
Leweston Pl. N16 —7F 33
Lewey Ho. E3 —4B 70
Lewgars Av. NW9 —6J 27
Lewing Clo. Orp —7J 145
Lewin Rd. SW14 —3K 99
Lewin Rd. SW16 —6H 121
Lewin Rd. Bexh —5E 110
Lewis Av. E17 —1C 34
Lewis Clo. N14 —7B 6
Lewis Cres. NW10 —5K 45
Lewis Gdns. N2 —2B 30
Lewis Gro. SE13 —4E 106
Lewisham. —3E 106
Lewisham Bus. Cen. SE14 —6K 87
Lewisham Cen. SE13 —4E 106
Lewisham Crematorium. SE6 —2H 125
Lewisham Heights. SE23 —1J 123
Lewisham High St. SE13 —6D 106
Lewisham Hill. SE13 —2E 106
Lewisham Model Mkt. SE13 —4E 106
(off Lewisham High St.)
Lewisham Pk. SE13 —5E 106
Lewisham Rd. SE13 —1D 106
Lewisham St. SW1 —2H 85 (7D 166)
(in two parts)
Lewisham Way. SE14 & SE4 —1B 106
Lewis Ho. E14 —1E 88
Lewis Rd. Mitc —2B 138
(in two parts)
Lewis Rd. Rich —5D 98
Lewis Rd. Sidc —3C 128
Lewis Rd. S'hall —2C 78
Lewis Rd. Sutt —4K 149
Lewis Rd. Well —3C 110
Lewis Silkin Ho. SE15 —6J 87
(off Lovelinch Clo.)
Lewis St. NW1 —6F 49
(in two parts)
Lewis Way. Dag —6H 57
Lexden Dri. Romf —6B 38
Lexden Rd. W3 —7H 63
Lexden Rd. Mitc —4H 139
Lexham Gdns. W8 —4J 83
Lexham Gdns. M. W8 —3K 83
Lexham Ho. Bark —1H 73
(off St Margarets)
Lexham M. W8 —4J 83
Lexham Wlk. W8 —3K 83
Lexington Apartments. EC1 —4D 68 (3F 163)
Lexington St. W1 —7G 67 (2B 166)
Lexington Way. Barn —4A 4
Lexton Gdns. SW12 —1H 121
Leyborne Av. W13 —2B 80
Leyborne Pk. Rich —1G 99
Leybourne Clo. Brom —6J 143
Leybourne Ho. E14 —6B 70
Leybourne Ho. SE15 —6J 87
Leybourne Rd. E11 —1H 53
Leybourne Rd. NW1 —7F 49
Leybourne Rd. NW9 —5G 27
Leybourne Rd. Uxb —1E 58
Leybourne St. NW1 —7F 49
Leybridge Ct. SE12 —5J 107
Leyburn Clo. E17 —4D 34
Leyburn Gdns. Croy —2E 152
Leyburn Gro. N18 —6B 18
Leyburn Rd. N18 —6B 18
Leydenhatch La. Swan —7J 129
Leyden Mans. N19 —7J 31
Leyden St. E1 —5F 69 (6J 163)
Leydon Clo. SE16 —1K 87
Leyes Rd. E16 —6B 72
Leyfield. Wor Pk —1A 148
Leyland Av. Enf —2F 9
Leyland Gdns. Wfd G —5F 21
Leyland Ho. E14 —7D 70
Leyland Rd. SE12 —5J 107
Leylang Rd. SE14 —7K 87
Leys Av. Dag —1J 75
Leys Clo. Dag —7K 57
(in two parts)
Leys Clo. Harr —5H 25
Leys Ct. SW9 —2A 104
Leysdown Av. Bexh —4J 111
Leysdown Ho. SE17 —5E 86
(off Madron St.)
Leysdown Rd. SE9 —2C 126
Leysfield Rd. W12 —3C 82
Leys Gdns. Barn —5K 5
Leyspring Rd. E11 —1H 53
Leys Rd. E. Enf —1F 9
Leys Rd. W. Enf —1F 9
Leys Sq. N3 —1K 29
Leys, The. N2 —4A 30
Leys, The. Harr —6F 27
Ley St. Ilf —2F 55
Leyswood Dri. Ilf —5J 37
Leythe Rd. W3 —2J 81
Leyton. —3E 52
Leyton Bus. Cen. E10 —2C 52
Leyton Ct. SE23 —1J 123
Leyton Grange Est. E10 —2C 52
Leyton Grn. Rd. E10 —6E 34
Leyton Ind. Village. E17 —7K 33
Leyton Orient F.C. —3D 52
Leyton Pk. Rd. E10 —3E 52
Leyton Rd. E15 —5E 52
Leyton Rd. SW19 —7A 120
Leytonstone. —1G 53
Leytonstone Rd. E15 —4G 53
Leyton Way. E11 —7G 35
Leywick St. E15 —2G 71
Liardet St. SE14 —6A 88
Liberia Rd. N5 —6B 50
Liberty Av. SW19 —1A 138
Liberty Ct. Bark —2B 74
Liberty M. N22 —1B 32
Liberty M. SW12 —6F 103
Liberty St. SW9 —1K 103
Libra Ct. E4 —4H 19
Libra Rd. E13 —2J 71
Library Ct. N17 —3F 33
Library Pde. NW10 —1A 64
(off Craven Pk. Rd.)
Library Pl. E1 —7H 69
Library St. SE1 —2B 86 (7A 168)
Library Way. Twic —7G 97
Lichfield Clo. Barn —3J 5
Lichfield Ct. Rich —4E 98
Lichfield Gdns. Rich —4E 98
Lichfield Gro. N3 —1J 29
Lichfield Rd. E3 —3A 70
Lichfield Rd. E6 —3B 72
Lichfield Rd. N9 —2B 18
Lichfield Rd. NW2 —4G 47
Lichfield Rd. Dag —4B 56
Lichfield Rd. Houn —3A 96
Lichfield Rd. N'wd —3J 23
Lichfield Rd. Rich —1F 99
Lichfield Rd. Wfd G —4B 20
Lichfield Ter. Rich —5E 98
Lickey Ho. W14 —6H 83
(off N. End Rd.)
Lidbury Rd. NW7 —6B 14
Lidcote Gdns. SW9 —2K 103
Liddall Way. W Dray —1B 76
Liddell Clo. Harr —3D 26
Liddell Gdns. NW10 —2E 64
Liddell Rd. NW6 —6J 47
Lidding Rd. Harr —5D 26
Liddington Rd. E15 —1H 71
Liddon Rd. E13 —3K 71
Liddon Rd. Brom —3A 144
Liden Clo. E17 —7B 34
Lidfield Rd. N16 —4D 50
Lidgate Rd. SE15 —7F 87
Lidiard Rd. SW18 —2A 120
Lidlington Pl. NW1 —2G 67
Lido Sq. N17 —2D 32
Lidyard Rd. N19 —1G 49
Lifetimes. —3C 152
(off Katharine St.)
Liffler Rd. SE18 —5J 91
Liffords Pl. SW13 —2B 100
Lifford St. SW15 —4F 101
Light App. NW9 —2B 28
Lightcliffe Rd. N13 —4F 17
Lighter Clo. SE16 —4A 88
Lighterman Ho. E14 —7E 70
Lighterman M. E1 —6K 69
Lightermans Rd. E14 —2C 88
Lighterman's Rd. E14 —2C 88
Lightermans Wlk. SW18 —4J 101
Lightfoot Rd. N8 —5J 31
Light Horse Ct. SW3 —6G 171
Lightley Clo. Wemb —1E 62
Ligonier St. E2 —4F 69 (3J 163)
Lilac Clo. E4 —6G 19
Lilac Ct. E13 —1A 72
Lilac Ct. Tedd —4K 115
Lilac Gdns. W5 —3D 80
Lilac Gdns. Croy —3C 154
Lilac Gdns. Hay —6G 59
Lilac Gdns. Romf —1K 57
Lilac Ho. SE4 —3C 106
Lilac Pl. SE11 —4K 85 (4G 173)
Lilac Pl. W Dray —7B 58
Lilac St. W12 —7C 64
Lilburne Gdns. SE9 —5C 108
Lilburne Rd. SE9 —5C 108
Lilburne Wlk. NW10 —6J 45
Lile Cres. W7 —5J 61
Lilestone Ho. NW8 —4B 66 (3B 158)
(off Frampton St.)
Lilestone St. NW8 —4C 66 (3C 158)
Lilford Ho. SE5 —2C 104
Lilford Rd. SE5 —2B 104
Lilian Barker Clo. SE12 —5J 107
Lilian Board Way. Gnfd —5H 43
Lilian Clo. N16 —3E 50
Lilian Gdns. Wfd G —1K 35
Lilian Rd. SW16 —1G 139
Lillechurch Rd. Dag —6B 56
Lilleshall Rd. Mord —6B 138
Lilley Clo. E1 —1G 87
Lilley La. NW7 —5E 12
Lillian Av. W3 —2G 81
Lillian Rd. SW13 —6C 82
Lillie Mans. W14 —6G 83
(off Lillie Rd.)
Lillie Rd. SW6 —6F 83
Lillieshall Rd. SW4 —3F 103
Lillie Yd. SW6 —6J 83
Lillington Gdns. Est. SW1 —4B 172
Lilliput Av. N'holt —1C 60
Lilliput Ct. SE12 —5K 107
Lilliput Rd. Romf —7K 39
Lily Clo. W14 —4F 83
(in two parts)
Lily Gdns. Wemb —2C 62
Lily Pl. EC1 —5A 68 (5K 161)
Lily Rd. E17 —6C 34
Lilyville Rd. SW6 —1H 101
Limberg Ho. SE8 —4B 88
Limborough Ho. E14 —5C 70
Limbourne Av. Dag —7F 39
Limburg Rd. SW11 —4C 102
Lime Av. W Dray —7B 58
Limeburner La. EC4 —6B 68 (1A 168)
Lime Clo. E1 —1G 87
Lime Clo. Brom —4C 144
Lime Clo. Buck H —2G 21
Lime Clo. Cars —2D 150
Lime Clo. Harr —2A 26
Lime Clo. Pinn —3H 23
Lime Clo. Romf —4J 39
Lime Ct. E11 —2G 53
(off Trinity Clo.)
Lime Ct. E17 —5E 34
Lime Ct. SE9 —2F 127
Lime Ct. Harr —6K 25
Lime Ct. Mitc —2B 138
Lime Cres. Sun —2A 132
Limecroft Clo. Eps —7K 147
Limedene Clo. Pinn —1B 24
Lime Gro. E4 —6G 19
Lime Gro. N20 —1C 14
Lime Gro. W12 —2E 82
Lime Gro. Hay —7F 59
Lime Gro. N Mald —3K 135
Lime Gro. Ruis —6K 23
Lime Gro. Sidc —6K 109
Lime Gro. Twic —6K 97
Limeharbour. E14 —3D 88
Limeharbour Ct. E14 —3D 88
Limehouse. —6B 70
Limehouse Causeway. E14 —7B 70
Limehouse Cut. E14 —5D 70
Limehouse Fields Est. E1 —5A 70
Limehouse Link. E14 —6A 70
Lime Kiln Dri. SE7 —6K 89
Limekiln Pl. SE19 —7F 123
Limerick Clo. SW12 —7G 103
Lime Rd. Eri —3F 93
Lime Rd. Rich —4F 99
Lime Row. Eri —3F 93
Limerston St. SW10 —6A 84 (7A 170)
Limes Av. E11 —4K 35
Limes Av. E12 —3C 54
Limes Av. N12 —4F 15
Limes Av. NW7 —6F 13
Limes Av. NW11 —7G 29
Limes Av. SE20 —7H 123
Limes Av. SW13 —2B 100
Limes Av. Cars —1D 150
Limes Av. Croy —3A 152
Limes Av., The. N11 —5A 16
Limes Clo. N11 —5B 16
Limes Clo. Ashf —5C 112
Limesdale Gdns. Edgw —2J 27
Limes Fld. Rd. SW14 —3A 100
Limesford Rd. SE15 —4K 105
Limes Gdns. SW18 —6J 101
Limes Gro. SE13 —4E 106
Limes Pl. Croy —7D 140
Limes Rd. Beck —2D 142
Limes Rd. Croy —6D 140
Limes, The. SW18 —6J 101
Limes, The. W2 —7J 65
(off Linden Gdns.)
Limes, The. Kes —2C 156
Limes, The. W Mol —4F 133
Limestone Wlk. Eri —2D 92
Lime St. E17 —4A 34
Lime St. EC3 —7E 68 (2G 169)
Lime St. Pas. EC3 —6E 68 (1G 169)
Limes Wlk. SE15 —4J 105
Limes Wlk. W5 —2D 80
Lime Ter. W7 —7J 61
Lime Tree Av. Esh & Th Dit —7H 133
Limetree Clo. SW2 —1K 121
Lime Tree Ct. S Croy —6C 152
Lime Tree Gro. Croy —3B 154
Lime Tree Pl. Mitc —1F 139
Lime Tree Rd. Houn —1F 97
Limetree Ter. SE6 —1B 124
Limetree Ter. Well —3A 110
Limetree Wlk. SW17 —5E 120
Lime Tree Wlk. Bush —1D 10
Lime Tree Wlk. Enf —1H 7
Lime Tree Wlk. W W'ck —4H 155
Lime Wlk. E15 —1G 71
Limewood Clo. E17 —4B 34
Limewood Clo. W13 —6B 62
Limewood Clo. Beck —5E 142
Limewood Ct. Ilf —5D 36
Limewood Rd. Eri —7J 93
Limpsfield Av. SW19 —2F 119
Limpsfield Av. T Hth —5K 139
Linacre Clo. SE15 —3H 105
Linacre Ct. W6 —5F 83
(off Talgarth Rd.)
Linacre Rd. NW2 —6D 46
Linale Ho. N1 —1E 162
Linberry Wlk. SE8 —4B 88
Linchmere Rd. SE12 —7H 107
Lincoln Av. N14 —3B 16
Lincoln Av. SW19 —3F 119
Lincoln Av. Romf —2K 57
Lincoln Av. Twic —2G 115
Lincoln Clo. SE25 —6G 141
Lincoln Clo. Gnfd —1G 61
Lincoln Clo. Harr —5D 24
Lincoln Ct. N16 —7D 32
Lincoln Ct. SE12 —3A 126
Lincoln Cres. Enf —5K 7
Lincoln Gdns. Ilf —7C 36
Lincoln Grn. Rd. Orp —5K 145
Lincoln Ho. SW3 —2D 84 (7E 164)
Lincoln Ho. SW9 & SE5 —7A 86
Lincoln M. NW6 —1H 65
Lincoln M. SE21 —2D 122
Lincoln Rd. E7 —6B 54
Lincoln Rd. E13 —4K 71
Lincoln Rd. E18 —1H 35
Lincoln Rd. N2 —3C 30
Lincoln Rd. SE25 —3H 141
Lincoln Rd. Enf —4K 7
Lincoln Rd. Felt —3D 114
Lincoln Rd. Harr —5D 24
Lincoln Rd. Mitc —5J 139
Lincoln Rd. N Mald —3J 135
Lincoln Rd. N'wd —3H 23
Lincoln Rd. Sidc —5B 128
Lincoln Rd. Wemb —6D 44
Lincoln Rd. Wor Pk —1D 148
Lincoln's Inn. —6K 67 (7H 161)
Lincolns Inn Fields. WC2 —6K 67 (7G 161)
Lincolns, The. NW7 —3G 13
Lincoln St. E11 —2G 53
Lincoln St. SW3 —4D 84 (4E 170)
Lincoln Way. Enf —5C 8
Lincoln Way. Sun —1G 131
Lincombe Rd. Brom —3H 125
Lindal Cres. Enf —4D 6
Lindal Rd. SE4 —5B 106
Lindbergh Rd. Wall —7J 151
Linden Av. NW10 —2F 65
Linden Av. Enf —1B 8
Linden Av. Houn —5F 97
Linden Av. Ruis —1J 41
Linden Av. T Hth —4B 140
Linden Av. Wemb —5F 45
Linden Clo. N14 —6B 6
Linden Clo. Ruis —1J 41
Linden Clo. Stan —5G 11
Linden Clo. Th Dit —7K 133
Linden Ct. W12 —1E 82
Linden Ct. Sidc —4J 127
Linden Cres. Gnfd —6K 43
Linden Cres. King T —2F 135
Linden Cres. Wfd G —6E 20
Lindenfield. Chst —2F 145
Linden Gdns. W2 —7J 65
Linden Gdns. W4 —5A 82
Linden Gdns. Enf —1B 8
Linden Gro. SE15 —3H 105
Linden Gro. SE26 —6J 123
Linden Gro. N Mald —3A 136
Linden Gro. Tedd —5K 115
Linden Ho. SE15 —3H 105
Linden Ho. Hamp —6E 114
Linden Lawns. Wemb —4F 45
Linden Lea. N2 —5A 30
Linden Leas. W W'ck —2F 155
Linden M. N1 —5D 50
Linden M. W2 —7J 65
Linden Pl. Mitc —4C 138
Linden Rd. N10 —4F 31
Linden Rd. N11 —2J 15
Linden Rd. N15 —4C 32
Linden Rd. Hamp —7E 114
Lindens, The. E17 —4D 34
(off Prospect Hill)
Lindens, The. N12 —5G 15
Lindens, The. W4 —1J 99
Lindens, The. New Ad —6E 154
Linden St. Romf —4K 39
Linden Wlk. N19 —2G 49
Linden Way. N14 —6B 6
Linden Way. Shep —5E 130
Lindeth Clo. Stan —6G 11
Lindfield Gdns. NW3 —5K 47
Lindfield Rd. W5 —4C 62
Lindfield Rd. Croy —6F 141
Lindfield St. E14 —6C 70
Lindhill Clo. Enf —2E 8
Lindholme Ct. NW9 —1A 28
(off Pageant Av.)
Lindisfarne Rd. SW20 —7C 118
Lindisfarne Rd. Dag —3C 56
Lindisfarne Way. E9 —4A 52
Lindley Ct. King T —1C 134
Lindley Est. SE15 —7G 87
Lindley Ho. SE15 —7G 87
(off Peckham Pk. Rd.)
Lindley Pl. Kew —1G 99
Lindley Rd. E10 —2E 52
Lindley St. E1 —5J 69
Lindore Rd. SW11 —4D 102
Lindores Rd. Cars —7A 138
Lindo St. SE15 —2J 105
Lind Rd. Sutt —5A 150
Lindrop St. SW6 —2A 102
Lindsay Clo. Chess —7E 146
Lindsay Clo. Stanw —5A 94
Lindsay Dri. Harr —6E 26
Lindsay Dri. Shep —6F 131
Lindsay Rd. Hamp H —4F 115
Lindsay Rd. Wor Pk —2D 148
Lindsay Sq. SW1 —5H 85 (5D 172)
Lindsell St. SE10 —1E 106
Lindsey Clo. Brom —3B 144
Lindsey Clo. Mitc —4J 139
Lindsey Ct. N13 —3F 17
(off Green Lanes)
Lindsey Gdns. Felt —7F 95
Lindsey Ho. W5 —4D 80
Lindsey M. N1 —7C 50
Lindsey Rd. Dag —4C 56
Lindsey St. EC1 —5B 68 (5B 162)
Lind St. SE8 —2C 106
Lindum Rd. Tedd —7C 116
Lindway. SE27 —5B 122
Lindwood Clo. E6 —6D 72
Linfield. WC1 —3K 67 (2G 161)
(off Sidmouth St.)
Linfield Clo. NW4 —4E 28
Linford Christie Stadium. —6C 64
Linford Rd. E17 —3E 34
Linford St. SW8 —1G 103
Lingard Ho. E14 —3E 88
Lingards Rd. SE13 —4E 106
Lingey Clo. Sidc —2K 127
Lingfield Av. King T —4E 134
Lingfield Clo. Enf —6K 7
Lingfield Clo. N'wd —1G 23
Lingfield Ct. N'holt —2E 60
Lingfield Cres. SE9 —4H 109
Lingfield Gdns. N9 —7C 8
Lingfield Ho. SE1 —7B 168
Lingfield Rd. SW19 —5F 119
Lingfield Rd. Wor Pk —3E 148
Lingham St. SW9 —2J 103
Lingholm Way. Barn —5A 4
Ling Rd. E16 —5J 71
Ling Rd. Eri —6J 93
Lingrove Gdns. Buck H —2E 20
Lings Coppice. SE21 —2D 122
Lingwell Rd. SW17 —3C 120
Lingwood. Bexh —2H 111
Lingwood Gdns. Iswth —7J 79
Lingwood Rd. E5 —7G 33
Linhope St. NW1 —4D 66 (3E 158)
Linkenholt Mans. W6 —4B 82
(off Stamford Brook Av.)
Linkfield. Hayes —6J 143
Linkfield. W Mol —3F 133
Linkfield Rd. Iswth —2K 97
Link Ho. E3 —2D 70
Link La. Wall —6H 151
Linklea Clo. NW9 —7F 13
Link Rd. E1 —7G 69 (2K 169)
Link Rd. N8 —3A 32
(in two parts)
Link Rd. N11 —4K 15
Link Rd. Dag —2H 75
Link Rd. Felt —7H 95
Link Rd. Wall —1E 150
Links Av. Mord —4J 137
(in two parts)
Linkscroft Av. Ashf —6D 112
Links Dri. N20 —1D 14
Links Gdns. SW16 —7A 122
Linkside. N12 —6D 14
Linkside. N Mald —2A 136
Linkside Clo. Enf —3E 6
Linkside Gdns. Enf —3E 6
Links Rd. NW2 —2B 46
Links Rd. SW17 —6E 120
Links Rd. W3 —6G 63
Links Rd. Ashf —5A 112
Links Rd. W W'ck —1E 154
Links Rd. Wfd G —5D 20
Links Side. Enf —3E 6
Links, The. E17 —4A 34
Link St. E9 —6J 51
Linksview. N2 —5D 30
(off Gt. North Rd.)
Links Vw. N3 —7C 14
Links Vw. Clo. Stan —7F 11
Links Vw. Ct. Hamp —4H 115
Links Vw. Rd. Croy —3C 154
Links Vw. Rd. Hamp H —5G 115
Linksway. NW4 —2F 29

Links Way—Longland Dri.

Links Way. Beck —6C 142
Links Way. N'wd —1E 22
Links Yd. E1 —5K 163
Link, The. SE9 —3E 126 (off William Barefoot Dri.)
Link, The. W3 —6H 63
Link, The. Enf —1F 9
Link, The. N'holt —5D 42
Link, The. Pinn —7A 24
Link, The. Tedd —6K 115
Link, The. Wemb —1C 44
Linkway. N4 —7C 32
Linkway. SW20 —4D 136
Link Way. Brom —7C 144
Linkway. Dag —4C 56
Link Way. Pinn —1B 24
Linkway. Rich —2B 116
Linkway, The. Barn —6E 4
Linkwood Wlk. NW1 —7H 49
Linley Ct. Sutt —4A 150
Linley Cres. Romf —3H 39
Linley Rd. N17 —2E 32
Linley Sambourne House. —3J 83 (off Stafford Ter.)
Linnell Clo. NW11 —6K 29
Linnell Dri. NW11 —6K 29
Linnell Ho. E1 —5F 69 (5J 163) (off Folgate St.)
Linnell Rd. N18 —5B 18
Linnell Rd. SE5 —2E 104
Linnet Clo. N9 —1E 18
Linnet Clo. SE28 —7C 74
Linnet Clo. Bush —1B 10
Linnet M. SW12 —7E 102
Linnett Clo. E4 —4K 19
Linom Rd. SW4 —4J 103
Linscott Rd. E5 —4J 51
Linsdell Rd. Bark —1G 73
Linsey Ct. E10 —1C 52 (off Grange Rd.)
Linsey St. SE16 —4G 87 (in two parts)
Linslade Clo. Houn —5C 96
Linslade Clo. Pinn —3K 23
Linslade Ho. E2 —1G 69
Linslade Ho. NW8 —4C 66 (3D 158) (off Paveley St.)
Linstead St. NW6 —7J 47
Linstead Way. SW18 —7G 101
Lintaine Clo. SW6 —6G 83
Linthorpe Av. Wemb —6C 44
Linthorpe Rd. N16 —7E 32
Linthorpe Rd. Cockf —3H 5
Linton Clo. SE7 —5A 90
Linton Clo. Mitc —7D 138
Linton Clo. Well —1B 110
Linton Ct. Romf —2K 39
Linton Gdns. E6 —6C 72
Linton Gro. SE27 —5B 122
Linton Ho. E14 —5C 70
Linton Rd. Bark —7G 55
Lintons, The. Bark —7G 55
Linton St. N1 —1C 68 (in two parts)
Lintott Ct. Stanw —6A 94
Linver Rd. SW6 —2J 101
Linwood Clo. SE5 —2F 105
Linwood Cres. Enf —1B 8
Linzee Rd. N8 —4J 31
Lion Av. Twic —1K 115
Lion Clo. SE4 —6C 106
Lion Clo. Shep —3A 130
Lion Ct. N1 —1K 67 (off Copenhagen St.)
Lion Ct. SE1 —1E 86 (5H 169) (off Magdalen St.)
Lionel Gdns. SE9 —5B 108
Lionel M. W10 —5G 65
Lionel Rd. SE9 —5B 108
Lionel Rd. N. Bren —3E 80
Lionel Rd. S. Bren —5F 81
Lion Ga. Gdns. Rich —3F 99
Liongate M. E Mol —3K 133
Lion Mills. E2 —2G 69
Lion Pk. Av. Chess —4G 147
Lion Rd. E6 —5D 72
Lion Rd. N9 —2B 18
Lion Rd. Bexh —4E 110
Lion Rd. Croy —5C 140
Lion Rd. Twic —1K 115
Lions Clo. SE9 —3B 126
Lion Way. Bren —7D 80
Lion Wharf Rd. Iswth —3B 98
Lion Yd. SW4 —4H 103
Liphook Cres. SE23 —7J 105
Lipton Clo. SE28 —7C 74
Lipton Rd. E1 —6K 69
Lisbon Av. Twic —2G 115
Lisbon Clo. E17 —2B 34
Lisburne Rd. NW3 —4D 48
Lisford St. SE15 —1F 105
Lisgar Ter. W14 —4H 83
Liskeard Clo. Chst —6G 127
Liskeard Gdns. SE3 —1J 107
Liskeard Ho. SE11 —5A 86 (5K 173) (off Kennings Way)
Lisle Clo. SW17 —4F 121
Lisle Ct. NW2 —3G 47
Lisle St. WC2 —7H 67 (2D 166)
Lismore. SW19 —5H 119 (off Woodside)
Lismore Cir. NW5 —5E 48
Lismore Clo. Iswth —2A 98
Lismore Ho. SE15 —3H 105
Lismore Rd. N17 —3D 32
Lismore Rd. S Croy —6E 152
Lismore Wlk. N1 —6C 50 (off Clephane Rd.)
Lisselton Ho. NW4 —4F 29 (off Belle Vue Est.)
Lissenden Gdns. NW5 —4E 48 (in two parts)
Lissenden Mans. NW5 —4E 48
Lisson Grn. Est. NW8 —4C 66
Lisson Grove. —5C 66 (5D 158)
Lisson Gro. NW8 & NW1 —4B 66 (3B 158)
Lisson Ho. NW1 —5C 66 (5C 158) (off Lisson St.)
Lisson St. NW1 —5C 66 (5C 158)
Lister Clo. W3 —5K 63
Lister Clo. Mitc —1C 138
Lister Ct. Harr —7B 26
Lister Gdns. N18 —5H 17
Listergate Ct. SW15 —4E 100
Lister Ho. E1 —5G 69
Lister Ho. Hay —4G 77
Lister Ho. Wemb —3J 45 (off Barnhill Rd.)
Lister Lodge. W2 —5J 65 (off Admiral Wlk.)
Lister M. N7 —4K 49
Lister Rd. E11 —1G 53
Lister Wlk. SE28 —7D 74
Liston Rd. N17 —1G 33
Liston Rd. SW4 —3G 103
Liston Way. Wfd G —7F 21
Listowel Clo. SW9 —7A 86
Listowel Rd. Dag —3G 57
Listria Pk. N16 —2E 50
Litchfield Av. E15 —6G 53
Litchfield Av. Mord —7H 137
Litchfield Ct. E17 —6C 34
Litchfield Gdns. NW10 —6C 46
Litchfield Rd. Sutt —4A 150
Litchfield St. WC2 —7H 67 (2D 166)
Litchfield Way. NW11 —5K 29
Lithgow's Rd. H'row A —4G 95
Lithos Rd. NW3 —6K 47
Little Acre. Beck —3C 142
Lit. Albany St. NW1 —2K 159 (in two parts)
Little Angel Theatre. —1B 68
Lit. Argyll St. W1 —6G 67 (1A 166)
Little Benty. W Dray —5A 76
Little Birches. Sidc —2J 127
Lit. Boltons, The. SW5 & SW10 —5K 83
Little Bornes. SE21 —4E 122
Littlebourne. SE13 —7G 107
Little Britain. EC1 —5B 68 (6B 162)
Littlebrook Clo. Croy —6K 141
Little Brownings. SE23 —2H 123
Littlebury Rd. SW4 —3H 103
Lit. Bury St. N9 —1J 17
Lit. Bushey La. Bush —1C 10
Lit. Cedars. N12 —4F 15
Lit. Chester St. SW1 —3F 85 (1J 171)
Little Cloisters. SW1 —3J 85 (1E 172)
Lit. College La. EC4 —7D 68 (off College St.)
Lit. College St. SW1 —3J 85 (1E 172)
Littlecombe. SE7 —6K 89
Littlecombe Clo. SW15 —6F 101
Lit. Common. Stan —3F 11
Littlecote Clo. SW19 —7G 101
Littlecote Pl. Pinn —1C 24
Little Ct. W W'ck —2G 155
Little Cft. SE9 —3E 108
Littledale. SE2 —6A 92
Lit. Dean's Yd. SW1 —1E 172
Little Dimocks. SW12 —2F 121
Lit. Dorrit Ct. SE1 —2C 86 (6D 168)
Little Ealing. —4G 81
Lit. Ealing La. W5 —4C 80
Lit. Edward St. NW1 —3F 67 (1K 159)
Little Elms. Hay —7F 77
Lit. Essex St. WC2 —2J 167
Lit. Ferry Rd. Twic —1B 116
Littlefield Clo. N19 —4G 49
Littlefield Clo. King T —2E 134
Littlefield Rd. Edgw —7D 12
Lit. Friday Rd. E4 —2B 20
Little Gearies. Ilf —4F 37
Lit. George St. SW1 —2J 85 (7E 166)
Little Grange. Gnfd —3A 62
Little Grn. Rich —4D 98
Lit. Green St. NW5 —4F 49
Littlegrove. E Barn —6H 5
Little Halliards. W on T —6J 131
Little Heath. —4B 38
Little Heath. SE7 —6C 90
Little Heath. Chad H —4B 38
Lit. Heath Rd. Bexh —1F 111
Littleheath Rd. S Croy —7H 153
Little Holt. E11 —5J 35
Little Ilford. —4E 54
Lit. Ilford La. E12 —4D 54
Lit. John Rd. W7 —6K 61
Little Larkins. Barn —6B 4
Lit. London Ct. SE1 —2F 87 (7K 169) (off Wolseley St.)
Lit. Marlborough St. W1 —1A 166
Littlemede. SE9 —3D 126
Littlemoor Rd. Ilf —3H 55
Littlemore Rd. SE2 —2A 92
Lit. Moss La. Pinn —2C 24
Lit. Newport St. WC2 —7H 67 (2D 166)
Lit. New St. EC4 —6A 68 (7K 161)
Lit. Orchard Clo. Pinn —2C 24
Lit. Park Dri. Felt —2C 114
Lit. Park Gdns. Enf —3H 7
Lit. Pluckett's Way. Buck H —1G 21
Lit. Portland St. W1 —6G 67 (7K 159)
Little Potters. Bush —1C 10
Lit. Queen's Rd. Tedd —6K 115
Lit. Redlands. Brom —2C 144
Little Rd. Hay —2H 77
Littlers Clo. SW19 —1A 138
Lit. Russell St. WC1 —5J 67 (6E 160)
Lit. St James's St. SW1 —1G 85 (5A 166)
Lit. St Leonard's. SW14 —3J 99
Lit. Sanctuary. SW1 —2H 85 (7D 166)
Lit. Smith St. SW1 —3H 85 (1D 172)
Lit. Somerset St. E1 —6F 69 (1J 169)
Little Stanmore. —1F 27
Littlestone Clo. Beck —6C 124
Little Strand. NW9 —2B 28
Little Thrift. Orp —4G 145
Lit. Titchfield St. W1 —5G 67 (6A 160)
Littleton. —3C 130
Littleton Av. E4 —1C 20
Littleton Common. —7E 112
Littleton Cres. Harr —2K 43
Littleton Ho. SW1 —5G 85 (6A 172) (off Lupus St.)
Littleton La. Shep —6A 130
Littleton Rd. Ashf —7E 112
Littleton Rd. Harr —2K 43
Littleton St. SW18 —2A 120
Lit. Trinity La. EC4 —7C 68 (2D 168)
Little Turnstile. WC1 —5K 67 (6G 161)
Lit. Warkworth Ho. Iswth —2B 98
Littlewood. SE13 —6E 106
Littlewood Clo. W13 —3B 80
Littlewood St. King T —2D 134
Livermere Ct. E8 —1F 69 (off Queensbridge Rd.)
Livermere Rd. E8 —1F 69
Liverpool Gro. SE17 —5C 86
Liverpool Rd. E10 —6E 34
Liverpool Rd. E16 —5G 71
Liverpool Rd. N7 & N1 —5A 50
Liverpool Rd. W5 —2D 80
Liverpool Rd. King T —7G 117
Liverpool Rd. T Hth —3C 140
Liverpool St. EC2 —5E 68 (6G 163)
Livesey Clo. King T —3F 135
Livesey Mus. —6H 87
Livesey Pl. SE15 —6G 87
Livingstone College Towers. E10 —6E 34
Livingstone Ct. E10 —6E 34
Livingstone Ct. W'stone —3K 25
Livingstone Ho. NW10 —7K 45
Livingstone Ho. SE5 —7C 86 (off Wyndam Rd.)
Livingstone Lodge. W2 —5J 65 (off Admiral Wlk.)
Livingstone Mans. W14 —6G 83 (off Queen's Club Gdns.)
Livingstone Pl. E14 —5E 88
Livingstone Rd. E15 —1E 70
Livingstone Rd. E17 —6D 34
Livingstone Rd. N13 —6D 16
Livingstone Rd. SW11 —3B 102
Livingstone Rd. Houn —4G 97
Livingstone Rd. S'hall —7B 60
Livingstone Rd. T Hth —2C 140
Livonia St. W1 —6G 67 (1B 166)
Lizard St. EC1 —3C 68 (2D 162)
Lizban St. SE3 —7K 89
Llandovery Ho. E14 —2E 88
Llanelly Rd. NW2 —2H 47
Llanover Rd. SE18 —6E 90
Llanover Rd. Wemb —3D 44
Llanthony Rd. Mord —5B 138
Llanvanor Rd. NW2 —2H 47
Llewellyn Ct. SE20 —1J 141
Llewellyn St. SE16 —2G 87
Lloyd Av. SW16 —1J 139
Lloyd Baker M. WC1 —3K 67 (off Lloyd Baker St.)
Lloyd Baker St. WC1 —3K 67 (2H 161) (in two parts)
Lloyd Ct. Pinn —5B 24
Lloyd M. Enf —1H 9
Lloyd Pk. Av. Croy —4F 153
Lloyd Pk. Ho. E17 —3C 34
Lloyd Rd. E6 —1D 72
Lloyd Rd. E17 —4K 33
Lloyd Rd. Dag —6F 57
Lloyd Rd. Wor Pk —3E 148
Lloyd's Av. EC3 —6E 68 (1H 169)
Lloyds Building. —6E 68 (1G 169)
Lloyd's Pl. SE3 —2G 107
Lloyd Sq. WC1 —3A 68 (1J 161)
Lloyd's Row. EC1 —3A 68 (2K 161)
Lloyd St. WC1 —3A 68 (1J 161)
Lloyds Way. Beck —5A 142
Lloyds Wharf. SE1 —7K 169
Lloyd Thomas Ct. N22 —7E 16
Loampit Hill. SE13 —2C 106
Loampit Vale. (Junct.) —3E 106
Loampit Va. SE13 —3D 106
Loanda Clo. E8 —1F 69
Loats Rd. SW2 —6J 103
Lobelia Clo. E6 —5C 72
Locarno Rd. W3 —1J 81
Locarno Rd. Gnfd —4H 61
Lochaber Rd. SE13 —4G 107
Lochaline St. W6 —6E 82
Lochan Clo. Hay —4C 60
Lochinvar St. SW12 —7F 103
Lochleven Ho. N2 —2B 30 (off Grange, The)
Lochmere Clo. Eri —6H 93
Lochmore Ho. SW1 —4E 84 (4H 171) (off Cundy St.)
Lochnagar St. E14 —5E 70
Lockbridge Ct. W9 —5J 65 (off Elmfield Way)
Lock Chase. SE3 —3G 107
Lock Clo. S'hall —2G 79
Lockesfield Pl. E14 —5D 88
Lockesley Dri. Orp —6K 145
Lockesley Sq. Surb —6D 134
Locket Rd. Harr —3J 25
Lockfield Av. Brim & Enf —2F 9
Lockgate Clo. E9 —5B 52
Lockhart Clo. N7 —6K 49
Lockhart Clo. Enf —5C 8
Lockhart St. E3 —4B 70
Lockhurst St. E5 —4K 51
Lockie Pl. SE25 —3G 141
Lockier Wlk. Wemb —3D 44
Lockington Rd. SW8 —1F 103
Lockmead Rd. N15 —6G 33
Lockmead Rd. SE13 —3E 106
Lock Rd. Rich —4C 116
Locksbottom. —3E 156
Locksfield Pl. E14 —5D 88
Locksfields. SE17 —4D 86 (off Catesby St.)
Lockside. E14 —7A 70 (off Narrow St.)
Locks La. Mitc —1D 138
Locksley Est. E14 —6B 70
Locksley St. E3 —5B 70
Locksmeade Rd. Rich —4C 116
Lockswood Clo. Barn —4J 5
Lock Vw. Ct. E14 —7A 70
Lockwood Clo. SE26 —4K 123
Lockwood Ho. SE11 —6A 86 (7J 173)
Lockwood Ind. Pk. N17 —3H 33
Lockwood Sq. SE16 —3H 87
Lockwood Way. E17 —2K 33
Lockwood Way. Chess —5G 147
Lockyer Est. SE1 —7F 169 (in two parts)
Lockyer Ho. SW8 —7H 85 (off Wandsworth Rd.)
Lockyer Ho. SW15 —3F 101
Lockyer St. SE1 —2D 86 (7F 169)
Locomotive Dri. Felt —1J 113
Locton Grn. E3 —1B 70
Loddiges Ho. E9 —7J 51
Loddiges Rd. E9 —7J 51
Loder St. SE15 —7J 87
Lodge Av. SW14 —3A 100
Lodge Av. Croy —3A 152
Lodge Av. Dag —1A 74
Lodge Av. Harr —4E 26
Lodge Clo. N18 —5H 17
Lodge Clo. Edgw —6A 12
Lodge Clo. Iswth —1B 98
Lodge Clo. Wall —1E 150
Lodge Ct. Wemb —6E 44
Lodge Dri. N13 —4F 17
Lodge Gdns. Beck —5B 142
Lodge Hill. Ilf —4C 36
Lodge Hill. Well —7B 92
Lodgehill Pk. Clo. Harr —2F 43
Lodge La. N12 —5F 15
Lodge La. Bex —6D 110
Lodge La. New Ad —6C 154
Lodge La. Romf —1G 39
Lodge Pl. Sutt —5K 149
Lodge Rd. NW4 —4E 28
Lodge Rd. NW8 —3B 66 (2B 158)
Lodge Rd. Brom —7K 125
Lodge Rd. Croy —6B 140
Lodge Rd. Wall —5F 151
Lodge Vs. Wfd G —6C 20
Lodge Way. Ashf —2A 112
Lodge Way. Shep —2E 130
Lodore Gdns. NW9 —5A 28
Lodore Grn. Uxb —3A 40
Lodore St. E14 —6E 70
Loft Ho. Pl. Chess —6C 146
Loftie St. SE16 —2G 87
Lofting Rd. N1 —7K 49
Loftus Rd. W12 —1D 82
Logan Clo. Enf —1E 8
Logan Clo. Houn —3D 96
Logan M. W8 —4J 83
Logan Pl. SW5 —4J 83
Logan Rd. N9 —2C 18
Logan Rd. Wemb —2D 44
Loggetts. SE21 —2E 122
Logs Hill. Chst & Brom —7C 126
Logs Hill Clo. Chst —1C 144
Lohmann Ho. SE11 —7J 173
Lois Dri. Shep —5D 130
Lolesworth Clo. E1 —5F 69 (6J 163)
Lollard St. SE11 —4K 85 (3H 173) (in two parts)
Loman St. SE1 —2B 86 (6B 168)
Lomas Clo. Croy —7E 154
Lomas St. E1 —5G 69
Lombard Av. Enf —1D 8
Lombard Av. Ilf —1J 55
Lombard Bus. Cen., The. SW11 —2B 102
Lombard Bus. Pk. Croy —7K 139
Lombard Ct. EC3 —7D 68 (2F 169)
Lombard Ct. W3 —1H 81
Lombard Ct. Romf —4J 39 (off Poplar St.)
Lombard La. EC4 —6A 68 (1K 167)
Lombard Rd. N11 —5A 16
Lombard Rd. SW11 —2B 102
Lombard Rd. SW19 —2K 137
Lombard Roundabout. (Junct.) —7K 139
Lombard St. EC3 —6D 68 (1F 169)
Lombard Trad. Est. SE7 —4K 89
Lombard Wall. SE7 —3K 89 (in two parts)
Lombardy Pl. W2 —7K 65
Lombardy Retail Pk. Hay —7K 59
Lomond Clo. N15 —5E 32
Lomond Clo. Wemb —7F 45
Lomond Gdns. S Croy —7A 154
Lomond Gro. SE5 —7D 86
Lomond Ho. SE5 —7D 86
Loncroft Rd. SE5 —6E 86
Londesborough Rd. N16 —4E 50
Londinium Tower. E1 —7F 69 (2K 169) (off W. Tenter St.)
London Aquarium. —2K 85 (6G 167)
London Arena. —3D 88
London Bri. SE1 & EC4 —1D 86 (4F 169)
London Bri. St. SE1 —1D 86 (5F 169)
London Bri. Wlk. SE1 —1D 86 (4F 169) (off Duke St. Hill)
London Broncos R.L.F.C. —5A 90 (Charlton Athletic Football Ground)
London Butterfly House. —1B 98
London Canal Mus. —2J 67
London City Airport. —1C 90
London City Airport. —1C 90
London City Airport. E16 —7C 72
London Commonwealth Institute. —3J 83
Londonderry Pde. Eri —7K 93
London Dungeon. —5F 169
London Eye. —2J 85 (6G 167)
London Fields E. Side. E8 —7H 51 (in two parts)
London Fields W. Side. E8 —7G 51
London Heathrow Airport. —3D 94
London Heathrow Airport. —3D 94
London-Heathrow Airport. H'row A —2A 94
London Ho. NW8 —2C 66 (off Avenue Rd.)
London Ho. WC1 —4K 67 (3G 161)
London Ind. Est., The. E6 —5E 72
London Ind. Pk., The. E6 —5F 73
London Knights Ice Hockey. —3D 88 (London Arena)
London La. E8 —7H 51
London La. Brom —7H 125
London Leopards Basketball. —3D 88 (London Arena)
London Master Bakers Almshouses. E10 —6D 34
London M. W2 —6B 66 (7B 158)
London Rd. E13 —2J 71
London Rd. SE1 —3B 86 (7A 168)
London Rd. SE23 —1H 123
London Rd. SW17 & Mitc —7D 120
London Rd. SW16 & T Hth —1K 139
London Rd. Bark —7F 55
London Rd. Brom —7H 125
London Rd. Cray —5K 111
London Rd. Enf —3J 7
London Rd. Eps & Ewe —7B 148
London Rd. Harr —2J 43
London Rd. Houn & Iswth —3G 97
London Rd. Iswth & Bren —2K 97
London Rd. Iswth & Twic —5A 98
London Rd. King T —2E 134 (in two parts)
London Rd. Mitc & Wall —7E 138
London Rd. Mord —5J 137
London Rd. Romf —6G 39
London Rd. Stai & Ashf —2A 112
London Rd. Stan —5H 11
London Rd. T Hth —5A 140
London Rd. Wemb —5E 44
London Road Roundabout. (Junct.) —6A 98
London Stile. W4 —5G 81
London St. EC3 —7E 68 (2H 169)
London St. W2 —6B 66 (7A 158)
London Ter. E2 —1K 163
London Towers Basketball. —6G 123 (Crystal Palace National Sports Centre)
London Transport Mus. —7J 67 (2F 167)
London Underwriting Cen. EC3 —7E 68
London Wall. EC2 —5C 68 (6D 162)
London Wall Bldgs. EC2 —6F 163
London Welsh Loins R.U.F.C. —3E 98
London Westland Heliport. —2B 102
London Wharf. E2 —1H 69 (off Wharf Pl.)
London Zoo. —2D 66
Lonesome. —1G 139
Lonesome Way. SW16 —1F 139
Long Acre. WC2 —7J 67 (2E 166)
Longacre Clo. Enf —3H 7
Long Acre Ct. W13 —5A 62
Longacre Pl. Cars —6E 150
Longacre Rd. E17 —1F 35
Longbeach Rd. SW11 —3D 102
Longberrys. NW2 —3H 47
Longboat Row. S'hall —6D 60
Longbridge Ho. Dag —4B 56 (off Gainsborough Rd.)
Longbridge Rd. Bark —6H 55
Longbridge Way. SE13 —5E 106
Longcroft. SE9 —3D 126
Longcrofte Rd. Edgw —7J 11
Long Deacon Rd. E4 —1B 20
Long Ditton. —1C 146
Longdon Wood. Kes —3C 156
Longdown Rd. SE6 —4C 124
Long Dri. W3 —6A 64
Long Dri. Gnfd —1F 61
Long Dri. Ruis —5A 42
Long Dri. W Dray —2A 76
Long Elmes. Harr —1F 25
Longfellow Rd. E17 —6B 34
Longfellow Rd. Wor Pk —2C 148
Longfellow Way. SE1 —4F 87
Long Fld. NW9 —7F 13
Longfield. Brom —1H 143
Longfield Av. E17 —4A 34
Longfield Av. NW7 —7H 13
Longfield Av. W5 —7C 62
Longfield Av. Wall —1E 150
Longfield Av. Wemb —1E 44
Longfield Cres. SE26 —3J 123
Longfield Dri. SW14 —5H 99
Longfield Dri. Mitc —7C 120
Longfield Est. SE1 —4F 87
Longfield Rd. W5 —6C 62
Longfield St. SW18 —7J 101
Longfield Wlk. W5 —6C 62
Longford Av. Felt —6G 95
Longford Av. S'hall —7F 61
Longford Av. Stai —1A 112
Longford Clo. Hamp H —4E 114
Longford Clo. Hanw —3C 114
Longford Clo. Hay —7B 60
Longford Ct. NW4 —4F 29
Longford Ct. Eps —4J 147
Longford Ct. S'hall —1E 78 (off Uxbridge Rd.)
Longford Gdns. Hay —7B 60
Longford Gdns. Sutt —3A 150
Longford Ho. Brom —5F 125 (off Brangbourne Rd.)
Longford Ho. Hamp —4E 114
Longford Rd. Twic —1E 114
Longford St. NW1 —4F 67 (3K 159)
Longford Wlk. SW2 —7A 104
Longford Way. Stai —1A 112
Longhayes Av. Romf —4D 38
Longhayes Ct. Romf —4D 38
Longheath Gdns. Croy —5J 141
Longhedge Ho. SE26 —4G 123 (off High Level Dri.)
Long Hedges. Houn —2E 96
Longhedge St. SW11 —2E 102
Longhill Rd. SE6 —2F 125
Longhook Gdns. N'holt —3K 59
Longhope Clo. SE15 —6E 86
Longhurst Rd. SE13 —5F 107
Longhurst Rd. Croy —6H 141
Longland Ct. SE1 —5G 87
Longland Dri. N20 —3E 14

236 A-Z Big London

Longlands—Lyndhurst Av.

Longlands. —3H 127
Longlands Ct. W11 —7H 65
(off Westbourne Gro.)
Longlands Ct. Sidc —3K 127
Longlands Pk. Cres. Sidc —3J 127
Longlands Rd. Sidc —3J 127
Long La. EC1 —5B 68 (6B 162)
Long La. N3 & N2 —1K 29
Long La. SE1 —2D 86 (7E 168)
Long La. Bexh —7D 92
Long La. Croy —6H 141
Long La. Hil —6D 40
Long La. Stai & Stanw —2B 112
Long La. Uxb —3C 58
Longleat Ho. SW1 —5H 85 (5C 172)
(off Rampayne St.)
Longleat Rd. Enf —5K 7
Longleat Way. Felt —7F 95
Longleigh Ho. SE5 —1E 104
(off Peckham Rd.)
Longleigh La. SE2 & Bexh —6C 92
Long Lents Ho. NW10 —1K 63
Longley Av. Wemb —1F 63
Longley Ct. SW8 —1J 103
Longley Rd. SW17 —6C 120
Longley Rd. Croy —7B 140
Longley Rd. Harr —5G 25
Long Leys. E4 —6J 19
Longley St. SE1 —4G 87
Longley Way. NW2 —3E 46
Longman Ho. E8 —1F 69
(off Haggerston Rd.)
Long Mark Rd. E16 —5B 72
Long Mead. NW9 —1B 28
Longmead. Chst —2E 144
Longmead Dri. Sidc —2D 128
Longmead Ho. SE27 —5C 122
Long Mdw. NW5 —5H 49
Long Mdw. Clo. W W'ck —7E 142
Longmeadow Rd. Sidc —1J 127
Longmead Rd. SW17 —5D 120
Longmead Rd. Hay —7H 59
Longmead Rd. Th Dit —7J 133
Longmoore St. SW1 —4G 85 (4A 172)
Longmore Av. Barn —6F 5
Longnor Est. E1 —3K 69
Longnor Rd. E1 —3K 69
Long Pond Rd. SE3 —1G 107
Longreach Ct. Bark —2H 73
Long Reach Rd. Bark —4K 73
Longridge Ho. SE1 —3C 86
Longridge La. S'hall —6F 61
Longridge Rd. SW5 —4J 83
Longridge Rd. Bark & Dag —7G 55
Longridge Rd. Rich —6F 99
Long Ridges. N10 —3E 30
(off Fortis Grn.)
Long Rd. SW4 —4F 103
Long's Ct. WC2 —3D 166
Longs Ct. Rich —4F 99
Longshaw Rd. E4 —3A 20
Longshore. SE8 —4B 88
Longshott Ct. SW5 —4J 83
(off W. Cromwell Rd.)
Longstaff Cres. SW18 —6J 101
Longstaff Rd. SW18 —6J 101
Longstone Av. NW10 —7B 46
Longstone Rd. SW17 —5F 121
Long St. E2 —3F 69 (1J 163)
Longthornton Rd. SW16 —2G 139
Longton Av. SE26 —4G 123
Longton Gro. SE26 —4H 123
Longview Vs. Romf —1F 39
Longview Way. Romf —1K 39
Longville Rd. SE11 —4B 86
Long Wlk. SE1 —3E 86 (7H 169)
Long Wlk. SE18 —6F 91
Long Wlk. SW13 —2A 100
Long Wlk. N Mald —3J 135
Longwalk Rd. Uxb —1D 76
Long Wall. E15 —3F 71
Longwood Dri. SW15 —6C 100
Longwood Gdns. Ilf —4D 36
Longworth Clo. SE28 —6D 74
Long Yd. WC1 —4K 67 (4G 161)
Loning, The. NW9 —4B 28
Lonsdale Av. E6 —4B 72
Lonsdale Av. Romf —6J 39
Lonsdale Av. Wemb —5E 44
Lonsdale Clo. E6 —4C 72
Lonsdale Clo. SE9 —3B 126
Lonsdale Clo. Edgw —5A 12
Lonsdale Clo. Pinn —1C 24
Lonsdale Clo. Uxb —5E 58
Lonsdale Ct. Surb —7D 134
Lonsdale Cres. Ilf —6F 37
Lonsdale Dri. Enf —4C 6
Lonsdale Gdns. SW16 —4K 139
Lonsdale Ho. W11 —6H 65
Lonsdale M. W11 —6H 65
(off Lonsdale Rd.)
Lonsdale M. Rich —1G 99
Lonsdale Pl. N1 —7A 50
Lonsdale Rd. E11 —6H 35
Lonsdale Rd. NW6 —1H 65
Lonsdale Rd. SE25 —4H 141
Lonsdale Rd. SW13 —1B 100
Lonsdale Rd. W4 —4B 82
Lonsdale Rd. W11 —6H 65
Lonsdale Rd. Bexh —2F 111
Lonsdale Rd. S'hall —3B 78
Lonsdale Sq. N1 —7A 50
Lonsdale Yd. W11 —7J 65
Loobert Rd. N15 —3E 32
Looe Gdns. Ilf —3F 37
Loop Rd. Chst —6G 127
Lopen Rd. N18 —4K 17
Lopez Ho. SW9 —3J 103
Lorac Ct. Sutt —7J 149
Lorain Clo. N12 —4E 14
Loraine Clo. Enf —5D 8
Loraine Ct. Chst —5F 127
Loraine Ho. Wall —4F 151
Loraine Rd. N7 —4K 49
Loraine Rd. W4 —6H 81
Lord Amory Way. E14 —2E 88
Lord Av. Ilf —4D 36
Lord Chancellor Wlk. King T —1J 135
Lordell Pl. SW19 —6E 118
Lorden Wlk. E2 —3G 69 (2K 163)
Lord Gdns. Ilf —4C 36
Lord Hills Bri. W2 —5K 65
Lord Hills Rd. W2 —5K 65
Lord Holland La. SW9 —2A 104
Lord Knyvetts Ct. Stanw —6A 94
Lord Napier Pl. W6 —5C 82
Lord N. St. SW1 —3J 85 (2E 172)
Lord Roberts M. SW6 —7K 83
Lord Robert's Ter. SE18 —5E 90
Lords Clo. SE21 —2C 122
Lords Clo. Felt —2C 114
Lord's Cricket Ground. —3B 66 (2B 158)
Lordship Gro. N16 —2D 50
Lordship La. N22 & N17 —2A 32
Lordship La. SE22 —4F 105
Lordship La. Est. SE21 —7G 105
Lordship Pk. N16 —2C 50
Lordship Pk. M. N16 —2C 50
Lordship Pl. SW3 —6C 84 (7C 170)
Lordship Rd. N16 —1D 50
Lordship Rd. N'holt —7C 42
Lordship Ter. N16 —2D 50
Lordsmead Rd. N17 —1E 32
Lord St. E16 —1C 90
Lords Vw. NW8 —3B 66 (2C 158)
(in two parts)
Lord Warwick St. SE18 —3D 90
Loreburn Ho. N7 —4K 49
Lorenzo St. WC1 —3K 67 (1G 161)
Loretto Gdns. Harr —4E 26
Loring Rd. N20 —2H 15
Loring Rd. SE14 —1A 106
Loring Rd. Isw th —2K 97
Loris Rd. W6 —3E 82
Lorn Ct. SW9 —2A 104
Lorne Av. Croy —7K 141
Lorne Clo. NW8 —3C 66 (2D 158)
Lorne Gdns. E11 —4A 36
Lorne Gdns. W11 —2F 83
Lorne Gdns. Croy —7K 141
Lorne Rd. E7 —4K 53
Lorne Rd. E17 —5C 34
Lorne Rd. N4 —1K 49
Lorne Rd. Harr —2K 25
Lorne Rd. Rich —5F 99
Lorne Ter. N3 —2H 29
Lorn Rd. SW9 —2K 103
Lorraine Ct. NW1 —7F 49
Lorraine Pk. Harr —7D 10
Lorrimore Rd. SE17 —6B 86
Lorrimore Sq. SE17 —6B 86
Lorton Ho. NW6 —1J 65
(off Kilburn Va.)
Lothair Rd. W5 —2D 80
Lothair Rd. N. N4 —6B 32
Lothair Rd. S. N4 —7A 32
Lothbury. EC2 —6D 68 (7E 162)
Lothian Av. Hay —5K 59
Lothian Clo. Wemb —4A 44
Lothian Rd. SW9 —1B 104
Lothrop St. W10 —3G 65
Lots Rd. SW10 —7A 84
Lotus Clo. SE21 —3D 122
Loubet St. SW17 —6D 120
Loudoun Av. Ilf —5F 37
Loudoun Rd. NW8 —1A 66
Loudwater Clo. Sun —4J 131
Loudwater Rd. Sun —4J 131
Loughborough Est. SW9 —3B 104
Loughborough Pk. SW9 —4B 104
Loughborough Rd. SW9 —2A 104
Loughborough St. SE11 —5K 85 (5H 173)
Lough Rd. N7 —5K 49
Loughton Way. Buck H —1G 21
Louisa Ct. Twic —2J 115
Louisa Gdns. E1 —4K 69
Louisa St. E1 —4K 69
Louise Bennett Clo. SE24 —4B 104
Louise Ct. N22 —1A 32
Louise Rd. E15 —6G 53
Louise White Ho. N19 —1H 49
Louis M. N10 —1F 31
Louisville Rd. SW17 —3E 120
Lousada Lodge. N14 —6B 6
(off Avenue Rd.)
Louvaine Rd. SW11 —4B 102
Lovage App. E6 —5C 72
Lovat Clo. NW2 —3B 46
Lovat La. EC3 —7E 68 (3G 169)
(in two parts)
Lovatt Clo. Edgw —6C 12
Lovatt Ct. SW12 —1F 121
Lovatt Dri. Ruis —5J 23
Lovat Wlk. Houn —7C 78
Loveday Rd. W13 —2B 80
Lovegrove St. SE1 —5G 87
Lovegrove Wlk. E14 —1E 88
Lovekyn Clo. King T —2E 134
Lovelace Av. Brom —6E 144
Lovelace Gdns. Bark —4A 56
Lovelace Gdns. Surb —7D 134
Lovelace Grn. SE9 —3D 108
Lovelace Ho. E8 —1F 69
(off Haggerston Rd.)
Lovelace Rd. SE21 —2C 122
Lovelace Rd. Barn —7H 5
Lovelace Rd. Surb —7C 134
Loveland Mans. Bark —7K 55
(off Upney La.)
Love La. EC2 —6C 68 (7D 162)
Love La. N17 —7A 18
Love La. SE18 —4E 90
Love La. SE25 —3H 141
(in two parts)
Love La. Bex —6F 111
Love La. Brom —3K 143
(off Elmfield Rd.)
Love La. Mitc —3C 138
(in two parts)
Love La. Mord —7J 137
Love La. Pinn —2B 24
Love La. Surb —2C 146
Love La. Sutt —6G 149
Love La. Wfd G —6J 21
Lovel Av. Well —2A 110
Lovelinch Clo. SE15 —6J 87
Lovell Ho. E8 —1G 69
(off Shrubland Rd.)
Lovell Pl. SE16 —3A 88
Lovell Rd. Rich —3C 116
Lovell Rd. S'hall —6F 61
Loveridge M. NW6 —6H 47
Loveridge Rd. NW6 —6H 47
Lovers Wlk. NW7 & N3 —6C 14
Lovers Wlk. SE10 —6F 89
Lovers' Wlk. W1 —1E 84 (4G 165)
Lovett Dri. Cars —7A 138
Lovett Way. NW10 —5J 45
Love Wlk. SE5 —2D 104
Lovibonds Av. W Dray —6B 58
Lowbrook Rd. Ilf —4F 55
Low Cross Wood La. SE21 —3F 123
Lowdell Clo. W Dray —6A 58
Lowden Rd. N9 —1C 18
Lowden Rd. SE24 —4B 104
Lowden Rd. S'hall —7C 60
Lowe Av. E16 —5J 71
Lowell Ho. SE5 —7C 86
(off Wyndham Est.)
Lowell St. E14 —6A 70
Lowen Rd. Rain —2K 75
Lwr. Addiscombe Rd. Croy —1E 152
Lwr. Addison Gdns. W14 —2G 83
Lwr. Belgrave St. SW1 —3F 85 (2J 171)
Lwr. Boston Rd. W7 —1J 79
Lwr. Broad St. Dag —1G 75
Lower Camden. Chst —7D 126
Lwr. Church St. Croy —2B 152
Lower Clapton. —4H 51
Lwr. Clapton Rd. E5 —3H 51
Lwr. Clarendon Wlk. W11 —6G 65
(off Clarendon Rd.)
Lwr. Common S. SW15 —3D 100
Lwr. Coombe St. Croy —4C 152
Lwr. Downs Rd. SW20 —1F 137
Lwr. Drayton Pl. Croy —2B 152
Lower Edmonton. —3B 18
Lower Feltham. —3H 113
Lower Fosters. NW4 —5E 28
(off New Brent St.)
Lwr. George St. Rich —5D 98
Lwr. Gravel Rd. Brom —1C 156
Lwr. Green W. Mitc —3C 138
Lwr. Grosvenor Pl. SW1 —3F 85 (1K 171)
Lwr. Grove Rd. Rich —6F 99
Lower Halliford. —7G 131
Lwr. Hall La. E4 —5F 19
(in two parts)
Lwr. Hampton Rd. Sun —3A 132
Lwr. Ham Rd. King T —5D 116
Lower Holloway. —5K 49
Lwr. James St. W1 —7G 67 (2B 166)
Lwr. John St. W1 —7G 67 (2B 166)
Lwr. Kenwood Av. Enf —5D 6
Lwr. Lea Crossing. E14 —7G 71
Lwr. Maidstone Rd. N11 —6B 16
Lower Mall. W6 —5D 82
Lwr. Mardyke Av. Rain —2J 75
Lower Marsh. SE1 —2A 86 (7J 167)
Lwr. Marsh La. King T —4F 135
(in two parts)
Lwr. Merton Ri. NW3 —7C 48
Lower Mill. Eps —7B 148
Lwr. Morden La. Mord —6E 136
Lwr. Mortlake Rd. Rich —4E 98
Lwr. Park Rd. N11 —5B 16
Lwr. Park Rd. Belv —4G 93
Lower Pk. Trad. Est. W3 —4J 63
Lower Place. —2J 63
Lwr. Place Bus. Cen. NW10 —2K 63
Lwr. Queen's Rd. Buck H —2G 21
Lwr. Richmond Rd. SW15 —3D 100
Lwr. Richmond Rd. Rich & SW14 —3G 99
Lower Rd. SE1 —2A 86 (6J 167)
Lower Rd. SE16 & SE8 —2J 87
(in two parts)
Lower Rd. Belv & Eri —3H 93
Lower Rd. Harr —1H 43
Lower Rd. Sutt —4A 150
Lwr. Sloane St. SW1 —4E 84 (4G 171)
Lower Sq. Isw th —3B 98
Lower Sq., The. Sutt —5K 149
Lower Strand. NW9 —2B 28
Lwr. Sunbury Rd. Hamp —2D 132
Lower Sydenham. —4K 123
Lwr. Sydenham Ind. Est. SE26 —5B 124
Lwr. Teddington Rd. King T —1D 134
Lower Ter. NW3 —3A 48
Lwr. Thames St. EC3 —7D 68 (3F 169)
Lowerwood Ct. W11 —6G 65
(off Westbourne Pk. Rd.)
Lwr. Wood Rd. Clay —6B 146
Lowestoft Clo. E5 —2J 51
(off Mt. Pleasant Hill)
Lowestoft M. E16 —2F 91
Loweswater Clo. Wemb —2D 44
Loweswater Ho. E3 —4B 70
Lowfield Rd. NW6 —7J 47
Lowfield Rd. W3 —6H 63
Low Hall Clo. E4 —7J 9
Low Hall La. E17 —6A 34
Low Hall Mnr. Bus. Cen. E17 —6A 34
Lowick Rd. Harr —4J 25
Lowlands Gdns. Romf —5H 39
Lowlands Rd. Harr —6J 25
Lowlands Rd. Pinn —7A 24
Lowman Rd. N7 —4K 49
Lowndes Clo. SW1 —3E 84 (2H 171)
Lowndes Ct. SW1 —3D 84 (1F 171)
Lowndes Ct. W1 —1A 166
Lowndes Pl. SW1 —3E 84 (2G 171)
Lowndes Sq. SW1 —2D 84 (7F 165)
Lowndes St. SW1 —3E 84 (1F 171)
Lownds Ct. Brom —2J 143
Lowood St. E1 —7H 69
Lowry Clo. Eri —4K 93
Lowry Cres. Mitc —2C 138
Lowry Ho. N17 —1F 33
(off Pembury Rd.)
Lowry Rd. Dag —5B 56
Lowshoe La. Romf —1G 39
Lowswood Clo. N'wd —1E 22
Lowther Dri. Enf —4D 6
Lowther Gdns. SW7 —2B 84 (1B 170)
Lowther Hill. SE23 —7A 106
Lowther Ho. E8 —1F 69
Lowther Ho. SW1 —5G 85 (6B 172)
(off Churchill Gdns.)
Lowther Rd. E17 —2A 34
Lowther Rd. N7 —5A 50
Lowther Rd. SW13 —1B 100
Lowther Rd. King T —1F 135
Lowther Rd. Stan —3F 27
Lowth Rd. SE5 —1C 104
Loxford. —5G 55
Loxford Av. E6 —2B 72
Loxford La. Ilf —5G 55
Loxford Rd. Bark —6F 55
Loxford Ter. Bark —6G 55
Loxham Rd. E4 —7J 19
Loxham St. WC1 —3J 67 (2F 161)
Loxley Clo. SE26 —5K 123
Loxley Rd. SW18 —1B 120
Loxley Rd. Hamp —4D 114
Loxton Rd. SE23 —1K 123
Loxwood Clo. Felt —1F 113
Loxwood Rd. N17 —3E 32
Lubbock Ho. E14 —7D 70
Lubbock Rd. Chst —7D 126
Lubbock St. SE14 —7J 87
Lucan Ho. N1 —1D 68
(off Colville Est.)
Lucan Pl. SW3 —4C 84 (4C 170)
Lucan Rd. Barn —3B 4
Lucas Av. E13 —1K 71
Lucas Av. Harr —2E 42
Lucas Ct. SE26 —5A 124
Lucas Ct. SW11 —1E 102
Lucas Rd. NW10 —7C 46
Lucas Rd. SE20 —6J 123
Lucas Sq. NW11 —6J 29
Lucas St. SE8 —1C 106
Lucerne Clo. N13 —3D 16
Lucerne Ct. Eri —3E 92
Lucerne Gro. E17 —4F 35
Lucerne M. W8 —1J 83
Lucerne Rd. N5 —4B 50
Lucerne Rd. Orp —7K 145
Lucerne Rd. T Hth —5B 140
Lucey Rd. SE16 —3G 87
Lucey Way. SE16 —3G 87
(in two parts)
Lucie Av. Ashf —6D 112
Lucien Rd. SW17 —4E 120
Lucien Rd. SW19 —2K 119
Lucinda Ct. Enf —5K 7
Lucknow St. SE18 —7J 91
Lucorn Clo. SE12 —6H 107
Luctons Av. Buck H —1F 21
Lucy Brown Ho. SE1 —1C 86 (5D 168)
(off Park St.)
Lucy Cres. W3 —5J 63
Lucy Gdns. Dag —3E 56
Luddesdon Rd. Eri —7G 93
Ludford Clo. NW9 —2A 28
Ludford Clo. Croy —3B 152
Ludgate B'way. EC4 —6B 68 (1A 168)
Ludgate Cir. EC4 —6B 68 (1A 168)
Ludgate Hill. EC4 —6B 68 (1A 168)
Ludgate Sq. EC4 —6B 68 (1B 168)
Ludham Clo. SE28 —6C 74
Ludlow Clo. Brom —3J 143
Ludlow Clo. Harr —4D 42
Ludlow Ct. W3 —2J 81
Ludlow Rd. W5 —4C 62
Ludlow Rd. Felt —4J 113
Ludlow St. EC1 —4C 68 (3C 162)
Ludlow Way. N2 —4A 30
Ludovick Wlk. SW15 —4A 100
Ludwick M. SE14 —7A 88
Luffield Rd. SE2 —3B 92
Luffman Rd. SE12 —3K 125
Lugard Ho. W12 —1D 82
Lugard Rd. SE15 —2H 105
Lugg App. E12 —3E 54
Luke St. EC2 —4E 68 (3G 163)
Lukin Cres. E4 —3A 20
Lukin St. E1 —6J 69
Lullingstone Clo. Orp —7B 128
Lullingstone Cres. Orp —7A 128
Lullingstone La. SE13 —6F 107
Lullingstone Rd. Belv —6F 93
Lullington Gth. N12 —5C 14
Lullington Gth. Brom —7G 125
Lullington Rd. SE20 —7G 123
Lullington Rd. Dag —7E 56
Lulot Gdns. N19 —2F 49
Lulworth. NW1 —7H 49
(off Wrotham Rd.)
Lulworth. SE17 —5D 86
(off Portland St.)
Lulworth Av. Houn —1F 97
Lulworth Av. Wemb —7C 26
Lulworth Clo. Harr —3D 42
Lulworth Cres. Mitc —2C 138
Lulworth Dri. Pinn —6B 24
Lulworth Gdns. Harr —2C 42
Lulworth Ho. SW8 —7K 85
Lulworth Rd. SE9 —2C 126
Lulworth Rd. SE15 —2H 105
Lulworth Rd. Well —2K 109
Lulworth Waye. Hay —6K 59
Lumen Rd. Wemb —2D 44
Lumiere Building, The. E7 —5B 54
(off Romford Rd.)
Lumley Clo. Belv —5G 93
Lumley Ct. WC2 —7J 67 (3F 167)
Lumley Flats. SW1 —5E 84 (5G 171)
(off Holbein Pl.)
Lumley Gdns. Sutt —5G 149
Lumley Rd. Sutt —5G 149
Lumley St. W1 —6E 66 (1H 165)
Lumsdon. NW8 —1K 65
(off Abbey Rd.)
Luna Rd. T Hth —3C 140
Lund Point. E15 —1E 70
Lundy Dri. Hay —4G 77
Lundy Wlk. N1 —6C 50
Lunham Rd. SE19 —6E 122
Luntley Pl. E1 —5G 69 (6K 163)
Lupin Clo. SW2 —2B 122
Lupin Clo. Croy —1K 153
Lupin Clo. Rush G —2K 57
Lupin Cres. Ilf —6F 55
Lupin Point. SE1 —7K 169
Lupton Clo. SE12 —3K 125
Lupton St. NW5 —4G 49
(in two parts)
Lupus St. SW1 —5F 85 (6K 171)
Luralda Gdns. E14 —5E 88
Lurgan Av. W6 —6F 83
Lurline Gdns. SW11 —1E 102
Luscombe Ct. Short —2G 143
Luscombe Way. SW8 —7J 85
Lushington Ho. W on T —6A 132
Lushington Rd. NW10 —2D 64
Lushington Rd. SE6 —4D 124
Lushington Ter. E8 —5G 51
(off Wayland Av.)
Lutea Ho. Sutt —7A 150
(off Walnut M.)
Luther Clo. Edgw —2D 12
Luther King Clo. E17 —6B 34
Luther Rd. Tedd —5K 115
Luton Ho. E13 —4J 71
(off Luton Rd.)
Luton Pl. SE10 —7E 88
Luton Rd. E13 —4J 71
Luton Rd. E17 —3B 34
Luton Rd. Sidc —3C 128
Luton St. NW8 —4B 66 (4B 158)
Lutton Ter. NW3 —4A 48
(off Heath St.)
Luttrell Av. SW15 —5D 100
Lutwyche Rd. SE6 —2B 124
Lutyens Ho. SW1 —5G 85 (6K 171)
(off Churchill Gdns.)
Luxborough Ho. W1 —5E 66 (5G 159)
(off Luxborough St.)
Luxborough La. Chig —3H 21
Luxborough St. W1 —5E 66 (5G 159)
Luxborough Tower. W1 —5G 159
Luxemburg Gdns. W6 —4F 83
Luxfield Rd. SE9 —1C 126
Luxford St. SE16 —4K 87
Luxmore St. SE4 —1B 106
Luxor St. SE5 —3C 104
Lyall Av. SE21 —4E 122
Lyall M. SW1 —3E 84 (2G 171)
Lyall M. W. SW1 —3E 84 (2G 171)
Lyall St. SW1 —3E 84 (2G 171)
Lyal Rd. E3 —2A 70
Lycett Pl. W12 —2C 82
Lychgate Mnr. Harr —7J 25
Lych Ga. Wlk. Hay —7H 59
(in two parts)
Lyconby Gdns. Croy —7A 142
Lydd Clo. Sidc —3J 127
Lydden Gro. SW18 —7K 101
Lydden Rd. SW18 —7K 101
Lydd Rd. Bexh —7F 93
Lydeard Rd. E6 —7D 54
Lydford. NW1 —1G 67
(off Royal College St.)
Lydford Clo. N16 —5E 50
(off Pellerin Rd.)
Lydford Rd. N15 —5D 32
Lydford Rd. NW2 —6E 46
Lydford Rd. W9 —4H 65
Lydhurst Av. SW2 —2K 121
Lydia Ct. N12 —6F 15
Lydney Clo. SE15 —7E 86
Lydney Clo. SW19 —2G 119
Lydon Rd. SW4 —3G 103
Lydstep Rd. Chst —4E 126
Lyford Rd. SW18 —7B 102
Lyford St. SE7 —4C 90
Lygon Ho. E2 —3F 69 (1K 163)
(off Gosset St.)
Lygon Ho. SW6 —1G 101
(off Fulham Pal. Rd.)
Lygon Pl. SW1 —3F 85 (2J 171)
Lyham Clo. SW2 —6J 103
Lyham Rd. SW2 —5J 103
Lyle Clo. Mitc —7E 138
Lyly Ho. SE1 —3D 86
(off Burbage Clo.)
Lyme Farm Rd. SE12 —4J 107
Lyme Gro. E9 —7J 51
Lymer Av. SE19 —5F 123
Lyme Rd. Well —1B 110
Lymescote Gdns. Sutt —2J 149
Lyme St. NW1 —7G 49
Lyme Ter. NW1 —7G 49
Lyminge Clo. Sidc —4K 127
Lyminge Gdns. SW18 —1C 120
Lymington Av. N22 —2A 32
Lymington Clo. E6 —5D 72
Lymington Clo. SW16 —2H 139
Lymington Ct. Sutt —3K 149
Lymington Dri. Ruis —2F 41
Lymington Gdns. Eps —5B 148
Lymington Rd. NW6 —6K 47
Lymington Rd. Dag —1D 56
Lyminster Clo. Hay —5C 60
Lympne. N17 —2D 32
(off Gloucester Rd.)
Lympstone Gdns. SE15 —7G 87
Lynbridge Gdns. N13 —4G 17
Lynbrook Clo. SE15 —7E 86
Lynbrook Clo. Rain —2K 75
Lynchen Clo. Houn —1K 95
Lynch Wlk. SE8 —6B 88
Lyncott Cres. SW4 —4F 103
Lyncourt. SE3 —2F 107
Lyncroft Av. Pinn —5C 24
Lyncroft Gdns. NW6 —5J 47
Lyncroft Gdns. W13 —2C 80
Lyncroft Gdns. Houn —5G 97
Lyncroft Mans. NW6 —5J 47
Lyndale. NW2 —4H 47
Lyndale. Th Dit —7J 133
Lyndale Av. NW2 —3H 47
Lyndale Clo. SE3 —6H 89
Lynde Ho. SW4 —3H 103
Lynde Ho. W on T —6A 132
Lynden Hyrst. Croy —2F 153
Lyndhurst Av. N12 —6J 15
Lyndhurst Av. NW7 —6F 13
Lyndhurst Av. SW16 —2H 139
Lyndhurst Av. Pinn —1K 23
Lyndhurst Av. S'hall —1F 79
Lyndhurst Av. Sun —3J 131

Lyndhurst Av.—Manbey Gro.

Lyndhurst Av. Surb —1H 147
Lyndhurst Av. Twic —1D 114
Lyndhurst Clo. NW10 —3K 45
Lyndhurst Clo. Bexh —3H 111
Lyndhurst Clo. Croy —3F 153
Lyndhurst Ct. E18 —1J 35
Lyndhurst Ct. NW8 —1B 66
(off Finchley Rd.)
Lyndhurst Ct. Sutt —7J 149
(off Grange Rd.)
Lyndhurst Dri. E10 —7E 34
Lyndhurst Dri. N Mald —7A 136
Lyndhurst Gdns. N3 —1G 29
Lyndhurst Gdns. NW3 —5B 48
Lyndhurst Gdns. Bark —6J 55
Lyndhurst Gdns. Enf —4K 7
Lyndhurst Gdns. Ilf —6H 37
Lyndhurst Gdns. Pinn —1K 23
Lyndhurst Gro. SE15 —2E 104
Lyndhurst Lodge. E14 —4F 89
Lyndhurst Ri. Chig —4K 21
Lyndhurst Rd. E4 —7K 19
Lyndhurst Rd. N18 —4B 18
Lyndhurst Rd. N22 —6F 17
Lyndhurst Rd. NW3 —5B 48
Lyndhurst Rd. Bexh —3H 111
Lyndhurst Rd. Gnfd —4F 61
Lyndhurst Rd. T Hth —4A 140
Lyndhurst Sq. SE15 —1F 105
Lyndhurst Ter. NW3 —5B 48
Lyndhurst Way. SE15 —1F 105
Lyndhurst Way. Sutt —7J 149
Lyndon Av. Sidc —5K 109
Lyndon Av. Wall —3E 150
Lyndon Rd. Belv —4G 93
Lyne Cres. E17 —1B 34
Lynegrove Av. Ashf —5E 112
Lyneham Wlk. E5 —5A 52
Lyneham Wlk. Pinn —3H 23
Lynette Av. SW4 —6F 103
Lynford Clo. Edgw —1J 27
Lynford Gdns. Edgw —3C 12
Lynford Gdns. Ilf —2K 55
Lynford Ter. N9 —1A 18
Lynhurst Cres. Uxb —7E 40
Lynhurst Rd. Uxb —7E 40
Lynmere Rd. Well —2B 110
Lyn M. E3 —3B 70
Lyn M. N16 —4E 50
Lynmouth Av. Enf —6A 8
Lynmouth Av. Mord —6F 137
Lynmouth Dri. Ruis —2K 41
Lynmouth Gdns. Gnfd —1B 62
Lynmouth Gdns. Houn —7B 78
Lynmouth Rd. E17 —6A 34
Lynmouth Rd. N2 —3D 30
Lynmouth Rd. N16 —1F 51
Lynmouth Rd. Gnfd —1B 62
Lynn Clo. Ashf —5F 113
Lynn Clo. Harr —2H 25
Lynne Clo. SE23 —7B 106
Lynnett Rd. Dag —2D 56
Lynne Way. NW10 —6A 46
Lynne Way. N'holt —2B 60
Lynn Ho. SE15 —6H 87
(off Friary Est.)
Lynn M. E11 —2G 53
Lynn Rd. E11 —2G 53
Lynn Rd. SW12 —7F 103
Lynn Rd. Ilf —7H 37
Lynn St. Enf —1J 7
Lynscott Way. S Croy —7B 152
Lynstead Ct. Beck —2A 142
Lynsted Clo. Bexh —5H 111
Lynsted Clo. Brom —2A 144
Lynsted Gdns. SE9 —3B 108
Lynton Av. N12 —4G 15
Lynton Av. NW9 —4B 28
Lynton Av. W13 —6A 62
Lynton Av. Romf —1G 39
Lynton Clo. NW10 —5A 46
Lynton Clo. Chess —4E 146
Lynton Clo. Iswth —4K 97
Lynton Cres. Ilf —6F 37
Lynton Est. SE1 —4G 87
Lynton Gdns. N11 —6C 16
Lynton Gdns. Enf —7K 7
Lynton Grange. N2 —3D 30
Lynton Ho. W2 —6A 66
(off Hallfield Est.)
Lynton Ho. Ilf —2G 55
Lynton Mans. SE1 —3A 86 (1J 173)
(off Kennington Rd.)
Lynton Mead. N20 —3D 14
Lynton Rd. E4 —5J 19
Lynton Rd. N8 —5H 31
(in two parts)
Lynton Rd. NW6 —2H 65
Lynton Rd. SE1 —4F 87
Lynton Rd. W3 —7G 63
Lynton Rd. Croy —6A 140
Lynton Rd. Harr —2C 42
Lynton Rd. N Mald —5K 135
Lynton Ter. W3 —6J 63
Lynton Wlk. Hay —3G 59
Lynwood Clo. E18 —1A 36
Lynwood Clo. Harr —3C 42
Lynwood Ct. King T —2H 135
Lynwood Dri. N'wd —1H 23
Lynwood Dri. Wor Pk —2C 148
Lynwood Gdns. Croy —4K 151
Lynwood Gdns. S'hall —6D 60
Lynwood Gro. N21 —1F 17
Lynwood Gro. Orp —7J 145
Lynwood Rd. SW17 —3D 120
Lynwood Rd. W5 —3D 62
Lynwood Rd. Th Dit —2A 146
Lyon Bus. Pk. Bark —2J 73
Lyon Ct. Ruis —1H 41
Lyon Ho. NW8 —4C 66 (4C 158)
Lyon Ind. Est. NW2 —2D 46
Lyon Meade. Stan —1C 26
Lyon Pk. Av. Wemb —6E 44
(in two parts)
Lyon Rd. SW19 —1A 138
Lyon Rd. Harr —6K 25
Lyonsdown. —5F 5
Lyonsdown Av. New Bar —6F 5
Lyonsdown Rd. Barn & New Bar —6F 5
Lyons Pl. NW8 —4B 66 (4A 158)
Lyon St. N1 —7K 49
Lyons Wlk. W14 —4G 83
Lyon Way. Gnfd —3J 61
Lyric Dri. Gnfd —4F 61
Lyric M. SE26 —4J 123
Lyric Rd. SW13 —1B 100
Lyric Theatre. —4E 82
Lysander Gdns. Surb —6F 135
Lysander Gro. N19 —1H 49
Lysander M. N19 —1G 49
Lysander Rd. Croy —6K 151
Lysander Rd. Ruis —2F 41
Lysias Rd. SW12 —6F 103
Lysia St. SW6 —7F 83
Lysons Wlk. SW15 —4C 100
Lytchet Rd. Brom —7J 125
Lytchet Way. Enf —1D 8
Lytchgate Clo. S Croy —7E 152
Lytcott Dri. W Mol —3D 132
Lytcott Gro. SE22 —5E 104
Lytham Clo. SE28 —6E 74
Lytham Ct. S'hall —6F 61
(off Whitecote Rd.)
Lytham Gro. W5 —3F 63
Lytham St. SE17 —5D 86
Lyttelton Clo. NW3 —7C 48
Lyttelton Ct. N2 —5A 30
Lyttelton Rd. E10 —3D 52
Lyttelton Rd. N2 —5A 30
Lyttleton Ct. Hay —4A 60
(off Dunedin Way)
Lyttleton Rd. N8 —3A 32
Lytton Av. N13 —1F 9
Lytton Clo. N2 —5B 30
Lytton Clo. N'holt —7D 42
Lytton Gdns. Wall —4H 151
Lytton Gro. SW15 —5F 101
Lytton Rd. E11 —7G 35
Lytton Rd. Barn & New Bar —4F 5
Lytton Rd. Pinn —1C 24
Lytton Strachey Path. SE28 —7B 74
Lyveden Rd. SE3 —7K 89
Lyveden Rd. SW17 —6D 120

Mabbett Ho. SE18 —6E 90
(off Nightingale Pl.)
Mabel Evetts Ct. Hay —7K 59
Maberley Cres. SE19 —7G 123
Maberley Rd. SE19 —1F 141
Maberley Rd. Beck —3K 141
Mabledon Ct. WC1 —3H 67 (2D 160)
(off Mabledon Pl.)
Mabledon Pl. NW1 —3H 67 (2D 160)
Mablethorpe Rd. SW6 —7G 83
Mabley St. E9 —5A 52
Mablin Lodge. Buck H —1F 21
Macaret Clo. N20 —7E 4
Macarthur Clo. E7 —6J 53
Macarthur Ter. SE7 —6B 90
Macaulay Ct. SW4 —3F 103
Macaulay Rd. E6 —2B 72
Macaulay Rd. SW4 —3F 103
Macaulay Sq. SW4 —4F 103
Macaulay Way. SE28 —1B 92
McAuley Clo. SE1 —3A 86 (1J 173)
McAuley Clo. SE9 —5F 109
Macauley M. SE13 —1E 106
Macbean St. SE18 —3F 91
Macbeth Ho. N1 —2E 68
Macbeth St. W6 —5D 82
McCall Clo. SW4 —2J 103
McCall Cres. SE7 —5C 90
McCall Ho. N7 —4J 49
McCarthy Rd. Felt —5B 114
M.C.C. Cricket Mus. —3B 66 (2A 158)
Macclesfield Ho. EC1 —3C 68 (2C 162)
(off Central St.)
Macclesfield Rd. EC1 —3C 68 (1C 162)
Macclesfield Rd. SE25 —5H 141
Macclesfield St. W1 —7H 67 (2D 166)
McCoid Way. SE1 —2C 86 (7C 168)
McCrone M. NW3 —6B 48
McCullum Rd. E3 —1B 70
McDermott Clo. SW11 —3C 102
McDermott Rd. SE15 —3G 105
Macdonald Av. Dag —3H 57
Macdonald Rd. E7 —4J 53
Macdonald Rd. E17 —2E 34
Macdonald Rd. N11 —5J 15
Macdonald Rd. N19 —2G 49
McDonough Clo. Chess —4E 146
McDowall Clo. E16 —5H 71
McDowall Rd. SE5 —1C 104
Macduff Rd. SW11 —1E 102
Mace Clo. E1 —1H 87
Mace Gateway. E16 —7J 71
McEntee Av. E17 —1A 34
Mace St. E2 —2K 69
McEwen Way. E15 —1F 71
Macfarlane La. Iswth —6K 79
Macfarlane Rd. W12 —1E 82
Macfarren Pl. NW1 —4E 66 (4H 159)
McGlashon Ho. E1 —4G 69 (4K 163)
(off Hunton St.)
McGrath Rd. E15 —5H 53
McGregor Ct. N1 —1H 163
MacGregor Rd. E16 —5A 72
McGregor Rd. W11 —6H 65
Machell Rd. SE15 —3J 105
McIndoe Ct. N1 —1D 68
(off Sherborne St.)
McIntosh Clo. Romf —3K 39
McIntosh Clo. Wall —7J 151
Macintosh Ho. W1 —5E 66 (5H 159)
(off Beaumont St.)
McIntosh Rd. Romf —3K 39
McIntyre Ct. SE18 —4C 90
(off Prospect Va.)
Mackay Ho. W12 —7D 64
(off White City Est.)
Mackay Rd. SW8 —3F 103
McKay Rd. SW20 —7D 118
McKay Trad. Est. W10 —4G 65
McKellar Clo. Bus H —2B 10
Mackennal St. NW8 —2C 66
Mackenzie Clo. W12 —7D 64
Mackenzie Ho. NW2 —3C 46
Mackenzie Rd. N7 —6K 49
Mackenzie Rd. Beck —2J 141
Mackenzie Wlk. E14 —1C 88
McKerrell Rd. SE15 —1G 105
Mackeson Rd. NW3 —4D 48
Mackie Rd. SW2 —7A 104
McKillop Way. Sidc —7C 128
Mackintosh La. E9 —5K 51
Macklin St. WC2 —6J 67 (7F 161)
Mackonochie Ho. EC1 —5A 68 (5J 161)
(off Baldwins Gdns.)
Mackrow Wlk. E14 —7E 70
Mack's Rd. SE16 —4G 87
Mackworth Ho. NW1 —3G 67 (1A 160)
(off Augustus St.)
Mackworth St. NW1 —3G 67 (1A 160)
Maclaren M. SW15 —4E 100
Maclean Rd. SE23 —6A 106
Macleod Rd. N21 —5D 6
McLeod Rd. SE2 —4B 92
McLeod's M. SW7 —4K 83
Macleod St. SE17 —5C 86
Maclise Ho. SW1 —4J 85 (4E 172)
(off Marsham St.)
Maclise Rd. W14 —3G 83
Macmillan Ct. S Harr —1E 42
McMillan Ho. SE4 —3A 106
(off Arica Rd.)
McMillan St. SE8 —6C 88
McNair Rd. S'hall —3F 79
Macnamara Ho. SW10 —7B 84
(off Worlds End Est.)
McNeil Rd. SE5 —2E 104
McNicol Dri. NW10 —2J 63
Macoma Rd. SE18 —6H 91
Macoma Ter. SE18 —6H 91
Maconochies Rd. E14 —5D 88
Macquarie Way. E14 —4D 88
McRae La. Mitc —7D 138
Macready Ho. W1 —5C 66 (6E 158)
(off Crawford St.)
Macready Pl. N7 —4J 49
Macroom Rd. W9 —3H 65
Macs Ho. E17 —3D 34
Mac's Pl. EC4 —6A 68 (7J 161)
Madame Tussaud's. —4E 66 (4G 159)
Maddams St. E3 —4D 70
Maddison Clo. Tedd —6K 115
Maddocks Clo. Sidc —5E 128
Maddock Way. SE17 —6B 86
Maddox St. W1 —7F 67 (2K 165)
Madeira Av. Brom —7G 125
Madeira Gro. Wfd G —6F 21
Madeira Rd. E11 —1F 53
Madeira Rd. N13 —4G 17
Madeira Rd. SW16 —5J 121
Madeira Rd. Mitc —4D 138
Madeley Rd. W5 —6D 62
Madeline Gro. Ilf —5H 55
Madeline Rd. SE20 —7G 123
Madge Gill Way. E6 —1C 72
(off High St. N.)
Madinah Rd. E8 —6G 51
Madison Cres. Bexh —7C 92
Madison Gdns. Bexh —7C 92
Madison Gdns. Brom —3H 143
Madras Pl. N7 —6A 50
Madras Rd. Ilf —4F 55
Madrid Rd. SW13 —1C 100
Madrigal La. SE5 —7B 86
Madron St. SE17 —5E 86
Mafeking Av. E6 —2C 72
Mafeking Av. Bren —6E 80
Mafeking Av. Ilf —7H 37
Mafeking Rd. E16 —4H 71
Mafeking Rd. N17 —2G 33
Mafeking Rd. Enf —3A 8
Magdala Av. N19 —2G 49
Magdala Rd. Iswth —3A 98
Magdala Rd. S Croy —7D 152
Magdalene Clo. SE15 —2H 105
Magdalene Gdns. E6 —4E 72
Magdalene Rd. Shep —4B 130
Magdalen Pas. E1 —7F 69 (2K 169)
Magdalen Rd. SW18 —1A 120
Magdalen St. SE1 —1E 86 (5G 169)
Magee St. SE11 —6A 86 (7J 173)
Magellan Ct. NW10 —7K 45
(off Stonebridge Pk.)
Magellan Pl. E14 —4C 88
Magnaville Rd. Bus H —1D 10
Magnet Rd. Wemb —2D 44
Magnin Clo. E8 —1G 69
Magnolia Clo. E10 —2C 52
Magnolia Clo. King T —6H 117
Magnolia Ct. N'holt —4C 60
Magnolia Ct. Rich —1H 99
Magnolia Ct. Sutt —7J 149
(off Grange Rd.)
Magnolia Ct. Uxb —6D 40
Magnolia Ct. Wall —5F 151
Magnolia Gdns. E10 —2C 52
Magnolia Gdns. Edgw —4D 12
Magnolia Ho. SE8 —6B 88
Magnolia Lodge. E4 —3J 19
Magnolia Lodge. W8 —3K 83
Magnolia Pl. SW4 —5J 103
Magnolia Pl. W5 —5D 62
Magnolia Pl. Harr —7F 27
Magnolia Rd. W4 —6H 81
Magnolia St. W Dray —4A 76
Magnolia Way. Eps —5J 147
Magpie All. EC4 —6A 68 (1K 167)
Magpie Clo. E7 —5H 53
Magpie Clo. NW9 —2A 28
Magpie Clo. Enf —1B 8
Magpie Hall Clo. Brom —6C 144
Magpie Hall La. Brom —7C 144
Magpie Hall Rd. Bus H —2D 10
Magpie Pl. SE14 —6A 88
Magri Wlk. E1 —5J 69
Maguire Dri. Rich —4C 116
Maguire St. SE1 —2F 87 (6K 169)
Mahatma Gandhi Ind. Est. SE24 —4B 104
Mahlon Av. Ruis —5K 41
Mahogany Clo. SE16 —1A 88
Mahon Clo. Enf —1A 8
Maida Av. E4 —7J 9
Maida Av. W2 —5A 66 (4A 158)
Maida Hill. —4H 65
Maida Rd. Belv —3G 93
Maida Vale. —3K 65
Maida Va. W9 —2K 65 (3A 158)
Maida Way. E4 —7J 9
Maiden Erlegh Av. Bex —1E 128
Maiden La. NW1 —7H 49
Maiden La. SE1 —1C 86 (5D 168)
Maiden La. WC2 —7J 67 (3F 167)
Maiden Pl. N19 —3G 49
Maiden Rd. E15 —7G 53
Maidenstone Hill. SE10 —1E 106
Maids of Honour Row. Rich —5D 98
Maidstone Av. Romf —2J 39
Maidstone Bldgs. SE1 —1C 86 (5D 168)
Maidstone Ho. E14 —6D 70
Maidstone Ho. N11 —6C 16
Maidstone Rd. Sidc —6D 128
Mail Coach Yd. E2 —3E 68 (1H 163)
Main Av. Enf —5A 8
Main Dri. Wemb —3D 44
Mainridge Rd. Chst —4E 126
Main Rd. Sidc —3H 127
Main St. Felt —5B 114
Mais Ho. SE26 —2H 123
Maismore St. SE15 —6G 87
Maisonettes, The. Sutt —5H 149
Maitland Clo. SE10 —7D 88
Maitland Clo. Houn —3D 96
Maitland Ct. W2 —7B 66 (2A 164)
(off Lancaster Ter.)
Maitland Ho. SW1 —6G 85 (7A 172)
(off Churchill Gdns.)
Maitland Pk. Est. NW3 —6D 48
Maitland Pk. Rd. NW3 —6D 48
Maitland Pk. Vs. NW3 —6D 48
Maitland Pl. E5 —4H 51
Maitland Rd. E15 —6H 53
Maitland Rd. SE26 —6K 123
Maitland Yd. W13 —1A 80
Maize Row. E14 —7B 70
Majendie Rd. SE18 —5H 91
Majestic Way. Mitc —2D 138
Major Rd. E15 —5F 53
Major Rd. SE16 —3G 87
Makepeace Av. N6 —2E 48
Makepeace Mans. N6 —2E 48
Makepeace Rd. E11 —4J 35
Makepeace Rd. N'holt —2C 60
Makinen Ho. Buck H —1F 21
Makins St. SW3 —4C 84 (4D 170)
Malabar Ct. W12 —7D 64
(off India Way)
Malabar St. E14 —2C 88
Malam Ct. SE11 —4A 86 (4J 173)
Malam Gdns. E14 —7D 70
Malbrook Rd. SW15 —4D 100
Malcolm Ct. E7 —6H 53
Malcolm Ct. NW4 —6C 28
Malcolm Ct. Stan —5H 11
Malcolm Cres. NW4 —6C 28
Malcolm Dri. Surb —1D 146
Malcolm Gavin Clo. SW17 —2C 120
Malcolm Ho. N1 —2E 68
(off Arden Est.)
Malcolm Pl. E2 —4J 69
Malcolm Rd. E1 —4J 69
Malcolm Rd. SE20 —7J 123
Malcolm Rd. SE25 —6G 141
Malcolm Rd. SW19 —6G 119
Malcolm Rd. Uxb —4B 40
Malcolmson Ho. SW1 —5H 85 (6C 172)
(off Aylesford St.)
Malcolm Way. E11 —5J 35
Malcombs Way. N14 —5B 6
Malden Av. SE25 —4H 141
Malden Av. Gnfd —5J 43
Malden Ct. N4 —6C 32
Malden Ct. N Mald —3D 136
Malden Cres. NW5 —6E 48
Malden Green. —1C 148
Malden Grn. Av. Wor Pk —1B 148
Malden Hill. N Mald —3B 136
Malden Hill Gdns. N Mald —3B 136
Malden Junction. (Junct.) —5B 136
Malden Pk. N Mald —6B 136
Malden Pl. NW5 —5E 48
Malden Rd. NW5 —5D 48
Malden Rd. N Mald & Wor Pk —5A 136
Malden Rd. Sutt —4E 148
Malden Way. N Mald —6K 135
Maldon Clo. E15 —5G 53
Maldon Clo. N1 —1C 68
Maldon Clo. SE5 —3E 104
Maldon Ct. E6 —1E 72
Maldon Ct. Wall —5G 151
Maldon Rd. N9 —3A 18
Maldon Rd. W3 —7J 63
Maldon Rd. Romf —7J 39
Maldon Rd. Wall —5F 151
Maldon Wlk. Wfd G —6F 21
Malet Pl. WC1 —4H 67 (4C 160)
Malet St. WC1 —4H 67 (4C 160)
Maley Av. SE27 —2B 122
Malford Ct. E18 —2J 35
Malford Gro. E18 —4H 35
Malfort Rd. SE5 —3E 104
Malham Clo. N11 —6K 15
Malham Rd. SE23 —1K 123
Malham Ter. N18 —6C 18
(off Dysons Rd.)
Malibu Ct. SE26 —3H 123
Mallams M. SW9 —3B 104
Mallard Clo. E9 —6B 52
Mallard Clo. NW6 —2J 65
Mallard Clo. W7 —2J 79
Mallard Clo. New Bar —6G 5
Mallard Clo. Twic —7E 96
Mallard Ct. E17 —3F 35
Mallard Ho. NW8 —2C 66
(off Barrow Hill Est.)
Mallard Path. SE28 —3H 91
(off Goosander Way)
Mallard Pl. N22 —2K 31
Mallard Pl. Twic —3A 116
Mallards. E11 —7J 35
(off Blake Hall Rd.)
Mallards Rd. Wfd G —7E 20
Mallard Wlk. Beck —5K 141
Mallard Wlk. Sidc —6C 128
Mallard Way. NW9 —7J 27
Mallard Way. Wall —7G 151
Mall Chambers. W8 —1J 83
(off Kensington Mall)
Mallet Dri. N'holt —5D 42
Mallet Rd. SE13 —6F 107
Mall Galleries. —4D 166
Mall Gallery. WC2 —6J 67
(off Thomas Neals Shop. Mall)
Malling Clo. Croy —6J 141
Malling Gdns. Mord —6A 138
Malling Way. Brom —7H 143
Mallinson Rd. SW11 —5C 102
Mallinson Rd. Croy —3H 151
Mallon Gdns. E1 —6F 69
(off Commercial St.)
Mallord St. SW3 —6B 84 (7B 170)
Mallory Clo. SE4 —4A 106
Mallory Gdns. E Barn —7K 5
Mallory St. NW8 —4C 66 (3D 158)
Mallow Clo. Croy —1K 153
Mallow Mead. NW7 —7B 14
Mallows, The. Uxb —3D 40
Mallow St. EC1 —4D 68 (3E 162)
Mall Rd. W6 —5D 82
Mall, The. E15 —7F 53
Mall, The. N14 —3D 16
Mall, The. SW1 —2G 85 (5D 166)
Mall, The. SW14 —5J 99
Mall, The. W5 —7E 62
Mall, The. Bexh —4G 111
Mall, The. Bren —6D 80
Mall, The. Brom —3J 143
Mall, The. Croy —2C 152
Mall, The. Dag —6G 57
Mall, The. Harr —6F 27
Mall, The. Surb —5D 134
Malmains Clo. Beck —4F 143
Malmains Way. Beck —4E 142
Malmesbury Clo. Pinn —4H 23
Malmesbury Rd. E3 —3B 70
Malmesbury Rd. E16 —5G 71
Malmesbury Rd. E18 —1H 35
Malmesbury Rd. Mord —7A 138
Malmesbury Ter. E16 —5H 71
Malmsey Ho. SE11 —5K 85 (5H 173)
Malpas Dri. Pinn —5B 24
Malpas Rd. E8 —5H 51
Malpas Rd. SE4 —2B 106
Malpas Rd. Dag —6D 56
Malsmead Ho. E9 —5B 52
(off Homerton Rd.)
Malta Rd. E10 —1C 52
Malta St. EC1 —4B 68 (3A 162)
Maltby Dri. Enf —1C 8
Maltby Rd. Chess —6G 147
Maltby St. SE1 —2F 87 (7J 169)
Malthouse Dri. W4 —6B 82
Malthouse Dri. Felt —5B 114
Malthouse Pas. SW13 —2B 100
(off Maltings Clo.)
Malthus Path. SE28 —1C 92
Malting Ho. E14 —7B 70
Maltings. W4 —5G 81
Maltings Clo. SW13 —2B 100
Maltings Lodge. W4 —6A 82
(off Corney Reach Way)
Maltings M. Sidc —3A 128
Maltings Pl. SE1 —7H 169
Maltings Pl. SW6 —1K 101
Malting Way. Iswth —3K 97
Malton M. SE18 —6J 91
Malton M. W10 —6G 65
Malton Rd. W10 —6G 65
Malton St. SE18 —6J 91
Maltravers St. WC2 —7K 67 (2H 167)
Malt St. SE1 —6G 87
Malva Clo. SW18 —5K 101
Malvern Av. E4 —7A 20
Malvern Av. Bexh —7E 92
Malvern Av. Harr —3C 42
Malvern Clo. SE20 —2G 141
Malvern Clo. W10 —5H 65
Malvern Clo. Mitc —3G 139
Malvern Clo. Surb —1E 146
Malvern Clo. Uxb —2C 40
Malvern Ct. SW7 —4B 84
(off Onslow Sq.)
Malvern Ct. W12 —2C 82
(off Hadyn Pk. Rd.)
Malvern Ct. Sutt —7J 149
Malvern Dri. Felt —5B 114
Malvern Dri. Ilf —4K 55
Malvern Dri. Wfd G —5F 21
Malvern Gdns. NW2 —2G 47
Malvern Gdns. Harr —4E 26
Malvern Ho. N16 —1F 51
Malvern M. NW6 —3J 65
Malvern Pl. NW6 —3H 65
Malvern Rd. E6 —1C 72
Malvern Rd. E8 —7G 51
Malvern Rd. E11 —2G 53
Malvern Rd. N8 —3A 32
Malvern Rd. N17 —3G 33
Malvern Rd. NW6 —3J 65
(in two parts)
Malvern Rd. Hamp —7E 114
Malvern Rd. Hay —7G 77
Malvern Rd. Surb —2E 146
Malvern Rd. T Hth —4A 140
Malvern Ter. N1 —1A 68
Malvern Ter. N9 —1A 18
Malvern Way. W13 —5B 62
Malwood Rd. SW12 —6F 103
Malyons Rd. SE13 —6D 106
Malyons Ter. SE13 —5D 106
Malyons, The. Shep —6F 131
Managers St. E14 —1E 88
Manatee Pl. Wall —3H 151
Manaton Clo. SE15 —3H 105
Manaton Cres. S'hall —6E 60
Manbey Gro. E15 —6G 53

Maneby Pk. Rd.—Markway

Manbey Pk. Rd. E15 —6G 53
Manbey Rd. E15 —6G 53
Manbey St. E15 —6G 53
Manbre Rd. W6 —6E 82
Manbrough Av. E6 —3E 72
Manchester Dri. W10 —4G 65
Manchester Gro. E14 —5E 88
Manchester Ho. SE17 —5C 86
Manchester M. W1 —6G 159
Manchester Rd. E14 —2E 88
Manchester Rd. N15 —6D 32
Manchester Rd. T Hth —3C 140
Manchester Sq. W1 —6E 66 (7G 159)
Manchester St. W1 —5E 66 (6G 159)
Manchester Way. Dag —4H 57
Manchuria Rd. SW11 —6E 102
Manciple St. SE1 —2D 86 (7E 168)
Mandalay Rd. SW4 —5G 103
Mandarin Ct. NW10 —6K 45
(off Mitchellbrook Way)
Mandarin St. E14 —7C 70
Mandarin Way. Hay —6C 60
Mandela Clo. NW10 —7J 45
Mandela Clo. W12 —7D 64
Mandela Ho. E2 —3F 69 (2J 163)
(off Virginia Rd.)
Mandela Ho. SE5 —2B 104
Mandela Rd. E16 —6J 71
Mandela St. NW1 —1G 67
Mandela St. SW9 —7A 86
(in two parts)
Mandela Way. SE1 —4E 86
Mandeville Clo. SE3 —7H 89
Mandeville Clo. SW19 —7G 119
Mandeville Ct. E4 —5F 19
Mandeville Dri. Surb —1D 146
Mandeville Ho. SE1 —5F 87
(off Rolls Rd.)
Mandeville Ho. SW4 —5G 103
Mandeville M. SW4 —4H 103
Mandeville Pl. W1 —6E 66 (7H 159)
Mandeville Rd. N14 —2A 16
Mandeville Rd. Iswth —2A 98
Mandeville Rd. N'holt —7E 42
Mandeville Rd. Shep —5C 130
Mandeville St. E5 —3A 52
Mandrake Rd. SW17 —3D 120
Mandrake Way. E15 —7G 53
Mandrell Rd. SW2 —5J 103
Manesty Ct. N14 —7C 6
(off Ivy Rd.)
Manette St. W1 —6H 67 (1D 166)
Manfred Rd. SW15 —5H 101
Manger Rd. N7 —6J 49
Mangold Way. Eri —3D 92
Manilla St. E14 —2C 88
Manister Rd. SE2 —3A 92
Manley Ct. N16 —3F 51
Manley Ho. SE11 —4A 86 (5J 173)
Manley St. NW1 —1E 66
Mann Clo. Croy —3C 152
Manneby Prior. N1 —2K 67 (1H 161)
(off Cumming St.)
Manningford Clo. EC1 —3B 68 (1A 162)
Manning Gdns. Harr —7D 26
Manning Pl. Rich —6F 99
Manning Rd. E17 —5A 34
Manning Rd. Dag —6G 57
Manningtree Clo. SW19 —1G 119
Manningtree Rd. Ruis —4K 41
Manningtree St. E1 —6G 69 (7K 163)
Mannin Rd. Romf —7B 38
Mannock Rd. N22 —3B 32
Mann's Clo. Iswth —5K 97
Manns Rd. Edgw —6B 12
Manny Shinwell Ho. SW6 —6H 83
(off Clem Attlee Ct.)
Manoel Rd. Twic —2G 115
Manor Av. E7 —4A 54
Manor Av. SE4 —2B 106
Manor Av. Houn —3B 96
Manor Av. N'holt —7D 42
Manor Brook. SE3 —4J 107
Manor Circus. (Junct.) —3G 99
Manor Clo. E17 —1A 34
Manor Clo. NW7 —5E 12
Manor Clo. NW9 —5H 27
Manor Clo. SE28 —7C 74
Manor Clo. Barn —4B 4
Manor Clo. Cray —4K 111
Manor Clo. Dag —6K 57
Manor Clo. Ruis —1H 41
Manor Clo. Wor Pk —1A 148
Manor Cotts. N2 —2A 30
Manor Cotts. N'wd —1H 23
Manor Cotts. App. N2 —2A 30
Manor Ct. E4 —1B 20
Manor Ct. E10 —1D 52
Manor Ct. N2 —5D 30
(off Aylmer Rd.)
Manor Ct. N14 —2C 16
Manor Ct. N20 —3J 15
(off York Way)
Manor Ct. SW2 —5K 103
Manor Ct. SW6 —1K 101
Manor Ct. SW16 —3J 121
Manor Ct. W3 —4G 81
Manor Ct. Bark —7K 55
Manor Ct. Bexh —4H 111
Manor Ct. Harr —6K 25
Manor Ct. King T —1G 135
Manor Ct. Twic —2G 115
Manor Ct. Wemb —5E 44
Manor Ct. W Mol —4E 132
Manor Ct. W W'ck —1D 154
Manor Ct. Rd. W7 —7J 61
Manor Cres. Surb —6G 135
Manor Deerfield Cotts. NW9 —5B 28
Manor Dene. SE28 —6C 74
Manordene Clo. Th Dit —1A 146
Manordene Rd. SE28 —6D 74
Manor Dri. N14 —1A 16
Manor Dri. N20 —4J 15
Manor Dri. NW7 —5E 12
Manor Dri. Eps —6A 148
Manor Dri. Esh —2A 146
Manor Dri. Felt —5B 114
Manor Dri. Sun —2J 131
Manor Dri. Surb —6F 135
Manor Dri. Wemb —4F 45
Manor Dri. N. N Mald & Wor Pk —7K 135
Manor Dri., The. Wor Pk —1A 148
Manor Est. SE16 —4H 87
Manor Farm Av. Shep —6D 130
Mnr. Farm Clo. Wor Pk —1A 148
Mnr. Farm Ct. E6 —3D 72
(off Holloway Rd.)
Mnr. Farm Dri. E4 —3B 20
Mnr. Farm Rd. SW16 —2A 140
Mnr. Farm Rd. Wemb —2D 62
Manorfield Clo. N19 —4G 49
(off Fulbrook M.)
Manor Fields. SW15 —6F 101
Manorfields Clo. Chst —3K 145
Manor Gdns. N7 —3J 49
Manor Gdns. SW4 —2G 103
(off Larkhall Ri.)
Manor Gdns. SW20 —2H 137
Manor Gdns. W3 —4G 81
Manor Gdns. W4 —5A 82
Manor Gdns. Hamp —7F 115
Manor Gdns. Rich —4F 99
Manor Gdns. Ruis —5A 42
Manor Gdns. S Croy —6F 153
Manor Gdns. Sun —1J 131
Manor Ga. N'holt —7C 42
Manorgate Rd. King T —1G 135
Manor Gro. SE15 —6J 87
Manor Gro. Beck —2D 142
Manor Gro. Rich —4G 99
Mnr. Hall Av. NW4 —2F 29
Mnr. Hall Dri. NW4 —2F 29
Manorhall Gdns. E10 —1C 52
Manor House. (Junct.) —1C 50
Manor Ho. NW1 —5C 66 (5D 158)
(off Marylebone Rd.)
Manor Ho. S'hall —3C 78
Manor Ho. Ct. W9 —4A 66
(off Warrington Gdns.)
Manor Ho. Ct. Shep —7D 130
Manor Ho. Dri. NW6 —7F 47
Manor Ho. Dri. N'wd —1D 22
Manor Ho. Est. Stan —6G 11
Mnr. Ho. Garden. E11 —6K 35
Mnr. Ho. Way. Iswth —3B 98
Manor La. SE13 & SE12 —5G 107
Manor La. Felt —2J 113
Manor La. Hay —6F 77
Manor La. Sun —2J 131
Manor La. Sutt —5A 150
Manor La. Ter. SE13 —4G 107
Manor M. NW6 —2J 65
(off Cambridge Rd., in two parts)
Manor M. SE4 —2B 106
Manor Mt. SE23 —1J 123
Manor Pde. N16 —2F 51
Manor Pde. NW10 —2B 64
(off High St.)
Manor Pde. Harr —6K 25
Manor Park. —4C 54
Manor Pk. SE13 —4F 107
Manor Pk. Chst —2H 145
Manor Pk. Rich —4F 99
Mnr. Park Clo. W W'ck —1D 154
Manor Park Crematorium. E7 —4A 54
Mnr. Park Cres. Edgw —6B 12
Mnr. Park Dri. Harr —3F 25
Mnr. Park Gdns. Edgw —5B 12
Mnr. Park Pde. SE13 —4F 107
(off Lee High Rd.)
Mnr. Park Rd. E12 —4B 54
Mnr. Park Rd. N2 —3A 30
Mnr. Park Rd. NW10 —1B 64
Mnr. Park Rd. Chst —1G 145
Mnr. Park Rd. Sutt —5A 150
Mnr. Park Rd. W W'ck —1D 154
Manor Pl. SE17 —5B 86
Manor Pl. Chst —2H 145
Manor Pl. Felt —1J 113
Manor Pl. Mitc —3G 139
Manor Pl. Sutt —4K 149
Manor Pl. W on T —7H 131
Manor Rd. E10 —7C 34
Manor Rd. E15 & E16 —2G 71
Manor Rd. E17 —2A 34
Manor Rd. N16 —2D 50
Manor Rd. N17 —1G 33
Manor Rd. N22 —6D 16
Manor Rd. SE25 —4G 141
Manor Rd. SW20 —2H 137
Manor Rd. W13 —7A 62
Manor Rd. Ashf —5B 112
Manor Rd. Bark —6K 55
Manor Rd. Barn —4B 4
Manor Rd. Beck —2D 142
Manor Rd. Bex —1H 129
Manor Rd. Chad H —6D 38
Manor Rd. Dag —6J 57
Manor Rd. Dart —4K 111
Manor Rd. E Mol —4H 133
Manor Rd. Enf —2H 7
Manor Rd. Harr —6A 26
Manor Rd. Hay —6J 59
Manor Rd. Mitc —4G 139
Manor Rd. Rich —4G 99
Manor Rd. Ruis —1F 41
Manor Rd. Sidc —3K 127
Manor Rd. Sutt —7H 149
Manor Rd. Tedd —5A 116
(in two parts)
Manor Rd. Twic —2G 115
Manor Rd. Wall —4F 151
Manor Rd. W on T —7H 131
Manor Rd. W W'ck —2D 154
Manor Rd. Wfd G & Chig —6J 21
Manor Rd. Ho. Harr —6A 26
Manor Rd. N. Wall —4F 151
Manorside. Barn —4B 4
Manorside Clo. SE2 —4C 92
Manor Sq. Dag —2C 56
Manor Va. Bren —5C 80
Manor Vw. N3 —2K 29
Manor Way. E4 —4A 20
Manor Way. NW9 —4A 28
Manor Way. SE3 —4H 107
Manor Way. Beck —2C 142
Manor Way. Bex —1G 129
Manor Way. Bexh —3K 111
Manor Way. Brom —6C 144
Manorway. Enf —7K 7
Manor Way. Harr —4F 25
Manor Way. Mitc —3G 139
Manor Way. Orp —4G 145
Manor Way. Rain —4K 75
Manor Way. Ruis —7G 23
Manor Way. S'hall —4B 78
Manor Way. S Croy —6E 152
Manor Way. Wfd G —5F 21
Manor Way. Wor Pk —1A 148
Manor Way Bus. Cen. Rain —5K 75
Manor Waye. Uxb —1A 58
Manor Way, The. Wall —4F 151
Manpreet Ct. E12 —5D 54
Manresa Rd. SW3 —5C 84 (6C 170)
Mansard Beeches. SW17 —5E 120
Mansard Clo. Pinn —3B 24
Manse Clo. Hay —6F 77
Mansel Gro. E17 —1C 34
Mansell Rd. W3 —2K 81
Mansell Rd. Gnfd —5F 61
Mansell St. E1 —6F 69 (1K 169)
Mansel Rd. SW19 —6G 119
Mansergh Clo. SE18 —7C 90
Manse Rd. N16 —3F 51
Manser Rd. Rain —3K 75
Mansfield Av. N15 —4D 32
Mansfield Av. Barn —6J 5
Mansfield Av. Ruis —1K 41
Mansfield Clo. N9 —6B 8
Mansfield Ct. E2 —1F 69
(off Whiston Rd.)
Mansfield Dri. Hay —4G 59
Mansfield Heights. N2 —5D 30
Mansfield Hill. E4 —7J 9
Mansfield M. W1 —5F 67 (6J 159)
Mansfield Pl. NW3 —4A 48
Mansfield Pl. S Croy —6D 152
Mansfield Rd. E11 —6K 35
Mansfield Rd. E17 —4B 34
Mansfield Rd. NW3 —5D 48
Mansfield Rd. W3 —4H 63
Mansfield Rd. Chess —5C 146
Mansfield Rd. Ilf —2E 54
Mansfield Rd. S Croy —6D 152
Mansfield St. W1 —5F 67 (6J 159)
Mansford St. E2 —2G 69
Manship Rd. Mitc —7E 120
Mansion Clo. SW9 —1A 104
(in two parts)
Mansion Gdns. NW3 —3K 47
Mansion House. —6D 68
Mansion Ho. Pl. EC4 —6D 68 (1E 168)
Mansion Ho. St. EC2 —1E 168
Mansions, The. SW5 —5K 83
Manson M. SW7 —4B 84 (4A 170)
Manson Pl. SW7 —4B 84 (4A 170)
Mansted Gdns. Romf —7C 38
Manston. N17 —2D 32
(off Adams Rd.)
Manston. NW1 —7G 49
(off Agar Gro.)
Manston Av. S'hall —4E 78
Manston Clo. SE20 —1J 141
Manstone Rd. NW2 —5G 47
Manston Gro. King T —5D 116
Manston Ho. W14 —3G 83
(off Russell Rd.)
Manthorp Rd. SE18 —5G 91
Mantilla Rd. SW17 —4E 120
Mantle Rd. SE4 —3A 106
Mantlet Clo. SW16 —7G 121
Mantle Way. E15 —7G 53
Manton Av. W7 —2K 79
Manton Clo. Hay —7G 59
Manton Rd. SE2 —4A 92
Mantua St. SW11 —3B 102
Mantus Clo. E1 —4J 69
Mantus Rd. E1 —4J 69
Manus Way. N20 —2F 15
Manville Gdns. SW17 —3F 121
Manville Rd. SW17 —2E 120
Manwood Rd. SE4 —5B 106
Manwood St. E16 —1D 90
Manygate La. Shep —7E 130
Manygate Mobile Home Est. Shep —6F 131
(off Mitre Clo.)
Manygates. SW12 —2F 121
Mapesbury Rd. NW2 —7G 47
Mapeshill Pl. NW2 —6E 46
Mapes Ho. NW6 —7G 47
Mape St. E2 —3H 69
(in two parts)
Maple Av. E4 —5G 19
Maple Av. W3 —1A 82
Maple Av. Harr —2F 43
Maple Av. W Dray —7A 58
Maple Clo. N16 —6G 33
Maple Clo. SW4 —6H 103
Maple Clo. Buck H —3G 21
Maple Clo. Hamp —6C 114
Maple Clo. Hay —3B 60
Maple Clo. Mitc —1F 139
Maple Clo. Orp —5H 145
Maple Clo. Ruis —6K 23
Maple Ct. E6 —5E 72
Maple Ct. SE6 —1D 124
Maple Ct. N Mald —3K 135
Maple Cres. Sidc —6A 110
Maplecroft Clo. E6 —6B 72
Mapledale Av. Croy —2G 153
Mapledene. Chst —5G 127
Mapledene Est. E8 —7G 51
Mapledene Rd. E8 —7F 51
Maple Gdns. Edgw —7F 13
Maple Gdns. Stai —2A 112
Maple Gro. NW9 —7J 27
Maple Gro. W5 —3D 80
Maple Gro. Bren —7B 80
Maple Gro. S'hall —5D 60
Maple Gro. Bus. Cen. Houn —4A 96
Maple Ho. E17 —3D 34
Maple Ho. SE8 —7B 88
(off Idonia St.)
Maplehurst. Brom —2G 143
Maplehurst Clo. King T —4E 134
Maple Ind. Est. Felt —3J 113
Maple Leaf Dri. Sidc —1K 127
Mapleleafe Gdns. Ilf —3F 37
Maple Leaf Sq. SE16 —2K 87
Maple Lodge. W8 —3K 83
Maple M. NW6 —2K 65
Maple M. SW16 —5K 121
Maple Pl. N17 —7B 18
Maple Pl. W1 —4G 67 (5B 160)
Maple Pl. W Dray —1A 76
Maple Rd. E11 —6G 35
Maple Rd. SE20 —1H 141
Maple Rd. Hay —3A 60
Maple Rd. Surb —6D 134
Maples Pl. E1 —5H 69
Maplestead Rd. SW2 —7K 103
Maplestead Rd. Dag —1B 74
Maples, The. Clay —7A 146
Maples, The. Tedd —7C 116
Maple St. W1 —5G 67 (5A 160)
Maple St. Romf —4J 39
Maplethorpe Rd. T Hth —4A 140
Mapleton Clo. Brom —6J 143
Mapleton Cres. SW18 —6K 101
Mapleton Cres. Enf —1D 8
Mapleton Rd. E4 —3K 19
Mapleton Rd. SW18 —6J 101
Mapleton Rd. Enf —2C 8
Maple Wlk. W10 —3F 65
Maple Way. Felt —3J 113
Maplin Clo. N21 —6E 6
Maplin Ho. SE2 —2D 92
(off Wolvercote Rd.)
Maplin Rd. E16 —6J 71
Maplin St. E3 —3B 70
Mapperley Clo. E11 —6H 35
Mapperley Dri. Wfd G —7B 20
Maran Way. Eri —3D 92
Marathon Ho. NW1 —5D 66 (5E 158)
(off Marylebone Rd.)
Marban Rd. W9 —3H 65
Marble Arch. (Junct.) —7D 66
Marble Arch. —2F 165
Marble Arch. W1 —7D 66 (2E 164)
Marble Clo. W3 —1H 81
Marble Dri. NW2 —1F 47
Marble Hill Clo. Twic —7B 98
Marble Hill Gdns. Twic —7B 98
Marble Hill House. —7C 98
Marble Ho. W9 —4H 65
Marble Quay. E1 —1G 87 (4K 169)
Marbrook Ct. SE12 —3A 126
March. NW9 —1B 28
(off Concourse, The)
Marchant Ct. SE1 —5F 87
Marchant Rd. E11 —2F 53
Marchant St. SE14 —6A 88
Marchbank Rd. W14 —6H 83
March Ct. SW15 —4D 100
Marchmont Rd. Rich —5F 99
Marchmont Rd. Wall —7G 151
Marchmont St. WC1 —4J 67 (3E 160)
March Rd. Twic —7A 98
Marchside Clo. Houn —1B 96
Marchwood Clo. SE5 —7E 86
Marchwood Cres. W5 —6C 62
Marcia Rd. SE1 —4E 86
Marcilly Rd. SW18 —5B 102
Marcon Ct. E8 —5H 51
(off Amhurst Rd.)
Marconi Rd. E10 —1C 52
Marconi Way. S'hall —6F 61
Marcon Pl. E8 —5H 51
Marco Polo Ho. SW8 —7F 85
Marco Rd. W6 —3E 82
Marcourt Lawns. W5 —4E 62
Marcus Ct. E15 —1G 71
Marcus Garvey M. SE22 —6H 105
Marcus Garvey Way. SE24 —4A 104
Marcus St. E15 —1G 71
Marcus St. SW18 —6K 101
Marcus Ter. SW18 —6K 101
Mardale Ct. NW7 —7H 13
Mardale Dri. NW9 —5K 27
Mardell Rd. Croy —5K 141
Marden Av. Brom —6H 143
Marden Ct. SE8 —6B 88
Marden Cres. Bex —5J 111
Marden Cres. Croy —6K 139
Marden Ho. E5 —5H 51
Marden Rd. N17 —2E 32
Marden Rd. Croy —6K 139
Marden Sq. SE16 —3H 87
Marder Rd. W13 —2A 80
Mardyke Ho. SE17 —4D 86
(off Mason St.)
Marechal Niel Av. Sidc —3H 127
Marechal Niel Pde. Sidc —3H 127
(off Main Rd.)
Maresby Ho. E4 —2J 19
Mares Fld. Croy —3E 152
Maresfield Gdns. NW3 —5A 48
Mare St. E8 —5H 51
Marfleet Clo. Cars —2C 150
Margaret Av. E4 —6J 9
Margaret Bondfield Av. Bark —7A 56
Margaret Bldgs. N16 —1F 51
Margaret Ct. W1 —7A 160
Margaret Ct. Barn —4G 5
Margaret Gardner Dri. SE9 —2D 126
Margaret Herbison Ho. SW6 —6H 83
(off Clem Attlee Ct.)
Margaret Ingram Clo. SW6 —6H 83
Margaret Lockwood Clo. King T —4F 135
Margaret Rd. N16 —1F 51
Margaret Rd. Barn —4G 5
Margaret Rd. Bex —6D 110
Margaret St. W1 —6F 67 (7K 159)
Margaretta Ter. SW3 —6C 84 (7C 170)
Margaretting Rd. E12 —1A 54
Margaret Way. Ilf —6C 36
Margaret White Ho. NW1 —3H 67 (1D 160)
(off Chalton St.)
Margate Rd. SW2 —5J 103
Margery Fry Ct. N7 —3J 49
Margery Pk. Rd. E7 —6J 53
Margery Rd. Dag —3D 56
Margery St. WC1 —3A 68 (2J 161)
Margin Dri. SW19 —5F 119
Margravine Gdns. W6 —5F 83
Margravine Rd. W6 —5F 83
Marham Dri. NW9 —1A 28
Marham Gdns. SW18 —1C 120
Marham Gdns. Mord —6A 138
Maria Clo. SE1 —4H 87
Marian Clo. Hay —4B 60
Marian Ct. E9 —5J 51
Marian Ct. Sutt —5K 149
Marian Pl. E2 —2H 69
Marian Rd. SW16 —1G 139
Marian Sq. E2 —2H 69
Marian St. E2 —2H 69
Marian Way. NW10 —7B 46
Maria Ter. E1 —5K 69
Maria Theresa Clo. N Mald —5K 135
Maribor. SE10 —7E 88
(off Burney St.)
Maricas Av. Harr —1H 25
Marie Lloyd Gdns. N19 —7J 31
Marie Lloyd Ho. N1 —2D 68 (1E 162)
(off Murray Gro.)
Marie Lloyd Wlk. E8 —6F 51
Mariette Way. Wall —7J 151
Marigold All. SE1 —3A 168
Marigold Clo. S'hall —7C 60
Marigold Rd. N17 —7D 18
Marigold St. SE16 —2H 87
Marigold Way. Croy —1K 153
Marina App. Hay —5C 60
Marina Av. N Mald —5D 136
Marina Clo. Brom —3J 143
Marina Dri. Well —2J 109
Marina Gdns. Romf —5H 39
Marina Way. Tedd —7D 116
Marine Dri. SE18 —4D 90
Marinefield Rd. SW6 —2K 101
Marinel Ho. SE5 —7C 86
Mariner Gdns. Rich —3C 116
Mariner Rd. E12 —4E 54
Mariners M. E14 —4F 89
Marine St. SE16 —3G 87 (7K 169)
Marion Av. Shep —5D 130
Marion Gro. Wfd G —5B 20
Marion Rd. NW7 —5H 13
Marion Rd. T Hth —5C 140
Marischal Rd. SE13 —3F 107
Maritime Ind. Est. SE7 —4K 89
Maritime Quay. E14 —5C 88
Maritime St. E3 —4B 70
Marius Pas. SW17 —2E 120
Marius Rd. SW17 —2E 120
Marjorie Gro. SW11 —4D 102
Marjorie M. E1 —6K 69
Mark Av. E4 —6J 9
Mark Clo. Bexh —1E 110
Mark Clo. S'hall —7F 61
Marke Clo. Kes —4C 156
Market Cen., The. S'hall —4K 77
Market Chambers. Enf —3J 7
(off Church St.)
Market Ct. W1 —7A 160
Market Entrance. SW8 —7G 85
Market Est. N7 —6J 49
Market Hill. SE18 —3E 90
Market La. Edgw —1J 27
Market Link. Romf —4K 39
Market M. W1 —1F 85 (5J 165)
Market Pde. E10 —6E 34
(off High Rd. Leyton)
Market Pde. E17 —3B 34
(off Forest Rd.)
Market Pde. N9 —2B 18
(off Winchester Rd.)
Market Pde. Felt —3C 114
Market Pde. Sidc —4B 128
Market Pavilion. E10 —3C 52
Market Pl. N2 —3C 30
Market Pl. NW11 —4K 29
Market Pl. SE16 —4G 87
(in two parts)
Market Pl. W1 —6G 67 (7A 160)
Market Pl. W3 —1J 81
Market Pl. Bexh —4G 111
Market Pl. Bren —7C 80
Market Pl. Enf —3J 7
Market Pl. King T —2D 134
Market Pl. S'hall —1D 78
Market Rd. N7 —6J 49
Market Rd. Rich —3G 99
Market Row. SW9 —4A 104
Market Sq. E14 —6D 70
Market Sq. Brom —2J 143
Market Sq., The. N9 —2C 18
(off Plevna Rd.)
Market St. E6 —2D 72
Market St. SE18 —4E 90
Market Ter. Bren —6E 80
(off Albany Rd.)
Market, The. Sutt —1A 150
Market Way. E14 —6D 70
Market Way. Wemb —5E 44
Markfield Gdns. E4 —7J 9
Markfield Rd. N15 —4G 33
Markham Ho. Dag —3G 57
(off Uvedale Rd.)
Markham Pl. SW3 —5D 84 (5E 170)
Markham Sq. SW3 —5D 84 (5E 170)
Markham St. SW3 —5C 84 (5D 170)
Markhole Clo. Hamp —7D 114
Markhouse Av. E17 —6A 34
Markhouse Pas. E17 —6B 34
(off Markhouse Rd.)
Markhouse Rd. E17 —6B 34
Mark La. EC3 —7E 68 (2H 169)
Mark Lodge. Cockf —4H 5
(off Edgeworth Rd.)
Markmanor Av. E17 —7A 34
Mark Rd. N22 —1B 32
Marksbury Av. Rich —3G 99
Marks Gate. —1E 38
Marks Lodge. Romf —5K 39
Mark Sq. EC2 —4E 68 (3G 163)
Marks Rd. Romf —5J 39
Markstone Ho. SE1 —2B 86 (7A 168)
(off Lancaster St.)
Mark St. E15 —7G 53
Mark St. EC2 —4E 68 (3G 163)
Markway. Sun —2A 132

Markwell Clo.—Mayfield Rd.

Markwell Clo. SE26 —4H 123
Markyate Rd. Dag —5B 56
Marlands Rd. Ilf —3C 36
Marlborough Av. E8 —1G 69
(in three parts)
Marlborough Av. N14 —3B 16
Marlborough Av. Edgw —3C 12
Marlborough Av. Ruis —6E 22
Marlborough Clo. N20 —3J 15
Marlborough Clo. SE17 —4C 86
Marlborough Clo. SW19 —6C 120
Marlborough Clo. Orp —6K 145
Marlborough Ct. W1 —2A 166
Marlborough Ct. W8 —4J 83
(off Pembroke Rd.)
Marlborough Ct. Buck H —2F 21
Marlborough Ct. Enf —5K 7
Marlborough Ct. Harr —4H 25
Marlborough Ct. N'wd —1H 23
Marlborough Ct. Wall —7G 151
Marlborough Cres. W4 —3K 81
Marlborough Dri. Ilf —3C 36
Marlborough Flats. SW3 —3D 170
Marlborough Gdns. N20 —3J 15
Marlborough Gdns. Surb —7D 134
Marlborough Gro. SE1 —5G 87
Marlborough Hill. NW8 —2A 66
Marlborough Hill. Harr —4H 25
Marlborough House. —1G 85 (5B 166)
Marlborough Ho. NW1 —4F 67 (3K 159)
(off Osnaburgh St.)
Marlborough La. SE7 —6A 90
Marlborough Mans. NW6 —5K 47
(off Canon Hill)
Marlborough M. SW2 —4K 103
Marlborough Pde. Uxb —4D 58
Marlborough Pk. Av. Sidc —7A 110
Marlborough Pl. NW8 —2A 66
Marlborough Rd. E4 —6J 19
Marlborough Rd. E7 —7A 54
Marlborough Rd. E15 —4G 53
Marlborough Rd. E18 —2J 35
Marlborough Rd. N9 —1A 18
Marlborough Rd. N19 —2H 49
(in two parts)
Marlborough Rd. N22 —7D 16
Marlborough Rd. SW1 —1G 85 (5B 166)
Marlborough Rd. SW19 —6C 120
Marlborough Rd. W4 —5J 81
Marlborough Rd. W5 —2D 80
Marlborough Rd. Ashf —5A 112
Marlborough Rd. Bexh —3D 110
Marlborough Rd. Brom —4A 144
Marlborough Rd. Dag —4B 56
Marlborough Rd. Felt —2B 114
Marlborough Rd. Hamp —6E 114
Marlborough Rd. Iswth —1B 98
Marlborough Rd. Rich —6F 99
Marlborough Rd. Romf —4G 39
Marlborough Rd. S'hall —3A 78
Marlborough Rd. S Croy —7C 152
Marlborough Rd. Sutt —3J 149
Marlborough Rd. Uxb —4D 58
Marlborough St. SW3 —4C 84 (4C 170)
Marlborough Yd. N19 —2H 49
Marlbury. NW8 —1K 65
(off Abbey Rd.)
Marler Rd. SE23 —1A 124
Marley Av. Bexh —6D 92
Marley Clo. N15 —4B 32
Marley Clo. Gnfd —3E 60
Marley Ho. W11 —7F 65
(off St Ann's Rd.)
Marley Wlk. NW2 —5E 46
Marlin Clo. Sun —6G 113
Marlingdene Clo. Hamp —6E 114
Marlings Clo. Chst —4J 145
Marlings Pk. Av. Chst —4J 145
Marlins Clo. Sutt —5A 150
Marloes Clo. Wemb —4D 44
Marloes Rd. W8 —3K 83
Marlow Clo. SE20 —3H 141
Marlow Ct. N14 —7B 6
Marlow Ct. NW6 —7F 47
Marlow Ct. NW9 —3B 28
Marlow Cres. Twic —6K 97
Marlow Dri. Sutt —2F 149
Marlowe Clo. Chst —6H 127
Marlowe Clo. Ilf —1G 37
Marlowe Ct. SW3 —4C 84 (4D 170)
Marlowe Gdns. SE9 —6E 108
Marlowe Rd. E17 —4E 34
Marlowe Sq. Mitc —4G 139
Marlowes, The. NW8 —1B 66
Marlowes, The. Dart —4K 111
Marlowe Way. Croy —2J 151
Marlow Gdns. Hay —3F 77
Marlow Ho. E2 —3F 69 (2J 163)
(off Calvert Av.)
Marlow Ho. SE1 —3F 87 (7J 169)
(off Maltby St.)
Marlow Ho. W2 —6K 65
(off Hallfield Est.)
Marlow Ho. Tedd —4A 116
Marlow Rd. E6 —3D 72
Marlow Rd. SE20 —3H 141
Marlow Rd. S'hall —3D 78
Marlow Way. SE16 —2K 87
Marl Rd. SW18 —4A 102
Marlton St. SE10 —5H 89
Marlwood Clo. Sidc —2J 127
Marmadon Rd. SE18 —4K 91
Marmion App. E4 —4H 19
Marmion Av. E4 —4G 19
Marmion Clo. E4 —4G 19
Marmion M. SW11 —3E 102
Marmion Rd. SW11 —4E 102
Marmont Rd. SE15 —1G 105
Marmora Rd. SE22 —6J 105
Marmot Rd. Houn —3B 96
Marne Av. N11 —4A 16
Marne Av. Well —3A 110
Marnell Way. Houn —3B 96
Marne St. W10 —3G 65
Marney Rd. SW11 —4E 102
Marnfield Cres. SW2 —1A 122
Marnham Av. NW2 —4G 47
Marnham Ct. Wemb —5C 44
Marnham Cres. Gnfd —3F 61
Marnock Ho. SE17 —5D 86
(off Brandon St.)
Marnock Rd. SE4 —5B 106
Maroon Ho. E14 —5A 70
Maroon St. E14 —5A 70
Maroons Way. SE6 —4C 124
Marqueen Towers. SW16 —7J 121
Marquess Rd. N1 —6D 50
Marquess Rd. N. N1 —6C 50
Marquess Rd. S. N1 —6C 50
Marquis Clo. Wemb —7F 45
Marquis Ct. N4 —1K 49
(off Marquis Rd.)
Marquis Ct. Bark —5J 55
Marquis Rd. N4 —1K 49
Marquis Rd. N22 —6E 16
Marquis Rd. NW1 —6H 49
Marrabon Clo. Sidc —1A 128
Marrick Clo. SW15 —4C 100
Marrick Ho. NW6 —1K 65
(off Mortimer Cres.)
Marriett Ho. SE6 —4E 124
Marrilyne Av. Enf —1G 9
Marriner Ct. Hay —7G 59
(off Barra Hall Rd.)
Marriott Clo. Felt —6F 95
Marriott Rd. E15 —1G 71
Marriott Rd. N4 —1K 49
Marriott Rd. N10 —1D 30
Marriott Rd. Barn —3A 4
Marriotts Clo. NW9 —6B 28
Marryat Ho. SW1 —5G 85 (6A 172)
(off Churchill Gdns.)
Marryat Pl. SW19 —4G 119
Marryat Rd. SW19 —5F 119
Marryat Sq. SW6 —1G 101
Marsala Rd. SE13 —4D 106
Marsden Rd. N9 —2C 18
Marsden Rd. SE15 —3F 105
Marsden St. NW5 —6E 48
(in two parts)
Marshall Clo. SW18 —6A 102
Marshall Clo. Harr —7H 25
Marshall Clo. Houn —5D 96
Marshall Dri. Hay —5H 59
Marshall Est. NW7 —4H 13
Marshall Ho. N1 —2D 68
(off Cranston Est.)
Marshall Ho. NW6 —2H 65
(off Albert Rd.)
Marshall Ho. SE1 —3E 86
(off Page's Wlk.)
Marshall Ho. SE17 —5D 86
Marshall Path. SE28 —7B 74
Marshall Rd. N17 —1D 32
Marshalls Clo. N11 —4A 16
Marshalls Dri. Romf —3K 39
Marshalls Gro. SE18 —4C 90
Marshall's Pl. SE16 —3F 87
Marshalls Rd. Romf —4K 39
Marshall's Rd. Sutt —4K 149
Marshall St. W1 —6G 67 (1B 166)
Marshall Way. E10 —3D 52
Marshalsea Rd. SE1 —2C 86 (6D 168)
Marsham Clo. Chst —5F 127
Marsham Ct. SW1 —3D 172
Marsham Ho. Eri —2D 92
Marsham St. SW1 —3H 85 (2D 172)
Marsh Av. Mitc —2D 138
Marshbrook Clo. SE3 —3B 108
Marsh Cen., The. E1 —6F 69 (7K 163)
(off Whitechapel High St.)
Marsh Clo. NW7 —3G 13
Marsh Ct. E8 —7F 51
(off St Philip's Rd.)
Marsh Dri. NW9 —6B 28
Marsh Farm Rd. Twic —1K 115
Marshfield St. E14 —3E 88
Marsh Ga. Bus. Cen. E15 —1E 70
Marshgate La. E15 —7D 52
Marshgate Path. SE28 —3G 91
Marshgate Trad. Est. E15 —7D 52
Marsh Grn. Rd. Dag —1G 75
Marsh Hall. Wemb —3E 45
Marsh Hill. E9 —5A 52
Marsh Ho. SW1 —5H 85 (6D 172)
(off Aylesford St.)
Marsh Ho. SW8 —1G 103
Marsh La. E10 —2B 52
Marsh La. N17 —1H 33
Marsh La. NW7 —3F 13
Marsh La. Stan —5H 11
Marsh Rd. Pinn —4C 24
Marsh Rd. Wemb —3D 62
Marshside Clo. N9 —1D 18
Marsh St. E14 —4D 88
Marsh Wall. E14 —1C 88
Marsh Way. Rain —3K 75
(in two parts)
Marshwood Ho. NW6 —1J 65
(off Kilburn Va.)
Marsland Clo. SE17 —5B 86
Marsom Ho. N1 —2D 68 (1E 162)
(off Provost Est.)
Marston Av. Chess —6E 146
Marston Av. Dag —2G 57
Marston Clo. NW6 —7A 48
Marston Clo. Dag —3G 57
Marston Ho. SW9 —2A 104
Marston Rd. Ilf —1C 36
Marston Rd. Tedd —5B 116
Marston Way. SE19 —7B 122
Marsworth Av. Pinn —1B 24
Marsworth Clo. Hay —5C 60
Marsworth Ho. E2 —1G 69
(off Whiston Rd.)
Martaban Rd. N16 —2F 51
Martello St. E8 —7H 51
Martello Ter. E8 —7H 51
Martell Rd. SE21 —3D 122
Martel Pl. E8 —6F 51
Marten Rd. E17 —2C 34
Martens Av. Bexh —4H 111
Martens Clo. Bexh —4J 111
Martha Ct. E2 —2H 69
Martham Clo. SE28 —7D 74
Martha Rd. E15 —6G 53
Martha St. E1 —6J 69
Marthorne Cres. Harr —2H 25
Martin Bowes Rd. SE9 —3D 108
Martinbridge Trad. Est. Enf —5B 8
Martin Clo. N9 —1E 18
Martin Clo. Uxb —2A 58
Martin Ct. E14 —2E 88
Martin Cres. Croy —1A 152
Martindale. SW14 —5J 99
Martindale Av. E16 —7J 71
Martindale Ho. E14 —7D 70
Martin Dale Ind. Est. Enf —3C 8
Martindale Rd. SW12 —7F 103
Martindale Rd. Houn —3C 96
Martin Dene. Bexh —5F 111
Martin Dri. N'holt —5D 42
Martineau Est. E1 —7J 69
Martineau Ho. SW1 —5G 85 (6A 172)
(off Churchill Gdns.)
Martineau M. N5 —4B 50
Martineau Rd. N5 —4B 50
Martingale Clo. Sun —4J 131
Martingales Clo. Rich —3D 116
Martin Gdns. Dag —4C 56
Martin Gro. Mord —3J 137
Martin Ho. SE1 —3C 86
Martin Ho. SW8 —7J 85
(off Wyvil Rd.)
Martin La. EC4 —7D 68 (2F 169)
(in two parts)
Martin Ri. Bexh —5F 111
Martin Rd. Dag —4C 56
Martins Clo. W W'ck —1F 155
Martins Mt. New Bar —4D 4
Martin's Rd. Brom —2G 143
Martins, The. Wemb —3F 45
Martin St. SE28 —1J 91
Martins Wlk. N10 —1E 30
Martin Way. SW20 & Mord —2G 137
Martlesham. N17 —2E 32
(off Adams Rd.)
Martlet Gro. N'holt —3B 60
Martlett Ct. WC2 —6J 67 (1F 167)
Martley Dri. Ilf —5F 37
Martock Clo. Harr —4A 26
Martock Gdns. N11 —5J 15
Marton Clo. SE6 —3C 124
Marton Rd. N16 —2E 50
Martynside. NW9 —1B 28
Martys Yd. NW3 —4B 48
Marvell Av. Hay —5J 59
Marvell Ho. SE5 —7D 86
(off Camberwell Rd.)
Marvels Clo. SE12 —2K 125
Marvels La. SE12 —2K 125
Marville Rd. SW6 —7H 83
Marvin St. E8 —6H 51
Marwell Clo. W W'ck —2H 155
Marwood Clo. Well —3B 110
Mary Adelaide Clo. SW15 —4A 118
Mary Ann Gdns. SE8 —6C 88
Maryatt Av. Harr —2F 43
Mary Bank. SE18 —4D 90
Mary Clo. Stan —4F 27
Mary Datchelor Clo. SE5 —1D 104
Maryfield Clo. Bex —3K 129
Mary Flux Ct. SW5 —5K 83
(off Bramham Gdns.)
Mary Grn. NW8 —1K 65
Mary Jones Ho. E14 —7C 70
Maryland Ho. E15 —6G 53
(off Manbey Pk. Rd.)
Maryland Ind. Est. E15 —5G 53
(off Maryland Rd.)
Maryland Pk. E15 —5G 53
Maryland Point. E15 —6G 53
(off Grove, The)
Maryland Rd. E15 —5F 53
Maryland Rd. N22 —6E 16
Maryland Rd. T Hth —1B 140
Maryland Sq. E15 —5G 53
Marylands Rd. W9 —4J 65
Maryland St. E15 —5F 53
Maryland Wlk. N1 —1C 68
(off Popham St.)
Maryland Way. Sun —2J 131
Mary Lawrenson Pl. SE3 —7J 89
Marylebone. —5E 66 (5H 159)
Marylebone Flyover. (Junct.) —5C 66
Marylebone Fly-Over. W2 & NW8 —5B 66 (6B 158)
Marylebone High St. W1 —5E 66 (5H 159)
Marylebone La. W1 —5E 66 (6H 159)
Marylebone M. W1 —5F 67 (6J 159)
Marylebone Pas. W1 —6G 67 (7B 160)
Marylebone Rd. NW1 —5C 66 (5D 158)
Marylebone St. W1 —5E 66 (6H 159)
Marylee Way. SE11 —4K 85 (4H 173)
Mary Macarthur Ho. W6 —6G 83
Mary Macarthur Ho. Dag —3G 57
(off Wythenshawe Rd.)
Maryon Gro. SE7 —4C 90
Maryon M. NW3 —4C 48
Maryon Rd. SE7 —4C 90
Maryon Rd. SE18 —4C 90
Mary Peters Dri. Gnfd —5H 43
Mary Pl. W11 —7G 65
Mary Rose Clo. Hamp —1E 132
Mary Rose Mall. E6 —5D 72
Mary Rose Way. N20 —1G 15
Mary Seacole Clo. E8 —1F 69
Mary Smith Ct. SW5 —4J 83
(off Trebovir Rd.)
Marysmith Ho. SW1 —5H 85 (5D 172)
(off Cureton St.)
Mary's Ter. Twic —7A 98
(in two parts)
Mary St. E16 —5H 71
Mary St. N1 —1C 68
Mary Ter. NW1 —1F 67
Maryville. Well —2K 109
Mary Wharrie Ho. NW3 —7D 48
Marzena Ct. Houn —6G 97
Masault Ct. Rich —4E 98
(off Kew Foot Rd.)
Masbro' Rd. W14 —3F 83
Mascalls Ct. SE7 —6A 90
Mascalls Rd. SE7 —6A 90
Mascotte Rd. SW15 —4F 101
Mascotts Clo. NW2 —3D 46
Masefield Av. S'hall —7E 60
Masefield Av. Stan —5E 10
Masefield Ct. New Bar —4F 5
Masefield Ct. Surb —7D 134
Masefield Cres. N14 —5B 6
Masefield Gdns. E6 —4E 72
Masefield Ho. NW6 —3J 65
(off Stafford Rd.)
Masefield La. Hay —4K 59
Masefield Rd. Hamp —4D 114
Masefield Way. Stai —1B 112
Mashie Rd. W3 —6A 64
Mashiters Hill. Romf —1K 39
Maskall Clo. SW2 —1A 122
Maskani Wlk. SW16 —7G 121
Maskell Rd. SW17 —3A 120
Maskelyne Clo. SW11 —1C 102
Mason Clo. E16 —7J 71
Mason Clo. SE16 —5G 87
Mason Clo. Bexh —3H 111
Mason Clo. Hamp —1D 132
Mason Rd. Sutt —5K 149
Mason Rd. Wfd G —4B 20
Mason's Arms M. W1 —6F 67 (1K 165)
Mason's Av. EC2 —6D 68 (7E 162)
Mason's Av. Croy —3C 152
Masons Av. Harr —4K 25
Masons Grn. La. W5 —4G 63
(in two parts)
Masons Hill. SE18 —4F 91
Masons Hill. Brom —3J 143
Masons Pl. EC1 —3C 68 (1C 162)
Masons Pl. Mitc —1D 138
Mason St. SE17 —4D 86
Mason's Yd. SW1 —1G 85 (4B 166)
Mason's Yd. SW19 —5F 119
Massey Clo. N11 —5A 16
Massey Ct. E6 —1A 72
(off Florence Rd.)
Massie Rd. E8 —6G 51
Massingberd Way. SW17 —4F 121
Massinger St. SE17 —4E 86
Massingham St. E1 —4K 69
Masson Av. Ruis —6A 42
Master Brewer. (Junct.) —6D 40
Master Gunners Pl. SE18 —7C 90
Masterman Rd. E6 —3C 72
Masters Dri. SE16 —5H 87
Master's St. E1 —5K 69
Masthouse Ter. E14 —4C 88
Mast Ho. Ter. E14 —4C 88
(in two parts)
Mastmaker Ct. E14 —2C 88
Mastmaker Rd. E14 —2C 88
Maswell Park. —5G 97
Maswell Pk. Cres. Houn —5G 97
Maswell Pk. Rd. Houn —5F 97
Matcham Ct. Twic —6D 98
(off Clevedon Rd.)
Matcham Rd. E11 —3G 53
Matchless Dri. SE18 —7E 90
Matfield Clo. Brom —5J 143
Matfield Rd. Belv —6G 93
Matham Gro. SE22 —4F 105
Matham Rd. E Mol —5H 133
Matheson Lang Ho. SE1 —7J 167
Matheson Rd. W14 —4H 83
Mathews Av. E6 —2E 72
Mathews Pk. Av. E15 —6H 53
Mathews Yd. WC2 —6J 67 (1E 166)
Mathieson Ct. SE1 —2B 86 (7B 168)
(off King James St.)
Matilda Clo. SE19 —7D 122
Matilda Ho. E1 —1G 87
(off St Katherine's Way)
Matilda St. N1 —1K 67
Matlock Clo. SE24 —4C 104
Matlock Clo. Barn —5A 4
Matlock Ct. SE5 —4D 104
Matlock Cres. Sutt —4G 149
Matlock Gdns. Sutt —4G 149
Matlock Pl. Sutt —4G 149
Matlock Rd. E10 —6E 34
Matlock St. E1 —6A 70
Matlock St. E14 —6A 70
Matlock Way. N Mald —1K 135
Maton Ho. SW6 —7H 83
(off Estcourt Rd.)
Matrimony Pl. SW8 —2G 103
Matson Ct. E4 —7B 20
Matson Ho. SE16 —3H 87
Matthew Clo. W10 —4F 65
Matthew Ct. E17 —3E 34
Matthew Ct. Mitc —5H 139
Matthew Parker St. SW1 —2H 85 (7D 166)
Matthews Ho. E14 —5C 70
Matthews Rd. Gnfd —5H 43
Matthews St. SW11 —2D 102
Matthews Wlk. E17 —1C 34
(off Chingford Rd.)
Matthias Rd. N16 —5E 50
Mattingley Way. SE15 —7F 87
Mattison Rd. N4 —6A 32
Mattock La. W13 & W5 —1B 80
Maud Cashmore Way. SE18 —3D 90
Maude Ho. E2 —2G 69 (1K 163)
(off Ropley St.)
Maude Rd. E17 —5A 34
Maude Rd. SE5 —1E 104
Maude Ter. E17 —5A 34
Maud Gdns. E13 —1H 71
Maud Gdns. Bark —2K 73
Maudlins Grn. E1 —1G 87 (4K 169)
Maud Rd. E10 —3E 52
Maud Rd. E13 —2H 71
Maudslay Rd. SE9 —3D 108
Maudsley Ho. Bren —5E 80
Maud St. E16 —5H 71
Maudsville Cotts. W7 —1J 79
Maud Wilkes Clo. NW5 —5G 49
Maugham Ct. W3 —3J 81
(off Palmerston Rd.)
Mauleverer Rd. SW2 —5J 103
Maundeby Wlk. NW10 —6A 46
Maunder Rd. W7 —1K 79
Maunsel St. SW1 —4H 85 (3C 172)
Maureen Ct. Beck —2J 141
Mauretania Building. E1 —7K 69
(off Jardine Rd.)
Maurice Av. N22 —2B 32
Maurice Bishop Ter. N6 —6E 30
(off View Rd.)
Maurice Brown Clo. NW7 —5A 14
Maurice Ct. Bren —7D 80
Maurice St. W12 —6D 64
Maurice Wlk. NW11 —4A 30
Maurier Clo. N'holt —1A 60
Mauritius Rd. SE10 —4G 89
Maury Rd. N16 —2G 51
Mavelstone Clo. Brom —1C 144
Mavelstone Rd. Brom —1B 144
Maverton Rd. E3 —1C 70
Mavis Av. Eps —5A 148
Mavis Clo. Eps —5A 148
Mavis Wlk. E6 —5C 72
(off Greenwich Cres.)
Mavor Ho. N1 —1K 67
(off Barnsbury Est.)
Mawbey Ho. SE1 —5F 87
Mawbey Pl. SE1 —5F 87
Mawbey Rd. SE1 —5F 87
Mawbey St. SW8 —7J 85
Mawdley Ho. SE1 —7A 168
Mawney. —4J 39
Mawney Clo. Romf —2H 39
Mawney Rd. Romf —2H 39
Mawson Clo. SW20 —2G 137
Mawson Ho. EC1 —5A 68 (5J 161)
(off Baldwins Gdns.)
Mawson La. W4 —6B 82
Maxden Ct. SE15 —3G 105
Maxey Gdns. Dag —4E 56
Maxey Rd. SE18 —4G 91
Maxey Rd. Dag —5E 56
Maxfield Clo. N20 —7F 5
Maximfeldt Rd. Eri —5K 93
Maxim Rd. N21 —6F 7
Maxim Rd. Eri —4K 93
Maxted Pk. Harr —7J 25
Maxted Rd. SE15 —3F 105
Maxwell Clo. Croy —1J 151
Maxwell Clo. Hay —7J 59
Maxwell Ct. SW4 —5H 103
Maxwell Rd. SW6 —7K 83
Maxwell Rd. Ashf —6E 112
Maxwell Rd. N'wd —1F 23
Maxwell Rd. Well —3K 109
Maxwell Rd. W Dray —4B 76
Maxwelton Av. NW7 —5E 12
Maxwelton Clo. NW7 —5E 12
Maya Angelou Ct. E4 —4K 19
Maya Clo. SE15 —2H 105
Mayall Rd. SE24 —5B 104
Maya Rd. N2 —4A 30
Maybank Av. E18 —2K 35
Maybank Av. Wemb —5K 43
Maybank Gdns. Pinn —5J 23
Maybank Rd. E18 —1K 35
May Bate Av. King T —1D 134
Maybells Commercial Est. Bark —2D 74
Mayberry Ct. Beck —7B 124
(off Copers Cope Rd.)
Mayberry Pl. Surb —7F 135
Maybourne Clo. SE26 —6H 123
Maybury Clo. Enf —1C 8
Maybury Clo. Orp —5F 145
Maybury Ct. W1 —5E 66 (6H 159)
(off Marylebone St.)
Maybury Ct. Harr —6H 25
Maybury Gdns. NW10 —6D 46
Maybury M. N6 —7G 31
Maybury Rd. E13 —4A 72
Maybury Rd. Bark —2K 73
Maybury St. SW17 —5C 120
Maychurch Clo. Stan —7J 11
May Clo. Chess —6F 147
Maycroft. Pinn —2K 23
Maycross Av. Mord —4H 137
Mayday Gdns. SE3 —2C 108
Mayday Rd. T Hth —6B 140
Maydwell Ho. E14 —5C 70
Mayerne Rd. SE9 —5B 108
Mayesbrook Rd. Bark —1K 73
Mayesbrook Rd. Ilf & Dag —3A 56
Mayesford Rd. Romf —7C 38
Mayes Rd. N22 —2K 31
Mayeswood Rd. SE12 —4A 126
Mayfair. —7F 67 (3J 165)
Mayfair Av. Bexh —1D 110
Mayfair Av. Ilf —2D 54
Mayfair Av. Romf —6D 38
Mayfair Av. Twic —7G 97
Mayfair Av. Wor Pk —1C 148
Mayfair Clo. Beck —1D 142
Mayfair Clo. Surb —1E 146
Mayfair Gdns. N17 —6H 17
Mayfair Gdns. Wfd G —7D 20
Mayfair M. NW1 —7D 48
(off Regents Pk. Rd.)
Mayfair Pl. W1 —1F 85 (4K 165)
Mayfair Ter. N14 —7C 6
Mayfield. Bexh —3F 111
Mayfield Av. N12 —4F 15
Mayfield Av. N14 —2C 16
Mayfield Av. W4 —4A 82
Mayfield Av. W13 —3B 80
Mayfield Av. Harr —5B 26
Mayfield Av. Wfd G —6D 20
Mayfield Clo. E8 —6F 51
Mayfield Clo. SE20 —1H 141
Mayfield Clo. SW4 —5H 103
Mayfield Clo. Ashf —6D 112
Mayfield Clo. Th Dit —1B 146
Mayfield Clo. Uxb —3D 58
Mayfield Cres. N9 —6C 8
Mayfield Cres. T Hth —4K 139
Mayfield Dri. Pinn —4D 24
Mayfield Gdns. NW4 —6F 29
Mayfield Gdns. W7 —6H 61
Mayfield Rd. E4 —2K 19
Mayfield Rd. E8 —7F 51
Mayfield Rd. E13 —4H 71
Mayfield Rd. E17 —2A 34
Mayfield Rd. N8 —5K 31
Mayfield Rd. SW19 —1H 137
Mayfield Rd. W3 —7H 63

Mayfield Rd.—Mersey Rd.

Mayfield Rd. W12 —2A 82
Mayfield Rd. Belv —4J 93
Mayfield Rd. Brom —5C 144
Mayfield Rd. Dag —1C 56
Mayfield Rd. Enf —2E 8
Mayfield Rd. S Croy —7D 152
Mayfield Rd. Sutt —6B 150
Mayfield Rd. T Hth —4K 139
Mayfield Rd. Flats. N8 —6K 31
Mayfields. Wemb —2G 45
Mayfields Clo. Wemb —2G 45
Mayflower Clo. SE16 —4K 87
Mayflower Clo. Ruis —6E 22
Mayflower Ct. SE16 —2H 87
Mayflower Ho. Bark —1H 73
(off Westbury Rd.)
Mayflower Rd. SW9 —3J 103
Mayflower St. SE16 —2J 87
Mayfly Clo. Eastc —7A 24
Mayfly Gdns. N'holt —3B 60
Mayford. NW1 —2G 67
(in three parts)
Mayford Clo. SW12 —7D 102
Mayford Clo. Beck —3K 141
Mayford Rd. SW12 —7D 102
May Gdns. Wemb —3C 62
Maygood St. N1 —2A 68
Maygrove Rd. NW6 —6H 47
Mayhew Clo. E4 —3H 19
Mayhew Ct. SE5 —4D 104
Mayhill Rd. SE7 —6K 89
Mayhill Rd. Barn —6B 4
Mayland Mans. Bark —7F 55
(off Whiting Av.)
Maylands Dri. Sidc —3D 128
Maylands Ho. SW3 —4C 84 (4D 170)
(off Elystan St.)
Maynard Clo. N15 —5E 32
Maynard Clo. SW6 —7K 83
Maynard Path. E17 —5E 34
Maynard Rd. E17 —5E 34
Maynards Quay. E1 —7J 69
Mayne Ct. SE26 —5H 123
Maynooth Gdns. Cars —7D 138
Mayo Ct. W13 —3B 80
Mayola Rd. E5 —4J 51
Mayo Rd. NW10 —6A 46
Mayo Rd. Croy —5D 140
Mayo Rd. W on T —7J 131
Mayow Rd. SE26 & SE23 —4K 123
Mayplace Clo. Bexh —3H 111
Mayplace La. SE18 —6F 91
(in two parts)
Mayplace Rd. E. Bexh & Dart —3H 111
Mayplace Rd. W. Bexh —4G 111
Maypole. —1K 129
Maypole Ct. S'hall —2D 78
(off Merrick Rd.)
May Rd. E4 —6H 19
May Rd. E13 —2J 71
May Rd. Twic —1J 115
Mayroyd Av. Surb —2G 147
May's Bldgs. M. SE10 —7E 88
May's Ct. SE10 —7F 89
Mays Ct. WC2 —7J 67 (3E 166)
Mays Hill Rd. Brom —2G 143
Mays La. Barn —1H 13
Maysoule Rd. SW11 —4B 102
Mays Rd. Tedd —5H 115
May St. W14 —5H 83
Mayswood Gdns. Dag —6J 57
Mayton St. N7 —3K 49
Maytree Clo. Edgw —3D 12
Maytree Ct. N'holt —3C 60
Maytree Gdns. W5 —2D 80
May Tree Ho. SE4 —3B 106
(off Wickham Rd.)
Maytree La. Stan —7F 11
Maytree Wlk. SW2 —2A 122
Mayville Est. N16 —5E 50
Mayville Rd. E11 —2G 53
Mayville Rd. Ilf —5F 55
May Wlk. E13 —2K 71
Mayward Ho. SE5 —1E 104
(off Peckham Rd.)
Maywood Clo. Beck —7D 124
Maze Hill. SE10 & SE3 —6G 89
Mazenod Av. NW6 —7J 47
Maze Rd. Rich —7G 81
Mead Clo. NW1 —7E 48
Mead Clo. Harr —1H 25
Mead Ct. NW9 —5J 27
Mead Cres. E4 —4K 19
Mead Cres. Sutt —3C 150
Meadcroft Rd. SE11 —6B 86 (7K 173)
(in two parts)
Meade Clo. W4 —6G 81
Meader Ct. SE14 —7K 87
Meadfield. Edgw —2C 12
(in two parts)
Mead Fld. Harr —3D 42
Meadfield Grn. Edgw —2C 12
Meadfoot Rd. SW16 —7G 121
Meadgate Av. Wfd G —5H 21
Mead Gro. Romf —3D 38
Mead Ho. W11 —1H 83
(off Ladbroke Rd.)
Mead Ho. La. Hay —4F 59
Meadhurst Pk. Sun —6G 113
Meadlands Dri. Rich —2D 116
Mead Lodge. W4 —2K 81
Meadow Av. Croy —6K 141
Meadow Bank. N21 —6E 6
Meadowbank. NW3 —7D 48
Meadow Bank. SE3 —3H 107
Meadowbank. Surb —6F 135
Meadowbank Clo. SW6 —7E 82
Meadowbank Gdns. Houn —1J 95
Meadowbank Rd. NW9 —7K 27
Meadowbrook Ct. Iswth —3J 97
Meadow Clo. E4 —1J 19
Meadow Clo. E9 —5B 52
Meadow Clo. SE6 —5C 124
Meadow Clo. SW20 —4E 136
Meadow Clo. Barn —6C 4
Meadow Clo. Bexh —5F 111
Meadow Clo. Chst —5F 127
Meadow Clo. Enf —1F 9
Meadow Clo. Esh —3A 146
Meadow Clo. Houn —6E 96
Meadow Clo. N'holt —2E 60
Meadow Clo. Rich —1E 116
Meadow Clo. Ruis —6H 23
Meadow Clo. Sutt —2A 150
Meadow Ct. N1 —2E 68
Meadow Ct. Houn —6F 97
Meadowcourt Rd. SE3 —4H 107
Meadowcroft. W4 —5G 81
(off Brooks Rd.)
Meadowcroft. Brom —3D 144
Meadowcroft Clo. N13 —2F 17
Meadowcroft Rd. N13 —2F 17
Meadow Dri. N10 —3F 31
Meadow Dri. NW4 —2E 28
Meadow Gdns. Edgw —6C 12
Meadow Gth. NW10 —6J 45
Meadow Hill. N Mald —6A 136
Meadow La. SE12 —3K 125
Meadowlea Clo. Harm —6A 76
Meadow M. SW8 —6K 85
Meadow Pl. SW8 —7J 85
Meadow Pl. W4 —7A 82
Meadow Rd. SW8 —7K 85
Meadow Rd. SW19 —7A 120
Meadow Rd. Ashf —5F 113
Meadow Rd. Bark —7K 55
Meadow Rd. Brom —2G 143
Meadow Rd. Dag —6F 57
Meadow Rd. Felt —2C 114
Meadow Rd. Pinn —4B 24
Meadow Rd. Romf —1J 57
Meadow Rd. S'hall —7D 60
Meadow Rd. Sutt —4C 150
Meadow Row. SE1 —3C 86
Meadows Clo. E10 —2C 52
Meadows Ct. Sidc —6B 128
Meadows End. Sun —1J 131
Meadowside. SE9 —4A 108
Meadowside. Twic —7D 98
Meadow Stile. Croy —3C 152
Meadowsweet Clo. E16 —5B 72
Meadowsweet Clo. SW20 —4E 136
Meadow, The. N10 —3F 31
Meadow, The. Chst —6G 127
Meadow Vw. Harr —1J 43
Meadow Vw. Sidc —7B 110
Meadowview Rd. SE6 —5B 124
Meadowview Rd. Bex —6E 110
Meadowview Rd. Eps —7A 148
Meadow Vw. Rd. Hay —4F 59
Meadow Vw. Rd. T Hth —5B 140
Meadow Wlk. E18 —4J 35
Meadow Wlk. Dag —6F 57
Meadow Wlk. Eps —6A 148
(in two parts)
Meadow Wlk. Wall —3F 151
Meadow Way. NW9 —5K 27
Meadow Way. Chess —5E 146
Meadow Way. Orp —3E 156
Meadow Way. Ruis —6K 23
Meadow Way. Wemb —4D 44
Meadow Waye. Houn —6C 78
Meadow Way, The. Harr —1J 25
Mead Path. SW17 —4A 120
Mead Pl. E9 —6J 51
Mead Pl. Croy —1C 152
Mead Plat. NW10 —6J 45
Mead Rd. Chst —6G 127
Mead Rd. Edgw —6B 12
Mead Rd. Rich —3C 116
Mead Row. SE1 —3A 86 (1J 173)
Meads Ct. E15 —6H 53
Meadside Clo. Beck —1A 142
Meads La. Ilf —7J 37
Meads Rd. N22 —2B 32
Meads Rd. Enf —1F 9
Meads, The. Edgw —6E 12
Meads, The. Mord —5C 138
Meads, The. Sutt —3G 149
Meads, The. Uxb —4A 58
Mead Ter. Wemb —4D 44
Mead, The. N2 —2A 30
Mead, The. W13 —5B 62
Mead, The. Beck —1E 142
Mead, The. Uxb —2C 40
Mead, The. Wall —6H 151
Mead, The. W W'ck —1F 155
Meadvale Rd. W5 —4B 62
Meadvale Rd. Croy —7F 141
Meadway. N14 —2C 16
Meadway. NW11 —6J 29
Mead Way. SW20 —4E 136
Meadway. Ashf —4C 112
Meadway. Barn & New Bar —4D 4
Meadway. Beck —1E 142
Mead Way. Brom —6H 143
Mead Way. Croy —2A 154
Meadway. Ilf —4J 55
Mead Way. Ruis —6F 23
Meadway. Surb —1J 147
Meadway. Twic —1H 115
Mead Way. Wfd G —5F 21
Meadway Clo. NW11 —6K 29
Meadway Clo. Barn —4D 4
Meadway Clo. Pinn —6A 10
Meadway Ct. NW11 —6K 29
Meadway Ct. W5 —4F 63
Meadway Ct. Dag —2F 57
Meadway Ct. Tedd —5C 116
Meadway Gdns. Ruis —6F 23
Meadway Ga. NW11 —6J 29
Meadway, The. SE3 —2F 107
Meadway, The. Buck H —1G 21
Meaford Way. SE20 —7H 123
Meakin Est. SE1 —3E 86
Meanley Rd. E12 —4C 54
Meard St. W1 —6H 67 (1C 166)
(in two parts)
Meath Rd. E15 —2H 71
Meath Rd. Ilf —3G 55
Meath St. SW11 —1F 103
Mechanics Path. SE8 —7C 88
Mecklenburgh Pl. WC1 —4K 67 (3G 161)
Mecklenburgh Sq. WC1 —4K 67 (3G 161)
Mecklenburgh St. WC1 —4K 67 (3G 161)
Medburn St. NW1 —2H 67
Medcroft Gdns. SW14 —4J 99
Medebourne Clo. SE3 —3J 107
Mede Ho. Brom —5K 125
(off Pike Clo.)
Medesenge Way. N13 —6G 17
Medfield St. SW15 —7C 100
Medhurst Clo. E3 —2A 70
Median Rd. E5 —5J 51
Medina Gro. N7 —3A 50
Medina Rd. N7 —3A 50
Medland Clo. Wall —1E 150
Medland Ho. E14 —7A 70
Medlar Clo. N'holt —2B 60
Medlar Ho. Sidc —3A 128
Medlar St. SE5 —1C 104
Medley Rd. NW6 —6J 47
Medora Rd. SW2 —7K 103
Medora Rd. Romf —4K 39
Medusa Rd. SE6 —6D 106
Medway Clo. Croy —6J 141
Medway Clo. Ilf —5G 55
Medway Ct. WC1 —3J 67 (2E 160)
(off Judd St.)
Medway Dri. Gnfd —2K 61
Medway Gdns. Wemb —4A 44
Medway Ho. NW8 —4C 66 (4C 158)
(off Penfold St.)
Medway Ho. SE1 —2D 86 (7F 169)
(off Hankey Pl.)
Medway Ho. King T —1D 134
Medway M. E3 —2A 70
Medway Pde. Gnfd —2K 61
Medway Rd. E3 —2A 70
Medway St. SW1 —3H 85 (2D 172)
Medwin St. SW4 —4K 103
Meek Rd. SW10 —7A 84
Meerbrook Rd. SE3 —3A 108
Meeson Rd. E15 —7H 53
Meeson St. E5 —4A 52
Meeting Fld. Path. E9 —6J 51
Meetinghouse All. E1 —1H 87
Meeting Ho. La. SE15 —1H 105
Mehetabel Rd. E9 —5J 51
Meister Clo. Ilf —1H 55
Melancholy Wlk. Rich —2C 116
Melanda Clo. Chst —5D 126
Melanie Clo. Bexh —1E 110
Melba Way. SE13 —1D 106
Melbourne Av. N13 —6E 16
Melbourne Av. W13 —1A 80
Melbourne Av. Pinn —3F 25
Melbourne Clo. SE20 —7G 123
Melbourne Clo. Orp —7J 145
Melbourne Clo. Uxb —4C 40
Melbourne Clo. Wall —5G 151
Melbourne Ct. N10 —7A 16
Melbourne Ct. W9 —4A 66
(off Clifton Rd.)
Melbourne Gdns. Romf —5E 38
Melbourne Gro. SE22 —4E 104
Melbourne Ho. W8 —1J 83
(off Kensington Pl.)
Melbourne Ho. Hay —4A 60
Melbourne Mans. W6 —6G 83
(off Musard Rd.)
Melbourne M. SE6 —7E 106
Melbourne M. SW9 —1A 104
Melbourne Pl. WC2 —6K 67 (1H 167)
Melbourne Rd. E6 —2D 72
Melbourne Rd. E10 —7D 34
Melbourne Rd. E17 —4A 34
Melbourne Rd. SW19 —1J 137
Melbourne Rd. Ilf —1F 55
Melbourne Rd. Tedd —6C 116
Melbourne Rd. Wall —5F 151
Melbourne Sq. SW9 —1A 104
Melbourne Way. Enf —6A 8
Melbray M. SW6 —2H 101
Melbreak Ho. SE22 —3E 104
Melbury Av. S'hall —3F 79
Melbury Clo. Chst —6C 126
Melbury Clo. Clay —6B 146
Melbury Ct. W8 —3H 83
Melbury Dri. SE5 —7E 86
Melbury Gdns. SW20 —1D 136
Melbury Ho. SW8 —7K 85
(off Richborne Ter.)
Melbury Rd. W14 —3H 83
Melbury Rd. Harr —5F 27
Melbury Ter. NW1 —4C 66 (4D 158)
Melchester. W11 —6H 65
(off Ledbury Rd.)
Melchester Ho. N19 —3H 49
(off Wedmore St.)
Melcombe Ct. NW1 —5D 66 (5E 158)
(off Melcombe Pl.)
Melcombe Gdns. Harr —6F 27
Melcombe Ho. SW8 —7K 85
(off Dorset Rd.)
Melcombe Pl. NW1 —5D 66 (5E 158)
Melcombe Regis Ct. W1 —5E 66 (6H 159)
(off Weymouth St.)
Melcombe St. NW1 —4D 66 (4F 159)
Meldex Clo. NW7 —6K 13
(off Prince of Wales Clo.)
Meldon Clo. SW6 —1K 101
Meldone Clo. Surb —7H 135
Meldrum Rd. Ilf —2A 56
Melfield Gdns. SE6 —4E 124
Melford Av. Bark —6J 55
Melford Clo. Chess —5F 147
Melford Ct. SE1 —3E 86
(off Fendall St.)
Melford Ct. SE22 —1G 123
Melford Pas. SE22 —7G 105
Melford Rd. E6 —4D 72
Melford Rd. E11 —2G 53
Melford Rd. E17 —4A 34
Melford Rd. SE22 —7G 105
Melford Rd. Ilf —2H 55
Melfort Av. T Hth —3B 140
Melfort Rd. T Hth —3B 140
Melgund Rd. N5 —5A 50
Melina Clo. Hay —5F 59
Melina Ct. SW15 —3C 100
Melina Pl. NW8 —3B 66 (2A 158)
Melina Rd. W12 —2D 82
Melior Ct. N6 —6G 31
Melior Pl. SE1 —2E 86 (6G 169)
Melior St. SE1 —2E 86 (6G 169)
Meliot Rd. SE6 —2F 125
Meller Clo. Croy —3J 151
Melling Dri. Enf —1B 8
Melling St. SE18 —6J 91
Mellish Clo. Bark —1K 73
Mellish Flats. E10 —7C 34
Mellish Gdns. Wfd G —5D 20
Mellish Ind. Est. SE18 —3B 90
Mellish St. E14 —3C 88
Mellison Rd. SW17 —5C 120
Mellitus St. W12 —5B 64
Mellor Clo. W on T —7D 132
Mellow La. E. Hay —4E 58
Mellow La. W. Uxb —3E 58
Mellows Rd. Ilf —3D 36
Mellows Rd. Wall —5H 151
Mells Cres. SE9 —4D 126
Mell St. SE10 —5G 89
Melody La. N5 —5C 50
Melody Rd. SW18 —5A 102
Melon Pl. W8 —2J 83
Melon Rd. E11 —3G 53
Melon Rd. SE15 —1G 105
Melrose Av. N22 —1B 32
Melrose Av. NW2 —5D 46
Melrose Av. SW16 —3K 139
Melrose Av. SW19 —2H 119
Melrose Av. Gnfd —2F 61
Melrose Av. Mitc —7F 121
Melrose Av. Twic —7F 97
Melrose Clo. SE12 —1J 125
Melrose Clo. Gnfd —2F 61
Melrose Clo. Hay —5J 59
Melrose Dri. S'hall —1E 78
Melrose Gdns. W6 —3E 82
Melrose Gdns. Edgw —3H 27
Melrose Gdns. N Mald —3K 135
Melrose Ho. E14 —3D 88
Melrose Ho. NW6 —3J 65
(off Carlton Va.)
Melrose Rd. SW13 —2B 100
Melrose Rd. SW18 —6H 101
Melrose Rd. SW19 —2J 137
Melrose Rd. W3 —3J 81
Melrose Rd. Pinn —4D 24
Melrose Ter. W6 —3E 82
Melrose Tudor. Wall —5J 151
(off Plough La.)
Melsa Rd. Mord —6A 138
Melthorne Dri. Ruis —3A 42
Melthorpe Gdns. SE3 —1C 108
Melton Clo. Ruis —1A 42
Melton Ct. SW7 —4B 84 (4B 170)
Melton Ct. Sutt —7A 150
Melton St. NW1 —3G 67 (2B 160)
Melville Av. SW20 —7C 118
Melville Av. Gnfd —5K 43
Melville Av. S Croy —5F 153
Melville Clo. Uxb —2F 41
Melville Ct. SE8 —4A 88
Melville Ct. W12 —3D 82
(off Goldhawk Rd.)
Melville Gdns. N13 —5G 17
Melville Ho. SE10 —1E 106
Melville Ho. New Bar —5G 5
Melville Pl. N1 —7C 50
Melville Rd. E17 —3B 34
Melville Rd. NW10 —7K 45
Melville Rd. SW13 —1C 100
Melville Rd. Romf —1H 39
Melville Rd. Sidc —2C 128
Melville Vs. Rd. W3 —1J 81
Melvin Rd. SE20 —1J 141
Melyn Clo. N7 —4G 49
Memel Ct. EC1 —4C 162
Memel St. EC1 —4C 68 (4C 162)
Memess Path. SE18 —6E 90
Memorial Av. E15 —3G 71
Memorial Clo. Houn —6D 78
Mendham Ho. SE1 —3E 86 (7G 169)
(off Cluny Pl.)
Mendip Clo. SE26 —4J 123
Mendip Clo. SW19 —2G 119
Mendip Clo. Hay —7F 77
Mendip Clo. Wor Pk —1E 148
Mendip Ct. SW18 —3A 102
Mendip Dri. NW2 —2G 47
Mendip Houses. E2 —3J 69
(off Welwyn St.)
Mendip Rd. SW11 —3A 102
Mendip Rd. Bexh —1K 111
Mendip Rd. Ilf —5J 37
Mendora Rd. SW6 —7G 83
Menelik Rd. NW2 —4G 47
Menlo Gdns. SE19 —7D 122
Menlo Lodge. N13 —3E 16
(off Crothall Clo.)
Menotti St. E2 —4G 69
Menteath Ho. E14 —6C 70
Mentmore Clo. Harr —6C 26
Mentmore Ter. E8 —7H 51
Meon Ct. Iswth —2J 97
Meon Rd. W3 —2J 81
Meopham Rd. Mitc —1G 139
Mepham Cres. Harr —7B 10
Mepham Gdns. Harr —7B 10
Mepham St. SE1 —1A 86 (5J 167)
Mera Dri. Bexh —4G 111
Merantun Way. SW19 —1K 137
Merbury Clo. SE13 —5F 107
Merbury Rd. SE28 —2J 91
Mercator Pl. E14 —5C 88
Mercator Rd. SE13 —4F 107
Mercer Clo. Th Dit —7A 134
Mercer Ho. SW1 —5F 85 (5J 171)
(off Ebury Bri. Rd.)
Merceron Houses. E2 —3J 69
(off Globe Rd.)
Merceron St. E1 —4H 69
Mercer Pl. Pinn —2A 24
Mercers Clo. SE10 —4H 89
Mercers Pl. W6 —4F 83
Mercers Rd. N19 —3H 49
(in two parts)
Mercer St. WC2 —6J 67 (1E 166)
Merchant Ind. Ter. NW10 —4J 63
Merchants Lodge. E17 —4C 34
(off Westbury Rd.)
Merchant St. E3 —3B 70
Merchiston Rd. SE6 —2F 125
Merchland Rd. SE9 —1G 127
Mercia Gro. SE13 —4E 106
Mercia Ho. SE5 —2C 104
(off Denmark Rd.)
Mercier Rd. SW15 —5G 101
Mercury. NW9 —1B 28
(off Concourse, The)
Mercury Cen. Felt —5J 95
Mercury Ct. E14 —4C 88
Mercury Ho. Bren —6C 80
(off Glenhurst Rd.)
Mercury Rd. Bren —6C 80
Mercury Way. SE14 —6K 87
Mercy Ter. SE13 —5D 106
Merebank La. Croy —5K 151
Mere Clo. SW15 —7F 101
Mere Clo. Orp —2E 156
Meredith Av. NW2 —5E 46
Meredith Clo. Pinn —1B 24
Meredith Ho. N16 —5E 50
Meredith M. SE4 —4B 106
Meredith St. E13 —3J 71
Meredith St. EC1 —3B 68 (2A 162)
Meredyth Rd. SW13 —2C 100
Mere End. Croy —7K 141
Mere Rd. Shep —6D 130
Mere Side. Orp —2E 156
Meretone Clo. SE4 —4A 106
Merevale Cres. Mord —6A 138
Mereway Rd. Twic —1H 115
Merewood Clo. Brom —2E 144
Merewood Rd. Bexh —2J 111
Mereworth Clo. Brom —5H 143
Mereworth Dri. SE18 —7F 91
Mereworth Ho. SE15 —6J 87
Merganser Ct. SE8 —6B 88
(off Edward St.)
Merganser Gdns. SE28 —3H 91
Meriden Clo. Brom —7B 126
Meriden Clo. Ilf —1G 37
Meriden Ct. SW3 —6C 170
Meridian Ga. E14 —2E 88
Meridian Pl. E14 —2E 88
Meridian Rd. SE7 —7B 90
Meridian Sq. E15 —7F 53
Meridian Trad. Est. SE7 —4K 89
Meridian Wlk. N17 —6K 17
Meridian Way. N18 & N9 —5D 18
Merifield Rd. SE9 —4A 108
Merino Clo. E11 —4A 36
Merino Pl. Sidc —6A 110
Merioneth Ct. W7 —5K 61
(off Copley Clo.)
Merivale Rd. SW15 —4G 101
Merivale Rd. Harr —7G 25
Merlewood Dri. Chst —1D 144
Merlewood Pl. SE9 —5D 108
Merley Ct. NW9 —1J 45
Merlin. NW9 —1B 28
(off Concourse, The)
Merlin Clo. Croy —4E 152
Merlin Clo. Mitc —3C 138
Merlin Clo. N'holt —3A 60
Merlin Clo. Wall —6K 151
Merlin Ct. Ruis —2F 41
Merlin Ct. Short —3H 143
Merlin Cres. Edgw —1F 27
Merlin Gdns. Brom —3J 125
Merling Clo. Chess —5C 146
Merlin Gro. Beck —4B 142
Merlin Rd. E12 —2B 54
Merlin Rd. Well —4A 110
Merlin Rd. N. Well —4A 110
Merlins Av. Harr —3D 42
Merlins Ct. WC1 —3A 68 (2J 161)
(off Margery St.)
Merlin St. WC1 —3A 68 (2J 161)
Mermaid Ct. SE1
—2D 86 (6E 168)
Mermaid Ct. SE16 —1B 88
Mermaid Ho. E14 —7E 70
Mermaid Tower. SE8 —6B 88
(off Abinger Gro.)
Meroe Ct. N16 —2E 50
Merredene St. SW2 —6K 103
Merriam Clo. E4 —5K 19
Merrick Ho. SE8 —4B 88
Merrick Rd. S'hall —3D 78
Merrick Sq. SE1 —3D 86 (7E 168)
Merridene. N21 —6G 7
Merrielands Cres. Dag —2F 75
Merrielands Retail Pk. Dag —1F 75
Merrilands Rd. Wor Pk —1E 148
Merrilees Rd. Sidc —1J 127
Merrilyn Clo. Clay —6A 146
Merriman Rd. SE3 —1A 108
Merrington Rd. SW6 —6J 83
Merrion Av. Stan —5J 11
Merritt Gdns. Chess —6C 146
Merritt Rd. SE4 —5B 106
Merritt's Bldgs. EC2 —4G 163
Merrivale. N14 —6C 6
Merrivale. NW1 —1G 67
(off Camden St.)
Merrivale Av. Ilf —4B 36
Merrow Ct. Mitc —2B 138
Merrow Rd. Sutt —7F 149
Merrow St. SE17 —5D 86
Merrow Wlk. SE17 —5D 86
Merrow Way. New Ad —6E 154
Merrydown Way. Chst —1C 144
Merryfield. SE3 —2H 107
Merryfield Gdns. Stan —5H 11
Merryfield Ho. SE9 —3A 126
(off Grove Pk. Rd.)
Merryfields. Uxb —2A 58
(in two parts)
Merryfields Way. SE6 —7D 106
Merry Hill. —1A 10
Merryhill Clo. E4 —7J 9
Merry Hill Mt. Bush —1A 10
Merryhills Ct. N14 —5B 6
Merryhills Dri. Enf —4C 6
Merryweather Ct. N19 —3G 49
Merryweather Ct. N Mald
—5A 136
Mersea Ho. Bark —6F 55
Mersey Ct. King T —1D 134
Mersey Rd. E17 —3B 34

Mersey Wlk. N'holt —2E 60
Mersham Dri. NW9 —5G 27
Mersham Pl. SE20 —1H 141
Mersham Rd. T Hth —3D 140
Merten Rd. Romf —7E 38
Merthyr Ter. SW13 —6D 82
Merton. —7K 119
Merton Av. W4 —4B 82
Merton Av. N'holt —5G 43
Merton Av. Uxb —7D 40
Merton Ct. Ilf —6C 36
Merton Ct. Well —2B 110
Merton Gdns. Orp —5F 145
Merton Hall Gdns. SW20 —1G 137
Merton Hall Rd. SW19 —7G 119
Merton High St. SW19 —7K 119
Merton Ind. Pk. SW19 —1K 137
Merton La. N6 —2D 48
Merton Lodge. New Bar —5F 5
Merton Mans. SE8 —1C 106
(off Brookmill Rd.)
Merton Mans. SW20 —2F 137
Merton Park. —2J 137
Merton Pk. Pde. SW19 —1H 137
Merton Pl. SW19 —1A 138
(off Nelson Gro. Rd.)
Merton Ri. NW3 —7C 48
(in two parts)
Merton Rd. E17 —5E 34
Merton Rd. SE25 —5G 141
Merton Rd. SW18 —6J 101
Merton Rd. SW19 —7K 119
Merton Rd. Bark —7K 55
Merton Rd. Enf —1J 7
Merton Rd. Harr —1G 43
Merton Rd. Ilf —7K 37
Merton Way. Uxb —7D 40
Merton Way. W Mol —4F 133
Mertoun Ter. W1 —5D 66 (7E 158)
(off Seymour Pl.)
Merttins Rd. SE15 & SE4 —5K 105
Meru Clo. NW5 —4E 48
Mervan Rd. SW2 —4A 104
Mervyn Av. SE9 —3G 127
Mervyn Rd. W13 —3A 80
Mervyn Rd. Shep —7E 130
Messaline Av. W3 —6J 63
Messent Rd. SE9 —5A 108
Messeter Pl. SE9 —6E 108
Messina Av. NW6 —7J 47
Messiter Ho. N1 —1K 67
(off Barnsbury Est.)
Metcalf Rd. Ashf —5D 112
Metcalf Wlk. Felt —4C 114
Meteor St. SW11 —4E 102
Meteor Way. Wall —7J 151
Metheringham Way. NW9 —1A 28
Methley St. SE11 —5A 86 (6K 173)
Methuen Clo. Edgw —7B 12
Methuen Pk. N10 —3F 31
Methuen Rd. Belv —4H 93
Methuen Rd. Bexh —4F 111
Methuen Rd. Edgw —7B 12
Methwold Rd. W10 —5F 65
Metro Bus. Cen., The. SE26 —6B 124
Metro Central Heights. SE1 —3C 86
(off Newington Causeway)
Metro Ind. Cen. Iswth —2J 97
Metropolis. SE11 —3B 86
(off Oswin St.)
Metropolitan Bus. Cen. N1 —7E 50
(off Enfield Rd.)
Metropolitan Clo. E14 —5C 70
Metropolitan Wharf. E1 —1J 87
Metro Trad. Est. Wemb —4H 45
Mews Pl. Wfd G —4D 20
Mews St. E1 —1G 87 (4K 169)
Mews, The. N1 —1C 68
Mews, The. N8 —3A 32
Mews, The. Ilf —5B 36
Mews, The. Romf —4K 39
Mews, The. Sidc —4A 128
Mews, The. Twic —6B 98
Mexborough. NW1 —1G 67
Mexfield Rd. SW15 —5H 101
Meyer Grn. Enf —1B 8
Meyer Rd. Eri —6K 93
Meymott St. SE1 —1B 86 (5A 168)
Meynell Cres. E9 —7K 51
Meynell Gdns. E9 —7K 51
Meynell Rd. E9 —7K 51
Meyrick Ho. E14 —5C 70
Meyrick Rd. NW10 —6C 46
Meyrick Rd. SW11 —3B 102
Miah Ter. E1 —1G 87
Miall Wlk. SE26 —4A 124
Micawber Av. Uxb —4C 58
Micawber Ct. N1 —3C 68 (1D 162)
(off Windsor Ter.)
Micawber Ho. SE16 —2G 87
(off Llewellyn St.)
Micawber St. N1 —3C 68 (1D 162)
Michael Cliffe Ho. EC1 —2A 162
Michael Faraday Ho. SE17 —5E 86
(off Beaconsfield Rd.)
Michael Gaynor Clo. W7 —1K 79
Michael Manley Ind. Est. SW8 —2G 103
(off Clyston St.)
Michaelmas Clo. SW20 —3E 136
Michael Rd. E11 —1H 53
Michael Rd. SE25 —3E 140
Michael Rd. SW6 —1K 101
Michael's Clo. SE13 —4G 107
Michael Stewart Ho. SW6 —6H 83
(off Clem Attlee Ct.)
Micheldever Rd. SE12 —6G 107
Michelham Gdns. Twic —3K 115
Michelle Ct. N12 —5F 15
Michelle Ct. W3 —7K 63
Michelsdale Dri. Rich —4E 98
Michelson Ho. SE11 —4H 173
Michel's Row. Rich —4E 98
Michigan Av. E12 —4D 54
Michigan Ho. E14 —3C 88
Michleham Down. N12 —4C 14
Mickledore. NW1 —2G 67 (1B 160)
(off Ampthill Est.)
Mickleham Clo. Orp —2K 145
Mickleham Gdns. Sutt —6G 149
Mickleham Rd. Orp —1K 145
Mickleham Way. New Ad —7F 155
Micklethwaite Rd. SW6 —6J 83
Midas Metropolitan Ind. Est. Mord —7E 136
Mid Beckton. —6D 72
Midcroft. Ruis —1G 41
Middle Dene. NW7 —3E 12
Middlefield. NW8 —1B 66
Middlefielde. W13 —5B 62
Middlefield Gdns. Ilf —6F 37
Middle Grn. Clo. Surb —6F 135
Middleham Gdns. N18 —6B 18
Middleham Rd. N18 —6B 18
Middle La. N8 —5J 31
Middle La. Tedd —6K 115
Middle La. M. N8 —5J 31
Middle Mill Hall. King T —3F 135
Middle Pk. Av. SE9 —6B 108
Middle Path. Harr —1H 43
Middle Rd. E13 —2J 71
Middle Rd. SW16 —2H 139
Middle Rd. E Barn —6H 5
Middle Rd. Harr —2H 43
Middle Row. W10 —4G 65
Middlesborough Rd. N18 —6B 18
Middlesex Bus. Cen. S'hall —2D 78
Middlesex County Cricket Club. —3B 66 (1B 158)
Middlesex Ct. W4 —5B 82
Middlesex Ct. Harr —5K 25
Middlesex Pas. EC1 —6B 162
Middlesex Pl. E9 —6J 51
(off Elsdale St.)
Middlesex Rd. Mitc —5J 139
Middlesex St. E1 —5E 68 (6H 163)
Middlesex Wharf. E5 —2J 51
Middle St. EC1 —5C 68 (5C 162)
Middle St. Croy —2C 152
(in two parts)
Middle Temple Hall. —2J 167
Middle Temple La. EC4 —6A 68 (1J 167)
Middleton Av. E4 —4G 19
Middleton Av. Gnfd —2H 61
Middleton Av. Sidc —6B 128
Middleton Bldgs. W1 —6A 160
Middleton Clo. E4 —3G 19
Middleton Dri. SE16 —2K 87
Middleton Dri. Pinn —3J 23
Middleton Gdns. Ilf —6F 37
Middleton Gro. N7 —5J 49
Middleton Ho. E8 —7F 51
Middleton Ho. SE1 —3D 86
(off Burbage Clo.)
Middleton Ho. SW1 —4H 85 (4D 172)
(off Causton St.)
Middleton M. N7 —5J 49
Middleton Rd. E8 —7F 51
Middleton Rd. NW11 —7J 29
Middleton Rd. Hay —5F 59
Middleton Rd. Mord & Cars —6K 137
Middleton Rd. N Mald —3J 135
Middleton St. E2 —3H 69
Middleton Way. SE13 —4F 107
Middleway. NW11 —5K 29
Middle Way. SW16 —2H 139
Middle Way. Eri —3E 92
Middle Way. Hay —4A 60
Middle Way, The. Harr —2K 25
Middle Yd. SE1 —1E 86 (4G 169)
Midfield Av. Bexh —3J 111
Midfield Pde. Bexh —3J 111
Midfield Way. Orp —7B 128
Midford Ho. NW4 —4F 29
(off Belle Vue Est.)
Midford Pl. W1 —4G 67 (4B 160)
Midholm. Wemb —1G 45
Midholm Clo. NW11 —4K 29
Midholm Rd. Croy —3A 154
Midhope Ho. WC1 —3J 67 (2F 161)
(off Midhope St.)
Midhope St. WC1 —3J 67 (2F 161)
Midhurst. SE26 —6J 123
Midhurst Av. N10 —3E 30
Midhurst Av. Croy —7A 140
Midhurst Gdns. Uxb —1E 58
Midhurst Hill. Bexh —6G 111
Midhurst Ho. E14 —6B 70
Midhurst Pde. N10 —3E 30
(off Fortis Grn.)
Midhurst Rd. W13 —2A 80
Midhurst Way. E5 —4G 51
Midland Cres. NW3 —6A 48
Midland Pde. NW6 —6K 47
Midland Pl. E14 —5E 88
Midland Rd. E10 —7E 34
Midland Rd. NW1 —2H 67 (1D 160)
Midland Ter. NW2 —3F 47
Midland Ter. NW10 —4A 64
(in two parts)
Midmoor Rd. SW12 —1G 121
Midmoor Rd. SW19 —1F 137
Midship Clo. SE16 —1K 87
Midship Point. E14 —2C 88
(off Quarterdeck, The)
Midstrath Rd. NW10 —4A 46
Midsummer Av. Houn —4D 96
Midway. Sutt —7H 137
Midway Ho. EC1 —1A 162
Midwinter Clo. Well —3A 110
Midwood Clo. NW2 —3D 46
Miers Clo. E6 —1E 72
Mighell Av. Ilf —5B 36
Milan Rd. S'hall —2D 78
Milborne Gro. SW10 —5A 84 (6A 170)
Milborne St. E9 —6J 51
Milborough Cres. SE12 —6G 107
Milburn Dri. W Dray —7A 58
Milcote St. SE1 —2B 86 (7A 168)
Mildenhall Rd. E5 —4J 51
Mildmay Av. N1 —6D 50
Mildmay Gro. N. N1 —5D 50
Mildmay Gro. S. N1 —5D 50
Mildmay Pk. N1 —5D 50
Mildmay Pl. N16 —5E 50
Mildmay Rd. N1 —5D 50
Mildmay Rd. Ilf —3F 55
Mildmay Rd. Romf —5J 39
Mildmay St. N1 —6D 50
Mildred Av. Hay —4F 77
Mildred Av. N'holt —5F 43
Mildred Rd. Eri —5K 93
Mildura Ct. N8 —4K 31
Mile End. —4B 70
Mile End Pk. —3A 70
Mile End Pl. E1 —4K 69
Mile End Rd. E1 & E3 —5J 69
Mile End, The. E17 —1K 33
Mile Rd. Wall —1F 151
Miles Bldgs. NW1 —5C 66 (5C 158)
(off Penfold Pl.)
Miles Dri. SE28 —1J 91
Miles Lodge. Harr —5H 25
Milespit Hill. NW7 —5J 13
Miles Pl. NW1 —5B 66
(off Penfold Pl.)
Miles Pl. Surb —4F 135
Miles Rd. N8 —3J 31
Miles Rd. Mitc —3C 138
Miles St. SW8 —6J 85 (7E 172)
Miles St. Bus. Est. SW8 —6J 85 (7F 173)
Milestone Clo. N9 —2B 18
Milestone Clo. Sutt —7B 150
Milestone Green. (3G 161) —4J 99
Milestone Rd. SE19 —6F 123
Miles Way. N20 —2H 15
Milfoil St. W12 —7C 64
Milford Clo. SE2 —6E 92
Milford Ct. S'hall —1E 78
Milford Gdns. Croy —5J 141
Milford Gdns. Edgw —7B 12
Milford Gdns. Wemb —4D 44
Milford Gro. Sutt —4A 150
Milford La. WC2 —7A 68 (2H 167)
Milford M. SW16 —3K 121
Milford Rd. W13 —1B 80
Milford Rd. S'hall —7E 60
Milford Towers. SE6 —7D 106
Milk St. E16 —1F 91
Milk St. EC2 —6C 68 (1D 168)
Milk St. Brom —6K 125
Milkwell Gdns. Wfd G —7E 20
Milkwell Yd. SE5 —1C 104
Milkwood Rd. SE24 —5B 104
Milk Yd. E1 —7J 69
Millais Av. E12 —5E 54
Millais Ct. N'holt —2B 60
(off Academy Gdns.)
Millais Gdns. Edgw —2G 27
Millais Ho. SW1 —4J 85 (4E 172)
(off Marsham St.)
Millais Rd. E11 —4E 52
Millais Rd. Enf —5A 8
Millais Rd. N Mald —7A 136
Millais Way. Eps —4J 147
Millard Clo. N16 —5E 50
Millard Ter. Dag —6G 57
Millbank. SW1 —3J 85 (2E 172)
Millbank Ct. SW1 —3E 172
Millbank Tower. SW1 —4E 172
Millbank Way. SE12 —5J 107
Millbourne Rd. Felt —4C 114
Mill Bri. Barn —6C 4
Millbrook Av. Well —4H 109
Millbrook Gdns. Chad H —6F 39
Millbrook Ho. SE15 —6G 87
(off Peckham Pk. Rd.)
Millbrook Pas. SW9 —3B 104
Millbrook Pl. NW1 —2G 67
(off Hampstead Rd.)
Millbrook Rd. N9 —1C 18
Millbrook Rd. SW9 —3B 104
Mill Clo. Cars —2E 150
Mill Corner. Barn —1C 4
Mill Ct. E10 —3E 52
Millcroft Ho. SE6 —4E 124
(off Melfield Gdns.)
Millender Wlk. SE16 —4J 87
Millennium Bridge. —7B 68 (3B 168)
Millennium Bus. Cen. NW2 —2D 46
Millennium Clo. E16 —6K 71
Millennium Dri. E14 —4F 89
Millennium Ho. E17 —5K 33
Millennium Pl. E2 —2H 69
Millennium Sq. SE1 —2F 87 (6K 169)
Millennium Way. SE10 —2G 89
Miller Av. Enf —1H 9
Miller Clo. Mitc —7D 138
Miller Clo. Pinn —2A 24
Miller Ct. Bexh —3J 111
Miller Rd. SW19 —6B 120
Miller Rd. Croy —1K 151
Miller's Av. E8 —5F 51
Millers Clo. NW7 —4H 13
Miller's Ct. W4 —5B 82
Millers Ct. Wemb —2E 62
(off Vicars Bri. Clo.)
Millers Grn. Clo. Enf —3G 7
Millers Mdw. Clo. SE3 —5H 107
Miller's Ter. E8 —5F 51
Miller St. NW1 —2G 67
(in two parts)
Millers Way. W6 —2E 82
Millers Wharf Ho. E1 —1G 87
(off St Katherine's Way)
Miller Wlk. SE1 —1A 86 (5K 167)
Millet Rd. Gnfd —3F 61
Mill Farm Av. Sun —7G 113
Mill Farm Bus. Pk. Houn —7C 96
Mill Farm Clo. Pinn —2A 24
Mill Farm Cres. Houn —1C 114
Millfield. N4 —2A 50
Millfield. King T —3F 135
Millfield. Sun —1F 131
Millfield Av. E17 —1A 34
Millfield La. N6 —1C 48
Millfield Pl. N6 —2E 48
Millfield Rd. Edgw —2J 27
Millfield Rd. Houn —1C 114
Millfields Rd. E5 —4J 51
Mill Gdns. SE26 —3H 123
Mill Grn. Mitc —7E 138
Mill Grn. Bus. Pk. Mitc —7E 138
Mill Grn. Rd. Mitc —7E 138
Millgrove St. SW11 —1E 102
Millharbour. E14 —2D 88
Mill Harbour. E14 —3D 88
Millhaven Clo. Romf —6B 38
Mill Hill. —5G 13
Mill Hill. SW13 —2C 100
Mill Hill Circus. (3G 161) —5G 13
Mill Hill Gro. W3 —1J 81
Mill Hill Ind. Est. NW7 —6G 13
Mill Hill Rd. SW13 —2C 100
Mill Hill Rd. W3 —2H 81
Mill Hill Ter. W3 —1H 81
Mill Hill Yd. W3 —2H 81
Mill Ho. Wfd G —5C 20
Millhouse Pl. SE27 —4B 122
Millicent Fawcett Ct. N17 —1F 33
Millicent Rd. E10 —1B 52
Milligan St. E14 —7B 70
Milling Rd. Edgw —7E 12
Millington Ho. N16 —3D 50
Millington Rd. Hay —3G 77
Mill La. E4 —3J 9
Mill La. NW6 —5H 47
Mill La. SE18 —5E 90
Mill La. Cars —4D 150
Mill La. Croy —3K 151
Mill La. Eps —7B 148
Mill La. Romf —6E 38
Mill La. Wfd G —5C 20
Millman M. WC1 —4K 67 (4G 161)
Millman Pl. WC1 —4K 67
(off Millman St.)
Millman St. WC1 —4K 67 (4G 161)
Millmark Gro. SE14 —2A 106
Millmarsh La. Brim & Enf —2F 9
Millmead Ind. Cen. N17 —3H 33
Mill Mead Rd. N17 —3H 33
Mill Meads. —2F 71
Mill Pl. E14 —6A 70
Mill Pl. Chst —1F 145
Mill Pl. King T —3F 135
Mill Plat. Iswth —2A 98
(in two parts)
Mill Plat Av. Iswth —2A 98
Millpond Est. SE16 —2H 87
Mill Ridge. Edgw —5A 12
Mill River Trad. Est. Enf —3F 9
Mill Rd. E16 —1K 89
Mill Rd. SW19 —7A 120
Mill Rd. Eri —7J 93
Mill Rd. Ilf —3E 54
Mill Rd. Twic —2G 115
Mill Row. N1 —1E 68
Mill Row. Bex —1H 129
Mills Clo. Uxb —2C 58
Mills Ct. EC2 —3G 163
Mills Gro. E14 —5E 70
Mills Gro. NW4 —3F 29
Millshot Clo. SW6 —1E 100
Mills Ho. E17 —3F 35
Millside. Cars —2D 150
Millside Pl. Iswth —2B 98
Millson Clo. N20 —2G 15
Mills Row. W4 —4K 81
Millstream Clo. N13 —5F 17
Millstream Rd. SE1 —2F 87 (7J 169)
Mill St. SE1 —2F 87 (7K 169)
Mill St. W1 —7F 67 (2A 166)
Mill St. King T —3E 134
Mill Trad. Est., The. NW10 —3J 63
Mill Va. Brom —2H 143
Mill Vw. Clo. Ewe —7B 148
Mill Vw. Gdns. Croy —3K 153
Millwall. —4C 88
Millwall Dock Rd. E14 —3C 88
Millwall F.C. —5J 87
Millway. NW7 —4F 13
Mill Way. Felt —5K 95
Millway Gdns. N'holt —6D 42
Millwood Rd. Houn —5G 97
Millwood St. W10 —5G 65
Mill Yd. E1 —7G 69
Milman Clo. Pinn —3B 24
Milman Rd. NW6 —2F 65
Milman's St. SW10 —6B 84 (7A 170)
Milne Gdns. SE9 —5C 108
Milne Ho. SE18 —4D 90
(off Ogilby St.)
Milner Dri. Twic —7H 97
Milner Pl. N1 —1A 68
Milner Pl. Cars —4E 150
Milner Rd. E15 —3G 71
Milner Rd. SW19 —1K 137
Milner Rd. Dag —2C 56
Milner Rd. King T —3D 134
Milner Rd. Mord —5B 138
Milner Rd. T Hth —3D 140
Milner Sq. N1 —7B 50
Milner St. SW3 —4D 84 (3E 170)
Milner Wlk. Sidc —2H 127
Milnthorpe Rd. W4 —6K 81
Milo Gdns. SE22 —6F 105
Milo Rd. SE22 —6F 105
Milroy Wlk. SE1 —1B 86 (4A 168)
Milson Rd. W14 —3F 83
Milstead Ho. E5 —5H 51
Milton Av. E6 —7B 54
Milton Av. N6 —7G 31
Milton Av. NW9 —3J 27
Milton Av. NW10 —1J 63
Milton Av. Barn —5C 4
Milton Av. Croy —7D 140
Milton Av. Sutt —3B 150
Milton Clo. N2 —5A 30
Milton Clo. SE1 —4F 87
Milton Clo. Hay —6J 59
Milton Clo. Sutt —3B 150
Milton Ct. EC2 —5D 68 (5E 162)
Milton Ct. SE14 —6B 88
Milton Ct. SW18 —5J 101
Milton Ct. Chad H —7C 38
Milton Ct. Twic —3J 115
Milton Ct. Uxb —3D 40
Milton Ct. Highwalk. EC2 —5D 68
(off Silk St.)
Milton Ct. Rd. SE14 —6A 88
Milton Cres. Ilf —7F 37
Milton Dri. Shep —4A 130
Milton Garden Est. N16 —4D 50
Milton Gdns. Stai —1B 112
Milton Gro. N11 —5B 16
Milton Gro. N16 —4D 50
Milton Ho. E17 —4C 34
Milton Ho. SE5 —7D 86
(off Elmington Est.)
Milton Ho. Sutt —3J 149
Milton Lodge. Sidc —4A 128
Milton Lodge. Twic —7K 97
Milton Mans. W14 —6G 83
(off Queen's Club Gdns.)
Milton Pk. N6 —7G 31
Milton Pl. N7 —5A 50
Milton Rd. E17 —4C 34
Milton Rd. N6 —7G 31
Milton Rd. N15 —4B 32
Milton Rd. NW7 —5H 13
Milton Rd. NW9 —7C 28
Milton Rd. SE24 —5B 104
Milton Rd. SW14 —3K 99
Milton Rd. SW19 —6A 120
Milton Rd. W3 —1K 81
Milton Rd. W7 —7K 61
Milton Rd. Belv —4G 93
Milton Rd. Croy —1D 152
Milton Rd. Hamp —7E 114
Milton Rd. Harr —4J 25
Milton Rd. Mitc —7E 120
Milton Rd. Sutt —3J 149
Milton Rd. Uxb —4D 40
Milton Rd. Wall —6G 151
Milton Rd. Well —1K 109
Milton St. EC2 —5D 68 (5E 162)
Milton Way. W Dray —4B 76
Milverton Dri. Uxb —4E 40
Milverton Gdns. Ilf —2K 55
Milverton Ho. SE23 —3A 124
Milverton Rd. NW6 —7E 46
Milverton St. SE11 —5A 86 (6K 173)
Milverton Way. SE9 —4E 126
Milward Wlk. E1 —5H 69
Milward Wlk. SE18 —6E 90
Mimosa Ho. Hay —5A 60
Mimosa Lodge. NW10 —5B 46
Mimosa Rd. Hay —5A 60
Mimosa St. SW6 —1H 101
Minard Rd. SE6 —7G 107
(in two parts)
Mina Rd. SE17 —5E 86
Mina Rd. SW19 —1J 137
Minchenden Ct. N14 —2C 16
Minchenden Cres. N14 —3B 16
Minchin Ho. E14 —6C 70
Mincing La. EC3 —7E 68 (2G 169)
Minden Rd. SE20 —1H 141
Minden Rd. Sutt —2H 149
Minehead Rd. SW16 —5K 121
Minehead Rd. Harr —3E 42
Mineral St. SE18 —4J 91
Minera M. SW1 —4E 84 (3G 171)
Minerva Clo. SW9 —7A 86
(in two parts)
Minerva Clo. Sidc —4J 127
Minerva Rd. E4 —7J 19
Minerva Rd. NW10 —4J 63
Minerva Rd. King T —2F 135
Minerva St. E2 —2H 69
Minet Av. NW10 —2A 64
Minet Dri. Hay —1J 77
Minet Gdns. NW10 —2A 64
Minet Gdns. Hay —1K 77
Minet Rd. SW9 —2B 104
Minford Gdns. W6 —2F 83
Mingard Wlk. N7 —2K 49
Ming St. E14 —7C 70
Minimax Clo. Felt —6J 95
Ministry Way. SE9 —2D 126
Miniver Pl. EC4 —2D 168
Mink Ct. Houn —2A 96
Minniedale. Surb —5F 135
Minnow St. SE17 —4E 86
Minnow Wlk. SE17 —4E 86
Minories. EC3 —6F 69 (1J 169)
Minshaw Ct. Sidc —4K 127
Minshill St. SW8 —1H 103
Minshull Pl. Beck —7C 124
Minson Rd. E9 —1K 69
Minstead Gdns. SW15 —7B 100
Minstead Way. N Mald —6A 136
Minster Av. Sutt —2J 149
Minster Ct. EC3 —2H 169
Minster Ct. W5 —4E 62
Minster Dri. Croy —4E 152
Minster Gdns. W Mol —4D 132
Minsterley Av. Shep —4G 131
Minster Pavement. EC3 —7E 68
(off Mincing La.)
Minster Rd. NW2 —5G 47
Minster Rd. Brom —7K 125
Minster Wlk. N8 —4J 31
Minstrel Gdns. Surb —4F 135
Mint Bus. Pk. E16 —5K 71
Mint Clo. Hil —3D 58
Mintern Clo. N13 —3G 17
Minterne Av. S'hall —4E 78
Minterne Rd. Harr —5F 27
Minterne Waye. Hay —6A 60
Mintern St. N1 —2D 68
Minton Ho. SE11 —3J 173
Minton M. NW6 —6K 47
Mint Rd. Wall —4F 151
Mint St. SE1 —2C 86 (6C 168)
Mint Wlk. Croy —3C 152
Mirabel Rd. SW6 —7H 83
Miranda Clo. E1 —5J 69
Miranda Ct. W3 —6F 63
Miranda Rd. N19 —1G 49
Mirfield St. SE7 —4B 90
Miriam Rd. SE18 —5J 91
Mirravale Trad. Est. Dag —7E 38
Mirren Clo. Harr —4D 42
Mirror Path. SE9 —3A 126
Misbourne Rd. Uxb —1C 58
Missenden. SE17 —5D 86
(off Roland Way)
Missenden Clo. Felt —1H 113
Missenden Gdns. Mord —6A 138
Missenden Ho. NW8 —3C 158
Mission Gro. E17 —5A 34
Mission Pl. SE15 —1G 105
Mission Sq. Bren —6E 80
Mission, The. E14 —6B 70
Mistletoe Clo. Croy —1K 153

Mistral—Morten Clo.

Mistral. SE5 —1E 104
Misty's Fld. W on T —7A 132
Mitali Pas. E1 —6G 69
(in two parts)
Mitcham. —3D 138
Mitcham Garden Village. Mitc —5E 138
Mitcham Ho. SE5 —1C 104
Mitcham Ind. Est. Mitc —1F 139
Mitcham La. SW16 —6G 121
Mitcham Pk. Mitc —4C 138
Mitcham Rd. E6 —3C 72
Mitcham Rd. SW17 —5D 120
Mitcham Rd. Croy —6J 139
Mitcham Rd. Ilf —7K 37
Mitcheldean Ct. SE15 —7E 86
(off Newent Clo.)
Mitchell. NW9 —1B 28
(off Concourse, The)
Mitchellbrook Way. NW10 —6K 45
Mitchell Clo. SE2 —5C 92
Mitchell Clo. Belv —3J 93
Mitchell Ho. W12 —7D 64
(off White City Est.)
Mitchell Rd. N13 —5H 17
Mitchell's Pl. SE21 —6E 104
(off Aysgarth Rd.)
Mitchell St. EC1 —4C 68 (3C 162)
(in two parts)
Mitchell Wlk. E6 —5C 72
(off Neats Ct. Rd.)
Mitchell Wlk. E6 —5D 72
(Lovage App.)
Mitchell Way. NW10 —6J 45
Mitchell Way. Brom —1J 143
Mitchison Rd. N1 —6D 50
Mitchley Rd. N17 —3G 33
Mitford Clo. Chess —6C 146
Mitford Rd. N19 —2J 49
Mitre Av. E17 —3C 34
Mitre Bri. Ind. Pk. W10 —4D 64
Mitre Clo. Brom —2H 143
Mitre Clo. Shep —6F 131
Mitre Clo. Sutt —7A 150
Mitre Ct. EC2 —7D 162
Mitre Rd. E15 —2G 71
Mitre Rd. SE1 —2A 86 (6K 167)
Mitre Sq. EC3 —6E 68 (1H 169)
Mitre St. EC3 —6E 68 (1H 169)
Mitre, The. E14 —7B 70
Mitre Way. NW10 —4D 64
Mitre Yd. SW3 —4C 84 (3D 170)
Moat Ct. SE9 —6D 108
Moat Ct. Sidc —3K 127
Moat Cres. N3 —3K 29
Moat Cft. Well —3C 110
Moat Dri. E13 —2A 72
Moat Dri. Harr —4G 25
Moat Dri. Ruis —7G 23
Moat Farm Rd. N'holt —6D 42
Moatfield. NW6 —7G 47
Moat Gdns. SE28 —7C 74
Moatlands Ho. WC1 —3J 67 (2F 161)
(off Cromer St.)
Moat Pl. SW9 —3K 103
Moat Pl. W3 —6H 63
Moat Side. Enf —4E 8
Moat Side. Felt —4A 114
Moat, The. N Mald —1A 136
Moberley Rd. SW4 —7H 103
Mobil Ct. WC2 —6K 67 (1H 167)
(off Clement's Inn)
Moby Dick. (Junct.) —4E 38
Modbury Gdns. NW5 —6E 48
Modder Pl. SW15 —4F 101
Model Bldgs. WC1 —2H 161
Model Cotts. SW14 —4J 99
Model Cotts. W13 —2B 80
Model Farm Clo. SE9 —3C 126
Modern Ct. EC4 —7A 162
Moelwyn. N7 —5H 49
Moelyn M. Harr —5A 26
Moffat Ct. SW19 —5J 119
Moffat Ho. SE5 —7C 86
Moffat Rd. N13 —6D 16
Moffat Rd. SW17 —4D 120
Moffat Rd. T Hth —2C 140
Mogden La. Iswth —5K 97
Mohammedi Pk. N'holt —1E 60
Mohmmad Khan Rd. E11 —1H 53
Moineau. NW9 —1B 28
(off Concourse, The)
Moira Clo. N17 —2E 32
Moira Rd. SE9 —4D 108
Mokswell Ct. N10 —1E 30
Moland Mead. SE16 —5K 87
Molasses Ho. SW11 —3A 102
(off Clove Hitch Quay)
Molasses Row. SW11 —3A 102
Mole Abbey Gdns. W Mol —3F 133
Mole Ct. Eps —4J 147
Molember Ct. E Mol —4J 133
Molember Rd. E Mol —5J 133
Molescroft. SE9 —3G 127
Molesey Av. W Mol —5D 132
Molesey Dri. Sutt —2G 149
Molesey Pk. Av. W Mol —5F 133
Molesey Pk. Clo. E Mol —5G 133
Molesey Pk. Rd. E Mol & W Mol —5F 133
Molesford Rd. SW6 —1J 101
Molesham Clo. W Mol —3F 133
Molesham Way. W Mol —3F 133
Molesworth Ho. SE17 —6B 86
(off Brandon Est.)
Molesworth St. SE13 —4E 106
Moliner Ct. Beck —7C 124
Mollis Ho. E3 —5C 70
Mollison Dri. Wall —7H 151
Mollison Way. Edgw —2F 27
Molly Huggins Clo. SW12 —7G 103
Molton Ho. N1 —1K 67
(off Barnsbury Est.)
Molyneux Dri. SW17 —4F 121
Molyneux St. W1 —5C 66 (6D 158)
Monarch Clo. Felt —7G 95
Monarch Clo. W W'ck —4H 155
Monarch Ct. N2 —5B 30
Monarch Dri. E16 —5B 72
Monarch M. E17 —6D 34
Monarch M. SW16 —5A 122
Monarch Pde. Mitc —2D 138
Monarch Pl. Buck H —2F 21
Monarch Rd. Belv —3G 93
Monarchs Way. Ruis —1G 41
Mona Rd. SE15 —2J 105
Monastery Gdns. Enf —2J 7
Mona St. E16 —5H 71
Monaveen Gdns. W Mol —3F 133
Moncks Row. SW15 —6H 101
(off West Hill Rd.)
Monck St. SW1 —3H 85 (2D 172)
Monclar Rd. SE5 —4D 104
Moncorvo Clo. SW7 —7C 164
Moncreiff Pl. SE15 —2G 105
Moncrieff Clo. E6 —6C 72
Moncrieff St. SE15 —2G 105
Mondial Way. Hay —7E 76
Monega Rd. E7 & E12 —6A 54
Moneyer Ho. N1 —2D 68 (1E 162)
(off Provost Est.)
Mongomery Ct. W4 —7J 81
Monica Ct. Enf —5K 7
Monica James Ho. Sidc —3A 128
Monica Shaw Ct. NW1 —2H 67 (1D 160)
(off Purchese St., in two parts)
Monier Rd. E3 —7C 52
Monivea Rd. Beck —7B 124
Monk Ct. W12 —1C 82
Monk Dri. E16 —7J 71
Monken Hadley. —2C 4
Monkfrith Av. N14 —6A 6
Monkfrith Clo. N14 —7A 6
Monkfrith Way. N14 —7K 5
Monkham's Av. Wfd G —5E 20
Monkham's Dri. Wfd G —5E 20
Monkham's La. Buck H —3E 20
Monkham's La. Wfd G —5D 20
(in two parts)
Monkleigh Rd. Mord —3G 137
Monk Pas. E16 —7J 71
(off Monk Dri.)
Monks Av. Barn —6F 5
Monks Av. W Mol —5D 132
Monks Clo. SE2 —4D 92
Monks Clo. Enf —2H 7
Monks Clo. Harr —2E 42
Monks Clo. Ruis —4B 42
Monks Cres. W on T —7K 131
Monksdene Gdns. Sutt —3K 149
Monks Dri. W3 —5G 63
Monks Orchard. —7A 142
Monks Orchard Rd. Beck —1C 154
Monks Pk. Wemb —6H 45
Monks Pk. Gdns. Wemb —7H 45
Monks Rd. Enf —2G 7
Monk St. SE18 —4E 90
Monks Way. NW11 —4H 29
Monks Way. Beck —6C 142
Monks Way. Orp —7G 145
Monks Way. W Dray —6A 76
Monkswood Gdns. Ilf —3E 36
Monkton Ho. E5 —5H 51
Monkton Rd. Well —2K 109
Monkton St. SE11 —4A 86 (3K 173)
Monkville Av. NW11 —4H 29
Monkville Pde. NW11 —4H 29
Monkwell Sq. EC2 —5C 68 (6D 162)
Monmouth Av. E18 —3K 35
Monmouth Av. King T —7C 116
Monmouth Clo. W4 —3J 81
Monmouth Clo. Mitc —4J 139
Monmouth Clo. Well —4A 110
Monmouth Ct. W7 —5K 61
(off Copley Clo.)
Monmouth Gro. W5 —4E 80
Monmouth Pl. W2 —6K 65
(off Monmouth Rd.)
Monmouth Rd. E6 —3D 72
Monmouth Rd. N9 —2C 18
Monmouth Rd. W2 —6J 65
Monmouth Rd. Dag —5F 57
Monmouth Rd. Hay —4G 77
Monmouth St. WC2 —6J 67 (1E 166)
Monnery Rd. N19 —3G 49
Monnow Rd. SE1 —5G 87
Mono La. Felt —2K 113
Monoux Almshouses. E17 —4D 34
Monoux Gro. E17 —1C 34
Monroe Cres. Enf —1C 8
Monroe Dri. SW14 —5H 99
Monro Gdns. Harr —7D 10
Monsell Rd. N4 —3A 50
Monson Rd. NW10 —2C 64
Monson Rd. SE14 —7K 87
Mons Way. Brom —6C 144
Montacute Rd. SE6 —7B 106
Montacute Rd. Bus H —1D 10
Montacute Rd. Mord —6B 138
Montacute Rd. New Ad —7E 154
Montagu Cres. N18 —4C 18
Montague Av. SE4 —4B 106
Montague Av. W7 —1K 79
Montague Clo. SE1 —1D 86 (4E 168)
Montague Clo. W on T —7K 131
Montague Ct. Sidc —3A 128
Montague Gdns. W3 —7G 63
Montague Pas. Uxb —7A 40
Montague Pl. E14 —7E 70
Montague Pl. WC1 —5H 67 (5D 160)
Montague Rd. E8 —5G 51
Montague Rd. E11 —2H 53
Montague Rd. N8 —5K 31
Montague Rd. N15 —4G 33
Montague Rd. SW19 —7K 119
Montague Rd. W7 —1K 79
Montague Rd. W13 —6B 62
Montague Rd. Croy —1B 152
Montague Rd. Houn —3F 97
Montague Rd. Rich —6E 98
Montague Rd. S'hall —4C 78
Montague Rd. Uxb —7A 40
Montague Sq. SE15 —7J 87
Montague St. EC1 —5C 68 (6C 162)
Montague St. WC1 —5J 67 (5E 160)
Montague Ter. Brom —4H 143
Montague Waye. S'hall —3C 78
Montagu Gdns. N18 —4C 18
Montagu Gdns. Wall —4G 151
Montagu Mans. W1 —5D 66 (5F 159)
Montagu M. N. W1 —5D 66 (6F 159)
Montagu M. S. W1 —6D 66 (7F 159)
Montagu M. W. W1 —6D 66 (7F 159)
Montagu Pl. W1 —5D 66 (6E 158)
Montagu Rd. N18 & N9 —5C 18
Montagu Rd. NW4 —6C 28
Montagu Rd. Ind. Est. N18 —4D 18
Montagu Row. W1 —5D 66 (6F 159)
Montagu Sq. W1 —5D 66 (6F 159)
Montagu St. W1 —6D 66 (7F 159)
Montalt Rd. Wfd G —4C 20
Montana Gdns. SE26 —5B 124
Montana Gdns. Sutt —5A 150
Montana Rd. SW17 —3E 120
Montana Rd. SW20 —1E 136
Montbelle Rd. SE9 —3F 127
Montcalm Clo. Brom —6J 143
Montcalm Clo. Hay —3K 59
Montcalm Ho. E14 —4C 88
Montcalm Rd. SE7 —7B 90
Montclare St. E2 —4F 69 (3J 163)
Monteagle Av. Bark —6G 55
Monteagle Ct. N1 —2E 68
Monteagle Way. E5 —3G 51
Monteagle Way. SE15 —3H 105
Montefiore St. SW8 —2F 103
Montego Clo. SE24 —4A 104
Montem Rd. SE23 —7B 106
Montem Rd. N Mald —4A 136
Montem St. N4 —1K 49
Montenotte Rd. N8 —5G 31
Monterey Clo. Bex —2J 129
Monterey Pl. Shop. Cen. NW7 —5F 13
Montesole Ct. Pinn —2A 24
Montesquieu Ter. E16 —6H 71
(off Clarkson Rd.)
Montevetro. SW11 —1B 102
Montford Pl. SE11 —5A 86 (6J 173)
Montford Rd. Sun —4J 131
Montfort Ho. E14 —3E 88
Montfort Pl. SW19 —1F 119
Montgolfier Wlk. N'holt —3C 60
Montgomery Clo. Mitc —4J 139
Montgomery Clo. Sidc —6K 109
Montgomery Rd. W4 —4J 81
Montgomery Rd. Edgw —6A 12
Montholme Rd. SW11 —6D 102
Monthope Rd. E1 —6K 163
(in two parts)
Montolieu Gdns. SW15 —5D 100
Montpelier Av. W5 —5C 62
Montpelier Av. Bex —7D 110
Montpelier Clo. Uxb —1C 58
Montpelier Ct. W5 —5D 62
Montpelier Gdns. E6 —3B 72
Montpelier Gdns. Romf —7C 38
Montpelier Gro. NW5 —5G 49
Montpelier M. SW7 —3C 84 (1D 170)
Montpelier Pl. E1 —6J 69
Montpelier Pl. SW7 —3C 84 (1D 170)
Montpelier Ri. NW11 —7G 29
Montpelier Ri. Wemb —1D 44
Montpelier Rd. N3 —1A 30
Montpelier Rd. SE15 —1H 105
Montpelier Rd. W5 —5D 62
Montpelier Rd. Sutt —4A 150
Montpelier Row. SE3 —2H 107
Montpelier Row. Twic —7C 98
Montpelier Sq. SW7 —2C 84 (7D 164)
Montpelier St. SW7 —3C 84 (1D 170)
Montpelier Ter. SW7 —2C 84 (7D 164)
Montpelier Va. SE3 —2H 107
Montpelier Wlk. SW7 —3C 84 (1D 170)
Montpelier Way. NW11 —7G 29
Montrave Rd. SE20 —6J 123
Montreal Pl. WC2 —7K 67 (2G 167)
Montreal Rd. Ilf —7G 37
Montrell Rd. SW2 —1J 121
Montrose Av. NW6 —2G 65
Montrose Av. Edgw —2J 27
Montrose Av. Sidc —7A 110
Montrose Av. Twic —7F 97
Montrose Av. Well —3H 109
Montrose Clo. Ashf —6E 112
Montrose Clo. Well —3K 109
Montrose Clo. Wfd G —4D 20
Montrose Ct. NW9 —2J 27
Montrose Ct. NW11 —4H 29
Montrose Ct. SE6 —1H 125
Montrose Ct. SW7 —2B 84 (7B 164)
Montrose Ct. Harr —5F 25
Montrose Cres. N12 —6F 15
Montrose Cres. Wemb —6E 44
Montrose Gdns. Mitc —2D 138
Montrose Gdns. Sutt —2K 149
Montrose Ho. E14 —3C 88
Montrose Pl. SW1 —2E 84 (7H 165)
Montrose Rd. Felt —6F 95
Montrose Rd. Harr —2J 25
Montrose Wlk. Stan —6G 11
Montrose Way. SE23 —1K 123
Montserrat Av. Wfd G —7A 20
Montserrat Clo. SE19 —5D 122
Montserrat Rd. SW15 —4G 101
Monument Gdns. SE13 —5E 106
Monument St. EC3 —7D 68 (2F 169)
Monument, The. —3F 169
Monument Way. N17 —3F 33
Monza St. E1 —7J 69
Moodkee St. SE16 —3J 87
Moody Rd. SE15 —1F 105
Moody St. E1 —3K 69
Moon Ct. SE12 —4J 107
Moon La. Barn —3C 4
Moon St. N1 —1B 68
Moorcroft. Edgw —1H 27
Moorcroft Gdns. Brom —5C 144
Moorcroft La. Uxb —5C 58
Moorcroft Rd. SW16 —3J 121
Moorcroft Way. Pinn —5C 24
Moordown. SE18 —7F 91
Moore Clo. SW14 —3J 99
Moore Clo. Mitc —2F 139
Moore Clo. Wall —7J 151
Moore Ct. N1 —1B 68
(off Gaskin St.)
Moore Cres. Dag —1B 74
Moorehead Way. SE3 —3J 107
Moore Ho. N8 —4J 31
(off Pembroke Rd.)
Mooreland Rd. Brom —7H 125
Moore Pk. Ct. SW6 —7K 83
(off Fulham Rd.)
Moore Pk. Rd. SW6 —7J 83
Moore Rd. SE19 —6C 122
Moore St. SW3 —4D 84 (3E 170)
Moore Wlk. E7 —4J 53
Moorey Clo. E15 —1H 71
Moorfield Av. W5 —4D 62
Moorfield Rd. N17 —2F 33
Moorfield Rd. Chess —5E 146
Moorfield Rd. Enf —1D 8
Moorfield Rd. Uxb —6A 58
Moorfields. EC2 —5D 68 (6E 162)
Moorfields Highwalk. EC2 —5D 68
(off Moor La., in two parts)
Moorgate. EC2 —6D 68 (7E 162)
Moorgate Pl. EC2 —7E 162
Moorgreen Ho. EC1 —1A 162
Moorhouse. NW9 —1B 28
Moorhouse Rd. W2 —6J 65
Moorhouse Rd. Harr —3D 26
Moorings, The. E16 —5A 72
(off Prince Regent La.)
Moorland Clo. Romf —1H 39
Moorland Clo. Twic —7E 96
Moorland M. N1 —7A 50
Moorland Rd. SW9 —4B 104
Moorlands. N'holt —1C 60
Moorlands Av. NW7 —6J 13
Moor La. EC2 —5D 68 (6E 162)
(in two parts)
Moor La. Chess —4E 146
Moormead Dri. Eps —5A 148
Moor Mead Rd. Twic —6A 98
Moor Pk. Gdns. King T —7A 118
Moor Pl. EC2 —5D 68 (6E 162)
Moorside Rd. Brom —3G 125
Moor St. W1 —6H 67 (1D 166)
Moot Ct. NW9 —5G 27
Morant Pl. N22 —1K 31
Morant St. E14 —7C 70
Mora Rd. NW2 —4E 46
Mora St. EC1 —3C 68 (2D 162)
Morat St. SW9 —1K 103
Moravian Clo. SW10 —6B 84 (7A 170)
Moravian Pl. SW10 —6B 84
Moravian St. E2 —2J 69
Moray Av. Hay —1H 77
Moray Clo. Edgw —2C 12
Moray Clo. Romf —1K 39
Moray M. N7 —2K 49
Moray Rd. N4 —2K 49
Moray Way. Romf —1K 39
Mordaunt Gdns. Dag —7E 56
Mordaunt Ho. NW10 —1K 63
Mordaunt Rd. NW10 —1K 63
Mordaunt St. SW9 —3K 103
Morden. —3K 137
Morden Ct. Mord —4K 137
Morden Ct. Pde. Mord —4K 137
Morden Gdns. Gnfd —5K 43
Morden Gdns. Mitc —4B 138
Morden Hall Rd. Mord —3K 137
Morden Hill. SE13 —2E 106
Morden La. SE13 —1E 106
Morden Park. —6G 137
Morden Rd. SE3 —2J 107
Morden Rd. SW19 —1K 137
Morden Rd. Mord & Mitc —4A 138
Morden Rd. Romf —7E 38
Morden Rd. M. SE3 —2J 107
Morden St. SE13 —1D 106
Morden Way. Sutt —7J 137
Morden Wharf Rd. SE10 —3G 89
Mordern Ho. NW1 —3D 158
Mordon Rd. Ilf —7K 37
Mordred Rd. SE6 —2G 125
Morecambe Clo. E1 —5K 69
Morecambe Gdns. Stan —4J 11
Morecambe St. SE17 —4C 86
Morecambe Ter. N18 —4J 17
(off Gt. Cambridge Rd.)
More Clo. E16 —6H 71
More Clo. W14 —4F 83
Morecoombe Clo. King T —7H 117
Moree Way. N18 —4B 18
Moreland Ct. NW2 —3J 47
Moreland St. EC1 —3B 68 (1B 162)
Moreland Way. E4 —3J 19
Morella Rd. SW12 —7D 102
Morello Av. Uxb —5D 58
Moremead Rd. SE6 —4B 124
Morena St. SE6 —7D 106
Moresby Av. Surb —7H 135
Moresby Rd. E5 —1H 51
Moresby Wlk. SW8 —2G 103
More's Garden. SW3 —6B 84
(off Cheyne Wlk.)
Moreton Av. Iswth —1J 97
Moreton Clo. E5 —2H 51
Moreton Clo. N15 —6D 32
Moreton Clo. NW7 —6K 13
Moreton Clo. SW1 —5B 172
Moreton Gdns. Wfd G —5H 21
Moreton Ho. SE16 —3H 87
Moreton Pl. SW1 —5G 85 (5B 172)
Moreton Rd. N15 —6D 32
Moreton Rd. S Croy —5D 152
Moreton Rd. Wor Pk —2C 148
Moreton St. SW1 —5G 85 (5B 172)
Moreton Ter. SW1 —5G 85 (5B 172)
Moreton Ter. M. N. SW1 —5G 85 (5B 172)
Moreton Ter. M. S. SW1 —5G 85 (5B 172)
Moreton Tower. W3 —1H 81
Morford Clo. Ruis —7K 23
Morford Way. Ruis —7K 23
Morgan Av. E17 —4F 35
Morgan Clo. Dag —7G 57
Morgan Ct. Ashf —5D 112
Morgan Ho. SW1 —4G 85 (4B 172)
(off Vauxhall Bri. Rd.)
Morgan Mans. N7 —5A 50
(off Morgan Rd.)
Morgan Rd. N7 —5A 50
Morgan Rd. W10 —5H 65
Morgan Rd. Brom —7J 125
Morgan Rd. Tedd —6J 115
Morgan's La. SE1 —1E 86 (5G 169)
Morgan's La. Hay —5F 59
Morgan St. E3 —3A 70
Morgan St. E16 —5H 71
Morgan Wlk. Beck —4D 142
Morgan Way. Wfd G —6H 21
Moriatry Clo. N7 —4J 49
Morie St. SW18 —5K 101
Morieux Rd. E10 —1B 52
Moring Rd. SW17 —4E 120
Morkyns Wlk. SE21 —3E 122
Morland Av. Croy —1E 152
Morland Clo. NW11 —1K 47
Morland Clo. Hamp —5D 114
Morland Clo. Mitc —3C 138
Morland Est. E8 —7G 51
Morland Gdns. NW10 —7K 45
Morland Gdns. S'hall —1F 79
Morland Ho. NW1 —2G 67 (1B 160)
(off Cranleigh St.)
Morland Ho. NW6 —1J 65
(off Brondesbury Rd.)
Morland Ho. SW1 —4J 85 (3E 172)
(off Marsham St.)
Morland Ho. W11 —6G 65
(off Lancaster Rd.)
Morland Rd. E17 —5K 33
Morland Rd. SE20 —6K 123
Morland Rd. Croy —1E 152
Morland Rd. Dag —7G 57
Morland Rd. Harr —5E 26
Morland Rd. Ilf —2F 55
Morland Rd. Sutt —5A 150
Morley Av. E4 —7A 20
Morley Av. N18 —4B 18
Morley Av. N22 —2A 32
Morley Ct. E4 —5G 19
Morley Ct. Short —4H 143
Morley Cres. Edgw —2D 12
Morley Cres. Ruis —2A 42
Morley Cres. E. Stan —2C 26
Morley Cres. W. Stan —3C 26
Morley Hill. Enf —1J 7
Morley Ho. N16 —2G 51
Morley Rd. E10 —1E 52
Morley Rd. E15 —2H 71
Morley Rd. SE13 —4E 106
Morley Rd. Bark —1H 73
Morley Rd. Chst —1G 145
Morley Rd. Romf —5E 38
Morley Rd. Sutt —1H 149
Morley Rd. Twic —6D 98
Morley St. SE1 —3A 86 (1K 173)
Morna Rd. SE5 —2C 104
Morning La. E9 —6J 51
Morningside Rd. Wor Pk —2D 148
Mornington Av. W14 —4H 83
Mornington Av. Brom —3A 144
Mornington Av. Ilf —7E 36
Mornington Clo. Wfd G —4D 20
Mornington Ct. NW1 —2G 67
(off Mornington Cres.)
Mornington Ct. Bex —1K 129
Mornington Cres. NW1 —2G 67
Mornington Cres. Houn —1K 95
Mornington Gro. E3 —3C 70
Mornington M. SE5 —1C 104
Mornington Pl. NW1 —2G 67
Mornington Rd. E4 —7K 9
Mornington Rd. E11 —7H 35
Mornington Rd. SE14 —7B 88
Mornington Rd. Ashf —5E 112
Mornington Rd. Gnfd —5F 61
Mornington Rd. Wfd G —4C 20
Mornington St. NW1 —2F 67
Mornington Ter. NW1 —1F 67
Mornington Wlk. Rich —4C 116
Morocco St. SE1 —2E 86 (7G 169)
Morpeth Gro. E9 —1K 69
Morpeth Mans. SW1 —4G 85 (3A 172)
(off Morpeth Ter.)
Morpeth Rd. E9 —1K 69
Morpeth St. E2 —3K 69
Morpeth Ter. SW1 —3G 85 (2A 172)
Morpeth Wlk. N17 —7C 18
Morrab Gdns. Ilf —3K 55
Morrel Ct. E2 —2G 69
(off Goldsmiths Row)
Morrell Clo. New Bar —3F 5
Morris Av. E12 —5D 54
Morris Blitz Ct. N16 —4F 51
Morris Clo. Croy —5A 142
Morris Ct. E4 —3J 19
Morris Gdns. SW18 —7J 101
Morris Ho. NW8 —4C 66 (4C 158)
(off Salisbury St.)
Morrish Rd. SW2 —7J 103
Morrison Av. N17 —3E 32
Morrison Bldgs. N. E1 —6G 69
(off Commercial Rd.)
Morrison Bldgs. S. E1 —6G 69
(off Commercial Rd.)
Morrison Ct. Barn —4B 4
(off Manor Way)
Morrison Rd. Bark —2E 74
Morrison Rd. Hay —3K 59
Morrison St. SW11 —3E 102
Morris Pl. N4 —2A 50
Morris Rd. E14 —5D 70
Morris Rd. E15 —4G 53
Morris Rd. Dag —2F 57
Morris Rd. Iswth —3K 97
Morriss Ho. SE16 —2H 87
(off Cherry Garden St.)
Morris St. E1 —6H 69
Morritt Ho. Wemb —5D 44
(off Talbot Rd.)
Morse Clo. E13 —3J 71
Morshead Mans. W9 —3J 65
(off Morshead Rd.)
Morshead Rd. W9 —3J 65
Morson Rd. Enf —6F 9
Morston Gdns. SE9 —4D 126
Mortain Ho. SE16 —4H 87
(off Roseberry St.)
Morten Clo. SW4 —6H 103

Morteyne Rd.—Nash Pl.

Morteyne Rd. N17 —1D 32
Mortgramit Sq. SE18 —3E 90
Mortham St. E15 —1G 71
Mortimer Clo. NW2 —2H 47
Mortimer Clo. SW16 —2H 121
Mortimer Ct. NW8 —2A 66 (1A 158)
(off Abercorn Pl.)
Mortimer Cres. NW6 —1K 65
Mortimer Cres. Wor Pk —3K 147
Mortimer Dri. Enf —6J 7
Mortimer Est. NW6 —1K 65
(off Mortimer Pl.)
Mortimer Ho. W11 —1F 83
(off Queensdale Cres.)
Mortimer Ho. W14 —4G 83
(off N. End Rd.)
Mortimer Mkt. WC1
—4G 67 (4B 160)
Mortimer Mkt. Cen. W1 —4G 67
Mortimer Pl. NW6 —1K 65
Mortimer Rd. E6 —3D 72
Mortimer Rd. N1 —7E 50
(in two parts)
Mortimer Rd. NW10 —3E 64
Mortimer Rd. W13 —6C 62
Mortimer Rd. Eri —6K 93
Mortimer Rd. Mitc —1D 138
Mortimer Sq. W11 —7F 65
Mortimer St. W1 —6G 67 (7K 159)
Mortimer Ter. NW5 —4F 49
Mortlake. —3K 99
Mortlake Clo. Croy —3J 151
Mortlake Crematorium. Rich —2J 99
Mortlake Dri. Mitc —1C 138
Mortlake High St. SW14 —3K 99
Mortlake Rd. E16 —6K 71
Mortlake Rd. Ilf —4G 55
Mortlake Rd. Rich —7G 81
Mortlake Ter. Rich —7G 81
(off Mortlake Rd.)
Mortlock Clo. SE15 —1H 105
Mortlock Ct. E7 —4B 54
Morton Clo. Wall —7K 151
Morton Ct. N'holt —5G 43
Morton Cres. N14 —4C 16
Morton Gdns. Wall —5G 151
Morton M. SW5 —4K 83
Morton Pl. SE1 —3A 86 (2J 173)
Morton Rd. E15 —7H 53
Morton Rd. N1 —7C 50
Morton Rd. Mord —5B 138
Morton Way. N14 —3B 16
Morvale Clo. Belv —4F 93
Morval Rd. SW2 —5A 104
Morven Rd. SW17 —3D 120
Morville St. E3 —2C 70
Morwell St. WC1 —5H 67 (6C 160)
Moscow Pl. W2 —7K 65
Moscow Rd. W2 —7J 65
Mosedale. NW1 —3G 67 (2K 159)
(off Cumberland Mkt.)
Moselle Av. N22 —2A 32
Moselle Clo. N8 —3K 31
Moselle Ho. N17 —7A 18
(off William St.)
Moselle Pl. N17 —7A 18
Moselle St. N17 —7A 18
Mossborough Clo. N12 —6E 14
Mossbury Rd. SW11 —3C 102
Moss Clo. E1 —5G 69
Moss Clo. Pinn —2D 24
Mossdown Clo. Belv —4G 93
Mossford Ct. Ilf —2F 37
Mossford Grn. Ilf —3F 37
Mossford La. Ilf —2F 37
Mossford St. E3 —4B 70
Moss Gdns. Felt —2J 113
Moss Gdns. S Croy —7K 153
Moss Hall Ct. N12 —6E 14
Moss Hall Cres. N12 —6E 14
Moss Hall Gro. N12 —6E 14
Mossington Gdns. SE16 —4J 87
Moss La. Pinn —1C 24
Mosslea Rd. SE20 —6J 123
(in two parts)
Mosslea Rd. Brom —5B 144
Mossop St. SW3 —4C 84 (3D 170)
Moss Rd. Dag —7G 57
Mossville Gdns. Mord —3H 137
Mosswell Ho. N10 —1E 30
Moston Clo. Hay —5H 77
Mostyn Av. Wemb —5F 45
Mostyn Gdns. NW10 —3F 65
Mostyn Gro. E3 —2C 70
Mostyn Rd. SW9 —1A 104
Mostyn Rd. SW19 —1H 137
Mostyn Rd. Edgw —7F 13
Mosul Way. Brom —6C 144
Mota M. N3 —1J 29
Motcomb St. SW1 —3E 84 (1G 171)
Moth Clo. Wall —7J 151
Mothers Sq. E5 —4H 51
Motley Av. EC2 —4G 163
Motley St. SW8 —2G 103
Motspur Park. —6C 136
Motspur Pk. N Mald —6B 136
Mottingham. —2C 126
Mottingham Gdns. SE9 —1B 126
Mottingham La. SE12 & SE9 —1A 126
Mottingham Rd. N9 —6E 8
Mottingham Rd. SE9 —2C 126
Mottisfont Rd. SE2 —3A 92
Mott St. E4 & Lou —1K 9
Moules Ct. SE5 —7C 86
Moulins Rd. E9 —7J 51
Moulsford Ho. N7 —5H 49
Moulton Av. Houn —2C 96
Moundfield Rd. N16 —6G 33
Mound, The. SE9 —3E 126
Mounsey Ho. W10 —3G 65
(off Third Av.)
Mountacre Clo. SE26 —4F 123
Mt. Adon Pk. SE22 —7G 105
Mountague Pl. E14 —7E 70
Mountain Ho. SE11 —4K 85 (4H 173)
Mt. Angelus Rd. SW15 —7B 100
Mt. Ararat Rd. Rich —5E 98
Mt. Arlington. Short —2G 143
(off Park Hill Rd.)
Mt. Ash Rd. SE26 —3H 123
Mount Av. E4 —3H 19
Mount Av. W5 —5C 62
Mount Av. S'hall —6E 60
Mountbatten Clo. SE18 —6J 91
Mountbatten Clo. SE19 —5E 122
Mountbatten Ct. Buck H —2G 21
Mountbatten Gdns. Beck —4A 142
Mountbatten Ho. N6 —7E 30
(off Hillcrest)
Mountbatten M. SW18 —7A 102
Mountbel Rd. Stan —1A 26
Mt. Carmel Chambers. W8 —2J 83
(off Pitt St. La.)
Mount Clo. W5 —5C 62
Mount Clo. Brom —1C 144
Mount Clo. Cars —7E 150
Mount Clo. Cockf —4K 5
Mountcombe Clo. Surb —7E 134
Mount Ct. SW15 —3G 101
Mount Ct. W W'ck —2G 155
Mt. Culver Av. Sidc —6D 128
Mount Dri. Bexh —5E 110
Mount Dri. Harr —5D 24
Mount Dri. Wemb —2J 45
Mountearl Gdns. SW16 —3K 121
Mt. Eaton Ct. W5 —5C 62
(off Mount Av.)
Mt. Echo Av. E4 —2J 19
Mt. Echo Dri. E4 —1J 19
Mt. Ephraim La. SW16 —3H 121
Mt. Ephraim Rd. SW16 —3H 121
Mt. Felix. W on T —7H 131
Mountfield Clo. SE6 —7F 107
Mountfield Rd. E6 —2E 72
Mountfield Rd. N3 —3H 29
Mountfield Rd. W5 —6D 62
Mountford Rd. E8 —5G 51
Mountford St. E1 —6G 69
Mountfort Cres. N1 —7A 50
Mountfort Ter. N1 —7A 50
Mount Gdns. SE26 —3H 123
Mount Gro. Edgw —3D 12
Mountgrove Rd. N5 —3B 50
Mounthurst Rd. Brom —7H 143
Mountington Pk. Clo. Harr —6D 26
Mountjoy Clo. EC2 —5C 68
(off Beech St.)
Mountjoy Clo. SE2 —2B 92
Mountjoy Ho. EC2 —6C 162
Mt. Lodge. N6 —6G 31
Mount M. Hamp —1F 133
Mt. Mills. EC1 —3B 68 (2B 162)
Mt. Nod Rd. SW16 —3K 121
Mt. Olive Ct. W7 —2J 79
Mount Pde. Barn —4H 5
Mount Pk. Cars —7E 150
Mount Pk. Av. Harr —2H 43
Mount Pk. Av. S Croy —7B 152
Mount Pk. Cres. W5 —6D 62
Mount Pk. Rd. W5 —5D 62
Mount Pk. Rd. Harr —3H 43
Mount Pk. Rd. Pinn —5J 23
Mount Pl. W3 —1H 81
Mt. Pleasant. N14 —7C 6
(off Wells, The)
Mt. Pleasant. SE27 —4C 122
Mt. Pleasant. WC1 —4A 68 (4J 161)
Mt. Pleasant. Barn —4H 5
Mt. Pleasant. Ilf —5G 55
Mt. Pleasant. Ruis —2A 42
Mt. Pleasant. Wemb —1E 62
Mt. Pleasant Cres. N4 —1K 49
Mt. Pleasant Hill. E5 —2H 51
Mt. Pleasant La. E5 —1H 51
Mt. Pleasant Pl. SE18 —4H 91
Mt. Pleasant Rd. E17 —2A 34
Mt. Pleasant Rd. N17 —2E 32
Mt. Pleasant Rd. NW10 —7E 46
Mt. Pleasant Rd. SE13 —6D 106
Mt. Pleasant Rd. W5 —4C 62
Mt. Pleasant Rd. N Mald —3J 135
Mt. Pleasant Vs. N4 —7K 31
Mt. Pleasant Wlk. Bex —5J 111
Mount Rd. NW2 —3D 46
Mount Rd. NW4 —6C 28
Mount Rd. SW19 —2J 119
Mount Rd. Barn —5H 5
Mount Rd. Chess —5F 147
Mount Rd. Dag —1F 57
Mount Rd. Felt —3C 114
Mount Rd. Hay —2J 77
Mount Rd. Mitc —2B 138
Mount Rd. N Mald —3K 135
Mount Row. W1 —7F 67 (3J 165)
Mountsfield Ct. SE13 —6F 107
Mountside. Stan —1K 25
Mounts Pond Rd. SE3 —2F 107
(in two parts)
Mount Sq., The. NW3 —3A 48
Mounts Rd. Bexh —5D 110
Mt. Stewart Av. Harr —7D 26
Mount St. W1 —7E 66 (3G 165)
Mount St. M. W1 —7F 67 (3J 165)
Mount Ter. E1 —5H 69
Mount, The. E5 —2H 51
(in two parts)
Mount, The. N20 —2F 15
Mount, The. NW3 —3A 48
Mount, The. W3 —1J 81
Mount, The. Bexh —5H 111
Mount, The. N Mald —3B 136
Mount, The. N'holt —5F 43
Mount, The. Wemb —2H 45
Mount, The. Wor Pk —4D 148
Mt. Vernon. NW3 —4A 48
Mount Vw. NW7 —3E 12
Mount Vw. W5 —4D 62
Mount Vw. Enf —1E 6
Mount Vw. S'hall —4B 78
Mountview Ct. N8 —4B 32
Mount Vw. Rd. E4 —7K 9
Mount Vw. Rd. N4 —7J 31
Mount Vw. Rd. NW9 —5K 27
Mount Vw. Rd. Clay —7B 146
Mountview Rd. Orp —7K 145
(in two parts)
Mount Vs. SE27 —3B 122
Mount Way. Cars —7E 150
Mount Wood. W Mol —3F 133
Movers Lane. (Junct.) —2J 73
Movers La. Bark —1H 73
Mowat Ct. Wor Pk —2B 148
(off Avenue, The)
Mowatt Clo. N19 —2H 49
Mowbray Ct. N22 —1A 32
Mowbray Ct. SE19 —7F 123
Mowbray Gdns. N'holt —1E 60
Mowbray Ho. N2 —2B 30
(off Grange, The)
Mowbray Pde. Edgw —4B 12
Mowbray Pde. N'holt —1E 60
Mowbray Rd. NW6 —7G 47
Mowbray Rd. SE19 —1F 141
Mowbray Rd. Edgw —4B 12
Mowbray Rd. New Bar —5F 5
Mowbray Rd. Rich —3C 116
Mowbrays Clo. Romf —1J 39
Mowbrays Rd. Romf —2J 39
Mowlem St. E2 —2H 69
Mowlem Trad. Est. N17 —7D 18
Mowll St. SW9 —7A 86
Moxon Clo. E13 —2H 71
Moxon St. W1 —5E 66 (6G 159)
Moxon St. Barn —3C 4
Moye Clo. E2 —2G 69
Moyers Rd. E10 —7E 34
Moylan Rd. W6 —6G 83
Moyle Ho. SW1 —5G 85 (6B 172)
(off Churchill Gdns.)
Moyne Ho. SW9 —5B 104
Moyne Pl. NW10 —2G 63
Moynihan Dri. N21 —5D 6
Moys Clo. Croy —6J 139
Moyser Rd. SW16 —5F 121
Mozart St. W10 —3H 65
Mozart Ter. SW1 —4E 84 (4H 171)
Muchelney Rd. Mord —6A 138
Mudlarks Way. SE10 & SE7 —3H 89
(in two parts)
Muggeridge Clo. S Croy —5D 152
Muggeridge Rd. Dag —4H 57
Muirdown Av. SW14 —4K 99
Muir Dri. SW18 —6C 102
Muirfield. W3 —6A 64
Muirfield Clo. SE16 —5H 87
Muirfield Cres. E14 —3D 88
Muirkirk Rd. SE6 —1E 124
Muir Rd. E5 —4G 51
Muir St. E16 —1C 90
Mulberry Av. Stai —1A 112
Mulberry Bus. Cen. SE16 —2K 87
Mulberry Clo. E4 —2H 19
Mulberry Clo. N8 —5J 31
Mulberry Clo. NW3 —4B 48
Mulberry Clo. NW4 —3E 28
Mulberry Clo. SE7 —6B 90
Mulberry Clo. SE22 —5G 105
Mulberry Clo. SW3 —6B 84 (7B 170)
Mulberry Clo. SW16 —4G 121
Mulberry Clo. Barn —4G 5
Mulberry Clo. N'holt —2C 60
Mulberry Ct. EC1 —3B 68 (2B 162)
(off Tompion St.)
Mulberry Ct. Bark —7K 55
Mulberry Ct. Surb —7D 134
Mulberry Ct. Twic —3K 115
Mulberry Cres. Bren —7B 80
Mulberry Cres. W Dray —2C 76
Mulberry Ho. SE8 —6B 88
Mulberry Ho. Short —1G 143
Mulberry Housing Co-operative. SE1
—4K 167
Mulberry La. Croy —1F 153
Mulberry M. SE14 —1B 106
Mulberry M. Wall —6G 151
Mulberry Pde. W Dray —3C 76
Mulberry Pl. E14 —7E 70
Mulberry Pl. W6 —5C 82
Mulberry Rd. E8 —7F 51
Mulberry St. E1 —6G 69
Mulberry Trees. Shep —7F 131
Mulberry Wlk. SW3 —6B 84 (7B 170)
Mulberry Way. E18 —2K 35
Mulberry Way. Belv —2J 93
Mulberry Way. Ilf —4G 37
Mulgrave Ct. Sutt —6K 149
(off Mulgrave Rd.)
Mulgrave Rd. NW10 —4B 46
Mulgrave Rd. SE18 —4D 90
Mulgrave Rd. SW6 —6H 83
Mulgrave Rd. W5 —3D 62
Mulgrave Rd. Belm & Sutt —7H 149
Mulgrave Rd. Croy —3D 152
Mulgrave Rd. Harr —2A 44
Mulholland Clo. Mitc —2F 139
Mulkern Rd. N19 —1H 49
Mullards Clo. Mitc —1D 150
Mullberry Pl. E14 —7E 70
(off Clove Cres.)
Mullen Tower. EC1 —4A 68 (4J 161)
(off Mt. Pleasant)
Muller Ho. SE18 —5E 90
Muller Rd. SW4 —6H 103
Mullet Gdns. E2 —3G 69
Mulletsfield. WC1 —3J 67
(off Cromer St.)
Mullins Path. SW14 —3K 99
Mullion Clo. Harr —1F 25
Mull Wlk. N1 —6C 50
(off Clephane Rd.)
Mulready Ho. SW1 —4J 85 (4E 172)
(off Marsham St.)
Mulready St. NW8 —4C 66 (4C 158)
Multimedia Ho. NW10 —4J 63
Multi Way. W3 —2A 82
Multon Rd. SW18 —7B 102
Mulvaney Way. SE1 —2D 86 (7F 169)
(in two parts)
Mumford Ct. EC2 —6C 68 (7D 162)
Mumford Rd. SE24 —5B 104
Muncaster Clo. Ashf —4C 112
Muncaster Rd. SW11 —5D 102
Muncaster Rd. Ashf —5D 112
Muncies M. SE6 —2E 124
Mundania Rd. SE22 —6H 105
Munday Ho. SE1 —3D 86
(off Deverell St.)
Munday Rd. E16 —7J 71
Munden St. W14 —4G 83
Mundford Rd. E5 —2J 51
Mundon Gdns. Ilf —1H 55
Mund St. W14 —5H 83
Mundy St. N1 —3E 68 (1G 163)
Mungo Pk. Clo. Bus H —2B 10
Munnery Way. Orp —3E 156
Munnings Gdns. Iswth —5H 97
Munro Dri. N11 —6B 16
Munro Ho. SE1 —7J 167
Munro M. W10 —5G 65
(in two parts)
Munro Ter. SW10 —7B 84
Munslow Gdns. Sutt —4B 150
Munster Av. Houn —5C 96
Munster Ct. SW6 —2H 101
Munster Ct. Tedd —6C 116
Munster Gdns. N13 —4G 17
Munster M. SW6 —7G 83
Munster Rd. SW6 —7G 83
Munster Rd. Tedd —6B 116
Munster Sq. NW1 —3F 67 (2K 159)
Munton Rd. SE17 —4C 86
Murchison Av. Bex —1D 128
Murchison Rd. E10 —2E 52
Murdock Clo. E16 —6H 71
Murdock St. SE15 —6H 87
Murfett Clo. SW19 —2G 119
Muriel Ct. E10 —7D 34
Muriel St. N1 —2K 67
(in two parts)
Murillo Rd. SE13 —4F 107
Murphy Ho. SE1 —3B 86 (7B 168)
(off Borough Rd.)
Murphy St. SE1 —2A 86 (7J 167)
Murray Av. Brom —3K 143
Murray Av. Houn —5F 97
Murray Ct. Harr —6K 25
Murray Ct. Twic —2H 115
Murray Cres. Pinn —1B 24
Murray Gro. N1 —2C 68 (1D 162)
Murray Ho. SE18 —4D 90
(off Rideout St.)
Murray M. NW1 —7H 49
Murray Rd. SW19 —6F 119
Murray Rd. W5 —4C 80
Murray Rd. N'wd —1G 23
Murray Rd. Rich —2B 116
Murray Sq. E16 —6J 71
Murray St. NW1 —7G 49
Murray Ter. NW3 —4A 48
Murray Ter. W5 —4D 80
Mursell Est. SW8 —1K 103
Musard Rd. W6 —6G 83
Musbury St. E1 —6J 69
Muscal. W6 —6G 83
(off Field Rd.)
Muscatel Pl. SE5 —1E 104
Muschamp Rd. SE15 —3F 105
Muschamp Rd. Cars —2C 150
Muscovy Ho. Eri —3E 92
(off Kale Rd.)
Muscovy St. EC3 —7E 68 (2H 169)
Museum Chambers. WC1
(off Bury Pl.) —5J 67 (6E 160)
Mus. in Docklands. —7C 70
Museum La. SW7 —2B 170
Mus. of Fulham Palace. —2G 101
Mus. of Gardening History.
—3K 85 (2G 173)
Mus. of London. —5C 68 (6C 162)
Mus. of Methodism.
—4D 68 (3F 163)
Mus. of Richmond. —5D 98
(off Whittaker Av.)
Mus. of Rugby, The. —6J 97
Museum Pas. E2 —3J 69
Museum St. WC1 —5J 67 (6E 160)
Musgrave Clo. Barn —1F 5
Musgrave Ct. SW11 —1C 102
Musgrave Cres. SW6 —7J 83
Musgrave Rd. Iswth —1K 97
Musgrove Rd. SE14 —1K 105
Musjid Rd. SW11 —2B 102
Musket Clo. E Barn —6G 5
Mus.of Artillery in the Rotunda.
—5D 90
Musquash Way. Houn —2A 96
Muston Rd. E5 —2H 51
Mustow Pl. SW6 —2H 101
Muswell Av. N10 —1F 31
Muswell Hill. —3F 31
Muswell Hill. N10 —3F 31
Muswell Hill B'way. N10 —3F 31
Muswell Hill Pl. N10 —4F 31
Muswell Hill Rd. N6 & N10 —6E 30
Muswell M. N10 —3F 31
Muswell Rd. N10 —3F 31
Mutrix Rd. NW6 —1J 65
Mutton Pl. NW1 —6E 48
Muybridge Rd. N Mald —2J 135
Myatt Rd. SW9 —1B 104
Myatts Fields S. SW9 —2A 104
(off St Lawrence Way)
Mycenae Rd. SE3 —7J 89
Myddelton Av. Enf —1K 7
Myddelton Clo. Enf —1A 8
Myddelton Gdns. N21 —7H 7
Myddelton Pk. N20 —3G 15
Myddelton Pas. EC1 —3A 68 (1K 161)
Myddelton Rd. N8 —3J 31
Myddelton Sq. EC1 —3A 68 (1K 161)
Myddelton St. EC1 —3A 68 (2K 161)
Myddleton Av. N4 —2C 50
Myddleton Ho. N1 —2A 68 (1J 161)
(off Pentonville Rd.)
Myddleton M. N22 —7D 16
Myddleton Rd. N22 —7D 16
Myers La. SE14 —6K 87
Mylis Clo. SE26 —4H 123
Mylius Clo. SE14 —7J 87
Mylne Clo. W6 —5C 82
Mylne St. EC1 —3A 68 (1J 161)
Myra St. SE2 —5A 92
Myrna Clo. SW19 —7C 120
Myron Pl. SE13 —3E 106
Myrtle Av. Felt —5G 95
Myrtle Av. Ruis —7J 23
Myrtleberry Clo. E8 —6F 51
(off Beechwood Rd.)
Myrtle Clo. E Barn —1J 15
Myrtle Clo. Uxb —5B 58
Myrtle Clo. W Dray —3B 76
Myrtledene Rd. SE2 —5A 92
Myrtle Gdns. W7 —1J 79
Myrtle Gro. Enf —1J 7
Myrtle Gro. N Mald —2J 135
Myrtle Rd. E6 —1D 72
Myrtle Rd. E17 —6A 34
Myrtle Rd. N13 —3H 17
Myrtle Rd. W3 —1J 81
Myrtle Rd. Croy —3C 154
Myrtle Rd. Hamp H —6G 115
Myrtle Rd. Houn —2G 97
Myrtle Rd. Ilf —2F 55
Myrtle Rd. Sutt —5A 150
Myrtle Wlk. N1 —2E 68 (1G 163)
Mysore Rd. SW11 —3D 102
Myton Rd. SE21 —3D 122
Mytton Ho. SW8 —7K 85
(off St Stephens Ter.)

Nadine Ct. Wall —7G 151
Nadine St. SE7 —5A 90
Nagasaki Wlk. SE7 —3K 89
Nagle Clo. E17 —2F 35
Nag's Head. (Junct.) —3J 49
Nags Head Ct. EC1 —4D 162
Nags Head La. Well —3B 110
Nags Head Rd. Enf —4D 8
Nags Head Shop. Cen. N7 —4K 49
Nailsworth Ct. SE15 —6E 86
(off Birdlip Clo.)
Nainby Ho. SE11 —4J 173
Nairne Gro. SE24 —5D 104
Nairn Rd. Ruis —6A 42
Nairn St. E14 —5E 70
Naish Ct. N1 —1J 67
(in three parts)
Naldera Gdns. SE3 —6J 89
Nallhead Rd. Felt —5A 114
Namba Roy Clo. SW16 —4K 121
Namton Dri. T Hth —4K 139
Nan Clark's La. NW7 —2G 13
Nankin St. E14 —6C 70
Nansen Ho. NW10 —7K 45
(off Stonebridge Pk.)
Nansen Rd. SW11 —3E 102
Nansen Village. N12 —4E 14
Nant Ct. NW2 —2H 47
Nantes Clo. SW18 —4A 102
Nantes Pas. E1 —5J 163
Nant Rd. NW2 —2H 47
Nant St. E2 —3H 69
Naoroji St. WC1 —3A 68 (2J 161)
Napier. NW9 —1B 28
Napier Av. E14 —5C 88
Napier Av. SW6 —3H 101
Napier Clo. SE8 —7B 88
Napier Clo. W14 —3G 83
Napier Clo. W Dray —3B 76
Napier Ct. N1 —2D 68
(off Cropley St.)
Napier Ct. SW6 —3H 101
(off Ranelagh Gdns.)
Napier Ct. Hay —4A 60
(off Dunedin Way)
Napier Gro. N1 —2C 68
Napier Pl. W14 —3H 83
Napier Rd. E6 —1E 72
Napier Rd. E11 —4G 53
Napier Rd. E15 —2G 71
(in two parts)
Napier Rd. N17 —3E 32
Napier Rd. NW10 —3D 64
Napier Rd. SE25 —4H 141
Napier Rd. W14 —3G 83
Napier Rd. Ashf —7F 113
Napier Rd. Belv —4F 93
Napier Rd. Brom —4K 143
Napier Rd. Enf —5E 8
Napier Rd. Iswth —4A 98
Napier Rd. H'row A —1A 94
Napier Rd. S Croy —7D 152
Napier Rd. Wemb —6D 44
Napier Ter. N1 —7B 50
Napier Wlk. Ashf —7F 113
Napoleon Rd. E5 —3H 51
Napoleon Rd. Twic —7B 98
Napton Clo. Hay —4C 60
Narbonne Av. SW4 —5G 103
Narborough Clo. Uxb —2E 40
Narborough St. SW6 —2K 101
Narcissus Rd. NW6 —5J 47
Nardini. NW9 —1B 28
(off Concourse, The)
Naresby Fold. Stan —6H 11
Narford Rd. E5 —3G 51
Narrow Boat Clo. SE28 —2H 91
Narrow St. E14 —7K 69
Narrow St. W3 —1H 81
Narrow Way. Brom —6C 144
Narvic Ho. SE5 —2C 104
Nascot St. W12 —6E 64
Naseby Clo. NW6 —7A 48
Naseby Clo. Iswth —1J 97
Naseby Ct. Sidc —4K 127
Naseby Rd. SE19 —6D 122
Naseby Rd. Dag —3G 57
Naseby Rd. Ilf —1D 36
Naseby Tower. SE14 —7A 88
(off Desmond St.)
Nash. —6J 155
Nash Clo. Sutt —3B 150
Nash Ct. E14 —1D 88
(off S. Colonnade, The)
Nash Ct. Kent —6B 26
Nashe Ho. SE1 —3D 86
(off Burbage Clo.)
Nash Grn. Brom —6J 125
Nash Ho. E17 —3D 34
Nash Ho. SW1 —5F 85 (6K 171)
(off Lupus St.)
Nash La. Kes —7J 155
Nash Pl. E14 —1D 88

244 A-Z Big London

Nash Rd.—Newton Rd.

Nash Rd. N9 —2D 18
Nash Rd. SE4 —4A 106
Nash Rd. Chad H & Romf —4D 38
Nash St. NW1 —3F 67 (1K 159)
Nash Way. Kent —6B 26
Nasmyth St. W6 —3D 82
Nassau Path. SE28 —1C 92
Nassau Rd. SW13 —1B 100
Nassau St. W1 —5G 67 (6A 160)
Nassington Rd. NW3 —4D 48
Natalie Clo. Felt —7F 95
Natalie M. Twic —3H 115
Natal Rd. N11 —6D 16
Natal Rd. SW16 —6H 121
Natal Rd. Ilf —4F 55
Natal Rd. T Hth —3D 140
Nathan Ct. N9 —7D 8
(off Causeyware Rd.)
Nathan Ho. SE11 —4A 86 (4K 173)
(off Reedworth St.)
Nathaniel Clo. E1 —5F 69 (6K 163)
Nathaniel Ct. E17 —7A 34
Nathans Rd. Wemb —1C 44
Nathan Way. SE28 —4H 91
National Army Mus. —6D 84 (7F 171)
National Film Theatre. —4H 167
National Gallery. —7H 67 (3D 166)
National Maritime Mus. —6F 89
National Portrait Gallery. —7H 67 (3D 166)
Nation Way. E4 —1K 19
Natural History Mus. —3B 84 (2A 170)
Nautilus Building, The. EC1
(off Myddelton Pas.) —3A 68 (1K 161)
Naval Ho. E14 —7F 71
Naval Row. E14 —7E 70
Naval Wlk. Brom —2J 143
Navarino Gro. E8 —6G 51
Navarino Mans. E8 —6G 51
Navarino Rd. E8 —6G 51
Navarre Rd. E6 —2C 72
Navarre St. E2 —4F 69 (3J 163)
Navenby Wlk. E3 —4C 70
Navestock Clo. E4 —3K 19
Navestock Cres. Wfd G —7F 21
Navestock Ho. Bark —2B 74
Navigation Dri. Enf —1H 9
Navigator Dri. S'hall —2G 79
Navy St. SW4 —3H 103
Nayland Ho. SE6 —4E 124
Naylor Gro. Enf —5E 8
Naylor Rd. N20 —2F 15
Naylor Rd. SE15 —7H 87
Nazareth Gdns. SE15 —2H 105
Nazrul St. E2 —3F 69 (1J 163)
Neagle Ho. NW2 —3E 46
(off Stoll Clo.)
Neal Av. S'hall —4D 60
Neal Clo. N'wd —1J 23
Nealden St. SW9 —3K 103
Neale Clo. N2 —3A 30
Neal St. WC2 —6J 67 (1E 166)
Neal's Yd. WC2 —6J 67 (1E 166)
Near Acre. NW9 —1B 28
Neasden. —3A 46
Neasden Clo. NW10 —5A 46
Neasden Junction. (Junct.) —4A 46
Neasden La. NW10 —3A 46
Neasden La. N. NW10 —3K 45
Neasham Rd. Dag —5B 56
Neate St. SE5 —6E 86
(in two parts)
Neath Gdns. Mord —6A 138
Neath Ho. SE24 —6B 104
(off Dulwich Rd.)
Neathouse Pl. SW1 —4G 85 (3A 172)
Neats Acre. Ruis —7F 23
Neatscourt Rd. E6 —5B 72
Nebraska St. SE1 —2D 86 (7E 168)
Neckinger. SE1 —3F 87 (7K 169)
Neckinger Est. SE16 —3F 87
Neckinger St. SE1 —2F 87 (7K 169)
Nectarine Way. SE13 —2D 106
Needham Ho. SE11 —4J 173
Needham Rd. W11 —6J 65
Needham Ter. NW2 —3F 47
Needleman St. SE16 —2K 87
Needwood Ho. N4 —1C 50
Neela Clo. Uxb —4D 40
Neeld Cres. NW4 —5D 28
Neeld Cres. Wemb —5G 45
Neeld Pde. Wemb —5F 45
Neil Clo. Ashf —5E 112
Neil Wates Cres. SW2 —1A 122
Nelgarde Rd. SE6 —7C 106
Nella Rd. W6 —6F 83
Nelldale Rd. SE16 —4J 87
Nellgrove Rd. Uxb —4D 58
Nell Gwynne Av. Shep —6F 131
Nello James Gdns. SE27 —4D 122
Nelson Clo. Croy —1B 152
Nelson Clo. Felt —1H 113
Nelson Clo. Romf —1H 39
Nelson Clo. Uxb —3D 58
Nelson Clo. W on T —7K 131
Nelson Ct. SE1 —2B 86 (6B 168)
Nelson Gdns. E2 —3G 69
Nelson Gdns. Houn —6E 96
Nelson Gro. Rd. SW19 —1A 138
Nelson Ho. SW1 —6G 85 (7B 172)
(off Dolphin Sq.)
Nelson Ind. Est. SW19 —1K 137
Nelson La. Uxb —3D 58
Nelson Mandela Clo. N10 —2E 30
Nelson Mandella Rd. SE3 —3A 108
Nelson Pas. EC1 —3C 68 (1D 162)
Nelson Pl. N1 —2B 68 (1B 162)
Nelson Pl. Sidc —4A 128
Nelson Rd. E4 —6J 19
Nelson Rd. E11 —4J 35
Nelson Rd. N8 —5K 31
Nelson Rd. N9 —2C 18
Nelson Rd. N15 —4E 32
Nelson Rd. SE10 —6E 88
Nelson Rd. SW19 —7K 119
Nelson Rd. Ashf —5A 112
Nelson Rd. Belv —5F 93
Nelson Rd. Brom —4A 144
Nelson Rd. Enf —6E 8
Nelson Rd. Harr —1H 43
Nelson Rd. Houn —6E 96
Nelson Rd. H'row A —1B 94
Nelson Rd. N Mald —5K 135
Nelson Rd. Sidc —4A 128
Nelson Rd. Stan —6H 11
Nelson Rd. Uxb —3D 58
Nelson Rd. M. SW19 —7K 119
Nelson's Column. —1J 85 (4D 166)
Nelson Sq. SE1 —2B 86 (6A 168)
Nelson's Row. SW4 —4H 103
Nelson St. E1 —6H 69
Nelson St. E6 —2D 72
(in two parts)
Nelson St. E16 —7H 71
(in two parts)
Nelsons Yd. NW1 —2G 67
(off Mornington Cres.)
Nelson Ter. EC1 —2B 68 (1B 162)
Nelson Wlk. SE16 —1A 88
Nelson Wlk. Eps —7G 147
Nemoure Rd. W3 —7J 63
Nene Gdns. Felt —2D 114
Nene Rd. H'row A —1D 94
Nene Rd. Roundabout. H'row A —1D 94
Nepaul Rd. SW11 —2C 102
Nepean St. SW15 —6C 100
Neptune Ct. E14 —4C 88
Neptune Rd. Harr —6H 25
Neptune Rd. H'row A —1E 94
Neptune St. SE16 —3J 87
Neptune Wlk. Eri —4K 93
Nero Ct. Bren —7D 80
Nesbit Rd. SE9 —4B 108
Nesbitt Clo. SE3 —3G 107
Nesbitts All. Barn —3C 4
Nesbitt Sq. SE19 —7E 122
Nesham St. E1 —1G 87
Ness St. SE16 —3G 87
Nesta Rd. Wfd G —6B 20
Nestles Av. Hay —3H 77
Nestor Av. N21 —6G 7
Netheravon Rd. W4 —4B 82
Netheravon Rd. W7 —1K 79
Netheravon Rd. S. W4 —5B 82
Netherbury Rd. W5 —3D 80
Netherby Gdns. Enf —4D 6
Netherby Rd. SE23 —7J 105
Nether Clo. N3 —7D 14
Nethercourt Av. N3 —6D 14
Netherfield Gdns. Bark —6H 55
Netherfield Rd. N12 —5E 14
Netherfield Rd. SW17 —3E 120
Netherford Rd. SW4 —2G 103
Netherhall Gdns. NW3 —6A 48
Netherhall Way. NW3 —5A 48
Netherlands Rd. Barn & New Bar —6G 5
Netherleigh Clo. N6 —1F 49
Nether St. N3 & N12 —1J 29
Netherton Gro. SW10 —6A 84
Netherton Rd. N15 —6D 32
Netherton Rd. Twic —5A 98
Netherwood. N2 —2B 30
Netherwood Rd. W6 —3F 83
Netherwood St. NW6 —7H 47
Nethewode Ct. Belv —3H 93
(off Lwr. Park Rd.)
Netley Clo. Cheam & Sutt —5F 149
Netley Clo. New Ad —7E 154
Netley Dri. W on T —7D 132
Netley Gdns. Mord —7A 138
Netley Rd. E17 —5B 34
Netley Rd. Bren —6E 80
Netley Rd. Ilf —5H 37
Netley Rd. Mord —7A 138
Netley St. NW1 —3G 67 (2A 160)
Nettlecombe. NW1 —7H 49
(off Agar Gro.)
Nettleden Av. Wemb —6G 45
Nettleden Ho. SW3 —4C 84 (4D 170)
(off Marlborough St.)
Nettlefold Pl. SE27 —3B 122
Nettlestead Clo. Beck —7B 124
Nettleton Ct. EC2 —5C 68
(off London Wall)
Nettleton Rd. SE14 —1K 105
Nettleton Rd. H'row A —1D 94
Nettleton Rd. Uxb —4B 40
Nettlewood Rd. SW16 —7H 121
Neuchatel Rd. SE6 —2B 124
Nevada Clo. N Mald —4J 135
Nevada St. SE10 —6E 88
Nevern Mans. SW5 —5J 83
(off Warwick Rd.)
Nevern Pl. SW5 —4J 83
Nevern Rd. SW5 —4J 83
Nevern Sq. SW5 —4J 83
Nevil Ho. SW9 —2B 104
(off Loughborough Est.)
Nevill Ct. EC4 —6A 68 (7K 161)
(off E. Harding St.)
Neville Av. N Mald —1K 135
Neville Clo. E11 —3H 53
Neville Clo. NW1 —2H 67
Neville Clo. NW6 —2H 65
Neville Clo. SE15 —1G 105
Neville Clo. W3 —2J 81
Neville Clo. Houn —2F 97
Neville Clo. Sidc —4K 127
Neville Ct. NW8 —1A 158
Neville Dri. N2 —6A 30
Neville Gdns. Dag —3D 56
Neville Gill Clo. SW18 —6J 101
Neville Ho. N11 —4K 15
Neville Ho. N22 —1K 31
(off Neville Pl.)
Neville Ho. Yd. King T —2E 134
Neville Pl. N22 —1K 31
Neville Rd. E7 —7J 53
Neville Rd. NW6 —2H 65
Neville Rd. W5 —4D 62
Neville Rd. Croy —7D 140
Neville Rd. Dag —2D 56
Neville Rd. Ilf —1G 37
Neville Rd. King T —2G 135
Neville Rd. Rich —3C 116
Nevilles Ct. NW2 —3C 46
Neville St. SW7 —5B 84 (5A 170)
Neville Ter. SW7 —5B 84 (5A 170)
Neville Wlk. Cars —7C 138
Nevill Rd. N16 —4E 50
Nevin Dri. E4 —1J 19
Nevin Ho. Hay —3E 76
Nevinson Clo. SW18 —6B 102
Nevis Rd. SW17 —2E 120
Nevitt Ho. N1 —2D 68
(off Cranston Est.)
New Acres Rd. SE28 —2J 91
(in three parts)
Newall Ho. SE1 —3C 86
(off Bath Ter.)
Newall Rd. H'row A —1E 94
Newark Cres. NW10 —3K 63
Newarke Ho. SW9 —2B 104
Newark Knok. E6 —6E 72
Newark Pde. NW4 —3C 28
Newark Rd. S Croy —6D 152
Newark St. E1 —5H 69
(in two parts)
Newark Way. NW4 —4C 28
New Ash Clo. N2 —3B 30
New Atlas Wharf. E14 —3C 88
(off Glengall Causeway)
New Barn Clo. Wall —6K 151
New Barnet. —4F 5
New Barn Rd. Swan —7K 129
New Barns Av. Mitc —4H 139
(in two parts)
New Barn St. E13 —4J 71
New Barns Way. Chig —3K 21
New Beckenham. —6B 124
New Bentham Ct. N1 —7C 50
(off Ecclesbourne Rd.)
Newbery Ho. N1 —7C 50
(off Northampton St.)
Newbold Cotts. E1 —6J 69
Newbolt Av. Sutt —5E 148
Newbolt Ho. SE17 —5D 86
(off Brandon St.)
Newbolt Rd. Stan —5E 10
New Bond St. W1 —6F 67 (1J 165)
Newborough Grn. N Mald —4K 135
New Brent St. NW4 —5E 28
Newbridge Point. SE23 —3K 123
(off Windrush La.)
New Bri. St. EC4 —6B 68 (1A 168)
New Broad St. EC2 —5E 68 (6G 163)
New B'way. W5 —7D 62
New B'way. Hamp —5H 115
New B'way. Uxb —3D 58
Newburgh Rd. W3 —1J 81
Newburgh St. W1 —6G 67 (1B 166)
New Burlington M. W1 —7G 67 (2A 166)
New Burlington Pl. W1 —7G 67 (2A 166)
New Burlington St. W1 —7G 67 (2A 166)
Newburn Ho. SE11 —5K 85 (5H 173)
(off Newburn St.)
Newburn St. SE11 —5K 85 (5H 173)
Newbury Clo. N'holt —6D 42
Newbury Ct. Sidc —4K 127
Newbury Gdns. Eps —4B 148
Newbury Ho. N22 —1J 31
Newbury Ho. SW9 —2B 104
Newbury Ho. W2 —6K 65
(off Hallfield Est.)
Newbury M. NW5 —6E 48
Newbury Park. —5G 37
Newbury Rd. E4 —6K 19
Newbury Rd. Brom —3J 143
Newbury Rd. Ilf —6J 37
Newbury Rd. H'row A —1B 94
Newbury St. EC1 —5C 68 (6C 162)
Newbury Way. N'holt —6C 42
New Bus. Cen., The. NW10 —3B 64
New Butt La. SE8 —7C 88
(in two parts)
New Butt La. N. SE8 —7C 88
(off Reginald Rd.)
New B'way Bldgs. W5 —7D 62
Newby. NW1 —3G 67 (2A 160)
(off Robert St.)
Newby Clo. Enf —2K 7
Newby Pl. E14 —7E 70
Newby St. SW8 —3F 103
New Caledonian Wharf. SE16 —3B 88
Newcastle Clo. EC4 —6B 68 (7A 162)
Newcastle Ct. EC4 —7C 68 (2D 168)
(off College Hill)
Newcastle Ho. W1 —5E 66 (5G 159)
(off Luxborough St.)
Newcastle Pl. W2 —5B 66 (5B 158)
Newcastle Row. EC1 —4A 68 (4K 161)
New Cavendish St. W1
—5E 66 (6H 159)
New Change. EC4 —6C 68 (1C 168)
New Chapel Sq. Felt —1K 113
New Charles St. EC1 —3B 68 (1B 162)
New Charlton. —4A 90
New Chu. Rd. SE5 —7C 86
(in two parts)
New City Rd. E13 —3A 72
New Clo. SW19 —3A 138
New Clo. Felt —5C 114
New Colebrooke Ct. Cars —7E 150
(off Stanley Rd.)
New College Ct. NW3 —6A 48
(off College Cres.)
New College M. N1 —7A 50
New College Pde. NW3 —6B 48
(off College Cres.)
Newcombe Gdns. SW16 —4J 121
Newcombe Pk. NW7 —5F 13
Newcombe Pk. Wemb —1F 63
Newcombe Ri. W Dray —6A 58
Newcombe St. W8 —1J 83
Newcomen Rd. E11 —3H 53
Newcomen Rd. SW11 —3B 102
Newcomen St. SE1 —2D 86 (6E 168)
New Compton St. WC2 —6H 67 (1D 166)
New Concordia Wharf. SE1
—2G 87 (6K 169)
New Ct. EC4 —2J 167
New Ct. N'holt —5F 43
Newcourt St. NW8 —2C 66 (1C 158)
New Covent Garden Market. —7H 85
New Coventry St. W1 —7H 67 (3D 166)
New Crane Pl. E1 —1J 87
Newcroft Clo. Uxb —5B 58
New Cross. —7B 88
New Cross. (Junct.) —1B 106
New Cross Gate. —1K 105
New Cross Gate. (Junct.) —1K 105
New Cross Rd. SE15 & SE14 —7J 87
Newdales Clo. N9 —2B 18
Newdene Av. N'holt —2B 60
Newdigate Ho. E14 —6B 70
Newell St. E14 —6B 70
New Eltham. —2G 127
New End. NW3 —4A 48
New End Sq. NW3 —4B 48
New England Ind. Est. Bark —2G 73
Newent Clo. SE15 —7E 86
New Era Est. N1 —1E 68
(off Phillipp St.)
New Farm Av. Brom —4J 143
New Farm La. N'wd —1G 23
New Fetter La. EC4 —6A 68 (7K 161)
Newfield Clo. Hamp —1E 132
Newfield Ri. NW2 —3D 46
New Forest La. Chig —6K 21
Newgale Gdns. Edgw —1F 27
New Garden Dri. W Dray —2A 76
Newgate. Croy —1C 152
Newgate Clo. Felt —2C 114
Newgate St. E4 —3B 20
Newgate St. EC1 —6B 68 (7B 162)
New Globe Wlk. SE1 —1C 86 (4C 168)
New Goulston St. E1 —6F 69 (7J 163)
New Grn. Pl. SE19 —6E 122
Newham Grn. N22 —1A 32
Newham's Row. SE1 —2E 86 (7H 169)
Newham Way. E16 & E6 —5H 71
Newhaven Clo. Hay —4H 77
Newhaven Cres. Ashf —5F 113
Newhaven Gdns. SE9 —4B 108
Newhaven La. E16 —4H 71
Newhaven Rd. SE25 —5D 140
New Heston Rd. Houn —7D 78
New Horizons Ct. Bren —6C 80
Newhouse Av. Romf —3D 38
Newhouse Clo. N Mald —7A 136
Newhouse Wlk. Mord —7A 138
Newick Clo. Bex —6H 111
Newick Rd. E5 —4H 51
Newing Grn. Brom —7B 126
Newington. —3C 86
Newington Barrow Way. N7 —3K 49
Newington Butts. SE11 & SE1 —4B 86
Newington Causeway. SE1
—3B 86 (7C 168)
Newington Ct. Bus. Cen. SE1 —7C 168
Newington Grn. N1 & N16 —5D 50
Newington Grn. Mans. N16 —5D 50
Newington Grn. Rd. N1 —6D 50
Newington Ind. Est. SE17 —4C 86
(off Crampton St.)
New Inn B'way. EC2 —4E 68 (3H 163)
New Inn Pas. WC2 —1H 167
New Inn Sq. EC2 —3H 163
New Inn St. EC2 —4E 68 (3H 163)
New Inn Yd. EC2 —4E 68 (3H 163)
New Jubilee Ct. Wfd G —7D 20
New Kelvin Av. Tedd —6J 115
New Kent Rd. SE1 —3C 86
New Kings Rd. SW6 —2H 101
New King St. SE8 —6C 88
Newland Ct. EC1 —2E 162
Newland Dri. Enf —1C 8
Newland Gdns. W13 —2A 80
Newland Ho. N8 —3J 31
(off Newland Rd.)
Newland Ho. N8 —3J 31
(off Newland Rd.)
Newland Rd. N8 —3J 31
Newlands. —5K 105
(Brockley)
Newlands. —3K 11
(Edgware)
Newlands. NW1 —3G 67 (1A 160)
(off Harrington St.)
Newlands Av. Th Dit —7J 133
Newlands Clo. Edgw —3K 11
Newlands Clo. S'hall —5C 78
Newlands Clo. Wemb —6C 44
Newlands Ct. SE9 —6E 108
Newlands Pk. SE26 —6J 123
Newlands Pl. Barn —5A 4
Newlands Quay. E1 —7J 69
Newlands Rd. SW16 —2J 139
Newlands Rd. Wfd G —2C 20
Newlands, The. Wall —7G 151
Newland St. E16 —1C 90
Newlands Way. Chess —5C 146
Newlands Wood. New Ad —7B 154
Newling Clo. E6 —6D 72
New London St. EC3 —2H 169
New Lydenburg Commercial Est. SE7
—3A 90
New Lydenburg St. SE7 —3A 90
Newlyn. NW1 —1G 67
(off Plender St.)
Newlyn Clo. Uxb —5C 58
Newlyn Gdns. Harr —7D 24
Newlyn Ho. Pinn —1D 24
Newlyn Rd. N17 —1F 33
Newlyn Rd. Barn —4C 4
Newlyn Rd. Well —2K 109
New Malden. —4A 136
Newman Pas. W1 —5G 67 (6B 160)
Newman Rd. E13 —3K 71
Newman Rd. E17 —5K 33
Newman Rd. Brom —1J 143
Newman Rd. Croy —1K 151
Newman Rd. Hay —7K 59
Newman Rd. Ind. Est. Croy —7K 139
Newman's Ct. EC3 —1F 169
Newmans La. Surb —6D 134
Newman's Row. WC2 —5K 67 (6H 161)
Newman St. W1 —5G 67 (6B 160)
Newman's Way. Barn —1F 5
Newman Yd. W1 —6G 67 (7C 160)
Newmarket Av. N'holt —5E 42
Newmarket Grn. SE9 —7B 108
Newmarsh Rd. SE28 —1K 91
Newmill Ho. E3 —4E 70
Newminster Rd. Mord —6A 138
New Mt. St. E15 —7F 53
Newnes Path. SW15 —4D 100
Newnet Clo. Cars —1D 150
Newnham Av. Ruis —1A 42
Newnham Clo. N'holt —6G 43
Newnham Clo. T Hth —2C 140
Newnham Gdns. N'holt —6G 43
Newnham Lodge. Belv —5G 93
(off Erith Rd.)
Newnham M. N22 —7E 16
Newnham Rd. N22 —1K 31
Newnhams Clo. Brom —3D 144
Newnham Ter. SE1 —3A 86 (1J 173)
Newnham Way. Harr —5E 26
New N. Pl. EC2 —4E 68 (3G 163)
New N. Rd. N1 —7C 50 (1F 163)
New N. Rd. Ilf —1G 37
New N. St. WC1 —5K 67 (5G 161)
Newnton Clo. N4 —7D 32
(in two parts)
New Oak Rd. N2 —2A 30
New Orleans Wlk. N19 —7H 31
New Oxford St. WC1
—6H 67 (7D 160)
New Pde. Ashf —4B 112
New Pde. Yiew —1A 76
New Pk. Av. N13 —3H 17
New Pk. Clo. N'holt —6C 42
New Pk. Est. N18 —5D 18
New Pk. Ho. N13 —4E 16
New Pk. Pde. SW2 —7J 103
(off New Pk. Rd.)
New Pk. Rd. SW2 —1H 121
New Pk. Rd. Ashf —5E 112
New Pl. New Ad —6C 154
New Pl. Sq. SE16 —3H 87
New Plaistow Rd. E15 —1G 71
New Pond Pde. Ruis —3J 41
Newport Av. E13 —4K 71
Newport Av. E14 —7F 71
Newport Ct. WC2 —7H 67 (2D 166)
Newport Lodge. Enf —5K 7
(off Village Rd.)
Newport Pl. WC2 —7H 67 (2D 166)
Newport Rd. E10 —2E 52
Newport Rd. E17 —4A 34
Newport Rd. SW13 —1C 100
Newport Rd. Hay —5F 59
Newport Rd. H'row A —1C 94
Newport St. SE11 —4K 85 (4G 173)
New Priory Ct. NW6 —7J 47
(off Mazenod Av.)
Newquay Cres. Harr —2C 42
Newquay Ho. SE11 —5A 86 (5J 173)
Newquay Rd. SE6 —2D 124
New Quebec St. W1 —6D 66 (1F 165)
New Ride. SW7 & SW1
—2B 84 (6C 164)
New River Ct. N5 —4C 50
New River Cres. N13 —4G 17
New River Head. EC1 —3A 68 (2K 161)
New River Wlk. N1 —7C 50
(off Canonbury Rd.)
New River Way. N4 —7D 32
New Rd. E1 —5H 69
New Rd. E4 —4J 19
New Rd. N8 —5J 31
New Rd. N9 —3B 18
New Rd. N17 —1F 33
New Rd. N22 —1C 32
New Rd. NW7 —7B 14
New Rd. SE2 —4D 92
New Rd. Bedf —1K 113
New Rd. Bren —6D 80
New Rd. Dag & Rain —2G 75
New Rd. Felt —6F 95
New Rd. Hanw —5C 114
New Rd. Harr —4K 43
New Rd. Hay —7E 76
New Rd. Houn —4F 97
New Rd. Ilf —2J 55
New Rd. King T —7G 117
New Rd. Mitc —1D 150
New Rd. Rich —4C 116
New Rd. Shep —3C 130
New Rd. Uxb —4E 58
New Rd. Well —2B 110
New Rd. W Mol —4E 132
New Rd. Hill. Kes & Orp —7C 156
New Rochford St. NW5 —5D 48
New Row. WC2 —7J 67 (2E 166)
Newry Rd. Twic —5A 98
Newsam Av. N15 —5D 32
Newsholme Av. N21 —5E 6
New Southgate. —5A 16
New Southgate Crematorium. N11
—3A 16
New Southgate Ind. Est. N11 —5B 16
New Spitalfields Market. —3C 52
New Spitalfields Mkt. E10 —3D 52
New Spring Gdns. Wlk. SE1
—5J 85 (6F 173)
New Sq. WC2 —6A 68 (7J 161)
New Sq. Felt —1E 112
New Sq. Pas. WC2 —7J 161
Newstead Clo. N12 —6H 15
Newstead Ct. N'holt —3C 60
Newstead Rd. SE12 —7H 107
Newstead Wlk. Cars —7A 138
Newstead Way. SW19 —4F 119
New St. EC2 —5E 68 (6H 163)
New St. Hill. Brom —5K 125
New St. Sq. EC4 —6A 68 (7K 161)
Newton Av. N10 —1E 30
Newton Av. W3 —2J 81
Newton Clo. E17 —6A 34
Newton Clo. Harr —2E 42
Newton Gro. W4 —4A 82
Newton Ho. E17 —3D 34
(off Prospect Hill)
Newton Ho. NW8 —1K 65
(off Abbey Rd.)
Newton Ho. SE20 —7K 123
Newton Ind. Est. Romf —4D 38
Newton Mans. W14 —6G 83
(off Queen's Club Gdns.)
Newton Point. E16 —6H 71
(off Clarkson Rd.)
Newton Rd. E15 —5F 53
Newton Rd. N15 —5G 33

A-Z Big London 245

Newton Rd.—Northumberland Gdns.

Newton Rd. NW2 —4E 46
Newton Rd. SW19 —7G 119
Newton Rd. W2 —6K 65
Newton Rd. Harr —2J 25
Newton Rd. Iswth —2K 97
Newton Rd. H'row A —1A 94
Newton Rd. Well —3A 110
Newton Rd. Wemb —7F 45
Newton St. WC1 —6J 67 (7F 161)
Newton's Yd. SW18 —5J 101
Newton Ter. Brom —6B 144
Newton Wlk. Edgw —1H 27
Newton Way. N18 —5H 17
New Tower Bldgs. E1 —1H 87
Newtown St. SW11 —1F 103
New Trinity Rd. N2 —3B 30
New Turnstile. WC2 —5K 67 (6G 161)
New Union Clo. E14 —3E 88
New Union St. EC2 —5D 68 (6E 162)
New Wanstead. E11 —6H 35
New Way Rd. NW9 —4A 28
New Wharf Rd. N1 —2J 67
Newyears Green. —7B 22
Newyears Grn. La. Hare —6A 22
New Zealand Av. W on T —7H 131
New Zealand Way. W12 —7D 64
Niagara Av. W5 —4C 80
Niagra Clo. N1 —2C 68
Nibthwaite Rd. Harr —5J 25
Nicholas Clo. Gnfd —2F 61
Nicholas Ct. W4 —6A 82
(off Corney Reach Way)
Nicholas Gdns. W5 —2D 80
Nicholas La. EC4 —7D 68 (2F 169)
(in two parts)
Nicholas Pas. EC4 —1F 169
Nicholas Rd. E1 —4J 69
Nicholas Rd. Croy —4J 151
Nicholas Rd. Dag —2F 57
Nicholas Way. N'wd —1E 22
Nichola Ter. Bexh —1E 110
Nicholay Rd. N19 —1H 49
Nichol Clo. N14 —1C 16
Nicholes Rd. Houn —4E 96
Nichol La. Brom —7J 125
Nicholl Ho. N4 —1C 50
Nicholls Av. Uxb —4C 58
Nichollsfield Wlk. N7 —5K 49
Nicholls Point. E13 —1J 71
(off Park Gro.)
Nicholl St. E2 —1G 69
Nichols Clo. N4 —1A 50
(off Osborne Rd.)
Nichols Clo. Chess —6C 146
Nichols Grn. W5 —5D 62
Nicholson Ct. E17 —4A 34
Nicholson Dri. Bush —1B 10
Nicholson Ho. SE17 —5D 86
Nicholson M. King T —4E 134
Nicholson Rd. Croy —1F 153
Nicholson St. SE1 —1B 86 (5A 168)
Nickelby Clo. SE28 —6C 74
Nickleby Clo. Uxb —6D 58
Nickleby Ho. SE16 —2G 87 (7K 169)
(off George Row)
Nicola Clo. Harr —2H 25
Nicola Clo. S Croy —6C 152
Nicol Clo. Twic —6B 98
Nicoll Ct. N10 —7A 16
Nicoll Ct. NW10 —1A 64
Nicoll Pl. NW4 —6D 28
Nicoll Rd. NW10 —1A 64
Nicolson. NW9 —1A 28
Nicosia Rd. SW18 —7C 102
Niederwald Rd. SE26 —4A 124
Nield Rd. Hay —2H 77
Nigel Clo. N'holt —1C 60
Nigel Ct. N3 —7E 14
Nigel Fisher Way. Chess —7C 146
Nigel Ho. EC1 —5A 68
(off Portpool La.)
Nigel M. Ilf —4F 55
Nigel Playfair Av. W6 —4D 82
Nigel Rd. E7 —5A 54
Nigel Rd. SE15 —3G 105
Nigeria Rd. SE7 —7A 90
Nighthawk. NW9 —1B 28
Nightingale Av. E4 —5B 20
Nightingale Av. Harr —1B 44
Nightingale Clo. E4 —4A 20
Nightingale Clo. W4 —6J 81
Nightingale Clo. Cars —2E 150
Nightingale Clo. Pinn —5A 24
Nightingale Ct. E14 —2E 88
Nightingale Ct. N4 —2K 49
(off Tollington Pk.)
Nightingale Ct. SW6 —1K 101
(off Maltings Pl.)
Nightingale Ct. Short —2G 143
Nightingale Dri. Eps —6H 147
Nightingale Gro. SE13 —5F 107
Nightingale Heights. SE18 —6F 91
Nightingale Ho. E1 —1G 87
(off Thomas More St.)
Nightingale Ho. N1 —1E 68
(off Wilmer Gdns.)
Nightingale Ho. SE18 —5E 90
(off Connaught M.)
Nightingale La. E11 —4K 35
Nightingale La. N8 —4J 31
Nightingale La. SW12 & SW4 —7D 102
Nightingale La. Brom —2A 144
Nightingale La. Rich —7E 98
Nightingale Lodge. W9 —5J 65
(off Admiral Wlk.)
Nightingale M. E3 —2K 69
Nightingale M. King T —3D 134
(off South La.)
Nightingale Pl. SE18 —6E 90
Nightingale Pl. SW10 —6A 84 (7A 170)
Nightingale Rd. E5 —3H 51
Nightingale Rd. N9 —6D 8
Nightingale Rd. N22 —7D 16
Nightingale Rd. NW10 —2B 64
Nightingale Rd. W7 —1K 79
Nightingale Rd. Cars —3D 150
Nightingale Rd. Hamp —5E 114
Nightingale Rd. Orp —6G 145
Nightingale Rd. W on T —7A 132
Nightingale Rd. W Mol —5F 133
Nightingale Sq. SW12 —7E 102
Nightingales, The. Stai —7B 94
Nightingale Va. SE18 —6E 90
Nightingale Wlk. SW4 —6F 103
Nightingale Way. E6 —5C 72
Nikols Wlk. SW18 —4K 101
Nile Clo. N16 —3F 51
Nile Path. SE18 —6E 90
Nile Rd. E13 —2A 72
Nile St. N1 —3C 68 (1D 162)
Nile Ter. SE15 —5F 87
Nimegen Way. SE22 —5E 104
Nimmo Dri. Bus H —1C 10
Nimrod. NW9 —1A 28
Nimrod Clo. N'holt —3B 60
Nimrod Pas. N1 —6E 50
Nimrod Rd. SW16 —6F 121
Nina Mackay Clo. E15 —1G 71
Nine Acres Clo. E12 —5C 54
Nine Elms. —7G 85
Nine Elms Clo. Felt —1H 113
Nine Elms La. SW8 —7G 85 (7C 172)
Nineteenth Rd. Mitc —4J 139
Ninhams Wood. Orp —4E 156
Ninth Av. Hay —7J 59
Nita Ct. SE12 —1J 125
Nithdale Rd. SE18 —7F 91
Nithsdale Gro. Uxb —3E 40
Niton Clo. Barn —6A 4
Niton Rd. Rich —3G 99
Niton St. SW6 —7F 83
Nobel Dri. Hay —1F 95
Nobel Ho. SE5 —2C 104
Nobel Rd. N18 —4D 18
Noble Corner. Houn —1E 96
Noble Ct. E1 —7H 69
(off Cable St., in two parts)
Noble Ct. Mitc —2B 138
Noblefield Heights. N2 —5C 30
Noble St. EC2 —6C 68 (7C 162)
Noel. NW9 —1A 28
Noel Ct. Houn —3D 96
Noel Coward Ho. SW1 —4G 85 (4B 172)
(off Vauxhall Bri. Rd.)
Noel Ho. NW3 —7B 48
Noel Park. —2B 32
Noel Pk. Rd. N22 —2A 32
Noel Rd. E6 —4C 72
Noel Rd. N1 —2B 68
Noel Rd. W3 —7G 63
Noel Sq. Dag —4C 56
Noel St. W1 —6G 67 (1B 166)
Noel Ter. SE23 —2J 123
Noel Ter. Sidc —4B 128
Nolan Way. E5 —4G 51
Nolton Pl. Edgw —1F 27
Nonsuch Pl. Sutt —7F 149
Nonsuch Wlk. Sutt —7F 148
(in two parts)
Nora Gdns. NW4 —4F 29
Norbiton. —2G 135
Norbiton Av. King T —1G 135
Norbiton Comn. Rd. King T —3H 135
Norbiton Hall. King T —2F 135
Norbiton Rd. E14 —6B 70
Norbreck Gdns. NW10 —3F 63
Norbreck Pde. NW10 —3E 62
Norbroke St. W12 —7B 64
Norburn St. W10 —5G 65
Norbury. —2K 139
Norbury Av. SW16 & T Hth —1K 139
Norbury Av. Houn —4H 97
Norbury Clo. SW16 —1A 140
Norbury Ct. Rd. SW16 —3J 139
Norbury Cres. SW16 —1K 139
Norbury Cross. SW16 —3J 139
Norbury Gdns. Romf —5D 38
Norbury Gro. NW7 —3F 13
Norbury Hill. SW16 —7A 122
Norbury Ri. SW16 —3J 139
Norbury Rd. E4 —5H 19
Norbury Rd. T Hth —2C 140
Norbury Trad. Est. SW16 —2K 139
Norcombe Gdns. Harr —6C 26
Norcombe Ho. N19 —3H 49
(off Wedmore St.)
Norcott Clo. Hay —4A 60
Norcott Rd. N16 —2G 51
Norcroft Gdns. SE22 —7G 105
Norcutt Rd. Twic —1J 115
Nordenfeldt Rd. Eri —5K 93
Norfield Rd. Dart —4J 129
Norfolk Av. N13 —6G 17
Norfolk Av. N15 —6F 33
Norfolk Clo. N2 —3C 30
Norfolk Clo. N13 —6G 17
Norfolk Clo. Barn —4K 5
Norfolk Clo. Twic —6B 98
Norfolk Ct. Barn —4B 4
Norfolk Cres. W2 —6C 66 (7C 158)
Norfolk Cres. Sidc —7J 109
Norfolk Gdns. Bexh —1F 111
Norfolk Gdns. Houn —5D 96
Norfolk Ho. SE8 —1C 106
Norfolk Ho. SE20 —1J 141
Norfolk Ho. SW1 —4H 85 (3D 172)
(off Page St.)
Norfolk Ho. Rd. SW16 —3H 121
Norfolk Mans. SW11 —1D 102
(off Prince of Wales Dri.)
Norfolk M. W10 —5H 65
(off Blagrove Rd.)
Norfolk Pl. W2 —6B 66 (7B 158)
(in two parts)
Norfolk Pl. Well —2A 110
Norfolk Rd. E6 —1D 72
Norfolk Rd. E17 —2K 33
Norfolk Rd. NW8 —1B 66
Norfolk Rd. NW10 —7A 46
Norfolk Rd. SW19 —7C 120
Norfolk Rd. Bark —7J 55
Norfolk Rd. Barn —3D 4
Norfolk Rd. Dag —5H 57
Norfolk Rd. Enf —6C 8
Norfolk Rd. Felt —1A 114
Norfolk Rd. Harr —5F 25
Norfolk Rd. Ilf —1J 55
Norfolk Rd. Romf —6J 39
Norfolk Rd. T Hth —3C 140
Norfolk Rd. Uxb —6A 40
Norfolk Row. SE1 —4K 85 (3G 173)
(in two parts)
Norfolk Sq. W2 —6B 66 (1B 164)
Norfolk Sq. M. W2 —1B 164
Norfolk St. E7 —5J 53
Norfolk Ter. W6 —5G 83
Norgrove St. SW12 —7E 102
Norhyrst Av. SE25 —3F 141
Norland Ho. W11 —1F 83
(off Queensdale Cres.)
Norland Pl. W11 —1G 83
Norland Rd. W11 —1F 83
(off Queensdale Cres.)
Norlands Cres. Chst —1F 145
Norland Sq. W11 —1G 83
Norland Sq. Mans. W11 —1G 83
(off Norland Sq.)
Norley Va. SW15 —1C 118
Norlington Rd. E10 & E11 —1E 52
Norman Av. N22 —1B 32
Norman Av. Felt —2C 114
Norman Av. S'hall —7C 60
Norman Av. Twic —7C 98
Normanby Clo. SW15 —5H 101
Normanby Rd. NW10 —4B 46
Norman Clo. N22 —1C 32
Norman Clo. Romf —1H 39
Norman Ct. N4 —7A 32
Norman Ct. NW10 —7C 46
Norman Ct. W13 —1B 80
(off Kirkfield Clo.)
Norman Ct. Ilf —7H 37
Norman Cres. Houn —7B 78
Norman Cres. Pinn —1A 24
Normand Gdns. W14 —6G 83
(off Greyhound Rd.)
Normand M. W14 —6G 83
Normand Rd. W14 —6H 83
Normandy Av. Barn —5C 4
Normandy Clo. SE26 —3A 124
Normandy Dri. Hay —6E 58
Normandy Rd. SW9 —1A 104
Normandy Ter. E16 —6K 71
Normandy Way. Eri —1K 111
Norman Gro. E3 —2A 70
Norman Hay Trad. Est. W Dray —7B 76
Norman Ho. SW8 —7J 85
(off Wyvil Rd.)
Norman Ho. Felt —2D 114
(off Watermill Way)
Normanhurst. Ashf —5C 112
Normanhurst Av. Bexh —1D 110
Normanhurst Dri. Twic —5A 98
Normanhurst Rd. SW2 —2K 121
Norman Pde. Sidc —2D 128
Norman Rd. E6 —4D 72
Norman Rd. E11 —2F 53
Norman Rd. N15 —5F 33
Norman Rd. SE10 —7D 88
Norman Rd. SW19 —7A 120
Norman Rd. Ashf —6F 113
Norman Rd. Belv —3H 93
Norman Rd. Ilf —5F 55
Norman Rd. Sutt —5J 149
Norman Rd. T Hth —5B 140
Norman's Clo. NW10 —6K 45
Normans Clo. Uxb —4B 58
Normansfield Av. Tedd —7C 116
Normanshire Av. E4 —4K 19
Normanshire Dri. E4 —4H 19
Norman's Mead. NW10 —6K 45
Norman St. EC1 —3C 68 (2D 162)
Normanton Av. SW19 —2J 119
Normanton Pk. E4 —2B 20
Normanton Rd. S Croy —5E 152
Normanton St. SE23 —2K 123
Norman Way. N14 —2D 16
Norman Way. W3 —5H 63
Normington Clo. SW16 —5A 122
Norrice Lea. N2 —5B 30
Norris. NW9 —1B 28
(off Concourse, The)
Norris Ho. N1 —1E 68
(off Colville Est.)
Norris St. SW1 —7H 67 (3C 166)
Norroy Rd. SW15 —4F 101
Norry's Clo. Cockf —4J 5
Norry's Rd. Cockf —4J 5
Norseman Clo. Ilf —1B 56
Norseman Way. Gnfd —1F 61
Norstead Pl. SW15 —2C 118
N. Access Rd. E17 —6K 33
North Acre. NW9 —1A 28
North Acton. —4K 63
N. Acton Rd. NW10 —2K 63
Northall Rd. Bexh —2J 111
Northampton Gro. N1 —5C 50
Northampton Pk. N1 —6C 50
Northampton Rd. EC1 —4A 68 (3K 161)
Northampton Rd. Croy —2G 153
Northampton Rd. Enf —4F 9
Northampton Row. EC1 —3K 161
Northampton Sq. EC1 —3B 68 (2A 162)
Northampton St. N1 —7C 50
Northanger Rd. SW16 —6J 121
N. Audley St. W1 —6E 66 (1G 165)
North Av. N18 —4B 18
North Av. NW10 —3E 64
North Av. W13 —5B 62
North Av. Cars —7E 150
North Av. Harr —6F 25
North Av. Hay —7J 59
North Av. Rich —1G 99
North Av. S'hall —7D 60
North Bank. NW8 —3C 66 (2C 158)
Northbank Rd. E17 —2E 34
North Beckton. —5C 72
N. Birkbeck Rd. E11 —3F 53
North Block. SE1 —2K 85
(off York Rd.)
Northborough Rd. SW16 —3H 139
Northbourne. Brom —7J 143
Northbourne Rd. SW4 —5H 103
N. Branch Av. NW10 —3E 64
Northbrook Dri. N'wd —1G 23
Northbrook Rd. N22 —7D 16
Northbrook Rd. SE13 —5G 107
Northbrook Rd. Barn —6B 4
Northbrook Rd. Croy —5D 140
Northbrook Rd. Ilf —2E 54
Northburgh St. EC1 —4B 68 (4B 162)
N. Carriage Dri. W2 —2C 164
North Cheam. —4F 149
Northchurch. SE17 —5D 86
(in three parts)
Northchurch Rd. N1 —7D 50
(in two parts)
Northchurch Rd. Wemb —6G 45
Northchurch Ter. N1 —7E 50
(in two parts)
N. Circular Rd. E4 —6G 19
N. Circular Rd. N3 —4H 29
N. Circular Rd. N13 —5F 17
N. Circular Rd. NW2 —3A 46
N. Circular Rd. NW4 —7E 28
N. Circular Rd. NW10 —2F 63
Northcliffe Clo. Wor Pk —3A 148
Northcliffe Dri. N20 —1C 14
North Clo. Bexh —4D 110
North Clo. Dag —1G 75
North Clo. Felt —6F 95
North Clo. Mord —4G 137
N. Colonnade, The. E14 —1C 88
N. Common Rd. W5 —7E 62
N. Common Rd. Uxb —5A 40
Northcote. Pinn —2A 24
Northcote Av. W5 —7E 62
Northcote Av. Iswth —5A 98
Northcote Av. S'hall —7C 60
Northcote Av. Surb —7H 135
Northcote M. SW11 —4C 102
Northcote Rd. E17 —4A 34
Northcote Rd. NW10 —7A 46
Northcote Rd. SW11 —5C 102
Northcote Rd. Croy —6D 140
Northcote Rd. N Mald —3J 135
Northcote Rd. Sidc —4J 127
Northcote Rd. Twic —5A 98
Northcott Av. N22 —1J 31
N. Countess Rd. E17 —2B 34
North Ct. SE24 —3B 104
North Ct. SW1 —3J 85 (2E 172)
(off Gt. Peter St.)
North Ct. W1 —5G 67 (5B 160)
North Cray. —5E 128
N. Cray Rd. Sidc & Bex —6E 128
North Cres. E16 —4F 71
North Cres. N3 —2H 29
North Cres. WC1 —5H 67 (5C 160)
Northcroft Ct. W12 —2C 82
Northcroft Rd. W13 —2B 80
Northcroft Rd. Eps —7A 148
North Crofts. SE23 —1H 123
Northcroft Ter. W13 —2B 80
N. Cross Rd. SE22 —5F 105
N. Cross Rd. Ilf —4G 37
Northdale Ct. SE25 —3F 141
North Dene. NW7 —3E 12
North Dene. Houn —1F 97
Northdene Gdns. N15 —6F 33
Northdown Clo. Ruis —3H 41
Northdown Gdns. Ilf —5J 37
Northdown Rd. Well —2B 110
Northdown St. N1 —2J 67 (1G 161)
North Dri. SW16 —4G 121
North Dri. Beck —4D 142
North Dri. Houn —2G 97
North Dri. Ruis —7G 23
N. East Pier. E1 —1H 87
North East Surrey Crematorium. Mord —6E 136
North End. —2A 48
North End. NW3 —2A 48
North End. Buck H —1F 21
North End. Croy —2C 152
N. End Av. NW3 —2A 48
N. End Cres. W14 —4H 83
N. End Ho. W14 —4G 83
N. End Pde. W14 —4G 83
(off N. End Rd.)
N. End Rd. NW11 —1J 47
N. End Rd. W14 & SW6 —4G 83
N. End Rd. Wemb —3G 45
N. End Way. NW3 —2A 48
Northern Av. N9 —2K 17
Northernhay Wlk. Mord —4G 137
Northern Perimeter Rd. H'row A —1D 94
Northern Perimeter Rd. W. H'row A —1A 94
Northern Rd. E13 —2K 71
Northesk Ho. E1 —4H 69
(off Tent St.)
N. Eyot Gdns. W6 —5B 82
Northey St. E14 —7A 70
North Feltham. —6K 95
N. Feltham Trad. Est. Felt —5K 95
Northfield Av. W13 & W5 —1B 80
Northfield Av. Pinn —4B 24
Northfield Clo. Brom —1C 144
Northfield Clo. Hay —3H 77
Northfield Cres. Sutt —4G 149
Northfield Gdns. Dag —4F 57
Northfield Ho. SE15 —6G 87
Northfield Ind. Est. NW10 —3G 63
Northfield Ind. Est. Wemb —1G 63
Northfield Pde. Hay —3G 77
Northfield Pk. Hay —3H 77
Northfield Path. Dag —4F 57
Northfield Rd. E6 —7D 54
Northfield Rd. N16 —7E 32
Northfield Rd. W13 —2B 80
Northfield Rd. Barn —3H 5
Northfield Rd. Dag —4F 57
Northfield Rd. Enf —5C 8
Northfield Rd. Houn —6B 78
Northfields. —3B 80
Northfields. SW18 —4J 101
Northfields Prospect Bus. Cen. SW18 —4J 101
Northfields Rd. W3 —5H 63
North Finchley. —5F 15
Northfleet Ho. SE1 —2D 86 (6E 168)
(off Tennis St.)
N. Flock St. SE16 —2G 87
N. Flower Wlk. W2 —3A 164
North Garden. E14 —1B 88
North Gdns. SW19 —7B 120
North Ga. NW8 —1C 158
Northgate. N'wd —1E 22
Northgate Bus. Pk. Enf —3C 8
Northgate Dri. NW9 —6A 28
Northgate Ho. E14 —7C 70
Northgate Ind. Est. Romf —1F 39
N. Glade, The. Bex —7F 111
N. Gower St. NW1 —3G 67 (2B 160)
North Grn. NW9 —7F 13
North Gro. N6 —7E 30
North Gro. N15 —5D 32
North Harrow. —5F 25
N. Hatton Rd. H'row A —1F 95
North Hill. N6 —6D 30
N. Hill Av. N6 —6E 30
North Hillingdon. —7E 40
North Ho. SE8 —5B 88
N. Hyde Gdns. Hay —4J 77
N. Hyde La. S'hall & Houn —5B 78
N. Hyde Rd. Hay —3G 77
Northiam. N12 —4D 14
(in two parts)
Northiam. WC1 —3J 67 (2F 161)
(off Cromer St.)
Northiam St. E8 & E9 —1H 69
Northington St. WC1 —4K 67 (4H 161)
North Kensington. —5F 65
Northlands St. SE5 —2C 104
North La. Tedd —6K 115
Northleach Ct. SE15 —6E 86
(off Birdlip Clo.)
North Lodge. New Bar —5F 5
N. Lodge Clo. SW15 —5F 101
North Mall. N9 —2C 18
(off Plevna Rd.)
North M. WC1 —4K 67 (4H 161)
North Mt. N20 —2F 15
(off High Rd.)
Northolm. Edgw —4E 12
Northolme Gdns. Edgw —1G 27
Northolme Rd. N5 —4C 50
Northolt. —7E 42
Northolt. N17 —2E 32
(off Griffin Rd.)
Northolt Av. Ruis —5K 41
Northolt Gdns. Gnfd —5K 43
Northolt Rd. Harr —4F 43
Northolt Rd. H'row A —1A 94
Northover. Brom —3H 125
North Pde. Chess —5F 147
North Pde. Edgw —2G 27
North Pde. S'hall —6E 60
(off North Rd.)
North Pk. SE9 —6D 108
North Pl. SW18 —5J 101
North Pl. Mitc —7D 120
North Pl. Tedd —6K 115
N. Pole La. Kes —6H 155
N. Pole Rd. W10 —5E 64
Northport St. N1 —1D 68
North Ride. W2 —7C 66 (3C 164)
North Ri. W2 —6C 66 (1D 164)
North Rd. N2 —2C 30
North Rd. N6 —7E 30
North Rd. N7 —6J 49
North Rd. N9 —1C 18
North Rd. SE18 —4J 91
North Rd. SW19 —6A 120
North Rd. W5 —3D 80
North Rd. Belv —3H 93
North Rd. Bren —6E 80
North Rd. Brom —1K 143
North Rd. Chad H —5E 38
North Rd. Edgw —1H 27
North Rd. Felt —6F 95
North Rd. Harr —7A 26
North Rd. Hay —5F 59
North Rd. Ilf —2J 55
North Rd. Rich —3G 99
North Rd. S'hall —7E 60
North Rd. Surb —6D 134
North Rd. W Dray —3B 76
North Rd. W W'ck —1D 154
Northrop Rd. H'row A —1G 95
North Row. W1 —7D 66 (2F 165)
N. Row Bldgs. W1 —7E 66 (2G 165)
(off North Row)
North Several. SE3 —2F 107
North Sheen. —3G 99
Northside Rd. Brom —1J 143
N. Side Wandsworth Comn. SW18 —5B 102
Northspur Rd. Sutt —3J 149
North Sq. N9 —2C 18
(off Hertford Rd.)
North Sq. NW11 —5J 29
Northstead Rd. SW2 —2A 122
North St. E13 —2K 71
North St. NW4 —5E 28
North St. SW4 —3G 103
North St. Bark —6F 55
(Barking Northern Relief Rd.)
North St. Bark —7G 55
(London Rd.)
North St. Bexh —4G 111
North St. Brom —1J 143
North St. Cars —3D 150
North St. Iswth —3A 98
North St. Romf —3K 39
N. Street Pas. E13 —2K 71
N. Tenter St. E1 —6F 69 (1K 169)
North Ter. SW3 —3C 84 (2C 170)
Northumberland All. EC3 —6E 68 (1H 169)
(in two parts)
Northumberland Av. E12 —1A 54
Northumberland Av. WC2 —1J 85 (4E 166)
Northumberland Av. Enf —1C 8
Northumberland Av. Iswth —1K 97
Northumberland Av. Well —4H 109
Northumberland Clo. Eri —7J 93
Northumberland Clo. Stanw —6A 94
Northumberland Cres. Felt —6G 95
Northumberland Gdns. N9 —3A 18
Northumberland Gdns. Brom —4E 144
Northumberland Gdns. Iswth —7A 80
Northumberland Gdns. Mitc —5H 139

246 A-Z Big London

Northumberland Gro.—Oast Lodge

Northumberland Gro. N17 —7C 18
Northumberland Heath. —7J 93
Northumberland Ho. SW1 —1J 85
(off Northumberland Av.)
Northumberland Pk. N17 —7A 18
Northumberland Pk. Eri —7J 93
Northumberland Pk. Ind. Est. N17 —7C 18
Northumberland Pl. W2 —6J 65
Northumberland Pl. Rich —5D 98
Northumberland Rd. E6 —6C 72
Northumberland Rd. E17 —7C 34
Northumberland Rd. Harr —5D 24
Northumberland Rd. New Bar —6F 5
Northumberland Row. Twic —1J 115
Northumberland St. WC2 —1J 85 (4E 166)
Northumberland Way. Eri —1J 111
Northumbria St. E14 —6C 70
N. Verbena Gdns. W6 —5C 82
Northview. N7 —3J 49
North Vw. SW19 —5E 118
North Vw. W5 —4C 62
North Vw. Pinn —7A 24
N. View Cres. NW10 —4B 46
Northview Dri. Wfd G —2B 36
N. View Rd. N8 —4H 31
North Vs. NW1 —6H 49
North Wlk. W8 —7K 65
(off Bayswater Rd.)
North Wlk. New Ad —6D 154
(in two parts)
North Way. N9 —2E 18
North Way. N11 —6B 16
North Way. NW9 —3H 27
Northway. NW11 —5K 29
Northway. Mord —3G 137
North Way. Pinn —4B 24
North Way. Uxb —7A 40
Northway. Wall —4G 151
Northway Cir. NW7 —4E 12
Northway Cres. NW7 —4E 12
Northway Gdns. NW11 —5K 29
Northway Rd. SE5 —3C 104
Northway Rd. Croy —6F 141
Northways Pde. NW3 —7B 48
(off College Cres.)
Northweald La. King T —5D 116
North Wembley. —3D 44
N. Western Commercial Cen. NW1 —7J 49
N. West Pier. E1 —1H 87
Northwest Pl. N1 —2A 68
North Wharf. E14 —1E 88
N. Wharf Rd. W2 —5B 66 (6A 158)
Northwick Av. Harr —6A 26
Northwick Circ. Harr —6C 26
Northwick Clo. NW8 —4B 66 (3A 158)
Northwick Clo. Harr —1B 44
Northwick Ho. W9 —3A 158
Northwick Pk. Rd. Harr —6K 25
Northwick Rd. Wemb —1D 62
Northwick Ter. NW8 —4B 66 (3A 158)
Northwick Wlk. Harr —7K 25
Northwold Dri. Pinn —2A 24
Northwold Est. E5 —2G 51
Northwold Rd. N16 & E5 —2F 51
N. Wood Ct. SE25 —3G 141
Northwood Gdns. N12 —5G 15
Northwood Gdns. Gnfd —5K 43
Northwood Gdns. Ilf —4E 36
Northwood Hills. —2J 23
Northwood Hills Cir. N'wd —1J 23
Northwood Ho. SE27 —4D 122
Northwood Pl. Eri —3F 93
Northwood Rd. N6 —7F 31
Northwood Rd. SE23 —1B 124
Northwood Rd. Cars —6E 150
Northwood Rd. H'row A —1A 94
Northwood Rd. T Hth —2B 140
Northwood Way. SE19 —6D 122
Northwood Way. N'wd —1J 23
North Woolwich. —1E 90
North Woolwich Old Station Mus. —2E 90
N. Woolwich Rd. E16 —1H 89
N. Worple Way. SW14 —3K 99
Norton Av. Surb —7H 135
Norton Clo. E4 —5H 19
Norton Clo. Enf —2C 8
Norton Folgate. E1 —5E 68 (5H 163)
Norton Folgate Houses. E1 —5F 69 (5J 163)
(off Puma Ct.)
Norton Gdns. SW16 —2J 139
Norton Ho. SW1 —3H 85 (2D 172)
(off Arneway St.)
Norton Ho. SW9 —2K 103
(off Aytoun Rd.)
Norton Rd. E10 —1B 52
Norton Rd. Dag —6K 57
Norton Rd. Wemb —6D 44
Norval Rd. Wemb —2B 44
Norway Ga. SE16 —3A 88
Norway Pl. E14 —6B 70
Norway St. SE10 —6D 88
Norway Wharf. E14 —6B 70
Norwich Ho. E14 —6D 70
Norwich M. Ilf —1A 56
Norwich Pl. Bexh —4G 111
Norwich Rd. E7 —5J 53
Norwich Rd. Dag —2G 75
Norwich Rd. Gnfd —1F 61
Norwich Rd. N'wd —3H 23
Norwich Rd. T Hth —3C 140
Norwich St. EC4 —6A 68 (7J 161)
Norwich Wlk. Edgw —7D 12
Norwood. —6E 122
Norwood Av. Romf —7K 39
Norwood Av. Wemb —1F 63
Norwood Clo. S'hall —4E 78
Norwood Clo. Twic —2H 115
Norwood Dri. Harr —6D 24
Norwood Gdns. Hay —4A 60
Norwood Gdns. S'hall —4D 78
Norwood Green. —4E 78
Norwood Grn. Rd. S'hall —4E 78
Norwood High St. SE27 —3B 122
Norwood Ho. E14 —7D 70
Norwood New Town. —6C 122
Norwood Pk. Rd. SE27 —5C 122
Norwood Rd. SE24 —1B 122
Norwood Rd. SE27 —2B 122
Norwood Rd. S'hall —3C 78
Norwood Ter. S'hall —4F 79
Notley St. SE5 —7D 86
Notson Rd. SE25 —4H 141
Notting Barn Rd. W10 —4F 65
Nottingdale Sq. W11 —1G 83
Nottingham Av. E16 —5A 72
Nottingham Ct. WC2 —6J 67 (1E 166)
Nottingham Ho. WC2 —6J 67 (1E 166)
Nottingham Pl. W1 —5E 66 (4G 159)
Nottingham Rd. E10 —6E 34
Nottingham Rd. SW17 —1D 120
Nottingham Rd. Iswth —2K 97
Nottingham Rd. S Croy —4C 152
Nottingham St. W1 —5E 66 (5G 159)
Nottingham Ter. NW1 —4G 159
Notting Hill. —7H 65
Notting Hill Ga. W11 —1J 83
Nottingwood Ho. W11 —7G 65
(off Clarendon Rd.)
Nova M. Sutt —1G 149
Novar Clo. Orp —7K 145
Nova Rd. Croy —1B 152
Novar Rd. SE9 —1G 127
Novello St. SW6 —1J 101
Nowell Rd. SW13 —6C 82
Nower Ct. Pinn —4D 24
Nower Hill. Pinn —4D 24
Noyna Rd. SW17 —3D 120
Nubia Way. Brom —3G 125
Nuding Clo. SE13 —3C 106
Nuffield Ct. Houn —7D 78
Nuffield Lodge. N6 —6G 31
Nuffield Lodge. W2 —5J 65
(off Admiral Wlk.)
Nugent Rd. N19 —1J 49
Nugent Rd. SE25 —3F 141
Nugents Ct. Pinn —1C 24
Nugent's Pk. Pinn —1C 24
Nugent Ter. NW8 —2A 66
Numa Ct. Bren —7D 80
Nun Ct. EC2 —6E 162
Nuneaton Rd. Dag —7E 56
Nunhead. —3H 105
Nunhead Cres. SE15 —3H 105
Nunhead Est. SE15 —4H 105
Nunhead Grn. SE15 —3H 105
Nunhead Gro. SE15 —3H 105
Nunhead La. SE15 —3H 105
Nunhead Pas. SE15 —3G 105
Nunnington Clo. SE9 —3C 126
Nunns Rd. Enf —2H 7
Nupton Dri. Barn —6A 4
Nurse Clo. Edgw —1J 27
Nursery App. N12 —6H 15
Nursery Av. N3 —2A 30
Nursery Av. Bexh —3F 111
Nursery Av. Croy —2K 153
Nursery Clo. SE4 —2B 106
Nursery Clo. SW15 —4F 101
Nursery Clo. Croy —2K 153
Nursery Clo. Enf —1E 8
Nursery Clo. Felt —7K 95
(in two parts)
Nursery Clo. Orp —7K 145
Nursery Clo. Romf —6D 38
Nursery Clo. Wfd G —5E 20
Nursery Ct. N17 —7A 18
Nursery Ct. W13 —5A 62
Nursery Gdns. Chst —6F 127
Nursery Gdns. Enf —1E 8
Nursery Gdns. Hamp —4D 114
Nursery Gdns. Houn —5D 96
Nursery Gdns. Sun —2H 131
Nursery La. E2 —1F 69
Nursery La. E7 —6J 53
Nursery La. W10 —5E 64
Nursery La. Uxb —4A 58
Nurserymans Rd. N11 —2K 15
Nursery Rd. E9 —6J 51
Nursery Rd. N2 —1B 30
Nursery Rd. N14 —7B 6
Nursery Rd. SW9 —4K 103
Nursery Rd. SW19 —2K 137
(Merton)
Nursery Rd. SW19 —7G 119
(Wimbledon)
Nursery Rd. Pinn —3A 24
Nursery Rd. Sun —2G 131
Nursery Rd. Sutt —4A 150
Nursery Rd. T Hth —4D 140
Nursery Row. Barn —3B 4
Nursery St. N17 —7A 18
Nursery Wlk. NW4 —3E 28
Nursery Wlk. Romf —7K 39
Nursery Waye. Uxb —1A 58
Nurstead Rd. Eri —7G 93
Nutbourne St. W10 —3G 65
Nutbrook St. SE15 —3G 105
Nutbrowne Rd. Dag —1F 75
Nutcroft Rd. SE15 —7H 87
Nutfield Clo. N18 —6A 18
Nutfield Clo. Cars —3C 150
Nutfield Gdns. Ilf —2K 55
Nutfield Gdns. N'holt —2A 60
Nutfield Rd. E15 —4E 52
Nutfield Rd. NW2 —3C 46
Nutfield Rd. SE22 —4F 105
Nutfield Rd. T Hth —4B 140
Nutfield Way. Orp —2E 156
Nutford Pl. W1 —6D 66 (7D 158)
Nuthatch Clo. Stai —1B 112
Nuthatch Gdns. SE28 —2H 91
(in two parts)
Nuthurst Av. SW2 —2K 121
Nutkin Wlk. Uxb —7A 40
Nutley Ter. NW3 —6A 48
Nutmead Clo. Bex —1J 129
Nutmeg Clo. E16 —4G 71
Nutmeg La. E14 —6F 71
Nuttall St. N1 —2E 68
Nutter La. E11 —6A 36
Nutt Gro. Edgw —2J 11
Nutt St. SE15 —7F 87
Nutty La. Shep —3E 130
Nutwell St. SW17 —5C 120
Nuxley Rd. Belv —6F 93
Nyanza St. SE18 —6H 91
Nye Bevan Est. E5 —3K 51
Nye Bevan Ho. SW6 —7H 83
(off St Thomas's Way)
Nylands Av. Rich —1G 99
Nymans Gdns. SW20 —3D 136
Nynehead St. SE14 —7A 88
Nyon Gro. SE6 —2B 124
Nyssa Clo. Wfd G —6J 21
Nyssa Ct. E15 —3G 71
(off Teasel Way)
Nyton Clo. N19 —1J 49

Oak Apple Ct. SE12 —1J 125
Oak Av. N8 —4J 31
Oak Av. N10 —7A 16
Oak Av. N17 —7J 17
Oak Av. Croy —1C 154
Oak Av. Enf —1E 6
Oak Av. Hamp —5C 114
Oak Av. Houn —7B 78
Oak Av. Uxb —2D 40
Oak Av. W Dray —3C 76
Oak Bank. New Ad —6E 154
Oakbank Av. W on T —7D 132
Oakbank Gro. SE24 —4C 104
Oakbrook Clo. Brom —4K 125
Oakbury Rd. SW6 —2K 101
Oak Clo. N14 —7A 6
Oak Clo. Sutt —2A 150
Oakcombe Clo. N Mald —1A 136
Oak Cottage Clo. SE6 —1H 125
Oak Cotts. W7 —2J 79
Oak Ct. SE15 —7F 87
(off Sumner Rd.)
Oak Cres. E16 —5G 71
Oakcroft Bus. Cen. Chess —4F 147
Oakcroft Clo. Pinn —2K 23
Oakcroft Rd. SE13 —2F 107
Oakcroft Rd. Chess —4F 147
Oakcroft Vs. Chess —4F 147
Oakdale. N14 —1A 16
Oakdale Av. Harr —5E 26
Oakdale Av. N'wd —2J 23
Oakdale Ct. E4 —5K 19
Oakdale Gdns. E4 —5K 19
Oakdale Rd. E7 —7K 53
Oakdale Rd. E11 —2F 53
Oakdale Rd. E18 —2K 35
Oakdale Rd. N4 —6C 32
Oakdale Rd. SE15 & SE4 —3J 105
Oakdale Rd. SW16 —5J 121
Oakdale Rd. Eps —7K 147
Oakdale Way. Mitc —7E 138
Oak Dene. SE15 —1H 105
Oakdene. W13 —5B 62
Oakdene Av. Chst —5E 126
Oakdene Av. Eri —6J 93
Oakdene Av. Th Dit —1A 146
Oakdene Clo. Pinn —1D 24
Oakdene Dri. Surb —7J 135
Oakdene M. Sutt —1H 149
Oakdene Pk. N3 —7C 14
Oakdene Rd. Orp —5K 145
Oakdene Rd. Uxb —2D 58
Oakden St. SE11 —4A 86 (3K 173)
Oake Ct. SW15 —5G 101
Oakeford Ho. W14 —3G 83
(off Russell Rd.)
Oakend Ho. N4 —7D 32
Oakenholt Ho. SE2 —1D 92
Oakenshaw Clo. Surb —7E 134
Oakes Clo. E6 —6D 72
Oakeshott Av. N6 —2E 48
Oakey La. SE1 —3A 86 (1J 173)
Oakfield. E4 —5J 19
Oakfield Av. Harr —3B 26
Oakfield Cen. SE20 —7H 123
Oakfield Clo. N Mald —5B 136
Oakfield Clo. Ruis —6H 23
Oakfield Ct. N8 —7J 31
Oakfield Ct. NW11 —7F 29
Oakfield Gdns. N18 —4K 17
Oakfield Gdns. SE19 —5E 122
(in two parts)
Oakfield Gdns. Beck —5D 142
Oakfield Gdns. Cars —1C 150
Oakfield Gdns. Gnfd —4H 61
Oakfield Ho. E3 —5C 70
Oakfield La. Kes —4A 156
Oakfield Lodge. Ilf —3F 55
(off Albert Rd.)
Oakfield Rd. E6 —1C 72
Oakfield Rd. E17 —2A 34
Oakfield Rd. N3 —1K 29
Oakfield Rd. N8 —6A 32
Oakfield Rd. N14 —3D 16
Oakfield Rd. SE20 —7H 123
Oakfield Rd. SW19 —3F 119
Oakfield Rd. Ashf —5D 112
Oakfield Rd. Croy —1C 152
Oakfield Rd. Ilf —3F 55
Oakfield Rd. Ind. Est. SE20 —7H 123
Oakfields Rd. NW11 —6G 29
Oakfield St. SW10 —6A 84
Oakford Rd. NW5 —4G 49
Oak Gdns. Croy —2C 154
Oak Gdns. Edgw —2H 27
Oak Glade. N'wd —1D 22
Oak Gro. NW2 —4G 47
Oak Gro. Ruis —7K 23
Oak Gro. Sun —7K 113
Oak Gro. W W'ck —1E 154
Oak Gro. Rd. SE20 —1J 141
Oakhall Ct. E11 —6K 35
Oakhall Dri. Sun —5H 113
Oak Hall Rd. E11 —6K 35
Oakham Clo. SE6 —2B 124
Oakham Clo. Barn —3J 5
Oakham Dri. Brom —4H 143
Oakhampton Rd. NW7 —7A 14
Oakhill. Clay —6A 146
Oakhill. Surb —7E 134
Oak Hill. Wfd G —7A 20
Oakhill Av. NW3 —4K 47
Oakhill Av. Pinn —2C 24
Oak Hill Clo. Wfd G —7A 20
Oakhill Ct. SE23 —6J 105
Oakhill Ct. SW20 —7F 119
Oak Hill Ct. Wfd G —7A 20
Oakhill Cres. Surb —7E 134
Oak Hill Cres. Wfd G —7A 20
Oakhill Dri. Surb —7E 134
Oak Hill Gdns. Wfd G —1G 35
Oakhill Gro. Surb —6E 134
Oak Hill Pk. NW3 —4K 47
Oak Hill Pk. M. NW3 —4A 48
Oakhill Path. Surb —6E 134
Oakhill Pl. SW15 —5J 101
Oakhill Rd. SW15 —5H 101
Oakhill Rd. SW16 —1J 139
Oakhill Rd. Beck —2E 142
Oakhill Rd. Surb —6E 134
Oakhill Rd. Sutt —3K 149
Oak Hill Way. NW3 —4A 48
Oak Ho. N2 —2B 30
Oak Ho. W10 —4G 65
(off Sycamore Wlk.)
Oakhouse Rd. Bexh —5G 111
Oakhurst Av. Barn & E Barn —7H 5
Oakhurst Av. Bexh —7E 92
Oakhurst Clo. E17 —4G 35
Oakhurst Clo. Chst —1D 144
Oakhurst Clo. Ilf —1F 37
Oakhurst Clo. Tedd —5J 115
Oakhurst Gdns. E4 —1C 20
Oakhurst Gdns. E17 —4G 35
Oakhurst Gdns. Bexh —7E 92
Oakhurst Gro. SE22 —4G 105
Oakhurst Rd. Eps —6J 147
Oakington Av. Harr —7E 24
Oakington Av. Hay —4F 77
Oakington Av. Wemb —3F 45
Oakington Ct. Enf —2G 7
(off Ridgeway, The)
Oakington Dri. Sun —2A 132
Oakington Mnr. Dri. Wemb —5G 45
Oakington Rd. W9 —4J 65
Oakington Way. N8 —7J 31
Oakland Pl. Buck H —2D 20
Oakland Rd. E15 —4F 53
Oaklands. N21 —2E 16
Oaklands. W13 —5A 62
Oaklands. Beck —1D 142
Oaklands Av. N9 —6C 8
Oaklands Av. Esh —7H 133
Oaklands Av. Iswth —6K 79
Oaklands Av. Sidc —7K 109
Oaklands Av. T Hth —4A 140
Oaklands Av. W W'ck —3D 154
Oaklands Clo. Bexh —5F 111
Oaklands Clo. Chess —4C 146
Oaklands Clo. Orp —6J 145
Oaklands Clo. Wemb —5D 44
Oaklands Ct. NW10 —1A 64
(off Nicoll Rd.)
Oaklands Ct. Wemb —5D 44
Oaklands Dri. Twic —7G 97
Oaklands Est. SW4 —6G 103
Oaklands Gro. W12 —1C 82
Oaklands M. NW2 —4F 47
(off Oaklands Rd.)
Oaklands Pk. Av. Ilf —2G 55
Oaklands Pas. NW2 —4F 47
(off Oaklands Rd.)
Oaklands Pl. SW4 —4G 103
Oaklands Rd. N20 —7C 4
Oaklands Rd. NW2 —4F 47
Oaklands Rd. SW14 —3K 99
Oaklands Rd. W7 —2K 79
Oaklands Rd. Bexh —4F 111
Oaklands Rd. Brom —7G 125
Oaklands Way. Wall —7H 151
Oakland Way. Eps —6A 148
Oak La. E14 —7B 70
Oak La. N2 —2B 30
Oak La. N11 —6C 16
Oak La. Iswth —4J 97
Oak La. Twic —7A 98
Oak La. Wfd G —4C 20
Oakleafe Gdns. Ilf —3F 37
Oaklea Pas. King T —3D 134
Oakleigh Av. N20 —2G 15
Oakleigh Av. Edgw —2H 27
Oakleigh Av. Surb —1G 147
Oakleigh Clo. N20 —3J 15
Oakleigh Ct. Barn —6H 5
Oakleigh Ct. Edgw —2J 27
Oakleigh Ct. S'hall —1D 78
Oakleigh Cres. N20 —2H 15
Oakleigh Gdns. N20 —1F 15
Oakleigh Gdns. Edgw —5A 12
Oakleigh M. N20 —1F 15
Oakleigh Park. —1G 15
Oakleigh Pk. Av. Chst —1E 144
Oakleigh Pk. N. N20 —1G 15
Oakleigh Pk. S. N20 —7H 5
Oakleigh Rd. Uxb —7E 40
Oakleigh Rd. N. N20 —2G 15
Oakleigh Rd. S. N11 —3K 15
Oakleigh Way. Mitc —1F 139
Oakleigh Way. Surb —1G 147
Oakley Av. W5 —7G 63
Oakley Av. Bark —7K 55
Oakley Av. Croy —4K 151
Oakley Clo. E4 —3K 19
Oakley Clo. E6 —6C 72
Oakley Clo. W7 —7J 61
Oakley Clo. Iswth —1H 97
Oakley Cres. EC1 —2B 68 (1B 162)
Oakley Dri. SE9 —1H 127
Oakley Dri. SE13 —6F 107
Oakley Dri. Brom —3C 156
Oakley Gdns. N8 —5K 31
Oakley Gdns. SW3 —6C 84 (7D 170)
Oakley Grange. Harr —3G 43
Oakley Ho. SW1 —4D 84 (3F 171)
Oakley Ho. W3 —7G 63
Oakley Pk. Bex —7C 110
Oakley Pl. SE1 —5F 87
Oakley Rd. N1 —7D 50
Oakley Rd. SE25 —5H 141
Oakley Rd. Brom —3C 156
Oakley Rd. Harr —6J 25
Oakley Sq. NW1 —2G 67
Oakley St. SW3 —6C 84 (7C 170)
Oakley Wlk. W6 —6F 83
Oakley Yd. E2 —3K 163
Oak Lodge. E11 —6J 35
Oak Lodge. W8 —3K 83
(off Chantry Sq.)
Oak Lodge Clo. Stan —5H 11
Oak Lodge Dri. W W'ck —7D 142
Oaklodge Way. NW7 —5G 13
Oakmead Av. Brom —6J 143
Oakmead Ct. Stan —4H 11
Oak Meade. Pinn —6A 10
Oakmead Gdns. Edgw —4E 12
Oakmead Pl. Mitc —1C 138
Oakmead Rd. SW12 —1E 120
Oakmead Rd. Croy —6H 139
Oakmede. Barn —4A 4
Oakmere Rd. SE2 —6A 92
Oakmont Pl. Orp —7H 145
Oak Pk. Gdns. SW19 —1F 119
Oak Pk. M. N16 —3F 51
Oak Pl. SW18 —5K 101
Oakridge Dri. N2 —3B 30
Oakridge La. Brom —5F 125
Oakridge Rd. Brom —4F 125
Oak Ri. Buck H —3G 21
Oak Rd. W5 —7D 62
Oak Rd. Eri —7J 93
Oak Rd. N Mald —2K 135
Oak Row. SW16 —2G 139
Oaks Av. SE19 —5E 122
Oaks Av. Felt —2C 114
Oaks Av. Romf —2J 39
Oaks Av. Wor Pk —3D 148
Oaks Cvn. Pk., The. Chess —3C 146
Oaksford Av. SE26 —3H 123
Oaks Gro. E4 —2B 20
Oakshade Rd. Brom —4F 125
Oakshaw Rd. SW18 —7K 101
Oakshott Ct. NW1 —2H 67 (1C 160)
(in two parts)
Oaks La. Croy —3J 153
(in two parts)
Oaks La. Ilf —5J 37
Oaks Rd. Croy —5H 153
Oaks Rd. Stai & Stanw —5A 94
Oaks Shop. Cen., The. W3 —1J 81
Oaks, The. E4 —7B 20
Oaks, The. N12 —4E 14
Oaks, The. NW10 —7D 46
Oaks, The. SE18 —5G 91
Oaks, The. Brom —6E 144
Oaks, The. Enf —3G 7
(off Bycullah Rd.)
Oaks, The. Hay —2E 58
Oaks, The. Mord —4G 137
Oaks, The. Ruis —7G 23
Oak St. Romf —5J 39
Oaks Way. Cars —7D 150
Oaksway. Surb —1D 146
Oakthorpe Ct. N13 —5H 17
Oakthorpe Pk. Est. N13 —5H 17
Oakthorpe Rd. N13 —5F 17
Oaktree Av. N13 —3G 17
Oak Tree Clo. W5 —6C 62
Oak Tree Clo. Stan —7H 11
Oak Tree Ct. W3 —7H 63
Oak Tree Ct. N'holt —2A 60
Oak Tree Dell. NW9 —5K 27
Oak Tree Dri. N20 —1E 14
Oak Tree Gdns. Brom —5K 125
Oaktree Gro. Ilf —5H 55
Oak Tree Ho. W9 —4J 65
(off Shirland Rd.)
Oak Tree Rd. NW8 —3C 66 (2B 158)
Oakview Gdns. N2 —4B 30
Oakview Gro. Croy —1A 154
Oakview Lodge. NW11 —7H 29
(off Beechcroft Av.)
Oakview Rd. SE6 —5D 124
Oak Village. NW5 —4E 48
Oak Vs. NW11 —6H 29
(off Hendon Pk. Row)
Oak Way. N14 —7A 6
Oak Way. SW20 —4E 136
Oak Way. W3 —1A 82
Oakway. Brom —2F 143
Oak Way. Croy —6K 141
Oak Way. Felt —1G 113
Oakway Clo. Bex —6E 110
Oakways. SE9 —6F 109
Oakwood. —6C 6
Oakwood. Wall —7F 151
Oakwood Av. N14 —7C 6
Oakwood Av. Beck —2E 142
Oakwood Av. Brom —3K 143
Oakwood Av. Mitc —2B 138
Oakwood Av. S'hall —7E 60
Oakwood Bus. Pk. NW10 —4K 63
Oakwood Clo. N14 —6B 6
Oakwood Clo. Chst —6D 126
Oakwood Clo. Wfd G —6H 21
Oakwood Ct. E6 —7C 54
Oakwood Ct. W14 —3H 83
Oakwood Ct. Harr —6H 25
Oakwood Cres. N21 —6D 6
Oakwood Cres. Gnfd —6A 44
Oakwood Dri. SE19 —6D 122
Oakwood Dri. Bexh —4J 111
Oakwood Dri. Edgw —6D 12
Oakwood Gdns. Ilf —2K 55
Oakwood Gdns. Sutt —2J 149
Oakwood La. W14 —3H 83
Oakwood Lodge. N14 —6B 6
(off Avenue Rd.)
Oakwood Pk. Rd. N14 —7C 6
Oakwood Pl. Croy —6A 140
Oakwood Rd. NW11 —4J 29
Oakwood Rd. SW20 —1C 136
Oakwood Rd. Croy —6A 140
Oakwood Rd. Pinn —2K 23
Oakwood Vw. N14 —6C 6
Oakworth Rd. W10 —5E 64
Oarsman Pl. E Mol —4J 133
Oasis, The. Brom —2A 144
Oast Ct. E14 —7B 70
Oast Lodge. W4 —7A 82
(off Corney Reach Way)

Ormanton Rd.—Palmerston Rd.

Ormanton Rd. SE26 —4G 123
Orme Ct. W2 —7K 65
Orme Ct. M. W2 —7K 65
(off Orme La.)
Orme Ho. E8 —1F 69
Orme La. W2 —7K 65
Ormeley Rd. SW12 —1F 121
Orme Rd. King T —2H 135
Ormerod Gdns. Mitc —2E 138
Ormesby Clo. SE28 —7D 74
Ormesby Way. Harr —6F 27
Orme Sq. W2 —7K 65
Ormiston Gro. W12 —1D 82
Ormiston Rd. SE10 —5J 89
Ormond Av. Hamp —1F 133
Ormond Av. Rich —5D 98
Ormond Clo. WC1 —5J 67 (5F 161)
Ormond Cres. Hamp —1F 133
Ormond Dri. Hamp —7F 115
Ormonde Ct. SW15 —4E 100
Ormonde Ga. SW3 —5D 84 (6F 171)
Ormonde Pl. SW1 —4E 84 (4G 171)
Ormonde Ri. Buck H —1F 21
Ormonde Rd. SW14 —3J 99
Ormonde Ter. NW8 —1D 66
Ormond M. WC1 —4J 67 (4F 161)
Ormond Rd. N19 —1J 49
Ormond Rd. Rich —5D 98
Ormond Yd. SW1 —1G 85 (4B 166)
Ormsby. Sutt —7K 149
Ormsby Gdns. Gnfd —2G 61
Ormsby Lodge. W4 —3A 82
Ormsby Pl. N16 —3F 51
Ormsby St. E2 —2F 69
Ormside St. SE15 —6J 87
Ornan Rd. NW3 —5C 48
Oronsay Wlk. N1 —7C 50
Orpen Wlk. N16 —3E 50
Orpheus St. SE5 —1D 104
Orpheus Tower. SE14 —7A 88
(off Desmond St.)
Orpington. —7K 145
Orpington Gdns. N18 —3K 17
Orpington Mans. N21 —1G 17
Orpington Rd. N21 —1G 17
Orpington Rd. Chst —3J 145
Orpwood Clo. Hamp —6D 114
Orsett M. W2 —6K 65
(in two parts)
Orsett St. SE11 —5K 85 (5H 173)
Orsett Ter. W2 —6K 65
Orsett Ter. Wfd G —7F 21
Orsman Rd. N1 —1E 68
Orton St. E1 —1G 87
Orville Rd. SW11 —2B 102
Orwell Clo. Hay —7G 59
Orwell Clo. Rain —5K 75
Orwell Ct. E8 —1G 69
(off Pownall Rd.)
Orwell Ct. N5 —4C 50
Orwell Rd. E13 —2A 72
Osbaldeston Rd. N16 —2G 51
Osberton Rd. SE12 —5J 107
Osbert St. SW1 —4H 85 (4C 172)
Osborn Clo. E8 —1G 69
Osborne Av. Stai —1B 112
Osborne Clo. Barn —3J 5
Osborne Clo. Beck —4A 142
Osborne Clo. Felt —5B 114
Osborne Ct. E10 —7D 34
Osborne Ct. W5 —5E 62
Osborne Gdns. T Hth —2C 140
Osborne Gro. E17 —4B 34
Osborne Gro. N4 —1A 50
Osborne M. E17 —4B 34
Osborne Pl. Sutt —5B 150
Osborne Rd. E7 —5K 53
Osborne Rd. E9 —6B 52
Osborne Rd. E10 —2D 52
Osborne Rd. N4 —1A 50
Osborne Rd. N13 —3F 17
Osborne Rd. NW2 —6D 46
Osborne Rd. W3 —3H 81
Osborne Rd. Belv —5F 93
Osborne Rd. Buck H —1E 20
Osborne Rd. Dag —5F 57
Osborne Rd. Enf —2F 9
Osborne Rd. Houn —3D 96
Osborne Rd. King T —7E 116
Osborne Rd. S'hall —6G 61
Osborne Rd. T Hth —2C 140
Osborne Rd. W on T —7J 131
Osborne Sq. Dag —4F 57
Osborne Ter. SW17 —5D 120
(off Church La.)
Osborn Gdns. NW7 —7A 14
Osborn La. SE23 —7A 106
Osborn St. E1 —5F 69 (6K 163)
Osborn Ter. SE3 —4H 107
Osbourne Ct. Harr —4F 25
Osbourne Ho. Twic —2G 115
Oscar Faber Pl. N1 —7E 50
Oscar St. SE4 —2C 106
(in two parts)
Oseney Cres. NW5 —5G 49
O'Shea Gro. E3 —1B 70
Osidge. —1A 16
Osidge La. N14 —1K 15
Osier Ct. Bren —6E 80
(off Ealing Rd.)
Osier Ct. Romf —6K 39
Osier Cres. N10 —1D 30
Osier M. W4 —6A 82
Osiers Rd. SW18 —4J 101
Osier St. E1 —4J 69
Osier Way. E10 —3D 52
Osier Way. Mitc —5D 138
Oslac Rd. SE6 —5D 124
Oslo Ct. NW8 —2C 66
(off Prince Albert Rd.)
Oslo Ho. SE5 —2C 104
(off Carew St.)
Oslo Sq. SE16 —3A 88
Osman Clo. N15 —6D 32
Osman Rd. N9 —3B 18
Osman Rd. W6 —3E 82
Osmond Clo. Harr —2G 43
Osmond Gdns. Wall —5G 151
Osmund St. W12 —5B 64
Osnaburgh St. NW1 —4F 67 (3K 159)
(Longford St.)
Osnaburgh Ter. NW1
—4F 67 (3K 159)
Osney Ho. SE2 —2D 92
Osney Wlk. Cars —6B 138
Osprey Clo. E6 —5C 72
Osprey Clo. E11 —4J 35
Osprey Clo. E17 —7F 19
Osprey Clo. Sutt —5H 149
Osprey Clo. W Dray —2A 76
Osprey Ct. Beck —7C 124
Osprey Est. SE16 —4A 88
(off Plough Way)
Osprey Est. SE16 —4A 88
(off Greenland Quay)
Osprey M. Enf —5D 8
Ospringe Clo. SE20 —7J 123
Ospringe Ho. SE1 —2A 86 (6K 167)
(off Wootton St.)
Ospringe Rd. NW5 —4G 49
Osram Ct. W6 —3E 82
Osram Rd. Wemb —3D 44
Osric Path. N1 —2E 68
Ossian M. N4 —7K 31
Ossian Rd. N4 —7K 31
Ossington Bldgs. W1
—5E 66 (5G 159)
Ossington Clo. W2 —7J 65
Ossington St. W2 —7J 65
Ossory Rd. SE1 —6G 87
Ossulston St. NW1 —2H 67 (1D 160)
Ossulton Pl. N2 —3A 30
Ossulton Way. N2 —4A 30
Ostade Rd. SW2 —7K 103
Ostell Cres. Enf —1H 9
Ostend Pl. SE1 —4C 86
Osten M. SW7 —3K 83
Osterley. —7H 79
Osterley Av. Iswth —7H 79
Osterley Clo. Orp —1K 145
Osterley Ct. Iswth —1H 97
Osterley Ct. N'holt —3A 60
(off Canberra Dri.)
Osterley Cres. Iswth —1J 97
Osterley Gdns. S'hall —2G 79
Osterley Gdns. T Hth —2C 140
Osterley Ho. E14 —6D 70
Osterley La. S'hall & Iswth —5E 78
(in two parts)
Osterley Lodge. Iswth —7J 79
(off Church Rd.)
Osterley Pk. House. —6H 79
Osterley Pk. Rd. S'hall —3D 78
Osterley Pk. Vw. Rd. W7 —2J 79
Osterley Rd. N16 —4E 50
Osterley Rd. Iswth —7J 79
Osterley Views. S'hall —1G 79
Oster Ter. E17 —5K 33
Ostliffe Rd. N13 —5H 17
Oswald Rd. S'hall —1C 78
Oswald's Mead. E9 —4A 52
Oswald St. E5 —3K 51
Oswald Ter. NW2 —3E 46
Osward Pl. N9 —2C 18
Osward Rd. SW17 —2D 120
Oswin St. SE11 —4B 86
Oswyth Rd. SE5 —2E 104
Otford Clo. SE20 —1J 141
Otford Clo. Bex —6H 111
Otford Clo. Brom —3E 144
Otford Cres. SE4 —6B 104
Otford Ho. SE1 —2D 86 (7F 169)
(off Staple St.)
Otford Ho. SE15 —6J 87
(off Lovelinch Clo.)
Othello Clo. SE11 —5B 86 (5K 173)
Otho Ct. Bren —7D 80
Otis St. E3 —3E 70
Otley App. Ilf —6F 37
Otley Dri. Ilf —5F 37
Otley Ho. N4 —3A 50
Otley Rd. E16 —6A 72
Otley Ter. E5 —3K 51
Ottawa Gdns. Dag —7K 57
Ottaway Ct. E5 —3G 51
Ottaway St. E5 —3G 51
Otterbourne Rd. E4 —3A 20
Otterbourne Rd. Croy —2C 152
Otterburn Gdns. Iswth —7A 80
Otterburn Ho. SE5 —7C 86
(off Sultan St.)
Otterburn St. SW17 —6D 120
Otterden St. SE6 —4C 124
Otterfield Rd. W Dray —7A 58
Otter Rd. Gnfd —4G 61
Otto Clo. SE26 —3H 123
Otto St. SE17 —6B 86
Otway Gdns. Bush —1D 10
Oulton Clo. E5 —2J 51
Oulton Clo. SE28 —6C 74
Oulton Cres. Bark —5K 55
Oulton Rd. N15 —5D 32
Ouseley Rd. SW12 —1D 120
Outer Circ. NW1 —3C 66 (1D 158)
Outgate Rd. NW10 —7B 46
Outram Pl. N1 —1J 67
Outram Rd. E6 —1C 72
Outram Rd. N22 —1H 31
Outram Rd. Croy —2F 153
Outwich St. EC3 —7H 163
Outwood Ho. SW2 —7K 103
(off Deepdene Gdns.)
Oval Ct. Edgw —7D 12
Oval Cricket Ground. —6K 85 (7H 173)
Oval House Theatre. —6A 86
Oval Mans. SE11 —6K 85 (7H 173)
Oval Pl. SW8 —7K 85
Oval Rd. NW1 —1F 67
Oval Rd. Croy —2D 152
Oval Rd. N. Dag —1G 75
Oval Rd. S. Dag —2H 75
Oval, The. E2 —2H 69
Oval, The. Sidc —7A 110
Oval Way. SE11 —5K 85 (6H 173)
Overbrae. Beck —6C 124
Overbrook Wlk. Edgw —7B 12
(in two parts)
Overbury Av. Beck —3D 142
Overbury Rd. N15 —6D 32
Overbury St. E5 —4K 51
Overcliff Rd. SE13 —3C 106
Overcourt Clo. Sidc —6B 110
Overdale Av. N Mald —2J 135
Overdale Rd. W5 —3C 80
Overdown Rd. SE6 —4C 124
Overhill Rd. SE22 —7G 105
Overhill Way. Beck —5F 143
Overlea Rd. E5 —7G 33
Overmead. SE9 —7H 109
Oversley Ho. W2 —5J 65
(off Alfred Rd.)
Overstand Clo. Beck —5C 142
Overstone Gdns. Croy —7B 142
Overstone Ho. E14 —6C 70
Overstone Rd. W6 —3E 82
Overstrand Mans. SW11 —1D 102
Overton Clo. NW10 —6J 45
Overton Clo. Iswth —1K 97
Overton Ct. E11 —7J 35
Overton Ct. Sutt —7J 149
Overton Dri. E11 —7J 35
Overton Dri. Romf —7C 38
Overton Ho. SW15 —7B 100
(off Tangley Gro.)
Overton Rd. E10 —1A 52
Overton Rd. N14 —5D 6
Overton Rd. SE2 —3C 92
Overton Rd. SW9 —2A 104
Overton Rd. Sutt —6J 149
Overton Rd. E. SE2 —3D 92
Overtons Yd. Croy —3C 152
Overy Ho. SE1 —2B 86 (7A 168)
Ovesdon Av. Harr —1D 42
Ovett Clo. SE19 —6E 122
Ovex Clo. E14 —2E 88
Ovington Gdns. SW3
—3C 84 (2D 170)
Ovington M. SW3 —2D 170
Ovington Sq. SW3 —3C 84 (2D 170)
Ovington St. SW3 —4C 84 (3D 170)
Owen Clo. SE28 —1C 92
Owen Clo. Croy —6D 140
Owen Clo. N'holt —3K 59
Owen Gdns. Wfd G —6H 21
Owen Ho. Twic —7B 98
Owenite St. SE2 —4B 92
Owen Mans. W14 —6G 83
(off Queen's Club Gdns.)
Owen Rd. N13 —5H 17
Owen Rd. Hay —3K 59
Owen's Ct. EC1 —3B 68 (1A 162)
Owen's Row. EC1 —3B 68 (1A 162)
Owen St. EC1 —2B 68 (1A 162)
(in two parts)
Owens Way. SE23 —7A 106
Owen Wlk. SE20 —1G 141
Owen Way. NW10 —6J 45
Owgan Clo. SE5 —7D 86
Oxberry Av. SW6 —2G 101
Oxendon St. W1 —7H 67 (3C 166)
Oxenford St. SE15 —3F 105
Oxenholme. NW1 —2G 67 (1A 160)
(off Harrington Sq.)
Oxenpark Av. Wemb —7E 26
Oxestall's Rd. SE8 —5A 88
Oxford & Cambridge Mans. NW1
—5C 66 (6D 158)
(off Old Marylebone Rd.)
Oxford Av. NW10 —3D 64
Oxford Av. SW20 —2G 137
Oxford Av. Hay —7H 77
Oxford Av. Houn —5E 78
Oxford Cir. W1 —6G 67 (1A 166)
(off Oxford St.)
Oxford Cir. Av. W1 —6G 67 (1A 166)
Oxford Clo. N9 —2C 18
Oxford Clo. Ashf —7E 112
Oxford Clo. Mitc —3G 139
Oxford Ct. EC4 —2E 168
Oxford Ct. W3 —6G 63
Oxford Ct. W4 —5H 81
Oxford Ct. W7 —5K 61
(off Copley Clo.)
Oxford Ct. Felt —4B 114
Oxford Cres. N Mald —6K 135
Oxford Dri. SE1 —1E 86 (5G 169)
Oxford Dri. Ruis —2A 42
Oxford Gdns. N20 —1G 15
Oxford Gdns. N21 —7H 7
Oxford Gdns. W4 —5G 81
Oxford Gdns. W10 —6E 64
Oxford Ga. W6 —4F 83
Oxford M. Bex —7G 111
Oxford Pl. NW10 —3K 45
(off Neasden La. N.)
Oxford Pl. NW10 —3K 45
(off Press Rd.)
Oxford Rd. E15 —6F 53
(in two parts)
Oxford Rd. N4 —1A 50
Oxford Rd. N9 —2C 18
Oxford Rd. NW6 —2J 65
Oxford Rd. SE19 —6D 122
Oxford Rd. SW15 —4G 101
Oxford Rd. W5 —7D 62
Oxford Rd. Cars —6C 150
Oxford Rd. Enf —5C 8
Oxford Rd. Harr —6G 25
Oxford Rd. Ilf —5G 55
Oxford Rd. Sidc —5B 128
Oxford Rd. Tedd —5H 115
Oxford Rd. Wall —5G 151
Oxford Rd. W'stone —3K 25
Oxford Rd. Wfd G —5G 21
Oxford Rd. N. W4 —5H 81
Oxford Rd. S. W4 —5G 81
Oxford Sq. W2 —6C 66 (1D 164)
Oxford St. W1 —6E 66 (1G 165)
Oxford Wlk. S'hall —1D 78
Oxford Way. Felt —4B 114
Oxgate Cen. NW2 —2D 46
Oxgate Ct. NW2 —2C 46
Oxgate Gdns. NW2 —3D 46
Oxgate La. NW2 —2D 46
Oxgate Pde. NW2 —2C 46
Oxhawth Cres. Brom —5E 144
Oxleas. E6 —6F 73
Oxleas Clo. Well —2H 109
Oxleay Rd. Harr —1E 42
Oxleigh Clo. N Mald —5A 136
Oxley Clo. SE1 —5F 87
Oxleys Rd. NW2 —3D 46
Oxlip Clo. Croy —1K 153
Oxlow La. Dag —4C 57
Oxonian St. SE22 —4F 105
Oxo Tower Wharf. —7A 68 (3K 167)
Oxo Tower Wharf. SE1 —7A 68
Oxted Clo. Mitc —3B 138
Oxtoby Way. SW16 —1H 139
Oystercatcher Clo. E16 —6K 71
Oystergate Wlk. EC4 —3E 168
Oyster Row. E1 —6J 69
Ozolins Way. E16 —6J 71

Pablo Neruda Clo. SE24 —4B 104
Pace Pl. E1 —6H 69
Pacific Clo. Felt —1H 113
Pacific Rd. E16 —6J 71
Packenham Ho. E2 —3F 69 (1K 163)
(off Wellington Row)
Packington Rd. W3 —3J 81
Packington Sq. N1 —1C 68
(in three parts)
Packington St. N1 —1B 68
Packmores Rd. SE9 —5H 109
Padbury. SE17 —5E 86
(off Bagshot St.)
Padbury Clo. Bedf & Felt —1F 113
Padbury Ct. E2 —3F 69 (2K 163)
Padbury Ho. NW8 —4C 66 (3D 158)
(off Tresham Cres.)
Padcroft Rd. W Dray —1A 76
Paddenswick Rd. W6 —3C 82
Paddington. —6B 66 (1A 164)
Paddington Clo. Hay —4B 60
Paddington Ct. W7 —5K 61
(off Copley Clo.)
Paddington Grn. W2
—5B 66 (5A 158)
Paddington St. W1 —5E 66 (5G 159)
Paddock Clo. SE3 —2J 107
Paddock Clo. SE26 —4K 123
Paddock Clo. N'holt —2E 60
Paddock Clo. Wor Pk —1A 148
Paddock Gdns. SE19 —6E 122
Paddock Lodge. Enf —5K 7
(off Village Rd.)
Paddock Pas. SE19 —6E 122
(off Paddock Gdns.)
Paddock Rd. NW2 —3C 46
Paddock Rd. Bexh —4E 110
Paddock Rd. Ruis —3B 42
Paddocks Clo. Harr —4F 43
Paddocks Grn. NW9 —1H 45
Paddocks, The. W5 —3D 80
(off Popes La.)
Paddocks, The. Cockf —3J 5
Paddocks, The. New Ad —6C 154
Paddocks, The. Wemb —2H 45
Paddock, The. NW9 —5G 27
Paddock, The. Uxb —4D 40
Paddock Way. Chst —7H 127
Padfield Rd. SE5 —3C 104
Padnall Ct. Romf —3D 38
Padnall Rd. Chad H & Romf —3D 38
Padstow Ho. E14 —7B 70
Padstow Rd. Enf —1G 7
Padstow Wlk. Felt —1H 113
Padua Rd. SE20 —1J 141
Pagden St. SW8 —1F 103
Pageant Av. NW9 —1K 27
Pageant Cres. SE16 —1A 88
Pageantmaster Ct. EC4 —1A 168
Pageant Wlk. Croy —3E 152
Page Clo. Dag —5E 56
Page Clo. Hamp —6C 114
Page Clo. Harr —6F 27
Page Cres. Croy —5B 152
Page Grn. Rd. N15 —5G 33
Page Grn. Ter. N15 —5F 33
Page Heath La. Brom —3B 144
Page Heath Vs. Brom —3B 144
Pagehurst Rd. Croy —7H 141
Page Mdw. NW7 —7J 13
Page Rd. Felt —6F 95
Pages Hill. N10 —2E 30
Pages La. N10 —2E 30
Page St. NW7 —1C 28
Page St. SW1 —4H 85 (3D 172)
Page's Wlk. SE1 —4E 86
Pages Yd. W4 —6B 82
Paget Av. Sutt —3B 150
Paget Clo. Hamp —4H 115
Paget Gdns. Chst —1F 145
Paget La. Iswth —3H 97
Paget Pl. King T —6J 117
Paget Pl. Th Dit —1A 146
Paget Ri. SE18 —6E 90
Paget Rd. N16 —1D 50
Paget Rd. Ilf —4F 55
Paget Rd. Uxb —4E 58
Paget St. EC1 —3B 68 (1A 162)
Paget Ter. SE18 —6F 91
Pagin Ho. N15 —5E 32
(off Braemar Rd.)
Pagitts Gro. Barn —1E 4
Pagnell St. SE14 —7B 88
Pagoda Av. Rich —3F 99
Pagoda Gdns. SE3 —2F 107
Paignton Rd. N15 —6E 32
Paignton Rd. Ruis —3J 41
Paines Clo. Pinn —3C 24
Paines La. Pinn —1C 24
Pain's Clo. Mitc —2F 139
Painsthorpe Rd. N16 —3E 50
Painswick Ct. SE15 —7F 87
(off Daniel Gdns.)
Painters Rd. Ilf —3K 37
Paisley Rd. N22 —1B 32
Paisley Rd. Cars —1B 150
Pakeman Ho. SE1 —2B 86 (6B 168)
(off Surrey Row)
Pakeman St. N7 —3K 49
Pakenham Clo. SW12 —1E 120
Pakenham St. WC1
—3K 67 (2H 161)
Pakington Ho. SW9 —2J 103
(off Stockwell Gdns. Est.)
Palace Av. W8 —2K 83
Palace Ct. NW3 —5K 47
Palace Ct. W2 —7K 65
(off Moscow Rd.)
Palace Ct. Harr —6E 26
Palace Ct. Gdns. N10 —3G 31
Palace Gdns. Buck H —1G 21
Palace Gdns. Enf —4J 7
Palace Gdns. M. W8 —1K 83
Palace Gdns. Shop. Cen. Enf —4J 7
Palace Gdns. Ter. W8 —1J 83
Palace Ga. W8 —2A 84
Palace Gates Rd. N22 —1H 31
Palace Grn. W8 —1K 83
Palace Grn. Croy —7B 154
Palace Gro. SE19 —7F 123
Palace Gro. Brom —1K 143
Palace Mans. W14 —4G 83
(off Hammersmith Rd.)
Palace M. E17 —4B 34
Palace M. SW1 —4H 171
Palace M. SW6 —7J 83
Palace M. Enf —3J 7
Palace Pde. E17 —4B 34
Palace Pl. SW1 —3G 85 (1A 172)
Palace Pl. Mans. W8 —2K 83
(off Kensington Ct.)
Palace Rd. N8 —5H 31
(in two parts)
Palace Rd. N11 —7D 16
Palace Rd. SE19 —7F 123
Palace Rd. SW2 —1K 121
Palace Rd. Brom —1K 143
Palace Rd. E Mol —3H 133
Palace Rd. King T —4D 134
Palace Rd. Ruis —4C 42
Palace Sq. SE19 —7F 123
Palace St. SW1 —3G 85 (1A 172)
Palace Vw. SE12 —2J 125
Palace Vw. Brom —3K 143
(in two parts)
Palace Vw. Croy —4B 154
Palace Vw. Rd. E4 —5J 19
Palamon Ct. SE1 —5F 87
(off Cooper's Rd.)
Palamos Rd. E10 —1C 52
Palatine Av. N16 —4E 50
Palatine Rd. N16 —4E 50
Palermo Rd. NW10 —2C 64
Palestine Gro. SW19 —1B 138
Palewell Comn. Dri. SW14 —5K 99
Palewell Pk. SW14 —5K 99
Palfrey Pl. SW8 —7K 85
Palgrave Av. S'hall —7E 60
Palgrave Gdns. NW1
—4C 66 (3D 158)
Palgrave Ho. SE5 —7C 86
(off Wyndham Est.)
Palgrave Ho. Twic —7G 97
Palgrave Rd. W12 —3B 82
Palissy St. E2 —3F 69 (2J 163)
(in two parts)
Pallant Ho. SE1 —3D 86
(off Tabard St.)
Pallant Way. Orp —3E 156
Pallett Way. SE18 —1C 108
Palliser Ct. W14 —5G 83
Palliser Rd. W14 —5G 83
Pall Mall. SW1 —1G 85 (5B 166)
Pall Mall E. SW1 —1H 85 (4D 166)
Pall Mall Pl. SW1 —5B 166
Palmar Cres. Bexh —3G 111
Palmar Rd. Bexh —2G 111
Palm Av. Sidc —6D 128
Palm Clo. E10 —3D 52
Palm Ct. SE15 —7F 87
(off Garnies Clo.)
Palmeira Rd. Bexh —3D 110
Palmer Av. Sutt —4E 148
Palmer Clo. Houn —1E 96
Palmer Clo. W W'ck —3F 155
Palmer Ct. NW10 —1K 63
(in two parts)
Palmer Cres. King T —3E 134
Palmer Gdns. Barn —5A 4
Palmer Pl. N7 —5A 50
Palmer Rd. E13 —4K 71
Palmer Rd. Dag —1D 56
Palmer's Ct. N11 —5B 16
(off Palmer's Rd.)
Palmers Green. —4F 17
Palmers Gro. W Mol —4E 132
Palmers La. Enf —1C 8
(in two parts)
Palmers Pas. SW14 —3J 99
(off Palmers Rd.)
Palmer's Rd. E2 —2K 69
Palmer's Rd. N11 —5B 16
Palmers Rd. SW14 —3J 99
Palmers Rd. SW16 —2K 139
Palmerston Cen. W'stone —3K 25
Palmerston Ct. Buck H —1F 21
Palmerston Ct. Surb —7D 134
Palmerston Cres. N13 —5E 16
Palmerston Cres. SE18 —6G 91
Palmerston Gro. SW19 —7J 119
Palmerston Ho. SE1 —2A 86 (7J 167)
(off Westminster Bri. Rd.)
Palmerston Ho. W8 —1J 83
(off Kensington Pl.)
Palmerston Mans. W14 —6G 83
(off Queen's Club Gdns.)
Palmerston Rd. E7 —6K 53
Palmerston Rd. E17 —3B 34
Palmerston Rd. N22 —7E 16
Palmerston Rd. NW6 —7H 47
(in two parts)
Palmerston Rd. SW14 —4J 99
Palmerston Rd. SW19 —7J 119
Palmerston Rd. W3 —3J 81
Palmerston Rd. Buck H —2E 20
Palmerston Rd. Cars —4D 150
Palmerston Rd. Croy —5D 140
Palmerston Rd. Harr —3J 25
Palmerston Rd. Houn —1K 97

Partridge Grn.—Pentire Rd.

Partridge Grn. SE9 —3E 126
Partridge Rd. Hamp —6D 114
Partridge Rd. Sidc —3J 127
Partridge Sq. E6 —5C 72
Partridge Way. N22 —1J 31
Pasadena Clo. Hay —2J 77
Pasadena Clo. Trad. Est. Hay —2K 77
Pascall Ho. SE17 —6C 86
(off Draco St.)
Pascal St. SW8 —7H 85
Pascoe Rd. SE13 —5F 107
Pasley Clo. SE17 —5B 86
Pasquier Rd. E17 —3A 34
Passage, The. W6 —3E 82
Passage, The. Rich —5E 98
Passey Pl. SE9 —6D 108
Passfield Dri. E14 —5D 70
Passfield Path. SE28 —7B 74
Passfields. SE6 —3D 124
Passfields. W14 —5H 83
(off Star St.)
Passing All. EC1 —4B 162
Passingham Ho. Houn —6E 78
Passmore Gdns. N11 —6C 16
Passmore St. SW1 —5E 84 (5G 171)
Pasteur Clo. NW9 —2A 28
Pasteur Ct. Harr —1B 44
Pasteur Gdns. N18 —5G 17
Paston Clo. E5 —3K 51
Paston Clo. Wall —3G 151
Paston Cres. SE12 —7K 107
Pastor Ct. N6 —6G 31
Pastor St. SE11 —4B 86
(in two parts)
Pasture Clo. Wemb —3B 44
Pasture Rd. SE6 —1H 125
Pasture Rd. Dag —4F 57
Pasture Rd. Wemb —2B 44
Pastures Mead. Uxb —6C 40
Pastures, The. N20 —1C 14
Patcham Ter. SW8 —1F 103
Patch Clo. Uxb —1B 58
Patching Way. Hay —5C 60
Pathway Ct. SE15 —6E 86
(off Newent Clo.)
Patent Ho. E14 —5D 70
Paternoster Row. EC4 —6B 68 (1C 168)
Paternoster Sq. EC4 —6B 68 (7B 162)
Paterson Ct. EC1 —2E 162
Pater St. W8 —3J 83
Pates Mnr. Dri. Felt —7F 95
Pathfield Rd. SW16 —6H 121
Path, The. SW19 —1K 137
Patience Rd. SW11 —2C 102
Patina Wlk. SE16 —1A 88
(off Capstan Way)
Patio Clo. SW4 —6H 103
Patmore Est. SW8 —1G 103
Patmore Ho. N16 —5E 50
Patmore Lodge. N6 —4D 30
Patmore St. SW8 —1G 103
Patmos Rd. SW9 —7B 86
Paton Clo. E3 —3C 70
Paton Ho. SW9 —2K 103
(off Stockwell Rd.)
Paton St. EC1 —3C 68 (2C 162)
Patricia Ct. Chst —1H 145
Patricia Ct. Well —7B 92
Patrick Coman Ho. EC1 —3B 68 (2A 162)
(off Finsbury Est.)
Patrick Connolly Gdns. E3 —3D 70
Patrick Pas. SW11 —2C 102
Patrick Rd. E13 —3A 72
Patriot Sq. E2 —2H 69
Patrol Pl. SE6 —6D 106
Patshull Pl. NW5 —6G 49
Patshull Rd. NW5 —6G 49
Patten All. Rich —5D 98
Pattenden Rd. SE6 —1B 124
Patten Ho. N16 —1C 50
Patten Rd. SW18 —7C 102
Patterdale. NW1 —3F 67 (2K 159)
(off Osnaburgh St.)
Patterdale Clo. Brom —6H 125
Patterdale Rd. SE15 —7J 87
Pattern Ho. EC1 —4B 68 (3A 162)
Patterson Ct. SE19 —7F 123
Patterson Rd. SE19 —6F 123
Pattinson Ct. E16 —5J 71
(off Fife Rd.)
Pattison Ho. SE1 —2C 86 (6D 168)
(off Redcross Way)
Pattison Rd. NW2 —3J 47
Pattison Wlk. SE18 —5G 91
Paul Byrne Ho. N2 —3A 30
Paul Clo. E15 —7G 53
Paul Ct. N18 —4B 18
(off Fairfield Rd.)
Paul Ct. Romf —5J 39
Paulet Rd. SE5 —2B 104
Paul Gdns. Croy —2F 153
Paulhan Rd. Harr —4D 26
Paulin Dri. N21 —7F 7
Pauline Cres. Twic —1G 115
Pauline Ho. E1 —5G 69
(off Old Montague St.)
Paul Julius Clo. E14 —7F 71
Paul Robeson Clo. E6 —3E 72
Pauls Ho. E3 —5B 70
Paul St. E15 —1G 71
Paul St. EC2 —4D 68 (4F 163)
Paul's Wlk. EC4 —7C 68 (2B 168)
Paultons Sq. SW3 —6B 84 (7B 170)
Paultons St. SW3 —6B 84 (7B 170)
Pauntley St. N19 —1G 49
Paved Ct. Rich —5D 98
Paveley Dri. SW11 —7C 84
Paveley Ho. N1 —2K 67
(off Priory Grn. Est.)
Paveley St. NW8 —3C 66 (2C 158)
Pavement M. Romf —7D 38
Pavement Sq. Croy —1G 153
Pavement, The. E11 —1E 52
(off Hainault Rd.)
Pavement, The. SW4 —4G 103
Pavement, The. W5 —3E 80
Pavement, The. Iswth —3A 98
(off South St.)
Pavet Clo. Dag —6H 57
Pavilion Lodge. Harr —1H 43
Pavilion M. N3 —3J 29
Pavilion Rd. SW1 —3D 84 (7F 165)
Pavilion Rd. Ilf —7D 36
Pavilion St. SW1 —3D 84 (2F 171)
Pavilion Ter. Ilf —5J 37
Pavilion, The. SW8 —7H 85
Pavilion Way. Edgw —7C 12
Pavilion Way. Ruis —2A 42
Pavillion Ter. W12 —6E 64
(off Wood La.)
Pawleyne Clo. SE20 —7J 123
Pawsey Clo. E13 —1K 71
Pawsons Rd. Croy —6C 140
Paxfold. Stan —5J 11
Paxford Rd. Wemb —2B 44
Paxton Clo. Rich —2F 99
Paxton Clo. W on T —7A 132
Paxton Ct. SE12 —3A 126
Paxton Ct. SE26 —4A 124
(off Adamsrill Rd.)
Paxton Pl. SE27 —4E 122
Paxton Rd. N17 —7A 18
Paxton Rd. SE23 —3A 124
Paxton Rd. W4 —6A 82
Paxton Rd. Brom —7J 125
Paxton Ter. SW1 —6F 85 (7K 171)
Payne Clo. Bark —7K 55
Payne Ho. N1 —1K 67
(off Barnsbury Est.)
Paynell Ct. SE3 —3G 107
Payne Rd. E3 —2D 70
Paynesfield Av. SW14 —3K 99
Paynesfield Rd. Bus H —1E 10
Payne St. SE8 —7B 88
Paynes Wlk. W6 —6G 83
Payzes Gdns. Wfd G —6C 20
Peabody Av. SW1 —5F 85 (5J 171)
Peabody Bldgs. E1 —2K 169
Peabody Bldgs. E2 —2H 69
(off Cambridge Cres.)
Peabody Bldgs. EC1 —4C 68 (4D 162)
(off Roscoe St.)
Peabody Bldgs. SW3 —7C 170
Peabody Clo. SE10 —1D 106
Peabody Clo. SW1 —7K 171
Peabody Clo. Croy —1J 153
Peabody Cotts. N17 —1E 32
Peabody Ct. EC1 —4C 68 (4D 162)
(off Roscoe St.)
Peabody Ct. SE5 —1D 104
(off Kimpton Rd.)
Peabody Est. E1 —7K 69
(off Glasmis Pl.)
Peabody Est. EC1 —4A 68 (4K 161)
(off Farringdon La.)
Peabody Est. EC1 —4C 68 (4K 161)
(off Whitecross St., in two parts)
Peabody Est. N1 —1C 68
Peabody Est. SE1 —5K 167
Peabody Est. SE1 —1A 86 (5K 167)
(Hatfield St.)
Peabody Est. SE1 —1C 86 (5K 167)
(Southwark St.)
Peabody Est. SE24 —7B 104
Peabody Est. SW1 —3B 172
Peabody Est. SW3 —6C 84 (7D 170)
Peabody Est. SW6 —6H 83
(off Lillie Rd.)
Peabody Est. SW11 —4C 102
Peabody Est. W6 —5E 82
Peabody Est. W10 —5E 64
Peabody Hill. SE21 —1B 122
Peabody Sq. SE1 —2B 86 (7A 168)
(in two parts)
Peabody Tower. EC1 —4C 68 (4D 162)
(off Golden La.)
Peabody Trust. SE17 —4D 86
(off Rodney Rd.)
Peabody Yd. N1 —1C 68
Peace Clo. N14 —5A 6
Peace Clo. SE25 —4E 140
Peace Clo. Gnfd —1H 61
Peace Gro. Wemb —3H 45
Peace St. SE18 —6E 90
Peaches Clo. Sutt —7G 149
Peachey Edwards Ho. E2 —3H 69
(off Teesdale St.)
Peachey La. Uxb —5A 58
Peach Rd. W10 —3F 65
Peach Tree Av. W Dray —6B 58
Peachum Rd. SE3 —6H 89
(in two parts)
Peachwalk M. E3 —2K 69
Peacock Av. Felt —1F 113
Peacock Ind. Est. N17 —7A 18
Peacock St. SE17 —4B 86
Peacock Wlk. E16 —6K 71
(off Mortlake Rd.)
Peacock Wlk. N6 —7F 31
Peacock Yd. SE17 —5B 86
(off Iliffe St.)
Peaketon Av. Ilf —4B 36
Peak Hill. SE26 —4J 123
Peak Hill Av. SE26 —4J 123
Peak Hill Gdns. SE26 —4J 123
Peak Ho. N4 —1C 50
(off Woodberry Down Est.)
Peak, The. SE26 —3J 123
Peal Gdns. W13 —3A 62
Peall Rd. Croy —6K 139
Peall Rd. Ind. Est. Croy —6K 139
Pearce Clo. Mitc —2E 138
Pearcefield Av. SE23 —1J 123
Pearce Rd. W Mol —3F 133
Pear Clo. NW9 —4K 27
Pear Clo. SE14 —7A 88
Pear Ct. SE15 —7F 87
(off Thruxton Way)
Pearcroft Rd. E11 —2F 53
Peardon St. SW8 —2F 103
Peareswood Gdns. Stan —1D 26
Pearfield Rd. SE23 —3A 124
Pearl Clo. E6 —6E 72
Pearl Clo. NW2 —7F 29
Pearl Rd. E17 —3C 34
Pearl St. E1 —1H 87
Pearmain Clo. Shep —5D 130
Pearman St. SE1 —3A 86 (1K 173)
Pear Pl. SE1 —2A 86 (6J 167)
Pear Rd. E11 —3F 53
Pearsall Ho. Uxb —6C 40
Pears Av. Shep —3G 131
Pearscroft Ct. SW6 —1K 101
Pearscroft Rd. SW6 —1K 101
Pearse St. SE15 —6E 86
Pearson's Av. SE14 —1C 106
Pearson St. E2 —2F 69
Pears Rd. Houn —3G 97
Peartree. SE26 —5A 124
Peartree Av. SW17 —3A 120
Pear Tree Av. W Dray —6B 58
Pear Tree Clo. E2 —1F 69
Pear Tree Clo. Chess —5G 147
Peartree Clo. Eri —1K 111
Peartree Clo. Mitc —2C 138
Pear Tree Ct. E18 —1K 35
Pear Tree Ct. EC1 —4A 68 (4K 161)
Peartree Gdns. Dag —4B 56
Peartree Gdns. Romf —2H 39
Pear Tree Ho. SE4 —3B 106
Peartree La. E1 —7J 69
Pear Tree Rd. Ashf —5E 112
Peartree Rd. Enf —3K 7
Peartrees. W Dray —7A 58
Pear Tree St. EC1 —4C 68 (3B 162)
Pear Tree Way. SE10 —4J 89
Peary Ho. NW10 —7K 45
Peary Pl. E2 —3J 69
Peas Mead Ter. E4 —4K 19
Peatfield Clo. Sidc —3J 127
Pebble Way. W3 —1H 81
(off Steyne Rd.)
Pebworth Rd. Harr —2A 44
Peckarmans Wood. SE26 —3G 123
Peckett Sq. N5 —4C 50
Peckford Clo. SW9 —2A 104
Peckford Pl. SW9 —2A 104
Peckham. —1G 105
Peckham Gro. SE15 —7E 86
Peckham High St. SE15 —1G 105
Peckham Hill St. SE15 —7G 87
Peckham Pk. Rd. SE15 —7G 87
Peckham Rd. SE5 & SE15 —1E 104
Peckham Rye. SE15 & SE22 —3G 105
Peckham Sq. SE15 —1G 105
Pecks Yd. E1 —5F 69
(off Hanbury St.)
Peckwater St. NW5 —5G 49
Pedhoulas. N14 —3D 16
Pedlar's Wlk. N7 —5K 49
Pedley Rd. Dag —1C 56
Pedley St. E1 —4F 69 (4K 163)
Pedro St. E5 —3K 51
Pedworth Gdns. SE16 —4J 87
Peebles Ct. S'hall —6G 61
(off Haldane Rd.)
Peek Cres. SW19 —5F 119
Peel Clo. E4 —2J 19
Peel Clo. N9 —3B 18
Peel Dri. Ilf —3C 36
Peel Gro. E2 —2J 69
(in two parts)
Peel La. NW9 —3C 28
Peel Pas. W8 —1J 83
(off Peel St.)
Peel Pl. Ilf —2C 36
Peel Precinct. NW6 —2J 65
Peel Rd. E18 —1H 35
Peel Rd. Harr & W'stone —3K 25
(in two parts)
Peel Rd. Wemb —3D 44
Peel St. W8 —1J 83
Peel Way. Uxb —5A 58
Peerglow Est. Enf —5D 8
Peerless St. EC1 —3D 68 (2E 162)
Pegamoid Rd. N18 —3D 18
Pegasus Clo. N5 —4D 50
Pegasus Ct. Bren —5F 81
Pegasus Ct. King T —3D 134
Pegasus Pl. SE11 —6A 86 (7J 173)
Pegasus Pl. SW6 —1J 101
Pegasus Tower. SE14 —7A 88
(off Woodpecker Rd.)
Pegasus Way. N11 —6A 16
Peggotty Way. Uxb —6D 58
Pegg Rd. Houn —7B 78
Pegley Gdns. SE12 —2J 125
Pegwell St. SE18 —7J 91
Pekin Clo. E14 —6C 70
Pekin Ho. E14 —6C 70
(off Pekin St.)
Pekin St. E14 —6C 70
Pelabon Ho. Twic —6D 98
(off Clevedon Rd.)
Peldon Ct. Rich —4F 99
Peldon Pas. Rich —4F 99
Peldon Wlk. N1 —1B 68
(off Popham St.)
Pelham Av. Bark —1K 73
Pelham Clo. SE5 —3E 104
Pelham Cotts. Bex —1H 129
Pelham Ct. SW3 —4C 84 (4C 170)
(off Fulham Rd.)
Pelham Ct. Sidc —3A 128
Pelham Cres. SW7 —4C 84 (4C 170)
Pelham Ho. W14 —4H 83
(off Mornington Av.)
Pelham Pl. SW7 —4C 84 (3C 170)
Pelham Rd. E18 —3K 35
Pelham Rd. N15 —4F 33
Pelham Rd. N22 —2A 32
Pelham Rd. SW19 —7J 119
Pelham Rd. Beck —2J 141
Pelham Rd. Bexh —3G 111
Pelham Rd. Ilf —2H 55
Pelham St. SW7 —4B 84 (3B 170)
Pelican Est. SE15 —1F 105
Pelican Ho. SE8 —4B 88
Pelican Pas. E1 —4J 69
Pelican Stairs. E1 —1J 87
Pelican Wlk. SW9 —4B 104
Pelier St. SE17 —6C 86
Pelinore Rd. SE6 —2G 125
Pella Ho. SE11 —5K 85 (5H 173)
Pellant Rd. SW6 —7G 83
Pellatt Gro. N22 —1A 32
Pellatt Rd. SE22 —5F 105
Pellatt Rd. Wemb —2D 44
Pellerin Rd. N16 —5E 50
Pelling St. E14 —6C 70
Pellipar Clo. N13 —3F 17
Pellipar Gdns. SE18 —5D 90
Pellipar Rd. SE18 —5D 90
Pelly Rd. E13 —1J 71
(in two parts)
Pelter St. E2 —3F 69 (1J 163)
(in two parts)
Pelton Rd. SE10 —5G 89
Pembar Av. E17 —3A 34
Pemberley Chase. W Ewe —5H 147
Pemberley Clo. W Ewe —5H 147
Pember Rd. NW10 —3F 65
Pemberton Gdns. N19 —3G 49
Pemberton Gdns. Romf —5E 38
Pemberton Ho. SE26 —4G 123
(off High Level Dri.)
Pemberton Pl. E8 —7H 51
Pemberton Rd. N4 —5A 32
Pemberton Rd. E Mol —4G 133
Pemberton Row. EC4 —6A 68 (7K 161)
Pemberton Ter. N19 —3G 49
Pembridge Av. Twic —1D 114
Pembridge Cres. W11 —7J 65
Pembridge Gdns. W2 —7J 65
Pembridge M. W11 —7J 65
Pembridge Pl. SW15 —5J 101
Pembridge Pl. W2 —7J 65
Pembridge Rd. W11 —7J 65
Pembridge Sq. W2 —7J 65
Pembridge Vs. W11 & W2 —7J 65
Pembroke Av. Enf —1C 8
Pembroke Av. Harr —3A 26
Pembroke Av. Pinn —1B 42
Pembroke Av. Surb —5H 135
Pembroke Bldgs. NW10 —3C 64
Pembroke Cen., The. Ruis —1H 41
Pembroke Clo. SW1 —2E 84 (7H 165)
Pembroke Cotts. W8 —3J 83
(off Pembroke Sq.)
Pembroke Ct. W7 —6K 61
(off Copley Clo.)
Pembroke Gdns. W14 —4H 83
Pembroke Gdns. Dag —3H 57
Pembroke Gdns. Clo. W8 —3J 83
Pembroke Hall. NW4 —3E 28
(off Mulberry Clo.)
Pembroke Ho. W2 —6K 65
(off Hallfield Est.)
Pembroke Ho. W3 —2J 81
(off Park Rd. E.)
Pembroke Lodge. Stan —6H 11
Pembroke M. E1 —4J 69
(off Wessex St.)
Pembroke M. E3 —3A 70
Pembroke M. N10 —1F 31
Pembroke M. W8 —3J 83
Pembroke Pde. Eri —5J 93
Pembroke Pl. W8 —3J 83
Pembroke Pl. Edgw —7B 12
Pembroke Pl. Iswth —2J 97
Pembroke Rd. E6 —5D 72
Pembroke Rd. E17 —5D 34
Pembroke Rd. N8 —4J 31
Pembroke Rd. N10 —1E 30
Pembroke Rd. N13 —3H 17
Pembroke Rd. N15 —5F 33
Pembroke Rd. SE25 —4E 140
Pembroke Rd. W8 —4H 83
Pembroke Rd. Brom —2A 144
Pembroke Rd. Eri —5J 93
Pembroke Rd. Gnfd —4F 61
Pembroke Rd. Ilf —1K 55
Pembroke Rd. Mitc —2E 138
Pembroke Rd. Ruis —1G 41
Pembroke Rd. Wemb —3D 44
Pembroke Sq. W8 —3J 83
Pembroke St. N1 —7J 49
(in two parts)
Pembroke Vs. W8 —4J 83
Pembroke Vs. Rich —4D 98
Pembroke Wlk. W8 —4J 83
Pembroke Way. Hay —3E 76
Pembrook M. SW11 —4B 102
Pembry Clo. SW9 —1A 104
Pembury Av. Wor Pk —1C 148
Pembury Clo. E5 —5H 51
Pembury Clo. Brom —7H 143
Pembury Ct. Hay —6F 77
Pembury Cres. Sidc —2E 128
Pembury Pl. E5 —5H 51
Pembury Rd. E5 —5H 51
Pembury Rd. N17 —1F 33
Pembury Rd. SE25 —4G 141
Pembury Rd. Bexh —7E 92
Pemdevon Rd. Croy —7A 140
Pemell Clo. E1 —4J 69
Pemerich Clo. Hay —5H 77
Pempath Pl. Wemb —2D 44
Penally Pl. N1 —1D 68
Penang St. E1 —1H 87
Penard Rd. S'hall —3F 79
Penarth Cen. SE15 —6J 87
Penarth St. SE15 —6J 87
Penberth Rd. SE6 —2E 124
Penbury Rd. S'hall —4D 78
Pencombe M. W11 —7H 65
Pencraig Way. SE15 —6H 87
Pendall Clo. Barn —4H 5
Penda Rd. Eri —7H 93
Pendarves Rd. SW20 —1E 136
Penda's Mead. E9 —4A 52
Pendell Av. Hay —7H 77
Pendennis Ho. SE8 —4A 88
Pendennis Rd. N17 —3D 32
Pendennis Rd. SW16 —4J 121
Penderel Rd. Houn —5E 96
Penderry Ri. SE6 —2F 125
Penderyn Way. N7 —4H 49
Pendle Ct. Uxb —1D 58
Pendle Ho. SE26 —3G 123
Pendle Rd. SW16 —6F 121
Pendlestone Rd. E17 —5D 34
Pendragon Rd. Brom —3H 125
Pendragon Wlk. NW9 —6A 28
Pendrell Ho. WC2 —6H 67 (1D 166)
(off New Compton St.)
Pendrell Rd. SE4 —2A 106
Pendrell St. SE18 —6H 91
Pendula Dri. Hay —4B 60
Pendulum M. E8 —5F 51
Penerley Rd. SE6 —1D 124
Penfield Lodge. W9 —5J 65
(off Admiral Wlk.)
Penfields Ho. N7 —6J 49
Penfold Clo. Croy —3A 152
Penfold La. Bex —2D 128
(in two parts)
Penfold Pl. NW1 —5C 66 (5C 158)
Penfold Rd. N9 —1E 18
Penfold St. NW8 & NW1 —4B 66 (4B 158)
Penford Gdns. SE9 —3B 108
Penford St. SE5 —2B 104
Pengarth Rd. Bex —5D 110
Penge. —7J 123
Penge Ho. SW11 —3B 102
Penge La. SE20 —7J 123
Penge Rd. E13 —1A 72
Penge Rd. SE25 & SE20 —3G 141
Penhall Rd. SE7 —4B 90
Penhill Rd. Bex —6C 110
Penhurst Pl. SE1 —1H 173
Penhurst Rd. Ilf —1F 37
Penifather La. Gnfd —3H 61
Peninsula Ct. E14 —3D 88
Peninsula Heights. SE1 —5J 85 (5F 173)
Peninsular Clo. Felt —6F 95
Peninsular Pk. Rd. SE7 —4J 89
Penistone Rd. SW16 —7J 121
Penketh Dri. Harr —3H 43
Penley Ct. WC2 —7K 67 (2H 167)
Penmayne Ho. SE11 —5A 86 (5K 173)
(off Kennings Way)
Penmon Rd. SE2 —3A 92
Pennack Rd. SE15 —6F 87
Pennant M. W8 —4K 83
Pennant Ter. E17 —2B 34
Pennard Rd. W12 —2E 82
Pennards, The. Sun —3A 132
Penn Clo. Gnfd —2F 61
Penn Clo. Harr —4C 26
Penn Ct. NW9 —3K 27
Penner Clo. SW19 —2G 119
Penners Gdns. Surb —7E 134
Pennethorne Clo. E9 —1J 69
Pennethorne Ho. SW11 —3B 102
Pennethorne Rd. SE15 —7H 87
Penn Gdns. Chst —2F 145
Penn Gdns. Romf —1G 39
Penn Ho. NW8 —4C 66 (4C 158)
(off Mallory St.)
Pennine Dri. NW2 —2F 47
Pennine La. NW2 —2G 47
Pennine Pde. NW2 —2G 47
Pennine Way. Bexh —1K 111
Pennine Way. Hay —7F 77
Pennington Clo. SE27 —4D 122
Pennington Ct. SE16 —1A 88
Pennington Dri. N21 —5D 6
Pennington St. E1 —7H 69
Pennington Way. SE12 —2K 125
Penniston Clo. N17 —2C 32
Penn La. Bex —5D 110
(in two parts)
Penn Rd. N7 —5J 49
Penn St. N1 —1D 68
Pennycroft. Croy —7A 154
Pennyfather La. Enf —3H 7
Pennyfields. E14 —7C 70
(in two parts)
Pennyford Ct. NW8 —4B 66 (3A 158)
(off St John's Wood Rd.)
Penny La. Shep —7G 131
Penny M. SW12 —7F 103
Pennymoor Wlk. W9 —4H 65
(off Ashmore Rd.)
Penny Rd. NW10 —3H 63
Penny Royal. Wall —6H 151
Pennyroyal Av. E6 —6E 72
Penpoll Rd. E8 —6H 51
Penpool La. Well —3B 110
Penrhyn Av. E17 —1B 34
Penrhyn Cres. E17 —1C 34
Penrhyn Cres. SW14 —4J 99
Penrhyn Gdns. King T —4D 134
Penrhyn Gro. E17 —1C 34
Penrhyn Rd. King T —4E 134
Penrith Clo. SW15 —5G 101
Penrith Clo. Beck —1D 142
Penrith Clo. Uxb —7A 40
Penrith Pl. SE27 —2B 122
Penrith Rd. N15 —5D 32
Penrith Rd. N Mald —4K 135
Penrith Rd. T Hth —2C 140
Penrith St. SW16 —6G 121
Penrose Gro. SE17 —5C 86
Penrose Ho. SE17 —5C 86
(in two parts)
Penrose St. SE17 —5C 86
Penryn Ho. SE11 —5K 173
Penryn St. NW1 —2H 67
Penry St. SE1 —4E 86
Pensbury Pl. SW8 —2G 103
Pensbury St. SW8 —2G 103
Pensford Av. Rich —2G 99
Penshurst. NW5 —6E 48
Penshurst Av. Sidc —6A 110
Penshurst Gdns. Edgw —5C 12
Penshurst Grn. Brom —5H 143
Penshurst Ho. SE15 —6J 87
(off Lovelinch Clo.)
Penshurst Rd. E9 —7K 51
Penshurst Rd. N17 —7A 18
Penshurst Rd. Bexh —1F 111
Penshurst Rd. T Hth —5B 140
Penshurst Wlk. Brom —5H 143
Penshurst Way. Sutt —7J 149
Pensilver Clo. Barn —4H 5
Penstemon Clo. N3 —6D 14
Pentagon, The. W13 —7A 62
Pentavia Retail Pk. NW7 —7G 13
Pentelow Gdns. Felt —6J 95
Pentire Rd. E17 —1F 35

Pentland Av.—Pitsea Pl.

Pentland Av. Edgw —2C 12
Pentland Av. Shep —5C 130
Pentland Clo. NW11 —2G 47
Pentland Gdns. SW18 —6A 102
Pentland Pl. N'holt —1C 60
Pentlands Clo. Mitc —3F 139
Pentland St. SW18 —6A 102
Pentland Way. Uxb —3E 40
Pentlow St. SW15 —3E 100
Pentlow Way. Buck H —1H 21
Pentney Rd. E4 —1A 20
Pentney Rd. SW12 —1G 121
Pentney Rd. SW20 —1G 137
Penton Gro. N1 —2A 68
Penton Ho. N1 —1J 161
Penton Ho. SE2 —1D 92
Penton Pl. SE17 —5B 86
Penton Ri. WC1 —3K 67 (1H 161)
Penton St. N1 —2A 68
Pentonville. —2K 67
Pentonville Rd. N1 —2K 67 (1F 161)
Pentrich Av. Enf —1B 8
Pentridge St. SE15 —7F 87
Pentyre Av. N18 —5J 17
Penwerris Av. Iswth —7G 79
Penwerris Ct. Houn —7G 79
Penwith Rd. SW18 —2J 119
Penwood Ct. Pinn —4D 24
Penwood Ho. SW15 —6B 100
Penwortham Ct. N22 —2K 31
Penwortham Rd. SW16 —6F 121
Penylan Pl. Edgw —7B 12
Penywern Rd. SW5 —5J 83
Penzance Ho. SE11 —5A 86 (5K 173)
(off Seaton Clo.)
Penzance Pl. W11 —1G 83
Penzance St. W11 —1G 83
Peony Ct. E4 —6B 20
Peony Gdns. W12 —7C 64
Peperfield. WC1 —3K 67 (2G 161)
(off Cromer St.)
Pepler Ho. W10 —4G 65
(off Wornington Rd.)
Pepler M. SE5 —5F 87
Peploe Rd. NW6 —2F 65
(in two parts)
Peplow Clo. W Dray —1A 76
Pepper Clo. E6 —5D 72
Peppercorn Clo. T Hth —2D 140
Peppermead Sq. SE4 —5C 106
Peppermint Clo. Croy —7J 139
Peppermint Pl. E11 —3G 53
Pepper St. E14 —3D 88
Pepper St. SE1 —2C 86 (6C 168)
Peppie Clo. N16 —2E 50
(in two parts)
Pepys Clo. Uxb —4D 40
Pepys Ct. SW4 —3F 103
Pepys Cres. E16 —1J 89
Pepys Cres. Barn —5A 4
Pepys Rd. SE14 —1K 105
Pepys Rd. SW20 —1E 136
Pepys St. EC3 —7E 68 (2H 169)
Perceval Av. NW3 —5C 48
Perceval Ct. N'holt —5E 42
Perceval Ho. W5 —7C 62
Percheron Clo. Iswth —3K 97
Perch St. E8 —4F 51
Percival Ct. N17 —7A 18
Percival David Foundation of Chinese Art. —3D 160
Percival Gdns. Romf —6C 38
Percival Rd. SW14 —4J 99
Percival Rd. Enf —4A 8
Percival Rd. Felt —2H 113
Percival St. EC1 —4B 68 (3A 162)
Percival Way. Eps —4K 147
Percy Av. Ashf —5C 112
Percy Bryant Rd. Sun —7G 113
Percy Bush Rd. W Dray —3B 76
Percy Cir. WC1 —3K 67 (1H 161)
Percy Gdns. Enf —5E 8
Percy Gdns. Hay —3G 59
Percy Gdns. Iswth —3A 98
Percy Gdns. Wor Pk —1A 148
Percy M. W1 —6C 160
Percy Pas. W1 —6C 160
Percy Rd. E11 —7G 35
Percy Rd. E16 —5G 71
Percy Rd. N12 —5F 15
Percy Rd. N21 —7H 7
Percy Rd. SE20 —1K 141
Percy Rd. SE25 —5G 141
Percy Rd. W12 —2C 82
Percy Rd. Bexh —2E 110
Percy Rd. Hamp —7E 114
Percy Rd. Ilf —7A 38
Percy Rd. Iswth —4A 98
Percy Rd. Mitc —7E 138
Percy Rd. Romf —3H 39
Percy Rd. Twic —1F 115
Percy St. W1 —5H 67 (6C 160)
Percy Way. Twic —1G 115
Percy Yd. WC1 —3K 67 (1H 161)
Peregrine Clo. NW10 —5K 45
Peregrine Ct. SE8 —6C 88
(off Edward St.)
Peregrine Ct. SW16 —4K 121
Peregrine Ct. Well —1K 109
Peregrine Gdns. Croy —2A 154
Peregrine Ho. EC1 —1B 162
Peregrine Rd. Sun —2H 131
Peregrine Way. SW19 —7E 118
Perham Rd. W14 —5G 83
Peridot St. E6 —5C 72
Perifield. SE21 —1C 122
Perimeade Rd. Gnfd —2C 62
Periton Rd. SE9 —4B 108
Perivale. —1C 62
Perivale Gdns. W13 —4B 62
Perivale Grange. Gnfd —3A 62
Perivale Ind. Pk. Gnfd —2B 62
Perivale La. Gnfd —3A 62
Perivale Lodge. Gnfd —3A 62
(off Perivale La.)
Perivale New Bus. Cen. Gnfd —2C 62
Perkin Clo. Wemb —5B 44
Perkins Ct. Ashf —5B 112
Perkins Ho. E14 —5B 70
Perkin's Rents. SW1
—3H 85 (2C 172)
Perkins Rd. Ilf —5H 37
Perkins Sq. SE1 —4D 168
Perks Clo. SE3 —3G 107
Perley Ho. E3 —5B 70
Perpins Rd. SE9 —6H 109
Perran Rd. SW2 —1B 122
Perran Wlk. Bren —5E 80
Perren St. NW5 —6F 49
Perrers Rd. W6 —4D 82
Perrin Clo. Ashf —5B 112
Perring Est. E3 —5C 70
Perrin Ho. NW6 —3J 65
Perrin Rd. Wemb —4B 44
Perrin's Ct. NW3 —4A 48
Perrin's La. NW3 —4A 48
Perrin's Wlk. NW3 —4A 48
Perronet Ho. SE1 —3B 86
(off Princess St.)
Perrott St. SE18 —4G 91
Perry Av. W3 —6K 63
Perry Clo. Rain —2K 75
Perry Clo. Uxb —6D 58
Perry Ct. E14 —5C 88
Perry Ct. N15 —6E 32
Perryfield Way. NW9 —6B 28
Perryfield Way. Rich —3B 116
Perry Gdns. N9 —3J 17
Perry Gth. N'holt —1A 60
Perry Hall Rd. Orp —6K 145
Perry Hill. SE6 —3B 124
Perry How. Wor Pk —1B 148
Perrymans Farm Rd. Ilf —6H 37
Perry Mead. Enf —2G 7
Perrymead St. SW6 —1J 101
Perryn Ct. Twic —6A 98
Perryn Ho. W3 —7A 64
Perryn Rd. SE16 —3H 87
Perryn Rd. W3 —1K 81
Perry Ri. SE23 —3A 124
Perry Rd. Dag —5F 75
Perry's Pl. W1 —6H 67 (7C 160)
Perry St. Chst —7H 127
Perry St. Gdns. Chst —6J 127
Perry St. Shaw. Chst —7J 127
Perry Va. SE23 —2J 123
Persant Rd. SE6 —2G 125
Perseverance Pl. SW9 —7A 86
Perseverance Pl. Rich —4E 98
Perseverance Works. E2
(off Kingsland Rd.) —3E 68 (1H 163)
Pershore Clo. Ilf —5F 37
Pershore Gro. Cars —6B 138
Pert Clo. N10 —7A 16
Perth Av. NW9 —7K 27
Perth Av. Hay —4A 60
Perth Clo. SE5 —4D 104
Perth Clo. SW20 —2B 136
Perth Ho. N1 —7K 49
Perth Rd. E10 —1A 52
Perth Rd. E13 —2K 71
Perth Rd. N4 —1A 50
Perth Rd. N22 —1B 32
Perth Rd. Bark —2H 73
Perth Rd. Beck —2E 142
Perth Rd. Ilf —6E 36
Perth Ter. Ilf —7G 37
Perwell Av. Harr —1D 42
Perystreete. SE23 —2J 123
Petavel Rd. Tedd —6J 115
Peter Av. NW10 —7D 46
Peterboat Clo. SE10 —4G 89
Peterborough Ct. EC4
—6A 68 (1K 167)
Peterborough Gdns. Ilf —7C 36
Peterborough M. SW6 —2J 101
Peterborough Rd. E10 —5E 34
Peterborough Rd. SW6 —2J 101
Peterborough Rd. Cars —6C 138
Peterborough Rd. Harr —1J 43
Peterborough Vs. SW6 —1K 101
Peter Butler Ho. SE1 —2G 87
(off Wolseley St.)
Petergate. SW11 —4A 102
Peterhead Ct. S'hall —6G 61
(off Osborne Rd.)
Peter Ho. SW8 —7J 85
(off Luscombe Way)
Peter James Bus. Cen. Hay —2J 77
Peter James Enterprise Cen. NW10
—3J 63
Peterley Bus. Cen. E2 —2H 69
Peters Clo. Dag —1D 56
Peters Clo. Stan —6J 11
Peters Clo. Well —2J 109
Peter Scott Vis. Cen., The. —1D 100
Peters Ct. W2 —6K 65
(off Porchester Rd.)
Petersfield Clo. N18 —5H 17
Petersfield Ri. SW15 —1D 118
Petersfield Rd. W3 —2J 81
Petersham. —1E 116
Petersham Clo. Rich —2D 116
Petersham Clo. Sutt —5H 149
Petersham Dri. Orp —2K 145
Petersham Gdns. Orp —2K 145
Petersham Ho. SW7 —4B 84 (3A 170)
(off Kendrick M.)
Petersham La. SW7 —3A 84
Petersham M. SW7 —3A 84
Petersham Pl. SW7 —3A 84
Petersham Rd. Rich —6D 98
Petersham Ter. Mitc —3J 151
(off Richmond Grn.)
Peter's Hill. EC4 —7C 68 (2C 168)
Peter's La. EC1 —5B 68 (5B 162)
Peter's Path. SE26 —4H 123
Peterstone Rd. SE2 —3B 92
Peterstow Clo. SW19 —2G 119
Peter St. W1 —7H 67 (2C 166)
Peterwood Pk. Croy —2K 151
Peterwood Way. Croy —2K 151
Petherton Ct. Harr —6K 25
(off Gayton Rd.)
Petherton Ho. N4 —1C 50
(off Woodberry Down Est.)
Petherton Rd. N5 —5C 50
Petiver Clo. E9 —7J 51
Petley Rd. W6 —6F 83
Peto Pl. NW1 —4F 67 (3K 159)
Peto St. N. E16 —6H 71
Peto St. S. E16 —7H 71
Petrie Clo. NW2 —6G 47
Petrie Ho. SE18 —6E 90
(off Woolwich Comn.)
Petros Gdns. NW3 —6A 48
Petticoat La. E1 —5E 68 (6J 163)
Petticoat Sq. E1 —6F 69 (7J 163)
Petticoat Tower. E1 —6F 69 (7J 163)
(off Petticoat Sq.)
Pettits Clo. Romf —2K 39
Pettits La. N. Romf —1K 39
Pettits Pl. Dag —5G 57
Pettits Rd. Dag —5G 57
Pettiward Clo. SW15 —4E 100
Pettley Gdns. Romf —5K 39
Pettman Cres. SE28 —3H 91
Pettsgrove Av. Wemb —5C 44
Pett's Hill. N'holt —5F 43
Petts La. Shep —4C 130
Pett St. SE18 —4C 90
Petts Wood. —5G 145
Petts Wood Rd. Orp —5G 145
Petty France. SW1 —3G 85 (1B 172)
Petworth Clo. N'holt —7D 42
Petworth Gdns. SW20 —3D 136
Petworth Gdns. Uxb —1E 58
Petworth Rd. N12 —5H 15
Petworth Rd. Bexh —5G 111
Petworth St. SW11 —1C 102
Petyt Pl. SW3 —6C 84
Petyward. SW3 —4C 84 (4D 170)
Pevensey Av. N11 —5C 16
Pevensey Av. Enf —2K 7
Pevensey Clo. Iswth —7G 79
Pevensey Ct. W3 —2H 81
Pevensey Rd. E7 —4H 53
Pevensey Rd. SW17 —4B 120
Pevensey Rd. Felt —1C 114
Peverel. E6 —6E 72
Peverel Ho. Dag —2G 57
Peveret Clo. N11 —5A 16
Peveril Dri. Tedd —5H 115
Peveril Ho. SE1 —3D 86
(off Rephidim St.)
Pewsey Clo. E4 —5H 19
Peyton Pl. SE10 —7E 88
Pharamond. NW2 —6F 47
Pharaoh Clo. Mitc —7D 138
Pheasant Clo. E16 —6K 71
Phelp St. SE17 —6D 86
Phelps Way. Hay —4H 77
Phene St. SW3 —6C 84 (7D 170)
Philadelphia Ct. SW10 —7A 84
(off Uverdale Rd.)
Philbeach Gdns. SW5 —5H 83
Phil Brown Pl. SW8 —3F 103
(off Wandsworth Rd.)
Philchurch Pl. E1 —6G 69
Philimore Clo. SE18 —5J 91
Philip Av. Romf —1K 57
Philip Clo. Romf —1K 57
Philip Ct. W2 —5B 66 (5A 158)
(off Hall Pl.)
Philip Gdns. Croy —2B 154
Philip Ho. NW6 —1K 65
(off Mortimer Pl.)
Philip La. N15 —4D 32
Philipot Path. SE9 —6D 108
Philippa Gdns. SE9 —5B 108
Philips Clo. Cars —1E 150
Philip St. E13 —4J 71
Philip Wlk. SE15 —3G 105
(in three parts)
Phillimore Gdns. NW10 —1E 64
Phillimore Gdns. W8 —2J 83
Phillimore Gdns. Clo. W8 —3J 83
Phillimore Pl. W8 —2J 83
Phillimore Ter. W8 —3J 83
(off Allen St.)
Phillimore Wlk. W8 —3J 83
Phillipp St. N1 —1E 68
(in two parts)
Phillips Ct. Edgw —6B 12
Philpot La. EC3 —7E 68 (2G 169)
Philpot Path. Ilf —3G 55
Philpots Clo. W Dray —7A 58
Philpot Sq. SW6 —3K 101
Philpot St. E1 —6H 69
Phineas Pett Rd. SE9 —3C 108
Phipps Bri. Rd. SW19 & Mitc
—2A 138
Phipps Hatch La. Enf —1H 7
Phipps Ho. W12 —7D 64
(off White City Est.)
Phipp St. EC2 —4E 68 (3G 163)
Phoebeth Rd. SE13 —5C 106
Phoenix Bus. Cen. E3 —5C 70
Phoenix Cen. Brom —4K 143
Phoenix Clo. E8 —1F 69
Phoenix Clo. W W'ck —2F 155
Phoenix Ct. E4 —3J 19
Phoenix Ct. E14 —4C 88
Phoenix Ct. NW1 —2H 67
(off Purchese St.)
Phoenix Ct. Houn —5B 96
Phoenix Ct. S Croy —5F 153
Phoenix Ct. Wemb —3H 45
Phoenix Dri. Kes —4B 156
Phoenix Ho. Sutt —4K 149
Phoenix Ind. Est. Harr —4K 25
Phoenix Pl. WC1 —4K 67 (3H 161)
Phoenix Rd. NW1 —3H 67 (1C 160)
Phoenix Rd. SE20 —6J 123
Phoenix St. WC2 —6H 67 (1D 166)
Phoenix Trad. Est. Gnfd —1C 62
Phoenix Trad. Pk. Bren —5D 80
Phoenix Way. Houn —6B 78
Phoenix Wharf Rd. SE1 —7K 169
Phoenix Yd. WC1 —2H 161
Phyllis Av. N Mald —5D 136
Physic Pl. SW3 —6D 84 (7E 170)
Piazza, The. WC2 —2F 167
Piazza, The. Uxb —7A 40
Picardy Manorway. Belv —3H 93
Picardy Rd. Belv —5G 93
Picardy St. Belv —3G 93
Piccadilly. W1 —1F 85 (5K 165)
Piccadilly Arc. SW1 —4A 166
Piccadilly Circus. —7H 67 (3C 166)
Piccadilly Cir. W1 —7H 67 (3C 166)
Piccadilly Pl. W1 —3B 166
Pickard St. EC1 —3B 68 (1B 162)
Pickering Av. E6 —2E 72
Pickering Clo. E9 —7K 51
Pickering Gdns. N11 —6K 15
Pickering Gdns. Croy —6F 141
Pickering Ho. W2 —6A 66
(off Hallfield Est.)
Pickering Ho. W5 —4C 80
(off Windmill Rd.)
Pickering M. W2 —6K 65
Pickering Pl. SW1 —5B 166
Pickering St. N1 —1B 68
Pickets Clo. Bus H —1C 10
Pickets St. SW12 —7F 103
Pickett Cft. Stan —1D 26
Picketts Lock La. N9 —2D 18
Picketts Lock La. Ind. Est. N9 —2F 19
Pickford Clo. Bexh —2E 110
Pickford La. Bexh —2E 110
Pickford Rd. Bexh —3E 110
Pickfords Wharf. N1 —2C 68
Pickfords Wharf. SE1
—1D 86 (4E 168)
Pickfords Yd. N17 —6A 18
Pickhurst Grn. Brom —7H 143
Pickhurst La. Brom —5G 143
Pickhurst Mead. Brom —7H 143
Pickhurst Pk. Brom —5G 143
Pickhurst Ri. W W'ck —7E 142
Pickwick Clo. Houn —5C 96
Pickwick Ho. SE16 —2G 87
(off George Row)
Pickwick Ho. W11 —1F 83
(off St Ann's Rd.)
Pickwick M. N18 —4K 17
Pickwick Pl. Harr —7J 25
Pickwick Rd. SE21 —7D 104
Pickwick St. SE1 —2C 86 (7C 168)
Pickwick Way. Chst —6G 127
Pickworth Clo. SW8 —7J 85
Picton Pl. W1 —6E 66 (1H 165)
Picton St. SE5 —7D 86
Pied Bull Yd. WC1 —6E 160
Piedmont Rd. SE18 —5H 91
Pield Heath. —5A 58
Pield Heath Av. Uxb —4C 58
Pield Heath Rd. Uxb —4A 58
Pier Head. E1 —1H 87
(off Wapping High St.)
Pier Ho. SW3 —7D 170
Piermont Pl. Brom —2C 144
Piermont Rd. SE22 —5H 105
Pier Pde. E16 —1E 90
(off Pier Rd.)
Pierpoint Building. E14 —2B 88
Pierrepoint Rd. W3 —7H 63
Pierrepont Arc. N1 —2B 68
(off Pierrepont Row)
Pierrepont Row. N1 —2B 68
(off Camden Pas.)
Pier Rd. E16 —2D 90
Pier Rd. Felt —5K 95
Pier St. E14 —4E 88
(in two parts)
Pier Ter. SW18 —4K 101
Pier Way. SE28 —3H 91
Pigeon La. Hamp —4E 114
Piggott St. E14 —6C 70
Pigott St. E14 —6C 70
Pike Clo. Brom —5K 125
Pike Clo. Uxb —1B 58
Pikemans Ct. SW5 —4J 83
(off W. Cromwell Rd.)
Pike Rd. NW7 —4E 12
Pike's End. Pinn —4K 23
Pikestone Clo. Hay —4C 60
Pikethorne. SE23 —2K 123
Pilgrimage St. SE1 —2D 86 (7E 168)
Pilgrim Clo. Mord —7K 137
Pilgrim Hill. SE27 —4C 122
Pilgrim Ho. SE1 —3D 86
(off Lansdowne Pl.)
Pilgrims Clo. N13 —4E 16
Pilgrims Clo. N'holt —5G 43
Pilgrim's La. NW3 —4B 48
Pilgrims M. E14 —7G 71
Pilgrim's Pl. NW3 —4B 48
Pilgrims Ri. Barn —5H 5
Pilgrim St. EC4 —6B 68 (1A 168)
Pilgrims Way. E6 —1C 72
Pilgrims Way. N19 —1H 49
Pilgrims Way. S Croy —5F 153
Pilgrim's Way. Wemb —1H 45
Pilkington Rd. SE15 —2H 105
Pillions La. Hay —4F 59
Pilot Clo. SE8 —6B 88
Pilot Ind. Cen. NW10 —4K 63
Pilsden Clo. SW19 —1F 119
Pilton Est., The. Croy —2B 152
Pilton Pl. SE17 —5C 86
(off Pingle St.)
Pilton Pl. Est. SE17 —5C 86
Pimento Ct. W5 —3D 80
Pimlico. —5G 85 (6A 172)
Pimlico Ho. SW1 —5F 85 (5J 171)
(off Ebury Bri. Rd.)
Pimlico Rd. SW1 —5E 84 (5G 171)
Pimlico Wlk. N1 —1G 163
Pinchin St. E1 —7G 69
Pincombe Ho. SE17 —5D 86
Pincott Pl. SE4 —3K 105
Pincott Rd. SW19 —7A 120
Pincott Rd. Bexh —5G 111
Pindar St. EC2 —5E 68 (5G 163)
Pindock M. W9 —4K 65
Pineapple Ct. SW1 —1B 172
Pine Av. E15 —5F 53
Pine Av. W W'ck —1D 154
Pine Clo. E10 —2D 52
Pine Clo. N14 —7B 6
Pine Clo. N19 —2G 49
Pine Clo. SE20 —1J 141
Pine Clo. Stan —4G 11
Pine Coombe. Croy —4K 153
Pine Ct. N21 —5E 6
Pine Ct. N'holt —4C 60
Pinecroft Ct. Well —7A 92
Pinecroft Cres. Barn —4B 4
Pine Dene. SE15 —1H 105
Pinefield Clo. E14 —7C 70
Pine Gdns. Ruis —1K 41
Pine Gdns. Surb —6G 135
Pine Glade. Orp —4D 156
Pine Gro. N4 —2J 49
Pine Gro. N20 —1C 14
Pine Gro. SW19 —5H 119
Pine Ho. W10 —4G 65
(off Droop St.)
Pinehurst Ct. W11 —6H 65
(off Colville Gdns.)
Pinehurst Wlk. Orp —7H 145
Pinemartin Clo. NW2 —3E 46
Pine M. NW10 —2F 65
Pine Pl. Hay —4H 59
Pine Ridge. Cars —7E 150
Pineridge Ct. Barn —4A 4
Pine Rd. N11 —2K 15
Pine Rd. NW2 —4E 46
Pines Rd. Brom —2C 144
Pines, The. N14 —5B 6
Pines, The. SE19 —7B 122
Pines, The. Sun —3J 131
Pines, The. Wfd G —3D 20
Pine St. EC1 —4A 68 (3K 161)
Pine Tree Clo. Houn —1K 95
Pine Tree Lodge. Short —4H 143
Pine Trees Dri. Uxb —4A 40
Pineview Ct. E4 —1K 19
Pine Wlk. Surb —6G 135
Pine Wood. Sun —1J 131
Pinewood Av. Pinn —6A 10
Pinewood Av. Sidc —1J 127
Pinewood Av. Uxb —6B 58
Pinewood Clo. Croy —3A 154
Pinewood Clo. Pinn —6A 10
Pinewood Ct. SW4 —6H 103
Pinewood Ct. Enf —3G 7
Pinewood Gro. W5 —6C 62
Pinewood Lodge. Bush —1C 10
Pinewood Pl. Eps —4K 147
Pinewood Rd. SE2 —6D 92
Pinewood Rd. Brom —4J 143
Pinewood Rd. Felt —3K 113
Pinfold Rd. SW16 —4J 121
Pinglestone Clo. W Dray —7A 76
Pinkcoat Clo. Felt —3K 113
Pinkerton Pl. SW16 —4H 121
Pinkham Mans. W4 —5G 81
Pinkham Way. N11 —7K 15
Pinkwell Av. Hay —4F 77
Pinkwell La. Hay —4E 76
Pinley Gdns. Dag —1B 74
Pinnace Ho. E14 —3E 88
Pinnacle Hill. Bexh —4H 111
Pinnacle Hill N. Bexh —3H 111
Pinnacle Pl. Stan —4G 11
Pinnell Rd. SE9 —4B 108
Pinner. —4C 24
Pinner Ct. NW8 —3A 158
Pinner Ct. Pinn —4E 24
Pinner Green. —2A 24
Pinner Grn. Pinn —2A 24
Pinner Gro. Pinn —4C 24
Pinner Hill Farm. Pinn —1K 23
Pinner Hill Rd. Pinn —1K 23
Pinner Pk. Pinn —2E 24
Pinner Pk. Av. Harr —3F 25
Pinner Pk. Gdns. Harr —2G 25
Pinner Rd. Harr —4E 24
Pinner Rd. N'wd & Pinn —1H 23
Pinner Rd. Pinn —4D 24
Pinner Vw. Harr —4G 25
Pinnerwood Park. —1A 24
Pinn Way. Ruis —7F 23
Pintail Clo. E6 —5C 72
Pintail Ct. SE8 —6B 88
(off Pilot Clo.)
Pintail Rd. Wfd G —7E 20
Pintail Way. Hay —5B 60
Pinter Ho. SW9 —2J 103
(off Grantham Rd.)
Pinto Way. SE3 —4K 107
Pioneer Mkt. Ilf —3F 55
(off Winston Way)
Pioneers Ind. Pk. Croy —1J 151
Pioneer St. SE15 —1G 105
Pioneer Way. W12 —6D 64
Piper Clo. N7 —5K 49
Piper Rd. King T —3G 135
Piper's Gdns. Croy —7A 142
Pipers Grn. NW9 —5J 27
Pipers Grn. La. Edgw —3K 11
(in two parts)
Pipewell Rd. Cars —6C 138
Pippin Clo. NW2 —3C 46
Pippin Clo. Croy —1B 154
Pippins Clo. W Dray —3A 76
Pippins Ct. Ashf —6D 112
Piquet Rd. SE20 —2J 141
Pirbright Cres. New Ad —6E 154
Pirbright Rd. SW18 —1H 119
Pirie Clo. SE5 —3D 104
Pirie St. E16 —1K 89
Pitcairn Clo. Romf —4G 39
Pitcairn Ho. E8 —7J 51
Pitcairn Rd. Mitc —7D 120
Pitcairn's Path. Harr —3G 43
Pitchford St. E15 —7F 53
Pitfield Cres. SE28 —1A 92
Pitfield Est. N1 —3E 68 (1G 163)
Pitfield St. N1 —3E 68 (1G 163)
Pitfield Way. NW10 —6J 45
Pitfield Way. Enf —1D 8
Pitfold Clo. SE12 —6J 107
Pitfold Rd. SE12 —6J 107
Pitlake. Croy —2B 152
Pitman Ho. SE8 —1C 106
Pitman St. SE5 —7C 86
(in two parts)
Pitmaston Ho. SE13 —2E 106
(off Lewisham Rd.)
Pitsea Pl. E1 —6K 69

Pitsea St.—Prentis Rd.

Pitsea St. E1 —6K 69
Pitshanger La. W5 —4B 62
Pitshanger Manor. —7D 62
Pitt Cres. SW19 —4K 119
Pittman Gdns. Ilf —5G 55
Pitt Rd. T Hth & Croy —5C 140
Pitt's Head M. W1 —1E 84 (5H 165)
Pittsmead Av. Brom —7J 143
Pitt St. W8 —2J 83
Pittville Gdns. SE25 —3G 141
Pixley St. E14 —6B 70
Pixton Way. Croy —7A 154
Place Farm Av. Orp —7H 145
Plaisterers Highwalk. EC2 —5C 68
(off Noble St.)
Plaistow. —7J 125
(Bromley)
Plaistow. —3K 71
(West Ham)
Plaistow Gro. E15 —1H 71
Plaistow Gro. Brom —7K 125
Plaistow La. Brom —7J 125
(in two parts)
Plaistow Pk. Rd. E13 —2K 71
Plaistow Rd. E15 & E13 —1H 71
Plaistow Wharf. E16 —1J 89
Plaine Ho. Short —2G 143
Plane St. SE26 —3H 123
Planetarium. —4E 66 (4G 159)
Planetree Ct. W6 —4F 83
(off Brook Grn.)
Plane Tree Cres. Felt —3K 113
Plane Tree Wlk. SE19 —6E 122
Plantagenet Clo. Wor Pk —4K 147
Plantagenet Gdns. Romf —7D 38
Plantagenet Ho. SE18 —3D 90
(off Leda Rd.)
Plantagenet Pl. Romf —7D 38
Plantagenet Rd. Barn —4F 5
Plantain Gdns. E11 —3F 53
(off Hollydown Way, in two parts)
Plantain Pl. SE1 —2D 86 (6E 168)
Plantation, The. SE3 —2J 107
Plantation Wharf. SW11 —3A 102
Plasel Ct. E13 —1K 71
(off Pawsey Clo.)
Plashet. —6C 54
Plashet Gro. E6 —1A 72
Plashet Rd. E13 —1J 71
Plassy Rd. SE6 —7D 106
Plate Ho. E14 —5D 88
Platina St. EC2 —3F 163
Plato Rd. SW2 —4J 103
Platt Halls. NW9 —2B 28
Platt's La. NW3 —4J 47
Platts Rd. Enf —1D 8
Platt St. NW1 —2H 67
Platt, The. SW15 —3F 101
Plawsfield Rd. Beck —1K 141
Plaxtol Clo. Brom —1A 144
Plaxtol Rd. Eri —7G 93
Plaxton Ct. E11 —3H 53
Playfair Ho. E14 —6C 70
Playfair Mans. W14 —6G 83
(off Queen's Club Gdns.)
Playfair St. W6 —5E 82
Playfield Av. Romf —1J 39
Playfield Cres. SE22 —5F 105
Playfield Rd. Edgw —2J 27
Playford Rd. N4 —2K 49
(in two parts)
Playgreen Way. SE6 —3C 124
Playground Clo. Beck —2K 141
Playhouse Yd. EC4 —6B 68 (1A 168)
Plaza Bus. Cen. Enf —2F 9
Plaza Pde. NW6 —2K 65
Plaza, The. W1 —6G 67 (7B 160)
Pleasance Rd. SW15 —5D 100
Pleasance, The. SW15 —4D 100
Pleasant Gro. Croy —3B 154
Pleasant Pl. N1 —7B 50
Pleasant Pl. S Harr —1H 43
Pleasant Row. NW1 —1F 67
Pleasant Vw. Eri —5K 93
Pleasant Way. Wemb —2C 62
Plender Pl. NW1 —1G 67
(off Plender St.)
Plender St. NW1 —1G 67
Pleshey Rd. N7 —4H 49
Plesman Way. Wall —7J 151
Plevna Cres. N15 —6E 32
Plevna Rd. N9 —3B 18
Plevna Rd. Hamp —1F 133
Plevna St. E14 —3E 88
Pleydell Av. SE19 —7F 123
Pleydell Av. W6 —4B 82
Pleydell Ct. EC4 —6A 68
(off Lombard La.)
Pleydell Est. EC1 —2D 162
Pleydell St. EC4 —1K 167
Plimsoll Clo. E14 —6D 70
Plimsoll Rd. N4 —3A 50
Plough Ct. EC3 —7D 68 (2F 169)
Plough Farm Clo. Ruis —6F 23
Plough La. SE22 —6F 105
Plough La. SW19 & SW17 —5K 119
Plough La. Purl —7J 151
Plough La. Tedd —5A 116
Plough La. Wall —4J 151
Plough La. Clo. Wall —5J 151
Ploughmans Clo. NW1 —1H 67
Ploughmans End. Iswth —5H 97
Plough Pl. EC4 —6A 68 (7K 161)
Plough Rd. SW11 —3B 102
Plough Rd. Eps —7K 147
Plough St. E1 —6F 69 (7K 163)
Plough Ter. SW11 —4B 102
Plough Way. SE16 —4K 87
Plough Yd. EC2 —4E 68 (4H 163)
Plover Ho. SW9 —7A 86
(off Brixton Rd.)
Plover Way. SE16 —3A 88
Plover Way. Hay —6B 60
Plowden Bldgs. EC4 —2J 167
Plowman Clo. N18 —5J 17
Plowman Way. Dag —1C 56
Plumber's Row. E1 —5G 69
Plumbridge St. SE10 —1D 106
Plum Clo. Felt —1J 113
Plum Gth. Bren —4D 80
Plum La. SE18 —7F 91
Plummer La. Mitc —2D 138
Plummer Rd. SW4 —7H 103
Plumpton Clo. N'holt —6E 42
Plumpton Way. Cars —3C 150
Plumstead. —4J 91
Plumstead Common. —6H 91
Plumstead Comn. Rd. SE18 —6F 91
Plumstead High St. SE18 —4H 91
Plumstead Rd. SE18 —4F 91
Plumtree Clo. Dag —6H 57
Plumtree Clo. Wall —7H 151
Plumtree Ct. EC4 —6B 68 (7A 162)
Plymouth Ho. Bark —7A 56
(off Keir Hardie Way)
Plymouth Rd. E16 —5J 71
Plymouth Rd. Brom —1K 143
Plymouth Wharf. E14 —4F 89
Plympton Av. NW6 —7H 47
Plympton Clo. Belv —3E 92
Plympton Pl. NW8 —4C 66 (4C 158)
Plympton Rd. NW6 —7H 47
Plympton St. NW8 —4C 66 (4C 158)
Plymstock Rd. Well —7C 92
Pocklington Clo. NW9 —2A 28
Pocklington Clo. W12 —3C 82
(off Goldhawk Rd.)
Pocklington Lodge. W12 —3C 82
Pocock Av. W Dray —3B 76
Pocock St. SE1 —2B 86 (6A 168)
Podmore Rd. SW18 —4A 102
Poet's Rd. N5 —5D 50
Poets Way. Harr —4J 25
Pointalls Clo. N3 —2A 30
Point Clo. SE10 —1E 106
Pointer Clo. SE28 —6D 74
Pointers Clo. E14 —5D 88
Pointers Cotts. Rich —2C 116
Point Hill. SE10 —7E 88
Point Pl. Wemb —7H 45
Point Pleasant. SW18 —4J 101
Point Ter. E7 —5K 53
(off Claremont Rd.)
Point, The. Ruis —4J 41
Point West. SW7 —4K 83
Poland St. W1 —6G 67 (1B 166)
Polebrook Rd. SE3 —3A 108
Pole Cat All. Brom —2H 155
Polecroft La. SE6 —2B 124
Polehamptons, The. Hamp —7G 115
Pole Hill Rd. E4 —7K 9
Pole Hill Rd. Uxb & Hayes —4D 58
Polesden Gdns. SW20 —2D 136
Polesworth Ho. W2 —5J 65
(off Alfred Rd.)
Polesworth Rd. Dag —7D 56
Police Sta. La. Bush —1A 10
Polish War Memorial. (Junct.) —7K 41
Pollard Clo. E16 —7J 71
Pollard Clo. N7 —4K 49
Pollard Ho. N1 —2K 67 (1G 161)
Pollard Rd. N20 —2H 15
Pollard Rd. Mord —5B 138
Pollard Row. E2 —3G 69
Pollards Cres. SW16 —3J 139
Pollards Hill E. SW16 —3K 139
Pollards Hill N. SW16 —3J 139
Pollards Hill S. SW16 —3J 139
Pollards Hill W. SW16 —3K 139
Pollard St. E2 —3G 69
Pollards Wood Rd. SW16 —3J 139
Pollard Wlk. Sidc —6C 128
Pollen St. W1 —6G 67 (1A 166)
Pollitt Dri. NW8 —4B 66 (3B 158)
Pollock Ho. W10 —4G 65
(off Kensal Rd.)
Pollock's Toy Mus. —5G 67 (5B 160)
Polperro Clo. Orp —6K 145
Polsted Rd. SE6 —7B 106
Polthorne Gro. SE18 —4G 91
Polworth Rd. SW16 —5J 121
Polygon Rd. NW1 —2H 67 (1C 160)
Polygon, The. NW8 —1B 66
(off Avenue Rd.)
Polygon, The. SW4 —4G 103
Polytechnic St. SE18 —4E 90
Pomell Way. E1 —6F 69 (7K 163)
Pomeroy Ho. W11 —6G 65
(off Lancaster Rd.)
Pomeroy St. SE14 —7J 87
Pomfret Rd. SE5 —3B 104
Pomoja La. N19 —2J 49
Pond Clo. N12 —6H 15
Pond Clo. SE3 —2H 107
Pond Cottage La. W W'ck —1C 154
Pond Cotts. SE21 —1E 122
Ponders End. —5D 8
Ponders End Ind. Est. Enf —5F 9
Ponder St. N7 —7K 49
(in two parts)
Pond Farm Est. E5 —3J 51
Pondfield Ho. SE27 —5C 122
Pondfield Rd. Brom —1G 155
Pondfield Rd. Dag —5H 57
Pond Grn. Ruis —2G 41
Pond Hill Gdns. Sutt —6G 149
Pond Ho. SW3 —4C 84 (4C 170)
Pond Lees Clo. Dag —7K 57
Pond Mead. SE21 —6D 104
Pond Path. Chst —6F 127
Pond Pl. SW3 —4C 84 (4C 170)
Pond Rd. E15 —2G 71
Pond Rd. SE3 —2H 107
Pondside Clo. Hay —6F 77
Pond Sq. N6 —1E 48
Pond St. NW3 —5C 48
Pond Way. Tedd —6C 116
Pondwood Ri. Orp —7J 145
Ponler St. E1 —6H 69
Ponsard Rd. NW10 —3D 64
Ponsford St. E9 —6J 51
Ponsonby Pl. SW1 —5H 85 (5D 172)
Ponsonby Rd. SW15 —7D 100
Ponsonby Ter. SW1 —5H 85 (5D 172)
Pontefract Ct. N'holt —5F 43
(off Newmarket Av.)
Pontefract Rd. Brom —5H 125
Ponton Rd. SW8 —7H 85 (7D 172)
Pont St. SW1 —3D 84 (2E 170)
Pont St. M. SW1 —3D 84 (2E 170)
Pontypool Pl. SE1 —2B 86 (6A 168)
Pool Clo. Beck —5C 124
Pool Clo. W Mol —5D 132
Pool Ct. SE6 —2C 124
Poole Clo. Ruis —2G 41
Poole Ct. Houn —2C 96
Poole Ct. Rd. Houn —2C 96
Poole Ho. SE11 —3J 173
Pool End. —5C 130
Pool End Clo. Shep —5C 130
Poole Rd. E9 —6K 51
Poole Rd. Eps —6K 147
Pooles Bldgs. WC1 —4J 161
Pooles Cotts. Rich —2D 116
Pooles La. SW10 —7A 84
Pooles La. Dag —2E 74
Pooles Pk. N4 —2A 50
Poole St. N1 —1D 68
Poole Way. Hay —3G 59
Pool Ho. NW8 —5B 66 (5C 158)
(off Penfold St.)
Poolmans St. SE16 —2K 87
Pool Rd. Harr —7H 25
Pool Rd. W Mol —5D 132
Poolsford Rd. NW9 —4A 28
Poonah St. E1 —6J 69
Pope Clo. SW19 —6B 120
Pope Clo. Felt —1H 113
Pope Rd. Brom —5B 144
Popes Av. Twic —2J 115
Popes Ct. Twic —2J 115
Popes Dri. N3 —1J 29
Popes Gro. Croy —3B 154
Popes Gro. Twic —2J 115
Pope's Head All. EC3 —6D 68 (1F 169)
Popes La. W5 —3D 80
Pope's Rd. SW9 —3A 104
Pope St. SE1 —2E 86 (7H 169)
Popham Clo. Hanw —3D 114
Popham Gdns. Rich —3G 99
Popham Rd. N1 —1C 68
Popham St. N1 —1B 68
(in two parts)
Pop-In Commercial Cen. Wemb —5H 45
Popinjays Row. Cheam —5F 149
(off Netley Clo.)
Poplar. —7D 70
Poplar Av. Mitc —1D 138
Poplar Av. S'hall —3F 79
Poplar Av. W Dray —7B 58
Poplar Bath St. E14 —7D 70
Poplar Bus. Pk. E14 —7E 70
Poplar Clo. E9 —5B 52
Poplar Clo. Pinn —1B 24
Poplar Ct. SW19 —5J 119
Poplar Ct. N'holt —2A 60
Poplar Ct. Twic —6C 98
Poplar Cres. Eps —6J 147
Poplar Farm Clo. Eps —6J 147
Poplar Gdns. SE28 —7C 74
Poplar Gdns. N Mald —2K 135
Poplar Gro. N11 —6K 15
Poplar Gro. W6 —2E 82
Poplar Gro. N Mald —2K 135
Poplar Gro. Wemb —3J 45
Poplar High St. E14 —7D 70
Poplar Ho. SE4 —4B 106
(off Wickham Rd.)
Poplar M. W12 —1E 82
(off Uxbridge Rd.)
Poplar Mt. Belv —4H 93
Poplar Pl. SE28 —7C 74
Poplar Pl. W2 —7K 65
Poplar Pl. Hay —7J 59
Poplar Rd. SE24 —4C 104
Poplar Rd. SW19 —2J 137
Poplar Rd. Ashf —5E 112
Poplar Rd. Sutt —1H 149
Poplar Rd. S. SW19 —3J 137
Poplars Av. NW2 —6E 46
Poplars Clo. Ruis —1G 41
Poplars Rd. E17 —6D 34
Poplars, The. N14 —5A 6
Poplar St. Romf —4J 39
Poplar Vw. Wemb —2D 44
Poplar Wlk. SE24 —3C 104
(in two parts)
Poplar Wlk. Croy —2C 152
Poplar Way. Felt —3J 113
Poplar Way. Ilf —4G 37
Poppins Ct. EC4 —6B 68 (1A 168)
Poppleton Rd. E11 —6G 35
Poppy Clo. Wall —1E 150
Poppy La. Croy —7J 141
Porchester Clo. SE5 —4C 104
Porchester Ct. W2 —7K 65
Porchester Gdns. W2 —7K 65
Porchester Gdns. M. W2 —6K 65
Porchester Ga. W2 —7K 65
(off Bayswater Rd., in two parts)
Porchester Mead. Beck —6C 124
Porchester M. W2 —6K 65
Porchester Pl. W2 —6C 66 (1D 164)
Porchester Rd. W2 —6K 65
Porchester Rd. King T —2H 135
Porchester Sq. W2 —6K 65
Porchester Ter. W2 —6A 66
Porchester Ter. N. W2 —6K 65
Porch Way. N20 —3J 15
Porcupine Clo. SE9 —2C 126
Porden Rd. SW2 —4K 103
Porlock Av. Harr —1G 43
Porlock Ho. SE26 —3G 123
Porlock Rd. W10 —4F 65
Porlock Rd. Enf —7A 8
Porlock St. SE1 —2D 86 (6F 169)
Porrington Clo. Chst —1D 144
Porson Ct. SE13 —3D 106
Portal Clo. SE27 —3A 122
Portal Clo. Ruis —4J 41
(in two parts)
Portal Clo. Uxb —7A 40
(in two parts)
Porta Way. E3 —4B 70
Portbury Clo. SE15 —1G 105
Port Cres. E13 —4K 71
Portcullis Ho. SW1 —7E 166
Portcullis Lodge Rd. Enf —3J 7
Portelet Ct. N1 —1E 68
(off De Beauvoir Est.)
Portelet Rd. E1 —3K 69
Porten Houses. W14 —3G 83
(off Porten Rd.)
Porten Rd. W14 —3G 83
Porter Rd. E6 —6D 72
Porters & Walters Almshouses. N22 —7E 16
(off Nightingale Rd.)
Porters Av. Dag —6B 56
Porter Sq. N19 —1J 49
Porter St. SE1 —1C 86 (4D 168)
Porter St. W1 —5D 66 (5F 159)
Porters Wlk. E1 —7H 69
(off Pennington St.)
Porters Way. W Dray —3B 76
Porteus Rd. W2 —5A 66 (5A 158)
Portgate Clo. W9 —4H 65
Porthcawe Rd. SE26 —4A 124
Porthkerry Av. Well —4A 110
Portia Ct. SE11 —5B 86
(off Opal St.)
Portia Ct. Bark —7A 56
Portia Way. E3 —4B 70
Porticos, The. SW3 —7A 170
Portinscale Rd. SW15 —5G 101
Portland Av. N16 —7F 33
Portland Av. N Mald —7B 136
Portland Av. Sidc —6A 110
Portland Clo. Romf —5E 38
Portland Commercial Est. Bark —2C 74
Portland Ct. SE1 —3D 86 (7E 168)
(off Gt. Dover St.)
Portland Cres. SE9 —2C 126
Portland Cres. Felt —4F 113
Portland Cres. Gnfd —4F 61
Portland Cres. Stan —2D 26
Portland Dri. Enf —1K 7
Portland Gdns. N4 —6B 32
Portland Gdns. Romf —5D 38
Portland Gro. SW8 —1K 103
Portland Ho. SW1 —3G 85
(off Stag Pl.)
Portland M. W1 —6G 67 (1B 166)
Portland Pl. SE25 —4G 141
(off Portland Rd.)
Portland Pl. W1 —4F 67 (4J 159)
Portland Ri. N4 —1B 50
Portland Ri. Est. N4 —1C 50
Portland Rd. N15 —4F 33
Portland Rd. SE9 —2C 126
Portland Rd. SE25 —4G 141
Portland Rd. W11 —7G 65
Portland Rd. Ashf —3A 112
Portland Rd. Brom —4A 126
Portland Rd. Hay —3G 59
Portland Rd. King T —3E 134
Portland Rd. Mitc —2C 138
Portland Rd. S'hall —3D 78
Portland Sq. E1 —1H 87
Portland St. SE17 —5D 86
Portland Ter. Rich —4D 98
Portland Wlk. SE17 —6D 86
Portman Av. SW14 —3K 99
Portman Clo. W1 —6D 66 (7F 159)
Portman Clo. Bex —1K 129
Portman Clo. Bexh —3E 110
Portman Dri. Wfd G —2B 36
Portman Gdns. NW9 —2K 27
Portman Gdns. Uxb —7C 40
Portman Ga. NW1 —4D 158
Portman Mans. W1 —5D 66 (5F 159)
(off Chiltern St.)
Portman M. S. W1 —6E 66 (1G 165)
Portman Pl. E2 —3J 69
Portman Rd. King T —2F 135
Portman Sq. W1 —6E 66 (7G 159)
Portman St. W1 —6E 66 (1G 165)
Portman Towers. W1 —6D 66 (7F 159)
Portmeadow Wlk. SE2 —2D 92
Portmeers Clo. E17 —6B 34
Portnall Rd. W9 —2H 65
Portnoi Clo. Romf —2K 39
Portobello Ct. Est. W11 —6H 65
Portobello M. W11 —7J 65
Portobello Rd. W10 —5G 65
Portobello Rd. W11 —6H 65
Portobello Road Market. —5G 65
Portpool La. WC1 —5A 68 (5J 161)
Portree Clo. N22 —7E 16
Portree St. E14 —6F 71
Portrush Ct. S'hall —6G 61
(off Whitecote Rd.)
Portsdown. Edgw —5B 12
Portsdown Av. NW11 —6H 29
Portsdown M. NW11 —6H 29
Portsea Hall. W2 —6D 66 (1D 164)
(off Portsea Pl.)
Portsea M. W2 —1D 164
Portsea Pl. W2 —6C 66 (1D 164)
Portslade Rd. SW8 —2G 103
Portsmouth Av. Th Dit —7A 134
Portsmouth M. E16 —1K 89
Portsmouth Rd. SW15 —7D 100
Portsmouth Rd. Th Dit & Surb —7A 134
Portsmouth St. WC2 —6K 67 (1G 167)
Portsoken St. EC3 —7F 69 (2J 169)
Portswood Pl. SW15 —6B 100
Portugal Gdns. Twic —2G 115
Portugal St. WC2 —6K 67 (1G 167)
Portway. E15 —1H 71
Portway Gdns. SE18 —7B 90
Pory Ho. SE11 —4K 85 (4H 173)
Poseidon Ct. E14 —4C 88
Postern Grn. Enf —2F 7
Postern, The. EC2 —6D 162
Post La. Twic —1H 115
Postmill Clo. Croy —3J 153
Post Office All. Hamp —2F 133
Post Office App. E7 —5K 53
Post Office Ct. EC4 —6D 68 (1F 169)
(off Barbican)
Post Office Way. SW8 —7H 85
Post Rd. S'hall —3F 79
Postway M. Ilf —3F 55
(in two parts)
Potier St. SE1 —3D 86
Potter Clo. Mitc —2F 139
Potteries, The. Barn —5D 4
Potterne Clo. SW19 —7F 101
Potters Clo. Croy —1A 154
Potters Fld. Enf —4K 7
(off Lincoln Rd.)
Potters Fields. SE1 —1E 86 (5H 169)
Potters Gro. N Mald —4J 135
Potters Heights Clo. Pinn —1K 23
Potter's La. SW16 —6H 121
Potters La. Barn —4D 4
Potters Lodge. E14 —5E 88
Potters Rd. SW6 —2A 102
Potter's Rd. Barn —4E 4
Potter St. N'wd —1J 23
Potter St. Pinn —1K 23
Pottery La. W11 —1G 83
Pottery Rd. Bex —2J 129
Pottery Rd. Bren —6E 80
Pottery St. SE16 —2H 87
Pott St. E2 —3H 69
Poulett Gdns. Twic —1A 116
Poulett Rd. E6 —2D 72
Poulner Way. SE15 —7F 87
(in two parts)
Poulters Wood. Kes —5B 156
Poulton Av. Sutt —3B 150
Poulton Clo. E8 —6H 51
Poultry. EC2 —6D 68 (1E 168)
Pound Clo. Surb —1C 146
Pound Grn. Bex —7G 111
Pound La. NW10 —6C 46
Pound Pk. Rd. SE7 —4B 90
Pound Pl. SE9 —6E 108
Pound St. Cars —5D 150
Pound Way. Chst —7G 127
Pountney Rd. SW11 —3E 102
Poverest. —5K 145
Poverest Rd. Orp —5K 145
Povey Ho. SE17 —4E 86
(off Tatum St.)
Powder Mill La. Twic —7D 96
Powell Clo. Chess —5D 146
Powell Clo. Edgw —6A 12
Powell Clo. Wall —7J 151
Powell Ct. E17 —3D 34
Powell Gdns. Dag —4G 57
Powell Rd. E5 —3H 51
Powell Rd. Buck H —1F 21
Powell's Wlk. W4 —6A 82
Powergate Bus. Pk. NW10 —3K 63
Power Rd. W4 —4G 81
Powers Ct. Twic —7D 98
Powerscroft Rd. E5 —4J 51
Powerscroft Rd. Sidc —6C 128
Powis Ct. W11 —6H 65
(off Powis Gdns.)
Powis Ct. Bus H —1C 10
(off Rutherford Way)
Powis Gdns. NW11 —7H 29
Powis Gdns. W11 —6H 65
Powis M. W11 —6H 65
Powis Pl. WC1 —4J 67 (4F 161)
Powis Rd. E3 —3D 70
Powis Sq. W11 —6H 65
(in two parts)
Powis St. SE18 —3E 90
Powis Ter. W11 —6H 65
Powlett Pl. NW1 —7E 48
Pownall Gdns. Houn —4F 97
Pownall Rd. E8 —1G 69
Pownall Rd. Houn —4F 97
Pownsett Ter. Ilf —5G 55
Powster Rd. Brom —5J 125
Powys Clo. Bexh —6D 92
Powys Ct. N11 —5D 16
Powys La. N14 & N13 —4D 16
Poynders Ct. SW4 —6G 103
Poynders Gdns. SW4 —7G 103
Poynders Rd. SW4 —6G 103
Poynings Rd. N19 —3G 49
Poynings Way. N12 —5D 14
Poyntell Cres. Chst —1H 145
Poynter Ct. N'holt —2B 60
(off Gallery Gdns.)
Poynter Ho. NW8 —4B 66 (3A 158)
(off Fisherton St.)
Poynter Ho. W11 —1F 83
(off Queensdale Cres.)
Poynter Rd. Enf —5A 8
Poynton Rd. N17 —2G 33
Poyntz Rd. SW11 —2D 102
Poyser St. E2 —2H 69
Praed M. W2 —6B 66 (7B 158)
Praed St. W2 —6B 66 (1A 164)
Pragel St. E13 —2A 72
Pragnell Rd. SE12 —2K 125
Prague Pl. SW2 —5J 103
Prah Rd. N4 —2A 50
Prairie St. SW8 —2E 102
Pratt M. NW1 —1G 67
Pratts Pas. King T —2E 134
Pratt St. NW1 —1G 67
Pratt Wlk. SE11 —4K 85 (3H 173)
Prayle Gro. NW2 —1F 47
Preachers Ct. EC1 —4B 68 (4B 162)
(off Charterhouse Sq.)
Prebend Gdns. W6 & W4 —4B 82
(in two parts)
Prebend Mans. W4 —4B 82
(off Chiswick High Rd.)
Prebend St. N1 —1C 68
Precinct Rd. Hay —7J 59
Precincts, The. Mord —6J 137
Precinct, The. N1 —1C 68
(in two parts)
Precinct, The. W Mol —3F 133
Premier Corner. W9 —2H 65
Premier Ct. Enf —1D 8
Premiere Pl. E14 —7C 70
Premier Ho. N1 —7B 50
Premier Pk. Rd. NW10 —2H 63
Premier Pl. SW15 —4G 101
Prendergast Rd. SE3 —3G 107
Prentice Ct. SW19 —5H 119
Prentis Rd. SW16 —4H 121

Prentiss Ct.—Quadrangle, The

Prentiss Ct. SE7 —4B 90
Presburg Rd. N Mald —5A 136
Presburg St. E5 —3K 51
Prescelly Pl. Edgw —1F 27
Prescot St. E1 —7F 69 (2K 169)
Prescott Av. Orp —6F 145
Prescott Clo. SW16 —7J 121
Prescott Ho. SE5 —6B 86
(off Hillingdon St.)
Prescott Pl. SW4 —3H 103
Presentation M. SW2 —2K 121
Preshaw Cres. Mitc —3C 138
President Dri. E1 —1H 87
President Ho. EC1 —3B 68 (2B 162)
Presidents Quay. E1 —4K 169
President St. EC1 —1C 162
Press Ho. NW10 —3K 45
Press Rd. NW10 —3K 45
Prestage Way. E14 —7E 70
Prestbury Rd. E7 —7A 54
Prestbury Sq. SE9 —4D 126
Prested Rd. SW11 —4C 102
Prestige Way. NW4 —5E 28
Preston. —1E 44
Preston Av. E4 —6A 20
Preston Clo. SE1 —4E 86
Preston Clo. Twic —3J 115
Preston Ct. New Bar —4F 5
Preston Ct. Sidc —4K 127
(off Crescent, The)
Preston Dri. E11 —5A 36
Preston Dri. Bexh —1D 110
Preston Dri. Eps —6A 148
Preston Gdns. NW10 —6B 46
Preston Gdns. Ilf —6C 36
Preston Hill. Harr —7E 26
Preston Ho. SE1 —3F 87
(off Stanworth St.)
Preston Ho. SE17 —4E 86
(off Preston Clo.)
Preston Ho. Dag —3G 57
(off Uvedale Rd.)
Preston Pl. NW2 —6C 46
Preston Pl. Rich —5E 98
Preston Rd. E11 —6G 35
Preston Rd. SE19 —6B 122
Preston Rd. SW20 —7B 118
Preston Rd. Shep —5C 130
Preston Rd. Wemb & Harr —1E 44
Preston's Rd. E14 —7E 70
Prestons Rd. Brom —3J 155
Preston Waye. Harr —1E 44
Prestwich Ter. SW4 —5G 103
Prestwick Clo. S'hall —5C 78
Prestwick Ct. S'hall —7G 61
(off Baird Av.)
Prestwood Av. Harr —4B 26
Prestwood Clo. SE18 —6A 92
Prestwood Clo. Harr —4B 26
Prestwood Gdns. Croy —7C 140
Prestwood Ho. SE16 —3H 87
(off Drummond Rd.)
Prestwood St. N1 —2C 68 (1D 162)
Pretoria Av. E17 —4A 34
Pretoria Clo. N17 —7A 18
Pretoria Cres. E4 —1K 19
Pretoria Rd. E4 —1K 19
Pretoria Rd. E11 —1F 53
Pretoria Rd. E16 —4H 71
Pretoria Rd. N17 —7A 18
Pretoria Rd. SW16 —6F 121
Pretoria Rd. Ilf —5F 55
Pretoria Rd. Romf —4J 39
Pretoria Rd. N. N18 —6A 18
Prevost Rd. N11 —2K 15
Price Clo. NW7 —6B 14
Price Clo. SW17 —3D 120
Price' Ct. SW11 —3B 102
Price Ho. N1 —1C 68
(off Britannia Row)
Price Rd. Croy —5B 152
Price's St. SE1 —1B 86 (5B 168)
Price's Yd. N1 —1K 67
Price Way. Hamp —6C 114
Prichard Ct. N7 —6K 49
Pricklers Hill. Barn —6E 4
Prickley Wood. Brom —1H 155
Priddy's Yd. Croy —2C 152
Prideaux Pl. W3 —7K 63
Prideaux Pl. WC1 —3K 67 (1H 161)
Prideaux Rd. SW9 —3J 103
Pridham Rd. T Hth —4D 140
Priestfield Rd. SE23 —3A 124
Priestlands Pk. Rd. Sidc —3K 127
Priestley Clo. N16 —7F 33
Priestley Gdns. Romf —6B 38
Priestley Ho. EC1 —4C 68 (3D 162)
(off Old St.)
Priestley Ho. Wemb —3J 45
(off Barnhill Rd.)
Priestley Rd. Mitc —2E 138
Priestley Way. E17 —3K 33
Priestley Way. NW2 —1C 46
Priest Pk. Av. Harr —2E 42
Priests Av. Romf —2K 39
Priest's Bri. SW14 & SW15 —3A 100
Priest's Ct. EC2 —7C 162
Prima Rd. SW9 —7A 86
Prime Meridian Line, The. —7F 89
Primrose Av. Enf —1J 7
Primrose Av. Romf —7B 38
Primrose Clo. SE6 —5E 124
Primrose Clo. Harr —3D 42
Primrose Clo. Wall —7F 139
Primrose Ct. SW12 —7H 103
Primrose Gdns. NW3 —6C 48
Primrose Gdns. Bush —1A 10
Primrose Gdns. Ruis —5A 42
Primrose Hill. —1E 66
Primrose Hill. EC4 —6A 68 (1K 167)
Primrose Hill Ct. NW3 —7D 48
Primrose Hill Rd. NW3 —7D 48
Primrose Hill Studios. NW1 —1E 66
Primrose La. Croy —1J 153
Primrose Mans. SW11 —1E 102
Primrose M. NW1 —7D 48
(off Sharpleshall St.)
Primrose M. SE3 —7J 89
Primrose Rd. E10 —1D 52
Primrose Rd. E18 —2K 35
Primrose Sq. E9 —7J 51
Primrose St. EC2 —5E 68 (5G 163)
Primrose Wlk. SE14 —7A 88
Primrose Wlk. Eps —7B 148
Primrose Way. Wemb —2D 62
Primula St. W12 —6C 64
Prince Albert Ct. NW8 —1D 66
(off Prince Albert Rd.)
Prince Albert Rd. NW1 & NW8 —3C 66 (1C 158)
Prince Arthur M. NW3 —4A 48
Prince Arthur Rd. NW3 —5A 48
Prince Charles Dri. NW4 —7E 28
Prince Charles Rd. SE3 —2H 107
Prince Charles Way. Wall —3F 151
Prince Consort Dri. Chst —1H 145
Prince Consort Rd. SW7 —3A 84 (1A 170)
Princedale Rd. W11 —1G 83
Prince Edward Mans. W2 —7J 65
(off Hereford Rd.)
Prince Edward Rd. E9 —6B 52
Prince George Av. N14 —5B 6
Prince George Rd. N16 —4E 50
Prince George's Av. SW20 —2E 136
Prince George's Rd. SW19 —1B 138
Prince Henry Rd. SE7 —7B 90
Prince Imperial Rd. SE18 —1D 108
Prince Imperial Rd. Chst —1F 145
Prince John Rd. SE9 —5C 108
Princelet St. E1 —5F 69 (5K 163)
Prince of Wales Clo. NW4 —4D 28
Prince of Wales Dri. SW8 —7F 85
Prince of Wales Dri. SW11 & SW8 —1C 102
Prince of Wales Mans. SW11 —1E 102
Prince of Wales Pas. NW1 —2A 160
Prince of Wales Rd. E16 —6A 72
Prince of Wales Rd. NW5 —6E 48
Prince of Wales Rd. SE3 —2H 107
Prince of Wales Rd. Sutt —2B 150
Prince of Wales Ter. W4 —5A 82
Prince of Wales Ter. W8 —2K 83
Prince Regent Ct. NW8 —2C 66
(off Avenue Rd.)
Prince Regent La. E13 & E16 —3K 71
Prince Regent M. NW1 —2A 160
Prince Regent Rd. Houn —3G 97
Prince Regent's Ga. NW8 —4C 66
Prince Rd. SE25 —5E 140
Prince Rupert Rd. SE9 —4D 108
Princes Arc. SW1 —4B 166
Princes Av. N3 —1J 29
Princes Av. N10 —3F 31
Princes Av. N13 —5F 17
Princes Av. N22 —1H 31
Princes Av. NW9 —4G 27
Princes Av. W3 —3G 81
Princes Av. Cars —7D 150
Prince's Av. Gnfd —6F 61
Princes Av. Orp —5J 145
Princes Av. Surb —1G 147
Princes Av. Wfd G —4E 20
Princes Cir. WC2 —6J 67 (7E 160)
Princes Clo. N4 —1B 50
Princes Clo. NW9 —4G 27
Princes Clo. SW4 —3G 103
Princes Clo. Edgw —5B 12
Princes Clo. Sidc —3D 128
Prince's Clo. Tedd —4H 115
Princes Ct. SE16 —3B 88
Prince's Ct. SW3 —3D 84 (1E 170)
(off Brompton Rd.)
Princes Ct. Wemb —5E 44
Princes Ct. Bus. Cen. E1 —7H 69
Princes Dri. Harr —3J 25
Prince's Gdns. SW7 —3B 84 (1B 170)
Princes Gdns. W3 —5G 63
Princes Gdns. W5 —4C 62
Prince's Ga. SW7 —2B 84 (7B 164)
(in six parts)
Prince's Ga. Ct. SW7 —2B 84 (7A 164)
Prince's Ga. M. SW7 —3B 84 (1B 170)
Princes La. N10 —3F 31
Prince's M. W2 —7K 65
Princes M. Houn —4E 96
Princes Pde. NW11 —6G 29
(off Golders Grn. Rd.)
Princes Pk. Av. NW11 —6G 29
Princes Pk. Av. Hay —7F 59
Princes Pk. Circ. Hay —7F 59
Princes Pk. Clo. Hay —7F 59
Princes Pk. La. Hay —7F 59
Princes Pk. Pde. Hay —7F 59
Princes Pl. SW1 —4B 166
Princes Pl. W11 —1G 83
Prince's Plain. Brom —7C 144
Prince's Ri. SE13 —2E 106
Princes Riverside Rd. SE16 —1K 87
Princes Rd. N18 —4D 18
Princes Rd. SE20 —6K 123
Princes Rd. SW14 —3K 99
Prince's Rd. SW19 —6J 119
Princes Rd. W13 —1B 80
Princes Rd. Ashf —5B 112
Princes Rd. Buck H —2F 21
Princes Rd. Felt —2H 113
Princes Rd. Ilf —4H 37
Princes Rd. Kew —1F 99
Princes Rd. King T —7G 117
Princes Rd. Rich —5F 99
Prince's Rd. Tedd —4H 115
Princessa Ct. Enf —5J 7
Princess Alice Ho. W10 —4E 64
Princess Alice Way. SE28 —2H 91
Princess Av. Wemb —2E 44
Princess Ct. N6 —7G 31
Princess Ct. W1 —5D 66 (6E 158)
(off Bryanston Pl.)
Princess Ct. W2 —7K 65
(off Queensway)
Princess Cres. N4 —2B 50
Princess La. Ruis —1G 41
Princess Louise Clo. W2 —5B 66 (5B 158)
Princess Mary Ho. SW1
(off Vincent St.) —4H 85 (3D 172)
Princess May Rd. N16 —4E 50
Princess M. NW3 —5B 48
Princess M. King T —3F 135
Princess Pde. Dag —2G 75
Princess Pde. Orp —3E 156
Princess Pk. Mnr. N11 —5K 15
Prince's Sq. W2 —7K 65
Princess Rd. NW1 —1E 66
Princess Rd. NW6 —2J 65
Princess Rd. Croy —6C 140
Princess St. SE1 —3B 86
Prince's St. EC2 —6D 68 (1E 168)
Princes St. N17 —6K 17
Princes St. W1 —6F 67 (1K 165)
Princes St. Bexh —3F 111
Princes St. Rich —4E 98
Princes St. Sutt —4B 150
Princes Ter. E13 —1K 71
Prince St. SE8 —6B 88
Princes Way. SW19 —7F 101
Princes Way. Buck H —2F 21
Princes Way. Croy —5K 151
Princes Way. Ruis —4C 42
Princes Way. W W'ck —4H 155
Prince's Yd. W11 —1G 83
(off Princedale Rd.)
Princethorpe Ho. W2 —5K 65
(off Woodchester Sq.)
Princethorpe Rd. SE26 —4K 123
Princeton Ct. SW15 —3F 101
Princeton M. King T —1G 135
Princeton St. WC1 —5K 67 (6G 161)
Principal Sq. E9 —5K 51
Pringle Gdns. SW16 —4G 121
(in two parts)
Pring St. W10 —7F 65
Printers Inn Ct. EC4 —6A 68 (7J 161)
Printers M. E3 —1A 70
Printer St. EC4 —6A 68 (7K 161)
Printinghouse La. Hay —2G 77
Printing Ho. Yd. E2 —3E 68 (1H 163)
Printon Ho. E3 —5B 70
Print Village. SE15 —2F 105
Priolo Rd. SE7 —5A 90
Prior Av. Sutt —7C 150
Prior Bolton St. N1 —6B 50
Prioress Rd. SE27 —3B 122
Prioress St. SE1 —3E 86
Prior Rd. Ilf —3E 54
Priors Cft. E17 —2A 34
Priors Fld. N'holt —6C 42
Priors Gdns. Ruis —5A 42
Priors Mead. Enf —1K 7
Prior St. SE10 —7E 88
Priory Av. E4 —3G 19
Priory Av. E17 —5C 34
Priory Av. N8 —4H 31
Priory Av. W4 —4A 82
Priory Av. Orp —6H 145
Priory Av. Sutt —4F 149
Priory Av. Wemb —4K 43
Priory Clo. E4 —3G 19
Priory Clo. E18 —1J 35
Priory Clo. N3 —1H 29
Priory Clo. N14 —5A 6
Priory Clo. N20 —7C 4
Priory Clo. SW19 —1K 137
Priory Clo. Beck —3A 142
Priory Clo. Chst —1D 144
Priory Clo. Hamp —1D 132
Priory Clo. Hay —7K 59
Priory Clo. Ruis —1H 41
Priory Clo. Stan —3E 10
Priory Clo. Sun —7J 113
Priory Clo. Wemb —4K 43
Priory Ct. E6 —1A 72
Priory Ct. E9 —5K 51
Priory Ct. E17 —2B 34
Priory Ct. EC4 —6B 68
(off Pilgrim St.)
Priory Ct. SW8 —1H 103
Priory Ct. Bush —1B 10
Priory Ct. Eps —7B 148
Priory Ct. Houn —3F 97
Priory Ct. Sutt —4G 149
Priory Ct. Wemb —2E 62
Priory Ct. Est. E17 —2B 34
Priory Cres. SE19 —7C 122
Priory Cres. Sutt —4F 149
Priory Cres. Wemb —3A 44
Priory Dri. SE2 —5D 92
Priory Dri. Stan —3E 10
Priory Field Dri. Edgw —4C 12
Priory Gdns. N6 —6F 31
Priory Gdns. SE25 —4F 141
Priory Gdns. SW13 —3B 100
Priory Gdns. W4 —4A 82
Priory Gdns. W5 —3E 62
Priory Gdns. Ashf —5F 113
Priory Gdns. Hamp —7D 114
Priory Gdns. Wemb —4A 44
Priory Grange. N2 —3D 30
(off Fortis Grn.)
Priory Grn. Est. N1 —2K 67
Priory Gro. SW8 —1J 103
Priory Gro. Barn —5D 4
Priory Hill. Wemb —4A 44
Priory Ho. E1 —5F 69 (5J 163)
(off Folgate St.)
Priory Ho. EC1 —4B 68 (3K 161)
(off Sans Wlk.)
Priory Ho. SW1 —5H 85 (5C 172)
(off Rampayne St.)
Priory La. SW15 —6A 100
Priory La. Rich —7G 81
Priory La. W Mol —4F 133
Priory Leas. SE9 —1C 126
Priory M. SW8 —1J 103
Priory Pk. SE3 —3H 107
Priory Pk. Rd. NW6 —1H 65
(in two parts)
Priory Pk. Rd. Wemb —4A 44
Priory Rd. E6 —1B 72
Priory Rd. N8 —4G 31
Priory Rd. NW6 —1K 65
Priory Rd. SW19 —7B 120
Priory Rd. W4 —3K 81
Priory Rd. Bark —7H 55
Priory Rd. Chess —3E 146
Priory Rd. Croy —7A 140
Priory Rd. Hamp —7D 114
Priory Rd. Houn —5G 97
Priory Rd. Rich —6G 81
Priory Rd. Sutt —4F 149
Priory St. E3 —3D 70
Priory Ter. NW6 —1K 65
Priory Ter. Sun —7J 113
Priory, The. SE3 —4H 107
(in two parts)
Priory, The. Croy —4A 152
Priory Vw. Bus H —1D 10
Priory Vs. N11 —6J 15
(off Colney Hatch La.)
Priory Wlk. SW10 —5A 84
Priory Way. Harr —4F 25
Priory Way. S'hall —3B 78
Priory Way. W Dray —6A 76
Pritchard Ho. E2 —2H 69
(off Ada Pl.)
Pritchard's Rd. E2 —1G 69
Priter Rd. SE16 —3G 87
Priter Way. SE16 —3G 87
Private Rd. Enf —5J 7
Probert Rd. SW2 —5A 104
Probyn Ho. SW1 —4H 85 (3D 172)
(off Page St.)
Probyn Rd. SW2 —2B 122
Procter Ho. SE5 —7D 86
(off Picton St.)
Procter St. WC1 —5K 67 (6G 161)
Proctor Clo. Mitc —1E 138
Proctor Ho. SE1 —5G 87
(off Avondale Sq.)
Proctors Clo. Felt —1J 113
Progress Bus. Pk., The. Croy —2K 151
Progress Cen., The. N9 —3K 17
Progress Cen., The. Enf —3E 8
Progress Way. N22 —1A 32
Progress Way. Croy —2K 151
Progress Way. Enf —5B 8
Project Pk. E3 —4F 71
Promenade App. Rd. W4 —7A 82
Promenade, The. W4 —2A 100
Promenade, The. Edgw —5B 12
Prospect Clo. SE26 —4H 123
Prospect Clo. Belv —4G 93
Prospect Clo. Houn —1D 96
Prospect Clo. Ruis —7B 24
Prospect Cotts. SW18 —4J 101
Prospect Cres. Twic —6G 97
Prospect Hill. E17 —4D 34
Prospect Ho. E17 —3E 34
(off Prospect Hill)
Prospect Ho. N1 —2A 68
(off Donegal St.)
Prospect Ho. SE1 —3B 86
(off Gaywood St.)
Prospect Pl. E1 —1J 87
Prospect Pl. N2 —4B 30
Prospect Pl. N7 —4J 49
Prospect Pl. N17 —7K 17
Prospect Pl. NW2 —3H 47
Prospect Pl. NW3 —4A 48
Prospect Pl. SW20 —7D 118
Prospect Pl. W4 —5K 81
Prospect Pl. Brom —3K 143
Prospect Pl. Romf —2J 39
Prospect Quay. SW18 —4J 101
(off Lightermans Wlk.)
Prospect Ring. N2 —3B 30
Prospect Rd. NW2 —3H 47
Prospect Rd. Barn —4D 4
Prospect Rd. Surb —6C 134
Prospect Rd. Wfd G —6F 21
Prospect St. SE16 —3H 87
Prospect Va. SE18 —4C 90
Prospect Wharf. E1 —7J 69
Prospero Rd. N19 —1H 49
Protea Clo. E16 —4H 71
Protheroe Ho. N17 —3F 33
Prothero Gdns. NW4 —5D 28
Prothero Ho. NW10 —7K 45
Prothero Rd. SW6 —7G 83
Prout Gro. NW10 —4A 46
Prout Rd. E5 —3H 51
Provence St. N1 —2C 68
Providence Clo. E9 —1K 69
Providence Ct. W1 —7E 66 (2H 165)
Providence La. Hay —7F 77
Providence Pl. N1 —1B 68
Providence Pl. Romf —1F 39
Providence Rd. W Dray —1A 76
Providence Row. N1 —1G 161
Providence Row Clo. E2 —3H 69
Providence Sq. SE1 —2G 87 (6K 169)
Providence Tower. SE16 —2G 87
(off Bermondsey Wall W.)
Providence Yd. E2 —3G 69 (1K 163)
(off Ezra St.)
Provost Est. N1 —1E 162
Provost Rd. NW3 —7D 48
Provost St. N1 —2D 68 (1E 162)
Prowse Av. Bus H —1B 10
Prowse Pl. NW1 —7G 49
Proyers Path. Harr —7B 26
Pruden Clo. N14 —2B 16
Prudent Pas. EC2 —7D 162
Prusom St. E1 —1H 87
Pryors, The. NW3 —3B 48
Public Record Office. —7H 81
Pudding La. EC3 —7D 68 (3F 169)
Pudding Mill La. E15 —1D 70
Puddle Dock. EC4 —7B 68 (2A 168)
(in two parts)
Puffin Clo. Beck —5K 141
Pugin Ct. N1 —7A 50
(off Liverpool Rd.)
Pulborough Rd. SW18 —7H 101
Pulborough Way. Houn —4A 96
Pulford Rd. N15 —6D 32
Pulham Av. N2 —4A 30
Pulham Ho. SW8 —7K 85
(off Dorset Rd.)
Pullen's Bldgs. SE17 —5B 86
(off Iliffe St.)
Puller Rd. Barn —2B 4
Pulleyns Av. E6 —3C 72
Pullman Ct. SW2 —1J 121
Pullman Gdns. SW15 —6E 100
Pullman M. SE12 —3K 125
Pullman Pl. SE9 —5C 108
Pulross Rd. SW9 —3K 103
Pulteney Clo. E3 —1B 70
Pulteney Gdns. E18 —3K 35
Pulteney Rd. E18 —3K 35
Pulteney Ter. N1 —1K 67
(in two parts)
Pulton Ho. SE4 —4A 106
(off Turnham Rd.)
Pulton Pl. SW6 —7J 83
Puma Ct. E1 —5F 69 (5J 163)
Pump All. Bren —7D 80
Pump Clo. N'holt —2E 60
Pump Ct. EC4 —6A 68 (1J 167)
Pump Ho. Clo. Brom —2G 143
Pumping Sta. Rd. W4 —7A 82
Pump La. SE14 —7J 87
Pump La. Hay —2H 77
Pump La. Ind. Est. Hay —2J 77
Pump Pail N. Croy —3C 152
Pump Pail S. Croy —3C 152
Punderson's Gdns. E2 —3H 69
Punjab La. S'hall —1D 78
Purbeck Av. N Mald —6B 136
Purbeck Dri. NW2 —2F 47
Purbeck Ho. SW8 —7K 85
(off Bolney St.)
Purbrook Est. SE1 —2E 86 (7H 169)
Purbrook St. SE1 —3E 86 (7H 169)
Purcell Cres. SW6 —7F 83
Purcell Ho. SW10 —6B 84
(off Milman's St.)
Purcell Mans. W14 —6G 83
(off Queen's Club Gdns.)
Purcell M. NW10 —7A 46
Purcell Rd. Gnfd —5F 61
Purcells Av. Edgw —5B 12
Purcell St. N1 —2E 68
Purchese St. NW1 —2H 67 (1D 160)
Purdon Ho. SE15 —1G 105
(off Peckham High St.)
Purdy Ct. Wor Pk —2C 148
Purdy St. E3 —4D 70
Purelake M. SE13 —3F 107
(off Marischal Rd.)
Purland Clo. Dag —1F 57
Purland Rd. SE28 —2K 91
Purleigh Av. Wfd G —6H 21
Purley Av. NW2 —2G 47
Purley Clo. Ilf —2E 36
Purley Pl. N1 —7B 50
Purley Rd. N9 —3K 17
Purley Rd. S Croy —7D 152
Purley Vw. Ter. S Croy —7D 152
(off Sanderstead Rd.)
Purley Way. Croy & Purl —7K 139
Purley Way Cen., The. Croy —2A 152
Purley Way Corner. Croy —7K 139
Purley Way Cres. Croy —7K 139
Purneys Rd. SE9 —4B 108
Purrett Rd. SE18 —5K 91
Purser Ho. SW2 —6A 104
(off Tulse Hill)
Pursers Cross Rd. SW6 —1H 101
(in two parts)
Purse Wardens Clo. W13 —1C 80
Pursley Rd. NW7 —7J 13
Purves Rd. NW10 —3D 64
Pusey Ho. E14 —6C 70
Putney. —4G 101
Putney Bri. SW15 & SW6 —3G 101
Putney Bri. App. SW6 —3G 101
Putney Bri. Rd. SW15 & SW18 —4G 101
Putney Comn. SW15 —3E 100
Putney Exchange Shop. Cen. SW15 —4F 101
Putney Gdns. Chad H —5B 38
Putney Heath. —6E 100
Putney Heath. SW15 —7D 100
Putney Heath La. SW15 —6F 101
Putney High St. SW15 —4F 101
Putney Hill. SW15 —7F 101
(in two parts)
Putney Pk. Av. SW15 —4C 100
Putney Pk. La. SW15 —4D 100
Putney Vale. —3C 118
Putney Vale Crematorium. SW15 —2C 118
Pycroft Way. N9 —4A 18
Pyecombe Corner. N12 —4C 14
Pylbrook Rd. Sutt —3J 149
Pylon Trad. Est. E16 —4G 71
Pylon Way. Croy —1J 151
Pym Clo. E Barn —5G 5
Pymers Mead. SE21 —1C 122
Pym Ho. SW9 —2A 104
Pymmes Brook Ho. N10 —7K 15
Pymmes Clo. N13 —5E 16
Pymmes Clo. N17 —1H 33
Pymmes Gdns. N. N9 —3A 18
Pymmes Gdns. S. N9 —3A 18
Pymmes Grn. Rd. N11 —4A 16
Pymmes Rd. N13 —6D 16
Pymms Brook Dri. Barn —4H 5
Pynchester Clo. Uxb —2C 40
Pyne Rd. Surb —1G 147
Pynfolds. SE16 —2H 87
Pynham Clo. SE2 —3B 92
Pynnacles Clo. Stan —5G 11
Pynnersmead. SE24 —5C 104
Pyramid Ho. Houn —2C 96
Pyrford Ho. SW9 —4B 104
Pyrland Rd. N5 —5D 50
Pyrland Rd. Rich —6F 99
Pyrmont Gro. SE27 —3B 122
Pyrmont Rd. W4 —6G 81
Pytchley Cres. SE19 —6C 122
Pytchley Rd. SE22 —3E 104

Quadrangle Clo. SE1 —4E 86
Quadrangle, The. SE24 —5C 104
Quadrangle, The. SW10 —1A 102
Quadrangle, The. W2 —6C 66 (7C 158)

Ramsey Clo. Gnfd —5H 43
Ramsey Ho. SW9 —7A 86
(off Vassall Rd.)
Ramsey Rd. T Hth —6K 139
Ramsey St. E2 —4G 69
Ramsey Wlk. N1 —6D 50
(off Handa Wlk.)
Ramsey Way. N14 —7B 6
Ramsfort Ho. SE16 —4H 87
(off Camilla Rd.)
Ramsgate Clo. E16 —1K 89
Ramsgate St. E8 —6F 51
Ramsgill App. Ilf —4K 37
Ramsgill Dri. Ilf —5K 37
Rams Gro. Romf —4E 38
Ram St. SW18 —5K 101
Ramulis Dri. Hay —4B 60
Rancliffe Gdns. SE9 —4C 108
Rancliffe Rd. E6 —2C 72
Randall Av. NW2 —2A 46
Randall Clo. SW11 —1C 102
Randall Clo. Eri —6J 93
Randall Ct. NW7 —7H 13
Randall Pl. SE10 —7E 88
Randall Rd. SE11 —5K 85 (4G 173)
Randall Row. SE11 —4K 85 (4G 173)
Randell's Rd. N1 —1J 67
(in two parts)
Randisbourne Gdns. SE6 —3D 124
Randle Rd. Rich —4C 116
Randlesdown Rd. SE6 —4C 124
(in two parts)
Randolph App. E16 —6A 72
Randolph Av. W9 —2K 65 (4A 158)
Randolph Clo. Bexh —3J 111
Randolph Clo. King T —5J 117
Randolph Cres. W9 —4A 66
Randolph Gdns. NW6 —2K 65
Randolph Gro. Romf —5C 38
Randolph M. W9 —4A 66
Randolph Rd. E17 —5D 34
Randolph Rd. W9 —4A 66
Randolph Rd. Brom —1D 156
Randolph Rd. S'hall —2D 78
Randolph St. NW1 —7G 49
Randon Clo. Harr —2F 25
Ranelagh Av. SW6 —3H 101
Ranelagh Av. SW13 —2C 100
Ranelagh Bri. W2 —5K 65
Ranelagh Clo. Edgw —4B 12
Ranelagh Dri. Edgw —4B 12
Ranelagh Dri. Twic —4B 98
Ranelagh Gdns. E11 —5A 36
Ranelagh Gdns. SW6 —3G 101
Ranelagh Gdns. W4 —7J 81
Ranelagh Gdns. W6 —4B 82
Ranelagh Gdns. Ilf —1D 54
Ranelagh Gdns. Mans. SW6 —3G 101
(off Ranelagh Gdns.)
Ranelagh Gro. SW1 —5E 84 (5H 171)
Ranelagh Ho. SW3 —5D 84 (5E 170)
(off Elystan Pl.)
Ranelagh M. W5 —2D 80
Ranelagh Pl. N Mald —5A 136
Ranelagh Rd. E6 —1E 72
Ranelagh Rd. E11 —4G 53
Ranelagh Rd. E15 —2G 71
Ranelagh Rd. N17 —3E 32
Ranelagh Rd. N22 —1K 31
Ranelagh Rd. NW10 —2B 64
Ranelagh Rd. SW1 —5G 85 (6B 172)
Ranelagh Rd. W5 —2D 80
Ranelagh Rd. S'hall —1B 78
Ranelagh Rd. Wemb —6D 44
Ranfurly Rd. Sutt —2J 149
Rangbourne Ho. N7 —5J 49
Rangefield Rd. Brom —5G 125
Rangemoor Rd. N15 —5F 33
Ranger's House. —1F 107
Ranger's Rd. E4 —1B 20
Rangers Sq. SE10 —1F 107
Range Way. Shep —7C 130
Rangeworth Pl. Sidc —3K 127
Rangoon St. EC3 —1J 169
Rankin Clo. NW9 —3A 28
Rankine Ho. SE1 —3C 86
(off Bath Ter.)
Ranleigh Gdns. Bexh —7F 93
Ranmere St. SW12 —1F 121
Ranmoor Clo. Harr —4H 25
Ranmoor Gdns. Harr —4H 25
Ranmore Av. Croy —3F 153
Ranmore Path. Orp —4K 145
Ranmore Rd. Sutt —7F 149
Rannoch Clo. Edgw —2C 12
Rannoch Rd. W6 —6E 82
Rannock Av. NW9 —7K 27
Ransome's Dock Bus. Cen. SW11 —7C 84
Ransom Rd. SE7 —4A 90
Ranston St. NW1 —5C 66 (5C 158)
Ranulf Rd. NW2 —4H 47
Ranwell Clo. E3 —1B 70
Ranworth Rd. N9 —2D 18
Ranyard Clo. Chess —3F 147
Rapesco Ho. SE14 —7A 88
(off Goodwood Rd.)
Raphael Dri. Th Dit —7K 133
Raphael St. SW7 —2D 84 (7E 164)
Rapley Ho. E2 —3G 69 (2K 163)
(off Turin St.)
Rashleigh Ct. SW8 —2F 103
Rashleigh Ho. WC1 —3J 67 (2E 160)
(off Thanet St.)
Rasper Rd. N20 —2F 15
Rastell Av. SW2 —2H 121
Ratcliff. —6A 70
Ratcliffe Clo. SE12 —7J 107
Ratcliffe Cross St. E1 —6K 69
Ratcliffe Ho. E14 —6A 70
Ratcliffe La. E1 —6A 70
Ratcliffe La. E14 —6A 70
Ratcliffe Orchard. E1 —7K 69
Ratcliff Rd. E7 —5A 54
Rathbone Ho. NW6 —1J 65
Rathbone Mkt. E16 —5H 71
Rathbone Pl. W1 —5H 67 (6C 160)
Rathbone Point. E5 —4G 51
Rathbone Sq. Croy —4C 152
Rathbone St. E16 —5H 71
Rathbone St. W1 —5G 67 (6B 160)
Rathcoole Av. N8 —5K 31
Rathcoole Gdns. N8 —5K 31
Rathfern Rd. SE6 —1B 124
Rathgar Av. W13 —1B 80
Rathgar Clo. N3 —2H 29
Rathgar Rd. SW9 —3B 104
Rathlin Wlk. N1 —6D 50
Rathmell Dri. SW4 —6H 103
Rathmore Rd. SE7 —5K 89
Rattray Ct. SE6 —2H 125
Rattray Rd. SW2 —4A 104
Raul Rd. SE15 —2G 105
Raveley St. NW5 —4G 49
(in two parts)
Raven Clo. NW9 —2A 28
Ravendale Rd. Sun —2H 131
Ravenet St. SW11 —1F 103
Ravenfield Rd. SW17 —3D 120
Ravenhill Rd. E13 —2A 72
Ravenings Pde. Ilf —1A 56
Ravenna Rd. SW15 —5F 101
Ravenor Ct. Gnfd —4F 61
Ravenor Pk. Rd. Gnfd —3F 61
Raven Rd. E18 —2A 36
Raven Row. E1 —5H 69
Ravensbourne Av. Brom —7F 125
Ravensbourne Av. Stai —1A 112
Ravensbourne Ct. SE6 —7C 106
Ravensbourne Gdns. W13 —5B 62
Ravensbourne Gdns. Ilf —1E 36
Ravensbourne Ho. NW8
(off Broadley St.) —5C 66 (5C 158)
Ravensbourne Ho. Brom —5F 125
Ravensbourne Pk. SE6 —7C 106
Ravensbourne Pk. Cres. SE6 —7B 106
Ravensbourne Pl. SE13 —2D 106
Ravensbourne Rd. SE6 —7B 106
Ravensbourne Rd. Brom —3J 143
Ravensbourne Rd. Twic —6C 98
Ravensbury Av. Mord —5A 138
Ravensbury Ct. Mitc —4B 138
(off Ravensbury Gro.)
Ravensbury Gro. Mitc —4B 138
Ravensbury La. Mitc —4B 138
Ravensbury Path. Mitc —4B 138
Ravensbury Rd. SW18 —2J 119
Ravensbury Rd. Orp —3K 145
Ravensbury Ter. SW18 —2K 119
Ravenscar. NW1 —1G 67
(off Bayham St.)
Ravenscar Rd. Brom —4G 125
Ravenscar Rd. Surb —2F 147
Ravens Clo. Brom —2H 143
Ravens Clo. Enf —2K 7
Ravens Clo. Surb —6D 134
Ravenscourt. Sun —1H 131
Ravenscourt Av. W6 —4C 82
Ravenscourt Clo. Ruis —7E 22
Ravenscourt Gdns. W6 —4C 82
Ravenscourt Pk. W6 —3C 82
Ravenscourt Pk. Barn —4A 4
Ravenscourt Pk. Mans. W6 —3D 82
(off Paddenswick Rd.)
Ravenscourt Pl. W6 —4D 82
Ravenscourt Rd. W6 —4D 82
(in two parts)
Ravenscourt Sq. W6 —3C 82
Ravenscraig Rd. N11 —4B 16
Ravenscroft Av. NW11 —7H 29
Ravenscroft Av. Wemb —1E 44
Ravenscroft Clo. E16 —5J 71
Ravenscroft Cotts. Barn —4D 4
Ravenscroft Cres. SE9 —3D 126
Ravenscroft Pk. Barn —3A 4
Ravenscroft Rd. E16 —5J 71
Ravenscroft Rd. W4 —4J 81
Ravenscroft Rd. Beck —2J 141
Ravenscroft St. E2 —2F 69 (1K 163)
Ravensdale Av. N12 —4F 15
Ravensdale Gdns. SE19 —7D 122
Ravensdale Rd. N16 —7F 33
Ravensdale Rd. Houn —3C 96
Ravensdon St. SE11 —5A 86 (6K 173)
Ravensfield Clo. Dag —4D 56
Ravensfield Gdns. Eps —5A 148
Ravenshaw St. NW6 —5H 47
Ravenshill. Chst —1F 145
Ravenshurst Av. NW4 —4E 28
Ravenside Clo. N18 —5E 18
Ravenside Retail Pk. N18 —5E 18
Ravenslea Rd. SW12 —7D 102
Ravensleigh Gdns. Brom —5K 125
Ravensmead Rd. Brom —7F 125
Ravensmede Way. W4 —4B 82
Ravens M. SE12 —5J 107
Ravenstone. SE17 —5E 86
Ravenstone Rd. N8 —3A 32
Ravenstone Rd. NW9 —6B 28
Ravenstone St. SW12 —1E 120
Ravens Way. SE12 —5J 107
Ravenswood. Bex —1E 128
Ravenswood Av. Surb —2F 147
Ravenswood Av. W W'ck —1E 154
Ravenswood Ct. King T —6H 117
Ravenswood Cres. Harr —2D 42
Ravenswood Cres. W W'ck —1E 154
Ravenswood Gdns. Iswth —1J 97
Ravenswood Ind. Est. E17 —4E 34
Ravenswood Rd. E17 —4E 34
Ravenswood Rd. SW12 —7F 103
Ravenswood Rd. Croy —3B 152
Ravensworth Rd. NW10 —3D 64
Ravensworth Rd. SE9 —3D 126
Ravent Rd. SE11 —4K 85 (3H 173)
Ravey St. EC2 —4E 68 (3G 163)
Ravine Gro. SE18 —6J 91
Rav Pinter Clo. N16 —7E 32
Rawalpindi Ho. E16 —4H 71
Rawchester Clo. SW18 —1H 119
Rawlings St. SW3 —4D 84 (3E 170)
Rawlins Clo. N3 —3G 29
Rawlins Clo. S Croy —7A 154
Rawlinson Ct. NW2 —7E 28
Rawlinson Ho. SE13 —4F 107
(off Mercator Rd.)
Rawlinson Point. E16 —5H 71
(off Fox Rd.)
Rawlinson Ter. N17 —3F 33
Rawnsley Av. Mitc —5B 138
Rawreth Wlk. N1 —1C 68
(off Basire St.)
Rawson St. SW11 —1E 102
(in two parts)
Rawsthorne Clo. E16 —1D 90
Rawsthorne Ct. Houn —4D 96
Rawstone Wlk. E13 —2J 71
Rawstorne Pl. EC1 —3B 68 (1A 162)
Rawstorne St. EC1 —3B 68 (1A 162)
Raybell Ct. Iswth —2K 97
Rayburne Ct. W14 —3G 83
Rayburne Ct. Buck H —1F 21
Ray Clo. Chess —6C 146
Raydean Rd. New Bar —5E 4
Raydons Gdns. Dag —4E 56
Raydons Rd. Dag —5E 56
Raydon St. N19 —2F 49
Rayfield Clo. Brom —6C 144
Rayford Av. SE12 —7H 107
Ray Gdns. Bark —2A 74
Ray Gdns. Stan —5G 11
Ray Gunter Ho. SE17 —5B 86
(off Marsland Clo.)
Ray Ho. N1 —1D 68
(off Colville Est.)
Rayleas Clo. SE18 —1F 109
Rayleigh Av. Tedd —6J 115
Rayleigh Clo. N13 —3J 17
Rayleigh Ct. N22 —1C 32
Rayleigh Ct. King T —2G 135
Rayleigh Ri. S Croy —6E 152
Rayleigh Rd. E16 —1K 89
Rayleigh Rd. N13 —3H 17
Rayleigh Rd. SW19 —1H 137
Rayleigh Rd. Wfd G —6F 21
Ray Lodge Rd. Wfd G —6F 21
Ray Massey Way. E6 —1C 72
(off High St. N.)
Raymead Av. T Hth —5A 140
Raymede Towers. W10 —5F 65
(off Treverton St.)
Raymere Gdns. SE18 —7H 91
Raymond Av. E18 —3H 35
Raymond Av. W13 —3A 80
Raymond Bldgs. WC1 —5K 67 (5H 161)
Raymond Clo. SE26 —5J 123
Raymond Ct. N10 —7A 16
Raymond Ct. Sutt —6K 149
Raymond Postage Ct. SE28 —7B 74
Raymond Rd. E13 —1A 72
Raymond Rd. SW19 —6G 119
Raymond Rd. Beck —4A 142
Raymond Rd. Ilf —7H 37
Raymond Way. Clay —6A 146
Raymouth Ho. SE16 —4J 87
(off Rotherhithe New Rd.)
Raymouth Rd. SE16 —4H 87
Raynald Ho. SW16 —3J 121
Rayne Ct. E18 —4H 35
Rayne Ho. W9 —4K 65
(off Delaware Rd.)
Rayners Clo. Wemb —5D 44
Rayners Cres. N'holt —3K 59
Rayners Gdns. N'holt —2K 59
Rayners Lane. —1D 42
Rayners La. Pinn & Harr —5D 24
Rayners Rd. SW15 —5G 101
Rayner Towers. E10 —7C 34
(off Albany Rd.)
Raynes Av. E11 —7A 36
Raynes Park. —4E 136
Raynes Pk. Bri. SW20 —2E 136
Raynham. W2 —6C 66 (7D 158)
(off Norfolk Cres.)
Raynham Av. N18 —6B 18
Raynham Rd. N18 —5B 18
Raynham Rd. W6 —4D 82
Raynham Ter. N18 —5B 18
Raynor Clo. S'hall —1D 78
Raynor Pl. N1 —7C 50
Raynton Clo. Harr —1C 42
Raynton Clo. Hay —4H 59
Raynton Dri. Hay —4H 59
Ray Rd. W Mol —5F 133
Rays Av. N18 —4D 18
Rays Rd. N18 —4D 18
Rays Rd. W W'ck —7E 142
Ray St. EC1 —4A 68 (4K 161)
Ray St. Bri. EC1 —4K 161
Ray Wlk. N7 —2K 49
Raywood Clo. Hay —7E 76
Reachview Clo. NW1 —7G 49
Read Clo. Th Dit —7A 134
Read Ct. E17 —6C 34
Reade Ct. W3 —3J 81
(off Stanley Rd.)
Reade Wlk. NW10 —7A 46
Read Ho. SE11 —7J 173
Reading Ho. SE15 —6G 87
(off Friary Est.)
Reading Ho. W2 —6A 66
(off Hallfield Est.)
Reading La. E8 —6H 51
Reading Rd. N'holt —5F 43
Reading Rd. Sutt —5A 150
Reading Way. NW7 —5A 14
Reads Clo. Ilf —3F 55
Reapers Clo. NW1 —1H 67
Reapers Way. Iswth —5H 97
Reardon Ct. N21 —2G 17
Reardon Path. E1 —1H 87
Reardon St. E1 —1H 87
Reaston St. SE14 —7K 87
Rebecca Ct. Sidc —4B 128
Reckitt Rd. W4 —5A 82
Record St. SE15 —6J 87
Recovery St. SW17 —5C 120
Recreation Av. Romf —5J 39
Recreation Rd. SE26 —4K 123
Recreation Rd. Brom —2H 143
Recreation Rd. Sidc —3J 127
Recreation Rd. S'hall —4C 78
Recreation Way. Mitc —3H 139
Rector St. N1 —1C 68
Rectory Bus. Cen. Sidc —4B 128
Rectory Clo. E4 —3H 19
Rectory Clo. N3 —1H 29
Rectory Clo. SW20 —3E 136
Rectory Clo. Shep —3C 130
Rectory Clo. Sidc —4B 128
Rectory Clo. Stan —6G 11
Rectory Clo. Surb —1C 146
Rectory Ct. E18 —1H 35
Rectory Ct. Felt —4A 114
Rectory Ct. Wall —4G 151
Rectory Cres. E11 —6A 36
(in two parts)
Rectory Farm Rd. Enf —1E 6
Rectory Fld. Cres. SE7 —7A 90
Rectory Gdns. N8 —4J 31
Rectory Gdns. SW4 —3G 103
Rectory Gdns. Beck —1C 142
(off Rectory Rd.)
Rectory Gdns. N'holt —1D 60
Rectory Grn. Beck —1B 142
Rectory Gro. SW4 —3G 103
Rectory Gro. Croy —2B 152
Rectory Gro. Hamp —4D 114
Rectory La. SW17 —6E 120
Rectory La. Edgw —6B 12
Rectory La. Sidc —4B 128
Rectory La. Stan —5G 11
Rectory La. Surb —1B 146
Rectory La. Wall —4G 151
Rectory Orchard. SW19 —4G 119
Rectory Pk. Av. N'holt —3D 60
Rectory Pl. SE18 —4E 90
Rectory Rd. E12 —5D 54
Rectory Rd. E17 —4D 34
Rectory Rd. N16 —2F 51
Rectory Rd. SW13 —2C 100
Rectory Rd. W3 —1H 81
Rectory Rd. Beck —2C 142
Rectory Rd. Dag —6H 57
Rectory Rd. Hay —6J 59
Rectory Rd. Houn —2A 96
Rectory Rd. Kes —7B 156
Rectory Rd. S'hall —3D 78
Rectory Rd. Sutt —3J 149
Rectory Sq. E1 —5K 69
Rectory Way. Uxb —2D 40
Reculver Ho. SE15 —6J 87
(off Lovelinch Clo.)
Reculver M. N18 —4B 18
Reculver Rd. SE16 —5K 87
Red Anchor Clo. SW3 —6B 84 (7B 170)
Redan Pl. W2 —6K 65
Redan St. W14 —3F 83
Redan Ter. SE5 —2B 104
Red Barracks Rd. SE18 —4D 90
Redberry Gro. SE26 —3J 123
Redbourne Av. N3 —1J 29
Redbourne Dri. SE28 —6D 74
Redbourne Ho. E14 —6B 70
Redbridge. —6B 36
Redbridge Enterprise Cen. Ilf —2G 55
Redbridge Gdns. SE5 —7E 86
Redbridge La. E. Ilf —6B 36
Redbridge La. W. E11 —6K 35
Redbridge Roundabout. (Junct.) —6B 36
Redburn St. SW3 —6D 84 (7E 170)
Redburn Trad. Est. Enf —6E 8
Redcar Clo. N'holt —5F 43
Redcar St. SE5 —7C 86
Redcastle Clo. E1 —7J 69
Red Cedars Rd. Orp —7J 145
Redchurch St. E1 —4F 69 (3J 163)
Redcliffe Clo. SW5 —5K 83
(off Old Brompton Rd.)
Redcliffe Gdns. SW5 & SW10 —5K 83
Redcliffe Gdns. W4 —7H 81
Redcliffe Gdns. Ilf —1E 54
Redcliffe M. SW10 —5K 83
Redcliffe Pl. SW10 —6A 84
Redcliffe Rd. SW10 —5A 84
Redcliffe Sq. SW10 —5K 83
Redcliffe St. SW10 —6K 83
Redcliffe Wlk. Wemb —3H 45
Redclose Av. Mord —5J 137
Redclyffe Rd. E6 —1A 72
Redcourt. Croy —3E 152
Redcroft Rd. S'hall —7G 61
Redcross Way. SE1 —2C 86 (6D 168)
Redding Ho. SE18 —3C 90
Reddings Clo. NW7 —4G 13
Reddings, The. NW7 —3G 13
Reddins Rd. SE15 —6G 87
Reddons Rd. Beck —7A 124
Redenham Ho. SW15 —7C 100
(off Ellisfield Dri.)
Rede Pl. W2 —6J 65
Redesdale Gdns. Iswth —7A 80
Redesdale St. SW3 —6C 84 (7D 170)
Redfern Av. Houn —7E 96
Redfern Ho. E15 —1H 71
(off Redriffe Rd.)
Redfern Rd. NW10 —7A 46
Redfern Rd. SE6 —7E 106
Redfield La. SW5 —4J 83
Redfield M. SW5 —4K 83
Redford Av. T Hth —4K 139
Redford Av. Wall —6J 151
Redford Clo. Felt —2H 113
Redford Wlk. N1 —1C 68
(off Popham St.)
Redgate Dri. Brom —2K 155
Redgate Ter. SW15 —6F 101
Redgrave Clo. Croy —6F 141
Redgrave Rd. SW15 —3F 101
Redgrave Ter. E2 —3G 69
(off Derbyshire St.)
Red Hill. Chst —5F 127
Redhill Ct. SW2 —2A 122
Redhill Dri. Edgw —2J 27
Redhill St. NW1 —2F 67 (1K 159)
Red Ho. La. Bexh —4D 110
Redhouse Rd. Croy —6H 139
Red Ho. Sq. N1 —7C 50
(off Ashby Gro.)
Redington Gdns. NW3 —4K 47
Redington Ho. N1 —2K 67
(off Priory Grn. Est.)
Redington Rd. NW3 —3K 47
Redland Gdns. W Mol —4D 132
Redlands. N15 —4D 32
Redlands. Tedd —6A 116
Redlands Ct. Brom —7H 125
Redlands Rd. Enf —1F 9
Redlands, The. Beck —2D 142
Redlands Way. SW2 —7K 103
Red La. Clay —6A 146
Redleaf Clo. Belv —6G 93
Redleaves Av. Ashf —6D 112
Redlees Clo. Iswth —4A 98
Red Leys. Uxb —7A 40
Red Lion Bus. Pk. Surb —3F 147
Red Lion Clo. SE17 —6D 86
(off Red Lion Row)
Red Lion Ct. EC4 —6A 68 (1K 167)
Red Lion Ct. SE1 —1C 86 (4D 168)
Red Lion Hill. N2 —2B 30
Red Lion La. SE18 —7E 90
Red Lion Pde. Pinn —3C 24
Red Lion Pl. SE18 —1E 108
Red Lion Rd. Surb —2F 147
Red Lion Row. SE17 —6C 86
Red Lion Sq. SW18 —5J 101
Red Lion Sq. WC1 —5K 67 (6G 161)
Red Lion St. WC1 —5K 67 (5G 161)
Red Lion St. Rich —5D 98
Red Lion Yd. W1 —4H 165
Red Lodge. W W'ck —1E 154
Red Lodge Cres. Bex —3K 129
Red Lodge Rd. Bex —3K 129
Red Lodge Rd. W W'ck —1E 154
Redman Clo. N'holt —2A 60
Redman Ho. EC1 —5A 68 (5J 161)
(off Bourne Est.)
Redman Ho. SE1 —2C 86 (7D 168)
(off Borough High St.)
Redman's Rd. E1 —5J 69
Redmead La. E1 —1G 87
Redmead Rd. Hay —4G 77
Redmond Ho. N1 —1K 67
(off Barnsbury Est.)
Redmore Rd. W6 —4D 82
Redo Ho. E12 —5E 54
(off Dore Av.)
Red Path. E9 —6A 52
Red Pl. W1 —7E 66 (2G 165)
Redpoll Way. Eri —3D 92
Red Post Hill. SE24 & SE21 —4D 104
Red Post Ho. E6 —7B 54
Redriffe Rd. E13 —1H 71
Redriff Est. SE16 —3B 88
Redriff Rd. SE16 —4K 87
Redriff Rd. Romf —2H 39
Redroofs Clo. Beck —1D 142
Redrose Trad. Cen. Barn —5G 5
Red Rover. (Junct.) —4C 100
Redruth Clo. N22 —7E 16
Redruth Ho. Sutt —7K 149
Redruth Rd. E9 —1J 69
Redstart Clo. E6 —5C 72
Redstart Clo. SE14 —7A 88
Redston Rd. N8 —4H 31
Redvers Rd. N22 —2A 32
Redvers St. N1 —3E 68 (1H 163)
Redwald Rd. E5 —4K 51
Redway Dri. Twic —7G 97
Redwing Path. SE28 —2H 91
Redwing Rd. Wall —6K 151
Redwood Clo. N14 —7C 6
Redwood Clo. SE16 —1A 88
Redwood Clo. Buck H —2E 20
Redwood Clo. Sidc —7A 110
Redwood Clo. Uxb —2D 58
Redwood Ct. N19 —7H 31
Redwood Ct. NW6 —7G 47
Redwood Ct. N'holt —3C 60
Redwood Ct. Surb —7D 134
Redwood Est. Houn —6K 77
Redwood Gdns. E4 —6J 9
Redwood Mans. W8 —3K 83
(off Chantry Sq.)
Redwood M. SW4 —3F 103
Redwoods. SW15 —1C 118
Redwood Wlk. Surb —1D 146
Redwood Way. Barn —5A 4
Reece M. SW7 —4B 84 (3A 170)
Reed Clo. E16 —5J 71
Reed Clo. SE12 —5J 107
Reede Gdns. Dag —5H 57
Reede Rd. Dag —6G 57
Reede Way. Dag —6H 57
Reedham Clo. N17 —4H 33
Reedham St. SE15 —2G 105
Reedholm Vs. N16 —4D 50
Reed Rd. N17 —2F 33
Reedsfield Clo. Ashf —4D 112
Reedsfield Rd. Ashf —4D 112
Reed's Pl. NW1 —7G 49
Reedworth St. SE11 —4A 86 (4K 173)
Reef Ho. E14 —3E 88
Reenglass Rd. Stan —4J 11
Rees Dri. Stan —4K 11
Rees Gdns. Croy —6F 141
Reesland Clo. E12 —6E 54
Rees St. N1 —1C 68
Reets Farm Clo. NW9 —6A 28
Reeves Av. NW9 —7K 27
Reeves Corner. Croy —2B 152
Reeves Ho. SE1 —2A 86 (7J 167)
(off Baylis Rd.)
Reeves M. W1 —7E 66 (3G 165)
Reeves Path. Hay —4H 77
Reeves Rd. E3 —4D 70
Reeves Rd. SE18 —6F 91
Reform Row. N17 —2F 33
Reform St. SW11 —2D 102
Regal Clo. E1 —5G 69
Regal Clo. W5 —5D 62
Regal Ct. N18 —5A 18
Regal Cres. Wall —3F 151
Regal Dri. N11 —5A 16
Regal La. NW1 —1E 66
Regal Pl. E3 —3B 70
Regal Pl. SW6 —7K 83
(off Maxwell Rd.)
Regal Row. SE15 —1J 105
Regal Way. Harr —6E 26

Regan Ho.—River Barge Clo.

Regan Ho. N18 —6A 18
Regan Way. N1 —2E 68 (1G 163)
Regatta Ho. Tedd —4A 116
Regatta Point. Bren —6F 81
Regency Clo. W5 —6E 62
Regency Clo. Hamp —5D 114
Regency Ct. Enf —5J 7
Regency Ct. Sutt —4K 149
Regency Ct. Tedd —6B 116
Regency Cres. NW4 —2F 29
Regency Dri. Ruis —1G 41
Regency Gdns. W on T —7A 132
Regency Ho. NW1 —4F 67 (3K 159)
(off Osnaburgh St.)
Regency Lawn. NW5 —3F 49
Regency Lodge. NW3 —7B 48
(off Adelaide Rd.)
Regency Lodge. Buck H —2G 21
Regency M. NW10 —6C 46
Regency M. Beck —7E 124
Regency M. Iswth —5J 97
Regency Pl. SW1 —4H 85 (3D 172)
Regency St. SW1 —4H 85 (3D 172)
Regency Ter. SW7 —5B 84
(off Fulham Rd.)
Regency Wlk. Croy —6A 142
Regency Wlk. Rich —5E 98
(off Grosvenor Av.)
Regency Way. Bexh —3D 110
Regent Av. Uxb —7D 40
Regent Bus. Cen. Hay —2K 77
Regent Clo. N12 —5F 15
Regent Clo. Harr —6E 26
Regent Clo. Houn —1K 95
Regent Ct. N3 —7E 14
Regent Ct. N20 —2F 15
Regent Ct. NW8 —2C 158
Regent Gdns. Ilf —7A 38
Regent Ho. W14 —4G 83
(off Windsor Way)
Regent Pl. SW19 —5A 120
Regent Pl. W1 —7G 67 (2B 166)
Regent Pl. Croy —1F 153
Regent Rd. SE24 —6B 104
Regent Rd. Surb —5F 135
Regents Av. N13 —5F 17
Regent's Bri. Gdns. SW8 —7J 85
Regents Canal Ho. E14 —6A 70
Regents Clo. Hay —5H 59
Regents Clo. S Croy —6E 152
Regents Clo. Stan —4K 11
Regents Ct. E8 —1F 69
(off Pownall Rd.)
Regents Ct. Brom —7H 125
Regent's Ct. King T —1E 134
(off Sopwith Way)
Regents Dri. Kes —5B 156
Regents Ho. Ga. E14 —7A 70
Regents M. NW8 —2A 66
Regent's Park. —2F 67 (1K 159)
Regent's Pk. —2D 66 (1F 159)
Regent's Pk. Est. NW1 —1A 160
Regent's Pk. Gdns. M. NW1 —1D 66
Regent's Pk. Ho. NW8 —3C 66 (2D 158)
(off Park Rd.)
Regent's Pk. Open Air Theatre. —3E 66 (2G 159)
Regents Pk. Rd. N3 —3H 29
Regent's Pk. Rd. NW1 —7D 48
(in two parts)
Regent's Pk. Ter. NW1 —1F 67
Regent's Pl. SE3 —2J 107
Regents Plaza. NW6 —2K 65
(off Kilburn High Rd.)
Regent Sq. E3 —3D 70
Regent Sq. WC1 —3J 67 (2F 161)
Regent Sq. Belv —4H 93
Regent's Row. E8 —1G 69
Regent St. NW10 —3F 65
Regent St. SW1 —7H 67
Regent St. W1 —6F 67 (7K 159)
Regent St. W4 —5G 81
Regents Wharf. E8 —1H 69
(off Wharf Pl.)
Regents Wharf. N1 —2K 67
Regina Clo. Barn —3A 4
Regina Ct. SE16 —2J 87
Regina Ho. SE20 —1K 141
Reginald Rd. E7 —7J 53
Reginald Rd. SE8 —7C 88
Reginald Rd. N'wd —1H 23
Reginald Sq. SE8 —7C 88
Regina Rd. N4 —1K 49
Regina Rd. SE25 —3G 141
Regina Rd. W13 —1A 80
Regina Rd. S'hall —4C 78
Regina Ter. W13 —1A 80
Regis Ct. N8 —4K 31
Regis Ct. NW1 —5D 66 (5E 158)
(off Melcombe Pl.)
Regis Ho. W1 —5E 66 (5H 159)
(off Beaumont St.)
Regis Pl. SW2 —4K 103
Regis Rd. NW5 —5F 49
Regnart Bldgs. NW1 —3B 160
Reid Clo. Pinn —4J 23
Reidhaven Rd. SE18 —4J 91
Reigate Av. Sutt —1J 149
Reigate Rd. Brom —3H 125
Reigate Rd. Ilf —2K 55
Reigate Way. Wall —5J 151
Reighton Rd. E5 —3G 51
Reinickendorf Av. SE9 —6G 109
Relay Rd. W12 —1E 82
Relf Rd. SE15 —3G 105
Reliance Arc. SW9 —4A 104
Reliance Sq. EC2 —3H 163
Relko Gdns. Sutt —5B 150
Relton M. SW7 —3C 84 (1D 170)
Rembrandt Clo. E14 —3F 89
Rembrandt Clo. SW1 —4G 171
Rembrandt Ct. Eps —6B 148
Rembrandt Rd. SE13 —4G 107
Rembrandt Rd. Edgw —2G 27
Remembrance Rd. E7 —4B 54
Remington Rd. E6 —6C 72
Remington Rd. N15 —6D 32
Remington St. N1 —2B 68 (1B 162)
Remnant St. WC2 —6K 67 (7G 161)
Remsted Ho. NW6 —1K 65
(off Mortimer Cres.)
Remus Building, The. EC1
(off Hardwick St.) —3A 68 (2K 161)
Remus Rd. E3 —7C 52
Rendle Clo. Croy —5F 141
Rendlesham Rd. E5 —4G 51
Rendlesham Rd. Enf —1G 7
Renforth St. SE16 —3J 87
Renfree Way. Shep —7C 130
Renfrew Clo. E6 —7E 72
Renfrew Ct. Houn —2C 96
Renfrew Ho. E17 —2B 34
Renfrew Rd. SE11 —4B 86 (3K 173)
Renfrew Rd. Houn —2B 96
Renfrew Rd. King T —7H 117
Renmuir St. SW17 —6D 120
Rennell St. SE13 —3E 106
Rennels Way. Iswth —2J 97
Renness Rd. E17 —3A 34
Rennets Clo. SE9 —5J 109
Rennets Wood Rd. SE9 —5H 109
Rennie Ct. SE1 —4A 168
Rennie Est. SE16 —4H 87
Rennie Ho. SE1 —3C 86
(off Bath Ter.)
Rennie St. SE1 —1B 86 (4A 168)
(in two parts)
Renown Clo. Croy —1B 152
Renown Clo. Romf —1G 39
Rensburg Rd. E17 —5K 33
Renshaw Clo. Belv —6F 93
Renters Av. NW4 —6E 28
Renton Clo. SW2 —6K 103
Renwick Ind. Est. Bark —2B 74
Renwick Rd. Bark —4B 74
Repens Way. Hay —4B 60
Rephidim St. SE1 —3E 86
Replingham Rd. SW18 —1H 119
Reporton Rd. SW6 —7G 83
Repository Rd. SE18 —6D 90
Repton Av. Hay —4F 77
Repton Av. Wemb —4C 44
Repton Clo. Cars —5C 150
Repton Ct. Beck —1D 142
Repton Ct. Ilf —1D 36
Repton Gro. Ilf —1D 36
Repton Ho. E14 —6A 70
Repton Ho. SW1 —4G 85 (4B 172)
(off Charlwood St.)
Repton Rd. Harr —4F 27
Repton St. E14 —6A 70
Repulse Clo. Romf —1G 39
Reservoir Clo. T Hth —4D 140
Reservoir Rd. N14 —5B 6
Reservoir Rd. SE4 —2A 106
Reservoir Rd. Ruis —4F 23
Resolution Wlk. SE18 —3D 90
Restell Clo. SE3 —6G 89
Restmor Way. Wall —2E 150
Reston Pl. SW7 —2A 84
Restons Cres. SE9 —6H 109
Restoration Sq. SW11 —1B 102
Restormel Clo. Houn —5E 96
Restormel Ho. SE11 —4J 173
Retcar Clo. N19 —2F 49
Retcar Pl. N19 —2F 49
(off Retcar Clo.)
Retford St. N1 —2E 68 (1H 163)
Retingham Way. E4 —2J 19
Retles Ct. Harr —7J 25
Retreat Clo. Harr —5C 26
Retreat Ho. E9 —6J 51
Retreat Pl. E9 —6J 51
Retreat Rd. Rich —5D 98
Retreat, The. NW9 —5K 27
Retreat, The. SW14 —3A 100
Retreat, The. Harr —7E 24
Retreat, The. Surb —6F 135
Retreat, The. T Hth —4D 140
Retreat, The. Wor Pk —2D 148
Reubens Ct. W4 —5H 81
(off Chaseley Dri.)
Reunion Row. E1 —7H 69
Reveley Sq. SE16 —2A 88
Revell Ri. SE18 —6K 91
Revell Rd. King T —2H 135
Revell Rd. Sutt —6H 149
Revelon Rd. SE4 —4A 106
Revelstoke Rd. SW18 —2H 119
Reventlow Rd. SE9 —1G 127
Reverdy Rd. SE1 —4G 87
Reverend Clo. Harr —3F 43
Revesby Rd. Cars —6B 138
Review Rd. NW2 —2B 46
Review Rd. Dag —1H 75
Rewell St. SW6 —7A 84
Rewley Rd. Cars —6B 138
Rex Av. Ashf —6C 112
Rex Clo. Romf —1H 39
Rex Pl. W1 —7E 66 (3H 165)
Reydon Av. E11 —5A 36
Reynard Clo. SE4 —3A 106
Reynard Clo. Brom —3E 144
Reynard Dri. SE19 —7F 123
Reynard Mills Trad. Est. Bren —5C 80
Reynard Pl. SE14 —6A 88
Reynardson Rd. N17 —7H 17
Reynolds Av. E12 —5E 54
Reynolds Av. Chad H & Romf —7C 38
Reynolds Av. Chess —7E 146
Reynolds Clo. NW11 —7K 29
Reynolds Clo. SW19 —1B 138
Reynolds Clo. Cars —1D 150
Reynolds Ct. Romf —3D 38
Reynolds Dri. Edgw —3F 27
Reynolds Ho. NW8 —2B 66
(off Wellington Rd.)
Reynolds Ho. SW1 —4H 85 (4D 172)
(off Erasmus St.)
Reynolds Pl. SE3 —7K 89
Reynolds Pl. Rich —6F 99
Reynolds Rd. SE15 —4J 105
Reynolds Rd. W4 —3J 81
Reynolds Rd. Hay —4A 60
Reynolds Rd. N Mald —7K 135
Reynolds Way. Croy —4E 152
Rheidol M. N1 —2C 68
Rheidol Ter. N1 —1C 68
Rheingold Way. Wall —7J 151
Rhein Ho. N8 —3J 31
(off Campsfield Rd.)
Rheola Clo. N17 —1F 33
Rhoda St. E2 —4F 69 (3K 163)
Rhodes Av. N22 —1G 31
Rhodes Ho. N1 —3D 68 (1E 162)
(off Provost Est.)
Rhodes Ho. W12 —1D 82
(off White City Est.)
Rhodesia Rd. E11 —2F 53
Rhodesia Rd. SW9 —2J 103
Rhodesmoor Ho. Ct. Mord —6J 137
Rhodes St. N7 —5K 49
Rhodeswell Rd. E14 —5A 70
Rhodrons Av. Chess —5E 146
Rhondda Gro. E3 —3A 70
Rhyl Rd. Gnfd —2K 61
Rhyl St. NW5 —6E 48
Rhys Av. N11 —7C 16
Rialto Rd. Mitc —2E 138
Ribble Clo. Wfd G —6F 21
Ribblesdale Av. N11 —6K 15
Ribblesdale Av. N'holt —6F 43
Ribblesdale Ho. NW6 —1J 65
(off Kilburn Va.)
Ribblesdale Rd. N8 —4K 31
Ribblesdale Rd. SW16 —6F 121
Ribbon Dance M. SE5 —1D 104
Ribchester Av. Gnfd —3K 61
Ribston Clo. Brom —1D 156
Ricardo Path. SE28 —1C 92
Ricardo St. E14 —6D 70
Ricards Rd. SW19 —5H 119
Riccall Ct. NW9 —1A 28
(off Pageant Av.)
Rice Pde. Orp —5H 145
Riceyman Ho. WC1 —3A 68 (2J 161)
(off Lloyd Baker St.)
Richard Burbidge Mans. SW13 —6E 82
(off Brasenose Dri.)
Richard Clo. SE18 —4C 90
Richard Fell Ho. E12 —4E 54
(off Walton Rd.)
Richard Ho. Dri. E16 —6B 72
Richards Av. Romf —6J 39
Richards Clo. Bush —1C 10
Richards Clo. Harr —5A 26
Richards Clo. Hay —6F 77
Richards Clo. Uxb —1C 58
Richards Fld. Eps —7K 147
Richard Sharples Ct. Sutt —7A 150
Richardson Clo. E8 —1F 69
Richardson Ct. SW4 —2J 103
(off Studley Rd.)
Richardson Rd. E15 —2G 71
Richardson's M. W1 —4A 160
Richards Pl. E17 —3C 34
Richard's Pl. SW3 —4C 84 (3D 170)
Richard St. E1 —6H 69
Richbell Pl. WC1 —5K 67 (5G 161)
Richborne Ter. SW8 —7K 85
Richborough Ho. SE15 —6J 87
(off Sharratt St.)
Richborough Rd. NW2 —4G 47
Richens Clo. Houn —2H 97
Riches Rd. Ilf —2G 55
Richfield Rd. Bush —1B 10
Richford Ga. W6 —3E 82
Richford Rd. E15 —1H 71
Richford St. W6 —2E 82
Rich Ind. Est. SE15 —6H 87
Richlands Av. Eps —4C 148
Rich La. SW5 —5K 83
Richmond. —5D 98
Richmond Av. E4 —5A 20
Richmond Av. N1 —1K 67
Richmond Av. NW10 —6E 46
Richmond Av. SW20 —1G 137
Richmond Av. Felt —6G 95
Richmond Av. Uxb —6D 40
Richmond Bri. Twic & Rich —6D 98
Richmond Bldgs. W1 —6H 67 (1C 166)
Richmond Circus. (Junct.) —4E 98
Richmond Clo. E17 —6B 34
Richmond Cotts. W14 —4G 83
(off Hammersmith Rd.)
Richmond Ct. SW1 —2D 84 (7F 165)
(off Sloane St.)
Richmond Ct. Mitc —3B 138
Richmond Ct. Wemb —3F 45
Richmond Cres. E4 —5A 20
Richmond Cres. N1 —1K 67
Richmond Cres. N9 —1B 18
Richmond Dri. Shep —6F 131
Richmond Gdns. NW4 —5C 28
Richmond Gdns. Harr —7E 10
Richmond Grn. Croy —3J 151
Richmond Gro. N1 —7B 50
(in two parts)
Richmond Gro. Surb —6F 135
Richmond Hill. Rich —6E 98
Richmond Hill Ct. Rich —6E 98
Richmond Ho. NW1 —2F 67 (1K 159)
(off Park Village E.)
Richmond Ho. SE17 —5D 86
(off Portland St.)
Richmond Mans. Twic —6D 98
Richmond M. W1 —6H 67 (1C 166)
Richmond M. Tedd —5K 115
Richmond Pde. Twic —6C 98
(off Richmond Rd.)
Richmond Pk. —1H 117
Richmond Pk. Rd. SW14 —5J 99
Richmond Pk. Rd. King T —1E 134
Richmond Pl. SE18 —4G 91
Richmond Rd. E4 —1A 20
Richmond Rd. E7 —5K 53
Richmond Rd. E8 —7F 51
Richmond Rd. E11 —2F 53
Richmond Rd. N2 —2A 30
Richmond Rd. N11 —6D 16
Richmond Rd. N15 —6E 32
Richmond Rd. SW20 —1D 136
Richmond Rd. W5 —2E 80
Richmond Rd. Croy —3J 151
Richmond Rd. Ilf —3G 55
Richmond Rd. Iswth —3A 98
Richmond Rd. King T —4D 116
Richmond Rd. New Bar —5E 4
Richmond Rd. T Hth —3B 140
Richmond Rd. Twic —7B 98
Richmond St. E13 —2J 71
Richmond Ter. SW1 —2J 85 (6E 166)
Richmond Way. E11 —2J 53
Richmond Way. W12 & W14 —2F 83
Richmount Gdns. SE3 —3J 107
Rich St. E14 —7B 70
Rickard Clo. NW4 —4D 28
Rickard Clo. SW2 —1A 122
Rickard Clo. W Dray —3A 76
Rickards Clo. Surb —2E 146
Rickett St. SW6 —6J 83
Rickman St. E1 —4J 69
Rickmansworth Rd. N'wd —1F 23
Rickmansworth Rd. Pinn —2K 23
Rick Roberts Way. E15 —1E 70
Rickthorne Rd. N19 —2J 49
Rickyard Path. SE9 —4C 108
Riddell Ct. SE5 —5F 87
Ridding La. Gnfd —5K 43
(in two parts)
Riddons Rd. SE12 —3A 126
Rideout St. SE18 —4D 90
Rider Clo. Sidc —6J 109
Ride, The. Bren —5B 80
Ride, The. Enf —3D 8
Ridgdale St. E3 —2D 70
Ridge Av. N21 —7H 7
Ridgebrook Rd. SE3 —3B 108
Ridge Clo. NW4 —2F 29
Ridge Clo. NW9 —4K 27
Ridge Clo. SE28 —2H 91
Ridge Ct. SE22 —7G 105
Ridge Crest. Enf —1E 6
Ridgecroft Clo. Bex —1J 129
Ridge Hill. NW11 —1G 47
Ridgemont Gdns. Edgw —4D 12
Ridgemount Av. Croy —1K 153
Ridgemount Clo. SE20 —7H 123
Ridgemount Gdns. Enf —3G 7
Ridge Rd. N8 —6K 31
Ridge Rd. N21 —1H 17
Ridge Rd. NW2 —3H 47
Ridge Rd. Mitc —7F 121
Ridge Rd. Sutt —1G 149
Ridges Yd. Croy —3B 152
Ridge, The. Barn —5C 4
Ridge, The. Bex —7F 111
Ridge, The. Surb —5G 135
Ridge, The. Twic —7H 97
Ridgeview Clo. Barn —6A 4
Ridgeview Rd. N20 —3E 14
Ridge Way. SE19 —6E 122
Ridgeway. Brom —2J 155
Ridge Way. Felt —3C 114
Ridgeway. Rich —6E 98
Ridge Way. Wfd G —4F 21
Ridgeway Av. Barn —6J 5
Ridgeway Dri. Brom —4K 125
Ridgeway E. Sidc —5K 109
Ridgeway Gdns. N6 —7H 31
Ridgeway Gdns. Ilf —5C 36
Ridgeway Rd. Iswth —7J 79
Ridgeway Rd. N. Iswth —7J 79
Ridgeway, The. E4 —2J 19
Ridgeway, The. N3 —7E 14
Ridgeway, The. N11 —4J 15
Ridgeway, The. N14 —2D 16
Ridgeway, The. NW7 —3H 13
Ridgeway, The. NW9 —4K 27
Ridgeway, The. NW11 —1H 47
Ridgeway, The. W3 —3G 81
Ridgeway, The. Croy —3K 151
Ridgeway, The. Kent —6C 26
Ridgeway, The. N Har —5D 24
(in two parts)
Ridgeway, The. Pot B & Enf —1E 6
Ridgeway, The. Ruis —7J 23
Ridgeway, The. Stan —6H 11
Ridgeway, The. W on T —7H 131
Ridgeway Wlk. N'holt —6C 42
(off Arnold Rd.)
Ridgeway W. Sidc —5J 109
Ridgewell Clo. N1 —1C 68
Ridgewell Clo. SE26 —4B 124
Ridgewell Clo. Dag —1H 75
Ridgmount Gdns. WC1 —5H 67 (5C 160)
Ridgmount Pl. WC1 —5H 67 (5C 160)
Ridgmount Rd. SW18 —5K 101
Ridgmount St. WC1 —5H 67 (5C 160)
Ridgway. SW19 —7E 118
Ridgway Ct. SW19 —6F 119
Ridgway Gdns. SW19 —7F 119
Ridgway Pl. SW19 —6G 119
Ridgway Rd. SW9 —3B 104
Ridgway, The. Sutt —7B 150
Ridgwell Rd. E16 —5A 72
Riding Ho. St. W1 —5F 67 (6K 159)
Ridings Av. N21 —4G 7
Ridings Clo. N6 —7G 31
Ridings, The. E11 —5J 35
Ridings, The. W5 —4F 63
Ridings, The. Barn —7G 5
Ridings, The. Ewe —7B 148
Ridings, The. Sun —1J 131
Ridings, The. Surb —5G 135
Riding, The. NW11 —7H 29
Ridler Rd. Enf —1K 7
Ridley Av. W13 —3B 80
Ridley Clo. Bark —7K 55
Ridley Ct. SW16 —6J 121
Ridley Rd. E7 —4A 54
Ridley Rd. E8 —5F 51
Ridley Rd. NW10 —2C 64
Ridley Rd. SW19 —7K 119
Ridley Rd. Brom —3H 143
Ridley Rd. Well —1B 110
Ridsdale Rd. SE20 —1H 141
Riefield Rd. SE9 —4G 109
Riesco Dri. Croy —6J 153
Riffel Rd. NW2 —5E 46
Rifle Ct. SE11 —6A 86 (7K 173)
Rifle Pl. W11 —1F 83
Rifle St. E14 —5D 70
Rigault Rd. SW6 —2G 101
Rigby Clo. Croy —3A 152
Rigby La. Hay —2E 76
Rigby M. Ilf —2E 54
Rigden St. E14 —6D 70
Rigeley Rd. NW10 —3C 64
Rigg App. E10 —1K 51
Rigge Pl. SW4 —4H 103
Riggindale Rd. SW16 —5H 121
Riley Ho. SW10 —7B 84
(off Riley St.)
Riley Rd. SE1 —3F 87 (7H 169)
Riley Rd. Enf —1D 8
Riley St. SW10 —6B 84
Rill Ho. SE5 —7D 86
(off Harris St.)
Rinaldo Rd. SW12 —7F 103
Ring Clo. Brom —7K 125
Ringcroft St. N7 —5A 50
Ringers Rd. Brom —3J 143
Ringford Rd. SW18 —5H 101
Ringles Ct. E6 —1D 72
Ringlet Clo. E16 —5K 71
Ringlewell Clo. Enf —2C 8
Ringmer Av. SW6 —1G 101
Ringmer Gdns. N19 —2J 49
Ringmer Pl. N21 —5J 7
Ringmer Way. Brom —5C 144
Ringmore Ri. SE23 —7H 105
Ring Rd. W12 —1E 82
Ringsfield Ho. SE17 —5C 86
(off Bronti Clo.)
Ringslade Rd. N22 —2K 31
Ringstead Rd. SE6 —7D 106
Ringstead Rd. Sutt —4B 150
Ring, The. W2 —7B 66 (2C 164)
Ring Way. N11 —6B 16
Ringway. S'hall —5B 78
Ringwold Clo. Beck —7A 124
Ringwood Av. N2 —2D 30
Ringwood Av. Croy —7J 139
Ringwood Clo. Pinn —3A 24
Ringwood Gdns. E14 —4C 88
Ringwood Gdns. SW15 —1C 118
Ringwood Rd. E17 —6B 34
Ringwood Way. N21 —1G 17
Ringwood Way. Hamp H —4E 114
Ripley Clo. Brom —5D 144
Ripley Clo. New Ad —6E 154
Ripley Ct. Mitc —2B 138
Ripley Gdns. SW14 —3K 99
Ripley Gdns. Sutt —4A 150
Ripley Ho. SW1 —6G 85 (7A 172)
(off Churchill Gdns.)
Ripley M. E11 —6G 35
Ripley Rd. E16 —6A 72
Ripley Rd. Belv —4G 93
Ripley Rd. Enf —1H 7
Ripley Rd. Hamp —7E 114
Ripley Rd. Ilf —2K 55
Ripley Vs. W5 —6C 62
Ripon Clo. N'holt —5E 42
Ripon Gdns. Chess —5D 146
Ripon Gdns. Ilf —6C 36
Ripon Rd. N9 —7C 8
Ripon Rd. N17 —3D 32
Ripon Rd. SE18 —6F 91
Rippersley Rd. Well —1A 110
Ripple Rd. Bark & Dag —7G 55
Ripple Road Junction. (Junct.) —1A 74
Rippleside. —1B 74
Rippleside Commercial Cen. Bark —2C 74
Ripplevale Gro. N1 —7K 49
Rippolson Rd. SE18 —5K 91
Ripston Rd. Ashf —5F 113
Risboro' Clo. N10 —3F 31
Risborough. SE17 —4C 86
Risborough Dri. Wor Pk —7C 136
Risborough Ho. NW8 —4C 66 (3D 158)
(off Mallory St.)
Risborough St. SE1 —2B 86 (6B 168)
Risdon St. SE16 —3J 87
Risedale Rd. Bexh —3J 111
Riseholme Ct. E9 —6B 52
Riseldine Rd. SE23 —6A 106
Rise Park. —1K 39
Rise Pk. Pde. Romf —2K 39
Rise, The. E11 —5J 35
Rise, The. N13 —4F 17
Rise, The. NW7 —6G 13
Rise, The. NW10 —4K 45
Rise, The. Bex —7C 110
Rise, The. Buck H —1G 21
Rise, The. Edgw —5C 12
Rise, The. Gnfd —5A 44
Rise, The. Uxb —2B 58
Risinghill St. N1 —2K 67
Risingholme Clo. Bush —1A 10
Risingholme Clo. Harr —1J 25
Risingholme Rd. Harr —2J 25
Risings, The. E17 —4F 35
Rising Sun Ct. EC1 —5B 162
Risley Av. N17 —1C 32
Rita Rd. SW8 —6J 85
Ritches Rd. N15 —5C 32
Ritchie Ho. E14 —6F 71
Ritchie Ho. N19 —1H 49
Ritchie Rd. Croy —6H 141
Ritchie St. N1 —2A 68
Ritchings Av. E17 —4A 34
Ritherdon Rd. SW17 —2E 120
Ritson Ho. N1 —1K 67
(off Barnsbury Est.)
Ritson Rd. E8 —6G 51
Ritter St. SE18 —6E 90
Ritz Pde. W5 —4F 63
Rivaz Pl. E9 —6J 51
Riven Ct. W2 —6K 65
(off Inverness Ter.)
Rivenhall Gdns. E18 —4H 35
River Ash Estate. —7H 131
River Av. N13 —3G 17
River Av. Th Dit —7A 134
River Av. Ind. Est. N13 —5F 17
River Bank. N21 —7H 7
River Bank. E Mol & W Mol —3J 133
River Bank. Th Dit —5K 133
River Bank. W Mol —3E 132
Riverbank Rd. Brom —3J 125
Riverbank Way. Bren —6C 80
River Barge Clo. E14 —2E 88

River Brent Bus. Pk.—Rose Av.

River Brent Bus. Pk. W7 —3J 79
River Clo. E11 —6A 36
River Clo. Ruis —6H 23
River Clo. S'hall —2G 79
River Ct. SE1 —7B 68 (3A 168)
River Ct. Surb —5D 134
(off Portsmouth Rd.)
Rivercourt Rd. W6 —4D 82
River Crane Way. Felt —2D 114
(off Watermill Way)
Riverdale. SE13 —4E 106
Riverdale Ct. N21 —5J 7
Riverdale Dri. SW18 —1K 119
Riverdale Gdns. Twic —6C 98
Riverdale Rd. SE18 —5K 91
Riverdale Rd. Bex —7F 111
Riverdale Rd. Eri —5H 93
Riverdale Rd. Felt —4C 114
Riverdale Rd. Twic —6C 98
Riverdale Shop. Cen. SE13 —3E 106
Riverdene. Edgw —3D 12
Riverdene Rd. Ilf —3E 54
Riverfleet. WC1 —3J 67 (1F 161)
(off Birkenhead St.)
River Front. Enf —3K 7
River Gdns. Cars —2E 150
River Gdns. Felt —5K 95
River Gdns. Bus. Cen. Felt —5K 95
River Gro. Pk. Beck —1B 142
Riverhead Clo. E17 —2K 33
Riverhill. Wor Pk —2K 147
Riverholme Dri. Eps —7K 147
Riverhope Mans. SE18 —3C 90
River Ho. SE26 —3H 123
River La. Rich —7D 98
Riverleigh Ct. E4 —5G 19
Rivermead. E Mol —3G 133
Rivermead. King T —5D 134
Rivermead Clo. Tedd —5B 116
Rivermead Ct. SW6 —3H 101
Rivermead Ho. E9 —5A 52
River Meads Av. Twic —3E 114
River Mt. W on T —7H 131
Rivernook Clo. W on T —5A 132
River Pk. Gdns. Brom —7F 125
River Pk. Rd. N22 —2K 31
River Pk. Trad. Est. E14 —3B 88
River Pl. N1 —7C 50
River Reach. Tedd —5C 116
River Rd. Bark —2J 73
River Rd. Buck H —1H 21
River Rd. Bus. Pk. Bark —3K 73
Riversdale Rd. N5 —3B 50
Riversdale Rd. Romf —1H 39
Riversdale Rd. Th Dit —5A 134
Riversfield Rd. Enf —3K 7
Rivers Ho. W4 —5G 81
(off Chiswick High Rd.)
Riverside. NW4 —7D 28
Riverside. SE7 —3K 89
Riverside. WC1 —3J 67 (1F 161)
(off Birkenhead St.)
Riverside. Rich —5D 98
Riverside. Shep —7G 131
Riverside. Sun —2B 132
Riverside. Twic —1B 116
Riverside Apartments. N13 —5E 16
Riverside Av. E Mol —5H 133
Riverside Bus. Cen. SW18 —1K 119
Riverside Clo. E5 —1J 51
Riverside Clo. W7 —4J 61
Riverside Clo. King T —4D 134
Riverside Clo. Wall —3F 151
Riverside Cotts. Bark —2H 73
Riverside Ct. E4 —6H 9
Riverside Ct. SE3 —4H 107
Riverside Ct. SE16 —1K 87
Riverside Ct. SW8 —6H 85 (7D 172)
Riverside Ct. Felt —7G 95
Riverside Ct. Iswth —2K 97
(off Woodlands Rd.)
Riverside Dri. NW11 —6G 29
Riverside Dri. W4 —7K 81
Riverside Dri. Mitc —5C 138
Riverside Dri. Rich —3B 116
Riverside Gdns. N3 —3G 29
Riverside Gdns. W6 —5D 82
Riverside Gdns. Enf —2H 7
Riverside Gdns. Wemb —2E 62
Riverside Ind. Est. Bark —3A 74
Riverside Ind. Est. Enf —6F 9
Riverside M. Croy —3J 151
Riverside Pl. N11 —3B 16
Riverside Pl. Stanw —6A 94
Riverside Rd. E15 —2E 70
Riverside Rd. N15 —6G 33
Riverside Rd. SW17 —4K 119
Riverside Rd. Sidc —3E 128
Riverside Rd. Stanw —5A 94
(in two parts)
Riverside, The. E Mol —3H 133
Riverside Wlk. N12 & N20 —3E 14
Riverside Wlk. SE10 —3G 89
(Morden Wharf Rd.)
Riverside Wlk. SE10 —2F 89
(Tunnel Av.)
Riverside Wlk. SW6 —3G 101
Riverside Wlk. W4 —6B 82
(off Chiswick Wharf)
Riverside Wlk. Barn —6A 4
Riverside Wlk. Iswth —3J 97
Riverside Wlk. King T —3D 134
Riverside Wlk. W W'ck —1D 154
Riverside Works. Bark —7F 55
Riverside Workshops. SE1 —1C 86 (4D 168)
(off Park St.)
Riverstone Ct. King T —1F 135
River St. EC1 —3A 68 (1J 161)
River Ter. W6 —5E 82
River Ter. WC2 —3G 167
Riverton Clo. W9 —3H 65
River Vw. Enf —3H 7
Riverview Gdns. SW13 —6D 82
River Vw. Gdns. Twic —2K 115
Riverview Gro. W4 —6H 81
Riverview Heights. SE16 —2G 87
(off Bermondsey Wall W.)
Riverview Pk. SE6 —2C 124
Riverview Rd. W4 —7H 81
Riverview Rd. Eps —4J 147
River Wlk. W6 —7E 82
River Wlk. W on T —6J 131
Riverway. N13 —5F 17
River Way. SE10 —3H 89
(in two parts)
River Way. Eps —5K 147
River Way. Twic —2F 115
River Wharf Bus. Pk. Belv —1K 93
Riverwood La. Chst —1H 145
Rivet Ho. SE1 —5F 87
(off Coopers Rd.)
Rivington Av. Wfd G —2B 36
Rivington Bldgs. EC2 —3E 68 (2G 163)
Rivington Ct. NW10 —1C 64
Rivington Cres. NW7 —7G 13
Rivington Pl. EC2 —3E 68 (2H 163)
Rivington St. EC2 —3E 68 (2G 163)
Rivington Wlk. E8 —1G 69
Rivulet Rd. N17 —7H 17
Rixon Ho. SE18 —6F 91
Rixon St. N7 —3A 50
Rixsen Rd. E12 —5C 54
Roach Rd. E3 —7C 52
Roads Pl. N19 —2J 49
Roan St. SE10 —6E 88
Robarts Clo. Pinn —6K 23
Robb Rd. Stan —6F 11
Robert Adam St. W1 —6E 66 (7G 159)
Roberta St. E2 —3G 69
Robert Bell Ho. SE16 —4G 87
(off Rouel Rd.)
Robert Clo. W9 —4A 66 (4A 158)
Robert Dashwood Way. SE17 —4C 86
Robert Gentry Ho. W14 —5G 83
Robert Jones Ho. SE16 —4G 87
(off Rouel Rd.)
Robert Keen Clo. SE15 —1G 105
Robert Lowe Clo. SE14 —7K 87
Roberton Dri. Brom —1A 144
Robert Owen Ho. N22 —1A 32
(off Progress Way)
Robert Owen Ho. SW6 —1F 101
Robert Runcie Ct. SW9 —4K 103
Roberts All. W5 —2D 80
Robertsbridge Rd. Cars —1A 150
Roberts Clo. SE9 —1H 127
Roberts Clo. SE16 —2K 87
Roberts Clo. Sutt —7F 149
Roberts Clo. W Dray —1A 76
Roberts Ct. N1 —1B 68
(off Essex Rd.)
Roberts Ct. SE20 —1J 141
(off Maple Rd.)
Roberts M. SW1 —3E 84 (1G 171)
Robertson Rd. E15 —1E 70
Robertson St. SW8 —3F 103
Roberts Pl. EC1 —4A 68 (3K 161)
Roberts Rd. E17 —1D 34
Roberts Rd. NW7 —6B 14
Roberts Rd. Belv —5G 93
Robert St. E16 —1F 91
Robert St. NW1 —3F 67 (2K 159)
Robert St. SE18 —5H 91
(in two parts)
Robert St. WC2 —7J 67 (3F 167)
Robert St. Croy —3C 152
Robeson St. E3 —5B 70
Robina Clo. Bexh —4D 110
Robina Clo. N'wd —1H 23
Robin Clo. NW7 —3F 13
Robin Clo. Hamp —5C 114
Robin Clo. Romf —1K 39
Robin Ct. E14 —3E 88
Robin Ct. SE16 —4G 87
Robin Cres. E6 —5B 72
Robin Gro. N6 —2E 48
Robin Gro. Bren —6C 80
Robin Gro. Harr —6F 27
Robin Hill Dri. Chst —6C 126
Robin Hood. (Junct.) —3A 118
Robinhood Clo. Mitc —3G 139
Robin Hood Dri. Harr —7E 10
Robin Hood Gdns. E14 —7E 70
(off Robin Hood La., in two parts)
Robin Hood Grn. Orp —5K 145
Robin Hood La. E14 —7E 70
Robin Hood La. SW15 —3A 118
Robin Hood La. Bexh —5E 110
Robinhood La. Mitc —3G 139
Robin Hood La. Sutt —5J 149
Robin Hood Rd. SW19 & SW15 —5C 118
Robin Hood Way. SW15 & SW20 —3A 118
Robin Hood Way. Gnfd —6K 43
Robin Ho. NW8 —2C 66
(off Barrow Hill Est.)
Robinia Cres. E10 —2D 52
Robins Ct. SE12 —3A 126
Robin's Ct. Beck —2F 143
Robinscroft M. SE10 —1E 106
Robins Gro. W W'ck —3J 155
Robinson Clo. E11 —3G 53
Robinson Ct. N1 —1B 68
(off St Mary's Path)
Robinson Cres. Bus H —1B 10
Robinson Ho. E14 —5C 70
Robinson Rd. E2 —2J 69
Robinson Rd. SW17 & SW19 —6C 120
Robinson Rd. Dag —4G 57
Robinson's Clo. W13 —5A 62
Robinson St. SW3 —6D 84 (7E 170)
Robinwood Pl. SW15 —4K 117
Robsart St. SW9 —2K 103
Robson Av. NW10 —7C 46
Robson Clo. E6 —6C 72
Robson Clo. Enf —2G 7
Robson Rd. SE27 —3B 122
Roby Ho. EC1 —4C 68 (3C 162)
(off Mitchell St.)
Roch Av. Edgw —2F 27
Rochdale Rd. E17 —7C 34
Rochdale Rd. SE2 —5B 92
Rochdale Way. SE8 —7C 88
Roche Ho. E14 —7B 70
Rochelle Clo. SW11 —4B 102
Rochelle St. E2 —3F 69 (2J 163)
(in two parts)
Rochemont Wlk. E8 —1G 69
(off Pownell Rd.)
Roche Rd. SW16 —1K 139
Rochester Av. E13 —1A 72
Rochester Av. Brom —2K 143
Rochester Av. Felt —2H 113
Rochester Clo. SW16 —7J 121
Rochester Clo. Enf —1K 7
Rochester Clo. Sidc —6B 110
Rochester Ct. NW1 —7G 49
(off Rochester Sq.)
Rochester Dri. Bex —6F 111
Rochester Dri. Pinn —5B 24
Rochester Gdns. Croy —3E 152
Rochester Gdns. Ilf —7D 36
Rochester Ho. SE1 —2D 86 (7F 169)
Rochester Ho. SE15 —6J 87
(off Sharratt St.)
Rochester M. NW1 —7G 49
Rochester M. W5 —4C 80
Rochester Pde. Felt —2J 113
Rochester Pl. NW1 —6G 49
Rochester Rd. NW1 —6G 49
Rochester Rd. Cars —4D 150
Rochester Rd. N'wd —3H 23
Rochester Row. SW1 —4G 85 (3B 172)
Rochester Sq. NW1 —7G 49
Rochester St. SW1 —3H 85 (2C 172)
Rochester Ter. NW1 —6G 49
Rochester Wlk. SE1 —4D 168
Rochester Way. SE3 & SE9 —1K 107
Rochester Way. Dart —7K 111
Rochester Way Relief Rd. SE3 & SE9 —1K 107
Roche Wlk. Cars —6B 138
Rochford. N17 —2E 32
(off Griffin Rd.)
Rochford Av. Romf —5C 38
Rochford Clo. E6 —2B 72
Rochford Wlk. E8 —7G 51
Rochford Way. Croy —6J 139
Rochfort Ho. SE8 —5B 88
Rock Av. SW14 —3K 99
Rockbourne M. SE23 —1K 123
Rockbourne Rd. SE23 —1K 123
Rock Clo. Mitc —2B 138
Rockell's Pl. SE22 —6H 105
Rockfield Ho. NW4 —4F 29
(off Belle Vue Est.)
Rockfield Ho. SE10 —6E 88
(off Welland St.)
Rockford Av. Gnfd —2A 62
Rock Gdns. Dag —5H 57
Rock Gro. Way. SE16 —4G 87
(in two parts)
Rockhall Rd. NW2 —4F 47
Rockhampton Clo. SE27 —4A 122
Rockhampton Rd. SE27 —4A 122
Rockhampton Rd. S Croy —6E 152
Rock Hill. SE26 —4F 123
Rockingham Clo. SW15 —4B 100
Rockingham St. SE1 —3C 86
Rockland Rd. SW15 —4G 101
Rocklands Dri. Stan —2B 26
Rockley Ct. W14 —2F 83
(off Rockley Rd.)
Rockley Rd. W14 —2F 83
Rockmount Rd. SE18 —5K 91
Rockmount Rd. SE19 —6D 122
Rocks La. SW13 —1C 100
Rock St. N4 —2A 50
Rockware Av. Gnfd —1H 61
Rockware Av. Bus. Cen. Gnfd —1H 61
Rockwell Gdns. SE19 —5E 122
Rockwell Rd. Dag —5H 57
Rockwood Pl. W12 —2E 82
Rocliffe St. N1 —2B 68
Rocombe Cres. SE23 —7J 105
Rocque Ho. SW6 —7H 83
(off Estcourt Rd.)
Rocque La. SE3 —3H 107
Rodale Mans. SW18 —6K 101
Rodborough Ct. W9 —4J 65
(off Hermes Clo.)
Rodborough Rd. NW11 —1J 47
Roden Gdns. Croy —6E 140
Rodenhurst Rd. SW4 —6G 103
Roden St. N7 —3K 49
Roden St. Ilf —3E 54
Roden Way. Ilf —3E 54
(off Roden St.)
Roderick Rd. NW3 —4D 48
Rodgers Ho. SW4 —7H 103
(off Clapham Pk. Est.)
Rodin Ct. N1 —1B 68
(off Essex Rd.)
Roding Av. Wfd G —6H 21
Roding Ho. N1 —1A 68
(off Barnsbury Est.)
Roding La. Buck H & Chig —1G 21
Roding La. N. Wfd G —6H 21
Roding La. S. Ilf & Wfd G —4B 36
Roding M. E1 —1G 87
Roding Rd. E5 —4K 51
Roding Rd. E6 —5F 73
Rodings Row. Barn —4B 4
(off Leecroft Rd.)
Rodings, The. Wfd G —6F 21
Roding Trad. Est. Bark —7F 55
Roding Vw. Buck H —1G 21
Rodmarton St. W1 —5D 66 (6F 159)
Rodmell. WC1 —3J 67 (2F 161)
(off Regent Sq.)
Rodmell Clo. Hay —4C 60
Rodmell Slope. N12 —5C 14
Rodmere St. SE10 —5G 89
Rodmill La. SW2 —7J 103
Rodney Clo. Croy —1B 152
Rodney Clo. N Mald —5A 136
Rodney Clo. Pinn —7C 24
Rodney Ct. NW8 —4A 66 (3A 158)
Rodney Ct. Barn —3C 4
Rodney Gdns. Pinn —5K 23
Rodney Gdns. W W'ck —4J 155
Rodney Ho. E14 —4D 88
Rodney Ho. N1 —2K 67
(off Donegal St.)
Rodney Ho. SW1 —5G 85 (6B 172)
(off Dolphin Sq.)
Rodney Ho. W11 —7J 65
(off Pembridge Cres.)
Rodney Pl. E17 —2A 34
Rodney Pl. SE17 —4C 86
Rodney Pl. SW19 —1A 138
Rodney Rd. E11 —4K 35
Rodney Rd. SE17 —4C 86
Rodney Rd. Mitc —3C 138
Rodney Rd. N Mald —5A 136
Rodney Rd. Twic —6E 96
Rodney St. N1 —2K 67 (1H 161)
Rodney Way. Romf —1H 39
Rodway Rd. SW15 —7C 100
Rodway Rd. Brom —1K 143
Rodwell Clo. Ruis —1A 42
Rodwell Pl. Edgw —6B 12
Rodwell Rd. SE22 —6F 105
Roe. NW9 —7G 13
Roebourne Way. E16 —1E 90
Roebuck Clo. Felt —4K 113
Roebuck Ho. SW1 —3G 85 (1A 172)
(off Palace Ho.)
Roebuck La. N17 —6A 18
Roebuck La. Buck H —1F 21
Roebuck Rd. Chess —5G 147
Roedean Av. Enf —1D 8
Roedean Clo. Enf —1D 8
Roedean Cres. SW15 —6A 100
Roe End. NW9 —4J 27
Roe Green. —4J 27
Roe Grn. NW9 —5J 27
Roehampton. —7C 100
Roehampton Clo. SW15 —4C 100
Roehampton Dri. Chst —6G 127
Roehampton Ga. SW15 —6A 100
Roehampton High St. SW15 —7C 100
Roehampton Lane. (Junct.) —1D 118
Roehampton La. SW15 —4C 100
Roehampton Va. SW15 —3B 118
Roe La. NW9 —4H 27
Roffey St. E14 —2E 88
Rogate Ho. E5 —3G 51
Roger Dowley Ct. E2 —2J 69
Roger Harriss Almshouses. E15 —1H 71
(off Gift La.)
Roger Reede's Almshouses. Romf —4K 39
Rogers Est. E2 —3J 69
Rogers Gdns. Dag —5G 57
Rogers Ho. SW1 —4H 85 (3D 172)
(off Page St.)
Roger's Ho. Dag —3G 57
Rogers Rd. E16 —6H 71
Rogers Rd. SW17 —4B 120
Rogers Rd. Dag —5G 57
Rogers Ruff. N'wd —1E 22
Roger St. WC1 —4K 67 (4H 161)
Rogers Wlk. N12 —3E 14
Rohere Ho. EC1 —3C 68 (2C 162)
Rojack Rd. SE23 —1K 123
Rokeby Gdns. Wfd G —1J 35
Rokeby Pl. SW20 —7D 118
Rokeby Rd. SE4 —2B 106
Rokeby Rd. Harr —3H 25
Rokeby St. E15 —1F 71
Rokell Ho. Beck —5D 124
(off Beckenham Hill Rd.)
Roker Pk. Av. Uxb —4A 40
Rokesby Clo. Well —2H 109
Rokesby Pl. Wemb —5D 44
Rokesly Av. N8 —5J 31
Roland Gdns. SW7 —5A 84 (5A 170)
Roland Ho. SW7 —5A 84 (5A 170)
(off Cranley M.)
Roland M. E1 —5K 69
Roland Rd. E17 —4F 35
Roland Way. SE17 —5D 86
Roland Way. SW7 —5A 84 (5A 170)
Roland Way. Wor Pk —2B 148
Roles Gro. Romf —4D 38
Rolfe Clo. Barn —4H 5
Rolinsden Way. Kes —5B 156
Rolland Ho. W7 —5J 61
Rollesby Rd. Chess —6G 147
Rollesby Way. SE28 —6C 74
Rolleston Av. Orp —6F 145
Rolleston Clo. Orp —7F 145
Rolleston Rd. S Croy —7D 152
Roll Gdns. Ilf —5E 36
Rollins St. SE15 —6J 87
Rollit Cres. Houn —5E 96
Rollit St. N7 —5A 50
Rolls Bldgs. EC4 —6A 68 (7J 161)
Rollscourt Av. SE24 —5C 104
Rolls Pk. Av. E4 —5H 19
Rolls Pk. Rd. E4 —5J 19
Rolls Pas. WC2 —7J 161
Rolls Rd. SE1 —5F 87
Rolt St. SE8 —6A 88
Rolvenden Gdns. Brom —7B 126
Rolvenden Pl. N17 —1G 33
Roman Clo. W3 —2H 81
Roman Clo. Felt —5A 96
Roman Clo. Rain —2K 75
Romanfield Rd. SW2 —7K 103
Roman Ho. EC2 —6D 162
Romanhurst Av. Brom —4G 143
Romanhurst Gdns. Brom —4G 143
Roman Ind. Est. Croy —7E 140
Roman Ri. SE19 —6D 122
Roman Rd. E2 & E3 —3J 69
Roman Rd. E3 —1B 70
Roman Rd. E6 —4B 72
Roman Rd. N10 —7A 16
Roman Rd. NW2 —3E 46
Roman Rd. W4 —4A 82
Roman Rd. Ilf —6F 55
Roman Sq. SE28 —1A 92
Roman Way. N7 —6K 49
Roman Way. SE15 —7J 87
Roman Way. Croy —2B 152
Roman Way. Enf —5A 8
Romany Gdns. E17 —1A 34
Romany Gdns. Sutt —7J 137
Roma Read Clo. SW15 —7D 100
Roma Rd. E17 —3A 34
Romayne Ho. SW4 —3H 103
Romberg Rd. SW17 —3E 120
Romborough Gdns. SE13 —5E 106
Romborough Way. SE13 —5E 106
Romero Clo. SW9 —3K 103
Romero Sq. SE3 —4A 108
Romeyn Rd. SW16 —3K 121
Romford Greyhound Stadium. —6J 39
Romford Rd. E15 & E7 —6G 53
Romford St. E1 —5G 69
Romilly Rd. N4 —2B 50
Romilly St. W1 —7H 67 (2D 166)
Romily Ct. SW6 —2G 101
Rommany Rd. SE27 —4D 122
(in two parts)
Romney Clo. N17 —1H 33
Romney Clo. NW11 —1A 48
Romney Clo. SE14 —7J 87
Romney Clo. Ashf —5E 112
Romney Clo. Chess —4E 146
Romney Clo. Harr —7E 24
Romney Ct. NW3 —6C 48
Romney Ct. W12 —2F 83
(off Shepherd's Bush Grn.)
Romney Dri. Brom —7B 126
Romney Dri. Harr —7E 24
Romney Gdns. Bexh —1F 111
Romney M. W1 —5E 66 (5G 159)
Romney Pde. Hay —2F 59
Romney Rd. SE10 —6F 89
Romney Rd. Hay —2F 59
Romney Rd. N Mald —6K 135
Romney Row. NW2 —2F 47
(off Brent Ter.)
Romney St. SW1 —3J 85 (2E 172)
Romola Rd. SE24 —1B 122
Romsey Gdns. Dag —1D 74
Romsey Rd. W13 —7A 62
Romsey Rd. Dag —1D 74
Romulus Ct. Bren —7D 80
Ronald Av. E15 —3G 71
Ronald Clo. Beck —4B 142
Ronald Ct. New Bar —3E 4
Ronald Ho. SE3 —4A 108
Ronaldshay. N4 —1A 50
Ronalds Rd. N7 —5A 50
(in three parts)
Ronalds Rd. Brom —1J 143
Ronaldstone Rd. Sidc —6J 109
Ronald St. E1 —6J 69
Rona Rd. NW3 —4E 48
Ronart St. W'stone —3K 25
Rona Wlk. N1 —6D 50
(off Ramsey Wlk.)
Rondel Ct. Bex —6E 110
Rondu Rd. NW2 —5G 47
Ronelean Rd. Surb —2F 147
Ron Leighton Way. E6 —1C 72
Ronver Rd. SE12 —1H 125
Rood La. EC3 —7E 68 (2G 169)
Rookby Ct. N21 —2G 17
Rook Clo. Wemb —3H 45
Rookeries Clo. Felt —3K 113
Rookery Clo. NW9 —5B 28
Rookery Cres. Dag —7H 57
Rookery Dri. Chst —1E 144
Rookery La. Brom —6B 144
Rookery Rd. SW4 —4G 103
Rookery Way. NW9 —5B 28
Rooke Way. SE10 —5H 89
Rookfield Av. N10 —4G 31
Rookfield Clo. N10 —4G 31
Rooksmead Rd. Sun —2J 131
Rooks Ter. W Dray —2A 76
Rookstone Rd. SW17 —5D 120
Rook Wlk. E6 —6B 72
Rookwood Av. N Mald —4C 136
Rookwood Av. Wall —4H 151
Rookwood Gdns. E4 —2C 20
Rookwood Ho. Bark —2H 73
Rookwood Rd. N16 —7F 33
Roosevelt Way. Dag —6K 57
Rootes Dri. W10 —5F 65
Ropemaker Rd. SE16 —2A 88
Ropemaker's Field. E14 —7B 70
Ropemakers Fields. E14 —7B 70
Ropemaker St. EC2 —5D 68 (5E 162)
Roper La. SE1 —2E 86 (7H 169)
Ropers Av. E4 —5J 19
Ropers Orchard. SW3 —6C 84
(off Danvers St.)
Roper St. SE9 —5D 108
Ropers Wlk. SW2 —7A 104
Roper Way. Mitc —2E 138
Ropery Bus. Pk. SE7 —4A 90
Ropery St. E3 —4B 70
Rope St. SE16 —4A 88
Rope Wlk. Sun —3A 132
Rope Wlk. Gdns. E1 —6G 69
Rope Yd. Rails. SE18 —3F 91
Ropley St. E2 —2G 69 (1K 163)
Rosa Alba M. N5 —4C 50
Rosa Av. Ashf —4C 112
Rosalind Ct. Bark —7A 56
(off Meadow Rd.)
Rosalind Ho. N1 —2E 68
(off Arden Ho.)
Rosaline Rd. SW6 —7G 83
Rosaline Ter. SW6 —7G 83
(off Rosaline Rd.)
Rosamond St. SE26 —3H 123
Rosamund Clo. S Croy —4D 152
Rosamun St. S'hall —4C 78
Rosary Clo. Houn —2C 96
Rosary Gdns. SW7 —4A 84
Rosary Gdns. Ashf —4D 112
Rosaville Rd. SW6 —7H 83
Roscoe St. EC1 —4C 68 (4D 162)
(in two parts)
Roscoe St. Est. EC1 —4C 68 (4D 162)
Roscoff Clo. Edgw —1J 27
Roseacre Clo. W13 —5B 62
Roseacre Clo. Shep —5C 130
Roseacre Rd. Well —3B 110
Rose All. EC2 —5E 68 (6H 163)
(off Bishopsgate)
Rose All. SE1 —1C 86 (4D 168)
Rose & Crown Ct. EC2 —7D 162
Rose & Crown Pas. Iswth —1A 98
Rose & Crown Yd. SW1 —1G 85 (4B 166)
Rose Av. E18 —2K 35

Rucklidge Pas.—St Anthony's Clo.

Rucklidge Pas. NW6 —2H 65
Rucklidge Pas. NW10 —2B 64
(off Rucklidge Av.)
Rudall Cres. NW3 —4B 48
Rudbeck Ho. SE15 —7G 87
(off Peckham Pk. Rd.)
Ruddington Clo. E5 —4A 52
Ruddock Clo. Edgw —7D 12
Ruddstreet Clo. SE18 —4F 91
Ruddy Way. NW7 —6G 13
Rudge Ho. SE16 —3G 87
(off Jamaica Rd.)
Rudgwick Ct. SE18 —4C 90
(off Woodville St., in two parts)
Rudgwick Ter. NW8 —1C 66
Rudland Rd. Bexh —3H 111
Rudloe Rd. SW12 —7G 103
Rudolf Pl. SW8 —6J 85 (7F 173)
Rudolph Rd. E13 —2H 71
Rudolph Rd. NW6 —2J 65
Rudyard Gro. NW7 —6D 12
Ruegg Ho. SE18 —6E 90
(off Woolwich Comn.)
Ruffetts Clo. S Croy —7H 153
Ruffetts, The. S Croy —7H 153
Ruffle Clo. W Dray —2A 76
Rufford Clo. Harr —6A 26
Rufford St. N1 —1J 67
Rufford Tower. W3 —1H 81
Rufforth Ct. NW9 —1A 28
(off Pageant Av.)
Rufus Clo. Ruis —3C 42
Rufus Ho. SE1 —3F 87 (7K 169)
(off Abbey St.)
Rufus St. N1 —3E 68 (2G 163)
Rugby Av. N9 —1A 18
Rugby Av. Gnfd —6H 43
Rugby Av. Wemb —5B 44
Rugby Clo. Harr —4J 25
Rugby Gdns. Dag —6C 56
Rugby Mans. W14 —4G 83
(off Bishop King's Rd)
Rugby Rd. NW9 —4H 27
Rugby Rd. W4 —2A 82
Rugby Rd. Dag —6B 56
Rugby Rd. Twic —5J 97
Rugby St. WC1 —4K 67 (4G 161)
Rugg St. E14 —7C 70
Rugless Ho. E14 —2E 88
Ruislip. —1G 41
Ruislip Clo. Gnfd —4F 61
Ruislip Common. —4E 22
Ruislip Ct. Ruis —2H 41
Ruislip Gardens. —3J 41
Ruislip Lido Railway. —4F 23
Ruislip Manor. —1J 41
Ruislip Rd. Gnfd —3E 60
Ruislip Rd. N'holt & S'hall —1A 60
Ruislip Rd. E. Gnfd & W7 —4H 61
Ruislip St. SW17 —4D 120
Rumball Ho. SE5 —7E 86
(off Harris St.)
Rumbold Rd. SW6 —7K 83
Rum Clo. E1 —7J 69
Rumford Ho. SE1 —3C 86
(off Tiverton St.)
Rumney Ct. N'holt —2B 60
(off Parkfield Dri.)
Rumsey Clo. Hamp —6D 114
Rumsey M. N4 —3B 50
Rumsey Rd. SW9 —3K 103
Runacres Ct. SE17 —5C 86
Runbury Circ. NW9 —2K 45
Runcorn Clo. N17 —4H 33
Runcorn Pl. W11 —7G 65
Rundell Cres. NW4 —5D 28
Rundell Tower. SW8 —1K 103
Runes Clo. Mitc —4B 138
Runnel Fld. Harr —3J 43
Running Horse Yd. Bren —6E 80
Runnymede. SW19 —1A 138
Runnymede Clo. Twic —6F 97
Runnymede Ct. SW15 —1C 118
Runnymede Cres. SW16 —1H 139
Runnymede Gdns. Gnfd —2J 61
Runnymede Gdns. Twic —6F 97
Runnymede Ho. E9 —4A 52
Runnymede Rd. Twic —6F 97
Runway, The. Ruis —5K 41
Rupack St. SE16 —2J 87
Rupert Av. Wemb —5E 44
Rupert Ct. W1 —7H 67 (2C 166)
Rupert Ct. W Mol —4E 132
(off St Peters Rd.)
Rupert Gdns. SW9 —2B 104
Rupert Ho. SE11 —4A 86 (4K 173)
Rupert Rd. N19 —3H 49
(in two parts)
Rupert Rd. NW6 —2H 65
Rupert Rd. W4 —3A 82
Rupert St. W1 —7H 67 (2C 166)
Rural Way. SW16 —7F 121
Ruscoe Rd. E16 —6H 71
Ruscombe Way. Felt —7H 95
Rusham Rd. SW12 —6D 102
Rushbrook Cres. E17 —1B 34
Rushbrook Rd. SE9 —2G 127
Rushbury Ct. Hamp —1E 132
Rushcroft Rd. E4 —7J 19
Rushcroft Rd. SW2 —4A 104
Rushden Clo. SE19 —7D 122
Rushdene. SE2 —3C 92
(in two parts)
Rushdene Av. Barn —7H 5
Rushdene Clo. N'holt —2A 60
Rushdene Cres. N'holt —2K 59
Rushdene Rd. Pinn —6B 24
Rushden Gdns. NW7 —6K 13
Rushden Gdns. Ilf —2E 36
Rushen Wlk. Cars —1B 150
Rushett Clo. Th Dit —1B 146
Rushett Rd. Th Dit —7B 134
Rushey Clo. N Mald —4K 135
Rushey Grn. SE6 —7D 106
Rushey Hill. Enf —4E 6
Rushey Mead. SE4 —5C 106
Rushford Rd. SE4 —6B 106
Rush Green. —1K 57
Rush Grn. Gdns. Romf —1J 57
Rush Grn. Rd. Romf —1H 57
Rushgrove Av. NW9 —5A 28
Rushgrove Pde. NW9 —5A 28
Rushgrove St. SE18 —4D 90
Rush Hill M. SW11 —3E 102
(off Rush Hill Rd.)
Rush Hill Rd. SW11 —3E 102
Rushley Clo. Kes —4B 156
Rushmead. E2 —3H 69
Rushmead. Rich —3B 116
Rushmead Clo. Croy —4F 153
Rushmead Clo. Edgw —2C 12
Rushmere Ct. Wor Pk —2C 148
Rushmere Pl. SW19 —5F 119
Rushmon Pl. Cheam —6G 149
Rushmon Vs. N Mald —4B 136
Rushmoor Clo. Pinn —4K 23
Rushmore Clo. Brom —3C 144
Rushmore Cres. E5 —4K 51
Rushmore Ho. W14 —3G 83
(off Russell Rd.)
Rushmore Rd. E5 —4J 51
(in three parts)
Rusholme Av. Dag —3G 57
Rusholme Gro. SE19 —5E 122
Rusholme Rd. SW15 —6F 101
Rushout Av. Harr —6B 26
Rush, The. SW19 —1H 137
(off Kingston Rd.)
Rushton Ho. SW8 —2H 103
Rushton St. N1 —2D 68
Rushworth Av. NW4 —3C 28
Rushworth Gdns. NW4 —3C 28
Rushworth St. SE1 —2B 86 (6B 168)
Rushy Mdw. La. Cars —3C 150
Ruskin Av. E12 —6C 54
Ruskin Av. Felt —6H 95
Ruskin Av. Rich —7G 81
(in two parts)
Ruskin Av. Well —2A 110
Ruskin Clo. NW11 —6K 29
Ruskin Ct. N21 —7E 6
Ruskin Ct. SE5 —3D 104
(off Champion Hill)
Ruskin Dri. Well —3A 110
Ruskin Dri. Wor Pk —2D 148
Ruskin Gdns. W5 —4D 62
Ruskin Gdns. Harr —5F 27
Ruskin Gro. Well —2A 110
Ruskin Ho. SW1 —4H 85 (4D 172)
(off Herrick St.)
Ruskin Mans. W14 —6G 83
(off Queen's Club Gdns.)
Ruskin Pk. Ho. SE5 —3D 104
Ruskin Rd. N17 —1F 33
Ruskin Rd. Belv —4G 93
Ruskin Rd. Cars —5D 150
Ruskin Rd. Croy —2B 152
Ruskin Rd. Iswth —3K 97
Ruskin Rd. S'hall —7C 60
Ruskin Wlk. N9 —2B 18
Ruskin Wlk. SE24 —5C 104
Ruskin Wlk. Brom —6D 144
Ruskin Way. SW19 —1B 138
Rusland Heights. Harr —4J 25
Rusland Pk. Rd. Harr —4J 25
Rusper Clo. NW2 —3E 46
Rusper Clo. Stan —4H 11
Rusper Ct. SW9 —2J 103
(off Clapham Rd.)
Rusper Rd. N22 & N17 —2B 32
Rusper Rd. Dag —6C 56
Russell Av. N22 —2A 32
Russell Clo. NW10 —7J 45
Russell Clo. SE7 —7A 90
Russell Clo. W4 —6B 82
Russell Clo. Beck —3D 142
Russell Clo. Bexh —4G 111
Russell Clo. Ruis —2A 42
Russell Ct. E10 —7D 34
Russell Ct. N14 —6C 6
Russell Ct. SE15 —2H 105
(off Heaton Rd.)
Russell Ct. SW1 —5B 166
Russell Ct. SW16 —5K 121
Russell Ct. WC1 —4J 67 (4E 160)
Russell Ct. New Bar —4F 5
Russell Ct. Wall —5G 151
(off Ross Rd.)
Russell Gdns. N20 —2H 15
Russell Gdns. NW11 —6G 29
Russell Gdns. W14 —3G 83
Russell Gdns. Ilf —7H 37
Russell Gdns. Rich —2C 116
Russell Gdns. W Dray —5C 76
Russell Gdns. M. W14 —2G 83
Russell Gro. NW7 —5F 13
Russell Gro. SW9 —7A 86
Russell Ho. E14 —6C 70
Russell Ho. SW1 —5G 85 (5A 172)
(off Cambridge St.)
Russell Kerr Clo. W4 —7J 81
Russell La. N20 —2H 15
Russell Lodge. E4 —2K 19
Russell Lodge. SE1 —3D 86
(off Spurgeon St.)
Russell Mead. Har W —1K 25
Russell Pde. NW11 —6G 29
(off Golders Grn. Rd.)
Russell Pl. NW3 —5C 48
Russell Pl. SE16 —3A 88
Russell Rd. E4 —4G 19
Russell Rd. E10 —6D 34
Russell Rd. E16 —6J 71
Russell Rd. E17 —3B 34
Russell Rd. N8 —6H 31
Russell Rd. N13 —6E 16
Russell Rd. N15 —5E 32
Russell Rd. N20 —2H 15
Russell Rd. NW9 —6B 28
Russell Rd. SW19 —7J 119
Russell Rd. W14 —3G 83
Russell Rd. Buck H —1E 20
Russell Rd. Enf —1A 8
Russell Rd. Mitc —3C 138
Russell Rd. N'holt —5G 43
Russell Rd. Shep —7E 130
Russell Rd. Twic —6K 97
Russell Rd. W on T —6J 131
Russell's Footpath. SW16 —5J 121
Russell Sq. WC1 —5J 67 (4E 160)
Russell St. WC2 —7J 67 (2F 167)
Russell Wlk. Rich —6F 99
Russell Way. Sutt —5K 149
Russell Yd. SW15 —4G 101
Russet Av. Shep —3G 131
Russet Clo. Uxb —4E 58
Russet Cres. N7 —5K 49
Russet Dri. Croy —1A 154
Russets Clo. E4 —4A 20
Russett Way. SE13 —2D 106
Russia Ct. EC2 —7D 162
Russia Dock Rd. SE16 —1A 88
Russia Row. EC2 —6C 68 (1D 168)
Russia Wlk. SE16 —2A 88
Russington Rd. Shep —6F 131
Rusthall Av. W4 —4K 81
Rusthall Clo. Croy —6J 141
Rustic Av. SW16 —7F 121
Rustic Pl. Wemb —4D 44
Rustic Wlk. E16 —6K 71
(off Lambert Rd.)
Rustington Wlk. Mord —7H 137
Ruston Av. Surb —7H 135
Ruston Gdns. N14 —6K 5
Ruston M. W11 —6G 65
Ruston Rd. SE18 —3C 90
Ruston St. E3 —1B 70
Rust Sq. SE5 —7D 86
Rutford Rd. SW16 —5J 121
Ruth Clo. Stan —4F 27
Ruth Ct. E3 —2A 70
Rutherford Clo. Sutt —6B 150
Rutherford Clo. Uxb —4B 58
Rutherford Ho. Wemb —3J 45
(off Barnhill Rd.)
Rutherford St. SW1 —4H 85 (3C 172)
Rutherford Tower. S'hall —6F 61
Rutherford Way. Bus H —1C 10
Rutherford Way. Wemb —4G 45
Rutherglen Rd. SE2 —6A 92
Rutherwyke Clo. Eps —6C 148
Ruth Ho. W10 —4G 65
(off Kensal Rd.)
Ruthin Clo. NW9 —6A 28
Ruthin Rd. SE3 —6J 89
Ruthven St. E9 —1K 69
Rutland Av. Sidc —7A 110
Rutland Clo. SW14 —3H 99
Rutland Clo. SW19 —7C 120
Rutland Clo. Bex —2D 128
Rutland Clo. Chess —6F 147
Rutland Ct. SE5 —4D 104
Rutland Ct. SE9 —2G 127
Rutland Ct. SW7 —7D 164
Rutland Ct. W3 —6G 63
Rutland Ct. Chst —1E 144
Rutland Ct. Enf —5C 8
Rutland Dri. Mord —6H 137
Rutland Dri. Rich —1D 116
Rutland Gdns. N4 —6B 32
Rutland Gdns. SW7 —2C 84 (7D 164)
Rutland Gdns. W13 —5A 62
Rutland Gdns. Croy —4E 152
Rutland Gdns. Dag —5C 56
Rutland Gdns. M. SW7
—2C 84 (7D 164)
Rutland Ga. SW7 —2C 84 (7D 164)
Rutland Ga. Belv —5H 93
Rutland Ga. Brom —4H 143
Rutland Ga. M. SW7 —7C 164
Rutland Gro. W6 —5D 82
Rutland Ho. W8 —3K 83
(off Marloes Rd.)
Rutland Ho. N'holt —6E 42
(off Farmlands, The)
Rutland M. NW8 —1K 65
Rutland M. E. SW7 —1D 170
Rutland M. S. SW7 —1C 170
Rutland M. W. SW7 —1C 170
Rutland Pk. NW2 —6E 46
Rutland Pk. SE6 —2B 124
Rutland Pk. Gdns. NW2 —6E 46
(off Rutland Pk.)
Rutland Pk. Mans. NW2 —6E 46
Rutland Pl. EC1 —4B 68 (5B 162)
Rutland Pl. Bush —1C 10
Rutland Rd. E7 —7B 54
Rutland Rd. E9 —1K 69
Rutland Rd. E11 —5K 35
Rutland Rd. E17 —6C 34
Rutland Rd. SW19 —7C 120
Rutland Rd. Harr —6G 25
Rutland Rd. Hay —4F 77
Rutland Rd. Ilf —3F 55
Rutland Rd. S'hall —5E 60
Rutland Rd. Twic —2H 115
Rutland St. SW7 —3C 84 (1D 170)
Rutland Wlk. SE6 —2B 124
Rutley Clo. SE17 —6B 86 (7K 173)
Rutlish Rd. SW19 —1J 137
Rutter Gdns. Mitc —4A 138
Rutters Clo. W Dray —2C 76
Rutt's Ter. SE14 —1K 105
Rutts, The. Bush —1C 10
Ruvigny Gdns. SW15 —3F 101
Ruxley. —7E 128
Ruxley Clo. Eps —5H 147
Ruxley Clo. Sidc —6D 128
Ruxley Corner Ind. Est. Sidc —6D 128
Ruxley Ct. Wor Pk —5J 147
Ruxley Cres. Clay —6B 146
Ruxley La. Eps —6H 147
Ruxley M. Eps —5H 147
Ruxley Ridge. Clay —7A 146
Ruxley Towers. Clay —7A 146
Ryalls Ct. N20 —3J 15
Ryan Clo. SE3 —4K 107
Ryan Clo. Ruis —1K 41
Ryan Ct. SW16 —7J 121
Ryan Dri. Bren —6A 80
Rycott Path. SE22 —7G 105
Rycroft Way. N17 —3F 33
Ryculff Sq. SE3 —2H 107
Rydal Clo. NW4 —2F 29
Rydal Ct. Edgw —5A 12
Rydal Ct. Wemb —7F 27
Rydal Cres. Gnfd —3B 62
Rydal Dri. Bexh —1G 111
Rydal Dri. W W'ck —2G 155
Rydal Gdns. NW9 —5A 28
Rydal Gdns. SW15 —5A 118
Rydal Gdns. Houn —6F 97
Rydal Gdns. Wemb —1C 44
Rydal Mt. Brom —4H 143
Rydal Rd. SW16 —4H 121
Rydal Water. NW1 —3G 67 (2A 160)
Rydal Way. Enf —6D 8
Rydal Way. Ruis —4A 42
Rydens Ho. SE9 —3A 126
Rydens Rd. W on T —7C 132
Ryde Pl. Twic —6D 98
Ryder Clo. Brom —5K 125
Ryder Ct. E10 —2D 52
Ryder Ct. SW1 —4B 166
Ryder Dri. SE16 —5H 87
Ryder M. E9 —5J 51
Ryder's Ter. NW8 —2A 66
Ryder St. SW1 —1G 85 (4B 166)
Ryder Yd. SW1 —1G 85 (4B 166)
Ryde Va. Rd. SW12 —2G 121
Rydon M. SW19 —7E 118
Rydons Clo. SE9 —3C 108
Rydon St. N1 —1C 68
Rydston Clo. N7 —7J 49
Rye Clo. Bex —6H 111
Ryecotes Mead. SE21 —1E 122
Ryecroft Av. Ilf —2F 37
Ryecroft Av. Twic —7F 97
Ryecroft Lodge. SW16 —6B 122
Ryecroft Rd. SE13 —5E 106
Ryecroft Rd. SW16 —6A 122
Ryecroft Rd. Orp —6H 145
Ryecroft St. SW6 —1K 101
Ryedale. SE22 —6H 105
Ryefield Av. Uxb —7D 40
Ryefield Ct. N'wd —2J 23
Ryefield Cres. N'wd —2J 23
Ryefield Path. SW15 —1C 118
Ryefield Pde. N'wd —2J 23
(off Joel St.)
Ryefield Rd. SE19 —6C 122
Rye Hill Pk. SE15 —4J 105
Rye Ho. SW1 —5F 85 (5J 171)
(off Ebury Bri. Rd.)
Ryeland Clo. W Dray —6A 58
Ryelands Cres. SE12 —6A 108
Rye La. SE15 —1G 105
Rye Pas. SE15 —3G 105
Rye Rd. SE15 —4K 105
Rye, The. N14 —7C 6
Rye Wlk. SW15 —5F 101
Rye Way. Edgw —6A 12
Ryfold Rd. SW19 —3J 119
Ryhope Rd. N11 —4A 16
Ryland Clo. Felt —4H 113
Rylandes Rd. NW2 —3C 46
Ryland Rd. NW5 —6F 49
Rylett Cres. W12 —2B 82
Rylett Rd. W12 —2B 82
Rylston Rd. N13 —3J 17
Rylston Rd. SW6 —6H 83
Rymer Rd. Croy —7E 140
Rymer St. SE24 —6B 104
Rymill St. E16 —1E 90
Rysbrack St. SW3 —3D 84 (1E 170)
Rythe Ct. Th Dit —7A 134

Saatchi Gallery. —1K 65
Sabah Ct. Ashf —4C 112
Sabbarton St. E16 —6H 71
Sabella Ct. E3 —2B 70
Sabine Rd. SW11 —3D 102
Sable Clo. Houn —3A 96
Sable St. N1 —7B 50
Sach Rd. E5 —2H 51
Sackville Av. Brom —1J 155
Sackville Clo. Harr —3H 43
Sackville Gdns. Ilf —1D 54
Sackville Ho. SW16 —3J 121
Sackville Rd. Sutt —7J 149
Sackville St. W1 —7G 67 (3B 166)
Sackville Way. SE22 —1G 123
Saddlebrook Pk. Sun —7G 113
Saddlers Clo. Pinn —6A 10
Saddlers M. SW8 —1J 103
Saddlers M. Hamp W —1C 134
Saddlers M. Wemb —4K 43
Saddlescombe Way. N12 —5D 14
Saddle Yd. W1 —1F 85 (4J 165)
Sadler Clo. Mitc —2D 138
Sadler Ho. EC1 —3B 68 (1K 161)
(off Spa Grn. Est.)
Sadlers Ride. W Mol —2G 133
Sadler's Wells Theatre.
—3A 68 (1K 161)
Saffron Av. E14 —7F 71
Saffron Clo. NW11 —6H 29
Saffron Clo. Croy —6J 139
Saffron Ct. E15 —5G 53
(off Maryland Pk.)
Saffron Ct. Felt —7E 94
Saffron Hill. EC1 —5A 68 (5K 161)
Saffron Rd. Romf —2K 39
Saffron St. EC1 —5A 68 (5K 161)
Saffron Way. Surb —1D 146
Saffron Wharf. SE1 —2F 87 (6K 169)
Sage Clo. E6 —5D 72
Sage St. E1 —7J 69
Sage Way. WC1 —2G 161
Sahara Ct. S'hall —7C 60
Saigasso Clo. E16 —6B 72
Sailmakers Ct. SW6 —2A 102
Sail St. SE11 —4K 85 (3H 173)
Saimel. NW9 —7G 13
(off Satchell Mead)
Sainfoin Rd. SW17 —2E 120
Sainsbury Rd. SE19 —5E 122
St Agatha's Dri. King T —6F 117
St Agatha's Gro. Cars —1D 150
St Agnes Clo. E9 —1J 69
St Agnes Pl. SE11 —6A 86 (7K 173)
St Agnes Well. EC1 —4D 68 (3F 163)
(off City Rd.)
St Aidans Ct. Bark —2B 74
St Aidan's Rd. SE22 —6H 105
St Aidan's Rd. W13 —2B 80
St Albans Av. E6 —3D 72
St Albans Av. W4 —4K 81
St Albans Av. Felt —5B 114
St Alban's Clo. NW11 —1J 47
St Albans Ct. EC2 —6D 162
St Alban's Cres. N22 —1A 32
St Alban's Cres. Wfd G —7D 20
St Alban's Gdns. Tedd —5A 116
St Alban's Gro. W8 —3K 83
St Alban's Gro. Cars —7C 138
St Alban's La. NW11 —1J 47
St Albans Mans. W8 —3K 83
(off Kensington Ct. Pl.)
St Alban's Pl. N1 —1B 68
St Albans Rd. NW5 —3E 48
St Alban's Rd. NW10 —1A 64
St Albans Rd. Ilf —1K 55
St Alban's Rd. King T —6E 116
St Alban's Rd. Sutt —4H 149
St Alban's Rd. Wfd G —7D 20
St Alban's St. SW1 —7H 67 (3C 166)
(in two parts)
St Albans Ter. W6 —6G 83
St Albans Vs. NW5 —3E 48
St Alban Tower. E4 —6G 19
St Alfege Pas. SE10 —6E 88
St Alfege Rd. SE7 —6B 90
St Alphage Garden. EC2
(in two parts) —5C 68 (6D 162)
St Alphage Highwalk. EC2 —6D 162
St Alphage Ho. EC2 —6E 162
St Alphage Wlk. Edgw —2J 27
St Alphege Rd. N9 —7D 8
St Alphonsus Rd. SW4 —4G 103
St Amunds Clo. SE6 —4C 124
St Andrews Av. Wemb —4A 44
St Andrews Chambers. W1
(off Wells St.) —5G 67 (6B 160)
St Andrew's Clo. N12 —4F 15
St Andrew's Clo. NW2 —3D 46
St Andrews Clo. SE16 —5H 87
(off Ryder Dri.)
St Andrews Clo. SE28 —6D 74
St Andrew's Clo. Iswth —1J 97
St Andrew's Clo. Ruis —2B 42
St Andrew's Clo. Shep —4F 131
St Andrew's Clo. Stan —2C 26
St Andrew's Ct. SW18 —2A 120
St Andrews Ct. Sutt —3C 150
St Andrews Dri. Stan —1C 26
St Andrews Gro. N16 —1D 50
St Andrew's Hill. EC4 —7B 68 (2B 168)
(in two parts)
St Andrew's Mans. W1 —5E 66 (6G 159)
(off Dorset St.)
St Andrews Mans. W14 —6G 83
(off St Andrews Rd.)
St Andrew's M. N16 —1E 50
St Andrew's M. SE3 —7J 89
St Andrews M. SW12 —1H 121
St Andrew's Pl. NW1 —4F 67 (3K 159)
St Andrew's Rd. E11 —6G 35
St Andrew's Rd. E13 —3K 71
St Andrew's Rd. E17 —2K 33
St Andrew's Rd. N9 —7D 8
St Andrew's Rd. NW9 —1K 45
St Andrew's Rd. NW10 —6D 46
St Andrew's Rd. NW11 —6H 29
St Andrew's Rd. W3 —7A 64
St Andrews Rd. W7 —2J 79
St Andrew's Rd. W14 —6G 83
St Andrew's Rd. Cars —3C 150
St Andrew's Rd. Croy —4C 152
St Andrew's Rd. Enf —3J 7
St Andrew's Rd. Ilf —7D 36
St Andrew's Rd. Romf —6K 39
St Andrew's Rd. Sidc —3D 128
St Andrew's Rd. Surb —6D 134
St Andrew's Rd. Uxb —1A 58
St Andrews Sq. W11 —6G 65
St Andrew's Sq. Surb —6D 134
St Andrews Tower. S'hall —7G 61
(off Baird Av.)
St Andrew St. EC4 —5A 68 (7K 161)
St Andrews Way. E3 —4D 70
St Andrew's Wharf. SE1
—2F 87 (6K 169)
St Anna Rd. Barn —5A 4
St Anne's Clo. N6 —3E 48
St Anne's Ct. NW6 —1G 65
St Anne's Ct. W1 —6H 67 (1C 166)
St Anne's Ct. W W'ck —4G 155
St Anne's Flats. NW1 —3H 67 (1C 160)
(off Doric Way)
St Anne's Gdns. NW10 —3F 63
St Anne's Pas. E14 —6B 70
St Anne's Rd. E11 —2F 53
St Anne's Rd. Wemb —5D 44
St Anne's Row. E14 —6B 70
St Anne's St. E14 —6B 70
St Anne's Trad. Est. E14 —6B 70
St Ann's. Bark —1G 73
St Ann's Ct. NW4 —3D 28
St Ann's Cres. SW18 —6K 101
St Ann's Gdns. NW5 —6E 48
St Ann's Hill. SW18 —5K 101
St Ann's Ho. WC1 —3A 68 (2J 161)
(off Margery St.)
St Ann's La. SW1 —3H 85 (2D 172)
St Ann's Pk. Rd. SW18 —6A 102
St Ann's Pas. E14 —6B 70
St Ann's Pas. SW13 —3A 100
St Ann's Rd. N9 —2A 18
St Ann's Rd. N15 —5B 32
St Ann's Rd. SW13 —2B 100
St Ann's Rd. W11 —7F 65
St Ann's Rd. Bark —1G 73
St Ann's Rd. Harr —6J 25
St Ann's Shop. Cen. Harr —6J 25
St Ann's St. SW1 —3H 85 (1D 172)
St Ann's Ter. NW8 —2B 66
St Ann's Vs. W11 —1F 83
St Ann's Way. S Croy —6B 152
St Anselm's Pl. W1 —7F 67 (2J 165)
St Anselm's Rd. Hay —2H 77
St Anthony's Av. Wfd G —6F 21
St Anthony's Clo. E1 —1G 87

St Anthony's Clo.—St Martin's le-Grand

St Anthony's Clo. SW17 —2C 120
St Anthony's Flats. NW1 —2H 67
(off Aldenham St.)
St Anthony's Way. Felt —4H 95
St Antony's Rd. E7 —7K 53
St Arvan's Clo. Croy —3E 152
St Asaph Rd. SE4 —3K 105
St Aubins Ct. N1 —1D 68
St Aubyn's Av. SW19 —5H 119
St Aubyn's Av. Houn —5E 96
St Aubyn's Rd. SE19 —6F 123
St Audrey Av. Bexh —2G 111
St Augustine's Av. W5 —2E 62
St Augustine's Av. Brom —5C 144
St Augustine's Av. S Croy —6C 152
St Augustines Av. Wemb —3E 44
St Augustine's Ho. NW1
(off Werrington St.) —3H 67 (1C 160)
St Augustine's Mans. SW1
(off Bloomburg St.) —4G 85 (4B 172)
St Augustine's Path. N5 —4C 50
St Augustine's Rd. NW1 —7H 49
St Augustine's Rd. Belv —4F 93
St Austell Clo. Edgw —2F 27
St Austell Rd. SE13 —2E 106
St Awdry's Rd. Bark —7H 55
St Awdry's Wlk. Bark —7G 55
St Barnabas Clo. SE22 —5E 104
St Barnabas Clo. Beck —2E 142
St Barnabas Ct. Har W —1G 25
St Barnabas Gdns. W Mol —5E 132
St Barnabas Rd. E17 —6C 34
St Barnabas Rd. Mitc —7E 120
St Barnabas Rd. Sutt —5B 150
St Barnabas Rd. Wfd G —1K 35
St Barnabas St. SW1 —5E 84 (5H 171)
St Barnabas Ter. E9 —5K 51
St Barnabas Vs. SW8 —1J 103
St Bartholomew's Clo. SE26 —4H 123
St Bartholomew's Ct. E6 —2C 72
(off St Bartholomew's Rd.)
St Bartholomew's Rd. E6 —2D 72
St Benedict's Clo. SW17 —5E 120
St Benet's Clo. SW17 —2C 120
St Benet's Gro. Cars —7A 138
St Benet's Pl. EC3 —7D 68 (2F 169)
St Bernards. Croy —3E 152
St Bernard's Clo. SE27 —4D 122
St Bernard's Rd. E6 —1B 72
St Blaise Av. Brom —2K 143
St Botolph Row. EC3 —6F 69 (1J 169)
St Botolph St. EC3 —6F 69 (7J 163)
St Brelades Ct. N1 —1E 68
St Briavel's Ct. SE15 —7E 86
(off Lynbrook Clo.)
St Bride's Av. EC4 —1A 168
St Bride's Av. Edgw —1F 27
St Bride's Church. —1A 168
St Brides Clo. Eri —2D 92
St Bride's Pas. EC4 —1A 168
St Bride St. EC4 —6B 68 (7A 162)
St Catherines Clo. Chess —6D 146
St Catherine's Clo. SW17 —2C 120
St Catherine's Ct. W4 —3A 82
St Catherines Ct. Felt —1J 113
St Catherine's Dri. SE14 —2K 105
St Catherine's Farm Ct. Ruis —6E 22
St Catherines M. SW3 —4D 84 (3E 170)
St Catherine's Rd. E4 —2H 19
St Catherine's Rd. Ruis —6F 23
St Catherines Tower. E10 —7D 34
St Cecilia's Clo. Sutt —1G 149
St Chads Clo. Surb —7C 134
St Chad's Gdns. Romf —7E 38
St Chad's Pl. WC1 —3J 67 (1F 161)
St Chad's Rd. Romf —7E 38
St Chad's St. WC1 —3J 67 (1F 161)
(in two parts)
St Charles Pl. W10 —5G 65
St Charles Sq. W10 —5F 65
St Christopher Rd. Uxb —6A 58
St Christopher's Clo. Iswth —1J 97
St Christophers Dri. Hay —7K 59
St Christopher's Gdns. T Hth —3A 140
St Christopher's Ho. NW1 —2G 67
(off Bridgeway St.)
St Christopher's M. Wall —5G 151
St Christopher's Pl. W1
—6E 66 (7H 159)
St Clair Clo. Ilf —2D 36
St Clair Dri. Wor Pk —3D 148
St Clair Rd. E13 —2K 71
St Clair's Rd. Croy —2E 152
St Clare Bus. Pk. Hamp —6G 115
St Clare St. EC3 —6F 69 (1J 169)
St Clement's Ct. EC4 —2F 169
St Clement's Ct. N7 —6K 49
St Clement's Heights. SE26 —3G 123
St Clement's La. WC2 —6K 67 (1H 167)
St Clements Mans. SW6 —6F 83
(off Lillie Rd.)
St Clement St. N7 —7A 50
St Clements Yd. SE22 —4F 105
St Cloud Rd. SE27 —4C 122
St Columbas Ho. E17 —4D 34
St Crispin's Clo. NW3 —4C 48
St Crispin's Clo. S'hall —6D 60
St Cross St. EC1 —5A 68 (5K 161)
St Cuthbert's Rd. NW2 —6H 47
St Cyprian's St. SW17 —4D 120
St David Clo. Uxb —5A 58
St Davids Clo. SE16 —5H 87
(off Masters Dri.)
St David's Clo. Wemb —3J 45
St David's Clo. W W'ck —7D 142
St David's Dri. Edgw —1F 27
St David's Pl. NW4 —7D 28
St David's Sq. E14 —5D 88
St Davids Sq. E14 —5D 88
St Denis Rd. SE27 —4D 122
St Dionis Rd. SW6 —2H 101
St Domingo Ho. SE18 —3D 90
(off Leda Rd.)
St Donatt's Rd. SE14 —1B 106
St Dunstan's. (Junct.) —6H 149
St Dunstan's All. EC3 —2G 169
St Dunstan's Av. W3 —7K 63
St Dunstan's Clo. Hay —5H 77
St Dunstan's Ct. EC4 —6A 68 (1K 167)
St Dunstan's Gdns. W3 —7K 63
St Dunstans Hill. EC3
—7E 68 (3G 169)
St Dunstan's Hill. Sutt —5G 149
St Dunstan's La. EC3
—7E 68 (3G 169)
St Dunstan's La. Beck —6E 142
St Dunstan's Rd. E7 —6K 53
St Dunstan's Rd. SE25 —4F 141
St Dunstan's Rd. W6 —5F 83
St Dunstan's Rd. W7 —2J 79
St Dunstan's Rd. Felt —3H 113
St Dunstan's Rd. Houn —2K 95
(in two parts)
St Edmund's Av. Ruis —6F 23
St Edmund's Clo. NW8 —1D 66
St Edmund's Clo. SW17 —2C 120
St Edmunds Clo. Eri —2D 92
St Edmund's Ct. NW8 —1D 66
(off St Edmund's Ter.)
St Edmund's Dri. Stan —1A 26
St Edmund's La. Twic —7F 97
St Edmund's Rd. N9 —7B 8
St Edmund's Rd. Ilf —6D 36
St Edmunds Sq. SW13 —6E 82
St Edmund's Ter. NW8 —1C 66
St Edward's Clo. NW11 —6J 29
St Edwards Ct. E10 —7D 34
St Edwards Ct. NW11 —6J 29
St Edwards Way. Romf —5K 39
St Egberts Way. E4 —1K 19
St Elizabeth Ct. E10 —7D 34
St Elmo Rd. W12 —1B 82
(in two parts)
St Elmos Rd. SE16 —2A 88
St Erkenwald M. Bark —1H 73
St Erkenwald Rd. Bark —1H 73
St Ermin's Hill. SW1 —1C 172
St Ervan's Rd. W10 —5H 65
St Eugene Ct. NW6 —1G 65
(off Salusbury Rd.)
St Fabians Tower. E4 —6G 19
St Fabian Tower. E4 —6G 19
St Faith's Clo. Enf —1H 7
St Faith's Rd. SE21 —1B 122
St Fidelis Rd. Eri —4K 93
St Fillans Rd. SE6 —1E 124
St Frances Way. Ilf —4H 55
St Francis Clo. Orp —6J 145
St Francis' Ho. NW1 —2H 67
(off Bridgeway St.)
St Francis Rd. SE22 —4E 104
St Francis Rd. Eri —4K 93
St Francis Tower. E4 —6G 19
(off Burnside Av.)
St Frideswides M. E14 —6E 70
(off Lodore St.)
St Gabriel's Clo. E11 —1K 53
St Gabriels Mnr. SE5 —1B 104
(off Cormont Rd.)
St Gabriels Rd. NW2 —5F 47
St George's Av. E7 —7K 53
St George's Av. N7 —4H 49
St George's Av. NW9 —4K 27
St George's Av. W5 —2D 80
St George's Av. S'hall —7D 60
St George's Bldgs. SE1 —3B 86
(off St George's Rd.)
St George's Cir. SE1 —3B 86
St George's Clo. NW11 —6H 29
St Georges Clo. SE28 —6D 74
St George's Clo. SW8 —1G 103
St George's Clo. Wemb —3A 44
St George's Ct. E6 —4D 72
St George's Ct. E17 —5F 35
St Georges Ct. EC4 —6B 68 (7A 162)
St George's Ct. SW15 —4H 101
St Georges Ct. Harr —6A 26
(off Kenton Rd.)
St George's Ct. Wemb —3H 45
St George's Dri. SW1 —4F 85 (4K 171)
St George's Dri. Uxb —3B 40
St George's Fields. W2 —6C 66 (1D 164)
St George's Gdns. Surb —2H 147
St George's Gro. SW17 —3B 120
St George's Ho. NW1 —2H 67
(off Bridgeway St.)
St Georges Ind. Est. N17 —7G 17
St George's Ind. Est. King T —5D 116
St George's La. EC3 —2F 169
St George's Mans. SW1
(off Causton St.) —5H 85 (5D 172)
St George's M. NW1 —7D 48
St George's M. SE1 —1K 173
St Georges Pde. SE6 —2B 124
St George's Path. SE4 —4C 106
(off Adelaide Av.)
St George's Pl. Twic —1A 116
St George's Rd. E7 —7K 53
St George's Rd. E10 —3E 52
St George's Rd. N9 —3B 18
St George's Rd. N13 —3E 16
St George's Rd. NW11 —6H 29
St George's Rd. SE1 —3A 86 (1K 173)
St George's Rd. SW19 —7H 119
(in two parts)
St George's Rd. W4 —2K 81
St George's Rd. W7 —1K 79
St George's Rd. Beck —1D 142
St George's Rd. Brom —2D 144
(in two parts)
St George's Rd. Dag —5E 56
St George's Rd. Enf —1A 8
St George's Rd. Felt —4B 114
St George's Rd. Ilf —7D 36
St George's Rd. King T —7G 117
St George's Rd. Mitc —3F 139
St George's Rd. Orp —6H 145
St Georges Rd. Rich —3F 99
St George's Rd. Sidc —6D 128
St George's Rd. Twic —5B 98
St George's Rd. Wall —5F 151
St George's Rd. W. Brom —2C 144
St George's Shop. & Leisure Cen. Harr
—6J 25
St George's Sq. E7 —7K 53
St Georges Sq. E14 —7A 70
St George's Sq. SE8 —4B 88
St George's Sq. SW1 —5H 85 (5C 172)
St George's Sq. N Mald —3A 136
St George's Sq. M. SW1 —5H 85 (6C 172)
St George's Ter. NW1 —7D 48
St George St. W1 —7F 67 (1K 165)
St George's Wlk. Croy —3C 152
St George's Way. SE15 —6E 86
St George's Wharf. SE1 —2F 87 (6K 169)
(off Shad Thames)
St Gerards Clo. SW4 —5G 103
St German's Pl. SE3 —1J 107
St German's Rd. SE23 —1A 124
St Giles Av. Dag —7H 57
St Giles Av. Uxb —4E 40
St Giles Cir. W1 —6H 67 (7D 160)
St Giles Clo. Dag —7H 57
St Giles Ct. WC2 —7E 160
St Giles High St. WC2 —6H 67 (7D 160)
St Giles Ho. New Bar —4F 5
St Giles Pas. WC2 —1D 166
St Giles Rd. SE5 —7E 86
St Giles Ter. EC2 —5C 68
(off Beech St.)
St Gothard Rd. SE27 —4D 122
(in two parts)
St Gregory Clo. Ruis —4A 42
St Helena Ho. WC1 —3A 68 (2J 161)
(off Margery St.)
St Helena Rd. SE16 —4K 87
St Helena St. WC1 —3A 68 (2J 161)
St Helens. Th Dit —7K 133
St Helen's Cres. SW16 —1K 139
St Helen's Gdns. W10 —5F 65
St Helen's Pl. EC2 —6E 68 (7G 163)
St Helen's Rd. SW16 —1K 139
St Helen's Rd. W13 —1B 80
St Helen's Rd. Eri —2D 92
St Helen's Rd. Ilf —6D 36
St Helier. —7C 138
St Helier Av. Mord —7A 138
St Helier Ct. N1 —1E 68
(off De Beauvoir Est.)
St Helier's Av. Houn —5E 96
St Helier's Rd. E10 —6E 34
St Hilda's Av. Ashf —5A 112
St Hilda's Clo. NW6 —1F 65
St Hilda's Clo. SW17 —2C 120
St Hilda's Rd. SW13 —6D 82
St Hubert's Ho. E14 —3C 88
St Hughes Clo. SW17 —2C 120
St Hugh's Rd. SE20 —1H 141
St James. SE14 —1A 106
St James Apartments. E17 —5A 34
(off High St.)
St James Av. N20 —3H 15
St James Av. W13 —1A 80
St James Av. Sutt —5J 149
St James Clo. N20 —3H 15
St James Clo. SE18 —5G 91
St James Clo. Barn —4G 5
St James Clo. N Mald —5B 136
St James Clo. Ruis —2A 42
St James Ct. E2 —3G 69
(off Bethnal Grn. Rd.)
St James Ct. E12 —2A 54
St James Ct. SE3 —1K 107
St James' Ct. SW1 —3G 85 (1B 172)
St James' Gdns. Wemb —7D 44
St James Ga. Buck H —1E 20
St James Gro. SW11 —2D 102
St James M. E14 —3E 88
St James M. E17 —5A 34
(off St James's St.)
St James Residences. W1
(off Brewer St.) —7H 67 (2C 166)
St James' Rd. E15 —5H 53
St James' Rd. N9 —2C 18
St James Rd. Cars —3C 150
St James Rd. Mitc —7E 120
St James' Rd. Surb —6D 134
St James Rd. Sutt —5J 149
St James's. —1H 85 (5C 166)
St James's. SW1 —1G 85
St James's App. EC2 —4E 68 (4G 163)
St James's Av. Beck —3A 142
St James's Av. Hamp H —5G 115
St James's Chambers. SW1
(off Ryder St.) —1G 85 (4B 166)
St James's Clo. NW8 —1D 66
(off St James's Ter M.)
St James's Clo. SW17 —2D 120
St James's Cotts. Rich —5D 98
St James's Ct. N18 —6A 18
(off Fore St.)
St James's Ct. Harr —6A 26
St James's Ct. King T —3E 134
St James's Cres. SW9 —3A 104
St James's Dri. SW17 & SW12 —1D 120
St James's Gdns. W11 —1G 83
St James's La. N10 —4F 31
St James's Mkt. SW1 —7H 67 (3C 166)
St James's Palace. —2G 85 (6B 166)
St James's Pk. —2H 85 (6C 166)
St James's Pk. Croy —7C 140
St James's Pas. EC3 —1H 169
St James's Pl. SW1 —1G 85 (5A 166)
St James's Rd. SE1 —6G 87
St James's Rd. SE16 —3G 87
St James's Rd. Croy —7B 140
St James's Rd. Hamp H —5F 115
St James's Rd. King T —2D 134
St James's Sq. SW1 —1G 85 (4B 166)
St James's St. E17 —5A 34
St James's St. SW1 —1G 85 (4A 166)
St James's Ter. NW8 —1D 66
(off Prince Albert Rd.)
St James's Ter. M. NW8 —1D 66
St James St. W6 —5E 82
St James's Wlk. EC1 —4B 68 (3A 162)
St James Ter. SW12 —1E 120
St James Way. Sidc —5E 128
St Jeromes Gro. Hay —6E 58
St Joan's Rd. N9 —2A 18
St John Fisher Rd. Eri —3D 92
St John's. —2C 106
St John's Av. N11 —5J 15
St John's Av. NW10 —1B 64
St John's Av. SW15 —5F 101
St Johns Chu. Rd. E9 —5J 51
St Johns Clo. N14 —6B 6
St John's Clo. N20 —3F 15
(off Rasper Rd.)
St John's Clo. SW6 —7J 83
St John's Clo. Wemb —5E 44
St John's Cotts. SE20 —7J 123
St John's Ct. N4 —2B 50
St John's Ct. N5 —4B 50
St John's Ct. SE13 —2E 106
St John's Ct. W6 —4D 82
(off Glenthorne Rd.)
St John's Ct. Buck H —1E 20
St John's Ct. Eri —4K 93
St John's Ct. Harr —6K 25
St John's Ct. Iswth —2K 97
St John's Ct. N'wd —1G 23
(off Murray Rd.)
St John's Cres. SW9 —3A 104
St Johns Dri. SW18 —1K 119
St John's Est. N1 —2D 68
St John's Est. SE1 —6J 169
St John's Gdns. W11 —7G 65
St John's Gate. —4A 162
St John's Gro. N19 —2G 49
St John's Gro. SW13 —2B 100
St John's Gro. Rich —4E 98
St John's Hill. SW11 —5B 102
St John's Hill Gro. SW11 —4B 102
St John's Ho. E14 —4E 88
St Johns Ho. SE17 —6D 86
(off Lytham St.)
St John's La. EC1 —4B 68 (4A 162)
St John's M. W11 —6J 65
St John's Pde. W13 —1B 80
St Johns Pde. Sidc —4A 128
(off Sidcup High St.)
St John's Pk. SE3 —7H 89
St John's Pk. Mans. N19 —3G 49
St John's Pas. SW19 —6G 119
St John's Path. EC1 —4A 162
St Johns Pathway. SE23 —1J 123
St John's Pl. EC1 —4B 68 (4A 162)
St John's Rd. E4 —4J 19
St John's Rd. E6 —1C 72
St John's Rd. E16 —6J 71
St John's Rd. E17 —2D 34
St John's Rd. N15 —6E 32
St John's Rd. NW11 —6H 29
St John's Rd. SE20 —6J 123
St John's Rd. SW11 —4C 102
St John's Rd. SW19 —7G 119
St John's Rd. Bark —1J 73
St John's Rd. Cars —3C 150
St John's Rd. Croy —3B 152
St John's Rd. E Mol —4H 133
St John's Rd. Eri —5K 93
St John's Rd. Felt —4C 114
St John's Rd. Hamp W —2C 134
St John's Rd. Harr —6K 25
St John's Rd. Ilf —7J 37
St John's Rd. Iswth —2K 97
St John's Rd. N Mald —3J 135
St John's Rd. Orp —6H 145
St John's Rd. Rich —4E 98
St John's Rd. Sidc —4B 128
St John's Rd. S'hall —3C 78
St John's Rd. Sutt —2K 149
St John's Rd. Well —3B 110
St John's Rd. Wemb —4D 44
St John's Sq. EC1 —4B 68 (4A 162)
St John's Ter. E7 —6K 53
St John's Ter. SE18 —6G 91
St John's Ter. SW15 —3A 118
(off Kingston Va.)
St John's Ter. W10 —4F 65
St John St. EC1 —2A 68 (1K 161)
St John's Va. SE8 —2C 106
St John's Vs. N11 —5J 15
(off Friern Barnet Rd.)
St John's Vs. N19 —2H 49
St John's Vs. W8 —3K 83
St John's Way. N19 —2G 49
St John's Wood. —2B 66
St John's Wood Ct. NW8 —2B 158
St John's Wood High St. NW8
—2B 66 (1C 158)
St John's Wood Pk. NW8 —1B 66
St John's Wood Rd. NW8
—4B 66 (3A 158)
St John's Wood Ter. NW8 —2B 66
St John's Yd. N17 —7A 18
St Joseph's Clo. W10 —5G 65
St Josephs Ct. SE7 —6K 89
St Joseph's Dri. S'hall —1C 78
St Joseph's Flats. NW1 —3H 67 (1C 160)
(off Drummond Cres.)
St Joseph's Gro. NW4 —4D 28
St Joseph's Rd. N9 —7C 8
St Joseph's St. SW8 —1F 103
St Joseph's Va. SE3 —3F 107
St Jude's Rd. E2 —2H 69
St Jude St. N1 —5E 50
St Julian's Clo. SW16 —4A 122
St Julian's Farm Rd. SE27 —4A 122
St Julian's Rd. NW6 —1J 65
St Katharine Docks. —1G 87 (3K 169)
St Katharine's Precinct. NW1 —2F 67
St Katharine's Way. E1 —1F 87 (4K 169)
(in two parts)
St Katherine's Rd. Eri —2D 92
St Katherine's Row. EC3 —2H 169
St Katherines Wlk. W11 —1F 83
(off St Ann's Rd.)
St Keverne Rd. SE9 —4C 126
St Kilda Rd. W13 —1A 80
St Kilda Rd. Orp —7K 145
St Kilda's Rd. N16 —1D 50
St Kilda's Rd. Harr —6J 25
St Kitts Ter. SE19 —5E 122
St Laurence Clo. NW6 —1F 65
St Lawrence Bus. Cen. Twic —2K 113
St Lawrence Clo. Edgw —7A 12
St Lawrence Cotts. E14 —1E 88
St Lawrence Ct. N1 —7D 50
(off De Beauvoir Est.)
St Lawrence Dri. Pinn —5K 23
St Lawrence Ho. SE1 —3E 86 (7H 169)
(off Purbrook St.)
St Lawrence St. E14 —1E 88
St Lawrence Ter. W10 —5G 65
St Lawrence Way. SW9 —2A 104
St Leonard M. N1 —2E 68
St Leonard's Av. E4 —6A 20
St Leonard's Av. Harr —5C 26
St Leonard's Clo. Well —3A 110
St Leonard's Ct. N1 —1F 163
St Leonards Ct. SW14 —3J 99
St Leonard's Gdns. Houn —1C 96
St Leonard's Gdns. Ilf —5G 55
St Leonard's Rd. E14 —5D 70
(in two parts)
St Leonard's Rd. NW10 —4K 63
St Leonard's Rd. SW14 —3H 99
St Leonard's Rd. W13 —7C 62
St Leonard's Rd. Clay —6A 146
St Leonard's Rd. Croy —3B 152
St Leonard's Rd. Surb —5D 134
St Leonard's Rd. Th Dit —6A 134
St Leonards Sq. NW5 —6E 48
St Leonards Sq. Surb —5D 134
St Leonard's St. E3 —3D 70
St Leonard's Ter. SW3 —5D 84 (6E 170)
St Leonard's Wlk. SW16 —7K 121
St Loo Av. SW3 —6C 84 (7D 170)
St Louis Rd. SE27 —4D 122
St Loy's Rd. N17 —2E 32
St Lucia Dri. E15 —1H 71
St Luke Clo. Uxb —6A 58
St Luke's. —4C 68 (3D 162)
St Luke's Av. SW4 —4H 103
St Luke's Av. Enf —1J 7
St Luke's Av. Ilf —5F 55
St Luke's Clo. EC1 —4C 68 (3D 162)
St Luke's Clo. SE25 —6H 141
St Lukes Ct. E10 —7D 34
(off Capworth St.)
St Luke's Est. EC1 —3D 68 (2E 162)
St Luke's M. W11 —6H 65
St Luke's Pas. King T —1F 135
St Luke's Path. Ilf —5F 55
St Luke's Rd. W11 —5H 65
St Luke's Rd. Uxb —1A 58
St Luke's Sq. E16 —6H 71
St Luke's St. SW3 —5C 84 (5D 170)
St Luke's Yd. W9 —2H 65
(in two parts)
St Malo Av. N9 —3D 18
St Margarets. —6B 98
St Margaret's. Bark —1G 73
St Margaret's Av. N15 —4B 32
St Margaret's Av. N20 —1F 15
St Margaret's Av. Ashf —5D 112
St Margaret's Av. Harr —3G 43
St Margaret's Av. Sidc —3H 127
St Margaret's Av. Sutt —3G 149
St Margarets Av. Uxb —4C 58
St Margarets Bus. Cen. Twic —6B 98
St Margarets Clo. EC2 —6D 68 (7E 162)
(off Lothbury)
St Margaret's Ct. N11 —4K 15
St Margarets Ct. SE1 —1C 86 (5D 168)
St Margarets Ct. SW15 —4D 100
St Margarets Ct. Edgw —5C 12
St Margaret's Cres. SW15 —5D 100
St Margaret's Dri. Twic —5B 98
St Margaret's Gro. E11 —3H 53
St Margaret's Gro. SE18 —6G 91
St Margaret's Gro. Twic —6A 98
St Margaret's La. W8 —3K 83
St Margaret's Pas. SE13 —3G 107
St Margarets Path. SE18 —5G 91
St Margaret's Rd. E12 —2A 54
St Margaret's Rd. N17 —3E 32
St Margaret's Rd. NW10 —3E 64
St Margarets Rd. SE4 —4B 106
(in two parts)
St Margaret's Rd. W7 —2J 79
St Margaret's Rd. Edgw —5C 12
St Margarets Rd. Iswth & Twic —4B 98
St Margaret's Rd. Ruis —6F 23
St Margarets Roundabout. (Junct.)
—6B 98
St Margaret's Ter. SE18 —5G 91
St Margaret St. SW1 —2J 85 (7E 166)
St Mark's Clo. SE10 —7E 88
St Marks Clo. SW6 —1J 101
St Marks Clo. Harr —7B 26
St Mark's Clo. New Bar —3E 4
St Marks Ct. E10 —7D 34
(off Capworth St.)
St Marks Ct. NW8 —2A 66
(off Abercorn Pl.)
St Marks Ct. W7 —2J 79
(off Lwr. Boston Rd.)
St Mark's Cres. NW1 —1E 66
St Mark's Ga. E9 —7B 52
St Mark's Gro. SW10 —7K 83
St Mark's Hill. Surb —6E 134
St Marks Ho. SE17 —6D 86
(off Lytham St.)
St Marks Ind. Est. E16 —1B 90
St Mark's Pl. SW19 —6H 119
St Mark's Pl. W11 —6G 65
St Mark's Ri. E8 —5F 51
St Mark's Rd. SE25 —4G 141
St Mark's Rd. W5 —1E 80
St Mark's Rd. W7 —2J 79
St Mark's Rd. W10 & W11 —5F 65
St Mark's Rd. Brom —3J 143
St Marks Rd. Enf —6A 8
St Marks Rd. Mitc —2D 138
St Mark's Rd. Tedd —7B 116
St Mark's Sq. NW1 —1E 66
St Mark St. E1 —6F 69 (1K 169)
St Martin Clo. Uxb —6A 58
St Martin's Almshouses. NW1 —1G 67
St Martin's App. Ruis —7G 23
St Martin's Av. E6 —2B 72
St Martin's Clo. NW1 —1G 67
St Martin's Clo. Enf —1C 8
St Martin's Clo. Eri —2D 92
St Martins Ct. N1 —1E 68
(off De Beauvoir Est.)
St Martin's Ct. WC2 —7J 67 (2E 166)
St Martins Est. SW2 —1A 122
St Martins La. WC2 —7J 67 (2E 166)
St Martins La. Beck —5D 142
St Martin's le-Grand. EC1
—6C 68 (7C 162)

St Martin's Pl.—Sandhurst Av.

St Martin's Pl. WC2 —7J 67 (3E 166)
St Martin's Rd. N9 —2C 18
St Martin's Rd. SW9 —2K 103
St Martin's St. WC2 —7H 67 (3D 166)
(in two parts)
St Martins Way. SW17 —3A 120
St Mary Abbot's Ct. W14 —3H 83
(off Warwick Gdns.)
St Mary Abbot's Pl. W8 —3H 83
St Mary Abbot's Ter. W14 —3H 83
St Mary at Hill. EC3 —7E 68 (3G 169)
St Mary Av. Wall —3E 150
St Mary Axe. EC3 —6E 68 (1G 169)
St Marychurch St. SE16 —2J 87
St Mary Graces Ct. E1 —7F 69 (3K 169)
St Marylebone Crematorium. N2 —3K 29
St Mary le-Park Ct. SW11 —7C 84
(off Parkgate Rd.)
St Mary Newington Clo. SE17 —5E 86
(off Surrey Sq.)
St Mary Rd. E17 —4C 34
St Mary's. Bark —1H 73
St Mary's App. E12 —5D 54
St Mary's Av. E11 —7K 35
St Mary's Av. N3 —2G 29
St Mary's Av. Brom —3G 143
St Mary's Av. Tedd —6K 115
St Mary's Av. Central. S'hall —4F 79
St Mary's Av. N. S'hall —4F 79
St Mary's Av. S. S'hall —4F 79
St Mary's Clo. N17 —1F 33
St Mary's Clo. Chess —7F 147
St Mary's Clo. Eps —7B 148
St Mary's Clo. Sun —4J 131
St Mary's Ct. E6 —4D 72
St Mary's Ct. SE7 —7B 90
St Mary's Ct. W5 —2D 80
St Mary's Ct. W12 —3B 82
St Mary's Ct. Wall —4G 151
St Mary's Cres. NW4 —3D 28
St Mary's Cres. Hay —7H 59
St Mary's Cres. Iswth —7H 79
St Mary's Dri. Felt —7E 94
St Mary's Est. SE16 —2J 87
(off St Marychurch St.)
St Mary's Flats. NW1 —3H 67 (1C 160)
St Mary's Gdns. SE11 —4A 86 (3K 173)
St Mary's Ga. W8 —3K 83
St Mary's Grn. N2 —2A 30
St Mary's Gro. N1 —6B 50
St Mary's Gro. SW13 —3D 100
St Mary's Gro. W4 —6H 81
St Mary's Gro. Rich —4F 99
St Mary's Ho. N1 —1B 68
(off St Mary's Path)
St Mary's Mans. W2 —5B 66 (5A 158)
St Mary's M. NW6 —7K 47
(in two parts)
St Marys M. Rich —2C 116
St Mary's Path. N1 —1B 68
St Mary's Pl. SE9 —6D 108
St Mary's Pl. W5 —2D 80
St Mary's Pl. W8 —3K 83
St Mary's Rd. E10 —3E 52
St Mary's Rd. E13 —2K 71
St Mary's Rd. N8 —4J 31
St Mary's Rd. N9 —1C 18
St Mary's Rd. NW10 —1A 64
St Mary's Rd. NW11 —7G 29
St Mary's Rd. SE15 —1J 105
St Mary's Rd. SE25 —3E 140
St Mary's Rd. SW19 —5G 119
St Marys Rd. W5 —2D 80
St Mary's Rd. Barn —7J 5
St Mary's Rd. Bex —1J 129
St Mary's Rd. Dit H —7C 134
St Mary's Rd. E Mol —5H 133
St Mary's Rd. Hay —7H 59
St Mary's Rd. Ilf —2H 55
St Mary's Rd. Surb —6D 134
St Mary's Rd. Wor Pk —2A 148
St Mary's Sq. W2 —5B 66 (5A 158)
St Mary's Sq. W5 —2D 80
St Mary's Ter. W2 —5B 66 (5A 158)
St Mary's Tower. EC1 —4C 68 (4D 162)
(off Fortune St.)
St Mary St. SE18 —4D 90
St Mary's Vw. Harr —5C 26
St Mary's Wlk. SE11 —4A 86 (3K 173)
St Mary's Wlk. Hay —7H 59
St Mary's Way. Chig —5K 21
St Matthew Clo. Uxb —6A 58
St Matthew's Av. Surb —1E 146
St Matthews Ct. E10 —7D 34
(off Capworth St.)
St Matthews Ct. N10 —2E 30
St Matthews Ct. SE1 —3C 86
(off Meadow Row)
St Matthew's Dri. Brom —3D 144
St Matthews Ho. SE17 —6D 86
(off Phelp St.)
St Matthew's Lodge. NW1 —2G 67
(off Oakley Sq.)
St Matthew's Rd. SW2 —4K 103
St Matthew's Rd. W5 —1E 80
St Matthew's Row. E2 —3G 69
St Matthew St. SW1 —3H 85 (2C 172)
St Matthias Clo. NW9 —5B 28
St Maur Rd. SW6 —1H 101
St Mellion Clo. SE28 —6D 74
St Merryn Clo. SE18 —7H 91
St Merryn Ct. Beck —7C 124
St Michael's All. EC3 —6D 68 (1F 169)
St Michael's Av. N9 —7D 8
St Michael's Av. Wemb —6G 45
St Michaels Clo. E16 —5B 72
St Michael's Clo. N3 —2H 29
St Michael's Clo. N12 —5H 15
St Michael's Clo. Brom —3C 144
St Michael's Clo. Eri —2D 92
St Michael's Clo. Wor Pk —2B 148
St Michaels Ct. E14 —5E 70
(off St Leonards Rd.)
St Michael's Ct. SE1 —2C 86 (7D 168)
(off Hulme Pl.)
St Michael's Cres. Pinn —6C 24
St Michael's Flats. NW1 —2H 67 (1C 160)
(off Aldenham St.)
St Michael's Gdns. W10 —5G 65
St Michael's Ri. Well —1B 110
St Michael's Rd. NW2 —4E 46
St Michael's Rd. SW9 —2K 103
St Michael's Rd. Ashf —5C 112
St Michael's Rd. Croy —1C 152
St Michaels Rd. W Mol —5A 132
St Michael's Rd. Wall —6G 151
St Michael's Rd. Well —3B 110
St Michael's St. W2 —6B 66 (7B 158)
St Michaels Ter. N6 —1E 48
(off South Gro.)
St Michael's Ter. N22 —1J 31
St Mildred's Ct. EC2 —6D 68 (1E 168)
St Mildreds Rd. SE6 —7G 107
St Mirren Ct. New Bar —5F 5
St Nicholas Cen. Sutt —5K 149
St Nicholas Clo. Uxb —6A 58
St Nicholas Dri. Shep —7C 130
St Nicholas' Flats. NW1
(off Werrington St.) —2H 67 (1C 160)
St Nicholas Glebe. SW17 —5E 120
St Nicholas Rd. SE18 —5K 91
St Nicholas Rd. Sutt —5K 149
St Nicholas Rd. Th Dit —6K 133
St Nicholas St. SE8 —1B 106
St Nicholas Way. Sutt —4K 149
St Nicolas La. Chst —1C 144
St Ninian's Ct. N20 —3J 15
St Norbert Grn. SE4 —4A 106
St Norbert Rd. SE4 —5K 105
St Olaf Ho. SE1 —4F 169
St Olaf's Rd. SW6 —7G 83
St Olaf Stairs. SE1 —4F 169
St Olave's Ct. EC2 —6D 68 (1E 168)
St Olave's Est. SE1 —2E 86 (6H 169)
St Olave's Gdns. SE11 —4A 86 (3J 173)
St Olave's Mans. SE11 —3J 173
St Olave's Rd. E6 —1E 72
St Olave's Ter. SE1 —6H 169
St Olaves Wlk. SW16 —2G 139
St Onge Pde. Enf —3J 7
(off Southbury Rd.)
St Oswald's Pl. SE11 —5K 85 (6G 173)
St Oswald's Rd. SW16 —1B 140
St Oswulf St. SW1 —4D 172
St Owen Ho. SE1 —3E 86
(off Fendall St.)
St Pancras. —3J 67 (1E 160)
St Pancras Commercial Cen. NW1
(off Pratt St.) —1G 67
St Pancras Ct. N2 —2B 30
St Pancras Way. NW1 —7G 49
St Patrick's Ct. E4 —7B 20
St Paul Clo. Uxb —5A 58
St Paul's All. EC4 —1B 168
St Paul's Av. NW2 —6D 46
St Paul's Av. SE16 —1K 87
St Paul's Av. Harr —4F 27
St Paul's Cathedral. —6C 68 (1B 168)
St Paul's Chyd. EC4 —6B 68 (1B 168)
(in two parts)
St Pauls Clo. SE7 —5B 90
St Paul's Clo. W5 —2F 81
St Paul's Clo. Ashf —5E 112
St Paul's Clo. Cars —1C 150
St Paul's Clo. Chess —4D 146
St Paul's Clo. Hay —5F 77
St Paul's Clo. Houn —2C 96
St Pauls Ct. SW4 —5H 103
St Pauls Ct. Houn —3C 96
St Pauls Courtyard. SE8 —7C 88
St Paul's Cray Rd. Chst —1H 145
St Paul's Cres. NW1 —7H 49
(in two parts)
St Paul's Dri. E15 —5F 53
St Paul's M. NW1 —7H 49
St Paul's Pl. N1 —6D 50
St Paul's Ri. N13 —6G 17
St Paul's Rd. N1 —6B 50
St Paul's Rd. N17 —7B 18
St Paul's Rd. Bark —1G 73
St Paul's Rd. Bren —6D 80
St Paul's Rd. Eri —7J 93
St Paul's Rd. Rich —3F 99
St Paul's Rd. T Hth —3C 140
St Paul's Shrubbery. N1 —6D 50
St Paul's Sq. Brom —2H 143
St Paul's Studios. W6 —5G 83
(off Talgarth Rd.)
St Pauls Ter. SE17 —6B 86
St Pauls Tower. E10 —7D 34
(off Beaumont Rd.)
St Paul St. N1 —1C 68
(in two parts)
St Pauls Vw. Apartments. EC1
(off Amwell St.) —3A 68 (2K 161)
St Paul's Wlk. King T —7G 117
St Pauls Way. E3 —5B 70
St Paul's Way. E3 —5B 70
St Paul's Way. N3 —7E 14
St Paul's Wood Hill. Orp —2J 145
St Peter's All. EC3 —6D 68 (1G 169)
(off Cornhill)
St Peter's Av. E2 —2G 69
St Peter's Av. E17 —4G 35
St Peters Av. N2 —7H 15
St Peter's Av. N18 —4B 18
St Petersburgh M. W2 —7K 65
St Petersburgh Pl. W2 —7K 65
St Peter's Cen. E1 —1H 87
(off Watts St.)
St Peters Chu. Clo. N1 —1B 68
(off Devonia Rd.)
St Peter's Clo. E2 —2G 69
St Peter's Clo. SW17 —2C 120
St Peters Clo. Bus H —1C 10
St Peter's Clo. Chst —7H 127
St Peter's Clo. Ilf —4J 37
St Peter's Clo. Ruis —2B 42
St Peter's Ct. NW4 —5E 28
St Peters Ct. W Mol —4E 132
St Peter's Gdns. SE27 —3A 122
St Peter's Gro. W6 —4C 82
St Peters Ho. SE17 —6D 86
St Peter's Ho. WC1 —3J 67 (2F 161)
(off Regent Sq.)
St Peters Pl. W9 —4K 65
St Peter's Rd. N9 —1C 18
St Peter's Rd. W6 —5C 82
St Peter's Rd. Croy —4D 152
St Peter's Rd. King T —2G 135
St Peter's Rd. S'hall —5E 60
St Peter's Rd. Twic —5B 98
St Peters Rd. Uxb —5A 58
St Peter's Rd. W Mol —4E 132
St Peter's Sq. E2 —2G 69
St Peter's Sq. W6 —4B 82
St Peter's St. N1 —1B 68
St Peter's St. S Croy —5D 152
St Peter's St. M. N1 —2B 68
(off St Peters St.)
St Peter's Ter. SW6 —7H 83
St Peter's Vs. W6 —4C 82
St Peter's Way. N1 —7E 50
St Peter's Way. W5 —5D 62
St Peter's Way. Hay —5F 77
St Peter's Wharf. W4 —5C 82
St Philip Ho. WC1 —3A 68 (2J 161)
(off Lloyd Baker St.)
St Philips Av. N2 —7H 15
St Philip's Av. Wor Pk —2D 148
St Philip's Ga. Wor Pk —2D 148
St Philip Sq. SW8 —2F 103
St Philip's Rd. E8 —6G 51
St Philips Rd. Surb —6D 134
St Philip St. SW8 —2F 103
St Philip's Way. N1 —1C 68
St Quentin Rd. Well —3K 109
St Quintin Av. W10 —5E 64
St Quintin Gdns. W10 —5E 64
St Quintin Rd. E13 —3K 71
St Raphael's Way. NW10 —5J 45
St Regis Clo. N10 —2F 31
St Regis Heights. NW3 —3K 47
St Richard's Ho. NW1 —3H 67 (1C 160)
(off Eversholt St.)
St Ronan's Clo. Barn —1G 5
St Ronan's Cres. Wfd G —7D 20
St Rule St. SW8 —2G 103
St Saviour's College. SE27 —4D 122
St Saviour's Ct. N10 —2F 31
(off Alexandra Pk. Rd.)
St Saviours Ct. Harr —5J 25
St Saviour's Est. SE1 —2F 87 (7J 169)
St Saviour's Rd. SW2 —5K 103
St Saviour's Rd. Croy —6B 140
St Saviour's Wharf. SE1
(off Shad Thames) —2F 87 (6K 169)
St Saviour's Wharf. SE1
(off Mill St.) —2F 87 (6K 169)
Saints Clo. SE27 —4B 122
Saints Dri. E7 —5B 54
St Silas Pl. NW5 —6E 48
St Simon's Av. SW15 —5E 100
St Stephen's Av. E17 —5E 34
St Stephen's Av. W12 —2D 82
(in two parts)
St Stephen's Av. W13 —6B 62
St Stephen's Clo. E17 —5D 34
St Stephen's Clo. NW8 —1C 66
St Stephen's Clo. S'hall —5E 60
St Stephens Ct. N8 —6K 31
St Stephens Ct. W13 —6B 62
St Stephen's Ct. Enf —6K 7
(off Park Av.)
St Stephen's Cres. W2 —6J 65
St Stephen's Cres. T Hth —3A 140
St Stephen's Gdns. SW15 —5H 101
St Stephen's Gdns. W2 —6J 65
(in two parts)
St Stephen's Gdns. Twic —6C 98
St Stephens Gro. SE13 —3E 106
St Stephens Ho. SE17 —6D 86
(off Lytham St.)
St Stephen's M. W2 —5J 65
St Stephens Pde. E7 —7A 54
St Stephen's Pas. Twic —6C 98
St Stephen's Rd. E3 —1A 70
St Stephen's Rd. E6 —7A 54
St Stephen's Rd. E17 —5D 34
St Stephen's Rd. W13 —6B 62
St Stephen's Rd. Barn —5A 4
St Stephen's Rd. Houn —6E 96
St Stephen's Rd. W Dray —1A 76
St Stephen's Row. EC4 —1E 168
St Stephen's Ter. SW8 —7K 85
St Stephen's Wlk. SW7 —4A 84
(off Southwell Gdns.)
St Swithins La. EC4 —7D 68 (2E 168)
St Swithun's Rd. SE13 —6F 107
St Theresa's Rd. Felt —4H 95
St Thomas Clo. Surb —1F 147
St Thomas Ct. E10 —7D 34
(off Beaumont Rd.)
St Thomas Ct. Bex —7G 111
St Thomas Ct. Pinn —1C 24
St Thomas Dri. Orp —7G 145
St Thomas Dri. Pinn —1C 24
St Thomas Gdns. Ilf —6G 55
St Thomas Rd. E16 —6J 71
St Thomas Rd. N14 —7C 6
St Thomas Rd. W4 —6J 81
St Thomas Rd. Belv —2J 93
St Thomas's Gdns. NW5 —6E 48
St Thomas's Pl. E9 —7J 51
St Thomas's Rd. N4 —2A 50
St Thomas's Rd. NW10 —1A 64
St Thomas's Sq. E9 —7J 51
St Thomas St. SE1 —1D 86 (5F 169)
St Thomas's Way. SW6 —7H 83
St Timothys M. Brom —1K 143
St Ursula Gro. Pinn —5B 24
St Ursula Rd. S'hall —6E 60
St Vincent Clo. SE27 —5B 122
St Vincent Ho. SE1 —3F 87
(off Fendall St.)
St Vincent Rd. Twic —6G 97
St Vincent St. W1 —5E 66 (6H 159)
St Wilfrid's Clo. Barn —5H 5
St Wilfrid's Rd. New Bar —5H 5
St Winefride's Av. E12 —5D 54
St Winifred's Rd. Tedd —6B 116
Sala Ho. SE3 —4K 107
Salamanca Pl. SE1 —4K 85 (4G 173)
Salamanca St. SE1 & SE11
—4K 85 (4F 173)
Salamander Clo. King T —5C 116
Salamander Quay. King T —1D 134
Salcombe Dri. Mord —1F 149
Salcombe Dri. Romf —6F 39
Salcombe Gdns. NW7 —6K 13
Salcombe Rd. E17 —7B 34
Salcombe Rd. N16 —5E 50
Salcombe Rd. Ashf —3A 112
Salcombe Way. Hay —3F 59
Salcombe Way. Ruis —2J 41
Salcott Rd. SW11 —5C 102
Salcott Rd. Croy —3J 151
Salehurst Clo. Harr —5E 26
Salehurst Rd. SE4 —6B 106
Salem Pl. Croy —3C 152
Salem Rd. W2 —7K 65
Sale Pl. W2 —5C 66 (6C 158)
Sale St. E2 —4G 69
Salford Ho. E14 —4E 88
Salford Rd. SW2 —1H 121
Salhouse Clo. SE28 —6C 74
Salisbury Av. N3 —3H 29
Salisbury Av. Bark —7H 55
Salisbury Av. Sutt —6H 149
Salisbury Clo. SE17 —4D 86
Salisbury Clo. Wor Pk —3B 148
Salisbury Ct. EC4 —6B 68 (1A 168)
Salisbury Ct. Cars —5D 150
Salisbury Ct. Enf —4J 7
(off London Rd.)
Salisbury Ct. N'holt —5F 43
(off Newmarket Av.)
Salisbury Gdns. SW19 —7G 119
Salisbury Gdns. Buck H —2G 21
Salisbury Hall Gdns. E4 —6H 19
Salisbury Ho. E14 —6D 70
Salisbury Ho. EC2 —5D 68 (6F 163)
(off London Wall)
Salisbury Ho. N1 —1B 68
(off St Mary's Path)
Salisbury Ho. SW1 —5H 85 (5D 172)
(off Drummond Ga.)
Salisbury Ho. SW9 —7A 86
(off Cranmer Rd.)
Salisbury Ho. Stan —6F 11
Salisbury Mans. N4 —5B 32
Salisbury M. SW6 —7H 83
Salisbury Pas. SW6 —7H 83
(off Dawes Rd.)
Salisbury Pavement. SW6 —7H 83
(off Dawes Rd.)
Salisbury Pl. SW9 —7B 86
Salisbury Pl. W1 —5D 66 (5E 158)
Salisbury Rd. E4 —3H 19
Salisbury Rd. E7 —6J 53
Salisbury Rd. E10 —2E 52
Salisbury Rd. E12 —5B 54
Salisbury Rd. E17 —5E 34
Salisbury Rd. N4 —5B 32
Salisbury Rd. N9 —3B 18
Salisbury Rd. N22 —1B 32
Salisbury Rd. SE25 —6G 141
Salisbury Rd. SW19 —7G 119
Salisbury Rd. W13 —2B 80
Salisbury Rd. Barn —3B 4
Salisbury Rd. Bex —1G 129
Salisbury Rd. Brom —5C 144
Salisbury Rd. Cars —6D 150
Salisbury Rd. Dag —6H 57
Salisbury Rd. Felt —1A 114
Salisbury Rd. Harr —5H 25
Salisbury Rd. Houn —3A 96
Salisbury Rd. Ilf —2J 55
Salisbury Rd. H'row A —5E 94
Salisbury Rd. N Mald —3K 135
Salisbury Rd. Pinn —4J 23
Salisbury Rd. Rich —4E 98
Salisbury Rd. S'hall —4C 78
Salisbury Rd. Wor Pk —4K 147
Salisbury Sq. EC4 —6A 68 (1K 167)
Salisbury St. NW8 —4C 66 (4C 158)
Salisbury St. W3 —2J 81
Salisbury Ter. SE15 —3J 105
Salisbury Wlk. N19 —2G 49
Salix Clo. Sun —7K 113
Salix Ct. N3 —6D 14
Salliesfield. Twic —6H 97
Sally Murray Clo. E12 —4E 54
(off Grantham Rd.)
Salmen Rd. E13 —2H 71
Salmond Clo. Stan —6F 11
Salmon La. E1 —6A 70
Salmon La. E14 —6A 70
Salmon M. NW6 —5J 47
Salmon Rd. Belv —5G 93
Salmons Rd. N9 —1B 18
Salmons Rd. Chess —6E 146
Salmon St. E14 —6B 70
Salmon St. NW9 —1H 45
Salomons Rd. E13 —5A 72
Salop Rd. E17 —6K 33
Saltash Clo. Sutt —4H 149
Saltash Rd. Ilf —1H 37
Saltash Rd. Well —1C 110
Saltcoats Rd. W4 —2A 82
Saltcroft Clo. Wemb —1H 45
Saltdene. N4 —1K 49
Salter Clo. Harr —4D 42
Salterford Rd. SW17 —6E 120
Salter Rd. SE16 —1K 87
Salters Ct. EC4 —1D 168
Salters Hall Ct. EC4 —7D 68
(off Cannon St.)
Salter's Hill. SE19 —5D 122
Salters Rd. E17 —4F 35
Salters Rd. W10 —4F 65
Salter St. E14 —7B 70
Salter St. NW10 —3C 64
Salterton Rd. N7 —3K 49
Salt Hill Clo. Uxb —5A 40
Saltley Clo. E6 —6C 72
Saltoun Rd. SW2 —4A 104
Saltram Clo. N15 —4F 33
Saltram Cres. W9 —3H 65
Saltwell St. E14 —7C 70
Saltwood Gro. SE17 —5D 86
Saltwood Ho. SE15 —6J 87
(off Lovelinch Clo.)
Salusbury Rd. NW6 —1G 65
Salutation Rd. SE10 —4G 89
Salvador. SW17 —5D 120
Salvia Gdns. Gnfd —2A 62
Salvin Rd. SW15 —3F 101
Salway Clo. Wfd G —7D 20
Salway Pl. E15 —6F 53
Salway Rd. E15 —6F 53
Samantha Clo. E17 —7B 34
Sam Bartram Clo. SE7 —5A 90
Sambrook Ho. SE11 —4J 173
Sambruck M. SE6 —1D 124
Samels Ct. W6 —5C 82
Samford Ho. N1 —1A 68
(off Barnsbury Est.)
Samford St. NW8 —4B 66 (4C 158)
Samira Clo. E17 —6C 34
Sam March Ho. E14 —6F 71
Samos Rd. SE20 —2H 141
Sampson Av. Barn —5A 4
Sampson Clo. Belv —3D 92
Sampson Ho. SE1 —1B 86 (4A 168)
Sampsons Ct. Shep —5E 130
Sampson St. E1 —1G 87
Samsbrooke Ct. Enf —6K 7
Samson St. E13 —2A 72
Samuda Est. E14 —3E 88
Samuel Clo. E8 —1F 69
Samuel Clo. SE14 —6K 87
Samuel Clo. SE18 —4C 90
Samuel Gray Gdns. King T —1D 134
Samuel Ho. E8 —1F 69
Samuel Johnson Clo. SW16 —4K 121
Samuel Jones Ind. Est. SE5 —7E 86
(off Peckham Gro.)
Samuel Lewis Bldgs. N1 —6A 50
Samuel Lewis Trust Dwellings. E8
—5G 51
Samuel Lewis Trust Dwellings. N15
—6E 32
Samuel Lewis Trust Dwellings. SE5
(off Warner Rd.) —1C 104
Samuel Lewis Trust Dwellings. SW3
(in two parts) —4C 170
Samuel Lewis Trust Dwellings. SW6
(off Vanston Pl.) —7J 83
Samuel Lewis Trust Dwellings. W14
(off Lisgar Ter.) —4H 83
Samuel Richardson Ho. W14 —4H 83
(off N. End Cres.)
Samuel's Clo. W6 —4E 82
Samuel St. SE15 —7F 87
Samuel St. SE18 —4D 90
Sancroft Clo. NW2 —3D 46
Sancroft Ho. SE11 —5H 173
Sancroft Rd. Harr —2K 25
Sancroft St. SE11 —5K 85 (5H 173)
Sanctuary Rd. H'row A —6C 94
Sanctuary St. SE1 —2C 86 (6D 168)
Sanctuary, The. SW1 —1D 172
Sanctuary, The. Bex —6D 110
Sanctuary, The. Mord —6J 137
Sandale Clo. N16 —3D 50
Sandall Clo. W5 —4E 62
Sandall Ho. E3 —2A 70
Sandall Rd. NW5 —6G 49
Sandall Rd. W5 —4E 62
Sandal Rd. N18 —5B 18
Sandal Rd. N Mald —5K 135
Sandal St. E15 —1G 71
Sandalwood Clo. E1 —4A 70
Sandal Wood Dri. Ruis —7E 22
Sandalwood Ho. Sidc —3K 127
Sandalwood Mans. W8 —3K 83
Sandalwood Rd. Felt —3K 113
Sandbach Pl. SE18 —4G 91
Sandbanks. Felt —1G 113
Sandbourne. NW8 —1K 65
(off Abbey Rd.)
Sandbourne. W11 —6J 65
(off Dartmouth Clo.)
Sandbourne Av. SW19 —2K 137
Sandbourne Rd. SE4 —2A 106
Sandbrook Clo. NW7 —6E 12
Sandbrook Rd. N16 —3E 50
Sandby Grn. SE9 —3C 108
Sandby Ho. NW6 —1J 65
Sandcliff Rd. Eri —4K 93
Sandcroft Clo. N13 —6G 17
Sandell's Av. Ashf —4E 112
Sandell St. SE1 —2A 86 (6J 167)
Sanderling Ct. SE8 —6B 88
(off Abinger Gro.)
Sanderling Ct. SE28 —7C 74
Sanders Clo. Hamp H —5G 115
Sanders Ho. WC1 —3A 68 (1J 161)
(off Gt. Percy St.)
Sanders La. NW7 —7K 13
(in three parts)
Sanderson Clo. NW5 —4F 49
Sanderstead Av. NW2 —2G 47
Sanderstead Clo. SW12 —7G 103
Sanderstead Rd. E10 —1A 52
Sanderstead Rd. S Croy —7D 152
Sanders Way. N19 —1H 49
Sandfield. WC1 —3J 67 (2F 161)
(off Cromer St.)
Sandfield Gdns. T Hth —3B 140
Sandfield Rd. T Hth —3B 140
Sandford Av. N22 —1C 32
Sandford Clo. E6 —4D 72
Sandford Ct. N16 —1E 50
Sandford Ct. New Bar —3E 4
Sandford Rd. E6 —3C 72
Sandford Rd. Bexh —4E 110
Sandford Rd. Brom —3J 143
Sandford Row. SE17 —5D 86
Sandford St. SW6 —7K 83
Sandgate Clo. Romf —7J 39
Sandgate Ho. E5 —5H 51
Sandgate Ho. W5 —5C 62
Sandgate La. SW18 —1C 120
Sandgate Rd. Well —7C 92
Sandgate St. SE15 —6H 87
Sandgate Trad. Est. SE15 —6H 87
(off Sandgate St.)
Sandham Ct. SW4 —1J 103
Sandhills. Wall —4H 151
Sandhills Mdw. Shep —7E 130
Sandhills, The. SW10 —6A 84 (7A 170)
(off Limerston St.)
Sandhurst Av. Harr —6F 25
Sandhurst Av. Surb —7H 135

262 A-Z Big London

Selkirk Rd. SW17 —4C 120
Selkirk Rd. Twic —2G 115
Sellers Hall Clo. N3 —7D 14
Sellincourt Rd. SW17 —5C 120
Sellindge Clo. Beck —7B 124
Sellons Av. NW10 —1B 64
Selsdon Av. S Croy —6D 152
Selsdon Clo. Romf —1J 39
Selsdon Clo. Surb —5E 134
Selsdon Ct. S'hall —6F 61
(off Dormers Ri.)
Selsdon Pk. Rd. S Croy —7K 153
Selsdon Rd. E11 —7J 35
Selsdon Rd. E13 —1A 72
Selsdon Rd. NW2 —2B 46
Selsdon Rd. SE27 —3A 122
Selsdon Rd. S Croy —5D 152
Selsdon Way. E14 —3D 88
Selsea Pl. N16 —5E 50
Selsey Cres. Well —1D 110
Selsey St. E3 —5C 70
Selsey St. E14 —5C 70
Selvage La. NW7 —5E 12
Selway Clo. Pinn —3K 23
Selwood Dri. Barn —5A 4
Selwood Pl. SW7 —5B 84 (5A 170)
Selwood Rd. Chess —4D 146
Selwood Rd. Croy —2H 153
Selwood Rd. Sutt —1H 149
Selwood Ter. SW7 —5B 84 (5A 170)
Selworthy Clo. E11 —5J 35
Selworthy Rd. SE6 —3B 124
Selwyn Av. E4 —6K 19
Selwyn Av. Ilf —6K 37
Selwyn Av. Rich —3E 98
Selwyn Clo. Houn —4C 96
Selwyn Ct. E17 —5C 34
(off Yunus Khan Clo.)
Selwyn Ct. SE3 —3H 107
Selwyn Ct. Edgw —7C 12
Selwyn Cres. Well —3B 110
Selwyn Rd. E3 —2B 70
Selwyn Rd. E13 —1K 71
Selwyn Rd. NW10 —7K 45
Selwyn Rd. N Mald —5K 135
Semley Ga. E9 —6B 52
Semley Ho. SW1 —4F 85
(off Semley Pl.)
Semley Pl. SW1 —4E 84 (4H 171)
Semley Rd. SW16 —2J 139
Senate St. SE15 —2J 105
Senator Wlk. SE28 —3H 91
Seneca Rd. T Hth —4C 140
Senga Rd. Wall —1E 150
Senhouse Rd. Sutt —3F 149
Senior St. W2 —5K 65
Senlac Rd. SE12 —1K 125
Sennen Rd. Enf —7A 8
Sennen Wlk. SE9 —3C 126
Senrab St. E1 —6K 69
Sentinel Clo. N'holt —4C 60
Sentinel Sq. NW4 —4E 28
September Ct. S'hall —1F 79
(off Dormers Wells La.)
September Ct. Uxb —2A 58
September Way. Stan —6G 11
Septimus Pl. Enf —5B 8
Sequoia Clo. Bus H —1C 10
Sequoia Gdns. Orp —7K 145
Sequoia Pk. Pinn —6A 10
Seraph Ct. EC1 —3C 68 (1B 162)
(off Moreland St.)
Serbin Clo. E10 —7E 34
Sergeant Ind. Est. SW18 —6K 101
Serica Ct. SE10 —7E 88
Serjeant's Inn. EC4 —6A 68 (1K 167)
Serle St. WC2 —6K 67 (7H 161)
Sermon La. EC4 —1C 168
Serpentine Gallery. —2B 84 (6A 164)
Serpentine Rd. W2 —1C 84 (5C 164)
Serviden Dri. Brom —1B 144
Servite Ho. Wor Pk —2B 148
(off Avenue, The)
Servius Ct. Bren —7D 80
Setchell Rd. SE1 —4F 87
Setchell Way. SE1 —4F 87
Seth St. SE16 —2J 87
Seton Gdns. Dag —7C 56
Settle Rd. E13 —2J 71
Settles St. E1 —5G 69
Settrington Rd. SW6 —2K 101
Seven Acres. Cars —2C 150
Seven Dials. WC2 —6J 67 (1E 166)
Seven Dials Ct. WC2 —6J 67
(off Short Gdns.)
Sevenex Pde. Wemb —5E 44
Seven Kings. —1J 55
Seven Kings Rd. Ilf —1J 55
Sevenoaks Clo. Bexh —4H 111
Sevenoaks Ct. N'wd —1E 22
Sevenoaks Rd. SE4 —6A 106
Sevenoaks Way. Sidc & Orp —7C 128
Seven Sisters. (Junct.) —5F 33
Seven Sisters. N15 —5F 33
Seven Sisters Rd. N7 & N4 —3K 49
Seven Sisters Rd. N15 —6D 32
Seven Stars Corner. W6 —3C 82
Seventh Av. E12 —4D 54
Seventh Av. Hay —1J 77
Severnake Clo. E14 —4C 88
Severn Ct. King T —1D 134
Severn Dri. Esh —2A 146
Severn Way. NW10 —5B 46
Severus Rd. SW11 —4C 102
Seville M. N1 —7E 50
Seville St. SW1 —2D 84 (7F 165)
Sevington Rd. NW4 —6D 28
Sevington St. W9 —4K 65
Seward Rd. W7 —2A 80
Seward Rd. Beck —2K 141
Sewardstone. —2K 9
Sewardstone Gdns. E4 —5J 9
Sewardstone Rd. E2 —2J 69
Sewardstone Rd. E4 —7J 9
Seward St. EC1 —3B 68 (3B 162)
Sewdley St. E5 —3K 51
Sewell Rd. SE2 —3A 92
Sewell St. E13 —3J 71
Sextant Av. E14 —4F 89
Seymer Rd. Romf —3K 39
Seymour Av. N17 —2G 33
Seymour Av. Eps —7F 133
Seymour Av. Mord —7F 137
Seymour Clo. E Mol —5G 133
Seymour Clo. Pinn —1D 24
Seymour Ct. E4 —2C 20
Seymour Ct. N10 —2E 30
Seymour Ct. N21 —6E 6
Seymour Ct. NW2 —2D 46
Seymour Dri. Brom —1D 156
Seymour Gdns. SE4 —3A 106
Seymour Gdns. Felt —4A 114
Seymour Gdns. Ilf —1D 54
Seymour Gdns. Ruis —1B 42
Seymour Gdns. Surb —5F 135
Seymour Gdns. Twic —7B 98
Seymour Ho. NW1 —3H 67 (2D 160)
(off Churchway)
Seymour Ho. WC1 —4J 67 (3E 160)
(off Tavistock Pl.)
Seymour Ho. Sutt —6K 149
(off Mulgrave Rd.)
Seymour M. W1 —6E 66 (7G 159)
Seymour Pl. SE25 —4H 141
Seymour Pl. W1 —5D 66 (6E 158)
Seymour Rd. E4 —1J 19
Seymour Rd. E6 —2B 72
Seymour Rd. E10 —1B 52
Seymour Rd. N3 —7E 14
Seymour Rd. N8 —5A 32
Seymour Rd. N9 —2C 18
Seymour Rd. SW18 —7H 101
Seymour Rd. SW19 —3F 119
Seymour Rd. W4 —4J 81
Seymour Rd. Cars —5E 150
Seymour Rd. E Mol —5G 133
Seymour Rd. Hamp H —5G 115
Seymour Rd. King T —1D 134
Seymour Rd. Mitc —7E 138
Seymour Rd. Ind. Est. E10 —1B 52
Seymour St. W2 & W1 —6D 66 (1E 164)
Seymour Ter. SE20 —1H 141
Seymour Vs. SE20 —1H 141
Seymour Wlk. SW10 —6A 84
Seymour Way. Sun —7H 113
Seyssel St. E14 —4E 88
Shaa Rd. W3 —7K 63
Shacklegate La. Tedd —4J 115
Shackleton Clo. SE23 —2H 123
Shackleton Ct. E14 —5C 88
Shackleton Ct. W12 —2D 82
Shackleton Ho. NW10 —7K 45
Shackleton Rd. S'hall —7D 60
Shacklewell. —4F 51
Shacklewell Grn. E8 —4F 51
Shacklewell Ho. E8 —4F 51
Shacklewell La. N16 —5F 51
Shacklewell Rd. N16 —4F 51
Shacklewell Row. E8 —4F 51
Shacklewell St. E2 —3F 69 (2K 163)
Shadbolt Clo. Wor Pk —2B 148
Shad Thames. SE1 —1F 87 (5J 169)
Shadwell. —7H 69
Shadwell Ct. N'holt —2D 60
Shadwell Dri. N'holt —3D 60
Shadwell Gdns. E1 —7J 69
(off Sutton St.)
Shadwell Pier Head. E1 —7J 69
Shadwell Pl. E1 —7J 69
(off Shadwell Gdns.)
Shadybush Clo. Bush —1B 10
Shaef Way. Tedd —7A 116
Shafter Rd. Dag —6J 57
Shaftesbury Av. W1 & WC2 —6J 67 (3C 166)
Shaftesbury Av. Enf —2E 8
Shaftesbury Av. Felt —6J 95
Shaftesbury Av. Harr & S Harr —1F 43
Shaftesbury Av. Kent —5D 26
Shaftesbury Av. New Bar —4F 5
Shaftesbury Av. S'hall —4E 78
Shaftesbury Circ. S Harr —1G 43
Shaftesbury Ct. E6 —6E 72
(off Sapphire Clo.)
Shaftesbury Ct. N1 —2D 68
(off Shaftesbury St)
Shaftesbury Ct. SW6 —1K 101
(off Maltings Pl.)
Shaftesbury Ct. SW16 —3H 121
Shaftesbury Cres. Stai —7A 112
Shaftesbury Gdns. NW10 —4A 64
Shaftesbury Lodge. E14 —6D 70
(off Upper N. St.)
Shaftesbury M. SE1 —3D 86
(off Falmouth Rd.)
Shaftesbury M. SW4 —5G 103
Shaftesbury M. W8 —3J 83
(off Stratford Rd.)
Shaftesbury Pde. S Harr —1G 43
Shaftesbury Pl. EC2 —5C 68
(off London Wall)
Shaftesbury Pl. W14 —4H 83
(off Warwick Rd.)
Shaftesbury Point. E13 —2J 71
(off High St.)
Shaftesbury Rd. E4 —1A 20
Shaftesbury Rd. E7 —7A 54
Shaftesbury Rd. E10 —1C 52
Shaftesbury Rd. E17 —6D 34
Shaftesbury Rd. N18 —6K 17
Shaftesbury Rd. N19 —1J 49
Shaftesbury Rd. Beck —2B 142
Shaftesbury Rd. Cars —7B 138
Shaftesbury Rd. Rich —3E 98
Shaftesburys, The. Bark —2G 73
Shaftesbury St. N1 —2C 68
(in two parts)
Shaftesbury Way. Twic —3H 115
Shaftesbury Waye. Hay —5A 60
Shafto M. SW1 —3D 84 (2F 171)
Shafton M. E9 —1K 69
Shafton Rd. E9 —1K 69
Shaftsbury Ct. SE5 —4D 104
Shafts Ct. EC3 —6E 68 (1G 169)
Shahjalal Ho. E2 —2G 69
(off Pritchards Rd.)
Shakespeare Av. N11 —5B 16
Shakespeare Av. NW10 —1K 63
Shakespeare Av. Felt —6J 95
Shakespeare Av. Hay —6J 59
(in two parts)
Shakespeare Ct. New Bar —3E 4
Shakespeare Cres. E12 —6D 54
Shakespeare Cres. NW10 —1K 63
Shakespeare Dri. Harr —6F 27
Shakespeare Gdns. N2 —4D 30
Shakespeare Ho. N14 —2C 16
Shakespeare Rd. E17 —2K 33
Shakespeare Rd. N3 —1J 29
Shakespeare Rd. NW7 —4G 13
Shakespeare Rd. SE24 —5B 104
Shakespeare Rd. W3 —1J 81
Shakespeare Rd. W7 —7K 61
Shakespeare Rd. Bexh —1E 110
Shakespeare's Globe Exhibition. —4C 168
Shakespeare's Globe Theatre. —1C 86 (4C 168)
Shakespeare Tower. EC2 —5D 162
Shakespeare Way. Felt —4A 114
Shakspeare M. N16 —4E 50
Shakspeare Wlk. N16 —4E 50
Shalcomb St. SW10 —6A 84 (7A 170)
Shalden Ho. SW15 —6B 100
Shaldon Dri. Mord —5G 137
Shaldon Dri. Ruis —3A 42
Shaldon Rd. Edgw —2F 27
Shalfleet Dri. W10 —7F 65
Shalford Ct. N1 —2B 68
(off Charlton Pl.)
Shalford Ho. SE1 —3D 86
Shalimar Gdns. W3 —7J 63
Shalimar Rd. W3 —7J 63
Shallons Rd. SE9 —4F 127
Shalstone Rd. SW14 —3H 99
Shalston Vs. Surb —6F 135
Shamrock Rd. Croy —6K 139
Shamrock St. SW4 —3H 103
Shamrock Way. N14 —1A 16
Shandon Rd. SW4 —6G 103
Shand St. SE1 —2E 86 (6H 169)
Shandy St. E1 —5K 69
Shanklin Ho. E17 —2B 34
Shanklin Rd. N8 —5H 31
Shanklin Way. SE15 —7F 87
Shannon Clo. NW2 —3F 47
Shannon Clo. S'hall —5B 78
Shannon Corner. (Junct.) —4C 136
Shannon Corner Retail Pk. N Mald —4C 136
Shannon Ct. N16 —3E 50
Shannon Gro. SW9 —4K 103
Shannon Pl. NW8 —2C 66
Shannon Way. Beck —6D 124
Shanti Ct. SW18 —1J 119
Shap Cres. Cars —1D 150
Shapland Way. N13 —5E 16
Shap St. E2 —2F 69
Shapwick Clo. N11 —5J 15
Shardcroft Av. SE24 —5B 104
Shardeloes Rd. SE14 —2B 106
Shard's Sq. SE15 —6G 87
Sharland Clo. T Hth —6A 140
Sharman Ct. Sidc —4A 128
(off Carlton Rd.)
Sharnbrooke Clo. Well —3C 110
Sharnbrook Ho. W14 —6J 83
Sharon Clo. Surb —1C 146
Sharon Gdns. E9 —1J 69
Sharon Rd. W4 —5K 81
Sharon Rd. Enf —2F 9
Sharpe Clo. W7 —5K 61
Sharp Ho. SW8 —3F 103
Sharp Ho. Twic —6D 98
Sharpleshall St. NW1 —7D 48
Sharpness Clo. Hay —5C 60
Sharpness Ct. SE15 —7F 87
(off Daniel Gdns.)
Sharp's La. Ruis —7F 23
Sharratt St. SE15 —6J 87
Sharsted St. SE17 —5B 86 (6K 173)
Sharvel La. N'holt —1K 59
Sharwood. WC1 —2K 67 (1H 161)
(off Penton Ri.)
Shaver's Pl. SW1 —3C 166
Shaw Av. Bark —2E 74
Shawbrooke Rd. SE9 —5A 108
Shawbury Rd. SE22 —5F 105
Shaw Clo. SE28 —1B 92
Shaw Clo. Bus H —2D 10
Shaw Ct. W3 —3J 81
(off All Saints Rd.)
Shaw Dri. W on T —7A 132
Shawfield Ct. W Dray —3A 76
Shawfield Pk. Brom —2B 144
Shawfield St. SW3 —5C 84 (6D 170)
Shawford Ct. SW15 —7C 100
Shawford Rd. Eps —6K 147
Shaw Gdns. Bark —2E 74
Shaw Ho. E16 —1E 90
(off Claremont St.)
Shaw Ho. Belv —5F 93
Shaw Path. Brom —3H 125
Shaw Rd. SE22 —4E 104
Shaw Rd. Brom —3H 125
Shaw Rd. Enf —1E 8
Shaws Cotts. SE23 —3A 124
Shaws Path. King T —1C 134
(off High St.)
Shaw Sq. E17 —1A 34
Shaw Way. Wall —7J 151
Shearing Dri. Cars —7A 138
Shearling Way. N7 —6J 49
Shearman Rd. SE3 —4H 107
Shears Ct. Sun —7G 113
Shears, The. (Junct.) —7G 113
Shearwater Ct. SE8 —6B 88
(off Abinger Gro.)
Shearwater Rd. Sutt —5H 149
Shearwater Way. Hay —6B 60
Sheaveshill Av. NW9 —4A 28
Sheaveshill Ct. NW9 —4K 27
Sheaveshill Pde. NW9 —4A 28
(off Sheaveshill Av.)
Sheen Comn. Dri. Rich —4G 99
Sheen Ct. Rich —4G 99
Sheen Ct. Rd. Rich —4G 99
Sheendale Rd. Rich —4F 99
Sheenewood. SE26 —4H 123
Sheen Ga. Gdns. SW14 —4J 99
Sheengate Mans. SW14 —4K 99
Sheen Gro. N1 —1A 68
Sheen La. SW14 —5J 99
Sheen Pk. Rich —4E 98
Sheen Rd. Orp —4K 145
Sheen Rd. Rich —5E 98
Sheen Way. Wall —5K 151
Sheen Wood. SW14 —5J 99
Sheepcote Clo. Houn —7J 77
Sheepcote La. SW11 —2D 102
Sheepcote Rd. Harr —6K 25
Sheepcotes Rd. Romf —4E 38
Sheephouse Way. N Mald —1K 147
Sheep La. E8 —1H 69
Sheep Wlk. Shep —5C 130
Sheep Wlk. M. SW19 —6F 119
Sheep Wlk., The. Wok —7B 130
Sheerness M. E16 —2F 91
Sheerwater Rd. E16 —5B 72
Sheffield Rd. H'row A —6E 94
Sheffield Sq. E3 —3B 70
Sheffield St. WC2 —6K 67 (1G 167)
Sheffield Ter. W8 —1J 83
Sheffield Way. H'row A —5F 95
Shelbourne Clo. Pinn —3D 24
Shelbourne Pl. Beck —7B 124
Shelbourne Rd. N17 —2H 33
Shelburne Dri. Houn —6E 96
Shelburne Rd. N7 —4K 49
Shelbury Clo. Sidc —3A 128
Shelbury Rd. SE22 —5H 105
Sheldon Av. N6 —7C 30
Sheldon Av. Ilf —2F 37
Sheldon Clo. SE12 —5K 107
Sheldon Clo. SE20 —1H 141
Sheldon Ct. SW8 —1J 103
(off Lansdowne Grn.)
Sheldon Ct. Barn —4E 4
Sheldon Rd. N18 —4K 17
Sheldon Rd. NW2 —4F 47
Sheldon Rd. Bexh —1F 111
Sheldon Rd. Dag —7E 56
Sheldon St. Croy —3C 152
Sheldrake Clo. E16 —1D 90
Sheldrake Ct. E6 —2C 72
(off St Bartholomew's Rd.)
Sheldrake Pl. W8 —2J 83
Sheldrick Clo. SW19 —2B 138
Shelduck Clo. E15 —5H 53
Shelduck Ct. SE8 —6B 88
(off Pilot Clo.)
Sheldwich Ter. Brom —6C 144
Shelford Pl. N16 —3D 50
Shelford Ri. SE19 —7F 123
Shelford Rd. Barn —6A 4
Shelgate Rd. SW11 —5C 102
Shell Clo. Brom —6C 144
Shellduck Clo. NW9 —2A 28
Shelley. N8 —3J 31
(off Boyton Rd.)
Shelley Av. E12 —6C 54
Shelley Av. Gnfd —3H 61
Shelley Clo. SE15 —2H 105
Shelley Clo. Edgw —4B 12
Shelley Clo. Gnfd —3H 61
Shelley Clo. Hay —5J 59
Shelley Ct. E10 —7D 34
(off Skelton's La.)
Shelley Ct. E11 —4K 35
(off Makepeace Rd.)
Shelley Ct. N19 —1K 49
Shelley Ct. SW3 —6D 84 (7F 171)
(off Tite St.)
Shelley Cres. Houn —1B 96
Shelley Cres. S'hall —6D 60
Shelley Dri. Well —1J 109
Shelley Gdns. Wemb —2C 44
Shelley Ho. SE17 —5C 86
(off Browning St.)
Shelley Ho. SW1 —6G 85 (7B 172)
(off Churchill Gdns.)
Shelley Rd. NW10 —1K 63
Shelley Way. SW19 —6B 120
Shellness Rd. E5 —5H 51
Shell Rd. SE13 —3D 106
Shellwood Rd. SW11 —2D 102
Shelmerdine Clo. E3 —5C 70
Shelson Av. Felt —3H 113
Shelton Rd. SW19 —1J 137
Shelton St. WC2 —6J 67 (1E 166)
(in two parts)
Shene Ho. EC1 —5A 68 (5J 161)
(off Bourne Est.)
Shenfield Ho. SE18 —1B 108
(off Portway Gdns.)
Shenfield Rd. Wfd G —7E 20
Shenfield St. N1 —2E 68 (1H 163)
(in two parts)
Shenley Av. Ruis —2H 41
Shenley Rd. SE5 —1E 104
Shenley Rd. Houn —1C 96
Shenstone. W5 —1C 80
Shenstone Clo. Dart —4K 111
Shepherd Clo. W1 —7E 66 (2G 165)
(off Lees Pl.)
Shepherdess Pl. N1 —3C 68 (1D 162)
Shepherdess Wlk. N1 —2C 68 (1D 162)
Shepherd Ho. E14 —6D 70
Shepherd Mkt. W1 —1F 85 (4J 165)
Shepherd's Bush. —2E 82
Shepherd's Bush Grn. W12 —2E 82
Shepherd's Bush Mkt. W12 —2E 82
Shepherd's Bush Pl. W12 —2F 83
Shepherd's Bush Rd. W6 —4E 82
Shepherd's Clo. N6 —6F 31
Shepherds Clo. Romf —5D 38
Shepherds Clo. Shep —6D 130
Shepherds Ct. W12 —2F 83
(off Shepherd's Bush Grn.)
Shepherds Grn. Chst —7H 127
Shepherd's Hill. N6 —6F 31
Shepherds La. E9 —6K 51
Shepherds Leas. SE9 —4G 109
Shepherd's Path. NW3 —5B 48
(off Lyndhurst Rd.)
Shepherds Path. N'holt —6C 42
(off Arnold Rd.)
Shepherds Pl. W1 —7E 66 (2G 165)
Shepherd St. W1 —1F 85 (5J 165)
Shepherds Wlk. NW2 —2C 46
Shepherd's Wlk. NW3 —5B 48
Shepherds Wlk. Bus H —2C 10
Shepherds Way. S Croy —7K 153
Shepiston La. Hay —4D 76
Shepley Clo. Cars —3E 150
Sheppard Clo. Enf —1C 8
Sheppard Clo. King T —4E 134
Sheppard Dri. SE16 —5H 87
Sheppard Ho. E2 —2G 69
(off Warner Pl.)
Sheppard Ho. SW2 —1A 122
Sheppard St. E16 —4H 71
Shepperton. —6E 130
Shepperton Bus. Pk. Shep —5E 130
Shepperton Ct. Shep —6D 130
Shepperton Ct. Dri. Shep —5D 130
Shepperton Film Studios. —3B 130
Shepperton Green. —4C 130
Shepperton Rd. N1 —1C 68
Shepperton Rd. Lale & Stai —4A 130
Shepperton Rd. Orp —6G 145
Sheppey Gdns. Dag —7C 56
Sheppey Rd. Dag —7B 56
Sheppey Wlk. N1 —6C 50
Shepton Houses. E2 —3J 69
(off Welwyn St.)
Sherard Ct. N7 —3J 49
Sherard Rd. SE9 —5C 108
Sheraton Bus. Cen. Gnfd —2C 62
Sheraton Ho. SW1 —6F 85 (7K 171)
(off Churchill Gdns.)
Sheraton St. W1 —6H 67 (1C 166)
Sherborne Av. Enf —2D 8
Sherborne Av. S'hall —4E 78
Sherborne Clo. Hay —6A 60
Sherborne Cres. Cars —7C 138
Sherborne Gdns. NW9 —3G 27
Sherborne Gdns. W13 —5B 62
Sherborne Gdns. Shep —7G 131
Sherborne Ho. SW1 —5F 85 (5K 171)
Sherborne Ho. SW8 —7K 85
(off Bolney St.)
Sherborne La. EC4 —7D 68 (2E 168)
Sherborne Rd. Bedf & Felt —1F 113
(in two parts)
Sherborne Rd. Chess —5E 146
Sherborne Rd. Orp —4K 145
Sherborne Rd. Sutt —2J 149
Sherborne St. N1 —1D 68
Sherboro Rd. N15 —6F 33
Sherbourne Ct. Sutt —6A 150
Sherbourne Pl. Stan —6F 11
Sherbrooke Clo. Bexh —4G 111
Sherbrooke Rd. SW6 —7G 83
Sherbrook Gdns. N21 —7G 7
Shere Clo. Chess —5D 146
Sheredan Rd. E4 —5A 20
Shere Ho. SE1 —7E 168
Shere Rd. Ilf —5E 36
Sherfield Clo. N Mald —4H 135
Sherfield Gdns. SW15 —6B 100
Sheridan Bldgs. WC2 —6J 67 (1F 167)
(off Martlett Ct.)
Sheridan Clo. Uxb —4E 58
Sheridan Ct. NW6 —7A 48
(off Belsize Rd.)
Sheridan Ct. W7 —7K 61
(off Milton Rd.)
Sheridan Ct. Harr —6H 25
Sheridan Ct. Houn —5C 96
Sheridan Ct. N'holt —5F 43
Sheridan Cres. Chst —2F 145
Sheridan Gdns. Harr —6D 26
Sheridan Ho. SE11 —4A 86 (4K 173)
(off Wincott St.)
Sheridan Lodge. Brom —4A 144
(off Homesdale Rd.)
Sheridan M. E11 —6K 35
(off High St.)
Sheridan Pl. SW13 —3B 100
Sheridan Pl. Hamp —1F 133
Sheridan Rd. E7 —3H 53
Sheridan Rd. E12 —5C 54
Sheridan Rd. SW19 —1H 137
Sheridan Rd. Belv —4G 93
Sheridan Rd. Bexh —3E 110
Sheridan Rd. Rich —3C 116
Sheridan St. E1 —6H 69
Sheridan Ter. N'holt —5F 43
Sheridan Wlk. NW11 —6J 29
Sheridan Wlk. Cars —5D 150
Sheridan Way. Beck —1B 142
Sheriden Pl. Harr —7J 25
Sheringham. NW8 —1B 66
Sheringham Av. E12 —4D 54
Sheringham Av. N14 —5C 6
Sheringham Av. Felt —3J 113
Sheringham Av. Romf —6J 39
Sheringham Av. Twic —1D 114
Sheringham Ct. Enf —3G 7
Sheringham Ct. Felt —3J 113
(off Sheringham Av.)
Sheringham Dri. Bark —5K 55
Sheringham Ho. NW1 —5C 66 (5C 158)
(off Lisson St.)
Sheringham Rd. N7 —6K 49
Sheringham Rd. SE20 —3J 141
Sheringham Tower. S'hall —7F 61
Sherington Av. Pinn —7A 10
Sherington Rd. SE7 —6K 89
Sherland Rd. Twic —1K 115
Sherlock Ct. NW8 —1B 66
(off Dorman Way)
Sherlock Holmes Mus. —4F 159
Sherlock M. W1 —5E 66 (5G 159)
Sherman Rd. Brom —1J 143
Shernhall St. E17 —3E 34
Sherrard Rd. E7 & E12 —6A 54
Sherrards Way. Barn —5D 4
Sherrick Grn. Rd. NW10 —5D 46
Sherriff Rd. NW6 —6J 47
Sherringham Av. N17 —2G 33
Sherrin Rd. E10 —4D 52
Sherrock Gdns. NW4 —4C 28

Sherry M.—Smith Ter.

Sherry M. Bark —7H 55
Sherston Ct. SE1 —4B 86
(off Newington Butts)
Sherston Ct. WC1 —2J 161
Sherwin Ho. SE11 —7J 173
Sherwin Rd. SE14 —1K 105
Sherwood. NW6 —7G 47
Sherwood Av. E18 —3K 35
Sherwood Av. SW16 —7H 121
Sherwood Av. Gnfd —6J 43
Sherwood Av. Hay —4K 59
Sherwood Av. Ruis —6G 23
Sherwood Clo. E17 —2B 34
Sherwood Clo. SW13 —3D 100
Sherwood Clo. W13 —1B 80
Sherwood Clo. Bex —6C 110
Sherwood Ct. SW11 —3A 102
Sherwood Ct. W1 —5D 66 (6E 158)
Sherwood Ct. S Harr —2F 43
Sherwood Gdns. E14 —4C 88
Sherwood Gdns. SE16 —5G 87
Sherwood Gdns. Bark —7H 55
Sherwood Pk. Av. Sidc —7A 110
Sherwood Pk. Rd. Mitc —4G 139
Sherwood Pk. Rd. Sutt —5J 149
Sherwood Rd. NW4 —3E 28
Sherwood Rd. SW19 —7H 119
Sherwood Rd. Croy —7H 141
Sherwood Rd. Hamp H —5G 115
Sherwood Rd. Harr —2G 43
Sherwood Rd. Ilf —4H 37
Sherwood Rd. Well —2J 109
Sherwood St. N20 —3G 15
Sherwood St. W1 —7G 67 (2B 166)
Sherwood Ter. N20 —3G 15
Sherwood Way. W W'ck —2E 154
Shetland Rd. E3 —2B 70
Shield Dri. Bren —6A 80
Shieldhall St. SE2 —4C 92
Shield Rd. Ashf —4E 112
Shifford Path. SE23 —3K 123
Shillaker Ct. W3 —1B 82
Shillibeer Pl. W1 —6D 158
Shillingford St. N1 —7B 50
Shilling Pl. W7 —2A 80
Shillingstone Ho. W14 —3G 83
(off Russell Rd.)
Shinfield St. W12 —6E 64
Shingle End. Bren —7C 80
Shinglewell Rd. Eri —7G 93
Shinners Clo. SE25 —5G 141
Ship All. W4 —6G 81
Ship & Mermaid Row. SE1 —2D 86 (6F 169)
Shipka Rd. SW12 —1F 121
Shiplake Ho. E2 —3F 69 (2J 163)
(off Arnold Cir.)
Ship La. SW14 —3J 99
Shipman Rd. E16 —6K 71
Shipman Rd. SE23 —2K 123
Ship St. SE8 —1C 106
Ship Tavern Pas. EC3 —7E 68 (2G 169)
Shipton Clo. Dag —3D 56
Shipton Ho. E2 —2F 69 (1K 163)
(off Shipton St.)
Shipton Rd. Uxb —4B 40
Shipton St. E2 —2F 69 (1K 163)
Shipway Ter. N16 —3F 51
Shipwright Rd. SE16 —2A 88
Shipwright Yd. SE1 —1E 86 (5G 169)
Ship Yd. E14 —5D 88
Shirburn Clo. SE23 —7J 105
Shirbutt St. E14 —7D 70
Shirebrook Rd. SE3 —3B 108
Shire Ct. Eps —7B 148
Shire Ct. Eri —3D 92
Shirehall Clo. NW4 —6F 29
Shirehall Gdns. NW4 —6F 29
Shirehall La. NW4 —6F 29
Shirehall Pk. NW4 —5F 29
Shire Horse Way. Iswth —3K 97
Shire La. Kes & Orp —7C 156
(in two parts)
Shire M. Whit —6G 97
Shire Pl. SW18 —7A 102
Shire Pl. Bren —7C 80
Shires, The. Ham —4E 116
Shirland M. W9 —3H 65
Shirland Rd. W9 —3H 65
Shirlbutt St. E14 —7D 70
Shirley. —2K 153
Shirley Av. Bex —7D 110
Shirley Av. Croy —1J 153
Shirley Av. Sutt —4B 150
Shirley Chu. Rd. Croy —3J 153
Shirley Clo. Houn —5G 97
Shirley Ct. SW16 —7J 121
Shirley Cres. Beck —4A 142
Shirley Dri. Houn —5G 97
Shirley Gdns. W7 —1K 79
Shirley Gdns. Bark —6J 55
Shirley Gro. N9 —7D 8
Shirley Gro. SW11 —3E 102
Shirley Heights. Wall —7G 151
Shirley Hills Rd. Croy —5J 153
Shirley Ho. SE5 —7D 86
(off Picton St.)
Shirley Ho. Dri. SE7 —7A 90
Shirley Oaks. —1K 153
Shirley Oaks Rd. Croy —1K 153
Shirley Pk. Croy —2J 153
Shirley Pk. Rd. Croy —1H 153
Shirley Rd. E15 —7G 53
Shirley Rd. W4 —2K 81
Shirley Rd. Croy —7H 141
Shirley Rd. Enf —3H 7
Shirley Rd. Sidc —3J 127
Shirley Rd. Wall —7G 151
Shirleys Clo. E17 —5D 34
Shirley St. E16 —6H 71
Shirley Way. Croy —3A 154
Shirlock Rd. NW3 —4D 48
Shobden Rd. N17 —1D 32
Shobroke Clo. NW2 —3E 46
Shoebury Rd. E6 —7D 54
Shoelands Ct. NW9 —3K 27
Shoe La. EC4 —6A 68 (7K 161)
Shooters Av. Harr —4C 26
Shooters Hill. —1E 108
Shooters Hill. SE18 & Well —1D 108
Shooters Hill Rd. SE3 & SE18 —7A 90
Shooters Hill Rd. SE10 & SE3 —1F 107
Shooters Rd. Enf —1G 7
Shoot Up Hill. NW2 —5G 47
Shore Bus. Cen. E9 —7J 51
Shore Clo. Felt —7J 95
Shore Clo. Hamp —6C 114
Shorediche Clo. Uxb —3B 40
Shoreditch. —3E 68 (2H 163)
Shoreditch Ct. E8 —7F 51
(off Queensbridge Rd.)
Shoreditch High St. E1 —4E 68 (4H 163)
Shore Gro. Felt —2D 114
Shoreham Clo. SW18 —5K 101
Shoreham Clo. Bex —1D 128
Shoreham Clo. Croy —6J 141
Shoreham Rd. E. H'row A —5A 94
Shoreham Rd. W. H'row A —5A 94
Shoreham Way. Brom —6J 143
Shore Ho. SW8 —3F 103
Shore M. E9 —7J 51
(off Shore Rd.)
Shore Pl. E9 —7J 51
Shore Rd. E9 —7J 51
Shorncliffe Rd. SE1 —5F 87
Shorndean St. SE6 —1E 124
Shorne Clo. Sidc —6B 110
Shornefield Clo. Brom —3E 144
Shornells Way. SE2 —4C 92
Shorrold's Rd. SW6 —7H 83
Shortcroft Mead Ct. NW10 —5C 46
(off Cooper Rd.)
Shortcroft Rd. Eps —7B 148
Shortcrofts Rd. Dag —6F 57
Shorter St. EC3 —7F 69 (2K 169)
Short Ga. N12 —4C 14
Short Hedges. Houn —1E 96
Short Hill. Harr —1J 43
Shortlands. —2G 143
Shortlands. W6 —4F 83
Shortlands. Hay —6F 77
Shortlands Clo. N18 —3J 17
Shortlands Clo. Belv —3F 93
Shortlands Gdns. Brom —2G 143
Shortlands Gro. Brom —3F 143
Shortlands Ho. E17 —5B 34
Shortlands Rd. E10 —7D 34
Shortlands Rd. Brom —3F 143
Shortlands Rd. King T —7F 117
Short La. Stai —7B 94
Short Path. SE18 —6F 91
Short Rd. E11 —2G 53
Short Rd. W4 —6A 82
Short Rd. H'row A —6A 94
Shorts Cft. NW9 —4H 27
Shorts Gdns. WC2 —6J 67 (1E 166)
Shorts Rd. Cars —4C 150
Short St. NW4 —4E 28
Short St. SE1 —2A 86 (6K 167)
Short Wall. E15 —3E 70
Short Way. N12 —6H 15
Short Way. SE9 —3C 108
Short Way. Twic —7G 97
Shotfield. Wall —6F 151
Shott Clo. Sutt —5A 150
Shottendane Rd. SW6 —1J 101
Shottery Clo. SE9 —3C 126
Shottfield Av. SW14 —4A 100
Shottsford. W11 —6J 65
(off Ledbury Rd.)
Shoulder of Mutton All. E14 —7A 70
Shouldham St. W1 —5C 66 (6D 158)
Showers Way. Hay —1J 77
Shrapnel Clo. SE18 —7C 90
Shrapnel Rd. SE9 —3D 108
Shrewsbury Av. SW14 —4J 99
Shrewsbury Av. Harr —4E 26
Shrewsbury Clo. Surb —2E 146
Shrewsbury Ct. EC1 —4D 162
Shrewsbury Cres. NW10 —1K 63
Shrewsbury Ho. SW8 —7H 173
Shrewsbury La. SE18 —1F 109
Shrewsbury M. W2 —5J 65
(off Chepstow Rd.)
Shrewsbury Rd. E7 —5B 54
Shrewsbury Rd. N11 —6B 16
Shrewsbury Rd. W2 —6J 65
Shrewsbury Rd. Beck —3A 142
Shrewsbury Rd. Cars —7C 138
Shrewsbury Rd. H'row A —6E 94
Shrewsbury St. W10 —4E 64
Shrewsbury Wlk. Iswth —3A 98
Shrewton Rd. SW17 —7D 120
Shroffold Rd. Brom —4G 125
Shropshire Clo. Mitc —4J 139
Shropshire Ct. W7 —6K 61
(off Copley Clo.)
Shropshire Pl. WC1 —4G 67 (4C 160)
Shropshire Rd. N22 —7E 16
Shroton St. NW1 —5C 66 (5D 158)
Shrubberies, The. E18 —2J 35
Shrubbery Clo. N1 —1C 68
Shrubbery Gdns. N21 —7G 7
Shrubbery Rd. N9 —3B 18
Shrubbery Rd. SW16 —4J 121
Shrubbery Rd. S'hall —1E 78
Shrubbery, The. E11 —5K 35
Shrubbery, The. Surb —1E 146
Shrubland Clo. N20 —1G 15
Shrubland Gro. Wor Pk —3E 148
Shrubland Rd. E8 —1G 69
Shrubland Rd. E10 —7C 34
Shrubland Rd. E17 —5C 34
Shrublands Av. Croy —3C 154
Shrublands Clo. SE26 —3J 123
Shrubsall Clo. SE9 —1C 126
Shuna Wlk. N1 —6D 50
Shurland Av. Barn —6G 5
Shurland Gdns. SE15 —7F 87
Shuters Sq. W14 —5H 83
Shuttle Clo. Sidc —7K 109
Shuttlemead. Bex —7F 111
Shuttle St. E1 —4G 69 (4K 163)
Shuttleworth Rd. SW11 —2C 102
Sibella Rd. SW4 —2H 103
Sibley Clo. Bexh —5E 110
Sibley Ct. Uxb —5E 58
Sibley Gro. E12 —7C 54
Sibthorpe Rd. SE12 —6K 107
Sibthorp Rd. Mitc —2D 138
Sibton Rd. Cars —7C 138
Sicilian Av. WC1 —6F 161
Sickle Corner. Dag —4H 75
Sidbury St. SW6 —1G 101
Sidcup. —4A 128
Sidcup By-Pass. Chst & Sidc —3H 127
Sidcup High St. Sidc —4A 128
Sidcup Hill. Sidc —4B 128
Sidcup Hill Gdns. Sidc —5C 128
Sidcup Pl. Sidc —5A 128
Sidcup Rd. SE12 & SE9 —5A 108
Sidcup Technical Cen. Sidc —6D 128
Siddeley Dri. Houn —3C 96
Siddons Ho. W2 —5B 66 (6B 158)
(off Harbet Rd.)
Siddons La. NW1 —4D 66 (4F 159)
Siddons Rd. N17 —1G 33
Siddons Rd. SE23 —2A 124
Siddons Rd. Croy —3A 152
Side Rd. E17 —5B 34
Sidewood Rd. SE9 —1H 127
Sidford Ho. SE1 —2J 173
Sidford Pl. SE1 —3A 86 (2H 173)
Sidgwick Ho. SW9 —2K 103
(off Lingham St.)
Sidings M. N7 —3A 50
Sidings, The. E11 —1E 52
Sidlaw Ho. N16 —1F 51
Sidmouth Av. Iswth —2J 97
Sidmouth Dri. Ruis —3J 41
Sidmouth Ho. SE15 —7G 87
(off Lympstone Gdns.)
Sidmouth Ho. W1 —6C 66 (7D 158)
(off Cato St.)
Sidmouth Pde. NW10 —7E 46
Sidmouth Rd. E10 —3E 52
Sidmouth Rd. NW2 —7E 46
Sidmouth Rd. Well —7C 92
Sidmouth St. WC1 —3K 67 (2F 161)
Sidney Av. N22 —5E 16
Sidney Boyd Ct. NW6 —7J 47
Sidney Elson Way. E6 —2E 72
Sidney Est. E1 —6J 69
(Bromhead St.)
Sidney Est. E1 —5J 69
(Wolsey St.)
Sidney Gdns. Bren —6D 80
Sidney Gro. EC1 —2B 68 (1A 162)
Sidney Miller Ct. W3 —1H 81
(off Crown St.)
Sidney Rd. E7 —3J 53
Sidney Rd. N22 —7E 16
Sidney Rd. SE25 —5G 141
Sidney Rd. SW9 —2K 103
Sidney Rd. Beck —2A 142
Sidney Rd. Harr —3G 25
Sidney Rd. Twic —6A 98
Sidney Rd. W on T —7J 131
Sidney Sq. E1 —5J 69
Sidney St. E1 —5H 69
Sidworth St. E8 —7H 51
Siebert Rd. SE3 —6J 89
Siemens Rd. SE18 —3B 90
Sienna Ter. NW2 —2C 46
Sigdon Pas. E8 —5G 51
Sigdon Rd. E8 —5G 51
Sigers, The. Pinn —6K 23
Sigmund Freud Statue. —6B 48
(off Adelaide Rd.)
Signmakers Yd. NW1 —1F 67
(off Delancey St.)
Sigrist Sq. King T —1E 134
Silbury Av. Mitc —1C 138
Silbury Ho. SE26 —3G 123
Silbury St. N1 —3D 68 (1E 162)
Silchester Rd. W10 —6F 65
Silecroft Rd. Bexh —1G 111
Silesia Bldgs. E8 —7H 51
Silex St. SE1 —2B 86 (7B 168)
Silicone Bus. Cen. Gnfd —2C 62
Silk Clo. SE12 —5J 107
Silk Ct. E2 —3G 69
(off Squirries St.)
Silkfield Rd. NW9 —5A 28
Silk Ho. NW9 —3K 27
Silk Mills Pas. SE13 —2D 106
Silk Mills Path. SE13 —2D 106
Silk Mills Sq. E9 —6B 52
Silks Ct. E11 —1H 53
Silkstream Pde. Edgw —1J 27
Silkstream Rd. Edgw —1J 27
Silk St. EC2 —5C 68 (5D 162)
Sillitoe Ho. N1 —1D 68
(off Colville Est.)
Silsoe Ho. NW1 —2F 67
Silsoe Rd. N22 —2K 31
Silver Birch Av. E4 —5G 19
Silverbirch Clo. N11 —6K 15
Silver Birch Clo. SE28 —1A 92
Silver Birch Clo. Dart —4K 129
Silver Birch Clo. Uxb —4A 40
Silver Birch Gdns. E6 —4D 72
Silverbirch Wlk. NW5 —6E 48
Silverburn Ho. SW9 —1B 104
(off Lothian Rd.)
Silver Chase Ct. Enf —1G 7
Silvercliffe Gdns. Barn —4H 5
Silver Clo. SE14 —7A 88
Silver Clo. Harr —7C 10
Silver Cres. W4 —4H 81
Silverdale. NW1 —3G 67 (1A 160)
(off Hampstead Rd.)
Silverdale. SE26 —4J 123
Silverdale. Enf —4D 6
Silverdale Av. Ilf —5J 37
Silverdale Cen., The. Wemb —1F 63
Silverdale Clo. W7 —1J 79
Silverdale Clo. N'holt —5D 42
Silverdale Clo. Sutt —4H 149
Silverdale Ct. EC1 —3B 162
Silverdale Dri. SE9 —2C 126
Silverdale Dri. Sun —2K 131
Silverdale Factory Cen. Hay —3J 77
Silverdale Gdns. Hay —2J 77
Silverdale Ind. Est. Hay —3J 77
Silverdale Rd. E4 —6A 20
Silverdale Rd. Bexh —2H 111
Silverdale Rd. Hay —2H 77
Silverdale Rd. Pet W —4G 145
Silverhall St. Iswth —3A 98
Silverholme Clo. Harr —7E 26
Silver Jubilee Way. Houn —2K 95
Silverland St. E16 —1D 90
Silver La. W W'ck —2F 155
Silverleigh Rd. T Hth —4K 139
Silvermead. E18 —1J 35
Silvermere Rd. SE6 —7D 106
Silver Pl. W1 —6G 67 (2B 166)
Silver Rd. SE13 —3D 106
(in two parts)
Silver Rd. W12 —7F 65
Silver Spring Clo. Eri —6H 93
Silverston Way. Stan —6H 11
Silver St. N18 —4J 17
Silver St. Enf —3J 7
Silverthorn. NW8 —1K 65
(off Abbey Rd.)
Silverthorne Rd. SW8 —2F 103
Silverthorn Gdns. E4 —2H 19
Silverton Rd. W6 —6F 83
Silvertown. —1B 90
Silvertown Way. E16 —6G 71
Silvertree La. Gnfd —3H 61
Silver Wlk. SE16 —1A 88
Silver Way. Hil —2D 58
Silver Way. Romf —3H 39
Silver Wing Ind. Est. Croy —6K 151
Silverwood Clo. Beck —7C 124
Silverwood Clo. N'wd —1E 22
Silvester Ho. W11 —6H 65
(off Basing St.)
Silvester Rd. SE22 —5F 105
Silvester St. SE1 —2D 86 (7E 168)
Silvocea Way. E14 —6F 71
Silwood Est. SE16 —4J 87
Silwood St. SE16 —4J 87
Simla Ho. SE1 —2D 86 (7F 169)
(off Kipling Est.)
Simmons Clo. N20 —2H 15
Simmons Clo. Chess —6C 146
Simmons La. E4 —2A 20
Simmons Rd. SE18 —5F 91
Simmons Way. N20 —2H 15
Simms Clo. Cars —2C 150
Simms Rd. SE1 —4G 87
Simnel Rd. SE12 —7K 107
Simon Clo. W11 —7H 65
Simon Ct. W9 —3J 65
(off Saltram Cres.)
Simonds Rd. E10 —2C 52
Simone Clo. Brom —1B 144
Simone Ct. SE26 —3J 123
Simon Peter Ct. Enf —2G 7
Simons Ct. N16 —2F 51
Simons Wlk. E15 —5F 53
Simpson Clo. N21 —5D 6
Simpson Dri. W3 —6K 63
Simpson Ho. NW8 —3C 66 (2C 158)
Simpson Ho. SE11 —5K 85 (6H 173)
Simpson Rd. Houn —6D 96
Simpson Rd. Rich —4C 116
Simpson's Rd. E14 —7D 70
Simpsons Rd. Brom —3J 143
Simpson St. SW11 —2C 102
Simpson Way. Surb —6C 134
Simrose Ct. SW18 —5J 101
Sims Wlk. SE3 —4H 107
Sinclair Ct. Croy —2E 152
Sinclair Dri. Sutt —7K 149
Sinclair Gdns. W14 —2F 83
Sinclair Gro. NW11 —6F 29
Sinclair Ho. WC1 —3J 67 (2E 160)
(off Sandwich St.)
Sinclair Mans. W14 —2F 83
(off Richmond Way)
Sinclair Pl. SE4 —6C 106
Sinclair Rd. E4 —5G 19
Sinclair Rd. W14 —2F 83
Sinclare Clo. Enf —1A 8
Singapore Rd. W13 —1A 80
Singer St. EC1 —3D 68 (2F 163)
Singleton Clo. SW17 —7D 120
Singleton Clo. Croy —7C 140
Singleton Rd. Dag —5F 57
Singleton Scarp. N12 —5D 14
Sinnott Rd. E17 —1K 33
Sion Ct. Twic —1B 116
Sion Rd. Twic —1B 116
Sippets Ct. Ilf —1H 55
Sipson. —6C 76
Sipson Clo. W Dray —6C 76
Sipson La. W Dray & Hay —6C 76
Sipson Rd. W Dray —3B 76
(in two parts)
Sipson Way. W Dray —7C 76
Sir Abraham Dawes Cotts. SW15 —4G 101
Sir Alexander Clo. W3 —1B 82
Sir Alexander Rd. W3 —1B 82
Sir Cyril Black Way. SW19 —7J 119
Sirdar Rd. N22 —3B 32
Sirdar Rd. W11 —7F 65
Sirdar Rd. Mitc —6E 120
Sir Henry Floyd Ct. Stan —2G 11
Sirinham Point. SW8 —6K 85
(off Meadow Rd.)
Sirius Building. E1 —7K 69
(off Jardine Rd.)
Sir John Soane's Mus. —6K 67 (7G 161)
Sir Nicholas Garrow Ho. W10 —4G 65
(off Kensal Rd.)
Sir Oswald Stoll Foundation, The. SW6 —7K 83
(off Fulham Rd.)
Sir Oswald Stoll Mans. SW6 —7K 83
(off Fulham Rd.)
Sir William Powell's Almshouses. SW6 —2G 101
Sise La. EC4 —1E 168
Sisley Rd. Bark —1J 73
Sispara Gdns. SW18 —6H 101
Sissinghurst Clo. Brom —5G 125
Sissinghurst Rd. Croy —7G 141
Sister Mabel's Way. SE15 —7G 87
Sisters Av. SW11 —3D 102
Sistova Rd. SW12 —1F 121
Sisulu Pl. SW9 —3A 104
Sittingbourne Av. Enf —6J 7
Sitwell Gro. Stan —5E 10
Siverst Clo. N'holt —6F 43
Sivill Ho. E2 —3F 69 (1K 163)
(off Columbia Rd.)
Siviter Way. Dag —7H 57
Siward Rd. N17 —1D 32
Siward Rd. SW17 —3A 120
Siward Rd. Brom —3K 143
Six Acres Est. N4 —2A 50
Six Bridges Ind. Est. SE1 —5G 87
Sixth Av. E12 —4D 54
Sixth Av. W10 —3G 65
Sixth Av. Hay —1H 77
Sixth Cross Rd. Twic —3G 115
Skardu Rd. NW2 —5G 47
Skeena Hill. SW18 —7G 101
Skeffington Rd. E6 —1D 72
Skeggs Ho. E14 —3E 88
Skelbrook St. SW18 —2A 120
Skelgill Rd. SW15 —4H 101
Skelley Rd. E15 —7H 53
Skelton Clo. E8 —6F 51
Skelton Rd. E7 —6J 53
Skelton's La. E10 —7D 34
Skelwith Rd. W6 —6E 82
Skerne Rd. King T —1D 134
Sketchley Gdns. SE16 —5K 87
Sketty Rd. Enf —3A 8
Skiers St. E15 —1G 71
Skiffington Clo. SW2 —1A 122
Skillen Lodge. Pinn —1B 24
Skinner Ct. E2 —2H 69
Skinner Pl. SW1 —4G 171
Skinners La. EC4 —7C 68 (2D 168)
Skinners La. Houn —1F 97
Skinner's Row. SE10 —1D 106
Skinner St. EC1 —3A 68 (2K 161)
Skip La. Hare —1A 40
Skipsey Av. E6 —3D 72
Skipton Clo. N11 —6K 15
Skipton Dri. Hay —3E 76
Skipton Ho. SE4 —4A 106
Skipwith Ho. EC1 —5A 68 (5J 161)
(off Bourne Est.)
Skipworth Rd. E9 —1J 69
Skomer Wlk. N1 —6C 50
Skyline Plaza Building. E1 —6G 69
(off Commercial Rd.)
Skylines. E14 —2E 88
Sky Peals Rd. Wfd G —7A 20
Sladebrook Rd. SE3 —3B 108
Slade Ct. New Bar —3E 4
Sladedale Rd. SE18 —5J 91
Slade Ho. Houn —6D 96
Sladen Pl. E5 —4H 51
Slades Clo. Enf —3F 7
Slades Dri. Chst —4F 127
Slades Gdns. Enf —2F 7
Slades Hill. Enf —3F 7
Slades Ri. Enf —3F 7
Slade, The. SE18 —6J 91
Slade Tower. E10 —2C 52
(off Leyton Grange Est.)
Slade Wlk. SE17 —6B 86
Slagrove Pl. SE4 —5C 106
Slaidburn St. SW10 —6A 84
Slaithwaite Rd. SE13 —4E 106
Slaney Ct. NW10 —7E 46
Slaney Pl. N7 —5A 50
Slater Clo. SE18 —5E 90
Slatter. NW9 —7G 13
Slattery Rd. Felt —1B 114
Sleaford Ind. Est. SW8 —7G 85
Sleaford St. SW8 —7G 85
Sledmere Ct. Felt —1G 113
Slewyn Ct. Wemb —3J 45
Slievemore Clo. SW4 —3H 103
Slindon Ct. N16 —3F 51
Slingsby Pl. WC2 —7J 67 (2E 166)
Slippers Pl. SE16 —3H 87
Sloane Av. SW3 —4C 84 (4D 170)
Sloane Ct. E. SW3 —5E 84 (5G 171)
Sloane Ct. W. SW3 —5E 84 (5G 171)
Sloane Gdns. SW1 —4E 84 (4G 171)
Sloane Sq. SW1 —4D 84 (4F 171)
Sloane St. SW1 —2D 84 (7F 165)
Sloane Ter. SW1 —4E 84 (3G 171)
Sloane Ter. Mans. SW1 —4E 84 (3G 171)
Sloane Wlk. Croy —6B 142
Slocum Clo. SE28 —7C 74
Sloman Ho. W10 —3G 65
(off Beethoven St.)
Slough La. NW9 —5J 27
Sly St. E1 —6H 69
Smaldon Clo. W Dray —3C 76
Smallberry Av. Iswth —2K 97
Smallbrook M. W2 —6B 66 (1A 164)
Smalley Clo. N16 —3F 51
Smalley Rd. Est. N16 —3F 51
(off Smalley Clo.)
Smallwood Rd. SW17 —4B 120
Smarden Clo. Belv —5G 93
Smarden Gro. SE9 —4D 126
Smart's Pl. N18 —5B 18
Smart's Pl. WC1 —6J 67 (7F 161)
Smart St. E2 —3K 69
Smeaton Clo. Chess —6D 146
Smeaton Ct. SE1 —3C 86
Smeaton Rd. SW18 —7J 101
Smeaton Rd. Wfd G —5J 21
Smeaton St. E1 —1H 87
Smedley St. SW8 & SW4 —2H 103
Smeed Rd. E3 —7C 52
Smiles Pl. SE13 —2E 106
Smith Clo. SE16 —1K 87
Smithfield St. EC1 —5B 68 (6A 162)
Smith Hill. Bren —6E 80
Smithies Ct. E15 —5E 52
Smithies Rd. SE2 —4B 92
Smith's Ct. W1 —2B 166
Smithson Rd. N17 —1D 32
Smiths Point. E13 —1J 71
(off Brooks Rd.)
Smith Sq. SW1 —3J 85 (2E 172)
Smith St. SW3 —5D 84 (5E 170)
Smith St. Surb —6F 135
Smith's Yd. SW18 —2A 120
Smith Ter. SW3 —5D 84 (6E 170)

Smithwood Clo.—Spa Rd.

Smithwood Clo. SW19 —1G 119
Smithy St. E1 —5J 69
Smock Wlk. Croy —6C 140
Smokehouse Yd. EC1 —5B 68 (5B 162)
(off St John St.)
Smoothfield. Houn —4E 96
Smugglers Way. SW18 —4K 101
Smyrk's Rd. SE17 —5E 86
Smyrna Rd. NW6 —7J 47
Smythe St. E14 —7D 70
Snakes La. Barn —3A 6
Snakes La. E. Wfd G —6F 21
Snakes La. W. Wfd G —5D 20
Snaresbrook. —5J 35
Snaresbrook Dri. Stan —4J 11
Snaresbrook Hall. E18 —4J 35
Snaresbrook Rd. E11 —4G 35
Snarsgate St. W10 —5E 64
Sneath Av. NW11 —7H 29
Snells Pk. N18 —6A 18
Sneyd Rd. NW2 —5E 46
Snowberry Clo. E11 —4F 53
Snowbury Rd. SW6 —2K 101
Snowden Av. Hil & Uxb —2D 58
Snowden Dri. NW9 —6A 28
Snowden St. EC2 —4E 68 (4G 163)
Snowdon Cres. Hay —3E 76
Snowdon Rd. H'row A —6E 94
Snowdown Clo. SE20 —1J 141
Snowdrop Clo. Hamp —6E 114
Snow Hill. EC1 —5B 68 (6A 162)
Snow Hill Ct. EC1 —6B 68 (7B 162)
(in two parts)
Snowman Ho. NW6 —1K 65
Snowsfields. SE1 —2D 86 (6F 169)
Snowshill Rd. E12 —5C 54
Snowy Fielder Waye. Iswth —2B 98
Soames St. SE15 —3F 105
Soames Wlk. N Mald —1A 136
Soane Ct. NW1 —7G 49
(off St Pancras Way)
Socket La. Hayes —6K 143
Soho. —6G 67 (1B 166)
Soho Sq. W1 —6H 67 (7C 160)
Soho St. W1 —6H 67 (7C 160)
Sojourner Truth Clo. E8 —6H 51
Solander Gdns. E1 —7J 69
Solar Ct. N3 —7E 14
Solarium Ct. SE1 —4F 87
(off Alscot Rd.)
Soldene Ct. N7 —5K 49
(off George's Rd.)
Solebay St. E1 —4A 70
Solent Ri. E13 —3J 71
Solent Rd. NW6 —5J 47
Solent Rd. H'row A —6B 94
Soley M. WC1 —3A 68 (1J 161)
Solna Av. SW15 —5E 100
Solna Rd. N21 —1J 17
Soloman Av. N18 —4B 18
Solomon's Pas. SE15 —4H 105
Solon New Rd. SW4 —4J 103
Solon New Rd. Est. SW4 —4J 103
Solon Rd. SW2 —4J 103
Solway Clo. E8 —6F 51
(off Queensbridge Rd.)
Solway Clo. Houn —3C 96
Solway Rd. N22 —1B 32
Solway Rd. SE22 —4G 105
Somaford Gro. Barn —6G 5
Somali Rd. NW2 —5H 47
Somerby Rd. Bark —7H 55
Somercoates Clo. Barn —3H 5
Somer Ct. SW6 —6J 83
(off Anselm Rd.)
Somerfield Ho. SE16 —5K 87
Somerfield Rd. N4 —2B 50
Somerford Clo. Eastc & Pinn —4J 23
Somerford Gro. N16 —4F 51
Somerford Gro. N17 —7B 18
(in two parts)
Somerford Gro. Est. N16 —4F 51
Somerford St. E1 —4H 69
Somerford Way. SE16 —2A 88
Somerhill Av. Sidc —7B 110
Somerhill Rd. Well —2B 110
Somerleyton Pas. SW9 —4B 104
Somerleyton Rd. SW9 —4A 104
Somersby Gdns. Ilf —5D 36
Somers Clo. NW1 —2H 67
Somers Cres. W2 —6C 66 (1C 164)
Somerset Av. SW20 —2D 136
Somerset Av. Chess —4D 146
Somerset Av. Well —5K 109
Somerset Clo. N17 —2D 32
Somerset Clo. N Mald —6A 136
Somerset Clo. Wfd G —1J 35
Somerset Ct. W7 —6K 61
(off Copley Clo.)
Somerset Ct. Buck H —2F 21
Somerset Est. SW11 —1B 102
Somerset Gdns. N6 —7E 30
Somerset Gdns. N17 —7K 17
Somerset Gdns. SE13 —2D 106
Somerset Gdns. SW16 —3K 139
Somerset Gdns. Tedd —5J 115
Somerset Hall. N17 —7K 17
Somerset House. —7K 67 (2G 167)
Somerset Lodge. Bren —6D 80
Somerset Rd. E17 —6C 34
Somerset Rd. N17 —3F 33
Somerset Rd. N18 —5A 18
Somerset Rd. NW4 —4E 28
Somerset Rd. SW19 —3F 119
Somerset Rd. W4 —3K 81
Somerset Rd. W13 —1B 80
Somerset Rd. Bren —6C 80
Somerset Rd. Harr —5G 25
Somerset Rd. King T —2F 135
Somerset Rd. New Bar —5E 4
Somerset Rd. S'hall —5D 60
Somerset Rd. Tedd —5J 115
Somerset Sq. W14 —2G 83
Somerset Waye. Houn —6C 78
Somersham Rd. Bexh —2E 110
Somers Pl. SW2 —7K 103
Somers Rd. E17 —4B 34
Somers Rd. SW2 —6K 103
Somers Town. —3H 67 (1C 160)
Somerton Av. Rich —3H 99
Somerton Rd. NW2 —3G 47
Somerton Rd. SE15 —4H 105
Somertrees Av. SE12 —2K 125
Somervell Rd. Harr —5D 42
Somerville Av. SW13 —6D 82
Somerville Point. SE16 —2B 88
Somerville Rd. SE20 —7K 123
Somerville Rd. Romf —6C 38
Sonderburg Rd. N7 —2K 49
Sondes St. SE17 —6D 86
Sonia Ct. Edgw —7A 12
Sonia Ct. Harr —6K 25
Sonia Gdns. N12 —4F 15
Sonia Gdns. NW10 —4B 46
Sonia Gdns. Houn —7E 78
Sonning Gdns. Hamp —6C 114
Sonning Ho. E2 —3F 69 (2J 163)
(off Swanfield St.)
Sonning Rd. SE25 —6G 141
Sontan Ct. Twic —1H 115
Soper Clo. E4 —5G 19
Soper Clo. SE23 —1K 123
Soper M. Enf —1H 9
Sophia Clo. N7 —6K 49
Sophia Rd. E10 —1D 52
Sophia Rd. E16 —6K 71
Sophia Sq. SE16 —7A 70
(off Sovereign Cres.)
Sopwith. NW9 —7G 13
Sopwith Av. Chess —5E 146
Sopwith Clo. King T —5F 117
Sopwith Rd. Houn —7A 78
Sopwith Way. SW8 —7F 85
Sopwith Way. King T —1E 134
Sorensen Ct. E10 —2D 52
(off Leyton Grange Est.)
Sorrel Clo. SE28 —1A 92
Sorrel Gdns. E6 —5C 72
Sorrel La. E14 —6F 71
Sorrell Clo. SE14 —7A 88
Sorrell Clo. SW9 —2A 104
Sorrento Rd. Sutt —3J 149
Sotheby Rd. N5 —3B 50
Sotheran Clo. E8 —1G 69
Sotheron Rd. SW6 —7K 83
Soudan Rd. SW11 —1D 102
Souldern Rd. W14 —3F 83
S. Access Rd. E17 —7A 34
South Acre. NW9 —2B 28
Southacre. W2 —6C 66 (1C 164)
(off Hyde Pk. Cres.)
Southacre Way. Pinn —1A 24
South Acton. —2H 81
S. Africa Rd. W12 —1D 82
Southall. —1D 78
Southall Ct. S'hall —7D 60
Southall Enterprise Cen. S'hall —2E 78
Southall Green. —3C 78
Southall La. Cran & Houn —6K 77
Southall Pl. SE1 —2D 86 (7E 168)
Southampton Bldgs. WC2 —5A 68 (6J 161)
Southampton Gdns. Mitc —5J 139
Southampton Pl. WC1 —5J 67 (6F 161)
Southampton Rd. NW5 —5D 48
Southampton Rd. H'row A —6A 94
Southampton Row. WC1 —5J 67 (5F 161)
Southampton St. WC2 —7J 67 (2F 167)
Southampton Way. SE5 —7D 86
Southampton Way. Stanw —6A 94
Southam St. W10 —4G 65
S. Audley St. W1 —7E 66 (3H 165)
South Av. E4 —7J 9
South Av. N2 —4K 29
South Av. NW10 —4E 64
South Av. Cars —7E 150
South Av. Rich —2G 99
South Av. S'hall —7D 60
South Av. Gdns. S'hall —7D 60
South Bank. Surb —6E 134
Southbank. Th Dit —7B 134
Southbank Bus. Cen. SW8 —6H 85 (7D 172)
Southbank Bus. Cen. SW11 —1D 102
South Bank Cen. —1K 85 (4H 167)
South Bank Centre. SE1 —1K 85
(off Belvedere Rd.)
S. Bank Ter. Surb —6E 134
South Barnet. —1K 15
South Beddington. —6H 151
S. Birkbeck Rd. E11 —3F 53
S. Black Lion La. W6 —5C 82
South Block. SE1 —2K 85
(off Westminster Bri. Rd.)
S. Bolton Gdns. SW5 —5A 84
Southborough. —5D 144
(Bromley)
Southborough. —1E 146
(Surbiton)
Southborough Clo. Surb —1D 146
Southborough Ho. SE17 —5E 86
(off Surrey Gro.)
Southborough La. Brom —5C 144
Southborough Rd. E9 —1K 69
Southborough Rd. Brom —3C 144
Southborough Rd. Surb —1E 146
S. Boundary Rd. E12 —3D 54
Southbourne. Brom —7J 143
Southbourne Av. NW9 —2J 27
Southbourne Clo. Pinn —7C 24
Southbourne Ct. NW9 —2J 27
Southbourne Cres. NW4 —4G 29
Southbourne Gdns. SE12 —5K 107
Southbourne Gdns. Ilf —5G 55
Southbourne Gdns. Ruis —1K 41
S. Branch Av. NW10 —4E 64
Southbridge Pl. Croy —4C 152
Southbridge Rd. Croy —4C 152
Southbridge Way. S'hall —2C 78
South Bromley. —6F 71
Southbrook M. SE12 —6H 107
Southbrook Rd. SE12 —6H 107
Southbrook Rd. SW16 —1J 139
Southbury. NW8 —1A 66
(off Loudoun Rd.)
Southbury Av. Enf —4B 8
Southbury Rd. Enf —3K 7
S. Carriage Dri. SW7 & SW1 —2B 84 (7B 164)
South Chingford. —5G 19
Southchurch Ct. E6 —2D 72
(off High St. S.)
Southchurch Rd. E6 —2D 72
S. Circular Rd. SW15 —4C 100
South Clo. N6 —7F 31
South Clo. Barn —3C 4
South Clo. Bexh —4D 110
South Clo. Dag —1G 75
South Clo. Mord —6J 137
South Clo. Pinn —7D 24
South Clo. Twic —3E 114
South Clo. W Dray —3B 76
S. Colonnade, The. E14 —1C 88
South Colonnade, The. E14 —1C 88
Southcombe St. W14 —4G 83
S. Common Rd. Uxb —6A 40
Southcote Av. Felt —2H 113
Southcote Av. Surb —7H 135
Southcote Ri. Ruis —7F 23
Southcote Rd. E17 —5K 33
Southcote Rd. N19 —4G 49
Southcote Rd. SE25 —5H 141
S. Countess Rd. E17 —3B 34
South Cres. E16 —4F 71
South Cres. WC1 —5H 67 (6C 160)
Southcroft Av. Well —3J 109
Southcroft Av. W W'ck —2E 154
Southcroft Rd. SW17 & SW16 —6E 120
S. Cross Rd. Ilf —5G 37
S. Croxted Rd. SE21 —3D 122
South Croydon. —5D 152
Southdean Gdns. SW19 —2H 119
South Dene. NW7 —3E 12
Southdene Ct. N11 —3A 16
Southdown. N7 —6J 49
Southdown Av. W7 —3A 80
Southdown Cres. Harr —1G 43
Southdown Cres. Ilf —5J 37
Southdown Dri. SW20 —7F 119
Southdown Rd. SW20 —1F 137
Southdown Rd. Cars —7E 150
South Dri. E12 —3C 54
South Dri. Ruis —1G 41
S. Ealing Rd. W5 —2D 80
S. Eastern Av. N9 —3A 18
S. Eaton Pl. SW1 —4E 84 (3H 171)
S. Eden Pk. Rd. Beck —6D 142
S. Edwardes Sq. W8 —3H 83
Southend. —4F 125
South End. W8 —3K 83
South End. Croy —4C 152
S. End Clo. NW3 —4C 48
Southend Clo. SE9 —6F 109
Southend Cres. SE9 —6F 109
S. End Grn. NW3 —4C 48
Southend La. SE26 & SE6 —4B 124
Southend Rd. E4 & E17 —5F 19
Southend Rd. E6 —7D 54
S. End Rd. NW3 —4C 48
Southend Rd. E18 & Wfd G —1J 35
Southend Rd. Beck —1C 142
S. End Row. W8 —3K 83
Southern Av. SE25 —3F 141
Southern Av. Felt —1J 113
Southerngate Way. SE14 —7A 88
Southern Gro. E3 —3B 70
Southern Rd. E13 —2K 71
Southern Rd. N2 —4D 30
Southern Row. W10 —4G 65
Southern St. N1 —2K 67
Southern Way. Romf —6G 39
Southernwood Retail Pk. SE1 —5F 87
Southerton Rd. W6 —4E 82
S. Esk Rd. E7 —6A 54
Southey Ho. SE17 —5C 86
(off Browning St.)
Southey M. E16 —1J 89
Southey Rd. N15 —5E 32
Southey Rd. SW9 —1A 104
Southey Rd. SW19 —7J 119
Southey St. SE20 —7K 123
Southfield. Barn —6A 4
Southfield Clo. Uxb —4C 58
Southfield Cotts. W7 —2K 79
Southfield Ct. E11 —3H 53
Southfield Gdns. Twic —4K 115
Southfield Pk. Harr —4F 25
Southfield Rd. N17 —2E 32
Southfield Rd. W4 —2K 81
Southfield Rd. Chst —3K 145
Southfield Rd. Enf —6C 8
Southfields. —1J 119
Southfields. NW4 —3D 28
Southfields. E Mol —6J 133
Southfields Av. Ashf —6D 112
Southfields Ct. Sutt —2J 149
Southfields M. SW18 —6J 101
Southfields Pas. SW18 —6J 101
Southfields Rd. SW18 —6J 101
South Gdns. SW19 —7B 120
South Gdns. Wemb —2G 45
Southgate. —1C 16
Southgate Av. Felt —4F 113
Southgate Cir. N14 —1C 16
Southgate Gro. N1 —7D 50
Southgate Ind. Est. N14 —7C 6
Southgate Rd. N1 —1D 68
S. Gipsy Rd. Well —3D 110
S. Glade, The. Bex —1F 129
South Grn. NW9 —1A 28
South Gro. E17 —5B 34
South Gro. N6 —1E 48
South Gro. N15 —5D 32
South Gro. Ho. N6 —1E 48
South Hackney. —7K 51
South Hampstead. —7A 48
South Harrow. —3G 43
S. Harrow Ind. Est. S Harr —2G 43
South Hill. Chst —6D 126
South Hill. N'wd —1G 23
S. Hill Av. Harr & S Harr —3G 43
S. Hill Gro. Harr —4J 43
S. Hill Pk. NW3 —4C 48
S. Hill Pk. Gdns. NW3 —3C 48
S. Hill Rd. Brom —3G 143
Southholme Clo. SE19 —1E 140
Southill Ct. Brom —5H 143
Southill La. Pinn —4K 23
Southill Rd. Chst —7C 126
Southill St. E14 —6D 70
S. Island Pl. SW9 —7K 85
South Kensington. —4B 84 (3B 170)
S. Kensington Sta. Arc. SW7 —4B 84
(off Pelham St.)
South Lambeth. —7J 85
S. Lambeth Pl. SW8 —5J 85 (7F 173)
S. Lambeth Rd. SW8 —6J 85
Southland Rd. SE18 —7K 91
Southlands Dri. SW19 —2F 119
Southlands Gro. Brom —3C 144
Southlands Rd. Brom —5A 144
Southland Way. Houn —5H 97
South La. King T —3D 134
(in two parts)
South La. N Mald —4K 135
South La. W. N Mald —4K 135
South Lodge. NW8 —2B 66 (1A 158)
South Lodge. SW7 —2C 84 (7D 164)
(off Knightsbridge)
South Lodge. Twic —6G 97
S. Lodge Av. Mitc —4J 139
S. Lodge Cres. Enf —4C 6
(in two parts)
S. Lodge Dri. N14 —4C 6
South London Crematorium. Mitc —2G 139
South London Gallery. —1E 104
(off Peckham Rd.)
Southly Clo. Sutt —3J 149
South Mall. N9 —3B 18
(off Plevna Rd.)
South Mead. NW9 —1B 28
South Mead. Eps —7B 148
South Meadows. Wemb —5F 45
Southmead Rd. SW19 —1G 119
S. Molton La. W1 —6F 67 (1J 165)
S. Molton Rd. E16 —6J 71
S. Molton St. W1 —6F 67 (1J 165)
Southmoor Way. E9 —6B 52
South Mt. N20 —2F 15
(off High Rd.)
South Norwood. —4F 141
South Norwood Country Pk. —4J 141
S. Norwood Hill. SE25 —1E 140
S. Oak Rd. SW16 —4K 121
Southold Ri. SE9 —3D 126
Southolm St. SW11 —1F 103
Southover. N12 —3D 14
Southover. Brom —5J 125
South Pde. SW3 —5B 84 (5B 170)
South Pde. W4 —4K 81
South Pde. Edgw —2G 27
South Pde. Wall —6G 151
S. Park Ct. Beck —7C 124
S. Park Cres. SE6 —1G 125
S. Park Cres. Ilf —3H 55
S. Park Dri. Ilf & Bark —2J 55
S. Park Gro. N Mald —4J 135
S. Park Hill Rd. S Croy —5D 152
S. Park M. SW6 —3K 101
S. Park Rd. SW19 —6J 119
S. Park Rd. Ilf —3H 55
S. Park Ter. Ilf —3J 55
S. Park Vs. Ilf —4J 55
S. Park Way. Ruis —6A 42
South Pl. EC2 —5D 68 (5F 163)
South Pl. Enf —5D 8
South Pl. Surb —7F 135
South Pl. M. EC2 —5D 68 (6F 163)
Southport Rd. SE18 —4H 91
S. Quay Plaza. E14 —2D 88
Southridge Pl. SW20 —7F 119
South Ri. W2 —2D 164
South Ri. Cars —7C 150
South Ri. Way. SE18 —5H 91
South Rd. N9 —1B 18
South Rd. SE23 —2K 123
South Rd. SW19 —6A 120
South Rd. W5 —4D 80
South Rd. Chad H —6E 38
South Rd. Edgw —1H 27
South Rd. Felt —5B 114
South Rd. Hamp —6C 114
South Rd. Harr —1A 44
South Rd. L Hth —5C 38
South Rd. S'hall —2D 78
South Rd. Twic —3H 115
South Rd. W Dray —3C 76
South Row. SE3 —2H 107
South Ruislip. —4A 42
Southsea Rd. King T —4E 134
S. Sea St. SE16 —3B 88
South Side. N15 —4F 33
South Side. W6 —3B 82
Southside Comn. SW19 —6E 118
Southside House. —6E 118
Southspring. Sidc —7H 109
South Sq. NW11 —6K 29
South Sq. WC1 —5A 68 (6J 161)
South St. W1 —1E 84 (4H 165)
South St. Brom —2J 143
South St. Enf —5D 8
South St. Iswth —3A 98
South St. Rain —2J 75
South St. Romf —5K 39
S. Tenter St. E1 —7F 69 (2K 169)
South Ter. SW7 —4C 84 (3C 170)
South Ter. Surb —6E 134
South Tottenham. —5F 33
Southvale. SE19 —6E 122
South Va. Harr —4J 43
Southvale Rd. SE3 —2G 107
South Vw. Brom —2A 144
Southview Av. NW10 —5B 46
Southview Clo. SW17 —5E 120
S. View Clo. Bex —6F 111
S. View Ct. SE19 —7C 122
Southview Cres. Ilf —6F 37
S. View Dri. E18 —3K 35
Southview Gdns. Wall —7G 151
Southview Pde. Rain —3K 75
S. View Rd. N8 —3H 31
Southview Rd. Brom —4F 125
South Vs. NW1 —6H 49
Southville. SW8 —1H 103
Southville Clo. Eps —7K 147
Southville Clo. Felt —1G 113
Southville Cres. Felt —1G 113
Southville Rd. Felt —1G 113
Southville Rd. Th Dit —7A 134
South Wlk. Hay —5F 59
South Wlk. W W'ck —3G 155
Southwark. —1C 86 (4D 168)
Southwark Bri. SE1 & EC4 —7C 68 (3D 168)
Southwark Bri. Bus. Cen. SE1 —1C 86 (5D 168)
(off Tower Bri. Rd.)
Southwark Bri. Office Village. SE1 —4D 168
Southwark Bri. Rd. SE1 —3B 86
Southwark Cathedral. —4E 168
Southwark Pk. Est. SE16 —3H 87
Southwark Pk. Rd. SE16 —4F 87
Southwark Pl. Brom —3D 144
Southwark St. SE1 —1B 86 (4A 168)
Southwater Clo. E14 —6B 70
Southwater Clo. Beck —7D 124
South Way. N9 —2D 18
South Way. N11 —6B 16
Southway. N20 —2D 14
Southway. NW11 —6K 29
Southway. SW20 —5E 136
South Way. Croy —3A 154
South Way. Harr —4E 24
South Way. Hayes —7J 143
Southway. Wall —4G 151
South Way. Wemb —5G 45
Southways Pde. Ilf —5E 36
Southwell Av. N'holt —6E 42
Southwell Gdns. SW7 —4A 84
Southwell Gro. Rd. E11 —2G 53
Southwell Ho. SE16 —4H 87
(off Anchor St.)
Southwell Rd. SE5 —3C 104
Southwell Rd. Croy —6A 140
Southwell Rd. Kent —6D 26
S. Western Rd. Twic —6A 98
S. W. India Dock Entrance. E14 —2E 88
S. W. India Dock Rd. E14 —2E 88
South West Middlesex Crematorium. Felt —1C 114
Southwest Rd. E11 —1F 53
S. Wharf Rd. W2 —6B 66 (7A 158)
Southwick M. W2 —6B 66 (7B 158)
Southwick Pl. W2 —6C 66 (1C 164)
Southwick St. W2 —6C 66 (7C 158)
Southwick Yd. W2 —1C 164
South Wimbledon. —6K 119
Southwold Dri. Bark —5A 56
Southwold Mans. W9 —3J 65
(off Widley Rd.)
Southwold Rd. E5 —2H 51
Southwold Rd. Bex —6H 111
Southwood Av. N6 —7F 31
Southwood Av. King T —1J 135
Southwood Clo. Brom —4D 144
Southwood Clo. Wor Pk —1F 149
Southwood Ct. EC1 —3B 68 (2A 162)
(off Wynyatt St.)
Southwood Ct. NW11 —5K 29
Southwood Dri. Surb —7J 135
South Woodford. —2J 35
S. Woodford to Barking Relief Rd. E11 & Bark —5B 36
Southwood Gdns. Esh —3A 146
Southwood Gdns. Ilf —4F 37
Southwood Hall. N6 —6F 31
Southwood Heights. N6 —7F 31
Southwood Ho. W11 —7G 65
(off Avondale Pk. Rd.)
Southwood La. N6 —1E 48
Southwood Lawn Rd. N6 —7E 30
Southwood Mans. N6 —6E 30
(off Southwood La.)
Southwood Pk. N6 —7E 30
Southwood Rd. SE9 —2F 127
Southwood Rd. SE28 —1B 92
Southwood Smith Ho. E2 —3H 69
(off Florida St.)
Southwood Smith St. N1 —1B 68
(off Old Royal Free Sq.)
S. Worple Av. SW14 —3A 100
S. Worple Way. SW14 —3K 99
Southwyck Ho. SW9 —4B 104
Sovereign Bus. Cen. Enf —3G 9
Sovereign Clo. E1 —7H 69
Sovereign Clo. W5 —5C 62
Sovereign Clo. Ruis —1G 41
Sovereign Ct. Houn —3E 96
Sovereign Ct. W Mol —4D 132
Sovereign Cres. SE16 —7A 70
Sovereign Gro. Wemb —3D 44
Sovereign Ho. SE18 —3D 90
(off Leda Rd.)
Sovereign M. E2 —2F 69
Sovereign Pk. NW10 —4H 63
Sovereign Pk. Trad. Est. NW10 —4H 63
Sovereign Rd. Bark —3C 74
Sowerby Clo. SE9 —5C 108
Space Waye. Felt —5J 95
Spa Clo. SE25 —1E 140
Spa Ct. SW16 —4K 121
Spafield St. EC1 —4A 68 (3J 161)
Spa Grn. Est. EC1 —3B 68 (1K 161)
Spa Hill. SE19 —1D 140
Spalding Ho. SE4 —4A 106
Spalding Rd. NW4 —7E 28
Spalding Rd. SW17 —5F 121
Spanby Rd. E3 —4C 70
Spaniards Clo. NW11 —1B 48
Spaniards End. NW11 —1A 48
Spaniards Rd. NW3 —2A 48
Spanish Pl. W1 —6E 66 (7H 159)
Spanish Rd. SW18 —5A 102
Spanswick Lodge. N15 —4B 32
Sparkbridge Rd. Harr —4J 25
Sparke Ter. E16 —6H 71
(off Clarkson Rd.)
Sparkford Gdns. N11 —5K 15
Sparks Clo. W3 —6K 63
Sparks Clo. Dag —2D 56
Sparks Clo. Hamp —6C 114
Spa Rd. SE16 —3F 87

266 A-Z Big London

Sparrick's Row—Stanley Sq.

Sparrick's Row. SE1 —2D 86 (6F 169)
Sparrow Clo. Hamp —6C 114
Sparrow Dri. Orp —7G 145
Sparrow Farm Dri. Felt —7A 96
Sparrow Farm Rd. Eps —4C 148
Sparrow Grn. Dag —3H 57
Sparrows Herne. Bush —1A 10
Sparrows La. SE9 —7G 109
Sparrows Way. Bush —1B 10
Sparsholt Clo. Bark —1J 73
(off Sparsholt Rd.)
Sparsholt Rd. N19 —1K 49
Sparsholt Rd. Bark —1J 73
Sparta St. SE10 —1E 106
Speakers Ct. Croy —1D 152
Speakman Ho. SE4 —3A 106
(off Arica Rd.)
Spearman Ho. E14 —6C 70
Spearman St. SE18 —6E 90
Spear M. SW5 —4J 83
Spearpoint Gdns. Ilf —5K 37
Spears Rd. N19 —1J 49
Speart La. Houn —7C 78
Spectacle Works. E13 —3A 72
Spedan Clo. NW3 —3A 48
Speed Highwalk. EC2 —5C 68
(off Silk St.)
Speed Ho. EC2 —5D 162
Speedway Ind. Est. Hay —2F 77
Speedwell Ho. N12 —4E 14
Speedwell St. SE8 —7C 88
Speedy Pl. WC1 —2E 160
Speer Rd. Th Dit —6K 133
Speirs Clo. N Mald —6B 136
Speke Hill. SE9 —3D 126
Speke Rd. T Hth —2D 140
Speke's Monument. —1B 84 (4A 164)
Speldhurst Clo. Brom —5H 143
Speldhurst Rd. E9 —7K 51
Speldhurst Rd. W4 —3K 81
Spellbrook Wlk. N1 —1C 68
Spelman Ho. E1 —5G 69 (6K 163)
(off Spelman St.)
Spelman St. E1 —5G 69 (5K 163)
(in two parts)
Spelthorne Gro. Sun —7H 113
Spelthorne La. Ashf —1E 130
Spence Clo. SE16 —2B 88
Spencer Av. N13 —6E 16
Spencer Av. Hay —5J 59
Spencer Clo. N3 —2J 29
Spencer Clo. NW10 —3F 63
Spencer Clo. Wfd G —5F 21
Spencer Dri. N2 —6A 30
Spencer Gdns. SE9 —5D 108
Spencer Gdns. SW14 —5J 99
Spencer Hill Rd. SW19 —7G 119
Spencer House. —5A 166
Spencer Ho. NW4 —5D 28
Spencer Mans. W14 —6G 83
(off Queen's Club Gdns.)
Spencer M. SW8 —1K 103
(off S. Lambeth Rd.)
Spencer M. W6 —6G 83
(off Queen's Club Gdns.)
Spencer Park. —5B 102
Spencer Pk. SW18 —5B 102
Spencer Pk. E Mol —5G 133
Spencer Pl. N1 —7B 50
Spencer Pl. Croy —7D 140
Spencer Ri. NW5 —4F 49
Spencer Rd. E6 —1B 72
Spencer Rd. E17 —2E 34
Spencer Rd. N8 —5K 31
(in two parts)
Spencer Rd. N11 —4A 16
Spencer Rd. N17 —1G 33
Spencer Rd. SW11 —4B 102
Spencer Rd. SW19 —6G 119
Spencer Rd. SW20 —1D 136
Spencer Rd. W3 —1J 81
Spencer Rd. W4 —7J 81
Spencer Rd. Brom —7H 125
Spencer Rd. E Mol —4G 133
Spencer Rd. Harr —2J 25
Spencer Rd. Ilf —1K 55
Spencer Rd. Iswth —1G 97
Spencer Rd. Mitc —3E 138
Spencer Rd. Mit J —7E 138
Spencer Rd. Rain —3K 75
Spencer Rd. S Croy —5E 152
Spencer Rd. Twic —3J 115
Spencer Rd. Wemb —2C 44
Spencer St. EC1 —3B 68 (2A 162)
Spencer St. S'hall —2B 78
Spencer Wlk. NW3 —4B 48
Spencer Wlk. SW15 —4F 101
Spenlow Ho. SE16 —3G 87
(off Jamaica Rd.)
Spenser Gro. N16 —5E 50
(in two parts)
Spenser M. SE21 —2D 122
Spenser Rd. SE24 —5B 104
Spenser St. SW1 —3G 85 (1B 172)
Spensley Wlk. N16 —3D 50
Speranza Rd. SE18 —5K 91
Sperling Rd. N17 —2E 32
Spert St. E14 —7A 70
Speyside. N14 —6B 6
Spey St. E14 —5E 70
Spey Way. Romf —1K 39
Spezia Rd. NW10 —2C 64
Spice Ct. E1 —7G 69
(off Asher Way)
Spice Quay Heights. SE1
—1F 87 (5K 169)
Spicer Clo. SW9 —2B 104
Spicer Clo. W on T —6A 132
Spicer Ct. Enf —3K 7
Spice's Yd. Croy —4C 152
Spigurnell Rd. N17 —1D 32
Spikes Bri. Rd. S'hall —6C 60
Spilsby Clo. NW9 —1A 28
Spindle Clo. SE18 —3C 90
Spindlewood Gdns. Croy —4E 152
Spindrift Av. E14 —4C 88
Spinel Clo. SE18 —5K 91
Spinnaker Ho. E14 —2C 88
Spinnells Rd. Harr —1D 42
Spinney Clo. Beck —4D 142
Spinney Clo. N Mald —5A 136
Spinney Clo. W Dray —7A 58
Spinney Clo. Wor Pk —2B 148
Spinney Dri. Felt —7E 94
Spinney Gdns. SE19 —5F 123
Spinney Gdns. Dag —5E 56
Spinney Oak. Brom —2C 144
Spinneys, The. Brom —2D 144
Spinney, The. N21 —7F 7
Spinney, The. SW13 —7D 82
Spinney, The. SW16 —3G 121
Spinney, The. Barn —2E 4
Spinney, The. Sidc —5E 128
Spinney, The. Stan —4K 11
Spinney, The. Sun —1J 131
Spinney, The. Sutt —4E 148
Spinney, The. Wemb —3A 44
Spire Ho. W2 —7A 66
(off Lancaster Ga.)
Spires Shop. Cen., The. Barn —3B 4
Spirit Quay. E1 —1G 87
Spitalfields. —5F 69 (5J 163)
Spitalfields. E1 —5F 69
Spital Sq. E1 —5E 68 (5H 163)
Spital St. E1 —5G 69 (5K 163)
Spital Yd. E1 —5E 68 (5H 163)
Spitfire Est., The. Houn —5A 78
Spitfire Rd. H'row A —6E 94
Spitfire Rd. Wall —7K 151
Spitfire Way. Houn —5A 78
Splendour Wlk. SE16 —5J 87
(off Verney Rd.)
Spode Ho. SE11 —2J 173
Spode Wlk. NW6 —5K 47
Spondon Rd. N15 —4G 33
Spoonbill Way. Hay —5B 60
Spooner Ho. Houn —6E 78
Spooners M. W3 —1K 81
Spooner Wlk. Wall —5J 151
Sportsbank St. SE6 —7E 106
Spottons Gro. N17 —1C 32
Spout Hill. Croy —5C 154
Spratt Hall Rd. E11 —6J 35
Spray La. Twic —6J 97
Spray St. SE18 —4F 91
Spreighton Rd. W Mol —4F 133
Spriggs Ho. N1 —7B 50
(off Canonbury Rd.)
Sprimont Pl. SW3 —5D 84 (5E 170)
Springall St. SE15 —7H 87
Springalls Wharf. SE16 —2G 87
(off Bermondsey Wall W.)
Spring Bank. N21 —6E 6
Springbank Rd. SE13 —6F 107
Springbank Wlk. NW1 —7H 49
Springbourne Ct. Beck —1E 142
(in two parts)
Spring Bri. M. W5 —7D 62
Springbridge Rd. W5 —7D 62
Spring Clo. Barn —5A 4
Spring Clo. Dag —1D 56
Spring Clo. La. Sutt —6G 149
Spring Corner. Felt —3J 113
Spring Cotts. Surb —5D 134
Spring Ct. NW6 —6H 47
Spring Ct. Eps —7B 148
Spring Ct. Rd. Enf —1F 7
Springcroft Av. N2 —4D 30
Springdale M. N16 —4D 50
Springdale Rd. N16 —4D 50
Spring Dri. Pinn —6J 23
Springfield. E5 —1H 51
Springfield. Bus H —1C 10
Springfield Av. N10 —3G 31
Springfield Av. SW20 —3H 137
Springfield Av. Hamp —6F 115
Springfield Clo. N12 —5E 14
Springfield Clo. Stan —3F 11
Springfield Ct. Ilf —5F 55
Springfield Ct. Wall —5F 151
Springfield Dri. Ilf —5G 37
Springfield Gdns. E5 —1H 51
Springfield Gdns. NW9 —5K 27
Springfield Gdns. Brom —4D 144
Springfield Gdns. Ruis —1K 41
Springfield Gdns. W W'ck —2D 154
Springfield Gdns. Wfd G —7F 21
Springfield Gro. SE7 —6A 90
Springfield Gro. Sun —1H 131
Springfield La. NW6 —1K 65
Springfield Mt. NW9 —5A 28
Springfield Pde. M. N13 —4F 17
Springfield Pl. N Mald —4J 135
Springfield Ri. SE26 —3H 123
(in two parts)
Springfield Rd. E4 —1B 20
Springfield Rd. E6 —7D 54
Springfield Rd. E15 —3G 71
Springfield Rd. E17 —6B 34
Springfield Rd. N11 —5A 16
Springfield Rd. N15 —4G 33
Springfield Rd. NW8 —1A 66
Springfield Rd. SE26 —5H 123
Springfield Rd. SW19 —5H 119
Springfield Rd. W7 —1J 79
Springfield Rd. Ashf —5B 112
Springfield Rd. Bexh —3H 111
Springfield Rd. Brom —4D 144
Springfield Rd. Harr —6J 25
Springfield Rd. Hay —1A 78
Springfield Rd. King T —3E 134
Springfield Rd. Tedd —5A 116
Springfield Rd. T Hth —1C 140
Springfield Rd. Twic —1E 114
Springfield Rd. Wall —5F 151
Springfield Rd. Well —3B 110
Springfields. New Bar —5E 4
(off Somerset Rd.)
Springfield Wlk. NW6 —1K 65
Springfield Wlk. Orp —7J 145
(off Andover Rd.)
Spring Gdns. N5 —5C 50
Spring Gdns. SW1 —1H 85 (4D 166)
Spring Gdns. Romf —5J 39
Spring Gdns. Wall —5G 151
Spring Gdns. W Mol —5F 133
Spring Gdns. Wfd G —7F 21
Spring Grove. —1J 97
Spring Gro. SE19 —7F 123
Spring Gro. W4 —5G 81
Spring Gro. Hamp —1F 133
Spring Gro. Mitc —1E 138
Spring Gro. Cres. Houn —1G 97
Spring Gro. Rd. Houn & Iswth —1F 97
Spring Gro. Rd. Rich —5F 99
Spring Hill. E5 —7G 33
Spring Hill. SE26 —4J 123
Springhill Clo. SE5 —3D 104
Spring Ho. WC1 —2J 161
Springhurst Clo. Croy —4B 154
Spring Lake. Stan —4G 11
Spring La. E5 —7H 33
Spring La. N10 —3E 30
Spring La. SE25 —6H 141
Spring M. W1 —5D 66 (5F 159)
Spring M. Eps —7B 148
Spring Park. —3C 154
Spring Pk. Av. Croy —2K 153
Spring Pk. Dri. N4 —1C 50
Springpark Dri. Beck —3E 142
Spring Pk. Rd. Croy —2K 153
Spring Pas. SW15 —3F 101
Spring Path. NW3 —5B 48
Spring Pl. N3 —3J 29
Spring Pl. NW5 —5F 49
Springpond Rd. Dag —5E 56
Springrice Rd. SE13 —6F 107
Spring Rd. Felt —3H 113
Spring Shaw Rd. Orp —1K 145
Spring St. W2 —6B 66 (1A 164)
Spring Ter. Rich —5E 98
Spring Tide Clo. SE15 —1G 105
Spring Va. Bexh —4H 111
Springvale Av. Bren —5D 80
Spring Va. Ter. W14 —3F 83
Spring Villa Rd. Edgw —7B 12
Spring Wlk. E1 —5G 69
Springwater. WC1 —5G 161
Springwater Clo. SE18 —1E 108
Springway. Harr —7H 25
Springwell Av. NW10 —1B 64
Springwell Clo. SW16 —4K 121
Springwell Ct. Houn —2B 96
Springwell Rd. SW16 —4A 122
Springwell Rd. Houn —2B 96
Springwood Cres. Edgw —2C 12
Sprowston M. E7 —6J 53
Sprowston Rd. E7 —5J 53
Spruce Ct. W5 —3E 80
Sprucedale Gdns. Croy —4K 153
Spruce Hills Rd. E17 —2E 34
Spruce Pk. Short —4H 143
Sprules Rd. SE4 —2A 106
Spurfield. W Mol —3F 133
Spurgeon Av. SE19 —1D 140
Spurgeon Rd. SE19 —1D 140
Spurgeon St. SE1 —3D 86
Spurling Rd. SE22 —4F 105
Spurling Rd. Dag —6F 57
Spurrell Av. Bex —4K 129
Spur Rd. N15 —4D 32
Spur Rd. SE1 —6J 167
Spur Rd. SW1 —2G 85 (7A 166)
Spur Rd. Edgw —4K 11
Spur Rd. Felt —4K 95
Spur Rd. Iswth —7A 80
Spurstowe Rd. E8 —6H 51
Spurstowe Ter. E8 —6H 51
Spurway Pde. Ilf —5D 36
(off Woodford Av.)
Square Rigger Row. SW11 —3A 102
Square, The. W6 —5E 82
Square, The. Cars —5E 150
Square, The. Ilf —7E 36
Square, The. Rich —5D 98
Square, The. Uxb —1F 77
Square, The. Wfd G —5D 20
Squarey St. SW17 —3A 120
Squire Gdns. NW8 —3B 66 (2A 158)
(off Grove End Rd.)
Squire's Bri. Rd. Shep —4B 130
Squires Ct. SW4 —1J 103
Squires Ct. SW19 —4J 119
Squires La. N3 —2K 29
Squires Mt. NW3 —3B 48
Squire's Rd. Shep —4C 130
Squires, The. Romf —6J 39
Squires Wlk. Ashf —7F 113
Squires Way. Dart —4K 129
Squires Wood Dri. Chst —7C 126
Squirrel Clo. Houn —3A 96
Squirrel Clo. Orp —7J 145
Squirrel M. W13 —7K 61
Squirrels Clo. N12 —4F 15
Squirrels Clo. Uxb —7C 40
Squirrels Ct. Wor Pk —2C 148
(off Avenue, The)
Squirrels Drey. Short —2G 143
(off Park Hill Rd.)
Squirrels Grn. Wor Pk —2B 148
Squirrel's La. Buck H —3G 21
Squirrels, The. SE13 —3F 107
Squirrels, The. Pinn —3D 24
Squirrels Trad. Est., The. Hay —3H 77
Squirries St. E2 —3G 69
Stable Clo. N'holt —2E 60
Stables Mkt., The. NW1 —7F 49
Stables M. SE27 —5C 122
Stables, The. W10 —6F 65
(off Bassett Rd.)
Stables, The. Buck H —1F 21
Stables Way. SE11 —5A 86 (5J 173)
Stable Wlk. N2 —1B 30
Stable Way. W10 —6E 64
Stable Yd. SW1 —6A 166
Stable Yd. SW15 —3E 100
Stable Yd. Rd. SW1 —2G 85 (6B 166)
Stableyard, The. SW9 —2K 103
Stacey Av. N18 —4D 18
Stacey Clo. E10 —5F 35
Stacey St. N7 —3A 50
Stacey St. WC2 —6H 67 (1D 166)
Stack Ho. SW1 —4E 84 (4H 171)
(off Cundy St.)
Stackhouse St. SW3 —1E 170
Stacy Path. SE5 —7E 86
Stadium Bus. Cen. Wemb —3H 45
Stadium Retail Pk. Wemb —3G 45
Stadium Rd. SE18 —7D 90
Stadium Rd. E. NW4 —7D 28
Stadium St. SW10 —7A 84
Stadium Way. Wemb —4F 45
Staffa Rd. E10 —1A 52
Stafford Clo. E17 —6B 34
(in two parts)
Stafford Clo. N14 —5B 6
Stafford Clo. NW6 —3J 65
(in two parts)
Stafford Clo. Sutt —6G 149
Stafford Ct. SW8 —7J 85
Stafford Ct. W7 —6K 61
(off Copley Clo.)
Stafford Cripps Ho. SW6 —6H 83
(off Clem Attlee Ct.)
Stafford Cross Bus. Pk. Croy —5K 151
Stafford Gdns. Croy —5K 151
Stafford Mans. SW1 —3G 85 (1A 172)
(off Stafford Pl.)
Stafford Mans. SW4 —4J 103
Stafford Pl. SW1 —3G 85 (1A 172)
Stafford Pl. Rich —7F 99
Stafford Rd. E3 —2B 70
Stafford Rd. E7 —7A 54
Stafford Rd. NW6 —3J 65
Stafford Rd. Harr —7B 10
Stafford Rd. N Mald —3J 135
Stafford Rd. Ruis —4H 41
Stafford Rd. Sidc —4J 127
Stafford Rd. Wall & Croy —6G 151
Staffordshire St. SE15 —1G 105
Stafford St. W1 —1G 85 (4A 166)
Stafford Ter. W8 —3J 83
Staff St. EC1 —3D 68 (2F 163)
Stag Clo. Edgw —2H 27
Stag Lane. (Junct.) —2B 118
Stag La. SW15 —3B 118
Stag La. Buck H —2E 20
Stag La. Edgw & NW9 —2H 27
Stag Pl. SW1 —3G 85 (1A 172)
Stags Way. Iswth —7K 79
Stainbank Rd. Mitc —3F 139
Stainby Clo. W Dray —3A 76
Stainby Rd. N15 —4F 33
Stainer Ho. SE3 —4A 108
Stainer St. SE1 —1D 86 (5F 169)
Staines Av. Sutt —2F 149
Staines Rd. Felt & Houn —1C 112
Staines Rd. Ilf —5G 55
Staines Rd. Twic —3E 114
Staines Rd. E. Sun —7J 113
Staines Rd. W. Ashf & Sun —6D 112
Staines Wlk. Sidc —6C 128
Stainford Clo. Ashf —5F 113
Stainforth Rd. E17 —4C 34
Stainforth Rd. Ilf —7H 37
Staining La. EC2 —6C 68 (7D 162)
Stainmore Clo. Chst —1H 145
Stainsbury St. E2 —2J 69
Stainsby Pl. E14 —6C 70
Stainsby Rd. E14 —6C 70
Stainton Rd. SE6 —6F 107
Stainton Rd. Enf —1D 8
Stalbridge Flats. W1 —6E 66 (1H 165)
(off Lumley St.)
Stalbridge St. NW1 —5C 66 (5D 158)
Stalham St. SE16 —3H 87
Stalham Way. Ilf —1F 37
Stambourne Way. SE19 —7E 122
Stambourne Way. W W'ck —2E 154
Stamford Brook Arches. W6 —4C 82
Stamford Brook Av. W6 —3B 82
Stamford Brook Gdns. W6 —3B 82
Stamford Brook Mans. W6 —4B 82
(off Goldhawk Rd.)
Stamford Brook Rd. W6 —3B 82
Stamford Clo. N15 —5G 33
Stamford Clo. NW3 —3A 48
(off Heath St.)
Stamford Clo. Harr —7D 10
Stamford Clo. S'hall —7E 60
Stamford Ct. W6 —4C 82
Stamford Dri. Brom —4H 143
Stamford Gdns. Dag —7C 56
Stamford Ga. SW6 —7K 83
Stamford Gro. E. N16 —1G 51
Stamford Gro. W. N16 —1G 51
Stamford Hill. —1F 51
Stamford Hill. N16 —2F 51
Stamford Lodge. N16 —7F 33
Stamford Rd. E6 —1C 72
Stamford Rd. N1 —7E 50
Stamford Rd. N15 —5G 33
Stamford Rd. Dag —1B 74
Stamford St. SE1 —1A 86 (5J 167)
Stamford Wharf. SE1 —7A 68
Stamp Pl. E2 —2F 69 (1J 163)
Stanard Clo. N16 —7E 32
Stanboard Way. E14 —3C 88
Stanborough Clo. Hamp —6D 114
Stanborough Pas. E8 —6F 51
Stanborough Rd. Houn —3H 97
Stanbridge Pl. N21 —2G 17
Stanbridge Rd. SW15 —3E 100
Stanbrook Rd. SE2 —2B 92
Stanbury Ct. NW3 —6D 48
Stanbury Rd. SE15 —2H 105
(in two parts)
Stancroft. NW9 —5A 28
Standale Gro. Ruis —5E 22
Standard Ind. Est. E16 —2D 90
Standard Pl. EC2 —2H 163
Standard Rd. NW10 —4J 63
Standard Rd. Belv —5G 93
Standard Rd. Bexh —4E 110
Standard Rd. Houn —3C 96
Standen Rd. SW18 —7H 101
Standfield Gdns. Dag —6G 57
Standfield Rd. Dag —5G 57
Standish Ho. SE3 —4K 107
(off Elford Clo.)
Standish Ho. W6 —4C 82
(off St Peter's Gro.)
Standish Rd. W6 —4C 82
Standlake Point. SE23 —3K 123
Stane Clo. SW19 —7K 119
Stane Pas. SW16 —5J 121
Stanesgate Ho. SE15 —7G 87
(off Friary Est.)
Stane Way. SE18 —7B 90
Stanfield Ho. NW8 —4B 66 (3B 158)
(off Frampton St.)
Stanfield Ho. N'holt —2B 60
(off Academy Gdns.)
Stanfield Rd. E3 —2A 70
Stanford Clo. Hamp —6D 114
Stanford Clo. Romf —6H 39
Stanford Clo. Ruis —6E 22
Stanford Clo. Wfd G —5H 21
Stanford Ct. SW6 —1K 101
Stanford Ho. Bark —2B 74
Stanford Pl. SE17 —4E 86
Stanford Rd. N11 —5J 15
Stanford Rd. SW16 —2H 139
Stanford Rd. W8 —3K 83
Stanford St. SW1 —4H 85 (4C 172)
Stanford Way. SW16 —2H 139
Stangate. SE1 —1H 173
Stangate Gdns. Stan —4G 11
Stangate Lodge. N21 —7E 6
Stanger Rd. SE25 —4G 141
Stanhill Cotts. Dart —7K 129
Stanhope Av. N3 —3H 29
Stanhope Av. Brom —1H 155
Stanhope Av. Harr —1H 25
Stanhope Clo. SE16 —2K 87
Stanhope Gdns. N4 —6B 32
Stanhope Gdns. N6 —6F 31
Stanhope Gdns. NW7 —5G 13
Stanhope Gdns. SW7 —4A 84 (3A 170)
Stanhope Gdns. Dag —3F 57
Stanhope Gdns. Ilf —1D 54
Stanhope Ga. W1 —1E 84 (5H 165)
Stanhope Gro. Beck —5B 142
Stanhope Ho. N11 —4A 16
(off Coppies Gro.)
Stanhope Ho. SE8 —7B 88
(off Adolphus St.)
Stanhope M. E. SW7 —4A 84 (3A 170)
Stanhope M. S. SW7 —4A 84
Stanhope M. W. SW7 —4A 84
Stanhope Pde. NW1 —3G 67 (1A 160)
Stanhope Pk. Rd. Gnfd —4G 61
Stanhope Pl. W2 —6D 66 (1E 164)
Stanhope Rd. E17 —5D 34
Stanhope Rd. N6 —6G 31
Stanhope Rd. N12 —5F 15
Stanhope Rd. Barn —6A 4
Stanhope Rd. Bexh —2E 110
Stanhope Rd. Cars —7E 150
Stanhope Rd. Croy —3E 152
Stanhope Rd. Dag —2F 57
Stanhope Rd. Gnfd —5G 61
Stanhope Rd. Sidc —4A 128
Stanhope Row. W1 —1F 85 (5J 165)
Stanhope St. NW1 —3G 67 (1A 160)
Stanhope Ter. W2 —7B 66 (2B 164)
Stanhope Ter. Twic —7K 97
Stanier Clo. W14 —5H 83
Stanlake M. W12 —1E 82
Stanlake Rd. W12 —1E 82
Stanlake Vs. W12 —1E 82
Stanley Av. Bark —3K 73
Stanley Av. Beck —2E 142
Stanley Av. Dag —1F 57
Stanley Av. Gnfd —1G 61
Stanley Av. N Mald —5C 136
Stanley Av. Wemb —7E 44
Stanley Bldgs. NW1 —2J 67
(off Stanley Pas.)
Stanley Clo. SW8 —6K 85
Stanley Clo. Wemb —7E 44
Stanley Cohen Ho. EC1 —4C 68 (4C 162)
(off Golden La. Est.)
Stanley Ct. W5 —5C 62
Stanley Ct. Cars —7E 150
Stanley Ct. Sutt —7K 149
Stanley Cres. W11 —7H 65
Stanleycroft Clo. Iswth —1J 97
Stanley Gdns. NW2 —5E 46
Stanley Gdns. W3 —2A 82
Stanley Gdns. W11 —7H 65
Stanley Gdns. Mitc —6E 120
Stanley Gdns. Wall —6G 151
Stanley Gdns. M. W11 —7H 65
(off Kensington Pk. Rd.)
Stanley Gdns. Rd. Tedd —5J 115
Stanley Gro. N17 —7A 18
Stanley Gro. SW8 —2E 102
Stanley Gro. Croy —6A 140
Stanley Ho. E14 —6C 70
Stanley Pk. Dri. Wemb —1F 63
Stanley Pk. Rd. Cars & Wall —7D 150
Stanley Pas. NW1 —2J 67
Stanley Rd. E4 —1A 20
Stanley Rd. E10 —6D 34
Stanley Rd. E12 —5C 54
Stanley Rd. E15 —1F 71
Stanley Rd. E18 —1H 35
Stanley Rd. N2 —3B 30
Stanley Rd. N9 —1A 18
Stanley Rd. N10 —7A 16
Stanley Rd. N11 —6C 16
Stanley Rd. N15 —4B 32
Stanley Rd. NW9 —7C 28
Stanley Rd. SW14 —4H 99
Stanley Rd. SW19 —6J 119
Stanley Rd. W3 —3J 81
Stanley Rd. Ashf —5A 112
Stanley Rd. Brom —4K 143
Stanley Rd. Cars —7E 150
Stanley Rd. Croy —7A 140
Stanley Rd. Enf —3K 7
Stanley Rd. Harr —2G 43
Stanley Rd. Houn —4G 97
Stanley Rd. Ilf —2H 55
Stanley Rd. Mitc —7E 120
Stanley Rd. Mord —4J 137
Stanley Rd. N'wd —1J 23
Stanley Rd. Orp —7K 145
Stanley Rd. Sidc —3A 128
Stanley Rd. S'hall —7C 60
Stanley Rd. Sutt —6K 149
Stanley Rd. Twic & Tedd —3H 115
Stanley Rd. Wemb —6F 45
Stanley Sq. Cars —7D 150

Stanley St.—Stoneyard La.

Stanley St. SE8 —7B 88
Stanley Ter. N19 —2J 49
Stanmer St. SW11 —1C 102
Stanmore. —5G 11
Stanmore Gdns. Rich —3F 99
Stanmore Gdns. Sutt —3A 150
Stanmore Hill. Stan —3F 11
Stanmore Lodge. Stan —4G 11
Stanmore Pk. Stan —5G 11
Stanmore Pl. NW1 —1F 67
Stanmore Rd. E11 —1H 53
Stanmore Rd. N15 —4B 32
Stanmore Rd. Belv —4J 93
Stanmore Rd. Rich —3F 99
Stanmore St. N1 —1K 67
Stanmore Ter. Beck —2C 142
Stannard Rd. E8 —6G 51
Stannary Pl. SE11 —6K 173
Stannary St. SE11 —6A 86 (7K 173)
Stannet Way. Wall —4G 151
Stansbury Ho. W10 —3G 65
(off Beethoven St.)
Stansfeld Rd. E6 —5B 72
Stansfield Ho. SE1 —4F 87
(off Balaclava Rd.)
Stansfield Rd. SW9 —3K 103
Stansfield Rd. Houn —2K 95
Stansgate Rd. Dag —2G 57
Stanstead Clo. Brom —5H 143
Stanstead Gro. SE6 —1B 124
Stanstead Mnr. Sutt —6J 149
Stanstead Rd. E11 —5K 35
Stanstead Rd. SE23 & SE6 —1K 123
Stanstead Rd. H'row A —6B 94
Stansted Cres. Bex —1D 128
Stanswood Gdns. SE5 —7E 86
Stanthorpe Clo. SW16 —5J 121
Stanthorpe Rd. SW16 —5J 121
Stanton Av. Tedd —6J 115
Stanton Clo. Eps —5H 147
Stanton Clo. Wor Pk —1F 149
Stanton Ho. SE10 —6E 88
(off Thames St.)
Stanton Rd. SE26 —4B 124
Stanton Rd. SW13 —2B 100
Stanton Rd. SW20 —1F 137
Stanton Rd. Croy —7C 140
Stanton Sq. SE26 —4B 124
Stanton Way. SE26 —4B 124
Stanway Ct. N1 —2E 68 (1H 163)
(in three parts)
Stanway Gdns. W3 —1G 81
Stanway Gdns. Edgw —5D 12
Stanway St. N1 —2E 68
Stanwell Clo. Stanw —6A 94
Stanwell Rd. Ashf —2A 112
Stanwell Rd. Felt —7D 94
Stanwick Rd. W14 —4H 83
Stanworth Ct. Houn —7D 78
Stanworth St. SE1 —3F 87 (7J 169)
Stanyhurst. SE23 —1A 124
Stapenhill Rd. Wemb —3B 44
Staple Clo. Bex —3K 129
Staplefield Clo. SW2 —1J 121
Stapleford. N17 —2E 32
(off Willan Rd.)
Stapleford Av. Ilf —5J 37
Stapleford Clo. E4 —3K 19
Stapleford Clo. SW19 —7G 101
Stapleford Clo. King T —2G 135
Stapleford Rd. Wemb —7D 44
Stapleford Way. Bark —3B 74
Staplehurst Rd. SE13 —5F 107
Staplehurst Rd. Cars —7C 150
Staple Inn. WC1 —6J 161
Staple Inn Bldgs. WC1 —5A 68 (6J 161)
Staples Clo. SE16 —1A 88
Staples Corner. (Junct.) —1D 46
Staples Corner Bus. Pk. NW2 —1D 46
Staples Ho. E6 —6E 72
(off Savage Gdns.)
Staple St. SE1 —2D 86 (7F 169)
Stapleton Gdns. Croy —5A 152
Stapleton Hall Rd. N4 —1K 49
Stapleton Rd. SW17 —3E 120
Stapleton Rd. Bexh —7F 93
Stapley Rd. Belv —5G 93
Stapylton Rd. Barn —3B 4
Star All. EC3 —2H 169
Star & Garter Hill. Rich —1E 116
Starboard Way. E14 —3C 88
Star Bus. Cen. Rain —5K 75
Starch Ho. La. Ilf —2H 37
Starcross St. NW1 —3G 67 (2B 160)
Starfield Rd. W12 —2C 82
Star Hill. Dart —5K 111
Star La. E16 —4G 71
Starling Clo. Buck H —1D 20
Starling Clo. Pinn —3A 24
Starling Ho. NW8 —2C 66
(off Barrow Hill Est.)
Starling Wlk. Hamp —5C 114
Starmans Clo. Dag —1E 74
Star Path. N'holt —2E 60
(off Brabazon Rd.)
Star Pl. E1 —7G 69 (3K 169)
Star Rd. W14 —6H 83
Star Rd. Iswth —2H 97
Star Rd. Uxb —4E 58
Star St. W2 —6C 66 (7B 158)
Starts Clo. Orp —3E 156
Starts Hill Rd. Farnb & Orp —3E 156
Starveall Clo. W Dray —3B 76
Star Yd. WC2 —6A 68 (7J 161)
Staten Gdns. Twic —1K 115
Statham Gro. N16 —4D 50
Statham Gro. N18 —5K 17
Station App. E4 —6A 20
Station App. E7 —4K 53
Station App. E11 —5J 35
Station App. E17 —5C 34
(in two parts)
Station App. E18 —2K 35
Station App. N11 —5A 16
Station App. N12 —4E 14
Station App. NW10 —3B 64
Station App. SE3 —3K 107
Station App. SE12 —6J 107
(off Burnt Ash Hill)
Station App. SE26 —5B 124
(Lower Sydenham)
Station App. SE26 —4J 123
(Sydenham)
Station App. SW6 —3G 101
Station App. SW14 —3J 99
Station App. SW16 —6H 121
(Estreham Rd.)
Station App. SW16 —5H 121
(Streatham High Rd.)
Station App. W7 —1J 79
Station App. Ashf —4B 112
Station App. B'hurst —2J 111
Station App. Beck —1C 142
Station App. Bex —1G 129
Station App. Bexh —2E 110
Station App. Bren —6C 80
Station App. Brom —3J 143
(off High St.)
Station App. Buck H —4G 21
Station App. Cars —4D 150
Station App. Cheam —7G 149
Station App. Chst —1E 144
(Chislehurst)
Station App. Chst —6C 126
(Elmstead Woods)
Station App. Gnfd —7G 43
Station App. Hamp —1E 132
Station App. Harr —7J 25
Station App. H End & Pinn —3C 24
Station App. Hay —3H 77
Station App. Hayes —1J 155
Station App. High Bar & New Bar —4F 5
Station App. King T —1G 135
Station App. Rich —1G 99
Station App. Ruis —1G 41
Station App. Shep —5E 130
Station App. S Croy —7D 152
Station App. S Ruis —5K 41
Station App. S'leigh —5C 148
Station App. Sun —1J 131
Station App. Well —2A 110
(in three parts)
Station App. Wemb —6B 44
Station App. W Dray —1A 76
Station App. W W'ck —7E 142
Station App. Wor Pk —1C 148
Station App. N. Sidc —2A 128
Station App. Rd. SE1 —2A 86 (7H 167)
Station App. Rd. W4 —7J 81
Station Av. SW9 —3B 104
Station Av. Eps —7A 148
Station Av. Kew —1G 99
Station Av. N Mald —3A 136
Station Clo. N3 —1J 29
Station Clo. N12 —4E 14
Station Clo. Hamp —1F 133
Station Ct. E10 —7D 34
(off Kings Clo.)
Station Cres. N15 —4D 32
Station Cres. SE3 —5J 89
Station Cres. Ashf —4A 112
Station Cres. Wemb —6B 44
Stationers' Hall Ct. EC4 —6B 68 (1B 168)
Station Est. Beck —3K 141
Station Est. Rd. Felt —1K 113
Station Garage M. SW16 —6H 121
Station Gdns. W4 —7J 81
Station Gro. Wemb —6E 44
Station Hill. Brom —2J 155
Station Ho. M. N9 —4B 18
Station Pde. E11 —5J 35
Station Pde. N14 —1C 16
Station Pde. NW2 —6E 46
Station Pde. SW12 —1E 120
Station Pde. W3 —6G 63
Station Pde. W4 —7J 81
Station Pde. W5 —1F 81
Station Pde. Ashf —4B 112
Station Pde. Bark —7G 55
Station Pde. Barn —4K 5
Station Pde. Bexh —2E 110
(off Pickford La.)
Station Pde. Buck H —4G 21
Station Pde. Dag —6G 57
Station Pde. Edgw —7K 11
Station Pde. Felt —1K 113
Station Pde. Harr —4F 43
(HA2)
Station Pde. Harr —2A 26
(HA3)
Station Pde. N Har —4F 43
Station Pde. N'holt —7E 42
Station Pde. Rich —1G 99
Station Pde. Sidc —2A 128
Station Pde. Sutt —6A 150
(off High St.)
Station Pas. E18 —2K 35
Station Pas. SE15 —1J 105
Station Path. E8 —6H 51
(off Graham Rd.)
Station Path. SW6 —3H 101
Station Pl. N4 —2A 50
Station Ri. SE27 —2B 122
Station Rd. E4 —1A 20
Station Rd. E7 —4J 53
Station Rd. E10 —3E 52
Station Rd. E12 —4C 54
Station Rd. E17 —6A 34
Station Rd. N3 —1J 29
Station Rd. N11 —5A 16
Station Rd. N17 —3G 33
Station Rd. N19 —3G 49
Station Rd. N21 —1G 17
Station Rd. N22 —2J 31
Station Rd. NW4 —6C 28
Station Rd. NW7 —6F 13
Station Rd. NW10 —2B 64
Station Rd. SE13 —3E 106
Station Rd. SE20 —6J 123
Station Rd. SE25 —4F 141
Station Rd. SW13 —2B 100
Station Rd. SW19 —1A 138
Station Rd. W5 —6F 63
Station Rd. W7 —1J 79
Station Rd. Ashf —4B 112
Station Rd. B'side —3H 37
Station Rd. Barn & New Bar —5E 4
Station Rd. Belv —3G 93
Station Rd. Bexh —3E 110
Station Rd. Brom —1J 143
Station Rd. Cars —4D 150
Station Rd. Chad H —7D 38
Station Rd. Chess —5E 146
Station Rd. Croy —1C 152
Station Rd. Edgw —6B 12
Station Rd. Hamp —1E 132
Station Rd. Hamp W —1C 134
Station Rd. Harr —4K 25
Station Rd. Hay —4G 77
(in three parts)
Station Rd. Houn —4F 97
Station Rd. Ilf —3F 55
Station Rd. King T —1G 135
Station Rd. N Mald —5D 136
Station Rd. N Har —5F 25
Station Rd. Shep —5E 130
Station Rd. Short —2G 143
Station Rd. Sidc —2A 128
Station Rd. Sun —7J 113
Station Rd. Tedd —6A 116
Station Rd. Th Dit —7K 133
Station Rd. Twic —1K 115
Station Rd. W Dray —2A 76
Station Rd. W W'ck —1E 154
Station Rd. N. Belv —3H 93
Station Sq. Orp —5G 145
Station St. E15 —7F 53
Station St. E16 —1F 91
Station Ter. NW10 —2F 65
Station Ter. SE5 —1C 104
Station Ter. M. SE3 —5J 89
Station Vw. Gnfd —1H 61
Station Way. SE15 —2G 105
Station Way. Buck H —4F 21
Station Way. Sutt —6G 149
Station Yd. Twic —7A 98
Staunton Ho. SE17 —4E 86
(off Tatum St.)
Staunton Rd. King T —6E 116
Staunton St. SE8 —6B 88
Staveley. NW1 —3G 67 (1A 160)
(off Varndell St.)
Staveley Clo. E9 —5J 51
Staveley Clo. N7 —4J 49
Staveley Clo. SE15 —1H 105
Staveley Gdns. W4 —1K 99
Staveley Rd. W4 —6J 81
Staveley Rd. Ashf —6F 113
Staverton Rd. NW2 —7E 46
Stave Yd. Rd. SE16 —1A 88
Stavordale Rd. N5 —4B 50
Stavordale Rd. Cars —7A 138
Stayner's Rd. E1 —4K 69
Stayton Rd. Sutt —3J 149
Steadfast Rd. King T —1D 134
Steadman Clo. Uxb —3C 40
Steadman Ct. EC1 —4C 68 (3D 162)
(off Old St.)
Steadman Ho. Dag —3G 57
(off Uvedale Rd.)
Stead St. SE17 —4D 86
Steam Farm La. Felt —4H 95
Stean St. E8 —1F 69
Stebbing Ho. W11 —1F 83
(off Queensdale Cres.)
Stebbing Way. Bark —2A 74
Stebondale St. E14 —4E 88
Stedham Pl. WC1 —7E 160
Stedman Clo. Bex —3K 129
Steedman St. SE17 —4C 86
Steeds Rd. N10 —1D 30
Steele Ho. E15 —2G 71
(off Eve Rd.)
Steele Rd. E11 —4G 53
Steele Rd. N17 —3E 32
Steele Rd. NW10 —2J 63
Steele Rd. W4 —3J 81
Steele Rd. Iswth —4A 98
Steele's M. N. NW3 —6D 48
Steele's M. S. NW3 —6D 48
Steele's Rd. NW3 —6D 48
Steele's Studios. NW3 —6D 48
Steele Wlk. Eri —7H 93
Steel's La. E1 —6J 69
Steelyard Pas. EC4 —3E 168
Steen Way. SE22 —5E 104
Steep Hill. SW16 —3H 121
Steep Hill. Croy —4E 152
Steeple Clo. SW6 —2G 101
Steeple Clo. SW19 —5G 119
Steeple Ct. E1 —4H 69
Steeplestone Clo. N18 —5H 17
Steeple Wlk. N1 —1C 68
(off Basire St.)
Steerforth St. SW18 —2A 120
Steers Mead. Mitc —1D 138
Steers Way. SE16 —2A 88
Stelfox Ho. WC1 —3K 67 (1H 161)
(off Penton Ri.)
Stella Rd. SW17 —6D 120
Stelling Rd. Eri —7K 93
Stellman Clo. E5 —3G 51
Stembridge Rd. SE20 —2H 141
Stephan Clo. E8 —1G 69
Stephendale Rd. SW6 —3K 101
Stephen Fox Ho. W4 —5A 82
(off Chiswick La.)
Stephen M. W1 —5H 67 (6C 160)
Stephen Pl. SW4 —3G 103
Stephen Rd. Bexh —3J 111
Stephens Ct. E16 —4H 71
Stephens Ct. SE4 —3A 106
Stephens Lodge. N12 —3F 15
(off Woodside La.)
Stephenson Ct. Cheam —7G 149
(off Station App.)
Stephenson Ho. SE1 —3C 86
Stephenson Rd. E17 —5A 34
Stephenson Rd. W7 —6K 61
Stephenson Rd. Twic —7E 96
Stephenson St. E16 —4G 71
Stephenson St. NW10 —3A 64
Stephenson Way. NW1 —4G 67 (3B 160)
Stephen's Rd. E15 —1G 71
Stephen St. W1 —5H 67 (6C 160)
Stepney. —5K 69
Stepney Causeway. E1 —6K 69
Stepney Grn. E1 —5J 69
Stepney High St. E1 —5K 69
Stepney Way. E1 —5H 69
Sterling Av. Edgw —4A 12
Sterling Clo. NW10 —7C 46
Sterling Gdns. SE14 —6A 88
Sterling Ho. SE3 —4K 107
Sterling Pl. W5 —4E 80
Sterling Rd. Enf —1J 7
Sterling St. SW7 —3C 84 (1D 170)
Sterling Way. N18 —5J 17
Stern Clo. Bark —2C 74
Sterndale Rd. W6 —3F 83
Sterne St. W12 —2F 83
Sternhall La. SE15 —3G 105
Sternhold Av. SW2 —2H 121
Sterry Cres. Dag —5G 57
Sterry Dri. Eps —4A 148
Sterry Dri. Th Dit —6J 133
Sterry Gdns. Dag —6G 57
Sterry Rd. Bark —1K 73
Sterry Rd. Dag —4G 57
Sterry St. SE1 —2D 86 (7E 168)
Steucers La. SE23 —1A 124
Stevannie Ct. Belv —5G 93
Steve Biko La. SE6 —4C 124
Steve Biko Rd. N7 —3A 50
Steve Biko Way. Houn —3E 96
Stevedale Rd. Well —2C 110
Stevedore St. E1 —1H 87
Stevenage Rd. E6 —6E 54
Stevenage Rd. SW6 —7F 83
Stevens Av. E9 —6J 51
Stevens Clo. Beck —6C 124
Stevens Clo. Bex —4K 129
Stevens Clo. Hamp —5C 114
Stevens Clo. Pinn —5A 24
Stevens Grn. Bus H —1B 10
Stevens La. Clay —7A 146
Stevenson Clo. SE16 —5G 87
Stevenson Clo. Barn —7G 5
Stevenson Ho. NW8 —1A 66
(off Boundary Rd.)
Stevens Rd. Dag —3B 56
Stevens St. SE1 —3E 86 (7H 169)
Steventon Rd. W12 —7B 64
Stewards Holte Wlk. N11 —4A 16
Steward St. E1 —5E 68 (5H 163)
(in two parts)
Stewart Av. Shep —4C 130
Stewart Clo. NW9 —6J 27
Stewart Clo. Chst —5F 127
Stewart Clo. Hamp —6C 114
Stewart Quay. Hay —2G 77
Stewart Rainbird Ho. E12 —5E 54
(off Parkhurst Rd.)
Stewart Rd. E15 —4F 53
Stewartsby Clo. N18 —5H 17
Stewart's Gro. SW3 —5B 84 (5B 170)
Stewart's Rd. SW8 —7G 85
Stewart St. E14 —2E 88
Stew La. EC4 —7C 68 (2C 168)
Steyne Ho. W3 —1J 81
(off Horn La.)
Steyne Rd. W3 —1H 81
Steyning Gro. SE9 —4D 126
Steynings Way. N12 —5D 14
Steyning Way. Houn —4A 96
Steynton Av. Bex —2D 128
Stickland Rd. Belv —4G 93
Stickleton Clo. Gnfd —3F 61
Stilecroft Gdns. Wemb —3B 44
Stile Hall Gdns. W4 —5G 81
Stile Hall Pde. W4 —5G 81
Stileman Ho. E3 —5B 70
Stile Path. Sun —3J 131
Stiles Clo. Brom —6D 144
Stiles Clo. Eri —5H 93
Stillingfleet Rd. SW13 —6C 82
Stillington St. SW1 —4G 85 (3B 172)
Stillness Rd. SE23 —6A 106
Stillwell Dri. Uxb —4B 58
Stilton Cres. NW10 —7K 45
Stilwell Roundabout. Uxb —7C 58
Stipularis Dri. Hay —4B 60
Stirling Av. Pinn —1B 42
Stirling Av. Shep —3G 131
Stirling Clo. SW16 —1H 139
Stirling Ct. W13 —7B 62
Stirling Gro. Houn —2G 97
Stirling Ho. SE18 —5F 91
Stirling Rd. E13 —2K 71
Stirling Rd. E17 —3A 34
Stirling Rd. N17 —1G 33
Stirling Rd. N22 —1B 32
Stirling Rd. SW9 —2J 103
Stirling Rd. W3 —3H 81
Stirling Rd. Harr —3K 25
Stirling Rd. Hay —7K 59
Stirling Rd. H'row A —6B 94
Stirling Rd. Twic —7E 96
Stirling Rd. Path. E17 —3A 34
Stirling Wlk. Surb —6H 135
Stirling Way. Croy —7J 139
Stiven Cres. Harr —3D 42
Stockbeck. NW1 —2G 67 (1B 160)
(off Ampthill Est.)
Stockbury Rd. Croy —6J 141
Stockdale Rd. Dag —2F 57
Stockdove Way. Gnfd —3K 61
Stocker Gdns. Dag —7C 56
Stock Exchange. —6D 68 (1F 169)
Stockfield Rd. SW16 —3K 121
Stockholm Ho. E1 —7G 69
(off Swedenborg Gdns.)
Stockholm Rd. SE16 —5J 87
Stockholm Way. E1 —1G 87
Stockhurst Clo. SW15 —2E 100
Stockingswater La. Enf —2G 9
Stockland Rd. Romf —6K 39
Stockleigh Hall. NW8 —2C 66
(off Prince Albert Rd.)
Stockley Clo. W Dray —2D 76
Stockley Country Pk. —7C 58
Stockley Farm Rd. W Dray —3D 76
Stockley Park. —1D 76
Stockley Rd. Uxb & W Dray —6C 58
Stockley Rd. W Dray —4D 76
Stock Orchard Cres. N7 —5K 49
Stock Orchard St. N7 —5K 49
Stockport Rd. SW16 —1H 139
Stocksfield Rd. E17 —3E 34
Stocks Pl. E14 —7B 70
Stock St. E13 —2J 71
Stockton Clo. New Bar —4F 5
Stockton Gdns. N17 —7H 17
Stockton Gdns. NW7 —3F 13
Stockton Ho. S Harr —1E 42
Stockton Rd. N17 —7H 17
Stockton Rd. N18 —6B 18
Stockwell. —2K 103
Stockwell Av. SW9 —3K 103
Stockwell Clo. Brom —2K 143
Stockwell Gdns. SW9 —1K 103
Stockwell Gdns. Est. SW9 —2J 103
Stockwell Grn. SW9 —2K 103
Stockwell Grn. Ct. SW9 —2K 103
Stockwell La. SW9 —2K 103
Stockwell M. SW9 —2K 103
Stockwell Pk. Cres. SW9 —2K 103
Stockwell Pk. Est. SW9 —2K 103
Stockwell Pk. Rd. SW9 —1K 103
Stockwell Pk. Wlk. SW9 —3A 104
Stockwell Rd. SW9 —2K 103
Stockwell St. SE10 —6E 88
Stockwell Ter. SW9 —1K 103
Stodart Rd. SE20 —1J 141
Stoddart Ho. SW8 —6K 85 (7H 173)
Stofield Gdns. SE9 —3B 126
Stoford Clo. SW19 —7G 101
Stokenchurch St. SW6 —1K 101
Stoke Newington. —3F 51
Stoke Newington Chu. St. N16 —3D 50
Stoke Newington Comn. N16 —2F 51
Stoke Newington High St. N16 —3F 51
Stoke Newington Rd. N16 —5F 51
Stoke Pl. NW10 —3B 64
Stoke Rd. King T —7J 117
Stokesby Rd. Chess —6F 147
Stokes Cotts. Ilf —1G 37
Stokes Ct. N2 —4C 30
Stokesley St. W12 —6B 64
Stokes Rd. E6 —4C 72
Stokes Rd. Croy —6K 141
Stokley Ct. N8 —4J 31
Stoll Clo. NW2 —3E 46
Stoms Path. SE6 —5C 124
Stonard Rd. N13 —3F 17
Stonard Rd. Dag —5B 56
Stondon Ho. E15 —1H 71
(off John St.)
Stondon Pk. SE23 —6A 106
Stondon Wlk. E6 —2B 72
Stonebanks. W on T —7J 131
Stonebridge. —1K 63
Stonebridge Pk. NW10 —7K 45
Stonebridge Rd. N15 —5F 33
Stonebridge Shop. Cen. NW10 —1K 63
Stonebridge Way. Wemb —6H 45
Stone Bldgs. WC2 —6H 161
Stonechat Sq. E6 —5C 72
Stone Clo. SW4 —2G 103
Stone Clo. Dag —2F 57
Stone Clo. W Dray —1B 76
Stonecot Clo. Sutt —1G 149
Stonecot Hill. Sutt —1G 149
Stone Cres. Felt —7H 95
Stonecroft Rd. Eri —7J 93
Stonecroft Way. Croy —7J 139
Stonecrop Clo. NW9 —3K 27
Stonecutter St. EC4 —6B 68 (7A 162)
Stonefield. N7 —2K 49
Stonefield Clo. Bexh —3G 111
Stonefield Clo. Ruis —5C 42
Stonefield St. N1 —1A 68
Stonefield Way. SE7 —7B 90
Stonefield Way. Ruis —4C 42
Stonegrove. —5A 12
Stonegrove. Edgw —4K 11
Stone Gro. Ct. Edgw —5A 12
Stonegrove Gdns. Edgw —5A 12
Stone Hall. W8 —3K 83
(off St Margarets's La.)
Stonehall Av. Ilf —6C 36
Stone Hall Gdns. W8 —3K 83
Stone Hall Pl. W8 —3K 83
Stone Hall Rd. N21 —7E 6
Stoneham Rd. N11 —5B 16
Stonehill Clo. SW14 —5K 99
Stonehill Ct. E4 —7J 9
Stonehill Green. —7J 129
Stonehill Rd. SW14 —5J 99
Stone Hill Rd. W4 —5G 81
Stonehills Ct. SE21 —3E 122
Stonehill Woods Pk. Sidc —6H 129
Stonehorse Rd. Enf —5D 8
Stonehouse. NW1 —1G 67
(off Plender St.)
Stone Ho. Ct. EC3 —7H 163
Stone Lake Ind. Pk. SE7 —4A 90
Stone Lake Retail Pk. SE7 —4A 90
Stoneleigh. —5C 148
Stoneleigh Av. Enf —1C 8
Stoneleigh Av. Wor Pk —4C 148
Stoneleigh B'way. Eps —5C 148
Stoneleigh Ct. Ilf —3C 36
Stoneleigh Cres. Eps —5B 148
Stoneleigh M. E3 —2A 70
Stoneleigh Pk. Av. Croy —6K 141
Stoneleigh Pk. Rd. Eps —6B 148
Stoneleigh Pl. W11 —7F 65
Stoneleigh Rd. N17 —3F 33
Stoneleigh Rd. Cars —7C 138
Stoneleigh Rd. Ilf —3C 36
Stoneleigh St. W11 —7F 65
Stoneleigh Ter. N19 —2F 49
Stonell's Rd. SW11 —6D 102
Stonemasons Clo. N15 —4D 32
Stonenest St. N4 —1K 49
Stone Pk. Av. Beck —4C 142
Stone Pl. Wor Pk —2C 148
Stone Rd. Brom —5H 143
Stones End St. SE1 —2C 86 (7C 168)
Stone St. Croy —5A 152
Stonewall. E6 —5E 72
Stonewold Ct. W5 —6D 62
Stoney All. SE18 —2E 108
Stoneyard La. E14 —7D 70

Stoneycroft Clo.—Sunnyside Rd.

Stoneycroft Clo. SE12 —7H 107
Stoneycroft Rd. Wfd G —6H 21
Stoneydeep. Tedd —4A 116
Stoneydown. E17 —4A 34
Stoneydown Av. E17 —4A 34
Stoneydown Ho. E17 —4A 34
(off Blackhorse Rd.)
Stoneyfields Gdns. Edgw —4D 12
Stoneyfields La. Edgw —5D 12
Stoney La. E1 —6F 69 (7H 163)
Stoney La. SE19 —6F 123
Stoney St. SE1 —1D 86 (4E 168)
Stonhouse St. SW4 —4H 103
Stonor Rd. W14 —4H 83
Stonycroft Clo. Enf —2F 9
Stopes St. SE15 —7F 87
Stopford Rd. E13 —1J 71
Stopford Rd. SE17 —5B 86
Stopher Ho. SE1 —2B 86 (7B 168)
(off Webber St.)
Store Rd. E16 —2E 90
Storers Quay. E14 —4F 89
Store St. E15 —5F 53
Store St. WC1 —5H 67 (6C 160)
Storey Ct. NW8 —2A 158
Storey Ho. E14 —7D 70
Storey Rd. E17 —4B 34
Storey Rd. N6 —6D 30
Storey's Ga. SW1 —2H 85 (7D 166)
Storey St. E16 —1E 90
Stories M. SE5 —2E 104
Stories Rd. SE5 —3E 104
Stork Rd. E7 —6H 53
Storksmead Rd. Edgw —7F 13
Stork's Rd. SE16 —3G 87
Stormont Rd. N6 —7D 30
Stormont Rd. SW11 —3E 102
Stormont Way. Chess —5C 146
Stormount Dri. Hay —2E 76
Storrington. WC1 —3J 67 (2F 161)
(off Regent Sq.)
Storrington Rd. Croy —1F 153
Story St. N1 —7K 49
Stothard St. E1 —4J 69
Stott Clo. SW18 —6B 102
Stoughton Av. Sutt —5F 149
Stoughton Clo. SE11
—4K 85 (4H 173)
Stoughton Clo. SW15 —1C 118
Stour Av. S'hall —3E 78
Stourcliffe Clo. W1 —6D 66 (1E 164)
Stourcliffe St. W2 —6D 66 (1E 164)
Stour Clo. Kes —4A 156
Stourhead Clo. SW19 —7F 101
Stourhead Gdns. SW20 —3C 136
Stourhead Ho. SW1 —5H 85 (5C 172)
(off Tachbrook St.)
Stour Rd. E3 —7C 52
Stour Rd. Dag —2G 57
Stourton Av. Felt —4D 114
Stowage. SE8 —6C 88
Stow Cres. E17 —7F 19
Stowe Cres. Ruis —6D 22
Stowe Gdns. N9 —1A 18
Stowe Ho. NW11 —6A 30
Stowell Ho. N8 —4J 31
(off Pembroke Rd.)
Stowe Pl. N15 —3E 32
Stowe Rd. W12 —2D 82
Stoxmead. Harr —1H 25
Stracey Rd. E7 —4J 53
Stracey Rd. NW10 —1K 63
Strachan Pl. SW19 —6E 118
Stradbroke Dri. Chig —6K 21
Stradbroke Gro. Buck H —1G 21
Stradbroke Gro. Ilf —3C 36
Stradbroke Pk. Chig —6K 21
Stradbroke Rd. N5 —4C 50
Stradbrook Clo. Harr —3D 42
Stradella Rd. SE24 —6C 104
Strafford Av. Ilf —2E 36
Strafford Rd. W3 —2J 81
Strafford Rd. Barn —3B 4
Strafford Rd. Houn —3D 96
Strafford Rd. Twic —7A 98
Strafford St. E14 —2C 88
Strahan Rd. E3 —3A 70
Straightsmouth. SE10 —7E 88
Straight, The. S'hall —2B 78
Strait Rd. E6 —7C 72
Strakers Rd. SE15 —4H 105
Strale Ho. N1 —1E 68
(off Whitmore Est.)
Strand. WC2 —7J 67 (3F 167)
Strand Ct. SE18 —5J 91
Strandfield Clo. SE18 —5J 91
Strand La. WC2 —7K 67 (2H 167)
Strand On The Green. —6G 81
Strand on the Grn. W4 —6G 81
Strand Pl. N18 —4K 17
Strand School App. W4 —6G 81
Strang Ho. N1 —1C 68
Strangways Ter. W14 —3H 83
Stranraer Rd. H'row A —6A 94
Stranraer Way. N1 —7J 49
Stranraer Way. Stanw —6A 94
Strasburg Rd. SW11 —1E 102
Stratfield Pk. Clo. N21 —7G 7
Stratford. —7F 53
Stratford Av. Uxb —2B 58
Stratford Cen., The. E15 —7F 53
Stratford Circus Arts Cen. —6F 53
Stratford Clo. Bark —7A 56
Stratford Clo. Dag —7J 57
Stratford Ct. N Mald —4K 135
Stratford Gro. SW15 —4F 101
Stratford Ho. Av. Brom —3C 144
Stratford Marsh. —7D 52
Stratford New Town. —5E 52
Stratford Office Village, The. E15 —7G 53
(off Romford Rd.)
Stratford Pl. W1 —6F 67 (1J 165)
Stratford Rd. E15 —1H 71
Stratford Rd. NW4 —4F 29
Stratford Rd. W8 —3J 83
Stratford Rd. Hay —4K 59
Stratford Rd. H'row A —6D 94
Stratford Rd. S'hall —4C 78
Stratford Rd. T Hth —4A 140
Stratford Shop. Cen. E15 —7F 53
(off Stratford Cen., The)
Stratford Studios. W8 —3J 83
Stratford Vs. NW1 —7G 49
Stratham Ct. N19 —3J 49
(off Alexander Rd.)
Strathan Clo. SW18 —6G 101
Strathaven Rd. SE12 —6K 107
Strathblaine Rd. SW11 —5B 102
Strathbrook Rd. SW16 —7K 121
Strathcona Rd. Wemb —2D 44
Strathdale. SW16 —5K 121
Strathdon Dri. SW17 —3B 120
Strathearn Av. Hay —7H 77
Strathearn Av. Twic —1F 115
Strathearn Pl. W2 —6C 66 (1C 164)
Strathearn Rd. SW19 —5J 119
Strathearn Rd. Sutt —5J 149
Stratheden Pde. SE3 —7J 89
Stratheden Rd. SE3 —1J 107
Strathfield Gdns. Bark —6H 55
Strathleven Rd. SW2 —5J 103
Strathmore Ct. NW8 —3C 66 (1C 158)
(off Park Rd.)
Strathmore Gdns. N3 —1K 29
Strathmore Gdns. W8 —1J 83
Strathmore Gdns. Edgw —2H 27
Strathmore Rd. SW19 —3J 119
Strathmore Rd. Croy —7D 140
Strathmore Rd. Tedd —4J 115
Strathnairn St. SE1 —4G 87
Strathray Gdns. NW3 —6C 48
Strath Ter. SW11 —4C 102
Strathville Rd. SW18 —2J 119
Strathyre Av. SW16 —3A 140
Stratton Clo. SW19 —2J 137
Stratton Clo. Bexh —3E 110
Stratton Clo. Edgw —6A 12
Stratton Clo. Houn —1E 96
Stratton Ct. Pinn —1D 24
(off Devonshire Rd.)
Strattondale St. E14 —3E 88
Stratton Dri. Bark —5J 55
Stratton Gdns. S'hall —6D 60
Stratton Rd. SW19 —2J 137
Stratton Rd. Bexh —3E 110
Stratton Rd. Sun —2H 131
Stratton St. W1 —1F 85 (4K 165)
Strauss Rd. W4 —2K 81
Strawberry Hill. —3K 115
Strawberry Hill. Twic —3K 115
Strawberry Hill Clo. Twic —3K 115
Strawberry Hill House. —3K 115
Strawberry Hill Rd. Twic —3K 115
Strawberry La. Cars —3E 150
Strawberry Ter. N10 —1D 30
Strawberry Va. N2 —1B 30
Strawberry Va. Twic —3A 116
(in two parts)
Streakes Fld. Rd. NW2 —2C 46
Streamdale. SE2 —6A 92
Stream La. Edgw —5C 12
Streamside Clo. N9 —1A 18
Streamside Clo. Brom —4J 143
Stream Way. Belv —6F 93
Streatfield Av. E6 —1D 72
Streatfield Rd. Harr —3C 26
Streatham. —4J 121
Streatham Clo. SW16 —2J 121
Streatham Common. —6J 121
Streatham Comn. N. SW16 —5J 121
Streatham Comn. S. SW16 —6J 121
Streatham Ct. SW16 —3J 121
Streatham High Rd. SW16 —4J 121
Streatham Hill. —1J 121
Streatham Hill. SW2 —2J 121
Streatham Ice Rink. —5J 121
Streatham Park. —4G 121
Streatham Pl. SW2 —7J 103
Streatham Rd. Mitc & SW16 —1E 138
Streatham St. WC1 —6J 67 (7E 160)
Streatham Vale. —7G 121
Streatham Va. SW16 —1G 139
Streathbourne Rd. SW17 —2E 120
Streatley Pl. NW3 —4A 48
Streatley Rd. NW6 —7H 47
Streeters La. Wall —3H 151
Streetfield M. SE3 —3J 107
Streimer Rd. E15 —2E 70
Strelley Way. W3 —7A 64
Stretton Mans. SE8 —5C 88
Stretton Rd. Croy —7E 140
Stretton Rd. Rich —2C 116
Strickland Ct. SE15 —3G 105
Strickland Ho. E2 —3F 69 (2K 163)
(off Chambord St.)
Strickland Row. SW18 —7B 102
Strickland St. SE8 —2C 106
Stride Rd. E13 —2H 71
Stringer Ho. N1 —1E 68
(off Whitmore Est.)
Strode Clo. N10 —7K 15
Strode Rd. E7 —4J 53
Strode Rd. N17 —2E 32
Strode Rd. NW10 —6C 46
Strode Rd. SW6 —7G 83
Strome Ho. NW6 —2K 65
(off Carlton Va.)
Strone Rd. E7 & E12 —6A 54
Strone Way. Hay —4C 60
Strongbow Cres. SE9 —5D 108
Strongbow Rd. SE9 —5D 108
Strongbridge Clo. Harr —1E 42
Stronsa Rd. W12 —2B 82
Strood Av. Romf —1K 57
Strood Ho. SE1 —2D 86 (7F 169)
(off Staple St.)
Stroud Cres. SW15 —3C 118
Stroudes Clo. Wor Pk —7A 136
Stroud Fld. N'holt —6C 42
Stroud Ga. Harr —4F 43
Stroud Green. —7K 31
Stroud Grn. Gdns. Croy —7J 141
Stroud Grn. Rd. N4 —1K 49
Stroud Grn. Way. Croy —7H 141
Stroudley Ho. SW8 —1G 103
Stroudley Wlk. E3 —3D 70
Stroud Rd. SE25 —6G 141
Stroud Rd. SW19 —3J 119
Stroud's Clo. Chad H —5B 38
Stroud Way. Ashf —6D 112
Strouts Pl. E2 —3F 69 (1J 163)
Strudwick Ct. SW4 —1J 103
(off Binfield Rd.)
Strutton Ground. SW1
—3H 85 (1C 172)
Strype St. E1 —5F 69 (6J 163)
Stuart Av. NW9 —7C 28
Stuart Av. W5 —1F 81
Stuart Av. Brom —1J 155
Stuart Av. Harr —3D 42
Stuart Av. W on T —7A 132
Stuart Clo. Uxb —6C 40
Stuart Cres. N22 —1K 31
Stuart Cres. Croy —3B 154
Stuart Cres. Hay —6E 58
Stuart Evans Clo. Well —3C 110
Stuart Gro. Tedd —5J 115
Stuart Ho. W14 —4G 83
(off Windsor Way)
Stuart Mantle Way. Eri —7K 93
Stuart Mill Ho. N1 —2K 67 (1G 161)
(off Killick St.)
Stuart Pl. Mitc —1D 138
Stuart Rd. NW6 —3J 65
(in two parts)
Stuart Rd. SE15 —4J 105
Stuart Rd. SW19 —3J 119
Stuart Rd. W3 —1J 81
Stuart Rd. Bark —7K 55
Stuart Rd. E Barn —7H 5
Stuart Rd. Harr —3K 25
Stuart Rd. Rich —2B 116
Stuart Rd. T Hth —4C 140
Stuart Rd. Well —1B 110
Stuart Tower. W9 —3A 66
(off Maida Va.)
Stubbs Ct. W4 —5H 81
(off Chaseley Dri.)
Stubbs Dri. SE16 —5H 87
Stubbs Ho. SW1 —4H 85 (4D 172)
(off Erasmus St.)
Stubbs M. Dag —4B 56
(off Marlborough Rd.)
Stubbs Point. E16 —4J 71
Stubbs Way. SW19 —1B 138
Stucley Pl. NW1 —7F 49
Stucley Rd. Houn —7G 79
Studdridge St. SW6 —2J 101
(in two parts)
Studd St. N1 —1B 68
Studholme Ct. NW3 —4J 47
Studholme St. SE15 —7H 87
Studio La. W5 —1D 80
Studio Pl. SW1 —7F 165
Studios Rd. Shep —3B 130
Studland. SE17 —5D 86
(off Portland St.)
Studland Clo. Sidc —3K 127
Studland Rd. SE26 —5K 123
Studland Rd. W7 —6H 61
Studland Rd. King T —6E 116
Studland St. W6 —4D 82
Studley Av. E4 —7A 20
Studley Clo. E5 —5A 52
Studley Ct. E14 —7F 71
Studley Ct. Sidc —5B 128
Studley Dri. Ilf —6B 36
Studley Est. SW4 —1J 103
Studley Grange Rd. W7 —2J 79
Studley Rd. E7 —6K 53
Studley Rd. SW4 —1J 103
Studley Rd. Dag —7D 56
Stukeley Rd. E7 —7K 53
Stukeley St. WC2 —6J 67 (7F 161)
Stumps Hill La. Beck —6C 124
Sturdee Ho. E2 —2G 69 (1K 163)
(off Horatio St.)
Sturdy Rd. SE15 —2H 105
Sturge Av. E17 —2D 34
Sturgeon Rd. SE17 —5C 86
Sturges Fld. Chst —6H 127
Sturgess Av. NW4 —7D 28
Sturge St. SE1 —2C 86 (6C 168)
Sturmer Way. N7 —5K 49
Sturminster Clo. Hay —6A 60
Sturminster Ho. SW8 —7K 85
(off Dorset Rd.)
Sturrock Clo. N15 —4D 32
Sturry St. E14 —6D 70
Sturt St. N1 —1D 162
Stutfield St. E1 —6G 69
Styles Gdns. SW9 —3B 104
Styles Ho. SE1 —6A 168
Styles Way. Beck —4E 142
Sudbourne Rd. SW2 —5J 103
Sudbrooke Rd. SW12 —6D 102
Sudbrook Gdns. Rich —3D 116
Sudbrook La. Rich —1E 116
Sudbury. —5B 44
Sudbury. E6 —6E 72
Sudbury Av. Wemb —3C 44
Sudbury Ct. E5 —4A 52
Sudbury Ct. SW8 —1H 103
Sudbury Ct. Dri. Harr —3K 43
Sudbury Ct. Rd. Harr —3K 43
Sudbury Cres. Brom —6J 125
Sudbury Cres. Wemb —5B 44
Sudbury Cft. Wemb —4K 43
Sudbury Gdns. Croy —4E 152
Sudbury Heights Av. Gnfd —5K 43
Sudbury Hill. Harr —2J 43
Sudbury Hill Clo. Wemb —4K 43
Sudbury Ho. SW18 —5K 101
Sudbury Rd. Bark —5K 55
Sudbury Towers. Gnfd —5J 43
Sudeley St. N1 —2B 68
Sudlow Rd. SW18 —5J 101
Sudrey St. SE1 —2C 86 (7C 168)
Suez Av. Gnfd —2K 61
Suez Rd. Enf —4F 9
Suffield Hatch. —4K 19
Suffield Ho. SE17 —5B 86
(off Berryfield Rd.)
Suffield Rd. E4 —3J 19
Suffield Rd. N15 —5F 33
Suffield Rd. SE20 —2J 141
Suffolk Ct. E10 —7C 34
Suffolk Ct. Ilf —6J 37
Suffolk Ho. SE20 —1K 141
(off Croydon Rd.)
Suffolk La. EC4 —7D 68 (2E 168)
Suffolk Pk. Rd. E17 —4A 34
Suffolk Pl. SW1 —1H 85 (4D 166)
Suffolk Rd. E13 —3J 71
Suffolk Rd. N15 —5D 32
Suffolk Rd. NW10 —7A 46
Suffolk Rd. SE25 —4F 141
Suffolk Rd. SW13 —7B 82
Suffolk Rd. Bark —7H 55
Suffolk Rd. Dag —5J 57
Suffolk Rd. Enf —5C 8
Suffolk Rd. Harr —6D 24
Suffolk Rd. Ilf —6J 37
Suffolk Rd. Sidc —6C 128
Suffolk Rd. Wor Pk —2B 148
Suffolk St. E7 —4J 53
Suffolk St. SW1 —7H 67 (3D 166)
Sugar Bakers Ct. EC3 —1H 169
Sugar Ho. La. E15 —2E 70
Sugar Loaf Wlk. E2 —3J 69
Sugar Quay. EC3 —3H 169
Sugar Quay Wlk. EC3 —7E 68 (3H 169)
Sugden Rd. SW11 —3E 102
Sugden Rd. Th Dit —1B 146
Sugden St. SE5 —6D 86
(off Depot St.)
Sugden Way. Bark —2K 73
Sulby Ho. SE4 —4A 106
(off Turnham Rd.)
Sulgrave Gdns. W6 —2E 82
Sulgrave Rd. W6 —3E 82
Sulina Rd. SW2 —7J 103
Sulivan Ct. SW6 —2J 101
Sulivan Enterprise Cen. SW6 —3K 101
Sulivan Rd. SW6 —3J 101
Sullivan Av. E16 —5B 72
Sullivan Clo. SW11 —3C 102
Sullivan Clo. W Mol —3F 133
Sullivan Ct. N16 —7F 33
Sullivan Cres. Hare —2A 22
Sullivan Ho. SE11 —4K 85 (4H 173)
(off Vauxhall St.)
Sullivan Ho. SW1 —6F 85 (7K 171)
(off Churchill Gdns.)
Sullivan Rd. SE11 —4B 86 (3K 173)
Sullivans Reach. W on T —7H 131
Sultan Rd. E11 —4K 35
Sultan St. SE5 —7C 86
Sultan St. Beck —2K 141
Sumatra Rd. NW6 —5J 47
Sumburgh Rd. SW12 —6E 102
Summer Av. E Mol —5J 133
Summercourt Rd. E1 —6J 69
Summerene Clo. SW16 —7G 121
Summerfield Av. NW6 —2G 65
Summerfield La. Surb —2D 146
Summerfield Rd. W5 —4B 62
Summerfields Av. N12 —6H 15
Summerfield St. SE12 —7H 107
Summer Gdns. E Mol —5J 133
Summer Hill. Chst —2E 144
Summerhill Gro. Enf —6K 7
Summerhill Rd. N15 —4D 32
Summerhill Vs. Chst —1E 144
(off Susan Wood)
Summerhill Way. Mitc —1E 138
Summerhouse Av. Houn —1C 96
Summerhouse Dri. Bex & Dart
—4K 129
Summerhouse Rd. N16 —2E 50
Summerland Gdns. N10 —3F 31
Summerland Grange. N10 —3F 31
Summerlands Av. W3 —7J 63
Summerlands Lodge. Orp —4E 156
Summerlee Av. N2 —4D 30
Summerlee Gdns. N2 —4D 30
Summerley St. SW18 —2K 119
Summer Rd. E Mol & Th Dit —5J 133
Summersby Rd. N6 —6F 31
Summers Clo. Sutt —7J 149
Summers Clo. Wemb —1H 45
Summers La. N12 —7G 15
Summers Row. N12 —6H 15
Summers St. EC1 —4A 68 (4J 161)
Summerstown. —3A 120
Summerstown. SW17 —3A 120
Summerton Way. SE28 —6D 74
Summer Trees. Sun —1K 131
Summerville Gdns. Sutt —6H 149
Summerwood Rd. Iswth —5K 97
Summit Av. NW9 —5K 27
Summit Bus. Pk. Sun —7J 113
Summit Clo. N14 —2B 16
Summit Clo. NW2 —5G 47
Summit Clo. NW9 —4K 27
Summit Clo. Edgw —7B 12
Summit Dri. Wfd G —2B 36
Summit Est. N16 —7G 33
Summit Rd. E17 —4D 34
Summit Rd. N'holt —7E 42
Summit Way. N14 —2A 16
Summit Way. SE19 —7E 122
Sumner Av. SE15 —1F 105
Sumner Bldgs. SE1 —4C 168
Sumner Ct. SW8 —7J 85
Sumner Est. SE15 —7F 87
Sumner Gdns. Croy —1A 152
Sumner Ho. E3 —5D 70
Sumner Pl. SW7 —4B 84 (4B 170)
Sumner Pl. M. SW7 —4B 84 (4B 170)
Sumner Rd. SE15 —6F 87
(in two parts)
Sumner Rd. Croy —1A 152
Sumner Rd. Harr —7G 25
Sumner Rd. S. Croy —1A 152
Sumner St. SE1 —1B 86 (4B 168)
Sumpter Clo. NW3 —6A 48
Sun All. Rich —4E 98
Sunbeam Cres. W10 —4E 64
Sunbeam Rd. NW10 —4J 63
Sunbury. —3A 132
Sunbury Av. NW7 —5E 12
Sunbury Av. SW14 —4K 99
Sunbury Av. Pas. SW14 —4A 100
Sunbury Common. —7H 113
Sunbury Ct. Barn —4B 4
Sunbury Ct. Island. Sun —3B 132
Sunbury Ct. M. Sun —2B 132
Sunbury Ct. Rd. Sun —2A 132
Sunbury Cres. Felt —4H 113
Sunbury Cross. (Junct.) —7J 113
Sunbury Cross Shop. Cen. Sun
—7H 113
Sunbury Gdns. NW7 —5E 12
Sunbury Ho. E2 —3F 69 (2J 163)
(off Swanfield St.)
Sunbury La. SW11 —1B 102
(in two parts)
Sunbury La. W on T —6J 131
Sunburylock Ait. W on T —4K 131
Sunbury Pk. Walled Garden. —3K 131
Sunbury Rd. Felt —3H 113
Sunbury Rd. Sutt —3F 149
Sunbury St. SE18 —3D 90
Sunbury Way. Hanw —5A 114
Sunbury Workshops. E2
(off Swanfield St.) —3F 69 (2J 163)
Sun Ct. EC3 —1F 169
Suncroft Pl. SE26 —3J 123
Sunderland Ct. SE22 —7G 105
Sunderland Ct. Stanw —6A 94
Sunderland Mt. SE23 —2K 123
Sunderland Rd. SE23 —1K 123
Sunderland Rd. W5 —3D 80
Sunderland Rd. H'row A —6A 94
Sunderland Ter. W2 —6K 65
Sunderland Way. E12 —2B 54
Sundew Av. W12 —7C 64
Sundew Clo. W12 —7C 64
Sundew Ct. Wemb —2E 62
(off Elmore Clo.)
Sundial Av. SE25 —3F 141
Sundorne Rd. SE7 —5A 90
Sundown Rd. Ashf —5E 112
Sundra Wlk. E1 —4K 69
Sundridge. —6A 126
Sundridge Av. Brom & Chst —1B 144
Sundridge Av. Well —2H 109
Sundridge Pde. Brom —7K 125
Sundridge Park. —7K 125
Sundridge Pl. Croy —1G 153
Sundridge Rd. Croy —7F 141
Sunfields Pl. SE3 —7K 89
Sunflower Dri. E8 —7F 51
Sungate Cotts. Romf —1F 39
Sun-in-the-Sands. (Junct.) —7K 89
Sun-in-the-Sands. SE3 —7J 89
Sunken Rd. Croy —5J 153
Sunkist Way. Wall —7J 151
Sunland Av. Bexh —4E 110
Sun La. SE3 —7K 89
Sunleigh Rd. Wemb —1E 62
Sunley Gdns. Gnfd —1A 62
Sunlight Clo. SW19 —6A 120
Sunlight Sq. E2 —3H 69
Sunmead Rd. Sun —3J 131
Sunna Gdns. Sun —2K 131
Sunningdale. N14 —5C 16
Sunningdale. W13 —5B 62
(off Hardwick Grn.)
Sunningdale Av. W3 —7A 64
Sunningdale Av. Bark —1H 73
Sunningdale Av. Felt —2C 114
Sunningdale Av. Ruis —1A 42
Sunningdale Clo. E6 —3D 72
Sunningdale Clo. SE16 —5H 87
(off Ryder Dri.)
Sunningdale Clo. SE28 —6E 74
Sunningdale Clo. Stan —6F 11
Sunningdale Clo. Surb —2E 146
Sunningdale Ct. Houn —6H 97
(off Whitton Dene)
Sunningdale Ct. S'hall —6G 61
(off Fleming Rd.)
Sunningdale Gdns. NW9 —5J 27
Sunningdale Gdns. W8 —3J 83
(off Stratford Rd.)
Sunningdale Lodge. Edgw —5A 12
(off Stonegrove)
Sunningdale Lodge. Harr —7J 25
(off Grove Hill)
Sunningdale Rd. Brom —4C 144
Sunningdale Rd. Sutt —3H 149
Sunningfields Cres. NW4 —2D 28
Sunningfields Rd. NW4 —3D 28
Sunninghill Ct. W3 —2J 81
Sunninghill Rd. SE13 —2D 106
Sunny Bank. SE25 —3G 141
Sunny Cres. NW10 —7J 45
Sunnycroft Rd. SE25 —3G 141
Sunnycroft Rd. Houn —2F 97
Sunnycroft Rd. S'hall —5E 60
Sunnydale. Orp —2E 156
Sunnydale Gdns. NW7 —6E 12
Sunnydale Rd. SE12 —5K 107
Sunnydene Av. E4 —5A 20
Sunnydene Av. Ruis —1J 41
Sunnydene Gdns. Wemb —6C 44
Sunnydene St. SE26 —4A 124
Sunnyfield. NW7 —4G 13
Sunnyfield Rd. Chst —3K 145
Sunny Gdns. Pde. NW4 —2D 28
Sunny Gdns. Rd. NW4 —2D 28
Sunny Hill. NW4 —3D 28
Sunnyhill Clo. E5 —4A 52
Sunnyhill Rd. SW16 —4J 121
Sunnyhurst Clo. Sutt —3J 149
Sunnymead Av. Mitc —3H 139
Sunnymead Rd. NW9 —7K 27
Sunnymead Rd. SW15 —5D 100
Sunnymede Av. Eps —7A 148
Sunnymede Dri. Ilf —5F 37
Sunny Nook Gdns. S Croy —6D 152
Sunny Rd., The. Enf —1E 8
Sunnyside. NW2 —3H 47
Sunnyside. SW19 —6G 119
Sunnyside. W on T —5A 132
Sunnyside Dri. E4 —7K 9
Sunnyside Houses. NW2 —3H 47
(off Sunnyside)
Sunnyside Pas. SW19 —6G 119
Sunnyside Rd. E10 —1C 52
Sunnyside Rd. N19 —7H 31
Sunnyside Rd. W5 —1G 80
Sunnyside Rd. Ilf —3G 55

Sunnyside Rd.—Tanglyn Av.

Sunnyside Rd. Tedd —4H 115
Sunnyside Rd. E. N9 —3B 18
Sunnyside Rd. N. N9 —3A 18
Sunnyside Rd. S. N9 —3A 18
Sunnyside Ter. NW9 —3K 27
Sunny Vw. NW9 —5K 27
Sunny Way. N12 —7H 15
Sun Pas. SE16 —3G 87
(off Old Jamaica Rd.)
Sunray Av. SE24 —4D 104
Sunray Av. Brom —6C 144
Sunray Av. Surb —2H 147
Sunrise Clo. Felt —3D 114
Sunrise Vw. NW7 —6G 13
Sun Rd. W14 —5H 83
Sunset Av. E4 —1J 19
Sunset Av. Wfd G —4C 20
Sunset Ct. Wfd G —7F 21
Sunset Gdns. SE25 —2F 141
Sunset Rd. SE5 —4C 104
Sunset Rd. SE28 —1A 92
Sunset Vw. Barn —2B 4
Sunshine Way. Mitc —2D 138
Sun St. EC2 —5D 68 (5F 163)
(in two parts)
Sun St. Pas. EC2 —5E 68 (6G 163)
Sun Wlk. E1 —7F 69 (3K 169)
Sunwell Clo. SE15 —1H 105
Surbiton. —6D 134
Surbiton Ct. Surb —6C 134
Surbiton Cres. King T —4E 134
Surbiton Hall Clo. King T —4E 134
Surbiton Hill Pk. Surb —5F 135
Surbiton Hill Rd. Surb —4E 134
Surbiton Pde. Surb —6E 134
Surbiton Rd. King T —4D 134
Surlingham Clo. SE28 —7D 74
Surma Clo. E1 —4G 69
Surrendale Pl. W9 —4J 65
Surrey Canal Rd. SE15 & SE14 —6J 87
Surrey County Cricket Club. —7H 173
Surrey Ct. N3 —2G 29
Surrey Cres. W4 —5G 81
Surrey Gdns. N4 —6C 32
Surrey Gro. SE17 —5E 86
Surrey Gro. Sutt —3B 150
Surrey La. SW11 —1C 102
Surrey La. Est. SW11 —1C 102
Surrey M. SE27 —4E 122
Surrey Mt. SE23 —1H 123
Surrey Quays Rd. SE16 —3J 87
Surrey Quays Shop. Cen. SE16 —3K 87
Surrey Rd. SE15 —5K 105
Surrey Rd. Bark —7J 55
Surrey Rd. Dag —5H 57
Surrey Rd. Harr —5G 25
Surrey Rd. W W'ck —1D 154
Surrey Row. SE1 —2B 86 (6A 168)
Surrey Sq. SE17 —5E 86
Surrey Steps. WC2 —7K 67
(off Surrey St.)
Surrey St. E13 —3K 71
Surrey St. WC2 —7K 67 (2H 167)
Surrey St. Croy —2C 152
Surrey Ter. SE17 —5E 86
Surrey Water Rd. SE16 —1K 87
Surridge Ct. SW9 —2J 103
(off Clapham Rd.)
Surridge Gdns. SE19 —6D 122
Surr St. N7 —5J 49
Susan Clo. Romf —3J 39
Susan Constant Ct. E14 —7F 71
Susan Lawrence Ho. E12 —4E 54
(off Walton Rd.)
Susannah St. E14 —6D 70
Susan Rd. SE3 —2K 107
Susan Wood. Chst —1E 144
Sussex Av. Iswth —3J 97
Sussex Clo. N19 —2J 49
Sussex Clo. Ilf —5D 36
Sussex Clo. N Mald —4A 136
Sussex Clo. Twic —6B 98
Sussex Cres. N'holt —6E 42
Sussex Gdns. N4 —5C 32
Sussex Gdns. N6 —5D 30
Sussex Gdns. W2 —7B 66 (2A 164)
Sussex Gdns. Chess —6D 146
Sussex Ga. N6 —5D 30
Sussex Lodge. W2 —6B 66 (1B 164)
(off Sussex Pl.)
Sussex Mans. SW7 —4A 170
Sussex Mans. WC2 —7J 67 (2F 167)
(off Maiden La.)
Sussex M. E. W2 —1B 164
Sussex M. W. W2 —7B 66 (2B 164)
Sussex Pl. NW1 —4D 66 (3E 158)
Sussex Pl. W2 —6B 66 (1B 164)
Sussex Pl. W6 —5E 82
Sussex Pl. Eri —7H 93
Sussex Pl. N Mald —4A 136
Sussex Ring. N12 —5D 14
Sussex Rd. E6 —1E 72
Sussex Rd. Cars —7D 150
Sussex Rd. Eri —7H 93
Sussex Rd. Harr —5G 25
Sussex Rd. Mitc —5J 139
Sussex Rd. N Mald —4A 136
Sussex Rd. Sidc —5B 128
Sussex Rd. S'hall —3B 78
Sussex Rd. S Croy —6D 152
Sussex Rd. Uxb —4E 40
Sussex Rd. W W'ck —1D 154
Sussex Sq. W2 —7B 66 (2B 164)
Sussex St. E13 —3K 71
Sussex St. SW1 —5F 85 (6K 171)
Sussex Ter. SE20 —7J 123
(off Graveney Gro.)
Sussex Wlk. SW9 —4B 104
(in two parts)
Sussex Way. N19 & N7 —1H 49
(in four parts)
Sussex Way. Barn & Cockf —5A 6
Sutcliffe Clo. NW11 —5K 29
Sutcliffe Rd. SE18 —6J 91
Sutcliffe Rd. Well —2C 110
Sutherland Av. W9 —4J 65
Sutherland Av. W13 —6B 62
Sutherland Av. Hay —4J 77
Sutherland Av. Orp —6K 145
Sutherland Av. Sun —2H 131
Sutherland Av. Well —4J 109
Sutherland Clo. Barn —4B 4
Sutherland Ct. N16 —3D 50
Sutherland Ct. NW9 —5H 27
Sutherland Ct. W9 —4J 65
(off Surrendale Pl.)
Sutherland Dri. SW19 —1B 138
Sutherland Gdns. SW14 —3A 100
Sutherland Gdns. Sun —2H 131
Sutherland Gdns. Wor Pk —1D 148
Sutherland Gro. SW18 —6G 101
Sutherland Gro. Tedd —5J 115
Sutherland Ho. W8 —3K 83
Sutherland Pl. W2 —6J 65
Sutherland Point. E5 —4H 51
(off Brackenfield Clo.)
Sutherland Rd. E3 —2B 70
Sutherland Rd. E17 —2K 33
Sutherland Rd. N9 —1C 18
Sutherland Rd. N17 —7B 18
Sutherland Rd. W4 —6A 82
Sutherland Rd. W13 —6A 62
Sutherland Rd. Belv —3G 93
Sutherland Rd. Croy —7A 140
Sutherland Rd. Enf —6E 8
Sutherland Rd. S'hall —6D 60
Sutherland Rd. Path. E17 —3K 33
Sutherland Row. SW1 —5F 85 (5K 171)
Sutherland Sq. SE17 —5C 86
Sutherland St. SW1 —5F 85 (5J 171)
Sutherland Wlk. SE17 —5C 86
Sutlej Rd. SE7 —7A 90
Sutterton St. N7 —6K 49
Sutton. —5K 149
Sutton Arc. Sutt —5K 149
Sutton Clo. Beck —1D 142
Sutton Clo. Lou —1H 21
Sutton Clo. Pinn —5J 23
Sutton Comn. Rd. Sutt —7H 137
Sutton Ct. SE19 —7F 123
Sutton Ct. W4 —6J 81
Sutton Ct. W5 —1E 80
Sutton Ct. Sutt —6A 150
Sutton Ct. Rd. E13 —3A 72
Sutton Ct. Rd. W4 —7J 81
Sutton Ct. Rd. Sutt —6A 150
Sutton Ct. Rd. Uxb —1D 58
Sutton Cres. Barn —5A 4
Sutton Dene. Houn —1F 97
Sutton Est. EC1 —2F 163
Sutton Est. W10 —5E 64
Sutton Est., The. N1 —7B 50
Sutton Est., The. SW3 —5C 170
Sutton Gdns. SE25 —5F 141
Sutton Gdns. Bark —1J 73
Sutton Grn. Bark —1J 73
Sutton Gro. Sutt —4B 150
Sutton Hall Rd. Houn —7E 78
Sutton La. Houn —3D 96
Sutton La. N. W4 —5J 81
Sutton La. S. W4 —6J 81
Sutton Pde. NW4 —4E 28
(off Church Rd.)
Sutton Pk. Rd. Sutt —6K 149
Sutton Pl. E9 —5J 51
Sutton Rd. E13 —4H 71
Sutton Rd. E17 —1K 33
Sutton Rd. N10 —1E 30
Sutton Rd. Bark —2J 73
Sutton Rd. Houn —1E 96
Sutton Row. W1 —6H 67 (7D 160)
Suttons Bus. Pk. Rain —3K 75
Sutton Sq. E9 —5J 51
Sutton Sq. Houn —1D 96
Sutton St. E1 —7J 69
Sutton's Way. EC1 —4C 68 (4D 162)
Sutton United F.C. —4J 149
Sutton Wlk. SE1 —1K 85 (5H 167)
Sutton Way. W10 —4E 64
Sutton Way. Houn —1D 96
Swaby Rd. SW18 —1A 120
Swaffham Way. N22 —7G 17
Swaffield Rd. SW18 —7K 101
Swain Clo. SW16 —6F 121
Swain Rd. T Hth —5C 140
Swains Clo. W Dray —2A 76
Swains La. N6 —1E 48
Swainson Rd. W3 —2B 82
Swains Rd. SW17 —7D 120
Swakeleys Dri. Uxb —4C 40
Swakeleys Rd. Ick & Uxb —4A 40
Swakeleys Roundabout. (Junct.) —4A 40
Swalecliffe Rd. Belv —5H 93
Swaledale Clo. N11 —6K 15
Swallands Rd. SE6 —3C 124
(in two parts)
Swallow Clo. SE14 —1K 105
Swallow Clo. Bush —1A 10
Swallow Clo. Eri —1K 111
Swallow Ct. SE12 —7J 107
Swallow Ct. W9 —5J 65
(off Admiral Wlk.)
Swallow Ct. Ilf —5F 37
Swallow Ct. Ruis —1A 42
Swallow Dri. NW10 —6K 45
Swallow Dri. N'holt —2E 60
Swallowfield Rd. SE7 —5K 89
Swallowfield Way. Hay —2F 77
Swallow Gdns. SW16 —5H 121
Swallow Ho. NW8 —2C 66
(off Barrow Hill Est.)
Swallow Pk. Cvn. Site. Surb —3F 147
Swallow Pas. W1 —6F 67
(off Swallow Pl.)
Swallow Pl. W1 —6F 67 (1K 165)
Swallow St. E6 —5C 72
Swallow St. W1 —7G 67 (3B 166)
Swanage Ho. SW8 —7K 85
(off Dorset Rd.)
Swanage Rd. E4 —7K 19
Swanage Rd. SW18 —6A 102
Swanage Waye. Hay —6A 60
Swan & Pike Rd. Enf —1H 9
Swan App. E6 —5C 72
Swanbourne. SE17 —4C 86
(off Wansey St.)
Swanbourne Ho. NW8 —4C 66 (3C 158)
(off Capland St.)
Swanbridge Rd. Bexh —1G 111
Swan Cen., The. SW17 —3K 119
Swan Clo. E17 —1A 34
Swan Clo. Croy —7E 140
Swan Clo. Felt —4C 114
Swan Ct. E14 —6B 70
Swan Ct. SW3 —5C 84 (6D 170)
Swan Ct. Iswth —3B 98
(off Swan St.)
Swandon Way. SW18 —5K 101
Swan Dri. NW9 —2A 28
Swanfield St. E2 —3F 69 (2J 163)
Swan La. EC4 —7D 68 (3F 169)
Swan La. N20 —3F 15
Swanley Ho. SE17 —5E 86
(off Kinglake Est.)
Swanley Rd. Well —1C 110
Swan Mead. SE1 —3E 86
Swan M. SW6 —1H 101
Swan M. SW9 —2K 103
Swann Ct. Iswth —3A 98
(off South St.)
Swan Pas. E1 —7F 69
(off Royal Mint Pl.)
Swan Pl. SW13 —2B 100
Swan Rd. SE16 —2J 87
Swan Rd. Felt —5C 114
Swan Rd. S'hall —6F 61
Swan Rd. W Dray —2A 76
Swanscombe Ho. W11 —1F 83
(off St Ann's Rd.)
Swanscombe Point. E16 —5H 71
(off Clarkson Rd.)
Swanscombe Rd. W4 —5A 82
Swanscombe Rd. W11 —1F 83
Swansea Ct. E16 —1F 91
Swansea Rd. Enf —4D 8
Swansea Rd. H'row A —6E 94
Swansland Gdns. E17 —1A 34
Swan St. SE1 —3C 86 (7D 168)
Swan St. SE18 —3B 90
(in two parts)
Swan St. Iswth —3B 98
Swanton Gdns. SW19 —1F 119
Swanton Rd. Eri —7G 93
Swan Wlk. SW3 —6D 84 (7E 170)
Swan Wlk. Shep —7G 131
Swan Way. Enf —2E 8
Swanwick Clo. SW15 —7B 100
Swan Yd. N1 —6B 50
Sward Rd. Orp —6K 145
Swathling Ho. SW15 —6B 100
(off Tunworth Cres.)
Swaton Rd. E3 —4C 70
Swaylands Rd. Belv —6G 93
Swaythling Clo. N18 —4C 18
Swedeland Ct. E1 —6H 163
Swedenborg Gdns. E1 —7H 69
Sweden Ga. SE16 —3A 88
Swedish Quays. SE16 —3A 88
Sweeney Cres. SE1 —2F 87 (7K 169)
Sweet Briar Grn. N9 —3A 18
Sweet Briar Gro. N9 —3A 18
Sweet Briar Wlk. N18 —4A 18
Sweetcroft La. Uxb —7B 40
Sweetland Ct. Dag —6B 56
Sweetmans Av. Pinn —3B 24
Sweets Way. N20 —2G 15
Swell Ct. E17 —6C 34
Swetenham Wlk. SE18 —5G 91
Swete St. E13 —2J 71
Sweyn Pl. SE3 —2J 107
Swift Clo. E17 —7F 19
Swift Clo. Harr —2F 43
Swift Clo. Hay —6H 59
Swift Ct. Sutt —7K 149
Swift Lodge. W9 —4J 65
(off Admiral Wlk.)
Swift Rd. Felt —3C 114
Swift Rd. S'hall —3E 78
Swiftsden Way. Brom —6G 125
Swift St. SW6 —1H 101
Swinbrook Rd. W10 —5G 65
Swinburne Ct. SE5 —4D 104
(off Basingdon Way)
Swinburne Cres. Croy —6J 141
Swinburne Rd. SW15 —4C 100
Swinderby Rd. Wemb —6E 44
Swindon Clo. Ilf —2J 55
Swindon Rd. H'row A —5E 94
Swindon St. W12 —1D 82
Swinfield Clo. Felt —3C 114
Swinford Gdns. SW9 —3B 104
Swingate La. SE18 —6J 91
Swinley Ho. NW1 —3F 67 (1K 159)
(off Redhill St.)
Swinnerton St. E9 —5A 52
Swinton Clo. Wemb —1H 45
Swinton Pl. WC1 —3K 67 (1G 161)
Swinton St. WC1 —3K 67 (1G 161)
Swires Shaw. Kes —4B 156
Swiss Cen. W1 —3C 166
Swiss Cottage. (Junct.) —7B 48
Swiss Cottage. NW3 —7B 48
Swiss Ct. WC2 —3D 166
Swiss Ter. NW6 —7B 48
Swithland Gdns. SE9 —4E 126
Swyncombe Av. W5 —4B 80
Swynford Gdns. NW4 —4C 28
Sybil M. N4 —6B 32
Sybil Phoenix Clo. SE8 —5K 87
Sybil Thorndike Casson Ho. SW5 —5J 83
(off Old Brompton Rd.)
Sybourn St. E17 —7B 34
Sycamore Av. E3 —1B 70
Sycamore Av. W5 —3D 80
Sycamore Av. Hay —7G 59
Sycamore Av. Sidc —6K 109
Sycamore Clo. E16 —4G 71
Sycamore Clo. N9 —4B 18
Sycamore Clo. SE9 —2C 126
Sycamore Clo. W3 —1A 82
Sycamore Clo. Barn —6G 5
Sycamore Clo. Cars —4D 150
Sycamore Clo. Edgw —4D 12
Sycamore Clo. Felt —3J 113
Sycamore Clo. N'holt —1C 60
Sycamore Clo. W Dray —7B 58
Sycamore Ct. E7 —6J 53
Sycamore Ct. NW6 —1J 65
(off Bransdale Clo.)
Sycamore Ct. Eri —5K 93
(off Sandcliff Rd.)
Sycamore Ct. Houn —4C 96
Sycamore Ct. N Mald —3A 136
Sycamore Gdns. N15 —4F 33
Sycamore Gdns. W12 —2D 82
Sycamore Gdns. Mitc —2B 138
Sycamore Gro. NW9 —7J 27
Sycamore Gro. SE6 —6E 106
Sycamore Gro. SE20 —1G 141
Sycamore Gro. N Mald —3K 135
Sycamore Hill. N11 —6K 15
Sycamore Ho. N2 —2B 30
(off Grange, The)
Sycamore Ho. W6 —2D 82
Sycamore Ho. Brom —2G 143
Sycamore Ho. Buck H —2G 21
Sycamore Lodge. W8 —3K 83
(off St Mary's Pl.)
Sycamore M. SW4 —3G 103
Sycamore M. Eri —5K 93
(off St John's Rd.)
Sycamore Rd. SW19 —6E 118
Sycamore St. EC1 —4C 68 (4C 162)
Sycamore Wlk. W10 —4G 65
Sycamore Wlk. Ilf —4G 37
Sycamore Way. Tedd —6C 116
Sycamore Way. T Hth —5A 140
Sydcote. SE21 —1C 122
Sydenham. —4J 123
Sydenham Av. N21 —5E 6
Sydenham Av. SE26 —5H 123
Sydenham Cotts. SE12 —2A 126
Sydenham Hill. SE23 & SE26 —1H 123
Sydenham Pk. SE26 —3J 123
Sydenham Pk. Mans. SE26 —3J 123
(off Sydenham Pk.)
Sydenham Pk. Rd. SE26 —3J 123
Sydenham Pl. SE27 —3B 122
Sydenham Ri. SE23 —2H 123
Sydenham Rd. SE26 —4J 123
Sydenham Rd. Croy —1C 152
Sydmons Ct. SE23 —7J 105
Sydner M. N16 —4F 51
Sydner Rd. N16 —4F 51
Sydney Clo. SW3 —4B 84 (4B 170)
Sydney Ct. Hay —4A 60
Sydney Cres. Ashf —6D 112
Sydney Gro. NW4 —5E 28
Sydney M. SW3 —4B 84 (4B 170)
Sydney Pl. SW7 —4B 84 (4B 170)
Sydney Rd. E11 —6K 35
Sydney Rd. N8 —4A 32
Sydney Rd. N10 —1E 30
Sydney Rd. SE2 —3C 92
Sydney Rd. SW20 —2F 137
Sydney Rd. W13 —1A 80
Sydney Rd. Bexh —4D 110
Sydney Rd. Enf —3J 7
(in two parts)
Sydney Rd. Felt —1J 113
Sydney Rd. Ilf —2G 37
Sydney Rd. Rich —4E 98
Sydney Rd. Sidc —4J 127
Sydney Rd. Sutt —4J 149
Sydney Rd. Tedd —5K 115
Sydney Rd. Wfd G —4D 20
Sydney St. SW3 —5C 84 (5C 170)
Sylvana Clo. Uxb —1B 58
Sylvan Av. N3 —2J 29
Sylvan Av. N22 —7E 16
Sylvan Av. NW7 —6F 13
Sylvan Av. Romf —6F 39
Sylvan Ct. N12 —3E 14
Sylvan Est. SE19 —1F 141
Sylvan Gdns. Surb —7D 134
Sylvan Gro. NW2 —4F 47
Sylvan Gro. SE15 —6H 87
Sylvan Hill. SE19 —1E 140
Sylvan Rd. E7 —6J 53
Sylvan Rd. E11 —5J 35
Sylvan Rd. E17 —5C 34
Sylvan Rd. SE19 —1F 141
Sylvan Wlk. Brom —3D 144
Sylvan Way. Dag —4B 56
Sylvan Way. W W'ck —4G 155
Sylverdale Rd. Croy —3B 152
Sylvester Av. Chst —6D 126
Sylvester Path. E8 —6H 51
Sylvester Rd. E8 —6H 51
Sylvester Rd. E17 —7B 34
Sylvester Rd. N2 —2A 30
Sylvester Rd. Wemb —5C 44
Sylvestrus Clo. King T —1G 135
Sylvia Ct. N1 —2D 68
Sylvia Ct. Wemb —7H 45
Sylvia Gdns. Wemb —7H 45
Sylvia Pankhurst Ho. Dag —3G 57
(off Wythenshawe Rd.)
Symes M. NW1 —2G 67
Symington Ho. SE1 —3D 86
(off Deverell St.)
Symington M. E9 —5K 51
Symister M. N1 —2G 163
Symons St. SW3 —4D 84 (4F 171)
Syon Ga. Way. Bren —7A 80
Syon House & Pk. —1C 98
Syon La. Iswth —6K 79
Syon Lodge. SE12 —7J 107
Syon Pk. Gdns. Iswth —7K 79
Syringa Ho. SE4 —3B 106

Tabard Ct. E14 —6E 70
(off Lodore St.)
Tabard Garden Est. SE1 —3D 86 (7E 168)
Tabard Ho. SE1 —3D 86 (7F 169)
(off Manciple St.)
Tabard St. SE1 —2D 86 (6D 168)
Tabernacle Av. E13 —4J 71
Tabernacle St. EC2 —4D 68 (4F 163)
Tableer Av. SW4 —5G 103
Tabley Rd. N7 —4J 49
Tabor Ct. Sutt —6G 149
Tabor Gdns. Sutt —6H 149
Tabor Gro. SW19 —7G 119
Tabor Rd. W6 —3D 82
Tachbrook Est. SW1 —5H 85 (6C 172)
Tachbrook M. SW1 —4G 85 (3A 172)
Tachbrook Rd. Felt —7H 95
Tachbrook Rd. S'hall —4B 78
Tachbrook Rd. W Dray —1A 76
Tachbrook St. SW1 —4G 85 (4B 172)
(in two parts)
Tack M. SE4 —3C 106
Tadema Ho. NW8 —4B 158
Tadema Rd. SW10 —7A 84
Tadmor Clo. Sun —4H 131
Tadmor St. W12 —1F 83
Tadworth Av. N Mald —4B 136
Tadworth Ho. SE1 —7A 168
Tadworth Rd. NW2 —2C 46
Taeping St. E14 —4D 88
Taffrail Ho. E14 —5D 88
Taffy's Row. Mitc —3C 138
Taft Way. E3 —3D 70
Tailworth St. E1 —5G 69 (6K 163)
(off Chicksand St.)
Tailworth St. Houn —2G 97
Tait Ct. SW8 —1J 103
(off Lansdowne Grn.)
Tait Ho. SE1 —1A 86 (5K 167)
(off Greet St.)
Tait Rd. Croy —7E 140
Takeley Clo. Romf —2K 39
Takhar M. SW11 —2C 102
Talacre Rd. NW5 —6E 48
Talbot Av. N2 —3B 30
Talbot Clo. N15 —4F 33
Talbot Ct. EC3 —2F 169
Talbot Ct. NW9 —3K 45
Talbot Cres. NW4 —5C 28
Talbot Gdns. Ilf —2A 56
Talbot Gro. Ho. W11 —6G 65
(off Lancaster Rd.)
Talbot Ho. E14 —6D 70
Talbot Pl. SE3 —2G 107
Talbot Rd. E6 —2E 72
Talbot Rd. E7 —4J 53
Talbot Rd. N6 —6E 30
Talbot Rd. N15 —4F 33
Talbot Rd. N22 —2G 31
Talbot Rd. SE22 —4E 104
Talbot Rd. W11 & W2 —6H 65
(in two parts)
Talbot Rd. W13 —1A 80
Talbot Rd. Ashf —5A 112
Talbot Rd. Cars —5E 150
Talbot Rd. Dag —6F 57
Talbot Rd. Harr —2K 25
Talbot Rd. Iswth —4A 98
Talbot Rd. S'hall —4C 78
Talbot Rd. T Hth —4D 140
Talbot Rd. Twic —1J 115
Talbot Rd. Wemb —6D 44
Talbot Sq. W2 —6B 66 (1B 164)
Talbot Wlk. NW10 —6A 46
Talbot Wlk. W11 —6G 65
Talbot Yd. SE1 —1D 86 (5E 168)
Talcott Path. SW2 —1A 122
Talfourd Pl. SE15 —1F 105
Talfourd Rd. SE5 —1F 105
Talgarth Mans. W14 —5G 83
(off Talgarth Rd.)
Talgarth Rd. W6 & W14 —5F 83
Talgarth Wlk. NW9 —5A 28
Talia Ho. E14 —3E 88
Talina Cen. SW6 —1A 102
Talisman Clo. Ilf —1B 56
Talisman Sq. SE26 —4G 123
Talisman Way. Wemb —3F 45
Tallack Clo. Harr —7D 10
Tallack Rd. E10 —1B 52
Tall Elms Clo. Brom —5H 143
Talleyrand Ho. SE5 —2C 104
(off Lilford Rd.)
Tallis Clo. E16 —6K 71
Tallis Gro. SE7 —6K 89
Tallis St. EC4 —7A 68 (2K 167)
Tallis Vw. NW10 —6K 45
Tall Trees. SW16 —3K 139
Talma Gdns. Twic —6J 97
Talmage Clo. SE23 —7J 105
Talman Gro. Stan —6J 11
Talma Rd. SW2 —4A 104
Talwin St. E3 —3D 70
Tamar Clo. E3 —1B 70
Tamar Ho. SE11 —5A 86 (5K 173)
(off Kennington La.)
Tamarind Ct. W8 —3K 83
(off St Margaret's La.)
Tamarind Yd. E1 —1G 87
(off Kennet St.)
Tamarisk Sq. W12 —7B 64
Tamar Sq. Wfd G —6E 20
Tamar St. SE7 —3C 90
Tamar Way. N17 —3G 33
Tamesis Gdns. Wor Pk —2A 148
Tamian Ind. Est. Houn —4A 96
Tamian Way. Houn —4A 96
Tamworth. N7 —6J 49
Tamworth Av. Wfd G —6B 20
Tamworth La. Mitc —2F 139
Tamworth Pk. Mitc —3F 139
Tamworth Pl. Croy —2C 152
Tamworth Rd. Croy —2B 152
Tamworth St. SW6 —6J 83
Tamworth Vs. Mitc —4F 139
Tancred Rd. N4 —7B 32
Tandem Cen. Retail Pk. SW19 —1B 138
Tandem Way. SW19 —1B 138
Tandridge Dri. Orp —7H 145
Tandridge Pl. Orp —7H 145
Tanfield Av. NW2 —4B 46
Tanfield Rd. Croy —4C 152
Tangier Rd. Rich —4G 99
Tangleberry Clo. Brom —4D 144
Tangle Tree Clo. N3 —2K 29
Tanglewood Clo. Croy —3J 153
Tanglewood Clo. Stan —2D 10
Tanglewood Clo. Uxb —4C 58
Tanglewood Way. Felt —3K 113
Tangley Gro. SW15 —6B 100
Tangley Pk. Rd. Hamp —5D 114
Tanglyn Av. Shep —5D 130

Tangmere—Theberton St.

Tangmere. N17 —2D 32
(off Willan Rd.)
Tangmere. WC1 —3K 67 (2G 161)
(off Sidmouth St.)
Tangmere Gdns. N'holt —2A 60
(in two parts)
Tangmere Gro. King T —5D 116
Tangmere Way. NW9 —2A 28
Tanhurst Ho. SW2 —7K 103
(off Redlands Way)
Tanhurst Wlk. SE2 —3D 92
Tankerton Houses. WC1 —3J 67 (2F 161)
(off Tankerton St.)
Tankerton Rd. Surb —2F 147
Tankerton St. WC1 —3J 67 (2F 161)
Tankerton Ter. Croy —6K 139
Tankerville Rd. SW16 —7H 121
Tankridge Rd. NW2 —2D 46
Tanner Ho. SE1 —2E 86 (7H 169)
(off Tanner St.)
Tanner Point. E13 —1J 71
(off Pelly Rd.)
Tanners Clo. W on T —6K 131
Tanners End La. N18 —4K 17
Tanner's Hill. SE8 —1B 106
Tanners La. B'side & Ilf —3G 37
Tanner St. SE1 —2E 86 (7H 169)
(in two parts)
Tanner St. Bark —6G 55
Tannery Clo. Beck —5K 141
Tannery Clo. Dag —3H 57
Tannington Ter. N5 —3B 50
Tannsfeld Rd. SE26 —5K 123
Tansley Clo. N7 —5H 49
Tanswell St. SE1 —2A 86 (7J 167)
Tansy Clo. E6 —6E 72
Tantallon Rd. SW12 —1E 120
Tant Av. E16 —6H 71
Tantony Gro. Romf —3D 38
Tanworth Gdns. Pinn —2K 23
Tanyard La. Bex —7G 111
Tanza Rd. NW3 —4D 48
Tapestry Clo. Sutt —7K 149
Tapley Ho. SE1 —2G 87 (7K 169)
(off Wolseley St.)
Taplow. SE17 —5D 86
(off Thurlow St.)
Taplow Ct. Mitc —4C 138
Taplow Ho. E2 —3F 69 (2J 163)
(off Palissy St.)
Taplow Rd. N13 —4H 17
Taplow St. N1 —2C 68 (1D 162)
Tappesfield Rd. SE15 —3J 105
Tapp St. E1 —4H 69
Tapster St. Barn —3C 4
Tara Ct. Beck —2D 142
Tarbert Rd. SE22 —5E 104
Tarbert Wlk. E1 —7J 69
Target Clo. Felt —6G 95
Target Ho. W13 —1B 80
(off Sherwood Clo.)
Target Roundabout. (Junct.) —1D 60
Tariff Cres. SE8 —4B 88
Tariff Rd. N17 —6B 18
Tarleton Ct. N22 —2A 32
Tarleton Gdns. SE23 —2H 123
Tarling Clo. Sidc —3B 128
Tarling Rd. E16 —6H 71
Tarling Rd. N2 —2A 30
Tarling St. E1 —6J 69
Tarling St. Est. E1 —6J 69
Tarn Bank. Enf —5D 6
Tarns, The. NW1 —3G 67 (1A 160)
(off Varndell St.)
Tarn St. SE1 —3C 86
Tarnwood Pk. SE9 —7D 108
Tarquin Ho. SE26 —4G 123
(off High Level Dri.)
Tarragon Clo. SE14 —7A 88
Tarragon Gro. SE26 —6K 123
Tarranbrae. NW6 —7G 47
Tarrant Pl. W1 —5D 66 (6E 158)
Tarrington Clo. SW16 —3H 121
Tartan Ho. E14 —6E 70
Tarver Rd. SE17 —5B 86
Tarves Way. SE10 —7D 88
Tash Pl. N11 —5A 16
Tasker Clo. Hay —7E 76
Tasker Ho. E14 —5B 70
Tasker Ho. Bark —2H 73
Tasker Rd. NW3 —5D 48
Tasman Ct. E14 —4D 88
Tasman Ct. Sun —7G 113
Tasmania Ter. N18 —6H 17
Tasman Rd. SW9 —3J 103
Tasman Wlk. E16 —6B 72
Tasso Rd. W6 —6G 83
Tasso Yd. W6 —6G 83
(off Tasso Rd.)
Tatam Rd. NW10 —7K 45
Tatchbury Ho. SW15 —6B 100
(off Tunworth Cres.)
Tate Britain. —4J 85 (4E 172)
Tate Modern. —1B 86 (4B 168)
Tate Rd. E16 —1D 90
(in two parts)
Tate Rd. Sutt —5J 149
Tatnell Rd. SE23 —6A 106
Tatsfield Ho. SE1 —3D 86 (7F 169)
(off Pardoner St.)
Tattersall Clo. SE9 —5C 108
Tatton Cres. N16 —7F 33
Tatum St. SE17 —4D 86
Tauheed Clo. N4 —2C 50
Taunton Av. SW20 —2D 136
Taunton Clo. Bexh —2K 111
Taunton Clo. Sutt —1J 149
Taunton Dri. N2 —2A 30
Taunton Dri. Enf —3F 7
Taunton Ho. W2 —6A 66
(off Hallfield Est.)
Taunton M. NW1 —4D 66 (4E 158)
Taunton Pl. NW1 —4D 66 (3E 158)
Taunton Rd. SE12 —5G 107
Taunton Rd. Gnfd —1F 61
Taunton Way. Stan —2E 26
Tavern Clo. Cars —7C 138
Taverners Clo. W11 —1G 83
Taverner Sq. N5 —4C 50
Taverners Way. E4 —1B 20
Tavern La. SW9 —2A 104
Tavern Quay. SE16 —4A 88
Tavistock Av. E17 —3K 33
Tavistock Av. Gnfd —2A 62
Tavistock Clo. N16 —5E 50
Tavistock Clo. Stai —7A 112
Tavistock Ct. WC1 —4H 67 (3D 160)
(off Tavistock Sq.)
Tavistock Ct. Croy —1D 152
(off Tavistock Rd.)
Tavistock Cres. W11 —5H 65
(in three parts)
Tavistock Cres. Mitc —4J 139
Tavistock Gdns. Ilf —4J 55
Tavistock Ga. Croy —1D 152
Tavistock Gro. Croy —7D 140
Tavistock Ho. WC1 —4H 67 (3D 160)
Tavistock M. E18 —4J 35
Tavistock M. W11 —6H 65
Tavistock Pl. E18 —4J 35
Tavistock Pl. N14 —7A 6
Tavistock Pl. WC1 —4J 67 (3E 160)
Tavistock Rd. E7 —4H 53
Tavistock Rd. E15 —6H 53
Tavistock Rd. E18 —3J 35
Tavistock Rd. N4 —6D 32
Tavistock Rd. NW10 —2B 64
Tavistock Rd. W11 —6H 65
(in two parts)
Tavistock Rd. Brom —4H 143
Tavistock Rd. Cars —1B 150
Tavistock Rd. Croy —1D 152
Tavistock Rd. Edgw —1G 27
Tavistock Rd. Uxb —5F 41
Tavistock Rd. Well —1C 110
Tavistock Rd. W Dray —1A 76
Tavistock Sq. WC1 —4H 67 (3D 160)
Tavistock St. WC2 —7J 67 (2F 167)
(in two parts)
Tavistock Ter. N19 —3H 49
Tavistock Tower. SE16 —3A 88
Tavistock Wlk. Cars —1B 150
Taviton St. WC1 —4H 67 (3C 160)
Tavy Bri. SE2 —2C 92
Tavy Bri. Cen. SE2 —2C 92
Tavy Clo. SE11 —5K 173
(in two parts)
Tawney Rd. SE28 —7B 74
Tawny Clo. W13 —1B 80
Tawny Clo. Felt —3J 113
Tawny Way. SE16 —4K 87
Tayben Av. Twic —6J 97
Taybridge Rd. SW11 —3E 102
Tay Bldgs. SE1 —7G 169
Tayburn Clo. E14 —6E 70
Tayfield Clo. Uxb —3E 40
Tayler Ct. NW8 —1B 66
(off Dorman Way)
Taylor Av. Rich —2H 99
Taylor Clo. N17 —7B 18
Taylor Clo. SE8 —6B 88
Taylor Clo. Hamp H —5G 115
Taylor Clo. Houn —1G 97
Taylor Ct. E15 —5E 52
Taylor Ct. SE20 —2J 141
(off Elmers End Rd.)
Taylor Rd. Mitc —7C 120
Taylor Rd. Wall —5F 151
Taylors Bldgs. SE18 —4F 91
Taylors Clo. Sidc —3K 127
Taylors Ct. Felt —2J 113
Taylors Grn. W3 —6A 64
Taylors La. NW10 —7A 46
Taylor's La. SE26 —4H 123
Taylors La. Barn —1C 4
Taylorsmead. NW7 —5H 13
Taymount Grange. SE23 —2J 123
Taymount Ri. SE23 —2J 123
Tayport Clo. N1 —7J 49
Tayside Ct. SE5 —4D 104
Tayside Dri. Edgw —3C 12
Taywood Rd. N'holt —3D 60
Teak Clo. SE16 —1A 88
Tealby Ct. N7 —5K 49
(off George's Rd.)
Teal Clo. E16 —5B 72
Teal Ct. NW10 —6K 45
Teal Ct. SE8 —6B 88
(off Abinger Gro.)
Teal Dri. N'wd —1E 22
Teale St. E2 —2G 69
Tealing Dri. Eps —4K 147
Teal Pl. Sutt —5H 149
Teasel Clo. Croy —1K 153
Teasel Way. E15 —3G 71
Tebworth Rd. N17 —7A 18
Teck Clo. Iswth —2A 98
Tedder Clo. Chess —5C 146
Tedder Clo. Ruis —5J 41
Tedder Clo. Uxb —7B 40
Tedder Rd. S Croy —7J 153
Teddington. —5A 116
Teddington Bus. Pk. Tedd —6K 115
(off Station Rd.)
Teddington Pk. Tedd —5K 115
Teddington Pk. Rd. Tedd —4K 115
Ted Roberts Ho. E2 —2H 69
(off Parmiter St.)
Tedworth Gdns. SW3 —5D 84 (6E 170)
Tedworth Sq. SW3 —5D 84 (6E 170)
Tees Av. Gnfd —2J 61
Tees Ct. W7 —6H 61
(off Hanway Rd.)
Teesdale Av. Iswth —1A 98
Teesdale Clo. E2 —2G 69
Teesdale Gdns. SE25 —2E 140
Teesdale Gdns. Iswth —1A 98
Teesdale Rd. E11 —6H 35
Teesdale St. E2 —2H 69
Teesdale Yd. E2 —2H 69
Teeswater Ct. Eri —3D 92
Tee, The. W3 —6A 64
Teevan Clo. Croy —7G 141
Teevan Rd. Croy —1G 153
Teignmouth Clo. SW4 —4H 103
Teignmouth Clo. Edgw —2F 27
Teignmouth Gdns. Gnfd —2A 62
Teignmouth Pde. Gnfd —2A 62
Teignmouth Rd. NW2 —5F 47
Teignmouth Rd. Well —2C 110
Telcote Way. Ruis —7A 24
Telecom Tower, The. —5G 67 (5A 160)
Telegraph Hill. NW3 —3K 47
Telegraph La. Clay —5A 146
Telegraph M. Ilf —1A 56
Telegraph Pas. SW2 —7J 103
Telegraph Path. Chst —5F 127
Telegraph Pl. E14 —4D 88
Telegraph Rd. SW15 —7D 100
Telegraph St. EC2 —6D 68 (7E 162)
Teleman Sq. SE3 —4K 107
Telephone Pl. SW6 —6H 83
Telfer Clo. W3 —2J 81
Telfer Ho. EC1 —3C 68 (2B 162)
(off Lever St.)
Telferscot Rd. SW12 —1H 121
Telford Av. SW2 —1H 121
Telford Clo. E17 —7A 34
Telford Clo. SE19 —6F 123
Telford Dri. W on T —7A 132
Telford Ho. SE1 —3C 86
(off Tiverton St.)
Telford Rd. N11 —5B 16
Telford Rd. NW9 —6C 28
Telford Rd. SE9 —2H 127
Telford Rd. W10 —5G 65
Telford Rd. S'hall —7F 61
Telford Rd. Twic —7E 96
Telfords Yd. E1 —7G 69
(off Pennington St.)
Telford Ter. SW1 —7A 172
Telford Way. W3 —5A 64
Telford Way. Hay —5C 60
Telham Rd. E6 —2E 72
Tell Gro. SE22 —4F 105
Tellson Av. SE18 —1B 108
Temeraire St. SE16 —2J 87
Tempelhof Av. NW4 —7E 28
Temperley Rd. SW12 —7E 102
Templar Ct. NW8 —2A 158
Templar Dri. SE28 —6D 74
Templar Ho. NW2 —6H 47
Templar Pl. Hamp —7E 114
Templars Av. NW11 —6H 29
Templars Cres. N3 —2J 29
Templars Dri. Harr —6C 10
Templars Ho. E15 —5D 52
Templar St. SE5 —2B 104
Temple. EC4 —2J 167
Temple Av. EC4 —7A 68 (2K 167)
Temple Av. N20 —7G 5
Temple Av. Croy —2B 154
Temple Av. Dag —1G 57
Temple Bar. —1J 167
Temple Chambers. EC4 —2K 167
Temple Clo. E11 —7G 35
Temple Clo. N3 —2H 29
Temple Clo. SE28 —3G 91
Templecombe Rd. E9 —1J 69
Templecombe Way. Mord —5G 137
Temple Ct. SW8 —7J 85
(off Thorncroft St.)
Templecroft. Ashf —6F 113
Temple Dwellings. E2 —2H 69
(off Temple St.)
Temple Fortune. —5H 29
Temple Fortune Hill. NW11 —5J 29
Temple Fortune La. NW11 —6H 29
Temple Fortune Pde. NW11 —5H 29
Temple Gdns. EC4 —7A 68 (2J 167)
(off Middle Temple La.)
Temple Gdns. N13 —2G 17
Temple Gdns. NW11 —6H 29
Temple Gdns. Dag —3D 56
Temple Gro. NW11 —6J 29
Temple Gro. Enf —2G 7
Temple Hall Ct. E4 —2A 20
Temple La. EC4 —6A 68 (1K 167)
Templeman Rd. W7 —5K 61
Templemead Clo. W3 —6A 64
Temple Mead Clo. Stan —6G 11
Templemead Ho. E9 —4A 52
Temple Mill La. E10 & E15 —4D 52
(in two parts)
Temple Mills. —4D 52
Temple Pde. Barn —7G 5
(off Netherlands Rd.)
Temple Pk. Uxb —3C 58
Temple Pl. WC2 —7K 67 (2H 167)
Temple Rd. E6 —1C 72
Temple Rd. N8 —4K 31
Temple Rd. NW2 —4E 46
Temple Rd. W4 —3J 81
Temple Rd. W5 —3D 80
Temple Rd. Croy —4D 152
Temple Rd. Houn —4F 97
Temple Rd. Rich —2F 99
Temple Sheen. SW14 —4J 99
Temple Sheen Rd. SW14 —4H 99
Temple St. E2 —2H 69
Templeton Av. E4 —4H 19
Templeton Clo. N15 —6D 32
Templeton Clo. N16 —5E 50
Templeton Clo. SE19 —1D 140
Templeton Pl. SW5 —4J 83
Templeton Rd. N15 —6D 32
Temple Way. Sutt —3B 150
Temple W. M. SE11 —3B 86
(off West Sq.)
Templewood. W13 —5B 62
Templewood Av. NW3 —3K 47
Templewood Gdns. NW3 —3K 47
Templewood Point. NW2 —2H 47
(off Granville Rd.)
Tempo Ho. N'holt —3B 60
Tempsford Clo. Enf —3H 7
Tempsford Ct. Harr —6K 25
Temsford Clo. Harr —2G 25
Tenbury Clo. E7 —5B 54
Tenbury Ct. SW12 —1H 121
Tenby Av. Harr —2B 26
Tenby Clo. N15 —4F 33
Tenby Clo. Romf —6E 38
Tenby Ct. E17 —5A 34
Tenby Gdns. N'holt —6E 42
Tenby Ho. W2 —6A 66
(off Hallfield Est.)
Tenby Ho. Hay —3E 76
Tenby Mans. W1 —5E 66 (5H 159)
(off Nottingham St.)
Tenby Rd. E17 —5A 34
Tenby Rd. Edgw —1F 27
Tenby Rd. Enf —4D 8
Tenby Rd. Romf —6E 38
Tenby Rd. Well —1D 110
Tench St. E1 —1H 87
Tenda Rd. SE16 —4H 87
Tendring Way. Romf —5C 38
Tenham Av. SW2 —1H 121
Tenison Ct. W1 —7G 67 (2A 166)
Tenison Way. SE1 —1K 85 (5H 167)
Tenniel Clo. W2 —7A 66
Tennis Ct. La. E Mol —3K 133
Tennison Rd. SE25 —4F 141
Tennis St. SE1 —2D 86 (6E 168)
Tenniswood Rd. Enf —1K 7
Tennyson. N8 —3J 31
(off Boyton Clo.)
Tennyson Av. E11 —7J 35
Tennyson Av. E12 —7C 54
Tennyson Av. NW9 —3J 27
Tennyson Av. N Mald —5D 136
Tennyson Av. Twic —1K 115
Tennyson Clo. Enf —5E 8
Tennyson Clo. Felt —6H 95
Tennyson Clo. Well —1J 109
Tennyson Ct. SW6 —1K 101
(off Maltings Pl.)
Tennyson Ho. SE17 —5C 86
(off Browning St.)
Tennyson Ho. Belv —5F 93
Tennyson Mans. W14 —6H 83
(off Queen's Club Gdns.)
Tennyson Rd. E10 —1D 52
Tennyson Rd. E15 —7G 53
Tennyson Rd. E17 —6B 34
Tennyson Rd. NW6 —1H 65
(in two parts)
Tennyson Rd. NW7 —5H 13
Tennyson Rd. SE20 —7K 123
Tennyson Rd. SW19 —6A 120
Tennyson Rd. W7 —7K 61
Tennyson Rd. Ashf —5A 112
Tennyson Rd. Houn —2G 97
Tennyson St. SW8 —2F 103
Tensing Rd. S'hall —3E 78
Tentelow La. S'hall —5E 78
Tenterden Clo. NW4 —3F 29
Tenterden Clo. SE9 —4C 126
Tenterden Dri. NW4 —3F 29
Tenterden Gdns. NW4 —3F 29
Tenterden Gdns. Croy —7G 141
Tenterden Gro. NW4 —3F 29
Tenterden Ho. SE17 —5E 86
(off Surrey Gro.)
Tenterden Rd. N17 —7A 18
Tenterden Rd. Croy —7G 141
Tenterden Rd. Dag —2F 57
Tenterden St. W1 —6F 67 (1K 165)
Tenter Ground. E1 —5F 69 (6J 163)
Tenter Pas. E1 —6F 69 (1K 169)
(off N. Tenter St.)
Tent Peg La. Pet W —5G 145
Tent St. E1 —4H 69
Terborch Way. SE22 —5E 104
Teredo St. SE16 —3K 87
(in two parts)
Terence Ct. Belv —6F 93
(off Charton Clo.)
Teresa M. E17 —4C 34
Teresa Wlk. N10 —5F 31
Terling Clo. E11 —3H 53
Terling Rd. Dag —2G 57
Terling Wlk. N1 —1C 68
(off Popham St.)
Terminal Ho. Stan —5J 11
Terminus Pl. SW1 —3F 85 (2K 171)
Terrace Av. NW10 —4E 64
Terrace Gdns. SW13 —2B 100
Terrace La. Rich —6E 98
Terrace Rd. E9 —7J 51
Terrace Rd. E13 —2J 71
Terrace Rd. W on T —7J 131
Terraces, The. NW8 —2B 66
(off Queen's Ter.)
Terrace, The. E4 —3B 20
(off Newgate St.)
Terrace, The. EC4 —1K 167
Terrace, The. N3 —2H 29
Terrace, The. NW6 —1J 65
Terrace, The. SE8 —4B 88
(off Longshore)
Terrace, The. SE23 —7A 106
Terrace, The. SW13 —2A 100
Terrace, The. Wfd G —6D 20
Terrace Wlk. SW11 —7H 171
Terrace Wlk. Dag —5E 56
Terrapin Rd. SW17 —3F 121
Terretts Pl. N1 —7B 50
(off Upper St.)
Terrick Rd. N22 —1J 31
Terrick St. W12 —6D 64
Terrilands. Pinn —3D 24
Territorial Ho. SE11 —4K 173
Terront Rd. N15 —4C 32
Tersha St. Rich —4F 99
Tessa Sanderson Pl. SW8 —3F 103
(off Daley Thompson Way)
Tessa Sanderson Way. Gnfd —5H 43
Testerton Wlk. W11 —7F 65
Testwood Ct. W7 —7J 61
Tetbury Pl. N1 —1B 68
Tetcott Rd. SW10 —7A 84
(in two parts)
Tetherdown. N10 —3E 30
Tetty Way. Brom —2J 143
Teversham La. SW8 —1J 103
Teviot Clo. Well —1B 110
Teviot Est. E14 —5D 70
Teviot St. E14 —4E 70
Tewkesbury Av. SE23 —1H 123
Tewkesbury Av. Pinn —5C 24
Tewkesbury Clo. N15 —6D 32
Tewkesbury Gdns. NW9 —3H 27
Tewkesbury Rd. N15 —6D 32
Tewkesbury Rd. W13 —1A 80
Tewkesbury Rd. Cars —1B 150
Tewkesbury Ter. N11 —6B 16
Tewson Rd. SE18 —5J 91
Teynham Av. Enf —6J 7
Teynham Ct. Beck —3D 142
Teynham Grn. Brom —5J 143
Teynton Ter. N17 —1C 32
Thackeray Av. N17 —2G 33
Thackeray Clo. SW19 —7F 119
Thackeray Clo. Harr —1E 42
Thackeray Clo. Iswth —2A 98
Thackeray Clo. Uxb —6D 58
Thackeray Ct. SW3 —5D 84 (5E 170)
Thackeray Ct. W14 —3G 83
(off Blythe Rd.)
Thackeray Dri. Romf —7A 38
Thackeray Ho. WC1 —3E 160
Thackeray Lodge. Felt —6F 95
Thackeray M. E8 —6G 51
Thackeray Rd. E6 —2B 72
Thackeray Rd. SW8 —2F 103
Thackeray St. W8 —3K 83
Thackrah Clo. N2 —2A 30
Thakeham Clo. SE26 —4H 123
Thalia Clo. SE10 —6F 89
Thame Rd. SE16 —2K 87
Thames Av. SW10 —1A 102
Thames Av. Dag —4G 75
Thames Av. Gnfd —2K 61
Thames Bank. SW14 —2J 99
Thamesbank Pl. SE28 —6C 74
Thames Barrier Ind. Area. SE18 —3B 90
(off Faraday Way)
Thames Barrier Vis. Cen. —3B 90
Thamesbrook. SW3 —5C 84
(off Dovehouse St.)
Thames Circ. E14 —4C 88
Thames Clo. Hamp —2F 133
Thames Ct. SE15 —7F 87
(off Daniel Gdns.)
Thames Ct. W7 —6J 61
(off Hanway Rd.)
Thames Cres. W4 —7A 82
Thames Ditton. —6A 134
Thames Ditton Miniature Railway. —1A 146
Thames Dri. Ruis —6E 22
Thames Exchange Building. EC4 —3D 168
Thames Eyot. Twic —1A 116
Thamesfield Ct. Shep —7E 130
Thamesfield M. Shep —7E 130
Thames Flood Barrier, The. —3A 90
Thamesgate Clo. Rich —4B 116
Thames Ga. Way. Dag —2F 75
Thameshill Av. Romf —2J 39
Thames Ho. EC4 —7C 68 (2D 168)
(off Up. Thames St.)
Thames Ho. SW1 —4J 85
(off Millbank)
Thameside. Tedd —7D 116
Thameside. W Mol —3F 133
Thameside Cen. Bren —6F 81
Thameside Ind. Est. E16 —2B 90
Thameside Wlk. SE28 —6A 74
Thames Lock. Sun —3A 132
Thamesmead. —1A 92
Thames Mead. W on T —7J 131
Thamesmead Central. —7A 74
Thamesmead East. —2G 93
Thamesmead North. —6C 74
Thames Mdw. Shep —7F 131
Thames Mdw. W Mol —2E 132
Thamesmead South. —2D 92
Thamesmead South West. —2K 91
Thamesmead West. —3H 91
Thamesmere Dri. SE28 —7A 74
Thames Pl. SW15 —3F 101
(in two parts)
Thamespoint. Tedd —7D 116
Thames Quay. E14 —2D 88
Thames Quay. SW10 —1A 102
(off Chelsea Harbour)
Thames Rd. E16 —1B 90
Thames Rd. W4 —6G 81
Thames Rd. Bark —3J 73
Thames Rd. Ind. Est. E16 —2B 90
Thames Side. King T —1D 134
Thames Side. Th Dit —6B 134
Thames St. SE10 —6D 88
Thames St. Hamp —1F 133
Thames St. King T —2D 134
(in two parts)
Thames St. Sun —4K 131
Thames St. W on T —7H 131
Thames Va. Clo. Houn —3E 96
Thamesview Houses. W on T —6J 131
Thames Village. W4 —1J 99
Thames Wlk. SW11 —7C 84
Thanescroft Gdns. Croy —3E 152
Thanet Ct. W3 —6G 63
Thanet Dri. Kes —3B 156
Thanet Ho. WC1 —3J 67 (2E 160)
Thanet Pl. Croy —4C 152
Thanet Rd. Bex —7G 111
Thanet St. WC1 —3J 67 (2E 160)
Thane Vs. N7 —3K 49
Thane Works. N7 —3K 49
Thant Clo. E10 —3D 52
Tharp Rd. Wall —5H 151
Thatcham Ct. N20 —7F 5
Thatcham Gdns. N20 —7F 5
Thatcher Clo. W Dray —2A 76
Thatchers Way. Iswth —5H 97
Thatches Gro. Romf —4E 38
Thavie's Inn. EC1 —6A 68 (7K 161)
Thaxted Ct. N1 —2D 68 (1F 163)
(off Fairbank Est.)
Thaxted Ho. Dag —7H 57
Thaxted Pl. SW20 —7F 119
Thaxted Rd. SE9 —3G 127
Thaxted Rd. Buck H —1H 21
Thaxton Rd. W14 —6H 83
Thayers Farm Rd. Beck —1A 142
Thayer St. W1 —6E 66 (6H 159)
Theatre Mus. —2F 167
Theatre Royal. —6F 53
Theatre Sq. E15 —6F 53
Theatre St. SW11 —3D 102
Theberton St. N1 —1A 68

Theed St.—Tolworth Rd.

Theed St. SE1 —1A 86 (5K 167)
Thelma Gdns. SE3 —1B 108
Thelma Gro. Tedd —6A 116
Theobald Cres. Harr —1G 25
Theobald Rd. E17 —7B 34
Theobald Rd. Croy —2B 152
Theobalds Av. N12 —4F 15
Theobalds Ct. N4 —3C 50
Theobald's Rd. WC1 —5K 67 (5G 161)
Theobald St. SE1 —3D 86
Theodora Way. Pinn —3H 23
Theodore Ct. SE13 —6F 107
Theodore Rd. SE13 —6F 107
Therapia La. Croy —7H 139
(in two parts)
Therapia Rd. SE22 —6J 105
Theresa Rd. W6 —4C 82
Therfield Ct. N4 —2C 50
Thermopylae Ga. E14 —4D 88
Theseus Wlk. N1 —1B 162
Thesiger Rd. SE20 —7K 123
Thessaly Ho. SW8 —7G 85
(off Thessaly Rd.)
Thessaly Rd. SW8 —7G 85
Thesus Ho. E14 —6E 70
Thetford Clo. N13 —6G 17
Thetford Gdns. Dag —1E 74
Thetford Ho. SE1 —3F 87 (7J 169)
(off Maltby St.)
Thetford Rd. Ashf —4A 112
Thetford Rd. Dag —7D 56
Thetford Rd. N Mald —6K 135
Thetis Ter. Rich —6G 81
Theydon Gro. Wfd G —6F 21
Theydon Rd. E5 —2J 51
Theydon St. E17 —7B 34
Thicket Cres. Sutt —4A 150
Thicket Gro. SE19 —7G 123
Thicket Gro. Dag —6C 56
Thicket Rd. SE20 —7G 123
Thicket Rd. Sutt —4A 150
Thicket, The. W Dray —6A 58
Third Av. E12 —4C 54
Third Av. E13 —3J 71
Third Av. E17 —5C 34
Third Av. W3 —1B 82
Third Av. W10 —3G 65
Third Av. Dag —1H 75
Third Av. Enf —5A 8
Third Av. Hay —1H 77
Third Av. Romf —6C 38
Third Av. Wemb —2D 44
Third Clo. W Mol —4G 133
Third Cross Rd. Twic —2H 115
Third Way. Wemb —4H 45
Thirleby Rd. SW1 —3G 85 (2B 172)
Thirleby Rd. Edgw —1K 27
Thirlestane Ct. N10 —2E 30
Thirlmere. NW1 —3F 67 (1K 159)
(off Cumberland Mkt.)
Thirlmere Av. Gnfd —3C 62
Thirlmere Gdns. Wemb —1C 44
Thirlmere Ri. Brom —6H 125
Thirlmere Rd. N10 —1F 31
Thirlmere Rd. SW16 —4H 121
Thirlmere Rd. Bexh —2J 111
Thirsk Clo. N'holt —6E 42
Thirsk Rd. SE25 —4D 140
Thirsk Rd. SW11 —3E 102
Thirsk Rd. Mitc —7E 120
Thistlebrook. SE2 —3C 92
Thistlecroft Gdns. Stan —1D 26
Thistledene. Th Dit —6J 133
Thistledene Av. Harr —3C 42
Thistle Gro. SW10 —5A 84
Thistle Ho. E14 —6E 70
Thistlemead. Chst —2F 145
Thistlewaite Rd. E5 —3H 51
Thistlewood Clo. N7 —2K 49
Thistleworth Clo. Iswth —7H 79
Thistleworth Marina. Iswth —4B 98
(off Railshead Rd.)
Thistley Clo. N12 —6H 15
Thistley Ct. SE8 —6D 88
Thomas A'Beckett Clo. Wemb —4K 43
Thomas Baines Rd. SW11 —3B 102
Thomas Burt Ho. E2 —3H 69
(off Canrobert St.)
Thomas Ct. E17 —5D 34
Thomas Cribb M. E6 —6E 72
Thomas Darby Ct. W11 —6G 65
(off Lancaster Rd.)
Thomas Dean Rd. SE26 —4B 124
Thomas Dinwiddy Rd. SE12 —2K 125
Thomas Doyle St. SE1 —3B 86 (7A 168)
Thomas England Ho. Romf —6K 39
(off Waterloo Gdns.)
Thomas Hewlett Ho. Harr —4J 43
Thomas Ho. Sutt —7K 149
Thomas La. SE6 —7C 106
Thomas More Highwalk. EC2 —5C 68
(off Beech St.)
Thomas More Ho. EC2 —6C 162
Thomas More Sq. E1 —7G 69
(off Thomas More St.)
Thomas More St. E1 —7G 69
Thomas More Way. N2 —3A 30
Thomas Neals Shop. Mall. WC2 —1E 166
Thomas N. Ter. E16 —5H 71
(off Barking Rd.)
Thomas Pl. W8 —3K 83
Thomas Rd. E14 —6B 70
Thomas Rd. Ind. Est. E14 —5C 70
(in two parts)
Thomas St. SE18 —4F 91
Thomas Turner Path. Croy —2C 152
(off George St.)
Thomas Wall Clo. Sutt —5K 149
Thomas Watson Cottage Homes. Barn
(off Leecroft Rd.) —4B 4
Thompson Av. Rich —3G 99
Thompson Clo. Ilf —2G 55
Thompson Rd. SE22 —6F 105
Thompson Rd. Dag —3F 57
Thompson Rd. Uxb —1A 58
Thompson's Av. SE5 —7C 86
Thomson Cres. Croy —1A 152
Thomson Ho. E14 —6C 70
Thomson Ho. SE17 —4E 86
(off Tatum St.)
Thomson Ho. SW1 —6D 172
Thomson Ho. S'hall —7C 60
(off Broadway, The)
Thomson Rd. Harr —3J 25
Thorburn Sq. SE1 —4G 87
Thorburn Way. SW19 —1B 138
Thoresby St. N1 —3C 68 (1D 162)
Thorkhill Gdns. Th Dit —1A 146
Thorkhill Rd. Th Dit —1A 146
Thornaby Gdns. N18 —6B 18
Thorn Av. Bus H —1B 10
Thorn Bank. Edgw —6B 12
Thornbury. NW4 —4D 28
(off Prince of Wales Clo.)
Thornbury Av. Iswth —7H 79
Thornbury Clo. N16 —5E 50
Thornbury Ct. W11 —7J 65
(off Chepstow Vs.)
Thornbury Ct. Iswth —7J 79
Thornbury Rd. SW2 —6J 103
Thornbury Rd. Iswth —7H 79
Thornbury Sq. N6 —1G 49
Thornby Rd. E5 —3J 51
Thorncliffe Rd. SW4 —6J 103
Thorncliffe Rd. S'hall —5D 78
Thorn Clo. Brom —6E 144
Thorn Clo. N'holt —3D 60
Thorncombe Rd. SE22 —5E 104
Thorncroft Rd. Sutt —5K 149
Thorncroft St. SW8 —7J 85
Thorndean St. SW18 —2A 120
Thorndene. SE28 —7B 74
Thorndene Av. N11 —1K 15
Thorndike Av. N'holt —1B 60
Thorndike Clo. SW10 —7A 84
Thorndike Ho. SW1 —5H 85 (5C 172)
(off Vauxhall Bri. Rd.)
Thorndike St. SW1 —4H 85 (4C 172)
Thorndon Clo. Orp —2K 145
Thorndon Gdns. Eps —5A 148
Thorndon Rd. Orp —2K 145
Thorne Clo. E11 —4G 53
Thorne Clo. E16 —6J 71
Thorne Clo. Ashf —7E 112
Thorne Clo. Eri —6H 93
Thorne Ho. E14 —3E 88
Thorne Ho. Clay —7B 146
Thorneloe Gdns. Croy —5A 152
Thorne Pas. SW13 —2A 100
Thorne Rd. SW8 —7J 85
Thornes Clo. Beck —3E 142
Thorne St. SW13 —3A 100
Thornet Wood Rd. Brom —3E 144
Thorney Ct. W8 —2A 84
(off Palace Ga.)
Thorney Cres. SW11 —7B 84
Thorneycroft Clo. W on T —6A 132
Thorney Hedge Rd. W4 —4H 81
Thorney St. SW1 —4J 85 (3E 172)
Thornfield Av. NW7 —1G 29
Thornfield Ct. NW7 —1G 29
Thornfield Ho. E14 —7C 70
Thornfield Pde. NW7 —7B 14
(off Holders Hill Rd.)
Thornfield Rd. W12 —2D 82
Thornford Rd. SE13 —5E 106
Thorngate Rd. W9 —4J 65
Thorngrove Rd. E13 —1K 71
Thornham Gro. E15 —5F 53
Thornham St. SE10 —6D 88
Thornhaugh M. WC1 —4H 67 (4D 160)
Thornhaugh St. WC1 —4H 67 (4D 160)
Thornhill Av. SE18 —7J 91
Thornhill Av. Surb —2E 146
Thornhill Bri. Wharf. N1 —1K 67
Thornhill Cres. N1 —7K 49
Thornhill Gdns. E10 —2D 52
Thornhill Gdns. Bark —7J 55
Thornhill Gro. N1 —7K 49
Thornhill Ho. W4 —5A 82
(off Wood St.)
Thornhill Houses. N1 —7A 50
Thornhill Rd. E10 —2D 52
Thornhill Rd. N1 —7A 50
Thornhill Rd. Croy —7C 140
Thornhill Rd. Surb —2E 146
Thornhill Rd. Uxb —4B 40
Thornhill Sq. N1 —7K 49
Thornhill Way. Shep —5C 130
Thornicroft Ho. SW9 —2K 103
(off Stockwell Rd.)
Thornlaw Rd. SE27 —4A 122
Thornley Clo. N17 —7B 18
Thornley Dri. Harr —2F 43
Thornsbeach Rd. SE6 —1E 124
Thornsett Pl. SE20 —2H 141
Thornsett Rd. SE20 —2H 141
Thornsett Rd. SW18 —1K 119
Thornsett Ter. SE20 —2H 141
(off Croydon Rd.)
Thorn Ter. SE15 —3J 105
Thornton Av. SW2 —1H 121
Thornton Av. W4 —4A 82
Thornton Av. Croy —6K 139
Thornton Av. W Dray —3B 76
Thornton Clo. W Dray —3B 76
Thornton Dene. Beck —2C 142
Thornton Gdns. SW12 —1H 121
Thornton Heath. —4C 140
Thornton Heath Pond. (Junct.) —5A 140
Thornton Hill. SW19 —7G 119
Thornton Ho. SE17 —4E 86
(off Townsend St.)
Thornton Pl. W1 —5D 66 (5E 158)
Thornton Rd. E11 —2F 53
Thornton Rd. N18 —3D 18
Thornton Rd. SW12 —7H 103
Thornton Rd. SW14 —4K 99
Thornton Rd. SW19 —6F 119
Thornton Rd. Barn —3B 4
Thornton Rd. Belv —4H 93
Thornton Rd. Brom —5J 125
Thornton Rd. Cars —1B 150
Thornton Rd. Croy & T Hth —7K 139
Thornton Rd. Ilf —4F 55
Thornton Rd. E. SW19 —6F 119
Thornton Row. T Hth —5A 140
Thornton's Farm Av. Romf —1J 57
Thornton St. SW9 —2A 104
Thornton Way. NW11 —5K 29
Thorntree Ct. W5 —5E 62
Thorntree Rd. SE7 —5B 90
Thornville Gro. Mitc —2B 138
Thornville St. SE8 —1C 106
Thornwell Ct. W7 —2J 79
(off Du Burstow Ter.)
Thornwood Clo. E18 —2K 35
Thornwood Ho. Buck H —1H 21
Thornwood Rd. SE13 —5G 107
Thornycroft Ho. W4 —5A 82
(off Fraser St.)
Thorogood Gdns. E15 —5G 53
Thorogood Way. Rain —1K 75
Thorold Ho. SE1 —2C 86 (6C 168)
(off Pepper St.)
Thorold Rd. N22 —7D 16
Thorold Rd. Ilf —2F 55
Thorparch Rd. SW8 —1H 103
Thorpebank Rd. W12 —1C 82
Thorpe Clo. SE26 —4K 123
Thorpe Clo. W10 —6G 65
Thorpe Ct. Enf —3G 7
Thorpe Cres. E17 —2B 34
Thorpedale Gdns. Ilf —4E 36
Thorpedale Rd. N4 —2J 49
Thorpe Hall Rd. E17 —1E 34
Thorpe Ho. N1 —1K 67
(off Barnsbury Est.)
Thorpe Pk. —4J 139
Thorpe Rd. E6 —1D 72
Thorpe Rd. E7 —4H 53
Thorpe Rd. E17 —2E 34
Thorpe Rd. N15 —6E 32
Thorpe Rd. Bark —7H 55
Thorpe Rd. King T —7E 116
Thorpewood Av. SE26 —2H 123
Thorpland Av. Uxb —3E 40
Thorsden Way. SE19 —5E 122
Thorverton Rd. NW2 —3G 47
Thoydon Rd. E3 —2A 70
Thrale Rd. SW16 —4G 121
Thrale St. SE1 —1C 86 (5D 168)
Thrasher Clo. E8 —1F 69
Thrawl St. E1 —5F 69 (6K 163)
Thrayle Ho. SW9 —3K 103
(off Benedict Rd.)
Threadgold Ho. N1 —6D 50
(off Dovercourt Est.)
Threadneedle St. EC2 —6D 68 (1F 169)
Three Barrels Wlk. EC4 —7C 68 (2D 168)
(off Queen St. Pl.)
Three Bridges Bus. Cen. S'hall —2G 79
Three Colt Corner. E2 & E1 —3K 163
Three Colts La. E2 —4H 69
Three Colt St. E14 —6B 70
Three Corners. Bexh —2H 111
Three Cups Yd. WC1 —6H 161
Three Kings Yd. W1 —7F 67 (2J 165)
Three Mill La. E3 —3E 70
Three Oak La. SE1 —2F 87 (6J 169)
Three Oaks Clo. Uxb —3B 40
Three Quays. EC3 —3H 169
Three Quays Wlk. EC3 —7E 68
Threshers Pl. W11 —7G 65
Thriffwood. SE26 —3J 123
Thrigby Rd. Chess —6F 147
Thring Ho. SW9 —2K 103
(off Stockwell Rd.)
Throckmorten Rd. E16 —6K 71
Throgmorton Av. EC2 —6D 68 (7F 163)
(in two parts)
Throgmorton St. EC2 —6D 68 (7F 163)
Throwley Clo. SE2 —3C 92
(in two parts)
Throwley Rd. Sutt —5K 149
Throwley Way. Sutt —4K 149
Thrupp Clo. Mitc —2F 139
Thrush Grn. Harr —4E 24
Thrush St. SE17 —5C 86
Thruxton Way. SE15 —7F 87
Thurbarn Rd. SE6 —5D 124
Thurland Ho. SE16 —4H 87
(off Camilla Rd.)
Thurland Rd. SE16 —3G 87
Thurlby Clo. Harr —6A 26
Thurlby Clo. Wfd G —5J 21
Thurlby Cft. NW4 —3E 28
(off Mulberry Clo.)
Thurlby Rd. SE27 —4A 122
Thurlby Rd. Wemb —6D 44
Thurleigh Av. SW12 —6E 102
Thurleigh Rd. SW12 —7D 102
Thurleston Av. Mord —5G 137
Thurlestone Av. N12 —6J 15
Thurlestone Av. Ilf —4K 55
Thurlestone Clo. Shep —6E 130
Thurlestone Ct. S'hall —6F 61
(off Howard Rd.)
Thurlestone Pde. Shep —6E 130
(off High St.)
Thurlestone Rd. SE27 —3A 122
Thurloe Clo. SW7 —4C 84 (3C 170)
Thurloe Ct. SW3 —4C 84 (4C 170)
(off Fulham Ct.)
Thurloe Pl. SW7 —4B 84 (3B 170)
Thurloe Pl. M. SW7 —3B 170
Thurloe Sq. SW7 —4C 84 (3C 170)
Thurloe St. SW7 —4B 84 (3B 170)
Thurlow Clo. E4 —6J 19
Thurlow Gdns. Wemb —5D 44
Thurlow Hill. SE21 —1C 122
Thurlow Ho. SW16 —3J 121
Thurlow Pk. Rd. SE21 —2B 122
Thurlow Rd. NW3 —5B 48
Thurlow Rd. W7 —2A 80
Thurlow St. SE17 —5D 86
(in two parts)
Thurlow Ter. NW5 —5E 48
Thurlow Wlk. SE17 —5E 86
(in two parts)
Thurlstone Rd. Ruis —3J 41
Thurnby Ct. Twic —3J 115
Thurnscoe. NW1 —1G 67
(off Pratt St.)
Thursland Rd. Sidc —5E 128
Thursley Cres. New Ad —7E 154
Thursley Gdns. SW19 —2F 119
Thursley Ho. SW2 —7K 103
(off Holmewood Gdns.)
Thursley Rd. SE9 —3D 126
Thurso Ho. NW6 —2K 65
Thurso St. SW17 —4B 120
Thurstan Dwellings. WC2
(off Newton St.) —6J 67 (7F 161)
Thurstan Rd. SW20 —7D 118
Thurston Ind. Est. SE13 —3D 106
Thurston Rd. SE13 —2D 106
Thurston Rd. S'hall —6D 60
Thurtle Rd. E2 —2F 69
Thwaite Clo. Eri —6J 93
Thyra Gro. N12 —6E 14
Tibbatts Rd. E3 —4D 70
Tibbenham Pl. SE6 —2C 124
Tibbenham Wlk. E13 —2H 71
Tibberton Sq. N1 —1C 68
Tibbet's Clo. SW19 —1F 119
Tibbet's Corner. (Junct.) —7F 101
Tibbet's Ride. SW15 —7F 101
Tiber Gdns. N1 —1J 67
Ticehurst Clo. Orp —7A 128
Ticehurst Rd. SE23 —2A 124
Tickford Clo. SE2 —2C 92
Tickford Ho. NW8 —3C 66 (2C 158)
Tidal Basin Rd. E16 —7H 71
Tidbury Ct. SW8 —7G 85
(off Stewart's Rd.)
Tidenham Gdns. Croy —3E 152
Tideside Ct. SE18 —3C 90
Tideswell Rd. SW15 —4E 100
Tideswell Rd. Croy —3C 154
Tideway Clo. Rich —4B 116
Tideway Ct. SE16 —1K 87
Tideway Ho. E14 —2C 88
Tideway Ind. Est. SW8 —6G 85
(off Kirtling St.)
Tideway Wlk. SW8 —6G 85 (7B 172)
Tidey St. E3 —5C 70
Tidford Rd. Well —2K 109
Tidworth Rd. E3 —4C 70
Tiepigs La. W W'ck & Brom —2G 155
Tierney Ct. Croy —2E 152
Tierney Rd. SW2 —1J 121
Tiffany Heights. SW18 —7J 101
Tiger La. Brom —4K 143
Tiger Way. E5 —4H 51
Tilbrook Rd. SE3 —3A 108
Tilbury Clo. SE15 —7F 87
Tilbury Rd. E6 —2D 72
Tilbury Rd. E10 —7E 34
Tildesley Rd. SW15 —6E 100
Tilehurst Point. SE2 —2D 92
Tilehurst Rd. SW18 —1B 120
Tilehurst Rd. Sutt —5G 149
Tile Kiln La. N6 —1F 49
Tile Kiln La. N13 —5H 17
(in two parts)
Tile Kiln La. Bex —2J 129
(in two parts)
Tile Kiln La. Hare —7D 22
Tile Kiln Studios. N6 —1G 49
Tile Yd. E14 —6B 70
Tileyard Rd. N7 —7J 49
Tilford Av. New Ad —7E 154
Tilford Gdns. SW19 —1F 119
Tilford Ho. SW2 —7K 103
(off Holmewood Gdns.)
Tilia Clo. Sutt —5H 149
Tilia Rd. E5 —4H 51
Tilia Wlk. SW9 —4B 104
Tilleard Ho. W10 —3G 65
(off Herries St.)
Tiller Rd. E14 —3C 88
Tillett Clo. NW10 —6J 45
Tillett Sq. SE16 —2A 88
Tillet Way. E2 —3G 69
Tillingbourne Gdns. N3 —3H 29
Tillingbourne Grn. Orp —4K 145
Tillingbourne Way. N3 —4H 29
Tillingham Way. N12 —4D 14
Tilling Rd. NW2 —1E 46
Tilling Way. Wemb —3D 44
Tillman St. E1 —6H 69
Tilloch St. N1 —7K 49
Tillotson Ct. SW8 —7H 85
(off Wandsworth Rd.)
Tillotson Rd. N9 —2A 18
Tillotson Rd. Harr —7A 10
Tillotson Rd. Ilf —7E 36
Tilney Ct. EC1 —4C 68 (3D 162)
Tilney Ct. Buck H —2D 20
Tilney Dri. Buck H —2D 20
Tilney Gdns. N1 —6D 50
Tilney Rd. Dag —6F 57
(in two parts)
Tilney Rd. S'hall —4A 78
Tilney St. W1 —1E 84 (4H 165)
Tilson Gdns. SW12 —7J 103
Tilson Ho. SW2 —7J 103
Tilson Rd. N17 —1G 33
Tilston Clo. E11 —3H 53
Tilton St. SW6 —6G 83
Tiltwood, The. W3 —7J 63
Tilt Yd. App. SE9 —6D 108
Timber Clo. Chst —2E 144
Timbercroft. Eps —4A 148
Timbercroft La. SE18 —6J 91
Timberdene. NW4 —2F 29
Timberdene Av. Ilf —1F 37
Timberland Clo. SE15 —7G 87
Timberland Rd. E1 —6H 69
Timber Mill Way. SW4 —3H 103
Timber Pond Rd. SE16 —1K 87
Timberslip Dri. Wall —7H 151
Timbers, The. Sutt —6G 149
Timber St. EC1 —4C 68 (3C 162)
Timberwharf Rd. N16 —6G 33
Timber Wharves Est. E14 —4C 88
Timbrell Pl. SE16 —1B 88
Time Sq. E8 —5F 51
Times Sq. Sutt —5K 149
Timothy Clo. SW4 —5G 103
Timothy Clo. Bexh —5E 110
Timothy Ho. Eri —2E 92
(off Kale Rd.)
Timothy Rd. E3 —5B 70
Timsbury Wlk. SW15 —1C 118
Tindal St. SW9 —1B 104
Tinderbox All. SW14 —3K 99
Tinniswood Clo. N5 —5A 50
Tinsley Rd. E1 —5J 69
Tintagel Cres. SE22 —4F 105
Tintagel Dri. Stan —4J 11
Tintagel Gdns. SE22 —4F 105
Tintern Av. NW9 —3H 27
Tintern Clo. SW15 —5G 101
Tintern Clo. SW19 —6A 120
Tintern Ct. W13 —7A 62
Tintern Gdns. N14 —7D 6
Tintern Ho. NW1 —2F 67 (1K 159)
(off Augustus St.)
Tintern Ho. SW1 —4F 85 (4J 171)
(off Abbots Mnr.)
Tintern Path. NW9 —6A 28
(off Fryent Gro.)
Tintern Rd. N22 —1C 32
Tintern Rd. Cars —1B 150
Tintern St. SW4 —4J 103
Tintern Way. Harr —1F 43
Tinto Rd. E16 —4J 71
Tinworth St. SE1 —5J 85 (5F 173)
Tippett Ct. E6 —2D 72
Tippetts Clo. Enf —1H 7
Tipthorpe Rd. SW11 —3E 102
Tipton Dri. Croy —4E 152
Tiptree Clo. E4 —3K 19
Tiptree Cres. Ilf —2E 36
Tiptree Dri. Enf —4J 7
Tiptree Rd. Ruis —4K 41
Tirlemont Rd. S Croy —7C 152
Tirrell Rd. Croy —6C 140
Tisbury Ct. W1 —2C 166
Tisbury Rd. SW16 —2J 139
Tisdall Pl. SE17 —4D 86
Tissington Ct. SE16 —4J 87
Titan Ct. Bren —5F 81
Titchborne Row. W2 —6C 66 (1D 164)
Titchfield Rd. NW8 —1C 66
Titchfield Rd. Cars —1B 150
Titchfield Wlk. Cars —7B 138
Titchwell Rd. SW18 —1B 120
Tite St. SW3 —5D 84 (6E 170)
Tithe Barn Clo. King T —1F 135
Tithe Barn Way. N'holt —2K 59
Tithe Clo. NW7 —1C 28
Tithe Clo. Hay —5H 59
Tithe Clo. W on T —6K 131
Tithe Farm Av. Harr —3E 42
Tithe Farm Clo. Harr —3E 42
Tithe Wlk. NW7 —1C 28
Titian Av. Bus H —1D 10
Titley Clo. E4 —5H 19
Titmus Clo. Uxb —6E 58
Titmuss Av. SE28 —7B 74
Titmuss St. W12 —2E 82
Tivendale. N8 —3J 31
Tiverton Av. Ilf —3E 36
Tiverton Dri. SE9 —1G 127
Tiverton Rd. N15 —6D 32
Tiverton Rd. N18 —5K 17
Tiverton Rd. NW10 —1F 65
Tiverton Rd. Edgw —2F 27
Tiverton Rd. Houn —2G 97
Tiverton Rd. Ruis —3J 41
Tiverton Rd. T Hth —5A 140
Tiverton Rd. Wemb —2E 62
Tiverton St. SE1 —3C 86
Tiverton Way. Chess —5D 146
Tivoli Ct. SE16 —1B 88
Tivoli Gdns. SE18 —4C 90
(in two parts)
Tivoli Rd. N8 —5H 31
Tivoli Rd. SE27 —5C 122
Tivoli Rd. Houn —4C 96
Toad La. Houn —4D 96
Tobacco Dock. E1 —7H 69
Tobacco Quay. E1 —7H 69
Tobago St. E14 —2C 88
Tobin Clo. NW3 —7C 48
Toby Ct. N9 —7D 8
(off Tramway Av.)
Toby La. E1 —4A 70
Toby Way. Surb —2H 147
Todd Ho. N2 —2B 30
(off Grange, The)
Todds Wlk. N7 —2K 49
Todhunter Ter. Barn —4D 4
Tokenhouse Yd. EC2 —6D 68 (7E 162)
Token Yd. SW15 —4G 101
Tokyngton. —6H 45
Tokyngton Av. Wemb —6G 45
Toland Sq. SW15 —5C 100
Tolcairn Ct. Belv —5G 93
Tolcarne Dri. Pinn —2J 23
Tolchurch. W11 —6H 65
(off Dartmouth Clo.)
Toley Av. Wemb —7E 26
Toll Bar Ct. Sutt —7K 149
Tollbridge Clo. W10 —4G 65
Tollesbury Gdns. Ilf —3H 37
Tollet St. E1 —4K 69
Tollgate Dri. SE21 —2E 122
Tollgate Dri. Hay —7B 60
Tollgate Gdns. NW6 —2K 65
Tollgate Ho. NW6 —2K 65
(off Tollgate Gdns.)
Tollgate Rd. E16 & E6 —5A 72
Tollgate Sq. E6 —5D 72
Tollhouse Way. N19 —2G 49
Tollington Pk. N4 —2K 49
Tollington Pl. N4 —2K 49
Tollington Rd. N7 —4K 49
Tollington Way. N7 —3J 49
Tolmers Sq. NW1 —4G 67 (3B 160)
(in two parts)
Tolpaide Ho. SE11 —4J 173
Tolpuddle Av. E13 —1A 72
(off Queens Rd.)
Tolpuddle St. N1 —2A 68
Tolsford Rd. E5 —5H 51
Tolson Rd. Iswth —3A 98
Tolverne Rd. SW20 —1E 136
Tolworth. —2H 147
Tolworth Clo. Surb —1H 147
Tolworth Gdns. Romf —5D 38
Tolworth Junction. (Junct.) —2H 147
Tolworth Pde. Chad H —5E 38
Tolworth Pk. Rd. Surb —2F 147
Tolworth Ri. N. Surb —1H 147
Tolworth Ri. S. Surb —2H 147
Tolworth Rd. Surb —2E 146

Trinity Rd.—Up. Hawkwell Wlk.

Trinity Rd. S'hall —1C 78
Trinity Sq. EC3 —7E 68 (2H 169)
Trinity St. E16 —5H 71
Trinity St. SE1 —2C 86 (7D 168)
(in two parts)
Trinity St. Enf —2H 7
Trinity Tower. E1 —7G 69
(off Vaughan Way)
Trinity Wlk. NW3 —6A 48
Trinity Way. E4 —6G 19
Trinity Way. W3 —7A 64
Trio Pl. SE1 —2C 86 (7D 168)
Tristan Sq. SE3 —3G 107
Tristram Clo. E17 —3F 35
Tristram Rd. Brom —4H 125
Triton Ho. E14 —4D 88
Triton Sq. NW1 —4G 67 (3A 160)
Tritton Av. Croy —4J 151
Tritton Rd. SE21 —3D 122
Triumph Clo. Hay —1E 94
Triumph Ho. Bark —3A 74
Triumph Rd. E6 —6D 72
Triumph Trad. Est. N17 —6B 18
Trocadero Entertainment Cen.
—7H 67 (3C 166)
Trocette Mans. SE1 —3E 86
(off Bermondsey St.)
Trojan Ct. NW6 —7G 47
Trojan Ind. Est. NW10 —6B 46
Trojan Way. Croy —3K 151
Troon Clo. SE16 —5H 87
Troon Clo. SE28 —6D 74
Troon St. E1 —6A 70
Trosley Rd. Belv —6G 93
Trossachs Rd. SE22 —5E 104
Trothy Rd. SE1 —4G 87
Trotman Ho. SE14 —1J 105
(off Pomeroy St.)
Trott Rd. N10 —7J 15
Trott St. SW11 —1C 102
Troughton Rd. SE7 —5K 89
Troutbeck. NW1 —2K 159
Troutbeck Rd. SE14 —1A 106
Trout Rd. W Dray —7A 58
Trouville Rd. SW4 —6G 103
Trowbridge Rd. E9 —6B 52
Trowlock Av. Tedd —6C 116
Trowlock Way. Tedd —6D 116
Troy Ct. SE18 —4F 91
Troy Ct. W8 —3J 83
(off Kensington High St.)
Troy Ind. Est. Harr —5K 25
Troy Rd. SE19 —6D 122
Troy Town. SE15 —3G 105
Trubshaw Rd. S'hall —3F 79
Truesdale Rd. E6 —6D 72
Trulock Ct. N17 —7B 18
Trulock Rd. N17 —7B 18
Truman Clo. Edgw —7C 12
Trumans Rd. N16 —5F 51
Trumble Gdns. T Hth —4B 140
Trumpers Way. W7 —3J 79
Trumpington Rd. E7 —4H 53
Trump St. EC2 —6C 68 (1D 168)
Trundlers Way. Bush —1D 10
Trundle St. SE1 —6C 168
Trundley's M. SE8 —5K 87
Trundley's Rd. SE8 —5K 87
Trundley's Ter. SE8 —4K 87
Truro Gdns. Ilf —7C 36
Truro Ho. Pinn —1D 24
Truro Rd. E17 —4B 34
Truro Rd. N22 —7D 16
Truro St. NW5 —6E 48
Truro Way. N'holt —3G 59
Truslove Rd. SE27 —5A 122
Trussley Rd. W6 —3E 82
Trust Wlk. SE21 —1B 122
Tryfan Clo. Ilf —5B 36
Tryon Cres. E9 —1J 69
Tryon St. SW3 —5D 84 (5E 170)
Trystings Clo. Clay —6A 146
Tuam Rd. SE18 —6H 91
Tubbs Rd. NW10 —2B 64
Tucklow Wlk. SW15 —7B 100
Tudor Av. E17 —7B 34
Tudor Av. Hamp —7E 114
Tudor Av. Wor Pk —3D 148
Tudor Clo. N6 —7G 31
Tudor Clo. NW3 —5C 48
Tudor Clo. NW7 —6H 13
Tudor Clo. NW9 —2J 45
Tudor Clo. SW2 —6K 103
Tudor Clo. Ashf —4A 112
Tudor Clo. Chess —5E 146
Tudor Clo. Chig —4K 21
Tudor Clo. Chst —1D 144
Tudor Clo. Hamp —5G 115
Tudor Clo. Pinn —5J 23
Tudor Clo. Sutt —5F 149
Tudor Clo. Wall —7G 151
Tudor Clo. Wfd G —5E 20
Tudor Ct. N1 —6E 50
Tudor Ct. N22 —7D 16
Tudor Ct. SE9 —4C 108
Tudor Ct. W3 —2G 81
Tudor Ct. Felt —4A 114
Tudor Ct. Sidc —3A 128
Tudor Ct. Stanw —6A 94
Tudor Ct. Tedd —6K 115
Tudor Ct. N. Wemb —5G 45
Tudor Ct. S. Wemb —5G 45
Tudor Cres. Enf —1H 7
Tudor Dri. King T —5D 116
Tudor Dri. Mord —6F 137
Tudor Enterprise Pk. Harr —3K 43
(HA1)
Tudor Enterprise Pk. Harr —3H 25
(HA3)
Tudor Est. NW10 —2H 63
Tudor Gdns. NW9 —2J 45
Tudor Gdns. SW13 —3A 100
Tudor Gdns. W3 —5G 63
Tudor Gdns. Harr —2H 25
Tudor Gdns. Twic —1K 115
Tudor Gdns. W W'ck —3E 154
Tudor Gro. E9 —7J 51
Tudor Ho. E9 —7J 51
Tudor Ho. W14 —4F 83
(off Windsor Way)
Tudor Ho. Pinn —2A 24
(off Pinner Hill Rd.)
Tudor Pde. SE9 —4C 108
Tudor Pde. Romf —7D 38
Tudor Pl. SE19 —7F 123
Tudor Pl. Mitc —7C 120
Tudor Rd. E4 —6J 19
Tudor Rd. E6 —1A 72
Tudor Rd. E9 —1H 69
Tudor Rd. N9 —7C 8
Tudor Rd. SE19 —7F 123
Tudor Rd. SE25 —5H 141
Tudor Rd. Ashf —6F 113
Tudor Rd. Bark —1K 73
Tudor Rd. Barn —3D 4
Tudor Rd. Beck —3E 142
Tudor Rd. Hamp —7E 114
Tudor Rd. Harr —2H 25
Tudor Rd. Hay —6F 59
Tudor Rd. Houn —4H 97
Tudor Rd. King T —7G 117
Tudor Rd. Pinn —2A 24
Tudor Rd. S'hall —7C 60
Tudor Sq. Hay —5F 59
Tudor Stacks. SE24 —4C 104
Tudor St. EC4 —7A 68 (2K 167)
Tudor Wlk. Bex —6E 110
Tudor Way. N14 —1C 16
Tudor Way. W3 —2G 81
Tudor Way. Orp —6H 145
Tudor Way. Uxb —6C 40
Tudor Well Clo. Stan —5G 11
Tudor Works. Hay —1B 78
Tudway Rd. SE3 —3K 107
Tufnell Park. —4G 49
Tufnell Pk. Rd. N19 & N7 —4G 49
Tufton Ct. SW1 —3J 85 (2E 172)
(off Tufton St.)
Tufton Gdns. W Mol —2F 133
Tufton Rd. E4 —4H 19
Tufton St. SW1 —3J 85 (1E 172)
Tugboat St. SE28 —2J 91
Tugela Rd. Croy —6D 140
Tugela St. SE6 —2B 124
Tulip Clo. E6 —5D 72
Tulip Clo. Croy —1K 153
Tulip Clo. Hamp —6D 114
Tulip Clo. S'hall —2G 79
Tulip Gdns. E4 —3A 20
Tulip Gdns. Ilf —6F 55
Tull St. Mitc —7D 138
Tulse Clo. Beck —3E 142
Tulse Hill. —1B 122
Tulse Hill. SW2 —6A 104
Tulse Hill Est. SW2 —6A 104
Tulse Ho. SW2 —6A 104
Tulsemere Rd. SE27 —2C 122
Tumbling Bay. W on T —6J 131
Tummons Gdns. SE25 —2E 140
Tunbridge Ho. EC1 —1K 161
Tuncombe Rd. N18 —4K 17
Tunis Rd. W12 —1E 82
Tunley Grn. E14 —5B 70
Tunley Rd. NW10 —1A 64
Tunley Rd. SW17 —1E 120
Tunmarsh La. E13 —3K 71
Tunnanleys. E6 —6E 72
Tunnel App. E14 —7A 70
Tunnel App. SE10 —2G 89
Tunnel App. SE16 —2J 87
Tunnel Av. SE10 —2F 89
(in two parts)
Tunnel Av. Trad. Est. SE10 —2F 89
Tunnel Gdns. N11 —7B 16
Tunnel Link Rd. H'row A —5C 94
Tunnel Rd. SE16 —2J 87
Tunnel Rd. E. H'row A —1D 94
Tunnel Rd. W. H'row A —1C 94
Tunstall Rd. SW9 —4K 103
Tunstall Rd. Croy —1E 152
Tunstall Wlk. Bren —6E 80
Tunstock Way. Belv —3E 92
Tunworth Clo. NW9 —6J 27
Tunworth Cres. SW15 —6B 100
Tun Yd. SW8 —2F 103
(off Silverthorne Rd.)
Tupelo Rd. E10 —2D 52
Tupman Ho. SE16 —2G 87
(off Scott Lidgett Cres.)
Turenne Clo. SW18 —4A 102
Turin Rd. N9 —7D 8
Turin St. E2 —3G 69 (2K 163)
Turkey Oak Clo. SE19 —7E 122
Turks Clo. Uxb —3C 58
Turk's Head Yd. EC1
—5B 68 (5A 162)
Turk's Row. SW3 —5D 84 (5F 171)
Turle Rd. N4 —2K 49
Turle Rd. SW16 —2J 139
Turlewray Clo. N4 —1K 49
Turley Clo. E15 —1G 71
Turnagain La. EC4 —7A 162
Turnage Rd. Dag —1E 56
Turnberry Clo. NW4 —2F 29
Turnberry Clo. SE16 —5H 87
(off Ryder Dri.)
Turnberry Quay. E14 —3D 88
Turnberry Way. Orp —7H 145
Turnbull Ho. N1 —1B 68
Turnbury Clo. SE28 —6D 74
Turnchapel M. SW4 —3F 103
Turner Av. N15 —4E 32
Turner Av. Mitc —1D 138
Turner Av. Twic —3G 115
Turner Clo. NW11 —6K 29
Turner Clo. SE5 —7B 86
Turner Clo. Hay —2E 58
Turner Clo. Wemb —5D 44
Turner Dri. NW11 —6K 29
Turner Ho. NW8 —2C 66
(off Townshend Est.)
Turner Ho. SW1 —4H 85 (4D 172)
(off Herrick St.)
Turner Ho. Twic —6D 98
(off Clevedon Rd.)
Turner Pl. SW11 —5C 102
Turner Rd. E17 —3E 34
Turner Rd. Edgw —2E 26
Turner Rd. N Mald —7K 135
Turner's All. EC3 —7E 68 (2G 169)
Turners Mdw. Way. Beck —1B 142
Turners Rd. E14 & E3 —5B 70
Turner St. E1 —5H 69
Turner St. E16 —6H 71
Turner's Way. Croy —2A 152
Turners Wood. NW11 —7A 30
Turneville Rd. W14 —6H 83
Turney Rd. SE21 —7C 104
Turnham Green. —5K 81
Turnham Grn. Ter. W4 —4A 82
Turnham Grn. Ter. M. W4 —4A 82
Turnham Rd. SE4 —5A 106
Turnmill St. EC1 —4B 68 (4A 162)
Turnpike Clo. SE8 —7B 88
Turnpike Ct. Bexh —4D 110
Turnpike Ho. EC1 —3B 68 (2B 162)
Turnpike La. N8 —4K 31
Turnpike La. Sutt —5A 150
Turnpike La. Uxb —3A 58
Turnpike Link. Croy —2E 152
Turnpike Pde. N8 —3B 32
(off Green Lanes)
Turnpike Way. Iswth —1A 98
Turnpin La. SE10 —6E 88
Turnstone Clo. E13 —3J 71
Turnstone Clo. NW9 —2A 28
Turnstone Clo. Ick —5D 40
Turpentine La. SW1 —5F 85 (5K 171)
Turpington Clo. Brom —6C 144
Turpington La. Brom —7C 144
Turpin Ho. SW11 —1F 103
Turpin Rd. Felt —6H 95
Turpin's La. Wfd G —5J 21
Turpin Way. N19 —2H 49
(in two parts)
Turpin Way. Wall —7F 151
Turquand St. SE17 —4C 86
Turret Gro. SW4 —3G 103
Turton Rd. Wemb —5E 44
Turville Ho. NW8 —4C 66 (3C 158)
(off Grendon St.)
Turville St. E2 —4F 69 (3J 163)
Tuscan Rd. SE18 —5H 91
Tuscany Ho. E17 —2B 34
Tuskar St. SE10 —6G 89
Tustin Est. SE15 —6J 87
Tutshill Ct. SE15 —7E 86
(off Newent Clo.)
Tuttlebee La. Buck H —2D 20
Tuttle Ho. SW1 —5H 85 (6C 172)
(off Aylesford St.)
Tweedale Ct. E15 —5E 52
Tweed Ct. W7 —6J 61
(off Hanway Rd.)
Tweeddale Gro. Uxb —3E 40
Tweeddale Rd. Cars —1B 150
Tweed Glen. Romf —1K 39
Tweed Ho. E14 —4E 70
Tweedmouth Rd. E13 —2K 71
Tweed Way. Romf —1K 39
Tweedy Clo. Enf —5A 8
Tweedy Rd. Brom —1J 143
Tweezer's All. WC2 —2J 167
Twelvetrees Cres. E3 & E16 —4E 70
(in two parts)
Twentyman Clo. Wfd G —5D 20
Twickenham. —1A 116
Twickenham Clo. Croy —3K 151
Twickenham Gdns. Gnfd —5A 44
Twickenham Gdns. Harr —7D 10
Twickenham Rd. E11 —2E 52
Twickenham Rd. Felt & Hanw —3D 114
Twickenham Rd. Iswth —5A 98
Twickenham Rd. Rich —4C 98
Twickenham Rd. Tedd —4A 116
(in two parts)
Twickenham Rugby Union Football
Ground. —6J 97
Twickenham Stadium Tours. —6J 97
Twickenham Trad. Est. Twic —6K 97
Twig Folly Clo. E2 —2K 69
Twigg Clo. Eri —7K 93
Twilley St. SW18 —7K 101
Twin Bridges Bus. Pk. S Croy —6D 152
Twine Clo. Bark —3B 74
Twine Ct. E1 —7J 69
Twineham Grn. N12 —4D 14
Twine Ter. E3 —4B 70
(off Ropery St.)
Twining Av. Twic —3G 115
Twinn Rd. NW7 —6B 14
Twin Tumps Way. SE28 —7A 74
Twisden Rd. NW5 —4F 49
Twybridge Way. NW10 —7J 45
Twycross M. SE10 —5G 89
Twyford Abbey Rd. NW10 —3F 63
Twyford Av. N2 —3D 30
Twyford Av. W3 —7G 63
Twyford Ct. N10 —3E 30
Twyford Ct. Wemb —2E 62
(off Vicars Bri. Clo.)
Twyford Cres. W3 —1G 81
Twyford Ho. N5 —3B 50
Twyford Ho. N15 —6E 32
(off Chisley Rd.)
Twyford Pl. WC2 —6K 67 (7G 161)
Twyford Rd. Cars —1B 150
Twyford Rd. Harr —1F 43
Twyford Rd. Ilf —5G 55
Twyford St. N1 —1K 67
Tyas Rd. E16 —4H 71
Tybenham Rd. SW19 —3J 137
Tyberry Rd. Enf —3C 8
Tyburn La. Harr —7K 25
Tyburn Way. W1 —7D 66 (2F 165)
Tyers Est. SE1 —6G 169
Tyers Ga. SE1 —2E 86 (7G 169)
Tyers St. SE11 —5K 85 (6G 173)
Tyers Ter. SE11 —5K 85 (6G 173)
Tyeshurst Clo. SE2 —5E 92
Tylecroft Rd. SW16 —2J 139
Tylehurst Gdns. Ilf —5G 55
Tyler Clo. E2 —2F 69
Tyler Rd. S'hall —3F 79
Tylers Ct. E17 —4C 34
(off Westbury Rd.)
Tyler's Ct. W1 —1C 166
Tylers Ct. Wemb —2E 62
Tylers Ga. Harr —6E 26
Tylers Path. Cars —4D 150
Tyler St. SE10 —5G 89
(in two parts)
Tylney Av. SE19 —5F 123
Tylney Rd. E7 —4A 54
Tylney Rd. Brom —2B 144
Tynan Clo. Felt —1J 113
Tyndale Ct. E14 —5D 88
Tyndale La. N1 —7B 50
Tyndale Mans. N1 —7B 50
(off Upper St.)
Tyndale Ter. N1 —7B 50
Tyndall Gdns. E10 —2E 52
Tyndall Rd. E10 —2E 52
Tyndall Rd. Well —3K 109
Tyne Ct. W7 —6J 61
(off Hanway Rd.)
Tyneham Clo. SW11 —3E 102
Tyneham Rd. SW11 —2E 102
Tyne Ho. King T —1D 134
Tynemouth Clo. E6 —6F 73
Tynemouth Dri. Enf —1B 8
Tynemouth Rd. N15 —4F 33
Tynemouth Rd. SE18 —5J 91
Tynemouth Rd. Mitc —7E 120
Tynemouth St. SW6 —2A 102
Tyne St. E1 —6F 69 (7K 163)
Tynley Av. SE19 —5F 123
Tynwald Ho. SE26 —3G 123
Type St. E2 —2K 69
Tyrawley Rd. SW6 —1K 101
Tyre La. NW9 —4A 28
Tyrell Clo. Harr —4J 43
Tyrell Ct. Cars —4D 150
Tyrell Ho. Beck —5D 124
(off Beckenham Hill Rd.)
Tyrols Rd. SE23 —1K 123
Tyrone Rd. E6 —2D 72
Tyron Way. Sidc —4J 127
Tyrrell Av. Well —5A 110
Tyrrell Ho. SW1 —6G 85 (7B 172)
(off Churchill Gdns.)
Tyrrell Rd. SE22 —4G 105
Tyrrell Sq. Mitc —1C 138
Tyrrel Way. NW9 —7B 28
Tyrwhitt Rd. SE4 —3C 106
Tysoe St. EC1 —3A 68 (2K 161)
Tyson Gdns. SE23 —7J 105
Tyson Rd. SE23 —7J 105
Tyssen Pas. E8 —6F 51
Tyssen Rd. N16 —3F 51
Tyssen St. E8 —6F 51
Tytherton Rd. N19 —3H 49

Uamvar St. E14 —5D 70
Uckfield Gro. Mitc —7E 120
Udall St. SW1 —4G 85 (4B 172)
Udney Pk. Rd. Tedd —6A 116
Uffington Rd. NW10 —1C 64
Uffington Rd. SE27 —4A 122
Ufford Clo. Harr —7A 10
Ufford Rd. Harr —7A 10
Ufford St. SE1 —2A 86 (6K 167)
Ufton Ct. N'holt —3B 60
Ufton Gro. N1 —7D 50
Ufton Rd. N1 —7D 50
(in two parts)
Uhura Sq. N16 —3E 50
Ujima Ct. SW16 —4J 121
Ullathorne Rd. SW16 —4G 121
Ulleswater Rd. N14 —4D 16
Ullin St. E14 —5E 70
Ullswater Ct. SW15 —4K 117
Ullswater Clo. Brom —7G 125
Ullswater Clo. Hay —2G 59
Ullswater Ct. Harr —7E 24
Ullswater Cres. SW15 —4K 117
Ullswater Rd. SE27 —2B 122
Ullswater Rd. SW13 —7C 82
Ulster Gdns. N13 —4H 17
Ulster Pl. NW1 —4F 67 (4J 159)
Ulster Ter. NW1 —3H 159
Ulundi Rd. SE3 —6G 89
Ulva Rd. SW15 —5F 101
Ulverscroft Rd. SE22 —5F 105
Ulverstone Rd. SE27 —2B 122
Ulverston Rd. E17 —2F 35
Ulysses Rd. NW6 —5H 47
Umberston St. E1 —6G 69
Umbria St. SW15 —6C 100
Umfreville Rd. N4 —6B 32
Undercliff Rd. SE13 —3C 106
Underhill. —5D 4
Underhill. Barn —5D 4
Underhill Ct. Barn —5D 4
Underhill Ho. E14 —5C 70
Underhill Pas. NW1 —1F 67
(off Camden High St.)
Underhill Rd. SE22 —5G 105
Underhill St. NW1 —1F 67
Underne Av. N14 —2A 16
Undershaft. EC3 —6E 68 (1G 169)
Undershaw Rd. Brom —3H 125
Underwood. New Ad —5E 154
Underwood Ct. E10 —1D 52
(off Leyton Grange Est.)
Underwood Rd. E1 —4G 69
Underwood Rd. E4 —5J 19
Underwood Rd. Wfd G —7F 21
Underwood Row. N1
—3C 68 (1D 162)
Underwood St. N1 —3C 68 (1D 162)
Underwood, The. SE9 —2D 126
Undine Rd. E14 —4D 88
Undine St. SW17 —5D 120
Uneeda Dri. Gnfd —1H 61
Unicorn Building. E1 —7K 69
(off Jardine Rd.)
Union Clo. E11 —4F 53
Union Cotts. E15 —7G 53
Union Ct. EC2 —7G 163
Union Ct. SW4 —2J 103
Union Ct. Rich —5E 98
Union Dri. E1 —4A 70
Union Gro. SW8 —2H 103
Union M. SW4 —2J 103
Union Rd. N11 —6C 16
Union Rd. SW8 & SW4 —2H 103
Union Rd. Brom —5B 144
Union Rd. Croy —7C 140
Union Rd. N'holt —2E 60
Union Rd. Wemb —6E 44
Union Sq. N1 —1C 68
Union St. E15 —1F 71
Union St. SE1 —1B 86 (5A 168)
Union St. Barn —3B 4
Union St. King T —2D 134
Union Theatre. —5B 168
Union Wlk. E2 —3E 68 (1H 163)
Union Yd. W1 —6F 67 (1K 165)
Unitair Cen. Felt —6E 94
Unit Workshops. E1 —6G 69
(off Adler St.)
Unity Clo. NW10 —6C 46
Unity Clo. SE19 —5C 122
Unity Clo. New Ad —7D 154
Unity M. NW1 —2H 67
Unity Way. SE7 —3B 90
Unity Wharf. SE1 —2F 87 (6K 169)
(off Mill St.)
University Clo. NW7 —7G 13
University Gdns. Bex —7F 111
University Pl. Eri —7J 93
University Rd. SW19 —6B 120
University St. WC1 —4G 67 (4B 160)
University Way. E16 —7E 72
Unwin Av. Felt —5F 95
Unwin Clo. SE15 —6G 87
Unwin Mans. W14 —6H 83
(off Queen's Club Gdns.)
Unwin Rd. SW7 —3B 84 (1A 170)
Unwin Rd. Iswth —3J 97
Upbrook M. W2 —6A 66 (1A 164)
Upcerne Rd. SW10 —7A 84
Upchurch Clo. SE20 —7H 123
Upcroft Av. Edgw —5D 12
Updale Rd. Sidc —4K 127
Upfield. Croy —3H 153
Upfield Rd. W7 —5K 61
Upgrove Mnr. Way. SE24 —7A 104
Uphall Rd. Ilf —5F 55
Upham Pk. Rd. W4 —4A 82
Uphill Dri. NW7 —5F 13
Uphill Dri. NW9 —5J 27
Uphill Gro. NW7 —4F 13
Uphill Rd. NW7 —4F 13
Upland M. SE22 —5G 105
Upland Rd. E13 —4J 71
Upland Rd. SE22 —5G 105
Upland Rd. Bexh —3F 111
Upland Rd. S Croy —5D 152
Upland Rd. Sutt —7B 150
Uplands. Beck —2C 142
Uplands Av. E17 —2K 33
Uplands Bus. Pk. E17 —3K 33
Uplands Clo. SW14 —5H 99
Uplands Ct. N21 —7F 7
(off Green, The)
Uplands End. Wfd G —7H 21
Uplands Pk. Rd. Enf —2F 7
Uplands Rd. N8 —5K 31
Uplands Rd. E Barn —1K 15
Uplands Rd. Romf —3D 38
Uplands Rd. Wfd G —7H 21
Uplands, The. Ruis —1J 41
Uplands Way. N21 —5F 7
Upnall Ho. SE15 —6J 87
Upney La. Bark —5J 55
Upnor Way. SE17 —5E 86
Uppark Dri. Ilf —6G 37
Up. Abbey Rd. Belv —4F 93
Up. Addison Gdns. W14 —2G 83
Up. Bardsey Wlk. N1 —6C 50
(off Douglas Rd. N.)
Up. Belgrave St. SW1
—3E 84 (1H 171)
Up. Berenger Wlk. SW10 —7B 84
(off Berenger Wlk.)
Up. Berkeley St. W2 —6D 66 (1E 164)
Up. Beulah Hill. SE19 —1E 140
Up. Blantyre Wlk. SW10 —7B 84
(off Blantyre Wlk.)
Up. Brighton Rd. Surb —6D 134
Up. Brockley Rd. SE4 —3B 106
Up. Brook St. W1 —7E 66 (2G 165)
Up. Butts. Bren —6C 80
Up. Caldy Wlk. N1 —7C 50
(off Caldy Wlk.)
Up. Camelford Wlk. W11 —6G 65
(off St Mark's Rd.)
Up. Cavendish Av. N3 —3J 29
Up. Cheyne Row. SW3 —7C 170
Upper Clapton. —2H 51
Up. Clapton Rd. E5 —2H 51
Up. Clarendon Wlk. W11 —6G 65
(off Clarendon Rd.)
Up. Dartrey Wlk. SW10 —7A 84
(off Whistler Wlk.)
Up. Dengie Wlk. N1 —1C 68
(off Baddow Wlk.)
Upper Edmonton. —5C 18
Upper Elmers End. —5B 142
Up. Elmers End Rd. Beck —4A 142
Up. Farm Rd. W Mol —4D 132
Upper Feilde. W1 —7E 66 (2G 165)
(off Park St.)
Upper Fosters. NW4 —4E 28
(off New Brent St.)
Up. Green E. Mitc —3D 138
Up. Green W. Mitc —2D 138
(in two parts)
Up. Grosvenor St. W1
—7E 66 (3G 165)
Up. Grotto Rd. Twic —2K 115
Upper Ground. SE1 —1A 86 (4J 167)
Upper Gro. SE25 —4E 140
Up. Grove Rd. Belv —6F 93
Up. Gulland Wlk. N1 —6C 50
(off Oronsay Wlk.)
Upper Halliford. —4G 131
Up. Halliford By-Pass. Shep —5G 131
Up. Halliford Grn. Shep —4G 131
Up. Halliford Rd. Shep —3G 131
Up. Hampstead Wlk. NW3 —4A 48
Up. Ham Rd. Rich —4D 116
Up. Handa Wlk. N1 —6D 50
(off Handa Wlk.)
Up. Hawkwell Wlk. N1 —1C 68
(off Maldon Rd.)

Up. Hilldrop Est.—Victoria Pk. Sq.

Up. Hilldrop Est. N7 —5H 49
Upper Holloway. —2G 49
Up. Holly Hill Rd. Belv —5H 93
Up. James St. W1 —7G 67 (2B 166)
Up. John St. W1 —7G 67 (2B 166)
Up. Lismore Wlk. N1 —6D 50
(off Clephane St.)
Upper Mall. W6 —5C 82
(in two parts)
Upper Marsh. SE1 —3K 85 (1H 173)
Up. Montagu St. W1 —5D 66 (5E 158)
Up. Mulgrave Rd. Sutt —7G 149
Up. North St. E14 —5C 70
Upper Norwood. —1E 140
Up. Palace Rd. E Mol —3G 133
Up. Park Rd. N11 —5A 16
Up. Park Rd. NW3 —5D 48
Up. Park Rd. Belv —4H 93
Up. Park Rd. Brom —1K 143
Up. Park Rd. King T —6G 117
Up. Phillimore Gdns. W8 —2J 83
Up. Ramsey Wlk. N1 —6D 50
(off Ramsey Wlk.)
Up. Rawreth Wlk. N1 —1C 68
(off Basire St.)
Up. Richmond Rd. SW15 —4B 100
Up. Richmond Rd. W. Rich & SW14 —4G 99
Upper Rd. E13 —3J 71
Upper Rd. Wall —5H 151
Upper Ruxley. —7F 129
Up. St Martin's La. WC2 —7J 67 (2E 166)
Up. Selsdon Rd. S Croy —7F 153
Up. Sheppey Wlk. N1 —6C 50
(off Skomer Wlk.)
Up. Sheridan Rd. Belv —4G 93
Upper Shirley. —4K 153
Up. Shirley Rd. Croy —2J 153
Upper Sq. Iswth —3A 98
Upper St. N1 —2A 68
Up. Sunbury Rd. Hamp —1C 132
Up. Sutton La. Houn —7E 78
Upper Sydenham. —3H 123
Up. Tachbrook St. SW1 —4G 85 (3B 172)
Up. Talbot Wlk. W11 —6G 65
(off Talbot Wlk.)
Up. Teddington Rd. King T —7C 116
Upper Ter. NW3 —3A 48
Up. Thames St. EC4 —7B 68 (2B 168)
Up. Tollington Pk. N4 —1A 50
(in two parts)
Upperton Rd. Sidc —5K 127
Upperton Rd. E. E13 —3A 72
Upperton Rd. W. E13 —3A 72
Upper Tooting. —3D 120
Up. Tooting Pk. SW17 —2D 120
Up. Tooting Rd. SW17 —4D 120
Up. Town Rd. Gnfd —4F 61
Up. Tulse Hill. SW2 —7K 103
Up. Vernon Rd. Sutt —5B 150
Upper Walthamstow. —4F 35
Up. Walthamstow Rd. E17 —4E 34
Up. Whistler Wlk. SW10 —7A 84
(off Worlds End Est.)
Up. Wickham La. Well —3B 110
Up. Wimpole St. W1 —5E 66 (5H 159)
Up. Woburn Pl. WC1 —3H 67 (2D 160)
Uppingham Av. Stan —1B 26
Upsdell Av. N13 —6F 17
Upshire Ho. E17 —2B 34
Upstall St. SE5 —1B 104
Upton. —5D 110
(Bexleyheath)
Upton. —7J 53
(Plaistow)
Upton Av. E7 —7J 53
Upton Clo. Bex —6F 111
Upton Ct. SE20 —7J 123
Upton Dene. Sutt —7K 149
Upton Gdns. Harr —5B 26
Upton La. E7 —7J 53
Upton Lodge. E7 —6J 53
Upton Lodge Clo. Bush —1B 10
Upton Park. —2B 72
Upton Pk. Rd. E7 —7K 53
Upton Rd. N18 —5B 18
Upton Rd. SE18 —6G 91
Upton Rd. Bexh & Bex —4E 110
Upton Rd. Houn —3E 96
Upton Rd. T Hth —2D 140
Upton Rd. S. Bex —6F 111
Upton Vs. Bexh —4E 110
Upway. N12 —6H 15
Upwey Ho. N1 —1E 68
Upwood Rd. SE12 —6J 107
Upwood Rd. SW16 —1J 139
Urlwin St. SE5 —6C 86
Urlwin Wlk. SW9 —1A 104
Urmston Dri. SW19 —1G 119
Urmston Ho. E14 —4E 88
Urquhart Ct. Beck —7B 124
Ursula Lodges. Sidc —5B 128
(off Eynswood Dri.)
Ursula M. N4 —1C 50
Ursula St. SW11 —1C 102
Urswick Gdns. Dag —7E 56
Urswick Rd. E9 —5J 51
Urswick Rd. Dag —7D 56
Usborne M. SW8 —7K 85
Usher Rd. E3 —1B 70
Usher-Walker Ho. E16 —4F 71
(off South Cres.)
Usk Rd. SW11 —4A 102
Usk St. E2 —3K 69
Utopia Village. NW1 —7E 48
Uvedale Rd. Dag —3G 57
Uvedale Rd. Enf —5J 7
Uverdale Rd. SW10 —7A 84
Uxbridge Rd. W5 & W3 —7E 62
Uxbridge Rd. W7 —1K 79
Uxbridge Rd. W12 —1B 82
Uxbridge Rd. W13 & W5 —1B 80
Uxbridge Rd. Felt —2A 114
Uxbridge Rd. Hamp —4E 114
Uxbridge Rd. Harr & Stan —7B 10
Uxbridge Rd. Hil & Uxb —3C 58
Uxbridge Rd. King T —4D 134
Uxbridge Rd. Pinn —2A 24
Uxbridge Rd. S'hall & W7 —1E 78
Uxbridge St. W8 —1J 83
Uxendon Cres. Wemb —1E 44
Uxendon Hill. Wemb —1F 45

Valance Av. E4 —1B 20
Valan Leas. Brom —3G 143
Vale Clo. N2 —3D 30
Vale Clo. W9 —3A 66
Vale Clo. Orp —4E 156
Vale Clo. Twic —3A 116
Vale Cotts. SW15 —3A 118
Vale Ct. W3 —1B 82
Vale Ct. W9 —3A 66
Vale Ct. New Bar —4E 4
Vale Cres. SW15 —4A 118
Vale Cft. Pinn —5C 24
Vale Dri. Barn —4C 4
Vale End. SE22 —4F 105
Vale Est., The. W3 —1A 82
Vale Gro. N4 —7C 32
Vale Gro. W3 —2K 81
Vale La. W3 —5G 63
Vale Lodge. SE23 —2J 123
Valence Av. Dag —1D 56
Valence Cir. Dag —3D 56
Valence House Mus. —3E 56
Valence Rd. Eri —7K 93
Valence Wood Rd. Dag —3D 56
Valencia Rd. Stan —4H 11
Valentia Pl. SW9 —4A 104
Valentine Av. Bex —2E 128
Valentine Ct. SE23 —2K 123
(in two parts)
Valentine Pl. SE1 —2B 86 (6A 168)
Valentine Rd. E9 —6K 51
Valentine Rd. Harr —3F 43
Valentine Row. SE1 —2B 86
Valentines Rd. Ilf —1F 55
Valentine's Way. Romf —2K 57
Vale Of Health. —3A 48
Vale of Health. NW3 —3B 48
Vale Pde. SW15 —3A 118
Valerian Way. E15 —3G 71
Valerie Ct. Sutt —7K 149
Vale Ri. NW11 —1H 47
Vale Rd. E7 —6K 53
Vale Rd. N4 —7C 32
Vale Rd. Brom —1E 144
Vale Rd. Eps —4B 148
Vale Rd. Mitc —3H 139
Vale Rd. Sutt —4K 149
Vale Rd. Wor Pk —3B 148
Vale Rd. N. Surb —2E 146
Vale Rd. S. Surb —2E 146
Vale Row. N5 —3B 50
Vale Royal. N7 —7J 49
Vale Royal Ho. WC2 —7H 67 (2D 166)
(off Charing Cross Rd.)
Valery Pl. Hamp —7E 114
Valeside Ct. Barn —4E 4
Vale St. SE27 —3D 122
Valeswood Rd. Brom —5H 125
Vale Ter. N4 —6C 32
Vale, The. N10 —1E 30
Vale, The. N21 —6E 6
Vale, The. NW11 —3F 47
Vale, The. SW3 —6B 84 (7A 170)
Vale, The. W3 —1K 81
Vale, The. Croy —2K 153
Vale, The. Felt —6K 95
Vale, The. Houn —6C 78
Vale, The. Ruis —4A 42
Vale, The. Sun —6J 113
Vale, The. Wfd G —7D 20
Valetta Gro. E13 —2J 71
Valetta Rd. W3 —2A 82
Valette Ct. N10 —4F 31
(off St James's La.)
Valette Ho. E9 —6J 51
Valette St. E9 —6J 51
Valiant Clo. N'holt —3B 60
Valiant Clo. Romf —2H 39
Valiant Ho. SE7 —5A 90
Valiant Way. E6 —5D 72
Vallance Rd. E2 & E1 —4G 69
Vallance Rd. N10 —2G 31
Vallentin Rd. E17 —4E 34
Valley Av. N12 —4G 15
Valley Clo. Pinn —2K 23
Valley Dri. NW9 —6G 27
Valleyfield Rd. SW16 —5K 121
Valley Fields Cres. Enf —2F 7
Valley Gdns. SW19 —7B 120
Valley Gdns. Wemb —7F 45
Valley Gro. SE7 —5A 90
Valleylink Est. Enf —6F 9
Valley M. Twic —2K 115
Valley Rd. SW16 —5K 121
Valley Rd. Belv —4H 93
Valley Rd. Brom & Short —2G 143
Valley Rd. Eri —4J 93
Valley Rd. Uxb —2A 58
Valley Side. E4 —2H 19
Valley Side. SE7 —5B 90
Valley Side Pde. E4 —2H 19
Valley Vw. Barn —6B 4
Valley Wlk. Croy —2J 153
Valliere Rd. NW10 —3C 64
Valliers Wood Rd. Sidc —1J 127
Vallis Way. W13 —5A 62
Vallis Way. Chess —4D 146
Valmar Rd. SE5 —1C 104
Valmar Trad. Est. SE5 —1C 104
Val McKenzie Av. N7 —3A 50
Valnay St. SW17 —5D 120
Valognes Av. E17 —1A 34
Valois Ho. SE1 —3F 87
(off Grange, The)
Valonia Gdns. SW18 —6H 101
Vambery Rd. SE18 —6G 91
Vanbrough Cres. N'holt —1A 60
Vanbrugh Clo. E16 —5B 72
Vanbrugh Ct. SE11 —4K 85
Vanbrugh Dri. W on T —7A 132
Vanbrugh Fields. SE3 —6H 89
Vanbrugh Hill. SE10 & SE3 —5H 89
Vanbrugh Pk. SE3 —7H 89
Vanbrugh Pk. Rd. SE3 —7H 89
Vanbrugh Pk. Rd. W. SE3 —7H 89
Vanbrugh Rd. W4 —3K 81
Vanbrugh Ter. SE3 —1H 107
Vanburgh Clo. Orp —7J 145
Vanburgh Ho. E1 —5F 69 (5J 163)
(off Folgate St.)
Vancouver Mans. Edgw —1H 27
Vancouver Rd. SE23 —2A 124
Vancouver Rd. Edgw —1H 27
Vancouver Rd. Hay —4K 59
Vancouver Rd. Rich —4C 116
Vanderbilt Rd. SW18 —1K 119
Vandome Clo. E16 —6K 71
Vandon Ct. SW1 —3G 85 (1B 172)
(off Petty France)
Vandon Pas. SW1 —3G 85 (1B 172)
Vandon St. SW1 —3G 85 (1B 172)
Van Dyck Av. N Mald —7K 135
Vandyke Clo. SW15 —7F 101
Vandyke Cross. SE9 —5C 108
Vandy St. EC2 —4E 68 (4G 163)
Vane Clo. NW3 —5B 48
Vane Clo. Harr —6F 27
Vanessa Clo. Belv —5G 93
Vanessa Way. Bex —3K 129
Vane St. SW1 —4G 85 (3B 172)
Van Gogh Clo. Iswth —3A 98
Van Gogh Ct. E14 —3F 89
Vanguard Building. E14 —2B 88
Vanguard Clo. E16 —5J 71
Vanguard Clo. Croy —1B 152
Vanguard Clo. Romf —2G 39
Vanguard St. SE8 —1C 106
Vanguard Trad. Est. E15 —1E 70
Vanguard Way. H'row A —2G 95
Vanguard Way. Wall —7J 151
Vanneck Sq. SW15 —5C 100
Vanoc Gdns. Brom —4J 125
Vansittart Rd. E7 —4H 53
Vansittart St. SE14 —7A 88
Vanston Pl. SW6 —7J 83
Vantage M. E14 —1E 88
(off Preston's Rd.)
Vantage W. W3 —4F 81
Vantrey Ho. SE11 —4J 173
Vant Rd. SW17 —5D 120
Varcoe Rd. SE16 —5H 87
Vardens Rd. SW11 —4B 102
Varden St. E1 —6H 69
Vardon Clo. W3 —6K 63
Vardon Ho. SE10 —1E 106
Varley Ho. NW6 —1J 65
(off Brondesbury Rd.)
Varley Pde. NW9 —4A 28
Varley Rd. E16 —6K 71
Varley Way. Mitc —2B 138
Varna Rd. SW6 —7G 83
Varna Rd. Hamp —1F 133
Varndell St. NW1 —3G 67 (1A 160)
Varsity Dri. Twic —5J 97
Varsity Row. SW14 —2J 99
Vartry Rd. N15 —6D 32
Vassall Rd. SW9 —7A 86
Vat Ho. SW8 —7J 85
(off Rita Rd.)
Vauban Est. SE1 —3F 87
Vauban St. SE16 —3F 87
Vaudeville Ct. N4 —2A 50
Vaughan Almshouses. Ashf —5D 112
(off Feltham Hill Rd.)
Vaughan Av. NW4 —5C 28
Vaughan Av. W6 —4B 82
Vaughan Clo. Hamp —6C 114
Vaughan Est. E2 —1J 163
Vaughan Gdns. Ilf —7D 36
Vaughan Ho. SE1 —2B 86 (6A 168)
(off Blackfriars Rd.)
Vaughan Ho. SW4 —7G 103
Vaughan Rd. E15 —6H 53
Vaughan Rd. SE5 —2C 104
Vaughan Rd. Harr —7G 25
Vaughan Rd. Th Dit —7B 134
Vaughan Rd. Well —2K 109
Vaughan St. SE16 —2B 88
Vaughan Way. E1 —7G 69
Vaughan Williams Clo. SE8 —7C 88
Vauxhall. —5J 85
Vauxhall Bri. SW1 & SE1 —5J 85 (6E 172)
Vauxhall Bri. Rd. SW1 —3G 85 (2A 172)
Vauxhall Cross. (Junct.) —5J 85
Vauxhall Cross. SE1 —5J 85 (6F 173)
Vauxhall Distribution Cen. SW8 —6H 85 (7C 172)
Vauxhall Gdns. S Croy —6C 152
Vauxhall Gro. SW8 —6K 85 (7G 173)
Vauxhall St. SE11 —5K 85 (5H 173)
Vauxhall Wlk. SE11 —5K 85 (5G 173)
Veals Mead. Mitc —1C 138
Vectis Gdns. SW17 —6F 121
Vectis Rd. SW17 —6F 121
Veda Rd. SE13 —4C 106
Vega Rd. Bush —1B 10
Veldene Way. Harr —3D 42
Velde Way. SE22 —5E 104
Vellum Dri. Cars —3E 150
Venables Clo. Dag —4H 57
Venables St. NW8 —4B 66 (5B 158)
Vencourt Pl. W6 —4C 82
Venetian Rd. SE5 —2C 104
Venetia Rd. N4 —6B 32
Venetia Rd. W5 —2D 80
Venice Ct. SE5 —7C 86
(off Bowyer St.)
Venner Rd. SE26 —6J 123
Venners Clo. Bexh —2K 111
Venn Ho. N1 —1K 67
(off Barnsbury Est.)
Venn St. SW4 —4G 103
Ventnor Av. Stan —1B 26
Ventnor Dri. N20 —3E 14
Ventnor Gdns. Bark —6J 55
Ventnor Rd. SE14 —7K 87
Ventnor Rd. Sutt —7K 149
Venture Clo. Bex —7E 110
Venture Ct. SE12 —7J 107
Venue St. E14 —5E 70
Venus Rd. SE18 —3D 90
Vera Av. N21 —5F 7
Vera Lynn Clo. E7 —4J 53
Vera Rd. SW6 —1G 101
Verbena Clo. E16 —4H 71
Verbena Gdns. W6 —5C 82
Verdant Ct. SE6 —7G 107
(off Verdant La.)
Verdant La. SE6 —7G 107
Verdayne Av. Croy —1K 153
Verdi Ho. W10 —2G 65
(off Herries St.)
Verdun Rd. SE18 —6A 92
Verdun Rd. SW13 —6C 82
Vereker Dri. Sun —3J 131
Vereker Rd. W14 —5G 83
Vere St. W1 —6F 67 (1J 165)
Veritas Ho. Sidc —2A 128
(off Station Rd.)
Verity Clo. W11 —7G 65
Ver Meer Ct. E14 —3F 89
Vermeer Gdns. SE15 —4J 105
Vermont Clo. Enf —4G 7
Vermont Ho. E17 —2B 34
Vermont Rd. SE19 —6D 122
Vermont Rd. SW18 —6K 101
Vermont Rd. Sutt —3K 149
Verne Ct. W3 —3J 81
(off Vincent Rd.)
Verney Gdns. Dag —4E 56
Verney Ho. NW8 —3B 158
Verney Rd. SE16 —6G 87
Verney Rd. Dag —4E 56
(in two parts)
Verney St. NW10 —3K 45
Verney Way. SE16 —5H 87
Vernham Rd. SE18 —6G 91
Vernon Av. E12 —4D 54
Vernon Av. SW20 —2F 137
Vernon Av. Wfd G —7E 20
Vernon Clo. Eps —6J 147
Vernon Ct. NW2 —3H 47
Vernon Ct. W5 —7C 62
Vernon Ct. Stan —1B 26
Vernon Cres. Barn —6K 5
Vernon Dri. Stan —1A 26
Vernon Ho. SE11 —6H 173
Vernon Ho. WC1 —5J 67 (6F 161)
(off Vernon Pl.)
Vernon M. E17 —5B 34
Vernon M. W14 —4G 83
(off Vernon St.)
Vernon Pl. WC1 —5J 67 (6F 161)
Vernon Ri. WC1 —3K 67 (1H 161)
Vernon Ri. Gnfd —5H 43
Vernon Rd. E3 —2B 70
Vernon Rd. E11 —1G 53
Vernon Rd. E15 —7G 53
Vernon Rd. E17 —5B 34
Vernon Rd. N8 —3A 32
Vernon Rd. SW14 —3K 99
Vernon Rd. Felt —2H 113
Vernon Rd. Ilf —1K 55
Vernon Rd. Sutt —5A 150
Vernon Sq. WC1 —3K 67 (1H 161)
Vernon St. W14 —4G 83
Vernon Yd. W11 —7H 65
Veroan Rd. Bexh —2E 110
Verona Dri. Surb —2E 146
Verona Rd. E7 —7J 53
Veronica Gdns. SW16 —1G 139
Veronica Ho. SE4 —3B 106
Veronica Rd. SW17 —2F 121
Veronique Gdns. Ilf —5G 37
Verran Rd. SW12 —7F 103
Versailles Rd. SE20 —7G 123
Verulam Av. E17 —6B 34
Verulam Bldgs. WC1 —5H 161
Verulam Ct. NW9 —7C 28
Verulam Ct. S'hall —6G 61
(off Haldane Rd.)
Verulam Rd. Gnfd —4E 60
Verulam St. WC1 —5A 68 (5J 161)
Verwood Dri. Barn —3J 5
Verwood Lodge. E14 —3F 89
Verwood Rd. Harr —2G 25
Veryan Ct. N8 —5H 31
Vesage Ct. EC1 —5A 68
(off Leather La.)
Vesey Path. E14 —6D 70
Vespan Rd. W12 —2C 82
Vessey Path. E14 —6D 70
Vesta Rd. SE4 —2A 106
Vestris Rd. SE23 —2K 123
Vestry Ct. SW1 —3H 85 (2D 172)
(off Monck St.)
Vestry House Mus. —4D 34
Vestry M. SE5 —1E 104
Vestry Rd. E17 —4D 34
Vestry Rd. SE5 —1E 104
Vestry St. N1 —3D 68 (1E 162)
Vevey St. SE6 —2B 124
Veysey Gdns. Dag —3G 57
Viaduct Bldgs. EC1 —5A 68 (6K 161)
Viaduct Pl. E2 —3H 69
Viaduct Rd. N2 —2B 30
Viaduct St. E2 —3H 69
Viaduct, The. E18 —2J 35
Viaduct, The. Wemb —1E 62
Vian St. SE13 —3D 106
Viant Ho. NW10 —7K 45
Vibart Gdns. SW2 —7K 103
Vibart Wlk. N1 —1J 67
(off Outram Pl.)
Vibia Clo. Stanw —7A 94
Vicarage Clo. Eri —6J 93
Vicarage Clo. N'holt —7D 42
Vicarage Clo. Ruis —7F 23
Vicarage Clo. Wor Pk —1A 148
Vicarage Ct. W8 —2K 83
Vicarage Ct. Beck —3A 142
Vicarage Ct. Felt —7E 94
Vicarage Ct. Ilf —5F 55
Vicarage Cres. SW11 —1B 102
Vicarage Dri. SW14 —5K 99
Vicarage Dri. Bark —7G 55
Vicarage Dri. Beck —1C 142
Vicarage Farm Ct. Houn —7D 78
Vicarage Farm Rd. Houn —2C 96
Vicarage Fields. W on T —6A 132
Vicarage Fld. Shop. Cen. Bark —7G 55
Vicarage Gdns. SW14 —5J 99
Vicarage Gdns. W8 —1J 83
Vicarage Gdns. Mitc —3C 138
Vicarage Ga. W8 —1K 83
Vicarage Gro. SE5 —1D 104
Vicarage La. E6 —3D 72
Vicarage La. E15 —7G 53
Vicarage La. Eps —7C 148
(in two parts)
Vicarage La. Ilf —1H 55
Vicarage M. NW9 —2K 45
Vicarage Pde. N15 —4C 32
Vicarage Pk. SE18 —5G 91
Vicarage Path. N8 —7J 31
Vicarage Rd. E10 —7C 34
Vicarage Rd. E15 —7H 53
Vicarage Rd. N17 —1G 33
Vicarage Rd. NW4 —6C 28
Vicarage Rd. SE18 —5G 91
(in two parts)
Vicarage Rd. SW14 —5J 99
Vicarage Rd. Bex —1H 129
Vicarage Rd. Croy —3A 152
Vicarage Rd. Dag —7H 57
Vicarage Rd. Hamp W —1C 134
Vicarage Rd. King T —2D 134
Vicarage Rd. Sun —5H 113
Vicarage Rd. Sutt —4K 149
Vicarage Rd. Tedd —5A 116
Vicarage Rd. Twic & Whit —2J 115
(Green, The)
Vicarage Rd. Twic & Whit —6G 97
(Kneller Rd.)
Vicarage Rd. Wfd G —7H 21
Vicarage Wlk. SW11 —1B 102
Vicarage Wlk. W on T —7J 131
Vicarage Way. NW10 —3K 45
Vicarage Way. Harr —7E 24
Vicars Bri. Clo. Wemb —2E 62
Vicar's Clo. E9 —1J 69
Vicars Clo. E15 —1J 71
Vicars Clo. Enf —2K 7
Vicar's Hill. SE13 —4D 106
Vicars Moor La. N21 —7F 7
Vicars Oak Rd. SE19 —6E 122
Vicar's Rd. NW5 —5E 48
Vicars Wlk. Dag —3B 56
Viceroy Clo. N2 —4C 30
Viceroy Ct. NW8 —2C 66
(off Prince Albert Rd.)
Viceroy Ct. Croy —1D 152
Viceroy Pde. N2 —3C 30
(off High Rd.)
Viceroy Rd. SW8 —1J 103
Vickers Clo. Wall —7K 151
Vickers Rd. Eri —5K 93
Vickers Way. Houn —5C 96
Vickery Ct. EC1 —4C 68 (3D 162)
(off Bartholomew Sq.)
Victor Cazalet Ho. N1 —1B 68
(off Gaskin St.)
Victor Gro. Wemb —7E 44
Victoria & Albert Mus. —3B 84 (2B 170)
Victoria Arc. SW1 —3F 85
(off Victoria St.)
Victoria Av. E6 —1B 72
Victoria Av. EC2 —5E 68 (6H 163)
Victoria Av. N3 —1H 29
Victoria Av. Barn —4G 5
Victoria Av. Hil & Uxb —6D 40
Victoria Av. Houn —5E 96
Victoria Av. Surb —6D 134
Victoria Av. Wall —3E 150
Victoria Av. Wemb —6H 45
Victoria Av. W Mol —3F 133
Victoria Bldgs. E8 —1H 69
(off Mare St.)
Victoria Clo. Barn —4G 5
Victoria Clo. Harr —6K 25
Victoria Clo. Hay —6F 59
Victoria Clo. W Mol —3E 132
Victoria Colonnade. WC1 —5J 67 (6F 161)
(off Southampton Row)
Victoria Cotts. E1 —5G 69
(off Deal St.)
Victoria Cotts. Rich —1F 99
Victoria Ct. E18 —3K 35
Victoria Ct. SE26 —6J 123
Victoria Ct. W3 —2G 81
Victoria Ct. Wemb —6G 45
Victoria Cres. N15 —5E 32
Victoria Cres. SE19 —6E 122
Victoria Cres. SW19 —7H 119
Victoria Dock Rd. E16 —6H 71
Victoria Dri. SW19 —7F 101
Victoria Embkmt. SW1 & WC2 —2J 85 (6F 167)
Victoria Gdns. W11 —1J 83
Victoria Gdns. Houn —1C 96
Victoria Gro. N12 —5G 15
Victoria Gro. W8 —3A 84
Victoria Gro. M. W2 —7J 65
Victoria Hall. E16 —1J 89
(off Wesley Av., in two parts)
Victoria Ho. E6 —6E 72
Victoria Ho. SW1 —4G 85 (5J 171)
(off Francis St.)
Victoria Ho. SW1 —5F 85 (3B 172)
(off Ebury Bri. Rd.)
Victoria Ho. SW8 —7J 85
(off S. Lambeth Rd.)
Victoria Ho. Edgw —6C 12
Victoria Ind. Est. W3 —5A 64
Victoria La. Barn —4C 4
Victoria La. Hay —5E 76
Victoria Mans. NW2 —7D 46
Victoria Mans. SW8 —7J 85
(off S. Lambeth Rd.)
Victoria M. NW6 —1J 65
Victoria M. SW4 —4F 103
Victoria M. SW18 —1A 120
Victorian Gro. N16 —4E 50
Victorian Rd. N16 —3E 50
Victoria Pde. Rich —1G 99
(off Sandycombe Rd.)
Victoria Pk. —1A 70
Victoria Pk. Ind. Cen. E9 —7C 52
(off Rothbury Rd.)
Victoria Pk. Rd. E9 —1J 69
Victoria Pk. Sq. E2 —3J 69

Victoria Pas.—Walpole Rd.

Victoria Pas. NW8 —3B 158
Victoria Pl. Rich —5D 98
Victoria Pl. Shop. Cen. SW1 —4F 85 (3K 171)
Victoria Point. E13 —2J 71
(off Victoria Rd.)
Victoria Retail Pk. Ruis —5B 42
Victoria Ri. SW4 —3F 103
Victoria Rd. E4 —1B 20
Victoria Rd. E11 —4G 53
Victoria Rd. E13 —2J 71
Victoria Rd. E17 —2E 34
Victoria Rd. E18 —2K 35
Victoria Rd. N4 —7K 31
Victoria Rd. N15 —4G 33
Victoria Rd. N18 & N9 —4A 18
Victoria Rd. N22 —1G 31
Victoria Rd. NW4 —4E 28
Victoria Rd. NW6 —2H 65
Victoria Rd. NW7 —5G 13
Victoria Rd. NW10 —5K 63
Victoria Rd. SW14 —3K 99
Victoria Rd. W3 —5K 63
Victoria Rd. W5 —5B 62
Victoria Rd. W8 —3A 84
Victoria Rd. Bark —6F 55
Victoria Rd. Barn & New Bar —4G 5
Victoria Rd. Bexh —4G 111
Victoria Rd. Brom —5B 144
Victoria Rd. Buck H —2G 21
Victoria Rd. Bush —1A 10
Victoria Rd. Chst —5E 126
Victoria Rd. Dag —5H 57
Victoria Rd. Eri —6K 93
(in two parts)
Victoria Rd. Felt —1K 113
Victoria Rd. King T —2F 135
Victoria Rd. Mitc —7C 120
Victoria Rd. Ruis —1J 41
Victoria Rd. Sidc —3K 127
Victoria Rd. S'hall —3D 78
Victoria Rd. Surb —6D 134
Victoria Rd. Sutt —5B 150
Victoria Rd. Tedd —6A 116
Victoria Rd. Twic —7B 98
Victoria Sq. SW1 —3F 85 (1K 171)
Victoria St. E15 —7G 53
Victoria St. SW1 —3G 85 (2K 171)
Victoria St. Belv —5F 93
Victoria Ter. N4 —1A 50
Victoria Ter. NW10 —4B 64
Victoria Ter. SW8 —2F 103
Victoria Ter. W5 —1D 80
Victoria Ter. Harr —1H 43
Victoria Vs. Rich —3F 99
Victoria Way. SE7 —5K 89
Victoria Way. Ruis —5B 42
Victoria Wharf. E14 —7A 70
Victoria Works. NW2 —2D 46
Victoria Yd. E1 —6G 69
Victor Rd. NW10 —3D 64
Victor Rd. SE20 —7K 123
Victor Rd. Harr —3G 25
Victor Rd. Tedd —4J 115
Victors Dri. Hamp —6C 114
Victors Way. Barn —3C 4
Victor Vs. N9 —3J 17
Victory Av. Mord —5A 138
Victory Bus. Cen. Iswth —4K 97
Victory Ct. W9 —4J 65
(off Hermes Clo.)
Victory Pl. E14 —7A 70
Victory Pl. SE17 —4D 86
Victory Pl. SE19 —7E 122
Victory Rd. E11 —4K 35
Victory Rd. SW19 —7A 120
Victory Rd. M. SW19 —7A 120
Victory Wlk. SE8 —1C 106
Victory Way. SE16 —2A 88
Victory Way. Houn —5A 78
Victory Way. Romf —2H 39
Vidler Clo. Chess —6C 146
Vienna Clo. Ilf —2B 36
View Clo. N6 —7D 30
View Clo. Harr —4H 25
View Ct. SE12 —3A 126
View Cres. N8 —5H 31
Viewfield Clo. Harr —7E 26
Viewfield Rd. SW18 —6H 101
Viewfield Rd. Bex —1C 128
Viewland Rd. SE18 —5K 91
View Rd. N6 —7D 30
View, The. SE2 —5E 92
Vigar Ct. Barn —3B 4
Viga Rd. N21 —6F 7
Vigilant Clo. SE26 —4G 123
Vignoles Rd. Romf —7G 39
Vigo St. W1 —7G 67 (3A 166)
Viking Clo. E3 —2A 70
Viking Ct. SW6 —6J 83
(off Halford Rd.)
Viking Gdns. E6 —4C 72
Viking Ho. SE5 —2C 104
(off Denmark Rd.)
Viking Pl. E10 —1B 52
Viking Rd. S'hall —7C 60
Viking Way. Eri —3J 93
Villacourt Rd. SE18 —7A 92
Village Arc. E4 —1A 20
Village Clo. E4 —5K 19
Village Clo. NW3 —5B 48
(off Belsize La.)
Village Ct. SE3 —3G 107
(off Hurren Clo.)
Village Heights. Wfd G —5C 20
Village M. NW9 —2K 45
Village Pk. Clo. Enf —6K 7
Village Rd. N3 —2G 29
Village Rd. Enf —5K 7
Village Row. Sutt —7J 149
Village, The. NW3 —2A 48
Village, The. SE7 —6A 90
Village Way. NW10 —4K 45
Village Way. SE24 —6D 104
Village Way. Ashf —4B 112
Village Way. Beck —2C 142
Village Way. Pinn —7C 24
Village Way E. Harr —7E 24
Villa Rd. SW9 —3A 104
Villas on the Heath. NW3 —3A 48
Villas Rd. SE18 —5G 91
(in three parts)
Villa St. SE17 —5D 86
Villa Wlk. SE17 —5D 86
(off Inville Rd.)
Villiers Av. Surb —5F 135
Villiers Av. Twic —1D 114
Villiers Clo. E10 —2C 52
Villiers Clo. Surb —4F 135
Villiers Gro. Sutt —7F 149
Villiers Path. Surb —5E 134
Villiers Rd. NW2 —6C 46
Villiers Rd. Beck —2K 141
Villiers Rd. Iswth —2J 97
Villiers Rd. King T —4F 135
Villiers Rd. S'hall —1D 78
Villiers St. WC2 —1J 85 (3E 166)
Vincam Clo. Twic —7E 96
Vincennes Est. SE27 —4D 122
Vincent Av. Surb —2J 147
Vincent Clo. SE16 —2A 88
Vincent Clo. Barn —3E 4
Vincent Clo. Brom —4K 143
Vincent Clo. Sidc —1J 127
Vincent Clo. W Dray —6C 76
Vincent Ct. N4 —1J 49
Vincent Ct. NW4 —4F 29
Vincent Ct. SW9 —1K 103
Vincent Ct. W1 —6D 66 (7E 158)
(off Seymour Pl.)
Vincent Ct. N'wd —1H 23
Vincent Dri. Shep —3G 131
Vincent Dri. Uxb —1B 58
Vincent Gdns. NW2 —3B 46
Vincent Ho. SW1 —4H 85 (4C 172)
(off Vincent Sq.)
Vincent M. E3 —2C 70
Vincent Rd. E4 —6A 20
Vincent Rd. N15 —4C 32
Vincent Rd. N22 —2A 32
Vincent Rd. SE18 —4F 91
Vincent Rd. W3 —3J 81
Vincent Rd. Croy —7E 140
Vincent Rd. Dag —7E 56
Vincent Rd. Houn —2B 96
Vincent Rd. Iswth —1H 97
Vincent Rd. King T —3G 135
Vincent Rd. Wemb —7F 45
Vincent Row. Hamp H —6G 115
Vincents Path. N'holt —6C 42
(off Arnold Rd.)
Vincent Sq. N22 —2A 32
Vincent Sq. SW1 —4H 85 (3C 172)
Vincent Sq. Mans. SW1 —4G 85 (3B 172)
(off Walcott St.)
Vincent St. E16 —5H 71
Vincent St. SW1 —4H 85 (3C 172)
Vincent Ter. N1 —2B 68
Vince St. EC1 —3D 68 (2F 163)
Vine Clo. Surb —6F 135
Vine Clo. Sutt —3A 150
Vine Clo. W Dray —4C 76
Vine Ct. E1 —5G 69
Vine Ct. Harr —6E 26
Vinegar All. E17 —4D 34
Vine Gdns. Ilf —5G 55
Vinegar St. E1 —1H 87
Vinegar Yd. SE1 —6G 169
Vine Gro. Uxb —7C 40
Vine Hill. EC1 —4A 68 (4J 161)
Vine La. SE1 —1E 86 (5H 169)
Vine La. Hil & Uxb —1B 58
Vine Pl. W5 —1E 80
(off Grange Pk.)
Vine Pl. Houn —4F 97
Viner Clo. W on T —6A 132
Vineries Bank. NW7 —5J 13
Vineries Clo. Dag —6F 57
Vineries Clo. W Dray —6C 76
Vineries, The. N14 —6B 6
Vineries, The. SE6 —1C 124
Vineries, The. Enf —3K 7
Vine Rd. E15 —7H 53
Vine Rd. SW13 —3B 100
Vine Rd. E Mol —4G 133
Vinery Way. W6 —3D 82
Vines Av. N3 —1K 29
Vine Sq. W14 —5H 83
(off Star Rd.)
Vine St. EC3 —6F 69 (1J 169)
Vine St. W1 —7G 67 (3B 166)
Vine St. Romf —4J 39
Vine St. Bri. EC1 —4A 68 (4K 161)
Vine Yd. SE1 —6D 168
Vineyard Av. NW7 —7B 14
Vineyard Clo. SE6 —1C 124
Vineyard Clo. King T —3F 135
Vineyard Gro. N3 —1K 29
Vineyard Hill Rd. SW19 —4H 119
Vineyard M. EC1 —3K 161
Vineyard Pas. Rich —5E 98
Vineyard Path. SW14 —3K 99
Vineyard Rd. Felt —3J 113
Vineyard Row. Hamp W —1C 134
Vineyards, The. Felt —3J 113
(off High St.)
Vineyards, The. Sun —3J 131
Vineyard, The. Rich —5E 98
Vineyard Wlk. EC1 —4A 68 (3J 161)
Viney Bank. Croy —7B 154
Viney Rd. SE13 —3D 106
Vining St. SW9 —4A 104
Vinlake Av. Uxb —3B 40
Vinopolis, City of Wine. —4D 168
Vinson Clo. Orp —7K 145
Vintners Ct. EC4 —7C 68
Vintners Hall. EC4 —7C 68 (2D 168)
(off Up. Thames St.)
Vintners Pl. EC4 —7C 68 (3D 168)
Vintry M. E17 —4C 34
Viola Av. SE2 —4B 92
Viola Av. Felt —6A 96
Viola Av. Stai —1A 112
Viola Sq. W12 —7B 64
Violet Av. Enf —1J 7
Violet Av. Uxb —5B 58
Violet Clo. E16 —4G 71
Violet Clo. SE8 —6B 88
Violet Clo. Wall —1E 150
Violet Gdns. Croy —5B 152
Violet Hill. NW8 —2A 66
Violet Hill Ho. NW8 —2A 66
(off Violet Hill)
Violet La. Croy —6B 152
Violet Rd. E3 —4D 70
Violet Rd. E17 —6C 34
Violet Rd. E18 —2K 35
Violet St. E2 —4H 69
V.I.P. Trading Est. SE7 —4A 90
Virgil Pl. W1 —5D 66 (6E 158)
Virgil St. SE1 —3K 85 (1H 173)
Virginia Clo. N Mald —4J 135
Virginia Clo. Romf —1J 39
Virginia Ct. WC1 —4H 67 (3D 160)
(off Burton St.)
Virginia Gdns. Ilf —2G 37
Virginia Ho. E14 —7E 70
Virginia Rd. E2 —3F 69 (2J 163)
Virginia Rd. T Hth —1B 140
Virginia St. E1 —7G 69
Virginia Wlk. SW2 —6K 103
Viscount Clo. N11 —6A 16
Viscount Ct. W2 —6J 65
(off Pembridge Vs.)
Viscount Dri. E6 —5D 72
Viscount Gro. N'holt —3B 60
Viscount Rd. Stanw —1A 112
Viscount St. EC1 —4C 68 (4C 162)
Viscount Way. H'row A —4G 95
Vista Av. Enf —2E 8
Vista Dri. Ilf —5B 36
Vista, The. SE9 —6B 108
Vista, The. Sidc —5K 127
Vista Way. Harr & Kent —6E 26
Vittoria Ho. N1 —1K 67
(off High Rd.)
Viveash Clo. Hay —3H 77
Vivian Av. NW4 —5D 28
Vivian Av. Wemb —5G 45
Vivian Comma Clo. N4 —3B 50
Vivian Ct. N12 —5E 14
Vivian Gdns. Wemb —5G 45
Vivian Mans. NW4 —5D 28
(off Vivian Av.)
Vivian Rd. E3 —2A 70
Vivian Sq. SE15 —3H 105
Vivian Way. N2 —5B 30
Vivien Clo. Chess —7E 146
Vivienne Clo. Twic —6D 98
Voce Rd. SE18 —7H 91
Voewood Clo. N Mald —6B 136
Vogans Mill. SE1 —2F 87 (6K 169)
Vogue Ct. Brom —1K 143
Vollasky Ho. E1 —5G 69 (5K 163)
(off Daplyn St.)
Voltaire Rd. SW4 —3H 103
Voltaire Way. Hay —7G 59
Volt Av. NW10 —3K 63
Volta Way. Croy —1K 151
Voluntary Pl. E11 —6J 35
Vorley Rd. N19 —2G 49
Voss Ct. SW16 —6J 121
Voss St. E2 —3G 69
Voyager Bus. Est. SE16 —3G 87
(off Spa Rd.)
Voyagers Clo. SE28 —6C 74
Vulcan Clo. E6 —6E 72
Vulcan Clo. Wall —7K 151
(off Handley Page Rd.)
Vulcan Ga. Enf —2F 7
Vulcan Rd. SE4 —2B 106
Vulcan Sq. E14 —4D 88
Vulcan Ter. SE4 —2B 106
Vulcan Way. N7 —6K 49
Vyner Rd. W3 —7K 63
Vyner St. E9 —1H 69
Vyner's Way. Uxb —5C 40
Vyne, The. Bexh —3H 111

Wadbrook St. King T —2D 134
Wadding St. SE17 —4D 86
Waddington Clo. Enf —4K 7
Waddington Rd. E15 —5F 53
Waddington St. E15 —6F 53
Waddington Way. SE19 —7C 122
Waddon. —3A 152
Waddon Clo. Croy —3A 152
Waddon Ct. Rd. Croy —3A 152
Waddon Marsh Way. Croy —1K 151
Waddon New Rd. Croy —3B 152
Waddon Pk. Av. Croy —4A 152
Waddon Rd. Croy —3A 152
Waddon Way. Croy —6A 152
Wade Ct. N10 —7A 16
Wade Ho. SE1 —2G 87 (7K 169)
(off Parkers Row)
Wade Ho. Enf —5J 7
Wades Gro. N21 —7F 7
Wades Hill. N21 —6F 7
Wades La. Tedd —5A 116
Wadeson St. E2 —2H 69
Wade's Pl. E14 —7D 70
Wadeville Av. Romf —6E 38
Wadeville Clo. Belv —6G 93
Wadham Av. E17 —7J 19
Wadham Clo. Shep —7E 130
Wadham Gdns. NW3 —1C 66
Wadham Gdns. Gnfd —6H 43
Wadham Rd. E17 —7J 19
Wadham Rd. SW15 —4G 101
Wadhurst Clo. SE20 —2H 141
Wadhurst Rd. SW8 —1G 103
Wadhurst Rd. W4 —3K 81
Wadley Rd. E11 —7G 35
Wadsworth Bus. Cen. Gnfd —2C 62
Wadsworth Clo. Enf —5E 8
Wadsworth Clo. Gnfd —2C 62
Wadsworth Rd. Gnfd —2B 62
Wager St. E3 —4B 70
Waggoners Roundabout. (Junct.) —1K 95
Waggon La. N17 —6B 18
Waggon M. N14 —1B 16
Waghorn Rd. E13 —1A 72
Waghorn Rd. Harr —3D 26
Waghorn St. SE15 —3G 105
Wagner St. SE15 —7J 87
Wagstaff Gdns. Dag —7C 56
Wagtail Clo. NW9 —2A 28
Wagtail Wlk. Beck —5E 142
Waight's Ct. King T —1E 134
Wainfleet Av. Romf —2J 39
Wainford Clo. SW19 —7F 101
Wainwright Gro. Iswth —4H 97
Waite Davies Rd. SE12 —7H 107
Waite St. SE15 —6F 87
Waithman St. EC4 —6B 68
(off Apothecary St.)
Wakefield Ct. SE26 —6J 123
Wakefield Gdns. SE19 —7E 122
Wakefield Gdns. Ilf —6C 36
Wakefield Ho. SE15 —1G 105
Wakefield M. WC1 —3J 67 (2F 161)
Wakefield Rd. N11 —5C 16
Wakefield Rd. N15 —5F 33
Wakefield Rd. Rich —5D 98
Wakefield St. E6 —1B 72
Wakefield St. N18 —5B 18
Wakefield St. WC1 —4J 67 (2F 161)
Wakeford Clo. SW4 —5G 103
Wakehams Hill. Pinn —3D 24
Wakeham St. N1 —6D 50
Wakehurst Rd. SW11 —5C 102
Wakeling Rd. W7 —5K 61
Wakeling St. E1 —6A 70
Wakeling St. E14 —6A 70
Wakelin Ho. N1 —7B 50
(off Sebbon St.)
Wakelin Ho. SE23 —7A 106
Wakelin Rd. E15 —2G 71
Wakeman Rd. NW10 —3E 64
Wakemans Hill Av. NW9 —5K 27
Wakering Rd. Bark —6G 55
(in two parts)
Wakerings, The. Bark —6G 55
Wakerley Clo. E6 —6D 72
Wakley St. EC1 —3B 68 (1A 162)
Walberswick St. SW8 —7J 85
Walbrook. EC4 —7D 68 (2E 168)
(in three parts)
Walbrook Ho. N9 —2D 18
(off Huntingdon Rd.)
Walbrook Wharf. EC4 —7C 68 (3D 168)
(off Bell Wharf La.)
Walburgh St. E1 —6H 69
Walcorde Av. SE17 —4C 86
Walcot Gdns. SE11 —3J 173
Walcot Rd. Enf —2G 9
Walcot Sq. SE11 —4A 86 (3K 173)
Walcott St. SW1 —4G 85 (3B 172)
Waldair Ct. E16 —2F 91
Waldeck Gro. SE27 —3B 122
Waldeck Rd. N15 —4B 32
Waldeck Rd. SW14 —3J 99
Waldeck Rd. W4 —6G 81
Waldeck Rd. W13 —6B 62
Waldeck Ter. SW14 —3J 99
(off Waldeck Rd.)
Waldegrave Av. Tedd —5K 115
Waldegrave Ct. Bark —1H 73
Waldegrave Gdns. Twic —2K 115
Waldegrave Pk. Twic —4K 115
Waldegrave Rd. N8 —3A 32
Waldegrave Rd. SE19 —7F 123
Waldegrave Rd. W5 —7F 63
Waldegrave Rd. Brom —4C 144
Waldegrave Rd. Dag —2C 56
Waldegrave Rd. Tedd —4K 115
Waldegrove. Croy —3F 153
Waldemar Av. SW6 —1G 101
Waldemar Av. W13 —1C 80
Waldemar Rd. SW19 —5J 119
Walden Av. N13 —4H 17
Walden Av. Chst —4D 126
Walden Av. Rain —2K 75
Walden Clo. Belv —5F 93
Walden Ct. SW8 —1H 103
Walden Gdns. T Hth —3K 139
Walden Ho. SW1 —4E 84 (4H 171)
(off Pimlico Rd.)
Walden Pde. Chst —6D 126
(in two parts)
Walden Rd. N17 —1D 32
Walden Rd. Chst —6D 126
Waldenshaw Rd. SE23 —1J 123
Walden St. E1 —6H 69
Walden Way. NW7 —6A 14
Waldo Clo. SW4 —5G 103
Waldo Ind. Est. Brom —3B 144
Waldo Pl. Mitc —7C 120
Waldorf Clo. S Croy —7B 152
Waldo Rd. NW10 —3C 64
(in two parts)
Waldo Rd. Brom —3B 144
Waldram Cres. SE23 —1J 123
Waldram Pk. Rd. SE23 —1K 123
Waldram Pl. SE23 —1J 123
Waldrist Way. Eri —2F 93
Waldron Gdns. Brom —3F 143
Waldronhyrst. S Croy —4B 152
Waldron M. SW3 —6B 84 (7B 170)
Waldron Rd. SW18 —3A 120
Waldron Rd. Harr —1J 43
Waldron's Path. S Croy —4C 152
Waldrons, The. Croy —4B 152
Waldrons Yd. S Harr —2H 43
Waldstock Rd. SE28 —7A 74
Waleran Clo. Stan —5E 10
Walerand Rd. SE13 —2E 106
Waleran Flats. SE1 —4E 86
Wales Av. Cars —5C 150
Wales Clo. SE15 —7H 87
Wales Farm Rd. W3 —5K 63
Waleton Acres. Wall —6G 151
Waley St. E1 —5A 70
Walfield Av. N20 —7E 4
Walford Ho. E1 —6H 69
Walford Rd. N16 —4E 50
Walfrey Gdns. Dag —7E 56
Walham Green. —1K 101
Walham Grn. Ct. SW6 —7K 83
(off Waterford Rd.)
Walham Gro. SW6 —7J 83
Walham Ri. SW19 —6G 119
Walham Yd. SW6 —7J 83
Walkato Lodge. Buck H —1F 21
Walkden Rd. Chst —5E 126
Walker Clo. N11 —4B 16
Walker Clo. SE18 —4G 91
Walker Clo. W7 —1J 79
Walker Clo. Felt —7H 95
Walker Clo. Hamp —6D 114
Walker Ho. NW1 —2H 67 (1C 160)
Walker's Ct. W1 —2C 166
Walkerscroft Mead. SE21 —1C 122
Walkers Pl. SW15 —4G 101
Walkford Way. SE15 —7F 87
Walkinshaw Ct. N1 —7C 50
(off Rotherfield St.)
Walks, The. N2 —3B 30
Walk, The. N13 —3F 17
(off Fox La.)
Walk, The. Sun —7H 113
Wallace Clo. SE28 —7D 74
Wallace Clo. Shep —4F 131
Wallace Clo. Uxb —2A 58
Wallace Collection. —6E 66 (7H 159)
Wallace Ct. NW1 —5C 66 (6D 158)
(off Old Marylebone Rd.)
Wallace Cres. Cars —5D 150
Wallace Ho. N7 —6K 49
(off Caledonian Rd.)
Wallace Rd. N1 —6C 50
Wallace Way. N19 —2H 49
(off St John's Way)
Wallasey Cres. Uxb —2C 40
Wallbrook Bus. Cen. Houn —3K 95
Wallbutton Rd. SE4 —2A 106
Wallcote Av. NW2 —1F 47
Wall Ct. N4 —1K 49
(off Stroud Grn. Rd.)
Wallend. —1E 72
Wall End Ct. E6 —1E 72
(off Wall End Rd.)
Wall End Rd. E6 —7D 54
Waller Dri. N'wd —2J 23
Waller Rd. SE14 —1K 105
Wallers Clo. Dag —1E 74
Wallers Clo. Wfd G —6J 21
Waller Way. SE10 —7D 88
Wallflower St. W12 —7B 64
Wallgrave Rd. SW5 —4K 83
Wallingford Av. W10 —5F 65
Wallington. —6G 151
Wallington Clo. Ruis —6E 22
Wallington Corner. Wall —4F 151
(off Manor Rd. N.)
Wallington Ct. Wall —6F 151
(off Stanley Pk. Rd.)
Wallington Green. (Junct.) —4F 151
Wallington Rd. Ilf —7K 37
Wallington Sq. Wall —6F 151
Wallis All. SE1 —6D 168
Wallis Clo. SW11 —3B 102
Wallis Ho. SE14 —1A 106
Wallis M. N8 —3A 32
(off Courcy Rd.)
Wallis Rd. E9 —6B 52
Wallis Rd. S'hall —6F 61
Wallis's Cotts. SW2 —7J 103
Wallman Pl. N22 —1K 31
Wallorton Gdns. SW14 —4K 99
Wallside. EC2 —6D 162
Wall St. N1 —6D 50
Wallwood Rd. E11 —7F 35
Wallwood St. E3 —5B 70
Wallwood St. E14 —5B 70
Walmar Clo. Barn —1G 5
Walmer Clo. E4 —2J 19
Walmer Clo. Romf —2H 39
Walmer Gdns. W13 —2A 80
Walmer Pl. W1 —5E 158
Walmer Rd. W10 —6E 64
Walmer Rd. W11 —7G 65
Walmer St. W1 —5D 66 (5E 158)
Walmer Ter. SE18 —4G 91
Walmgate Rd. Gnfd —1B 62
Walmington Fold. N12 —6D 14
Walm La. NW2 —6E 46
Walney Wlk. N1 —6C 50
Walnut Av. W Dray —3C 76
Walnut Clo. SE8 —6B 88
Walnut Clo. Cars —5D 150
Walnut Clo. Hay —7G 59
Walnut Clo. Ilf —4G 37
Walnut Ct. E17 —4E 34
Walnut Ct. W5 —2E 80
Walnut Ct. W8 —3K 83
(off St Mary's Pl.)
Walnut Fields. Eps —7B 148
Walnut Gdns. E15 —5G 53
Walnut Gro. Enf —5J 7
Walnut M. Sutt —7A 150
Walnut Rd. E10 —2C 52
Walnut Tree Av. Mitc —3C 138
Walnut Tree Clo. SW13 —1B 100
Walnut Tree Clo. Chst —1H 145
Walnut Tree Clo. Shep —3E 130
Walnut Tree Cotts. SW19 —5G 119
Walnut Tree Ho. SW10 —6K 83
(off Tregunter Rd.)
Walnut Tree Rd. SE10 —5G 89
(in two parts)
Walnut Tree Rd. Bren —6E 80
Walnut Tree Rd. Dag —2E 56
Walnut Tree Rd. Houn —6D 78
Walnut Tree Rd. Shep —2E 130
Walnut Tree Wlk. SE11 —4A 86 (3J 173)
Walnut Way. Buck H —3G 21
Walnut Way. Ruis —6A 42
Walpole Av. Rich —2F 99
Walpole Clo. W13 —2C 80
Walpole Ct. W14 —3F 83
(off Blythe Rd.)
Walpole Ct. Twic —2J 115
Walpole Cres. Tedd —5K 115
Walpole Gdns. W4 —5J 81
Walpole Gdns. Twic —2J 115
Walpole Ho. SE1 —2A 86 (7J 167)
(off Westminster Bri. Rd.)
Walpole Lodge. W5 —1C 80
Walpole M. NW8 —1B 66
Walpole M. SW19 —6B 120
Walpole Pl. SE18 —4F 91
Walpole Pl. Tedd —5K 115
Walpole Rd. E6 —7A 54
Walpole Rd. E17 —4A 34
Walpole Rd. E18 —1H 35

Walpole Rd.—Watson St.

Walpole Rd. N17 —2C 32
(in two parts)
Walpole Rd. SW19 —6B 120
Walpole Rd. Brom —5B 144
Walpole Rd. Croy —2D 152
Walpole Rd. Surb —7E 134
Walpole Rd. Tedd —5K 115
Walpole Rd. Twic —2J 115
Walpole St. SW3 —5D 84 (5E 170)
Walrond Av. Wemb —5E 44
Walsham Clo. N16 —1G 51
Walsham Clo. SE28 —7D 74
Walsham Ho. SE14 —2K 105
Walsham Ho. SE17 —5D 86
(off Blackwood St.)
Walsham Rd. SE14 —2K 105
Walsham Rd. Felt —7K 95
Walsingham. NW8 —1B 66
Walsingham Gdns. Eps —4A 148
Walsingham Lodge. SW13 —1C 100
Walsingham Mans. SW6 —7K 83
(off Fulham Rd.)
Walsingham Pk. Chst —2H 145
Walsingham Pl. SW11 —6E 102
Walsingham Rd. E5 —3G 51
Walsingham Rd. W13 —1A 80
Walsingham Rd. Enf —4J 7
Walsingham Rd. Mitc —5D 138
Walsingham Wlk. Belv —6G 93
Walston Ho. SW1 —5H 85 (5C 172)
(off Aylesford St.)
Walter Ct. W3 —6J 63
(off Lynton Ter.)
Walter Grn. Ho. SE15 —1J 105
(off Lausanne Rd.)
Walter Hurford Pde. E12 —4E 54
Walter Rodney Clo. E6 —6D 54
Walters Clo. SE17 —4D 86
(off Brandon St.)
Walters Ho. SE11 —6B 86
(off Brandon Est.)
Walters Rd. SE25 —4E 140
Walters Rd. Enf —4D 8
Walter St. E2 —3K 69
Walter St. King T —1E 134
Walters Way. SE23 —6K 105
Walters Yd. Brom —2J 143
Walter Ter. E1 —6K 69
Walterton Rd. W9 —4H 65
Walter Wlk. Edgw —6D 12
Waltham Av. NW9 —6G 27
Waltham Av. Hay —3E 76
Waltham Dri. Edgw —2G 27
Waltham Ho. NW8 —1A 66
Waltham Pk. Way. E17 —1C 34
Waltham Rd. Cars —7B 138
Waltham Rd. S'hall —3C 78
Waltham Rd. Wfd G —6H 21
Walthamstow. —4C 34
Walthamstow Av. E4 —6G 19
Walthamstow Bus. Cen. E17 —2E 34
Walthamstow Greyhound Stadium. —7J 19
Waltham Way. E4 —3G 19
Waltheof Av. N17 —1D 32
Waltheof Gdns. N17 —1D 32
Walton Av. Harr —5D 42
Walton Av. N Mald —4B 136
Walton Av. Sutt —3H 149
Walton Bri. Shep & W on T —7G 131
Walton Bri. Rd. Shep —7G 131
Walton Clo. E5 —3K 51
Walton Clo. NW2 —2D 46
Walton Clo. SW8 —7J 85
Walton Clo. Harr —4H 25
Walton Ct. New Bar —5F 5
Walton Cft. Harr —4J 43
Walton Dri. NW10 —6K 45
Walton Dri. Harr —4H 25
Walton Gdns. W3 —5H 63
Walton Gdns. Felt —4H 113
Walton Gdns. Wemb —2E 44
Walton Grn. New Ad —7D 154
Walton Ho. E2 —4F 69 (3J 163)
Walton Ho. E4 —5H 19
(off Chingford Mt. Rd.)
Walton Ho. E17 —3D 34
(off Drive, The)
Walton La. Shep —7F 131
Walton La. Wey & W on T —7G 131
Walton-On-Thames. —7J 131
Walton Pl. SW3 —3D 84 (1E 170)
Walton Rd. E12 —4E 54
(in three parts)
Walton Rd. E13 —2A 72
Walton Rd. N15 —4F 33
Walton Rd. E Mol & W Mol —4D 132
Walton Rd. Harr —4H 25
Walton Rd. Romf —1F 39
Walton Rd. Sidc —2C 128
Walton Rd. W on T & W Mol —5A 132
Walton St. SW3 —4C 84 (3D 170)
Walton St. Enf —1J 7
Walton Way. W3 —5H 63
Walton Way. Mitc —4G 139
Walt Whitman Clo. SE24 —4B 104
Walworth. —5C 86
Walworth Pl. SE17 —5C 86
Walworth Rd. SE1 & SE17 —4C 86
Walwyn Av. Brom —3B 144
Wanborough Dri. SW15 —1D 118
Wanderer Dri. Bark —3C 74
Wandle Bank. SW19 —7B 120
Wandle Bank. Croy —3J 151
Wandle Ct. Croy —3J 151
Wandle Ct. Eps —4J 147
Wandle Ct. Gdns. Croy —3J 151
Wandle Ho. NW8 —5C 66 (5C 158)
(off Penfold St.)
Wandle Ho. Brom —5H 125
Wandle Pk. Trad. Est., The. Croy —2B 152
Wandle Rd. SW17 —2C 120
Wandle Rd. Bedd —3C 152
Wandle Rd. Croy —3J 151
Wandle Rd. Mord —4A 138
Wandle Rd. Wall —3F 151
Wandle Side. Croy —3K 151
Wandle Side. Wall —3F 151
Wandle Way. SW18 —1K 119
Wandle Way. Mitc —5D 138
Wandon Rd. SW6 —7K 83
(in two parts)
Wandsworth. —5K 101
Wandsworth Bri. SW6 & SW18 —3K 101
Wandsworth Bri. Rd. SW6 —1K 101
Wandsworth Common. —1D 120
Wandsworth Comn. W. Side. SW18 —5A 102
Wandsworth Gyratory.(Junct.) —5K 101
Wandsworth High St. SW18 —5J 101
Wandsworth Plain. SW18 —5K 101
Wandsworth Rd. SW8 —3F 103 (7E 172)
Wandsworth Shop. Cen. SW18 —6K 101
Wangey Rd. Chad H & Romf —7D 38
Wangford Ho. SW9 —4B 104
(off Loughborough Pk.)
Wanless Rd. SE24 —3C 104
Wanley Rd. SE5 —4D 104
Wanlip Rd. E13 —4K 71
Wannock Gdns. Ilf —1F 37
Wansbeck Ct. Enf —3G 7
(off Waverley Rd.)
Wansbeck Rd. E9 & E3 —7B 52
Wansdown Pl. SW6 —7K 83
Wansey St. SE17 —4C 86
Wansford Rd. Wfd G —1A 36
Wanstead. —5K 35
Wanstead Clo. Brom —2A 144
Wanstead Gdns. Ilf —6B 36
Wanstead La. Ilf —6C 36
Wanstead Pk. Av. E12 —1B 54
Wanstead Pk. Rd. Ilf —6B 36
Wanstead Pl. E11 —6J 35
Wanstead Rd. Brom —2A 144
Wansunt Rd. Bex —1J 129
Wantage Rd. SE12 —5H 107
Wantz Rd. Dag —4H 57
Wapping. —1H 87
Wapping Dock St. E1 —1H 87
Wapping High St. E1 —1G 87
Wapping La. E1 —7H 69
Wapping Wall. E1 —1J 87
Warbank La. King T —7B 118
Warbeck Rd. W12 —2D 82
Warberry Rd. N22 —2K 31
Warboys App. King T —6H 117
Warboys Cres. E4 —5K 19
Warboys Rd. King T —6H 117
Warburton Clo. N1 —6E 50
(off Culford Rd.)
Warburton Clo. Harr —6C 10
Warburton Ct. Ruis —2J 41
Warburton Ho. E8 —1H 69
(off Warburton St.)
Warburton Rd. E8 —1H 69
Warburton Rd. Twic —1F 115
Warburton St. E8 —1H 69
Warburton Ter. E17 —2D 34
Wardalls Gro. SE14 —7J 87
Wardalls Ho. SE8 —6B 88
(off Staunton St.)
Ward Clo. Eri —6K 93
Ward Clo. S Croy —6E 152
Wardell Clo. NW7 —7F 13
Wardell Fld. NW9 —1A 28
Warden Av. Harr —1D 42
Warden Rd. NW5 —6E 48
Wardens Gro. SE1 —1C 86 (5C 168)
Wardle St. E9 —5K 51
Wardley St. SW18 —7K 101
Wardo Av. SW6 —1G 101
Wardour M. W1 —1B 166
Wardour St. W1 —6G 67 (7B 160)
Ward Point. SE11 —4A 86 (4J 173)
Ward Rd. E15 —1F 71
Ward Rd. N19 —3G 49
Ward Rd. SW19 —1A 138
Wardrobe Pl. EC4 —1B 168
Wardrobe Ter. EC4 —2B 168
Wardrobe, The. Rich —5D 98
(off Old Pal. Yd.)
Wards Rd. Ilf —7H 37
Ware Ct. Sutt —4H 149
Wareham Clo. Houn —4F 97
Wareham Ho. SW8 —7K 85
Waremead Rd. Ilf —5F 37
Warepoint Dri. SE28 —2H 91
Warfield Rd. NW10 —3F 65
Warfield Rd. Felt —7G 95
Warfield Rd. Hamp —1F 133
Warfield Yd. NW10 —3F 65
(off Warfield Rd.)
Wargrave Av. N15 —6F 33
Wargrave Ho. E2 —3F 69 (2J 163)
(off Navarre St.)
Wargrave Rd. Harr —3G 43
Warham Rd. N4 —5A 32
Warham Rd. Harr —2K 25
Warham Rd. S Croy —5B 152
Warham St. SE5 —7B 86
Waring & Gillow Est. W3 —4G 63
Waring Rd. Sidc —6C 128
Waring St. SE27 —4C 122
Warkworth Gdns. Iswth —7A 80
Warkworth Rd. N17 —7J 17
Warland Rd. SE18 —7H 91
Warley Av. Dag —7F 39
Warley Av. Hay —6J 59
Warley Clo. E10 —1B 52
Warley Rd. N9 —2D 18
Warley Rd. Hay —6J 59
Warley Rd. Ilf —1E 36
Warley Rd. Wfd G —7E 20
Warley St. E2 —3K 69
Warlingham Rd. T Hth —4B 140
Warlock Rd. W9 —4H 65
Warlters Clo. N7 —4J 49
Warlters Rd. N7 —4J 49
Warltersville Mans. N19 —7J 31
Warltersville Rd. N19 —7J 31
Warmington Clo. E5 —3K 51
Warmington Rd. SE24 —6C 104
Warmington St. E13 —4J 71
Warmington Tower. SE14 —1A 106
Warminster Gdns. SE25 —2G 141
Warminster Rd. SE25 —2G 141
Warminster Sq. SE25 —2G 141
Warminster Way. Mitc —1F 139
Warmley Ct. SE15 —6E 86
(off Newent Ct.)
Warmsworth. NW1 —1G 67
(off Pratt St.)
Warndon St. SE16 —4K 87
Warneford Rd. Harr —3D 26
Warneford St. E9 —1H 69
Warne Pl. Sidc —6B 110
Warner Av. Sutt —2G 149
Warner Clo. E15 —5G 53
Warner Clo. NW9 —7B 28
Warner Clo. Hamp —5D 114
Warner Clo. Hay —7F 77
Warner Ho. NW8 —3A 66
Warner Ho. SE13 —2D 106
(off Russett Way)
Warner Pde. Hay —7F 77
Warner Pl. E2 —2G 69
Warner Rd. E17 —4A 34
Warner Rd. N8 —4H 31
Warner Rd. SE5 —1C 104
Warner Rd. Brom —7H 125
Warners Clo. Wfd G —5D 20
Warners La. Rich —4D 116
Warners Path. Wfd G —5D 20
Warner St. EC1 —4A 68 (4J 161)
Warner Ter. E14 —5C 70
(off Broomfield)
Warner Yd. EC1 —4J 161
Warnford Ho. SW15 —6A 100
(off Tunworth Cres.)
Warnford Ind. Est. Hay —2G 77
Warnham. WC1 —3K 67 (2G 161)
(off Sidmouth St.)
Warnham Ct. Rd. Cars —7D 150
Warnham Ho. SW2 —7K 103
(off Up. Tulse Hill)
Warnham Rd. N12 —5H 15
Warple M. W3 —2A 82
Warple Way. W3 —1A 82
(in two parts)
Warren Av. E10 —3E 52
Warren Av. Brom —7G 125
Warren Av. Rich —4H 99
Warren Av. S Croy —7K 153
Warren Clo. N9 —7E 8
Warren Clo. SE21 —7C 104
Warren Clo. Bexh —5G 111
Warren Clo. Hay —5A 60
Warren Clo. Wemb —2D 44
Warren Ct. N17 —3G 33
(off High Cross Rd.)
Warren Ct. W5 —5C 62
Warren Ct. Beck —7C 124
Warren Ct. Croy —1E 152
Warren Cres. N9 —7A 8
Warren Cutting. King T —7K 117
Warrender Rd. N19 —3G 49
Warrender Way. Ruis —7J 23
Warren Dri. Gnfd —4F 61
Warren Dri. Ruis —7B 24
Warren Dri. N. Surb —1H 147
Warren Dri. S. Surb —1J 147
Warren Dri., The. E11 —7A 36
Warren Farm Cotts. Romf —4F 39
Warren Fields. Stan —4H 11
Warren Footpath. Twic —1C 116
Warren Gdns. E15 —5F 53
Warren La. SE18 —3F 91
Warren La. Stan —2F 11
Warren M. W1 —4G 67 (4A 160)
Warren Pk. King T —6J 117
Warren Pk. Rd. Sutt —6B 150
Warren Pl. E1 —6K 69
(off Caroline St.)
Warren Pond Rd. E4 —1C 20
(in two parts)
Warren Ri. N Mald —1K 135
Warren Rd. E4 —2K 19
Warren Rd. E10 —3E 52
Warren Rd. E11 —6A 36
(in two parts)
Warren Rd. NW2 —2B 46
Warren Rd. SW19 —6C 120
Warren Rd. Ashf —7G 113
Warren Rd. Bexh —5G 111
Warren Rd. Brom —2J 155
Warren Rd. Bus H —1B 10
Warren Rd. Croy —1E 152
Warren Rd. Ilf —5H 37
Warren Rd. King T —6J 117
Warren Rd. Sidc —3C 128
Warren Rd. Twic —6G 97
Warren Rd. Uxb —4A 40
Warrens Shawe La. Edgw —2C 12
Warren St. W1 —4F 67 (4A 160)
Warren Ter. Romf —4D 38
(in two parts)
Warren, The. E12 —4C 54
Warren, The. Hay —6J 59
Warren, The. Houn —7D 78
Warren, The. Wor Pk —4K 147
Warren Wlk. SE7 —6A 90
Warren Way. NW7 —6B 14
Warren Wood Clo. Brom —2H 155
Warriner Gdns. SW11 —1D 102
Warrington Cres. W9 —4A 66
Warrington Gdns. W9 —4A 66
Warrington Pl. E14 —1E 88
(off Yabsley S)
Warrington Rd. Croy —3B 152
Warrington Rd. Dag —2D 56
Warrington Rd. Harr —5J 25
Warrington Rd. Rich —5D 98
Warrington Sq. Dag —2D 56
Warrior Sq. E12 —4E 54
Warsaw Clo. Ruis —6K 41
Warspite Ho. E14 —4D 88
Warspite Rd. SE18 —3C 90
Warton Rd. E15 —7E 52
Warwall. E6 —6F 73
Warwick. W14 —4H 83
(off Kensington Village)
Warwick Av. W9 & W2 —4K 65
Warwick Av. Edgw —3C 12
Warwick Av. Harr —4D 42
Warwick Chambers. W8 —3J 83
(off Pater St.)
Warwick Clo. Barn —5G 5
Warwick Clo. Bex —7F 111
Warwick Clo. Bus H —1D 10
Warwick Clo. Hamp —7G 115
Warwick Ct. W7 —6K 61
(off Copley Clo.)
Warwick Ct. WC1 —5K 67 (6H 161)
Warwick Ct. Brom —2G 143
Warwick Ct. Harr —3J 25
Warwick Ct. New Bar —5E 4
(off Station Rd.)
Warwick Ct. N'holt —5E 42
(off Newmarket Av.)
Warwick Cres. W2 —5A 66
Warwick Cres. Hay —4H 59
Warwick Dene. W5 —1E 80
Warwick Dri. SW15 —3D 100
Warwick Est. W2 —5K 65
Warwick Gdns. N4 —5C 32
Warwick Gdns. W14 —3H 83
Warwick Gdns. Barn —1C 4
Warwick Gdns. Ilf —1F 55
Warwick Gdns. Th Dit —5K 133
Warwick Gdns. T Hth —3A 140
Warwick Gro. E5 —2H 51
Warwick Gro. Surb —7F 135
Warwick Ho. SW9 —2A 104
Warwick Ho. St. SW1 —1H 85 (4D 166)
Warwick La. EC4 —6B 68 (7B 162)
Warwick Lodge. Twic —3F 115
Warwick Pde. Harr —2B 26
Warwick Pas. EC4 —6B 68 (1B 168)
(off Old Bailey)
Warwick Pl. W5 —2D 80
Warwick Pl. W9 —5A 66
Warwick Pl. Th Dit —6A 134
Warwick Pl. N. SW1 —4G 85 (4A 172)
Warwick Rd. E4 —5H 19
Warwick Rd. E11 —5K 35
Warwick Rd. E12 —5C 54
Warwick Rd. E15 —6H 53
Warwick Rd. E17 —1B 34
Warwick Rd. N11 —6C 16
Warwick Rd. N18 —4K 17
Warwick Rd. SE20 —3H 141
Warwick Rd. W5 —2D 80
Warwick Rd. W14 & SW5 —4H 83
Warwick Rd. Ashf —5A 112
Warwick Rd. Barn —4E 4
Warwick Rd. Houn —3K 95
Warwick Rd. King T —1C 134
Warwick Rd. N Mald —3J 135
Warwick Rd. Sidc —5B 128
Warwick Rd. S'hall —3D 78
Warwick Rd. Sutt —4A 150
Warwick Rd. Th Dit —5K 133
Warwick Rd. T Hth —3A 140
Warwick Rd. Twic —1J 115
Warwick Rd. Well —3C 110
Warwick Rd. W Dray —2A 76
Warwick Row. SW1 —3G 85 (1K 171)
Warwickshire Path. SE8 —7B 88
Warwickshire Rd. N16 —4E 50
Warwick Sq. EC4 —6B 68 (7B 162)
Warwick Sq. SW1 —5G 85 (5A 172)
Warwick Sq. M. SW1 —4G 85 (4A 172)
Warwick St. W1 —7G 67 (2B 166)
Warwick Ter. E10 —5F 35
(off Lea Bri. Rd.)
Warwick Ter. SE18 —6H 91
Warwick Way. SW1 —5F 85 (5J 171)
Warwick Yd. EC1 —4C 68 (4D 162)
Washington Av. E12 —4D 54
Washington Clo. E3 —3D 70
Washington Ho. E17 —2B 34
(off Priory Ct.)
Washington Rd. E6 —7A 54
Washington Rd. E18 —2H 35
Washington Rd. SW13 —7C 82
Washington Rd. King T —2G 135
Washington Rd. Wor Pk —2D 148
Wasps R.U.F.C. —1D 82
(Queens Park Rangers Football Ground)
Wastdale Rd. SE23 —1K 123
Watchfield Ct. W4 —5J 81
Watcombe Cotts. Rich —6G 81
Watcombe Pl. SE25 —5H 141
Watcombe Rd. SE25 —5H 141
Waterbank Rd. SE6 —3D 124
Waterbeach Rd. Dag —6C 56
Water Brook La. NW4 —5E 28
Watercress Pl. N1 —7E 50
Waterdale Rd. SE2 —6A 92
Waterden Cres. E15 —5C 52
Waterden Rd. E15 —5C 52
Waterer Ho. SE6 —4E 124
Waterer Ri. Wall —6H 151
Waterfall Clo. N14 —3B 16
Waterfall Cotts. SW19 —6B 120
Waterfall Rd. N11 & N14 —4A 16
Waterfall Rd. SW19 —6B 120
Waterfall Ter. SW17 —6C 120
Waterfall Wlk. N14 —3A 16
Waterfield Clo. SE28 —1B 92
Waterfield Clo. Belv —3G 93
Waterfield Gdns. SE25 —4D 140
Waterford Ho. W11 —7H 65
(off Kensington Pk. Rd.)
Waterford Rd. SW6 —7K 83
(in two parts)
Water Gdns. Stan —6G 11
Water Gdns., The. W2 —6C 66 (7D 158)
Watergardens, The. King T —6J 117
Watergate. EC4 —7B 68 (2A 168)
Watergate St. SE8 —6C 88
Watergate Wlk. WC2 —1J 85 (4F 167)
Waterhall Av. E4 —4B 20
Waterhall Clo. E17 —1K 33
Waterhead. NW1 —3G 67 (1A 160)
(off Varndell St.)
Waterhouse Clo. E16 —5B 72
Waterhouse Clo. NW3 —5B 48
Waterhouse Clo. W6 —4F 83
Waterhouse Sq. EC1 —5A 68 (6J 161)
Wateridge Clo. E14 —3C 88
Water La. E15 —6G 53
Water La. EC3 —7E 68 (3H 169)
Water La. N9 —1C 18
Water La. NW1 —7F 49
Water La. SE14 —7J 87
Water La. Ilf —3J 55
Water La. King T —1D 134
Water La. Rich —5D 98
Water La. Sidc —2F 129
(in two parts)
Water La. Twic —1A 116
Water Lily Clo. S'hall —2G 79
Waterloo Bri. WC2 & SE1 —7K 67 (3G 167)
Waterloo Clo. E9 —5J 51
Waterloo Clo. Felt —1H 113
Waterloo Gdns. E2 —2J 69
Waterloo Gdns. Romf —6K 39
Waterloo Pas. NW6 —7H 47
Waterloo Pl. SW1 —1H 85 (4C 166)
Waterloo Pl. Cars —3D 150
(off Wrythe La.)
Waterloo Pl. Kew —6G 81
Waterloo Pl. Rich —4E 98
Waterloo Rd. E6 —7A 54
Waterloo Rd. E7 —5H 53
Waterloo Rd. E10 —7C 34
Waterloo Rd. NW2 —1C 46
Waterloo Rd. SE1 —1K 85 (4H 167)
Waterloo Rd. Ilf —2G 37
Waterloo Rd. Romf —5K 39
Waterloo Rd. Sutt —5B 150
Waterloo Ter. N1 —7B 50
Waterlow Ct. NW11 —7K 29
Waterlow Rd. N19 —1G 49
Waterman Building. E14 —2B 88
Watermans Clo. King T —7E 116
Watermans Ct. Bren —6D 80
(off High St.)
Watermans M. W5 —7E 62
Waterman St. SW15 —3F 101
Waterman's Wlk. EC4 —3E 168
Watermans Wlk. SE16 —2A 88
Waterman Way. E1 —1H 87
Watermead. Felt —1G 113
Watermead Ho. E9 —5A 52
Watermead La. Cars —7D 138
Watermeadow La. SW6 —2A 102
Watermead Rd. SE6 —4E 124
Watermead Way. N17 —3G 33
Watermen's Sq. SE20 —7J 123
Water M. SE15 —4J 105
Watermill Bus. Cen. Enf —2G 9
Watermill Clo. Rich —3C 116
Water Mill Ho. Felt —2E 114
Watermill La. N18 —5K 17
Watermill Way. SW19 —1B 138
Watermill Way. Felt —2D 114
Watermint Quay. N16 —7G 33
Water Rd. Wemb —1F 63
Waters Edge. SW6 —1E 100
Watersedge. Eps —4J 147
Watersfield Way. Edgw —7J 11
Waters Gdns. Dag —5G 57
Waterside. E17 —6J 33
Waterside. Beck —1B 142
Waterside Bus. Cen. Iswth —4B 98
Waterside Clo. E3 —1B 70
Waterside Clo. SE16 —2G 87
Waterside Clo. Bark —4A 56
Waterside Clo. N'holt —3D 60
Waterside Clo. Surb —2E 146
Waterside Dri. W on T —5J 131
Waterside Ho. E14 —2D 88
Waterside Pl. NW1 —1E 66
Waterside Point. SW11 —7C 84
Waterside Rd. S'hall —3E 78
Waterside Trad. Cen. W7 —3J 79
Waterside Way. SW17 —4A 120
Watersmeet Way. SE28 —6C 74
Waterson St. E2 —3E 68 (1H 163)
Waters Pl. SW15 —2E 100
Watersplash Clo. King T —3E 134
Watersplash La. Hay —4J 77
(in two parts)
Watersplash Rd. Shep —5C 130
Waters Rd. SE6 —3G 125
Waters Rd. King T —2H 135
Waters Sq. King T —3H 135
Water St. WC2 —2J 167
Water Tower Clo. Uxb —5A 40
Water Tower Hill. Croy —4D 152
Water Tower Pl. N1 —1A 68
Waterworks Corner. (Junct.) —1G 35
Waterworks La. E5 —2K 51
Waterworks Rd. SW2 —6K 103
Waterworks Yd. Croy —3C 152
Watery La. SW20 —2H 137
Watery La. Hay —5G 77
Watery La. N'holt —2A 60
Watery La. Sidc —6B 128
Wates Way. Mitc —6D 138
Wateville Rd. N17 —1C 32
Watford By-Pass. Edgw —4C 12
Watford Clo. SW11 —1C 102
Watford Rd. E16 —5J 71
Watford Rd. Harr & Wemb —7A 26
Watford Way. NW4 —4C 28
Watford Way. NW7 & NW4 —4F 13
Watkin Rd. Wemb —3H 45
Watkins Ct. N'wd —1H 23
Watkinson Rd. N7 —6K 49
Watling. —7E 12
Watling Av. Edgw —1J 27
Watling Ct. EC4 —1D 168
Watling Farm Clo. Stan —1H 11
Watling Gdns. NW2 —6G 47
Watling Ga. NW9 —4A 28
Watlings Clo. Croy —6A 142
Watling St. EC4 —6C 68 (1D 168)
Watling St. SE15 —6E 86
Watling St. Bexh —4H 111
Watlington Gro. SE26 —5A 124
Watney Cotts. SW14 —3J 99
Watney Mkt. E1 —6H 69
Watney Rd. SW14 —3J 99
Watney's Rd. Mitc —5H 139
Watney St. E1 —6H 69
Watson Av. E6 —7E 54
Watson Av. Sutt —2G 149
Watson Clo. N16 —5D 50
Watson Clo. SW19 —6C 120
Watson's M. W1 —5C 66 (6D 158)
Watsons Rd. N22 —1K 31
Watson's St. SE8 —7C 88
Watson St. E13 —2K 71

Watsons Yd.—Westbrooke Cres.

Watsons Yd. NW2 —2C 46
Wattisfield Rd. E5 —3J 51
Watts Clo. N15 —5E 32
Watts Gro. E3 —5C 70
Watts La. Chst —1F 145
Watts La. Tedd —5A 116
Watts Point. E13 —1J 71
(off Brooks Rd.)
Watts Rd. Th Dit —7A 134
Watts St. E1 —1H 87
Watts St. SE15 —1F 105
Wat Tyler Ho. N8 —3J 31
(off Boyton Rd.)
Wat Tyler Rd. SE10 & SE3 —2E 106
Wauthier Clo. N13 —5G 17
Wavell Dri. Sidc —6J 109
Wavel M. N8 —4H 31
Wavel M. NW6 —7K 47
Wavel Pl. SE26 —4F 123
Wavendon Av. W4 —5K 81
Waveney Av. SE15 —4H 105
Waveney Clo. E1 —1G 87
Waveney Ho. SE15 —4H 105
Waverley Av. E4 —4G 19
Waverley Av. E17 —3F 35
Waverley Av. Surb —6H 135
Waverley Av. Sutt —2K 149
Waverley Av. Twic —1D 114
Waverley Av. Wemb —5F 45
Waverley Clo. E18 —1A 36
Waverley Clo. Brom —5B 144
Waverley Clo. Hay —4F 77
Waverley Clo. W Mol —5E 132
Waverley Ct. NW6 —7G 47
Waverley Ct. SE26 —5J 123
Waverley Ct. Enf —3H 7
Waverley Cres. SE18 —5H 91
Waverley Gdns. E6 —5C 72
Waverley Gdns. NW10 —2F 63
Waverley Gdns. Bark —2J 73
Waverley Gdns. Ilf —2G 37
Waverley Gdns. N'wd —1J 23
Waverley Gro. N3 —3G 29
Waverley Ind. Est. Harr —3H 25
Waverley Pl. N4 —2B 50
Waverley Pl. NW8 —2B 66
Waverley Rd. E17 —3E 34
Waverley Rd. E18 —1A 36
Waverley Rd. N8 —6J 31
Waverley Rd. N17 —7C 18
Waverley Rd. SE18 —5G 91
Waverley Rd. SE25 —4H 141
Waverley Rd. Enf —3G 7
Waverley Rd. Eps —5D 148
Waverley Rd. Harr —2C 42
Waverley Rd. S'hall —7E 60
Waverley Vs. N17 —2F 33
Waverley Way. Cars —6C 150
Waverton Ho. E3 —1B 70
Waverton Rd. SW18 —7A 102
Waverton St. W1 —1E 84 (4J 165)
Wavertree Ct. SW2 —1J 121
Wavertree Rd. E18 —2J 35
Wavertree Rd. SW2 —1K 121
Waxlow Cres. S'hall —6E 60
Waxlow Ho. Hay —5B 60
Waxlow Rd. NW10 —2J 63
Waxwell Clo. Pinn —2B 24
Waxwell Farm Ho. Pinn —2B 24
Waxwell La. Pinn —2B 24
Wayborne Gro. Ruis —6E 22
Waye Av. Houn —1J 95
Wayfarer Rd. N'holt —3B 60
Wayfield Link. SE9 —6H 109
Wayford St. SW11 —2C 102
Wayland Av. E8 —5G 51
Wayland Clo. E8 —5G 51
Wayland Ho. SW9 —2A 104
(off Robsart St.)
Waylands. Hay —5F 59
Waylands Mead. Beck —1D 142
Waylett Ho. SE11 —6J 173
Waylett Pl. SE27 —3B 122
Waylett Pl. Wemb —4D 44
Wayman Ct. E8 —6H 51
Wayne Kirkum Way. NW6 —5H 47
Waynflete Av. Croy —3B 152
Waynflete Sq. W10 —7F 65
Waynflete St. SW18 —2A 120
Wayside. NW11 —1G 47
Wayside. SW14 —5J 99
Wayside. New Ad —6D 154
Wayside Clo. N14 —6B 6
Wayside Ct. Twic —6C 98
Wayside Ct. Wemb —3G 45
Wayside Gdns. Dag —5G 57
Wayside Gro. SE9 —4D 126
Wayside M. Ilf —5E 36
Weald Clo. SE16 —5H 87
Weald Clo. Brom —2C 156
Weald La. Harr —2H 25
Weald Ri. Harr —7E 10
Weald Rd. Uxb —2C 58
Weald Sq. E5 —2G 51
Wealdstone. —3J 25
Wealdstone Rd. Sutt —2H 149
Weald, The. Chst —6D 126
Weald Way. Hay —3G 59
Weald Way. Romf —6H 39
Wealdwood Gdns. Pinn —6A 10
Weale Rd. E4 —3A 20
Weall Ct. Pinn —4C 24
Weardale Gdns. Enf —1J 7
Weardale Rd. SE13 —4F 107
Wearmouth Ho. E3 —5B 70
Wear Pl. E2 —3H 69
(in two parts)
Wearside Rd. SE13 —4D 106
Weatherbury. W2 —6J 65
(off Talbot Rd.)
Weatherbury Ho. N19 —3H 49
(off Wedmore St.)
Weatherley Clo. E3 —5B 70
Weaver Clo. E6 —7F 73
Weaver Clo. Croy —4F 153
Weavers Clo. Iswth —4J 97
Weavers Ho. E11 —6J 35
(off New Wanstead)
Weavers La. SE1
—1E 86 (5H 169)
Weavers Ter. SW6 —6J 83
(off Micklethwaite Rd.)
Weaver St. E1 —4G 69
Weavers Way. NW1 —1H 67
Weaver Wlk. SE27 —4C 122
Webb Clo. W10 —4E 64
Webber Row. SE1 —2B 86 (1K 173)
(in two parts)
Webber St. SE1 —2A 86 (6K 167)
Webb Est. E5 —7G 33
Webb Gdns. E13 —4J 71
Webb Ho. SW8 —7H 85
Webb Ho. Dag —3G 57
(off Kershaw Rd.)
Webb Ho. Felt —3C 114
Webb Pl. NW10 —3B 64
Webb Rd. SE3 —6H 89
Webbscroft Rd. Dag —4H 57
Webb's Rd. SW11 —4D 102
Webbs Rd. Hay —3K 59
Webb St. SE1 —3E 86
Webheath. NW6 —7H 47
(off Netherwood St.)
Webster Gdns. W5 —1D 80
Webster Rd. E11 —3E 52
Webster Rd. SE16 —3G 87
Wedderburn Rd. NW3 —5B 48
Wedderburn Rd. Bark —1J 73
Wedgewood Ct. Bex —7F 111
Wedgewood Ho. SW1 —5F 85 (6K 171)
(off Churchill Gdns.)
Wedgewood M. W1 —6H 67 (1D 166)
Wedgwood Ho. SE11 —2J 173
Wedgwood Wlk. NW6 —5K 47
(off Dresden Clo.)
Wedgwood Way. SE19 —7C 122
Wedlake St. W10 —4G 65
Wedmore Av. Ilf —1E 36
Wedmore Ct. N19 —2H 49
Wedmore Gdns. N19 —2H 49
Wedmore M. N19 —3H 49
Wedmore Rd. Gnfd —3H 61
Wedmore St. N19 —3H 49
Weech Rd. NW6 —4J 47
Weedington Rd. NW5 —5E 48
Weedon Ho. W12 —6C 64
Weekley Sq. SW11 —3B 102
Weigall Rd. SE12 —5J 107
Weighhouse St. W1 —6E 66 (1H 165)
Weighton M. SE20 —2H 141
Weighton Rd. SE20 —2H 141
Weighton Rd. Harr —1H 25
Weihurst Ct. Sutt —5C 150
Weihurst Gdns. Sutt —5B 150
Weirdale Av. N20 —2J 15
Weir Hall Av. N18 —6J 17
Weir Hall Gdns. N18 —5J 17
Weir Hall Rd. N18 & N17 —5J 17
Weir Rd. SW12 —7G 103
Weir Rd. SW19 —3K 119
Weir Rd. Bex —7H 111
Weir Rd. W on T —6J 131
Weir's Pas. NW1 —3H 67 (1D 160)
Weiss Rd. SW15 —3F 101
Welbeck Av. Brom —4J 125
Welbeck Av. Hay —4K 59
Welbeck Av. Sidc —1A 128
Welbeck Clo. N12 —5G 15
Welbeck Clo. Eps —7C 148
Welbeck Clo. N Mald —5B 136
Welbeck Ct. W14 —4H 83
(off Addison Bri. Pl.)
Welbeck Ho. W1 —6F 67 (7J 159)
(off Welbeck St.)
Welbeck Rd. E6 —3B 72
Welbeck Rd. Barn —6H 5
Welbeck Rd. Harr —1F 43
Welbeck Rd. Sutt & Cars —2B 150
Welbeck St. W1 —5E 66 (6H 159)
Welbeck Vs. N21 —2H 17
Welbeck Wlk. Cars —1B 150
Welbeck Way. W1 —6F 67 (7J 159)
Welbourne Rd. N17 —3F 33
Welby Ho. N19 —7H 31
Welby St. SE5 —1B 104
Welch Pl. Pinn —1K 23
Welcome Ct. E17 —7C 34
(off Boundary Rd.)
Weldon Clo. Ruis —6K 41
Weldon Ct. N21 —5E 6
Weldon Dri. W Mol —4D 132
Weld Pl. N11 —5A 16
(in two parts)
Welfare Rd. E15 —7G 53
Welford Clo. E5 —3K 51
Welford Ct. NW1 —7F 49
(off Castlehaven Rd.)
Welford Ct. SW8 —2G 103
Welford Pl. SW19 —4G 119
Welham Rd. SW17 & SW16 —5E 120
Welhouse Rd. Cars —1C 150
Wellacre Rd. Harr —6B 26
Wellan Clo. Sidc —5B 110
Welland Ct. SE6 —2B 124
(off Oakham Clo.)
Welland Gdns. Gnfd —2K 61
Welland Ho. SE15 —4J 105
Welland M. E1 —1G 87
Wellands Clo. Brom —2D 144
Welland St. SE10 —6E 88
Well App. Barn —5A 4
Wellbrook Rd. Orp —4E 156
Wellby Ct. E13 —1A 72
Well Clo. SW16 —4K 121
Well Clo. Ruis —3C 42
Wellclose Sq. E1 —7G 69
(in two parts)
Wellclose St. E1 —7G 69
Wellcome Cen. for Medical Science.
—3C 160
Well Cottage Clo. E11 —6A 36
Well Ct. EC4 —6C 68 (1D 168)
(in two parts)
Welldon Ct. Harr —5J 25
Welldon Cres. Harr —5J 25
Weller Ho. SE16 —2G 87
(off George Row)
Wellers Ct. NW1 —2J 67 (1E 160)
Weller St. SE1 —2C 86 (6C 168)
Wellesley Av. W6 —3D 82
Wellesley Clo. SE7 —5A 90
Wellesley Ct. NW2 —2C 46
Wellesley Ct. W9 —3A 66
Wellesley Ct. Sutt —1G 149
Wellesley Ct. Rd. Croy —2D 152
Wellesley Cres. Twic —2J 115
Wellesley Gro. Croy —2D 152
Wellesley Ho. NW1 —3H 67 (2D 160)
(off Churchway)
Wellesley Ho. SW1 —5F 85 (5J 171)
(off Ebury Bri. Rd.)
Wellesley Lodge. Sutt —7J 149
(off Worcester Rd.)
Wellesley Mans. W14 —5H 83
(off Edith Vs.)
Wellesley Pde. Twic —3J 115
Wellesley Pk. M. Enf —2G 7
Wellesley Pas. Croy —2C 152
Wellesley Pl. NW1 —3H 67 (2C 160)
Wellesley Pl. NW5 —5E 48
Wellesley Rd. E11 —5J 35
Wellesley Rd. E17 —6C 34
Wellesley Rd. N22 —2A 32
Wellesley Rd. NW5 —5E 48
Wellesley Rd. W4 —5G 81
Wellesley Rd. Croy —1C 152
Wellesley Rd. Harr —5J 25
Wellesley Rd. Ilf —2F 55
Wellesley Rd. Sutt —6A 150
Wellesley Rd. Twic —3H 115
Wellesley St. E1 —5K 69
Wellesley Ter. N1 —3C 68 (1D 162)
Wellfield Av. N10 —3F 31
Wellfield Rd. SW16 —4J 121
Wellfield Wlk. SW16 —5K 121
(in two parts)
Wellfit St. SE24 —3B 104
Wellgarth. Gnfd —6B 44
Wellgarth Rd. NW11 —1K 47
Well Gro. N20 —1F 15
Well Hall Pde. SE9 —4D 108
Well Hall Rd. SE9 —3C 108
Well Hall Roundabout. (Junct.) —4D 108
Well Hall Roundabout. SE9 —4D 108
Wellhouse La. Barn —4A 4
Wellhouse Rd. Beck —4C 142
Welling. —3B 110
Welling High St. Well —3B 110
Wellington. N8 —4J 31
(in two parts)
Wellington Av. E4 —2H 19
Wellington Av. N9 —3C 18
Wellington Av. N15 —6F 33
Wellington Av. SE18 —3F 91
Wellington Av. Houn —5E 96
Wellington Av. Pinn —1D 24
Wellington Av. Sidc —6A 110
Wellington Av. Wor Pk —3E 148
Wellington Bldgs. SW1
—5E 84 (6H 171)
Wellington Clo. SE14 —1K 105
Wellington Clo. W11 —6J 65
Wellington Clo. Dag —7J 57
Wellington Clo. W on T —7H 131
Wellington Ct. NW8 —2B 66
(off Wellington Rd.)
Wellington Ct. SW1 —2D 84 (7E 164)
(off Knightsbridge)
Wellington Ct. SW6 —1K 101
(off Maltings Pl.)
Wellington Ct. Hamp —5H 115
Wellington Ct. Pinn —1D 24
(off Wellington Rd.)
Wellington Ct. Stanw —7A 94
Wellington Cres. N Mald —3J 135
Wellington Dri. Dag —7J 57
Wellington Est. E2 —2J 69
Wellington Gdns. SE7 —6A 90
Wellington Gdns. Twic —4H 115
Wellington Gro. SE10 —7F 89
Wellington Ho. W5 —3E 62
Wellington Ho. N'holt —7E 42
(off Farmlands, The)
Wellington Mans. E10 —1C 52
Wellington M. N7 —6K 49
(off Roman Way)
Wellington M. SE7 —6A 90
Wellington M. SE22 —4G 105
Wellington M. SW16 —3H 121
Wellington Mus. —2E 84 (6H 165)
Wellington Pde. Sidc —5A 110
Wellington Pk. Est. NW2 —1C 46
Wellington Pas. E11 —5J 35
(off Wellington Rd.)
Wellington Pl. E11 —5J 35
Wellington Pl. N2 —5C 30
Wellington Pl. NW8 —3B 66 (1B 158)
Wellington Rd. E6 —1D 72
Wellington Rd. E7 —4H 53
Wellington Rd. E10 —1A 52
Wellington Rd. E11 —5J 35
Wellington Rd. E17 —4A 34
Wellington Rd. NW8 —2B 66 (1B 158)
Wellington Rd. NW10 —3F 65
Wellington Rd. SW19 —2J 119
Wellington Rd. W5 —3C 80
Wellington Rd. Ashf —5A 112
Wellington Rd. Belv —5F 93
Wellington Rd. Bex —5D 110
Wellington Rd. Brom —4A 144
Wellington Rd. Croy —7B 140
Wellington Rd. Enf —5K 7
Wellington Rd. Felt —5G 95
Wellington Rd. Hamp & Twic —5H 115
Wellington Rd. Harr —3J 25
Wellington Rd. Pinn —1D 24
Wellington Rd. N. Houn —3D 96
Wellington Rd. S. Houn —4D 96
Wellington Row. E2 —3F 69 (1K 163)
Wellington Sq. SW3 —5D 84 (5E 170)
Wellington St. SE18 —4E 90
Wellington St. WC2 —7K 67 (2G 167)
Wellington St. Bark —1G 73
Wellington Ter. E1 —1H 87
Wellington Ter. N8 —3A 32
(off Turnpike La.)
Wellington Ter. W2 —7J 65
Wellington Ter. Harr —1H 43
Wellington Way. E3 —3C 70
Welling United F.C. —3C 110
Welling Way. SE9 & Well —3G 109
Well La. SW14 —5J 99
Wellmeadow Rd. SE13 & SE6 —6G 107
(in two parts)
Wellmeadow Rd. W7 —4A 80
Wellow Wlk. Cars —1B 150
Well Pl. NW3 —3B 48
Well Rd. NW3 —3B 48
Well Rd. Barn —5A 4
Wells Clo. N'holt —3A 60
Wells Ct. NW6 —2J 65
(off Cambridge Av.)
Wells Dri. NW9 —1K 45
Wells Gdns. Dag —5H 57
Wells Gdns. Ilf —7C 36
Wells Ho. EC1 —3A 68 (1K 161)
(off Spa Grn. Est.)
Wells Ho. W5 —1D 80
(off Grove Rd.)
Wells Ho. Bark —7A 56
(off Margaret Bondfield Av.)
Wells Ho. Brom —5K 125
(off Pike Clo.)
Wells Ho. Rd. NW10 —5A 64
Wellside Clo. Barn —4A 4
Wellside Gdns. SW14 —4J 99
Wells M. W1 —5G 67 (6B 160)
Wellsmoor Gdns. Brom —3E 144
Wells Pk. Rd. SE26 —3G 123
Wells Path. N'holt —3G 59
Wellsprings Cres. Wemb —3H 45
Wells Ri. NW8 —1D 66
Wells Rd. W12 —2E 82
Wells Rd. Brom —2D 144
Wells Sq. WC1 —3K 67 (2G 161)
Wells St. W1 —5G 67 (6A 160)
Wellstead Av. N9 —7E 8
Wellstead Rd. E6 —2E 72
Wells Ter. N4 —2A 50
Wells, The. N14 —7C 6
Well St. E9 —7J 51
Well St. E15 —6G 53
Wells Way. SE5 —6D 86
Wells Way. SW7 —3B 84 (1A 170)
Wells Yd. N7 —5A 50
Well Wlk. NW3 —4B 48
Wellwood Rd. Ilf —1A 56
Welsby Ct. W5 —5C 62
Welsford St. SE1 —4G 87
(in two parts)
Welsh Clo. E13 —3J 71
Welshpool Ho. E8 —1G 69
Welshpool St. E8 —1G 69
(in two parts)
Welshside Wlk. NW9 —6A 28
Welstead Ho. E1 —6H 69
(off Cannon St. Rd.)
Welstead Way. W4 —4B 82
Weltje Rd. W6 —4C 82
Welton Ct. SE5 —1E 104
Welton Rd. SE18 —7J 91
Welwyn Av. Felt —6H 95
Welwyn St. E2 —3J 69
Welwyn Way. Hay —4G 59
Wembley. —5E 44
Wembley Arena. —4G 45
Wembley Arena. —4G 45
Wembley Commercial Cen. Wemb
—2D 44
Wembley Conference Centre. —4G 45
Wembley Hill Rd. Wemb —3F 45
Wembley Park. —3G 45
Wembley Pk. Bus. Cen. Wemb —4H 45
Wembley Pk. Dri. Wemb —4F 45
Wembley Retail Pk. Wemb —4H 45
Wembley Rd. Hamp —1E 132
Wembley Stadium. —5G 45
Wembley Stadium Ind. Est. Wemb
—4H 45
Wembley Way. Wemb —6H 45
Wemborough Rd. Stan —1B 26
Wembury M. N6 —7G 31
Wembury Rd. N6 —7F 31
Wemyss Rd. SE3 —2H 107
Wendela Ct. Harr —2J 43
Wendell Rd. W12 —3B 82
Wendle Ct. SW8 —6J 85 (7E 172)
Wendling Rd. Sutt —1B 150
Wendon St. E3 —1B 70
Wendover. SE17 —5E 86
(in two parts)
Wendover Clo. Hay —4C 60
Wendover Ct. NW2 —3J 47
Wendover Ct. NW10 —4H 63
Wendover Ct. W1 —5E 66 (6G 159)
(off Chiltern St.)
Wendover Dri. N Mald —6B 136
Wendover Ho. W1 —5E 66 (6G 159)
(off Chiltern St.)
Wendover Rd. NW10 —2B 64
Wendover Rd. SE9 —3B 108
Wendover Rd. Brom —4K 143
Wendover Way. Well —5A 110
Wendy Clo. Enf —6A 8
Wendy Way. Wemb —1E 62
Wenham Ho. SW8 —7G 85
(off Ascalon St.)
Wenlake Ho. EC1 —4C 68 (3C 162)
(off Old St.)
Wenlock Barn Est. N1 —2D 68
(off Wenlock St.)
Wenlock Ct. N1 —2D 68 (1F 163)
Wenlock Gdns. NW4 —4D 28
Wenlock Rd. N1 —2C 68 (1D 162)
Wenlock Rd. Edgw —7C 12
Wenlock St. N1 —2C 68 (1D 162)
Wennington Rd. E3 —2K 69
Wensdale Ho. E5 —2G 51
Wensley Av. Wfd G —7C 20
Wensley Clo. SE9 —6D 108
Wensleydale Av. Ilf —2C 36
Wensleydale Gdns. Hamp —7F 115
Wensleydale Pas. Hamp —1E 132
Wensleydale Rd. Hamp —6E 114
Wensley Rd. N18 —6C 18
Wentland Clo. SE6 —2F 125
Wentland Rd. SE6 —2F 125
Wentway Ct. W13 —4K 61
(off Ruislip Rd. E.)
Wentworth Av. N3 —7D 14
Wentworth Clo. N3 —7E 14
Wentworth Clo. SE28 —6D 74
Wentworth Clo. Ashf —4D 112
Wentworth Clo. Hayes —2J 155
Wentworth Clo. Mord —7J 137
Wentworth Clo. Surb —2D 146
Wentworth Ct. W6 —6G 83
(off Laundry Rd.)
Wentworth Ct. Twic —3J 115
Wentworth Cres. SE15 —7G 87
Wentworth Cres. Hay —3F 77
Wentworth Dri. Pinn —5J 23
Wentworth Dwellings. E1
(off Wentworth St.) —6F 69 (7J 163)
Wenthier Clo. Hay —2F 59
Wentworth Gdns. N13 —3G 17
Wentworth Hill. Wemb —1F 45
Wentworth M. E3 —4A 70
Wentworth Pk. N3 —7D 14
Wentworth Pl. Stan —6G 11
Wentworth Rd. E12 —4B 54
Wentworth Rd. NW11 —6H 29
Wentworth Rd. Barn —3A 4
Wentworth Rd. Croy —7A 140
Wentworth Rd. S'hall —4A 78
Wentworth St. E1 —6F 69 (7J 163)
Wentworth Way. Pinn —4C 24
Wenvoe Av. Bexh —2H 111
Wepham Clo. Hay —5B 60
Wernbrook St. SE18 —6G 91
Werndee Rd. SE25 —4G 141
Werneth Hall Rd. Ilf —3E 36
Werrington St. NW1 —2G 67 (1B 160)
Werter Rd. SW15 —4G 101
Wesleyan Pl. NW5 —4F 49
Wesley Av. E16 —1J 89
Wesley Av. NW10 —3K 63
Wesley Av. Houn —2C 96
Wesley Clo. N7 —2K 49
Wesley Clo. SE17 —4B 86
Wesley Clo. Harr —2G 43
Wesley Rd. E10 —7E 34
Wesley Rd. N2 —1C 30
Wesley Rd. NW10 —1J 63
Wesley Rd. Hay —7J 59
Wesley's House Mus. —4D 68 (4F 163)
Wesley Sq. W11 —6G 65
Wesley St. W1 —5E 66 (6H 159)
Wessex Av. SW19 —3J 137
Wessex Clo. Ilf —6J 37
Wessex Clo. King T —1H 135
Wessex Ct. Barn —4A 4
Wessex Ct. Beck —1A 142
Wessex Ct. Stanw —6A 94
Wessex Dri. Pinn —1C 24
Wessex Gdns. NW11 —1G 47
Wessex Ho. SE1 —5F 87
Wessex La. Gnfd —3H 61
Wessex St. E2 —3J 69
Wessex Way. NW11 —1G 47
Westacott. Hay —5G 59
Westacott Clo. N19 —1H 49
West Acton. —6G 63
West App. Orp —5G 145
W. Arbour St. E1 —6K 69
West Av. E17 —4D 34
West Av. N2 —3K 29
West Av. N3 —6D 14
West Av. NW4 —5F 29
West Av. Hay —7H 59
West Av. Pinn —6D 24
West Av. S'hall —7D 60
West Av. Wall —5J 151
W. Avenue Rd. E17 —4C 34
West Bank. N16 —7E 32
West Bank. Bark —1F 73
West Bank. Enf —2H 7
Westbank Rd. Hamp H —6G 115
West Barnes. —4D 136
W. Barnes La. N Mald & SW20
—5C 136
West Beckton. —6B 72
West Bedfont. —6B 94
Westbeech Rd. N22 —3A 32
Westbere Dri. Stan —5J 11
Westbere Rd. NW2 —4G 47
West Block. SE1 —2K 85
(off Addington St.)
Westbourne Av. W3 —6K 63
Westbourne Av. Sutt —2G 149
Westbourne Bri. W2 —5A 66
Westbourne Clo. Hay —4A 60
Westbourne Cres. W2 —7B 66 (2A 164)
Westbourne Cres. M. W2 —2A 164
Westbourne Dri. SE23 —2K 123
Westbourne Gdns. W2 —6K 65
Westbourne Green. —6H 65
Westbourne Gro. W11 & W2 —7H 65
Westbourne Gro. M. W11 —6J 65
Westbourne Gro. Ter. W2 —6K 65
Westbourne Ho. SW1 —5F 85 (5J 171)
Westbourne Ho. Houn —6E 78
Westbourne Pde. Hil —4D 58
Westbourne Pk. Pas. W2 —5J 65
(off Alfred Rd., in two parts)
Westbourne Pk. Rd. W11 & W2 —6G 65
Westbourne Pk. Vs. W2 —5J 65
Westbourne Pl. N9 —3C 18
Westbourne Rd. N7 —6K 49
Westbourne Rd. SE26 —6K 123
Westbourne Rd. Bexh —7D 92
Westbourne Rd. Croy —6F 141
Westbourne Rd. Felt —3H 113
Westbourne Rd. Uxb —4D 58
Westbourne St. W2 —7B 66 (2A 164)
Westbourne Ter. SE23 —2K 123
(off Waldram Pk. Rd.)
Westbourne Ter. W2 —6A 66
Westbourne Ter. M. W2 —6A 66
Westbourne Ter. Rd. W2
—5K 65 (1A 164)
Westbourne Ter. Rd. Bri. W2 —5A 66
(off Westbourne Ter. Rd.)
Westbridge Clo. W12 —2C 82
Westbridge Rd. SW11 —1B 102
West Brompton. —6K 83
Westbrook Av. Hamp —7D 114
Westbrook Clo. Barn —3G 5
Westbrook Cres. Cockf —3G 5
Westbrooke Cres. Well —3C 110

Westbrooke Rd.—Wheelock Clo.

Westbrooke Rd. Sidc —2H 127
Westbrooke Rd. Well —3B 110
(in two parts)
Westbrook Rd. SE3 —1K 107
Westbrook Rd. Houn —7D 78
Westbrook Rd. T Hth —1D 140
Westbrook Sq. Barn —3G 5
Westbury Av. N22 —3B 32
Westbury Av. S'hall —4E 60
Westbury Av. Wemb —7E 44
Westbury Clo. Ruis —7J 23
Westbury Clo. Shep —6D 130
Westbury Ct. Bark —1H 73
(off Westbury Rd.)
Westbury Gro. N12 —6D 14
Westbury Ho. E17 —4B 34
Westbury La. Buck H —2F 21
Westbury Lodge Clo. Pinn —3B 24
Westbury Pl. Bren —6D 80
Westbury Rd. E7 —6K 53
Westbury Rd. E17 —4B 34
Westbury Rd. N11 —6D 16
Westbury Rd. N12 —6D 14
Westbury Rd. SE20 —1K 141
Westbury Rd. W5 —6E 62
Westbury Rd. Bark —1H 73
Westbury Rd. Beck —3A 142
Westbury Rd. Brom —1B 144
Westbury Rd. Buck H —2F 21
Westbury Rd. Croy —6D 140
Westbury Rd. Felt —1B 114
Westbury Rd. Ilf —2E 54
Westbury Rd. N Mald —4K 135
Westbury Rd. Wemb —7E 44
Westbury St. SW8 —2G 103
(off Portslade Rd.)
Westbury Ter. E7 —6K 53
W. Carriage Dri. W2 —7C 66 (3C 164)
W. Central St. WC1 —6J 67 (7E 160)
W. Centre Av. NW10 —4D 64
West Chantry. Harr —1F 25
Westchester Dri. NW4 —3F 29
West Clo. N9 —3A 18
West Clo. Ashf —4A 112
West Clo. Cockf —4K 5
West Clo. Gnfd —2G 61
West Clo. Hamp —6C 114
West Clo. Wemb —1F 45
Westcombe Av. Croy —7J 139
Westcombe Ct. SE3 —7H 89
Westcombe Dri. Barn —5D 4
Westcombe Hill. SE3 —7J 89
Westcombe Lodge Dri. Hay —5F 59
Westcombe Pk. Rd. SE3 —6G 89
W. Common Rd. Brom & Kes —1J 155
W. Common Rd. Uxb —5A 40
Westcoombe Av. SW20 —1B 136
Westcote Ri. Ruis —7E 22
Westcote Rd. SW16 —5G 121
West Cotts. NW6 —5J 47
Westcott Clo. N15 —6F 33
Westcott Clo. Brom —5D 144
Westcott Clo. New Ad —7D 154
Westcott Cres. W7 —6J 61
Westcott Ho. E14 —7C 70
Westcott Rd. SE17 —6B 86
West Ct. E17 —4C 34
West Ct. Houn —7G 79
West Ct. Wemb —2C 44
Westcroft Clo. NW2 —4G 47
Westcroft Clo. Enf —1D 8
Westcroft Gdns. Mord —3H 137
Westcroft Rd. Cars & Wall —4E 150
Westcroft Sq. W6 —4C 82
Westcroft Way. NW2 —4G 47
W. Cromwell Rd. W14 & SW5 —5H 83
W. Cross Cen. Bren —6A 80
W. Cross Route. W10 —7F 65
W. Cross Way. Bren —6B 80
Westdale Pas. SE18 —6F 91
Westdale Rd. SE18 —6F 91
Westdean Av. SE12 —1K 125
W. Dean Clo. SW18 —6K 101
West Dene. Sutt —6G 149
Westdown Rd. E15 —4E 52
Westdown Rd. SE6 —7C 106
West Drayton. —2A 76
W. Drayton Pk. Av. W Dray —3A 76
W. Drayton Rd. Uxb —6D 58
West Dri. SW16 —4G 121
West Dri. Harr —6C 10
West Dri. Sutt —7F 149
West Dri. Gdns. Harr —6C 10
West Dulwich. —2D 122
West Ealing. —7B 62
W. Ealing Bus. Cen. W13 —7A 62
W. Eaton Pl. SW1 —4E 84 (3G 171)
W. Eaton Pl. M. SW1 —2G 171
W. Ella Rd. NW10 —7A 46
West End. —2B 60
W. End Av. E10 —5F 35
W. End Av. Pinn —4B 24
Westend Clo. NW10 —7J 45
W. End Ct. NW6 —7K 47
W. End Ct. Pinn —4B 24
W. End Gdns. N'holt —2A 60
W. End La. NW6 —5J 47
W. End La. Barn —4A 4
W. End La. Hay —7E 76
W. End La. Pinn —3B 24
W. End Rd. Ruis & N'holt —2G 41
W. End Rd. S'hall —1C 78
Westerdale Rd. SE10 —5J 89
Westerfield Rd. N15 —5F 33
Westergate. W5 —5E 62
Westergate Rd. SE2 —6E 92
Westerham. NW1 —1G 67
(off Bayham St.)
Westerham Av. N9 —3J 17
Westerham Dri. Sidc —6B 110
Westerham Ho. SE1 —3D 86
(off Law St.)
Westerham Lodge. Beck —7C 124
(off Park Rd.)
Westerham Rd. E10 —7D 34
Westerham Rd. Kes —7B 156
Westerley Cres. SE26 —5B 124
Western Av. NW11 —6F 29
Western Av. W5 & W3 —4F 63
Western Av. Dag —6J 57
Western Av. Gnfd & W5 —2H 61
Western Av. Uxb & N'holt —6E 40
Western Av. Bus. Pk. W3 —4H 63
Western Beach Apartments. E16 —7J 71
Western Circus. (Junct.) —7B 64
Western Ct. N3 —6D 14
Western Ct. NW6 —2H 65
Western Ct. W3 —6K 63
Western Dri. Shep —6F 131
Western Gdns. W5 —7G 63
Western International Mkt. S'hall —4K 77
Western La. SW12 —7E 102
Western Mans. New Bar —5E 4
(off Gt. North Rd.)
Western M. W9 —4H 65
Western Pde. New Bar —5D 4
Western Pl. SE16 —2J 87
Western Rd. E13 —2A 72
Western Rd. E17 —5E 34
Western Rd. N2 —4D 30
Western Rd. N22 —2K 31
Western Rd. NW10 —4J 63
Western Rd. SW9 —3A 104
Western Rd. W5 —7D 62
Western Rd. SW19 & Mitc —1B 138
Western Rd. S'hall —4A 78
Western Rd. Sutt —5J 149
Western Ter. W6 —5C 82
(off Chiswick Mall)
Western Vw. Hay —2H 77
Westernville Gdns. Ilf —7G 37
Western Way. SE28 —3H 91
Western Way. Barn —6D 4
West Ewell. —7A 148
Westferry Cir. E14 —1C 88
Westferry Rd. E14 —7B 70
Westfield Clo. NW9 —3J 27
Westfield Clo. SW10 —7A 84
Westfield Clo. Enf —3F 9
Westfield Clo. Sutt —4H 149
Westfield Dri. Harr —4D 26
Westfield Gdns. Harr —4D 26
Westfield Ho. SW18 —1K 119
Westfield La. Harr —5D 26
(in two parts)
Westfield Pk. Pinn —1D 24
Westfield Pk. Dri. Wfd G —6H 21
Westfield Rd. NW7 —3E 12
Westfield Rd. W13 —1A 80
Westfield Rd. Beck —2B 142
Westfield Rd. Bexh —3J 111
Westfield Rd. Croy —2B 152
Westfield Rd. Dag —4E 56
Westfield Rd. Mitc —2C 138
Westfield Rd. Surb —5D 134
Westfield Rd. Sutt —4H 149
Westfield Rd. W on T —7C 132
Westfields. SW13 —3B 100
Westfields Av. SW13 —3A 100
Westfields Rd. W3 —5H 63
Westfield St. SE18 —3B 90
Westfield Way. E1 —3A 70
Westfield Way. Ruis —3G 41
W. Garden Pl. W2 —6C 66 (1D 164)
West Gdns. E1 —7H 69
West Gdns. SW17 —6C 120
Westgate. W5 —3E 62
Westgate Ct. SE12 —1J 125
(off Burnt Ash Hill)
Westgate Ct. SW9 —3A 104
(off Canterbury Cres.)
Westgate M. W10 —4G 65
(off West Row)
Westgate Rd. SE25 —4H 141
Westgate Rd. Beck —2D 142
Westgate St. E8 —1H 69
Westgate Ter. SW10 —5K 83
Westglade Ct. Kent —5D 26
West Green. —4B 32
W. Green Pl. Gnfd —1H 61
W. Green Rd. N8 —4B 32
West Gro. SE10 —1E 106
West Gro. Wfd G —6F 21
Westgrove La. SE10 —1E 106
W. Halkin St. SW1 —3E 84 (1G 171)
W. Hallowes. SE9 —1B 126
W. Hall Rd. Rich —1H 99
West Ham. —1J 71
W. Ham La. E15 —7F 53
West Hampstead. —6K 47
W. Hampstead M. NW6 —6K 47
West Ham United F.C. —2B 72
W. Harding St. EC4 —6A 68 (7K 161)
West Harrow. —7G 25
W. Hatch Mnr. Ruis —1H 41
Westhay Gdns. SW14 —5H 99
West Heath. —6D 92
W. Heath Av. NW11 —1J 47
W. Heath Clo. NW3 —3J 47
W. Heath Ct. NW11 —1J 47
W. Heath Dri. NW11 —1J 47
W. Heath Gdns. NW3 —3J 47
W. Heath Rd. NW3 —2J 47
W. Heath Rd. SE2 —6C 92
West Hendon. —7C 28
West Hill. —6H 101
West Hill. SW15 & SW18 —7F 101
West Hill. Harr —2J 43
West Hill. Wemb —1F 45
W. Hill Ct. N6 —3E 48
Westhill Pk. N6 —2D 48
(in two parts)
W. Hill Rd. SW18 —6H 101
W. Hill Way. N20 —1E 14
Westholm. NW11 —4K 29
W. Holme. Eri —1J 111
Westholme. Orp —7J 145
Westholme Gdns. Ruis —1J 41
Westhope Ho. E2 —4G 69
(off Derbyshire St.)
Westhorne Av. SE12 & SE9 —7J 107
Westhorpe Gdns. NW4 —3E 28
Westhorpe Rd. SW15 —3E 100
West Ho. Clo. SW19 —1G 119
West Ho. Cotts. Pinn —4B 24
Westhurst Dri. Chst —5F 127
W. India Av. E14 —1C 88
W. India Dock Rd. E14 —7B 70
(in two parts)
W. India Ho. E14 —7C 70
West Kensington. —4H 83
W. Kensington Ct. W14 —5H 83
(off Edith Vs.)
W. Kensington Mans. W14 —5H 83
(off Beaumont Cres.)
West Kilburn. —3H 65
Westlake Clo. N13 —3F 17
Westlake Clo. Hay —4C 60
Westlake Rd. Wemb —2D 44
Westland Clo. Stanw —6A 94
Westland Ct. N'holt —3B 60
(off Seasprite Clo.)
Westland Dri. Brom —2H 155
Westland Ho. E16 —1E 90
(off Rymill St.)
Westland Pl. EC1 —3D 68 (1E 162)
Westlands Clo. Hay —4J 77
Westlands Ter. SW12 —6G 103
West La. SE16 —2H 87
Westlea Rd. W7 —3A 80
Westleigh Av. SW15 —5D 100
Westleigh Ct. E11 —5J 35
Westleigh Dri. Brom —1C 144
Westleigh Gdns. Edgw —1G 27
Westlington Clo. NW7 —6C 14
W. Lodge Av. W3 —1G 81
W. Lodge Ct. W3 —1G 81
West London Crematorium. NW10 —4D 64
Westmacott Dri. Felt —1H 113
Westmacott Ho. NW8 —4B 66 (4B 158)
(off Hatton St.)
West Mall. W11 —1J 83
(off Palace Gdns. Ter.)
Westmead. SW15 —6D 100
West Mead. Eps —6A 148
West Mead. Ruis —4A 42
Westmead Corner. Cars —4C 150
Westmead Rd. Sutt —4B 150
Westmere Dri. NW7 —3E 12
W. Mersea Clo. E16 —1K 89
West M. N17 —7C 18
West M. SW1 —4A 172
Westmill Ct. N4 —2C 50
(off Brownswood Rd.)
Westminster. —2J 85 (7E 166)
Westminster Abbey. —3H 85 (7E 166)
Westminster Abbey Chapter House. —1E 172
Westminster Av. T Hth —2B 140
Westminster Bri. SW1 & SE1 —2J 85 (7F 167)
Westminster Bri. Rd. SE1 —2K 85 (7F 167)
Westminster Bus. Sq. SE11 —5K 85 (6G 173)
Westminster Clo. Felt —1J 113
Westminster Clo. Ilf —2H 37
Westminster Clo. Tedd —5A 116
Westminster Ct. E11 —6J 35
(off Cambridge Pk.)
Westminster Dri. N13 —5D 16
Westminster Gdns. E4 —1B 20
Westminster Gdns. SW1
(off Marsham St.) —4J 85 (3E 172)
Westminster Gdns. Bark —2J 73
Westminster Gdns. Ilf —2G 37
Westminster Hall. —7E 166
Westminster Ho. Har W —7E 10
Westminster Ind. Est. SE18 —3B 90
Westminster Mans. SW1 —3H 85 (2D 172)
Westminster Pal. Gdns. SW1 —2C 172
Westminster R.C. Cathedral. —3G 85 (2A 172)
Westminster Rd. N9 —1C 18
Westminster Rd. W7 —1J 79
Westminster Rd. Sutt —2B 150
Westmoat Clo. Beck —7E 124
West Molesey. —4E 132
Westmoor Gdns. Enf —2E 8
Westmoor Rd. Enf —2E 8
Westmoor St. SE7 —3A 90
Westmoreland Av. Well —3J 109
Westmoreland Dri. Sutt —7K 149
Westmoreland Pl. SW1 —5F 85 (6K 171)
Westmoreland Pl. W5 —5D 62
Westmoreland Pl. Brom —3J 143
Westmoreland Rd. NW9 —3F 27
Westmoreland Rd. SE17 —6D 86
(in two parts)
Westmoreland Rd. SW13 —1B 100
Westmoreland Rd. Brom —5G 143
Westmoreland St. W1 —5E 66 (6H 159)
Westmoreland Ter. SW1 —5F 85 (6K 171)
Westmoreland Wlk. SE17 —6D 86
(in three parts)
Westmorland Clo. E12 —2B 54
Westmorland Clo. Twic —6B 98
Westmorland Ct. Surb —7D 134
Westmorland Rd. E17 —6C 34
Westmorland Rd. Harr —5F 25
Westmorland Sq. Mitc —5J 139
(off Westmorland Way)
Westmorland Ter. SE20 —7H 123
Westmorland Way. Mitc —4H 139
Westmount Ct. W5 —6F 63
Westmount Rd. SE9 —2D 108
West Norwood. —3B 122
West Norwood Crematorium. SE27 —3C 122
West Oak. Beck —1F 143
Westoe Rd. N9 —2C 18
Weston Av. Th Dit —7J 133
Weston Av. W Mol —3C 132
Westonbirt Ct. SE15 —6F 87
(off Ebley Clo.)
Weston Ct. N4 —3C 50
Weston Dri. Stan —1B 26
West One Ho. W1 —5G 67 (6A 160)
(off Wells St.)
Westone Mans. Bark —7K 55
(off Upney La.)
Weston Gdns. Iswth —1J 97
Weston Green. —7J 133
Weston Grn. Dag —4F 57
Weston Grn. Rd. Esh & Th Dit —7J 133
(in two parts)
Weston Gro. Brom —1H 143
Weston Ho. E9 —1J 69
(off King Edward's Rd.)
Weston Ho. NW6 —7G 47
Weston Pk. N8 —6J 31
Weston Pk. King T —2E 134
Weston Pk. Th Dit —7J 133
Weston Ri. WC1 —3K 67 (1H 161)
Weston Rd. W4 —3J 81
Weston Rd. Brom —7H 125
Weston Rd. Dag —4E 56
Weston Rd. Enf —2J 7
Weston St. SE1 —2E 86 (7F 169)
(in three parts)
Weston Wlk. E8 —7H 51
Westover Hill. NW3 —2J 47
Westover Rd. SW18 —7A 102
Westow Hill. SE19 —6E 122
Westow St. SE19 —6E 122
West Pk. SE9 —2C 126
West Pk. Av. Rich —1G 99
W. Park Clo. Houn —6D 78
W. Park Clo. Romf —5D 38
W. Park Rd. Rich —1G 99
W. Park Rd. S'hall —1G 79
West Parkside. SE10 —2G 89
West Pier. E1 —1H 87
West Pl. SW19 —5E 118
West Point. E14 —7B 70
West Point. SE1 —5G 87
Westpoint Trad. Est. W3 —5H 63
Westpole Av. Barn & Cockf —4K 5
Westport Ct. Hay —4A 60
Westport Rd. E13 —4K 71
Westport St. E1 —6K 69
W. Poultry Av. EC1 —5B 68 (6A 162)
West Quarters. W12 —6C 64
West Quay. SW10 —1A 102
W. Quay Dri. Hay —5C 60
West Ramp. H'row A —1C 94
W. Ridge Gdns. Gnfd —2G 61
West Ri. W2 —2D 164
West Rd. E15 —1H 71
West Rd. N2 —2B 30
West Rd. N17 —6C 18
West Rd. SE1 —2K 85 (6H 167)
West Rd. SW3 —5D 84 (6F 171)
West Rd. SW4 —5H 103
West Rd. W5 —5E 62
West Rd. Barn —1K 15
West Rd. Chad H —6D 38
West Rd. Felt —6F 95
West Rd. King T —1J 135
West Rd. Rush G —7K 39
West Rd. W Dray —3B 76
Westrow. SW15 —6E 100
West Row. W10 —4G 65
Westrow Dri. Bark —5A 56
Westrow Gdns. Ilf —2K 55
West Ruislip. —2E 40
W. Ruislip Ct. Ruis —2F 41
(off Ickenham Rd.)
W. Sheen Va. Rich —4F 99
Westside. N2 —3D 30
West Side. NW4 —2D 28
W. Side Comn. SW19 —5E 118
Westside Ct. W9 —4J 65
(off Elgin Av.)
West Smithfield. EC1 —5B 68 (6A 162)
West Sq. SE11 —3B 86 (2K 173)
West St. E2 —2H 69
West St. E11 —3G 53
West St. WC2 —6H 67 (1D 166)
West St. Bexh —3F 111
West St. Bren —6C 80
West St. Brom —1J 143
West St. Cars —3D 150
West St. Croy —4C 152
West St. Eri —4K 93
West St. Harr —1H 43
West St. Sutt —5K 149
West St. La. Cars —4D 150
W. Temple Sheen. SW14 —5H 99
W. Tenter St. E1 —6F 69 (1K 169)
West Ter. Sidc —1J 127
West Towers. Pinn —6B 24
Westvale M. W3 —2A 82
West Vw. NW4 —4E 28
Westview. W7 —6J 61
West Vw. Felt —7E 94
W. View Clo. NW10 —5B 46
Westview Clo. W10 —6E 64
Westview Cres. N9 —7K 7
Westview Dri. Wfd G —2B 36
Westville Rd. W12 —2C 82
Westville Rd. Th Dit —1A 146
West Wlk. E Barn —7K 5
West Wlk. Hay —1J 77
Westward Rd. E4 —5G 19
Westward Way. Harr —6E 26
W. Warwick Pl. SW1 —4G 85 (4A 172)
Westway. N18 —4J 17
West Way. NW10 —3K 45
Westway. SW20 —3D 136
Westway. W2 —5H 65 (6A 158)
Westway. W10 & W9 —5H 65
Westway. W12 & W10 —7B 64
West Way. Croy —2A 154
West Way. Edgw —6C 12
West Way. Houn —1D 96
Westway. Orp —5H 145
West Way. Pinn —4B 24
West Way. Ruis —1H 41
West Way. Shep —6F 131
West Way. W W'ck —6F 143
Westway Clo. SW20 —3D 136
Westway Ct. N'holt —1E 60
Westway Cross Retail Pk. Gnfd —1J 61
W. Way Gdns. Croy —2K 153
Westways. Eps —4B 148
West Ways. N'wd —2J 23
Westwell M. SW16 —6J 121
Westwell Rd. SW16 —6J 121
Westwell Rd. App. SW16 —6J 121
Westwick. King T —2G 135
(off Chesterton Ter.)
Westwick Gdns. W14 —2F 83
Westwick Gdns. Houn —2K 95
West Wickham. —1E 154
Westwood Av. SE19 —1C 140
Westwood Av. Harr —4F 43
Westwood Clo. Brom —2B 144
Westwood Clo. Ruis —6D 22
Westwood Ct. Gnfd —5H 43
Westwood Ct. Wemb —4B 44
Westwood Gdns. SW13 —3B 100
Westwood Hill. SE26 —5G 123
Westwood La. Sidc —5A 110
Westwood La. Well —3K 109
Westwood Pk. SE23 —7H 105
Westwood Pk. Trad. Est. W3 —5H 63
Westwood Pl. SE26 —4G 123
Westwood Rd. E16 —1K 89
Westwood Rd. SW13 —3B 100
Westwood Rd. Ilf —1K 55
West Woodside. Bex —1E 128
Wetheral Dri. Stan —1B 26
Wetherby Clo. N'holt —6F 43
Wetherby Gdns. SW5 —4A 84
Wetherby Mans. SW5 —5K 83
(off Earl's Ct. Sq.)
Wetherby M. SW5 —5K 83
Wetherby Pl. SW7 —4A 84
Wetherby Rd. Enf —1H 7
Wetherby Way. Chess —7E 146
Wetherden St. E17 —7B 34
Wetherell Rd. E9 —1K 69
Wetherill Rd. N10 —1E 30
Wetland Cen., The. —1D 100
Wevco Wharf. SE16 —6H 87
Wevell Ho. N6 —7E 30
(off Hillcrest)
Wexford Rd. SW12 —7D 102
Weybourne St. SW18 —2A 120
Weybridge Ct. SE16 —5H 87
(off Argyle Way)
Weybridge Point. SW11 —2D 102
Weybridge Rd. T Hth —4A 140
Wey Ct. Eps —4J 147
Weydown Clo. SW19 —1G 119
Weyhill Rd. E1 —6G 69
Weylands Clo. W on T —7D 132
Weylond Rd. Dag —3F 57
Weyman Rd. SE3 —1A 108
Weymarks, The. N17 —6J 17
Weymouth Av. NW7 —5F 13
Weymouth Av. W5 —3C 80
Weymouth Clo. E6 —6F 73
Weymouth Ct. E2 —2F 69
(off Weymouth Ter.)
Weymouth Ct. Sutt —7J 149
Weymouth Ho. SW8 —7K 85
(off Bolney St.)
Weymouth M. W1 —5F 67 (5J 159)
Weymouth Rd. Hay —3G 59
Weymouth St. W1 —5E 66 (6H 159)
Weymouth Ter. E2 —2F 69 (1K 163)
Weymouth Wlk. Stan —6F 11
Whadcoat St. N4 —2A 50
Whalebone Av. Romf —6F 39
Whalebone Ct. EC2 —7E 162
Whalebone Gro. Romf —6F 39
Whalebone La. E15 —7G 53
Whalebone La. N. Romf —1E 38
Whalebone La. S. Romf & Dag —7F 39
Whales Yd. E15 —7G 53
(off West Ham La.)
Wharfdale Clo. N11 —6K 15
Wharfdale Rd. N1 —2J 67
Wharfedale Ct. E5 —4K 51
Wharfedale Gdns. T Hth —4K 139
Wharfedale Ho. NW6 —1K 65
(off Kilburn Va.)
Wharfedale St. SW10 —5K 83
Wharf La. Twic —1A 116
Wharf Pl. E2 —1H 69
Wharf Rd. E15 —1F 71
Wharf Rd. N1 —2C 68 (1C 162)
Wharf Rd. NW1 —1H 67
Wharf Rd. Enf —6F 9
Wharf Rd. Ind. Est. Enf —6F 9
Wharfside Rd. E16 —5G 71
Wharf St. E16 —5G 71
Wharf, The. EC3 —1F 87 (4H 169)
Wharncliffe Dri. S'hall —1H 79
Wharncliffe Gdns. SE25 —2E 140
Wharncliffe Rd. SE25 —2E 140
Wharton Clo. NW10 —6A 46
Wharton Cotts. WC1 —3A 68 (2J 161)
Wharton Ho. SE1 —3F 87 (7J 169)
(off Maltby St.)
Wharton Rd. Brom —1K 143
Wharton St. WC1 —3K 67 (2H 161)
Whateley Rd. SE20 —7K 123
Whateley Rd. SE22 —5F 105
Whatley Av. SW20 —3F 137
Whatman Ho. E14 —6B 70
Whatman Rd. SE23 —7K 105
Wheatfields. E6 —6F 73
Wheatfields. Enf —1F 9
Wheatfield Way. King T —2E 134
Wheathill Rd. SE20 —3H 141
Wheatland Ho. SE22 —3E 104
Wheatlands. Houn —6E 78
Wheatlands Rd. SW17 —3E 120
Wheatley Clo. NW4 —2C 28
Wheatley Cres. Hay —7J 59
Wheatley Gdns. N9 —2K 17
Wheatley Ho. SW15 —7C 100
(off Ellisfield Dri.)
Wheatley Mans. Bark —7A 56
(off Bevan Av.)
Wheatley Rd. Iswth —3K 97
Wheatley St. W1 —5E 66 (6H 159)
Wheat Sheaf Clo. E14 —4D 88
Wheatsheaf Clo. N'holt —5C 42
Wheatsheaf La. SW6 —7E 82
Wheatsheaf La. SW8 —7J 85
(in two parts)
Wheatsheaf Ter. SW6 —7H 83
Wheatstone Clo. Mitc —1C 138
Wheatstone Rd. W10 —5G 65
Wheatstone Rd. Eri —5K 93
Wheeler Clo. Wfd G —6J 21
Wheeler Gdns. N1 —1J 67
(off Outram Pl.)
Wheelers Cross. Bark —2H 73
Wheelers Dri. Ruis —6E 22
Wheel Farm Dri. Dag —3J 57
Wheel Ho. E14 —5D 88
Wheelock Clo. Eri —7H 93

A-Z Big London 279

Wheelwright St. N7 —7K 49
Whelan Way. Wall —3H 151
Wheler Ho. E1 —4F 69 (4J 163)
(off Quaker St.)
Wheler St. E1 —4F 69 (4J 163)
Whellock Rd. W4 —3A 82
Whenman Av. Bex —2J 129
Whernside Clo. SE28 —7C 74
Whetstone. —2F 15
Whetstone Clo. N20 —2G 15
Whetstone Pk. WC2 —6K 67 (7G 161)
Whetstone Rd. SE3 —2A 108
Whewell Rd. N19 —2J 49
Whidborne Clo. SE8 —2C 106
Whidborne Ho. WC1 —3J 67 (2F 161)
(off Whidborne St.)
Whidborne St. WC1 —3J 67 (2F 161)
Whimbrel Clo. SE28 —7C 74
Whimbrel Way. Hay —5B 60
Whinchat Rd. SE28 —3H 91
Whinfell Clo. SW16 —5H 121
Whinyates Rd. SE9 —3C 108
Whipps Cross. E11 —6H 35
Whipps Cross. E17 —5F 35
Whipps Cross Ho. E17 —5F 35
(off Wood St.)
Whipps Cross Rd. E11 —5F 35
(in two parts)
Whiskin St. EC1 —3B 68 (2A 162)
Whisperwood Clo. Harr —1J 25
Whistler Gdns. Edgw —2F 27
Whistler M. SE15 —7F 87
Whistler M. Dag —5B 56
(off Fitzstephen Rd.)
Whistlers Av. SW11 —7B 84
Whistler St. N5 —5B 50
Whistler Tower. SW10 —7A 84
(off Worlds End Est.)
Whistler Wlk. SW10 —7B 84
Whiston Ho. N1 —7B 50
(off Richmond Gro.)
Whiston Rd. E2 —2F 69
(in two parts)
Whitbread Clo. N17 —1G 33
Whitbread Rd. SE4 —4A 106
Whitburn Rd. SE13 —4D 106
Whitby Av. NW10 —3H 63
Whitby Ct. N7 —4J 49
Whitby Gdns. NW9 —3G 27
Whitby Gdns. Sutt —2B 150
Whitby Ho. NW8 —1A 66
(off Boundary Rd.)
Whitby Pde. Ruis —2A 42
Whitby Rd. SE18 —4D 90
Whitby Rd. Harr —3G 43
Whitby Rd. Ruis —3K 41
Whitby Rd. Sutt —2B 150
Whitby St. E1 —4F 69 (3J 163)
(in two parts)
Whitcher Clo. SE14 —6A 88
Whitcher Pl. NW1 —6G 49
Whitchurch Av. Edgw —7A 12
Whitchurch Clo. Edgw —6A 12
Whitchurch Gdns. Edgw —6A 12
Whitchurch Ho. W10 —6F 65
(off Kingsdown Clo.)
Whitchurch La. Edgw —7J 11
Whitchurch Pde. Edgw —7B 12
Whitchurch Rd. W11 —7F 65
Whitcomb Ct. SW1 —3D 166
Whitcomb St. WC2 —7H 67 (3D 166)
White Acre. NW9 —2A 28
Whiteadder Way. E14 —4D 88
Whitear Wlk. E15 —6F 53
Whitebarn La. Dag —1G 75
Whitebeam Av. Brom —7E 144
Whitebeam Clo. SW9 —7K 85
White Bear Pl. NW3 —4B 48
White Bear Yd. EC1 —4A 68 (4J 161)
(off Clerkenwell Rd.)
White Bri. Av. Mitc —3B 138
Whitebridge Clo. Felt —6H 95
White Butts Rd. Ruis —3B 42
Whitechapel. —5G 69 (6K 163)
Whitechapel High St. E1
—6F 69 (7K 163)
Whitechapel Rd. E1 —5G 69 (7K 163)
White Church La. E1 —6G 69 (7K 163)
White Church Pas. E1 —6G 69 (7K 163)
(off White Church La.)
White City. —7D 64
White City. —6E 64
White City Clo. W12 —7E 64
White City Est. W12 —7D 64
White City Rd. W12 —7E 64
White Conduit St. N1 —2A 68
Whitecote Rd. S'hall —6G 61
Whitecroft Clo. Beck —4F 143
Whitecroft Way. Beck —5E 142
Whitecross Pl. EC2 —5D 68 (5F 163)
Whitecross St. EC1 —4C 68 (3D 162)
Whitefield Av. NW2 —1E 46
Whitefield Clo. SW18 —6G 101
Whitefoot La. Brom —4E 124
Whitefoot Ter. Brom —3G 125
Whitefriars Av. Harr —2J 25
Whitefriars Ct. N12 —5G 15
Whitefriars Dri. Harr —2H 25
Whitefriars St. EC4 —6A 68 (1K 167)
Whitefriars Trad. Est. Harr —3H 25
White Gdns. Dag —6G 57
Whitegate Gdns. Harr —7E 10
Whitehall. —6G 149
Whitehall. SW1 —1J 85 (5E 166)
Whitehall Ct. SW1 —1J 85 (5E 166)
(in two parts)
Whitehall Cres. Chess —5D 146
Whitehall Gdns. E4 —1B 20
Whitehall Gdns. SW1 —5E 166
Whitehall Gdns. W3 —1G 81
Whitehall Gdns. W4 —6H 81
Whitehall La. Buck H —2D 20
Whitehall Lodge. N10 —3E 30
Whitehall Pk. N19 —1G 49
Whitehall Pk. Rd. W4 —6H 81
Whitehall Pl. E7 —5J 53
Whitehall Pl. SW1 —1J 85 (5E 166)
Whitehall Pl. Wall —4F 151
Whitehall Rd. W7 —2A 80
Whitehall Rd. E4 & Wfd G —2B 20
Whitehall Rd. Brom —5B 144
Whitehall Rd. Harr —7J 25
Whitehall Rd. T Hth —5A 140
Whitehall St. N17 —7A 18
White Hart Clo. Hay —6F 77
White Hart Ct. EC2 —6G 163
White Hart La. N22 & N17 —1K 31
White Hart La. NW10 —6B 46
White Hart La. SW13 —3A 100
White Hart La. Romf —1G 39
White Hart Rd. SE18 —4J 91
White Hart Roundabout. N'holt —2B 60
White Hart Slip. Brom —2J 143
White Hart St. SE11 —5A 86 (5K 173)
White Hart Yd. SE1 —1D 86 (5E 168)
Whitehaven Clo. Brom —4J 143
Whitehaven St. NW8 —4C 66 (4C 158)
Whitehead Clo. N18 —5J 17
Whitehead Clo. SW18 —7A 102
Whitehead's Gro. SW3 —4C 84 (4D 170)
White Heart Av. Uxb —5E 58
Whiteheath Av. Ruis —7E 22
White Heather Ho. WC1 —3J 67 (2F 161)
(off Cromer St.)
White Heron M. Tedd —6K 115
Whitehorn Av. W Dray —7A 58
White Horse All. EC1 —5A 162
White Horse Hill. Chst —4E 126
White Horse La. E1 —4K 69
Whitehorse La. SE25 —4D 140
Whitehorse M. SE1 —3A 86 (1K 173)
White Horse Rd. E1 —5A 70
(in two parts)
White Horse Rd. E6 —3D 72
Whitehorse Rd. Croy & T Hth —7C 140
White Horse St. W1 —1F 85 (5K 165)
White Horse Yd. EC2 —6D 68 (7E 162)
White Ho. SW4 —7H 103
(off Clapham Pk. Est.)
White Ho. SW11 —1B 102
White Ho. Dri. Stan —4H 11
White Ho. Dri. Wfd G —6C 20
Whitehouse Est. E10 —6E 34
Whitehouse La. Enf —1H 7
White Ho., The. NW1 —3K 159
Whitehouse Way. N14 —2A 16
White Kennett St. E1 —6E 68 (7H 163)
Whitelands Ho. SW3 —5D 84 (5F 171)
(off Cheltenham Ter.)
Whiteledges. W13 —6C 62
Whitelegg Rd. E13 —2H 71
Whiteley Rd. SE19 —5D 122
Whiteleys Cen. W2 —6K 65
Whiteley's Cotts. W14 —4H 83
Whiteleys Pde. Uxb —4D 58
Whiteley's Way. Hanw —3E 114
White Lion Ct. EC3 —1G 169
White Lion Ct. SE15 —6J 87
White Lion Ct. Iswth —3B 98
White Lion Hill. EC4 —7B 68 (2B 168)
White Lion St. N1 —2A 68
White Lodge. SE19 —7B 122
White Lodge. W5 —5C 62
White Lodge Clo. N2 —6B 30
White Lodge Clo. Sutt —7A 150
White Lyon Ct. EC2 —5C 162
Whiteoak Ct. Chst —6E 126
White Oak Dri. Beck —2E 142
White Oak Gdns. Sidc —7K 109
Whiteoaks La. Gnfd —3H 61
White Orchards. N20 —7C 4
White Orchards. Stan —5F 11
White Post La. E9 —7B 52
White Post St. SE15 —7J 87
White Rd. E15 —7G 53
Whites Av. Ilf —6J 37
White's Grounds. SE1
—2E 86 (7H 169)
White's Grounds Est. SE1 —6H 169
White's Mdw. Brom —4E 144
White's Row. E1 —5F 69 (6J 163)
Whites Sq. SW4 —4H 103
Whitestile Rd. Bren —5C 80
Whitestone La. NW3 —3A 48
Whitestone Wlk. NW3 —3A 48
White St. S'hall —2B 78
Whiteswan M. W4 —5A 82
Whitethorn Av. W Dray —1B 76
Whitethorn Gdns. Croy —2H 153
Whitethorn Gdns. Enf —5J 7
Whitethorn Pas. E3 —4C 70
Whitethorn Pl. W Dray —1B 76
Whitethorn St. E3 —5C 70
Whitewebbs Way. Orp —1K 145
Whitfield Ho. NW8 —4C 66 (4C 158)
(off Salisbury St.)
Whitfield Pl. W1 —4A 160
Whitfield Rd. E6 —7A 54
Whitfield Rd. SE3 —1F 107
Whitfield Rd. Bexh —7F 93
Whitfield St. W1 —4G 67 (4A 160)
Whitford Gdns. Mitc —3D 138
Whitgift Av. S Croy —5B 152
Whitgift Cen. Croy —2C 152
Whitgift Ho. SE11 —4K 85 (3G 173)
Whitgift Sq. Croy —2C 152
Whitgift St. SE11 —4K 85 (3G 173)
Whitgift St. Croy —3C 152
Whiting Av. Bark —7F 55
Whitings. Ilf —5J 37
Whitings Rd. Barn —5A 4
Whitings Way. E6 —5E 72
Whitland Rd. Cars —1B 150
Whitley Clo. Stanw —6A 94
Whitley Ho. SW1 —6G 85 (7B 172)
(off Churchill Gdns.)
Whitley Rd. N17 —2E 32
Whitlock Dri. SW19 —7G 101
Whitman Rd. E3 —4A 70
Whitmead Clo. S Croy —6E 152
Whitmore Clo. N11 —5A 16
Whitmore Est. N1 —1E 68
Whitmore Gdns. NW10 —2E 64
Whitmore Ho. E2 —1E 68
(off Whitmore Est.)
Whitmore Rd. N1 —1E 68
Whitmore Rd. Beck —3B 142
Whitmore Rd. Harr —7G 25
Whitnell Way. SW15 —5E 100
Whitney Av. Ilf —4B 36
Whitney Rd. E10 —7D 34
Whitney Wlk. Sidc —6E 128
Whitstable Clo. Beck —1B 142
Whitstable Clo. Ruis —2G 41
Whitstable Ho. W10 —6F 65
(off Silchester Rd.)
Whitstable Pl. Croy —4C 152
Whittaker Av. Rich —5D 98
Whittaker Pl. Rich —5D 98
(off Whittaker Av.)
Whittaker Rd. E6 —7A 54
Whittaker Rd. Sutt —3H 149
Whittaker St. SW1 —4E 84 (4G 171)
Whittaker Way. SE1 —4G 87
Whitta Rd. E12 —4B 54
Whittell Gdns. SE26 —3J 123
Whittingham. N17 —7C 18
Whittingham Ct. W4 —7A 82
Whittingstall Rd. SW6 —1H 101
Whittington Av. EC3 —6E 68 (1G 169)
Whittington Av. Hay —5H 59
Whittington Ct. N2 —5D 30
Whittington M. N12 —4F 15
(off Fredericks Pl.)
Whittington Rd. N22 —7D 16
Whittington Way. Pinn —5C 24
Whittlebury Clo. Cars —7D 150
Whittle Clo. E17 —6A 34
Whittle Clo. S'hall —6F 61
Whittle Rd. Houn —7A 78
Whittle Rd. S'hall —2F 79
Whittlesea Clo. Harr —7B 10
Whittlesea Path. Harr —1G 25
Whittlesea Rd. Harr —7B 10
Whittlesey St. SE1 —1A 86 (5J 167)
Whitton. —7G 97
Whitton Av. E. Gnfd —5J 43
Whitton Av. W. N'holt & Gnfd —5F 43
Whitton Clo. Gnfd —6B 44
Whitton Dene. Houn & Iswth —5G 97
Whitton Dri. Gnfd —6A 44
Whitton Mnr. Rd. Iswth —6G 97
Whitton Rd. Houn —4F 97
Whitton Rd. Twic —6J 97
Whitton Road Roundabout. (Junct.)
—6K 97
Whitton Wlk. E3 —3C 70
Whitton Waye. Houn —6E 96
Whitwell Rd. E13 —3J 71
Whitworth Ho. SE1 —3C 86
Whitworth Rd. SE18 —7E 90
Whitworth Rd. SE25 —3E 140
Whitworth St. SE10 —5G 89
Whorlton Rd. SE15 —3H 105
Whymark Av. N22 —3A 32
Whytecroft. Houn —7B 78
Whyteville Rd. E7 —6K 53
Whytlaw Ho. E3 —5B 70
Wickersley Rd. SW11 —2E 102
Wickers Oake. SE19 —4F 123
Wicker St. E1 —6H 69
Wicket Rd. Gnfd —3A 62
Wickets, The. Ashf —4A 112
Wicket, The. Croy —5C 154
Wickfield Ho. SE16 —2H 87
(off Wilson Gro.)
Wickford St. E1 —4J 69
Wickford Way. E17 —4K 33
Wickham Av. Croy —2A 154
Wickham Av. Sutt —5E 148
Wickham Chase. W W'ck —1F 155
Wickham Clo. E1 —5J 69
Wickham Clo. Enf —3C 8
Wickham Clo. N Mald —5B 136
Wickham Ct. Rd. W W'ck —2E 154
Wickham Cres. W W'ck —2E 154
Wickham Gdns. SE4 —3B 106
Wickham La. SE2 & Well —5A 92
Wickham M. SE4 —2B 106
Wickham Rd. E4 —7K 19
Wickham Rd. SE4 —4B 106
Wickham Rd. Beck —2D 142
Wickham Rd. Croy —2J 153
Wickham Rd. Harr —2H 25
Wickham St. SE11 —5K 85 (5G 173)
Wickham St. Well —2J 109
Wickham Way. Beck —4E 142
Wick La. E3 —1C 70
(in two parts)
Wickliffe Av. N3 —2G 29
Wickliffe Gdns. Wemb —2H 45
Wicklow Ho. N16 —1F 51
Wicklow St. WC1 —3K 67 (1G 161)
Wick M. E9 —6A 52
Wick Rd. E9 —6K 51
Wick Rd. Tedd —7B 116
Wicks Clo. SE9 —4B 126
Wick Sq. E9 —6B 52
Wicksteed Clo. Bex —3K 129
Wicksteed Ho. SE1 —3C 86
Wicksteed Ho. Bren —5F 81
Wickway Ct. SE15 —6F 87
(off Cator St.)
Wickwood St. SE5 —2B 104
Widdecombe Av. S Harr —2C 42
Widdenham Rd. N7 —4K 49
Widdin St. E15 —7G 53
Widecombe Gdns. Ilf —4C 36
Widecombe Rd. SE9 —3C 126
Widecombe Way. N2 —5B 30
Widegate St. E1 —5E 68 (6H 163)
Widenham Clo. Pinn —5A 24
Wide Way. Mitc —3H 139
Widewing Clo. Tedd —7B 116
Widford Ho. N1 —2B 68
(off Colebrooke Rd.)
Widgeon Clo. E16 —6K 71
Widley Rd. W9 —3J 65
Widmer Ct. Houn —2C 96
Widmore. —3A 144
Widmore Green. —1A 144
Widmore Lodge Rd. Brom
—2B 144
Widmore Rd. Brom —2J 143
Widmore Rd. Uxb —4D 58
Wigan Ho. E5 —1H 51
Wigeon Path. SE28 —3H 91
Wigeon Way. Hay —6C 60
Wiggins Mead. NW9 —7G 13
Wigginton Av. Wemb —6H 45
Wightman Rd. N8 & N4 —4A 32
Wigley Rd. Felt —2B 114
Wigmore Ct. W13 —1A 80
(off Singapore Rd.)
Wigmore Hall. —7J 159
Wigmore Pl. W1 —6F 67 (7J 159)
Wigmore Rd. Cars —2B 150
Wigmore St. W1 —6E 66 (7H 159)
Wigmore Wlk. Cars —2B 150
Wigram Ho. E14 —7D 70
Wigram Rd. E11 —6A 36
Wigram Sq. E17 —3E 34
Wigston Clo. N18 —5K 17
Wigston Rd. E13 —4K 71
Wigton Gdns. Stan —1E 26
Wigton Pl. SE11 —5A 86 (6K 173)
Wigton Rd. E17 —1B 34
Wilberforce Rd. N4 —2B 50
Wilberforce Rd. NW9 —6C 28
Wilberforce Way. SW19 —6F 119
Wilbraham Ho. SW8 —7J 85
(off Wandsworth Rd.)
Wilbraham Pl. SW1 —4D 84 (3F 171)
Wilbury Way. N18 —5J 17
Wilby M. W11 —1H 83
Wilcox Clo. SW8 —7J 85
(in two parts)
Wilcox Gdns. Shep —3A 130
Wilcox Ho. E3 —5B 70
Wilcox Pl. SW1 —3G 85 (2B 172)
Wilcox Rd. SW8 —7J 85
Wilcox Rd. Sutt —4K 149
Wilcox Rd. Tedd —4H 115
Wild Ct. WC2 —6K 67 (1G 167)
(in two parts)
Wildcroft Gdns. Edgw —6J 11
Wildcroft Mnr. SW15 —7E 100
Wildcroft Rd. SW15 —7E 100
Wilde Clo. E8 —1G 69
Wilde Pl. N13 —6G 17
Wilde Pl. SW18 —7B 102
Wilder Clo. Ruis —1K 41
Wilderness M. SW4 —4F 103
Wilderness Rd. Chst —7F 127
Wilderness, The. E Mol —5G 133
Wilderness, The. Hamp —4F 115
Wilde Rd. Eri —7H 93
Wilderton Rd. N16 —7E 32
Wildfell Rd. SE6 —7D 106
Wild Goose Dri. SE14 —1J 105
Wild Hatch. NW11 —6J 29
Wild's Rents. SE1 —3E 86 (7G 169)
Wild St. WC2 —6J 67 (1F 167)
Wildwood Clo. SE12 —7H 107
Wildwood Gro. NW3 —1A 48
Wildwood Ri. NW11 —1A 48
Wildwood Rd. NW11 —6K 29
Wildwood Ter. NW11 —1A 48
Wilford Clo. Enf —3J 7
Wilfred Ct. N15 —5D 32
(off South Gro.)
Wilfred Owen Clo. SW19 —6A 120
Wilfred St. SW1 —3G 85 (1A 172)
Wilfrid Gdns. W3 —5J 63
Wilkes Rd. Bren —6E 80
Wilkes St. E1 —5F 69 (5K 163)
Wilkie Ho. SW1 —5H 85 (5D 172)
(off Cureton St.)
Wilkie Way. SE22 —1G 123
Wilkins Clo. Hay —5H 77
Wilkins Clo. Mitc —1C 138
Wilkins Ho. SW1 —6F 85 (7K 171)
(off Churchill Gdns.)
Wilkinson Clo. Uxb —1D 58
Wilkinson Ct. SW17 —4B 120
Wilkinson Ho. N1 —2D 68
(off Cranston Est.)
Wilkinson Rd. E16 —6A 72
Wilkinson St. SW8 —7K 85
Wilkinson Way. W4 —2K 81
Wilkin St. NW5 —6E 48
Wilkin St. M. NW5 —6F 49
Wilks Gdns. Croy —1A 154
Wilks Pl. N1 —2E 68
Willan Rd. N17 —2D 32
Willan Wall. E16 —7H 71
Willard St. SW8 —3F 103
Willcocks Clo. Chess —3E 146
Willcott Rd. W3 —1H 81
Will Crooks Gdns. SE9 —4A 108
Willenfield Rd. NW10 —2J 63
Willenhall Av. New Bar —6F 5
Willenhall Ct. New Bar —6F 5
Willenhall Dri. Hay —7G 59
Willenhall Rd. SE18 —5F 91
Willersley Av. Sidc —1K 127
Willersley Clo. Sidc —1K 127
Willesden. —6C 46
Willesden Green. —6D 46
Willesden La. NW2 & NW6 —6E 46
Willes Rd. NW5 —6F 49
Willett Clo. N'holt —3A 60
Willett Clo. Orp —6J 145
Willett Ho. E13 —2K 71
(off Queens Rd. W.)
Willett Pl. T Hth —5A 140
Willett Rd. T Hth —5A 140
Willett Way. Orp —5H 145
William Allen Ho. Edgw —7A 12
William Banfield Ho. SW6 —2H 101
(off Munster Rd.)
William Barefoot Dri. SE9 —4E 126
William Blake Ho. SW11 —1C 102
William Bonney Est. SW4 —4H 103
William Booth Rd. SE20 —1G 141
William Carey Way. Harr —6J 25
William Channing Ho. E2 —3H 69
(off Canrobert St.)
William Clo. N2 —3B 30
William Clo. SE13 —3E 106
William Clo. Romf —1J 39
William Clo. S'hall —2G 79
William Cobbett Ho. W8 —3K 83
(off Scarsdale Pl.)
William Ct. W5 —5C 62
William Covell Clo. Enf —1E 6
William Dromey Ct. NW6 —7H 47
William Dunbar Ho. NW6 —2H 65
(off Albert Rd.)
William Dyce M. SW16 —4H 121
William Ellis Way. SE16 —3G 87
(off St James's Rd.)
William Evans Ho. SE8 —4K 87
(off Bush Rd.)
William Fenn Ho. E2 —3G 69 (1K 163)
(off Shipton Rd.)
William IV St. WC2 —7J 67 (3E 166)
William Gdns. SW15 —5D 100
William Gibbs Ct. SW1 —3H 85 (2C 172)
(off Old Pye St.)
William Gunn Ho. NW3 —5C 48
William Guy Gdns. E3 —3D 70
William Henry Wlk. SW8
—6H 85 (7C 172)
William Hunt Mans. SW13 —6E 82
William Margrie Clo. SE15 —2G 105
William M. SW1 —2D 84 (7F 165)
William Morley Clo. E6 —1B 72
William Morris Clo. E17 —3B 34
William Morris Gallery. —3C 34
William Morris Ho. W6 —6F 83
William Morris Way. SW6 —3A 102
William Paton Ho. E16 —6K 71
William Pike Ho. Romf —6K 39
(off Waterloo Gdns.)
William Pl. E3 —2B 70
William Rathbone Ho. E2 —3H 69
(off Florida St.)
William Rd. NW1 —3F 67 (2K 159)
William Rd. SW19 —7G 119
William Rd. Sutt —5A 150
William Rushbrooke Ho. SE16 —4G 87
(off Rouel Rd.)
Williams Av. E17 —1B 34
William Saville Ho. NW6 —2H 65
(off Denmark Rd.)
Williams Clo. N8 —6H 31
Williams Clo. SW6 —7G 83
Williams Gro. N22 —1A 32
Williams Gro. Surb —6C 134
Williams Ho. NW2 —3E 46
(off Stoll Clo.)
William's La. SW14 —3J 99
Williams La. Mord —5A 138
William Smith Ho. Belv —3G 93
(off Ambrook Rd.)
Williamson Clo. SE10 —5H 89
Williamson Ct. SE17 —5C 86
Williamson Rd. N4 —6B 32
Williamson St. N7 —4J 49
Williamson Way. NW7 —6B 14
William Sq. SE16 —7A 70
(off Sovereign Cres.)
Williams Rd. W13 —1A 80
Williams Rd. S'hall —4C 78
Williams Ter. Croy —6A 152
William St. E10 —6D 34
William St. N17 —7A 18
William St. SW1 —2D 84 (7F 165)
William St. Bark —7G 55
William St. Cars —3C 150
William White Ct. E13 —1A 72
(off Green St.)
William Wood Ho. SE26 —3J 123
(off Shrublands Clo.)
Willifield Way. NW11 —4H 29
Willingale Clo. Wfd G —6F 21
Willingdon Rd. N22 —2B 32
Willingham Clo. NW5 —5G 49
Willingham Ter. NW5 —5G 49
Willingham Way. King T —3G 135
Willington Ct. E5 —3A 52
Willington Rd. SW9 —3J 103
Willis Av. Sutt —6C 150
Willis Ct. T Hth —6A 140
Willis Ho. E14 —7D 70
Willis Rd. E15 —2H 71
Willis Rd. Croy —7C 140
Willis Rd. Eri —4J 93
Willis St. E14 —6D 70
Will Miles Ct. SW19 —7A 120
Willmore End. SW19 —1K 137
Willoughby Av. Croy —4K 151
Willoughby Dri. Rain —7K 57
Willoughby Gro. N17 —7C 18
Willoughby Highwalk. EC2 —5D 68
(off Moor La.)
Willoughby Ho. EC2 —5E 162
Willoughby La. N17 —6C 18
Willoughby Pk. Rd. N17 —7C 18
(in two parts)
Willoughby Pas. E14 —1C 88
Willoughby Rd. N8 —3A 32
Willoughby Rd. NW3 —4B 48
Willoughby Rd. King T —1F 135
Willoughby Rd. Twic —5C 98
(in two parts)
Willoughbys, The. SW15 —3A 100
Willoughby St. WC1 —6E 160
Willoughby Way. SE7 —4K 89
Willow Av. SW13 —2B 100
Willow Av. Side —6A 110
Willow Av. W Dray —7B 58
Willow Bank. SW6 —3G 101
Willow Bank. Rich —3B 116
Willow Bri. Rd. N1 —6C 50
Willowbrook. Hamp H —5F 115
Willowbrook Est. SE15 —7G 87
Willow Brook Rd. SE15 —7F 87
Willowbrook Rd. S'hall —3E 78
Willowbrook Rd. Stai —2A 112
Willow Bus. Cen., The. Mitc —6D 138
Willow Bus. Pk. SE26 —3J 123
Willow Clo. SE6 —1H 125
Willow Clo. Bex —6F 111
Willow Clo. Bren —6C 80
Willow Clo. Brom —5D 144
Willow Clo. Buck H —3G 21
Willow Cotts. Hanw —3C 114
Willow Cotts. Rich —6G 81
Willow Ct. E11 —2G 53
(off Trinity Clo.)
Willow Ct. EC2 —3G 163
Willow Ct. NW6 —7G 47
Willow Ct. W4 —7A 82
(off Corney Reach Way)
Willow Ct. Edgw —4K 11
Willow Ct. Harr —1K 25
Willowcourt Av. Harr —5B 26
Willowdene. N6 —7D 30

Willowdene—Wishart Rd.

Willowdene. SE15 —7H 87
Willow Dene. Bus H —1D 10
Willow Dene. Pinn —2B 24
Willowdene Clo. Twic —7G 97
Willowdene Ct. N20 —7F 5
(off High Rd.)
Willow Dri. Barn —4B 4
Willow End. N20 —2D 14
Willow End. Surb —1E 146
Willow Farm La. SW15 —3D 100
Willowfields Clo. SE18 —5J 91
Willow Gdns. Houn —1E 96
Willow Gdns. Ruis —2H 41
Willow Grange. Sidc —3B 128
Willow Grn. NW9 —1A 28
Willow Gro. E13 —2J 71
Willow Gro. Chst —6E 126
Willow Gro. Ruis —2H 41
Willowhayne Dri. W on T —7K 131
Willowhayne Gdns. Wor Pk —3E 148
Willow Ho. W10 —4F 65
(off Maple Wlk.)
Willow Ho. Brom —2G 143
Willow La. SE18 —4D 90
Willow La. Mitc —5D 138
Willow Lodge. SW6 —1F 101
Willowmead Clo. W5 —5D 62
Willow Mt. Croy —3E 152
Willow Pl. SW1 —4G 85 (3B 172)
Willow Rd. E12 —3D 54
Willow Rd. NW3 —4B 48
Willow Rd. W5 —2E 80
Willow Rd. Enf —3K 7
Willow Rd. N Mald —4J 135
Willow Rd. Romf —6E 38
Willow Rd. Wall —7F 151
Willows Av. Mord —5K 137
Willows Clo. Pinn —2A 24
Willowside Ct. Enf —3G 7
Willows Ter. NW10 —2B 64
(off Rucklidge Av.)
Willows, The. E6 —7D 54
Willows, The. Beck —1C 142
Willow St. E4 —1A 20
Willow St. EC2 —4E 68 (3G 163)
Willow St. Romf —4J 39
Willow Tree Clo. E3 —1A 70
Willow Tree Clo. SW18 —1K 119
Willow Tree Clo. Hay —4A 60
Willowtree Clo. Uxb —3E 40
Willow Tree Ct. Sidc —5A 128
Willow Tree Ct. Wemb —5D 44
Willow Tree La. Hay —4A 60
Willow Tree Wlk. Brom —1K 143
Willowtree Way. T Hth —1A 140
Willow Va. W12 —1C 82
Willow Va. Chst —6F 127
Willow Vw. SW19 —1B 138
Willow Wlk. E17 —5B 34
Willow Wlk. N2 —2B 30
Willow Wlk. N15 —4B 32
Willow Wlk. N21 —6E 6
Willow Wlk. SE1 —3E 86
Willow Wlk. Ilf —2F 55
Willow Wlk. Orp —3E 156
Willow Wlk. Sutt —3H 149
Willow Way. N3 —7E 14
Willow Way. SE26 —3J 123
Willow Way. W11 —7F 65
Willow Way. Eps —6K 147
Willow Way. Sun —4J 131
Willow Way. Twic —2F 115
Willow Way. Wemb —3A 44
Willow Wood Cres. SE25 —6E 140
Willow Wren Wharf. S'hall —4K 77
Willrose Cres. SE2 —5B 92
Willsbridge Ct. SE15 —6F 87
Wills Cres. Houn —6F 97
Wills Gro. NW7 —5H 13
(in two parts)
Wilman Gro. E8 —7G 51
Wilmar Clo. Hay —4F 59
Wilmar Gdns. W W'ck —1D 154
Wilmcote Ho. W2 —5K 65
(off Woodchester Sq.)
Wilment Ct. NW2 —3E 46
Wilmer Clo. King T —5F 117
Wilmer Cres. King T —5F 117
Wilmer Gdns. N1 —1E 68
(in two parts)
Wilmer Lea Clo. E15 —7F 53
Wilmer Pl. N16 —2F 51
Wilmer Way. N14 —5C 16
Wilmington Av. W4 —7K 81
Wilmington Ct. SW16 —7J 121
Wilmington Gdns. Bark —6H 55
Wilmington Sq. WC1 —3A 68 (2J 161)
(in two parts)
Wilmington St. WC1 —3A 68 (2J 161)
Wilmot Clo. N2 —2A 30
Wilmot Clo. SE15 —7G 87
Wilmot Pl. W7 —1J 79
Wilmot Rd. E10 —2D 52
Wilmot Rd. N17 —3D 32
Wilmot Rd. Cars —5D 150
Wilmot St. E2 —4H 69
Wilmot St. NW1 —7G 49
Wilmount St. SE18 —4F 91
Wilna Rd. SW18 —7A 102
Wilsham St. W11 —1F 83
Wilshaw Ho. SE8 —7C 88
Wilshaw St. SE14 —1C 106
Wilsmere Dri. Har W —7D 10
Wilsmere Dri. N'holt —6C 42
Wilson Av. Mitc —1C 138
Wilson Clo. S Croy —5D 152
Wilson Clo. Wemb —7F 27
Wilson Dri. Wemb —7F 27
Wilson Gdns. Harr —7G 25
Wilson Gro. SE16 —2H 87
Wilson Rd. E6 —3B 72
Wilson Rd. SE5 —1E 104
Wilson Rd. Chess —6F 147
Wilson Rd. Ilf —7D 36
Wilson's Av. N17 —2F 33
Wilson's Pl. E14 —6B 70
Wilson's Rd. W6 —5F 83
Wilson St. E17 —5E 34
Wilson St. EC2 —5D 68 (5F 163)
Wilson St. N21 —7F 7
Wilson Wlk. W6 —4B 82
(off Prebend Gdns.)
Wilstone Clo. Hay —4C 60
Wiltern Ct. NW2 —6G 47
Wilthorne Gdns. Dag —7H 57
Wilton Av. W4 —5A 82
Wilton Clo. W Dray —6A 76
Wilton Cres. SW1 —2E 84 (7G 165)
Wilton Cres. SW19 —7H 119
Wilton Dri. Romf —1J 39
Wilton Est. E8 —6G 51
Wilton Gdns. W Mol —3E 132
Wilton Gro. SW19 —1H 137
Wilton Gro. N Mald —6B 136
Wilton M. SW1 —3E 84 (1H 171)
Wilton Pde. Felt —1K 113
Wilton Pl. SW1 —2E 84 (7G 165)
Wilton Pl. Harr —6K 25
Wilton Rd. N10 —2E 30
Wilton Rd. SE2 —4C 92
Wilton Rd. SW1 —3F 85 (2A 172)
Wilton Rd. SW19 —7C 120
Wilton Rd. Cockf —4J 5
(in two parts)
Wilton Rd. Houn —3B 96
Wilton Row. SW1 —2E 84 (7G 165)
Wilton Sq. N1 —1D 68
Wilton St. SW1 —3F 85 (1J 171)
Wilton Ter. SW1 —3E 84 (1G 171)
Wilton Vs. N1 —1D 68
(off Wilton Sq.)
Wilton Way. E8 —6G 51
Wiltshire Clo. NW7 —5G 13
Wiltshire Clo. SW3 —4D 84 (3E 170)
Wiltshire Ct. N4 —1K 49
(off Marquis Rd.)
Wiltshire Ct. Ilf —6G 55
Wiltshire Ct. S Croy —5C 152
Wiltshire Gdns. N4 —6C 32
Wiltshire Gdns. Twic —1G 115
Wiltshire La. Pinn —3H 23
Wiltshire Rd. SW9 —3A 104
Wiltshire Rd. Orp —7K 145
Wiltshire Rd. T Hth —3A 140
Wiltshire Row. N1 —1D 68
(off Bridport Pl.)
Wilverley Cres. N Mald —6A 136
Wimbart Rd. SW2 —7K 103
Wimbledon. —6H 119
Wimbledon. —3G 119
(All England Tennis Club)
Wimbledon Bri. SW19 —6H 119
Wimbledon Clo. SW20 —7F 119
Wimbledon Common. —5C 118
Wimbledon Common Postmill. —3E 118
Wimbledon Common Windmill Mus. —3E 118
Wimbledon F.C. —4E 140
(Crystal Palace Football Ground)
Wimbledon Greyhound Stadium. —4A 120
Wimbledon Hill Rd. SW19 —6G 119
Wimbledon Lawn Tennis Mus. —3G 119
(Wimbledon All Endland Lawn Tennis & Croquet Club)
Wimbledon Mus. of Local History. —6G 119
Wimbledon Park. —3J 119
Wimbledon Pk. Rd. SW19 & SW18 —2G 119
Wimbledon Pk. Side. SW19 —3F 119
Wimbledon Rd. SW17 —4A 120
Wimbledon Stadium Bus. Cen. SW17 —3K 119
Wimbolt St. E2 —3G 69
Wimborne Av. Hay —6K 59
Wimborne Av. Orp & Chst —4K 145
Wimborne Av. S'hall —4E 78
Wimborne Clo. SE12 —5H 107
Wimborne Clo. Buck H —2E 20
Wimborne Clo. Wor Pk —1E 148
Wimborne Ct. SW12 —3G 121
Wimborne Ct. N'holt —6E 42
Wimborne Dri. NW9 —3G 27
Wimborne Dri. Pinn —7B 24
Wimborne Gdns. W13 —5B 62
Wimborne Ho. NW1 —4C 66 (4D 158)
(off Harewood Av.)
Wimborne Ho. SW8 —7K 85
(off Dorset Rd.)
Wimborne Rd. N9 —2B 18
Wimborne Rd. N17 —2E 32
Wimborne Way. Beck —3K 141
Wimbourne Ct. N1 —2D 68
(off Wimbourne St.)
Wimbourne St. N1 —2D 68
Wimpole Clo. Brom —4A 144
Wimpole Clo. King T —2F 135
Wimpole M. W1 —5F 67 (5J 159)
Wimpole Rd. W Dray —1A 76
Wimpole St. W1 —5F 67 (6J 159)
Wimshurst Clo. Croy —1J 151
Winans Wlk. SW9 —2A 104
Wincanton Ct. N11 —6K 15
(off Martock Gdns.)
Wincanton Cres. N'holt —5E 42
Wincanton Gdns. Ilf —3F 37
Wincanton Rd. SW18 —7H 101
Winchcombe Bus. Cen. SE15 —6E 86
Winchcombe Ct. SE15 —6E 86
(off Longhope Clo.)
Winchcombe Rd. Cars —7B 138
Winchcomb Gdns. SE9 —3B 108
Winchelsea Av. Bexh —7F 93
Winchelsea Clo. SW15 —5F 101
Winchelsea Cres. W Mol —2F 133
Winchelsea Rd. E7 —3J 53
Winchelsea Rd. N15 —3E 32
Winchelsea Rd. NW10 —1K 63
Winchelsey Ri. S Croy —6F 153
Winchendon Rd. SW6 —1H 101
Winchendon Rd. Tedd —4H 115
Winchester Av. NW6 —1G 65
Winchester Av. NW9 —3G 27
Winchester Av. Houn —6D 78
Winchester Clo. E6 —6D 72
Winchester Clo. SE17 —4B 86
Winchester Clo. Brom —3H 143
Winchester Clo. Enf —5K 7
Winchester Clo. King T —7H 117
Winchester Ct. W8 —2J 83
Winchester Dri. Pinn —5B 24
Winchester Ho. SE18 —7B 90
(off Portway Gdns.)
Winchester Ho. SW3 —7B 170
Winchester Ho. SW9 —7A 86
Winchester Ho. W2 —6A 66
(off Hallfield Est.)
Winchester Ho. Bark —7A 56
(off Keir Hardie Way)
Winchester Pk. Brom —3H 143
Winchester Pl. E8 —5F 51
Winchester Pl. N6 —1F 49
Winchester Rd. E4 —7K 19
Winchester Rd. N6 —7F 31
Winchester Rd. N9 —1A 18
Winchester Rd. NW3 —7B 48
Winchester Rd. Bexh —2D 110
Winchester Rd. Brom —3H 143
Winchester Rd. Felt —3D 114
Winchester Rd. Harr —4E 26
Winchester Rd. Hay —7G 77
Winchester Rd. Ilf —3H 55
Winchester Rd. N'wd —2H 23
Winchester Rd. Twic —6B 98
Winchester Rd. W on T —7J 131
Winchester Sq. SE1 —4E 168
Winchester St. SW1 —5F 85 (5K 171)
Winchester St. W3 —1J 81
Winchester Wlk. SE1 —1D 86 (4E 168)
Winchet Wlk. Croy —6J 141
Winchfield Clo. Harr —6C 26
Winchfield Ho. SW15 —6B 100
Winchfield Rd. SE26 —5A 124
Winch Ho. E14 —3D 88
Winch Ho. SW10 —7A 84
(off King's Rd.)
Winchilsea Cres. W Mol —2G 133
Winchilsea Ho. NW8 —3B 66 (2B 158)
(off St John's Wood Rd.)
Winchmore Hill. —7F 7
Winchmore Hill Rd. N14 & N21 —1C 16
Winchmore Vs. N21 —7E 6
(off Winchmore Hill Rd.)
Winchstone Clo. Shep —4B 130
Winckley Clo. Harr —5F 27
Wincott St. SE11 —4A 86 (4K 173)
Wincrofts Dri. SE9 —4H 109
Windall Clo. SE19 —1G 141
Windborough Rd. Cars —7E 150
Windermere. NW1 —3F 67 (2K 159)
(off Albany St.)
Windermere Av. N3 —3J 29
Windermere Av. NW6 —1G 65
Windermere Av. SW19 —3K 137
Windermere Av. Ruis —7A 24
Windermere Av. Wemb —7C 26
Windermere Clo. Felt —1H 113
Windermere Clo. Orp —3E 156
Windermere Clo. Stai —1A 112
Windermere Ct. SW13 —6B 82
Windermere Ct. Wemb —7C 26
Windermere Gdns. Ilf —5C 36
Windermere Gro. Wemb —1C 44
Windermere Hall. Edgw —5A 12
Windermere Ho. E3 —4B 70
Windermere Ho. New Bar —4E 4
Windermere Point. SE15 —7J 87
(off Old Kent Rd.)
Windermere Rd. N10 —1F 31
Windermere Rd. N19 —2G 49
Windermere Rd. SW15 —4A 118
Windermere Rd. SW16 —1G 139
Windermere Rd. W5 —3C 80
Windermere Rd. Bexh —2J 111
Windermere Rd. Croy —1F 153
Windermere Rd. S'hall —5D 60
Windermere Rd. W W'ck —2G 155
Windermere Way. W Dray —1A 76
Winders Rd. SW11 —2C 102
(in two parts)
Windfield Clo. SE26 —4K 123
Windham Rd. Rich —3F 99
Winding Way. Dag —3C 56
Winding Way. Harr —4J 43
Windlass Pl. SE8 —4A 88
Windlesham Gro. SW19 —1F 119
Windley Clo. SE23 —2J 123
Windmill. WC1 —5K 67 (5G 161)
(off New North St.)
Windmill Av. S'hall —1G 79
Windmill Bus. Cen. S'hall —1G 79
Windmill Bus. Village. Sun —1G 131
Windmill Clo. SE1 —4G 87
(off Beatrice Rd.)
Windmill Clo. SE13 —2E 106
Windmill Clo. Sun —7G 113
Windmill Clo. Surb —1C 146
Windmill Ct. NW2 —6G 47
Windmill Ct. W5 —4C 80
(off Windmill Rd.)
Windmill Dri. SW4 —5F 103
Windmill Dri. Kes —4A 156
Windmill Gdns. Enf —3F 7
Windmill Grn. Shep —7G 131
(off Walton La.)
Windmill Gro. Croy —6C 140
Windmill Hill. NW3 —3A 48
Windmill Hill. Enf —3G 7
Windmill Hill. Ruis —7H 23
Windmill La. E15 —6F 53
Windmill La. Bus H —1D 10
Windmill La. Gnfd —5G 61
Windmill La. S'hall & Iswth —1G 79
Windmill La. Surb —6B 134
Windmill M. W4 —4A 82
Windmill Pas. W4 —4A 82
Windmill Ri. King T —7H 117
Windmill Rd. N18 —4J 17
Windmill Rd. SW18 —6B 102
Windmill Rd. SW19 —4D 118
Windmill Rd. W4 —4A 82
Windmill Rd. W5 & Bren —4C 80
Windmill Rd. Croy —7C 140
Windmill Rd. Hamp H —5F 115
Windmill Rd. Mitc —5G 139
Windmill Rd. Sun —1G 131
Windmill Rd. W. Sun —2G 131
Windmill Row. SE11 —5A 86 (6J 173)
Windmill St. W1 —5H 67 (6C 160)
(in two parts)
Windmill St. Bus H —1D 10
Windmill Ter. Shep —7G 131
Windmill Wlk. SE1 —1A 86 (5K 167)
Windmill Way. Ruis —1H 41
Windover Av. NW9 —4K 27
Windrose Clo. SE16 —2K 87
Windrush. SE28 —1B 92
Windrush. N Mald —4H 135
Windrush Clo. N17 —1E 32
Windrush Clo. SW11 —4B 102
Windrush Clo. W4 —1J 99
Windrush Clo. Uxb —4B 40
Windrush La. SE23 —3K 123
Windrush Rd. NW10 —1K 63
Windsock Clo. SE16 —4B 88
Windsor Av. E17 —2A 34
Windsor Av. SW19 —1A 138
Windsor Av. Edgw —4C 12
Windsor Av. N Mald —5J 135
Windsor Av. Sutt —3G 149
Windsor Av. Uxb —1D 58
Windsor Av. W Mol —3E 132
Windsor Cen., The. N1 —1B 68
(off Windsor St.)
Windsor Clo. N3 —2G 29
Windsor Clo. SE27 —4C 122
Windsor Clo. Bren —6B 80
Windsor Clo. Chst —5F 127
Windsor Clo. Harr —3E 42
Windsor Clo. N'wd —2J 23
Windsor Ct. N12 —5J 15
Windsor Ct. N14 —7B 6
Windsor Ct. NW3 —4J 47
Windsor Ct. NW11 —6G 29
(off Golders Grn. Rd.)
Windsor Ct. SW3 —5C 84 (5D 170)
(off Jubilee Pl.)
Windsor Ct. SW11 —2B 102
Windsor Ct. W2 —7K 65
(off Moscow Rd.)
Windsor Ct. W10 —6F 65
(off Darfield Way)
Windsor Ct. Pinn —3B 24
Windsor Ct. Sun —7J 113
Windsor Cres. Harr —3E 42
Windsor Cres. Wemb —3H 45
Windsor Dri. Barn —6J 5
Windsor Gdns. W9 —5J 65
Windsor Gdns. Croy —3J 151
Windsor Gdns. Hay —3F 77
Windsor Gro. SE27 —4C 122
Windsor Hall. E16 —1K 89
(off Wesley Av., in two parts)
Windsor Ho. N1 —2C 68
Windsor Ho. NW1 —1K 159
Windsor Ho. N'holt —6E 42
(off Farmlands, The)
Windsor M. SE6 —1E 124
Windsor M. SE23 —1A 124
Windsor M. SW18 —7A 102
(off Wilna Rd.)
Windsor Pk. Rd. Hay —7H 77
Windsor Pl. SW1 —3G 85 (3B 172)
Windsor Rd. E4 —4J 19
Windsor Rd. E7 —5K 53
Windsor Rd. E10 —2D 52
Windsor Rd. E11 —1J 53
Windsor Rd. N3 —2G 29
Windsor Rd. N7 —3J 49
Windsor Rd. N13 —3F 17
Windsor Rd. N17 —2G 33
Windsor Rd. NW2 —6D 46
Windsor Rd. W5 —7E 62
(in two parts)
Windsor Rd. Barn —6A 4
Windsor Rd. Bexh —4E 110
Windsor Rd. Dag —3E 56
Windsor Rd. Harr —1G 25
Windsor Rd. Houn —2K 95
Windsor Rd. Ilf —4F 55
Windsor Rd. King T —7E 116
Windsor Rd. Rich —2F 99
Windsor Rd. S'hall —3D 78
Windsor Rd. Sun —6J 113
Windsor Rd. Tedd —5H 115
Windsor Rd. T Hth —2B 140
Windsor Rd. Wor Pk —2C 148
Windsors, The. Buck H —2H 21
Windsor St. N1 —1B 68
Windsor Ter. N1 —3C 68 (1D 162)
Windsor Wlk. SE5 —2D 104
Windsor Way. W6 —4F 83
Windsor Wharf. E9 —6C 52
Windspoint Dri. SE15 —6H 87
Windus Rd. N16 —1F 51
Windus Wlk. N16 —1F 51
Windy Ridge. Brom —1C 144
Windy Ridge Clo. SW19 —5F 119
Wine Clo. E1 —7J 69
Wine Office Ct. EC4 —6A 68 (7K 161)
Winery La. King T —3F 135
Winford Ct. SE15 —1H 105
Winford Ho. E3 —7B 52
Winford Pde. S'hall —6F 61
(off Brunel Pl.)
Winforton St. SE10 —1E 106
Winfrith Rd. SW18 —7A 102
Wingate Cres. Croy —6J 139
Wingate Rd. W6 —3D 82
Wingate Rd. Ilf —5F 55
Wingate Rd. Sidc —6C 128
Wingate Trad. Est. N17 —7B 18
Wingfield Ct. Sidc —2K 127
Wingfield Ho. E2 —3F 69 (2J 163)
(off Virginia Rd.)
Wingfield Ho. NW6 —2K 65
(off Tollgate Gdns.)
Wingfield M. SE15 —3G 105
Wingfield Rd. E15 —4G 53
Wingfield Rd. E17 —5D 34
Wingfield Rd. King T —6F 117
Wingfield St. SE15 —3G 105
Wingfield Way. Ruis —6K 41
Wingford Rd. SW2 —6J 103
Wingmore Rd. SE24 —3C 104
Wingrave. SE17 —4D 86
(in three parts)
Wingrave Rd. W6 —6E 82
Wingreen. NW8 —1K 65
(off Abbey Rd.)
Wingrove. E4 —7H 9
Wingrove Ct. Romf —5J 39
Wingrove Rd. SE6 —2G 125
Wings Clo. Sutt —4J 149
Winicotte Ho. W2 —5B 66 (5B 158)
(off Paddington Grn.)
Winifred Pl. N12 —5F 15
Winifred Rd. SW19 —1J 137
Winifred Rd. Dag —2E 56
Winifred Rd. Eri —5K 93
Winifred Rd. Hamp H —4E 114
Winifred St. E16 —1D 90
Winifred Ter. E13 —2J 71
(off Victoria Rd.)
Winifred Ter. Enf —7A 8
Winkfield Rd. E13 —2K 71
Winkfield Rd. N22 —1A 32
Winkley Ct. N10 —4F 31
(off St James's La.)
Winkley Ct. S Harr —3E 42
Winkley St. E2 —2H 69
Winlaton Rd. Brom —4F 125
Winmill Rd. Dag —3F 57
Winnett St. W1 —7H 67 (2C 166)
Winningales Ct. Ilf —2C 36
Winnings Wlk. N'holt —6C 42
Winnington Clo. N2 —6B 30
Winnington Ho. SE5 —7C 86
(off Wyndham Est.)
Winnington Rd. N2 —6B 30
Winnock Rd. W Dray —1A 76
Winn Rd. SE12 —1J 125
Winns Av. E17 —3B 34
Winns Comn. Rd. SE18 —6J 91
Winns M. N15 —4E 32
Winns Ter. E17 —3C 34
Winsbeach. E17 —2F 35
Winscombe Cres. W5 —4D 62
Winscombe St. NW5 —3F 49
Winscombe Way. Stan —5F 11
Winsford Rd. SE6 —3B 124
Winsford Ter. N18 —5J 17
Winsham Gro. SW11 —5E 102
Winsham Ho. NW1 —3H 67 (1D 160)
(off Churchway)
Winslade Rd. SW2 —5J 103
Winslade Way. SE6 —7D 106
Winsland M. W2 —6B 66 (7A 158)
Winsland St. W2 —6B 66 (7A 158)
Winsley St. W1 —6G 67 (7B 160)
Winslow. SE17 —5E 86
Winslow Clo. NW10 —3A 46
Winslow Clo. Pinn —6K 23
Winslow Gro. E4 —2B 20
Winslow Rd. W6 —6E 82
Winslow Way. Felt —3B 114
Winsmoor Ct. Enf —3G 7
Winsor Park. —5F 73
Winsor Ter. E6 —5E 72
Winstanley Est. SW11 —3B 102
Winstanley Rd. SW11 —3B 102
Winstead Gdns. Dag —5J 57
Winston Av. NW9 —7A 28
Winston Churchill's Britain at War Experience. —5G 169
Winston Clo. Harr —6E 10
Winston Clo. Romf —4H 39
Winston Ct. Brom —1K 143
(off Widmore Rd.)
Winston Ct. Harr —7A 10
Winston Ho. N1 —2D 68
(off Cherbury St.)
Winston Ho. W13 —2A 80
(off Salisbury Rd.)
Winston Ho. WC1 —3D 160
Winston Rd. N16 —4D 50
Winston Wlk. W4 —3K 81
Winston Way. Ilf —3F 55
Winter Av. E6 —1C 72
Winterbourne Ho. W11 —7G 65
(off Portland Rd.)
Winterbourne Rd. SE6 —1B 124
Winterbourne Rd. Dag —2C 56
Winterbourne Rd. T Hth —4A 140
Winter Box Wlk. Rich —5F 99
Winterbrook Rd. SE24 —6C 104
Winterburn Clo. N11 —6K 15
Winterfold Clo. SW19 —2G 119
Wintergreen Clo. E6 —5C 72
Winterleys. NW6 —2H 65
(off Albert Rd.)
Winter Lodge. SE16 —5G 87
(off Fern Wlk.)
Winter's Ct. E4 —3J 19
Winterslow Ho. SE5 —2C 104
(off Flaxman Rd.)
Winters Rd. Th Dit —7B 134
Winterstoke Gdns. NW7 —5H 13
Winterstoke Rd. SE6 —1B 124
Winterton Ct. SE20 —2G 141
Winterton Pl. SW10 —6A 84 (7A 170)
Winterwell Rd. SW2 —5J 103
Winthorpe Rd. SW15 —4G 101
Winthrop St. E1 —5H 69
Winthrop Wlk. Wemb —3E 44
Winton Av. N11 —7B 16
Winton Clo. N9 —7E 8
Winton Gdns. Edgw —7A 12
Winton Rd. Orp —4E 156
Winton Way. SW16 —5A 122
Wirrall Ho. SE26 —3G 123
Wirral Wood Clo. Chst —6E 126
Wisbeach Rd. Croy —5D 140
Wisbech. N4 —1K 49
(off Lorne Rd.)
Wisborough Rd. S Croy —7F 153
Wisden Ho. SW8 —6K 85 (7H 173)
Wisdom Ct. Iswth —3A 98
(off South St.)
Wisdons Clo. Dag —1H 57
Wise La. NW7 —5H 13
Wise La. W Dray —4A 76
Wiseman Rd. E10 —2C 52
Wise Rd. E15 —1F 71
Wiseton Rd. SW17 —1C 120
Wisham Wlk. N13 —6D 16
Wishart Rd. SE3 —2B 108

Wisley Ho.—Woolf Ct.

Wisley Ho. SW1 —5H 85 (5C 172)
(off Rampayne St.)
Wisley Rd. SW11 —5E 102
Wisley Rd. Orp —7A 128
Wisteria Clo. NW7 —5G 13
Wisteria Clo. Ilf —5F 55
Wisteria Dri. NW7 —6G 13
Wisteria Gdns. Wfd G —5D 20
Wisteria Rd. SE13 —4F 107
Witanhurst La. N6 —1E 48
Witan St. E2 —3H 69
Witham Ct. E10 —3D 52
Witham Rd. SE20 —3J 141
Witham Rd. W13 —1A 80
Witham Rd. Dag —5G 57
Witham Rd. Iswth —1H 97
Witherby Clo. Croy —5E 152
Witherington Rd. N5 —5A 50
Withers Clo. Chess —6C 146
Withers Mead. NW9 —1B 28
Withers Pl. EC1 —4C 68 (3D 162)
Witherston Way. SE9 —2E 126
Withycombe Rd. SW19 —7F 101
Withy La. Ruis —5E 22
Withy Mead. E4 —3A 20
Witley Ct. WC1 —4K 160
Witley Cres. New Ad —6E 154
Witley Gdns. S'hall —4D 78
Witley Ho. SW2 —7J 103
Witley Ind. Est. S'hall —4D 78
Witley Rd. N19 —2G 49
Witney Clo. Uxb —4B 40
Witney Path. SE23 —3K 123
Wittenham Way. E4 —3A 20
Wittering Clo. King T —5D 116
Wittersham Rd. Brom —5H 125
Wivenhoe Clo. SE15 —3H 105
Wivenhoe Ct. Houn —4D 96
Wivenhoe Rd. Bark —2A 74
Wiverton Rd. SE26 —6J 123
Wixom Ho. SE3 —4A 108
Wix Rd. Dag —1D 74
Wix's La. SW4 —3F 103
Woburn. W13 —5B 62
(off Clivedon Ct.)
Woburn Clo. SE28 —6D 74
Woburn Clo. SW19 —6A 120
Woburn Ct. E18 —2J 35
Woburn Ct. SE16 —5H 87
(off Masters Dri.)
Woburn Ct. Croy —1C 152
Woburn M. WC1 —4H 67 (4D 160)
Woburn Pl. WC1 —4J 67 (4E 160)
Woburn Rd. Cars —1C 150
Woburn Rd. Croy —1C 152
Woburn Sq. WC1 —4H 67 (4D 160)
Woburn Tower. N'holt —3B 60
(off Broomcroft Av.)
Woburn Wlk. WC1 —3H 67 (2D 160)
Wodehouse Av. SE5 —1F 105
Wodehouse Ct. W3 —3J 81
(off Vincent Rd.)
Woffington Clo. King T —1C 134
Woking Clo. SW15 —4B 100
Wolcot Ho. NW1 —2G 67 (1B 160)
(off Aldenham St.)
Woldham Pl. Brom —4A 144
Woldham Rd. Brom —4A 144
Wolds Dri. Orp —4E 156
Wolfe Clo. Brom —6J 143
Wolfe Clo. Hay —3K 59
Wolfe Cres. SE7 —5B 90
Wolfe Cres. SE16 —2K 87
Wolfe Ho. W12 —7D 64
(off White City Est.)
Wolferton Rd. E12 —4D 54
Wolffe Gdns. E15 —6H 53
Wolfington Rd. SE27 —4B 122
Wolfram Clo. SE13 —5G 107
Wolftencroft Clo. SW11 —3C 102
Wollaston Clo. SE1 —4C 86
Wollett Ct. NW1 —7G 49
(off St Pancras Way)
Wolmer Clo. Edgw —4B 12
Wolmer Gdns. Edgw —3B 12
Wolseley Av. SW19 —2J 119
Wolseley Gdns. W4 —6H 81
Wolseley Rd. E7 —7K 53
Wolseley Rd. N8 —6H 31
Wolseley Rd. N22 —1K 31
Wolseley Rd. W4 —4J 81
Wolseley Rd. Harr & W'stone —3J 25
Wolseley Rd. Mitc —7E 138
Wolseley Rd. Romf —7K 39
Wolseley St. SE1 —2G 87 (7K 169)
Wolsey Av. E6 —3E 72
Wolsey Av. E17 —3B 34
Wolsey Av. Th Dit —5K 133
Wolsey Clo. SW20 —7D 118
Wolsey Clo. Houn —4G 97
Wolsey Clo. King T —1H 135
Wolsey Clo. S'hall —3G 79
Wolsey Clo. Wor Pk —4C 148
Wolsey Cres. Mord —7G 137
Wolsey Cres. New Ad —7E 154
Wolsey Dri. King T —5E 116
Wolsey Dri. W on T —7B 132
Wolsey Gro. Edgw —7E 12
Wolsey M. NW5 —6G 49
Wolsey Rd. N1 —5D 50
Wolsey Rd. Ashf —4A 112
Wolsey Rd. E Mol —4H 133
Wolsey Rd. Enf —2C 8
Wolsey Rd. Hamp H —6F 115
Wolsey Rd. Sun —7H 113
Wolsey Spring. King T —7J 117
Wolsey St. E1 —5J 69
Wolsey Way. Chess —5G 147
Wolsley Clo. Dart —5K 111
Wolstonbury. N12 —5D 14
Wolvercote Rd. SE2 —2D 92
Wolverley St. E2 —3H 69
Wolverton. SE17 —5E 86
(in two parts)
Wolverton Av. King T —1G 135
Wolverton Gdns. W5 —7F 63
Wolverton Gdns. W6 —4F 83
Wolverton Rd. Stan —6G 11
Wolverton Way. N14 —5B 6
Wolves La. N22 & N13 —7F 17
Womersley Rd. N8 —6K 31
Wonersh Way. Sutt —7F 149
Wonford Clo. King T —1A 136
Wontner Clo. N1 —7C 50
Wontner Rd. SW17 —2D 120
Wooburn Clo. Uxb —4D 58
Woodall Clo. E14 —7D 70
Woodall Ho. N22 —1A 32
Woodall Rd. Enf —6E 8
Woodbank Rd. Brom —3H 125
Woodbastwick Rd. SE26 —5K 123
Woodberry Av. N21 —2F 17
Woodberry Av. Harr —4F 25
Woodberry Clo. Sun —6J 113
Woodberry Cres. N10 —3F 31
Woodberry Down. N4 —7C 32
Woodberry Down Est. N4 —7C 32
(in two parts)
Woodberry Gdns. N12 —6F 15
Woodberry Gro. N4 —7C 32
Woodberry Gro. N12 —6F 15
Woodberry Gro. Bex —3K 129
Woodberry Way. E4 —7K 9
Woodberry Way. N12 —6F 15
Woodbine Clo. Twic —2H 115
Woodbine Gro. SE20 —7H 123
Woodbine Gro. Enf —1J 7
Woodbine La. Wor Pk —3D 148
Woodbine Pl. E11 —6J 35
Woodbine Rd. Sidc —1J 127
Woodbines Av. King T —3D 134
Woodbine Ter. E9 —6J 51
Woodborough Rd. SW15 —4D 100
Woodbourne Av. SW16 —3H 121
Woodbourne Clo. SW16 —3J 121
Woodbourne Gdns. Wall —7F 151
Woodbridge Clo. N7 —2K 49
Woodbridge Ct. Wfd G —7H 21
Woodbridge Ho. E11 —1H 53
Woodbridge Rd. Bark —5K 55
Woodbridge St. EC1 —4B 68 (3A 162)
(in two parts)
Woodbrook Rd. SE2 —6A 92
Woodburn Clo. NW4 —5F 29
Woodbury Clo. E11 —4K 35
Woodbury Clo. Croy —2F 153
Woodbury Ho. SE26 —3G 123
Woodbury Pk. Rd. W13 —4B 62
Woodbury Rd. E17 —4D 34
Woodbury St. SW17 —5C 120
Woodchester Sq. W2 —5K 65
Woodchurch Clo. Sidc —3H 127
Woodchurch Dri. Brom —7B 126
Woodchurch Rd. NW6 —7J 47
Wood Clo. E2 —4G 69
Wood Clo. NW9 —7K 27
Wood Clo. Harr —7H 25
Woodclyffe Dri. Chst —2E 144
Woodcock Ct. Harr —7E 26
Woodcock Dell Av. Harr —7D 26
Woodcock Hill. Harr —5C 26
Woodcock Ho. E14 —5C 70
Woodcocks. E16 —5A 72
Woodcombe Cres. SE23 —1J 123
Woodcote Av. NW7 —6K 13
Woodcote Av. T Hth —4B 140
Woodcote Av. Wall —7F 151
Woodcote Clo. Enf —6D 8
Woodcote Clo. King T —5F 117
Woodcote Ct. Sutt —6J 149
Woodcote Dri. Orp —7H 145
Woodcote Grn. Wall —7G 151
Woodcote Ho. SE8 —6B 88
(off Prince St.)
Woodcote M. Wall —6F 151
Woodcote Pl. SE27 —5B 122
Woodcote Rd. E11 —7J 35
Woodcote Rd. Wall & Purl —6F 151
Wood Ct. Eri —7K 93
Wood Crest. Sutt —7A 150
(off Christchurch Pk.)
Woodcroft. N21 —1F 17
Woodcroft. SE9 —3D 126
Woodcroft. Gnfd —6A 44
Woodcroft Av. NW7 —6F 13
Woodcroft Av. Stan —1A 26
Woodcroft Cres. Uxb —1D 58
Woodcroft M. SE8 —4A 88
Woodcroft Rd. T Hth —5B 140
Wood Dene. SE15 —1H 105
(off Queen's Rd.)
Wood Dri. Chst —6C 126
Woodedge Clo. E4 —1C 20
Wood End. —5H 59
(Hayes)
Wood End. —5H 43
(Northolt)
Woodend. SE19 —6C 122
Wood End. Hay —6G 59
Woodend. Sutt —2A 150
Wood End Av. Harr —4F 43
Wood End Clo. N'holt —5H 43
Woodend Gdns. Enf —4D 6
Wood End Gdns. N'holt —5G 43
Wood End Green. —5G 59
Wood End Grn. Rd. Hay —5F 59
Wood End La. N'holt —6F 43
(in two parts)
Woodend Rd. E17 —2E 34
Wood End Rd. Harr —4H 43
Woodend, The. Wall —7F 151
Wood End Way. N'holt —5G 43
Wooder Gdns. E7 —4J 53
Wooderson Clo. SE25 —4E 140
Woodfall Av. Barn —5C 4
Woodfall Rd. N4 —2A 50
Woodfall St. SW3 —5D 84 (6E 170)
Woodfarrs. SE5 —4D 104
Wood Fld. NW3 —5D 48
Woodfield Av. NW9 —4A 28
Woodfield Av. SW16 —3H 121
Woodfield Av. W5 —4C 62
Woodfield Av. Cars —6E 150
Woodfield Av. Wemb —3C 44
Woodfield Clo. SE19 —7C 122
Woodfield Clo. Enf —4K 7
Woodfield Cres. W5 —4C 62
Woodfield Dri. E Barn —1K 15
Woodfield Gdns. N Mald —5B 136
Woodfield Gro. SW16 —3H 121
Woodfield Ho. SE23 —3K 123
(off Dacres Rd.)
Woodfield La. SW16 —3H 121
Woodfield Pl. W9 —4H 65
Woodfield Ri. Bush —1C 10
Woodfield Rd. W5 —4C 62
Woodfield Rd. W9 —5H 65
Woodfield Rd. Houn —2K 95
Woodfield Way. N11 —7C 16
Woodford. —6E 20
Woodford Av. Ilf —3B 36
Woodford Bridge. —6H 21
Woodford Bri. Rd. Ilf —3B 36
Woodford Ct. W14 —2F 83
(off Shepherd's Bush Grn.)
Woodford Cres. Pinn —2K 23
Woodforde Ct. Hay —5F 77
Woodford Green. —6D 20
Woodford Hall Path. E18 —1H 35
Woodford Ho. E18 —4J 35
Woodford New Rd. E17 & E18 —4G 35
Woodford Pl. Wemb —1E 44
Woodford Rd. E7 —3K 53
Woodford Rd. E18 —4J 35
Woodford Side. —5C 20
Woodford Trad. Est. Wfd G —2B 36
Woodford Wells. —3E 20
Woodgate Av. Chess —5D 146
Woodgate Dri. SW16 —7H 121
Woodger Rd. W12 —2E 82
Woodget Clo. E6 —6C 72
Woodgrange Av. N12 —6G 15
Woodgrange Av. W5 —1G 81
Woodgrange Av. Enf —6B 8
Woodgrange Av. Harr —5C 26
Woodgrange Clo. Harr —5D 26
Woodgrange Gdns. Enf —6B 8
Woodgrange Mans. Harr —5D 26
Woodgrange Rd. E7 —5K 53
Woodgrange Ter. Enf —6B 8
Wood Green. —2K 31
Wood Green Shop. City. N22 —2A 32
Woodhall. NW1 —3G 67 (2A 160)
(off Robert St.)
Woodhall Av. SE21 —3F 123
Woodhall Av. Pinn —1C 24
Woodhall Clo. Uxb —5A 40
Woodhall Dri. SE21 —3F 123
Woodhall Dri. Pinn —1B 24
Woodham Ct. E18 —4H 35
Woodham Rd. SE6 —3E 124
Woodhatch Clo. E6 —5C 72
Woodhaven Gdns. Ilf —4G 37
Woodhayes Rd. SW19 —7E 118
Woodheyes Rd. NW10 —5K 45
Woodhill. SE18 —4C 90
Woodhill Cres. Harr —6D 26
Woodhouse Av. Gnfd —2K 61
Woodhouse Clo. Gnfd —1K 61
Woodhouse Clo. Hay —3G 77
Woodhouse Gro. E12 —6C 54
Woodhouse Rd. E11 —3H 53
Woodhouse Rd. N12 —6G 15
Woodhurst Av. Orp —6G 145
Woodhurst Rd. SE2 —5A 92
Woodhurst Rd. W3 —7J 63
Woodington Clo. SE9 —6E 108
Woodin St. E14 —5D 70
Woodison St. E3 —4A 70
Woodknoll Dri. Chst —1D 144
Woodland App. Gnfd —6A 44
Woodland Clo. NW9 —6J 27
Woodland Clo. SE19 —6E 122
Woodland Clo. Eps —6A 148
Woodland Clo. Ick —2D 40
Woodland Clo. Wfd G —3E 20
Woodland Ct. E11 —6J 35
(off New Wanstead)
Woodland Cres. SE10 —6G 89
Woodland Cres. SE16 —2K 87
Woodland Gdns. N10 —5F 31
Woodland Gdns. Iswth —3J 97
Woodland Gro. SE10 —5G 89
Woodland Hill. SE19 —6E 122
Woodland Ri. N10 —4F 31
Woodland Ri. Gnfd —6A 44
Woodland Rd. E4 —1K 19
Woodland Rd. N11 —5A 16
Woodland Rd. SE19 —5E 122
Woodland Rd. T Hth —4A 140
Woodlands. —2J 97
Woodlands. NW11 —5G 29
Woodlands. SW20 —4E 136
Woodlands. Harr —4E 24
Woodlands. Short —4H 143
Woodlands Art Gallery. —6J 89
Woodlands Av. E11 —1K 53
Woodlands Av. N3 —7F 15
Woodlands Av. W3 —1H 81
Woodlands Av. N Mald —1J 135
Woodlands Av. Romf —7E 38
Woodlands Av. Ruis —7A 24
Woodlands Av. Sidc —1J 127
Woodlands Av. Wor Pk —2B 148
Woodlands Clo. NW11 —5G 29
Woodlands Clo. Brom —2D 144
Woodlands Clo. Clay —7A 146
Woodlands Ct. SE23 —7H 105
Woodlands Ct. Brom —1H 143
Woodlands Ct. Harr —5K 25
Woodlands Dri. Stan —6E 10
Woodlands Dri. Sun —2A 132
Woodlands Gdns. E17 —4G 35
Woodlands Ga. SW15 —5H 101
Woodlands Gro. Iswth —2J 97
Woodlands Ho. NW6 —7G 47
Woodlands Pde. Ashf —6E 112
Woodlands Pk. Bex —4K 129
Woodlands Pk. Rd. N15 —5B 32
Woodlands Pk. Rd. SE10 —6G 89
Woodlands Rd. E11 —2G 53
Woodlands Rd. E17 —3E 34
Woodlands Rd. N9 —1D 18
Woodlands Rd. SW13 —3B 100
Woodlands Rd. Bexh —3E 110
Woodlands Rd. Brom —2C 144
Woodlands Rd. Enf —1J 7
Woodlands Rd. Harr —5K 25
Woodlands Rd. Ilf —3G 55
Woodlands Rd. Iswth —3H 97
Woodlands Rd. S'hall —1B 78
Woodlands Rd. Surb —7D 134
Woodlands St. SE13 —7F 107
Woodlands, The. N5 —4C 50
Woodlands, The. N12 —6F 15
Woodlands, The. N14 —1A 16
Woodlands, The. SE13 —7F 107
Woodlands, The. SE19 —7C 122
Woodlands, The. Harr —2J 43
Woodlands, The. Iswth —2K 97
Woodlands, The. Stan —5G 11
Woodlands, The. Wall —7F 151
Woodland St. E8 —6F 51
Woodlands Way. SW15 —5H 101
Woodland Ter. SE7 —4C 90
Woodland Wlk. NW3 —5C 48
Woodland Wlk. SE10 —5G 89
Woodland Wlk. Brom —4G 125
(in two parts)
Woodland Wlk. Eps —6G 147
Woodland Way. N21 —2F 17
Woodland Way. NW7 —6F 13
Woodland Way. SE2 —4D 92
Woodland Way. Croy —1A 154
Woodland Way. Mitc —7E 120
Woodland Way. Mord —4H 137
Woodland Way. Orp —4G 145
Woodland Way. Surb —2H 147
Woodland Way. W W'ck —4D 154
Woodland Way. Wfd G —3E 20
Wood La. N6 —6F 31
Wood La. NW9 —7K 27
Wood La. W12 —6E 64
Wood La. Dag —4C 56
Wood La. Iswth —6J 79
Wood La. Ruis —1F 41
Wood La. Stan —3F 11
Wood La. Wfd G —4C 20
Woodlawn Clo. SW15 —5H 101
Woodlawn Cres. Twic —2F 115
Woodlawn Dri. Felt —2B 114
Woodlawn Rd. SW6 —7F 83
Woodlawns. Eps —7K 147
Woodlea Dri. Brom —5G 143
Woodlea Rd. N16 —3E 50
Woodleigh. E18 —1J 35
Woodleigh Av. N12 —6H 15
Woodleigh Gdns. SW16 —3J 121
Woodley Clo. SW17 —7D 120
Woodley La. Cars —3C 150
Wood Lodge Gdns. Brom —7C 126
Wood Lodge La. W W'ck —3E 154
Woodman Pde. E16 —1E 90
(off Woodman St.)
Woodmans Gro. NW10 —5B 46
Woodman's M. W12 —5D 64
Woodmansterne Rd. SW16 —7G 121
Woodmansterne Rd. Cars —7C 150
Woodman St. E16 —1E 90
(in two parts)
Wood Mead. N17 —6B 18
Woodmere. SE9 —1D 126
Woodmere Av. Croy —7J 141
Woodmere Clo. SW11 —3E 102
Woodmere Clo. Croy —7K 141
Woodmere Ct. N14 —7A 6
Woodmere Gdns. Croy —7K 141
Woodmere Way. Beck —5F 143
Woodnook Rd. SW16 —5F 121
Woodpecker Clo. N9 —6C 8
Woodpecker Clo. Bush —1B 10
Woodpecker Clo. Harr —1K 25
Woodpecker Mt. Croy —7A 154
Woodpecker Rd. SE14 —6A 88
Woodpecker Rd. SE28 —7C 74
Woodquest Av. SE24 —5C 104
Wood Retreat. SE18 —7H 91
Wood Ride. Barn —1G 5
Wood Ride. Orp —4H 145
Woodridge Clo. NW2 —3D 46
Woodridge Clo. Enf —1F 7
Woodridings Av. Pinn —1D 24
Woodridings Clo. Pinn —1C 24
Woodridings Ct. N22 —1H 31
Woodriffe Rd. E11 —7F 35
Wood Ri. Pinn —5J 23
Wood Rd. Shep —4C 130
Woodrow. SE18 —4D 90
Woodrow Av. Hay —5H 59
Woodrow Clo. Gnfd —7B 44
Woodrow Ct. N17 —7C 18
Woodrush Clo. SE14 —7A 88
Woodrush Way. Romf —4D 38
Woodseer St. E1 —5F 69 (5K 163)
Woodsford. SE17 —5D 86
(off Portland St.)
Woodsford Sq. W14 —2G 83
Woodshire Rd. Dag —3H 57
Woodside. —6G 141
Woodside. N10 —3E 30
Wood Side. NW11 —5J 29
Woodside. SW19 —6H 119
Woodside. Buck H —2F 21
Woodside Av. N6 & N10 —5D 30
Woodside Av. N12 —4F 15
Woodside Av. SE25 —6H 141
Woodside Av. Chst —5G 127
Woodside Av. Esh —7J 133
Woodside Av. Wemb —1E 62
Woodside Clo. Bexh —4K 111
Woodside Clo. Ruis —6F 23
Woodside Clo. Stan —5G 11
Woodside Clo. Surb —7J 135
Woodside Clo. Wemb —1E 62
Woodside Ct. E12 —1A 54
Woodside Ct. N12 —4E 14
Woodside Ct. W5 —1E 80
Woodside Ct. Rd. Croy —7G 141
Woodside Cres. Sidc —3J 127
Woodside Dri. Dart —4K 129
Woodside End. Wemb —1E 62
Woodside Gdns. E4 —6J 19
Woodside Gdns. N17 —2E 32
Woodside Grange. N12 —4D 14
Woodside Grange Rd. N12 —4E 14
Woodside Grn. SE25 —6G 141
(in two parts)
Woodside Gro. N12 —3F 15
Woodside La. N12 —3F 15
Woodside La. Bex —6D 110
Woodside M. SE22 —5F 105
Woodside Pde. Sidc —3J 127
Woodside Park. —4D 14
Woodside Pk. SE25 —6H 141
Woodside Pk. Av. E17 —4F 35
Woodside Pk. Rd. N12 —4E 14
Woodside Pl. Wemb —1E 62
Woodside Rd. E13 —4A 72
Woodside Rd. N22 —7E 16
Woodside Rd. SE25 —6H 141
Woodside Rd. Bexh —4K 111
Woodside Rd. Brom —5C 144
Woodside Rd. King T —7E 116
Woodside Rd. N Mald —2K 135
Woodside Rd. Sidc —3J 127
Woodside Rd. Sutt —3A 150
Woodside Rd. Wfd G —4D 20
Woodside Way. Croy —6J 141
Woodside Way. Mitc —1F 139
Woods M. W1 —7D 66 (2G 165)
Woodsome Rd. NW5 —3E 48
Wood's Pl. SE1 —3E 86
Woodspring Rd. SW19 —2G 119
Woods Rd. SE15 —1H 105
Woodstead Gro. Edgw —6K 11
Woods, The. Uxb —4D 40
Woodstock Av. NW11 —7G 29
Woodstock Av. W13 —3A 80
Woodstock Av. Iswth —5A 98
Woodstock Av. S'hall —3D 60
Woodstock Av. Sutt —7H 137
Woodstock Clo. Bex —1F 129
Woodstock Clo. Stan —2E 26
Woodstock Ct. SE11 —5K 85 (5H 173)
Woodstock Ct. SE12 —6J 107
Woodstock Cres. N9 —6C 8
Woodstock Dri. Uxb —4A 40
Woodstock Gdns. Beck —1D 142
Woodstock Gdns. Hay —5H 59
Woodstock Gdns. Ilf —2A 56
Woodstock Grange. W5 —1E 80
Woodstock Gro. W12 —2F 83
Woodstock La. N. Surb —2C 146
Woodstock La. S. Clay & Chess —5B 146
Woodstock M. W1 —6H 159
Woodstock Ri. Sutt —7H 137
Woodstock Rd. E7 —7A 54
Woodstock Rd. E17 —2F 35
Woodstock Rd. N4 —1A 50
Woodstock Rd. NW11 —7H 29
Woodstock Rd. W4 —4A 82
Woodstock Rd. Cars —5E 150
Woodstock Rd. Croy —3D 152
Woodstock Rd. Wemb —1F 63
Woodstock St. W1 —6F 67 (1J 165)
Woodstock Ter. E14 —7D 70
Woodstock, The. (Junct.) —7H 137
Woodstock Way. Mitc —2F 139
Woodstone Av. Eps —5C 148
Wood Street. (Junct.) —3E 34
Wood St. E16 —7K 71
Wood St. E17 —3E 34
Wood St. EC2 —6C 68 (7D 162)
Wood St. W4 —5A 82
Wood St. Barn —4A 4
Wood St. King T —2D 134
Wood St. Mitc —7E 138
Woodsyre. SE26 —4F 123
Woodthorpe Rd. SW15 —4D 100
Woodthorpe Rd. Ashf —5A 112
Woodtree Clo. NW4 —2F 29
Wood Va. N10 —5G 31
Wood Va. SE23 —1H 123
Woodvale Av. SE25 —3F 141
Wood Va. Est. SE23 —7J 105
Woodvale Wlk. SE27 —5C 122
Woodvale Way. NW11 —3F 47
Woodview Av. E4 —4K 19
Woodview Clo. N4 —7B 32
Woodview Clo. SW15 —4K 117
Woodville. SE3 —1K 107
Woodville Clo. SE12 —5J 107
Woodville Clo. Tedd —4A 116
Woodville Ct. SE19 —1F 141
Woodville Gdns. NW2 —7F 29
Woodville Gdns. W5 —6E 62
Woodville Gdns. Ilf —3F 37
Woodville Gdns. Ruis —7E 22
Woodville Gdns. Surb —7D 134
Woodville Gro. Well —3A 110
Woodville Ho. SE1 —3F 87
(off Grange Wlk.)
Woodville Rd. E11 —1H 53
Woodville Rd. E17 —4B 34
Woodville Rd. E18 —2K 35
Woodville Rd. N1 —5E 50
Woodville Rd. NW6 —2H 65
Woodville Rd. NW11 —7F 29
Woodville Rd. W5 —6D 62
Woodville Rd. Barn & New Bar —3E 4
Woodville Rd. Mord —4J 137
Woodville Rd. Rich —3B 116
Woodville Rd. T Hth —4C 140
Woodville St. SE18 —4C 90
Woodville, The. W5 —6D 62
(off Woodville Rd.)
Woodward Av. NW4 —5C 28
Woodward Clo. Clay —6A 146
Woodwarde Rd. SE22 —6E 104
Woodward Gdns. Dag —7C 56
Woodward Gdns. Stan —7E 10
Woodward Rd. Dag —7B 56
Woodward's Footpath. Twic —6G 97
Wood Way. Orp —2E 156
Woodway Cres. Harr —6A 26
Woodwell St. SW18 —5A 102
Wood Wharf. SE10 —6E 88
Wood Wharf Bus. Pk. E14 —1D 88
(in two parts)
Woodyard Clo. NW5 —5E 48
Woodyard La. SE21 —7E 104
Woodyates Rd. SE12 —6J 107
Woolacombe Rd. SE3 —1A 108
Woolacombe Way. Hay —4G 77
Wooler St. SE17 —5D 86
Woolf Clo. SE28 —1B 92
Woolf Ct. W3 —3J 81
(off Vincent Rd.)

Woolf M.—Zoffany St.

Woolf M. WC1 —4H 67 (3D 160)
(off Burton Pl.)
Woolgar M. N16 —5E 50
(off Gillett St.)
Woollaston Rd. N4 —6B 32
Woolley Ho. SW9 —3B 104
(off Loughborough Rd.)
Woolmead Av. NW9 —7C 28
Woolmer Gdns. N18 —5B 18
Woolmer Rd. N18 —5B 18
Woolmore St. E14 —7E 70
Woolneigh St. SW6 —3K 101
Woolridge Way. E9 —7J 51
Wool Rd. SW20 —6D 118
Woolstaplers Way. SE16 —3G 87
Woolston Clo. E17 —2K 33
Woolstone Rd. SE23 —2A 124
Woolwich. —3E 90
Woolwich Chu. St. SE18 —3C 90
Woolwich Comn. SE18 —6E 90
Woolwich Dockyard Ind. Est. SE18 —3C 90
Woolwich High St. SE18 —3E 90
Woolwich Ind. Est. SE28 —3J 91
(Hadden Rd.)
Woolwich Ind. Est. SE28 —3K 91
(Kellner Rd.)
Woolwich Mnr. Way. E6 & E16 —4D 72
Woolwich New Rd. SE18 —5E 90
Woolwich Rd. SE10 & SE7 —5H 89
Woolwich Rd. SE2 & Belv —6D 92
Woolwich Rd. Bexh —3G 111
Wooster Gdns. E14 —6F 71
Wooster M. Harr —3G 25
Wooster Pl. SE1 —4D 86
(off Searles Rd.)
Wootton Gro. N3 —1J 29
Wootton St. SE1 —1A 86 (5K 167)
Worbeck Rd. SE20 —2H 141
Worcester Av. N17 —7B 18
Worcester Clo. NW2 —3D 46
Worcester Clo. Croy —2C 154
Worcester Clo. Mitc —2E 138
Worcester Ct. N12 —5E 14
Worcester Ct. W7 —6K 61
(off Copley Clo.)
Worcester Ct. Harr —3J 25
Worcester Ct. Wor Pk —3A 148
Worcester Cres. NW7 —3F 13
Worcester Cres. Wfd G —4E 20
Worcester Dri. W4 —2A 82
Worcester Dri. Ashf —5D 112
Worcester Gdns. Gnfd —6H 43
Worcester Gdns. Ilf —7C 36
Worcester Gdns. Wor Pk —3A 148
Worcester Ho. SE11 —3A 86 (2J 173)
(off Kennington Rd.)
Worcester Ho. SW9 —7A 86
(off Cranmer Rd.)
Worcester Ho. W2 —6A 66
(off Hallfield Est.)
Worcester M. NW6 —6K 47
Worcester Park. —1C 148
Worcester Pk. Rd. Wor Pk —3K 147
Worcester Rd. E12 —4D 54
Worcester Rd. E17 —2K 33
Worcester Rd. SW19 —5H 119
Worcester Rd. Sutt —7J 149
Worcesters Av. Enf —1B 8
Wordsworth Av. E12 —7C 54
Wordsworth Av. E18 —3H 35
Wordsworth Av. Gnfd —3H 61
Wordsworth Ct. Harr —7J 25
Wordsworth Dri. Cheam & Sutt —4E 148
Wordsworth Ho. NW6 —3J 65
(off Stafford Rd.)
Wordsworth Pde. N15 —4B 32
Wordsworth Pl. NW3 —5D 48
Wordsworth Rd. N16 —4E 50
Wordsworth Rd. SE1 —4F 87
Wordsworth Rd. SE20 —7K 123
Wordsworth Rd. Hamp —4D 114
Wordsworth Rd. Wall —6G 151
Wordsworth Rd. Well —1J 109
Wordsworth Wlk. NW11 —4J 29
Wordsworth Way. W Dray —4A 76
Worfield St. SW11 —7C 84
Worgan St. SE11 —5K 85 (5G 173)
Worgan St. SE16 —4K 87
Worland Rd. E15 —7G 53
World Bus. Cen. H'row A —1E 94
World of Silk. —5K 111
(off Bourne Rd.)
World's End. —3E 6
Worlds End Est. SW10 —7B 84
World's End La. N21 & Enf —5E 6
World's End Pas. SW10 —7B 84
(off Worlds End Est)
World's End Pl. SW10 —7B 84
(off Worlds End Est.)
Worlidge St. W6 —5E 82
Worlingham Rd. SE22 —4F 105
Wormholt Rd. W12 —7C 64
Wormwood St. EC2 —6E 68 (7G 163)
(in two parts)
Wornington Rd. W10 —4G 65
(in two parts)
Wornum Ho. W10 —2G 65
(off Kilburn La.)
Woronzow Rd. NW8 —1B 66
Worple Av. SW19 —7F 119
Worple Av. Iswth —5A 98
Worple Clo. Harr —1D 42
Worple Rd. SW20 & SW19 —2E 136
Worple Rd. Iswth —4A 98
Worple Rd. M. SW19 —6H 119
Worple St. SW14 —3K 99
Worple Way. Harr —1D 42
Worple Way. Rich —5E 98
Worship St. EC2 —4D 68 (4F 163)
Worslade Rd. SW17 —4B 120
Worsley Bri. Rd. SE26 & Beck —4B 124
Worsley Ho. SE23 —2H 123
Worsley Rd. E11 —4G 53
Worsopp Dri. SW4 —5G 103
Worthfield Clo. Eps —7K 147
Worth Gro. SE17 —5D 86
Worthing Clo. E15 —1G 71
Worthing Rd. Houn —6D 78
Worthington Clo. Mitc —4F 139
Worthington Ho. EC1 —3A 68 (1K 161)
(off Myddelton Pas.)
Worthington Rd. Surb —1F 147
Wortley Rd. E6 —7B 54
Wortley Rd. Croy —7A 140
Worton Ct. Iswth —4J 97
Worton Gdns. Iswth —2H 97
Worton Hall Ind. Est. Iswth —4J 97
Worton Rd. Iswth —4H 97
Worton Way. Iswth —2H 97
Wotton Ct. E14 —7F 71
Wotton Rd. NW2 —3E 46
Wotton Rd. SE8 —6B 88
Wouldham Rd. E16 —6H 71
Wragby Rd. E11 —3G 53
Wrampling Pl. N9 —1B 18
Wrangthorn Wlk. Croy —4A 152
Wray Av. Ilf —3E 36
Wrayburn Ho. SE16 —2G 87
(off Llewellyn St.)
Wray Cres. N4 —2J 49
Wrayfield Rd. Sutt —3F 149
Wray Rd. Sutt —7H 149
Wraysbury Clo. Houn —5C 96
Wrays Way. Hay —4G 59
Wrekin Rd. SE18 —7G 91
Wren Av. NW2 —5E 46
Wren Av. S'hall —4D 78
Wren Clo. E16 —6H 71
Wren Clo. N9 —1E 18
Wren Cres. Bush —1B 10
Wren Gdns. Dag —5D 56
Wren Ho. SW1 —5H 85 (6C 172)
(off Aylesford St.)
Wren Landing. E14 —1C 88
Wrenn Ho. SW13 —6E 82
Wren Path. SE28 —3H 91
Wren Rd. SE5 —1D 104
Wren Rd. Dag —5D 56
Wren Rd. Sidc —4C 128
Wren's Av. Ashf —4E 112
Wren's Pk. Ho. E5 —2H 51
Wren St. WC1 —4K 67 (3H 161)
Wrentham Av. NW10 —2F 65
Wrenthorpe Rd. Brom —4G 125
Wrenwood Way. Pinn —4K 23
Wrestlers Ct. EC3 —7G 163
Wrexham Rd. E3 —2C 70
Wricklemarsh Rd. SE3 —2K 107
(in two parts)
Wrigglesworth St. SE14 —7K 87
Wright Clo. SE13 —4F 107
Wright Gdns. Shep —5C 130
Wright Rd. N1 —6E 50
Wright Rd. Houn —7A 78
Wrights All. SW19 —6E 118
Wrights Clo. Dag —4H 57
Wrights Grn. SW4 —4H 103
Wright's La. W8 —3K 83
Wrights Pl. NW10 —6J 45
Wright's Rd. E3 —2B 70
(in two parts)
Wrights Rd. SE25 —3E 140
Wrights Row. Wall —4F 151
Wrights Wlk. SW14 —3K 99
Wrigley Clo. E4 —5A 20
Writtle Ho. NW9 —2B 28
Wrotham Ho. SE1 —3D 86
(off Law St.)
Wrotham Ho. Beck —7B 124
(off Sellindge Clo.)
Wrotham Rd. NW1 —7G 49
Wrotham Rd. W13 —1C 80
Wrotham Rd. Barn —2B 4
Wrotham Rd. Well —1C 110
Wrottesley Rd. NW10 —2C 64
Wrottesley Rd. SE18 —6G 91
Wroughton Rd. SW11 —5D 102
Wroughton Ter. NW4 —4D 28
Wroxall Rd. Dag —6C 56
Wroxham Gdns. N11 —7C 16
Wroxham Rd. SE28 —7D 74
Wroxham Way. Ilf —1F 37
Wroxton Rd. SE15 —2J 105
Wrythe Grn. Cars —3D 150
Wrythe Grn. Rd. Cars —3D 150
Wrythe La. Cars —1A 150
Wrythe, The. —3D 150
Wulfstan St. W12 —5B 64
Wyatt Clo. SE16 —2B 88
Wyatt Clo. Bush —1C 10
Wyatt Clo. Felt —1B 114
Wyatt Clo. Hay —5J 59
Wyatt Ct. Wemb —7E 44
Wyatt Dri. SW13 —6D 82
Wyatt Ho. NW8 —4B 66 (4B 158)
(off Frampton St.)
Wyatt Ho. SE3 —2H 107
Wyatt Ho. Twic —6D 98
Wyatt Pk. Rd. SW2 —2J 121
Wyatt Rd. E7 —6J 53
Wyatt Rd. N5 —3C 50
Wyatts La. E17 —3E 34
Wybert St. NW1 —4G 67 (3A 160)
Wyborne Ho. NW10 —7J 45
Wyborne Way. NW10 —7J 45
Wyburn Av. Barn —3C 4
Wyche Gro. S Croy —7D 152
Wych Elm Lodge. Brom —7H 125
Wych Elm Pas. King T —7F 117
Wycherley Clo. SE3 —7H 89
Wycherley Cres. New Bar —6E 4
Wychombe Studios. NW3 —6D 48
Wychwood Av. Edgw —6J 11
Wychwood Av. T Hth —3C 140
Wychwood Clo. Edgw —6J 11
Wychwood Clo. Sun —6J 113
Wychwood End. N6 —7G 31
Wychwood Gdns. Ilf —4D 36
Wychwood Way. SE19 —6D 122
Wyclif Ct. EC1 —3B 68 (2A 162)
(off Wyclif St.)
Wycliffe Clo. Well —1K 109
Wycliffe Rd. SW11 —2E 102
Wycliffe Rd. SW19 —6K 119
Wyclif St. EC1 —3B 68 (2A 162)
Wycombe Gdns. NW11 —2J 47
Wycombe Ho. NW8 —4C 66 (3C 158)
(off Grendon St.)
Wycombe Pl. SW18 —6A 102
Wycombe Rd. N17 —1G 33
Wycombe Rd. Ilf —5D 36
Wycombe Rd. Wemb —1G 63
Wydehurst Rd. Croy —7G 141
Wydell Clo. Mord —6F 137
Wydeville Mnr. Rd. SE12 —4K 125
Wye Clo. Ashf —4D 112
Wye Clo. Orp —7K 145
Wye Clo. Ruis —6E 22
Wye Ct. W13 —5B 62
(off Malvern Way)
Wyemead Cres. E4 —2B 20
Wye St. SW11 —2B 102
Wyevale Clo. Pinn —3J 23
Wyfields. Ilf —1F 37
Wyfold Ho. SE2 —2D 92
(off Wolvercote Rd.)
Wyfold Rd. SW6 —7G 83
Wyhill Wlk. Dag —7J 57
Wyke Clo. Iswth —6K 79
Wyke Gdns. W7 —3A 80
Wykeham Av. Dag —6C 56
Wykeham Clo. W Dray —5C 76
Wykeham Ct. N11 —2K 15
(off Wykeham Rd.)
Wykeham Ct. NW4 —5E 28
(off Wykeham Rd.)
Wykeham Grn. Dag —6C 56
Wykeham Hill. Wemb —1F 45
Wykeham Ri. N20 —1B 14
Wykeham Rd. NW4 —4E 28
Wykeham Rd. Harr —4B 26
Wyke Rd. E3 —7C 52
Wyke Rd. SW20 —2E 136
Wylchin Clo. Pinn —3H 23
Wyldes Clo. NW11 —1A 48
Wyldfield Gdns. N9 —2A 18
Wyld Way. Wemb —6H 45
Wyleu St. SE23 —7A 106
Wylie Rd. S'hall —3E 78
Wyllen Clo. E1 —4J 69
Wymans Way. E7 —4A 54
Wymering Mans. W9 —3J 65
(off Wymering Rd., in two parts)
Wymering Rd. W9 —3J 65
Wymond St. SW15 —3E 100
Wynan Rd. E14 —5D 88
Wynash Gdns. Cars —5C 150
Wynaud Ct. N22 —6E 16
Wyncham Av. Sidc —1J 127
Wyncham Ho. Sidc —2A 128
(off Longlands Rd.)
Wynchgate. N14 & N21 —1C 16
Wynchgate. Harr —7D 10
Wynchgate. N'holt —5D 42
Wyncroft Clo. Brom —3D 144
Wyndale Av. NW9 —6G 27
Wyndcliff Rd. SE7 —6K 89
Wyndcroft Clo. Enf —3G 7
Wyndham Clo. Sutt —7J 149
Wyndham Ct. W7 —4A 80
Wyndham Cres. N19 —3G 49
Wyndham Cres. Houn —6E 96
Wyndham Deedes Ho. E2 —2G 69
(off Hackney Rd.)
Wyndham Est. SE5 —7C 86
Wyndham Ho. E14 —2D 88
Wyndham M. W1 —5D 66 (6E 158)
Wyndham Pl. W1 —5D 66 (6E 158)
Wyndham Rd. E6 —7B 54
Wyndham Rd. SE5 —7C 86
Wyndham Rd. W13 —3B 80
Wyndham Rd. Barn —1J 15
Wyndham Rd. King T —7F 117
(in two parts)
Wyndham St. W1 —5D 66 (5E 158)
Wyndham Yd. W1 —5D 66 (6E 158)
Wyneham Rd. SE24 —5D 104
Wynell Rd. SE23 —3K 123
Wynford Ho. N1 —2K 67
(off Priory Grn. Est.)
Wynford Pl. Belv —6G 93
Wynford Rd. N1 —2K 67
Wynford Way. SE9 —3D 126
Wynlie Gdns. Pinn —2K 23
Wynndale Rd. E18 —1K 35
Wynne Ho. SE14 —1K 105
Wynne Rd. SW9 —2A 104
Wynnstay Gdns. W8 —3J 83
Wynter St. SW11 —4A 102
Wynton Gdns. SE25 —5F 141
Wynton Pl. W3 —6H 63
Wynyard Ho. SE11 —5H 173
Wynyard Ter. SE11 —5K 85 (5H 173)
Wynyatt St. EC1 —3B 68 (2A 162)
Wyre Gro. Edgw —3C 12
Wyre Gro. Hay —4J 77
Wyresdale Cres. Gnfd —3K 61
Wyteleaf Clo. Ruis —6E 22
Wythburn Ct. W1 —6D 66 (7E 158)
(off Wythburn Pl.)
Wythburn Pl. W1 —6D 66 (1E 164)
Wythenshawe Rd. Dag —3G 57
Wythens Wlk. SE9 —6F 109
Wythes Clo. Brom —2D 144
Wythes Rd. E16 —1C 90
Wythfield Rd. SE9 —6D 108
Wyvenhoe Rd. Harr —4G 43
Wyvern Est. N Mald —4C 136
Wyvil Rd. SW8 —7J 85
Wyvis St. E14 —5D 70

Xylon Ho. Wor Pk —2D 148

Yabsley St. E14 —1E 88
Yalding Rd. SE16 —3G 87
Yale Clo. Houn —5D 96
Yale Ct. NW6 —5K 47
Yaohan Plaza. NW9 —3K 27
Yarborough Rd. SW19 —1B 138
Yardley Clo. E4 —5J 9
Yardley Ct. Sutt —4E 148
Yardley La. E4 —5J 9
Yardley St. WC1 —3A 68 (2J 161)
(in two parts)
Yarlington Ct. N11 —5K 15
(off Sparkford Gdns.)
Yarmouth Cres. N17 —5H 33
Yarmouth Pl. W1 —1F 85 (5J 165)
Yarnfield Sq. SE15 —1G 105
Yarnton Way. SE2 & Eri —2C 92
Yarrow Cres. E6 —5C 72
Yarrow Ho. E14 —3E 88
Yateley St. SE18 —3B 90
Yates Ho. E2 —3G 69
(off Roberta St.)
Yeading. —4A 60
Yeading Av. Harr —2C 42
Yeading Fork. Hay —5A 60
Yeading Gdns. Hay —5K 59
Yeading Ho. Hay —5B 60
Yeading La. Hay & N'holt —6K 59
Yeading Wlk. N Har —5D 24
Yeames Clo. W13 —6A 62
Yeate St. N1 —7D 50
Yeatman Rd. N6 —6D 30
Yeats Clo. NW10 —5A 46
Yeats Clo. SE13 —2F 107
Yeend Clo. W Mol —4E 132
Yeldham Rd. W6 —5F 83
Yelverton Lodge. Twic —7C 98
Yelverton Rd. SW11 —2B 102
Yenston Clo. Mord —6J 137
Yeoman Clo. E6 —7F 73
Yeoman Clo. SE27 —3B 122
Yeoman Ct. SE1 —5F 87
(off Cooper's Rd.)
Yeoman Ct. Houn —7D 78
Yeoman Rd. N'holt —7C 42
Yeomans Acre. Ruis —6J 23
Yeomans M. Iswth —6H 97
Yeoman's Row. SW3 —3C 84 (2D 170)
Yeoman St. SE8 —4A 88
Yeomans Way. Enf —2D 8
Yeoman's Yd. E1 —2K 169
Yeo St. E3 —5D 70
Yeovilton Pl. King T —5C 116
Yerbury Rd. N19 —3H 49
(in two parts)
Yester Dri. Chst —7C 126
Yester Pk. Chst —7D 126
Yester Rd. Chst —7C 126
Yew Av. W Dray —7A 58
Yew Clo. Buck H —2G 21
Yewdale Clo. Brom —6G 125
Yewfield Rd. NW10 —6B 46
Yew Gro. NW2 —4F 47
Yews, The. Ashf —3D 112
Yew Tree Clo. N21 —7F 7
Yewtree Clo. N22 —1G 31
Yewtree Clo. N Har —4F 25
Yewtree Clo. Well —1A 110
Yew Tree Clo. Wor Pk —1A 148
Yew Tree Ct. NW11 —5H 29
(off Bridge La.)
Yew Tree Ct. Sutt —7A 150
(off Walnut M.)
Yew Tree Gdns. Chad H —5E 38
Yew Tree Gdns. Romf —5K 39
Yew Tree Lodge. SW16 —4G 121
Yew Tree Lodge. Romf —5K 39
(off Yew Tree Gdns.)
Yew Tree Rd. W12 —7B 64
Yewtree Rd. Beck —3B 142
Yew Tree Rd. Uxb —1B 58
Yew Trees. Shep —4B 130
Yew Tree Wlk. Houn —5D 96
Yew Wlk. Harr —1J 43
Yiewsley Ct. W Dray —1A 76
Yoakley Rd. N16 —2E 50
Yoke Clo. N7 —6J 49
Yolande Gdns. SE9 —5C 108
Yonge Pk. N4 —3A 50
York Av. SE17 —5C 86
York Av. SW14 —5J 99
York Av. W7 —1J 79
York Av. Hay —5E 58
York Av. Sidc —2J 127
York Av. Stan —1B 26
York Bri. NW1 —4E 66 (3G 159)
York Bldgs. WC2 —7J 67 (3F 167)
York Clo. E6 —6D 72
York Clo. SE5 —2C 104
(off Lilford Rd.)
York Clo. W7 —1J 79
York Clo. Mord —4K 137
York Ct. N14 —3D 16
York Ga. N14 —7D 6
York Ga. NW1 —4E 66 (4G 159)
York Gro. SE15 —1J 105
York Hill. SE27 —3B 122
York Ho. SE1 —3K 85 (2H 173)
York Ho. W1 —5D 66 (5E 158)
(off York St.)
York Ho. Enf —1J 7
York Ho. Wemb —4F 45
York Ho. Pl. W8 —2K 83
Yorkland Av. Well —3K 109
York Mans. SW5 —5K 83
(off Earl's Ct. Rd.)
York Mans. SW11 —1E 102
(off Prince Of Wales Dri.)
York Mans. W1 —5E 66 (5G 159)
(off Chiltern St.)
York M. NW5 —5F 49
York M. Ilf —3E 54
York Pde. Bren —5D 80
York Pl. SW11 —3B 102
York Pl. WC2 —3F 167
York Pl. Dag —6J 57
York Pl. Ilf —2E 54
York Pl. Mans. W1 —5D 66 (5F 159)
(off Baker St.)
York Ri. NW5 —3F 49
York Rd. E4 —4H 19
York Rd. E7 —6J 53
York Rd. E10 —3E 52
York Rd. E17 —5K 33
York Rd. N11 —6C 16
York Rd. N18 —6C 18
York Rd. N21 —7J 7
York Rd. SE1 —2K 85 (7H 167)
York Rd. SW18 & SW11 —4A 102
York Rd. SW19 —6A 120
York Rd. W3 —6J 63
York Rd. W5 —3C 80
York Rd. Bren —5D 80
York Rd. Croy —7A 140
York Rd. Houn —3F 97
York Rd. Ilf —3E 54
York Rd. King T —7F 117
York Rd. New Bar —5F 5
York Rd. N'wd —2J 23
York Rd. Rain —7K 57
York Rd. Rich —5F 99
York Rd. Sutt —6J 149
York Rd. Tedd —4J 115
Yorkshire Clo. N16 —3E 50
Yorkshire Gdns. N18 —5C 18
Yorkshire Grey. —5B 108
Yorkshire Grey. SE9 —5B 108
Yorkshire Grey Pl. NW3 —4A 48
Yorkshire Grey Yd. WC1 —6G 161
Yorkshire Pl. E14 —6A 70
Yorkshire Rd. E14 —6A 70
Yorkshire Rd. Mitc —5J 139
Yorkshire St. E14 —6A 70
York Sq. E14 —6A 70
York St. W1 —5D 66 (6E 158)
York St. Bark —1G 73
York St. Mitc —7E 138
York St. Twic —1A 116
York St. Chambers. W1 —5D 66 (6E 158)
(off York St.)
York Ter. Enf —1H 7
York Ter. Eri —1J 111
York Ter. E. NW1 —4E 66 (4H 159)
York Ter. W. NW1 —4E 66 (4G 159)
Yorkton St. E2 —2G 69
York Way. N7 & N1 —6H 49 (1F 161)
York Way. N20 —3J 15
York Way. Chess —7E 146
York Way. Felt —3C 114
(in two parts)
York Way Ct. N1 —1J 67
(off Tiber Gdns.)
York Way Est. N7 —6J 49
Young Ct. NW6 —7G 47
Youngmans Clo. Enf —1H 7
Young Rd. E16 —6A 72
Youngs Bldgs. EC1 —3D 162
Youngs Ct. SW11 —1E 102
Youngs Rd. Ilf —5H 37
Young St. W8 —2K 83
Young Vic Theatre, The. —6K 167
Yoxley App. Ilf —6G 37
Yoxley Dri. Ilf —6G 37
Yukon Rd. SW12 —7F 103
Yuletide Clo. NW10 —7A 46
Yunus Khan Clo. E17 —5C 34

Zampa Rd. SE16 —5J 87
Zander Ct. E2 —3G 69
Zangwill Rd. SE3 —1B 108
Zealand Av. W Dray —7A 76
Zealand Ho. SE5 —2C 104
(off Denmark Rd.)
Zealand Rd. E3 —2A 70
Zenith Lodge. N3 —7E 14
Zennor Rd. SW12 —1G 121
Zennor Rd. Ind. Est. SW12 —1G 121
Zenoria St. SE22 —4F 105
Zermatt Rd. T Hth —4C 140
Zetland Ho. W8 —3K 83
(off Marloes Rd.)
Zetland St. E14 —5D 70
Zion Pl. T Hth —4D 140
Zion Rd. T Hth —4D 140
Zoar St. SE1 —1C 86 (4C 168)
Zoffany St. N19 —2H 49

HOSPITALS and HOSPICES
covered by this atlas
with their map square reference

N.B. WhereHospitals and Health Centresre not named on the map, the reference given is for the road in which they are situated.

ACTON HOSPITAL —2G **81**
Gunnersbury La.
LONDON
W3 8EG
Tel: 020 83831133

ASHFORD HOSPITAL —2A **112**
London Rd., ASHFORD
TW15 3AA
Tel: 01784 884488

ATHLONE HOUSE —1D **48**
Hampstead La.
LONDON
N6 4RX
Tel: 020 83485231

ATKINSON MORLEY'S HOSPITAL —7D **118**
31 Copse Hill, LONDON
SW20 0NE
Tel: 020 89467711

BARKING HOSPITAL —7K **55**
Upney La.
BARKING
IG11 9LX
Tel: 0208 9838000

BARNES HOSPITAL —3A **100**
South Worple Way
LONDON
SW14 8SU
Tel: 020 88784981

BARNET HOSPITAL —4A **4**
Wellhouse La.
BARNET
EN5 3DJ
Tel: 020 82164000

BECKENHAM HOSPITAL —2B **142**
379 Croydon Rd.
BECKENHAM
BR3 3QL
Tel: 020 82896600

BECONTREE DAY HOSPITAL —2E **56**
508 Becontree Av.
DAGENHAM
RM8 3HR
Tel: 0208 9841234

BELVEDERE DAY HOSPITAL —1C **64**
341 Harlesden Rd.
LONDON
NW10 3RX
Tel: 020 84593562

BELVEDERE PRIVATE CLINIC —5C **92**
Knee Hill
LONDON
SE2 0AT
Tel: 020 83114464

BETHLEM ROYAL HOSPITAL, THE —7C **142**
Monks Orchard Rd.
BECKENHAM
BR3 3BX
Tel: 020 87776611

BLACKHEATH BMI HOSPITAL, THE —3H **107**
40-42 Lee Ter.
LONDON
SE3 9UD
Tel: 020 83187722

BOLINGBROKE HOSPITAL —5C **102**
Bolingbroke Gro.
LONDON
SW11 6HN
Tel: 020 72237411

BRITISH HOME & HOSPITAL FOR INCURABLES —5B **122**
Crown La.
LONDON
SW16 3JB
Tel: 020 86708261

BROMLEY HOSPITAL —4K **143**
Cromwell Av.
BROMLEY
BR2 9AJ
Tel: 020 82897000

BUSHEY BUPA HOSPITAL —1E **10**
Heathbourne Rd.
Bushey Heath
BUSHEY
WD23 1RD
Tel: 020 89509090

CAMDEN MEWS DAY HOSPITAL —6G **49**
1-5 Camden Mews
LONDON
NW1 9DB
Tel: 020 75304780

CARSHALTON WAR MEMORIAL HOSPITAL —6D **150**
The Park
CARSHALTON
SM5 3DB
Tel: 020 86475534

CASSEL HOSPITAL, THE —4D **116**
1 Ham Comn.
RICHMOND
TW10 7JF
Tel: 020 89408181

CENTRAL MIDDLESEX HOSPITAL —3J **63**
Acton La.
LONDON
NW10 7NS
Tel: 020 89655733

CHADWELL HEATH HOSPITAL —5B **38**
Grove Rd.
ROMFORD
RM6 4XH
Tel: 020 89838000

CHARING CROSS HOSPITAL —6F **83**
Fulham Palace Rd.
LONDON
W6 8RF
Tel: 020 88461234

CHASE FARM HOSPITAL —1F **7**
127 The Ridgeway
ENFIELD
EN2 8JL
Tel: 020 83666600

CHELSEA & WESTMINSTER HOSPITAL —6A **84**
369 Fulham Rd., LONDON
SW10 9NH
Tel: 020 87468000

CLAYPONDS HOSPITAL —4E **80**
Sterling Pllace
LONDON
W5 4RN
Tel: 020 85604011

CLEMENTINE CHURCHILL HOSPITAL, THE —3K **43**
Sudbury Hill
HARROW
HA1 3RX
Tel: 020 88723872

COLINDALE HOSPITAL —2A **28**
Colindale Av.
LONDON
NW9 5HG
Tel: 020 89522381

COTTAGE DAY HOSPITAL —3C **120**
Springfield University Hospital
61 Glenburnie Rd.
LONDON
SW17 7DJ
Tel: 020 86826514

CROMWELL HOSPITAL, THE —4K **83**
162-174 Cromwell Rd.
LONDON
SW5 0TU
Tel: 020 74602000

DEVONSHIRE HOSPITAL, THE —5E **66** (5H **159**)
29-31 Devonshire St.
LONDON
W1N 1RF
Tel: 020 74867131

EALING HOSPITAL —1H **79**
Uxbridge Rd.
SOUTHALL
UB1 3HW
Tel: 020 89675000

EAST HAM MEMORIAL HOSPITAL —7B **54**
Shrewsbury Rd., LONDON
E7 8QR
Tel: 0208 5865000

EASTMAN DENTAL HOSPITAL & DENTAL INSTITUTE, THE —4K **67** (3G **161**)
256 Gray's Inn Rd., LONDON
WC1X 8LD
Tel: 020 79151000

EDENHALL MARIE CURIE CENTRE —5B **48**
11 Lyndhurst Gardens
LONDON
NW3 5NS
Tel: 020 77940066

EDGWARE COMMUNITY HOSPITAL —7C **12**
Burnt Oak Broadway
EDGWARE
HA8 0AD
Tel: 020 89522381

ERITH & DISTRICT HOSPITAL —6K **93**
Park Cres.
ERITH
DA8 3EE
Tel: 020 83022678

FARNBOROUGH HOSPITAL —4E **156**
Farnborough Comn.
ORPINGTON
BR6 8ND
Tel: 01689 814000

FINCHLEY MEMORIAL HOSPITAL —7F **15**
Granville Rd.
LONDON
N12 0JE
Tel: 020 83493121

FLORENCE NIGHTINGALE DAY HOSPITAL —5C **66** (5D **158**)
1B Harewood Row
LONDON
NW1 6SE
Tel: 020 7259940

FLORENCE NIGHTINGALE HOSPITAL —5C **66** (5D **158**)
11-19 Lisson Gro.
LONDON
NW1 6SH
Tel: 020 72583828

GAINSBOROUGH CLINIC, THE —3A **86**
22 Barkham Ter.
LONDON
SE1 7PW
Tel: 020 79285633

GARDEN HOSPITAL, THE —3E **28**
46-50 Sunny Gardens Rd.
LONDON
NW4 1RP
Tel: 020 84574500

GOODMAYES HOSPITAL —5A **38**
Barley La.
ILFORD
IG3 8XJ
Tel: 020 89838000

GORDON HOSPITAL —4H **85** (4C **172**)
Bloomburg St.
LONDON
SW1V 2RH
Tel: 020 87468733

GREAT ORMOND STREET HOSPITAL FOR CHILDREN —4J **67** (4F **161**)
Great Ormond St.
LONDON
WC1N 3JH
Tel: 020 74059200

GREENWICH & BEXLEY COTTAGE HOSPICE —5C **92**
185 Bostall Hill, LONDON
SE2 0QX
Tel: 020 83122244

GREENWICH DISTRICT HOSPITAL —5H **89**
Vanbrugh Hill
LONDON
SE10 9HE
Tel: 020 88588141

GROVELANDS PRIORY HOSPITAL —1D **16**
The Bourne
LONDON
N14 6RA
Tel: 020 88828191

GUY'S HOSPITAL —2D **86** (5E **168**)
St Thomas St.
LONDON
SE1 9RT
Tel: 020 79555000

GUY'S NUFFIELD HOUSE —2D **5F** (6E **169**)
Newcomen St.
LONDON
SE1 1YR
Tel: 020 79554257

HAMMERSMITH & NEW QUEEN CHARLOTTE'S HOSPITAL —6D **64**
Du Cane Rd.
LONDON
W12 0HS
Tel: 020 83831000

HARLEY STREET CLINIC, THE —5F **67** (5J **159**)
35 Weymouth St., LONDON
W1N 4BJ
Tel: 020 79357700

HAYES GROVE PRIORY HOSPITAL —2J **155**
Prestons Rd.
BROMLEY
BR2 7AS
Tel: 020 84627722

HEART HOSPITAL, THE —5E **66** (6H **159**)
16-18 Westmoreland St.
LONDON
W1G 8PH
Tel: 020 75738888

HIGHGATE PRIVATE HOSPITAL —6D **30**
17 View Rd.
LONDON
N6 4DJ
Tel: 020 83414182

HILLINGDON HOSPITAL —5B **58**
Pield Heath Rd.
UXBRIDGE
UB8 3NN
Tel: 01895 238282

HOLLY HOUSE HOSPITAL —2E **20**
High Rd.
BUCKHURST HILL
IG9 5HX
Tel: 0208 5053311

HOMERTON HOSPITAL —5K **51**
Homerton Row
LONDON
E9 6SR
Tel: 020 85105555

HORNSEY CENTRAL HOSPITAL —5H **31**
Park Rd.
LONDON
N8 8JL
Tel: 020 82191700

HOSPITAL FOR TROPICAL DISEASES —4G **67** (4B **160**)
Mortimer Market, Capper St.
LONDON
WC1E 6AU
Tel: 020 73879300

HOSPITAL OF ST JOHN & ST ELIZABETH —2B **66**
60 Grove End Rd.
LONDON
NW8 9NH
Tel: 020 72865126

KING EDWARD VII'S HOSPITAL FOR OFFICERS —5E **66** (5H **159**)
5-10 Beaumont St.
LONDON
W1N 2AA
Tel: 020 74864411

KING GEORGE HOSPITAL —5A **38**
Barley La.
ILFORD
IG3 8YB
Tel: 020 89838000

KING'S COLLEGE HOSPITAL —2D **104**
Denmark Hill
LONDON
SE5 9RS
Tel: 020 77374000

KING'S COLLEGE HOSPITAL, DULWICH —4E **104**
East Dulwich Gro., LONDON
SE22 8PT
Tel: 020 77374000

KING'S OAK BMI HOSPITAL, THE —1F **7**
The Ridgeway
ENFIELD
EN2 8SD
Tel: 020 83709500

KINGSBURY COMMUNITY HOSPITAL —4G **27**
Honeypot La.
LONDON
NW9 9QY
Tel: 020 89031323

KINGSTON HOSPITAL —1H **135**
Galsworthy Rd.
KINGSTON UPON THAMES
KT2 7QB
Tel: 020 85467711

LATIMER DAY HOSPITAL —5G **67** (5A **160**)
40 Hanson St.
LONDON
W1W 6UL
Tel: 020 73809187

LEWISHAM UNIVERSITY HOSPITAL —5D **106**
Lewisham High St.
LONDON
SE13 6LH
Tel: 020 83333000

LISTER HOSPITAL, THE —5F **85** (6J **171**)
Chelsea Bridge Rd.
LONDON
SW1W 8RH
Tel: 020 77303417

LONDON BRIDGE HOSPITAL —1D **86** (4F **169**)
27 Tooley St.
LONDON
SE1 2PR
Tel: 020 74073100

LONDON CHEST HOSPITAL —2J **69**
Bonner Rd.
LONDON
E2 9JX
Tel: 020 73777000

LONDON CLINIC, THE —4E **66** (4H **159**)
20 Devonshire Pl.
LONDON
W1N 2DH
Tel: 020 79354444

LONDON FOOT HOSPITAL —4G **67** (4A **160**)
33 & 40 Fitzroy Sq.
LONDON
W1P 6AY
Tel: 020 75304500

LONDON INDEPENDENT HOSPITAL —5K **69**
1 Beaumont Sq.
LONDON
E1 4NL
Tel: 020 77900990

LONDON LIGHTHOUSE —6G **65**
111-117 Lancaster Rd.
LONDON
W11 1QT
Tel: 020 77921200

LONDON WELBECK HOSPITAL —5E **66** (6H **159**)
27 Welbeck St.
LONDON
W1G 8EN
Tel: 020 72242242

MAITLAND DAY HOSPITAL —4J **51**
143-153 Lower Clapton Rd.
LONDON
E5 8EQ
Tel: 020 89195600

MAUDSLEY HOSPITAL, THE —2D **104**
Denmark Hill
LONDON
SE5 8AZ
Tel: 020 77036333

MAYDAY UNIVERSITY HOSPITAL —6B **140**
Mayday Rd.
THORNTON HEATH
CR7 7YE
Tel: 020 84010300

MEADOW HOUSE HOSPICE —2H **79**
Ealing Hospital, Uxbridge Rd.
SOUTHALL
UB1 3HW
Tel: 020 8967 5179

MEMORIAL HOSPITAL —2E **108**
Shooters Hill
LONDON
SE18 3RZ
Tel: 020 88565511

MIDDLESEX HOSPITAL, THE —5G **67** (6B **160**)
Mortimer St.
LONDON
W1N 8AA
Tel: 020 76368333

MILDMAY MISSION HOSPITAL —3F **69** (2J **163**)
Hackney Rd., LONDON
E2 7NA
Tel: 020 76136300

MOLESEY HOSPITAL —5E **132**
High St.
WEST MOLESEY
KT8 2LU
Tel: 020 89414481

MOORFIELDS EYE HOSPITAL —3D **68** (2E **162**)
162 City Rd., LONDON
EC1V 2PD
Tel: 020 72533411

MORLAND ROAD DAY HOSPITAL —7G **57**
Morland Rd.
DAGENHAM, RM10 9HU
Tel: 0208 5932343

NATIONAL HOSPITAL FOR NEUROLOGY &
NEUROSURGERY (FINCHLEY), THE —4C **30**
Great North Rd.
LONDON
N2 0NW
Tel: 020 78373611

NATIONAL HOSPITAL FOR NEUROLOGY &
NEUROSURGERY, THE —4J **67** (4F **161**)
Queen Sq.
LONDON
WC1N 3BG
Tel: 020 78373611

NELSON HOSPITAL —2H **137**
Kingston Rd.
LONDON
SW20 8DB
Tel: 020 82962000

NEW VICTORIA HOSPITAL —1A **136**
184 Coombe La. West
KINGSTON UPON THAMES
KT2 7EG
Tel: 020 89499000

NEWHAM GENERAL HOSPITAL —4A **72**
Glen Rd.
LONDON
E13 8SL
Tel: 020 74764000

NORTH LONDON HOSPICE —3F **15**
47 Woodside Av.
LONDON
N12 8TT
Tel: 020 83438841

NORTH LONDON NUFFIELD HOSPITAL, THE —2F **7**
Cavell Dri.
ENFIELD
EN2 7PR
Tel: 020 83662122

NORTH MIDDLESEX HOSPITAL, THE —5K **17**
Sterling Way
LONDON
N18 1QX
Tel: 020 88872000

NORTHWICK PARK HOSPITAL —7A **26**
Watford Rd.
HARROW
HA1 3UJ
Tel: 020 88643232

NORTHWOOD & PINNER COMMUNITY HOSPITAL—1J **23**
Pinner Rd.
NORTHWOOD
HA6 1DE
Tel: 01923 824182

OBSTETRIC HOSPITAL, THE —4G **67** (4B **160**)
Huntley St.
LONDON
WC1E 6DH
Tel: 020 73879300

OLDCHURCH HOSPITAL —6K **39**
Oldchurch Rd.
ROMFORD
RM7 0BE
Tel: 01708 746090

PARKSIDE HOSPITAL —3F **119**
53 Parkside
LONDON
SW19 5NX
Tel: 020 89718000

PENNY SANGHAM DAY HOSPITAL —3D **78**
Osterley Pk. Rd.
SOUTHALL
UB2 4EU
Tel: 020 85719676

PLAISTOW HOSPITAL —2A **72**
Samson St.
LONDON
E13 9EH
Tel: 020 85866200

PORTLAND HOSPITAL FOR WOMEN & CHILDREN,
THE —4F **67** (4K **159**)
209 Great Portland St.
LONDON
W1N 6AH
Tel: 020 75804400

PRINCESS GRACE HOSPITAL —4E **66** (4G **159**)
42-52 Nottingham Pl.
LONDON
W1M 3FD
Tel: 020 74861234

PRINCESS LOUISE HOSPITAL —5F **65**
St. Quintin Av.
LONDON
W10 6DL
Tel: 020 89690133

QUEEN ELIZABETH HOSPITAL —7C **90**
Stadium Rd.
LONDON
SE18 4QH
Tel: 020 88565533

QUEEN MARY'S HOSPITAL —3A **48**
23 East Heath Rd.
LONDON, NW3 1DU
Tel: 020 74314111

QUEEN MARY'S HOSPITAL —6A **128**
Frognal Av.
SIDCUP
DA14 6LT
Tel: 020 83022678

QUEEN MARY'S HOSPITAL FOR CHILDREN —1A **150**
Wrythe La.
CARSHALTON
SM5 1AA
Tel: 020 82962000

QUEEN MARY'S UNIVERSITY HOSPITAL —6C **100**
Roehampton La.
LONDON
SW15 5PN
Tel: 020 87896611

REDFORD LODGE PSYCHIATRIC HOSPITAL —2B **18**
15 Church St.,
LONDON, N9 9DY
Tel: 020 89561234

RICHARD HOUSE CHILDREN'S HOSPICE —7B **72**
Richard House Dri.
LONDON
E16 3RG
Tel: 020 75110222

Hospitals & Hospices

RICHMOND HEALTHCARE HAMLET —3E **98**
Kew Foot Rd.
RICHMOND
TW9 2TE
Tel: 020 89403331

RODING HOSPITAL (BUPA) —3B **36**
Roding La. South
ILFORD
IG4 5PZ
Tel: 020 85511100

ROEHAMPTON PRIORY HOSPITAL —4B **100**
Priory La.
LONDON
SW15 5JJ
Tel: 020 88768261

ROYAL BROMPTON HOSPITAL —5C **84** (5C **170**)
Sydney St.
LONDON
SW3 6NP
Tel: 020 73528121

ROYAL BROMPTON HOSPITAL (ANNEXE) —5B **84** (5B **170**)
Fulham Rd.
LONDON
SW3 6HP
Tel: 020 73528121

ROYAL FREE HOSPITAL, THE —5C **48**
Pond St.
LONDON
NW3 2QG
Tel: 020 77940500

ROYAL HOSPITAL FOR NEURO-DISABILITY —6G **101**
West Hill
LONDON
SW15 3SW
Tel: 020 87804500

ROYAL LONDON HOMOEOPATHIC HOSPITAL, THE —5J **67** (5F **161**)
Great Ormond St.
LONDON
WC1N 3HR
Tel: 020 78378833

ROYAL LONDON HOSPITAL (MILE END) —4K **69**
Bancroft Rd.
LONDON
E1 4DG
Tel: 020 73777920

ROYAL LONDON HOSPITAL (WHITECHAPEL) —5H **69**
Whitechapel Rd.
LONDON
E1 1BB
Tel: 020 73777000

ROYAL MARSDEN HOSPITAL (FULHAM), THE —5B **84** (5B **170**)
Fulham Rd., LONDON
SW3 6JJ
Tel: 020 73528171

ROYAL NATIONAL ORTHOPAEDIC HOSPITAL —2G **11**
Brockley Hill
STANMORE
HA7 4LP
Tel: 020 89542300

ROYAL NATIONAL ORTHOPAEDIC HOSPITAL (OUTPATIENTS)
—4F **67** (4K **159**)
45-51 Bolsover St.
LONDON
W1P 8AQ
Tel: 020 89542300

ROYAL NATIONAL THROAT, NOSE & EAR HOSPITAL
—3K **67** (1G **161**)
330 Gray's Inn Rd.
LONDON
WC1X 8DA
Tel: 020 79151300

ROYAL NATIONAL THROAT, NOSE & EAR HOSPITAL - SPEECH &
LANGUAGE UNIT —5C **62**
10 Castlebar Hill
LONDON
W5 1TD
Tel: 020 89978480

ST ANDREW'S AT HARROW —2J **43**
Bowden House Clinic
London Rd.
HARROW
HA1 3JL
Tel: 020 89667000

ST ANDREW'S HOSPITAL —4D **70**
Devas St., LONDON
E3 3NT
Tel: 020 74764000

ST ANN'S HOSPITAL —5C **32**
St Ann's Rd., LONDON
N15 3TH
Tel: 020 84426000

ST ANTHONY'S HOSPITAL —2F **149**
London Rd.
LONDON
SM3 9DW
Tel: 020 83376691

ST BARTHOLOMEW'S HOSPITAL —5B **68** (6B **162**)
West Smithfield, LONDON
EC1A 7BE
Tel: 020 73777000

ST BERNARD'S HOSPITAL —2H **79**
Uxbridge Rd.
SOUTHAL
UB1 3EU
Tel: 020 89675000

ST CHARLES HOSPITAL —5F **65**
Exmoor St.
LONDON
W10 6DZ
Tel: 020 89692488

ST CHRISTOPHER'S HOSPICE —5J **123**
51-59 Lawrie Pk. Rd.
LONDON
SE26 6DZ
Tel: 020 87789252

ST CLEMENT'S HOSPITAL —3B **70**
2A Bow Rd.
LONDON
E3 4LL
Tel: 020 73777000

ST GEORGE'S HOSPITAL (TOOTING) —5B **120**
Blackshaw Rd.
LONDON
SW17 0QT
Tel: 020 86721255

ST HELIER HOSPITAL —1A **150**
Wrythe La.,
CARSHALTON
SM5 1AA
Tel: 020 82962000

ST JOHN'S AND AMYAND HOUSE —7A **98**
Strafford Rd.
TWICKENHAM
TW1 3AD
Tel: 020 87449943

ST JOHN'S HOSPICE —2B **66** (1A **158**)
Hospital of St John & St Elizabeth
60 Grove End Rd.
LONDON
NW8 9NH
Tel: 020 72865126

ST JOSEPH'S HOSPICE —1H **69**
Mare St.,
LONDON
E8 4SA
Tel: 020 85256000

ST LUKE'S HOSPITAL FOR THE CLERGY —4G **67** (4A **160**)
14 Fitzroy Sq.
LONDON
W1T 6AH
Tel: 020 73884954

ST LUKE'S KENTON GRANGE HOSPICE —5H **25**
Kenton Grange
Kenton Rd.
HARROW
HA3 0YG
Tel: 020 83828000

ST LUKE'S WOODSIDE HOSPITAL —4E **30**
Woodside Av.
LONDON
N10 3HU
Tel: 020 82191800

ST MARY'S HOSPITAL —6B **66** (7B **158**)
Praed St., LONDON
W2 1NY
Tel: 020 77256666

ST PANCRAS HOSPITAL —1H **67**
4 St Pancras Way,
LONDON
NW1 0PE
Tel: 020 75303500

ST RAPHAEL'S HOSPICE —1F **149**
St Anthony's Hospital
London Rd.
SUTTON
SM3 9DW
Tel: 020 83354575

ST THOMAS' HOSPITAL —3K **85** (1G **173**)
Lambeth Palace Rd.
LONDON
SE1 7EH
Tel: 020 79289292

SHIRLEY OAKS HOSPITAL —7J **141**
Poppy La., CROYDON
CR9 8AB
Tel: 020 86555500

SLOANE HOSPITAL, THE —1F **143**
125-133 Albemarle Rd.
BECKENHAM
BR3 5HS
Tel: 020 84666911

SOUTH LONDON AND MAUDSLEY TRUST —3J **103**
108 Landor Rd.,
LONDON,   SW9 9NT
Tel: 020 74116100

SOUTHWOOD HOSPITAL —7E **30**
70 Southwood La.,
LONDON
N6 5SP
Tel: 020 83408778

SPRINGFIELD UNIVERSITY HOSPITAL —3C **120**
61 Glenburnie Rd.
LONDON
SW17 7DJ
Tel: 020 86826000

SURBITON HOSPITAL —6E **134**
Ewell Rd.
SURBITON
KT6 6EZ
Tel: 020 83997111

TEDDINGTON MEMORIAL HOSPITAL —6J **115**
Hampton Rd.
TEDDINGTON
TW11 0JL
Tel: 020 84088210

THORPE COOMBE HOSPITAL —3E **34**
714 Forest Rd.
LONDON
E17 3HP
Tel: 020 85208971

TOLWORTH HOSPITAL —2G **147**
Red Lion Rd.
SURBITON
KT6 7QU
Tel: 020 83900102

TRINITY HOSPICE —4F **103**
30 Clapham Comn. N. Side
LONDON
SW4 0RN
Tel: 020 77871000

UNITED ELIZABETH GARRETT ANDERSON & SOHO HOSPITALS
FOR WOMEN —3H **67** (2D **160**)
144 Euston Rd., LONDON
NW1 2AP
Tel: 020 73872501

UNIVERSITY COLLEGE HOSPITAL —4G **67** (4B **160**)
Gower St.
LONDON
WC1E 6AU
Tel: 020 73879300

UPTON DAY HOSPITAL —4E **110**
14 Upton Rd.
BEXLEYHEATH
DA6 8LQ
Tel: 020 83017900

WELLINGTON HOSPITAL, THE —3B **66** (1B **158**)
8a Wellington Pl., LONDON
NW8 9LE
Tel: 020 75865959

WEST MIDDLESEX UNIVERSITY HOSPITAL —2A **98**
Twickenham Rd.
ISLEWORTH
TW7 6AF
Tel: 020 85602121

WESTERN OPHTHALMIC HOSPITAL —5D **66** (5E **158**)
153 Marylebone Rd.
LONDON
NW1 5QH
Tel: 020 78866666

WHIPPS CROSS HOSPITAL —6F **35**
Whipps Cross Rd.
LONDON, E11 1NR
Tel: 020 85395522

WHITTINGTON NHS TRUST —2G **49**
Highgate Hill
LONDON, N19 5NF
Tel: 020 72723070

WILLESDEN COMMUNITY HOSPITAL —7C **46**
Harlesden Rd.
LONDON
NW10 3RY
Tel: 020 84591292

RAIL, CROYDON TRAMLINK, DOCKLANDS LIGHT RAILWAY AND LONDON UNDERGROUND STATIONS

with their map square reference

Abbey Wood Station. Rail —3C 92
Acton Central Station. Rail —1K 81
Acton Main Line Station. Rail —6J 63
Acton Town Station. Tube —2G 81
Addington Village Station. CT —6C 154
Addiscombe Station. CT —1G 153
Albany Park Station. Rail —2D 128
Aldgate East Station. Tube —6F 69 (7K 163)
Aldgate Station. Tube —6F 69 (1J 169)
Alexandra Palace Station. Rail —2J 31
All Saints Station. DLR —7D 70
Alperton Station. Tube —1D 62
Ampere Way Station. CT —1K 151
Anerley Station. Rail —1H 141
Angel Road Station. Rail —5D 18
Angel Station. Tube —2A 68
Archway Station. Tube —2G 49
Arena Station. CT —5J 141
Arnos Grove Station. Tube —5B 16
Arsenal Station. Tube —3A 50
Ashford Station. Rail —4B 112
Avenue Road Station. CT —2K 141

Baker Street Station. Tube —4D 66 (4F 159)
Balham Station. Rail & Tube —1F 121
Bank Station. Tube & DLR —6D 68 (1E 168)
Barbican Station. Rail & Tube —5C 68 (5C 162)
Barking Station. Rail & Tube —7G 55
Barkingside Station. Tube —3H 37
Barnehurst Station. Rail —2J 111
Barnes Bridge Station. Rail —2B 100
Barnes Station. Rail —3C 100
Barons Court Station. Tube —5G 83
Battersea Park Station. Rail —7F 85
Bayswater Station. Tube —7K 65
Beckenham Hill Station. Rail —5E 124
Beckenham Junction Station. Rail & CT —1C 142
Beckenham Road Station. CT —1A 142
Beckton Park Station. DLR —7D 72
Beckton Station. DLR —5E 72
Becontree Station. Tube —6D 56
Beddington Lane Station. CT —6G 139
Belgrave Walk Station. CT —4B 138
Bellingham Station. Rail —3D 124
Belsize Park Station. Tube —5C 48
Belvedere Station. Rail —3H 93
Bermondsey Station. Tube —3G 87
Berrylands Station. Rail —4H 135
Bethnal Green Station. Rail —4H 69
Bethnal Green Station. Tube —3J 69
Bexley Station. Rail —1G 129
Bexleyheath Station. Rail —2E 110
Bickley Station. Rail —3C 144
Bingham Road Station. CT —1G 153
Birkbeck Station. CT —3J 141
Blackfriars Station. Rail & Tube —7B 68 (2A 168)
Blackheath Station. Rail —3H 107
Blackhorse Lane Station. CT —7G 141
Blackhorse Road Station. Rail & Tube —4K 33
Blackwall Station. DLR —7E 70
Bond Street Station. Tube —6F 67 (1J 165)
Borough Station. Tube —2C 86 (7D 168)
Boston Manor Station. Tube —4A 80
Bounds Green Station. Tube —6C 16
Bow Church Station. DLR —3C 70
Bow Road Station. Tube —3C 70
Bowes Park Station. Rail —7D 16
Brent Cross Station. Tube —7F 29
Brentford Station. Rail —6C 80
Brimsdown Station. Rail —2F 9
Brixton Station. Rail & Tube —4A 104
Brockley Station. Rail —3A 106
Bromley North Station. Rail —1J 143
Bromley South Station. Rail —3J 143
Bromley-by-Bow Station. Tube —3E 70
Brondesbury Park Station. Rail —1G 65
Brondesbury Station. Rail —7H 47
Bruce Grove Station. Rail —2F 33
Buckhurst Hill Station. Tube —2G 21
Burnt Oak Station. Tube —1J 27
Bush Hill Park Station. Rail —6A 8

Caledonian Road & Barnsbury Station. Rail —7K 49
Caledonian Road Station. Tube —6K 49
Cambridge Heath Station. Rail —2H 69
Camden Road Station. Rail —7G 49
Camden Town Station. Tube —1F 67
Canada Water Station. Tube —2J 87
Canary Wharf Station. DLR —1C 88
Canning Town Station. Rail, DLR & Tube —6G 71
Cannon Street Station. Rail & Tube —7D 68 (2E 168)
Canonbury Station. Rail —5C 50
Canons Park Station. Tube —7K 11
Carshalton Beeches Station. Rail —6D 150
Carshalton Station. Rail —4D 150
Castle Bar Park Station. Rail —5K 61
Catford Bridge Station. Rail —7C 106
Catford Station. Rail —7C 106
Chadwell Heath Station. Rail —7D 38
Chalk Farm Station. Tube —7E 48
Chancery Lane Station. Tube —5A 68 (6J 161)
Charing Cross Station. Rail & Tube —1J 85 (4E 166)
Charlton Station. Rail —5A 90
Cheam Station. Rail —7G 149
Chessington North Station. Rail —5E 146
Chessington South Station. Rail —7D 146
Chingford Station. Rail —1B 20
Chislehurst Station. Rail —2E 144
Chiswick Park Station. Tube —4J 81
Chiswick Station. Rail —7J 81
Church Street Station. CT —2C 152
City Thameslink Station. Rail —6B 68 (7A 162)
Clapham Common Station. Tube —4G 103
Clapham High Street Station. Rail —3H 103
Clapham Junction Station. Rail —3C 102
Clapham North Station. Tube —3J 103
Clapham South Station. Tube —6F 103
Clapton Station. Rail —2H 51
Clock House Station. Rail —1A 142
Cockfosters Station. Tube —4K 5
Colindale Station. Tube —3A 28
Colliers Wood Station. Tube —7B 120
Coombe Lane Station. CT —5J 153
Covent Garden Station. Tube —7J 67 (1F 167)
Cricklewood Station. Rail —4F 47
Crofton Park Station. Rail —5B 106
Crossharbour Station. DLR —3D 88
Crouch Hill Station. Rail —7K 31
Crystal Palace Station. Rail —6G 123
Custom House Station. Rail & DLR —7K 71
Cutty Sark Station. DLR —6E 88
Cyprus Station. DLR —7E 72

Dagenham Dock Station. Rail —3F 75
Dagenham East Station. Tube —5J 57
Dagenham Heathway Station. Tube —6F 57
Dalston Kingsland Station. Rail —5E 50
Denmark Hill Station. Rail —2D 104
Deptford Bridge Station. DLR —1C 106
Deptford Station. Rail —7C 88
Devons Road Station. DLR —4D 70
Dollis Hill Station. Tube —5C 46
Drayton Green Station. Rail —6K 61
Drayton Park Station. Rail —4A 50
Dundonald Road Station. CT —7H 119

Ealing Broadway Station. Rail & Tube —7D 62
Ealing Common Station. Tube —1F 81
Earl's Court Station. Tube —4K 83
Earlsfield Station. Rail —1A 120
East Acton Station. Tube —6B 64
East Croydon Station. Rail & CT —2D 152
East Dulwich Station. Rail —4E 104
East Finchley Station. Tube —4C 30
East Ham Station. Tube —7C 54
East India Station. DLR —7F 71
East Putney Station. Tube —5G 101
Eastcote Station. Tube —7A 24
Eden Park Station. Rail —5C 142
Edgware Road Station. Tube —5C 66 (6C 158)
Edgware Station. Tube —6C 12
Edmonton Green Station. Rail —2B 18
Elephant & Castle Station. Rail & Tube —4C 86
Elmers End Station. Rail & CT —4K 141
Elmstead Woods Station. Rail —6C 126
Eltham Station. Rail —5D 108
Elverson Road Station. DLR —2D 106
Embankment Station. Tube —1J 85 (4F 167)
Enfield Chase Station. Rail —3H 7
Enfield Town Station. Rail —3K 7
Erith Station. Rail —5K 93
Essex Road Station. Rail —7C 50
Euston Square Station. Tube —4G 67 (3B 160)
Euston Station. Rail & Tube —3H 67 (2C 160)
Ewell West Station. Rail —7A 148

Fairlop Station. Tube —1H 37
Falconwood Station. Rail —4H 109
Farringdon Station. Rail & Tube —5B 68 (5A 162)
Feltham Station. Rail —1K 113
Fenchurch Street Station. Rail —7E 68 (2J 169)
Fieldway Station. CT —7D 154
Finchley Central Station. Tube —1J 29
Finchley Road & Frognal Station. Rail —5A 48
Finchley Road Station. Tube —6A 48
Finsbury Park Station. Rail & Tube —2A 50
Forest Gate Station. Rail —5J 53
Forest Hill Station. Rail —2J 123
Fulham Broadway Station. Tube —7J 83
Fulwell Station. Rail —4H 115

Gallions Reach Station. DLR —7F 73
Gants Hill Station. Tube —6E 36
George Street Station. CT —2C 152
Gipsy Hill Station. Rail —5E 122
Gloucester Road Station. Tube —4A 84
Golders Green Station. Tube —1J 47
Goldhawk Road Station. Tube —2E 82
Goodge Street Station. Tube —5H 67 (5C 160)
Goodmayes Station. Rail —1A 56
Gordon Hill Station. Rail —1G 7
Gospel Oak Station. Rail —4E 48
Grange Park Station. Rail —5G 7
Gravel Hill Station. CT —6A 154
Great Portland Street Station. Tube —4F 67 (4K 159)
Green Park Station. Tube —1G 85 (4K 165)
Greenford Station. Rail & Tube —1H 61
Greenwich Station. Rail & DLR —7D 88
Grove Park Station. Rail —3K 125
Gunnersbury Station. Rail & Tube —5H 81

Hackbridge Station. Rail —2F 151
Hackney Central Station. Rail —6H 51
Hackney Downs Station. Rail —5H 51
Hackney Wick Station. Rail —6C 52
Hadley Wood Station. Rail —1F 5
Hammersmith Station. Tube —4E 82
Hampstead Heath Station. Rail —4C 48
Hampstead Station. Tube —4A 48
Hampton Court Station. Rail —4J 133
Hampton Station. Rail —1E 132
Hampton Wick Station. Rail —1C 134
Hanger Lane Station. Tube —3E 62
Hanwell Station. Rail —7J 61
Harlesden Station. Rail & Tube —2K 63
Harringay Green Lanes Station. Rail —6B 32
Harringay Station. Rail —6A 32
Harrington Road Station. CT —3J 141
Harrow & Wealdstone Station. Rail & Tube —4J 25
Harrow-On-The-Hill Station. Rail & Tube —6J 25
Hatton Cross Station. Tube —4H 95
Haydons Road Station. Rail —5A 120
Hayes & Harlington Station. Rail —3H 77
Hayes Station. Rail —1J 155
Headstone Lane Station. Rail —1F 25
Heathrow Terminal 4 Station. Tube —5E 94
Heathrow Terminals 1, 2, 3 Station. Tube —3D 94
Hendon Central Station. Tube —5D 28
Hendon Station. Rail —6C 28
Herne Hill Station. Rail —6B 104
Heron Quays Station. DLR —1C 88
High Barnet Station. Tube —4D 4
High Street, Kensington Station. Tube —2K 83
Highams Park Station. Rail —6A 20
Highbury & Islington Station. Rail & Tube —6B 50
Highgate Station. Tube —6F 31
Hillingdon Station. Tube —5D 40
Hither Green Station. Rail —6G 107
Holborn Station. Tube —6K 67 (6G 161)
Holland Park Station. Tube —1H 83
Holloway Road Station. Tube —5K 49
Homerton Station. Rail —6K 51
Honor Oak Park Station. Rail —6K 105
Hornsey Station. Rail —4K 31
Hounslow Central Station. Tube —3F 97
Hounslow East Station. Tube —2G 97
Hounslow Station. Rail —5F 97
Hounslow West Station. Tube —2C 96
Hyde Park Corner Station. Tube —2E 84 (6H 165)

Ickenham Station. Tube —4E 40
Ilford Station. Rail —3F 55
Island Gardens Station. DLR —5E 88
Isleworth Station. Rail —2K 97

Kennington Station. Tube —5B 86
Kensal Green Station. Rail & Tube —3E 64
Kensal Rise Station. Rail —2F 65
Kensington Olympia Station. Rail & Tube —3G 83
Kent House Station. Rail —1A 142
Kentish Town Station. Rail & Tube —5G 49
Kentish Town West Station. Rail —6F 49
Kenton Station. Rail & Tube —6B 26
Kew Bridge Station. Rail —5F 81
Kew Gardens Station. Rail & Tube —1G 99
Kidbrooke Station. Rail —3K 107
Kilburn High Road Station. Rail —1K 65
Kilburn Park Station. Tube —2J 65
Kilburn Station. Tube —6H 47
King's Cross St Pancras Station. Tube —3J 67 (1E 160)
King's Cross Station. Rail —2J 67
King's Cross Thameslink Station. Rail —3J 67 (1G 161)
Kingsbury Station. Tube —5G 27
Kingston Station. Rail —1E 134
Knightsbridge Station. Tube —2D 84 (7F 165)

Ladbroke Grove Station. Tube —6G 65
Ladywell Station. Rail —5D 106
Lambeth North Station. Tube —3A 86 (1J 173)
Lancaster Gate Station. Tube —7B 66 (2A 164)
Latimer Road Station. Tube —7F 65
Lebanon Road Station. CT —2E 152
Lee Station. Rail —6J 107
Leicester Square Station. Tube —7J 67 (2D 166)
Lewisham Station. Rail & DLR —3E 106
Leyton Midland Road Station. Rail —1E 52
Leyton Station. Tube —3E 52
Leytonstone High Road Station. Rail —2G 53
Leytonstone Station. Tube —1G 53
Limehouse Station. Rail & DLR —6A 70
Liverpool Street Station. Rail & Tube —5E 68 (6G 163)
Lloyd Park Station. CT —4F 153
London Bridge Station. Rail & Tube —1D 86 (5F 169)
London Fields Station. Rail —7H 51
Loughborough Junction Station. Rail —3B 104
Lower Sydenham Station. Rail —5B 124

Maida Vale Station. Tube —3K 65
Malden Manor Station. Rail —7A 136
Manor House Station. Tube —7C 32
Manor Park Station. Rail —4B 54
Mansion House Station. Tube —7C 68 (2D 168)
Marble Arch Station. Tube —6D 66 (1F 165)
Maryland Station. Rail —6G 53
Marylebone Station. Rail & Tube —4D 66 (4E 158)
Maze Hill Station. Rail —6G 89
Merton Park Station. CT —1J 137
Mile End Station. Tube —4B 70
Mill Hill Broadway Station. Rail —6F 13

Rail, Croydon Tramlink, Docklands Light Railway & London Underground Stations

Mill Hill East Station. Tube —7B **14**
Mitcham Junction Station. Rail & CT —5E **138**
Mitcham Station. CT —4C **138**
Monument Station. Tube —7D **68** (2F **169**)
Moorgate Station. Rail & Tube —5D **68** (6E **162**)
Morden Road Station. CT —2K **137**
Morden South Station. Rail —5J **137**
Morden Station. Tube —3K **137**
Mornington Crescent Station. Tube —2G **67**
Mortlake Station. Rail —3J **99**
Motspur Park Station. Rail —5D **136**
Mottingham Station. Rail —1D **126**
Mudchute Station. DLR —4D **88**

Neasden Station. Tube —5A **46**
New Barnet Station. Rail —5G **5**
New Beckenham Station. Rail —7B **124**
New Cross Gate Station. Rail & Tube —1A **106**
New Cross Station. Rail & Tube —7B **88**
New Eltham Station. Rail —1G **127**
New Malden Station. Rail —3A **136**
New Southgate Station. Rail —5A **16**
Newbury Park Station. Tube —6H **37**
Norbiton Station. Rail —1G **135**
Norbury Station. Rail —1K **139**
North Acton Station. Tube —5K **63**
North Dulwich Station. Rail —5D **104**
North Ealing Station. Tube —6F **63**
North Greenwich Station. Tube —2G **89**
North Harrow Station. Tube —5F **25**
North Sheen Station. Rail —4G **99**
North Wembley Station. Rail & Tube —3D **44**
North Woolwich Station. Rail —2E **90**
Northfields Station. Tube —3C **80**
Northolt Park Station. Rail —4F **43**
Northolt Station. Tube —6E **42**
Northumberland Park Station. Rail —7C **18**
Northwick Park Station. Tube —7B **26**
Northwood Hills Station. Tube —2J **23**
Norwood Junction Station. Rail —4G **141**
Notting Hill Gate Station. Tube —1J **83**
Nunhead Station. Rail —2J **105**

Oakleigh Park Station. Rail —7G **5**
Oakwood Station. Tube —5B **6**
Old Street Station. Rail & Tube —4D **68** (3F **163**)
Osterley Station. Tube —7H **79**
Oval Station. Tube —6A **86**
Oxford Circus Station. Tube —6G **67** (7A **160**)

Paddington Station. Rail & Tube —6B **66** (1A **164**)
Palmers Green Station. Rail —4E **16**
Park Royal Station. Tube —4G **63**
Parsons Green Station. Tube —1J **101**
Peckham Rye Station. Rail —2G **105**
Penge East Station. Rail —6J **123**
Penge West Station. Rail —6H **123**
Perivale Station. Tube —2A **62**
Petts Wood Station. Rail —5G **145**
Phipps Bridge Station. CT —3B **138**
Piccadilly Circus Station. Tube —7H **67** (3C **166**)
Pimlico Station. Tube —5H **85** (5C **172**)
Pinner Station. Tube —4C **24**
Plaistow Station. Tube —2H **71**
Plumstead Station. Rail —4H **91**
Ponders End Station. Rail —5F **9**
Poplar Station. DLR —7D **70**
Preston Road Station. Tube —1E **44**
Prince Regent Station. DLR —7A **72**
Pudding Mill Lane Station. DLR —1D **70**
Putney Bridge Station. Tube —3H **101**
Putney Station. Rail —4G **101**

Queen's Road (Peckham) Station. Rail —1J **105**
Queens Park Station. Rail & Tube —2H **65**
Queensbury Station. Tube —3F **27**
Queenstown Road (Battersea) Station. Rail —1F **103**
Queensway Station. Tube —7K **65**

Ravensbourne Station. Rail —7F **125**
Ravenscourt Park Station. Tube —4D **82**
Rayners Lane Station. Tube —7D **24**
Raynes Park Station. Rail —2E **136**
Rectory Road Station. Rail —3F **51**
Redbridge Station. Tube —6B **36**
Regent's Park Station. Tube —4F **67** (4J **159**)
Richmond Station. Rail & Tube —4E **98**
Roding Valley Station. Tube —4G **21**
Rotherhithe Station. Tube —2J **87**
Royal Albert Station. DLR —7C **72**
Royal Oak Station. Tube —5K **65**
Royal Victoria Station. DLR —7J **71**
Ruislip Gardens Station. Tube —4J **41**
Ruislip Manor Station. Tube —1J **41**
Ruislip Station. Tube —1G **41**
Russell Square Station. Tube —4J **67** (4E **160**)

St Helier Station. Rail —6J **137**
St James Street, Walthamstow Station. Rail —5A **34**
St James's Park Station. Tube —2H **85** (1C **172**)
St John's Wood Station. Tube —2B **66**
St Johns Station. Rail —2C **106**
St Margarets Station. Rail —6B **98**
St Pancras Station. Rail —3J **67** (1E **160**)
St Paul's Station. Tube —6C **68** (7C **162**)
Sanderstead Station. Rail —7D **152**
Sandilands Station. CT —2F **153**
Selhurst Station. Rail —5E **140**
Seven Kings Station. Rail —1J **55**
Seven Sisters Station. Rail & Tube —5E **32**
Shadwell Station. DLR —7H **69**
Shepherd's Bush Station. Tube —2F **83**
Shepherd's Bush Station. Tube —1E **82**
Shepperton Station. Rail —5E **130**
Shoreditch Station. Tube —4F **69** (4K **163**)
Shortlands Station. Rail —2G **143**
Sidcup Station. Rail —2A **128**
Silver Street Station. Rail —4A **18**
Silvertown & City Airport Station. Rail —1C **90**
Sloane Square Station. Tube —4E **84** (4G **171**)
Snaresbrook Station. Tube —5J **35**
South Acton Station. Rail —3J **81**
South Bermondsey Station. Rail —5J **87**
South Croydon Station. Rail —5D **152**
South Ealing Station. Tube —3D **80**
South Greenford Station. Rail —3J **61**
South Hampstead Station. Rail —7A **48**
South Harrow Station. Tube —3G **43**
South Kensington Station. Tube —4B **84** (3B **170**)
South Kenton Station. Rail & Tube —1C **44**
South Merton Station. Rail —3H **137**
South Quay Station. DLR —2D **88**
South Ruislip Station. Rail & Tube —5A **42**
South Tottenham Station. Rail —5F **33**
South Wimbledon Station. Tube —7K **119**
South Woodford Station. Tube —2K **35**
Southall Station. Rail —2D **78**
Southbury Station. Rail —4C **8**
Southfields Station. Tube —1H **119**
Southgate Station. Tube —1C **16**
Southwark Station. Tube —1B **86** (5A **168**)
Stamford Brook Station. Tube —4B **82**
Stamford Hill Station. Rail —7E **32**
Stanmore Station. Tube —4J **11**
Stepney Green Station. Tube —4K **69**
Stockwell Station. Tube —2J **103**
Stoke Newington Station. Rail —2F **51**
Stonebridge Park Station. Rail & Tube —7H **45**
Stoneleigh Station. Rail —5C **148**
Stratford (Low Level) Station. Rail —7F **53**
Stratford Station. Rail, Tube & DLR —7F **53**
Strawberry Hill Station. Rail —3K **115**
Streatham Common Station. Rail —7H **121**
Streatham Hill Station. Rail —2J **121**
Streatham Station. Rail —5H **121**
Sudbury & Harrow Road Station. Rail —5B **44**
Sudbury Hill Station. Tube —4J **43**
Sudbury Hill, Harrow Station. Rail —4J **43**
Sudbury Town Station. Tube —6B **44**
Sunbury Station. Rail —1J **131**
Sundridge Park Station. Rail —7K **125**
Surbiton Station. Rail —6E **134**
Surrey Quays Station. Tube —4K **87**
Sutton Common Station. Rail —2K **149**
Sutton Station. Rail —6A **150**
Swiss Cottage Station. Tube —7B **48**
Sydenham Hill Station. Rail —3F **123**
Sydenham Station. Rail —4J **123**
Syon Lane Station. Rail —7A **80**

Teddington Station. Rail —6A **116**
Temple Station. Tube —7K **67** (2H **167**)
Thames Ditton Station. Rail —7K **133**
Therapia Lane Station. CT —7J **139**
Thornton Heath Station. Rail —4C **140**
Tolworth Station. Rail —2H **147**
Tooting Bec Station. Tube —3E **120**
Tooting Broadway Station. Tube —5C **120**
Tooting Station. Rail —6D **120**
Tottenham Court Road Station. Tube —6H **67** (7D **160**)
Tottenham Hale Station. Rail & Tube —3H **33**
Totteridge & Whetstone Station. Tube —2F **15**
Tower Gateway Station. DLR —7F 69 (2J **169**)
Tower Hill Station. Tube —7F **69** (2J **169**)
Tufnell Park Station. Tube —4G **49**
Tulse Hill Station. Rail —2B **122**
Turnham Green Station. Tube —4A **82**
Turnpike Lane Station. Tube —3B **32**
Twickenham Station. Rail —7A **98**

Upney Station. Tube —7K **55**
Upper Halliford Station. Rail —2G **131**
Upper Holloway Station. Rail —2H **49**
Upton Park Station. Tube —1A **72**

Vauxhall Station. Rail & Tube —5J **85**
Victoria Coach Station Station. Bus —4F **85** (4J **171**)
Victoria Station. Rail & Tube —3F **85** (3K **171**)

Waddon Marsh Station. CT —1K **151**
Waddon Station. Rail —4A **152**
Wallington Station. Rail —6F **151**
Walthamstow Central Station. Rail & Tube —5C **34**
Walthamstow Queens Road Station. Rail —5C **34**
Wandle Park Station. CT —2A **152**
Wandsworth Common Station. Rail —1D **120**
Wandsworth Road Station. Rail —2G **103**
Wandsworth Town Station. Rail —4K **101**
Wanstead Park Station. Rail —4K **53**
Wanstead Station. Tube —6K **35**
Wapping Station. Tube —1J **87**
Warren Street Station. Tube —4G **67** (3A **160**)
Warwick Avenue Station. Tube —4A **66**
Waterloo East Station. Rail —1A **86** (5K **167**)
Waterloo International Station. Rail —2K **85** (6H **167**)
Waterloo Station. Rail & Tube —2A **86** (6J **167**)
Wellesley Road Station. CT —2D **152**
Welling Station. Rail —2A **110**
Wembley Central Station. Rail & Tube —5E **44**
Wembley Park Station. Tube —3G **45**
Wembley Stadium Station. Rail —5F **45**
West Acton Station. Tube —6G **63**
West Brompton Station. Rail & Tube —6J **83**
West Croydon Station. Rail & CT —1C **152**
West Drayton Station. Rail —1A **76**
West Dulwich Station. Rail —2D **122**
West Ealing Station. Rail —7B **62**
West Finchley Station. Tube —6E **14**
West Ham Station. Tube —3G **71**
West Ham Station. Rail —3G **71**
West Hampstead Station. Rail —6J **47**
West Hampstead Station. Tube —6K **47**
West Hampstead Thameslink Station. Rail —6J **47**
West Harrow Station. Tube —6G **25**
West India Quay Station. DLR —7C **70**
West Kensington Station. Tube —5H **83**
West Norwood Station. Rail —4B **122**
West Ruislip Station. Rail & Tube —2E **40**
West Sutton Station. Rail —4J **149**
West Wickham Station. Rail —7E **142**
Westbourne Park Station. Tube —5H **65**
Westcombe Park Station. Rail —5J **89**
Westferry Station. DLR —7C **70**
Westminster Station. Tube —2J **85** (7F **167**)
White City Station. Tube —7E **64**
White Hart Lane Station. Rail —7A **18**
Whitechapel Station. Tube —5H **69**
Whitton Station. Rail —7G **97**
Willesden Green Station. Tube —6E **46**
Willesden Junction Station. Rail & Tube —3B **64**
Wimbledon Chase Station. Rail —2G **137**
Wimbledon Park Station. Tube —3J **119**
Wimbledon Station. Rail, CT & Tube —6H **119**
Winchmore Hill Station. Rail —7G **7**
Wood Green Station. Tube —2A **32**
Wood Street, Walthamstow Station. Rail —4F **35**
Woodford Station. Tube —6E **20**
Woodgrange Park Station. Rail —5B **54**
Woodside Park Station. Tube —4E **14**
Woodside Station. CT —6H **141**
Woolwich Arsenal Station. Rail —4F **91**
Woolwich Dockyard Station. Rail —4D **90**
Worcester Park Station. Rail —1C **148**